a

EMMET
ON
TITLE

EMMET'S

NOTES ON

PERUSING TITLES

AND ON

PRACTICAL

CONVEYANCING

SIXTEENTH EDITION

By

J. T. FARRAND, LL.D.

Solicitor (Hons.)
Professor of Law at the University of Manchester

Consultant Editor

J. GILCHRIST SMITH, LL.D

Solicitor (Hons.)

LONDON
OYEZ PUBLISHING LIMITED
————
1974

©

OYEZ PUBLISHING LIMITED
OYEZ HOUSE, 237 LONG LANE
LONDON SE1 4PU

1974

SBN 85120208 X

First published 1895
Second Edition 1896
Third Edition 1897
Fourth Edition 1899
Fifth Edition 1903
Sixth Edition 1912
Seventh Edition 1915
Eighth Edition 1920
Ninth Edition 1921
Tenth Edition 1923
Eleventh Edition (*in two volumes*) . . . 1926–27
Twelfth Edition (*in two volumes*) . . . 1930–31
Thirteenth Edition (*in two volumes* . . . 1949–50
Fourteenth Edition (*in two volumes*) . . . 1955–56
Fifteenth Edition 1967
Sixteenth Edition 1974

MADE AND PRINTED IN GREAT BRITAIN BY
OYEZ PRESS LIMITED,
PRINTING SUBSIDIARY OF
THE SOLICITORS LAW STATIONERY SOCIETY, LIMITED.
AT THEIR WORKS, OYEZ HOUSE, BREAMS BUILDINGS,
FETTER LANE, LONDON, E.C.4

PREFACE TO THE SIXTEENTH EDITION

IT IS my vain conceit that I have been privileged to edit a book the scope and purpose of which everyone professionally concerned with conveyancing already appreciates without calling for further and better particulars in a Preface. Equally it is confidently believed that the fact of multitudinous and major developments in conveyancing law and practice during the last seven or so years is sufficiently well understood by potential users for no enumeration to be necessary here by way of justification for a new edition. The fifteenth edition was published in 1967 and the intervening period has needed two substantial supplements simply to preserve the utility of the text. This sixteenth edition purports to deal with the relevant and available cases and statutes as at the beginning of November, 1973, but with a few subsequent interpolations. From time to time no doubt supplements will again be needed and published.

The last edition prepared by the late Lewis E. Emmet was the twelfth published in 1930-31. The two following editions were prepared unaided by James Gilchrist Smith and, of course, through his inherently Herculean labours, he not only re-established post-war the reputation of *Emmet* but made the book very much his own. Probably the true depth of Dr. Smith's influence could only be comprehended by someone as closely involved with him and with the work as I was fortunate enough to become as joint editor of the fifteenth edition. Unhappily, due to the increasing demands of practice and of public and private life, Dr. Smith has found it impossible to undertake the full part he would have wished in the preparation of the present edition. Nevertheless, he was persuaded to remain as consultant editor and the contributions which he has been able to make in that capacity naturally proved invaluable.

In this edition, under its new management, some attempt has been made to counter the otherwise inevitable inflation of the contents. Deliberately excluded have been certain topics on the periphery of practical conveyancing which enjoy full treatment in their own practitioners' books ; in particular, there are now no Chapters on Wills, Family Provision, Intestacy or Powers of Appointment (Personal Representatives and Trustees are not lost but incorporated as appropriate in Chapter 9 : Parties to Deeds). It should be said that this approach accords with the informal instructions of several solicitors to say nothing of the trenchant advice of sundry reviewers. Rationalised somewhat perhaps, but surely still undoubtedly recognisable as the old *Emmet!*

Beyond this, one major innovation is embodied in Chapter 24 : Taxation, where I have tried to do for its subject-matter what Dr. Smith achieved for Town and Country Planning and Compulsory Purchase in the thirteenth edition (1949-50). This Chapter on Taxation is supposed to contain not an elementary introduction but an advanced and detailed account of the rules and principles as seen strictly from the point of view of the conveyancer. Throughout endeavours are made to anticipate the impact of charging provisions upon ordinary transactions in land and to foresee and answer the taxing questions arising. The bulk of the Chapter, concerning Capital Gains Tax, Income Tax and Value Added Tax, represents new writing save that much of it, now fairly extensively revised, first appeared in article form in the *Solicitors' Journal*, producing a gratifying number of requests for more permanent and accessible reproduction ; only the parts on Stamps and Estate Duty have been retained from earlier editions. It is hoped that the text can stand judgment by tax experts whilst appealing to the conveyancing practitioner.

Finally, I have a measure of sincere gratitude to offer : firstly, to that nearly silent minority of readers who gently submit constructive criticism of enormous assistance to editors—please continue ; and secondly, to Arnold Monahan of the publishers without whose careful supervision this edition might merely have blushed unseen.

J. T. FARRAND.

January, 1974.

CONTENTS

*[A summary of the contents of subdivided chapters appears
at the head of such chapters]*

TABLE OF CASES

PAGE

b

PAGE

Jenkin's Contract, *Re* [1917] W.N. 49...................................653, 660
Jenkins and Randall (H. E.) & Co.'s Contract, *Re* [1903] 2 Ch. 362 ; 72 L.J. Ch.
    693 ; 88 L.T. 628..170, 765
Jenner *v.* Jenner (1866), L.R. 1 Eq. 361 ; 35 L.J. Ch. 329 ; 14 W.R. 305 ; 12 Jur.
    (N.S.) 138.. 447
Jennings *v.* Jordan (1881), 6 App. Cas. 698 ; 51 L.J. Ch. 129 ; 45 L.T. 593 ; 30
    W.R. 369 ; *varying* S.C. *sub nom.* Mills *v.* Jennings (1880), 13 Ch. D. 639 1016
—— *v.* Tavener [1955] 1 W.L.R. 932 ; [1955] 2 All E.R. 769 ; 99 Sol. J. 543.... 72
Jennings' Trustee *v.* King [1952] 1 Ch. 899 ; 2 All E.R. 608 ; 96 Sol. J. 648 ;
    2 T.L.R. 469 ; W.N. 431.. 251
Jervis *v.* Berridge (1873), L.R. 8 Ch. 351 ; 42 L.J. Ch. 518 ; 28 L.T. 481 ; 21 W.R.
    395.. 40
Jeune *v.* Queens Cross Properties, Ltd. [1973] 3 All E.R. 97................... 878
Joel *v.* Montgomery and Taylor [1967] 2 W.L.R. 21 ; [1967] Ch. 272 ; [1966]
    3 All E.R. 763 ; 110 Sol. J. 809... 200
—— *v.* Swaddle [1957] 1 W.L.R. 1094 ; [1957] 3 All E.R. 325 ; 101 Sol. J. 850.. 907
John *v.* John [1898] 2 Ch. 573 ; *on appeal* [1898] 2 Ch. 577...................328, 388
John's Assignment Trusts, *Re*, Niven *v.* Niven [1970] 1 W.L.R. 955 ; 114 Sol. J.
    396 ; [1970] 2 All E.R. 210.....................................363, 367, 776
John Griffiths Cycle Corporation, Ltd. *v.* Humber & Co., Ltd. [1899] 2 Q.B. 414 ;
    68 L.J.Q.B. 959 ; 81 L.T. 310 ; *revsd. on other grounds, sub nom.* Humber
    & Co. *v.* John Griffiths Cycle Co. (1901), 85 L.T. 141.................. 48
Johns *v.* Ware [1899] 1 Ch. 359 ; 68 L.J. Ch. 155 ; 80 L.T. 112 ; 47 W.R. 202 ;
    6 Mans. 38.. 530
Johnson, *Re*, Cowley *v.* Public Trustee [1915] 1 Ch. 435 ; 84 L.J. Ch. 393 ; 112 L.T.
    935 ; 59 Sol. J. 333... 675
—— *v.* Clarke [1928] Ch. 847 ; 97 L.J. Ch. 337 ; 139 L.T. 552 ; 72 Sol. J. 556.... 230
—— *v.* Humphrey [1946] 1 All E.R. 460 ; 174 L.T. 324 ; 90 Sol. J. 211........ 50, 65
—— *v.* Smart (1860), 2 Gitt. 151 ; 2 L.T. 307 ; 6 Jur. (N.S.) 815............... 94
—— *v.* Try (W.S.) (1946), 62 T.L.R. 355 ; 27 T.C. 167, 174.................... 1103
—— *v.* Warwick (1856), 17 C.B. 516 ; 25 L.J.C.P. 102 ; 26 L.T. (O.S.) 220 ; 139
    E.R. 1176.. 412
Johnson and Tustin, *Re* (1885), 18 Ch. D. 109 ; 54 L.J. Ch. 889 ; 53 L.T. 281 ;
    1 T.L.R. 579 ; 33 W.R. 737......................................126, 142
Johnson's Settled Estates, *Re* (1913), 59 Sol. J. 717 ; W.N. 222................. 720
Johnston *v.* Heath [1970] 1 W.L.R. 1567 ; 114 Sol. J. 866 ; [1970] 3 All E.R. 915 ;
    [1970] T.R. 183 ; 46 T.C. 463...........................1094, 1095, 1108
Johnstone *v.* Holdway [1963] 1 Q.B. 601 ; [1963] 2 W.L.R. 147 ; 107 Sol. J. 55.. 504
Joliffe *v.* Baker (1883), 11 Q.B.D. 255....................................... 96
Jones, *Re*, *ex parte* Jones (1881), 18 Ch. D. 109 ; 50 L.J. Ch. 673 ; 45 L.T. 193 ; 29
    W.R. 747.. 351
—— *Re* (1884), 26 Ch. D. 736 ; 53 L.J. Ch. 807 ; 50 L.T. 466 ; 32 W.R. 735....729, 741
—— *Re*, Farrington *v.* Forrester [1893] 2 Ch. 461 ; 62 L.J. Ch. 996 ; 69 L.T. 45 ;
    3 R. 498.. 471
—— *Re*, Jones *v.* Cusack-Smith [1931] 1 Ch. 375 ; 100 L.J. Ch. 129 ; 144 L.T. 642
                                                  299, 772, 775
—— *Re*, Lambert *v.* Colbourn [1928] W.N. 227.............................. 1174
—— (E. B.) (deceased), *Re*, Public Trustee *v.* Jones [1934] Ch. 315 ; 103 L.J. Ch.
    102 ; 150 L.T. 400 ; 78 Sol. J. 82.................................... 432
—— *v.* Barnett [1900] 1 Ch. 370 ; 69 L.J. Ch. 242 ; 82 L.T. 37 ; 16 T.L.R. 178 ;
    48 W.R. 278.. 183
—— *v.* Bates [1938] 2 All E.R. 237 ; 158 L.T. 507 ; 82 Sol. J. 314 ; 158 T.L.R. 648 ;
    102 J.P. 291 ; 36 L.G.R. 227.. 519
—— *v.* Bone (1870), L.R. 9 Eq. 674 ; 39 L.J. Ch. 405 ; 23 L.T. 304 ; 18 W.R.
    489 ; 34 J.P. 468.. 853
—— *v.* Browne (1945), 146 E.G. 9... 605
—— *v.* Challenger [1961] 1 Q.B. 176 ; [1960] 2 W.L.R. 695 ; [1960] 1 All E.R. 785 ;
    104 Sol. J. 328.. 776
—— *v.* Clifford (1876), 3 Ch. D. 779 ; 45 L.J. Ch. 809 ; 35 L.T. 937 ; 24 W.R. 979 80
—— *v.* Consolidated Anthracite Collieries, Ltd., and Dynevor (Lord) [1916] 1 K.B.
    123 ; 85 L.J.K.B. 465 ; 114 L.T. 288...........................494, 871
—— *v.* Daniel [1894] 2 Ch. 332 ; 63 L.J. Ch. 562 ; 70 L.T. 588 ; 42 W.R. 687 ;
    8 R. 579.. 35
—— *v.* Davies (1902), 86 L.T. 447 ; 66 J.P. 439 ; 20 Cox C.C. 184 ; *sub nom.*
    Davies *v.* Jones, 46 Sol. J. 319 ; 18 T.L.R. 367...................... 526

PAGE

d

d2

TABLE OF STATUTES

[Figures in bold type indicate where the text of an enactment is printed]

e

f

f2

TABLE OF RULES

[Figures in bold type indicate where the text of the Rule is quoted]

ABBREVIATIONS

A.E.A.	. .	Administration of Estates Act.
A.H.A.	. .	Agricultural Holdings Act.
F.A.	. . .	Finance Act.
I.C.T.A.	. .	Income and Corporation Taxes Act.
L.C.A.	. .	Land Charges Act.
L.P.A.	. .	Law of Property Act.
L.R.A.	. .	Land Registration Act.
L.R.R.	. .	Land Registration Rules.
S.A.	. . .	Stamp Act.
S.L.A.	. .	Settled Land Act.
T.A.	. . .	Trustee Act.

[The year will be indicated in the text; e.g., L.P.A. 1925 or L.P.A. 1969 as appropriate.]

Co. Litt.	. .	Coke on Littleton.
Dart.	. . .	Dart on Vendors and Purchasers (8th ed., 1929).
Gale	. . .	Gale's Law of Easements (13th ed., 1959).
K. & E.	. .	Key and Elphinstone's Conveyancing Precedents (15th ed., 1953).
Prideaux	. .	Prideaux's Precedents in Conveyancing (25th ed., 1958–1959).
Theobald	. .	Theobald on Wills (12th ed., 1963).
W. & C.	. .	Wolstenholme and Cherry's Conveyancing Statutes (12th ed., 1932).
Williams V. & P.	. .	Williams on Vendor and Purchaser (4th ed., 1936).

[Except when another edition is expressly referred to, references are in all cases to the editions stated above.]

MATTERS BEFORE CONTRACT

PART 1. GENERAL PRINCIPLES

Practice.—The practice of making searches and inquiries on behalf of a person proposing to buy land, before a contract is entered into, is now well established. The three main reasons why a purchaser's solicitor should adopt this practice are as follows :—

(1) In order to obtain information to enable the purchaser to decide whether to bind himself by a contract and to enable the solicitor to determine whether any special provisions need be inserted in the contract. In general, it is not the duty of a solicitor to ascertain facts on the basis of which the client will decide whether to buy ; that should be done by the client himself or by his surveyor or other agent. Nevertheless, it may be convenient to obtain information on such matters as the rents recoverable and the application of statutory provisions as to security of tenure.

(2) There are now many statutory restrictions on the use and enjoyment of land, the effect of which can be investigated most conveniently by the purchaser's solicitor. An example is whether planning permission will be necessary for the development proposed by the purchaser under the Town and Country Planning legislation (as to which, see *post*, p. 1181 *et seq*.). Many of these restrictions are not matters of title which will enable the purchaser to rescind the contract if he later discovers their existence, for instance, in the course of his solicitor's investigation of title. Consequently, unless the purchaser is prepared to take the risk that they may adversely affect him, or the contract is prepared so that he will have a special right of rescission if a relevant matter is discovered after signature of the contract, inquiries must be made prior to contract.

(3) Registration of any instrument or matter under the provisions of the L.C.A. 1972 is deemed to constitute actual notice of such instrument or matter to all persons and for all purposes connected with the land affected: L.P.A. 1925, s. 198. The extent to which this section gives notice to a prospective purchaser and the effect of L.P.A. 1969, ss. 24 and 25, are considered *post*, at p. 4 *et seq*. It is sufficient to note here that unless special provision is made in the contract, local land charges searches and possibly some land charges searches should be made before contract to ensure that there is no entry which might inconvenience the purchaser.

There are three classes of searches and inquiries which may have to be made, namely (i) local and other land charges searches, (ii) inquiries of local authorities, (iii) inquiries of the vendor and others. Each class is considered in detail below (pp. 6 *et seq.*, 9 *et seq.*), and the necessity for insurance immediately on making of the contract is then discussed (p. 29 *et seq.*).

Obligations of solicitor.—How far a solicitor is under an obligation to make the customary searches and inquiries before contract cannot perhaps be stated with complete certainty. Probably the question would be decided by a court on evidence as to what action is usually taken having regard to the nature of the property, and particularly to any special instructions of the client or any special knowledge of the solicitor as to matters likely to require investigation. Accordingly it is thought to follow from the fact that the practice is now well established of making searches and inquiries before contract that there is a general obligation on a solicitor to do so. Indeed, it has been indicated judicially and specifically that a solicitor has a duty not only to make but also to pursue vigorously at least some particular preliminary inquiries on behalf of a prospective purchaser on pain of liability for negligence in not complying with conveyancing practice (see *per* Danckwerts, J., in *Goody* v. *Baring* [1956] 1 W.L.R. 448, at p. 465 ; also *per* Russell, L.J., in *Hill* v. *Harris* [1965] 2 Q.B. 601, at p. 618). However, although practice may dictate such a general obligation, it may remain difficult to say which particular individual searches and inquiries must be made before contract (the two cases cited concerned, respectively, recoverable rents where the property was let and covenants in superior leases where the property was leasehold). The Solicitors' Remuneration Order, 1972, does not in terms refer to this matter, but there surely can be no doubt that the work involved is comprehended.

Two points are clear :—

(1) The question of a solicitor's obligations before contract cannot arise where the purchaser does not consult his solicitor until after he has signed a contract ; common examples occur on sale by auction and where estate agents and others procure the signature of a contract.

(2) Where the purchaser's solicitor does make inquiries, before or after the contract, he is under a duty to communicate to his client any information he obtains which may affect the client's actions or decisions. For instance, in *Lake* v. *Bushby* [1949] 2 All E.R. 964, the purchaser's solicitors were aware that the purchaser proposed to convert a building into a bungalow ; when the local land charges search was returned, they were informed that plans had not been approved for the erection of the building ; the solicitors obtained a statement from the vendor that he would obtain the necessary approval, but they failed to inform the purchaser of its absence ; Pritchard, J., held that they were liable to the purchaser in damages. See also *Sykes* v. *Midland Bank Executor and Trustee Co., Ltd.* [1971] 1 Q.B. 113, where the Court of Appeal held that a solicitor instructed to advise on a leasehold title had been negligent in not drawing his client's attention to clauses in an unusual form which might have affected his client's interests as he knew them (although in the special circumstances of that case only nominal damages were awarded for the breach of duty).

It is suggested that if a client presses his solicitor to approve a contract and wishes to enter into it before the solicitor has made the usual inquiries or searches, the solicitor should, for his own protection, obtain an authority in writing absolving him from responsibility.

In the absence of specific instructions a solicitor who acts on sale of land does not undertake the duty of advising the client whether the transaction is a prudent one, for instance as to reasonableness of the price (*Bowage* v. *Harold Michelmore & Co.* (1962), 106 Sol. J. 512 ; 183 E.G. 233). Nor would it be a solicitor's duty in general to advise on business questions, such as whether to surrender a lease, or even to remind a client of material dates for action, such as for the exercise of an option (see *Yager* v. *Fishman & Co. and Teff & Teff* [1944] 1 All E.R. 552, C.A.).

However, contrast *Stinchcombe & Cooper, Ltd.* v. *Addison, Cooper, Jesson & Co.* (1971), 115 Sol. J. 368, where solicitors were held liable in damages for failure fully to inform and warn their client ; Brightman, J., is reported as saying that " the contract was no ordinary contract for sale ; it was one which would automatically terminate or was capable of being terminated unilaterally if the purchaser failed to perform certain acts within a specified time and time was therefore, in a real sense, of the essence. It was the solicitor's duty, on or shortly after receiving the contract from the local authority, either to supply a copy to the plaintiffs or inform them of the exchange of contracts or the date thereof. Additionally, it was their duty, on receiving the letter from the local authority in June 1965, to warn the plaintiffs of what was needed in order to obtain a conveyance of the land and that they were in jeopardy of losing the contract." Again in *Neushul* v. *Mellish and Harkavy* (1967), 111 Sol. J. 399, a solicitor was held liable in damages for not advising one client that the other party to a transaction, another client for whom he had acted before, was untrustworthy ; Danckwerts, L.J., is reported as saying that " although he accepted that the duty normally owed by a solicitor to his client only extended to legal advice, he might also undertake to advise on business matters, and he then owed a duty to advise competently, fully and not misleadingly. It was often difficult in a given situation to disentangle legal and business or practical advice, and a solicitor who was carrying out a transaction for a client was not justified in expressing no opinion when it was plain that the client was rushing into an unwise, not to say disastrous, adventure." See also *Spector* v. *Ageda* [1971] 3 W.L.R. 498.

Further, where it is apparent that a purchaser will require a mortgage advance to enable him to complete the purchase, his solicitor is under a duty to *warn the client of the risk* involved in signing a contract before ascertaining that a sufficient advance will be available, but there is no duty to ensure availability of the advance (*Buckland* v. *Mackesy* (1968), 112 Sol. J. 841). To a considerable extent this decision may have depended on the particular facts, but it seems clear that the courts require a solicitor to advise in a businesslike manner although the decision whether to take a risk is that of the client. See generally the survey of a solicitor's duty of care by Alec Samuels in the *Law Society's Gazette*, vol. 69, No. 31, p. 661 *et seq.*

Solicitor acting for both parties.—Over the years a not inconsiderable number of judicial opinions have been reported criticising the practice of one solicitor acting for both vendor and purchaser in the same transaction, the criticism being on account of the potential conflict of interests involved. See *per* Scrutton, L.J., in *Moody* v. *Cox and Hatt* [1917] 2 Ch. 71, at p. 91 ;

per Danckwerts, J., in *Goody* v. *Baring* [1956] 1 W.L.R. 448, at p. 450 ; *per* Danckwerts, L.J., in *Gavaghan* v. *Edwards* [1961] 2 Q.B. 220, at p. 225, and in *Smith* v. *Mansi* [1963] 1 W.L.R. 26, at p. 30 ; also *Neushul* v. *Mellish and Harkavy* (1967), 111 Sol. J. 399. These *dicta* were fully examined in the 15th Edition of this book at pp. 3–6 in the light of the views then variously expressed and indicated by the Council of The Law Society. Now, however, the position has been crystallised by a Practice Rule in the following terms :—

" (1) A solicitor or two or more solicitors practising in partnership or association shall not act for both vendor and purchaser on a transfer of land for value at arm's length or for both lessor and lessee on the grant of a lease for value at arm's length.

(2) Provided no conflict of interest appears and the vendor and lessor is not a builder or developer selling or leasing as such this rule shall not apply if—

(*a*) the parties are associated companies ; or

(*b*) the parties are related by blood, adoption or marriage ; or

(*c*) both parties are established clients (which expression shall include persons related by blood, adoption or marriage to established clients) ; or

(*d*) on a transfer of land the consideration is less than £1,000 ; or

(*e*) there are no other solicitors in the vicinity whom the client can reasonably be expected to consult ; or

(*f*) two associated firms or two offices of the same firm are respectively acting for the parties, provided that—

(i) the respective firms or offices are in different localities, and

(ii) neither party was referred to the firm or office acting for him from an associated firm or from another office of the same firm, and

(iii) the transaction is dealt with or supervised by a different solicitor in full-time attendance at each firm or office."

This rule was published in the *Law Society's Gazette*, vol. 69, No. 43, at p. 1117, together with the strategic explanation that the lack of precise definition of such expressions as " established clients ", " vicinity " and " locality " was intentional so as not to facilitate circumvention.

Necessity for searches before contract.—Searches before contract were for many years generally thought to be necessary in principle on account of *dicta* of Eve, J., at first instance (not referred to on appeal) in *Re Forsey and Hollebone's Contract* [1927] 2 Ch. 379, at p. 387. There he said of an undisclosed planning resolution : " Even if it were an incumbrance, it was an incumbrance of which the purchaser, under s. 198 of the L.P.A. 1925, had notice of a nature which precluded him from repudiating his purchase." Thus, in the (*obiter*) opinion of the learned judge, the effect of s. 198 was to fix a purchaser with notice of any instrument or matter duly registered (as the resolution was) under the L.C.A. 1925 even though he had not searched before entering into the contract. This opinion was subjected to considerable criticism (see especially H. W. R. Wade in the *Cambridge Law Journal*, April, 1954, p. 89 *et seq.*, whose views were outlined in the 15th Edition of this book at p. 7). Nevertheless the making of full land charge searches before exchange of contracts had to be advised as the better practice (see Law Society's Digest, 1954, Opinion No. 135). However, the so-called rule in *Re Forsey and Hollebone* was largely reversed in 1969.

The L.P.A. 1969, s. 24 (1), provides that a purchaser's knowledge of a registered land charge at the time of the contract is to be determined by reference to " his actual knowledge " without regard to s. 198 of the 1925 Act. The quoted expression is undefined, except that subs. (4) provides that " any knowledge acquired in the course of a transaction by a person who is acting therein as counsel, or as a solicitor or other agent, for another shall be treated as the knowledge of that other." Thus it appears that imputed (but not constructive) notice may constitute actual knowledge on the part of a purchaser (cf. L.P.A. 1925, s. 199 (1) (ii) (a) and (b)). In other words, so far as concerns registered land charges, the vendor's duty of disclosure of latent defects in title is not qualified by the mere fact of registration. Accordingly, in this respect it can be said that there is strictly now no necessity for land charge searches before contract.

Four points with regard to the L.P.A. 1969, s. 24 (1), should be observed :—

(1) The word " purchaser " is defined as including " a lessee, mortgagee or other person acquiring or intending to acquire an estate or interest in land " (subs. (3)).

(2) The expression " registered land charge " means any instrument or matter registrable under the L.C.A. 1925 (see now the 1972 consolidating Act) *but expressly excluding local land charges* (s. 24 (3) of the 1969 Act). Accordingly the so-called rule in *Re Forsey and Hollebone* would appear to apply still in relation to registered local land charges, so that it is necessary to continue the common conveyancing practice of making searches for these before contract.

(3) Any provision of the contract purporting to exclude s. 24 or to restrict consequential remedies is rendered void where the purchaser " had not received notice and did not otherwise actually know " of the relevant registered land charge (subs. (2)). It is difficult to say what is intended by the reference to " notice " in that subsection.

(4) The L.P.A. 1969, s. 24 (1), expressly does *not* apply where title is registered (see further the following paragraph).

Registered conveyancing.—The necessity for pre-contract searches (apart from local land charges) would *not* appear to apply in any case to registered titles. The reason is the absence of any provision that the registration constitutes " actual notice . . . to all persons and for all purposes " (i.e., as in the L.P.A. 1925, s. 198). Instead protection by entry on the register gives notice, not before subsequent contracts, but only " to all persons deriving title from the proprietor " (*per* Simonds, J., in *White* v. *Bijou Mansions, Ltd.* [1937] Ch. 610, at p. 610 ; on appeal [1938] Ch. 851 ; compare the report at [1937] 3 All E.R. 269, at p. 274). Thus in *Re Stone and Saville's Contract* [1963] 1 W.L.R. 163, which concerned an undisclosed restrictive covenant entered on the charges register of the vendor's title, there was no suggestion at all that disclosure was therefore unnecessary. However, if the usual practice is followed of supplying with the draft contract copies of the entries on the charges register, then a prospective purchaser would no doubt be fixed with notice thereof. It is true that The Law Society's Conditions of Sale (1973 Revision), General Condition No. 7 (3), provides apparently generally that in such a case the purchaser should not be fixed with notice ; this provision would be effective to preserve the purchaser's rights as against his vendor but would not confer any protection or priority as against persons whose interests appear in the copy entries.

Matrimonial homes.—As a result, therefore, of the above provisions, land charge searches (other than local land charges) before contract are not necessary as a matter of law in unregistered or registered conveyancing. Nevertheless, as a matter of practice, it may still be thought advisable to make a land charge search before contract (against the vendor's name or of the registered title as appropriate) where the purchase is to be of a dwelling-house from one spouse. The point is that the other spouse may have protected by registration a statutory right of occupation (as a Class F land charge or by entry of a notice or caution) and, although the so-called rule in *Re Forsey and Hollebone* was never applicable (see s. 4 of the Matrimonial Homes Act, 1967), no purchaser would wish to become involved in the complex procedure for removal of such registration (cf. *Wroth* v. *Tyler* [1973] 2 W.L.R. 405, where in fact the registration occurred after exchange of contracts).

PART 2.   SEARCHES AND INQUIRIES OF LOCAL AUTHORITIES

Local land charge searches.—Search in the appropriate local register should be made before contract unless it is intended that the contract shall incorporate one of the special conditions designed to avoid the necessity for doing so. Such a search is equally necessary in the case of registered land since local land charges constitute overriding interests (L.R.A. 1925, s. 70 (1) (i)). With effect from 1st April, 1974, all local land charges outside London are registered in district council registers (Local Government Act, 1972, s. 212) ; the registration of local land charges in Greater London is, as from 1st October, 1964, carried on by the town clerks of the new London boroughs and of the City of London. See further, *post*, p. 627. For the reasons there appearing it will not normally be essential to make further similar searches before completion except perhaps on behalf of a mortgagee. Care should be taken to advise the purchaser of entries disclosed by the search certificate (*Lake* v. *Bushby* [1949] 2 All E.R. 964, *ante*, p. 2).

Additional inquiries of local authorities.—There are many ways in which the actions of a local authority may adversely affect property. Forms of additional inquiries have been agreed by the Council of The Law Society with bodies representing local authorities, and it is thought that all authorities answer the appropriate form. Practice may vary as to the giving of further information but probably most clerks to local authorities will endeavour to answer reasonable questions.

At the time of preparing this edition, these agreed forms were undergoing revision. As from 1st April, 1974, local searches are to be made with the district council, not with the (new) county council ; see *post*, p. 353. Consequently the intention is that additional enquiries should be sent to district councils which would obtain from the county council such information as is necessary to answer questions relating to the functions of the county council.

The Council of The Law Society have expressed the opinion that a purchaser's solicitor should make inquiries of local authorities on agreed forms and should take reasonable steps to follow up the results of such inquiries and to inform the purchaser of any risks resulting from unsatisfactory answers (see *Law Society's Gazette*, vol. 46, p. 67, and vol. 69, p. 1164).

These forms have for long stated that replies are furnished after appropriate inquiries and in the belief that they are in accordance with information available to the officers of the council, but on the understanding that neither the council nor any officer of the council is legally responsible therefor.

However, it has been held that this disclaimer of liability for errors in replies to the agreed forms related only to exemption from contractual liability and did not exclude liability for the tort of negligence (*Coats Patons (Retail), Ltd.* v. *Birmingham Corporation* (1971), 115 Sol. J. 757). As a consequence of this decision a new form of disclaimer of liability was adopted unilaterally by local authorities with a view to securing full protection against any responsibility for their errors (see Council Note in *Law Society's Gazette*, vol. 68, at p. 398). But after strong resistance from and prolonged negotiations with the Council of The Law Society, the local government bodies agreed to withdraw that new form of disclaimer and to rely on the old disclaimer as interpreted in the *Coats Patons* case (see *Law Society's Gazette*, vol. 69, No. 45, p. 1164). Indeed it is to make this clear that the words " except for negligence " have been added to the end of the disclaimer (*loc. cit.*).

The use of the standard forms is so widespread that any detailed explanation of them here would be unnecessary.

Register of planning applications.—Every local planning authority must keep a register containing particulars of applications for planning permission and of decisions of the authority or of the Minister in respect of such applications, and such registers are available for inspection by the public (Town and Country Planning Act, 1971, s. 34). The Town and Country Planning General Development Order, 1973, art. 17, requires Part I of the register to contain copies of applications and plans and drawings submitted with them until the matter has been disposed of. Thereafter Part II will contain as a permanent record the same details as before. There is no provision for official searches in this register, but the Minister of Town and Country Planning suggested that local planning authorities should supply extracts by post (Circular 47 of 1948). The current Law Society forms of additional inquiry to accompany local searches ask whether there are any, and if so what, entries in this register.

If planning permission has been refused or granted conditionally only, or such a permission has been revoked or modified, it may be necessary to inquire of the vendor whether any compensation became payable under the provisions of the Town and Country Planning Act, 1971, ss. 146 or 164 (or earlier similar legislation). On the carrying out by the purchaser of certain development (assuming permission for it can be obtained) there may be a liability to repay the compensation (1971 Act, s. 159), if a notice of payment has been entered in the local land charges register. There is a difficulty, however, that when the intending purchaser makes his local search the compensation may still be under negotiation or otherwise outstanding, in which case there will be no entry in the register, but one may be made before the purchaser wishes to develop. Therefore inquiry should be made as to the effect of any refusal, conditional grant, revocation or modification of planning permission. See further, *post*, p. 1181 *et seq.*

Special inquiries of local authorities.—In addition to the local land charges register the following registers and other particulars are kept by local authorities :—

(i) Registers of rents of regulated tenancies and of furnished lettings under the Rent Act, 1968, ss. 43 and 74, also the Housing Finance Act, 1972, ss. 39, 40 and 41.

(ii) Register of applications for planning permission. See above.

(iii) Statement of admitted rights of way made under the Highways Act, 1959, s. 34 (6).

(iv) List of streets maintainable at the public expense, kept by urban authorities (Highways Act, 1959, s. 38 (6), as amended by Local Government Act, 1972, Sched. 21, para. 15).

(v) Map of public sewers and certain other sewers (Public Health Act, 1936, s. 32).

(vi) Map of land subject to access agreements or orders under the National Parks and Access to the Countryside Act, 1949, Pt. V, kept by local planning authorities (*ibid.*, s. 78).

Questions on many of these matters are asked on the standard forms of inquiry of local authorities.

Conditions avoiding preliminary searches and inquiries.—The practice of making searches and inquiries before entering into a contract, however necessary in the interests of the purchaser, causes delay. Consequently, certain standard forms of conditions of sale were introduced containing provisions designed to make searches and local authority inquiries before contract unnecessary. These provisions did not need to form part of a contract based on the relevant forms of conditions but could be incorporated if the parties thought fit ; they have not been used frequently.

The principle behind such provisions is that the vendor should disclose matters about which the purchaser would otherwise inquire, in or prior to the contract, and if he does not do so the purchaser has the right to call on the vendor to remove such matters, or, in the alternative, the right to rescind the contract. Where the contract gives him such rights the purchaser is safe in deferring the corresponding inquiries until he investigates title. On the other hand, if one of these forms of condition is to be used the vendor should endeavour to disclose all incumbrances, notices, entries, etc., within the specified classes, preferably in the special conditions. It is thought that any relevant ones should normally appear from earlier search certificates and other documents or should be known to the vendor. The main reason why these conditions are seldom used is because vendors' solicitors are doubtful whether they can be sure of making full disclosure without themselves carrying out searches and inquiries ; the danger is that non-disclosure would give the purchaser the right to rescind and so there may be doubt as to whether the contract is firm until the purchaser makes searches before completion. Accordingly, the 1973 Revision of The Law Society's Conditions of Sale is drafted on the assumption that the purchaser will make all appropriate searches and inquiries before exchange of contracts. Therefore there is no such provision to be opted for. Instead, by Condition 2, the purchaser will only be able to rescind where, after negotiations began and before the contract was made, the vendor received notice in writing of any closing, demolition or clearance order or any compulsory acquisition affecting the property and the purchaser did not also receive such a notice.

The 18th edition of the National Conditions of Sale retains from earlier editions the general condition designed to avoid preliminary searches and inquiries. If the special conditions make it applicable, General Condition 13 provides that if, immediately before the making of the contract, the property is affected by any matter to which the condition applies, and the vendor has not disclosed such matter to the purchaser in the Special Conditions or otherwise by writing, then the purchaser may by notice in writing (referred to as a " Condition 13 notice ") *expressly referring to the condition* require the vendor to accept as a term of the contract that the vendor will cause the said matter to be effectively cancelled, removed or vacated on or before completion. This condition applies to the following :—

" (i) any matter entered in a register of local land charges other than either a matter to which paragraph (3) of condition 16 applies or a matter of general application over the district of any local planning or other authority ;

(ii) any closing order, demolition order or clearance order ;

(iii) any order or proposal, of which the vendor has had notice by writing or advertisement, for the compulsory acquisition or requisitioning of the property ;

(iv) any other matter mentioned in the Special Conditions as a matter to which this condition shall apply."

Unless within ten days from the receipt of the Condition 13 notice (exclusive of the day of such receipt) or within such longer time as the notice may prescribe, the vendor communicates in writing his acceptance of the term that the matter shall be cancelled, the contract is rescinded and time is of the essence of the condition. If the matter is one which cannot be removed there can be no object in the vendor purporting to undertake the obligation of doing so.

Assuming that one of the offending matters was not disclosed by the vendor, National Condition 13 (3) requires that the purchaser's notice must be given within twenty-eight days from the date of the contract. Thus, it is necessary for the purchaser to make his local search and inquiries within that period of twenty-eight days, which seems reasonably adequate.

PART 3. INQUIRIES OF VENDOR AND OTHERS

General note.—It is now common practice to address to the vendor's solicitor certain questions before entering into a contract. The conditions of sale, designed to avoid searches and local authority inquiries before contract, are not intended to affect this practice (although by appropriate additions to the relevant condition it might in some cases be possible to render inquiries of the vendor similarly unnecessary).

It is difficult to give a comprehensive account of the purposes of these inquiries. In the first place they may well cover the same ground as investigations by the purchaser or his surveyor or other agent ; as far as possible they should be drafted in such a way as to avoid this. Secondly, the searches and inquiries which are necessary depend largely on the nature of the property to be purchased. To some extent they overlap the so-called requisitions on title which might be made at a later stage. Except as to matters of title, however, a vendor's obligations appear to be limited so far as concerns answers to requisitions ; see further, *post*, p. 133. Therefore, there is obvious advantage in asking for information before signing a contract when the purchaser need not proceed if he is not satisfied with the answers given.

Answers to preliminary inquiries, like answers to requisitions, should refer to the knowledge of the vendor. It is not sufficient for a vendor's solicitor to reply to the best of his own knowledge, unless, perhaps, the matter is one more likely to be known by the solicitor than by his client. As there is no binding obligation to answer preliminary inquiries a solicitor who receives replies limited to the knowledge of the vendor's solicitor is in difficulty. It is wise to ask that further replies should be given by or on behalf of the vendor. It can be argued that a solicitor who fails to do so may be liable for negligence if his client suffers loss which would have been avoided by a statement of the vendor's knowledge. Compare the remarks as to requisitions, at p. 134, *post*.

A standard form of Enquiries before Contract (form Con. 29 (long)) published by Oyez Publishing, Ltd., and a shorter form (intended for use in relatively simple cases when many of the questions asked by the longer form would not be appropriate) are available. Opinions differ as to the exact scope of such preliminary inquiries and the circumstances of the transaction should be considered carefully, particularly before using that shorter (or any similar) form ; appropriate additions should be made to meet the requirements of a particular transaction. Against this, the unnecessary use of the long form (or failure to delete unnecessary questions) may well cause irritation and result in generally less helpful answers.

Inquiries as to planning matters are now so important and involve so many complicated rules that they are considered separately below.

Answers are representations only.—An answer to a question addressed to the vendor or his solicitor before contract will normally be a representation only on the part of the vendor. The answer forms no part of the contract for sale itself, so it cannot give rise to a breach of that contract as a misdescription. Again in *Mahon* v. *Ainscough* [1952] 1 All E.R. 337, the Court of Appeal held that a vendor's solicitor's answer, " I understand not," to a preliminary inquiry as to whether the property had suffered war damage, did not amount to a warranty ; it was pointed out that the standard form of preliminary inquiry which had been used contained a note to the effect that it was also necessary to inspect the property and make other inquiries and so it could hardly be argued that a reply was intended to be a warranty. The conclusion to be drawn from this case would be that one cannot rely greatly on answers to such inquiries. If it is proposed to rely on them the vendor should be called on to insert a term in the contract warranting their accuracy.

However, a wrong statement in answer to a preliminary inquiry may amount to a misrepresentation (see *Gilchester Properties, Ltd.* v. *Gomm* [1948] 1 All E.R. 493, as to the rents of the property). The consequences of an innocent misrepresentation, in terms of the remedies available to the purchaser, have become much more serious for a vendor since the Misrepresentation Act, 1967 (see *post*, p. 91) so even greater care is necessary when answering preliminary inquiries.

In this connection, the Council of The Law Society suggested (*Law Society's Gazette*, vol. 65, p. 468) that, *first*, a total disclaimer of responsibility attached to the whole of the answers would not be in the client's interest or in accordance with good conveyancing practice ; *secondly*, replies to the standard inquiries should be headed with a notice in the following form : " Replies to these inquiries are believed to be correct but their accuracy is not guaranteed, and they do not obviate the need to make appropriate searches, inquiries and inspections." The Council pointed out (i) that the note would not necessarily exclude liability for misrepresentation, but it might assist the vendor in showing that the purchaser had not relied on the representation ; (ii) it may be necessary further to qualify individual replies ; (iii) circumspection is necessary where the vendor's solicitor replies on factual matters

without reference to the vendor or without clear information from the vendor
or his agents ; (iv) where a reply contains a statement of belief, there must
exist good grounds for expressing the belief.

Further it should be observed that if the replies are qualified by some such
phrase as " so far as the vendor knows " then there is authority for saying
that they will not constitute sufficiently definite statements of fact to amount
to representations or, of course, misrepresentations (see *per* Romer, J., in
Gilchester Properties, Ltd. v. *Gomm* [1948] 1 All E.R. 493, at p. 495).

Following the 1967 Act, the current editions of the standard conditions of
sale now contain some general attempts to deal with misrepresentations at
this stage from a vendor's point of view. The National Conditions of Sale,
18th ed., Condition 17, has been extended to provide that "no error, misstatement or omission *in any preliminary answer concerning the property* . . .
shall annul the sale . . . " (italics supplied) ; the condition further proceeds
with a restriction upon the recovery of damages or compensation and with a
definition of "preliminary answer" which would appear to include any
statement made in any circumstances by the vendor or by the estate agents
or even solicitors acting for him. Equally, The Law Society's Conditions of
Sale, 1973 Revision, Condition 13, is expressed as extending similar protective
cover to "replies to any inquiry oral or written made with respect to the
property in the course of the negotiations leading to the contract." Reference
may further and generally be made to the discussion, *inter alia*, of certain
specially drafted conditions relating to vendors' possible misrepresentations
by John Adams in the *Law Society's Gazette*, vol. 67, at pp. 257 and 318.

This indicates the change of conveyancing practice. Nevertheless, the
question is how far these conditions have any effect. Section 3 of the 1967
Act enacts that any provision in any agreement excluding or restricting
either the liability or the remedies for misrepresentation of a party to a
contract shall be of no effect, but concludes "except to the extent (if any)
that, in any proceedings arising out of the contract, the court or arbitrator
may allow reliance on it as being fair and reasonable in the circumstances
of the case." Thus it is, at least, arguable that an exclusion clause (i.e., a
condition of sale as above) contained in a formal contract for the sale and
purchase of land, the terms of which have been approved by the solicitors
acting for each party, should as a rule not be disallowed.

A. INQUIRIES ON PLANNING MATTERS

General summary.—The effect of the Town and Country Planning Acts
on land proposed to be purchased is often a matter of great moment. The
problems which may concern the solicitor for a prospective purchaser may be
classified as follows :—

(1) What is the history of the land on planning matters ? This may
involve inquiries on the following topics :—

   (a) Has there been any infringement of planning law in the development of the land that may render a purchaser subject to
   enforcement proceedings ? "Development" may be by way
   of (i) building or other operations, or (ii) a material change of
   use ; see *post*, p. 1181.

   (b) Are there any restrictions, conditional permissions or other
   matters which may adversely affect the use of the land ?
   See pp. 16, 17.

(c) Was any claim made for compensation for depreciation in land value, and if so what is the "unexpended balance of established development value?" This question will arise only in the case of property which had a development value in 1948, and may still have value for development or further development. See *post*, p. 1203.

(2) What are the proposals of the local planning authority? This, in turn, raises two problems :—

(a) What development will be permitted? A firm answer can be obtained only by making application for planning permission for a particular development, but the development or structure plan may give useful information ; see *post*, pp. 16–17.

(b) Does the development or structure plan indicate any intention of the local planning authority to take adverse action under planning powers, or can such intention be ascertained otherwise? See *post*, p. 16.

There is apparently no implied obligation on the part of a vendor to disclose general restrictions on the purposes for which the property may be used, even though the present user is not lawful (*Mitchell* v. *Beacon Estates (Finsbury Park), Ltd.* (1949), 1 P. & C.R. 32 ; also cases noted in *Conveyancer N.S.*, vol. 14, p. 307). It is the business of the purchaser " if he does not protect himself by an express warranty, to satisfy himself that the premises are fit for the purposes for which he wants to use them, whether that fitness depends on the state of their structure, the state of the law, or on any other relevant circumstances " (*per* Devlin, J., in *Edler* v. *Auerbach* [1950] 1 K.B. 359, at p. 374, approved by the Court of Appeal in *Hill* v. *Harris* [1965] 2 Q.B. 601). Accordingly, it would appear clear that the vendor under an open contract cannot be required to show that the existing use of the land is an authorised one or that any buildings have been erected in accordance with planning restrictions. Therefore, if it is important for the purchaser to have information on these matters, he should take care to get it before he enters into a contract or should stipulate in the contract that it will be provided.

The inquiries a solicitor should make must vary very greatly according to the nature of the property. If, for instance, it is a dwelling-house in a residential area which is known to have been used as such for many years without any material alterations to it, and the purchaser wishes to use it as a residence, there is little or no reason for preliminary inquiries on planning matters. On the other hand very great care will be needed in dealing with business premises which have in the past been used for various different purposes and where the purpose for which they will be required in the future is doubtful ; compare, for instance, *London Investment and Mortgage Co., Ltd.* v. *Ember Estates, Ltd.* (1950), 1 P. & C.R. 188. Solicitors can protect the interests of their clients only by considering carefully the exact effect of the Town and Country Planning Acts on the particular property proposed to be purchased and by framing inquiries and endeavouring to obtain provisions in contracts appropriate to the circumstances of each case.

The inquiries a solicitor should make on reporting to a bank on title are specified in the *Law Society's Gazette*, vol. 63, p. 185.

Standard conditions of sale.—It is useful to remember that if the National Conditions of Sale, 18th ed., are used, the Special Conditions may express the property to be sold on the footing of a specified "authorised" use (i.e., a use which is established or permitted or for which permission is not required). If this is done and it appears before completion that the specified use is not an authorised use for the purpose of the Town and Country Planning enactments in force, the purchaser may rescind by virtue of National Condition 15 (3). Thus inquiries as to the relevant planning matters may be deferred until after contract *except* as to development other than changes of use. In other cases it is not wise to enter into a contract without inquiring as to any possible contravention of planning law which may adversely affect the purchaser. In particular, it should be noticed that the 1973 Revision of the Law Society's Conditions of Sale contains no similar provision (cp. General Condition 22 (3) of the 1953 edition, indicated in the 15th Edition of this book at p. 21).

Inquiries as to planning contraventions.—The purchaser will wish to know the purpose for which the property is being used and whether this is in accordance with planning restrictions. In the previous edition of this book (15th Edition, at p. 21) it was possible to reach the conclusion that (with trivial exceptions) it was sufficient to inquire as to development during the preceding four years only. The reason was that the period for service of an enforcement notice by a planning authority was four years from the carrying out of development without permission or from alleged failure to comply with a limitation or condition subject to which permission was granted (see Town and Country Planning Act, 1962, s. 45). Unfortunately, this relatively satisfactory state of affairs has ceased because, under the relevant provisions of the Town and Country Planning Act, 1968 (now ss. 87 and 88 of the 1971 Act), the four-year time limit for service of an enforcement notice ceased to have effect as regards certain notices. The new rules are set out *post*, p. 1201 *et seq.*

The main results for present purposes are :—

(i) Development by way of change of use only (other than to use as a single dwelling-house) will never be made lawful by lapse of time unless it occurred before the end of 1963. Thus inquiries as to changes of use must be made back to 1963 (except that four years will still suffice as to a single dwelling-house).

(ii) An enforcement notice relating to building or other operations may be served only within four years from the date of the breach of planning control. Thus, inquiries as to possible breaches relating to "operations" need only be made (as before) in respect of the preceding four years.

The opinion has sometimes been expressed that inquiries should be made on planning matters back to 1948 however difficult that may be in practice. One ground for that opinion is that the legislation does not make contravening development lawful after expiration of the period during which an enforcement notice may be served. This is true, but it is not considered that a purchaser could be adversely affected if it is too late for the authority to serve an enforcement notice because :—

(a) Although an injunction can sometimes be obtained to prevent contravening development it is reasonable to assume that a court would not exercise its discretion to grant an injunction after the expiration of the statutory period (compare *A.-G.* v. *Bastow* [1957] 1 Q.B. 514 ; *A.-G.* v. *Smith* [1958] 2 Q.B. 173).

(b) There is no other remedy for contravention of planning restrictions.

(c) Development charges can no longer be imposed even if one should
have been paid (but was not) in respect of development between
1st July, 1948, and 18th November, 1952. Section 74 (1) of the
Town and Country Planning Act, 1947 (which authorised land to be
charged) was repealed by the 1962 Act. Any charge previously
imposed will not bind a purchaser unless it is registered as a land
charge Class A (1947 Act, s. 74 (5)) and so would appear on a search
certificate.

It follows that the intending purchaser should ascertain the use to which
the land was put four years ago or in 1963 as appropriate and whether any
operations have been carried out or any material change has taken place in
the use of the land since that date which would amount to " development."
The definition of development and the circumstances in which planning
permission is required are stated in the chapter on Town and Country
Planning, post, p. 1181 et seq.

If permission was necessary the intending purchaser can ascertain by
searching the register of planning applications (ante, p. 7) whether it has
been obtained and whether any conditions were attached. In practice, a
separate search is not usually necessary as the agreed forms of additional
inquiry to be sent with local searches ask as to entries in the register ; see
ante, p. 7. Unauthorised development may result in an enforcement
notice being served on the purchaser under s. 87 of the 1971 Act. Unless
such a notice has taken effect before he searches, the only ways in which
he can ascertain whether one may be served on him are by inquiring whether
development has taken place and by inspecting the property to see if there
has been recent development.

Generally, service of an enforcement notice for breach of planning control
before 1st July, 1948, ceased to be possible after 1st July, 1951 (1947 Act,
s. 75 (1), proviso). Conditions imposed on permissions and consents granted
under the Town and Country Planning Acts or the Restriction of Ribbon
Development Acts, 1935 and 1943, may adversely affect the purchaser. In
practice these are usually registered as local land charges although that step
does not seem to be necessary (Rose v. Leeds Corporation [1964] 1 W.L.R.
1393, post, p. 629). Whether or not they are so registered the answers to the
usual additional inquiries made with local searches (ante, p. 6) disclose
entries in the planning register. Thus, the prospective purchaser who makes
searches and additional inquiries of local authorities before contract will know
of permissions granted and should ascertain whether any of them were
subject to any, and if so what, conditions or limitations. A permission
granted ten years ago may, for example, be subject to a time limit of twelve
years and so be of little value to a purchaser.

Unfortunately there is a complication that conditions imposed on permissions and consents granted under earlier planning legislation, including
the Restriction of Ribbon Development Act, 1935, and the Restriction of
Ribbon Development (Temporary Development) Act, 1943, remain enforceable. The better opinion appears to be that these should be registered in
the register of local land charges, in which case they will appear on the
search certificate, but this view is not universally held. Consequently it has
been suggested that, if the land adjoins a road which may have been affected
by those Acts, to remove doubt a supplementary inquiry might be made of

the planning authority whether all such conditions have been registered, and if not, whether any affect the particular property (*Solicitors' Journal*, vol. 97, p. 630).

In the following two special cases inquiries back to 1948 may be helpful to a purchaser :—

(i) Ascertainment of the use and extent of development which was lawful on 1st July, 1948, may be necessary to determine the extent of enlargement permitted without planning consent (Town and Country Planning Act, 1971, Sched. 8).

(ii) In connection with industrial premises it may be useful to know the authorised use in 1948 in order that the purchaser may take advantage of the Town and Country Planning General Development Order, 1973, Sched. 1, Class VIII.

Inquiries as to possible development by operations during the last four years can usually be made easily by inspection of the property and inquiry of the vendor. Otherwise inquiries may have to be made of tenants and others but the local planning authority are usually not able (even if willing) to say whether development has occurred ; that may have happened without the matter coming to their notice. If an abstract of title is available before contract it may give useful information.

The Council of The Law Society has recommended that the vendor's solicitor should supply to the purchaser's solicitor copies of all " outstanding planning permissions including any site layout or access plans, . . . i.e., all permissions, which have never been implemented by development and permissions which have been implemented within the preceding four years." The Council considered that there was " no obligation upon a vendor's solicitor to supply copies of spent permissions, i.e., temporary permissions which have expired by effluxion of time, or permissions which have been implemented by development completed more than four years previously." Copies of outstanding permissions granted to the vendor, or in his possession, should be supplied by the vendor's solicitor to the purchaser's solicitor free of charge ; copies of any other outstanding permissions required by the purchaser should be supplied by the vendor's solicitor at the cost of the purchaser (*Law Society's Gazette*, vol. 63, p. 21). As the exact terms of permissions (particularly regarding limitations or conditions) rarely appear in answers to additional inquiries of local authorities, such copies should be obtained from the vendor or otherwise unless there is no doubt about the granting of an adequate unconditional permission.

It is questionable whether the distinction between permissions implemented within the last four years, and other permissions, was ever sound. A permission granted over four years ago although implemented might be most important, for instance, because it contained onerous conditions or was limited so as to be operative for a specified period only—perhaps over four years. And, of course, the four-year time limit is no longer generally applicable to development by change of use.

Information or answers given informally by an official of a planning authority as to the authorised use should not, it is thought, in practice be relied on even though they may operate to estop the council from alleging that the facts are different (see *Wells* v. *Minister of Housing* [1967] 1 W.L.R. 1000 and *Lever (Finance), Ltd.* v. *Westminster (City) London Borough Council* [1971] 1 Q.B. 222 ; cp. *Southend-on-Sea Corporation* v. *Hodgson (Wickford), Ltd.* [1962] 1 Q B. 416 ; also *Norfolk County Council* v. *Secretary of State for the Environment* (1973), 117 Sol. J. 650).

Information from local searches.—Reasons have already been given why a search in the local land charges register should be made before contract (*ante*, p. 4 *et seq.*).

The following information on planning matters will appear from the search :—

(i) Whether any buildings have been listed as being of special architectural or historic interest (Town and Country Planning Act, 1971, s. 54).

(ii) Whether a notice has been served requiring the proper maintenance of waste land (*ibid.*, s. 65).

(iii) Any revocation or modification of planning permission (*ibid.*, s. 45).

(iv) Any order requiring the discontinuance of an existing use or the alteration or removal of a building (*ibid.*, s. 51).

(v) Any tree preservation order (*ibid.*, s. 60).

(vi) Whether any enforcement notice has taken effect requiring unauthorised development to be discontinued (*ibid.*, s. 87).

(vii) Any payment of compensation in respect of which a liability for repayment may arise on subsequent development ; see below.

A notice may be entered in the local land charges register of compensation paid under certain provisions of the Town and Country Planning Acts in respect of the refusal, conditional grant, revocation or modification of planning permission. Understandably, it is provided that no person may carry out thereafter " new development " of certain classes until repayment of the compensation has been made or secured. The classes are as follows :—

1. Development of a residential, commercial or industrial character consisting wholly or mainly of houses, flats, shop or office premises or industrial buildings.

2. The winning and working of minerals.

3. Development " to which, having regard to the probable value of the development, it is in the opinion of the Minister reasonable that this section should apply " (1971 Act, s. 152 (2)).

In practice purchasers will not often be concerned as it is unlikely that permission will be given enabling such development to take place if there has already been a refusal or conditional grant of such a nature that compensation has become payable. A purchaser may be warned of the possibility by his inquiry as to previous planning applications and by registration of the compensation payment, or his further inquiry as to any outstanding payment ; see *ante*, p. 12.

Future planning proposals.—A person who proposes to buy land for development will be well advised to make application for planning permission before entering into a contract if there is any doubt about the grant of permission. Anyone who genuinely hopes to acquire an interest in land may make a valid application (*Hanily* v. *Minister of Local Government and Planning* [1952] 2 Q.B. 444). Where permission is granted (unless it provides otherwise) it enures for the benefit of the land and of all persons for the time being interested therein (1971 Act, s. 33 (1)). A further reason for obtaining planning permission at an early stage is the advantage that may thereby be obtained on subsequent compulsory purchase ; see *post*, p. 1208.

It may be advisable to inspect the development or structure plan on behalf of a purchaser as it contains such matters as allocation of areas of land for use for agricultural, residential, industrial or other purposes, and designates certain land as subject to compulsory purchase (1971 Act, ss. 6–21). As a result, it provides a guide to the classes of development which are likely to be permitted on any land, but it will not be conclusive, as a planning authority must also have regard to other material considerations in considering applications for planning permission (*ibid.*, s. 29 (1)). The agreed forms of additional inquiry ask, however, as to whether the plan, or proposals for alterations or additions thereto (i) designate the property as subject to compulsory acquisition, (ii) indicate the primary use for the area in which the property is situated (in which case particulars of that use are requested), or (iii) indicate any other matter which specifically affects the property (in which case short particulars are requested). It follows that in normal cases all essential information is obtained from the customary form of inquiries of a local authority.

It does not follow that the local planning authority will object to a use of premises for some purpose other than that indicated as the primary one for the area. Thus, a limited number of shops in appropriate positions may be necessary in a residential area. Further, if there is a valid existing use the local planning authority can require it to cease only on payment of compensation (Town and Country Planning Act, 1971, ss. 51 and 170). Consequently, a prospective purchaser will not normally be concerned if he finds that the existing use of the premises does not accord with the primary use of the area. An application for planning permission might be wise, however, if an extension of the premises or other development was proposed.

Specific proposals, for instance, allocation of land for road widening, require serious consideration by a prospective purchaser. Although they will normally be carried out only after payment of full compensation, his possession may be disturbed and difficulty may be experienced with mortgagees.

As to how far it is safe to rely on an informal statement by an official of the local planning authority that permission is unnecessary, see the cases cited *post*, pp. 1187–1188.

B. INQUIRIES OTHER THAN ON PLANNING MATTERS

General inquiries.—An inquiry is often made of the vendor as to whether there are any outgoings, other than the usual rates and taxes. It appears that the vendor is obliged in any case to disclose any tithe redemption annuity; see *post*, p. 103.

It is common practice to ask whether the property is subject to any easement or public or other similar right or, in the case of registered land, any overriding interest. The extent of the obligation to disclose these is considered *post*, p. 97. As a vendor is not in general obliged to disclose patent defects in title, and as reliance on covenants for title may not be possible, particularly if easements or other adverse rights over the land were created many years ago, a purchaser must make adequate inspections and inquiries, particularly as the vendor's answer to questions on these subjects may be non-committal. Some assistance may be gained from maps kept by the local authority under the Highways Act, 1959, s. 34, or the National Parks and Access to the Countryside Act, 1949 ; see *ante*, pp. 7–8.

The standard forms of inquiry of the appropriate local authority ask whether the property is drained into a public sewer. It may be necessary, however, to inquire of the vendor whether rights of drainage exist over intermediate land. Where the answer of the local authority indicates that there is a combined drainage agreement, the vendor should be asked to supply a copy. As services such as water, gas and electricity are not usually mentioned in particulars of sale, it is wise to endeavour to ascertain whether they are provided directly to the property by statutory undertakers, as otherwise it is necessary to know whether easements or other rights exist. The fact that the vendor is himself unaware of such matters is some indication that no problem has arisen in the past.

It is useful to ask for particulars of all notices affecting the property served on the vendor. Very many different types of notice may have been served, for example under public health, housing and planning legislation. In the case of an old property an important type of notice which is likely is a sanitary notice under the Public Health Act, 1936, s. 93. Even if such a notice has not been complied with, no reference to the fact will appear on the local search but it will be disclosed in answer to the usual additional inquiries.

Prior to purchase of land in a compulsory registration area, and possibly in some other cases, it is advisable to ascertain whether the title to the land or any part of it has been registered or a caution against first registration or a priority notice has been lodged. This should be done by forwarding to the Land Registry an official index search on printed form 96. Generally no fee is payable although bulk applications affecting numerous properties will be charged for according to the actual cost of the work invo!ved (see Ruoff and Roper, Registered Conveyancing, 3rd ed., p. 55). A plan need not be provided in compulsory areas if a description by street number enables the land to be identified on the maps kept at the registry.

Tenancies and licences.—Conditions of sale commonly state expressly whether the property is sold with vacant possession or subject to tenancies, particulars of which are given. In the absence of express provision it is usually implied that the sale is with vacant possession ; see *post*, p. 199. In practice, it is necessary that the purchaser should satisfy himself as to any tenancies and the incidents thereof. In any case, a tenant's occupation may be notice to a purchaser of his rights subject to the provisions of the L.C.A. 1972 (*Hunt* v. *Luck* [1902] 1 Ch. 428 ; L.R.A. 1925, s. 70 (1) (*g*) ; see *post*, pp. 166–167). Further, it now appears that the rights of a licensee may in some circumstances remain binding on a purchaser of the land and so it may be necessary to inquire as to the existence of licences to occupy or use the land. A purchaser should, therefore, inspect the property with a view to ascertaining evidence on such matters and call for and examine all leases, tenancy agreements and licences, with particular reference to the performance of covenants, and the termination of tenancies and licences.

The National Conditions of Sale, 18th ed., General Condition 18, states that, copy leases having been made available, the purchaser is deemed to have notice of and to take subject to all the existing tenancies and the rights of the tenants notwithstanding any partial or incomplete statement in the Special Conditions. Comparably, The Law Society's Conditions of Sale, 1973 Revision, General Condition 3 (2) (3), provides that, where the property is sold subject to any lease or tenancy, the vendor shall furnish full particulars but that the sale shall not be affected by any partial, incomplete or inaccurate statement in the contract with reference thereto if honestly made. This latter set of conditions, unlike the former, on the face of it does not appear to envisage pre-contract disclosure of particulars by the vendor, although this should be the practice. It appears clear that neither condition would be construed as imposing on the purchaser a tenancy quite different from any one of which copies or particulars had been supplied by the vendor (see *Pagebar Properties, Ltd.* v. *Derby Investment Holdings, Ltd.* [1973] 1 All E.R. 65). Further it seems possible that both conditions would be ineffective with regard to any statements amounting to misrepresentations as being provisions excluding or restricting liability (see s. 3 of the Misrepresentation Act, 1967 ; this point was not adverted to in the last cited case).

Leaseholds.—When instructed by an intending purchaser of leasehold property the solicitor should ask him if he is satisfied that the property is in a fair state of repair, and should tell him that if it is not he may, directly the lessor gets to know that he has purchased, get a notice from him to put the property into repair. In this connection it is important to bear in mind that the production of the last receipt for ground rent is not necessarily evidence that a covenant for repair has been carried out. Section 45 (2) of the L.P.A. 1925 only provides that on production of the last receipt for ground rent a purchaser must assume that the covenants and provisions have been performed and observed, if the contrary does not appear. But it may appear, and in that case the production of the receipt means nothing. See further at p. 102.

If the current Law Society's Conditions of Sale, 1973 Revision, or the National Conditions of Sale, 18th ed., are incorporated in the contract the purchaser will be deemed to purchase with full notice of the actual state of repair and will be required to take the property as it stands (Law Society's General Condition 4 (2) (*a*) ; National Condition 12 (3)). As to consequent modifications of the covenants for title, see *post*, p. 471.

Also it may be desirable to inquire as to the possibility of a Schedule D income tax charge arising on assignments of a lease granted for a term of fifty years or less at an undervalue (i.e., under s. 81 (1) of I.C.T.A. 1970 : see *post*, p. 1130). If there is any substantial doubt about this matter, the facts should be submitted to the inspector of taxes for a certificate, in effect, as to the amount of any charge (i.e., under s. 81 (2), *ibid.*).

Minerals.—It may be important to ascertain whether the minerals are included in the property sold, and, if not, whether there is a provision that compensation will be allowed in case of subsidence. Even if the minerals are not sold with the land, the owner of such minerals (not being the owner of the surface) who claims the right to cause the surface to subside, must generally show that he has been granted, either in express terms or by necessary implication, a right so to do. See further, *post*, p. 500 *et seq.*

If minerals are not included in the property sold or any right to withdraw support exists, the contract should state that such is the case. Unless the contract states otherwise, all mines and minerals (with the exceptions of gold, silver, petroleum and coal) are deemed included in the sale, and a vendor who is not able to convey other minerals will not be able to make a good title (*Bellamy* v. *Debenham* [1891] 1 Ch. 412 ; *Re Jackson and Haden's Contract* [1906] 1 Ch. 412).

All coal and mines of coal are now vested in the National Coal Board and the rights to withdraw support vested in the Board are specified in the Coal Act, 1938, Sched. 2, Pt. II. See p. 501. In dealing with land under which coal is known, or thought, to exist, solicitors will no doubt bear in mind the rules relating to withdrawal of support and will advise intending purchasers as occasion demands. The ownership of coal and of mines of coal is now a matter of general law presumed to be known to purchasers, and so no express mention of such ownership need be inserted in contracts for sale of land. As the right (if any) of the National Coal Board to withdraw support depends on the state of affairs existing on 1st January, 1939, if any such right exists the contract may have to be made subject to it. See further at p. 502.

The Coal-Mining (Subsidence) Act, 1957, provides for the execution of remedial works and the making of payments in respect of damage caused by subsidence resulting from the working of coal. Certain notices, which can be served pursuant to the Act, may be of particular concern to a purchaser and, if a building is likely to be, or to have been, affected by subsidence, inquiries should be made of the vendor whether notices have been served, and any necessary information should be obtained from the National Coal Board.

The main matters of concern to a purchaser are :—

(i) Notice to the Board of the occurrence of damage (*ibid.*, s. 2 (1)).

(ii) Notice by the Board of their decision whether they will pay compensation instead of executing remedial works where that option is open to the Board (*ibid.*, s. 2 (2)).

(iii) Notice of the Board's decision to do emergency works only because further damage is likely (*ibid.*, s. 3).

(iv) Requirement by the Board that preventive works be carried out (*ibid.*, s. 4).

On purchase of an active or closed tip inquiries should be made as to the possible application of the Mines and Quarries (Tips) Act, 1969, e.g., if instability of a disused tip causes action by a local authority.

Agricultural land.—Under s. 30 of the Agricultural Holdings Act, 1948, *post*, p. 958, a current notice to quit may become void on the making of the contract for sale of the holding unless the tenant will agree that the notice shall remain in force.

As a result of the complicated provisions of the Agriculture Act, 1947, s. 86, the consent of the Minister of Agriculture, Fisheries and Food may have to be obtained to the sale of a *part* only of an " agricultural unit " (defined *ibid.*, s. 109 (2)). If this is not done the Minister may, within three years thereafter, purchase the land compulsorily. Consent may be refused only if the Minister is satisfied that it is expedient so to do in order to avoid a less efficient use of the land for agriculture (*ibid.*, s. 86 (4)). The section has not yet come into force at the time of writing.

An intending purchaser may wish to know what claims for compensation may be made and a general inquiry should be addressed to the vendor. The rules as to compensation are outlined in the part on Agricultural Tenancies, *post*, p. 942.

Streets and roads.—One of the inquiries customarily made of the appropriate local authority is whether the roadways (including footpaths) abutting on the property are maintained at the public expense. If they are not a prospective purchaser must be warned as to potential liability, particularly if the authority resolve to make up a street or road under statutory powers. It is important to remember that the definition of a " private street " in the Highways Act, 1959 (under which local authorities require them to be made up or make them up, and, in either case, take them over) is a " street not being a highway maintainable at the public expense " and includes land deemed to be such by virtue of a declaration under s. 206 ; " street " includes a cul-de-sac, a footpath or an alley (*ibid.*, ss. 213, 295).

Standard additional enquiries ask whether a local authority have resolved to make up roadways not maintainable at public expense at the cost of frontagers or to adopt them without cost to frontagers, and search in the local land charges register discloses any provisional and final apportionment of cost.

It is particularly important, where adjoining roads and streets have not become repairable by the public, to ascertain whether land being purchased is, or may be, affected by the " advance payments code " in the Highways Act, 1959, ss. 192 to 199, which replaces the New Streets Act, 1951, as amended.

This code applies in all outer London boroughs, in all counties in which the code was in force before 1st April, 1974 (boroughs and urban districts and those rural districts to which it had been applied by order of the Secretary of State for the Environment), and in any parish or community in which it is thereafter adopted (1959 Act, s. 192 (5), as amended by Local Government Act, 1972, Sched. 21). Broadly the intention is to ensure that before buildings are erected either (i) the streets are made up, or (ii) a deposit or security is given to the local authority for the cost, or (iii) an agreement for making up and taking them over is entered into pursuant to s. 40 (*post*, p. 23.) No work may be done for the erection of a building for which plans are required to be deposited in accordance with building regulations if the building will have a frontage on to a private street, unless the owner has paid to the local authority or secured tc the satisfaction of the authority the payment of the sum estimated as representing the cost, appropriate to the frontage of the building, of making the street to the standard required for adoption as a highway repairable by the public (*ibid.*, ss. 192 (1), 1973, as amended by the Public Health Act, 1961, s. 11 (2), Sched. 1, Pt. III, and Local Government Act, 1972, Sched. 21, para. 70). No deposit or security is required, however, in certain cases, for instance where—

   (i) the street is already substantially built up, or is not likely to become joined to a highway in a reasonable time ;

  (ii) the local authority grant exemption because it is not likely to become joined to a highway maintainable at the public expense in a reasonable time ; or

 (iii) the authority are satisfied that more than three-quarters of the frontage of the street, or of a relevant part not less than one hundred yards in length, consists, or is likely to consist, of industrial premises *and* that their private street works powers are unlikely to be exercised in a reasonable time ; or

 (iv) where an agreement has been made *by any person* under s. 40 of the Highways Act, 1959, as to which, see *post*, p. 23 (*ibid.*, s. 193 (2)).

For the present purpose the words " private street " include land shown as a proposed street on plans deposited with respect to [the building] either under building regulations or on an application for planning permission (*ibid.*, s. 213 (1), as amended by the Public Health Act, 1961, s. 11 (2), Sched. 1, Pt. III).

The local authority may serve an amending notice reducing the sum to be paid or secured if they revise their estimate of cost (*ibid.*, s. 193 (3)). Where this step is taken, but payment has already been made, or security given, the local authority must refund any excess payment to the *owner for the time being* of the land ; if the person whose property is security is for the time being owner the security must be released, otherwise the security must be realised and the excess paid to the owner for the time being (*ibid.*, s. 193 (6)).

According to the Quarter Sessions Appeal Committee decision in *Cruse* v. *Tidswell*, reported and discussed in the *Conveyancer, N.S.*, vol. 22, p. 120 *et seq.*, a notice requiring payment or security relates to a particular frontage. If this is so on amended plans being passed affecting the same frontage the local authority need not serve a further notice.

Notices served by an authority requiring payment or security and certain other matters mentioned *post*, p. 627 *et seq.*, are registrable in the local land charges register and so a purchaser is warned.

Where a sum has been paid or secured the liability of the owner or any subsequent owner in respect of the carrying out of street works under the private street works code is discharged *but to the extent of the sum paid or secured only* (*ibid.*, s. 195 (1)). Any further sum payable when the street works are eventually carried out will be recoverable from the then owner under the normal private street works procedure. On the other hand, if, when the street is declared to be a highway maintainable at the public expense, the sum paid or secured is found to exceed the total liability in respect of the carrying out of street works, or there is no liability because the street was not made up at the expense of the local authority, the excess or the sum paid, as the case may be, must be refunded to the *person who is for the time being the owner*. If the sum was secured and the person whose property is security is for the time being the owner, the security must be released to the extent of the excess, or wholly, as the case may be. If the sum was secured and the person whose property is security is not for the time being the owner (e.g., if the land has been sold since security was given by means of a charge on other property) the amount of the excess or, as the case may be, the whole sum, must be paid to the *owner for the time being* and the local authority may realise the security for the purpose of recovering the amount so paid (*ibid.*). Where the proposal to build is abandoned after payment on account of street charges, repayment must be made in a similar manner to the *owner for the time being* (*ibid.*, s. 196 (1)).

The obligation to make a refund *to the owner for the time being* often has unexpected results. If a builder has made a deposit or given security he should not covenant to make up the road without providing that any repayment of the whole or part of the sum paid or secured will be refunded to him ; compare the remarks *post*, p. 23.

Where land in respect of which a sum has been paid or secured is subsequently divided into two or more parts, so that two or more owners incur liability in respect of the street works, the sum is treated as apportioned between those owners according to their respective frontages (*ibid.*, s. 196 (2)).

The two essential points are, first, that payment or security may not completely discharge a future liability for street works and, secondly, that any repayment by the local authority of the whole or part of the sum will be to the owner for the time being. Therefore, if building land is sold after payment has been made or security given, the price should be increased on account of the value to the purchaser of the payment or security (just as a higher price would be paid if the adjoining street had been made up). Similarly, if an owner who has made a payment or given security erects on the land and sells houses, the purchaser of each house may safely pay a price based on the assumption that any future liability for street charges will be largely, if not entirely, discharged. Compare *Henshall* v. *Fogg* [1964] 1 W.L.R. 1127, C.A.

It often happens that after a sum has been paid or secured certain street works are carried out otherwise than at the expense of the local authority, for instance, under covenant by the builder of houses fronting the street. Under the 1951 Act the local authority were not able to refund any sum deposited with them, or to release security, unless the street was declared repairable by the public, in which case refund was made to the owner for the time being as stated above. In practice a builder often made the deposit or gave security and undertook in favour of purchasers of houses to make up the roads. In these cases it was inconvenient that repayment should be to the purchasers who did not wish to be concerned in any way with road charges. Further, there was no power to recompense the builder if he did part, but not all, of the necessary road works. To avoid these difficulties the Highways Act, 1959, s. 194 (1), provides that where a sum has been paid or secured and street works are subsequently carried out to the satisfaction of, but otherwise than at the expense of the authority, the authority "*may* refund to the person at whose expense the works are carried out the whole or such proportion of that sum or, as the case may be, release the whole or such part of the security, as in their opinion represents the amount by which the liability of the owner of that land in respect of street works has been reduced as a result of the carrying out of the said street works." It will be noted that a local authority are not obliged to do this. Moreover, where the person at whose expense the works are carried out is not the owner for the time being, that owner must be notified of the proposal and given an opportunity of making representations (*ibid.*).

Where a sum has been paid or secured and *thereafter* the local authority exempt the street or a relevant part thereof from the statutory requirements, the local authority must refund that sum to the *person who is for the time being the owner* of the land (apportioned if necessary) or release the security (*ibid.*, s. 192 (4)).

Where street works have been executed the local authority may, by notice to be fixed up in the street, declare the street, or a relevant part thereof, to be a highway maintainable at public expense (Highways Act, 1959, s. 202). The Act also contains provision for the making up under the private street works code and the taking over of the street at the request of a majority of frontagers (*ibid.*, s. 203 (1)).

A failure by the vendor or a predecessor to make a payment or to give security would not render a purchaser liable to any penalty, but before contract, in an appropriate case, it is advisable to inquire whether this has been done, and (if applicable) what is the value apportioned to the frontage of the land being purchased. The purchaser will then know the extent to which he will be protected against a demand by the local authority on account of street charges. There is no need to mention in contracts or conveyances the fact that a payment has been made or security given, as the Act operates to transfer the benefit to the purchaser even if he does not know of it.

Agreements as to street works.—It has been noted above that it is not necessary to make a deposit or give security for road charges in cases in which an agreement is made with the local authority under the Highways Act, 1959, s. 40, for the making up of the street (*ibid.*, s. 192 (3) (*d*)). In practice many builders prefer to enter into an agreement and so avoid the need to make payments or give security. Such an agreement may be entered into even after a sum has been paid or secured and may provide for the refund of such sum or any part thereof or for the release of security (1959 Act, s. 194 (3)).

In practice such agreements are normally adequate protection for purchasers of houses but some doubt has been thrown on their enforceability by the highway authority ; see the discussions in *Solicitors' Journal*, vol. 108, pp. 126, 183, 195 and 611. Nevertheless, the better opinion seems to be that the authority can enforce them and, provided adequate security is given (for instance by bond executed by an insurance company) a purchaser may reasonably rely on the existence of the agreement ; if the builder is of good financial standing the insertion in the conveyance of a covenant to make up the road to the satisfaction of the highway authority, and to maintain it to that satisfaction until declared a highway repairable by the public is a useful further safeguard.

The Council of The Law Society have drawn attention to a number of points concerning a purchaser or mortgagee, for example, that an agreement should be expressed to be made under s. 40, whether the builder is expressed to be obliged to construct and maintain the road to the satisfaction of the authority, whether they may do work in default and whether the authority undertake to adopt the road when completed (*Law Society's Gazette*, vol. 62, p. 537). Accordingly the Council recommend that the vendor's solicitor should, free of charge—

(i) supply a copy of the agreement and bond or an abstract or extract showing at least the main essentials, together with a copy of the site plan, or (if it is large) at least an extract covering the material part ;

(ii) produce the vendor's duplicate or counterpart of the agreement for inspection with the deeds, and allow it to be included in an acknowledgment for production of deeds ;

(iii) if so required authorise the authority to give any particulars required by the purchaser or his mortgagee and to allow inspection of the originals.

These recommendations are limited to the text of the agreement and the site plan and do not extend to constructional specifications and drawings.

The Building Societies Association has issued a circular drawing attention to the chief problems affecting societies, as mortgagees ; the suggestions are discussed in the *Solicitors' Journal*, vol. 108, pp. 811, 812.

Such agreements do not normally require registration but if they contain an option for the local authority to acquire the developer's estate in the land over which the highway will exist they should be registered as estate contracts in the land charges register and an entry will remain until the interest is acquired. Few agreements contain such a provision ; the usual terms as to dedication of a road to the public and adoption by the authority as a highway repairable by the public provide no reason for registration.

Public utilities street works.—The main object of the Public Utilities Street Works Act, 1950, is to regulate the relations between highway authorities and statutory undertakers. The following provisions are the only ones likely to require consideration in the course of conveyancing practice.

A local authority may declare any street not repairable by the public to be a " prospectively maintainable highway " (*ibid.*, Sched. 2, para. 1). The declaration must be registered in the local land charges register (*ibid.*, para. 2) and so it will be disclosed on a purchase of land fronting on the street. It indicates that the street is likely to be taken over at some time in the future as a highway repairable by the public, but its only direct effect is to enable the local authority to consider plans of statutory undertakers affecting the street and to exercise various powers under the Act (see, for instance, *ibid.*, s. 3 (1), as read with s. 2 (1) (*a*)). The local authority who have made such a declaration are obliged to ensure that the rights of frontagers are protected (*ibid.*, ss. 9, 2 (5) (*b*)), and so the making of a declaration will not normally be in any way contrary to the interests of the frontagers.

Special inquiries.—There are many ways in which land can be affected by statutory provisions which are unlikely to affect small parcels of land, but which may need attention. Examples are—

(i) agreements with statutory water undertakers regarding works on the land (these are registrable as land charges : Water Act, 1945, s. 15, as amended by Water Act, 1973, Sched. 8, para. 49) ;

(ii) on sale and purchase of a disused tip associated with a mine or quarry the possible consequences of action under the Mines and Quarries (Tips) Act, 1969, should be considered. For example, contribution orders for expenses of remedial action for danger may be made against any person who has had an estate or interest in the previous twelve years (*ibid.*, s. 19) ;

(iii) forestry dedication covenants (these are probably registrable in Class D as restrictive covenants ; Forestry Act, 1967, s. 5) ;

(iv) orders and directions creating rights over land or controlling the use of land for the purposes of an aerodrome ; these are registrable as local land charges (Civil Aviation Act, 1949, ss. 24, 26, 33 ; Civil Aviation Act, 1962, s. 22 ; Airports Authority Act, 1965, s. 17 (4), Sched. 4, Pt. II) ; a right in or in relation to land granted or agreed to be granted by the Board of Trade (now Department of Trade and Industry) after 25th October, 1968, is not enforceable by virtue of s. 23 (7) of the 1949 Act (which grants powers in connection with civil aviation) against a purchaser for money or money's worth of a legal estate unless before completion the grant or agreement has been registered in the appropriate local land charges register (Civil Aviation Act, 1968, s. 21) ;

(v) access agreements or orders under the National Parks and Access to the Countryside Act, 1949 ; maps indicating land subject to these are kept by local planning authorities (*ibid.*, s. 78) ; agreements between landowners on the one hand and the Countryside Commission or a local authority on the other hand made under the Countryside Act, 1968, are binding on successors in title (*ibid.*, s. 45 (3)) : consequently a purchaser of land which might be affected should make a specific inquiry as to the existence of any such agreement ;

(vi) coast protection works schemes, which are registrable as local land charges (Coast Protection Act, 1949, s. 8 (8)) ; a river board or other authority who do work pursuant to the Coastal Flooding (Emergency Provisions) Act, 1953, may be entitled to have the work left in place and to maintain it (*ibid.*, s. 5 (1)) ;

(vii) licences for felling trees granted by the Forestry Commissioners may contain conditions for securing the stocking or re-stocking of the same or other land (Forestry Act, 1967, s. 12 (1) ; Trees Act, 1970, s. 2) ; such conditions are enforceable against the fee simple owner for the time being and so become a burden on the land which should be disclosed by a vendor (*ibid.*, ss. 24, 26). In the absence of express agreement to the contrary, costs of complying with conditions are recoverable from the person who applied for the licence. Consequently, a purchaser who takes subject to such conditions, and is required to comply with them, may have a personal action against the vendor who obtained a felling licence, but did not comply fully with all conditions. The Forestry Act, 1967, s. 24, enables conditions to be enforced against the "owner." This term is defined by s. 34 of the 1967 Act as the person in whom for the time being is vested the legal estate in fee simple, except (i) where all persons appearing to the Minister to be concerned agree, with the approval of the Minister, that some other person shall be treated as the owner, and (ii) the Agricultural Land Tribunal determine that some other person shall be treated as owner ;

(viii) orders made by a Minister for the removal, re-siting or alteration of an object obstructing an airfield used for defence purposes (Land Powers (Defence) Act, 1958, ss. 10, 11) ; on purchase of land outside a built-up area it would seem advisable to inquire whether it is within two miles of such an airfield and, if so, to ascertain whether an order has been, or is likely to be, made ;

(ix) wayleave orders vesting in a Minister rights to instal and use oil pipe lines and accessory works (Land Powers (Defence) Act, 1958, s. 17) ; these orders are registrable in the register of local land charges ;

(x) compulsory rights orders granting temporary rights of use and occupation of land for opencast coal operations (Opencast Coal Act, 1958, s. 4) ; these orders are registrable in the register of local land charges ;

(xi) on purchase of land adjoining a railway line enquiry should be made whether the British Railways Board remains liable, pursuant to the Railway Clauses Consolidation Act, 1845, s. 68, to maintain fences ; in many cases the company contracted out of this liability by payment of compensation to adjoining owners. If the vendor is unaware enquiry should be made of the Board. The matter is explained in the *Law Society's Gazette*, vol. 58, p. 743.

There is a good account of the answers to various questions likely to be raised by a purchaser of riparian land in the *Justice of the Peace*, vol. 121, p. 345 *et seq.* An explanation of the potential liabilities is contained in the *Law Society's Gazette*, vol. 58, p. 517. The Land Drainage Act, 1961 (now amended by Water Act, 1973, Sched. 8, paras. 72–75), was passed more recently under which drainage rates and drainage charges can be levied for a variety of purposes ; their operation is not limited to agricultural land, and they may be imposed on such land even if it is not within an internal drainage district.

A river authority may arrange with the owner of chargeable land for drainage charges to be levied on the owner instead of on the occupier (Agriculture (Miscellaneous Provisions) Act, 1968, s. 25). A 10 per cent. discount is payable to the owner in certain circumstances (*ibid.*, s. 25 (2)). Notice must be given to the occupier who is obliged to pay the amount of the charges to the owner ; alternatively he may prevent or determine the arrangement if he wishes (*ibid.*, s. 25 (3)).

Section 35 of that Act requires every drainage board to prepare and keep up to date a register containing prescribed information in respect of the drainage hereditaments in their district and a map thereof ; both will be available for public inspection.

Other problems which do not arise frequently but may require particular investigation are as follows :—

(a) Particular inquiries may be necessary if an intending purchaser proposes to abstract water from an " inland water " or from underground strata or to discharge sewage or trade effluent to a stream. With minor exceptions (for instance, for domestic or agricultural purposes) a licence from the river authority is necessary for abstraction of water (Water Resources Act, 1963, s. 23) and inquiry should be made whether a vendor holds a licence and as to the terms. A register of applications for licences is kept by each river authority (ibid., s. 53).

There are awkward provisions in the 1963 Act, s. 32, as to succession to licences to abstract water. If the original holder (i) occupies the whole of the land specified in the licence on which the water is used, (ii) dies or (for instance, on sale) ceases to occupy any part of that land, and (iii) immediately thereon someone else (" the successor ") occupies the whole then (other than on death of the original holder) the successor becomes holder of the licence. However, the successor ceases to be holder of the licence one month after the date when he became occupier unless within that period he has given to the river authority notice of the change in occupation. Thus on sale of the whole with vacant possession, provided due notice is given, the purchaser can be sure of having a licence ; otherwise he must apply for a licence, if he wishes to continue to abstract water. See the Water Resources (Succession to Licensee) Regulations, 1969 (S.I. 1969 No. 976).

Similarly, consent is necessary for the making of a new discharge, or continuance of a discharge existing before 1st June, 1963, of trade or sewage effluent, but consent enures for the benefit of subsequent owners or occupiers (Rivers (Prevention of Pollution) Acts, 1951 and 1961). A register of any *conditions* imposed on consents is kept by river authorities (1951 Act, s. 7 (7)), but not of consents themselves. These matters are further discussed by Professor J. F. Garner in the *Conveyancer N.S.*, vol. 27, p. 489 *et seq.*

Whether or not abstraction is proposed it is advisable to inquire as regards riparian land, or land in an internal drainage district, whether there is any special liability such as a drainage rate or an order prohibiting use of land in a way that might result in pollution. Inquiries should be forwarded to the clerk of the water authority (Water Act, 1973, Pt. II).

Further enquiries which may be made of water authorities are considered in a useful article in *Solicitors' Journal*, vol. 111, p. 422.

(b) On purchase of land of appreciable area it may be advisable to inquire whether there is any liability of the owner for the time being to meet the cost of repair of the chancel of the parish church, for instance, as lay impropriator of a tithe rentcharge. In *Chivers and Sons Ltd.* v. *Air Ministry* [1955] Ch. 585, it was held that a purchaser of part of land, which had been allotted under the Inclosure Act, 1833, in lieu of rectorial or great tithes, was liable to repair the chancel. That liability rested on the several owners of parts of the rectorial property in proportion to the areas owned by each. In that case the abstract showed that the land had been awarded in lieu of rectorial property but a shorter title might well not make any reference to the matter. As a vendor may not know of the liability (which may, but rarely does, apply to ecclesiastical property other than the chancel of a church), and is unlikely to be liable on covenants for title in the conveyance on failure to disclose it, a purchaser of land of appreciable area and in a neighbourhood in which such a liability might be expected should make his own inquiries.

A liability to repair attached to the ownership of tithe rent-charge is indicated on the Record of Ascertainments prepared by the former Tithe Redemption Commission; some parishes hold copies of this record. The liability may arise in a few other cases, however, as in the case quoted in the last paragraph. The Tithe Redemption Commission prepared a memorandum on Chancel Repair and a copy can be obtained from the Controller, Tithe Redemption Office, Inland Revenue, Barrington Road, Worthing, Sussex ; reference should be made to this in cases of doubt.

The matter is also discussed in the *Law Times*, vol. 220, pp. 237, 263 and 293 ; there is a very useful summary of the reasons causing the liability to attach to land, *ibid.*, p. 294.

(c) On purchase of rural land it may be advisable to inquire of the county council whether any enclosure award may affect the land. Investigation of the contents of such awards is usually a lengthy task but unexpected burdens, such as rights of way or public rights over the land occasionally come to light. Compare *Wyld* v. *Silver* [1963] Ch. 243.

If any question may arise as to whether land is common land or a town or village green or as to rights of common over such land the provisions as to registration thereof contained in the Commons Registration Act, 1965, should be considered. All such land and rights must be registered between 2nd January, 1967, and 31st March, 1970, and provision is made for the vesting of unclaimed land, for instance, in the local authority. Final registration of such land and rights will be conclusive evidence of matters registered (*ibid.*, s. 10).

Provisional registration, however, is not merely not conclusive evidence, but is no evidence at all of those matters (*Cooke* v. *Amey Gravel Co., Ltd.* [1972] 1 W.L.R. 1310 ; see also *Thorne Rural District Council* v. *Bunting* [1972] 2 W.L.R. 517).

A special form (Form 21, obtainable free from the county council) is provided by the Commons Registration (General Regulations), 1966, for a requisition for an official search in the Register of Common Land or of Town or Village Greens. See further a Council statement at *Law Society's Gazette*, vol. 68, p. 132 (also p. 195).

(d) On purchase of premises by a medical practitioner from another practitioner practising under the National Health Service Act it must be remembered that sale of goodwill is an offence and a substantial excess of consideration on sale of the property could amount to sale of goodwill (National Health Service Act, 1946, s. 35 (3)). A certificate that no valuable consideration has been given for the goodwill may be obtained from the medical practices committee (*ibid.*, s. 35 (9)). The title to the property is not affected by the absence of a certificate even if the consideration is substantially increased but solicitors for both vendor and purchaser should advise their clients on the matter and take instructions whether to apply for a certificate. See generally *Conveyancer N.S.*, vol. 21, p. 50 *et seq.*

(e) It may be necessary to inquire as to the existence of any pipe-line constructed pursuant to the Pipe-lines Act, 1962 (as extended by the Gas Act, 1972). There is no provision for registration of the existence of a pipe-line or works, but a map showing the route (but not exact position : Pipe-lines (Limits of Deviation) Regulations, 1962), is deposited with local authorities, which is open to inspection. Rights of owners of such pipe-lines seem to be easements (or statutory equivalents) on the authority of Re Salvin's Indenture [1938] 2 All E.R. 498 and are overriding interests. A pipe-line should be excepted from the parcels on a subsequent conveyance or transfer of the land through which it runs and noted on a registered title. It is not clear whether rights of support for a pipe-line may be gained by prescription or implication.

(f) Where premises change hands and an application for an electricity supply is received from the new consumer the appropriate electricity board, wherever possible, declares that the new system of supply shall be the standard a.c. system. Where fixed plant or apparatus such as lifts, circulating pumps, motors, etc., are installed which had previously been supplied from the direct current system (d.c.) the Board offer, where possible, a supply of alternating current and, if they give a temporary d.c. supply, it is on condition that the new consumer shall make the installation suitable for a.c. within a specified time and indemnify the Board in respect of costs incurred. In respect of premises on non-standard a.c. supply, a new consumer may be required to take a standard supply and to bear any consequential expenses. If premises being purchased may have a supply which is not standard a.c. it is desirable to ascertain from the Board's district office the nature of any future electricity supplies (Law Society's Gazette, vol. 64, p. 248 ; it is understood that all Boards, except South Wales, have consumers on non-standard supplies totalling about 500,000 in number).

(g) On purchase or mortgage of land (i) intended for building or (ii) on which a building is being erected or (iii) on which there is a building not connected to a public sewer, if the land abuts upon a highway, questions should be asked of the local authority as to the existence of any resolution under the Public Health Act, 1961, s. 12 or 13 (or any similar local legislation). The reason is that such legislation may require a proportion of the cost of sewering of a highway to be paid by a frontager but a local land charge is not registrable until the building has been erected and notice requiring payment has been served. See Law Society's Gazette, vol. 66, p. 590.

PART 4. INSURANCE

Before contract, a solicitor must bear in mind that, immediately the contract is signed by the purchaser, the property is at the risk of the purchaser, for instance, as regards fire. It follows that if before completion the property should be burned down and the property is not insured, the purchaser would still have to pay the purchase-money and receive only a heap of ashes (Rayner v. Preston (1881), 18 Ch. D. 1). The property may, of course, have been insured by the vendor but, if so, the benefit of such insurance would not pass to the purchaser unless it had been expressly assigned to him (ibid. ; Castellain v. Preston (1883), 11 Q.B.D. 380). It may be that, under the Fire Prevention

(Metropolis) Act, 1774, if a vendor has insured a house or other building which is burnt down before completion the purchaser can require the insurance company to apply the insurance money in rebuilding. This enactment applies elsewhere than in the metropolis (*Ex parte Gorely* (1864), 4 De G. J. & S. 477), but it is not entirely clear that it applies in the present case, so that reliance should not be placed on it.

In practice, however, the purchaser will often take the benefit of the vendor's insurance even if there is no express assignment of it. It is provided by s. 47 of the L.P.A. 1925 as follows :—

" 47.—(1) Where after the date of any contract for sale or exchange of property, money becomes payable under any policy of insurance maintained by the vendor in respect of any damage to or destruction of property included in the contract, the money shall, on completion of the contract, be held or receivable by the vendor on behalf of the purchaser and paid by the vendor to the purchaser on completion of the sale or exchange, or so soon thereafter as the same shall be received by the vendor.

(2) This section applies only to contracts made after the commencement of this Act, and has effect subject to—

(*a*) any stipulation to the contrary contained in the contract,

(*b*) any requisite consents of the insurers,

(*c*) the payment by the purchaser of the proportionate part of the premium from the date of the contract."

It will be seen that to obtain the benefit of s. 47 the consent of the insurance company has to be obtained, but most policies contain terms indicating the consent of the company. As there may be delay in ascertaining whether the vendor has a policy and what are its terms, and even as to whether the insurers might for some reason be able to repudiate it, unless the value of the property is considerable and the premium a matter of moment it is usually better to insure straight away. Whether a purchaser's solicitor has authority to effect an insurance without the express consent of his client is doubtful, however. It is possible to assign the benefit of an insurance policy to a purchaser or to agree to hold the policy on trust for him provided the consent of the insurance office is obtained, but reliance on s. 47 appears to achieve the same object without such express provision.

Most companies include in policies of fire insurance a term that if at the time of damage the insured has contracted to sell his interest the purchaser, on completion, shall be entitled to the benefit of the policy. It would seem that a purchaser could not sue the company on such a clause as he is not a party to the contract (compare *Beswick* v. *Beswick* [1968] A.C. 58) ; but no doubt most companies would readily pay to the purchaser and the vendor could have no objection on receiving the full purchase price. In any case the term is presumably a consent of the insurers for the purposes of the L.P.A. 1925, s. 47, and so the purchaser would obtain the benefit of any sums payable.

General Condition 6 of The Law Society's Conditions of Sale, 1973 Revision, and National Condition 21, 18th ed., both provide that the vendor is not bound to keep on foot any insurance nor to give to the purchaser notice of any premium being or becoming due. The purchaser may insist on having his name indorsed on the policy as a person interested, in which event he must pay a proportion of the premium from the date of the contract.

The Council of The Law Society have drawn attention to the fact that " most householders' comprehensive policies do not provide cover, where a house is left unfurnished, against burglary, housebreaking, larceny or theft, or attempts thereat or certain types of malicious damage, nor against bursting or overflowing of water tanks, apparatus or pipes or breakage of fixed glass or sanitary fittings." They point out that losses from these causes may arise if a vendor vacates a house a few days before the purchaser goes into occupation. Apparently an additional premium would be payable if cover against these risks were required and granted (*Law Society's Gazette*, vol. 62, p. 478). The problems arising are fully considered, but no entirely satisfactory solution found, by Mr. J. E. Adams in *Law Society's Gazette*, vol. 68, p. 224.

Insurance of leaseholds.—In the case of leasehold property one must remember that the original lease may contain a covenant that the lessee must insure in a certain fire office, or in some other responsible fire insurance office to be approved by the lessor. In such a case the lessor can refuse to approve a particular office, even though there is no doubt as to its position and responsibility (*Tredegar (Lord)* v. *Harwood* [1929] A.C. 72). If the lease contains such a covenant a vendor who has not insured will be in breach of his covenant and so it is likely that the lease will be voidable. In such a case the purchaser of the lease could not be compelled to complete and so would not be concerned to insure against damage.

If compliance with the requirements of the lease may take some time, use of s. 47 of the L.P.A. 1925 may well be advisable.

CHAPTER TWO

THE CONTRACT

PART 1. FORMATION OF CONTRACT

IN essence, for the formation of any contract, there must be an agreement between the parties which is supported by consideration, certain in its terms, and intended to be binding in law. The detailed rules as to formation will have to be sought elsewhere, only a few points and illustrations of relevance to conveyancers being noted here.

Intention.—If there is in other respects an enforceable contract, the intention to create legal relations will generally be inferred (*Chalmers* v. *Pardoe* [1963] 1 W.L.R. 677). However, there may be no such inference where an arrangement is made for sharing a house, for instance between relatives (*Balfour* v. *Balfour* [1919] 2 K.B. 571). Nevertheless the circumstances of a particular case may show that the parties intended a binding agreement which will then be enforced (*Palmer* v. *Clark* [1960] 1 W.L.R. 286), although the equitable remedies of specific performance or injunction may not be available (*Thompson* v. *Park* [1944] K.B. 408).

There is a presumption that arrangements within a family are not intended to create legal relations (*Balfour* v. *Balfour, ante ; Jones* v. *Padavatton* [1969] 1 W.L.R. 328). This presumption was applied by the Court of Appeal in *Gould* v. *Gould* [1970] 1 Q.B. 275, concerning an agreement as to maintenance, but an exactly contrary presumption was applied, also by the Court of Appeal, in *Merritt* v. *Merritt* [1970] 1 W.L.R. 1121, where the spouses were separated, and an agreement to transfer a freehold house was held enforceable.

The parties may expressly or impliedly negative any intention to be bound, most commonly by making it clear that, even though all the terms of a draft contract may have been approved by or on behalf of the parties, there will be no concluded agreement until a formal contract has been made (*Coope* v. *Ridout* [1921] 1 Ch. 291 ; *Eccles* v. *Bryant* [1948] Ch. 93 ; see further *post*, p. 34).

Consideration.—A contract for the sale of land is almost invariably supported by *executory* consideration, i.e., mutual promises to convey and to pay the price respectively. There is a distinction between *executed* consideration, which would involve an act (that is, conveyance or payment) by one party in return for the other's promise, and *past* consideration where the one party's act precedes the other's promise which is thus a mere expression

of gratitude and does not create a contract. For example, in *Re McArdle*
[1951] Ch. 669, various improvements were made to a house and after all the
work was finished the owners signed a document agreeing to reimburse the
sums spent ; this was held not a binding contract.

Certainty of terms.—The court must be able to say precisely what the
parties have agreed. Thus a contract for sale " subject to answers to
preliminary enquiries and subject to searches " is liable to fail for uncertainty
(*Smith and Olley* v. *Townsend* (1949), 1 P. & C.R. 26). Again there will be no
contract if anything is left to be settled by agreement between the parties
(*May & Butcher* v. *The King* [1934] 2 K.B. 17, 21n ; compare *Foley* v.
Classique Coaches, Ltd. [1934] 2 K.B. 1), for example, if it is expressly agreed
that " the date fixed for completion is to be agreed between the parties "
(see the county court decision in *Gavaghan* v. *Edwards* [1961] 2 Q.B. 220).
However, an agreement to grant a lease containing " such other covenants
and conditions as shall be reasonably required " by the proposed lessor has
been held by the Court of Appeal to be not too vague to be specifically
enforceable (*Sweet & Maxwell, Ltd.* v. *Universal News Services, Ltd.* [1964]
2 Q.B. 699). Indeed, in that case the formula used was described as " a
convenient and effective means of dealing with the position where the parties
have agreed on the main points, but have not yet settled the details, and wish
to make a binding agreement immediately " (*per* Pearson, L.J., *ibid.*, p. 733).

Further, compare *King's Motors (Oxford), Ltd.* v. *Lax* [1969] 1 W.L.R. 426
(where an option in a lease for a further term " at such rental as may be
agreed upon between the parties " was void for uncertainty) with *Smith* v.
Morgan [1971] 1 W.L.R. 803 (where an option in a conveyance for the
purchase of adjoining land " at a figure to be agreed upon " was valid and
binding) and *Brown* v. *Gould* [1972] Ch. 53 (where an option to renew a
lease " at a rent to be fixed having regard to the market value at the time of
exercising this option, taking into account to the advantage of the tenant
any increased value of such premises attributable to structural improvements
made by the tenant " was held to provide a sufficient formula to be valid
and enforceable). In this last cited case, Megarry, J., collected an anthology
of warnings (at *ibid.*, pp. 56–57) which itself indicates the apparently growing
reluctance of the courts to hold void for uncertainty any provision which was
intended to have legal effect. However, the actual decision has been strongly
criticised (see Mr. J. E. Adams in the *Law Society's Gazette*, vol. 68, pp. 484
and 529, dealing with all the above recent cases). Also not every judge is
prepared to accept the same approach (see *Lee-Parker* v. *Izzet (No. 2)* [1972]
1 W.L.R. 775, where Goulding, J., held void for uncertainty a sale " subject
to the purchaser obtaining a satisfactory mortgage ").

Offer.—Agreement between the parties is traditionally thought of in two
parts as the due acceptance of an offer. The offer must be a definite promise
to be bound, not for example a mere statement of intention (*Harris* v.
Nickerson (1873), L.R. 8 Q.B. 286, advertising an auction sale) nor mere
information (*Harvey* v. *Facey* [1893] A.C. 552, quotation of lowest price). The
courts are not quick to treat an ambiguously worded document as an offer
(*Clifton* v. *Palumbo* [1944] 2 All E.R. 497). However, both *Harvey* v. *Facey*
and *Clifton* v. *Palumbo* were distinguished by the Court of Appeal in *Bigg* v.
Boyd Gibbins, Ltd. [1971] 1 W.L.R. 913, where a letter saying : " For a quick
sale I would accept £26,000 . . . " was held to constitute an offer capable of
acceptance so as to create a binding contract of which specific performance
was ordered.

Withdrawal of offer.—An offer may be effectively withdrawn by the offeror so long as knowledge of the withdrawal is received by the offeree before any acceptance (*Dickenson* v. *Dodds* (1876), 2 Ch. D. 463). There may still be withdrawal notwithstanding a promise to keep the offer open for a specified time (*Routledge* v. *Grant* (1828), 4 Bing. 653). But if there is a binding contract to keep the offer open, i.e., the promise is either supported by consideration or made under seal, then withdrawal of the offer would be a breach of that contract (see further *Option to Purchase, post*, p. 73).

Acceptance.—The agreement between the parties is constituted by the due communication to the offeror of an unconditional acceptance. If any new conditions are introduced, the purported " acceptance " amounts only to a counter-offer destroying the original offer and leaving the parties merely in a state of negotiation (*Hyde* v. *Wrench* (1840), 3 Beav. 334 ; *secus* a mere inquiry for information : *Stevenson* v. *McLean* (1880), 5 Q.B.D. 346). Where there is an acceptance but with added words, it becomes a question of construction as to whether those words make the acceptance conditional or not. Illustrations from the cases may help.

Unconditional : binding contracts were found where (i) a letter accepted an offer and appointed a meeting to arrange for a formal contract to be drawn up (*Rouse* v. *Ginsberg* (1911), 55 Sol. J. 632) ; (ii) a letter accepted the offer but stated that the writer had requested his solicitors " to forward the agreement for purchase " (*Rossiter* v. *Miller* (1878), 3 App. Cas. 1124) ; (iii) the acceptance stated that the writer had asked his solicitors " to prepare contract," or to " prepare the necessary documents " (*Bonnewell* v. *Jenkins* (1878), 8 Ch. D. 70 ; *Bolton Partners* v. *Lambert* (1888), 41 Ch. D. 295) ; (iv) the acceptance used the words " such lease to be approved in the customary way by my solicitor " (*Chipperfield* v. *Carter* (1895), 72 L.T. 487) ; (v) an agreement contained the words : " This is a provisional agreement until a fully legalised agreement drawn up by a solicitor and embodying all the conditions herewith stated is signed " (*Branca* v. *Cobarro* [1947] K.B. 854) ; and (vi) the words were, " formal contract to be signed in due course embodying these terms," and here notwithstanding that certain matters of detail had to be left over to be settled by a later agreement (*Ronald Frankau Productions, Ltd.* v. *Bell* (1927), 164 L.T. News. 504).

Conditional.—Examples of words held to incorporate a condition, with the result that it was decided that there was not a binding contract, are as follows : (i) " subject to the approval of a detailed contract to be entered into " (*Page* v. *Norfolk* (1894), 70 L.T. 781) ; (ii) " subject to the preparation by my solicitor of a formal agreement " (*Lloyd* v. *Nowell* [1895] 2 Ch. 744) ; (iii) " subject to surveyor's report " (*Marks* v. *Board* (1930), 46 T.L.R. 424 ; *Graham and Scott* v. *Oxlade* [1950] 2 K.B. 257) ; (iv) " subject to agreement stating fully the conditions being prepared and signed " (*Watson* v. *McAllum* (1902), 87 L.T. 547) ; (v) " subject to formal contract to embody such reasonable provisions as my solicitors may approve " (*Rossdale* v. *Denny* [1921] 1 Ch. 57) ; (vi) " please instruct your solicitor to forward the contract to me " (*Hucklesby* v. *Hook* (1900), 82 L.T. 117) ; (vii) " subject to formal contract to be prepared by the vendors' solicitors if the vendors shall so require " (*Riley* v. *Troll* [1953] 1 All E.R. 966 ; this case appears to have been decided on the construction of the exact words used and so it may not be very valuable as a precedent). If an offer be accepted subject to a term which, even if it were not referred to, would be implied by law, this will not prevent the acceptance from making a binding contract. In *Simpson* v.

Hughes (1897), 76 L.T. 237, the purchaser, in accepting, added : " I should
like to know from what time Mr. *H* wishes the purchase to date " ; and it
was held that this did not prevent the contract being binding, as the law
implied that the contract would be completed within a reasonable time.

In *Hudson* v. *Buck* (1877), 7 Ch. D. 683, it was held that if a contract for
the purchase of a lease was stated to be made subject to the approval of
the title by the purchaser's solicitors, the vendor could not enforce specific
performance if the purchaser's solicitors in good faith disapproved of the
title.   This rule has been confirmed by Maugham, J., in *Curtis Moffat, Ltd.*
v. *Wheeler* [1929] 2 Ch. 224, and by Farwell, J., in *Caney* v. *Leith* [1937]
2 All E.R. 532.   In this last-mentioned case, Farwell, J., reviewed the
authorities and drew the distinction between a provision making it clear
that the purchaser's solicitor is to investigate title in the usual manner,
in which case there is a binding contract, and a provision that the contract
is to be conditional on approval (compare *Edginton* v. *Clark* [1964] 1 Q.B. 367
and *Re Longlands Farm* [1968] 3 All E.R. 552, at p. 555).

In *Richard West and Partners (Inverness), Ltd.* v. *Dick* [1969] 2 Ch. 424,
a contract to purchase " conditional upon planning consent being granted "
was held binding by the Court of Appeal because on the facts the condition
had been satisfied despite certain conditions being attached to the consent.
Contrast *Hargreaves Transport, Ltd.* v. *Lynch* [1969] 1 W.L.R. 215, C.A.
(outline planning permission held insufficient)

Where the party making an offer stipulates a particular method of
acceptance (for example a letter to a stated address posting of which is deemed
to be acceptance) but does not stipulate that this shall be the sole means of
acceptance, the offer can be accepted by any other means of communication
provided it is not less advantageous to the party who made the offer
(*Manchester Diocesan Council for Education* v. *Commercial & General
Investments, Ltd.* [1970] 1 W.L.R. 241).   Whether an offer becomes incapable
of acceptance by reason of delay depends on whether the party to whom the
offer was made should be treated as having refused it by his conduct (see
authorities cited *ibid.*, p. 247).

Sometimes, instead of referring to a more formal document to be drawn
up, the vendor in his letter of acceptance encloses a formal contract for the
purchaser's signature.   In such a case, whether or not there is a completed
contract depends on whether the form of contract contains any new term
which has not already been agreed upon.   If it does not contain any new
term, the agreement will be binding, although the formal document remains
unsigned (*Jones* v. *Daniel* [1894] 2 Ch. 332 ; *Filby* v. *Hounsell* [1896] 2 Ch. 737,
at p. 742 ; see also *Rossiter* v. *Miller* (1878), 3 App. Cas. 1124 ; *Bonnewell*
v. *Jenkins* (1878), 8 Ch. D. 70).

Subject to contract.—The proposition is well known that the effect of
the insertion of the words " subject to contract " is that the matter is left
merely in the stage of negotiation until a formal contract is made ; see *Winn*
v. *Bull* (1877), 7 Ch. D. 29, where the words were, " subject to the preparation
and approval of a formal contract," *Spottiswoode, Ballantyne & Co.* v. *Doreen
Appliances, Ltd.* [1942] 2 K.B. 32, where the words were, " subject to the
terms of a formal agreement," *Chillingworth* v. *Esche* [1924] 1 Ch. 97, where
the words were, " subject to a proper contract to be prepared by the vendor's
solicitors," *Lockett* v. *Norman-Wright* [1925] Ch. 56, where the words were,
" subject to suitable agreements being arranged between your solicitors and
mine," and *Wilson* v. *Balfour* (1929), 45 T.L.R. 625, where Eve, J., held that
the words " subject to contract " in the circumstances meant, " subject to

the execution by the parties of a formal contract " (see also *George Trollope & Sons* v. *Martyn Bros.* [1934] 2 K.B. 436). For the same reason an agreement to grant a lease " subject to the terms of a lease " does not constitute a binding contract (*Raingold* v. *Bromley* [1931] 2 Ch. 307 ; see also *H. C. Berry, Ltd.* v. *Brighton and Sussex B.S.* [1939] 3 All E.R. 217).

This proposition has been somewhat undermined by modern decisions. In *Griffiths* v. *Young* [1970] Ch. 675, a solicitor's letter expressly contemplating " subject to contract " negotiations was held by the Court of Appeal to have been superseded by a subsequent unconditional offer and acceptance over the telephone ; the suspensive condition embodied in the words " subject to contract " was treated as having been waived so as to produce immediately an informal but a binding contract (as to the requisite evidence in writing, see p. 40). Thus an agreement " subject to contract " did not subsist solely by reference to a formal exchange, which some conveyancers may find surprising (e.g., the solicitors in the case itself had actually continued to conduct an ineffectual correspondence about a formal contract). Although a submission along substantially similar lines had been rejected at first instance in another case (see *D'Silva* v. *Lister House Development, Ltd.* [1971] Ch. 17, at p. 29), it has since been applied and even elaborated by the Court of Appeal. The majority decision in *Law* v. *Jones* [1973] 2 All E.R. 437 has emphasised that the unilateral insertion of the words " subject to contract " into correspondence between the solicitors acting does not negative the effect of any existing binding agreement, whether oral or written, made between the parties. Further, causing a problem for the practitioner, it has been decided that such " subject to contract " correspondence can constitute a memorandum within s. 40 (1) of the L.P.A. 1925, and so render an oral agreement enforceable (*Griffiths* v. *Young, ante ; Law* v. *Jones, ante*). However, a differently constituted Court of Appeal has held that inclusion of the words " subject to contract " effectively prevented correspondence from satisfying the statute (*Tiverton Estates, Ltd.* v. *Wearwell, Ltd.* (1973), *The Times*, 21st November, purporting to follow *Thirkell* v. *Cambi* [1919] 2 K.B. 590 in preference to *Law* v. *Jones*). The Council of The Law Society has in consequence stated that " The problem has now been solved " (*Law Society's Gazette*, vol. 70, p. 2637). There are difficulties in accepting this view that, in effect, *Law* v. *Jones* has been overruled by *Tiverton Estates*. Only the House of Lords can overrule a Court of Appeal decision, and the decision in *Law* v. *Jones* received implicit approval from the House of Lords in that the Appellate Committee refused leave to appeal (*The Times*, 6th July, 1973) ; no notice of appeal was lodged within the week allowed in *Tiverton Estates* (*Law Society's Gazette*, vol. 70, p. 2609). Moreover, the two cases strictly concerned different questions : an action for specific performance in *Law* v. *Jones* ; an application by motion for cancellation of a caution in *Tiverton Estates*. And *Griffiths* v. *Young, ante*, which raises much the same problem, was said to be justifiable on other grounds (*per* Lord Denning, M.R., in *Tiverton Estates*). Consequently the safer practice must be to assume that *Law* v. *Jones* may still be fully applicable.

It should be appreciated that in normal circumstances it would be difficult if not impossible to find that the prior oral agreement was intended to be binding. Such a finding was not challenged on appeal in *Law* v. *Jones, ante*, but normally the prior agreement will itself be made " subject to contract ", either expressly or *semble* by implication from conduct (see *per* Danckwerts, J., in *Smith* v. *Mansi* [1963] 1 W.L.R. 26, at p. 31 ; also *per* Stamp, J., in *Goldsmith (F.) (Sidelesmere), Ltd.* v. *Baxter* [1970] Ch. 85, at pp. 89–90). In the normal case, therefore, no question of the L.P.A. 1925, s. 40 (1), memorandum should arise. Nevertheless, a serious practical problem remains. Conveyancing practitioners must be able to rely with complete confidence on their clients' agreements remaining non-binding or at least unenforceable until the formal constitution of a contract for sale, usually by exchange. It had been thought that this position was secured in all cases by the use of the words " subject to contract ", but it now appears possible that these words do not avoid entirely the risk of inadvertent memoranda within the L.P.A. 1925, s. 40. Various suggestions for achieving the desired position, i.e., a state of negotiation until exchange, by other means have been suggested in letters to legal journals ; indeed Russell, L.J., dissenting in *Law* v. *Jones, ante,* had already indicated communication by telephone coupled with the omission of signatures from letters (see [1973] 2 All E.R., at p. 441f). However, it is considered that the simplest and most effective method is that suggested by Mr. D. Herbert Jones (see *Solicitors' Journal,* (1973), vol. 117, at pp. 568 and 604), namely to deny that there is any contract. That such a denial would effectively prevent the correspondence from constituting a memorandum was in fact said, very nearly directly, by both Buckley, L.J., and Orr, L.J., in *Law* v. *Jones, ante* (see [1973] 2 All E.R., at pp. 445 and 447 respectively). Mr. Herbert Jones proposed adding to letters the words : " The existence of a binding oral agreement in this matter [or : in the above terms] between our clients is denied ". Whilst this formula should prove entirely effective, it is thought that a contraction of it might be more useful : the words " contract denied " could in practice simply replace the present formula " subject to contract " with a view to achieving the expected and desired effect. However, it will, of course, be necessary to consider in each case whether the denial of a contract is to the advantage or prejudice of a client's interests.

Further, a similar point is that the consequences of the words " subject to contract " are applicable but qualified where the agreement is for a term of years and the transaction proceeds directly towards grant of the lease itself. The first rule is that a state of negotiation continues and there will be no contract to enforce until exchange of lease and counterpart (see *per* Harman, J., in *Hollington Bros., Ltd.* v. *Rhodes* [1951] 2 T.L.R. 691, at p. 694 ; also *D'Silva* v. *Lister House Development, Ltd.* [1971] Ch. 17). But the second prevailing rule is that if the grantor actually executes the lease as an unconditional deed then it is immediately binding as such even without any exchange (see *Beesly* v. *Hallwood Estates, Ltd.* [1961] Ch. 105, and *D'Silva* v. *Lister House Development, Ltd., ante*). This conflict in rules clearly constitutes a trap in practice which may be fallen into whenever the efficient preparation for completion involves the execution of documents under seal in advance, i.e., particularly where a company is concerned (see further the editorial comment in *Conveyancer N.S.* (1970), vol. 34, pp. 145–147 ; also as to escrows, *post,* p. 591).

Another point is that the words " subject to contract " do not necessarily negative the possibility of some collateral liability subsisting between the parties (e.g., in quasi-contract). For example, where a prospective purchaser has requested the prospective vendor to make alterations to the property and has agreed (expressly or, presumably, by implication) to accept responsibility for the cost, then if the negotiations for a contract of sale break down the cost of the alterations made can nevertheless be recovered from the prospective purchaser (see *Brewer Street Investments, Ltd.* v. *Barclays Woollen Co., Ltd.* [1954] 1 Q.B. 428, C.A.). This would clearly be so if the blame for the breakdown of negotiations could be placed on the prospective purchaser alone and apparently would remain true if no blame attached to either party, but not if the blame was the prospective vendor's alone since he would also be taking the benefit of the alterations (see *ibid.*).

Making of formal contract.—Where a formal contract is drawn up by the solicitor for the vendor and approved by the solicitor for the purchaser an appointment may be made at which a part of the contract signed by each party is handed over to the other, but most commonly parts will be exchanged by post. Where such procedure is adopted neither party will be bound until the exchange has been made. Thus, in *Eccles* v. *Bryant and Another* [1948] Ch. 93, the vendor's solicitors wrote to the purchaser's solicitors stating that the vendors had signed their part and were ready to exchange. The purchaser's solicitors replied that they would obtain the purchaser's signature to his part and forward it to the vendor's solicitors. Shortly afterwards a letter containing a part of the contract was posted to the vendor's solicitors which crossed in the post a letter from the vendor's solicitors repudiating the contract. In an action by the purchaser for specific performance, it was held that no contract was formed until the parts were exchanged.

On exchange by post it is not certain whether the exchange is regarded as taking place when the later of the two parts to be forwarded is put in the post or when it is received by the other party (cf. *Household Fire & Carriage Accident Insurance Co.* v. *Grant* (1879), 4 Ex. D. 216 ; also *Holwell Securities, Ltd.* v. *Hughes* [1973] 2 All E.R. 476). General Condition 5 (2) of the 1973 Revision of The Law Society's Conditions of Sale now provides that the contract is made when " the last part is actually posted." The 1953 edition of the same Conditions, where applicable, provides that the test is the time of actual delivery at the premises of the person or firm to whom it is addressed.

If the contract is contained in one document, for instance where the same solicitor acts for both parties, or an estate agent's form is signed, there is no question of exchange of parts and the contract is complete when signed by both parties (*Smith* v. *Mansi* [1963] 1 W.L.R. 26 ; but see *ante*, p. 3, as to a solicitor acting for both parties).

The Council of The Law Society have expressed the opinion (*Law Society's Gazette*, vol. 68, p. 358) that " where a prospective purchaser has agreed to purchase subject to contract there is nothing unprofessional in the vendor's solicitor forwarding draft contracts to more than one prospective purchaser even if the vendor states that he will sell to the purchaser who returns a signed contract first provided that the vendor's solicitor discloses the facts to each prospective purchaser or his solicitor." If such disclosure is not authorised by the vendor, it is considered by the Council that the vendor's solicitor should refuse to continue to act in the matter.

Expedited procedure.—The Council of The Law Society have conferred with the professional bodies representing surveyors, valuers, auctioneers, and land and estate agents, with a view to devising a procedure designed to expedite the signing of contracts for the sale of land by private treaty (*Law Society's Gazette*, vol. 59, p. 203). The Council urge solicitors to do their share in making that practice as effective as possible.

The first step suggested is that, in suitable cases, as soon as an agent receives instructions to dispose of a property by sale he will request the client to give instructions to his solicitor to prepare a draft contract and to take other appropriate steps. Secondly, a form of Preliminary Sale Information has been agreed and it is recommended that it should be completed by the agent as

far as possible, immediately following his inspection of the property and
consultation with the vendor, and forthwith sent to the vendor's solicitor in
duplicate.   The agent should inform the solicitor by letter of the name and
address of the purchaser and his solicitor, the price, who holds the deposit
and in what capacity and of any arrangements as to fixtures and fittings.

The form is " not intended to relieve the vendor's solicitor from checking
any matters which it is his duty to investigate." This can be done by sending
a copy of the form to the client, obtaining confirmation and instructions on
additional points such as the date when vacant possession can be given.
To expedite matters the vendor's solicitor should, with his first letter to the
purchaser's solicitor, give particulars of the local authorities and, if possible,
provide a plan to enable the usual searches and inquiries to be made.   The
Council " do not favour the practice of a vendor's solicitor preparing a form
of contract for the vendor's agent to place before a prospective purchaser for
signature.   It is their view . . . that no step should be taken which in any
way could induce or lead a purchaser to sign a binding contract without
first obtaining legal advice " (*Law Society's Gazette*, vol. 53, p. 19, and vol. 63,
p. 267).

Registration of contract.—A contract by an estate owner or by a person
entitled at the date of the contract to have a legal estate conveyed to him to
convey or create a legal estate is registrable as an estate contract in the land
charges register (L.C.A. 1972, s. 2 (4) ; see further, *post*, p. 599).   Registration
should be in the name of the estate owner, that is, the owner of the *legal* estate
intended to be affected (L.C.A. 1972, ss. 3 (1), 17 (1) ; L.P.A. 1925, ss. 1 (1),
205 (1) (*v*)).

A contract which is not duly registered will be void against a purchaser of
a legal estate for money or money's worth (L.C.A. 1972, s. 4 (6)).   In practice
contracts are often not registered if it is thought that they are likely to be
completed reasonably speedily.   On the other hand, it would be wise to
register, for instance, (i) if the good faith of the vendor is doubted, (ii) where
a dispute arises between vendor and purchaser, (iii) where the vendor delays
completion, or (iv) where the price is to be paid by instalments and the
estate is not to be conveyed to the purchaser until the last instalment has
been paid.   Another case where it may be desirable to register an estate
contract occurs where a conveyance, by inadvertence, has, since 1925, been
made direct to an infant and there is likely to be some delay in the execution
of a vesting deed and trust instrument under s. 27 of the S.L.A. 1925 ; or
where a mortgage has since that date been made direct to an infant, as it
operates as an agreement to execute such mortgage on his attaining full age
(L.P.A. 1925, s. 19 (6) ; see further *post*, p. 336).

Registered land.—If title to the land sold is registered, the purchaser can
protect his contract on the register either by a notice or a restriction, each of
which require the vendor's co-operation in lodging his land certificate, or else
by a caution which requires no such co-operation (L.R.A. 1925, ss. 49 (1) (*c*),
58 (1) and 54 respectively ; see further *post*, p. 618).   However, often in
practice the land will be subject to a registered charge and the land certificate
will already be deposited at H.M. Land Registry (L.R.A. 1925, s. 65), so that
the purchaser will not need to fall back on a caution but will be able to obtain
the entry of a notice.   Alternatively once occupation is taken under the
contract for sale the purchaser will be protected by having an " overriding
interest " (L.R.A. 1925, s. 70 (1) (*g*) ; *Bridges* v. *Mees* [1957] Ch. 475 ;
Lee-Parker v. *Izzet* (*No.* 2) [1972] 1 W.L.R. 775 ; see further *post*, p. 188).

Otherwise, if not protected on the register or as an overriding interest, the purchaser's rights are liable to be overridden by a registered disposition for valuable consideration (L.R.A. 1925, ss. 20 (1) and 23 (1)). Whether or not protection should be sought depends on almost exactly the same considerations as in unregistered conveyancing (see above).

PART 2. NECESSITY FOR WRITTEN MEMORANDUM

Essentials of memorandum.—The L.P.A. 1925, s. 40 (re-enacting, in part, the Statute of Frauds, 1677, s. 4), provides as follows :—

"40. (1) *No action may be brought* upon any contract for the sale or other disposition of land or *any interest in land*, unless *the agreement* upon which such action is brought, *or some memorandum or note thereof, is in writing, and signed by the party to be charged or by some other person* thereunto by him lawfully authorised.

"(2) This section applies to contracts whether made before or after the commencement of this Act and does not affect the law relating to *part performance*, or *sales by the court.*"

"*No action may be brought.*"—If a plaintiff in an action alleges, as an essential part of his case, that a contract within s. 40 exists, he must be in a position to prove the existence of a sufficient memorandum or that circumstances exist in which a memorandum is unnecessary (*Delaney* v. *Smith* (*T. P.*), *Ltd.* [1946] K.B. 393). However, the statute must be specifically pleaded ; if it be not so pleaded as a defence, then the absence of the writing required by the statute will not be a bar to success (see *North* v. *Loomes* [1919] 1 Ch. 378). If it is proved that a document which would constitute a sufficient memorandum has been lost, secondary evidence of its contents may be given, and this will comply with the requirements of s. 40 (*Barber* v. *Rowe* [1948] 2 All E.R. 1050).

The Statute of Frauds was not allowed to be used as an instrument to help the fraud of one of the parties (*Heard* v. *Pilley* (1869), L.R. 4 Ch. 548) ; and parol evidence was admissible, where the result of excluding such evidence would have been to cover a fraud (*Re Duke of Marlborough ; Davis* v. *Whitehead* [1894] 2 Ch. 133 ; *Rochefoucauld* v. *Boustead* [1897] 1 Ch. 196). As stated in *Jervis* v. *Berridge* (1873), L.R. 8 Ch. 351, at p. 360, " the Statute of Frauds is a weapon of defence, not offence, and does not make any signed instrument a valid contract by reason of the signature, if it is not such according to the good faith and real intention of the parties." These cases equally apply to s. 40 (1) of the L.P.A. 1925.

The doctrine of part performance constitutes the commonest example of a fraud making parol evidence admissible as above ; see further *post*, p. 52 *et seq.*

"*any interest in land.*"—This expression does not include an agreement in connection with tenant's fixtures (*Lee* v. *Gaskell* (1876), 1 Q.B.D. 700 ; *Thomas* v. *Jennings* (1896), 66 L.J.Q.B. 5) ; nor an agreement to construct a road (*Jameson* v. *Kinmell, etc., Co.* (1931), 47 T.L.R. 595). It includes an agreement to grant or assign a lease (*Thursby* v. *Eccles* (1900), 70 L.J.Q.B. 91), an agreement to pay a lessee a sum of money to surrender his lease and arrange with the lessor to accept the person paying the money as tenant (*Smart* v. *Harding* (1855), 15 C.B. 652), an agreement to charge land (*Whitmore* v. *Farley* (1881), 45 L.T. 99) (probably) an agreement to assign an undivided share in land, that is a share in the proceeds of sale of land subject to a trust for sale (*Cooper* v. *Critchley* [1955] Ch. 431 ; cf. *Irani Finance, Ltd.* v. *Singh*

[1971] Ch. 59, at p. 79), and a right of shooting over land and taking game (*Webber* v. *Lee* (1882), 9 Q.B.D. 315). For a useful discussion, see *Conveyancer N.S.*, vol. 20, pp. 12 to 14.

With regard to timber and growing crops, the rule is that *fructus naturales* (natural crops), as opposed to *fructus industriales* (cultivated crops), are to be regarded as " land " within s. 40 (1), unless necessarily to be severed on sale ; see further *Conveyancer N.S.*, vol. 22, p. 137 *et seq.*

" agreement . . . or some memorandum or note thereof."—All the terms of the contract are often not contained in any one document but in several documents, e.g., in correspondence between the parties. However, a sufficient memorandum may be constituted by several documents in two cases. First, if the several documents can be seen to refer to the same transaction when laid side by side and are all signed by or on behalf of the defendant, then they can be read together without any further evidence being needed to connect them (*Sheers* v. *Thimbleby & Son* (1879), 76 L.T. 709). This may even be so where the defendant has signed only one of the documents provided that they " manifestly " refer to the same transaction (*Burgess* v. *Cox* [1951] Ch. 383).

The second case involves starting from an incomplete document signed by the defendant and following up references in it by parol evidence until documents together constituting a complete memorandum have been collected. An authoritative explanation of the rule is " that there should be a document signed by the party to be charged which, while not containing in itself all the necessary ingredients of the required memorandum, does contain some reference, express or implied, to some other document or transaction. Where any such reference can be spelt out of a document so signed, then parol evidence may be given to identify the other document referred to, or as the case may be, to explain the other transaction, and to identify any document relating to it. If by this process a document is brought to light which contains in writing all the terms of the bargain so far as not contained in the document signed by the party to be charged, then the two documents can be read together so as to constitute a sufficient memorandum for the purposes of s. 40 of the Law of Property Act, 1925. The laying of documents side by side may no doubt lead to the conclusion as a matter of *res ipsa loquitur* that the two are connected. But before a document signed by the party to be charged can be laid alongside another document to see if between them they constitute a sufficient memorandum, there must, I conceive, be found in the document signed by the party to be charged some reference to some other document or transaction " (Jenkins, L.J., in *Timmins* v. *Moreland Street Property Co., Ltd.* [1958] Ch. 110, at p. 130 ; see also *Stokes* v. *Whicher* [1920] 1 Ch. 411 ; *Cave* v. *Hastings* (1881), 7 Q.B.D. 12, and *Fowler* v. *Bratt* [1950] 2 K.B. 96, at pp. 101–2 ; see further an article at *Conveyancer N.S.*, vol. 22, p. 275). However, in *Timmins* v. *Moreland Street Properties*, *ante*, no sufficient memorandum was in fact found by the Court of Appeal. In the case the document signed by the defendant was a cheque for the deposit payable to the plaintiff's solicitors. At an interview the cheque for the deposit was given to the plaintiff, who signed and handed to the defendant's agent a receipt which stated the amount of the deposit and described the property. It was decided that the receipt could not be used to supply essential terms missing from the cheque as there was no reference, either express or implied, in the cheque to any other document or transaction. It appears from the judgments of Jenkins and Romer, L.JJ., that if the cheque had been in favour of the plaintiff,

2A

rather than his solicitors, it might have been possible to read it together with the plaintiff's receipt, i.e., as " manifestly " referring to the same transaction (see *Burgess* v. *Cox, ante*).

It was decided in *Timmins* v. *Moreland Street Property Co., Ltd.* [1958] Ch. 110, in the words of Jenkins, L.J., at p. 123, that : " where two documents relied on as a memorandum are signed and exchanged at one and the same meeting as part of the same transaction, so that they may fairly be said to have been to all intents and purposes contemporaneously signed, the document signed by the party to be charged should not be treated as incapable of referring to the other document merely because the latter, on a minute investigation of the order of events at the meeting, is found to have come second in the order of preparation and signing."

To enable the document or documents together forming the contract to be enforced, it or they must contain the following particulars :—

(1) The names of the vendor and purchaser, or a reference to or description of them sufficient to identify them.

(2) A description of the property sufficient to identify it.

(3) The consideration (when the price has been agreed it must be mentioned in the memorandum : *Re Kharaskhoma, etc., Syndicate, Ltd.* [1897] 2 Ch. 451, at p. 464) or the means of ascertaining it. The price will not be deemed to have been fixed if there remains a dispute as to terms of payment (*Neale* v. *Nerrett* [1930] W.N. 189). However, a contract will be valid and the memorandum sufficient in this respect if it leaves the court to supply the machinery of valuation. Thus an agreement to sell land expressly at a " fair price " or a " reasonable valuation " will be valid and enforceable (Grant, M.R., in *Milnes* v. *Gery* (1807), 14 Ves. 400, at p. 407 ; followed in *Brown* v. *Gould* [1972] Ch. 53 ; see also *Morgan* v. *Milman* (1853), 3 De G.M. & G. 24, at pp. 34 and 37 ; *Talbot* v. *Talbot* [1968] Ch. 1, at p. 12).

(4) Any other material terms arranged between the parties, except such as are implied by law (*Blackburn* v. *Walker* [1920] W.N. 291).

Whether it is necessary that the memorandum should acknowledge the existence of a contract has recently become unclear. It is clear that a writing which denies the existence of a contract cannot be relied on as within the L.P.A. 1925, s. 40 (*Thirkell* v. *Cambi* [1919] 2 K.B. 590), but whether the words " subject to contract " amount to such a denial has produced conflicting Court of Appeal decisions. In *Law* v. *Jones* [1973] 2 All E.R. 437, the view was taken that it is the terms agreed on, not the fact of agreement, which must be found recorded in writing and it was held that the words " subject to contract " did not prevent there being a sufficient memorandum (following *Griffiths* v. *Young* [1970] Ch. 675, C.A.). But in *Tiverton Estates, Ltd.* v. *Wearwell, Ltd.* (1973), *The Times*, 21st November, a completely contrary decision was reached : the writing must acknowledge the existence of the contract, and the words " subject to contract " are equivalent to a denial. As to which decision should prevail see further p. 36, *ante*.

" *is in writing.*"—No special form of writing is necessary (*Hill* v. *Hill* [1947] Ch. 231) and no intention of satisfying s. 40 (1) need have been present : " the question is not one of intention of the party who signs the document, but simply one of evidence against him " (*Re Hoyle* [1893] 1 Ch. 84, at p. 99 ; see also *per* Sargant, J., in *Daniels* v. *Trefusis* [1914] 1 Ch. 788, at p. 799). Thus sufficient memoranda are often found in receipts for deposits (for instance, *Davies* v. *Sweet* [1962] 2 Q.B. 300 ; compare *Timmins* v. *Moreland*

Street Property Co., Ltd. [1958] Ch. 110) and especially in correspondence (*Smith-Bird* v. *Blower* [1939] 2 All E.R. 406). This last-cited case shows that a letter written by a party to his own solicitor may amount to a sufficient memorandum, and will not be privileged unless written for the purpose of obtaining legal advice (see also *Smith* v. *Mansi* [1963] 1 W.L.R. 26).

The contract itself need not be made in writing so long as there is at least a written memorandum of it (*Re Holland* [1902] 2 Ch. 360), which memorandum may be informal and unintended (see above). Further, such a memorandum may be made either at the time of or at any time after the contract is entered into provided only that it is made before the particular action on the contract commenced, that is, by the time the writ was issued (*Lucas* v. *Dixon* (1889), 22 Q.B.D. 357 ; *Farr, Smith & Co.* v. *Messers, Ltd.* [1928] 1 K.B. 397). What is more, a written offer which shows an intention to contract may be a sufficient memorandum even if it is accepted by word of mouth and notwithstanding the fact that it is necessarily made before the contract it " evidences " came into existence (*Parker* v. *Clark* [1960] 1 W.L.R. 286). It would not be sufficient, however, to rely on a document stating the terms of a proposed agreement, such as the engrossment of a contract in writing, if that document did not itself show an intention to contract *at that stage* (*Munday* v. *Asprey* (1880), 13 Ch. D. 855, which may not be of general application ; see *per* Buckley, L.J., in *Law* v. *Jones* [1973] 2 All E.R. 437, at p. 446).

" *sales by the court.*"—In the case of a sale by the court the absence of writing is no objection. The direction and supervision of the court are considered sufficient safeguard against fraud.

Distinction between validity and enforceability of contract.—The rules which determine whether a binding contract has been made apply to contracts for the sale of land in the same way as they apply to other contracts. A common error is to consider whether an adequate memorandum exists to satisfy the requirements of s. 40 (1) of the L.P.A. 1925 before deciding that a valid contract has been formed. This error is avoided if one remembers that the absence of a sufficient memorandum (and of circumstances rendering the contract enforceable in spite of that absence) means only that the contract is *unenforceable by action*. Whether a contract exists must, therefore, be considered before it is material to inquire whether that contract can be enforced. Thus if, in a contract to grant a lease, no date is fixed for the commencement of the proposed term, there being no concluded agreement, a claim for specific performance will not succeed (*Edwards* v. *Jones* (1921), 124 L.T. 740 ; *Harvey* v. *Pratt* [1965] 1 W.L.R. 1025). The distinction between validity and enforceability was well illustrated by *Griffiths* v. *Young* [1970] Ch. 675, where the written evidence contained the expression " subject to contract " but the oral evidence showed that its effect had been waived and the Court of Appeal held there to be a valid and enforceable contract ; but cp. *Law* v. *Jones* [1973] 2 All E.R. 437, C.A., and *Tiverton Estates, Ltd.* v. *Wearwell, Ltd.* (1973), *The Times*, 21st November, C.A., in relation to a prior oral agreement (*ante*, pp. 36, 42).

The case of *Low* v. *Fry* (1935), 51 T.L.R. 322, shows very clearly that a contract of purchase may be valid although not enforceable by action because not evidenced in writing as required by s. 40. In that case an oral agreement for purchase of a house was made and the purchaser gave a cheque for about half the purchase-money as part payment of the price. Before the cheque was presented the purchaser decided not to go on with the transaction and stopped the cheque. In an action to recover on the cheque the vendor was successful, although there was no written evidence of the contract. Again in *Monnickendam* v. *Leanse* (1923), 39 T.L.R. 445, a deposit paid under an oral contract was forfeited by the vendor. In each of these cases, there was a valid contract effectively enforced by the vendor *otherwise* than by action and therefore not within L.P.A. 1925, s. 40 (1).

Names or descriptions of parties.—The Statute of Frauds was satisfied if the parties were so described that their identities could not fairly be disputed, although their names were not actually mentioned (*Potter* v. *Duffield* (1874), L.R. 18 Eq. 4; *Cohen* v. *Roche* [1927] 1 K.B. 169). For instance, where the party sought to be bound was referred to in the contract as " you," and this word referred to the person who had paid a deposit, and this person was admittedly the person to be bound, it was held that there was a sufficient description (*Carr* v. *Lynch* [1900] 1 Ch. 613; *Stokes* v. *Whicher* [1920] 1 Ch. 411). " The proprietor " was considered sufficient; also " the trustee for sale " (*Sale* v. *Lambert* (1874), L.R. 18 Eq. 1; *Catling* v. *King* (1877), 5 Ch. D. 660; *Coombs* v. *Wilkes* [1891] 3 Ch. 77; *Rossiter* v. *Miller* (1878), 3 App. Cas. 1124); also " owner " and " mortgagee " (*Jarrett* v. *Hunter* (1886), 34 Ch. D. 182); also " executors " (*Hood* v. *Lord Barrington* (1868), L.R. 6 Eq. 218), or " personal representatives " (*Towle* v. *Topham* (1877), 37 L.T. 308; *Fay* v. *Miller, Wilkins & Co.* [1941] Ch. 360). In *Commins* v. *Scott* (1875), L.R. 20 Eq. 11, the word " vendors " appeared from the contract to mean the company in possession, who were the owners entitled to sell, and it was held that the vendors were sufficiently described. *Commins* v. *Scott* was followed by Stamp, J., in *F. Goldsmith (Sicklesmere), Ltd.* v. *Baxter* [1970] Ch. 85, as showing that it is not essential to the validity of a contract made on behalf of a limited company that the company should be described with precision (specific performance was ordered of a contract for sale where the plaintiff-vendor had been named in the memorandum as " Goldsmith Coaches (Sicklesmere), Ltd.").

But the word " vendor " by itself, without anything else to connect it with the person entitled to sell, was not considered a sufficient description, because it was not sufficiently specific (*Catling* v. *King, ante; Sale* v. *Lambert, ante; Butcher* v. *Nash* (1889), 61 L.T. 72). Such descriptions as "landlord" (*Coombs* v. *Wilkes, ante*); " my client," or " my principal " (*Rossiter* v. *Miller, ante; Allen & Co., Ltd.* v. *Whiteman* (1920), 123 L.T. 773), were not deemed sufficient, as being too general. In the latter case the vendors' agent had forwarded to the intending purchaser the auction particulars, wherein the sale was stated to be by order of the mortgagees. In the contract, however, the vendors were referred to as " our clients." It was held that although the expression " our clients " was not a sufficient description, the reference in the auction particulars got over the difficulty. In *Lovesy* v. *Palmer* [1916] 2 Ch. 233, the description of one of the parties as " your client " in a letter addressed to his solicitor was held to be insufficient.

In considering whether both parties can be found in the document purporting to be the contract, either by description or by name, the signatures will be considered part of the document (*Stokell* v. *Niven* (1889), 61 L.T. 18).

A letter beginning " Dear Sir," and signed by the defendant, and containing all material terms except the name of the plaintiff, was held to be incorporated with its envelope addressed to the plaintiff (*Rearce* v. *Gardner* [1897] 1 Q.B. 688). In a case where the envelope was lost, evidence was admitted to show that the letter was contained in an envelope addressed to the plaintiff (*Last* v. *Hucklesby* [1914] W.N. 157).

If the memorandum states the names of the contracting parties, though one may be known to the other to be the agent of an undisclosed principal, the statute will be satisfied (*Filby* v. *Hounsell* [1896] 2 Ch. 737).

Also in *Davies* v. *Sweet* [1962] 2 Q.B. 300, the Court of Appeal held that a memorandum will be sufficient, even though one of the parties to the contract is not identified, provided it does identify some person who will be bound by the contract, such as an agent who has incurred personal liability. In the case, the vendor's estate agent signed the receipt for the deposit on his own headed notepaper. Apart from not identifying the vendor, the receipt contained all the terms of the agreement for sale which had been concluded orally by the estate agent with the purchaser. The estate agent was held to have incurred personal liability under the rule that where an agent contracts in his own name without mentioning the agency both he and his principal (the vendor) are bound even though the other party knows of the agency (see *Basma* v. *Weekes* [1950] A.C. 441). Consequently the receipt was a sufficient memorandum for the contract to be enforceable against the vendor.

Description of property.—Although the description of the property may be vague, yet if it contains sufficient internal information to enable the property to be ascertained with exactness, parol evidence will be admitted for that purpose ; but parol evidence cannot be called in to *make* a description where there is none in the contract ; for instance, a contract to sell " my property in *A B* Street," if the vendor had more than one property in *A B* Street, would fail for want of certainty (*Plant* v. *Bourne* [1897] 2 Ch. 281). Parol evidence was allowed to identify properties described as : " Mr. Ogilvie's house " (*Ogilvie* v. *Foljambe* (1817), 3 Mer. 53) ; " the property in Cable Street " (*Bleakley* v. *Smith* (1840), 11 Sim. 150) ; " the Mill property including cottages in Esher Village " (*McMurray* v. *Spicer* (1868), L.R. 5 Eq. 527) ; " the property purchased for £420 at the Sun Inn, Paxton, on the above date, Mr. George Cotterell, Paxton, owner " (*Shardlow* v. *Cotterell* (1881), 20 Ch. D. 90) ; also " 24 acres of land, freehold, and all appurtenances thereto at Totmonslow, in the parish of Draycott, in the county of Stafford, and all the mines and minerals thereto appertaining " (*Plant* v. *Bourne, ante*).

The case of *Auerbach* v. *Nelson* [1919] 2 Ch. 383 is a very instructive one. The receipt for the deposit which evidenced the contract between the parties was as follows : " 21/11/1918. Received of Mr. Auerbach, 197 High Street, Shoreditch, £10 on account of house being sold for £500 from Mr. M. Nelson, Nelson Lodge, 143 Victoria Park Road. Possession to be taken in 6 weeks after date. (Signed) Morris Nelson. 21/11/1918." It was held that the memorandum was sufficient. There was, it was decided, on the face of the contract a sufficiently definite description of the thing sold and therefore parol evidence could be given to show to what that description referred ; the Statute of Frauds did not require the property to be described in such a way that it would be wholly unnecessary to resort to parol evidence.

A physical description of the property will be sufficient without mention of the estate or interest being sold because this aspect is governed by implied terms (*Timmins* v. *Moreland Street Property Co., Ltd.* [1958] Ch. 110).

Signature of memorandum.—The object of the signature is to identify the party in the contract, *and not to authenticate the contract* (*Re Hoyle* [1893] 1 Ch. 84). The word in the subsection is " signed " and not " subscribed," and therefore if one of the parties (or his authorised agent) *writes out* an agreement containing, in a part of the document which governs the whole, his name, but does not sign it, this name written in the agreement may be a sufficient signature (*Caton* v. *Caton* (1867), L.R. 2 H.L. 127 ; *Evans* v. *Hoare* [1892] 1 Q.B. 593 ; *Brooks* v. *Billingham* (1912), 56 Sol. J. 503 ; *Leeman* v. *Stocks* [1951] Ch. 941). On the other hand, if such document merely contains the name of the party to be charged, and is not written or dictated by him, there will be no sufficient signature as there is no recognition by him of his name to satisfy the statute (*Hucklesby* v. *Hook* (1900), 82 L.T. 117). Similarly, if an intention can be gathered that the parties are actually to sign—for instance, an agreement ending with " As witness our hands "—this will prevent the name in the body being a signature (*Hubert* v. *Turner* (1842), 11 L.J.C.P. 78).

The approval of a draft conveyance by the solicitor of one of the parties will not take the case out of the section.

A signature by initials is a sufficient signature. Parol evidence will be allowed to prove the identity of the person signing (*Chichester* v. *Cobb* (1866), 14 L.T. 433). The signature to a telegram form is a sufficient signature to the contract contained in a telegram (*McBlain* v. *Cross* (1871), 25 L.T. 804).

A signed letter containing an admission of the bargain was held to be sufficient to satisfy the statute, although in the letter the writer repudiated his liability (*Daniels* v. *Trefusis* [1914] 1 Ch. 788). A signed offer which sufficiently sets forth particulars may be accepted by parol (*Reuss* v. *Picksley* (1866), L.R. 1 Ex. 342 ; *Filby* v. *Hounsell* [1896] 2 Ch. 737 ; *Parker* v. *Clark* [1960] 1 W.L.R. 286). But as a memorandum must, to satisfy the statute, be signed by " the party to be charged," the party signing can alone have the contract enforced against him (*Seton* v. *Slade* (1802), 7 Ves. 265 ; *Lever* v. *Koffler* [1901] 1 Ch. 543). That is to say, the other party not signing may enforce the contract provided that he is prepared to perform his part of the contract (*Auerbach* v. *Nelson* [1919] 2 Ch. 383).

Signature by solicitor or counsel.—A solicitor may not sign the writing (whether constituting the contract itself, or only a memorandum of it) which makes an enforceable contract within L.P.A. 1925, s. 40 (1), unless this is within his authority received from his client. Whether he has such authority or not is, as always, a question of fact or construction or both. But certainly no implication that he has authority to sign the contract itself appears to arise merely from the solicitor-client relationship, although instructions to a solicitor to act would seem sufficient for him to sign a memorandum of an already negotiated oral contract (*North* v. *Loomes* [1919] 1 Ch. 378). Thus in *Horner* v. *Walker* [1923] 2 Ch. 218, it was held that a letter signed by the lessee's solicitor purporting to enclose an engrossment of the lease formed an adequate memorandum. The lessee's solicitor had authority to carry out the transaction in the usual way and so had authority to sign the letter although no-one thought that it might be treated as a memorandum of the oral agreement for the lease. It is thought that the same rule would be applied to a letter sending requisitions or a draft conveyance if the documents together contain all the terms of the contract. Similarly in *Gavaghan* v. *Edwards* [1961] 2 Q.B. 220, a note of a telephone conversation with the purchaser, confirming what he had already agreed with the vendor, made by the solicitor acting for both parties on a copy letter, was held to amount, with the copy letter, to a memorandum binding on the purchaser. In this case, Danckwerts, L.J., said (at p. 226) that " from the way in which the instructions are given to the solicitor, he may by implication be entitled to sign a memorandum which will bind his client." Against this, the courts have not been prepared to find that the giving of instructions to a solicitor to act in a transaction which is still in a state of negotiation (for example, to prepare or approve a draft contract where the parties have agreed "subject to contract" : see *ante*, p. 35) confers any authority to conclude or sign the contract itself (*Smith* v. *Webster* (1876), 3 Ch. D. 49 ; *Bowen* v. *Duc d'Orleans* (1900), 16 T.L.R. 226 ; and see *Daniels* v. *Trefusis* [1914] 1 Ch. 788, at p. 798). In practice, therefore, it is probably better to assume that a solicitor's authority to sign the contract itself can only be given to him expressly whilst his authority to sign a memorandum of a contract may be implied.

In a case where a vendor signed a contract and handed it to his solicitor to exchange for the duplicate and the solicitor made unauthorised alterations to make it correspond with the part produced by the purchaser it was intimated that if the matter had stopped there the contract would not have been binding on the client, but as the vendor afterwards ratified the alterations, it was held that such ratification operated retrospectively (*Koenigsblatt* v. *Sweet* [1923] 2 Ch. 314). See also *Griffiths* v. *Young* [1970] Ch. 675 and *Law* v. *Jones* [1973] 2 All E.R. 437 as to an oral contract being sufficiently evidenced by a solicitor's letters even though these letters contained the words "subject to contract," and *Tiverton Estates, Ltd.* v. *Wearwell, Ltd.* (1973), *The Times*, 21st November, to the contrary (*ante*, pp. 36 and 42).

In *Grindell* v. *Bass* [1920] 2 Ch. 487, counsel signed a defence in an action, containing an admission of a verbal contract, and all the terms thereof. It was held that the document was a sufficient memorandum for the purposes of the statute. It did not matter that the fact that a memorandum within the statute would thereby be brought into existence was not present either to the minds of counsel or client ; counsel, being the authorised agent to sign the particular document, was an agent "thereunto lawfully authorised" within the meaning of the statute. See also *Farr, Smith & Co.* v. *Messers, Ltd.* [1928] 1 K.B. 397, and *H. Clark (Doncaster), Ltd.* v. *Wilkinson* [1965] Ch. 694.

Signature by auctioneer.—An auctioneer has an implied authority to sign a contract on behalf of the highest bidder at a sale by auction, but the signature must be made at the time or as soon after the sale as can reasonably be considered a part of the transaction (*Sims* v. *Landray* [1894] 2 Ch. 318 ; *Van Praagh* v. *Everidge* [1903] 1 Ch. 434). In *Chaney* v. *Macklow* [1929] 1 Ch. 461, the purchaser refused to sign the contract, and left the auction room. The auctioneer returned to his own office about three miles away, and when told that the purchaser had not called to sign the contract, he signed it himself on behalf of the purchaser. It was held by the Court of Appeal that it was impossible to fix the exact moment at which the implied authority of an auctioneer to sign a contract on behalf of a purchaser ceased, but that Maugham, J., having come to the conclusion that the signature of the auctioneer could fairly be held to be part of the transaction, that decision could not be interfered with. Signing the next day might be sufficient if there was good reason for the delay (*Chaney* v. *Maclow, ante*), but signing a week later would not be sufficient (*Bell* v. *Balls* [1897] 1 Ch. 663).

The signature must be made by the auctioneer in the capacity of agent for the purchaser (*Dewar* v. *Mintoft* [1912] 2 K.B. 373). An auctioneer's clerk has no such authority, though the authority may be conferred on him by word, sign or otherwise (*Bell* v. *Balls, ante*).

The auctioneer is also the agent of the vendor and has authority to sign a memorandum on his behalf. It appears that the authority to sign for the vendor is not so limited as to time as is the authority to sign for the purchaser

(*McMeekin* v. *Stevenson* [1917] 1 Ir. R. 348), and is not conditional on receipt of the deposit from the purchaser (*Phillips* v. *Butler* [1945] Ch. 358). See also *Richards* v. *Phillips* [1969] 1 Ch. 39.

Signature by other agent.—The authority to an agent to sign a contract need not be in writing (*Yonge* v. *Toynbee* [1910] 1 K.B. 215 ; *Daniels* v. *Trefusis* [1914] 1 Ch. 788).

In determining whether an agent has authority to sign a contract, the point is not whether the principal had authorised the agent expressly to sign the particular document forming a record of the contract, but whether the agent was acting within the scope of his authority. If he was, the signature is binding (*John Griffiths Cycle Corporation, Ltd.* v. *Humber & Co., Ltd.* [1899] 2 Q.B. 414 ; *Daniels* v. *Trefusis, ante ; Re Drabble Bros.* [1930] 2 Ch. 211).

A general authority to find a purchaser does not authorise an agent *to sign a contract* on behalf of the proposed vendor. His business is to get offers and submit them to his employer for acceptance (*Thuman* v. *Best* (1907), 97 L.T. 239 ; *Lewcock* v. *Bromley* [1920] W.N. 346 ; *Keen* v. *Mear* [1920] 2 Ch. 574).

Whether an authority to *sell* implies the power to sign a contract must be regarded as doubtful. In *Rosenbaum* v. *Belson* [1900] 2 Ch. 267, the authority was in these terms : " Please sell for me my houses . . . , and I agree to pay you . . . commission . . . on the purchase price accepted." Buckley, J., said : " This is an authority to sell. A sale *prima facie* means a sale effectual in point of law, including the execution of a contract where the law requires a contract in writing. I do not find anything in the circumstances of this case which induces me to say that the word ' sell ' here means less than this." The contract which the agent would in these circumstances be empowered to sign would be an " open contract," and not a contract containing any special condition as to title (*Keen* v. *Mear, ante*) ; but the vendor would be bound even by a special contract, if he should subsequently approve of and adopt it (*ibid.*). However, in *Wragg* v. *Lovett* [1948] 2 All E.R. 968, Lord Greene, M.R., said, at p. 969 : " we must not be understood as suggesting that when a vendor merely authorises a house agent to ' sell ' at a stated price he must be taken to be authorising the agent to do more than agree with an intending purchaser, the essential (and, generally, the most essential) term, i.e., the price. The making of a contract is no part of an estate agent's business, and although, on the facts of an individual case, the person who employs him may authorise him to make a contract, such an authorisation is not lightly to be inferred from vague or ambiguous language." This case was decided on the finding of fact that the agent had authority to make the contract which he entered into, and, consequently, the above quotation appears to be *obiter*. It is not in accord with the decision in *Rosenbaum* v. *Belson, ante*, which, unfortunately, was not considered.

If an agent enters into a contract in his own name so as to bind himself personally, there is a good contract, and parol evidence can be given to show that he is contracting as agent for an undisclosed principal, and the principal when so disclosed or discovered can both sue and be sued upon it *even though the other party knew the agent was acting as such* (*Filby* v. *Hounsell* [1896] 2 Ch. 737 ; *Drughorn (Fred), Ltd.* v. *Rederiaktiebolaget Trans-Atlantic* [1919] A.C. 203 ; *Basma* v. *Weekes* [1950] A.C. 441). But evidence of authority of an outside principal is not admissible if such evidence would contradict some term in the contract itself. For instance, where one of the parties is described in the contract as " the owner," or as " proprietor," evidence is not admissible to show that somebody else is the owner or proprietor (*Humble* v. *Hunter* (1848), 12 Q.B. 310 ; *Formby Brothers* v. *Formby* [1910] W.N. 48).

Where an agent contracts for an undisclosed principal, and he is sued, and judgment is obtained against him, this judgment against the agent, although it may be unsatisfied, will bar any action against the principal (*R.M.K.R.M. Somasundaram Chetty* v. *M.R.M.V.L. Supramanian Chetty* [1926] A.C. 761).

On the other hand, where the agent expressly contracted only as agent on behalf of an undisclosed or unnamed principal and not so as to bind himself personally, the principal can only sue on the contract if his name appears in the memorandum thereof or his identity, from the description of him therein appearing, cannot fairly be disputed (*Lovesy* v. *Palmer* [1916] 2 Ch. 233 ; *Keen* v. *Mear, ante*).

Where an agent contracts professedly on behalf of a named principal, whose authority he has, and signs the contract as agent, he is not personally liable (*James (Arthur) & Co.* v. *John Weston & Co., Ltd.* (1929), 73 Sol. J. 484). Where a person signs a contract " as agent " for another, he is to be taken to contract as an agent only, and is not personally liable even though in the body of the contract he purports to be the principal (*Universal Steam Navigation Co.* v. *James McKelvie & Co.* [1923] A.C. 492). A signature " for " a named person is equivalent to a signature " as agent for " that person and so avoids any personal liability on the agent (*Kimber Coal Co.* v. *Stone and Rolfe, Ltd.* [1926] A.C. 414).

Although a person may have signed a contract without express or implied authority, the principal can, if he wishes, adopt and ratify the act, in which case he will be bound just as much as if he had himself signed the contract (*Koenigsblatt* v. *Sweet* [1923] 2 Ch. 314). Ratification may be defined to be the adoption by one person of acts done by another on his behalf but without his authority. Where, however, an offer has been accepted by an agent subject to ratification by his principal, there is no contract until ratification and at any time before ratification the offer may be withdrawn (*Watson* v. *Davies* [1931] 1 Ch. 455). But suppose an unauthorised person should accept an offer unconditionally on behalf of someone alleged to be his principal and then the offer is withdrawn. May the alleged principal ratify the acceptance after such withdrawal ? This was the case in *Bolton Partners* v. *Lambert* (1888), 41 Ch. D. 295, and it was held by the Court of Appeal that the ratification related back to the acceptance, and therefore the withdrawal was inoperative. This decision was followed by a Divisional Court in *Re Tiedemann and Ledermann Frères* [1899] 2 Q.B. 66, but doubt was thrown on it by the Privy Council in *Fleming* v. *Bank of New Zealand* [1900] A.C. 577.

Memorandum must contain all material terms.—It is not sufficient that the memorandum should show on its face a valid contract ; it must evidence the contract actually made between the parties. Thus, in *Smith* v. *MacGowan* [1938] 3 All E.R. 447, a solicitor, on the defendant's instructions, purchased three separate lots of freehold property at an auction. One memorandum was signed by the solicitor, by which the defendant was expressed to agree to purchase all three lots at a certain price. It was held that, as the agent had no authority to combine the separate agreements into one agreement, the memorandum did not correctly evidence any of the three contracts and so did not satisfy the requirements of the statute.

The rule is that a contract which is required by statute to be evidenced by writing, and which is wholly in writing, cannot be contradicted, varied or added to by parol evidence. But where the contract is partly in writing and partly oral the rule does not apply and evidence can be given by the party to be charged to prove that the written document does not contain all the terms and is therefore unenforceable (*De Lassalle* v. *Guildford* [1901] 2 K.B. 215 ; *Hutton* v. *Watling* [1948] 1 All E.R. 803). See also *Lloyd, Ltd.* v. *Sturgeon Falls Pulp Co., Ltd.* (1901) 85 L.T. 162 ; *Bristol Tramways* v. *Fiat Motors, Ltd.* [1901] 2 K.B. 831, and cases therein referred to.

In the latter circumstances the fact that the written document does not contain all the terms agreed on will be a good defence to an action for specific performance, and the defendant will be allowed to bring extrinsic evidence to prove the omission (*Johnson* v. *Humphrey* [1964] 1 All E.R. 460 ; *Beckett* v. *Nurse* [1948] 1 K.B. 535). It appears, however, that if the term omitted is solely for the benefit of the plaintiff, he may waive it and insist on performance of the contract in accordance with the written document (*Smith* v. *Wheatcroft* (1878), 9 Ch. D. 223 ; *North* v. *Loomes* [1919] 1 Ch. 378). In *North* v. *Loomes, ante,* the memorandum took the form of a receipt, and it was alleged that the receipt omitted a term of the oral contract that the defendant would pay the plaintiff's costs. The learned judge stated that the term was one of insufficient importance to have been referred to in the receipt and was a term exclusively for the benefit of the party suing, who was entitled to waive the benefit of the term and to sue on the agreement as recorded in the receipt. See also *Johnson* v. *Humphrey, ante.*

No question of waiver by a vendor of terms in his favour can arise unless he can first establish that there was a concluded contract (*Allsop* v. *Orchard* [1923] 1 Ch. 323). In *Hawkins* v. *Price* [1947] Ch. 645, Evershed, J., pointed out that there may well be a difference between " cases, on the one hand, in which the memorandum is the contract or purports to be a record of it, and cases, on the other hand, where the contract sued on is oral and the question is whether some document such as a receipt for a deposit (which does not on the face of it purport to be an agreement) sufficiently satisfies the statute." The learned judge stated, in a case where the memorandum set up was a receipt for a deposit, that if the term omitted from the memorandum was " really an essential part of the bargain " the contract was unenforceable. He decided that a term as to vacant possession was for the benefit of both parties, and so, without deciding how far the qualification illustrated in *North* v. *Loomes* extended, the case did not fall within it. It appears, however, that there may be cases in which, on the facts, it is found that the date of possession is not vital, in which cases the omission of it will not render a memorandum insufficient (*Fowler* v. *Bratt* [1950] 2 K.B. 96).

The converse case, namely where the term omitted is solely for the benefit of the defendant, has appeared even more doubtful. Can the plaintiff enforce the contract on the basis that he submits to performing the omitted term ? In *Martin* v. *Pycroft* (1852), 22 L.J. Ch. 94, the plaintiff sued for specific performance of an agreement for a sub-lease contained in a written document. The defendants alleged that though not in the document it was part of the arrangement that the plaintiff should pay the defendants a premium of £200. The plaintiff assented and submitted to pay the £200. The Court of Appeal decided that it would be contrary to all proper principles to allow the defendants to resist specific performance by setting up the added term. On this authority the rule was accepted in Williams on Vendor and Purchaser (4th ed., 1939, vol. I, p. 5), that if the plaintiff submits to performing the omitted term he may enforce the contract. Nevertheless, Harman, J., in *Burgess* v. *Cox* [1951] Ch. 383, decided that there was no such rule and that a plaintiff could not enforce a contract within the L.P.A. 1925, s. 40, by endeavouring to prove a term not in the memorandum. The decision in *Burgess* v. *Cox* was criticised and the rule stated in Williams supported by " R. E. M." in the *Law Quarterly Review*, vol. 67, p. 229 *et seq.*, and now these criticisms, the decision in *Martin* v. *Pycroft* and the rule accepted in Williams have been followed (in preference to *Burgess* v. *Cox*) by Plowman, J., in *Scott* v. *Bradley* [1971] 1 Ch. 850 (where the plaintiff, submitting to perform the missing term that he pay half the defendants' costs, was held entitled to specific performance).

Any terms which are not expressly agreed between the parties, but which are implied into their agreement, need not be contained in the memorandum for it to be sufficient. Thus, although the parties may have agreed on the basis that the freehold interest to be sold is subject to a lease, the memorandum need not mention that lease. There is an implication that the interest to be sold is the fee simple in possession free from incumbrances. Nevertheless, this implication may be impliedly rebutted and the purchaser will be compelled to accept a title subject to the lease as it is an irremovable incumbrance known to him prior to the contract (*Timmins* v. *Moreland Street Property Co., Ltd.* [1958] Ch. 110) : compare the explanation, *post*, p. 101.

Rectification.—Another exception to the " all terms " rule exists where the equitable remedy of rectification is applicable. If any of the provisions of the prior oral agreement are omitted from the memorandum thereof due to a mistake common to both parties, then the court may, in one action, both rectify the memorandum and decree specific performance of the true agreement : *Craddock, Bros. Ltd* v. *Hunt* [1923] 2 Ch. 136 (see also *United States* v. *Motor Trucks, Ltd.* [1924] A.C. 196, at p. 201). Further, after a recent re-examination of this remedy by the Court of Appeal, it now appears that there is jurisdiction to rectify on the basis of a common continuing intention of the parties, such intention having some outward expression, even though no prior concluded agreement existed (see *Joscelyne* v. *Nissen* [1970] 2 Q.B. 86). Consequently, considerable inroads into the " all terms " rule of s. 40 (1) could be achieved with sales of land where the negotiations customarily proceed throughout on a basis of various common continuing intentions expressed in correspondence up to a formal exchange of contracts. See further, *post*, 84.

Parol evidence of the sense in which words are used.—It is well settled that if the language of a written contract has a definite and unambiguous meaning parol evidence is not admissible to show that the parties meant something different from what they had said. But if the description of the subject-matter is susceptible of more than one interpretation, evidence is admissible to show what were the facts to which the contract relates. If there are circumstances which the parties must be taken to have had in view in entering into the contract it is necessary that the court which construes the contract should have the circumstances before it (*Charrington & Co., Ltd.* v. *Wooder* [1914] A.C. 71).

Variation, abandonment or rescission of contract.—Where it is alleged that there has been a *variation* of a written contract by a new parol contract which incorporates some of the terms of the old contract, the new contract must be looked at in its entirety, and if the terms of the *new contract* when thus considered are such that, by reason of s. 40 of the L.P.A. 1925, they cannot be given in evidence unless in writing, then, being an unenforceable contract, it cannot operate to effect a variation of the original contract (*Noble* v. *Ward* (1867), 15 L.T. 672 ; *Morris* v. *Baron & Co.* [1918] A.C. 1). But, notwithstanding that the proposed variation cannot be given in evidence, if the parties have so acted that it would be fraudulent to insist on the carrying out of the terms of the old contract, the party wishing to abide by the new contract would be entitled to ask for the assistance of the court on the equitable ground of part performance.

It was held in *Hartley* v. *Hymans* [1920] 3 K.B. 475, that, in the case of a contract which requires to be evidenced by writing, *the waiver* of a stipulation which is of the essence of the contract cannot be made by parol. In *Levey and Co.* v. *Goldberg* [1922] 1 K.B. 688, the defendant, by a contract in writing, agreed to buy from the plaintiffs certain goods to be delivered within a defined period. At the oral request of the defendant the plaintiffs withheld delivery during that period. The defendant afterwards refused to accept delivery and, in the action commenced by the plaintiffs to enforce the agreement, contended that there had been a parol variation of the written contract which was unenforceable as it was not in writing. It was held that the forbearance by the plaintiffs, at the request of the defendant, did not constitute a variation of the contract, and that the plaintiffs were entitled to maintain their action. See also *British and Bennington's, Ltd.* v. *N. W. Cachar Tea Co., Ltd.* [1923] A.C. 48 ; and *Royal Exchange Assurance* v. *Hope* [1928] Ch. 179.

For many years there was confusion as to what amounted to variation and what to rescission. It was decided in *Morris* v. *Baron & Co., ante,* that the test as to whether there is a rescission or only a variation is whether there is an intention *in any event* to rescind independent of any further intention which may exist to substitute a second contract, and not merely the desire for an alteration, however sweeping in terms, which still leaves the first contract subsisting. See also *Fisher, Ltd.* v. *Eastwoods, Ltd.* [1936] 1 All E.R. 421. Also distinguished must be mere further negotiations which, if they prove to be abortive, do not affect the original contract in any way (*Davies* v. *Sweet* [1962] 2 Q.B. 300).

Parol evidence is admissible to prove a total abandonment of an agreement required to be in writing (*Morris* v. *Baron & Co., ante*). Although a new oral agreement may itself be incapable of being sued on, that agreement may have the effect of rescinding the original agreement, where there is a clear intention to rescind as distinguished from an intention to vary (*ibid.*).

PART 3.   PART PERFORMANCE

The equitable doctrine of part performance was, shortly, as follows. When the contract had been partly performed by the parties thereto, and acts had been done which must, from their nature, have been referable to the contract, equities arose which could not be administered unless the contract was regarded. In such a case the court had jurisdiction, notwithstanding the Statute of Frauds, to inquire into the actual contract which had been made, and having discovered by parol evidence the terms of that contract, to enforce its performance (*Lester* v. *Foxcroft* (1801), and notes thereon, 2 White and Tudor's Leading Cases, 9th ed., p. 410 *et seq.* ; *Caton* v. *Caton* (1866), L.R. 1 Ch. 137, at p. 148). It was said in *Höhler* v. *Aston* [1920] 2 Ch. 420, that where there was a contract, although not in writing, the Statute of Frauds could not be pleaded with success where one of the parties had incurred expense or altered his position on the faith of the agreement.

Section 4 of the Statute of Frauds, so far as it relates to contracts for the sale of land, was repealed and reproduced as s. 40 of the L.P.A. 1925 (quoted, *ante*, p. 40), with the express addition, declaratory of the law, that the section is not to affect the law relating to part performance. The law, therefore, not only remains the same, but has received statutory recognition. All the cases decided on the Statute of Frauds apply to s. 40.

Existence of valid contract essential.—It will be seen that the rule assumes that there is a contract in existence. Lord Brougham, in *Thynne* v. *Glengall* (1848), 2 H.L. Cas. 131, 158, said : " There can be no part performance where there is no completed agreement in existence." But it is not necessary that the agreement should be in writing. If the agreement is by word of mouth oral evidence will usually be admitted to prove the existence of the contract. Where one or more of the material terms of an alleged contract cannot be determined, either by interpretation or as being of a kind which the law will imply, there is no contract *even though there has been an act of part performance*, and the court cannot grant specific performance or damages (*Stimson* v. *Gray* [1929] 1 Ch. 629). In that case a proposed purchaser signed an agreement to purchase premises subject to taking his conveyance " in the model form of conveyance specially prepared." No form had been prepared and the wrong form had been sent. It was held that if the court, as in the case in question, is unable to determine all the material terms of the alleged contract, it is impossible to say that there is a binding contract which the court can enforce. Similarly, where the contract is so ambiguously or inexactly drawn as a whole, or in some important particular, that it is impossible to determine its meaning, the contract will be void. For instance, in *Pearce* v. *Watts* (1875), L.R. 20 Eq. 492, a contract was entered into for the sale of an estate, the vendor reserving " the necessary land for making a railway through the estate," and it was held that the reservation made the contract void for uncertainty. See also *Re Vince ; ex parte Baxter* [1892] 2 Q.B. 478.

What acts amount to part performance.—The act of part performance relied on must be that of the party seeking to enforce the contract, and not of the party sought to be charged. To take the case out of the statute so that the contract may be enforced in spite of the absence of a written memorandum (*a*) the act must be unequivocally referable to the contract, (*b*) it must be such an act as would render the non-performance a fraud, and (*c*) the contract must be one which can be enforced by the court.

An act which, though in truth done in pursuance of a contract, admits of explanation without supposing a contract, will not be deemed to constitute an act of part performance, taking the case out of the statute (*Dale* v. *Hamilton* (1846), 5 Hare 369). For instance, the payment of a deposit, or even the payment of the whole purchase-money, is not considered an act of part performance which would let in oral evidence. The reason is that it cannot be said to have any necessary connection with the kind of contract in question (*Clinan* v. *Cooke* (1802), 1 Sch. & Lef. 41 ; *Hughes* v. *Morris* (1852), 2 De G.M. & G. 349 ; *Maddison* v. *Alderson* (1883), 8 App. Cas. 467). Similarly, the mere payment of rent in advance under an oral agreement for a lease is not regarded as an adequate act of part performance (*Chaproniere* v. *Lambert* [1917] 2 Ch. 356). On the other hand, it was decided in *Miller & Aldworth, Ltd.* v. *Sharp* [1899] 1 Ch. 622, that the payment of increased rent by a tenant in possession pursuant to an oral agreement to grant a further lease at such increased rent was in itself a sufficient part performance to take the case out of the statute and to let in parol evidence of the agreement.

In practice, the acts which are most often successfully relied on as acts of part performance are the delivery of possession by the vendor or the taking of possession by the purchaser. Delivery of possession complies with the necessary conditions (*Maddison* v. *Alderson* (1883), 8 App. Cas. 467 ; see also *Kingswood Estate Co., Ltd.* v. *Anderson* [1963] 2 Q.B. 169, and *Wakeham* v. *Mackenzie* [1968] 1 W.L.R. 1175). The reason is that the court, finding a stranger in acknowledged possession of the land who would *prima facie* be a trespasser, could only explain his being there by the supposition of an antecedent contract (*Hodson* v. *Heuland* [1896] 2 Ch. 428 ; *Biss* v. *Hygate* [1918] 2 K.B. 314). But the delivery of the keys for the purpose of making alterations is not necessarily an act of part performance (*Brown* v. *Strong* (1907), 122 L.T. News. 367). So, if the purchaser is also the tenant, his possession might be referable to his tenancy as well as to his contract of purchase, and therefore is not a sufficient part performance (*Wills* v. *Stradling* (1797), 3 Ves. 378). In *Daniels* v. *Trefusis* [1914] 1 Ch. 788, the purchaser requested the vendor to give notice to the tenants in order to obtain early possession, and the action of the vendor in giving such notice was held to constitute part performance by the vendor.

An example of a case in which a purchaser's act of taking possession was considered as part performance such as to enable him to give evidence of a parol contract is to be found in *Brough* v. *Nettleton* [1921] 2 Ch. 25. *B* entered into a parol agreement with *N* to take a house on lease with an option of purchase during the term. *B* took possession and later gave notice of his intention to exercise the option. *N* denied that he had given an option and pleaded the Statute of Frauds. It was held that the taking possession by *B* constituted part performance and entitled him to *give evidence of the entire contract*, including the option of purchase.

The carrying out of substantial alterations or improvements may be sufficient part performance even if there is no delivery of possession. Thus, in *Dickinson* v. *Barrow* [1904] 2 Ch. 339, the defendant agreed orally to buy land with a dwelling-house to be built on it by the plaintiffs. During construction the defendant visited the premises and at her request certain alterations were made. It was held that the acts done by the plaintiffs were acts of part performance and that parol evidence of the contract was admissible in an action for specific performance of the contract. See also *Rawlinson* v. *Ames* [1925] Ch. 96. In *Broughton* v. *Snook* [1938] Ch. 505, the plaintiff entered into possession and carried out substantial alterations, following an oral contract for purchase of the fee simple. At that time the land was subject to a tenancy but the acts had been done with the consent of the defendant landlord. It was held that they amounted to part performance. The delivery of an abstract of title is not an act which can be considered to be part performance (*Whaley* v. *Bagnel* (1765), 1 Bro. P.C. 345).

PART 4. CONDITIONS OF SALE

Difference between particulars and conditions.—It was stated by Malins, V.-C., in *Torrance* v. *Bolton* (1872), L.R. 8 Ch. 118, that " the proper office of the particulars is to describe the subject-matter of the contract ; that of the conditions to state the terms on which it is sold." Warrington, J., in *Blaiberg* v. *Keeves* [1906] 2 Ch. 175, at p. 184, said that it was not the function of the particulars to deal with the title at all ; that had to be dealt with on evidence, and it was the function of the conditions to state what evidence of title the purchaser was to have.

Nevertheless, the Council of The Law Society has drawn attention to the fact that " the proper description of the subject-matter involves not only a physical description, but also a description of the exact estate or interest sold and of every charge upon it or right restricting the purchaser's absolute enjoyment of it ; these matters should appear in the particulars and not merely in the conditions. Reference should accordingly be made in the particulars to onerous covenants, easements and the like, whether or not they are also mentioned in the conditions " (*Law Society's Gazette*, vol. 49, p. 29).

In *Robins* v. *Evans* (1863), 2 H. & C. 410, it was decided that a misrepresentation in the particulars cannot be cured by information given in the conditions. In that case certain ground rents had been sold by auction. They were described in the particulars as including £4 4s. garden rent secured on certain land and residences. It turned out that the garden rent was not in the nature of a ground rent issuing out of the land, but a gross sum payable under a covenant. There was information in the conditions which showed the proper position. It was held that notwithstanding the condition the purchaser was entitled to rescind the contract and recover his deposit.

The distinction may have some relevance to conditions for payment of compensation for error. In *Re Courcier and Harrold's Contract* [1923] 1 Ch. 565, the conditions provided that " If any error, mis-statement or omission shall be discovered in the *particulars*, the same shall not annul the sale, nor shall any compensation be allowed by the vendor in respect thereof." Sargant, J., held that " this general condition cannot be construed so narrowly as to exclude from its purview omissions in the part of the documents under which the sale was effected divided off and headed 'Conditions of Sale '." If the learned judge intended to hold that the word " particulars " must be taken to include the " conditions of sale " it would seem that this part of the judgment was not in agreement with previous decisions, or with the practice of conveyancers. In *Re Beyfus and Masters' Contract* (1888), 39 Ch. D. 110, there was a condition that compensation should be made for errors of description of the *property*. It was held that the condition did not extend to defects in the *title* to the property, as where the land sold was described in the particulars as leasehold, whereas it was only held on an underlease.

Open contracts.—Conditions of sale are so often made that it is sometimes forgotten that a code of rules is implied by law in an " open " contract, that is, where there are no conditions. An open contract is formed if agreement is reached as to the parties, the property and the price. In considering what conditions should be inserted in a contract, and in construing conditions, it is essential to start by ascertaining the conditions which will be implied if no provision to the contrary is contained in the contract.

The following miscellaneous conditions will be implied where there is no condition to the contrary :—

    (a) That the sale is of an estate in fee simple in possession free from incumbrances. If the property on inspection is vacant and the contract is silent as to tenancies, it is implied that vacant possession will be given on completion (see *Cook* v. *Taylor* [1942] Ch. 349).

(b) That the vendor will show a good title. The rules as to how title should be deduced on a sale of registered land are stipulated by statute and mostly may not be varied by the contract (L.R.A. 1925, s. 110).

(c) That the purchase shall be completed as soon as a good title has been shown to the property and that a good title shall be shown within a reasonable time.

(d) That a vendor shall have the right to retain documents of title if he retains any part of the land to which they relate (L.P.A. 1925, s. 45 (9) (a)). And he may retain an instrument creating a trust which is still subsisting, or an instrument relating to the appointment or discharge of trustees of a subsisting trust (L.P.A. 1925, s. 45 (9) (b)).

(e) That such acknowledgments and undertakings as the purchaser is entitled to shall be made at his expense, except that the vendor shall bear the expense of perusal and execution by himself and persons other than the purchaser (L.P.A. 1925, s. 45 (8)).

(f) That the inability of the vendor to give an acknowledgment for production of deeds shall be no objection to title if the purchaser will have an equitable right to production thereof (L.P.A. 1925, s. 45 (7)).

(g) A condition fixing the meaning in contracts of the words " month " and " person," and the use of expressions of number and gender. It is provided by s. 61 of the L.P.A. 1925 that in all deeds, contracts, wills, orders and other instruments made or coming into operation after 1925, unless the context otherwise requires :—

   (i) " Month " means calendar month.

   (ii) " Person " includes a corporation.

   (iii) The singular includes the plural and *vice versa*. This makes unnecessary such expressions as " the person or persons claiming under him " ; " the trustees or trustee," etc.

   (iv) The masculine includes the feminine and *vice versa*. This does away with such expressions as " his, her or their."

(h) Time is not considered to be " of the essence of the contract " unless there is an express condition that it is to be so, or unless the circumstances are such as to show that the parties intended it to be so (L.P.A. 1925, s. 41).

Conditions which will be void by statute.—

(a) A condition that a purchaser of a legal estate in land shall accept a title made with the concurrence of any person entitled to an equitable interest, if a title can be made free from such equitable interest without such concurrence under a trust for sale, or under the L.P.A., or the S.L.A., or any other statute (L.P.A. 1925, s. 42 (1), (8)).

(b) A condition that a purchaser of a legal estate in land shall pay the costs of obtaining a vesting order or the appointment of trustees of a settlement, or the appointment of trustees of a conveyance on trust for sale ; or of preparing a conveyance on trust for sale, or a vesting instrument for bringing into force the provisions of the S.L.A. or the stamping or execution thereof (L.P.A. 1925, s. 42 (2), (8)).

(c) A condition that an outstanding legal estate is to be traced or got in by or at the expense of a purchaser, or that no objection is to be taken on account of an outstanding legal estate (L.P.A. 1925, s. 42 (3), (8)).

(d) A condition that a purchaser of a legal estate who is entitled to have it discharged from a *registered* equitable interest which will not be over-reached by the conveyance to him, shall not require such registration to be cancelled or the person entitled to the equitable interest to concur in the conveyance, and, in either case, free of expense to the vendor (L.P.A. 1925, s. 43 (1), (2)).

(e) A condition made with a view to preventing a purchaser employing his own solicitor (L.P.A. 1925, s. 48).

(f) A condition that a purchaser shall not be entitled to have a power of attorney affecting the title or a copy of the material portions thereof delivered to him, free of expense (L.P.A. 1925, s. 125 (2), (3) ; Law of Property (Amendment) Act, 1926 ; Powers of Attorney Act, 1971, s. 11 (3)).

(g) A condition varying certain of the statutory provisions applying as between a vendor and purchaser of registered land (L.R.A. 1925, s. 110).

(h) A condition excluding or restricting any liability or remedy for mis-representation before contract, except to the extent that the court (or arbitrator) may allow reliance on it as being fair and reasonable in the circumstances of the case (Misrepresentation Act, 1967, s. 3).

(i) A condition purporting to exclude the statutory provision that as against the vendor any question as to registered land charges is to be determined by reference to a purchaser's actual knowledge (L.P.A. 1969, s. 24 (2)).

Contract to convey an undivided share.—As, since 1925, a legal estate cannot subsist or be created in an undivided share in land (L.P.A. 1925, s. 1 (6)), it is provided by s. 42 (6) of the same Act that any contract to convey an undivided share in land will be deemed to be sufficiently complied with by the conveyance of a corresponding share in the proceeds of sale of the land in like manner as if the contract had been to convey that corresponding share. See also *Cooper* v. *Critchley* [1955] Ch. 431 ; cf. *Irani Finance, Ltd.* v. *Singh* [1971] Ch. 59.

General conditions of sale.—Most contracts for the sale of land are made subject to standard general conditions of sale, such as those in The Law Society's Conditions of Sale, 1973 Revision, or the National Conditions of Sale, 18th ed. It is not necessary to reproduce these forms. Most of the important conditions contained in them will be found discussed in relation to the topic with which they deal.

Conditions as to title.—Special conditions as to title are often made and the following are some common provisions :—

(a) *That the vendor shall give a free conveyance.* This will not prevent the purchaser from investigating the title.

(b) *That the vendor expressly agrees by the contract that a good title shall be shown.* In this case the fact that the purchaser may know of a defect in the title is no answer by the vendor.

(c) *That the purchaser agrees to accept the title of the vendor.* Even in this case the purchaser has the right to assume that the vendor has disclosed all that he ought to have disclosed, and if he has not done so the condition is not binding.

(d) *That the vendor contracts to sell the land subject to such title as he has himself, such condition not stating whether or not the title is a good holding one.* In such a case the vendor is bound to convey the right or interest free from an existing incumbrance.

(e) *That the vendor agrees to sell " all the estate, interest and title which is at the date of this contract vested in him."* These were the words in a decided case, and notwithstanding that there was a mortgage on the property of which the purchaser was unaware, it was held that the purchaser had to take the property subject to the mortgage and could not require the vendor to pay off the mortgage.

An express representation by the vendor in regard to his title relieves the purchaser from an investigation of the facts of the case, and it is no defence to say that the purchaser had the means of discovery, and might with reasonable care have discovered that the statement was untrue.

See generally Chapter 5, Part I, *post.*

Condition preventing a purchaser employing his own solicitor.—The effect of s. 48 (1) of the L.P.A. 1925 is that any condition made on the sale of any interest in land to the effect that the conveyance (including a demise or sub-demise when the sale is carried out in that form) to, or the registration of the title of, the purchaser, shall be prepared or carried out at the expense of the purchaser by the solicitor for the vendor, and any condition which might restrict a purchaser in the selection of a solicitor to act on his behalf, is void. But this is not to affect any right reserved to a vendor to furnish a form of conveyance to a purchaser from which the draft can be prepared, or to charge a reasonable fee therefor, or, where a perpetual rent-charge is reserved as the only consideration in money or money's worth, to stipulate that the draft conveyance is to be prepared by his solicitor at the expense of the purchaser.

In the opinion of the Council of The Law Society a reasonable fee to be charged by a vendor's solicitor for a form of draft conveyance should not exceed the out-of-pocket expenses of the vendor's solicitor for providing the form ; where the same form is used for more than a few sales, the fee for repro-duction should be nominal only, and half a guinea (presumably now its decimalised equivalent) might be a reasonable fee where the conveyance is not of great length and has no complex plan (*Law Society's Gazette,* vol. 52, pp. 310, 311 ; *ibid.,* vol. 62, p. 184).

In the Council's view " the practice of providing a form of conveyance in estate development or otherwise is normally to assist the vendor by ensuring conformity and therefore high charges cannot be justified. In the Council's view, subject as above mentioned, the practice is unobjectionable, but would not generally be appropriate on the sale of a single property " (*ibid.,* vol. 62, p. 184).

Where, on the reservation of a perpetual rent-charge as the only considera-tion, it is stipulated that the draft conveyance is to be prepared by the vendor's solicitor at the expense of the purchaser, the Council consider that " the vendor's solicitor should, as a matter of good conveyancing practice, not seek to charge the purchaser for a copy of the conveyance (which would include the grant of the rent-charge) any more than a purchaser's solicitor in the usual run of sales and purchases would ask payment of the vendor for a carbon copy of the conveyance, which is normally supplied as a matter of courtesy" (*ibid.*). This suggestion refers only to the supply of a copy of the conveyance. It is understood that the Council do not intend to recommend that anything less than the proper charge should be made for drafting the conveyance where, on account of the rent-charge, the contract provides that the vendor's solicitor shall do that work and may charge the cost to the purchaser.

Similarly, any covenant contained in, or entered into with reference to, any lease or underlease or any agreement therefor made with a view to preventing a purchaser of the interest of the lessee or underlessee employing his own solicitor to prepare his conveyance, or which in any way restricts his right to have his own solicitor to carry out the transaction, is void (L.P.A. 1925, s. 48 (2), (4)). " Provided that, where any covenant or stipulation is rendered void by this subsection, there shall be implied in lieu thereof a covenant or stipulation that the lessee or underlessee or tenant shall register with the lessor or his solicitor within six months from the date thereof, or as soon after the expiration of that period as may be practicable, all conveyances and devolutions (including probates or letters of administration) affecting the lease or underlease and pay a fee of one guinea in respect of each registration, and the power of entry (if any) on breach of any covenant contained in the lease or underlease [agreement or tenancy : s. 48 (4)] shall apply and extend to the breach of any covenant so to be implied " (L.P.A. 1925, s. 48 (2), proviso).

Except where a sale is carried out by demise or sub-demise, the right of the solicitor for the lessor to prepare a lease or underlease or any agreement therefor or other tenancy will remain the same (L.P.A. 1925, s. 48 (3), (4)).

The general object of s. 48 appears to be to make void any condition made to prevent a person choosing his own solicitor, but there is generally nothing to prevent a vendor making a condition that a purchaser shall pay his, the vendor's, solicitor's charges for deducing title and perusing and completing the deed of purchase on his, the vendor's, behalf.

Condition requiring purchaser to assume facts.—A condition requiring the purchaser to assume certain facts can be disregarded as to facts the vendor knows to be untrue (*Re Banister* (1879), 12 Ch. D. 131 ; *Beyfus* v. *Lodge* [1925] Ch. 350), and even as to facts the vendor knows *may* be untrue (*Wilson* v. *Thomas* [1958] 1 W.L.R. 422, where the facts to be assumed depended on the proper construction, with the aid of extrinsic evidence, of a latent ambiguity in a will) ; but not as to facts the vendor believes to be true, although, as a matter of fact, they are not true (*Re Sandbach and Edmondson's Contract* [1891] 1 Ch. 99) ; or possibly as to facts the vendor knows nothing about one way or another (*Re Banister, ante*).

Contract of sale to tenant.—An agreement to purchase does not, *prima facie*, operate as a surrender by the intending purchaser of a tenancy he may hold (*Doe d. Gray* v. *Stanion* (1836), 1 M. & W. 695). On the other hand, an agreement to purchase may contain an express term surrendering the tenancy or a surrender may be implied from provisions in it. Thus, in *Turner* v. *Watts* (1927), 44 T.L.R. 105, 337, a provision that interest should accrue from the date of the agreement on the amount of the purchase price was considered, with other terms, to show an intention to surrender an existing tenancy held by the purchaser. See the explanation in *Leek and Moorlands Building Society* v. *Clark* [1952] 2 Q.B. 788, 791. Similarly, if there is a subsisting statutory tenancy of a house it continues even after the tenant has contracted to buy unless there is something in the contract to indicate that the right of occupation which is to continue is referable to something other than the statute which previously supported it.

Thus, in *Nightingale* v. *Courtney* [1954] 1 Q.B. 399, it was held that a vendor who rescinded on account of the purchaser's failure to complete could not obtain an order for possession as the former statutory tenancy of the purchaser was not surrendered on the making of the contract to purchase.   In that case, however, the contract was expressed to be subject to the tenancy and other circumstances indicated an intention that the tenancy should continue.

A solicitor acting for a landlord on sale of a house to a tenant who can claim the protection of the Rent Acts might, therefore, insert in the draft contract a special condition that the tenancy, whether contractual or statutory, is thereby surrendered and thereafter the former tenant will remain as licensee only.   It is advisable to state that he shall pay interest on the balance of the purchase-money from the date of contract until completion and thus show clearly that he holds as purchaser.   Where these steps are taken the vendor will be able to obtain possession if the purchaser fails to complete.   On the other hand, such a special condition should be resisted by the purchaser, if possible.   It may place him in a difficult position if, for instance, the vendor is unable to make a good title, or has a power to rescind the contract.

Precautions may also have to be taken on sale of a house to a relative of the tenant, for instance his wife or child, or on sale to the tenant and his wife jointly, to ensure that a contractual or statutory tenancy does not continue. A mortgagee from the purchaser or purchasers will be particularly concerned. It now seems to be settled that an express surrender by the tenant would put an end even to a statutory tenancy (*Nightingale* v. *Courtney* [1954] 1 Q.B. 399 ;   *Foster* v. *Robinson* [1951] 1 K.B. 149 ;   *Collins* v. *Claughton* [1959] 1 W.L.R. 145 ;   compare *dicta* of Greene, M.R., in *Brown* v. *Draper* [1944] K.B. 309).   An alternative procedure is to make a contract of sale by the owner with the tenant subject to the tenancy, and a further contract of sale by the former tenant with the relative with vacant possession.   One conveyance by sub-purchase could then be prepared in which the former tenant would convey free from any tenancy.

An agreement for the sale of a house to a tenant who is protected by the Rent Acts is often made at a price much below the vacant possession value. Such a tenant, if he intends to leave the house, may endeavour to buy it first in order to resell at an increased price.   If the tenant made a positive misstatement to the owner before contract that he wanted the house for his own occupation, that misstatement may amount to a condition, in which case the owner would be able to rescind the contract on finding the true facts before completion (*Wybrow* v. *Jope* (1951), 157 *Estates Gazette* 311). On the other hand, rescission cannot be obtained where the tenant honestly intended to reside in the house at the time when he made such a statement to the owner, but later decided to move because his circumstances changed (*Wragg* v. *Lovett* [1948] 2 All E.R. 968).

How far damages can be claimed after completion, where the tenant has made a positive statement of his intention, is doubtful, even following the Misrepresentation Act, 1967.   In particular, it is difficult to prove that the tenant's statement of his intention was untrue when it was made.   Consequently, if the owner is selling on the understanding that the purchaser

proposes to continue to reside in the house, it may be advisable to reserve
to the vendor an option to re-purchase at a specified price in the event of the
purchaser wishing to sell within a certain period. Such an option should be
protected as an estate contract by registration under the L.C.A. 1972 or by
entry of notice on the register of title. There is a good discussion of the
matter in the *Law Times*, vol. 212, p. 337 *et seq.*, where it is suggested that the
purchaser should further be required to undertake not to grant a protected
tenancy under the Rent Acts during the period of the option. See also the
discussion of various provisions intended to reserve a benefit to the vendor
in the event of the purchaser wishing to resell, in the *Solicitors' Journal*,
vol. 96, pp. 19, 76 and 103.

Payment of deposit.—No term is implied into a contract for the sale of
land that the purchaser should pay a deposit (*Binks* v. *Rokeby* (1818),
2 Swanst. 222, at pp. 225–226 ; *Doe d. Gray* v. *Stanion* (1836), 1 M. & W.
695, at p. 701). In practice, however, it is customary to include in the
contract a condition for the payment of a deposit of 10 per cent. of the
purchase price (see Condition 5 (1) of the Law Society's Conditions of Sale,
1973 Revision). Indeed, a vendor's solicitor will not normally conclude the
exchange of contracts until a deposit has been paid, since such payment
provides a most effective remedy for his client, i.e., forfeiture of the deposit,
as to which see *post*, p. 226.

A deposit will usually be paid not to the vendor himself but to some *third
party*, most frequently to an estate agent or to the vendor's solicitors (this
latter is provided for by Condition 5 (1) of the Law Society's Conditions of
Sale, 1973 Revision). The question then arises of the capacity in which such a
third party holds the deposit, that is, whether as stakeholder or as an agent of
the vendor. The capacity may be, and mostly is, expressly agreed (see also
Condition 5 (1) of the Law Society's Conditions of Sale, 1973 Revision).
Otherwise, the presumption is that the vendor's solicitor holds any deposit
as an agent for the vendor (*Edgell* v. *Day* (1865), L.R. 1 C.P. 80 ; *Ellis* v.
Goulton [1893] 1 Q.B. 350 ; *Law Society's Digest*, Opinion No. 61). However,
if there is no such express agreement, there is an established presumption
that an auctioneer holds a deposit as stakeholder (*Harington* v. *Hoggart* (1830),
1 B. & Ad. 577 ; *Furtado* v. *Lumley* (1890), 54 J.P. 407) whilst it has recently
been held that an estate agent takes a deposit as agent of the vendor (*Goding*
v. *Frazer* [1967] 1 W.L.R. 286, Sachs, J., not following *dicta* to the contrary
of Denning, L.J., in *Brodard* v. *Pilkington* [1953] C.P.L. 275, at p. 276, and
of Goddard, L.C.J., in *R.* v. *Pilkington* (1958), 42 Cr. App. R. 233, at p. 235 ;
see also *Ryan* v. *Pilkington* [1959] 1 W.L.R. 403, at pp. 408 and 414). It
seems clear that an estate agent instructed to find a purchaser will be acting
within his implied or apparent authority in taking the deposit expressly
either as a stakeholder or as the vendor's agent (*Ryan* v. *Pilkington, ante*,
where the deposit was expressly taken in the latter capacity). However,
Ryan v. *Pilkington* has been accepted by a majority of the Court of Appeal
as authority that an estate agent is at all material times, at any rate during
the pre-contract period, the agent of the vendor who therefore bears the
risk of default over any deposit held by virtue of that agency (*Burt* v. *Claude
Cousins & Co., Ltd. and Shaw* [1971] 2 Q.B. 426).

A *stakeholder* may be said to be the agent of both parties to the contract :
he will be bound to pay the deposit to the vendor either on completion of
the sale or on forfeiture and to the purchaser if it becomes returnable, but
until any of these events occur he may not pay the deposit to either party

without the other's consent (*Collins* v. *Stimson* (1883), 11 Q.B.D. 142, at p. 144). However, where a purchaser is affirming a contract for sale, the vendor cannot claim payment of a deposit in the hands of a stakeholder so long as there are outstanding incumbrances on the property it is the vendor's duty to discharge (*Skinner* v. *The Trustee of the Property of Reed* [1967] Ch. 1194). Consequently an auctioneer's lien only attaches to so much of the deposit he holds as is not needed to discharge incumbrances (*ibid.*). In practice, if there is a dispute the court will declare which of the parties can give a good receipt to the stakeholder (see, for example, *Smith* v. *Hamilton* [1951] Ch. 174).

A stakeholder is entitled to retain any interest earned by the deposit pending payment to the appropriate party (*Harington* v. *Hoggart* (1830), 1 B. & Ad. 577, at pp. 586–587 ; *Smith* v. *Hamilton, ante*, at p. 184 ; *Law Society's Digest*, Opinion No. 63). This established proposition as to retention of interest has now been applied to an estate agent holding a pre-contract deposit expressly as stakeholder even though no contract for sale was ever concluded (*Potters* v. *Loppert* [1973] 2 W.L.R. 469).

If the deposit is not recoverable from the stakeholder (for instance, on account of his bankruptcy) the loss is borne by the vendor in any case where a binding contract has been concluded (*Rowe* v. *May* (1854), 18 Beav. 613 ; *Barrow* v. *White* (1862), 2 J. & H. 587) and also *semble* where the vendor in fact nominated the person as stakeholder, as is the usual case with estate agents and presumably also with the vendor's solicitor (*Goding* v. *Frazer* [1967] 1 W.L.R. 286 ; applying *Annesley* v. *Muggridge* (1816), 1 Madd. 593, relating to an auctioneer). Otherwise where no binding contract has been concluded and where the stakeholder is the purchaser's or a joint nomination, it would appear that the purchaser should bear the loss (compare *Chillingworth* v. *Esche* [1924] 1 Ch. 97). In any event, a purchaser apparently has no lien on the land in respect of a deposit held by a stakeholder (*Combe* v. *Swaythling* [1947] Ch. 625). There is some difference of opinion as to whether it is proper for a trustee or other person in a fiduciary capacity to agree to payment of the deposit to a stakeholder, and some writers affirm that he is under a duty to ensure that the deposit is paid to his agent. The respective views are discussed by a learned writer in the *Law Times*, vol. 224, p. 36, who reaches the conclusion that the trustee's liability, if he allowed payment to a stakeholder, would depend on the facts of the case.

If the deposit-holder is the *agent of the vendor*, he is bound to pay the deposit to the vendor on demand and any action by the purchaser to recover it must be brought against the vendor (*Edgell* v. *Day* (1865), L.R. 1 C.P. 80 ; *Ellis* v. *Goulton* [1893] 1 Q.B. 350), except apparently before a binding contract is concluded where the deposit-holder is an agent *by implication* since he is then deemed to be authorised by the vendor to pay it over to the purchaser on, in effect, a simple demand after which it becomes money had and received to the use of the purchaser (*Goding* v. *Frazer* [1967] 1 W.L.R. 286 ; *Burt* v. *Claude Cousins & Co., Ltd., and Shaw* [1971] 2 Q.B. 426, C.A. ; relating particularly to estate agents). Also the deposit-holder, as an agent, is accountable to the vendor for any interest earned by the deposit (*Harington* v. *Hoggart* (1830), 1 B. & Ad. 577, at p. 586). If the deposit is not recoverable from an agent of the vendor, the purchaser can recover it from the vendor even though no binding contract has been concluded (*Ryan* v. *Pilkington* [1959] 1 W.L.R. 403 ; *Burt* v. *Claude Cousins & Co., Ltd., and Shaw* [1971] 2 Q.B. 426, C.A. ; cf. *Barrington* v. *Lee* [1972] 1 Q.B. 326, C.A., where judgment had already been obtained against agents). Also where the deposit-holder is the vendor's agent, the purchaser will have a lien on the land for the deposit and costs (*Whitbread & Co., Ltd.* v. *Watt* [1902] 1 Ch. 835).

Payment of price by instalments.—Contracts for sale of land sometimes provide that the price shall be paid by instalments, the purchaser being allowed into possession before completion which is dependent on payment of all instalments. As the purchaser may default it is customary to add a term permitting the vendor to rescind and retain instalments already paid if the purchaser makes default in payment of any one, time to be of the essence. There is considerable doubt as to whether the provision for forfeiture may be a penalty against which relief can be given in equity: see *Steedman* v. *Drinkle* [1916] 1 A.C. 275, and *Stockloser* v. *Johnson* [1954] 1 Q.B. 476. It appears from the judgments of Somervell and Denning, L.JJ., in the last-mentioned case, that (i) where there is no forfeiture clause if part of the purchase-money is paid and the purchaser defaults, then so long as the vendor keeps the contract open the purchaser cannot recover the money paid, but once the vendor rescinds the purchaser can recover money paid, the vendor having an action for damages (see *Mayson* v. *Clouet* [1924] A.C. 980, *post*, p. 227) ; (ii) where there is a forfeiture clause, or if the money was expressly paid as deposit, the purchaser who has defaulted may have relief in equity from the forfeiture, on terms. It is not easy, however, to say when the forfeiture clause will be regarded as penal, or when retention of the money would be unconscionable and, apparently, both of these conditions must exist before relief will be granted. Consequently, in the present state of the authorities there are so many doubts that provisions for payment of the price by instalments may be unsatisfactory. Nevertheless, precedents may be found in the *Conveyancer N.S.*, vol. 18, p. 683 *et seq.* See further a penetrating article by B. M. Hoggett in *Conveyancer N.S.*, vol. 36, p. 325 *et seq.* ; also *Lee-Parker* v. *Izzet* (*No.* 2) [1972] 2 All E.R. 800 which illustrates unsatisfactorily how instalment arrangements may be used for what is in substance a rental situation.

Sale conditional on obtaining a mortgage.—In 1959 the 17th edition of the National Conditions of Sale introduced a new general condition (No. 9) aimed at enabling the contract to be made conditional upon the purchaser arranging a mortgage (as to the risks of exchanging contracts before a mortgage is arranged, see *Buckland* v. *Mackesey* (1968), 112 Sol. J. 841, where the purchaser lost his deposit and sued his solicitor). Although this condition was attributable to popular demand (see the explanation at 105 Sol. J. 497) it was apparently little used in practice and has now been omitted altogether from the latest 18th edition of the National Conditions. The difficulties attending such a condition have recently been illustrated in a case where the formal contract included the special conditon : " This sale is subject to the purchaser obtaining a satisfactory mortgage " (*Lee-Parker* v. *Izzet* (*No.* 2) [1972] 2 All E.R. 800). Goulding, J., held that the condition was void for uncertainty and that this avoided the whole contract. He said (*ibid.*, p. 803 g/h) : " . . . it seems to me that in the circumstances of the present case the concept of a satisfactory mortgage is too indefinite for the court to give it a practical meaning. Everything is at large, not only matters like rate of interest and ancillary obligations, on which evidence might establish what would be usual or reasonable, but also on these two most essential points—the amount of the loan and the terms of repayment." Goulding, J., was able to follow specifically the decision of Russell, J., in

Re Rich's Will Trusts (1962), 106 Sol. J. 75, that a contract for sale providing that the vendor's solicitors should " be instructed to obtain and fix a suitable mortgage advance in this property " thereby failed for uncertainty (both followed generally *Scammell* v. *Ouston* [1941] A.C. 251 concerning the vagueness of " on hire-purchase terms "). However, he differed directly from a decision of Goff, J., in earlier proceedings involving somewhat similar words (in *Lee-Parker* v. *Izzet* [1971] 1 W.L.R. 1688, relating to different parties and properties). The case is reported on other points, but it is noted (in brackets at [1971] 3 All E.R. 1099, p. 1105, but not at all in the W.L.R.) that Goff, J., rejecting a submission that the contract failed for uncertainty, held that " ' arranging . . . a satisfactory mortgage ' meant a mortgage to the satisfaction of the purchaser acting reasonably." This objective approach might well commend itself as a means of binding the parties but the position in practice seems unsatisfactory since it cannot yet be said that this approach will prevail. Clearly a condition is required drafted in terms which are certain beyond argument or litigation. Mr. J. E. Adams has suggested the following apparently satisfactory wording :—

" conditional upon the Purchaser receiving within . . . days from the date of this contract an offer of a mortgage advance of not less than £ . . . over a period of . . . years from the . . . Building Society (the Purchaser having already made application for such an advance) such offer to be at the normal rate of interest and subject to no abnormal conditions."

It will often be in the interest of a purchaser to seek the inclusion of this term. The disadvantage to the vendor is that he must wait some time before he knows whether the contract is firm. Vendors may be inclined to agree, however, for instance where the price is largely dependent on the maximum advance a building society will make to a satisfactory borrower on the security of the property.

Conditions as to repair of leaseholds.—If the Law Society's Conditions of Sale, 1973 Revision, are incorporated in the contract, the purchaser will be deemed to purchase with full notice of the actual state of repair and will be required to take the property as it stands except where it is to be constructed or converted by the vendor (General Condition 4 (2) (*a*)). In such a case the covenants on the part of the assignor implied either by the L.P.A. 1925, s. 76 (1) (B) and Sched. 2, Pt. II, or by the L.R.A. 1925, s. 24 (1), in the assignment must be modified by a proviso to the effect that they shall *not* be deemed to imply that the repairing covenant has been performed (*Butler* v. *Mountview Estates, Ltd.* [1951] 2 K.B. 563 ; *Re King* [1962] 1 W.L.R. 632, 655 ; on appeal [1963] Ch. 459 ; see further Dr. E. O. Walford's article in the *Conveyancer N.S.*, vol. 15, p. 141). This modification is now provided for by General Condition 8 (4).

It follows that where there is a repairing covenant which has not been performed a vendor's solicitor should ensure that terms similar to those in the Law Society's Conditions are contained in the contract (see National Conditions of Sale, 18th ed., Conditions 12 (3) and 10 (7) respectively to like effect). On the other hand, the purchaser's solicitor should point out to his client the risk that such terms will leave him with the burden of carrying out the repairs. Compare the discussion of liability under an open contract *post*, p. 102.

Sale by grant of lease or underlease.—Where, by virtue of a specific stipulation, the interest sold is leasehold for a term of years *to be granted* by the vendor, the National Conditions of Sale, 18th ed., Condition 19 (1) provides that the lease or underlease and counterpart shall be prepared by the *vendor's* solicitor " in accordance (as nearly as the circumstances admit) with a form or draft *annexed to the contract or otherwise sufficiently identified by the signatures of the parties or their solicitors.*" Thus, it is essential to agree and identify the form before a contract of this kind is made. The Law Society's Conditions of Sale, 1973 Revision, Condition 11 (1), merely refers to the draft conveyance being prepared on behalf of the purchaser " save where the sale is by way of grant of lease " without anywhere entitling or obliging the vendor to draft the lease.

In transactions of this nature it will usually be advisable for the intending lessee to contract on the basis that the lessor will deduce title to the freehold and to any intermediate leasehold interest ; the reason why this is so and the form in which the term can be drawn are discussed at p. 143 *et seq., post.* In addition, notwithstanding the Costs of Leases Act, 1958, it is probably advisable to provide expressly in the contract for the payment of costs and stamp duty arising.

Conditions as to time for completion.—If there is no provision in either the special or the general conditions of sale fixing a date for completion, then " the law implies that completion is to take place within a reasonable time. What is a reasonable time has to be measured by the legal business which has to be performed in connection with the investigation of title and the preparation of the necessary conveyancing documents " (*Johnson* v. *Humphrey* [1946] 1 All E.R. 460, at p. 463 ; *Simpson* v. *Hughes* (1897), 66 L.J. Ch. 334). This is a question of fact (*Re Stone and Saville's Contract* [1962] 1 W.L.R. 460).

Usually, however, a completion date will be stated as a special condition of sale and if not so stated will be governed by the general conditions of sale incorporated. Examples are : " the first working day after the expiration of five weeks from the date of the contract " (Law Society's Conditions of Sale, 1973 Revision, No. 15 (1)) ; or " the first working day after the expiration of five weeks from the delivery of the abstract of title " which must be delivered " within fourteen days next after the date of the contract " (National Conditions of Sale, 18th ed., Conditions 4 (1) and 8 (1)). These general conditions are not inconsistent with (and so will apply despite) a special condition as to the completion date which has not been filled in on exchange of contracts (*Smith* v. *Mansi* [1963] 1 W.L.R. 26). But if the contract provides that completion should take place when possession of the property is given, but does not fix when possession should be given, there is no implication of a reasonable time and the contract will not be enforceable (*Johnson* v. *Humphrey, ante ;* as to vacant possession, see *post*, p. 199 ; see also *Gavaghan* v. *Edwards* [1961] 2 Q.B. 220 as to an agreement to agree the completion date).

As to remedies on delay see *post*, p. 213 *et seq.*

Time for conditions.—Where a contract is made conditional on certain steps being taken or certain circumstances existing, for example, the purchaser obtaining a mortgage (see *ante*, p. 63) or the vendor securing the renewal of a lease, the question may arise of the time by which the condition must be fulfilled. The following rules were laid down in *Aberfoyle Plantations, Ltd.* v. *Cheng* [1960] A.C. 115 : " (1) Where a conditional contract of sale fixes a date for the completion of the sale, then the condition must be fulfilled by that date. (2) Where a conditional contract of sale fixes no date for

3

completion of the sale, then the condition must be fulfilled within a reasonable time. (3) Where a conditional contract of sale fixes (whether specifically or by reference to the date fixed for completion) the date by which the condition is to be fulfilled, then the date so fixed must be strictly adhered to, and the time allowed is not to be extended by reference to equitable principles."

If, however, the condition on its true construction is not a condition precedent to the formation of a contract of sale but only a matter of title, then the time for its fulfilment is not the date fixed for completion but the date at which title has in fact to be established (*Property and Bloodstock, Ltd.* v. *Emerton* [1968] Ch. 94, concerning the standard provision in a contract for the sale of leasehold property that the landlords' consent be obtained). See also *Re Longlands Farm* [1968] 3 All E.R. 552, in which the rules laid down in *Aberfoyle Plantations, Ltd.* v. *Cheng* were applied.

PART 5. CONTRACTS BY CORRESPONDENCE

In general the rules already stated apply to contracts by correspondence. It is convenient to set out separately, however, the rules governing the formation of such contracts. Further, there is a special statutory provision as to the conditions to be implied.

Formation of contract by correspondence.—" Where it is sought to make out a binding contract from correspondence, the whole of it should be looked at, and, if once a definite offer has been made and it has been accepted without qualification, and it appears that the letters of offer and acceptance contain all the terms agreed on between the parties, the complete contract thus arrived at cannot be affected by subsequent negotiations without the consent of both " (*Bellamy* v. *Debenham* (1890), 45 Ch. D. 481). See also *Perry* v. *Suffields, Ltd.* [1916] 2 Ch. 187 ; *Hussey* v. *Horne-Payne* (1879), 4 App. Cas. 311 ; *Mason* v. *von Buch* (1899), 15 T.L.R. 430 ; *Davies* v. *Sweet* [1962] 2 Q.B. 300 ; and most recently *Bigg* v. *Boyd Gibbins, Ltd.* [1971] 1 W.L.R. 913. But where there is subsequent correspondence continuing the negotiation on an important point, this may show that the contract was not complete (*Bellamy* v. *Debenham, ante*). It was held in *Ronald Frankau Productions, Ltd.* v. *Bell* (1927), 164 L.T. News. 504, that any indication from correspondence as to the views of parties, after signing the document, on its legal operation, was wholly irrelevant to its construction and would therefore have to be disregarded. When, looking at the whole of the correspondence, it appears that it was intended by the parties to have a formal contract, unless that formal contract has been executed, the parties would not be deemed to have got beyond the stage of negotiations (*Re Langherne House* (1928), 165 L.T. News. 512). See further, *ante*, p. 32.

Where the contract has been effected by correspondence, an acceptance of an offer is complete from the time of posting such acceptance (*Henthorn* v. *Fraser* [1892] 2 Ch. 27 ; *James* v. *Institute of Chartered Accountants* (1907), 98 L.T. 225) ; even though the letter be lost in the post, and never actually reached the person making the offer (*Household Fire Insurance Co.* v. *Grant* (1879), 4 Ex. D. 216).

A withdrawal of an offer, in order to be effectual, must be made before the offer is clinched by the posting of the letter of acceptance (*Re London and Northern Bank* [1900] 1 Ch. 220). The withdrawal of an offer does not date back to the time of posting, and is not effectual until brought to the mind of the person to whom the offer was made (*Henthorn* v. *Fraser, ante*).

Conditions implied in contracts by correspondence.—It is provided by s. 46 of the L.P.A. 1925 that the Lord Chancellor may prescribe forms of conditions of sale of land, and the forms so prescribed, subject to any modification, or any stipulation or intention to the contrary, expressed in the correspondence, apply to contracts by correspondence.

In other words, unless it is stated in the correspondence that these conditions are not to apply, they will automatically apply.

The Act contains no definition of the word "correspondence." The popular meaning of the word is a contract arrived at by the parties by letters through the post or by hand. It would probably apply to the case where an offer was made by word of mouth and accepted by a letter through the post or by hand delivery, and to the case where the offer was made by letter through the post or by hand and accepted by word of mouth. Sometimes a contract is made by word of mouth, and by arrangement each of the parties writes to the other referring to the contract so made and confirming the terms in writing. It is doubtful whether the expression would cover this case.

The following is the form prescribed, which is somewhat out of date :—

STATUTORY FORM OF CONDITIONS OF SALE

1. *Date fixed for completion.*—The date for completion shall, unless otherwise agreed, be the first day after the expiration of seven weeks from the time when the contract is made, or if that day is a Sunday, Christmas Day, Good Friday or Bank Holiday, the next following working day.

2. *Place for completion.*—Completion shall take place at the office of the vendor's solicitors, or if the vendor so requires at the office of the solicitors of his mortgagees, if any.

3. *Possession and apportionment of outgoings.*—(1) The purchaser paying his purchase-money or, where a deposit is paid, the balance thereof, shall, as from the date fixed for completion (but subject to the execution of any conveyance which ought to be executed by him), be let into possession, or into receipt of rents and profits, and shall, as from that date, pay all outgoings, and up to that date all current rents, and all rates, taxes, and other outgoings shall (if necessary) be apportioned, and the balance shall be paid by or allowed to the purchaser on actual completion, and for this purpose the purchaser shall be liable to pay to the vendor a proportionate part of the current rents accrued in respect of the property up to the date fixed for completion :

Provided that all rates shall be apportioned, so far as practicable, according to the period for which they are intended to provide, and not as running from the dates when the same are made or allowed.

(2) Where as respects any rate the date fixed for completion falls between the expiration of the period for which the last rate was made and the making of a new rate, the new rate shall, for the purposes of this condition, be deemed to have been made at the same rate in the pound as that at which the last rate was made, and shall be calculated from day to day.

4. *Interest on purchase-money.*—(1) If from any cause whatever (save as hereinafter mentioned), the completion of the purchase is delayed beyond the date fixed for completion, the purchase-money, or where a deposit is paid, the balance thereof, shall bear interest at the rate of £5 per cent. per annum, from the date fixed for the completion to the day of actual payment thereof.

(2) Provided that, if delay in completion arises from any other cause than the purchaser's own act or default the purchaser may—

(a) at his own risk, deposit the purchase-money, or where a deposit is paid, the balance thereof, at any bank in England or Wales, in his own name or otherwise, and

(b) give notice in writing forthwith of such deposit to the vendor or his solicitors,

and in that case the vendor shall be bound to accept the interest, if any, allowed thereon, as from the date of such deposit, in lieu of the interest accruing after the date of the deposit, which would otherwise be payable to him under this condition.

(3) No interest shall become payable by the purchaser if delay in completion is attributable to—

(a) a refusal by the vendor to deduce title in accordance with the contract, or to give an authority to inspect the register kept under the Land Registration Act, 1925, or to convey ; or

(b) any other wilful act or default of the vendor or his Settled Land Act trustees.

(4) The vendor shall as from the date when interest becomes payable under this condition, have the option (to be exercised by notice in writing) of taking an apportioned part of the rents and profits, less apportioned outgoings, up to the date of actual completion, in lieu of the interest otherwise payable under this condition ; and, if the said option is exercised, the same payments, allowances and apportionments shall be made as if the date fixed for completion had been the date of actual completion.

The said option shall not be exercisable in any case in which sub-clause (2) of this clause applies.

5. *Delivery of abstract.*—(1) The vendor shall deliver to the purchaser or his solicitor—

(a) an abstract of the title to the property sold, or

(b) in the case of land registered with an absolute or good leasehold title, the particulars and information which ought to be furnished in lieu of an abstract, with a written authority to inspect the register.

and, in either case, within fourteen days from the date when the contract was made.

(2) Where land is registered with a possessory or qualified title, the abstract (if any) shall only relate to estates, rights, and interests, subsisting or capable of taking effect prior to the date of first registration, or excluded from the effect of first registration, and dealings therewith, and subject as aforesaid, the foregoing provisions relating to absolute or good leasehold titles shall apply.

6. *Requisitions.*—(1) The purchaser shall within fourteen days after the actual delivery of the abstract, or of the said particulars and information whether or not delivered within the time prescribed, send to the solicitors of the vendor a statement in writing of all the objections and requisitions (if any) to or on—

(a) the title or evidence of title,

(b) the abstract or the said particulars and information,

(c) the contract as respects matters not thereby specifically provided for and subject thereto the title shall be deemed accepted.

(2) All objections and requisitions not included in any statement sent within the time aforesaid, and not going to the root of the title, shall be deemed waived.

(3) An abstract or the said particulars and information though in fact imperfect, shall be deemed perfect, except for the purpose of any objections or requisitions, which could not have been taken or made on the information therein contained.

(4) An answer to any objection or requisition shall be replied to, in writing, within seven days after delivery thereof and, if not so replied to, shall be considered satisfactory.

7. *Power to rescind.*—(1) If the purchaser shall take or make any objection or requisition, which the vendor is unable to remove or comply with, and the purchaser shall not withdraw such objection or requisition within ten days after being required, in writing, so to do, the vendor may, by notice in writing delivered to the purchaser or his solicitor and notwithstanding any intermediate negotiations, rescind the contract.

(2) This condition does not apply so as to prevent the enforcement by a purchaser of any right conferred on him by s. 42 of the Law of Property Act, 1925.

(3) If the contract is so rescinded the vendor shall, within one week after default is made in complying with the requirement to withdraw the objection or requisition, repay to the purchaser his deposit money (if any), but without interest, and the purchaser shall return forthwith all abstracts and papers in his possession, belonging to the vendor, and shall not make any claim on the vendor for costs, compensation or otherwise.

8. *Preparation of conveyance.*—(1) The conveyance or instrument of transfer to the purchaser shall be prepared by him and at his own expense, and the draft thereof shall be delivered at the office of the solicitors of the vendor at least ten days before the date fixed for completion, for perusal and approval on behalf of the vendor and other necessary parties (if any).

(2) The engrossment of such conveyance or transfer, for execution by the vendor and other necessary parties (if any), shall be left at the said office within four days after the draft has been returned approved on behalf of the vendor and other necessary conveying parties (if any).

(3) Delivery of a draft or of an engrossment shall not prejudice any outstanding requisition.

9. *Power for vendor to resell after notice.*—(1) If the purchaser shall neglect or fail to perform his part of the contract the vendor may give to the purchaser or to his solicitor at least twenty-one days' notice in writing specifying the breach and requiring the purchaser to make good the default before the expiration of the notice.

(2) If the purchaser does not comply with the terms of the said notice—

(*a*) the deposit money, if any, shall, unless the court otherwise directs, be forfeited to the vendor, or, in the case of settled land, to his Settled Land Act trustees ;

(*b*) the vendor may resell the property without previously tendering a conveyance or instrument of transfer to the purchaser ;

and the following provisions shall apply.

(3) Any resale may be made, by auction or private contract, at such time, subject to such conditions, and in such manner generally as the vendor may think proper, and the defaulting purchaser shall have no right to any part of the purchase-money thereby arising.

PART 6. COLLATERAL CONTRACTS

Representations.—In practice, before a contract for the sale and purchase of land is concluded, each of the parties, particularly the vendor, will usually have made to the other various representations relating to the land and purporting to be of fact or intention. These representations can be classified, according to their legal consequences if incorrect, as follows :

(1) as a mere representation giving rise to no contractual liability although damages may be recoverable in tort or rescission obtained (see further Misrepresentation, *post*, p. 87) ;

(2) as a term of the principal contract for the sale and purchase of the land, which may give rise to the ordinary remedies for breach (see *post*, p. 218). It is necessary, if the term is a subsidiary one and so technically a " warranty " rather than a condition of the contract, not to confuse the present classification with the next classification, in which a collateral contract may be called a " warranty " but in the sense simply of a binding promise (see *per* Denning, L.J., in *Oscar Chess, Ltd.* v. *Williams* [1957] 1 W.L.R. 370) ;

(3) as a separate contract, collateral to the principal contract.

Collateral contracts.—A representation falls into this third class only if all the elements of a binding contract are present, that is, it must amount to an agreement supported by consideration and intended to be binding. Usually the consideration is found, if at all, in the fact that the other party would not otherwise enter into the principal contract : " It is evident, both on principle and on authority, that there may be a contract the consideration for which is the making of some other contract. ' If you will make such and such a contract I will give you one hundred pounds,' is in every sense of the word a complete legal contract. It is collateral to the main contract, but each has an independent existence, and they do not differ in respect of their possessing to the full the character and status of a contract " (*per* Lord Moulton in *Heilbut, Symons & Co.* v. *Buckleton* [1913] A.C. 30, at p. 47). Also there must be " evidence of an intention by one or both parties that there should be contractual liability in respect of the accuracy of the statement," which intention, however, " can only be deduced from the totality of the evidence " (*ibid.*, p. 51).

Thus it may be said that collateral contracts depend on the court being able to attribute *ex post facto* the appropriate intention to the parties. In fact these contracts may be better understood if thought of as a device developed to avoid the following otherwise inconvenient consequences : (i) " that an innocent misrepresentation gives no right to damages " (*per* Lord Moulton, *loc. cit.*, p. 48 ; see now s. 2 of the Misrepresentation Act, 1967, giving a right to damages, and compare *Hedley Byrne & Co., Ltd.* v. *Heller & Partners* [1964] A.C. 465) ; (ii) that the principal contract will be unenforceable if the memorandum of it omits one of its terms (L.P.A. 1925, s. 40 (1)), a collateral contract not needing to be evidenced in writing (*Jameson* v. *Kinmell Bay Land Co.* (1931), 47 T.L.R. 593) ; (iii) that extrinsic evidence is not admissible to vary or add to the terms of a written contract (*Goss* v. *Lord Nugent* (1833), 5 B. & Ad. 58, at p. 64), but is admissible to establish a collateral contract (*City and Westminster Properties* (1934), *Ltd.* v. *Mudd* [1959] Ch. 129) ; (iv) that those terms which are part of the contract for the sale of land, and not collateral to it, merge in the conveyance on completion ; and (v) that the representation may have been made by a person not a party to the principal contract against whom there would, apart from a collateral contract, be no action in contract (see *Andrews* v. *Hopkinson* [1957] 1 Q.B. 229, and cases there cited) and in respect of whose misrepresentation there might be no action in tort (*Armstrong* v. *Strain* [1951] 1 T.L.R. 856, *affd.* [1952] 1 K.B. 232).

Examples.—In practice the distinctions between the three classes of representation are difficult to make, depending as they do on the parties' unexpressed intentions. Some brief examples from decided cases may, therefore, help. In *De Lassalle* v. *Guildford* [1901] 2 K.B. 215, a prospective tenant refused to complete the lease by handing over his signed counterpart unless he was assured that the drains were in good order ; the Court of Appeal held that the assurance constituted a contract collateral to the lease and, the drains not being in good order, the lessor was liable for breach of it. In *Saunders* v. *Cockrill* (1902), 87 L.T. 30, a vendor of a house in course of erection agreed to supply and fix certain drains and stoves and to complete the house in a proper and workmanlike manner ; after the conveyance to him the purchaser discovered defects in the building and was held entitled to recover damages for breach of contract. In *Jameson* v. *Kinmell Bay Land Co.* (1931), 47 T.L.R. 593, a prospective purchaser of a building plot was promised orally on behalf of the vendor that a road marked on a plan shown to him would be constructed ; the road was not constructed and the purchaser was held able to recover damages for breach of the collateral contract. In *Hodges* v. *Jones* [1935] Ch. 657, similarly a plan was produced to a prospective purchaser of a plot on an estate on which an adjoining strip of land was marked " Tennis Courts " but no oral promise was made ; an injunction was sought to stop garages being built on the strip, but Luxmoore, J., held that no collateral contract had been established. Again, in *London County Properties, Ltd.* v. *Berkeley Property Co., Ltd.* [1936] 2 All E.R. 1039, a prospective purchaser of a block of flats was told " There are no disputes and rents are paid promptly with very few immaterial exceptions " ; this was untrue but was held by the Court of Appeal to amount to a mere representation not a collateral contract. See also *Gilchester Properties, Ltd.* v. *Gomm* [1948] 1 All E.R. 493, where a false statement as to the rents of property was held to be an innocent misrepresentation only. Answers to preliminary inquiries are usually representations only and do not amount to collateral contracts, that is, they are not " warranted " true (see *Mahon* v. *Ainscough* [1952] 1 All E.R. 739). Again in *Hill* v. *Harris* [1965] 2 Q.B. 601, statements in discussions and letters relating to the user of premises permitted by a head lease were found to be made only in the course of negotiations and to be superseded by the terms of the lease eventually entered into ; it was also held that the estate agents concerned had no authority at all to make any express warranties on this point.

Implied warranty that a house shall be habitable.—In one case in particular, a collateral contract may be found without there being any express representation. Where a builder agrees to sell a plot of land and to build a house thereon, or merely to build a house, there is an implied agreement that the house when built shall be reasonably fit for habitation (*De Lassalle* v. *Guildford* [1901] 2 K.B. 215). In *Miller* v. *Cannon Hill Estates, Ltd.* [1931] 2 K.B. 113, the purchaser had been shown a " show house " on a building estate and told that the house to be built on the plot purchased by him would be completed in a similar manner. After conveyance the purchaser found that the house was defective, and particularly that it was so damp t hat it was unfit for habitation. An oral assurance had been given that the workmanship and materials used would be of the best, and it was held that this amounted to a warranty, on which an action would lie. In any event, Swift, J. (at p. 120), pointed out that even if there had not been an express undertaking it would have been implied that the house when completed would be habitable. On the sale of a house in the course of erection, the warranty implied is that it will be completed in a manner making it fit for occupation (*Perry* v. *Sharon Development Co., Ltd.* [1937] 4 All E.R. 390) and covers materials already used at the date of the contract (*Hancock* v. *B. W. Brazier* [1966] 1 W.L.R. 1317).

The warranty requires that foundations shall be reasonably fit. For instance, there is a breach if they are built in a place or manner such that they settle in consequence of the extraction of moisture from the soil by roots of neighbouring poplars (*Jennings* v. *Tavener* [1955] 1 W.L.R. 932). An express (or, apparently, implied) warranty to build in a proper manner implies that proper materials shall be used (*Hancock* v. *B. W. Brazier* [1966] 1 W.L.R. 1317).

The implied warranty is not broken where the parties have expressly agreed that the house should be completed in accordance with plans and specifications and a defect appears even though that was done properly and with good materials (*Lynch* v. *Thorne* [1956] 1 W.L.R. 303). This decision turned on the fact that the provision in the contract was " sufficiently explicit to debar the owner notwithstanding the defective nature of the work " (Edmund Davies, L.J., in *Billyack* v. *Leyland Construction Co., Ltd.* [1968] 1 W.L.R. 471, at p. 475). It was distinguished by Thesiger, J., in a case where the builder, instead of working precisely to the approved specification, actually worked to another improved, but still defective, specification ; he held that there was in consequence room to imply the warranty (*King* v. *Victor Parsons & Co.* [1972] 1 W.L.R. 801 ; this implication was admitted on appeal : (1972), *The Times,* 17th November).

It is possible that the vendor may be protected by a condition (described by Harman, L.J., as " rash " so far as purchasers were concerned) that inspection by the local authority building surveyor should be " conclusive evidence that the property has been satisfactorily completed " (*Richards (Builders), Ltd.* v. *White* (1963), 107 Sol. J. 828). However, a provision that a habitation certificate should be conclusive evidence of completion of the house has since been construed as defining only the date when the purchaser had to pay and was not conclusive that work had been properly carried out (*Billyack* v. *Leyland Construction Co., Ltd.* [1968] 1 W.L.R. 471). Further, it should be borne in mind in such cases that substantial liability may be found on the part of the local authority or its building surveyor in the tort of negligence or breach of statutory duty (see *Dutton* v. *Bognor Regis U.D.C.* [1972] 2 W.L.R. 299, C.A.). Again, inclusion in a contract of a clause rendering the builder liable to remedy defects notified within a specified time does not prevent the purchaser from relying later on the implied warranty ; that warranty is excluded only by clear words (*Hancock* v. *B. W. Brazier* [1966] 1 W.L.R. 1317).

The implied warranty does not arise on the sale of a completed house even if the house is on a building estate and has been completed immediately before the contract is made (*Hoskins* v. *Woodham* [1938] 1 All E.R. 692). However, the Defective Premises Act, 1972, which came into force on 1st January, 1974 (s. 7 (2)), does purport to impose a " duty to build dwellings properly " which is not confined, like the implied warranty, to houses sold in course of construction. This statutory duty is owed *by* " a person *taking on work* for or in connection with the provision of a dwelling . . ." (s. 1 (1)). The italicised words are undefined but the subsection subsequently makes clear that professional men may be included ; it is thought that the statutory duty is clearly imposed upon surveyors, architects and such like. The duty is owed *to* (*a*) the person ordering the dwelling, and (*b*) " every person who acquires an interest (whether legal or equitable) in the dwelling " (s. 1 (1) of the 1972 Act). Thus the benefit of the duty will " run with the land " which the benefit of the implied warranty does not. Building properly within the actual terms of the statutory duty, despite mention of " a work-manlike or, as the case may be, professional manner, with proper materials," appears to mean little more in the end than the implied requirement of fitness for habitation outlined above (s. 1 (1)). The statute actually provides that its duties are " in addition to any duty a person may owe apart from [the Act] " (s. 6 (2)). The warranty of fitness for habitation implied at common law is exceeded in at least two respects : under the statute, first, successors in title may benefit (s. 1 (1) (*b*)), and second, contracting out is virtually forbidden (s. 6 (3) ; see also s. 1 (2), (3) as to the consequences of building in accordance with defective instructions or specifications). However, the statutory liability will be superseded where the dwelling is constructed or first sold with the benefit of an " approved scheme " (s. 2 ; e.g., the National House-Builders Registration Council Certificates and Agreements). Further, it should be borne in mind that a majority of the Court of Appeal has given the considered opinion that a builder-vendor of land can incur liability in tort for negligence in building, even to subsequent purchasers (*Dutton* v. *Bognor Regis U.D.C.* [1972] 2 W.L.R. 299) and that this opinion receives independent but direct support from s. 3 of the Defective Premises Act, 1972. Consequently, it may be found that, in practice, many questions of contractual liability under the implied warranty become academic in the light of the statutory or tortious liabilities.

PART 7. OPTION TO PURCHASE

Nature.—An option to purchase may be said to constitute an offer to sell which the prospective vendor is contractually precluded from withdrawing so long as the option remains exercisable (see *per* Buckley, J., in *Beesley* v. *Hallwood Estates, Ltd.* [1960] 1 W.L.R. 549, at p. 556, affirmed on other grounds [1961] Ch. 105). See also *Mountford* v. *Scott* (1973), 117 Sol. J. 584, as to specific performance being the appropriate remedy.

Enforcement.—The question of enforcement has for long depended largely upon whether or not the option is void for infringing the perpetuity rule. However, certain changes have been made in the application of this rule to options granted by instruments taking effect after 15th July, 1964, only (Perpetuities and Accumulations Act, 1964, ss. 9, 10 and 15 (5)). Accordingly it is necessary to state separately the position apart from and under that Act.

Apart from 1964 Act.—Between the original parties, the option is enforce-able on a basis of privity of contract and as creating personal obligations (assuming it to be otherwise enforceable, e.g., evidenced in writing as required by L.P.A. 1925, s. 40 (1)). Consequently, as between the parties (and, of course, their respective personal representatives) the rule against perpe-tuities has no application (*Hutton* v. *Watling* [1948] Ch. 26 and cases there cited ; on appeal on another point [1948] Ch. 398). Enforcement of an

option by or against successors of the original parties, however, depends not
on privity of contract but on whether the benefit or burden respectively
of the option has been effectively passed.

Benefit.—An option, unless its exercise is in terms restricted, is a chose in
action the benefit of which may be assigned by the grantee to anyone he
chooses, such an assignment being either express or implied (*Griffith* v. *Pelton*
[1958] Ch. 205, where the benefit of an option to purchase the reversion granted
to the " lessee," defined to include " assigns," was held to pass impliedly on
an assignment of the lease ; a petition for leave to appeal was dismissed by the
House of Lords [1958] 1 W.L.R. 65 ; see also *Re Button's Lease* [1964] Ch. 263).
The assignee of the benefit can then enforce the option, as a contractual right
against the original grantor personally, or his estate if he is dead, without
reference again to the perpetuity rule (*South Eastern Rly. Co.* v. *Assoc.
Portland Cement Manufacturers (1900), Ltd.* [1910] 1 Ch. 12). As to enforcement
against successors of the original grantor, see below.

Burden.—The rule is well-known that the burden of a contract cannot be
assigned apart from a novation. However, an option to purchase land creates
not only personal obligations but also a contingent equitable interest in the
land (*Griffith* v. *Pelton, ante*, at p. 225). Consequently, as an equitable
interest, the burden of the option is able to pass to and bind successors in
title to the land. But where enforcement of the option rests solely on this
basis, the perpetuity rule becomes relevant. In other words, an option to
purchase land will be void as against the grantor's successors in title unless
its exercise is restricted to the perpetuity period (*L. & S.W. Rly. Co.* v.
Gomm (1882), 20 Ch. D. 562 ; *Woodall* v. *Clifton* [1905] 2 Ch. 257, at p. 266 ;
Worthing Corpn. v. *Heather* [1906] 2 Ch. 532). In addition, protection of the
option by registration may be necessary ; see below.

If the burden has *not* passed, i.e., if the land has been sold to a purchaser
against whom the option is void, damages for breach of contract may still
be recoverable from the original grantor of the option (*Wright* v. *Dean*
[1948] 2 All E.R. 415) ; which damages may include loss of profit from an
intended development (*Cottrill* v. *Steyning B.S.* [1966] 1 W.L.R. 753). There
appears to be no duty to mitigate the damages by protecting the option by
registration (*ibid.*). Consequently it is advisable that the solicitor for the
grantor of an option should ensure that the grantee registers it so that it will
bind any subsequent purchaser (cf. *Du Sautoy* v. *Symes* [1967] Ch. 1146).
However, it should be noted that the grantor may be entitled to be indemnified
by the purchaser who has not complied with the exercise of the option because
it was void against him (*Eagon* v. *Dent* [1965] 3 All E.R. 334, where an
indemnity against tenant's claims had been given under the National
Conditions of Sale, Condition 18 (3), 17th ed., repeated in 18th ed. ; see also
The Law Society's Conditions of Sale, 1973 Revision, Condition 4 (2) (*d*)).

Under 1964 Act.—The changes made by ss. 9 and 10 of the Perpetuities
and Accumulations Act, 1964, in the application of the perpetuity rule to
options to purchase land granted after 15th July, 1964 (s. 15 (5)) are as
follows. Section 9 (1) provides that an option to purchase the reversion on a
lease should be valid notwithstanding the rule against perpetuities provided
that it is exercisable only by the lessee or his successors in title and ceases
to be exercisable one year after the determination of the lease (overruling,
in effect, *Woodall* v. *Clifton, ante*). Section 9 (2) provides that other options

to purchase land for valuable consideration should be limited to a perpetuity period of twenty-one years (except for the option of a public or local authority to purchase land which has ceased to be used for religious purposes).

Section 10 must be particularly noted for it applies the perpetuity rule to options (and other contracts) which, apart from the Act, could have been enforced without reference to the rule, i.e., against the original parties. The section provides that if a disposition would be treated as void as between third parties for infringing the perpetuity period (presumably twenty-one years in the present context : see s. 9 (2) above), then it is also to be void as between the original parties (overruling in effect *Hutton* v. *Watling, ante*).

Protection by registration.—An option to purchase unregistered land including a right of pre-emption, or any other like right, made or assigned after 1925, should be registered as an estate contract at the Land Charges Registry since otherwise it will be void against a purchaser of a legal estate for money or money's worth (L.C.A. 1972, s. 2 (4), Class C (iv), and s. 4 (6) ; see further *post*, p. 599). Reference should also be made, as to indemnity despite non-registration, to *Eagon* v. *Dent, ante*.

If title to the land is registered, the option should similarly be protected by entry on the register normally of a notice, or else of a caution or restriction (L.R.A. 1925, ss. 49 (1) (c), 59 (2), 54 and 58 (1) ; see further *post*, p. 618), *unless* the grantee or his successors are in possession of the land, when adequate protection against future registered proprietors will be afforded to the option as an overriding interest (L.R.A. 1925, s. 70 (1) (g) ; *Webb* v. *Pollmount* [1966] Ch. 584 ; but see Registered Land Practice Notes, 1972, p. 30, No. 50, where it is suggested that notwithstanding this last decision it is still desirable for such options to be noted on the register).

Exercise of option.—" It is well-established that an option for the purchase or re-purchase of property must in all cases be exercised strictly within the time limited for the purpose. The reason for this, as I understand it, is that an option is a species of privilege for the benefit of the party on whom it is conferred. That being so, it is for that party to comply strictly with the conditions stipulated for the exercise of the option " (*per* Willmer, L.J., in *Hare* v. *Nicoll* [1966] 2 W.L.R. 441, at p. 446, following *Lord Ranelagh* v. *Melton* (1864), 2 Dr. & Sm. 278 ; *Dibbins* v. *Dibbins* [1904] 1 Ch. 305). This will not be so, if the conduct of the grantor has been conducive to delay (*Bruner* v. *Moore* [1904] 1 Ch. 305 ; *Riddell* v. *Durnford* [1893] W.N. 30) or has constituted a waiver or estoppel in respect of non-compliance with any stipulated conditions (compare *West Country Cleaners (Falmouth), Ltd.* v. *Saly* [1966] 1 W.L.R. 1485, where mere silence was not sufficient). However, any variation of the option, as by extending the period for its exercise, must be evidenced in writing within s. 40 (1) of the L.P.A. 1925 in order to be relied on (*Richards* v. *Creighton Griffiths (Investments), Ltd.* (1972), 225 E.G. 2104). Also, it has been held that an option exercisable by notice in writing is not effectively exercised by posting a letter which is never actually received by the grantor (*Holwell Securities, Ltd* v. *Hughes* (1973), *The Times*, 6th November C.A., distinguishing *Henthorn* v. *Fraser* [1892] 2 Ch. 27).

For particular rules affecting options to purchase in leases, also options to renew, see chapter on Leases, *post*, p. 802.

Title on exercise of option.—A point often overlooked is that the exercise of an option creates a binding contract which, unless provision is made to the contrary, is an open contract. The grantor of the option would probably not be advised to enter into an open contract and so it is necessary to consider whether any conditions of sale should be made applicable to the exercise of the option.

It is normally implied that on the exercise of an option to purchase the grantee is entitled to a conveyance of the fee simple free from incumbrance with vacant possession (*Re Crosby's Contract* [1949] 1 All E.R. 830 ; see, however, *Fowler* v. *Willis* [1922] 2 Ch. 514, *post*, p. 108).

First refusal—pre-emption.—Sometimes the owner of land promises another that he, the owner, will give him " the first refusal " to buy such owner's property, without mentioning any price. This does not mean that the owner will sell the property to such person, as he may not wish to sell it to any person. If the owner does determine to sell he is under an obligation to offer the property to the person to whom he made the promise, at the price at which, if such person does not wish to buy, he intends to sell to some other person. But he must not offer the property at a certain price, and, on receiving a refusal, sell to someone else at a less price (*Manchester Ship Canal Co.* v. *Manchester Racecourse Co.* [1900] 2 Ch. 352 ; [1901] 2 Ch. 37 ; *Ryan* v. *Thomas* (1911), 55 Sol. J. 364).

In *Gardner* v. *Coutts & Co.* [1968] 1 W.L.R. 173, Cross, J., held that an agreement for consideration between a landowner and his neighbour that if the landowner should wish to sell the land, and in any event on his death the neighbour should have an option to purchase it for a stated sum, impliedly precluded the landowner from giving the land away in his lifetime without first offering it to the neighbour. Compare *Du Sautoy* v. *Symes* [1967] Ch. 1146, where a clause was construed as conferring both an option to purchase and a right of pre-emption as separate rights, the former continuing to subsist despite the lapse of the latter.

Whether a right of pre-emption at a fixed or ascertainable price in the event of the vendor wishing to sell creates an interest in land has been regarded as doubtful. However, the better view now appears to be that it does create an interest in land, albeit contingent, which may be enforceable against third parties (see to this effect the decision of Ungoed-Thomas, J., in *Williams* v. *Andrews* (1971), 221 E.G. 1158, where in fact the right in terms only bound the original transferee). This view may be supported by two statutory references whereby such rights are put on the same footing as options to purchase. First, protection by registration is made requisite by the express inclusion also of a right of pre-emption as an estate contract (L.C.A. 1972, s. 2 (4), Class (iv)). Second, the clear inference can be drawn that rights of pre-emption are ordinarily subject to the perpetuity rule with the period being twenty-one years (see Perpetuities and Accumulations Act, 1964, s. 9 (2) proviso, which expressly excludes certain rights of pre-emption : *exclusio unius est inclusio alterius ;* also *ibid.*, s. 10, as to contractual rights generally). See also L.P.A. 1925, s. 186. But against this view, in *Manchester Ship Canal Co.* v. *Manchester Racecourse Co.* [1901] 2 Ch. 37 (especially at p. 50) the Court of Appeal decided that a right of " first refusal " did not amount to an interest in land and so would not bind an intending purchaser with notice. This was followed in *Murray* v. *Two Strokes, Ltd.* [1973] 1 W.L.R. 823, where Goulding, J., held that in consequence a right of " first refusal " did not constitute a " minor interest " capable of binding third parties under the L.R.A. 1925. Nevertheless, these last-mentioned cases could be distinguished on the point that no price had been mentioned or indicated for the " first refusal."

Grant of option by trustees, etc.—Tenants for life, trustees for sale, and personal representatives may grant options to purchase. Section 51 of the S.L.A. 1925 empowers *a tenant for life* at any time, either with or without consideration (that is, other than the price fixed), to grant by writing an option to purchase the settled land or any part thereof, or any easement, right or privilege over or in relation to the same, at a price fixed at the time of the granting of the option. Such option must be made exercisable within an agreed number of years not exceeding ten and the price must be the best which, having regard to all the circumstances, can reasonably be obtained. A tenant for life being a trustee (S.L.A. 1925, s. 107) should not agree for the price to be fixed by a valuer (*Thomas* v. *Williams* (1883), 24 Ch. D. 558). The consideration for the grant of the option (if any) will be deemed capital money (S.L.A. 1925, s. 51 (5)), and must be paid to two trustees or a trust corporation (S.L.A. 1925, s. 94). One month's notice of the intention to grant the option must be given to the trustees of the settlement and their solicitor, but a purchaser dealing in good faith with a tenant for life is not concerned to see that such notice has been given (S.L.A. 1925, s. 101).

Trustees for sale have, in relation to land, all the powers of a tenant for life, and therefore have the power to grant such an option (L.P.A. 1925, s. 28 (1), as amended). Personal representatives also have all the powers of a tenant or life and trustees for sale (A.E.A. 1925, s. 39).

CHAPTER THREE

MISTAKE

Introductory.—In this Chapter is considered the extent to which a mistake made by the parties, or by one of them, may affect an otherwise apparently concluded and binding contract for the sale of land. Certain other factors which may affect the validity of such a contract are dealt with in the succeeding Chapter on Misrepresentation, Misdescription and Non-disclosure. Although any one of these other factors may also be the cause of a mistake, it is necessary to keep them strictly separate since they can, at most, result only in a *voidable* contract, whilst a mistake can result in a contract which is *void*. The principal importance of this distinction between a contract valid unless and until avoided and a contract *void ab initio* is in the effect on third party rights, these being acquirable under the former before avoidance but not at all under the latter.

The somewhat harsh consequences of a contract void for mistake, as well as certain other aspects, may be mitigated in accordance with equitable principles. Therefore, it is expedient to treat separately the position of mistake (1) at common law, and (2) in equity.

The topic of mistake in the law of contract, lacking any definitive judicial statement, has attracted considerable academic controversy. Consequently, since neither the rules nor even the terminology of the topic are entirely settled, it is proposed in this Chapter to offer a utilitarian outline only, supported so far as possible with illustrations in a conveyancing context (further reference, if desired, may be made, for example, to Cheshire and Fifoot's Law of Contract, 8th ed., Pt. IV, Ch. 1, p. 201 *et seq.*, wherein much modern journal literature on the topic is cited).

A. AT COMMON LAW

General rule.—It is essential to emphasise that, as the general rule, a mistake by either of the parties does *not* affect the creation or validity of a contract at all. Thus a mistake of motive or judgment on the part of the purchaser, for instance, as to an element in the value of the land such as the existence of minerals beneath it, will generally constitute a case of *caveat emptor*. Lord Atkin illustrated and explained this as follows : " *A* agrees to take a house on lease or to buy from *B* an unfurnished dwelling-house. The house is in fact uninhabitable. *A* would never have entered into the bargain if he had known the fact. *A* has no remedy and the position is the same whether *B* knew the facts or not, so long as he made no representation or gave no warranty. *A* buys a roadside garage business from *B* abutting on a public thoroughfare ; unknown to *A* but known to *B*, it has already been decided to construct a by-pass road which will divert substantially the whole of the traffic from passing *A's* garage. Again *A* has no remedy. All these cases involve hardship on *A* and benefit to *B*, as most people would say unjustly. They can be supported on the ground that it is of paramount importance that contracts should be observed, and that if parties honestly comply with the essentials of the formation of contracts—i.e., *agree in the same terms on the same subject-matter*—they are bound, and must rely on the stipulations of the contract for protection from the effect of facts unknown to them " (*Bell* v.

Lever Brothers, Ltd. [1932] A.C. 161, at p. 224). Again, in *Dewar* v. *Mintoft* [1912] 2 K.B. 373, a man made a bid at an auction and the property was immediately knocked down to him ; even though he afterwards explained that he had not intended to buy the property but merely as a friendly action to start the bidding, he was nonetheless held bound by the contract (see also *Van Praagh* v. *Everidge* [1902] 2 Ch. 266, reversed on other grounds [1903] 1 Ch. 434).

Of course, not only purchasers may make mistakes. In *Wood* v. *Scarth* (1855), 2 K. & J. 33 ; (1858), 1 F. & F. 293, *S* offered in writing to lease a public house to *W* at a rent of £63 per annum ; *W* accepted this offer by letter after an interview with *S's* clerk ; even though *S* had intended that a premium of £500 should be paid in addition and mistakenly thought that his clerk had told *W* that, the contract was nonetheless held valid. Again, in *Okhill* v. *Whittaker* (1847), 16 L.J. Ch. 454, a vendor sold a leasehold property for the unexpired residue of the term, thinking this to be eight years and fixing the price accordingly ; even though the lease actually had twenty years to run, the vendor was still held bound.

Exceptions where mistake of fact can affect a contract.—Notwithstanding the general rule, in certain exceptional cases, because there has been a mistake, no contract will have been created.

For all these cases the rule is that the mistake must have been one of fact, not one of law—*ignorantia juris haud excusat*. For example, in a slightly different context, in *Brothers and Knight* v. *Chant* [1917] 1 K.B. 771, a landlord and tenant agreed to an increase in rent of 6d. a week which was paid for some time notwithstanding that under the Rent Restriction Acts in force the increase was not valid ; even so, the tenant was held unable to recover the increase already paid. See also *Finck* v. *Tranter* [1905] 1 K.B. 427, where a tenant, who had paid rent to an equitable mortgagee, with notice of this capacity, was held unable to recover the payments because the equitable mortgagee's lack of a legal title to claim the rent amounted to a mistake of law.

Unfortunately, the distinction between mistakes of fact and mistakes of law is not always clear, in that some " facts " are conclusions drawn from law (for example, that persons are married : see *Galloway* v. *Galloway* (1914), 30 T.L.R. 531, where a separation deed was declared a nullity). Thus in *Cooper* v. *Phibbs* (1867), L.R. 2 H.L. 149, the House of Lords set aside a contract by a person to take a lease of a salmon fishery in Ireland which he himself already owned as tenant in tail, both parties mistakenly thinking that by virtue of a private Act of Parliament and a particular deed the prospective lessor was the owner. Lord Westbury explained (*ibid.*, p. 170) : " It is said ' *Ignorantia juris haud excusat*,' but in that maxim the word ' *jus* ' is used in the sense of denoting general law, the ordinary law of the country. But when the word ' *jus* ' is used in the sense of denoting a private right, that maxim has no application. Private right of ownership is a matter of fact ; it may be the result also of a matter of law ; but if parties contract under a mutual mistake and misapprehension as to their relative and respective rights, the result is that that agreement is likely to be set aside as having proceeded upon a common mistake. Now, that was the case with these parties—the respondents believed themselves to be entitled to the property, the petitioner believed that he was a stranger to it, the mistake is discovered, and the agreement cannot stand." See also *Newsome* v. *Graham* (1829), 10 B. & C. 234, where a tenant's mistake as to who was the landlord entitled to payment of rent was held to be one of fact.

However, some of the cases are difficult to reconcile. Thus a mistake in the construction or effect of a written document will amount to one of general law (*Rogers* v. *Ingham* (1876), 3 Ch. D. 351 ; *Ord* v. *Ord* [1923] 2 K.B. 432 ; *Hill* v. *Krishenstein* [1920] 3 Ch. 351). Again, in *Solle* v. *Butcher* [1950] 1 K.B. 671, a flat was damaged during the last war and afterwards repaired and altered ; the flat was then let, both parties mistakenly thinking that the alterations were sufficiently extensive to make it a new flat outside the Rent Restriction Acts ; the majority of the Court of Appeal held this to be a mistake of fact, whilst Jenkins, L.J., dissenting, regarded it as one of law.

(i) *Same fundamental mistake.*—The exceptional cases in which a mistake can operate to affect the creation of a contract may be put into three classes. The first of these classes of operative mistake arises when the parties do in fact reach agreement " in the same terms on the same subject-matter " but do so only on the basis of something as to which they both make the same mistake ; provided that this " something " is fundamental to their agreement, there will be no contract—it will be void (*Couturier* v. *Hastie* (1856), 5 H.L.C. 673). The commonest example of this occurs where the subject-matter of the contract in fact does not exist—*res extincta* (as in *Couturier* v. *Hastie*, *ante*). This, however, would be a rare event with contracts for the sale of land, although illustrations in a conveyancing context can be found. Thus in *Strickland* v. *Turner* (1852), 7 Ex. 208, a contract was entered into for the sale of the life interest in property of a person then thought by both of the parties to be alive, but who was in fact dead, and it was held that the purchaser, having completed the purchase, was entitled to recover his purchase-money ; if the contract had not been completed, the purchaser would on the same principle have been entitled to recover any deposit paid. See also *Pritchard* v. *Merchant's*, *etc.*, *Life Assurance Society* (1858), 3 C.B. (N.S.) 622, where a beneficiary paid a premium to revive a lapsed life insurance policy when the assured had already died, and *Scott* v. *Coulson* [1903] 2 Ch. 249.
" Corresponding to mistake as to the existence of the subject-matter is mistake as to title in cases where, unknown to the parties, the buyer is already the owner of that which the seller purports to sell to him. The parties intend to effect a transfer of ownership ; such a transfer is impossible ; the stipulation is *naturali ratione inutilis* " (Lord Atkin in *Bell* v. *Lever Bros., Ltd.* [1942] A.C. 161, at p. 218, citing *Cooper* v. *Phibbs* (1867), L.R. 2 H.L. 149, mentioned above). Thus, in *Cochrane* v. *Willis* (1865), L.R. 1 Ch. 58, the assignee of a tenant for life agreed to sell to the remainderman timber on the estate which he, as assignee, was entitled to cut ; in fact the tenant for life had died and the agreement was held void. For other cases concerning this sort of mistake, that is as to *res sua*, see *Bingham* v. *Bingham* (1748), 1 Ves. Sen. 126 ; *Jones* v. *Clifford* (1876), 3 Ch. D. 779, and *Debenham* v. *Sawbridge* [1901] 2 Ch. 98, 109 ; also *Bligh* v. *Martin* [1968] 1 W.L.R. 804.

Whether this first class of operative mistake extends beyond *res extincta* and *res sua* to render void contracts made on the basis of mistakes as to other fundamental matters is not settled. The judgments of the House of Lords as a whole in the leading case of *Bell* v. *Lever Bros., Ltd.* [1942] A.C. 161 are somewhat ambiguous, and the text books on the law of contract are divided, for instance, Cheshire and Fifoot, 8th ed., pp. 209–213, prefers the narrower extent whilst Chitty on Contract, 22nd ed., paras. 197 and 203 to 207, would not so restrict the class. This, however, is not the place in which to pursue the discussion.

(ii) *Parties at cross purposes.*—The second class of operative mistake arises where the parties do *not* in fact reach agreement because they are at cross purposes. There is no correspondence between the offer and the acceptance, no *consensus ad idem*, and therefore again there will be no contract (*Raffles* v. *Wickelhaus* (1864), 2 H. & C. 906 ; *Scriven* v. *Hindley* [1913] 3 K.B. 564). An example given in Williams on Vendor and Purchaser, 4th ed., vol. II, p. 756, is : " If *A* sells to *B* his farm called the Grange, and *A* has two farms of that name, one in Essex and one in Hampshire, and *A* intended to sell his farm in Essex, but *B* meant to buy the farm in Hampshire, there is no true consent and no contract between the parties." Another example may be seen in *Higginson* v. *Clowes* (1808), 15 Ves. 516, where the particulars of sale of a property by auction as to including or excluding timber were ambiguous, the vendor meaning them in one way and the purchaser construing them in another, and it was held that specific performance could not be decreed on either construction.

It must be emphasised, however, that this class of mistake is to be approached objectively. As a rule no subjective enquiry will be made by the courts into what the parties actually intended. Consequently, for a mistake of this class to be operative there must also be some ambiguity in the terms of the contract—for if the parties " agree in the same terms on the same subject-matter " they will be bound in contract even though they were at cross purposes (see, for example, *Rosse* v. *Pim* [1953] 2 Q.B. 450, and Misdescription, *post*, p. 93). Thus, in *Tamplin* v. *James* (1880), 15 Ch. D. 215, property clearly described by reference to a plan was bought at an auction, the purchaser mistakenly thinking that a garden plot was included. He was nonetheless held bound by the contract. Of course, if the ambiguity is not patent but is latent (as in the example given in Williams on Vendor and Purchaser, *ante*) then in accordance with the ordinary rule extrinsic evidence of the parties' actual intentions does become admissible ; compare *Re Jackson* [1933] Ch. 237. Further, where there is ambiguity in the contract, which cannot be resolved, and no evidence of cross purposes, then the contract is liable to fail anyway for uncertainty of terms.

(iii) *Unilateral mistake.*—This last class of operative mistake again arises where the parties do *not* in fact reach agreement, but here correspondence between the offer and the acceptance is lacking because of a mistake made by one of the parties alone. The contract will be void if, and only if, the other party knew of the mistake (see *per* Hannen, J., in *Smith* v. *Hughes* (1871), L.R. 6 Q.B. 597, at p. 610, and *Hartog* v. *Colin and Shields* [1939] 3 All E.R. 566). Without the other party's knowledge, a unilateral mistake comes within the general rule above, that is, it does not affect the contract at all. Unlike the second class, this third class of mistake has necessarily to be approached subjectively. The courts must inquire as to the other party's actual knowledge, although a person will be taken to have known what a reasonable man would in the circumstances have known (*Hartog* v. *Colin and Shields, ante*).

Further, for a unilateral mistake to be operative, it must be fundamental in the sense of relating to the terms of the offer or of the acceptance constituting the contract, and not merely to the quality of the subject-matter of the contract (*Smith* v. *Hughes, ante*). Thus in *Webster* v. *Cecil* (1861), 30 Beav. 62, Cecil, having refused to sell certain land to Webster for £2,000, wrote to him offering to sell it for £1,250, which Webster accepted by return of post ; knowledge that Cecil had intended to write £2,250 was imputed to Webster so that the contract was void for mistake. The commonest case before the

courts concerns one party's mistake as to the other's identity or personality.
At this point a considerable academic controversy over conflicting cases is
encountered, a discussion of which would be outside the scope of this book ;
see Cheshire and Fifoot's Law of Contract, 8th ed., pp. 224–231 (the 7th ed.
was cited as an authority by Megaw, L.J., in *Lewis* v. *Averay* [1972] 1 Q.B.
198). It may, however, be stressed here that it is *not* enough for the
plaintiff to show that though he made an agreement with the defendant, he
would not have done had he realised the defendant's identity. The plaintiff
must show that the identity of the other party, and not merely certain of his
attributes, was an essential element of the contract into which the plaintiff
was prepared to enter. Having said this, it becomes apparent that the other
party's identity will very rarely be an element of the contract for the sale of
land (but see a note at (1964), 108 Sol. J. 510). The concern in conveyancing
is much more likely to be with the attribute of ability, respectively, to convey
or to pay, which will not affect the creation of the contract (compare *Dennant*
v. *Skinner and Collom* [1948] 2 K.B. 164). Thus in *Nash* v. *Dix* (1898),
78 L.T. 445, the trustees of a Congregational Chapel which was for sale
declined an offer to buy because it was made on behalf of a committee of
Roman Catholics. That committee then told the plaintiff, the manager of a
company, that if he bought the chapel they would buy it from him at £100
profit. The trustees contracted to sell to the plaintiff, but refused to proceed
on learning the facts. It was admitted that the plaintiff knew that the trustees
thought that he was buying for his company. North, J., held this immaterial
and granted specific performance on the ground that the trustees had not
cared whether they sold to the plaintiff or his company (compare *Archer* v.
Stone (1888), 78 L.T. 34, but contrast *Sowler* v. *Potter* [1940] 1 K.B. 271,
more fully reported at [1939] 4 All E.R. 478). In this case the defendant
changed her name by deed poll and took a lease from the plaintiff which he
would not have granted to her had he known her true identity because she
had been convicted of an offence making her an undesirable tenant. Tucker, J.,
held the lease void for mistake but his decision has been criticised (see Dr. A. L.
Goodhart, *Law Quarterly Review*, vol. 57, p. 228, and Denning, L.J., in *Solle*
v. *Butcher* [1950] 1 K.B. 671, at p. 691) ; the better view appears to be that
the lease should not have been void but voidable for fraud.

Mistake in signing written contract.—This is essentially an example of the
class of unilateral mistake just discussed, but it is traditionally treated
separately. The rule is that if a person is misled into signing a document
containing a contract fundamentally different from that which he contemplated, then the plea of *non est factum* will be available to him and the contract
will, in effect, be void (see the leading case of *Saunders* v. *Anglia Building
Society* [1971] A.C. 1004). Thus in *Foster* v. *Mackinnon* (1869), L.R. 4
C.P. 704, the defendant who was told he was signing a guarantee, as he had
done before, whilst actually he was endorsing a bill of exchange, was held not
liable to an indorsee of the bill. See also *Lewis* v. *Clay* (1897), 67 L.J. Q.B.
224, where a person who thought himself to be a witness to a private family
document actually signed a promissory note.
The mistake as to a written contract held void has usually been induced
by fraud (not necessarily that of the other party) but this is not the essential
element : a contract " is invalid not merely on the ground of fraud, where
fraud exists, but on the ground that the mind of the signer did not accompany
the signature ; in other words, that he never intended to sign, and therefore
in contemplation of law never did sign, the contract to which his name is

appended " (*per* Byles, J., in *Foster* v. *Mackinnon* (1869), L.R. 4 C.P. 704, at p. 711). Nevertheless it appears that the plea of *non est factum* will not succeed unless there has been a misrepresentation inducing the mistaken belief as to the class and character of the document (*Hasham* v. *Zenab* [1960] A.C. 316, at p. 335 ; *Mercantile Credit Co., Ltd.* v. *Hamblin* [1965] 2 Q.B. 242).

It is now clear that the plea has very limited availability for persons of full capacity. Although it is not restricted to the blind and illiterate, it is unlikely to be established by anyone who simply signs a document without informing himself of its meaning and cannot in any case be relied on if there were, in his signing, any carelessness or negligence, not in any technical sense and not operating by way of estoppel (*Saunders* v. *Anglia Building Society* [1971] A.C. 1004). Further the distinction previously adopted between the nature and the contents of the document has been rejected as unsatisfactory : what is essential, for the plea to succeed in this respect, is merely that a radical or fundamental overall difference be shown between the document as it is and as it was believed to be (*Saunders* v. *Anglia Building Society, ante,* in which the difference between a deed of gift and an assignment on sale was found to be insufficient).

Lastly, note that whenever the facts may or may not support a plea of *non est factum,* it is advisable to consider also (i) whether the contract may be void in the ordinary way for unilateral mistake, see above, (ii) whether the written contract may be open to rectification (see *post,* p. 84), and (iii) whether remedies may be available for misrepresentation or misdescription (see *post,* pp. 87, 93).

B. IN EQUITY

In general, equity follows the common-law rules as to the effect, or more usually, the non-effect of a mistake on the validity of a contract (*Hitchcock* v. *Giddings* (1817), 4 Price 135, 141 ; *Preston* v. *Luck* (1884), 27 Ch. D. 497). Thus in *Powell* v. *Smith* (1872), L.R. 14 Eq. 85, a lessor's agent had agreed to the grant of a lease for seven or fourteen years, which the lessor mistakenly took to mean a lease determinable at his, rather than the tenant's option after seven years, and specific performance was nonetheless decreed ; see also *Tamplin* v. *James* (1880), 15 Ch. D. 215, and *Van Praagh* v. *Everidge* [1902] 2 Ch. 266. Nonetheless, equity may interfere by adding, as it were, an element of discretion to the common-law position in the following two alternatives. It should be noted, however, that this equitable jurisdiction to interfere is, as yet, neither predictable in exercise nor supported by final authority.

First, where a contract would be void at common law for mistake, equity may impose terms on the parties in setting the contract aside (*Cooper* v. *Phibbs* (1867), L.R. 2 H.L. 149, where the term imposed was a lien for money already expended on improvements).

Secondly, where a contract would be valid at common law, equity may still set the contract aside, although not so as to affect any third parties' interests ; see the judgment of Denning, L.J., in *Solle* v. *Butcher* [1950] 1 K.B. 671, at p. 695 ; followed in *Magee* v. *Pennines Insurance Co., Ltd.* [1969] 2 Q.B. 507, C.A. Thus in *Huddersfield Banking Co., Ltd.* v. *Henry Lister & Son, Ltd.* [1895] 2 Ch. 273, mortgagees concurred in the sale by the mortgagor's liquidator of certain looms in a mill after an inspection had shown that the looms were not attached and so not fixtures, but the concurrence was set aside on it turning out that the looms had been attached at the date of the mortgage and since separated without authority. In *Solle* v. *Butcher, ante,* a lease valid at common law was set aside in equity for mistake but not *simpliciter,* the court imposing terms designed to avoid an unjust position ; Denning, L.J. (at p. 693), laid down the principle in these terms : " A contract is also liable in equity to be set aside if the parties were under a common misapprehension either as to facts or as to their relative and respective rights, provided that the misapprehension was fundamental and that the party seeking to set it aside was not himself at fault." This was followed more recently by Goff, J., in *Grist* v. *Bailey* [1967] Ch. 532, where a purchaser sought specific performance of a contract for sale of a house subject to a tenancy, at a price of £850 ; both parties had thought there was a statutory tenancy whereas in fact the tenant left without claiming any such tenancy ; the vacant possession value was £2,250. Rescission of the contract was ordered but on condition that the vendor entered into a fresh contract at a proper vacant possession price, if required.

In addition, the equitable remedy of specific performance (see *post,* p. 288), being discretionary, may be refused on the ground of mistake, even though the contract remains valid at common law (see *per* Bacon, V.-C., in *Burrow* v. *Scammell* (1881), 19 Ch. D. 175, at p. 182, and in *Paget* v. *Marshall* (1884), 28 Ch. D. 255, at p. 263). In *Paget* v. *Marshall, ante,* in offering to let certain houses the plaintiff had intended to, but did not, reserve to himself his own shop in one of the houses and the court gave the defendant a choice of submitting to rectification or of losing the lease.

However, where the mistake has not been contributed to by the other party, specific performance will not be refused " unless the case is one of considerable harshness and hardship " (*per* Kay, J., in *Goddard* v. *Jeffreys* (1881), 45 L.T. 674). Thus in *Van Praagh* v. *Everidge* [1902] 2 Ch. 266 (reversed on another point at [1903] 1 Ch. 434) a builder bought a piece of land in mistake for another piece and it was held that since the land bought could be built on there was insufficient hardship to justify a refusal of specific performance to the vendor. Contrast *Bray* v. *Briggs* (1872), 26 L.T. 817, where again a builder bought land but found that building was prohibited by Act of Parliament and the court did refuse to enforce the contract against him on the ground that this would entail hardship amounting to injustice. Specific performance was refused against a vendor who had instructed his auctioneer to sell subject to the reservation of a right of way and the auctioneer forgot to make the reservation (*Manser* v. *Back* (1848), 6 Hare 443), and in a case where the auctioneer had made a mistake in the reserve price (*Day* v. *Wells* (1861), 30 Beav. 220).

Rectification.—In addition, the courts enjoy an equitable jurisdiction to rectify a written contract, in general, whenever the parties have reached agreement but a mistake has been made in reducing that agreement to writing—it is then the writing and not the contract that is rectified (see *per* Jones, V.-C., in *Mackenzie* v. *Coulson* (1869), L.R. 8 Eq. 368, at p. 375). For example, if a vendor orally agrees to sell a house without the adjoining yard but the formal contract in writing includes the yard, then the latter will be rectified (see *Craddock Brothers, Ltd.* v. *Hunt* [1923] 2 Ch. 136, where a subsequent conveyance according with the formal contract was also rectified).

To be more particular, the jurisdiction to rectify depends on the following conditions :—

(i) As a rule, there must have been a prior concluded agreement between the parties going beyond mere negotiations (see *per* Denning, L.J., in *Frederick*

E. Rose (London), Ltd. v. *William H. Pim & Co., Ltd.* [1953] 2 Q.B. 450, at p. 461). However, it now appears clear that there is jurisdiction to rectify on the basis of a common continuing intention of the parties, which intention has some outward expression, even though no prior concluded contract existed (*Joscelyne* v. *Nissen* [1970] 2 Q.B. 86, in which the jurisdiction to rectify was re-examined by the Court of Appeal; see also *per* Clauson, J., in *Shipley U.D.C.* v. *Bradford Corpn.* [1936] Ch. 375 ; on appeal *ibid.*, p. 399 ; *per* Simonds, J., in *Crane* v. *Hegeman Harris & Co., Inc.* [1939] 1 All E.R. 662, at p. 664 ; on appeal [1939] 4 All E.R. 68 ; *per* Harman, L.J., in *Earl* v. *Hector Whaling* [1961] 1 Ll. R. 459, at p. 470 ; also *Carlton Contractors, Ltd.* v. *Bexley Corpn.* (1962), 106 Sol. J. 391). Further reference may be made to *Wilson* v. *Wilson* [1969] 1 W.L.R. 1470 in which Buckley, J., ordered rectification of a conveyance declaring a beneficial joint tenancy contrary to the common intention of the parties concerned ; and *Lloyd* v. *Stanbury* [1971] 1 W.L.R. 535, in which no common intention of the parties was established as to the exclusion of a piece of land from a contract for sale. The requirement stipulated in *Joscelyne* v. *Nisson, ante,* of " some outward expression of accord " has been doubted by Leonard Bramley, Q.C., in the *Law Quarterly Review,* vol. 87, p. 532 *et seq.*

(ii) As a rule, for there to be rectification, the written contract must fail to represent the prior concluded agreement or common intention because of a mistake of *both* parties (*Sells* v. *Sells* (1860), 1 Dr. & Sm. 42 ; *Mortimer* v. *Shortall* (1842), 2 Dr. & War. 363, at p. 372). Thus it is not sufficient that one party was not told by his agent of the term sought to be inserted (*Fowler* v. *Scottish Equitable Life Insurance Society* (1858), 28 L.J. Ch. 225). However, there are two clear exceptions to this rule, where there may be rectification despite the mistake being made by only one of the parties. The first is where the other party has taken advantage of the mistaken party in a way fraudulent to the eyes of equity (*Ball* v. *Storie* (1823), 1 Sim. & St. 210, at p. 219 ; *May* v. *Platt* [1900] 1 Ch. 618, at p. 623). The second exception is stated in Snell's Equity (now 27th ed., at p. 614) : " By what appears to be a species of equitable estoppel, if one party to a transaction knows that the instrument contains a mistake in his favour but does nothing to correct it, he (and those claiming under him) will be precluded from resisting rectification on the ground that the mistake is unilateral and not common." This statement was quoted with approval by Pennycuick, J., in *A. Roberts & Co., Ltd.* v. *Leicestershire C.C.* [1961] Ch. 555, at p. 570, but with some uncertainty as to whether the principle ought correctly to be rested on estoppel or on fraud. In addition, there are some cases in which a party who knew or suspected a mistake was given the option of rectification or cancellation of the contract (*Garrard* v. *Frankel* (1862), 30 Beav. 445 ; *Harris* v. *Pepperell* (1867), L.R. 5 Eq. 1 ; *Bloomer* v. *Spittle* (1872), L.R. 13 Eq. 427 ; *Paget* v. *Marshall* (1884), 28 Ch. D. 255 ; compare *Solle* v. *Butcher* [1950] 1 K.B. 671). These cases have been criticised (for example in Williams on Vendor and Purchaser, 4th ed., vol. II, pp. 784–791) and it has been pointed out judicially that in them the defendant's conduct, though not so stigmatised, was in fact treated as equivalent to fraud (*per* Farwell, J., in *May* v. *Platt* [1900] 1 Ch. 616, at p. 623).

The burden of proof lies on the party who alleges that the written contract does not represent the parties' prior agreement or intention (*Tucker* v. *Bennett* (1887), 38 Ch. D. 1). This is a heavy burden which can only be discharged by clear evidence not only of the mistake in the written contract but also that the rectified writing will accord with the prior agreement or intention (*Fowler* v.*Fowler* (1859), 4 De G. & J. 250; *Fredensen* v. *Rothschild* [1941] 1 All E.R. 430).

(iii) Next, for there to be rectification, it must be shown that the written contract was intended to represent the agreement or common intention of the parties ; that is, the original agreement or intention must have continued unchanged up to its reduction to writing (*Breadalbane* v. *Chandos* (1837), 2 My. & Cr. 711 ; *Fowler* v. *Fowler* (1859), 4 De G. & J. 250).

(iv) Lastly, for there to be rectification, it must be a case for the exercise of equity's discretion (*Beale* v. *Kyte* [1907] 1 Ch. 564 ; claim barred by *laches* or acquiescence). Thus the contract must still be capable of performance (*Borrowman* v. *Rossell* (1864), 16 C.B. (N.S.) 58 ; *Caird* v. *Moss* (1886), 33 Ch. D. 22). Again a document will not be rectified where there is no issue between the parties (*Whiteside* v. *Whiteside* [1950] Ch. 65 ; purpose of claiming rectification only to obtain taxation advantage ; cp. *Re Colebrook's Conveyance* [1973] 1 All E.R. 132, where the taxation advantage was only incidental). Nor, as with any other equitable remedy, will rectification be ordered to the prejudice of a *bona fide* purchaser for value of a legal estate or even equitable interest without notice of the claim to rectification, this claim being a mere equity (*Smith* v. *Jones* [1954] 1 W.L.R. 1089 ; rectification of a tenancy agreement refused as against a subsequent purchaser of the reversion who had inspected and relied on the agreement).

Parol evidence.—Rectification constitutes an established exception to the rule that parol evidence is inadmissible to add to, contradict or vary the terms of a written contract (*Murray* v. *Parker* (1854), 1 Beav. 305 ; *Lovell and Christmas, Ltd.* v. *Wall* (1911), 104 L.T. 85). Again there may be rectification of a written contract to accord with a prior oral agreement notwithstanding the statutory requirements of evidence in writing in the L.P.A. 1925, s. 40, *ante*, p. 40. " The statute only provides that no agreement not in writing and not duly signed shall be sued on ; but where the written instrument is rectified there is a writing which satisfies the statute, the jurisdiction of the court to rectify being outside the prohibition of the statute " (*United States* v. *Motor Trucks, Ltd.* [1924] A.C. 196, at p. 201). Then the court may in one and the same action order specific performance of the written contract as rectified (*Craddock Bros., Ltd.* v. *Hunt* [1923] 2 Ch. 136 ; *United States* v. *Motor Trucks, Ltd., ante*).

CHAPTER FOUR

MISREPRESENTATION MISDESCRIPTION AND NON-DISCLOSURE

IN this chapter are considered certain important factors which may affect the validity of a contract for the sale of land other than Mistake (as to which see Chapter 3, *ante*, p. 78). These factors, unlike mistake, will never render the contract void *ab initio*, but will at most make it voidable, in this context almost always at the instance of the purchaser.

PART 1. MISREPRESENTATION

For any misrepresentations that became part of the contract for sale itself, see Part 2, Misdescription, *post*, 93 ; for misrepresentations that amount to collateral contracts, see *ante*, p. 70 ; for misrepresentations causing mistake, see *ante*, p. 78.

Certain additional consequences of practical importance have been imposed by the Misrepresentation Act, 1967, upon the position as a result of misrepresentation in equity and at common law. Accordingly, it appears sensible to state first the position apart from that statute and then to give the additions made in 1967.

A. IN EQUITY AND AT COMMON LAW

Requirements for rescission.—A purchaser may in equity rescind a contract for the sale of land on the ground of misrepresentation where a *false statement of fact made by the vendor to the purchaser induced the purchaser to enter into the contract.* These requirements may be further considered individually :

False.—There may be misrepresentation even though what is actually stated is literally true if a false impression is created because of what is not stated, i.e., a half-truth (*Peek* v. *Gurney* (1873), L.R. 6 H.L. 377, at p. 403). An example of this would be where a vendor states that the property is let but omits to state that the tenants have given notice to quit (*Dimmock* v. *Hallett* (1866), 2 Ch. App. 21). Again if the statement was true when made, but becomes untrue before the contract is made, the vendor may be guilty of misrepresentation unless he corrects it (*With* v. *O'Flanagan* [1935] Ch. 575). If what is stated is ambiguous, the burden is on the purchaser to prove that he reasonably understood it in a false sense (*Arkwright* v. *Newbold* (1881), 17 Ch. D. 301 ; *Low* v. *Bouverie* [1891] 3 Ch. 82, at pp. 101 and 106).

If the statement is false, it is immaterial that the vendor honestly believed it to be true (*Redgrave* v. *Hurd* (1881), 20 Ch. D. 14), except that if he did not, or if he owed a duty of care, the purchaser may have common-law remedies in addition (see Damages, below).

Statement.—A misrepresentation may be made not only by words but also by conduct, " a nod or a wink, or a shake of the head or a smile " (Lord Campbell in *Walters* v. *Morgan* (1861), 3 De G. F. & J. 718, at p. 723 ; *R.* v. *Barnard* (1837), 7 C. & P. 784). An example given by Williams on Vendor and Purchaser, 4th ed., vol. II, p. 764, despite being said in an earlier edition of the present work to be " an extreme case," actually occurred in *Ridge* v. *Crawley* (1959), 173 E.G. 959, where a vendor who had had cracks in the walls outside filled and inside papered over, so that faulty foundations would be difficult to detect, was held by the Court of Appeal to be guilty of misrepresentation by conduct.

Silence, however, even as to a material fact, does not generally constitute a misrepresentation, *caveat emptor* being the rule (*per* Lord Atkin in *Bell* v. *Lever Bros., Ltd.* [1932] A.C. 161, at p. 227 ; *Turner* v. *Green* [1895] 2 Ch. 205). Nonetheless, in certain exceptional cases there may be a duty to disclose all material facts, with rescission as the consequence of non-disclosure. This is so where a fiduciary relationship exists between the parties to a contract, e.g., parent and child, principal and agent, trustee and beneficiary (see *Tate* v. *Williamson* (1866), 2 Ch. App. 55). It would also be so where the contract required *uberrima fides*, e.g., a contract of insurance, but a contract for the sale of land is not of this sort (*Walters* v. *Morgan* (1861), 3 De G.F. & J. 718, at p. 723), although disclosure of certain matters is necessary for other reasons (see Part 3, Non-Disclosure, *post*, p. 97).

Fact.—For rescission, the misrepresentation must be of fact and *not* of law, intention or opinion. The difficult distinction between fact and law is dealt with *ante*, p. 79. A statement of intention will normally amount to a promise as to the future which can consequently only be enforced if it forms part of a valid contract (see *per* Mellish, L.J., in *Beattie* v. *Ebury* (1872), 7 Ch. App. 777, at p. 804 ; also *Maddison* v. *Alderson* (1883), 8 App. Cas. 467). If, however, the stated intention is not, in fact, held then there will be a clear misrepresentation of existing fact (see *per* Bowen, L.J., in *Edgington* v. *Fitzmaurice* (1885), 29 Ch. D. 459, at p. 483).

The distinction between a statement of fact and the expression of an opinion may be illustrated by *Bisset* v. *Wilkinson* [1927] A.C. 117, where a vendor of the land which had never before been used as a sheep farm told a prospective purchaser that it would carry 2,000 sheep and this was held to be an honest if mistaken expression of opinion and not a representation as to the actual carrying capacity. Against this such statements as that the length of the garden is approximately forty feet, that the cellars are dry or that the premises are sanitary are obviously more than mere expressions of opinion (*Bellotti* v. *Chequers Developments Ltd.* [1936] 1 All E.R. 89 ; *Lamare* v. *Dixon* (1873), L.R. 6 H.L. 414 ; and *Whittington* v. *Seale-Hayne* (1900), 82 L.T. 49). Nevertheless such statements as " a desirable residence for a family of distinction " or " fertile and improvable " are equally obviously not statements of fact (see *Magennis* v. *Fallon* (1828), 2 Mol. 561, at p. 588, and *Dimmock* v. *Hallett* (1866), 2 Ch. App. 21).

However, as Bowen, L.J., said in *Smith* v. *Land and House Property Corporation* (1884), 28 Ch. D. 7, at p. 15, " It is often fallaciously assumed that a statement of opinion cannot involve a statement of fact. In a case where the facts are equally well known to both parties, what one of them says to the other is frequently nothing but an expression of opinion . . . But if the facts are not equally well known to both sides, then a statement of opinion by one who knows the facts best involves very often a statement of material fact, for he impliedly states he knows facts which justify his opinion." In that case, the vendor had described the occupier as " a most desirable tenant " although the rent was considerably in arrear, and the purchaser was held able to rescind. This was followed in *Brown* v. *Raphael* [1958] Ch. 636 where the particulars of sale at an auction of a reversion stated that the life tenant was " believed to have no aggregable estate," and the purchaser was permitted to rescind, there being a substantial aggregable estate, because of the implication that the vendor had reasonable grounds for his belief ; the Court of Appeal also indicated that the appearance of solicitors' names at the end of the particulars would imply that the belief was based on competent advice.

By the vendor.—For rescission, the misrepresentation must have been made by the vendor, except that he would be liable as a principal for a misrepresentation made by his agent on his behalf (*Lloyd* v. *Grace, Smith & Co.* [1912] A.C. 716 ; see also *Gosling* v. *Anderson* (1972), *The Times*, 6th February).

To the purchaser.—To be entitled to rescission, the purchaser must be able to show that the misrepresentation was made to him and was intended to be acted on by him (*Peek* v. *Gurney* (1873), L.R. 6 H.L. 377 ; compare *Andrews* v. *Mockford* [1896] 1 Q.B. 372). Reference should also be made to *Gross* v. *Lewis Hillman, Ltd.* [1970] Ch. 445, where the Court of Appeal decided that a sub-purchaser was not entitled to rescind as against the original vendor on account of a misrepresentation made only to the original purchaser even though the sub-purchaser had known of the misrepresentation and had taken a conveyance of the property directly from the original vendor.

Induced.—The misrepresentation need not be the sole reason inducing the purchaser to enter into the contract (*Reynell* v. *Sprye* (1851), 1 De G.M. & G. 660, at p. 708 ; *Edgington* v. *Fitzmaurice* (1885), 29 Ch. D. 459), but it must be at least one of the reasons inducing him, i.e., for rescission there must have been a material misrepresentation (*Smith* v. *Chadwick* (1882), 20 Ch. D. 27, at pp. 44–45). Thus an over-statement of the length of a garden by four feet only was a material misrepresentation where the purchaser wanted to build a garage (*Bellotti* v. *Chequers Developments, Ltd.* [1936] 1 All E.R. 89 ; compare *Watson* v. *Burton* [1957] 1 W.L.R. 19 as to a misdescription in area, *post*, p. 93).

There is no such inducement if the purchaser (*a*) was unaware of the misrepresentation (*Horsfall* v. *Thomas* (1862), 1 H. & C. 90) ; (*b*) knew it was untrue (*Begbie* v. *Phosphate Sewage Co.* (1875), L.R. 10 Q.B. 491) ; or (*c*) did not rely on it, e.g., relying instead on his own survey report or judgment (*Attwood* v. *Small* (1838), 6 Cl. & Fin. 232 ; *Smith* v. *Chadwick, ante*). Note, however, that there will still be inducement notwithstanding that the purchaser may have had every opportunity of discovering the truth ; e.g., if a vendor misrepresents the contents of a lease, it is no defence for him to say that inspection of the lease was expressly invited but not accepted (see *per* Jessel, M.R., in *Redgrave* v. *Hurd* (1881), 20 Ch. D. 1, at p. 14).

Rescission must be equitable.—A purchaser will lose his equitable right to rescind for misrepresentation in the following circumstances :

(i) If a third party acquires, in good faith and for value, an interest in the subject-matter of the contract without notice of the right to rescind

(*White* v. *Garden* (1851), 10 C.B. 919 ; *Scholefield* v. *Templer* (1859), 4 De
G. & J. 429 ; see also *Re L. G. Clarke* [1967] Ch. 1121) ; contrast Mistake
where a contract is rendered void not voidable, *ante*, p. 78.

(ii) If it becomes impossible to restore the parties to their pre-contract
position (*Clarke* v. *Dickson* (1858), E.B. & E. 148), e.g., if the subject-matter
of the contract has been substantially altered (*Vigers* v. *Pike* (1842), 8 Cl. &
Fin. 562, mine worked out) ; note that the courts are apparently ready to
relax this *restitutio in integrum* rule in a case of fraud (see *Spence* v. *Craword*
[1939] 3 All E.R. 271, at p. 288 ; also *Hilton* v. *Hilton* [1917] 1 K.B. 813).

(iii) If the purchaser expressly or impliedly affirms the contract, which
may be evidenced by a lapse of time without action after knowledge of the
misrepresentation (*Clough* v. *L.N.W.R.* (1871), L.R. 7 Ex. 26, at p. 35) ;
note too that : " It behoves the purchaser either to verify or, as the case
may be, to disprove the representation within a reasonable time, or else
stand or fall by it " (*per* Jenkins, L.J., in *Leaf* v. *International Galleries*
[1950] 2 K.B. 86).

(iv) Unless the misrepresentation was fraudulent, if the contract has
been completed by execution of a conveyance or lease of the land (*Wilde* v.
Gibson (1848), 1 H.L.C. 605, at pp. 632–633 : conveyance ; *Angel* v. *Jay*
[1911] 1 K.B. 666 : lease ; *Armstrong* v. *Jackson* [1917] 2 K.B. 822, at
p. 825). This rule had been so much criticised, more particularly in relation
to contracts for the sale of goods, that its application had become somewhat
uncertain (see especially *per* Denning, L.J., in *Solle* v. *Butcher* [1950] 1 K.B.
671, at p. 696, and in *Leaf* v. *International Galleries* [1950] 2 K.B. 86, at
p. 90 ; but compare *Edler* v. *Auerbach* [1950] 1 K.B. 309, *Long* v. *Lloyd* [1958]
1 W.L.R. 753 and *Senanayake* v. *Cheng* [1966] A.C. 63). However, for all
practical purposes, the uncertainty has ended with the express reversal of
the rule by the Misrepresentation Act, 1967, s. 1, *post*.

Damages.—An innocent misrepresentation did not give rise to common-
law remedies but only to an intervention of equity ; consequently the purchaser had only the choice of avoiding or affirming the contract *without*
damages or any reduction in the price (*Heilbut, Symms & Co.* v. *Buckleton*
[1913] A.C. 30, at p. 51 ; *Gilchester Properties, Ltd.* v. *Gomm* [1948] 1 All E.R.
493), although he might if he rescinded claim an indemnity against any
obligations necessarily created by the contract (as to the distinction between
damages and indemnity, see *Whittington* v. *Seal-Hayne* (1900), 82 L.T. 49).
This position again has now in substance been replaced by the Misrepresentation Act, 1967, s. 2, *post*, under which damages may be obtained.

However, if the misrepresentation was fraudulent—that is, if the vendor
did not honestly believe it to be true (see *per* Lord Herschell in *Derry* v.
Peek (1889), 14 App. Cas. 337, at pp. 374 and 379)—then the purchaser, in
addition to any other remedies, may recover damages for the tort of deceit
(*Briess* v. *Woolley* [1954] A.C. 333, at pp. 353–354).

Again, if a duty of care was owed in the making of statements, a misrepresentation may give rise to the recovery of damages for the tort of
negligence (*Hedley Byrne & Co.* v. *Heller and Partners, Ltd.* [1964] A.C. 465).
A duty of care will be owed in " all these relationships where it is plain that
the party seeking information or advice was trusting the other to exercise
such a degree of care as the circumstances required, where it was reasonable
for him to do that, and where the other gave the information or advice when
he knew or ought to have known that the inquirer was relying on him "

(*per* Lord Reid, *ibid.*, p. 486). It is doubtful that this duty extends to the lay vendor making statements to a prospective purchaser (see Lords Morris and Hodson, *ibid.*, pp. 502 and 514 ; also Denning, L.J., dissenting, in *Candler* v. *Crane, Christmas & Co.* [1951] 2 K.B. 164) ; that it would not so extend appears clearly indicated by the Privy Council decision in *Mutual Life and Citizens' Assurance Co., Ltd.* v. *Evatt* [1971] A.C. 793. Nonetheless, the duty might be held to attach to a vendor's solicitor making such statements (e.g., replying to preliminary inquiries) so that the safest course to adopt in practice appears to be to make any statements " without responsibility " (as in *Hedley Byrne & Co.* v. *Heller & Partners, ante* ; see a note as to insurance in the *Law Society's Gazette*, vol. 60, p. 740).

B. UNDER THE MISREPRESENTATION ACT, 1967

The Misrepresentation Act, 1967, introduced certain considerable extensions of the law as stated in the preceding paragraphs. The Act came into operation on 22nd April, 1967 (s. 6 (2)), and does not apply in relation to any misrepresentation or contract of sale which is made before that date (s. 5).

First, it is provided that a contract may be rescinded for innocent misrepresentation notwithstanding (*a*) that the misrepresentation has become a term of the contract (i.e., a misdescription) or (*b*) that the contract has been performed (s. 1). Thus a purchaser of land will no longer lose his right to rescind merely because the contract has been completed by execution of a conveyance or lease of the land (compare para. (iv) on p. 90, *ante*). It is assumed that the possibility of such rescission will not be a matter of concern to any other person acquiring an interest in the land in good faith and for value without notice of the right to rescind. Indeed, s. 1 of the 1967 Act only enables a purchaser to rescind after completion for innocent misrepresentation " if otherwise he would be entitled to rescind," so that in the ordinary case of a mortgage also being completed it would appear that rescission may still not be available (compare para. (i) on p. 89, *ante*).

Secondly, the court (or arbitrator) is given a discretion, in any proceedings where it is claimed that a contract ought to be or has been rescinded for innocent misrepresentation to declare the contract subsisting and award damages in lieu of rescission (s. 2 (2)). The court (or arbitrator) must be of opinion that it is equitable to award damages in lieu of rescission, having regard to the nature of the misrepresentation and the loss that would be caused by it if the contract were upheld, as well as to the loss that rescission would cause to the other party (s. 2 (2)). It is quite impossible to predict the circumstances in which or the frequency with which this discretionary power will be exercised, but it may be suggested that it should prove equitable in most cases to award damages in lieu of rescission where a contract for the sale or other disposition of land has been completed.

Thirdly, the 1967 Act makes damages recoverable notwithstanding that the misrepresentation was not fraudulent unless the person making the misrepresentation proves that he had reasonable grounds to believe and did believe up to the time the contract was made that the facts represented were true (s. 2 (1)) ; damages were awarded by the Court of Appeal under this subsection in *Gosling* v. *Anderson* (1972), *The Times*, 16th February). In effect, this provision imposes on the lay vendor the duty of care laid down in the *Hedley Byrne* case, mentioned on p. 90, *ante*. However, the statutory liability differs from that in the tort of negligence in that (*a*) it is not dependent on any special relationship between the parties, (*b*) it only applies where a contract has been entered into after a misrepresentation made by another party to the contract, and (c) it cannot be avoided by attaching any such statement as "without responsibility" (see below). Since the burden of proof will be upon him, a vendor of land should be extremely careful in making statements to prospective purchasers. However, the Act contains no definition of misrepresentation itself, so that this must be decided by reference to the pre-Act law. In particular attention is drawn to p. 10, *ante*, as to replies to preliminary enquiries.

It is worth noticing that the provisions of the Act so far mentioned all apply "where a person has entered into a contract *after* a misrepresentation has been made to him" (ss. 1, 2 (1), (2)). It is presumed that the common-law element of inducement (see p. 89, *ante*) is to be found implicit in the context although not made explicit. If so, the Act would appear to be of no assistance to the cautious purchaser who has not relied on his vendor but obtained instead his own survey report.

Finally, it is enacted that any provision in any agreement excluding liability or remedies for misrepresentation shall be of no effect "except to the extent (if any) that in any proceedings arising out of the contract, the court or arbitrator may allow reliance on it as being fair and reasonable in the circumstances of the case" (s. 3). Thus exclusion clauses are not absolutely prohibited and it is, at least, arguable that one contained in a contract for the sale of land the terms of which have been approved by the solicitors of both parties should not be disallowed. This prohibition of exclusion clauses expressly applies whether the agreement containing it was made before or after 22nd April, 1967 (ss. 3, 6 (2)). Presumably this prevails over the later unqualified provision that "nothing in this Act shall apply in relation to any misrepresentation or contract of sale which is made before [22nd April, 1967]" (s. 5).

Although in their previous editions no attempt was made to deal with mis-statements prior to the contract, both the 1973 Revision of The Law Society's Conditions of Sale (Condition 13 (2)) and the 18th edition of the National Conditions of Sale (Condition 17) do purport to exclude some at least of the purchaser's remedies for, in effect, misrepresentations. Their success must depend upon the exception in s. 3 of the 1967 Act mentioned in the previous paragraph.

Reference may further be made to the full consideration of the implications of the 1967 Act to the conveyancer by Mr. J. E. Adams in the *Law Society's Gazette*, vol. 67, pp. 183, 256 and 318.

False trade descriptions.—It is "an offence for any person in the course of any trade or business . . . recklessly to make a statement which is false as to . . . the provision in the course of any trade or business of any services . . ." (s. 14 (1) of the Trade Descriptions Act, 1968). In *Breed* v. *Cluett* [1970] 2 Q.B. 459 it was decided that such a "statement" is not confined to statements inducing a contract but could apply to ones subsequently made (distinquished on this point in *Hall* v. *Wickens Motors, Ltd.* [1972] 1 W.L.R. 1418). In *Breed* v. *Cluett*, *ante*, the false statement was that a bungalow was covered by the House Builders Registration Council ten-year guarantee. The court decided that evidence should have been given whether in fact that guarantee included "provision of services" but in the circumstances there was no such evidence. However, it appears clear that the obligations do include provision of services. There was no decision that the section refers to sale of land (as the point that it may not was not taken before the justices) but it is thought that contracts for sale of land have no exemption. If these conclusions are correct vendors who sell in course of trade must take particular care both before and after the contract. However, it has been decided that s. 14 (1) of the 1968 Act does not apply to a statement which amounts to a promise as to what a person will do in the future but only to a false statement as to what he has done (*Beckett* v. *Cohen* [1973] 1 All E.R. 120). In that case, a builder agreed to build a garage for a customer and during the course of negotiations undertook to complete the work within ten days, which he failed to do ; it was held that this could not be a false statement but was really a breach of warranty which Parliament never contemplated being turned into a criminal offence. It was also indicated that the question of whether the work of a builder in such circumstances amounted to the provision of services may be open to fuller argument and a decision in another case. As to the award of compensation, i.e., not merely penalties, in respect of an offence, see ss. 1–5 of the Criminal Justice Act, 1972.

PART 2. MISDESCRIPTION

Meaning.—Misdescription means that the vendor is unable to convey to the purchaser property corresponding exactly with that described in the contract for sale. It follows that a misdescription necessarily involves the committal of a breach of contract by the vendor. This indicates the essential distinction between a misdescription and misrepresentation : a misdescription only occurs in the contract itself giving rise to common-law remedies, whilst a misrepresentation occurs before and induces the contract, giving rise normally only to equitable remedies. Of course, this distinction is often not so clear in practice because a misrepresentation as to the property may be repeated in the contract. If so, apart from statute, the purchaser was, as a rule, restricted to his remedies for the misdescription into which the misrepresentation has merged (*per* Branson, J., in *Pennsylvania Shipping Co.* v. *Cie. Nat. de Navigation* [1936] 2 All E.R. 1167, at p. 1171 ; also *Leaf* v. *International Galleries* [1950] 2 K.B. 86). However, the Misrepresentation Act, 1967, s. 1, provides that a contract may be rescinded for innocent misrepresentation notwithstanding that the misrepresentation has become a term of the contract. It would appear to follow that in such a case the purchaser has available the two courses of pursuing both the misrepresentation and the misdescription.

Some illustrations of the many possible sorts of misdescription may be given. There may be a physical inaccuracy, such as an over-statement of the area of the land (*Watson* v. *Burton* [1957] 1 W.L.R. 19), or a legal inaccuracy such as describing leasehold land as freehold or land held by underlease as leasehold, or *vice versa* (*Russ and Brown's Contract* [1934] Ch. 34 ; *Re Thompson and Cottrell's Contract* [1943] Ch. 97 ; but compare *Becker* v. *Partridge* [1966] 2 Q.B. 155, where it was doubted whether calling a sub-underlease an underlease would amount to a misdescription). Again, four freehold houses were held to be misdescribed as " freehold decontrolled tenancies " where two rooms in one of the houses were still subject to the Rent Acts (*Ridley* v. *Oster* [1939] 1 All E.R. 618). Further, to amount to a misdescription, the description need not be positively inaccurate but may simply be misleading. Thus a description of land as " registered " *simpliciter* will not suffice where the vendor has only a possessory title (*Re Brine and Davies' Contract* [1935] Ch. 388). Again, in a more recent case, land was sold subject to and with the benefit of a protected tenancy, and although the particulars of sale stated the rent payable correctly as at the date of the contract, mention was neglected of a prospective abatement of the rent in consequence of a certificate of disrepair (*Re Englefield Holdings, Ltd. and Sinclair's Contract* [1962] 1 W.L.R. 1119).

However, for there to be a misdescription there must be a statement which purports to be of fact (compare Mistake and Misrepresentation, *ante*, pp. 78, 87). A mistaken opinion, even though written into the particulars of sale, will not give rise to a misdescription. Thus the following adjectival expressions used in the particulars, namely, " valuable and extensive," " in a first-class position," and even " suitable for development," have been dismissed by Wynn Parry, J., " with no disrespect as typical auctioneers' ' puff ' "not to be regarded as part of the contract (in *Watson* v. *Burton, ante*, at pp. 21 and 24). Again a statement that a house was " well built " (*Kennard* v. *Ashman* (1894), 10 T.L.R. 213) or was " substantial " (*Johnson* v. *Smart* (1860), 2 Giff. 151), would be considered in the nature of a commendatory statement and would not amount to a misdescription.

Equally, it is thought that a description as " building land " would probably be held by the courts to refer only to the quality of the land itself and not to amount to a statement that planning permission for building of any particular class has been obtained. Nevertheless, until the matter has come before the courts it would be wise (unless the conditions of sale deal expressly with planning matters) to avoid such descriptions in case the absence of planning permission might make them misdescriptions. The case of *Charles Hunt, Ltd.* v. *Palmer* [1931] 2 Ch. 287, mentioned at p. 107, might be cited by analogy, but, as it refers to restrictive covenants which cannot be known by the purchaser to exist unless they are disclosed, the analogy is far from complete. See also the discussion in the *Solicitors' Journal*, vol. 92, at p. 479.

Such words as " more or less," " or thereabouts," etc., will be held to apply only to small mistakes (*Whittemore* v. *Whittemore* (1869), L.R. 8 Eq. 602 ; *Re Terry and White's Contract* (1886), 32 Ch. D. 14) ; particularly if the quantity be given, not merely, for instance, in acres, but in acres, roods and perches, as the particularity of the statement would convey the notion of actual admeasurement (*Hill* v. *Buckley* (1811), 17 Ves. 394). But where the particulars of sale stated that the property was let at £30 per year, and it was afterwards found that the rates and taxes were payable by the landlord, the purchaser was allowed compensation (*Bos* v. *Helsham* (1866), L.R. 2 Ex. 72 ; see also *Barnes* v. *Wood* (1860), L.R. 8 Eq. 424).

A " clear yearly rent " means a rent clear of all outgoings, etc., usually borne by the tenant, but subject to such—e.g., land tax—as are borne by the landlord (*Earl of Tyrconnell* v. *Duke of Ancaster* (1754), 2 Ves. Sen. 499 ; *Re Edwards and Daniel Sykes & Co.* (1890), 62 L.T. 445). " Annual rental " means gross annual rental (*ibid.*).

Contracts for the sale of registered land often describe the property sold as " the land comprised in " a specified title number. A purchaser's solicitor should ensure that the title in question in fact comprises the land his client intended to buy since without a more particular description in the contract there can be no misdescription.

Effect of misdescription.—Under an open contract, the rules as to the effect of a misdescription appear to be as follows :—

(1) If the misdescription is substantial the vendor will be unable to enforce the contract, even with an abatement of the price (*Flight* v. *Booth* (1834), 1 Bing. (N.C.) 370 ; see also *Re Weston and Thomas's Contract* [1907] 1 Ch. 244

—purchaser not compelled to accept personal indemnity from vendor). A misdescription will be substantial if it is as to a point " . . . so far affecting the subject matter of the contract that it may be reasonably supposed that, but for such misdescription, the purchaser might never have entered into the contract at all " (*per* Tindal, C.J., in *Flight* v. *Booth, ante,* at p. 377). This is not simply a question of value ; Eve, J., has said : " A vendor could not fulfil a contract to sell Whiteacre by conveying Blackacre, although he might prove to demonstration that the value of the latter was largely in excess of the value of the former. Value, no doubt, is an element to be taken into account in determining whether an error in description is substantial or material, but it is certainly not the only element, nor, in my opinion, the dominant one " (*Lee* v. *Rayson* [1917] 1 Ch. 613, at p. 618). It seems clear that the question whether a misdescription is substantial or not is one of fact for the court to decide in the circumstances of each particular case (*Watson* v. *Burton* [1957] 1 W.L.R. 19). Thus although in this case a 40 per cent. overstatement of the area sold was held to be a substantial misdescription, a different decision as to a similar overstatement had been reached in an earlier case where the purchaser had apparently wanted what he saw without relying on the stated area for the price that he would pay (*Re Fawcett & Holmes' Contract* (1889), 42 Ch. D. 150). Again, the facts of *Dyer* v. *Hargrave* (1805), 10 Ves. 505, are typical of many cases which arise in practice. On the sale of a farm by auction, the particulars described the house as being in good repair, the farm as being in a high state of cultivation, and all within a ring fence ; none of these descriptions was true but the vendor was nonetheless held able to enforce the contract subject to compensation, the Master of the Rolls saying, in effect, that not every variation from the contract description would enable a purchaser to resist specific performance and particularly not where he had seen the property, had an idea of its condition and lost nothing but money by the misdescription. In *McQueen* v. *Farquhar* (1805), 8 R.R. 212, on the sale of a large estate, a purchaser was compelled to complete where the deficiency in description was six acres ; and similarly in *Leslie* v. *Thompson* (1851), 20 L.J. Ch. 561, where the deficiency was ten acres. In all these cases, in other words, the misdescription was held not to be substantial.

(2) If the misdescription is *not* substantial, then, provided that the misdescription was made innocently, the vendor will be able to enforce the contract, although subject to an abatement of the price by way of compensation for the insubstantial deficiency (*Jacobs* v. *Revell* [1900] 2 Ch. 858). This is so even though the purchaser would prefer to rescind (*Re Brewer and Hankin's Contract* (1899), 80 L.T. 127).

(3) The purchaser's position is stronger than the vendor's. Whether the misdescription is substantial or not, the purchaser " may elect to take all he can get, and to have a proportionate abatement from the purchase-money " (Viscount Haldane in *Rutherford* v. *Acton-Adams* [1915] A.C. 866, at p. 870). In other words, the vendor may be compelled to convey whatever he can and to suffer compensation, even though the purchaser will not thereby get the property as described in the contract.

However, Viscount Haldane's proposition will not apply where the misdescription is as to a defect in title preventing the vendor from conveying without committing a breach of contract with a third party (*Lipman's Wallpaper, Ltd.* v. *Mason & Hodghton, Ltd.* [1969] 1 Ch. 20). Nor can the proposition ever be applied where the vendor has and effectively exercises a right of rescission of the contract (*ibid.*).

Further, the purchaser will be taken to have waived any compensation by way of an abatement of the price (see (2) and (3) above), if he fails to make a claim before completion (*Joliffe* v. *Baker* (1883), 11 Q.B.D. 255), unless the misdescription was not discoverable before completion (*Clayton* v. *Leech* (1889), 41 Ch. D. 103 ; and see further *post*, p. 203). Nonetheless, after completion, and assuming the misdescription to be embodied in the conveyance, the purchaser would probably be able to sue the vendor on his implied covenants for title (*Re Wallis and Barnard's Contract* [1899] 2 Ch. 515). Also the purchaser will not be entitled to compensation either if it is not open to fair assessment (*Rudd* v. *Lascelles* [1900] 1 Ch. 815—restrictive covenants ; as to the mode of assessment, see *Re Chifferiel* (1880), 40 Ch. D. 54, and *Aspinalls to Powell and Scholefield* (1889), 60 L.T. 595) or if he was aware of the misdescription at the date of the contract (*Castle* v. *Wilkinson* (1870), L.R. 5 Ch. 534).

(4) If the misdescription is *against* the vendor, i.e., more property is described in the contract than intended, the vendor cannot claim an increase in price by way of compensation (*Re Lindsay and Forder's Contract* (1895), 72 L.T. 832). However, if such a misdescription were substantial, the court might refuse specific performance in respect of the whole on the ground of hardship (*Manser* v. *Back* (1848), 6 Hare 443, where an auctioneer forgot to sell subject to the reservation of a right of way ; see also Jessel, M.R.'s, judgment in *Cato* v. *Thompson* (1882), 9 Q.B.D. 616). Nonetheless, in a case of hardship, the purchaser would still be able to obtain specific performance in respect of what the vendor intended to sell, but only if he does not also claim compensation in respect of the rest (*Alvanley* v. *Kinnaird* (1849), 2 Mac. & G. 1). Alternatively, instead of seeking specific performance at all, the purchaser would be entitled to recover substantial damages for loss of bargain (see *Lloyd* v. *Stanbury* [1971] 1 W.L.R. 535).

Conditions of sale as to misdescription.—The Statutory Conditions of Sale (*ante*, p. 67) implied in contracts by correspondence unless an intention to the contrary is shown, do not contain any condition as to misdescription. Condition 7 (1) provides, however, that if the purchaser shall take or make any objection or requisition which the vendor *is unable* to remove or comply with, and the purchaser shall not withdraw such objection or requisition within ten days after being required in writing so to do, the vendor may rescind the contract. In commenting on this condition, J. M. Lightwood in Williams on Vendor and Purchaser, 4th ed., vol. II, at p. 1234, expressed the view that the condition might be exercised in a case where the vendor had by an innocent error sold more, in quantity, estate or title, than he had the right to convey, but that it could not be exercised in a case where the vendor had knowingly or recklessly sold more than he was entitled to convey ; see further *post*, p. 221.

Otherwise, conditions of sale directed to the consequences of a misdescription are most commonly found to be to the following effect (cf. generally Condition 13 (2) of The Law Society's Conditions of Sale, 1973 Revision, and Condition 17 (1) of the National Conditions of Sale, 18th ed.) :—

First, *that no misdescription shall annul the sale.* The purport of this condition is that the vendor should be able to enforce the contract despite rule (1) above. However, the condition will *not* have this effect : the purchaser will still be able to avoid the contract, recovering his deposit and costs, where the misdescription is substantial (*Flight* v. *Booth, ante* ; *Jacobs* v. *Revell, ante* ; also *Re Courcier and Harrold's Contract* [1923] 1 Ch. 565 ; and *Watson* v. *Burton, ante*).

Secondly, *that the purchaser or the vendor, as appropriate, shall be entitled to compensation, to be settled by an arbitrator, for any misdescription pointed out before completion.* It follows from what has been said above that this condition will be applicable where the misdescription is not substantial or where the purchaser chooses not to avoid the contract, and not otherwise. The only significant alteration of the general law seems to be that the condition provides for compensation for the vendor where the misdescription is against him (compare rule (4) above).

Had the condition simply provided for compensation without any restriction to misdescription pointed out before completion, a claim could be made under it for misdescriptions discovered even after completion (*Palmer* v. *Johnson* (1884), 13 Q.B.D. 351 ; compare the position under rule (3) above where there is no express provision for compensation).

Thirdly, *that the purchaser shall not be entitled to compensation for any misdescription.* If the misdescription is substantial, the vendor will still be unable to enforce the contract against the purchaser (*Jacobs* v. *Revell, ante,* and *Lee* v. *Rayson, ante*), and this is so even though the vendor is willing to waive the exclusion of compensation (*Watson* v. *Burton, ante*). Therefore, the application of this condition is limited to preventing the purchaser from obtaining compensation if *he* asks for specific performance (*Re Terry and White's Contract* (1886), 32 Ch. D. 14) or from recovering damages for breach of contract (see *Curtis* v. *French* [1929] 1 Ch. 253).

PART 3.   NON-DISCLOSURE

Introductory.—The general rule of contract is that a vendor is under no duty to disclose material facts to a prospective purchaser (*Bell* v. *Lever Bros.* [1932] A.C. 161), and this applies to contracts for the sale of land (*Terrene Ltd.* v. *Nelson* [1937] 3 All E.R. 739, at p. 744). Thus in *Greenhalgh* v. *Brindley* [1901] 2 Ch. 324, a vendor sold a house with windows overlooking a stranger's land. The vendor did not disclose that he enjoyed access of light only by the stranger's licence. When the purchaser ascertained the facts he refused to complete. The vendor brought an action for specific performance and obtained his decree. However, there is a term implied into a contract for the sale of land that a good title should be shown by the vendor (*Re Ossemsley Estate, Ltd.* [1937] 3 All E.R. 774, at p. 778), i.e., that he is selling the fee simple free from incumbrances (*Hughes* v. *Parker* (1841), 8 M. & W. 244). The implication of such a term does not arise if the purchaser has knowledge, actual or constructive, at the time of the contract of any irremediable defect in the vendor's title (*per* Romer, L.J., in *Timmins* v. *Moreland Street Property Co. Ltd.* [1958] Ch. 110, at p. 132). Consequently it may be said that a prospective vendor of land has a duty of disclosure to the extent necessary to prevent the implied term arising. In other words, a vendor should disclose to prospective purchasers any defects in his title which are latent and not patent.

Distinction between patent and latent defects.—A *patent* defect is a defect which a purchaser might himself have discovered by a reasonable inspection of the property, provided he *could* have inspected the property if he had wished to do so ; for instance, the ruinous condition of the buildings

4

(*Cook* v. *Waugh* (1860), 2 Giff. 201), or an obvious right of way (*Yandle & Sons* v. *Sutton* [1922] 2 Ch. 199), or a public footpath (*Bowles* v. *Round* (1800), 5 Ves. 508). A *latent* defect may be said to be a defect which a purchaser could not have discovered by the exercise of reasonable care by the inspection of the property.

For instance, a right of way (*Ashburner* v. *Sewell* [1891] 3 Ch. 405), or a public footpath not obviously apparent (*Yandle* v. *Sutton, ante*), may, under the circumstances, be latent defects which it would be the duty of the vendor to disclose.

Duty of disclosure of defects in quality.— A vendor is only bound to disclose a *latent defect* in the quality of the land sold if the defect is of such a nature as materially to interfere with the enjoyment of the property as promised by the contract or promised in any statement previously made to induce the purchaser to enter into the contract, or to interfere with user of the land for any purpose for which, to the knowledge of the vendor, it was purchased (*Shepherd* v. *Croft* [1911] 1 Ch. 521 ; see p. 99).

Subject to the above duty, the vendor is under no obligation to disclose to a purchaser any defects, *latent or patent* (even though known to him), in the quality of the land sold, except that some of the decisions can be explained on the ground that a defect in physical quality also involves a defect in title (*Re Brewer and Hankin's Contract* (1899), 80 L.T. 127, public sewer ; *Re Belcham and Gawley's Contract* [1930] 1 Ch. 56, sewers vested in local authority). Further, a vendor is not bound to disabuse the purchaser of any erroneous belief which the purchaser has formed, and which the vendor knows he has formed, as to the quality of the property purchased. The result is that, provided the vendor has not been guilty of any acts of deception, such as concealing or covering up a defect or diverting the purchaser from inspection and inquiry, and subject to the equitable jurisdiction of the court in Mistake (as to which, see p. 83), he " may well sell a house which has got dry rot in all the woodwork, and is badly drained, to a purchaser, who knows nothing of these defects, but believes to the knowledge of the vendor that the house is in good repair and well drained, and yet the purchaser will not be entitled to claim the rescission of the contract "—or compensation, or any other legal or equitable relief (see Williams on Vendor and Purchaser, 4th ed., vol. II, pp. 758–761, 764–766).

As to the obligations upon a builder-vendor by virtue of implied warranty, tort or statutory duty, see p. 71, *ante*.

It is important to bear in mind that if certain of the standard forms of conditions of sale are used it may be essential for a vendor to disclose also certain matters not strictly concerned with his title, otherwise the purchaser may be able to rescind the contract ; see *ante*, p. 80 *et seq.*

Effect of non-disclosure.—The position of the parties where a latent defect of title which should have been disclosed by the vendor is discovered after the contract is very similar to the position where a misdescription is discovered (see *ante*, p. 94). Indeed, some of the illustrating cases given below apply equally to both. Thus the rules appear to be as follows : (1) If the non-disclosure is of a substantial defect, the vendor will be unable to enforce the contract (*Phillips* v. *Caldcleugh* (1868), L.R. 4 Q.B. 159) ; " substantial " here has the same meaning as with misdescription, i.e., of the purchaser not getting what was intended (see below). (2) If the defect is not substantial the vendor can enforce the contract subject to a reduction in the price by way of compensation (*Re Belcham and Gawley's Contract*

[1930] 1 Ch. 56). (3) The purchaser may, where the defect is substantial, either avoid the contract or obtain specific performance with a reduction in price (*Rudd* v. *Lascelles* [1900] 1 Ch. 815) ; also he may be able to recover damages for breach of the implied term that a good title will be shown (*Baines* v. *Tweddle* [1959] Ch. 679). See also L.P.A. 1925, s. 183, *post*, p. 103.

Some illustrations of these rules may be helpful. In *Re Brewer and Hankin's Contract* (1899), 80 L.T. 127, a purchaser, after entering into a contract for the purchase of a villa with a garden at the back, discovered that there was a public sewer passing under the garden, but at some distance from the house, and there was a manhole used for the purpose of obtaining access to the sewer. *Both the vendor and the purchaser were ignorant* of the existence of the sewer. It was held that the existence of the sewer did not so alter the character of the piece of land that the purchaser had the right to say, " I do not get that which was intended to be sold to me," and that he could not be released from his contract to take the property, but that as there was a condition in the contract that compensation should be paid in case of error, compensation was allowed. The case differed from *Re Puckett and Smith's Contract* (below) in that the property was not sold as building land.

On the other hand, in *Re Puckett and Smith's Contract* [1902] 2 Ch. 258, land was sold as building land, and it was stated in the particulars of sale that the property " has a valuable *prospective building element*." In addition the vendors had informed the intending purchaser that the property was capable of development. After contract, but before completion, he discovered that a culvert ran across the land a short distance from the surface although there was no indication of it on the plan shown to the purchaser, and *the vendors were unaware of its existence*. The purchaser had not noticed anything when he inspected the property before agreeing to buy, and he could not by any reasonable inspection have found out the existence of the defect. It was held that the culvert was such a substantial defect as to alter the nature of the thing which he intended to buy, and so, in the circumstances, the purchaser was not bound to complete.

In *Shepherd* v. *Croft* [1911] 1 Ch. 521, the question was whether the facts brought the case within *Re Puckett and Smith's Contract* or *Re Brewer and Hankin's Contract*. The contract stated that the property had certain building advantages, consisting of extensive road frontages, and that excellent building sites could be formed, but that the property was sold subject to all drainage, sewer and other easements (if any) affecting the same. It was admitted that there was an invisible underground watercourse well known to the vendor, and Parker, J., held that it was a *latent* defect. The purchaser having refused to complete, the vendor commenced an action for specific performance. The judge said that in order to see whether the case was within *Flight* v. *Booth* (1834), 1 Bing. (N.C.) 370 (see at pp. 94–95), he had to ask himself whether, if specific performance were granted, *the purchaser would be getting something substantially different from that which the vendor had contracted to give her*. If this should be so, then, according to the decision in *Flight* v. *Booth*, the purchaser would have the right to rescind the contract, notwithstanding a condition in the contract that if any error or mis-statement be contained in the particulars or conditions the same should not annul the sale. If, on the other hand, the purchaser would be getting, if he were to decree specific performance, substantially what the vendor contracted to give her, the decision in *Flight* v. *Booth* would have no application. For the purpose of answering the question he was bound to consider the terms of the contract itself, and, if the purchaser purchased for any particular purpose *which was known to the vendor* then he had to consider that purpose. The property offered was a residential property with certain specified building advantages, and in the learned judge's opinion, notwithstanding the existence of the underground watercourse, if he were to decree specific performance, the purchaser would get substantially what the vendor contracted to give her. Therefore, it was a case which was not within *Flight* v. *Booth*, but it was analogous to *Re Brewer and Hankin's Contract* rather than *Re Puckett and Smith's Contract*. There may, however, the judge said, be *latent* defects which, though not such as to give in equity the right to rescission, may yet affect the value of the property. In his opinion, the value of the property in the case before him was to some extent affected by the existence of the watercourse, and so he made a decree for specific performance with a reduction of the purchase-money by way of compensation.

See also *Pemsel and Wilson* v. *Tucker* [1907] 2 Ch. 191, and *Simpson* v. *Gilley* (1922), 92 L.J. Ch. 194, considered in *Re Belcham and Gawley's Contract* [1930] 1 Ch. 56. In the latter case the vendors were aware that under the property sold there were two sewers vested in the local authority, but no reference was made to them in the particulars of sale. Maugham, J., held that the existence of the two sewers did not cause the property to be substantially different from that agreed to be sold, and therefore the purchaser was not entitled to rescission, but that he was entitled to compensation payable under a condition in the contract.

Whether the vendor was aware of the defect does not seem to be important. *Shepherd* v. *Croft* was a case in which the vendor was aware of it, but the judgment followed the decision in *Re Brewer and Hankin's Contract*, in which the vendor was ignorant of the defect. In any case a purchaser would have to take the property with all its defects (*Re Puckett and Smith's Contract, ante*), unless the defect made the land useless for the purpose for which the purchaser bought the land, for instance, to build on, and the vendor was aware at the time of his entering into the contract of the purpose for which the purchaser was buying the property. In such a case the purchaser could not be compelled to complete even with compensation, notwithstanding that the contract may have contained the clause that errors should not annul the sale and that no compensation should be allowed (*ibid.*).

Again in *Re Leyland and Taylor* [1900] 2 Ch. 625, it was held that a notice to carry out private street works served by the local authority need not be disclosed to the purchaser, on the ground that an inspection of the property would show that such a notice might at any time be served. It would have been otherwise if the fact not disclosed was one which the purchaser could not be supposed to have reasonably ascertained, for instance, a party-wall notice on which an award had been made (*Carlish* v. *Salt* [1906] 1 Ch. 335). See also *Re Englefield Holdings, Ltd. and Sinclair's Contract* [1962] 1 W.L.R. 1119, where a house was sold subject to a protected tenancy and it was held the vendor was bound to disclose that a certificate of disrepair had been served.

Remedies before completion.—The purchaser must seek his remedies, of avoiding the contract or of compensation by way of a reduction in price, before completion (compare Misrepresentation, *ante*, p. 90). Non-disclosure amounts to the breach of a term of the contract, i.e., that vendor can show a good title, which will on completion merge into the conveyance (see Merger, *post*, p. 203). However, rights of action may be available to the purchaser after completion under the usual implied covenants for title (L.P.A. 1925, s. 76, *post*, p. 466).

Patent defects.—There is no duty on the vendor to disclose any *patent* defect in the quality of freehold land (*Yandle & Sons* v. *Sutton* [1922] 2 Ch. 199). The reason is that a purchaser will be deemed to have constructive notice of all *patent* defects in the condition of the property which he could have discovered by reasonable inspection.

Purchaser's knowledge.—As already mentioned, the vendor need not normally disclose any latent defects of title of which the purchaser knew when he entered into the contract. The reason is that the purchaser's knowledge (actual or constructive : see " Patent defects," above) rebuts the implication that the vendor should show a good title (*Timmins* v. *Moreland Street Property Co., Ltd.* [1958] Ch. 110, at p. 132). However, a distinction must be made between an irremovable defect and a removable defect, since only knowledge of the former rebuts the implication of a good title (*ibid.*). Despite knowledge of a removable defect, e.g., a mortgage, the purchaser can still require the vendor to remove the defect before completion subject to any stipulation to the contrary (*Re Gloag and Miller's Contract* (1883), 23 Ch. D. 320). Note that if the contract includes an *express* term that a good title should be conveyed, then unlike an implied term this cannot be rebutted by the purchaser's knowledge of an irremovable defect (*Cato* v. *Thompson* (1882), 9 Q.B.D. 616, restrictive covenants ; also *Re Gloag and Miller's Contract, ante*).

The practice of sending a full abstract of title with the draft contract, which appears to be on the increase, raises the question whether this could constitute a sufficient disclosure by the vendor of any latent defects in title shown in the abstract. It is possible to argue that the purchaser will have constructive knowledge at least of such defects and that (as with patent defects) this will rebut the implication that the vendor should show a good title. Consequently, it would seem advisable for the purchaser's solicitors, receiving an abstract with the draft contract and not wishing to investigate the title before a contract is concluded, at least to point out before contract that the title has not been investigated and even, if an important defect is seen or suspected, to insist on the inclusion in the contract of an *express* term that a good title should be shown (as to which see above).

As to the effect of a purchaser having notice of the defect in question by virtue of its registration under the L.C.A. 1972 or L.R.A. 1925, see *ante*, p. 4 *et seq.*

As to disclosure of tenancies and licences to which the property is subject, see p. 18, *ante*.

Non-binding interests.—The duty to disclose latent defects in title cannot extend to anything which will not be binding on the purchaser (see *Smith* v. *Colburne* [1914] 2 Ch. 533). Nevertheless it may occasionally be in a vendor's best interests to disclose matters even though the purchaser will not be bound by them. For example, it may be that the vendor himself will remain personally liable and so will wish to make disclosures with a view to securing an indemnity covenant from the purchaser (see Law Society's Conditions of Sale, 1973 Revision, Condition 4 (2) (*d*) ; cp. *Eagon* v. *Dent* [1965] 3 All E.R. 334 concerning an unregistered option to renew a tenancy).

Overriding interests.—Where registered land is sold, the vendor would appear to be under a duty to disclose any " overriding interests " (see L.R.A. 1925, s. 70, and *post*, p. 184) which come within the meaning of latent defects in title, and need not disclose any which amount to patent defects.

Leaseholds held subject to covenant to repair.—The rule that a purchaser is deemed to have notice of all patent defects in the condition of the property does not apply to leasehold property where there is a covenant to repair. Even if the purchaser knows that the property is out of repair, contrary to the lessee's covenants, he can require the property to be put into repair *in the absence of a condition to the contrary (Barnett* v. *Wheeler* (1841), 7 M. & W. 364). As to disclosure of the contents of the lease, see *post*, p. 145.

The distinction mentioned above between a removable defect and an irremovable defect is applicable (*Cato* v. *Thompson* (1882), 9 Q.B.D. 616 ; *Re Wallis and Barnard's Contract* [1899] 2 Ch. 515 ; *Re Allen and Driscoll's Contract* [1904] 2 Ch. 226). Even the taking of possession of leasehold property with knowledge of the non-performance of a covenant to repair or paint the property, which is a removable defect, will not, *in the absence of a condition to the contrary*, prevent the purchaser requiring the vendor to remove such defect or objecting to complete if it is not removed (*Re Gloag and Miller's Contract* (1883), 23 Ch. D. 320 ; *Ellis* v. *Rogers* (1885), 29 Ch. D. 661 ; *Re Judge and Sheridan's Contract* (1907), 96 L.T. 451 ; *Re Martin* (1912), 106 L.T. 381). In *Re Highett and Bird's Contract* [1903] 1 Ch. 287, the leasehold house purchased was so badly out of repair that the vendor had been served with an order under the London Building Acts, requiring him to do repairs. There were cracks in the building of which the purchaser was aware, but it was held that the obligation to make a good title to leaseholds was not removed by the knowledge of the purchaser that the title was bad by reason of a breach of the covenant, and that the vendor must pay for the repairs. See also *Re Allen and Driscoll's Contract* [1904] 2 Ch. 226, at p. 230 ; and *Re Taunton and West of England P. B. Building Society and Roberts' Contract* [1912] 3 Ch. 381, a case where a covenant to paint had not been complied with.

The principle of *Re Highett and Bird's Contract* was not applied, however, in the case of *Lockhart's, Ltd.* v. *Bernard Rosen & Co.* [1922] 1 Ch. 433. In that case the purchasers agreed to purchase leasehold premises, known by them to be in a bad state, at a low price, subject to the consent of the superior landlord and to the *premises being taken in their existing condition.* The lessor required, as a condition of giving consent, that the property should be put into repair, which the purchasers refused to do. The vendors executed the repairs and they were held, from the date of the contract, to be trustees for the purchasers of the premises in their then state of disrepair and were granted specific performance on the footing that the purchasers indemnified them against the money spent on the property. Further it has been held by the High Court of Eire in *Re Flynn and Newman's Contract* [1948] Ir. R. 104 that disrepair which was a breach of covenant, but which, in the absence of a proviso for re-entry, could not be a ground of forfeiture, was not a defect of title, but of subject-matter only. Consequently, it was decided that if the terms of the lease were known to the purchaser before he entered into the contract and he had the opportunity of inspecting the property there was no breach of the vendor's obligations of disclosure and the purchaser could not compel him to carry out the repairs.

Conditions of sale of leaseholds affected by repairing covenants are discussed *ante*, p. 64 ; in practice it is usual to provide that the purchaser will take the property as it stands.

Land Tax.—Land tax was not an incumbrance and did not need to be referred to in the contract. Land tax has now been abolished with effect from 25th March, 1963 (F.A. 1963, s. 68). This does not affect any compulsory redemption of tax under the F.A. 1949, where this became due before 25th March, 1963, but no redemption payment will become due where land changes hands on or after that date. As respects outstanding land tax, all official functions are transferred to the general commissioners of income tax and to the collectors of taxes (*ibid.*).

Tithe redemption annuity.—Under the Tithe Act, 1936, tithe rent-charge was extinguished on 2nd October, 1936, and its place was taken by tithe redemption annuities charged on the land and payable to the Crown for sixty years. It is provided by s. 13 (8) of the Act that an annuity is deemed to be an incumbrance for the purposes of the L.P.A. 1925, s. 183, but by s. 13 (10) of the Act that an annuity is not, for the purposes of the L.C.A., deemed to be a registrable land charge. Although s. 183 of the L.P.A. 1925 deals only with fraudulent concealment of incumbrances, the better opinion appears to be that s. 13 (8) means that a vendor must disclose any tithe redemption annuity to which the land is subject (see J. M. Lightwood in the *Law Journal*, vol. 82, p. 437 ; compare *Law Notes*, vol. 62, p. 48).

The functions of the Tithe Redemption Commission were transferred to the Board of Inland Revenue with effect from 1st April, 1960 (Tithe Redemption Commission (Transfer of Functions and Dissolution) Order, 1959).

The records of the Tithe Redemption Office are open to personal inspection free of charge ; certain postal applications are dealt with subject to charge. The reference number, with the county and tithe district should be stated if possible ; a plan showing the boundaries is essential for identification *in all cases ;* a postal address is inadequate. See *Law Society's Gazette*, vol. 60, p. 391, and the pamphlet " Conditions concerning the Inspection of Tithe Documents and the Supply of Copies and Extracts Therefrom " obtainable free of charge from the Tithe Redemption Office, Inland Revenue (H), East Block, Barrington Road, Worthing, Sussex. See also *Solicitors' Journal*, vol. 110, p. 795.

It is understood that if information is requested by post about tithe redemption annuity only, quoting the name of the present owner, no fee is charged. If other information is requested, normally as to corn rents and corn rent annuities, a fixed fee of two pounds is charged. The matter is discussed in the *Solicitors' Journal*, vol. 108, p. 366, where it is pointed out that corn rent annuities are believed to be restricted to certain areas, but there is no published list of these areas.

Schemes for the apportionment and redemption of corn and similar rents may be made by the Commissioners of Inland Revenue pursuant to the Corn Rents Act, 1963 ; see also Tithe Act, 1936, s. 30 (2), as amended by *ibid.*, s. 2 regarding extinguishment.

See, further, as to redemption after completion, *post*, p. 636.

Fraudulent concealment and falsification.—Such frauds are, fortunately, rare, but a note must be made of the L.P.A. 1925, s. 183 (1), which provides :—

" 183.—(1) Any person disposing of property or any interest therein for money or moneys' worth to a purchaser, or the solicitor or other agent of such person, who—

    (a) conceals from the purchaser any instrument or incumbrance material to the title ; or (*b*) falsifies any pedigree upon which the title may depend in order to induce the purchaser to accept the title offered or produced ;

with intent in any of such cases to defraud, is guilty of a misdemeanour punishable by fine, or by imprisonment for a term not exceeding two years, or by both.''

Where title is made to a legal estate there is no need to disclose instruments relating to incumbrances which will be overreached (L.P.A. 1925, s. 10 (1) ; see *post*, p. 130). It is submitted that a solicitor would be liable even where an incumbrance was prior to the root of title *if intent to defraud were established* (cf. *Smith* v. *Robinson* (1879), 13 Ch. D. 148.). No prosecution may be commenced without the leave of the Attorney General (L.P.A. 1925, s. 183 (4)).

Any such person, solicitor or agent is liable to an action for damages by the purchaser or persons deriving title under him for loss sustained by reason of such concealment or of any claim by a person under such pedigree whose right was concealed (*ibid.*, s. 183 (2) and (3)), provided such person, solicitor or agent had the intent to defraud mentioned in s. 183 (1) (*District Bank, Ltd.* v. *Luigi Grill, Ltd.* [1943] Ch. 78).

CHAPTER FIVE

DEDUCTION AND
INVESTIGATION OF TITLE

PART 1. TITLE TO BE DEDUCED

Duty of vendor.—The principal term of a contract for the sale of land is that the vendor should show a good title (*per* Jessel, M.R., in *Lysaght* v. *Edwards* (1876), 2 Ch. 499, at p. 507). The *prima facie* implication is that the vendor is entitled to and is selling the land in fee simple absolute in possession free from incumbrances (*Hughes* v. *Parker* (1841), 8 M. & W. 244 ; *Re Ossemsley* [1937] 3 All E.R. 774, at p. 778 ; *Timmins* v. *Moreland Street*

4A

Properties, Ltd. [1958] Ch. 110). A like implication appears to arise where the sale is of *registered* land, namely, that the vendor is registered as the proprietor of the freehold estate with an absolute title which he is selling free from any incumbrances or other entries on the register and from overriding interests (*Re Brine and Davies' Contract* [1935] Ch. 388 ; *Re Stone and Saville's Contract* [1963] 1 W.L.R. 163).

Nonetheless, any such implications may be rebutted by the purchaser's pre-contract knowledge to the contrary, and the vendor's resulting duty to disclose certain defects in his title has been considered under Non-Disclosure, *ante*, p. 97.

Further, a vendor may wish to insert a condition in the contract dealing with any defect in his title, designed to " safeguard himself against any undue trouble to which he might be put by inquiries about facts which took place some time ago " (Simonds, J., in *Re Holmes* [1944] Ch. 53, at p. 57). If so, the rule is that the condition must not mislead the purchaser in any way (*Re Banister* (1879), 12 Ch. D. 131). " The vendor's title is a matter which is exclusively within his own knowledge and he is bound to state it fairly ; and his suppression of a fact material to the title may, according to the degree in which it affects the title, be a ground for rescinding the contract or for resisting its specific performance " (Williams on Vendor and Purchaser, 4th ed., vol. II, p. 763). The vendor will only be able to rely on the condition if he has made a sufficiently full disclosure to enable the purchaser to consider and determine whether it is worth his while to accept the particular defective title by entering into the contract (*Re Haedicke and Lipski's Contract* [1901] 2 Ch. 606). " There is no doubt that by a clearly drawn special condition which is put in the contract by a vendor who acts in good faith, and which discloses a possible defect in the title, the purchaser may be compelled to accept the title offered by the vendor ; but the vendor must have disclosed the defects of which he knew " (*per* Danckwerts, L.J., giving the judgment of the Court of Appeal in *Becker* v. *Partridge* [1966] 2 Q.B. 155, at pp. 171–172).

Examples are numerous. In *Phillips* v. *Caldcleugh* (1868), L.R. 4 Q.B. 159, the contract contained a condition that the title should commence with a certain deed, and that the purchaser should not investigate or take any objection in respect of the title before the date of that deed. The purchaser ascertained that the property was subject to certain restrictive covenants created by a deed earlier in date than the root of title, and it was held that the purchaser was entitled to have an unencumbered freehold title, and that the condition did not protect the vendors. The purchaser was therefore entitled to rescind the contract and recover the deposit. In *Upperton* v. *Nickolson* (1871), L.R. 6 Ch. 436, where land was described in the contract as freehold, but in fact it was enfranchised copyhold, the minerals having been reserved to the lord of the manor, it was decided that there was a fatal objection to the title.

A condition that the property is sold subject to any general incumbrances or defects in title which may exist will not be sufficient to enable the vendor to enforce the contract where there are in fact incumbrances or defects known to him but not disclosed to the purchaser (*Nottingham Patent Brick and Tile Co.* v. *Butler* (1886), 16 Q.B.D. 778 ; restrictive covenants). Further, such a condition will apparently not be sufficient where there are incumbrances or defects of which the vendor ought reasonably to have known (*Heywood* v. *Mallalieu* (1883), 25 Ch. D. 357, where the vendor's solicitor would have discovered the existence of an easement if he had made fuller inquiries into certain claims). Thus in *Becker* v. *Partridge* [1966] 2 Q.B. 155, a contract for the sale of an underlease provided that the vendor's title "has been accepted . . . and the purchaser shall raise no requisition or objection thereon"; the purchaser discovered that there were breaches of covenants in the superior lease giving grounds for forfeiture ; the vendor had no actual knowledge of these breaches but had constructive notice because his solicitor, although entitled to, had neglected to inspect the superior lease on the grant of the underlease ; accordingly, notwithstanding the contractual provision, the purchaser was entitled to rescission.

The inclusion of a term in the contract that any error or omission in the particulars shall not annul the sale nor entitle the purchaser to compensation does not affect these rules. Such a term does not compel the purchaser to accept a defect in title such as that caused by the existence of restrictive covenants (*Phillips* v. *Caldcleugh, ante ; Nottingham Patent Brick and Tile Co.* v. *Butler, ante*).

In *Re Courcier and Harrold's Contract* [1923] 1 Ch. 565, the contract contained a condition that the property should not be used (*inter alia*) as a school, hospital, nursing home or public workshop, and also a condition that if any error, misstatement or omission should be discovered in the particulars, the same should not annul the sale, nor should any compensation be allowed by the vendor in respect thereof. It turned out that the restrictions on the user of the property were incorrectly set out, as the words " or public institution or charity nor for holding public meetings nor for public worship " ought to have been inserted instead of the words " public workshop." It was held, however, that the purchaser had sufficient notice of the restrictions, and that, in any case, the omission was an error, " misstatement or omission " within the condition set out above. Apparently, such a condition may apply to an error in the particulars " with regard to a matter of right as well as of physical content " provided it does not make the property produced entirely different from that sold (Williams on Vendor and Purchaser, 4th ed., vol. I, pp. 729, 730).

Effect of express representation as to title.—An express representation by a vendor in regard to his title to the land relieves the purchaser from an investigation of the facts of the case, as he is entitled to rely on such statement, and it is no defence to say that he (the purchaser) had the means of discovery, and might with reasonable care have discovered that the statement was untrue (*Redgrave* v. *Hurd* (1881), 20 Ch. D. 1). For instance, if a vendor states that the lease contains no covenant not to carry on certain trades, even though the lease be produced at the sale or the purchaser otherwise be given an opportunity of inspecting it, the purchaser is entitled to rely on the statement (*ibid.*).

Thus, in *Hunt (Charles), Ltd.* v. *Palmer* [1931] 2 Ch. 287, the particulars of sale of two leasehold shops described them as " valuable business premises." In fact, the lease contained a covenant restricting the lessee from carrying on any other trade or business than that of a ladies' outfitter, fancy draper, or the manufacture of ladies' clothing. The purchaser wanted the premises to use as a dairy. The conditions contained a condition as to the lease being open for inspection before the sale and that the purchaser should be deemed to have notice of the covenants in it. It was held by Clauson, J., that as the vendors had described the premises as valuable business premises, the purchaser was induced by that description to buy them and he was entitled to require that the premises should fairly answer that description.

The fact that the purchaser must be deemed to have had notice of the covenant was not relevant. The action for specific performance against the purchaser was therefore dismissed. See also *Allen* v. *Smith* [1924] 2 Ch. 308 and compare *Simmons* v. *Pennington and Son* [1955] 1 W.L.R. 183.

But although there be an express representation by the vendor, the purchaser would not be entitled to take advantage of it if it can be shown that he was well aware of the real facts of the case (*Eaglesfield* v. *Londonderry* (1875), 4 Ch. D. 693 ; *Smith* v. *Chadwick* (1884), 9 App. Cas. 187) ; or that he stated in terms or showed clearly by his conduct that he did not rely on the representation (*Redgrave* v. *Hurd* (1881), 20 Ch. D. 1). But mere constructive notice will not be an answer to misrepresentation (*Jones* v. *Rimmer* (1880), 14 Ch. D. 588).

Sale of such title as the vendor has.—Even where a purchaser agrees to accept a vendor's title, he has a right to assume that the vendor has disclosed all that it was his duty to have disclosed, and the condition can only be read as precluding objection on that footing (*Re Haedicke and Lipski's Contract* [1901] 2 Ch. 666 ; *Becker* v. *Partridge* [1966] 2 Q.B. 155). And a vendor who contracts to sell only such right or interest, if any, as he has, is bound to convey such right or interest free from an existing incumbrance (*Goold* v. *Birmingham, Dudley and District Bank* (1888), 58 L.T. 560). Compare *Fowler* v. *Willis* [1922] 2 Ch. 514, where a lease contained an option of purchase in favour of the tenant of " all the estate interest and title which is at the date of these presents vested in the landlords " for the sum of £3,000. The tenant exercised his option, and only on receipt of the abstract did he discover that at the date of the lease there was a mortgage on the property for £500. The purchaser contended that the vendors must convey the property free from the mortgage on the ground that the words were used as a general description of the quality of the estate the vendors possessed, but the court held otherwise. It is difficult to agree with the decision.

Purchaser to assume that a state of facts exists.—A condition requiring a purchaser to assume what the vendor knows is not true can be disregarded on the ground that it is misleading, and the vendor cannot enforce specific performance (*Re Sandbach and Edmondson's Contract* [1891] 1 Ch. 99). This is also so if the vendor knows only that what has to be assumed *may* not be true (*Wilson* v. *Thomas* [1958] 1 W.L.R. 422, where the state of facts to be assumed depended on the proper construction, with the aid of extrinsic evidence, of a latent ambiguity in a will). But the condition would not be considered misleading if the vendor believed to be true what he asked the purchaser to assume, although his belief was untrue and unsupported by any evidence (*ibid.*). The utmost that can be asked of a purchaser is that he shall assume something of which the vendor knows nothing. It follows that if the vendor knows, or from the state of his title ought to know, that what he asks the purchaser to assume is not correct, the condition would be misleading (*Re Banister* (1879), 12 Ch. D. 131 ; *Hammond* v. *Best* (1879), 40 L.T. 769). In *Beyfus* v. *Lodge* [1925] Ch. 350, there was a condition that the production of the last receipt for the rent due under two leases should be *conclusive* evidence that the covenants had been observed up to the date of completion. The vendor had received notices to put the property in repair which had not been complied with. It was held that the vendor could not derive any assistance from the condition, *as it bound the purchaser to assume a state of affairs which the vendor knew to be untrue without fairly bringing the facts to the attention of the purchaser.* See also *Re Tower's Contract*

[1924] W.N. 331, where it was held that the condition in the contract under which the vendors were to be free of liability to make compensation for a misdescription did not extend to a misstatement, of the inaccuracy of which the vendors must have been aware at the time it was made.

Contract as to how title to be made.—Although the contract states that title shall be made by the vendor in a particular way or particular capacity the purchaser cannot object to a good title made otherwise unless there was a warranty as to how it would be made. In *Re Spencer and Hauser's Contract* [1928] Ch. 598, the vendors were both executors and trustees for sale of a will. They intended to sell as executors as they had not assented to the devise to themselves as trustees. Unfortunately, by error, they were stated in the contract as selling in the capacity of trustees for sale. The purchaser objected that this was not the title which the vendors had contracted to give, and refused to complete. Tomlin, J., held that the purchaser must accept the title from the vendors as personal representatives. The learned judge took the view that it would be a strange construction to place upon any contract to say that it was a warranty by the vendor that he was making title in any particular form, and that he could not hold that the contract did anything more than indicate the way in which the vendors were contemplating making a title.

This decision is easily understandable and businesslike, but the later decision of Eve, J., in *Green* v. *Whitehead* [1930] 1 Ch. 38, causes some uncertainty. In that case joint tenants entitled to land beneficially agreed to sell as statutory trustees, but the conveyance offered was executed by an attorney for one of them. The delegation to the attorney by a trustee was not effective (see now s. 25 of the T.A. 1925, as amended by s. 8 of the Powers of Attorney Act, 1971). Consequently, it was decided that a good title had not been offered although the vendors could validly have made title as beneficial owners, in which case an attorney could have executed a conveyance for one of them. There does not seem to be anything in this decision contrary to *Re Spencer and Hauser's Contract, ante,* which was not, however, apparently cited to Eve, J., as it is essentially a decision on the particular title offered at all material times, namely, in pursuance of the trust for sale.

A condition as to the title may, however, amount to a warranty as to the evidence to be provided in support of it, in which case the vendor cannot comply by showing a good title according to the rules applicable to an open contract. This was so in *George Wimpey & Co., Ltd.* v. *Sohn* [1967] Ch. 487, where the vendors undertook to sell such interest as they had in certain land to be supported by a statutory declaration of undisputed possession for twenty years. It was not open to the vendors to show a title under the Limitation Act, 1939, by twelve years' adverse possession (even if they had been able to do that).

If the vendor cannot himself make title he is not able to compel the purchaser to accept a title made by another ; to do so would be to force a different contract on the purchaser. In *Re Bryant and Barningham's Contract* (1890), 44 Ch. D. 218, the vendors had contracted to sell as trustees for sale. On investigation it was found that such trust for sale only arose on the death of a tenant for life. The vendors then proposed that a title should be made by the tenant for life under the then S.L.A. The purchaser objected, and the Court of Appeal agreed with his objection, *on the ground that the life-tenant was not bound to agree on request.* On the other hand, in

Re Baker and Selmon's Contract [1907] 1 Ch. 238, the vendor sold land as trustee under a will *at the request of the beneficiaries.* The land was not vested in him as trustee for sale and he had no power of sale. When the defect was found out the beneficiaries agreed to join in the conveyance to the purchaser, and it was held that he must accept a title so made. The explanation of this decision seems to be that, on the facts, the vendor was selling as agent for the beneficiaries who were bound to join in because of their request. (See also *Re Atkinson and Horsell's Contract* [1912] 2 Ch. 1, and *Re Head's Trustees and Macdonald* (1890), 45 Ch. D. 310.) In addition, it has been held that a purchaser is unable to object where title is actually in a company of which the vendor is the controlling shareholder (*Elliott* v. *Pierson* [1948] Ch. 452, at p. 457 ; also *Jones* v. *Lipman* [1962] 1 W.L.R. 832).

Right of purchaser to legal estate in fee simple.—As the legal estate is the basis of post-1925 conveyancing, there are a number of statutory provisions enabling the purchaser to call for it, as follows :—

(i) The L.P.A. 1925, s. 42 (3), provides : " A stipulation contained in any contract for the sale or exchange of land made after [1925] to the effect that an *outstanding legal estate* is to be traced or got in by or at the expense of a purchaser or that no objection is to be taken on account of an outstanding legal estate, shall be void."

(ii) The L.P.A. 1925, s. 42 (4) (ii), provides : " If the subject matter of any contract for the sale or exchange of land is an *equitable interest capable of subsisting as a legal estate,* and the vendor has power to vest such legal estate in himself or in the purchaser or to require the same to be so vested, the contract shall be deemed to extend to such legal estate."

(iii) The L.P.A. 1925, s. 42 (4) (iii), provides : " If the subject matter of any contract for the sale or exchange of land is an *entailed interest* in possession and the vendor has power to vest in himself or in the purchaser the fee simple in the land (or, if the entailed interest is an interest in a term of years absolute, such term) or to require the same to be so vested, the contract shall be deemed to extend to the fee simple in the land or the term of years absolute." See also *Re Alefounder's Will Trusts* [1927] 1 Ch. 360, *post.*

Title to settled land.—The detailed rules relating to settlements are set out in the chapter on Settled Land, *post,* p. 664 ; the form of an abstract of title to settled land is indicated in the L.P.A. 1925, Sched. 6, Specimen No. 1, and reference is made *post,* p. 689, to the statements a purchaser must accept as true.

In general, title is made by the tenant for life or by the person having the same powers pursuant to the S.L.A. 1925, and a conveyance by such a person of a legal estate will, if the necessary steps are taken, overreach the equitable interests under the settlement ; see *post,* p. 173. It is necessary to note, however, that in some cases title may be made otherwise than by virtue of the statutory overreaching powers of the tenant for life.

It is provided by s. 42 of the L.P.A. 1925 as follows :—

" 42.—(1) A stipulation that a purchaser of a legal estate in land shall accept a title made *with the concurrence of any person* entitled to an equitable interest shall be void, if a title can be made discharged from the equitable interest without such concurrence—

(*a*) under a trust for sale ; or

(b) under this Act, or the Settled Land Act, 1925, or any other statute.

(2) A stipulation that a purchaser of a legal estate in land shall pay or contribute towards the costs of or incidental to—

(a) obtaining a vesting order, or the appointment of trustees of a settlement, or the appointment of trustees of a conveyance on trust for sale ; or

(b) the preparation stamping or execution of a conveyance on trust for sale, or of a vesting instrument for bringing into force the provisions of the Settled Land Act, 1925 ;

shall be void."

*   *   *   *   *

" (8) A vendor shall not have any power to rescind a contract by reason only of the enforcement of any right under this section."

Notwithstanding s. 42 (1), there is nothing to prevent a vendor and a purchaser agreeing to give and accept a title in the same way as before 1926. All a purchaser wants is the legal estate in the land free from all charges and claims.   If he can be given this at comparatively small expense, why should the vendor be forced to adopt, at great expense, the cumbersome method of making title by vesting deed and appointment of trustees to receive the purchase-money, or by creating a settlement with trustees, under s. 2 (2) of the L.P.A. 1925, as amended ?

In practice, s. 42 (1) is often ignored.   This result is not due entirely to the common sense and goodwill of the profession, for there are two other matters which have considerably helped.   One is s. 1 of the Law of Property (Amendment) Act, 1926, and the other is the decision in Re Alefounder's Will Trusts [1927] 1 Ch. 360.

Before 1926, a good deal of land was held subject to jointures in favour of wives or portions in favour of younger children, and when it became necessary to sell parts of the land it was usually arranged that the purchaser should take the land subject to the charge, but with an indemnity.   The land was not then settled land (Re Carnarvon's Chesterfield S.E. [1927] 1 Ch. 138), and could not be sold clear of the family charge, unless, of course, the incumbrancers joined.   Immediately the S.L.A. 1925 came into operation all such land became settled land under s. 1 (1) (v) of the Act, and each parcel of land so sold became the subject of a separate settlement (Re Ogle's S.E. [1927] 1 Ch. 229).   The person entitled to the land became a person having the powers of a tenant for life under s. 20 (1) (ix) of the S.L.A. 1925, with the result that he could not deal with the land until he had obtained a vesting deed under s. 13 of the Act, and trustees had been discovered or appointed to receive the purchase-money.   This was so extremely inconvenient that the matter was put right by the Law of Property (Amendment) Act, 1926, providing in effect that in such a case the owner of the land could sell, or deal with the land, as if it were not settled land.   That is to say, he is allowed to sell subject to the charge, but the land still, technically, remains settled land.   The result of this is that on the death of the purchaser, technically speaking, a grant should be made to the trustees of the settlement creating the charge as special personal representatives.   But it is generally accepted that this course would be highly inconvenient in practice, and that it is not improper, in view of the highly technical aspect, for the executor to state in the oath to lead to probate that there is no settled land.   This enables a grant of probate to be made to the general executors who can make a perfectly good title to the land under the decision in *Re Bridgett and Hayes' Contract* [1928] 1 Ch. 163, as to which see p. 183.

In *Re Alefounder's Will Trusts, ante*, Astbury, J., decided that s. 13 of the S.L.A. 1925 (which is the section which makes it necessary to have a vesting deed and trustees to receive purchase-money, as a condition of being able to deal effectively with settled land), applies only in the case of settled land. Consequently if, before a vesting deed has been executed, the settlement comes to an end, the land ceases to be settled land, and the section is no longer applicable to it. Therefore, if the land is, for instance, charged with the payment of an annuity, and in consequence has become settled land, and the vendor can arrange to pay off or satisfy the annuitant or arrange for him to execute a deed discharging the land therefrom, the land will cease to be settled land, and the owner can sell and convey as an ordinary absolute owner. See also chapter on Settled Land, *post*, p. 664.

It seems better to have the interest discharged by a separate document, as otherwise it would be necessary to bring the equitable interest on the title. But the late Mr. Lightwood, in a learned article in the *Cambridge Law Journal*, vol. 3, at p. 59, considered that notwithstanding this advantage, the practice of joining the equitable owner is too convenient to be abandoned.

Rights of purchaser where a land charge has been registered.—It is provided by s. 43 of the L.P.A. 1925, as follows :—

" 43.—(1) Where a purchaser of a legal estate is entitled to acquire the same discharged from an equitable interest which is protected by registration as a pending action, annuity, writ, order, deed of arrangement or land charge, and which will not be overreached by the conveyance to him, he may, notwithstanding any stipulation to the contrary, require—

(a) that the registration shall be cancelled ; or

(b) that the person entitled to the equitable interest shall concur in the conveyance ;

and in either case free of expense to the purchaser.

(2) Where the registration cannot be cancelled or the person entitled to the equitable interest refuses to concur in the conveyance, this section does not affect the right of any person to rescind the contract."

Where the equitable interest was registered the practice is to get the registration cancelled ; see further, *post*, p. 174.

A vendor selling as tenant for life can overreach the following equitable interests, notwithstanding that they are registered as a land charge, that is to say, an annuity, a limited owner's charge, or a general equitable charge, within the meaning of the L.C.A. 1972 (S.L.A. 1925, s. 72 (3)). Therefore, in these cases, there is no necessity for the registration to be cancelled, or for the person entitled to be joined in the document. See further at p. 174, and see pp. 176 and 179 as to whether trustees for sale and personal representatives have similar powers.

PART 2. ROOT OF TITLE

General rule as to fifteen years' title.—With a few minor exceptions, fifteen years is the time now prescribed for the commencement of title if no other time is agreed. The L.P.A. 1925, s. 44 (1), provided :—

" After [1925] *thirty years* shall be substituted for forty years as the period of commencement of title which a purchaser of land may require ;

nevertheless earlier title than thirty years may be required in cases similar to those in which earlier title than forty years might immediately before [1926] be required."

Now the L.P.A. 1969, s. 23, provides that s. 44 (1) of the 1925 Act should have effect in its application to contracts made after 1969 " as if it specified *fifteen years* instead of thirty years as the period of commencement of title which may be so required." The change follows directly from the recommendations in the Law Commission's Report " Transfer of Land—Interim Report on Root of Title to Freehold Land " (Law Com. No. 9, 15th December, 1966).

The Building Societies Association have stated the view that, whilst a solicitor should in no way be discouraged from accepting a fifteen-year title in the normal owner-occupier case, where the land to be mortgaged involves building finance (including that for housing societies), then " a period longer than fifteen years is desirable " (see *Law Society's Gazette*, vol. 67, pp. 516-517).

The risk of there being land charges registered against the names of estate owners outside the shortened statutory period of title, which names a purchaser will not know to search against, has been dealt with by the provision of compensation (s. 25 of the 1969 Act noted *post*, p. 161).

It does not necessarily follow that the date of commencement will be exactly fifteen years or exactly the time agreed. The old conveyancing rule was that on sale of a legal estate the first abstracted deed (in the absence of a condition to the contrary) should purport to deal with the entire legal and equitable estates in the property or should at least afford *prima facie* evidence that the title to such legal and equitable estates was, at the date of such deed, consistent with the title as subsequently deduced (*Re Cox and Neve's Contract* [1891] 2 Ch. 109). The principle of this rule still remains good. That is to say, if you are selling a legal estate in land, the deed commencing the title should purport to deal with the whole legal estate, and if you are selling an equitable interest, similarly the deed starting the title should purport to deal with the whole equitable interest. Therefore a fifteen years' title means a title deduced for fifteen years and for so much longer as it is necessary to go back in order to arrive at a proper root of title (see *post*, p. 114).

The chief cases in which, in the absence of a condition to the contrary, an earlier title than fifteen years can be asked for are sales of advowsons, leaseholds, and reversionary interests. See further at p. 120.

Registered titles.—The fifteen years' period of title prescribed by the L.P.A. 1925, s. 44 (1), as amended by the L.P.A. 1969, s. 23, *ante*, is not, as the general rule, applicable where title to the land sold is registered under the L.R.A. 1925-1971. The purchaser is concerned only with the present position of the vendor's title as it appears on the register, he is not concerned with the history of the title at all, not even with the conveyance or transfer to the vendor (compare Registered Land Practice Notes 1972, p. 22, No. 27 distinguishing the decision in *Lee* v. *Barrey* [1957] Ch. 251 by which purchasers might have been concerned with the plans on earlier transfers). As to the method of deducing a registered title, see *post*, p. 131 *et seq.* If, however, the vendor is not registered with an absolute title, that is he holds a possessory or qualified title, the purchaser will be concerned to investigate the pre-registration title, as to which the register is not conclusive, just as in un-registered conveyancing (L.R.A. 1925, s. 110 (2) ; *Re Brine and Davies'*

Contract [1935] Ch. 388). In addition, a purchaser will, of course, be concerned to investigate any overriding interests, as to which see *post*, p. 184.

Contracts for a short title.—A purchaser is not deemed to have notice of any matters on the title prior to a proper root of title within the L.P.A. 1925, s. 44 (1), as amended by the L.P.A. 1969, s. 23, *ante*, unless he actually investigates or inquires about such matters (L.P.A. 1925, s. 44 (6)). But a purchaser may be offered a shorter title even than the present statutory fifteen years and if he agrees to it he will have constructive notice of any matters which an investigation of the title for the full period would have disclosed ; see further *post*, pp. 164–165.

Where a short title is offered, it is important to remember that, whatever document is fixed upon as the root of title, it is necessary that it should be a document which deals with the whole legal and equitable title to the property (see above). In some cases it is necessary, and in all cases it is better, to describe the nature of the document so fixed as the root. A purchaser is entitled to assume, where he is being asked to accept title for less than the statutory period, unless there is something in the contract to the contrary, that the document commencing the title was one where the title would have been investigated. " On a voluntary conveyance the prior title is not likely to be investigated. You do not look a gift horse in the mouth." Baggallay, L.J., in *Re Marsh and Earl Granville* (1882), 24 Ch. D. 11 said, at p. 22, that : " Any stipulation inserted in a contract for the purpose of limiting the period for which a title shall be shown must give a perfectly fair description of the nature of that which is to form the root of title ; and if the root of title is an instrument, whether a deed of conveyance, commonly so called, or a deed of settlement, or a will, or whatever it may be, its nature must, if that stipulation is to have effect, be fairly and clearly stated . . . If the stipulation had provided that the title should commence with an indenture dated the [date given], which was *a voluntary settlement*, stating its effect, and mentioning the power of revocation, it would have been for the consideration of the purchaser whether he would submit to be bound by a stipulation of that kind. As the stipulation stands he, *prima facie*, would suppose that the indenture referred to was a conveyance to a purchaser for value, the inference from which would be that at that time the title was investigated and approved of. I do not, however, rest my judgment on the ground that that would be the idea conveyed to the purchaser in the present case, but on the ground that he ought to have had an opportunity of deciding whether he would accept a title of this description as a root of title when the title was to commence within the statutory period. There was not, in my opinion, such a full and explicit description of the deed given as he was entitled to."

It will be seen, therefore, that a voluntary conveyance may be a perfectly good root of title although it may be less than fifteen years old provided that a full description is given of its nature, and of any special provisions therein which a purchaser ought to know.

Instrument forming root of title.—An instrument to be a good root of title " must be an instrument of disposition dealing with or proving on the face of it (without the aid of extrinsic evidence) the ownership of the whole legal and equitable estate in the property sold, containing a description by which the property can be identified and showing nothing to cast any doubt on the title of the disposing parties " (Williams on Vendor and Purchaser, 4th ed., vol. I, p. 124). That the root should also deal on the face of it with the equitable estate in the property sold may now be more of an exception than a rule. This is because, since 1925, the legal estate has become the basis of conveyancing, the general policy of the 1925 property legislation being to keep equities off the title largely by means of the overreaching provisions (see *post*, p. 172). Consequently, for example, a post-1925 conveyance on trust for sale or vesting deed under a strict settlement may be acceptable as a good root of title even though not dealing with the equitable estate. Nevertheless, for any case in which equitable interests are not overreached (and such cases are envisaged by the property legislation, see, e.g., L.P.A. 1925, ss. 10 and 43, and the Law of Property (Amendment) Act, 1926, s. 1) the old rule remains, namely, that the root must deal on the face of it with the whole legal and equitable estate.

Document exercising a power.—A document which depends entirely for its effect on an earlier document must be regarded as casting a doubt on the title of the disposing party and therefore is not a good root. Thus, a document exercising a power, whether of appointment, sale, attorney or otherwise, is not in itself a good root of title (*Re Copelin's Contract* [1937] 4 All E.R. 447 ; *Re Holmes* [1944] Ch. 53 ; L.P.A. 1925, s. 45 (1), *post*, pp. 120, 121). Nonetheless, such a document may be made a good root by describing its nature fully in the contract (*Re Marsh and Earl Granville* (1882), 24 Ch. D. 11).

Mortgage.—A conveyance in fee by way of mortgage is a good root of title (Williams on Vendor and Purchaser, 4th ed., vol. I, p. 124). " Before 1926, a mortgage for a long term of years was not a good root of title on sale of the fee simple unless the mortgage deed contained matter from which it could be presumed that the mortgagor was seised in fee simple of the mortgaged land. Strictly speaking, the same considerations apply to a mortgage made of the fee simple, on or after January 1, 1926, either by a demise for a term of years or by a charge by way of legal mortgage . . . But where such a mortgage contains recitals or statements showing that the mortgagor is entitled in fee simple at law to the mortgaged land and is mortgaging the fee simple in the manner permitted by [the L.P.A. 1925], it is thought that the mortgage deed, when sufficiently old, would form a good root of title " (*ibid.*). It is often said that from the point of view of a purchaser a mortgage is a better root of title than a conveyance on sale because purchasers will accept doubtful titles more often than will mortgagees. This is perfectly true, but, in practice, difficulty sometimes arises because mortgages are often not expressed to be subject to such matters as restrictive covenants which affect the land.

Transfer of mortgage.—A transfer of mortgage in which the mortgagor concurs and a new equity of redemption is reserved is a good root of title, but a transfer of a mortgage without reserving a new equity of redemption, or without the mortgagor's concurrence, is not a good root of title (*ibid.*).

Conveyance of equity.—A conveyance on sale of the equity of redemption of mortgaged property was formerly not regarded as a good root of title. The reason was that before 1926 the mortgagor, having conveyed the legal estate to the mortgagee, had an equitable interest only. It may be that, where the conveyance of the " equity " is after 1925, as the mortgagor still holds the legal fee simple it will be regarded as a good root of title. Nevertheless, as it is necessary to trace devolution of the mortgagee's estate it is probably better to treat the mortgage as the root of title.

Wills, grants and assents.—A general devise, for example a devise of " all my freehold property to *A B*," has never been a good root of title, as there is, on the face of it, nothing to show that the property sold belonged to the testator at the time of his death. An earlier root of title must be adopted, for instance the conveyance to the testator (*Parr* v. *Lovegrove* (1857), 4 Drew. 170). In the case of a specific devise where the death took place before 1898 the legal estate in the land devised passed directly to the devisee, and he alone could confer a title. Therefore a will containing a devise of, e.g., " my freehold house in which I now reside to *A B* " would be a good root of title.

On the death of a beneficial owner after 1897 and before 1926, the legal estate in the land devised beneficially did not pass to the devisee, but vested, like a chattel real, in the personal representatives of the deceased (Land Transfer Act, 1897, s. 1), and only the equitable interest, subject to debts and administration expenses, passed to the devisee (*ibid.*, s. 2); the personal representatives' assent or conveyance was therefore necessary to vest the legal estate in the devisee (*ibid.*, s. 3; *Re Pix* [1901] W.N. 165). It was not necessary, however, that the assent should be in writing; any act from which an assent could be assumed was sufficient, for instance, allowing the devisee to take possession of the property the subject of the devise (*Attenborough* v. *Solomon* [1913] A.C. 76 ; *Wise* v. *Whitburn* [1924] 1 Ch. 460).

The effect of the assent was to make the devise in the will operative (*Attenborough* v. *Solomon, ante*). Therefore a specific devise in the will of a person dying after 1897 and before 1926 may be a good root of title, and a purchaser would be entitled to an abstract or copy of the portion of the will showing the devise, particulars of probate and of the assent, if in writing, and if not, a statement of the facts relied on as constituting the assent.

Since 1925, an assent, to be effectual, must be in writing and must contain the name of the person in whose favour it is made and must be signed by the executors (A.E.A. 1925, s. 36 (4)), even if the assent is in their own favour (*Re King's Will Trusts* [1964] Ch. 542). Where, after 1925, land is vested in personal representatives, and their duties and obligations have come to an end, they can be required (after the expiration of a year from the death), when called on, to execute an assent or conveyance in favour of a specific devisee under a will (A.E.A. 1925, ss. 36 (10) and 44).

It is important to note that after 1925 an assent relates back to the date of the death of the testator (A.E.A. 1925, s. 36 (2)). After 1897 and before 1926 an assent passed the legal estate in the land to the devisee by making the devise in the will operative (*Attenborough* v. *Solomon* [1913] A.C. 76); but since 1925 the legal estate passes by virtue of the assent itself (A.E.A. 1925, s. 36 (2)). The will operates to pass the equitable interest only, and has not to be abstracted. It follows that, if death took place after 1925, a will cannot become a good root of title. A written assent duly executed after 1925 may be a good root of title ; such a document complies with the requirements in spite of the fact that it was not given for value. However, it is probable that the probate or letters of administration should also be produced to show both the title to assent and the absence of endorsements (A.E.A. 1925, s. 36 (5), and *Re Miller and Pickersgill's Contract* [1931] 1 Ch. 511).

Voidable conveyances.—There are a number of statutory provisions whereby a conveyance, particularly if voluntary, may be set aside. As a rule, however, potential liability to avoidance under these provisions does not prevent the conveyance being a good root of, or link in, title. The reason is that the provisions all contain, in effect, saving qualifications in favour of a *bona fide* purchaser for value without notice. In addition to the provisions outlined in the immediately following paragraphs, see s. 42 of the Bankruptcy Act, 1914, *post*, p. 252.

Conveyances in fraud of creditors.—This subject is most likely to arise in connection with voluntary conveyances and settlements. The rule is now contained in the L.P.A. 1925, s. 172 (1), which provides :—

" 172.—(1) Save as provided in this section, every *conveyance* of property, made . . . with intent to defraud creditors, shall be voidable, at the instance of any person thereby prejudiced."

" *Save as provided in this section.*"—The section does not affect the operation of a disentailing assurance, or the law of bankruptcy (*ibid.*, s. 172 (2)), nor does it extend to " any estate or interest in property conveyed for valuable consideration and in good faith or upon good consideration and in good faith to any person not having, at the time of the conveyance, notice of the intent to defraud creditors " (*ibid.*, s. 172 (3)). The reference both to valuable and to good consideration separately is odd and suggests that creditors may be defeated by a conveyance for natural love and affection. However, in *Re Eicholz* [1959] Ch. 708, apparently without argument, valuable and good consideration seemed to be treated as synonymous.

The words of s. 172 (3), construed literally, mean that the *vendor* must have acted in good faith. They were taken from the old Act, 13 Eliz. I, c. 5, under which the courts held that the words were to be deemed to mean that *the purchaser only* was to be without notice of the fraud, and it is assumed that the old decisions apply to s. 172.

The reference in s. 172 (3) to " notice " includes constructive notice and the burden of proof under that subsection lies on the transferee whereas under subs. (1) it is on the person seeking to avoid the conveyance (*Lloyds Bank, Ltd.* v. *Marcan* [1973] 3 All E.R. 754, C.A.).

" *conveyance.*"—This word includes " a mortgage, charge, lease, assent, vesting declaration, vesting instrument, disclaimer, release, and every other assurance . . . by any instrument except a will " (L.P.A. 1925, s. 205 (1)) but, apparently, does not include an assurance which is not in writing (*Rye* v. *Rye* [1962] A.C. 496 which seems inconsistent with *Re Eicholz* [1959] Ch. 708). The whole of the circumstances surrounding the execution of the conveyance must be looked at to ascertain whether the conveyance was in fact executed with intent to defraud creditors (*Re Holland ; Gregg* v. *Holland* [1902] 2 Ch. 360) ; the test being whether the transaction was entered into in good faith, or was a mere contrivance for the personal benefit of the settlor, or of others whom he wished improperly to favour (*Maskelyne and Cook* v. *Smith* [1903] 1 K.B. 671 ; *Re David and Adlard* [1914] 2 K.B. 694 ; *Cornish* v. *Clark* (1872), L.R. 14 Eq. 184). The court is not bound to presume an intent to defeat creditors merely because they are defeated as a consequence of the settlement, if it appears from the evidence that the settlor had not, in fact, such an intent (*Re Wise ; ex parte Mercer* (1886), 17 Q.B.D. 290). See also *Re Lane-Fox* [1900] 2 Q.B. 508. However, although intention is a question of fact provable by direct evidence, the requisite intent to defraud can be inferred from surrounding circumstances or even imputed on the basis that a man must be presumed to intend the natural consequence of his acts (*Lloyds Bank, Ltd.* v. *Marcan* [1973] 3 All E.R. 754, C.A.). The word " defraud " here has been held to carry the meaning of " depriving creditors of timely recourse to property which would otherwise be applicable for their benefit," for example, not only by an outright conveyance but also by the grant of a lease at a full rack-rent (*ibid.*).

A deed of arrangement will not necessarily be voidable either because it contains provisions in favour of the debtor, or because a particular creditor is intentionally excluded from its operation (*Maskelyne and Cook* v. *Smith, ante*) ; and a conveyance to a creditor with the intention of preferring such creditor over others is not fraudulent under the statute, unless the debtor is himself benefited by the conveyance (*Re Lloyd's Furniture Palace, Ltd.* [1925] Ch. 853).

A voluntary conveyance *with a power of revocation* will be deemed to be on the face of it fraudulent (*Tarback* v. *Marbury* (1705), 2 Vern. 510) ; and as the trustee in bankruptcy may exercise all powers in respect of property which might have been exercised by the bankrupt for his own benefit, he may exercise the power of revocation (Bankruptcy Act, 1914, s. 38 ; *Re Tarn* (1893), 9 T.L.R. 489).

If an intent on the part of all the parties to the transaction to delay, hinder, or defraud creditors is clear, the settlement will be voidable, even if made for valuable consideration (*Re Pennington ; ex parte Pennington* (1888), 5 Morr. 268 ; *Golden* v. *Gillam* (1882), 51 L.J. Ch. 503 ; *Hemingway* v. *Braithwaite* (1889), 61 L.T. 224 ; *Spirett* v. *Willows* (1869), L.R. 4 Ch. 407 ; *Re Lane-Fox ; ex parte Gimlett* [1900] 2 Q.B. 508 ; *Re Fasey* [1923] 2 Ch. 1). But, unless the intention to defeat creditors is apparent, such intent to defeat creditors must be shown, also that the assignees had notice of the fraud (*Gonville's Trustee* v. *Patent Caramel Co., Ltd.* [1921] 1 K.B. 599). The fact that the settlement contained a covenant by the husband to settle all his after-acquired property will not of itself be evidence of fraud on the part of the wife (*Clough* v. *Samuel* [1905] A.C. 442) ; and a marriage settlement can only be avoided as against the wife when it can be shown, or implied with certainty, that she was a party to the fraud (*Parnell* v. *Stedman* (1883), Cab. & El. 153). Whether an assignment of leaseholds, in form voluntary, will be a conveyance for value within the section, owing to the liability on the part of the assignee to pay the rent and perform the covenants of the lease, seems doubtful (*Re Ridler* (1882), 22 Ch. D. 74 ; *contra, Harris* v. *Tubb* (1889), 42 Ch. D. 79).

Even though a settlement is voidable under the section not only will purchasers for value without notice, taking directly under the settlement, be protected, but also persons who have, without notice of the fraud, purchased an interest derived under it (*Halifax Joint Stock Banking Co.* v. *Gledhill* [1891] 1 Ch. 31).

Voluntary dispositions with intent to defraud purchasers.—The L.P.A. 1925, s. 173, provides :—

" 173.—(1) Every voluntary disposition of land made with intent to defraud a subsequent purchaser is voidable at the instance of that purchaser.

(2) For the purposes of this section, no voluntary disposition, whenever made, shall be deemed to have been made with intent to defraud by reason only that a subsequent conveyance for valuable consideration was made, if such subsequent conveyance was made after the twenty-eighth day of June, eighteen hundred and ninety-three."

The mere fact that a disposition was made voluntarily does not mean that a subsequent conveyance for valuable consideration will upset it. On the other hand, if the voluntary disposition was made with the intention of

defrauding a subsequent purchaser for value, that purchaser will be able to
upset the earlier conveyance.   If at the present time a conveyance be made for
inadequate consideration, but still for consideration, with a view to defrauding
a subsequent purchaser, the question may arise whether such disposition for
an inadequate consideration can be considered " a voluntary disposition".

Dispositions to avoid spouse's claims.—Where proceedings for financial
provision under the Matrimonial Proceedings and Property Act, 1970, are
brought by a person against his or her spouse or former spouse, that person
may apply to the court to restrain or set aside any disposition which such
spouse is about to make or has made with the intention (which may be
presumed within three years) of defeating the claim for financial relief
(s. 16 of the 1970 Act).   However, it is expressly provided that the section
does not apply to a disposition made for valuable consideration (other than
marriage) to a person who, at the time of the disposition, acted in relation to
it in good faith and without notice of any intention of defeating a claim for
financial provision (*ibid.*, subs. (2)).   Further, even if the immediate disposition
by the spouse is ordered to be set aside this will not have the result of nullifying
subsequent intermediate dispositions to which the section does not apply as
above (*National Provincial Bank, Ltd.* v. *Hastings Car Mart, Ltd.* (*No.* 2)
[1964] Ch. 128 ; affd. [1964] Ch. 665).   Thus a *bona fide* purchaser for value
will not be concerned with these provisions unless he has notice of the motives
behind the disposition, but what will constitute such notice is difficult to say
in the absence of any decision (mere occupation by a deserted wife apparently
does not : *ibid.*).   Since here marriage is not valuable consideration, an otherwise voluntary settlement on remarriage would be liable to be set aside.

Section 16 of the 1970 Act does not apply to a disposition made more than
three years before 1st August, 1971 (*ibid.*, subs. (5)).

Inclosure award.—An inclosure award is not a good root of title.   The
reason is that lands allotted under Inclosure Acts become subject to the same
title and tenure as the property in respect of which they were allotted, and
therefore the purchaser can ask for an abstract to be supplied prior to and
up to the date of the award.   The Commissioners had no jurisdiction to
determine title (*Jacomb* v. *Turner* [1892] 1 Q.B. 47) ; but if the award has
been acted on for a great number of years without dispute, the court would
presume that it was valid (*Micklethwait* v. *Vincent* (1893), 69 L.T. 57).

Disentailing deed.—The reason that a disentailing deed is not a good root
of title is that, even when it affected a legal estate (as it might before 1926),
it showed ownership merely of an estate tail and not of the fee simple.   A
purchaser can therefore require an abstract of the deed creating the estate
tail (Williams on Vendor and Purchaser, 4th ed., vol. I, p. 126).

Vesting instruments.—A vesting deed or assent executed to give effect to
a post-1925 settlement may provide a good root of title.   It seems that a
first vesting instrument executed after 1925 for the purposes of a settlement
existing before 1926 may also be a good root of title under an open contract
if it passed a legal estate.   On the other hand, there may be doubt whether a
deed which merely declared that the legal estate was already vested in the
tenant for life can be regarded as a good root of title under an open contract.
It would be unfortunate if a distinction had to be drawn between a vesting
deed which transfers the legal estate and one which merely declares the
person in whom it is already vested.   It may be, however, that traditional
definitions of a good root of title require revision in the light of the 1925

legislation. Pending a decision of a court, if it is proposed that a vesting instrument will be the root of title the root should be fixed by a condition of sale describing it with accuracy. If a vesting deed is a root of title, then the question arises whether inquiries need be made by a purchaser from a tenant for life under the settlement as to matters before such root of title ; this problem is considered *post*, p. 689 *et seq*.

Leaseholds.—In the case of a sale of leaseholds a purchaser is entitled to an abstract or copy of the lease, however old, and fifteen years' title to it back from date of purchase (*Frend* v. *Buckley* (1870), L.R. 5 Q.B. 213 ; *Williams* v. *Spargo* [1893] W.N. 100). As he may not, unless the contract stipulates otherwise, investigate the freehold title or any prior leasehold title, this right may be of little value to him especially if the lease is recent. See further, *post*, p. 143. Where, therefore, the lease is a recent one, a purchaser's solicitor should, if he is consulted before the signing of the contract, insist on being satisfied that the person who granted the lease had power to do so. The interest of such person might have been mortgaged and the statutory power of leasing excluded (*Dudley Building Society* v. *Emerson* [1949] Ch. 707). Most building societies will require title to the freehold to be deduced where a recent lease is to be mortgaged, unless the lessor is a public authority or of similar standing (*Law Society's Gazette*, vol. 60, p. 479).

A lease made under a power is not itself a good root of title. When a lease granted in exercise of a power is sold, a special stipulation should always be made that the title shall commence with the lease *and it should be stated that such lease was granted in exercise of a power*. In such a case it is better expressly to stipulate further that the instrument creating the power shall not be required to be abstracted or produced (Williams, Contract of Sale of Land, p. 62).

Reversionary interest or interest in remainder.—The only legal estates in remainder or reversion which can now subsist or be created in land are those subsisting or created in reversion or remainder expectant on the determination of a term of years absolute. All other estates in reversion or remainder can take effect only as equitable interests (L.P.A. 1925, ss. 1 and 3). A purchaser can ask for an abstract of the document creating the interest, however old, and then thirty years' title back from the date of the purchase.

Sale of an advowson.—On a sale of an advowson a title for at least 100 years must be shown, together with a list of the presentations made during that period. See the Benefices Act, 1898, s. 1, and the Benefices Act, 1898 (Amendment) Measure, 1923.

Documents before the root of title.—The general rule is contained in s. 45 (1) of the L.P.A. 1925, that " *a purchaser* of any property shall not (*a*) require the production, or any abstract or copy, of any deed, will, or other document, dated or made before the time prescribed by law, or stipulated for the commencement of the title, *even though the same creates a power subsequently exercised by an instrument abstracted* in the abstract furnished to the purchaser ; or (*b*) require any information, or make any requisition, objection, or inquiry, with respect to any such deed, will, or document, or the title prior to that time, notwithstanding that any such deed, will, or other document, or that prior title, is recited, agreed to be produced, or noticed."

The particular difficulty which arises when a tenant for life under a pre-1926 settlement sells and the first vesting instrument after 1925 becomes the root of title is discussed *post*, p. 689 *et seq.*

" *purchaser*."—This word includes a mortgagee and a lessee (L.P.A. 1925, **s.** 205 (1) (xxi)).

" *even though the same creates a power*," *etc.*— A document exercising a power is not in itself a good root of title, and is not made a good root of title by the above subsection. The reason is that s. 45 (1), *ante*, only operates as if it were a special condition in a contract (*ibid.*, subs. (11)), and, as a result, such condition has no effect unless the nature of the document is mentioned in the contract (*Re Marsh and Earl Granville* (1882), 24 Ch. D. 11, referred to at p. 114). Such a document would be a perfectly good root of title if the nature of the document were fully described in the contract. In addition to describing the nature of the document, it would be better to stipulate expressly that such document shall be accepted as a good root of title (Williams on Vendor and Purchaser, 4th ed., vol. I, pp. 86 and 126). The practical result of not stating the nature of the document would be that specific performance of the contract would not be granted if this remedy had to be resorted to.

Where there is on the title a document exercising a power of appointment, although the solicitor for the purchaser (in the absence of a stipulation) cannot insist (by reason of s. 45 (1) of the L.P.A. 1925) on being supplied with a copy of the document containing the power to appoint, or on inspecting it, he should make every effort to ascertain the terms of the power. Usually, the solicitor for the vendor will give the information, by way of courtesy. The appointment may be defective for various reasons, for instance, it may have been effected by a will, whereas the power to appoint might have stipulated that it should be made by deed, or with the consent of some person.

Section 58 of the L.P.A. 1925 contains a provision to the effect that the mere fact that an instrument is expressed to be " supplemental " to a previous instrument is not to operate to give any right to an abstract or production of such previous instrument, and that a purchaser may accept the same evidence that the previous instrument does not affect the title as if it had *merely been mentioned* in the supplemental instrument.

Purchaser's knowledge of pre-root defect.—Since L.P.A. 1925, s. 45 (1), *ante*, only operates as if it were a special condition in a contract (*ibid.*, subs. (11) ; *Nottingham Patent Brick Co.* v. *Butler* (1886), 16 Q.B.D. 778), if the purchaser actually learns of a defect in the pre-root title (e.g., by the vendor of his own accord allowing inspection of earlier deeds) then he will not be compelled by an order of specific performance to take a clearly bad title (*Re Scott and Alvarez* [1895] 2 Ch. 603 (second appeal) ; *Smith* v. *Robinson* (1879), 13 Ch. D. 148). However, the purchaser would apparently remain bound at law to damages and forfeiture of his deposit (*ibid.*), although this latter is subject to L.P.A. 1925, s. 49 (2), *post*, p. 227. Also the purchaser would apparently be compelled to take a title which, although not clearly bad, is made doubtful by pre-root matters (*Re Scott and Alvarez* [1895] 1 Ch. 596 (first appeal) ; compare *Re National Provincial Bank and Marsh* [1895] 1 Ch. 190, at p. 192).

Documents abstracted although before root of title.—Exceptions to the above general rule, apart from the purchaser's knowledge of pre-root defects, are contained in the proviso to s. 45 (1) of the L.P.A. 1925, and are as follows :—

" Provided that this sub-section shall not deprive a purchaser of the right to require the production, or any abstract or copy of—

    (i) *any power of attorney* under which any abstracted document is executed ; or

    (ii) *any document* creating or disposing of an interest, power or obligation which is not shown to have ceased or expired, and *subject to which* any part of *the property is disposed of* by an abstracted document ; or

    (iii) any document creating any limitation or trust by reference to which any part of the property is disposed of by an abstracted document."

" *any power of attorney.*"—A purchaser is therefore entitled to an abstract or copy of a power of attorney under which any abstracted instrument was executed, whatever the date thereof ; for instance, even if that instrument, being the root of title, was more than fifteen years old (*Re Copelin's Contract* [1937] 4 All E.R. 447). The L.P.A. 1925, s. 125 (2), as amended by the Law of Property (Amendment) Act, 1926, and the Powers of Attorney Act, 1971, s. 11 (3), provides that if there is a power of attorney affecting the title, and the purchaser will not on completion have the original handed to him, he can require, notwithstanding any condition to the contrary, that a copy thereof, or of the material portions thereof, be delivered to him free of expense, except in the case of land or a charge registered under the L.R.A. 1925–1971.

" *any document . . . subject to which . . . the property is disposed of.*"— Examples are as follows :—

    (i) A plan on a deed dated before the root of title by reference to which the property is later described. In this case a purchaser is entitled to a copy of the plan at the expense of the vendor, as the reference has the effect of incorporating in the deed containing the reference the description of the property contained in the deed referred to.

    (ii) Restrictive covenants contained in a deed dated before the date of the root of title, and still remaining effective.

    (iii) Interests and powers still affecting the property sold created before the date of the root of title, unless they will be overreached by the conveyance to the purchaser, as to which, see p. 172 *et seq.*

    (iv) A purchaser can require abstracts or copies of leases or agreements in writing with tenants, notwithstanding that they may have been made before the date of the root of title, provided that they remain effective. Although a purchaser is not entitled to an abstract or copy of expired leases (whether they expired before or after the date of the document forming the root of title), he is entitled to an abstract or copy of a *surrendered* lease, although the surrender was before the date of the root of title. The reason is that the purchaser is entitled to be satisfied that the surrender was effectual at law. If a new lease is, for any reason, invalid, the old lease may revive (*Knight* v. *Williams* [1901] 1 Ch. 256).

PART 3. ABSTRACTS OF TITLE

A. PREPARATION AND CONTENTS

Right of purchaser to an abstract.—In the absence of any condition of sale to the contrary, a purchaser of land is entitled at the vendor's expense to an abstract of title, delivery of the title deeds instead not being sufficient (*Horne* v. *Wingfield* (1841), 3 Man. & G. 33, and see below). This entitlement is expressly confirmed by General Condition 8 of the National Conditions of Sale, 18th ed., and by General Condition 7 of The Law Society's Conditions of Sale, 1973 Revision. An agreement to take a free conveyance is not a waiver of such right (*Re Pelly and Jacob's Contract* (1899), 80 L.T. 45). On a sale of property in lots, a purchaser of two or more lots, held wholly or partly under the same title, is entitled to one abstract only of the common title, except at his own expense (L.P.A. 1925, s. 45 (5)). There is no impropriety in the delivery of a carbon copy of an abstract if reasonably legible (*Law Society's Digest*, Opinion No. 88). Also it has been held that a vendor satisfied his obligations where he supplied not abstracts but full copies of certain documents since at the time it was difficult to obtain the services of skilled persons to abstract documents (*Bond* v. *Bassett* (1917), 87 L.J. Ch. 160, at p. 163).

It sometimes happens on small purchases that a vendor hands over the deeds and refuses to consult a solicitor. The following is the Opinion of the Council of The Law Society (*Law Society's Digest*, Opinion No. 93 as amended in Fourth (Cumulative) Supplement) as to the procedure which should be adopted :—

" The Committee expressed the opinion that in circumstances where a purchaser's solicitor was requested to accept title deeds in lieu of a proper abstract from a vendor who was not legally represented, it was the duty of that solicitor to insist on the delivery of a complete abstract and that if the vendor should fail to produce one, whether prepared by himself or by another solicitor, and had not requested the purchaser's solicitor to act on his behalf, the purchaser's solicitor should suggest to his client that he had three possible courses open to him, namely, (a) to persuade the vendor to consult a solicitor, or (b) to instruct him (the purchaser's solicitor) to prepare the abstract and pay him for the extra work occasioned ; (c) to register the contract as an estate contract and to take such proceedings as were necessary to compel the vendor to deduce his title."

The Council of The Law Society have also expressed the opinion that the abstract of title is to be delivered unconditionally, the vendor's solicitors being unable to require the purchaser's solicitor to hold it to their order pending completion (*Law Society's Digest*, Opinion No. 95 (b) in Fourth (Cumulative) Supplement).

In recent years the practice has arisen of supplying photographic (or other similarly produced) copies of documents of title in place of an abstract. The Council of The Law Society have now expressed the following opinion :—

1. Subject to due compliance with the requirements set out below, and to the exception specified in para. 5 hereof regarding copies made by photographic or sensitised paper process, an unregistered title may be deduced by supplying an epitome of the title accompanied by copies (which may be machine-made facsimile copies) of the documents shown in the epitome, as an alternative to an abstract of title in traditional form. The Council wish to emphasise however that care must always be taken

to ensure that the copy documents supplied are of satisfactory quality to meet the essential requirements of this method of deducing title. Copies of unsatisfactory quality will *not* satisfy these requirements.

2. The epitome should be typed, preferably on foolscap paper or the nearest convenient size, and be headed with the name or a short identification of the property. In preparing it the following points should be observed :—

(a) It should list all material documents events and matters which would normally be shown on an abstract in traditional form, stating the date and nature of each and with names of the parties to documents.

(b) It should show the evidence of title offered in respect of each document or event, i.e., whether by copy attached, or included in a traditional abstract or copy thereof attached, or as the case may be.

(c) Where part of the title deduced is in the form of a traditional abstract and part consists of copy documents, the epitome should set out in the appropriate sequence the details as above in respect of each document and event included in such abstract so as to show each link in the whole title.

(d) It is also helpful if each document and event is given a consecutive number in the epitome, and the relative copy document numbered to correspond. This numbering should be continued when additions are made on subsequent transactions.

(e) Against each copy document the epitome should show whether or not the original or a typed and examined copy of it will be handed over at completion. The recipient needs to know this from the outset so as to ascertain whether the provisions of para. 5 below apply.

(f) Where the epitome shows an event or a matter of record of which no copy document (such as a probate, death certificate or order of court) is offered as evidence, the relevant particulars should be set out on a separate sheet in the same way as in a traditional abstract, and be included with the copy documents supplied. Inclusion in the epitome is not sufficient by itself. The epitome is not the evidence of title, but only an index, and is unsuitable for marking as examined or checked.

3. Each copy document supplied with the epitome (including a copy from a traditional abstract) *must* comply with the following requirements :—

(a) It must show the text in black on non-glossy white paper so it can be easily read and suitably marked when examined against the original or checked by other evidence, and so that working notes can be made on it.

(b) It must be sufficiently durable and permanent to remain serviceable and clearly legible throughout the likely period of need as evidence of the title. It must be remembered that in the case of copies or extracts of documents creating continuing rights or burdens such as easements, covenants and other matters, and also plans, which are likely to be mentioned by reference in subsequent documents, this period may be far longer than the actual length of title normally deduced. Copies which are liable to fade or become seriously discoloured, or are made on paper too thin to withstand frequent handling, are quite unsuitable.

(c) The copying must be clear and " definite " so as to show all detail and be easily legible and also be suitable for further copies to be reproduced from it. Copies which are blurred or faint, or with excessive discolouration or "fogging" of the background, or made from a document which is itself unsuitable for such copying, should not be offered or accepted.

(d) A copy of a plan must show all details appearing on the original, including measurements, T-marks, etc., and must be coloured to correspond with the original. A copy on which the colouring of the original has come out black or so heavily darkened as to obliterate details, or render correct colouring impossible, should not be offered or accepted.

(e) If on account of size it is necessary to copy in sections and join them together by means of adhesive tape on the front of the sheet, they must be joined accurately with a transparent and matt-surface tape which will not discolour with age, so that no detail will become obscured and markings can be made over it.

(f) In addition to the text and plan (if any) each copy must show the stamping as on the original, and also all memoranda and other material indorsed on the original.

4. An epitome of the title as indicated above, with the requisite set of copy documents which are either typewritten or copied by an electro-static, gelatine-transfer or dual spectrum process, and comply with the requirements set out in para. 3 above, will be deemed a proper method of deducing title which the purchaser or other recipient may be required to accept in lieu of a traditional typed abstract.

5. In general, copy documents produced by a photographic or sensitised paper process cannot at present be regarded as satisfying the requirement of sufficient permanence, even if they satisfy the other requirements indicated above, and therefore cannot be deemed a proper method of deducing title, whether as a copy of a traditional abstract or as copy documents with an epitome. However, and as an exception to the general rule, if the originals of *all* the documents concerned, or typed and examined copies or extracts of the material parts thereof, will be handed over on completion of the transaction, then such copies will nevertheless be deemed to satisfy the requirements of deducing title for that transaction and a purchaser or other recipient may be required to accept them as such, provided that the copies comply with the other requirements as above.

6. The requirements laid down in paras. 3, 4 and 5 above for copy documents apply equally to a copy of an abstract in traditional form as a means of deducing title if produced by machine-copying from another abstract. It should not be regarded as a proper abstract unless it complies with such requirements including (in the case of a photographic or similar copy) that under para. 5 as to all the original documents, or typed and examined copies or extracts, being handed over."

(*Law Society's Digest*, Opinion No. 94 in Fourth (Cumulative) Supplement.)

Abstract when one solicitor acts for both parties.—It seems hardly necessary to point out that where the same solicitor acts for both a vendor and a purchaser, or both a mortgagor and a mortgagee, in the absence of any agreement to the contrary, it is the duty of the solicitor to prepare and put with the deeds a proper abstract of title, that is, such an abstract as, if the purchaser or mortgagee had been separately represented, he would have been entitled to (see *Law Society's Digest*, Opinion Nos. 78 and 238 ; as to the propriety of acting for more than one party, see, *ante*, p. 30).

Vendor must furnish abstract at his own expense.—The expense of obtaining the deeds and all other costs incurred for the purpose of preparing the abstract fall on the vendor (*Re Johnson and Tustin* (1885), 30 Ch. D. 42 ; *Re Ebsworth and Tidy* (1889), 42 Ch. D. 23 ; *Re Stamford, etc., Banking Co. and Knight's Contract* [1900] 1 Ch. 287). Section 45 (4) of the L.P.A. 1925, *post*, p. 141, presupposes that the vendor has furnished a proper abstract and its purpose is to limit the vendor's liability for the expenses of any verification of the abstract which the purchaser may consider necessary or advisable.

Contents of abstracts.—The general rule is that "every instrument must be abstracted, which is subsequent to the instrument forming the root of title, and has been executed or has taken effect during the period for which title is required to be shown, and has been dealt with or affected or may hereafter affect the estate contracted to be sold " (Williams, Vendor and Purchaser, 4th ed., vol. I, p. 48 ; see further, *op. cit.*, p. 127 *et seq.*).

Abstracting mortgages.—A legal mortgage should be abstracted, as the purchaser is entitled to know its contents and to satisfy himself that it has been duly discharged (*Heath* v. *Crealock* (1875), L.R. 10 Ch. 22). Nevertheless, in the case of a puisne mortgage, that is a legal mortgage of land which is not protected by deposit of the deeds, if it has been discharged and the entry protecting it removed from the land charges register before the date of the contract it will not be necessary to abstract the mortgage. The reason is that it will not affect a purchaser even if he has notice of it (L.P.A. 1925, ss. 97, 198, 199 ; L.C.A. 1972, s. 4 (5)). Notwithstanding that a second mortgage has been registered as a puisne mortgage or general equitable charge, a first mortgagee holding the deeds can, when exercising his power of sale, overreach it (L.C.A. 1972, s. 13 (2)) and pass the fee simple (L.P.A. 1925, s. 88 (1)). It will not, therefore, be necessary to abstract a second or subsequent mortgage on such a sale.

Where a vendor has given an equitable charge, for example to a bank, which is not registered because it is protected by deposit of the deeds relating to the legal estate, and it is intended to pay it off on completion of the purchase and hand the deeds (including the discharged charge) to the purchaser, it is the general practice not to abstract the equitable charge (although, strictly, it may be that a vendor should do so ; see *Drummond* v. *Tracy* (1860), John. 608, 612). But if the charge contained an agreement to execute a legal mortgage when called on, then such agreement might have been registered as an estate contract under L.C.A. 1972, s. 2 (4), Class C (iv), and if so, the charge should be abstracted. The Council of The Law Society have expressed the opinion that an equitable charge with a receipt endorsed, which was not disclosed in the abstract, should, nevertheless, be handed over to the purchaser on completion with the other documents of title (*Law Society's Digest*, Opinion No. 194).

If the purchaser will not get the charge and deeds because they relate also to other property, difficulties arise about which there has been considerable controversy (see, for instance, the *Conveyancer O.S.*, vol. 16, pp. 27, 41, 82 and 121, and the *Law Journal*, vol. 86, pp. 39, 76 and 88). Such equitable charges are usually made in favour of a bank and often come to light (if for no other reason) because the vendor is a company and registration has been effected in the Companies Register. Where many small portions of land are sold it is inconvenient to have to request the bank to execute a sealed release every time, and, in any case, banks often refuse to execute acknowledgments for the production of the deeds. The difficulty may be met by the manager of the local branch of the bank giving a letter acknowledging that as regards the particular property the bank has no claim, and that it holds the deeds relating to that particular property as agent for the owner. Such a letter would appear to be an effective discharge because a reconveyance or receipt under seal has never been necessary for the discharge of an equitable mortgage or charge, and the practice is so common that a bank could not deny the authority of a manager to give such a letter. It is doubtful, however, whether it renders valid an acknowledgment and undertaking as to the deeds given by the vendor, as such acknowledgment and undertaking must be given by the person retaining possession thereof (L.P.A. 1925, s. 64 (1)). It is thought that most solicitors accept the letter and acknowledgment by the vendor, and the late Mr. J. M. Lightwood expressed his agreement (*Law Journal*, vol. 86, p. 76) although a contrary opinion was stated by " E. H. B." in the same magazine (vol. 103, pp. 83, 84). Even if the bank will not give such a letter permission will usually be given to endorse on the deeds a memorandum of the sale. If this is done it is customary to treat the vendor's acknowledgment as sufficient.

Perhaps the practice can be justified on the ground that even if the acknowledgment is not effective under the L.P.A. 1925, s. 64 (1), the purchaser will have an *equitable* right to production and a subsequent purchaser must accept this as sufficient (L.P.A. 1925, s. 45 (7) ; see further, chapter on Custody of Deeds, *post*, p. 650). Also the practice avoids the alternative difficulty that if an effective acknowledgment were to be taken from the bank it would also bring notice of the equitable charge on to the legal title to be investigated unnecessarily by subsequent purchasers. See further a full discussion of the theoretical problems arising in the *Conveyancer N.S.*, vol. 26, p. 445 *et seq.*

When rent-charge should be abstracted.—A rent-charge in possession issuing out of or charged on land being either perpetual or for a term of years absolute is a legal interest (L.P.A. 1925, s. 1 (2) (*b*)), and must be abstracted. A rent-charge for any other estate, for instance, a rent-charge for life or in reversion, will be an equitable interest only, and will normally be created only in connection with settled land. See S.L.A. 1925, s. 1 (1) (v). If this is the case it can be overreached and need not be abstracted.

Apportionment of ground rent or rent-charge.—The Council of The Law Society have expressed the opinion (*Law Society's Gazette*, vol. 46, p. 131) that " Where a sale takes place of part only of (*a*) a leasehold interest in property under a long lease at a ground rent, or (*b*) a freehold interest in property which is subject to the payment of a perpetual rent-charge, the following conveyancing practice should be adopted if the ground rent or rent-charge is apportioned, so that subsequent purchasers either of the part originally sold or of the part retained may be aware of the terms of the express or implied covenants of indemnity—

(1) the vendor should retain a duplicate of the deed effecting the apportionment ; and

(2) on subsequent sales, either of the part of the property originally sold or of the part retained, the deed effecting the apportionment should be abstracted even if it be dated prior to the root of title."

The Council have also drawn attention to the necessity for making full inquiries regarding the collection of apportioned rents in all cases where property being purchased is subject to a ground rent or rent-charge. It is pointed out that hardship may result if a purchaser (for instance of a plot of land which was the last to be developed) is not made fully aware of a liability to collect apportioned parts of a ground rent or rent-charge from adjoining owners and to pay the whole to the freeholder or owner of the rent-charge (*Law Society's Gazette*, vol. 57, p. 399).

Certificates of search.—The Council of The Law Society have expressed the opinion that certificates of a land charge search are not documents of title, but that it is " a convenient practice for them to be included in abstracts of title " (*Law Society's Digest*, Opinion No. 90). This appears to imply that a vendor is not obliged to abstract them, but it is suggested that he should abstract all certificates of search from 1st January, 1926, which he has in his possession. The purchaser is also entitled to production of all such certificates free of expense to him (L.P.A. 1925, s. 45 (4) (*b*)).

There is no provision in the Acts making it necessary for anyone to search. Therefore, if in any case a search was not made, the purchaser cannot require the vendor to make one against previous owners (*Law Society's Digest*, Opinion No. 129). If the purchaser wants such a certificate he must make the search himself. The late author of this book was of the opinion that the solicitor should get his client's authority if he omits to make any searches, and that if he did not do so he might become personally liable. The property may, however, have changed hands many times since 1925 and the expense of making searches against all estate owners may be considerable, particularly if the land is in Yorkshire. In such circumstances, if the value of the property is small, it is believed that many solicitors are of the opinion that it is sufficient if they search in the names of the estate owners since the last transaction for value on which searches can reasonably be expected to have been made. Although earlier searches are frequently omitted in order to save expense to purchasers a solicitor doing so may expose himself to a claim for negligence (compare the observations of Danckwerts, J., in *Goody* v. *Baring* [1956] 1 W.L.R. 448, at p. 456) but the risk is undoubtedly slight and liability is by no means certain if the solicitor acted reasonably and in accordance with general practice. See further as to compensation for undisclosed land charges by virtue of the L.P.A. 1969, s. 25, *post*, p. 161.

Statements of facts on which title depends.—Where the vendor's title depends upon the existence of a fact or facts, it is sufficient to state such fact or facts. Proof thereof is " verification " within s. 45 (4) of the L.P.A. 1925, and must be paid for by the purchaser (*Re Wright and Thompson's Contract* [1920] 1 Ch. 191). For instance, where the vendor is selling as heir at law, it is sufficient to state in the abstract the fact of his being the heir at law. *Proof* of the heirship, if not in the vendor's possession, must be paid for by the purchaser (*Re Conlon and Faulkener's Contract* [1916] 1 Ir. R. 241). Descent to the heir is abolished when the death took place after 1925 (A.E.A. 1925, s. 45) ; but the heir can still take by gift as *persona designata*, and in a few other cases. See p. 328 *et seq*.

Documents to be abstracted in chief.—" All documents forming part of the title should be abstracted in *chief* ; the introduction of them merely as recitals in other abstracted instruments is clearly improper. The omission to abstract a document in chief might proceed from a desire to avoid noticing matters of a suspicious character occurring in such document, but which are not noticed in the recital " (Dart on Vendors and Purchasers, 6th ed., p. 335, quoted with approval by North, J., in *Re Stamford, etc., Banking Co. and Knight's Contract* [1900] 1 Ch. 287). The reason is that a recital of a conveyance or assignment in another document amounts merely to the opinion of the person who prepared the recital that the deed recited has such and such an effect. But a purchaser is entitled to be put in the position that he may judge for himself as to the effect of the deed. He is therefore entitled to have substantially abstracted the words of the deed itself, as only in this way can he so satisfy himself. There may be cases where the form of the deed may be important. Before 1926 there were many such cases. For instance, it was important to see that proper words of limitation were used and, in the case of a will, the exact words might be of vital importance. See *Re Ebsworth and Tidy's Contract* (1889), 42 Ch. D. 23.

It follows that the rule is that the wording of all the material parts of an abstracted document must be given in full, whilst the inclusion of immaterial parts, e.g., any common covenants or overreachable trusts, may be merely mentioned (*Burnaby* v. *Equitable Reversionary Interests Society* (1885), 28 Ch. D. 416). Equally endorsements on documents are often material, especially since 1925, and if so must be fully abstracted, e.g., of assents or of the appointment of new trustees (see *Re Miller and Pickersgill* [1931] 1 Ch. 511). The Council of The Law Society have expressed the opinion that coloured copies of plans on abstracted documents should always be attached to the abstract (but compare *Blackburn* v. *Smith* (1848), 25 Ex. 783, at p. 792).

Time for delivery of abstract.—Under an open contract the due date for delivery of an abstract of title by the vendor is within a reasonable time, except that apparently a purchaser may by giving a reasonable notice fix a date (*Compton* v. *Bagley* [1892] 1 Ch. 313). However, a time for delivery of the abstract is in practice generally specified by the conditions of sale (for instance, fourteen days by General Condition 8 (1) of the National Conditions of Sale, 18th ed.). Also, in practice, the abstract of title may be delivered with the vendor's part of the contract on exchange (this is now provided for by General Condition 7 (1) of The Law Society's Conditions of Sale, 1973 Revision). Further, the increasing practice of delivering a full abstract with the draft contract, which is consequently shorter, should be noted. This practice was deprecated for a number of cogent reasons in a letter in the *Law Society's Gazette*, vol. 59, p. 757, but would appear to lead safely to speedier conveyancing in a sufficient majority of cases.

Although, as a rule, time is not of the essence with regard to delivery of an abstract (*Roberts* v. *Berry* (1853), 3 De G.M. & G. 291), nonetheless, wilful non-delivery of the abstract by the day named in the conditions, or within a reasonable time, if no day is named, entitles the purchaser to refuse to carry out the contract (*Compton* v. *Bagley* [1892] 1 Ch. 313) ; but the acceptance of the abstract without objection after the day named in a condition for its delivery operates as a waiver of the condition (*Hipwell* v. *Knight* (1835), 4 L.J. Ex. 52).

If there is a condition that objections to title are to be taken within a certain time from delivery of an abstract, time will run only from delivery of a perfect abstract, i.e., an abstract as perfect as the vendor could furnish at the time of delivery (*Hobson* v. *Bell* (1839), 8 L.J. Ch. 241 ; *Morley* v. *Cook* (1842), 2 Hare 106, 111). However, not only is an abstract presumed to be perfect unless the contrary is shown by the purchaser (*Gray* v. *Fowler* (1873), L.R. 8 Ex. 249) but conditions of sale tend to provide that time should run from the *actual* delivery of an abstract whether or not perfect and whether or not itself delivered within the due time (see General Conditions 8 (2), (3) and (5) and 10 (1) and (3) respectively of the sets of conditions cited above).

Epitomes of abstracts in the Law of Property Act, 1925.—The epitomes (referred to in the L.P.A. 1925, s. 206 (2), as " examples ") are contained in the Sixth Schedule. They were printed in full, with explanations, in several editions of this book, including the 14th. It is thought that they have served their purpose (which was to indicate how abstracts should be framed in order that they might accord with the 1925 legislation) and consequently they have been omitted from the present edition.

B. DOCUMENTS WHICH NEED NOT BE ABSTRACTED

The L.P.A. 1925 imposes the following important limit on the general rule as to the contents of an abstract (see *ante*, p. 126) :—

" 10.—(1) Where title is shown to a legal estate in land, it shall be deemed not necessary or proper to include in the abstract of title an instrument relating only to interests or powers which will be overreached by the conveyance of the estate to which title is being shown ; but nothing in this Part of this Act affects the liability of any person to disclose an equitable interest or power which will not be so overreached, or to furnish an abstract of any instrument creating or affecting the same."

The interests or powers which can be overreached are considered in some detail *post*, p. 172 *et seq*.

Settled land.—The general rule is that a purchaser is not entitled to an abstract of or to any information concerning the trust instrument but is concerned solely with the vesting instruments which alone affect the legal estate. However, the precise extent of this general rule and the cases in which a purchaser may be concerned with the trust instruments are fully considered *post*, p. 689, which should be referred to. As to the effect of errors in vesting instruments, see *post*, p. 684.

Appointments of new trustees.—A purchaser of settled land is not concerned with the actual appointment or discharge of new trustees of the settlement, whether made by deed or by an order of court. He is only concerned with *the deed of declaration, and with the memorandum, and these two documents will be the only documents which will have to be abstracted.* See further as to such appointments, *post*, p. 719.

Where a trust for sale has been effected by two documents, it is sufficient to abstract the appointment of new trustees of the conveyance of the legal estate on trust for sale ; see further *post*, p. 793.

Wills.—The reason why wills of persons dying after 1925 need not normally be abstracted is that they operate only in equity. The *legal estate* vested in a testator at the date of his death passes, by virtue of ss. 1 and 3 of the A.E.A. 1925, to his personal representatives notwithstanding any specific devise or bequest of freehold or leasehold property contained in his will. The document to be abstracted is, therefore, if death took place after 1925, the probate and not the will, and in the case of an intestacy, the letters of administration. The probate or letters of administration are each conveyancing evidence of the death of the testator or intestate, the appointment of the executors or administrators and of the legal estate having vested in them.

As a guide to what should be abstracted, see Specimen No. 2 of Abstracts given in Sched. 6 to the L.P.A. 1925. Unless essential it is wiser *not* to mention the contents of the will, as to do so may lead the purchaser to compare the terms of the will with the abstract when he examines the probate. The less the purchaser knows of the contents of the will the better (*Re Duce and Boots' Cash Chemists* [1937] Ch. 642 ; discussed *post*, p. 417).

In the case of a sale by trustees for sale, all that should be abstracted would be the probate, the assent by the executors to the devise to the trustees and any memorandum of the assent endorsed on the probate. Nevertheless, where the assent is expressed to be *on the trusts of the will* the will must be abstracted so far as necessary to indicate those trusts. In practice, they will usually include an immediate binding trust for sale and so no interests arising under the trust for sale need be mentioned (*post*, p. 176). In this instance in abstracting the will one is merely abstracting a document which (by reason of the reference in the assent) forms part of the assent.

See further *post*, p. 179.

Discharged mortgages.—It is sometimes contended that, after a *legal* mortgage has been paid off and a reconveyance executed, the mortgage and reconveyance need not be abstracted, on the ground that the title has by the reconveyance been brought back to its original state. This view cannot be supported, and they should be abstracted. See further, *ante*, p. 126, as to puisne mortgages and equitable charges.

Disentailing deeds.—A disentailing assurance executed after 1925 has not to be abstracted because it only affects the equitable interest.

C. REGISTERED TITLES

It is fundamental that abstracts of title of the sort required in *un*registered conveyancing, i.e., showing the history of the title, should have no place where title to the land is registered under the L.R.A. 1925-1971. Indeed s. 110 (3) of that Act provides that " notwithstanding any stipulation to the contrary, it shall not be necessary for the vendor to furnish the purchaser with any abstract or other written evidence of title, or any copy or abstract of the land certificate, or of any charge certificate."

Vendor's obligations.—Instead s. 110 (1) of the Act makes the positive provision that, again " notwithstanding any stipulation to the contrary," on a sale or other disposition of registered land, the vendor is obliged to furnish the purchaser with the following documents :—

First, "*with an authority to inspect the register.*" Without such an authority the register cannot be inspected, and the authority also confers the right to take pencil copies, to obtain office copies and to make official searches (L.R.A. 1925, s. 112; L.R.R. 1925, rr. 287–297 and Schedule, Form 80; also L.R. (Official Searches) R. 1969; and see *post*, p. 138). The authority to inspect usually takes the form of a letter from the vendor's solicitor addressed to the registrar quoting the title number and authorising inspection by the purchaser or his solicitor (Ruoff, Land Registration Forms, 2nd ed., Precedent No. 18, at p. 62). This does not enable the purchaser to give a similar authority to a prospective mortgagee or his solicitor (Ruoff and Roper, Registered Conveyancing, 3rd ed., pp. 343, 707). Consequently it is a convenient practice for the vendor to give an authority both to the purchaser and to any mortgagee who may advance money to the purchaser in connection with the particular purchase.

Secondly, " *with a copy of the subsisting entries on the register and of any filed plans and copies or abstracts of any documents or any part thereof noted on the register.*" These need only be furnished " if required " (s. 110 (1)), but the insertion of a condition into the contract not to require them would appear to be ineffective. This obligation on the vendor does not extend to filed settlements (s. 110 (1), proviso (*b*)); nor does it extend to anything not affecting the land to be dealt with (s. 110 (1); for example, on a sale of part of the land in a title, matters affecting the remainder of the land); nor does it extend to charges or incumbrances which will be discharged or overridden on completion (s. 110 (1)). Filed abstracts or copies referred to by the register are, as between vendor and purchaser, to be assumed to be correct and to contain all material portions of the original without production of the original (s. 110 (4)). All expenses are to be borne by the vendor unless the purchase price does not exceed £1,000 when, in the absence of any stipulation to the contrary, the expenses are to be borne by the purchaser requiring the copies, etc. (s. 110 (1), proviso (*a*)). In practice, whatever the strict position, office copies of anything relevant are almost always supplied by the vendor at his own expense (the fees are negligible) on exchange of contracts as a matter of course and this practice has been recommended strongly as standard procedure by the Council of The Law Society (see *Law Society's Gazette*, vol. 70, p. 1281). The Council Note adds (*ibid.*) (1) that a mere photo-copy of the land and charge certificate will not suffice as it may be incomplete and carries no protection (cp. L.R.A. 1925, s. 113); and (2) that the whole of the pre-registration register should be withheld until after exchange of contracts where the previous price is not to be revealed (i.e., rather than cutting it out).

Exceptions.—The above two obligations on a vendor are expressed not to apply where the sale or disposition of the registered land is to " a lessee or chargee " (L.R.A. 1925, s. 110; compare L.P.A. 1925, s. 44 (2), *post*, p. 143). It is also provided that, " subject to any stipulation to the contrary," title to anything as to which the register is not conclusive or which is excepted from the effect of registration must be deduced by the vendor at his own expense as in unregistered conveyancing (s. 110 (2)). This provision applies primarily to the pre-registration position of a " possessory " title, to " overriding interests," and to incumbrances entered on the register as subsisting on first registration (L.R.R. 1925, r. 160).

Also, if the vendor is not the registered proprietor but is selling on the basis of his entitlement to be registered (i.e., under L.R.A. 1925, s. 37, and L.R.R. 1925, rr. 72, 81 and 170), then the purchaser should, of course, ascertain that the vendor is in fact entitled to be registered. Usually, this means either that there is a subsale, when he will inspect the contract of sale and transfer to his vendor, or else that the sale is by a personal representative, when he will inspect the grant to his vendor as the personal representative of a deceased registered proprietor. Such an inspection is probably sufficient in practice for a purchaser to accept a transfer from his vendor without more (Ruoff and Roper, Registered Conveyancing, 3rd ed., at pp. 340–341). Nonetheless, it should be noted that a purchaser would be within his rights in insisting on the vendor procuring either his own registration as proprietor before the transfer or else a disposition directly from the registered proprietor (s. 110 (5) ; this also applies " notwithstanding any stipulation to the contrary "). However, it has been held that where an easement over unregistered land is appurtenant to registered land, there is no obligation on a vendor of the registered land to procure registration of himself as proprietor of the easement before completion ; s. 110 (5) does not apply (*Re Evans' Contract* [1970] 1 W.L.R. 583).

As to verification and searches in respect of registered titles, see *post*, pp. 138 and 625 respectively.

PART 4. REQUISITIONS ON TITLE

Conditions enabling vendor to rescind on making of requisitions, see p. 221.

Nature of requisitions.—As the name itself indicates, requisitions on title are questions concerning the *title* to the land. It is stated, however, in Williams on Vendor and Purchaser, 4th ed., vol. I, at p. 212 : " Besides the requisitions, properly so called, asking for the production of some particular piece of evidence to complete the title, it is generally desirable for the purchaser's advisers to make certain inquiries of the vendor respecting the property sold." An instance taken is that if the property is sold subject to all easements, tenancies, etc., an inquiry should be made whether any such exist. It is interesting to note that in this most authoritative work such inquiries are not described as requisitions but as " Inquiries supplemental to Requisitions on title." See *ibid.*, vol. II, p. 1262, and further below.

Many matters which were formerly raised as requisitions on title are now dealt with by means of inquiries before contract. Nevertheless, " it is still the duty of a purchaser's solicitor to make the appropriate requisitions and inquiries after the formal contract is signed, even if the preliminary inquiries have been so complete that it is only necessary to ask whether the answers thus received are still complete and accurate " (Danckwerts, J., in *Goody* v. *Baring* [1956] 1 W.L.R. 448, at p. 456).

A vendor, to the best of his information, is bound to answer all specific questions put to him in respect of the property which he has contracted to sell, or the title thereto, unless his *prima facie* liability in this respect is expressly negatived by the conditions. *Re Ford and Hill* (1879), 10 Ch. D. 365, decides nothing more than that a vendor need not reply to a requisition made for the purpose of negativing the existence of incumbrances. It was stated in Dart on Vendors and Purchasers, 8th ed., 1929, at p. 1010, that the decision merely negatives the right of a purchaser to make inquiries from the vendor with regard to matters the suppression of which by the vendor's solicitor would constitute a misdemeanour ; it has no application to matters which affect the property but which it is not customary to notice in the abstract, such as easements not created by express grant, paving charges, notices to remove dangerous structures and the like. Sir Benjamin Cherry, in his " Lectures," 1926, at p. 121, said " *Re Ford and Hill* only applies to protect the vendor's solicitors from insinuations that they have improperly

omitted to abstract something material which is known to them ; also that
if the vendor's solicitors object to answer the requisition personally, they
should be required to ask their client to answer the requisition." See also
Wilkes v. *Spooner* [1911] 2 K.B. 473, 486 ; *Re Chafer and Randall's Contract*
[1916] 2 Ch. 8, 15.   For a narrower view of the proper scope of requisitions,
see *Solicitors' Journal*, vol. 111, pp. 591, 592.

It is as well to remember, when requisitions are being drafted, the warning
contained in Williams on Vendor and Purchaser, 4th ed., vol. I, p. 222,
that " the conveyancer should, as a rule, be guided, in making requisitions on
title, by the countenance he would expect his contention to receive from the
court in proceedings either to enforce specific performance or to recover the
deposit.   He should, therefore, make no frivolous or unnecessary requisitions
and he should be chary of asking for anything which he considers the other
party not bound to concede."   Thus, for example, questions should not be
asked about matters apparent on inspection of the property ; the purchaser
should inspect it for himself.   Many questions are, therefore, better put to
the vendor as inquiries *before* contract ; if the vendor does not answer them
the purchaser can then decide whether to enter into the contract, see *ante*,
p. 9.   Some such inquiries may properly be repeated by way of requisitions
in order to ensure that if there is any concealment or falsification, the purchaser
will have the benefit of the L.P.A. 1925, s. 183 ; and see *Goody* v. *Baring*,
ante.   On the other hand, it is usually wrong to repeat all such inquiries ;
the vendor would often be entitled to give the common form answer " if
any (such rights) exist the purchaser takes subject thereto."

Where questions are properly asked affecting the land the vendor's solicitor
should not give the reply one often sees, namely (there are none such) " *so
far as I am aware*."   He should answer to the vendor's knowledge, not the
solicitor's, and a reply such as that quoted should not be accepted.   Where
necessary the vendor's solicitor should confirm the accuracy of his answer
with his client before replying to the requisitions.   Indeed the view is expressed
in the *Solicitors' Journal*, vol. 104, p. 4, that a reply which refers only to the
vendor's solicitor's knowledge should not be accepted " unless the question
is one which, it is reasonable to expect, is outside the personal knowledge of
the vendor."   It is there argued, by analogy with *Goody* v. *Baring* [1956]
1 W.L.R. 448, that a purchaser's solicitor who accepts such an answer (other
than in the circumstances mentioned) with the result that his client suffers
loss, will be liable for negligence.

Various matters on which requisitions are usual.—When the answer
to the usual requisition : " Are there any tenancy agreements in writing ? "
is " Yes," the purchaser should inspect them to see that they are stamped
and to see that they contain no unusual agreement.   The purchaser is entitled
to have tenancy agreements stamped at the vendor's expense (*Smith* v. *Wyley*
(1852), 16 Jur. 1136 ; *Coleman* v. *Coleman* (1898), 79 L.T. 66).

Should a land charge search show that there is a charge in respect of estate
duty, the purchaser is entitled to require the vendor to supply him with a
certificate under s. 11 of the F.A. 1894, of the discharge thereof (*Re Conlon
and Faulkener's Contract* [1916] 1 Ir. R. 241).

Where an objection to the title is purely theoretical and of no practical
importance and the vendor offers to give an indemnity, the objection of the
purchaser must be considered to be sufficiently answered (*Re Heaysman's and
Tweedy's Contract* (1893), 69 L.T. 89).   See also *Manning* v. *Turner* [1957]
1 W.L.R. 91, where specific performance would have been decreed against

the purchaser despite an encumbrance (a potential estate duty charge) had the vendor effected " an indemnity policy issued by a reputable insurance company insuring against the risk involved."

The matters as to which requisitions should be raised vary so much that a comprehensive list cannot be drawn. Many solicitors use printed forms of standard requisitions to which appropriate additions can be made. This system has the advantages of saving time and of preventing the purchaser's solicitor from overlooking a requisition which has to be made in most cases. However, it also has the serious disadvantage of causing many requisitions to be made which are in no way appropriate to the property being sold in the particular transaction. The result is, very often, that requisitions and the answers thereto are regarded by the solicitors for both purchaser and vendor as formalities and the replies of the vendor's solicitor would frequently be better described as " evasions " than as " answers." If printed forms are used they should be amended to meet the circumstances of the transaction.

Registered titles.—Notwithstanding that titles to land registered under the L.R.A. 1925 may be free from technical defects, requisitions will still have to be raised wherever the title shown on the register does not accord with that provided for, expressly or impliedly, by the contract for sale ; for example, where the vendor is registered with only a possessory and not an absolute title (*Re Brine and Davies' Contract* [1935] Ch. 388), or where the charges register refers to a restrictive covenant not mentioned in the contract (*Re Stone and Saville's Contract* [1963] 1 W.L.R. 163 ; see useful summary by F. R. Crane in the *Conveyancer N.S.*, vol. 2, pp. 49–50 ; compare Ruoff and Roper, Registered Conveyancing, 3rd ed., at pp. 345–346).

In addition, requisitions should, of course, be raised in respect of any matters as to which the register of title is not conclusive. This applies particularly to overriding interests (see further *post*, p. 184).

Time for making requisitions.—The day of delivery of the abstract is excluded from the time given for sending in requisitions (*Blackburn* v. *Smith* (1848), 2 Ex. 783). If the vendor does not deliver his abstract (that is, an abstract as perfect as he can furnish at the time of delivery) within the time mentioned in the contract, after the purchaser has requested him to do so, the purchaser can refuse to carry out his contract, or, if he wishes to proceed, he need not deliver his requisitions within the limited time, even though it is stipulated in the conditions that time in that respect shall be of the essence of the contract (*Upperton* v. *Nickolson* (1871), L.R. 6 Ch. 436). An abstract may be as perfect as the vendor can at the time of delivery make it, even though it shows a defective title, but not if it shows that the vendor has no title at all (*Want* v. *Stallibrass* (1873), L.R. 8 Ex. 175).

A condition limiting the time for sending in requisitions on the title only applies to matters disclosed by the abstract (*Re Cox and Neve's Contract* [1891] 2 Ch. 109 ; *Re Ossemsley Estates, Ltd.* [1937] 3 All E.R. 774).

General Condition 10 of The Law Society's Conditions of Sale, 1973 Revision, allows fourteen days only from the delivery of the abstract for the requisitions, time being of the essence of the condition. Any not sent within that time *and not going to the root of title* are deemed waived. Condition 8 of the National Conditions of Sale, 18th ed., provides that the purchaser shall have fourteen days from the delivery of the abstract in which to deliver his requisitions and in this respect time is of the essence of the contract *notwithstanding that the abstract may not have been delivered within due time.*

If the requisition goes to the root of the title, that is, the power of the vendor to sell or to give to the purchaser what it is intended by the contract he shall have, a condition limiting the time will not preclude the purchaser from making it after the time has expired (*Warde* v. *Dixon* (1858), 28 L.J. Ch. 315; *Re Tanqueray-Willaume and Landau* (1882), 20 Ch. D. 465; *Saxby* v. *Thomas* (1891), 64 L.T. 65). For instance, a purchaser can make a requisition in respect of a restrictive covenant, although he has allowed the time to pass (*Re Cox and Neve's Contract, ante*); or in respect of a right of way (*Simpson* v. *Gilley* (1922), 128 L.T. 622). But if a purchaser should find, after the time had gone by for making requisitions, that a deed was wrongly stamped, it is thought that the purchaser could not insist on the vendor stamping the deed, notwithstanding s. 117 of the Stamp Act, 1891.

So, if the objection is one of " conveyance," as distinguished from one of " title," the purchaser need not make it within the time limited for sending in requisitions (*Re Scott and Eave's Contract* (1902), 86 L.T. 617). In fact, whenever there is a matter of conveyancing and not a matter of title, it is the duty of the vendor to do everything that he is enabled to do by force of his own interest and also by force of the interest of others whom he can compel to concur in the conveyance, without it being necessary for the purchaser to make a requisition at all (*Bain* v. *Fothergill* (1874), L.R. 7 H.L. 158). At the same time, as a matter of practice, it is always better to mention the matter in the requisitions; for instance, the payment off of a mortgage on the property (*Re Daniel; Daniel* v. *Vassall* [1917] 2 Ch. 405), or the obtaining of the consent of a lessor to an assignment of leaseholds where it is necessary (*Day* v. *Singleton* [1899] 2 Ch. 320). It is arguable that General Condition 10 of The Law Society's Conditions of Sale, 1973 Revision, is expressed so widely that requisitions as to matters of conveyance would in fact also have to be raised within the fourteen days' period (see Walford, Sale of Land, 2nd ed., at p. 49), but this view is not acted on in practice.

In addition, requisitions may be raised out of time as to any matter affecting the title and *not* discoverable from the face of the abstract (*Warde* v. *Dixon* (1858), 28 L.J. Ch. 315). This would apply, for example, where incumbrances (e.g., restrictive covenants) are discovered as a result of the purchaser's own searches and inquiries elsewhere (*Re Haedicke and Lipski's Contract* [1901] 2 Ch. 666, at p. 669).

If requisitions are improperly raised out of time, it is inadvisable for a solicitor simply to reply to them as a matter of courtesy since this might amount to a waiver of the vendor's right to insist on the time-limits (see *Cutts* v. *Thodey* (1842), 6 Jur. 1027; *Lane* v. *Debenham* (1853), 11 Hare 188). To avoid any liability the client's authority should be sought before replying although it might be sufficient to state in replying that the time-limits are not to be taken as waived.

Times for replies and observations.—The usual sets of conditions of sale do not specify any particular time within which a vendor must reply to his purchaser's requisitions. However, where a vendor has failed to reply to a requisition within a reasonable time, the purchaser wishing to insist upon a reply should serve a notice on the vendor fixing a time within which the vendor is to reply and which is to be of the essence (see *per* Upjohn, L.J., in *Re Stone and Saville's Contract* [1963] 1 W.L.R. 163, at p. 171). Service of such a notice will not be necessary where the vendor has acted so that the only reasonable inference is that he is not going to reply, for instance, by serving a notice to complete whilst there are outstanding requisitions (*ibid.*).

It is usually provided in practice that the purchaser's observations on the vendor's replies to requisitions must be made within seven days, time being of the essence (General Condition 10 (4) and (5) of The Law Society's Conditions of Sale, 1973 Revision, and General Condition 8 (2) and (3) of the National Conditions of Sale, 18th ed.). Otherwise the implication appears to be that the purchaser has the same time for his observations as for his original requisitions. Also if the vendor's reply to an original requisition has had to take the form of a supplementary abstract of title, then further requisitions on the abstract are regarded as original requisitions for which the purchaser has the appropriate time (*Re Ossemsley* [1937] 3 All E.R. 774).

PART 5. VERIFICATION AND ACCEPTANCE

A. VERIFICATION OF ABSTRACT

In addition to delivering an abstract of title, a vendor of land is bound to verify it by producing evidence to support it. In other words having shown a good title on the face of the abstract by way of statement, the vendor must go on to show a good title in the full sense by proving that the statements are true (see *per* Cottenham, L.C., in *Southby* v. *Hutt* (1837), 2 My. & Cr. 207, at pp. 212 and 213).

Production of documents.—First, therefore, to verify the abstract the vendor must produce the abstracted documents. As to this the Council of The Law Society has reminded solicitors of the importance of the examination of an abstract against the deeds, stating that " the practice of examining the deeds and marking the abstract, whether the vendor and purchaser are separately represented or represented by the same solicitor, is one which should always be carried out, however small the purchase money may be. It should be done before the time for requisitions expires so that any queries may be raised ; if a solicitor omits to do so, or is out of time, he may well be guilty of negligence and must accept full responsibility for any adverse consequences " (*Law Society's Digest*, Opinion No. 95 (*a*) in Fourth (Cumulative) Supplement ; cf. Opinion No. 89). However, some doubt may be expressed as to whether it is necessary to mark the abstract if the deeds will be handed over on completion, and many solicitors do not. Also the far from uncommon practice is to leave inspection of the deeds until the time of completion itself. This practice is clearly inconvenient in the occasional cases where an objection is found in that delay in completion is almost unavoidably caused. But, despite the Council's view above, it is not thought that the practice would result in queries being precluded (see *Pagebar Properties, Ltd.* v. *Derby Investment Holdings, Ltd.* [1972] 1 W.L.R. 1500, where inspection of the documents of title on the last day allowed by a vendor's notice to complete revealed a misstatement in the contract and Goulding, J., held that the purchaser was entitled to a reasonable opportunity to consider the newly disclosed matter and thereafter obtain specific performance). The established rule is that, notwithstanding conditions as to the time for requisitions, a purchaser may always object to any defect in title not discoverable from the face of the abstract of title itself (*Warde* v. *Dixon* (1858), 28 L.J. Ch. 315) ; defects only discoverable on inspection of the deeds would appear to come within the rule (see *Southby* v. *Hutt* (1837), 2 My. & Cr. 207). This sort of difficulty can be avoided, of course, and much time and trouble saved, if photographic copies of the deeds are supplied instead of a traditional abstract (see further as to this *ante*, p. 123).

Production of the original is, of course, accepted in practice as sufficient proof of an abstracted document (or production of the counterpart on a sale subject to a lease : *Magdalen Hospital* v. *Knotts* (1878), 8 Ch. D. 709, affirmed (1879), 4 App. Cas. 324). Due execution of the document, which strictly should also be proved, is almost always presumed (*Law Society's Digest*, Opinion No. 125) but should not be if there is some circumstance casting doubt on the document (*Hobson* v. *Bell* (1839), 2 Beav. 17). In particular the purchaser should ascertain that the documents are produced from proper custody, which appears to be any place where the documents might reasonably be expected to be found (see *per* Parke, B., in *Croughton* v. *Blake* (1843), 12 M. & W. 205, at p. 208 ; also Tindal, C.J., in *Meath* v. *Winchester* (1736), 4 Cl. & Fin. 445, at p. 450).

Where the vendor is unable to produce any of the documents because they have been destroyed or lost, he is permitted instead to produce secondary evidence of the contents of the documents (*Re Halifax Commercial Banking Co. and Wood* (1898), 79 L.T. 336 ; *Halkett* v. *Dudley* [1907] 1 Ch. 590). Here, however, the due execution of the missing documents has to be proved, not presumed (*Bryant* v. *Buck* (1827), 4 Russ. 1). Again, the loss of the documents must be proved (*Re Duthy and Jesson* [1898] 1 Ch. 419), although a statutory declaration as to this will usually suffice (*Hart* v. *Hart* (1841), 1 Hare 1). Due stamping of such missing documents will be presumed (*ibid.*).

Events.—As to events stated in the abstract of title, the position is stated in Williams on Vendor and Purchaser, 4th ed., vol. I, p. 170, as follows : " In the matters of pedigree, to prove the facts of birth, marriage and death, the purchaser is in the first instance entitled to require certificates of baptism or birth, of marriage and of burial [it is usual to accept a grant of probate or administration or a death certificate as evidence] but if these cannot be found the vendor may not only have recourse to other evidence admissible in litigation, as statements of deceased members of the family or entries in a family bible or register, but in default of such testimony he may proffer statutory declarations of living members of the family, or even of strangers."

Registered titles.—It has already been seen that in registered conveyancing the vendor delivers not a traditional abstract of title, but instead an authority to inspect the register together with copies of the entries in the register and of certain documents, etc., noted thereon (L.R.A. 1925, s. 110, *ante*, p. 131). The place of the title deeds is taken by the register and the verification of title could take the form of the purchaser (or his solicitor) personally examining the copies, etc., delivered to him against the register. The much more common practice, however, is for the purchaser to be satisfied with seeing the vendor's land certificate (or a charge certificate) or else an office copy of the register (each of which constitute admissible evidence of the entries in the register, etc. : L.R.A. 1925, ss. 78 and 113) and with making an official search as to entries on the register since the last date noted as being when the land certificate was last officially made to correspond with the register or since the date of the office copy (see further, *post*, p. 625). This practice is supported by the following statement supplied by the Chief Land Registrar at the request of the Council of The Law Society and published in the *Law Society's Gazette*, vol. 56, at p. 395 : " The advantages of obtaining a certificate of the result of an official search of the register of title are that it gives the applicant up-to-date information as to the entries on the register ; it gives fifteen working days' priority for the application (transfer, lease or charge) in respect of which the search is made ; if there is a mistake in the certificate of the result of the search, indemnity is payable for any resulting loss ; it is applied for by post and attendance at the registry is not necessary ; no fee is payable ; and the great majority of the certificates of the results of searches are issued within two days of the receipt of the applications for them.

" Personal searches of the register are subject to the following disadvantages. They can only be made by attendance at H.M. Land Registry . . . ; the register which it desired to inspect may not be available immediately as it may have to be obtained from another office of the Registry outside London ; a personal search confers no priority for the transaction in respect of which it is made ; if an entry on the register or the existence of a pending application is overlooked, no indemnity is payable out of the Land Registry insurance fund and the solicitor concerned is solely liable for any loss his client may suffer ; the fee for a personal search is one shilling but to that must be added the costs of travelling to the Registry and a proportion of the salary of the person making the search." However, a case in which a personal search would have proved preferable to the official search made was *Parkash* v. *Irani Finance Co., Ltd.* [1970] Ch. 101 (where an official search had failed to disclose a caution which was nevertheless effective against the purchaser who, presumably, had to rely instead on indemnity).

Re-sales and sub-sales.—It may happen that a purchaser of registered land may contract to sell (or let) part or all of the land to a third party before the Land Registry has had time to complete the registration of his purchase. In the case of such a re-sale or sub-sale (or letting) it will obviously not be possible to verify title by production of a land (or charge) certificate or office copy showing the purchaser as registered proprietor of the land. In such a case, however, the sub-purchaser (or lessee) may verify the purchaser's title by taking the following steps (Registered Land Practice Notes 1972, pp. 33 and 8, No. 17 and No. 38). First, he should obtain from the purchaser an office copy (*not* an ordinary copy) of the original vendor's register (the purchaser should already possess this or be authorised to apply for it). Secondly, the sub-purchaser (or lessee) should at once apply for an official search based on this office copy (as to searches, see further *post*, p. 625). The certificate of the result of this search will not only certify the state of the register so far as it exists, but will also reveal the presence in the Registry of the transfer to the purchaser and state whether it is in order and whether or not it contains restrictive covenants or easements affecting the land in question. Thirdly, possessing this information, the sub-purchaser (or lessee) should ascertain the precise terms of the transfer to the purchaser. And finally, a second official search will be necessary before completion to secure the usual priority (see *post*, p. 625).

Developing building estates.—Where the procedure set out *post*, pp. 648–649, has been adopted by a developing vendor (involving principally official approval of the estate layout plan by the Land Registry) the method of verification is as follows (see Registered Land Practice Leaflet No. 7 and Registered Land Practice Notes, 1972, p. 14, No. 51).

In the first place, office copies of the entries in the register should be obtained by application on Form A44 either by the vendor for delivery to the purchaser or by the purchaser himself with the vendor's authority. Then to establish that the plot with which the purchaser is concerned is comprised in the vendor's title, application should be made on Form 101 for a certificate of official inspection of the filed plan (see L.R. (Official Searches) Rules, 1969, r. 12 (1)). This form of application requires a description of the property being purchased primarily by reference to its plot number on the approved estate plan (although names of roads, plan numbers and floor levels should be indicated where appropriate). The resulting certificate will state whether the plot is within the title and whether it is affected by any colour or other reference shown on the filed plan (see L.R. (Official Searches) Rules, 1969, r. 12 (2) and Form 102). Whilst this certificate confers no priority, any errors should lead to indemnity (i.e., within L.R.A. 1925, s. 83 (3)). However, it is emphasised that the certificate does not take the place of an office copy of the entries on the register, which must still be obtained and perused.

Since this certificate takes the place of a copy of the filed plan, strictly the purchaser could require the vendor to make the application and pay the fee for each plot in order to supply it as he is obliged to under L.R.A. 1925, s. 110 (1) (see *ante*, p. 131). But it would be better conveyancing practice for the purchaser to make this application, regarding it as resulting in an official search.

However, since the certificate does not indicate the full extent of the land in the vendor's title, it is also necessary for the purchaser's solicitor to be satisfied that the vendor has power to grant the easements provided for in the contract (for example, rights of way over roads and passageways, rights of drainage and rights of using water, gas and electricity supplies and other utilities). Assuming a draft of the standard form of transfer proposed was submitted for approval as recommended (see *post*, pp. 648–649), in the Land Registry's letter signifying approval an assurance will be given (if practicable) that any easements granted in the standard form will be registered as appurtenant. " If the vendor supplies each purchaser with a copy of the Registry's letter a purchaser who relies upon this assurance is thereby relieved of the duty of investigating in detail the vendor's power to grant the easements that he purports to grant " (Registered Land Practice Notes, 1972, p. 9, No. 39).

If no such assurance has been given as to easements, then if the grant is sufficiently specific (e.g., of a right of way over a particular road) it may be possible for the Land Registry to confirm in a Form 102 certificate that the land affected is also within the vendor's title (*ibid.*). Failing this, however, it is considered that the only proper expedient is to require the vendor to supply a copy of the filed plan on the register of his title ; the Forms 101 and 102 procedure is merely an optional alternative to the otherwise obligatory provisions of s. 110 (1) of the L.R.A. 1925 (*ante*, p. 131), and should not be adopted in case of any doubt to the possible prejudice of a purchaser.

In addition to the above, the usual search as to adverse entries and for priority will have to be made before completion (see *post*, p. 625). " When the estate layout plan has been officially approved, the application for an official search in form 94B should describe the land searched by reference to the plot number on the estate plan so saving the cost and trouble of having to provide separate plans." (Ruoff and Roper, Registered Conveyancing, 3rd ed., p. 364.)

Expense of verifying abstract.—At common law the vendor was bound, at his own expense, to produce all abstracted deeds for examination by or on behalf of the purchaser and to adduce proper evidence of all facts material to the title (Williams on Vendor and Purchaser, 4th ed., vol. I, p. 157). This rule continues to apply to documents and evidence in the possession of the vendor, his mortgagee or trustee. Otherwise, s. 45 (4) of the L.P.A. 1925 provides :—

" 45.—(4) On a sale of any property, the following expenses shall be borne by the purchaser where he requires them to be incurred for the purpose of verifying the abstract *or any other purpose*, that is to say—

(a) the expenses of the production and inspection of all Acts of Parliament, inclosure awards, records, proceedings of courts, court rolls, deeds, wills, probates, letters of administration, and other documents, not in the possession of the vendor or his mortgagee or trustee, and the expenses of all journeys incidental to such production or inspection ; and

(b) the expenses of searching for, procuring, making, verifying and producing all certificates, declarations, evidences, and information not in the possession of the vendor or his mortgagee or trustee, and all attested, stamped, office, or other copies or abstracts of, or extracts from, any Acts of Parliament or other documents aforesaid, not in the possession of the vendor or his mortgagee or trustee ;

and where the vendor or his mortgagee or trustee retains possession of any document, the expenses of making any copy thereof, attested or unattested, which a purchaser requires to be delivered to him, shall be borne by that purchaser."

" or any other purpose."—For example, where a change of name and address causes doubt as to the identity of a vendor the expense of obtaining a statutory declaration in proof falls on the purchaser (Law Society Council Opinion No. 940 (a) ; *Law Society's Digest*, Fourth Supplement).

Where the deeds are in London, a country solicitor should employ his London agents to examine the deeds, as the cost of sending a clerk to London would not be allowed on taxation as against the client, although undertaken at the request of the client, unless it had been first expressly explained to him what the usual and proper practice is (*Alsop* v. *Lord Oxford* (1833), 1 Myl. & K. 564). This only applies where the deeds are in London, and not where the deeds are in a country town (*Hughes* v. *Wynne* (1836), 8 Sim. 85).

If it is inconvenient for the purchaser's solicitor to make a journey it is customary to instruct a solicitor practising near the vendor's solicitor to examine the deeds and mark the abstract and later to complete as agent for the purchaser's solicitor. The Council of The Law Society have commented as follows on the practice of asking the *vendor's* solicitor to examine the deeds and mark the abstract : " The Council, while not suggesting that the practice is improper, does not consider it desirable or necessary except in special circumstances where the normal procedure of instructing an independent solicitor agent is impracticable. Where, nevertheless, the vendor's solicitor is instructed to act as agent, the Council recommends that he should be specifically asked and agree to act as agent and should be paid an appropriate fee for so doing ; he should moreover exercise as high a degree of care in the matter as he would have exercised had the abstract been entirely new to him " (*Law Society's Gazette*, vol. 54, p. 389).

As to expenses in connection with registered titles, see L.R.A. 1925, s. 110 (1), proviso (a), *ante*, p. 132.

Purchaser's entitlement.—Notwithstanding the above rule as to expense, the purchaser has certain substantial rights in this respect against the vendor.

First, the vendor can be compelled to bear any expense incurred in obtaining production of documents for the purpose of preparing the abstract of title in the first place (*Re Johnson and Tustin* (1885), 30 Ch. D. 42). Secondly, the vendor can be called upon to account for the documents not being in his own possession since the purchaser has constructive notice of the rights of any other person in possession (L.P.A. 1925, s. 13, and *post*, p. 164). Thirdly, the vendor must bear the expenses of obtaining possession of documents for the purpose of handing them over on completion (*Re Duthy and Jesson's Contract* [1898] 1 Ch. 419 ; as to the custody of deeds, see *post*, p. 650). And fourthly, the purchaser, albeit at his own expense (see L.P.A. 1925, s. 45 (4), above), is entitled to demand that the vendor should procure the production, so far as this is not impossible, of any of the documents of title he wishes to examine, in whomsoever's possession they may be (see *per* Parker, J., in *Halkett* v. *Dudley* [1907] 1 Ch. 590, at pp. 603–4). Nevertheless this last entitlement is denied to a purchaser by General Condition 11 (3) of the National Conditions of Sale, 18th ed. (cf. General Condition 7 (2) of The Law Society's Conditions of Sale, 1973 Revision, which contains no such denial.)

B. ACCEPTANCE OF TITLE

Waiver.—By accepting the vendor's title, the purchaser is taken to have waived any objections he might otherwise have had to the title as abstracted (*Burnell* v. *Brown* (1820), 1 Joc. & W. 168 ; *Bown* v. *Stenson* (1857), 24 Beav. 631). This waiver will not, however, extend to any matter not appearing on the face of the abstract (see *per* Romilly, M.R., in *Bousfield* v. *Hodges* (1863), 33 Beav. 90, at p. 94 ; *Turquand* v. *Rhodes* (1868), 37 L.J. Ch. 830 ; *Southby* v. *Hutt* (1837), 2 My. & Cr. 207). Nor will the waiver extend to removable defects in title and mere matters of conveyance (see *per* Fry, J., in *Re Gloag amd Miller's Contract* (1883), 23 Ch. D. 320, at pp. 327–8).

By conduct.—An acceptance of title by the purchaser may be by express words. But in practice the acceptance will usually be deemed to have occurred by virtue of conditions of sale as to the time for delivery of requisitions and of observations on the replies thereto (see *ante*, pp. 135, 136). Also, the acceptance may be implied from conduct on the part of the purchaser showing that he intended to waive any objections he might have had to the vendor's title. This essentially involves the performance by the purchaser of acts which a prudent purchaser would not normally perform until the vendor had shown a good title so that the contract would be bound to be completed (*Haydon* v. *Bell* (1838), 1 Beav. 337 ; *Hyde* v. *Warden* (1877), 3 Ex. D. 72). At the same time, any implication of acceptance of the title from such conduct may be nullified if the purchaser continued to insist upon his objections to the title (*Burroughs* v. *Oakley* (1819), 3 Swanst. 159).

An obvious example of conduct which, in accordance with the above, may imply acceptance of the title would be payment of the purchase-money. Another more common example would be the purchaser's submission of a draft conveyance for approval, although it should be noted that this on its own would probably not be conclusive (*Burroughs* v. *Oakley*, *ante*, at p. 171). In practice, the draft conveyance is often submitted at the same time as the purchaser's requisitions on title are sent with a covering letter stating that it is submitted subject to the vendor's replies to the requisitions being satisfactory ; this would, of course, completely nullify any implied acceptance of the title (see, e.g., *Re Spollon and Long's Contract* [1936] Ch. 713).

Another common example of conduct which may imply acceptance of the title is the purchaser's taking possession of the land (see *per* Romilly, M.R., in *Bown* v. *Stenson* (1857), 24 Beav. 631, at p. 637 ; also *Burroughs* v. *Oakley*, ante at p. 169), but the mere act of taking possession on its own is probably not conclusive (*Re Barrington* (1835), 2 Mont. & A. 146 ; *Simpson* v. *Sadd* (1854), 4 De G. M. & G. 665). If possession is taken by virtue of a condition in the contract for sale, acceptance of the title cannot be presumed (*Bolton* v. *London School Board* (1878), 7 Ch. D. 766 ; *Boxhall* v. *Jackson* (1825), 2 L.J. (o.s.) Ch. 100 ; *Stevens* v. *Guppy* (1828), 3 Russ. 171 ; and see General Condition 14 (1) of The Law Society's Conditions of Sale, 1973 Revision, and General Condition 7 (3) of the National Conditions of Sale, 18th ed.). Where the contract contains no such condition, a purchaser would be ill-advised to take possession without *either* first obtaining a letter from the vendor or his solicitor confirming that such possession will not prejudice any questions arising on the title *or else* stating his objection to the title on taking possession and continuing to insist upon it (*Rellie* v. *Pyke* [1936] 1 All E.R. 345).

PART 6. TITLE TO LEASEHOLDS

Title a purchaser or lessee can require.—The statutory limitations governing an open contract are contained in s. 44 (2), (3), (4) and (5) of the L.P.A. 1925, given below :—

" 44.—(2) Under a contract to grant or assign a term of years, whether derived or to be derived out of freehold or leasehold land, the intended lessee or assign shall not be entitled to call for *the title to the freehold.*

(3) Under a contract to sell and assign a term of years derived out of a leasehold interest in land, the intended assign shall not have the right to call for the title to the *leasehold reversion.*

(4) On a contract to grant a lease for a term of years to be derived out of a leasehold interest, with a leasehold reversion, the intended lessee shall not have the right to call for the title to that reversion.

(5) Where by reason of any of the three last preceding subsections, an intending lessee or assign is not entitled to call for the title to the freehold or to a leasehold reversion, as the case may be, he shall not, where the contract is made after the commencement of this Act, be deemed to be affected with notice of any matter or thing of which, if he had contracted that such title should be furnished, he might have had notice."

" *the title to the freehold.*"—The view of the Council of The Law Society is that on the granting of a lease at a ground rent and a premium, and, possibly, in other circumstances, it is reasonable that the lessor should be asked to deduce title at the lessee's expense ; if this is agreed without provision being made as to the incidence of the lessor's solicitor's charges, costs of deduction and investigation of title should be borne by the parties respectively incurring them (*Law Society's Digest*, Opinion No. 1200 (*a*) in Fourth (Cumulative) Supplement).

The Council consider that it would be difficult to define those leases where such investigation ought to be allowed and those where it ought to be precluded, and that the present system " however theoretically dangerous to a lessee, ought to remain unchanged." The Council state that " they feel sure that in the future, as in the past, solicitors acting for lessors will not put obstacles in the way of lessees who, because of the length of the term, the premium to be paid, the money to be expended by them or some other special reason, seek to satisfy themselves that the proposed lessor is in fact entitled to grant the lease " (*Law Society's Gazette*, vol. 55, p. 151).

A lessee who succeeds in investigating the freehold title to unregistered land, for instance, because he paid a substantial premium, should endeavour to obtain an acknowledgment of his right to production of the deeds and an undertaking for safe custody.   If these are inserted in the lease express provision should be made enabling an assignee of the term or a sub-lessee to call for the deeds.   Otherwise it may be argued that an assignee is a " lessee at a rent " and so debarred by the L.P.A. 1925, s. 64 (3), from exercising the rights purported to be granted.

"*leasehold reversion.*"—It was decided in *Gosling* v. *Woolfe* [1893] 1 Q.B. 39 (better reported at 68 L.T. 89) on the similar words in s. 3 of the Conveyancing Act, 1881, that the words " leasehold reversion " meant the reversion of that leasehold interest out of which the term of years contracted to be sold or assigned was derived.   Therefore, if *A* (the freeholder) leases to *B*, and *B* underleases to *C*, and *C* then agrees to sell to *D*, *D* is entitled to a copy or abstract of *C's* underlease but not to a copy or abstract of the lease to *B* ; but compare the remarks of Romer, L.J., in *Drive Yourself Hire Co. (London), Ltd.* v. *Strutt* [1954] 1 Q.B. 250, at p. 278.   The effect of s. 44 of the L.P.A. 1925, on each of the above transactions, if carried out under open contracts, would be as follows :—

B could not call on *A* to show any title (s. 44 (2)).

C could require *B* to supply a copy or abstract of the lease granted by *A* but could not require him to show *A*'s title to grant the lease (s. 44 (2)).

D can require *C* to supply a copy or abstract of the underlease from *B* to *C* but cannot require any information about *A*'s title or about the lease from *A* to *B* (s. 44 (3)).

Equally, if *C* had contracted instead to grant a sub-underlease to *D*, *D* would have been entitled again to call for the underlease from *B* to *C* (compare *Becker* v. *Partridge* [1966] 2 Q.B. 155).

If at some time in the future *D* assigns the underlease to *E*, who in turn agrees by an open contract to assign to *F*, *E* will have to abstract the underlease from *B* to *C* and the assignments of it by *C* to *D* and by *D* to *E*.   The rule is that an assignee can always call for an abstract of the last underlease and of assignments of it *back to a good root of title at least fifteen years old* (*Williams* v. *Spargo* [1893] W.N. 100).   Thus, in course of time, early assignments will drop out of the title.

In the example given it is usually considered advisable that *D*, the purchaser of the underlease, should have an abstract or copy of the lease from *A* to *B* in order that he may satisfy himself that *B* was in a position to grant the underlease, and provision to this effect is often contained in conditions of sale (see, for an example, *post*, p. 146).

A further danger is that a superior lease may contain burdensome covenants, for instance, restricting businesses which may be carried on.   In *Hill* v. *Harris* [1965] 2 Q.B. 601, Russell, L.J., said (*obiter*) that a solicitor acting for an intending sub-lessee is guilty of negligence if he does not " take the ordinary conveyancing precaution . . . of finding out by inspection of the head lease what were the covenants."   See also *Becker* v. *Partridge, ante,* where a solicitor made the " terrible mistake " of not inspecting the superior lease and so failed to discover the requirement of consent to an underletting. Apparently even if there is no right to investigate a head lease it should be called for and, if inspection is refused, the client warned of the danger.

On a contract for sale of an underlease, by which the underlease is made the root of title, it is not an objection to title that the headlease had, before the contract, been disclaimed under the Bankruptcy Act, 1914, s. 54 (1) (*Re Thompson and Cottrell's Contract* [1943] Ch. 97).

Registered title.—Where the leasehold title is registered under the L.R.A. 1925–1971 the vendor nonetheless will have possession of the lease itself, this being returned after noting in the Property Register (rr. 21, 310, and 5 of the L.R.R. 1925). Accordingly the lease remains the essential root of title as in unregistered conveyancing, the register only replacing the subsequent chain of title, and the purchaser must be given the usual notice of its contents (see below).

Whether or not a purchaser of registered leaseholds should be concerned to investigate any superior title depends on the quality of his vendor's title. An absolute leasehold title means that the registrar has investigated and approved the title not only to the leasehold but also to the freehold and any intermediate leaseholds (L.R.A. 1925, s. 8 (1), proviso (i)). Therefore, where the vendor is registered with an absolute title the purchaser need never concern himself with any superior titles. However, if the vendor is registered with the currently more common good leasehold title, this means that the registrar has only investigated and approved the leasehold title itself (L.R.A. 1925, s. 8 (1), proviso (ii)). In such a case, therefore, the purchaser is as much concerned with the superior title as in unregistered conveyancing (see above).

Notice of contents of lease.—In the case of a purchase of leaseholds under an open contract, although a purchaser who has notice of a lease is deemed in a general way to have notice of the contents thereof, he is not deemed to have notice of covenants of an unusual character (see *per* Tomlin, J., in *Melzak* v. *Lilienfeld* [1926] Ch. 480, at pp. 490–492), even though such covenants are common in the neighbourhood (*Midgley* v. *Smith* [1893] W.N. 120); unless the vendor has brought them to the knowledge of the purchaser or the purchaser has had a reasonable opportunity of inspecting them (*Reeve* v. *Berridge* (1888), 20 Q.B.D. 523 ; *Re White and Smith's Contract* [1896] 1 Ch. 637 ; *Re Haedicke and Lipski's Contract* [1901] 2 Ch. 666 ; *Molyneux* v. *Hawtrey* [1903] 2 K.B. 487). It is not enough to offer inspection of the lease in the sale room only (*Dougherty* v. *Oates* (1900), 45 Sol. J. 119). If the particulars are so drawn as to mislead the purchaser, the vendor will not be allowed to say that the purchaser could have discovered the error if he had inspected the lease (*Re Davis and Cavey* (1888), 40 Ch. D. 601).

In the absence of a condition to the contrary, where property is described as held under a lease, a good title is not made unless the lease is the head lease (*Charles Hunt, Ltd.* v. *Palmer* [1931] 2 Ch. 287 ; *Camberwell and South London Building Society* v. *Holloway* (1879), 13 Ch. D. 754 ; *Cunningham* v. *Shackleton* (1935), 79 Sol. J. 381 ; *Re Beyfus and Masters' Contract* (1888), 39 Ch. D. 110 ; *Broom* v. *Phillips* (1896), 74 L.T. 459 ; *Re Russ and Brown's Contract* [1934] Ch. 34) ; even although the condition states that the purchaser shall be deemed to have notice of the contents of the lease (*ibid.*) ; unless he knew that he was only to get an underlease (*Flood* v. *Pritchard* (1879), 40 L.T. 873). Also, apart from any condition to the contrary, a purchaser may object to the title where the covenants in a head lease are more onerous than those in the underlease sold (*Darlington* v. *Hamilton* (1854), Kay 550, at pp. 558–9). Again a purchaser of an underlease should be given notice before the contract where the head lease comprises more property than that sold, since this fact would subject the purchaser to the risk of forfeiture due to the acts of persons over whom he has no control (*Re Lloyds Bank, Ltd. and Lillington's Contract* [1912] 1 Ch. 601). However, any objection to the lack of express notice will be weakened by the fact that the property sold is part of a house so that it is practically obvious that it would almost certainly be the subject of a letting of the whole house (*Becker* v. *Prichard* [1966] 2 Q.B. 155).

In *Re Moody and Yates* (1885), 30 Ch. D. 344, on a sale of leaseholds at a *peppercorn* rent, the lease contained the ordinary covenant that the lessee would complete the houses to the satisfaction of the lessor's surveyor. It was held on s. 3 (6) of the Conveyancing Act, 1881, now replaced by s. 45 (4) of the L.P.A. 1925, that the surveyor's certificate was a link in the title, and should be obtained at the vendor's expense.

In the absence of a condition to the contrary, a covenant in a lease not to assign without licence is an unusual covenant, and is an objection to title where the purchaser has not had a reasonable opportunity of inspecting such lease (*Reeve* v. *Berridge* (1888), 20 Q.B.D. 523) ; and in such a case a purchaser is entitled to repudiate his contract (*Hyde* v. *Warden* (1877), 3 Ex. D. 72 ; *Bishop* v. *Taylor* (1891), 64 L.T. 529 ; *Melzak* v. *Lilienfeld* [1926] Ch. 480 ; *Becker* v. *Partridge* [1966] 2 Q.B. 155). Where the leasehold title is registered under the L.R.A. 1925 an entry will have been made on the register excepting from the effect of registration the rights arising on an assignment without the lessor's licence required under such a covenant (L.R.A. 1925, s. 8 (2) ; L.R.R. 1925, r. 45).

Where there is no condition on the matter it is the duty of the vendor to try to obtain the consent of the lessor, and if he refuses or wilfully neglects to do so he is liable to pay general damages for the loss of his bargain to the purchaser (*Day* v. *Singleton* [1899] 2 Ch. 320). Note that the purchaser is by implication bound to co-operate in the obtaining of the vendor's consent, e.g., by giving references for himself (see *per* Harman, L.J., in *Scheggia* v. *Gradwell* [1963] 1 W.L.R. 1049, at p. 1062). Where a lessor refuses to give his consent, although such refusal is unreasonable, and the vendor could therefore assign without such consent, the title will not be forced on a purchaser (*Re Marshall and Salt's Contract* [1900] 2 Ch. 202), unless either the vendor has previously brought an action and obtained a declaration that he is entitled to assign without licence (*Young* v. *Ashley Gardens, etc., Ltd.* [1903] 2 Ch. 112) or else *semble* the lessor's refusal is with certainty unreasonable (*White* v. *Hay* (1895), 72 L.T. 281 ; see also *per* Maugham, J., in *Curtis Moffat, Ltd.* v. *Wheeler* [1929] 2 Ch. 224, at p. 236). See also *Lipmans Wallpaper, Ltd.* v. *Mason & Hodghton, Ltd.* [1969] 1 Ch. 20.

Conditions of sale.—The Statutory Conditions of Sale contain nothing at all relevant to leasehold titles. The National Conditions of Sale, 18th ed., General Condition 10, deals only with aspects of leasehold sales other than the investigation of title. However, The Law Society's Conditions of Sale, 1973 Revision, General Condition 8 (1), does deal with title and makes an attempt to recognise reasonable practice. It restates the open contract rule that the root of title should be the lease which is being sold but in addition provides that where that lease was granted not more than fifteen years before the contract and for a term exceeding twenty-one years then, in effect, the freehold title must be deduced as well for at least fifteen years (i.e., the statutory period ; see *ante*, p. 112). Further, the condition brings in superior leasehold titles for investigation where an underlease is being sold of appropriate age and length, and also entitles the purchaser to require an abstract or copy of the immediately superior lease in all cases. Obviously a vendor unwilling or, especially, unable to comply with these considerable concessions to purchasers would be well-advised to modify this condition (i.e., by a special condition of sale). The condition, as revised, does not apply, in any case, where the vendor is registered with absolute leasehold title.

PART 7. POSSESSORY TITLE

Title of mortgagee by possession and extinguishment of mortgagor's title, see chapter on Mortgages, *post*, p. 970.

Possessory title and " overriding interests " under L.R.A. 1925–1971, see *post*, p. 187.

Proof of title by possession.—A purchaser under an open contract can be compelled to accept a title depending on parol evidence of adverse possession (*Games* v. *Bonnor* (1884), 54 L.J. Ch. 517). Also it was decided in *Re Atkinson and Horsell's Contract* [1912] 2 Ch. 1 that even where the contract stated that the title should commence with a certain document, a purchaser could be compelled to accept a possessory title commencing at a later date. It was also decided in that case that a vendor has to do more than show forty (now fifteen) years' possession. He must also show who were rightfully entitled, and that such possession has effectually barred their claims. Contrast *George Wimpey & Co., Ltd.* v. *Sohn* [1967] Ch. 487, where a condition of sale as to the title amounted to a warranty that particular evidence of title would be provided, with the consequence that the purchaser could not be compelled to take a title based on adverse possession. An agreement to accept a possessory title merely points to the evidence by which it is to be supported and the vendor must still prove the full statutory period of title, although part of the period may be a documentary title and part only possessory (*Douglass* v. *London and North Western Railway Co.* (1857), 3 Kay & J. 173 ; *Jacobs* v. *Revell* [1900] 2 Ch. 858 ; *Ecclesiastical Commissioners* v. *Parr* [1894] 2 Q.B. 420 ; L.P.A. 1925, s. 44 (1)). See also *Jacobs* v. *Revell* [1900] 2 Ch. 858.

A purchaser who agrees to accept a title based on evidence of possession only should obtain the clearest possible statements, by statutory declaration, of the date on which, and the circumstances in which, possession was taken, and of the title claimed to be extinguished so far as it is known ; see further, *Law Journal*, vol. 103, pp. 743, 744.

A right of action to recover land is not deemed to accrue unless the land is in the possession of some person in whose favour the period of limitation can run ; the right accrues on dispossession if that person has *adverse* possession on that date (Limitation Act, 1939, ss. 5 (1), 10 (1)). Acts of user committed on land " which do not interfere and are consistent with the purpose to which the owner intends to devote it, do not amount to a ' dispossession ' of him " (*Leigh* v. *Jack* (1879), 5 Ex. D. 264). Thus it was decided in *Williams Brothers Direct Supply, Ltd.* v. *Raftery* [1958] 1 Q.B. 159 that cultivation of land during and since the last war, and the erection of sheds, did not bar the title of an owner who had desired to develop the land but who had been prevented from doing so by war-time conditions and planning restrictions. Again in *George Wimpey & Co., Ltd.* v. *Sohn* [1967] Ch. 487, it was held that merely fencing a piece of land was too equivocal to support a claim of adverse possession in that the fence might have been intended to exclude only the public and not the true owner. Possession held by a tenant becomes adverse after expiration of the period covered by the last payment of rent (*Hayward* v. *Chaloner* [1968] 1 Q.B. 107).

Proof of title by evidence of possession is not admissible as an alternative where deeds forming part of the modern title have been lost or destroyed, secondary evidence of the documentary title being required in such a case (*Re Halifax Commercial Banking Co., Ltd., and Wood* (1898), 79 L.T. 183, 536 (C.A.) ; see further *post*, p. 657).

Effect of twelve years' possession.—Twelve years' uninterrupted adverse possession does not necessarily confer a good title ; it is essential in the absence of a condition in the contract to the contrary that the abstract of title should show the interests which existed in the land and that the effect of the adverse possession has been to bar the claims of the persons entitled to those interests (*Games* v. *Bonnor* (1884), 54 L.J. Ch. 517). It has been decided that the effect of s. 34 of the Real Property Limitation Act, 1833, was to extinguish the title of the dispossessed owner, not to transfer it to the squatter (*Fairweather* v. *St. Marylebone Property Co., Ltd.* [1963] 2 A.C. 510 (H.L.)). In other words that statute did not, nor does the Limitation Act, 1939, s. 16, by which s. 34 is replaced, directly give the intruder any title, but prevented the former owner asserting his title. The title acquired by the wrongdoer is a new, independent fee simple which prevails against all comers who cannot show a better title (e.g., it will not prevail against a lessor where only the lessee's title has been defeated). However, a restrictive covenant is binding in equity on the wrongdoer (*Re Nisbet and Pott's Contract* [1906] 1 Ch. 386).

Actions for the recovery of land must be brought within the following periods after the accrual of the right (as to which, see Limitation Act, 1939, ss. 5 to 10)—actions by the Crown to recover foreshore within sixty years ; other actions by the Crown within thirty years ; by any spiritual or eleemosynary corporation sole within thirty years ; by any other person within twelve years (1939 Act, s. 4, replacing, with amendments, Crown Suits Act, 1769, s. 1 ; Real Property Limitation Act, 1833, s. 29 ; Real Property Limitation Act, 1874, s. 1).

A vendor who has received the full purchase price becomes a bare trustee for the purchaser. Consequently, if the purchaser has possession for twelve years the vendor's title is barred under the Limitation Act, 1939, s. 10 (1) (*Bridges* v. *Mees* [1957] Ch. 475 ; see also *post*, p. 187, as to particular rules affecting registered land, and an article by M. J. Goodman in *Conveyancer N.S.*, vol. 29, p. 356, as to the position of certain other beneficiaries).

Effect of disability of person entitled and of acknowledgment of title. —Rights of action to recover land may not be barred even after the expiration of these periods if *on the date when a right of action accrued* the person to whom it accrued was under disability, as a further period of six years is allowed after cessation of disability or death of the person to whom the right accrued (Limitation Act, 1939, s. 22, replacing Real Property Limitation Act, 1874, s. 3), provided that no action to recover land may be brought under this section after the expiration of thirty years from the date on which the right accrued (s. 22, proviso (c), replacing Real Property Limitation Act, 1874, s. 5). As to what is " disability," see 1939 Act, s. 31 (2). Further, where any right of action to recover land has accrued and the person in possession acknowledges the title of the person to whom the right of action has accrued, the right is deemed to have accrued on *and not before* the date of the acknowledgment (*ibid.*, s. 23 (1), replacing Real Property Limitation Act, 1833, s. 14). To have this effect, an acknowledgment must be in writing and signed by the person making it but may be made by an agent (*ibid.*, s. 24, replacing Real Property Limitation Act, 1833, s. 14). If made by a person in possession such an acknowledgment binds all other persons in possession during the ensuing period of limitation (*ibid.*, s. 25 (1)). Subsequent acknowledgment does not restore a title which has once been barred (*Sanders* v. *Sanders* (1881), 19 Ch. D. 373 ; *Kibble* v. *Fairthorne* [1895] 1 Ch. 219 ; *Beamish* v. *Whitney* [1909] Ir. R. 360 ; *Nicholson* v. *England* [1926] 2 K.B. 93).

Where before 1926 a legal mortgage was paid off but no reconveyance executed, it was held that the mortgagor became tenant at will of the premises and, therefore, that the legal estate of the mortgagee was extinguished at the expiration of thirty years (*Sands to Thompson* (1883), 22 Ch. D. 614). If such were the circumstances on 31st December, 1925, the legal estate would under the transitional provisions have vested in the mortgagor (L.P.A. 1925, Sched. 1, Pt. II, para. 6 (*d*)). When, after 1925, money secured by a mortgage has been discharged, the mortgage term will become a satisfied term and will cease. See also chapter on Mortgages, *post*, p. 970.

Future estates.—Some difficulty has been caused with regard to the effect of adverse possession on future estates as a result of s. 1 of the L.P.A. 1925, by which the only future estate which can exist *at law* is a term of years absolute. The Limitation Act, 1939, s. 6 (1) (replacing Real Property Limitation Act, 1833, s. 3, and Real Property Limitation Act, 1874, s. 2), provides that, subject to certain exceptions (as to which see s. 6 (3) regarding interests expectant on estates tail), " the right of action to recover any land shall, in a case where the estate or interest claimed was an estate or interest in reversion or remainder or any other future estate or interest and no person has taken possession of the land by virtue of the estate or interest claimed, be deemed to have accrued on the date on which the estate or interest fell into possession by the determination of the preceding estate or interest." Subsection (2) of s. 6 then enacts that—

" 6.—(2) If the person entitled to the preceding estate or interest, not being a term of years absolute, was not in possession of the land on the date of the determination thereof, no action shall be brought by the person entitled to the succeeding estate or interest after the expiration of twelve years from the date on which the right of action accrued to the person entitled to the preceding estate or interest, or six years from the date on which the right of action accrued to the person entitled to the succeeding estate or interest, whichever period last expires : "

There is a proviso extending the periods if the Crown or a spiritual or eleemosynary corporation sole is entitled to the succeeding estate.

If land is held for two or more persons in succession for freehold estates (e.g., for *A* for life and after his death for *B*), then, unless the land is subject to a trust for sale, it must be settled land and the legal estate vested in the tenant for life or statutory owners (S.L.A. 1925, s. 1 (1) (i)), and the tenant for life or statutory owners will hold on trust for the persons entitled to equitable interests. The general rule was formerly that if the right of a trustee was barred the adverse possessor obtained the legal estate subject to any equities.

In the Limitation Act, 1939, an endeavour has been made to solve these difficulties. In the first place, both legal and equitable estates and interests in land and interests in the proceeds of sale of land held on trust for sale are land for the purposes of the Act (s. 31 (1)). Secondly, s. 7 (1) contains special rules affecting settled land and land held on trust. (It will be noted that, except in the case of a term of years absolute and the reversion following it, the provisions of s. 6 (1) as to future interests, mentioned above, operate only by virtue of s. 7.) The effect of these rules is as follows :—

(1) Subject to s. 19 (1) (which relates to actions by beneficiaries where there has been fraud or similar dealing by trustees), the Act applies to equitable interests in land and in the proceeds of sale of land held on trust for sale, in like manner as it applies to legal estates (s. 7 (1)).

(2) If the period during which a tenant for life or statutory owner can bring an action has expired, his legal estate is not extinguished so long as the right of action to recover the land of any person entitled to a beneficial interest has not accrued or has not been barred (s. 7 (2)).

(3) Where land is held on trust, including a trust for sale, and the period during which the trustees may bring an action has expired, the estate of the trustees is not extinguished so long as the right of action to recover the land of any person entitled to a beneficial interest in the land or proceeds of sale has not accrued or has not been barred (s. 7 (3)).

(4) Statutory owners and trustees may bring an action to recover the land on behalf of any person entitled to a beneficial interest *in possession* whose right has not been barred notwithstanding that, apart from this provision, the right of the statutory owners or trustees would have been barred (s. 7 (4)).

It is important to note that the effect of s. 7 is that a purchaser is not safe in accepting a title obtained by adverse possession, unless it is proved that the land was not formerly settled or held on trust for sale, or unless the equitable title is shown and proved extinguished.

PART 8.   TITLE TO LAND FORMERLY COPYHOLD

It is provided by s. 44 (6) of the L.P.A. 1925, replacing s. 3 (2) of the Conveyancing Act, 1881, that where land of copyhold or customary tenure has been converted into freehold by enfranchisement, then, under a contract to sell and convey the freehold, the purchaser shall not have the right to call for the title to make the enfranchisement. The subsection only affects the title of the lord to the freehold, and will not prevent the purchaser requiring the vendor to show his title to a good root of title at least thirty years back from the date of the contract, notwithstanding that the enfranchisement deed and part of the copyhold title may come within that period.

Land enfranchised by the Law of Property Act, 1922, was after enfranchisement held under the same title as that under which it was held at the commencement of the Act (Act of 1922, Sched. 12, para. 1 (e)), and the enfranchisement did not affect the rights of any person in the land (for instance, a mortgagee), or deprive a tenant of any commonable right or right to minerals, etc., and those rights continue to attach upon the land enfranchised as nearly as may be as if the freehold had been comprised in the instrument or disposition under which that person claims (*ibid.*, paras. (2), (4), (5)). The land remains subject to the lord's rights of sporting, and his rights in regard to mines, minerals, fairs, markets, rights of chase or warren, piscaries, or other rights of hunting, shooting, fishing, fowling, or otherwise taking game, fish, or fowl (*ibid.*, para. (5)), until such rights are extinguished.

Consequently, it is still necessary, when selling freehold property formerly copyhold, to state in the conditions that the land was formerly copyhold. For, in the absence of such a condition, that is to say, if the property is simply described as freehold, and the right of the lord to the minerals still remains in existence, the purchaser may object to the title (*Upperton* v. *Nickolson* (1871), L.R. 6 Ch. 436 ; *Bellamy* v. *Debenham* [1891] 1 Ch. 412 ; *Re Jackson and Haden's Contract* [1906] 1 Ch. 412). See further, below.

The freehold title should be made to commence with the deed of enfranchisement, where the enfranchisement was made before 1926 ; and, notwithstanding that the earlier title may be recited in the deed of enfranchisement the purchaser will not be entitled to make a requisition thereon (L.P.A. 1925, s. 45 (1)).

Where the manorial incidents formerly affecting the land have been extinguished, the purchaser of the freehold will not have the right to call for the title of the person entering into any compensation agreement, or giving a receipt for the compensation money, to enter into such agreement or to give such receipt, and will not be deemed to be affected with notice of any matter or thing of which, if he had contracted that such title should be furnished, he might have had notice (L.P.A. 1925, s. 44 (7)).

A. TRANSACTIONS BEFORE 1926

Surrender and admittance.—A sale of copyhold land before 1926 was carried out by a surrender by the vendor to the lord of the manor, followed by admittance of the purchaser. The surrender was often preceded by a covenant to surrender, which was deemed to be a " conveyance " within the definition contained in s. 7 (5) of the Conveyancing Act, 1881.

Consequently, the covenants for title implied by the use of the words " beneficial owner," " mortgage," etc., were implied when used in such a conveyance. A covenant to surrender itself passed an equitable interest in the land but not the legal estate.

Although it was the admittance which passed the legal estate, it was the surrender and not the admittance which governed the estate taken. It was therefore essential that the surrender should contain proper words of limitation. For instance, if the surrender was for life, either expressly, or by implication of law by reason of the want of proper words of limitation, although the admittance might be in fee, only a life interest passed (Scriven on Copyholds, 7th ed., pp. 141, 142). But the words " in fee simple," " in tail," etc., were inapplicable to surrenders or admittances, as s. 51 of the Conveyancing Act, 1881, allowing their use, only applied to " deeds." Different manors had different customs as to the words which were sufficient to pass the legal estate.

After long uninterrupted possession consistent with there having been a surrender, a surrender was, before 1926, as between vendor and purchaser, generally presumed (Scriven on Copyholds, 7th ed., p. 115) ; and in some cases an admittance was implied (*ibid.*, pp. 138 to 140 ; *Ecclesiastical Commissioners* v. *Parr* [1894] 2 Q.B. 420). The court will not readily presume an enfranchisement (*Beighton* v. *Beighton* [1895] W.N. 119).

With some few exceptions, such as executory and contingent estates, a married woman's equitable estates, and an estate as tenant in tail, equitable estates in copyholds could not be surrendered, but had to be passed by deed.

Copyhold surrenders did not require registration under the Acts governing registration in deeds registers, but enfranchisement deeds did. See *R*. v. *Middlesex Registrar* (1888), 21 Q.B.D. 555 ; Yorkshire Registries Act, 1884, s. 28. A lease, being a common-law assurance, required registration under the local Acts if the property was within their districts, but a devise did not (Sugden's Vendors and Purchasers, p. 732).

B.   STATUTORY ENFRANCHISEMENT

It should be noticed that most of the provisions of the L.P.A. 1922 referred to in the following pages were repealed on 1st January, 1970, by the Statute Law (Repeals) Act, 1969, Schedule, Pt. III (in particular repealed were ss. 128 to 136, ss. 138 to 143 and Schedules 12 to 14). However, since these provisions will have affected titles within their scope before their repeal, the following account is retained in this edition for the benefit of conveyancers investigating such titles.

It is provided by the L.P.A. 1922, s. 128 (1), that " as from [1st January, 1926] every parcel of copyhold land shall by virtue of this Act be enfranchised and cease to be of copyhold or customary tenure and land so enfranchised is in this Act referred to as enfranchised land." The expression " copyhold land " as used in this subsection is defined by s. 189 of the L.P.A. 1922 as including customary land or customary freehold land where the freehold was in the lord and not in the customary tenant ; land of copyhold tenure held for life or lives or for years, whether or not determinable with life, where the tenant had by custom a perpetual right of renewal ; land held in free tenure for life or lives or for years, whether or not determinable with life (but subject to custom), where the tenant had by custom a perpetual right of renewal.

Where the freehold of customary land was in the tenant there was no occasion for enfranchisement.

Where copyhold land was held under a grant by the lord as copyhold for a life or lives or for years *without a right of perpetual renewal* the interest of the tenant became converted into a leasehold interest ; see *post*, pp. 157–158. Otherwise, every parcel of copyhold land (this included the mines and minerals : L.P.A. 1922, s. 188 (1)) automatically became, at the beginning of 1926, by virtue of the L.P.A. 1922, enfranchised and became freehold free from the incidents referred to in the next note ; but the land remained subject to certain *manorial incidents* having a money value, until they became extinguished under the provisions of the Act (L.P.A. 1922, s. 128 (1), (2)) ; also to certain rights and liabilities of the tenant and the lord not deemed to be *manorial incidents*. It is proposed to take these matters in order.

Incidents which ceased on 1st January, 1926.—Certain incidents ceased automatically both as regards copyholds proper and as regards customary freeholds where the freehold was in the tenant. These are referred to in Sched. 12, para. (1), to the L.P.A. 1922, and are as follows :—

(a) Liability for forfeiture for the conveyance or attempted conveyance of an estate of freehold in the land, and for alienation without licence (see L.P.A. 1922, s. 128 (2) (c) ; Sched. 12, para. (1) (a)). As to other forfeitures, see below. Schedule 12 does not apply to leaseholds within s. 133 of the L.P.A. 1922.

(b) Customary suits and services and liability to do fealty. There is, however, an exception in the case of services incident to Grand and Petty Sergeanty under s. 136 of the L.P.A. 1922.

(c) In place of the lord's right to escheat, the Crown or the Duchy of Lancaster or the Duke of Cornwall may become entitled to the land as *bona vacantia* under the provisions of the A.E.A. 1925, ss. 45 (1) (d), 46 (1) (vi).

(d) The land is not subject to the custom of borough English, or of gavelkind, or to any other customary mode of descent, or to any custom relating to dower or freebench or tenancy by the curtesy, or to any other custom whatsoever, but is governed as to descent on death and intestacy or partial intestacy and devolution on death by the provisions of Pt. IV of the A.E.A. 1925.

The land is held under the same title as that under which it was held on 31st December, 1925, and is not subject to any estate, right, charge, or interest affecting the manor (L.P.A. 1922, Sched. 12, para. (1) (e)). Generally, the rights or interests of any person in the enfranchised land under a will, settlement, mortgage or otherwise by purchase continued to attach upon the land enfranchised in the same way as nearly as might be as if the freehold had been comprised in the instrument or disposition under which that person claimed (L.P.A. 1922, Sched. 12, para. (2)).

Incidents to which land remained temporarily subject.—Certain manorial incidents, such as quit rents, fines, rights as to timber and forfeitures (other than forfeitures for conveyance or attempted conveyance and for alienation without licence) were only temporary, and have now come to an end, but until they became extinguished the enfranchised land remained subject in like manner as if the land had not been enfranchised (L.P.A. 1922, s. 128 (2)).

To protect the lord, it was provided by s. 129 (1), (2), of the L.P.A. 1922 that so long as any of such manorial incidents remained unextinguished, an assurance of the land or of any interest therein became void so far as regards the grant or conveyance of the legal estate unless it was produced to the steward within six months. On such production and on payment of all manorial dues up to date, including any fines, reliefs, or heriots payable in respect of the transaction, the steward endorsed the assurance with his certificate of production. See further below.

There were three ways in which such manorial incidents might be extinguished, namely :—

(1) By agreement in writing as to the compensation between the lord and tenant made within ten years from 1st January, 1926.

(2) By a notice requiring the ascertainment of the compensation served by the lord on the tenant or by the tenant on the lord, if made within the same period ; except that the lord was not entitled to serve the notice until 1st January, 1931.

(3) By simply waiting until the expiration of ten years from 1st January, 1926, as, after the expiration of that period, if no agreement had been entered into, or notice given, all manorial incidents ceased.

The extinguishment took effect immediately on the signing of the agreement, the giving of the notice, or the expiration of the ten years (L.P.A. 1922, s. 138 (1)).

Section 138 (3) of the L.P.A. 1922 provides that an agreement as to the compensation might be effected by the persons who on a sale would be able to dispose of the manorial incidents and the land affected thereby respectively, or might be effected under Pt. II of the Copyhold Act, 1894, as applied by the 1922 Act, by the persons who, if the land had not been enfranchised, would have been entitled to effect an enfranchisement with the consent of the Minister of Agriculture. A tenant for life and a statutory owner were persons able on a sale to dispose of the manorial incidents and the land affected under s. 138 (3), (5) of the 1922 Act. Reference may also be made to ss. 38 (ii), 62 (3), 71 (1) and 73 (1) of the S.L.A. 1925 as to powers of tenants for life and to the L.P.A. 1925, s. 28 (1), and the A.E.A. 1925, s. 39, as to the powers of trustees for sale and personal representatives.

The form of compensation agreement contained in Pt. I of Sched. 13 might be used, with such variations as the circumstances of each case required, and is deemed sufficient (L.P.A. 1922, s. 138 (1)).

Where the compensation agreement provided for the creation of a compensation rent-charge payable by equal annual instalments, the agreement operated by virtue of the Act as a grant by all necessary parties of an annual terminable rent-charge of the agreed amount issuing out of the land agreed to be charged therewith of the like nature and with the like incidents as if the agreement had been effected under the Copyhold Act, 1894, as amended (L.P.A. 1922, s. 138 (6)). The agreement should be registered as a puisne mortgage under the L.C.A. 1972, s. 2 (4), Class C (i).

Where no agreement was made or notice served before the expiration of ten years from 1st January, 1926, then, upon the expiration of those ten years, the manorial rights became automatically extinguished unless the Minister by order extended the period (L.P.A. 1922, s. 138 (1)). The lord or the tenant might during certain specified periods (now expired) apply to the Minister of Agriculture and Fisheries to determine the amount of compensation to be paid by the tenant to the lord for the extinguishment of the manorial incidents ; if no application was made during one of those periods, no compensation is payable in respect of the extinguishment of manorial incidents (L.P.A. 1922, s. 140 ; Postponement of Enactments (Miscellaneous Provisions) Act, 1939, s. 3 ; Postponement of Enactments, etc. (Manorial Incidents Extinguishment) Order, 1949).

A certificate under the seal of the Minister stating that the compensation for extinguishment has been duly ascertained to be the amount stated in the certificate is conclusive evidence of the facts so stated (L.P.A. 1922, s. 139 (2) (a)).

Rights and liabilities to which the land remains subject.—There are certain rights and liabilities of the tenant and the lord which are excluded from the effect of the enfranchisement. It is specially provided by the L.P.A., 1922, Sched. 12, para. (7), that a right preserved to the lord is not to be deemed a manorial incident unless it is otherwise agreed. These exceptional rights and liabilities are as follows :—

(i) *Commonable rights of a tenant.*—The enfranchisement did not deprive a tenant of any commonable right to which he was entitled in respect of the enfranchised land, and any such right will continue attached to the land (L.P.A. 1922, Sched. 12, para. (4)).

(ii) *Mines and minerals.*—Notwithstanding that mines and minerals became freehold, the enfranchisement did not affect any right of the lord or tenant in or to any mines, minerals, limestone, lime, clay, stone, gravel, pits, or quarries, or any right of entry, right of working, or similar right (*ibid.*, para. (5)). Before 1926, the property in the minerals was usually in the lord, but the tenant had possession. The result was that unless there was a custom to the contrary, the lord could not get the minerals without the consent of the tenant (*Inland Revenue Commissioners* v. *Joicey* (*No.* 2) [1913] 2 K.B. 580).

(iii) *Rights of lord as regards fairs and markets and sporting rights.*—All rights, franchises, royalties or privileges of the lord in respect of any fairs, markets, rights of chase or warren, piscaries, or other rights of hunting, shooting, fishing, fowling, or otherwise taking game, fish or fowl are preserved (L.P.A. 1922, Sched. 12, para. (5)).

(iv) *Liability for maintenance of dykes, etc.*—It is also provided by the L.P.A. 1922, Sched. 12, para. (6), that the enfranchisement will not affect any liability for the construction, maintenance, cleansing or repair of any dykes, ditches, canals, sea or river walls, piles, bridges, levels, ways and other works required for the protection or general benefit of any land.

It is provided by the L.P.A. 1922, Sched. 12, para. (7), that the rights mentioned above (which were not extinguished by the Act) will not be deemed to be " manorial incidents " unless it is otherwise agreed. The provisions as to agreement in respect of these rights are contained in s. 138 (12) of the L.P.A. 1922, which provides that the lord and the tenant may in writing agree that any of these rights shall be treated as a manorial incident, and be extinguished as if it were a manorial incident.

General rules as to vesting of enfranchised land.—As the provisions of the L.P.A. 1922, Pt. V, relating to copyholds were not consolidated in the L.P.A. 1925, in order to determine the final vesting of the legal estate on 1st January, 1926, it is often necessary to refer first to the 1922 Act (as amended by the L.P. (Amendment) Act, 1924) and then to the L.P.A. 1925, Sched. 1, or the S.L.A. 1925, Sched. 2. Section 202 of the L.P.A. 1925 provides that for giving effect to that Act, the enfranchisement of copyhold land effected by the 1922 Act, as amended, will be deemed to have been effected immediately *before* the commencement of that Act.

The fact that a person had been admitted tenant on the court rolls, and therefore in the eye of the law before 1926 was entitled to the legal estate, was not conclusive as to the vesting of the land. The reason was that, particularly in the case of mortgagees, the real owner was often not admitted until it was necessary to enable him to make a title to the legal estate.

It should also be noted that the words " lord " and " tenant " as used in the Acts for the purpose of defining the proper person to sell property, and therefore to enter into compensation agreements, was often not the lord of the manor, or the person admitted on the court rolls of the manor on 31st December, 1925. For instance, in the case of settled land, although the trustees of the settlement may have been admitted, the legal estate did not vest in them on 1st January, 1926, but in the tenant for life, and the latter would be the person to sell and to enter into a compensation agreement, after he had obtained a vesting deed.

Persons in whom enfranchised land vested.—This matter is dealt with by the L.P.A. 1922, Sched. 12, para. (8), as amended by the L.P. (Amendment) Act, 1924, as follows :—

(*a*) If there was a copyholder in fee (not being a mortgagee) the freehold estate in fee simple vested (subject as provided in the Schedule) in that person. " Copyholder in fee " means the person who was admitted in respect of the inheritance (L.P.A. 1922, s. 189). But it may remain necessary to consider the provisions as to vesting in Pts. II to VIII of Sched. 1 to the L.P.A. 1925 or, when the land was settled, the provisions of the S.L.A. 1925, Sched. 2. Thus where the person admitted was the beneficial owner, he took the legal estate. If the persons admitted were personal representatives or trustees for sale then they took that estate. Where the land was settled, then the legal estate vested in the tenant for life or statutory owner. If the property was in mortgage, then the mortgagee took a term of years or a sub-term under para. (1) (*f*) of Sched. 12 to the L.P.A. 1922 (see at p. 158), and under Pt. VII or VIII of Sched. 1 to the L.P.A. 1925.

(*b*) If there was no copyholder in fee (that is, where there was no person admitted on the court rolls), then, according to the L.P.A. 1922, Sched. 12, para. (8) (*b*), the fee simple vested (subject as provided in the Schedule) in the person who, immediately before 1st January, 1926, had the best right to be admitted as copyholder in fee, otherwise than as a mortgagee, and if the last person who was admitted as copyholder in fee (being a trustee) had died before 1st January, 1926 (whether or not having disposed of the land by will), his personal representative, if any, was deemed to have had a better right to be admitted than the devisee or customary heir. Once again it is essential to go further and determine the effect of the L.P.A. 1925, Sched. 1, or the S.L.A. 1925, Sched. 2, in the manner mentioned in para. (*a*). For an example, see *Re King's Theatre, Sunderland* [1929] 1 Ch. 483.

(*c*) In the case of manors in which it was the practice of admitted copyholders to grant derivative interests (such as leases) to persons who were admitted in respect of those interests, the enfranchisement of the land enured for the benefit of every person having any customary estate or interest in the land, and every such person became entitled (without prejudice to the provisions of the L.P.A. 1925 and S.L.A. 1925) to a legal estate (if the interest was capable of subsisting as a legal estate) or equitable interest in the enfranchised land corresponding to his former customary or other estate or interest, but so that a mortgagee took only a term of years absolute (L.P.A. 1922, Sched. 12, para. (8) (*c*)).

(*d*) Where the copyhold land was subject to interests affecting the fee simple which were under the L.P.A. 1925 capable of subsisting at law, but were not capable of being overreached by virtue of a subsisting trust for sale or a settlement (such as a second mortgage or a perpetual rent-charge), the persons entitled took (subject to the terms of years absolute of prior mortgagees) *legal estates* in the enfranchised land corresponding to their former *equitable* or other interests (L.P.A. 1922, Sched. 12, para. (8) (*d*)).

(*e*) If there was a person entitled to a perpetually renewable lease in the copyhold land (not being a mortgagee) the freehold estate in fee simple vested (subject as provided in the Schedule) in that person as if he had been a copyholder in fee (L.P.A. 1922, Sched. 12, para. (8) (*e*)).

(*f*) If the copyholder in fee was a mortgagee the freehold estate in fee simple vested (subject to the terms of years absolute of any mortgagees) in the person entitled to the equity of redemption.

(*g*) If the copyholder in fee, or other person entitled to an interest corresponding to a legal estate, was a trustee for a corporation or other person absolutely and beneficially entitled, the freehold estate in fee simple or other corresponding legal estate vested in the corporation or other person so entitled.

(*h*) If a person had, under the Limitation Acts, acquired a customary estate corresponding to a legal estate, then a legal estate corresponding to the customary estate so acquired vested in him.

Then comes a long proviso (that is, to para. (8) of Sched. 12 to the L.P.A. 1922), dealing principally with the vesting of copyhold land in particular cases at the commencement of the Act, and the effect of which is, shortly, as follows :—

(i) Where the copyhold land was on 1st January, 1926, or by virtue of the S.L.A. 1925, *settled land,* the freehold estate in fee simple or derivative legal estate vested in the tenant for life of full age or statutory owner (including a personal representative entitled to the settled land) upon the trusts and subject to the powers and provisions of the settlement.

(ii) Where the copyhold land or an equitable interest therein capable of subsisting as a legal estate was vested in an infant, the freehold estate in fee simple or derivative legal estate, as the case might be, vested in the personal representatives or trustees of the settlement, or other persons who, under the L.P.A. 1925, Sched. 1, Pt. III, or the S.L.A. 1925, Sched. 2, para. 3, became entitled to the legal estate of the infant. See further, *post,* p. 334 *et seq.*

(iv) Where the copyhold land was held in undivided shares, the entirety of the freehold estate in fee simple vested in trustees for sale in accordance with the L.P.A. 1925, Sched. 1, Part IV, *ante,* p. 305 *et seq.*

(v) Where the copyhold land was subject to a trust for sale, or was made so subject by the 1925 legislation, the freehold estate in fee simple (subject to the terms of mortgagees) vested in the trustees for sale under the provisions of the L.P.A. 1925, Sched. 1, Pt. II.

Copyhold land subject to an existing lease.—It is provided, in effect, by the L.P.A. 1922, Sched. 12, para. (3), that where the land was at the commencement of the Act, or by virtue of the Act, subject to any existing lease, for a term of years absolute into which the copyhold estate was converted should be the reversion immediately expectant on the lease, and any lease otherwise than for a term of years absolute took effect in equity only. But, in the case of manors in which it was the practice for copyholders in fee to grant derivative interests to persons admitted as copyholders of the manor in respect of those interests, this paragraph applied only in respect of leases taking effect out of the estate of the copyholder in fee.

Copyhold land granted for life or for years, with a right of perpetual renewal.—Section 135 of the L.P.A. 1922 provided that where copyhold land was held for life or lives or for years and the tenant had a perpetual right of renewal, then Pt. V of the Act applied as if the person who at the commencement of the Act was the admitted tenant or had the best right to be admitted in respect of such renewable interest had been admitted, or (as the case might be) had the best right to be admitted, in respect of the inheritance. If the last admitted tenant died before the commencement of the Act his personal representatives and not the person entitled by the custom of the manor were deemed to have had the best right to be admitted. The land so enfranchised vested in accordance with the provisions of Sched. 12 to the L.P.A. 1922 and the L.P.A. 1925, Sched. 1, Pts. II and VIII, or the S.L.A. 1925, Sched. 2.

Effect of enfranchisement on equitable interests.—In the case of the *beneficial interest*, with a few exceptions there was no alteration in the law, and the persons who were beneficially entitled before 1926 continued after 1925 to have the same interests ; see the detailed provision of the L.P.A. 1922, Sched. 12, para. (2). The most important exception is in the special case of the old fee simple conditional on the birth of issue. This became an ordinary estate tail in equity ; for an explanation see the 13th Edition of this book, pp. 1250, 1251.

Effect of enfranchisement on mortgages.—It is provided by the L.P.A. 1922, Sched. 12, para. (1) (*f*), that every mortgage of the copyhold estate in the land should become a mortgage of the land for a term of years absolute in accordance with the provisions of Pt. I of the Act, which provisions were replaced by the L.P.A. 1925, Sched. 1, Pts. VII and VIII, *post*, p. 1033 *et seq.*

Title to enfranchised copyholds.—The purchaser under an open contract can require the copyhold title if and so far as it may still be necessary to go back to a good root of title at least as old as the statutory period of title.

However, on the sale of freehold land which was formerly copyhold, the contract ought to state whether the rights of the lord in the mines and minerals, and other rights of the lord not coming within the expression " manorial incidents " used in the Acts and preserved to him (see p. 154) are existing, or have by agreement between him and the tenant been treated as " manorial incidents " and become extinguished. See the following cases : *Upperton* v. *Nickolson* (1871), L.R. 6 Ch. 436 ; *Bellamy* v. *Debenham* [1891] 1 Ch. 412 ; *Re Jackson and Haden's Contract* [1906] 1 Ch. 412. Knowledge by a purchaser that the land has formerly been of copyhold tenure will not give him constructive notice that the rights in the minerals are excepted (*Bellamy* v. *Debenham, ante*). See further, as to the rights of the lord and the tenant in the mines and minerals, at p. 154.

The rights of the lord in mines and minerals, and other matters mentioned at p. 154, which were not otherwise extinguished, may have been extinguished by agreement. But, under a contract to sell the freehold, the purchaser will not have the right to call for the title of the lord of the manor or other person entering into any compensation agreement or giving a receipt for the compensation money to enter into such agreement or to give such receipt, and will not be deemed to be affected with notice of any matter or thing of which, if he had contracted that such title should be furnished, he might have had notice (L.P.A. 1925, s. 44 (7)). The effect of this subsection is to make the compensation agreement conclusive as to the right to give a receipt for the compensation money, and a purchaser is not entitled to an abstract of the lord's title.

It is not now necessary for a purchaser's solicitor to inquire of the steward whether there are any fines or fees unpaid, because any that may be outstanding will have become barred by lapse of time (L.P.A. 1922, s. 130 (5)).

So long as any of the manorial incidents saved by the L.P.A. 1922, s. 128, *ante*, p. 153, remained unextinguished (that is, until a compensation agreement was made, or until automatic extinguishment took place on 1st January, 1936), every assurance of any land or any interest therein had to be produced to the steward of the manor within six calendar months of its execution, or within such extended period as the court might for any special reason allow (*ibid.*, s. 129 (1)). An " assurance " is defined as not including a will or a grant or assignment of a lease or tenancy for a year or less or from year to year, but including an assent, an order of a court and a vesting declaration ; where an assurance by a personal representative was produced the probate or letters of administration also had to be produced (*ibid.*, s. 129 (9)). In default of such production it was provided that the assurance should become void so far as regards the grant or conveyance of a legal estate (*ibid.*, s. 129 (1)). Nevertheless (even if within the period for which title is deduced), it is not now necessary for a purchaser to ensure that an assurance made during the relevant period was produced and endorsed by the steward with a certificate under *ibid.*, s. 129 (2), because the effect of non-production would merely be to leave the *legal* estate outstanding. As the latest date when production could be necessary was 31st December, 1935, any outstanding legal estate will now have vested in the person entitled in equity under the Limitation Act, 1939 (compare *Sands to Thompson* (1883), 22 Ch. D. 614 ; *Re Cussons, Ltd.* (1904), 73 L.J. Ch. 296).

Registered land.—In the property register of the title to enfranchised copyholds, a statement will be entered that the land was formerly copyhold of a named manor and that the mines and minerals and other of the lord's rights excepted from the enfranchisement are not included in the registration (see further as to such mines and minerals Ruoff and Roper, Registered Conveyancing, 3rd ed., p. 242). " Rights of fishing and sporting, seignorial and manorial rights of all descriptions (until extinguished) and franchises " are overriding interests (L.R.A. 1925, s. 70 (1) (*j*)).

Power to inspect court rolls.—Any person interested in enfranchised land may, on payment of the fee prescribed by the Lord Chancellor, inspect at any reasonable hour any court rolls of the manor of which the land was held ; and court rolls will (even after the manorial incidents have been extinguished) for the purposes of s. 14 of the Evidence Act, 1851, be deemed to be documents of such a public nature as to be admissible in evidence on their mere production from the proper custody (L.P.A. 1922, s. 144).

Under the L.P.A. 1922, s. 144A (inserted by the Law of Property (Amendment Act, 1924), all manorial documents are under the charge of the Master of the Rolls, but they are to remain in the possession or under the control of the lord for the time being of the manor. He is not entitled to destroy or damage wilfully such documents, and the Master of the Rolls may from time to time make inquiries for the purpose of ascertaining that such documents are in the proper custody, and are being properly preserved, or may direct that any manorial documents which are not being properly preserved be transferred to the Public Record Office. Nothing contained in the section is to prejudice or affect the right of any person to the production and delivery of copies of any manorial documents.

PART 9. DOCTRINE OF NOTICE

Notice of a lease ; see p. 145.

Notice to purchaser of an irremovable defect in title ; see p. 97.

Generally.—As a rule, both at law and in equity, where there are competing interests in any property, they will rank for priority according to their order of creation (*Cave* v. *Cave* (1880), 15 Ch. D. 639).   The two primary exceptions to this rule in the context of title to land are found, first, in the machinery whereby certain interests may be " overreached " on a sale (see Part 10, *post,* p. 172), and secondly, in the well-known doctrine that the *bona fide* purchaser for value of a legal estate takes free from all existing equitable interests (*not* legal estates or interests, these being binding independently of notice) of which he has no notice (*Pilcher* v. *Rawlins* (1872), 7 Ch. App. 259).

Recent examples of interests prevailing on the basis of being first in time are to be found in *McCarthy & Stone, Ltd.* v. *Julian S. Hodge & Co., Ltd.* [1971] 1 W.L.R. 1547 (where an equitable interest acquired by virtue of contract for sale of land retained priority over the interest subsequently created by an equitable mortgage) and in *Barclays Bank, Ltd.* v. *Taylor* [1973] 2 W.L.R. 293 (where the Court of Appeal held that an equitable mortgage had priority over a purchaser's equitable interest as it was first in time, notwithstanding that title to the land was registered).

Notice given by registration.—The L.P.A. 1925, s. 198, provides as follows :—

" 198.—(1) The registration of any instrument or matter under the provisions of the Land Charges Act, 1925, or any enactment which it replaces, in any register kept at the land registry *or elsewhere,* shall be deemed to constitute actual notice of such instrument or matter, and of the fact of such registration, to all persons and for all purposes connected with the land affected, as from the date of registration or other prescribed date and so long as the registration continues in force.

(2) This section operates without prejudice to the provisions of this Act respecting the making of further advances by a mortgagee, and applies only to instruments and matters required or authorised to be registered under the Land Charges Act, 1925."

See now the L.C.A. 1972, largely replacing the L.C.A. 1925.

" *or elsewhere.*"—Section 198 (1) must be read with s. 205 (3) of the L.P.A. 1925, which provides that references to registration under the Land Charges Act apply to any registration made under any other statute which is by that Act to have effect as if the registration had been made under that Act.   An example of such a reference is to be found in s. 3 (7) (8) of the L.C.A. 1972, whereby a land charge for securing money created by a company before 1st January, 1970 (or at any time as a floating charge) is sufficiently protected by registration under s. 95 of the Companies Act, 1948, in place of registration under the L.C.A. 1972 and has effect as if it were registered under the L.C.A. 1972.   However, company charges (not being floating charges) created on or after that date, in order to bind purchasers for value, must be protected by deposit of documents or else by registration under the L.C.A. 1972.   Registration within s. 95 of the Companies Act, 1948, is still required, but does not suffice alone.

With regard to the effect of the L.P.A. 1925, s. 198 (1), as between prospective vendors and purchasers of land, the effect of s. 24 of the L.P.A. 1969 on the so-called rule in *Re Forsey and Hollebone's Contract* [1927] 2 Ch. 379 has already been discussed at pp. 4–5.

Section 198 of the L.P.A. 1925, applies only to instruments and matters *required or authorised* to be registered under the L.C.A. (L.P.A. 1925, s. 198 (2)). Therefore, the registration of a matter which does not fall within one of the classes properly registrable (as to which see *post*, p. 595 *et seq.*) does not by virtue of this section give notice to persons dealing with the land.

The section operates without prejudice to the provisions of the Act respecting the making of further advances by a mortgagee. This reference is to s. 94 (2) of the L.P.A. 1925, which provides, in effect, that where a prior mortgage is made expressly for securing a current account or other further advances, the prior mortgagee will not be deemed to have notice of a later incumbrance, merely by reason of the fact that it was registered as a land charge or in a local deeds registry, unless it was so registered at the date of the original advance or when the last search (if any) by or on behalf of the mortgagee was made, whichever last happened. See chapter on Mortgages, *post*, p. 970.

Undisclosed land charges.—The L.P.A. 1925, s. 198, has produced unfortunate results. A purchaser is deemed to have actual notice of matters even if they were registered against prior owners soon after 1925. The root of title may, however, be after 1925 and so he may not even know the names of the persons against whom registration might have been effected, say, in 1926.

However, the unfortunate results referred to (which would have been even more serious since the reduction in the statutory period of title to fifteen years from thirty years) have now been mitigated in a financial sense following recommendations of the Law Commission (" Transfer of Land—Report on Land Charges Affecting Unregistered Land," Law. Com. No. 18). The L.P.A. 1969, s. 25, makes provision for compensation to be paid (by the Chief Land Registrar) where a purchaser has suffered loss because he had " no actual knowledge " of a registered land charge binding the land until after completion (being post-1969). It is a pre-condition that the registered land charge, in essence, could not have been discovered by searching against the names of the estate owners revealed in a perfect abstract covering the full period of title accepted by the purchaser (not being shorter than the new statutory period of fifteen years).

The section applies in relation to instruments or matters (other than local land charges) registered under the L.C.A. (s. 25 (10) of the 1969 Act) and affords compensation not only following purchases but also following exchanges, mortgages, grants of sub-leases, compulsory purchases and conveyances under the Leasehold Reform Act, 1967 (s. 25 (9) of the 1969 Act). It is inapplicable by nature to transfers of registered land and does not cover the cases where the purchaser's ignorance of whom to search against is due to the statutory restrictions on the investigation of leasehold titles (see p. 143 *et seq.*, *ante* ; s. 25 (9), (10) of the 1969 Act).

The question whether a person had actual knowledge of a land charge is determined for the purposes of these compensation provisions without any reference to the deemed actual notice imposed by the L.P.A. 1925, s. 198 (s. 25 (2) of the 1969 Act). However, any knowledge (the word " actual " is

6

here oddly omitted) acquired in the course of the transaction by such a person's counsel, solicitor or other agent will be treated as his knowledge (s. 25 (11), *ibid.*).

Where compensation has once been claimed under s. 25 of the 1969 Act, the Chief Land Registrar is empowered to amend the register and its alphabetical index so as to ensure that the charge concerned never again remains undisclosed (Land Charges (No. 2) Rules, 1972).

Accordingly the general position as to land charges not disclosed to a purchaser before contract is as follows : *First*, a purchaser is expected to discover by searching before completion any charge registered against estate owners named in the root of title or subsequent title deeds and then to exercise his contractual rights against the vendor. *Secondly*, any other registered land charges which the purchaser did not discover before completion and which bind him afterwards, give rise to compensation from, in effect, the State which imposed the flawed system of registration against names.

Notice given by registration in the Yorkshire Registries.—As to the closing of the Yorkshire deeds registries in consequence of the extension to their areas of compulsory registration of title, see L.P.A. 1969, s. 16, and *post*, p. 611 *et seq.* At the time of writing, the East Riding Register alone still survives. It is provided by s. 197 of the L.P.A. 1925 as follows :—

" 197.—(1) The registration in a local deeds registry of a memorial of any instrument *transferring or creating a legal estate* or charge by way of legal mortgage, shall be deemed to constitute *actual notice of the transfer or creation* of the legal estate or charge by way of legal mortgage, to all persons and for all purposes whatsoever, as from the date of registration or other prescribed date, and so long as the registration continues in force.

(2) The registration of a memorial of an instrument not required to be registered does not operate to give notice of such instrument or of the contents thereof.

(3) This section operates without prejudice to the provisions of this Act respecting the making of further advances by a mortgagee, and only applies to land within the jurisdiction of the registry." (This refers to s. 94 (2) of the L.P.A. 1925).

Note that provision has been made for the repeal of this section on the closing of the Yorkshire deeds registries : L.P.A. 1969, s. 15 (2) and Sched. 2, Pt. I.

" *transferring or creating a legal estate.*"—As a result of the L.P.A. 1925, s. 11, as to which see *post*, p. 612, the only documents requiring registration in a local deeds registry after 1925 were those operating to transfer or create a legal estate, or to create a charge thereon by way of legal mortgage.

" *actual notice of the transfer or creation.*"—The result is that registration of such a document in one of the Yorkshire Registries gave notice *of the transfer or creation of the legal estate or charge by way of legal mortgage.* It is noteworthy that the Act does not state that notice is thereby given of all the contents of the document ; this point may be open to argument.

A *puisne* mortgage (as to which see *post*, p. 598) is a legal mortgage, and therefore, when affecting land in, now, the East Riding of Yorkshire, must be registered by way of memorial in the local deeds registry and not as a land charge. If the land is partly in the area and partly out, it must be registered as a land charge at the Land Registry as well as by memorial in the local deeds registry.

Rules regarding the Middlesex Deeds Register.—Sections 11 and 197 of the L.P.A. 1925 formerly applied to the Middlesex Deeds Register as they apply to the Yorkshire Deeds Registers, but by the Middlesex Deeds Act, 1940, s. 1 (1), that register was closed. The Land Registration Act, 1936, s. 2, had provided that no memorial of any instrument made after 31st December, 1936, could be registered except certain entries of discharge of mortgages.

The closing of the register does not affect the consequences under the Middlesex Deeds Acts of any failure to register a memorial of an instrument capable of registration. Under the Middlesex Registry Act, 1708, a conveyance of land in Middlesex was void against a subsequent purchaser or mortgagee for value unless a memorial was registered before the memorial of the subsequent purchase or mortgage was registered, although a subsequent purchaser or mortgagee could not get priority if he had actual notice of the unregistered instrument.

In the case, however, of a purchase which takes place after 9th July, 1940, if the purchaser has no notice of a transaction a memorial of which was duly registered, he will have the same rights as if the memorial had not been registered (Middlesex Deeds Act, 1940, s. 1 (2)). A person suffering loss as a result of s. 1 (2) is entitled to indemnity out of public funds unless he has caused or substantially contributed to the loss by his act, neglect or default (*ibid.*, s. 3 (1) and (2)).

By the Middlesex Deeds Act, 1940, and the L.P.A. 1925, s. 97, *puisne* mortgages of land will rank, if made after 1925, according to date of registration under the *L.C.A.*, *even if they had previously been registered by memorial.* There is provision for indemnity of a person suffering loss as a result of this change (Act of 1940, s. 3).

Actual knowledge of unregistered charges or documents.—It must now be regarded as settled that a purchaser for value who has actual and admitted knowledge of a land charge, say a restrictive covenant, which ought to have been registered but which has not been registered, is not bound by the covenant by reason of such actual notice. This is the result of s. 199 (1) (i) of the L.P.A. 1925, which provides :—

" 199.—(1) A purchaser shall not be prejudicially affected by notice of—

(i) any instrument or matter capable of registration under the provisions of the Land Charges Act, 1925, or any enactment which it replaces, which is void or not enforceable as against him under that Act or enactment, by reason of the non-registration thereof."

Although there is no binding decision on s. 199, Harman, J., said, *obiter*, in *Hollington Brothers, Ltd.* v. *Rhodes* [1951] 2 All E.R. 578, that matters which are void and which are stated by the L.P.A. 1925, s. 199, not to prejudice a purchaser cannot be validated by an equitable doctrine of notice. Further, the decision in *Re Monolithic Building Co.* [1915] 1 Ch. 643, provides authority for this view. The Companies (Consolidation) Act, 1908, s. 93 (now Companies Act, 1948, s. 95), made an unregistered mortgage of a company void against the liquidator and creditors. The Court of Appeal held that a registered mortgagee had priority over an unregistered mortgagee even though he took with *actual* notice. Cozens-Hardy, M.R., said : " It is not fraud to take advantage of legal rights."

It must be remembered that " purchaser " in s. 199 means " a purchaser in good faith for *valuable consideration* and includes a lessee, mortgagee or

other person who for valuable consideration acquires an interest in property "
(L.P.A. 1925, s. 205 (1) (xxi)).　Also it should be appreciated that there may
be a collateral liability on indemnity covenants notwithstanding the statutory
consequences of non-registration (see *Eagon* v. *Dent* [1965] 3 All E.R. 334).

The provision of s. 199 (1) (i), that if a charge be not registered a purchaser
will not be affected, applies to *local* land charges in the same way as it does
to other land charges.　See further, *post*, p. 627.

Notice from possession of deeds.—If deeds are in the hands of some
person other than the vendor, or the person who ought to hold them, the
purchaser is thereby placed on inquiry as to the reason for this, and he has
constructive notice of the facts which such inquiry would disclose (*Spencer* v.
Clarke (1878), 47 L.J. Ch. 692).

So, if a purchaser omits to use ordinary care in making inquiry for the
deeds, or omits to insist upon the deeds being handed to him when he is
entitled to possession of them, he will be deemed to be guilty of conduct
which will amount to evidence of a fraudulent intention to escape notice of
some third parties' claims (*Northern Counties of England Fire Insurance
Co.* v. *Whipp* (1884), 26 Ch. D. 482).　Since this decision the doctrine of
carelessness has been considerably extended, and it is now unnecessary
to prove a fraudulent intent ; it is sufficient to show " gross negligence."
In *Oliver* v. *Hinton* [1899] 2 Ch. 264, Lindley, M.R., said : " To deprive a
purchaser for value without notice of a prior incumbrance of the protection
of the legal estate it is not, in my opinion, essential that he should have been
guilty of fraud ; it is sufficient that he has been guilty of such gross negligence
as would render it unjust to deprive the prior incumbrancer of his priority."
In that case the agent of the purchaser inquired about the deeds, and the
vendor told him that he held them, but that they could not be handed over
on completion because they also related to other property.　Under these
circumstances, it was clearly the duty of the agent to ask to see the deeds.
He omitted to do so, and it turned out afterwards that they were in the
possession of an equitable mortgagee.　This case was followed in *Walker* v.
Linom [1907] 2 Ch. 104, in which Parker, J., decided that a legal mortgagee
will be postponed notwithstanding that he may have been perfectly honest,
if he has been guilty of such negligence as to make it inequitable for him to
rely on his legal estate so as to deprive a prior incumbrancer of his priority.
In *Hudston* v. *Viney* [1921] 1 Ch. 98, " gross negligence " was defined as
" at least, carelessness of so aggravated a nature as to amount to the neglect
of precautions which an ordinary reasonable man would have observed, and
to indicate an attitude of mental indifference to obvious risks."　In that case,
a legal mortgage was taken by a bank without investigation of title, and it
subsequently appeared that there was a prior equitable charge on the
property.　It was held that there had been some negligence, but not sufficient
to deprive the bank of priority.

Section 13 of the L.P.A. 1925 provides that the Act " shall not prejudicially
affect the right or interest of any person arising out of or consequent on the
possession by him of any documents relating to a legal estate in land, *nor
affect any question arising out of or consequent upon any omission to obtain*
or any other absence of possession by any person of any documents relating
to a legal estate in land."

Constructive notice by acceptance of a short title.—It is provided by
s. 44 (8) of the L.P.A. 1925 that a purchaser will not be deemed to be or ever

to have been affected with notice of any matter or thing of which, if he had investigated the title or made inquiries in regard to matters prior to the period of commencement of title fixed by the Act, or by any other statute, or by any rule of law, he might have had notice, unless he actually makes such investigation or inquiries. But a purchaser who accepts less than a fifteen years' title will be deemed to have constructive notice of matters he would have discovered if he had insisted on having a full legal title (*Re Cox and Neve's Contract* [1891] 2 Ch. 109 ; *Oliver* v. *Hinton* [1899] 2 Ch. 264 ; *Re Nisbet and Pott's Contract* [1906] 1 Ch. 386). A solicitor, therefore, should not accept less than a full legal title without his client's authority.

It is provided by s. 44 (5) of the L.P.A. 1925 that where by reason of subss. (2), (3) and (4) of the section (see p. 143), an intending lessee or assign is not entitled to call for the title to the freehold or to a leasehold reversion, as the case may be, he will not, where the contract is made after 1925, be deemed to be affected with notice of any matter or thing of which, if he had contracted that such title should be furnished, he might have had notice. This subsection overrules the decision in *Patman* v. *Harland* (1881), 17 Ch. D. 353, on this point. Where a lessee escapes from liability under subs. (5) of s. 44, the burden of proving that he had actual notice of a covenant entered into before 1926 lies on the person alleging that he had such notice (*Shears* v. *Wells* [1936] 1 All E.R. 832). However, Simonds, J., has observed that the L.P.A. 1925, s. 198, " appears, notwithstanding the unqualified language of s. 44 (5), to affect a lessee with notice of all those charges which are registered under the Land Charges Act, 1925 " (*White* v. *Bijou Mansions, Ltd.* [1937] Ch. 610, at p. 621 ; on appeal [1938] Ch. 351). Consequently the effect of s. 44 (5) is probably to enable a lessee to have priority only over such equitable interests as are not registrable and registered under the L.C.A. 1972, e.g., pre-1926 restrictive covenants or equitable mortgages of the reversion protected by deposit of documents.

This apparent injustice is not rectified by the L.P.A. 1969 in its provisions relating to undisclosed land charges (see *ante*, p. 161, as to s. 25). No compensation is made available to purchasers of leaseholds in respect of unknown land charges registered against freehold or superior leasehold estate owners (see s. 25 (10) of the 1969 Act). Also, although the compensation provisions are made available to the grantee of an underlease, they are withheld from the grantee of a lease out of the freehold (see s. 25 (9) of the 1969 Act ; the underlessee's claims for compensation are confined to land charges registered against the immediately superior leasehold title, which he can investigate : see s. 25 (10)).

Statutory limits on doctrine of constructive notice.—It is provided by s. 199 (1) (ii) of the L.P.A. 1925 that—

" 199.—(1) A purchaser shall not be prejudicially affected by notice of—

*   *   *   *   *

(ii) any *other* instrument or matter or any fact or thing unless—

      (*a*) it is within his own knowledge, or would have come to his knowledge if such inquiries and inspections had been made as ought reasonably to have been made by him ; or

      (*b*) in the same transaction with respect to which a question of notice to the purchaser arises, it has come to the knowledge of his counsel, as such, or of his solicitor or other agent, as such, or would have come to the knowledge of his solicitor or other agent, as such, if such inquiries and inspections had been made as ought reasonably to have been made by the solicitor or other agent."

The word " other " in supplied italics distinguishes the instruments or matters within s. 199 (1) (ii) from the instruments or matters which are void for non-registration and are referred to in s. 199 (1) (i), set out at p. 163.

As to when the knowledge of his solicitor is notice to the client under sub-para. (b), see p. 171.

Analysis of a wife's account, with a view to discovering whether she has an equitable interest in the matrimonial home, is not an inquiry which ought reasonably to be made within s. 199 (1) (ii) by a bank lending money to and taking a legal charge from the husband (Caunce v. Caunce [1969] 1 W.L.R. 286).

Another statutory limit on the doctrine is to be found in the T.A. 1925, s. 28, which provides as follows :—

" 28.   A trustee or personal representative acting for the purposes of more than one trust or estate shall not, in the absence of fraud, be affected by notice of any instrument, matter, fact or thing in relation to any particular trust or estate if he has obtained notice thereof merely by reason of his acting or having acted for the purposes of another trust or estate."

It is thought that s. 28 extends to actual knowledge. For instance, the trustee may have a notice in writing among his papers to which his attention has been recently drawn in connection with Trust No. 1, but it may convey no meaning to him in relation to Trust No. 2 ; if so, there would be no fraud.

A purchaser is not bound to investigate the title to land prior to a good root of title fifteen or more years old, and, if he does not make any inquiry into the earlier title, he will not be deemed to have notice of defects on such earlier title ; see p. 114. So also in the case of leasehold property where he is not by law entitled to call for or investigate the title to the freehold or leasehold reversion (see p. 143) he is not deemed to have notice of anything of which, if he had contracted that such title should be furnished, he might have had notice ; see p. 165.

The provisions of s. 199 (2) of the L.P.A. 1925, which replaces s. 3 (2) of the Conveyancing Act, 1882, sometimes cause misunderstanding. They are as follows :—

" 199.—(2) Paragraph (ii) of the last subsection shall not exempt a purchaser from any liability under, or any obligation to perform or observe, any covenant, condition, provision, or restriction contained in any instrument under which his title is derived, mediately or immediately ; and such liability or obligation may be enforced in the same manner and to the same extent as if that paragraph had not been enacted."

The subsection would not appear to make any alteration in the law as it would exist if the subsection had not been included in s. 199, and its purpose is difficult to understand. The general effect of this subsection is that a purchaser of the fee simple will be bound by provisions in any deed forming part of the title *unless either he escapes as a purchaser without notice, or the equitable interest is overreached under the statutory provisions, or is defeated* by reason of non-registration or otherwise.

Implied notice from occupation of land.—A purchaser will have constructive notice of any rights reasonably discoverable from inspection of the property and, in particular, from inquiry of any occupier as to his interest and the terms on which he holds it (*Hunt* v. *Luck* [1902] 1 Ch. 428). Therefore, a purchaser should carefully ascertain the nature of the tenancies affecting the property ; and if there are any leases or agreements in writing, copies or an abstract should be asked for. It is expressly enacted by s. 14 of the L.P.A. 1925 that Pt. I of that Act shall not prejudicially affect the interest of any person in possession or in actual occupation of land to which he may be entitled in right of such possession. However,'it must be borne in mind that s. 199 (1) (i) is not contained in Pt. I of the L.P.A. 1925 so that if the occupier's interest or rights happen to be registrable under the L.C.A. 1972 but are not so registered then they will be void as against a purchaser despite the occupation (and see s. 4 of the L.C.A. 1972). This applies especially to the common case of occupation by virtue of an agreement for a lease which is registrable as an " estate contract " (L.C.A. 1972, s. 2 (4), Class C (iv), and s. 4 (6)). The purchaser may also assume that a written agreement correctly sets out the rights as between landlord and tenant (*Smith* v. *Jones* [1954] 1 W.L.R. 1089). In that case it was decided that an action by a tenant for rectification of a tenancy agreement will not succeed against a subsequent purchaser who has inspected it.

But a tenant's occupation is not notice *of his lessor's title* or rights. It was contended in *Hunt* v. *Luck, ante,* that if the proposed purchasers had inquired of the tenants, " To whom do you pay your rents ? " they would have ascertained that some other person than the person who proposed to give a title to the land was the true owner, and that they, not having made this inquiry, were affected by constructive notice of the true owner's title. It was also held, in the same case, that it is not the duty of a purchaser or mortgagee to inquire of the tenants to whom they pay their rents either under s. 3 of the Conveyancing Act, 1882 (now replaced by s. 199 (1) (ii) of the L.P.A. 1925), or under the law as it stood independently of that Act.

Stamp, J., has held that a purchaser (or mortgagee) will not be affected with constructive notice of the equitable interests of any persons (such as spouses) who may be resident on the property and whose presence is wholly consistent with the title of the vendor (or mortgagor) being a sole legal owner and himself in occupation (*Caunce* v. *Caunce* [1969] 1 W.L.R. 286 ; considered by Stephen Cretney in *Solicitors' Journal,* vol. 113, p. 397). However, since then the Court of Appeal has considered a case in which the vendor was sole legal owner and himself in occupation but in reality held the house on a resulting trust for the benefit of a lady who was also in occupation, and has indicated a rather different conclusion (*Hodgson* v. *Marks* [1971] Ch. 892). In fact, title to the land in question was registered and the lady was held to have an overriding interest within s. 70 (1) (*g*) of the L.R.A. (see p. 188, *post*). Nevertheless, Russell, L.J., is reported as observing more generally that " I do not consider that it is correct in law to say that any rights of a person who is in occupation will be overridden whenever the vendor is, or appears to be, also in occupation." He further indicated that whether a person other than the vendor was in occupation of unregistered land for the purpose of constructive notice . . . " must depend on the circumstances, and a wise purchaser or lender will take no risks . . . Reliance on the untrue *ipse dixit* of the vendor will not suffice " (at [1971] Ch., pp. 932 and 935). The obvious practical difficulties for purchasers becoming involved in intricate and controversial inquiries of deciding what it is reasonable to pursue had already been underlined by Lord Wilberforce in *National Provincial Bank, Ltd.* v. *Ainsworth* [1965] A.C. 1175, at p. 1250.

In *McCarthy & Stone, Ltd.* v. *Julian S. Hodge* [1971] 1 W.L.R. 1547, Foster, J., held that a purchaser's building activities on the land sufficed to give constructive notice of his equitable interest under the contract of sale to a subsequent equitable mortgagee, notwithstanding a contention that these activities were consistent with the vendor-mortgagor's title.

It now appears that a person having a licence to use land may hold an equitable interest enforceable against a purchaser other than one who takes a legal estate for value without notice (*Errington* v. *Errington* [1952] 1 K.B. 290 ; also *per* Lord Denning, M.R., in *Inwards* v. *Baker* [1965] 2 Q.B. 29, at p. 32 and in *Binions* v. *Evans* [1972] 2 W.L.R. 729). Consequently, as licences are apparently not registrable, it is necessary that a purchaser should ascertain whether any person is in possession, or has other rights, by virtue of a licence not immediately revocable. See the conclusions drawn by Professor F. R. Crane after a very full discussion in the *Conveyancer N.S.*, vol. 16, p. 323 *et seq.* and vol. 31, p. 332 *et seq.*

Recent decisions have also suggested that a tenancy granted by a purchaser/mortgagor between contract and completion may in some cases be binding on a mortgagee advancing part of the purchase-money. See the discussion in the chapter on Mortgages, *post*, p. 970. It follows that, on the present state of the authorities, a mortgagee should inquire whether anyone is in possession under the authority of such a tenancy.

As to the rights of every person in occupation of the land where title to it is registered under the L.R.A. 1925–1971 being " overriding interests," see *post*, p. 188.

Effect of notice of document.—Notice of a document *necessarily* affecting the title, or which is stated to affect the title, is notice of its contents, unless inspection of the deed could not be obtained (*Patman* v. *Harland* (1881), 17 Ch. D. 353). Thus in *Hooper* v. *Bromet* (1904), 90 L.T. 234, a sub-purchaser of a plot of land on a building estate was told that the original deed of conveyance was lost. He was shown a copy, but it was eventually found that the copy did not disclose a restrictive covenant contained in the original deed. It was held that the purchaser, having notice of the deed, was affected by notice of its actual contents. A distinction is drawn between documents which must necessarily affect the title and those which might or might not do so. To the latter class the rule is not applicable (*English and Scottish Mercantile Investment Trust* v. *Brunton* [1892] 2 Q.B. 700 ; *Re Alms Corn Charity* [1901] 2 Ch. 750).

Acknowledgments for production, etc., should, therefore, be carefully examined and information as to the contents of the deeds mentioned therein obtained where possible.

Notice, of trusts affecting mortgage money.—Even before 1926 a purchaser could not go behind a recital in a transfer of mortgage evidently framed for the purpose of keeping notice of a trust off the title ; e.g., a recital that the trustees were entitled in equity (*Re Harman and Uxbridge and Rickmansworth Railway Co.* (1883), 24 Ch. D. 720). But if by a slip it was disclosed that the mortgage money belonged to mortgagees as trustees under a settlement or a will, and the trusts on which they held it were also disclosed, from which it appeared that they were not the original trustees, the purchaser could ask for the title of the trustees to be traced from the date of the settlement (*Re Blaiberg and Abraham's Contract* [1899] 2 Ch. 340). This was a very inconvenient decision, and s. 113 of the L.P.A. 1925 was passed to meet it. By subss. (1), (2), of this section it is provided as follows :—

" 113.—(1) A person dealing in good faith with a mortgagee, or with the mortgagor if the mortgage has been discharged released or postponed as to the whole or any part of *the mortgaged property*, shall not be concerned with any trust at any time affecting the mortgage money or the income thereof, *whether or not he has notice of the trust*, and may assume unless the contrary is expressly stated in the instruments relating to the mortgage—

(a) that the mortgagees (if more than one) are or were entitled to the mortgage money on a joint account ; and

(b) that the mortgagee has or had power to give valid receipts for the purchase money or mortgage money and the income thereof (including any arrears of interest) and to release or postpone the priority of the mortgage debt or any part thereof or to deal with the same or the mortgaged property or any part thereof ;

without investigating the equitable title to the mortgage debt or the appointment or discharge of trustees in reference thereto.

(2) This section applies to mortgages made before or after the commencement of this Act, *but only as respects dealings effected after such commencement.*"

The fact that a transfer of a mortgage was stamped 10s. (*sic*) only did not give the purchaser notice of a trust, *whether the stamp has been adjudicated or not* (L.P.A. 1925, s. 112, replacing Conveyancing Act, 1911, s. 13).

Recitals to keep trusts off the title.—The rule that a recital may be framed to keep notice of a trust off the title was not confined to mortgages, but applied and still applies to a *conveyance* of land. If, therefore, there is a recital that *A* and *B* are trustees for *C* absolutely, a purchaser is under no obligation to inquire as to the creation of the trust or to require proof that the alleged trustees were the duly constituted trustees and able to give a receipt for the purchase-money without the joinder of the parties beneficially entitled (*Re Chafter and Randall's Contract* [1916] 2 Ch. 8 ; *Re Soden and Alexander's Contract* [1918] 2 Ch. 258).

It may, however, be dangerous to keep trusts off the title. Thus, in *Re King's Settlement* [1931] 2 Ch. 294, a settlor, in order to keep trusts of a settlement off the title, conveyed property to grantees in consideration of love and affection, and such grantees at the same time executed a deed poll declaring trusts in favour of the settlor and others. The deeds were handed to the grantees, except the deed poll, which was held by the settlor's solicitor. The grantees, as absolute owners, created equitable incumbrances on the property. It was held by Farwell, J., that as the conveyance to the grantees contained a direct misrepresentation implying that the grantees were absolute owners, the settlor and other beneficiaries were estopped from denying this statement against the equitable incumbrancers, and the prior equity of the beneficiaries was therefore postponed.

But it was also decided in *Re Soden and Alexander's Contract* that if, in the case of a conveyance, the trusts were disclosed, or even if it appeared from the recital that the property was held in trust for a person under a deed or a will, this made it necessary to require evidence that the trustees proposing to convey were the duly constituted trustees of the settlement. This has now to be read with the post-1925 law. For where the land is settled

land any power of sale given by the settlement to the trustees thereunder
has to be construed as given to the tenant for life or statutory owners
(S.L.A. 1925, ss. 108, 109) ; and on a sale by such tenant for life or statutory
owners the purchaser has to assume that the trustees of the settlement referred
to in the last or only vesting deed are the trustees thereof and have been
properly appointed, except in the cases mentioned in s. 110 (2) of the S.L.A.
1925. See at p. 689.

Recital giving notice of a breach of trust.—When trust moneys have,
in breach of trust, been invested in the purchase of land, a purchaser from
the trustees will get a good title under s. 23 of the L.P.A. 1925 on the ground
that the land has become subject to an implied trust for sale. Section 23
provides that where land has, either before or after the commencement of
the Act, become subject to an express or *implied* trust for sale, such trust
will, so far as regards the safety and protection of any purchaser thereunder,
be deemed to be subsisting *until the land has been conveyed* to or under the
direction of the persons interested in the proceeds of sale. So that even if
a purchaser has actual notice that the parties beneficially entitled have all
attained a vested interest in the property, and are all of age, he will still
get a good title so long as the property has not been actually conveyed to
them.

Similarly, when trust moneys have, in breach of trust, been invested on
mortgage, a purchaser from the trustees under their power of sale will get
a good title, as the trustees will only be doing their duty in remedying the
breach of trust by realising the fund (*Re Jenkins and Randall* [1903] 2 Ch. 362 ;
L.P.A. 1925, s. 23).

A purchaser is not affected with notice of matters which he could not have
learned without inquiring into the truth of recitals contained in the documents
of title, or otherwise going behind the documents themselves (*Earl of
Gainsborough* v. *Whatcombe Terra Cotta Clay Co.* (1885), 54 L.J. Ch. 991).

The danger of unnecessary recitals is also illustrated by *Re Duce and Boots
Cash Chemists (Southern), Ltd.'s Contract* [1937] Ch. 642, where a recital in an
assent contained details of the will which gave the purchaser notice that the
land was settled within the S.L.A. 1925 ; the conveyancing machinery of that
Act had not been complied with and Bennett, J., held that the purchaser
was unable, because of the recital, to accept the assent as " sufficient evidence "
of its own propriety under A.E.A. 1925, s. 36 (7).

Notice of a document or fact from an indorsement.—When purchasing
from personal representatives it has now become the established practice
to insert a recital in the conveyance to the effect that the personal representatives have not executed an assent or conveyance of the legal estate affecting
the property. But this is not sufficient. For any person in whose favour
an assent or conveyance will not protect the purchaser (*ibid.*, s. 36 (6)). The
on or annexed to the probate or letters of administration, at the cost of the
deceased's estate (A.E.A. 1925, s. 36 (5)) and, if that has been done, the
statement by the personal representatives that they have not given or made
an assent or conveyance will not protect the purchaser (*ibid.*, s. 36 (6)) The
solicitor, therefore, should always insist on the probate or letters of administration being produced to him (*Re Miller and Pickersgill's Contract* [1931]
1 Ch. 511).

A purchaser should also be on the look-out for indorsements indicating
that part of the property has been sold off.

A purchaser who does not take the deeds is entitled to require that a memorandum should be indorsed on a deed selected by him giving notice of any restrictive covenants and grants of easements over land retained by the vendor. This is provided for by s. 200 of the L.P.A. 1925, a portion of which is given below. It will be noticed, however, that such an indorsement does not make it unnecessary to register a restrictive covenant or an *equitable* easement as a land charge. It is expedient that notice of legal estates should be indorsed, not to protect them, but to prevent their being overlooked when an abstract is prepared.

The section of the L.P.A. 1925 is given below :—

" 200.—(1) Where land having a common title with other land is disposed of to a purchaser (other than a lessee or a mortgagee) who does not hold or obtain possession of the documents forming the common title, such purchaser, notwithstanding any stipulation to the contrary, may require that a memorandum giving notice of any provision contained in the disposition to him restrictive of user of, or giving rights over, any other land comprised in the common title, shall, where practicable, be written or indorsed on, or, where impracticable, be permanently annexed to some one document selected by the purchaser but retained in the possession or power of the person who makes the disposition, and being or forming part of the common title.

(2) The title of any person omitting to require an indorsement to be made or a memorandum to be annexed shall not, by reason only of this enactment, be prejudiced or affected by the omission.

(3) This section does not apply to dispositions of registered land.

(4) Nothing in this section affects the obligation to register a land charge in respect of—

(a) any restrictive covenant or agreement affecting freehold land ; or

(b) any estate contract ; or

(c) any equitable easement, liberty or privilege."

When knowledge of solicitor constructive notice to client.—The rule is that a purchaser is deemed to have notice of an instrument, matter, fact or thing if, *in the same transaction with respect to which a question of notice to the purchaser arises*, it has come to the knowledge of his solicitor, as such, or would have come to the knowledge of his solicitor, as such, if such inquiries and inspections had been made as ought reasonably to have been made by the solicitor (L.P.A. 1925, s. 199 (1) (ii) (b)). The purchaser is not deemed to have notice when the solicitor would certainly conceal the fact from the client : for instance, his own fraud (*Kennedy* v. *Green* (1834), 3 Myl. & K. 699 ; *Lloyds Bank Limited* v. *Pearson* [1901] 1 Ch. 865 ; compare *Dixon* v. *Winch* [1900] 1 Ch. 736).

Notice to the solicitor of trustees or mortgagees of an assignment or mortgage is not sufficient. The notice to be effectual must be communicated to the trustees or mortgagees (*Saffron Walden Second Benefit Building Society* v. *Rayner* (1880), 14 Ch. D. 406). In the same case the Court of Appeal strongly discountenanced the view that there is such a thing as a permanent office of solicitor, or that a solicitor who happens to be in the habit of acting for a person is his agent so as to bind him by receiving notices or information.

In another case, where s. 3 of the Conveyancing Act, 1882 (now represented by s. 199 (1) (ii) of the L.P.A. 1925), was much discussed, the same solicitor acted for mortgagor and mortgagee, and the court refused to impute to the mortgagee notice either of facts known to the mortgagor or of facts which had come to the knowledge of the solicitor when acting in *previous* transactions for other mortgagees of the same property (*Re Cousins* (1885), 31 Ch. D. 671). See also *Thorne* v. *Heard* [1895] A.C. 495.

For a case where it was held that such inquiry as ought reasonably to have been made by the solicitor had not been made, see *Re Alms Corn Charity* [1901] 2 Ch. 750. A person cannot escape the consequences of constructive notice by employing a dishonest solicitor (*Berwick & Co.* v. *Price* [1905] 1 Ch. 632).

Registered land.—The doctrine of notice, in effect, plays no part in conveyancing under the L.R.A. 1925–1971. This is because of the so-called " curtain principle " that " the register is the sole source of information for proposing purchasers, who need not, and indeed, must not, concern themselves with trusts and equities which lie behind the curtain " (Ruoff, The Torrens System, p. 11). This principle is carried out by s. 74 of the L.R.A. 1925 which provides that no person " dealing with a registered estate . . . shall be affected by notice of a trust express, implied or constructive," and by ss. 20 (1) and 23 (1) of the same Act which provide that registration should confer the legal estate on a transferee subject to any entries on the register and to overriding interests " but free from all other estates and interests whatsoever." Thus, as Cross, J., has said, " It must, however, be borne in mind, first, that it is vital to the working of the land registration system that notice of something which is not on the register of title in question shall not affect a transferee unless it is an overriding interest . . ." (*Strand Securities, Ltd.* v. *Caswell* [1965] Ch. 373, at p. 390 ; on appeal *ibid.*, p. 958 ; see also *per* Simonds, J., in *White* v. *Bijou Mansions, Ltd.* [1937] Ch. 610, at p. 620 ; affirmed [1938] Ch. 351 and *per* Bridge, J., in *Miles* v. *Bull* (*No.* 2) [1969] 3 All E.R. 1585, at pp. 1589–1590). As to protection by entries on the register, see *post*, p. 618, and as to " overriding interests," see *post*, p. 184.

PART 10. INTERESTS OVERREACHABLE ON CONVEYANCE OF LEGAL ESTATE

Meaning of expression " overreached."—When the expression " overreached " is used, it does not mean that the interest or power is destroyed, but that it is passed on to and becomes a charge on the consideration money ; and it is only when this passing on can be effected that the principle of " overreaching " can be applied. For instance, the principle of overreaching could not be applied to a restrictive covenant affecting land made after 1925 not registered as a land charge. In such a case it is obvious that the restrictive covenant could not be passed on to the purchase-money or other consideration, and the result would be that the purchaser, mortgagee or lessee would take the land free from the covenant, and the covenant would be destroyed. But where an equitable interest becomes void because it was not registered, it is often described as having been " overreached."

Overreaching of legal estates and interests.—Note first that there is nothing in s. 10 (1) of the L.P.A. 1925 (*ante*, p. 130) to suggest that the powers of overreaching are limited to equitable interests and powers. The general rule is that a purchaser takes subject to legal estates and interests authorised to subsist or be created under the L.P.A. 1925, notwithstanding that he may have no notice thereof, either express or implied, for they have the same incidents as legal estates subsisting at the commencement of the Act (L.P.A. 1925, s. 1 (4) ; a list of such legal estates and interests will be found in L.P.A. 1925, s. 1 and s. 7 (1) and (2), as amended by the Law of Property (Amendment) Act, 1926). But, like most other general rules, it has its exceptions.

A first mortgagee can, in the exercise of his power of sale, overreach legal estates vested in his mortgagor or in subsequent mortgagees, notwithstanding that the purchaser may have express notice of the subsequent mortgages, and although they have been registered as land charges (L.P.A. 1925, ss. 88, 89 and 104 ; L.C.A. 1972, s. 13). The overreached mortgages will not therefore have to be abstracted. In the case of a further charge, a legal mortgage may be overreached by a prior mortgagee " tacking," under the provisions of s. 94 of the L.P.A. 1925 ; see further, chapter on Mortgages, *post*, p. 970.

It is possible for an equitable mortgage to overreach, or, to be more accurate, to obtain by registration priority over an unregistered legal mortgage (L.P.A. 1925, s. 97).

Another exception is that a tenant for life, in the exercise of his powers under the S.L.A., can overreach a legal term of years unless it has priority to the settlement (S.L.A. 1925, s. 1 (1) (*b*), and s. 72 (2) (i)), or money has actually been raised on the security of the term (S.L.A. 1925, s. 72 (2) (ii)).

Overreaching of equitable interests and powers.—The chief statutory provisions dealing with this subject, in addition to s. 10 (1) of the L.P.A. 1925, are ss. 2 (1), 2 (2) (as amended by the Law of Property (Amendment) Act, 1926), 42 and 43 of the same Act, and ss. 21, 72 and 109 of the S.L.A. 1925, and these are dealt with under appropriate headings in the following pages.

A. OVERREACHING POWERS IN THE SETTLED LAND ACT, 1925

General rule.—Section 2 (1) of the L.P.A. 1925 introduces the subject :—

" 2.—(1) A conveyance to a purchaser of a legal estate in land shall overreach any equitable interest or power affecting that estate, whether or not he has notice thereof, if—

(i) the conveyance is made under the *powers conferred by the Settled Land Act*, 1925, or any *additional powers* conferred by a settlement, and the equitable interest or power is capable of being overreached thereby, and the statutory requirements respecting the payment of capital money arising under the settlement are complied with ; "

" *powers conferred by the Settled Land Act*, 1925."—These are considered in detail in the chapter on Settled Land, *post*, p. 664.

" *additional powers.*"—As to these being conferred on and exercisable by the tenant for life, see the S.L.A. 1925, s. 109 (considered in the chapter on Settled Land, *post*, p. 664).

Effect of conveyance, etc., by tenant for life.—On the completion of any transaction by a tenant for life, the conveyance, to the extent to which it is expressed or intended to operate and can operate under the S.L.A. 1925, is effectual (subject to the exceptions mentioned below) to pass the land conveyed, or the easements, rights, privileges or other interests created, *discharged from all the limitations, powers, and provisions of the settlement, and from all estates, interests, and charges subsisting or to arise thereunder* (S.L.A. 1925, s. 72 (2)). The " settlement," for this purpose, means the compound settlement if there is one and a transaction is made under it. It must be remembered that the expression " tenant for life " includes a person (not being a statutory owner) who has the powers of a tenant for life under the S.L.A. 1925, and also (where the context requires) one of two or more persons who together constitute the tenant for life, or have the powers of a tenant for life (see S.L.A. 1925, s. 117 (1) (xxviii)).

Section 72 confers on the tenant for life greater powers of overreaching than s. 2 (1) (i) of the L.P.A. 1925 would lead one to suppose, for the latter subsection specifically refers to equitable interests or powers only, whereas s. 72 (2) confers the power to overreach (with certain exceptions) *all* interests and powers subsisting or to arise *under the settlement*, that is, not only equitable interests and powers, but legal interests and powers as well. Special attention is drawn, however, to the fact that the subsection does not (except in the special cases mentioned in s. 72 (3), *post*) give the power to overreach interests created before the date of the settlement.

Nevertheless the power of overreaching of a tenant for life is limited to the extent of the estate or interest vested in him (*ibid.*, s. 72 (1)). For instance, if the equity of redemption in property was the only interest vested in him, he could deal only with this interest. Provided, however, that any further interest was comprised in the settlement, the power of the tenant for life extends to any such interest *declared* to be vested in him by the last or only vesting instrument. As to when a purchaser of a legal estate must assume that such declarations are correct, see the S.L.A. 1925, s. 110 (2), *post*, p. 689. To have the effect of overreaching equitable interests and powers " subsisting or to arise under the settlement," the transaction must be effected by a deed. This is the general rule, but there is one exception, namely, in the case of a lease made in writing only and not by deed (S.L.A. 1925, s. 72 (4) ; S.L.A. 1925, s. 42 (5) (ii) ; chapter on Leases, *post*, p. 801).

Equitable charges overreached although registered.—The S.L.A. 1925, s. 72 (3), provides :—

" (3) Notwithstanding registration under the Land Charges Act, 1925, of—

(a) *an annuity within the meaning of Part II* of that Act ;

(b) *a limited owner's charge or a general equitable charge* within the meaning of that Act ;

a disposition under this Act operates to overreach such annuity or charge which shall, according to its priority, take effect as if limited by the settlement."

The general rule is that a purchaser will take subject to a charge on the land which has been registered as a land charge (L.C.A. 1972, s. 4 ; S.L.A. 1925, s. 72 (2) (iii) (b)). The above exception to this rule is provided for by s. 13 of the L.C.A. 1972 to the effect that the registration of any charge, annuity, or other interest under the L.C.A. 1972 is not to prevent the charge, annuity or interest being overreached under any provision contained in any other statute except where otherwise provided by that other statute.

" *annuity within the meaning of Part II.*"—This class of annuity is very rare. No further examples can arise since 1925. See further, *post*, p. 609.

" *limited owner's charge.*"—See *post*, p. 598.

" *general equitable charge.*"—This is a land charge Class C (iii), defined by the L.C.A. 1972, s. 2 (4), as a residual category to cover equitable charges not otherwise registrable ; see *post*, p. 599. It includes, for example, an equitable mortgage of land which, because it is a second or subsequent charge, is not protected by deposit of the documents relating to the legal estate.

Charges and interests which a tenant for life cannot overreach.—The S.L.A. 1925, s. 72 (2), contains the following exceptions to the tenant for life's overreaching powers :—

" (i) *all legal estates and charges by way of legal mortgage having priority to the settlement.*"—Therefore, a tenant for life cannot overreach a legal mortgage created before the date of the settlement, or a legal mortgage created after the date of the settlement under the provisions of s. 16 (1) (ii) of the S.L.A. 1925. If before the date of the settlement an advance had been made on the security of an equitable charge on the property, then so long as it remained a purely equitable charge it would be overreachable by a tenant for life. To meet such a case s. 16 (1) (ii) provides that whenever any person of full age is entitled to require a legal estate in the settled land to be vested in him *in priority* to the settlement, the estate owner shall be bound, if so requested in writing, to create such legal estate as may be required for giving legal effect to the rights of the person so entitled.

" (ii) *all legal estates and charges by way of legal mortgage which have been conveyed or created for securing money actually raised at the date of the deed.*"—It was decided in *Re Dickin and Kelsall* [1908] 1 Ch. 213 (on similar wording in the Settled Land Act, 1882) that this exception is merely an exception out of the words " estates, interests and charges subsisting or to arise thereunder " in subs. (2) of s. 72 of the S.L.A. 1925. Therefore as a rule it will only exclude legal estates conveyed or created for securing money, etc., under s. 16 (1) (iii), or under the Law of Property (Amendment) Act, 1926, s. 1. The interest of a tenant for life or other beneficiary under a settlement is only an equitable interest and can on this ground be overreached.

" (iii) all leases and grants at fee farm rents or otherwise, and all grants of easements, rights of common, or other rights or privileges which—

(*a*) were before the date of the deed [i.e., before the date of the conveyance, etc., by the tenant for life] granted or made for value in money or money's worth, or agreed so to be, by the tenant for life or statutory owner, or by any of his predecessors in title, or any trustees for them, under the settlement, or under any statutory power, or are at that date otherwise binding on the successors in title of the tenant for life or statutory owner ; and

(*b*) are at the date of the deed protected by registration under the Land Charges Act, 1925, if *capable of registration thereunder.*"

" *if capable of registration.*"—The principle is that the tenant for life cannot overreach interests previously created for value under statutory powers. For instance, he cannot, on sale of the fee simple, overreach a lease which he has properly granted earlier. Nevertheless, interests which were capable of registration and were not registered are overreached, as they would be on conveyance by an absolute owner. For instance, an agreement for a lease, which should be registered as an estate contract (L.C.A. 1972, s. 2 (4), Class C (iv)), will, if it has not been registered, be overreached by a conveyance made by the tenant for life for value. Similarly, a legal easement would not be overreached, but an unregistered equitable easement might be.

Overreaching powers exercisable by special settlement.—An absolute owner holding his land subject to certain equitable interests or powers can arrange for the land to be conveyed free therefrom under the provisions of s. 21 of the S.L.A. 1925. This section provides, in effect, that where a person is beneficially entitled in possession to a legal estate subject to any equitable interests or powers, he may by deed (which shall have effect as a principal vesting deed) declare that the legal estate is vested in him on trust to give effect to all equitable interests and powers affecting the legal estate, and that deed shall be executed by two or more individuals approved or appointed by the court, or a trust corporation, who shall be stated to be the trustees of the settlement for the purposes of the Act. Thereupon the person so entitled and each of his successors in title being an estate owner shall have the powers of a tenant for life and the land shall be deemed to be settled land. A sale under S.L.A. 1925 powers may then overreach certain equitable interests having priority to the settlement, but there are the same exceptions to this section as to s. 2 (2) of the L.P.A. 1925, *post*, p. 178.

It is thought that this section is never used. The interests or powers may be such that the land is already settled land under S.L.A. 1925, s. 1 (1) (v), and the owner has already the powers of a tenant for life. There may be other cases to which the section will apply, but it is thought that, if there are, the owner will choose the mode of overreaching contained in s. 2 (2) of the L.P.A. 1925, *post*, p. 178.

B. OVERREACHING POWERS OF TRUSTEES FOR SALE

It is provided by s. 2 (1) of the L.P.A. 1925 that " a *conveyance to a purchaser* of a legal estate in land shall overreach any equitable interest or power affecting that estate, whether or not he has notice thereof, if the conveyance is made by *trustees for sale* and the equitable interest or power is at the date of the conveyance capable of being overreached by such trustees under the provisions of subsection (2) of this section [see p. 178] or independently of that subsection, and the statutory requirements respecting the payment of capital money arising under a disposition upon trust for sale are complied with."

" *conveyance to a purchaser*."—" Conveyance " includes a mortgage, charge, lease, assent, vesting declaration, vesting instrument, disclaimer, release and every other assurance of property or of an interest therein by an instrument, except a will (L.P.A. 1925, s. 205 (1) (ii)) ; and " purchaser," for this purpose, means a person who acquires an interest in or charge on property for money or money's worth, and in reference to a legal estate includes a chargee by way of legal mortgage (L.P.A. 1925, s. 205 (1) (xxi)).

" *trustees for sale*."—The L.P.A. 1925, s. 205 (1) (xxix), defines this phrase as meaning the persons (including a personal representative) holding land on trust for sale. The definition of a trust for sale is considered in the chapter on Settled Land, *post*, p. 673 *et seq.*

The overreaching powers arising independently of the L.P.A. 1925, s. 2 (2), i.e., those of ordinary trustees holding on ordinary trusts for sale (whether arising expressly from a deed or will or by implication of statute), will be considered first, and the powers arising under that subsection, i.e., those of approved trustees holding on special trusts for sale, discussed afterwards.

Ordinary trustees.—The statutory requirements referred to in s. 2 (1) (ii) are contained in s. 27 (2) of the L.P.A. 1925, which provides that, notwithstanding anything to the contrary in the instrument (if any) creating a trust for sale of land or in the settlement of the net proceeds, the proceeds of sale or other capital money shall not be paid to or applied by the direction of fewer than two persons as trustees for sale, except where the trustee is a trust corporation.

If these requirements are complied with, the trustees can overreach all equitable interests arising *under* the trust for sale. This is made clear by s. 27 (1), which provides that a purchaser of legal estate from trustees for sale shall not be concerned with the trusts affecting the proceeds of sale of land subject to a trust for sale, or affecting the rents and profits of the land until sale, *whether or not those trusts are declared by the same instrument by which the trust for sale is created.*

The more difficult problem is whether *ordinary* trustees for sale can overreach any interests having *priority* to the trust. Sir Benjamin Cherry took the view that such trustees have powers to overreach interests corresponding to those which are conferred on a tenant for life. In his lectures on " The New Property Acts," at p. 48, he says : " at least that is the view I have hitherto adopted though it is open to the court to hold that, having regard to the express overreaching powers referred to in s. 27 of the Law of Property Act, the powers conferred by s. 72 of the Settled Land Act are not applicable and are not required by trustees for sale."

The importance of the matter is this. If, as Sir Benjamin Cherry argued, trustees for sale have the powers which are given to a tenant for life by s. 72 of the S.L.A. 1925 then they can, by virtue of s. 72 (3), overreach annuities, limited owners' charges and general equitable charges *even though these interests have priority to the trust for sale and even though they are registered as land charges.* If, on the other hand, trustees for sale do *not* have the overreaching powers specified in s. 72 of the S.L.A. 1925, then they can overreach equitable interests arising under the trust for sale but not any interests having priority to it (L.P.A. 1925, s. 27 (1)).

Section 28 (1) would, at first sight, appear quite clearly to give trustees for sale the powers in s. 72 of the S.L.A. 1925. It reads : " Trustees for sale shall, in relation to land . . . have *all* the powers of a tenant for life " And that this means what it says was the decision of the Court of Appeal in connection with other powers in *Re Wellsted's Will Trusts* [1949] Ch. 296 (followed by Danckwerts, J., in *Re Simmons* [1956] Ch. 125). Yet the matter is not free from doubt. The late Mr. J. M. Lightwood, in the *Law Journal*, vol. 73, p. 164, wrote : " Under s. 28 (1), trustees for sale have the powers of a tenant for life, but this does not give them his conveyancing powers. A conveyance by the trustees operates only as an exercise of the trust for sale, and in order to obtain overreaching powers they must be guaranteed trustees so as to be able to take advantage of the powers conferred by s. 2 (2) of the Law of Property Act."

The difference of opinion is interesting but not of great practical importance. It is usually more convenient to obtain a release of prior equitable interests than to overreach them ; and so the extent of the overreaching powers of ordinary trustees for sale is an academic rather than a practical problem, although it might be important if, for example, the person entitled to an equitable interest could not be traced.

Trustees for sale holding on the statutory trusts which arose under the L.P.A. 1925, Sched. 1, Pt. IV, where land was held, immediately before 1926, in undivided shares, have a special power to overreach certain charges formerly affecting undivided shares although such charges existed before the trust for sale arose (L.P.A. 1925, Sched. 1, Pt. IV, para. 1 (1), (3) and (4)). This is an extension of the normal overreaching powers.

Where persons become entitled to settled land in possession in undivided shares the land has to be vested in the trustees of the settlement on trust for sale (S.L.A. 1925, s. 36 (1) and (2)). The overreaching powers of such trustees are greater than those of ordinary trustees for sale and are dealt with at p. 312.

Approved trustees.—We have seen (*ante*, p. 177) that ordinary trustees for sale can overreach interests taking effect under the trust for sale, but they cannot, with a few possible exceptions, affect interests having priority to the trust for sale. The L.P.A. 1925, s. 2 (2), as amended by the Law of Property (Amendment) Act, 1926, has made provision for the creation of special trusts for sale with the object of overreaching prior equities. The idea is that on a sale by the trustees the purchaser takes free from any equitable interest and that interest becomes enforceable against the purchase-money in the hands of the trustees. It is believed that the section is rarely used and there are a number of reasons for this. Usually it will be easier to obtain a release of an equitable interest, or, if this cannot be done, a sum of money can be paid into court in discharge (L.P.A. 1925, s. 50). The provision is as follows : —

" 2.—(2) Where the legal estate affected is subject to a trust for sale, then if at the date of a conveyance made after [1925] under the trust for sale or the powers conferred on the trustees for sale, the trustees (whether original or substituted) are either—

(*a*) two or more individuals approved or appointed by the court or the successors in office of the individuals so approved or appointed ; or

(*b*) a trust corporation,

any equitable interest or power *having priority to the trust for sale* shall, notwithstanding any stipulation to the contrary, be overreached by the conveyance, and shall, according to its priority, take effect as if created or arising by means of a primary trust affecting the proceeds of sale and the income of the land until sale."

Various exceptions to the operation of the subsection, that is, equitable interests which an estate owner cannot overreach, notwithstanding that the trustees have been approved by the court, are contained in subs. (3), which provides as follows :—

" 2.—(3) The following equitable interests and powers are excepted from the operation of sub-section (2) of this section, namely—

(i) Any equitable interest protected by a deposit of documents relating to the legal estate affected ;

(ii) The benefit of any covenant or agreement restrictive of the user of land ;

(iii) Any easement, liberty, or privilege over or affecting land and being merely an equitable interest (in this Act referred to as an ' equitable easement ') ;

(iv) The benefit of any contract (in this Act referred to as an ' estate contract ') to convey or create a legal estate, including a contract conferring either expressly or by statutory implication a valid option to purchase, a right of pre-emption, or any other like right ;

(v) Any *equitable interest protected by registration* under the Land Charges Act, 1925, other than—

(*a*) an annuity within the meaning of Part II of that Act ;

(*b*) a limited owner's charge or a general equitable charge within the meaning of that Act."

" *equitable interest protected by registration* " (under now the L.C.A. 1972).— There can be no overreaching *even under a special trust for sale* of equitable interests protected by registration *other than* annuities, limited owner's charges and general equitable charges. The reason why these are allowed to be overreached, although they may have been registered as land charges, is that no injustice will be done to the parties interested, as it will be just the same to them whether their interests are secured by the land itself or by the purchase-money and the income thereof. In practice these will be the only interests which can be overreached, the exceptions to the operation of the subsection being otherwise so complete.

It will be noted that to obtain the benefit of the L.P.A. 1925, s. 2 (2), if the land is not already subject to a trust for sale one will have to be created for the purpose. If the land is already held on trust for sale by a trust corporation, that corporation can sell and the subsection will operate without further formality. If the trustees holding on trust for sale are individuals, they will have to be approved by the court.

C. OVERREACHING POWERS OF PERSONAL REPRESENTATIVES

No distinction need be drawn between executors and administrators, as the A.E.A. 1925, s. 21, provides that, subject to any limitations contained in the grant, administrators have the same rights and liabilities as executors.

An executor has always had power to overreach beneficial interests arising under the will of the deceased, a power which he needs in order to administer the estate for payment of debts, etc. Thus an executor can make a good title to freehold or leasehold property although it be specifically devised or bequeathed (*Graham* v. *Drummond* [1896] 1 Ch. 968), unless, before 1926, he had done or allowed any act which amounted to an assent to the bequest to the beneficiaries or, after 1925, he had assented in writing, in either of which cases his power to sell would have ceased (*Stevenson* v. *Liverpool Corporation* (1874), L.R. 10 Q.B. 81 ; *Wise* v. *Whitburn* [1924] 1 Ch. 460 ; A.E.A. 1925, s. 36).

The powers of personal representatives are increased by the A.E.A. 1925, s. 39. In substance it confers on them, primarily for the purposes of administration, all the powers, discretions and duties conferred or imposed by law on trustees holding land on trust for sale (*including power to overreach equitable interests and powers as if the same affected the proceeds of sale*) ; and all the powers conferred by statute on trustees for sale.

The exact circumstances in which this section operates are doubtful. The important point to note here is that, until personal representatives have made an assent, they have power by a conveyance to a purchaser for value to overreach all interests created by the testator's will, notwithstanding that by the terms of the will a property may have been charged with an annuity or a legacy (*Parker* v. *Judkin* [1931] 1 Ch. 475) and notwithstanding that the purchaser has notice by the terms of the will having been abstracted (*ibid.*). A purchaser will not be concerned to inquire whether or not the executor is conveying for purposes of administration, since, under s. 36 (8) of the A.E.A. 1925, a conveyance of a legal estate by a personal representative is not to be invalidated simply because the purchaser has notice that all the debts, liabilities, funeral and testamentary or administration expenses, duties, and legacies of the deceased have been discharged or provided for. Further, by subs. (6) of the same section, a statement in writing by the personal representative that he has not given or made any assent or conveyance in respect of a legal estate is, in favour of a purchaser, made sufficient evidence of the fact unless notice of a previous assent or conveyance has been placed on or annexed to the grant ; but this protection is without prejudice to any previous disposition made in favour of another purchaser.

Section 33 (1) of the A.E.A. 1925, which applies on the death of a person intestate, provides that the estate shall be held by the personal representatives (*a*) as to the real estate upon trust to sell the same ; and (*b*) as to the personal estate upon trust to call in, sell and convert into money such part thereof as may not consist of money, with power to postpone such sale and conversion for such a period as the personal representatives, without being liable to account, may think proper. By virtue of this provision they would enjoy the overreaching powers of trustees for sale. However, the estate, in the first instance, passes to the administrators on the issue of the grant and they have overreaching powers which are required for purposes of administration in their capacity of personal representatives. Then even after the administration is completed, it seems that the legal estate can only become vested in the administrators in their new capacity of trustees for sale by means of a formal assent in their own favour in that capacity within s. 36 (4) of the A.E.A. 1925 (*Re King's Will Trusts* [1964] Ch. 542 ; also *Re Yerburgh* [1928] W.N. 208). In the meantime they will still have the sufficient overreaching powers of personal representatives.

It must be borne in mind that the overreaching powers of personal representatives are not dependent, as are the powers of trustees for sale, on payment of the purchase-money to at least two trustees or a trust corporation. The L.P.A. 1925, s. 27 (2), as amended by the Law of Property (Amendment) Act, 1926, provides that the provision contained therein that capital money must not be paid to less than two persons as trustees, except where the trustee is a trust corporation, is not to affect the right of a sole personal representative as such to give valid receipts for or direct the application of the proceeds of sale or other capital money.

Abstract on sale by personal representatives or beneficiary.—A result of the above provisions is that where personal representatives have sold and conveyed a legal estate after 1925 (whether or not the death was before 1926 : ss. 36 (12) and 39 (3) of the A.E.A. 1925), the will should not appear on the abstract of title since any interests created by it will have been over-reached. In other words, the will operates only in equity. Further, s. 36 (7) of the A.E.A. 1925 provides, in effect, that an assent or conveyance by a personal representative in respect of a legal estate shall, in favour of a purchaser (unless there is an endorsement to the contrary on the probate or administration), be taken as *sufficient* evidence that the person in whose favour the assent or conveyance is given or made is the person entitled to have the legal estate conveyed to him.

It follows that, when a person sells after an assent in his favour in respect of the legal estate made after 1925 (whether or not the death was before 1926 : s. 36 (12) of the A.E.A. 1925), the purchaser will only be entitled to an abstract showing the grant of probate or letters of administration and the assent, together with any relevant memoranda endorsed on the probate or administration. He is not entitled to satisfy himself that the vendor was entitled under the will to have an assent made to him nor concerned to know the terms of the will. What is more, it would even be unwise for the purchaser to make any inquiry as to these matters, for s. 36 (7) of the A.E.A. 1925 makes the assent *not conclusive* evidence that it is made in favour of the proper person but only *sufficient*. This means that the purchaser is protected " unless and until, upon a proper investigation by a purchaser of his vendor's title, facts come to the purchaser's knowledge which indicate the contrary. When that happens, in my judgment, the vesting assent cannot be, and ought not to be, accepted, as sufficient evidence of something which the purchaser has reason to believe is contrary to the fact, still less so when, as in the present case, he knows it to be contrary to the fact " (*per* Bennett, J., in *Re Duce and Boots', etc., Ltd.* [1937] Ch. 642, at p. 650 ; will recited in full in the assent). Consequently, to avoid inquiry, neither the assent nor the abstract should give any reason for the making of the assent ; it is immaterial how the beneficial title of the estate owner arose.

D. INTERESTS OVERREACHED ON SALE BY MORTGAGEE

Once more the matter is introduced by the L.P.A. 1925, s. 2, it being provided by s. 2 (1) (iii) that a conveyance to a purchaser of a legal estate in land shall overreach any equitable interest or power affecting that estate, whether or not he has notice thereof, if the conveyance is made by a mortgagee in the exercise of his paramount powers, and the equitable interest or power is capable of being overreached by such conveyance, and any capital money arising from the transaction is paid to the mortgagee.

The overreaching powers apply to legal estates as well as to equitable interests as the L.P.A. 1925, s. 104 (1), provides as follows :—

" 104.—(1) A mortgagee exercising the power of sale conferred by this Act shall have power, by deed, to convey the property sold, for such estate and interest therein as he is by this Act authorised to sell or convey or may be the subject of the mortgage, freed from all estates, interests, and rights to which the mortgage has priority, but subject to all estates, interests and rights which have priority to the mortgage."

As to the estate authorised to be conveyed in the case of freehold mortgages, the L.P.A. 1925, s. 88, provides as follows :—

" 88.—(1) Where an estate in fee simple has been mortgaged by the creation of a term of years absolute limited thereout or by a charge by way of legal mortgage and the mortgagee sells under his statutory or express power of sale—

(*a*) the conveyance by him shall operate to vest in the purchaser the fee simple in the land conveyed subject to any legal mortgage having priority to the mortgage in right of which the sale is made and to any money thereby secured, and thereupon

(b) *the mortgage term or the charge by way of legal mortgage and any
subsequent mortgage term or charges shall merge or be extinguished*
as respects the land conveyed ;

and such conveyance may, as respects the fee simple, be made in the name
of the estate owner in whom it is vested.

*   *   *   *   *

(5) In the case of a sub-mortgage by sub-demise of a long term (less
a nominal period) itself limited out of an estate in fee simple, the foregoing
provisions of this section shall operate as if the derivative term, if any,
created by the sub-mortgage had been limited out of the fee simple, and so
as to enlarge the principal term and extinguish the derivative term created
by the sub-mortgage as aforesaid, and to enable the sub-mortgagee to
convey the fee simple or acquire it by foreclosure, enlargement, or otherwise
as aforesaid."

As regards leasehold mortgages the L.P.A. 1925, s. 89, provides as
follows :—

" 89.—(1) Where a term of years absolute has been mortgaged by the
creation of another term of years absolute limited thereout or by a charge
by way of legal mortgage and the mortgagee sells under his statutory or
express power of sale—

(a) the conveyance by him shall operate to convey to the purchaser
not only the mortgage term, if any, but also (unless expressly
excepted with the leave of the court) the leasehold reversion affected
by the mortgage, subject to any legal mortgage having priority
to the mortgage in right of which the sale is made and to any money
thereby secured, and thereupon

(b) *the mortgage term, or the charge by way of legal mortgage and any
subsequent mortgage term or charge,* shall merge in such leasehold
reversion or be extinguished unless excepted as aforesaid ;

and such conveyance may, as respects the leasehold reversion, be made
in the name of the estate owner in whom it is vested.

Where a licence to assign is required on a sale by a mortgagee, such
licence shall not be unreasonably refused."

Subsection (5) of s. 89 is similar to subs. (5) of s. 88, above. To deal
with a particular difficulty affecting leaseholds there is the following
provision, however :—

" 89.—(6) This section . . . does not apply where the mortgage term does
not comprise the whole of the land included in the leasehold reversion
unless the rent (if any) payable in respect of that reversion *has been
apportioned* as respects the land affected, or the rent is of no money value
or no rent is reserved, and unless the lessee's covenants and conditions
(if any) have been apportioned, either expressly or by implication, as
respects the land affected.   In this subsection references to an apportionment *include an equitable apportionment made without the consent of the
lessor.*"

If premises comprised in a lease have been mortgaged by the lessee a
mortgagee selling part of the premises under his power of sale can make an
equitable apportionment of the rent (L.P.A. 1925, s. 190).   It follows, therefore, that by doing this the mortgagee can convey the head term held by the
mortgagor even when he is selling part only of the land mortgaged.

It will be noticed that the conveyance " may " be made in the name of the estate owner but this is very rarely done. It certainly is not necessary that the conveyance should be so made, for it is provided by s. 9 (1) (e) of the L.P.A. 1925 that every conveyance made under any power reserved or conferred by the Act which is made or executed for the purpose of conveying a legal estate is to operate to convey the legal estate in like manner as if the same had been a conveyance executed by the estate owner of the legal estate to which the conveyance relates.

Sections 88 and 89 of the L.P.A. 1925 should also be read with s. 42 (4) (i) and (5) of the L.P.A. 1925 given below :—

" 42.—(4) If the subject matter of any contract for the sale or exchange of land—

(i) is a mortgage term and the vendor has power to convey the fee simple in the land, or, in the case of a mortgage of a term of years absolute, the leasehold reversion affected by the mortgage, the contract shall be deemed to extend to the fee simple in the land or such leasehold reversion ;

*   *   *   *   *

(5) This section does not affect the right of a mortgagee of leasehold land to sell his mortgage term only if he is unable to convey or vest the leasehold reversion expectant thereon."

E. INTERESTS OVERREACHED ON CONVEYANCE UNDER ORDER OF COURT

It is provided by s. 2 (1) (iv) of the L.P.A. 1925 that a conveyance to a purchaser of a legal estate in land shall overreach any equitable interest or power affecting that estate, whether or not he has notice thereof, if the conveyance is made under an order of the court and the equitable interest or power is bound by such order, and any capital money arising from the transaction is paid into, or in accordance with the order of, the court.

For the protection of a purchaser, it is provided by s. 204 (1) of the L.P.A. 1925 that an order of the court under any statutory or other jurisdiction will not, as against a purchaser, be invalidated on the ground of want of jurisdiction, or of want of any concurrence, consent, notice or service, whether the purchaser has notice of any such want or not. But in spite of the apparent width of the subsection a purchaser would be entitled to the concurrence in his conveyance of all persons having a *legal* interest, whether parties to the suit or not, though he would not be entitled to the concurrence of any persons bound by the proceedings whose interests were merely equitable (*Re Hall Dare's Contract* (1882), 46 L.T. 755 ; *Mostyn* v. *Mostyn* [1893] 3 Ch. 376 ; *Re Whitham* (1901), 84 L.T. 585). The subsection will not enable the court to sell the property of *A*, when it supposed it was selling the property of *B*, *A* not being a party to the proceedings (*Jones* v. *Barnett* [1900] 1 Ch. 370).

An order of the court under the section applies to a grant of probate or administration. In *Re Bridgett and Hayes' Contract* [1928] 1 Ch. 163, a grant of probate had been made to the general executor of the will of a tenant for life, and the question arose as to whether the legal estate in the land in question had become vested in the trustees of the settlement as the special executors deemed to be appointed by the tenant for life under s. 22 (1) of the A.E.A. 1925. It was decided that the trusts of the settlement had come to an end, and that the general executor was the person to whom the grant ought to have been made. But Romer, J., said that, whether that was so or not, *the fact of the probate having been granted to the general executor* vested the legal estate in the executor, and that the purchaser would be protected under s. 204 (1) of the L.P.A. 1925.

A vesting order made by any court for the purpose of vesting, conveying, or creating a legal estate, will operate to convey or create the legal estate disposed of in like manner as if the same had been a conveyance executed by the estate owner of the legal estate to which the order relates (L.P.A. 1925, s. 9 (1)) ; and where the order is made in favour of a purchaser, the provisions of the Act relating to a conveyance of a legal estate to a purchaser will apply thereto (*ibid.*, subs. (2)).

Where the purchase-money is paid into court it is provided by s. 203 (1) of the L.P.A. 1925 that such payment will effectually exonerate therefrom the person making the payment.

PART 11. OVERRIDING INTERESTS

Mention of such interests on the register.—The expression " overriding interests " means all those interests, incumbrances, rights and powers which are enforceable against a proprietor of registered land even though not mentioned on the register and subject to which registered dispositions necessarily take effect (L.R.A. 1925, ss. 3 (xvi), 5 (*b*), 9 (*c*), 20 (1) (*b*), 23 (1) (*c*) and 70 (1)). Before dealing further with these interests, the provisions concerning their mention on the register may be noted. Although, by definition, overriding interests strictly cease to be such when entered on the register (*ibid.*, s. 3 (xvi)), it is clear, of course, that they continue to bind the land and also that they are not confined to those interests which cannot be protected on the register (*Bridges* v. *Mees* [1957] Ch. 475 ; *Re Dances Way, West Town, Hayling Island* [1962] Ch. 490, at p. 507 ; also *Webb* v. *Pollmount* [1966] Ch. 584).

There are four provisions dealing directly with the mention of overriding interests on the register, as follows :—

First, there is the provision that " Where at the time of first registration any easement, right, privilege, or benefit created by an instrument and appearing on the title adversely affects the land, the registrar shall enter a note thereof on the register " (s. 70 (2) of the L.R.A. 1925). This is not a happily drafted provision ; although the interests referred to are gathered together in a phrase used throughout the 1925 property legislation (see, e.g., s. 1 (2) (*a*) of the L.P.A. 1925, and s. 3 (viii) of the L.R.A. 1925), it is not a phrase appearing either to cover or even to be amongst the list of overriding interests, which has a more specific enumeration (see particularly para. (*a*) and (*j*) of s. 70 (1) of the L R.A. 1925, *post*). However, where the subsection is applicable, the registrar apparently has no discretion as to entry. Diplock, L.J., has said : " This is a mandatory provision and is not in my view qualified by r. 41 which deals with easements, rights or privileges created by an instrument, without being restricted to those which appear on the title. These shall, but only if the registrar thinks fit, be entered in the register. It seems to me that the *discretionary* power to enter easements created by an instrument is limited to those which do not appear on the title : where they do appear on the title, it is a mandatory duty under s. 70 (2) to enter them " (in *Re Dances Way, West Town, Hayling Island* [1962] Ch. 490, at p. 508). However, r. 199 of the L.R.R. 1925 does relieve the registrar from the burden of entering on the register matters of a " trivial or obvious character " or "likely to cause confusion or inconvenience."

Secondly, it is provided that : " Where the existence of any overriding interest mentioned in this section is proved to the satisfaction of the registrar or admitted, he may (subject to any prescribed exception) enter notice of the same or of a claim thereto on the register . . ." (s. 70 (3) of the L.R.A. 1925). This is a better drafted provision, clearly covering all overriding interests whenever created and wherever appearing. Further there is no question that this second provision is discretionary and the " any prescribed exception " can be taken as referring to r. 199 of the L.R.R. 1925 (mentioned above).

Thirdly, the express creation by a registered proprietor of any interest in the land, overriding or not, cannot be completed at law off the register (see ss. 19 (2) and 22 (2) of the L.R.A. 1925). There are exceptions provided for, particularly short leases (see para. (*k*), *post*), and notice of easements, etc. (see para. (*a*), *post*) is only required to be entered against the title of the servient land. Exceptions apart, however, in cases of express creation, there can, it is thought, be no discretion in the registrar as to whether or not the disposition should be completed by registration.

Fourthly, there is the qualification that registered land is subject to overriding interests only " unless under the provisions of this Act the contrary is expressed on the register " (s. 70 (1) of the L.R.A. 1925 ; see also ss. 5 (*b*), 9 (*c*), 20 (1) (*b*) and 23 (1) (*c*)). The only relevant provision of the Act is the proviso to s. 70 (1), which is restricted to freedom from land tax, tithe, etc. (see para. (*e*), *post*). Nonetheless, the L.R.R. 1925 do set out the procedure for satisfying the registrar of freedom from all or any of the overriding interests (r. 197). Even thus widened, however, it has been judicially suggested that the registrar's ability to put negative information on the register is limited : " . . . for on the true construction of r. 197 an entry on the register of freedom from an overriding interest can only be made where there has been a previous entry of the existence of such a liability and evidence is produced that such a liability has been discharged " (*per* Diplock, L.J., in *Re Dances Way, West Town, Hayling Island* [1962] Ch. 490, at p. 510). However, in Ruoff and Roper, Registered Conveyancing, 3rd ed., at p. 120, it is said : " With the greatest respect, the rule contains no such limitation and appears to apply to any overriding interest, whether or not it has been previously noted on the register."

Overriding interests classified.—Having noted what information may appear about overriding interests on the register, it is now appropriate to deal with the individual interests that come within this class. The various types of overriding interests are set out below in italics in the words of the L.R.A. 1925, s. 70 (1) :—

(a) " *Rights of common, drainage rights, customary rights (until extinguished), public rights, profits à prendre, rights of sheepwalk, rights of way, watercourses, rights of water, and other easements not being equitable easements required to be protected by notice on the register.*"

An easement may be equitable because it was created either otherwise than " for an interest equivalent to an estate in fee simple absolute in possession or a term of years absolute " (s. 1 (2) (*a*) of the L.P.A. 1925, e.g., for life or determinable) or by an instrument not under seal (s. 52 (1) of the same Act ; cf. *Mason* v. *Clarke* [1955] A.C. 778). In addition, in registered conveyancing, the express grant of an easement will operate only in equity unless and until it is completed by registration (ss. 19 (2) and 22 (2) of the L.R.A. 1925). Further, reference should be made to the restrictive proposition that " an ' equitable easement ' is a proprietary interest in land such as would before 1926 have been recognised as capable of being conveyed or created at law, but which since 1926 [*sic*] only takes effect as an equitable interest " (*per* Lord Denning, M.R., in *E. R. Ives Investment, Ltd.* v. *High* [1967] 2 Q.B. 379, at p. 395 ; see also *per* Cross, J., in *Poster* v. *Slough Estates, Ltd.* [1969] 1 Ch. 495, at p. 507, confining this definition to pre-1926 easements or profits ; cf. generally *Shiloh Spinners, Ltd.* v. *Harding* [1973] 1 All E.R. 90, H.L., and Paul Jackson at *Conveyancer N.S.*, vol. 33, p. 135).

Equitable easements over *un*registered land will normally bind a purchaser of a legal estate only if he takes with notice of them, which for easements created after 1925 involves exclusively registration under the L.C.A. 1972 (see s. 2 (5), Class D (iii), and s. 4 (6) of that Act and s. 199 (1) of the L.P.A. 1925). Similarly, but perhaps deceptively so, provision has been made that a person entitled to an equitable easement over registered land " *may* apply to the registrar to register notice " thereof " and when so registered every proprietor and the persons deriving title under him shall be deemed to be affected with notice " thereof (see ss. 3 (ix), 48 (1), 49 (1) (*c*) and 59 (2) of the L.R.A. 1925 and r. 190 of the L.R.R. 1925). It is arguable that this is not a provision, nor is there any other in the Act or Rules, by which equitable easements are " *required* to be protected by notice on the register " within the exception from para. (*a*) of s. 70 (1) above. Also, it may be pointed out that rr. 250, 257 and 258 variously appear to treat equitable easements as on an equal footing with legal easements as overriding interests. Consequently, the view has been expressed that " It is apparent that equitable rights [*sic*] were not intended to operate as overriding interests, but it does not appear that there are any provisions which limit the generality of the Act and Rules already cited, and it is submitted, therefore, that at present equitable easements are in law overriding interests " (Potter, Registered Land Conveyancing, p. 11). However, it should be noted that Ruoff and Roper, Registered Conveyancing, 3rd ed., at p. 102, regard it as beyond argument that equitable easements are not overriding interests. They say that the word " required " in para. (*a*) above can only mean that an equitable easement must always be protected by notice on the register to be enforceable against a purchaser and so has not got the characteristics of an overriding interest. It is thought that this latter view is preferable as according more with the principles of registration of title. Nevertheless it may simply not be open on a proper construction of the statute and indeed the one judicial decision so far reported actually adopts the Potter approach to this point (see *Payne* v. *Adnams* [1971] C.L.Y. 6486), but unhappily this was only a county court case which was not very fully reported.

    (*b*) " *Liability to repair highways by reason of tenure, quit-rents, crown rents, heriots and other rents and charges (until extinguished) having their origin in tenure.*"

    (*c*) " *Liability to repair the chancel of any church.*"

Reference may be made to a case concerning this liability in unregistered conveyancing : *Chivers & Sons, Ltd.* v. *Air Ministry and Queen's College, Cambridge* [1955] Ch. 585.

(d) " *Liability in respect of embankments, and sea and river walls.*"

(e) " [*Land tax, tithe rentcharge,*] *payments in lieu of tithe, and charges or annuities payable for the redemption of tithe rentcharges.*"

See s. 13 (11) of the Tithe Act, 1936, and s. 32 of the F.A. 1962 (as to compulsory redemption of tithe redemption annuities on a change of ownership) ; note also the abolition of land tax by s. 68 of the F.A. 1963.

(f) " *Subject to the provisions of this Act, rights acquired or in course of being acquired under the Limitation Acts.*"

There are special rules applicable to the acquisition of title under the Limitation Act, 1939. Although adverse possession affects registered land in the same manner as it affects unregistered land, the estate of the registered proprietor is not extinguished as a result of the adverse possession, but is held by the registered proprietor *in trust* for the person who has acquired title by possession, but without prejudice to the interests of any other person whose interest is not extinguished (L.R.A. 1925, s. 75 (1)).   The L.R.A. 1925, s. 75, does not amount to a statutory grant of title but merely recognises the negative effect of the Limitation Act which applies to registered land in a similar manner.   Consequently a squatter who has acquired title to either unregistered or registered land cannot claim the benefit of an easement by implied grant, such as a way of necessity (*Wilkes* v. *Greenway* (1890), 6 T.L.R. 449 ; *Palace Court Garages* (*Hampstead*), *Ltd.* v. *Steiner*, unreported but noted in the *Law Journal*, vol. 108, p. 274).   Any person who claims to have acquired a title in this way may apply to be registered as proprietor, and if the registrar is satisfied as to the applicant's title he must enter the applicant as proprietor with absolute, good leasehold, qualified or possessory title, as the case may require, but without prejudice to any estate or interest protected by an entry on the register which may not have been extinguished. Any such registration will have the same effect as the registration of a first proprietor, but the proprietor, the applicant or any other person interested may apply to the court for the determination of any question arising (L.R.A. 1925, s. 75 (2), (3)).   The registrar has a discretion in special circumstances to compensate any purchaser or person deriving title under him whose title, being registered or protected on the register, is prejudicially affected by any such entry (L.R.A. 1925, s. 74 (4)).

An applicant for compensation may appeal to the court from the decision of the registrar as to indemnity, and in determining whether indemnity is to be awarded and the amount thereof regard must be made to whether the applicant and his predecessors in title have by negligence caused or contributed to the loss (L.R.A., 1936, s. 3).

An adverse possessor is entitled to have the register rectified even against a person with an absolute title (*Chowood* v. *Lyall* (*No.* 2) [1930] 2 Ch. 156) and without indemnity being paid to the latter (*Re Chowood's Registered Land* [1933] Ch. 574 ; see also *Re Boyle's Claim* [1961] 1 W.L.R. 339).   Thus, if an adverse possessor's rights are overriding interests binding purchasers, the position will approximate, as surely intended, to that in unregistered conveyancing (cf. s. 12 of the L.P.A. 1925).   However, para. (*f*), above, is expressly made " subject to the provisions of this Act."   One of these provisions is that no one dealing with registered land " shall be affected with notice of a trust expressed implied or constructive " (s. 74).   Since an adverse possessor becomes entitled under a trust the question may be raised whether he is therefore excluded from having an overriding interest (see Potter, Registered Land Conveyancing, at p. 12). In *Re Chowood*, *ante*, Clauson, J., said in his judgment (at p. 581) : " It was suggested that the words ' subject to the provisions of this Act ' affect the matter ; I cannot see why. The reference seems to be to s. 75 [*sic*] . . .", but he dealt no further with this question (the counsel who made the suggestion clearly had a different point in mind : see *ibid.*, at p. 576). But more recently, Harman, J., although not adverting to this question, has held in the clearest possible terms that the rights of the adverse possessor *are* overriding interests binding purchasers of the registered land (*Bridges* v. *Mees* [1957] Ch. 475, where a person who had agreed to buy land from a company and who took possession was held to have acquired title by adverse possession and so was entitled to a transfer or to rectification of the register as against a subsequent purchaser from the company).

(g) " *The rights of every person in actual occupation of the land or in receipt of the rents and profits thereof, save where inquiry is made of such person and the rights are not disclosed.*"

The word " land " in this paragraph does not refer to an estate in land, but to the physical land (*Webb* v. *Pollmount* [1966] Ch. 584).

This paragraph constitutes by far the most important class of overriding interests, if only in that it has occasioned the most litigation in a comparatively unlitigated field. The paragraph has received judicial explanation as " a statutory application to registered land of the well known rule protecting the rights of persons in occupation " (*National Provincial Bank, Ltd.* v. *Ainsworth* [1965] A.C. 1175, at p. 1259 ; see also *Grace Rymer Investments Ltd.* v. *Waite* [1958] Ch. 831, at p. 849, *Mornington Permanent Building Society* v. *Kenway* [1953] Ch. 382, at p. 386, and *Woolwich Equitable Building Society* v. *Marshall* [1952] Ch. 1, at p. 9). The rule referred to is that a purchaser has constructive notice of anything detectable from an inspection of the property and in particular of anything that would be revealed by reasonable enquiry of any occupier (*Hunt* v. *Luck* [1902] 1 Ch. 428 ; see further *ante*, pp. 166–167).

However, relating para. (g) to the *Hunt* v. *Luck* rule brings some difficulties in its train. First, although still nominally preserved (s. 14 of the L.P.A. 1925), the uncertainties of the equitable doctrine of notice were largely abandoned in 1925, for unregistered conveyancing, in favour of the certainty of protection by registration (s. 199 (1) (i) of the same Act, and s. 4 of the L.C.A. 1972). Consequently, the application of the rule in registered conveyancing represents a considerable difference between the two systems. The second difficulty is that para. (g) is very widely drawn and might, as a result, have protected more rights than did the *Hunt* v. *Luck* rule. In particular, unlike that rule, the paragraph is not qualified by any requirement about enquiry of an occupier as to his rights being reasonable (i.e., for constructive notice). Nevertheless, in nature the rights capable of protection apparently do not differ as between registered and unregistered conveyancing. Making an authoritative analysis in the House of Lords, Lord Wilberforce has said that : " To ascertain what ' rights ' come within [para. (g)], one must look outside [the L.R.A. 1925], and see what rights affect purchasers under the general law. To suppose that [para. (g)] makes any right, of howsoever a personal character, which a person in occupation may have, an overriding interest by which a purchaser is bound, would involve two consequences : first, that [the L.R.A. 1925] is, in this respect, bringing about a substantive change in real property law by making personal rights bind purchasers ; second, that there is a difference *as to the nature of the rights by which a purchaser may be bound* between registered and unregistered land . . . One may have to accept that there is a difference between unregistered land and registered land as regards what kind of notice binds a purchaser, or what kind of enquiries a purchaser has to make. But there is no warrant in the terms of this paragraph or elsewhere in the Act for supposing that the nature of the rights which are to bind a purchaser is to be different, excluding personal rights in one case, including them in another. The whole frame of s. 70, with the list that it gives of interests, or rights, which are overriding, shows that it is made against a background of interests or rights whose nature and whose transmissible character is known, or ascertainable, *aliunde*, i.e., under other statutes or under the common law " (*National Provincial Bank, Ltd.* v. *Ainsworth* [1965] A.C. 1175, at p. 1261).

Actual occupation.—It is perhaps most convenient to consider the application of para. (*g*) of s. 70 (1) of the L.R.A. 1925 by taking the cases of various potential occupiers of land. However, it should be emphasised that for the rights of such persons to be even *prima facie* overriding interests they must be " in actual occupation of the land or in receipt of the rents and profits thereof." Thus the regular parking of a car on a strip of land has been held not to come within the paragraph as not amounting to actual occupation either in whole or in respect of any defined part or time (*Epps* v. *Esso Petroleum Co., Ltd.* [1973] 2 All E.R. 465). Again a lessee who allowed his stepdaughter and her family to occupy his flat on their own account and not as his caretaker or servant and without sharing occupation or receiving a token rent was not protected within para. (*g*) (*Strand Securities, Ltd.* v. *Caswell* [1965] Ch. 958). Nonetheless it is clear from the judgments of the Court of Appeal in this case that a person can be in actual occupation of land for the purposes of para. (*g*) through the agency of another person (in *National Provincial Bank, Ltd.* v. *Ainsworth, ante*, the House of Lords, notwithstanding arguments to the contrary, was prepared to assume that a deserted wife, rather than her husband, was in actual occupation). Also it should be noted that the relevant date for occupation is apparently not that of inspection or completion, but of registration (*Re Boyle's Claim* [1961] 1 W.L.R. 339).

More recently, in *Hodgson* v. *Marks* [1971] Ch. 892 the Court of Appeal held that a person could be " in actual occupation of the land " within para. (*g*) notwithstanding that the vendor was or appeared to be also in occupation. At first instance, Ungoed-Thomas, J., had attached a special construction to the words of the paragraph by which the occupation would not only have to be actual but also apparent to a purchaser (see at p. 916). By withholding any endorsement of this construction and in reversing his decision, the Court of Appeal deliberately preferred a policy of protecting occupiers rather than purchasers of registered land (see *per* Russell, L.J., at p. 932, giving in effect the judgment of the court). Thus the case at least suggests that physical occupation without pre-supposing a right to occupy will suffice for the paragraph (see also *Lee-Parker* v. *Izzet (No. 2)* [1972] 1 W.L.R. 775). This seems especially so since the word " land " in the paragraph is apparently to be construed as referring not at all to any estate in the land but to the physical land itself and as including part of the land (see at [1971] Ch., p. 931 ; also *Webb* v. *Pollmount* [1966] Ch. 584). For an examination of the implications of *Hodgson* v. *Marks, ante*, reference should be made to Ian Leeming at *Conveyancer N.S.*, vol. 35, at p. 255 *et seq.* (also compare the result of earlier proceedings in *Marks* v. *Attallah*

(1966), 110 Sol. J. 709). Further in *London and Cheshire Insurance Co.,
Ltd.* v. *Laplagrene Property Co., Ltd.* [1971] Ch. 499, the gloss has been added
that if a person had an overriding interest within para. (*g*) by virtue of his
actual occupation at the date of registration he does not lose the priority
and protection thereby gained merely through subsequent cessation of occupation. This case again underlines the time-factor : occupation on the one
material day, namely the date of registration, is alone enough for an overriding
interest (see *Re Boyle's Claim, ante*).

Tenants.—The case of tenants is taken first, because occupation by such
persons led to the development of the *Hunt* v. *Luck* rule in unregistered
conveyancing from which para. (*g*) derives. However, if their lease happens
to be for twenty-one years or less, para. (*k*), below, provides them with the
more appropriate class of overriding interest. Again leases *not* within that
paragraph should, and generally will, be completed almost immediately by
registration (see ss. 19 (2) and 22 (2) of the L.R.A. 1925 ; this assumes the
lessor to be a registered proprietor ; otherwise see s. 123 of that Act).
Nonetheless, the present paragraph could effectively provide protection in
the period between execution and registration of these latter leases (see
Land Registry Practice Notes 1972, pp. 14, 15, No. 24 (*c*) (ii)).

Additionally, a " lease containing an absolute prohibition against all
dealings therewith *inter vivos* " is not to be registered (s. 8 (2) of the L.R.A.
1925). Such leases appear rare, and their terms seem unlikely to exceed
twenty-one years when the tenants will have overriding interests within
para. (*k*), below. But if not within para. (*k*), the occupier under such a
lease would have an overriding interest within the present paragraph (see
Ruoff and Roper, Registered Conveyancing, 3rd ed., p. 111). Also it would
appear that tenants at will or at sufferance may have their rights protected
as overriding interests within this paragraph (see *ibid.*). Presumably those
with Rent Act rights also would fall within this protection (see *ibid.*, and
per Lord Denning, M.R., in *National Provincial Bank, Ltd.* v. *Hastings Car
Mart, Ltd.* [1964] Ch. 665, at p. 689), as do certain lessees whose leases have
been preserved by statute beyond their contractual end (see s. 2 (5) of the
Leasehold Property (Temporary Provisions) Act, 1951).

The rights of tenant-occupiers protected as overriding interests appear
to extend past those " touching and concerning the land " to carry also those
purely collateral to the landlord-tenant relationship ; this, at least, was the
rule even under the *Hunt* v. *Luck* rule. A more difficult point is whether
the tenant's hidden equities (if any) also amount to overriding interests.
In *un*registered conveyancing, notice is confined to what it would be reasonable to inquire about, and purchasers have been held entitled not to inquire
beyond the lease itself, nor need they inquire of the tenant if the document
correctly represents his rights (*Smith* v. *Jones* [1954] 1 W.L.R. 1089). Against
this, as already mentioned, the registered position depends not at all on the
inquiry being reasonable (or even made) but at most on the truthfulness of
the reply. Thus the conclusion seems to be that this unqualified paragraph
embraces *all* the rights of a tenant-occupier. See further in support *Webb* v.
Pollmount [1966] Ch. 584, and *Lee-Parker* v. *Izzet* (*No.* 2) [1972] 2 All E.R.
800, below.

Contracts.—The next sort of occupier is the person who takes possession
before completion of a contract to grant him a legal estate, leasehold or
freehold. In *un*registered conveyancing such a person can only protect
himself from subsequent purchasers by registering his " estate contract "

under the L.C.A. 1972 (s. 2 (4), Class C (iv), and s. 4 (6)), nothing else now amounting to notice (see s. 199 of the L.P.A. 1925). Alternatively such a person may find his priority accidentally preserved by the doctrines of tenancy by estoppel and feeding the estoppel (i.e., if he would actually have had the legal estate but for the fact that his grantor had not yet got it to grant, then the grantor anyway will be estopped from denying he had the legal estate and also when and if the grantor does get the legal estate the existing estoppel will at once be fed giving the grantee an actual legal estate a *scintilla temporis* at least before any other purchaser or mortgagee can get one : see *Church of England Building Society* v. *Piskor* [1954] Ch. 553). These doctrines would seem to be applicable to registered land, notwithstanding that nobody gets a legal estate before registration and that everything (i.e., conveyance and mortgage) is likely to be lodged for registration simultaneously, since the *scintilla temporis* can be found in the order in which the column headed " nature and priority of applications " is completed on the cover form, the conveyance preceding the mortgage (ss. 19 (1) and 22 (1) of the L.R.A. 1925, with rr. 83 and 84 of the L.R.R. 1925). In fact the doctrines have already been applied to registered land at first instance, but only on the basis of a recital in the mortgage (*Woolwich Equitable Building Society* v. *Marshall* [1952] Ch. 1), and the problem created by simultaneous registration has received only judicial mention, without decision, from the Court of Appeal (in *City Permanent Building Society* v. *Miller* [1952] Ch. 840 ; cf. *Grace Rymer Investments, Ltd.* v. *Waite* [1958] Ch. 831).

Estoppel aside, in registered conveyancing, the intention of the legislature almost certainly was that contracts for sale or lease should create at most mere minor interests not binding purchasers unless protected on the register, i.e., to equate exactly with " estate contracts " in unregistered conveyancing (see, e.g., s. 107 (1) of the L.R.A. 1925). Nonetheless, it has now been decided that only where the person with a contract has *not* gone into occupation is he vulnerable unless protected on the register (as in *City Permanent Building Society* v. *Miller* [1952] Ch. 840). This difference from the *un*registered position first emerged in 1951 when Danckwerts, J., held that a tenancy agreement plus occupation constituted an overriding interest binding a subsequent mortgagee (*Woolwich Equitable Building Society* v. *Marshall* [1952] Ch. 1). Having been followed by Vaisey, J. (in *Mornington Permanent Building Society* v. *Kenway* [1953] Ch. 382), this ruling was more recently adopted by the Court of Appeal (in *Grace Rymer Investments, Ltd.* v. *Waite* [1958] Ch. 381). In 1957 this was extended from tenancy agreements to contracts for sale plus occupation (in *Bridges* v. *Mees* [1957] Ch. 475) ; Harman, J., held that any subsequent purchaser would take subject to such an occupier's rights, which were " an equitable estate in the land existing under the contract . . . and the right to bring an action against the [vendor] for specific performance by a conveyance of the legal estate " (*ibid.*, p. 486). In this case also the learned judge expressly rejected the argument that the present paragraph, preserving the rights of those in occupation, should be limited to such rights as could not be protected on the register (*ibid.*, p. 487). This decision was applied by Ungoed-Thomas, J., in *Webb* v. *Pollmount* [1966] Ch. 584, where he held that an option to purchase the reversion granted by a lease of registered land bound a purchaser of that reversion as an overriding interest within para. (*g*), the lessee being in actual occupation, even though not protected by notice or caution on the register.

This is all so well established now that it seems to have become a matter of common ground or concession that contractual rights of the " estate contract " sort are overriding interests within para. (*g*) (see *per* Goff, J., in *Lee-Parker* v. *Izzet* [1971] 1 W.L.R. 1688, at p. 1691 g ; and *per* Goulding, J., in *Lee-Parker* v. *Izzet* (*No.* 2) [1972] 2 All E.R. 800, at p. 802 g). Instead, such questions may be raised as " whether [the purchaser's] rights in derogation of the written contract (arising as the case may be under an antecedent oral contract, a claim for rectification, or a waiver of rights . . .) are overriding interests within s. 70 (1) (*g*) . . ." (see *per* Goulding, J., in *Lee-Parker* v. *Izzet* (*No.* 2) [1972] 2 All E.R. 800, at p. 803 d/e, where no judicial views were expressed since the point did not strictly arise on the facts).   Indeed, in the same case, as an alternative, equitable relief was claimed by an occupier on the footing that she had expended money at the request of the alleged vendor under the belief induced by him that in the quality of purchaser she was the beneficial owner of the premises and it was not denied by the plaintiffs (mortgagees) that an equity of this character would be binding on them as an overriding interest (see *per* Goulding, J., *loc. cit.* at p. 804 e/f).   It should be emphasized that in each of these last cited cases the approach was adopted of considering first whether the occupiers' claimed rights could enjoy protection and priority as overriding interests and only afterwards whether the rights existed and were enforceable in substance (in the latter case, for example, the alleged contract was in the end held void for uncertainty).

Another aspect of the protection of contractual rights as overriding interests can occur where the *vendor* remains in occupation after completion.   Thus the unpaid vendor's lien may enjoy priority as against the purchasers' mortgagees (or subsequent purchasers), even though the vendor's continued occupation is as tenant under a lease-back transaction (this was conceded in *London and Cheshire Insurance Co. Ltd.* v. *Laplagrene Property Co., Ltd.* [1971] Ch. 499, see at pp. 502/H–503/A, as following from *Webb* v. *Pollmount, Ltd.*, *ante*).   The reader will appreciate that in unregistered conveyancing such a lien would call for protection either by retention of the title deeds or by registration as a " general equitable charge " (see L.C.A. 1972, ss. 2 (4), Class C (iii) and 4 (5)).

Beneficiaries.—Next, a beneficiary under a trust may be found in actual occupation of registered land.   However, it may be argued that since such an occupier's rights are clearly within the definition of " minor interests " (see s. 3 (xv) of the L.R.A. 1925) he could not by bringing himself within " the generality of the wording " of para. (*g*) be " thereby given a stronger position than he would otherwise have " (Potter, Registered Land Conveyancing, at p. 13).   Also, of course, there is s. 74 of the Act providing that no-one dealing with registered land " shall be affected with notice of a trust express implied or constructive."

Unfortunately, this argument faces certain difficulties.   Thus the definition of " minor interests " (s. 3 (xv)) expressly excludes overriding interests. Again, the rights of a beneficiary in occupation under a bare trust have already been held to be within this overriding interest first in *Bridges* v. *Mees* [1957] Ch. 475 (where the bare trust was constituted either because of adverse possession or because of a contract for sale plus payment of the price) and now more recently in *Hodgson* v. *Marks* [1971] Ch. 892 (where the Court of Appeal decided that a beneficiary who remained in actual occupation of a house and for whom the registered proprietor held as a bare trustee under a resulting trust had an overriding interest within para. (*g*) and did nothing to abandon the rights thereby protected unless on inquiry she failed to reveal them). From these cases it would appear that notice has nothing at all to do with overriding interests. If occupying beneficiaries under bare trusts are within the protection of para. (*g*)—and they must surely be within however the bare trust arose—it may be asked why not also where there is either a strict settlement or a trust for sale ? For the former, however, the Act provides that " the successive or other interests created by or arising under a settlement shall . . . take effect as minor interests, *and not otherwise* " (s. 86 (2)). But what about the more common trust for sale ?

No question arises, of course, where the overreaching machinery has been operated by payment to two trustees in compliance usually with the restriction on the register (s. 27 of the L.P.A. 1925 and s. 58 (3) of the L.R.A. 1925). For in such cases an occupying beneficiary's only rights would be against the proceeds of sale, beating the air so far as any purchaser of land is concerned. Consequently the only case requiring consideration is where a sole unrestricted proprietor appears on the register and is selling as beneficial owner whilst in fact a trust for sale subsists (e.g., because of contributions to the purchase price ; compare *Bull* v. *Bull* [1955] 1 Q.B. 234). In *un*registered conveyancing the answer would depend on notice, the *bona fide* purchaser for value of a legal estate taking free of any equitable interest of which he had no notice (see *Pilcher* v. *Rawlins* (1872), L.R. 7 Ch. App. 259). In registered conveyancing, however, para. (*g*) appears to make the consequences of occupation absolute rather than a mere matter of constructive notice (and see, to this effect, *per* Ungoed-Thomas, J., in *Webb* v. *Pollmount* [1966] Ch. 584, at p. 598). Accordingly, one learned writer has already submitted " . . . with some hesitation, that in the absence of any restriction or other entry on the register, a beneficiary in possession under a trust for sale can claim an overriding interest, but a beneficiary in possession of settled land cannot. This result is anomalous and probably accidental " (F. R. Crane, *Conveyancer N.S.*, vol. 22, at p. 24). If this submission were to be accepted by the courts, the conveyancing consequences would be extremely inconvenient, for in practice in the circumstances envisaged no inquiries are made of other occupiers as to whether they claim equitable interests. A more acceptable conclusion would be that the specific provision of s. 74 of the L.R.A. 1925, i.e., that no purchaser of registered land is affected with notice of any trust, should prevail over para. (*g*) despite the decisions in *Bridges* v. *Mees, ante,* and *Hodgson* v. *Marks, ante.* Further, in an interesting article by Mr. D. J. Hayton at *Conveyancer N.S.*, vol. 33, p. 254 *et seq.*, it has been argued that the interest of a beneficiary under a trust for sale is simply not in nature capable of being an overriding interest (referring to *National Provincial Bank, Ltd.* v. *Ainsworth,* mentioned *ante,* pp. 188–189). The central point made was that such a beneficiary's interest was not of a known transmissible character because it was not an interest in the land at all but merely in the proceeds of sale (which is certainly true : *Irani Finance, Ltd.* v. *Singh* [1971] Ch. 59). However, it is to be observed that the *rights* of such a beneficiary go beyond a mere interest in the proceeds of sale, and do attach to the land itself, according to substantive real property law, being transmissible so as to bind a purchaser, for example, if the overreaching machinery is not properly worked. Also it must be noticed that if the trust for sale in question is not express but is imposed by statute because of beneficial co-ownership (i.e., under the L.P.A. 1925, ss. 34–36, as in *Bull* v. *Bull,* the case envisaged *ante*), then the interest of any person in actual occupation of the land is in fact expressly preserved from the otherwise prejudicial effects of the statutory conversion (i.e., by s. 14 of the L.P.A. 1925). Accordingly there appears room for further argument on the point.

7

Licensees.—Apart from persons who have legal estates or equitable interests in the registered land, there may, of course, be occupiers who have no proprietary interest of this sort, in particular licensees. In *National Provincial Bank, Ltd.* v. *Ainsworth* [1965] A.C. 1175, all the members of the House of Lords adopted the following view of Russell, L.J., expressed, whilst dissenting, in the Court of Appeal : " It seems to me that [s. 70 of the L.R.A. 1925] in all its parts is dealing with rights in reference to land which have the quality of enduring through different ownerships of the land, according to normal conceptions of the title to real property." Following from this the actual decision in the case was that a deserted wife in occupation had no such rights as to amount to an overriding interest binding purchasers (see further *post*, p. 364).

However, the extent to which a licence can be either irrevocable or binding on third parties is not yet settled in *un*registered conveyancing. That constructive notice arising from occupation in cases of a licence coupled with an interest or with an equity will affect the licensor's successors in title may be established in so far as the Court of Appeal is concerned (see the judgment of Lord Denning, M.R., in *Bendall* v. *McWhirter* [1952] 2 Q.B. 466, at p. 485 and in *Binions* v. *Evans* [1972] 2 All E.R. 70, at pp. 75–77 ; also *Inwards* v. *Baker* [1965] 2 Q.B. 29 and *Ward* v. *Kirkland* [1966] 1 W.L.R. 601). If this is correct then such a licensee's right would clearly, it is thought, be of a nature to be protected as an overriding interest (as held in a county court case, *Dovto Properties, Ltd.* v. *Astell*, reported in *Conveyancer N.S.*, vol. 28, at p. 270). But considerable doubt now exists because in the *National Provincial Bank* case, *ante*, Lord Upjohn and Lord Wilberforce each expressly reserved for later decision the question whether any licensee at all could have an interest in land capable of binding purchasers (see also the observations of Goff, J., in *Re Solomon* [1967] Ch. 573, at pp. 583–6).

(*h*) " *In the case of a possessory, qualified or good leasehold title, all estates, rights, interests and powers excepted from the effect of registration.*"

All three of these titles are capable of conversion into absolute titles (see s. 77 of the L.R.A. 1925). Then, of course, this class of overriding interests becomes inapplicable.

(*i*) " *Rights under local land charges unless and until registered or protected on the register in the prescribed manner.*"

Local land charges here have the same meaning as in the L.C.A. 1925, s. 15 (see s. 3 (ix) of the L.R.A. 1925). They can be, but generally are not, protected by notice on the register and, if to secure money, must be registered before realisation (see L.R.A. 1925, ss. 49 (1) (*c*) and 59 (2), and L.R.R. 1925, r. 155). In practice, therefore, the same searches in the local authorities' registers are made with exactly the same consequences as in unregistered conveyancing.

(*j*) " *Rights of fishing and sporting, seignorial and manorial rights of all descriptions (until extinguished) and franchises.*"

As to the manorial rights which may still exist, see *ante*, p. 154.

(*k*) " *Leases for any term or interest not exceeding twenty-one years, granted at a rent without taking a fine.*"

These leases can, as a rule, only be protected as overriding interests and nothing else, since mention of them on the register is expressly prohibited (see ss. 8 (1) (*a*), 19 (2) (*a*), 22 (1) (*a*) and 48 (1) of the L.R.A. 1925 ; cf. s. 70 (3) thereof). In the L.R.A. 1925 the word " lease " is defined as including an agreement for a lease unless the context otherwise requires (s. 3 (x)). Consequently, the question arose whether agreements for leases could be overriding interests within this paragraph (see, e.g., Potter, Registered Land Conveyancing, pp. 15–16). However, the Court of Appeal has decided in *City Permanent Building Society* v. *Miller* [1952] Ch. 840, that the use of the word " granted " in para. (*k*) clearly indicates the actual creation of a term of years at law. Accordingly, no mere agreement for a lease (unsupported by occupation ; see para. (*g*), *ante*) can be an overriding interest, protection by notice on the register being needed instead (s. 49 (1) (*c*) of the L.R.A. 1925). However, para. (*k*) does not require that the lease take effect in possession (compare s. 54 (2) of the L.P.A. 1925). Consequently it is thought that reversionary and other non-occupation leases may come within the paragraph (contrast Ruoff and Roper, Registered Conveyancing, 3rd ed., at pp. 115–117, which appears to envisage only occupation leases). Thus the present Act's predecessor did expressly limit this overriding protection to occupation leases and made separate provision for the protection by notice of reversionary leases (see ss. 18 and 50 of the Land Transfer Act, 1875) ; since the present Act does neither, it can be deduced that an amendment was intended. Again, although the statutory definition of " lease " is of no assistance (see s. 3 (x)), the obvious inference is that a " term of years absolute " is meant (see s. 8 (1) (*a*)), and this expression is defined to include reversionary leases (s. 3 (xxvii)). Note that the term of the lease is not to exceed twenty-one years ; i.e., a lease with only twenty-one years or less to run of a longer term will not be within para. (*k*). Also the lease must be granted " at a rent without taking a fine." In connection with this, questions have arisen over payments expressed to be of rent in advance and as yet the Court of Appeal has given no clear answer. For example, in *City Permanent Building Society* v. *Miller*, *ante*, the alleged lease acknowledged receipt of " the sum of £228 being three years' rent at 30s. per week in advance." Harman, J., at first instance held this to be a fine and Hodson, L.J., on appeal agreed with him. However, Evershed, M.R., expressed no view, whilst Jenkins, L.J., reserved for some future occasion the question whether the payment was a fine but also expressed the view that the lease was not at a rent. Further, although " rent " in advance has been held at first instance to be a premium or fine for other purposes (*Hughes* v. *Waite* [1957] 1 W.L.R. 713), the point has since twice come before the Court of Appeal still without a clear answer (see *Woods* v. *Wise* [1955] 2 Q.B. 29 and *Grace Rymer Investments, Ltd.* v. *Waite* [1958] Ch. 851).

It may be mentioned that although a lease may itself be within para. (*k*), it does not apparently follow that all the rights granted to the tenant by it are also within this paragraph (compare *Webb* v. *Pollmount* [1966] Ch. 584, relating to an option to purchase the reversion).

(*l*) " *In respect of land registered before* [1926], *rights to mines and minerals, and rights of entry, search, and user, and other rights and reservations incidental to or required for the purpose of giving full effect to the enjoyment of rights to mines and minerals or of property in mines or minerals being rights which, where the title was first registered before the first day of January, eighteen hundred and ninety-eight, were created before that date, and where the title was first registered after the thirty-first day of December, eighteen hundred and ninety-seven, were created before the date of first registration.*"

A purchaser who is registered as proprietor of the fee simple obtains an interest in the land which includes the mines and minerals (L.R.A. 1925,

s. 3 (viii), (xiv)). On the other hand, no indemnity is payable under the L.R.A. 1925 on account of any mines or minerals or the existence of any rights to work or get mines or minerals unless a note is entered on the register that they are included in the registered title (L.R.A. 1925, s. 83 (5) (*b*)). It is important, therefore, on first registration that such a note should be made. The severance of mines and minerals after registration could be effected only by a registered disposition which would have the effect of causing a note to be made on the register that minerals were excluded.

Overriding interests under later legislation.—Other statutes have made the following also overriding interests :—

    (i) Tithe redemption annuities (Tithe Act, 1936, s. 13 (11)).

   (ii) Rights in respect of coal vested in the National Coal Board (Coal Act, 1938, s. 41).

  (iii) Rights of certain lessees whose leases have been preserved beyond their contractual end (Leasehold Property (Temporary Provisions) Act, 1951, s. 2 (5)).

CHAPTER SIX

POSITION PENDING COMPLETION AND COMPLETION OF PURCHASE

Purchase by sitting tenant, see *ante*, p. 59.

Date of completion, see *ante*, p. 65.

PART 1. RIGHTS AND DUTIES PENDING COMPLETION

THE result of a binding contract for sale of land of which specific performance would be granted is that the purchaser becomes the equitable owner of the property, although, until completion, the vendor remains the legal owner. The vendor must, therefore, manage the property with much the same degree of care as a trustee owes to beneficiaries (*Clarke* v. *Ramuz* [1891] 2 Q.B. 456 ; *Royal Bristol Permanent Building Society* v. *Bomash* (1887), 35 Ch. D. 390 ; *Golden Bread Co.* v. *Hemmings* [1922] 1 Ch. 162 ; *Cumberland Consolidated Holdings, Ltd.* v. *Ireland* [1946] K.B. 264). The vendor's duty of care is not restricted to the preservation of the property from physical destruction. It includes care in its management having regard to the interests of the purchaser. For instance, if agricultural land becomes vacant after contract but before completion the vendor should consult the purchaser as to whether it should be relet and, if the purchaser wishes, should refrain from doing so provided that the purchaser indemnifies him against loss (*Egmont* v. *Smith* (1877), 6 Ch. D. 469). Similarly, the vendor should not, without consulting the purchaser, create a new tenancy of business premises which would be subject to statutory control (*Abdulla* v. *Shah* [1959] A.C. 124) and it is wise to consult with the purchaser whatever is the nature of the property. On the other hand the vendor is a trustee of the property sold and any physical accretions thereto only ; he is not a trustee of financial benefits not expressly included in the sale, e.g., compensation payable under the Compensation (Defence) Act, 1939, s. 2 (1) (*b*) (*Re Hamilton-Snowball's Conveyance* [1959] Ch. 308). Equally the risk of loss from any cause not attributable to the default of the vendor lies on the purchaser (*Rayner* v. *Preston* (1881), 18 Ch. D. 1, fire ; *Cass* v. *Rudele* (1693), 2 Vern. 280, earthquake ; *Paine* v.

Meller (1801), 6 Ves. 349, fire; *Killner* v. *France* [1946] 2 All E.R. 83, bombing; and see a practice note in the *Law Society's Gazette*, vol. 55, p. 775, drawing attention to the risks of larceny, malicious damage, burst pipes and " overflowing of water apparatus " where the vendor vacates the property before completion). It is for this reason that a purchaser should insure as soon as he has entered into a binding contract; see *ante*, p. 29.

Duty of vendor to repair.—The duty of the vendor extends to the carrying out of all ordinary repairs necessary to prevent deterioration to the property pending completion (*Royal Bristol Building Society* v. *Bomash, ante; Phillips* v. *Silvester* (1872), L.R. 8 Ch. 173). Similarly, the vendor must not permit damage to the property (*Clarke* v. *Ramuz* [1891] 2 Q.B. 456) or damage it himself, for instance, by removing a valuable ornate door (*Phillips* v. *Lamdin* [1949] 2 K.B. 33) and he must maintain agricultural land in a proper state of cultivation (*Lord* v. *Stephens* (1835), 1 Y. & C. Ex. 222).

If completion is delayed beyond the date fixed by the contract because the vendor has not shown a good title or is otherwise in default, the liability to do repairs remains with the vendor until a good title is shown (*Sherwin* v. *Shakspear* (1854), 5 De G.M. & G. 517; *Regent's Canal Co.* v. *Ware* (1857), 23 Beav. 575), but if completion is delayed by default of the purchaser he will have no remedy if, after he has become in default, the property is allowed to fall into disrepair (*Minchin* v. *Nance* (1841), 4 Beav. 332). What is more, the vendor is not entitled to be indemnified for his expenditure in respect of any repairs to the property, since unlike an ordinary trustee the vendor has rights of his own over the property (see below) so that he might himself have benefited from the repairs (see *per* Simonds, J., in *Re Watford Corporation's and Ware's Contract* [1943] Ch. 82, at p. 85). However, it has been suggested that, if the state of the property is such that permanent improvements of a substantial nature are necessary in order to prevent deterioration, a vendor who carries them out will be entitled to recover the cost from the purchaser (*Phillips* v. *Silvester* (1872), L.R. 8 Ch. 173, at p. 176, also *Bolton Partners* v. *Lambert* (1888), 41 Ch. D. 295, at p. 302). But it is arguable that this suggestion goes no further than saying that a vendor may make the purchaser choose between paying for such improvements or permitting the deterioration to continue (*Golden Bread Co.* v. *Hemmings* [1922] 1 Ch. 162).

Rights of vendor.—The obligations of the vendor as trustee for the purchaser are subject to certain valuable rights in his own favour (*Lysaght* v. *Edwards* (1876), 2 Ch. D. 499; *Re Watford Corporation and A. S. Ware's Contract* [1943] Ch. 83). Thus, in the absence of a contrary provision in the contract, the vendor is entitled to retain possession of the property until the transaction is completed by payment of the purchase-money (*Gedye* v. *Montrose* (1858), 26 Beav. 45; *Phillips* v. *Silvester, ante*). If the contract provides that possession shall be given on a certain date this is assumed to mean that a good title shall first be shown, unless the contract clearly shows otherwise (*Tilley* v. *Thomas* (1869), L.R. 3 Ch. 61). What is more, if the vendor parts with possession of or conveys the land before actual completion, he will still have an equitable lien over the land until he receives the purchase price (*Winter* v. *Lord Anson* (1827), 3 Russ. 488; *Nives* v. *Nives* (1880), 15 Ch. D. 649; *Re Birmingham* [1959] Ch. 523). A vendor who undertakes by the contract to lend to the purchaser part of the price to be secured by a legal mortgage has an equitable mortgage between contract and completion and his lien as unpaid vendor merges in this except as to the part of the purchase price to be paid in cash on completion (*Capital Finance Co., Ltd.* v. *Stokes* [1969] 1 Ch. 261). See *post*, p. 633, as to the particular danger of this rule where the purchaser is a company and *post*, p. 464, as to the position where the lien passes by subrogation.

If the property is let, a vendor selling under an open contract is entitled to receive the rents and profits and to keep them until completion actually takes place, although he may then have to account to the purchaser for the rents and profits accrued due after the date when a good title was shown (see p. 205). Similarly, the vendor may, subject to any provision in the contract, up to the proper time for completion gather crops for his own benefit in proper course of husbandry (*Webster* v. *Donaldson* (1865), 11 Jur. (N.S.) 404).

PART 2. VACANT POSSESSION

When purchaser can claim vacant possession.—In Williams on Vendor and Purchaser, 4th ed., vol. I, p. 202, it is stated that " a purchaser buying land by private contract and desiring to obtain actual possession on completion should expressly stipulate for *vacant* possession, especially if the land is described as being in the occupation of a tenant." Nevertheless, it is submitted, *op. cit.*, p. 201, that where the contract expressly or impliedly undertakes conveyance of the fee simple, free from incumbrances (as to which, see *ante*, p. 105), " it is *prima facie* a term of the contract that the purchaser shall on completion be put into actual (and not constructive) possession." See also, *per* Goff, J., in *Horton* v. *Kurzke* [1971] 1 W.L.R. 769, at pp. 771–772.

The question is really one of the intention of the parties as shown by the contract (*Lake* v. *Dean* (1860), 28 Beav. 607 ; *Hughes* v. *Jones* (1861), 3 De G. F. & J. 307, 314 ; *Re Crosby's Contract* [1949] 1 All E.R. 830). In *Cook* v. *Taylor* [1942] Ch. 349, where the contract was silent as to tenancies, it was held to be implied that vacant possession would be given on completion. In that case some importance was attached to the fact that the property was seen to be vacant on inspection, but Simons, J., said, in general terms, that " where a contract is silent as to vacant possession, and silent as to any tenancy to which the property is subject, there is impliedly a contract that vacant possession will be given on completion." See also *Hughes* v. *Jones*, *ante*, where it was decided that if the effect of a contract is that the vendor has undertaken to convey the property free from incumbrances, the purchaser will be entitled to require vacant possession on completion. A lease would prevent the vendor giving actual possession of the property, and if it is not referred to in the contract the purchaser will be entitled to require that the land be conveyed free therefrom. General Condition 3 (1) of the 1973 Revision of The Law Society's Conditions of Sale renders a special condition for vacant possession unnecessary.

Meaning of phrase "vacant possession."—An undertaking that vacant possession will be given is usually taken to mean that possession will be given free from any occupation by the vendor or a third party and free from any claim to a right to possession of the premises. Thus, in *Cleadon Trust, Ltd.* v. *Davis* (1944), 143 *Estates Gazette* 611, it was held that vacant possession was not given because the land was occupied by persons who had formerly been tenants, but whose tenancies had expired. See also *Engell* v. *Fitch* (1869), L.R. 4 Q.B. 559, and *James Macara, Ltd.* v. *Barclay* [1945] K.B. 148, where it was held that, although there was no physical occupation, the existence of a right of a third party to take possession prevented a vendor from giving vacant possession. Vacant possession is not given if a physical impediment exists such as the existence of a quantity of rubbish in the cellars of a building, which substantially interferes with the enjoyment of the right to possession of a substantial part of the premises (*Cumberland Consolidated Holdings, Ltd.* v. *Ireland* [1946] K.B. 264, followed in *Norwich Union Life Insurance Society* v. *Preston* [1957] 1 W.L.R. 813 as to a house left full of furniture). As to the steps and procedure whereby a vendor obtains vacant possession of property he wishes to sell, see *Re 9 Orpen Road, Stoke Newington* [1971] 1 W.L.R. 166.

Merger on completion.—In *Hissett* v. *Reading Roofing Co., Ltd.* [1969] 1 W.L.R. 1757, a contract for the sale of property comprising offices, depot space and a flat had contained a special condition for vacant possession on completion, yet a protected tenant remained in occupation of the flat and the purchaser succeeded in an action for damages for breach of contract. Stamp, J., rejected the argument put for the vendor that the contractual term for vacant possession had disappeared by merger into the conveyance ; he took the view that this was not a matter with which the conveyance was concerned (see *post*, p. 203 ; *semble* the result would be the same even though the term for vacant possession was implied rather than express).

Compulsory purchase.—Where a compulsory purchase order is made and notice to treat served after contract but before completion, the question arises whether the purchaser may claim that the contract has been frustrated and that, as a result, he is not obliged to complete. In *Hillingdon Estates Co., Ltd.* v. *Stonefield Estates, Ltd.* [1952] Ch. 627, it was decided that, as the purchasers were treated as owners in equity as soon as a binding contract was made, the service of a notice to treat did not affect the vendors, whose sole interest was to receive the purchase-money. It followed that the risk of compulsory purchase properly fell on the purchasers, who were not entitled to rescind. In the *Solicitors' Journal*, vol. 96, p. 691, it was suggested that this decision might not be binding in a case in which time was not of the essence of the contract and no long delay or other circumstance was available to raise a right to specific performance ; the present editor would not be inclined to rely on this suggestion since, for one thing, the right to specific performance clearly arises independently of any delay (see *Marks* v. *Lilley* [1959] 1 W.L.R. 749, at p. 753, and *Hasham* v. *Zenab* [1960] A.C. 316, at p. 329).

Possession before completion.—A purchaser who is allowed to enter into possession of premises before completion, paying a periodic sum, may be a tenant or a licensee. Both The Law Society's Conditions of Sale, 1973 Revision (Condition 14), and the National Conditions (18th ed., Condition 7 (1)) provide that if the purchaser is authorised to take possession before completion otherwise than under a pre-contract lease or tenancy (i.e., whether under the contract or by virtue of a subsequent agreement) he shall occupy as licensee of the vendor and not as a tenant. However, The Law Society's Condition now provides that where the purchaser is authorised to enter into a dwelling-house solely to decorate or repair it, without leaving personal chattels upon it, there is no entry into possession.

These general conditions are not applicable to an agreement for a lease where rent is paid in advance on taking possession (*Joel* v. *Montgomery & Taylor* [1967] Ch. 272). Under an open contract the purchaser who pays a periodic sum for use of premises will normally be a tenant (*Francis Jackson Developments, Ltd.* v. *Stemp* [1943] 2 All E.R. 601) as, apparently, will a purchaser who pays interest on the balance of the price in accordance with an arrangement made *subsequent* to the contract (*Finch* v. *Thorpe* (1950), decided in a county court and reported in the *Law Journal*, vol. 100, p. 472) ; but if interest is paid *pursuant* to the contract, such payments appear referable to the relationship of vendor and purchaser and not to be construed as rent.

A special condition of sale providing that the vendor should " allow the purchasers to enter into occupation pending completion " was construed as meaning *lawfully* allow, with the consequence that interdependent provisions were inapplicable where a necessary licence was not yet forthcoming (*Cantor Art Services, Ltd.* v. *Kenneth Bieber Photography, Ltd.* [1969] 1 W.L.R. 1226, C.A., concerning a contract to assign leasehold property and intermediate liability to pay rent).

As to the risks run by a vendor who allows a purchaser to go into possession before completion, see *Maskell* v. *Ivory* [1970] 1 Ch. 502 (also articles by Mr. Trevor M. Aldridge in the *Solicitors' Journal*, vol. 114, pp. 544 and 584). In that case, under a contract for the sale of a farmhouse and some adjoining land the purchaser, without ever completing, had gone into possession, carried on his business of plastic manufacturer and caused such extensive alterations that the land, allegedly, was no longer usable for agricultural purposes, the only permitted use under the planning legislation. The vendor sought an order that the purchaser, who had accepted title, lodge the balance of the purchase price in court, but only obtained an order in terms which gave the purchaser an option of going out of possession (*ibid.*). Conversely, a person allowed into possession as purchaser under a contract for sale which subsequently turns out to be void (e.g., for uncertainty) may be entitled to equitable relief in respect of expenditure on repairs or improvements to the property (such a claim was made but on the facts did not succeed in *Lee-Parker* v. *Izzet* (*No.* 2) [1972] 1 W.L.R. 775 ; see also *Lee-Parker* v. *Izzet* [1971] 1 W.L.R. 1688 ; cf. *Lloyd* v. *Stanbury* [1971] 1 W.L.R. 535, *post*, p. 226).

PART 3. DEATH OF VENDOR OR PURCHASER BEFORE COMPLETION

Generally.—The death of either, or even both, of the parties does not avoid a contract for the sale of land, which remains enforceable by or against the personal representatives of the deceased party (*Hoddel* v. *Pugh* (1864), 33 Beav. 489 ; *Baden* v. *Pembroke* (*Countess*) (1868), 2 Vern. 52). Indeed, personal representatives have a duty to perform all the enforceable contracts of the deceased (*Re Rushbrooke's Will Trusts* [1948] 1 Ch. 421). In suing the personal representatives for damages or specific performance, no devisee should be joined in the action unless the personal representatives have already assented or the court so orders.

Death of vendor.—If a vendor contracts, as absolute owner, to sell freehold or leasehold land and dies before completion of the sale, the legal estate in the land and his equitable or beneficial interest in the purchase-money and right of lien on the property therefor pass to his personal representatives (A.E.A. 1925, ss. 1 and 3). They are the persons to complete the contract and convey the legal estate in the land to the purchaser (*ibid.*, s. 2).

7A

If the vendor left a will which was executed *after the date of the contract* and thereby specifically devised the property the subject of the contract the specific devise amounts to an indication of an intention to pass to the devisee whatever interest the testator had in the property at the date of his will (*Weeding* v. *Weeding* (1861), 1 J. & H. 424 ; *Re Pyle* [1895] 1 Ch. 724). Even where the will containing the specific devise was executed before the date of the contract, if the testator after the contract executed a codicil confirming the specific devise, this would equally entitle the specific devisee to the purchase-money (*Re Pyle, ante*). The same rule would seem to apply where the testator devised part of the property (*Drant* v. *Vause* (1842), 1 Y. & C.C.C. 580 ; *Weeding* v. *Weeding, ante ; Re Calow* [1928] Ch. 710). Where, however, there was no specific devise of the property or of the testator's interest therein or the specific devise of the property was made in a will executed before the date of the contract, and was not brought up to date by a codicil, then the personal representatives would take the purchase-money as personal estate, and would hold it, subject to their rights as personal representatives, for the benefit of the residuary legatee under the will (*Weeding* v. *Weeding, ante ; Re Carrington* [1932] 1 Ch. 1).

On sale by a vendor as tenant for life or person having the powers of a tenant for life, or statutory owner, the contract remains binding on and enures for the benefit of the settled land, and is enforceable against and by every successor in title for the time being of such tenant for life or statutory owner, and may be carried into effect by such successor (S.L.A. 1925, s. 90 (2), (3)). It is also provided by s. 63 of the same Act that a tenant for life may make any disposition which is necessary or proper for giving effect to a contract entered into by a predecessor in title, and which, if made by that predecessor, would have been valid as against his successors in title. This includes a person entitled before the land was settled. Where on the death of the tenant for life the settlement came to an end, the legal estate would pass to the general personal representatives of the former tenant for life under the decision in *Re Bridgett and Hayes' Contract* [1928] Ch. 163 (as to which see the chapter on Settled Land, *post*, p. 664), and they would be the persons to complete any outstanding contract.

Death of purchaser.—In equity a purchaser is considered the owner of the land as from the time when the contract becomes enforceable. If the purchaser devised the property, the interest of the purchaser in the first instance would pass to his executors for purposes of administration, and, subject thereto, the devisee under the will would be entitled to the beneficial interest in the land ; as a result of the provisions of s. 35 of the A.E.A. 1925, however, he would have to find the balance of the purchase-money, unless the will contained a contrary intention. Section 35 (1) provides that where a person dies possessed of an interest in property, which at the time of his death is charged with the payment of money, *including a lien for unpaid purchase-money*, and the deceased has not by will, deed, or other document signified a contrary intention, the interest so charged shall, as between the different persons claiming through the deceased, be primarily liable for the payment of the charge, and every part of the said interest, according to its value, shall bear a proportionate part of the charge on the whole thereof. It must be noted, in particular, that a direction to pay " mortgage debts " will not extend to a vendor's lien for unpaid purchase-money (*Re Beirnstein* [1925] Ch. 12). Note also the decision in *Re Birmingham* [1959] Ch. 523, where the testatrix, after contracting to buy a house, wrote to her solicitors that she wished to leave the house to her daughter and executed a codicil reciting the contract and giving the house to her daughter. The testatrix died before completion and it was held that the daughter took subject to a charge for the unpaid balance of the purchase-money, on the ground that neither the letter nor the codicil signified a contrary intention for the purposes of s. 35. The decision is difficult to understand as most people would regard the intention as clearly stated.

Registered title.—It is worth noticing that it is open to the personal representatives of a deceased registered proprietor to transfer the land in question without first procuring their own registration as proprietors (L.R.A. 1925, s. 37, and L.R.R. 1925, r. 170). However, although such a procedure is acceptable to H.M. Land Registry and to most practitioners, a purchaser is entitled if he wishes to insist on the personal representatives procuring their own registration (L.R.A. 1925, s. 110 (5)).

PART 4.   PLACE FOR COMPLETION

In practice, because of the value of both title deeds and purchase-money, completion is usually carried out in person by the solicitors acting for each party and rarely by post. If the contract contains no condition in this respect, the place at which the completion strictly should be carried out would appear to be governed by the following rule : namely, that any person bound to make tender, as the purchaser is of both the purchase-money and the engrossed conveyance for execution, must seek out his tenderee to do so (*Reading Trust, Ltd.* v. *Spero* [1930] 1 K.B. 492, at pp. 513–4). The only limitation on this rule seems to be that the place where the vendor chooses to await tender should be within England or Wales (*ibid.* ; *Re Young and Harston's Contract* (1885), 31 Ch. D. 168). In practice, however, the only proper place for completion is thought to be at the office either of the vendor's solicitor or, when appropriate, of his mortgagee's solicitor (and see *Law Society's Digest*, Opinions Nos. 165–168 and 172, and 174 (*a*) in the Fourth Cumulative Supplement) and this will usually be provided for by the general conditions of sale (National Conditions of Sale, 18th ed., Condition 4 (2), and The Law Society's Conditions of Sale, 1973 Revision, Condition 15 (1)).

PART 5.   MERGER OF CONTRACT IN CONVEYANCE

Where there are matters in a contract which it is the intention of the parties shall be carried out notwithstanding the execution of the conveyance and the completion of the purchase, such as putting the drains right, or doing certain repairs, a cautious purchaser should get the vendor to sign a memorandum on the contract that he will do such matters, notwithstanding that the purchase-money has been paid and the deed handed over and the purchase completed. Alternatively, the contract may provide that there shall be no merger of any terms to which effect is not given by the conveyance. Of course, if the matter to be done is a serious one, such as completing the building of the house purchased, the purchaser should arrange to keep back a portion of the purchase-money until it has been done.

Should such a memorandum or provision not have been made and a dispute arises after the completion of the purchase as to the position of the parties, the question to be answered will be whether the informal document, the contract, has been merged in the formal and more important document, the deed under seal, so as to prevent the purchaser making a claim. This will depend on what the intention of the parties was on entering into the contract (*Barclays Bank, Ltd.* v. *Beck* [1952] 2 Q.B. 47). A contract comes to an end when the terms of it have been performed. If the contract provides that something shall be done in addition to matters connected with the completion of the purchase, then there are two contracts, just as much as if they were written out on two separate pieces of paper : the one to complete the purchase and the other to do repairs or whatever the contract provides should be done. When the vendor executes the conveyance and completes the purchase he completes one of the contracts and the completed contract merges in the conveyance (*Knight Sugar Co.* v. *Alberta Railway Co.* [1938] 1 All E.R. 266). But he still remains liable on the other contract and this separate contract does not merge in the conveyance.

Bowen, L.J., in *Palmer* v. *Johnson* (1884), 13 Q.B.D. 351, said : " When one is dealing with a deed by which the property has been conveyed, one must see if it covers the whole ground of the preliminary contract. One must construe the preliminary contract by itself, and see whether it was intended to go on to any and what extent after the formal deed had been executed." So, Lord Alverstone, in *Saunders* v. *Cockrill* (1902), 87 L.T. 30, said : " The rule is that if the contract is collateral and is independent, and is in addition to the description of the property, an action can be brought despite the completion of the conveyance." See also the judgment of Lord Campbell, C.J., in *Dale* v. *Humphrey* (1857), 7 El. & Bl. 266, at p. 274. Thus, in *Lawrence* v. *Cassel* [1930] 2 K.B. 83, there was a written agreement to sell a house in course of erection with an undertaking to complete it in accordance with plans and specifications. In an action brought after completion alleging defective building work, it was held that the terms of the contract as to building had not become merged in the conveyance.

Again, where property was contracted to be sold with vacant possession but there is a protected tenant of part, the term as to vacant possession is not merged in the conveyance and damages may be recovered thereafter for breach of contract (*Hissett* v. *Reading Roofing Co., Ltd.* [1969] 1 W.L.R. 1757).

An example of the class of cases on the other side is *Greswolde-Williams* v. *Barneby* (1900), 83 L.T. 708. In that case the agreement in effect warranted the mansion house to be in perfect order as to drainage and otherwise. After the completion of the purchase it was ascertained that the drainage was far from perfect, and an action for damages was brought. It was held that the action could not be maintained. Wills, J., said, in effect, that if the preliminary contract was intended to be superseded by the conveyance the former merged in the latter. It is not easy to agree with this decision. The contract could have been divided into two distinct parts just as much as if there were two separate agreements, and it was the intention that the conveyance should be a discharge of the contract as regards the one part only, not being the warranty as to the drains.

If it is intended that any obligation contained in a contract should continue to have effect after completion, then, unless it is clearly collateral to the main contract which is carried out by the conveyance, the safest course is to repeat the provision in the conveyance in the form of a covenant.

Note finally that the above general rule as to merger applies equally to sales of land with a registered title subject to the point that the merger then depends on both execution of the transfer and registration taking place (see ss. 19 (1) and 22 (1) of the L.R.A. 1925, and *Knight Sugar Co.* v. *Alberta*

Railway Co., *ante*, where the Privy Council were concerned with the somewhat different provisions of the Land Titles Act, 1906, of Alberta ; see case notes in the *Conveyancer N.S.*, vol. 2, p. 262 and at [1962] B.T.R. 388).

PART 6. APPORTIONMENT OF RENT AND OUTGOINGS AND PAYMENT OF INTEREST

The general rule is that the vendor becomes entitled to interest as soon as he ceases to be entitled to keep the rents and profits for his own benefit, for, as Wilberforce, J., has said " on general principle it is not right that the purchaser both should have the income of the property from the date of the contract [*sic*] and in addition should be relieved from paying interest on the purchase-money " (*Re Hewitt's Contract* [1963] 1 W.L.R. 1298, at pp. 1301-2). Consequently, it is considered advisable to discuss these matters together.

Rent and interest under open contract.—Under an open contract completion should take place as soon as a good title is shown, and after that time the vendor receives the rents and profits as a trustee and must account for them to the purchaser when completion takes place (*Re Highett and Bird's Contract* [1903] 1 Ch. 287 ; *Bennett* v. *Stone* [1903] 1 Ch. 509).

It follows that, under such a contract, if the purchase is not completed at the proper time, that is when a good title has been shown, the purchaser must pay interest, apparently at the rate currently applicable to all equitable apportionment, namely 4 per cent. per annum, on the balance of the purchase price from that time until completion (see *per* Leach, V.-C., in *Esdaile* v. *Stephenson* (1822), 1 Sim. & St. 122, at p. 123 ; *Monro* v. *Taylor* (1852), 21 L.J. Ch. 525 ; also *Halkett* v. *Dudley* [1907] 1 Ch. 590, 606). As the purchaser is entitled to rents and profits from this time no hardship is caused by this rule, except that the rate of interest is inadequate at the present time.

Correspondingly, a vendor who remains in occupation must make allowance to the purchaser of a fair occupation rent from the date when the purchaser has to pay interest to the date of actual completion (*Metropolitan Railway Company* v. *Defries* (1877), 2 Q.B.D. 387), unless the delay in completion has been the fault of the purchaser and the vendor has been obliged to remain in possession for the protection of the property and not for his own benefit (*Dakin* v. *Cope* (1827), 2 Russ. 170, 181-2 ; *Leggot* v. *Metropolitan Railway Co.* (1870), L.R. 5 Ch. 716). As to ascertaining the amount of a fair occupation rent, see *Sherwin* v. *Shakspear* (1854), 5 De G.M. & G. 517, 532 and 538-9, and *Metropolitan Railway Company* v. *Defries*, *ante*, at p. 387.

Rent and interest where date fixed for completion.—A day is usually fixed for completion by the contract, but even if this has been done, the vendor is entitled to retain possession or to take rents and profits until the actual time when the transaction is completed, and even though delay was due to the state of his title (*Gedye* v. *Montrose* (1858), 26 Beav. 45) unless the contract expressly provides otherwise. But if completion is delayed, then when it does take place the purchaser will be entitled to the rents and profits as from the day fixed for completion and he will usually have to pay interest on the balance of the purchase-money from that day (*Esdaile* v. *Stephenson* (1822), 1 Sim. & St. 122).

Delay vendor's fault.—If delay in completion is the fault of the vendor he is not allowed to profit from his own wrong, so that where the interest would exceed the rents and profits the purchaser may insist on the vendor being satisfied with the rents and profits until completion takes place (*Paton* v. *Rogers* (1822), 6 Madd. 275 ; *Jones* v. *Mudd* (1827), 4 Russ. 118). As Wilberforce, J., more recently said, " where the sale is delayed by the vendor's default the general rule is that the vendor, instead of getting the interest, must be satisfied with the interim rent and profits ; but he does not lose both ways " (in *Re Hewitt's Contract* [1963] 1 W.L.R. 1298, at p. 1302). See further below as to conditions in the contract relating to the vendor's " wilful default." In any case, if the purchaser is not responsible for the delay the purchaser may place the balance of the purchase-money on deposit and give notice to the vendor of the deposit, and he will then be liable only for such interest as is actually received from the deposit (*Regents Canal Co.* v. *Ware* (1857), 23 Beav. 575, 587). See, however, the remarks made, *post*, p. 208, as to the fact that interest is not now normally paid in respect of money on deposit withdrawable on demand.

Provision for payment of interest if completion delayed.—A common provision in contracts is that the purchaser shall pay interest *if from any cause whatever* the purchase shall not be completed on the day fixed. The rule is that in such cases interest is payable as provided except where there is bad faith, vexatious conduct, or gross negligence on the part of the vendor, disentitling him, in the view of the court, to the benefit of the stipulation. Therefore, delay arising from mere accident, or from something which the vendor could not have guarded against, or from difficulties ocasioned by the state of the title, is not enough to exempt the purchaser from the payment of interest pursuant to the contract, even though the difficulties may be such as to justify him in refusing to complete until they are removed. Thus the purchaser was obliged to pay interest in all the following cases : where the abstract was not delivered in time (*Rowley* v. *Adams* (1850), 12 Beav. 476) ; where delay was due to the death of the vendor (*Bannerman* v. *Clarke* (1856), 3 Drew. 632) ; where delay was caused by the state of the vendor's title (*Vickers* v. *Hand* (1859), 26 Beav. 630) ; where it was necessary to institute a suit for the rectification of the power under which the vendor was selling (*Lord Palmerston* v. *Turner* (1864), 10 L.T. 364) ; where the vendor had to institute a partition action to enable him to sell (*Williams* v. *Glenton* (1866), L.R. 1 Ch. 200).

The better opinion is that a purchaser who enters into a contract containing such a term cannot discharge himself from his liability to pay interest by appropriating the unpaid purchase-money, for instance by paying it into a bank. See *Re Riley to Streatfield* (1886), 34 Ch. D. 386 ; Williams on Vendor and Purchaser, 4th ed., vol. I, p. 78 ; but to the contrary, see *Re Monckton and Gilzean* (1884), 27 Ch. D. 555 and *Re Golds' and Norton's Contract* (1885), 52 L.T. 321. It is more clear that, despite payment into a bank, interest will still be payable by a purchaser whose own act or default caused the delay in completion (see *De Visme* v. *De Visme* (1849), 1 Mac. & G. 336 ; *Pearlberg* v. *May* [1951] Ch. 699).

A condition which has given rise to much litigation is that requiring the purchaser to pay interest if completion is delayed from any cause *other than wilful default on the part of the vendor*. The purchaser will be relieved from payment of interest under this condition only if he can prove (*a*) that the vendor has been in default, (*b*) that such default was wilful, and (*c*) that the wilful default was the direct cause of the delay in completion.

The vendor is guilty of wilful default if his conduct, either by his acts or neglects, can be considered unreasonable from the point of view of the purchaser. The fact that the vendor has made an honest mistake will not, unless it is persisted in after it has been pointed out, prevent him from obtaining interest from the purchaser. Similarly, the purchaser must pay interest although the delay arose from a defect in the title not known to the vendor. It appears that where the vendor is not guilty of wilful default the purchaser cannot escape liability for payment of interest by appropriating the amount of the unpaid purchase-money and giving notice to the vendor (*Re Riley to Streatfield, ante*, but see the cases to the contrary cited above).

" ' Default ' is a purely relative term, just like negligence—it means nothing more, nothing less, than not doing what is reasonable under the circumstances —not doing something which you ought to do, having regard to the relations which you occupy towards the other persons interested in the transaction. The other word which it is sought to define is 'wilful.' As used in courts of law it generally implies nothing blameable, but merely that, there being a person who is acting as a free agent, that which has been done arises from the spontaneous act of his will " (Bowen, L.J., in *Re Young and Harston's Contract* (1885), 31 Ch. D. 168, where it was held that a vendor was guilty of wilful default by going abroad two days before the time known by him to have been fixed for completion). This definition makes it clear that a default may be " wilful " even though " moral delinquency, intentional delay, wilful obstruc- tion on the part of the vendor may all be absent " (*Re Hetling and Merton's Contract* [1893] 3 Ch. 269, 281). But as a definition of " default " itself, Wilberforce, J., after quoting the first sentence, has said of it : " That, with great respect, does not seem to me to enlighten the matter to any great extent. It simply transfers the basic interpretation to another set of considerations, namely, what one ought to do. One is still faced with the question of deciding what in fact the vendor ought to do in relation to this matter " (*Re Hewitt's Contract* [1963] 1 W.L.R. 1298, at p. 1303). The learned judge proceeded to draw a distinction, in effect, between difficulties foreseen by the vendor, who hoped but failed to overcome them, and unforeseen occurrences, only delay caused by the former being due to wilful default (he followed *dicta* in *Re Hetling and Merton's Contract, ante*).

An honest mistake or oversight on the part of a vendor is not wilful default by him. An example of such a mistake is a misstatement of the title to part of the property by neglect to look at the deeds (*Re Mayor of London and Tubbs' Contract* [1894] 2 Ch. 524). Where, however, the vendor persists in a mistake when it is called to his attention his default will be regarded as wilful (*Bennett v. Stone* [1903] 1 Ch. 509), although this may not be the case where the question at issue was a difficult one so that the vendor's action could not be regarded as clearly mistaken.

Examples of wilful default are : the omission to deliver an abstract until after the time fixed for completion (*Wallis* v. *Sarel* (1852), 5 De G. & S. 429) ; the failure of the vendor to obtain the concurrence of necessary parties (*Re Earl of Strafford and Maples* [1896] 1 Ch. 235).

Alternative forms of condition are (i) that the purchaser shall pay interest if delay arises from some cause other than *default on the part of the vendor* and (ii) that the purchaser shall pay interest unless the delay arises from a cause *other than the neglect or default of the purchaser*. The definition of Bowen, C.J., in *Re Young and Harston's Contract, ante*, is relevant to either of these forms. Further, the error in *Re Mayor of London and Tubbs' Contract, ante*, provides an example of default, although it was not regarded as wilful.

In the case of *Re Bayley-Worthington and Cohen's Contract* [1909] 1 Ch. 648, the condition was that the purchaser should not be called on to pay interest if the delay was not caused by his neglect or default. The purchaser had made an objection going to the root of title but the House of Lords ultimately decided that the objection was not well founded. It was held by Parker, J., that the delay resulting from these proceedings was caused by the default of the purchaser.

Deduction of tax.—The long-standing practice of deducting income tax from interest payable on delay in completion can no longer be followed. By virtue of the Income and Corporation Taxes Act, 1970, ss. 52–56, interest payable on the balance of purchase monies should now on completion be paid gross, without deduction of tax. This does not apply, and tax should be deducted, if the interest is paid (*a*) by a company or local authority, or (*b*) by a partnership of which a company is a member, or (*c*) to a vendor whose usual place of abode is outside the United Kingdom (s. 54 of the 1970 Act). Where interest is paid gross on the balance of purchase monies on completion of the purchase of a dwelling-house, the purchaser will be entitled to tax relief in respect of it (under F.A. 1972, s. 75 (3) and Sched. 9). See further Practice Notes in the *Law Society's Gazette*, vol. 67, p. 89, vol. 68, p. 510.

Conditions of sale as to interest.—The relevant provision in The Law Society's Conditions of Sale, 1973 Revision, is General Condition 16, the effect of which (except where the purchaser was authorised to take possession before completion, when Condition 14 applies) is as follows :—

First.—Interest at the rate specified or at the rate of 2 per cent. per annum above Bank of England minimum lending rate at the date of the contract on the balance of the purchase-money is payable from the day fixed for completion to the day of actual payment if completion is delayed from any cause (except as stated below). Where, however, delay arises from any cause other than default of the purchaser, the purchaser may place the money on *deposit* account, giving notice to the vendor, in which case the interest (if any) from the deposit only is payable unless and until further delay arises from the purchaser's default. As the purchaser is required to make a deposit at interest it would appear that the necessity for notice of withdrawal is accepted and so the vendor must thereafter give at least that length of notice to complete. See the comments in the *Conveyancer N.S.*, vol. 18, pp. 213, 214.

Second.—No interest is payable so long as delay in completion is attributable to default of the vendor.

Third.—The condition, however, gives the *vendor* the option of taking the rents and profits less outgoings, apportioned if necessary, up to the date of actual completion in lieu of his right to interest. This option is not available, however, where the purchaser was entitled to, and has, deposited the balance of the purchase price as above.

Fourth.—Express provision is made for the vendor to pay a fair occupation rent as from the contractual completion until actual completion, so long as the delay was the vendor's fault ; the rent is to be at an annual rate of 2½ times the gross annual value of the property.

It is now vital to note that this form of condition (which occurs equally in Condition 6 of the National Conditions of Sale, 18th ed.) has been held " clearly to link the right to income (less outgoings) with the right to receive interest, and to make it plain that the vendor can exercise the option to take the income of the property only in a case where, if he did not exercise the option, he would have been entitled to interest " (*Re Hewitt's Contract* [1963] 1 W.L.R. 1298, at p. 1302, concerning General Condition 7 in the 1953 edition, but appearing equally applicable to the present condition). In other words, if the delay is due to the vendor's default, then under such a condition the purchaser can both keep the interest and claim the income. Accordingly, it is suggested that solicitors acting for vendors might, if delay by the vendor should be contemplated, adopt the practice of drafting special amendments to any such general condition in order to provide that the vendor should not lose both interest and income.

A special condition stating merely that interest shall be paid at a certain rate is not inconsistent with standard conditions (such as those in The Law Society's and National forms) incorporated so far as they are not inconsistent ; in such circumstances the special condition fixes the rate but interest is payable only in accordance with the general conditions (*Re Debenham and Mercer's Contract* [1944] 1 All E.R. 364).

Rent and interest when purchaser in possession.—Where the purchaser is in possession as tenant of the vendor, in the absence of a condition to the contrary, it appears that the purchaser must pay interest from the date of the contract and is not thereafter accountable for the rent. The reason is that, in equity, the purchaser is considered to be entitled as owner from the date of the contract. This is the view taken in Williams on Vendor and Purchaser, 4th ed., vol. I, p. 564, although the matter is not beyond doubt ; contrast the argument by the late Mr. Lewis E. Emmet in the 11th Edition of this work at pp. 208, 209. The circumstances in which a tenancy is surrendered by an agreement to purchase are considered *ante*, p. 59.

Where the purchaser enters into possession under the terms of the contract, or there is an agreement whereby he takes possession thereafter, there will normally be express provision for payment of interest, otherwise interest should be paid from the taking of possession (*Fludyer* v. *Cocker* (1806), 12 Ves. 25). This rule applies even where delay arises from the neglect of the vendor and even where there is no income from the property or any real beneficial occupation (*Ballard* v. *Shutt* (1880), 15 Ch. D. 122). Further, a purchaser in possession cannot avoid paying interest by depositing the purchase-money (*Re Priestley's Contract* [1947] Ch. 469 ; but compare *Kershaw* v. *Kershaw* (1869), L.R. 9 Eq. 56). See also General Conditions 14 (2) and 16 of The Law Society's Conditions of Sale, 1973 Revision, and General Conditions 7 (1) (ii) and (iv) and 6 (1) proviso (ii) of the National Conditions of Sale, 18th ed.

Apportionment of rents.—Even if the purchase is completed at the contractual time, it will usually be necessary to apportion rents and outgoings. In the absence of a condition to that effect in the contract the vendor cannot require the purchaser to pay to him an apportioned part of rent accruing at the time of completion until the purchaser actually receives such rents.

Where a yearly rent is payable by quarterly instalments on the usual quarter days the apportionment should be on the basis of the number of days in the current quarter. Condition 5 (4) of the 18th edition of the National Conditions of Sale provides for apportionment of rents according to the period in respect of which they are payable, and that " apportionment of yearly items (whether or not the same are payable by equal quarterly, monthly or other instalments) shall be according to the relevant number of days relatively to the number of days in the full year." See an article by the late Dr. E. O. Walford in the *Conveyancer N.S.*, vol. 15, p. 17, discussing certain Opinions of the Council of The Law Society ; also an article in *ibid.*, vol. 26, p. 287, considering the difficulty confronting the owner of a block of houses who desires to dispose of them piecemeal when a large rent is charged upon the whole of the houses.

Liability for outgoings.—Under an open contract, the vendor must bear all expenses and outgoings which are a charge on the property, down to the time when a good title to the property is first made out, and, as from that time, all such expenses and outgoings must be borne by the purchaser (*Re Bettesworth and Richer* (1888), 37 Ch. D. 535 ; *Barsht* v. *Tagg* [1900] 1 Ch. 231, at p. 234 ; *Stock* v. *Meakin* [1900] 1 Ch. 683 ; *Baxendale* v. *North Lambeth Liberal Club, Ltd.* [1902] 2 Ch. 427 ; *Re Highett and Bird* [1902] 2 Ch. 214, at p. 217 ; [1903] 1 Ch. 287). Where the contract fixes a date for completion, but otherwise the contract is an open one, the vendor is similarly liable up to the time fixed for completion (*Re Waterhouse's Contract* (1900), 44 Sol. J. 645).

But where such expenses and outgoings are not a charge on the property but are merely recoverable by suing the owner thereof for the time being personally, the vendor ought to pay them if they fall due before the time for completion (Williams on Vendor and Purchaser, 4th ed., vol. I, p. 562 ; *Egg* v. *Blayney* (1888), 21 Q.B.D. 107) ; and in some circumstances the purchaser may be entitled to refuse to complete until such outgoings are paid (Williams, *loc. cit.* ; *Re Bettesworth and Richer* (1888), 37 Ch. D. 535, where there were exceptional charges—not current rates).

Rates payable to local authorities are not charged on the property ; they are payable by the occupier (General Rate Act, 1967, s. 16 ; but see *ibid.*, s. 17 and Sched. 1, as to unoccupied property). Thus, a subsequent purchaser, or a receiver appointed by a mortgagee, is not liable to meet arrears (*Liverpool Corporation* v. *Hope* [1938] 1 K.B. 751). A person who occupies for part only of the period for which the rate is made is, in general, liable only for an apportioned part of the rate (1967 Act, s. 18). If he is liable to pay the whole rate because he was in occupation when the rate was made he may reclaim a proportion on going out of occupation unless he has previously recovered the excess from an incoming occupier (*ibid.*). The consequence is that on sale with vacant possession either the rates may be apportioned or (if the vendor has paid the whole sum due for the period) he may make a reclaim (which is advisable if the property has been vacant and so no sum is due during that time).

An owner of premises which are let may be assessed (i) compulsorily if the property is below a certain rateable value and the local authority have so resolved (*ibid.*, s. 55) ; (ii) by agreement if rent is recoverable at intervals shorter than quarterly (*ibid.*, s. 56). In these cases default in payment may result in action by the authority against the tenant who may deduct the amount from rent payable or may be obliged to pay future rent to the authority (*ibid.*, ss. 59, 61 and 62). Consequently, if premises have a rateable value of £56 or less a purchaser should inquire whether the local authority assess the owner, and, if rent is payable at intervals shorter than quarterly, he should ask whether the vendor has entered into a " compounding agreement." On receiving an affirmative answer to either question it is wise to call for evidence that there are no arrears, otherwise the purchaser may be compelled to suffer a reduction in rent until they are discharged.

If the vendor may be a person of low income who receives a rebate from rates under s. 49 of the 1967 Act, apportionment should not be carried out without consultation with the rating authority (*Law Society's Gazette*, vol. 64, pp. 246, 247). In such cases it will normally be best for the vendor to reclaim any overpayment so that apportionment becomes unnecessary.

In other cases, the occupier resident in a dwelling-house now has the right to pay rates by instalments (s. 50 of the 1967 Act). However, this, even if there are arrears, would not appear capable of adversely affecting a purchaser in any way (see *ibid.*, Sched. 10, para. 6 (*b*)) and the need for apportionment remains as before.

Local legislation may cause difficulty with regard to water rates but, in general, the rules are similar (Water Act, 1945, s. 38 (2), Sched. 3, para. 54 ; *East London Waterworks Co.* v. *Kellerman* [1892] 2 Q.B. 72). An occupier cannot be deprived of water until arrears due from a former occupier are discharged (*Sheffield Waterworks Co.* v. *Wilkinson* (1879), 4 C.P.D. 410).

In most cases there is a provision in the contract for apportionment of outgoings. For instance, Condition 15 (2) of The Law Society's Conditions of Sale, 1973 Revision, and Condition 5 of the National Conditions of Sale, 18th ed., both provide for apportionment of outgoings.

The " expenses " referred to in the first part of this note are covered by the expression " outgoings " in the above condition (see *Tubbs* v. *Wynne* [1897] 1 Q.B. 74 ; *Barsht* v. *Tagg* [1900] 1 Ch. 231 ; *Stock* v. *Meakin* [1900] 1 Ch. 683 ; *Calder's Yeast Co., Ltd.* v. *Stockdale* [1928] 1 Ch. 340) ; but a condition in a contract that the vendor will pay all " outgoings " does not, generally speaking, include payments of a capital nature (*Re Jacobs' and Stedman's Contract* [1942] Ch. 400).

Certain payments, for instance charges for street works, are of such a nature that they cannot be apportioned. These may have been incurred, for instance, by a local authority under the Public Health Act, 1875, or the Private Street Works Act, 1892. However, the relevant provisions of these two Acts have been repealed, and replaced by the Highways Act, 1959. This Act expressly states that charges resulting from the making of streets in accordance with " the Code of 1875 " arise " as from the date of the completion of the works " (1959 Act, ss. 190, 264 (1), Sched. 18).

Unfortunately s. 181 (2), which deals with charges imposed after work has been done by the local authority by the procedure described as the " Code of 1892," does not state expressly from what date the charge takes effect. *Stock* v. *Meakin* [1899] 2 Ch. 496 ; [1900] 1 Ch. 683 decided that the charge under the 1892 Act arose on completion of the works and so the cost fell on the vendor if they were completed before the date of the contract. The judgment in the Court of Appeal gave two main reasons. The first was that the charge under the 1892 Act operated " to the like effect " as that under the 1875 Act (which was stated to be from the date of completion). There is no similar wording in the 1959 Act. Secondly, the court considered that the 1892 Act was so worded that the charge was intended to be operative from completion of the works and not from final apportionment (which occurred on an arbitrary date fixed by the local authority). This reasoning seems similarly applicable to the 1892 Code in the 1959 Act and, although there is an element of doubt, it appears that the date of completion of the works provides the test also where works are done under the 1892 Code contained in the 1959 Act.

The liability for such payments of a capital nature is usually determined by the contract and reference should be made, when applicable, to General Condition 2 of The Law Society's Conditions of Sale, 1973 ed., and to General Condition 5 of the National Conditions of Sale, 18th ed.

Undertakings given on completion.—A purchaser will often accept an undertaking by the vendor's solicitor when he would not accept an undertaking by the vendor himself. If the undertaking is signed by the vendor's solicitor it should make clear whether the solicitor accepts liability personally. The opinion of the Council of The Law Society is that an undertaking expressed to be made " on behalf of the vendor " involves the solicitor in personal liability and that more clear words are needed if the solicitor wishes to avoid this (*Law Society's Gazette*, vol. 45, p. 56) and that " solicitors should not give undertakings which they are not in a position to implement personally, or in a matter where circumstances beyond the control of the solicitor may well supervene to make implementation impossible, e.g., where there is a possibility of bankruptcy " (*Law Society's Gazette*, vol. 54, p. 215).

Forms of undertaking to be given when banks release title deeds or a land certificate to enable solicitors to deal with conveyancing and other transactions have been agreed between The Law Society and the clearing banks. They are set out in the *Law Society's Gazette*, vol. 58, p. 681 ; see also *ibid.*, vol. 66, p. 491, where procedure on change of solicitor is outlined.

As to enforcement of such undertakings, see *Re A Solicitor* [1966] 1 W.L.R. 1604 and *Geoffrey Silver & Drake* v. *Baines* [1971] 1 Q.B. 396.

As to undertakings to discharge mortgages, see *post*, p. 266.

Tax treatment of receipts and outgoings.—Rents and other income from land are, in general, charged to income tax under Schedule A ; see the account, *post*, p. 1115 *et seq.* The Income and Corporation Taxes Act, 1970, s. 86, now provides, in effect, that any tax liability is to be apportioned as between a vendor and purchaser of land with the receipts and outgoings concerned.

In a statement published in full in *Law Society's Gazette*, vol. 61, p. 701, and *Solicitors' Journal*, vol. 108, p. 752, the Board of Inland Revenue state that they are advised that (on account of the trustee relationship between vendor and purchaser under an enforceable contract) apportionments of rents, etc., receivable, and outgoings payable, between contract and completion " fall to be taken into account." The I.C.T.A. 1970, s. 86 (1), recognises this rule, but " modifies its operation for tax purposes in relation to rent payable in advance, in so far as the timing of the adjustment is concerned." The Board point out that the section provides that the part of the rent which is attributed beneficially to the purchaser is to be treated as receivable on his behalf, *immediately after* the time to which the apportionment falls to be made, e.g., on the day after the date fixed for completion, if the conditions provide that the purchaser is entitled to rent as from that date (instead of the date when the rent is receivable from the tenant). The subsection applies similarly to receipts other than rent, and to outgoings.

Section 86 (2) provides for similar adjustments in computing tax liability of vendor and purchaser in the case of apportionable rents, etc., receivable or outgoings payable in advance before the contract was entered into. The parties are treated as if the contract was entered into first and s. 86 (1) applies accordingly.

Section 86 (3) applies to apportionable rents, etc., receivable and outgoings payable by the purchaser *after* completion. It provides that in arriving at the tax liability of the purchaser the amount apportioned to the vendor is to be deducted from the receipt or outgoing and in arriving at that of the vendor it is to be treated as a revenue receipt or outgoing *receivable or payable by him immediately before the time to which the apportionment is made*, e.g., the date fixed for completion if the conditions provide for the vendor to be entitled to rent to that date.

The section applies to ground rents, rent-charges and to property let furnished where the rent is assessed under Case VI (see *post*, p. 1135). It does not apply to transfers otherwise than on sale, e.g., on death, bankruptcy or by way of gift ; accordingly where a personal representative, or a trustee in bankruptcy, contracts to sell, rent *received by the deceased or the bankrupt* cannot be treated for tax purposes as apportioned to the purchaser.

PART 7. DELAY IN COMPLETION

The preceding parts of this chapter deal, *inter alia*, with the position of the parties, their rights and liabilities, where there has been delay but the contract has been eventually completed. In this part the position is considered where there is delay and the contract has not yet been completed.

For the conditions, express or implied, as to the date on which completion of the contract ought to take place, see *ante*, p. 65 (compare the rules relating to conditional contracts, *ante*, pp. 65–66).

Time of the essence.—The first thing to consider is whether in regard to the particular contract time is of the essence of the contract. Usually, delay in the completion of the sale or purchase on the day fixed by the contract for the completion is not of the essence of the contract either at law or in equity (*Stickney* v. *Keeble* [1915] A.C. 386 and L.P.A. 1925, s. 41) ; but time may be of the essence of the contract where from the nature of the property or the surrounding circumstances the value of the property must necessarily increase or diminish according to the effluxion of time (*Stickney* v. *Keeble, ante*). For instance, time is of the essence in the case of a sale of a reversion which may become an estate in possession during the delay (*Newman* v. *Rogers* (1793), 4 Bro. C.C. 391) ; where the interest purchased is determinable with life (*Withy* v. *Cottle* (1823), Turn. & R. 78) ; where the property is of a wasting nature, as a leasehold property for a short unexpired term (*Hudson* v. *Temple* (1860), 30 L.J. Ch. 251), where the property consists of a public-house sold as a going concern (*Coslake* v. *Till* (1826), 1 Rus. 376, in which case the delay of a single day was held to relieve the vendor from the contract) ; (probably) where the property consists of a brickfield with modern machinery and arrangements for making wire-cut bricks (*Harold Wood Brick Co., Ltd.* v. *Ferris* [1935] 2 K.B. 198) ; on sale of working mines (*MacBryde* v. *Weekes* (1856), 22 Beav. 533), a public-house or licensed premises, or a shop or business as a going concern (*Cowles* v. *Gale* (1871), L.R. 7 Ch. 12 ; *Powell* v. *Marshall, Parkes & Co.* [1899] 1 Q.B. 710). In all these cases the date of completion fixed by the contract was deemed to be of the essence of the contract.

In *Lock* v. *Bell* [1931] 1 Ch. 35 there was a contract for the sale of an interest in licensed premises whereby it was provided that the completion should take place " on or about " a certain date. It was held by Maugham, J., that the words used had the same effect as " on or before " and that time was of the essence, and, as completion had not been effected on or about the date mentioned, the claim of the plaintiff that the deposit should be forfeited must be allowed. However, in *James Macara, Ltd.* v. *Barclay* [1945] K.B. 148, at p. 156, the Court of Appeal took the view that the words " on or before " did *not* have the effect of making the time for completion of the essence. It is a question of the construction of the particular contract.

Even where the date for completion was not originally of the essence (either by express provision or in accordance with the above-mentioned rules), if delay has been unreasonable, the other party can treat the contract as broken, without first giving notice as mentioned below (*Farrant* v. *Olver* [1922] W.N. 471).

Also the equitable remedy of specific performance may be sought, even where time was not of the essence and there has been no unreasonable delay, because this depends not on a breach of the contract but on the duty in equity of performing it. Thus in *Marks* v. *Lilley* [1959] 1 W.L.R. 749, a vendor who issued his writ for specific performance thirty-three days after the date fixed for completion without first making time of the essence was allowed his costs, the purchaser having completed shortly after issue of the writ. Vaisey, J., decided that the vendor was justified in issuing the writ as the purchaser was in default in equity. Again in *Hasham* v. *Zenab* [1960] A.C. 316, an order for specific performance was obtained *before* the completion date where the purchaser had repudiated the contract. Also in *Eva* v. *Morrow*, an unreported decision noted in the *New Law Journal*, vol. 116, p. 1657, a writ was issued for specific performance before a notice to complete had expired, but it was held that to succeed the plaintiff was only required to be ready and willing to complete at the date of issue ; the defendant's objection that an error in the certificate of value precluded the plaintiff from being so ready was rejected since the engrossment of the conveyance was in the form approved by the defendant's solicitors.

Notice to complete.—It is, however, always better, following delay, to make time of the essence of the contract by giving the other party notice fixing a reasonable date and stating that if the purchase or sale be not completed within that time the contract will be considered broken, except for the purpose of obtaining the relief or damages to which the party giving the notice may be entitled. If time was not initially of the essence, one party cannot, by serving notice to complete, make it of the essence, unless there has already been such delay on the part of the other as to render it fair that, if steps were not immediately taken to complete, the person giving notice should be relieved from his contract (*Green* v. *Sevin* (1879), 13 Ch. D. 589).

The position was well summarised by Danckwerts, J., in *Re Barr's Contract* [1956] Ch. 551, at p. 556 : " Apart from the provisions of any plain and clear conditions of sale, the law about making time of the essence of the contract for the purpose of completion . . . is subject to the following conditions : first of all, the vendor must be able, ready and willing to proceed to completion . . . Secondly, at the time when the vendor purports to make time of the essence, the purchaser must be guilty of such default as to entitle the vendor to rescind the contract subject to its being done by a reasonabls notice. Thirdly, once the right to serve a notice of the kind in question hae arisen, the time allowed by the notice must be a reasonable time." What is reasonable is, as always, a question of fact. In *Smith* v. *Hamilton* [1951] Ch. 174, Harman, J., said that fourteen days' notice was not enough. Then in *Re Engall's Agreement* [1953] 1 W.L.R. 977, at p. 979, Vaisey, J., doubted whether a twenty-one days' notice given by vendors twenty-one days after the completion date was long enough where the draft conveyance had not been submitted for approval. And in *Re Barr's Contract, ante,* it was held that a notice requiring the purchasers to complete within twenty-eight days served by the vendors the day after the completion date was not, on the facts, reasonable. Nevertheless, in *Ajit* v. *Sammy* [1967] A.C. 255, in the circumstances a mere six days' notice was sufficient. Clearly in serving a notice to complete regard must be had to all the circumstances of the case, amongst which Danckwerts, J., included (*Re Barr, ante,* at p. 558) " the practical considerations of the ability in the circumstances of the purchaser to find the money, having regard to reasonable behaviour as well as mere conveyancing matters, though it is quite true that conveyancing difficulties may be some of the circumstances." *Re Roger Malcolm Development, Ltd.'s Contract* (1960), 176 E.G. 1237, seems to provide authority for the proposition that the question whether the time allowed by a notice to complete is reasonable must be " judged by matters known to the vendor or knowledge of which ought to be imputed to him."

A party who has made time of the essence by serving notice to complete must himself be ready to complete on the day fixed. If he is not then ready, he will not be able to claim specific performance when he is ready and it is open to the other party to rescind (*Re Sandwell Park Colliery* [1929] 1 Ch. 277 ; *Finkielkraut* v. *Monahan* [1949] 2 All E.R. 234 ; *Re Prestbury Investment, Ltd.* (1961), 177 E.G. 75).

Before serving a notice to complete on behalf of a vendor care must be taken to ensure that the vendor has deduced a good title and carried out all his obligations ; the notice amounts to an assertion by the vendor that he has performed the duties required of him before completion (*Re Stone and Saville's Contract* [1963] 1 W.L.R. 163). In this case the vendor had not answered a requisition pointing out that a good title had not been made for the reason mentioned. Thereafter, it was not necessary for the purchaser to deliver a notice making time of the essence of the contract as regards the vendor's default in answering the requisition. It followed that there was then a breach by the vendor of his obligations such as to entitle the purchaser to rescind the contract. See also *Horton* v. *Kurzke* [1971] 1 W.L.R. 769 (where a vendor who had improperly served a notice to complete was ordered to pay the purchaser's costs of an action for specific performance) and *Pagebar Properties, Ltd.* v. *Derby Investments Holdings, Ltd.* [1973] 1 All E.R. 65 (*post,* p. 216).

Where it is the purchaser who is in default, after receiving such a notice, the vendor is entitled to treat the contract as repudiated by the purchaser, and to resell the property and claim as damages the difference between the contract price and the price realised by the resale (*Harold Wood Brick Co.* v. *Ferris* [1935] 2 K.B. 198). As to when the vendor can retain the deposit, see at p. 226.

Where it is the vendor who is in default, the purchaser may treat the contract as repudiated and recover the deposit, or any other sum paid on account of the purchase-money, with interest thereon, and he will, until paid, have an equitable lien on the property therefor (*Whitbread & Co., Ltd.* v. *Watt* [1902] 1 Ch. 835 ; unless held by a stakeholder : *Combe* v. *Swaythling* [1947] Ch. 625). Alternatively, he can take a conveyance when the vendor is ready and able to convey, and recover damages for the vendor's breach of contract in delaying completion (*Phillips* v. *Lamdin* [1949] 2 K.B. 33). In that case it was decided that such damages may be recovered even after completion has taken place, but a learned writer in the *Solicitors' Journal*, vol. 94, p. 90, has given reasons for submitting that this decision is not supported by earlier authority, and should be treated with caution.

Conditions of sale.—In practice most contracts will incorporate general conditions of sale which attempt, at least, to provide for the problems caused by delay in completion. In particular, after earlier unsatisfactory attempts, the National Conditions of Sale, in its 17th ed., succeeded in substantially solving the problems with General Condition 22 which has naturally been reproduced with the same number and very slight amendments in the current 18th ed. Further, this condition has now been followed in substance in the 1970 ed. (revised in 1973) of The Law Society's Conditions of Sale, General Condition 19.

The successful National Condition 22 provides in effect as follows : At any time on or after the completion date *either party*, being ready and willing to fulfil his own outstanding obligations under the contract, may give to the other party notice in writing requiring completion of the contract in conformity with this condition. Condition 22 (2) provides that on service of such notice it shall become a term of the contract, *in respect of which time shall be of the essence*, that the party to whom the notice is given shall complete within twenty-eight days after service of the notice (exclusive of the day of service). The condition does not confer on the vendor an express right to resell but Condition 22 (3) provides that if the purchaser refuses or fails to complete in conformity with the condition, and the vendor thereafter re-sells the property within six months of the expiration of the twenty-eight days, then the vendor shall be entitled (upon crediting the deposit) to recover from the purchaser the amount of any loss occasioned by expenses of or incidental to such resale or by diminution of the price.

The courts have now made it clear that there is no room left for doubt as to the operation and efficacy of this condition. Thus Ungoed-Thomas, J., has held that " time automatically becomes of the essence of the contract " under the condition, so making it unnecessary for him to go into all the circumstances of the case to see whether the period of notice was reasonable (*Cumberland Court (Brighton), Ltd.* v. *Taylor* [1964] Ch. 29 ; see also the decision of Buckley, J., to the same effect in *Innisfail Laundry, Ltd.* v. *Dawe* (1963), 107 Sol. J. 437). Again, the vacation of a purchaser's registration of an estate contract has been summarily ordered following the expiry of a notice to complete under The Law Society's Condition 19 on the basis that no triable or arguable point remained as to the validity of the contract (*Hooker* v. *Wyle* [1973] 3 All E.R. 707). See also *Babacomp, Ltd.* v. *Rightside, Ltd.* [1973] 3 All E.R. 873 as to the efficacy of an informal notice.

It has, however, now been held that a vendor in breach of his contractual obligations, e.g., because of a misdescription or failure to deliver an abstract of title, could not be regarded as " ready and willing " to complete within National Condition 22 (*Pagebar Properties, Ltd.* v. *Derby Investment Holdings, Ltd.* [1973] 1 All E.R. 65). This is obviously sensible, but Goulding, J., went on (*loc. cit.*) to blur slightly the certainty of the condition by adding " But even if the notice was valid, if a purchaser without any fault on his part, only discovered the existence of [a breach] in the last day for completion, and at the moment of completion, he must have a reasonable opportunity to consider the matter." In the case, this merely meant taking instructions over a weekend, but in practice one cannot always predict what will amount to a reasonable opportunity.

Further, there is also a matter of distinction to be noticed. The Law Society's Conditions (1973 Revision, Condition 19 (6)) concludes by providing, in effect, that a party who has served a notice to complete will not be prejudiced by allowing the other party an extension of " one or more specifically stated periods of time " : time will remain of the essence of the new period. The National Conditions contain no similar provision, so that in this small respect at least The Law Society Conditions are the better for making explicit beyond argument the application of the decision in *Lock* v. *Bell* [1931] 1 Ch. 35. However, it must be appreciated that generally the mere fact that a valid notice to complete has been given and not been complied with does not mean that time will be of the essence of any appointment for completion which might result from further negotiation (*Luck* v. *White* (1973), 117 Sol. J. 486).

REMEDIES FOR BREACH OF CONTRACT

PART 1. GENERAL RULES

THE remedies for breach of a contract to sell land are concisely stated at p. 1003 of vol. II of Williams on Vendor and Purchaser, 4th ed., as follows : " Where the stipulation broken goes to the whole root of the consideration— as on breach of one of the main duties of the contract—the injured party's remedies are either to rescind the contract and sue for restitution to his former position, or to affirm the contract and sue either for damages for the breach or for the specific performance of the agreement. Besides these remedies by action, it is open to him to adopt the special mode of procedure by vendor and purchaser summons." [It might be added, to make the statement complete, " Provided that where by the act of the party aggrieved by the breach it has become impossible completely to restore the parties to their former position, that party shall have no right to rescind the contract, but shall only be entitled to affirm it and pursue his remedies thereunder " (Williams, Contract of Sale of Land, p. 119).] " Where a breach has been committed of a stipulation which is not essential, the appropriate remedy is usually an action for damages for the particular breach, but that will not preclude any further proceedings which may be necessary to enforce the main duty of the contract either at law or in equity." A breach of one of the main duties of the contract also has the effect of discharging the other party from his obligation to perform his part of the contract (*General Bill-Posting Co., Ltd.* v. *Atkinson* [1908] 1 Ch. 537).

" A breach of contract may be committed, not only by the failure to perform some obligation under the contract at the time when it ought to be fulfilled, but also by the renunciation of performance of the contract ; and this may occur in two ways. If either party absolutely refuses, or if by his own act he makes it impossible for him to carry out his part of the agreement, the other is entitled at his election either to treat such renunciation of performance as a breach of contract, and at once to rescind or sue upon the contract accordingly, or else to treat the agreement as still subsisting, wait till the time is gone by for the renouncing party to perform the acts promised and then sue him for the breach occasioned by such non-performance "

(Williams on Vendor and Purchaser, 4th ed., vol. II, p. 994). This passage was quoted by Wynn Parry, J., in *Thorpe* v. *Fasey* [1949] Ch. 649, who decided that there is no distinction between the nature of the repudiation which is required to constitute an anticipatory breach and that which is required where the alleged breach occurs after the time for performance has arisen. See also *White and Carter (Councils), Ltd.* v. *McGregor* [1962] A.C. 413, where a majority of the House of Lords held that one party need not only passively disregard the other's renunciation, but could actively complete his own part of the contract even though this would increase rather than mitigate the loss and the damages recoverable ; this decision has been criticised (e.g., Dr. A. L. Goodhart in the *Law Quarterly Review*, vol. 78, p. 263) and its application to contracts for the sale of land is far from clear.

There may be a difference in the position of a purchaser when he is resisting the equitable remedy of specific performance and when he is seeking to enforce one of the remedies given by the common law for breach of the contract. The reason is that there may be defences to an action for specific performance, for instance, mistake causing hardship of the kind discussed *ante*, p. 84, which could not be set up in common-law proceedings. See further, Williams on Vendor and Purchaser, 4th ed., vol. II, p. 994 ; *Best* v. *Hamand* (1879), 12 Ch. D. 1 ; *Nottingham Patent Brick & Tile Co.* v. *Butler* (1886), 16 Q.B.D. 778 ; *Re Davis and Cavey* (1888), 40 Ch. D. 601 (followed in *Charles Hunt, Ltd.* v. *Palmer* [1931] 2 Ch. 287) ; *Re National Provincial Bank of England and Marsh* [1895] 1 Ch. 190 ; *Re Scott and Alvarez's Contract* [1895] 1 Ch. 596 ; 2 Ch. 603 ; and *Beyfus* v. *Lodge* [1925] Ch. 350.

In the same action the plaintiff may claim the equitable remedy (specific performance), and the defendant the common-law remedy (rescission of contract and return of deposit), with the result that the claim of the plaintiff has to be decided by the rules of equity and the claim of the defendant by the rules of law. Similarly, on the breach of a contract, the party affirming it can, in the same action, claim the common-law remedy of damages, and, in the alternative, the equitable remedy, namely, specific performance (*Cornwall* v. *Henson* [1900] 2 Ch. 298), and can choose at the hearing which of the remedies he will ask for. For instance, in *Farrant* v. *Olver* [1922] W.N. 471, a purchaser refused or neglected to complete for a considerable time after the date fixed, and the vendor commenced an action for specific performance, and, in the alternative, for rescission and forfeiture of the deposit, and obtained the order he finally elected to ask for, namely, that the contract be rescinded and the deposit forfeited. See also *Glover* v. *Broome* [1926] W.N. 46.

PART 2. RESCISSION OF CONTRACT

Rescission for misrepresentation, misdescription and non-disclosure, see *ante*, p. 87.

It is pointed out in the *Conveyancer N.S.*, vol. 19, p. 116 *et seq.*, that " rescission " has three fundamentally different meanings, namely (i) " the setting aside of the contract in equity (in or out of court) for misrepresentation, duress or undue influence " ; (ii) " the discharge at common law of the innocent party by the other's breach " ; (iii) " rescission by agreement."

Where either party to a contract commits a breach affecting one of the main duties thereof, this discharges the other from his obligations thereunder, and he may at his election either (1) rescind, or (2) affirm the contract and sue upon it for damages for the breach or for specific performance of the contract. If he elects to rescind he will be entitled to take proceedings in equity to assert such right and to secure complete restitution. He will also be entitled, independently of the contract, to sue at law to recover any money paid or property transferred by him thereunder. Thus, a purchaser rescinding the contract for the vendor's failure to show a good title may recover his deposit or any other sum paid on account of the purchase-money with interest, and a vendor who has delivered over possession before completion and rescinds for the purchaser's failure to pay the price, may recover possession of the land sold (Williams on Vendor and Purchaser, 4th ed., vol. II, pp. 1004, 1005, 1009, and cases there referred to). Further, either party lawfully rescinding the contract for the other's breach will be entitled to recover the expenses he has incurred in discharge of any obligation imposed on him by the contract, such as the investigation of title, and he will have an equitable lien on the land for the moneys to which he is entitled, similar to and enforceable in the same manner as the vendor's lien for unpaid purchase-money (ibid., pp. 1005, 1006).

It is important to bear in mind the difference between cases of rescission of the contract, and cases where the contract has been broken but remains in being ; the party who rescinds a contract cannot get damages for the breach of it, as there is no contract in existence for breach of which damages can be given (Williams on Vendor and Purchaser, 4th ed., vol. II, p. 1013). In *Harold Wood Brick Co.* v. *Ferris* [1935] 1 K.B. 613, Swift, J., treated the matter as one of rescission and yet allowed damages. This was a slip. In the Court of Appeal ([1935] 2 K.B. 198), however, the contract was treated as not rescinded but as broken by the purchaser, and damages were allowed. Therefore, although the same result was arrived at, it was by different reasoning. In *Barber* v. *Wolfe* [1945] Ch. 187, the vendor obtained a decree for specific performance and, later, an order rescinding the contract in lieu of specific performance. The purchaser had been in possession, and, on the motion for rescission, the vendor claimed a sum as damages for breach of contract or, alternatively, that the purchaser was bound to pay an occupation rent. It was held that the effect of rescission was to rescind the contract *ab initio* so that no such claims could be made. Again in *Lowe* v. *Hope* [1970] Ch. 94, where part only of the agreed deposit had been paid, the vendor was held unable, following rescission of the contract, to recover the balance. It may, however, still be arguable that damages can be obtained even after a party has given notice to rescind *under a term in the contract ;* see the *Law Journal*, vol. 98, p. 200.

Where, under the terms of the contract, part of the land has been conveyed to the purchaser but the purchaser later makes default in taking a conveyance of the balance, the vendor cannot rescind ; if a contract is rescinded at all, it must be rescinded *in toto* (*Thorpe* v. *Fasey* [1949] Ch. 649). It is argued in an article in the *Solicitors' Journal*, vol. 96, p. 775, that following gross delay by a purchaser, the purchaser loses his right to specific performance and, simultaneously, the vendor acquires the right to sue for damages *or* rescind and forfeit the deposit. The suggestion is made that, following gross delay, the vendor should not rescind, but should inform the purchaser that his delay has amounted to repudiation ; by doing this the vendor retains his right to damages in addition to the deposit.

Purchaser's right of rescission.—The breach of contract by the vendor in failing to show a good title releases the purchaser from any obligation to perform his part of the agreement and gives him the right to rescind.

If he takes advantage of this right at once, without making requisitions on title or acting otherwise under the contract in such a way as to affirm it, then the contract ceases to have effect and so the vendor cannot take advantage of any term in the contract under which he may rescind (*Bowman* v. *Hyland* (1878), 8 Ch. D. 588). The purchaser may then recover the deposit with interest on it and his expenses of investigating title (*Re Bryant and Barningham's Contract* (1890), 44 Ch. D. 218). The issue of a summons claiming a declaration that the vendor has failed to discharge his obligations and the return of the deposit does not amount to affirmation of the contract and so does not prevent the purchaser from alleging that the contract is at an end (*Re Stone and Saville's Contract* [1963] 1 W.L.R. 163 ; distinguishing *Re Atkinson and Horsell's Contract* [1912] 2 Ch. 1).

It is sufficient for the purchaser to show that the vendor has no title whatever (*Bowman* v. *Hyland, ante ; Re Terry and White's Contract* (1886), 32 Ch. D. 14) ; or that the vendor knew that he could not convey what he contracted to convey, and so, in concealing this, was guilty of fraud (*Re National Provincial Bank of England and Marsh* [1895] 1 Ch. 190). But a purchaser cannot rescind if the vendor can compel an assurance by one who has a good title, for instance, by a limited company in which he holds the majority of shares (*Elliott* v. *Pierson* [1948] Ch. 452).

If the vendor neglects to disclose incumbrances or defects in title of which he is aware, or of which he ought to be aware, the purchaser can rescind (*Re Cox and Neve's Contract* [1891] 2 Ch. 109, 118 ; *Re Ebsworth and Tidy's Contract* (1889), 42 Ch. D. 23 ; *Re Nisbett and Pott's Contract* [1906] 1 Ch. 386) ; though not if they are no longer enforceable (*Hepworth* v. *Pickles* [1900] 1 Ch. 108). As to the general position, if the matters in question are registered under the L.C.A. 1972, see *ante*, pp. 4–5, dealing with the effect of s. 24 of the L.P.A. 1969.

Vendor's right of rescission under contract.—Contracts for the sale of land tend in practice to contain a condition, in effect, allowing the vendor to rescind if the purchaser should insist on any requisition which the vendor is unable or unwilling to comply with, although the exact wording varies (see, e.g., General Condition 18 of The Law Society's Conditions of Sale, 1973 Revision, and Condition 9 of the National Conditions of Sale, 18th ed.). If the contract contains the words " should the purchaser *make* any requisition," etc., the right of the vendor to rescind arises directly the requisition is made, without giving the purchaser any *locus pœnitentiœ* (*Re Starr-Bowkett Building Society and Sibun's Contract* (1889), 42 Ch. D. 375). But if the words are " should the purchaser *insist* " (*Duddell* v. *Simpson* (1866), L.R. 2 Ch. 102), or " *persist*," a vendor cannot refuse to answer reasonable requisitions (*Re Dames and Wood* (1885), 29 Ch. D. 626 ; *Mawson* v. *Fletcher* (1870), L.R. 6 Ch. 91 ; *Procter* v. *Pugh* [1921] 2 Ch. 256) ; in such cases the vendor cannot rescind if the purchaser at once withdraws his objection.

A vendor must not use his right of rescission under a contract unreasonably (*Quinion* v. *Horne* [1906] 1 Ch. 596) ; that is to say, " he must exercise the power *bona fide* for the purpose for which it was made part of the contract " (*Bowman* v. *Hyland* (1878), 8 Ch. D. 588). A vendor cannot rescind if he has no title to any part of the property sold and thus escape his liability to recoup to the purchaser his expenses of investigating the title (*Re Deighton and Harris' Contract* [1898] 1 Ch. 458) ; it is otherwise if a good title can be made to part of the property sold (*Re Jackson and Haden's Contract* [1906] 1 Ch. 412). *Re Jackson and Haden* is an instructive case. The vendor had impliedly represented that he was the owner of the mines by not excepting them from his description of the property sold. He acted in good faith, thinking that everybody knew that the mines under the land did not belong to the surface owner. There was no fraud, but he had knowledge of the limitations of his title. It was held that he was not entitled to the benefit of the condition for rescission.

The applicable principles, as recently outlined by the Privy Council, are that " a vendor in seeking to rescind, must not act arbitrarily, or capriciously, or unreasonably. Much less can he act in bad faith. He may not use the power of rescission to get out of a sale *brevi manu*, since by so doing he makes a nullity of the whole elaborate and protracted transaction. Above all, perhaps, he must not be guilty of ' recklessness ' in entering into his contract, a term frequently resorted to in discussion of the legal principle and which their lordships understand to connote an unacceptable indifference to the situation of a purchaser who is allowed to enter into a contract with the expectation of obtaining a title which the vendor has no reasonable anti-cipation of being able to deliver. A vendor who has so acted is not allowed to call off the whole transaction by resorting to the contractual right of rescission " (*Selkirk* v. *Romar Investments, Ltd.* [1963] 1 W.L.R. 1415, at pp. 1422-3 ; on the facts of the case the vendor was allowed to rescind instead of complying with the purchaser's requisition calling for unobtainable evidence to establish that a predecessor had died intestate before 1914 and who his heir at law was). An example of a reckless vendor occurred in *Baines* v. *Tweddle* [1959] Ch. 679, where it was held that on the refusal by the vendor's mortgagees (whose mortgage extended also to other land) to join in the conveyance to the purchaser the vendor could not rescind the contract pursuant to a condition of sale ; this was because the vendor had not sought the concurrence of the mortgagees before contracting to sell free from the mortgage and so had acted recklessly. As to the amount of recklessness necessary to disqualify a vendor from rescinding, see further *Merrett* v. *Schuster* [1920] 2 Ch. 240, where the vendor *bona fide* believed that he could carry out his contract, and it was held that he could not be said to have acted recklessly. Another example where a vendor is not held to have acted recklessly is where he has acted on mistaken advice (*Re Milner and Organ's Contract* (1920), 89 L.J. Ch. 315 ; see also *Baines* v. *Tweddle, ante,* but compare *Selkirk* v. *Romar Investments, Ltd., ante,* where the vendor was a limited company and only the actions of its solicitor were considered).

In *Re Des Reaux and Setchfield's Contract* [1926] Ch. 178, the vendor, when he entered into the contract, knew that he was not in a position to make a good title, but thought he might be able to do so before completion. The purchaser suggested that the vendor should make an application to the court for an order which would have given him the power, but the vendor refused on the ground of expense, and gave the purchaser notice to rescind under a power in the contract. It was held that the vendor had acted recklessly in entering into the contract before he had the power to make a title, that his refusal to make an application was unreasonable, and that the notice to rescind was void. The above cases have largely concerned the vendor's pre-contract knowledge and actions. Note, however, that the Privy Council has observed that " no doubt recklessness in entering into the contract may not be the only thing to be regarded when a vendor's right to exercise a contractual power of rescission is brought into question. It is the *use* of that right that is not to be arbitrary or without reason, and courts have expressed themselves from time to time as being unwilling to allow a vendor to call the whole contract off in the face of some requisition to which he takes what is merely a capricious or fanciful objection " (*Selkirk* v. *Romar Investments, Ltd., ante*, at p. 1424).

If the condition giving the right to rescind refers to a requisition as to *title* only, the vendor cannot rescind if the requisition be only a matter of *conveyance*, for instance, the discharge of a mortgage (*Re Jackson and Oakshott's Contract* (1880), 14 Ch. D. 851) ; or the appointment of trustees for the purposes of the Settled Land Acts (*Hatten* v. *Russell* (1888), 38 Ch. D. 334 ; L.P.A. 1925, s. 42 (2)).

Under a contract containing a condition that misdescription shall not annul the sale, but shall be the subject of compensation, and also containing a condition for rescission, the purchaser cannot insist upon compensation if the vendor chooses to exercise his right to rescind the contract (*Ashburner* v. *Sewell* [1891] 3 Ch. 405 ; *Re Terry and White's Contract* (1886), 32 Ch. D. 14).

If a vendor brings an action for specific performance, so long as that plea is on the record, he cannot claim to rescind under a power contained in the contract (*Public Trustee* v. *Pearlberg* [1940] 2 K.B. 1).

The relevant provision in The Law Society's Conditions of Sale, 1973 Revision, is General Condition 18, which refers to a requisition which the vendor is " unable or, *on the ground of unreasonable expense or other reasonable ground*, unwilling to remove or comply with." See also National Conditions of Sale 18th ed., Condition 9.

Rescission after completion.—To succeed in a claim *under the contract* for rescission *after* conveyance of the property, it appears that in general fraud or unfair dealing has had to be proved, and there must be no undue delay (*Kennedy* v. *Panama, etc., Mail Co.* (1867), L.R. 2 Q.B. 580 ; *Brownlie* v. *Campbell* (1880), 5 App. Cas. 925 (H.L. Sc.) ; *Seddon* v. *North Eastern Salt Co., Ltd.* [1905] 1 Ch. 326 ; cf. *Solle* v. *Butcher* [1950] 1 K.B. 671). However, rescission even for innocent misrepresentation is now possible despite completion by virtue of the Misrepresentation Act, 1967, s. 1 ; see *ante*, p. 91 *et seq.* Mistake, short of a total failure of consideration, would not be sufficient. See *Soper* v. *Arnold* (1888), 37 Ch. D. 102 ; 14 App. Cas. 429 ; *Re Tyrell* (1900), 82 L.T. 675 ; *Debenham* v. *Sawbridge* [1901] 2 Ch. 98 ; *May* v. *Platt* [1900] 1 Ch. 616, 623 ; *Rutherford* v. *Acton-Adams* [1915] A.C. 866. But where the defect can be classed as a defect in the title, compensation may be recovered under the covenants for title implied in the conveyance (*May* v. *Platt, ante ; Eastwood* v. *Ashton* [1913] 2 Ch. 39 ; [1914] 1 Ch. 68 ; [1915] A.C. 900).

PART 3. DAMAGES

Wherever there is a breach of contract for the sale or purchase of land, a right of action *at law* for damages arises against the party who commits the breach (*Laird* v. *Pim* (1841), 7 M. & W. 474 ; *York Glass Co., Ltd.* v. *Jubb* (1924), 131 L.T. 559, affirmed on appeal 42 T.L.R. 1). As to the amount of damages recoverable, the general common-law rule is that where a party sustains a loss by reason of a breach of contract, he is entitled, so far as money can do it, to be placed in the same situation as if the contract had been performed (*Robinson* v. *Harman* (1848), 1 Ex. 850). In pursuance of this rule, Megarry, J., has more recently held that the damages should be assessed as at the date of the hearing, rather than as at the earlier date of the breach (*Wroth* v. *Tyler* [1973] 2 W.L.R. 405, assuming specific performance to be an available alternative ; see also *Grant* v. *Dawkins* [1973] 3 All E.R.

897). Whilst this may be necessary to put the purchaser into the appropriate money situation, it may produce hardship for a vendor in times of rapid inflation of property prices (see further J. E. Adams in the *Law Society's Gazette*, vol. 70, No. 22, pp. 1919–1920).

It was decided in *Hadley* v. *Baxendale* (1854), 9 Ex. 341, that the damages " should be such as may fairly and reasonably be considered either arising naturally, i.e., according to the usual course of things, from such breach of the contract itself, or such as may reasonably be supposed to have been in the contemplation of both parties at the time they made the contract, as the probable result of the breach of it." If special circumstances under which the contract was actually made were communicated by the plaintiff to the defendant, and so known to both parties, the damages which he would reasonably contemplate would be the amount of the injury which would ordinarily follow from a breach of contract under these special circumstances. But if the special circumstances were unknown to the party breaking the contract he would only be supposed to have had in his contemplation the amount of the injury which would arise generally, that is in cases not affected by special circumstances, from such a breach of contract. In applying this rule a knowledge that a purchaser intends to use property in a particular manner is not normally imputed to a vendor (*Diamond* v. *Campbell-Jones* [1961] Ch. 22). In *Steyning* v. *Littlehampton Building Society* [1966] 1 W.L.R. 753, it was held that a vendor who in fact knows that the purchaser intends to develop for profit must pay damages assessed by reference to the profits both parties contemplated that the purchaser would make. The purchaser's right to damages may be limited by what is commonly known as the rule in *Bain* v. *Fothergill* (1874), L.R. 7 H.L. 158, and so the rights of vendor and purchaser respectively are considered separately.

Damages awarded to vendor.—The vendor can claim the full loss which he has sustained by the purchaser's breach (*Laird* v. *Pim* (1841), 7 M. & W. 474, 478 ; *York Glass Co., Ltd.* v. *Jubb* (1924), 131 L.T. 559, affirmed on appeal, 42 T.L.R. 1), and such damages will consist of the difference between the price which the purchaser would have paid if he had completed the contract and the price which the vendor afterwards obtains, plus the expenses of the resale (*Noble* v. *Edwardes* (1877), 5 Ch. D. 378, 393 ; *Keck* v. *Faber* (1915), 60 Sol. J. 253), but less the deposit (if any). The vendor must give credit for the deposit, notwithstanding that the contract contained a stipulation that, if the purchaser failed to comply with the condition, the deposit should be forfeited (*Howe* v. *Smith* (1884), 27 Ch. D. 89 ; *Shuttleworth* v. *Clews* [1910] 1 Ch. 176). But the fact that, by reason of the loss of the contract which the purchaser failed to perform, the vendor obtains the benefit of another contract which is of value to him, does not entitle the purchaser to the benefit of the latter contract (*Jamal* v. *Moolla Dawood, Sons & Co.* [1916] 1 A.C. 175) ; for the loss to be ascertained is the loss at the date of the breach (*ibid.*).

To obtain damages the vendor must prove that he was able and willing to give a good title, and had offered to convey the land (*Noble* v. *Edwardes, ante*).

Damages awarded to purchaser.—It was decided in *Flureau* v. *Thornhill* (1776), 2 W. Bl. 1078, that, owing to the difficulties and uncertainty of the English law of real property, the parties must be taken to have contracted on the understanding that if the purchase should go off by reason of the inability of the vendor (without his own fault) to make a good title, the purchaser should not be entitled to damages for the loss of his bargain but only to the return of his deposit with interest and expenses incurred in investigating the title. This would appear to be so even although the vendor knew that he could not make a good title (*Bain* v. *Fothergill* (1874), L.R. 7 H.L. 158). However, any false representations as to title might give rise to an action for damages in tort, i.e., for deceit, or under the Misrepresentation Act, 1967.

In *Keen* v. *Mear* [1920] 2 Ch. 574, two partners were entitled to property, and one thought he had the authority of the other to sell it, but the other partner refused to sign the conveyance and consequently the sale went off. The partner who sold did his best to persuade his co-partner to confirm the sale, but without success. In a claim for damages by the purchaser it was held that the selling partner had acted in good faith, and that in those circumstances the case fell within the rule in *Bain* v. *Fothergill*, and that the purchaser was not entitled to damages for loss of bargain. Similarly, a person who agrees to grant a lease but finds himself unable to do so, because there are restrictive covenants binding on him, is not able to give the title he contracted for, and so is liable only to return the deposit with interest and to pay the expenses of investigating title (*J. W. Cafes, Ltd.* v. *Brownlow Trust, Ltd.* [1950] 1 All E.R. 894).

However, Megarry, J., has held that the statutory charge in favour of a spouse arising under the Matrimonial Homes Act, 1967 (see *post*, p. 370), being imposed generally and in no way dependent on the vicissitudes of a particular title to property, did not fall within the spirit and intendment of the rule in *Bain* v. *Fothergill* (*Wroth* v. *Tyler* [1973] 2 W.L.R. 405). Accordingly, a husband, unable to perform his contract to sell a house with vacant possession because his wife, having statutory rights of occupation, would not concur, was held unable to rely on the rule to limit the measure of damages (*ibid.*).

But *if the vendor can make a good title and will not* do what he can and ought to do to obtain one, he can be made to pay damages for loss of bargain, in addition to the repayment of the deposit, with interest (*Engell* v. *Fitch* (1869), L.R. 4 Q.B. 659 ; *Jones* v. *Gardiner* [1902] 1 Ch. 191). Other cases where general damages were allowed on this ground are *Day* v. *Singleton* [1899] 2 Ch. 320, where the vendor deliberately omitted to get the licence of the lessor to the sale of leasehold property ; *Re Daniel* [1917] 2 Ch. 405, where the vendor did not get the mortgagee of the property to join in the conveyance on payment off of his mortgage ; *Thomas* v. *Kensington* [1942] 2 K.B. 181, where the facts were similar ; *Goffin* v. *Houlder* (1920), 90 L.J. Ch. 488, where the vendor so acted as to put it out of her power to complete ; and *Braybrooks* v. *Whaley* [1919] 1 K.B. 435, where the vendor was a mortgagee with a power of sale, but was not in possession, and to make a good title it was necessary that he should make an application to the court under the Courts (Emergency Powers) Act, 1914, for leave to realise his security. The vendor sold the property without first making the necessary application and refused to complete. It was held that damages for loss of the bargain were payable.

Damages are *not* assessed as at the date of the contract where the market value of the land has subsequently altered. Thus if that value has risen by the date of the breach, damages will be assessed as at that date (see *Diamond* v. *Campbell-Jones* [1961] Ch. 22 ; see also *Engell* v. *Fitch* (1869), L.R. 4 Q.B. 659). But if that value has further risen since the date of the breach, then the damages will be assessed as at the date of the hearing (*Wroth* v. *Tyler* [1973] 2 W.L.R. 405, assuming specific performace to be still an available alternative claim).

8

Such damages for loss of the bargain are normally confined to the difference (if any) between the purchase price and the value of the property. If the purchaser does obtain such damages he cannot claim, in addition, his conveyancing costs in the transaction so far incurred (*Re Daniel* [1917] 2 Ch. 405). From this, logically it would follow that the vendor could claim to deduct from the damages any costs and stamp duty that the purchaser would have paid had the transaction been completed, and the Court of Appeal has conceded that this might be an appropriate deduction in some cases, although disallowing it on the facts (*Ridley* v. *De Geerts* [1945] 2 All E.R. 654). In *Beard* v. *Porter* [1948] 1 K.B. 321, the vendor failed to give the vacant possession he had promised by the contract. The damages awarded to the purchaser were made up of the difference in value between the purchase price and the value of the house subject to the tenancy, solicitors' charges and stamp duty incurred in buying another house, and a sum paid for lodgings before the second house was bought. See also *Lloyd* v. *Stanbury* [1971] 1 W.L.R. 535, where Brightman, J., said that the damages which a disappointed purchaser was entitled to recover included expenditure incurred prior to the contract representing (i) legal costs of approving and executing the contract and (ii) the costs of performing an act required to be done under the contract notwithstanding that the act was performed in anticipation of the execution of the contract. The learned judge added that, on general principles, the purchaser would be entitled to damages for any loss which ought to be regarded as within the contemplation of the parties, but subject to an important limitation : a purchaser allowed into possession before completion who elected to repudiate the contract could *not* recover money spent on improvements to the property. This case has since been approved by the Court of Appeal in *Anglia Television, Ltd.* v. *Reed* [1972] 1 Q.B. 60 (which did not itself relate to a sale of land).

Where a vendor delays completion unreasonably, otherwise than as a result of a defective title or other conveyancing difficulty, a purchaser who can prove that he has suffered loss in consequence may be able to recover damages for the delay, notwithstanding that there is a term in the contract as to payment of interest on delay (*Jones* v. *Gardiner* [1902] 1 Ch. 191 ; *Phillips* v. *Lamdin* [1949] 2 K.B. 33 ; but compare *Smith* v. *Hamilton* [1951] Ch. 174).

If the purchaser cannot prove any actual loss as a result of the breach he is nevertheless entitled, by way of damages, to his costs incurred in the abortive transaction, and to recover his deposit with interest on it for the time during which he lost the use of it (*Wallington* v. *Townsend* [1939] Ch. 588).

PART 4. FORFEITURE OF DEPOSIT

Payment of deposit, see *ante*, p. 61.

A distinction must be made between the case where a sum of money has been paid by way of deposit and the case where the money has been paid not as a deposit, but as purchase-money. The principal object of a vendor requiring the payment of a deposit is to prevent the purchaser from unreasonably running off his contract (*Howe* v. *Smith* (1884), 27 Ch. D. 89 ; *Holford* v. *Trim* [1921] W.N. 243), although, if the transaction goes through, it is also part payment of the purchase-money. If the purchaser neglects or unreasonably refuses to carry out his part of the contract the vendor has a right to an order to rescind and for forfeiture of the deposit although the contract contains no express stipulation as to what is to become of it in the event of the purchaser making default ; and the fact that the deposit was placed in the hands of a third party as stakeholder makes no difference (*Hall* v. *Burnell* [1911] 2 Ch. 551 ; *Monnickendam* v. *Leanse* (1923), 39 T.L.R. 445 ; *Barber* v. *Wolfe* [1945] 1 All E.R. 399).

In *Mayson* v. *Clouet* [1924] A.C. 980, the contract provided that the purchase-money should be paid by a deposit and the balance by instalments, and in default *the deposit* was to be forfeited. On default in payment of the last instalment, the vendor rescinded the contract. It was held that the rights of the parties depended on the contract, and that although the purchaser could not recover the deposit he could recover the instalments paid by him.

If part only of the agreed deposit has been paid the vendor, in rescission of the contract, cannot recover the balance (*Lowe* v. *Hope* [1970] Ch. 94).

Where there is no binding contract but the proposed purchaser has paid a deposit, and afterwards changes his mind and determines not to proceed with the purchase, he can recover such deposit (*Chillingworth* v. *Esche* [1924] 1 Ch. 97). The reason is that the parties have not bound themselves to carry out *any* bargain : it was a part payment of the purchase-money and paid only in anticipation of a final bargain. On the other hand, in *Monnickendam* v. *Leanse*, *ante*, where on a contract for the sale of a house a memorandum was drawn up which did not satisfy s. 4 of the Statute of Frauds (now L.P.A. 1925, s. 40, *ante*, p. 40), and a sum of money was paid as a deposit by the purchaser, on such purchaser repudiating the agreement it was held that he was not entitled to recover the deposit. See also *Low* v. *Fry* (1935), 51 T.L.R. 322, mentioned at p. 43. It is sometimes thought that *Monnickendam* v. *Leanse* conflicts with *Chillingworth* v. *Esche*. This is not the case. In *Chillingworth* v. *Esche* there was no contract and so the deposit was recovered. In *Monnickendam* v. *Leanse* the purchaser could not recover because there was a valid contract, although it could not be enforced by action because there was no sufficient memorandum to satisfy the requirements of s. 4.

Conditions of sale often provide that, if the purchaser neglects or fails to complete on the day fixed, the deposit shall be forfeited and the vendor may resell. Except where time was of the essence of the contract, the vendor may not exercise these rights unless the purchaser has failed to complete on the day fixed *or within a reasonable time thereafter* (*Smith* v. *Hamilton* [1951] Ch. 174). See further, the discussion of the rules as to notices to complete, *ante*, p. 214, and, particularly, the statement of the effect of The Law Society's and the National Conditions of Sale.

Settled land.—If on a sale under the S.L.A. 1925 the deposit is forfeited, or the purchaser allows the vendor to keep the deposit in consideration of his being released from completing the contract, the tenant for life cannot keep the money, as it is capital, unless the court otherwise orders (S.L.A. 1925, s. 90 (5) ; *Re Foster's Settled Estates* [1922] 1 Ch. 348 ; *Re Ward's Settled Estate* [1919] W.N. 51).

Power to order repayment of deposit.—It is provided by s. 49 (2) of the L.P.A. 1925 that :—

" 49.—(2) Where the court refuses to grant specific performance of a contract, or in any action for the return of a deposit, the court may, if it thinks fit, order the repayment of any deposit."

In *Charles Hunt, Ltd.* v. *Palmer* [1931] 2 Ch. 287 the vendor claimed specific performance of a contract for sale, and the purchaser counter-claimed for relief under the subsection. Clauson, J., dismissed the claim, but, in exercise of his discretionary power conferred by the subsection, declared the purchaser entitled to give a valid receipt for the deposit to the auctioneer, who held it. The subsection is in very wide terms, but in a footnote to p. 31 of vol. I, Williams on Vendor and Purchaser, 4th ed., it " is submitted, however, that the court has no jurisdiction under this enactment to order the return of the deposit where the vendor has a rightful claim (apart from the enactment) to retain the amount, or part of the amount, of the deposit not as *forfeited*, but either in reduction or on account of damages or (when such is adjudged to be the parties' true contract) as liquidated damages," and the learned writer refers to several cases in support of his submission.

A further limitation on the court's jurisdiction was indicated by Vaisey, J., in *James Macara, Ltd.* v. *Barclay* [1944] 2 All E.R. 31, at p. 32 (affirmed on other grounds at [1945] K.B. 148), namely that " while the court may order the return of the whole of the deposit, it is not, at any rate in terms, authorised to order the return of less than the whole."

PART 5. SPECIFIC PERFORMANCE

In Fry on Specific Performance, 6th ed., p. 19, the learned author said : " There is an observation often made with regard to the jurisdiction in specific performance which remains to be noticed. It is said to be in the discretion of the court. The meaning of this proposition is not that the court may arbitrarily or capriciously perform one contract and refuse to perform another, but that the court has regard to the conduct of the plaintiff and to circumstances outside the contract itself, and that the mere fact of the existence of a valid contract is not conclusive in the plaintiff's favour " See *Hexter* v. *Pearce* [1900] 1 Ch. 341 and *Re Hare and O'More* [1901] 1 Ch. 93.

It is important to remember that specific performance cannot be granted where there is no concluded contract, and this is so even if there have been acts which might bring in the doctrine of part performance. See *ante,* p. 52.

When specific performance will not be granted.—The following is a list of some of the chief cases in which the court will refuse specific performance, although the contract is valid :—

(i) *where the title is doubtful ;* see further, *post,* p. 229 ;

(ii) *where such an order would be prejudicial to the rights of third parties ;* for instance, if the order would assist in a breach of trust (*Willmott* v. *Barber* (1880), 15 Ch. D. 96 ; applied in *Warrington* v. *Miller* [1973] 2 W.L.R. 654, C.A., where a breach of covenant in a head lease would have ensued) ; but specific performance will be ordered against a party to a contract who has it in his power to compel a third party, such as a company under his control, to convey (*Jones* v. *Lipman* [1962] 1 W.L.R. 832) ; if a company in which land is vested is a mere sham an order for specific performance of a contract with the main shareholder may also be made against that company (*ibid.*) ;

(iii) *where a party has insisted and acted upon a mistaken construction in such a way as to amount to a final election.* In such a case the court will generally refuse to grant specific performance in any form, and dismiss the action (*Clowes* v. *Higginson* (1813), 1 Ves. & B. 524). But the fact that a vendor has insisted on a wrong interpretation of the contract down to and at the trial will not take away his right to elect to have specific performance of the contract as rightly interpreted, the purchaser's offer, contained in his defence, to complete on those terms not having been withdrawn (*Berners* v. *Fleming* [1925] Ch. 264). In other cases where, in an action for specific performance, the plaintiff contends that the terms of the contract were *XYZ*, and the defendant contends that they were *XY*, the fact that the plaintiff turns out to be in the wrong will not generally prevent him waiving the term *Z* and obtaining specific performance according to what the defendant admits to be the true construction (*Preston* v. *Luck* (1884), 27 Ch. D. 497);

(iv) *where the party asking for specific performance has been guilty of some act or default which would make it inequitable to grant him the relief asked for.* For instance, where the contract is voidable on account of its having been induced by misrepresentation, the person who was deceived could elect to avoid the contract, and this would be a good defence to an application for specific performance by the vendor;

(v) *where specific performance would impose real hardship on the other party.* See generally *ante*, p. 84. In *Wroth* v. *Tyler* [1973] 2 W.L.R. 405, Megarry, J., held that the court would be slow to decree specific performance where this would require the vendor to embark upon difficult or uncertain litigation in order to secure any requisite consent or obtain vacant possession where the outcome of any litigation depended on disputed facts, difficult questions of law or the exercise of a discretionary jurisdiction;

(vi) *where the party asking for specific performance has been guilty of delay.* The ordinary period of six years for the enforcement of contracts does not apply either to actions for specific performance or to equity's discretion to refuse relief (Limitation Act, 1939, ss. 2 (1) and (7) and 29). As a result the old equitable doctrine of *laches*—delay defeats equities —remains applicable (see *Eads* v. *Williams* (1854), 4 De G.M. & G. 674, at pp. 691–2). Therefore if there is any delay in seeking a decree of specific performance, which usually means that an action must be commenced within one year, no decree may be obtainable (*Huxham* v. *Llewellyn* (1873), 21 W.R. 570; but see *Du Sautoy* v. *Symes* [1967] Ch. 1146). There is, however, one notable exception to this: lapse of time does not bar a purchaser's claim to specific performance if, during the period of delay, he has been in possession with the vendor's concurrence pursuant to a contract under which he is equitable owner of the land and which he has not abandoned (*Williams* v. *Greatrex* [1957] 1 W.L.R. 31).

Doubtful titles.—The long-standing rule is that the court will not force a doubtful title upon an unwilling purchaser under an open contract (*Pryke* v. *Waddingham* (1852), 10 Hare 1; *Mullings* v. *Trinder* (1870), L.R. 10 Eq. 449). This occurs where the vendor's title has not been shown to be either good or bad, the doubt arising because of uncertainty as to the law at some point or as to the application of the law or, more commonly, as to some fact or construction on which the title depends (e.g. as to whether a vendor had taken without notice of an adverse equitable interest: *Nottingham Patent Brick Co.* v. *Butler* (1885), 15 Q.B.D. 261; *Re Handman and Wilcox* [1902] 1 Ch. 599; or as to who was the heir at law of a predecessor in title who may or may not

have died intestate : *Selkirk* v. *Romar Industries, Ltd.* [1963] 1 W.L.R. 1415).
Then the rule has been that the vendor can only obtain specific performance
if he first pursues the litigation or inquiry for evidence necessary to disperse
the doubt and clear his title not just against the purchaser but also, as it were,
against the world.   Thus in *Re Nichols and Van Joel's Contract* [1910] 1 Ch. 43,
a vendor whose title depended upon the construction of a will issued a vendor
and purchaser summons and was given the option, which he accepted, of
having that summons stand over until he could have the point of construction
settled on an originating summons ; the point was settled in the vendor's
favour but he was nonetheless held liable to pay the purchaser's costs of the
vendor and purchaser summons because his title had been doubtful.

However, the tendency of the courts appears to be to decide any doubt,
so far as this is at all possible, at least as between the vendor and the purchaser
(*Alexander* v. *Mills* (1870), 6 Ch. App. 124 ; *Smith* v. *Colbourne* [1914] 2
Ch. 533).   Thus in *Johnson* v. *Clarke* [1928] Ch. 847, the purchaser received
notice of a claim that the vendors had given an option in respect of the property
and so refused to complete ; on the vendor seeking specific performance
Maugham, J., came to the conclusion that the claim had no reasonable
chance of success and refused to compel the vendor to commence an action
to determine the claim.

The above cases were very fully considered by Roxburgh, J., in *Wilson* v.
Thomas [1958] 1 W.L.R. 422.   He thought that they were not inconsistent
although some of the *dicta* in them may be.   His view was that questions of
law, including questions of mere construction, should be decided as between
vendor and purchaser on the authority of *Smith* v. *Colbourne*.   Nevertheless,
questions of fact, or mixed fact and law, should not be so decided, and, if
they give rise to doubt, should enable a purchaser to rescind (unless the vendor
resolves the questions at his own cost) as decided in *Re Nichols and Van
Joel's Contract*.   In *Wilson* v. *Thomas* the question could not be decided
without admitting extrinsic evidence to resolve a latent ambiguity in a will
and so the vendor's action for specific performance failed.   *Johnson* v. *Clarke*
was distinguished because there the court had before it all evidence necessary
to settle the problem.

As to the purchaser obtaining a decree of specific performance against the
vendor where the title, or some aspect of it, is doubtful see *Wroth* v. *Tyler*
[1973] 2 W.L.R. 405, *ante*.

PART 6.   VENDOR AND PURCHASER SUMMONS

A vendor and purchaser summons is a method of settling disputes between
vendor and purchaser on matters arising under a contract other than the
validity thereof, for instance where the vendor refuses to answer or to conform to the purchaser's requisitions.   Statutory provision for this procedure
is contained in the L.P.A. 1925, s. 49, re-enacting and extending the Vendor
and Purchaser Act, 1874, s. 9, as follows :—

" 49.—(1) A vendor or purchaser of any interest in land, or their
representatives respectively, may apply in a summary way to the court,
in respect of any requisitions or objections, or any claim for compensation,
or any other question arising out of or connected with the contract (not
being a question affecting the existence or validity of the contract), and
the court may make such order upon the application as to the court may
appear just, and may order how and by whom all or any of the costs of
and incident to the application are to be borne and paid.

(2) . . .

(3) This section applies to a contract for the sale or exchange of any interest in land."

The application is made by originating summons, and must be entitled " In the matter of the Agreement and in the matter of the Law of Property Act, 1925," and in the body of the summons the section (that is, s. 49) under which the application is made must be specified.   Evidence may be given by affidavit and the deponents may be cross-examined (*Re Burroughs, Lynn and Sexton* (1877), 5 Ch. D. 601).

When the procedure is available.—Speaking generally, the procedure on a vendor and purchaser summons is only available when no question arises as to the existence or validity of the contract.   But even where the validity of the contract is not admitted, if a point arises between the vendor and the purchaser which would have to be settled if the contract should turn out to be good, the court has jurisdiction to try such question (*Re Hughes and Ashley's Contract* [1900] 2 Ch. 595).

The validity of a notice to rescind (*Re Jackson and Woodburn's Contract* (1887), 37 Ch. D. 44) ; questions arising on the form of the conveyance (*Re Cooper and Crondace's Contract* (1904), 90 L.T. 258) ; or the question whether mistake on the part of the vendor enables him to rescind (*Re Wallis and Barnard's Contract* [1899] 2 Ch. 515), may be decided

The procedure is not suitable in cases where the vendor's title depends upon a question of construction involving real difficulty—for instance, as to the proper construction of a deed or a will.   In such a case the proper mode of settling the question is by a " construction " summons (*Re Nichols and Van Joel's Contract* [1910] 1 Ch. 43 ; *Re Hogan and Marnell's Contract* [1919] 1 Ir. R. 422).   The reason is that an order made under a vendor and purchaser summons would only be binding as between the vendor and purchaser, and by forcing the title on the purchaser the result might be to force a lawsuit on him (see *Horton* v. *Kurzke* [1971] 1 W.L.R. 769).   The court has no power to compel the vendor to clear his title by having the point settled in such a way as would become binding on all parties interested, but in one case (*Re Nichols and Van Joel's Contract*, *ante*) the court got over the difficulty by offering to adjourn the summons to enable the vendor to clear his title, but the vendor was ordered to pay the costs, and more recently this case was followed but the vendor declined the offer (*Wilson* v. *Thomas* [1958] 1 W.L.R. 422).

Orders which can be made.—The summons may, apparently, ask the court to make a general declaration as to whether the vendor has or has not made out a good title (*Re Burroughs, Lynn and Sexton* (1877), 5 Ch. D. 601 ; *Re Hargreaves and Thompson's Contract* (1886), 32 Ch. D. 454 ; Williams on Vendor and Purchaser, 4th ed., vol. II, p. 1071), notwithstanding the observation of Kekewich, J., in *Re Wallis and Barnard's Contract*, *ante*, that the summons should not ask for a general declaration that a good title has been or has not been shown, but whether a particular requisition has or has not been sufficiently answered.

It would seem that the court has jurisdiction not only to answer any particular question properly submitted to it, but also to direct such things to be done as would be the natural consequence of the court's decision ; for instance, to make an order rescinding the contract, and to order the vendor to return the deposit with interest, and to pay the purchaser's costs of investigating the title, and the costs of the summons (*Re Hargreaves and Thompson's Contract, ante ; Re Higgins and Percival* (1888), 59 L.T. 213 ; *Re Marshall and Salt's Contract* [1900] 2 Ch. 202 ; *Re Hare and O'More's Contract* [1901] 1 Ch. 93 ; *Re Walker and Oakshott's Contract* [1901] 2 Ch. 383). But there is no absolute rule that, in all cases where a good title has not been shown, an order must be made for the return of the deposit (*Re Hargreaves and Thompson's Contract, ante*) ; and in *Re Davis and Cavey* (1888), 40 Ch. D. 601, the court refused to order the return of the deposit, but without prejudice to the purchaser's right to recover the same by action.

It does not appear, however, that the court has ever made an order for specific performance on a vendor and purchaser summons.

A purchaser's summons may be dismissed without costs, if it is held that he was fairly entitled to submit the question to the court (*Re Baker and Selmon's Contract* [1907] 1 Ch. 238).

CHAPTER EIGHT

DATE OF DEED

Generally.—It is presumed that the date, if any, actually appearing on a deed is the date it took effect, but this presumption is open to rebuttal (see *per* Patterson, J., in *Browne* v. *Burton* (1847), 17 L.J.Q.B. 49, at p. 50). A deed takes effect from the date of its execution being completed by delivery so that it is that date which should appear (see *per* Evershed, M.R., in *Universal Permanent Building Society* v. *Cooke* [1952] Ch. 95, at p. 101). The execution of a deed is completed, for present purposes, on its delivery by the last party whose execution is essential to its validity ; e.g., execution of a deed of conveyance is commonly completed on delivery by the vendor even without any execution by the purchaser (*Bishop of Crediton* v. *Bishop of Exeter* [1905] 2 Ch. 455 and *Naas* v. *Westminster Bank, Ltd.* [1940] A.C. 366 ; compare *Sinclair* v. *I.R.C.* (1942), 24 T.C. 432).

Escrows.—Where a document is delivered as an escrow, it does not take effect as a deed until the condition of its delivery is performed (*Degoze* v. *Rowe* (1591), Moore K.B. 300). On performance of the condition, however, the deed is regarded as having been executed and takes effect retrospectively as at the date of delivery as an escrow (*Graham* v. *Graham* (1791), 1 Ves. 272 ; *per* Farwell, L.J., in *Foundling Hospital* v. *Crane* [1911] 2 K.B. 367, at p. 377 ; *Re Duke of Devonshire's Settlement* (1952), 31 A.T.C. 399 ; and *per* Cross, J., in *Windsor Refrigerator Co., Ltd.* v. *Branch Nominees, Ltd.* [1961] Ch. 375 ; also J. G. Monroe, " The Dating of a Document," at [1960] B.T.R., p. 180). Nevertheless, in practice, a document delivered as an escrow will almost always be dated as on the day when its condition is fulfilled, and this is apparently accepted as correct for stamp duty purposes (see *per* Lord Denning, M.R., and Diplock, L.J., in *Wm. Cory & Son, Ltd.* v. *I.R.C.* [1964] 1 W.L.R. 1322, at pp. 1341 and 1346 respectively, and *per* Lord Reid on appeal : *ibid.* [1965] A.C. 1088, at pp. 1107–8).

Same date.—Where two deeds relating to the same subject-matter—e.g., a conveyance and a mortgage—both bear the same date or were, in fact, both executed on the same day, then the position is that " the court must inquire which was in fact executed first, but that if there is anything in the deeds themselves to show an intention, either that they shall take effect *pari passu* or even that the later deed shall take effect in priority to the earlier, in that case the court will presume that the deeds were executed in such order as to give effect to the manifest intention of the parties " (Fry, J., in *Gartside* v. *Silkestone Coal and Iron Co.* (1882), 21 Ch. D. 762, at pp. 767–8 ; see also *Church of England Building Society* v. *Piskor* [1954] Ch. 553 and *Weg Motors, Ltd.* v. *Hales* [1962] Ch. 49).

No date.—It follows from the rule as to a deed taking effect from the date of its execution being completed that the lack of a date does not affect the validity of a deed and that parol evidence is admissible to show the correct date (see *per* Astbury, J., in *Morrell* v. *Studd and Millington* [1913] 2 Ch. 648, at p. 658).

Registered conveyancing.—As indicated by the headings to the prescribed forms in the Schedule to the L.R.R. 1925, a transfer of registered land must be dated. Since such transfers must also be executed as deeds, the same principles apply to the dating as in unregistered conveyancing (*R.* v. *Edwards* [1947] K.B. 392 ; s. 27 (3) of the L.R.A. 1925, as explained in *Grace Rymer Investments, Ltd.* v. *Waite* [1958] Ch. 831).

Note, however, that the legal estate in registered land does not pass as at the date of the transfer but only on the date of registration (ss. 19 (1) and 22 (1) of the L.R.A. 1925, and see *Smith* v. *Express Dairy* [1954] J.P.L. 45 and *Lever Finance, Ltd.* v. *Needleman's Trustee* [1956] Ch. 375). More accurately, the legal estate is passed retrospectively as on the day on which the instrument or application for registration was delivered to H.M. Land Registry, and as a rule such delivery governs priority (r. 83 (2) of the L.R.R. 1925). However, where two or more instruments or applications relating to the same land, or to the same charge, are delivered *at the same time by the same person*, they rank for purposes of priority in such order as may be directed by, or inferred from, the instruments or applications, and in default, as may be required in writing by the person delivering them (r. 84). It was pointed out by Cross, J., at first instance in *Strand Securities, Ltd.* v. *Caswell* [1965] Ch. 373, at p. 387, that this rule is not applicable where applications are made at the same time (i.e., delivered on the same day) by different persons, with the result that neither would have precedence. But in such a case it would appear that the order of priority *inter se* could invariably be inferred from the nature of the instruments concerned, there merely being no one person to direct the order. This view seems the one taken by Russell and Harman, L.JJ., on appeal, *ibid.* [1965] Ch. 958, at pp. 991 and 982 (and see the parenthesis in r. 83 (2) ; *contra Conveyancer N.S.*, vol. 29, p. 252). In other words, the position in such a case is as if two deeds in unregistered conveyancing bear the same date (see p. 233).

PARTIES TO DEEDS

INTRODUCTORY

General rule.—In determining who should be joined as a party to any particular deed the general rule is simply as follows : all necessary parties should be joined, but no unnecessary parties even though they may be willing to join (*Corder* v. *Morgan* (1811), 18 Ves. 344). The persons who are the necessary parties will depend on the intended function of the particular deed. In this connection, two established principles must normally be borne in mind, first, that property can only be transferred by deed to a person who is a party thereto, and secondly, that only a person who is a party to a deed can be bound or benefited by a covenant or other obligation created thereby. These principles are, of course, subject to a number of substantial exceptions, some of which are noted below.

Further, if any person owns an interest in an estate which is to be conveyed free from any such interest, then whether or not that person is a necessary party to the deed of conveyance depends on whether or not his interest is overreachable (see as to this, *ante*, p. 172). If the person's interest is over-reachable, then he should not be joined as a party. What is more, a contractual stipulation that a purchaser (for money or moneys' worth) of a legal estate in land should accept a conveyance made with the concurrence of a person entitled to an overreachable equitable interest would be void (s. 42 (1), (9) of the L.P.A. 1925). If the interest cannot be overreached, e.g., because it is legal and not equitable (see s. 1 (1), (2) of the L.P.A. 1925), then the owner thereof must be joined if the property is to be conveyed free from the interest.

In addition to joining the grantor and grantee, any covenantor and covenantee, and the owners of interests which cannot be overreached, it may be that the consideration money has to be paid to some third person (or persons). The commonest example of this is payment to the vendor's Settled Land Act trustees (see s. 18 (1) (*b*) (*c*) of the S.L.A. 1925). In such a case, the appropriate third person (or persons) should be joined in the deed to give a receipt for the consideration money (as to Consideration and Receipts, see Chapter 11, *post*, p. 454).

Conveyance to self.—Before 1926 if a person desired to convey freehold property to himself, it could be done, but only by means of a conveyance to uses under the Statute of Uses. When the Statute of Uses was repealed (s. 207 and Sched. 7 to the L.P.A. 1925) it was provided by s. 72 (3) of the L.P.A. 1925 that after 1925 a person may convey land to or vest land in himself. Indeed, in some circumstances it is essential for a person to convey land to himself ; e.g. an assent by a personal representative in his own favour whether beneficially or in trust (see s. 36 (4) of the A.E.A. 1925 ; *Re King's Will Trusts* [1964] Ch. 542). When a tenant for life purchases part of the estate under s. 68 of the S.L.A. 1925, the trustees should convey in his name to him : see *Re Tennant's Will Trusts* [1970] Ch. 75.

A conveyance of leasehold property by the owner to himself jointly with another person since 1859 has been good (Lord St. Leonard's Act, 1859, s. 21 ; now replaced by s. 72 (1) of the L.P.A. 1925) ; and a conveyance of freehold property by the owner to himself jointly with another person since 1881 has been good (Conveyancing Act, 1881, s. 50 ; now replaced by s. 72 (2) of the L.P.A. 1925).

In conveyances made after 31st December, 1881, a conveyance of freehold land or a thing in action by a husband to his wife, and by a wife to her husband, alone or jointly with another person, has been good (L.P.A. 1925, s. 72 (2), replacing s. 50 of the Conveyancing Act, 1881). The word " conveyance " in the L.P.A. 1925 includes " a lease " (s. 205 (1) (ii)). See also *Sutherland* v. *Sutherland* [1893] 3 Ch. 169 ; *Gilbey* v. *Rush* [1906] 1 Ch. 11. So, a tenant for life may lease to his wife if he acts in good faith (*ibid.; Middlemas* v. *Stevens* [1901] 1 Ch. 574).

Two or more persons (whether or not being trustees or personal representatives) may convey, and will be deemed always to have been capable of conveying, any property vested in them to any one or more of themselves in like manner as they could have conveyed such property to a third party ; *provided that*, if the persons in whose favour the conveyance is made are, by reason of any fiduciary relationship or otherwise, precluded from validly carrying out the transaction, the conveyance will be liable to be set aside (L.P.A. 1925, s. 72 (4)). See *Green* v. *Whitehead* [1930] 1 Ch. 38.

Section 72 of the L.P.A. 1925 was considered by the House of Lords in *Rye* v. *Rye* [1962] A.C. 496, in which the majority based their decision on the ground that it is still not possible in law, despite the section, for one person to grant a lease to himself, or for one or more persons to grant a lease of land to themselves in any circumstances, largely because of the contractual nature of a lease.

A person could not before 1926 covenant with himself, and therefore he could not covenant with himself and another or others (*Napier* v. *Williams* [1911] 1 Ch. 361). By virtue of s. 82 (1) of the L.P.A. 1925 he is now able to do so. This subsection provides that " any covenant, whether express or implied [this includes the implied covenants for title] or agreement entered into by a person with himself and one or more other persons shall be construed and be capable of being enforced in like manner as if the covenant or agreement had been entered into with the other person or persons alone." Subsection (2) makes the section retrospective. This is important, as the mistake used often to be made, for instance, in transfers of mortgages by trustees to continuing and new trustees by conveying " as mortgagees." The subsection validates these mistakes.

Sub-purchasers.—A purchaser is entitled to insist upon the conveyance being to his nominee, for example, to a sub-purchaser (in any number of lots, provided that the purchaser meets any additional expenses), unless the purchaser's personal qualifications are material. If the conveyance is to be subject to obligations, the vendor can insist on the purchaser joining as a party to guarantee observance of the obligations (*Curtis Moffat, Ltd.* v. *Wheeler* [1929] 2 Ch. 224). As far as the implied covenants for title are concerned a sub-purchaser does not need to have the purchaser join as a party provided the conveyance is expressed to be by his direction as beneficial owner (see s. 76 (2) of the L.P.A. 1925).

The entitlement of the purchaser referred to in the preceding paragraph is expressly negated by Condition 11 (4) of the 1973 Revision of The Law Society's Conditions of Sale and also by Condition 4 (3) of the 18th edition of the National Conditions of Sale. The primary reason for this was clearly the now defunct betterment levy consequence of sub-sales. It is thought that without this reason the new conditions are in this respect unduly favourable for vendors and Condition 11 (4) might therefore justifiably be struck out on behalf of purchasers.

Exceptions.—As indicated, there exist a number of exceptional cases in which non-parties may be affected, adversely or otherwise, by the provisions of a deed. For example, this is so in cases of agency (see Attorneys, *post*, p. 239), deeds poll, trusts, privity of estate, the benefit of covenants at common law, and the benefit and burden of restrictive covenants in equity (see generally Chapter 15, *post*, p. 544). See also the effect of ss. 56 (in particular), 63 and 204 of the L.P.A. 1925 discussed *post*, pp. 546 and 542 and *ante*, p. 183, respectively.

Description of parties.—Where a person or a corporation is once properly described, a subsequent error in referring to the name is immaterial, unless it causes uncertainty, by producing a doubt, as to the identity of the party. Parol evidence may be adduced to correct an erroneous description of the parties (*Re Howgate and Osborn's Contract* [1902] 1 Ch. 451), or to identify the parties, although it is of paramount importance to bear in mind the indicia of identity afforded by the deed itself (*Fung Ping Shan* v. *Tong Shun* [1918] A.C. 403, at p. 406). For example, where a firm is made a party, evidence is admissible to show who constituted the firm at that date (*Carruthers* v. *Sheddon* (1815), 6 Taunt. 14); where a firm carried on business as " W. W.", evidence was allowed to show who were the partners constituting the firm (*Wray* v. *Wray* [1905] 2 Ch. 349).

In the case of a corporation it is sufficient if it is described by a name which sufficiently identifies it, although the full corporate name be not given (*Croydon Hospital* v. *Farley* (1816), 6 Taunt. 467), as in the case of an error in the name of a contracting company (*F. Goldsmith (Sicklesmere), Ltd.* v. *Baxter* [1970] Ch. 85; see also *per* Lord Hodson in *Saunders* v. *Anglia Building Society* [1971] A.C. 1004).

As to the importance assumed by the description of the parties in title deeds for the purpose of land charges searches, see *post*, p. 596.

In all deeds, contracts, wills, orders, assents and other instruments made or coming into operation after 1925, unless the context otherwise requires, " person " includes a corporation; the singular includes the plural, and *vice versa*; and the masculine includes the feminine, and *vice versa* (L.P.A. 1925, ss. 61, 83).

Infants.—Persons expressed to be parties to any conveyance will, until the contrary is proved, be presumed to be of full age at the date thereof (L.P.A. 1925, s. 15). It is assumed that the effect of this section is that it will not be accounted as negligence on the part of a purchaser's solicitor to assume, without making inquiries, that a person is of full age and that he will not be deemed to have notice if he does not inquire. An infant cannot hold a legal estate in land (L.P.A. 1925, s. 1 (6)) ; nor can he be a tenant for life or person having the powers of a tenant for life (see words " of full age " in ss. 19 and 20 of the S.L.A. 1925). See further, *post*, p. 334, and chapter on Settled Land, *post*, p. 664.

ALIENS

An alien is a person who is not a British subject, a British protected person or a citizen of Eire (British Nationality Act, 1948, s. 32 (1) ; see also the British Nationality Acts of 1958 and 1965).

Since 1870 (except between 22nd December, 1919, and 23rd December, 1922 : Aliens Restriction (Amendment) Act, 1919) an alien has been able to buy, hold and sell, and give a good title to property of every description, except British ships, in the same manner as a British subject (Naturalisation Act, 1870, repealed and replaced by Status of Aliens Act, 1914, s. 17 ; British Nationality Act, 1948, Sched. 4, Pt. II).

As regards the period from 1919 to 1922, the 1919 Act provided, in effect, that it was not lawful for a former enemy alien, either in his own name or in the name of a trustee, to acquire any land or any interest in land within the United Kingdom, and if any such land or interest should be acquired in contravention of the Act, the Board of Trade might by order vest the property in the Public Trustee. Should such a conveyance appear on the title it would be as well to inquire from the Department of Trade and Industry (as successor of the Board of Trade) whether such an order had been made.

During the last war the Board of Trade had power to vest in the Custodian of Enemy Property such enemy property as might be prescribed (Trading with the Enemy Act, 1939, s. 7 (1) ; see also Enemy Property Act, 1953).

ATTORNEYS

In pursuance of recommendations of The Law Commission (Law Com. No. 30) the Powers of Attorney Act, 1971, introduces a considerably more rational and reliable scheme of provisions, particularly with regard to protection against revocation of a power and with regard to delegation by trustees. The Act, which came into force on 1st October, 1971 (s. 11 (4)), repeals altogether the important ss. 123, 124, 125 (1), 126, 127, 128 and 129 of the L.P.A. 1925 (which sections were largely derived from the Conveyancing Acts of 1881 and 1882) and also repealed is s. 29 of the T.A. 1925 and s. 25 thereof is substantially amended.

For an account of these superseded provisions and a consideration of the practical difficulties which led to the reforms, reference may be made to pp. 246–255 of the 15th Edition of this work. The following paragraphs deal with the current position, in particular because the important provisions of the 1971 Act have some retrospective operation.

Reference generally may be made with advantage to the articles by Mr. C. K. Liddle and Mr. J. E. Adams in the *Law Society's Gazette*, vol. 68, at pp. 434 and 437 respectively, and also to certain letters in *ibid*. at pp. 481, 482 and 524.

Construction of powers of attorney.—A purchaser should satisfy himself that the execution of the deed in question—conveyance, lease, etc.—was authorised by the power (*Danby* v. *Coutts* (1885), 29 Ch. D. 500) ; and also that the power is under seal (*Powell* v. *London and Provincial Bank* [1893] 2 Ch. 555), unless the deed is to be or was executed in the donor's presence (*R.* v. *Longnor* (*Inhabitants*) (1833), 4 B. & Ad. 647).

Powers of attorney tend to be construed strictly, so that it must be shown that, " on a fair construction of the whole instrument, the authority in question is to be found within the four corners of the instrument either in express terms or by necessary implication " (*Re Bryant ; Powis and Bryant* v. *Banque de Peuple* [1893] A.C. 170, at p. 177). For instance, a power of attorney " to ask, demand, sue for, recover, and receive all sums of money . . . owing or payable " to the donor of the power " by virtue of any security and to give, sign and execute receipts, releases and other discharges for the same . . . also to sell any real and personal property now or hereafter *belonging to* " the donor, was held not to authorise the attorney to exercise a statutory power of sale vested in the donor as mortgagee in possession of real estate (*Re Dowson and Jenkin's Contract* [1904] 2 Ch. 219). Again, a power of attorney to sell property at a particular place " whether owned solely or jointly with any other person " was held to confer no power in respect of land held by the donor as trustee for sale (*Green* v. *Whitehead* [1930] 1 Ch. 38).

Such general words as " and do and execute and perform any other act, matter or thing in or about the premises," will only confer such additional authority as is necessary to carry out the powers specifically conferred (*Hawksley* v. *Outram* (1892), 67 L.T. 804 ; *Jacobs* v. *Morris* [1902] 1 Ch. 816 ; *Australian Bank of Commerce, Ltd.* v. *Perel* [1926] A.C. 737).

Execution of powers of attorney.—By virtue of s. 1 (1) of the Powers of Attorney Act, 1971, all powers of attorney must now be signed *and sealed* (not merely those empowering the attorney to execute deeds ; cf. *Powell* v. *London and Provincial Bank* [1893] 2 Ch. 555). Somewhat oddly the subsection does not also require delivery so as to bring the position patently into line with the execution of deeds generally. The signing and sealing will ordinarily be by the donor of the power, but now may alternatively be " by the direction and in the presence of " the donor when two witnesses must be present and attest (subss. (1) and (2) ; cf. s. 9 of the Wills Act, 1837). This alternative caters for potential donors of powers who are physically incapable of executing documents although of sound mind. These new provisions do not prejudice any other special statutory requirements (e.g., s. 25 (3) of the T.A. 1925, as amended, see below) and do not affect the rules relating to corporations (s. 1 (3) of the 1971 Act).

Abolition of filing of powers of attorney.—As from 1st October, 1971, the requirements as to the filing of instruments or copies contained in s. 125 of the L.P.A. 1925, and s. 219 of the Judicature Act, 1925, are inapplicable, as also are the requirements in s. 25 of the T.A. 1925 : filing is no longer possible or permitted (s. 2 (1) of the 1971 Act). However, the right to search for, and obtain copies of powers of attorney already filed is preserved (s. 2 (2) of the 1971 Act).

By s. 4 (1) of the Evidence and Powers of Attorney Act, 1940, office copies of filed powers are sufficient evidence of the contents of the power and of the fact of filing ; as to proof see further below.

Proof of powers of attorney.—Although s. 4 of the Evidence and Powers of Attorney Act, 1940 (see above) remains unaffected, the 1971 Act, s. 3, now authorises proof of the contents of a power of attorney by means of a duly certified "photocopy." The precise provisions of this section which may be useful in the deduction of title are as follows :—

" 3.—(1) The contents of an instrument creating a power of attorney may be proved by means of a copy which—

(a) is a reproduction of the original made with a photographic or other device for reproducing documents in facsimile ; and

(b) contains the following certificate or certificates signed by the donor of the power or by a solicitor or stockbroker, that is to say—

(i) a certificate at the end to the effect that the copy is a true and complete copy of the original ; and

(ii) if the original consists of two or more pages, a certificate at the end of each page of the copy to the effect that it is a true and complete copy of the corresponding page of the original.

(2) Where a copy of an instrument creating a power of attorney has been made which complies with subsection (1) of this section, the contents of the instrument may also be proved by means of a copy of that copy if the further copy itself complies with that subsection, taking references in it to the original as references to the copy from which the further copy is made.

(3) In this section ' stockbroker ' means a member of any stock exchange within the meaning of the Stock Transfer Act 1963 or the Stock Transfer Act (Northern Ireland) 1963."

Irrevocability of powers of attorney.—Sections 4 and 5 of the 1971 Act replace, with greatly simplified form and effect, the obscure and complex protective provisions in ss. 124, 126, 127 and 128 of the L.P.A. 1925. The precise terms of the new provisions are of importance and are as follows :—

" *Powers of attorney given as security*

4.—(1) Where a power of attorney is expressed to be irrevocable and is given to secure—

(a) a proprietary interest of the donee of the power ; or

(b) the performance of an obligation owed to the donee,

then, so long as the donee has that interest or the obligation remains undischarged, the power shall not be revoked—

(i) by the donor without the consent of the donee ; or

(ii) by the death, incapacity or bankruptcy of the donor or, if the donor is a body corporate, by its winding up or dissolution.

(2) A power of attorney given to secure a proprietary interest may be given to the person entitled to the interest and persons deriving title under him to that interest, and those persons shall be duly constituted donees of the power for all purposes of the power but without prejudice to any right to appoint substitutes given by the power.

(3) This section applies to powers of attorney whenever created."

This section, which operates to some extent retrospectively (see subs. (3)), unlike s. 5 below, still requires an expression of irrevocability (subs. (1)).

In substance, subs. (1) primarily gives some statutory effect to the common-law rule of irrevocability where an agent's authority is " coupled with an interest " (see *per* Wilde, C.J., in *Smart* v. *Sandars* (1848), 5 C.B. 895, at p. 917). It should be noticed that, although a deed is required (s. 1 (1) of the 1971 Act), this section does not make valuable consideration a necessary element (cf. *Raleigh* v. *Atkinson* (1840), 6 M. & W. 670).

A power of attorney given to an equitable mortgagee to facilitate sale (see *post*, p. 1030) is a clear example of a case within this section.

" *Protection of donee and third persons where power of attorney is revoked*

5.—(1) A donee of a power of attorney who acts in pursuance of the power at a time when it has been revoked shall not, by reason of the revocation, incur any liability (either to the donor or to any other person), if at that time he did not know that the power had been revoked.

(2) Where a power of attorney has been revoked and a person, without knowledge of the revocation, deals with the donee of the power, the transaction between them shall, in favour of that person, be as valid as if the power had then been in existence.

(3) Where the power is expressed in the instrument creating it to be irrevocable and to be given by way of security then, unless the person dealing with the donee knows that it was not in fact given by way of security, he shall be entitled to assume that the power is incapable of revocation except by the donor acting with the consent of the donee and shall accordingly be treated for the purposes of subsection (2) of this section as having knowledge of the revocation only if he knows that it has been revoked in that manner.

(4) Where the interest of a purchaser depends on whether a transaction between the donee of a power of attorney and another person was valid by virtue of subsection (2) of this section, it shall be conclusively presumed in favour of the purchaser that that person did not at the material time know of the revocation of the power if—

(*a*) the transaction between that person and the donee was completed within twelve months of the date on which the power came into operation ; or

(*b*) that person makes a statutory declaration, before or within three months after the completion of the purchase, that he did not at the material time know of the revocation of the power.

(5) Without prejudice to subsection (3) of this section, for the purposes of this section knowledge of the revocation of a power of attorney includes knowledge of the occurrence of any event (such as the death of the donor) which has the effect of revoking the power.

(6) In this section ' purchaser ' and ' purchase ' have the meanings specified in section 205 (1) of the Law of Property Act 1925.

(7) This section applies whenever the power of attorney was created but only to acts and transactions after the commencement of this Act."

Subsection (3) of this section is obviously allied to s. 4 : the former provision protects the donee of a security power, whilst the present provision protects third parties relying on such a power. In this respect, s. 126 of the L.P.A. 1925 is replaced by subs. (3), but with certain notable changes : *First*, subs. (3) substitutes " by way of security " for " for valuable consideration " ;

Second, the power now need only be expressed to be by way of security whereas previously it had in fact to be for valuable consideration ; *Third*, a third party is now protected notwithstanding that the power has been revoked with the donee's consent but without the third party's knowledge ; and *Fourth*, it is now beyond argument that a third party is not protected if he knew of a revoking event (see subs. (5)) ; under s. 126 this depended on the element of good faith in the statutory definition of "purchaser." It is thought that the words "know" and "knowledge" used throughout s. 5 of the 1971 Act are intended to be construed as meaning actual notice of a revocation or other matter and as excluding any deemed, constructive or imputed notice thereof (but see subs. (5)).

Otherwise, s. 5 is drafted to confer upon a purchaser protection at least equal to that under s. 127 of the L.P.A. 1925. It will be observed that there is no repetition of the old requirement that the power should be expressed to be irrevocable for a fixed limited period. Nevertheless, the one-year period does reappear in subs. (4) (*a*) as the condition for a conclusive presumption. Equally, if the one-year period is not available, a purchaser must still look to a statutory declaration. But instead of one given by the donee (as under s. 124 (2) of the L.P.A. 1925), which was pointless if fraud was involved, the statutory declaration is to be given by the third party who dealt with the donee and, in effect, confirms that he enjoyed the protection of subs. (2).

Subsection (1) of s. 5 above replaces s. 124 (1) of the L.P.A. 1925, in providing protection for the donee of a power of attorney.

Section 6 of the 1971 Act provides certain additional protection for transferees under stock exchange transactions.

Purchaser entitled to copy of power of attorney.—As regards instruments executed after 1925, and notwithstanding any stipulation to the contrary, a purchaser of any interest in or charge upon land (not being land or a charge registered under the L.R.A. 1925), will be entitled to have any instrument creating a power of attorney which affects his title, or a copy thereof, or of the material portions thereof, delivered to him free of expense (L.P.A. 1925, s. 125 (2), as amended by the Law of Property (Amendment) Act, 1926 and by the 1971 Act ; also s. 45 (1) of the L.P.A. 1925) ; and no right to rescind a contract is to arise by reason of the enforcement of such provision (L.P.A. 1925, s. 125 (3)).

Execution by attorney under power.—It is provided by s. 7 (1) of the 1971 Act, in effect, that the donee of a power of attorney may, if he thinks fit, execute any instrument or thing in and with his own name and signature, and under his own seal, where sealing is required, by the authority of the donor of the power ; and any document or thing so executed and done shall be as effectual in law as if it had been executed or done by the donee of the power in the name and with the signature and seal of the donor thereof. By s. 7 (3) of the 1971 Act it is also provided that *the section is to operate without prejudice to any statutory direction* that an instrument is to be executed in the name of an estate owner. This refers to s. 7 (4) of the L.P.A. 1925, which provides that : "Where any such power for disposing of or creating a legal estate is exercisable by a person who is not the estate owner, the power shall, when practicable be exercised in the name and on behalf of the estate owner" (see also s. 8 (1) of the L.P.A. 1925 and s. 29 (5) of the S.L.A. 1925).

It is better to sign in the name of the principal so that there can be no risk of not complying with s. 7 (3) of the 1971 Act, but if the attorney wishes to take advantage of the section to execute the deed in his own name, there should be a statement that he has executed the deed as attorney for his principal (*Re Whitley Partners, Ltd.* (1886), 32 Ch. D. 337). That is, he will sign his name and then add : " As attorney for and on behalf of the said [principal]."

Otherwise the principal should be made a party to the deed, and the deed should be prepared exactly as if the principal was going to execute it. The attorney may, in all cases, if he so desires, execute the deed in the name of the principal. The form will be " *AB* (principal) by *CD* (the attorney)." The attestation clause will be " Signed Sealed and Delivered by the said (principal) by *CD* his attorney duly authorised by deed dated, etc., in the presence of."

Since now the power of attorney must be under seal, it is advisable to state in the attestation clause that the power was given to him by deed, although it is not necessary to give the date and parties to the deed.

However, it seems that the execution of the deed would be valid even though the attorney wrote his principal's name by way of signature without anything being added anywhere to show that it was done by virtue of a power of attorney (*L.C.C.* v. *Agricultural Food Products, Ltd.* [1955] 2 Q.B. 218). Nonetheless, this would be bad practice in that it might mislead (see *per* Denning, L.J., *ibid.*).

Powers granted by and to corporations.—As an alternative to the above, to execute a conveyance as attorney of a corporation, the attorney should sign the name of the corporation in the presence of a witness and affix *his own seal* (L.P.A. 1925, s. 74 (3) ; and see s. 7 (2) of the 1971 Act which removes any doubt as to there being alternatives). A corporation acting under a power of attorney may execute by an officer appointed for that purpose, by the board of directors, council or other governing body, and he will execute in the name of the donor of the power (L.P.A. 1925, s. 74 (4)). A purchaser may safely accept the execution of an instrument by a person who appears to be an officer so appointed (L.P.A. 1925, s. 74 (4)).

The board of directors, council or other governing body of a corporation aggregate may, by resolution or otherwise, appoint an agent either generally or in any particular case, to execute on behalf of the corporation any agreement or other *instrument not under seal* in relation to any matter within the powers of the corporation (L.P.A. 1925, s. 74 (2)).

Trustees and powers of attorney.—A tenant for life and a statutory owner are deemed to be trustees for the parties entitled under the settlement (S.L.A. 1925, s. 16 (1) (i) and s. 107 (1)), and, therefore, in exercising the powers of the S.L.A. 1925 by attorney they will be deemed to be in the position and to have the duties and liabilities of a trustee for those parties. " Tenant for life " includes a person who has the powers of a tenant for life (S.L.A. 1925, s. 117 (xxviii)). "Trustee," where the context admits, includes a personal representative (T.A. 1925, s. 68 (17)).

By the *rules of equity*, a trustee must himself exercise his discretionary powers and cannot delegate them to another, but he can appoint an attorney to carry into effect a discretion which he has already exercised (*Offen* v. *Harman* (1859), 29 L.J. Ch. 307). If, therefore, a trustee wishes to appoint an attorney to execute a deed to pass the legal estate and to receive trust money, the power must be specially given, and must refer to the particular transaction. It follows that a power of attorney given by a trustee authorising the attorney to execute deeds and give receipts *generally*, although given in the widest terms, will not be sufficient (*Re Hetling and Merton's Contract* [1893] 3 Ch. 269 ; *Day* v. *Woolwich Equitable Building Society* (1888), 40 Ch. D. 491).

The rule applies although the trustees are only statutory trustees. For instance, it applies to owners who, being entitled to land before 1926 as joint tenants or tenants in common, became trustees for sale on 1st January, 1926, by virtue of the transitional provisions and sell as such (*Green* v. *Whitehead* [1930] 1 Ch. 38). Nevertheless, it is considered that two or more persons who are solely entitled at law and in equity may appoint an attorney to convey the legal estate, and that a purchaser from an attorney so appointed who conveys for the joint tenants as beneficial owners cannot object to the validity of the appointment on the ground that it is made by trustees for sale.

However, " the law is not that trustees cannot delegate ; it is that trustees cannot delegate unless they have authority to do so " (see *per* Viscount Radcliffe in *Pilkington* v. *I.R.C.* [1964] A.C. 612, at p. 639, concerning the power of advancement conferred by s. 32 of the T.A. 1925). Note in particular, therefore, the following three statutory exceptions to the rule that a trustee cannot delegate the exercise of his discretionary power :—

(*a*) *Exception as regards property outside the United Kingdom.*—It is provided by s. 23 (2) of the T.A. 1925 (as to which, see *Re Vickery* [1931] 1 Ch. 572), as follows :—

" 23.—(2) Trustees or personal representatives may appoint any person to act as their agent or attorney for the purpose of selling, converting, collecting, getting in, and executing and perfecting insurances [this is a misprint in the Act for ' assurances ' : see *per* Eve, J., in *Green* v. *Whitehead, ante*] of, or managing or cultivating, or otherwise administering any property, real or personal, moveable or immoveable, subject to the trust or forming part of the testator's or intestate's estate, in any place *outside the United Kingdom or executing or exercising any discretion* or trust or power vested in them in relation to any such property, and such ancillary powers, and with and subject to such provisions and restrictions as they may think fit, including a power to appoint substitutes, and shall not, by reason only of their having made such appointment, be responsible for any loss arising thereby."

(*b*) *Exception for short-term delegations.*—Section 25 of the T.A. 1925 has been substantially amended by s. 8 of the 1971 Act which substitutes the following five subsections for the original subss. (1)–(8) ; (in addition it renumbers the original subss. (9) and (10) as (6) and (7), and then substitutes a new subs. (8) for the original subs. (11)) :—

" 25.—(1) Notwithstanding any rule of law or equity to the contrary, a trustee may, by power of attorney, delegate for a period not exceeding twelve months the execution or exercise of all or any of the trusts, powers and discretions vested in him as trustee either alone or jointly with any other person or persons.

(2) The persons who may be donees of a power of attorney under this section include a trust corporation but not (unless a trust corporation) the only other co-trustee of the donor of the power.

(3) An instrument creating a power of attorney under this section shall be attested by at least one witness.

(4) Before or within seven days after giving a power of attorney under this section the donor shall give written notice thereof (specifying the date

on which the power comes into operation and its duration, the donee of the power, the reason why the power is given and, where some only are delegated, the trusts, powers and discretions delegated) to—

> (a) each person (other than himself), if any, who under any instrument creating the trust has power (whether alone or jointly) to appoint a new trustee ; and
>
> (b) each of the other trustees, if any ;

but failure to comply with this subsection shall not, in favour of a person dealing with the donee of the power, invalidate any act done or instrument executed by the donee.

(5) The donor of a power of attorney given under this section shall be liable for the acts or defaults of the donee in the same manner as if they were the acts or defaults of the donor."

The substituted provisions apply whenever the trusts, powers or discretions arise (s. 9 (4) of the 1971 Act, not invalidating anything done under s. 25 in its original form before 1st October, 1971) and expressly apply also to personal representatives as well as to tenants for life and statutory owners (subs. (8)).

Two fundamental amendments should be noted : *first*, the substituted subsections are in *no* way dependent upon the trustee's absence abroad, but the period of delegation cannot now exceed twelve months (cp. s. 36 (1) of the T.A. 1925, *post*, p. 790) ; *second*, there is a new condition (in the substituted subs. (4)) that notice be given, in effect, to the persons who can appropriately consider the replacement of the delegating trustee if he comes within s. 36 (1) of the T.A. 1925 (*post*, p. 790). As already noted, the requirement of filing the power of attorney has been abolished (s. 2 of the 1971 Act). Otherwise, in particular it should be observed that the delegating trustee's liability is preserved (subs. (5)).

Further, it remains clear that the section authorises the power to be given in general terms merely referring to the instrument creating the trust (cp. *Re Donoughmore and Hackett* [1918] 1 Ir. R. 359).

Infants.—A power of attorney given by an infant is void (*Zouch d. Abbot* v. *Parsons* (1765), 3 Burr. 1794 ; *Allen* v. *Allen* (1842), 2 Dr. & War. 307), except that he can validly appoint an agent to do any specific act or acts which would legally bind him (*Ewer* v. *Jones* (1846), 9 Q.B. 623). For instance, by s. 21 of the L.P.A. 1925 a married infant is empowered to give valid receipts for all income to which he may be entitled as if the infant were of full age, and so he could appoint an agent to do this on his behalf.

An infant cannot appoint an agent to make a disposition of his property so as to bind him irrevocably ; a disposition by an agent for an infant is voidable just as a disposition by the infant himself would be, so long as it is avoided within a reasonable time after attaining full age (*per* Lord Denning, M.R., in *G (A)* v. *G (T)* [1970] 2 Q.B. 643).

An infant could, before 1926, be *appointed* an attorney (Co. Litt. 52a), and could bind his principal (*Watkins* v. *Vince* (1818), 2 Stark. 368 ; *Re D'Angibau* (1880), 15 Ch. D. 228, 246). He could convey the legal estate in land under a power given to him to sell and convey, provided he had no interest himself in the property sold (*King* v. *Bellord* (1863), 1 H. & M. 343, at p. 347).

Statutory form of general power.—Schedule 1 to the 1971 Act sets out a form of general power of attorney (see below). If that form or one to the like effect is used, it will operate to confer on the donee(s) " authority to do on behalf of the donor anything which he can lawfully do by an attorney " (s. 10 (1) of the 1971 Act). This does *not* apply, however, to any functions which the donor has as a trustee or personal representative or as a tenant for life or statutory owner within the S.L.A. 1925 (s. 10 (2) of the 1971 Act). The Law Commission included these provisions in its recommendations to encourage greater standardisation of powers of attorney. The simple form in Sched. 1 is as follows :—

" FORM OF GENERAL POWER OF ATTORNEY FOR PURPOSES OF SECTION 10

THIS GENERAL POWER OF ATTORNEY is made this   day of by AB of

I appoint CD of

[*or* CD of

and EF of

jointly *or* jointly and severally] to be my attorney[s] in accordance with section 10 of the Powers of Attorney Act 1971.

IN WITNESS etc.,   "

Registration.—On presentation for registration of an instrument executed by an attorney either (i) the original power or a certified copy or (ii) a document complying with the Evidence and Powers of Attorney Act, 1940, s. 4, must be lodged. If the transaction was not completed within one year of the coming into operation of the power there must be lodged a statutory declaration by the person dealing with the donor of the power that the declarant did not at completion know of revocation of the power or the occurrence of any event (such as death, bankruptcy or other incapacity of the donor) which had the effect of revoking the power. Similarly if it was expressed to be irrevocable and to be given by way of security the declaration must be that at completion the declarant did not know that the power was not given by way of security nor that the power had been revoked by the donor acting with the consent of the donee (Land Registration (Powers of Attorney) Rules, 1971).

BANKRUPTS

Bankruptcy of tenant for life under S.L.A. 1925, see *post*, p. 742.

Re-entry on bankruptcy of lessee, see *post*, p. 893.

Bankrupt's entailed interests in land, see *post*, p. 439.

Receiving order, adjudication and appointment of trustee.—A receiving order has not the effect of divesting the debtor's property (*Rhodes* v. *Dawson* (1886), 16 Q.B.D. 548 ; *Re Sartoris* [1892] 1 Ch. 11) ; until adjudication the property remains vested in the bankrupt (*Re Smith, ex parte Mason* [1893] 1 Q.B. 323 ; Bankruptcy Act, 1914, s. 53 (1)). On adjudication the bankrupt's *own* property vested in the official receiver, and continues in him until a trustee is appointed (*ibid.*, s. 53 (1), (2), (3) ; L.P.A. 1925, s. 7 (3) ; *Rhodes* v. *Dawson, ante*) ; and he has power to sell (*Turquand* v. *Board of Trade* (1886), 11 App. Cas. 286).

On the appointment of a trustee, the bankrupt's *own* property forthwith vests in such trustee without any conveyance as from the date of the certificate given by the Department of Trade and Industry (Bankruptcy

Act, 1914, ss. 19 (4), 53 (3)). The title of the trustee relates back to the time of the act of bankruptcy on which the receiving order was made, or, if there are several acts proved, to the time of the first of the acts proved to have been committed within three months preceding the date of presentation of the petition (*ibid.*, s. 37 ; *Re Foulds ; ex parte Learoyd* (1878), 10 Ch. D. 3). The certificate of the Department of Trade and Industry is conclusive evidence of the appointment (Bankruptcy Act, 1914, ss. 19 (4), 143) ; it is deemed to be a conveyance or assignment of property, and, so far as it affects land in Yorkshire, required registration in the local deeds registry (*ibid.*, s. 53 (4)), as it passes a legal estate (L.P.A. 1925, s. 11 ; see *post*, p. 612). During any vacancy in the office of trustee the official receiver will act as trustee (Bankruptcy Act, 1914, s. 78 (4)).

A purchaser from a trustee should, therefore, require proof of adjudication. This is conclusively proved by production of a copy of the *London Gazette* containing a notice thereof (Bankruptcy Act, 1914, s. 137), but it is customary to accept an office copy of the order of adjudication. The purchaser should also call for production of the certificate of the trustee's appointment issued by the Department of Trade and Industry.

When, instead of an order of adjudication, a composition or scheme of arrangement is approved by the court, and a trustee appointed to manage the debtor's property, the property vests in such trustee, and he has the same powers as a trustee in bankruptcy (*ibid.*, s. 16 (17), (18)). In the absence of fraud a certificate of the official receiver that a scheme has been accepted and approved is conclusive (*ibid.*, s. 16 (14)). If the court approves a composition after adjudication, it may make an order annulling the bankruptcy and vesting the property in the bankrupt or such other person as the court may appoint, on such conditions as the court may declare (*ibid.*, s. 21 (2)).

Administration order.— An order for administration in bankruptcy of a deceased debtor's estate vests the property in the official receiver as trustee, with power to realise, until the appointment of a trustee by the creditors (Bankruptcy Act, 1914, s. 130 (4)). This section was repealed by the A.E.A. 1925, but has been revived by the Expiring Laws Act, 1925.

Settled land.—The *legal estate* in settled land does not vest in the trustee in bankruptcy of an estate owner unless and until the estate owner becomes absolutely and beneficially entitled to the settled land free from all limitations, powers and charges taking effect under the settlement (S.L.A. 1925, s. 103). The *equitable* or beneficial interest of the bankrupt, on the other hand, passes to the trustee.

Bankrupt's trust property.—Property held by a bankrupt on trust for any other person does not pass to the trustee (Bankruptcy Act, 1914, s. 38). The exemption applies to *implied* as well as to *express* trusts (*Re Whitehead* (1885), 14 Q.B.D. 419). As to this exemption, Roxburgh, J., has said : " The words ' on trust for any other person,' in my judgment, are of very wide import . . . If it can be said of any asset that though the title is in the bankrupt, a beneficial interest therein resides in some person other than the bankrupt, even though the bankrupt himself may also have a beneficial interest therein, the asset does not vest in the trustee [in bankruptcy], though the beneficial interest, if any, which the bankrupt himself has would vest in the trustee [in bankruptcy] " (*Re a Solicitor* [1952] 1 Ch. 328, at p. 332).

The decision of the Court of Appeal in *St. Thomas' Hospital Governors* v. *Richardson* [1910] 1 K.B. 271, which is often cited to the contrary was not, in fact, cited to Roxburgh, J., and should be distinguished on the ground that the circumstances there considered were of a trustee having either the entire or at least a substantial priority of beneficial interest (see *per* Farwell, L.J., at p. 284 ; compare *Morgan* v. *Swansea U.D.S.A.* (1878), 9 Ch. D. 582, and *Re Caine's Mortgage Trusts* [1918] W.N. 370 ; see further *Solicitors' Journal*, vol. 109, p. 263 *et seq.*).

Bankruptcy renders a person " unfit " to continue to act as a trustee within the meaning of s. 36 (1) of the T.A. 1925 (*Re Roche* (1842), 2 Dr. & War. 287 ; *Re Hopkins* (1881), 19 Ch. D. 61, at p. 63) ; and, therefore, another trustee can be appointed in his place (see *post*, p. 790). The court can, if it thinks fit, remove a bankrupt trustee from his trusteeship (whether he consents or not), and appoint another trustee in his place, and vest the property in such new trustee (T.A. 1925, ss. 41, 44, 49 ; see *post*, p. 799). If the bankrupt is one of several trustees he remains in office until he is removed, for instance, pursuant to the T.A. 1925, s. 36 (1) (*b*). Consequently, it seems that if one of two or more persons who are entitled as joint tenants upon trust for sale for themselves (either as joint tenants or tenants in common) should become bankrupt he will remain one of the trustees although his equitable interest will pass to the trustee.

Disclaimer of property.—The Bankruptcy Act, 1914, s. 54, permits the trustee in bankruptcy to disclaim onerous property, but this rarely applies to freehold land. Although disclaimer can be carried out if the land is burdened with onerous covenants, restrictive covenants rarely will so reduce the value as to justify disclaimer. In *Re Mercer and Moore* (1880), 14 Ch. D. 287, the land was subject to a fee farm rent and restrictive covenants and disclaimer was permitted on these accounts but not because there was also a charge by equitable mortgage.

If the owner enters into a *contract* to sell freeholds or leaseholds and becomes bankrupt, the trustee cannot disclaim such contract unless he is able to, and in fact, disclaims the freehold or leasehold interest, as contracts of sale are not themselves capable of being disclaimed by virtue of s. 54 of the Bankruptcy Act, 1914. For the disclaimer would have the effect, not of getting rid of burdensome property in the hands of the bankrupt and of the trustee representing him, but of divesting from a purchaser an interest which had already passed to him (*Re Bastable* [1901] 2 K.B. 518 ; *Pearce* v. *Bastable's Trustee in Bankruptcy* [1901] 2 Ch. 122).

A trustee cannot disclaim a lease without the leave of the court, except in the cases prescribed by general rule 278 of the Bankruptcy Rules, 1952 (Bankruptcy Act, 1914, s. 54 (3)). See further, chapter on Leases, *post*, p. 839. If the trustee disclaims the whole lease then the purchaser can apply for an order under s. 54 of the Bankruptcy Act, 1914, vesting the property in him on terms ; if he does not disclaim, the purchaser can compel specific performance of the contract (*Pearce* v. *Bastable's Trustee, ante*).

A disclaimer under s. 54 must be in writing and signed by the trustee ; a disclaimer signed by his solicitor would not be sufficient (*Wilson* v. *Wallani* (1880), 5 Ex. D. 155).

Purchase from an insolvent before receiving order.—It is provided by s. 37 (1) of the Bankruptcy Act, 1914, that the bankruptcy of a debtor is deemed to have relation back to and to commence at the time of the act of bankruptcy being committed on which a receiving order is made against him, or, if the bankrupt is proved to have committed more acts of bankruptcy than one, to have relation back to and to commence at the time of the first of the acts of bankruptcy proved to have been committed by the bankrupt *within three months next preceding the date of the presentation of the bankruptcy petition.*

Nevertheless, the effect of the Bankruptcy Act, 1914, s. 45, is that, subject to the provisions of the Act as to the avoidance of certain settlements, assignments and preferences, nothing in the Act is to invalidate any conveyance or assignment by the bankrupt, or any contract, dealing or transaction by or with the bankrupt *bona fide* for valuable consideration, *before the date of the receiving order,* provided that the purchaser had no notice of any available act of bankruptcy committed by the bankrupt. The section applies although the transaction itself may be an act of bankruptcy (*Shears* v. *Goddard* [1896] 1 Q.B. 406), but not if the transaction was fraudulent on the part of the person dealing with the bankrupt. For instance, it was held in *Re Jukes* [1902] 2 K.B. 58 that a similar section would not protect a creditor who took over the whole of the debtor's property in satisfaction of a past debt, knowing that there were other creditors. See also *Re Simms* [1930] 2 Ch. 22. It has been held that, although a fraudulent assignment, amounting to an act of bankruptcy by the bankrupt, to an assignee without notice is protected by s. 45, this protection does not extend to a *bona fide* assignee from an original assignee who had notice, nor to any subsequent assignee even if he were both *bona fide* and without notice (*Re Gunsbourg* [1920] 2 K.B. 426).

The result of ss. 37 (1) and 45 is that if *A* purchases from *B* (who afterwards becomes bankrupt), for valuable consideration, *bona fide* and without notice of any available act of bankruptcy committed by *B*, the purchaser will get a good title. Even if *A* had notice of an act of bankruptcy, but allowed three months from the date of such act to pass before taking a conveyance, the conveyance would be good, providing that no proceedings had, in the meantime, been commenced for the purpose of making *B* a bankrupt. The point occurs when a purchase is made from a trustee of a deed of assignment for the benefit of creditors. A voluntary settlement also may be an act of bankruptcy (Bankruptcy Act, 1914, s. 42 (1) ; see p. 252).

It is provided by s. 5 (8) of the L.C.A. 1972 that a petition in bankruptcy will not bind a purchaser of a legal estate in good faith for money or money's worth, *without notice of an available act of bankruptcy,* unless it is for the time being registered as a pending action ; by subs. (9), that as respects any transfer or creation of a legal estate, a petition in bankruptcy which is not for the time being registered as a pending action *shall not be notice or evidence of any act of bankruptcy therein alleged ;* and by s. 6 (6) of the same Act, that the title of a trustee in bankruptcy acquired after 1925 shall be void as against a purchaser of a legal estate *in good faith* for money or money's worth *without notice of an available act of bankruptcy* claiming under a conveyance made *after the date of registration* of the petition in bankruptcy, unless, at the date of the conveyance, either the registration of the petition is in force, or a receiving order is registered.

Purchase from an insolvent after receiving order.—Although the bankrupt's property remains vested in him until adjudication, the effect of a receiving order is to prevent him from dealing with it even in favour of a person who has no notice of the bankruptcy. But it is provided by s. 6 (5) of the L.C.A. 1972 that a receiving order in bankruptcy shall be void as against a purchaser of the legal estate in land in good faith, for money or money's worth, *without notice of an available act of bankruptcy*, unless it is registered in the register of writs and orders at the Land Registry. See also L.C.A. 1972, s. 6 (6), mentioned in the last paragraph.

It is also important to note that under s. 8 of the L.C.A. 1972 the registration of receiving orders and petitions in bankruptcy ceases to have effect at the expiration of five years from the date of registration, or if renewed, at the expiration of five years from the date of renewal. The result of this is that for this purpose a purchaser of land need only search for five years.

A trustee in bankruptcy can give a good receipt for purchase-money as he is " a trust corporation " by virtue of the Law of Property (Amendment) Act, 1926.

Property acquired after adjudication.—Property acquired by a bankrupt after adjudication, but before discharge, vests in the trustee (Bankruptcy Act, 1914, s. 38 ; *Re Pascoe* [1944] Ch. 219). But the Bankruptcy Act, 1914, s. 47 (1), provides that all transactions by a bankrupt with any person dealing with him *bona fide* and for value (see *Re Bennett* [1907] 1 K.B. 149), in respect of property, whether real or personal, *acquired by the bankrupt after the adjudication*, will, if completed before any intervention by the trustee, be valid against the trustee, and any estate or interest in such property which by virtue of the Act was vested in the trustee will determine and pass in such a manner and to such extent as may be required for giving effect to any such transaction. The section applies (although it does not state this specifically) whether or not the purchaser has notice of the prior act of bankruptcy (*Hosack* v. *Robins* (*No.* 2) [1918] 2 Ch. 339). But the view was expressed in the *Law Journal*, vol. 67, p. 72, that as the subsection does not contain the words '' whether with or without knowledge of the bankruptcy," it is doubtful whether a person with knowledge of the bankruptcy can be said to be dealing with the bankrupt *bona fide* within the section. The section enacts the rule known as that in *Cohen* v. *Mitchell* (1890), 25 Q.B.D. 262, which was formerly expressed in terms including these words. The late author of this book submitted that notice is immaterial so long as the trustee has not intervened. If such submission is correct, it is unnecessary to consider whether or not registration of the petition or receiving order would, under the L.P.A. 1925, s. 198, be notice for this purpose. It may be noted that in *Dyster* v. *Randall and Sons* [1926] Ch. 932, Lawrence, J., stated (at p. 940) that the subsection applies whether or not the parties dealing with the bankrupt have knowledge of the bankruptcy, and quoted *Cohen* v. *Mitchell*, *ante*, in support.

When once the trustee has intervened, he will not be allowed to withdraw (*Hill* v. *Settle* [1917] 1 Ch. 319).

Purchaser's act of bankruptcy.—The commission of an act of bankruptcy by a purchaser, after contract but before the date fixed for completion, cannot be treated by the vendor as an anticipatory breach entitling him to repudiate the contract (*Jennings' Trustee* v. *King* [1952] 1 Ch. 899). Even after the day fixed for completion the vendor, in such a case, may not treat the contract as though time were of its essence and so he may not rescind on account of the purchaser's failure to complete on the due date (*ibid.*). The vendor has two alternatives. First, he may wait for three months after the act of bankruptcy ; if no petition is presented within that time he may safely complete, as the act of bankruptcy will no longer be available to found a petition. Secondly, he may, when the day fixed for completion has passed, petition himself and serve on the trustee, when appointed, a notice to elect whether to disclaim or adopt the contract.

If, in such a case, time had been of the essence, apparently the vendor might have repudiated the contract (*Powell* v. *Marshall, Parkes & Co.* [1899] 1 Q.B. 710, in which the act of bankruptcy was that of the vendor).

Disclaimer of contract to purchase.—The trustee in bankruptcy has power to disclaim the contract under s. 54 of the Bankruptcy Act, 1914, if he considers it an unprofitable contract, and he is allowed twelve months after his appointment to make up his mind. He may disclaim notwithstanding that he has endeavoured to sell or has taken possession of the property or exercised any act of ownership in relation thereto. But the vendor can compel the trustee to elect either to proceed or to disclaim by first giving him notice, for it is provided by s. 54 (4) that a trustee shall not be entitled to disclaim in any case where an application in writing has been made to him to decide whether he will disclaim or not, and he has, for a period of twenty-eight days or such extended period as the court may allow, declined or neglected to give notice whether he disclaims or not; and, if he does not within that period in fact disclaim, he will be deemed to have adopted the contract.

Specific performance will not be enforced against the trustee in bankruptcy of a purchaser without his consent (*Holloway* v. *York* (1877), 25 W.R. 627 ; *Pearce* v. *Bastable's Trustee in Bankruptcy* [1901] 2 Ch. 122, 125). If the trustee disclaims or fails to pay the full amount of the purchase-money the vendor can retain the deposit (*Re Barrell* (1875), L.R. 10 Ch. 512).

Discharge and annulment.—The bankrupt is entitled to any property acquired by or devolving on him after his discharge (*Re Croom ; England* v. *Provincial Assets Co., Ltd.* [1891] 1 Ch. 695) ; but such discharge does not divest any property already vested in the trustee. If a lease is not disclaimed by the trustee but the bankrupt remains in possession after his discharge the landlord can recover from the bankrupt rent accruing after the discharge (*Metropolis Estates Co., Ltd.* v. *Wilde* [1940] 2 K.B. 536).

On annulment of the bankruptcy, the property of the bankrupt vests in the person appointed by the court, or in default, reverts to the bankrupt on such conditions, if any, as the court orders (Bankruptcy Act, 1914, ss. 21 (2) and 29 (2)). If the court makes no order the property revests in the bankrupt (*Flower* v. *Lyme Regis Corporation* [1921] 1 K.B. 488).

Purchase by member of committee of inspection.—Although no member of the committee of inspection may purchase the bankrupt's property without leave of the court (Bankruptcy Rules, 1952, r. 349), it would seem that the partner of a member may purchase for his own benefit (*Re Gallard* [1897] 2 Q.B. 8). As to when leave will be given, see *Re Spink, ex parte Slater* (*No.* 2) (1913), 108 L.T. 811.

Effect of bankruptcy on a voluntary settlement or conveyance.—By the Bankruptcy Act, 1914, s. 42 (1), any settlement (the word " settlement " includes any conveyance or transfer) of property is declared *void*, as against the trustee in bankruptcy of the settlor, if the settlor becomes bankrupt within two years after the date of the settlement, and also if he becomes bankrupt within ten years of that date, *unless* the parties claiming under the settlement can prove that the settlor was, at the time of making the settlement, able to pay all his debts without the aid of the property comprised therein, and that the interests of the settlor in such property passed to the trustee of such settlement on the execution thereof. There are the following exceptions to the operation of s. 42 (1) :—

(1) a marriage settlement made before and in consideration of marriage ;

(2) a settlement in favour of the wife or children of the settlor, if of property of the settlor coming to him after marriage in right of his wife ; and

(3) a conveyance or mortgage in favour of *a purchaser* or incumbrancer *in good faith* and for valuable consideration.

It was decided in *Re Mathieson* [1927] 1 Ch. 283 that the exercise by a bankrupt in favour of his wife of a general power of appointment which he had under a marriage settlement was *not* " a settlement of property " within the subsection, as the property appointed was not available for paying the debts of the " settlor " at the time of its execution. In *Re Schebsman* [1944] Ch. 83 it had been agreed that *S* should cease to be employed by a company and should not compete with it, and, in consideration, the company should make certain payments to the wife and daughter of *S*. On the bankruptcy of *S*, it was held that the arrangement did *not* amount to a settlement within s. 42 (1).

On the other hand, in *Re A Debtor, ex parte The Official Receiver* [1965] 1 W.L.R. 1498, where the bankrupt had provided the whole of the purchase price of a house, apart from a substantial mortgage advance, which was conveyed to his wife there was held to be a settlement notwithstanding that it was she alone who had entered into the contract to purchase and who had charged the house by way of legal mortgage. Stamp, J., said that s. 42 (1) must be construed in a commercial sense and that he could not hold that the section " may be defeated by the conveyancing machinery adopted for carrying out a transaction that would otherwise be within it."

In *Shrager* v. *March* [1908] A.C. 402, the settlement was effected by the settlor declaring himself a trustee of the property, and it was held that although there was no transfer of the legal estate, yet the interest of the settlor had passed to the trustee of the settlement within the meaning of the closing words of the subsection.

In *Re Bower Williams* [1927] 1 Ch. 441, certain shares devolved on the husband by reason of his wife dying intestate, and it was held that such shares had accrued to him " in right of his wife " within the meaning of the words in the second exception.

A person is *a purchaser in good faith* within the meaning of the third exception if he himself acts in good faith, and it is not necessary that both parties should so act (*Mackintosh* v. *Pagose* [1895] 1 Ch. 505). The release of a right or the compromise of a claim may suffice to constitute a person " a purchaser " for this purpose (*Re Pope, ex parte Dicksee* [1908] 2 K.B. 169 ; *Re Collins* (1914), 112 L.T. 87 ; *Re Pole* [1931] 2 Ch. 174). So, an agreement to accept the liability of a mortgage debt and interest on property assigned, and to indemnify the assignor, will also make the assignee a " purchaser " (*Re Charters* [1923] B. & C.R. 94). But on an assignment of leaseholds (otherwise voluntary) the liability of the volunteer to pay the rent and perform the covenants is not sufficient to bring the case within the third exception (*Ex parte Hillman* (1879), 10 Ch. D. 622). And in *Re a Debtor, ante,* Stamp, J., said that in this third exception the word " purchaser " means a buyer in the ordinary commercial sense and not a purchaser in the legal sense of the word. Consequently, the valuable consideration within the meaning of the exception is a consideration moving to the bankrupt which replaces the property extracted from his creditors. Therefore, in the case, the wife was held not to have given consideration within the exception by entering into the mortgage.

The word " *void* " in the above subsection is construed as meaning " voidable " ; further, the subsection does not say that such settlements are to be void generally, but only against the trustee in bankruptcy. A settlement cannot be void against a trustee until there is in existence a trustee against whom it can be void (*Re Carter and Kenderdine's Contract* [1897] 1 Ch. 776). Therefore, a voluntary settlement is not void as against the settlor's trustee in bankruptcy from the date of the settlement, but only from the date when the title of the trustee accrues. Consequently, if before that date (or after that date, *Re Hart, ex parte Green* [1912] 3 K.B. 6) there has been a *bona fide* sale for value of the property to a purchaser, whether from the trustees of the settlement or the volunteers claiming under it, the purchaser will have a good title against the trustee (*Re Brall* [1893] 2 Q.B. 381 ; *Re Carter and Kenderdine, ante*) unless he has notice of the bankruptcy (*Re Shrager* (1913), 108 L.T. 346). Registration under the L.C.A. 1972 of a petition or receiving order would give such notice (L.P.A. 1925, s. 198) and so, on a purchase from one who acquired under a voluntary settlement which is still liable to be set aside it is most important to search up to date against the name of the donor.

The subsection only makes the settlement *void* as against the trustee in bankruptcy. It does not *pass* the property to the trustee. It merely puts things in the position they would have been in if the settlement had not been made, and the property would, therefore, pass to persons (if any) entitled subject to the settlement (*Sanguinetti* v. *Stuckey's Bank* [1895] 1 Ch. 176 ; approved in *Re Farnham* [1895] 2 Ch. 799).

Effect of bankruptcy on covenants in consideration of marriage.— By the Bankruptcy Act, 1914, s. 42 (2), it is provided that any covenant or contract made by a settlor *in consideration of marriage,* either for the future payment of money for the benefit of the settlor's wife or husband, or children, or for the future settlement on or for the settlor's wife or husband or children, of property, *wherein the settlor had not at the date of the marriage any estate or interest* (not being property in right of the settlor's wife or husband), will, if the settlor is adjudged bankrupt, *and the covenant or contract has not then been executed,* be void against the trustee in bankruptcy, except for the purpose of claiming a dividend, but any such claim to dividend will be postponed until all claims of the other creditors for valuable consideration in money have been satisfied.

It is also provided by subs. (3) of the same section that, *if the covenant or contract has been executed,* any payment of money (not being payment of premiums on a policy of life assurance) or transfer of property will be void against the trustee in bankruptcy of the settlor, unless—

(a) the payment or transfer was made more than two years before the date of the commencement of the bankruptcy ;

(b) at the date of the payment or transfer the settlor was able to pay all his debts without the aid of the money so paid or property transferred ;

(c) the payment or transfer was made in pursuance of a covenant or contract to pay or transfer money or property expected to come to the settlor from or on the death of a particular person named in the covenant or contract, and was made within three months after the money or property came into the possession or under the control of the settlor.

The fact that the payment or transfer is declared void does not prevent the parties claiming for dividend.

As to what will amount to a sufficient equitable transfer of property so as to be protected on the ground that the covenant or contract was executed more than two years before the settlor was adjudged bankrupt, see *Re Lind* [1915] 2 Ch. 345 ; *Re Dent* [1923] 1 Ch. 113.

Effect of bankruptcy on settlements generally.—If property settled by a husband was acquired through his wife, the bankruptcy of the husband will not uspet it. In *Mackintosh* v. *Pogose* [1895] 1 Ch. 505, a wife allowed her separate property to be used for the purposes of her husband's business, as a loan. The husband settled part of the property upon trust under which he took a life interest, with a proviso for cesser on his bankruptcy. The husband having become bankrupt, in an action by the trustee in bankruptcy, it was held that the bankruptcy did not upset the settlement, and that the proviso for cesser was operative.

Although a person will not be allowed to settle his own property on himself until bankruptcy and then over, he may settle his property on himself for life or until he shall assign, charge or do some act by which the property becomes vested in some other person, and then over. For instance, in a case where a settlement contained a somewhat similar provision, with a gift over to the wife, and a judgment creditor obtained the appointment of a receiver of the income, it was held that the gift over to the wife took effect. Shortly after the appointment of the receiver the husband became bankrupt, but the trustee in bankruptcy did not succeed in his claim, because at the date of the bankruptcy the settlor had no interest, such interest having come to an end on the appointment of the receiver (*Re Detmold* (1889), 40 Ch. D. 585). See also *Re Burroughs-Fowler* [1916] 2 Ch. 251, a case where the interest was forfeitable *on bankruptcy*, and the trustee in bankruptcy on this ground, therefore, succeeded in his claim.

Conveyances in fraud of creditors or purchasers.—Section 172 of the L.P.A. 1925 provides that conveyances made with intent to defraud creditors shall be voidable at the instance of any person prejudiced, but the section does not extend to any estate or interest conveyed for value and in good faith or upon good consideration and in good faith to any person not having, at the time of the conveyance, notice of the intent to defraud creditors. " Good " consideration is normally taken to exist where the conveyance is to a near relative towards whom the grantor is assumed to have natural love and affection, or where there is some moral duty, as in a conveyance to a charity (*Sharington* v. *Strotton* (1565), 1 Plowd. 298). However, it was clearly assumed in *Re Eicholz* [1959] Ch. 708 that nothing but valuable consideration (e.g. money or marriage) could amount to good consideration within the L.P.A. 1925, s. 172. If the conveyance was voluntary the fact that it necessarily resulted in defeating creditors is sufficient proof that it was so intended (*Freeman* v. *Pope* (1870), L.R. 5 Ch. 538). The section is of general application and is not limited to cases where the person conveying subsequently becomes bankrupt ; it is mentioned here for convenience but discussed more fully *ante*, p. 117. See also the similar provisions of s. 173 of the L.P.A. 1925, dealt with in the same place, under which any *voluntary* disposition of land made with intent to defraud a subsequent purchaser is voidable at the instance of that purchaser.

By the Bankruptcy Act, 1914, s. 44 (1), as amended by the Companies Act, 1947, s. 115 (3), every conveyance or transfer of property, or charge thereon made by any person unable to pay his debts as they become due from his own money in favour of any creditor, or of any person in trust for any creditor, with a view to giving such creditor, or any surety or guarantor for the debt due to such creditor, a preference over the other creditors, will, if the person making the same is adjudged bankrupt on a bankruptcy petition presented within six months after the date of making the same, be deemed fraudulent and void as against the trustee in the bankruptcy. By subs. (2) it is provided that the section is not to affect the rights of any person making title in good faith and for valuable consideration through or under a creditor of the bankrupt. The phrase " with a view to giving " refers to the intention of the debtor, which is a matter of fact (*Re Eric Holmes* (*Property*), *Limited* [1965] Ch. 1052).

A trustee, who had misappropriated trust funds, by a deed executed two days before a receiving order was made against him, conveyed an estate upon trust to raise money thereon, with a view to it being applied in making good the breaches of trust committed by him in respect of the trust estates mentioned in the deed. He executed this deed with the object of *shielding himself* as far as possible from liability to any proceedings to which he might be exposed by reason of the breaches of trust referred to in the deed, and not with the object of giving a preference. The execution of the deed was not communicated to the *cestuis que trust*. It was held that the deed was not a fraudulent preference, and that it was binding on the trustee in bankruptcy of the grantor (*Sharp* v. *Jackson* [1899] A.C. 419).

Bankruptcy of mortgagor.—A mortgagee may give the trustee notice in writing *setting a value on his security* and requiring him to elect whether he will or will not exercise his power of redeeming the security or requiring it to be realised, and if the trustee does not within six months signify his election to exercise his power, he will not be entitled to exercise it ; and the equity of redemption or any other interest in the property comprised in the security which is vested in the trustee will thereupon vest in the mortgagee, *and the amount of his debt will be reduced by the amount at which the security has been valued* (Bankruptcy Act, 1914, Sched. 2, para. 13 (c)). It is the italicised words of the sub-paragraph which make it a condition of giving notice that the mortgagee shall first set a value on his security and give notice thereof to the trustee. A mortgagee cannot, when the mortgage deed has been executed after 1925, exercise a power of sale on the ground that the mortgagor has committed an act of bankruptcy or been adjudged bankrupt, without leave of the court (L.P.A. 1925, s. 110).

If leaseholds have been mortgaged by the bankrupt and the trustee should disclaim the lease, the lessor will be entitled to an order under s. 54 of the Bankruptcy Act, 1914, declaring that, unless the mortgagee accepts an order vesting the property in him subject to the same liabilities as the bankrupt was liable to at the date of the bankruptcy petition, or if the court thinks fit, subject only to the same liabilities and obligations as if the lease had been assigned to him at that date, he will lose his security (*Re Baker ; ex parte Lupton* [1901] 2 K.B. 628 ; *Re Holmes ; ex parte Ashworth* [1908] 2 K.B. 816). An order of court vesting disclaimed property is exempt from stamp duty.

Bankruptcy of proprietor of registered land.—As soon as practicable after registration of a petition in bankruptcy under the L.C.A. 1972 (as to which, see *post*, p. 605), the registrar must register a creditors' notice against the title of any proprietor of any registered land or charge which appears to be affected (L.R.A. 1925, s. 61 (1)), such entry being made in the proprietorship register (L.R.R. 1925, r. 179). Such a notice protects the rights of creditors, and, unless cancelled in the meantime, remains in force until a bankruptcy inhibition is registered or the trustee in bankruptcy is registered as proprietor (*ibid.*). Purchasers and others dealing in registered land are protected by the rule that, until a creditors' notice is registered, a bankruptcy petition does not, as respects any registered disposition for money or money's worth of any registered land or charge, give notice of any act of bankruptcy alleged therein (L.R.A. 1925, s. 61 (2)). As soon as practicable after registration of a receiving order under the L.C.A. 1972 (as to which, see *post*, p. 607), the registrar must enter a bankruptcy inhibition against the title of any proprietor of any registered land or charge which appears to be affected (L.R.A. 1925, s. 61 (3)), and such entry is also made in the proprietorship register (L.R.R. 1925, r. 180). The effect of entry of a bankruptcy inhibition is that no dealing affecting the registered land or charge of the proprietor, other than the registration of the trustee in bankruptcy, may be entered on the register until the inhibition is vacated, but this rule operates, of course, without prejudice to dealings with or in right of interests or charges having priority over the estate or charge of the bankrupt proprietor (L.R.A. 1925, s. 61 (4)).

On the adjudication in bankruptcy of the proprietor of registered land or a charge, his registered estate or interest, *if belonging to him beneficially*, and whether acquired before or after the date of adjudication, vests in the trustee in bankruptcy in accordance with the Bankruptcy Act, 1914, s. 53, as to which see *ante*, p. 247 (L.R.A. 1925, s. 61 (5)). On production of evidence that the land or charge is part of the property of the bankrupt divisible among his creditors, the trustee is entitled to be registered as proprietor in his place and the official receiver is entitled to be registered pending appointment of a trustee (L.R.A. 1925, s. 42 (1)). The official receiver may be registered on production of an office copy of the adjudication order together with a certificate signed by the official receiver that the registered land or charge is part of the property of the bankrupt divisible among his creditors ; if some other person is subsequently appointed trustee, such person may be registered as proprietor in place of the official receiver on production of an office copy of the certificate by the Department of Trade and Industry of his appointment as trustee (L.R.R. 1925, rr. 174, 175). Where, however, the official receiver has not been registered as proprietor, the trustee may be registered on production of office copies of the adjudication order and of the certificate of the appointment of the trustee, with a certificate signed by the trustee that the land or charge is part of the property of the bankrupt divisible amongst his creditors (L.R.R. 1925, r. 176). A note of the capacity in which the official receiver or trustee holds is added in the register (L.R.R. 1925, r. 177).

If the trustee disclaims a registered lease under the Bankruptcy Act, 1914, s. 54, as to which, see *post*, p. 839, and an order is made vesting the lease

9

in any person, the order will direct the alteration of the register, and, on being served with such order, the registrar must alter the register accordingly (L.R.A. 1925, s. 42 (2)).

A purchaser in good faith for money or money's worth without notice of an available act of bankruptcy, or of a receiving order or adjudication, who is registered as proprietor, obtains a good title as against the trustee in bankruptcy, unless a creditors' notice or bankruptcy inhibition was registered, notwithstanding that an available act of bankruptcy has been committed by the person making the disposition (L.R.A. 1925, s. 61 (6)). By the Bankruptcy Act, 1914, s. 47 (*ante*, p. 251), all transactions by a bankrupt with any person dealing with him *bona fide* and for value, in respect of property acquired by the bankrupt *after* adjudication, will, if completed before any intervention by the trustee, be valid against the trustee. The L.R.A. 1925, s. 61 (8), provides that nothing in that section prejudicially affects a registered disposition of any registered land or charge acquired by the bankrupt after adjudication which would have been valid by virtue of the Bankruptcy Act, 1914, s. 47, if the land or charge had not been registered, *if neither a creditors' notice nor a bankruptcy inhibition is registered against the bankrupt proprietor.*

The registrar has a discretion to take the action he thinks advisable after making such inquiry and giving such notices as he deems necessary, when he receives notice of such matters as the vacation of registration of a bankruptcy petition, or rescission of a receiving order, or annulment of the bankruptcy (L.R.R. 1925, r. 181). Provision is made for registration of the official receiver if a trustee in bankruptcy vacates office, and a new trustee in bankruptcy may be registered on production of an office copy of the certificate of his appointment (L.R.R. 1925, r. 183). As to the divesting of the estate of the official receiver or a trustee, see L.R.R. 1925, r. 184.

Where a scheme of arrangement has been approved by the court, the official receiver or other trustee may be registered as proprietor of any registered land or charge vested in the trustee under the provisions thereof, upon production of an office copy of the scheme, a certificate of the official receiver or other trustee that the registered land or charge was part of the property vested in him under the provisions of the scheme, and, in the case of a trustee other than the official receiver, an office copy of the certificate by the Department of Trade and Industry of his appointment as trustee (L.R.R. 1925, r. 178).

There is no express provision in the L.R.A. 1925 for the procedure on execution of a deed of arrangement under the Deeds of Arrangement Act, 1914 (as to which, see *post*, p. 608), other than an incidental reference in s. 59 (1). Most such deeds except from any immediate conveyance property the title to which is registered, declare that registered property shall be held by the debtor in trust for the trustee and require him to execute any necessary documents. The trustee under the deed should apply for entry of a caution in order that the debtor shall not deal with the property without notice to the trustee. In order that the trustee may be registered as proprietor the debtor should execute a transfer in his favour which should be lodged at the registry with (i) the land or charge certificate, and (ii) the deed of assignment (which will be returned) and a certified copy. Evidence, in the form of an endorsement on the deed or a certificate by the trustee, must be provided that the deed has been duly registered under s. 2 of the 1914 Act with the registrar at the Department of Trade and Industry. In proof that requisite assents to the deed have been given there should be lodged either an office copy of the statutory declaration filed with the registrar of the Department of Trade and Industry or a certificate in writing of the trustee. It is also necessary to give a certificate of the value of the registered property and pay the *ad valorem* fee.

BUILDING SOCIETIES

As to mortgages generally, see chapter on this subject, *post*, p. 970.

Mortgage by personal representatives.—A mortgage by personal representatives to a building society is perfectly good to the extent of the money actually advanced. The question came before the court in *Thorne* v. *Thorne* [1893] 3 Ch. 196, where an executor obtained an advance from a building society for the purpose of the administration of the estate. The deed contained a covenant by him to pay principal and interest and all subscriptions, fines, etc., and a provision that the mortgage should not be redeemed except on payment of all other mortgages made by him to the society. It was held that as regards the estate of the testator no liability in respect of the shares could be enforced, and the consolidation clause was void, but that the mortgage was good to the extent of the money actually advanced, together with reasonable interest.

Power to take collateral security.—A builder or other person may enter into an agreement (known as a "pooling agreement") with a building society that the society should advance on mortgage to purchasers of houses a high proportion of the value of the houses, on the vendor depositing a sum of money with the building society by way of guarantee that the purchasers will meet their obligations under the mortgages. In *Halifax Building Society* v. *Salisbury* [1939] 4 All E.R. 427, a claim was made that a mortgage was void on the ground that an advance was made of a greater percentage of the value of a house than would have been made if there had been no pooling agreement. It was contended that under the Building Societies Act, 1874, s. 13 (now substantially re-enacted by the Building Societies Act, 1962, s. 1 (1)), the building society could advance only on the security of freehold, copyhold, or leasehold property and because part of the advance was on the security provided by the pooling agreement the whole security was void. This contention failed, the reason for the decision being that the advance was made on the security of the property and the taking of collateral security was not *ultra vires*.

In *Bradford Third Equitable Benefit Building Society* v. *Borders* [1941] 2 All E.R. 205, it was alleged that collateral security on a pool rendered the mortgage illegal under the Building Societies Act, 1874, s. 13, and the rules of the society. Further, damages were claimed from the society for fraudulent misrepresentation in a brochure issued by the builders stating that the house would be thoroughly inspected by the society's surveyor, and would be of good materials. The Court of Appeal held that the mortgagor could recover damages from the building society ([1940] Ch. 202), but the House of Lords decided that the society had not itself made any false representation. The contention that the mortgage money was irrecoverable because it was outside the powers of the building society to take such security was not upheld.

As to the income taxation consequences of a "pooling agreement", see *post*, p. 1099.

Limits on collateral security.—The difficulties made apparent by the above cases have given rise to statutory rules. The Building Societies Act, 1962, s. 26, re-enacting the Building Societies Act, 1939, s. 2, provides :—

" 26.—(1) In determining the amount of an advance . . . the society shall not have power to take into account the value of any additional security taken by the society for the advance, except security of a class specified in the Third Schedule to this Act.

(2) Where a charge upon a policy of life assurance is taken as additional security for such an advance, the value of the policy shall be assessed at an amount not exceeeding the surrender value thereof at the time when the advance is made.

(3) Where a guarantee given in pursuance of a continuing arrangement (not being such a guarantee as is mentioned in paragraph 3 of the Third Schedule to this Act) is taken as additional security for such an advance, the advance shall not exceed the amount of the purchase price for the defraying of which the advance is made, the basic advance shall not exceed eighty per cent. of that amount and the excess advance shall not exceed twenty per cent. of that amount."

The " basic advance " means the maximum amount the society would consider proper to advance upon the security of the estate if no other security were taken, and the " excess advance " means the amount by which the advance exceeds the basic advance (*ibid.*, s. 129 (1)).

The securities specified in Sched. 3 are as follows :—

1. A charge upon a policy of life assurance.

2. A guarantee by an assurance company.

3. A guarantee by a local authority under the Housing (Financial Provisions) Act, 1958, s. 45, and similar earlier powers (see also Building Societies (Additional Security) Order, 1963).

4. A charge given by the member on money deposited with the society or upon trustee investments.

5. Certain charges or securities of public utility undertakings if made in favour of societies carrying on business for the purpose of facilitating the acquisition of houses by persons employed by public utility undertakings.

6. A guarantee, not being in pursuance of a continuing arrangement, accepted with the written consent of the member and supported by a charge upon money deposited or upon trustee investments.

7. A charge upon money deposited in accordance with arrangements approved by the Chief Registrar of Friendly Societies which also provide for guarantee by an assurance company.

8. A guarantee in pursuance of a continuing arrangement for guarantee of sums due to the society which complies with the conditions of Pt. I of Sched. 4 to the 1962 Act.

A " continuing arrangement " is defined in s. 129 (1), and means an arrangement of the kind described above as a " pooling agreement." The conditions contained in Pt. I of Sched. 4 are too detailed to be set out here ; they fix the amount which must be deposited by way of guarantee, and the circumstances in which deposits may be withdrawn.

Notices to borrower of additional security.—Where security for an advance to a member is taken from another person and the advance is for the purpose of defraying the purchase price of freehold or leasehold property, then no sums are recoverable in respect of the advance or of any security given therefor, except by leave of the court, unless, before any contract requiring the member to repay the advance is entered into, the society gives to the member notice in writing in the prescribed form, stating the basic advance and the excess advance (if any) ; " basic advance " and " excess advance " are defined above (Building Societies Act, 1962, s. 28). The section does not apply, however, to an advance to an individual where the only security taken from a third party is a guarantee by an individual not secured by a charge on property (*ibid.*, s. 28 (1) proviso). If at the time that a contract for the acquisition of freehold or leasehold estate is made there is in force between a society and any person having a financial interest in the disposition of the estate an arrangement by which, in the event of the society making an excess advance for the purpose of its being used in defraying the purchase price a person will, or may, provide additional security, then a notice in writing must be given before the contract is made to the person by whom the estate is to be acquired. Such notice must be in the prescribed form, and if it is not given the purchaser may rescind the contract and recover the deposit (*ibid.*, s. 29).

It would appear from the wording of s. 29 that if such an arrangement exists but the prescribed notice is not given to the purchaser, then the purchaser can rescind the contract *even though he never intended to borrow any money from the building society in question* or even though he intended to borrow a small sum only. There would seem to be a right of rescission for any purchaser if any building society has entered into an arrangement of the kind specified with a vendor but the appropriate notice is not served on the purchaser.

Warranty in absence of notice to borrower.—The Building Societies Act, 1962, s. 30 (re-enacting s. 9 of the 1939 Act), provides as follows :—

" 30. Where a building society makes to a member an advance for the purpose of its being used in defraying the purchase price of freehold or leasehold estate, the society shall be deemed to warrant to the member that the purchase price is reasonable *unless, before any contract requiring the member to repay the advance is entered into, the society gives to the member a notice* in writing, in the prescribed form, stating that the making of the advance implies no such warranty."

If a person having a financial interest in the disposition of any estate or in the erection of any building thereon, or his servant or agent, makes any representation that the making of an advance by a society upon the security of that estate implies any assurance to the person to whom the advance is made that the estate is sufficient security for the amount of the advance, then, unless he satisfies the court that he had reasonable grounds for believing the representation to be true, that person is liable to a fine not exceeding one hundred pounds or to imprisonment for a term not exceeding three months or to both (Building Societies Act, 1962, s. 31).

Exercise of power of sale.—The Building Societies Act, 1962, s. 36, imposes on societies duties which may be more onerous than those imposed on other mortgagees (see *post*, p. 989). Section 36 (1) is as follows :—

" 36.—(1) Where any freehold or leasehold estate has been mortgaged to a building society as security for an advance, and a person sells that estate in exercise of a power (whether statutory or express) exercisable by virtue of the mortgage, it shall be his duty—

(a) in exercising that power, to take reasonable care to ensure that the price at which the estate is sold is the best price which can reasonably be obtained ;

(b) and within twenty-eight days from the completion of the sale, to send by registered post to the mortgagor, at the mortgagor's last known address, a notice containing the prescribed particulars of the sale."

In *Reliance Permanent Building Society* v. *Harwood-Stamper* [1944] Ch. 362, Vaisey, J., said that the duty of a mortgagee other than a building society was to act in good faith and take reasonable precautions to obtain a proper price, but not necessarily the best price obtainable. He decided that the effect of the similar provision in the 1939 Act was to put a building society in the position of a fiduciary vendor, who is under a duty to secure the best price possible, subject to three qualifications ; first, it might decide in its own interest the time when it would sell ; secondly, the powers in the L.P.A. 1925, s. 101, to sell in lots, etc., exist ; and, thirdly, the society has the protection of the L.P.A. 1925, s. 106 (3). In the case in question the society had not sold by auction or advertised the sale, but put the property in the hands of one agent only. In the circumstances it was decided that the society had just fulfilled its obligations. The grant by a building society of an option to purchase at a specified price is not invalidated by the section if the grant of such an option was reasonably necessary to obtain the best price (*Cottrill* v. *Steyning and Littlehampton Building Society* [1966] 2 All E.R. 296n).

The Building Societies Act, 1962, s. 36, does not give any protection to a purchaser from a building society selling under its powers. Consequently, the title of a purchaser might be challenged by the mortgagor if he could show that the purchaser had not given the best price reasonably obtainable. Compare the protection afforded a purchaser in respect of a similar duty as to price by s. 110 (1) of the S.L.A. 1925 (see *post*, p. 734). Whether a purchaser would be protected by the L.P.A. 1925, s. 104 (2) (d), referred to *post*, p. 993, is doubtful.

Most building society mortgages contain an express power of sale. It has been doubted whether the power in the L.P.A. 1925, s. 101, and earlier statutory powers in similar terms, apply to building society mortgages (*Re Thompson and Holt's Contract* (1890), 44 Ch. D. 492, and *Walsh* v. *Derrick* (1903), 19 T.L.R. 209). The general opinion is that the power does apply and such was assumed to be the case by Vaisey, J., in his judgment in *Reliance Permanent Building Society* v. *Harwood-Stamper*, ante.

Second mortgage.—Building societies are prohibited from advancing money on a second mortgage (Building Societies Act, 1962, s. 32). Although this section does not prevent a society which has a first mortgage from taking a second mortgage on other land by way of further security for the same debt (*Hayes Bridge Estate* v. *Portman Building Society* [1936] 2 All E.R. 1400), there would appear to be no object in so doing as the society may not take into account the second mortgage in determining the amount of the advance on first mortgage (Building Societies Act, 1962, s. 26, *ante*, p. 260).

An advance may be made, however, notwithstanding the existence of a prior charge acquired by a local authority under an Act of Parliament or

under an instrument made under an Act, being a charge which takes effect
by virtue of the Act or instrument (*ibid.*, Sched. 5). Examples of such
charges are those acquired on default in payment for street works (Highways
Act, 1959, s. 264) or under the advance payments code in the Highways
Act, 1959, ss. 192 to 198.

Transfer of mortgage.—It seems to be doubtful whether a building
society can, in the absence of provision in the mortgage deed that the powers
may be exercised by its *assigns*, transfer a mortgage *without the consent of
the mortgagor*. In the Irish case of *Ulster Building Society* v. *Glenton* (1888),
21 Ir. R. 124, it was decided that this could be done ; but in *Re Rumney and
Smith's Contract* [1897] 2 Ch. 351, none of the judges was prepared without
further argument to follow the Irish decision, and the court pointed out that
in the latter case the mortgagor had consented to the transfer. The point
was referred to in *Sun Permanent Benefit Building Society* v. *Western Suburban,
etc., Building Society* [1920] 2 Ch. 144 ; on appeal [1921] 2 Ch. 438, but the
case was decided on other grounds. It seems to have been assumed in that
case that, if the definition of " society " in the mortgage had included
" assigns," this would have justified a transfer without the consent of the
mortgagor.

It is quite clear, however, that where in the mortgage deed a power of
sale is expressly given to " the trustees or trustee for the time being of the
society," only the persons coming within this description could exercise that
power (*Re Rumney and Smith's Contract, ante*).

The statutory right of a mortgagor entitled to redeem to require the
mortgagee, instead of reconveying or surrendering, to transfer (s. 95 of
the L.P.A. 1925) is discussed *post*, p. 1005. Section 115 (2) of the L.P.A. 1925
(which provides that where on the discharge of a mortgage it appears from
the receipt that the money was paid off by a person not entitled to the equity,
the receipt will act as a transfer) is explained at p. 1010, *post*.

Transfer of equity of redemption by mortgagor.—Most building
societies have rules as to this. See, for instance, *West Bromwich Building
Society* v. *Bullock* [1936] 1 All E.R. 887, in which the original mortgagor's
liability on the personal covenant for repayment after a transfer was determined in accordance with a proper construction of the society's rules as to the
obtaining of a release from the board of the society.

Union of building societies.—Provision for union of societies or for
the transfer of the engagements of one society to another is made by the
Building Societies Act, 1962, ss. 18, 19 and 20, re-enacting earlier provisions
(including the Building Societies Act, 1874, s. 33, and the Building Societies
Act, 1877, s. 5 ; and see *Northern Rock B.S.* v. *Davies* [1969] 1 W.L.R.
1742 as to the general effect of union). The instrument of union or transfer
of engagements forms a part of the title to any property previously mortgaged
but later released or reconveyed by the joint acquiring society ; it is not
sufficient merely to abstract the registrar's receipt of the notice of union
or transfer of engagement (*Re Fryer and Hampson's Contract* [1929] W.N. 45).

Statutory receipts.—The subject of statutory receipts is dealt with in
the chapter on Mortgages, *post*, p. 1006, and only those rules particular to
building societies are discussed here.

The right of a purchaser to inquire as to the validity of a receipt on a mortgage to a building society may be restricted by the contract. Thus The Law Society's Conditions of Sale, 1973 Revision, provide :—

" 9.—Where a title includes a mortgage or legal charge in favour of a Building or Friendly Society or a society registered under the Industrial and Provident Societies Acts, or any trustees or other persons on behalf of such a society, no evidence shall be required in relation to the rules, constitution or incorporation of the society and the purchaser shall assume that any receipt given on the discharge of every such mortgage or legal charge and purporting to be executed in the manner required by the statute relating to the society was duly executed by all proper persons and is valid and effectual."

On payment or discharge of all moneys the society may endorse on or annex to the mortgage :—

(a) a receipt under seal, countersigned by a person acting under authority of the board, in the form contained in Sched. 6 ; *or*

(b) a reconveyance to the mortgagor ; *or*

(c) a reconveyance to such person of full age, and on such trusts, if any, as the mortgagor may direct (Building Societies Act, 1962, s. 37 (1)).

For the purposes of this section " mortgagor " means the person for the time being entitled to the equity of redemption (*ibid.*, s. 37 (5)).

Such a receipt in that form endorsed on, or annexed to, a mortgage (not being a charge or incumbrance registered under the L.R.A. 1925–1971) operates in accordance with the L.P.A. 1925, ss. 115 (1), (3), (6) and (8) in like manner as a receipt which fulfils the requirements of s. 115 (1), i.e., states the name of the person who pays the money (1962 Act, s. 37 (2)).

The following is the form specified in Sched. 6 (being the form in the Schedule to the Building Societies Act, 1874, as amended by the Building Societies Act, 1960, s. 20) :—

" The   Building Society hereby acknowledge to have received all moneys intended to be secured by the within [*or* above] written deed.

In witness whereof the seal of the society is hereto affixed this   day of   by order of the board of directors [*or* committee of management] in presence of

> { By authority of the board of directors
>   [*or* committee of management].

> { [*Other witnesses, if any, required by the*
>   *rules of the Society.*] "

An endorsed or annexed receipt *not* in the scheduled form may still have effect pursuant to the L.P.A. 1925, s. 115 (9), and may be executed under seal and countersigned as required by s. 37 (1) (a) of the 1962 Act (*ibid.*, s. 37 (3)).

The result is that a society may use either the scheduled form or a form stating the payer's name and both forms normally have the same effect, namely, that set out in s. 115. The only difference is that the scheduled form, which does not state the name of the payer, cannot operate as a transfer pursuant to s. 115 (2) ; this is no disadvantage as that subsection is unnecessary and likely to cause confusion. However, the L.P.A. 1925, s. 115 (7), provides that where a mortgage consists of a mortgage and a further charge, or more than one deed, it is sufficient for the purpose of s. 115 if the receipt refers to all the deeds whereby the mortgage money is secured or to the aggregate amount of the money thereby secured and for the time being owing, and is endorsed on, written at the foot of, or annexed to, one of the mortgage deeds. The better opinion is that this subsection does not apply if a receipt is taken in the 1962 Act form in which case a receipt should be endorsed on or annexed to each further charge.

If a receipt is taken in the scheduled form care must be taken to adhere strictly to that form because only if that is done will the receipt operate under s. 37 (1) (although it can be argued that any proof of discharge is adequate under the L.P.A. 1925, s. 116, discussed in the chapter on Mortgages, *post*, p. 1006).

If the land is in Yorkshire and the mortgage has been registered (as it should have been) in the local deeds registry, the receipt should be registered therein so as to clear the register ; see further *post*, p. 616.

Former rules as to receipts.—Before the Building Societies Act, 1962, came into operation on 1st October, 1962, there was a difference of opinion as to whether a receipt in the form contained in the Schedule to the 1874 Act took effect in the manner specified in the L.P.A. 1925, s. 115, or took effect as stated in s. 42 of the 1874 Act. Section 42 (as amended by the Building Societies Act, 1960, s. 20) provided as follows :—

" When all moneys intended to be secured by any mortgage or further charge given to a society under this Act in England or Ireland have been fully paid or discharged, the society may endorse upon or annex to such mortgage or further charge a reconveyance of the mortgaged property . . . or a receipt under the seal of the society, countersigned by any person acting under the authority of the board of directors or committee of management of the society, in the form specified in the schedule to this Act, and such receipt shall vacate the mortgage or further charge or debt, and vest the estate of and in the property therein comprised in the person for the time being entitled to the equity of redemption, without any reconveyance or re-surrender whatever . . ."

If s. 42 governed the consequences of a receipt in the scheduled form certain doubts might arise as to the person in whom the estate vested, for instance, if a second mortgage had been created.

Section 115 (9) of the L.P.A. 1925 provided as follows :—

" 115.—(9) The provisions of this section relating to the *operation* of a receipt shall (*in substitution for the like statutory provisions* relating to receipts given by or on behalf of a building [or] friendly society) apply to the discharge of a mortgage made to any such society, *provided that the receipt is executed in the manner required by the statute relating to the society*, but nothing in this section shall render a receipt given by or on behalf of any such society liable to any stamp duty which would not have been otherwise payable."

The opinion which is believed to be generally accepted is that s. 115 (9) caused a receipt in the scheduled form to operate as specified in s. 115 (and not in accordance with s. 42). On that basis the doubts caused by s. 41 could

9A

not arise after 1925 ; some evidence that this was the intention is provided by the fact that the 1962 Act expressly incorporated the relevant consequences of s. 115. The doubt now rarely arises and it is sufficient to refer to the full discussion in the 12th, 13th and 14th Editions of this book.

Vacation of mortgage on sale of the property.—A vendor whose property is subject to a building society mortgage is often unable to repay the amount owing under the mortgage until he receives the purchase price. In such circumstances it is often arranged that the purchaser's solicitor shall pay to the building society the amount owing under the mortgage, the balance of the purchase price only being handed to the vendor's solicitor. Building societies usually refuse to have a statutory receipt executed ready for handing over on repayment of the amount owing, and so it is customary for the building society's solicitor, or the vendor's solicitor, to undertake to have a vacating receipt endorsed and executed.

This practice has been criticised on the ground that the mortgagor is entitled to have the mortgage discharged at the moment of repayment and that the purchaser should not have to accept an incomplete title pending its vacation. The Council of The Law Society have expressed the opinion that the practice for a vendor's solicitor on completion to give an undertaking relating to the discharge of an existing building society mortgage facilitates conveyancing and should be accepted by a purchaser's solicitors (*Law Society's Gazette*, vol. 67, p. 753). The Council further recommend the use of the following form of undertaking : " In consideration of your today completing the purchase of . . . we hereby undertake forthwith to pay over to the. . . building society the money required to redeem the mortgage/legal charge dated . . . and to forward the receipted mortgage/legal charge to you as soon as it is received by us from the . . . building society." It is important to notice that this opinion and recommendation is limited to *building society* mortgages and is not applicable in the case of bank or private mortgages (see *Conveyancer N. S.*, vol. 35, pp. 305–307).

However, reference should be made to correspondence criticising the above form of undertaking (*Law Society's Gazette*, vol. 68, p. 76 ; also at *Solicitors' Journal*, vol. 115, pp. 170, 230). The primary objection is that the form does not specify any time within which the undertaking must be implemented. It is pointed out, in effect, that unless the receipted mortgage/legal charge can be shown by the purchaser's solicitors to have reached the vendor's solicitors the undertaking is valueless. Reference may also be made to *Law Society's Gazette*, vol. 68, p. 135, where Mr. D. M. Schayek points out the difficulties which such a practice as that indicated above could cause if time were of the essence of the contract, either originally or by virtue of a notice to complete.

Further, it has been found that some practitioners cautiously amend the recommended form to relate to " the sum presently stated by the Society as sufficient to redeem . . . " (see a full consideration of the topic by J. E. Adams at *Law Society's Gazette* (1973), vol. 70, No. 4 and 5, pp. 1346 and 1360).

It is felt that there is substance in these criticisms of the suggested form and practice of giving undertakings and, whilst recognising that in very many individual cases no practical risk is run, in general the view is still preferred that the purchaser's solicitor should not be asked to accept such an undertaking, and that if he does accept it without the express and irrevocable authority of his client he may be held liable for negligence if, for any reason the mortgage is not duly vacated. Nevertheless, such undertakings are very frequently offered and accepted, but it should be emphasised that the strictly correct procedure would still be for the building society to hand over the deeds with the vacated mortgage to the purchaser's solicitor on payment of the sum due (see *Rourke* v. *Robinson* [1911] 1 Ch. 480).

Registered land.—It is expressly provided by the L.R.A. 1925, s. 25 (1) (*b*), that a proprietor of any registered land may by deed charge the registered land in favour of a building society in accordance with the rules of the society. In practice, the ordinary form of the building society's mortgage will be used, although a charge in Form 45 in the Schedule to the L.R.R. 1925 is possible. Application for registration must be accompanied by the mortgage, and a copy certified by the secretary or solicitor of the society, and by the land certificate.

There is a special rule that upon the registration of a charge in favour of a building society, friendly society, or industrial and provident society, the instrument of charge may, if desired, be delivered to them after registration upon their delivering at the registry a copy verified by the secretary or solicitor as a correct copy (L.R.R. 1925, r. 92). Where this is done, in practice, the original mortgage deed is bound into an ordinary charge certificate and the normal entries made, the certified copy being filed in the registry. Such a mortgage will generally be discharged by endorsement of the usual statutory receipt, although the discharge may be in Form 53 in the Schedule to the L.R.R. 1925 if wished (r. 152).

CHAPEL TRUSTEES

Acquisition of land.—Sales and gifts of land for chapel purposes amount to charitable dispositions, but since the repeal of the Mortmain and Charitable Uses Acts, 1888 and 1891, by the Charities Act, 1960, most of the former restrictions on assurances to trustees for such purposes no longer apply. In addition, any past infringement of these restrictions will most probably have been validated by the provisions of s. 38 (2) of the 1960 Act, *post*, p. 270. Most religious bodies have model deeds which should be followed in conveying land to or for the body.

The Places of Worship Sites Act, 1873, s. 1, enabled persons seised in fee simple beneficially and being in possession to grant by way of gift an area not exceeding one acre as a site for a church, chapel or place of divine worship, or for the residence of a minister or for a burial place. It was provided that on use for another purpose or on cesser of the intended use for a year the site reverted to the lands from which it was severed. A conveyance for such a purpose did not necessarily operate under that Act and must be construed to see whether it was so intended (*Imperial Tobacco Co., Ltd.* v. *Wilmott and others* [1964] 1 W.L.R. 902).

Appointment of new trustees.—Appointments of trustees for chapel purposes were formerly often made under the Trustees Appointment Acts, 1850 to 1890, which have now been repealed by the Charities Act, 1960, Sched. 7, Pt. 1. Those Acts provided that where land was conveyed in trust for any body of persons associated for religious purposes, as a place of religious worship, a minister's house, rooms for the transaction of their business or a burial ground or for similar purposes for several congregations, the conveyance *vested the property without any conveyance or assurance* not only in the original grantees but *in their successors in office* for the time being appointed in the mode prescribed by the conveyance or any separate deed of trust, or if no mode was prescribed or the power had lapsed, in the mode agreed upon by the body of persons (1850 Act, s. 1). Every such appointment of a new trustee had to be evidenced by deed in statutory form executed by the chairman of the meeting at which the appointment was made in the presence of the meeting and attested by two witnesses (*ibid.*, s. 3, Sched. ; 1869 Act, s. 1 ; 1890 Act, s. 2). The provision for vesting the property in continuing trustees (if any) and their successors was effectual to vest the land where the appointment was made under any other statutory power, that is, now, the T.A. 1925, s. 36 (1890 Act, s. 4). For the purpose of any sale or mortgage persons purporting or appearing to have been appointed under the Trustees Appointment Acts were, after the expiration of six months, deemed to be duly appointed and, where an appointment could be made by persons present at a meeting, a memorandum in the form in the Schedule to the 1850 Act stating that the meeting was duly constituted was made conclusive evidence that an appointment was duly made (1890 Act, ss. 6, 7).

These Acts were repealed by the Charities Act, 1960, s. 35 of which provides a new method for the appointment of charity trustees (dealt with *post*, pp. 276–277). As to the trusts and vesting of title of shared church buildings, see s. 2 of the Sharing of Church Buildings Act, 1969 (also s. 7 as to the sharing of residential buildings).

Disposition of land.—Prior to the Charities Act, 1960, charity trustees might not sell, mortgage or charge the estate or make certain leases *without the consent of the Charity Commissioners* except in certain cases. By the Charitable Trusts Act, 1853, s. 62, consent of the Charity Commissioners to such transactions was not necessary if they related to places of worship registered under the Places of Worship Registration Act, 1855, and *bona fide* used as such. The Charitable Trusts (Places of Religious Worship) Amendment Act, 1894, s. 4, extended such exemption to gardens and other lands connected with registered buildings, Sunday school houses, and other land or buildings certified by the Charity Commissioners to be held upon the same trusts and to be so connected with a registered building that they could not conveniently be separated therefrom.

In practice it was almost invariably found that trust deeds were so drawn that one of the exemptions contained in the Charitable Trusts Act, 1853, s. 62, was applicable and, therefore, the consent of the Charity Commissioners was unnecessary. Further, attention is drawn, in particular, to the Methodist Church Union Act, 1929, which provided that lands held upon trust for the Wesleyan Methodist Church, the Primitive Methodist Church and the United Methodist Church should be held in trust for the Methodist Church, but otherwise on existing trusts ; to the Methodist Church Act, 1939, constituting trustees for Methodist Church purposes ; to the Calvinistic Methodist or Presbyterian Church of Wales Act, 1933, establishing a Properties Board for that church to act as custodian trustee and to which properties belonging to the church were transferred ; and to the Baptist and Congregational Trusts Act, 1951, enabling the adoption of certain model trusts and their amendment, and the appointment as trustee of certain Baptist or Congregational trust corporations.

Except for purposes of investigation of title these provisions are not now important in view of the Charities Act, 1960, s. 38 (2), *post*, p. 270.

CHARITIES 269

CHARITIES

Chapel lands ; see *ante,* p. 267.

Church lands ; see *post,* p. 278.

Nationalisation of hospitals ; see *post,* p. 1216.

Definition of a charity.—A consideration of what is meant in law by a charity would be outside the scope of this book. It may be noted only that " no comprehensive definition of legal charity has been given either by the legislature or in judicial utterance " (see *per* Viscount Simonds in *I.R.C.* v. *Baddeley* [1955] A.C. 572, at p. 583) and that no definition was attempted even in the recent Charities Act, 1960. However, it may be convenient to quote the classification of charitable purposes given in Lord Macnaghten's speech in *Commissioners of Income Tax* v. *Pemsel* [1891] A.C. 531, at p. 583, as follows : " ' Charity ' in its legal sense comprises four principal divisions : trusts for the relief of poverty ; trusts for the advancement of education ; trusts for the advancement of religion ; and trusts for other purposes beneficial to the community, not falling under any of the preceding heads." For a discussion of this classification and the relevant cases, see, e.g., Snell's Equity, 27th ed., p. 142 *et seq.* In addition, reference may be made to the Recreational Charities Act, 1958, and to the Charitable Trusts (Validation) Act, 1954 (applying only to trusts contained in instruments taking effect before 16th December, 1952, but causing a few modern cases).

For purposes of conveyancing it may suffice to conclude by noting that any trust or undertaking is for all purposes other than rectification of the register to be conclusively presumed to be or to have been a charity at any time when it is or was on the register of charities established and maintained under the Charities Act, 1960 (see ss. 4 and 5). Further, it has been held that this statutory presumption will apply to any pre-registration time at which the trusts or purposes were the same as at registration (*Re Murawski's Will Trusts* [1971] 1 W.L.R. 707). Any person affected by the registration may apply for removal of the trust or undertaking from the register on the ground that it is not really a charity, and appeals are provided for (s. 5). The converse, an absence of registration, does not create any non-charitable presumption.

Conveyances to charities.—As many charities are incorporated, it was formerly necessary to remember that if land was assured to a corporation in mortmain otherwise than by statutory authority or on licence of the Crown, the land was forfeited to the Crown (Mortmain and Charitable Uses Act, 1888, s. 1 (1)). A Royal Charter incorporating a charity usually authorised the charity to hold a limited quantity of land. Statutory authorities were contained, for instance, in the Charitable Trustees Incorporation Act, 1872, s. 1, and in the Companies Act, 1948, s. 14 (1). However, the general restriction is no longer in force as the 1888 Act has been repealed by the Charities Act, 1960, Sched. 7.

The Mortmain and Charitable Uses Act, 1888, s. 4 (1), formerly provided that " Subject to the savings and exceptions contained in this Act, every assurance of *land* to or for the benefit of any charitable uses . . . shall be made in accordance with the requirements of this Act, and unless so made shall be void." As regards assurances made after 1925, some of these requirements were revoked or varied by s. 29 (4) of the S.L.A. 1925.

Now the 1888 Act has been repealed by the Charities Act, 1960, Sched. 7. Moreover, if in 1960 possession had been taken by the charity, their title would be preserved notwithstanding the 1888 Act by s. 38 (2) of the 1960 Act which provides as follows :—

" (2) No right or title to any property shall be defeated or impugned, and no assurance or disposition of property shall be treated as void or voidable, by virtue of any of the [Mortmain and Charitable Uses Acts, 1888 and 1891, Mortmain and Charitable Uses Act Amendment Act, 1892, or any Acts amending those Acts including the Education Act, 1944, s. 87, and the Companies Act, 1948, ss. 14 and 408], or of any other enactment relating to mortmain, if at the [29th July, 1960], the possession is in accordance with that right or title or with that assurance or disposition, and no step has been taken to assert a claim by virtue of any enactment :

Provided that this subsection shall not validate any assurance or disposition so as to defeat a right or title acquired by adverse possession before the passing of this Act."

The requirements of the 1888 Act, s. 4, as amended by s. 29 of the S.L.A. 1925, where the conveyance was made after 1925, were (broadly) as follows :—

(i) The assurance had to take effect in possession immediately.

(ii) The assurance had to be made within twelve months before the assurer's death, unless for full and valuable consideration.

(iii) It had to be without power of revocation, reservation, condition or provision, for the benefit of the assurer or any person claiming under him other than certain specified reservations such as a nominal rent, or mines or minerals, or any easement or covenants as regards buildings, or roads, or other stipulations for the benefit of the assurer.

(iv) Assurances executed before 1926 had to be executed before two witnesses, except in the case of copyholds, and to be enrolled at the Central Office within six months. Where assurances were executed after 1925, or if the charitable uses were declared by a separate instrument, the instrument had to be sent to the offices of the Charity Commissioners within six months or within such extended period as the Commissioners might allow. The subsection did not extend to registered dispositions of registered land, or to assurances or instruments required by s. 87 of the Education Act, 1944, to be sent to the Minister of Education, or to assurances which were exempt from the requirement of being sent to the Minister by virtue of the Education (Miscellaneous Provisions) Act, 1953.

Charitable dispositions of land by will.—Since the Charities Act, 1960, there has been no restriction on gifts of land by will to charities.

The Mortmain and Charitable Uses Act, 1891, formerly provided that any property of a testator dying after 5th August, 1891, might be given by will for any charitable use, subject as regards gifts of land to the provision that, except in the case mentioned below, any land must be sold within one year from the death of the testator, or such extended period as might be determined by the High Court, or any judge, or by the Charity Commissioners (1891 Act, ss. 5, 6 ; *Re Gorham's Charity Trust* [1939] Ch. 410). The exception was that the court or the Charity Commissioners might sanction the retention of the land if they were satisfied that the land was required for actual occupation for the purposes of the charity and not as an investment (1891 Act, s. 8).

Section 7 of the 1891 Act rendered valid bequests in favour of charities of personal estate to be laid out in the purchase of land, and provided that such bequests should be held to the charitable use as though there had been no direction to purchase land. In this respect s. 38 (3) of the 1960 Act provides that the repeal of the 1891 Act should have effect in relation to wills of persons dying before 29th July, 1960, so as to abrogate any requirement to sell land then unsold, but not so as to enable effect to be given to a direction to lay out personal estate in land without an order under s. 8 of that Act or so as to affect the power to make such an order.

Powers of trustees in connection with land.—It is provided by s. 29 of the S.L.A. 1925 as follows :—

" 29.—(1) For the purposes of this section, all land vested or to be vested in trustees on or for charitable, ecclesiastical, or public trusts or purposes shall be deemed to be settled land, and the trustees shall, without constituting them statutory owners, have in reference to the land, all the powers which are by this Act conferred on a tenant for life and on the trustees of a settlement.

In connection only with the exercise of those powers, and not so as to impose any obligation in respect of or to affect—

(a) the mode of creation or the administration of such trusts ; or

(b) the appointment or number of trustees of such trusts ;

the statute or other instrument creating the trust or under which it is administered shall be deemed the settlement, and the trustees shall be deemed the trustees of the settlement, and, *save where the trust is created by a will coming into operation* after the commencement of this Act, *a separate instrument shall not be necessary* for giving effect to the settlement.

Any conveyance of land held on charitable, ecclesiastical or public trust shall state that the land is held on such trusts, and, where a purchaser has notice that the land is held on charitable, ecclesiastical, or public trusts, he shall be bound to see that any consents or orders requisite for authorising the transaction have been obtained."

All such powers are exercisable subject to such consents or orders, if any, being obtained as would have been requisite if the S.L.A. 1925 had not been passed and if the transaction were being effected under an express power (S.L.A. 1925, s. 29 (2)). For necessary consents on sale, mortgage, or lease, see *post*, p. 272 *et seq.*

In *Re Higgs* [1927] W.N. 316, a house was vested in trustees upon trust to permit the minister for the time being officiating at a certain church to reside there. It was held by Romer, J., that the house was not limited in trust for these ministers in succession within the meaning of the S.L.A. 1925, s. 1, but was really limited in trust for the benefit of the church, and was, therefore, held upon a charitable trust, and s. 29 was applicable. Under that section the trustees would have the powers of a tenant for life, and if necessary, proper proceedings could be taken by means of which the house could be sold. If the house should be sold, then the proceeds of sale would have to be the subject-matter of a scheme. Section 29 (1) does not apply to a consecrated church or consecrated land (*Re St. Swithin's, Norwich* [1960] P. 77).

It is difficult to state the effect of the S.L.A. 1925, s. 29, and it is believed that in practice it is rarely used ; most transactions are justified by express powers in the trust instruments or by powers in the Charities Act, 1960. In *Re Booth and Southend-on-Sea Estates Company's Contract* [1927] 1 Ch. 579, it was decided that if a charity has a trust deed of its own, giving power to trustees, or even to a single trustee, to buy and sell property and to give a good discharge for purchase-money, there is nothing in s. 29 to prevent them or him exercising their or his powers under the deed.

Consent of Charity Commissioners to sale, mortgage or lease.—It is provided by s. 29 of the Charities Act, 1960, as follows :—

" 29.—(1) Subject to the exceptions provided for by this section, no property forming part of the permanent endowment of a charity shall, without an order of the court or of the Commissioners, be mortgaged or charged by way of security for the repayment of money borrowed, nor, in the case of land in England or Wales, be sold, leased or otherwise disposed of.

(2) Subsection (1) above shall apply to any land which is held by or in trust for a charity and is or has at any time been occupied for the purposes of the charity, as it applies to land forming part of the permanent endowment of a charity ; but a transaction for which the sanction of an order under subsection (1) above is required by virtue only of this subsection shall, notwithstanding that it is entered into without such an order, be valid in favour of a person who (then or afterwards) in good faith acquires an interest in or charge on the land for money or money's worth.

(3) This section shall apply notwithstanding anything in the trusts of a charity, but shall not require the sanction of an order—

(a) for any transaction for which general or special authority is expressly given (without the authority being made subject to the sanction of an order) by any statutory provision contained in or having effect under an Act of Parliament or by any scheme legally established ; or

(b) for the granting of a lease for a term ending not more than twenty-two years after it is granted, not being a lease granted wholly or partly in consideration of a fine ; or

(c) for any disposition of an advowson.

(4) This section shall not apply to an *exempt charity*, nor to any charity which is *excepted by order or regulations*."

Where freehold land is sold by a charity to a tenant who has compelled enfranchisement in pursuance of the Leasehold Reform Act, 1967, the accepted view appears to be that the consent of the Charity Commissioners is not required provided the procedure of the 1967 Act has been followed (see *Solicitors' Journal*, vol. 112, pp. 749, 750). There is some difficulty in taking this view in that the 1967 Act contains no express authority which could be said to satisfy s. 29 (3) (a) of the Charities Act, 1960. However, there is little doubt that the view can be safely acted upon in practice.

" *Exempt charities* " are defined in Sched. 2 and the Exempt Charities Order, 1962 ; they include certain universities and colleges, the Church Commissioners and a registered society within the meaning of the Industrial and Provident Societies Act, 1965, or of the Friendly Societies Act, 1896.

" *excepted by order or regulations.*"—A charity for the advancement of religion is excepted as regards any sale of its land of certain classes if " it is certified on behalf of the charity at the time of the sale that the proceeds of the sale are to be applied in or towards the provision of other land or premises to be used in place of the land sold " (Charities (Religious Premises) Regulations, 1962, reg. 1). The reference to other land or premises is to be construed as including a reference to the repayment of money borrowed for that purpose (*ibid.*) and so a temporary loan for purchase may be obtained pending sale of old premises. The certificate might well be given by recital in the conveyance so that a record is preserved. The classes of land affected consist of land which has not been used during the period of three years immediately preceding the sale (or, where the land was acquired during that period, since the land was acquired by or for the charity) otherwise than as one or more of the following (*a*) a place of worship ; (*b*) a burial ground ; (*c*) a Sunday school ; (*d*) a church hall ; (*e*) a residence for a minister of religion ; (*f*) a residence for a caretaker of a place or places listed above ; (*g*) the curtilage of a place or places listed above. In the cases (*e*) and (*f*) if the religion is not Christianity, the reference includes a school or hall of similar kind (*ibid.*, reg. 2). It seems necessary to prove and record the facts of use ; in most cases this will best be done by statutory declaration.

Provided the land has not been used in the previous three years (or since acquisition if more recent) otherwise than as a place of worship, burial ground, Sunday school, church hall, residence for a minister or a caretaker of one of the specified places, land of which the Friends Trusts Limited, the Fellowship of Independent Evangelical Churches or the Properties Board of the Calvinistic Methodist Church of Wales or the Presbyterian Church of Wales is a trustee may similarly be sold or otherwise disposed of without the necessity for an order of the court or the Charity Commissioners (Charities (Society of Friends, etc.) Regulations, 1962).

The provision in s. 29 (2) validating certain transactions in favour of persons who acquire in good faith has important consequences. It appears to mean that there is no need for persons such as purchasers of land to inquire as to whether the land was occupied by the charity, although a contrary view may be held on the ground that a person who does not inquire is not acting in good faith. Inquiry must be made as to whether land is part of the permanent endowment because if it is (unless the transaction falls within subs. (3) or the charity is exempt) a good title is not given unless an order of the court or of the Charity Commissioners is obtained. Where the proceeds of sale would properly be expended as income of the charity, the land is not part of the permanent endowment and so there is no need to obtain consent (unless the land is or has been occupied by the charity, although in this instance a *bona fide* purchaser is not concerned).

A charity is deemed to have a permanent endowment unless all property held for the purposes of the charity may be expended for those purposes without distinction between capital and income, and " permanent endowment " means " property held subject to a restriction on its being so expended " (Charities Act, 1960, s. 45 (3)).

By analogy to s. 29 of the 1855 Act, it seems that a sale is made when the contract is entered into. Consequently, if the consent of the Charity Commissioners is necessary but has not been obtained at that time the contract is unlawful and a deposit paid can be recovered (*Milner* v. *Staffordshire Congregational Union* [1956] Ch. 275). There are precedents of contracts of sale subject to consent being obtained within a specified period, for example, six months. The effect of a contract drawn in this way was left open (*ibid.*, p. 282) but there are *dicta* in a later case indicating that a contract conditional on consent would *not* be effective (see *per* Buckley, J., in *Manchester Diocesan*

Council for v. *Education Commercial and General Investment, Ltd.* [1970]
1 W.L.R. 241, at p. 247 ; the *Milner* case was distinguished since a special
section relating to the charity's property in the later case actually envisaged
a conditional contract for sale). Accordingly, in practice consent should be
obtained before a contract is signed. This is particularly so since any dealing
not complying with the section is wholly void, not merely voidable (*Bishop of
Bangor* v. *Parry* [1891] 2 Q.B. 277).

Advice of Charity Commissioners.—In any case of doubt the wise course is
to consult the Commissioners. Section 24 of the Charities Act, 1960, provides
that on the written application of any charity trustee the Commissioners
may give him their opinion or advice on any matter affecting the performance
of his duties as such. A trustee who acts upon the opinion or advice
given by the Commissioners is deemed to have acted in accordance with his
trust unless either (*a*) he knew or had reasonable cause to suspect that the
opinion or advice was given in ignorance of material facts or (*b*) the decision
of the court had been obtained on the matter or proceedings were pending
to obtain one.

Official Custodian of Charities.—Prior to the Charities Act, 1960, the
Secretary of the Board of Charity Commissioners was a corporation sole by
the name of " the Official Trustee of Charity Lands," and any charity lands
might be vested in him by an order of a court or judge or by an order of the
Charity Commissioners without any conveyance (Charitable Trusts Act, 1853,
ss. 47 and 48 ; Charitable Trusts Amendment Act, 1855, s. 15 ; Charitable
Trusts Act, 1860, s. 2). These Acts have been repealed but s. 3 (1) of the 1960
Act constitutes an " official custodian for charities " who is the successor of
the official trustee (*ibid.*, s. 48 (6)). The court may by order vest any property
held by or in trust for a charity in the official custodian or authorise or require
the persons in whom any such property is vested to transfer it to him (*ibid.*,
s. 16 (1)). Where any personal property is held by or in trust for a charity
it may, with the agreement of the official custodian, be transferred to him ;
for this purpose " personal property " extends to any real security, i.e., money
invested upon mortgage, but does not include an interest in land otherwise
than by way of security only (*ibid.*, s. 16 (2)). Thus only pure personalty,
and not, e.g., leaseholds, can be transferred to the official custodian without
an order of the court. The vesting of the legal estate in charity lands in
the official custodian does not prevent the trustees of the charity from
exercising rights of ownership over the lands, and such trustees, subject to any
necessary consents, may sell, exchange, mortgage, lease and otherwise dispose
of lands as freely as if they were not vested in the official custodian. It is
not necessary for the official custodian to execute personally any conveyance
or other assurance, where the transaction (*a*) has been authorised by the
court or the Commissioners or (*b*) is a lease for a term ending not more than
twenty-two years after it is granted (not granted in consideration of a fine)
or an acceptance of a surrender of a lease. The official custodian should be
named as a party to the deed but it will be executed in his name and on his
behalf by the charity trustees under s. 17 (2) of the 1960 Act. All such
trustees should execute unless two or more of them have been authorised
to do so pursuant to s. 34 (see further below).

A transaction (other than such a lease as is described at (*b*) in the last
paragraph) relating to land vested in the official custodian which does *not*
require the authority of the court or the Commissioners (e.g., a sale of land not

part of the permanent endowment and not occupied for the purposes of the charity) will have to be carried out by deed executed by the official custodian unless an order authorising the transaction has in fact been obtained. The custodian trustee is bound to act at the request of the managing trustees provided no breach of trust is involved and no personal liability falls on him (s. 4 (2) of the Public Trustee Act, 1906). The main advantage of having land vested in the official custodian is that when new managing trustees have to be appointed it is not necessary to vest the land in them, and so, on a subsequent sale, the title is simplified.

In addition, charity trustees can enter into obligations binding land vested in the official custodian as if it were vested in them ; and any covenant, agreement or condition which is enforceable by or against the official custodian by reason of the land being vested in him, is enforceable by or against the charity trustees as if the land were vested in them (Charities Act, 1960, s. 17 (3)). Consequently, the official custodian should not be joined as a party to any action to enforce, e.g., restrictive covenants the benefit or burden of which is annexed to the charity land.

It is expressly provided that the charity trustees are not authorised to impose any personal liability on the official custodian (ibid., subs. (5)), and that the latter may, without liability, permit documents of title relating to the trust property to be in the possession of the charity trustees (ibid., subs. (6)).

Execution of instruments.—Since the number of trustees holding land on charitable trusts is permitted to exceed the normal four (Trustee Act, 1925, s. 34 (3)), conveyancing could be considerably complicated were there not also special provisions enabling instruments to be executed without the concurrence of all the trustees. Apart from the case-law rule that trustees of a charity could act by a majority (Re Whiteley [1910] 1 Ch. 66), it was provided by s. 12 of the Charitable Trusts Act, 1869, that a majority of such trustees present at a duly constituted meeting could execute deeds and do anything necessary to carry out any disposition of any property of the charity with the same effect as if all the trustees had acted. The principal difficulty of this provision in practice was that it afforded no protection to a purchaser if the meeting had not in fact been duly constituted, so that evidence of this, usually by way of statutory declaration, had to be called for. Now, however, s. 12 of the 1869 Act has been repealed and replaced by the simpler provisions of s. 34 of the Charities Act, 1960, as follows :—

" 34.—(1) Charity trustees may, subject to the trusts of the charity, confer on any of their body (not being less than two in number) a general authority, or an authority limited in such manner as the trustees think fit, to execute in the names and on behalf of the trustees assurances or other deeds or instruments for giving effect to transactions to which the trustees are a party ; and any deed or instrument executed in pursuance of an authority so given shall be of the same effect as if executed by the whole body.

(2) An authority under subsection (1) above—

(a) shall suffice for any deed or instrument if it is given in writing or by resolution of a meeting of the trustees, notwithstanding the want of any formality that would be required in giving an authority apart from that subsection ;

(b) may be given so as to make the powers conferred exerciseable by any of the trustees, or may be restricted to named persons or in any other way ;

(c) subject to any such restriction, and until it is revoked, shall, notwithstanding any change in the charity trustees, have effect as a continuing authority given by and to the persons who from time to time are of their body.

(3) In any authority under this section to execute a deed or instrument in the names and on behalf of charity trustees there shall, unless the contrary intention appears, be implied authority also to execute it for them in the name and on behalf of the official custodian for charities or of any other person, in any case in which the charity trustees could do so.

(4) Where a deed or instrument purports to be executed in pursuance of this section, then in favour of a person who (then or afterwards) in good faith acquires for money or money's worth an interest in or charge on property or the benefit of any covenant or agreement expressed to be entered into by the charity trustees, it shall be conlusively presumed to have been duly executed by virtue of this section.

(5) The powers conferred by this section shall be in addition to and not in derogation of any other powers."

It would appear that the authority within this section could be conferred by a majority of the trustees (see *Re Whiteley* [1910] 1 Ch. 66), and that it may extend beyond conveyancing instruments to include, e.g., cheques.

Trustees of charitable and public trusts as trust corporations.— It is provided by s. 3 (1) of the Law of Property (Amendment) Act, 1926, in effect, that for the purposes of the 1925 Acts the expression " trust corporation " includes (*inter alia*), in relation to charitable, ecclesiastical and public trusts, any local or public authority prescribed by the Lord Chancellor, and any other corporation constituted under the laws of the United Kingdom or any part thereof which satisfies the Lord Chancellor that it undertakes the administration of any such trusts without remuneration, or that by its constitution it is required to apply the whole of its net income after payment of outgoings for charitable, ecclesiastical, or public purposes, and is prohibited from distributing, directly or indirectly, any part thereof by way of profits amongst any of its members, and is authorised by him to act in relation to such trusts as a trust corporation.

Appointment of new trustees of a charity.—The restrictions on the number of trustees of settlements or dispositions on trust for sale of land contained in the T.A. 1925, s. 34, do not apply in the case of land vested in trustees for charitable, ecclesiastical or public purposes, or where the proceeds of sale are held for like purposes (T.A. 1925, s. 34 (3) (a), (b)). The powers of appointing new trustees contained in the Conveyancing Act, 1881, s. 31, and in the T.A. 1925, s. 36 (as to which, see *post*, p. 790), apply to charities (*Re Coates to Parsons* (1886), 34 Ch. D. 370) and, in practice, used to take the place of the Trustees Appointment Acts, 1850, 1869 and 1890. Now, however, where the trusts of a charity provide for the appointment or discharge of trustees by resolution of a meeting of the trustees, members or other persons, a memorandum declaring a trustee to have been so appointed or discharged is sufficient evidence of that fact if it is signed either at the meeting by the person presiding or in some other manner directed by the meeting, and is attested by two persons present at the meeting (Charities Act, 1960, s. 35 (1)). Such a memorandum, if executed as a deed, operates under the T.A. 1925, s. 40, to vest the property as if the appointment or discharge were by deed (s. 35 (2) of the 1960 Act). Where a document purports to have been signed and attested in this way then on proof (by evidence or as a presumption) of the signature, the document is presumed to have been so signed and attested unless the contrary is shown (*ibid.*, s. 35 (3)). Subsection (2) applies only to memoranda made after 1960 but the remainder of the section applies to a memorandum made at any time (*ibid.*, s. 35 (4)).

It is also provided that the Trustees Appointment Acts, 1850, 1869 and 1890, should cease to have effect, except that where their provisions still applied to land at the end of 1960 they should continue to have effect " as if contained in the conveyance or other instrument declaring the trusts on which the land [was] then held " (s. 35 (6) of the 1960 Act ; compare *ibid.*, s. 48 (2) and Sched. 7, Pt. I). Those Acts applied to land held for closely defined purposes of a religious or educational character (1850 Act, s. 1 ; School Sites Act, 1852, s. 1 ; 1869 Act, s. 1 ; 1890 Act, s. 2) and their provisions are outlined *ante*, pp. 267–268. In particular, note that under them a memorandum of appointment of a trustee in due form was conclusive evidence that the appointment was duly made (1850 Act, s. 3 ; 1890 Act, s. 7). It is questionable, however, whether this provision should still be relied on since it no longer has statutory effect (see subs. (6) of s. 35 of the 1960 Act, *ante*). Consequently, it would appear better practice to use the new method wherever applicable rather than the procedure under the old Trustees Appointment Acts.

Nonetheless, two limitations on the new method of appointment under s. 35 of the Charities Act, 1960, should be noted. First, the method is only available where the trusts of the charity provide for trustees to be appointed or discharged by resolution, so that a purchaser ought to investigate the trusts to this extent. Second, the memorandum is only evidence of the appointment or discharge and not that the persons named are the only trustees, so that a purchaser ought to require the usual conveyancing evidence, e.g., of deaths, as to who are the continuing trustees in whom the property is vested.

Registered land.—Where the Land Registration Acts, 1925–1971, apply, the managing trustees (or charitable corporation) will be registered as proprietors unless the legal estate is vested in the official custodian of charities who will be registered as proprietor notwithstanding that the managing trustees have the powers of disposition (L.R.A. 1925, s. 98 ; L.R.R. 1925, r. 60 ; see *ante*, p. 274). Further, where there can be no dealing with the land without the consent of the Charity Commissioners or the Secretary of State for Education and Science (Charities Act, 1960, s. 29, and *ante*, p. 272 ; a certificate as to the necessity of consent can be given in cases of doubt under L.R.R. 1925, r. 61), then a restriction preventing dealings without such consent must be entered on the register (L.R.R. 1925, r.r. 60c, 123 (2) and 124, and Schedule, Form 12). The restriction may be qualified, e.g., conditional as to occupation, when the registrar will act on a certificate from the solicitor to the charity. In addition where the new method of appointing or discharging trustees by resolution is available (i.e., under s. 35 of the Charities Act, 1960 ; see above) then the trustees will normally be registered as proprietors collectively (i.e., as " The trustees of the [named] Charity ") together with a restriction referring to the requirements of s. 35 of the 1960 Act. Here the registrar will require with an application for registration either a certified copy of any memorandum or a certificate from the clerk or solicitor to the charity.

School sites.—Under the School Sites Act, 1841, s. 2 (replacing the School Sites Act, 1836), absolute and limited owners were empowered to grant up to one acre of land as a school site, but it was provided that on the land ceasing to be used for the purposes of the Act it should " revert to and become a portion of the said estate." No estate is expressly mentioned in the section and a parcel of land may revert to the grantor even though he did not own neighbouring land and even though he sold for value (*Re Cawston's Conveyance* [1940] Ch. 27). Usually conveyances were made to the vicar and wardens under s. 7 of the 1841 Act ; in other cases it may be difficult to decide whether the Act applied. See *Dennis* v. *Malcolm* [1934] Ch. 244. It was decided in *Re Ingleton Charity* [1956] Ch. 585 that the vicar and wardens remain trustees of the trusts declared by the original grant even if the reverter has occurred and they have, thereafter, acquired title by lapse of time. Consequently, even after they have so acquired title they may sell only in pursuance of the appropriate statutory powers. An example of the operation of an express reverter clause on property ceasing to be used as a school is provided by *Bankes* v. *Salisbury Diocesan Council of Education* [1960] Ch. 631.

The Education Act, 1944, s. 86 (2), contains provision for the avoiding of reverter to a grantor in certain cases in order that a scheme under the Endowed Schools Acts, 1869 to 1948, may make provision for the sale of land. See further, *Solicitors' Journal*, vol. 96, p. 174.

On sale under s. 14 of the 1841 Act, it seems that a good title will be obtained, notwithstanding the statutory right of reverter, provided that right has not attached at the date of the sale. Thus evidence is required that even at the date of the conveyance the premises were still used as a school pursuant to the trusts ; provision is necessary for vacant possession to be given later. See the explanation of the practice of the Land Registry in Ruoff and Roper, Registered Conveyancing, 3rd vol., at pp. 252–253.

CHURCH AUTHORITIES

It is not proposed to deal here with the acquisition of land by Church of England authorities, because any necessary information can be obtained from the Church Commissioners, and conveyances to such authorities are usually dealt with by solicitors conversant with the technicalities. Perhaps it should be noted that the Church Commissioners came into being on 1st April, 1948, and took over the functions of Queen Anne's Bounty and the Ecclesiastical Commissioners (Church Commissioners Measure, 1947). All property of those bodies vested in the Commissioners without any conveyance, but subject to any existing trust or mortgage or charge or any existing lease or tenancy (*ibid.*, s. 2). Note also that the Church Commissioners and any institution which is administered by them are exempt from the mandatory provisions of the Charities Act, 1960 (Sched. 2, para. (*f*)).

Sales and leases of church lands may be effected under various statutory powers. There is no authority on the matter, but the better opinion appears to be that an incumbent has the powers of a tenant for life and trustees of the settlement under the S.L.A. 1925. However, it has been held that the S.L.A. 1925, s. 29, does not apply to consecrated land and buildings, such as churches, which are vested in an incumbent for the duration of his incumbency (*Re St. Swithin's, Norwich* [1960] P. 77 ; it was not found necessary to express any view as to the application of the S.L.A. 1925 to secular property).

The incumbent of an ecclesiastical benefice, with the consents of the bishop and patron, may let any part of the glebe or other lands of the benefice at the best rent for farming purposes for fourteen years, or on an improving lease for twenty years, provided the parsonage house and ten acres of land adjoining it are reserved and provided specified covenants are inserted (Ecclesiastical Leases Act, 1842, ss. 1, 2). The lease should be indorsed with a receipt for a counterpart or attested copy signed by the lessor and should be executed by the bishop and patron (*ibid.*, s. 4). A power for ecclesiastical corporations, aggregate or sole, with a few exceptions, with the consent of the Church Commissioners and of the patron, to grant building leases for ninety-nine years is contained in the Ecclesiastical Leasing Act, 1842, s. 1. Such ecclesiastical corporations may also, with the same consents, if the Church Commissioners are satisfied that it will be to the permanent advantage of the estate, lease, sell or exchange any part of the property, but no sale can be authorised unless one month's notice has been given to the bishop (Ecclesiastical Leasing Act, 1858, s. 1).

The incumbent of a benefice may sell any part of the glebe with the approval of the Minister of Agriculture, Fisheries and Food and on notice being given to the bishop of the diocese, to the patron, to the parishioners, to the clerk of the county council and to the clerk of the parish or borough or urban district council. See the Glebe Lands Act, 1888, and the Sale of Glebe Land Rules, 1927, which contain detailed provision as to the procedure which must be adopted. The power contained in the 1888 Act to sell does not apply to the parsonage house or the appurtenances thereto, or such part of the glebe as is necessary to the convenient enjoyment of the house (*ibid.*, ss. 2, 3 (1)), or where the land is subject to a lease for a term exceeding twenty-one years or let at less than two-thirds of the rack-rent, or where the incumbent is not in possession of the full rents and profits (*ibid.*, s. 5 (2)).

An incumbent or, during a vacancy, the bishop, may sell the residence, house and appurtenances annexed to a benefice with any land contiguous thereto belonging to the benefice, although not more than twelve acres may be sold in any one benefice (Parsonages Measure, 1938, s. 1 (1), (3) (i)), and the consents of the Church Commissioners, the Diocesan Dilapidations Board, and the bishop are necessary (*ibid.*, s. 1 (3) (ii)). Alternatively, instead of a sale, the same authorities may exchange the residence house (Church Property (Miscellaneous Provisions) Measure, 1960, s. 1). There is also a power to sell lands annexed to a benefice under the Church Building Act, 1839, ss. 15, 16, 17, with the consent of the Church Commissioners, and certain other consents.

Any land may be sold pursuant to a scheme for the union of benefices made by the Church Commissioners and confirmed by Order in Council under the Union of Benefices Act, 1860, or the Union of Benefices Measures, 1923 and 1936. When a direction for sale under the Measures comes into operation the property to be sold vests in the Church Commissioners for the purpose of being disposed of in accordance with the scheme (Union of Benefices Measure, 1923, s. 22).

Lands acquired by the Ecclesiastical Commissioners, or the Church Building Commissioners, or the Church Commissioners for churches, churchyards or houses for ecclesiastical persons, which, in the opinion of the Church Commissioners and the bishop, are not required for the purposes for which they were acquired may, if acquired for value and except in the case of consecrated ground, be sold by the Church Commissioners (New Parishes Measure, 1943, s. 13). In addition, s. 17 of the Church Property (Miscellaneous Provisions) Measure, 1960, enables sale or exchange of land acquired by the Commissioners or the Church Building Commissioners for the purposes specified (except for houses). If the land is vested in the Commissioners, the consent of the incumbent, if any, and the bishop is required ; if it is vested in the incumbent, the consent of the Commissioners and the bishop must be obtained. If the land or building was acquired for value before 4th February, 1943, and has been held for less than twenty years it must be offered to the person from whom it was acquired (1943 Measure, s. 17 (2) as substituted). On sale under this section the proceeds must be paid to the Commissioners (*ibid.*, s. 17 (4)).

In an area covered by a reorganisation scheme under the Reorganisation Areas Measure, 1944, all church lands (other than a churchyard or burial ground used for burials) may be sold under the terms of a scheme, and if not vested in the Church Commissioners or the Diocesan Board of Finance the lands will vest in one of those bodies for the purpose of disposition in accordance with the scheme (Reorganisation Areas Measure, 1944, s. 32).

A parochial church council may acquire, by gift or otherwise, any property for any ecclesiastical purpose affecting the parish, but (except in the case of a lease for not more than one year) land may be acquired only with the consent of the diocesan authority and must be vested in that authority (Parochial Church Councils (Powers) Measure, 1956, ss. 5, 6). Such land may be sold, exchanged or let (other than a letting of land held on a short lease) only with the consent of the diocesan authority.

Although there is power for a parochial church council to borrow money, there is no power for such a council to charge anything as security for a loan (*Mulholland* v. *St. Peter, Roydon* [1969] 1 W.L.R. 1842).

A pamphlet containing practical notes concerning the acquisition of property by parochial church councils and certain model precedents has been published by the Church Information Office and may be referred to with advantage.

There is nothing to prevent trusts for parochial purposes being constituted without reference to the diocesan authority or the parochial church council and such trusts will be subject to the usual rules affecting charitable trusts ; see *ante*, p. 269.

Note, however, that notwithstanding the various consents required by statute and referred to in the preceding paragraphs, the incumbent, being the fee simple owner, may grant a licence which will be enforceable in equity if expenditure is incurred on the strength of it (*Ward* v. *Kirkland* [1966] 1 W.L.R. 601, applying *Inwards* v. *Baker* [1965] 2 Q.B. 29). Even though this equity may, in effect, take effect as an interest in property, this is due to the court's action and the licence itself does not amount to a disposition without necessary consents (*ibid.*).

CLUB TRUSTEES

Acquisition of land.—No unusual difficulty is likely to arise in the case of a proprietary club, in respect of which the property is vested in a proprietor, the members having certain rights of user. In the cases of both proprietary clubs and members' clubs (in which the property is vested in the members or in trustees for them) it is convenient to register the club as a limited company.

Land acquired by a members' club, which is not incorporated, is usually conveyed to a number of trustees as joint tenants on behalf of the club. It is advisable to disclose the trust in the conveyance so that there can be no claim for estate duty on the death of a trustee. It is then probably unnecessary to confine the trust within the rule against perpetuities (*Re Drummond* [1914] 2 Ch. 90), but it may be better practice to do so to meet the contention that the trust is for the members for the time being rather than just for the present members. The trustees do not hold beneficially, and so they would not become trustees for sale under the L.P.A. 1925, s. 36 (1). It follows that there may be more than four trustees (T.A. 1925, s. 34 (1)). To avoid difficulty when it is desired to sell, the conveyance to the trustees should require them to hold or dispose of the land as directed by the committee, but provide that no purchaser, dealing in good faith, shall be concerned with any such directions.

On change in the nature and purpose of a club it is a question of degree whether there is a dissolution of the old club (in which case property is held on trust for the then members) or the same club continues (in which case property is held on trust for members from time to time of the continuing club (*Abbatt* v. *Treasury Solicitor* [1969] 1 W.L.R. 1575)).

Appointment of new trustees.—The rules of the club will probably determine how new trustees should be appointed, and this is likely to be by resolution at a meeting. As such an appointment is not by deed, the implied vesting declaration in the T.A. 1925, s. 40, will not operate and it is necessary for all surviving trustees to join in a conveyance to the new trustees. A method of avoiding this difficulty is by providing in the rules for nomination of new trustees by a majority of the committee and for appointment of the trustees so nominated by the chairman of the meeting. The appointment can then be made by the chairman by deed under the T.A. 1925, s. 36, with the advantage of the implied vesting declaration under the T.A. 1925, s. 40. In this way the necessity for the concurrence of all existing trustees is avoided. If the club is a registered friendly society under the Friendly Societies Act, 1896, once property has been vested in the trustees, it remains vested in the trustees for the time being without any conveyance (Friendly Societies Act, 1896, s. 50, as slightly amended by the 1971 Act, Sched. 2).

Disposition of land.—If the land was conveyed to trustees on an express trust for sale they will dispose of the land in pursuance of that trust for sale. Similarly, if the land was conveyed to the trustees as joint tenants, apparently beneficially and without disclosing the trust, it would appear to a purchaser that the land became held on trust for sale under the L.P.A. 1925, s. 36 (1), and presumably a purchaser who accepted a title on this assumption would be protected against any claim by members of the club. Where, as is usual, the conveyance was to trustees as joint tenants, to hold as the committee of the club may direct, the purchaser should ensure that any necessary resolution has been passed, except so far as inquiry may be rendered unnecessary by provision in the trust deed for his protection. In this case a purchaser is not concerned to inquire as to the authority for any sale (Friendly Societies Act, 1896, s. 47 (1)).

CONVICTS

A convict is not now subject to any special disability, and is able to appoint an attorney to act for him. Various statutory restrictions were repealed as from 18th April, 1949, by the Criminal Justice Act, 1948, s. 70 (1); the rules laid down by the Forfeiture Act, 1870, as regards dealings by convicts (i.e., persons against whom sentence of death or penal servitude was pronounced for treason or felony: *ibid.*, s. 6) with their property before 18th April, 1949, are to be found in the 13th Edition of this book at pp. 266, 267.

Trust and mortgage estates have never been affected by the trustee or mortgagee becoming a convict (*Re Levy and Debenture Corporation* (1894), 38 Sol. J. 530). It was provided by s. 65 of the T.A. 1925, replacing s. 48 of the Trustee Act, 1893, with a slight variation, that property vested in any person on any trust or by way of mortgage should not, in case of that person becoming a convict within the meaning of the Forfeiture Act, 1870, vest in the administrator, but should remain in the trustee or mortgagee, or pass to his co-trustee in right of survivorship or devolve on his personal representative as if he had not become a convict. The court, however, had power to appoint a new trustee in substitution for a convict trustee, and to make a vesting order on the appointment of such new trustee (T.A. 1925, ss. 41, 44 and 49, replacing Trustee Act, 1893, ss. 25, 26 and 32). The legal estate in settled land vested in a convict as tenant for life remained vested in him in the capacity of a trustee (S.L.A. 1925, s. 107 (1)), and, since 1949, his beneficial interest also remains in him.

CO-OWNERS (JOINT TENANTS AND TENANTS IN COMMON)

Nature of a joint tenancy.—For the creation of a joint tenancy, there are two essential requirements. First and negatively, there must be an absence of any " words of severance " in the conveyance, or other limitation, of the property. There will be such " words of severance " whenever there is the slightest indication of an intention that the grantees are to take distinct shares. Thus, the expression " in equal shares " clearly indicates a tenancy in common and not a joint tenancy (*Re Davies* [1950] 1 All E.R. 120) and further examples are given below. In practice it is usual and desirable to express the intention to create a joint tenancy positively and clearly by some such words as " jointly " or " as joint tenants." Then any indications which might in themselves have created a tenancy in common will be overridden. Note, however, that the contradictory expression " jointly and severally " indicates a joint tenancy in a deed (*Slingsby's Case* (1587), 5 Co. Rep. 18*b*, at p. 19*a*) but a tenancy in common in a will (*Perkins* v. *Baynton* (1781), 1 Bro. C.C. 118).

Secondly and positively, for the creation of a joint tenancy, what are known as the " four unities " must be present. That is to say, there must be unity of (*a*) *possession*, i.e., each tenant is as much entitled to possession of any part of the property as the others ; (*b*) *interest*, i.e., each tenant has an interest which is the same in extent, nature and duration as that of the others, e.g., all fee simples or all life interests ; (*c*) *title*, i.e., each tenant must hold under the same document or act, e.g., the same conveyance or all simultaneously entering into adverse possession (*Ward* v. *Ward* (1871), 6 Ch. App. 789) ; and (*d*) *time*, i.e., the interest of each tenant must vest at the same time, e.g., not a right to X for life, remainder to the heirs of Y and Z where Y and Z die at different times during X's life.

In addition it should be noted that where a joint tenancy might otherwise have been created as above, in certain circumstances an equitable presumption will arise in favour of a tenancy in common : see *post*, p. 295 *et seq.*

Since 1925 a legal estate in land can only be held by several persons as joint tenants (L.P.A. 1925, s. 1 (6)).   Then, unless the land is settled land within the meaning of the S.L.A. 1925 (as to which see *post*, p. 665), the legal estate will necessarily be held on trust for sale, this trust being either express or imposed by statute (L.P.A. 1925, ss. 34, 35 and 36 ; and see *Re Buchanan-Wollaston's Conveyance* [1939] Ch. 738 and *Bull* v. *Bull* [1955] 1 Q.B. 234). The proceeds of sale may be held on trust by the joint tenants for themselves or any other persons beneficially in equity either as joint tenants or as tenants in common.

The unique characteristic of a joint tenancy, as opposed to a tenancy in common, is the *right of survivorship*.   The interest of a joint tenant does not pass under his will or as on his intestacy but accrues automatically on his death to the survivors or survivor (this latter would then hold as sole owner). Thus the A.E.A. 1925, s. 1 (1), provides that real estate to which a deceased person was entitled for an interest *not* ceasing on his death should devolve on his personal representatives, and s. 3 (4) of that Act explains that " the interest of a deceased person under a joint tenancy where another tenant survives the deceased *is* an interest ceasing on his death."

Consequently, a joint tenant cannot dispose of his interest or sever the tenancy by his will.   However, he has full powers of independent disposition of his beneficial interest *inter vivos* and the joint tenancy can also be turned into a tenancy in common (except of a *legal* estate in land) during the lifetime of the tenants ; as to severance, see *post*, p. 302.   Note that if there are more than two joint tenants and one of them severs the equitable joint tenancy, the remaining interests will still be held as joint tenants ; also if one of them disposes of his equitable interest to a third party, the third party becomes a tenant in common of that interest ; but if one of them releases his interest, legal or equitable, to all the others, they continue to hold as the joint tenants (see L.P.A. 1925, s. 36 (2)).   A joint tenancy may be determined by union of all interests beneficially in one tenant, either as the sole survivor (see *Re Cook* [1948] Ch. 212) or by release to the one of the interests of all the other tenants.

Nature of a tenancy in common.—It is stated in Cheshire's Modern Law of Real Property, 11th ed., p. 335, that " A tenancy in common arises (i) where land is limited to two or more persons with words of severance showing an intention, even in the slightest degree, that the donees are to take separate shares [examples of which are given below], or (ii) where equity reads what is at law a joint tenancy as a tenancy in common [for an example, where land is bought by partners, see p. 381, *post*], or (iii) where one joint tenant disposes of his interest to a stranger or acquires an interest greater than that of his co-tenants " [see p. 302, *post*].   Although a *legal* estate cannot now be held by tenants in common these rules apply to the creation of equitable interests in common.   The following expressions, having words of severance, have been held to create a tenancy in common :—

To *A* and *B* as tenants in common.

To *A* and *B* equally.

To *A* and *B* in equal shares.

To *A* and *B* respectively.

To *A* and *B* share and share alike.

Between *A* and *B*.

Among *A*, *B* and *C*.

Even though there may be no such clear words of severance, the grant or gift construed as a whole may nonetheless indicate that a tenancy in common was intended. Thus maintenance and advancement clauses indicated that the beneficiaries were to be tenants in common (*Bennett* v. *Houldsworth* (1911), 104 L.T. 304 ; *Re Woolley* [1903] 2 Ch. 206 ; *Re Dunn ; Carter* v. *Barrett* [1916] 1 Ch. 97 ; *Re Ward ; Partridge* v. *Hoare-Ward* [1920] 1 Ch. 334). The reason is that these powers show an intention on the part of the testator to divide the property, and are inconsistent with the beneficiaries taking as joint tenants. Also, for example, a gift to *A* and *B* on the condition that they should pay *C* an annuity " in equal shares " created a tenancy in common, the intention being presumed that the gift should correspond to the obligation (*Re North* [1952] Ch. 397).

Where there is a gift to a compound class consisting of children and the issue of any deceased child who should have died leaving issue, there must be double words of severance, if a tenancy in common is to be imported not only among the children, but also among the grandchildren (*Re Brooke* [1953] 1 W.L.R. 439). This rule does not apply where the gift is in such a condensed form that words of division can readily be construed as applying not only to the original class of children, but to any substituted issue (*Crosthwaite* v. *Dean* (1879), 40 L.T. 837 ; *Re Froy ; Froy* v. *Froy* [1938] Ch. 566).

The expression " jointly and severally," which involves a contradiction in terms, has been solved by the courts holding that the first word prevails in a deed and the last in a will (*Slingsby's Case* (1587), 5 Co. Rep. 18b ; *Perkins* v. *Baynton* (1781), 1 Bro. C.C. 118 ; *Cookson* v. *Bingham* (1853), 17 Beav. 262).

Further, if the evidence of intention is clear, a conveyance may be rectified by substituting the words " tenants in common " for the words " joint tenants " (*Re Colebrook's Conveyances* [1973] 1 All E.R. 132, where an incidental tax advantage was no bar to rectification).

Before 1926 it was sometimes impossible to sell land held by a number of persons as tenants in common without the aid of the court, for instance, because one was an infant or had not been heard of for a number of years. The scheme of the 1925 legislation was (i) to remove the difficulties incidental to the legal estate in land being held by persons as tenants in common, (ii) to prevent the creation of tenancies in common of the *legal estate* in the future ; and (iii) to enable land to be sold in such a way that the purchaser is not concerned with the beneficial interests, which are transferred to the proceeds of sale. A legal estate is not now allowed to subsist or to be created in an undivided share in land, and provision is made whereby land held in undivided shares should always be subject to a trust for sale so that a purchaser can deal with the trustees without having to investigate the title to shares.

Nevertheless, until sale, the equitable tenants in common are concurrently entitled to possession as if they were legal tenants in common (*Re Warren* [1932] 1 Ch. 42 ; *Bull* v. *Bull* [1955] 1 Q.B. 234, considered critically in the *Conveyancer N.S.*, vol. 19, p. 146 ; see also *per* Lord Denning, M.R., in *Bedson* v. *Bedson* [1965] 2 Q.B. 666, at p. 678), but this was described as " a strange claim after 1st January, 1926 " by Lord Upjohn in *Williams* v. *Holland* [1965] 1 W.L.R. 739. However, a tenant in common taking under a will would have no answer to a personal representative's application for possession for the purposes of administration (*Williams* v. *Holland, ante*). Further, if one tenant in common takes more than his fair share of possession it appears that he will have to give credit for this in an action for account or on the ultimate distribution of the proceeds of sale (*Bull* v. *Bull, ante,* and *Williams* v. *Holland, ante*).   *Bull* v. *Bull* was distinguished by the Court of Appeal in *Barclay* v. *Barclay* [1970] 2 Q.B. 677 where there was an express testamentary direction for sale before the gift in shares so that the beneficiaries were only tenants in common of the proceeds and none had any interest in or right to remain in possession of the land.   See further P.V.B. at *Law Quarterly Review,* vol. 86, pp. 443–444 ; also *Irani Finance, Ltd.* v. *Singh* [1971] Ch. 59 in which *dicta* in both the above cases were criticised by the Court of Appeal.

A. TRANSITIONAL PROVISIONS

Joint tenancy.—What happened to the legal and equitable estate in land held in joint tenancy on 31st December, 1925, will now be considered.

(i) *Land held by beneficial owners as joint tenants.*—A special transitional provision in regard to beneficial joint tenancies may be found contained in the L.P.A. 1925, Sched. 1, Pt. II, para. 6 (*b*), as follows :—

" Where the land is at the commencement or by virtue of this Act or any Act coming into operation at the same time subject or is by virtue of any statute made subject to a trust for sale, the legal estate affected shall vest in the trustees for sale (including personal representatives holding land on trust for sale) but subject to any mortgage term subsisting or created by this Act."

The words " made subject to a trust for sale " bring in s. 36 (1) of the L.P.A. 1925, which provides that " Where a legal estate (not being settled land) is beneficially limited to or held in trust for any persons as joint tenants, the same shall be held on trust for sale, in like manner as if the persons beneficially entitled were tenants in common, but not so as to sever their joint tenancy in equity."

So that the result was that, where persons were beneficially entitled to the legal and equitable estates in the land as joint tenants on 1st January, 1926, *and the land was not settled land,* the legal estate still remained in them, but they held such legal estate as trustees for sale for the benefit of themselves as equitable joint tenants.   But where a joint tenancy was subject to a family charge within S.L.A. 1925, s. 1 (1) (v), this special transitional provision was not applicable, the land being settled (*Re Gaul and Houlston's Contract* [1928] Ch. 689, where both at first instance and in the Court of Appeal it was assumed, *obiter* and *per incuriam* it is submitted, that there were no transitional provisions relating to beneficial joint tennats ; for the transitional provisions relating to settled land, see *post,* p. 695).

The terms of the " trust for sale " referred to in the above provisions, on which the property is to be held, are contained in s. 35 of the L.P.A. 1925, as to which see *post,* p. 307.

Notwithstanding that the joint tenants who, on 1st January, 1926, became trustees for sale, consisted of more than four persons, the legal estate remained in them all, and they could all act (T.A. 1925, s. 34 (1)).

(ii) *Land held on trust for persons beneficially entitled as joint tenants.*— Where the legal estate in the land was held by trustees for persons beneficially entitled as joint tenants on 1st January, 1926, such legal estate vested in the joint tenants upon trust for sale (L.P.A. 1925, Sched. 1, Pt. II, paras. 3 and 6 (*d*) ; *Re King's Theatre* [1929] 1 Ch. 483).

(iii) *Land held by joint tenants which was settled land.*—An express transitional provision is contained in the L.P.A. 1925, Sched. 1, Pt. II, para. 6 (*c*) as follows :—

" Where at the commencement of this Act or by virtue of any statute coming into operation at the same time the land is settled land, the legal estate affected shall vest in the tenant for life or statutory owner entitled under the Settled Land Act, 1925, to require a vesting deed to be executed in his favour, or in the personal representative, if any, in whom the land may be vested or the Public Trustee, as the case may require, but subject to any mortgage term subsisting or created by this Act."

Therefore, on 1st January, 1926, the legal estate automatically vested in the joint tenants for life entitled under the S.L.A. to require a vesting deed to be executed in their favour, but subject to any mortgage term subsisting or created by the Act. As the legal estate was vested by the Act and not by the vesting deed, the vesting deed will state that fact. Notwithstanding that the legal estate was vested by the Act, a vesting deed is, as a rule, still necessary before the land can be dealt with (S.L.A. 1925, s. 13).

Who are " the persons entitled " under the Act to require a vesting deed to be executed ? The answer is in s. 19 (2) of the same Act. This subsection provides that " If in any case there are two or more persons of full age so entitled as joint tenants, they together constitute the tenant for life for the purposes of this Act."

A tenant for life will be deemed to be such notwithstanding that under the settlement or otherwise the settled land, or his estate or interest therein, is incumbered or charged in any manner or to any extent, and notwithstanding any assignment by operation of law or otherwise of his estate or interest under the settlement (S.L.A. 1925, s. 19 (4)).

There is no restriction as to the number of persons who may be tenants for life of land as joint tenants. Tenants for life are certainly trustees for the other persons interested in the settled land, but they are not trustees in the sense in which the word " trustees " is used in s. 34 of the T.A. 1925.

(iv) *Land held by infants as joint tenants.*—There are several cases which come within this heading. They will be found dealt with under the heading of Infants, *post*, p. 334 *et seq.*

Tenancy in common.—Now the transitional provisions applying where the legal and equitable estate in land was held by tenants in common on 31st December, 1925, will be considered. It is provided by s. 1 (6) of the L.P.A. 1925 that a legal estate cannot now subsist in an undivided share in land, and s. 205 (1) (ix) of the same Act states that the word " land " is to include " land of any tenure [e.g., leaseholds as well as freeholds : *Re Brooker* [1926] W.N. 93] . . . but not an undivided share in land." Therefore provision had to be made for the cases where persons held the legal estate in land as tenants in common on 31st December, 1925.

Accordingly the L.P.A. 1925, s. 39, provides that for the purpose of effecting the transition from the old to the new law, the provisions set out in Pt. IV of Sched. 1 to the L.P.A. 1925 shall have effect " for subjecting land held in undivided shares to trusts for sale."

The L.P.A. 1925, Sched. 1, Pt. IV, is introduced by the following words :—

" 1. Where, immediately before the commencement of this Act, *land is held at law or in equity in undivided shares vested in possession*, the *following provisions* shall have effect :— "

In determining which of the sub-paragraphs of para. 1 of Pt. IV is applicable to any particular case the opening words of para. 1 of Pt. IV must be repeated before each. The result is that in each case the land must be considered as it was immediately before the commencement of the L.P.A. 1925, that is, on 31st December, 1925. For example " settled land " in sub-paras. (2) and (3) of para. 1 means settled land under the Settled Land Acts, 1882 to 1890, and not settled land under the S.L.A. 1925 (*Re Ryder and Steadman's Contract* [1927] 2 Ch. 62).

Note also that the transitional provisions contained in the L.P.A. 1925, Sched. 1, Pt. II, paras. 2, 3 and 4, apply only where the person is entitled " *immediately after* the commencement of this Act— " whilst the transitional provisions contained in Pt. IV of the same schedule operate as from " *immediately before* the commencement of this Act—." Consequently, Pt. IV operates before Pt. II of Sched. 1 to the L.P.A. 1925, and if persons have become trustees for sale on the statutory trusts under Pt. IV, they then come within the exception in Pt. II " not vested in trustees for sale," and the case does not come within Pt. II at all (*Re Forster* [1929] 1 Ch. 146).

" *land is held . . . in undivided shares*."—Partnership property held by partners before 1926 was held by them upon trust for sale under Pt. IV (*Re Fuller's Contract* [1933] Ch. 652 ; see *post*, p. 381). It has not yet been decided whether coparceners held in undivided shares for the purposes of Pt. IV of the L.P.A., although a clear opinion to this effect is expressed in Megarry & Wade, Real Property, 3rd ed., p. 443. Coparceners are in a peculiar position, being neither tenants in common nor joint tenants, but holding a position intermediate between these two classes (*ibid.*, p. 441 *et seq.*). Joint tenants who have not severed do not hold in undivided shares (*Re King's Theatre* [1929] 1 Ch. 483). Where on 31st December, 1925, there was a trust to divide income among a class of persons, the land was *held in undivided shares* under Pt. IV, and was not settled land (*Re Robins* [1928] Ch. 721).

" *held at law or in equity*."—Part IV, therefore, applies in the case of trustees, personal representatives and mortgagees holding a legal estate as well as in the case of beneficiaries holding only an equitable interest.

" *vested in possession*."—This means, not in remainder. A person may have let the land and, therefore, not be in actual possession of the land, but for the purposes of Pt. IV he would be deemed to be in possession. If the land was not vested in possession it would be settled land (*Re Bird* [1927] 1 Ch. 210). In *Re Earl of Stamford and Warrington* [1927] 2 Ch. 217, Russell, J., stated that the expression " vested in possession " involved the absence of any antecedent estate of freehold, and the immediate beneficial enjoyment of possession, either physical or notional (i.e., by receipt of the rents and profits). He held that land limited for a long term to trustees on trust to accumulate the income and discharge incumbrances on other settled estates and subject thereto on trust under separate settlements for persons in undivided shares was not within Pt. IV, the legal estate instead being vested in the trustees as statutory owners under Pt. II, paras. 5 and 6 (*c*), of Sched. 1 to the L.P.A. 1925, and s. 23 (1) (*b*) of the S.L.A. 1925.

See also *Re Price* [1929] 2 Ch. 400, *Re House* [1929] 2 Ch. 166, *Re Dawson's Settled Estate* [1928] Ch. 421, *Re Myhill* [1928] Ch. 100, and *Re Stevens and Dunsby's Contract* [1928] W.N. 187.

The imposition of the statutory trusts operated as a conversion of real estate into personalty. This may have unexpected results where a testator has devised realty to one person and personalty to another. See *Re Kempthorne* [1930] 1 Ch. 268.

"*following provisions.*"—There are four separate sub-paragraphs in para. 1 of Pt. IV. These should be read in numerical order in relation to any particular case, so that, for example, if the case is covered by sub-paragraph (1) there is no need to look further even though, *prima facie*, it might also be covered by sub-para. (3) (*Re Dawson's Settled Estate* [1928] Ch. 421 ; *Re Barrat* [1929] 1 Ch. 336).

(1) *Entirety vested in trustees or personal representatives in trust for persons in undivided shares.*—The L.P.A. 1925, Sched. 1, Pt. IV, para. 1 (1), provides as follows :—

> "(1) If the entirety of the land is vested in trustees or personal representatives (whether subject or not to incumbrances affecting the entirety or an undivided share) *in trust for persons entitled in undivided shares*, then—
>
> > (*a*) if the land is subject to incumbrances affecting undivided shares or to incumbrances affecting the entirety which under this Act or otherwise are not secured by legal terms of years absolute, the entirety of the land shall vest free from such incumbrances in such trustees or personal representatives and be held by them upon the *statutory trusts ;* and
> >
> > (*b*) in any other case, the land shall be held by such trustees or personal representatives upon the *statutory trusts ;*
>
> subject in the case of personal representatives, to their rights and powers for the purposes of administration."

"*statutory trusts*" are explained, *post*, p. 307.

"*in trust for persons entitled in undivided shares.*"—This phrase is used in the general sense of having a present interest therein and is not confined to the case of persons entitled absolutely in undivided shares. In *Re Myhill* [1928] Ch. 100, real estate was held on 31st December, 1925, in trust in undivided shares in possession, as to three undivided fourth shares for persons for life, and as to the other fourth part for others absolutely, and it was held that the entirety of the land was held in trust for persons entitled in undivided shares, some holding for life, and some absolutely, and that the case, therefore, fell within para. 1 (1).

Another point was decided in *Re Myhill*. On 31st December, 1925, the legal estate in the land was vested in *one trustee*, and the learned judge decided that under the Interpretation Act, 1889, the plural included the singular, and that, accordingly, the legal estate remained vested in the single trustee, but that to enable him to make a good title and give a good receipt it would be necessary to appoint another trustee to act with him.

An example of land vesting in a personal representative under para. 1 (1) occurred in *Re Collins* [1929] 1 Ch. 201. In that case a testator, who died in 1917, devised real estate to his widow on trust for her own use for life and then for his children. The widow died in 1923, having by her will appointed X

as her sole executrix. It was held by Maugham, J., that, having regard
to s. 31 of the Wills Act, 1837, the widow was legal owner in trust for the
persons entitled in undivided shares, and that *X*, as her executrix, was the
person in whom the legal estate vested on 1st January, 1926, on the statutory
trusts for the children under para. 1 (1) (*b*) of Pt. IV.

Paragraph 1 (1), however, does not apply where several shares were
vested in the same persons as trustees but upon different trusts. In *Re
Hayward* [1928] Ch. 367, the land was, immediately before 1926, divided
into three shares, each of which was vested in the same persons as trustees
upon three different trusts. An order had been made in 1927 appointing
new trustees in the place of the Public Trustee, it being assumed, when the
order was made, that the entirety of the land had become vested in the Public
Trustee under para. 1 (4) of Pt. IV. The report contains no argument,
but it appears that the court took the view that, where undivided shares
were vested in the same trustees upon different trusts or under different
settlements, the entirety of the land was not vested in the trustees so as to
bring the case within para. 1 (1) of Pt. IV.

It sometimes happens that all the trustees died before 1926, and, there
having been no necessity for a sale, no fresh trustees were appointed. If,
in such a case, representation had been taken out to the estate of the last
surviving trustee before 1926, the legal estate would be in his executors
or administrators, but if no probate or administration had been taken out
before 1926, the legal estate would have passed to the Public Trustee under
para. 1 (4), and, to enable the land to be dealt with, trustees would have to
be appointed to take the legal estate out of the Public Trustee.

(2) *Entirety vested in not more than four persons in undivided shares.*—The
L.P.A. 1925, Sched. 1, Pt. IV, para. 1 (2), provides as follows :—

> " (2) If the entirety of the land (*not being settled land*) is vested absolutely
> and beneficially in not more than four persons of full age entitled
> thereto in undivided shares free from incumbrances affecting
> undivided shares, but subject or not to incumbrances affecting the
> entirety, it shall, by virtue of this Act, vest in them as joint tenants
> upon the statutory trusts."

" *not being settled land.*"—In this sub-paragraph and in para. 1 (3) " settled
land " means settled land under the 1882 to 1890 Settled Land Acts, and
not settled land under the S.L.A. 1925 (see above, p. 287).

It will be noted that the sub-paragraph did not apply—

(i) unless there were not more than four persons of full age entitled
in undivided shares in possession. This is similar to s. 34 (2) of
the T.A. 1925, which provides that in the case of dispositions on trust
for sale of land coming into operation after 1925, the number of
trustees shall not in any case exceed four ;

(ii) where any of the parties was an infant ; and

(iii) where any of the owners of undivided shares had incumbered his
share (although a mortgage of the whole of the land would not have
prevented this sub-paragraph from applying).

In these three cases where the sub-paragraph did not apply, the legal
estate vested in the Public Trustee under para. 1 (4), until trustees were
appointed in his place.

10

(3) *Entirety being settled land under one settlement.*—The L.P.A. 1925, Sched. 1, Pt. IV, para. 1 (3), provides as follows :—

" (3) *If the entirety of the land is settled land* (whether subject or not to incumbrances affecting the entirety or an undivided share) *held under one and the same settlement,* it shall, by virtue of this Act, vest free from incumbrances affecting undivided shares, and from incumbrances affecting the entirety, which under this Act or otherwise are not secured by a legal [mortgage, and free from any interests, powers, and charges subsisting under the settlement, which have priority to the interests of the persons entitled to the undivided shares] *in the trustees (if any) of the settlement* as joint tenants upon the statutory trusts.

Provided that if there are no such trustees, then—

(i) *pending their appointment, the land shall,* by virtue of this Act, *vest (free as aforesaid) in the Public Trustee* upon the statutory trusts ;

(ii) the Public Trustee shall not be entitled to act in the trust, or charge any fee, or be liable in any manner, unless and until requested in writing to act by or on behalf of persons interested in more than an undivided half of the land or the income thereof ;

(iii) after the Public Trustee has been so requested to act, and has accepted the trust, no trustee shall (except by an order of the court) be appointed in the place of the Public Trustee without his consent ;

(iv) if, before the Public Trustee has accepted the trust, trustees of the settlement are appointed, the land shall, by virtue of this Act, vest (free as aforesaid) in them as joint tenants upon the statutory trusts ;

(v) if, before the Public Trustee has accepted the trust, the persons having power to appoint new trustees are unable or unwilling to make an appointment or if the tenant for life having power to apply to the court for the appointment of trustees of the settlement neglects to make the application for at least three months after being requested by any person interested in writing so to do, or if the tenants for life of the undivided shares are unable to agree, any person interested under the settlement may apply to the court for the appointment of such trustees."

The amendment made by the Law of Property (Amendment) Act, 1926, is contained in square brackets.

" *If the entirety of the land is settled land* " means settled land under the Settled Land Acts, 1882 to 1890 (*Re Ryder and Steadman's Contract* [1927] 2 Ch. 62).

The general effect of para. 1 (3), as amended, appears to be to create a paramount trust for sale, the exercise of which will overreach the limitations of the settlement, where the entirety of the land was settled land under the Settled Land Acts, 1882 to 1890 (*Re Flint* [1927] 1 Ch. 570). Thus, the amendment appears to have given the trustees of the settlement under the earlier Settled Land Acts the same powers as are given to trustees of a settlement (as defined in s. 36 (1) of the S.L.A. 1925) by subs. (2) of s. 36. These two subsections read together provide, in effect, that if and when, after 1925, land is held in trust for persons entitled in possession under a trust instrument in undivided shares, the trustees of the settlement (if the settled land is not already vested in them) may require the estate owner in whom the settled land is vested to convey the land to them, or assent to the land vesting in them as joint tenants upon the statutory trusts, subject to any incumbrances affecting the settled land which were secured by a legal mortgage, but free from any incumbrances affecting the undivided shares, or not secured as aforesaid.

When settled land becomes subject to a paramount trust for sale the settlement is brought to an end, with the result that the land ceases to be settled land (S.L.A. 1925, s. 3).

If there is only one trustee, the land cannot vest in him under this sub-paragraph, because it is required to vest in " trustees . . . as joint tenants " (*Re Price* [1929] 2 Ch. 400, notwithstanding s. 1 of the Interpretation Act, 1889 ; contrast *Re Myhill* under sub-para. (1)).

Attention is drawn here to para. 4, which was introduced by the Law of Property (Amendment) Act, 1926, because this paragraph is really in the nature of an exception to sub-para. (3) of para. 1 of Pt. IV. The paragraph is discussed *post*, p. 294.

Land held, before 1926, by trustees on trust to secure a family charge, and subject thereto on trust for tenants in common, was not then settled land, and therefore did not come within para. 1 (3), but within para. 1 (1) ; and land held, before 1926, by tenants in common absolutely (that is, without the interposition of a trust), subject to a family charge, was also not settled land, and came within para. 1 (2), and not within para. 1 (3).

In *Re Colyer's Farningham Estate* [1927] 2 Ch. 677, land was, on 31st December, 1925, held on trust for *A* and *B* as tenants in common, with a gift over, subject to a special power of appointment ; Tomlin, J., held that the land vested in the trustees of the settlement under sub-para. (3). In *Re Higgs and May's Contract* [1927] 2 Ch. 249, on 31st December, 1925, land was held under a will on trust for the testator's children, subject to a proviso that when all the children except two were dead, the trustees should sell and divide the proceeds between the two surviving children, and the children of the deceased children ; Eve, J., held that the legal estate in the land vested in the trustees under sub-para. (3). In neither of these cases was the question argued as to whether para. 1 (1) applied ; and, in view of the later decision in *Re Dawson's Settled Estates* [1928] 1 Ch. 421, it appears that the assumption in these cases that the land vested in the trustees under para. 1 (3) was wrong, as it vested under para. 1 (1).

" *settled land . . . held under one and the same settlement.*"—If the land was held under more than one settlement, it vested in the Public Trustee under para. 1 (4) (*Re Hayward* [1928] Ch. 367).

" *in the trustees (if any) of the settlement.*"—In *Re Catchpool* [1928] Ch. 429, it was decided that these words meant the trustees (if any) under the 1882 to 1890 Settled Land Acts, and not the trustees under the S.L.A. 1925. In that case, on 31st December, 1925, the land was held by the personal representative of the last surviving trustee of a will in trust for a person for life, and afterwards for persons in undivided shares. It was held that as there were no trustees under the Settled Land Acts, 1882 to 1890 (cp. S.L.A. 1925, s. 30 (3)), the legal estate in the land had vested under the proviso next.

" *Provided that if there are no such trustees . . . pending their appointment, the land shall . . . vest . . . in the Public Trustee.*"—If, before the Public

Trustee had accepted the trust, trustees of the settlement for the purposes of the S.L.A. 1925 were appointed, the land, by virtue of the Act, vested in them as joint tenants on the statutory trusts. But directly the land vested in them on the statutory trusts, the settlement came to an end, and the land ceased to be settled land. As to appointment of new trustees, where there were none, or of an additional trustee to make the number up to two, so as to enable the land to be vested in them for the purposes of para. 1 (3), see *Re Catchpool* [1928] Ch. 429 ; *Re Price* [1929] 2 Ch. 400.

(4).—*Land to which previous sub-paragraphs do not apply.*—A residuary provision is contained in the L.P.A. 1925, Sched. 1, Pt. IV, para. 1 (4), as amended in 1926, to this effect :—

" (4) In any case to which the foregoing provisions of this Part of this Schedule do not apply, the entirety of the land shall vest (*free as aforesaid*) in the Public Trustee upon the statutory trusts."

There is a proviso to this paragraph as a result of which—

(i) the Public Trustee is not entitled to act in the trust unless requested in writing by persons interested in more than an undivided half of the land or the income thereof ;

(ii) *persons interested in more than an undivided half of the land or the income thereof may appoint new trustees in the place of the Public Trustee with the consent of any incumbrancers of undivided shares* (but so that a purchaser shall not be concerned to see whether any such consent has been given) and thereupon the land by virtue of the Act vests in the persons so appointed (*free as aforesaid*) upon the statutory trusts ; or such persons may (without such consent as aforesaid), apply to the court for the appointment of trustees and thereupon the land vests (*free as aforesaid*) in the trustees as joint tenants upon the statutory trusts ;

(iii) if the persons interested in more than an undivided half do not either request the Public Trustee to act, or apply to the court for the appointment of trustees in his place, within three months from the time when they have been requested in writing by any person interested so to do, then any person interested may apply to the court for the appointment of trustees in the place of the Public Trustee and thereupon the land vests (*free as aforesaid*) in the trustees upon the statutory trusts.

"*free as aforesaid.*"—This means free from incumbrances affecting undivided shares or incumbrances, not being legal mortgages, affecting the entirety.

"*persons interested in more than an individed half of the land or the income thereof.*"—It was decided in *Re Cliff and English Electric Co.'s Contract* [1927] 2 Ch. 94, that persons holding an undivided share on trust for sale are " persons interested " for the purposes of this proviso, and that the expression must not be limited to persons " beneficially interested." But bare trustees of an undivided share would not be " persons interested " (*Re Forster* [1929] 1 Ch. 146).

"*may appoint new trustees in the place of the Public Trustee.*"—Directly the L.P.A. 1925 came into operation the question whether trustees could appoint one or more of themselves naturally arose, and the opinion of eminent conveyancers was that although at one time (*Montefiore* v. *Guedella* [1903] 2 Ch. 723 ; *Re Sampson* [1906] 1 Ch. 435) the courts were against such an appointment, the provisions of s. 36 (1) of the T.A. 1925 allowing this to be done when the appointment was made under the statutory power must be taken as an indication that in future the stricter rule will not be pressed. And, in practice, this view has been generally acted on. It is thought, therefore, that a purchaser may safely accept such an appointment as good.

" *with the consent of any incumbrancers of undivided shares.*"—It is not clear whether the words mean only the incumbrancers of the shares of the actual appointors, or the incumbrancers of *all* the undivided shares. But, as all such appointments will now have been completed, in view of the fact that a purchaser is not concerned to see whether any such consent has been given, it is of little consequence.

Miscellaneous provisions.—There are various other provisions in para. 1 of Pt. IV of Sched. 1 to the L.P.A. 1925, to the following effect :—

(i) Where all the undivided shares in land were vested in the same mortgagees for securing the same mortgage money and the rights of redemption affecting the land were the same as might have been subsisting if the entirety had been mortgaged before the undivided shares were created, the land vested in the mortgagees as joint tenants for a legal term of years absolute subject to cesser on redemption by the trustees for sale in whom the right of redemption became vested, and the mortgage was deemed an incumbrance affecting the entirety (sub-para. (7)).

(ii) Part IV did not, except where expressly provided, prejudice incumbrancers of the entirety of the land and, so far as the nature of the incumbrance admitted, the land vested in them for legal terms of years absolute but not so as to affect priority (sub-para. (8)).

(iii) The trust for sale vested in persons who hold the entirety of the land is not exercisable without the consent of any incumbrancer whose incumbrance is divested by this Part, but a purchaser is not concerned as to such consent (sub-para. (9)).

(iv) In Pt. IV " incumbrance " did not include a legal rent-charge affecting the entirety, land tax, tithe rent-charge or any similar charge on the land not created by an instrument (sub-para. (10) as amended in 1926).

Undivided shares falling into possession after 1925.—Paragraph 1 dealt with the cases of undivided shares vested *in possession* at the commencement of the L.P.A. 1925. Paragraph 2 of Pt. IV of Sched. 1 to the L.P.A. 1925, deals with undivided shares *created before* but *falling into possession after* the commencement of the L.P.A. 1925, as follows :—

" 2. Where undivided shares in land, created before the commencement of this Act, fall into possession after such commencement, and the land is not settled land when the shares fall into possession, the personal representatives (subject to their rights and powers for purposes of administration) or other estate owners in whom the entirety of the land is vested shall, by an assent or a conveyance, give effect to the foregoing provisions of this Part of this Schedule in like manner as if the shares had fallen into possession immediately before the commencement of this Act, and in the meantime the land shall be held on the statutory trusts."

In the ordinary case of the termination of a life interest followed by a tenancy in common s. 36 of the S.L.A. 1925 applies (*Re Cugny* [1931] 1 Ch. 305 ; see *post*, p. 309). This paragraph is only supplemental to that section and designed to cover any case not within it.

Party structures and open spaces.—These, not being suitable objects of an unqualified trust for sale, are dealt with by Pt. V of Sched. 1 to the L.P.A. 1925 (see pp. 487 and 491, *post*), and para. 3 of Pt. IV provides :—

" 3. This Part of this Schedule shall not save as hereinafter mentioned apply to party structures and open spaces within the meaning of the next succeeding Part of this Schedule."

Land held by tenants for life in undivided shares, the entirety of which, after cesser of their interests, is limited to devolve together.—Paragraph 4 of Pt. IV of Sched. 1 to the L.P.A. 1925 provides as follows :—

" 4. Where, immediately before the commencement of this Act, there are two or more tenants for life of full age entitled *under the same settlement* in undivided shares, and *after the cesser of all their interests in the income of the settled land, the entirety of the land is limited so as to devolve together* (not in undivided shares), their interests shall, but without prejudice to any beneficial interest, be converted into a joint tenancy, and the joint tenants and the survivor of them shall, until the said cesser occurs, constitute the tenant for life for the purposes of the Settled Land Act, 1925, and this Act."

This rule, introduced by the Law of Property (Amendment) Act, 1926, is very important. It forms an exception to sub-para. (3) of para. 1 of Pt. IV, which is set out at p. 290, *ante*. By sub-para. (3), if, immediately before 1926, the entirety of land held in undivided shares was settled land, it *vested in the trustees* of the settlement (if any) as joint tenants *upon the statutory trusts*. But the effect of the amendment is that in the case therein mentioned the entirety of the land vested on 1st January, 1926, not in the trustees of the settlement, *but in the tenants for life*, and the survivor of them. A purchaser from such tenants for life must therefore be careful to see that a vesting deed has been executed in their favour, otherwise they will not be able to pass the legal estate (S.L.A. 1925, s. 13).

"*under the same settlement.*"—It will be noted that the paragraph only applies where the tenants for life become entitled in this way.

"*after the cesser of all their interests . . . the entirety of the land is limited so as to devolve together.*"—To come within the paragraph the land must necessarily devolve *together*. A power of appointment may prevent the paragraph applying, as in the case of *Re Colyer's Farningham Estate* [1927] 2 Ch. 677.

In *Re Higgs and May's Contract* [1927] 2 Ch. 249, Eve, J., held that land settled on an ultimate trust for sale and division of the proceeds could not be described as land so limited as to devolve as an undivided whole (followed in *Re Robins* [1928] Ch. 721).

In *Re Barrat* [1929] 1 Ch. 336, where the last survivor of the tenants for life would become absolutely entitled to the property, Maugham, J., held that para. 4 only applied where the entirety of the land was limited so as to devolve on some person *other than* one of the tenants for life originally or previously.

Position of a mortgagee of an undivided share.—Section 102 (1) of the L.P.A. 1925 provides that a person who was, before 1926, a mortgagee of an undivided share in land shall have the same power to sell his share in the proceeds of sale of the land and in the rents and profits thereof until sale, as, independently of the Act, he would have had in regard to his share in the land ; and shall also have a right to require the trustees for sale in whom

the land is vested to account to him for the income attributable to that share
or to appoint a receiver to receive the same from such trustees corresponding
to the right which, independently of the Act, he would have had to take
possession or to appoint a receiver of the rents and profits attributable to the
same share.

B. JOINT TENANCIES CREATED AFTER 1925

Legal estate (except in settled land) held on trust for sale.—This is
the general effect of s. 36 (1) of the L.P.A. 1925, which provides as follows :—

"Where a legal estate (not being settled land) is beneficially limited
to or held in trust for any persons as joint tenants, the same shall be held
on trust for sale, in like manner as if the persons beneficially entitled were
tenants in common, but not so as to sever their joint tenancy in equity."

See generally the Chapter on Trusts for Sale, *post*, p. 763.

Before proceeding, it should be noted that this provision does not purport
to impose the statutory trust for sale in all cases of joint tenancies created
after 1925.   The subsection is expressed to relate only to equitable or
beneficial joint tenancies and not to bare legal joint tenancies.   Accordingly,
where neither a tenancy in common nor a beneficial joint tenancy is involved,
e.g., a conveyance of the legal estate to *A* and *B* who take as trustees for *C*,
there should be no trust for sale and no settled land.   See further *Conveyancer
N.S.*, vol. 9, p. 72 *et seq.*

The words " *as if the persons beneficially entitled were tenants in common* "
in s. 36 (1) above apply by implied cross-reference the provisions of s. 34 of the
L.P.A. 1925.   Subsection (2) of s. 34 provides that as regards a conveyance
to persons as tenants in common where the persons to whom the conveyance
is made are of full age the conveyance is to operate as if the land had been
expressed to be conveyed to the grantees, or if there are more than four
grantees, to the first four named in the conveyance, as joint tenants *upon the
statutory trusts*, and so as to give effect to the rights of the persons who would
have been entitled to the shares had the conveyance operated to create those
shares (see L.P.A. 1925, s. 35, *post*, p. 307).

Apart from ss. 34 to 36 of the L.P.A. 1925, if on a purchase, property were to
be conveyed to two or more persons as joint tenants and the purchase-money
were to be advanced in equal shares, they would take as joint tenants in
equity as well as at law (*Robinson* v. *Preston* (1858), 27 L.J. Ch. 395).   Now,
the grantees, or, if there are more than four grantees, the first four named
in the conveyance, take the legal estate as joint tenants on trust for sale
for the benefit of themselves as joint tenants in equity, unless, of course,
the conveyance states that they are to take the proceeds as tenants in
common.   Again, apart from ss. 34 to 36 of the L.P.A. 1925, if property were
to be conveyed to two or more persons as joint tenants and the purchase-
money were to be paid by them in *un*equal shares, or if the property were
to be purchased for trading purposes, or out of money belonging to them
as partners, they would hold the *legal* estate as joint tenants, but in *equity*
they would be presumed to be entitled to the property in the shares in which
the purchase-money was paid by them or to which they were entitled by
the terms of the partnership arrangement (*Lake* v. *Gibson* (1729), 1 Eq. Cas.
Abr. 290 ; on appeal *Lake* v. *Craddock* (1732), 2 P. Wms. 158 ; and see
Bull v. *Bull* [1955] 1 Q.B. 234, and *Diwell* v. *Farnes* [1959] 1 W.L.R. 624,
also Snell's Equity, 25th ed., pp. 34 and 35).   This equitable presumption
could, of course, be rebutted by the parties' declarations or other admissible
evidence of intention (*Shephard* v. *Cartwright* [1955] A.C. 431).   Now, where

the presumption is not rebutted, the grantees, or if there are more than four grantees, the first four named in the conveyance, will take the legal estate as joint tenants on trust for sale for themselves as tenants in common in equity in the shares to which they are entitled.

Also where property was conveyed by way of mortgage, to two or more persons as joint tenants, it was immaterial whether the money was advanced equally or unequally, in equity the mortgagees would be presumed entitled as tenants in common (*Morley* v. *Bird* (1798), 3 Ves. 629, at p. 631) and this presumption was not rebutted by a joint account clause alone (*Re Jackson ; Smith* v. *Sibthorpe* (1887), 56 L.T. 562 ; see now L.P.A. 1925, s. 111). This will still be so, except that the property will vest in the grantees, or if there are more than four mortgagees in the first four named in the mortgage, for a term of years absolute (as provided by L.P.A. 1925, ss. 85, 86) as joint tenants subject to cesser on redemption in like manner as if the mortgage money had belonged to them on a joint account, *but without prejudice to the beneficial interests in the mortgage money and interest* (L.P.A. 1925, s. 34 (2)).

Registered land.—The L.R.A. 1925, s. 58 (3), provides that, subject to general rules, in the case of joint proprietors, a restriction is obligatory unless it is shown that the joint proprietors are entitled for their own benefit, or can give valid receipts for capital, or that one of them is a trust corporation. Such restrictions are considered *post*, p. 623 ; they provide that, when the number of joint proprietors has been reduced to one, unless such proprietor is a trust corporation, no registered disposition under which capital money arises shall be made except under an order of the registrar or an order of the court. See also L.R.R. 1925, r. 213. It is understood that no restriction beyond that required by s. 58 (3) is now normally entered even if the joint proprietors are mere trustees with others. In any event no person dealing with a registered estate is affected with notice of a trust (L.R.A. 1925, s. 74).

Two or more joint tenants who are solely entitled beneficially will be registered without any restriction. The result is that on the death of one or more leaving a sole survivor, that survivor will be able to sell without appointing another trustee to act jointly with him (compare the position in the case of unregistered land, *post*, p. 300). If the joint tenancy has been severed, an appropriate restriction should have been entered ; if this was not done a purchaser from the survivor will get a good title. However, as an alternative to a restriction, it has been held that a caution can be lodged to protect a beneficial interest in the proceeds of sale of land held on trust for sale (*Elias* v. *Mitchell* [1972] Ch. 652).

Conveyance of freehold land to joint tenants.—When such a conveyance has to be drawn, and the solicitor is in a position to choose the form, it is customary to adopt some form whereby the vendor, as beneficial owner, conveys unto the purchasers in fee simple as " joint tenants." Then comes a declaration that the purchasers shall stand possessed of the premises upon trust to sell the same and to stand possessed of the net proceeds and the net rents in trust for the purchasers as joint tenants beneficially—that is, a declaration in much the same terms as those implied by s. 35 of the L.P.A. 1925 (given in full at p. 307). This is followed by a clause granting to the purchasers (and the trustees for the time being) unrestricted powers of mortgaging the premises and of leasing or otherwise dealing with them as an absolute beneficial owner in fee simple would have. Despite doubts as to its necessity, it used also to be the practice, *ex abundanti cautela*, to restrict these

powers to the perpetuity period. Now, however, such restriction is clearly
unnecessary, statute having declared that the administrative powers of
trustees are not to be invalidated by the rule against perpetuities (Perpetuities
and Accumulations Act, 1964, s. 8, applying also to the exercise after the Act
of powers conferred before the Act).

Further it is possible to convey the property to the purchasers in fee simple
as joint tenants without mentioning a trust for sale or any administrative
powers. By ss. 34 and 36 (1) of the L.P.A. 1925 such a conveyance would
operate to vest the legal estate in the purchasers, or, if more than four, in the
first four named, as joint tenants in fee simple on trust for sale, and it would
also operate to vest in them the equitable estate. The equitable estate
would consist of their joint interest in the net proceeds of sale, and of the net
rents and profits until sale of the land. The terms of the trust for sale on
which they would hold the legal estate in the land and the rents are set out in
s. 35 of the L.P.A. 1925, and are given in full at p. 307. As trustees for the
sale of land, the purchasers would have " all the powers of a tenant for life
and of the trustees of a settlement under the Settled Land Act, 1925, including
in relation to the land the power of management conferred by that Act during
a minority " (s. 28 (1) of the L.P.A. 1925 ; whether or not there is a minority :
Re Gray [1927] 1 Ch. 242). As to these extensive powers, see *post*, pp. 733
and 777. For discussion of the pros and cons of abandoning what are
known as the " usual joint tenancy clauses," see *Law Society's Gazette*,
vol. 60, p. 419, and *Law Times*, vol. 234, p. 463, and for a form, see Parker's
Modern Conveyancing Precedents at p. 22. The estate duty consequences are
outlined below. The joint purchasers would, in effect, have all the powers
of an absolute owner by virtue of their beneficial entitlement, but exercise
of these powers on this basis would involve bringing the equities on to the
title.

Land Registry transfers.—It is not the practice to include the " usual
joint tenancy clauses " of *un*registered conveyancing in transfers of registered
land to beneficial joint tenants. Instead the names of the transferees are
simply inserted as such in the appropriate form of transfer with, at most,
the following *habendum* added " to hold unto themselves as joint tenants
beneficially." The explanation for this practice appears to be the fact that
any person dealing with the joint registered proprietors is not only not affected
with notice of any trust but is also entitled to assume that they have full
powers of disposition unless a restriction indicating the contrary has been
entered on the register (Ruoff and Roper, Registered Conveyancing,
3rd ed., at p. 406 ; L.R.A. 1925, s. 74). Such a restriction (i.e., to dispositions
authorised by the S.L.A. 1925 ; L.R.R. 1925, Sched., Form 10) is not normally
entered by the registry without an application being made and it is not
thought necessary to apply for it simply because the administrative powers
of the trustees are not extended.

Estate duty.—The inclusion of an express trust for sale is in general not
now attended by the slight disadvantage that on the death of a joint tenant his
beneficial interest is in personalty so that an option to pay estate duty by
instalments is not available (see F.A. 1894, s. 6 (8), as to realty and L.P.A.
1925, s. 16 (4), as to statutory trusts for sale). It is now provided by F.A.
1971, s. 62 (2) (c), that the option to pay by instalments (yearly or half-yearly
over eight years) applies also to—

" the following property situate in England and Wales, that is to say any
leasehold estate or interest in land, *and any property which is treated as*

personal property for estate duty purposes by reason only of being held on trust for sale, not being in any case an estate, interest or right by way of mortgage or other security."

However, it has been queried whether this provision as drafted is apt to apply where leasehold land is held on trust for sale, since the beneficial interests are then personalty anyway (see Alan Prichard, *Conveyancer N.S.*, vol. 36, at pp. 184–185). Nevertheless, it is doubted by the present writer that the courts or the revenue will actually be found to discriminate between trusts for sale on this basis. Further, it is understood that the Estate Duty Office practice now is to value beneficial interests on the same basis whether subsisting behind an express or a statutory trust for sale. Also it should be noted that where there is a statutory trust for sale of freehold land, estate duty may be a charge on the beneficial interests thereunder, e.g., following a severance of the equitable joint tenancy (see L.P.A. 1925, s. 16 (4), and F.A. 1894, s. 9 (1)). Accordingly it is considered that there is no longer any valid estate duty reason for avoiding an express trust for sale. See further as to estate duty on the death of a joint tenant, *post*, p. 1174 ; also as to the capital gains tax position, *post*, p. 1041.

Protection of purchasers from joint tenants.—The joint tenants could sell the land and make good title thereto, either as trustees for sale or as beneficial owners. If they sold, mortgaged or leased as trustees for sale, under s. 28 (1) of the L.P.A. 1925, they could overreach any equitable interests or powers by the Act made to attach to the net proceeds of sale as if created by a trust affecting those proceeds (L.P.A. 1925, s. 2).

The purchasers, mortgagees or lessees from the joint tenants would be fully protected by s. 27 (1) of the L.P.A. 1925, which provides that a purchaser (which includes a mortgagee and lessee) of a legal estate from trustees for sale shall not be concerned with the trusts affecting the proceeds of sale of land subject to a trust for sale (whether made to attach to such proceeds by virtue of the Act or otherwise) or affecting the rents and profits of the land until sale. It is also provided, by s. 23 of the L.P.A. 1925, that where land has become subject to an express or *implied trust for sale*, such trust shall, as far as regards the safety and protection of any purchaser thereunder, be deemed to be subsisting until the land has been conveyed to or under the direction of the persons interested in the proceeds of sale.

The joint tenants could alternatively sell as beneficial owners. For they, having both the legal and equitable estates vested in them, would have absolute dominion over the property and could deal with it at their will. But it is important to observe that where the persons entitled as joint tenants sell, mortgage or lease the land by virtue of their being beneficially entitled *to both* the legal and equitable estates, the *conveyance, mortgage or lease would not overreach* the equitable interests and powers by the Act made to attach to the net proceeds of sale, as it would if made under the statutory trust for sale. In other words, a purchaser in whose favour title is made in this way relies on having the concurrence of all persons entitled to equitable interests in the property or relies on taking free from such interests, because he has no notice of them, instead of overreaching those interests.

In practice, where beneficial joint tenants are selling, it will usually be stipulated in the contract whether they are doing so as trustees for sale or as beneficial owners. However, it should be noted that this may inconveniently restrict them to making title in the stipulated capacity without any alternative (see *Green* v. *Whitehead* [1930] 1 Ch. 38 ; compare *Re Spencer and Hauser's Contract* [1928] Ch. 598, at p. 608). The general rule is that where trustees are selling in exercise of a trust for sale, the purchaser is not entitled to insist upon having the beneficiaries joined in the conveyance to give the full covenants for title " as beneficial owners " (*Cottrell* v. *Cottrell* (1866), L.R. 2 Eq. 330 ; and see L.P.A. 1925, s. 42). Consequently, where joint tenants, as is usual, deduce their title as trustees with a view to overreaching any equitable entitlement, they can only be required to give the lesser covenants for title " as trustees," notwithstanding their beneficial ownership (with which, in any case, the purchaser will not have concerned himself ; L.P.A. 1925, s. 27). Only if they contract to or actually make title as beneficial owners can they be required to covenant in that capacity. Note also the additional covenants for title implied on behalf of the husband in respect of the wife where a husband and wife both convey as beneficial owners (L.P.A. 1925, s. 76 (3)).

Lease to joint tenants.—It must not be forgotten that a lease creates a " term of years absolute," which is a legal estate (L.P.A. 1925, ss. 1 (1) and 205 (1) (xxvii)). Consequently, a lease to joint tenants beneficially gives rise to a trust for sale of the leasehold interest (L.P.A. 1925, s. 36 (1)), and there cannot be more than four joint tenants who will hold the legal estate as trustees for sale, unless the land is held for charitable purposes (T.A. 1925, s. 34).

Power of joint tenants to mortgage.—Where persons of full age hold land as joint tenants on the statutory trusts for sale for themselves there is no doubt that they can sell, mortgage, or deal with the land in any way they think fit, for in that case they have absolute dominion over the property. In theory they are trustees with a statutory power of sale, but as beneficiaries who are *sui juris* and together absolutely entitled they can effectively authorise an extension of their statutory powers where necessary to achieve anything that they may wish (see *Saunders* v. *Vautier* (1841), Cr. & Ph. 240 ; cf. *Re Brockbank* [1948] Ch. 206 ; L.P.A. 1925, s. 26 (3), as re-enacted in 1926, and *Re Jones* [1931] 1 Ch. 375). However, if the joint tenants have sought their power to mortgage from their alternative capacity as the beneficial owners and it is not a case covered by their powers as trustees, then the mortgagee would be bound to investigate their equitable entitlement for his own protection. Consequently, it is better practice for joint tenants to mortgage where possible in exercise of their ordinary powers as trustees, for then as regards the protection of a purchaser or mortgagee, it is provided by s. 17 of the T.A. 1925 that no purchaser or mortgagee paying or advancing money on a mortgage *purporting* to be made under any trust vested in trustees is to be concerned to see that such money is wanted, or that no more than is wanted is raised, or otherwise as to the application thereof.

It is not necessary to go beyond this, but there are certain other provisions giving trustees for sale power to mortgage. For instance, s. 16 (1) of the T.A. 1925 provides that " Where trustees are authorised . . . by law to pay or apply capital money subject to the trust for any purpose or in any manner, they shall have . . . power to raise the money required by . . . mortgage of all or any part of the trust property for the time being in possession." Subsection (2) provides that the above is not to apply to charity trustees or to S.L.A. trustees, not being also the statutory owners. That is to say, the subsection *does apply* to trustees when they are statutory owners.

Then there is s. 28 (1) of the L.P.A. 1925, as amended, which gives trustees for sale, in relation to land and to the proceeds of sale, all the powers of a tenant for life under the S.L.A. 1925 and the trustees of a settlement, and enacts that, provided such power is exercised with such consents (if any) as would have been required on a sale under the trust for sale, it will operate to overreach any equitable interests or powers which are by virtue of the Act or otherwise made to attach to the proceeds of sale as if created by a trust affecting those proceeds. The power of a life tenant to mortgage is contained in s. 71 of the S.L.A. 1925, but is somewhat limited, in particular not including raising the purchase price in the first place of the land.

Where beneficial joint tenants have mortgaged property to secure a loan and one of them is adjudicated bankrupt, the mortgagee having realised the security for an insufficient amount to repay the loan may prove in the bankruptcy but only for half the balance of the loan (*Re A Debtor* [1971] 2 W.L.R. 1477).

As to the ability of beneficial joint tenants validly to mortgage the land rendering proper a charging order in respect of joint liabilities, see *National Westminster Bank, Ltd.* v. *Allen* [1971] 2 Q.B. 218, dealt with *post*, p. 608.

Power of a surviving joint tenant to sell, mortgage or lease.—At one time a doubt was raised as to whether a surviving joint tenant, for instance, a husband or a wife, could sell by virtue of his or her beneficial ownership, and whether or not it was necessary to appoint another trustee to make a good title. As several times pointed out by Sir Benjamin Cherry, there was no substance in the doubt, and to remove doubt it was enacted by the Law of Property (Amendment) Act, 1926, that at the end of s. 36 (2) of the L.P.A. 1925 the following words should be inserted, that is to say : " Nothing in this Act affects the right of a survivor of joint tenants, who is solely and beneficially interested, to deal with his legal estate as if it were not held on trust for sale." It will be borne in mind that when the sale, etc., is made by the surviving joint tenant under this provision he can only make title to the land subject to the equities subject to which he or she holds the land.

One danger to a purchaser taking a conveyance from a surviving joint tenant of his supposed beneficial interest in the whole used to be that the deceased joint tenant (or tenants) might have dealt with his share, for instance, mortgaged it, and thereby severed the joint tenancy and turned it into a tenancy in common in equity. The result would be that the survivor would *not* be solely and beneficially interested so that the legal estate would still be held on trust for sale. A statutory declaration by the survivor that there had been no severance, or a recital to the same effect, was often obtained and accepted as sufficient evidence, but as the survivor might not always have notice of a severance if it occurred in such a way as by mortgage of a share, a purchaser was not completely protected. Further, it was not certain whether death duties might be charged on the estate of the deceased joint tenant and whether they would be void against a purchaser if not registered as land charges ; see the *Law Journal*, vol. 98, p. 185. Consequently for many years, notwithstanding the addition to s. 36 (2), careful conveyancers advised that a new trustee be appointed, in which case equitable interests and death duties were overreached, the trust for sale being deemed to subsist still in favour of purchasers (L.P.A. 1925, s. 23), and such an appointment could be incorporated in the conveyance to the purchaser.

Although the appointment of an additional trustee to receive the proceeds of sale came to be generally accepted as good conveyancing practice (see *Law Society's Gazette*, vol. 52, p. 159), controversy continued to rage both as to the strict necessity for such an appointment and as to whether a purchaser was entitled to insist upon such an appointment (see the 14th Edition of this book, vol. 1, p. 325, and p. 63 *et seq.* of the Third Supplement thereto). Now, however, the controversy has been rendered completely academic by the provisions of the Law of Property (Joint Tenants) Act, 1964. Section 1 (1) of that Act provides that, for the purposes of L.P.A. 1925, s. 36 (2), as amended, " the survivor of two or more joint tenants shall, *in favour of a purchaser of the legal estate*, be deemed to be solely and beneficially interested if he conveys as beneficial owner or the conveyance includes a statement that he is so interested." Presumably the words " if he conveys " mean " if he purports to convey." The customary expression of capacity " as beneficial owner " will now serve the dual purpose of incorporating the implied covenants for title and obviating the need to appoint an additional trustee. The provision is also applied with the necessary modifications in relation to a conveyance by the personal representative of such a survivor (s. 1 (2) of the 1964 Act). Further, the provision is made retrospective in that s. 1 of the Act is deemed to have come into force on 1st January, 1926 (*ibid.*, s. 2) ; and in the unlikely event of a conveyance by a survivor executed before the passing of the Act omitting to state the survivor's beneficial capacity, then a statement signed by the vendor or by his personal representative as to this is to be treated as if it were included in the conveyance (*ibid.*, s. 2).

It must be noted that protection is given only to a purchaser of the legal estate for valuable consideration (*ibid.*, ss. 1 (1), 4 (1) ; L.P.A. 1925, s. 205 (1) (xxi)).

These provisions of the 1964 Act will not apply if, before the conveyance in question, either (*a*) a memorandum of severance (that is to say, a note signed by one or more of the joint tenants and recording severance of the joint tenancy in equity on a specified date) had been endorsed on or annexed to the conveyance to the joint tenants ; or else (*b*) a receiving order, or a petition for one, against any of the joint tenants had been registered under the L.C.A. 1925 and 1972 so as to give the purchaser notice (*ibid.*, s. 1, proviso). In addition, it is expressly enacted that the 1964 Act does not apply to registered land (s. 3), presumably because the absence from the register of a restriction against sales by a sole proprietor is regarded as sufficient protection for purchasers (see *ante*, p. 296).

But if the sole surviving joint tenant was not beneficially interested, either initially or there is a memorandum of severance as above, that is, if he was a trustee for other persons, then to make a title he would have to appoint another trustee. On his death without having sold the land, leaving only one personal representative, such personal representative would have to appoint another trustee to act with him to enable a good receipt to be given (T.A. 1925, s. 18 (2) ; s. 14 (2)). But if he died leaving two personal representatives, they could make a good title, unless the person having power to appoint trustees should have appointed other trustees (T.A. 1925, s. 18 (2)). When personal representatives act as trustees it would seem that they should sign a written assent to the legal estate vesting in themselves as trustees (A.E.A. 1925, s. 36 (4) ; *Re King's Will Trusts* [1964] Ch. 542 ; compare *Re Stirrup's Contract* [1961] 1 W.L.R. 449 ; see further *post*, p. 417).

Sale of share of one of joint tenants.—A familiar case is where *A* and *B* are joint tenants of land and *A* wishes to sell his share to a stranger. This should be effected by an assignment of his equitable interest to the purchaser (*Cooper* v. *Critchley* [1955] Ch. 431). The effect of such an assignment would be to sever the joint tenancy (see next note) and the purchaser will, after the assignment, hold as tenant in common with *B*.   There will therefore be no right of survivorship, either in *B* or the purchaser.   *A* and *B* will still remain trustees notwithstanding the sale.   If so desired, the purchaser could be appointed a trustee in the place of *A* (who would by the same deed retire from the trust) and the legal estate be conveyed by *A* and *B* to *B* and the purchaser.

An assignment of leaseholds by one joint tenant to another before 1926 without the consent of the lessor was a breach of a covenant not to assign without the lessor's consent having been first obtained.

By virtue of the provisions of s. 137 of the L.P.A. 1925, a purchaser of the equitable interest of a joint tenant in the land will now have the advantage of being able, *as of right*, to make inquiries of the remaining joint tenants, whether they have received any notices of any dealings with the share, as, being trustees, they come within that section.   The section extends the rule in *Dearle* v. *Hall* (1828), 3 Russ. 1, to equitable interests in land and capital money.   This rule is that priority of right will depend upon priority of notice of dealings with the equitable interests or capital money.   The notice has to be in writing, and any person interested is entitled upon payment of costs to require to see all notices (L.P.A. 1925, s. 137 (8)).   Note also that where the legal title to the land is registered the rule in *Dearle* v. *Hall*, *ante*, has been superseded by the " minor interests index," priorities being regulated by the order of the priority cautions or inhibitions lodged therein (L.R.A. 1925, s. 102 (2) ; L.R.R. 1925, r. 299 ; *post*, p. 624).

Conveyances by joint tenants to one or more of themselves are discussed *post*, p. 536.

Severance of joint tenancy.—Since 31st December, 1925, *the legal estate* in land may not be held by persons as tenants in common ; see *post*, p. 305. It follows that a severance of the legal estate held by persons as joint tenants is not allowed, as this would create a tenancy in common.   But one joint tenant can sever his equitable joint tenancy, and can also release his equitable interest to the other joint tenant or joint tenants.   And it would appear that tenants for life holding as joint tenants can, for the period of the joint lives, sever their equitable interests in the income and that this does not create undivided shares in the settled land, hence no trust for sale arises and the land remains settled land.   They can make such arrangements as they think fit as to sharing the income.   One of several joint tenants cannot disclaim his interest although he may release both his legal estate and his equitable interest to the other joint tenants (*Re Schär* [1950] 2 All E.R. 1069 ; also L.P.A. 1925, s. 36 (2), below).

Subsections (2) and (3) of s. 36 of the L.P.A. 1925, which deal with the matter, are given below :—

" 36.—(2) *No severance* of a joint tenancy of a legal estate, so as to create a tenancy in common in land, *shall be permissible*, whether by operation of law or otherwise, *but this subsecton does not affect the right of a joint tenant to release his interest to the other joint tenants*, or the right to sever a joint tenancy in an equitable interest whether or not the legal estate is vested in the joint tenants :

Provided that, where a legal estate (not being settled land) is vested in joint tenants beneficially, and any tenant *desires to sever the joint tenancy in equity*, he shall give to the other joint tenants a notice in writing of such desire or do such *other acts or things as would, in the case of personal estate, have been effectual to sever the tenancy in equity,* and thereupon under the trust for sale affecting the land the net proceeds of sale, and the net rents and profits until sale, shall be held upon the trusts which would have been requisite for giving effect to the beneficial interests if there had been an actual severance. [See p. 300 for words added by the Law of Property (Amendment) Act, 1926.]

(3) Without prejudice to the right of a joint tenant to release his interest to the other joint tenants no severance of a mortgage term or trust estate, so as to create a tenancy in common, shall be permissible."

As regards the giving of a notice in writing, the provisions of the L.P.A. 1925, s. 196, apply (see *post,* p. 836), including subs. (4) of s. 196 which refers only to serving and not also to giving notice (*Re 88 Berkeley Road, London, N.W.*9 [1971] Ch. 648, where one beneficial joint tenant managed to effect a severance by serving a notice received by herself, and never by the other joint tenant, through the use of a recorded delivery).

As regards the " other acts or things as would, in the case of personal estate, have been effectual to sever the tenancy in equity," the old cases on severance, when the legal estate could be severed, will still apply, but limited to severance of the equitable interest.

The words in the proviso " where a legal estate . . . is vested in joint tenants beneficially " appear to mean that a notice of severance is valid only if the persons who are entitled beneficially also hold the legal estate. If this is so a notice cannot be used to effect severance where the legal estate is held by some only of the beneficial joint tenants or by other trustees for them. Whether the court would adopt this strict construction is doubtful (compare the comment in Megarry & Wade, Real Property, 3rd ed., p. 421) but an attempt to sever by notice in such circumstances would be unwise.

Severance by one joint tenant does not affect the joint tenancy as between others.

Stirling, J., in *Re Wilks ; Child* v. *Bulmer* [1891] 3 Ch. 59, said that a joint tenancy may be severed either (1) by a disposition made by one of the joint owners, amounting at law or in equity to an assignment of the share of that owner ; or (2) by mutual agreement between the joint owners ; and that, without going so far as to say there was no other way of severing a joint tenancy, he thought the act of a joint tenant to amount to a severance must be such as to preclude him from claiming by survivorship any interest in the subject-matter of the joint tenancy. A third manner in which severance may take place would appear to be as a result of a course of dealing with the property sufficient to intimate that the interests of all were mutually treated as a tenancy in common (*Williams* v. *Hensman* (1861), 30 L.J. Ch. 878 ; *Re Denny* (1947), 177 L.T. 291).

A joint tenancy could also be severed by operation of law, as, for instance, where one of several joint tenants for life acquires the reversion by descent or by purchase (*Wiscot's Case* (1599), 2 Co. Rep. 60*b*). Similarly there is a severance by operation of law where a joint tenancy vests in the trustee in bankruptcy of the joint tenant ; compare the reasoning in *Re Butler's Trusts* (1888), 38 Ch. D. 286.

An agreement for sale of the entirety entered into by all the joint tenants did not operate to sever the joint tenancy in the purchase-money (*Re Hayes' Estate* [1920] 1 Ir. R. 207) ; but a *contract* for the sale by a joint tenant of his share to a stranger in equity severed the tenancy (*Kingsford* v. *Ball* (1852), 2 Giff. App. 1). A mortgage by a joint tenant of his entire interest had the effect of severing the joint tenancy both at law and in equity (*Re Sharer ;*

Abbott v. *Sharer* (1912), 57 Sol. J. 60). A *lease* for years by one joint tenant severed the tenancy if the property was leasehold, but not if the property was freehold.

Where the matrimonial home is held by spouses as joint tenants in equity, issue by one of them of a summons under the Married Women's Property Act, 1882, s. 17, asking for an order for sale and distribution of the proceeds, coupled with an affidavit in support operates to sever the joint tenancy (*Re Draper's Conveyance* [1969] 1 Ch. 486).

Even an equitable joint tenancy cannot be severed by will (see *ante*, p. 283). It is necessary that severance should be *inter vivos*, but this can be done by an irrevocable agreement that in consideration of one of the joint tenants making a will in favour of the other, the other would make a will in his favour (*In the Estate of Heys* [1914] P. 192).

A covenant to settle after-acquired property severed an estate of joint tenancy coming to husband and wife after the date of the covenant (*Burnaby* v. *Equitable Reversionary Interest Society* (1885), 28 Ch. D. 416 ; *Re Hewett ; Hewett* v. *Hallett* [1894] 1 Ch. 362). See also *Goddard* v. *Lewis* (1909), 101 L.T. 528, where many cases as to " severance " are cited.

Finally, a novel restriction on severance has recently been suggested by Lord Denning, M.R., in *Bedson* v. *Bedson* [1965] 2 Q.B. 666 in respect of a matrimonial home. He said (at p. 678) that : " So long as the house is in the possession of the husband and wife as joint tenants or one of them, there can be no severance of their equitable interests ; . . . Neither of them can sell his or her equitable interest separately. If he or she could do so, it would mean that the purchaser could insist on going into possession himself—with the other spouse there—which is absurd. It would mean also that one of them could, of his own head, destroy the right of survivorship which was the essence of the joint tenancy. That cannot be correct." Nonetheless, this suggestion seems of doubtful soundness and was, indeed, described by Russell, L.J., dissenting in the case, as being " without the slightest foundation in law or equity " (*ibid.*, p. 690 ; see also strong criticism by R.E.M. in *Law Quarterly Review*, vol. 82, p. 29 *et seq.*). Further, the *dicta* of Lord Denning, M.R., quoted above were not followed in *Radziej* v. *Radziej* [1967] 1 W.L.R. 659, where Baker, J., held that a notice of severance was effective to produce an equitable tenancy in common even where the beneficial joint tenancy previously subsisting in the house had been created by a post-nuptial settlement. Also in *Re Draper's Conveyance* [1969] 1 Ch. 486, Plowman, J., expressed preference for the view of Russell, L.J. Nevertheless, the Master of the Rolls has recently cited his own *dicta* with evident approval in *Jackson* v. *Jackson* [1971] 1 W.L.R. 1539 (at p. 1542), as did Bagnall, J., in *Cowcher* v. *Cowcher* [1972] 1 All E.R. 943, at p. 949 b/c.

Tenancies by entireties.—Such tenancies ceased to exist at the end of 1925 and so a brief note only is required.

Before the Married Women's Property Act, 1882, in consequence of the doctrine that husband and wife were one, a grant to a husband and wife, in terms which would normally have given rise to a joint tenancy, created a tenancy with certain peculiar incidents, known as a " tenancy by entireties." One of such peculiar incidents was that neither the husband nor the wife could deal with the fee simple in the property without the consent of the other. On the death of either, without having made any joint disposition, the whole went to the survivor.

The effect of the 1882 Act was to enable a wife to own property separately from her husband and so a limitation after that Act, to husband and wife jointly, made them joint tenants (*Thornley* v. *Thornley* [1893] 2 Ch. 229), the wife taking her share as separate property.

It was provided by Pt. VI of Sched. 1 to the L.P.A. 1925, that " Every tenancy by entireties existing immediately before [1926] shall, but without prejudice to any beneficial interest, as from [1st January, 1926], be converted into a joint tenancy." The result was that the legal estate vested in the husband and wife as joint tenants on trust for sale but that the beneficial interest was not affected (L.P.A. 1925, s. 36 ; Sched. 1, Pt. II, para. 6 (*b*)).

Grants before 1926 to husband and wife and a third party.— There was also a further rule as a result of the fiction that husband and wife were one person, that if there was a grant to a husband and wife and a third party as joint tenants, the husband and wife took one-half as tenants by the entireties, and the third party the other half. As between the husband and wife taken together as one person, and the third party, there was a joint tenancy.

If such a grant was made after 1882 the husband and wife still took only one-half, but they took it as joint tenants ; in other words, the unity of husband and wife was dissolved by the Married Women's Property Act, 1882, only as regards the rights of property *inter se* (*Re Jupp* (1888), 39 Ch. D. 148 ; compare *Cambridge Law Journal*, November, 1959, p. 252). But the rule as to husband and wife being one did not apply where an intention could be collected from a will that the testator intended them to take separately (*Re Dixon ; Byram* v. *Tull* (1889), 42 Ch. D. 306) ; or where the gift was made to them as a class (*Re Gue ; Smith* v. *Gue* (1892), 67 L.T. 823).

As regards dispositions made or coming into operation after 1925, it is provided by s. 37 of the L.P.A. 1925 that " A husband and wife shall, for all purposes of acquisition of any interest in property, under a disposition made or coming into operation after the commencement of this Act, be treated as two persons." The effect of this section will be that as regards dispositions made or coming into operation after 1925 to a husband, wife and stranger, each will now get one-third in equity, either as joint tenant or tenant in common with the others, according to the terms of the gift or disposition. The legal estate will be held by them as joint tenants on trust for sale under s. 36 (1) of the L.P.A. 1925.

C. UNDIVIDED SHARES IN LAND SINCE 1925

Generally.—A *legal estate in land* cannot, since 1925, be held by two or more persons as tenants in common : it is provided by s. 1 (6) of the L.P.A. 1925 that " A *legal estate* is not capable of subsisting or of being created in an undivided share in land." Further, by s. 36 (2) of the same Act, no severance of a joint tenancy of a legal estate, so as to create a tenancy in common in land, is permissible, whether by operation of law or otherwise, but a joint tenancy of *an equitable interest* may be severed, whether or not the legal estate is vested in the joint tenants. An equitable interest in land includes an interest or charge in the proceeds of sale of land (L.P.A. 1925, s. 205 (1) (x)).

A contract to convey an undivided share in land after 1925 will be deemed to have been sufficiently complied with by the conveyance of a corresponding share in the proceeds of sale in the land (L.P.A. 1925, s. 42 (6)).

Section 36 (4) of the S.L.A. 1925 provides that " An undivided share in land shall not be capable of being created except under a trust instrument or under the Law of Property Act, 1925, and shall then only take effect behind a trust for sale." The way it can be created under the L.P.A. 1925 is stated in s. 34 (2), (3) and (4)). Subsection (3) deals with the creation by will and is mentioned at p. 308. It is provided by subs. (2), in effect, that if an attempt is made, after 1925, to create a tenancy in common in land in the same way as it was proper to do before 1926, and the persons are of full age, the conveyance shall operate as if the land had been expressed to be conveyed to the grantees, or if there are more than four grantees, to the first four named in the conveyance, as *joint tenants* upon the statutory trusts and so as to give effect to the rights of the persons who would have been entitled to the shares had the conveyance operated to convey those shares. The subsection also contains a proviso that where the conveyance is made by way of mortgage the land shall vest in the grantees or such four of them as aforesaid for a term of years absolute (as provided by the Act) as *joint tenants* subject to cesser on redemption in like manner as if the mortgage money had belonged to them on a joint account, but without prejudice to the beneficial interests in the mortgage money and interest. And subs. (4) of s. 34 provides that " Any disposition purporting to make a settlement of an undivided share in land shall only operate as a settlement of a corresponding share of the net proceeds of sale and of the rents and profits until sale of the entirety of the land."

It will be noted that s. 34 (2) of the L.P.A. 1925, above, only applies where the conveyance of the land in undivided shares is made directly to the beneficiaries themselves. The other way, referred to in s. 36 (4) of the S.L.A. 1925, by which an undivided share in land can be created is under a trust instrument behind a trust for sale. This covers the cases (i) where the conveyance is made to trustees on trust for beneficiaries in equal shares, but without the interposition of an express trust for sale, and (ii) where the conveyance is to trustees for sale and to stand possessed of the proceeds of sale for persons in shares. In both cases the number of trustees must not exceed four. See s. 34 (1) and (2) of the T.A. 1925 and the L.P.A. 1925, s. 3 (1) (*b*) (ii). Thus, although there may be any number of persons entitled to a share in the proceeds of sale, there must never be more than four persons holding the legal estate. When the land is conveyed directly to the beneficiaries, only four can hold the legal estate as trustees for themselves and any others ; and where the land is conveyed to trustees on an express trust for sale on trust to hold the proceeds for beneficiaries, there must never be more than four of such trustees ; and where the land is given to trustees on trust for persons in undivided shares, without an express trust for sale, the law will imply a trust for sale, but the number of trustees must not exceed four.

The proper way to create an interest in land in persons as tenants in common, *inter vivos*, is to convey the legal estate to not more than four trustees as *joint tenants* on trust to sell, and to stand possessed of the net proceeds of sale (and of the rents and profits) on trust for the persons intended to be benefited, as *tenants in common*. For although a tenancy in common can no longer be created in a legal estate, it can still be created in the equitable interest in the land, that is, in the proceeds of sale thereof.

In *Bull* v. *Bull* [1955] 1 Q.B. 234 the purchase price of a house was provided by *A* and *B*, but the house was conveyed to *A* alone. Consequently a resulting trust was presumed and it was held that *A* and *B* were equitable tenants in common and that *A* held the legal estate on " the statutory trusts for sale."

The Court of Appeal thus brought conveyances of this sort within the general scheme of the 1925 property legislation, although without analysing the relevant sections (L.P.A. 1925, ss. 1 (6), 34 to 38, and S.L.A. 1925, s. 36) which do not expressly cover the case. See also *Re Rayleigh Weir Stadium* [1954] 1 W.L.R. 786, *Cook* v. *Cook* [1962] P. 235, and *Waller* v. *Waller* [1967] 1 W.L.R. 451 (a husband and wife case); cf. *Re Buchanan-Wollaston's Conveyance* [1939] Ch. 738 where a trust for sale was found by straining the statutory language in another way. However, there appears to be no doubt that such a single trustee (i.e., *A* above) could effectively convey the legal estate as beneficial owner to a *bona fide* purchaser for value without notice of the equitable interest giving rise to the trust for sale (that is, despite the provisions as to payment to two trustees, L.P.A. 1925, s. 27 (2), and T.A. 1925, s. 14 (2) ; see *Pilcher* v. *Rawlins* (1872), L.R. 7 Ch. 259 ; *Re King's Settlement* [1931] 2 Ch. 294, and *Law Society's Gazette*, vol. 52, p. 311). Unfortunately in many cases of the *Bull* v. *Bull* type a purchaser may not be able to rely on this last point. If the other equitable tenant in common (i.e., *B* above) happens to be in possession or actual occupation of the property, this would, *prima facie*, fix all prospective purchasers with at least constructive notice of the equitable interest in question (*Nelthorpe* v. *Holgate* (1844), 1 Coll. 203, at p. 215 ; *Penny* v. *Watts* (1849), 1 Mac. & G. 150, at p. 164 ; L.P.A. 1925, s. 14 ; L.R.A. 1925, s. 70 (1) (*g*)). In these circumstances, a good title could only be conferred by way of the statutory overreaching machinery, that is, appointment of a second trustee, consent of beneficiary and, perhaps, application to the court under s. 30 of the L.P.A. 1925. However, as to the binding effect of such occupation, see the discussion of *Caunce* v. *Caunce* [1969] 1 W.L.R. 286, and *Hodgson* v. *Marks* [1971] Ch. 892, *ante*, p. 167.

There are two sets of " statutory trusts," namely, (i) those contained in s. 35 of the L.P.A. 1925, and (ii) those contained in s. 36 (6) of the S.L.A. 1925. Those in s. 35 are the trusts implied when the grant is made direct to the parties as in s. 34 of the L.P.A. 1925, above ; and those in s. 36 (6) of the S.L.A. 1925, although nearly similar, apply only when *settled land* becomes held in trust for persons entitled in possession in undivided shares (S.L.A. 1925, s. 36 (1) and (2)). A statutory trust for sale can only subsist in the absence of an express trust for sale (*Re McKee* [1931] 2 Ch. 145). The " statutory trusts " contained in s. 35 of the L.P.A. 1925 are as follows :—

" upon trust to sell the same and to stand possessed of the net proceeds of sale, after payment of costs, and of the net rents and profits until sale after payment of rates, taxes, costs of insurance, repairs and other outgoings, upon such trusts, and subject to such powers and provisions, as may be requisite for giving effect to the rights of the persons (including an incumbrancer of a former undivided share or whose incumbrance is not secured by a legal mortgage) interested in the land."

By the Law of Property (Amendment) Act, 1926, s. 7 and Sched., the following words were added to the L.P.A. 1925, s. 35 :—

" Where—

(*a*) an undivided share was subject to a settlement, and

(*b*) the settlement remains subsisting in respect of other property, and

(*c*) the trustees thereof are not the same persons as the trustees for sale,

then the statutory trusts include a trust for the trustees for sale to pay the proper proportion of the net proceeds of sale or other capital money attributable to the share to the trustees of the settlement to be held by them as capital money arising under the Settled Land Act, 1925."

This amendment to s. 35 is declaratory, and it reconverts proceeds of sale arising under the statutory trusts into land.

As to overreaching powers of trustees holding under these trusts, see *ante*, p. 176.

Registered land.—As a legal estate cannot since 1925 be held by two or more persons as tenants in common (L.P.A. 1925, ss. 1 (6), 34 (2), (3), (4) ; S.L.A. 1925, s. 36 (4)) it is provided by the L.R.A. 1925, s. 78 (4), that no entry other than a caution against dealings with the entirety shall be made in the register as respects the title to an undivided share in land. It has been held that a beneficial tenant in common is entitled to lodge such a caution (*Elias* v. *Mitchell* [1972] Ch. 652, relating to L.R.A. 1925, s. 54 (1)). As to whether such a tenant in common can have an overriding interest by virtue of actual occupation within L.R.A. 1925, s. 70 (1) (*g*), see *ante*, p. 193.

Where, in the case of land belonging to persons in undivided shares, the entirety was registered before 1926 and the persons entitled to the undivided shares were registered as proprietors, the registrar was obliged, on the occasion of the first dealing affecting the title after 1925, to rectify the register by entering as the proprietor of the entirety the persons in whom the legal estate vested by virtue of the L.P.A. 1925 (L.R.A. 1925, s. 78 (1)). The position where the title to an *undivided share* was registered before 1926 although the entirety of the land was not registered is dealt with by L.R.A. 1925, s. 78 (2), and the L.R.R. 1925, r. 248.

Tenancy in common in chattels.—A legal tenancy in common can still be created in chattels ; the restriction only applies to the legal estate in land. When furniture or pictures or collections of stamps or such-like chattels have been bequeathed among several persons as a class, it sometimes happens that several want one thing and a difficulty arises as to the division. Section 188 of the L.P.A. 1925 is likely to be useful in such a case. It provides that where any chattels belong to persons in undivided shares, the persons interested in a moiety or upwards may apply to the court for an order for division of the chattels or any of them according to a valuation or otherwise, and the court may make such order and give any consequential directions as it thinks fit.

Devise to persons as tenants in common.—The words which, in a will, create a tenancy in common have been mentioned *ante*, p. 283. A devise, bequest or testamentary appointment, coming into operation after 1925, of land *to two or more persons in undivided shares* will operate as a devise, bequest or appointment of the land to the trustees (if any) of the will for the purposes of the S.L.A. 1925, or, if there are no such trustees, then to the personal representatives of the testator, and in each case (but without prejudice to the rights and powers of the personal representatives for purposes of administration) upon the statutory trusts (L.P.A. 1925, s. 34 (3)). The statutory trusts referred to are those contained in s. 35 of the L.P.A. 1925, set out above.

In *Re House* [1929] 2 Ch. 166, it was decided that a devise coming into operation after 1925 in trust for a period during lives to divide the income amongst certain persons, followed by a gift to another class of persons on the determination of that period, *was a devise of land in undivided shares* within the meaning of the L.P.A. 1925, s. 34 (3).   As the will contained a devise to two or more persons in undivided shares within the language of s. 34 (3) it operated as a devise of the land to the trustees of the will for the purposes of the S.L.A. 1925, upon the statutory trusts.   Further, as there was a future power of sale in the trustees, they were the trustees of the will for the purposes of the S.L.A. 1925, and the persons in whose favour the executor of the will was required to assent in respect of the land.

A will only passes an equitable interest, and, as in the case of any other devise, the legal estate, in the first instance, passes to the personal representatives, and subject to their requiring it for the purposes of administration they will, in due course, assent to such legal estate vesting in the persons entitled (A.E.A. 1925, ss. 1, 10, 22, 23 and 24).

Undivided shares in settled land falling into possession.—It is provided by s. 36 (1) of the S.L.A. 1925 that if and when, after 1925, settled land is held in trust for persons entitled in possession under a trust instrument in undivided shares the trustees of the settlement (if the settled land is not already vested in them) may require the estate owner in whom the settled land is vested (but in the case of a personal representative subject to his rights and powers for purposes of administration), at the cost of the trust estate, to convey the land to them, or assent to the land vesting in them *as joint tenants*, and in the meantime the land is to be held on the same trusts as if it had vested in the trustees.

It has been noted (*ante*, p. 293) that this subsection operates where land has been settled on a tenant for life and after his death limited to two or more persons in undivided shares.   On the death of the tenant for life his personal representatives, subject to their rights for purposes of administration, must execute an assent as required by s. 36 (1) in favour of the trustees of the settlement (*Re Cugny's Will Trusts* [1931] 1 Ch. 305).   In *Re Thomas* [1939] 1 Ch. 513, it was argued that following *Re Bridgett and Hayes' Contract* [1928] Ch. 163 and *Re Alefounder's Will Trusts* [1927] 1 Ch. 360, in such circumstances the settlement came to an end on the death of the tenant for life and so the land was no longer " settled land " within the meaning of the S.L.A. 1925, s. 36 (1).   This argument did not succeed, and Bennett, J., held, following *Re Cugny*, that the general personal representative of the life tenant must execute an assent in favour of the trustee of the settlement.   On the other hand the settlement appears to have come to an end as defined in *Re Bridgett and Hayes*, with the result that the land vests in the *general* (and not the *special*) personal representatives of the tenant for life.   *Re Bridgett and Hayes* and *Re Cugny* cannot, in logic, stand together.   However, both decisions are well established and it must be assumed that each case governs the particular issue decided by it.   Thus it is clear that where the trustees of the settlement have taken a conveyance under s. 36 (1) they hold the land on the statutory trusts, the land not being settled land for any purpose other than the interpretation of s. 36 (1) (Megarry & Wade, Real Property, 3rd ed., p. 437).

If all other interests under the settlement have come to an end the tenants in common will probably desire to have the land vested in themselves, in which case the simplest procedure would be for the personal representatives of the tenant for life to assent in their favour, being of full age and not more than four in number, as joint tenants on trust for sale and to hold the proceeds for themselves as tenants in common.   The trustees of the settlement need not be concerned.

The words " *and in the meantime* " refer to the period from the time when the land ceases to be settled land to the time when the land is conveyed to the trustees for sale.

" *persons entitled in possession.*"—There must be two persons at least who have become entitled in possession. It is not sufficient if one person has become so entitled to possession but others are only entitled in remainder. In the latter case the persons to sell or mortgage, etc., would be the trustees of the settlement as statutory owners (*Re Bird* [1927] 1 Ch. 210).

" *to be held on the same trusts.*"—That is, on the statutory trusts contained in subs. (6) of s. 36 of the S.L.A. 1925, as appears from subs. (2) of the section. Subsection (2) provides that when the settled land so held in trust in undivided shares is or becomes vested in the trustees of the settlement, the land must be held by them (subject to any incumbrances affecting the settled land which are secured by a legal mortgage, but freed from any incumbrances affecting the undivided shares or not secured as aforesaid, and from any interests, powers, and charges subsisting under the trust instrument which have priority to the trust for the persons entitled to the undivided shares) upon the statutory trusts.

The statutory trusts for the purposes of s. 36 of the S.L.A. 1925 are defined by subs. (6) as follows :—

" upon trust to sell the same, with power to postpone the sale of the whole or any part thereof, and to stand possessed of the net proceeds of sale, after payment of costs, and of the net rents and profits until sale, after payment of rates, taxes, costs of insurance, repairs and other outgoings, upon such trusts and subject to such powers and provisions as may be requisite for giving effect to the rights of the persons interested in the settled land."

As to overreaching powers of trustees holding on these trusts, see *ante*, p. 176.

Partition.—As, since 1925, the legal estate in land cannot be held by persons as tenants in common, but must be vested in trustees (who may be the beneficial owners entitled to the proceeds of sale) as joint tenants on trust for sale, the Partition Acts no longer applied, and they were repealed by Sched. 10 to the Law of Property (Amendment) Act, 1924, and Sched. 7 to the L.P.A. 1925. But *the trustees*, in whom the legal estate is vested, *can partition* the land among the parties entitled under s. 28 (3) of the L.P.A. 1925 ; and should this subsection not apply the court has power to confer on the trustees the necessary power (T.A. 1925, s. 57 (1) ; also Variation of Trusts Act, 1958).

It is provided by the proviso to s. 3 (1) (*b*) (ii) of the L.P.A. 1925 that if the proceeds of sale are held in trust for persons of full age in undivided shares absolutely free from incumbrances affecting undivided shares, those persons may require (subject to effect being given by way of legal mortgage to incumbrances affecting the entirety) the land to be vested in any of them (not exceeding four) as joint tenants on trust for sale.

If, on the other hand, the parties prefer that the land should be partitioned between them, provision is made for this by s. 28 (3) of the L.P.A. 1925 as follows :—

" 28.—(3) Where the net proceeds of sale have under the trusts affecting the same become absolutely vested in persons of full age in undivided shares (whether or not such shares may be subject to a derivative trust) the trustees for sale may, with the consent of the persons, if any, of full age, not being annuitants, interested in possession in the net rents and profits of the land until sale—

    (a) partition the land remaining unsold or any part thereof ; and

    (b) provide (by way of mortgage or otherwise) for the payment of any equality money.''

The trustees for sale give effect to such partition by conveying the land in severalty (subject or not to any legal mortgage created for raising equality money) to persons of full age and either absolutely or on trust for sale or, where any part of the land becomes settled land, by a vesting deed, or partly in one way and partly in another in accordance with the rights of the persons interested under the partition (*ibid.*).

" *consent of the persons . . . interested in possession.*"—A purchaser is not concerned to see or inquire whether any such consent has been given (*ibid.*), but only with consents which are, by the disposition, made requisite to the exercise of the trust for sale (L.P.A. 1925, s. 26 (1)). If a share in the net proceeds belongs to a person suffering from mental disorder, the consent of his receiver is sufficient to protect the trustees for sale, and if a share in the net proceeds is affected by an incumbrance the trustees for sale may either give effect thereto or provide for the discharge thereof by means of the property allotted in respect of such share, as they may consider expedient (*ibid.*, s. 28 (3), proviso, as amended by the Mental Health Act, 1959, Sched. 7). If a share in the net proceeds is absolutely vested in an infant, the trustees for sale may act on his behalf and retain land (to be held on trust for sale) or other property to represent his share, but in other respects the foregoing power applies as if the infant had been of full age (L.P.A. 1925, s. 28 (4)). It appears that a receiver by way of equitable execution of a tenant in common's share would not be a person " interested " within the subsection (see *Stevens* v. *Hutchinson* [1953] Ch. 299, applied by the Court of Appeal in *Irani Finance, Ltd.* v. *Singh* [1971] Ch. 59 ; but cf. *Elias* v. *Mitchell* [1972] Ch. 652), but that a trustee in bankruptcy would be such a person (*Re Solomon* [1967] Ch. 573).

As a purchaser is not concerned to see that the necessary consents have been obtained it will not be proper to join the consenting parties in the conveyances. The consents will be kept off the title altogether. For the same reason the co-owners will not have to be parties to the deeds. But if there should be an equitable mortgage on any of the shares, the mortgagee can require the trustees to give him a legal mortgage to take effect in priority to the trust for sale as a condition of his giving his consent or, in the alternative, to pay him off. See L.P.A. 1925, s. 3 (1) (*b*) (i), (ii), and subs. (2) ; s. 35 and s. 102.

If the legal estate is vested in a sole trustee there is nothing in the L.P.A. 1925, s. 27 (2), which would require another trustee to be appointed in order to partition, *provided no capital money is to arise on the transaction.* If a mortgage is made for the purpose of raising equality money under s. 28 (3) (*b*), then one individual trustee will not be able to give a good receipt for it. Although the L.P.A. 1925, s. 28 (3), refers to " trustees for sale " the plural includes the singular, there being no contrary intention shown : Interpretation Act, 1889, s. 1 (1) (*b*).

It has been held that this statutory power to partition is not exercisable where one or more of the shares remain settled by the original disposition of the entirety and not merely by virtue of a derivative settlement (*Re Thomas*

[1930] 1 Ch. 194). In that case also a power to appropriate contained in the original disposition was held not to come within subs. (1) of the same section, as amended by the Law of Property (Amendment) Act, 1926 (which provides that where settled land is vested in the trustees upon the statutory trusts, such trustees shall also have all the additional or larger powers (if any) conferred on them by the settlement), as the power was overridden by the statutory trusts. It was held, however, that the court could authorise the trustees to effect partition under s. 57 of the T.A. 1925 if such a course was expedient (see now Variation of Trusts Act, 1958).

It was held by Eve, J., in *Re Brooker ; Public Trustee* v. *Young* [1934] Ch. 610 that the words of s. 28 (3) of the L.P.A. 1925, *ante*, " become absolutely vested in persons of full age in undivided shares " included personal representatives and trustees as well as persons absolutely entitled to beneficial interests ; and, referring to *Re Thomas, ante*, he said that all that Farwell, J., decided in that case was that the words do not extend to a case where the proceeds are only vested in life-tenants. See also *Re Gorringe & Braybons, Ltd.'s Contract* [1934] Ch. 614n.

Powers of overreaching equitable interests by virtue of the statutory trusts for sale.—This subject is dealt with *ante*, at p. 176, and it is convenient here to mention here some only of the rules affecting statutory trusts which arise when land is held in undivided shares.

The statutory trusts conferred by s. 36 (6) of the S.L.A. 1925 arise when land formerly settled ceases to be such by reason of a trust taking effect for two or more persons in undivided shares in possession (S.L.A. 1925, s. 36 (1) and (2)). In such a case it has been suggested that the former Settled Land Act trustees obtain a paramount trust for sale giving them the overreaching power which they would obtain if they were trustees for sale within the meaning of s. 2 (2) of the L.P.A. 1925, as amended (as to which, see p. 178). This view has not been accepted by all writers (see, e.g., J. M. Lightwood, *Law Journal*, vol. 73, p. 356), but the provisions of the L.P.A. 1925, s. 2 (2), are rarely invoked because it is easier to obtain release of an equitable interest, so the point is almost academic.

The overreaching powers of trustees holding on the statutory trusts in the L.P.A. 1925, s. 35, appear to depend on the provision bringing the statutory trusts into operation. If, for instance, a legal estate is purported to be conveyed, after 1925, to two persons of full age in undivided shares, those persons hold upon the statutory trusts (L.P.A. 1925, s. 34 (2)). There is no power vested in such trustees to overreach any interest having priority to the conveyance, whether legal or equitable (see L.P.A. 1925, s. 35 ; s. 3 (6)). Where, on the other hand, the statutory trusts have come into operation by virtue of Pt. IV of Sched. 1 to the L.P.A. each paragraph must be looked at to see what incumbrances remain binding on the land after it has vested in accordance with the relevant paragraph (L.P.A. 1925, Sched. 1, Pt. IV, para. 1 (1), (3) and (4) ; see *ante*, p. 287 *et seq*.). There is no doubt, of course, about the power of two or more trustees for sale to overreach an equitable interest which arises under the trust for sale.

Appointment of new trustees of the " statutory trusts."—First, where immediately before 1926 the entirety of the land was vested in the trustees of a will in trust for persons entitled in undivided shares, it became vested in them on the " statutory trusts " (L.P.A. 1925, Sched. 1, Pt. IV, para. 1 (1), *ante*, p. 288). Then, when a vacancy arises in the trust, the question arises whether it is necessary to have two appointments, that is, one appointment of a new trustee of the will and a separate appointment of the same person to be the new trustee of the statutory trusts.

The better opinion clearly appears that it is only *necessary* to have one appointment, namely, an appointment of a new trustee of the will, the new trustees of the will becoming also trustees of the statutory trusts (see *Re Wilson* (an unreported decision of Astbury, J.) mentioned in the *Law Journal*, vol. 67, p. 137 ; *Law Journal*, vol. 72, p. 105 ; *Solicitors' Journal*, vol. 75, pp. 688, 694).

Notwithstanding this, it is considered *advisable* to make one deed do, but to make the deed both an appointment under the trust instrument and an appointment under the statutory trusts. To effect this it will be necessary to recite that the document is intended both as an appointment under the trust instrument and an appointment under the statutory trusts. Then, as regards the parties, if the trust instrument nominates a person or persons to exercise the power of appointment given in the instrument, to prevent the point being raised that such power did not include a power to appoint a trustee of the statutory trusts, it would be better to join not only the person or persons expressly given the power to appoint, but also the only other person or persons who might be considered necessary, that is, the surviving or continuing trustee or trustees (see T.A. 1925, s. 36 (1) (*b*)) ; and for the latter to confirm the appointment.

Power of trustees for sale to join with other owners of undivided shares in sale.—Trustees for sale of an undivided share in the proceeds of sale of land directed to be sold, or personal representatives, are given power by s. 24 of the T.A. 1925 to execute or exercise any trust or power vested in them in relation to such share, in conjunction with the persons entitled to or having power in that behalf over the other share or shares, and, notwithstanding that one or more of the trustees or personal representatives may be entitled to or interested in any such other share, either in his or their own right or in a fiduciary capacity.

CORPORATIONS AND COMPANIES

A. CORPORATIONS SOLE

Definition.—The definition given by Blackstone is : " *A corporation sole* consists of one person only and his successors in some particular station, who are incorporated by law in order to give them some legal capacities and advantages, particularly that of perpetuity, which in their natural persons they could not have." By this device, after the first grant, the property passes to the persons holding the office from time to time, without the necessity of periodic conveyances. A bishop is a corporation sole, and so is every archdeacon, rector and vicar, but a Roman Catholic bishop is not a corporation sole (*Kehoe* v. *Lansdowne* [1893] A.C. 451). Other corporations sole are the Crown (Co. Litt. 15*b*) ; the Solicitor to the Treasury (Treasury Solicitor Act, 1876, s. 1) ; the Public Trustee (Public Trustee Act, 1906, s. 1 (2)) ; the Official Custodian for Charities (Charities Act, 1960, s. 3).

Vacancy in the office of a corporation sole.—Before 1926 a grant of lands to a corporation sole was void unless the corporator to whom the grant was made was in office at the date of the grant (Norton on Deeds, 1st ed.,

p. 302 ; 2nd ed., p. 332). This has been remedied by s. 180 (2) of the L.P.A. 1925, which provides, in effect, that where, either before 1926 or after 1925, there is or has been a vacancy in the office of a corporation sole at the time when, if there had been no vacancy, any interest in or charge on property would have been acquired by the corporation, such interest shall, *notwithstanding such vacancy*, vest and be deemed to have vested in the successor to such office on his appointment as a corporation sole, but without prejudice to the right of such successor to disclaim that interest or charge.

Conveyance of freeholds to a corporation sole.—A grant of land *in fee simple* to a corporation sole could always have been made if the proper word of limitation was used, namely, " successors." If this word were not used, only a life interest passed to the person representing the corporation for the time being, in his personal capacity, but he had to hold it on trust for the corporation and its successors. For instance, the word "heirs" would only have created an estate for life in such representative and so the words " in fee simple " would have had no larger effect (*contra* Megarry & Wade, Real Property, 3rd ed., at p. 55, notes 14 and 15). There was an exception in the case of a grant to the Crown. In that case no words of limitation were ever necessary.

Since 1925, to pass the fee simple to a corporation sole it is unnecessary to use *any* word of limitation, provided that the conveyance is made to the corporation by his corporate designation and no contrary intention appears (L.P.A. 1925, s. 60 (2)). It is advised that in conveyances to a rector or vicar of a parish, if his name is used in the operative part of the conveyance, it will still be expedient to use the word " successors " to show that he is not to take as an individual. This will not be necessary when the corporation designation is used, as in the case of a conveyance to the Public Trustee.

Conveyance of leaseholds to a corporation sole.—Before 1926 there was no way by which *leaseholds* could be vested in a corporation sole in his corporate capacity. If *A* were a corporation sole, and a lease were made or assigned to him and his successors, the word " successors " was rejected, " yet his executors or administrators shall have it in *autre droit* " (Norton on Deeds, 2nd ed., p. 327). In other words, the effect of an assignment of leaseholds to a corporation sole before 1926 was to vest the estate in the holder of the office as a trustee for the corporation and its successors. On his death the legal estate did not pass to the successors of the corporation, but to the personal representatives of the holder of the office, and they held it as trustees for the corporation and its successors.

It is now provided by s. 180 (1) of the L.P.A. 1925 that where either after 1925 or before 1926 any *property* or any interest therein is or *has been vested in a corporation sole* (including the Crown), the same shall, unless and until otherwise disposed of by the corporation, pass and devolve to and vest in and be deemed always to have passed and devolved to or vested in the successors from time to time of such corporation. " Property " is defined in s. 205 (1) (xx) of the L.P.A. 1925 as including " any thing in action, and any interest in real or personal property."

Also now it is provided by s. 3 (5) of the A.E.A. 1925 that " On the death of a corporator sole his interest in the corporation's real and personal estate shall be deemed to be an interest ceasing on his death and shall devolve to his successor."

Corporation sole as trustee.—It was held in *Bankes* v. *Salisbury Diocesan Council* [1960] Ch. 631, that there is no principle that a conveyance to a corporation sole, whether or not jointly, could not take effect when a trust was imposed.

B. CORPORATIONS AGGREGATE

Definition.—A corporation aggregate consists of several persons incorporated by Royal Charter or under Act of Parliament, such as the mayor, aldermen and burgesses of a borough, or a joint stock company incorporated under one of the Companies Acts. The rules affecting local authorities are discussed *post*, p. 353, and some special rules applicable to limited companies formed under one of the Companies Acts are mentioned *post*, p. 317.

In all deeds, contracts, wills, orders, assents and other instruments made or coming into operation after 1925, unless the context otherwise requires, " person " includes a corporation (L.P.A. 1925, s. 61).

Power of corporation to hold land.—Prior to the operation of the Charities Act, 1960, there were certain restrictions on conveyances of land to corporations " in mortmain." These have been repealed by the Charities Act, 1960, s. 38 and Sched. 7, and s. 38 (2) provides that " no right or title to any property shall be defeated or impugned, and no assurance or disposition of property shall be treated as void or voidable, by virtue of [the Mortmain and Charitable Uses Act, 1891, and the Mortmain and Charitable Uses Amendment Act, 1892] or of any other enactment relating to mortmain, if at [29th July, 1960] the possession is in accordance with that right or title or with that assurance or disposition, and no step has been taken to assert a claim by virtue of any such enactment. Provided that this subsection shall not validate any assurance or disposition so as to defeat a right or title acquired by adverse possession before [29th July, 1960] ". Consequently it is unnecessary to deal with the old rules which can be found in the 14th Edition of this book, Vol. 1, p. 278.

The proviso to s. 38 (2) would appear to apply where a conveyance to trustees was not only void under the Mortmain and Charitable Uses Acts, but the trustees actually held the land on trusts other than those imposed by the conveyance. Although there would be no period of limitation in respect of the trusts under the conveyance, since the trustees were in possession of the trust property (Limitation Act, 1939, s. 19 (1) (*b*)), the repeal of the Acts is not to revive and enable the enforcement of such trusts.

Further it is apparent that foreign or overseas corporations (i.e., companies incorporated outside Great Britain) are now under no automatic disqualification or restriction in English law from holding land in the United Kingdom. Nor is the power to do so now confined to those companies with a place of business within Great Britain which have delivered the required documents to the registrar of companies (s. 408 of the Companies Act, 1948, was repealed by s. 38 (1) of the Charities Act, 1960).

Contracts by corporations.—The Corporate Bodies' Contracts Act, 1960, now provides (s. 1 (1)) that any person with authority, express or implied, may make a contract on behalf of a corporation by signed writing if that would be required of private persons and otherwise by parol. A contract made in this way may be similarly varied or discharged (*ibid.*, s. 1 (2)).

Corporate body as joint tenant.—A body corporate, since 9th August, 1899, has been capable of acquiring and holding any real or personal property in joint tenancy in the same manner as if it were an individual, and, on its dissolution, the property will devolve on the other joint tenant, whether it be another body corporate or an individual (Bodies Corporate (Joint Tenancy) Act, 1899).

Dissolution of a corporation.—The Companies Act, 1948, s. 323 (1), enables the liquidator of a company, with the leave of the court, to disclaim land of any tenure burdened with onerous covenants. On disclaimer such land vests in the Crown. No liability is imposed on the Crown in respect of any rent-charge unless the Crown has taken possession or control of the land or entered into occupation (*ibid.*, ss. 324, 326) and it appears that, unless the Crown enters, there is no liability on covenants or otherwise (*Attorney-General* v. *Parsons* [1956] A.C. 421).

In *Re Nottingham General Cemetery Co.* [1955] Ch. 683, it was decided that, having regard to the special Act incorporating the company, the cemetery land was land burdened with onerous covenants within the meaning of s. 323 (1). The liquidator was, therefore, permitted to disclaim notwithstanding the fact that the special Act prohibited the company from disposing of the land.

On dissolution of a corporation, leaseholds belonging to the corporation vest in the Crown as *bona vacantia* (*Re Sir Thomas Spencer Wells* [1933] Ch. 29). The destination of freeholds is doubtful, but they would appear to pass to the Crown by escheat (*ibid.*, at p. 54 ; *Re Strathblaine Estates, Ltd.* [1948] Ch. 228). In the case of a company formed under the Companies Acts, on dissolution all its property, real and personal, now passes to the Crown as *bona vacantia* (Companies Act, 1948, s. 354), but the title of the Crown may be disclaimed by notice signed by the Treasury Solicitor (Companies Act, 1948, s. 355). If an order is made by the court under the Companies Act, 1948, s. 352, declaring the dissolution to have been void, no order is needed to revest any property in the company (*Re C. W. Dixon, Ltd.* [1947] Ch. 251).

Section 354 excepts property held by the company on trust for others, and it was held in *Re Strathblaine Estates, Ltd., ante*, that the legal estate in such property can be vested in the beneficiaries under the T.A. 1925, s. 44 (ii) (*c*), below. The L.P.A. 1925, s. 181, provides that where by reason of the dissolution of a corporation a legal estate in any property has *determined*, the court may by order create a corresponding estate and vest it in the person who would have been entitled to it had it remained subsisting. It would not appear that a legal estate does *determine* on dissolution of a corporation (*Re Strathblaine Estates, Ltd., ante*) so that s. 181 would not seem to have any effect, although it might be considered that the legal estate had determined if the Treasury Solicitor had disclaimed under the Companies Act, 1948, s. 355. It is provided by the L.P.A. 1925, s. 7, that a fee simple vested in a corporation which is liable to determine by reason of the dissolution of the corporation, is, for the purposes of the Act, a fee simple absolute.

Section 36 (3) of the T.A. 1925, provides that " Where a corporation being a trustee is or has been dissolved, either before or after the commencement of this Act, then, for the purposes of this section and of any enactment replaced thereby, the corporation shall be deemed to be and to have been from the date of the dissolution incapable of acting in the trusts or powers reposed in or conferred on the corporation."

See also s. 41 (1) of the T.A. 1925, which provides, generally, that the court may make an order appointing a new trustee in substitution for a trustee who is a corporation which has been dissolved. Section 44 (ii) (c) provides that where a trustee entitled to or possessed of any land or interest therein, whether by way of mortgage or otherwise, or entitled to a contingent right therein, either solely or jointly with any other person, *being a corporation, has been dissolved*, the court may make a vesting order vesting the land or interest therein in any such person and for any such estate or interest as the court may direct, or releasing or disposing of the contingent right to such person as the court may direct.

For a discussion of the rules relating to the property of a dissolved company see the *Solicitors' Journal*, vol. 91, p. 93, and vol. 99, p. 479 *et seq.*

C. COMPANIES FORMED UNDER THE COMPANIES ACTS

The Companies Act, 1948, applies to limited companies formed or registered or re-registered under former Acts, provided that reference, express or implied, to the date of registration of a company shall be construed as a reference to the date at which the company was registered under a former Act (Companies Act, 1948, ss. 377 to 381).

A company which has been struck off the register for failure to file annual returns may be restored (Companies Act, 1948, s. 353) and an order may be made that particulars of a legal charge purported to have been created after striking off may (for example if there has been no subsequent change and the company is solvent) be deemed to have been duly delivered (*Re Boxco, Ltd.* [1970] 1 Ch. 442). Apparently striking off was discovered when an attempt was made to register particulars. It is not apparent why the fact of striking off was not discovered by search before the creation of the legal charge ; the period between the striking off and the date of charge was only about six weeks.

Certificate of incorporation.—A certificate of incorporation given by the registrar is conclusive evidence that the company was authorised to be and is duly registered and incorporated, and, therefore, the validity of the memorandum of association of a limited company cannot be disputed (Companies Act, 1948, s. 15 (1) ; *McGlade* v. *Royal London Mutual Insurance Society, Ltd.* [1910] 2 Ch. 169 ; *Cotman* v. *Brougham* [1918] A.C. 514, 521 ; *Hammond* v. *Prentice Brothers, Ltd.* [1920] 1 Ch. 201) ; and the certificate is also conclusive evidence that the registration and incorporation were duly effected on the day mentioned in the certificate (*Jubilee Cotton Mills, Ltd.* v. *Lewis* [1924] A.C. 958).

Non-trading companies.—A non-trading company has no implied power to borrow (*Baroness Wenlock* v. *River Dee Co.* (1885), 10 App. Cas. 354). For instance, a building society (*Blackburn Benefit Building Society* v. *Cunliffe Brooks* (1882), 22 Ch. D. 61) ; or a school board (*R.* v. *Sir Charles Reed* (1880), 5 Q.B.D. 483) ; or a literary and scientific institution (*Re Badger* [1905] 1 Ch. 568) cannot, in the absence of express authority, borrow.

Contracts of companies.—It is provided by s. 32 (1) of the Companies Act, 1948, that (a) a contract which if made between private persons would be required to be in writing, and under seal, may be made on behalf of the company in writing under the common seal of the company ; (b) a contract which if made between private persons would be required to be in writing, signed by the parties to be charged therewith, may be made on behalf of the company in writing signed by any person acting under its authority, express or implied ; (c) a contract which if made between private persons would by law be valid although made by parol only, and not reduced into writing, may be made by parol on behalf of the company by any person acting under its authority, express or implied. By s. 32 (2) a contract so made is effectual in law, and binds the company and its successors and all other parties thereto ; and by subs. (3) of the same section a contract so made may be varied or discharged in the same manner in which it is authorised by that section to be made.

Section 74 (2) of the L.P.A. 1925, provides that the board of directors of a corporation aggregate (including a limited company) may, by resolution or otherwise, *appoint an agent*, either generally or in any particular case, to execute on behalf of the corporation any agreement or other *instrument not under seal* in relation to any matter within the powers of the corporation. But if the instrument to be executed by the agent has to be under seal, then it will be necessary to give him this power by a power of attorney under seal.

Power to buy, sell and mortgage.—The powers of a corporation formed under statutory authority, such as that provided by the Companies Acts, are limited to the achievement of certain specified purposes. Therefore, it must be ascertained whether the company has power to enter into any particular transaction (but see below as to the protection of purchasers, etc.). To ascertain this, the main purpose for which the company was incorporated must first be determined ; then the special powers in the memorandum of association for effectuating that purpose must be looked for ; and then, if the act is not within either the main purpose or the special powers expressly given by the memorandum, the inquiry remains whether the act is incidental or consequential to the main purpose, and is a thing reasonably to be done for effectuating it. See the Companies Act, 1948, ss. 6 and 8 (1), (2) ; *Re Patent File Co.* (1871), L.R. 6 Ch. 83 ; *General Auction Estate Co.* v. *Smith* [1891] 3 Ch. 432 ; *Re Kingsbury Collieries, Ltd. and Moore's Contract* [1907] 2 Ch. 259.

The memorandum of association of a company is invariably drawn in wide terms, such as to include power to purchase, sell or take on lease any land. If such power were not included expressly, then it is apprehended that the company would have power to acquire land and dispose of it only if such transactions were incidental to the expressed objects of the company. There does not appear, however, to be any reported case in which a purchase or sale of land has been held to be *ultra vires*. In any case it is usually accepted that even if purchase by a company was not within its powers, it would be held, on a resale by the company, that such resale passed a good title to the purchaser, by analogy to the case of a trustee making an un-authorised purchase then reselling. See Williams on Vendor and Purchaser, 4th ed., vol. II, p. 918.

In *General Auction Estate Co.* v. *Smith, ante*, the company was a trading company. The company had no express power to borrow by the memorandum or articles, but it was held that as the borrowing was properly incidental to the course and conduct of the business, the company had an implied power to borrow.

Speaking generally, when a company proposes to raise money by an ordinary mortgage of the property of the company, or by the issue of debentures, it should be ascertained from the memorandum and articles, first, whether the company has power to borrow; secondly, whether the directors have authority to exercise the company's borrowing powers without a resolution of the company; thirdly, whether there is any limit on the amount which may be borrowed, and, if so, whether that limit has been reached; and, fourthly, whether the company or the directors have power to secure the repayment of the money borrowed by a mortgage or charge on all or any part of the assets of the company. If the memorandum is silent, a power to borrow will, as we have seen above, be implied if it be properly incident to the course and conduct of the business for its proper purposes.

Two points of some general importance here were raised by the modern decision of the Court of Appeal in *Bell Houses, Ltd.* v. *City Wall Properties, Ltd.* [1966] 2 Q.B. 656. Firstly, it was held that, where a company's objects include the carrying on of businesses which in the opinion of the directors can advantageously be carried on in connection with its main business, then the honestly formed opinion of the directors as to this prevents any such other business from being *ultra vires*. Secondly, it was found " unnecessary to consider the interesting, important and difficult question which would arise were the contract *ultra vires*, namely whether, the plaintiff company having fully performed its part under the contract, the defendants could successfully take the point that the contract was *ultra vires* the plaintiff company and so avoid payment " (*per* Salmond, L.J., at pp. 693, 694). The question was apparently not argued but the suggestion of such a defence clearly was not favoured (but compare *Re Staines U.D.C.* [1969] 1 Ch. 10 in which this *dictum* was distinguished and an *ultra vires* covenant held to mean an absence of consideration for a defendant's promise).

Protection of purchasers, etc.—Recently the *ultra vires* doctrine has become considerably qualified, to the benefit of conveyancers, by the following provision of the European Communities Act, 1972 (s. 9 (1)) :—

" In favour of a person dealing with a company in good faith, any transaction decided on by the directors shall be deemed to be one which it is within the capacity of the company to enter into, and the power of the directors to bind the company shall be deemed to be free of any limitation under the memorandum or articles of association ; and a party to a transaction so decided on shall not be bound to inquire as to the capacity of the company to enter into it or as to any such limitation on the power of the directors, and shall be presumed to have acted in good faith unless the contrary is proved."

This provision came into force on 1st January, 1973 (s. 9 (9) of the Act) and does not appear to have retrospective operation. Previously the position was that purchasers and other persons dealing with a limited company were deemed to have notice of the contents of its articles of association, and, therefore, of the extent of the powers given thereby to the directors. The production thereof, therefore, had to be required (*Royal British Bank* v. *Turquand* (1856), 25 L.J.Q.B. 317). Thus the number of necessary inquiries and requisitions has clearly been reduced : in principle, it should suffice in practice to call for a copy of the directors' resolution.

However, the new provision (s. 9 (1) of the European Communities Act, 1972, above) is not entirely without its difficulties. *First*, although good faith is to be presumed, there is no relevant definition so that it could become a matter of uncertain argument as to the point at which a failure to make inquiries amounts to bad faith. *Second*, the protection depends upon a decision of the directors which must mean the board of directors and it seems unclear how far the situation is covered where a single director or other person, e.g., the secretary, acts with the authority of the board. *Third*, valuable consideration is not expressly an element of the protection but it may be suggested that voluntary transactions are outside the provision on the grounds that a donee would be put on inquiry sufficiently to show an absence of good faith. *Fourth*, no provision is made for successors in title : following an *ultra vires* transaction, how is a subsequent purchaser to be affected by his own or an original absence of good faith?

Apart from these points, it is to be observed that this qualification of the *ultra vires* doctrine only defeats the company itself as against persons within s. 9 (1) of the European Communities Act, 1972. It does not operate, for example, to protect the directors as against shareholders. Nor would it operate to prevent any other person relying on the doctrine as against the company (cf. *Re Staines U.D.C.* [1967] 1 Ch. 10).

Further, even before 1973, a purchaser or other person dealing with a limited company was not concerned with matters which come under the heading of private regulations, or what are sometimes termed " matters of indoor management " ; he was entitled to assume that where the articles of association give a power to do the act proposed to be done, all such regulations have been complied with, although, as a matter of fact, they may not have been. This is known as the rule in *Royal British Bank* v. *Turquand* (1856), 25 L.J.Q.B. 317. For example, under the rule, a mortgagee from a company would not be affected by the fact that the mortgage had been sealed at a meeting of directors at which no quorum was present (*County of Gloucester Bank* v. *Rudry Merthyr, etc., Colliery Co.* [1895] 1 Ch. 629 ; see also *Duck* v. *Tower Galvanising Co.* [1901] 2 K.B. 314, where debentures issued under the seal of a company were held valid even though there had been no meeting or resolutions of the company or the board). Again, a company would be unable to avoid a transaction entered into on behalf of the company by a director (or other officer) within the scope of whose duties and powers the transaction would ordinarily come but who had not in fact been formally authorised to enter into the transaction (*Kreditbank Cassel* v. *Schenkers, Ltd.* [1927] 1 K.B. 826 ; compare *Houghton & Co.* v. *Northard* [1928] A.C. 1 ; *Freeman & Lockyer* v. *Buckhurst Park Properties (Mangal), Ltd.* [1964] 2 Q.B. 480 ; and *Panorama Developments (Guildford), Ltd.* v. *Fidelis Furnishing Fabrics, Ltd.* [1971] 2 Q.B. 711).

It is thought that this rule still stands substantially unaffected by s. 9 (1) of the European Communities Act, 1972, except, of course, that there should be fewer occasions calling for reliance on it. Reliance on s. 9 (1) should suffice in most cases without more.

However, there are exceptions to the rule in *Royal British Bank* v. *Turquand*, *ante*, as follows :—

(1) Where the person dealing with the company actually knew that some matter of indoor management had not been complied with (see *Howard* v. *Patent Ivory Co.* (1888), 38 Ch. D. 156, power to borrow up to a specified sum exceeded ; *Morris* v. *Kanssen* [1946] A.C. 459, director dealing with his company). This exception used to apply also where there was constructive notice only of such non-compliance, but it appears clear that this is now precluded by s. 9 (1) of the European Communities Act, 1972, so long as good faith is present.

(2) Where a document, relied on as the company's, is forged (*Ruben* v. *Great Fingall Consolidated* [1906] A.C. 439). This should be unaffected by the 1972 provision.

(3) Where the person dealing with the company has never inspected the provision in question in the articles of association. For example, he cannot rely on a provision in them under which an authority might have been conferred on an officer of the company who would not normally have the authority in question (*Roma Corporation, Ltd.* v. *Proved Tin, Ltd.* [1952] 2 Q.B. 147 ; see also *South London Greyhound Racecourses, Ltd.* v. *Wake* [1931] 1 Ch. 496, a provision, which had not been inspected, that the sealing and attestation of documents should be conclusive evidence of genuineness could not be relied upon in a case of forgery). This would appear to remain so except where it is the board of directors which has decided on and carried out a transaction beyond its powers. The 1972 provision appears to contain nothing relevant to the protection of third persons where a director or secretary purporting to act for the company has not been duly authorised to do so by the board of directors.

Debentures.—Section 85 (1) of the L.P.A. 1925 provides that a legal mortgage of freehold property can only be made by a demise or by a charge by deed by way of legal mortgage ; and s. 86 (1) provides that a legal mortgage of leaseholds can only be made by a sub-demise or charge by way of legal mortgage. By ss. 85 (3) and 86 (3) it is provided that the sections respectively are to apply to mortgages expressed to be made by way of trust for sale. Therefore, a trust deed to secure debenture or debenture stock must be made by demise or sub-demise respectively, or charge by way of legal mortgage.

Most memoranda of association contain one or more principal objects and a number of subsidiary powers, such as a power to borrow. As borrowing under a power so worded is not an independent activity a loan for a purpose known by the lender to be *ultra vires* is tainted with the illegality and a security given for it is void. Although a lender is deemed to know of the contents of the memorandum he is not bound to inquire as to the purpose of the loan but, if in fact he knows, he must ensure that it is authorised by the objects clause (*Introductions, Ltd.* v. *National Provincial Bank, Ltd.* [1970] Ch. 199). How far this is affected by s. 9 (1) of the European Communities Act, 1972, above, will depend on whether the knowledge of the lender in question can be taken to signify an absence of good faith.

When lending money on the security of debentures, it is sometimes important to see that the issue of such debentures was not defective on the ground that any of the directors who issued them held any office of profit under the company other than that of managing director or manager. For, if the company is governed by Table A in the Companies Act, 1929, and cl. 72 (*b*) to this effect was not negatived in the articles, the acceptance of such an office vacates the office of director. The words in Table A in the Companies Act, 1929, were, " without the consent of the company in general meeting holds any other office of profit under the company except that of managing director or manager." As to the meaning of these words, see *Star Steam Laundry Company, Ltd.* v. *Dukas* (1913), 108 L.T. 367. The appointment as solicitor to a company is not such an office of profit (*Re Harper's Ticket Machine, Ltd.* [1912] W.N. 263). If the company is governed

11

by Table A in the Companies Act, 1948, there is no provision similar to cl. 72 (*b*) in Table A of the 1929 Act (see Companies Act, 1948, Sched. 1, para. 84 (3)).

But, although a resolution that debentures be issued is invalid because the articles of association make it improper that certain persons should have been the directors to pass it, yet, in the events which have happened, the company may be estopped from alleging the invalidity of the debentures, as was the case in *Victor's, Ltd.* v. *Lingard* [1927] 1 Ch. 323. See also *Webb* v. *Commissioners of Herne Bay* (1870), L.R. 5 Q.B. 642.

Floating charges.—The issue of debentures as a floating security does not in general interfere with the company's power of disposition, so long as there is no receiver or winding-up order. See *Governments Stock, etc., Investment Co.* v. *Manila Railway Co.* [1897] A.C. 81. For it is well settled that by creating a charge upon its assets generally by way of floating security a company is not, in the absence of any stipulation to the contrary, prohibited from creating specific charges on specific portions of its assets in the ordinary course of business, as otherwise it would be prevented from effectually carrying on that business, the carrying on of which was contemplated by the parties to the security (Warrington, L.J., in *Re Automatic Bottle Makers, Ltd.* [1926] Ch. 412, at p. 421). But where a debenture trust deed creating a general floating charge over all the undertaking and assets of the company, both present and future, reserves power to the company in the ordinary course of its business to create specific charges over any of those assets, then a second general floating charge over *all the property* comprised in the first charge but ranking *pari passu* with or in priority to that charge is, under the general law, incompatible with the first charge and ranks subject to it (*Smith* v. *English and Scottish Mercantile Investment Trust* [1896] W.N. 86 ; *Re Benjamin Cope & Sons* [1914] 1 Ch. 800 ; *Re Automatic Bottle Makers, Ltd., ante*). There is, however, no principle of law which forbids the creation of a second floating charge over *part only* of those assets ranking *pari passu* with, or in priority to, the earlier floating charge, so long as the later floating charge is within the limits of the power reserved (*Re Automatic Bottle Makers, Ltd., ante*).

A company by a trust deed gave debenture-holders a general floating charge on all the company's property, both present and future, and it was provided that the company should not create any mortgage or charge in respect of such property in priority to or ranking *pari passu* with the debentures. The company *afterwards purchased* certain freehold property and obtained part of the purchase-money by a charge on the property. It was held that the company only obtained an equity of redemption over the property and that the charge had priority over the debentures (*Re Connolly Brothers, Ltd.* (*No.* 2) [1912] 2 Ch. 25). On the other hand if the debenture had contained a *fixed* charge by way of legal mortgage on (for example) all freehold property it would affect any freeholds subsequently purchased ; compare *Church of England Building Society* v. *Piskor* [1954] Ch. 553. In such a case on sale by the company the concurrence of the debenture-holder would be essential to release the charge.

The power of sale implied in mortgages since the Conveyancing Act, 1881, is not implied in the debentures of a joint stock company creating a floating charge (*Blaker* v. *Herts & Essex Waterworks Co.* (1889), 41 Ch. D. 399 ; *Deyes* v. *Wood* [1911] 1 K.B. 806). The circumstances in which leave of the court under the Courts (Emergency Powers) Act, 1943, was formerly required on sale by a receiver for debenture-holders were discussed in *Re Northern Garage, Ltd.* [1946] Ch. 188.

A charge for the purpose of securing debentures must be registered with the registrar of companies (Companies Act, 1948, s. 95 (2) (*a*)) ; as must any charge on land (*ibid.*, s. 95 (2) (*d*)) ; but a charge for any rent or other periodical sum issuing out of land does not need to be so registered (Companies Act, 1948, s. 95 (2) (*d*)). The fact that a registered debenture-holder had notice of a previous unregistered mortgage will not prevent his debenture having priority (*Re Monolithic Building Co. ; Tacon v. The Company* [1915] 1 Ch. 643).

Investigation of title after floating charge.—Floating charges affect all the company's property and so should be abstracted ; it is then for the purchaser to satisfy himself as to the circumstances in which they become fixed. If a charge is discovered, for instance, on searching, it should be examined to ensure that it is a floating charge and not a fixed charge such as can be released only with the concurrence of the mortgagee. A purchaser is entitled to reasonable evidence that a floating charge has not crystallised. If (as is unusual) that is to happen at the expiration of a period, or on default in making a payment, then the evidence must show that the period has not expired or (as the case may be) there has been no default (*Re Horne and Hellard* (1885), 29 Ch. D. 736). In the normal case in which there is no express limit to the " floating " of the charge (even though the debenture may state that business may be carried on until default is made) it does not crystallise until the debenture-holder intervenes, the business ceases or winding up commences. Evidence that the charge has not so crystallised should be called for (*Edward Nelson & Co.* v. *Faber & Co.* [1903] 2 K.B. 367), for instance by statutory declaration of an officer (at the cost of the purchaser : L.P.A. 1925, s. 45 (4)) unless the company is so well known that it is unnecessary.

Further reference may be made generally to a useful article by Mr. G. N. Benson at *Law Society's Gazette*, vol. 66, p. 713, and to correspondence arising at *ibid.*, vol. 66, p. 777 and vol. 67, p. 107.

Fraudulent preferences.—By the Companies Act, 1948, s. 320, any convey-ance, mortgage, execution or other act relating to property made or done by or against a company within six months before commencement of winding up, which in the case of an individual, had it been made or done within six months before bankruptcy would be a fraudulent preference, is, in the event of the company being wound up, invalid as a fraudulent preference. See Bankruptcy Act, 1914, s. 44, *ante*, p. 256.

Powers on winding up.—On a winding-up order by the court, the court may appoint a liquidator or liquidators (Companies Act, 1948, s. 237). Until such appointment the official receiver will become the provisional liquidator with power to act as such until he or another person becomes liquidator (*ibid.*, s. 239 (*a*)) ; where a liquidator is not appointed by the court, the official receiver will be the liquidator (*ibid.*, s. 239 (*d*)) ; and the official receiver will be the liquidator during any vacancy (*ibid.*, s. 239 (*e*)).

Where winding up is by order of the court the order for winding up and the order appointing the liquidator should be abstracted and recited in a convey-ance by the liquidator on behalf of the company. Although practice varies it would seem that on compulsory winding up proof must be given that a liquidator (other than the official receiver) has notified his appointment to the registrar of companies and given security to the satisfaction of the Department of Trade and Industry ; he is not capable of acting as liquidator (and so apparently cannot give a valid discharge for purchase price) until the steps have been taken (Companies Act, 1948, s. 240). Where winding up is under supervision the special resolution for winding up and appointing the liquidator together with the order that winding up should continue under supervision of the court should be abstracted and recited. In the normal case of members' voluntary winding up it is proper to abstract and recite the special resolution for winding up, the statutory declaration by directors of solvency and the appointment of the liquidator ; in the case of a creditors' voluntary winding up the relevant matters are the resolution for winding up and the resolution of the meeting of creditors appointing the liquidator.

Assets, including freeholds, are often transferred (particularly on members' voluntary winding up) by the liquidator to members in satisfaction of their interests. For precedents of such conveyances, see Encyclopædia of Forms, 4th ed., vol. 6, p. 1738 *et seq.*, and note the opinion there expressed (p. 1738, note 10) that the liquidator may not act in this way unless the memorandum or articles of association contains an express power enabling this procedure. The accuracy of this opinion is doubted ; the Companies Act, 1948, s. 302, does not require assets to be sold, and division between members (after satisfaction of liabilities) appears to be within the powers of a liquidator to distribute property " among the members according to their rights and interests " unless the articles provide otherwise.

The liquidator in a winding-up by the court has power, without the sanction of the court, to sell the real and personal property of the company by public auction or private contract, to transfer the whole thereof to any person or company, or to sell the same in parcels ; also to execute in the name and on behalf of the company all deeds, receipts and other documents, and for that purpose, when necessary, to use the company's seal (*ibid.*, s. 245 (2)). The court will not interfere with the exercise of this power of sale unless it is established that the liquidator did not exercise his discretion *bona fide* or had acted in a way in which no reasonable liquidator could have acted (*Leon* v. *York-O-Matic, Ltd.* [1966] 1 W.L.R. 1450). No power of leasing is expressly given to the liquidator by the 1948 Act. However, it is thought that, provided the purposes of the company in its memorandum of association include dealing in land, a prospective tenant can safely assume that the grant of a lease by a liquidator is within his power " to carry on the business of the company so far as may be necessary for the beneficial winding-up thereof " (*ibid.*, s. 245 (1) (*b*)).

Where a company is being wound up voluntarily, its corporate state and corporate powers continue until it is dissolved (*ibid.*, proviso to s. 281) ; and the liquidator can, without the sanction of the court, exercise all the powers referred to in the last paragraph given to the liquidator in a winding-up by the court (*ibid.*, s. 303 (1) (*b*)).

Where an order is made for a winding up subject to supervision, the liquidator may, subject to any restrictions imposed by the court, exercise all the powers referred to in the last two paragraphs, without the sanction of the court, in the same manner as if the company were being wound up altogether voluntarily (*ibid.*, s. 315 (1)).

Neither an order for winding up a company by or under the supervision of the court, nor a voluntary winding up, divests the company of its property. Although, therefore, the liquidator sells for the company and gives a receipt for the money, the company should be made a party to the deed and its seal used to pass the estate. It is considered that all the liquidators should join in the deed. This view that company liquidators should be joined as parties to deeds of conveyance has been questioned as illogical if, as is generally the case, the property in question remains vested in the company (see D. I. Marcus, *Law Society's Gazette*, vol. 67, p. 329). Nevertheless, the view expressed above is adhered to on the grounds that, whilst the company clearly must be joined to convey the property, the liquidator should be joined in practice in order to demonstrate the exercise of his statutory powers both of selling and of giving a receipt on behalf of the company (see s. 245 (2) (*a*), (*b*) of the Companies Act, 1948 ; *Re Ebsworth and Tidy's Contract* (1889), 42 Ch. D. 23 ; also correspondence in particular at *Law Society's Gazette*, vol. 69, pp. 626 and 714). If for any special reason (for instance, where property is vested in trustees for the company) it is desired that any particular property should be vested in the liquidator, power is given to the court by s. 244 of the Companies Act, 1948, on the application of the liquidator, by order to direct that all or any part of the property belonging to the company or held by trustees on its behalf shall vest in the liquidator by his official name, and thereupon the property to which the order relates shall vest accordingly.

Registered land.—Since a licence in mortmain is now unnecessary (see *ante*, p. 269), a transfer of registered land to a company or corporation will be accepted in the ordinary form used for transfers to individuals (L.R.R., 1925, Sched., Form 19 ; compare r. 121 and Form 35). When an application for registration as proprietor of land (or of a charge) by a company is made a certified copy of its memorandum and articles of association should be produced to the registrar (L.R.R. 1925, r. 259 ; alternatively a certificate by the company's solicitor may be accepted in the form given in Ruoff's Land Registration Forms, 2nd ed., Precedent No. 40, p. 86). If the powers of disposition of the company are limited in a way which would affect a purchaser in *un*registered conveyancing, an entry protecting the limitation must be made on the register usually in the form of an appropriate restriction (L.R.R. 1925, r. 123 (4)).

Since the property of a company does not pass from the company on the making of an order for winding up by or under the supervision of the court, or on a voluntary winding up (see *ante*, p. 323), less complicated rules apply in this case than on the bankruptcy of an individual (see *ante*, p. 257). Any resolution or order appointing a liquidator may be filed and referred to on the register and, when so registered, is deemed to be in force until cancelled or superseded (L.R.R. 1925, r. 185). A liquidator should apply for this to be done, forwarding the land or charge certificate, as the case may be, together with a copy of the order appointing him, or, in the case of a voluntary winding up, of any necessary resolutions. Any transfer of the registered land or charge would then be executed by both the company and the liquidator, as in the case of a conveyance of unregistered land (Ruoff's Land Registration Forms, 2nd ed., Precedent No. 38, p. 84).

An application to register a transfer to a company incorporated outside Great Britain should be accompanied by a certified copy of the instrument of its constitution (plus a certified translation where necessary) in order to satisfy the registry about the powers of the company to hold and deal with land. It will also be necessary for such a company to furnish to the registry " a place of address in the United Kingdom " (L.R.A. 1925, s. 79 (1)). Reference may also be made to L.R.R. 1925, s. 315 (2), whereby three addresses, including that of a solicitor, may be entered on the register : it is not expressly provided that all three of these addresses must be in the United Kingdom (but this is simply inferred in Ruoff and Roper, Registered Conveyancing, 3rd ed., p. 20, from s. 79 (1), *ante*). Otherwise, such a company is treated no differently from companies incorporated under the Companies Acts.

FRIENDLY SOCIETIES

Appointment of trustees.—The Friendly Societies Act, 1896, s. 25, provides that every registered society and branch shall have one or more trustees, and the section also contains provisions as to the appointment of such trustee or trustees. A corporate body may be appointed as sole trustee (*Re Pilkington Brothers, Ltd. Workmen's Pension Fund* [1953] 1 W.L.R. 1084).

All property belonging to a registered society vests in the trustees for the time being of the society, for the use and benefit of the society and its members, and the property of a registered branch vests either in the trustees for the time being of the branch, or, if the rules so provide, in the trustees of the society for the time being on similar uses (1896 Act, s. 49).

Upon the death, resignation or removal of a trustee, the property vests in the succeeding trustees, either solely or together with any surviving or continuing trustees, and, until the appointment of succeeding trustees, in such surviving or continuing trustees only, or in the executors or administrators of the last surviving or continuing trustee, subject to the same trusts, without conveyance or assignment (1896 Act, s. 50, as amended by the Friendly Societies Act, 1971, Sched. 2).

It is understood that where a change of trustees appears on the title, a common practice is for the purchaser to accept the certificate of the secretary of the society, that, for instance, "*A* [one of the trustees] died on the   day of   , and that *B* has been duly appointed in his place, and that the present trustees of the society are *B* and *C*." It is not necessary to ask for the production of the receipt of the registrar of friendly societies for the copy resolution sent to him, as provided by s. 25 of the 1896 Act, because the appointment is complete without such copy resolution being sent, and the neglect to send it is a matter of penalty only (*Beckett* v. *Willetts* (1857), 5 W.R. 622). Nevertheless, purchasers often ask for production of that receipt.

Power to buy, sell and mortgage.—A registered society may (if the rules so provide) purchase, or take on lease, land, in the names of its trustees, and may also sell or mortgage the same (Friendly Societies Act, 1896, s. 47 (1), but compare s. 44 (1) (*d*) *ibid.*, which confers a power to invest in land without reference to the rules so providing). A purchaser or mortgagee is not bound to inquire as to the authority of the society to sell or mortgage, and the receipt of the trustees will be a good discharge (*ibid.*, s. 47 (1)). In any case, even if the rules provide that the society may not purchase land, the trustees will hold any land actually conveyed to the society on trust to sell it as land purchased in breach of trust (*Re Patten and Edmonton Union* (1883), 52 L.J. Ch. 787).

Dissolution.—Trustees of a dissolved society remain trustees for the purposes of division of the society's assets, and can give a good title to a purchaser of such assets.

Statutory receipts.—Section 53 (1) of the Act provides that " A receipt under the hands of the trustees of a registered society or branch, countersigned by the secretary, for all sums of money secured to the society or branch by any mortgage or other assurance, being in the form prescribed by this Act, if endorsed upon or annexed to the mortgage or other assurance, shall vacate the mortgage or assurance and vest the property therein comprised in the person entitled to the equity of redemption of that property, without reconveyance or re-surrender." Section 98 (4) prescribed that such a receipt " shall be in the form set forth in Part III of [Sched. 2], or in any form specified in the rules of the society or branch or any schedule thereto . . ." The form set out in Sched. 2 is as follows :—

" The trustees of the   Society [or the   branch of the Society] hereby acknowledge to have received all moneys intended to be secured by the within [or above] written deed.

Signed [Signatures of trustees].

Trustees.

Countersigned [Signature of secretary].

Secretary."

It will be seen that the above form of receipt is exactly the same as a statutory receipt formerly prescribed by the Building Societies Act, 1874, and its effect is the same. The matter is discussed *ante*, p. 263 *et seq.* The form does not include a place for the date and it is sometimes suggested that the addition of a date invalidates the form so that it cannot take effect under the 1896 Act ; it is considered that the suggestion is ill-founded. Nevertheless, if the receipt is in the appropriate form it may operate under the L.P.A. 1925, s. 115, " provided that the receipt is executed in the manner required by the statute relating to the society " (L.P.A. 1925, s. 115 (9)). The word " execute " here means execute or sign as the statute requires. In the case of a friendly society the trustees of the society sign, and the secretary countersigns.

If the friendly society is being wound up, there will be no secretary. In this case a reconveyance will have to be taken.

A statutory receipt under the Friendly Societies Act, 1896, or one given by trustees of a society under the L.P.A. 1925, s. 115, was made exempt from stamp duty by s. 33 (*a*) of the 1896 Act (as applied by s. 115 (9)), which provides that stamp duty shall not be chargeable upon a receipt given by a registered society or branch in respect of money payable by virtue of its rules or of that Act. This would not have covered the case where the mortgage was expressed to be paid off by a person who was not entitled to the immediate equity of redemption, and so the receipt operates as a transfer. It was decided in *Old Battersea Building Society* v. *Commissioner of Inland Revenue* [1898] 2 Q.B. 294, as regards a building society, that when on the discharge of a mortgage by a member, a reconveyance was taken instead of a statutory receipt, the document was also exempt from stamp duty. There has been no decision as regards a friendly society, but the principle involved would appear to be the same. However, see now as to the repeal of the relevant stamp duties, *post*, p. 1167.

The general rules as to statutory receipts on mortgages are dealt with in the chapter on Mortgages, *post*, p. 1006.

If The Law Society's Conditions of Sale, 1973 Revision, govern the contract, a purchaser must assume that any statutory receipt on the title has been executed by all proper persons and was valid and effectual (General Condition 9 ; *ante*, p. 264).

Unregistered society.—There are still in existence sick and funeral societies, or semi-friendly societies which have not been registered under the Friendly Societies Acts. When a trustee of such a society dies or retires, a new trustee should be appointed as if he were an ordinary trustee. If there are any mortgages belonging to the society they should be transferred as in the case of an ordinary trustee, otherwise the legal estate would remain in the old trustees or trustee. This is sometimes overlooked, the parties being under the impression that the appointment of a new trustee is all that is necessary to pass to him the legal estate.

Registered land.—On application for registration, the rules of a friendly society must be produced to the registrar (L.R.R. 1925, r. 259). The transfer should be made in favour of the society's trustees who will be entered on the register as the proprietors. Assuming that the rules of the society do not limit the society's powers of disposition (see above), no restriction need be entered. However, the registrar will require satisfying that any transfers or other instruments have been executed by the trustees for the time being. In this respect he will be satisfied if the execution by the trustees is witnessed by the secretary of the society. Otherwise a certificate as to the present trustees will be required from either the secretary or the solicitor of the society.

HEIRS AND HEIRESSES (COPARCENERS);
ESCHEAT FOR WANT OF HEIRS

Sale by an heir before 1926.—Where a sale by the heir-at-law of a person who died before 1926 appears on the title it will still be necessary to consider the laws of descent. In such a case, if death took place after 1897, the legal estate would, on administration being taken out, have vested in the administrator, and to enable the heir to sell as heir he should have obtained a *conveyance* thereof from such administrator (Land Transfer Act, 1897, s. 3). An *assent* would not have passed the legal estate to him.

The reader may occasionally come across a case where the document purporting to transfer the legal estate to the heir was in the form of an " assent " instead of a conveyance, or for some other reason the legal estate was outstanding on 31st December, 1925. In such a case it is thought that the legal estate vested in the heir on 1st January, 1926, by virtue of para. 3 of Pt. II of Sched. 1 to the L.P.A. 1925. If, however, the deceased's widow was then still alive and entitled to dower which had not been assigned by metes and bounds it is thought that this paragraph did not vest the legal estate in the heir.

If the heir was also the administrator and he had not done anything to bring his powers as an administrator to an end, he could, of course, have sold as administrator and have passed the legal estate, as it would have been in him in that capacity. But if the heir, being also the administrator, *sold as heir*, to enable him to pass the legal estate he should have executed a deed poll, as administrator, declaring that he henceforth held in his own right as heir and no longer as administrator.

Where death took place after 1897, it was provided that any real property should vest in the deceased's personal representative (Land Transfer Act, 1897, s. 1 (1)). However, despite this, unless and until an administrator was appointed, the legal estate vested in the deceased's heir (see *per* North, J., in *John* v. *John* [1898] 2 Ch. 573, at p. 576, also *Re Griggs* [1914] 2 Ch. 547).

Nonetheless, the better view is that the heir could not make a good title without taking out a grant, he being in the meantime in the position of a trustee and the administrator's title, when appointed, relating back to death (*Re Pryse* [1904] P. 301, 305).

Where the land was in Yorkshire and the heir was selling as heir, one would also expect to find that an affidavit of intestacy had been registered at the deeds registry. The reason was that an heir-at-law who claimed any estate or interest in lands in Yorkshire which would be defeated by the existence of a will, might, when six months from the death had elapsed, but not before, register an affidavit of intestacy ; and when this affidavit had been registered, an assurance for valuable consideration from him, duly registered, had priority over an assurance from the devisee under any will of the supposed intestate not then registered (Yorkshire Registries Act, 1884, s. 12). It was not, of course, necessary for the heir to register an affidavit of intestacy when the sale was by the administrator, although he himself was the administrator, for an administrator could give a good title to a purchaser, although a will afterwards turned up (*Hewson* v. *Shelley* [1914] 2 Ch. 13). See further at p. 614.

It was not necessary before 1926 to register letters of administration at the Middlesex or Yorkshire Deeds Registries.

A purchaser ought to ascertain, if the deceased intestate left a widow entitled to dower, that her claim was satisfied.

Canons of descent.—The old canons of descent are summarised at p. 331. These canons, with tenancy by the curtesy, dower, freebench and escheat, were, in general, abolished with regard to the real estate of every person dying after 1925 by the A.E.A. 1925, s. 45 (1).

Although a person may still in a few instances take as heir by descent, and in any case as heir by purchase, such interest will only be a *beneficial or equitable interest*. The legal estate will have passed to the personal representatives and they will be able to give a good title to a purchaser of the land *free from any claims of an heir*. It will, therefore, be of no interest to a purchaser of the legal estate in land whether or not any particular person takes as heir.

There are several exceptions to the abolition by s. 45 (1) of the canons of descent which are summarised in Sched. 9, para. 1, to the Law of Property (Amendment) Act, 1924. The Inheritance Act, 1833, as amended by s. 19 of the Law of Property Amendment Act, 1859, " remains in force for the purpose (so far as applicable) of ascertaining the devolution of entailed interests as equitable interests, and of ascertaining the persons who are to take equitable interests as heirs by purchase [that is, otherwise than by descent], but in other respects ceases to apply (save in the case of a lunatic or defective provided for by the [Law of Property Act, 1922]) on intestacies " (Law of Property (Amendment) Act, 1924, Sched. 9, para. 1).

The Inheritance Act, 1833, as amended, therefore, *still remains in force* for the purpose of—

(i) ascertaining the devolution of entailed interests ;

(ii) ascertaining the persons who are to take equitable interests as *heirs by purchase* ; and

(iii) ascertaining who are the equitable heirs of a person of unsound mind or defective, dying intestate, who, since 1925, has been incapable of making a will.

11A

(i) *Devolution of entailed interests as equitable interests.*—An interest in tail or in tail male or in tail female or in tail special may now only be created in equity, and by way of trust (L.P.A. 1925, s. 130 (1)). By subs. (4) of the same section it is provided that " In default of and subject to the execution of a disentailing assurance or the exercise of the testamentary power conferred by this Act, an entailed interest (to the extent of the property affected) shall devolve *as an equitable interest*, from time to time, upon the persons who *would have been successively entitled thereto as the heirs of the body* (either generally or of a particular class) of the tenant in tail or other person, or as tenant by the curtesy, if the entailed interest had, before [1926] been limited in respect of freehold land governed by the general law in force immediately before such [date] and such law had remained unaffected."

Tenancy by the curtesy still exists as respects past and future entailed interests (L.P.A. 1925, s. 130 (4) ; S.L.A. 1925, s. 20 (1) (vii) ; *post*, p. 428).

(ii) *Persons who take equitable interests as heirs by purchase.*—It is provided by s. 51 (1) of the A.E.A. 1925 that " Nothing in this part of this Act affects the right of any person to take *beneficially, by purchase, as heir* either general or special." " By purchase "—that is, otherwise than by descent (Inheritance Act, 1833, s. 1).

It is also provided by s. 132 (1) of the L.P.A. 1925 that a limitation of real or personal property in favour of the heir, either general or special, of a deceased person which, if limited in respect of freehold land before 1926, would have conferred on the heir an estate in the land by purchase, will operate to confer a corresponding *equitable* interest in the property on the person who would, if the *general law* in force immediately before such date had remained unaffected, have answered the description of the heir, either general or special, of the deceased in respect of his freehold land, either at the death of the deceased or at the time named in the limitation, as the case may require. *The canons of descent will therefore have to be referred to for the purpose of ascertaining such heir* ; these canons are summarised below. Note that the interest is conferred on the heir according to the *general law* and so a person who, before 1926, would be customary heir would not take an interest under the subsection.

A gift to the person who on the death of a living person should succeed to his title cannot be distinguished from a gift to the heir of a living person, which confers no immediate interest, contingent or otherwise, on any person (*Re Earl of Midleton's Will Trusts* [1969] 1 Ch. 600, applying *Re Parsons* (1890), 45 Ch. D. 51, and not following *Re Duke of St. Albans' Will Trusts* [1963] Ch. 365).

There is a particular case where under a provision in the L.P.A. 1925 an heir may take an equitable interest by purchase caused by the abolition of the rule in *Shelley's* case (1581), 1 Co. Rep. 93*b*, by s. 131 of the L.P.A. 1925, and the substitution of a new rule. The effect of the rule in *Shelley's* case was that when an ancestor by any gift or conveyance took an estate of freehold and in the same gift or conveyance an estate was limited either mediately or immediately to his heirs in fee or in tail, the words " the heirs " were construed as words of limitation of the estate of the ancestor. The simplest example was a gift to *A* for his life and after his death to his heirs. This gave *A* an estate in fee simple. If, instead of the word " heirs," the words had been " heirs of the body," then *A* would have taken an estate tail.

The L.P.A. 1925, s. 131, provides in effect that where, by any instrument coming into operation after 1925, an interest in any property is given to the heir or heirs or issue or any particular heir or any class of the heirs or issue of any person *in words which would, under the rule in Shelley's case, have operated to give to that person an interest in fee simple or an entailed interest, such words shall operate in equity as words of purchase and not of limitation,* and in the case of an interest in any property given to an heir or heirs or any particular heir or class of heirs, the same person or persons will take as would in the case of freehold land have answered that description under the general law in force before 1926. Consequently, a gift to *A* for his life and after his death to his heirs, instead of giving *A* an estate in fee simple, as formerly, gives *A* only an estate for life, and, subject thereto, an estate in fee simple to the heir, both estates being equitable.

(iii) *Persons of unsound mind or defective.*—If a person of unsound mind or defective of full age at the end of 1925, unable by reason of his incapacity to make a will, dies intestate after that date without having recovered his testamentary capacity, his *beneficial* interest in real estate (not including leaseholds) devolves in accordance with the *general* law in force before 1926 (A.E.A. 1925, s. 51 (2)). See further, *post*, p. 418.

Rules of Inheritance to Real Estate on Death Before 1st January, 1926

1. Descent is traced from the " purchaser," the person last entitled being considered to have been the " purchaser " of the land unless it is proved that he inherited the same (Inheritance Act, 1833, s. 2). " Purchaser " is defined as the person who last acquired the land otherwise than by descent (*ibid.*, s. 1).

2. On total failure of heirs of the purchaser descent is traced from the person last entitled as if he had been the purchaser (Law of Property Amendment Act, 1858, s. 19).

3. Descent is traced lineally to the issue of the purchaser *ad infinitum.*

4. Males in equal degree of relationship are preferred to females.

5. If there are two or more males in equal degree of relationship the eldest inherits, but if there are two or more females they inherit together as coparceners ; see below.

6. Lineal descendants of a deceased person in line of descent stand in the place of that person. For instance, issue of an elder son take before a younger son or his issue.

7. On failure of issue descent is to the nearest lineal ancestor (Inheritance Act, 1833, s. 6).

8. None of the maternal ancestors nor any of their descendants may inherit until all paternal ancestors and their descendants have failed ; no female paternal ancestor nor any of her descendants may inherit until all male paternal ancestors and their descendants have failed ; no female maternal ancestor nor any of her descendants may inherit until all male maternal ancestors and their descendants have failed (Inheritance Act, 1833, s. 7). But on failure of male paternal ancestors and their descendants the mother of the *more* remote paternal ancestor, or her descendants, take in preference to the mother of a less remote male paternal ancestor, or her descendants ; and on failure of male maternal ancestors, and their descendants, the mother of the more remote male maternal ancestor, and her descendants, take in preference to the mother of a less remote male maternal ancestor, and her descendants (*ibid.*, s. 8).

9. Relations of the half blood take next after any relation in the same degree of the whole blood, and his issue, where the common ancestor is a male, but next after the common ancestor where such common ancestor is a female (*ibid.*, s. 9).

10. As to dower, see 15th Edition, at p. 357, and as to curtesy, see *post*, p. 428. On death after 1st September, 1890, leaving a widow but no issue, the widow might take an interest in realty under the Intestates' Estates Act, 1890.

NOTE.—*Rules 1 to 6, inclusive, apply to descent of entailed interests on death after 1925 provided the entail has not been barred or devised ; see post, pp. 435, 436.*

Coparcenary.—This could happen in two cases, namely, (i) where a person seised of a fee simple estate died intestate without sons but leaving two or more female heirs, (ii) where a person was seised of an estate tail (other than an estate in tail male) and died leaving only female heirs. In both these cases the female heirs took an estate in coparcenary. Thus, if a person died intestate leaving an estate in fee simple, and there were no sons but three daughters, living at his death, the three daughters took as coparceners. On the death of one of the daughters her interest did not pass to the survivors, as in joint tenancy, but passed to her devisee, or to her heir if she did not leave a will. If the original deceased owner died leaving, besides the three daughters, issue (whether male or female) of a deceased female who would have been entitled to a share of the land as coparcener had she been living, such issue were entitled to that share in coparcenary with the other females. Such issue took not as heirs, but by representation by the common law. In other words, under the old law the lineal issue stood in the place of their ancestor (*Cooper* v. *France* (1850), 14 Jur. 214 ; *Re Baker ; Pursey* v. *Holloway* (1898), 79 L.T. 343).

The estate in coparcenary only arose when the females took by *descent*. If they took by *devise*, unless there were words of division, they took as joint tenants (*Owen* v. *Gibbons* [1902] 1 Ch. 636).

This interest had some of the incidents of a joint tenancy, but more of the incidents of a tenancy in common. Each coparcener could dispose of her share in the land by deed or will. An estate in coparcenary was dissolved by the alienation of one coparcener, which changed the estate into a tenancy in common. The alienee held as tenant in common with the other coparcener or coparceners, but the remaining coparceners, if there were more than one, continued between themselves to hold in coparcenary as regards their shares. On her death after 1897, without having disposed of her interest, the legal estate passed to her personal representative under the Land Transfer Act, 1897, and the beneficial interest to her devisee or the issue and all other to her descendants (*Re Matson* [1897] 2 Ch. 509).

The next question is as to what happened on 1st January, 1926, to the legal estate then held by tenants in coparcenary. The answer to this will be found in Pt. IV of Sched. 1 to the L.P.A. 1925. Part IV is headed " Provisions subjecting land held in undivided shares to a trust for sale," and appears to apply to coparceners as if they were tenants in common. See further, *ante*, p. 278. Speaking generally, if the coparceners were seised in fee simple, and there were not more than four of them, and none of their shares were mortgaged, the legal estate vested in them upon trust for sale, under para. 1 (2) of Pt. IV, for the benefit of themselves subject to the peculiar incidents attached to an interest held by coparceners. If there were more than four coparceners, or if any of them had mortgaged her share, then the legal estate vested in the Public Trustee, under para. 1 (4) of Pt. IV, until trustees were appointed in his place.

Coparcenary cannot arise on a death after 1925 except as an equitable interest and then in two cases only : (i) in the case of a person of unsound mind or defective dying intestate in consequence of his incapacity to make a will (see (iii) at p. 331) ; and (ii) in the case where a tenant in tail dies intestate as regards his entailed interest without having executed a deed of disentailment (see (i) at p. 330).

Escheat.—Escheat happened when an owner of freehold property (for a *legal* estate therein) died intestate and without heirs. In such case the property escheated to the lord of the fee.

Since the Intestates' Estates Act, 1884, on the death of an owner of an *equitable* estate in fee simple intestate and without heirs, such equitable estate also escheated (s. 4 ; *Re Wood; A.-G.* v. *Anderson* [1896] 2 Ch. 596); also where a person left a will (where there was no heir), if the trusts were incapable of being executed (s. 7).

The fact that escheat for want of heirs is abolished does not mean that the Crown or the Duchy of Lancaster or the Duke of Cornwall get nothing. In default of any person taking an absolute interest they take the residuary estate of the intestate as *bona vacantia* in lieu of such right to escheat. It is provided by s. 46 (1) (vi) of the A.E.A. 1925 that in default of any person taking an absolute interest under the new table of distribution of the estate of an intestate, the residuary estate of the intestate shall belong to the Crown or to the Duchy of Lancaster or to the Duke of Cornwall for the time being, as the case may be, as *bona vacantia*, and in lieu of any right to escheat. See, for instance, *Re Mitchell* [1954] Ch. 525.

The late Mr. T. Cyprian Williams, in the *Solicitors' Journal*, vol. 75, p. 847, pointed out that although the A.E.A. 1925 abolished escheat for want of heirs it did not abolish the right of the lord of the fee on the determination of the tenant's estate in fee simple owing to some other cause. For instance, on the disclaimer by a trustee in bankruptcy under the Bankruptcy Act, 1914, s. 54, of the bankrupt's freeholds in fee simple, which are subject to onerous covenants, the immediate lord of the fee is entitled (if no vesting order be made by the court under subs. (6)) to enter on the land as his escheat (*British General Insurance Co., Ltd.* v. *A.-G.* [1945] L.J.N.C.C.R. 113).

INDUSTRIAL AND PROVIDENT SOCIETIES

These societies are governed by the Industrial and Provident Societies Act, 1965. Two aspects only of the law relating to such societies need be mentioned here.

Statutory receipts on mortgages.—A statutory receipt can be given under the 1965 Act or under s. 115 of the L.P.A. 1925. It is thought better to take the receipt under the L.P.A. so that it is not necessary to rely on the references in the 1965 Act to the provisions of s. 115.

The section of the Industrial and Provident Societies Act, 1965, which deals with the matter is s. 33, and it provides that a receipt in full, signed by two members of the committee, and countersigned by the secretary (or, if the society is in liquidation, signed by the liquidator or liquidators for the time being, described as such) of a registered society, for all moneys secured to the society on any property, and being in one of the forms set out in Part I of Sched. 3 to the Act, *or in any other form specified in the rules of the society,* if endorsed on or annexed to the mortgage or assurance, shall be deemed to be a receipt which fulfils the requirements of the L.P.A. 1925, s. 115, for the purposes of :—

(a) subs. (1) thereof so far as it relates to the operation of such a receipt as is mentioned in that subsection ;

(b) if, but only if, the receipt states the name of the person who pays the money, subs. (2) ;

(c) subss. (3), (6), (8), (10) and (11) ;

(d) where consistent with the terms of the form authorised and used, subs. (7).

The first form given in Sched. 3 to the Act is as follows :—

" The   , Limited, hereby acknowledges to have received all moneys intended to be secured by the [within (or above) written] [annexed] deed [and by a further charge dated, etc., *or otherwise as required*].

Dated this   day of   .

⎱
⎰ Members of the Committee.

Secretary."

The second form is similar but makes provision for naming the person making payment. Section 35 provides that on payment of all moneys intended to be secured to a registered society on the security of any property, the debtor or his successor or representatives are *entitled* to a receipt in the appropriate form in Sched. 3.

There is no express provision in the 1965 Act that a statutory receipt should be exempt from stamp duty but it is understood that the Adjudication Department agreed that it was exempt " by long-standing practice." It was exempt from receipt duty by the Stamp Act, 1891 (exemption 11 " receipt " in Schedule to the Act). See further as to stamps, *post*, p. 1167.

Purchase of land.—It is provided by s. 30 of the Industrial and Provident Societies Act, 1965, that a registered society may (unless its registered rules direct otherwise), hold, purchase or take on lease in its own name, any land, and may sell, exchange, mortgage or lease any such land, and no purchaser, assignee, mortgagee or tenant shall be bound to inquire as to the authority for any such dealing, and the receipt of the society shall be a good discharge.

As regards registered land reference may be made to the notes relating to Friendly Societies, *ante*, p. 328, which are largely applicable here too.

INFANTS

Introductory.—The Family Law Reform Act, 1969, s. 1 (1), reduced the age of majority from twenty-one to eighteen as from 1st January, 1970. This applies for any rule of law and (subject to a contrary intention being indicated) for the construction of " full age," " infant," " infancy," " minor," " minority " and similar expressions in (a) any statutory provision whenever made, and (b) any deed, will or other instrument made on or after 1st January, 1970 (*ibid.*, subs. (2)). This reduction applies also for tax purposes (F.A. 1969, s. 16 ; see now the I.C.T.A. 1970, ss. 48 (4) and 437 ; see also the Representation of the People Act, 1969, s. 7, as to elections).

Section 12 of the Family Law Reform Act, 1969, expressly enables the use of the term " minor " as a description of a person who is not of full age, but does not render it incorrect to refer to such a person as an " infant." Presumably the intention was that a preference for the term " minor " should be inferred, but if so, the present writer does not share it.

Before 1926 an infant could purchase, acquire, hold and dispose of a legal or equitable estate in land, but a purchase or sale by him could be avoided at his election on his attaining twenty-one, or within a reasonable time thereafter ; and, if he died before that age, this right passed to his personal representatives (*Burnaby* v. *Equitable Reversionary Interest Society* (1885), 28 Ch. D. 416 ; *Whittingham* v. *Murdy* (1889), 60 L.T. 956). There was an exception in the case of a male infant of the age of twenty years, and of a female infant of the age of seventeen years, who had executed a marriage settlement with the sanction of the court under the Infant Settlements Act, 1855. In this case he or she could make a binding contract. The powers conferred by this Act are still operative, except that the court cannot sanction a legal estate being vested in an infant. See further, *post*, p. 346.

Since 1925 it has been made impossible for an infant to hold a legal estate in land either beneficially (L.P.A. 1925, s. 1 (6)), or as a mortgagee (L.P.A. 1925, s. 19 (6)), or as a personal representative (Judicature Act, 1925, s. 165), or trustee (L.P.A. 1925, s. 19 (4)), or otherwise to be an estate owner. For it is expressly provided by s. 1 (6) of the L.P.A. 1925 that " a legal estate is not . . . capable of being held by an infant." It will also be seen from the wording of ss. 19 and 20 of the S.L.A. 1925 that an infant cannot be a tenant for life within the meaning of that Act, or have the powers of a tenant for life. On the other hand a legal estate can be vested in trustees for his benefit, and his interests can be properly safeguarded. See at p. 343 *et seq.* Also it is worth noticing that the persons expressed to be parties to any conveyance are (rebuttably) presumed to be of full age at the date of the conveyance (L.P.A. 1925, s. 15).

There has been no major alteration in the law relating to the power of an infant to acquire, hold and dispose of an *equitable* interest in land. A special rule applies, however, on the death of an infant unmarried entitled under a settlement to a vested equitable interest in fee simple in land ; see *post*, p. 347.

Transitional provisions.—As an infant cannot since 1925 hold a legal estate the question arises as to the vesting of any such legal estate held by an infant on 31st December, 1925. The answer is to be found in the transitional provisions of the S.L.A. 1925 and the L.P.A. 1925. These transitional provisions are still of interest for purposes of investigation of title, but a legal estate was rarely vested in an infant before 1926 and as over forty years have expired since they took effect it is thought that they will be of interest on very few occasions indeed in the future. Consequently they are not dealt with in detail in this edition and reference may be made to the 14th Edition, vol. 1, p. 296 *et seq.* Very briefly the broad effect was :—

(i) Where the legal estate in land belonging to an infant, whether absolutely or for life, was on 1st January, 1926, vested in personal representatives it remained in the personal representatives for the purposes of administration, subject to any mortgage term then subsisting or created by the Act (L.P.A. 1925, Sched. 1, Pt. II, para. 6 (c) ; see also S.L.A. 1925, ss. 1 (1) (ii) (d), (2), 3, 26, 117 (1) (ix), Sched. 2, para. 2).

(ii) Where an infant, or two or more infants, was or were on 31st December, 1925, beneficially entitled or jointly entitled, to land in possession, or would, if of full age, have been a tenant or tenants for life, and the land was not vested in personal representatives, it vested in the trustees of the settlement (L.P.A. 1925, Sched. 1, Pt. III, para. 1 ; S.L.A. 1925, Sched. 2, para. 3 ; see also ibid., ss. 20 (1), 23 and 26).

(iii) Where an infant was on 31st December, 1925, beneficially entitled in possession to land for an estate in fee simple or for a term of years absolute, *jointly* with a person or persons of full age, the legal estate vested in that other person or those other persons on the statutory trusts (L.P.A. 1925, Sched. 1, Pt. III, para. 2). Compare L.P.A. 1925, Sched. 1, Pt. II, paras. 3 and 6 (b) ; S.L.A. 1925, s. 36 and *Re King's Theatre, Sunderland* [1929] 1 Ch. 483. If there had been a tenancy in common the land would have vested in the Public Trustee under the L.P.A. 1925, Sched. 1, Pt. IV, para. 4.

(iv) Where land, before 1926, was held in trust for infants as tenants in common contingently on their attaining twenty-one, and one only of the infants had attained twenty-one, the legal estate vested in the trustees of the settlement as statutory owners (S.L.A. 1925, s. 1 (1) (iii) and 23 ; *Re Bird* [1927] 1 Ch. 210). If more than one, but not all of them, had attained twenty-one, the legal estate vested in the trustees on the statutory trusts (L.P.A. 1925, Sched. 1, Pt. IV, para. 1 (1) ; *Re Pedley* [1927] 2 Ch. 168 ; *Re Myhill* [1928] Ch. 100).

(v) Where an infant on 31st December, 1925, was the tenant for life or had the powers of a tenant for life, together with another person of full age, the legal estate vested in the person of full age as tenant for life of the entirety (L.P.A. 1925, Sched. 1, Pt. II, para. 6 (c) ; S.L.A. 1925, s. 19 (3)).

(vi) Where the land was on 31st December, 1925, vested in an infant sole personal representative, trustee, trustee for sale or mortgagee, or where it would on 1st January, 1926, have become so vested if the infant had been of full age, the legal estate vested in the Public Trustee, pending appointment of trustees in his place by the parents or guardians of the infant (L.P.A. 1925, Sched. 1, Pt. III, para. 3).

(vii) Where the land was on 31st December, 1925, vested in two or more personal representatives, trustees, trustees for sale or mortgagees, one of whom was an infant, or where on 1st January, 1926, it would have become so vested if the infant had been of full age, the legal estate vested in the other person or persons of full age on similar trusts (mentioned above) as in the case of an infant being sole trustee (L.P.A. 1925, Sched. 1, Pt. III, para. 4).

Conveyance after 1925 of a legal estate to an infant or infants.—If a conveyance [this does not include a will (S.L.A. 1925, s. 117 (1) (v))] of a legal estate in land is by mistake or otherwise made to an infant alone, or to two or more infants jointly, for his or their own benefit, it will operate only as an *agreement for valuable consideration* to execute a settlement by means of a principal vesting deed and a trust instrument in favour of the infant or infants and in the meantime to hold the land in trust for the infant or infants (L.P.A. 1925, s. 19 (1) ; S.L.A. 1925, s. 27 (1)). The infant gets an equitable interest by the subsection. To protect the infant or infants the document should be registered as an estate contract under the L.C.A. 1972, s. 2 (4), Class C (iv) ; see *post*, p. 599.

The words " for valuable consideration " were inserted, it is assumed, to ensure that the agreement could be enforced in the case where the conveyance happened to be voluntary since otherwise there would be " no equity to perfect an imperfect gift." The meaning of the S.L.A. 1925, s. 27 (1), was the subject of an interesting discussion by the late Dr. Harold Potter in the *Conveyancer N.S.*, vol. 19, pp. 1, 48.

If a conveyance were made by error to an infant, and it became necessary during the minority to convey, mortgage, or lease the land, it would not be correct for the settlor, in whom the legal estate would then be vested, to convey, mortgage or lease the land in his own name and keep from the person with whom he was dealing all knowledge of the agreement for a settlement. The correct way would be for him to execute a trust deed appointing trustees and stating the nature of the trusts which the trustees were appointed to carry out. Two individual trustees or a trust corporation would have to be appointed. The settlor could be one of the trustees if he wished. Having done that he would have to execute a vesting deed to vest the legal estate in such trustees. It is not absolutely necessary that there should be two documents. The trust deed could both appoint trustees and declare the trusts and vest the legal estate in them. Only when it is desired to keep the trusts off the title would it be necessary to have two documents. The trustees would then be in a position to deal with the land as statutory owners under s. 23 of the S.L.A. 1925.

If the settlement was in favour of a single infant, then, on his attaining full age and becoming absolutely entitled to the settled land beneficially, free from all limitations, powers, and charges taking effect under the settlement, he would be entitled to require the trustees of the settlement, in whom the settled land was vested, to convey the land to him. But if there were two or more infants jointly entitled, then, when the first attained full age, the legal estate would still remain in the trustees and only when both or all the infants attained full age and became absolutely entitled free from the limitations, etc., under the settlement, would they be entitled to require the trustees to convey the legal estate to them as joint tenants (S.L.A. 1925, s. 7 (5)).

The above rules apply where the conveyance was made to an infant alone, or to two or more infants jointly. It has been suggested that an attempted conveyance to two or more infants as tenants in common is void as an undivided share in land cannot be created except as provided in the S.L.A. 1925 or the L.P.A. 1925 (L.P.A. 1925, s. 34 (1)). The means provided are the S.L.A. 1925, s. 36 (4), where a trust instrument is executed, and the L.P.A. 1925, s. 34 (2), which relates only to conveyances to persons of full age. The opinion of the late author of this book was, however, that if a conveyance was made to two or more infants as tenants in common the settlor would hold the land on trust for sale and to stand possessed of the proceeds of sale and of the rents and profits until the sale for the benefit of the infants as tenants in common. For s. 34 (4) of the L.P.A. 1925 provides that " any *disposition* [this includes a devise or bequest, L.P.A. 1925, s. 205 (1) (ii)] purporting to make a settlement of an undivided share in land shall only operate as a settlement of a corresponding share of the net proceeds of sale and of the rents and profits until sale of the entirety of the land." In other words, an undivided share cannot be settled as land but only as money. Further, there is now authority for the view that the legal estate will be held on the statutory trusts for sale wherever the circumstances would create undivided shares even though the case may not precisely comply with the provisions of the S.L.A. 1925 or the L.P.A. 1925 (*Bull* v. *Bull* [1955] 1 Q.B. 234). To enable the land to be dealt with, another trustee would have to be appointed to act with the settlor, or, if he did not wish to act, then two individual trustees or a trust corporation would have to be appointed, and the entirety of the land vested in them upon the statutory trusts.

Conveyance of a legal estate to an infant jointly with a person of full age.—If a conveyance ["conveyance" does not include "a will," L.P.A. 1925, s. 205 (1) (ii)] of a legal estate in land is made to an infant, jointly with one or more other persons of full age, it will operate to vest the legal estate in the other person or persons on the statutory trusts, but not so as to sever any joint tenancy in the net proceeds of sale or in the rents and profits until sale, *or affect the right of a tenant for life or statutory owner to have settled land vested in him* (L.P.A. 1925, ss. 19 (2), 35).

As " the other person or persons " take on the statutory trusts the land will not be settled land, and during the minority such trustees for sale will be the persons to make title.

Conveyance to an infant and a person of full age for life.—Such a conveyance is dealt with by s. 19 (3) of the S.L.A. 1925, which provides that if in any case there are two or more persons beneficially entitled under a settlement to possession of settled land *for life* as joint tenants and they are not all of full age, such one or more of them as is or are for the time being of full age is or (if more than one) together constitute the tenant for life for the purposes of the Act, but the subsection does not affect the beneficial interests of such of them as are not for the time being of full age.

When the infant attains full age, or, where there is more than one infant, as each infant attains full age, he will be entitled to require the person or persons in whom the settled land is vested to convey the land to him and the other person or persons who, together with him or them, constitute the tenant for life as joint tenants for life (S.L.A. 1925, s. 7 (3)).

Mortgage of land to an infant.—If a legal mortgage or transfer of a legal mortgage of land be made to an infant after 1925, it will operate only as an agreement for valuable consideration to execute a proper conveyance when the infant attains full age, and in the meantime to hold any beneficial interest in the mortgage debt in trust for the persons for whose benefit the conveyance was intended to be made. But if the mortgage is made to the infant and another person or other persons of full age, it will operate as if the infant had not been named therein, but without prejudice to any beneficial interest in the mortgage debt intended to be thereby provided for the infant (L.P.A. 1925, s. 19 (6)).

It is provided by s. 46 of the T.A. 1925, that where any person entitled to or possessed of any *interest in land*, or entitled to a contingent right in land, by way of security for money, is an infant, the court may make an order vesting or releasing or disposing of the interest in the land or the right in like manner as in the case of a trustee under disability.

Devise or bequest of land to an infant or infants.—Although on the death of a testator who has devised or bequeathed land to an infant or infants absolutely or for life, the land becomes settled land (S.L.A. 1925, s. 1 (1) (ii) (*d*)), the legal estate therein will, in the first instance, vest in his personal representatives for the purposes of administration, and in the case of a minority will remain in them during such minority. During this period they have the widest possible powers of selling, mortgaging and leasing. For this purpose " land " does not include an undivided share in land (S.L.A. 1925, s. 117 (1) (ix) ; *Re Bird* [1927] 1 Ch. 210).

It is provided by the L.P.A. 1925, s. 27 (2), as amended, that *a sole personal representative can give valid receipts for*, or direct the application of, proceeds of sale or other capital money. In practice, this provision is limited to executors, because in the case of an administration, where there is an infant beneficiary, the court will not grant administration to less than two administrators (Judicature Act, 1925, s. 160 (1)). And, although there is no provision against the granting of probate to a sole executor, the court will, on the application of a person interested, when there is a minority, appoint one or more personal representatives in addition to the original personal representative (*ibid.*, s. 160 (2)).

As regards *a purchaser* (including a mortgagee or lessee : S.L.A. 1925, s. 117 (1) (xxi), A.E.A. 1925, s. 55 (1) (xviii)), it is provided by s. 110 (3) of the S.L.A. 1925 that a purchaser of the legal estate in settled land from a personal representative shall be entitled to act on the assumption that, if the capital money payable in respect of the transaction is paid to the personal representative, such representative is acting under his statutory or other powers and requires the money for the purposes of administration. Other provisions for the protection of a purchaser are contained in S.L.A. 1925, ss. 18 (2) and 36 (8) ; A.E.A. 1925, ss. 24 and 39.

Moreover, whether personal representatives have or have not completed their duties as pure personal representatives, they can, under s. 26 of the S.L.A. 1925, sell, convey, mortgage and lease the land of an infant under the direction of the S.L.A. 1925 trustees of the settlement created by the will of the testator. Section 26 (1) provides as follows :—

" 26.—(1) Where an infant [or two or more infants entitled jointly : see subss. (4), (5)] is beneficially entitled in possession to land for an estate in fee simple or for a term of years absolute or would if of full age be a tenant for life of or have the powers of a tenant for life over *settled land*, then during the minority of the infant—

> (*a*) if *the settled land* is vested in a personal representative the personal representative, until a principal vesting instrument has been executed pursuant to the provisions of this Act ; and
>
> (*b*) in every other case, the *trustees of the settlement ;*

shall have, in reference to the settled land and capital money, all the powers conferred by this Act and the settlement on a tenant for life, and on the trustees of the settlement."

If the settled land is vested in a personal representative, then, if and when during the minority the infant, if of full age, would have been entitled to have the legal estate vested in him, a principal vesting instrument must, if the trustees of the settlement so require, be executed for vesting the legal estate in themselves (S.L.A. 1925, s. 26 (2)). In the meantime the personal representatives must, during the minority, give effect to the directions of the trustees of the settlement, and are not concerned with the propriety of any conveyance directed to be made by those trustees if it appears to be a proper conveyance under the powers conferred by the S.L.A. 1925 or by the settlement, and the capital money, if any, arising under the conveyance is paid to or by the direction of the trustees or into court (*ibid.*). A purchaser dealing with the personal representative and paying the capital money, if any, to him is not concerned to see that the money is paid to trustees of the settlement or into court, or to inquire whether the personal representative is liable to give effect to any such directions, or whether any such directions have been given (*ibid.*).

In practice the trustees never ask for the legal estate to be vested in them, and everything which is required to be done in connection with the land is done by the personal representatives under the direction of the trustees. As a matter of fact, the point does not very often arise because in the majority of cases the personal representatives and the S.L.A. 1925 trustees are the same persons. When the executors so act under the direction of the trustees, provided the legal estate remains in them, they will be deemed to be acting as " statutory owners " and as such have all the powers conferred by the S.L.A. 1925 and the settlement on a tenant for life and on the trustees of the settlement. The expression " statutory owners " is defined in s. 117 (1) (xxvi) of the S.L.A. 1925 as the trustees of the settlement or other persons who, during a minority, have the powers of a tenant for life under that Act.

If an infant died while engaged on war service or outside the United Kingdom at a time when it was not practicable to return for a reason connected with the war, then any act done in purported exercise of the powers contained in the S.L.A. 1925, s. 26, *after the infant's death* in favour of a person without actual notice of the death was *as valid as if the infant had still been alive* (Execution of Trusts (Emergency Provisions) Act, 1939, s. 5).

Section 26 (2) has effect during successive minorities until a person of full age becomes entitled to require the settled land to be vested in him (S.L.A. 1925, s. 26 (3)). The section does not apply where an infant is beneficially entitled in possession to land for an estate in fee simple or for a term of years absolute jointly with a person of full age (for which case provision is made in the L.P.A. 1925), *but it applies to two or more infants entitled as aforesaid jointly, until one of them attains full age* (S.L.A. 1925, s. 26 (4)). Further, the section does not apply where an infant would, if of full age, constitute the tenant for life or have the powers of a tenant for life *together with another person of full age*, but it applies to two or more infants who would, if all of them were of full age, together constitute the tenant for life or have the powers of a tenant for life, until one of them attains full age (S.L.A. 1925, s. 26 (5)).

" *settled land.*"—A will under which land is limited in trust for an infant, in possession, for an estate in fee simple or for a term of years absolute, is a settlement (S.L.A. 1925, s. 1 (1) (ii) (*d*)). Section 26 does not apply, for instance, to the case where the testator has devised the land to trustees on trust for sale and to stand possessed of the proceeds, and until sale of the rents, for the benefit of an infant (S.L.A. 1925, s. 1 (7)).

" *trustees of the settlement.*"—These words are defined by s. 117 (1) (xxiv) of the S.L.A. 1925 to mean the trustees of the settlement for the purposes of the S.L.A. 1925 however appointed or constituted. See the discussion *post*, p. 713, as to the persons who are such trustees.

Powers of special personal representatives over land of an infant.—Special personal representatives are only appointed where the land vested in a deceased person as tenant for life was settled previously to his death and not by his will. The case occurs when land has been settled on a tenant for life and on his death given to an infant. Until the infant attains full age the land will remain settled land within ss. 22 and 23 of the A.E.A. 1925 and s. 162 of the Judicature Act, 1925, and, on the death of the tenant for life, special personal representatives will have to be appointed. It is provided by s. 22 (1) of the A.E.A. 1925 that a testator may appoint, and in default of such express appointment shall be deemed to have appointed, as his special executors in regard to settled land, that is, land vested in him which was settled previously to his death and not by his will, the persons, if any, who are at his death the trustees of the settlement thereof, and probate may be granted to such trustees specially limited to the settled land. But it might be that the tenant for life did not make a will. In that case it is provided by s. 162 (1) of the Judicature Act, 1925, that in regard to land settled previously to the death of the deceased and not by his will, administration with the will annexed may be granted to the trustees of the settlement, and where the deceased died wholly intestate administration will be granted to such trustees, if any, and if willing to act. It must be borne in mind that these sections apply only where the land remained settled land on the death of the tenant for life. For instance, if on the death of the tenant for life the land was devised to trustees for sale and to stand possessed of the proceeds, and until sale, of the rents, for the benefit of the infant, then the settlement would have come to an end and the land would have ceased to be settled land (*Re Bridgett and Hayes' Contract* [1928] Ch. 163).

In the above case, provided that on the death of the tenant for life the land remained settled land, the special personal representatives would be the persons to make title on a sale, mortgage, or lease. It is specially provided by s. 24 (1) of the A.E.A. 1925 that such special personal representatives may dispose of the settled land without the concurrence of the general personal representatives.

Land devised or bequeathed to trustees for sale for the benefit of an infant.—A testator may devise land to trustees upon trust for sale and to stand possessed of the proceeds of sale, and in the meantime until sale, of the rents, in trust for the benefit of an infant, which is now the usual way of settling land for the benefit of an infant. It is much better to adopt this course than to make the land settled land and thereby bring in all the complications of vesting assents and special representation.

Immediately on the death of the testator the legal estate passes to the executors, and, where the settlement provides that the infant shall become absolutely entitled on his attaining full age, the trustees, unless the infant was very young when the testator died, will usually be advised to allow the legal estate to remain in the executors until the infant attains that age. For, under s. 39 of the A.E.A. 1925, executors have, for the purposes of administration, or during the minority of any beneficiary, all the powers, discretions and duties conferred or imposed by law on trustees holding land upon an effectual trust for sale (including power to overreach equitable interests and powers as if the same affected the proceeds of sale) ; and all the powers conferred by statute on trustees for sale. So that, even when their duties as executors have come to an end, so long as the minority continues, and they have not assented to the legal estate vesting in the trustees, they can exercise the above powers. But if the settlement is to remain in force after the infant attains full age, then, when the executors have finished their duties, it will be best for them to execute an assent vesting the legal estate in the trustees.

When the trustees get the legal estate, their powers will be derived from s. 28 of the L.P.A. 1925. This section provides that trustees for sale shall, in relation to land, have all the powers of a tenant for life and the trustees of a settlement under the S.L.A. 1925, including the powers of management conferred by that Act [s. 102] during a minority. The section also provides that the powers conferred thereby shall be exercised with such consents (if any) as would have been required on a sale under the trust for sale, and when exercised shall operate to overreach any equitable interests or powers which are by virtue of the Act or otherwise made to attach to the net proceeds of sale as if created by a trust affecting those proceeds. In any event a purchaser of a legal estate from trustees for sale is not concerned with the trusts affecting the proceeds of sale *whether or not those trusts are declared by the same instrument by which the trust for sale is created* (L.P.A. 1925, s. 27 (1)). So that, even if a purchaser becomes aware of the beneficial trusts by reason of his inspecting the will for the purpose of satisfying himself that there is no limitation in the document of the power of the trustees to sell, he will not be affected by such knowledge.

Devise and bequest to trustees for the benefit of a class of infants, as tenants in common.—This case would come within s. 34 (3) of the L.P.A. 1925, which provides that a devise, bequest or testamentary appointment, coming into operation after 1925, of land to two or more persons in undivided shares shall operate as a devise, bequest or appointment of the land to the trustees (if any) of the will for the purposes of the S.L.A. 1925, or, if there are no such trustees, then to the personal representatives of the testator, and in each case (but without prejudice to the rights and powers of the personal representatives for purposes of administration) upon the statutory trusts set out in s. 35 of the same Act.

Land held on the death of a tenant for life for infants as tenants in common in possession.—This case comes within s. 36 (1) of the S.L.A. 1925 which provides that if, after 1925, *settled land* [that is, land which was settled land immediately before the trust for sale arose] is held in trust for *persons entitled in possession* under a trust instrument in undivided shares, the trustees of the settlement (if the settled land is not already vested in them) may require the estate owner in whom the settled land is vested (but in the case of a personal representative subject to his rights and powers for purposes of administration), at the cost of the trust estate, to convey the land to them, or assent to the land vesting in them as joint tenants. When the settled land is or becomes vested in such trustees, the land is held by them (subject to any incumbrances affecting the settled land which are secured by a legal mortgage, but freed from any incumbrances affecting the undivided shares or not secured as aforesaid, *and from any interests, powers and charges subsisting under the trust instrument which have priority to the trust for the persons entitled to the undivided shares*) upon the statutory trusts for sale (S.L.A. 1925, s. 36 (2)).

For instance, to take a simple case, land may be settled on *A*, a widow, for life, and, on her death, for the benefit of her two infant children, in undivided shares. While the tenant for life lives, the land will be settled land, but on the death of the tenant for life the land will cease to be settled land because the gift to the infants as tenants in common causes a trust for sale to arise. In other words, on the death of the tenant for life, the land is held in trust for infants entitled in possession, under a trust instrument [the will], and the trustees thereof for the purposes of the S.L.A. 1925, if such settled land was not already vested in them, may require the estate owner in whom the settled land was vested, that is the personal representatives of the deceased tenant for life (subject to their rights and powers for purposes of administration) to vest the land in them as joint tenants on the statutory trusts. The statutory trusts are given in subs. (6) of the same section referred to *ante*, p. 310.

It will be noted that for the case to come within s. 36 of the S.L.A. 1925, the interest of the infants in the land on the death of the tenant for life must be an interest in possession, that is, not in remainder (S.L.A. 1925, s. 117 (1) (xix)). Such interest must also not be contingent, because, until two persons, at least, become entitled in possession, the interest could not be said to be held in undivided shares, and therefore in such case the trustees would not take on trust for sale, but as statutory owners. Nevertheless, in such capacity of statutory owners they could exercise all the powers of a tenant for life. See S.L.A. 1925, s. 26, at p. 733, and *Re Bird* [1927] 1 Ch. 210.

Appointment of trustees of infant's interest.—It is provided by s. 42 (1) of the A.E.A. 1925 that where an infant is *absolutely entitled* under a will or on an intestacy to a devise or legacy, or to the residue of the estate of the deceased, or any share therein, *and such interest is not under the will (if any) of the deceased devised or bequeathed to trustees* for the infant, the personal representatives may appoint a trust corporation, or two or more individuals not exceeding four (whether or not including themselves or one of them) to be the trustees of such devise, legacy, residue or share for the infant, and to be trustees of any land devised or any land being of forming part of such residue or share, for the purposes of the S.L.A. 1925, and of the statutory provisions relating to the management of land during a minority, and may execute or do any assurance [the document will be a vesting assent] or thing requisite for vesting the same in the trustee or trustees so appointed ; also that on such appointment the personal representatives, as such, shall be discharged from all further liability, and such interest may be retained in its existing condition or state of investment, or may be converted into money, and such money may be invested in any authorised investment.

It will be noted that this subsection only applies where (i) the infant is absolutely entitled, and (ii) such interest is not under the will (if any) of the deceased devised or bequeathed to trustees for the infant.

It may also be noted that unless and until an appointment is made within s. 42 (1), a personal representative will retain the capacity and liability of such, not becoming a trustee despite the completion otherwise of his administration (*Harvell* v. *Foster* [1954] 2 Q.B. 367 ; see further *post*, p. 393).

If the infant became entitled under an intestacy he would not normally be absolutely entitled, because by reason of s. 47 of the A.E.A. 1925 his interest would only be contingent on his attaining full age or marrying under that age. The subsection therefore would only apply where the infant has married before attaining full age (*Re Wilks* [1935] Ch. 645, 650). The subsection also would not apply where the surviving spouse on an intestacy took a life interest (*Re Yerburgh* [1928] W.N. 208).

If the infant is not absolutely entitled the personal representatives are not able to take advantage of the A.E.A. 1925, s. 42 (1), but they may find it advisable to make an appropriation under the A.E.A. 1925, s. 41, *post*, p. 401.

Settlement of land inter vivos on an infant.—If it is desired to give an infant an interest in land *inter vivos*, one way is to make a settlement by means of a *vesting deed and trust instrument*, and the other way is to convey the land to two or more trustees *on trust for sale*, and to declare the trusts by the same or a separate deed. As regards the first case a settlement *inter vivos* must be created by the procedure explained *post*, p. 680. In particular, the S.L.A. 1925, s. 4 (1), required that a settlement of a *legal estate* in land *inter vivos* shall be effected by two deeds, namely, a vesting deed and a trust instrument, and if effected in any other way shall not operate to transfer or create a legal estate.

Consequently, if a settlor, intending to effect a settlement of the legal estate in land in favour of an infant, conveyed the same to two trustees in fee simple on trust for an infant [not on trust for sale] as was done before 1926, the conveyance would not pass the legal estate to the trustees, and it would remain in the settlor. The conveyance would be deemed to be a trust instrument (S.L.A. 1925, s. 9 (1) (iii)). Therefore, to put matters right it would be necessary for the trustees to execute a vesting deed in favour of themselves as statutory owners, when, under s. 9 (2) of the same Act, such vesting deed would operate to vest the legal estate in themselves as joint tenants and enable them to deal with the land. A vesting instrument made under this subsection operates, without a conveyance, to get in any outstanding legal estate. It will be remembered that it is provided by s. 13 of the S.L.A. 1925 that, until a vesting deed has been executed, no disposition of the settled land *inter vivos* will take effect, except in favour of a purchaser of a legal estate without notice that such statutory owners have become entitled to require a vesting instrument to be made in their favour.

As we know, an infant cannot hold a legal estate in land, or be a tenant for life under the S.L.A. 1925, and if the land be by mistake conveyed to him for an estate in fee or for a term absolute, or as tenant for life, the result would be that the land would become settled land, and the document creating the interest would be the settlement (S.L.A. 1925, s. 1 (1) (i) (*d*)) ; and the trustees thereof the trustees for the purposes of the S.L.A. (S.L.A. 1925, s. 30). The land remains settled land during the minority (s. 3). Under the general scheme of the S.L.A. 1925, *ibid.*, when there is no tenant for life of the settlement, the trustees of the settlement for the purposes of the S.L.A. become statutory owners (S.L.A. 1925, s. 117 (1) (xxvi)), and as such, entitled to require the persons in whom the legal estate is vested to vest it in them, to enable them to deal with the land (S.L.A. 1925, ss. 4 and 7).

Where an infant is beneficially entitled in possession to land for an estate in fee simple or for a term of years absolute or would, if of full age, be a tenant for life or have the powers of a tenant for life over settled land, then, during the minority of the infant, the trustees have the powers conferred by the Act and the settlement on a tenant for life, and on the trustees of the settlement (S.L.A. 1925, s. 26 (1)). This includes the powers of management given by s. 102 of the S.L.A. 1925 ; and also any additional or larger powers conferred by the settlement (see S.L.A. 1925, ss. 108 and 109).

If the other mode be adopted, that is, if the legal estate in the land be conveyed to trustees on trust for sale, with power of postponement, and to hold the net proceeds of sale, and, until sale, the rents and profits thereof for the benefit of the infant, the land will not be settled land and no vesting deed will have to be executed (S.L.A. 1925, s. 1 (7), introduced by the Law of Property (Amendment) Act, 1926).

Section 27 (1) of the L.P.A. 1925 provides that a purchaser of a legal estate from trustees for sale shall not be concerned with the trusts affecting the proceeds of sale, " *whether or not those trusts are declared by the same instrument by which the trust for sale is created.*" The quoted words show that a settlement by way of trust for sale will not be void if made by one document. In a marriage settlement or other complicated settlement it will usually be more convenient to have two deeds, one declaring the trusts and the other conveying the legal estate to the trustees, but in a simple settlement, such as the one we are now considering [a settlement on an infant] only one deed will be necessary.

In this case the trustees get their powers under s. 28 (1) of the L.P.A. 1925, as amended. This subsection gives trustees for sale, in relation to land and to the proceeds of sale, all the powers of a tenant for life and the trustees of a settlement under the S.L.A. 1925, including, in relation to the land, the powers of management conferred by that Act during a minority [that is, the powers of management given by s. 102 of the S.L.A. 1925, referred to below]. The powers conferred by this subsection must be exercised with such consents (if any) as would have been required under a sale under the trust for sale.

Section 28 (4) of the L.P.A. 1925 provides that if a share in the net proceeds is absolutely vested in an infant, the trustees for sale may act on his behalf and retain land (to be held on trust for sale) or other property to represent his share.

It is thought much better when preparing a settlement for the benefit of an infant to effect the object of the settlor by creating a trust for sale, so as to prevent the land becoming settled land, with all the complications which settled land entails, especially as it will have been seen that the trustees have as full powers as statutory owners have when the land has been made settled land.

Management of land during minority.—If and so long as any person entitled to a beneficial interest *in possession* affecting land is an infant, the trustees appointed for the purpose by the settlement, or if there are none appointed, the trustees of the settlement have powers of management given by s. 102 of the S.L.A. 1925 (*ibid.*, s. 102 (1)). This section must be read with s. 26 of the S.L.A. 1925, mentioned at p. 339. The section applies where any person is *contingently* entitled to land if he became entitled *under an instrument coming into operation after* 1925, but subject to any prior interests or charges and only until that person's interest vests, or, if it vests during his minority, until he attains full age (*ibid.*, s. 102 (5) and (6)).

The same powers are conferred on trustees for sale (L.P.A. 1925, s. 28 (1)), and on personal representatives (A.E.A. 1925, s. 39).

This section will save many an application to court for directions. It gives power to fell timber, or cut underwood in the usual course for sale or for repairs ; to erect, pull down, rebuild and repair houses, and other buildings and erections ; to continue the working of mines, minerals and quarries which have usually been worked ; to drain or otherwise improve the land or any part thereof ; to insure against loss by fire ; to make allowances to and arrangements with tenants and others ; to determine tenancies, and to accept surrenders of leases and tenancies ; and generally to deal with the land in a proper and due course of management ; but so that, where the infant is impeachable for waste, the trustees shall not commit waste, and shall cut timber on the same terms only, and subject to the same restrictions, on and subject to which the infant could, if of full age, cut the same.

Receipts by married infant.—A married infant has power to give valid receipts for all *income* (including statutory accumulations of income made during the minority) to which the infant may be entitled, in like manner as if the infant were of full age (L.P.A. 1925, s. 21). The expression " statutory accumulations " refers to s. 31 of the T.A. 1925, and particularly to subs. (2) thereof, which provides, in effect, that the trustees during an infancy are to accumulate the residue of the income not expended, in the way of compound interest, by investing the same and the resulting income in authorised investments, and to hold those accumulations as therein particularly mentioned.

It is also provided by the A.E.A. 1925, s. 47 (1) (ii), that when an infant marries, such infant is to be entitled to give valid receipts for the *income* of the infant's share or interest under an intestacy.

Where a testator directs that a legacy or share of residue can be paid to a person under full age, for instance, on marriage under that age, the personal representatives or trustees obtain a good discharge from the beneficiary notwithstanding his infancy (*Re Deneker* [1895] W.N. 28). Nevertheless, the representatives or trustees may, in their discretion, withhold payment until the beneficiary has attained full age (*Re Somech* [1957] Ch. 165).

Marriage settlements.—The Infant Settlements Act, 1855, outlined below, together with s. 27 (3) of the S.L.A. 1925, has been repealed *except* in relation to anything done before 1st January, 1970 (Family Law Reform Act, 1969, s. 11 (*a*)).

By the Infant Settlements Act, 1855, an infant could, upon or in contemplation of his or her marriage, if a male when over twenty years of age, and if a female when over seventeen years of age, with the sanction of the Chancery Division of the High Court (Judicature Act, 1925, s. 56 (1)), execute a valid and binding settlement or contract for settlement *of all or any part of any property to which he or she was entitled* or over which he or she had any power of appointment, and execute such power of appointment, unless it was expressly declared that the power shall not be exercised by an infant.

It was provided by s. 27 (3) of the S.L.A. 1925 that " Nothing in this Act affects the powers conferred by the Infant Settlements Act, 1855, provided that a legal estate in land is not vested in an infant." As an infant cannot hold a legal estate in land or be a tenant for life under the S.L.A. 1925, the Act affected only the equitable interest of an infant. See, as to power of an infant to deal with his equitable interests, at p. 348 *et seq.*

The Act applied to a post-nuptial settlement (*Re Sampson and Wall* (1884), 25 Ch. D. 482 ; *Buckmaster* v. *Buckmaster* (1887), 35 Ch. D. 21 ; *Hemingway* v. *Braithwaite* (1889), 61 L.T. 224), whether or not the infant was a ward of the court (*Re Adams* [1943] Ch. 155).

A marriage settlement made by an infant, *without the leave of the court,* was not void, but only voidable ; and if it was for the benefit of the infant, like any other conveyance by an infant, it became binding if not repudiated within a reasonable time of the infant attaining majority or on his death by his personal representatives (*Edwards* v. *Carter* [1893] A.C. 360 ; *Viditz*

v. *O'Hagan* [1899] 2 Ch. 569 ; [1900] 2 Ch. 87 ; *Davenport* v. *Marshall* [1902]
1 Ch. 82 ; *Carnell* v. *Harrison* [1916] 1 Ch. 328). See further at p. 348.

**Death of an infant unmarried when entitled to a freehold interest
under a settlement.**—It is provided by s. 51 (3) of the A.E.A. 1925 that where
an infant dies after 1925 without having been married, and independently
of that section he would, at his death, have been equitably entitled under
a settlement (including a will) to a vested estate in fee simple or absolute
interest in freehold land or in any property settled to devolve therewith or
as freehold land, such infant will be deemed to have had an entailed interest,
and the settlement will be construed accordingly. As the infant is assumed
in the subsection to have died unmarried he cannot have had legitimate
children, and, as he generally could not make a will, his interest in the property
would cease at his death, and revert, in default of a gift over, to the settlor ;
or if the settlement was effected by a will, would fall into the residue. It
would appear that realty held by trustees *for sale* for an infant is excluded
from the subsection by virtue of the doctrine of conversion. Also it would
appear that leasehold land (and other personalty) is not within the subsection
unless held by trustees upon trust to devolve with or as freehold land.
Further, the better view is that the provision of L.P.A. 1925, s. 176, that an
infant cannot dispose of his entailed interests by will, prevails over the
exceptional privilege enabling infants to devise realty otherwise conferred
by ss. 1 and 3 of the Wills (Soldiers and Sailors) Act, 1918.

The question has been raised, whether an attempted conveyance of a legal
estate in fee simple to an infant, which operates as an *agreement to make a
settlement* under the S.L.A. 1925, s. 27 (1) (*ante*, p. 336), is a " settlement "
within the meaning of the A.E.A. 1925, s. 51 (3). The late Mr. J. M.
Lightwood, in the *Law Journal*, vol. 69, p. 22, expressed the view that it was
not and that s. 51 (3) would not apply to a legal estate so purported to be
granted to the infant. In spite of this opinion, it is thought that the beneficial
interest of an infant under s. 27 (1) is such that there is a settlement within
the S.L.A. 1925, s. 1 (1) (ii) (*d*). See further, *Law Journal*, vol. 69, pp. 37, 49.

In *Re Taylor ; Pullan* v. *Taylor* [1931] 2 Ch. 242, the question arose
whether the word " settlement " in s. 51 (3) included a notional settlement
arising under an intestacy occurring before 1926 by reason of the provision
contained in s. 1 (2) of the S.L.A. 1925. Farwell, J., held that it did include
such a notional settlement. The intestate died in September, 1925, seised of
freehold property, leaving a widow and three infant children, including
Sydney, the eldest son, and another son, Harry. The widow took out
administration in November, 1925. The position on 1st January, 1926,
when the S.L.A. 1925 came into operation, was that Sydney was entitled as
heir subject to his mother's right to dower under the notional settlement
deemed to have been made by the intestate. Sydney died in 1930, still an
infant and unmarried, and the reversion devolved on the next eldest son,
Harry, as under the old law, and Harry being still under age had only an
entailed interest until twenty-one or marriage, when his estate would become
absolute.

A similar result would not happen where the intestacy occurred after
1925, because normally the freeholds of an intestate now pass to the
administrator on trust for sale, and to divide the proceeds amongst the
persons entitled under the A.E.A. 1925.

But s. 51 (3) of the A.E.A. 1925, above, must be read with s. 53 (*a*) of the
T.A. 1925, which provides that where an infant is beneficially entitled to any

property the court may, with a view to the application of the capital or income thereof for the maintenance, education or benefit of the infant, make an order appointing a person to convey such property. The late author of this work expressed the opinion that the terms are wide enough to enable the court for the benefit of the infant to make an order to convey for the express purpose of barring the entailed interest which the infant takes by implication under s. 51 (3) of the A.E.A. 1925, above. Such opinion would seem to have been strengthened by the decision of Clauson, J., in *Re Gower's Settlement* [1934] 1 Ch. 365, where it was held that the T.A. 1925, s. 53, enabled the court to sanction the execution on behalf of an infant tenant in tail in remainder of a disentailing assurance.

Infant's interest under intestacy.—On the death of a person intestate after 1925, his child or children, or the issue of a child or children dying in his lifetime, only obtain an interest in his residuary estate on condition of attaining full age or marrying under that age. Until then their interest is contingent. This is the effect of s. 47 (1) of the A.E.A. 1925, which provides that the personal representatives shall hold such interest " In trust, in equal shares if more than one, for all or any the children or child of the intestate, living at the death of the intestate, who attain the age of [eighteen] years or marry under that age, and for all or any of the issue living at the death of the intestate who attain the age of [eighteen] years or marry under that age of any child of the intestate who predeceases the intestate, such issue to take . . . in equal shares if more than one, the share which their parent would have taken if living at the death of the intestate . . . " (as amended by the Family Law Reform Act, 1969, s. 3 (2)).

Power of an infant to deal with equitable interests in land.—There has been no alteration in the law as to the power of an infant to acquire, hold and deal with an equitable interest in land, although his interest in land is not always quite the same as before 1926, for, as we have seen, he loses his freehold equitable interest under a settlement if he dies an infant without having been married, and (above) he only obtains an interest in the proceeds of sale of land which forms part of the residue of the estate of an intestate, if he attains full age or marries under that age.

Before 1926 a sale and conveyance by an infant of his equitable interest in land was not void but voidable, and he could either avoid or ratify it on attaining his majority (*Burnaby* v. *Equitable, etc., Society* (1885), 28 Ch. D. 416; *Edwards* v. *Carter* [1893] A.C. 360; *Hamilton* v. *Hamilton* [1892] 1 Ch. 396; *Viditz* v. *O'Hagan* [1899] 2 Ch. 569; [1900] 2 Ch. 87). The avoidance or ratification could be made verbally or even by conduct (*Re Birchall* (1889), 40 Ch. D. 436).

Such conveyance became automatically binding if not repudiated within a reasonable time after attaining his majority (*Edwards* v. *Carter, ante*), and so s. 2 of the Infants' Relief Act, 1874, providing that no action shall be brought upon any ratification made after full age of any contract made during infancy, did not apply (Williams on Vendor and Purchaser, 4th ed., vol. II, pp. 859, 860). If the infant died while an instrument was voidable, his representatives could elect to repudiate it (*ibid.*). In the case of a reversionary interest, the repudiation by the infant had to be made within a reasonable time of his attaining his majority and not from the time of the falling into possession of the interest (*Carnell* v. *Harrison* [1916] 1 Ch. 328).

If the infant or the person representing him avoided the sale of the equitable interest the conveyance became void, and the equitable interest re-vested in him or them without any conveyance, and, in the absence of fraud, he or they could not be obliged to repay the purchase-money (Williams on Vendor and Purchaser, 4th ed., vol. II, pp. 849–851). And this would seem to be the case although the purchaser might in the meantime have sold the property. Therefore, if a person purchased land of an infant, believing him to be of full age, and then sold it to another, the infant, unless he had been guilty of fraud, could avoid his conveyance, and recover such equitable interest either from the second purchaser or from the original buyer (Williams on Vendor and Purchaser, 4th ed., vol. II, pp. 849, 850).

An infant or his representatives (on his death) could in the same way ratify or avoid *his* purchase of an equitable interest in land. If the infant or his representatives avoided his purchase, the equitable interest re-vested in the vendor or his successors in interest without any conveyance (Williams on Vendor and Purchaser, 4th ed., vol. II, p. 847). At one time it was thought that the test as to whether the infant could recover the price was whether he or his representatives could put the vendor in the same position as he was in when he sold (*Valentini* v. *Canali* (1889), 24 Q.B.D. 166), but it would seem from the reasoning in *Steinberg* v. *Scala* (*Leeds*), *Ltd.* [1923] 2 Ch. 452, that, to entitle the infant to recover, he would have to prove that there was an absolute failure of the consideration for which the money was paid. Thus, where an infant took a lease at a premium and entered into possession of the premises during his infancy, although only for a short time, it was held that he could not recover the premium on avoiding the lease on obtaining his majority (*Holmes* v. *Blogg* (1818), 8 Taunt. 508).

Section 1 of the Infants' Relief Act, 1874, made void contracts by way of mortgage by infants to secure the repayment of money lent. Therefore a mortgage by an infant of his equitable interest in land was void and the money lent could not be recovered, although it might have been spent in improving the property ; nevertheless the infant may be ordered to make repayment as a condition of recovering possession of the property (*Thurstan* v. *Nottingham Building Society* [1902] 1 Ch. 1 ; [1903] A.C. 6).

If an infant is entitled to an equitable interest in fee simple in possession, the legal estate will be subject of a settlement (S.L.A. 1925, s. 1 (1) (ii) (*d*)). The infant can sell his equitable interest subject to his right to repudiate the sale on attaining full age. It would appear that the purchaser would then acquire an equitable fee simple subject to defeasance if the infant later avoids the conveyance. This interest of the purchaser would seem to be a determinable fee within the S.L.A. 1925, s. 1 (1) (ii) (*c*), with the result that the land would remain settled. See a discussion of this in the *Solicitors' Journal*, vol. 82, p. 207.

Lease to an infant.—Roche, J., in *Davies* v. *Beynon-Harris* (1931), 47 T.L.R. 424, decided that a lease granted to an infant was a contract for an interest in permanent property, and was, therefore, binding on him unless he repudiated it within a reasonable time after attaining his majority. The effect of the L.P.A. 1925 was that the purported conveyance of a legal estate to an infant merely acted as a covenant by the grantor to execute a settlement when called upon. This created a beneficial interest, and if the infant had taken advantage of it after attaining full age the principles of equity would not allow him to avoid the necessary obligations on his part (e.g., payment of the rent reserved).

Contract by an infant.—An infant may avoid a contract for sale or purchase of land (*Flight* v. *Bolland* (1828), 4 Russ. 298 ; *Edwards* v. *Carter* [1893] A.C. 360), notwithstanding the Infants' Relief Act, 1874, for that Act does not apply to a contract for the sale of an interest in land (*Duncan* v. *Dixon* (1890), 44 Ch. D. 211). Such contracts, by which an interest in property of a permanent nature is acquired by the infant, remain binding unless he repudiates either during infancy or within a reasonable time of attaining full age. Until such repudiation, however, the infant remains bound to discharge any obligations arising under the contract (*North Western Railway* v. *M'Michael* (1850), 5 Ex. 114). Ratification is unnecessary and so the Infants' Relief Act, 1874, s. 2, has no application.

A contract by an infant for the sale of a *legal* estate in land would be construed as a contract to sell any equitable interest in the land which the infant might have, subject to his right of repudiation above referred to.

A person can, even while an infant, sue the other party of full age for damages for breach of contract. The reason is that *at law* the other party is bound, and the *remedy at law* is damages. On the other hand, where the remedy is in equity, the rule is different. In equity to enable a party to enforce a contract there must be mutuality. The other party of full age could not enforce the equitable remedy of specific performance, and in consequence of this want of mutuality the infant could not specifically enforce the contract (*Flight* v. *Bolland* (1828), 4 Russ. 298 ; *Lumley* v. *Ravenscroft* [1895] 1 Q.B. 683).

An infant can rescind a contract during his minority if it is to his advantage to do so, and may recall such repudiation within a reasonable time after he comes of age, on the ground that such repudiation would not be binding any more than the document repudiated (*North Western Railway* v. *M'Michael* (1850), 5 Ex. 114, 127). In *Waterman* v. *Fryer* [1922] 1 K.B. 632, it was assumed that an infant cannot assent to a revocation of a contract unless such revocation is for his benefit. The effect of rescission is to put an end to the infant's future liability and it is only reasonable that he ought to be able to get rid of the liability *at once*, instead of the liability going on until he becomes of full age, by showing that it was a contract prejudicial to him (see *North Western Railway* v. *M'Michael, ante*). As regards any contract for the *benefit* of the infant there would be no desire to rescind it, and as regards a contract not for his benefit there would be little likelihood of the infant repudiating his repudiation after attaining his majority. But should it be alleged that he had done so, the court would require the very strongest evidence of the fact (*Rawlins* v. *Birkett* (1856), 25 L.J. Ch. 837). In *Steinberg* v. *Scala* (*Leeds*), *Ltd.* [1923] 2 Ch. 452, an infant paid £250 in respect of some shares in a company, but when the company made a further call on her she rescinded the contract, and it was not disputed that, as under the circumstances of that particular case it was for the benefit of the infant that the contract should be rescinded, she was entitled to do so. In the same action the infant applied for the return of the £250, but it was held that to entitle her to recover it would have to be proved that there was an absolute failure of consideration for which the money was paid. This is not the same as the case of an action to recover a deposit paid by an infant to secure the performance of a contract, for in this case immediately the contract became rescinded there remained no consideration for the payment of such deposit and the infant could recover it (*Corpe* v. *Overton* (1833), 10 Bing. 252).

Infant agent.—An infant can act as an agent and can bind his principal in the same manner as if he were of full age (*Re Seager ; Seeley* v. *Briggs* (1889), 60 L.T. 665). See *ante*, p. 246, as to appointment of an infant as an attorney and as to appointment of an attorney by an infant. Note here, however, that Denning, L.J., has stated broadly that the appointment by an infant of an agent (whether or not by power of attorney) has always been held void (in *Shephard* v. *Cartwright* [1953] Ch. 728, at p. 755 ; reversed on another point at [1955] A.C. 431 ; see criticisms of the statement in the *Law Quarterly Review*, vol. 69, p. 446 and the *Modern Law Review*, vol. 18, p. 461).

Fraud of infant.—If an infant, by fraudulently representing himself to be of full age, causes another to complete a sale of property, the transaction is avoidable in equity (though not at law), and a court of equity will rescind the transaction and order the restitution of such property fraudulently obtained (*Re Jones* (1881), 18 Ch. D. 109 ; see further *Modern Law Review*, vol. 22, p. 273) ; and, in the case of a mortgage, will order the infant to repay what is owing as a condition of his obtaining the assistance of the court in declaring the invalidity of the mortgage and recovering possession of the property (*Thurstan* v. *Nottingham Building Society* [1902] 1 Ch. 1 ; [1903] A.C. 6). So where an infant has sold land on the faith of his statement that he was of full age, he would not be helped by the court to recover possession except on the terms of refunding the purchase-money (*Hannah* v. *Hodgson* (1861), 30 L.J. Ch. 738). But there must be an actual representation made either by the infant's positive assurance that he was of age or by the infant's active concealment of the facts, and mere silence as to his age will not be sufficient.

But where no question of restitution arises, a fraudulent infant cannot be compelled to refund money advanced. In *Leslie, Ltd.* v. *Shiell* [1914] 3 K.B. 607, an infant obtained a loan by a fraudulent misrepresentation that he was of full age. In an action by the moneylenders it was held that the infant was not liable to refund the money, either as damages for fraudulent misrepresentation or as " money had and received," or on the ground that the infant was compelled in equity to refund the moneys which he had obtained by fraud.

Infant executor.—The appointment in a will by a testator of an infant to be an executor will not operate to transfer any interest in the property of the deceased to the infant or to constitute him a personal representative for any purpose *unless* and until probate is granted to him after he has attained full age (Judicature Act, 1925, s. 165 (2)). Where an infant is a sole executor of a will it is provided by subs. (1) of the same section that administration with the will annexed will be granted to his guardian, or to such other person as the court thinks fit, *until the infant attains full age :* at which time, and not before, probate of the will may be granted to him.

It will be noted that the administration with the will annexed will cease to have operation directly the infant attains full age, but that although the infant attains full age, he has no power to act until probate of the will has been granted to him.

If an infant is appointed as one of several executors probate will be granted to the other or others, power being reserved to the infant to prove when he attains full age. See further, rr. 31 and 32 of the Non-Contentious Probate Rules, 1954.

Infant trustee.—As to the effect of an infant being a sole trustee, or one of several trustees, in whom the legal estate in land was vested on 31st December, 1925, see at p. 336. Since 1925 the appointment of an infant to be a trustee in relation to any settlement or trust will be void, but without prejudice to the power to appoint a new trustee to fill the vacancy (L.P.A. 1925, s. 20).

Section 36 of the T.A. 1925 provides that where a trustee is an infant a new trustee can be appointed in his place. Where it is found impracticable or difficult to appoint a new trustee without the aid of the court, the court has power to appoint under s. 41 of the T.A. 1925, and to make a vesting order under s. 44 (ii) (*a*) or s. 51 (1) (*a*) of the same Act.

If a conveyance of a legal estate in land should be made to an infant alone or to two or more persons jointly, both or all of whom are infants, on any trusts, it would operate as a declaration of trust and would not be effectual to pass any legal estate (L.P.A. 1925, s. 19 (4)) ; but a conveyance of a legal estate in land to an infant jointly with one or more other persons of full age on any trusts would operate as if the infant had not been named therein, but, of course, without prejudice to any beneficial interest in the land intended to be thereby provided for the infant (*ibid.*, subs. (5)).

Registered land.—A purported disposition of registered land or a registered charge to an infant made after 1925, or by the will of a proprietor dying after 1925, does not entitle the infant to be registered as proprietor until he attains full age, but in the meantime operates only as a declaration, binding on the proprietor or his personal representatives, that the registered land or charge is to be held on trust to give effect to minor interests in favour of the infant corresponding with the interests which the disposition purports to transfer or create. The disposition, or a copy or extract, must be deposited at the registry, and, unless and until the tenant for life, statutory owners, personal representatives or trustees for sale are registered as proprietors, it must be protected by a restriction or otherwise on the register (L.R.A. 1925, s. 111 (1)). The effect of this provision is similar to that in the S.L.A. 1925, s. 27 (1), applicable to unregistered land (*ante*, pp. 336–337). The provisions of the L.R.A. 1925 as to the vesting of land in infants are similar to the rules mentioned *ante*, at p. 336 *et seq.*, in the case of unregistered land. For instance, if a disposition is made to an infant jointly with another person of full age, that other person, during the minority, is entitled to be registered as proprietor (L.R.A. 1925, s. 111 (1), proviso). Where an infant becomes entitled under a will or on an intestacy to registered land or a charge, the land or charge will not be transferred by the personal representative to the infant until he attains full age (L.R.A. 1925, s. 111 (2)). If an infant becomes entitled to the benefit of a registered charge the charge must, during the minority, be registered in the names of the personal representatives, trustees, or other persons who would have been able to dispose of it if the charge had affected unregistered land (L.R.A. 1925, s. 111 (3)).

Where, by reason of minority or otherwise, the land is settled land, the provisions mentioned in the chapter on Settled Land (*post*, p. 759) apply.

In reliance, no doubt, on the presumption as to full age (see L.P.A. 1925, s. 15), birth certificates are *not* required to be produced with an application for registration. Consequently, it is not impossible for an infant to become registered as a proprietor. If such a case comes to light an application, by letter, for rectification of the register (i.e., in favour of the statutory owners, etc., or to strike the name of an infant co-owner) and in the meantime for entry of an appropriate restriction should be made. However, it would appear that a purchasing transferee from an infant registered proprietor who obtains registration of the disposition will be protected against the defect in his transferor's title (see *Morelle* v. *Wakeling* [1955] 2 Q.B. 379, at p. 411, as to the effect of L.R.A. 1925, ss. 20 and 23 ; overruled on other points by *A.-G.* v. *Parsons* [1956] A.C. 421 ; see also *Gibbs* v. *Messer* [1891] A.C. 248, at p. 254).

LITERARY AND SCIENTIFIC INSTITUTIONS

These are defined by the Literary and Scientific Institutions Act, 1854, s. 33, as institutions " established for the promotion of science, literature, the fine arts, for adult instruction, the diffusion of useful knowledge, the foundation or maintenance of libraries or reading rooms for general use among the members or open to the public, of public museums and galleries of paintings and other works of art, collections of natural history, mechanical and philosophical inventions, instruments or designs." Whether an institution falls within the definition is normally a question of fact which can best be proved by statutory declaration exhibiting a copy of the constitution, rules, or other documents stating the objects.

There are a number of powers enabling conveyances to such institutions to be made by persons having limited interests (*ibid.*, s. 1), by the Duchy of Lancaster and the Duchy of Cornwall (*ibid.*, ss. 2 and 3) subject to reverter if the land ceases to be used for the purposes of the institution (*ibid.*, s. 4). Powers of conveyance are also granted to certain corporations and commissioners (*ibid.*, s. 6).

Where the institution is not incorporated the grant, whether taking effect under the Act or otherwise, may be made to any corporation or to trustees for the purposes of the institution (*ibid.*, s. 11). The Charities Act, 1960, s. 35, *ante*, p. 277 (which relates to the transfer and evidence of title to property vested in trustees), applies in relation to any institution to which the Literary and Scientific Institutions Act, 1854, applies, as it applies in relation to a charity.

LOCAL AUTHORITIES

Generally.—The Local Government Act, 1972, creates, with effect from 1st April, 1974, a new structure for local government and allocates functions among new authorities. England (exclusive of Greater London and the Isles of Scilly) is divided into counties which contain districts ; certain counties are known as metropolitan counties and contain metropolitan districts, and the allocation of functions differs in certain respects between metropolitan and non-metropolitan counties. A district may be given borough status by charter ; the name is affected but not the functions. The structure of local government within Greater London is not materially changed. Rural parishes continue in existence. As the former administrative counties, boroughs, urban and rural districts and urban parishes cease to exist and boundaries of the new authorities differ greatly from the old ones, complex provisions have been made for transfer of property which will give rise to conveyancing problems. Further, there will in future be one local search only (with the district council) and, it is understood, additional inquiries will be sent to the district council only ; see *ante*, p. 6.

All property, or interests in property, owned by the former local authorities outside Greater London (except property of a rural parish which was not

12

divided) was transferred on 1st April, 1974, by Order made pursuant to the
Local Government Act, 1972, s. 254, to the appropriate new authority.
A general order known as the Local Authorities (England) (Property, etc.)
Order, 1973, provided for transfers (including those to passenger transport
executives and (by virtue of the Water Act, 1973) to regional water authorities) and extended to the property of joint boards, to fire service property
and to the police, magistrates' courts and probation and after-care services.
However, property vested in area health authorities was transferred under
separate statutory provision in the National Health Services Reorganisation
legislation.   Authorities may reach agreement between themselves on the
transfer of property otherwise than in accordance with the general rules of
the main order and there is provision for resolution of disputes ; supplemental
orders will provide for the vesting of the property affected.

Where property was held immediately before 1st April, 1974, as sole
trustee, exclusively for charitable purposes, by a local authority for an area
outside Greater London (other than the parish council, parish meeting or
representative body of an existing rural parish in England) the property
vested on the same trusts in a new local authority (Local Government Act,
1972, s. 210 (1)).   In general the vesting is in the most appropriate new
authority having regard to the area which has the benefit of the charitable
trust (*ibid.*, s. 210 (2), (5)) ; there is special provision for vesting of property
of educational charities in the (new) local education authority (*ibid.*, s. 210 (3)).

Particular undertakings and properties are expressly transferred, for
example a road passenger transport undertaking of a borough or an urban
or rural district wholly comprised in a metropolitan county is transferred to
the passenger transport executive for the county (Local Authorities (England)
(Property, etc.) Order, 1973, art. 5 and Sched. 1).   Detailed provision is
made, for example, for transfer of specified classes of property (*ibid.*, art. 6
and Sched. 3) and for residual transfer of property (*ibid.*, art. 12 and Sched. 5)
which cannot be conveniently copied here but it may assist if two basic
principles are mentioned.

The first principle is that property held by one of the former authorities
for the purposes of a particular function immediately before 1st April, 1974
(whether situate within or outside that authority's area) was transferred to
the new authority which, from that date, became responsible for that function
and whose area includes the former authority's area.   The following property
is deemed to be held for the purposes of that function for which the property
is chiefly used, namely, (i) property held for the purposes of more than one
function, (ii) property held for the purposes of what was formerly one function
but which was divided by the 1972 Act, and (iii) " general purpose " property
which was used wholly or mainly in connection with a particular function.

The second principle is that other property was transferred to a " legatee "
authority ;   where a former authority's area was not divided there is a
" general legatee " authority.   For example, for a former county council
the " general legatee " authority is the new county council for the county
whose area includes the area of the existing county.   Property so transferred
included " general purpose " property which was not used wholly or mainly
in connection with a particular function.   Where the area of a former authority was divided between two or more of the new authorities one " residuary
legatee " authority was specified.   Property situated within the area of the
former (divided) authority by which it was held was normally transferred
to the new county or district in which the property is situated (according
to the two main principles stated above).   Special provision was made for

property situated outside the area of the former (divided) authority. Transfer did not itself affect the continuance of user of property ; corporate land (as defined by the Local Government Act, 1933) held by a borough was normally transferred to the new authority for the function for which it was mainly used.

Fortunately, it will not be necessary for a solicitor acting, for example, on purchase of property from a local authority to investigate the purpose for which the property was held by the former authority immediately prior to 1st April, 1974, or otherwise to investigate in detail the statutory transfer made by the 1972 Act. Article 3 of the Local Authorities (England) (Property, etc.) Order, 1973 (which applies to councils of the new counties and districts and parish authorities) provides that if the authority proposes to sell, lease or otherwise dispose of land transferred to them by that order (other than the particular undertakings and properties specified in art. 5 and thus clearly defined), they must not less than thirty days before completion give notice to the " relevant authorities ". " Relevant authorities " are the councils of any county or district or the authority of any parish in which any part of the area of the authority giving the notice is comprised. Thus, the notice is given to any other authority who might claim the property. No claim by a relevant authority that any land was transferred to them by the Order affects the title of the purchaser, lessee or other disponee unless within twenty-one days of the giving of the notice the relevant authority have (a) where the title is registered, lodged a caution, or (b) otherwise given notice by recorded delivery to the authority who served the notice that they dispute the transfer to such authority. At the expiration of thirty days from the giving of the notice of the proposal to dispose of the land the authority giving it must certify to the purchaser, lessee or other disponee, or to such persons as have been nominated by him, that they have given a necessary notice and (where the land is not registered) that no claim has been made that transfer is disputed. Lodging of a caution by a " disputing " authority is without prejudice to the Land Registration (Official Searches) Rules, 1969. Thus, if a purchaser, lessee or other disponee obtains the prescribed certificate and, where the title is registered, searches in the usual way, he will obtain a good title notwithstanding any possible claim by another local authority.

Contracts.—The general rule of the common law was that a contract with a local authority, being a body corporate, would not be enforceable by or against the authority unless it was under the common seal of the authority (*Ludlow Corporation* v. *Charlton* (1840), 6 M. & W. 815). There were several exceptions to this rule which were not of great importance in the context of sales of land ; see also L.P.A. 1925, s. 74 (2). The equitable doctrine of part-performance and the authorisation of an agent under the common seal to contract could, when appropriate, have been relied on ; see the 14th Edition of this work, vol. I, p. 329.

Now, however, this rule and the exceptions have become of academic interest only. The Corporate Bodies' Contracts Act, 1960, s. 1 (1), provides that contracts may be made on behalf of any body corporate as follows :—

" (a) a contract which if made between private persons would be by law required to be in writing, signed by the parties to be charged therewith, may be made on behalf of the body corporate in writing signed by any person acting under its authority, express or implied, and (*b*) a contract which if made between private persons would by law be valid although made by parol only, and not reduced into writing, may be made by parol on behalf of the body corporate by any person acting under its authority, express or implied."

A contract so made may be varied or discharged in the same manner (*ibid.*, s. 1 (3)).

A person entering into a contract with a local authority is not bound to inquire as to whether the standing orders of the authority which apply to the contract have been complied with (Local Government Act, 1972, s. 135 (4)). Non-compliance with any such orders will not invalidate any contract entered into by or on behalf of the authority (*ibid.*).

Acquisition of land by agreement.—A principal council, i.e., the council of a county, Greater London, a district or a London borough, has power to acquire by agreement any land, whether situated inside or outside the council's area, for the purpose of (*a*) any of their statutory functions, or (*b*) the benefit, or development of their area (Local Government Act, 1972, ss. 120 (1), 270 (1) ; taking the place as from 1st April, 1974, of ss. 157, 158 and 176 of the 1933 Act). This power extends to any interest in land and any easement or right in, to or over land (*ibid.*, s. 270 (1)). The acquisition may be made notwithstanding that the land is not immediately required for the purpose of the acquisition and until so required may be used for the purposes of any of the council's functions (*ibid.*, s. 120 (2)). Parish and community councils have the same powers of acquisition of land by agreement as principal councils (*ibid.*, s. 124). See further the Local Authorities (Land) Act, 1963.

It is sometimes difficult for a person dealing with a local authority to know what is the purpose for which land is acquired and so to determine whether power exists, but persons dealing with local authorities are rarely concerned to inquire. A vendor who receives the purchase-money need not concern himself whether the authority has power to acquire the land. It is generally accepted that a purchaser from a local authority would get a good title even if the authority never had power to acquire the land, just as a trustee selling land bought in breach of trust can pass a good title. See Williams on Vendor and Purchaser, 4th ed., vol. II, p. 918.

It must be remembered that a body, such as a local authority, possessing statutory powers, cannot fetter itself in the exercise of those powers, and so a restrictive covenant which would prevent the use of land for the purpose for which statutory power to acquire the land has been given, is void (*Ayr Harbour Trustees* v. *Oswald* (1883), 8 App. Cas. 623). This rule will, however, rarely invalidate a restrictive covenant. A covenant will be valid if it leaves the local authority with power to use the land for the essential purpose for which the authority acquired the land, even though it prevents user for a subsidiary purpose which would otherwise have been within the powers of the authority (*Stourcliffe Estates Co., Ltd.* v. *Bournemouth Corporation* [1910] 2 Ch. 12).

As to restrictive covenants already binding on the land, see section on Compulsory Acquisition, *post*, p. 1214.

Costs on sale to local authority.—Where acquisition of land by local authorities by agreement takes place under the power contained in the Local Government Act, 1972, s. 120 (1), the provisions of Pt. I of the Compulsory

Purchase Act, 1965 (other than s. 31) are applicable. One important result is that, in the absence of agreement between the parties to the contrary, the acquiring authority are liable to pay the vendor's costs of deducing title and conveying the land (Compulsory Purchase Act, 1965, s. 23; *Re Burdekin* [1895] 2 Ch. 136). Part I of the 1965 Act clearly appears not to apply where acquisition takes place by agreement under the Housing Act, 1957 (compare s. 38 (1) of and Sched. 6 to the 1965 Act). Whether such costs would be payable by the local authority in such a case on the grounds that the Lands Clauses Consolidation Act, 1845, s. 82, was incorporated into the Housing Act, 1957, has been a matter on which opinions differ (*Law Journal*, vol. 98, pp. 58, 150; *Conveyancer N.S.*, vol. 13, pp. 9, 176, and vol. 15, p. 4). It is thought that the better view is that the Lands Clauses Acts were *not* incorporated into the 1957 Housing Act (compare s. 63 of the Housing Act, 1925).

Disposal of land.—A principal council, i.e., the council of a county, Greater London, a district or a London borough, have as a general rule power to dispose of any of their land in any manner they wish (Local Government Act, 1972, ss. 123 (1), 270 (1); s. 123 is derived from ss. 164 and 165 of the 1933 Act and s. 26 of the Town and Country Planning Act, 1959). To this general rule there are exceptions: first, public trust land in excess of 250 square yards cannot be disposed of under this section; second, except for a short tenancy (i.e., term not exceeding seven years), the consent of the appropriate Minister is required if the disposal will be at less than the best rent reasonably obtainable or if the land is part of an open space within the Town and Country Planning Act, 1971, or if the land was acquired under compulsory powers (directly or indirectly) within the previous ten years and has not been appropriated subsequently (Local Government Act, 1972, s. 123 (2), (3), (4), (5)). Parish and community councils have the same power of disposal (*ibid.*, s. 127). Reference should also be made to *Hauxwell* v. *Barton-upon-Humber U.D.C.* [1973] 2 All E.R. 1022 as to the inability of a local authority to dispose of land held on charitable trusts.

On a disposition after 15th August, 1959, a person dealing with or claiming under a local authority is not concerned to inquire whether any necessary consent has been given and will acquire a good title in any event (Local Government Act, 1972, s. 128 (2), replacing Town and Country Planning Act, 1959, s. 29). If, before 16th August, 1959, a local authority purported to sell or lease land in circumstances in which Ministerial consent was necessary, without having obtained that consent, the conveyance or lease was void and, as they acted *ultra vires*, the authority cannot be estopped from asserting that it was invalid (*Rhyl U.D.C.* v. *Rhyl Amusements, Ltd.* [1959] 1 W.L.R. 465). Thus, it may be necessary on investigation of title to inquire as to the grant of consent in respect of a disposition by a local authority before that date.

Sale, etc., of houses.—The disposal by local authorities of houses provided by them under statutory powers is facilitated by the Housing Act, 1957; it is no longer necessary that the local authority should obtain the best price or the best rent, but the necessity for the consent of the Secretary of State for the Environment remains (ss. 104, 106; Town and Country Planning Act, 1968, s. 39). However, a purchaser is not now concerned with Ministerial consent and a good title is obtained even if consent is lacking (s. 29 of the 1959 Act).

Very often the purchase price will be advanced wholly or mainly by the vendor authority. The manner in which this may be secured is considered in a note in the *Solicitors' Journal*, vol. 97, p. 73.

The Council of The Law Society have expressed the view that a solicitor acting for a local authority should not offer to draw the conveyance for a purchaser and have stated their opinion on various points as to the making of charges by private solicitors and by solicitors who are clerks to local authorities. See further, *Law Society's Gazette*, vol. 50, p. 199.

Restrictions on resale of houses.—The Housing Act, 1957, s. 104, provides that, where a house has been sold by a local authority subject to the prescribed conditions, certain provisions of the Building Materials and Housing Act, 1945, as amended by the Housing Act, 1949, shall apply. The result is that during the specified period of five years from the date of the completion of the sale it is an offence to let or agree to let the house at a rent beyond the maximum determined or to sell or agree to sell it at a price in excess of the price at which it was sold by the authority, plus an allowance, agreed with the authority or determined by the Minister, for improvements (1945 Act, s. 7). For this purpose a " sale " means a contract followed by a conveyance (*Lewis* v. *Wallace* (1947), 177 L.T. 362) and such a sale takes place where the contract is completed, it being immaterial for present purposes that registration is also required at H.M. Land Registry (*R.* v. *Edwards ; ex parte Joseph* [1947] K.B. 392). The commission of an offence under the Act does not affect the title to any property or the operation of any contract (*ibid.*, s. 7 (8)), except that the court may vary contracts after conviction of a lessor or vendor (*ibid.*, s. 7 (7)).

If no criminal proceedings have been brought against a vendor who agreed to sell at an excessive price, or if the court has not varied the contract, there is authority for saying that the vendor can compel the purchaser to complete at the price agreed. See *Pateman* v. *Wilson* [1952] C.P.L. 727; *Solicitors' Journal*, vol. 97, p. 21 ; and *Maynard* v. *Chappell* [1953] C.P.L. 81.

The exchange of a controlled price house for another house may constitute an offence if the value of that other house in the market exceeds the maximum permitted price. See the discussion in the *Solicitors' Journal*, vol. 95, pp. 480, 556.

Registered land.—The application by a local authority for first registration of title to land must contain a statement of the particular statute(s) under the authority of which the land was acquired, unless this is apparent from the conveyance to the authority. A transfer of land the title to which is already registered should be made in the prescribed Form 35 in the Schedule to L.R.R. 1925 and state the statute under the authority of which the land is being acquired (r. 121 (2)). In either case a restriction will usually be entered that, except under an order of the registrar, no disposition is to be registered unless made in accordance with the stated Act or some other Act or authority.

Where a purchaser acquires land from a local authority in an area of compulsory registration of title, arrangements have been made by the Chief Land Registrar for the authority to give a certificate as to title in an agreed form, instead of a normal deduction of title (see *Solicitors' Journal* (1972), vol. 116, p. 908). Since this certificate will contain a statement of relevant incumbrances which will be accepted without question, land charges searches against the local authority are not required, where an application for first registration of title is to be made.

MARRIED WOMEN

A. GENERALLY

The Law Reform (Married Women and Tortfeasors) Act, 1935, placed married women in almost the same position as unmarried women so far as concerns their interests in property. For some years it has been necessary to know the old law in order that the validity of documents appearing on titles could be considered. However, it is thought that the time has now come for omission of the statement of the special rules affecting property (not including trust property) of a woman married before 1st January, 1883, and acquired by her before that date and not made her separate property (see pp. 344–347 of the 15th Edition of this book).

As regards property acquired after 1882 by a woman married before 1883 and property belonging to a woman married after 1882 at marriage or acquired thereafter, the Married Women's Property Act, 1882, ss. 1, 2 and 5, provided that a married woman could acquire, hold and (unless restrained from anticipation) dispose of the whole legal and beneficial estate without the concurrence of her husband or acknowledgment, as her separate property, as if she were a *feme sole*. There was an exception where the property was included in a marriage settlement, the settlement being construed as if the Married Women's Property Act, 1882, had not been passed ; see notes on Marriage Settlements at p. 360.

The exception " unless restrained from anticipation," of course, referred to her beneficial interest only. A married woman could dispose of property as tenant for life under the S.L.A. 1925, notwithstanding a restraint on anticipation.

These sections of the 1882 Act were repealed by the Law Reform (Married Women and Tortfeasors) Act, 1935, and the phrase " separate " property is no longer used. Section 1 of that Act provided that a married woman should be capable of acquiring, holding and disposition of any property in all respects as if she were a *feme sole*. Further, by s. 2 (1) of that Act all property which immediately before 2nd August, 1935, was the separate property of a married woman or held for her separate use in equity, or belonged at the time of her marriage to a woman married after 2nd August, 1935, or, after 2nd August, 1935, was acquired by or devolved upon a married woman, belonged to her in all respects as if she were a *feme sole* and might be disposed of accordingly. It was provided, however, that nothing in that subsection should render inoperative any restriction upon anticipation or alienation attached to the enjoyment of any property by virtue of any Act passed before 2nd August, 1935, or any instrument executed before 1st January, 1936 (*ibid.*, s. 2 (1) proviso). After 16th December, 1949, for reasons given below, this proviso ceased to have effect.

The effect of these sections is that since 1935 most of the property of a married woman belongs to her as if she were not married ; it is not now properly described as her *separate* property and the unrepealed provisions of the Married Women's Property Acts, 1882 and 1893, are amended accordingly. There were two exceptions, however.

First, the 1935 Act does not apply where both the coverture began and the property in question (not being held for her separate use) was acquired by the married woman before 1st January, 1883 (s. 4 (1) (a)). In this rare event the rules stated at pp. 345 and 346 of the 15th Edition of this book will govern the disposition thereof.

Secondly, the proviso saved certain restraints on anticipation for a time. See next paragraph.

Restraint on anticipation.—The Law Reform (Married Women and Tortfeasors) Act, 1935, s. 2 (2), provided that any instrument executed on or after 1st January, 1936, in so far as it purported to attach to the enjoyment of any property by a woman any restriction upon anticipation or alienation which could not have been attached to the enjoyment of that property by a man, should be void. Section 2 (3) defined the dates on which certain instruments were deemed to have been executed for this purpose ; see also *Re Heath* [1949] Ch. 170.

Section 2 (2) and (3) were repealed by the Married Women (Restraint upon Anticipation) Act, 1949. Section 1 (1) of the 1949 Act provides that no restriction upon anticipation or alienation attached to the enjoyment of any property by a woman which could not have been attached to the enjoyment of that property by a man shall be of any effect after 16th December, 1949. This provision applies whatever is the date of the passing, execution or coming into operation of the Act or instrument containing the restriction (*ibid.*, s. 1 (2)).

Thus, it is no longer possible to attach such restraints to the enjoyment of property by married women ; in place thereof it is usually possible to give to married women, as to any other persons, interests on " protective trusts " (see s. 33 of the T.A. 1925).

Between 1925 and 1949 the imposition of a restraint on anticipation did not prevent a married woman selling, mortgaging or dealing with land to which she was entitled in fee or for a term of years absolute, subject thereto. It was provided by s. 1 (1) (iv) of the S.L.A. 1925 that any instrument under which land was limited to or in trust for a married woman of full age in possession for an estate in fee simple or a term of years absolute *or any other interest* with a restraint on anticipation created a settlement. A married woman so entitled to land subject to a restraint on anticipation, if of full age and entitled in possession, had the powers of a tenant for life under the S.L.A. 1925 (*ibid.*, s. 20 (1) (x)). See also S.L.A. 1925, s. 25 (1), (2). But these powers were given her for the purpose of dealing with the property as a trustee only ; the restraint might attach to her interest in the proceeds of sale or mortgage and in the investments for the time being representing the same. The S.L.A. 1925, ss. 1 (1) (iv), 20 (1) (x) and 25 (2), have been repealed by the Married Women (Restraint upon Anticipation) Act, 1949, as they are now unnecessary.

If the married woman wished to deal with her beneficial interest which she was restrained from anticipating, the court had power, for her benefit and with her consent, to make an order binding her interest in such property (L.P.A. 1925, s. 169).

Settlement by wife.—Where a wife makes a settlement on her marriage and enters into a covenant to settle after-acquired property, although she be an infant at the date of the settlement, but dies without having done any act to avoid it, it will be binding in favour of those within the marriage consideration (*Burnaby* v. *Equitable Reversionary Interest Society* (1885), 28 Ch. D. 416 ; *Re Kay's Settlement* [1939] Ch. 329). If such a settlement is made without the sanction of the court and the husband brings no property into the settlement, then the wife within a reasonable time after attaining full age has a choice whether to avoid or to ratify the settlement (*Edwards* v. *Carter* [1893] A.C. 360). If, however, the husband has also settled property then the equitable doctrine of election will apply ; i.e., the wife would be unable to repudiate the settlement to recover her own property and also benefit from the property settled by her husband, this latter being used instead to compensate any beneficiaries disappointed by her repudiation (*Re Vardon's Trusts* (1885), 31 Ch. D. 275).

A post-nuptial settlement by a married woman will, unless there is consideration, have effect as a voluntary settlement, and be good or bad in accordance with the ordinary rules affecting voluntary settlements (*Re Cook's Settlement Trusts* [1965] Ch. 902).

Settled land.—Under s. 61 (2) of the Settled Land Act, 1882, where the wife was tenant for life, but did not hold the estate for her separate use, the concurrence of her husband (for instance, to a conveyance) was necessary. But all the powers given by the S.L.A. 1925, to a tenant for life could be exercised by a married woman of full age whether or not she was entitled to her estate or interest for her separate use or as her separate property, and her husband was not a necessary party (S.L.A. 1925, s. 25 (1)).

Power of husband and wife to convey or lease to each other.— After 1881, freehold land or a thing in action may be conveyed by a husband to his wife, or by a wife to her husband, alone or jointly with another person (L.P.A. 1925, s. 72 (2), replacing Conveyancing Act, 1881, s. 50). The word " conveyance " in s. 72 (2) includes a lease (*ibid.*, s. 205 (1) (ii)), and, therefore, a wife may grant a lease out of her freeholds to her husband, and a husband may grant a lease to his wife : but see *Rye* v. *Rye* [1962] A.C. 496.

After 1882, a married woman can contract with her husband and she can also convey to her husband as if she were a *feme sole*, and without the intervention of a trustee (Married Women's Property Act, 1882, s. 1 ; Law Reform (Married Women and Tortfeasors) Act, 1935, s. 1, Sched. 2 ; *Ramsay* v. *Margrett* [1894] 2 Q.B. 18 ; *Re Cuno* (1889), 43 Ch. D. 12). Nevertheless, it should be noted that it is not always easy to establish the necessary intention to create binding legal obligations where there is an agreement between husband and wife (*Balfour* v. *Balfour* [1919] 2 K.B. 571 ; *Spellman* v. *Spellman* [1961] 1 W.L.R. 921).

So also a husband who is a tenant for life under the S.L.A. 1925 may grant a lease to his wife under that Act (*Sutherland* v. *Sutherland* [1893] 3 Ch. 169 ; *Gilbey* v. *Rush* [1906] 1 Ch. 11) ; but there must be absolute good faith (*Sutherland* v. *Sutherland, ante ; Middlemas* v. *Stevens* [1901] 1 Ch. 574).

Gifts between husband and wife.—Not only is a husband able to make a gift to his wife, but he has for long been presumed in equity to have intended a gift or advancement if ever he transfers any property to her. Equally if a husband purchases property and has the purchase completed by a conveyance in his wife's name a presumption of advancement has arisen (*Gascoigne* v. *Gascoigne* [1918] 1 K.B. 223). Again, the same presumption has arisen where the conveyance of the property is taken in both their names, i.e., *prima facie* they become beneficial joint tenants with the right of survivorship (see, e.g., *Re Hicks* (1917), 117 L.T. 360). The presumption has also been extended to apply where property is purchased in the name of a prospective wife, provided the marriage is duly solemnised (*Moate* v. *Moate* [1948] 2 All E.R. 486). Further the fact of the marriage being dissolved or voidable (as opposed to void *ab initio*) has not destroyed the presumption of advancement which arose at the date of the conveyance (*Silver* v. *Silver* [1958] 1 W.L.R. 259).

12A

However, it has now been authoritatively pronounced that the presumption of advancement between husband and wife has little place in modern circumstances (*Pettitt* v. *Pettitt* [1970] A.C. 777). See also Lord Diplock in *Gissing* v. *Gissing* [1971] A.C. 886, at p. 907 ; and the Court of Appeal decision in *Falconer* v. *Falconer* [1970] 1 W.L.R. 1333. It is thought that in practical terms, this can be taken as indicating that the presumption will be very readily found to be rebutted rather than that it will no longer arise.

It has always been accepted that, when the presumption of advancement does arise, it can be rebutted by evidence of the actual intention of the husband-purchaser, the onus of proof being on him. The clearest and commonest evidence is, of course, to include an express declaration in the conveyance of the legal estate. Otherwise the court considers all the circumstances of the case ; " the acts and declarations of the parties before or at the time of the purchase, or so immediately after it as to constitute a part of the transaction, are admissible in evidence either for or against the party who did the act or made the declaration ; subsequent acts and declarations are only admissible as evidence against the party who made them and not in his favour " (Snell's Equity, 26th ed., p. 195, approved by Viscount Simonds in *Shephard* v. *Cartwright* [1955] A.C. 431, at p. 445). However, a husband was not allowed to rebut the presumption of advancement where the evidence for the purpose involved his own illegality or fraud or other acts against public policy (*Gascoigne* v. *Gascoigne, ante ; Re Emery's Investment Trust* [1959] Ch. 410). Again a husband was unable to rebut the presumption of advancement by giving evidence that a property (which was to become the matrimonial home) had been conveyed to his wife to defeat potential creditors of his business, even though he acted honestly and on the advice of his solicitors (*Tinker* v. *Tinker* [1970] P. 136, C.A. ; nevertheless the court had power to vary the conveyance as a post-nuptial settlement within s. 17 of the Matrimonial Causes Act, 1965, see p. 368). However, this decision was distinguished, and a resulting trust imputed, where property was transferred between spouses to mitigate estate duty but from the wife to the husband and at the instance of the husband (*Heseltine* v. *Heseltine* [1971] 1 W.L.R. 342, C.A.).

Particular reference must be made to the nowadays common case of property purchased out of a joint bank account. The *prima facie* position was recently stated by Stamp, J., in *Re Bishop* [1965] Ch. 450 as follows : " Now, where a husband and wife open a joint account at a bank on terms that cheques may be drawn on the account by either of them, then, in my judgment, in the absence of facts or circumstances which indicate that the account was intended, or was kept, for some specific or limited purposes, each spouse can draw on it not only for the benefit of both spouses, but for his or her own benefit. Each spouse, in drawing money out of the account, is to be treated as doing so with the authority of the other and, in my judgment, if one of the spouses purchases a chattel for his own benefit or an investment in his or her own name, that chattel or investment belongs to the person in whose name it is purchased or invested : for in such a case there is, in my judgment, no equity in the other spouse to displace the legal ownership of the one in whose name the investment is purchased. What is purchased is not to be regarded as purchased out of a fund belonging to the spouses in the proportions in which they contribute to the account or in equal proportions, but of a pool or fund of which they were, in law and in equity, joint tenants." See also *Re Young* (1885), 28 Ch. D. 705. As indicated by Stamp, J., this *prima facie* position can be displaced by evidence

of a contrary intention, for example, that the husband alone was to benefit
(see *Hoddinott* v. *Hoddinott* [1949] 2 K.B. 406) or that " a common purse and
a pool of their resources " was intended so that a purchase in the name of
one spouse alone would nevertheless be held as to one half in trust for the
other (see *Jones* v. *Maynard* [1951] Ch. 572).

Further, the presumption that a joint account belongs to both the spouses
jointly and beneficially will be rebutted by evidence that the account was
established by one spouse for convenience only, and may be rebutted by the
presumption of a resulting trust if the wife was the sole contributor (*Heseltine*
v. *Heseltine* [1971] 1 W.L.R. 342, C.A. ; also *Thompson* v. *Thompson* (1970),
114 Sol. J. 455). However, even if a joint account was initially opened by
one spouse for convenience only, it does not follow that this character is
stamped on the account immutably : the spouse's intention may change
and in consequence a sole beneficial interest be converted into a joint beneficial
interest (*Re Figgis* [1969] 1 Ch. 123, 145).

It may also be mentioned that the Married Women's Property Act, 1964,
now makes provision for any question arising as to the right of a husband
or wife to money derived from any allowance made by the husband for the
expenses of the matrimonial home or for similar purposes, or to any property
acquired out of such money. The money or property, in the absence of any
agreement between them to the contrary, is to be treated as belonging to
the husband and wife in equal shares (*ibid.*, s. 1 ; compare *Hoddinott* v.
Hoddinott [1949] 2 K.B. 406 and see Bromley's Family Law, 4th ed., at
pp. 362–363, for problems created by the provision). In *Re John's Assignment
Trusts* [1970] 1 W.L.R. 955, Goff, J., *obiter*, indicated the view that s. 1 of
the 1964 Act could not be applied retrospectively and also that moneys
paid to discharge a mortgage on the matrimonial home might be within the
section.

Against all this, where a wife transfers property to her husband or
purchases property and puts it in her husband's name, no presumption of
advancement arises. Instead the onus of proving a gift is on the husband
(*Rich* v. *Cockell* (1804), 9 Ves. 369) since *prima facie* he holds as trustee on a
resulting trust for his wife (*Mercier* v. *Mercier* [1903] 2 Ch. 98). Further, if
a wife were to mortgage her property for the purposes of paying her husband's
debts, she would be presumed to be lending, not giving him the money and
entitled to have the mortgage discharged by him (*Hudson* v. *Carmichael*
(1854), Kay 613). However, these presumptions of a resulting trust and
of a loan may be rebutted by evidence of the wife's contrary intention in
just the same way as the presumption of advancement by a husband may
be ; see above.

Although a fiduciary relationship giving rise to a presumption of undue
influence may be found to exist between an engaged couple, so that in equity
transactions between them are liable to be set aside (*Zamet* v. *Hyman* [1961]
1 W.L.R. 1442) as a rule no presumption of undue influence arises when a
gift is made by a wife to her husband (*Hawes* v. *Bishop* [1909] 2 K.B. 390).
Nevertheless, transactions between spouses may, of course, be avoided if
positive evidence of undue influence can be adduced (*Bank of Montreal* v.
Stuart [1911] A.C. 120). Further since the courts tend to scrutinise very
carefully the conduct of the husband receiving gifts from his wife it may be
that the solicitor confronted with such a case should always insist on the wife
obtaining independent advice and otherwise refuse to act (*ibid.* ; *Shears
and Sons, Ltd.* v. *Jones* [1922] 2 Ch. 802).

Property interests and transactions entered into *inter se* by engaged couples have now been subjected to the same rules as for married couples in cases where the engagement is terminated (s. 2 of the Law Reform (Miscellaneous Provisions) Act, 1970, which expressly refers to applications under s. 17 of the Married Women's Property Act, 1882, and to the new rule under s. 37 of the Matrimonial Proceedings and Property Act, 1970 : see *post*, p. 369). Also the recovery of gifts made between engaged persons is provided for irrespective of which of them broke off the engagement (*ibid.*, s. 3). This Act came into force on 1st January, 1971 (*ibid.*, s. 7 (3)).

B. THE MATRIMONIAL HOME

Rights in matrimonial home.—Where a married woman enjoys with her husband a clearly defined interest in the matrimonial home, whether as a joint tenant of the legal estate or only as a joint tenant or tenant in common of the equitable interest, and whether arising by express declaration or by implication of equity, then the rules applicable are those applying in general to any other property held on trust for sale (*Rawlings* v. *Rawlings* [1964] P. 398 ; *Silver* v. *Silver* [1958] 1 W.L.R. 259 ; *Waller* v. *Waller* [1967] 1 W.L.R. 451 ; L.P.A. 1925, s. 30 ; and especially *ante*, p. 306 and *post*, p. 763).

As to beneficial interests in the matrimonial home arising by implication of equity, particular reference should be made to *Gissing* v. *Gissing* [1971] A.C. 886, H.L. It is clear that a direct cash contribution of a not insubstantial amount to the purchase price (or to the deposit, mortgage repayments or even legal charges) will give the contributing spouse a beneficial interest. However, the *quantum* of this beneficial interest will not necessarily be governed, as before, by the maxim "Equity is Equality"; the court is to attempt to calculate proportions of contributions where possible (*Gissing* v. *Gissing*, *ante*, followed in *Falconer* v. *Falconer* [1970] 1 W.L.R. 1333, C.A. ; cp. *Chapman* v. *Chapman* [1969] 1 W.L.R. 1367, C.A. ; *Cracknell* v. *Cracknell* [1971] P. 356, C.A., and *Hargrave* v. *Newton* [1971] 1 W.L.R. 1611, C.A.).

The position where there have been *indirect* cash contributions to the purchase was left in some doubt despite (or perhaps because of) a number of *dicta* in the speeches directed to the point (*Gissing* v. *Gissing*, *ante* ; compare Lord Reid and Lord Pearson, apparently favouring a lack of distinction between direct and indirect contributions, with Lord Dilhorne and Lord Diplock to the contrary). Nevertheless, Lord Denning, M.R., trying "to distil" what was said in the House of Lords, has since pronounced that : "The financial contribution may be *direct*, as where it is actually stated to be a contribution towards the price [or the mortgage] instalments. It may be *indirect*, as where both go out to work, and one pays the housekeeping and the other the mortgage instalments. It does not matter which way round it is. It does not matter who pays what. So long as there is a substantial financial contribution to the family expenses, it raises the inference of a trust" (in *Falconer* v. *Falconer* [1970] 1 W.L.R. 1333, see also *Davis* v. *Vale* [1971] 1 W.L.R. 1022, C.A., and *Hargrave* v. *Newton* [1971] 1 W.L.R. 1611, C.A.). Further, the Court of Appeal has held that no agreement, express or implied, between the spouses as to their beneficial shares is necessary : it is sufficient if a wife's contribution to family expenses relieves her husband of other expenditure so that he is indirectly helped with mortgage payments (*Hazell* v. *Hazell* [1972] 1 W.L.R. 301). It was also held that indirect contributions of this sort need not be expressly referable to the acquisition of the house (*ibid.*, where the wife had merely gone out to work and suffered a reduction of her housekeeping allowance). However, it is open to doubt whether this distillation of principles in the Court of Appeal accords at all consistently with the approach adopted in the House of Lords in *Gissing* v. *Gissing, ante.* Reference may be made to the first instance decision in *Cowcher* v. *Cowcher* [1972] 1 W.L.R. 425, where Bagnall, J., re-examined the principles at length and concluded by emphasising the importance of there being evidence of the actual, subjective intention or agreement of the spouses as to the creation and *quantum* of their beneficial interests where there are indirect contributions (see a critical note by J. M. Eekelaar at (1972), *Law Quarterly Review*, vol. 88, p. 333). Nevertheless, Lord Denning, M.R., has since found occasion to reaffirm the approach of looking only to whether the acquisition was, in effect, by the " joint efforts " of the spouses and, if so, of imputing or imposing a trust (*Kowalczuk* v. *Kowalczuk* [1973] 1 W.L.R. 930). In that case, the house had in fact been acquired by the husband alone long before the marriage so that the wife could only obtain an interest through subsequent contributions if they were directly referable to improvements within s. 37 of the Matrimonial Proceedings and Property Act, 1970 (see *post*, p. 369).

Incidentally, it should be observed that the Court of Appeal has held that the same principles as for husband and wife apply where man and mistress acquire property by joint efforts with the intention of setting up home together (*Cooke* v. *Head* [1972] 1 W.L.R. 518).

Where a trust has arisen by virtue of indirect contributions (e.g., joint efforts in building up a business out of the profits of which property was purchased) so that property in one spouse's name is held for both spouses beneficially, it is irrelevant to the other spouse's claim that the one spouse has died leaving a will (*Re Cummins* [1972] Ch. 62, C.A.). The principle must be the same, *a fortiori*, in the case of direct contributions.

As to contribution through improvements, see below.

Where the interests in the matrimonial home, or other property, are not clearly defined, so that there are conflicting claims between husband and wife, then recourse may be had to the procedure provided by s. 17 of the Married Women's Property Act, 1882 (as amended). Section 17 provides that " in any question between husband and wife as to the title to or possession of property, either party . . . may apply by summons or otherwise in a summary way to any judge of the High Court of Justice . . . [or of the county court] . . . and the judge . . . may make such order with respect to the property in dispute . . . *as he thinks fit*, or may direct such application to stand over from time to time, and any inquiry touching the matters in question to be made in such manner *as he shall think fit* . . ." ; this includes a power to order a sale of the property (Matrimonial Causes (Property and Maintenance) Act, 1958, s. 7 (7)). Further an application may also be made where a spouse has had, but no longer has, possession or control of property in which the other had a beneficial interest, the court's jurisdiction extending to any property which represents the property in question and to ordering payment of a sum of money (1958 Act, s. 7 (1), (2) and (3)). Section 17 of the 1882 Act (as extended by s. 7 of the 1958 Act) has been further extended so that its procedure is available to the parties to a marriage notwithstanding dissolution or annulment, provided the application is made within three years thereafter (s. 39 of the Matrimonial Proceedings and Property Act, 1970).

This procedure under s. 17 was formerly regarded as of more importance since there used to be an assumption that no alternative proceedings, e.g., in tort, were available to a husband against his wife (based on *obiter* observations of Goddard, L.J., in *Bramwell* v. *Bramwell* [1942] 1 K.B. 370, at p. 374). This assumption, which had been doubted (e.g., in *Short* v. *Short* [1960] 1 W.L.R. 833), can no longer subsist in view of the Law Reform (Husband and Wife) Act, 1962, enabling spouses to sue one another in tort. Further, questions used to be raised as to the extent of the discretion of the court under s. 17 of the 1882 Act. However, it is now established that the courts' powers under the section are substantially the same as in any other proceedings where the ownership of property is in question. In other words, " the court has a discretion to be exercised in the interest of the parties to restrain or postpone the enforcement of legal rights, but not to vary agreed or established rights to property in an endeavour to achieve a kind of palm tree justice " (*per* Lord Hodson in *National Provincial Bank, Ltd.* v. *Ainsworth* [1965] A.C. 1175, at pp. 1220–1 ; see also *per* Romer, L.J., in *Cobb* v. *Cobb* [1955] 1 W.L.R. 731, at pp. 736–7). In *Pettit* v. *Pettit* [1970] A.C. 777, the members of the House of Lords all restated and reaffirmed the view of s. 17 of the 1882 Act enunciated in the *National Provincial Bank* case, namely, that that section is procedural only and confers no jurisdiction on the courts to change the property rights of the spouses.

Thus if, as would be the better practice, a conveyance to husband and wife expressly declares trusts of the beneficial interests or alternatively if the parties' intention as to these interests can be established *aliunde* on the available evidence—e.g., by the equitable presumption of advancement or by equity favouring equality—then no further question of the court's discretion, under s. 17 or otherwise, arises (*Wilson* v. *Wilson* [1963] 1 W.L.R. 601, and *per* Lord Upjohn in *National Provincial Bank, Ltd.* v. *Ainsworth* [1965] A.C. 1175, at p. 1236). However, it would appear that such an express declaration of trusts should go further than the usual joint tenancy clauses if it is to be certain to exclude the court's discretion. In *Bedson* v. *Bedson* [1965] 2 Q.B. 666, a husband purchased the property and had it conveyed into the names of himself and his wife with an express declaration, in the usual form, of the trust for sale and that they were joint tenants in respect of the proceeds. Following an application by the wife under s. 17, the members of the Court of Appeal, whilst accepting that there was no jurisdiction to vary established rights, took differing views of the effect of this declaration : Lord Denning, M.R., considered that it raised no presumption at all as to the parties' beneficial entitlement, so that their intention must be sought from the evidence (in fact, he found that equal shares were intended) ; Davies, L.J., considered that the declaration raised a presumption, which might be (but in fact he found was not) rebutted by the evidence, that the beneficial entitlement stated was intended ; Russell, L.J., considered that the declaration was conclusive as to parties' entitlement. It is thought that this last approach was more consistent with the House of Lords' approach in *National Provincial Bank, Ltd.* v. *Ainsworth* [1965] A.C. 1175 and the *dicta* of Lord Denning, M.R., and of Davies, L.J., limiting the effect of an express declaration of trust, have since been treated as unduly influenced by the erroneous view of s. 17 of the 1882 Act adopted in the Court of Appeal. In *Pettit* v. *Pettit* [1970] A.C. 777, Lord Upjohn said : " In the first place, the beneficial ownership of the property in question must depend on the agreement of the parties determined at the time of its acquisition. If the property in question is land there must be a lease or conveyance which shows how it was acquired. If that document declares not merely in whom the legal title is to vest but in whom the beneficial title is to vest *that necessarily concludes the question of title as between the spouses for all time,* and in the absence of fraud or mistake at the time of the transaction the parties cannot go behind it at any time thereafter even on death or the break-up of the marriage." This passage was applied by Goff, J., in *Re John's Assignment Trusts* [1970] 1 W.L.R. 955. Reference should also be made to *Re Solomon* [1967] Ch. 573, where a matrimonial home purchased by the husband was conveyed to the parties with the usual joint tenancy clause, but the transaction was carried into effect by the wife acting under a power of attorney, the husband being abroad at the time and unaware (so he claimed) that the purchase was in joint names. Nonetheless, the face value of the transaction was not challenged and Goff, J., felt obliged to proceed on the footing that it was what it purported to be, i.e., a case of an ordinary beneficial joint tenancy.

In *Radziej* v. *Radziej* [1967] 1 W.L.R. 659, Baker, J., suggested that a notice given by one party to a marriage severing a beneficial joint tenancy might prevent that party denying, in proceedings under s. 17 of the Married Women's Property Act, 1882, that the other party had a right to an equal share in the property. See also *Re Draper's Conveyance* [1969] 1 Ch. 486.

Notwithstanding that the court's discretion is more limited than has sometimes been suggested (compare, e.g., *per* Lord Denning in *Hine* v. *Hine* [1962] 1 W.L.R. 1124, at pp. 1127–1128, that the court's discretion " transcends all rights, legal and equitable," which can no longer be regarded as good law), nevertheless the section is not without general utility. Apart from affording a summary procedure for determining the parties' rights in the first place, the section can be treated " as conferring on the court power, without disturbing established property rights, not to allow those rights to be fully enforced where to do so would run counter to the duties of one spouse to another " (*per* Lord Wilberforce in *National Provincial Bank, Ltd.* v. *Ainsworth* [1965] A.C. 1175, at p. 1246). Thus the court has intervened by injunction to restrain a husband from entering into a contract for the sale of the matrimonial home when his wife and children were living there until the husband provided suitable alternative accommodation (*Lee* v. *Lee* [1952] 2 Q.B. 489n ; and see *per* Tucker, L.J., in *Stewart* v. *Stewart* [1948] 1 K.B. 507, at p. 513 ; also *Hutchinson* v. *Hutchinson* [1947] 2 All E.R. 792). These cases were followed by the Court of Appeal in *Halden* v. *Halden* [1966] 1 W.L.R. 1481, where it had been contended that a non-cohabitation clause in a wife's maintenance order ends the court's jurisdiction to make an order restraining sale of the matrimonial home by a husband. Lord Denning, M.R., said : " Whatever the position may be as to a subsequent purchaser, it seems to me quite plain that as between husband and wife, if the husband deserts his wife, leaving her in the house, he has not a right to turn her out. She has not to show a legal or equitable interest in herself. It is sufficient for her to say : ' I am his wife and I am under the roof which he provided.' He is not entitled to turn her out except by order of the court ; and that will not be given in the ordinary way unless he provides alternative accommodation for her." Indeed, the majority in *Bedson* v. *Bedson* [1965] 2 Q.B. 666, having found in one way or another that the wife in desertion was entitled to an equal share of the proceeds, refused to allow her to enforce her right and realise her interest. This entirely accords with the extent of the court's discretion under s. 17 as now established by the House of Lords (see above, also *post*, p. 775, as to the L.P.A. 1925, s. 30).

However, even to this more limited and acceptable extent, it must be observed that s. 17 is only applicable as between husband and wife themselves (or if the wife dies, her personal representatives : s. 23 of the 1882 Act), not as between their respective successors in title (*per* Lord Wilberforce in *National Provincial Bank, Ltd.* v. *Ainsworth* [1965] A.C. 1175, at p. 1246). Further if the court does determine that it was not the parties' intention, express or implied, that the wife should have a beneficial interest in the matrimonial home under a trust, then " she has no proprietary rights in the house by virtue of her status as a wife . . . If her husband leaves her, the right which she had to be left undisturbed is a personal right and does not attach itself to any specific piece of property which may at a given time be the home in which the spouses have lived together " (*per* Lord Hodson in *National Provincial Bank, Ltd.* v. *Ainsworth* [1965] A.C. 1175, at p. 1220). However, reference must now be made to the provisions of the Matrimonial Homes Act, 1967, below, p. 370.

It should not be overlooked that the court does have power to refuse to give effect to sham or fraudulent sales (*Ferris* v. *Weaven* [1952] 2 All E.R. 233 ; *Rutter* v. *Nicholas* (1964), 108 Sol. J. 579 ; L.P.A. 1925, ss. 172 and 173 ; and Bankruptcy Act, 1914, s. 42). In particular, it should be remembered that the court has a statutory power to set aside any disposition made by a husband with the intention or effect of defeating his wife's claim for financial relief (Matrimonial Proceedings and Property Act, 1970, s. 16). See further *ante*, p. 119.

Further, the limitations established in the House of Lords on the court's jurisdiction under s. 17 of the Married Women's Property Act, 1882, may be regarded as of considerably less importance now. The reason lies in the much wider powers conferred on the court on divorce, nullity and judicial separation by s. 4 of the Matrimonial Proceedings and Property Act, 1970. "It can be anticipated that many of the hard-fought disputes between spouses as to title to the matrimonial home which are now brought under s. 17 . . . will not now arise. Instead, the wife, the spouse who most usually seeks to establish a beneficial interest under the 1882 Act, will be able to ask for the house to be transferred to her name under s. 4. This power, coupled with the protection afforded by the Matrimonial Homes Act, 1967, should go a long way towards protecting a spouse's—and children's—legitimate desire to keep the home " (Jennifer Levin, LL.M., at *Conveyancer N.S.*, vol. 34, p. 385).

Section 4 of the 1970 Act has replaced, with retrospective effect and much wider provisions, s. 17 of the Matrimonial Causes Act, 1965 (see *Williams* v. *Williams* [1971] P. 271, in which it was held that the implication of retro-spection seemed necessary to give reasonable efficacy to the Act ; followed in *Powys* v. *Powys* [1971] P. 340). The new section confers jurisdiction on the court on or after granting a decree of divorce, nullity or judicial separation to order either party to transfer or settle any property for the benefit of the other party or of any child of the family (s. 4 (*a*), (*b*)). In addition, power is conferred to vary any ante-nuptial or post-nuptial settle-ment, now including testamentary settlements (s. 4 (*c*)). Also the court may make an order extinguishing or reducing the interest of either party under such a settlement (s. 4 (*d*) ; cf. *Jones* v. *Jones* [1972] 3 All E.R. 289, as to a tenancy in common). A considerable number of guidelines are expressly indicated as to the circumstances to which the court must have regard to making an order (s. 5). But these are very generally expressed and no order of priority is given, so it remains to be seen how the courts will be able to use them, but it is thought that little difference in practice will be seen (see *Wachtel* v. *Wachtel* [1973] 2 W.L.R. 84 ; *Mesher* v. *Mesher*

(1973), *The Times*, 13th February ; *Trippas* v. *Trippas* [1973] 2 W.L.R. 585 ; and *Harnett* v. *Harnett* [1973] 2 All E.R. 593 ; also *Cuzner* v. *Underdown* (1973), 117 Sol. J. 465).

A settlement or transfer made in pursuance of an order under s. 4 of the 1970 Act remains liable to be avoided under s. 42 of the Bankruptcy Act, 1914, see *ante*, p. 252 (s. 23 of the 1970 Act).

Reference may be made to two decisions under the replaced s. 17 of the 1965 Act. In *Spizewski* v. *Spizewski* [1970] 1 W.L.R. 522, a very practical approach was adopted by the Court of Appeal : the wife was in desertion and so her interest was extinguished from the date of desertion but the house was charged with payment to her by instalments of a lump sum. See also *Smith* v. *Smith* [1970] 1 W.L.R. 155, where the variation of a settlement was the only effective means of providing financial protection for the wife, since there was little possibility of obtaining periodical payments from the husband who had departed to New Zealand.

Improvements.—The principle that contributions by a spouse to the improvement of property conferred a proprietary interest of uncertain quantum so that the court had jurisdiction to make an order of substance under s. 17 of the Married Women's Property Act, 1882, was first promulgated by the Court of Appeal (see *Appleton* v. *Appleton* [1965] 1 W.L.R. 25 and *Jansen* v. *Jansen* [1965] P. 478). It was then disapproved in the House of Lords (*Pettit* v. *Pettit* [1970] A.C. 777 ; also *Gissing* v. *Gissing* [1971] A.C. 886). That disapproval has, with statutory assistance, been survived and the law is now to be found enshrined in s. 37 of the Matrimonial Proceedings and Property Act, 1970, as follows :—

" It is hereby declared that where a husband or wife contributes in money or money's worth to the improvement of real or personal property in which or in the proceeds of sale of which either or both of them has or have a beneficial interest, the husband or wife so contributing shall, if the contribution is of a substantial nature and subject to any agreement between them to the contrary express or implied, be treated as having then acquired by virtue of his or her contribution a share or an enlarged share, as the case may be, in that beneficial interest of such an extent as may have been agreed or, in default of such agreement, as may seem in all the circumstances just to any court before which the question of the existence or extent of the beneficial interest of the husband or wife arises (whether in proceedings between them or in any other proceedings)."

Attention is drawn particularly to the following points about this section :—

(1) As an expressly declaratory provision this is of retrospective effect (as in *Davis* v. *Vale* [1971] 1 W.L.R. 1022, C.A.).

(2) Since the section refers to " money or money's worth," it will apply whether the spouse pays a contractor, or provides materials, or does the work himself.

(3) The section is *not* confined to the matrimonial home and so could extend, for example, to a share in a business.

(4) The familiar, although often difficult, distinction between improvements and repairs (as often for tax purposes) will have to be drawn for the purposes of this section.

(5) As the contribution (but not necessarily, it seems, the improvement) must be of a substantial nature, a spouse will still " not be entitled to

a share in the house simply by doing the 'do-it-yourself' jobs which husbands often do" (*per* Lord Denning, M.R., in *Button* v. *Button* [1968] 1 W.L.R. 457, at p. 461).

(6) The contribution must be identifiable with the relevant improvement, as well as substantial; mere general contributions, which would be taken into account by the court in making financial provision, are not sufficient (*Harnett* v. *Harnett* [1973] 2 All E.R. 593).

(7) The principle is only applicable in the absence of a contrary agreement "express or implied". This limitation would appear to indicate the real effect of the section, namely, a shifting in the burden of proof of an appropriate agreement from the spouse alleging the existence of a beneficial interest (as before the Act) to the spouse denying such existence. *Quaere:* does such an agreement (or an agreement as to *quantum*) require written evidence under s. 40 of the L.P.A. 1925 ?

(8) The *quantum* of the beneficial interest acquired is left, in the absence of agreement, to the discretion of the court. Reference may be made to *Davis* v. *Vale* [1971] 1 W.L.R. 1022 where there had been contributions to the purchase as well as to the improvement of the matrimonial home and the Court of Appeal upheld an equal division.

(9) Since a contributing spouse who started with no interest in the property is given a share in the beneficial interest hitherto belonging wholly to the other spouse, the result in conveyancing terms should be to constitute the latter a trustee for sale of the legal estate to hold the proceeds for both spouses as tenants in common in equity. Thus a situation akin to that in *Bull* v. *Bull* [1955] 1 Q.B. 234 will be produced in a manner which is both novel and imprecise and there may well arise in an acute form those conveyancing difficulties adverted to *ante*, pp. 306–307.

Further it should be noticed that the Court of Appeal has not allowed itself to be inhibited by the fact that its principle, having been disapproved in the House of Lords, was only revived by statute for " a husband or a wife " (see s. 37, *ante*). In one case a mistress and in another a mother-in-law, having contributed substantially to the improvement of property, were held to have beneficial interests therein (see *Cooke* v. *Head* [1972] 1 W.L.R. 518 and *Hussey* v. *Palmer* [1972] 1 W.L.R. 1286).

C. MATRIMONIAL HOMES ACT, 1967

This is yet another aspect of this topic where the ideas of the Court of Appeal have, with statutory assistance, survived a squashing clash with those of the House of Lords. For some thirteen years it had been thought probable that the successors in title of a husband might be adversely affected by the " equity " of a deserted wife even though she had no proprietary rights. Now, however, all those cases cited in the 14th Edition of this book (pp. 344–345) and in the Supplements thereto (beginning with *Bendall* v. *McWhirter* [1952] 2 Q.B. 466), which decided or suggested that, if a deserted wife remained in occupation of a matrimonial home which belonged to her husband, she had a right good against third parties, such as a purchaser or mortgagee from him, to continue in occupation, have been overruled or disapproved by the House of Lords (*National Provincial Bank, Ltd.* v. *Ainsworth* [1965] A.C. 1175). Further, since the deserted wife's " equity " has now been shown beyond doubt not to be a property right able to endure through different ownerships, it followed also that it was not an " overriding interest " within s. 70 of the L.R.A. 1925 (*ibid.* ; see *ante*, p. 188 *et seq.*). Consequently, conveyancers no longer had any necessity to pursue indelicate enquiries on behalf of purchasers or mortgagees into the matrimonial affairs of vendors or mortgagors. But this immunity proved short-lived.

On 1st January, 1968, " there came into force the provisions of the Matrimonial Homes Act, 1967, designed no doubt to provide a statutory substitute for the supposed deserted wife's equity, the creature of the courts which the House of Lords had strangled " (*per* Bridge, J., in *Miles* v. *Bull* (*No.* 2) [1969] 3 All E.R. 1585, at p. 1587). This Act is of considerable concern to conveyancers and accordingly a full account of it is attempted here.

The object of the Matrimonial Homes Act, 1967, is to give a spouse rights of occupation in respect of the matrimonial home not only as against the other spouse but also as against third parties, such as subsequent purchasers, provided the rights are properly protected. See generally Professor F. R. Crane in *Conveyancer N.S.*, vol. 32, p. 85.

Rights of occupation.—The statutory rights of occupation are conferred only where, *first*, one spouse is " entitled to occupy a dwelling-house by virtue of any estate or interest or contract or by virtue of any enactment giving him or her the right to remain in occupation," *and secondly* " the other spouse is not so entitled " (s. 1 (1)). It is, of course, the latter spouse who gets the statutory rights and whether husband or wife is entirely irrelevant, but for the purposes of exposition the former spouse will hereinafter be called " *H* " and the latter spouse " *W*."

Before applying the rules regarding the statutory right of occupation one should not overlook that it is *prima facie* a husband's duty at common law to provide a home for his wife and children. Unless the wife has misbehaved she is entitled to remain in the matrimonial home whether it is owned jointly or solely by the husband. This is a personal right against the husband only but in an extreme case the court may even order the husband to leave the house so that it can be occupied by the wife (*Gurasz* v. *Gurasz* [1970] P. 11, *per* Lord Denning, M.R., and Edmund Davies, L.J. ; see also *Hall* v. *Hall* [1971] 1 W.L.R. 404 and *Jones* v. *Jones* [1971] 1 W.L.R. 396 ; but compare *Tarr* v. *Tarr* [1972] 2 W.L.R. 1068, H.L., *post*, p. 373). Nor could a husband be treated as a trespasser in the former matrimonial home belonging to the wife so long as the marriage remained undissolved and there was no court order that he leave (*Morris* v. *Tarrant* [1971] 2 W.L.R. 630).

Clearly the statutory rights of occupation can arise in a variety of situations. Principally in mind, no doubt, will be the case where *H* owns beneficially the legal freehold. But a difficulty may occur even here. In the vast majority of such cases *H* will have acquired his ownership with the assistance of a mortgage advance and it is now well established that a legal mortgagee has an unqualified right to take possession immediately (see *post*, p. 996 *et seq.*). *H*, as mortgagor, is certainly in lawful occupation, but can it be said that he is " *entitled* to occupy " a mortgaged dwelling-house ? Clearly *H* will be so entitled if there is some such provision in the mortgage as an attornment clause, and other subsections in the 1967 Act envisaging the existence of a mortgage can be confined to this circumstance (see ss. 1 (5), 2 (8)). However, in *Hastings and Thanet Building Society* v. *Goddard* [1970] 1 W.L.R. 1544 the Court of Appeal drew attention to the question (without expressing an opinion on it) of whether a mortgagor-spouse remained entitled to occupy the dwelling-house *after* an order for possession against him and the issue of a warrant for possession. It was not apparently doubted that before then the mortgagor-spouse was entitled to occupy.

The 1967 Act will also apply where *H* owns beneficially a legal leasehold estate (e.g., a weekly tenancy) and where his occupation is by virtue of a statutory tenancy or even purely contractual. Further, the Act would appear to apply where *H* is a tenant for life for the purposes of the S.L.A. 1925. However, the Act would appear *not* to apply where *H* is merely permitted to occupy under the provisions of a trust for sale (contrast *Re Herklots' Will Trusts* [1964] 1 W.L.R. 583 where there was a direction as to occupation ; see *post*, pp. 656, 721).

As the 1967 Act was originally enacted, the statutory rights simply did not arise at all if *W* had any like entitlement to occupy. The consequence was that the Act was inapplicable in many of the common cases of co-ownership by *H* and *W* (see *Gurasz* v. *Gurasz* [1970] P. 11). However, a new subs. (9) to s. 1 of the 1967 Act was inserted by s. 38 of the Matrimonial Proceedings and Property Act, 1970, as follows :—

" It is hereby declared that a spouse who has an equitable interest in a dwelling-house or in the proceeds of sale thereof, not being a spouse in whom is vested (whether solely or as a joint tenant) a legal estate in fee simple or a legal term of years absolute in the dwelling-house, is to be treated for the purposes only of determining whether he or she has rights of occupation under this section as not being entitled to occupy the dwelling-house by virtue of that interest."

Although s. 38 of the 1970 Act came into force on 1st August, 1970 (s. 43 (2)), as a declaratory provision the subsection must have retrospective effect. However, it still seems that the 1967 Act is *not* applicable to the common case where the *legal estate* has been conveyed to the spouses *H* and *W* jointly to hold on trust for sale for themselves. This case involves the legal estate being vested in the spouses as joint tenants and is in terms excluded from the new subsection (notwithstanding that it was just this case that inspired the insertion : see *Gurasz* v. *Gurasz, ante*). Accordingly, the new subsection operates to make the Act applicable in cases where the legal estate is vested in one spouse, say *H*, alone but both spouses (or even *semble W* alone) are entitled in equity (see *ante*, p. 364 *et seq.*).

Presumably the reference to a contract in the subsection (s. 1 (1) of the 1967 Act) does not include the marriage contract itself which anyway gives a wife occupation rights over the matrimonial home, albeit these are not proprietary rights (see p. 364 *et seq.*) ; if there were such inclusion, it would render the Act largely nugatory (see *Law Society's Gazette*, vol. 64, p. 544).

In the Act, " dwelling-house " is defined as including " any building or part thereof which is occupied as a dwelling, and any yard, garden, garage or outhouse belonging to the dwelling-house and occupied therewith " (s. 1 (7)). The present tense of this definition makes it arguable that the statutory rights cannot subsist in respect of a house, although it was once occupied as a dwelling, if it no longer is, e.g., if it is used for business purposes or *semble* if it is vacant, more than merely temporarily. It will be observed that there is no requirement as to length of occupation of the building. Conversely, it is provided that the Act will not apply to a dwelling-house which " has at no time been a matrimonial home of the spouses in question " (s. 1 (8)). That the dwelling-house is no longer the spouses' matrimonial home appears irrelevant so long as it once was. That several dwelling-houses, without limit in number, may qualify by this test appears equally irrelevant (but see s. 3 below).

These last points may at first sight seem purely academic in that W, the spouse claiming the statutory rights, is likely actually to be in occupation of the house in question. This is true, but the statutory " rights of occupation " are defined to go beyond this case. The rights conferred on W by the Act are as follows (s. 1 (1)) :—

" (a) if in occupation, a right not to be evicted or excluded from the dwelling-house or any part thereof by the other spouse except with the leave of the court given by an order under this section ;

(b) if not in occupation, a right with the leave of the court so given to enter into and occupy the dwelling-house."

The Court of Appeal has held that an interim order can be made permitting a return under para. (b) above : *Baynham* v. *Baynham* [1968] 1 W.L.R. 1890 ; Lord Denning, M.R., underlined the extent of the rights newly conferred by the 1967 Act, commenting (at p. 1895) : " Previously a wife who herself left the home was not protected. The deserted wife's equity, as it was called, only applied to a wife who was herself in occupation when the husband had deserted her." Further, the Court of Appeal has now decided that a spouse who is not in occupation is able to register a class F land charge (see below) even before the leave of the court has been obtained within para. (b) above (*Watts* v. *Waller* [1972] 3 W.L.R. 315, C.A., overruling *Rutherford* v. *Rutherford* [1970] 1 W.L.R. 1479).

In addition to giving its leave as above, the court (which means the High Court or a county court : s. 1 (6)) may on the application of either spouse declare, enforce, restrict or terminate the statutory rights of occupation or regulate " the exercise by either spouse of the right to occupy the dwelling-house " (s. 1 (2)). From the quoted words it is apparent that the court's jurisdiction under the Act extends beyond the statutory rights thereby created to cover also exercise (at least) of the existing rights of H. However, in *Tarr* v. *Tarr* [1972] 2 W.L.R. 1068, the House of Lords decided that an order that a spouse should vacate his property and not re-enter without leave was not within the jurisdiction conferred by this subsection since such an order would not regulate but would prohibit the exercise altogether of his rights of occupation.

The court's discretion is virtually unfettered ; it may make " such order as it thinks just and reasonable " having regard to all the circumstances including the conduct, needs, financial resources and children of the spouses (s. 1 (3)). Without limiting the generality of this, the court is specifically empowered (a) to except part of the dwelling-house from the statutory rights of occupation (e.g., a part used for H's trade, business or professional purposes) ; (b) to order W to make periodical payments to H in respect of occupation under the Act ; (c) to impose obligations on H or W as to repairs or maintenance or discharge of liabilities on the dwelling-house (s. 1 (3)).

The statutory rights of occupation conferred on W are not of unlimited duration. The rights will continue only so long as the marriage subsists and H retains his right to occupy the dwelling-house (s. 1 (8) ; this is subject to the provisions for protection as against third parties outlined below).

Thus W's rights appear to expire if an order for possession becomes effective against H, whether on the application of a landlord (as in *Penn* v. *Dunn*

[1970] 2 Q.B. 686, C.A.) or of a mortgagee (as suggested in *Hastings and Thanet Building Society* v. *Goddard* [1970] 1 W.L.R. 1544, C.A.).

Further, the Act expressly provides that *W* may " by a release in writing release [the statutory] rights " (s. 6 (1), which allows also a release of part only of the dwelling-house). From the wording, the intention must be assumed that such a release requires the support neither of a seal nor of consideration to be valid and effective (cp. ss. 52 (1) and 205 (1) (ii) of the L.P.A. 1925). It is not clear, however, whether a conditional release or revival of the statutory rights is possible. The question has been encountered of the effect of a release of the rights by *W* purportedly only as against a particular person (e.g., by a clause in a second mortgage). It is thought that such a limited release is not envisaged by the provisions of the 1967 Act and so might well be effective absolutely for all purposes. The correct procedure in such cases is that mentioned later of *W* merely agreeing in writing that some other charge should have priority (i.e., under s. 6 (3) of the 1967 Act).

Creation of charge.—Before coming to the mechanics of protection, it is vital to note the substantive provision whereby *W's* statutory rights of occupation become enforceable not only against *H* but also against third parties. This provision is twofold : first, that the statutory rights are to be a charge on the estate or interest by virtue of which *H* is entitled to occupy the dwelling-house ; and secondly that the charge is to have the like priority as if it were an equitable interest created at the *latest* of (*a*) the date when *H* acquired the estate or interest ; (*b*) the date of the marriage; or (*c*) 1st January, 1968 (s. 2 (1)). An important point not to be overlooked is that this charge does not arise in all the cases in which *W* may have statutory rights, but only where *H* has an estate or interest (i.e., omitting the contractual or statutory entitlement to occupy mentioned in s. 1 (1), to which a charge would be inappropriate). Further, it would appear that if *H* has merely an equitable estate or interest in the dwelling-house a charge upon it would be equally liable to be overreached on a sale of the legal estate. This may not be a serious weakness ; if *H* is entitled under a bare trust, his interest would not be over- reachable ; if *H's* interest is under a trust for sale, as mentioned earlier, he would probably only be permitted to occupy and not " entitled " within the Act (the present problem would arise, however, if *H* happened to be an equitable joint tenant or tenant in common with someone other than *W*— as occurred, indeed, in *Bull* v. *Bull* [1955] 1 Q.B. 234 itself). Some difficulty might be experienced where *H* has both the legal estate and an equitable interest in deciding by virtue of which estate or interest he is entitled to occupy, since this decides also on which estate or interest the charge will be. For example, if *H* is a tenant for life within the S.L.A. 1925, is *W's* charge on the legal estate vested in him or on the equitable interest qualifying him to be tenant for life ? If the latter, then surely it is overreachable on a sale by *H*. And it is thought that this is the correct answer : *H* is entitled to occupy the house by virtue of his equitable interest under the settlement not by virtue of his legal estate under the 1925 Act. However, in *Miles* v. *Bull* [1969] 1 Q.B. 258, also *Miles* v. *Bull* (*No.* 2) [1969] 3 All E.R. 1585, the legal estate had been vested in *H* and his brother, " the joint owners " who conducted a farming partnership and who sold " as beneficial owners " so presumably the equitable position was that they were tenants in common (see *ante*, p. 283) ; nevertheless there was no suggestion that *W's* charge might only be on *H's* equitable interest under the statutory trust for sale and so overreachable.

Additionally, the 1967 Act provides for the ending of the charge on the death of *H* or on the termination of the marriage *unless* a contrary court order had been made during the subsistence of the marriage (s. 2 (2)). Also any court order within s. 1 above in effect becomes part of the charge (s. 2 (3)). More important perhaps is the provision that the charge is *not* to be defeated by *H* surrendering his estate or interest so that it disappears by merger (s. 2 (4)).

Protection by registration.—This elevation of *W's* statutory rights of occupation to the level of an equitable charge suffices, of course, without more to secure priority over anyone later taking a mere equitable interest from *H* or taking a legal estate or interest as a volunteer. But more is necessary to ensure that the charge does not succumb to a *bona fide* purchaser for value of a legal estate and without notice. Indeed it will be most important in conveyancing practice to consider the provisions of the 1967 Act from the point of view of just such a purchaser. The short answer is that full protection is afforded to *W* by way only of registration, and this is still, so it seems, notwithstanding the fact of any court order with regard to the statutory rights.

If title to the dwelling-house is unregistered, *W's* charge is registrable under the L.C.A. 1972, s. 2 (7), as a Class F land charge (s. 2 (5) of the 1967 Act as amended).

Registration, renewal of registration, or cancellation, should be applied for on the forms now specified in Sched. 2 to the Land Charges (No. 2) Rules, 1972.

If title to the dwelling-house is registered, *W's* statutory rights will *not* amount to an overriding interest and her charge can only be protected by entry of a notice or caution under the L.R.A.1925 (s. 2 (7) of the 1967 Act).

Application for registration or renewal of registration of a notice or caution should be made on forms 99 and 100, respectively, which are prescribed under the Land Registration (Matrimonial Homes) Rules, 1967. The Land Registry do *not* notify the registered proprietor where a caution is registered or a notice entered (see Chief Land Registrar's letter in *Solicitors' Journal*, vol. 112, p. 210 ; also Ruoff and Roper, Registered Conveyancing, 3rd ed. at p. 784) but this negative practice has suffered pointed criticism in the courts (i.e. in *Watts* v. *Waller* [1972] 3 W.L.R. 365, C.A., and *Wroth* v. *Tyler* [1973] 2 W.L.R. 405).

The consequences will be the usual ones of binding purchasers if properly protected and of being void against them if not. But it must be noted that this protection by registration of *W's* charge is only possible where *H* is entitled to occupy the dwelling-house by virtue of a *legal* estate and not otherwise (this is made explicit by s. 2 (7) of the 1967 Act, and follows from reading s. 2 (5) thereof, as amended, with ss. 3 (1) and 17 (1) of the L.C.A. 1972).

Notwithstanding due protection by registration, *W's* charge will still be void against *H's* trustee in bankruptcy or the trustees of a conveyance for the benefit of *H's* creditors or *H's* personal representatives if his estate is insolvent (s. 2 (5)). Another miscellaneous point is that registration of *W's* charge is not to prevent " tacking " when appropriate (s. 2 (8), so that *W* may be well advised to give express notice to *H's* bank in case he has given security for an overdraft ; see *post*, p. 1021 *et seq.*), and *W* is in any case permitted to agree in writing that any other charge or interest should enjoy priority to hers (s. 6 (3), which would enable *H* to grant a mortgage without *W* releasing her rights). Of more practical importance is the provision that although *W*. may have statutory rights of occupation, and therefore an equitable charge, in respect of two or more of *H's* dwelling-houses, only one charge may be protected by registration at any one time (s. 3). This enables *W* to change her mind and choose her place of protection, for the last charge registered at any given time prevails, any earlier registrations having to be cancelled automatically (s. 3).

Estoppel.—Before moving on from these provisions for the registration of the charge which represents and protects *W's* statutory right of occupation, it is necessary to mention the remarkable suggestion that such registration may in itself work to *W's* detriment (made in an interesting article, " Some Practical Aspects of the Matrimonial Homes Act, 1967," by J. E. Adams in *Law Society's Gazette*, vol. 65, pp. 362, 421 and 488). The starting point for the suggestion is the undeniable proposition that it would be preferable for *W* to claim a beneficial equitable interest in the dwelling-house if at all possible ; this would give her proprietary rights and a share of the proceeds of sale, not merely a right to occupy subject to the court's discretion. After this it is pointed out, as also earlier here, that the statutory rights of occupation are only conferred on *W* if she has no other right to occupy the dwelling-house. Therefore, it is said, the risk of protecting *W's* statutory rights by registration as a land charge is that an estoppel may be created against the later establishment of an equitable interest : " The estoppel would arise from the assertion, implicit on the registration . . . of . . .the absence of any interest which gives occupational rights to [*W*] " (*loc. cit.*, p. 367).

However, with respect, this estoppel suggestion does appear to lack any sufficient foundation. In the first place, for there to be an effective estoppel, an " implicit assertion " would not be enough ; a clear definite statement of a particular fact is required and the extraction of a proposition by inference from some other statement or conduct with a view to estoppel is not permissible (see *per* Bowen, L.J., in *Onward Building Society* v. *Smithson* [1893] 1 Ch. 1, at p. 14). In the second place, the person seeking to establish an estoppel by representation would have to show that the statement was made to him with the intention that he should change his position on the strength of it which he has to his prejudice (see *General Finance Co.* v. *Liberator Society* (1878), 10 Ch. D. 15, at p. 25, also *Canadian Pacific Railway* v. *R.* [1931] A.C. 414, at p. 429). It is hardly likely that *H* could show any of this. Accordingly, it is not considered that practitioners need hesitate before registering as a charge any statutory rights of occupation claimed by *W* ; after all, registration alone can never be conclusive as to the validity or otherwise of the protected interest.

Position of purchaser.—If *W's* statutory rights of occupation (if any) are not duly protected by registration as a land charge, a purchaser of the dwelling-house from *H* for valuable consideration, whether or not making the usual pre-completion searches, is simply not affected. In one of the comparatively few cases so far concerning the Act— *Miles* v. *Bull* [1969] 1 Q.B. 258— a Class F land charge was registered the day after completion of the sale by *H* of the dwelling-house ; Megarry, J., observed : " Registration of the land charge in the present case, however, could do nothing to protect the wife, completion having taken place ; in any event, the land being registered land, what was required was a notice or caution against the title under s. 2 (7) of the 1967 Act." Thus, the registration was both late and undue. And, in further proceedings in the same case, Bridge, J., reached a decision to the same effect : a transferee of registered land takes subject to entries on the register and overriding interests but "free from all other estates and interests whatsoever" by virtue of s. 20 (1) of the L.R.A. 1925, and this embraces freedom from any unregistered rights arising under the 1967 Act (*Miles* v. *Bull* (*No.* 2) [1969] 3 All E.R. 1585).

If, however, there is such a charge duly protected then the 1967 Act deals with the position of the purchaser as against *H* by implying a term into the contract for sale (s. 4 (1) ; this is subject to the expression of a contrary intention : subs. (3) ; but applies also to contracts for exchange or for leases or underleases : subss. (4), (5)). The implied term is that "the vendor will before completion procure the cancellation of the registration of the charge at his expense" (s. 4 (1), not applying if the vendor is entitled to sell free of the charge, e.g., a prior mortgagee exercising his power of sale). The term is only to be implied into a contract for sale "whereby the vendor agrees to give vacant possession of the dwelling-house on completion of the contract on completion" (s. 4 (1)). There seems no good reason for assuming that this requires an express provision for vacant possession in the contract (as at *Law Society's Gazette*, vol. 65, p. 5) ; if the contract were open in this respect it would still be one whereby the vendor agrees to give vacant possession, albeit impliedly (see *ante*, pp. 55 and 199).

The intended effect of this implied term was, no doubt, to exclude any possible application of *Re Forsey and Hollebone's Contract* [1927] 2 Ch. 379 in any case where the registration of *W's* charge had been made *before* the date of the contract of sale by *H*. This provision indeed was apparently introduced into the Act at the instance of The Law Society based on the assumption that in practice pre-contract land charge searches may *not* be made on behalf of purchasers notwithstanding *Re Forsey and Hollebone* (see *Law Society's Gazette*, vol. 64, at p. 546). However, it is now clear that *Re Forsey and Hollebone* can have no such application as would compel pre-contract searches (see s. 24 of the Law of Property Act, 1969, outlined *ante*, pp. 4–5). Nevertheless it is still prudent and advisable for a vendor's (i.e., *H's*) solicitor both to make appropriate searches and to arrange for any release of *W's* statutory rights before exchange of contracts (cf. *Law Society's Gazette*, vol. 65, at p. 5). Taking these steps would forestall any difficulties which would otherwise be caused by an unsuspected registration on behalf of *W* at the time of the contract, although the difficulties arising from a registration after contract and before completion could not be thus avoided (see *Wroth* v. *Tyler* [1973] 2 W.L.R. 405).

In this latter case of a registration on behalf of *W* between contract and completion, her charge would bind the purchaser from *H* after completion notwithstanding that the contract with *H* was itself protected by registration as an "estate contract" before the date of *W's* registration (see s. 4 (8) of the L.C.A. 1972 ; also J. E. Adams in *Law Society's Gazette*, vol. 65, pp. 442, 545). However, such a purchaser should discover the registration by means of the customary pre-completion searches when he would be entitled to refuse to complete unless and until the registration were cancelled. The basis of this entitlement would be either the term implied by s. 4 (1) of the 1967 Act (see above ; arguably this is not confined to cases of pre-contract registration) or else because of a breach of the express or implied term of the contract that *H* is selling free from incumbrances (see *ante*, pp. 55 and 105 *et seq.*). However, if *W* will not consent or co-operate in the cancellation, the court will be slow to grant a decree of specific performance which would require *H* to apply to the court against *W* under s. 1 (2) of the 1967 Act, especially as the outcome would depend upon the application of such phrases as " just and reasonable " in s. 1 (3) of the Act (*Wroth* v. *Tyler* [1973] 2 W.L.R. 405). In effect, *W* would appear to constitute or involve an irremovable defect in title, but not so as to preclude recovery by the purchaser from *H* of substantial damages for breach of contract (*ibid.*; see further *ante*, p. 223). Other problems in practice may be experienced where there happens to be a charge registered protecting *W*'s statutory rights of occupation and *W*, unexpectedly perhaps, refuses to co-operate in the cancellation. It is thought that a purchaser from *H* would not be able immediately to rescind the contract on the arrival of the contractual completion date, unless time was of the essence (see J. E. Adams, *Law Society's Gazette*, vol. 65, at p. 488 *et seq.*). A reasonable time thereafter would have to be allowed to *H* to procure the cancellation, whether with *W*'s co-operation or in pursuance of a court order terminating her statutory rights of occupation (s. 5 (1) (*c*) ; also a death or divorce would do for present purposes : s. 5 (1) (*a*), (*b*)). However, the better practice to adopt would appear to be to follow the usual procedure of serving a notice to complete (see *ante*, pp. 213–217).

Even where *W* is willing to co-operate, the purchaser may have to be satisfied with less than actual cancellation of the registration. It is provided that if on completion there is delivered to the purchaser or his solicitor an application by *W* for the cancellation of the registration of her charge (prescribed form L.C. 21), then the term implied by the Act as to *H* procuring cancellation shall be deemed to have been performed (s. 4 (2)). This will prove an effective and reliable procedure in practice because of the Act's later provision that *W*'s statutory rights constituting the charge should be deemed to have been released on the delivery of such an application to a purchaser (or lessee) or his solicitor on completion (s. 6 (2)). A purchaser's mortgagee would be equally protected by virtue of the delivery, but in any case it is also provided that the rights are deemed released on the lodging of *W*'s application for cancellation of the registration at H.M. Land Registry (s. 6 (2)). It should be noted, however, that these provisions for a deemed release apply only where there has first been a contract for sale or lease of the dwelling-house ; so in this respect at least a prior contract should not be dispensed with.

Miscellaneous.—So far as third parties other than purchasers from *H* are concerned, it is also provided that any payment or tender made or anything else done by *W* in or towards satisfaction of any liability of *H* in respect of rent, rates, mortgage payments or other outgoings affecting the dwelling-house shall be as good as if made or done by *H* (s. 1 (5)) ; but this is without prejudice to any claim of *W* against *H* to an interest in the house). To this is added the point that *W*'s occupation under the 1967 Act is to be treated as possession by *H* for the purposes of the Rent Acts (s. 1 (5) of the 1967 Act ; see also *Penn* v. *Dunn* [1970] 2 Q.B. 686, C.A.). Presumably *W*'s occupation under the 1967 Act, although not protecting her statutory rights as an overriding interest, would suffice by way of constructive occupation to protect the rights of *H* within s. 70 (1) (*g*) of the L.R.A. 1925, although this cannot be said to be clear (see *ante*, p. 188 *et seq.*). Lastly, under the present subheading it may be merely mentioned that a court granting a decree of divorce or nullity is given jurisdiction also to make an order dealing specifically with cases where the Rent Acts apply to the dwelling-house (s. 7 ; see also *Maynard* v. *Maynard* [1969] P. 88).

Duty of solicitor.—The Council of The Law Society have published a lengthy consideration of the question of when a solicitor acting in connection with the purchase of a dwelling-house should explain to W the nature of her statutory rights and when he should advise her to register the charge protecting these rights (*Law Society's Gazette*, vol. 65, pp. 3-5). First, the Council distinguish cases in which the solicitor clearly either is or is not acting for W (e.g., where she herself separately consults a solicitor) when the professional duty of giving advice will be equally clear. Then the Council deals with what will surely be the commonest case of a simple purchase of matrimonial home in H's name and the solicitor " at least feels that he should regard [W] as relying on him to look after her interests " (*loc. cit.*, p. 4). The Council take the view that : " In such a case, provided there is no reason for the solicitor to believe that the parties are otherwise than happily married it does not seem that, in practice, any serious problem need arise " (*ibid.*). The solicitor's duty then is to inform W of her statutory rights but it is *not* his duty to go on and advise her to register a land charge. In addition to this the Council point out that if in such a case the solicitor is aware of matrimonial troubles he runs the risk of suffering a conflict in the duty he owes to H and W respectively in advising not only as to the registration of a charge but also perhaps as to any steps which may be taken to avoid the registration (*loc. cit.*, pp. 4-5 ; see also H. W. A. Thirlway, *Solicitors' Journal*, vol. 112, p. 203).

Since this pronouncement by the Council of The Law Society, a judicial indication of a solicitor's duties in connection with the 1967 Act has been forthcoming. In *Miles* v. *Bull* [1969] 1 Q.B. 258, Megarry, J., observed that " the Act of 1967 contains nothing to require prior notice of any proposed transaction to be given to the occupying spouse . . . those advising such a spouse should, accordingly, consider whether a precautionary registration should be made as soon as the matrimonial affairs reach a stage in which there appears to be any risk of a dealing with the home to the disadvantage of the occupying spouse."

NEW TOWNS

Acquisition of land.—A development corporation established for the purposes of a new town may acquire land by agreement for the exercise of its functions with the consent of the Secretary of State for the Environment, or alternatively may be authorised to acquire land by compulsory purchase order submitted to and confirmed by him (New Towns Act, 1965, s. 7 (1)). The land in respect of which such powers may be exercised comprises (*a*) any land within the area of the new town, whether or not it is proposed to develop that particular land, (*b*) any land adjacent to that area which the corporation require for purposes connected with the development of the new town, and (*c*) any land, whether adjacent to that area or not, which it requires for the provision of services for the purpose of the new town (*ibid.*). The procedure for making and confirming a compulsory purchase order is that laid down in Sched. 3 to the New Towns Act, 1965 ; see further *post*, p. 1208. As to registration of compulsory purchase orders as local land charges, see *post*, p. 627 *et seq.*

Where any land within the area covered by a designation order as the site of a new town has not been acquired by the development corporation within seven years from the date on which that order became operative, any owner of that land may by notice in writing served on the corporation require it to purchase his interest in the land ; thereupon the corporation will be deemed to have been authorised to acquire that interest compulsorily and to have served notice to treat in respect thereof on the date of service of the purchase notice (New Towns Act, 1965, s. 11).

Disposal of land.—A development corporation may, subject to any directions by the Secretary of State, dispose of any land acquired by it to such persons, in such manner and subject to such covenants or conditions as it considers expedient for securing the development of the new town or for purposes connected therewith (New Towns Act, 1965, s. 18 (1)). However, the corporation has no power to dispose of land by way of gift, mortgage or charge, but otherwise the disposal may be in any manner whether by way of sale, exchange or lease, by the creation of any easement, right or privilege or otherwise, except that the transfer of the freehold in any land or the grant of a lease for a term exceeding ninety-nine years requires the consent of the Secretary of State (subs. (3) and (1), proviso, of s. 18). Power to override easements and other rights is conferred by s. 19 of the New Towns Act, 1965, and provisions is made by s. 23 for the extinguishment of public rights of way.

Commission for New Towns.—Where the Secretary of State is satisfied, after consulting the local authorities where the new town is situated, that the purposes for which the development corporation was established have been substantially achieved, he must by order direct that the property of the corporation should vest in the Commission for the New Towns on a specified date (New Towns Act, 1965, s. 41 (1)). On such transfer date, by virtue of the aforesaid order, and without further assurance, all the property, rights, liabilities and obligations of the development corporation (other than certain excepted property) vest in the Commission (*ibid.*, s. 41 (2) and Sched. 10, para. 1 (1)).

The Commission is a body corporate having perpetual succession and a common seal and incorporated for the purposes of taking over, holding, managing and turning to account the property previously vested in the corporation (*ibid.*, ss. 35 and 36).

The Commission has power, subject to the 1965 Act and to any direction by the Secretary of State, with a view to the better fulfilment of its statutory purposes by the improvement of any of its towns, or to the convenience or welfare of persons residing, working, or carrying on business there, *inter alia*, to acquire, hold, manage and turn to account land situated in or near the town, or any interest in or right over such land, and to dispose of any property for such purposes and in such manner as the Commission thinks fit (*ibid.*, s. 36 (3) ; disposal is subject to like restrictions as disposal by a development corporation : *ibid.*, s. 37 (3) ; see above).

PARTNERS

Partnership property.—Unless the partnership agreement provides to the contrary, all property and rights and interests in property originally brought in as capital of the partnership or acquired, whether by purchase or otherwise, on account of the firm or for the purposes and in the course of the partnership business, is partnership property (Partnership Act, 1890, s. 20 (1)). Further, unless the contrary intention appears, property bought with money belonging to the firm is deemed to have been bought on account of the firm (*ibid.*, s. 21). Also the presumption appears to be that land occupied by partners is partnership property although this does not follow as a matter of law (*Davies* v. *Davies* [1894] 1 Ch. 393). Partnership property must be held and applied by the partners exclusively for the purposes of the partnership and in accordance with the partnership agreement (*ibid.*, s. 20 (1)). In addition, it will be recalled that in equity where partners acquire property they are presumed to hold it as beneficial tenants in common (*Lake* v. *Craddock* (1732), 3 P. Wms. 158). This presumption may arise even though the property was not purchased but was devised to persons who used it for trade (*Jackson* v. *Jackson* (1804), 9 Ves. 591 ; *Morris* v. *Barret* (1829), 3 Y. & J. 384).

Title to partnership land.—On a sale before 1926, if the purchaser had notice that the land was partnership land, he was bound to ensure that all persons interested in equity under the partnership agreement joined in the conveyance to him. See Williams on Vendor and Purchaser, 4th ed., vol. I, p. 500. In order to avoid difficulties caused by this rule, land was often conveyed to partners on an express trust for sale and, if this had been done, a good title could be obtained from the trustees without the concurrence of the persons entitled in equity. Consequently, where freehold or leasehold property formed part of partnership property on 31st December, 1925, it may have been conveyed to the partners as joint tenants upon an express trust for sale, as part of their partnership property, or merely as part of their partnership property, without any express trust for sale. In the latter case, however, the legal estate would nonetheless be held by the partners on an *implied* trust for sale (*Re Bourne* [1906] 2 Ch. 427 ; Partnership Act, 1890, ss. 20 (2) and 22). Accordingly, in either case, after 31st December, 1925, the legal estate would remain vested in the partners as trustees, either on the express trust for sale or upon the statutory trusts (L.P.A. 1925, Sched. 1, Pt. IV, para. 1 (1) ; *Re Fuller's Contract* [1933] Ch. 652 ; also *Elias* v. *Mitchell* [1972] 2 W.L.R. 740). Purchasers, therefore, are no more concerned with the equitable position than on purchase from other trustees for sale.

Since 1925 it has been the practice to convey land to not more than four persons (usually the partners themselves) as joint tenants on trust to sell and to hold the proceeds as part of the partnership property. Even if there is no express trust for sale in a conveyance to partners, whether the conveyance is expressed to be made to them as joint tenants or as part of the partnership property, there will be a trust for sale implied by law (L.P.A. 1925, ss. 34 (1), (2), 36 (1) ; *Re Bourne* [1906] 2 Ch. 427). The point sometimes arises whether a surviving partner can make a good title to land. Suppose there were three partners originally, say, *A*, *B* and *C*. On the death of *A* the legal estate would vest in *B* and *C*, and on the death of *B* it would vest in *C*. As *C* would hold on either the express trust for sale, if there was one, or, if not, on the statutory trusts, there are two ways in which the conveyance could be made : (i) to appoint another trustee and then both convey ; or (ii) for the surviving partner to convey as beneficial owner, the personal representatives of *A* and *B* joining in to release the land from their claims as representing the estates of *A* and *B*. However, it would appear clear that (i) is the more proper way, since any stipulation in a contract for sale requiring the purchaser to accept way (ii) would be void (L.P.A. 1925, s. 42 (1)).

Mortgages of partnership land.—It is provided by s. 16 of the T.A. 1925 that where trustees are authorised by the instrument, if any, creating the trust, *or by law* to pay or apply capital money subject to the trust for any purpose or in any manner, they are to have and are to be deemed always to have had power to raise the money required by sale, conversion, calling in or mortgage of all or any part of the trust property for the time being in possession. The section applies notwithstanding anything to the contrary contained in the instrument, if any, creating the trust. Partners have *by law* an implied power to mortgage the assets of the partnership for purposes of the partnership and to give a receipt (*Re Bourne* [1906] 2 Ch. 427).

Section 17 of the same Act provides that no purchaser or mortgagee paying or advancing money on a sale or mortgage purporting to be made under any trust or power vested in trustees shall be concerned to see that such money is wanted, or that no more than is wanted is raised, or otherwise as to the application thereof.

Partners have also power to mortgage partnership land as having the powers of a tenant for life under s. 28 (1) of the L.P.A. 1925, which provides that trustees for sale shall in relation to land have all the powers of a tenant for life, and the trustees of a settlement under the S.L.A. 1925. These powers are contained in s. 71 of the S.L.A. 1925 but are limited to the purposes therein mentioned.

It is better, however, to insert in a conveyance to partners an express power to mortgage, in particular because the statutory powers do not include raising the initial purchase price of property to be acquired. But in the majority of cases the partner trustees will be also the actual beneficial owners, that is, the persons entitled to the proceeds of sale of the land under the express or implied trust for sale. In that case they can as absolute owners mortgage the land in any way they think fit. The mortgage should recite the fact that they are beneficially entitled.

Parol evidence to identify partners.—Parol evidence is admissible to show who constituted a firm at any particular date (*Carruthers* v. *Sheddon* (1815), 6 Taunt. 14). Freehold property was purchased out of partnership assets and conveyed to " William Wray," under which name several persons carried on the partnership business, and it was held that the deed passed the legal estate to all the partners constituting the firm (*Wray* v. *Wray* [1905] 2 Ch. 349).

Conveyance by a person to himself jointly with another person.— In conveyances made after 12th August, 1859, leasehold property, and, in conveyances made after 31st December, 1881, freehold land may be conveyed by a person to himself jointly with another person by the like means by which it might be conveyed by him to another person (L.P.A. 1925, s. 72 (1), replacing s. 21 of the Law of Property Amendment Act, 1859 ; and s. 72 (2) of L.P.A. 1925, replacing s. 50 of the Conveyancing Act, 1881). These subsections are useful when a partner wishes to convey his own property to himself and a co-partner ; also in the case where a surviving partner (not beneficially entitled to the whole of the property) wishes to appoint another trustee for sale to enable the property to be dealt with, for the appointment operates as a conveyance by himself to himself and another although it contains no vesting declaration (T.A. 1925, s. 40).

Section 72 (3) provides that after 1925 " a person may convey land to or vest land in himself," while subsection (4) of s. 72 also provides that two or more persons (whether or not being trustees) may convey, and are to be deemed always to have been capable of conveying, any property vested in them to any one or more of themselves in like manner as they could have conveyed such property to a third party ; provided that if the persons in whose favour the conveyance is made are, by reason of any fiduciary relationship or otherwise, precluded from validly carrying out the transaction, the conveyance will be liable to be set aside. On the winding up of a partnership it is often desired to divide up the properties forming part of the partnership assets, and this subsection enables this to be done. Before 1926 the transaction would have been carried out by a conveyance to a grantee to uses, but as the Statute of Uses has been repealed, it became necessary to make this provision.

It is likely that such conveyances will contain covenants. Before 1926 a covenant by one person with himself and another or others, to be good, should have been made with the " other " or " others " only. This point was not always appreciated, with the consequence that at the end of 1925 many apparent covenants were void. The principle equally applied in the case of covenants for title *implied* by the use of such words as " beneficial owner." See such cases as *Napier* v. *Williams* [1911] 1 Ch. 361 ; *Boyce* v. *Edbrooke* [1903] 1 Ch. 836 ; and *Ellis* v. *Kerr* [1910] 1 Ch. 529. This difficulty was overcome by s. 82 of the L.P.A. 1925, which enacts that any covenant, whether express or implied, or agreement entered into by a person with himself and one or more other persons, will be construed and be capable of being enforced in like manner as if the covenant or agreement had been entered into with the other person or persons alone. The section is retrospective. See further at pp. 550–551.

Nevertheless, one person may not grant a lease to himself nor may two or more persons (for example, partners) grant a lease to all of themselves (*Rye* v. *Rye* [1962] A.C. 496 ; *post*, p. 805).

PERSONAL REPRESENTATIVES

A. APPOINTMENT AND DEVOLUTION OF OFFICE

Dealing with property without representation.—It is often perfectly in order to administer a small estate without taking out representation. Certain enactments (specified in Sched. 1 to the Administration of Estates (Small Payments) Act, 1965), such as the Navy and Marines (Property of Deceased) Act, 1865, ss. 5, 6 and 8, the Friendly Societies Act, 1896, s. 58, the Local Government Superannuation Act, 1953, s. 25, the Building Societies Act, 1962, s. 46 (1), and the Industrial and Provident Societies Act, 1965, s. 25, authorise disposal of property on death without probate or other proof of title to persons appearing to be beneficially entitled, relatives or certain other persons, subject to a limit of £500 (*ibid.*, ss. 1 and 3). Other enactments (listed in Sched. 2 to that Act) such as the Trade Union Act Amendment Act, 1876, s. 10, the Friendly Societies Act, 1896, ss. 56 and 57, the Trustee Savings Banks Regulations, 1929, and the Industrial and Provident Societies Act, 1965, s. 23 (3) (*c*), enable a person by nomination to dispose of property on his death up to a limit of £500 (Administration of Estates (Small Payments) Act, 1965, s. 2). See also ss. 65 and 66 of the Merchant Shipping Act, 1894, and s. 9 of the National Savings Bank Act, 1971.

Certain local Acts also enable property to be disposed of on death without a grant of representation. The Administration of Estates (Small Payments) Order, 1967, makes amendments and repeals to such Acts and raises the limit of value of the property to £500.

In other cases, the strict consequence of taking any step towards the administration of a deceased's estate without taking out representation is to

incur liability as an executor *de son tort* (*New York Breweries Co.* v. *A.-G.*
[1899] A.C. 62 ; A.E.A. 1925, ss. 28 and 55 (1) (xi)). Of course, if the estate
duty minimum principal value is not exceeded and only proper payments are
made, such liability is by no means necessarily a serious matter (see s. 28 (*b*)
of the A.E.A. 1925 ; also *In the Estate of Biggs* [1966] P. 118). It is true that
a penalty of £100 would become exigible under the Stamp Act, 1815, s. 37,
but the alternative penalty, which, if any, appears to be exacted in practice,
under the Customs and Inland Revenue Act, 1881, s. 40, would not be relevant
unless estate duty were in fact chargeable. However, it may be noted that
the rule prohibiting a personal representative from purchasing any assets of
the estate applies in general to a non-proving executor who has done acts
of administration (see *Holder* v. *Holder* [1968] Ch. 353, where in special
circumstances the rule was not applied). Further, such an executor, having
intermeddled with the deceased's estate, cannot renounce probate, but it
does not follow that he will always be compelled to take a grant : the court
has jurisdiction to pass over even an intermeddling executor and direct the
grant of letters of administration (*In the Estate of Biggs, ante*).

Who can be executor.—Anybody duly appointed can be an executor,
including a corporation sole or aggregate, except an infant during infancy or
a person suffering from mental disorder (see Non-Contentious Probate Rules,
1954, rr. 31–36). If a person appointed executor should become bankrupt
before the death of the testator, a receiver would be appointed, as it would
be assumed that if the testator had known that such person had become
bankrupt he would have appointed some other person (*Bowen* v. *Phillips*
[1897] 1 Ch. 174). Where there is a solvent executor willing to act, the court
will restrain the bankrupt executor from acting, but will not appoint a
receiver (*ibid.*). The court has also power under the Judicial Trustees Act,
1896, to remove a trustee in a suitable case, and appoint a judicial trustee in
his place. Under s. 1 (2) of this Act *an executor* is "a trustee," and the
administration of the property of a deceased person is a "trust" (*Re Ratcliff*
[1898] 2 Ch. 352). See also Public Trustee Act, 1906, ss. 3 and 6, as to
transferring estates to the Public Trustee, after grant of probate.

The practicability of appointing as executors (and trustees) the partners
of a firm of solicitors as at the date of the testator's death has been upheld
in *Re Horgan* [1971] P. 50, in which case Latey, J., expressed approval of
a clause to achieve such an appointment suggested by Mr. R. T. Oerton
(see *Law Society's Gazette*, vol. 64, pp. 244 and 343 ; also *Law Society's
Gazette*, vol. 67, pp. 3, 46 and especially 340, where further drafting improvements are proposed).

Appointment of executor.—Even if a person has not been expressly
appointed as executor, he will be held to be executor "according to the tenor"
of the will if that appears to have been the testator's intention. Thus trustees
nominated to carry out the will have been held to be executors according to
the tenor (*In the Goods of Russell* [1892] P. 380).

The Judicature Act, 1925, s. 160 (2), provides that if there is only one
personal representative (not being a trust corporation), then, during the
minority of a beneficiary or the subsistence of a life interest and until the
estate is fully administered, the court may, on the application of any person
interested or of the guardian, committee or receiver of any such person,
appoint one or more personal representatives in addition to the original
personal representative. Therefore, it will be generally wise to appoint two

executors to save expense in the future. But, should only one executor be appointed, or should there be only one surviving executor, he will have full power to act until another executor or executors has or have been appointed under the above section.

If the testator is tenant for life of settled land, which will continue to be settled after his death, it will be as well that he should appoint the trustees of the settlement to be special executors as regards such settled land. See *post*, p. 710. It is not absolutely necessary that he should do this, for if he should not do so he will be *deemed* to have so appointed them. The advantage is that it will draw the attention of the solicitor who will be acting at the death to the fact that there is settled land.

There is a tendency to confuse the capacities of executor and trustee, no doubt because the same persons are usually both executors and trustees. It is always necessary to have an executor (or administrator) to administer an estate, but there is no need to appoint trustees unless some form of trust is constituted. The distinction between the two capacities is important because there must be at least two individual trustees for sale to give a good receipt for capital (L.P.A. 1925, s. 27 (1)), but this does not affect the right of a sole executor to give a good receipt (*ibid.*). Further, the rules as to assents (*post*, p. 409) are sometimes difficult to apply unless the distinction is kept in mind.

Priority of right to probate and administration with the will annexed. —It is provided by r. 19 of the Non-Contentious Probate Rules, 1954, that where the deceased died on or after 1st January, 1926, the priority of right to a grant of probate or administration with the will annexed is as follows :—

(1) Executors.

(2) Residuary legatees or devisees in trust.

(3) Residuary legatees or devisees for life.

(4) Ultimate residuary legatees or devisees, or, where the residue is not wholly disposed of, the persons entitled upon an intestacy (including the Treasury Solicitor when claiming *bona vacantia* on behalf of the Crown).

(5) The legal personal representatives of persons indicated in (4).

(6) Legatees or devisees, or creditors.

(7) Contingent residuary or specific legatees or devisees, or persons, having no interest in the estate, who would have been entitled to a grant had the deceased died wholly intestate.

It must be noted that a grant of administration with the will annexed may be made even if executors were appointed by the will, for instance, if they have died without proving the will, or if they renounce, or if a last surviving executor who has proved dies intestate without having completed the administration of the estate.

Priority of right to administration.—It is provided by r. 21 of the Non-Contentious Probate Rules, 1954, that where the deceased died on or after 1st January, 1926, *wholly* intestate, the priority of right to a grant of administration is as follows :—

(1) Surviving spouse.

13

(2) Children, or the issue of a child who has died during the lifetime of the deceased.

(3) Father or mother.

(4) Brothers and sisters of the whole blood, or the issue of a deceased brother or sister of the whole blood.

The Non-Contentious Probate (Amendment) Rules, 1969, made amendments to the 1954 Rules consequential upon the provisions of s. 14 of the Family Law Reform Act, 1969. Rule 21 of the 1954 Rules as amended confers upon illegitimate children and their parents the same priorities for the purposes of grants of administration as are enjoyed by legitimate children and their parents. Further the Non-Contentious Probate (Amendment) Rules, 1971, applied the provisions of the Adoption Act, 1958, to the determination of entitlement to a grant just as they apply to the devolution of property on intestacy.

If no person in any of classes (2) to (4) survived, then on death of a person after 1952 wholly intestate without leaving a surviving spouse the priority of right to a grant is as follows :—

(5) Brothers and sisters of the half blood, or the issue of deceased brothers and sisters of the half blood.

(6) Grandparents.

(7) Uncles and aunts of the whole blood, or the issue of deceased uncles and aunts of the whole blood.

(8) Uncles and aunts of the half blood, or the issue of deceased uncles and aunts of the half blood.

In default of any person having a beneficial interest, the Treasury Solicitor is entitled to a grant if he claims *bona vacantia* on behalf of the Crown (*ibid.*, r. 21 (3)). Further, if all the persons nominated have been cleared off a grant may be made to a creditor (*ibid.*, r. 21 (4)).

The personal representative of a person in any of the eight classes mentioned has the same right as the person he represents, but (i) unless the registrar directs otherwise a grant is made to a living person in preference to the representatives of a deceased person entitled in the same degree ; (ii) persons in classes (2) to (8) are preferred to the representatives of a spouse who has died without taking a beneficial interest in the whole estate (*ibid.*, rr. 21 (5), 25 (3)).

Where several persons are equally entitled to a grant it may be made to the first applicant or applicants, without notice to the others ; a dispute is brought by summons before a registrar of the principal registry (*ibid.*, r. 25 (1), (2)).

Number of personal representatives.—Probate or administration will not be granted to more than four persons in respect of the same property (Judicature Act, 1925, s. 160 (1)). For instance, where a testator appointed four general executors, and a fifth person as literary executor, in respect of certain papers, the court refused to grant probate save and except the papers to the four on the ground that one of the five must renounce (*In the Estate of Holland* [1936] 3 All E.R. 13).

Where there is a minority or if a life interest arises under a will (for instance, where no executor is appointed) or intestacy, administration will not be granted to less than two individuals or to a trust corporation, with or without an individual (Judicature Act, 1925, s. 160 (1)). But this subsection must be read with s. 162 (1) of the same Act (as amended by s. 9 of the Administration of Justice Act, 1928), which provides as follows :—

" 162.—(1) In granting administration the High Court shall have regard to the rights of all persons interested in the estate of the deceased person or the proceeds of sale thereof, and, in particular, administration with the will annexed may be granted to a devisee or legatee, and in regard to land settled previously to the death of the deceased and not by his will, may be granted to the trustees of the settlement, and any such administration may be limited in any way the court thinks fit :

Provided that—

(a) Where the deceased died wholly intestate as to his estate, administration shall be granted to some one or more persons interested in the residuary estate of the deceased, if they make an application for the purpose, and as regards lands settled previously to the death of the deceased, be granted to the trustees, if any, of the settlement if willing to act ; and

(b) If, by reason of the insolvency of the estate of the deceased or of any other *special circumstances*, it appears to the court to be necessary or expedient to appoint as administrator some person other than the person who, but for this provision, would by law have been entitled to the grant of administration, the court may in its discretion, notwithstanding anything in this Act, appoint as administrator such person as it thinks expedient, and any administration granted under this provision may be limited in any way the court thinks fit."

" *special circumstances.*"—In *In the Goods of Edwards-Taylor* [1951] P. 24, Willmer, J., said he was attracted to the contention that these words relate only to circumstances in connection with the estate itself or the administration of the estate. See also *In the Estate of Biggs* [1966] P. 118, where Rees, J., exercising his jurisdiction under the section took into account the lack of competency and willingness to act of the person primarily entitled ; and *Re Newsham* [1967] P. 230, where the deceased's widow had a claim in respect of personal injuries against his estate and under a policy of insurance so that her position might be prejudiced if she were appointed administrator.

In *Re S (deceased)* [1968] P. 302, the person appointed a sole executrix and beneficiary had been convicted of manslaughter of the deceased and sentenced to life imprisonment ; she was passed over, and letters of administration with the will annexed granted to those entitled on intestacy, under s. 162 (1).

For the purposes of s. 162 (1) a former wife or husband by or on whose behalf an application for maintenance under the Matrimonial Causes Act, 1965, s. 26, is proposed to be made is deemed to be a person interested in the estate (*ibid.*, ss. 25 (4), 28 (2)).

Section 160 (1), *ante*, does not prevent probate being granted to a single *executor*, nor does it prevent a grant of administration *pendente lite* to a sole administrator (*Re Lindley* [1953] P. 213). But it is provided by s. 160 (2) of the same Act that where there is only one personal representative, that is, either executor or administrator (not being a trust corporation), during the minority of a beneficiary, or the subsistence of a life interest, and until the estate is fully administered, the court may, on the application of any person interested or of the guardian or receiver of any such person, appoint one or more personal representatives in addition to the original personal representative. Section 160 (2) is not limited to cases of dishonesty or incompetence and the jurisdiction may be exercised where the court considers the appointment of an additional representative to be in the interests of the beneficiaries. See the unreported case of *Re Mears*, explained by Mr. Hubert A. Rose in the *Law Journal*, vol. 83, p. 319. It should be noted that unless an application is made for appointment of an additional representative a sole or last surviving personal representative can give a good title to freeholds even if there is a minority or life interest.

The proviso to the Judicature Act, 1925, s. 162, deals with the class of persons who are suitable for appointment as administrators and not with the number of such persons. Consequently, it does not alter the rule in s. 160 (1) that, where there is a life interest, administration must not be granted to less than two individuals (*Re Hall* [1950] P. 156).

Power to grant representation of real and personal estate separately. —It is provided by s. 155 (1) of the Judicature Act, 1925, that probate or administration in respect of the real estate of a deceased person, or any part thereof, may be granted either separately or together with probate or administration of his personal estate, and may also be granted in respect of real estate only where there is no personal estate, or in respect of a trust estate only ; and a grant of administration to real estate may be limited in any way the court thinks proper. But where the estate of the deceased is known to be insolvent, the grant of representation to the estate will not be severed except as regards a trust estate (*ibid.*).

Devolution of property on death before 1926.—On the death of a person after 31st December, 1897, and before 1926, by virtue of ss. 1 and 2 of the Land Transfer Act, 1897, the legal and equitable estates in his freehold property, and the equitable estate in his lands of copyhold or customary tenure, that is, in those to which he had not been admitted tenant on the court rolls (*Re Somerville and Turner's Contract* [1903] 2 Ch. 583), and any real estate over which he had, and exercised, a power of appointment by will, passed to his executor, if he made a will (and before probate : *Pemberton* v. *Chapman* (1857), 26 L.J.Q.B. 117), or, if he died intestate, to his heir-at-law, until administration was granted (*John* v. *John* [1898] 2 Ch. 573). On administration being granted, the estate passed from the heir to the administrator (*Re Griggs ; ex parte London School Board* [1914] 2 Ch. 547). See further, *ante*, p. 328.

Estates tail did not pass to the personal representatives because they could not be disposed of by the will of the testator, but passed under the entail.

Leaseholds passed to executors by the general law. On intestacy they vested in the President of the Probate Division of the High Court of Justice (Court of Probate Act, 1858, s. 19) and, on administration being granted, they vested in the administrator. A sale made by the person who afterwards became administrator, before he actually obtained the grant, would, if for the benefit of the estate, have been upheld, and the administration construed to have operated retrospectively as from the date of the death (*In the Goods of Pryse* [1904] P. 301).

Freehold trust and mortgage estates vested in any person solely became vested in his personal representative(s) notwithstanding any testamentary disposition, in like manner as if the same were a chattel real (Conveyancing Act, 1881, s. 30).

Where the deceased died before 1926, one of two or more executors or administrators can give a good title to personalty, including leaseholds, and to freeholds held on trust or by way of mortgage (Conveyancing Act, 1881, s. 30 ; *Jacomb* v. *Harwood* (1751), 2 Ves. Sen. 265), but all personal representatives, other than executors who did not prove, must join in to convey other realty (Land Transfer Act, 1897, s. 2 (2) ; Conveyancing Act, 1911, s. 12).

A personal representative of a sole or last surviving trustee was able (in the absence of any direction to the contrary and except as to certain copyholds) to exercise powers given to that trustee in the case of a trust constituted after 1881 (Conveyancing Act, 1911, s. 8 (1)).

Devolution of property on death after 1925.—Where the deceased has left a will, the legal estate in his own property passes to his general executors immediately on his death (A.E.A. 1925, ss. 1 and 3). Where there is an intestacy it passes to the President of the Family Division of the High Court (*ibid.*, ss. 9 and 55 (1) (*xv*) as amended by Administration of Justice Act, 1970, s. 1, Sched. 2, para. 5) ; on administration being granted, the estate then passes to the administrators (*ibid.*, s. 9).

The same rule applies to all freehold and leasehold land held by the deceased in trust or by way of mortgage or security, and also to any interest in land passing under any gift contained in his will which operates as an appointment under a general power to appoint by will, or operates under the testamentary power conferred by s. 176 of the L.P.A. 1925 (as to which, see *post*, pp. 441–442) to dispose of an entailed interest (A.E.A. 1925, ss. 1 and 3).

It is often necessary to serve a notice to quit on personal representatives, for instance where the deceased held premises on a weekly tenancy. If the deceased left a will, the notice should be served on the executors. If he died intestate and no grant of representation has been taken out, then the tenancy, even though only a weekly one, vests in the President. A notice can be served on the President by sending it by post to him c/o the Treasury Solicitor, 3 Central Buildings, Matthew Parker Street, London, S.W.1 (Practice Direction [1965] 1 W.L.R. 1237) ; see further, *post*, p. 837.

A conveyance of " real estate " (which includes leaseholds ; see s. 3 (1) (i) below) cannot be made, if the deceased died after 1925, without the concurrence of all the personal representatives, or an order of the court, except that executors who have not proved need not join in even if power has been reserved for them to prove, and that special representatives for settled land are not concerned with other estate, and *vice versa* (A.E.A. 1925, ss. 2 (2), 24).

The sections may now be considered in more detail. Section 1 (1) of the A.E.A. 1925 provides that *real estate* to which a deceased person was entitled for an interest not *ceasing on his death* is, notwithstanding any testamentary disposition thereof, to devolve from time to time on the personal representative of the deceased, in like manner as before 1926 chattels real devolved on a personal representative.

" *Real estate* " is defined by the A.E.A. 1925, s. 3, to mean :—

" (i) Chattels real, and land in possession, remainder, or reversion, and every interest in or over land to which a deceased person was entitled at the time of his death ; and,

(ii) Real estate held on trust (including settled land) or by way of mortgage or security, but not money to arise under a trust for sale of land, nor money secured or charged on land."

Note that " money to arise under a trust for sale of land," and " money secured or charged on land," passes to the executor by the ordinary law. The exception in s. 3, above, only means that the words " real estate " do not include them.

" *ceasing on his death.*"—This refers to any interest which the deceased may in his lifetime have held with others as joint tenants. In such a case his interest would, of course, pass to the surviving joint tenants. So, if the deceased did not devise or bequeath any entailed interest held by him in possession, the interest would pass under the entail and would be " an interest ceasing on his death " and would not pass to his personal representatives. As to the power under the L.P.A. 1925, s. 176, to devise or bequeath entailed property, see *post*, pp. 441–442.

It must be noted that the definition of " real estate " includes settled land. As to the vesting of land, which remains settled land, in special personal representatives, see *post*, p. 710. Section 55 (1) (xi) of the A.E.A. 1925 defines " executor " as including a person deemed to be appointed executor as respects settled land.

It will be seen, therefore, that the general personal representatives have complete control of the estate so long as they require such control for the purposes of administration, and a testator has no power to pass the legal estate to, or to create a legal estate in favour of, a beneficiary, by his will. Any interests devised or bequeathed take effect as equitable interests ; only where the subject of the purchase is this equitable interest is the purchaser entitled to an abstract of the will. See *ante*, p. 116.

Registered titles.—" Although the legal estate in registered property is at all times deemed to be vested in the registered proprietor, it is obvious that when he dies the legal estate can no more remain vested in him than it can be *in nubibus*. Nor, of course, can the register be altered as he expires. Thus, as the Land Registration Acts say nothing about what happens on the death of a proprietor, it may be assumed that the general law applies and that the property of a testator vests in his executor and that of an intestate in the President of the Family Division " (Ruoff and Roper, Registered Conveyancing, 3rd ed., p. 627). Accordingly, on the death of the sole proprietor, or the survivor of joint proprietors, of any registered land or charge, his personal representative is entitled to be registered as proprietor with the addition of the words " executor (or administrator) of (name) deceased " (L.R.A. 1925, s. 41 (1) ; L.R.R. 1925, r. 168 (1)). On the death of a person registered in this way as a personal representative, his personal representative will not be entitled to be registered unless there is a proper chain of representation (i.e., under A.E.A. 1925, s. 7, below).

In the case of land settled previously to the death of the proprietor which remains settled land, the special personal representatives are entitled to be registered (L.R.R. 1925, r. 168 (2)).

It is not essential, however, that the personal representative should be registered as proprietor, as he may transfer the registered land or charge or dispose of it by way or assent or appropriation or vesting assent, without being himself registered (L.R.A. 1925, s. 37 (1) ; L.R.R. 1925, r. 170 (1)).

On the death of one of two or more joint proprietors the registrar will remove his name from the register on proof of death (L.R.R. 1925, r. 172). If any restriction was entered it will remain unless application is made for its removal. This can be done by letter accompanied by evidence of the equitable title showing that the survivor of the joint tenants can give a good receipt for capital money.

Devolution of office of executor.—It is provided by s. 5 of the A.E.A. 1925 that where a person appointed executor by a will—

(i) survives the testator but dies without having taken out probate of the will ; or

(ii) is cited to take out probate of the will and does not appear to the citation ; or

(iii) renounces probate of the will ;

his rights in respect of the executorship wholly cease, and the representation to the testator and the administration of his real and personal estate devolve in like manner as if that person had not been appointed executor.

On the renunciation or death of an executor the right to representation passes to the surviving executors or executor who prove or proves. On the renunication or death of *all* the executors or of a sole executor, without proving the will, administration with the will annexed must be taken out to make a title (*Wyman* v. *Carter* (1871), L.R. 12 Eq. 309).

But if an executor has proved the will, and dies, his executor becomes executor of the former testator by representation (A.E.A. 1925, s. 7 (1) ; see below), and he cannot renounce (*Brooke* v. *Haymes* (1868), L.R. 6 Eq. 25).

A renunciation of probate by an executor is equivalent to a disclaimer of any interest conferred by the appointment of executor in the testator's estate, real or personal, and makes his concurrence in any disposition of the testator's real estate unnecessary (*Re Birchall* (1889), 40 Ch. D. 436). But when an executor is also the trustee of a will, renunciation of probate will not alone amount to a disclaimer of his office of trustee and the trusts attached to it (although it may be some evidence thereof) *unless* the administration of the estate and the carrying out of the trusts are so combined that one cannot be performed without the other (*Re Gordon* (1877), 6 Ch. D. 531). It has been held that where the trustees of a will are also executors, the taking out of probate will amount to an acceptance of the trust (*Mucklow* v. *Fuller* (1821), Jac. 198).

Renunciation of probate or administration may be retracted at any time on order of a registrar of the principal registry, but leave may be given to an executor to retract after a grant has been made to some other person entitled in a lower degree only in exceptional circumstances (Non-Contentious Probate Rules, 1954, r. 35 (3)). Where an executor who has renounced probate has been permitted to withdraw the renunciation and prove the will, the probate will take effect and be deemed always to have taken effect without prejudice to the previous acts and dealings of and notices to any other personal representative who had previously proved the will or taken out letters of administration, and a memorandum of the subsequent probate must be endorsed on the original probate or letters of administration.

Section 7 of the A.E.A. 1925 provides a " chain " of office of executor as follows :—

" 7.—(1) An executor of a sole or last surviving executor of a testator is the executor of that testator.

This provision shall not apply to an executor who does not prove the will of his testator, and, in the case of an executor who on his death leaves surviving him some other executor of his testator who afterwards proves the will of that testator, it shall cease to apply on such probate being granted.

(2) So long as the chain of such representation is unbroken, the last executor in the chain is the executor of every preceding testator.

(3) The chain of such representation is broken by—

(a) an intestacy ; or

(b) the failure of a testator to appoint an executor ; or

(c) the failure to obtain probate of a will ;

but is not broken by a temporary grant of administration if probate is subsequently granted."

Therefore, if two or more persons are appointed executors, and all prove the will, on the death of one or more of them, the office survives to the survivors or survivor, and on the death of the last survivor, or on the death of a sole executor after proving, to *his* executor (A.E.A. 1925, s. 7) ; but, if he died intestate, administration *de bonis non* would have to be taken out to the estate of the original testator. On the other hand, if such surviving or sole executor was also trustee *and had assented to the devise or bequest to himself* of such estate as trustee, the estate will have passed to the trustee's own personal representatives (whether executors or administrators) before 1926 under s. 30 of the Conveyancing Act, 1881 ; and after 1925 under the A.E.A. 1925, s. 3 (1) (ii). See also T.A. 1925, s. 18 (2), *post*, p. 768.

In the case of an executor who on his death leaves surviving him some other executor of his testator who afterwards proves the will of that testator, the provision that the executor of a sole or last surviving executor of a testator is the executor of that testator ceases to apply on such probate being granted (A.E.A. 1925, s. 7 (1), *ante*). If *A*, *B* and *C* are appointed executors, and *A* and *B* prove the will and power to prove is reserved to *C* : then if *A* dies first, and then *B* dies, having appointed an executor, and then *C*, to whom power has been reserved, takes out probate, the representation continues through him. But, if *C* dies *without proving*, the representation to the testator will be traced through *B*, the surviving acting executor (*In the Goods of Lorimer* (1862), 6 L.T. 612). If one of two executors proves, and the power is reserved to the other to prove, on the death of the proving executor, *his executor* becomes representative of the original testator until probate is granted to the non-proving executor and without the need for citation of the non-proving executor (A.E.A. 1925, s. 7 (1), *ante*). If, however, it is desired to obtain a grant of administration in respect of the estate of the original testator a citation must first be served on the non-proving executor (*Re Reid* [1896] P. 129).

The statement in s. 7 that the chain of representation is not broken by a temporary grant of administration, refers to cases where an executor may be disabled from acting on account of his suffering from mental disorder or having become afflicted with serious illness, in which cases, sometimes, a temporary grant with the will annexed is made (see *In the Goods of Frengley* [1915] 2 Ir. R. 1). Such temporary grants will not break the chain of executorship.

Death of administrator.—On the death of one administrator, the office survives to the remaining administrators or administrator, and on the death of the last surviving administrator or on the death of a sole administrator, an administrator *de bonis non* to the intestate's estate must be appointed. But if such last surviving administrator or sole administrator has completed the administration of the estate, and assented, he then holds the estate in a different capacity, that is, as trustee. The consequence of this is that the estate devolves as a trust estate, that is, it passes on his death to *his* personal representative or representatives and there is no need for a grant of administration *de bonis non* to the original estate. See next paragraph.

When personal representatives become trustees.—The office of personal representative (either executor or administrator) and the office of trustee have always been distinct offices. There is often confusion of language on this point, as wills normally appoint the same persons as executors and trustees. Danckwerts, J., in *Re Cockburn's Will Trusts* [1957] Ch. 438 said, at pp. 439, 440 : " Whether persons are executors or administrators, once they have completed the administration in due course, they become trustees holding for the beneficiaries either on an intestacy or under the terms of the will, and are bound to carry out the duties of trustees, though in the case of personal representatives they cannot be compelled to go on indefinitely acting as trustees, and are entitled to appoint new trustees in their place . . . if they do not appoint new trustees to proceed to execute the trusts of the will, they will become trustees in the full sense." (Contrast *Harvell* v. *Foster* [1954] 2 Q.B. 367 as to administrators where there are minority or life interests.) Personal representatives should not appoint new trustees until they have assented in writing in their own favour as trustees, although both assent and appointment can be combined in one document. If there is no written assent within s. 36 (4) of the A.E.A. 1925, it appears that the personal representatives continue to hold any legal estates in land as such, the appointment being ineffective to pass them under s. 40 (1) of the T.A. 1925 (*Re King's Will Trusts* [1964] Ch. 542 ; this decision can be criticised on the grounds mentioned *post*, p. 418).

The point is important because a sole or last surviving personal representative selling a legal estate in land under his statutory powers can give a good title, whereas a good receipt can be given only by at least two trustees or a trust corporation. It is also important if a sole or last surviving administrator dies. If he still holds land as such it will be necessary to take out a grant *de bonis non*, but if an effective assent has been made in his own favour, so that he holds as trustee, the legal estate will pass to his personal representatives (A.E.A. 1925, s. 3 (1) (ii)), who are given power to act in the trust by the T.A. 1925, s. 18 (2).

Section 33 (1) of the A.E.A. 1925, provides that, on the death of a person intestate as to any real or personal estate, such estate shall be held by his personal representatives upon trust for sale, but Romer, J., has held in *Re Yerburgh* [1928] W.N. 208, that this is subject to their rights and powers as personal representatives, that is, that this trust for sale only comes into operation when their duties of personal representatives have come to an end, and they have assented to themselves as trustees. As to the powers of personal representatives, see below.

Where a settlement is created by will *and there are no trustees for the purposes of the S.L.A.* 1925, of such settlement, or the trustees are not willing to act, then the general personal representatives of the deceased will, until other trustees

13A

are appointed, be by virtue of the S.L.A. 1925, the trustees of the settlement (S.L.A. 1925, s. 30 (3)). See further, *post*, p. 714. A direct gift to an infant by a will without the interposition of trustees is an example of the case where a settlement has been made by a will and there are no trustees under the S.L.A. 1925. See further *ante*, p. 343.

B. DUTIES AND POWERS

General rules.—The *duties* (as opposed to the powers) of personal representatives, hitherto largely dependent on common law and equity, have now been rendered statutory in extremely general terms. A new s. 25 of the A.E.A. 1925 has been substituted by s. 9 of the Administration of Estates Act, 1971, as follows :—

" 25. The personal representative of a deceased person shall be under a duty to—

(a) collect and get in the real and personal estate of the deceased and administer it according to law ;

(b) when required to do so by the court, exhibit on oath in the court a full inventory of the estate and when so required render an account of the administration of the estate to the court ;

(c) when required to do so by the High Court, deliver up the grant of probate or administration to that court."

As to *powers*, it is provided by s. 21 of the A.E.A. 1925 that—

" 21. Every person to whom *administration* of the real and personal estate of a deceased person is granted, shall, subject to the limitations contained in the grant, have the same rights and liabilities and be accountable in like manner *as if he were the executor* of the deceased."

Therefore, in the following notes no distinction will be made between executors and administrators. An executor can make a good title to freehold or leasehold property, although it be specifically devised or bequeathed (*Graham* v. *Drummond* [1896] 1 Ch. 968) ; unless, before 1926, he had done or allowed any act which amounted to an assent to the gift to the beneficiaries, or, after 1925, he had assented in writing, in either of which cases his power to sell would have ceased (*Stevenson* v. *Mayor of Liverpool* (1874), L.R. 10 Q.B. 81 ; *Wise* v. *Whitburn* [1924] 1 Ch. 460 ; A.E.A. 1925, s. 36). See further, p. 409 *et seq.*

Before 1926 one of two or more executors or administrators could assign leaseholds, but since 1925 all the proving executors, or all the administrators, must join in a conveyance of freeholds or an assignment of leaseholds, except under an order of court (A.E.A. 1925, s. 2 (2)).

Where probate is granted to one or some of two or more persons named as executors, whether or not power is reserved to the others or other to prove, all the powers which are by law conferred on the personal representative may be exercised by the proving executor or executors for the time being and shall be as effectual as if all the persons named as executors had concurred therein (*ibid.*, s. 8 (1)). Every person in the chain of representation to a testator (as to which, see *ante*, pp. 391–392) has the same rights in respect of the real and personal estate of that testator as the original executor would have had if living (*ibid.*, s. 7 (4)).

Date of operation of powers.—The date when executors and administrators respectively get their powers is not the same. The powers of an executor can be exercised before obtaining probate, as they are derived from the will and not from the probate; the probate is merely evidence of the will (*Pemberton* v. *Chapman* (1857), 26 L.J.Q.B. 117); but a purchaser cannot be compelled to pay his purchase-money until the executor has obtained probate, because until the evidence of title exists the executor cannot give a complete indemnity (*Mewton* v. *Metropolitan Railway Co.* (1861), 5 L.T. 542 ; *Re Stevens* [1897] 1 Ch. 422). But the rights and powers of an administrator are derived wholly from the letters of administration. On the grant of administration, however, the title of the administrator relates back to the date of death for purposes connected with the protection or preservation of the estate from wrongful injury in the interval (*In the Goods of Pryse* [1904] P. 301 ; *Long* v. *Burgess* [1950] 1 K.B. 115). This doctrine enables administrators to sue in respect of matters arising before the grant, but relation back does not take place for other purposes. For instance, a writ issued by a person as administrator, before a grant is obtained by him, is a nullity (*Ingall* v. *Moran* [1944] K.B. 160 ; *Hilton* v. *Sutton Steam Laundry* [1946] K.B. 56 ; *Burns* v. *Cambell* [1951] W.N. 582), and a notice to quit served on the President of, now, the Family Division before the date of the grant remains valid against the administrator (*Long* v. *Burgess*, *ante*). The same rules apply in the case of an administrator *cum testamento annexo* (*Boxall* v. *Boxall* (1884), 27 Ch. D. 220). Contrast *Stebbings* v. *Holst & Co.*, *Ltd.* [1953] 1 All E.R. 925 where a writ before grant issued as " widow and administratrix " was held valid as to the former capacity, ignoring the latter.

The result is that an intending administrator has no rights justifying him in entering into a contract of sale before he has obtained a grant. Although an executor may validly contract before obtaining probate he may in some cases have doubt whether he can obtain probate in time. If either decides to contract before obtaining a grant, but in due course is unable to make title, he may not be obliged to pay damages for reasons given *ante*, p. 383. Nevertheless it is wise to insert in the contract a clause such as that suggested in the *Conveyancer N.S.*, vol. 22, p. 84, making the contract conditional on the obtaining of a grant (which the vendor undertakes to endeavour to obtain) and enabling either party to rescind if the vendor fails to do so before the date fixed for completion.

Powers of management.—Section 39 of the A.E.A. 1925 is one of the most important of the sections in the Act, and is therefore given in full :—

" 39.—(1) In dealing with the real and personal estate of the deceased his personal representatives shall, for purposes of administration, or *during a minority* of any beneficiary or the subsistence of any life interest, or until the period of distribution arrives, have—

    (i) the same powers and discretions, including power to raise money by mortgage or charge (whether or not by deposit of documents), as a personal representative had before the commencement of this Act, with respect to personal estate vested in him, and such power of raising money by mortgage may in the case of land be exercised by way of legal mortgage ; and

    (ii) all the powers, discretions and duties conferred or imposed by law on *trustees holding land upon an effectual trust for sale* (including power to overreach equitable interests and powers as if the same affected the proceeds of sale) ; and

(iii) all the powers conferred by statute on trustees for sale, and so that every contract entered into by a personal representative shall be binding on and be enforceable against and by the personal representative for the time being of the deceased, and may be carried into effect, or be varied or rescinded by him, and, in the case of a contract entered into by a predecessor, as if it had been entered into by himself.

(2) Nothing in this section shall affect the right of any person to require an assent or conveyance to be made.

(3) This section applies whether the testator or intestate died before or after the commencement of this Act."

Despite some conflict of views, the position appears to be that personal representatives have these full powers under s. 39 so long only as they are acting as such. After they have completed the administration and assented in their own favour as trustees, they derive their powers from s. 28 of the L.P.A. 1925 to the exclusion of s. 39 of the A.E.A. 1925 (*Re Trollope's Will Trusts* [1927] 1 Ch. 596, 604, 605). Thus in *Re Yerburgh* [1928] W.N. 208, Romer, J., held that the trust for sale imposed on personal representatives by s. 33 of the A.E.A. 1925 on an intestacy operates subject entirely to the powers conferred on them for the purposes of administration by s. 39. As to the necessity for a formal assent in respect of a legal estate in land by personal representatives in their own favour as trustees see *Re King's Will Trusts* [1964] Ch. 542, *post*, p. 418.

In practice, the mere fact of completion of the administration is of little importance where a personal representative has not yet assented to the legal estate passing to himself as trustee or to a beneficiary, since a purchaser will not be concerned to inquire whether or not he is conveying for purposes of administration, and, under s. 36 (8) of the A.E.A. 1925, he will get a good title even if he has notice that all the debts, liabilities, funeral and testamentary or administration expenses, duties and legacies of the deceased have been discharged or provided for. And, by subs. (6) of the same section, recital in a conveyance by the personal representative that he has not given or made an assent or conveyance in respect of a legal estate affords some protection to the purchaser in the absence of an indorsement on the grant, see *post*, p. 415.

" *during a minority.*"—The reduction in the age of majority from twenty-one to eighteen does not affect the meaning of " minority " in s. 39 (1) of the A.E.A. 1925 where the beneficiary's interest arose under a will or codicil made before 1970 or on a death intestate before 1970 (Family Law Reform Act, 1969, Sched. 3, para. 6).

" *trustees holding land upon an effectual trust for sale.*"—There is considerable doubt as to the meaning of the word " effectual." Some writers have stated that it means a special trust for sale under the L.P.A. 1925, s. 2 (2), and, in consequence, that personal representatives can overreach certain equitable interests even if they arose in the testator's lifetime without the appointment of the representatives being approved by the court. This opinion was held by the late J. M. Lightwood (see, for instance, *Law Journal*, vol. 80, p. 396). The point is not of great importance as such overreaching powers are rarely of value. It would seem unreasonable that representatives should have such a power and, in the absence of authority, it is wise to assume that an ordinary trust for sale is meant. In any case the A.E.A. 1925, s. 39 (1) (ii), means that representatives have the powers of a tenant for life under the S.L.A. 1925 (L.P.A. 1925, s. 28).

Power of single personal representative to act.—A single personal representative, or the survivor of several representatives, has the same powers of disposition of real or personal estate as two or more (A.E.A. 1925, ss. 2 (1), 3 (1) (ii)). Further, s. 2 (2) provides that where probate is granted to one or some of two or more persons named as executors, whether or not power is reserved to the other or others to prove, any conveyance of the real estate (which includes leaseholds) may be made by the *proving executor* or executors for the time being without an order of the court, and will be as effectual as if all the persons named as executors had concurred therein. It is expressly provided by s. 27 (2) of the L.P.A. 1925, as amended by the Law of Property (Amendment) Act, 1926, that the provision contained therein that capital money must not be paid to less than two persons as trustees for sale, except where the trustee is a corporation, *is not to affect the right of a sole personal representative as such* to give valid receipts for or direct the application of the proceeds of sale or other capital money.

Purchase by personal representative or his wife.—A personal representative owes fiduciary obligations to the persons beneficially entitled and care should be taken not to allow him to purchase from himself, as such a transaction will be set aside by the court. This equitable rule applies also to a non-proving executor who has performed acts of administration disentitling him from renunciation (but compare *Holder* v. *Holder* [1968] Ch. 353, where there were special circumstances validating the transaction).

The above rule would *not*, however, appear to prevent even a sole personal representative exercising in his own favour powers of appropriation conferred *either* by s. 41 of the A.E.A. 1925 (which is " not . . . expressed to be subject to the equitable principle and there appears to be nothing so to limit the generality of its wording " ; *Conveyancer N.S.*, vol. 6, at p. 109) ; *or* by the general law and preserved by subs. (6) of s. 41 (for which there is direct authority in *Barclay* v. *Owen* (1889), 60 L.T. 220, 222 ; *Re Beverley* [1901] 1 Ch. 681 ; and *Re Bythway* (1911), 104 L.T. 411). However, this proposition has yet to be tested by the courts in the light of the decision that such an appropriation is in substance a sale and purchase (*Jopling* v. *I.R.C.* [1940] 2 K.B. 282). Further where a surviving spouse is *not* a sole personal representative it is expressly provided that the rule that a trustee may not be a purchaser of trust property does not prevent such spouse from " purchasing out of the estate of an intestate " an interest in the matrimonial home (Intestates' Estates Act, 1952, Sched. 2, para. 5 (1)). From this it might be inferred that the equitable rule does apply to prevent an appropriation being required in the case of a surviving spouse being the sole personal representative. But more probably the permissive provision is directed not to an ordinary appropriation under s. 41, but to the extension in favour of surviving spouses which allows an appropriation of the matrimonial home to be partly in return for a payment of money (*ibid.*, para. 5 (2)). See further *Solicitors' Journal*, vol. 107, pp. 503, 525.

In *Re Pennant's Will Trusts* [1970] Ch. 75 the testator's widow was one of the personal representatives and life tenant. The personal representatives sold to the life tenant at a valuation and it was held (i) that the transaction

was valid under the S.L.A. 1925, s. 68 (2), even though the parties did not
have this power in mind and (ii) the life tenant, being one of the trustees,
should be a conveying party.

Powers of personal representatives to mortgage.—Under s. 2 (1) of the
A.E.A. 1925, personal representatives have all such powers of dealing with the
estate as were before 1926 exercisable by them. They could, at common
law, unless the will peremptorily required an absolute sale, mortgage the assets
vested in them in order to raise any money required to pay debts (*Re Morgan*
(1881), 18 Ch. D. 93 ; *Re O'Donnell* [1905] 1 Ir. R. 406), or to pay administration expenses (*Re Whistler* (1887), 35 Ch. D. 561), or to facilitate the division
of the estate (*Re O'Donnell, ante*). See also *Earl Vane* v. *Rigden* (1870),
L.R. 5 Ch. 663, 670.

It is now provided by s. 39 (1) (i) of the A.E.A. 1925 that personal representatives shall, for purposes of administration, or during a minority of any
beneficiary or the subsistence of any life interest, or until the period of
distribution arrives, have power to raise money by mortgage or charge
(whether or not by deposit of documents) as a personal representative had
before 1926, with respect to personal estate vested in him, and that such
power of raising money by mortgage may, in the case of land, be exercised
by way of legal mortgage. The reason why power is specially given to personal
representatives to mortgage or charge by way of deposit of documents is that
trustees are not generally allowed to do so.

So, under s. 39 (1) (ii) and (iii) of the A.E.A. 1925, as read with the L.P.A.
1925, s. 28 as amended, personal representatives have all the powers of
trustees for sale, which include the powers of tenants for life and trustees of a
settlement under the S.L.A. 1925 and so include powers of mortgaging,
shifting incumbrances, and varying the terms of a mortgage deed, and
entering into a contract to mortgage which will bind their successors in title
(*post*, p. 747 *et seq.*). As to power of trustees to mortgage, see *post*, p. 780.

Personal representatives have power under s. 40 of the A.E.A. 1925 to raise
money for giving effect to beneficial interests. The section provides that for
giving effect to beneficial interests the personal representatives may limit or
demise land for a term of years absolute, with or without impeachment for
waste, to trustees on usual trusts for raising or securing any principal sum and
the interest thereon for which the land, or any part thereof, is liable, and may
limit or grant a rent-charge for giving effect to any annual or periodical sum
for which the land or the income thereof or any part thereof is liable. They
have also power to mortgage on any partition in order to raise money to
make the partition equal (L.P.A. 1925, s. 28 (3)). Similarly, under s. 48 (2)
of the A.E.A. 1925, as amended by the Intestates' Estates Act, 1952, they
have power to raise by mortgage certain sums payable to a surviving spouse
on intestacy.

Under s. 16 (3) of the L.P.A. 1925, personal representatives have also all the
powers which are by any statute conferred for raising death duties for which
they are accountable ; see the powers given by s. 9 of the F.A. 1894 and the
S.L.A. 1925, s. 71 (1) (i).

It was decided in *Thorne* v. *Thorne* [1893] 3 Ch. 196, however, that an
executor, unless he is expressly authorised by the will, is not entitled on
behalf of the estate to execute a mortgage in favour of a building society,
and any mortgage so given would not bind the estate so as to charge it with
the executor's liabilities as a shareholder. But if the advance was made in

good faith to executors in that capacity, and the mortgage was not merely a colourable device for securing an advance to the executors in their personal capacity, the mortgage would be good and would bind the estate to the extent of the money advanced and reasonable interest thereon.

As regards trustees (and therefore as regards personal representatives : A.E.A. 1925, s. 39 (1) (i)), it is provided by s. 17 of the T.A. 1925 that no mortgagee, paying or advancing money on a mortgage purporting to be made under any trust or power vested in trustees, shall be concerned to see that such money is wanted or that no more than is wanted is raised, or otherwise as to the application thereof. It is also provided by s. 110 (3) of the S.L.A. 1925 that a purchaser (which includes a mortgagee) of a legal estate in settled land from a personal representative shall be entitled to act on the assumption, if the capital money payable under the transaction is paid to a personal representative, that such personal representative is acting under his statutory or other powers and requires the money for purposes of administration.

The fact that a mortgagee may have notice that all the deceased's debts, liabilities, funeral and testamentary or administration expenses, duties and legacies have been paid will not invalidate any mortgage or make it incumbent on the mortgagee to inquire the purpose for which the personal representative is mortgaging (A.E.A. 1925, s. 36 (8)).

Powers of leasing.—Powers of leasing in general are discussed *post*, p. 822, but it is relevant to note here that personal representatives who hold a number of properties comprised in one lease often wish to sell the properties separately by means of underleases. In such cases it is often convenient to reserve an improved ground rent on the making of each underlease except the last ; in any case the last transaction should be carried out by an assignment of the lease, subject to, but with the benefit of, the underleases. It appears that such underleases can be regarded as conveyancing devices for carrying out what are, in substance, sales, and that the transactions are within the powers of personal representatives. There is a useful discussion of the matter in the *Law Journal*, vol. 100, p. 675, where *Re Judd* [1906] 1 Ch. 684, *Re Chaplin and Staffordshire Potteries Contract* [1922] 2 Ch. 824, *Re Webb* [1897] 1 Ch. 144, and A.E.A. 1925, s. 36 (7), are quoted in support of this view.

Power to carry on the business of the deceased.—The position of executors who carry on the business of their testator, notwithstanding that they do so under directions contained in the will, is not a very happy one, for they make themselves personally liable to the creditors even if they avowedly contract as representatives (*Liverpool Borough Bank* v. *Walker* (1859), 4 De G. & J. 24). In such cases they are entitled to be indemnified out of the assets in respect of liabilities properly incurred in carrying on the business (in priority to the claims of the creditors of the testator where they have carried on for such reasonable time as is necessary to sell the business as a going concern : *Dowse* v. *Gorton* [1891] A.C. 190, 199). Their right to indemnity includes interest at 4 per cent. where the executors have advanced money themselves to pay debts (*Re Bracey* [1936] W.N. 207).

Except for the purpose of winding-up or selling, an executor has no power, in the absence of a provision in the will enabling him to do so, to carry on a business (*Collinson* v. *Lister* (1855), 20 Beav. 356). Nevertheless, he may be bound to complete contracts entered into by the testator and it is his duty to do whatever may be required to preserve the business as an asset (*ibid.*; *Strickland* v. *Symons* (1884), 22 Ch. D. 666, 671). Even if he is authorised by the will to carry on a business he is not entitled to employ any of the testator's assets other than those in the business at the date of death and any directed by the will to be employed (*Re Hodson* (1818), 3 Madd. 138 ; *Cutbush* v. *Cutbush* (1839), 1 Beav. 184). Executors are not compelled to carry out directions to carry on a business, and an executor places himself in that position by his own choice, judging for himself whether it is safe to contract that sort of responsibility (*Ex parte Garland* (1804), 10 Ves. 110, 119).

In *Re Chancellor* (1884), 26 Ch. D. 42, a testator left his estate upon trust for sale with power to postpone, and until sale to pay the profits to his widow ; although the will contained no reference to his business it was held that the executors had power to carry it on (for nearly two years) with a view to its sale as a going concern. In *Re Crowther* [1895] 2 Ch. 56, the will contained an express reference to the testator's business and a general power to the executors to postpone sale " for such period as to them shall seem expedient," and it was held that there was an implied power to carry on the business until sale even for several years. But a general power to postpone the sale of the business, and to sell it with all convenient speed, will not authorise the business to be carried on for an indefinite time (*Re Smith* [1896] 1 Ch. 171). Further it must be noted that the power to carry on the business with a view to its winding-up or sale as a going concern does not make the business an authorised investment. In consequence, the rule in *Howe* v. *Lord Dartmouth* (1802), 7 Ves. 137, will be applicable where the business forms part of the residuary estate left to persons in succession unless expressly excluded (*Re Berry* [1962] Ch. 97, where a hotel business was sold one year after death having made a seasonal profit and a seasonal loss, but the life tenant was held entitled to a flat income of 4 per cent. of the proceeds of sale ; in *Re Chancellor*, above, payment of the profits to the widow was held justified by a direction in the will relating to the income of the estate pending sale).

The safest way, if there is a doubt as to the solvency of the business, is to get the consent of the creditors to carry it on. Even though directed by the will to continue the business, the executor's right to indemnity must be subject to the rights of creditors, unless the creditors have assented to the continuance of the business, in which case the executor is entitled to be indemnified in priority to their claims. But although the consent of a creditor has not been expressly obtained, if it could be proved that he had knowledge that the business was being carried on and had acquiesced in their doing so, the executors would have a right of indemnity out of the testator's estate as against such creditor (*Re Oxley* [1914] 1 Ch. 604 ; *Re East* [1914] W.N. 187) ; mere standing by with knowledge that the business is being carried on does not amount to acquiescence, however (*Re Oxley, ante*).

In view of the power to postpone the sale of the estate given by s. 33 of the A.E.A. 1925, it is thought clear that administrators would be justified in carrying on a business for the purpose of winding-up or sale as a going concern. Their right of indemnity would, however, extend only to assets employed in the business at the date of death.

It is often difficult to advise a testator as to the best thing to be done when he wants his business carried on. If it is his intention to give the business to a son or other relative, one way is to give the business directly to such son or relative subject to the debts, with power to the executors to make him a certain limited advance out of the general estate to enable him to carry on, such advance to be paid back as arranged, and to make such beneficiary a special executor of the business.

Where a testator appointed his partner in a business his executor, it was held that there was no objection to such surviving partner purchasing and taking over the share of the deceased partner, on the ground that the conflict of interest and duty had been brought about the by testator himself (*Hordern* v. *Hordern* [1910] A.C. 465). Where personal representatives continue in the place of the deceased as a partner, profits are regarded as being earned at the end of the customary accounting period and are not apportioned as between persons entitled under the deceased's will (*Re Robbins* [1941] Ch. 434).

Power to appropriate.—This power is given by s. 41 of the A.E.A. 1925, which applies whether the deceased died intestate or not (s. 41 (9)). It is often convenient to make an appropriation in satisfaction of the surviving spouse's statutory legacy. The personal representative is empowered to appropriate any part of the real or personal estate, including things in action, of the deceased, *other than property specifically devised or bequeathed* (where there is a will), in the actual condition or state of investment thereof at the time of appropriation in or towards satisfaction of any legacy bequeathed by the deceased, or of any other interest or share in his property, whether settled or not, *as to the personal representative may seem just and reasonable*, according to the respective rights of the persons interested in the property of the deceased (s. 41 (1)). The section also extends to property over which a testator exercises a general power of appointment, including the statutory power to dispose of entailed interests, and authorises the setting apart of a fund to answer an annuity by means of the income of that fund or otherwise (s. 41 (9)).

As to personal representatives exercising this power in respect of their own interests, see *ante*, p. 397.

When the proposed appropriation is to be made for the benefit of a person absolutely and beneficially entitled in possession, the consent of that person must be obtained (s. 41 (1), proviso (ii) (*a*)). If the share is settled, the consent of either the trustee (not being also the personal representative) or of the person entitled to the income is required (*ibid.*, proviso (ii) (*b*)). Where the person whose consent is required is an infant or is incapable by reason of mental disorder within the meaning of the Mental Health Act, 1959, of managing and administering his property and affairs the consent can be given on his behalf by his parents or parent, or by his guardian or receiver, or if, in the case of an infant, there is no guardian, then by the court on the application by his next friend (*ibid.*, proviso (ii)). Where no receiver is acting for a person suffering from mental disorder then, if the appropriation is of an investment authorised by law or by the will, if any, of the deceased, for the investment of money subject to the trust, no consent will be required on behalf of the said person (*ibid.*, proviso (iv) ; Mental Health Act, 1959, Sched. 7). If the person whose consent is necessary cannot be found or ascertained, no consent will be necessary, and, as regards any person who may become interested but who may not at the time of the appropriation be born, no consent will be necessary, except as regards settled shares, in which case it will only be necessary to get the consent of the trustees of the settlement, if the executors are not themselves the trustees (*ibid.*, proviso (iii)). If, independently of the personal representatives, there are no trustees and no person of full age and capacity entitled to income, then no consent will be required provided that the appropriation is of an authorised investment (*ibid.*, proviso (v)). But in making the appropriation the executors must have regard to the rights of such persons as cannot be found or may afterwards come into existence (s. 41 (5)).

For the purposes of such appropriation the personal representative may ascertain and fix the value of the respective parts of the real and personal estate and the liabilities of the deceased as he may think fit, and must for that purpose employ a duly qualified valuer in any case where such employment may be necessary ; and may make any conveyance or assent which may be requisite for giving effect to the appropriation (s. 41 (3)).

Although it is provided by s. 41 (2) that any property appropriated under the powers conferred shall afterwards be treated as an authorised investment, and may be retained or dealt with accordingly, personal representatives will be advised not to rely on this provision, for the whole tenor of the section is to put responsibility on them to look after the interests of all the parties. Consequently, where the property to be appropriated is land they should, in all cases, get a valuation, and, to be on the safe side, it would also be better not to agree to an appropriation unless it is a trustee's security, or such security is authorised by the terms of the will, when there is one. But as regards a purchaser from the person in whose favour the property has been appropriated, it is specially provided that the appropriation shall be deemed to have been made in accordance with the requirements of the section and after all requisite consents, if any, had been given (s. 41 (7)).

In addition, in exercising the power of appropriation, personal representatives should bear in mind that there will probably be deemed to have been a disposition of the appropriated assets for the purposes of capital gains tax (F.A. 1965, s. 25 (3) (8) ; and see *New Law Journal*, vol. 116, at p. 62 ; as to the advantages of appropriating where there are several life tenants, see [1965] B.T.R. 341 *et seq.*).

If it is wished that the trustees should have a power of appropriation, a special power for this purpose should be given by the will, as the statutory power of appropriation under s. 41, above, is only exercisable by personal representatives ; but trustees for sale have, in practice, a general power of appropriation. See *post*, p. 779.

Appropriation of matrimonial home.—Under the A.E.A. 1925, s. 41, personal representatives may, with certain consents, appropriate any part of the estate in or towards satisfaction of any interest or share in the property of the deceased. This power has often been used to appropriate the matrimonial home in satisfaction of the statutory legacy of a surviving spouse, but personal representatives cannot be compelled to exercise it. On death intestate after 1952 the I.E.A. 1952, Sched. 2, enables a surviving husband or wife to *require* an interest in a dwelling-house comprised in the residuary estate which was the " matrimonial home " to be appropriated in or towards satisfaction of any absolute interest of the surviving husband or wife in accordance with the A.E.A. 1925, s. 41. A house is treated as the " matrimonial home," and so the right is exercisable, if the surviving husband or wife was resident in the house at the time of the intestate's death, even if the intestate was not so resident. The right is not exercisable, however, in respect of a tenancy which would determine or could be determined by the landlord by notice within the period of two years from the death of the intestate.

By claiming this right instead of relying on the power of appropriation in the A.E.A. 1925, s. 41, stamp duty which would be payable on appropriation can be saved (compare *Jopling* v. *Inland Revenue Commissioners* [1940] 2 K.B. 282).

The " absolute interests " of the surviving spouse against which appropriation may be made are the statutory legacy of £15,000 or £40,000, as the case may be, the surviving spouse's absolute half interest in the balance where the intestate left no issue, and the capital value of a life interest which the surviving spouse had elected to have redeemed (I.E.A. 1952, Sched. 2, para. 1 (4)).

In making the appropriation the personal representatives must have regard to the requirements of the A.E.A. 1925, s. 41, as to valuation (*ante*, p. 402) ; appropriation may be partly in satisfaction of an interest in the estate of the intestate and partly in return for a payment of money by the surviving spouse (Sched. 2, para. 5 (2)).

Where part of a building was occupied as a separate dwelling-house, appropriation of that part may be claimed unless an interest in the whole of the building is comprised in the residuary estate, in which case the rule next stated will apply. Appropriation may be claimed only where the court so orders, on being satisfied that it is not likely to diminish the value of other assets or make them more difficult to dispose of, in the following cases, namely, where (*a*) the house forms part of a building and an interest in the whole is comprised in the residuary estate, or (*b*) the house is held with agricultural land an interest in which is comprised in the residuary estate, or (*c*) the whole or a part of the house was at the time of death used as an hotel or lodging house, or (*d*) part of the house was at the time of death used for purposes other than domestic (I.E.A. 1952, Sched. 2, para. 2).

This right to appropriation of the matrimonial home does not, however, amount to an equitable interest in property by itself giving the spouse *locus standi* in any proceedings relating to the property (*Lall* v. *Lall* [1965] 1 W.L.R. 1249).

Notification of the claim must be given within twelve months from the first taking out of a general grant of representation with respect to the estate and cannot be given after the death of the surviving husband or wife (I.E.A. 1952, Sched. 2, para. 3 (1)). The period may, however, be extended by the court in the same circumstances as the period for election to have redemption of a life interest (I.E.A. 1952, Sched. 2, para. 3 (3) ; A.E.A. 1925, s. 47A (5)). Except where the surviving spouse is sole personal representative the right is exercisable by notifying the personal representative or representatives, or where the surviving spouse is one of them, the remainder, in writing (I.E.A. 1952, Sched. 2, para. 3 (1) (*c*)). Notification is not revocable except with the consent of the personal representatives (*ibid.*, para. 3 (2)).

In order to enable a surviving spouse to judge whether it is advantageous to claim an appropriation, he or she may require the personal representative to have the relevant interest in the house valued in accordance with the A.E.A. 1925, s. 41, and to inform him or her of the result (I.E.A. 1952, Sched. 2, para. 3 (2)).

Sale of matrimonial home.—Unless the personal representative is obliged to sell the house for payment of debts owing to want of other assets, he may not dispose of the deceased's interest in it until after the expiration of the period of twelve months during which the surviving spouse may claim appropriation, except with the written consent of the surviving spouse (I.E.A. 1952, Sched. 2, para. 4 (1)). In the case of the " mixed " properties mentioned above, where appropriation can be claimed only with the consent of the court, the personal representatives may apply for a decision as to whether the spouse can call for appropriation ; if the court decides that the spouse cannot do so, it may authorise disposal of the deceased's interest within the period of twelve months (I.E.A. 1952, Sched. 2, para. 4 (2)). On the other hand, where the court extends the period during which the right to claim appropriation exists, it may apply the restriction on disposition to the extended period. Where the surviving spouse is sole personal representative or one of two or more personal representatives, this restriction on disposition does not apply ; there is no need for it as his or her concurrence in sale is necessary.

A purchaser, lessee, mortgagee or other person who, in good faith, acquires an interest for value need not inquire whether a surviving spouse has any right to require appropriation (A.E.A. 1925, s. 55 (1) (xviii) ; I.E.A. 1952, Sched. 2, paras. 4 (5) and 7 (2)).

Appropriation of matrimonial home where surviving spouse is personal representative.—Usually the surviving spouse will be either sole personal representative or one of several. Where he or she is one of two or more personal representatives, an appropriation of the matrimonial home may be made in his or her favour notwithstanding the rule that a trustee may not be a purchaser of trust property (I.E.A. 1952, Sched. 2, para. 5 (1)). Effect will normally be given to the appropriation by a simple assent from the personal representative to the surviving husband or wife, and a purchaser will not be concerned to look to the adequacy of consideration or any other circumstances affecting the appropriation (A.E.A. 1925, ss. 36 (7), 41 (7)).

Where the surviving spouse is a sole personal representative the I.E.A. 1952, Sched. 2, has no application. He or she may use the power in the A.E.A. 1925, s. 41, and if an assent is executed in his or her own favour without recitals or other explanatory matter, the better opinion appears to be that a purchaser must accept it as passing the legal estate. The sole personal representative would remain liable to challenge by another person beneficially interested, but if the house is competently valued this need not cause concern.

Reference may be made generally to an article in the *Solicitors' Journal*, vol. 107, pp. 503, 525.

Powers of general personal representatives when land ceases to be settled.—The question has been asked whether, when the legal estate in settled property vested in a tenant for life has on his death passed to his general personal representatives in consequence of the settlement having come to an end (as to which, see *post*, p. 708), such general personal representative has, in relation to the land, the same powers as he has in relation to the land to which his testator or intestate was beneficially entitled. In particular, has he power to confer a good title on a purchaser ? There are two aspects of this. On the one hand, it is fairly confidently considered that a purchaser in good faith for value from such a general personal representative would be adequately protected anyway (*Re Bridgett and Hayes' Contract* [1928] Ch. 163 ; *In the Estate of Taylor* [1929] P. 260 ; and see s. 110 (3) of the S.L.A. 1925 and ss. 14 and 17 of the T.A. 1925, *post*, pp. 405–406). However, the contrary has been argued by Sir Lancelot Elphinstone who, in effect, took the view that, because of the limits of such a general personal representative's powers mentioned below, a purchaser would not be regarded as being in good faith unless the purpose of the sale is inquired about and expressed in the conveyance (*Conveyancer N.S.*, vol. 23, p. 360 *et seq.* ; *ibid.*, vol. 24, pp. 43 *et seq.* and 314 *et seq.*). This view is differed from in that a mere failure to inquire would not appear to be such actual notice of any irregularities as to constitute bad faith (and see " The Conveyancer," *Law Times*, vol. 229, pp. 32 and 237). It is, indeed, not the usual practice to make any such inquiries but to assume that the vendor (i.e., the general personal representative) is acting properly in selling and conveying and that in the absence of something more positive protection is available.

On the other hand, the general personal representative's powers in respect of such land do appear somewhat limited. His primary duty is to vest the legal estate in the person next entitled (s. 7 (5) of the S.L.A. 1925). This, however, is subject to payment of death duties (s. 8 (3) (*b*), (5), (6) of the S.L.A. 1925 ; s. 16 of the L.P.A. 1925) but *not* apparently subject to the rights and powers of personal representatives for purposes of administration (para. (*a*) of s. 8 (3) of the S.L.A. 1925 applies only to the settlor-testator's personal representative). Consequently a general personal representative strictly has no power to sell or mortgage otherwise than to pay death duties unless all those beneficially entitled effectively consent (see Sir Lancelot Elphinstone, *op. cit.*). In any other case such representative risks incurring liability for breach of trust notwithstanding that his conveyance confers a good title on the purchaser (see above). Consequently the safer practice may be for the general personal representative never to sell at the instance of the person next entitled but instead to vest the legal estate in him by assent or conveyance (see s. 110 (5) of the S.L.A. 1925,) and let him sell for himself.

Protection to persons dealing with personal representatives.—A purchaser may accept a title from personal representatives although he may have actual notice that all debts have, as a matter of fact, been discharged. For, by s. 36 (8) of the A.E.A. 1925, it is provided that a conveyance of a legal estate by a personal representative to a purchaser will not be invalidated by reason only that the purchaser may have notice that all the debts, liabilities, funeral and testamentary or administration expenses, duties and legacies of the deceased have been discharged or provided for. The reason is that a purchaser is not interested in the contents of the will, or as to the persons beneficially interested therein, or under an intestacy, and for all he knows there may be a minority or a life interest, during which, of course, their powers would exist notwithstanding that all the debts had been paid.

Before 1926, the fact that the assent need not be in writing was always a source of anxiety to the solicitor. The personal representatives themselves might not have been sure whether or not they had done anything which might, without any intention to do so, have amounted to an assent, and therefore have had the effect of terminating their powers. But now, unless there has been an assent in writing conforming to s. 36 of the A.E.A. 1925, or a conveyance, the purchaser may feel safe however long the sale may be after the death of the testator or intestate. But the purchaser should get a statement in his conveyance that there has been no dealing with the legal estate, and should inspect the probate or administration to see that there are no indorsements thereon to the contrary ; see *post*, p. 415.

Section 14 of the T.A. 1925 makes the receipt in writing of a personal representative a good discharge, and s. 17 of the same Act provides that no purchaser or mortgagee, paying or advancing money on a sale or mortgage purporting to be made under (*inter alia*) any trust or power vested in trustees [and therefore in personal representatives], will be concerned to see that such money is wanted, or that no more than is wanted is raised, or otherwise as to the application thereof.

When the subject of the purchase from personal representatives is settled land the purchaser gets protection under the S.L.A. 1925, s. 110 (3). This subsection provides that a purchaser is entitled to act on the assumption that if the capital money payable in respect of the transaction is paid to the personal representative, such personal representative is acting under his statutory or other powers and requires the money for purposes of administration ; and in any other case, that the personal representative is acting under his statutory or other powers.

The effect of *Re Bridgett and Hayes' Contract* [1928] Ch. 163, *post*, p. 708, as explained in *In the Estate of Taylor* [1929] P. 260, at p. 263, is that a purchaser of settled land from a personal representative to whom a general grant (not excluding settled land) had been made is protected by s. 204 of the L.P.A. 1925, the grant being an order of the court. This would seem to be the case even though the general grant had been subsequently varied, and a grant limited to the settled land made to special personal representatives.

Conveyances (including assents : A.E.A. 1925, s. 55 (1) (iii)) of any interest in real or personal estate made to a purchaser by a person to whom probate or letters of administration have been granted are valid, notwithstanding any subsequent revocation or variation of the probate or administration (A.E.A. 1925, s. 37 (1)). Further, any person making any payment or disposition in good faith under a representation is protected in so doing, notwithstanding any defect or circumstance whatsoever affecting the validity of the representation (*ibid.*, s. 27 (1)). There is a corresponding provision in the A.E.A. 1925, s. 27 (2), to the effect that where a representation is revoked, all payments and dispositions made in good faith to a personal representative under the representation before revocation are a valid discharge ; and the personal representative who acted under the revoked representation may reimburse himself in respect of any payments or dispositions made by him which the person to whom representation is afterwards granted might have properly made.

Protection against liability in respect of leasehold property.— If personal representatives take possession of leaseholds they become *personally* liable, by privity of estate, on the covenants in the leases. Provided they apply to the court before making an assignment, however, they will be permitted to retain a fund in order to indemnify themselves as the T.A. 1925, s. 26, below, covers only their liability as personal representatives (*Re Owers* [1941] Ch. 389). But they are not entitled to indemnity out of property in respect of which they have already executed an assent (*Re Bennett* [1943] 1 All E.R. 467).

Even though personal representatives do not take possession they must ensure that all future liability of the estate will be met before distributing the estate, otherwise they may become personally liable. Such liability exists if the deceased was the original lessee or an assignee who covenanted to indemnify the assignor. This difficulty is met by the T.A. 1925, s. 26, as amended by the Law of Property (Amendment) Act, 1926, Schedule, which provides, in effect, that a personal representative may convey [this word includes an assent : T.A. 1935, s. 68 (3)] the property demised or underleased to a purchaser, legatee, devisee or other person entitled to call for the same, and distribute the estate of the testator or intestate without being personally liable in respect of any subsequent claim under the lease or underlease or under any indemnity given in respect thereof, provided that he first satisfies all liabilities under the lease or underlease which may have accrued, and been claimed, up to the date of assignment, and, where necessary, sets apart a sufficient fund to answer any future claim that may be made in respect of any fixed and ascertained sum which the lessee agreed to lay out on the property, although the period for laying out the same may not have arrived.

The section operates without prejudice to the right of the lessor or the persons deriving title under him to follow the assets or the trust property into the hands of the persons amongst whom the same may have been respectively distributed.

It was decided in *Re Lawley* [1911] 2 Ch. 530, under the provisions in the Law of Property (Amendment) Act, 1859, that the personal representative was not protected where money was paid to an assignee of onerous leaseholds to take an assignment. Under that Act it was necessary for the lease to be assigned to a " purchaser " and it may be that under the wider wording of the present provision a personal representative would be protected in such a case.

Protection by advertisement.—It is provided by s. 27 of the T.A. 1925, as amended by the Law of Property (Amendment) Act, 1926, in effect, that, with a view to the conveyance to or distribution among the persons entitled to any real or personal property, personal representatives may give notice by advertisement in the *Gazette* and in a newspaper circulating in the district *in which the land is situated*, and such other like notices, including notices elsewhere than in England and Wales, as would, in any special case, have been directed by a court of competent jurisdiction in an action for administration, of their intention to make such conveyance (this word includes an assent, see *ante*) or distribution as aforesaid, and requiring any person interested to send to the personal representatives within the time, *not being less than two months*, fixed in the notice, or, where more than one notice is given, in the last of the notices, particulars of his claim in respect of the property to which the notice relates. At the expiration of the time fixed by the notice, the personal representatives may convey or distribute the property to or among the persons entitled thereto, having regard only to the claims, whether formal or not, of which they then had notice, and will not, as respects such property, be liable to any person of whose claim they have not had notice at the time of conveyance or distribution. It may incidentally be noticed that, even without advertisement, similar protection is provided where personal representatives distribute assets without inquiry as to or notice of the claims arising from illegitimate relationships (s. 17 of the Family Law Reform Act, 1969 ; see ss. 14 and 15 thereof).

There is an important proviso to s. 27 of the T.A. 1925 to the effect that *nothing in the section is to free the personal representatives from any obligation to make searches or obtain official certificates of search similar to those which an intending purchaser would be advised to make or obtain.* The meaning of this is not clear. As a purchaser would make at least a local land charges search and a search, in the name of the deceased, in the land charges register, a personal representative who does not do so will be deemed to have notice of any matter he would have found by searching (for instance, a charge registered by the local authority or a charge by the deceased to secure money) and in respect of such matters will not be protected by the T.A. 1925,

s. 27. Consequently, the Council of The Law Society (*Law Society's Gazette*, vol. 31, p. 62) have expressed the view that representatives should make these searches before assenting in respect of land. The Council also suggested that search should be made in the names of the representatives themselves in case anything has been registered against them without their knowledge, but, with due respect, it is doubtful if this is necessary ; registration of an incumbrance which is unknown to the representative is almost impossible. It is doubted whether there is any settled practice on these matters but, unless the representatives are members of the deceased's family or otherwise ready to take the slight risk involved, at least the limited searches mentioned above should be made before an assent.

It is desired to draw special attention to the following points, namely : (i) that to protect the personal representatives the advertisement must be in a paper circulating in the district where the land is situate ; if, therefore, the deceased had land some considerable distance from the place where he lived, it may be necessary to advertise also in a paper circulating there ; (ii) in the case of personal estate, other than leaseholds, notice in the *London Gazette* is all that is required, save in the special cases ; (iii) it may be difficult to be certain if the case is a special one and, if so, what notices would be directed by the court, and so it may be necessary to apply to the court to state what notices are necessary as was done in *Re Letherbrow* [1935] W.N. 34 ; (iv) " the section applies equally to the claims of beneficial owners as to the claims of creditors . . . advertisements for creditors or for persons beneficially interested . . . should be re-cast so as to . . . indicate to normal people that it is not merely the claims of creditors which are required to be sent in, but also those of beneficiaries " (Danckwerts, J., in *Re Aldhous* [1955] 1 W.L.R. 459–462 ; see also *Law Society's Gazette*, vol. 52, p. 307).

Personal representatives and trustees distributing an estate, otherwise than under order of the court, are always subject to the danger that a receiving order may have been made against one of the beneficiaries (Bankruptcy Act, 1914, ss. 45, 46) and however carefully searches are made there is always a slight danger that payment may be made between the date of the receiving order and its registration.

Protection in regard to constructive notice.—A personal representative acting for the purposes of more than one estate will not, in the absence of fraud, be affected by notice of any instrument, matter, fact or thing in relation to any particular estate if he has obtained notice thereof merely by reason of his acting or having acted for the purposes of another estate (T.A. 1925, s. 28).

Notice would not be imputed to the client by reason of his solicitor having notice where such solicitor was party to the fraud and therefore would certainly conceal the fact from his client (*Cave* v. *Cave* (1880), 15 Ch. D. 639). See further, *ante*, p. 171. Trustees or personal representatives may convey or distribute any property to or among persons entitled without having ascertained that no adoption order has been made which might affect distribution, and they are not liable to a person of whose claim they have not had notice, although such person may follow the property (Adoption Act, 1958, s. 17 (3)). Similar protection is provided where personal representatives distribute assets without inquiry as to or notice of the claims arising from illegitimate relationships (s. 17 of the Family Law Reform Act, 1969).

Protection against claims for estate duty.—Personal representatives and trustees who wish to be sure that no further claim will be made against them for estate duty, for instance because additional free estate belonging to a life tenant is discovered resulting in an increase in the estate rate of duty, should apply for a determination of the estate duty payable in respect of the property. On payment of that duty the property and the applicant, so far as regards that property, are discharged from any further claim and the Commissioners give a certificate to that effect under the F.A. 1894, s. 11 (2), as amended by the F.A. 1907, s. 14, and F.A. 1969, Sched. 21, Pt. V. See *Law Society's Gazette*, vol. 45, p. 55. A certificate will not be issued unless all values have been accepted ; a certificate may be obtained even where the value of the estate is such that no estate duty is payable (*Law Society's Gazette*, vol. 56, p. 479).

Contraventions of planning law.—First, it must be noted that a local planning authority may recover from the owner of premises any expenses incurred in taking steps required (i) either by an enforcement notice (Town and Country Planning Act, 1971, s. 91), or (ii) by a listed building enforcement notice in restoring a building of special architectural or historic interest (*ibid.*, s. 99). For these purposes " owner " is defined as including a person who, as trustee for another, is entitled to receive the rack rent, or who would be so entitled if the land were so let (*ibid.*, s. 290 (1)). Consequently, a personal representative or trustee of the will of a deceased person may become under an obligation to pay such expenses, whether contravention occurred before or after death of the deceased person. There is, however, a provision that where a local planning authority claim to recover expenses in taking such steps from a person as being owner of premises and that person proves that he is receiving rent merely as agent or trustee for some other person and that he has not, since service on him of a demand for payment, had in his hands on behalf of that other person sufficient money to discharge the whole of the demand, his liability shall be limited to the total amount of money he has had in his hands since the demand, and the authority may recover the balance from the person on whose behalf the rent was received (Public Health Act, 1936, s. 294, as applied by the Town and Country Planning Act, 1971, s. 91 (3) (4)).

C. ASSENTS

Assents before 1926.—One great difference between an assent affecting land under the law before 1926 and the law after 1925 is that the assent to pass the legal estate must now be *in writing*, whereas before 1926 the assent might be *implied*. It was often a question of law, and not only a question of fact, whether or not what had happened amounted to an assent, and therefore whether or not the legal estate had passed out of the executors into the devisee or legatee under the will. If it had, the powers of the executors would have ceased to exist.

Another difference between an assent affecting the legal estate in land under the law before 1926, and the law after 1925, is that before 1926 when an assent was given by an executor it passed the legal estate to the devisee or legatee under the will by virtue of the devise or bequest in such will, and the assent only operated to carry out such devise or bequest (*Attenborough* v. *Solomon* [1913] A.C. 76). Since 1925 the legal estate passes by virtue of the assent itself and the will passes only an equitable interest. See the words of s. 36 (2) of the A.E.A. 1925 : " The assent shall operate to vest . . ." See below. Section 36 (1) of the A.E.A. 1925 gives power to assent to a personal representative but does not empower a trustee to assent.

Before 1926 the fact of the executor allowing the life tenant to take the rents amounted to an assent to a bequest in remainder (*Stevenson* v. *Mayor of Liverpool* (1874), L.R. 10 Q.B. 81). In *Wise* v. *Whitburn* [1924] 1 Ch. 460, a testator bequeathed a leasehold house to his executors and trustees upon trust to permit his wife to occupy it during her life, with remainders over. The executors allowed the widow to reside in the house for ten years, that is until she died. A purchaser from the executors had notice of the fact, and it was held that the legacy had been assented to soon after the testator's death and the effect was to strip the executors of their title as such and to clothe them with a title as trustees so that they had no power to sell as executors. But, generally, when personal representatives were selling to pay debts, the purchaser was entitled to assume, when the legatee was not in possession, that there had been no assent (*Re Venn and Furze's Contract* [1894] 2 Ch. 101).

Where the executors and trustees were the same persons, and, as trustees, they purported to exercise a trust for sale, their action was itself sufficient evidence that they had, as executors, assented to the devise or bequest to themselves as trustees. They already had the legal estate in themselves as executors, and it was only the change of character in which they held such legal estate which had to be implied by their acts.

One often used to see in conveyances an attempted conveyance by persons as " executors and trustees." This was inartistic, as persons could not be executors and trustees at the same time. But it was effectual, as the word not required would be treated as surplusage. In *Re Milner and Organ's Contract* (1920), 89 L.J. Ch. 315, the vendors purported to sell a freehold farm " as trustees " under a will, but found that their trust for sale was not exercisable until a future date. They then offered to sell as personal representatives, but the purchaser objected that by purporting to sell as trustees there was proof that their powers as legal personal representatives had come to an end, and the judge took this view also and allowed the contract to be rescinded. See also *Re Spencer and Hauser's Contract* [1928] Ch. 598 and *Green* v. *Whitehead* [1930] 1 Ch. 38, mentioned *ante*, p. 109.

As before 1926, an *administrator* could not make an assent as regards real estate to the heir, it followed that when the heir was entitled on intestacy, the administrator had to *convey* the estate to him (Land Transfer Act, 1897, s. 3 (1)) unless the heir happened also to be the administrator in which case the proper course was for him to execute a deed poll declaring that he held such legal estate free from his office as administrator. But as s. 36 of the A.E.A. 1925 applies where the death occurred before 1926, if the heir became entitled before that date and the assent is made after 1925, such assent will be sufficient without a conveyance.

Form and effect of assent.—Since 1925 the " assent " to the vesting of the legal estate in land must be in writing, signed by the personal representatives, and must name the person in whose favour it is given. The exact wording of s. 36 (1) and (4) of the A.E.A. 1925 is given below :—

" 36.—(1) *A personal representative* may assent to the vesting, in any person who (whether by devise, bequest, devolution, appropriation *or otherwise*) may be entitled thereto, either beneficially or as a trustee or personal representative, of *any estate or interest in real estate to which the testator or intestate was entitled* or over which he exercised a general power of appointment by his will, including the statutory power to dispose of entailed interests, and *which devolved upon the personal representative.*

(4) An assent to the *vesting of a legal estate* shall be in writing, signed by the personal representative, and shall *name the person in whose favour it is given* and shall operate to vest in that person the legal estate to which it relates ; and an assent not in writing or not in favour of a named person shall not be effectual to pass a legal estate."

" *a personal representative.*"—Administrators may now assent ; the application in *Re Dalley* (1926), 70 Sol. J. 839, was made on this supposition ; and see the definition in s. 55 (1) (xi) of the A.E.A. 1925. (The Land Transfer Act, 1897, s. 3 (1), enabled a personal representative to pass freeholds to a *devisee* by assent and so an administrator could assent in favour of a devisee if the deceased had left a will, but could not pass freeholds to the *heir* in this way. A conveyance to the heir was necessary ; compare *ante*, p. 116.) An assent cannot be made by trustees as such (cf. *Re Rosenthal* [1972] 1 W.L.R. 1273).

" *or otherwise.*"—There is some doubt whether these words allow an executor to make an assent in favour of a purchaser from a beneficiary under a will. The point, of course, turns on whether the words must be construed as *ejusdem generis* with the words preceding them, or as having an independent meaning. Until there is a decision on the matter, it will be better to complete the transaction by a conveyance and not by an assent. In either case it would be necessary to pay *ad valorem* stamp duty on the document, based on the purchase-money. In *G.H.R. Co.* v. *Commissioners* [1943] K.B. 303, the testator had sold property and received the purchase-money but died before executing a conveyance. His executor assented in favour of the purchaser and the assent was treated as a valid one but chargeable with *ad valorem* duty. See *post*, p. 1156. On the other hand, a subsequent purchaser need not inquire whether the person in whose favour the assent was made was a devisee or purchaser and he is not concerned with *ad valorem* stamp duty.

" *any estate or interest in real estate.*"—These words include leasehold but not (*semble*) the proceeds of sale of land to arise under a trust for sale (A.E.A. 1925, ss. 3 (1), 55 (1) (xix) ; see *Irani Finance, Ltd.* v. *Singh* [1971] Ch. 59 ; cp. *Elias* v. *Mitchell* [1972] Ch. 652). As to whether they include a mortgage debt, see *post*, p. 1005 (an assent in respect of a registered charge is expressly authorised : L.R.R. 1925, r. 170 (1)). It follows that an assent affecting pure personalty can be made only by virtue of the common-law rules and so cannot validly be made by an administrator ; see Williams on Assents, pp. 95, 96. Further reference may be made to an article by Alan Prichard concerning " Assents and Assignments to a Tenant in Common of a Remaining Share " at *Conveyancer N.S.*, vol. 37, p. 42 *et seq.*

" *to which the testator or intestate was entitled.*"—It has been suggested that these words mean " beneficially entitled to " and that the personal representatives of a sole or last surviving trustee cannot pass the property to a beneficiary by an assent, but should execute a conveyance. It should be noted that the subsection earlier mentions an assent in favour of a person " entitled thereto, either beneficially *or as a trustee.*" Consequently the suggestion would appear mistaken, as the word " entitled " would not be used in two different senses in one subsection. In view of the doubt, however expressed, the use of an assent cannot be recommended, but the opinion of the late J. M. Lightwood in the *Law Journal*, vol. 82, p. 309, was that an assent could be made by the personal representatives of a sole or last surviving trustee.

" *which devolved upon the personal representatives.*"—If a person beneficially entitled dies before an assent is made in his favour the personal representatives of the original testator or intestate may assent in favour of the personal representatives of the beneficiary. Normally it will be more convenient to assent directly in favour of the person beneficially entitled on the second death but there may be difficulties if the property could be required in the administration of the second estate. If the assent is in favour of the personal representatives of the original beneficiary it seems that they will not be able to execute a valid assent to the person ultimately entitled beneficially because they did not acquire the *legal* estate by devolution ; s. 36 (1) relates to " any estate . . . to which the testator or intestate was entitled . . . and which *devolved* upon the personal representatives " (*Re Stirrup's Contract* [1961] 1 W.L.R. 449). Although this reasoning was questioned by Sir Lancelot Elphinstone in the *Conveyancer N.S.*, vol. 25, p. 490 *et seq.*, to be safe the representatives should execute a conveyance or assignment. If, however, the purported assent is under seal and the intention to transfer the legal estate is manifest, it may be effective to pass the legal estate because the requirements of the L.P.A. 1925, s. 52 (1), are complied with even though its form is not that usually adopted for a conveyance (*Re Stirrup's Contract, ante*).

" *vesting of a legal estate.*"—An assent to the vesting of equitable interests in land, or to things in action and chattels personal need not be in writing, and the law existing before 1926 still applies to these, so that assent may be implied from conduct but cannot be made by an administrator in the case of pure personalty. Solicitors should, even in these cases, advise that the assent be in writing, as the advantages are obvious.

" *name the person in whose favour it is given.*"—It has been suggested that the assentee should be named and not merely described, for instance as " the beneficiary," even if that description is defined elsewhere in the document. It is thought that this suggestion is unreasonable.

It would appear that an *executor* can assent before probate and that the assent will be effectual even though he dies without taking out probate, since he derives his powers from the will (see *ante*, pp. 394–395 ; also *Johnson* v. *Warwick* (1856), 17 C.B. 516). However, an assent relating to a legal estate in land is better not made until after probate so that notices thereof may be endorsed on the probate (A.E.A. 1925, s. 36 (5)). An *administrator* can only assent after the grant of administration. The assent will, unless a contrary intention appears, relate back to the death of the deceased (A.E.A. 1925, s. 36 (2)).

An assent in respect of pure personalty may be made by one of several executors. In the case of real estate, including leaseholds, all personal representatives must sign the assent (A.E.A. 1925, ss. 2 (2), 55 (1) (iii)). All personal representatives who proved the will or took out letters of administration must concur in an assent affecting land (A.E.A. 1925, s. 2 (2)), but executors who have not proved need not join in, even though power has been reserved to them to prove (A.E.A. 1925, s. 8 (1)). On the death of one or

more of the personal representatives the right to execute an assent passes
to the other or others (A.E.A. 1925, s. 2 (1)). As to the death of a sole or
surviving executor or administrator, see p. 391 *et seq.*

Personal representatives may, as a condition of giving an assent or making
a conveyance, require security for the payment of liabilities affecting the
estate, but they will not be justified in refusing to give an assent merely
by reason of the subsistence of any such liabilities if reasonable arrangements
have been made for discharging them ; and an assent may be given subject
to any legal estate or charge by way of legal mortgage (A.E.A. 1925, s. 36 (10)).
This subsection gives the representatives a power only and they cannot be
compelled, for instance, to assent subject to a mortgage if they prefer to sell
and discharge the mortgage out of the proceeds of sale (*Williams* v. *Holland*
[1965] 1 W.L.R. 739). The A.E.A. 1925, s. 43 (1), will often prove
useful. It provides that a personal representative, before giving an
assent in favour of any person entitled, may permit that person to take
possession of the land, and that such possession shall not prejudicially
affect the right of the personal representative to take or resume possession
nor his power to convey the land as if he were in possession thereof. By
acting under this subsection the personal representative is enabled to keep
back the final assent until the estate is cleared of all liabilities and at the same
time not withhold possession from the tenant for life or other person entitled.
Although no mesne profits will be recoverable from a beneficiary in possession,
if one of several co-beneficiaries has enjoyed beneficial occupation rent-free
credit for this may have to be given on the ultimate distribution of the estate
(*Williams* v. *Holland, ante* ; see also *Bull* v. *Bull* [1955] 1 Q.B. 234 and
Barclay v. *Barclay* [1907] 2 Q.B. 677, noted *post*, p. 776).

Contents and execution of assents.—" Before 1926, it was held that a
devisee could not require an assent to describe the land devised in more precise
terms than those comprised in the will : *Re Pix* [1901] W.N. 165. But the
importance which is now given to assents as principal vesting instruments
requires that an assent should contain proper parcels, sufficient on comparison
with the earlier documents of title to identify the property, and that, in
particular, an assent should never describe the property by reference to any
document, such as a will, which affects merely the equitable title " (Key
and Elphinstone's Precedents in Conveyancing, 15th ed., vol. I, p. 239).

It is not usually necessary to make an assent subject to restrictive
covenants because the failure to mention them will not impose any liability
on the personal representatives ; their covenants for title are limited to
their own acts only (L.P.A. 1925, s. 76 (1) (F)). On the other hand, it may be
desirable, particularly in the case of leaseholds, to take an indemnity from
the devisee against future liability on covenants. It has been suggested that
the personal representatives could require this unless it could be shown that
the estate would not be liable. For instance, the estate would not be liable
if the deceased was not the original lessee, and had not entered into such
a covenant with a prior assignee (*Moule* v. *Garret* (1872), L.R. 7 Ex. 101 ;
Bonner v. *Tottenham and Edmonton Building Society* [1899] 1 Q.B. 161 ;
and see *post*, p. 842 *et seq.*). Again, the executors might be protected under
s. 26 of the T.A. 1925, in which case they could not ask for such a covenant
of indemnity ; see at p. 406. Where the benefit of a restrictive covenant
would pass by a conveyance without mention, it would equally pass by an
assent without mention ; compare *post*, p. 559. Even though personal
representatives have executed an assent without passing the benefit of a

restrictive covenant, they will hold the benefit as bare trustees for the person equitably entitled to the land, for instance a devisee, who may sue on the covenant or assign the benefit of it (*Newton Abbot Co-operative Society, Ltd.* v. *Williamson and Treadgold, Ltd.* [1952] Ch. 286). The use of recitals in assents is considered *post*, p. 417.

Assents by trust corporations are often executed under the hand of an agent, in reliance on the L.P.A. 1925, s. 74 (2), which enables a corporation aggregate to appoint an agent to execute an instrument not under seal. Some doubt has been expressed as to whether an assent executed in this way passes a good title as s. 74 (2) does not enable the general exercise of a discretion to be delegated, and it may be that the corporation could be required to provide evidence that the particular assent has been authorised or to execute an assent under seal. See further, the *Law Times*, vol. 207, p. 259, and a justification of the practice of signature by an agent, *ibid.*, vol. 209, p. 182.

The statutory covenants implied by a person conveying as " personal representative " will be implied by the use of such words in an assent, in the same way as in a conveyance by deed (A.E.A. 1925, s. 36 (3) ; an unnecessary provision since L.P.A. 1925, s. 76, is not confined to deeds and expressly applies to post-1925 assents : subs. (8)).

Registered land.—Where title to the land is registered, an ordinary assent should be in Form 56 and a vesting assent should be in Form 57 (L.R.A. 1925, s. 41 (4) ; L.R.R. 1925, r. 170 (3) ; as to alternatives and additions, see *ibid.*, r. 74). The appropriate form should be forwarded with (i) a statement of value by the solicitor on Form 87, (ii) the land or charge certificate, (iii) the probate or letters of administration, (iv) Form A.4, (v) certificate of non-liability to death duty ; in practice, only a photostat or certified copy of the grant will be lodged. Also, as already noted *ante*, p. 133, the personal representative of a deceased proprietor may, without himself being registered, transfer or otherwise dispose of any registered land or charge of the deceased in the usual way (L.R.R. 1925, r. 170 (1) ; L.R.A. 1925, s. 37 (1)). On delivery of a transfer, assent, appropriation or vesting assent, accompanied by probate or letters of administration, the registrar will register the person named in the instrument for that purpose as proprietor and enter any restriction contained in the instrument, for instance in a vesting assent affecting settled land (L.R.R. 1925, r. 170 (4)). The registrar is never concerned with the terms of any will of the deceased proprietor and he is entitled to assume that the personal representative is acting correctly and within his powers (L.R.R. 1925, r. 170 (5)).

Acknowledgment for production in assent.—Since 1925 an acknowledgment of the right to production of the probate or letters of administration should be contained in an assent, together with an acknowledgment in respect of any title deeds retained if, for instance, a devisee takes part only of the deceased's land (*Re Miller & Pickersgill's Contract* [1931] 1 Ch. 511). Where a devisee assents in his own favour an acknowledgment is not valid as it must be given in favour of *another* (L.P.A. 1925, s. 64 (1)) ; see *post*, p. 658. There would seem to be no objection to an acknowledgment in the usual form in an assent to several persons of whom a personal representative is one, but an acknowledgment in an assent to a person who is one of the personal representatives is probably invalid ; consequently it is advisable to insert an express covenant for production in the old form. The statutory forms of assent given in the L.P.A. 1925, Sched. 5 (Forms 8 and 9), are deficient in that they do not contain an acknowledgment.

Registered land.—It has been suggested that an acknowledgment for production of the probate or letters of administration is strictly necessary where the personal representative of a deceased registered proprietor assents or transfers without first himself obtaining registration (Potter, Registered Land Conveyancing, pp. 69, 70). The point is that the grant will have to be lodged in order for the transferee's subsequent application for registration to succeed (L.R.R. 1925, r. 170 (4)), so that he ought to enable himself to call for its production. However, in Ruoff and Roper, Registered Conveyancing, 3rd ed., p. 634, it is denied that an acknowledgment is necessary in such a case and asserted (without citing any authority) that : " Not only would a personal representative who refused to deposit the grant (or evidence of it) at the Land Registry to enable an assent to be registered be acting in derogation of his assent, but he can also be made to produce the grant, regardless of whether he had given an acknowledgement " (contrast the limited right to production conferred by A.E.A. 1925, s. 36 (5), below). The better practice would appear to be, for a transferee for value at least, to require the deposit of the grant at the Land Registry before completion unless a solicitor's undertaking to make the deposit after completion is forthcoming, i.e., instead of insisting upon an acknowledgment for production.

Indorsement on grant : protection of purchaser.—Subsection (5) of s. 36 of the A.E.A. 1925 provides as follows :—

" 36.—(5) Any person in whose favour an assent or conveyance of a legal estate is made by a personal representative may require that notice of the assent or conveyance be written or indorsed on or permanently annexed to the probate or letters of administration, at the cost of the estate of the deceased, and that the probate or letters of administration be produced, at the like cost, to prove that the notice has been placed thereon or annexed thereto."

This subsection only applies to assents and conveyances made after 1925 (*ibid.*, s. 36 (12)). It is extremely important that in every case where a personal representative assents to a devise or bequest in a will, a memorandum of the transaction should be indorsed on the probate or letters of administration. The estate has to pay the small cost. On the other hand, although customary, it is not essential to make an indorsement on a sale by a personal representative. The distinction arises as a result of the following provision in s. 36 (6) :—

" 36.—(6) A statement in writing by a personal representative that he has not given or made an assent or conveyance in respect of a legal estate, shall, in favour of a purchaser, *but without prejudice to any previous disposition made in favour of another purchaser* deriving title mediately or immediately under the personal representative, be sufficient evidence that an assent or conveyance has not been given or made in respect of the legal estate to which the statement relates, unless notice of a previous assent or conveyance affecting that estate has been placed on or annexed to the probate or administration.

A conveyance by a personal representative of a legal estate to a purchaser accepted on the faith of such a statement shall (*without prejudice as aforesaid* and unless notice of a previous assent or conveyance affecting that estate has been placed on or annexed to the probate or administration) operate to transfer or create the legal estate expressed to be conveyed in like manner as if no previous assent or conveyance had been made by the personal representative."

Thus, a devisee must see that an indorsement is made ; if he does not he may lose his estate by reason of a subsequent conveyance by the personal representative containing a statement that there has been no previous assent or conveyance (and see *Law Society's Digest*, Opinion No. 642, that the solicitor acting for the personal representatives should make the endorsement without being requested as a matter of good conveyancing practice). But a purchaser from a representative need not make an indorsement ; he is protected by the words of the subsection given in italics, although it is convenient and customary to make an indorsement.

No useful purpose is served by a statement in a statutory receipt given by personal representatives of a mortgagee that there has been no previous assent or conveyance as the mortgagor is not a "purchaser" within the A.E.A. 1925, s. 36 (6). Consequently, it is not necessary to indorse a memorandum on the probate or letters of administration. Compare the remarks, *post*, p. 661, as to acknowledgment of the probate or letters of administration. Similarly, it does not seem necessary to include in an assent relating to registered land a statement that the personal representative has not made any previous assent or conveyance. A search will disclose whether there has been any previous assent or conveyance which has been registered; a previous assent or conveyance which has not been registered will not affect a devisee who obtains registration (see Ruoff and Roper, Registered Conveyancing, 3rd ed., pp. 634–635).

If the person in whose favour an assent has been made has omitted to have an indorsement made, the question arises whether a purchaser from him can compel him to do so. Apparently the purchaser cannot insist, because once the sale has taken place a subsequent assent or conveyance by the personal representatives, even in favour of a person taking without notice of the earlier assent, would not prejudice the purchaser.

Personal representatives may change. For instance, a grant *de bonis non* may be taken out on death of an administrator, or an executor of an executor may become representative of the original testator under the rules mentioned *ante*, p. 391. It appears that a statement by any personal representative (in the absence of an indorsement) protects a purchaser from him against any assent by a previous personal representative of the deceased. The definition of personal representative in the A.E.A. 1925, s. 55 (1) (xi), is " the executor, original or by representation, or administrator *for the time being.*" Although there is no judicial authority on the point, if this definition is read into s. 36 (6) then that subsection would appear to make the statement of one representative cover actions of earlier ones.

Protection of purchaser from devisee.—Section 36 (7) provides, in effect, that (unless there is an indorsement to the contrary on the probate or administration) an assent or conveyance by a personal representative in respect of a legal estate shall, in favour of a purchaser for money or money's worth, be taken as *sufficient evidence* that the person in whose favour the assent or conveyance is given or made is the person entitled to have the legal estate conveyed to him and upon the proper trusts, if any. It follows that when a person who becomes entitled to property under an assent sells, the purchaser will only be entitled to an abstract showing the probate or letters of administration and the assent. He cannot claim to satisfy himself that the vendor was entitled under a will to have an assent made to him, as the purchaser is not entitled to know the terms of the will. See *ante*, p. 180.

" *sufficient evidence.*"—This does *not* mean that the assent is conclusive that it is made in favour of the proper person. In *Re Duce and Boots Cash Chemists (Southern), Limited's Contract* [1937] Ch. 642, the abstract of title and a recital in the assent both showed that the land was settled, and so should have been vested in the tenant for life, but the land was nevertheless vested in the remaindermen entitled in fee simple. It was held that a purchaser was entitled to object to the title. The conclusion seems to be that a purchaser may assume that the person named in the assent is the person entitled to have the property vested in him unless, upon a proper investigation of the title, facts come to his knowledge indicating the contrary. On the other hand, a purchaser of a legal estate should not examine the will (and would seem to be protected even if it is abstracted and indicates that rights exist to which effect was not given by the assent); the will does not form any part of the title. Nor should such a purchaser question an assent because it is in favour of someone not apparently entitled on intestacy. He should take advantage of the " curtain " provided by s. 36 (7) unless doubt arises by virtue of the documents in front of that curtain.

It is the practice of some solicitors when preparing an assent to include recitals showing the devolution of the title, as was the practice before 1926, but it is a mistake to do so. Speaking generally, an assent should contain no recitals but the mere fact of the assent. If this is done, a purchaser must accept the assent and is not entitled to require proof that the person making it had power to do so, or that the person assented to was the person entitled to have the assent made to him. The case of *Re Duce and Boots Cash Chemists (Southern) Limited's Contract, ante,* shows the danger of unnecessary recitals. Reasons why a few recitals may be advisable are given in Williams' Law Relating to Assents, p. 50 *et seq.,* but it is thought that in most cases recitals are better omitted altogether. There is no object in reciting that no previous assent or conveyance has been given ; only a *purchaser for money or money's worth* obtains protection from such a statement (A.E.A. 1925, s. 36 (6), (11)).

If the deceased has granted an option to purchase land difficulty may arise because the proceeds of sale payable on exercise of the option may pass to a legatee and not the devisee of the land (*Lawes* v. *Bennett* (1785), 1 Cox Eq. Cas. 167). The better opinion seems to be that in such circumstances the devisee is entitled subject to an executory limitation within the meaning of the S.L.A. 1925, s. 1 (1) (notwithstanding the fact that the interest ceases as a result of the exercise of a contractual right it seems that the fee simple is subject to a " disposition " over) ; on this basis the land is settled. The personal representatives should, therefore, execute a vesting assent in favour of the devisee as tenant for life. See the discussions in the *Law Society's Gazette,* vol. 58, pp. 159, 161 and 271, and *Solicitors' Journal,* vol. 105, pp. 337, 338.

Assent by personal representatives in their own favour.—Personal representatives are often also entitled to the legal estate in part or all of their deceased's land in some other capacity, commonly as beneficiaries or trustees for sale. It is clear that such personal representatives can assent in their own favour (see L.P.A. 1925, s. 72, Sched. 5, Form 9) and that in any case a formal written assent would be desirable. But the difficult question arises of whether an assent in writing is essential or whether in such a case an implied assent is still possible as before 1926. The answer depends on s. 36 (4) of the A.E.A. 1925, which provides that an assent not in writing " shall not be effectual to *pass* a legal estate". For many years the better opinion of conveyancers was that this provision did not apply to the present case since this involves only a change in the capacity in which an already vested legal estate is held and not a passing (see, e.g., the 14th Edition of this book, vol. II, p. 474 ; Gibson's Conveyancing, 19th ed., p. 23, cp. now 20th ed., p. 22). The decided cases relevant to this view were few, inconclusive and generally of little authority (see, e.g., *Re Hodge* [1940] Ch. 260 ; also *Harris* v. *Harris* [1942] L.J. N.C.R. 119 and *Hurley* v. *Simmonds* (1956), 107 L.J. 60, and *Conveyancer N.S.*, vol. 21, p. 167, both in the county court), but the view was none the less accepted and acted upon in practice. However, a decision at first instance upset this practice. Pennycuick, J., in *Re King's Will Trusts* [1964] Ch. 542 held that an assent by a personal representative in his own favour involved both a vesting and a divesting of the legal estate, which could not be distinguished from a passing, so that such an assent was within the contemplation of s. 36 (4) of the A.E.A. 1925, and required to be in writing. The decision has been strongly criticised, in particular because its conflict with previously established conveyancing practice is likely to render defective existing titles (see *Solicitors' Journal*, vol. 108, pp. 698 and 719 ; *Conveyancer N.S.*, vol. 28, p. 298 ; *Law Society's Gazette*, vol. 63, p. 145). Of course, so long as the decision stands it cannot safely be ignored by practitioners who must, therefore, insist on a formal written assent in such circumstances.

Mention may also be made of the common practice of persons who are both the personal representatives and the trustees of the deceased by deed appointing new or additional trustees without first making a formal written assent in respect of any legal estate in land in their own favour. The better view was that no objection could be taken to a title made in this way since an assent would be read into the appointment by virtue of s. 40 (1) (*b*) of the T.A. 1925 (see 14th Edition, vol. II, at p. 474). However, this view also was rejected in *Re King's Will Trusts*, *ante*, on the ground that s. 40 is applicable only to property already vested in the appointor as trustee. Thus, although the appointment itself will be valid, a written assent by the personal representative is still necessary in favour of the new trustees. This aspect of the decision has also suffered much criticism (see the articles cited) in particular as conflicting with the principle of *Re Stirrup's Contract* [1961] 1 W.L.R. 449, *ante*, p. 412 (not apparently even cited to Pennycuick, J.). But again, of course, *Re King's Will Trusts*, *ante*, must be accepted as correct by practitioners. In this connection reference should also be made to *Re Pennant's Will Trusts* [1970] Ch. 75 (noted *post*, pp. 743 and 797) in which Buckley, J., adopted the less strict and more helpful approach of not allowing the statutory conveyancing machinery to defeat the clear and legitimate intentions of the parties. See further Professor F. R. Crane's Case Note in the *Conveyancer N.S.*, vol. 33, at p. 339. Reference may be made to a precedent of a confirmatory conveyance for such case given in the *Conveyancer N.S.*, vol. 29, p. 750, Form 19.

PERSONS SUFFERING FROM MENTAL DISORDER

Transactions by persons suffering from mental disorder personally.—It is not often that a solicitor has to consider the effect of a sale or purchase of property of a person suffering from mental disorder which has not been effected under an order of court. First the ground may be cleared by saying that the *voluntary* conveyance of a person suffering from mental disorder, even though no receiver is acting, is absolutely void (*Elliot* v. *Ince* (1857), 7 De G.M. & G. 475 ; *Manning* v. *Gill* (1872), L.R. 13 Eq. 485).

A person suffering from mental disorder where no receiver has been appointed under s. 105 of the Mental Health Act, 1959, can, during a lucid interval, make a binding conveyance of his property for *valuable consideration*, or may purchase property if he is capable of understanding the effect of the deed (*Selby* v. *Jackson* (1844), 6 Beav. 192 ; *Jenkins* v. *Morris* (1880), 14 Ch. D. 674 ; *Drew* v. *Nunn* (1879), 4 Q.B.D. 661).

As regards the power of such a person to enter into a binding contract, Lord Esher, M.R., in *Imperial Loan Co.* v. *Stone* [1892] 1 Q.B. 599, stated that when a person enters into an ordinary contract for valuable consideration and afterwards alleges that he was so insane at the time that he did not know what he was doing, though he proves that to be so, the contract is as binding on him as if he had been fully sane, unless he also prove that, at the time of making the contract, the person he contracted with knew him to be so insane as not to know what he was doing. These rules were applied in the more recent case of *Broughton* v. *Snook* [1938] Ch. 505. See also *York Glass Co., Ltd.* v. *Jubb* (1925), 134 L.T. 36. In that case the medical evidence on behalf of the person suffering from mental disorder was that anyone bargaining with him must have realised that he was insane. The evidence of the selling parties who were present when the bargain was made that they had no suspicion that he was otherwise than normal was accepted, however, and the agreement was upheld.

However, it has been suggested that in this sort of case equitable relief may more readily be found available to render the contract voidable on the grounds of fraud or undue influence where no relief appears available under the above-cited common-law authorities (see further A. H. Hudson in *Conveyancer N.S.*, vol. 25, at p. 319 *et seq.*, and G. H. L. Fridman in *Law Quarterly Review*, vol. 79, at p. 509 *et seq.*).

If no action be taken in the lifetime of a person suffering from mental disorder to upset a contract entered into by him, his personal representatives would have the same power to upset it, neither more nor less, than he had (*Matthews* v. *Baxter* (1873), L.R. 8 Ex. 132).

But a person whose estate has been affected by the appointment of a receiver under s. 105 of the Mental Health Act, 1959, cannot exercise any power of disposition, *inter vivos*, over his own property, even during a lucid interval, because upon the making of the order his property passes out of his control, and any disposition is inconsistent with that control, and therefore void (*Re Marshall* [1920] 1 Ch. 284). In this respect the position was the same in the case of a person of unsound mind so found by inquisition before the 1959 Act (*Re Walker* [1905] 1 Ch. 160).

Dealings under an order of court.—Pursuant to Part VIII of the Mental Health Act, 1959, the court may do or secure the doing of all things necessary or expedient for administering the patient's affairs (*ibid.*, s. 102), and in particular may make orders or give directions or authorities for (*inter alia*) " the sale, exchange, charging or other disposition of or dealing with any property of the patient ; the acquisition of any property in the name or on behalf of the patient ; the settlement of any property of the patient . . . the exercise of any power (including a power to consent) vested in the patient, whether beneficially, or as guardian or trustee or otherwise " (*ibid.*, s. 103 ; see also ss. 17 and 18 of the Administration of Justice Act, 1969, as to making wills). The functions of the judge under that Part are exercisable " where after considering medical evidence he is satisfied that a person is incapable, by reason of mental disorder, of managing and administering his property and affairs " (1959 Act, s. 101).

The L.P.A. 1925, s. 22 (as substituted by the Mental Health Act, 1959) provides as follows :—

" 22.—(1) Where a legal estate in land (whether settled or not) is vested in a person suffering from mental disorder, either solely or jointly with any other person or persons, his receiver or (if no receiver is acting for him) any person authorised in that behalf shall, under an order of the authority having jurisdiction under Part VIII of the Mental Health Act, 1959, or of the court, or under any statutory power, make or concur in making all requisite dispositions for conveying or creating a legal estate in his name and on his behalf.

(2) If land held on trust for sale is vested, either solely or jointly with any other person or persons, in a person who is incapable, by reason of mental disorder, of exercising his functions as trustee, a new trustee shall be appointed in the place of that person, or he shall be otherwise discharged from the trust, before the legal estate is dealt with under the trust for sale or under the powers vested in the trustees for sale."

Conveyances by receiver.—Conveyances, leases and other grants are executed by a receiver appointed by an order made under the Mental Health Act, 1959, s. 105. The normal course on sale of the property of a person suffering from mental disorder is for the receiver to obtain an order and then to enter into a contract in accordance with it. In special circumstances, however (for instance, where an exceptionally advantageous offer is received), a receiver may enter into a provisional agreement and later apply for the approval of the master.

On sale by private treaty a contract is entered into by the receiver " acting on behalf of the vendor pursuant to an order of the Court of Protection dated . . ." The contract must contain a term to the effect that if the approval of the court is not obtained it shall be void. The court require insertion of a special condition which states (*inter alia*) that an office copy of the order authorising sale or of the relevant portion thereof will be handed over on completion and shall be deemed to be conclusive evidence of authority to sell. The procedure is set out in detail in Receivership under the Mental Health Act, 1959 (Oyez Practice Notes, No. 39), 4th ed., p. 63 *et seq.* Precedents of conveyances are contained in those notes ; it is usual to recite the order authorising sale subject to approval of the court and that the deed has been settled and approved by the court. After the draft has been approved by the court it is engrossed but not executed by the receiver until it has been sealed by the court. Such sealing is evidence that the document has been settled and approved (Court of Protection Rules, 1960, r. 85 (1)).

Purchases on behalf of persons suffering from mental disorder.—Where a purchase of freeholds on behalf of a person suffering from mental disorder is desirable the Court of Protection will (on proof of the need and of value) issue an order approving a provisional contract and authorising a conveyance (Mental Health Act, 1959, s. 103 (1) (c)).

The receiver will enter into a conditional agreement as on a sale and obtain an order adopting the contract on summons. The draft conveyance is settled and approved by the court and the engrossment is sealed by the court before execution by the receiver. Unless the order contains such a provision it appears sufficient that the person suffering from mental disorder should be a party to the conveyance, the habendum being in his favour without any trust. In order to avoid the need for solicitors acting for receivers on the sale or purchase of property to advance money for stamp duty and similar expenses, arrangements have been made by The Law Society with the Court of Protection for the provision in advance of sums required. See *Law Society's Gazette*, vol. 46, p. 130, and vol. 50, p. 31.

Registered land.—If unregistered land within a compulsory area for registration of title is acquired for a person suffering from mental disorder, the receiver should make the application for first registration in the name of the patient. The receiver must lodge a copy of the order appointing him and also a copy of the order authorising the purchase (Ruoff and Roper, Registered Conveyancing, 3rd ed., pp. 160–161). A restriction of the powers of a patient registered as proprietor will *not* be entered on the register of his title unless an express application is made (*ibid.*). However restraint will be derived from the fact of the receiver retaining the land certificate until the patient is restored to the management of his affairs. The position as to claiming indemnity from the Land Registry insurance fund if loss is suffered because of the lack of a registration is not entirely clear, but presumably if rectification is ordered against the patient, as is more probable, any claim for indemnity by him or on his behalf would be debarred (see *ibid.*).

Where a person suffering from mental disorder is the proprietor of registered land or a registered charge, his receiver may exercise, in the name and on behalf of the patient, all the powers which he could otherwise exercise for himself. However, such powers can only be exercised by the receiver if duly conferred by an order of the court and a copy of every such order must be filed with H.M. Land Registry and may be referred to on the register (L.R.A. 1925, s. 111 (5), as substituted by s. 149 (1) and Sched. 7 to the Mental Health Act, 1959). In practice, no reference to such an order will be made on the register.

If the receiver and not the patient is registered as a proprietor, a restriction will be entered to the effect that, except under an order of the registrar, no disposition by the proprietor is to be registered unless made pursuant to an order of the court.

Settlement of property.—The Mental Health Act, 1959, s. 102 (1), provides that the judge may, with respect to the property and affairs of a patient, secure the doing of all such things as appear necessary or expedient " (a) for the maintenance or other benefit of the patient, (b) for the maintenance or other benefit of members of the patient's family, (c) for making provision for other persons or purposes for whom or which the patient might be expected to provide if he were not mentally disordered, or (d) otherwise for administering the patient's affairs." For the purpose of para. (b) the " family " consists only of persons for whom the patient might *prima facie* be expected to provide and so excludes collaterals such as nephews and nieces (*Re D.M.L.* [1965] Ch. 1133 ; *Re L.* (*W.J.G.*) [1966] Ch. 135). In appropriate circumstances the patient might have been expected to provide for collateral relations by arrangements designed to reduce liability to estate duty (*ibid.* ; contrast *Re R.H.C.* [1963] 1 W.L.R. 1095), whereupon provision can be made pursuant to s. 102 (1) (c). Similarly provision may be made for an illegitimate son under s. 102 (1) (c) if the evidence shows that the applicant might have been expected to provide for him (*Re T.B.* [1967] Ch. 247). The word "benefit" in the subsection is not confined to material benefits (*Re W.* (*E.E.M.*) [1971] 1 Ch. 123). As to how the court should deal with the possibility of undue influence where there is an application for the order of a settlement desired by the patient, see *Re C.M.G.* [1970] Ch. 574.

The Mental Health Act, 1959, s. 103, enacts that the judge may (except when the patient is an infant, in which case the T.A. 1925, s. 53, below, applies), order the settlement of any property of the patient (including the making of a gift out of the property) and may make such consequential vesting or other orders as the case may require to such persons and for such purposes as are mentioned in s. 102 (1) (b) and (c). Where such a settlement has been made and the Lord Chancellor or a nominated judge is satisfied, at any time before the death of the patient, that " any material fact was not disclosed when the settlement was made, or that there has been any substantial change in circumstances," he may by order vary the settlement (*ibid.*, s. 103 (4)). A settlement need not reserve a power of revocation if the patient should recover (*Re C.W.M.* [1951] 2 K.B. 714). In *Re C.* [1960] 1 W.L.R. 92 a settlement was made in order to prevent a person suffering from mental disorder from squandering his capital when his receiver was discharged.

An application for a settlement may be made by the receiver or any person who under any will or codicil of the patient or on intestacy may become entitled to any property of the patient or any interest therein or any person for whom the patient might be expected to provide if he was not mentally disordered (Court of Protection Rules, 1960, r. 21). The practice is for the application to be made by the person who would benefit under the settlement unless, in the opinion of the court, there is reason for it to be made by someone else.

Settled land.—The special powers formerly contained in the S.L.A. 1925, s. 28, have been repealed by the Mental Health Act, 1959, Sched. 8. Apparently, it is intended that the powers of a patient who is tenant for life of settled land should be exercised pursuant to an order made under s. 103 (1) (j) of the 1959 Act which refers to " the exercise of any power (including a power to consent) vested in the patient, whether beneficially, or as guardian or trustee, or otherwise."

Where freehold land is vested in the patient pursuant to the S.L.A. 1925, sale can be made by the procedure applicable where the patient is absolute owner. Unless previously given by the patient notices required to be given by the S.L.A. 1925, will be directed by order. Similarly the receiver may be given power to manage and let property of which the patient is tenant for life for periods not exceeding three years without further reference to the court provided a reasonable rent is obtained and no option of renewal or purchase is given. It is usually necessary to obtain specific authority on summons to grant a lease for a term exceeding three years. If approval is given terms are negotiated and a draft lease is then submitted for approval.

Infant's property.—Section 53 of the T.A. 1925 provides that where an infant is beneficially entitled to *any property* the court may, with a view to the application of the capital or income thereof for his maintenance, education or benefit, make an order appointing a person to convey such property.

Appointment of a new trustee.—It is provided by s. 36 (1) of the T.A. 1925, that where a trustee, either original or substituted and whether appointed by a court or otherwise, is unfit to act, or is incapable of acting [a person of unsound mind is " unable to act," *Re East* (1873), L.R. 8 Ch. 735 ; and " incapable of acting," *Re Blake* [1887] W.N. 173 ; see also *Re Lemann's Trusts* (1883), 22 Ch. D. 633, and *Re Weston's Trusts* [1898] W.N. 151], then, subject to the restrictions imposed by the Act on the number of trustees—

(a) the person or persons nominated for the purpose of appointing new trustees by the instrument, if any, creating the trust ; or

(b) if there is no such person, or no such person able and willing to act, then the surviving or continuing trustees or trustee for the time being, or the personal representatives of the last surviving or continuing trustee ;

may, by writing, appoint one or more other persons (whether or not being the persons exercising the power) to be a trustee or trustees in the place of the trustee being unfit or being incapable, as aforesaid.

Nevertheless, it is further provided by the T.A. 1925, s. 36 (9), as substituted by the Mental Health Act, 1959, Sched. 7, as follows :—

" (9) Where a trustee is incapable, by reason of mental disorder within the meaning of the Mental Health Act, 1959, of exercising his functions as trustee and is also entitled in possession to some beneficial interest in the trust property, no appointment of a new trustee in his place shall be made by virtue of paragraph (b) of subsection (1) of this section unless leave to make the appointment has been given by the authority having jurisdiction under Part VIII of the Mental Health Act, 1959."

This is, of course, for the protection of the patient, otherwise an unsuitable trustee might be appointed. In favour, however, of a purchaser of a legal estate, a statement contained in any instrument coming into operation after 1925 by which a new trustee is appointed for any purpose connected with land, to the effect that a trustee is unfit to act, or is incapable of acting, or that he is not entitled to a beneficial interest in the trust property in possession, will be conclusive evidence of the matter stated (T.A. 1925, s. 38 (1)) ; and, in favour of such purchaser, any appointment of a new trustee depending on that statement, and any vesting declaration, express or implied, consequent on the appointment, will be valid (*ibid.*, subs. (2)).

A purchaser should therefore always be particular to see that the document contains a statement that the person suffering from mental disorder had no beneficial interest in the property.

It is also provided by s. 41 (1) of the T.A. 1925 (as amended by the Mental Health Act, 1959, Sched. 7), that the court may, whenever it is expedient to appoint a new trustee, and it is found inexpedient, difficult or impracticable to do so without the assistance of the court, make an order appointing a new trustee or new trustees either in substitution for or in addition to any existing trustee or trustees, or although there is no existing trustee ; *and in particular the court may make an order in the case of a trustee who is incapable by reason of mental disorder within the meaning of the Mental Health Act, 1959, of exercising his functions as trustee.*

The T.A. 1925, s. 54, is re-enacted by the Mental Health Act, 1959, Sched. 7, as follows :—

" 54.—(1) Subject to the provisions of this section, the authority having jurisdiction under Part VIII of the Mental Health Act, 1959, shall not have power to make any order, or give any direction or authority, in relation to a patient who is a trustee if the High Court has power under this Act to make an order to the like effect.

(2) Where a patient is a trustee and a receiver appointed by the said authority is acting for him or an application for the appointment of a receiver has been made but not determined, then, except as respects a trust which is subject to an order for administration made by the High Court, the said authority shall have concurrent jurisdiction with the High Court in relation to—

(a) mortgaged property of which the patient has become a trustee merely by reason of the mortgage having been paid off;

(b) matters consequent on the making of provision by the said authority for the exercise of a power of appointing trustees or retiring from a trust;

(c) matters consequent on the making of provision by the said authority for the carrying out of any contract entered into by the patient;

(d) property to some interest in which the patient is beneficially entitled but which, or some interest in which, is held by the patient under an express, implied or constructive trust.

The Lord Chancellor may make rules with respect to the exercise of the jurisdiction referred to in this subsection.

(3) In this section ' patient ' means a patient as defined by section one hundred and one of the Mental Health Act, 1959, or a person as to whom powers are exercisable and have been exercised under section one hundred and four of that Act."

The procedure is now governed by the Court of Protection Rules, 1960.

RAILWAYS

Nationalisation of railways.—The undertakings of railway companies vested in the British Transport Commission on 1st January, 1948 (Transport Act, 1947, ss. 12 13, 25 ; Sched. 3, Pt. I). On such vesting the property of the companies vested in the Commission and, as from that date, the Commission had the rights and were subject to the liabilities of the companies (*ibid.*, s. 14 (2)).

On 1st January, 1963, the property rights and liabilities comprised in the part of the Transport Commission's undertaking which constituted its railway system (except so much of it as was carried on by the London Transport Executive or was within certain harbours) and any property rights and liabilities which were not transferred to other bodies, were transferred to the British Railways Board (Transport Act, 1962, s. 31, Sched. 3, Pt. I). Powers of compulsory acquisition of land are conferred on the British Railways Board, the London Transport Board, the British Transport Docks Board and the British Waterways Board by *ibid.*, s. 15.

A brief note on the powers of the former railway companies is included for purposes of investigation of title.

Until 1949, the power of a railway company to alienate land was acquired under the provisions of the Lands Clauses Consolidation Act, 1845, which Act was deemed to be incorporated in a railway company's special Act, unless expressly excluded. These provisions were never applied to British Rail(ways) : s. 59 of the British Transport Commission Act, 1949.

The 1845 Act dealt with three classes of property :—

1. Land acquired for the special purposes of the undertaking.

2. Land taken for extraordinary purposes under s. 45.

3. Superfluous lands within ss. 127–129.

1. *Land acquired for the special purposes of the undertaking.*—A company could not alienate the land for any purposes outside its special Act (*Foster* v. *London, Chatham & Dover Railway Co.* [1895] 1 Q.B. 711, and cases there cited).

2. *Land taken for extraordinary purposes under s.* 45.—There seemed to be no restriction on the power of the company to sell (s. 13 ; see also *City of Glasgow Union Railway Co.* v. *Caledonian Railway Co.* (1871), L.R. 2 Sc. & Div. 160).

3. *Superfluous lands within ss.* 127–129.—There were very special provisions as to this class of property. Section 127 of the 1845 Act provided that lands acquired by the promoters of the undertaking, which should not be required for the purposes thereof, were to be sold as superfluous lands within the prescribed period ; or, if no period were prescribed, within ten years after the expiration of the time limited by the special Act for the completion of the works ; and, in default of such sale, such superfluous lands were to vest in the owners of the adjoining land. But s. 128 of the same Act provided that, before superfluous lands were sold, they must, unless such lands were situate within a town, or were lands built upon, or used for building purposes, first be offered for sale to the person then entitled to the lands, if any, from which the same were originally severed ; or, if such person refused to purchase them or could not be found, then the like offer was to be made to the person or persons whose land immediately adjoined the land so proposed to be sold. See *Best* v. *Hamand* (1879), 12 Ch. D. 1.

This right of pre-emption had to be registered as a land charge, otherwise a company could, on a sale of superfluous land, defeat the right (L.C.A. 1925, s. 10 (1), Class C (iv) ; see now L.C.A. 1972). The right devolved upon future owners of the estate from which superfluous lands were severed (*Coventry* v. *London, Brighton and South Coast Railway Co.* (1867), L.R. 5 Eq. 104).

A right of pre-emption could be *released*. It is provided by s. 186 of the L.P.A. 1925 that all statutory and other rights of pre-emption affecting a legal estate are to be and to be deemed always to have been capable of release, and unless released are to remain in force as equitable interests only. It is also provided by s. 58 (2) of the S.L.A. 1925 that *a tenant for life* may, with the consent in writing of the trustees of the settlement, at any time, by deed or writing, either with or without consideration in money or otherwise, release any land from a right of pre-emption affecting the same for the benefit of the settled land, or any part thereof.

The company must have sold absolutely, without reserving to itself any interest in the land (Lands Clauses Consolidation Act, 1845, s. 128 ; *London and South Western Railway Co.* v. *Gomm* (1882), 20 Ch. D. 562) ; but this did not prevent the company imposing on the purchaser such covenants as most conduced to its own advantage (s. 128 ; *Re Higgins and Hitchman's Contract* (1882), 21 Ch. D. 95).

14A

SOLICITORS

Obligations of solicitor before contract, see p. 2 *et seq.*

Purchase or lease from or sale to client.—A fiduciary relationship subsists between a solicitor and his client ; consequently in equity a presumption of undue influence arises with regard to transactions between them. Since this presumption is rebuttable, a solicitor is not wholly incapacitated from purchasing or taking a lease from his client, but the onus of upholding the validity of the transaction will rest upon the solicitor, that is, he must prove that the client was fully informed of all the material facts, understood the transaction, and that the transaction itself, both as to price and otherwise, was a fair one (*Wright* v. *Carter* [1903] 1 Ch. 27 ; *Allison* v. *Clayhills* (1907), 97 L.T. 709 ; see also Eldon, L.C., in *Montesquieu* v. *Sandys* (1811), 18 Ves. 302, 313). The same principle applies even though the relationship of solicitor and client has ceased, so long as the confidence arising from such former relationship may be presumed to have continued (*Demarara Bauxite Co.* v. *Hubbard* [1923] A.C. 673).

Where a solicitor purchases and takes a conveyance in the name of a nominee, the concealment will vitiate the sale, although fair and proper in other respects (*McPherson* v. *Watt* (1877), 3 App. Cas. 254).

The same rule applies when the solicitor is *selling* to a client. The fact that the solicitor-vendor is not dealing with property belonging to himself, but is acting as trustee for and owes a duty to beneficiaries to get the best price, does not relieve the solicitor from his duty to disclose all material facts, for instance, valuations in the possession of the solicitor-vendor showing the property to be of less value than the price obtained (*Moody* v. *Cox and Hatt* [1917] 2 Ch. 71).

Useful summaries of the relevant cases are collected in the *Law Society's Digest,* Opinions Nos. 334 to 350.

Mortgage by a client to a solicitor.—A solicitor may not take from a client a mortgage containing a power of sale exercisable without previous notice to the mortgagor, unless he has first clearly explained to the client the unusually stringent character of the power of sale ; and the burden of proving that such explanation was given rests upon the solicitor (*Cockburn* v. *Edwards* (1881), 18 Ch. D. 449). In that case the solicitor sold the property under his power of sale, without giving notice to the mortgagor, and it was held that the mortgagor was entitled to damages and costs. In *Pooley's Trustee* v. *Whetham* (1886), 55 L.T. 333, a client entered into an agreement with his solicitor in which he admitted that he was indebted to the solicitor in a certain sum made up principally of costs and interest and agreed to pay the sum on a fixed date, and in default that the solicitor was to be at liberty, without giving him any notice, to realise certain securities which he lodged with him. The money was not paid on the agreed date, and the solicitor realised the securities without giving the client any notice. It was held, distinguishing *Cockburn* v. *Edwards,* above, that the agreement was not an ordinary mortgage, but an agreement for giving time to the client, and, therefore, the solicitor had not committed a breach of duty to his client in not explaining that the power of sale was in an unusual form. For summaries of the applicable cases see *Law Society's Digest,* Opinions Nos. 352 to 364.

As to the duty owed by a solicitor when making a loan to a client, see *Spector* v. *Ageda* [1971] 3 W.L.R. 498. In all ordinary circumstances a solicitor ought to refuse to act for a person in a transaction to which the solicitor is himself a party with an adverse interest (*per* Megarry, J., *ibid.*, at p. 512).

Gifts by a client to a solicitor otherwise than by will.—A gift by a client to a solicitor will be invalid unless the client can be shown to have been wholly free from the influence of the solicitor in making the gift. It is difficult for the solicitor to discharge the burden of proof on him unless he can show that the donor has previously had competent and independent advice in the matter (*Liles* v. *Terry* [1895] 2 Q.B. 679 ; *Wright* v. *Carter* [1903] 1 Ch. 27) ; though the transaction may be not only free from fraud, but the most moral in its nature (*Wright* v. *Proud* (1806), 13 Ves. 136). The rule is equally applicable to a gift to a solicitor's wife, and the fact that she may be a relative of the donor, or that the gift is to her for her separate use is, therefore, immaterial (*Liles* v. *Terry, ante*). The same rule applies where the gift is to a solicitor's son (*Barron* v. *Willis* [1899] 2 Ch. 578 ; [1900] 2 Ch. 121 ; [1902] A.C. 271, under heading *Willis* v. *Barron*, reversed on facts). As to what amounts to competent and independent advice, see *Wright* v. *Carter, ante*.

After the relation of solicitor and client has come to an end, and any influence arising from such relation has ceased to exist, the client may, provided he is advised of and knows of his right to impeach and recall the gift, ratify what he has done ; but such ratification must be fixed, deliberate and unbiased determination that the transaction shall not be impeached (*Tyars* v. *Alsop* (1889), 61 L.T. 8).

For further cases and summaries on this aspect, see *Law Society's Digest*, Opinions Nos. 366 to 378a.

Subsequent purchasers.—It is not sufficiently precise to say that a solicitor is totally incapacitated from transacting, whether by sale, mortgage or gift with his client unless the presumption of undue influence be rebutted. As with trustee and beneficiary, the true rule is that the transaction is *voidable* within a reasonable time at the instance of the client (*Campbell* v. *Walker* (1800), 5 Ves. 678). Accordingly, subsequent *bona fide* purchasers for value of the property without notice of the client's equitable rights will take free of them (*Pilcher* v. *Rawlins* (1872), 7 Ch. App. 259), whilst a purchaser who becomes aware of a previous dealing with the property between solicitor and client must make the same objections as if he had discovered a purchase of trust property by a trustee (see, for example, *Pilkington* v. *Wood* [1953] Ch. 770).

Registered land.—On an application for registration under the L.R.A. 1925 following a voidable dealing between solicitor and client, it appears that H.M. Land Registry will ask no questions and that the registration will be completed with absolute title in the normal way (Ruoff and Roper, Registered Conveyancing, 3rd ed., p. 168). However, the solicitor-proprietor, not being " entitled for his own benefit " will have the estate vested in him subject to his client's "minor interests" (L.R.A. 1925, ss. 5 (c) and 9 (d)). Further, transferees from the solicitor-proprietor " *without* valuable consideration " will also be subject to these minor interests (L.R.A. 1925, ss. 20 (4) and 23 (5)). In either such case, rectification of the register without indemnity would be available (L.R.A. 1925, ss. 82 and 83, as amended by the Land Charges and Land Registration Act, 1971, ss. 2, 3, 14 (2), Sched. 2).

TENANTS BY THE CURTESY

Before 1926 there were four requisites to the existence of an estate by the curtesy, that is, life estate of a widower in the whole of a deceased wife's freeholds :—

1. Marriage (subsisting at the time of the wife's death).

2. Seisin (in possession, unless such possession could not possibly be obtained) of the wife for an estate of inheritance at her death. The " possession " had to be sole possession ; that is, the wife had not to be seised jointly with another person.

3. Issue born alive in the wife's lifetime and capable at the time of birth of inheriting. It was not necessary that the child should be alive at the wife's death.

4. Death of the wife intestate.

Where an estate as tenant by the curtesy can still be claimed (see below), these requisites still hold good, except that No. 2 should read " equitable estate of inheritance."

The right to curtesy extended to the wife's *equitable*, as well as to her *legal*, estates in fee, including those held by her for her separate use (*Eager* v. *Furnivall* (1881), 17 Ch. D. 115) ; but not if she had disposed of them in her lifetime or by will (*Cooper* v. *Macdonald* (1877), 7 Ch. D. 288). The Married Women's Property Act, 1882, did not affect the right of the husband to curtesy (*Hope* v. *Hope* [1892] 2 Ch. 336). Divorce took away the right to curtesy.

Curtesy attached to land of which the wife was tenant in tail, provided that a child was born capable of taking under the entail, although the wife might eventually die without issue (*Paine's Case* (1587), 3 Rep. 34a).

It is now provided by s. 45 (1) of the A.E.A. 1925 that with regard to the real estate and personal inheritance of every person dying after 1925 tenancy by the curtesy and every other estate and interest of a husband in real estate as to which his wife dies intestate, whether arising under the general law or by custom or otherwise, should be abolished except on descent or devolution of an entailed interest. By s. 130 (4) of the L.P.A. 1925, where a wife being entitled to an entailed interest dies without having executed a disentailing assurance and without having disposed of the interest by her will, the husband will take an equitable estate by the curtesy if the conditions above mentioned are fulfilled.

A tenant by the curtesy is a person having the powers of a tenant for life (S.L.A. 1925, s. 20 (1) (vii)) ; and, by subs. (3) of the same section, " the estate or interest of a tenant by the curtesy shall be deemed to be an estate or interest arising under a settlement made by his wife." The personal representatives of the intestate will be the trustees of the settlement until other trustees are appointed (S.L.A. 1925, s. 30 (3)).

TENANTS IN TAIL AND ENTAILED INTERESTS

If any land stands limited after 1925 in trust for any person in possession for an entailed interest there is a settlement for the purposes of the S.L.A. 1925 (*ibid.*, s. 1 (1) (ii) (*a*)). Questions arising on the title to a legal estate in settled land are considered in the chapter on Settled Land, *post*, p. 664. It is, however, convenient to deal here with the law relating to estates tail, and their modern equivalent, entailed interests.

A. ESTATES TAIL EXISTING BEFORE 1926

Words of limitation in deeds.—Before 1882, at common law, to create an estate tail by deed it was necessary to use the word "heirs" plus some words of procreation (i.e., words confining "heirs" to descendants of the original grantee). An example of an effective expression would be the words "heirs of his body," also "heirs of his flesh," "heirs from him proceeding." For further examples and certain qualifications of the common-law rule, see Megarry and Wade, Real Property, 3rd ed., p. 57 *et seq.* Under s. 51 of the Conveyancing Act, 1881, it became sufficient in the limitation of an estate in tail, to use the words "in tail" without such words as "heirs of his body"; and in the limitation of an estate in tail male or in tail female, to use the words "in tail male," or "in tail female," as the case requires, without such words as "heirs male of his body" or "heirs female of his body." Since 1st January, 1926, the law has continued the same, as s. 51 of the Conveyancing Act, 1881, has been re-enacted by s. 60 of the L.P.A. 1925.

In dealing with an equitable estate created before 1926 the language used by the settlor had to bear the same construction as in the case of a legal estate, if strict conveyancing language with a definite legal meaning had been used by the settlor. If, on the other hand, strict conveyancing language had not been used in the limitation of an equitable estate then it was sufficient that the instrument should disclose, as a matter of construction, a clear intention as to the quantum of the interest which was intended to be given (*Re Bostock's Settlement* [1921] 2 Ch. 469). Thus in *Re Arden ; Short* v. *Camm* [1935] Ch. 326, the intention of the settlor to pass the fee simple was held to be sufficiently shown by his use of the word "absolutely." And, even where, following *Re Bostock*, above, the court would have been bound to construe the language used according to the strict rules, it might have been that, in an action for rectification of the settlement, the court could have found sufficient evidence of the true intention of the settlor to enable it to rectify the settlement by inserting the words of limitation necessary to give effect to the intention (*Banks* v. *Ripley* [1940] Ch. 719). This law now applies only where the document was executed before 1926. Since 1925 an entailed interest cannot be created by an executory or any other document without technical words of limitation (L.P.A. 1925, s. 130 (1), mentioned at p. 431).

Words of limitation in wills before 1926.—The following are some expressions which under the old law were sufficient in the case of freehold property to create an estate tail by will, but which under the new law will create absolute fee simple or other interests corresponding to those which, if the property had been personal estate, would have been created therein by similar expressions :

To *A* and his issue (*Relham-Clinton* v. *Duke of Newcastle* [1903] A.C. 111).

To *A* or his issue (*Re Clerke ; Clowes* v. *Clerke* [1915] 2 Ch. 301 ; *Re Whitehead* [1920] 1. Ch. 298 ; *Re Hayden* [1931] 2 Ch. 333).

To *A* and his children, *A* having no children at the time of the execution of the will, the word "children" being construed as a word of limitation and not of purchase (*Wild's Case* (1599), 6 Co. Rep. 16*b*).

To *A* and his heirs lawfully begotten (*Good* v. *Good* (1857), 7 El. & Bl. 295).

To *A* and her descendants (*Re Sleeman* [1929] W.N. 16).

Transitional provisions.—Under the 1925 conveyancing Acts a tenancy in tail, or an " entailed interest," cannot be a legal estate (L.P.A. 1925, s. 1 (1)), and can only be created as an equitable interest (L.P.A. 1925, s. 130 (1), (7)). Therefore, to bring the old law into line with the new law, all estates tail existing as legal estates before 1926 were converted into equitable interests on 1st January, 1926 (L.P.A. 1925, ss. 1 and 39, and Pt. I of Sched. 1).

Accordingly, where on 31st December, 1925, there was under a settlement a legal tenant in tail in possession, on 1st January, 1926, his legal estate in tail in possession was converted into an equitable entailed interest in possession (L.P.A. 1925, Sched. 1, Pt. I). The settlement under which he became entitled became the " trust instrument " for the purposes of the S.L.A. 1925 (Sched. 2, para. 1 (1)) ; and the land settled land (S.L.A. 1925, s. 2). The tenant in tail in possession became the tenant for life within the meaning of the S.L.A. 1925, and under the provisions contained in the L.P.A. 1925, Sched. 1, Pt. II, paras. 3, 5 and 6 (c), the legal estate in fee simple became vested in such tenant in tail in possession as tenant for life, but only as trustee for himself as owner of the equitable entailed interest, with remainders over (S.L.A. 1925, s. 107). As such tenant for life he obtained the wide powers of tenants for life under the S.L.A. 1925 (ss. 20 (1), 117 (1) (xxviii)) ; but to enable him to exercise such powers he had first to obtain a vesting instrument stating that legal estate was vested in him (S.L.A. 1925, s. 13). This instrument he was entitled to require the trustees of the settlement to execute in his favour (S.L.A. 1925, Sched. 2, para. 1 (2)). The tenant in tail in possession, so long as the trusts of the settlement had not come to an end, and the trustees for the purposes of the S.L.A. 1925, had not been released, would be the person to make title to the settled land as tenant for life under the Act.

But it might have been that, on 31st December, 1925, all the trusts of the settlement had come to an end. In this case the tenant in tail in possession could have barred the entail and thus become entitled to the absolute fee simple free from the settlement and the land would then have ceased to be settled land. Consequently no vesting deed would have been necessary, because a vesting deed is only necessary so long as the land remained settled land (*Re Alefounders' Will Trusts* [1927] 1 Ch. 360).

B. ENTAILED INTERESTS AFTER 1925

Summary of alterations in the law.—(i) All estates tail existing on 31st December, 1925, were converted into equitable interests ; after that date an estate can only be created as an equitable interest. Such interests are now known as " entailed interests."

(ii) Entailed interests can now be created in *personal property* as well as in real property.

(iii) Entailed interests can only be created by a settlement or agreement for a settlement, *inter vivos*, or by a will.

(iv) To enable an entailed interest in real or personal property to be created, technical words of limitation must now be used, whether the entailed interest is created *inter vivos* or by a will. These technical words will be the words which had be to used to create an estate tail by deed in freehold property before 1926.

(v) The power of a settlor under s. 32 of the Fines and Recoveries Act, 1833, to appoint special protectors of a settlement, has now been abolished.

But where a person is entitled to an entailed interest on the death of a life-tenant, such life-tenant will still be the protector of the settlement, and if such tenant in tail in remainder should convey his interest without the consent of the life-tenant, he would only create a *base fee*.

(vi) When an entailed interest had been barred by means of a disentailing deed before 1926, such deed had to be enrolled. Enrolment has now been done away with.

(vii) A tenant in tail in possession and the owner of a *base fee* in possession, of full age, may now devise or bequeath his or her interest as if he or she had barred the entail.

Creation by strict settlement.—In the case of a strict settlement, there is no trust for sale and successive interests are given to the members of a family, the object being to keep the land in one family as long as the rule against perpetuities will allow. A strict settlement is a " settlement " within the meaning of the S.L.A. 1925, and the law and practice in connection there-with are governed by the provisions of the S.L.A. 1925, which means that there have to be vesting instruments, special representation, and the settlement and the land become subject to many highly technical rules. The result is that the practice is to settle land by way of a trust for sale.

Section 130 (6) of the L.P.A. 1925 states that an entailed interest shall only be capable of being created by a *settlement of real or personal property or the proceeds of sale thereof* (including the will of a person dying after the com-mencement of the Act), or by an *agreement for a settlement* in which the trusts to affect the property are sufficiently declared.

The authorised method of creating a *strict settlement* of land, *inter vivos*, is given in s. 4 (1) of the S.L.A. 1925, *post*, p. 680. It is provided by s. 9 (1) (iii) of the S.L.A. 1925 that an instrument *inter vivos* intended to create a settle-ment of a legal estate in land which does not comply with the requirements of the Act with respect to the method of effecting such a settlement, shall be deemed to be a trust instrument.

It is also provided by s. 9 (1) (iv) of the S.L.A. 1925, in effect, that a settle-ment of an entailed interest or a *base fee* [as to what is a base fee, see at p. 438] or any corresponding interest in leasehold land in remainder on the death of a life-tenant, shall not be deemed to be a trust instrument until the interest settled takes effect free from all equitable interests and powers under every prior settlement. Until that event happens a vesting deed need not be executed. Therefore, should there be a settlement prior to the settlement creating an entailed interest, the latter instrument will not become a trust instrument until such latter instrument takes effect free from all equitable interests and powers under the prior instrument, and until then a vesting deed will not have to be executed.

If entailed interests are granted to the first and other sons of a named person, it is implied that they are to take successively, even though this word has been omitted from the limitation (*Re Gosset* [1943] Ch. 351).

Words of limitation.—Strict words of limitation are now necessary to create an entailed interest, whether by a document *inter vivos* or by will. The L.P.A. 1925, s. 130 (1), provides :—

" 130.—(1) An interest in tail or in tail male or in tail female or in tail special (in this Act referred to as an ' entailed interest ') may be created by way of trust in any *property, real or personal, but only by the like expressions* as those by which before the commencement of this Act a similar estate tail could have been created by deed (*not being an executory instrument*) in freehold land, and *with the like results*, including the right to bar the entail either absolutely or so as to create an interest equivalent to a base fee, and accordingly all statutory provisions relating to estates tail in real property shall apply to entailed interests in personal property.

Personal estate so entailed (not being chattels settled as heirlooms) may be invested, applied and otherwise dealt with as if the same were capital money or securities representing capital money arising under the Settled Land Act, 1925, from land settled on the like trusts."

" *property, real or personal.*"—The following special rule as to settlement of personalty is contained in the L.P.A. 1925, s. 130 (3) :—

" (3) Where personal estate (including the proceeds of sale of land directed to be sold and chattels directed to be held as heirlooms) is, after the commencement of this Act, directed to be enjoyed or held with, or upon trusts corresponding to trusts affecting, land in which, either before or after the commencement of this Act an entailed interest has been created, and is subsisting, such direction shall be deemed sufficient to create a corresponding entailed interest in such personal estate."

Therefore, in this case technical words of limitation are not necessary, but it was held by Clauson, J., in *Re E. B. Jones, deceased* [1934] 1 Ch. 315, that in the case of a will, before the subsection operates, one must find a direction that the property is to be held upon trusts *corresponding to trusts affecting land*. In other words, there must be a use of the actual words mentioned in the subsection. They were not used in the will before him and so the old law applied, namely, that an absolute interest was created.

" *but only by the like expressions.*"—For the expressions which, before 1926, were sufficient to create an estate tail by deed, see *ante*, p. 429.

" *not being an executory interest.*"—" Executory " means that something remains to be done to complete the gift ; for instance, a direction in a will giving instructions or short heads from which the trustee is subsequently to model a formal settlement would be " executory." " Executed " means that nothing remains to be done to complete the gift. A contract is usually an executory document and the deed carrying out the terms of the contract is the executed document.

" *with the like results.*"—Thus, an entailed interest in personalty is subject to the same rules of law, statutory and otherwise (for instance as to disposition of income pending birth of a person who would be entitled in possession) as applied to estates tail in realty before 1926 (*Re Crossley's Settlement Trusts* [1955] Ch. 627).

Effect of informal expressions.—The L.P.A. 1925, s. 130 (2), provides :—

" Expressions contained in an instrument coming into operation after [1925] which, in a will, or executory instrument coming into operation before [1926] would have created an entailed interest in freehold land, but would not have been effectual for that purpose in a deed not being an executory instrument, shall (*save as provided by the next succeeding section*) operate in equity, in regard to property real or personal, to create absolute, fee simple or other interests corresponding to those which, if the property affected had been personal estate, would have been created therein by similar expressions before the commencement of this Act."

This subsection may not be straightforward to construe since there is some dispute as to what would have been the corresponding interests in a bequest of personalty ; see *Cambridge Law Journal*, vol. 6, p. 67, and *ibid.*, vol. 9, pp. 46, 185 and 190.   At least it is clear that no entail can arise because personalty could not be entailed before 1926 (but compare *Re Compton* [1944] 2 All E.R. 255).   Otherwise, an expression such as " to *A* and his issue " may give an absolute interest either to *A* jointly with such of his issue as are living when the gift takes effect or else to *A* alone (Hawkins and Ryder on the Construction of Wills, p. 256 *et seq.*).

" *save as provided by the next succeeding section.*"—These words, in s. 130 (2), refer to the abolition of the rule in *Shelley's Case* (1581), 1 Co. Rep. 93*b*, by s. 131 ; see *ante*, p. 330.

Creation of entailed interest by way of trust for sale.—A trust for sale with a settlement of the proceeds is equally suitable as a strict settlement, for the purpose of keeping the land in one family as long as possible.   For since 1925 it has been made possible by s. 130 (1) of the L.P.A. 1925 to create an entailed interest in *personalty*.   Therefore, the trustees could be directed to hold the proceeds of sale upon such trusts as to create the same entailed interests as are customary in a strict settlement but this is certainly not frequently done.   Settlements on trust for sale have long contained different trusts and taxation considerations now usually cause very different terms to be adopted.

The great advantage which a settlement by way of trust for sale has is undoubtedly that it is not affected by the provisions of the S.L.A. 1925 as to vesting deeds, special grants, etc. (S.L.A. 1925, s. 1 (7)).   But it is very important to be sure that what appears, on the face of it, to be a trust for sale is in fact a trust for sale as defined by s. 205 (1) (xxix) of the L.P.A., 1925.

Interest of a tenant in tail of an undivided share in the proceeds of sale of the entirety.—Put shortly, s. 35 of the L.P.A. 1925 provides that, for the purposes of the Act, land held upon the "statutory trusts" shall be held upon trust to sell the same and to stand possessed of the net proceeds of sale and of the net rents and profits until sale upon such trusts as may be requisite for giving effect to the rights of the persons interested in the land ; and s. 36 (6) of the S.L.A. 1925, is in similar terms.   The effect of these provisions is to effect a statutory conversion, in equity, of the land into money, so that the beneficial interest therein devolves as personal estate.   It was held in *Re Price* [1928] Ch. 579 that where land was held in undivided shares, and one of the undivided shares was held in tail, the imposition of the statutory trusts, by converting the share into personalty, destroyed the entail and gave to the tenant in tail of that share an absolute interest in the share of the proceeds of sale and not an entailed interest in such share.   But, by the statutory trusts (s. 35 of the L.P.A. 1925), the proceeds of sale are to be held upon such trusts as are requisite for giving effect to the rights of the persons interested in the land.   This decision appears to have been wrong.   At any rate the result was so obviously unlooked for that it was corrected by the Law of Property (Entailed Interests) Act, 1932. which provides by s. 1 that at the end of s. 36 (6) of the S.L.A. 1925, and of s. 35 of the L.P.A. 1925 the following words shall be inserted :—

" And the right of a person who, if the land had not been made subject to a trust for sale by virtue of this Act, would have been entitled to an entailed interest in an undivided share in the land, shall be deemed to be a right to a corresponding entailed interest in the net proceeds of sale attributable to that share."

It was decided in *Re Hind*; *Bernstone* v. *Montgomery* [1933] 1 Ch. 208, that the expression " entailed interest " in the above Act does not include a *base fee*.

The Act was to be deemed to have come into operation on 1st January, 1926, except in the cases mentioned therein.

Sale of personal chattels.—Subsection (5) of s. 130 of the L.P.A. 1925 provides for the sale of personal chattels when they have been *settled without reference to settled land*. A distinction must be made between chattels *settled with reference to land* and those *settled without reference to land*. The former class is dealt with by s. 67 of the S.L.A. 1925, which ensures that heirlooms shall not be sold without the consent of the court. Section 130 (5) is as follows :—

" (5) Where personal chattels are settled *without reference to settled land* on trusts creating entailed interests therein, the trustees, with the consent of the usufructuary for the time being if of full age, may sell the chattels or any of them, and the net proceeds of any such sale shall be held in trust for and shall go to the same persons successively, in the same manner and for the same interests, as the chattels sold would have been held and gone if they had not been sold, and the income of investments representing such proceeds of sale shall be applied accordingly."

It must be noted that before 1926 an entailed interest could not be created in personalty unless it was directed to be laid out in the purchase of land and so converted into realty. In *Re Hope's Will Trusts* [1929] 2 Ch. 136, a testator who died before 1926 by his will settled certain chattels, including three family portraits, to be held upon trusts which should as nearly as the rules of law and equity permitted correspond with the limitations of real estate in tail, and set out such limitations at length, *but settled no real estate upon the same limitations*, and it was held by Eve, J., that the testator had attempted to create an entailed interest in the chattles but had not succeeded, and that the trustees of his will had no power to sell them under the above subs. (5). But the court, deeming it " expedient " within the meaning of the word in s. 57 of the T.A. 1925, made an order authorising the sale of the portraits by the trustees under that section.

Creation of entailed interest by agreement.—It is not thought that the power to create an entailed interest by an agreement for a settlement will often be used, as an agreement is not a suitable medium for creating an entailed interest.

However, should it be attempted to create an entailed interest by an agreement, the question arises whether technical words of limitation are necessary, so long as the intention is shown to create an entailed interest. The words of subs. (6) of s. 130 of the L.P.A. 1925 are : " or by an agreement for a settlement in which the trusts to affect the property are *sufficiently declared*." These words seem to take the case out of subs. (1) of the section, which provides that an entailed interest can only be created by the use of technical words. If this is so, then the intention to create an entailed interest must be clearly shown. To be on the safe side it will be better, even in an agreement, to use the same technical words as would be used in a deed or a will.

Creation of entailed interest by will.—It is provided by s. 130 of the L.P.A. 1925, that an entailed interest may be created (*inter alia*) by the will of a person dying after 1925, but only by the like expressions as those by which before 1926 a similar estate tail could have been created by deed (not being an executory instrument) in freehold land.

All the matter contained in the note as to the manner of creating an entailed interest by a strict settlement by deed, set out at p. 680 *et seq.*, applies equally to a will. The procedure to be adopted when a settlement is so created by will is discussed *post*, p. 685.

The distinction between a will creating an entailed interest and a will devising or bequeathing an entailed interest must be borne in mind. In the latter case which in effect bars the entail it is not necessary to use words of limitation, but only to refer specifically either to the property or to the instrument under which it was acquired or to entailed property generally (L.P.A. 1925, s. 176 (1)).

Settlement by tenant in tail in remainder.—If a tenant in tail in remainder executes a settlement of his interest in remainder on himself for life with remainders over, and in due course the tenant for life dies, but the land still remains subject to the widow's jointure or to a term to secure portions for younger children under the prior settlement, the settlement made by him of his interest in tail in remainder will not be a trust instrument because the interest settled *is not free from all equitable interests and powers* under the prior settlement (S.L.A. 1925, s. 9 (1)). But immediately the settled interest becomes free from such equitable interests by the death of the widow and payment of the younger children's portions, the settlement made by the tenant in tail will become a trust instrument, and a vesting deed under subs. (2) of s. 9 of the S.L.A. 1925 should be executed by the trustees of the settlement, declaring that the legal estate in the settled land shall vest or is vested in the person being the tenant for life or statutory owner, and such deed will, unless the legal estate is already so vested, operate to convey or vest the legal estate in the settled land to or in such person or persons, and, if more than one, as joint tenants. And, the prior settlement having come to an end, the trustees of such prior settlement should then execute a deed of discharge under s. 17 (1) of the S.L.A. 1925, in which there should be a statement that the land is settled land by virtue of the vesting deed and the trust instrument referred to or is held on trust for sale by virtue of a conveyance, as the case may require.

It will be noted that the section says : " and such deed shall, unless the legal estate is already so vested [for instance, vested in the trustees of the latter settlement who are entitled to it as statutory owners] operate to convey or vest the legal estate in the settled land to or in the person or persons aforesaid." If the trustees of the prior settlement and the trustees of the later settlement should happen to be the same persons, probably a new vesting deed would not be necessary (but compare *Re King's Will Trusts* [1964] Ch. 542).

C. DEVOLUTION OF ENTAILED INTERESTS

The devolution of an entailed interest where the tenant in tail has not barred the entail, or devised or bequeathed it by will, is provided for by s. 130 (4) of the L.P.A. 1925, given below :—

" (4) In default of and subject to the execution of a disentailing assurance or the exercise of the testamentary power conferred by this Act, an entailed interest (*to the extent of the property affected*) shall devolve as an equitable interest, from time to time, upon the persons who would have been successively entitled thereto as the heirs of the body (either generally or of a particular class) of the tenant in tail or other person, or as tenant by the curtesy, if the entailed interest had, before the commencement of this Act, been limited in respect of freehold land governed by the general law in force immediately before such commencement, and such law had remained unaffected."

"*to the extent of the property affected.*"—This refers to the case where leasehold property is being entailed. The entailed interest can only remain operative while the term remains existing.

A statement of the old canons of descent of an estate tail is contained in the section on Heirs, *ante*, p. 329.

Although heirship, in general, was abolished by s. 45 (1) of the A.E.A. 1925, subs. (2) thereof provided that " Nothing in this section affects the descent or devolution of an entailed interest." The effect of this subsection is also to save curtesy both as regards past and future interests since 1925, but apparently not dower. As the " heir " has to be ascertained according to the old canons of descent, the Inheritance Act, 1833, as amended by the Law of Property Amendment Act, 1859, was kept alive by the Law of Property (Amendment) Act, 1924, Sched. 9, para. 1.

Part IV of the A.E.A. 1925 deals with the devolution and distribution of the property of an intestate generally, but it is specially provided by s. 51 (4) of that Act that Pt. IV thereof shall not affect the devolution of an entailed interest.

An entailed interest of a deceased person, if not disposed of under the testamentary power conferred by statute, is deemed to be *an interest ceasing on his death*, within the meaning of A.E.A. 1925, s. 3 (3), and does not pass to the personal representatives of the deceased tenant in tail and will not be liable for his debts. If, however, the deceased had any further or other interest in the same property in remainder or reversion which was capable of being disposed of by his will, such further or other interest would not be deemed to be an interest so ceasing (*ibid.*).

Death of devisee of an entailed interest in testator's lifetime.— It is provided by s. 32 of the Wills Act, 1837, in effect that where any person, to whom any real estate shall have been devised for an estate tail or an estate in *quasi*-tail shall die in the testator's lifetime, leaving issue living at the testator's death who could inherit, there will be no lapse, but the devise will take effect as if the death of such person had happened immediately after the death of the testator, unless a contrary intention appears from the will.

Section 130 (1) of the L.P.A. 1925, provides that, *inter alia*, " all statutory provisions relating to estates tail in real property shall apply to entailed interests in personal property." It follows, therefore, that as an entailed interest can now be created in personal property (*ibid.*), where personal property is bequeathed to a person for an interest in tail, and such person dies in the testator's lifetime leaving issue who could inherit, s. 32 will apply, and the bequest will not lapse, unless there is a contrary intention in the will.

D. BARRING THE ENTAIL

General rules.—It is provided by s. 130 (1) of the L.P.A. 1925 in effect, that an entailed interest may, after 1925, be created by way of trust (that is, as an equitable interest) in any property, real or personal, and with the like results, *including the right to bar the entail either absolutely or so as to create an interest equivalent to a base fee, and that accordingly all statutory provisions relating to estates tail in real property* [the Fines and Recoveries Act, 1833, as amended] shall apply to entailed interests in personal property.

No particular form of disentailing deed was prescribed by the Fines and Recoveries Act, but it had to be a *deed* which, if the tenant in tail had been possessed of an absolute fee simple, would have been sufficient to convey the fee (ss. 15, 20, and see *Re St. Albans' Will Trust* [1963] Ch. 365). Before 1926 a tenant in tail contracted to disentail and sell the land and died before the deed was executed, and it was held that the contract became void (*Bankes* v. *Small* (1887), 36 Ch. D. 716). A deed will therefore still be necessary although the interest to be conveyed is only equitable. When the interest falls into possession legal effect will be given to the disentailing deed by an assent or vesting instrument.

As disentailing assurances of land will operate only in equity, it will still be necessary to employ a grantee, so as to comply with the Fines and Recoveries Act, 1833 ; and such grantee (being now a trustee of an equitable interest) should always execute the deed, otherwise it might be rendered inoperative by disclaimer (see *Peacock* v. *Eastland* (1870), L.R. 10 Eq. 17).

The reason is that he is no longer a mere conduit pipe taking no disclaimable interest. A declaration of trust was held not to be sufficient to bar the entail (*Carter* v. *Carter* [1896] 1 Ch. 62).

A mortgage in fee barred the entail (1833 Act, s. 21) unless the proviso for redemption revived the trusts of the settlement or contained a new set of limitations by way of resettlement (*Re Oxenden's Settled Estates ; Oxenden* v. *Chapman* (1904), 74 L.J. Ch. 234). As all legal mortgages have now to be by demise or sub-demise no difficulty will arise in the future on this point.

The deed purporting to bar the entail had to be enrolled within six months after execution (1833 Act, s. 41) otherwise its effect was to convey the tenant in tail's own life interest only. Enrolment has now been abolished : see *post*, p. 441. As to the manner in which the consent of the protector has to be given, see *post*, p. 441.

If the lands were within a Middlesex or Yorkshire registry district, the deed had to be there registered. Registration became unnecessary after 1925, as an entailed interest is only an equitable interest (L.P.A. 1925, s. 11).

Where a solicitor is consulted by a tenant in tail regarding the interest of that tenant, it may be the solicitor's duty to advise that the entail may be barred. In *Otter* v. *Church, Adams, Tatham & Co.* [1953] 1 W.L.R. 156, the solicitor had given the impression in a letter to the tenant's mother that the tenant in tail was absolutely entitled and there was a particular danger of his early death ; in the circumstances the solicitor was held to have been guilty of negligence.

Tenant in tail in possession free from family charges.—With certain exceptions (see *post*, p. 440), a tenant in tail in possession, and also the owner of a *base fee* in possession, may by a deed *inter vivos* bar the entail and create a fee simple or term of years absolute, according as the property is freehold or leasehold, in himself, without the consent of anyone. And now he can also dispose of his interest in tail by his will in like manner as if, after barring the entail, he had been tenant in fee simple or absolute owner thereof for an equitable interest. See *post*, at p. 441. The effect of disentailment by a tenant in tail in possession, when the settlement is thereby brought to an end, is illustrated by *Re Alefounder's Will Trusts* [1927] 1 Ch. 360 ; it is not then necessary to obtain a vesting deed before sale.

The decision in *Re Alefounder's Will Trusts* does not apply where the tenant in tail has obtained a vesting deed. In that case s. 18 (1) (*a*) of the S.L.A. 1925 provides, in effect, that so long as land remains the subject of a vesting instrument, and the trustees have not been discharged, then any disposition by the tenant for life other than a disposition authorised by the Act shall be void, except for the purpose of conveying the beneficial interest of the tenant for life. If, therefore, the tenant in tail conveyed the land to a purchaser in fee simple, the effect would be that the land would be disentailed, but the purchaser would only get an equitable interest in the land. Certainly such purchaser could require the legal estate to be conveyed to him by the persons in whom it was then vested under subs. (2) of s. 18, but no purchaser would be advised to take such a title, and probably he could not be compelled to do so ; see s. 42 (4) (iii) of the L.P.A. 1925. If the tenant in tail desired to use the money himself, he could make title as tenant for life and then bring the settlement to an end and make the money his own by disentailing the purchase-money. Another way, but not so good a way as the last, would be for the tenant in tail himself to execute a disentailing deed and then call for a conveyance of the legal estate under s. 18 (2), above. He would then become absolute owner in fee simple and could deal with the land in any way he thought fit.

Tenant in tail in possession, subject to family charges.—If the tenant in tail in possession held his estate subject to family charges under the settlement, then the settlement would be still existing, and to enable him to convey the property free from those charges he would have to convey as tenant for life under the S.L.A. 1925. This he could do assuming the legal estate had been vested in him by vesting deed or assent.

Barring an entail in remainder with the consent of the protector.— The effect of a tenant in tail in remainder executing a deed barring the entail with the consent of the tenant for life, in possession, the protector, is to give the former a fee simple absolute, barred against not only his own issue, but against the claims of other persons whose interests take effect after the determination or in defeasance of the entailed interest, but subject, of course, to the prior life interest and to any jointure charged on the land and any term vested in the trustees for the purpose of raising money (*Millbank* v. *Vane* [1893] 3 Ch. 79 ; *Cardigan* v. *Curzon-Howe* [1901] 2 Ch. 479).

Barring an entail in remainder without the consent of the protector.— The rule is that a tenant in tail in remainder can only, without the consent of the protector, *partially* bar the entail. That is to say, he would acquire an estate in fee simple which would defeat his own issue, but would not defeat the claims of persons entitled to take interests in the property upon the determination of the entailed interest by failure of his issue or otherwise (Fines and Recoveries Act, 1833, s. 34). The interest which he would thus obtain was called " a base fee," which is defined by s. 1 of the 1833 Act as " that estate in fee simple into which an estate is converted where the issue in tail are barred, but persons claiming estates by way of remainder or otherwise are not barred " (*Re Drummond and Davies' Contract* [1891] 1 Ch. 524). Strictly speaking, since 1925, the interest acquired would not be a " base fee," but an equitable interest equivalent to a base fee.

Before the interest comes into possession, the base fee can be enlarged into an equitable fee simple by getting the consent to the disentail of the protector (Fines and Recoveries Act, 1833, s. 19). Also, after the base fee has come into possession it can be enlarged into a fee simple (*ibid.*) ; this may be done notwithstanding that the interest has been parted with to a purchaser (*Bankes* v. *Small* (1887), 36 Ch. D. 716).

If the owner of an equitable interest equivalent to a base fee becomes absolutely entitled to the remainder or reversion expectant thereon, such interest will become enlarged into a fee simple (Fines and Recoveries Act, 1833, s. 39). The effect of the Limitation Act, 1939, s. 11, is that when a person has been in possession of a base fee for twelve years after the original tenant in tail might have barred the remainders without the consent of anyone, the base fee will become a fee simple. And now, by s. 176 (1) and (3) of the L.P.A. 1925, the owner of a base fee *in possession* can dispose of the property by will, referring specifically either to the property or to the instrument under which it was acquired, or to entailed property generally, in like manner as if, after barring the entail, he had been tenant in fee simple or absolute owner thereof for an equitable interest at his death.

Bankrupt's entailed lands.—On the bankruptcy of a tenant in tail, the trustee is empowered to deal with the property in the same manner as the bankrupt might have dealt with it (Bankruptcy Act, 1914, s. 55 (5)). Section 103 of the S.L.A. 1925 provides that the legal estate in settled land shall not vest in the trustee in bankruptcy of an estate owner until the estate owner becomes absolutely and beneficially entitled to the settled land free from the settlement. Assuming there were no prior interests under the settlement the bankrupt could have attained this position by barring the entail. Therefore the trustee can do so ; when he has barred the entail he can deal with the legal estate. So also, if a person adjudicated a bankrupt could, if he had not been a bankrupt, enlarge his base fee into a fee simple, the trustee in bankruptcy can do so with the consent of the protector, if any (Bankruptcy Act, 1914, s. 55 (5)). It follows that the trustee cannot disentail after the death of the debtor tenant in tail.

The tenant in tail, although a bankrupt, can sell as tenant for life under the S.L.A. 1925 (s. 104); and, if he should refuse to act, an order of court could be obtained enabling the S.L.A. 1925 trustees to act as statutory owners (S.L.A. 1925, s. 24). See also s. 38 (2) (*b*) of the Bankruptcy Act, 1914, giving the trustee power to exercise all powers in or over property which the debtor could have executed for his own benefit.

Married woman's entailed lands.—If a married woman tenant in tail who had acquired her interest before 1883 and was married before that date wished to bar the entail, she could only do so with the concurrence of the husband and by an acknowledged deed (Fines and Recoveries Act, 1833, s. 2 ; *Cooper* v. *Macdonald* (1877), 7 Ch. D. 288). Since 1925 the concurrence of the husband will still be necessary, but not acknowledgment (L.P.A. 1925, s. 167 (1), now repealed).

The estate or interest of a married woman tenant in tail in possession, when she was married after the passing of the Married Women's Property Act, 1882, or if married before that date, acquired such property after that date, is her own property and she can bar the entail without her husband's concurrence or acknowledgment (Law Reform (Married Women and Tortfeasors) Act, 1935, s. 2). A restraint on anticipation did not prevent a married woman barring the entail.

Infant's entailed lands.—An infant cannot execute a disentailing assurance, except as mentioned below.   Although an infant may lose his interest under a settlement in land if he dies under age unmarried (see A.E.A. 1925, s. 51 (3)), the court can, under s. 53 of the T.A. 1925, make an order appointing a person to convey the property.   The section provides (*inter alia*) that, where an infant is beneficially entitled to any property, the court may, with a view to the application of the capital or income thereof for the maintenance, education or benefit of the infant, make an order appointing a person to convey such property.   See also *ibid.*, s. 44 (ii) (*a*).

An infant could before 1970 execute a disentailing settlement under the provisions of the Infant Settlements Act, 1855 (repealed by Family Law Reform Act, 1969, s. 11 (*a*), but not retrospectively), that is, with the consent of the court, but should he or she die under age, the disentailing assurance would become void (*ibid.*, s. 2 ; *Re Scott ; Scott* v. *Hanbury* [1891] 1 Ch. 298).

Cases where the tenant in tail cannot bar the entail.—The power to bar the entail, or to devise the land as if the entail had been barred, does not extend to a tenant in tail who is by statute restrained from barring the entail, or to a tenant in tail after possibility of issue extinct, or to the case where the land was granted by the Crown for services with a reversion to the Crown (Fines and Recoveries Act, 1833, s. 18, repealed in error, but re-enacted by the Expiring Laws Act, 1925 ; L.P.A. 1925, s. 176 (2)).

Barring the entail created by way of trust for sale.—An entailed interest may now be created as an equitable interest in personal property, and such entail may be barred either absolutely or so as to create an interest equivalent to a base fee, and all statutory provisions relating to estates tail in real property will apply to entailed interests in personal property (L.P.A. 1925, s. 130 (1)).   Also a settlement by way of trust for sale is specially excepted from the provisions of the S.L.A. 1925 (s. 1 (7)), with the result that the legal estate is vested in the trustees of the settlement and not, as in the case of settled land, in the tenant for life.   No vesting instruments, therefore, are required where the land is held on trust for sale.

The disentailing deed would be a deed by which the tenant in tail would assign the proceeds of sale of the property entailed, or the stocks or shares entailed, unto trustees to hold the same unto the trustees discharged from all equitable interests in tail of the tenant in tail, and from all estates, rights, interests and powers to take effect upon the determination or in defeasance of any such interest of the tenant in tail in trust for the tenant in tail absolutely.

The protector of the settlement.—Before the passing of the Fines and Recoveries Act, 1833, a tenant in tail in remainder could, by suffering " a recovery " (provided he got the consent of the person who was in actual possession of the land), fully bar the entail against his issue and persons entitled on failure thereof.   But if the person in possession would not give his consent he could only bar the entail by means of a " fine " so as to bar his own issue, that is, so as to create a *base fee*.   This would have the effect of creating an estate to last as long as he and his issue lived, and on his death and the death of all his issue the land would revert to the grantor or his heirs. The deed purporting to bar the entail had to be enrolled.   If this was not done the deed would have no effect under the statute and would only pass his own beneficial life interest.

When fines and recoveries were abolished by the 1833 Act, it was thought wise to retain the obligation to obtain the consent of the person in possession, as otherwise tenants in remainder might ruin family estates. By s. 22 of the Fines and Recoveries Act, 1833, *if the settlor did not appoint a special protector* (which office is now abolished), then, if there should be under the *same* settlement any estate for years determinable on a life, or any greater estate, prior to the estate tail, the owner of such prior estate, or the first of such prior estates, if more than one, is *the protector*, and for the purposes of the Act is deemed to be the owner, although he may have incumbered such estate, or even absolutely disposed of it, or lost it by bankruptcy or any other act or default. Where there was both a trustee and a *cestui que trust* of the estate of freehold in possession, the *cestui que trust* was deemed to be the protector of the settlement (*Clarke* v. *Chamberlin* (1880), 16 Ch. D. 176).

Where the entailed interest is preceded by a discretionary trust of income during the life of a beneficiary neither the trustees of those trusts nor the discretionary objects are protectors of the settlement; neither does the court become protector under s. 33 of the Fines and Recoveries Act, 1833, so that the tenant in tail may disentail without any consent (*Re Darnley's Will Trusts* [1970] 1 W.L.R. 405).

The consent of the protector can be given either by the disentailing deed or by a separate deed.

Section 32 of the Fines and Recoveries Act, 1833, provided that a settlor might by the settlement appoint any person or persons, not exceeding three, to be special protector or protectors of the settlement. The deed of appointment, as also any deed by which a protector relinquished his office, had to be enrolled within six months of its execution (*ibid.*). This office of special protector survived to the others or other or the death or retirement of one of the persons nominated by the settlor, unless the settlement expressly provided to the contrary, and it was not necessary that the original number should be filled up (*Cohen* v. *Bayley-Worthington* [1908] A.C. 97). The section has now been repealed as respects settlements *made or coming into operation after* 1925, by Sched. 1 to the Law of Property (Amendment) Act, 1924, and the repeal was repeated in Sched. 7 to the L.P.A. 1925.

Abolition of enrolment.—The L.P.A. 1925, s. 133 (repealed in 1969) provided that every assurance or instrument executed or made after 1925, which, under the provisions of ss. 41, 46, 58, 59, 71 and 72 of the Fines and Recoveries Act, 1833, would have been required to be enrolled in the Central Office, will be as effectual for all purposes, without such enrolment, as if it had been duly enrolled within the time prescribed by the said Act for such enrolment. " Assurance " includes a vesting order operating as a disentailing assurance, whether made for barring an estate tail or enlarging a base fee or otherwise. The section applies to entailed interests authorised to be created by the Act as well as to estates tail created before the commencement of the Act.

Power of tenant in tail in possession to bar entail by will.—Before 1926 a tenant in tail could not dispose by will of property of which he was tenant in tail (Fines and Recoveries Act, 1833, s. 40). This is now altered. By s. 176 (1) of the L.P.A. 1925 it is provided that " a tenant in tail of full age shall have power to dispose by will, by means of a devise or bequest *referring* *specifically either to the property or to the instrument under which it was acquired or to entailed property generally—*

(a) of all property of which he is tenant in tail *in possession* at his death ; and

(b) of money (including the proceeds of property directed to be sold) subject to be invested in the purchase of property, of which if it had been so invested he would have been tenant in tail in possession at his death ;

in like manner as if, after barring the entail, he had been tenant in fee simple or absolute owner thereof for an equitable interest at his death, but, subject to and in default of any such disposition by will, such property shall devolve in the same manner as if this section had not been passed." The gift would be in some such form as: " I devise and bequeath the residue of my property, including property in which I have an entailed interest in possession to, etc."

The subsection applies to estates tail created before 1926 as well as to entailed interests authorised to be created by the Act, but does not extend to a tenant in tail who is by statute restrained from barring or defeating his estate tail, or to a tenant in tail after possibility of issue extinct, and does not render any interest which is not disposed of by the will of the tenant in tail liable for his debts or other liabilities (*ibid.*, subs. (2)). The section only applies to wills *executed after* 1925, or confirmed or republished by codicil executed after that date (*ibid.*, subs. (4)).

The expression " tenant in tail " as used above includes an owner of a base fee in possession who has power to enlarge the base fee into a fee simple without the concurrence of any other person (*ibid.*, subs. (3)).

There are two important points to note in s. 176 (1) of the L.P.A. 1925 :—

(1) The subsection only applies where the tenant in tail is in possession. If the tenant in tail requires the consent of the protector to bar the entail he has no power to dispose of the property by will.

(2) The devise or bequest must refer specifically either to the property or the instrument under which it was acquired or to entailed property generally. Therefore, a general devise or bequest would not pass the property. In *Acheson* v. *Russell* [1951] Ch. 67 the testator was entitled to a farm as to one equal undivided third share thereof in fee simple in possession and as to the other two equal undivided third shares thereof as tenant in tail general in possession. By his will he gave " all my one-third share and all other my estate and interest in [the farm] and in the proceeds thereof " to a beneficiary. Vaisey, J., held that the words of the will referred specifically to the two undivided third shares and so the gift operated under s. 176 (1).

It is provided by s. 32 of the A.E.A. 1925 that the real and personal estate of which a deceased person, in pursuance of the statutory power to dispose of entailed interests, disposes by his will, will be assets for payment of his debts and liabilities, and any disposition by will inconsistent with this enactment will be void as against his creditors.

On the death of a tenant in tail who has exercised his testamentary power of disposition, the interest dealt with passes in the first place to his personal representatives (A.E.A. 1925, ss. 1, 3 (2)), and when they have completed administration they will assent in favour of the person or persons beneficially entitled.

TENANTS PUR AUTRE VIE

Before 1926 the estate of a tenant *pur autre vie* was an estate of freehold (*Doe d. Blake* v. *Luxton* (1795), 6 Term Rep. 289) which might exist at law, but since 1925 it can only exist as an equitable interest (L.P.A. 1925, s. 1 (1)). A tenant *pur autre vie* may hold land for the term of another man's life, or for the term of several concurrent lives ; or for the term of his own life and the lives of others ; and in the latter case on his death in the lifetime of the others or either of them the estate will not determine. If he, in his lifetime, had assigned his estate it would continue in favour of the assignee until the death of the survivor. If he had not assigned his estate, it would on his death pass to the special occupant until the death of the survivor (*Utty Dale's Case* (1590), Cro. Eliz. 182).

The estate may arise by express limitation or by assignment of an existing life estate. It can also be created by way of lease, at a rent, for the life of another or lives of others. No words of limitation were ever necessary for the creation of an estate *pur autre vie*, and, if used, would not alter the *quantum* of estate passing. But words of limitation affected the devolution on intestacy of the *legal and equitable* estate before the Land Transfer Act, 1897, that is, before 1898, and of the *equitable estate* after that date and before 1926. The rules as to such devolution are now very rarely of concern to conveyancers and so they are not set out ; reference may be made to the 14th Edition of this book, vol. 2, p. 91. It is sufficient to note that if a tenant *pur autre vie* died after 1st January, 1898, the estate, whether disposed of by will or not, passed to the personal representatives as though it were a chattel real, and was applicable like other real estate in their hands, as assets for the payment of debts, and subject thereto they held it for the persons beneficially entitled, that is to say, the devisee if there was a will, and if not the heir as special occupant, and if the heir did not take as special occupant then it would be divisible among the next of kin as personal estate under the old Statute of Distributions. See *Re Sheppard* [1897] 2 Ch. 67 ; *Re Inman* [1903] 1 Ch. 241.

Now by s. 45 (1) of the A.E.A. 1925 all existing modes of devolution by (*inter alia*) *special occupancy* of real estate are abolished. By ss. 1 and 3 such *real estate* devolves on the personal representatives whether the grant was made with or without the word " heirs."

A tenant *pur autre vie* is one of the persons under s. 20 of the S.L.A. 1925 who have the powers of a tenant for life. He comes under definition (v), " a tenant for life of another, not holding merely under a lease at a rent," and not under definition (vi). But an assignee from the tenant *pur autre vie* of his equitable interest cannot exercise the powers of a tenant for life. Such powers still remain exercisable by the tenant for life, subject to this, that if the assignment were made for value before 1926 he may not do any act which would prejudice the rights of the assignee, and in that case the assignee's rights will not be affected without his consent (S.L.A. 1925, s. 104 (1), (3)). But if the assignee should be the remainderman and the tenant for life has surrendered his life interest to him with intent to extinguish it, then the powers of the life tenant *would* become exercisable by the assignee remainderman (S.L.A., s. 105 (1) ; *Re Carnarvon's Settled Estates* [1927] 1 Ch. 138). See also s. 111 of the S.L.A. 1925, *post* p. 736.

TRADE UNIONS (AND EMPLOYERS' ASSOCIATIONS)

Any eligible organisation of workers or of employers may apply for registration as, respectively, a trade union or an employers' association under the Industrial Relations Act, 1971 (ss. 67 and 68, 71 and 72). A certificate of such registration will be issued specifying, *inter alia*, the organisation's registered name (s. 73). On receipt of such a certificate, the organisation, whether or not already a body corporate, becomes a body corporate by the name so specified, having perpetual succession and a common seal (s. 74 (1)). On incorporation in this way, " all property and funds, of whatsoever nature, for the time being held by any person in trust for the organisation shall vest in the organisation [by statute] . . . and without further assurance " (s. 74 (3)). Apart from the provisions of the 1971 Act, all the property of a registered trade union had to be vested in trustees for the use and benefit of the trade union and the members thereof (see Trade Union Act, 1871, s. 8, now repealed). Such trustees are divested of the property and any liability or obligation on them in their capacity as trustees is transferred to the organisation on incorporation under the 1971 Act (s. 74 (3)). See also s. 84 of the 1971 Act, as to the special register for organisations which either were already registered under the Companies Act, 1948, or are incorporated by charter or letters patent : the provisions of s. 74 of the 1971 Act indicated above do not have effect in relation to organisations on the special register (s. 86).

A registered trade union or employers' association must have rules which, *inter alia*, comply with certain statutory requirements (Industrial Relations Act, 1971, s. 75 (1) (c), referring to Sched. 4). One requirement is that the rules must " make provision as to the purposes for which, and the manner in which, any property or funds of the organisation are authorised to be applied or invested " (*ibid.*, Sched. 4, para. 19). Accordingly any person dealing with a registered organisation should inspect the rules to ascertain that the proposed transaction comes within such provision (s. 9 of the European Communities Act, 1972, which restricts the *ultra vires* doctrine for companies, has no application to trade unions or employers' associations ; see *ante*, p. 319).

On application by such an organisation for registration as proprietor of land under the L.R.A. 1925–1971, a copy of the rules certified as true by its secretary or solicitor must be supplied (Ruoff and Roper, Registered Conveyancing, 3rd ed., pp. 186, 463–465). A restriction will be entered on the register indicating any limitation on the powers of the organisation to dispose of, or deal with, its land (*ibid.*). Subsequently, any purchaser or other person taking a disposition from such an organisation as registered proprietor which does not infringe the restriction should, it is thought, get a good title without need to investigate the organisation's rules (i.e., in reliance on ss. 20 (1) and 22 (1) of the L.R.A. 1925).

Any organisation of workers or of employers which does not register under the 1971 Act appears to be left with the status subsisting before the Act, which will generally be as an unincorporated association. However, it is provided that civil proceedings may be brought by or against such an unregistered organisation in the name of the organisation and that enforcement may be " against any property belonging to, or held in trust for, the organisation, to the like extent and in the like manner as if the organisation were a body corporate " (s. 154 of the Industrial Relations Act, 1971).

UNIVERSITIES AND COLLEGES

Oxford, Cambridge and Durham universities, and the colleges and halls therein (and the public schools of Winchester and Eton) have the same powers of sale and exchange as a tenant for life under the S.L.A. 1925, by virtue of the Universities and College Estates Act, 1925, ss. 1 to 5 (the consent of the Minister of Agriculture, Fisheries and Food, and payment of the purchase money to him is no longer normally required except as to the schools : see Universities and College Estates Act, 1964). The 1925 Act also confers similar powers of leasing (ss. 6 to 13 ; cf. *Eton College* v. *Minister of Agriculture, Fisheries and Food* [1964] Ch. 274). See further *Law Society's Gazette*, vol. 61, p. 673.

Other universities, university colleges, and connected institutions are not within the above Acts and as a rule are not limited in their powers of disposition.

Most universities, and many university colleges and institutions, are classed as " exempt charities " and so able to dispose of their land without the consent of the Charity Commissioners (Charities Act, 1960, ss. 4, 45 and Sched. 2 ; and Exempt Charities Order, 1962).

On first registration under the L.R.A. 1925 of land in the names of any of the bodies mentioned in the first paragraph of this section, a restriction will be entered that except under order of the registrar no disposition is to be registered unless it is made in accordance with the 1925 and 1964 Acts.

CHAPTER TEN

RECITALS

Recital framed to keep notice of trusts off title, see p. 169.

Recital disclosing a breach of trust, see p. 170.

Recitals generally.—A useful note in the *Law Times*, vol. 175, p. 419, stated that " the insertion of recitals is justified, it would appear, on three grounds : First, they may be necessary to explain the circumstances in which the deed is to operate and the intention of the parties . . . The second reason for inserting recitals is that they may operate by estoppel, and so strengthen the grantee's title . . . The third ground . . . is that it is desired to record some fact or matter so as to obtain the benefit of s. 45 (6) of the Law of Property Act, 1925 . . . If any particular recital is not required on one of the above grounds, it should be omitted." This is a very sound summary. See also Williams on Vendor and Purchaser, 4th ed., vol. I, p. 649, where it is stated that if the vendor has proved that he is absolutely entitled to the whole estate contracted for in the land sold, recitals may be dispensed with altogether ; but even in such a case it is probably as well to insert a recital of the seisin of the vendor (see *post*, p. 449). The second and third grounds mentioned above are dealt with in later paragraphs. A vendor can refuse to execute a deed containing incorrect recitals (*Mansfield* v. *Childerhouse* (1876), 4 Ch. D. 82 ; *Hartley* v. *Burton* (1868), L.R. 3 Ch. 365).

Recitals twenty years old as evidence.—Recitals, statements and descriptions of facts, matters, and parties contained in deeds, instruments, Acts of Parliament or statutory declarations twenty years old at the date of the contract are, in the absence of any condition to the contrary, and unless and except so far as they are proved to be inaccurate, to be taken to be sufficient evidence of the truth of such facts, matters and descriptions (L.P.A. 1925, s. 45 (6), (10), replacing Vendor and Purchaser Act, 1874, s. 2 ; see *Re Marsh and Earl Granville* (1882), 24 Ch. D. 11).

The recital is only evidence of so much of the deed as is stated in the recital (*Gillett* v. *Abbott* (1838), 3 N. & P. 24). The much discussed decision of Malins, V.-C., in *Bolton* v. *London School Board* (1878), 7 Ch. D. 766, that a recital of the vendor's seisin contained in a deed twenty years old was sufficient evidence, and that the then forty years' title could not be asked for by the purchaser was dissented from in *Re Wallis and Grout's Contract* [1906] 2 Ch. 206 (but see *dicta* of the Privy Council in *Selkirk* v. *Romar Investments, Ltd.* [1963] 1 W.L.R. 1415, at pp. 1419 to 1420, apparently more consistent with the earlier decision). However, this discussion has become of little more than academic interest in view of the reduction of the period of title from thirty years to fifteen years (L.P.A. 1925, s. 44 (1), as affected by L.P.A. 1969, s. 23).

Effect of recital on the construction of a deed.—The leading case as regards the construction of recitals is *Re Moon, ex parte Dawes* (1886),

17 Q.B.D. 275, in which the following rules, in effect, were laid down by Lord Esher, M.R. (at p. 286)—

(a) if the recitals are clear but the operative part of a deed ambiguous, the recitals govern (see also *Orr* v. *Mitchell* [1893] A.C. 238, at p. 254 ; *Crouch* v. *Crouch* [1912] 1 K.B. 378) ;

(b) if the recitals are ambiguous but the operative part of a deed clear, the operative part governs ; and

(c) if the recitals and operative parts are both clear, but are inconsistent with each other, the operative part is to be preferred (see also *MacKenzie* v. *Duke of Devonshire* [1896] A.C. 400 ; *Re Sassoon ; Inland Revenue Commissioners* v. *Raphael and Ezra* [1935] A.C. 96).

Referring to *Re Moon, ex parte Dawes*, Norton on Deeds, 2nd ed., at p. 197, states : " It follows that a specific description of property, or a specific statement of what is intended to be done, contained in the operative part, will not be controlled by a general description, or a general or ambiguous statement, contained in the recitals." It was said by Brett, L.J. (as Lord Esher, M.R., then was), in *Leggott* v. *Barrett* (1880), 15 Ch. D. 306, at p. 311, that " If there is any doubt about the construction of the governing words of that document, the recital may be looked at in order to determine what is the true construction ; but if there is no doubt about the construction, the rights of the parties are governed entirely by the operative part of the writing or the deed."

General words of grant may be restricted by the recitals. It was held in *Jenner* v. *Jenner* (1866), L.R. 1 Eq. 361, that a conveyance of " all other the freehold hereditaments, if any, in the county of York, of or to which the grantor was seised," was restricted by a recital showing the intention that only the specified property was to pass. And a conveyance of " all that the one equal eighth part or share, or other the part or share " was restricted by the recitals to one eighth share (*Gray* v. *Earl of Limerick* (1848), 2 De G. & Sm. 370).

The operative part of a power of attorney appointed *X* and *Y* to be attorneys without limiting the duration of their powers, but such operative part was preceded by a recital that the donor was going abroad, and desired to appoint attorneys to act in his absence. It was held that the recital limited the exercise of the powers to the period of the donor's absence from this country (*Danby* v. *Coutts* (1885), 29 Ch. D. 500).

A covenant for title will not be limited by the fact that a defect in the title appears from the recitals (*Page* v. *Midland Railway Co.* [1894] 1 Ch. 11).

If the language of a covenant is ambiguous, the recitals can be looked at for an explanation of the ambiguity (*Re Coghlan ; Broughton* v. *Broughton* [1894] 3 Ch. 76 ; *Crouch* v. *Crouch* [1912] 1 K.B. 378).

The most striking instances of the generality of the operative words being controlled by the recitals usually occur in the case of releases. See the cases collected in Norton on Deeds, pp. 192, 193 ; 2nd ed., pp. 208–210.

A recital may have the effect of a covenant.—A recital that something is *intended* to be done will amount to a covenant to do that thing unless there is an express covenant to which the recital can be referred (*Dawes* v. *Tredwell* (1881), 18 Ch. D. 354 ; *Buckland* v. *Buckland* [1900] 2 Ch. 534 ; *Stephens* v. *Junior Army and Navy Stores, Ltd.* [1914] 2 Ch. 516).

A deed contained a recital that it was intended to be a part of all future contracts for sale of plots forming part of a building estate that the several purchasers should execute the deed, and be bound by the stipulations contained in it. The deed also contained a covenant by such purchasers to conform to such stipulations, but *no covenant by the vendor*. It was held that the effect of the recital operated as a covenant by the vendor not to authorise the use of the unsold lots in a manner inconsistent with the stipulations (*Mackenzie* v. *Childers* (1889), 43 Ch. D. 265). See also *Sampson* v. *Easterby* (1829), 9 B. & C. 505 ; *Buckland* v. *Buckland, ante ; Re Cadogan and Hans Place Estate, Ltd., ex parte Willis* (1895), 73 L.T. 387.

Estoppel by recital.—Although a grant only operates on the estate or interest of the grantor, and will pass no more than he is by law enabled to convey, yet where a man unequivocally recites that he is the owner of an estate, and affects to convey it for valuable consideration, when in reality he has not such an estate, if by any means he afterwards acquires such estate, he will be estopped from saying that he had not such estate at the time of his execution of the deed (*Re Bridgwater's Settlement; Partridge* v. *Ward* [1910] 2 Ch. 342 ; *Lovett* v. *Lovett* [1898] 1 Ch. 82 ; *Cumberland Court (Brighton), Ltd.* v. *Taylor* [1964] Ch. 29).

A clear and unambiguous statement, although incorrect, contained in a recital, acts as an estoppel against the party making it and against persons claiming under him (*Bensley* v. *Burdon* (1830), 8 L.J. (o.s.) Ch. 85 ; *Stroughill* v. *Buck* (1850), 14 Q.B. 781). Whether a statement is intended to be made by all parties to a deed or one only of them depends on the construction of the deed ; recitals of title are clearly statements by a vendor but not by a purchaser (*Stroughill* v. *Buck, ante ; Greer* v. *Kettle* [1938] A.C. 156, at p. 170). As to the benefit of estoppel, it has been said that the doctrine of estoppel " can have no operation except in the case of third parties who are innocent of fraud and who have become owners for value " (*General Finance, etc., Co.* v. *Liberator Society* (1878), 10 Ch. D. 15, at p. 24). Thus taking the benefit of an estoppel does not depend on executing, or even being a party, to the deed containing the recital or other statement ; the principle is that estoppel operates in favour of persons, such as successors in title, acting on the faith of the misrepresentation (*Re King's Settlement* [1931] 2 Ch. 294, where the immediate grantee knew the truth). Again a recital will not operate as an estoppel or constitute evidence of the facts stated where the party making it was under the undue influence of the party benefiting (*Allie* v. *Katah* [1963] 1 W.L.R. 202). The estoppel does not arise out of the grant, but out of the recital which leads up to the grant and, therefore, the statement must be express, precise and direct (*Heath* v. *Crealock* (1875), L.R. 10 Ch. 22, at p. 30 ; *General Finance, etc., Co.* v. *Liberator Society, ante ; Re Maddy's Estate* [1901] 2 Ch. 820). For instance, a general statement, as that a grantor is " seised of *or otherwise well entitled to* " land, would not act as an estoppel (*Heath* v. *Crealock, ante*) ; or that " the vendor is well entitled in fee at law or in equity " (*Onward Building Society* v. *Smithson* [1893] 1 Ch. 1) ; though a recital that the vendor *is* seised would constitute an estoppel (*Cumberland Court (Brighton), Ltd.* v. *Taylor* [1964] Ch. 29). The usual implied covenants for title are not sufficiently precise statements to raise an estoppel so as to prevent the person giving the covenants from setting up the true facts (*Onward Building Society* v. *Smithson, ante ;* see also *Re King's Settlement, ante*).

A purchaser, therefore, would be well advised to see that he gets in his conveyance a recital of the seisin of the vendor, whenever the facts allow. A form commonly adopted is that the vendor is " seised of the property

hereinafter described for an estate in fee simple free from incumbrances."
Having regard to the definition of the estates existing at law in the L.P.A.
1925, s. 1 (1), it seems better to recite that the vendor is seised for an estate
in fee simple *absolute in possession,* or that the vendor is the estate owner in
respect of the fee simple. The advantage of such a recital is that if the vendor
had not then the legal estate but afterwards acquired it, it would pass by the
estoppel without any further conveyance ; a grant alone without the recital
would not have this effect, being only an innocent conveyance (Williams,
Real Property, 23rd ed., p. 689 ; *Re Harper's Settlement* [1919] 1 Ch. 270).
See also below.

The doctrine of estoppel by recital applies to an easement, and it was held
in *Poulton* v. *Moore* [1915] 1 K.B. 400 that a statement by the owner that
she *was* entitled to the easement was a sufficiently precise and particular
statement to effect an estoppel. The grant of an estate does not amount to
a statement that the grantor has the estate he purports to grant (*Heath* v.
Crealock, ante).

There is no estoppel where the statement is a mutual mistake between
the parties (*Empson's Case* (1870), L.R. 9 Eq. 597 ; *Williams* v. *Pinckney*
(1897), 77 L.T. 700 ; *Greer* v. *Kettle* [1938] A.C. 156). If a statement in a
deed is true, but not the whole truth, the person making it is not estopped
from proving the whole truth (*Lovett* v. *Lovett* [1898] 1 Ch. 82). So, an
incorrect recital in a conveyance of the vendor's earlier title will not preclude
the grantee from showing what interest really passed by the vendor's grant
(*Trinidad Asphalte Co.* v. *Coryat* [1896] A.C. 587, at p. 593). The doctrine
will not be extended (*General Finance, etc., Co.* v. *Liberator Society* (1878),
10 Ch. D. 15, at p. 21.)

Recital by vendor that he is seised free from incumbrances.—In
Williams on Vendor and Purchaser, 3rd ed., vol. I, p. 613, it was stated, in
effect, that in the absence of express stipulation to the contrary, a vendor
of land is not bound to give, in the conveyance of the land, any manner of
warranty of title other than is afforded by the usual qualified covenants for
title. For this reason, it was further stated there that if the conveyance as
prepared on the purchaser's behalf purports to assure the land to be held by
him " free from incumbrances," the vendor should strike out these words, as
they might import an unrestricted warranty at common law that the lands
were free from incumbrances. Mr. T. Cyprian Williams, however, in an
explanatory article in the *Solicitors' Journal,* vol. 70, p. 355, drew attention
to the fact that such statement refers only to the conveyance of land " free
from incumbrances " *in the testatum or habendum.* He intimated that
the above objection does not apply to a *recital* that the property is free
from incumbrances, and that if a vendor of land has by the contract agreed
to sell the land in fee simple free from incumbrances he cannot reasonably
object to a recital in the conveyance that he is seised of the land sold for an
unincumbered estate in fee simple. It will be remembered that a contract
for the sale of land is assumed to be for the sale of an estate in fee simple in
possession free from incumbrances unless the contract expressly or impliedly
stipulates to the contrary. See *ante,* p. 105.

The nature of the interest properly described by the word " incumbrance "
is a matter of some doubt. It is very common for a recital to state that the
vendor is seised " subject as hereinafter is mentioned but otherwise free
from incumbrances," and for the operative part of the deed to convey the
land subject, for example, " to the exceptions reservations and covenants

15

contained in a deed dated," etc. (the word "reservations" commonly refers to the earlier creation of rights of way or other easements : see *post*, p. 493). On the other hand, many solicitors do not consider such matters as restrictive covenants and easements to amount to incumbrances and, therefore, they will, when acting for a vendor, allow the deed to recite that the vendor is seised free from incumbrances, although the land is subject to restrictive covenants or easements. As to the effect of restrictions on development under the Town and Country Planning Acts, see *post*, p. 1181.

The meaning given to the word " incumbrance " in the L.P.A. 1925, s. 205 (1), suggests that it applies only to charges on land involving the payment of money, such as mortgages and annuities, but this subsection states only that the word *includes* the interests specified and it does not provide a complete definition. In any case, the meaning given in s. 205 (1) is for the purpose of the L.P.A. 1925 only and does not apply if the context requires otherwise. In conveyancing practice the word is given a much wider meaning. A vendor who has expressly or impliedly contracted to sell free from incumbrances does not carry out his obligations if he shows title subject to restrictive covenants or to easements not apparent on inspection. For these reasons a vendor's solicitor should assume that the word " incumbrance " has a wide meaning and should not permit his client to execute a deed containing an unqualified recital that he is seised free from incumbrances if he holds subject to any interest the existence of which would mean that a vendor selling under an open contract could not show a good title. The view is held despite the decision of Danckwerts, J., in *District Bank, Ltd.* v. *Webb* [1958] 1 W.L.R. 148, that a recital that vendors were " seised in unincumbered fee simple in possession upon trust for sale " was not sufficiently clear and unambiguous to estop the vendors from denying the validity of a lease in favour of one of them. Danckwerts, J., said (at p. 149) : " I am not satisfied that a lease was an incumbrance to these parties. It is true that in certain circumstances a lease may be regarded as an incumbrance, but it seems to me that an incumbrance, normally, is something in the nature of a mortgage and not something in the nature of a lease or a tenancy, and since, on the authorities, an unambiguous representation must be shown if an estoppel is to be created, it seems to me that in that respect the recital is not sufficient for the plaintiff bank's purpose [of impugning the validity of the lease]." However, it may be observed, first, that the facts of this case were somewhat special, and second, that the learned judge can be taken as confining his *dicta* to those facts by the words " to these parties," " in certain circumstances," and " normally." Certainly if a vendor contracts, expressly or impliedly, to convey free from incumbrances he will not have shown a good title if a binding lease subsists. Consequently, it is usual in practice to treat a lease as an incumbrance when drafting both recitals and the grant in a conveyance.

Recitals should be continued without a break.—To take a simple case—a conveyance, say to *A*, appears on the abstract ; then a mortgage by *A* ; then a document discharging the mortgage. One often comes across a later conveyance containing a recital of the conveyance, then omitting the mortgage and deed of discharge, and then reciting some other deed executed by *A*, as if *A* had been entitled during the whole period. This is not good conveyancing. For a purchaser should be satisfied that the mortgage has been properly discharged and that the legal estate got back into *A*, and the omission is apt to prevent him considering the point. It was stated in an old but valuable practical book on conveyancing, Bythewood and Jarman's System of Conveyancing, 4th ed., 1888, vol. V, at pp. 138 and 148, in effect, that when once the recitals are begun they should be continued without a break down to the date of the transaction in hand, except, of course, where, in reciting the title to leaseholds, the original lease is recited and the later title without detail is referred to under the description of " divers mesne assignments and acts in the law " or some similar or appropriate phrase.

Recital of reason of vacancy in a trust.—It is provided by s. 38 of the T.A. 1925 that a statement, contained in any instrument coming into operation after 1925, by which a new trustee is appointed for any purpose connected with land, to the effect that a trustee has remained out of the United Kingdom for more than twelve months or refuses or is unfit to act, or is incapable of acting, or that he is *not entitled to a beneficial interest* in the *trust property in possession*, will, in favour of a purchaser of a legal estate, be conclusive evidence of the matter stated ; and that in favour of such purchaser any appointment of a new trustee depending on that statement, and any *vesting declaration, express or implied*, consequent on the appointment, will be valid.

" *not entitled to a beneficial interest.*"—These words refer to s. 36 (9) of the T.A. 1925, which provides that, where a trustee is incapable by reason of mental disorder within the meaning of the Mental Health Act, 1959, of exercising his functions as a trustee, and is also entitled in possession to some beneficial interest in the trust property, no appointment of a new trustee in his place shall be made by the continuing trustee or trustees, under this section, unless leave has been given to make the appointment.

" *vesting declaration, express or implied.*"—See T.A. 1925, s. 40, *post*, p. 796.

Although s. 38 is in wide terms it would seem that it was intended primarily to apply to a statement contained in an appointment of a new *trustee for sale*, because special provision is made as regards a statement contained in a deed of declaration as to persons being trustees for the purposes of the S.L.A. This latter provision is contained in s. 35 (3) of the S.L.A. 1925, given below :—

" 35.—(3) A statement contained in any such deed of declaration as is mentioned in this section to the effect that the person named in the principal vesting instrument as the person for the time being entitled to appoint new trustees of the settlement is unable or unwilling to act, or that a trustee has remained outside the United Kingdom for more than twelve months, or refuses or is unfit to act, or is incapable of acting, shall in favour of a purchaser of a legal estate be conclusive evidence of the matter stated."

Recital in appointment of trustees of infant's lands in the place of the Public Trustee.—It is provided by para. 3 (1) (i) of Sched. 2 to the S.L.A. 1925 that where on 1st January, 1926, an infant is beneficially entitled to land, the same shall vest in the trustees of the settlement (if any) and, if none, in the Public Trustee, until trustees are appointed in his place. The father and mother have the first privilege of making the appointment. It is also provided by sub-para. (iv) as follows :—

" Provided that in favour of a purchaser a statement in the deed of appointment that the father or mother or both are dead or are unable or unwilling to make the appointment shall be conclusive evidence of the fact stated."

Recital that personal representative has not assented.—A statement in writing by a personal representative that he has not given or made an assent or conveyance in respect of a legal estate, will, in favour of a purchaser (but without prejudice to any previous disposition made in favour of another purchaser deriving title mediately or immediately under the personal representative), be sufficient evidence that an assent or conveyance has not been given or made in respect of the legal estate to which the statement relates, unless notice of a previous assent or conveyance affecting that estate has been placed on or annexed to the probate or administration ; and a conveyance by him of a legal estate to a purchaser accepted on the faith of such a statement will (without prejudice as aforesaid and unless notice of a previous assent or conveyance has been placed on, etc., the probate or administration as before mentioned) operate to transfer or create the legal estate expressed to be conveyed in like manner as if no previous assent or conveyance had been made by the personal representative (A.E.A. 1925, s. 36 (6)).

The statement can be made in the form of a recital in the conveyance, such as : " The vendor (who has not made any previous assent or conveyance in respect of the legal estate hereinafter conveyed) as the personal representative of the said *A B* deceased has agreed to sell, etc." The purchaser must, however, be careful to inspect the probate or administration to satisfy himself that there is no indorsement or annexed statement of a previous assent or conveyance, as provided by the subsection. See section on Personal Representatives, *ante*, p. 415.

Document stated to be supplemental to another document.—It is provided by s. 58 of the L.P.A. 1925 that *any instrument* expressed to be supplemental to a previous *instrument* is to be read and have effect as if the supplemental instrument contained a full recital of the previous instrument. The section goes on to provide that it is not to operate to give any right to an abstract or production of any such previous instrument, and that a purchaser may accept the same evidence that the previous instrument does not affect the title as if it had merely been mentioned in the supplemental instrument.

Recitals of planning matters.—Although the right to develop the land which a purchaser will obtain is severely restricted by the Town and Country Planning Acts, this restriction is a matter of general law and is not an incumbrance on the particular land being sold. Consequently, it is proper, in appropriate circumstances, to continue to recite that the vendor is seised free from incumbrances, without mentioning the use to which the property may lawfully be put.

There may, however, be a few cases in which recitals of facts which become material as a result of the Town and Country Planning Acts should be inserted in conveyances. For instance, in certain special cases it may be agreed between the parties that the vendor will covenant that the user of the property is in accordance with planning restrictions and that, where necessary, permission has been obtained for any development which may have taken place. A recital should, in such a case, be inserted stating the purpose for which the property is used and that the vendor has agreed to enter into the necessary covenants which will be contained in the body of the deed. Such a recital would be properly inserted on the ground that it is necessary in order to explain the circumstances of the deed and the intention of the parties.

It has been suggested that a recital of the nature of the user of the property may be useful because, in the event of a dispute as to whether development has occurred, such a recital could be used as evidence being the statement of the vendor who was likely to have precise knowledge of the nature of the user. See, for instance, L.P.A. 1925, s. 45 (6), and Civil Evidence Act, 1968, s. 2. The possibility that a purchaser might wish to use a recital as evidence seems so remote that it will not normally be worth inserting recitals for this purpose, even assuming that vendors will be prepared to make the statements involved in such recitals ; in most cases other evidence of user could be obtained if required. Further, the rule now is that development by way of change of use only will normally never be made lawful by lapse of time (see s. 87 (3) of the Town and Country Planning Act, 1971 ; i.e., the four years time limit is no longer applicable). In consequence there is in general no point in providing evidence of the actual use as at the date of a conveyance.

Registered land.—In general, a transfer of registered land does not and should not include any recitals, these being regarded as inconsistent with the principles upon which the register is kept (see Ruoff, Concise Land Registration Practice, pp. 74–75). However, this is only true as a general rule in the commonest case of transfer by a beneficial owner of the whole of land registered with absolute title. In other cases, recitals may, where appropriate, serve much the same purposes as in unregistered conveyancing.

CHAPTER ELEVEN

CONSIDERATION AND RECEIPTS

PART 1.   THE CONSIDERATION

Statement of the consideration.—The Stamp Act, 1891, provides that all facts and circumstances affecting the liability of any instrument to duty, or the amount of duty, are to be fully and truly set forth in the instrument ; and that any person who, with intent to defraud, executes an instrument in which they are not so set forth, or is employed in the preparation of an instrument and omits so to set them forth, shall incur a fine (s. 5). As to the consideration on which stamp duty should be paid in various circumstances, see section on Stamps, at p. 1151.

The Council of The Law Society are of the opinion that unless arranged beforehand a purchaser's solicitor should not ask the vendor's solicitor to accept a cheque in payment of a purchase price. The duty of the vendor's solicitor is to obtain cash or a bank draft, and acceptance of a cheque without the vendor's authority will make his solicitor personally liable. Apart from failure to meet a cheque for financial reasons there are other possible causes of difficulty, for example, an error in preparing the cheque or " death of the drawer before clearance in the case of a one-man practice." Working arrangements are often made, particularly where the consideration is small, but the risks should be appreciated. See *Law Society's Gazette*, vol. 66, pp. 406 and 761.

At any rate where the consideration stated is nominal, and possibly in other cases, evidence is admissible to show that the true consideration was something more than the consideration stated in a document, whether under hand or under seal (*Turner* v. *Forwood* [1951] 1 All E.R. 746).

It has been stated that if the consideration be much *smaller* than in previous deeds, this may put the purchaser on inquiry as to whether the whole of the property is intended to be conveyed, and particularly so if the description of the property in the parcels is at all general or ambiguous. As values have appreciated so much in recent years, the rule is probably now of little importance.

Purchase of reversionary interest at undervalue.—Before 1868 the vendor of a reversionary interest could have the transaction set aside if he could prove that the consideration given was inadequate. It is provided by s. 174 (1) of the L.P.A. 1925, re-enacting the Sales of Reversions Act, 1867, that " No acquisition made in good faith, without fraud or unfair dealing, of any *reversionary interest* in real or personal property, for money or money's worth, shall be liable to be opened or set aside merely on the ground of undervalue. In this subsection ' reversionary interest ' includes an expectancy or possibility." Subsection (2) provides that " This section does not affect the jurisdiction of the court to set aside or modify unconscionable bargains."

It will be noticed that a purchaser may still be called upon to prove that no unfair advantage was taken. In every case, therefore, the solicitor, when acting for both parties, should insist on having the vendor advised by an independent solicitor, who should attest the document and state in the attestation clause that the vendor has been so advised. It would also be a wise course for that solicitor to write out a statement giving an account of the interview, and, in particular, as to what he said to the vendor and the replies of the vendor, to be kept as evidence, because there is always the danger of other persons, not knowing the true facts, persuading him to try to get the transaction set aside, especially if the reversion falls into possession earlier than was expected.

Voluntary conveyances.—When perusing an abstract the consideration should always be noticed to see whether the document can be classed as a voluntary conveyance. But a deed which appears to be a voluntary conveyance may be shown by extrinsic evidence to have been given for valuable consideration (*Re Holland ; Gregg* v. *Holland* [1902] 2 Ch. 360 ; *Re Davies* [1921] 3 K.B. 628).

In any case, consideration is not, of course, essential to a deed ; a legal estate may be passed and any contract contained in a deed enforced at law even though the transaction was entirely voluntary (*Pratt* v. *Barker* (1828), 1 Sim. 1). Further, such statutory provisions as there are which may adversely affect voluntary conveyances (e.g., s. 172 of the L.P.A. 1925 ; s. 42 of the Bankruptcy Act, 1914 ; s. 16 of the Matrimonial Proceedings and Property Act, 1970 ; see *ante*, p. 116 *et seq.*) at most render them voidable so that a *bona fide* purchaser for value of the legal estate without notice cannot be prejudiced. Such purchasers are also protected by the L.P.A. 1925, s. 173, which deals with voluntary dispositions of land made with intent to defraud a subsequent purchaser. It is provided that every voluntary disposition of land made with intent to defraud a subsequent *purchaser* shall be voidable at the instance of that purchaser. Consequently, as a general rule, no objection should be raised to voluntary conveyances which have been abstracted since these will generally be perfectly good links in title. The possible liability of a purchaser to estate duty on the subsequent death of a donor is considered *post*, p. 1176.

Sale by fiduciary owners in consideration of a rent-charge.—The power to sell in consideration of a rent-charge is conferred on tenants for life and statutory owners by s. 39 of the S.L.A. 1925, which provides that a sale may be made by a tenant for life in consideration, wholly or partially, of a perpetual rent, or a terminable rent consisting of principal and interest combined, payable yearly or half-yearly, to be secured upon the land sold. In the case of a terminable rent, the conveyance—which will take the form of a subsidiary vesting deed (S.L.A. 1925, s. 10)—must distinguish the part attributable to principal and that attributable to interest; and the part attributable to principal will be capital money arising under the Act. The conveyance must contain a covenant by the purchaser for payment of the rent, and a duplicate of the conveyance must be executed by the purchaser and delivered to the tenant for life or statutory owner, of which execution and delivery the execution of the conveyance by the tenant for life or statutory owner will be sufficient evidence. By an amendment made by the Law of

Property (Amendment) Act, 1926, it is provided that the statutory powers and remedies for the recovery of the rent are to apply in such cases.

Trustees for sale could not, before 1926, sell for a rent-charge (*Reid* v. *Shergold* (1805), 10 Ves. 370, 380) except when selling under the Lands Clauses Consolidation Acts Amendment Act, 1860. But trustees for sale now have all the powers of a tenant for life under the S.L.A. 1925 (L.P.A. 1925, s. 28 (1)), and so they also have this power. On the same ground, personal representatives have this power under s. 39 of the A.E.A. 1925.

The statutory remedies for the recovery of annual sums charged on land are contained in s. 121 of the L.P.A. 1925, to which the reader is referred. The section gives power, if at any time the annual sum is unpaid for twenty-one days, to enter into and distrain on the land charged and dispose of any distress found in payment of the amount owing, and after the annual sum is in arrear for forty days to take possession of the land itself and receive the rents until receipt of the amount required.

Sale by fiduciary owners at valuation.—Trustees cannot usually sell at a price to be fixed by valuation or arbitration and a tenant for life is a trustee of the S.L.A. powers (S.L.A. 1925, s. 107 (1) ; *Re Earl of Wilton's Settled Estate* [1907] 1 Ch. 50). But s. 49 (2) of the S.L.A. 1925 provides that a sale of land may be made by a tenant for life subject to a stipulation that all or any of the timber and other trees, pollards, tellers, underwood, saplings and plantations on the land sold or any articles attached to the land shall be taken by the purchaser at a valuation, and the amount of the valuation shall form part of the price of the land, and shall be capital money accordingly. Before 1926, trustees for sale of land could not agree to sell timber or fixtures at a price to be fixed by valuation, as that would have been a delegation of their discretion to decide what price they would accept (*Re Wilton's Settled Estate, ante*). But now, trustees for sale have, by s. 28 (1) of the L.P.A. 1925, and personal representatives have, by s. 39 of the A.E.A. 1925, all the powers of a tenant for life.

Sale of settled land to a company in consideration of fully paid securities.—It is provided by s. 39 (5) of the S.L.A. 1925 that the consideration on a sale to any company *incorporated by special Act of Parliament, or by provisional order confirmed by Parliament, or by any other order, scheme or certificate having the force of an Act of Parliament*, may, with the consent of the tenant for life, consist, wholly or in part, of fully paid securities of any description of the company, and such securities must be vested in the trustees of the settlement and will be subject to the provisions of the Act relating to securities representing capital money arising under the Act, and may be retained and held by the trustees in like manner as if they had been authorised by the Act for the investment of capital money. This subsection does not apply to an ordinary limited company, as incorporation under the Companies Act depends on registration.

Sale of part of leasehold property.—On sale of part of land comprised in a lease, it is necessary to apportion the rent. Apportionment at law can be effected only with the concurrence of the lessor, which is not usually obtained. The practice is to agree the apportionment only between the vendor and purchaser of the leasehold interest, which apportionment takes effect in equity only. Under the L.P.A. 1925, s. 190 (3), if, in such circumstances, the rent is charged exclusively on the land conveyed or exclusively on the land retained, or is apportioned between the two, then without prejudice to the rights of the lessor such charge or apportionment becomes binding as between the vendor and purchaser and their respective successors in title.

The result is that the lessor is able to distrain on any part of the land in respect of the whole of the rent and can enforce a right of re-entry on breach of covenant arising out of the use of any part of the land. The vendor and purchaser of part of the land comprised in the lease and their respective successors in title are protected, however, by covenants implied in the conveyance. The purchaser for value is deemed to covenant for himself and persons deriving title under him that he will pay the apportioned rent and observe and perform the covenants contained in the lease so far as the same relate to the land conveyed and will indemnify the vendor (L.P.A. 1925, s. 77 (1) (*d*) and Sched. 2, Pt. X). Correspondingly, a vendor who conveys or is expressed to convey as beneficial owner is deemed to covenant that he or the persons deriving title under him will pay the balance of the rent and observe and perform all the covenants contained in the lease so far as the same relate to the land demised, which remains vested in the vendor, and will indemnify the purchaser (*ibid.*). See further, *post*, p. 856.

When the whole of the leasehold property is sold in plots it is customary to carry out sale by means of underleases, but to assign the lease to the purchaser of one plot subject to the underleases. On the grant of each sub-lease, the seller covenants with the under-lessee to pay the rent and perform the covenants so far as they relate to the remainder of the property. Further, the seller remains liable for the defaults of the sub-lessees under his implied covenants for title with the assignee of the lease. He is protected, however, by the implied covenant to indemnify given by each sub-lessee. If the seller of such plots was personally liable under the lease (that is, if he was the original lessee or had entered into a covenant to indemnify a former lessee) he does not avoid liability to the lessor by an assignment of the balance of the term, but if he is sued by the lessor he will have a remedy on the express or implied covenants given in his favour by sub-lessees or the assignee.

When the whole of the land is sold in lots the lease may be assigned to the purchaser of the largest plot on terms that he will grant sub-leases to other purchasers. If it is desired to avoid delay in carrying out the various transactions, it may be convenient for the seller to reserve the right to determine which purchaser shall take an assignment of the balance of the term.

Registered land.—The prescribed forms of transfer of registered land commence (with a few exceptions) with " In consideration of —— pounds (£   ) . . ." and accordingly require, *prima facie*, a money consideration to be stated (see Schedule to L.R.R. 1925, Form 19 *et seq.*). However, H.M. Land Registry would not object to a voluntary transfer commencing, e.g., "In consideration of my natural love and affection for . . ." (see Precedent No. 31 on p. 78 of Ruoff, Land Registration Forms). A disposition made without valuable consideration is subject *so far as the immediate transferee is concerned* not only to the entries on the register and any overriding interests but also to any minor interests (L.R.A. 1925, ss. 20 (4) and 23 (5)). Apart from this, when registered such a disposition has *in all respects* the same effect as if it had been made for valuable consideration (*ibid.*). As a result subsequent transferees for value are not concerned.

PART 2. RECEIPTS

Receipt in deed evidence of payment.—A receipt for consideration
money or securities in the body of a deed is a sufficient discharge to the
person paying or delivering the same, without any further receipt being
endorsed on the deed (L.P.A. 1925, s. 67), and a receipt for consideration money
or other consideration in the body of a deed or endorsed thereon will, in
favour of *a subsequent purchaser, not having notice that the money or other
consideration thereby acknowledged to be received was not in fact paid or given*
wholly or in part, be sufficient evidence of the payment or giving of the
whole amount thereof (L.P.A. 1925, s. 68).   Both these sections apply to deeds
executed after 31st December, 1881, and since a Land Registry transfer is
a deed (see *Chelsea and Walham Green B.S.* v. *Armstrong* [1951] Ch. 853, 857)
they apply in registered conveyancing also.

In order for the L.P.A. 1925, s. 68, to be applicable, it is *not* essential
that the purchaser should see the original deed containing the receipt :
it will suffice if he sees an accurate copy (whether photographed or typed)
or even record of the deed including the receipt (*London and Cheshire Insurance
Co., Ltd.* v. *Laplagrene Property Co. Ltd.* [1971] Ch. 499).   However, the statement in the proprietorship register where title to land is registered, using
the words : " Price paid £——, " does not suffice since it records not receipt
but rather cost (*ibid.*).   Accordingly it appears that, despite the potential
applicability of the L.P.A. 1925, s. 68, in registered conveyancing, a purchaser
of registered land will rarely if ever be able to rely on the section since it is not
the practice to inspect the instrument of transfer (containing a receipt) which
led to the vendor's registration.   Also any unpaid vendor's lien will require
other protection than constructive notice arising from the absence of a receipt
to be enforceable in any case : see *post*, pp. 459–460.

In order to constitute a receipt within the L.P.A. 1925, ss. 67 and 68,
express words acknowledging the receipt of the consideration are necessary,
such as " of which sum *A* hereby acknowledges the receipt."   A mere statement that money has been expended or paid is insufficient (*Renner* v. *Tolley*
(1893), 68 L.T. 815) but will probably raise an estoppel against the vendor
to much the same effect as the sections (*Rimmer* v. *Webster* [1902] 2 Ch. 163).
The sections apply even in the case of a purchase by a solicitor from a client
or a mortgage from a client to a solicitor (*Powell* v. *Browne* (1907), 97 L.T. 854).

A copyhold surrender was not considered to be a " deed " within the
Conveyancing Act, 1881, and the practice, therefore, was to endorse a
receipt.

The word " purchaser " in s. 68 includes an equitable mortgagee (*Lloyds
Bank, Ltd.* v. *Bullock* [1896] 2 Ch. 192) and a transferee of a mortgage
(*Bickerton* v. *Walker* (1885), 31 Ch. D. 151).   The fact that the mortgagee
acted as the solicitor for the transferee on the transfer would not affect the
transferee with constructive notice (*Bateman* v. *Hunt* [1904] 2 K.B. 530).
Therefore, if a vendor who has not received the whole of his purchase-money
should be so unwise as to hand the purchaser the conveyance containing the
receipt, and the purchaser deposits it with an equitable mortgagee who has
no notice of the lien, the mortgagee would have priority over such lien
(*Rice* v. *Rice* (1854), 2 Drew. 73 ; *Lloyds Bank, Ltd.* v. *Bullock, ante*) unless
it was registered as a land charge.

Receipt in deed authority for payment to solicitor.—It is provided by
s. 69 of the L.P.A. 1925 that where a solicitor produces a deed, having in the

body thereof or endorsed thereon a receipt for consideration money or other consideration, the deed being executed, or the endorsed receipt being signed, by the person entitled to give a receipt for that consideration, the deed will be a *sufficient* authority to the person liable to pay or give the same for his paying or giving the same to the solicitor, without the solicitor producing any separate or other direction or authority in that behalf from the person who executed or signed the deed or receipt. Again this will apply to a Land Registry transfer.

The solicitor must be acting for the person signing the receipt (*Re Hetling and Merton's Contract* [1893] 3 Ch. 269 ; *Day* v. *Woolwich, etc., Society* (1888), 40 Ch. D. 491). It appears that the section does not authorise payment to the London agent of the solicitor for the person giving the receipt (*Law Society's Digest*, Opinion No. 164).

The view is expressed in Williams on Vendor and Purchaser, 4th ed., vol. I, p. 743, that payment to the solicitor's managing clerk would have the same protection, but the Council of The Law Society have expressed a contrary opinion (*Law Society's Digest*, Opinion No. 163). Certainly, in practice, payment of purchase-money is frequently made to managing clerks and it would seem reasonable that the same protection should be given as if payment had been made to the solicitor himself.

The Council of The Law Society have drawn attention to the fact that the L.P.A. 1925, s. 69, gives protection only where there is a receipt for purchase money in a deed ; it does not apply, for instance, to a sale of chattels passing by delivery. In such a case a purchaser's solicitor should call for written authority before handing over purchase-money to the vendor's solicitor (*Law Society's Gazette*, vol. 46, p. 167). The Council also state that, in the absence of prior arrangement, a cheque for purchase-money should not be offered on completion, but cash or a banker's draft should be produced (*ibid.*).

It is also provided by s. 23 (3) (*a*) of the T.A. 1925 that a *trustee* may appoint a solicitor to be his agent to receive and give a discharge for any money or valuable consideration or property receivable by the trustee under the trust, by permitting the solicitor to have the custody of, and to produce a deed having in the body thereof or endorsed thereon a receipt for such money or valuable consideration or property, the deed being executed, or the endorsed receipt being signed by, the person entitled to give a receipt for that consideration ; and (s. 23 (3) (*b*)) the production of any such deed by the solicitor is to have the same statutory validity and effect as if the person appointing the solicitor had not been a trustee.

It was said in *Re Hetling and Merton, ante,* that an earlier provision similar to s. 23 (3) (*a*) did not authorise the payment of purchase-money to the solicitor of an attorney under a power of attorney, unless such power appointed the solicitor to receive purchase-money. It is suggested in Williams on Vendor and Purchaser, 4th ed., vol. I, p. 742, however, that this construction is too narrow and that the execution of a deed by an attorney is a sufficient authority for payment to the solicitor who produces it.

As to the revocation of the solicitor's authority by the death of a trustee, see *Re Sheppard* [1911] 1 Ch. 50.

Absence of receipt in deed.—If a receipt for consideration money is neither included in the body of a deed nor endorsed thereon, then generally speaking this is now only of concern to the person making payment of the consideration money. Being unable to rely on ss. 67 and 69 of the L.P.A. 1925, he should obtain a separate receipt by way of discharge and, where relevant, require production of an authority for payment to a solicitor or any other agent. The absence of a receipt clause in a title deed will not, since 1925, in itself be a defect in title of concern to subsequent purchasers. Such absence in a deed before 1926 might have given constructive notice of an earlier unpaid vendor's lien (see *post*, p. 464). Now, however, a purchaser will not be affected by such a lien unless it is protected either by retention of the title deeds or else by registration under the L.C.A. 1972 (see *post*, p. 599).

In registered conveyancing, such a lien would have to be protected by deposit of the land certificate (L.R.A. 1925, s. 66) or by entry of a notice or caution on the register (L.R.A. 1925, ss. 49, 54).

If not so protected a transferee for value will, on registration as proprietor, take free from it (L.R.A. 1925, ss. 20 (1), 23 (1)), *unless* the vendor has remained in occupation so that his lien is protected as an overriding interest (L.R.A. 1925, s. 70 (1) (*g*) ; *London and Cheshire Insurance Co., Ltd.* v. *Laplagrene Property Co., Ltd.* [1971] Ch. 499).

Receipts by trustees generally.—It is provided by s. 14 (1) of the T.A. 1925 as amended by the Law of Property (Amendment) Act, 1926, that the receipt in writing of a trustee for any money, securities, or other personal property or effects payable, transferable, or deliverable to him under any trust or power will be a sufficient discharge to the person paying, transferring, or delivering the same and will effectually exonerate him from seeing to the application or being answerable for any loss or misapplication thereof. But the section is not, except where the trustee is a trust corporation, to enable a sole trustee to give a valid receipt for—

(*a*) the proceeds of sale or other capital money arising under a trust for sale of land ;

(*b*) capital money arising under the S.L.A. 1925 (*ibid.*, s. 14 (2)).

The section applies notwithstanding anything to the contrary in the instrument (if any) creating the trust (*ibid.*, subs. (3)).

The word " trustee " includes an implied and a constructive trustee and, where the context admits, a personal representative (T.A. 1925, s. 68 (17)) ; also a bare trustee selling by the direction of the beneficiaries, because in such cases trustees become trustees for sale (*Re British Land Co. and Allen's Contract* (1900), 44 Sol. J. 593). As to receipts by sole personal representatives, see *post*, p. 462. See also s. 3 (1) of the Law of Property (Amendment) Act, 1926, defining the meaning of the expression " trust corporation," mentioned *ante*, p. 276.

Where there is more than one trustee, all the trustees should join to give a receipt, as one trustee cannot empower one of his co-trustees to receive purchase-money on behalf of all (*Lee* v. *Sankey* (1873), L.R. 15 Eq. 204 ; *Re Flower and Metropolitan Board of Works* (1884), 27 Ch. D. 592). Under s. 25 of the T.A. 1925 as amended, a trustee may appoint someone other than his co-trustee to act as his attorney (see *ante*, p. 245).

Receipts by trustees for sale.—It is provided by s. 27 (2) of the L.P.A. 1925, as amended by the Law of Property (Amendment) Act, 1926, that notwithstanding anything to the contrary in the instrument (if any) creating a trust for sale of land or in the settlement of net proceeds, the proceeds of sale or other capital money must not be paid to or applied by the direction of fewer than two persons as trustees for sale, except where the trustee is a trust corporation, but this subsection is *not to affect the right of a sole personal* *representative as such to give valid receipts* for, or direct the application of, the proceeds of sale or other capital money aforesaid ; nor, except where capital money arises on the transaction, to render it necessary to have more than one trustee.

It is also provided by s. 17 of the T.A. 1925 that no purchaser or mortgagee, paying or advancing money on a sale or mortgage purporting to be made under any trust or power vested in trustees, will be concerned to see that such money is wanted, or that no more than is wanted is raised, or otherwise as to the application thereof.

Receipts by trustees under the S.L.A.—It is provided by s. 18 (1) (*b*) of the S.L.A. 1925 that *if any capital money is payable* in respect of a transaction, a conveyance to a purchaser of the land will take effect under the Act only if the capital money is paid to or by the direction of the trustees of the settlement or into court ; and by subs. (1) (*c*) that notwithstanding anything to the contrary in the vesting instrument, or the trust instrument, capital money must not, except where the trustee is a trust corporation, be paid to or by the direction of fewer persons than two as trustees of the settlement.

Under s. 75 (1) of the S.L.A. 1925, the tenant for life has the option to require capital money arising under the Act to be paid either to the trustees of the settlement or into court. This section presupposes that there are trustees for the purposes of the Act in existence, and it is thought that the tenant for life cannot require the purchaser to pay the money into court where he, the purchaser, has notice of the fact that there are no trustees (*Re Fisher and Grazebrook's Contract* [1898] 2 Ch. 660).

It is also provided by s. 94 (1) of the S.L.A. 1925 that, notwithstanding anything in the Act, capital money arising under the Act must not be paid to fewer than two persons as trustees of a settlement, unless the trustee is a trust corporation ; and by subs. (2) that, subject as aforesaid, the provisions of the Act referring to the trustees of a settlement apply to the *surviving or continuing trustees or trustee* of the settlement for the time being.

It is further provided by s. 95 of the S.L.A. 1925 that the receipt or direction in writing of or by the trustees of the settlement, or where a sole trustee is a trust corporation, of or by that trustee, or of or by the personal representatives of the last surviving or continuing trustee, for or relating to any money or securities paid or transferred to or by the direction of the trustees, trustee or representatives, as the case may be, effectually discharges the payer or transferor therefrom, and from being bound to see to the application or being answerable for any loss or misapplication thereof, and, in case of a mortgagee or other person advancing money, from being concerned to see that any money advanced by him is wanted for any purpose of the Act, or that no more than is wanted is raised.

Receipts by personal representatives.—The powers and duties of personal representatives and trustees are, of course, quite distinct. The duty of the personal representatives is to clear the estate from liabilities, and only when such duties have been finished do the duties and powers of trustees come into force. Usually the personal representatives and the trustees are the same persons. When personal representatives are selling in their capacity as such, they can give a good receipt. When the estate is cleared, and they have *assented* to the legal estate vesting in the trustees, or in themselves where they are the trustees, such trustees or they themselves as trustees then come under the headings already dealt with.

As regards a sale of *settled land*, it is specially provided by s. 110 (3) of the S.L.A. 1925 as follows :—

" 110.—(3) A purchaser of a legal estate in settled land from a personal representative shall be entitled to act on the following assumptions :—

(i) If the capital money, if any, payable in respect of the transaction is paid to the personal representative, that such representative is acting under his statutory or other powers and requires the money for purposes of administration ;

(ii) If such capital money is, by the direction of the personal representative, paid to persons who are stated to be the trustees of a settlement, that such persons are the duly constituted trustees of the settlement for the purposes of this Act, and that the personal representative is acting under his statutory powers during a minority ;

(iii) In any other case, that the personal representative is acting under his statutory or other powers."

Where land was settled before his death it vests in the personal representatives of the tenant for life and before they execute an assent it may be expedient to sell some land to pay death duties or charges affecting the settled land. On the other hand, if the land is settled by the will, the title of the personal representatives is paramount to the settlement and so they can similarly sell before assenting. The S.L.A. 1925, s. 94, relates only to trustees as such.

A sole personal representative can give a valid receipt. It is provided by s. 27 (2) of the L.P.A. 1925, as amended, that " this subsection [the subsection provides that proceeds of sale or capital money shall not be paid to fewer than two persons or to a trust corporation] does not affect the right *of a sole personal representative* as such to give valid receipts for, or direct the application of, proceeds of sale or other capital money . . ." See also s. 2 (1) (iii) of the same Act, by which power is given to *a sole personal representative* to overreach equitable interests and powers " in the exercise of *his* paramount powers."

This power of a sole personal representative to give a valid receipt *applies to a sole administrator* as well as to a sole executor. It was at one time suggested that as regards a sole administrator, these provisions must be read with s. 33 (1) of the A.E.A. 1925, the effect of which, it was contended, was to make administrators trustees for sale, and thus bring in s. 14 (2) (*a*) of the T.A. 1925, set out at p. 460, and prevent a sole administrator having power to give a valid receipt. But this could not be so, for on a grant of administration the legal estate vests in the sole administrator, and only when he had completed his administrative duties does he become a trustee for sale under s. 33. When this happens he should in his capacity of personal representative expressly assent in writing to the vesting of the legal estate in himself as trustee for sale otherwise he continues to hold it in his capacity of personal representative. This was made quite clear in *Re King's Will Trusts* [1964] Ch. 54, as to which, see *ante*, p. 418. The point, however, does not often arise, because it is provided by s. 160 (1) of the Judicature Act, 1925, that *administration* shall, if there is a minority or if a life interest arises under the will or intestacy, be granted either to a trust corporation, with or without an individual, or to not less than two individuals.

As regards a sole executor, it is provided by the A.E.A. 1925, s. 2 (2), in effect, that, where only one executor is appointed and proves the will, or if more than one executor is appointed but only one of them proves the will, such sole proving executor can act alone whether or not power is reserved to the other or others to prove. But this must be read with s. 160 (2) of the Judicature Act, 1925, which provides that if there is only one personal representative (not being a trust corporation), then during the minority of a beneficiary or the subsistence of a life interest and until the estate is fully administered, the court may, on the application of any person interested or of the guardian, committee or receiver of any such person, appoint one or more personal representatives in addition to the original personal representative in accordance with probate rules and orders. This subsection applies to an administrator, but, as stated above, there will usually be two administrators appointed.

Receipts by mortgagees.—It is provided by s. 107 (1) of the L.P.A. **1925,** replacing s. 22 (1) of the Conveyancing Act, 1881, that the receipt in writing of a mortgagee will be a sufficient discharge for any money arising under the power of sale conferred by the Act, or for any money or securities comprised in his mortgage, or arising thereunder ; and a person paying or transferring the same to the mortgagee is not to be concerned to inquire whether any money remains due under the mortgage. The receipt would be a discharge even if the mortgage had, in fact, been satisfied ; unless the person paying had actual notice that no money was due, in which case probably the above subsection would not be any protection (*Dicker* v. *Angerstein* (1876), 3 Ch. D. 600 ; *Hockey* v. *Western* [1898] 1 Ch. 350).

Where before 1926 the mortgagees were trustees and the trusts of the settlement were disclosed, a purchaser could ask for the title of the trustees from the date of the settlement, so that he might be satisfied that the mortgagees proposing to give the receipt had the power to give it (*Re Blaiberg and Abrahams' Contract* [1899] 2 Ch. 340). This was a very inconvenient decision, and it has now been remedied by s. 113 of the L.P.A. 1925 which provides, in effect, that a person dealing in good faith with a mortgagee is not to be concerned with any trust at any time affecting the mortgage money or the income thereof, *whether or not he has notice of the trust,* and may assume that, unless the contrary is expressly stated in the instruments relating to the mortgage, the mortgagees (if more than one) are or were entitled to the mortgage money on a joint account ; and that the mortgagee has or had full power to give valid receipts for the purchase-money or mortgage money and the income thereof, without investigating the equitable title to the mortgage debt or the appointment or discharge of trustees in reference thereto.

Joint account clause in mortgages.—The provision as to this (in addition to the provision contained in s. 113 of the L.P.A. 1925, referred to in the last note) is contained in s. 111 of the L.P.A. 1925, given below :—

" 111.—(1) Where—

(a) in a mortgage, or an obligation for payment of money, or a transfer of a mortgage or of such an obligation, the sum, or any part of the sum, advanced or owing is expressed to be advanced by or owing to more persons than one out of money, or as money, belonging to them on a joint account ; or

(b) a mortgage, or such an obligation, or such a transfer is made to more persons than one, jointly ;

the mortgage money, or other money or money's worth, for the time being due to those persons on the mortgage or obligation, shall, as between them and the mortgagor or obligor, be deemed to be and remain money or money's worth belonging to those persons on a joint account ; and the receipt in writing of the survivors or last survivor of them, or of the personal representative of the last survivor, shall be a complete discharge for all money or money's worth for the time being due, notwithstanding any notice to the payer of a severance of the joint account.

(2) This section applies if and so far as a contrary intention is not expressed in the mortgage, obligation, or transfer, and has effect subject to the terms of the mortgage, obligation, or transfer, and to the provisions therein contained.

(3) This section applies to any mortgage, obligation or transfer made after the thirty-first day of December eighteen hundred and eighty-one."

Lien of vendor for unpaid purchase-money and of purchaser for deposit.—When a vendor delivers up possession of land, or executes a conveyance containing a receipt for the purchase-money, without having received the whole of the purchase-money, he has still a lien on the land for the balance, as against the immediate purchaser and also against persons taking under him as volunteers (even without notice), including the trustee in his bankruptcy, or under a deed of assignment for the benefit of his creditors (*Ex parte Hanson* (1806), 12 Ves. 346).

A purchaser also has a lien on the land for a deposit paid on a contract (*Whitbread and Co.* v. *Watt* [1902] 1 Ch. 835 ; *Kitton* v. *Hewett* [1904] W.N. 21).

The doctrine of lien equally applies to personal estate, such as a reversionary interest in a trust fund (*Re Stucley ; Stucley* v. *Kekewich* [1906] 1 Ch. 67). The doctrine does not apply when it can be shown that the intention of the parties was that there should be no lien, as by the vendor taking a mortgage of land for the purchase-money (*Re Albert, etc., Co.* (1870), L.R. 11 Eq. 164, at p. 179).

The lien of an unpaid vendor may be abandoned or merged if he has contracted to take a legal mortgage on lending the price (*Capital Finance Co., Ltd.* v. *Stokes* [1969] 1 Ch. 261, C.A. ; distinguished in *Coptic Ltd.* v. *Bailey* [1972] 2 W.L.R. 1061, where a vendor's lien was held able to survive despite the existence of legal mortgages and to pass by subrogation from the vendor to two successive mortgagees).

It should also be noticed that a person who provides the purchase-money for land may be entitled by subrogation to the vendor's lien even where the repayment of a loan by the purchaser would be unenforceable (see *Congresbury Motors, Ltd.* v. *Anglo-Belge Finance Co., Ltd.* [1971] Ch. 81 ; applied in *Coptic, Ltd.* v. *Bailey, ante*).

A lien should be registered as a land charge when it is not secured by a deposit of documents, as it comes within the definition of " a general equitable charge " in the L.C.A. 1972, s. 2 (4), Class C (iii), *post*, p. 599. A lien unsecured by a deposit of documents and not registered as a land charge will be void against a subsequent purchaser for value of the land or any interest therein (L.C.A. 1972, s. 4 (5)), even though the purchaser has notice thereof.

A lien unsecured by a deposit of documents, even when registered as a land charge, can be overreached under the curtain clauses on a sale by a tenant for life, and, possibly, on a sale by trustees for sale or personal representatives, as this is one of the cases where no injustice will be caused by transferring the charge to the purchase-money, for the owner of the lien will only want his money. See *ante*, p. 172 *et seq.*, and also L.C.A. 1972, s. 13, which provides, in effect, that registration of any charge under the Act is not to prevent the charge being overreached under any provision contained in any other statute, except where otherwise provided by that statute.

In the case of registered land, the lien may be protected by deposit of the land or charge certificate (L.R.A. 1925, s. 66) and this may further be protected by notice on the register (L.R.R. 1925, rr. 239 to 242 ; L.R.A. 1925, s. 54). If not so protected, transferees for value will, on registration as proprietors, take free from it (L.R.A. 1925, ss. 20 (1) and 23 (1)) unless the vendor remains in occupation so that his lien is protected as an overriding interest within L.R.A. 1925, s. 70 (1) (g) (*London and Cheshire Insurance Co., Ltd.* v. *Laplagrene Property Co., Ltd.* [1971] Ch. 499). See also *Abbey National B.S.* v. *Davis Contractors, Ltd.* (1972), 225 E.G. 1917.

The mode of enforcing the lien of a vendor is to apply for an order for sale of the property (*Williams* v. *Aylesbury Railway Co.* (1873), 21 W.R. 819 ; see also L.P.A. 1925, ss. 90, 91 and 205 (1) (xvi)). As to enforcing the lien of a vendor when the purchase-money is to be paid by instalments and default has been made, see *Nives* v. *Nives* (1880), 15 Ch. D. 649.

CHAPTER TWELVE

COVENANTS FOR TITLE

Implied covenants on sale of part of leasehold property, see *ante*, p. 456, *and post*, p. 856.

Covenants to which the purchaser is entitled.—A vendor who agrees to sell freehold land as beneficial owner must enter into the four qualified covenants for title which are implied by the use of the words " beneficial owner " in the conveyance ; see *post*, p. 468. It used to be thought that a vendor selling under compulsion, for instance, under the Lands Clauses Consolidation Act, 1845, could not be asked to give covenants for title (*Baily* v. *De Crespigny* (1869), L.R. 4 Q.B. 180). However, it has now been decided that in this respect a compulsory purchase should stand in the same position as a contractual purchase under an open contract (*Re King* [1962] 1 W.L.R. 632, reversed on other points at [1963] 2 Q.B. 459 ; and see *Harding* v. *Metropolitan Railway Co.* (1872), L.R. 7 Ch. 154).

If it appears from the conditions that the vendor is a trustee, a purchaser cannot insist on further covenants than that he has done no act to incumber (*Worley* v. *Frampton* (1846), 5 Hare 560) ; see *post*, p. 472. Where trustees are selling under a *trust for sale* the purchaser cannot ask the beneficiaries to join to give covenants for title (L.P.A. 1925, s. 23 ; and see *Cottrell* v. *Cottrell* (1866), L.R. 2 Eq. 330). Where the trustees are themselves beneficially entitled to the proceeds of sale it is sometimes suggested that they should convey as beneficial owners. The contract will usually provide whether or not this shall be done ; if it does not it is thought that the purchaser cannot insist on the trustees conveying as beneficial owners. The purchaser will rely on the overreaching powers of the trustees and he will not be concerned to inquire whether they are also beneficially entitled (L.P.A. 1925, s. 27 (1)).

In the case of a tenant for life selling under the Settled Land Acts, 1882 to 1890, the former practice was for him to convey as " beneficial owner," limited to the acts and defaults of himself and those claiming under him. After 1925 a tenant for life should merely convey " as trustee " save where he is absolutely and beneficially entitled, subject only to equitable interests which will be overreached by the conveyance ; in this case he should convey as beneficial owner without qualification. For a tenant for life is a trustee of the legal estate (S.L.A. 1925, s. 16) and a trustee in relation to the exercise by him of his powers as such (*ibid.*, s. 107) or of any additional or wider powers given by the settlement (*ibid.*, ss. 108, 109).

General rules as to covenants for title.—The implied covenants for title extend to a defect even though appearing on the face of a conveyance or of which the purchaser has notice outside the conveyance (*Page* v. *Midland Railway* [1894] 1 Ch. 11). In *Great Western Railway Co.* v. *Fisher* [1905] 1 Ch. 316, a vendor conveyed property free from an easement, which easement appeared from the conveyance and was known *aliunde* by the purchaser to be existing. The person entitled to the easement having recovered damages for the blocking up of such easement against the purchaser, it was held that the vendor was liable to repay him under his implied covenants for title.

See *ante*, p. 223, as to claiming compensation for defects in title ascertained *after* completion of purchase, under the implied covenants for title.

It is provided by s. 76 (6) of the L.P.A. 1925, in effect, that the benefit of the implied covenants for title shall be annexed and incident to, and shall go with, the estate or interest of the implied covenantee, and shall be capable of being enforced by every person in whom that estate or interest is, for the whole or any part thereof, from time to time vested. The effect of the subsection is to make the benefit of the covenants run with the land *provided* that the successor in title has the same estate or interest as the original covenantee. For example, a lessee would not be able to enforce covenants for title given by his lessor's predecessors in title. This is not really open to objection. However, it also follows, logically, that since 1925 a mortgagee cannot claim the benefit of the covenants for title given by the mortgagor's predecessors in title (L.P.A. 1925, s. 85 (1) ; see A.M. Prichard in the *Conveyancer N.S.*, vol. 28, p. 205 *et seq.*). These latter covenants will, of course, become enforceable after foreclosure or exercise of the mortgagee's power of sale.

Under the L.P.A. 1925, s. 76 (1), the appropriate covenants for title are implied only where a person " conveys and is expressed to convey " in one of the specified capacities. The question therefore arises whether this means that the person conveying must not merely be expressed to have a particular capacity but must also actually have that capacity. For example, are no covenants implied if a person who conveys " as beneficial owner " later turns out to be a trustee or to have no title at all ? Since the intention behind s. 76 was to save the trouble of expressing the covenants in full and since if they were expressed in full the grantor's actual capacity would be irrelevant, it is submitted that the words " conveys and is expressed to convey " ought to be construed as " expressly purports to convey " so as not to alter the position. Unfortunately in *Fay* v. *Miller Wilkins & Co.* [1941] Ch. 360, at pp. 363 and 366, Lord Greene, M.R., and Clauson, L.J., each expressed the view that the covenants would not be implied unless the vendor actually held the capacity in which he was expressed to convey. This was later cited as authority by Harman, J., in *Pilkington* v. *Wood* [1953] Ch. 770, at p. 777, for saying ". . . it being a *sine qua non* that the covenantor must be in fact, as well as being expressed to be, the beneficial owner " (see also *per* Megarry, J., in *Re Robertson's Application* [1969] 1 W.L.R. 109, at p. 112). However, in these cases these views were arguably *obiter dicta* and also they conflict not only with the idea behind s. 76 (see above) but also with existing direct authority which was not considered in the cases. See *David* v. *Sabin* [1893] 1 Ch. 523, *Re Ray* [1896] 1 Ch. 468, *Wise* v. *Whitburn* [1924] 1 Ch. 460, and *Parker* v. *Judkin* [1931] 1 Ch. 475 all of which afford support for submission that the actual capacity held by the vendor is irrelevant. Nevertheless, in the light of the obvious trend in the more modern cases, in some circumstances it might be advisable in practice to make express provision that the covenants shall be implied. For instance, where the contract gives the impression that the vendor is beneficial owner but it later appears that he is a trustee, he can apparently be required to give covenants for title as beneficial owner. In such a case it would be wise to state expressly that he shall give the same covenants as if he had conveyed and had been expressed to convey as beneficial owner. See generally the discussion by M. J. Russell in the *Conveyancer N.S.*, vol. 32, p. 123 *et seq.*

It is important to bear in mind that the object of inserting in conveyances a reference to the fact that the vendor conveys as beneficial owner, trustee, or as the case may be, is to imply appropriate covenants for title. The use of inappropriate words (e.g., that the vendor conveys as personal representative when he holds as trustee) does not invalidate the conveyance, since the rule is that the clear intention of the parties prevails over inaccurate technical words (*Re Stirrup's Contract* [1961] 1 W.L.R. 449). Thus if persons who have been appointed executors and trustees of a will convey land forming part of the estate " as trustees " without first expressly assenting as personal representatives in their own favour as trustees, the conveyance should nonetheless be accepted as valid and effective to pass the legal estate (see *ibid.*; also A.E.A. 1925, s. 36 (7); distinguish *Re King's Will Trusts* [1964] Ch. 542).

If a conveyance as prepared by the purchaser's solicitor contains a statement *in the testatum or habendum* that the land is conveyed in fee simple " free from incumbrances," these words should be objected to by the vendor, as they might import an absolute warranty of title at common law, to which a purchaser is not entitled (see *Ex parte Stanford* (1886), 17 Q.B.D. 259, 271 ; Williams on Vendor and Purchaser, 4th ed., vol. I, p. 665 ; see also *ante*, p. 449).

The word " give " or " grant " does not, in a deed made after 1st October, 1845, imply any covenant in law, *save where otherwise provided by statute* (L.P.A. 1925, s. 59 (2)). The words in italics refer to Lands Clauses Consolidation Act, 1845, s. 132, which provides, in effect, that the use of the word " grant " in a conveyance by a company under that Act shall imply covenants for title similar to those under s. 76 (1) of the L.P.A. 1925.

Covenants implied by use of the words " beneficial owner."—The covenants for title implied in a conveyance for valuable consideration by the use of the words " beneficial owner " are *qualified* covenants and do not give an absolute warranty of title. For this purpose, " conveyance " does not include a lease (L.P.A. 1925, s. 76 (5)). It will be noted that these covenants for title are not implied in a voluntary conveyance.

The liability of the covenantor is qualified (except in the case of a mortgage, see below) to extend only to a breach of the covenants caused by the acts or omissions of the following persons : (*a*) the covenantor himself ; (*b*) anyone " through whom he derives title " *otherwise than by purchase for value ;* (*c*) any person conveying by the covenantor's direction or " claiming by, *through* or under " either the covenantor or a person within (*b*) above ; and (*d*) any person claiming in trust for him (see *per* Lindley, L.J., in *David* v. *Sabin* [1893] 1 Ch. 523).

"*through.*"—Note the slight variation in meaning of this word : in class (*b*) above it covers predecessors in title in fee simple whilst in (*c*) above it does not cover successors in title in fee simple but only persons with derivative interests such as lessees or mortgagees (see *ibid.*, at pp. 530 and 540).

"*otherwise than by purchase for value.*"—This means that the covenantor is liable for the acts and omissions not only of himself but also of every person through whom he derives title since the last conveyance for value (which, in this context, does not include marriage). Often, of course, the conveyance to the covenantor will have been for value so that his liability is in effect confined to his own acts and omissions. But, for example, in *Stoney* v. *Eastbourne R.D.C.* [1927] 1 Ch. 367, the land in question had been in the covenantor's family since the last conveyance for value in 1782. In that case the plaintiff's action failed only because it could not be shown whether the defect in question arose before or after that date and the onus

of proof was on him. See also *Howard* v. *Maitland* (1883), 11 Q.B.D. 695.
As to what amounts to an act or omission within the terms of the covenants,
see *Eastwood* v. *Ashton* [1915] A.C. 900, below, and *Chivers & Sons, Ltd.*
v. *Air Ministry* [1955] Ch. 585, deciding that these qualified covenants
do not require a vendor to indemnify the purchaser against a liability imposed
on the owner for the time being of the land because of the transaction for
value by which the vendor had acquired the land (contrast *Stock* v. *Meakin*
[1900] 1 Ch. 683, *post,* p. 470, where also the vendor could not have prevented
the imposition of the liability but was required to indemnify the purchaser
on the ground that he had omitted to discharge it).

On the other hand, the covenants for title implied in a mortgage (including
a charge) as " beneficial owner " are absolute, that is they are not limited to
the acts and omissions of the persons mentioned above.

These four principal covenants for title, the results of which are stated
more fully below (and see further M. J. Russell in the *Conveyancer N.S.*, vol. 34,
p. 178 *et seq.*), are, briefly, as follows :—

1. That the vendor has, with the concurrence of any other person
conveying by his direction, full power to convey the subject-matter
expressed to be conveyed subject as it is expressed to be conveyed.

2. That the purchaser shall have quiet enjoyment and possession
without any lawful interruption.

3. That the property is free from all adverse estates, incumbrances,
claims and demands other than those subject to which the conveyance
is expressly made.

4. That the vendor and any person conveying by his direction will,
at the request and cost of the purchaser, execute and do all assurances
and things for further assuring the subject-matter of the conveyance.

Full power to convey.— This covenant is broken " if the land assured remains
subject to any outstanding estate, interest, mortgage, charge or claim,
whether at law or in equity, to which the conveyance was not expressly
made subject, and which was created or caused by any act, omission or
sufferance of any person comprehended in the covenant " (Williams on
Vendor and Purchaser, 4th ed., vol. II, p. 1078). In *Eastwood* v. *Ashton* [1915]
A.C. 900, a vendor, as beneficial owner, conveyed a farm described by a plan
endorsed on the conveyance. This plan included a small piece of land which,
it was afterwards ascertained, the vendor had no power to sell, as he had lost
his title to it by *allowing the adjoining owners to gain a title by prescription.*
The covenant is that " notwithstanding anything by him . . . omitted, or
knowingly suffered, he has full power to convey." It was held by the House
of Lords that the omission of the vendor to prevent the acquisition of an
adverse title to the strip of land constituted a breach of the implied covenant.
It will be noticed that the vendor must have had a title originally (*Thackeray* v.
Wood (1865), 6 B. & S. 766). For instance, if a squatter sold the land before
he had acquired a full title under the Limitation Act, 1939, it could not be said
that he had had a title, and he therefore would not be liable under the implied
covenant. See further the discussion in *Conveyancer N.S.*, vol. 18, p. 362
et seq., also *ibid.*, vol. 28, p. 188.

The covenant is broken if the vendor has conveyed an estate the whole of
which has not been surrendered prior to or by the conveyance containing
the covenant. Thus, in *David* v. *Sabin* [1893] 1 Ch. 523, the vendor had
granted a lease to a person who mortgaged his interest by sub-demise. The
lessee later surrendered his term without disclosing the mortgage. The

vendor was held to be liable on his covenants for title even though the outstanding interest, namely, the mortgage by sub-demise, was unknown to him.

Quiet enjoyment.—The covenant for quiet enjoyment implied in a *conveyance* for valuable consideration, other than a mortgage, is, substantially, that the property will be held without any lawful interruption or disturbance by the vendor or anyone claiming under him or claiming under a person for whose acts he is responsible. The cases dealing with the construction of a covenant for quiet enjoyment contained or implied in a lease are mentioned in the chapter on Leases, *post*, p. 870 ; they should be referred to as regards the construction of the similar covenant in a conveyance of freeholds.

There appears to be a distinction between the case where a vendor, having sold land with the benefit of the usual implied covenants for title, afterwards acquires adjoining property, and does some act thereon which interferes with the full enjoyment by the purchaser (or his assigns) of the land sold to him, and the case where the vendor was already at the time of the sale the owner of adjoining land on which he does such an act. In the former case, the vendor cannot be restricted in the use of the land later acquired, as otherwise a covenant for quiet enjoyment would have the effect of enlarging the original grant, which could not be allowed (*Davis* v. *Town Properties Investments Co.* [1903] 1 Ch. 797). As regards the latter case, the point would turn on whether or not the act complained of amounted to a derogation by the vendor from his grant (*Harmer* v. *Jumbil, etc., Ltd.* [1921] 1 Ch. 200).

Free from incumbrances.—This amounts to an undertaking (qualified as mentioned above) that there are no " estates, incumbrances, claims and demands, other than those subject to which the conveyance is expressly made ".

Any contravention of planning restrictions which may have taken place before the purchase may result in an enforcement notice being served on the purchaser under the Town and Country Planning Acts ; see *post*, p. 1021. It would seem that if the vendor was expressed to convey as beneficial owner any contravention of planning law by him which occasioned the demand in the enforcement notice would constitute a breach of his covenant for freedom from incumbrances. The covenant refers to claims and demands even though they may not also fall within the definition of the word "incumbrances". An enforcement notice served on a purchaser as a result of a contravention of planning law by the vendor would appear to be a claim or demand occasioned by the vendor even though it is served after completion. " It is important to mark that the regular covenant for freedom from incumbrances is, *not* that the lands conveyed *are* free from incumbrances, but that they shall be quietly enjoyed free from the incumbrances specified " (Williams on Vendor and Purchaser, 4th ed., vol. II, p. 1080).

Money due for paving expenses charged on the land falls within the covenant for freedom from incumbrances (*Stock* v. *Meakin* [1900] 1 Ch. 683 ; *Re Allen and Driscoll* [1904] 2 Ch. 226), although not a matter of title to be investigated as such. Similarly, it is thought that a contravention of planning control is not a matter of title but, *if followed by service of an enforcement notice,* and more particularly if steps are taken by the planning authority in default, might be held to constitute a breach of a covenant for freedom from incumbrances, claims and demands. Although conflicting judicial opinions have been expressed as to the acts which amount to a breach, the writers have not found any decision which would prevent the court from deciding that an enforcement notice consequent on the vendor's contravention (or the contravention of one for whose acts he is responsible) amounts to a breach of such a covenant, and a decision to this effect would appear to be within the words of the L.P.A. 1925, Sched. 2, Pt. I, and to do justice between vendor and purchaser.

In order that the vendor shall not become liable under his covenants for title, it is essential that the property should be conveyed *expressly* subject to any incumbrance if the existence of such an incumbrance might otherwise make him liable ; it is not sufficient that the purchaser should know of the incumbrance (see *ante*, p. 466). But it should be noted that even a vendor who conveys for value as beneficial owner gives *qualified* covenants only, and so the existence of an order (such as a tree preservation order : Town and Country Planning Act, 1971, s. 60), would not constitute an incumbrance " made occasioned or suffered " by the vendor or any person for whose acts he might be responsible under the usual qualified covenants. Therefore it is not necessary to make the conveyance subject to such orders. For the same reasons it would not appear necessary to convey subject to any conditions imposed by the local planning authority on a grant of planning permission.

Further assurance.—This covenant requires a vendor who has not conveyed all the estate expressed to be conveyed, to execute or do such lawful assurances and things for further assuring the subject-matter of the conveyance as shall be reasonably required. Such further assurances are, however, at the cost of the purchaser. Under this covenant the vendor can be compelled to convey to the purchaser any outstanding estate or interest necessary to give effect to the original conveyance to the purchaser, even if that estate or interest had been later acquired by the vendor for value (*Otter* v. *Vaux* (1856), 26 L.J. Ch. 128). A common example used to be the request that an entail be barred where an owner of a base fee had purported to convey the fee simple (*Bankes* v. *Small* (1887), 36 Ch. D. 716). A more modern example though not common under the covenant, would be the request that an outstanding mortgage or charge be discharged (see *Re Jones* [1893] 2 Ch. 461, 471).

Covenants implied in conveyance of leaseholds.—In a conveyance of leaseholds for value, other than a mortgage, there is implied, in addition to the covenants applicable on a similar conveyance of freeholds (*ante*, p. 468 *et seq.*), a further covenant by a person who conveys and is expressed to convey as beneficial owner, that the lease is still valid and in full force, and that all rents reserved by, and all the covenants, conditions, and agreements contained in the lease, and on the part of the lessee and persons deriving title under him to be paid, observed and performed, have been paid, observed and performed up to the time of the conveyance (L.P.A. 1925, s. 76 (1) (*b*) ; Sched. 2, Pt. II). This covenant is also qualified so that it extends only to acts and omissions of the grantor and of persons through whom he derives title, otherwise than by purchase for value (*ibid.*).

It often happens that there has been a breach of a repairing covenant prior to the sale of leaseholds. Common-form conditions of sale usually provide that a purchaser shall be deemed to have full notice of the actual state and condition of the property and shall take it as it stands ; see, for example, General Condition 4 (2) (*a*) of The Law Society's Conditions of Sale, 1973 Revision, and condition 12 (3) of the National Conditions of Sale, 18th ed. A vendor who contracted to sell on these terms might, however, appear to become liable in damages to the purchaser by reason of the implied covenant for title mentioned above. To remove any doubt, General Condition 8 (4) of The Law Society's

Conditions of Sale, 1973 Revision, provides that the covenants implied by statute should not extend to any past breach of covenant to repair to which the purchaser is precluded from objecting (see also General Condition 10 (7) of the National Conditions of Sale, 18th ed.). The conveyance should contain a reservation to this effect. Even if this is overlooked, however, rectification of the conveyance might later be obtained (*Butler* v. *Mountview Estates, Ltd.* [1951] 1 All E.R. 693 ; *Re King* [1962] 1 W.L.R. 632, reversed on other points at [1963] 2 Q.B. 459).

The covenants in an assignment regarding the future payment of rent, and the future performance of the covenants in the lease, are considered in the chapter on Leases, *post*, p. 856, and, as regards assignments of part of the leasehold land, *ante*, p. 456.

Covenants implied by use of other words.—A person who is expressed to convey by way of settlement " as settlor " gives a covenant for further assurance only (L.P.A. 1925, s. 76 (1), Sched. 2, Pt. V). A person who is expressed to convey (whether or not for value) as trustee, mortgagee, personal representative, committee or receiver of a person of unsound mind, or a defective, or under an order of the court, covenants only that he personally has not charged, affected or encumbered the subject-matter of the conveyance (L.P.A. 1925, s. 76 (1), Sched. 2, Pt. VI).

A mortgagor who is expressed to convey or charge as " beneficial owner " gives covenants similar to those mentioned *ante*, p. 468, but in this case they are absolute and not qualified (L.P.A. 1925, s. 76 (1) (*c*) and (*d*)). No covenants are implied by the use of the words " as mortgagor ".

Registered land.—For the purpose of introducing the covenants for title implied under the L.P.A. 1925, s. 76, the vendor may, in a Land Registry disposition, be expressed to execute, transfer or charge as beneficial owner, settlor, trustee, mortgagee, personal representative, etc. ; i.e., the form of transfer may contain the appropriate words in order to incorporate the covenants for title (L.R.R. 1925, r. 76 ; L.R.A. 1925, s. 144 (1) (xxxi)). These implied covenants for title will be of obvious value if the transferor is only registered with a possessory or qualified title, since protection may be required in case of rights and interests subsisting prior to or excepted from registration (see L.R.A. 1925, ss. 6, 7 and 20 (2) and (3)). Equally, if the transferor is registered with a good leasehold title protection may be needed in respect of the enforcement of any right or interest adversely affecting the lessor's title (L.R.A. 1925, s. 23 (2)). However, where the transferor is registered with an absolute title, the view has often been authoritatively expressed that the implied covenants for title perform no useful function (see Ruoff and Roper, Registered Conveyancing, 3rd ed., p. 310). This view is clearly correct so far as *registrable* interests are concerned, since the transferee is not affected by such interests unless they are registered when not only will he in the usual way have notice of their existence but also the implied covenants for title take effect as if the transfer was expressly made subject to the interests (L.R.R. 1925, r. 77 (1) (*a*)). Also this view is quite acceptable so far as concerns overriding interests *of which the transferee has notice*, since again the covenants take effect as if the transfer was expressly made subject to them (L.R.R. 1925, r. 77 (1) (*b*)). Unfortunately, considerable academic controversy has arisen so far as concerns, in this context, overriding interests *of which the transferee does not have notice.*

The matter was fully discussed in the *Solicitors' Journal*, vol. 105, p. 800 *et seq.* where it was submitted that such implied covenants for title are *not* " effective protection in the case of undisclosed overriding interests," and so " the mere insertion of the words ' as beneficial owner ' in a transfer for value of freehold land registered with absolute title is probably pointless," and concluded that a proviso expressly extending the implied covenants to cover overriding interests should be contained in every such transfer. It is doubtful whether a vendor should be advised to agree to this extension and he cannot be compelled unless there is a term in the contract. Compare the note in the *Solicitors' Journal*, vol. 105, p. 985. The practical view seems to be that overriding interests are outside the protection of registration and inquiries should be made, for instance by preliminary inquiries, inspection and questions to tenants or others.

In *Re King* [1962] 1 W.L.R. 632, Buckley, J., expressed the opinion that " on a conveyance of registered land the same rules must apply [as to the covenants for title which, in the absence of special stipulation, a vendor can be required to give] as if the conveyance were of unregistered land, although, if the title be registered as absolute, the grantee may often not insist on any covenant for title ". Consequently, under an open contract, a purchaser who knows that the vendor is selling as personal representative cannot require the vendor to give covenants more onerous than that in the L.P.A. 1925, Sched. 2, Pt. VI. Thus the covenant implied by the L.R.A. 1925, s. 24 (1) (a) (that, notwithstanding anything done, omitted or suffered by the transferor, the rents, covenants and conditions of the lease on his part have been paid, performed and observed) may be limited (*Re King, ante ;* on appeal [1963] 2 Q.B. 459).

CHAPTER THIRTEEN

PARCELS

PART 1. PARCELS GENERALLY

Conditions negativing right to require evidence of identity and of boundaries.—Under an open contract, an obligation will be on the vendor to prove the identity of the property sold with that to which the documents of title relate (*Flower* v. *Hartopp* (1843), 6 Beav. 476). If the contract description differs from the title deeds' description, the purchaser will be entitled to require further evidence establishing that the latter comprises the former (*ibid.*). However, in practice there will usually be conditions of sale dealing with the point. Thus General Condition 12 of The Law Society's Conditions of Sale, 1973 Revision, provides as follows :—

" 12. The purchaser shall accept such evidence of identity as may be gathered from the descriptions in the documents abstracted plus a statutory declaration made where required at the purchaser's expense that the property has been held and enjoyed for at least twelve years in accordance with the title shown but the vendor shall not be required to define exact boundaries, fences, ditches, hedges or walls or separately identify parts of the property held under different titles."

Attention is drawn also to Condition 12 (1) and (2) of the National Conditions of Sale, 18th ed., which has a substantially similar effect.

In *Flower* v. *Hartopp* (1843), 6 Beav. 476, the condition was that " no further evidence of identity of the parcels shall be required, than what is afforded by the abstract, or the deeds, instruments or other documents therein abstracted," and the descriptions in the documents differed among themselves and from the description in the particulars of sale. The purchaser was held entitled to have what he had bought distinguished, as without that it could not be said by the vendor that he had proved by the instruments the parcels described in the particulars. In *Curling* v. *Austin* (1862), 2 Dr. & Sm. 129, it was provided that " the purchaser is not to require any further proof of the identity of the property than is furnished by the title deeds themselves." Kindersley, V.-C., held in effect that, although the purchaser was precluded from calling for any other evidence, the condition would not enable the vendor to force the title on the purchaser if the deeds failed to show identity. These decisions were followed in *Re Bramwell* [1969] 1 W.L.R. 1659 where National Condition 12 (1) was held not to apply where the relevant document of title did not contain any description of a part of the land (Condition 12 (1) remains the same exactly in

the 18th as in the 17th edition of the National Conditions of Sale). As to
the right of a purchaser to require the boundaries of land of different tenures
to be shown, in the absence of a condition such as those above, see *Monro* v.
Taylor (1848), 8 Hare 51, and *Dawson* v. *Brinckman* (1850), 3 M. & G. 53.

Ordnance maps.—A reference to the ordnance survey map should mention
the edition, as the numbers of reference are not always the same in different
editions (and see further a letter in *Law Society's Gazette*, vol. 58, p. 562). In
the ordnance survey map a line marks the *centre* of hedges without regard to
the ownership of such hedges and the ditches beyond, if there be any, and
areas are calculated accordingly. See *Fisher* v. *Winch* [1939] 1 K.B. 666
and *post*, p. 490 ; judicial notice is taken of this practice (*Davey* v. *Harrow
Corporation* [1958] 1 Q.B. 60). The consent of the Controller of H.M.
Stationery Office is necessary for the making of a plan based on the ordnance
survey and the present rules regarding licences for reproduction are explained
in the *Law Society's Gazette*, vol. 53, p. 19, vol. 54, p. 83, vol. 60, p. 177, and
vol. 62, p. 122. Applications for licences should be made by letter addressed
to the Director-General, Ordnance Survey Office, Romsey Road, Maybush,
Southampton SO9 4DH. The Law Society emphasise that these licences
cover reproductions made within the licensee's own office only and that any
reproductions undertaken by printing firms are subject to normal royalties.

Plans attached to particulars and conditions of sale.—Plans attached
to particulars and conditions of sale should be so framed as to convey clear
information *not only to a lawyer* but to the class of persons who frequent
sales by auction (*Dykes* v. *Blake* (1838), 4 Bing. (N.C.) 463), and, if a purchaser
is deceived, even without any intentional suppression, the court will grant
him relief, provided he acted reasonably (*Bascomb* v. *Beckwith* (1869), 20 L.T.
862 ; *Denny* v. *Hancock* (1870), 23 L.T. 686). For instance, where the plan
did not disclose a footway over the property, this was held to amount to a
misrepresentation, although a footway is a patent defect, and the purchaser
was granted relief on the ground that when the vendor has been guilty of
misrepresentation the effect of notice is excluded, as the purchaser is justified
in relying on the vendor's statement (*Dykes* v. *Blake, ante*).

Where land is sold for building purposes, and on the plan attached to the
particulars intended roads on adjacent land are shown, this will not bind
the vendor to make such roads (*Tucker* v. *Vowles* [1893] 1 Ch. 195 ; *Whitehouse*
v. *Hugh* [1906] 2 Ch. 283).

Plans often contain notes that they are for identification purposes only
and not part of a contract, but it is doubtful whether such notes are effective.
In *Re Lindsay and Forder's Contract* (1895), 72 L.T. 832, a plan annexed
to particulars of sale had endorsed thereon a note that " this plan is simply
prepared as a guide to intending purchasers, and its accuracy in regard to
area, measurement, abuttals, or otherwise is in no way guaranteed," and
it was held that, notwithstanding the note, it formed part of the contract,
and that the purchaser was entitled to a conveyance of the whole of the
land coloured on the plan. However, it has been suggested that a note to
the effect that a plan attached to the contract was for reference only and that
no guarantee of its accuracy was given would enable the vendor to correct
the plan on proper evidence before completion (*Re Sparrow and James'
Contract* (1902), reported at [1910] 2 Ch. 60).

Purchaser entitled to copy plan referred to in abstract.—A reference
to a plan in an abstracted document makes it a part of the description. It

is as much a part of the title as the original document on which it is endorsed or to which it is annexed. A purchaser can, therefore, insist on having a copy (*Llewellyn* v. *Earl of Jersey* (1843), 11 M. & W. 183 ; *Brown* v. *Wales* (1872), L.R. 15 Eq. 142, at p. 147). The purchaser is also entitled to a copy of the plan although it is endorsed on a deed dated before the root of title if it is referred to in a deed dated after the root of title. See L.P.A. 1925, s. 45 (1), proviso (ii), p. 122. But the Council of The Law Society have expressed the opinion that where a vendor of a large piece of land has divided it into lots for sale, a purchaser of one of the lots is entitled only to an extract from a large plan on the conveyance to the vendor, provided that the particulars in the abstract and the extract are sufficient to identify the plot referred to in the contract (*Law Society's Digest*, Opinion No. 84).

Description in conveyance.—The following rule is stated in Williams on Vendor and Purchaser, 4th ed., vol. I, p. 651 : " . . . it appears that the purchaser is entitled to have inserted in the conveyance such a description of the property sold as will clearly identify the land intended to be assured. If, therefore, the description of the property sold contained in the contract is misleading, inadequate or obsolete, the purchaser should insert in the draft conveyance an accurate description of the land, according to its present condition, prepared from his own surveyor's report ; and it is thought that in these circumstances the vendor could not refuse to convey the land by the new description." This passage was approved by Swinfen Eady, J., in *Re Sansom and Narbeth's Contract* [1910] 1 Ch. 741, at p. 749, and by Farwell, J., in *Re Sharman and Meade's Contract* [1936] Ch. 755, at p. 758. See also the remarks of Eve, J., in *Monighetti* v. *Wandsworth Borough Council* (1908), 73 J.P. 91, 92, and of Swinfen Eady, J., in *Re Sansom and Narbeth's Contract*, *loc. cit.*, at p. 747. The vendor is assumed to know what is meant by the description in the contract and, if he does, he must be able to say whether the purchaser's description is correct or not ; he should either admit its correctness or point out where it is incorrect (*Re Sansom and Narbeth's Contract, ante*).

When purchaser entitled to have a plan on the conveyance.—The purchaser's right to take a conveyance by plan depends on his general right to determine the form of the conveyance. After quoting the passage from Williams mentioned in the last paragraph, Swinfen Eady, J., in *Re Sansom and Narbeth's Contract, ante*, said, at p. 749 : " I consider that, in all simple cases *in which a plan would assist the description*, the purchaser has a right to have a plan on the conveyance. I am not, however, prepared to say that in every case the purchaser is entitled to have a description by plan. In the case of a considerable estate where the contract does not contain any plan, if a plan were to be insisted on showing the abuttals, hedges, ditches, streams and boundaries at every point, the form of the conveyance, so far as regards the accuracy of the plan, might lead to much litigation—that is, if the exact boundaries had to be defined at every point before the conveyance was agreed between the parties. It will be sufficient for the determination of the present case to hold that in this case and in ordinary simple cases the purchaser, as part of the rule that he is entitled to take the conveyance in his own form, is entitled to have a plan on his conveyance, and is entitled to a conveyance by reference to that plan."

The headnote to *Re Sansom and Narbeth's Contract* merely stated that " In simple cases a purchaser is entitled to have land conveyed to him by reference to a plan on his conveyance." This seems to overlook the words stated above in italics, although it must be noted that there was nothing in the facts reported to show that a plan assisted the description in any material respect. In *Re Sharman and Meade's Contract, ante,* the property consisted of a house with a forecourt and a small court in the rear, and was one of a row of houses. It was held that a description stating the boundaries and the number of the house was sufficient and that the purchaser was not entitled to require the vendor to agree to a plan. Farwell, J., did not throw any doubt on the decision in *Re Sansom and Narbeth,* but laid down the rule in these words : " If in order that there shall be a sufficient and satisfactory identification of the land sold, a plan is necessary, then beyond all doubt, in my view, the vendor is bound to convey the land by reference to a plan. But, in my judgment, if it is possible to convey the property by a sufficient and satisfactory identification without a plan, and if the use of a plan throws upon the vendor an expense which is not necessary, then it is not right to say that a purchaser can insist upon a vendor going to that additional and unnecessary expense."

When preparing a conveyance by reference to a plan the solicitor should remember that a statement that the plan is " for the purpose of delineation only," means only that the plan is not true to scale (*Re Freeman and Taylor's Contract* (1907), 97 L.T. 39) ; also that a vendor is not entitled to qualify the conveyance by reference to a plan, by adding the words, " by way of elucidation and not of warranty," where the property cannot be accurately defined without a plan, if the vendor cannot show that the plan is inaccurate (*Re Sparrow and James' Contract* (1902), reported at [1910] 2 Ch. 60).

When mortgagees, who are paid off, or trustees join in a conveyance on sale, they are not, as a rule, bound to convey by any other description than that by which the land was conveyed to them (*Mostyn* v. *Mostyn* [1893] 3 Ch. 376 ; but see *Re Sansom and Narbeth's Contract, ante,* where the vendors were trustees).

The Council of The Law Society have expressed the opinion that the signing of plans annexed to documents is good conveyancing practice, and for such purposes a form of memorandum on the plan clearly identifying the document to which the plan is annexed is desirable (*Law Society's Digest,* Opinion No. 157).

Registered land.—The L.R.A. 1925, s. 76, provides that "registered land may be described (*a*) by means of a verbal description and a filed plan or general map, based on the ordnance map ; or (*b*) by reference to a deed or other document, a copy or extract whereof is filed at the registry, containing a sufficient description, and a plan or map thereof ; or (*c*) otherwise as the applicant for registration may desire, and the registrar, or, if the applicant prefers, the court, may approve, regard being had to ready identification of parcels, correct descriptions of boundaries, and, so far as may be, uniformity of practice." However, parcels clauses are, in fact, included in the prescribed forms of transfer of registered land, i.e., in the instruments the preparation of which are of direct concern to the solicitor. (For details of the descriptions, plans or maps kept by H.M. Land Registry, see rr. 272–285 of the L.R.R. 1925, and pp. 46–64 of Ruoff and Roper, Registered Conveyancing, 3rd ed. ; as from 1st January, 1969, land measurements based on the metre, the millimetre and the hectare will gradually replace the imperial system ; the procedure is explained in Registered Land Practice Notes 1972, p. 20, No. 52.)

If the *whole* of the land, freehold or leasehold, comprised in the title is to be transferred, then the prescribed description is " the land comprised in the title above referred to " (L.R.R. 1925, r. 98 and Schedule, Forms 19 and 32). Where there is a dealing prior to registration (e.g., under L.R.A. 1925, s. 37, or L.R.R. 1925, r. 73) so that the title number in the heading to the transfer is left blank, then instead of the words " the title above referred to " a reference to the last preceding document of title containing a description of the land must be inserted. If *part* only of the land comprised in a title is to be transferred, the prescribed parcels clause is : " . . . the land shown and edged with red on the accompanying plan and known as [and—*if it is desired that a particular verbal description be entered on the register*—described in the Schedule hereto] being part of the land comprised in the title above referred to " (L.R.R. 1925, rr. 98, 117 and Schedule, Forms 20 and 34). However, where sufficient particulars (by parcel number or otherwise) to enable the land to be fully identified on the general map, ordnance map, or filed plan, can be furnished without need for an accompanying plan (e.g., in built-up areas), these particulars may be introduced into the transfer instead of the reference to a plan. Nonetheless, where the part of the land comprised in a registered title is a flat or maisonette the Chief Land Registrar apparently proposes insisting upon compliance in all instances with the following provision of L.R.R. 1925, r. 54, that " on the registration of a proprietor of a flat or floor, or part of a flat or floor, of a house or of a cellar or tunnel or other underground space apart from the surface, a plan shall be furnished of the surface under or over which the tenement to be registered lies, and such further verbal or other description as the registrar may deem necessary, together with notes of any appurtenant rights of access, whether held in common with others or not, or obligations affecting other tenements for the benefit of the tenement the title to which is being registered ". However, there is a proviso to r. 54 that " if the applicant leaves in the registry a reference to the general map showing with sufficient accuracy the land affected by his application, it shall not be necessary for him to leave, deposit, or furnish any plan ". Despite this the official view is that the main provision of r. 54 is " for all practical purposes mandatory in requiring a plan " (Registered Land Practice Notes, 1972, p. 13, No. 46).

With reference to developing building estates sold off in plots (see the indicated procedure *post*, pp. 648–649) each instrument of transfer should be accompanied by a plan of the property concerned. Mere reference to a plot number on the approved estate plan would not be sufficient, although an extract from the plan could be used provided its details enable the position of the land sold to be ascertained on the vendor's filed plan ; also " T " marks and other references in the transfer should be shown on the plan.

Where a plan is used on an instrument of transfer it must be signed by the transferor (or duly sealed where a corporation transfers) and also signed by or on behalf of the transferee, e.g. by his solicitor who should describe himself as such (L.R.R. 1925, rr. 79, 113 and Schedule, Form 20). It is apparently not regarded as permissible by H.M. Land Registry to incorporate a plan into a transfer (or other registered disposition) of part of the land in a title " for the purpose of identification only " (Registered Land Practice Notes, 1972, p. 12, No. 45). This is clearly a common-sense view in that the registered conveyancing system as a whole is based on plans, but strictly speaking it is thought that these words would have effect only as between the transferor and the transferee and that in view of the " general boundaries " rule

(L.R.R. 1925, r. 278), filed plans have only the function of identifying and not of delineating the land (see further *post*, p. 482).

The question has arisen whether the parties' own plans attached to the conveyance or transfer should be bound into the land certificate as a matter of course. The registry is not prepared to do this in all cases, having regard to the fact that a number of plans received are merely rough freehand drawings or otherwise inadequate. In such cases, however, as those of overlapping floors or party walls where solicitors and their clients have taken the trouble to have detailed plans prepared on large scales, which approximate almost to architectural drawings, the Chief Land Registrar is ready to consider using such plans either as an adjunct to or in substitution for the filed plan (Registered Land Practice Notes, 1972, p. 20, No. 6). Also, when a conveyance or transfer creates restrictive covenants or easements which are described by reference to colours or hatching shown on the deed plan, the Chief Land Register is well aware of the desirability of reproducing the identical colours or hatchings on the filed plan and every effort is made to do so. However, for many very years the registry has, by convention, used certain colours for particular situations and it is impracticable to depart from these usages. Thus the registry uses (*inter alia*) the following colour reference on the filed plan :—

Red edging to show the extent of the registered plan.

Green edging to indicate land removed from title.

Green tinting to show excluded islands of land within the land edged red.

Brown tinting for land over which the registered land has the benefit of right of way.

Blue tinting for the part of the registered land subject to a right of way.

Subject to the continued use of these colours for the purposes described, the Chief Land Registrar will, whenever it is possible, endeavour to use on filed plans the same references as are used on deed plans. In some cases, however, it will clearly not be possible to do so as, for example, where more than one pre-registration deed containing restrictive covenants has used the same colour reference for different parts of the land, or where a deed uses colours that are already shown on the filed plan.

If solicitors can be persuaded to adopt the same references as the registry for the situations referred to above they will ensure, to that extent, that those references will be reproduced on the filed plan, provided they do not already appear there.

In addition, it is suggested that where additional references are required for deed plans solicitors should have regard to colours already in use on the filed plan and, subject thereto, draw on additional references in the following order :—

Tinting in pink, blue, yellow and mauve.

Edging the desired area with a blue, yellow or mauve band.

Hatching in colour (not black or green).

Numbering or lettering of small self-contained areas.

(Registered Land Practice Notes, 1972, p. 18, No. 29). It is the practice in the registry to make enlargements of plans wherever the colourings are not plainly visible in plans drawn to the normal scale. In any case where the plan issued is thought to be on too small a scale, it will always be considered on request with a view to providing a plan on a larger scale (*ibid.*, p. 20, No. 5). Field numbers and areas are not shown on the filed plan (*ibid.*, p. 19, No. 12, which gives the Chief Land Registrar's reason for the practice).

Construction of parcels.— One of the most important of the rules for the construction of parcels is that, where the different portions of the description of the property are not consistent, that portion which defines the property clearly and definitely will be accepted, and the remainder rejected, under the maxim *falsa demonstratio non nocet* (see *Llewellyn* v. *Earl of Jersey* (1843), 11 M. & W. 183 ; *Eastwood* v. *Ashton* [1915] A.C. 900, at p. 914). In applying the maxim it is immaterial in what part of the description the incorrect description occurs (*Cowen* v. *Truefitt* [1899] 2 Ch. 309).

"In construing a deed purporting to assure a property, if there be a description of the property sufficient to render certain what is intended, the addition of a wrong name or an erroneous statement as to quantity, occupancy, locality, or an erroneous enumeration of particulars, will have no effect " (Norton on Deeds, 2nd ed., p. 214). In *Lambe v. Reaston* (1813), 5 Taunt. 207, the property was described in the wrong parish though otherwise the description was correct, and the incorrect part of the description was rejected and the property held to pass under the remainder of the description. On the other hand, as stated in the marginal note to *Roe d. Conolly* v. *Vernon* (1804), 5 East 51, " where a grant is in *general* terms, there the addition of a particular circumstance *will* operate by way of restriction and modification of such grant." This exception was defined by Joyce, J., in *Re Brocket* [1908] 1 Ch. 185, at p. 196, in the following well-chosen words : "It is quite clear, to my mind, that if there be a conveyance of real estate described in general terms followed by a definite and specific enumeration of particulars, as by a schedule with or without plan, which enumeration omits something which might otherwise have been covered by the general description, then, generally speaking, the designation by schedule and plan would not be read as an imperfect enumeration to be disregarded as '*falsa demonstratio,*' but as restrictive of the prior general description."

A general description of a property as being bounded by the property of another will not be sufficient to exclude what is not so bounded if the previous description of the property was sufficient to include it (*Francis* v. *Hayward* (1882), 22 Ch. D. 177, 181).

If no definite conclusion can be reached from the parts or the whole of the description, the recitals and other parts of the deed can be looked to for expressions of the intention of the parties ; if these cannot be found, extrinsic evidence can in some few cases be used, e.g., to show to what property the description applies (*Fox* v. *Clarke* (1874), 9 Q.B. 565), or to show what is included in the strict words of the deed, but such evidence will not be admissible if it tends to vary or contradict the deed. For instance, conditions of sale were not admitted to restrict the parcels in *Doe d. Norton* v. *Webster* (1840), 12 A. & E. 442 ; nor to enlarge them in *Williams* v. *Morgan* (1850), 15 Q.B. 782 ; nor to import a reservation into the conveyance (*Teebay* v. *Manchester, etc., Railway Co.* (1883), 24 Ch. D. 572) ; nor to *make* a description where there was none (*Plant* v. *Bourne* [1897] 2 Ch. 281). Evidence of user may be given to show the sense in which the parties used the language in a deed when there is a latent ambiguity in the deed (*Watcham* v. *A.-G. of the East African Protectorate* [1919] A.C. 533).

Effect of reference to a plan.—Despite the general rule that a plan can only be relied on where there are words in the conveyance incorporating the plan by reference into the parcels clause, Cross, J., has held that a plan can be looked at where there is no such reference provided (i) the verbal description in the conveyance is not clear, and (ii) the plan physically forms part of the conveyance, as by being bound up with it or drawn on it (*Leachman* v. *L. & K. Richardson, Ltd.* [1969] 1 W.L.R. 1129).

It may be said generally that, if the contents and linear admeasurements are stated, or if a clear and sufficient independent description of the property in the body of or schedule to the deed is given, a plan will only operate as an explanation of this description, and will not be allowed to contradict such description. This is particularly the case if the plan was stated to be for " purposes of identification only "; see *per* Jenkins, L.J., in *Hopgood* v. *Brown* [1955] 1 W.L.R. 231, at p. 228, and compare *Law Times*, vol. 211, pp. 36, 180. If the boundary does not exist prior to preparation of the plan, but is pegged out or otherwise indicated in reliance on the plan, the words " for purposes of identification only " can have little or no meaning. In any case an express agreement to be bound by a particular marking out of the land will bind a party agreeing (*Taylor* v. *Parry* (1840), 1 Man. & G. 604). The unreported decision of the Court of Appeal in *Webb* v. *Nightingale* indicates that an agreement on the position of a peg may be binding on the parties even though the peg is wrongly placed and was intended to be inserted in accordance with a boundary on a plan which is for identification only ; see the discussion of the decision in the *Law Journal*, vol. 107, pp. 358, 359. *Webb* v. *Nightingale* was followed by Foster, J., in *Willson* v. *Greene* [1971] 1 W.L.R. 635, where correctly placed pegs, showing a kinked boundary, prevailed over a plan, incorporated for identification only, which incorrectly showed a straight boundary.

In *Taylor* v. *Parry* (1840), 1 Scott. (N.R.) 576, the plan was on such a small scale that a boundary could not be accurately traced, and as the land was sufficiently described in the body of the deed, the plan was not allowed to control the description. See also *Fox* v. *Clarke* (1874), L.R. 9 Q.B. 565, 570. In *Willis* v. *Watney* (1881), 51 L.J. Ch. 181, the parcels referred to a house and the yards usually occupied therewith delineated on a plan and thereon coloured, together with " all yards . . . appertaining and with the same . . . occupied." A yard which had been enjoyed with the messuage was delineated on the plan, but not coloured. It was held that the yard passed by the description in the deed. In *Mellor* v. *Walmesley* [1905] 2 Ch. 164, the exact dimensions of the land were given in the parcels and marked on the plan. But it was in addition stated that the land was bounded on the west by the seashore. This statement was incorrect, and it was held that these words must be rejected. In *Gregg* v. *Richards* [1926] Ch. 521 the Court of Appeal held that a right of way passed by the description in the deed, although it was not coloured on the plan referred to in the parcels. Boundaries of plots shown on a plan are assumed to be uniform and regular unless there is clear indication otherwise (*Hopgood* v. *Brown* [1955] 1 W.L.R. 213).

But if the plan is clear, and the description in the body of the deed not clear, and more particularly where the reference to the plan is in such words as " all which premises are more particularly described in the plan endorsed on," etc., the description in the plan will prevail (*Eastwood* v. *Ashton* [1915] A.C. 900 ; *Wallington* v. *Townsend* [1939] Ch. 588). Compare the old case of *Doe d. Smith* v. *Galloway* (1833), 5 B. & Ad. 43, where the property was described by words but stated to be " now in the occupation of one *R. S.*" All the land so described was not in the occupation of *R. S.* but it was held

16

that the whole passed. But, as was said in *Eastwood* v. *Ashton, ante,* a description by occupation is so inconclusive, and so liable to error, that it will readily yield to any more accurate description.

Plans attached to conveyances are normally intended to show boundaries at ground level only. In *Truckell* v. *Stock* [1957] 1 W.L.R. 161 property had been conveyed by the description " all that land dwelling-house office garages outbuildings and premises . . . delineated . . . on the plan attached hereto . . . being known as No. 45 East Street." Below ground level certain footings protruded beyond the boundary line marked on the plan, which indicated the outside of a side wall. It was decided that those footings, and certain eaves which also extended beyond the line shown on the plan (but not the column of air between them), passed to the purchaser. As the plan correctly indicated the boundary at ground level it was consistent with the verbal description which passed subsidiary parts of the house. It appears to follow that the decision would have been the same even if the conveyance had stated that the property was " more particularly " described on the plan. Unfortunately, the judgments do not refer to the decision in *Laybourn* v. *Gridley* [1892] 2 Ch. 53. It is doubtful whether this must be regarded as overruled or whether it can be distinguished on the ground that the plan was stated to refer particularly to dimensions abuttals and boundaries. Reference may also be made to the extreme case which occurred recently in *Grigsby* v. *Melville* [1973] 3 All E.R. 455, where it was contended that, since the plan attached to a conveyance of a cottage was merely of the boundaries as they existed at ground level, a cellar wholly beneath the cottage was not conveyed. This contention was rejected by the Court of Appeal, notwithstanding that the only practical access was from retained land and that easements and quasi-easements had been excepted and reserved to the vendor. But this was rather more than a mere projection case, of the *Truckell* v. *Stock* (*ante*) sort.

If the description is by reference to a plan on an earlier conveyance it appears that the same land will be conveyed even if minor adjustments of boundaries have been made in the meantime (*Hopgood* v. *Brown* [1955] 1 W.L.R. 213).

Registered land.—Questions of construction similar to those arising in unregistered conveyancing could in theory at least arise as to any inconsistency between the verbal description in the property register of a title and the plan it refers to (see L.R.R. 1925, r. 3, and L.R.A. 1925, s. 76). There are, of course, no such words as " for the purposes of identification only " to limit the effect of reference to the plan. However, L.R.R. 1925, r. 285, provides that the registrar " shall decide any conflict between the verbal particulars and the filed plan or General Map." Again, there might be inconsistencies between the verbal description and the special accompanying plan on a transfer of part of the land comprised in a title where also no words limiting the plan's effect are used (see *ante*, p. 481), but here any question of construction will be for decision by the court and not by the registrar since the conflict is not with the " filed plan or General Map " within r. 285. In such cases as these, the dual function of the instrument of transfer with its plan appears. On the one hand, it immediately provides the material for entries on the register. On the other hand, it may in the future afford the basis of a claim for rectification of the register since it determines the rights between the parties themselves.

In *Lee* v. *Barrey* [1957] Ch. 251, the transfer correctly indicated a boundary containing an angle as agreed by the parties, but the filed plan, and the copy attached to the land certificate, showed the boundary as a straight line. The Court of Appeal decided that the land certificate could not be set up to overturn the plain effect of the bargain, and it was not necessary to rectify the register, a declaration as to the correct boundary being given.

Registered Land Practice Notes, 1972, p. 22, No. 27, points out that, notwithstanding this decision, it is not necessary for a solicitor acting for a subsequent purchaser to examine the plan on a previous transfer. The registry " portrays as accurately as possible on its maps the position of physical features including boundary fences, hedges and walls and where none such exist reproduces the boundaries depicted on the conveyance or transfer plan with all available detail. Consequently, where the conveyance or transfer plan shows boundaries which do not agree with those actually existing on the ground, the registry will consider the need for having either the deed plan or the boundaries altered so that the two correspond and thus give effect to the intentions of the parties. If the plan is altered (as will usually be the case) all parties concerned must sign a new plan or the altered plan under a statement that it correctly represents their intentions . . . Where, however, the deed plan is so badly drawn or so ambiguous that the registry cannot decide whether or not it represents the fenced boundaries, the application will either be cancelled or the registry will submit a draft filed plan for approval by all parties before completing the registration. Where there are no physical features defining the boundaries of the land, the conveyance or transfer plan will always be treated as the governing factor and the existence of survey pegs which do not conform with the boundaries shown on the deed plan will be ignored by the registry ".

It is stated that the registry neglected to apply these principles to the transaction in *Lee* v. *Barrey*, but that it is extremely improbable that the circumstances will be repeated. Moreover, it is stated that " should actual monetary loss occur because the registry makes a mistake in drawing its maps a claim for compensation would lie under the provisions of the L.R.A. 1925, s. 83, notwithstanding that the land was registered with general boundaries."

Conveyance of a flat or part of a building.—It is quite ͵clear that a flat, or other part of a building divided horizontally, can be conveyed freehold. There are a few examples of long standing, for instance in Lincoln's Inn, and precedents are to be found, e.g., in the *Conveyancer N.S.*, vol. 19, p. 651. Various problems affecting lifts (for instance, whether they are fixtures), and the nature of repairing obligations are discussed in the *Conveyancer N.S.*, vol. 19, p. 467 *et seq.*

In such conveyances it is usually necessary to include restrictive covenants as to the user of the various parts. No real difficulty arises in this respect, as normally conveyances will form part of a building scheme and so restrictive covenants will be enforceable by and against future purchasers ; see further, *post*, p. 565. Also it will almost always be necessary for easements to be created on the conveyance. In addition to the rights of access to the flat itself, the flat owner will require access to other parts of the building for the purpose of repairs (see below), laying cables, etc., and the usual rights of passage and running of water, soil, gas, electricity, etc. Further, certain aspects of enjoyment may have to be catered for, e.g., rights to light, to use the garden (*Re Ellenborough Park* [1956] Ch. 131), even to use a lavatory

(see *Miller* v. *Emcer Products, Ltd.* [1956] Ch. 304). However, the most
important problem arises out of the need to grant rights of support from
below and beside and of shelter from above for the benefit of a flat and to
reserve such rights over the property conveyed. There can be no doubt
but that the grant of a flat carries with it by implication rights of support
over portions of the building retained by the vendor (L.P.A. 1925, s. 62 ;
Hansford v. *Jago* [1921] 1 Ch. 322 ; see further, *post,* p. 511). There might
appear to be doubt regarding the implied reservation of easements for the
reasons given *post,* p. 508, but it seems that rights of support over portions
of the building would be regarded as easements of necessity and so reservation
also would be implied. Consequently, it would not seem strictly necessary
to make express grants and reservations, although it may be advisable to
reserve to a vendor rights of support if there is any doubt as to the extent
of their enjoyment, and rights of access and of light which may not always
be " necessary " in the strict sense of the word.

Conveyances of parts of buildings divided horizontally have long been
unpopular, particularly on account of the difficulty of providing adequately
for maintenance of other parts. The grant of a right of support does not
require the servient owner to take positive action to carry out necessary
repairs (*Sack* v. *Jones* [1925] Ch. 235), although it does entitle the dominant
owner to enter and take the necessary steps to ensure that the support
continues by effecting repairs (*Bond* v. *Nottingham Corporation* [1940]
Ch. 429). Further, repairs may be necessary to common parts of the property,
such as passageways and staircases. It is possible to include covenants
that the respective parties will carry out repairs, but a practical difficulty
is that the burden of such positive covenants does not pass with the land
to future successors in title (*Austerberry* v. *Oldham Corporation* (1885),
29 Ch. D. 750 ; see *post,* p. 544). To some extent personal covenants may
be effective as a person bound would probably obtain an indemnity from
any purchaser to whom he sells, but in time they become unsatisfactory.
In some cases it is possible to form a service company to maintain parts of
the building in common use, and precedents can be found in the *Conveyancer
N.S.,* vol. 17, p. 501 *et seq.* Another suggestion is that the conveyance of the
freehold interest should reserve a rent-charge sufficient to meet the expenses
of maintenance of the main structure and of the parts thereof used in common ;
see, for instance, the *Conveyancer N.S.,* vol. 14, p. 350 *et seq.* (although
different suggestions are made *ibid.,* vol. 19, p. 3 *et seq.*) and the *Law Journal,*
vol. 102, p. 578. The decision in *Halsall* v. *Brizell* [1957] Ch. 169, *post,* p. 554
(to the effect that a successor in title cannot refuse to perform positive
covenants if he claims benefits under the same provisions), has particular
application to covenants affecting flats. It may be possible to make rights
and liabilities interdependent so that no successor in title dare repudiate
obligations for fear of losing essential benefits.

In many cases it is preferable to dispose of flats for long terms of years
only. The advantage is, of course, that the burden of positive covenants
can be made to run with a leasehold interest. At the same time a rent can
be reserved, if required, to meet expenses of maintenance of the structure by
the lessor. As to the taxation position, see *post,* p. 1115 *et seq.*

Registered land.—Where large houses are converted into flats the registry
takes pains to ensure that complete particulars of the rights and easements
granted and reserved on the sale of each flat are referred to on the registers
of both the vendor's and purchaser's titles. These particulars are made

available to interested persons in one of two ways according to circumstances. Either (i) they may be set out verbatim on the register, or (ii) they may be entered by reference to the documents creating them. In this case copies of the material documents are, wherever practicable, bound up in the respective land or charge certificates, but where this is not so the registers show clearly the title numbers under which the documents are filed. In complicated cases the registry sometimes consults with the solicitors concerned in an endeavour to frame the entries in the register to meet their requirements. It is not practicable or desirable to bind up in the land certificate of a developing building estate copies of transfers of part (which often run into hundreds) by which easements are granted and reserved (Registered Land Practice Notes, 1972, p. 23, No. 19). In cases where solicitors and their clients have taken the trouble to have detailed plans prepared on large scales, e.g., of overlapping floors or party walls, which approximate almost to architectural drawings, the registrar is ready to consider using such plans either as an adjunct to or in substitution for the filed plan (ibid., p. 20, No. 6). See further as to plans on transfers, ante, p. 477.

Maps or plans as evidence of boundaries, etc.—Although it is provided by the Tithe Act, 1836, s. 64, that the map or plan annexed to the instrument of tithe apportionment shall be deemed satisfactory evidence of the accuracy of such plan, it was decided in Wilberforce v. Hearfield (1877), 5 Ch. D. 709, that tithe commutation maps were never intended by the legislature to be evidence of the title to the land, and therefore not evidence of boundaries between two adjoining owners. See also Frost v. Richardson (1910), 103 L.T. 22, 416. The same reasoning applies in the case of an ordnance survey map (Tisdall v. Parnell (1863), 14 Ir. C.L.R. 1, at p. 28 ; Coleman v. Kirkcaldy [1882] W.N. 103), but see post, p. 490.

An inclosure award plan may be some evidence against the owner of the land comprised in an inclosure award (Frost v. Richardson, ante) ; but it is not conclusive evidence (Collis v. Amphlett [1918] 1 Ch. 232 ; [1920] A.C. 271).

In A.-G. v. Antrobus [1905] 2 Ch. 188, it was held that a tithe map was admissible in evidence on the question whether there was or was not a public road across land. The reason given was that the commissioners had power under the Tithe Act, 1836, to examine witnesses on oath and that it is certainly to the interest of anyone who has land, part of which is not titheable, to put forward his claim and establish it if he can ; if it was a road it would not be titheable. This case was distinguished in Stoney v. Eastbourne Rural District Council [1927] 1 Ch. 367. It was held in that case that, although the map was satisfactory evidence of the matters therein stated within the meaning of s. 64 of the Tithe Act, 1836, it could not be accepted as evidence of the non-existence of a public footpath which might have been but was not inserted in it ; a public footpath, where the cultivation of the soil was not prevented, would not reduce liability to tithe.

It was held in Copestake v. West Sussex County Council [1911] 2 Ch. 331 that a tithe map is not admissible as evidence of the extent of a public right of way, though it may be evidence that part of the land was not used at the time when the map was made for such purposes as to make it titheable.

Construction of particular words.—The most suitable word by which to describe the land comprised in a conveyance was considered by " The Conveyancer," in the Law Times, vol. 176, p. 44. The writer pointed out that " hereditaments " refers to property which descends to an heir and so is not appropriate since 1925, and that "*tenements*" is an obsolete word. He concluded that the most suitable word was the simple one "*lands,*" particularly as it is given a wide definition by the L.P.A. 1925, s. 205 (1) (ix), for the purposes of that Act (and see further as to statutory definition of "land" articles in the *Conveyancer N. S.*, vol. 20, p. 10, and the *Conveyancer N.S.*, vol. 21, p. 141). The word "*premises*" strictly means that which has been described before, and so should not be used in the parcels, but may properly be used later in referring to the parcels (*Gardiner* v. *Sevenoaks R.D.C.* [1950] 2 All E.R. 84, 85). However, the word may be taken to mean "appurtenances" as in the phrase "mansion house, gardens and premises" (*Lethbridge* v. *Lethbridge* (1862), 31 L.J. Ch. 737), or may even have its informal meaning of buildings (*County Hotel Co.* v. *L.N.W. Railway Co.* [1918] 2 K.B. 251 ; see further, *Law Times*, vol. 217, p. 29).

The words "*house,*" "*messuage*" and "*cottage,*" although they will not necessarily include all lands commonly occupied therewith, will include such lands commonly occupied therewith as are reasonably necessary, as distinguished from being a matter of pleasure ; for instance, outbuildings, orchard, garden and courtyard (*St. Thomas's Hospital* v. *Charing Cross Railway Co.* (1861), 1 J. & H. 400 ; *Re Willis* [1911] 2 Ch. 563).

In *Doe d. Clements* v. *Collins* (1788), 2 Term Rep. 498, it was held that a coal pen on the opposite side of a public road passed as part of a house, on the ground (as explained by Turner, L. J., in *Steele* v. *Midland Railway Co.* (1846), 14 L.T. 3) that it was necessary for the convenient use and occupation of the house. See also *Caledonian Railway Co.* v. *Turcan* [1898] W.N. 18. On the other hand, in *Pulling* v. *London, Chatham and Dover Railway Co.* (1864), 10 L.T. 741, it was held that lands adjoining a house used simply for the purposes of pleasure and for keeping cows did not constitute part of the house.

The word "*farm*" will include the principal dwelling-house and all arable land, meadow, pasture, wood, etc., belonging to or occupied with it (*Whitfield* v. *Langdale* (1875), 1 Ch. D. 61). As to the meaning of the word "*bungalow,*" see *Ward* v. *Paterson* [1929] 2 Ch. 396. A grant of a "*wood*" will carry the soil, but not a grant of "*trees*" (*Stanley* v. *White* (1811), 14 East 332). Therefore, by an exception in a lease of the woods and underwoods growing or being on the property demised, the soil itself on which they grow is excepted (*Whilster* v. *Raslow* (1619), Cro. Jac. 487).

"*Timber.*" It was said by Eve, L.J., in *Re Tower's Contract* [1924] W.N. 331, that when persons entered into a formal contract to sell property for a large sum, and included in the parcels a quantity of timber of such importance as to be valued at £500, he was of opinion that they used the word "timber" in its primary meaning, that was to say, as referring to trees which were recognised as timber throughout the whole country, namely, oak, ash and elm. It might be, of course, that, according to the custom of a particular locality, other trees, such as beech, were included as timber.

The meaning of the words "gateway" and "room" are considered in the *Law Times*, vol. 217, pp. 28, 29.

Construction of the abbreviation "etc."—In *Re Walmsley and Shaw's Contract* [1917] 1 Ch. 93, there was a contract for the sale of two plots of land "and buildings, material, etc." The question in the case was whether these words included a right of way not appurtenant. It was held that upon the construction of the contract the word "etc." referred to "material," and was limited to something of the same character and, therefore, did not carry the right of way ; but that if the word could be extended to include property of the same character and nature as " land and buildings," the most it could be held to include would be rights appurtenant to land and buildings. In effect this was applying the *ejusdem generis* rule. See also the decision of the House of Lords in *Ambatielos* v. *Anton Jurgens Margarine Works* [1923] A.C. 175.

Meaning of "adjoining" and "adjacent."—It was said by Buckley, L.J., in *Cave* v. *Horsell* [1912] 3 K.B. 533, at p. 544, that " There are three words ' adjoining,' ' adjacent,' and ' contiguous,' which lie not far apart in the meaning which they convey. But of no one of them can its meaning be stated with exactitude and without exception . . . Any one of the three may by its context be shown to convey ' *neighbouring* ' without the necessity of physical contact." In *Re Ecclesiastical Commissioners for England's Conveyance* [1936] Ch. 430, Luxmoore, J., said, at p. 440 : " When used in conjunction with the word ' land,' the word ' adjoining ' in its primary sense means that which lies near so as to touch in some part the land which it is said to adjoin. Of necessity it denotes contiguity . . . The word ' adjacent ' when used in contradistinction to the word ' adjoining ' means I think that which lies near but is not in actual contact with land." Thus, in *Vale & Sons* v. *Moorgate Street Buildings, Ltd.* (1899), 80 L.T. 487, a landlord who owned a large block of buildings had covenanted with the tenant of a shop at the end of the block not to " permit any of his tenants of his or their adjoining premises " to carry on upon such premises the business of a tobacconist. A shop was opened at the far end of the block, but the court held that the covenant had not been broken. See also *Derby Motor Cab Co.* v. *Crompton and Evans Union Bank* (1913), 29 T.L.R. 673 ; *Ind, Coope & Co., Ltd.* v. *Hamblin* (1900), 84 L.T. 168 ; *Harrow* v. *Marylebone District Property Co., Ltd.* (1902), 86 L.T. 4 ; *Foster* v. *Lyons and Co.* [1927] 1 Ch. 219, at p. 223.

But the use of the word " any " in addition to the word " adjoining " may entirely alter its meaning. In *Cave* v. *Horsell, ante*, a landlord who owned a row of shops had covenanted with the tenant of one of the shops not to let " any of the *adjoining* shops belonging to me on the Limes Estate " for the purpose of furniture dealers. The breach complained of was in regard to one of the shops, but such shop was not next door. The majority of the court held that as the word " any " imported plurality, the object of the parties was that the scope of the covenant should not be limited to shops in actual physical contact with the plaintiffs' shop.

As regards the word " *adjacent*," in *Wellington Corporation* v. *Lower Hutt Corporation* [1904] A.C. 773, Sir Arthur Wilson, in delivering the judgment of the Judicial Committee, said : " ' adjacent ' is not a word to which a precise and uniform meaning is attached by ordinary usage. It is not confined to places adjoining, and it includes places close to or near. What degree of proximity would justify the application of the word is entirely a question of circumstances."

Party walls.—The purchaser should ascertain the ownership of the walls and fences, and whether any of them are party walls.

Before 1926, a conveyance, by the owner of two houses separated by a wall, of one of the houses passed an undivided moiety of such wall, so that the owners of the houses became tenants in common thereof (*Wiltshire* v. *Sidford* (1827), 1 Man. & Ry. K.B. 404). In *Watson* v. *Gray* (1880), 14 Ch. D. 192, 195, Fry, J., said that the term " party wall " was rather a popular than a legal one, and that the expression appeared to be used in four different senses : (1) A wall erected on land belonging to the owners of adjoining lands, in equal moieties as tenants in common, as the term was applied in *Wiltshire* v. *Sidford, ante,* and in *Cubitt* v. *Porter* (1828), 8 B. & C. 257 ; (2) a wall divided into longitudinal halves, one half standing on the land of each of two adjoining owners, as in *Matts* v. *Hawkins* (1813), 5 Taunt. 20 ; (3) a wall which belonged entirely to one of two owners of adjoining lands, but which was subject to an easement of user belonging to the other owner as it is used in many Building Acts, and (4) a wall longitudinally divided, each moiety being subject to an easement of user by the owner of the other moiety.

A legal estate in land cannot now be held by persons as tenants in common and party walls in the first class mentioned by Fry, J. (to which class walls are presumed to belong as mentioned above), at the end of 1925 were dealt with by s. 39 (5) and Sched. 1, Pt. V, of the L.P.A. 1925. For the purpose of effecting the transition from the law existing prior to 1926, to the law enacted by the L.P.A. 1925, s. 39 and Sched. 1, Pt. V, provided that where, *before* 1926, a party wall or other party structure was held in undivided shares, the ownership thereof " shall be deemed to be severed vertically as between the respective owners, and the owner of each part shall have such rights to support and of user over the rest of the structure as may be requisite for conferring rights corresponding to those subsisting at the commencement of this Act " ; and any person interested may apply to the court for an order declaring the rights and interests of the persons interested.

As regards walls or structures made party walls or party structures *after* 1925, it is provided by s. 38 (1) of the L.P.A. 1925 that where under a disposition or other arrangement which, if a holding in undivided shares had been permissible, would have created a tenancy in common, a wall or other structure is or is expressed to be made a party wall or structure, that structure is to be and remain severed vertically as between the respective owners, and the owner of each part is to have such rights to support and user over the rest of the structure as may be requisite for conferring rights corresponding to those which would have subsisted if a valid tenancy in common had been created ; and that any person interested may apply to the court for an order declaring the rights and interests of the persons interested. The effect, therefore, of both the transitional provisions and s. 38 (1) is to turn what would otherwise be a wall of the first class into a wall of the fourth class mentioned.

Conveyances declaring walls or fences to be party walls or fences frequently provide that each party shall pay one-half of the cost of repairs. This may imply a covenant, but it would appear safer to insert an express covenant to this effect, the benefit of which could be expressly assigned in future conveyances. Choices open to the conveyancer in providing for the ownership of walls or fences are considered by J. E. Adams in the *Law Society's Gazette,* vol. 68, p. 275 *et seq.,* where the following formula is recommended : " party structures repaired and maintained at the equally shared expense of the respective party owners."

In the absence of express provision, neither owner is bound to execute repairs which may be necessary to ensure the continued enjoyment of the right of support by the other owner, but either owner is entitled to repair the half of the other owner to enable him to enjoy his right of support (*Jones* v. *Pritchard* [1908] 1 Ch. 630 ; *Sack* v. *Jones* [1925] Ch. 235 ; also *Bond* v. *Nottingham Corpn.* [1940] Ch. 429, 439). However, such an owner has been held unable by action, at law or in equity, to compel his co-tenant to contribute to the expense (*Leigh* v. *Dickeson* (1883), 12 Q.B.D. 194 ; on appeal (1884), 15 Q.B.D. 60 ; also *Mayfair Property Co.* v. *Johnston* [1894] 1 Ch. 508, at p. 515). On the other hand, neither owner is entitled to do any positive act which may cause damage to the party wall. For instance, in *Broder* v. *Saillard* (1876), 2 Ch. D. 692, the plaintiff's house was rendered damp by percolation from an artificial rockery or mound of earth placed against his house, and it was held to be an actionable nuisance. See also note on " Right of support," *post*, p. 520 *et seq.*

It is important to remember that (exceptionally as it involves expenditure) the right to have a wall or fence kept in repair is an easement which may pass under the L.P.A. 1925, s. 62 (*Crow* v. *Wood* [1971] 1 Q.B. 77).

Boundary where river runs between two estates.—The bed of a *tidal* river at any point at which the water flows and reflows regularly belongs to the Crown, the boundary on each side being medium high water, unless it can be proved that the Crown has made a grant to some person (*A.-G.* v. *Lonsdale* (1868), L.R. 7 Eq. 377 ; see also *Government of Penang* v. *Beng Hong Oon* [1971] 3 All E.R. 1163). As to *non-tidal* rivers, in *Blount* v. *Layard* [1891] 2 Ch. 681n, Bowen, L.J., said at p. 689n : " The natural presumption is, that a man whose lands abut on a river owns the bed of the river up to the middle of the stream, and, if he owns the land on both sides, the presumption is that the whole bed of the river belongs to him unless it is a tidal river. There is also a presumption that the owner of the bed of the river has the right to fish in the stream, and to prevent other persons from fishing there. But these are presumptions of fact, which may be rebutted."

Gradual accretions to either bank belong to that riparian owner, the boundary in the middle being automatically adjusted (*Foster* v. *Wright* (1878), 4 C.P.D. 438). But if a river suddenly changes its course the boundary remains where it was before (*Ford* v. *Lacey* (1861), 7 H. & N. 151). These presumptions do not apply to lakes (*Marshall* v. *Ulleswater Steam Navigation Co., Ltd.* (1863), 3 B. & S. 732) or to artificial watercourses, such as canals (*Chamber Colliery Co.* v. *Rochdale Canal Co.* [1895] A.C. 564) ; nor will the presumptions carry ownership of islands up to the middle of a non-tidal river, the riparian owner's boundary being the middle of the stream between the bank and the island (*Great Torrington Commons Conservators* v. *Moore Stevens* [1904] 1 Ch. 347).

Ownership of hedge and ditch.—When two estates are separated by a hedge and a single ditch, the presumption is, in default of evidence, that both ditch and hedge belong to the owner of the land on which the hedge is planted. " The rule is this : No man making a ditch can cut into his neighbour's soil, but usually he cuts it to the very extremity of his own land : he is of course bound to throw the soil which he digs out upon his own land ; and often, if he likes it, he plants a hedge on the top of it : therefore, if he afterwards cuts beyond the edge of the ditch, which is the extremity of his land, he cuts into his neighbour's land, . . . no rule about four feet or eight feet has anything to do with it " (Lawrence, J., in *Vowles* v. *Miller* (1810), 3 Taunt. 137, at pp. 137, 138 ; for an illustration, see *Weston* v. *Lawrence Weaver, Ltd.* [1961] 1 Q.B. 402 ; also *A.-G.* v. *Beynon* [1970] Ch. 1).

Probably this doctrine does not arise when it is not known that the ditch is artificial (*Marshall* v. *Taylor* [1895] 1 Ch. 641). For instance, the ditch may have been a watercourse formed by nature, in which case the presumption would not apply (*ibid.*). When the presumption arises it will not be rebutted

16A

unless the evidence to the contrary is very clear. In one case, the adjacent owner had for nearly fifty years trimmed the hedge and cleaned the ditch, but there was no evidence of knowledge on the part of the owner, and it was held that the presumption was not rebutted (*Henniker* v. *Howard* (1904), 90 L.T. 157 ; contrast *Jones* v. *Price* [1965] 2 Q.B. 618, where maintenance of a hedge for fifty years was held more indicative of ownership than of a prescriptive servient obligation to repair). A title may be acquired to a ditch against the owner by lapse of time (*Marshall* v. *Taylor, ante*).

The presumption does not arise if the position of the boundary can be ascertained from the title deeds. Thus, in *Fisher* v. *Winch* [1939] 1 K.B. 666, the Court of Appeal decided that, where the limits and acreage of land conveyed were *described by reference to the ordnance survey map*, the boundary was in the position which is delineated on that map, and admitted evidence which showed that the boundary for the purposes of that map is taken to be the centre line of a hedge. See also *Rouse* v. *Gravelworks, Ltd.* [1940] 1 K.B. 489, 493 ; *Davey* v. *Harrow Corporation* [1958] 1 Q.B. 60, and notes as to ordnance maps, *ante*, p. 475. In the unreported decision in *Jarvis* v. *Aris*, 14th July, 1961, referred to in an interesting article on the subject in the *Law Times* (vol. 232, pp. 229, 230) the Court of Appeal held that, where a ditch does not pass by conveyance because the plan refers to the boundaries as on the ordnance map, it cannot be claimed to pass by virtue of the L.P.A. 1925, s. 62 (1), *post*, p. 511.

If there is no ditch, or where the former existence of a ditch cannot be proved, there is no presumption of law that the owner of a hedge is entitled to four or any other number of feet as " ditch width " on the further side of his land (*Collis* v. *Amphlett* [1920] A.C. 271) ; but compare *White* v. *Taylor* (*No. 2*) [1969] 1 Ch. 160, where waste-land on one side was as good as a ditch for the purpose of preserving ownership of a hedge.

Boundaries of registered land.—Wherever practicable the boundaries of all freehold land and all requisite details in relation to these (e.g., declarations as to the ownership of fences) are to be entered on the register or filed plan or general map (L.R.A. 1925, s. 76, and Registered Land Practice Notes, 1972, p. 19, No. 34, which see further as to the entry of " T " marks).

The boundaries shown on the filed plan or general map are only general boundaries and follow the ordnance survey map through the centres of hedges. In the case of agricultural land, this is frequently incorrect, having regard to the " hedge and ditch " rule. The explanation of the registry's practice is to be found in r. 278 in cases where the boundaries have not been fixed. Under r. 278 of the L.R.R. 1925, the filed plan or general map of a registered property is deemed to indicate its general boundaries only and the exact line of the boundary of the registered land is left undetermined—as, for instance, whether it includes a hedge or wall and ditch or runs along the centre of a wall or fence, or its inner or outer face, or how far it runs within or beyond it (Registered Land Practice Notes, 1972, pp. 21 and 22, Nos. 13 and 27).

If it is desired to indicate on the filed plan or general map, or otherwise to define in the register, the precise position of boundaries, notice must be given to the owners and occupiers of the adjoining lands of the intention to ascertain and fix the boundary, with such plan, or tracing, or extract from the proposed verbal description as may be necessary to show clearly the fixed boundary proposed to be registered (L.R.R. 1925, r. 276). Any dispute will be determined by the registrar subject to appeal to the court (L.R.R.

1925, r. 298). When the position and description of the boundaries have been determined, the necessary particulars are added to the filed plan or general map, and a note that they have been fixed is made in the property register (L.R.R. 1925, r. 277). The plan or general map is then deemed to define accurately the fixed boundaries (ibid.).

Ownership of open spaces, common yards and gardens.—Where at the end of 1925 *an open space* of land (with or without any building *used in common* for the purposes of any adjoining land) *was held in undivided shares,* in right whereof each owner had rights of access and user over the open space, the ownership thereof vested in the Public Trustee on the statutory trusts, but these " shall be executed only with the leave of the court, and, subject to any order of the court to the contrary, each person who would have been a tenant in common shall, until the open space is conveyed to a purchaser, have rights of access and user over the open space corresponding to those which would have subsisted if the tenancy in common had remained subsisting "; and any person interested can apply to the court for an order declaring the rights and interests under the Act of the persons interested in any such open space and the court may make such order as it thinks fit (L.P.A. 1925, s. 39 ; Sched. 1, Pt. V, para. 2).

It was held by Tomlin, J., in *Re Bradford City Premises* [1928] Ch. 138, that the expression " an open space of land " means any land which is unbuilt upon, and that the word " building " in the bracketed words meant a building on the space. A small yard and ashes place at the rear of two houses in White Abbey Road, Bradford, were immediately before 1926 held in undivided shares by the owners of the houses with rights of access and user over the same. It was held that the yard and ashes place were an open space within the meaning of the paragraph, and had vested in the Public Trustee, and leave was given to the Public Trustee to sell the same. During the hearing of the case it was mentioned by Mr. H. H. King, as *amicus curiae,* that the history of the paragraph was that the closing of the bracket had been accidentally shifted from after " building " to its present position, but the learned judge said that he must deal with the paragraph as he found it.

In *Re Townsend* [1930] 2 Ch. 338, the question again arose in connection with a railway siding consisting partly of freehold land vested in trustees of a will and partly of leasehold land held by trustees of a lease containing a declaration of trust, but neither set of trustees held on trust for sale or had any power of sale. Immediately before 1926 the persons entitled to the siding and the user thereof were the two sets of trustees and certain tenants paying rents. Eve, J., said that without criticising the decision in *Re Bradford City Premises,* and the construction put upon the expression " an open space," he had come to the conclusion that the rights of access and user were personal rights under the trusts and that no part of the siding was " an open space " vested in undivided shares in right whereof each owner had rights of access and user thereof, and so the land had not vested in the Public Trustee.

It will be noticed that the above paragraph deals only with open spaces existing on 1st January, 1926 ; after 1925 no undivided share can be created of a legal estate (L.P.A. 1925, ss. 1 (6) and 34). It is suggested that, as a matter of conveyancing, the best way to deal with the matter now is to convey the open space to one person, and for that person to grant all the other persons entitled legal easements in common under s. 187 (2) of the L.P.A. 1925.

Ownership of roads.—The general presumption is that the owner of land adjoining a road is owner of the soil of one-half of the road and that such soil passes by a conveyance of land abutting on the road. This rule applies to streets in towns as much as to streets in the country (*Re White's Charities* [1898] 1 Ch. 659 ; *London and North Western Railway Co.* v. *Mayor and Corporation of the City of Westminster* [1902] 1 Ch. 269) ; also to a private road (*Smith* v. *Howden* (1863), 14 C.B. (N.S.) 398). The presumption does not apply where a railway is the boundary. Consequently, a grant of the land and minerals on each side of a railway will not pass the minerals under the railway (*Thompson* v. *Hickman* [1907] 1 Ch. 550).

The presumption may, of course, be rebutted, but it is not rebutted by the land being described as bounded on one side by the road, or containing an area which can be satisfied without including half the road, or by the land being referred to as coloured on a plan whereon the half of the road is not coloured (Norton on Deeds, p. 232 ; 2nd ed., p. 252 ; *Berridge* v. *Ward* (1861), 10 C.B. (N.S.) 400 ; *Micklethwait* v. *Newlay Bridge Co.* (1886), 33 Ch. D. 133 ; *Pryor* v. *Petre* [1894] 2 Ch. 11). The fact that a private road leads to the lands of one only of two adjoining proprietors will not be sufficient to rebut the presumption (*Smith* v. *Howden, ante*).

The presumption can be rebutted by showing that it must be inferred from the surrounding circumstances that it was not intended to pass the site of the moiety of the street (*Mappin Brothers* v. *Liberty & Co., Ltd.* [1903] 1 Ch. 118). The circumstance from which this intention can generally be inferred is that the grantor would require the land for some purpose ; for instance, to make a street. The following are examples of cases where the presumption is considered to be rebutted, namely :—

(1) Where the conveyance of the land refers to the road as an intended road, on the ground that the grantor must retain the soil to enable him to construct the road and dedicate it to the public (*Leigh* v. *Jack* (1879), 5 Ex. D. 264). The presumption, of course, applies where the street is already dedicated (*Re White's Charities* [1898] 1 Ch. 659).

(2) Where roads are set out under an Inclosure Act (*R.* v. *Wright* (1832), 3 B. & Ad. 681 ; but see *Ecroyd* v. *Coulthard* [1897] 2 Ch. 554).

(3) Where the land conveyed forms part of a building estate it is doubtful whether the presumption applies ; if it does it is easily rebutted (*Plumstead Board of Works* v. *British Land Co.* (1874), L.R. 10 Q.B. 16). This case was reversed on appeal (L.R. 10 Q.B. 203) on a different point, and no opinion was given on this point, but it was more recently applied by Brightman, J., in *Giles* v. *County Building Constructors (Hertford), Ltd.* (1971), 22 P. & C.R. 264 (see also *Beckett* v. *Leeds Corporation* (1872), 7 Ch. App. 421 ; *Leigh* v. *Jack* (1879), 5 Ex. D. 264).

Whether the presumption applies to leases seems doubtful. Certainly in *Doe d. Pring* v. *Pearsey* (1827), 7 B. & C. 304, at p. 307, Holroyd, J., said that it does ; and in *Haynes* v. *King* [1893] 3 Ch. 439, it was so held, but the matter was not fully argued. In *Landrock* v. *Metropolitan District Railway Co.* [1886] W.N. 195 the question was expressly reserved. The point came up again in *Mappin Brothers* v. *Liberty & Co., Ltd. and A.-G.* [1903] 1 Ch. 118, but was again reserved. It is submitted that the presumption must apply on the ground that " it is a law by which you ascertain the parcel of a grant " (*Tilbury* v. *Silva* (1890), 45 Ch. D. 98, at p. 109, a case of the bed of a river, but where the same principle applies).

The common-law rule is that the owner of the soil of a highway has a right to everything above and beneath it subject only to public rights of passage, and may exercise all rights of ownership consistent with such public rights. Certain statutes, however, have vested roads and streets in local authorities. For instance, the effect of the Highways Act, 1959, s. 226 is, with certain exceptions, to vest in the highway authority highways maintainable at the public expense, together with the material and scrapings thereof. The effect is not to transfer the ownership of the land forming the site of a road to the local authority, but to vest in the authority *the surface* of such a thickness—or perhaps it would be more accurate to say " the surface and so much of the actual soil of the road " (*Foley's Charity Trustees* v. *Dudley Corporation* [1910] 1 K.B. 317)—as it may require for the purpose of doing to the road that which is necessary for it as a road (*Coverdale* v. *Charlton* (1878), 4 Q.B.D. 104, 118 ; *Finchley Electric Light Co.* v. *Finchley Urban District Council* [1903] 1 Ch. 437 ; *Baird* v. *Tunbridge Wells Corporation* [1894] 2 Q.B. 867 ; *Singh* v. *Arjun Lal* [1937] 4 All E.R. 5 (P.C.)). The local authority holds a legal estate in the surface thickness, i.e., a fee simple determinable on the land ceasing to be used as a highway (L.P.A. 1925, s. 7 (1), and *Tithe Redemption Commission* v. *Runcorn U.D.C.* [1954] Ch. 383).

If a highway is bounded by hedges or fences the whole of the area between the hedges or fences which is capable of being used is presumed to have been dedicated to the public provided such presumption is reasonable in the circumstances ; in deciding whether it is reasonable, regard must be had to such matters as the width of margins at the side of a metalled road, and the regularity of the line of hedges (*Hinds and Diplock* v. *Brecon County Council* [1938] 4 All E.R. 24). The preliminary question is whether the fences had been put up by reference to the highway ; if they had there is a rebuttable presumption of law that the highway extends to the whole space between them (*A.-G.* v. *Beynon* [1970] Ch. 1). Fences are taken to have been put up by reference to the highway in the absence of contrary indication (*ibid.*). But a ditch which is not adapted for the exercise of the public's right of passage is presumed not to form part of the highway (*Chorley Corporation* v. *Nightingale* [1906] 2 K.B. 637 ; *Hanscombe* v. *Bedfordshire County Council* [1938] Ch. 944). The problem of the ownership of land at the site of a made-up highway and questions affecting the use which may be made of highway verges were considered in the *Solicitors' Journal*, vol. 101, p. 218.

Exceptions and reservations.—The distinction between an *exception* and a *reservation* is sometimes overlooked. By *exception* is meant something excepted out of that which is granted and is actually *in esse* at the time of the grant, such as an exception of mines and minerals or timber trees. The effect of an exception is not to include in the grant that which is excepted (*Doe d. Douglas* v. *Lock* (1835), 2 A. & E. 705). For this reason *an exception has always had effect notwithstanding that the grantee had not executed the deed.* Exceptions are properly placed directly after the parcels, whilst reservations should be placed in the habendum although in practice, of course, they tend also to be placed after the parcels, the whole being introduced by some such words as " Except and reserving . . .".

By *reservation* is meant some benefit to be newly created, that is, a reservation of a thing *not in esse* at the time of the grant. Originally the term only applied to a reservation of services to be provided by a tenant, such as paying rent (see *per* Denning, L.J., in *Mason* v. *Clarke* [1954] 1 Q.B. 461, at p. 466 ; on appeal [1955] A.C. 778), but it has obtained an extended meaning and can be properly applied to some incorporeal right which the grantor desires re-granted for his benefit over the thing granted, such as a right of way (*Durham and Sunderland Railway Co.* v. *Walker* (1842), 2 Q.B. 940 ; *Jones* v. *Consolidated Anthracite Collieries, Ltd.* [1916] 1 K.B. 123, 135). Nevertheless, such words as " saving and reserving " will, when the intention is clear, be construed as equivalent to " saving and excepting." In *Duke of Sutherland* v. *Heathcote* [1891] 3 Ch. 504 ; [1892] 1 Ch. 475, the words in the deed were, " saving and reserving nevertheless to the said [*G* and *T*] and to their heirs and assigns, full and free liberty by all necessary and convenient ways and means to search for, get, dig, drain, and carry away, the coal, ironstone, and minerals which may or shall be found within the several lands hereby granted and exchanged." It was held that as there was no context in the deed showing a clear intention to except the minerals, these words did not operate as an exception but as a regrant of a licence to get the coal, but not of an exclusive licence. Lindley, L.J., said that to construe the reservation clause as an exception would be to violate well-settled rules of conveyancing, and that no conveyancer intending to except mines and minerals from a conveyance would express his intention by reserving a liberty to get minerals. See also *A.-G. for New South Wales* v. *Dickson* [1904] A.C. 273, where the word " reserving " was held to operate as an exception. This may be compared with *British Railways Board* v. *Glass* [1965] Ch. 538, where the Court of Appeal held that the words in a conveyance following " save and except " on their true construction conferred a general right of way, i.e., strictly a reservation or regrant and not an exception. Again in *Re Dances Way, West Town, Hayling Island* [1962] Ch. 490 the Court of Appeal emphasised that the technical conveyancing phrase " excepting and reserving " is not necessarily of such significance that it will govern the construction of all that immediately follows it so as to convert existing rights into new grants (existing rights ought strictly to be introduced by " subject to " after the habendum : *Scotson* v. *Jones* (1961), unreported but noted in the *Law Times*, vol. 231, p. 187). More recently, the general words : " Except and reserving unto the vendor such rights and easements or quasi rights and quasi easements as may be enjoyed in connection with the . . . adjoining property ", were *not* construed as excluding from the conveyance of a cottage the cellar underneath even though it had been used for storage in connection with the adjoining property (*Grigsby* v. *Melville* [1973] 3 All E.R. 455, C.A.).

As regards the general construction of an exception, Stirling, L.J., in *Savill Bros., Ltd.* v. *Bethell* [1902] 2 Ch. 523, said : " It is a settled rule of construction that where there is a grant and an exception out of it, the exception is to be taken as inserted for the benefit of the grantor and to be construed in favour of the grantee. If then the grant be clear, but the exception be so framed as to be bad for uncertainty, it appears to us that on this principle the grant is operative and the exception fails." As a reservation is now effective without any regrant (L.P.A. 1925, s. 65 (1), *post*, p. 495), the same rule applies to a reservation which, in case of doubt, is construed against the grantor (*Cordell* v. *Second Clanfield Properties, Ltd.* [1969] 1 Ch. 9 ; but compare *Bulstrode* v. *Lambert* [1953] 1 W.L.R. 1064, 1068).

Reservation effective although purchaser does not execute.—Before 1926, a reservation was not effective *at law unless the deed was executed by the grantee* or it was made by way of use under s. 62 of the Conveyancing Act, 1881. If the deed was executed by the grantee the reservation operated as if the grantor had granted the whole property to the grantee and the grantee had then granted back to the grantor the particular right which the grantor had bargained to possess (*Wickham* v. *Hawker* (1840), 7 M. & W. 63 ; *Thellusson* v. *Liddard* [1900] 2 Ch. 635, 645). If, before 1926, the grantee should not have executed the deed, still, *in equity*, he was bound to give effect to a so-called reservation on the principle that where a person named in a deed, whether as a party thereto or not, had, without executing the deed, accepted some benefit assured to him, he was obliged to give effect to all the conditions on which the benefit was therein expressed to be conferred (*May* v. *Belleville* [1905] 2 Ch. 605).

As s. 62 of the 1881 Act was repealed in 1925, it was necessary to make special provision, which was effected by s. 65 (1) of the L.P.A. 1925, as follows :—

" 65.—(1) A reservation of a legal estate shall operate at law without any execution of the conveyance by the grantee of the legal estate out of which the reservation is made, or any regrant by him, so as to create the legal estate reserved, and so as to vest the same in possession in the person (whether being the grantor or not) for whose benefit the reservation is made."

This subsection apparently applies even though the reservation is not contained in a deed but in one of the exceptions to the L.P.A. 1925, s. 52 (which otherwise requires a deed for the creation of a legal estate) such as a valid lease under hand (*Mason* v. *Clarke* [1955] A.C. 778). However, it has been suggested that the subsection does *not* apply to a transfer of registered land on the grounds that this is not a " conveyance . . . of the legal estate " (this not passing until registration), but this suggestion has not been accepted on behalf of H.M. Land Registry and in practice it is unlikely that a reservation in a transfer of registered land would be objected to because of non-execution by the transferee. A registered proprietor is expressly empowered to transfer the land subject to reservations (L.R.A. 1925, ss. 18 (1) (*d*) and 21 (1) (*c*)) but it is thought that any reservation operating as a regrant of an incorporeal hereditament would require completion by registration to be effective at law (L.R.A. 1925, s. 19 (2)).

It is also provided by s. 65 (2) of the L.P.A. 1925 that, after 1925, a conveyance of a legal estate expressed to be made subject to another legal estate not in existence immediately before the date of the conveyance shall operate as a reservation, unless the contrary intention appears.

PART 2. MINES AND MINERALS

Definitions.—It is most difficult to formulate definitions from the decided cases since certain differences of judicial opinions have been expressed.

In *Hext* v. *Gill* (1872), L.R. 7 Ch. 699, Mellish, L.J., said at p. 712 that the result of the earlier authorities was this : " a reservation of ' minerals ' includes every substance which can be got from underneath the surface of the earth for the purpose of profit, unless there is something in the context or in the nature of the transaction to induce the court to give it a more limited meaning." However, James, L.J., in the same case, while concurring with Mellish, L.J., said that but for these authorities he should have thought that what was meant by " mines " and " minerals " in a grant was a question of what those words meant in the vernacular of the mining world and commercial world and landowners at the date of the grant. Again, in *Re Todd and North Eastern Railway* [1903] 1 K.B. 603, Lord Halsbury said : " I think it absolutely wrong to say that the question whether a thing can be worked at a profit or not is to determine whether it is a mineral or not."

In *Waring* v. *Foden* [1932] 1 Ch. 276, the question was whether certain gravel, the subject of a lease, and which was only about ten inches below the surface of almost all the land, was included in a reservation of " all mines, minerals and mineral substances " but to be got " by underground workings only." These last words showed that it was not the intention of the parties to include gravel which was obtained by quarrying from the surface, and it was admitted that there were seams of coal, ironstone and fireclay at a considerable depth below the surface. Besides, gravel was the ordinary soil of the neighbourhood. It was held, therefore, that the gravel was not within the limits of the reservation (see also *Duke of Hamilton* v. *Graham* (1871), L.R. 2 H.L. (Sc.) 166). In *Waring* v. *Foden*, Lawrence, L.J., said that " the decision in *Hext* v. *Gill* was followed by a sharp difference of judicial opinion on the question whether the true principle was that laid down by Mellish, L.J., or that suggested by James, L.J. This difference of opinion was finally settled by the [*North British Railway* v. *Budhill Coal and Sandstone Co.* [1910] A.C. 116 and *Caledonian Railway Co.* v. *Glenboig Fireclay Co.* [1911] A.C. 290] cases in which the House of Lords definitely decided that the view suggested by James, L.J., was the right view . . . The two main principles to be gathered from these pronouncements are, first, that the word ' mineral ' when found in a reservation out of a grant of land means substances exceptional in use, in value and in character (such as, for instance, the china clay in *Great Western Railway Co.* v. *Carpalla United China Clay Co.* [1910] A.C. 83) and does not mean the ordinary soil of the district which if reserved would practically swallow up the grant (such as, for instance, the sandstone in the *Budhill* case) ; and, secondly, that in deciding whether or not in a particular case exceptional substances are ' minerals,' the true test is what that word means in the vernacular of the mining world, the commercial world, and land owners at the time of the grant, and whether the particular substance was so regarded as a mineral. Further, it is to be noted that the fact that certain substances can be worked for the purpose of profit may have a bearing upon the question, whether they have been recognised as included in the term ' minerals,' but does not necessarily determine that they have been ordinarily understood to be so included. It follows from the decisions in the *Budhill* and *Glenboig* cases that the question whether a given substance is or is not a ' mineral ' within the meaning of the instrument in which it is mentioned is a question of fact to be decided according to the circumstances of the particular case."

It was held in *Waring* v. *Foden* that the expressions " minerals and mineral substances " meant as nearly the same thing as two expressions can mean, and that the use of the words " mineral substances " in no way enlarged the reservation.

The expression " mines of coal, ironstone, slate or other minerals," used in s. 77 of the Railways Clauses Consolidation Act, 1845, was held equivalent to the expression " mines and minerals " in common use with conveyancers (*Great Western Railway Co.* v. *Carpalla United China Clay Co., ante*). The expression may also include anything exceptional in use, character or value, provided that it is included in the word " minerals " as understood in the vernacular of the mining world, the commercial world and the landowner (*Caledonian*

Railway Co. v. *Glenboig Fireclay Co., ante).* Section 77 was not affected by the Mines (Working Facilities and Support) Act, 1923. So where a bed of clay underlies the surface, and is the ordinary soil of the whole district, such clay, though it might elsewhere be " a mineral," is not a mineral within the meaning of s. 77 (*Glasgow Corporation* v. *Farie* (1888), 13 App. Cas. 657 ; *Great Western Railway Co.* v. *Blades* [1901] 2 Ch. 624). Therefore, sandstone, where it is the ordinary rock of the district, is not a " mineral " (*North British Railway Co.* v. *Budhill Coal and Sandstone Co.* [1910] A.C. 116). China clay is not the ordinary soil of a district and is, therefore, a mineral within the meaning of the section (*Great Western Railway Co.* v. *Carpalla United China Clay Co., ante).* Limestone and freestone ordinarily got by surface workings are minerals within the section (*Midland Railway Co.* v. *Robinson* (1889), 15 App. Cas. 19).

" Mines and minerals " are defined in s. 205 (1) (ix) of the L.P.A. 1925 and s. 3 (xiv) of the L.R.A. 1925 for the purposes of those Acts to " include any strata or seam of minerals or substances in or under any land and powers of working and getting the same, but not an undivided share thereof."

Exceptions of mines and minerals.—By an exception of *mines*, the stratum is reserved, and the owner can use it for any purpose he thinks fit, e.g., he may make a road through it for the conveyance of the produce of adjoining mines (*Duke of Hamilton* v. *Graham* (1871), L.R. 2 H.L. (Sc.) 166) ; but in the case of an exception of *minerals* without more, only the minerals can be taken, and the chamber containing the minerals is comprised in the grant and not in the exception, and the grantor has no interest whatever in the space which his working creates (*Ramsay* v. *Blair* (1876), 1 App. Cas. 701). But the exception may contain words which may extend the meaning. For instance, in the case last mentioned, the words were, " the whole coal, stone, quarries, and all other metals and minerals," and it was held that the effect of these words was to except the whole of the land under the surface.

An exception of mines and minerals will carry with it a reservation of all powers necessary for working the minerals without these powers being expressly reserved (*Aspden* v. *Seddon* (1875), L.R. 10 Ch. 394) ; but not so as to damage the surface, even though this restriction would destroy the value of the right (*Mundy* v. *Duke of Rutland* (1883), 23 Ch. D. 81). In *General Accident, Fire & Life Assurance Corporation, Ltd.* v. *British Gypsum, Ltd.* [1967] 1 W.L.R. 1215, Plowman, J., held that the exception and reservation of all mines and minerals together with full powers by means of underground workings or operations only to win, work and carry away the mines and minerals, included the right to search for minerals by implication from the word " win " but that this was restricted to underground searching and gave no right to enter on the surface of the land.

Where land is sold for the erection of a house, with an exception of minerals, the grantee may, *prima facie*, notwithstanding the exception, dig out the foundations of his house (*Robinson* v. *Milne* (1884), 53 L.J. Ch. 1070).

Title to mines and minerals other than under an exception.—Mines and minerals pass with freehold land without mention, except in the case of land purchased by companies or public authorities under certain statutory powers, such as a purchase formerly made by a railway company under the provisions of the Railways Clauses Consolidation Act, 1845, or by a water-works company under the Water Act, 1945, Sched. 3, Pt. IV, re-enacting certain provisions in the Waterworks Clauses Act, 1847.

In the case of copyhold land, the property in the mines and minerals was, before 1926, usually in the lord of the manor, but the copyholder had possession. The result was that neither the lord nor the tenant could get the minerals without the consent of the other and when the landlord had got them the space left belonged to the copyhold tenant (*Eardley* v. *Granville* (1876), 3 Ch. D. 826). The effect of the general enfranchisement of copyhold and customary land on 1st January, 1926, was to make the mines and minerals freehold, but the enfranchisement did not affect the rights of the lord or the tenants in reference to the getting of the same. By s. 138 (2) of the L.P.A. 1922, it was provided, in effect, that the lord and the tenant might in writing agree that the rights of the lord in the mines and minerals were extinguished as if they were manorial incidents. It was foreseen that if one of the parties should stick out for terms the result might be that the minerals could not be worked. To prevent such a thing happening, provision was made in the Mines (Working Facilities and Support) Act, 1923, Pt. I, as amended by the Railway and Canal Commission (Abolition) Act, 1949, s. 1 (1), for the High Court to give the necessary power.

For removing doubts, it is declared by s. 162 (1) (*d*) (i) of the L.P.A. 1925 that the rule of law relating to perpetuities does not apply, and shall be deemed never to have applied to any grant, exception or reservation of any right of entry on, or user of, the surface of land or of any easements, rights or privileges over or under land for the purpose of winning, working, inspecting, measuring, converting, manufacturing, carrying away, and disposing of mines and minerals.

A lease for however long a period does not pass to the lessee the right to work unopened mines without special power being given (*Astry* v. *Ballard* (1677), 2 Lev. 185). In the very rare case of an open mine being leased without any special provision as to the working thereof and paying therefor, the lessee would be entitled to work and sell the minerals.

Sometimes, instead of a lease giving an *estate* in the land, a mere licence to enter and to get minerals is given. In this case the right to get the minerals will not pass an *exclusive* right, unless the language is clear. When the grant is not exclusive, the owner of the surface has a right to work them, so long as he does not disturb the grantee in any working which he is carrying on at the time (*Duke of Sutherland* v. *Heathcote* [1892] 1 Ch. 475).

Provisions as to mines and minerals on sale of former copyholds.— In dealing with freehold property formerly of copyhold or customary tenure, it should be considered whether the vendor can sell the minerals. See last note. Knowledge by a purchaser that land has formerly been of copyhold tenure will not give him constructive notice that the minerals are excepted (*Bellamy* v. *Debenham* [1891] 1 Ch. 412). A vendor, therefore, should be especially careful to state in the contract the fact that the property was formerly copyhold and whether or not the mines and minerals are included in the sale. If he should omit to do this the purchaser may object to the title (*Upperton* v. *Nickolson* (1871), L.R. 6 Ch. 436 ; *Re Jackson and Haden's Contract* [1906] 1 Ch. 412).

Sales of mines and minerals separately from the surface.—(i) *By a tenant for life.*—See *post*, p. 733.

(ii) *By trustees for sale.*—A trustee could not before 1926, unless he had power under the instrument creating the trust, sell the land and minerals separately without the sanction of the court (Trustee Act, 1893, s. 44 ;

Re Skinner [1896] W.N. 68). But if the instrument creating the trust empowered the trustees to sell the whole *or part* of the hereditaments, it would seem that this would have been sufficient power, as a " part of land " refers quite as much to a horizontal section as to a vertical section (*Re Pearons's Will* (1900), 83 L.T. 626 ; *Re Eardley and Birk's Settlement* (1908), 124 L.T. News. 503).

Since 1925 trustees for sale have the power to sell the minerals separately from the land under s. 28 (1) of the L.P.A. 1925, which provides that trustees for sale shall, in relation to land, have all the powers of a tenant for life and the trustees of a settlement under the S.L.A. 1925.

(iii) *By personal representatives.*—Even before 1926, personal representatives could sell the minerals separately from the surface in the course of administration if in the neighbourhood this means of disposing of the estate would be the best for the estate (*Re Chaplin* [1922] 2 Ch. 824). Since 1925, by s. 39 of the A.E.A. 1925, when read with s. 28 (1) of the L.P.A. 1925, they are granted all the powers of a tenant for life under s. 50 of the S.L.A. 1925 and so personal representatives have the like powers, in addition to their power at common law.

(iv) *By mortgagees.*—Before 1926, mortgagees had power to sell the minerals separately from the land without the consent of the court where the mortgage deed was executed after 1911 (Conveyancing Act, 1911, s. 4). Where the mortgage deed was executed before 1911, it was necessary to get the consent of the court (Trustee Act, 1893, Amendment Act, 1894, s. 3, extending s. 44 of the Trustee Act, 1893) and the court was given power by s. 92 of the L.P.A. 1925 to authorise a sale of the mines and minerals separately from the surface " and thenceforth the powers so conferred shall have effect as if the same were contained in the mortgage." Now, by s. 101 (2) of the L.P.A. 1925, a mortgagee is given the fullest power to sell the mines and minerals separately from the surface where the mortgage deed was executed after 1911.

Registered land.—After 1925, the title to mines and minerals will *prima facie* be included whenever the title to land is registered since the definition of " land " now expressly includes mines and minerals (L.R.A. 1925, s. 3 (viii)). In the case of land registered before 1926 rights to mines and minerals and certain associated rights created before 1898 are overriding interests (*ibid.*, s. 70 (1) (*b*)). Also all rights and title of the National Coal Board to unworked coal, mines of coal and allied mineral substances and ancillary rights constitute overriding interests (Coal Act, 1938, ss. 3, 15, 41 ; Coal Industry Nationalisation Act, 1946, ss. 5, 8 and Sched. 1). Express provision is made for the registration of mines and minerals severed from the land, with the appurtenant rights of access and rights incidental to the working (L.R.R. 1925, rr. 50 and 53). Further, when surface land is being registered and it appears from the documents or any other source that all or any of the mines and minerals are severed from the land, a note will be entered in the property register of the title to the surface to the effect that such mines and minerals are excepted from the registration (L.R.R. 1925, r. 196). Otherwise, if the mines and minerals have been opened and worked by the owner of the land or his predecessors in title or if in any case it is satisfactorily proved that the mines and minerals are vested in the registered proprietor a note may be added to the property register to the effect that they are included in the registration (L.R.R. 1925, r. 195). Without such a note no mines and minerals are deemed to be included in the registered title for the purposes of claiming indemnity on rectification of the register in respect of mines and minerals (L.R.A. 1925, s. 83 (5) (*b*)). Statutory forms are prescribed (but not published and printed) both for the transfer of land excepting mines and minerals and for the transfer of mines and minerals without the surface land (L.R.R. 1925, rr. 111 and 112 and Schedule, Forms 25, 26, 27, 28, 29 and 30).

Power to let down the surface.—An owner of minerals other than coal (not being also the owner of the surface) who claims the right to cause the surface and buildings thereon to subside, must show that, either in express terms or by necessary implication, he has been granted a licence to do so.

" The result seems to be that in all cases where there has been a severance in title and the upper and lower strata are in different hands, the surface owner is entitled of common right to support for his property in its natural position and in its natural condition without interference or disturbance by or in consequence of mining operations, unless such interference or disturbance is authorised by the instrument of severance either in express terms or by necessary implication " (Lord Macnaghten in *Butterknowle Colliery Company* v. *Bishop Auckland Industrial Co-operative Society* [1906] A.C. 305, 313 ; see also *Beard* v. *Moira Colliery Co.* [1915] 1 Ch. 257).

The burden of establishing that the instrument of severance gave the right to let down the surface is on the mineral owner and will not be discharged by showing that such instrument gave full powers of working minerals in general terms (*Warwickshire Coal Co.* v. *Corporation of Coventry* [1934] Ch. 488). A provision in the instrument of severance for compensation for damage does not raise an inference that support may be withdrawn on payment of compensation if the compensation clause is capable of being satisfied by reference to acts done on the surface (*New Sharlston Collieries Co., Ltd.* v. *Earl of Westmorland* (1900), 82 L.T. 725), but if entry on the surface is prohibited it is reasonable to infer that the clause relates to subsidence caused by underground working (*Aspden* v. *Seddon* (1875), L.R. 10 Ch. 394).

This right to the support of the surface is a legal right and not an easement (*Davies* v. *Powell Duffryn Steam Coal Co.* [1921] W.N. 161). As to rights of support generally, see p. 520.

Previously to the decision of Astbury, J., in *Welldon* v. *Butterley Colliery Co., Ltd.* [1920] 1 Ch. 130, the courts, including the House of Lords, based their decisions on the assumption that it was possible to extract minerals without causing subsidence. It was thought to have been proved in that case that however the workings are carried out, sooner or later, subsidence will result, but such does not seem to be the inevitable conclusion. See *Warwickshire Coal Co., Ltd.* v. *Corporation of Coventry* [1934] Ch. 488, at p. 518. The decision in *Welldon* v. *Butterley Colliery Co., Ltd.*, was on the construction of an Inclosure Act, but the same principle applies to a claim under a deed. In that case the Act reserved the rights of the owners of coal under the commons and gave them full powers of carrying it away, without making satisfaction in as full a manner as if the Act had not been passed. It was proved that long before the Act the coal had been worked by a system which inevitably caused subsidence. Astbury, J., held that, having regard to the common practice known to all parties at the date of the Act, a similar system of mining was authorised to be carried on even though it inevitably caused subsidence. The learned judge held further that apart from these special circumstances the Legislature had given a power to get the coal and that as it was proved that all systems caused subsidence, they were entitled to cause subsidence. In *Warwickshire Coal Co., Ltd.* v. *Corporation of Coventry, ante,* the Court of Appeal approved the ground of decision first given by Astbury, J., but pointed out that the second proposition above mentioned was contrary to the authorities, and that in the absence of express or implied authority to cause subsidence, if subsidence is inevitable the mineral owner may be obliged to leave his mines unworked. See also *Consett Industrial and Provident Society* v. *Consett Iron Co.* [1922] 2 Ch. 135.

A power to enter and work the minerals " in as full and ample a way as if these presents had not been made and executed," was held to amount to a reservation of the right to let down the surface (*Davies* v. *Powell Duffryn Steam Coal Co.* [1921] W.N. 161).

A lessee of a colliery cannot excuse himself for letting down the surface by proving that no damage would have been caused if previous lessees had not worked out the coal above his workings (*Manley* v. *Burn* [1916] 2 K.B. 121).

Statutory vesting of coal and rights of support.—The effect of the Coal Act, 1938, the Coal (Concurrent Leases) Act, 1942, the Coal Act, 1943, and the Coal Industry Nationalisation Act, 1946, has been to place coal (as defined for this purpose in the 1938 Act, s. 3 (4)) in a special position. All coal and mines of coal are now vested in the National Coal Board. The rights to withdraw support which are held by the National Coal Board are specified in Pt. II of Sched. 2 to the 1938 Act. The provisions of this part are most complex. The following is a brief summary intended to state the main rules likely to be of importance in conveyancing practice and it should not be taken as complete without reference to the Acts :—

(*a*) Where on 1st January, 1939, the fee simple in coal or a mine was vested in a person other than the person in whom the fee simple in the land supported thereby was vested and a right to withdraw support (other than a right granted under the Mines (Working Facilities and Support) Act, 1923) was annexed to the coal or mine the Board have a similar right to withdraw support.

(*b*) If the ownership of the mines and surface were severed on 1st January, 1939, but the person entitled to the mines had no right to withdraw support, then no right has passed to the Board.

(*c*) If the fee simple in both land supported and coal was on 1st January, 1939, vested in the same person but a term of years was then subsisting in the coal with a right to withdraw support (not granted under the 1923 Act), such right vests in the Board and is *not* limited to the term of years but remains as long as any coal is ungotten. If the lease contained a provision, intended to protect land from subsidence, that the lessee should not work certain coal without consent, then nevertheless the Board may work such coal but must make compensation for, or make good, any damage (Coal Act, 1943, s. 11, Sched. 2 ; S.R. & O., 1947, No. 395).

(*d*) Where on 1st January, 1939, the fee simple in the coal and the fee simple in the land supported thereby were vested in the same person and no coal mining lease was subsisting, the Board have a right to withdraw support from the land so far as may be reasonably requisite for the working of the coal, subject to an obligation either to pay proper compensation for damage or, with the consent (not to be unreasonably withheld) of the person otherwise entitled to compensation, to make good that damage. This last-mentioned right to withdraw support is, however, limited to the extent to which the owners of the coal on 1st January, 1939, were competent to grant it by virtue of their interests in the land. On first exercising or granting to a lessee the benefit of a right vested in them under this paragraph the Board must give public notice that they propose so to do by advertisement in the *London Gazette* and in one or more newspapers circulating in the locality. After first publication of such a notice, before construction of any buildings or works is begun on land liable to be damaged by the exercise of the right to which the notice relates, the building owner must notify the Board of the proposal to construct them, and, if requested, must produce plans and specifications. The Board may then make certain requirements as to the construction of foundations on paying any extra cost incurred. If an owner fails to give notice to the Board, the obligation to pay compensation for damage mentioned in this paragraph is limited to damage which could not have been avoided by reasonable and proper precautions taken in the design and construction of the foundations.

The National Coal Board became under an obligation to carry out repairs to or to make payments in respect of, structural damage caused to dwelling-houses of rateable value not exceeding £32 by the withdrawal of support from land as the result of the working and getting of coal (Coal-Mining (Subsidence) Act, 1950). This problem is now dealt with by the Coal-Mining (Subsidence) Act, 1957. Unlike the 1950 Act, the Act of 1957 is not confined to damage to small dwelling-houses but covers subsidence damage to any building or structure and also to certain works and to land as such. Also the 1957 Act provides for payment in respect of death or disablement in certain cases. Generally, the 1957 Act is only concerned with damage occurring after 31st July, 1957, but it does contain special provisions relating to certain damage occurring before that date but after 31st December, 1955, to property within the curtilage of a dwelling-house to which the 1950 Act did not apply. The rights under these Acts do not interfere with any rights which already exist, for instance, to claim compensation on withdrawal of support ; if the surface owner has rights both under the Act and independent of it, he may elect to rely on either but may not pursue both (1950 Act, s. 14 (1) ; 1957 Act, s. 6 (1)).

Conveyance of land under which coal is known or believed to exist.— As the vesting of coal in the National Coal Board was by statutory authority, no reference to such vesting need be made in a conveyance of land, which would formerly have been presumed to include the coal under it if a contrary intention had not been expressed.

As we have seen above, certain rights to withdraw support dependent on the state of affairs on 1st January, 1939, may be vested in the National Coal Board. In the circumstances mentioned in paragraphs (*a*) and (*c*), above, the vendor must ensure that he contracts to sell subject to these rights and that the conveyance is expressed to be made subject to them. In the circumstances mentioned in paragraph (*d*), however, it would appear that the rights of the National Coal Board are dependent on general rules of law assumed to be known by a purchaser and, consequently, that a contract or conveyance need not refer to these rights.

Statutory grant of right to work minerals.—The Mines (Working Facilities and Support) Act, 1966, replacing Pt. I of the Mines (Working Facilities and Support) Act, 1923, gives power to the High Court to confer a right to work minerals and certain ancillary rights such as a right to let down the surface.

None of these rights is to be granted unless it is shown that it is not reasonably practicable to obtain the right in question by private arrangement for any of certain specified reasons, for instance, that the persons having power to grant the right cannot be ascertained or that the person having such power unreasonably refuses to grant the right or demands terms which are unreasonable (1966 Act, s. 3). It is not unreasonable to require that a lease of minerals should contain a covenant to work them diligently (*Glassbrook Bros., Ltd.* v. *Leyson* [1933] 2 K.B. 91).

The procedure is to send to the appropriate Minister an application for the grant of such a right. The Minister will consider the application, and unless he is of opinion that a *prima facie* case is not made out, refer the matter to the High Court, who are given very wide powers, including power to make an order conferring rights on a tenant for life or other persons in a fiduciary position. See *Re Markham Main Colliery, Ltd.* (1926), 134 L.T. 253. The court may order compensation to be paid on account of anticipated future subsidence (*Re National Coal Board's Application* [1960] Ch. 192, not following *Re Beckermet Mining Co., Ltd.* [1938] 1 All E.R. 389).

A right to search for coal may be conferred on the National Coal Board under this Part (*ibid.*, s. 1). The Act applies, with amendments, to petroleum (Petroleum (Production) Act, 1934, s. 3, as amended by 1966 Act, Sched. 2 ; and see Continental Shelf Act, 1964, s. 9).

Railway companies and waterworks companies.—Mines and minerals did not pass to a *railway company* and do not pass to a *waterworks company* by a conveyance of the land, except such parts as are necessary to be dug or carried away in the construction of its works, unless expressly purchased and mentioned (Railways Clauses Consolidation Act, 1845, ss. 77, 78 ; Water Act, 1945, Sched. 3, Pt. IV, para. 11, substantially re-enacting Waterworks Clauses Act, 1847, s. 18 ; *Great Western Railway Co.* v. *Bennett* (1867), L.R. 2 H.L. 27 ; *Lord Provost of Glasgow* v. *Farie* (1888), 13 App. Cas. 657 ; *Midland Railway Co.* v. *Robinson* (1889), 15 App. Cas. 19).

PART 3. EASEMENTS

Nature of easements.—An easement cannot be granted otherwise than for the benefit of a dominant tenement, that is, it cannot be granted in *gross* (*Rangeley* v. *Midland Railway Co.* (1868), L.R. 3 Ch. 306 ; *Thorpe* v. *Brumfitt* (1873), L.R. 8 Ch. 650 ; *Hawkins* v. *Rutter* [1892] 1 Q.B. 668, 671 ; *King* v. *David Allen & Sons Billposting, Ltd.* [1916] 2 A.C. 54). On the same principle an easement cannot be acquired by prescription unless it is appurtenant to a dominant tenement (*Shuttleworth* v. *Le Fleming* (1865), 19 C.B. (N.S.) 687).

The rights of owners of neighbouring houses to the enjoyment of a pleasure ground may be valid easements appurtenant to those houses (*Re Ellenborough Park* [1956] Ch. 131). The preservation of open spaces may be achieved by the grant of easements more effectively than by restrictive covenants alone, particularly as easements are not liable to modification on the ground that they may be regarded as obsolete. Other rights which have been held to amount to easements are a right to use a neighbour's kitchen for washing (*Heywood* v. *Mallalieu* (1883), 25 Ch. D. 357), a right to use a lavatory (*Miller* v. *Emcer Products, Ltd.* [1956] Ch. 304), a right to construct and maintain a ventilation duct (*Wong* v. *Beaumont Property Trust* [1965] 1 Q.B. 573) and a right to enter on adjoining land to repair an outside wall (*Ward* v. *Kirkland* [1966] 1 W.L.R. 601), but not a right to have a structure protected from the weather (*Phipps* v. *Pears* [1965] 1 Q.B. 76, strongly criticised by R.E.M. in *Law Quarterly Review*, vol. 80, p. 318 *et seq.*). See further the exposition in *Conveyancer N.S.*, vol. 28, p. 450.

Rights of statutory undertakers created by statute to lay and maintain pipes, cables, etc., are *sui generis* and not easements (see *Conveyancer N.S.*, vol. 20, p. 208 *et seq.*), although easements for similar purposes may be expressly granted.

In the case of a statutory undertaker, such as a water company, it seems that the whole of the corporeal and incorporeal hereditaments of the company may constitute the dominant tenement, and so a right to lay pipes or wires granted to such a company may be an easement if it is of benefit to such dominant tenement (*Re Salvin's Indenture* [1938] 2 All E.R. 498, but this decision was criticised in the *Conveyancer N.S.*, vol. 14, pp. 267, 268). As a matter of good practice the dominant tenement should be identified in a grant or reservation of an easement, such as a right of way, but if that is not done extrinsic evidence is admissible to identify it (*Johnstone* v. *Holdway* [1963] 1 Q.B. 601). If the words in a deed of grant are clear, extrinsic evidence is not admissible, but where identification of the dominant tenement is not clear or sufficient the court must construe the words in the light of surrounding circumstances as to which evidence may be given (*The Shannon, Ltd.* v. *Venner, Ltd.* [1965] Ch. 682). There is a rebuttable presumption that, in the absence of identification, land conveyed by a deed granting the easement is the dominant tenement (*ibid.*).

There is no objection to granting a *personal licence* to use land independently of the possession of any tenement by the grantee, for instance, a right to pass over the land. Such a licence is not, of course, an easement, and the remedy for disturbance would be on the contract, if any. Whether such a licence may be enforceable against successors in title of the licensor is still the subject of controversy. It seems that a person acquiring title under the licensor, other than a purchaser of a legal estate for value without notice, may be restrained in equity from revoking the licence against a licensee who has entered into occupation and so has an equity to specific performance (see *per* Lord Denning, M.R., in *Inwards* v. *Baker* [1965] 2 Q.B. 29, at p. 37 ; also *Hopgood* v. *Brown* [1955] 1 W.L.R. 213 ; *Armstrong* v. *Sheppard and Short* [1959] 2 Q.B. 384 ; *Ward* v. *Kirkland* [1966] 1 W.L.R. 601, and cases cited).

Legal easements.—A legal easement is required by s. 1 (2) (*a*) of the L.P.A. 1925 to be " an easement, right, or privilege in or over land for an interest equivalent to an estate in fee simple absolute in possession or a term of years absolute " (and see L.R.A. 1925, s. 3 (xi)).

Also the express grant of a legal easement requires an instrument under seal (L.P.A. 1925, s. 52 (1)). In addition, in registered conveyancing, the express grant of an easement will operate only in equity unless and until it is completed by registration (L.R.A. 1925, ss. 19 (2) and 22 (2)).

A legal easement passes by a conveyance of the land to which it is annexed without express mention, quite irrespective of s. 62 of the L.P.A. 1925, as to which, see at p. 511 (see *per* Joyce, J., in *Godwin* v. *Schweppes, Ltd.* [1902] 1 Ch. 926, at p. 932 ; also L.R.R. 1925, rr. 256 and 257, and L.R.A. 1925, s. 72). A legal easement cannot be overreached, because it has all the incidents of a legal estate (L.P.A. 1925, s. 1 (4)), and for the same reason it is not necessary to register it as a land charge under the L.C.A. 1972 ; a purchaser of the servient land will take subject thereto whether or not he has notice thereof. In registered conveyancing, legal easements are enforceable against registered proprietors, again independently of notice or the L.C.A. 1972, by virtue of being overriding interests (L.R.A. 1925, s. 70 (1) (*a*)).

Section 205 (1) (ix) of the L.P.A. 1925 defines " land " as including an easement, and by s. 1 (6) of the same Act a legal estate in land is not capable of subsisting or of being created in an undivided share in land (see also L.R.A. 1925, s. 3 (viii) and (xi)). The exercise of an easement in common is not the same as the holding of an undivided share in a legal estate ; in any case it is provided by the L.P.A. 1925, s. 187 (2), that : " Nothing in this Act affects the right of a person to acquire, hold or exercise an easement, right or privilege over or in relation to land for a legal estate in common with any other person, or the power of creating or conveying such an easement, right or privilege." For instance, the owners of adjoining properties may have a common right to use a yard (see at p. 491) ; or a party wall (see at p. 487) ; or a road.

Equitable easements.—All easements which are not legal easements will be equitable easements (but see further the discussion in *Poster* v. *Slough Estates, Ltd.* [1969] 1 Ch. 495 ; *Shiloh Spinners, Ltd.* v. *Harding* [1973] 1 All E.R. 90, H.L. ; also Paul Jackson in the *Conveyancer N.S.*, vol. 33, p. 135 *et seq.*). For instance, an easement granted in connection with land to a person for his life would be an equitable easement, as it would not be an interest in land held for an estate in fee simple or for a term of years absolute.

Only equitable easements created since 1925 can be registered as land charges (L.C.A. 1972, s. 2 (5), Class D (iii)), and even when such an easement is assigned after 1925 it is not necessary to register it, as s. 4 (7) of the L.C.A. 1972 does not apply in this case. An equitable easement created before 1926 will not bind a purchaser of a legal estate for value if he has no notice thereof, but it will bind him if he has notice (L.P.A. 1925, s. 2 (5)).

An equitable easement created *after* 1925 will be void against a purchaser for money or money's worth of a legal estate in the land charged therewith, unless it is registered as a land charge in the appropriate register before the completion of the purchase (L.C.A. 1972, s. 4 (6)). If an equitable easement created after 1925 is not registered, the fact that the purchaser has notice of it will not prevent the easement being void as against him (L.P.A. 1925, s. 199 (1) (i)). An equitable easement cannot be overreached if it is registered as a land charge (L.P.A. 1925, s. 2 (3) ; S.L.A. 1925, ss. 21 (2), 72 (2) (iii) (*b*)).

In addition to registering an equitable easement created after 1925 as a land charge, it will be a wise precaution, where the purchaser does not get the deeds, to have a memorandum of the charge indorsed on one of the recent deeds. A *purchaser is entitled to require* this by virtue of s. 200 (1) of the L.P.A. 1925, but it is expressly provided by subs. (2) that the title of the person omitting to require such an indorsement is not to be prejudiced by the omission, and by subs. (4) that nothing in the section is to affect the obligation to register an easement as a land charge.

Similarly, in registered conveyancing provisions have been made that a person entitled to an equitable easement over registered land " may apply to the registrar to register notice " thereof " and when so registered, every proprietor and the persons deriving title under him shall be deemed to be affected with notice " thereof (see L.R.A. 1925, ss. 3 (ix), 48 (1), 49 (1) (c) and 59 (2) ; L.R.R. 1925, r. 190). Further it is provided that " equitable easements required to be protected by notice on the register " are not over-riding interests (L.R.A. 1925, s. 70 (1) (a)). It has been submitted that since the above provisions enable rather than require protection by notice and that as there are no other provisions positively requiring such protection, therefore " at present equitable easements are in law overriding interests " (Potter, Registered Land Conveyancing, pp. 11 and 268 ; see also L.R.R. 1925, rr. 250, 257 and 258, which variously appear to treat legal and equitable easements as on the same footing in being overriding interests). However, it is stated quite firmly in Ruoff and Roper, Registered Conveyancing, 3rd ed., p. 102, that " the word ' required ' and those following it [i.e., in s. 70 (1) (a)] can only mean that equitable easements must always be protected by notice on the register in order to be enforceable against a purchaser and that consequently they have not got the characteristics of overriding interests." Nevertheless, the contrary view was accepted by Judge Duveen in holding that an equitable easement did amount to an overriding interest (*Payne* v. *Adnams* [1971] C.L.Y. 6486).

Quasi-easements.—A quasi-easement is a user of one tenement belonging to *A* for the benefit of another tenement also belonging to him, which could in law constitute an easement if the tenements were owned by different persons. Although a quasi-easement is often referred to as an easement, it is not strictly speaking an easement for, as the two tenements are in the same ownership, all the acts which the owner does are referred to his ownership (*Bolton* v. *Bolton* (1879), 11 Ch. D. 968, *per* Fry, J., at p. 970). See also at pp. 511–513.

Although an easement will be extinguished by the union of the ownership of the dominant and servient tenements where the estates are equal in nature, if the estates are not of the same duration the easement will revive on their severance, as in the meantime the right is only suspended (*Simper* v. *Foley* (1862), 2 J. & H. 555).

Where quasi-easements have existed for the benefit of certain land over other land in the same ownership and either the land for the benefit of which the quasi-easements existed, or the land over which they existed, is sold, the question arises whether easements are created corresponding to the quasi-easements which previously existed. If such easements are *expressly* created on the severance of the ownership of the land the position is clear, and ideally the contract should contain appropriate special conditions providing for this ; otherwise assistance may be sought from General Condition 4 (2) (c) of The Law Society's Conditions of Sale, 1973 Revision, if incorporated. However, in certain circumstances easements corresponding to the former quasi-easements are held to be created *impliedly*. These circumstances must be examined, but in so doing it must be noted that in most *conveyances* the " general words " mentioned in the L.P.A. 1925, s. 62, are *deemed to be included*, and easements may be created by these words. See *post*, p. 511 *et seq*.

Implied grant or reservation of easements.—Two general rules were laid down by Thesiger, L.J., in *Wheeldon* v. *Burrows* (1879), 12 Ch. D. 31, 49, in these words : " The first of these rules is, that on the grant by the owner of a tenement of part of that tenement as it is then used and enjoyed, there will pass to the grantee all those continuous and apparent easements (by which, of course, I mean quasi-easements), or, in other words, all those easements which are necessary to the reasonable enjoyment of the property granted, and which have been and are at the time of the grant used by the owners of the entirety for the benefit of the part granted. The second proposition is that, if the grantor intends to reserve any right over the tenement granted, it is his duty to reserve it expressly in the grant. Those are the general rules governing cases of this kind, but the second of those rules is subject to certain exceptions." For convenience, the two rules will be dealt with separately and a note added as to the exceptions to the rules.

(1) *Implied grant of continuous and apparent quasi-easements on sale of quasi-dominant tenement.*—An example of the first proposition in *Wheeldon* v. *Burrows* would occur where two tenements are severed, and at the time of severance a formed road exists over one (the quasi-servient) tenement for the apparent use of the other (the quasi-dominant) tenement, such formed road *being necessary for the reasonable and convenient enjoyment* of the quasi-dominant tenement, a right to use such formed road will pass by implied grant with the quasi-dominant tenement, even where the only " apparent sign " is the state of the road on the quasi-servient tenement itself. See also *Pyer* v. *Carter* (1857), 1 H. & N. 916 ; *Ewart* v. *Cochrane* (1861), 7 Jur. (N.S.) 925. The word " *necessary* " in the above statement must not be confused with the word " necessity " in the expression " easements of necessity," which expression is used later in dealing with implied *reservations* of easements. When used as above it means, as there indicated, " *necessary for the reasonable and convenient enjoyment*," etc., but the expression " easement of necessity " in dealing with an implied *reservation* means " an easement without which the property retained *cannot be used at all*, and not one merely necessary to the reasonable enjoyment of that property " (Stirling, L.J., in *Union Lighterage Co.* v. *London Graving Dock Co.* [1902] 2 Ch. 557, at p. 673). See also *Aldridge* v. *Wright* [1929] 2 K.B. 117 ; *post*, p. 508, and Norton on Deeds, 2nd ed., p. 281.

Fry, L.J., in *Bayley* v. *Great Western Railway Co.* (1884), 26 Ch. D. 434, said, at p. 457 : " If one person owns both Whiteacre and Blackacre, and if *there be a made and visible road* over Whiteacre, and that has been used for the purpose of Blackacre in such a way that, if [the] two tenements belonged to several owners there would have been an easement in favour of Blackacre over Whiteacre, and the owner aliened Blackacre to a purchaser, retaining Whiteacre, then the grant of Blackacre either ' with all rights usually enjoyed with it ' or ' with all rights appertaining to Blackacre,' or *probably the mere grant* of Blackacre itself *without general words*, carried a right of way over Whiteacre."

The words " continuous and apparent " must be read together ; they refer to easements accompanied by evidence of their existence which can be seen on inspection (*Pyer* v. *Carter* (1857), 1 H. & N. 916, at p. 922 ; *Brown* v. *Alabaster* (1887), 37 Ch. D. 490) ; it is not necessary that the easement be continuously in use (*Borman* v. *Griffith* [1930] 1 Ch. 493, at p. 499). See further, *Watts* v. *Kelson* (1871), L.R. 6 Ch. 166 ; *Allen* v. *Taylor* (1880), 16 Ch. D. 355 ; *Schwann* v. *Cotton* [1916] 2 Ch. 459 ; *Hansford* v. *Jago* [1921] 1 Ch. 322. More recently in *Ward* v. *Kirkland* [1966] 1 W.L.R. 601, Ungoed-Thomas, J., held that an easement to enter on land to repair a wall could not be validly created by implied grant as it was not " continuous and apparent " within the rule (but see L.P.A. 1925, s. 62, *post*, p. 511).

The application of this first proposition in registered conveyancing is somewhat uncertain in that neither the L.R.A. 1925 nor the L.R.R. 1925 contains any provision in terms referring to it. However, it is provided that registration as proprietor confers the legal estate in the land " together with all rights, privileges and appurtenances belonging or appurtenant thereto " (L.R.A. 1925, s. 20 (1) ; see further L.R.R. 1925, r. 251) and the view is generally taken that this is adequate for the implied grant of easements (see Ruoff and Roper, Registered Conveyancing, 3rd ed., p. 104). The point is largely academic in that the " general words " implied under the L.P.A. 1925, s. 62, are expressly provided for and operate sufficiently (see *ibid.*, also L.R.A. 1925, ss. 19 (3) and 22 (3), *post*, p. 516).

(2) *Implied reservation of easements of necessity.*—On the ground that a vendor cannot derogate from his own grant, in the absence of express stipulation, as a rule the grantor of part of a tenement retains no rights over the part granted (*Wheeldon* v. *Burrows* (1879), 12 Ch. D. 31 ; *Liddiard* v. *Waldron* [1934] 1 K.B. 435 ; see also *Grigsby* v. *Melville* [1973] 3 All E.R. 455, C.A., where it was held that there could not be an implied exception of a cellar). A mistake in not *reserving* easements in a conveyance will not be rectified unless such mistake is mutual (*Slack* v. *Hancock* (1912), 107 L.T. 14). As indicated, Thesiger, L.J., recognised that his second proposition is subject to certain exceptions : " one of these exceptions is the well-known exception which attaches to cases of what are called ways of necessity ; and I do not dispute for a moment that there may be, and probably are, certain other exceptions " (*Wheeldon* v. *Burrows, ante,* at p. 49).

The " easements of necessity," referred to in the judgment in *Wheeldon* v. *Burrows, ante,* mean easements without which the property retained cannot be used at all, and not those merely necessary to the reasonable enjoyment of the property (*Union Lighterage Co.* v. *London Graving Dock Co.* [1902] 2 Ch. 557 ; *Ray* v. *Hazeldine* [1904] 2 Ch. 17, a case of light (see at p. 523) ; *Hansford* v. *Jago* [1921] 1 Ch. 322 ; *Liddiard* v. *Waldron* [1934] 1 K.B. 435).

For instance, if a vendor has no access to the portion retained except through the property sold, the reservation of a right of way over the land sold will be implied (*Clark* v. *Cogge* (1607), Cro. Jac. 170 ; *Corporation of London* v. *Riggs* (1880), 13 Ch. D. 798 ; *Titchmarsh* v. *Royston Water Co., Ltd.* (1889), 81 L.T. 673). But this right of way will not necessarily be a right of way for all purposes, but only for the purposes of the enjoyment of the land in the condition in which it happened to be at the time when the right first arose (*Maguire* v. *Browne* [1921] 1 Ir. R. 148). Whether or not the right of way ceases if the necessity subsequently ceases is a difficult and unsettled question : cesser was stated to be the rule in one case (*Holmes* v. *Goring* (1824), 2 Bing. 76, at p. 83) but doubted in another (*Proctor* v. *Hodgson* (1855), 10 Ex. 824, at p. 828). So, a right which is necessary for the enjoyment of adjoining property retained by a vendor will be impliedly regranted where the intention to enjoy or use the adjoining land in a manner making the right necessary is communicated to the purchaser, or is well-known to him. For instance, where a vendor sells land to a purchaser with notice that the adjoining land of the vendor is to be laid out in building in such a way that the only means of access will be over the land sold, the vendor will be entitled to an implied regrant of such a right of way over the land sold, although omitted to be reserved in the conveyance (*Davies* v. *Sear* (1869), L.R. 7 Eq. 427 ; *Cory* v. *Davies* [1923] 2 Ch. 95).

Another example occurs where a man builds two houses adjoining each other and so that one cannot stand without the support of the other, and then conveys one of such houses. In this case there is in law an implied reservation and regrant to him of a right of lateral support for the house retained (*Richards* v. *Rose* (1853), 9 Ex. 218 ; *Rigby* v. *Bennett* (1882), 21 Ch. D. 559 ; *Howarth* v. *Armstrong* (1897), 77 L.T. 62). Where a lease provides for a particular use of the premises and that can be made only if an easement is granted then that easement is one of necessity impliedly granted (*Wong* v. *Beaumont Property Trust, Ltd.* [1965] 1 Q.B. 173).

The decision in *Aldridge* v. *Wright* [1929] 2 K.B. 117, provides a good example of the application of the rules. Two adjoining houses with their respective gardens, Nos. 28 and 30, were the property of one man. He conveyed No. 30 to the predecessor in title of the plaintiff, and later conveyed No. 28 to the predecessor in title of the defendant. The occupier of No. 28 had, for some time, used a way across the garden of No. 30, leading to a passage, to the back of both houses for the purpose of taking in coals and removing dust, and she claimed an easement of way over the garden of No. 30. It was held that, as there had been an absolute conveyance to the plaintiff's predecessor in title of her house and garden, without any right of way being expressly reserved, the matter being one of implied reservation, and not of implied grant, the principle laid down in *Wheeldon* v. *Burrows* applied, and the plaintiff could not claim any easement which had not been expressly reserved, other than a way of necessity, which this was not.

It is not usually necessary to rely on the implied *grant* of an easement of necessity, as a case which might fall within head (2) will usually also fall within head (1), *ante*, p. 507. Nevertheless, similar rules apply to implied grants as to implied reservations of easements if necessary.

A way of necessity may be impliedly granted although the land sold is not entirely surrounded by land retained if the remainder of the adjoining land is owned by other persons who cannot be compelled by the purchaser to give him a legal right of way (*Barry* v. *Hasseldine* [1952] Ch. 835).

Other exceptional cases in which reservation of easement is implied.— Greer, L.J., gave, in his judgment in *Aldridge* v. *Wright, ante,* at p. 130, the following list of exceptions to the general rules laid down in *Wheeldon* v. *Burrows* and quoted *ante*, pp. 506–507. He said : " I have endeavoured, and I hope I have succeeded in the attempt, to extract from the decisions a sufficiently accurate description of the circumstances and considerations upon which these exceptions depend :—

(1) Where the owner of a house and adjoining land expressly sells the house and with it an apparent easement, such as a right to light or a physically defined right of way, and at the same time sells the land, both purchasers being aware of the simultaneous conveyances, there is, in the conveyance of the land, a reservation of the right to the easement. If it were not so the express or implied grant of the apparent easement would be nugatory (*Allen* v. *Taylor* (1880), 16 Ch. D. 355).

(2) If an agreement, by which a lessee of a continuous building or series of buildings assigns part of the same, cannot have effect given to its provisions without implying the reservation of a particular easement, such reservation will not be deemed to be in derogation of the assignor's grant but will be held to be impliedly excluded from the grant (*Russell* v. *Watts* (1885), 10 App. Cas. 590).

(3) If the owner of two adjoining properties, *A* and *B*, grants to the tenant of *A* a tenancy from year to year with a right of way during his tenancy over *B*, and subsequently leases *B*, the lease of *B* is subject to a reservation of the right of way which has *ex hypothesi* been granted to the tenant of *A* if it is shown that the lessee of *B* was aware of a long continued exercise of the right by the tenant of *A* (*Thomas* v. *Owen* (1887), 20 Q.B.D. 225). It is not clear from the report of this case how the tenant of *A* obtained his right of way, but it is clear from the judgment of the court delivered by Fry, L.J., that the tenant of *A* had, before the lease of *B*, acquired from his landlord by grant express or implied the right of using the road in question. Fry, L.J., points out (20 Q.B.D. 230) that the plaintiff and his predecessors in title had acquired the right to use the road as an easement of the farm occupied by him, and that no demise could be made of the soil of the road free from that right ' without derogating from the grant to the plaintiff under which his then subsisting tenancy was constituted.' See also *Westwood* v. *Heywood* [1921] 2 Ch. 130. [It was stated by the Court of Appeal in *Liddiard* v. *Waldron* [1934] 1 K.B. 435, that *Thomas* v. *Owen* laid down no general principle ; it was a decision on its own special facts, and the doctrine that a man cannot derogate from his own grant was applied to those facts. Greer, L.J., confirmed (p. 447), that the first sentence of this paragraph was a correct summary of *Thomas* v. *Owen*].

(4) Where an owner executes contemporaneous conveyances of adjoining plots with the houses erected on them, and there exists a made road across the land of one plot to an entrance to the house on the other plot, and it is proved that the road was constructed for the use of both houses, there will be implied a grant in the one conveyance of a right to use the road and a corresponding reservation in the other conveyance (*Nicholls* v. *Nicholls* (1899), 81 L.T. 811). The decision of Russell, J., in *Hansford* v. *Jago* [1921] 1 Ch. 322, appears to me to depend upon the same considerations as the decision in *Nicholls* v. *Nicholls, ante.*

(5) A similar exception arises for a similar reason where building leases are granted contemporaneously to different owners who undertake to build in accordance with a general plan which provides for the construction of a road for the convenient mutual use of the occupiers of each of the houses which are to be built in accordance with the plan. There is then implied in the lease of each of the plots a right of way over that part of the road which is on the other plots, and a corresponding reservation to the lessor of an easement so as to enable him to give effect to his grant of an easement to each of the lessees (*Cory* v. *Davies* [1923] 2 Ch. 95).

So far as I have been able to find, the exceptions to the rule in *Wheeldon* v. *Burrows* have not been carried beyond those above stated.''

It seems that the court will not readily extend the scope of these exceptions, although it may be that the exceptions could be stated in general terms as being those cases in which an implied reservation is necessary to give effect to the common intention of the parties as to the user of the land in some definite and particular manner (*Pwllbach Colliery Co.* v. *Woodman* [1915] A.C. 634 ; *Re Webb* [1951] Ch. 808 ; see also *White* v. *Taylor (No. 2)* [1969] 1 Ch. 460).

Implied reservations in registered conveyancing.—The question of an implied reservation on a transfer of registered land is even less certain than that of an implied grant. Further, where such reservations would otherwise be possible (i.e., because of necessity or some other exception) the question is not merely of academic interest. Neither the L.R.A. 1925 nor the L.R.R. 1925 contains any express or other clarifying provision, although s. 108 of the Act appears to envisage, without explaining, the creation of easements for the benefit of registered land in the same way entirely as in unregistered conveyancing. Consequently, it is thought that whilst a reservation may be implied as under the above rules unless and until the reservation, being a " disposition," is completed by registration (see L.R.A. 1925, s. 19 (2)), the easement in question remains equitable (as to which, see *ante*, p. 505).

Contemporaneous sales of two properties.—The rule was stated in Norton on Deeds, 2nd ed., at p. 297, as follows : " Where two properties belonging to the same owner are sold at the same time, and each purchaser has notice of the sale to the other, the right to any continuous and apparent quasi-easements in respect of either property is the same as if it had been conveyed first."

It will be noted that Greer, L.J., in *Aldridge* v. *Wright, ante*, in his exceptions, numbers (1) and (4), stated particular instances of contemporaneous sales and concluded that in other cases the rules in *Wheeldon* v. *Burrows* would apply. Two or more conveyances can never be precisely contemporaneous and it would appear that in cases other than those he specified Greer, L.J., was of the opinion that the rules in *Wheeldon* v. *Burrows* would apply according to the order in which the conveyances were executed. The rule as to contemporaneous conveyances is, however, usually expressed in terms similar to those used in Norton, above ; see, for instance, Cheshire, Modern Real Property, 11th ed., p. 523. The main authorities on the matter are *Compton* v. *Richards* (1814), 1 Pr. 27 ; *Swansborough* v. *Coventry* (1832), 9 Bing. 305 ; *Allen* v. *Taylor* (1880), 16 Ch. D. 355 ; *Rigby* v. *Bennett* (1882), 21 Ch. D. 559 ; *Nicholls* v. *Nicholls* (1899), 81 L.T. 811 ; *Hansford* v. *Jago* [1921] 1 Ch. 322 ; *Aldridge* v. *Wright* [1929] 2 K.B. 117 ; and *Borman* v. *Griffith* [1930] 1 Ch. 493.

Devise of properties to different persons.—In *Schwann* v. *Cotton* [1916] 2 Ch. 459, Cozens-Hardy, M.R., at p. 466, said : " The decision of Chitty, J., in *Phillips* v. *Low* [1892] 1 Ch. 47, is an express authority on this point. He applied to the case of a devise of two portions of property by the same will the well-established doctrine where there are two conveyances of the same date, and held that there is an implied grant where one of the two properties is so constructed as that parts of it involve a necessary dependence, in order to its enjoyment in the state in which it was when devised, upon the adjoining tenement."

Rights impliedly granted by a conveyance.—The law in connection with the " general words " implied by s. 62 of the L.P.A. 1925 in a conveyance of land alone, and also in a conveyance of land having houses and other buildings thereon, in the absence of any expressed intention to the contrary, is of vital importance in practical conveyancing. The material parts of the section are as follows :—

" 62.—(1) *A conveyance of land* shall be deemed to include and shall by virtue of this Act operate to convey, with the land, all buildings, erections, fixtures, commons, hedges, ditches, fences, ways, waters, watercourses, liberties, privileges, easements, rights, and advantages whatsoever, appertaining or reputed to appertain to the land, or any part thereof, or at the time of conveyance, demised, occupied, or enjoyed with, or reputed or known as part or parcel of or appurtenant to the land or any part thereof.

(2) *A conveyance of land, having houses or other buildings thereon*, shall be deemed to include and shall by virtue of this Act operate to convey, with the land, houses, or other buildings, all outhouses, erections, fixtures, cellars, areas, courts, courtyards, cisterns, sewers, gutters, drains, ways, passages, lights, watercourses, liberties, privileges, easements, rights, and advantages whatsoever, appertaining or reputed to appertain to the land, houses, or other buildings conveyed, or any of them, or any part thereof, or, at the time of conveyance, demised, occupied, or enjoyed with, or reputed or known as part or parcel of or appurtenant to, the land, houses, or other buildings conveyed, or any of them, or any part thereof.''

The section applies to conveyances made after 31st December, 1881 (*ibid.*, s. 62 (6)), but does not create any better title to any right than the vendor is able to convey (*ibid.*, s. 62 (5)) and applies only so far as a contrary intention is not expressed in the conveyance (*ibid.*, s. 62 (4)). Section 62 will not operate to convey an easement which the vendor has no power to grant expressly (*Beddington* v. *Atlee* (1887), 35 Ch. D. 317 ; *Quicke* v. *Chapman* [1903] 1 Ch. 659) ; nor a right to an extent inconsistent with the intention to be implied from the circumstances arising at the time of the contract, and known to the purchaser (*Godwin* v. *Schweppes, Ltd.* [1902] 1 Ch. 926 ; *Re Walmsley and Shaw's Contract* [1917] 1 Ch. 93 ; see also *White* v. *Taylor* (*No.* 2) [1969] 1 Ch. 160).

A consideration of the history of this section will, it is thought, help the practitioner to grasp its effect. It was always clear that all rights and easements which were strictly *appurtenant* to land passed with the land, on a conveyance, without the use of any special words. But to enable a purchaser to enjoy fully the benefit of his purchase it might and may be necessary that he should have various *quasi-easements and privileges* granted to him as well. The rules of law as to what quasi-easements and privileges will be granted or reserved by implication, without special mention, have been gradually built up (see p. 506 *et seq.*) by the decisions of the courts, but long before the passing of s. 6 of the Conveyancing Act, 1881, it was usual to insert in conveyances a long list of what were known as '' general words '' very much the same as those set out above in s. 62, so as to make sure that not only appurtenances but quasi-easements and privileges should pass to the purchaser. In order to shorten deeds, s. 6 of the Conveyancing Act, 1881, which s. 62 of the L.P.A. 1925 has replaced, gave by implication all that the old general words used to give.

The vital point is that the object of both these sections was to shorten deeds, and not to alter the rights of the parties under a contract. Therefore if, under the terms of the contract, the purchaser is not entitled to the benefit of these statutory general words, the vendor is entitled to insert in the conveyance to the purchaser words restricting the generality of such general words (which without such restriction would be implied) to the actual rights to which the purchaser was entitled under the contract (*Re Peck and London School Board* [1893] 2 Ch. 315).

Thus, the general words pass more rights than are implied by the word " appurtenances." Therefore it follows that, if the *contract* provides that the property with the " appurtenances " is sold, the vendor can insist upon a clause being inserted in the conveyance excluding other rights than appurtenances (*ibid.*). But see *Hansford* v. *Jago*, referred to below, as to use of the word in the *conveyance*, and bear in mind that rights other than appurtenances may be implied into the contract under the rule in *Wheeldon* v. *Burrows* (see below) so entitling the purchaser to their inclusion in the conveyance.

It is important to note that the " general words " are deemed to be included in a " conveyance " ; but not in an agreement or contract. " Conveyance " includes a " mortgage, charge, lease, assent, vesting declaration, vesting instrument, disclaimer, release, and every other assurance of property, or of an interest therein, by any instrument except a will " (L.P.A. 1925, s. 205 (1) (ii)). In *Borman* v. *Griffith* [1930] 1 Ch. 493, Maugham, J., said that *a contract for a lease* exceeding a term of three years was not within the term " assurance of property, or of an interest therein," and that accordingly the contract for lease in the case, *not being under seal*, could not be construed as if the general words of s. 62 of the L.P.A. 1925 were therein included. A document under hand letting property for one year only is, however, a lease to which s. 62 applies (*Wright and Another* v. *Macadam* [1949] 2 K.B. 744), but it appears that the general words in s. 62 cannot be imported into the grant of a mere oral tenancy which is not within the definition of a " conveyance " (*Rye* v. *Rye* [1962] A.C. 496).

In practice the section normally operates to pass to a purchaser of part of land those rights which the vendor exercised for the benefit of that part over a part retained. Such rights were not previously easements (see *ante*, p. 506), but were *quasi*-easements and usually fall within the words " rights and advantages . . . reputed to appertain to the land . . . conveyed." Apart from quasi-easements, the section does not deal with anything that is not part and parcel of the land conveyed. Thus the section did not operate to pass two greenhouses which were on the land conveyed but which were not fixtures (i.e., they were not therefore " erections " within subss. (1) and (2) : *H. E. Dibble, Ltd.* v. *Moore* [1970] 2 Q.B. 181).

It is most important that if a quasi-easement is not mentioned in the contract, and it is not impliedly granted, a solicitor acting for a vendor who is selling part of his land should take care to make any necessary alteration to the draft conveyance to prevent an easement passing as a result of the general words mentioned above. It is sometimes suggested that if s. 62 of the L.P.A. 1925 passes to the purchaser more than he is entitled to under the contract, a rectification of the conveyance can be obtained. Although rectification was obtained in such cases as *Clark* v. *Barnes* [1929] 2 Ch. 368 (see p. 514, *post*), it is doubtful if it could be obtained in a case in which no agreement as to easements had been made by the parties and in which s. 62 was just as likely to carry out their intentions as was the rule in *Wheeldon* v. *Burrows*.

The rights impliedly granted or reserved in a *contract* are determined by the rule in *Wheeldon* v. *Burrows* (1879), 12 Ch. D. 31, *ante*, p. 506 *et seq.* In the interesting case of *Borman* v. *Griffith* [1930] 1 Ch. 493, notwithstanding that Maugham, J., decided that a contract for a lease exceeding a term of three years, not under seal, was not a " conveyance " within s. 62, he held that the plaintiff was entitled to a right of way. The learned judge said that the position of the court in granting specific performance of the contract

17

was the same, in effect, so far as regarded rights of way, as if there had been, before the Conveyancing Act, 1881, a conveyance of the property without mentioning rights of way ; in other words, the doctrine that a grantor might not derogate from his own grant would be applicable. The plaintiff being entitled to specific performance, the court would decide that the tenant must be given all such rights of way as, according to the doctrine of the court in regard to implied grants, would pass upon a conveyance or a demise.

The section applies only if and so far as a contrary intention is not expressed in the conveyance and has effect subject to the terms of the conveyance (L.P.A. 1925, s. 62 (4)). In *Hansford* v. *Jago* [1921] 1 Ch. 322, a conveyance was made of a cottage " with the garden outbuildings and appurtenances," and it was contended that the effect of the use of the word " appurtenances " was to show a contrary intention. Russell, J., said that it would be a very strong thing to say that when an Act of Parliament provides that a conveyance is to be deemed to include a large number of matters, unless a contrary intention is expressed, the mere fact that the draftsman has elected to include one or two of these matters expressly in the conveyance should operate as an indication of an intention that the remainder should not be included. He held that it was not sufficient. See also *Broomfield* v. *Williams, post*, at pp. 523, 524. A contrary intention will not readily be taken to be shown by common-form provisions in a conveyance which might, at first sight, appear to be contrary to the words deemed to be included by s. 62 (*Hapgood* v. *Martin and Son, Ltd.* (1934), 152 L.T. 72).

In *Clark* v. *Barnes* [1929] 2 Ch. 368, the purchaser was not by the terms of the contract entitled to a certain right of way, but as in the conveyance to him of the property no words had been inserted by the vendor to limit the implication of the grant of the right of way, it passed to the purchaser. Luxmoore, J., said that he was *satisfied from the evidence that at the date of the contract it was mutually understood* that the purchaser was not to have the benefit of such right of way ; as by the conveyance the general words referred to in the section passed the right of way, and there had been a mutual mistake, the vendor was entitled to have the conveyance rectified. Note that in this case there was a *mutual* mistake. Rectification will not usually be granted where the mistake is only on the part of one of the parties. See *ante*, p. 84.

The lesson to be learned is that the solicitor for a vendor and purchaser respectively, when settling the form of contract, should carefully consider what rights or quasi-easements his client requires to enable him to have the full enjoyment of the property purchased, or retained, as the case may be, and should make provision accordingly. And, later, the vendor should, when settling the draft conveyance to the purchaser, see that proper words are inserted limiting the generality of s. 62, if the purchaser is not entitled by the contract to the full benefit of the section.

The general words in s. 62 seem to be explicit enough to revive easements which have become extinct by unity of possession, and to pass quasi-easements (as defined *ante*, p. 506), which have been first created by the grantor during unity of ownership, provided they are apparent and continuous, or even if they are discontinuous, if they are necessary for the enjoyment of the right granted or necessary to give effect to the common intention as to the purpose for which the land is to be used, and have been and were at the time of the conveyance used and enjoyed by the vendor for the benefit of the property sold (*Watts* v. *Kelson* (1871), L.R. 6 Ch. 166, at p. 172 ; *Kay* v. *Oxley* (1875), L.R. 10 Q.B. 360 ; *Barkshire* v. *Grubb* (1881), 18 Ch. D. 616 ;

Birmingham, etc., Banking Co. v. *Ross* (1888), 38 Ch. D. 295 ; *Pollard* v. *Gare* [1901] 1 Ch. 834 ; *International Tea Stores* v. *Hobbs* [1903] 2 Ch. 165 ; *Re Walmsley and Shaw's Contract* [1917] 1 Ch. 93 ; *Pwllbach Colliery Co., Ltd.* v. *Woodman* [1915] A.C. 634 ; *Bayley* v. *Great Western Railway Co.* (1884), 26 Ch. D. 434 ; and see *Burrows* v. *Lang* [1901] 2 Ch. 502 ; *Lewis* v. *Meredith* [1913] 1 Ch. 571 ; *Long* v. *Gowlett* [1923] 2 Ch. 177). More recently in *Ward* v. *Kirkland* [1966] 1 W.L.R. 601, Ungoed-Thomas, J., held that a quasi-easement which was not continuous and apparent within the rule in *Wheeldon* v. *Burrows* (1879), 12 Ch. D. 31 (*ante*, p. 507) but which had in fact been enjoyed, even if by permission, could be validly transformed into an easement by virtue of the L.P.A. 1925, s. 62. See further an article by Mr. Paul Jackson in *Conveyancer N.S.*, vol. 30, p. 340 *et seq.*

As regards the words " enjoyed with " in s. 62 of the L.P.A. 1925, a quasi-easement to come within those words must be such a right as has been used under circumstances leading to an expectation that the enjoyment would be continued (*Birmingham, etc., Banking Co.* v. *Ross, ante ; Bartlett* v. *Tottenham* [1932] 1 Ch. 114) ; even if such right was precarious, if there had been actual user (*International Tea Stores* v. *Hobbs, ante ; Hansford* v. *Jago* [1921] 1 Ch. 322 ; *Westwood* v. *Heywood* [1921] 2 Ch. 130 ; *Wright and Another* v. *Macadam* [1949] 2 K.B. 744 ; *Goldberg* v. *Edwards* [1950] Ch. 247) ; provided the user had been by the occupier of that part of the land for the benefit of which the claim is made altogether apart from the ownership or occupation of the other part of the land (*Long* v. *Gowlett, ante ; Ward* v. *Kirkland, ante*).

A profit enjoyed by a tenant over other land of his landlord does not establish a reputation of a right appurtenant to the holding so as to fall within the words " appertaining or reputed to appertain to the land " on subsequent conveyance of the holding (*White* v. *Taylor (No. 2)* [1969] 1 Ch. 160).

The implied general words are wide enough to cover the case of a profit *à prendre*, and therefore a right to depasture sheep on a sheep walk will pass with land to which the right appertains without express mention (*White* v. *Williams* [1922] 1 K.B. 727), but they do not include matters of general enjoyment, such as the parking of a car in a road near to a house, on a lease of which house the right to park was alleged to have passed as a result of s. 62 of the L.P.A. 1925 (*Le Strange* v. *Pettefar* (1939), 161 L.T. 300). They may pass the right to use a shed for the storage of coal for the purposes of a flat (*Wright and Another* v. *Macadam* [1949] 2 K.B. 744). But a matter of personal contract, such as the supply of hot water and central heating, is not within the words " privileges, easements, rights, and advantages " in s. 62 as these words refer to rights such as are capable of being granted by a lease or conveyance (*Regis Property Co., Ltd.* v. *Redman* [1956] 2 Q.B. 612). Thus more recently in *Phipps* v. *Pears* [1965] 1 Q.B. 76, Lord Denning, M.R., said that " in order for s. 62 to apply, the right or advantage must be one which is known to the law, in this sense, that it is capable of being granted at law so as to be binding on all successors in title, even those who take without notice " ; he added that neither a fine view nor protection from the weather would fall within this. Again in *Green* v. *Ashco Horticulturist* [1966] 1 W.L.R. 889 (at p. 897), Cross, J., said there were two sets of circumstances which may prevent s. 62 from operating : " In the first place, the section can only operate if the kind of user relied on could have been the subject of a grant of a legal right ; and secondly, the section will not operate if at the time of the conveyance or lease in question it was, or should have been, apparent to the grantee or lessee that the enjoyment which he claims

to have been converted into a right by the section was only temporary."
In the case it was held that a permission to use a back entrance on, in effect,
convenient occasions only was not capable of being turned into a legal right.
See also *Crow* v. *Wood* [1971] 1 Q.B. 77 where the Court of Appeal held that
a right to have one's neighbour keep up the fences or walls is a right in the
nature of an easement, or is an " advantage," capable of being granted at
law and so able to pass under s. 62.

The statutory general words will be implied on a sale by a mortgagee of
part of the tenement (*Born* v. *Turner* [1900] 2 Ch. 211 ; L.P.A. 1925, s. 101 (2)).

Registered Conveyancing.—The L.R.A. 1925, s. 19 (3), provides that " the
general words implied in conveyances under the Law of Property Act, 1925,
shall apply, so far as applicable thereto, to dispositions of a registered estate "
(see also ss. 22 (3) and 20 (1) and L.R.R. 1925, r. 251). Thus the implied
general words may operate on the registration of a transfer of part to create
automatically legal easements, which will be overriding interests so far as
the servient tenement is concerned (L.R.A. 1925, s. 70 (1), (2), and L.R.R.
1925, r. 258), and which may be noted as appurtenant to the dominant
tenement in its property register (L.R.R. 1925, rr. 251–257). If the purchaser
is not entitled to all rights which would be passed by the implied general
words, then the vendor should ensure that an entry to the contrary is made
on the register by insisting that the question be dealt with expressly in the
transfer.

Meaning of " appurtenances."—It is unnecessary to consider the old
authorities on the subject because the tendency of modern cases is to carry
out the intention of the parties and to give secondary extended meanings
to words which are capable of having more than one meaning, for instance,
the word " *appurtenances.*" In its primary meaning it will only pass what
is strictly appurtenant ; thus, in *Bolton* v. *Bolton* (1879), 11 Ch. D. 968,
it was held that a contract for the sale of land " with the appurtenances "
did not pass rights of way which were not strictly appurtenant. See also
Re Walmsley and Shaw's Contract [1917] 1 Ch. 93, but compare *Borman* v.
Griffith [1930] 1 Ch. 493 (see p. 513). In *Hansford* v. *Jago* [1921] 1 Ch. 322,
Russell, J., in commenting on the decision in *Bolton* v. *Bolton*, said, at p. 330 :
" All the decision comes to is that that particular contract was a contract for
the sale of the land and its appurtenances in the strict sense." The secondary
meaning of the word " appurtenances " is " usually held or enjoyed therewith " ; very little context is necessary for the court to hold that the
secondary meaning was intended. It is quite clear from the celebrated
case of *Wheeldon* v. *Burrows* (1879), 12 Ch. D. 31 (see *ante*, p. 506), that on the
grant of part of a tenement all those continuous and apparent easements over
the part retained by the grantor, which are necessary to the enjoyment of the
part granted, and have before and up to the time of the grant been used
therewith, passed to the grantee. In fact, the rule ought to be, and probably
now is, that the word " appurtenances " should always be given its secondary
meaning when the result of the construction of the word in its primary
sense would be inconsistent with the obvious intention of the parties to be
implied from the circumstances existing and known to the parties at the time
of the contract. The following further cases show the modern spirit : *Watts*
v. *Kelson* (1871), L.R. 6 Ch. 166 ; *Kay* v. *Oxley* (1875), L.R. 10 Q.B. 360, 369 ;
Barkshire v. *Grubb* (1881), 18 Ch. D. 616 ; *Broomfield* v. *Williams* [1897]
1 Ch. 602 ; *Hansford* v. *Jago* [1921] 1 Ch. 322 ; *Westwood* v. *Heywood* [1921]
2 Ch. 130 ; *Trim* v. *Sturminster R D.C.* [1938] 2 K.B. 508.

Meaning of " appertaining."—" Appertaining " originally meant and included only such rights as were attached to the land by reason of the fact that it had at one time been part of a manor over which such rights existed. Such rights also pass with the land without mention. One difference between something appendant and something appurtenant was, and still is, that " Appendants are ever by prescription ; but appurtenants may be created in some cases at this day " (*Baring* v. *Abingdon* [1982] 2 Ch. 374).

If the word " appertaining " has acquired a secondary meaning, it is only when used in connection with " appurtenances," such as " appurtenant and appertaining." The reason for this is that when the word is used with another word it shows that it is not intended that it should have its usual meaning, but that it is used for extending the meaning of the word with which it is used. See the old case of *Hill* v. *Grange* (1555), 1 Plow. 164, referred to in Norton on Deeds, 2nd ed., p. 278.

Repairs to right of way.—Apart from any provision in the grant, it is clear that there is no obligation at law on the grantee of a right of way to effect repairs to the way (*Duncan* v. *Louch* (1845), 4 L.T. (o.s.) 356 ; see also *Weston* v. *Weaver* [1961] 1 Q.B. 402). Nor is there any obligation on the grantor either to keep the way in repair (*Duncan* v. *Louch, ante*) or even to use his land so as to minimise the cost of any repairs that the grantee may wish to carry out (*Birkenhead Corporation* v. *L.N.W.R. Co.* (1885), 15 Q.B.D. 572).

If, however, the grant of the right of way is made, as is commonly the case with shared ways, subject to the grantee being responsible for or contributing to the cost of repairs, this would appear to impose an obligation enforceable not only against the grantee but also against his successors in title wishing to use the way (*Halsall* v. *Brizell* [1957] Ch. 169 ; see also *Re Ellenborough Park* [1956] Ch. 131).

Further, where a servient owner constructed ramps on the right of way (to slow traffic) which were not in themselves a disturbance of the right, they were held to become a disturbance in consequence of the disrepair of the road surface (*Saint* v. *Jenner* [1972] 3 W.L.R. 888, C.A.). It followed that a liability to maintain the road surface would fall on the servient owner who constructed the ramps and on his successors in title keeping the ramps (*ibid.*).

Extent of right of way.—A grant of a right of way for horses and carriages will give a right of way for motor cars (*White* v. *Grand Hotel Eastbourne, Ltd.* [1913] 1 Ch. 113), and proof of user by horses and carriages sufficient to establish the right to an easement will give a right to use the way by motor vehicles (*Lock* v. *Abercester, Ltd.* [1939] Ch. 861). A grant of a right of way " with or without horses carts and agricultural machines and implements " to a dominant tenement which, at the time of the grant, was mainly agricultural land, authorises use of the way by motor lorries removing large quantities of sand from the dominant tenement (*Kain* v. *Norfolk & Baker (Hauliers), Ltd.* [1949] Ch. 163).

The grant in 1901 of a right " with or without horses carts and carriages to pass and re-pass through over and along the yard " was held by the Court of Appeal to include a right to stop for the purpose of loading and unloading motor vans (*McIlraith* v. *Brady* [1968] 1 Q.B. 468).

A grant of way simply to " *A B* his heirs and assigns " was held before 1926 to include the *licensees* of *A B* (*Hammond* v. *Prentice Bros., Ltd.* [1920] 1 Ch. 201).

The following summary of the law was made by Sir George Jessel, M.R., in *Cannon* v. *Villars* (1878), 8 Ch. D. 415, at pp. 420, 421 : " As I understand, the grant of a right of way *per se* and nothing else may be a right of footway, or it may be a general right of way, that is a right of way not only for people on foot but for people on horseback, for carts, carriages and other vehicles. Which it is, is a question of construction of the grant, and that construction will, of course, depend on the circumstances surrounding, so to speak, the execution of the instrument. Now, one of those circumstances, and a very material circumstance, is the nature of the *locus in quo* over which the right of way is granted. If we find a right of way granted over a metalled road with pavement on both sides existing at the time of the grant, the presumption would be that it was intended to be used for the purpose for which it was constructed, which is obviously the passage not only of foot passengers, but of horsemen and carts. Again, if we find the right of way granted along a piece of land capable of being used for the passage of carriages, and the grant is of a right of way to a place which is stated on the face of the grant to be intended to be used or to be actually used for a purpose which would necessarily or reasonably require the passing of carriages, there again it must be assumed that the right of way was intended to be effectual for the purpose for which the place was designed to be used, or was actually used . . . If, on the other hand, you find that the road in question over which the grant was made was paved only with flagstones, and that it was only four or five feet wide, over which a wagon or cart or carriage ordinarily constructed could not get, and that it was only a way used to a field or close, or something on which no erection was, there, I take it, you would say that the physical circumstances showed that the right of way was a right for foot passengers only. It might include a horse under some circumstances, but could not be intended for carts or carriages."

In *Todrick* v. *Western National Omnibus Co.* [1934] Ch. 190, 561, it was held that a reservation of a right of way to a house and garages along a narrow roadway held up by a retaining wall, and passing through a narrow archway, did not authorise the user of the way for the passage of omnibuses. On the other hand, in *Robinson* v. *Bailey* [1948] 2 All E.R. 791, the grant in general terms of a right of way over a road on a building estate was held to justify the use of the road by lorries carrying building materials, although the materials were being stored on one of the plots of the estate, and were not merely for the building of a house on that plot. A right granted over land wide enough for a vehicle is not restricted to use by pedestrians only because at the time of the grant the gate into it was too narrow to permit passage of a vehicle (*Keefe* v. *Amor* [1965] 1 Q.B. 334, distinguishing *Bulstrode* v. *Lambert* [1953] 1 W.L.R. 1064). Again the grant of " a right of crossing the railway to the extent of twelve feet in width on the level with all manner of cattle " was held by a majority of the Court of Appeal to confer a general right of way, not one limited to the agricultural or domestic user contemplated at the time (*British Railways Board* v. *Glass* [1965] Ch. 538) ; the surrounding circumstances were looked at as well as the words of the grant and of particular importance was the circumstance that the level crossing afforded the only means of access to the dominant tenement. See also *Finch* v. *Great Western Railway* (1879), 5 Ex. D. 254, and compare *Taff Vale Railway* v. *Gordon Canning* [1909] 3 Ch. 48.

Even a grant " at all times and for all purposes " does not authorise excessive user which would be an unreasonable interference with rights of others such as those entitled to a like right (*Jelbert* v. *Davis* [1968] 1 W.L.R.

589). But, in considering whether there is excessive user within the principle that the owner of the dominant tenement is not entitled to increase the burden on the servient tenement, a distinction has to be drawn between a mere increase in user and user of a different kind, the former not being within the principle (*per* Plowman, J., in *Woodhouse & Co., Ltd.* v. *Kirkland (Derby), Ltd.* [1970] 1 W.L.R. 1185).

If it is intended that a way should be used only for a limited purpose, such as agriculture, the limitation should be stated, because in the event of ambiguity in the words used they will be construed against the grantor. Thus, in *Hurt* v. *Bowmer* [1937] 1 All E.R. 797, it was held that the words " as at present enjoyed " referred to the quality of the user, which was for both foot and vehicular traffic, and did not limit the extent to which the way could be used. See also *Kain* v. *Norfolk* [1949] Ch. 163, *ante*, p. 517.

It has been said that the grantee of a right of way cannot use it for access to a close other than that for which it is granted (*Henning* v. *Burnet* (1852), 8 Ex. 187 ; *Harris* v. *Flower* (1904), 74 L.J. Ch. 127) ; but when the use is not particularly defined, so that it can fairly be contended that the intention is to make it part of a larger close, then the right of way will be deemed to be appurtenant to the whole of such close (*Thorpe* v. *Brumfitt* (1873), L.R. 8 Ch. 650 ; *Callard* v. *Beeney* (1930), 142 L.T. 45).

A right of way can be made appurtenant to land with which it has no physical contiguity provided the right is beneficial in respect of the ownership of that land (*Bailey* v. *Stephens* (1862), 12 C.B. (N.S.) 91 ; *Todrick* v. *Western National Omnibus Co.* [1934] Ch. 190, 561).

Public rights of way.—The law relating to public rights of way is not strictly relevant to the present discussion, but a short note on the effect of some modern statutes may be of assistance to readers.

All highways, including footpaths, if not created as such by statute, are created by dedication. Proof of dedication is a matter of some difficulty, particularly where persons in possession of the land in recent years have been life-tenants or other limited owners. Under the Highways Act, 1959, s. 34 (which re-enacted the Rights of Way Act, 1932, s. 1 (1), as amended by the National Parks and Access to the Countryside Act, 1949, s. 58), if a way has been used by the public for twenty years as of right and without interruption it is deemed to have been dedicated as a public highway unless there is sufficient evidence that there was no intention to dedicate (see *A.-G.* v. *Honeywill* [1972] 1 W.L.R. 1506 as to user with vehicles). The construction of s. 1 (1) of the 1932 Act and the question how far authorities decided under the Prescription Act, 1832, could be relied on, were considered in *Merstham Manor, Ltd.* v. *Coulsdon and Purley U.D.C.* [1937] 2 K.B. 77. The change made by the 1932 Act as to what is proof of dedication was discussed in *Jones* v. *Bates* [1938] 2 All E.R. 237. The period of twenty years is a period next before the time when the right of the public to use a way has been brought into question (1959 Act, s. 34 (2)), but user during such period may be relied on even though it came to an end before the Act came into force (*A.-G. and Newton Abbot R.D.C.* v. *Dyer* [1947] Ch. 67). As to the nature of acts which will amount to interruption, see *Lewis* v. *Thomas* [1950] 1 K.B. 438. See also *Fairey* v. *Southampton County Council* [1956] 2 Q.B. 439, where *A.-G. and Newton Abbot R.D.C.* v. *Dyer* was followed and it was decided that the right was first " brought into question " when the owner first refused to allow the public to use the path.

A landowner who wishes to prevent the acquisition of rights by the public may do so by putting up a notice visible to those using the way, inconsistent with the dedication of the way (*ibid.*, s. 34 (3)), and, if this is torn down or defaced, by a notice in writing to the local authority. Alternatively, the owner may deposit with the local authority a map with a statement of the ways he admits to have been dedicated. If the owner or his successors then, at least once every six years, deposit statutory declarations that no additional ways, other than such as are specified, have been dedicated, such declarations will be sufficient evidence to negative the intention to dedicate other ways unless a contrary intention is proved (*ibid.*, s. 34 (6)).

The Highways Act, 1959, does not prevent proof of dedication by any evidence which would have been sufficient before the Act was passed (*ibid.*, s. 34 (9)); the Act directs the court to have regard to maps and other relevant documents when considering questions of dedication (*ibid.*, s. 35) although not for the purpose of determining the extent of a highway (*Webb* v. *Eastleigh Building Society* (1958), *Current Law*, May, 1958, No. 128); the rights of reversioners to prevent acquisition of public rights are reserved (*ibid.*, s. 36).

Right of support.—The right of support, whether lateral or vertical, for the soil in its natural state, which every owner of land is entitled to as an incident of ownership, is not an easement but a common-law right wholly independent of any grant by one person to another (*Dalton* v. *Angus* (1881), 6 App. Cas. 740; *Butterknowle Colliery Co.* v. *Bishop Auckland Industrial Co-operative Co.* [1906] A.C. 305, 313; *Warwickshire Coal Co.* v. *Corporation of Coventry* [1934] Ch. 488). But an owner of land has no natural right as an incident of his ownership to the support of his land *with the extra weight thereon of buildings*. He may obtain such a right by twenty years' uninterrupted enjoyment for a building proved to have been newly built or altered so as to increase the pressure at the beginning of that time; and it will be deemed to have been so acquired if the enjoyment has been peaceable and without deception or concealment, and so open that it must be known that some support is being enjoyed by the building (*Dalton* v. *Angus, ante*). The right of such extraordinary support is an easement which can be acquired under s. 2 of the Prescription Act, 1832 (*Lemaitre* v. *Davies* (1881), 19 Ch. D. 281, at p. 291; see also *Southwark and Vauxhall Water Co.* v. *Wandsworth Board of Works* [1898] 2 Ch. 603, at p. 612; *Gateley* v. *Martin* [1900] 2 Ir. R. 269).

A purchaser can also obtain a right of support of land weighted with buildings by implied grant. For instance, if the owner of two houses should, at the same time, sell one house to one purchaser and the other to another purchaser, or if he should sell one house to a purchaser and retain the other, although no reference to any right of support be made in the conveyances or conveyance, a right of support will be implied for each of the houses, both in the case of the house sold to each of the two purchasers and in the case of the sale of the one house; also a similar right of support for the benefit of the vendor in the case where he retains one of the houses. The reason is that a vendor cannot derogate from his grant and must be assumed to have intended that the purchasers or purchaser should take such rights as would enable them or him properly to enjoy the property conveyed. And, in the case of the vendor, a reservation and regrant would be implied on the ground that it was an easement of necessity. See at p. 508 *et seq.* See also *Richards* v. *Rose* (1853), 9 Ex. 218; *Gayford* v. *Nicholls* (1854), 9 Ex. 702; *Russell* v. *Watts* (1885), 10 App. Cas. 590.

So also if a vendor sells land for the express purpose of its being built upon by the purchaser or his assigns, he will be considered to have impliedly granted such a right of support from his adjoining land to the land sold and the buildings thereon when erected (*Rigby* v. *Bennett* (1882), 21 Ch. D. 559 ; *Grosvenor Hotel Co.* v. *Hamilton* [1894] 2 Q.B. 836).

There is no natural right to support of a *building* by a building, and even if the grant of such a right be expressed or implied neither owner is under any obligation to do the repairs which may be necessary to ensure the continuation of support for the building of the other owner (*Peyton* v. *London Corporation* (1829), 9 B. & C. 715 ; *Southwark & Vauxhall Water Co.* v. *Wandsworth Board of Works* [1898] 2 Ch. 603, at p. 612). However, where a right of support has been created in respect of a building " the owner of the dominant tenement is not bound to sit by and watch the gradual deterioration of the support constituted by his neighbour's building. He is entitled to enter and take the necessary steps to ensure that the support continues by effecting repair and so forth to the part of the building which gives the support " (*Bond* v. *Nottingham Corporation* [1940] Ch. 429, at pp. 438–9).

There appears to be no right of support of buildings from subterranean water (the exception does not apply to sand or silt), and, therefore, if a man by draining his land lets down the land adjoining, the owner of the latter does not appear to have any right of action (*Popplewell* v. *Hodgkinson* (1869), L.R. 4 Ex. 248 ; *Jordesen* v. *Sutton, etc., Gas Co.* [1899] 2 Ch. 217 ; *Trinidad Asphalte Co.* v. *Ambard* [1899] A.C. 594 ; *Fletcher* v. *Birkenhead Corporation* [1906] 1 K.B. 605). But see *Shelfer* v. *City of London Electric Lighting Co.* [1895] 1 Ch. 287, as to when the building has been erected for over twenty years. Further a right of action will lie where the operation complained of consists first in causing a solid support to liquefy and then in removing the resulting liquid (*Lotus, Ltd.* v. *British Soda Co., Ltd.* [1972] Ch. 123, which concerned the pumping of brine resulting from the solution of salt beds ; Pennycuick, V.C., distinguished *Popplewell* v. *Hodgkinson* as relating to the pumping of water only). But, so far as water alone is concerned, it is clear that this may be abstracted from under a man's own land, to whatever extent he pleases, and without liability, notwithstanding that this may result in the abstraction of water percolating under his neighbour's land and thereby cause him injury, by settlement in buildings or otherwise (*Langbrook Properties, Ltd.* v. *Surrey County Council* [1970] 1 W.L.R. 161).

As to rights of support on severance of minerals from the surface, see *ante*, p. 500, and as to the rights of the National Coal Board to withdraw support provided by mines of coal, see *ante*, p. 501.

Where a right of support has been interfered with, no right of action accrues until some actual damage has resulted (*Backhouse* v. *Bonomi* (1861), 9 H.L. Cas. 503). The law as to claiming damages for withdrawal of support is in a very unsatisfactory state. A client comes to the office and complains that his neighbour is excavating close to his boundary, and says he is afraid that the result will be that he will have cracks in the wall of his house, or even worse damage, and asks the solicitor to apply for an injunction. But the solicitor has to tell him it cannot be done, and that until some damage results, or possibly unless damage must inevitably result, he has no remedy. A further defect in the law occurs where a person excavates and then sells the property, and damage occurs. The owner of the land damaged has no cause of action against the purchaser, and he can only claim damage against the original excavator. Such excavator may have sold all his property and

at the time of the damage be a man of straw.   See *Darley Main Colliery Co.*
v. *Mitchell* (1886), 11 App. Cas. 127 ;   *Greenwell* v. *Low Beechburn Coal Co.*
[1897] 2 Q.B. 165 ;   *West Leigh Colliery Co., Ltd.* v. *Tunnicliffe and Hampson,*
Ltd. [1908] A.C. 27, and *Hall* v. *Duke of Norfolk* [1900] 2 Ch. 493.

In *Backhouse* v. *Bonomi*, *ante*, Lord Cranworth said : " It has been supposed
that the right of the party whose land is interfered with is a right to what is
called the pillars of support.   In truth, his right is a right to the ordinary
enjoyment of his land, and until that ordinary right is interfered with he has
nothing of which to complain."

In *Upjohn* v. *Seymour Estates* [1938] 1 All E.R. 614, defendants demolished
a house, taking proper steps under the London Building Act with respect to
a party wall.   Although certain shores were put up, the *defendants'* half of
the wall collapsed leaving exposed certain apertures in plaintiff's half by
reason of which the plaintiff's stock was damaged.   It was held that there
was no trespass by the defendants as the half which had fallen belonged to
the defendants as a result of the L.P.A. 1925, s. 38 (1) (as to which, see *ante*,
p. 488), but that the plaintiff's right of support and user over that half
included protection of the apertures, which rights had been infringed whereby
damage had been caused to the plaintiffs.

A building which is subject to an easement of support in favour of an
adjoining building could not be demolished, either by the owner or the local
authority, under a clearance order made under the Housing Act, 1957,
without providing support for the adjoining building (*Bond* v. *Nottingham
Corporation* [1940] Ch. 429).

Easements in respect of artificial watercourses.—In *Wood* v. *Wood*
(1849), 3 Ex. 748, Pollock, C.B., said at p. 777 : " The right to artificial watercourses, as against the party creating them, surely must depend upon the
character of the watercourse, whether it be of a permanent or temporary
nature, and upon the circumstances under which it is created.   The enjoyment
for twenty years of a stream diverted or penned up by permanent embankments clearly stands upon a different footing from the enjoyment of a flow of
water originating in the mode of occupation or alteration of a person's property,
and presumably of a temporary character, and liable to variation."   In
Bartlett v. *Tottenham* [1932] 1 Ch. 114, the question was whether the owner
of land which formerly formed part of a larger piece of land was entitled to
the benefit of an overflow of water from a tank on the remainder of the land
from which it had been separated.   It was contended first that under s. 62
of the L.P.A. 1925 " waters " and " watercourses " had passed to the plaintiffs
by their conveyance, and that the case was covered by *Wheeldon* v. *Burrows*
(1879), 12 Ch. D. 31 (*ante*, p. 506).   In answer to this Lawrence, L.J., said
that this rule did not apply because the overflow was not an easement used
by the owner of the entirety for the benefit of the part conveyed.   The judge
distinguished the facts of *Watts* v. *Kelson* (1871), L.R. 6 Ch. 166, 172, and
Schwann v. *Cotton* [1916] 2 Ch. 459.   In the former case the watercourse
was constructed by the common owner for the benefit of both tenements,
and in the latter the pipe was laid by the common owner for the sole benefit
of the tenement granted.   The plaintiff also contended, in the alternative,
that he was entitled to insist on the continuance of the overflow by prescription.   Lawrence, L.J., pointed out that the overflow was of a temporary
nature, and being only of a permissive character it could never become a
foundation for the presumption of a grant.   The judge also pointed out
that in *Arkwright* v. *Gell* (1839), 5 M. & W. 203, the water pumped from

mines had flowed over a man's land for upwards of sixty years, and it was held that this gave him no right to the continuance of the flow. In the present case, the overflow was only temporary and the plaintiff had no claim.

The general result seems to be that a right to have the benefit of an artificial watercourse or drain can only be successfully claimed by prescription when user has been " as of right," as where it can be proved that it was constructed for the joint benefit of two owners or for the benefit of the particular land in respect of which it is claimed. This will be the case where the right claimed is to take water from a pipe constructed to supply several properties (*Beauchamp* v. *Frome R.D.C.* [1938] 1 All E.R. 595). Otherwise mere enjoyment of the benefit for upwards of twenty years will give no right.

A grant of a right to lay and maintain drains, sewers, pipes and cables (with rights to enter on the servient land) was considered in *Simmons* v. *Midford* [1969] 2 Ch. 415. It was decided : (i) a drain pipe laid pursuant to the grant is normally not intended to form part of the freehold and so (in absence of express agreement) belongs to the person providing it is appurtenant to his land ; (ii) even if it had been intended that the pipe should form part of the freehold, the person laying it is entitled to its exclusive use and can prevent the servient freeholder from using it.

The words used and circumstances of each case must be considered but these rules would normally apply in the common case of a grant on sale of part of land of the grantor for building purposes. The grantor should, therefore, consider whether he should provide expressly as to the capacity of pipes to be laid and for his right to make connections.

Right of light.—On perusing the title to building land it is important to consider whether the adjoining owners have any rights of light which may prevent the purchaser building according to plans on which he may have based his calculations as to price ; see *Pemsel and Wilson* v. *Tucker* [1907] 2 Ch. 191.

The court is entitled to take into account the nature of the locality and also modern lighting standards in an action for infringement of a right of light (*Ough* v. *King* [1967] 1 W.L.R. 1547). See further the discussion of *Newham* v. *Lawson* (1971), 22 P. & C.R. 852, by E. P. Merritt in *Conveyancer N.S.*, vol. 36, p. 15 *et seq*.

There is no natural right of light, as in the case of a right of support. The right has to be obtained by grant or acquired by prescription. Therefore, apart from (*a*) the necessity for planning permission, byelaw approval or consent under the Building Acts, (*b*) grants or agreements, express or implied, (*c*) questions of acquiescence, and (*d*) questions of prescription, a person may build over the whole of his own land, right up to the verge, though by so doing he completely blocks up his neighbour's light.

If the owner of a house, the windows of which overlook adjoining land also belonging to such owner, grants the house alone to a purchaser, without expressly reserving the right to obstruct the access of light to the house, he *impliedly* grants to the purchaser a right of light to the windows of the house over his other land ; consequently, neither the owner nor any person claiming under him can so build upon the other land as to obstruct the access of light to the purchaser's windows (*Broomfield* v. *Williams* [1897] 1 Ch. 602 ; *Cable* v. *Bryant* [1908] 1 Ch. 259).

The same principle extends to the case where the erection of a house is contemplated by *both* parties at the date of the grant (*Bailey* v. *Icke* (1891), 64 L.T. 789). But if land unbuilt upon is simply conveyed, the mere intention on the part of the purchaser to build upon it will not be sufficient to give him a grant of lights (*Robinson* v. *Grave* (1873), 21 W.R. 569). So, if a person owns a house and also adjoining land unbuilt upon, and at the same time sells the house to one person and the land to another, each purchaser being aware of the sale to the other, the purchaser of the house will get an implied right of light over the land sold to the other purchaser (*Compton* v. *Richards* (1814), 1 Price 27 ; *Allen* v. *Taylor* (1880), 16 Ch. D. 355). But where the two sales are independent of each other and not a part of one transaction, and the owner of a house and of adjoining land sells first the land and then the house, and on the sale of the land he omits to reserve a right of light for the house, the purchaser of such land can build upon it so as to obstruct the access of light to the house (*Wheeldon* v. *Burrows* (1879), 12 Ch. D. 31 ; *Beddington* v. *Atlee* (1887), 35 Ch. D. 317 ; *Ray* v. *Hazeldine* [1904] 2 Ch. 17). The owner of two adjoining tenements granted one to a purchaser without expressly reserving any rights over the other. The purchaser built a wall blocking out all light from the owner's window ; it was held that there was no implied reservation of the right of light to the window (*Ray* v. *Hazeldine, ante*). As to implied grant and reservation of easements generally, see *ante*, p. 506 *et seq*.

The above general rule is also applicable to devises. Where a testator, being seised of a house with windows and a field adjoining over which the light required for the windows passed, devised the house to one person and the field to another, it was held that the right to light over the field was comprised in the devise of the house (*Phillips* v. *Low* [1892] 1 Ch. 47).

So, if the land is conveyed under a building scheme which pre-supposes that the adjoining land will be built on, the grantee will not acquire an unrestricted right of light (*Godwin* v. *Schweppes, Ltd.* [1902] 1 Ch. 926). But a mere statement on a plan that the adjoining land of the vendor is building land will not prevent a right of light passing (*Broomfield* v. *Williams* [1897] 1 Ch. 602 ; *Pollard* v. *Gare* [1901] 1 Ch. 834), and, speaking generally, the general rule does not apply where an implied grant of the right to light would be inconsistent with the intention to be implied from the circumstances existing at the time of grant and known to the grantee (*Birmingham, Dudley and District Banking Co.* v. *Ross* (1888), 38 Ch. D. 295).

The principle does not apply where the vendor of the house is not the owner of the adjoining ground. In that case there is no implied warranty that the windows are entitled to the access of light over such land (*Greenhalgh* v. *Brindley* [1901] 2 Ch. 324 ; *Smith* v. *Colbourne* [1914] 2 Ch. 533). The mere fact of there being windows in an adjoining house overlooking a purchased property will not be taken to be constructive notice of any agreement giving a right to the access of light to them (*Allen* v. *Seckham* (1878), 11 Ch. D. 790).

A right of light to a dwelling-house, workshop or other building (including a greenhouse : *Clifford* v. *Holt* [1899] 1 Ch. 698) may be acquired under the Prescription Act, 1832, ss. 3, 4, when the access of light has been enjoyed without interruption for twenty years next before some action wherein the claim is brought into question. No act or other matter is deemed to be an interruption within the meaning of the statute, however, unless it is acquiesced in for one year after the party interrupted has notice thereof. The result is that an indefeasible right cannot be obtained until the right has been brought into question in some suit (*Hyman* v. *Van den Bergh* [1907] 2 Ch. 516 ; [1908] 1 Ch. 167). But as an interruption must have been acquiesced in for one year, it follows that after nineteen years have passed there cannot be such an interruption ; but before bringing an action for the purpose of getting an obstruction removed it is necessary to wait until the expiration of the twentieth year (*Bridewell Hospital* v. *Ward* (1892), 62 L.J. Ch. 270).

Although there could not be an *interruption* after nineteen years, the person over whose land the right was enjoyed might prevent the acquisition of an easement by commencing an action questioning the claim at any time before twenty years expired. The commencement of such an action was not an interruption but was the event marking the date down to which the requisite period of user must be shown (*Reilly* v. *Orange* [1955] 2 Q.B. 112).

For the purpose of proceedings in actions begun after 1962 (and certain actions begun earlier) in so far as it falls to be determined whether premises are entitled to a right to light, and whether anything done before 1st January, 1963, may constitute an infringement, the period of twenty years mentioned in the Prescription Act, 1832, s. 3, is changed to twenty-seven years (Rights of Light Act, 1959, s. 1 (1) (2)).

There is a peculiarity as regards rights of light which should be referred to. In the case of other easements a leaseholder cannot acquire an easement against his landlord. In *Morgan* v. *Fear* [1907] A.C. 425, adjacent buildings were occupied by lessees holding under a common lessor, and it was held that a right to light may be acquired in respect of one building as against the other, and that such right will enure in favour of one lessee and his successors against the adjoining lessee and their common landlord.

A reservation in a lease empowering the lessor to build to any height upon the adjoining land to that demised, notwithstanding that such building might obstruct any lights on the land thereby demised, was held to prevent the lessee from acquiring a right to light under s. 3 of the Prescription Act, 1832 (*Foster* v. *Lyons* [1927] 1 Ch. 219).

A right is not acquired under these sections if user has been " by some consent or agreement expressly made or given for that purpose by deed or writing." For other phrases which, if inserted in leases, will amount to consent to enjoyment of the right to light with the result that no prescriptive right is acquired under the Prescription Act, 1832, s. 3, see *Haynes* v. *King* [1893] 3 Ch. 439 ; *Willoughby* v. *Eckstein* [1937] Ch. 167.

The effect of an agreement as to access of light and, in particular, the results of repudiation of such an agreement, are considered in the *Law Journal*, vol. 105, p. 374 *et seq.*

When the owner of property containing " ancient lights " intends to pull the property down and erect another building in its place, it is most important, if he wishes to preserve such rights for his new building, that he should keep evidence of the exact position of the old lights, otherwise he may find that he cannot claim the benefits as regards the lights placed in the new building in substitution for the old lights (*News of the World, Ltd.* v. *Allen Fairhead & Sons, Ltd.* [1931] 2 Ch. 402).

In recent years there has been a danger that adjoining owners may acquire rights of light, by prescription, over vacant sites which could not be developed as a result of restrictions on building. Formerly, the only way in which the acquisition of such rights could be prevented was by the erection of an obstruction to the light (unless, of course, adjoining owners would accept a licence which would prevent the acquisition of a right to light) but the erection of a hoarding as an obstruction might itself need planning permission. This difficulty has been overcome by the Rights of Light Act, 1959. For the purpose of preventing a right to light being acquired, the owner of land over which light passes may apply in prescribed form (which must be accompanied by a certificate of the Lands Tribunal) to the local authority for the registration of a notice in the local land charges register (*ibid.*, s. 2). The effect of registration of a notice is the same as if access to light had been obstructed to a specified extent (*ibid.*, s. 3). Although the procedure is somewhat cumbersome involving an application to the Lands Tribunal for a certificate that adequate notice of the proposed application has been given to persons likely to be affected by registration (or that, on grounds of exceptional urgency, the notice should be registered forthwith), an alternative to the physical obstruction of light is provided. Taken in conjunction with the extension of the period necessary for acquisition of a right to light in the Prescription Act, 1832, s. 3, these rules are particularly valuable in preventing adverse rights over war damaged land. In practice the threat of action may often persuade the person enjoying the light to enter into an agreement which will prevent a right being acquired.

Right of fishing.—When the owner of a fishery is also the riparian owner, a lease by him of the riparian land presumptively carries with it a right to fish in the river *ex adverso* the land *usque ad medium filum aquae* (*Jones* v. *Davies* (1902), 86 L.T. 447) ; and to defeat this presumption it is necessary to reserve in the lease a right to fish in the river. See also *ante*, p. 489.

Perpetuity rule and future easements.—In *Dunn* v. *Blackdown Properties, Ltd.* [1961] Ch. 433, Cross, J., held that the grant of a right to use the sewers and drains " now passing or hereafter to pass " under the servient tenement was invalid as infringing the perpetuity rule where there was no sewer or drain in existence at the date of the grant (he also held that the L.P.A. 1925, s. 162 (1) (d) (iv), related only to rights of construction, etc., ancillary to a valid easement). The decision has been criticised (see, e.g., Sir Lancelot Elphinstone in the *Solicitors' Journal*, vol. 109, p. 2), but so long as it stands it means that any grant of an easement to arise in the future must, to be acceptably valid, comply with the perpetuity rule. *Dunn* v. *Blackdown Properties, Ltd.* was followed by Plowman, J., in *Newham* v. *Lawson* (1971), 115 Sol. J. 446, with regard to the purported grant of a right to light where the building was not then erected. It may, however, be possible that what looks at first sight like a future easement may be construed as an immediate grant, e.g., a right of way over a defined route where a road is to be constructed.

The Perpetuities and Accumulations Act, 1964, omits any provision expressly relating to this problem but does appear to offer some indirect assistance. Firstly, when drafting the grant of future easements it will be possible to use the 80 years period instead of either 21 years or the " royal lives " formulae (see s. 1 (1) of the Act and compare the suggestion in the *Law Society's Gazette* (1964), vol. 61, at p. 61). And secondly, it seems probable that any grant of a future easement made after 16th July, 1964, and not expressly confined within the perpetuity period may on the facts be saved by the new " wait and see " rule (see ss. 3 and 15 (5) of the Act).

Extinguishment of easements.—Apart from extinguishment by statute, easements may be extinguished in two ways, first by express or implied release, and secondly by unity of seisin of the dominant and servient tenements. An easement or profit may be abandoned but this occurs only where there is a fixed intention never to exercise the right again (*Tehidy Minerals, Ltd.* v. *Norman* [1971] 2 Q.B. 528). These matters cannot be dealt with in full here, but will be found discussed in Cheshire, Modern Real Property, 11th ed., p. 541 *et seq.*

PART 4. FIXTURES

Generally.—Questions relating to fixtures have to be considered from
many points of view : for instance, as between vendor and purchaser, as
between landlord and tenant (and different considerations arise when the
tenancy is an agricultural one), and as between mortgagee and mortgagor.

Let us start by considering the degree of affixation which is, in general,
necessary to make an article a fixture so as to pass with the land on a transfer
thereof. The expression " in general " is used because there are cases
where an article may be a fixture although it is not affixed to the soil or
to a building. The classical statement of the law by Lord Blackburn,
in *Holland* v. *Hodgson* (1872), L.R. 7 C.P. 328, at p. 334, is often quoted.
The learned judge said : " There is no doubt that the general maxim of
the law is, that what is annexed to the land becomes part of the land ; but
it is very difficult, if not impossible, to say with precision what constitutes
an annexation sufficient for this purpose. It is a question which must
depend on the circumstances of each case, and mainly on two circumstances,
as indicating the intention, viz., the *degree of annexation and the object of
the annexation.* When the article in question is no further attached to the
land than by its own weight, it is generally to be considered a mere chattel :
see *Wiltshear* v. *Cottrell* (1853), 1 El. & Bl. 674, and the cases there cited.
But even in such a case, if the intention is apparent to make the articles part
of the land, they do become part of the land : see *D'Eyncourt* v. *Gregory*
(1866), L.R. 3 Eq. 382 [see also below]. Thus, blocks of stone placed one
on the top of another without any mortar or cement for the purpose of
forming a dry stone wall would become part of the land, though the same
stones, if deposited in a builder's yard and for convenience sake stacked on
the top of each other in the form of a wall, would remain chattels. On the
other hand, an article may be very firmly fixed to the land, and yet the
circumstances may be such as to show that it was never intended to be part
of the land, and then it does not become part of the land. The anchor of a
large ship must be very firmly fixed in the ground in order to bear the strain
of the cable, yet no one could suppose that it became part of the land even
though it should chance that the shipowner was also the owner of the fee
of the spot where the anchor was dropped. An anchor similarly fixed in
the soil for the purpose of bearing the strain of the chain of a suspension
bridge would be part of the land. Perhaps the true rule is, that articles not
otherwise attached to the land than by their own weight are not to be
considered as part of the land, unless the circumstances are such as to show
that they were intended to be part of the land, the onus of showing that they
were so intended lying on those who assert that they have ceased to be
chattels, and that, on the contrary, an article which is affixed to the land even
slightly is to be considered as part of the land, unless the circumstances are
such as to show that it was intended all along to continue a chattel, the onus
lying on those who contend that it is a chattel."

The fact that a chattel may sink into the ground (*Huntley* v. *Russell*
(1849), 13 Q.B. 572), or is set in a place prepared for it in the ground
(*Re Richards* (1869), L.R. 4 Ch. 630, at p. 638), is not sufficient to make it a
fixture. But where the article is so firmly fixed in the ground that it cannot
be removed except by digging, such as an advertisement hoarding, it has
been held that it would become a fixture and could not be distrained on for
rent (*Provincial Bill Posting Co.* v. *Low Moor Iron Co.* [1909] 2 K.B. 344);

though, as against his landlord, the tenant who put it up would be entitled to remove it at the end of the tenancy (*ibid.*).

But attachment to the soil or building is not essential to make an article a fixture, if a clear intention can be shown to make the article a part of the land or house. Two cases are often referred to to substantiate this proposition, namely, *D'Eyncourt* v. *Gregory* (1866), L.R. 3 Eq. 382, and *Monti* v. *Barnes* [1901] 1 K.B. 205. In the former case it was held that where sculptured statues, or ornamental vases and stone garden seats, merely held in position by their own weight, were essentially part of the architectural design of a house or its grounds, they were fixtures. In the latter case it was held that dog grates substituted for ordinary fixed grates must be considered fixtures. Greenhouses not attached to land, standing on their own weight on dollies, are not fixtures (*Dibble* v. *Moore* [1970] 2 Q.B. 181). See also *Holland* v. *Hodgson* (1872), L.R. 7 C.P. 328, 335 ; *Wake* v. *Hall* (1883), 8 App. Cas. 195, at p. 205 ; *Leigh* v. *Taylor* [1902] A.C. 157, at p. 161 ; *Re Hulse* [1905] 1 Ch. 406, at p. 411.

The object and purpose of the annexation must be inferred from the circumstances of each case (*Leigh* v. *Taylor, ante*) ; but direct evidence of intention on the part of the person fixing the chattel does not appear to be admissible (see *Hobson* v. *Gorringe* [1897] 1 Ch. 182). If, however, the article cannot be removed without great damage to the land or building, this test is conclusive, and it is immaterial to inquire into the object of the annexation (*Wake* v. *Hall, ante,* 8 App. Cas., at p. 204). As regards trade fixtures, the article affixed is deemed to be a fixture if it is placed in its position permanently and in order to make the land or building more valuable for the special purpose for which it is used (*Hobson* v. *Gorringe, ante*) ; but although the effect of such an annexation may be to make the article a fixture, the question whether a tenant can, as between landlord and tenant, remove it at the end of the tenancy is determined by other considerations.

Where machinery is a fixture, portions of it which are removable, but which are an essential part of it, are also fixtures (*Sheffield and South Yorkshire P.B. Society* v. *Harrison* (1884), 15 Q.B.D. 358 ; see also s. 62 of the L.P.A. 1925, at p. 511). But in *Jordan* v. *May* [1947] K.B. 427, although a generating plant was held to be a fixture, storage batteries attached to it by wires were considered not to be so essential a part of it as to be themselves fixtures.

As between vendor and purchaser.—When a vendor occupies the property sold, he must not, in the absence of a condition to the contrary, after signing the contract, remove any fixtures annexed to the property, although they may be such as, between landlord and tenant, could be removed (*Gibson* v. *Hammersmith & City Railway Co.* (1863), 32 L.J. Ch. 337 ; *Colegrave* v. *Dias Santos* (1823), 2 B. & C. 76 ; see also Adkin and Bowen on Fixtures, 3rd ed., pp. 127, 128). In *Phillips* v. *Lamdin* [1949] 2 K.B. 33, at the time when a purchaser viewed the property it contained an ornate door matching a mantelpiece which was attributed to the design of the brothers Adam. The vendor removed the door before the purchaser took possession and substituted a plain one. It was held that the vendor must replace the door. Similarly, growing crops pass to the purchaser, subject to the right of the vendor to gather them in proper course of husbandry before the proper time for completion (*Webster* v. *Donaldson* (1865), 11 Jur. (N.S.) 404). A vendor is not entitled, in the absence of provision in the contract, to remove, or to require the purchaser to pay for, timber or other trees, or, apparently, such things as rose trees and herbaceous plants. There is occasional doubt as to whether an external television aerial fixed to a chimney stack or a roof passes to a purchaser as a fixture. As they can usually be detached without damage many vendors remove them or call for payment of their value although it could possibly be argued that they are fixtures.

If, therefore, the vendor intends that the purchaser shall pay for fixtures in addition to the property, he should be careful to see that the contract contains a clear condition on the point. There are several ways of providing for the payment for the fixtures, but it is probably best to state in the contract the amount which the purchaser is to pay for the fixtures. A condition that chattels (or, presumably, fixtures) shall be paid for at a valuation to be determined by the vendor's agent as sole valuer should *not*, in the opinion of the Council of The Law Society, be inserted (*Law Society's Gazette*, vol. 50, p. 308).

In determining what items pass with land on conveyance account must be taken of the L.P.A. 1925, s. 62 (*ante*, p. 511) by virtue of which a conveyance of land is deemed to include all " buildings, erections, fixtures." Neither the " fixtures " nor the word " erections " includes greenhouses which stand on their weight on dollies (*Dibble* v. *Moore* [1970] 2 Q.B. 181).

Gas fittings are not in practice treated as fixtures, though they may be included on a sale of a house with " fixtures " (*Sewell* v. *Angerstein* (1868), 18 L.T. 300). Electric lamps are not fixtures (*British Economical Lamp Co.* v. *Empire, Mile End, Ltd.* (1913), 29 T.L.R. 386).

Assignment or mortgage of fixtures.—An *assignment or mortgage* of the following articles, even if they are described in a schedule, need not be registered as a bill of sale, as they are not " *trade machinery* " within the meaning of s. 5 of the Bills of Sale Act, 1878 ; that is to say :—

(*a*) Fixed motive power, such as water wheels, steam engines, steam boilers, donkey engines, and other fixed appurtenances of the said motive powers ;

(*b*) Fixed power machinery, such as shafts, wheels, drums and their fixed appurtenances, which transmit the action of the motive powers to the other machinery, fixed and loose ; and

(*c*) Pipes for steam, gas and water in a factory or workshop (see *Topham* v. *Greenside Glazed Fire-brick Co., Ltd.* (1887), 37 Ch. D. 281).

As between mortgagee and mortgagor.—Fixtures pass to a mortgagee, whether legal or equitable, of the land, and whether they were attached before or after the mortgage ; a mortgagor, even though in possession of the land, has no right to remove " tenant's " fixtures. But if fixtures have been attached after the date of the mortgage under an agreement with the mortgagor which allows a third party to remove them in certain events, that third party may be permitted to do so even against the mortgagee. See *post*, p. 530. What are fixtures must, for this purpose, be determined by the general rules given above at p. 527. Thus, in *Vaudeville Electric Cinema, Ltd.* v. *Muriset* [1923] 2 Ch. 74, seats in a cinema which were fixed to the floor by screws were considered as fixtures so attached to the land as to pass with the land by a mortgage deed, although they were not referred to in the deed. This case should be contrasted with that of *Lyon & Co.* v. *London City and Midland Bank* [1903] 2 K.B. 135. In the latter case the chairs attached to the floor of a place of entertainment were the property of a person who let them out for hire, and they were only so let out for hire for a comparatively short time, and, therefore, the annexation or fixing of the chairs to the building could never have been intended to have the effect of depriving the person who let them out of his property, and make them the property of the person who was hiring them. Consequently, they were held *not* to be fixtures. The two cases show that the question turns less on *how* articles are attached than on the *intention* with which they were attached.

In *Hulme* v. *Brigham* [1943] K.B. 152, it was held that printing machines, not attached to the freehold but secured by their own weight, although attached to electric motors which, in turn, were attached to the freehold, did not pass to a mortgagee of the freehold.

Mortgagee selling fixtures apart from land.—A mortgagee could not under the power to sell the mortgaged property " or any part thereof," implied by the Conveyancing Act, 1881, and, therefore, cannot now under s. 101 (1) of the L.P.A. 1925, which contains the same words, sell trade machinery *apart* from the land to which it is affixed (*Re Yates; Batcheldor* v. *Yates* (1888), 38 Ch. D. 112). If, however, the fixtures are mentioned and assigned, and further dominion is given over the fixtures than a mortgage without mention of them would give (for instance, if an express power be given to sell them separately from the land), the deed will be void as regards such fixtures for want of registration as a bill of sale (*Small* v. *National Provincial Bank of England* [1894] 1 Ch. 686). The position is the same where the mention of the fixtures has the effect of carrying *more* fixtures than would pass without the mention of them (*Re Brooke* [1894] 2 Ch. 600). The rule applies to freeholds as well as leaseholds (*Johns* v. *Ware* [1899] 1 Ch. 359). The deed would not be void *in toto*, but only as regards the fixtures so mentioned and assigned (*Re Burdett, ex parte Byrne* (1888), 58 L.T. 708 ; *Re Isaacson* [1895] 1 Q.B. 333).

The above statement is not affected by s. 88 (4) and s. 89 (4) of the L.P.A. 1925, which provide in effect that where a mortgage includes fixtures, any statutory power of sale and any right to foreclose or take possession is to extend to the absolute or other interest therein affected by the charge. These subsections only mean that when the fixtures are sold with the land the mortgagee can give a good title thereto.

Mortgages of land and fixtures the subject of a hiring agreement.— If the property on which a trade fixture has been affixed is in *mortgage*, further questions may arise as to whether such fixture can, if the mortgagee objects, be removed from the property.

It is now settled that a mortgage of freehold or leasehold land on which is affixed, at the date of the mortgage, a trade fixture belonging to a third party, placed there under a hiring agreement of which he had no notice, can take possession of the fixture under his mortgage, and hold it against the original unpaid owner (*Hobson* v. *Gorringe* [1897] 1 Ch. 182, followed in *Reynolds* v. *Ashby & Son* [1904] A.C. 466 ; *Ellis* v. *Glover & Hobson, Ltd.* [1908] 1 K.B. 388). If the fixture is affixed *after* the date of the mortgage, and the mortgage can be taken to have authorised its removal, as, for instance, if the agreement is one usual in the mortgagor's trade, the person who has let it on hire can take it away so long as the mortgagor remains in possession (*Gough* v. *Wood* [1894] 1 Q.B. 713) ; but this right comes to an end immediately the mortgagee takes possession (*Hobson* v. *Gorringe, ante ; Reynolds* v. *Ashby & Son, ante*). But the person who has let it on hire would not have such a right if the mortgagor had entered into a covenant with the mortgagee not to remove anything from the land (*Ellis* v. *Glover and*

Hobson, Ltd., ante). As to what will amount to a taking of possession for the above purposes, see *Re Morrison, Jones & Taylor, Ltd.* [1914] 1 Ch. 50.

The above rule only applies as between the mortgagee and a third party. If the fixture is the property of the mortgagor and has been affixed by him, although only for the purposes of his trade, it will not be removable by him as against his own mortgagee *(Gough* v. *Wood, ante).* There appears to be an exception in the case of a mortgagor removing fixtures in the ordinary way of carrying on his business. For instance, a nurseryman would be allowed to sell and remove his plants, trees and shrubs, on the ground that the mortgagee by leaving the mortgagor in possession impliedly authorised him to carry on his business (*ibid.*; *Huddersfield Banking Co.* v. *Lister* [1895] 2 Ch. 273).

In the case of a mere floating charge, the mortgagee only gets a right to seize the property existing at the time when payment is enforced. Where, therefore, fixtures had been sold before a bank's charge had crystallised, it was held that they had thereby passed to the purchaser and that the bank had no claim (*Hamer* v. *London, City & Midland Bank, Ltd.* (1918), 118 L.T. 571).

If the mortgagor becomes bankrupt it would appear that trade fixtures put up since the date of the mortgage, so far as they are affixed to the freehold, go with it to the mortgagee and not to the trustee in bankruptcy (*Climie* v. *Wood* (1868), L.R. 3 Ex. 257 ; (1869), L.R. 4 Ex. 328).

If a mortgagor being in possession lets the property to a tenant and the tenant brings trade fixtures on to the property, the fixtures remain the property of the tenant even though the mortgagee takes possession (*Sanders* v. *Davis* (1885), 15 Q.B.D. 218).

In the case of an equitable mortgage, the equitable rights created by a hire-purchase agreement have priority over the equitable rights of a subsequent equitable mortgagee (*Re Samuel Allen & Sons, Ltd.* [1907] 1 Ch. 575 ; *Re Morrison, Jones & Taylor, Ltd.* [1914] 1 Ch. 50).

CHAPTER FOURTEEN

HABENDUM

PART 1. FORM AND CONSTRUCTION OF HABENDUM

General rule for construction.—Before considering some of the chief rules for the construction of the habendum, the reader is asked to bear in mind a most important and sometimes overriding rule, namely, that a deed must be construed in such manner that each part of it may, if possible, be effectual. As was said in an old case : " Every part of the deed ought to be compared with the other and one entire sense ought to be made thereof " (*Throckmerton* v. *Tracy* (1555), 1 Plow. 145, at p. 161). So, repugnant words may be rejected. " The result of all the authorities is that when a court of law can clearly collect from the language within the four corners of the deed or instrument in writing the real intention of the parties, they are bound to give effect to it by supplying anything necessarily to be inferred from the terms used, and by rejecting as superfluous whatever is repugnant to the intention so discerned . . ." : per Kelly, C.B., in *Gwyn* v. *Neath Canal Co.* (1868), L.R. 3 Ex. 209, at p. 215.

Function of the habendum.—It was never essential to have an habendum in a deed, and, before 1926, it was incorrect to have an habendum in a deed which operated merely by declaration of use, such as a deed purporting to exercise a power of appointment, a covenant to stand seised, or a bargain and sale.

When an habendum is used, its primary function is to fix the *quantum* of the estate which the grantee is to have. The premises fix what property is to pass and the habendum the estate therein to be taken by the grantee. Where the deed contained no habendum, the grantee took the *quantum* of estate mentioned in the premises (*Goodtitle d. Dodwell* v. *Gibbs* (1826), 5 B. & C. 709) ; but if no *quantum* was mentioned, he took an estate for life by implication of law (*Altham's Case* (1610), 8 Co. Rep. 150*b* ; *Re Whiston's Settlement* [1894] 1 Ch. 661). Since 1925, if no *quantum* is mentioned, the fee simple, or other the whole interest of the grantor, will pass unless a contrary intention appears (L.P.A. 1925, s. 60 (1) ; see *post*, p. 537). Despite this, it is a useful practice still to include an habendum, such as " To hold the property unto the Purchaser in fee simple," or other appropriate words, for two reasons. First, it makes the parties' intentions explicit, so preventing a contrary intention from inadvertently appearing on a construction of the deed as a whole. Secondly, it prevents any questions arising as to the application of the usual implied covenants for title (see *May* v. *Platt* [1900] 1 Ch. 616 and *post*, p. 537).

Habendum not to abridge the estate granted by the premises.—It would appear that although the habendum will be allowed to carry the limitation of the estate farther than the premises do, it will not be allowed to *abridge* the estate *expressly granted by the premises*. Thus, in *Kendal* v. *Micfield* (1740), Barn, Ch. Rep. 46, an estate was granted to *A* for life, habendum to him and his heirs, and it was held that the fee simple passed ; but where the estate was granted to *A* and his heirs, habendum to *A* for life, the habendum was held to be void, as repugnant in attempting to limit a smaller estate than that already granted by the premises (*Throckmerton* v. *Tracy* (1555), 1 Plow. 145). So, a grant to *M & Co.*, their heirs, successors and assigns, to hold unto and to the use of *M & Co.*, their successors and assigns (without the word " heirs "), was held to convey the fee (*Re Fayle and The Irish Feather Company's Contract* [1918] 1 Ir. R. 13).

But where no estate is expressly granted by the premises the case is different. For " if by your premises you have given no certain nor express estate than that otherwise the law would give, you may alter and abridge, nay, you may utterly frustrate it by the habendum " (*Stukeley* v. *Butler* (1614), Hob. 168).

It is stated in Norton on Deeds, 2nd ed., p. 317, that : " If words of limitation are added to the grantee's name both in the premises and in the habendum, the limitation in the habendum will, if possible, be considered as explanatory of that in the premises ; but if the limitations are repugnant, the estate given by the premises *cannot be abridged* by the habendum." It is further there stated that : " This rule only applies where there are words of limitation added to the grantee's name in the premises."

Where a grant was made to *A* and his heirs, habendum to *A* and the heirs of his body, it was held that *A* took an estate tail (*Altham's Case* (1610), 8 Co. Rep. 150b). At first sight, this case seems to contradict the rule that the habendum must not restrict the estate given in the premises, for *A* got the fee simple in the premises; which estate was restricted by the habendum to an estate tail ; but apparently the case came within the other part of the rule, namely, that the habendum explained *what* heirs were intended.

Habendum may not extend parcels.—A result of the rule that the office of the habendum is to limit the *quantum* of estate is that it *cannot introduce any new parcels*. Therefore, if more parcels are enumerated in the habendum than are comprised in the grant, the habendum will be void as to such additional parcels (Norton on Deeds, 2nd ed., p. 311). The rule does not affect such parcels as are *in effect included* in the grant, although they are only specifically included in the habendum. The example given in Preston on Abstracts, at p. 40, is ; " If there be a grant of a manor, with the appurtenances, an advowson which is appendant will pass inclusively ; and though the habendum be in these words, ' to hold the manor together with the advowson,' the advowson will be effectually granted by force of the grant, and not of the habendum ; for it was in effect comprehended in the granting part or premises of the deed." Again, it would appear that the expression in the habendum of what would in any case be implied into the premises (e.g., under the L.P.A. 1925, s. 62) may, within the general rule for construction, simply serve to make the parties' intentions clear (see *Gregg* v. *Richards* [1926] 1 Ch. 521, 533).

On the other hand, the omission of any parcels mentioned in the premises out of the habendum will leave the deed to operate as if there had not been any habendum as regards those premises.

Different grantee in habendum and premises.—If no person is mentioned as grantee in the premises, the person mentioned as grantee in the habendum takes the estate limited by the habendum (*Butler* v. *Dodton* (1579), Cary 86, at p. 122 ; Norton on Deeds, 2nd ed., p. 310).

Where a person was mentioned as grantee in the premises, another person mentioned in the habendum but not in the premises could not take an immediate interest in the land granted ; but he could take an estate in remainder or by way of use declared on the estate limited in the habendum (*Sammes' Case* (1609), 13 Co. Rep. 54 ; Norton on Deeds, p. 287 ; 2nd ed., p. 314). For instance, a demise to *A*, habendum to *A* and *B*, carried the whole estate to *A*, and *B* got nothing (*Reynold* v. *Kingman* (1587), Cro. Eliz. 115) ; but a conveyance to *A* and his heirs, to hold to the use of *A* and *B* and their heirs as tenants in common, before 1926, gave *A* and *B* legal estates under the Statutes of Uses (*Sammes' Case, ante ; Lowcock* v. *Overseers of Broughton* (1884), 12 Q.B.D. 369).

Registered conveyancing.—No habendum is included in the prescribed form of transfer of registered freehold land (see L.R.R. 1925, Sched., Form 19). Words fixing the *quantum* of the estate to be taken by the transferee do not need to be incorporated into such a transfer. What is expressed to be transferred is " the land comprised in the title above mentioned " and this means the fee simple, not because of the L.P.A. 1925, s. 60 (1), but because only freehold land will be comprised in such title. The prescribed form of transfer of registered leasehold land is the same with the addition of " for the residue of the term granted by the registered lease " (*ibid.*, Form 32).

Limitation to commence from a future date.—Feoffments, grants and other assurances at common law did not admit of a limitation to commence *in futuro*, except by way of terms of years, or by way of remainder expectant on a prior *vested estate* of freehold. At common law, that is to say, there had to be continuous seisin. Therefore, such future limitations of freehold interests were void. But covenants to stand seised to uses, and bargains and sales, and trusts, did admit of such future limitations. The reason why a deed made to operate as a covenant to stand seised to uses, or a bargain and sale, could be limited to commence *in futuro*, was that the freehold remained with the covenantor, or with the bargainor, and thus the freehold was not placed in abeyance. Terms of years could always on their creation be limited to commence *in futuro*.

A grant " unto and to the use of *A* and his heirs, to commence one year from the date of the grant," being a common-law grant, and not a grant operating under the Statute of Uses (see at p. 540), was void as infringing the rule at common law (*Boddington* v. *Robinson* (1875), L.R. 10 Ex. 270 ; *Savill Brothers, Ltd.* v. *Bethell* [1902] 2 Ch. 523) ; whereas a grant to *A* and his heirs, to the use of *B* and his heirs, to commence one year from the date of the grant was perfectly good as it operated under the Statute of Uses (*Buckhurst Peerage Case* (1876), 2 App. Cas. 1 ; *Savill Brothers, Ltd.* v. *Bethell, ante*).

But there is another rule, under which sometimes the difficulty was overcome, namely, that if the habendum is void, but the premises contain an express limitation, the habendum will be rejected, and the grant in the premises will operate. For instance, in the leading case of *Goodtitle d. Dodwell* v. *Gibbs* (1826), 5 B. & C. 709, the conveyance was to a person and his heirs, to hold to him, his heirs and assigns after the death of another person, and it was held that the habendum was void as purporting to give an estate *in futuro*, and was therefore rejected, but it was further held that the express grant *in præsenti* operated. See more fully in Norton on Deeds, 2nd ed., pp. 308, 309, 423–425 ; Challis, Real Property, 3rd ed., p. 104 *et seq.*

Lands and interests therein are now incapable of being conveyed by feoffment, or by bargain and sale (L.P.A. 1925, s. 51 (1)), but the old law, as to common-law grants *in futuro* being void, still remains good. And, as the Statute of Uses has been repealed, a *legal estate* to commence from a future date can no longer be created under that statute. See also s. 1 (1) (*a*) of the L.P.A. 1925 by which a fee simple absolute must take effect in possession to be a legal estate. As, however, by s. 4 (1) of the L.P.A. 1925, all interests in land which under the Statute of Uses could have been created as legal estates can now be created as equitable interests, it follows that *equitable interests* may be created to take effect from a future date.

See *post*, p. 811, as to the provision in s. 149 of the L.P.A. 1925 that terms of years absolute to commence from a future date are capable of taking effect at law or in equity from the date fixed for the commencement of the term without actual entry.

Conveyance subject to restrictive covenants.—A purchaser is entitled to have the conveyance expressed to be subject only to the restrictive covenants (if any) referred to in the contract, even though the purchaser will become bound by other covenants (*Hardman* v. *Child* (1885), 28 Ch. D. 712 ; *Re Wallis and Barnard's Contract* [1899] 2 Ch. 515 ; *Re Cooper and Crondace's Contract* (1904), 90 L.T. 258).

Where easements over the land sold have previously been granted or reserved the habendum should be expressed to be subject to those easements. A repetition of a reservation in an earlier deed is mistaken and might even grant additional rights to a third party. See the discussion of the unreported decision in *Scotson* v. *Jones* in the *Law Times*, vol. 231, p. 187, but compare *Re Dances Way, West Town, Hayling Island* [1962] Ch. 490 in which the Court of Appeal emphasised that the phrase " Excepting and reserving . . ." is not necessarily of such significance that it will govern the construction of all that immediately follows so as to convert existing rights into new grants.

Conveyance by a person to himself solely or jointly.—A person may now convey land to or vest land in himself (L.P.A. 1925, s. 72 (3)). Before 1926 the interposition of a trustee to uses was necessary to effect this. See further *post*, p. 541.

Since 12th August, 1859, *leaseholds* could and can be assigned by a person to himself jointly with another person by the like means by which they might be assigned by him to another person (L.P.A. 1925, s. 72 (1), replacing s. 21 of the Law of Property (Amendment) Act, 1859).

In conveyances made after 31st December, 1881, freehold land, or a thing in action, could and can be conveyed by a person to himself jointly with another person, by the like means by which it might be conveyed by him to another person (L.P.A. 1925, s. 72 (2), replacing s. 50 of the Convey-ancing Act, 1881). Before that date the conveyance was effected by the interposition of a trustee to uses.

It should be noted, however, that notwithstanding s. 72 and despite the wide definitions of " conveyance " and " convey " in the L.P.A. 1925 (s. 205

(1) (ii)), the House of Lords has decided that it is still not possible in law for one person to grant a lease of land to himself or for two or more persons to grant a lease of land to all of themselves in any circumstances (*Rye* v. *Rye* [1962] A.C. 496). The primary reason for this decision appeared to be that contractual obligations are necessarily involved in a lease and require a difference in parties for there to be any enforcement.

Conveyance by two or more persons to one or more of themselves.— Two or more persons (whether or not being trustees or personal representatives) may convey any property vested in them to any one or more of themselves in like manner as they could have conveyed such property to a third party ; provided that if the persons in whose favour the conveyance is made are, by reason of any fiduciary relationship or otherwise, precluded from validly carrying out the transaction, the conveyance will be liable to be set aside (L.P.A. 1925, s. 72 (4)).

In connection with this subject, reference may be made to s. 36 (2) of the L.P.A. 1925, which expressly reserves the rights of a joint tenant to release his interest to the other joint tenant or joint tenants. The question has been raised whether a sale by one joint tenant to another is voidable by reason of the fact that it would be a case of one trustee selling to another trustee and so come within the latter part of s. 72 (4), above. Thus it was held at first instance in *Green* v. *Whitehead* [1930] 1 Ch. 38 that statutory trustees came within the rule that a joint tenant who is a statutory trustee must himself exercise his discretionary powers as a trustee and cannot delegate them to another. But as the trustees are also the beneficial owners, the sale can be carried out alternatively and effectively as a sale by one beneficiary to another (see *Cooper* v. *Critchley* [1955] 1 Ch. 431 as to the form of the contract). The equitable title of the trustee beneficiary would have to be recited. The transaction would be carried out by a release under s. 36 (2) of the L.P.A. 1925, on the execution of which the trust for sale would automatically come to an end under s. 23 of the L.P.A. 1925. A form of release is given in Hallett's Conveyancing Precedents, at p. 278, under the title " Conveyance on sale by one of two joint tenants to the other of his share in the proceeds of sale." See further, *Law Journal*, vol. 101, p. 384.

Husband and wife.—A conveyance to a husband and wife will take effect as if they were two persons (L.P.A. 1925, s. 37). See note " Tenancy by Entireties," at p. 304, and see also p. 305. A husband may convey property to his wife, and a wife may convey property to her husband (L.P.A. 1925, s. 72 (2)).

Before the Married Women's Property Act, 1882, a grant of freeholds by a husband to a wife or by a wife to her husband was void unless a trustee or grantee to uses was interposed ; and an assignment of leaseholds was also void unless the husband had constituted himself a trustee (*Baddeley* v. *Baddeley* (1878), 9 Ch. D. 113 ; *Fox* v. *Hawks* (1879), 13 Ch. D. 822 ; *Re Breton's Estate* (1881), 17 Ch. D. 416). See also p. 359.

Limitation to an infant.—An infant cannot hold a legal estate (L.P.A. 1925, s. 1 (6)). But a conveyance may be made by mistake to an infant, either beneficially or as a trustee, or as a mortgagee, and in any of these cases alone or jointly with a person of full age. The effect of such a conveyance is discussed at p. 336 *et seq.*

PART 2. WORDS OF LIMITATION

Words of limitation not now necessary to pass the fee simple.—
A conveyance (which includes a mortgage, charge, assent, vesting declaration, vesting instrument, disclaimer, release, and every other assurance of property by an instrument except a will ; L.P.A. 1925, s. 205 (1) (ii)) of freehold land executed after 1925 to any person without words of limitation, or any equivalent expression, will pass to the grantee the fee simple or other the whole interest which the grantor had power to convey in such land, *unless a contrary intention appears* in the conveyance (L.P.A. 1925, s. 60 (1)). In view of the words, "unless a contrary intention appears," it is best to continue the practice of using the expression " in fee simple," so as to make it clear that it is intended to pass the fee. It may also be advisable to include the words to ensure that the covenants for title are implied. The L.P.A. 1925, s. 76 (1), *ante*, p. 467, refers to the subject-matter *expressed* to be conveyed. By virtue of s. 60 (1), the subject-matter expressed to be conveyed is the fee simple *or other the whole interest of the grantor* and some conveyancers argue that the subsection will not operate fully (i.e., to protect the grantee in case the grantor has only some lesser interest than the fee simple) unless the words " in fee simple " (or other appropriate words) are used.

A grant to " *A* and his heirs " would still be effective to pass the fee simple (*Re McElligott* [1944] Ch. 216), but the form is obsolete.

Before 1926, a conveyance of freehold land to an individual, as distinguished from a corporation, without words of limitation, passed only an estate for life (*Re Hudson ; Kuhne* v. *Hudson* (1895), 72 L.T. 892 ; *Re Whiston's Settlement* [1894] 1 Ch. 661). To pass the fee simple to an individual by a deed before 1882, the necessary words of limitation were " and his heirs." Even the word " heir " in the singular would not have been sufficient, and would only have created an estate for life (*Chambers* v. *Taylor* (1836), 2 Myl. & Cr. 376 ; *Re Davison's Settlement ; Cattermole Davison* v. *Munby* [1913] 2 Ch. 498). So, a conveyance " to the use of *A* and his children," or " to the use of *A* and his issue," or " to the use of *A* and his assigns for ever," passed merely a life estate. From 1882 to 1926, by virtue of s. 51 of the Conveyancing Act, 1881, the words " in fee simple " were sufficient to pass the fee simple to an individual although the word " heirs " was still effectual. But the words " *in fee* " without the additional word " *simple* " were not sufficient and passed only an estate for life (*Re Ethell and Mitchell & Butler's Contract* [1901] 1 Ch. 945).

If, however, a purchaser through a mistake of this kind acquired by the conveyance a less estate at law than he was entitled to under the contract, he was, in equity, entitled to have the conveyance rectified by the court (*Re Ethell's Contract, ante*). Further, a document, such as a settlement, may be rectified by the insertion of appropriate words of limitation necessary to carry out the intention of the parties if there is sufficient evidence of that intention ; and the terms of the document itself may alone provide such sufficient evidence although there is no extrinsic evidence of intention (*Banks* v. *Ripley* [1940] Ch. 719).

But there were always certain special kinds of documents which by their nature or by statutory provision did not require words of limitation to pass to an individual the legal fee simple. For instance, no words of limitation were required in the following cases :—

(1) A release by one joint tenant to another.

(2) A release by one partner to another.

(3) A partition between co-partners.

(4) A vesting declaration under s. 12 of the Trustee Act, 1893 (re-enacting s. 34 of the Conveyancing Act, 1881), now s. 40 (3) of the T.A. 1925.

(5) A statutory transfer of mortgage under s. 27 of the Conveyancing Act, 1881, now replaced by s. 118 (1) of the L.P.A. 1925.

(6) An assurance of personal property subject to a trust for conversion into realty (*Re Monckton's Settlement* [1913] 2 Ch. 636).

Effect of transitional provisions.—It is provided by Sched. 1, Pt. II, para. 3, to the L.P.A. 1925 that " where immediately after [1925] any person is entitled, subject or not to the payment of the costs of tracing the title and of conveyance, to require any legal estate (not vested in trustees for sale) to be conveyed to or otherwise vested in him, such legal estate shall, by virtue of this Part of this Schedule, vest in manner hereinafter provided." In effect, para. 6 (*d*) of the same Part enacts that the legal estate affected shall vest in the person of full age who, immediately after 1925, is entitled (subject or not to the payment of costs) to require the legal estate to be vested in him, but subject to any mortgage term subsisting or created by the Act.

If in a conveyance of freehold property executed before 1926 the necessary words of limitation were by mistake omitted, the purchaser obtained only an estate for life, but was entitled to have the conveyance rectified (*Fitzgerald* v. *Fitzgerald* [1902] 1 Ir. R. 477 and see above). It has been argued that such a purchaser became entitled, on 1st January, 1926, to the benefit of paras. 3 and 6 (*d*) and so the legal estate (i.e., the fee simple absolute in possession) which remained vested in the vendor passed to the purchaser, and no action for rectification or any conveyance was necessary to put matters right. But doubts have been expressed (e.g., in Williams, Contract of Sale of Land, p. 207) on the ground that it cannot be said that the equitable owner is entitled to have the legal estate vested in him, as an order of court directing rectification is required before he will be in that position.

Absence of words of limitation in transfer of equitable interest.— As a general rule in the case of an *executed* trust the same strict words of limitation had to be used before 1926 in order to create an equitable estate in fee simple or fee tail as if a legal estate were being limited (*Re Bostock's Settlement* [1921] 2 Ch. 469). It has long been held that in an *executory* trust, however, strict words of limitation were not essential and equity would, even before 1926, look to the true intention of the settlor and order the final trust to be created by words appropriate to carry out that intention. In *Re Arden ; Short* v. *Camm* [1935] Ch. 326, the word " absolutely " had been used in an appointment, made in 1901, of an equitable interest. The appointment constituted an executed trust, but nevertheless Clauson, J., held that the word " absolutely " showed that the limitation was not framed in strict conveyancing language, and, consequently, that it was sufficient that the instrument should disclose a clear intention as to the *quantum* of interest intended to be given. The learned judge therefore held that an equitable fee simple passed. It will be noted that the same problem will not arise on limitations made after 1925 (L.P.A. 1925, s. 60 (1), p. 537).

Abolition of the rule in Shelley's Case.—The rule in *Shelley's Case* was that " Where the ancestor takes an estate of freehold, whether by limitation or resulting use, and in the same instrument an estate is limited by way of remainder, either mediately or immediately, to his ' heirs ' or ' heirs of the body,' the word ' heirs ' is a word of limitation and not of purchase, and therefore the ancestor takes an estate in fee simple or in tail, as the case may be " (Norton on Deeds, 2nd ed., pp. 354, 355).

The simplest example is a gift to *A B* for his life and after his decease to his heirs, which formerly gave *A B* a fee simple estate which he might alienate by deed or will so that his heir might not take any interest. Similarly a gift to *A B* for his life and after his decease to the heirs of his body gave *A B* an estate tail which he could bar. The rule had no application to the old form of limitation of the fee simple, that is, " to *A* and his heirs," in which case no interest was expressed to be given to the heirs (*Re McElligott* [1944] Ch. 216). Similarly, the rule did not apply to a limitation, in the customary form of settlement, to a person for life with remainder to his first and other sons successively according to seniority in tail male. In such a case (as has always been thought) the person mentioned took a life interest and the sons entailed interests as purchasers (*Re Williams' Will Trusts* [1952] Ch. 828).

The test was whether the word " heirs " was used as a general term including all who could inherit from the ancestor, or as a specific description of an individual to be ascertained at the ancestor's death ; in the latter case the rule did not apply. Thus, in *Re Routledge* [1942] Ch. 457, Bennet, J., held that the rule did not apply to a limitation " to the use of the heirs male of the body of [a person] living at his decease, his heirs and assigns for ever," as the wording showed that the object of the gift was to be ascertained at a particular point of time.

The rule is rendered obsolete (except as to deeds executed, or wills in operation, before 1926) by the L.P.A. 1925, s. 131, which provides as follows :—

" 131. Where by any instrument coming into operation after [1925] an interest in any property is expressed to be given to the heir or heirs or issue or any particular heir or any class of the heirs or issue of any person in words which, but for this section, would, under the rule of law known as the rule in Shelley's case, have operated to give to that person an interest in fee simple or *an entailed interest*, such *words shall operate in equity as words of purchase and not of limitation*, and shall be construed and have effect accordingly, and in the case of an interest in any property expressed to be given to an heir or heirs or any particular heir or class of heirs, *the same person or persons shall take as would in the case of freehold land have answered that description under the general* law in force before [1926]."

The effect of the section is that the word " heir " and the other words in the section will have the effect of conferring on the person or persons coming within such expressions, as ascertained by the old canons of descent, an absolute gift of the property. The section relates to property, not merely to land, by reason of the assimilation effected by s. 130.

Although an estate for life is now only an equitable interest, s. 131 will apply, if following the grant of such interest, the remainder is limited to the " heirs " or " heirs of the body " of the grantee. In such a case the ancestor will take a life interest with remainder to the appropriate heir, the land becoming settled land.

Conveyance to corporation.—The necessity for appropriate words of limitation on a conveyance to a corporation sole before 1926, and the present rule, are discussed *ante*, p. 314.

No words of limitation were ever required to pass an estate in fee simple in the case of a *corporation aggregate*. The words " successors or assigns," or " in fee simple," were often used, but they were meaningless (*Re Woking Urban District Council* [1914] 1 Ch. 300, 307 ; *Re Albert Road* [1916] 1 Ch. 289).

PART 3. STATUTE OF USES

General effect of the Statute of Uses.—The history leading up to the passing of the Statute of Uses is of insufficient practical importance to be given here. The effect of the statute, in its simplest form, and reading the singular to include the plural, was that where any person was *seised* of hereditaments to the use of [that is, on trust for] any *other* person or corporation, such other person or corporation was deemed to be seised of the like estate in the hereditaments that they had in the use [that is, they obtained a legal estate instead of a mere equitable estate].

The first point which will be noted is that the grantee to uses had to be *seised*, that is, have an estate of freehold. This at once excluded copyholds and leaseholds from the operation of the statute, and left them to be governed by the rules of common law. Therefore, uses declared in respect thereof only passed equitable estates. For instance, an assignment of an existing term of years to *A*, to the use of *B*, vested the legal estate in *A*, while the declaration of the use gave *B* merely an equitable estate. But a term of years could be created by a declaration of use on an estate of freehold. For instance, if a fee simple was limited to *A* and his heirs, to the use of *B* for a term of years, *B* got the legal estate in the term of years by the statute, because *A*, the grantee, *was* seised for an estate of freehold to the use of *B* (*Fox's Case* (1609), 8 Rep. 93*f*).

The next point to note is that the statute was confined to cases where one person was seised to the use of *another* person. Therefore, a grant to " *A* and his heirs, to the use of *B* and his heirs," vested the legal estate in *B*. But the ordinary limitation in a conveyance of freeholds, namely, " to *A* and his heirs, to the use of *A* and his heirs," or " unto and to the use of *A* and his heirs," or " in fee simple," vested the legal estate in *A*, by the rules of common law and not by force of the statute (*Orme's Case* (1872), L.R. 8 C.P. 281 ; *Savill Bros., Ltd.* v. *Bethell* [1902] 2 Ch. 523).

Case law engrafted an exception on the rule that to come within the statute one person must be seised to the use of another person, in the case where the estate declared in the grantee's favour by the uses was *less* than that which would be taken at common law by the same grant. For instance, in the case of a grant to *A* and his heirs to the use of himself and the heirs of his body, at common law he took the fee simple on the ground that by virtue of the premises, before the habendum came into operation, the grantee became seised of the fee simple, and, therefore, the limitation in the habendum of a lesser estate would be rejected as repugnant, but case law made the rule that the declared estate should apply, and that his estate should be thereby limited to an estate tail (*Sammes' Case* (1609), 13 Co. Rep. 54).

On the other hand, if the estate declared by the use was a larger estate than the estate of which the grantee to uses was seised, the *cestui que use* only got an estate equivalent to the estate of which the grantee was seised (*Orme's Case, ante*), because the uses flowed from the " seisin," which word means " an estate of freehold." Therefore, a grant to *A* simply (without the word " heirs "), to the use of *B* and his heirs, gave *B* only an estate for the life of *A*. This rule applied only where the estate was taken under the statute, that is, where the grantee to uses and the *cestui que use* were different persons (*Jenkins* v. *Younge* (1631), Cro. Car. 230). Where they were the same persons, the grant operated as we have seen, at common law, and a grant to *A* simply, to the use of *A* and his heirs, gave *A* the fee simple.

The doctrine that a *use must not be limited on a use* applied equally to a common-law conveyance as to a conveyance under the statute. For example, under a common-law conveyance, " unto and to the use of *A* and his heirs, to the use of *B* and his heirs," *A* took the legal estate and *B* only an equitable estate. So, by a conveyance under the statute " to *A* and his heirs, to the use of *B* and his heirs, to the use of *C* and his heirs," *B* took the legal estate and *C* the equitable estate (*Peacock* v. *Eastland* (1870), 22 L.T. 706).

A deed executed before 1926, purporting to exercise a power of appointment, should merely have declared the use, as the deed executing the power was construed as if written in the deed granting the power, and as one document. Therefore, if *A* having a power of appointment wished to exercise it in favour of *C*, *A* should merely have appointed that the hereditaments go, remain, and be to the use of *C* and his heirs ; in which case *C* took by virtue of the statute. Deeds exercising powers of appointment are often met with where, under similar circumstances, *A* appoints " unto and to the use of *C* and his heirs." This was an unscientific way of effecting the appointment, nevertheless *C* effectually got the estate, but under the common law and not by the statute (*Orme's Case* (1872), L.R. 8 C.P. 281).

If *A*, however, appointed unto *B* and his heirs, to the use of *C* (another person) and his heirs, *B* would take the legal estate under the statute, and *C* only an equitable interest, as the latter use would be a use on a use.

Another example of the different construction of a grant, whether construed at common law or under the statute, was a grant of an estate of freehold to commence from a future date. At common law a limitation to commence from a future date was generally void ; but such a limitation framed to take effect under the Statute of Uses would have been perfectly good.

The repeal of the Statute of Uses.—The Statute of Uses was repealed by the L.P.A. 1925, s. 207 and Sched. 7. A few changes in the law which may be of practical importance and which were made necessary by its repeal are here noted.

At common law a person could not convey land to or vest it in himself, but this could be effected by a conveyance to uses. It is now provided by s. 72 (3) of the L.P.A. 1925 that " After the commencement of this Act a person may convey land to or vest land in himself."

Before 1926, when it became necessary to execute a conveyance to confirm a title, the conveyance was made under the provisions of the Statute of Uses, that is by a conveyance to uses. It is now provided by s. 66 of the L.P.A. 1925 that a deed containing a declaration by the estate owner that his estate shall devolve in such a manner as may be requisite for confirming any interests intended to affect his estate and capable under the Act of subsisting as legal estates which, at some prior date, were expressed to have been transferred or created, and any dealings therewith which would have been legal if those interests had been legally and validly transferred or created, shall, to the extent of the estate of the estate owner, but without prejudice to the restrictions imposed by the Act in the case of mortgages, operate to give legal effect to the interests so expressed to have been transferred or created and to the subsequent dealings aforesaid. A form of deed for confirming legal estates which have not been validly created is given in Sched. 5 to the L.P.A. 1925, and is Form No. 7 therein.

Before 1926, if there was no consideration, it was necessary to use the words " unto *and to the use of* " in the operative part of a conveyance to a stranger in order to prevent a resulting use to the grantor which would have been executed by the Statute of Uses with the consequence that no estate would have passed to the grantee. No resulting use occurred, however, if the voluntary assurance was in favour of a son or other person towards whom the grantor stood *in loco parentis* (*Re Luby's Estate* (1908), 43 Ir. L.T. 141). Resulting uses cannot now be created, for a legal estate cannot pass by implication. There can be a resulting trust, but it is provided by s. 60 (3) of the L.P.A. 1925 that " in a voluntary conveyance a resulting trust for the grantor shall not be implied merely by reason that the property is not expressed to be conveyed for the use or benefit of the grantee."

Before 1926 a reservation was not effective at law unless the deed was executed by the grantee or it was made by way of use under the Conveyancing Act, 1881, s. 62. As a result of the repeal of the Statute of Uses provision was made by the L.P.A. 1925, s. 65 (1), that a reservation shall be effective at law although the conveyance is not executed by the grantee. See *ante*, p. 494.

PART 4. IMPLIED ALL-ESTATE CLAUSE

The section of the L.P.A. 1925 dealing with the " *all-estate* " clause is given in full, as it may be important to refer to the exact words :—

" 63.—(1) Every conveyance is effectual to pass all the estate, right, title, interest, claim, and demand which the conveying parties respectively have, in, or on the property conveyed, or expressed or intended so to be, or which they respectively have power to convey in, to, or on the same.

(2) This section applies only if and as far as a contrary intention is not expressed in the conveyance, and has effect subject to the terms of the conveyance and to the provisions therein contained.

(3) This section applies to conveyances made after the thirty-first day of December, eighteen hundred and eighty-one."

When a person having several estates and interests in land joins in conveying all his estate and interest therein to a purchaser, every estate or interest vested in him will pass by that conveyance, although not vested in him in the character in which he was made a party to the conveyance (*Drew* v. *Earl of Norbury* (1846), 3 Jo. & Lat. 267, at p. 284 ; *Taylor* v. *London and County Banking Co.* [1901] 2 Ch. 231). Of course, the whole deed must be considered, and particularly the recitals, to determine the true intention. The case where difficulty most often arises is where the person conveying is entitled to one estate as trustee or as personal representative, and another as beneficiary. In *Fausset* v. *Carpenter* (1831), 2 Dow. & Cl. 232, the House of Lords decided that in such a case only the beneficial interest passed, on the ground that it could not have been intended to pass the trust interest, as to do so would have been a breach of trust. It is stated in Norton on Deeds, 2nd ed., p. 304, however that : " It is submitted that the decision in *Fausset* v. *Carpenter* is erroneous, as the fact of the conveyance by the trustee being a breach of trust did not appear on the face of the conveyance ; it was necessary to look out of the deed in order to ascertain that fact."

Although not decided on s. 63 support for the view in Norton is derived from the advice of the Judicial Committee of the Privy Council in *Byraj Nopani* v.

Pura Sundari Dasse (1914), 41 Indian Appeals 189. In that case an executor who was also beneficially interested in his testator's estate, together with other of the beneficiaries, sold and conveyed part of it to a purchaser. The executor did not purport to convey as executor, and the deed stated that all the estate, right and title of the vendor was conveyed. It was held that the effect of the deed was to pass to the purchaser the whole title vested in the executor, and that it was not proper to infer from the conduct of the parties that the intention was only to convey the beneficial interest, as such an inference would be contrary to the terms of the conveyance.

Section 63, however, may have its limitations. For instance, it was held in *Hanbury* v. *Bateman* [1920] 1 Ch. 313, on the similar section in the Conveyancing Act, 1881, that a deed purporting to *convey* would not have the effect of exercising a power of appointment, notwithstanding the fact that in the interpretation clause the word " conveyance " included " appointment." Sargant, J., did not think one could read the definition clause of the Act so as to provide that a conveyance should operate not only to convey everything that the person could convey, but also to appoint everything he could appoint. More recently in *Re Stirrup* [1961] 1 W.L.R. 449, Wilberforce, J., stated that s. 63 of the L.P.A. 1925, read in conjunction with the definition of " conveyance " in s. 205 (1) (ii) as including an assent, served " to produce the result that an assent, provided that it is under seal, is effective to pass whatever estate the conveying party has " (*Hanbury* v. *Bateman, ante,* was not apparently cited).

Registered conveyancing.—The L.R.A. 1925, ss. 20 (1) and 23 (1), provide that registration should confer on the proprietor the legal estate together with " the appropriate rights and interests which would, under the Law of Property Act, 1925, have been transferred if the land had not been registered." These words would appear wide enough to allow the " all-estate " clause to be implied as by s. 63 of the L.P.A. 1925.

CHAPTER FIFTEEN

COVENANTS

PART 1. COVENANTS GENERALLY

Covenants for title, see p. 466.

Covenants in leases, see chapter on Leases, *post*, p. 841.

Principles governing the enforceability of covenants.—A busy solicitor when confronted with a problem relating, for instance, to the enforceability of a restrictive covenant, is inclined to think solely of the detailed rules governing that branch of the law. An adequate appreciation of those rules and their correct application to the problem in question demand, however, that certain general principles shall be known and constantly borne in mind. Before proceeding to examine in some detail the law relating to covenants it may be of assistance to readers if these principles are summarised briefly (quotations are taken from Megarry & Wade, Law of Real Property, 3rd ed., p. 725 *et seq.*).

" 1. *If there is privity of contract, all covenants are enforceable.*"—This statement may appear to be too obvious to justify mention. On the other hand in framing covenants, particularly positive ones, it is as well to remember that the parties themselves will be bound whether or not persons deriving title under them will be entitled to the benefit or subject to the burden of the covenants.

" 2. *If there is privity of estate, but not privity of contract, only covenants which touch and concern the land are enforceable.*"—Privity of estate means that there is tenure between the parties, i.e., that a relationship of landlord and tenant exists between them." The particular rules governing covenants in leases are dealt with in the chapter on Leases.

" 3. *If there is privity neither of contract nor of estate, then with two exceptions, no covenants are enforceable.*"—The two exceptions are :—

" *First, even the common law allowed the benefit of a covenant to be assigned.*"
—On the other hand the *burden* will not pass *at law*. See further *post*, p. 552.

" *Secondly, equity allows the transmission of both the benefit and the burden of restrictive covenants.*"—As the *burden* can pass in equity under this rule, if the covenant is restrictive, the solutions to most problems arising between vendor and purchaser turn on its application. The rule is, therefore, considered in detail *post*, p. 555 *et seq.*

These rules " should be applied in the given order : if there is privity of contract, there is no need to look further ; and if there is privity of estate, there is no need to consider whether the covenant is restrictive."

Provisions which constitute covenants.—No formal words are necessary to make a covenant (*Mackenzie* v. *Childers* (1889), 43 Ch. D. 265). Every obligation which, on a fair construction of the language of a deed, is imposed upon one of the parties thereto amounts to an express covenant by him to perform that obligation, provided the language shows an intention that there should be an agreement between the covenantor and the covenantee to do or not to do the particular thing referred to (*Re Cadogan and Hans Place Estate, Ltd. ; ex parte Willis* (1895), 73 L.T. 387). Pickford, L.J., in *Westacott* v. *Hahn* [1918] 1 K.B. 495, said, at p. 504 : " A great number of authorities beginning in early days were cited to us, but I do not think they are of much assistance . . . *covenant is a matter of intention* . . . *any words will make a covenant*, whether participial or not, if it can be clearly seen that such was the intention of the parties." See also Norton on Deeds, 2nd ed., p. 534.

A covenant may be implied from a recital (*Re Weston* [1900] 2 Ch. 164) ; see *ante*, p. 447. But where a deed contains *express* covenants, no other covenants on the same subject-matter can be implied (*Line* v. *Stephenson* (1838), 5 Bing. (N.C.) 183 ; *Dawes* v. *Tredwell* (1881), 18 Ch. D. 345). For instance, a covenant to repair may in some cases imply a covenant to build that which has to be repaired. But where there is an express covenant to build and also a covenant to repair, if the covenant to build cannot be enforced, the covenant to repair cannot be taken to imply an additional covenant to build (*Stephens* v. *Junior Army and Navy Stores, Ltd.* [1914] 2 Ch. 516). So, an express covenant for quiet enjoyment in a deed will supersede any implied covenant for quiet enjoyment (*Mills* v. *United Counties Bank, Ltd.* [1912] 1 Ch. 231).

If the language of a covenant is ambiguous, the recitals can be looked at for an explanation of the ambiguity (*Re Coghlan ; Broughton* v. *Broughton* [1894] 3 Ch. 76). But ambiguous words in a covenant will be construed most strongly against the covenantor. This point sometimes arises in the case of a restrictive covenant, where such covenant has not made it clear as to the particular land which the covenant is intended to protect or the particular land which is to be subject to the covenant.

A court does not imply restrictions unless it is satisfied that they were fairly within the contemplation of the parties to the contract judging from the terms in which they are therein expressed. In *Holford* v. *Acton Urban Council* [1898] 2 Ch. 240 conditions of sale provided that purchasers should covenant with the vendor to erect shops and dwelling-houses, but the court refused to imply a negative stipulation that nothing but shops and dwelling-houses should be erected. See also *Re Rutherford's Conveyance* [1938] Ch. 396, where land was expressed to be conveyed subject to certain restrictions, but there was no covenant to observe them and the purchaser did not execute the deed. It was held that although the deed created an equitable obligation

18

as between vendor and purchaser to observe the restrictions no covenant could be implied for the benefit of land retained by the vendor.

A covenant may be so vaguely worded as to be void for uncertainty (*National Trust* v. *Midlands Electricity Board* [1952] Ch. 380).

Persons who may take the benefit of, or be bound by, covenants.— The common-law rule that a person cannot sue on a covenant in a deed to which he is not a party applied only to deeds *inter partes*. A covenant in an indenture not *inter partes* expressed to be made with a person not a party can be sued on by the covenantee as if the indenture were a deed poll. Thus a mortgagee who is not a party to the registered transfer of land subject to the mortgage may sue on a covenant by the transferee, as a registered transfer is in the nature of a deed poll rather than a deed *inter partes* (*Chelsea & Walham Green Building Society* v. *Armstrong* [1951] Ch. 853).

Even as regards indentures *inter partes*, however, a material exception to the common-law rule is made by the L.P.A. 1925, s. 56 (1), which provides that a person may take the benefit of any condition, right of entry, covenant or agreement over or respecting *land or other property*, although he may not be named as a party to the conveyance or other instrument (L.P.A. 1925, s. 56 (1)). But to claim the benefit of the covenant the proposed taker thereof must have been in existence at the date of the deed (*Kelsey* v. *Dodd* (1881), 52 L.J. Ch. 34), and he must have been a person with whom, although he was not a party to the deed, the covenant was purported to be made (*White* v. *Bijou Mansions, Ltd.* [1938] Ch. 351 ; *Zetland* (*Marquess*) v. *Driver* [1939] Ch. 1). An option to purchase land is an " agreement . . . respecting land " within s. 56 (1) (*Stromdale and Ball, Ltd.* v. *Burden* [1952] Ch. 223). Before a person can enforce a covenant under this subsection he must be " a person who falls within the scope and benefit of the covenant according to the true construction of the document in question " (Greene, M.R., in *White* v. *Bijou Mansions, Ltd.*, *ante*). The judgments in the House of Lords in *Beswick* v. *Beswick* [1968] A.C. 58 indicate that the operation of s. 56 is limited to realty and that the section confers rights only on persons who lost rights at common law because they were not named as parties in a deed. It is now clear that s. 56 (1) has not radically altered the common-law rule as to privity of contract.

Thus, in *Re Ecclesiastical Commissioners for England's Conveyance* [1936] Ch. 430, a house had been conveyed by the Commissioners to one who entered into covenants with the Commissioners and their successors and also with their assigns, owners for the time being of lands adjoining or adjacent to the land conveyed. Before the date of this conveyance the Commissioners had conveyed several adjacent plots to various purchasers. Luxmoore, J., decided that the covenant with the Commissioners' assigns, owners for the time being of adjoining or adjacent lands, denoted the hereditaments intended to be benefited, and, therefore, that the owners of such hereditaments, even though they purchased before the conveyance containing the covenants, were covenantees. It followed that the persons deriving title under them could sue on the covenants.

A covenant contained in a deed will, in equity, bind a person who has accepted the benefit of the deed, although he may not have executed it (*Webb* v. *Spicer* (1849), 13 Q.B. 886 ; *Formby* v. *Barker* [1903] 2 Ch. 539 ; and see *Halsall* v. *Brizell* [1957] Ch. 169).

If a trustee or personal representative enters into a personal covenant, to which is added a proviso that he shall not be liable under the covenant,

the proviso will be void as being repugnant. But there is no objection to
a proviso limiting the liability of a covenantor, provided it only limits it
and does not destroy it (*Williams* v. *Hathaway* (1877), 6 Ch. D. 544;
Re Tewkesbury Gas Co. [1912] 1 Ch. 1). For instance, where trustees borrowed
money and covenanted " as such trustees but not otherwise," Buckley, L.J.,
was of opinion that the covenant did not bind the trustees personally, but
only in respect of the trust funds in their hands (*Re Robinson's Settlement ;
Gant* v. *Hobbs* [1912] 1 Ch. 717). The decision to the contrary in *Watling*
v. *Lewis* [1911] 1 Ch. 414 will probably not be followed. It was decided
in *Farhall* v. *Farhall* (1871), L.R. 7 Ch. 123, that a covenant " as executor "
made the covenantor personally liable, but it is thought that, if the point
comes again before the court, a different conclusion will be reached.

Provisions of the 1925 legislation as to form of covenants.—The
provisions of the 1925 Acts have done much to simplify the *form* of covenants
when contained in a deed executed after 1925. Sections 78 and 79 of the
L.P.A. 1925 provide as follows :—

" 78.—(1) A covenant *relating to any land of the covenantee* shall be
deemed to be made with the covenantee and his successors in title and the
persons deriving title under him or them, and shall have effect as if such
successors and other persons were expressed.

For the purposes of this subsection in connection with *covenants restrictive
of the user of land* ' successors in title ' shall be deemed to include the
owners and occupiers for the time being of the land of the covenantee
intended to be benefited.

(2) This section applies to covenants made after the commencement of
this Act, but the repeal of section fifty-eight of the Conveyancing Act, 1881,
does not affect the operation of covenants to which that section applied.

79.—(1) A covenant relating to any land of a covenantor or capable
of being bound by him, shall, unless a *contrary intention* is expressed, be
deemed to be made by the covenantor on behalf of himself his successors in
title *and the persons deriving title under him* or them, and, subject as
aforesaid, shall have effect as if such successors and other persons were
expressed.

This subsection extends to a covenant to do some act relating to the
land, notwithstanding that the subject-matter may not be in existence
when the covenant is made.

(2) For the purposes of this section in connection with covenants
restrictive of the user of land ' successors in title ' shall be deemed to
include the owners and occupiers for the time being of such land.

(3) This section applies only to covenants made after the commencement
of this Act."

It may be said, therefore, that a covenant in a deed executed after 1925,
by *A* with *B* simply, will have the same effect (at least—it may have a greater
effect, see the next following paragraphs) as if the covenant had been
expressed in the following full form : " *A* hereby, on behalf of himself and
his successors in title and the persons deriving title under him or them,
covenants with *B* and his successors in title and the persons deriving title
under him or them." And, in the case of a restrictive covenant, the expression
" successors in title " will also include the owners and occupiers for the time
being of the land.

18

"*relating to any land of the covenantee.*"—In *Smith* v. *River Douglas Catchment Board* [1949] 2 K.B. 500, there was a covenant with the owner of land that the board would construct and maintain new banks to a stream to prevent flooding. The Court of Appeal decided that the covenant " touched and concerned " land which was ascertainable with reasonable accuracy, and that the parties intended that the benefit should run with the land. Consequently, the covenant was one the benefit of which ran with the land and a successor in title of the covenantee could sue on the covenant under the L.P.A. 1925, s. 78 (1).

One of the persons who successfully sued on the covenant in *Smith* v. *River Douglas Catchment Board, ante*, was a purchaser from the original covenantee and the other a lessee from that purchaser. Although the point does not appear to have been pressed in argument, the court decided that the lessee was a person deriving title under the covenantee and so could sue on the covenant. If this is so the L.P.A. 1925, s. 78, has amended the common-law rule that only a successor who took the same estate as the covenantee obtained the benefit of the covenant. See the case of *Williams* v. *Unit Construction Co., Ltd.*, formerly unreported, but of which a report now appears in the *Conveyancer N.S.*, vol. 19, p. 262.

The judgments in the House of Lords in *Beswick* v. *Beswick* [1968] A.C. 58 may be taken as casting some doubt on *Smith* v. *River Douglas Catchment Board* and *Williams* v. *Unit Construction Co., Ltd.* as to this point although it was not directly considered in the case ; since the L.P.A. 1925 is a consolidating statute the presumption would be that s. 78 deals merely with drafting without altering substantive rights.

" *covenants restrictive of the user of land.*"—See, as to this provision, *post*, p. 555.

" *contrary intention.*"—For successors in title to be bound by a restrictive covenant, the first essential is that the original parties must not have intended the burden to be purely personal to the covenantor (see *Re Fawcett & Holme's Contract* (1889), 42 Ch. D 150). Accordingly, for the burden to run, the covenantor should be expressed to covenant, for example, " for himself, his successors and assigns " (see *Powell* v. *Hemsley* [1909] 2 Ch. 252). It is true that since 1925 a covenantor is deemed to covenant to this effect, but only " unless a contrary intention is expressed " (L.P.A. 1925, s. 79 (1)). This has been widely construed to mean " unless an indication to the contrary is to be found in the instrument, and that such an indication may be sufficiently contained in the wording and context of the instrument even though the instrument contains no provision expressly excluding successors in title from its operation " (*per* Pennycuick, J., in *Re Royal Victoria Pavilion Ramsgate* [1961] Ch. 581, at p. 589). In that case a covenant by an assignor of a leasehold interest to " procure " a certain state of affairs in connection with the property retained was regarded as a personal covenant only. Accordingly, it would appear better practice, where the burden is intended to run, not to rely on s. 79 (1) but to express the covenant to be for successors in title also. However, compare *Sefton* v. *Tophams, Ltd.* [1964] 1 W.L.R. 1408 (on appeal [1966] 2 W.L.R. 814) where successors in title were not expressly included in the covenant but it was held as a matter of construction that no contrary intention to s. 79 (1) was shown so that *prima facie* the burden could run ; in fact the covenant in question would not have been enforceable against the covenantee's successors in title since the covenantor retained no land capable of being benefited (*L.C.C.* v. *Allen* [1914] 3 K.B. 642).

" *deemed to be made by the covenantor* . . . *and the persons deriving title under him.*"—It has been suggested that the effect of s. 79 (1) was to alter the rule in *Austerberry* v. *Corporation of Oldham* (1885), 29 Ch. D. 750, namely, that a covenant to do something of a positive nature involving expense, in connection with freehold property, is not binding on an assign. This is not so. The effect of the section is simply to imply the words mentioned therein, in the covenant, so as to save the draftsman the labour of writing them in. Such a covenant, with the implied words fully written in, would not before 1926 have altered the rule in the above case, and therefore it will not alter it now. In other words, the subsection has not the effect of making a covenant run with the land, if, before the L.P.A. 1925, the use of the further words in a covenant would not have made such covenant run with the land.

The discussion in the *Conveyancer N.S.*, vol. 19, p. 261 *et seq.*, initiated by Mr. W. Lyon Blease, gives emphasis to the question whether, if a lessee is a successor in title for the purposes of s. 78, he is also a successor for the purposes of s. 79. It is difficult to suggest that a different meaning can be given to the same words in the two sections. On the other hand if the same meaning is given it can be argued that, on the basis of *Smith* v. *River Douglas Catchment Board, ante*, a lessee is bound by positive covenants given by the freeholder and a sub-lessee (for instance, a mortgagee by demise) is bound by positive covenants given by a lessee. On this problem being drawn to their attention, the Court of Appeal in *Williams* v. *Unit Construction Co., Ltd., ante*, decided that they were bound by the decision in *Smith's* case on the construction of s. 78 but expressed no view regarding s. 79.

It is suggested that the true view is that both ss. 78 and 79 deal only with drafting and do not in any way alter the rules as to when the benefit and the burden of covenants pass. If this is so, the lessee in *Smith's* case should not have recovered damages. It must be admitted, however, first that the Court of Appeal have decided that they are bound by their own decision on s. 78 and, secondly, justice appears to be done by allowing a lessee to take the benefit of a covenant on the freehold title. A relevant consideration may be that a benefit can be taken under the L.P.A. 1925, s. 56 (*ante*, p. 546), but there is no corresponding rule as to the burden ; see Denning, L.J.'s judgment in *Smith's* case [1949] 2 K.B., at p. 517. This may enable the court to distinguish between s. 78 and s. 79.

As a result of the judgments in the House of Lords in *Beswick* v. *Beswick* [1968] A.C. 58, it is now arguable that s. 78 deals only with drafting (see *ante*, p. 548), but s. 79, unlike s. 78, was in fact a new section in 1925 and so could be taken as introducing changes in law.

Another provision which may assist in shortening deeds is the L.P.A. 1925, s. 80 (3), as follows :—

" 80.—(3) The benefit of a covenant relating to land entered into after the commencement of this Act may be made to run with the land *without the use of any technical expression* if the covenant is of such a nature that the benefit could have been made to run with the land before the commencement of this Act."

" *without the use of any technical expression.*"—This is a reference to the necessity for the use, before 1926, of the word " assigns," in covenants affecting leasehold property, to make a covenant relating to a thing not then in existence, run with the land. The theory was that the law would not annex a covenant to a thing not in existence, unless *the intention* to do so was shown by the expression of the parties, and the use of the word " assigns " in the covenant was deemed to show such an intention. This point has been covered by the provision in s. 79 (1) of the L.P.A. 1925.

Another useful section is s. 81 of the L.P.A. 1925. This section makes it now unnecessary in a covenant with *several covenantees* to state that the covenant is made with each of them. It provides, in effect, that any covenant made with two or more jointly, to pay money, or to make a conveyance, or to do any other act for their benefit, will be deemed to include and imply an obligation to do the act for the benefit of the survivor or survivors of them, and for the benefit of any other person to whom the right to sue on the covenant devolves, *and, where made after 1925, will be construed as being also made with each of them.* The section applies to a covenant made after 31st December, 1881 ; it replaces s. 60 of the Conveyancing Act, 1881, except the words in italics, which were new. For the effect of the section, see *Josselson* v. *Borst* [1938] 1 K.B. 723.

Covenant by a person with himself and another or others jointly.—

Before 1926, a person could not covenant with himself and another or with himself and others jointly (*Ellis* v. *Kerr* [1910] 1 Ch. 529 ; *Napier* v. *Williams* [1911] 1 Ch. 361). In consequence of this rule many covenants were void, especially covenants implied by law. Section 82 (1) of the L.P.A. 1925 provides that any covenant, whether express or implied, or agreement entered into by a person with himself and one or more other persons is to be construed and to be capable of being enforced in like manner as if the covenant or agreement had been entered into with the other person or persons alone. The section applies to covenants or agreements entered into *before or after* the commencement of the Act, and to covenants *implied* by statute in the case of, e.g., a person who conveys or is expressed to convey to himself and one or more other persons.

In *Ridley* v. *Lee* [1935] Ch. 591, as part of a building scheme, three tenants in common, in 1907, sold certain plots to one of themselves, *B*, who entered into various covenants with himself and the others as vendors. It was pointed out by Luxmoore, J., that if the covenants had in the first instance been entered into between *B* and the two other persons, they would not have enured for the benefit of the whole of the interests in the land retained, because the two other persons were only two out of three tenants in common, and covenants in such form would not have created that mutuality of obligation which is the essential ingredient for the enforcement of a building scheme by one purchaser from the common vendors against another purchaser from them (*Elliston* v. *Reacher* [1908] 2 Ch. 374, at p. 385 ; see *post*, p. 565). There was, therefore, no building scheme, and there was nothing in s. 82 of the L.P.A. 1925 which compelled the learned judge to hold that what was insufficient to create such a scheme in 1907, must by reason of that section be deemed, from 1st January, 1926, to have constituted a building scheme as from the earlier date. It is interesting to consider how far the same reasoning might be applicable to covenants made by a person with himself and others, after 1925, with the intention of creating a building scheme. After 1925, the legal estate in the land would be held by the persons interested as joint tenants. In spite of *Ridley* v. *Lee* it is thought that covenants which by s. 82 are deemed made with the other *joint* tenants would be held to enure for the benefit of the whole of the land retained. See also *Re Pinewood Estate, Farnborough* [1958] Ch. 280.

But where the person entering into the covenant is a tenant for life of settled land, s. 82 must be read with s. 68 of the S.L.A. 1925. This latter section, after providing that certain dispositions of settled land may be made to the tenant for life or a purchase may be made from him of land to be made subject to the limitations of the settlement, provides that in every such case the trustees of the settlement shall have power to enforce any covenants by the tenant for life, or, *where the tenant for life is himself one of the trustees,* then the other or others of them shall have such power. A covenant for the benefit of settled land made by a person, not a tenant for life, should be made with the tenant for life, and not with the trustees of the settlement, as the legal estate is vested in the tenant for life, and, on his death, the covenant devolves with the legal estate (L.P.A. 1925, s. 80 (2)).

Restrictive and positive covenants contrasted.—It is essential to make clear the distinction between a positive covenant and a negative (or restrictive) covenant. A positive covenant is a covenant which involves the payment of money or the doing of anything of an active character. An example of a positive covenant is where the owner in fee enters into a covenant to erect a house, or to fence a plot of land, or to pay for the making of a road, or to do any other act involving expense (or, as it has been said, " involving putting his hand in his pocket ").

A negative or restrictive covenant is a covenant *not* to do something on or concerning the land of the covenantor for the benefit of land belonging to the covenantee (*Formby* v. *Barker* [1903] 2 Ch. 539). If a covenant is in terms positive it will be construed as restrictive if it is restrictive in substance (*Catt* v. *Tourle* (1869), L.R. 4 Ch. 654 ; *Clegg* v. *Hands* (1890), 44 Ch. D. 503). For instance, a covenant to give the first refusal of land is equivalent to a covenant not to sell the land without giving the first refusal (*Manchester Ship Canal Co.* v. *Manchester Racecourse Co.* [1901] 2 Ch. 37 ; *Ryan* v. *Thomas* (1911), 55 Sol. J. 364).

Where the covenant is partly restrictive and partly not, the court will in a proper case enforce the restrictive portion of the covenant (*Clegg* v. *Hands, ante*).

PART 2. PASSING OF THE BENEFIT OF COVENANTS AT LAW

Position of original parties to covenants.—A person in whose favour a covenant has been made can enforce the covenant against the covenantor even after the covenantee has sold the land intended to be benefited by the covenant (*Stokes* v. *Russell* (1790), 3 Term Rep. 678), although after sale of his interest he will have a right to nominal damages only (*L.C.C.* v. *Allen* [1914] 3 K.B. 642, at p. 660 ; and see *Tophams, Ltd.* v. *Sefton* [1967] A.C. 50, where the covenantee was expressly not to remain liable after all interest had been parted with). Further, the personal representative of the covenantee will have a right of action for damages for a breach committed after the death of the covenantee (*Formby* v. *Barker* [1903] 2 Ch. 539, at p. 549). Even a *positive* covenant is binding for all time as against the covenantor personally, and against his estate after his death (*S.E. Railway Co.* v. *Associated Portland Cement Manufacturers* (1900), *Ltd.* [1910] 1 Ch. 12). These rules are of particular importance in connection with *positive* covenants because, of course, the burden of such covenants cannot run with the land (except between landlord and tenant) as it may, in certain circumstances, in the case of *restrictive* covenants.

The benefit of covenants may pass at law.—The benefit of a covenant, *whether positive or restrictive*, will run at law with land to which it relates provided the covenant is one which affects *per se*, and not merely from collateral circumstances, the nature, quality or value of the land and has been entered into with a person holding a legal estate in the land (*Rogers* v. *Hosegood* [1900] 2 Ch. 388, at pp. 395, 404), and provided the assignee who seeks to enforce the covenant has the same legal estate as the original covenantee (*Webb* v. *Russell* (1789), 3 Term Rep. 393 ; *Westhoughton U.D.C.* v. *Wigan Coal & Iron Co.* [1919] 1 Ch. 159, at p. 171). A good example of this is the passing of the benefit of the usual implied covenants for title. The rule applies to both freehold and leasehold property (*Kingdon* v. *Nottle* (1815), 4 M. & S. 53 ; *Campbell* v. *Lewis* (1820), 3 B. & Ald. 392). See also *Dyson* v. *Forster* [1909] A.C. 98 ; *Shayler* v. *Woolf* [1946] 1 All E.R. 464, affirmed on other grounds [1946] Ch. 320, and the discussion in the *Conveyancer N.S.*, vol. 18, p. 546 *et seq.*

The judgments of the Court of Appeal in *Smith* v. *River Douglas Catchment Board* [1949] 2 K.B. 500, the facts of which are given briefly *ante*, p. 548, follow *Rogers* v. *Hosegood*, *ante*, and state that the benefit will run if (i) the covenant shows that the parties so intended, (ii) the covenantee had an interest in the land to be benefited, (iii) that land is described so as to be ascertainable with reasonable accuracy (but with the help of extrinsic evidence if necessary), (iv) the covenant touches and concerns the land. Requirements (iii) and (iv) apply also to the passing of the benefit of *restrictive* covenants *in equity* (which rules are applicable when it is necessary to rely on them in order that the *burden* may pass) ; these requirements are, therefore, discussed *post*, p. 559 *et seq.*

The benefit of a covenant may run with the land of the covenantee, although the burden of the covenant does not run with the land of the covenantor (*Rogers* v. *Hosegood*, *ante*). So that, to enable a covenant to be enforced at law, it has to be shown not only that the person proposing to enforce it is entitled to the benefit of the covenant, but that the person he proposes to sue is liable under the covenant, which can rarely be done.

The benefit of a covenant to pay a rent-charge does not run with the rent-charge.—The Court of Appeal has decided that such a covenant is a covenant in gross and does not run with the rent-charge, and is therefore ineffectual as against assigns of the land (*Grant* v. *Edmondson* [1931] 1 Ch. 143). The reasons given for the decision are not convincing, but see the reasons suggested in Elphinstone, Covenants Affecting Land, p. 134. It is clear, however, that an action of debt may be brought against the *terre tenant* for non-payment of the rent-charge, if the land is freehold (*Thomas* v. *Sylvester* (1873), L.R. 8 Q.B. 368) ; but not if the land is leasehold (*Re Herbage Rents* [1896] 2 Ch. 811).

The burden of covenants does not pass at law (except between landlord and tenant).—*At law* the burden of a covenant does not run with the land (*Austerberry* v. *Oldham Corporation* (1885), 29 Ch. D. 750 ; *Re Fitzherbert-Brockholes Agreement* [1940] Ch. 51 ; *Cator* v. *Newton* [1940] 1 K.B. 415), except in the case of a covenant which, upon the true construction of it, amounts to a grant of an easement (*Rowbotham* v. *Wilson* (1860), 8 H.L. Cas. 348, at p. 362) ; or a rent-charge (*Morland* v. *Cook* (1868), L.R. 6 Eq. 252 ; *Austerberry* v. *Oldham Corporation*, *ante*) ; and except covenants in a lease as between landlord and tenant (as to which see chapter on Leases).

As the burden does not run with the land, it follows that the covenant cannot be enforced against an assign at law. In fact, it operates (unless the covenant is restrictive) merely as a covenant personal to the person making it. But, of course, as against that person the covenant remains binding for all time in favour of the covenantee (*South Eastern Railway Co.* v. *Associated Portland Cement Manufacturers* [1910] 1 Ch. 12). An assign is not bound by such a covenant, notwithstanding that the covenant was made by the covenantor for his assigns, or that the assign has express notice of the covenant (*ibid.*), or that under the L.P.A. 1925, s. 79 (1), the covenant was deemed to be made on behalf of the covenantor, his successors in title, and the persons deriving title under him (as to this, see *ante*, p. 547).

Positive covenants : covenants for indemnity.—Since the burden of restrictive covenants may pass with land in equity, it is in respect of positive covenants that the rule at law, that the burden of a covenant does not pass with a freehold estate, is of greatest importance. How then is a vendor who sells part of his land to ensure that positive burdens, such as the duty to make a roadway, are imposed on owners for the time being of the land sold ? Such burdens cannot be satisfactorily imposed on freehold land and for this reason long terms of years are often granted because positive covenants in leases can be enforced as long as there is privity of estate, provided the covenants touch and concern the land.

Nevertheless, in practice, positive covenants are often imposed on sales of freeholds and they are not altogether ineffective. The covenantor remains personally liable on a covenant even after he has parted with all interest in the land. Therefore, if a purchaser covenants that he will, for instance, erect and for ever maintain a fence he will be liable to be sued for damages if the fence falls into disrepair after he has resold the land ; the covenant will be deemed to have been made by the covenantor on behalf of himself, his successors in title and the persons deriving title under him or them (L.P.A. 1925, s. 79 (1)).

In practice, on reselling, the covenantor will invariably ensure that the conveyance contains a covenant whereby the purchaser from him undertakes to indemnify him against any future breach of the covenants in question, and such covenants for indemnity are obtained on each successive conveyance. For example, under General Condition 11 (2) of The Law Society's Conditions of Sale, 1973 Revision, if, after completion, the vendor will remain liable in respect of a breach of an existing restrictive or positive covenant relating to the property sold, the purchaser must covenant to indemnify him in respect thereof, provided the property was, in the contract, *expressed to be sold subject* to the covenant in question. See also General Condition 19 (5) and (6) of the National Conditions of Sale, 18th ed. By threat to sue the original covenantor, who will seek indemnity against the purchaser from him, who in turn will seek indemnity, and so on, even positive covenants can be binding for long periods, provided the successive owners are solvent. In time, however, it becomes impossible to trace one of the parties or his representatives, or to follow his assets, or a party is found to be insolvent and not worth suing, and so the system breaks down.

In addition, two rather esoteric ways of enforcing positive obligations may be mentioned. Firstly, the Court of Appeal, after a full consideration of the authorities, has reaffirmed the anomalous rule that a landowner can acquire *by prescription* a legal right to have a boundary hedge repaired by the owner of neighbouring land and his successors in title, provided it can be shown that the neighbour and his predecessors in title had carried out repairs as a matter of obligation, e.g., not for his own benefit or as owner of the hedge ; at the same time it was emphasised that such a legal right *cannot* be created *by agreement* (*Jones* v. *Price* [1965] 2 Q.B. 618 ; see also *Crow* v. *Wood* [1971] 1 Q.B. 77). Secondly, the possibility of an action in tort by the covenantee against a purchaser from the covenantor is suggested by the judgments both at first instance and in the Court of Appeal in *Sefton* v. *Tophams, Ltd.* [1965] Ch. 1140 (on appeal, *sub nom. Tophams, Ltd.* v. *Sefton* [1967] A.C. 50). The tort suggested is that of interfering with the contractual relations between the covenantor and the covenantee and would apparently be committed by a purchase from the covenantor with a view to breach of the covenant provided the covenantor suffers damage.

It is possible that some obligations of a positive nature may be imposed by means of a fluctuating rent-charge. Provided that the rent-charge vests immediately it does not break the perpetuity rule because the amount may vary from year to year (*Beachway Management, Ltd.* v. *Wisewell* [1971] Ch. 610). It is essential that the *quantum* should be capable of being rendered certain by an agreed formula ; in that case it depended on rateable value from time to time. Unless the rating system is drastically altered a formula of this nature is likely to be satisfactory to ensure compliance with many obligations.

Further a successor in title of a covenantor may be obliged to perform a positive covenant because such performance may be an essential condition of the exercise by him of a right. For example, in *Halsall* v. *Brizell* [1957] Ch. 169 land was sold in building plots, the vendors retaining the roads and sewers together with a promenade and sea wall. By a deed of covenant the purchasers of plots covenanted that they and their respective heirs, executors, administrators and assigns would pay a due proportion of the expenses of maintenance of the roads, sewers, promenade and sea wall. The burden of this positive covenant did not run with the title to the plots.

In the circumstances it was found that the owners of the houses erected on these plots of land had no right to use the roads and sewers otherwise than under a deed of covenant. Consequently, Upjohn, J., decided that if the present owner of one of the houses wished to use the roads, as he clearly did, then he must also, as a condition of the exercise of his rights under the deed, accept the burden of making the payments prescribed by the deed. Thus, on the principle that a man cannot take the benefit under a deed without subscribing to the obligations thereunder, the positive covenants were enforceable against successors in title.

It is suggested that this decision does not apply as often as is assumed in some comments. It will usually be found, for example, that after a number of years roads have been dedicated to the public even if the liability for their maintenance has not passed to the local authority. Similarly drainage pipes will often be found to have become public sewers vested in the local authority under the Public Health Acts, so that they can be used irrespective of private rights under deeds containing covenants. For these and other similar reasons it will not be often that a successor in title will be obliged to rely on rights granted by the deed purporting to impose the burden of covenants on him. Probably, in practice, the decision will be most useful in framing or enforcing covenants relating to flats.

The fact that a subsequent purchaser's title depends on a deed containing positive covenants does not, on this principle, make the covenants enforceable against him. Once a conveyance has been executed the legal estate has passed ; the purchaser and his successors rely on their title and not on rights arising in the future and so they cannot be compelled to elect between rights and obligations expressed in the deed.

Statutory provisions regarding covenants for indemnity.—The L.P.A. 1925 contains various provisions regarding covenants for indemnity which are of greatest importance in connection with leaseholds, but which may affect freeholds.

It is provided by s. 189 (2) of the L.P.A. 1925 that the benefit of all covenants and powers given by way of indemnity against a rent or any part thereof, payable in respect of land, or against the breach of any covenant or condition in relation to land, is and is to be deemed always to have been annexed to the land to which the indemnity is intended to relate, and *may be enforced by the estate owner for the time being of the whole or any part of that land, notwithstanding that the benefit may not have been expressly apportioned or assigned to him or to any of his predecessors in title.*

Various covenants are implied in a conveyance of freehold land subject to a rent-charge, as follows :—

(a) In a conveyance for value, other than a mortgage, of the entirety of the land, a covenant by the purchaser with the vendor to pay the rent-charge and to observe the covenants, agreements and conditions contained in the document creating it and to indemnify the vendor in respect thereof (L.P.A. 1925, s. 77 (1) (a) ; Sched. 2, Pt. VII).

(b) In a conveyance for value, other than a mortgage, of part of the land, subject to a part of the rent-charge which has been apportioned *without* the consent of the owner thereof, similar covenants to those mentioned above as regards such apportioned part and also similar covenants by the vendor regarding the balance of the rent-charge (L.P.A. 1925, s. 77 (1) (b) ; Sched. 2, Pt. VIII).

When part of land affected by a rent-charge is sold and the rent-charge is charged exclusively on the land conveyed, or on the land retained or apportioned between the land conveyed and the land retained *without the consent of the owner of the rent-charge* (that is, where the apportionment is equitable only), such charge or apportionment is binding between the grantor and the grantee and their respective successors in title (L.P.A. 1925, s. 190 (1)). In the event of default of the person liable under such charge or apportionment causing loss or damage to the owner for the time being of other land affected by the entire rent-charge, rights to distrain or take the income of the land in respect of which default occurs are granted by the L.P.A. 1925, s. 190 (2).

PART 3. RESTRICTIVE COVENANTS

Nature of restrictive covenants.—We have seen that at common law the burden of a covenant will not pass with freehold land. In equity, both the benefit and the burden of a *restrictive* covenant may pass. The rule, in courts of equity, was that an assign of the legal estate for value was not entitled to use the land in a manner inconsistent with the contract entered into by his vendor, and with notice of which he purchased (*London and South Western Railway Co.* v. *Gomm* (1882), 20 Ch. D. 562, at p. 583).

The distinction between positive and restrictive covenants was drawn *ante,* p. 551, but we must note that, although a covenant is a restrictive one, it may be so framed as to amount to a purely personal covenant. For instance, a covenant that " the said *G F* . . . shall only erect messuages " of a certain description was held a mere personal covenant by *G F* not binding on his assigns (*Re Fawcett and Holmes's Contract* (1889), 42 Ch. D. 150). So, a covenant by a purchaser " for himself, his executors, administrators and assigns " [in the pre-1926 style] that *he* will not do a particular act, was not equivalent to a covenant by him " for himself, his heirs, executors, administrators and assigns that he, his executors, administrators and assigns will not do," the particular act, and a restrictive covenant in the former form did not impose liability on the covenantor for the acts of his assigns (*Powell* v. *Hemsley* [1909] 1 Ch. 680 ; [1909] 2 Ch. 252). And see as to the operation of the L.P.A. 1925, s. 79, *ante*, p. 547 *et seq.*

Notice.—The theory was that a restrictive covenant (as regards freeholds) created an equitable burden on the land in the nature of a negative easement, and that an assign or lessee took the estate subject to such equitable burden, subject to this, that if he acquired the legal estate for value without notice, he took the estate free from the burden of the covenant (*Wilkes* v. *Spooner* [1911] 2 K.B. 473). This is known as the doctrine in *Tulk* v. *Moxhay* (1848), 2 Ph. 774. In that case it was said by Cottenham, L.C., that " the question *is not whether the covenant runs with the land*, but whether a party shall be permitted to use the land in a manner inconsistent with the contract entered into by his vendor, and with notice of which he purchased." In *London and South Western Railway Co.* v. *Gomm*, *ante*, Jessel, M.R., referring to *Tulk* v. *Moxhay*, said, at p. 583 : " This is an equitable doctrine establishing an exception to the rules of common law which did not treat such a covenant as running with the land . . . The purchaser took the estate subject to the equitable burden, with the qualification that if he acquired the legal estate for value without notice he was freed from the burden. That qualification, however, did not affect the nature of the burden ; the notice was required merely to avoid the effect of the legal estate, and did not create the right, and if the purchaser took only an equitable estate he took subject to the burden, whether he had notice or not."

The rule applied to a purchaser for value who was in a position to demand a conveyance of the legal estate, for instance, the owner of an equity of redemption, in the same way as it applied to a purchaser for value who acquired the legal estate.

But if a purchaser only gets the *equitable estate*, he will be bound by a restrictive covenant whether he has notice of it or not (*Mander* v. *Falcke* [1891] 2 Ch. 554). Also, if he gets the legal estate, but is not a purchaser for value, he will be bound (*Re Nisbet and Potts' Contract* [1906] 1 Ch. 386).

When a purchaser has bought land *bona fide* without notice of restrictive covenants, another purchaser (including a lessee : *Holloway* v. *Hill* [1902] 2 Ch. 612) from him will not be bound by such covenants, *even though he has notice thereof* (*Nottingham Patent Brick Co.* v. *Butler* (1886), 16 Q.B.D. 778 ; *Rowell* v. *Satchell* [1903] 2 Ch. 212, at p. 220 ; *Wilkes* v. *Spooner* [1911] 2 K.B. 473). However, this does not necessarily mean that the restrictive covenants are extinguished once the land otherwise burdened by them comes into the hands of such a purchaser without notice, since it would appear that they may revive against subsequent owners who do not claim by purchase from him, e.g., against squatters (see *St. Marylebone Property Co., Ltd.* v. *Fairweather* [1963] A.C. 510 ; as to revival see also *Marten* v. *Flight Refuelling, Ltd.* [1962] Ch. 115).

These rules have not been changed by the 1925 legislation. It is expressly provided by the L.P.A. 1925, s. 2 (5), that " so far as regards the following interests *created before the commencement of this Act* . . . namely (*a*) the benefit of any covenant or agreement restrictive of the user of the land . . . a purchaser of a legal estate shall only take subject thereto if he has notice thereof . . . " It will be noted that in this subsection " a purchaser " means a purchaser in good faith for money or money's worth, and includes a lessee, mortgagee or other person who for money or money's worth acquires an interest in property ; and in reference to a legal estate includes a chargee by way of legal mortgage ; and where the context so requires, includes an intending purchaser (*ibid.*, s. 205 (1) (xxi)).

A purchaser will not be deemed to be affected with notice of a restrictive covenant created before 1926 which could only be discovered by investigating the title previous to fifteen years, the time fixed by s. 44 (1) of the L.P.A. 1925, as affected by s. 23 of the L.P.A. 1969, unless he actually investigates such earlier title (*ibid.*, subs. (8)). But if he accepts a shorter title he will be deemed to have notice of such a restrictive covenant if it would have been disclosed by investigating the title for fifteen years (*Re Cox and Neve's Contract* [1891] 2 Ch. 109).

Registration of restrictive covenants created after 1925.—A restrictive covenant or agreement, not being a covenant or agreement made between a lessor and lessee, entered into after 1925, will not be binding on a purchaser of the legal estate in the land for money or money's worth, notwithstanding that he may have actual notice thereof, unless it is registered as a land charge in the appropriate register. Such registration gives actual notice to all persons for all purposes of such covenant. The material provisions of the L.C.A. 1972 and the L.P.A. 1925 are given below.

The reason why a restrictive covenant or agreement between a lessor and lessee need not be registered as a land charge is that a purchaser is expected to look at the lease to ascertain what restrictions have been made to affect the land as between landlord and tenant. Nevertheless, this exception may cause difficulty if the covenant binds other land retained by the landlord ; see *post*, p. 601. As regards any other restrictions affecting the land, to be binding on a purchaser of leaseholds they will have to be registered as a land charge, and he is expected to be able, like any other person interested, to search the appropriate register (but see s. 44 of the L.P.A. 1925, and *per* Simonds, J., in *White* v. *Bijou Mansions, Ltd.* [1937] Ch. 610, at p. 621 ; on appeal [1938] Ch. 351).

It is provided by s. 2 (5), Class D (ii), of the L.C.A. 1972 that one of the classes of charges on, or obligations affecting, land which may be registered as land charges in the register of land charges is a restrictive covenant, namely, a covenant or agreement (other than a covenant or agreement made between a lessor and lessee) restrictive of the user of land entered into after 1925. The above must be read with s. 4 (6) of the L.C.A. 1972 and s. 199 (1) of the L.P.A. 1925, given below :—

" 4.—(6) . . . a land charge of Class D, created or entered into on or after 1st January 1926 shall *be void* as against a purchaser for money or money's worth of a legal estate in the land charged with it, unless the land charge is registered in the appropriate register before the completion of the purchase."

[A " purchaser " is defined in the L.C.A. 1972, s. 17 (1), as meaning " any person (including a mortgagee or lessee) who, for valuable consideration, takes any interest in land or in a charge on land "].

(L.P.A. 1925) " 199.—(1) A purchaser shall not be prejudicially affected by notice of—

(i) any instrument or matter capable of registration under the provisions of the Land Charges Act, 1925, or any enactment which it replaces which is void or not enforceable as against him under that Act or enactment, by reason of the non-registration thereof."

If, therefore, a restrictive covenant (except as between lessor and lessee) created after 1925, is not registered as a land charge, it is void as against a purchaser (including a lessee and mortgagee) of the legal estate for money or money's worth, even although he has express notice thereof. On the other hand an assign of the equitable interest in the land burdened with a restrictive covenant, and an assign of the legal estate not for value, will still be liable, and whether or not he has notice thereof.

A purchaser is, of course, *personally* liable under his restrictive covenant with his vendor, although such covenant is not registered as a land charge.

Section 198 (1) of the L.P.A. 1925 is a vital subsection :—

" 198.—(1) The registration of any instrument or matter under the provisions of the Land Charges Act, 1925, or any enactment which it replaces, in any register kept at the land registry *or elsewhere*, shall be deemed to constitute actual notice of such instrument or matter, and of the fact of such registration, to all persons and for all purposes connected with the land affected, as from the date of registration or other prescribed date so long as the registration continues in force."

It was stated by Eve, J., in *Re Forsey and Hollebone's Contract* [1927] W.N. 181, that by virtue of the above subsection registration under the L.C.A. constituted notice to a purchaser at the date when he entered into his contract, but this statement was invalidated by s. 24 of the L.P.A. 1969 ; see the discussion, *ante*, p. 4.

The fact that registration of a restrictive covenant as a land charge gives a purchaser notice thereof, does not necessarily make him liable thereunder. Before 1926, even if a person *had* notice of a restrictive covenant, this, in practice, would not affect him *unless* there was a person in existence entitled to the benefit of the covenant who could enforce it. There is no alteration in the law on this point. See *Tophams, Ltd.* v. *Sefton* [1967] A.C. 50 where the restrictive covenants were registered before completion of the contract for sale in question but the covenantee retained no land enabling him to enforce them in equity. The only effect of the above sections is (i) that if the restrictive covenant is not registered as a land charge it is void against a purchaser of the legal estate for money or money's worth ; and (ii) if it is so registered, a purchaser gets statutory notice, and is in no different position from a person affected with notice under the old law. And the provisions contained in ss. 78 (1), 79 (1), (2) of the L.P.A. 1925 (*ante*, p. 547), as regards a restrictive covenant being deemed to have been made with the covenantee (as to the benefit), and with the covenantor (as to the burden), and his successors in title, owners and occupiers for the time being of the land, probably do not make a covenant run with the land if the insertion of those words in a covenant made before 1926 would not have made it run with the land. And the provision in s. 80 (4) of the L.P.A. 1925, that " For the purposes of this section, a covenant runs with the land when the benefit or burden of it, whether at law or in equity, passes to the successors in title of the covenantee or the covenantor, as the case may be " is only declaratory of the existing law.

Where a vendor or a purchaser, as the case may be, is entitled to the benefit of a restrictive covenant, but does not get the deed containing the covenant enuring for his benefit, he is entitled to, and should, see that a memorandum is indorsed on a deed selected by him giving notice of the restrictions. See s. 200 of the L.P.A. 1925. The indorsement does not make it unnecessary to register the restriction as a land charge. The object is to prevent the restriction being overlooked when the abstract is being prepared on a future sale.

It may be necessary to consider whether a particular covenant in a deed executed after 1925, made in connection with a restrictive covenant contained in a deed executed before 1926, is so framed as to constitute a fresh restrictive covenant, and thus require registering as a land charge. A covenant certainly does not require to be registered if it merely amounts to a covenant of indemnity such as the covenants in *Harris* v. *Boots, Cash Chemists (Southern), Ltd.* [1904] 2 Ch. 376, and *Reckitt* v. *Cody* [1920] 2 Ch. 452. In *Reckitt* v. *Cody* the distinction was made between a covenant to observe and perform the restrictive covenants under which the vendor bought and a direct covenant with the vendor to do or abstain from doing specified acts, and it was pointed out that in the former case the covenant was merely a covenant of indemnity, and in the latter case it would be *a covenant which the vendor could enforce independently of the question whether he was being sued by his covenantees.* If the covenant is in the latter form it is thought that it should be registered.

It is thought that occasionally solicitors do not register restrictive covenants imposed on the sale of land, even though the vendor retains land to which the benefit of the covenants is annexed. The restrictive covenants considered in *Tophams, Ltd.* v. *Sefton* [1967] A.C. 50 were entered into in 1949 but not registered until 1964 and only then it is assumed because of the chance that publicity attended the covenantor's contract to sell. The effect of non-registration will be that as soon as the purchaser resells the land the covenants will become void. Registration is neither difficult nor expensive, and there seems to be no excuse for such an omission.

Persons who take the benefit of restrictive covenants.—A person in whose favour a restrictive covenant has been made can, of course, enforce the covenant against the covenantor. See *ante*, p. 551. But even the original covenantee cannot, after he has sold the land intended to be benefited by the covenant, enforce such a covenant *against a person on whom the burden of performing the covenant has passed by virtue of the rule in Tulk* v. *Moxhay* (*Formby* v. *Barker* [1903] 2 Ch. 539 ; *L.C.C.* v. *Allen* [1914] 3 K.B. 642 ; *Chambers* v. *Randall* [1923] 1 Ch. 149 ; *Torbay Hotel, Ltd.* v. *Jenkins* [1927] 2 Ch. 225 ; *Tophams Ltd.* v. *Sefton* [1967] A.C. 50).

The more difficult question is whether a subsequent purchaser of the land intended to be benefited by a restrictive covenant can enforce the covenant. The benefit of a covenant may run with the dominant land *at law*, but the burden will not run with the servient land *at law*. If a subsequent purchaser of the dominant land wishes to enforce a restrictive covenant against a person on whom he alleges the burden has been imposed by the equitable rule in *Tulk* v. *Moxhay*, *ante*, he must prove that the benefit has passed to him in accordance with the equitable rules (*Re Union of London and Smith's Bank Conveyance* [1933] Ch. 611).

The benefit of a restrictive covenant will pass in equity on a conveyance of freehold land if the following conditions are fulfilled :—

(i) *The covenantee must have retained land capable of being benefited* (*Formby* v. *Barker* [1903] 2 Ch. 539) ; *such land must be ascertainable with reasonable certainty* (*Renals* v. *Cowlishaw* (1879), 11 Ch. D. 866 ; *Re Union of London and Smith's Bank Conveyance, ante*) ; *and the covenant must "touch and concern" such land.*

The test that a covenant must "touch and concern" the land was first applied to covenants between landlord and tenant and the meaning of the phrase is considered further *post*, p. 841. It means that the covenant must be one beneficial to the owner of the land as such owner, and not merely one which will benefit him in some other capacity. Lord Macnaghten said, in *Dyson* v. *Forster* [1909] A.C. 98, at p. 102 : "The question is, does this covenant affect the nature, quality, or value of the land, or is it a covenant simply collateral ? " The words "with reference to the subject-matter" in the L.P.A. 1925, s. 142, have the same meaning (*Barnes* v. *City of London Real Property Co.* [1918] 2 Ch. 18).

In *Marquess of Zetland* v. *Driver* [1939] Ch. 1, Farwell, J., in the Court of Appeal, said : "The covenant must be one that touches or concerns the land, by which is meant that it must be imposed for the benefit or to enhance the value of the land retained by the vendor or some part of it." See further, Elphinstone, Covenants Affecting Land, art. 51, p. 55.

See also *Re Gadd's Land Transfer* [1966] Ch. 56 in which it was held that the mere retention of a service road on a developed building estate was sufficient to enable the enforcement of a covenant that only one private dwelling-house should be erected on adjoining plots since this significantly affected user of the road and the obligations inherent in excessive user.

At first sight one might have thought that a covenant against competing on the covenantor's land with a business conducted on the covenantee's land would affect the value of the latter land from collateral circumstances rather than *per se* (see *Wilkes* v. *Spooner* [1911] 2 K.B. 473, at p. 485). None the less, such a covenant has in fact been held enforceable between successors of the original parties (*Newton Abbot Co-operative Society, Ltd.* v. *Williamson & Treadgold* [1952] Ch. 286 ; see also *Re Royal Victoria Pavilion, Ramsgate* [1961] Ch. 581). However, it has more recently been held that the common law doctrine avoiding contracts in restraint of trade does apply to a restraint on the use of a particular piece of land, and not only to restraints on the activities of a particular person or company, even though the covenant in question be contained in a mortgage of the land (*Esso Petroleum Co.* v. *Harper's Garage* [1968] A.C. 269).

The decision in *Esso Petroleum Co.* v. *Harper's Garage, ante*, raises the question of exactly how far the common-law doctrine of restraint of trade inhibits the equitable rules as to restrictive covenants. It was argued that such covenants are subject to the common-law doctrine but would never in fact be found unreasonable. This was rejected in the House of Lords, where the majority view was expressed that restrictive covenants would not be subject to the restraint of trade doctrine at all, *provided* they satisfied the test of the covenantor being a person with *no* previous right to be on the land (as is a purchaser in the ordinary case). This test may not always prove acceptable, for example, if the restrictive covenant is imposed on a tenant buying the reversion or on a vendor in respect of adjoining land retained. Accordingly the less precise minority view of Lord Wilberforce may be preferable, namely, that since the common-law doctrine of restraint of trade is based on public policy, it will not apply to transactions which have " passed into the accepted and normal currency of commercial or contractual or conveyancing relations." Nevertheless, the majority test was applied by the Court of Appeal, in respect of covenants in a lease which were accordingly valid as the lessee had not previously been in possession, in *Cleveland Petroleum Co., Ltd.* v. *Dartstone, Ltd.* [1969] 1 W.L.R. 116.

(ii) *The benefit of the covenant must have been assigned to the purchaser or annexed to land acquired by him.*

In *Reid* v. *Bickerstaff* [1909] 2 Ch. 305, at pp. 319, 320, Cozens-Hardy, M.R., stated the rule as follows: " If on a sale of part of an estate the purchaser covenants with the vendor, his heirs and assigns, not to deal with the purchased property in a particular way, *a subsequent purchaser of part of the estate* [retained by the vendor] does not take the benefit of the covenant unless (a) he is an express assignee of the covenant, as distinct from assignee of the land, or (b) the restrictive covenant is expressed to be for the benefit and protection of the particular parcel purchased by the subsequent purchaser. In the case of (a) the subsequent purchaser can, of course, sue. In the case of (b) the benefit of the covenant passes to the purchaser, whether he knew of its existence or not . . . But unless either (a) or (b) can be established, it remains for the vendor to enforce or abstain from enforcing the restrictive covenant."

It is a question of construction of a covenant whether the right to pass the benefit by express assignment is excluded by annexation of the benefit (*Stilwell* v. *Blackman* [1968] Ch. 508). " Express assignment of the benefit of a restrictive covenant can only be forbidden if it is positively excluded ; and automatic assignment of the benefit with the passing of the covenantee's land can only be permitted if it is positively included " (*ibid., per* Ungoed-Thomas, J.).

Thus, the benefit may pass :—

(a) *By express assignment* to a person who, by the same transaction, acquires an interest in the land or part of the land benefited by the covenant (*Re Union of London and Smith's Bank Conveyance* [1933] Ch. 611 ; *Russell* v. *Archdale* [1964] Ch. 38). Express assignment of the benefit of a covenant may be made on sale of part of the land benefited notwithstanding that the benefit was annexed to the whole (but not to part only) of that land (*Stilwell* v. *Blackman, ante*). If the vendor has sold the whole or any part of his land to a purchaser who has not taken an assignment of the benefit of covenant at the time of the sale the purchaser cannot obtain the benefit of it by a subsequent assignment (*Chambers* v. *Randall* [1923] 1 Ch. 149 ; *Re Union of London and Smith's Bank Conveyance, ante*). An assignment of the benefit taking effect in equity only is sufficient (*Newton Abbot Co-operative Society, Ltd.* v. *Williamson & Treadgold, Ltd.* [1952] Ch. 286). Where there has been an *express* assignment of the benefit to a purchaser, it was decided in the *Newton Abbot* case that evidence of surrounding circumstances may be sufficient to show that the land to be benefited was ascertainable with reasonable certainty, but this decision is questioned by Sir Lancelot Elphinstone in an article in the *Law Quarterly Review*, vol. 68, p. 353. Nevertheless, the decision was approved by Wilberforce, J., in *Marten* v. *Flight Refuelling, Ltd.* [1962] Ch. 115. In the last mentioned case the second plaintiff was the original covenantee and the first plaintiff the person for whose benefit in equity the covenant was taken. Consequently, the question whether the benefit of the covenant might pass to a subsequent purchaser did not arise. However, before determining that a successor in title of the land restricted was bound in equity it was necessary to decide that the covenant was taken for the benefit of ascertainable land. In arriving at this decision Wilberforce, J., considered that he was entitled to have regard to surrounding and attendant circumstances.

Roxburgh, J., suggested in *Russell* v. *Archdale, ante,* that if such express assignment of the benefit of a covenant entered into before 1926 took place after 1925 it might be argued that the assignment was a charge on land requiring registration as a land charge, although the covenant was not registrable. It is not thought that this argument is sound and Roxburgh, J., did not express any opinion on it. The basis of the argument appears to be that the assignment effects a charge, as the covenant ceases to be enforceable in the absence of assignment. See the note of the proceedings in which the question was raised in *Solicitors' Journal,* vol. 100, pp. 679, 680.

(b) *If the benefit of the covenant was annexed to land and an interest in that land is conveyed to a purchaser.* In this case the benefit will pass with the land even if the purchaser, at the time when he bought, was unaware of the existence of the covenant.

Thus Romer, L.J., expressed the rule in these words in *Re Union of London and Smith's Bank Conveyance, ante,* at p. 628 : " A purchaser from the original covenantee of land retained by him when he executed the conveyance containing the covenant will be entitled to the benefit of the covenant if the conveyance shows that the covenant was intended to enure for the benefit of that particular land. It follows that, if what is being acquired by the purchaser was only part of the land shown by the conveyance as being intended to be benefited, it must also be shown that the benefit was intended to enure to each portion of that land." Thus, phrases such as " for the benefit of land shown on the plan," " land I am retaining known as my X estate," " the vendor's adjoining and neighbouring land " are not sufficient to annex the benefit to each and every part thereof (*Russell* v. *Archdale* [1964] Ch. 38, not following *dicta* of Romer, L.J., in *Drake* v. *Gray* [1936] Ch. 451). These cases were followed in *Re Jeff's Transfer* (*No.* 2) [1966] 1 W.L.R. 841, where Stamp, J., held that a covenant expressed to be " for the benefit of the Chorleywood Estate (Loudwater) belonging to the vendor " could not be construed as being for the benefit of each and every part of the retained land so as to pass by virtue of annexation and without any express assignment to the purchasers of parts of it.

In *Re Selwyn's Conveyance* [1967] Ch. 674, restrictive covenants had been entered into for the benefit of " the adjoining or neighbouring land part of *or lately part of* the Selwyn estate " ; Goff, J., held that the italicised words did not cause the annexation to fail for uncertainty but even showed an intention to benefit each and every part of the estate by envisaging parts in different ownerships.

The annexation to land of the benefit of a covenant takes place where the intention so to do is shown by the instrument creating the covenant (*Re Heywood's Conveyance ; Cheshire Lines Committee* v. *Liverpool Corporation* [1938] 2 All E.R. 230). Covenants are often imposed expressly for the benefit of land described by plan or otherwise. In such cases no question can arise (*Reid* v. *Bickerstaff* [1909] 2 Ch. 305). A covenant expressed to be made for the benefit of the owner of specified land is thereby annexed to that land (*Drake* v. *Gray, ante ; Re Ecclesiastical Commissioners' Conveyance* [1936] Ch. 430) ; a covenant for the benefit of " the vendor's adjoining and neighbouring land " is also sufficient to annex the benefit provided that such land can be ascertained (*Russell* v. *Archdale* [1964] Ch. 38). Whatever method is used it is essential that the land to be benefited should be clearly identified (*Newton Abbot Co-operative Society* v. *Williamson, ante*). It is not sufficient merely that the deed imposing the covenant showed by its language an intention that the parties should be mutually bound by the covenants (*Re Pinewood Estate, Farnborough* [1958] Ch. 280).

If the covenant is so properly worded, the benefit of the covenant becomes annexed to and passes with such land to subsequent assignees by a mere grant of the reserved land, in the same manner as an easement appurtenant thereto will pass with land, without express mention, or proof of special bargain, and even although the purchaser is unaware of the existence of the covenant (*Rogers* v. *Hosegood* [1900] 2 Ch. 388). This would appear to be so although such covenant was not made with the person having the legal estate. In a conveyance from *C & Co.* and their mortgagees to *B*, *B* covenanted with *C & Co.* (not with the mortgagees having the legal estate) to erect on the land only one house, and declared that the covenant was to enure for the benefit of *C & Co.*, their heirs and assigns, as regards any of their adjoining lands, and it was held that this was a covenant which concerned *C & Co.'s* adjoining land, and being declared to be for its benefit, became annexed to and passed with the land to subsequent assignees (*Rogers* v. *Hosegood, ante*).

Re Union of London and Smith's Bank Conveyance [1933] Ch. 611, provides a good illustration. A covenant was made in favour of certain purchasers, their heirs and assigns, or other the owners or owner for the time being of land coloured on a plan or any part or parts thereof. It was held that this covenant was annexed to the land described so that the benefit would run with it. On the other hand, covenants in the same conveyance by the purchasers in favour of the vendors " their successors and assigns " were held not to have been annexed to any land of the vendors. That words apt to annex the benefit had been used in the first case was one reason why it was held that the intention to annex the benefit of the other covenants was not shown. A covenant with a person and his assigns refers to assigns of the covenant and not of any land belonging to the covenantee, and so does not attach the benefit to that land unless the covenant contains other words connecting the word " assigns " with the land (*Renals* v. *Cowlishaw* (1879), 11 Ch. D. 866 ; *Re Union of London and Smith's Bank Conveyance, ante*). For lists of cases in which the benefit was annexed, and of cases in which the benefit was not annexed, see Elphinstone, Covenants Affecting Land, p. 58 *et seq.*

For the benefit of a covenant to be validly so annexed to land, that land must have been capable of being benefited by the covenant. In *Re Ballard's Conveyance* [1937] Ch. 473, the covenant in question was with the owner of the Childwickbury Estate, which comprised 1,700 acres. Clauson, J., held that, while the covenant might touch and concern a small part of the estate, it could not touch and concern the greater part of it. There were no words such as " or any part thereof," which might have shown an intention to annex the covenant to part of the land and so it was held that the covenant could not be treated as being annexed to such part of the land as was touched and concerned by it.

In *Marquess of Zetland* v. *Driver* [1939] Ch. 1, a covenant had been made for the benefit of such part or parts of lands subject to a settlement as might remain unsold or as should be sold with the express benefit of the covenant. The lands comprised in the settlement included a small parcel of land contiguous to the land on which the covenant was imposed, a number of scattered parcels of land in the neighbourhood and a larger undeveloped estate, part of which was more than a mile from the restricted land.   The Court of Appeal distinguished *Re Ballard's Conveyance, ante,* on the ground that in that case the covenant was expressed to run with the whole estate, whereas in the present case it was for the benefit of the whole or any part or parts of the unsold property.   The provision that the benefit should be annexed to the settled land until sale and thereafter only if it was expressly assigned was held to be valid.   The essence of the decision was that the covenant was, by the words used, annexed to the parts of the settled estate capable of being benefited by it and so passed by a conveyance of such parts.   The court distinguished *Re Ballard's Conveyance* but did not express any opinion as to the correctness of the decision.   In fact, professional opinion tends to criticise it.   For instance, Sir Lancelot Elphinstone, in his Covenants Affecting Land, at p. 60, argues that the decision is wrong because the annexation could have been construed as effective as regards such part of the land as was in fact touched and concerned by the covenant.   Compare also *Marten* v. *Flight Refuelling, Ltd.* [1962] Ch. 115, where a covenant was held able to benefit the whole of the Crichel Estate, which comprised 7,500 acres.

The result is that when a vendor of a large estate sells a part of it and imposes on that part restrictive covenants he should take care to express the covenants as being for the benefit of the whole or any part or parts of the retained land.   In construing covenants in which this has not been done *Re Ballard's Conveyance, ante,* must be regarded as an authority, but one which may well be overruled if the point comes before a higher court.

(*c*) *Where the dominant and servient lands were both part of a building scheme in respect of which the covenant was made.*   The passing of both the benefit and the burden of covenants constituting building schemes are subject to special rules which are set out below.

Statutory powers of local and other authorities to enforce covenants. —It is provided by the Housing Act, 1957, s. 151, that where (*a*) a local authority have sold or exchanged land acquired by them under the Act and the purchaser has entered into a covenant with the local authority concerning the land ; or (*b*) an owner of any land has entered into a covenant with the local authority concerning the land for the purposes of any of the provisions of the Act ; the authority shall have power to enforce the covenant against the persons deriving title under the covenantor, notwithstanding that the authority are not interested in any land for the benefit of which the covenant was entered into. This section does not refer expressly to *restrictive* covenants, but its object is to change the general rule (*ante,* p. 559) that a covenantee must retain land capable of being benefited, and, as that rule applies only to restrictive covenants, it seems that the section would not make the burden of a *positive* covenant pass with the land.

Statutory water undertakers may enforce an agreement as to water rights against successors in title of an owner if the agreement is expressed to be so enforceable without regard to equitable rules as to the passing of the burden ; such an agreement should be registered under the L.C.A. 1972 (Water Act, 1945, s. 15).

A local planning authority has power to enter into an agreement with any person interested in land for the purpose of restricting or regulating the development or use of the land. Such an agreement may be enforced by the local planning authority against persons deriving title under the owner *as if the local planning authority were possessed of adjacent land and as if the agreement had been expressed to be made for the benefit of that land* (Town and Country Planning Act, 1971, s. 52).

Somewhat similar provisions enable the Forestry Commissioners and the Nature Conservancy to enforce a forestry dedication covenant and a restriction contained in an agreement with the Nature Conservancy, respectively, against the successors of the covenantor although they do not retain adjoining land capable of being benefited (Forestry Act, 1967, s. 5 (2) ; National Parks and Access to the Countryside Act, 1949, s. 16 (4)). See also National Trust Act, 1937, s. 8.

An agreement for use of land for a cattle-grid or by-pass will bind the interest of any person who is a party to the agreement notwithstanding any devolution of that interest (Highways Act, 1959, s. 92 (3), Sched. 24, para. 12).

Rights under an agreement with the Countryside Commission or a local authority made pursuant to the Countryside Act, 1968, are binding on successors in title (*ibid.*, s. 45 (3)).

Mutual restrictive covenants under a general building scheme.—
Where there is a general building scheme in connection with a defined area and there is an intention appearing that all purchasers shall be bound by defined restrictive covenants designed for their mutual benefit, such covenants, although they may be entered into with the vendor only, can be enforced in equity (provided that when made after 1925 they are registered as a land charge ; see *post*, p. 569) by and against all persons who take as purchasers under the scheme.

The basic question which determines whether or not individual purchasers can enforce the covenants against each other is whether the intention shown was that the covenants were to be for the benefit of the several purchasers *inter se*, and not merely for the protection of the vendor in respect of his remaining property (*Lawrence* v. *South County Freeholds* [1939] Ch. 656). Thus in *Baxter* v. *Four Oaks Properties, Ltd.* [1965] Ch. 816, Cross, J., said that " what came to be called ' building schemes ' were enforced by the courts if satisfied that it was the intention of the parties that the various purchasers should have rights *inter se*, even though no attempt was made to bring them into direct contractual relations." Such intention can be gathered from any circumstances which can throw light upon what the intention was (*Nottingham Patent Brick and Tile Co.* v. *Butler* (1886), 16 Q.B.D. 778). If a vendor had no property remaining, this would be a strong element in favour of the presumption that the covenants were for the benefit of the purchasers against each of the other purchasers (*ibid.*). This will be so even though the covenants be expressed to be entered into with the vendor only (*Mackenzie* v. *Childers* (1889), 43 Ch. D. 265) ; and even though the covenants were also for the protection of the vendor's remaining land. But, as stated in Dart, 8th ed., at p. 645 : " the fact that the several purchasers were not aware at the date of their common purchase, of the existence of any such covenants, seems to be almost conclusive evidence of an intention that the covenants were not entered into for the benefit of the purchasers *inter se*, but for the advantage of the vendor himself." This passage was referred to with approval by Farwell, J., in *Osborne* v. *Bradley* [1903] 2 Ch. 446, where the learned judge stated that in order to arrive at the inference that a building scheme was intended, he would have to find that all the purchasers intended to contract one with another, as they purchased, to abide by the various covenants which were made applicable to the whole estate ; and also, where the vendor retained a number of plots, that he, the vendor, intended to enter into similar covenants. It would not be reasonable to draw the inference that a number of persons, coming in and buying, intend to be bound to an unknown number of unknown persons in respect of an estate which, so far as it has been sold, *was undefined*, and to undertake liabilities to them and to accept a corresponding benefit from them ; in that case neither the persons, nor the estate, nor the lots in respect of which those covenants were entered into or undertaken, were in any way stated.

The validity of a power to waive covenants in a building scheme was considered in *Pearce* v. *Maryon-Wilson* [1935] Ch. 188. The plaintiff, the lessee of a house comprised in what was assumed to be a building scheme, alleged that there was an implied condition in the scheme that the common lessor could not exercise a power given to him by the covenants to consent to use of premises for purposes other than as private dwelling-houses, in such a way as to depreciate substantially the value of the remainder of the estate. It was held that there was no such implied condition and that the common lessor could authorise whatever user he thought fit.

The question whether a power reserved to the vendor to waive any of the covenants with regard to unsold lots, as occurred in *Osborne* v. *Bradley*, *ante*, prevented there being a building scheme, came up in the later case of *Elliston* v. *Reacher* [1908] 2 Ch. 374, at pp. 384, 387, where there was a similar clause. Although in the earlier case Farwell, J., decided that, having regard to the clause, there was no building scheme, Parker, J., in *Elliston* v. *Reacher*, did not think this was sufficient to negative the intention, otherwise clear, so far as the various lots were sold subject to the common restrictions. In the same case Parker, J., also laid down certain tests which have often been quoted, and which have been found helpful. He said that it must be proved (1) that both the plaintiffs and defendants derived title under a common vendor ; (2) that previously to selling the lands to which the plaintiffs and defendants were respectively entitled the vendor laid out his estate or a definite portion thereof (including the lands purchased by the plaintiffs and defendants respectively) for sale in lots subject to restrictions intended to be imposed on all the lots, and which, though varying in detail as to particular lots, were consistent, and consistent only with some general scheme of development ; (3) that these restrictions were intended by the common vendor to be *and were* for the benefit of all the lots intended to be sold, whether or not they were also intended to be *and were* for the benefit of other land retained by the vendor ; and (4) that both the plaintiffs and defendants, or their predecessors in title, purchased their lots from the common vendor upon the footing that the restrictions subject to which the purchases were made were to enure for the benefit of the other lots included in the general scheme, whether or not they were also to enure for the benefit of other lands retained by the vendors. The case went to the Court of Appeal ([1908] 2 Ch. 665), and the decision of Parker, J., was affirmed. As to the vendor having reserved power to alter the covenants, Cozens-Hardy, J., said that he did not deny that the insertion of such a power was an element to be considered, but that out of many building schemes which he had seen it was altogether exceptional not to see some power reserved to the vendor to abstract certain property from the scheme.

In connection with the second test above, in *Baxter* v. *Four Oaks Properties, Ltd.* [1965] Ch. 816 (at p. 828) Cross, J., observed that, unlike the case before him, " *Elliston* v. *Reacher* was not a case in which there was direct evidence, afforded by the execution of a deed of mutual covenant, that the parties intended a building scheme. The question was whether one could properly infer that intention in all the circumstances. In such a case, no doubt the fact that the common vendor did not divide his estate into lots before beginning to sell it is an argument against there having been an intention on his part and on the part of the various purchasers that there should be a building scheme, since it is, perhaps, *prima facie* unlikely that a purchaser of a plot intends to enter into obligations to an unknown number of subsequent purchasers. I cannot believe, however, that Parker, J., was intending to lay it down that the fact that the common vendor did not bind himself to sell off the defined area to which the common law [i.e., of the building scheme] was to apply in lots of any particular size but proposed to sell off parcels of various sizes according to the requirements of the various purchasers must, as a matter of law, preclude the court from giving effect to the clearly proved intention that the purchasers were to have rights *inter se* to enforce the provisions of the common law [i.e., of the building scheme]." Cross, J., purported to find support for his decision that, in effect, a deed of mutual covenant prevailed over the omission to lay out the estate in plots, in the judgment of Simonds, J., in *Lawrence* v. *South County Freeholds* [1939] Ch. 656 (where absence of a plan of lots proved fatal), who said (at p. 674) that " it may, no doubt, be urged that even without a division of the building estate into plots, there may be sufficient evidence of a building scheme and I do not wish to rule out some exceptional case."

It now appears clear that proof of each specific requirement as stated in *Elliston* v. *Reacher* (p. 566) may not be essential (for instance, prior laying out in lots) if on construction of the conveyancing documents it is apparent that purchasers of parcels were intended to have mutual rights so that there was a common intention and common interest between purchasers to " lay down a local law involving reciprocal rights and obligations " (see *Re Dolphin's Conveyance* [1970] 1 Ch. 654 and the discussion by G. H. Newsom, Q.C., in *Solicitors' Journal*, vol. 114, p. 796, where it is pointed out that phrases such as " building scheme " suggest too narrow a scope and that one might better refer to a " scheme of reciprocal rights and obligations " or " a scheme of local law " (to be shortened in practice to a " scheme ") ; but compare also the more critical consideration by P.V.B. in the *Law Quarterly Review*, vol. 86, at pp. 445–447). Reference should also be made to *Brunner* v. *Greenslade* [1971] Ch. 997, in which Megarry, J., also adopted basically the approach of looking to the elements of community of interest and reciprocity of obligation in holding that where there was a scheme of development what bound plot-owners *inter se* was an equity independent of any contractual obligation. See also, however, *Eagling* v. *Gardner* [1970] 2 All E.R. 838, in which Ungoed-Thomas, J., applied the principles as laid down in *Elliston* v. *Reacher* by Parker, J.

As regards the words " *and were* " in the third test of Parker, J., in *Elliston* v. *Reacher*, above, it was held in *Lord Northbourne* v. *Johnston & Son* [1922] 2 Ch. 309 that where in the case of a building estate restrictive covenants are entered into for the purpose of preserving the general residential character of the estate, it is *not* incumbent on the plaintiff, on each occasion of enforcing such covenants, to show that the covenants are, in fact, beneficial to any portions of the retained estate. All that is necessary is to prove that they were imposed for the benefit of the estate as a whole.

In *Reid* v. *Bickerstaff* [1909] 2 Ch. 305, Cozens-Hardy, M.R., said that the principal essentials of a building scheme are that there must be a defined area within which the scheme is operative ; that reciprocity is the foundation of the idea of a scheme ; and that a purchaser of one parcel cannot be subject to an implied obligation to purchasers of an undefined and unknown area. *Not only must the area be defined, but the obligations to be imposed within that area must be defined.* Those obligations need not be identical. For example, there might be houses of a certain value in one part and houses of a different value in another part. *A building scheme is not*, he said, *created by the mere fact that the owner of an estate sells it in lots and takes varying covenants from various purchasers.* There must be notice to the various purchasers of what he ventured to call the local law imposed by the vendors upon a definite area. See also *Willé* v. *St. John* (*No.* 1) [1910] 1 Ch. 84, 325 ; *Milbourne* v. *Lyons* [1914] 2 Ch. 231 ; *Kelly* v. *Barrett* [1924] 2 Ch. 379 ; *Mayner* v. *Payne* [1914] 2 Ch. 555 ; *Torbay Hotel, Ltd.* v. *Jenkins* [1927] 2 Ch. 225 ; *Baxter* v. *Four Oaks Properties, Ltd.* [1965] Ch. 816 ; and *Re Wembley Park Estate Co., Ltd.'s Transfer* [1968] Ch. 491.

Much the same principle has been applied in the case of the letting of flats, when the intention is that each lessee is to have the benefit of covenants governing the common user of the property. In *Hudson* v. *Cripps* [1896] 1 Ch. 265, the lessor proposed to turn certain residential flats into one single club. A lessee of another flat obtained an injunction against the lessor on the ground that it was proved that there was in existence a common purpose revealed in the original intention of the lessor and accepted in good faith by the lessees, and that the proposed letting by the lessor would be a breach of this common intention. See also *Gedge* v. *Bartlett* (1900), 17 T.L.R. 43 ; *Jaeger* v. *Mansions Consolidated, Ltd.* (1902), 87 L.T. 690 ; *Newman* v. *Real Estate Debenture Corporation, Ltd.* [1940] 1 All E.R. 131 ; *Pearce* v. *Maryon-Wilson* [1935] Ch. 188.

Such a letting scheme will not be inferred, however, in regard to a house which was originally built as one dwelling and never physically split into separate dwelling-houses, although separate floors were sub-let as flats. Such a case arose in *Kelly* v. *Battershell* [1949] 2 All E.R. 830, where it was held that the covenants in the sub-leases were inserted to ensure that the terms of the head lease were not infringed, and not by reason of a letting scheme.

Where a building estate is offered for sale by public auction, the particulars and conditions (in the absence of a condition to the contrary) constitute an invitation to the public to come in and purchase on the footing that the whole of the property offered for sale is to be bound by a general law affecting the character of the buildings to be erected thereon (*Spicer* v. *Martin* (1888), 14 App. Cas. 12). In *Re Birmingham and District Land Co. and Allday* [1893] 1 Ch. 342, part of a building estate was put up for sale by auction in lots, subject to conditions as to building. One lot only was sold, and it was held that the purchaser was entitled to the benefit of the contract implied in the restrictive conditions against the unsold lots, and to have the same expressed in his conveyance. See also *Holford* v. *Acton Urban Council* [1898] 2 Ch. 240.

Where purchasers holding under a building scheme release the covenants with a view to entering into new ones, the benefit or burden of those new covenants passes according to the rules usually affecting covenants in general without regard to the former building scheme which has ceased (*Re Pinewood Estate, Farnborough* [1958] Ch. 280).

Registration of covenants in connection with building schemes.—A difficulty has come to light which does not appear to have been appreciated when the 1925 legislation was drafted. It is not usual to have a mutual deed of covenant (as in *Baxter* v. *Four Oaks Properties, Ltd.* [1965] Ch. 816), but instead the common vendor imposes covenants on each purchaser in the conveyance to that purchaser, and there is usually no express covenant entered into by the common vendor. If all plots on the building scheme are sold and the common vendor registers the same covenants against all purchasers no difficulty arises. On the other hand, the common vendor may omit to register covenants against some purchaser. In this case it might be thought that any covenants imposed on that purchaser would, on a future resale by him, become void and thereby a purchaser of another plot would be prejudiced. If, of course, the common vendor enters into express covenants binding the land retained by him, any purchaser can register these and make himself safe. If the vendor does not expressly enter into any covenants there does not seem to be anything which can be registered against him. It may be argued that the implied obligation binding on the vendor to hold retained land subject to the common restrictions (*Re Birmingham & District Land Co. and Allday* [1893] 1 Ch. 342 ; *Davis* v. *Leicester Corporation* [1894] 2 Ch. 208) is itself a " covenant or agreement restrictive of the user of land " within the meaning of the L.C.A. 1972, s. 2 (5), Class D (ii), and so itself registrable. But how is a purchaser to know exactly which plots are retained ? It is just possible that registration might properly be effected against the whole building estate. The editors of this volume are not aware that registration in this way has ever been attempted.

A more satisfactory conclusion in practice would be that reached by the late J. M. Lightwood in his " Conveyancer's Letter " in the *Law Journal*, vol. 78, p. 39. Mr. Lightwood argued that the implied obligation on the vendor is not within the definition of a " restrictive covenant " in the L.C.A. 1925, s. 10 (1), Class D (ii), and so is not registrable at all. The result is, Mr. Lightwood wrote, " that the Land Charges Register is not concerned with restrictions arising under building schemes except when they are embodied in an express covenant or agreement. In that case the covenantee should register them against the covenantor . . . So far as the building scheme raises ' reciprocity of obligation ' between the purchasers there is nothing to register and the obligations are not void for want of registration." However, this conclusion does not appear acceptable in principle : there are always express covenants entered into by each individual purchaser ; all that equity does is extend the range of persons to whom the *benefit* of these easements may pass ; registration is concerned with the persons to whom the *burden* may pass ; statute provides that a restrictive covenant which is registrable but not registered is void against a purchaser of a legal estate in the land for money's worth ; and Harman, J., has said " I do not see how that which is void and which is not to prejudice the purchaser can be validated by some equitable doctrine " (*Hollington Bros.* v. *Rhodes* [1951] 2 All E.R. 578, at p. 580). There is a full discussion of the problem in the *Conveyancer N.S.*, vol. 20, p. 370 *et seq.*

Sale of land subject to existing restrictive covenants.—A purchaser is entitled to have his conveyance made subject only to the restrictive covenants (if any) referred to in the contract ; the conveyance need not be *expressed* to be subject to any other covenants even if the purchaser will take subject to them in consequence of his having notice of them (*Re Wallis and Barnard's Contract* [1899] 2 Ch. 515 ; see also *Re Cooper and Crondace's Contract* (1904), 90 L.T. 258).

If a purchaser has agreed to buy land subject to existing restrictive covenants which will be enforceable against him he will not be granted an order for specific performance of the contract unless he is prepared to enter into a covenant to indemnify the vendor against any breach of those covenants (*Re Poole and Clarke's Contract* [1904] 2 Ch. 173), but if the vendor will not remain liable on the covenants he cannot insist on having a covenant for indemnity from the purchaser (*Re Poole and Clarke's Contract, ante ; Re Cooper and Crondace's Contract, ante ; Harris v. Boots, Cash Chemists (Southern), Ltd.* [1904] 2 Ch. 376). See further, Elphinstone, Covenants Affecting Land, p. 148. General Condition 11 (2) of The Law Society's Conditions of Sale, 1973 Revision, provides that if the vendor, or any estate of which the vendor is personal representative or trustee, will, after completion, remain liable in respect of any existing restrictive or positive covenant and, in the contract, the property is *expressed to be sold subject thereto*, the purchaser shall enter into a covenant for indemnity. See also General Condition 19 (5) of the National Conditions of Sale, 18th ed., the wording of which appears not as satisfactory.

The vendor will remain liable on the covenants if he was himself the covenantor and did not limit his liability to the time during which the land was vested in him, or if he agreed to indemnify one who was liable. Covenants for indemnity should be limited so as to apply only so far as the restrictive covenants are then enforceable ; if this is not done a purchaser who wishes to allege that the covenants have been waived, or otherwise have ceased to have effect, may be met with the reply that they were revived by the terms of the covenant he gave to the vendor. Under ss. 77 and 189 of the L.P.A. 1925, covenants of indemnity, which formerly were treated as personal covenants, are made to run with the land. It was held in *Reckitt v. Cody* [1920] 2 Ch. 452 that no action will lie under a covenant of indemnity until the person entitled to the benefit of the covenant has actually taken steps to enforce the restriction. See also generally as to covenants of indemnity at p. 553 *et seq.*

PART 4. COVENANTS IN REGISTERED CONVEYANCING

Hitherto this Chapter has not distinguished between covenants relating to unregistered land and those relating to land the title to which is registered. In fact, there is no substantive difference in this respect in the rules applying in the two systems of conveyancing. A proprietor of registered land has power to impose by covenant any obligation as to user of the land but only " so far as the law permits " (L.R.A. 1925, s. 40 (1)). Accordingly the general rules already dealt with as to the running of the benefit and of the burden of covenants relating to land apply equally here (see *Cator v. Newton* [1940] 1 K.B. 415).

Forms.—A form is prescribed for transfers of registered land imposing restrictive covenants (L.R.R. 1925, r. 135, and Schedule, Form 43). This form requires the use of the prescribed form of transfer of part of freehold land (i.e., *ibid.*, Form 20) with the addition of the following words " And *C D* hereby covenants with *A B* for the benefit of the remainder of the land comprised in the above title number as follows, namely ", after which the form sets out some elementary examples. This prescribed form is not always adequate (e.g., it is not appropriate for building schemes, *ante*, p. 565, nor would it appear sufficient to annex the benefit to each and every part of the remainder of the land : *Re Jeff's Transfer (No.* 2) [1966] 1 W.L.R. 841) and in practice its use is not insisted upon (see Ruoff, Land Registration Forms, 2nd ed., pp. 65–70, Precedents 22 and 23).

Notice.—In registered conveyancing, the function of registration under the L.C.A. 1972 is fulfilled by the entry of a notice of the restrictive covenant on the charges register of the servient land (L.R.A. 1925, s. 50 (1) and L.R.R. 1925, rr. 7 (*c*) and 212) for which no application is strictly speaking necessary (L.R.A. 1925, s. 40 (3)). As with registration under the L.C.A. 1972, the effect of such an entry is thereafter to give notice to all concerned (L.R.A. 1925, s. 50 (2), also ss. 20 (1) and 52 (1)), including lessees who may not be entitled to see the lessor's title (*White* v. *Bijou Mansions* [1937] Ch. 610 ; on appeal [1938] Ch. 351). If there is no such entry, the restrictive covenant will be defeated by a registered disposition for valuable consideration (L.R.A. 1925, s. 20 (1) (*a*) and (4) ; *Hodges* v. *Jones* [1935] Ch. 657). Here, however, the " valuable consideration " apparently need not be in money or money's worth (L.R.A. 1925, s. 3 (xxxi), compare L.C.A. 1972, s. 4 (6)).

The equitable doctrine of notice, which still applies in unregistered conveyancing in respect of covenants made either before 1926 or between a lessor and a lessee (*ante*, p. 557), appears to be excluded from registered conveyancing. There is here no exception for covenants made before 1926 from the provisions as to entry of a notice, so that such an entry should normally be made on first registration (see L.R.A. 1925, s. 50 (1)). Against this, covenants made between a lessor and a lessee are excepted from the provisions as to entry of a notice (*ibid.* ; see also *Newman* v. *Real Estate Debenture Corporation* [1940] 1 All E.R. 131). But notwithstanding this exception, the position if there is no entry of a notice in the charges register is that a registered disposition for valuable consideration of the lessor's estate (but not of the lessee's estate) would, irrespective of notice, still defeat the covenant (L.R.A. 1925, ss. 20 (1) and 23 (1)).

Registered Land Practice Notes, 1972, pp. 26–27, No. 55, deals with the entry of notice of unregistered restrictive covenants on first registration of title. If the applicant for first registration believes that such a covenant is unenforceable he may request that notice of it be omitted and must support the request with a clear official certificate of a search, correctly applied for in all respects, in the Land Charges Department.

Positive covenants.—Entry of a notice in the charges register is merely deemed to give notice and does not operate to validate any covenant otherwise unenforceable (L.R.A. 1925, s. 52 (2) ; *Willé* v. *St. John* [1910] 1 Ch. 325) and there may be rectification of the register by cancellation of the notice (L.R.A. 1925, s. 82 ; *Re Sunnyfield* [1932] 1 Ch. 79). Therefore the mere entry of a notice will not cause the burden of a positive covenant to run with the land (*Cator* v. *Newton* [1940] 1 K.B. 45). Accordingly notice of covenants the burden of which does not run and which are thus purely personal should not be entered on the register as though affecting the land (see *per* Farwell, J., in *Barnes* v. *Cadogan Developments, Ltd.* [1930] 1 Ch. 479, at p. 486).

However, notwithstanding the above, the practice is for a note to be made in the proprietorship register of the burden of positive covenants created *after* first registration and a copy of them sewn up in the land or charge certificate (Registered Land Conveyancing Practice Notes, 1972, p. 29, No. 21). The reason is that otherwise the existence of such covenants contained in a document retained at H.M. Land Registry (see L.R.R. 1925, r. 90) might be overlooked by the vendor and a covenant for indemnity in consequence not taken from the purchaser (as to which see L.R.R. 1925, r. 110).

Benefit of covenants.—Conversely to the above, it is not the practice to enter the benefit of covenants on the register of title to the covenantee's land (Registered Conveyancing Practice Notes, 1972, pp. 28–29, No. 18 ; compare L.R.R. 1925, r. 2 (2) (*c*)). " If, however, in a particular case a special request is made for the purpose, a note will be entered on the register that a transfer or a conveyance contains covenants which were expressed to be imposed for the benefit of the land in the title " (*ibid.*).

PART 5. CONSTRUCTION OF VARIOUS COVENANTS

Covenants which are usually found in leases are dealt with in the chapter on that subject, although certain covenants are common both in conveyances of freeholds and in leases. A few particular covenants which often cause difficulty when found in conveyances will be mentioned here.

Covenant to submit plans before building.—In an action to compel the defendant to pull down and remove a house for breach of covenant first to submit plans, Eve, J., said : " I think that the covenant . . . involves a negative contract that no building shall be commenced until plans have been submitted to and approved by the vendor . . . In my opinion the covenant was broken once and for all when the house was erected contrary to it ; . . . The defendant, therefore, cannot be liable on the footing of a continuing breach " (*Powell* v. *Hemsley* [1909] 1 Ch. 680, at pp. 687, 688 ; affirmed [1909] 2 Ch. 252). Nominal damages only would be awarded if the only breach was a failure to submit plans (*ibid.*), but if buildings are erected that would not have been approved an injunction may be granted (*Goolden* v. *Anstee* (1868), 18 L.T. 989).

Covenant to contribute to the cost of road repairs.—A covenant is often inserted in a conveyance that a purchaser shall pay a rateable proportion of the cost of maintaining and repairing a road. Such a covenant refers to the cost of maintaining the road at a standard of repair existing or contemplated at the date of the conveyance and does not render the covenantor liable to contribute to the cost of making the road fit for heavier traffic existing at some later time (*Barton* v. *Alliance Economic Investment Co., Ltd.* (1935), 179 L.T. News. 256). Such a covenant may not, for example, impose a liability to contribute towards extensive reconstruction necessary to bring the road up to a standard fit for it to be taken over by the local authority (*Scott* v. *Brown* (1904), 69 J.P. 89). And see *Halsall* v. *Brizell* [1957] Ch. 169 where such a covenant was enforceable against the covenantor's successors in title (see *ante*, p. 554), but an additional assessment based on user was disallowed.

Difficulties often arise from undertakings by builders to bear road charges. In practice the interest of a purchaser, for instance of a house, is to obtain a covenant that the builder will make the road up to the standard required by the local authority and pay all charges arising before the road becomes repairable by the public. In *Richardson* v. *St. Meryl Estates, Ltd.*, reported in the *Estates Gazette*, 27th April, 1957, at p. 521, a covenant " to make, form and complete a proper road " and to indemnify the purchaser against road-making charges until its adoption by the local authority, was said by Lynskey, J., to give a purchaser " ample protection." Unfortunately, the covenant in issue in that case omitted any reference to indemnity. Two years was considered reasonable for compliance with the covenant, and as more than twelve years had elapsed thereafter, action to enforce the covenant was statute-barred. With regard to building works at the present time, or carried out recently, see the requirements of the Highways Act, 1959, ss. 192 to 198, *ante*, p. 21, which may protect a purchaser, and *Henshall* v. *Fogg* [1964] 1 W.L.R. 1127. Where a builder covenants to indemnify a purchaser against road charges and has also made a deposit under the " advance payments code " in the Highways Act, 1959, ss. 192 to 199, it may be necessary in the interest of the builder to insert a covenant that the purchaser will repay to him any sum by which the payment (with interest) may exceed the road charges ultimately incurred. If the road is made up by the street authority but the cost is less than the sum deposited and interest then the excess must be paid to the *owner for the time being* (Highways Act, 1959, s. 195 (1) (*a*)).

Private dwelling-house.—A covenant to use premises as a private dwelling-house only is broken by using them as a school (*Wickenden* v. *Webster* (1856), 25 L.J.Q.B. 264), or a charitable institution for board and education of children (*German* v. *Chapman* (1877), 7 Ch. D. 271), or a boarding house (*Hobson* v. *Tulloch* [1898] 1 Ch. 424), or for receiving paying guests (*Thorn* v. *Madden* [1925] Ch. 847 ; *Tendler* v. *Sproule* [1947] 1 All E.R. 193) ; or as a hospital for surgical tuberculosis (*Frost* v. *King Edward VII Welsh National Association for Prevention of Tuberculosis* [1918] 2 Ch. 180 ; on appeal 35 T.L.R. 138).

A lease contained a covenant that a house should not be used " for any purpose whatsoever other than for the purpose of a private dwelling-house, wherein no business of any kind is carried on." It was held that the sub-letting of three rooms of the first floor of the house to a sub-tenant was a breach of the covenant ; and that the words " wherein no business of any kind is carried on " must be construed as adding to the stringency of the covenant that the house should be used as a dwelling-house (*Barton* v. *Keeble* [1928] Ch. 517). Where there is nothing more than a covenant against user otherwise than as a private dwelling-house, a sub-division into two or more dwelling-houses is a breach of that covenant (*Barton* v. *Keeble, ante ; Dobbs* v. *Linford* [1953] 1 Q.B. 48). These decisions were followed more recently where a covenant " not at any time . . . [to] use [certain land] or any part thereof or any messuage or building now erected or hereafter to be erected thereon or on any part thereof for any purpose other than that of a single private dwelling-house . . . " was construed as *not* permitting the erection of a second dwelling-house on the land (*Re Enderick's Conveyance* [1973] 1 All E.R. 843). In that case the reference to " on any part " and to buildings to be erected were treated as unnecessary additions which did not curtail the general prohibition. It may be, however, that other covenants show that a sub-letting of part of the premises is contemplated. In such a case the covenant against user otherwise than as a private dwelling-house is construed in such a way as not to prevent sub-letting as two or more dwelling-houses (*Downie* v. *Turner* [1951] 2 K.B. 112, as explained in *Dobbs* v. *Linford, ante*). As to use as flats, see further, *A.-G.* v. *Mutual Tontine Westminster Chambers Association* (1876), 35 L.T. 224 ; *Kimber* v. *Adams* [1900] 1 Ch. 412 ; *Rogers* v. *Hosegood* [1900] 2 Ch. 388 ; *Ilford Park Estates, Ltd.* v. *Jacobs* [1903] 2 Ch. 522 ; *Day* v. *Waldron* (1919), 120 L.T. 634 ; *Barton* v. *Reed* [1932] 1 Ch. 362.

In *Jenkins* v. *Price* [1908] 1 Ch. 10, it was held that a covenant as to residence impliedly prohibited any assignment to a limited company. As to "paying guests," see *Thorn* v. *Madden* [1925] Ch. 847, and at p. 575. A covenant to erect private dwelling-houses only does not prevent the erection of stables (*Russell* v. *Baber* (1870), 18 W.R. 1021 ; *Blake* v. *Marriage* (1893), 9 T.L.R. 569) ; and therefore would not, it is thought, prevent the erection of a garage for the sole use of the owner of the dwelling-house. See also *Baxter* v. *Four Oaks Properties, Ltd.* [1965] Ch. 816 where a covenant that " No dwelling-house or other building shall be used . . . otherwise than as a private residence " was said not to be a covenant against erecting a block of flats, but only against using the building as flats.

What is a " business " and a " trade " ?—The word " trade " means buying and selling (*Doe d. Weatherell* v. *Bird* (1834), 2 Ad. & E. 161). The word " business " has a wider meaning and comprises occupations which are not carried on by an open exhibition of buying and selling and almost anything which is an occupation as distinguished from a pleasure (*Wickenden* v. *Webster* (1856), 25 L.J.Q.B. 264) ; although it was said by Denman, C.J., that every trade is a business (*Doe d. Weatherell* v. *Bird, ante*). In *Rolls* v. *Miller* (1884), 27 Ch. D. 71, at p. 87, Pearson, J., compared " business " to domestic life. He said : " that is a business which is carried on by any person in addition to, and diverse from, his ordinary domestic life. This, of course, makes the covenant tantamount to a covenant ' to use the premises as a private dwelling-house only '." The decision in *Doe d. Mackenzie* v. *Baylis* (1851), 17 L.T. (o.s.) 172, does not quite fit in with this definition. In that case ladies occupying premises formed a sisterhood and received boarders whose friends had abandoned them because of their change of faith, and it was held that they were *not* carrying on a business. They certainly could not have been said to have been using the premises as a dwelling-house only. The word " business " normally includes a profession such as the medical profession (*Re Williams' Will Trusts* [1953] Ch. 138).

The question whether letting premises as flats was " a business " came before Luxmoore, J., in *Barton* v. *Reed* [1932] 1 Ch. 362. In that case the lease contained a covenant by the lessee that he would not use the premises for, *inter alia*, " the carrying thereon any trade business or manufactory." Luxmoore, J., said that the sub-letting of premises in suites of apartments with or without the provision of any other service was " a business." But later on in his judgment the learned judge said that the fact that the under-lessee retained control of an important portion of the premises and was under liability to supply certain services like the provision of hot water and so on, constituted the carrying on of a business. This seems rather to limit the first more general statement of the judge. On the facts before him he decided that there was a breach of covenant.

In *Doe d. Bish* v. *Keeling* (1813), 1 M. & S. 95, it was held that three factors constituted a school a business : the invitation to the public, the circumstance that there would be more people about than in the case of a private house, and the fact that all manner of persons would resort to the house. But see *Rolls* v. *Miller* (1884), 27 Ch. D. 71, at p. 85, where it was held that advertising was not a necessary attribute of a business.

It does not appear to be essential that there should be *payment* in order to constitute a business. On the other hand payment does not necessarily make an occupation a business (*Rolls* v. *Miller, ante*). In that case it was held that the use of a house as a charitable home was carrying on the business of a lodging house. In *Bramwell* v. *Lacy* (1879), 10 Ch. D. 691, it was held that a hospital for poor persons who were charged according to their means, but no profit made, was a business. In *Thorn* v. *Madden* [1925] Ch. 847, it was held that the receiving of paying guests, although they were limited to friends of the tenant or vouched for by her friends, was a business. An important element in the case was that the defendant was " of set purpose occupying a house which she is aware is beyond her means." Indeed, the judge (Tomlin, J.), in the same case indicated that if a friend desiring to visit a friend suggested a visit, and the reply was : " I cannot afford to keep you, but I shall be delighted to see you if you will pay," there would be no breach of covenant.

If a covenant prohibits the carrying on of some specified trade upon the property, it is broken by carrying on that trade, although only as ancillary to another trade (*Fitz* v. *Iles* [1893] 1 Ch. 77 ; *Buckle* v. *Fredericks* (1890), 44 Ch. D. 244). But there is an exception when the trades of the plaintiff and defendant overlap. In such a case a covenant not to carry on the plaintiff's trade would not be broken by *bona fide* sales by the defendant of certain articles the sale of which formed part of the plaintiff's trade (*Lumley* v. *Metropolitan Railway Co.* (1876), 34 L.T. 774 ; *Stuart* v. *Diplock* (1889), 43 Ch. D. 343 ; *Bailey* v. *Skinner, etc.* (1898), 42 Sol. J. 780). On this ground it was held in *Lewis (A.) and Company (Westminster), Ltd.* v. *Bell Property Trust, Ltd.* [1940] Ch. 345, that the sale of cigarettes at the cashier's desk of a tea-shop did not amount to a breach of a covenant not to use the premises for the business of the sale of tobacco, cigars and cigarettes. See also *Labone* v. *Litherland U.D.C.* [1956] 1 W.L.R. 522.

The keeping of a local post office is not " trading " (*Frampton* v. *Gillison* (1927), 70 Sol. J. 965) ; but in *Westripp* v. *Baldock* [1939] 1 All E.R. 279 it was found, as a fact, that the business of a jobbing builder involved buying and selling of materials and therefore it was held that it amounted to the carrying on of a trade. Letting the gable ends of a house as a bill-posting station is a breach of a covenant not to carry on any trade or business upon the premises (*Tubbs* v. *Esser* (1909), 26 T.L.R. 145).

General words are not usually construed as limited to matters *ejusdem generis* with the named trade (*Wanton* v. *Coppard* [1899] 1 Ch. 92).

A restrictive covenant relating to trade or business may be void as being in unreasonable restraint of trade. Lord Denning, M.R., explained in *Petrofina, Ltd.* v. *Martin* [1966] Ch. 146, at p. 170, as follows : " No doubt in our law of land a covenant can be placed on a piece of land so as to prevent any trade being carried on there or any particular kind of trade. To such a case the doctrine of restraint of trade has no application. But when we come to covenants which restrict a tradesman in the way in which he may carry on his trade on his own land, then we get into the realm of contract. And the doctrine of restraint of trade does apply." See also *Esso Petroleum Co.* v. *Harper's Garage* [1968] A.C. 269.

Offensive trades.—A covenant not to carry on " any other offensive or noisy trade, business or profession whatsoever," may be broken by the use of the property as a private hospital (*Pembroke* v. *Warren* [1896] 1 Ir. R. 76). As to a public hospital, see *Tod-Heatly* v. *Benham* (1888), 40 Ch. D. 80 ; and also *Frost* v. *King Edward VII Welsh National Association for Prevention of Tuberculosis* [1918] 2 Ch. 180.

In construing the word " offensive," the situation of the property must be taken into consideration and the question whether any similar trade was carried on at the time of granting a lease. For instance, in *Devonshire* (*Duke*) v. *Brookshaw* (1899), 81 L.T. 83, a fish-frying business was under the circumstances of that case held to be offensive. See also *Errington* v. *Birt* (1911), 105 L.T. 373 ; *Adams* v. *Ursell* [1913] 1 Ch. 269. The business of a butcher is not necessarily of an offensive nature (*Cleaver* v. *Bacon* (1887), 4 T.L.R. 27) ; nor that of a slaughter-house (*Rapley* v. *Smart* (1893), 10 T.L.R. 174) ; nor a laundry business (*Knight* v. *Simmonds* [1896] 2 Ch. 294). For, as was said in *Devonshire* (*Duke*) v. *Brookshaw, ante*, some trades are necessarily offensive, others can be carried on without giving offence, but become offensive unless carried on with great care.

A covenant not to carry on any trade or business or occupation whereby any disagreeable noise or nuisance should be occasioned would prevent the carrying on of a boys' school (*Wanton* v. *Coppard* [1899] 1 Ch. 92).

"Erection," "building," "hoarding."—A petrol pump (*Mackenzie* v. *Abbott* (1926), 24 L.G.R. 444) ; a scaffolding (*R.* v. *Whittingham* (1840), 9 C. & P. 234) ; a cistern bricked up to the brim (*Bidder* v. *Trinidad Petroleum Co.* (1868), 17 W.R. 153) ; or a booth on wheels (*Williams* v. *Weston-super-Mare U.D.C.* (*No.* 2) (1910), 103 L.T. 9), may be an " erection." In *Paddington Corporation* v. *A.-G.* [1906] A.C. 1, Halsbury, L.C., said, at p. 3 : " there may be found a great variety of cases where, with reference to the subject-matter of the covenant and the meaning of what was in question between the parties, a screen or some erection of that nature might be considered a ' building ' with reference to some covenants and might not be considered a building with reference to others . . . It is impossible to give any definite meaning to [the word ' building '] in the loose language which is used in some cases ; anything which is in the nature of a building might be within one covenant and the same erection might not be a building with reference to another covenant." See *Foster* v. *Fraser* [1893] 3 Ch. 158, where it was held that the hoarding in question was not " a building " ; also *Wilson* v. *Queen's Club* [1891] 3 Ch. 522 ; and *Urban Housing Company, Ltd.* v. *Oxford Corporation* [1940] Ch. 70, where it was held that a wall was not " a building." In *Nussey* v. *Provincial Billposting Co.* [1909] 1 Ch. 734, it was held that the advertisement hoarding in the case was " a building," also that bill-posting was an offensive trade within a covenant not to erect any building for the carrying on of any noisy, noisome or offensive trade.

A purchaser covenanted not to erect on land " any buildings whatsoever " with certain exceptions. The defendants bought the land with notice of the covenant, but commenced to erect an advertisement hoarding. Maugham, J., held that the hoarding was " a building " within the covenant and granted a mandatory injunction ordering the defendants to pull down the hoarding (*Stevens* v. *Willing & Co., Ltd.* [1929] W.N. 53). The erection of a wooden shed about seven feet in length and in width on a concrete base was held not to amount to a breach of a covenant not to erect a building, in *Gardiner* v. *Walsh* [1936] 3 All E.R. 870. Poles to carry an overhead electricity supply are not " buildings " (*National Trust* v. *Midlands Electricity Board* [1952] W.N. 47).

" Permit."—In *Tophams, Ltd.* v. *Sefton* [1967] 1 A.C. 50 a bare majority of the House of Lords (reversing the Court of Appeal) held that a covenant not to cause or permit land to be used otherwise than for horse racing would *not* be breached by a sale with knowledge that the purchaser intended to use the land for housing.

PART 6.   ENFORCEMENT, RELEASE AND MODIFICATION OF RESTRICTIVE COVENANTS

Effect of change of character of neighbourhood.—Where a restrictive covenant is otherwise enforceable in equity and, either by permission or acquiescence or by a change of circumstances, the property becomes so changed that the character of the place or neighbourhood is altered, and the object for which the restrictive covenant was originally entered into is at an end, then equity in the exercise of its discretion will not permit the covenant to be enforced (*Duke of Bedford* v. *British Museum Trustees* (1822), 2 Myl. & K. 552 ; *German* v. *Chapman* (1877), 37 L.T. 685 ; *Sayers* v. *Collyer* (1884), 28 Ch. D. 103 ; *Knight* v. *Simmonds* [1896] 2 Ch. 294 ; *Sobey* v. *Sainsbury* [1913] 2 Ch. 513). But the court requires very strict evidence of changes in the character of the neighbourhood before holding that a person has in consequence lost his right to enforce restrictive regulations (*Meredith* v. *Wilson* (1893), 69 L.T. 336 ; *Ramuz* v. *Leigh-on-Sea Conservative Club, Ltd.* (1915), 31 T.L.R. 174 ; *Westripp* v. *Baldock* [1939] 1 All E.R. 279). In *Chatsworth Estates Co.* v. *Fewell* [1931] 1 Ch. 224, Farwell, J., said that in order to succeed on this ground the defendant must show such a complete change in the character of the neighbourhood as to render the covenants valueless to the plaintiffs, so that the action to enforce them would be unmeritorious, not *bona fide*, and merely brought from some ulterior purpose. See further, *Solicitors' Journal*, vol. 92, p. 570.

The statutory power of the Lands Tribunal to declare restrictive covenants obsolete is discussed *post*, p. 579.

Acquiescence on the part of persons seeking to enforce covenants.— The right to enforce a covenant may be lost by reason of the conduct of the person seeking to enforce it, which may bring him within the doctrine of "*acquiescence.*" Lord Eldon, in *Dann* v. *Spurrier* (1802), 7 Ves. 231, at p. 235, said that the circumstance of looking on is in many cases as strong as using terms of encouragement. See also the following cases : *De Bussche* v. *Alt* (1878), 8 Ch. D. 286, at p. 314 ; *Kelsey* v. *Dodd* (1881), 52 L.J. Ch. 34 ; *Sayers* v. *Collyer* (1884), 28 Ch. D. 103 ; *Knight* v. *Simmonds, ante ; Civil Service Musical Instrument Association* v. *Whiteman* (1899), 80 L.T. 685 ; *Hepworth* v. *Pickles* [1900] 1 Ch. 108 ; *Osborne* v. *Bradley* [1903] 2 Ch. 446.

There is no rule that if a restrictive covenant for the preservation of a building estate is not enforced in all cases it cannot be enforced in equity in any case (*Knight* v. *Simmonds, ante*) ; and acquiescence in a breach of minor importance will not disentitle a person from enforcing the observance of the covenant as regards other and more essential matters (*Osborne* v. *Bradley, ante*). If the person who is endeavouring to enforce the covenant has himself been guilty of a breach, he cannot in equity enforce such covenant, unless the breach is only a slight or trivial one and such person does not insist that he is entitled to continue it (*Western* v. *MacDermott* (1866), 15 L.T. 641 ; *Hooper* v. *Bromet* (1904), 90 L.T. 234 ; *Sobey* v. *Sainsbury* [1913] 2 Ch. 513 ; *Kelsey* v. *Dodd, ante*).

19

In *Chatsworth Estates Co.* v. *Fewell* [1931] 1 Ch. 224, above referred to, another of the equitable defences was that the change in the character of the neighbourhood was brought about by the acts or omissions of the plaintiffs or their predecessors. Farwell, J., said that in order to succeed on this ground the defendant must make out a sort of estoppel by showing that the plaintiffs' acts and omissions were such as to justify a reasonable person in believing that the covenants were no longer enforceable. See *Russell* v. *Archdale* [1962] 2 All E.R. 305, at p. 313, as to the grant of a revocable licence not amounting to acquiescence (not reported on this point at [1964] Ch. 38).

Where a covenant affecting real property has been openly and uninterruptedly broken for more than twenty years, a waiver or release of such covenant will be presumed (*Hepworth* v. *Pickles* [1900] 1 Ch. 108).

Unity of seisin.—It is thought that unity of seisin of the whole of the land benefited and of the whole of the land subject to the burden of a covenant in the same person causes the covenant to be destroyed so that it will not revive if the lands again pass into separate ownerships (but compare *Marten* v. *Flight Refuelling, Ltd.* [1962] Ch. 115 as to the revival of covenants after requisitioning).

Merger.—Where restrictive covenants were entered into by a lessor in respect of adjoining land of the lessor, the subsequent purchase by a lessee of the freehold reversion on his lease expressly with intent to merge the lease in the freehold was held to render the covenants unenforceable (*Golden Lion Hotel (Hunstanton), Ltd.* v. *Carter* [1965] 1 W.L.R. 1189, distinguishing *Birmingham Joint Stock Co.* v. *Lea* (1877), 36 L.T. 843, on the ground that in that case the covenant had been expressly kept alive).

Power of tenant for life to release restrictive covenants.—A tenant for life may, with the consent in writing of the trustees of the settlement either with or without giving or taking any consideration in money or otherwise, compromise, compound, abandon, submit to arbitration, or otherwise settle any claim, dispute or question in regard to (*inter alia*) *restrictive covenants relating to the settled land*, and for such purpose may enter into, give, execute and do such agreements, assurances, *releases*, and other things as the tenant for life may, with such consent as aforesaid, think proper (S.L.A. 1925, s. 58 (1)). A tenant for life may also, with such consent as aforesaid, by deed or writing, either with or without consideration *release, waive or modify* any covenant or *restriction imposed on any other land for the benefit of the settled land*, or any part thereof, or release any other land from any right or privilege affecting the same for the benefit of the settled land or any part thereof (*ibid.*, subs. (2)).

It is also provided by s. 97 (*a*) of the S.L.A. 1925 that trustees of a settlement, or any of them, will not be liable for giving any such consent.

Power of trustees for sale and personal representatives to release restrictive covenants.—Trustees for sale have this power under the L.P.A. 1925, s. 28 (1), which provides that " trustees for sale shall in relation to land . . . have all the powers of a tenant for life and the trustees of a settlement under the S.L.A. 1925 . . ."

Personal representatives hold their power under the A.E.A. 1925, s. 39, which provides that " in dealing with the real and personal estate of the deceased, his personal representatives shall, for purposes of administration, or during a minority of any beneficiary or the subsistence of any life interest, or until the period of distribution arrives, have . . . all the powers, discretions and duties conferred or imposed by law on trustees holding land upon an effectual trust for sale . . . and all the powers conferred by statute on trustees for sale . . ."

Modification of restrictive covenants affecting freehold land.—This important power is contained in the L.P.A. 1925, s. 84 (1), which has been substantially amended by s. 28 of the L.P.A. 1969, in pursuance of the Law Commission's recommendations based on the opinion that the original provisions of the section " have proved to be of limited value, for the grounds on which modification or discharge can be ordered are extremely narrow : and any tendency to adopt a liberal interpretation of them has been discouraged by the courts " (" Transfer of Land, Report on Restrictive Covenants," Law Com., No. 11, para. 25, p. 11).

Accordingly, in the following paragraphs, s. 84 is printed in full and commented upon as amended by the 1969 Act. The amendments, except as mentioned, apply to restrictions whenever created, but do not affect proceedings pending when they came into force on 1st January, 1970 (s. 28 (11) of the 1969 Act.) See generally the discussion of the amendments by George Newsom, Q.C., at [1970] J.P.L. 424 *et seq.*

" 84 —(1) The Lands Tribunal shall (without prejudice to any concurrent jurisdiction of the court) have power from time to time, on the application of any person interested in any freehold land affected by any restriction arising under covenant or otherwise as to the user thereof or the building thereon, by order wholly or partially to discharge or modify any such restriction on being satisfied—

(*a*) that by reason of changes in the character of the property or the neighbourhood or other circumstances of the case which the Lands Tribunal may deem material, the restriction ought to be deemed obsolete ; or

(*aa*) that (in a case falling within subsection (1A) below) the continued existence thereof would impede some reasonable user of the land for public or private purposes or, as the case may be, would unless modified so impede such user ; or

(*b*) that the persons of full age and capacity for the time being or from time to time entitled to the benefit of the restriction, whether in respect of estates in fee simple or any lesser estates or interests in the property to which the benefit of the restriction is annexed, have agreed, either expressly or by implication, by their acts or omissions, to the same being discharged or modified ; or

(*c*) that the proposed discharge or modification will not injure the persons entitled to the benefit of the restriction ;

and an order discharging or modifying a restriction under this subsection may direct the applicant to pay to any person entitled to the benefit of the restriction such sum by way of consideration as the Tribunal may think it just to award under one, but not both, of the following heads, that is to say, either—

(i) a sum to make up for any loss or disadvantage suffered by that person in consequence of the discharge or modification ; or

(ii) a sum to make up for any effect which the restriction had, at the
time when it was imposed, in reducing the consideration then
received for the land affected by it."

As to the "concurrent jurisdiction of the court," the enforcement of
restrictive covenants, being an equitable remedy, is in the discretion of the
court.   Thus a plaintiff may have defeated his claim to relief by acquiescence
in the breach of covenant (*German* v. *Chapman* (1877), 7 Ch.D. 271) or inactive
delay (*Gaskin* v. *Balls* (1879), 13 Ch. D. 324) but not by a revocable licence
(*Russell* v. *Archdale* [1962] 2 All E.R. 305, at p. 313D, not reported on this
point in the *Law Reports*).   In particular, a restrictive covenant will not be
enforced where the character of the neighbourhood has so completely changed
that there is no longer any value left in the covenant at all (*Chatsworth
Estates Co.* v. *Fewell* [1931] 1 Ch. 224 ; also *Westripp* v. *Baldock* [1939] 1 All
E.R. 279, as to the evidence required).   See also the Housing Act, 1957,
s. 165, with regard to the conversion of a house into several tenements despite
a covenant to the contrary (*Alliance Economic Investment Co.* v. *Berton* (1923),
92 L.J.K.B. 750 ; *Stack* v. *Church Commissioners for England* [1952] 1 All
E.R. 1352) ; also Town and Country Planning Act, 1971, s. 127.

The power conferred on the Lands Tribunal to discharge or modify
covenants remains discretionary even though the tribunal is satisfied that the
case falls within this subsection (*Driscoll* v. *Church Commissioners for England*
[1957] 1 Q.B. 330).   The tribunal has jurisdiction to modify a covenant the
day after it is made but in its discretion is justified in refusing, and is likely
to refuse to do so so shortly after the covenant has been freely negotiated
(*Cresswell* v. *Proctor* [1968] 1 W.L.R. 906).

Again, the power conferred by this subsection is available even where
the applicant was the original covenantor, although relief will not then
readily be given (*Ridley* v. *Taylor* [1956] 1 W.L.R. 611 ; also *Re Rudkin's
Application* (1963), 16 P. & C.R. 75).   A person who has entered into a
binding contract to purchase conditional upon the making of an order under
this subsection is regarded as being a " person interested " in the land (*Re
Pioneer Properties, Ltd. and Goodman's Application* [1956] J.P.L. 613).   Issue
of a writ to enforce forfeiture of the lease does not debar the tenant from
applying as a person interested (*Driscoll* v. *Church Commissioners for England*
[1957] 1 Q.B. 330).

The subsection does not apply only to " freehold land," see subs. (12), *post*,
as to leasehold land.

Despite the words " land affected by any restriction," the Lands Tribunal
has jurisdiction to modify a covenant even though the restrictions it imposes
merely bind the covenantor personally and even though positive obligations
were also imposed (*Shepherd Homes, Ltd.* v. *Sandham (No. 2)* [1971] 1 W.L.R.
1062).

The word " obsolete " in para. (*a*) of this subsection means that the original
purpose of the covenant can no longer be served ; it does not necessarily
involve showing that the covenant has become absolutely valueless (*cf.*
para. (*c*)) : *Re Truman, Hanbury, Buxton & Co., Ltd.'s Application* [1967]
1 Q.B. 261.

Paragraph (*aa*) was newly inserted in this subsection by s. 28 (2) of the
L.P.A. 1969, in place of what had been the second limb of para. (*a*), reading
as follows : " or that the continued existence thereof would impede the reasonable user of the land for public or private purposes without securing practical
benefits for other persons . . ."   This limb required evidence that the restriction
was no longer necessary for any reasonable purpose of the person who was

enjoying the benefit of it (*Re Henderson's Conveyance* [1940] Ch. 835, 846) and that the user proposed by the applicant for discharge or modification is the only reasonable user available (*Re Ghey and Galton's Application* [1957] 2 Q.B. 650, 663). Now all that will have to be shown is that *some* reasonable user would be impeded, but see the elaboration of this requirement in subs. (1A), *infra.*

In para. (*b*) the expression " agreed," it is thought, refers not only to a *consensus ad idem* between the parties but also to a mere acquiescence.

The reference to " persons entitled to the benefit " in para. (*c*) (see also para. (*b*)) in practice required the Lands Tribunal to assume in most cases that anyone who appeared as an objector was entitled to the benefit of the restriction without undertaking an investigation into the title of individual objectors (*Re Purkiss' Application* [1962] 1 W.L.R. 902). See now subs. (3A), *infra*, which is, *inter alia*, directed to this point. Further, Russell, L.J., has expressed the view that para. (*c*) was merely designed to cover the case of the vexatious or frivolous objection to extended user (*Ridley* v. *Taylor* [1965] 1 W.L.R. 611). In *Gee* v. *The National Trust for Places of Historic Interest or Natural Beauty* [1966] 1 W.L.R. 170, C.A., it was held that the National Trust could not successfully oppose in reliance on para. (*c*) an application to modify a restrictive covenant made with it under s. 8 of the National Trust Act, 1937, unless the amenities or beauty of the district would be injured. See also *Re Gadd's Land Transfer, Cornmill Developments, Ltd.* v. *Bridle Lane (Estates), Ltd.* [1966] Ch. 56.

The subsection as originally worded permitted the Lands Tribunal to make the discharge or modification subject to the payment by the applicant of compensation to any person suffering loss in consequence of the order. However, the requirements of the original three paragraphs were so stringent that only the very rare case for compensation could occur. Now the provisions enabling the award of compensation have been promoted from a parenthesis, renamed (i.e., consideration) and extensively rewritten. Head (i) would appear aimed largely at subs. (1A), *post*. Head (ii) would appear to reflect the only two modern cases in which compensation had been ordered (*Re Gateshead County Borough's Application* (1960), 12 P. & C.R. 265, and *Re Watson's Application* (1965), 17 P. & C.R. 176) ; problems may arise in cases where the benefit has already run with land or with parts of it and the effect of inflation cannot be predicted.

Subsection (1A) reads as follows:—

" (1A) Subsection (1) (*aa*) above authorises the discharge or modification of a restriction by reference to its impeding some reasonable user of land in any case in which the Lands Tribunal is satisfied that the restriction, in impeding that user, either—

(*a*) does not secure to persons entitled to the benefit of it any practical benefits of substantial value or advantage to them ; or

(*b*) is contrary to the public interest ;

and that money will be an adequate compensation for the loss or disadvantage (if any) which any such person will suffer from the discharge or modification."

This subsection was inserted by s. 28 (2) of the L.P.A. 1969 ; see the case and comment in the note to subs. (1) (*aa*), *ante.*

As to para. (*a*) of this subsection, *ante*, compare *Ridley* v. *Taylor* [1965] 1 W.L.R. 170.

As to para. (*b*) of this subsection, *ante*, see also subs. (1B), *post*, which also emphasises the new importance of the public interest aspects of restrictive covenants.

The fact of " adequate compensation " will clearly have to be shown by every applicant relying on these new grounds. Presumably the test of when money will be adequate compensation can only be objective but may in any case prove difficult to assess and apply (cf. *Rudd* v. *Lascelles* [1900] 1 Ch. 815). Obviously, however, an applicant who proposes in any degree to render his neighbour's house uninhabitable will remain unassisted.

" (1B) In determining whether a case is one falling within subsection (1A) above, and in determining whether (in any such case or otherwise) a restriction ought to be discharged or modified, the Lands Tribunal shall take into account the development plan and any declared or ascertainable pattern for the grant or refusal of planning permissions in the relevant areas, as well as the period at which and context in which the restriction was created or imposed and any other material circumstances."

This subsection also was inserted by s. 28 (2) of the L.P.A. 1969. By the reference to subs. (1A), its application is confined to ground (*aa*) in subs. (1), notwithstanding that the evidence it envisaged might well have been relevant to ground (*a*).

As to " development," and as to planning permission, see generally, *post*, p. 1181 *et seq.* It is not thought to be the practice for a *pattern* of planning permissions to be *declared* as apparently contemplated by this subsection.

The sort of evidence the admission of which this subsection now makes mandatory was not previously regarded with invariable favour in the courts (see *per* Harman, J., in *Bell* v. *Norman C. Ashton, Ltd.* (1956), 7 P. & C.R. 359, at p. 369).

" (1c) It is hereby declared that the power conferred by this section to modify a restriction includes power to add such further provisions restricting the user of or the building on the land affected as appear to the Lands Tribunal to be reasonable in view of the relaxation of the existing provisions, and as may be accepted by the applicant ; and the Lands Tribunal may accordingly refuse to modify a restriction without some such addition."

This subsection also was inserted by s. 28 (2) of the L.P.A. 1969.

" (2) The court shall have power on the application of any person interested—

(*a*) to declare whether or not in any particular case any freehold land is, or would in any given event be, affected by a restriction imposed by any instrument ; or

(*b*) to declare what, upon the true construction of any instrument purporting to impose a restriction, is the nature and extent of the restriction thereby imposed and whether the same is, or would in any given event be, enforceable and if so by whom.

Neither subsections (7) and (11) of this section nor, unless the contrary is expressed, any later enactment providing for this section not to apply to any restrictions shall affect the operation of this subsection or the operation for purposes of this subsection of any other provisions of this section."

This subsection is printed as amended by s. 28 (4) of the L.P.A. 1969. The principal change effected by the amendments is that the court now has a limited jurisdiction under this subsection to determine future or hypothetical questions of the enforceability of covenants, e.g., where a proposed development may or may not be a breach (*cf. Re Gadd's Land Transfer, Cornmill Developments, Ltd.* v. *Bridle Lane (Estates), Ltd.* [1966] Ch. 56).

As to the evidence required to show that the land is not affected by a building scheme, see *Re Sunnyfield* [1932] 1 Ch. 79. See further *Re Freeman-Thomas Indenture* [1957] 1 W.L.R. 568 where Harman, J., stated that the court has a discretion to make an order even if it is satisfied that no person can enforce the covenant (cf. *Law Times*, vol. 223, pp. 204, 205). Also *Re Ecclesiastical Commissioners for England's Conveyance* [1936] Ch. 430 ; *Re Spencer Flats, Ltd.* [1937] Ch. 86 ; *Re Rutherford's Conveyance, Goadby* v. *Bartlett* [1938] Ch. 396. As to costs, see *Re Jeffkins' Indentures* [1965] 1 W.L.R. 375 ; *Re Jeff's Transfer (No. 2)* [1966] 1 W.L.R. 841 ; and *Re Wembley Park Estate Co., Ltd.'s Transfer, London Sephardi Trust* v. *Baker* [1968] Ch. 491.

" (3) The Lands Tribunal shall, before making any order under this section, direct such enquiries, if any, to be made of any government department or local authority, and such notices, if any, whether by way of advertisement or otherwise, to be given to such of the persons who appear to be entitled to the benefit of the restriction intended to be discharged, modified, or dealt with as, having regard to any enquiries, notices or other proceedings previously made, given or taken, the Lands Tribunal may think fit."

This subsection is printed as amended by s. 28 (1) (*a*) and (5) of the L.P.A. 1969.

Under the L.C.A. 1925, s. 15 (7), such local authority restrictions become " local land charges."

" (3A) On an application to the Lands Tribunal under this section the Lands Tribunal shall give any necessary directions as to the persons who are or are not to be admitted (as appearing to be entitled to the benefit of the restriction) to oppose the application, and no appeal shall lie against any such direction ; but rules under the Lands Tribunal Act, 1949, shall make provision whereby, in cases in which there arises on such an application (whether or not in connection with the admission of persons to oppose) any such question as is referred to in subsection (2) (*a*) or (*b*) of this section, the proceedings on the application can and, if the rules so provide, shall be suspended to enable the decision of the court to be obtained on that question by an application under that subsection, or by means of a case stated by the Lands Tribunal, or otherwise, as may be provided by those rules or by rules of court."

This subsection was inserted by s. 28 (6) of the L.P.A. 1969, and came into force on 1st July, 1970 (Law of Property Act, 1969 (Commencement) Order, 1970).

It deals with the unsatisfactory situation revealed by the decision in *Re Purkiss's Application* [1962] 1 W.L.R. 902, in that the Lands Tribunal had either to assume the covenant to be valid and enforceable and give a determination as to modification or discharge which might turn out to be a nullity, or else, if the validity or enforceability of the covenant was in doubt, to adjourn the proceedings until the court had decided the matter on an application under subs. (2) of this section, *ante*. A procedure is now provided to enable all issues of law (e.g., as to annexation or imposition of a covenant onto particular land and enforceability by or against particular owners or occupiers) to be raised and conclusively determined, by the courts if necessary, before the Lands Tribunal considers the issue of modification or discharge of the covenant.

(4) [*This subsection was repealed by the Lands Tribunal Act*, 1949, *s*. 10, *Sched*. 2.]

" (5) Any order made under this section shall be binding on all persons, whether ascertained or of full age or capacity or not, then entitled or thereafter capable of becoming entitled to the benefit of any restriction, which is thereby discharged, modified or dealt with, and whether such persons are parties to the proceedings or have been served with notice or not."

This subsection is reproduced as modified by the Lands Tribunal Act, 1949, s. 10, Sched. 2.

As to requiring the Tribunal to state a case for the decision of the Court of Appeal where any person is aggrieved by the decision as being erroneous in point of law, see s. 3 (4) of the 1949 Act ; cf. *Re* 108 *Lancaster Gate and Law of Property Act*, 1925, *Application for Discharge of Restriction* [1933] Ch. 419 and *Re Henderson's Conveyance* [1940] Ch. 835.

" (6) An order may be made under this section notwithstanding that any instrument which is alleged to impose the restriction intended to be discharged, modified, or dealt with, may not have been produced to the court or the Lands Tribunal, and the court or the Lands Tribunal may act on such evidence of that instrument as it may think sufficient."

In many cases persons bound by a building scheme within *Spicer* v. *Martin* (1888), 14 App. Cas. 12, will not have possession of the documents imposing the restriction.

" (7) This section applies to restrictions whether subsisting at the commencement of this Act or imposed thereafter, but this section does not apply where the restriction was imposed on the occasion of a disposition made gratuitously or for a nominal consideration for public purposes."

To give power to vary restrictive covenants imposed when a public or charitable trust was created was beyond the scope of this section ; such matters were left to the jurisdiction of the Charity Commissioners.

" (8) This section applies whether the land affected by the restrictions is registered or not, but, in the case of registered land, the Land Registrar shall give effect on the register to any order under this section in accordance with the Land Registration Act, 1925."

See the L.R.A. 1925, ss. 46 (Discharge of restriction noted as incumbrance), 82 (Rectification of the register) ; also L.R.R. 1925, r. 212.

The subsection is printed as slightly amended by s. 28 (7) of the L.P.A. 1969.

" (9) Where any proceedings by actions or otherwise are taken to enforce a restrictive covenant, any person against whom the proceedings are taken, may in such proceedings apply to the court for an order giving leave to apply to the Lands Tribunal under this section, and staying the proceedings in the meantime."

An action to recover possession of leasehold land, under a power of re-entry, for breach of a restrictive covenant contained in the lease is not an action " to enforce a restrictive covenant " within this subsection : *Iveagh* v. *Harris* [1929] 2 Ch. 142.

Semble, the court will normally give leave to apply to the Lands Tribunal if the applicant can show a *prima facie* case, for the section gives the Tribunal a jurisdiction which the court does not possess, i.e., to modify a restrictive covenant : *Feilden* v. *Byrne* [1926] Ch. 620 ; *Richardson* v. *Jackson* [1954] 1 W.L.R. 447. The applicant must also have proceeded without unreasonable delay : *Richardson* v. *Jackson, ante.*

As to the terms on which the court will grant a stay of proceedings, see *Hanning* v. *Gable-Jeffreys Properties, Ltd.* [1965] 1 W.L.R. 1390.

(10) [*This subsection was repealed by the Lands Tribunal Act, 1949, s. 10, Sched. 2.*]

" (11) This section does not apply to restrictions imposed by the Commissioners of Works under any statutory power for the protection of any Royal Park or Garden or to restrictions of a like character imposed upon the occasion of any enfranchisement effected before the commencement of this Act in any manor vested in His Majesty in right of the Crown or the Duchy of Lancaster, nor (subject to subsection (11A) below) to restrictions created or imposed—

(*a*) for naval, military or air force purposes,

(*b*) for civil aviation purposes under the powers of the Air Navigation Act, 1920, or of section 19 or 23 of the Civil Aviation Act, 1949."

This subsection was saved from the operation of the Requisitioned Land and War Works Act, 1945, s. 38 (3) (amended by s. 28 (10) of the L.P.A. 1969), and is printed as slightly amended by s. 28 (8) of the L.P.A. 1969.

The Commissioners of Works are now embodied in the Secretary of State for the Environment. For the statutory powers appropriate, see the L.P.A. 1922, s. 137, *ante.*

This section also does not apply (i) to a forestry dedication covenant (Forestry Act, 1967, s. 5 (2) (*b*)) ; (ii) to a restriction on the exercise of rights over land contained in an agreement with the Nature Conservancy (National Parks and Access to the Countryside Act, 1949, s. 16 (4)) ; (iii) to a restriction entered into under the Countryside Act, 1968, s. 15, in favour of the Natural Environment Research Council ; (iv) to certain covenants enforceable by Ministers under the Defence Acts, 1842 to 1935 (Requisitioned Land and War Works Act, 1945, s. 84 (3)).

See further the new subsection (11A), *post.*

" (11A) Subsection (11) of this section—

(*a*) shall include the application of this section to a restriction falling within subsection (11) (*a*), and not created or imposed in connection with the use of any land as an aerodrome, only so long as the restriction is enforceable by or on behalf of the Crown ; and

(*b*) shall exclude the application of this section to a restriction falling within subsection (11) (*b*), or created or imposed in connection with the use of any land as an aerodrome, only so long as the restriction is enforceable by or on behalf of the Crown or any public or international authority."

This subsection was inserted by s. 28 (9) of the Law of Property Act, 1969.

" (12) Where a term of more than forty years is created in land (whether before or after the commencement of this Act) this section shall, after the expiration of twenty-five years of the term, apply to restrictions affecting

19A

such leasehold land in like manner as it would have applied had the land been freehold :

Provided that this subsection shall not apply to mining leases."

This subsection is printed as amended by the Landlord and Tenant Act, 1954, s. 52 (1), which substituted " forty " and " twenty-five " for the original " seventy " and " fifty " respectively.

The twenty-five years starts from the date of the lease and not from the commencement of the term if such term is made to start before the date of the lease : *Cadogan (Earl)* v. *Guinness* [1936] Ch. 515. See also *Ridley* v. *Taylor* [1965] 1 W.L.R. 611, where the Court of Appeal exercised its discretion against modification of certain leasehold covenants by analogy with this subsection because, although more than twenty-five years of the term had expired, less than twenty-five years had elapsed since the covenant had been expressly affirmed by the tenant in a licence. Further in that case Harman, L.J., expressed the view that it should be more difficult to persuade the court to exercise its discretion in leasehold than in freehold cases.

See also *Iveagh* v. *Harris* [1929] 2 Ch. 142, mentioned in note to subsection (9), *ante*.

(13) [*This subsection was added by the Administration of Justice Act*, 1932, *s. 6, but later repealed by the Lands Tribunal Act*, 1949, *s. 10, Sched. 2.*]

Discharge and modification of restrictions under special statutory authority.—Where either (i) a house cannot readily be let as a single tenement owing to changes in the character of the neighbourhood, but it could readily be let if converted into two or more tenements, or (ii) planning permission has been granted under the Town and Country Planning Act, 1947, for the use as two or more separate dwelling-houses of a building previously used as a single dwelling-house, the county court may, on such terms as it thinks just, vary any covenant affecting the house (Housing Act, 1957, s. 165 ; *Alliance Economic Investment Co.* v. *Berton* (1923), 92 L.J.K.B. 750). This is a very useful power when dealing with old houses that can best be let as flats ; " conversion " may take place although there are no structural alterations (*Stack* v. *Church Commissioners* [1952] 1 All E.R. 1352).

Notwithstanding any provision to the contrary in any lease or tenancy or in any covenant, contract or undertaking relating to the use to be made of any land, it is lawful for the occupier of any land to keep, otherwise than by way of trade or business, hens or rabbits in any place on the land and to erect or place and maintain such buildings or structures as are reasonably necessary for that purpose, provided that nothing is done prejudicial to health or causing a nuisance (Allotments Act, 1950, s. 12). It should be noted that this restriction on the enforcement of covenants, etc., applies to any land, not merely to allotments ; it is one easily overlooked in practice.

Where a local authority have taken possession of land by virtue of a lease or authorisation under the War Damaged Sites Act, 1949, they may use the land for the purposes of their statutory functions, or a lessee from them may use the land, notwithstanding any right restrictive of the user of the land. A person thereby injured may recover compensation from the local authority (War Damaged Sites Act, 1949, s. 4 (3)).

CHAPTER SIXTEEN

EXECUTION OF DEEDS

Form of deed.—The formalities necessary to constitute a deed at common law were stated as follows : "... there are but three things of the essence and substance of a deed, that is to say, writing in paper or parchment, sealing and delivery " (*Goddard's* case (1584), 2 Co. Rep. 4*b*, 5*a*). To these, the L.P.A. 1925, s. 73, has added that where an individual executes a deed, he shall either sign or place his mark upon the same and sealing alone shall not be deemed sufficient. For corporations see s. 74 of the L.P.A. 1925, *post*, p. 589.

Provided it is legible, the "writing" referred to in *Goddard's* case, *ante*, may apparently be made in any way at all (*Geary* v. *Physic* (1826), 4 L.J. (o.s.) K.B. 147 : pencil ; *R.* v. *Middlesex Registers* (1845), 7 Q.B. 156 : lithograph ; *Foster* v. *Mentor Life Assurance Co.* (1854), 23 L.J.Q.B. 145 : print). Against this, however, it appears that only "paper or parchment" will suffice (see Co. Litt. 35*b* ; 229*a*). The paper or parchment need only be signed, sealed and delivered by one of the parties in order for it to be a deed (*I.R.C.* v. *Angus* (1889), 23 Q.B.D. 579, 581 and 582).

To these formal requirements, Norton on Deeds, 2nd ed., p. 3, adds the requirement of substance that the writing must be one "whereby an interest, right or property passes, or an obligation binding on some person is created, or which is in affirmance of some act whereby an interest, right or property has passed." This would exclude such documents as degree or share certificates (*South London Greyhound Racecourses, Ltd.* v. *Wake* [1931] 1 Ch. 496, 503). Whether or not this requirement is satisfied is primarily a question of the parties' intention. Thus, in *Re Stirrup* [1961] 1 W.L.R. 449, at p. 454, Wilberforce, J., said that "provided the sole formal requirement of being under seal is complied with, any document, since 1925, at any rate, is effective to pass a legal estate, provided the intention so to pass it can be ascertained." In that case an instrument in form an assent was held able to operate as a conveyance, since the manifest intention of the parties is not to be defeated by the fact that a wrong technical name or method has been used. But contrast *Re King's Will Trusts* [1964] Ch. 542, in which a deed appointing trustees was not allowed to operate either as an assent or as a conveyance of the legal estate by personal representatives despite their intention (see further *ante*, p. 418).

A Land Registry transfer (or other disposition of registered land) is, of course, a "writing" on "paper" and must be signed, sealed and delivered (see the prescribed forms in the Schedule to the L.R.R. 1925 ; see also s. 38 (1) of the L.R.A. 1925). Also it creates, at least, "an obligation binding on some person." Consequently a Land Registry transfer clearly is to be regarded as a deed (see *per* Vaisey, J., in *Chelsea and Walham Green Building Society* v. *Armstrong* [1951] Ch. 853, at p. 857). Note, however, that such a transfer despite being a deed is not in itself effective to pass the legal estate in the registered land : this passes only on registration (L.R.A. 1925, ss. 19 (1) and 22 (1) ; see also *Smith* v. *Express Dairy* [1954] J.P.L. 45 and *Lever Finance, Ltd.* v. *Needleman's Trustees* [1956] Ch. 375 ; more accurately, the legal estate is passed retrospectively as on the day on which the application for registration was delivered at H.M. Land Registry : L.R.R. 1925, r. 83 (2)).

Signing, sealing and delivery.—Instead of signing, the executing party may place his mark on the deed (L.P.A. 1925, s. 73) or even, it would appear, rubber stamp a facsimile signature on it or do anything else of this sort which makes patent his intention to authenticate the deed (compare *Goodman* v. *Eban* [1954] 1 Q.B. 550).

A *seal* need not consist of wax nor of a wafer. Any kind of impression will be sufficient (*Re Smith ; Oswell* v. *Shepherd* (1892), 67 L.T. 64). For instance, an impression made with ink by means of a wooden block is sufficient (*R.* v. *St. Paul, Covent Garden* (1845), 7 Q.B. 232). Indeed, a permanent impression is not absolutely necessary. For instance, in *National Provincial Bank of England* v. *Jackson* (1886), 33 Ch. D. 1, at p. 11, it was said by Cotton, L.J., that " If the finger be pressed on the ribbon that may amount to a sealing." Where the deed does not show any trace of a seal, the fact that it is stated in the attestation clause that the deed *was* sealed would not be sufficient evidence by itself of such sealing (*National Provincial Bank of England* v. *Jackson, ante ;* see the explanation therein of *Re Sandilands* (1871), L.R. 6 C.P. 411 ; *Re Balkis Consolidated Co., Ltd.* (1888), 58 L.T. 300).

In *Stromdale and Ball, Ltd.* v. *Burden* [1952] Ch. 223, Danckwerts, J., said : " meticulous persons executing a deed may still place their finger on the wax seal or wafer on the document, but it appears to me that at the present day if a party signs a document bearing wax or wafer or other indication of a seal with the intention of executing the document as a deed, that is sufficient adoption or recognition of the seal to amount to due execution as a deed." Further the learned judge pointed out that the document was described as a deed, it stated that the parties had set their hands and seals thereunto and it contained the usual words " signed sealed and delivered " ; it seemed to him, therefore, the clearest case of estoppel possible. However, the weight of earlier authority is against any estoppel or presumption of due execution arising from the traditional formulae of the *testatum* and the *testimonium* (see *National Provincial Bank of England* v. *Jackson, ante ; Re Balkis Consolidated Co., Ltd., ante ;* and *Re Smith* (1892), 67 L.T. 64).

The registration of a memorial of a deed in a Yorkshire deeds registry is not evidence of the execution of the deed (*Re Halifax Commercial Banking Co. and Wood* (1898), 79 L.T. 536).

In the case of a deed more than twenty years old coming from an unsuspected repository there is a presumption in favour of its due execution (*Re Airey ; Airey* v. *Stapleton* [1897] 1 Ch. 164 ; Evidence Act, 1938, s. 4 ; cf. Civil Evidence Act, 1968, s. 6 (1)). Such presumption, however, only goes to the fact of execution, and therefore where a deed was executed by an attorney it was held that there was no presumption that the attorney was duly authorised by the power to execute the deed (*ibid.*).

In ordinary everyday practice if a deed on the face of it appears to have been duly executed and attested and there are no suspicious circumstances, the fact of such due execution is accepted without inquiries or further proof (*Law Society's Digest*, Opinion No. 125). If, however, the original deed has been lost and only a copy is produced, and the deed is vital to the title, then, in the absence of a condition to the contrary, the vendor should be required to prove the execution (*Re Halifax Commercial Banking Co. and Wood, ante*).

A person who is a party to a deed in more than one capacity probably need not execute more than once but the better practice is to execute separately for each capacity (*Young* v. *Schuler* (1883), 11 Q.B.D. 651). A party who holds more than one interest in the same capacity need execute once only in order to pass all interests unless a contrary intention appears (*Drew* v. *Earl of Norbury* (1846), 3 Jo. & Lat. 267, at p. 284; L.P.A. 1925, s. 63, *ante*, p. 542).

Where a deed is not necessary, an instrument intended to be such, but ineffective because it has not been delivered, may operate as an instrument in writing (*Windsor Refrigerator Co., Ltd.* v. *Branch Nominees, Ltd.* [1961] Ch. 375).

Execution of deed by corporation aggregate.—It is provided by s. 74 of the L.P.A. 1925, as follows :—

" 74.—(1) In favour of a purchaser a deed shall be deemed to have been duly executed by a corporation aggregate if its seal be affixed thereto in the presence of and attested by its clerk, secretary or other permanent officer or his deputy, and a member of the board of directors, council or other governing body of the corporation, and where a seal purporting to be the seal of a corporation has been affixed to a deed, attested by persons purporting to be persons holding such offices as aforesaid, the deed shall be deemed to have been executed in accordance with the requirements of this section, and to have taken effect accordingly.

* * * * *

(6) Notwithstanding anything contained in this section, any mode of execution or attestation authorised by law or by practice or the statute, charter, memorandum or articles, deed of settlement or other instrument constituting the corporation or regulating the affairs thereof, shall (in addition to the modes authorised by this section) be as effectual as if this section had not been passed."

Whenever a trading company or other corporation, therefore, has executed a deed so as to conform to subs. (1), above, a purchaser need not inspect the articles of association of the company or other authority to see how the seal ought to be affixed or to satisfy himself that it has been properly affixed. It will be noted that the protection given by the above section does not extend to anyone other than a " purchaser " as defined by the L.P.A. 1925, s. 205 (1) (xxi). It is unfortunate that similar protection is not given to all persons dealing in good faith with a company.

As s. 74 applies only to deeds executed after 1925 and does not protect all persons dealing with corporations aggregate it is often necessary to inspect the articles of association or other authority for the purpose of ascertaining how the seal should be affixed, and to see that it has been so affixed (*D'Arcy* v. *Tamar, etc., Railway Co.* (1866), L.R. 2 Ex. 158). But if the seal appears to have been affixed in accordance with the articles or other authority, no duty will rest on the purchaser to ascertain whether the affixing of the seal was duly authorised by the minutes of the directors, or that the secretary or directors were properly appointed : all these details are merely matters of the internal management of the company with which a purchaser has no concern (*Allen* v. *Sea, Fire and Life Assurance Society* (1850), 19 L.J.C.P. 305 ; *County of Gloucester Bank* v. *Rudry Methyr Steam, etc., Colliery Co.* [1895] 1 Ch. 629 ; *Re Fireproof Doors, Ltd.* ; *Umney* v. *The Company* [1916] 2 Ch. 142 ; *Dey* v. *Pullinger Engineering Co.* [1921] 1 K.B. 77 ; *Parker* v. *Judkin* [1931] 1 Ch. 475). See further, *ante*, p. 317 *et seq.*

If the articles of association of a company require that the seal shall be affixed in the presence of two directors and the seal is affixed in the presence of one director only, the document would (subject to the protection given by the L.P.A. 1925, s. 74, *ante*, where applicable) be construed as an agreement, in the same way as a lease void at law would be construed as an agreement (*Re Fireproof Doors, Ltd. ; Umney* v. *The Company, ante*).

There has been a conflict of authority as to whether a separate act of delivery is necessary to constitute the deed of a corporation. In *Beesly* v. *Hallwood Estates, Ltd.* [1960] 1 W.L.R. 549 (apparently approved on this point by the Court of Appeal at [1961] Ch. 105), Buckley, J., said : " The sealing of a deed by a corporate body, in my judgment, *prima facie*, imports delivery of that deed." The true rule thus appeared to be that delivery is necessary (*Windsor Refrigerator Co., Ltd.* v. *Branch Nominees, Ltd.* [1961] Ch. 88 ; *Mowatt* v. *Castle Steel & Iron Works Co.* (1886), 34 Ch. D. 58) but *prima facie* sealing imports delivery unless the company indicates a contrary intention or such an intention can be implied (*Merchants of the Staple* v. *Bank of England* (1887), 21 Q.B.D. 160, 165). Now *Beesly* v. *Hallwood Estates, Ltd.*, has been followed on this point by the Court of Appeal in *Vincent* v. *Premo Enterprises (Voucher Sales), Ltd.* [1969] 2 Q.B. 609, and by Buckley, J., in *D'Silva* v. *Lister House Development, Ltd.* [1971] Ch. 17. It appears clear from the judgments in these cases that once a document has been sealed by a company within s. 74 of the L.P.A. 1925 it will be treated as executed either as a deed immediately binding or else as an escrow.

It is preferable that sealing shall be in the presence of the secretary or other permanent officer and a director whereupon the deed is deemed duly executed in favour of a purchaser by the L.P.A. 1925, s. 74. If the sealing is, for instance in the presence of two directors as authorised by Table A (where applicable), the doubt certainly arises. The Court of Appeal in *Beesly* v. *Hallwood Estates, Ltd.*, held that conditional delivery as an escrow is possible and so even where s. 74 applies the purchaser must consider whether the delivery was conditional just as on purchase from an individual.

As to the power of the liquidator in a winding up to execute deeds in the name and on behalf of the company, see p. 324.

Attestation.—The execution of a deed is invariably attested, but it is not necessary to the validity of a deed, except in a few special cases, for instance, the execution of certain powers of appointment. However, it should be noted that the prescribed forms for dispositions of registered land do in fact include attestation clauses (see Schedule to L.R.R. 1925) so that it is arguable that attestation here is essential. The obvious value of an attestation clause is that, assuming it to be in proper form, it provides evidence of due execution even without production of the witness or any recollection by him (see *Hope* v. *Harman* (1847), 16 Q.B. 751n and *Stromdale & Ball, Ltd.* v. *Burden* [1952] Ch. 223 ; but compare *National Provincial Bank Ltd.* v. *Jackson* (1886), 33 Ch. D. 1). On a sale the purchaser is not entitled to require that the conveyance to him be executed in his presence or that of his solicitor as such but he is entitled at his own cost to have the execution to be attested by some person appointed by him, who may, if he thinks fit, be his solicitor (L.P.A. 1925, s. 75). This right is very rarely exercised (see *Law Society's Digest*, Opinion No. 125).

It should be remembered that a party to a deed cannot be a witness (*Seal* v. *Claridge* (1881), 7 Q.B.D. 516). Where an individual attests the execution of a deed he signs as witness, but in the case of a company, directors or a secretary in whose presence the seal of the company is affixed do not attest as witnesses but as part of the operation of the actual sealing (*Shears* v. *Jacob* (1866), L.R. 1 C.P. 513 ; Norton on Deeds, 2nd ed., p. 21) and so a director or secretary may authenticate sealing by the company even if he is a party (see also *Windsor Refrigerator Co., Ltd.* v. *Branch Nominees, Ltd., ante*).

Delivery as an escrow.—" There are two sorts of delivery . . . one absolute, and the other conditional, that is, an escrow, to be the deed of the party when, and if, certain conditions are performed " (Farwell, L.J., in *Foundling Hospital* v. *Crane* [1911] 2 K.B. 367, at p. 377). On performance of the condition the deed is deemed, for purposes of title, to have been executed retrospectively to the date of delivery as an escrow and the legal estate (if applicable) passed as on that date (*Graham* v. *Graham* (1791), 1 Ves. 272 ; *Foundling Hospital* v. *Crane* [1911] 2 K.B. 367). This rule does not, however, create rights or liabilities in respect of intermediate rents or outgoings ; compare *ante*, p. 205.

Whether a deed was, in fact, executed as an escrow is entirely a matter of intention. As was said by Parke, B., in *Bowker* v. *Burdekin* (1843), 11 M. & W. 128, at p. 147 : " You are to look at all the facts attending the execution, to all that took place at the time, and to the result of the transaction and therefore, though it is in form an absolute delivery, if it can reasonably be inferred that it was delivered not to take effect as a deed till a certain condition was performed, it will nevertheless operate as an escrow." When the condition has been performed the escrow automatically becomes a deed without any further delivery, notwithstanding that the person who executed the deed as an escrow has in the meantime died (*Copeland* v. *Stephens* (1818), 1 B. & Ald. 593, at p. 606).

If a deed is sealed subject to the carrying out of instructions which can be revoked by the grantor it is not thereby delivered as an escrow. As there is an overriding power in the grantor to recall it, there is no delivery of it whatever. The carrying out of revocable instructions cannot be regarded as a condition of delivery (*Windsor Refrigerator Co., Ltd.* v. *Branch Nominees, Ltd.* [1961] Ch. 88 ; [1961] Ch. 375). Consequently if a party to a deed wishes to execute it but retain the right to recall it he must grant to some other person a sealed authority to deliver it on his behalf. On the other hand if a deed is delivered as an escrow (that is, on terms, expressed or implied, that it shall have no effect until a certain time has arrived or a condition has been performed) it is not recallable and on performance of the condition it becomes binding (*Beesly* v. *Hallwood Estates, Ltd.* [1961] Ch. 105). Thus a vendor who has so delivered a conveyance may find that the legal estate has passed to the purchaser on payment of the price (or, apparently, tender of it : *Beesly* v. *Hallwood Estates, Ltd., ante*) even if the vendor has decided after execution by him that he does not wish to proceed. At this point a comparatively recent *obiter dictum* uttered in the House of Lords must be mentioned. Lord Denning, M.R., in the Court of Appeal had put the case of a conveyance which is executed by the vendor but delivered in escrow, saying that so soon as the condition (payment of the price) were performed the sale was complete : *Cory (Wm.) & Son, Ltd.* v. *I.R.C.* [1964] 1 W.L.R. 1322, at p. 1341. But in the course of allowing an appeal Lord Reid expressly referred to this instance of an executed conveyance delivered in escrow and shortly said : " In my understanding there would then be nothing binding : both parties would have a *locus poenitentiae* " ([1965] A.C. 1088, at pp. 1107–8). However, in view of all the earlier established authorities, none of which were apparently cited, with the greatest respect this can only be disregarded as *per incuriam* pending a direct consideration by the House of Lords (but see also Diplock, L.J., dissenting in the Court of Appeal at [1964] 1 W.L.R. 1322, at p. 1346, explained by J. G. M. at [1964] B.T.R., p. 285).

The decisions in the *Beesly* and *Windsor Refrigerator* cases have caused much controversy as to the efficacy, or wisdom, of the standard practice whereby the solicitor for a vendor arranges for his client (and any other necessary party) to execute a deed of conveyance before completion and hands it over to the solicitor for the purchaser on completion. Clearly in such a case the vendor does not intend the legal estate to pass until the price has been paid and so delivery is not absolute. If delivery is meant to be as an escrow then it must be appreciated that it is irrevocable (*Beesly* v. *Hallwood Estates, ante*) since the carrying out of revocable instructions cannot be regarded as a condition of delivery (*Windsor Refrigerator Co., Ltd.* v. *Branch Nominees, Ltd., ante*). It is normally assumed that delivery becomes absolute only when, on actual completion, the deed is handed over. But if the deed is an escrow the conditions of delivery must be capable of definition even though they may be implied; certainly a lay vendor gives no thought to them. If the only condition of delivery is payment of the price then the purchaser can obtain the legal estate merely by paying (or, perhaps, even tendering) the price even if, for some reason, the vendor does not then wish to complete. (See further *Solicitors' Journal*, vol. 106, pp. 987, 1023 and 1046 and *Conveyancer N.S.*, vol. 25, p. 126 *et seq.*).

For these reasons it has been argued that the theoretically proper procedure is for the vendor to give his solicitor a power of attorney to deliver the conveyance on completion. However logically sound, adoption of this view would be most inconvenient and difficult to explain to a vendor and solicitors continue to adopt their customary practice. As the two decisions leave a number of points unresolved and do not expressly deal with the position as between vendor and purchaser the editors of this volume consider that solicitors are justified in retaining the conventional procedure although they should bear in mind that in the event of a dispute a purchaser who knows that the conveyance has been executed as an escrow may attempt to comply with conditions so as to obtain the legal estate. As the court would have to decide whether delivery was conditional and, normally, to decide what conditions were to be implied it is to be hoped that they could, and would, imply such conditions as would give effect to the normal intentions of a vendor.

Reference should be made to three more recent cases contributing to the law relating to this topic. In *Vincent* v. *Premo Enterprises (Voucher Sales), Ltd.* [1969] 2 Q.B. 609, the Court of Appeal considered the requirement of " delivery " generally and then held that a counterpart lease had been delivered conditionally, as an escrow, by a company in accordance with the intention of one of its directors although the counterpart was merely sent to the company's solicitors, and not exchanged for the lease, and the intention as to a conditional delivery was not then known to the other side. In consequence the company was unable to withdraw from the transaction on the ground that no exchange had taken place but was bound by the lease on performance of the particular condition contemplated, and it was held that this could be and was, performed at the court hearing in which delivery or not was in issue. It is thought that this decision lends considerable support to the reasoning in the two preceding paragraphs.

In *D'Silva* v. *Lister House Development, Ltd.* [1971] Ch. 17, Buckley, J., considered in particular the ascertainment of the relevant intention where it is alleged that a company has executed a document as an escrow. He held that he was concerned with the intention of the executing parties, which meant, in effect, the director and secretary of the company authorised to attest the affixing of the common seal, and that the intention of the employees of the company who happened to manage that part of the business which involved the transaction in question was not relevant.

In *Plymouth Corporation* v. *Harvey* [1971] 1 W.L.R. 549 Plowman, J., held ineffective a surrender of a lease delivered in escrow by a tenant to a third party, the condition of the escrow being the tenant's failure to comply with certain covenants in the lease. This was treated as being merely a device designed to avoid the L.P.A. 1925, s. 146, and as remaining in substance a forfeiture within that section.

To deliver an instrument as an escrow, it is not necessary that such instrument should be delivered to a person not a party to it (*London Freehold and Leasehold Property Co.* v. *Baron Suffield* [1897] 2 Ch. 608). Nevertheless, if the deed appears to have been duly executed and is in proper custody (such as that of the grantee) a heavy burden of proving delivery as an escrow is on the party asserting that it was so delivered (*Rowley* v. *Rowley* (1854), Kay 242). If a conveyance is delivered by a vendor at a time when part only of the purchase price has been paid, in the absence of direct evidence it will be assumed to have been delivered as an escrow pending payment of the balance (*Thompson* v. *McCullough* [1947] K.B. 447). A statutory receipt can be delivered as an escrow (*Lloyds Bank, Ltd.* v. *Bullock* [1896] 2 Ch. 192).

If a deed has been delivered on the clear understanding that another party will execute it and meanwhile the party who delivered it will not otherwise be bound, and that other party fails to so do with the result that to treat it as having been delivered would be to cause substantial injustice to the party who delivered it, the deed would not, in equity, be binding on the person delivering it (*Luke* v. *South Kensington Hotel Co.* (1879), 11 Ch. D. 121 ; *Naas* v. *Westminster Bank, Ltd.* [1940] A.C. 366).

Effect of failure to execute deed.—A party who takes the benefit of a deed is bound by it in equity though he does not execute it (*Webb* v. *Spicer* (1849), 13 Q.B. 886 ; *Witham* v. *Vane* (1881), 44 L.T. 718). See also *Naas* v. *Westminster Bank, Ltd.* [1940] A.C. 366, mentioned above.

As to the necessity, before 1926, for a purchaser to execute a deed containing a reservation of an easement to make it operate at law as a regrant to the vendor of the easement, see *ante*, p. 494.

Alterations.—The presumption (which may be rebutted) is that an alteration appearing in a deed was made *before* execution (*Doe d. Tatum* v. *Catomore* (1851), 16 Q.B. 745 ; *Re Spollon and Long's Contract* [1936] Ch. 713). An alteration or addition for the purpose of correcting an obvious error made after execution will not avoid a deed ; for instance, the filling in of the date of the deed, or the names of the occupiers of the property conveyed, or the agreed date in the proviso for redemption (see *Keane* v. *Smallbone* (1855), 17 C.B. 179 ; *Aldous* v. *Cornwell* (1868), L.R. 3 Q.B. 573 ; *Adsetts* v. *Hives* (1863), 9 L.T. 110) ; or even altering the date of a deed when it is done to carry out the intention of the parties (*Bishop of Crediton* v. *Bishop of Exeter* [1905] 2 Ch. 455). In *Re Howgate and Osborn's Contract* [1902] 1 Ch. 451, the name " William Gray " had been erased after execution, and the words " Edward Thomas Gray " inserted, and parol evidence was allowed to show that the name " William Gray " had been inserted in error and afterwards corrected, and the deed was upheld.

A *material* alteration made in a deed after its execution, without the consent of the parties, avoids the deed to the extent that the covenants contained in it cannot be enforced by a party who made the alteration or whose servant or agent made it (*Ellesmere Brewery Co.* v. *Cooper* [1896] 1 Q.B. 75) ; but when once an estate has been conveyed by a deed, the deed has done its work, and a subsequent alteration of the deed cannot operate to reconvey the estate (*Lord Ward* v. *Lumley* (1860), 5 H. & N. 656). Whether a deed would now be held to be avoided by a material alteration made by a stranger is doubtful. The strict rule of common law was that it did become void (*Pigot's Case* (1614), 11 Co. Rep. 26b), but more recent cases suggest that this unreasonable rule would not now be followed. See *Hutchins* v. *Scott* (1837), 6 L.J. Ex 186 ; *Davidson* v. *Cooper* (1844), 13 L.J. Ex. 276 ; *Henfree* v. *Bromley* (1805), 6 East 309.

If a deed is altered in a material part after execution, with the consent of the parties, *so as to effect a new contract between the parties*, the deed requires restamping (*London, Brighton and South Coast Railway* v. *Fairclough* (1841), 2 Man. & G. 674).

As a matter of practice, a principal should always make it an absolute rule of the office that no deed or document should be executed or signed until it has been examined with the draft, and marked by the two clerks who have done the examining, and, in addition, a principal should always, after the examination, himself glance through the engrossment. Where there are any alterations the principal should give express instructions to the person who will witness the execution or signing of the document to initial such alterations.

PROTECTION BY REGISTRATION

PART 1. UNREGISTERED LAND

A. LAND CHARGES

General Note.—There may be charges, liabilities and interests affecting land which will not be disclosed by the abstract, and which even an inspection of the property will not bring to light. The object of the L.C.A. 1972 (which consolidated the enactments relating to the registration of land charges, etc. ; i.e., L.C.A. 1925 to the Land Registration and Land Charges Act, 1971) is to compel persons claiming any such charges, etc., to register them, by providing that unless they do so their claims will be void as against purchasers for value of the land. But there are certain interests which do not come within any of the classes of interests which can be registered, for instance, equitable interests arising under a trust for sale or a settlement. The reason why registration was not required in these cases is that a purchaser who pays the purchase-money to two individual trustees or to a trust corporation is fully protected because the conveyance to him will overreach such interests, and the beneficial owner is also protected because his interest is transferred to the purchase-money. However, unfortunately, certain other rights affecting land exist which have been held to be within neither the system of registration nor the system of overreaching.

By s. 1 (1) of the L.C.A. 1972 the following five registers are to continue to be kept :—

(*a*) a register of land charges (see below) ;

(*b*) a register of pending actions (see *post*, p. 605) ;

(*c*) a register of writs and orders affecting land (see *post*, p. 607) ;

(*d*) a register of deeds of arrangement affecting land (see *post*, p. 608) ;

(*e*) a register of annuities (see *post*, p. 609).

A sixth register was created by the Agricultural Credits Act, 1928 (see *post*, p. 610). These registers are dealt with *seriatim* in the following pages.

(a) **Register of land charges.**—The L.C.A. 1972, s. 3 (1), contains a provision which is sometimes overlooked, namely, that a land charge registered after

1925 shall be registered in the name of the estate owner (that is, the owner of the *legal* estate—L.C.A. 1972, s. 17 (1) ; L.P.A. 1925, ss. 1 (1) and 205 (1) (v)) whose estate is intended to be affected. Thus, if *A*, who has agreed to purchase a legal estate in land, contracts to resell to *B*, then an estate contract registered in *A's* name will not be effective. It is arguable that the registration in *A's* name only remains in suspense, becoming fully effective when *A* acquires the legal estate, particularly since *B* may not know the name (or even of the existence) of the original vendor. Against this it can be said that the L.C.A. 1972 does not cater for inchoate registrations of this sort (see R. G. Rowley, *Conveyancer N.S.*, vol. 19, at p. 105, and further J. E. Adams, *ibid.*, vol. 35, at p. 155). Accordingly the only reliable practice is that in the meantime both contracts should be registered in the name of the original vendor. There is doubt whether registration is effective if made after the person against whom it is made has ceased to be the estate owner. The better opinion seems to be that the wording of the L.C.A. 1972 is such that the registration is void (*Law Society's Gazette*, vol. 63, p. 74). This would be so if the estate owner has lost his legal estate in the meantime by disposal *inter vivos*, bankruptcy or death. Even if registration were not itself valid for this reason, it would be if an effective priority notice has been entered as the registration would relate back to the creation of the charge ; see *post*, p. 610. The matter is discussed *ibid.*, pp. 447, 573, 723.

Although the L.C.A. 1972, s. 3 (1), requires that registration shall be in " the name of the estate owner " registration in a name which may fairly be described as a version of the proper names of an estate owner is not a nullity. Such a registration would be void under the L.C.A. 1972, s. 10 (4), against a purchaser who obtained a nil certificate on searching in the correct name. Nevertheless the registration may be effective against a subsequent purchaser who fails to apply for an *official* search or applies for an official search in the wrong name (*Oak Co-operative Building Society* v. *Blackburn* [1968] Ch. 370, C.A.). In that case registration was in the name Frank but the correct name of the estate owner was Francis. The court took a very practical view of the procedure and the judgment is of great interest not least on account of its description of the register. It provides an additional reason for making official searches rather than personal ones. A personal search in the correct name would not give protection against a registration which could not be found because it was in the wrong name if, under this decision, registration in the wrong name was valid.

It is necessary, also, to remember that the following provisions refer to charges or obligations in respect of " *land* " which does not include an undivided share in land (L.C.A. 1972, s. 17 (1) ; see *Re Rayleigh Weir Stadium* [1954] 1 W.L.R. 786 and *Irani Finance, Ltd.* v. *Singh* [1971] Ch. 59).

The Land Charges (No. 2) Rules, 1972 (which consolidate, replace and amend all previous rules) provide that the relevant particulars to be recorded in the register include " the county and parish, place or district in which land charged is situated together with short descriptions identifying land so far as practicable " (r. 3 and Sched. 1). Similarly the form for application for registration of a land charge (L.C. 4) has a marginal note (5) that " a short description sufficient to identify the land may if practicable be added " (*ibid.*, Sched. 2). In many cases a plan may appear the best means of doing this, but it is provided generally that no application should be accompanied or supported by any deed, document or plan (Land Charges (No. 2) Rules, 1972, r. 19 (2)).

Classes of land charges.—The register is divided by the L.C.A. 1972, s. 2, into the following classes :

Class A.—The cases in this class are principally land charges of the type which were land charges within the meaning of the Land Charges Registration and Searches Act, 1888, that is to say, charges obtained under the provisions of the class of Acts of Parliament known as " Improvement Acts ". The 1888 Act is repealed but land charges registered under it have effect as if registered under the L.C.A. The following is the general provision of the L.C.A. 1972, s. 2 (2) :

" A Class A land charge is—

(*a*)   a rent or annuity or principal money payable by instalments or otherwise, with or without interest, which is not a charge created by deed but is a charge upon land (other than a rate) created pursuant to the application of some person under the provisions of any Act of Parliament, for securing to any person either the money spent by him or the costs, charges and expenses incurred by him under such Act, or the money advanced by him for repaying the money spent or the costs, charges and expenses incurred by another person under the authority of an Act of Parliament."

Alternatively and more specifically it is provided that a Class A land charge is such a rent or annuity or principal money payable as in para. (*a*) (above) and is a charge created under certain specified enactments (L.C.A. 1972, s. 2 (2) (*b*), referring to Sched. 2). The enactments specified are : Tithe Act, 1918, ss. 4 (2), 6 (1) (charge of consideration money for redemption of tithe rent charge) ; Tithe Annuities Apportionment Act, 1921, s. 1 (charge of apportioned part of tithe redemption annuity) ; Landlord and Tenant Act, 1927, Sched. 1, para. (7) (charge in respect of improvement to business premises) ; Land Drainage Act, 1930, s. 9 (5) (charge in respect of sum paid in commutation of certain obligations to repair banks, water-courses, etc.) ; Tithe Act, 1936, s. 30 (1) (charge for redemption of corn rents, etc.) ; Civil Defence Act, 1939, ss. 18 (4), 19 (1) (charge in respect of civil defence works) ; Agricultural Holdings Act, 1948, ss. 72, 73, 74 (charges in respect of sums due to tenant or occupier of agricultural holdings) and s. 82 (charge in favour of landlord of agricultural holding in respect of compensation for or cost of certain improvements) ; Corn Rents Act, 1963, s. 1 (5) (charge under a scheme for the apportionment or redemption of corn rents or other payments in lieu of tithes).

Class B.—This class includes any charge on land (not being a local land charge) of any of the general kinds described in Class A, para. (*a*), above, created otherwise than pursuant to the application of any person (L.C.A. 1972, s. 2 (3)).

There are not many charges operating under Class B, in view of the exception " not being a local land charge."

Class C.—This class consists of the following (L.C.A. 1972, s. 2 (4)), namely—

(i) a puisne mortgage ;

(ii) a limited owner's charge ;

(iii) a general equitable charge ;

(iv) an estate contract.

(i) *Puisne mortgages.*—A puisne mortgage is a " *legal* mortgage which is not protected by a deposit of documents relating to the legal estate affected " (L.C.A. 1972, s. 2 (4) (i)).

No authority is known but it is assumed that the deposit must be of those deeds which would, in fact, protect the mortgagee.

The L.C.A. 1972 makes special provision in regard to this kind of land charge. By s. 3 (3) it is provided that a puisne mortgage created before 1926 may be registered as a land charge before any transfer of the mortgage is made. Unless this is done a mortgage not protected by a deposit of documents relating to the legal estate does not, as against a purchaser in good faith without notice, obtain any benefit by reason of being converted into a legal mortgage by Sched. 1 to the L.P.A. 1925 (L.P.A. 1925, Sched. 1, Pt. VII, para. 6, and Pt. VIII, para. 5). If, therefore, the certificate of search does not disclose the registration of such a charge the purchaser will not be concerned therewith unless he has notice thereof (L.P.A. 1925, s. 2 (5)). But such a charge created before 1926 and acquired under a transfer made after 1925 *must* be registered within one year after the transfer ; otherwise it will be void against a purchaser for value of the land charged therewith or any interest in such land (L.P.A. 1925, s. 2 (5) ; L.C.A. 1972, s. 4 (7)).

A puisne mortgage created after 1925 must be registered as a land charge, otherwise it will be void as against a purchaser for value, including a mortgagee or lessee, of the land charged therewith or of any interest in such land (L.C.A. 1972, ss. 4 (5), 17 (1)). So, a puisne mortgage created after 1925 and not registered will lose priority against a mortgage which has been registered or is protected by the deposit of the documents, in consequence of the provision contained in s. 97 of the L.P.A. 1925 that mortgages (other than mortgages or charges of registered land) not protected by a deposit of documents will rank according to the date of registration as a land charge. See further, *post*, p. 1018.

Section 13 (2) of the L.C.A. 1972 is important. It provides that the registration of a puisne mortgage or charge as a land charge shall not operate to prevent that mortgage or charge being overreached in favour of a prior mortgagee, or a person deriving title under him, where, by reason of a sale, foreclosure, or otherwise, the right of the puisne mortgagee or subsequent chargee to redeem is barred.

(ii) *A limited owner's charge.*—This class of charge is defined (L.C.A. 1972, s. 2 (4) (ii)) as follows :—

> " an equitable charge acquired by a tenant for life or statutory owner under the Finance Act, 1894, or any other statute, by reason of the discharge by him of any death duties or other liabilities and to which special priority is given by the statute."

In practice, a limited owner's charge is not often registered, as the person entitled will generally have control of the fund and can refund himself. The chief charge under this heading is under s. 9 (6) of the F.A. 1894, under which a person who, having a limited interest in land, pays the estate duty thereon will be entitled to a charge for the money so paid, and for the expense of registering the charge.

Where the charge has been created *before* 1926 and transferred after 1925, the transferee will not be able to enforce the land charge as against a purchaser for value, including a mortgagee or lessee, of the land charged therewith, or of any interest in the land, unless the charge is registered as a land charge within one year of the transfer (L.C.A. 1972, ss. 4 (7), 17 (1)).

Where the charge is created *after* 1925 it will be void against a subsequent purchaser for value, including a mortgagee or lessee, unless it is registered as a land charge before the completion of the purchase (*ibid.*, ss. 4 (5), 17 (1)).

(iii) *A general equitable charge.*—This class of charge is defined as :—

" any equitable charge which—

(*a*) is not secured by a deposit of documents relating to the legal estate affected ;

(*b*) does not arise or affect an interest arising under a trust for sale or a settlement ;

(*c*) is not a charge given by way of indemnity against rents equitably apportioned or charged exclusively on land in exoneration of other land, and against the breach or non-observance of covenants or conditions ; and

(*d*) is not included in any other class of land charge."

A contract for the division of the proceeds of sale of land, where there is no loan that could stand charged on the land, is not registrable as a " general equitable charge " under the L.C.A. (*Thomas* v. *Rose* [1968] 1 W.L.R. 1797).

A general equitable charge includes an annuity created after 1925, also an annuity created before 1926 and transferred after 1925, but *not* an annuity created before 1926, which should be registered under Class E.

If the charge is protected by the deposit of the deeds it has not to be registered. The object of registration is to protect the person entitled to the charge, but if he has the deeds he will already be protected (L.P.A. 1925, s. 13). So, where the charge relates to an interest arising under a trust for sale or under a settlement it is not necessary to register it. In this case the person entitled to the charge is sufficiently protected, because all capital money has to be paid to two trustees or to a trust corporation.

The effect of non-registration is dealt with *post*, p. 602.

(iv) *Estate contract.*—An estate contract is defined in the L.C.A. 1972, s. 2 (4) (iv), as—

" a contract by an estate owner or by a person entitled at the date of the contract to have a legal estate conveyed to him to convey or create a legal estate, including a contract conferring either expressly or by statutory implication a valid option to purchase, a right of pre-emption or any other like right."

It includes an option to renew a lease (*Beesly* v. *Hallwood Estates, Ltd.* [1960] 1 W.L.R. 549), a right of pre-emption under s. 128 of the Lands Clauses Consolidation Act, 1845, and a notice to treat with charity trustees for redemption of a rent-charge (Charities Act, 1960, s. 27 (7)).

In *Turley* v. *Mackay* [1944] Ch. 37, an unusual form of agency agreement provided that if the plaintiff wished to dispose of certain property he should do so only in such manner as the defendant should think fit. It was held that the agreement meant that the plaintiff was bound to create a legal estate in favour of such third person as the defendant should direct and so it was properly registered as an estate contract. However, *Turley* v. *MacKay* was distinguished by Megarry, J., in *Thomas* v. *Rose* [1968] 1 W.L.R. 1797, who held, in relation to another most unusual agency agreement, that a contract providing for the making of a further contract to convey and create a legal estate is not itself an " estate contract " registrable under the L.C.A.

That constant care is necessary in deciding what will amount to an estate contract is further illustrated by the case of *Sharp* v. *Coates* [1949] 1 K.B. 285. There a tenant from year to year sub-let the land and agreed that if the reversion became absolutely vested in him he would grant to the under-lessee a term for ten years. It was held that the tenant from year to year was an " estate owner " (L.C.A. 1972, s. 17 (1) ; L.P.A. 1925, ss. 1 (1) and 205 (1) (v) and (xxvii)) and therefore that the agreement constituted an estate contract. As it had not been registered it was void against a purchaser of the reversion from the tenant from year to year who later acquired such reversion. Similarly, it has been held that an agreement to create a weekly tenancy at a future date, made at a time when the intended landlord had agreed to buy the property but had not completed the purchase, is an estate contract which may become void for non-registration even if not made in writing (*Coventry Permanent Economic Building Society* v. *Jones* [1951] 1 All E.R. 901 ; *Universal Permanent Building Society* v. *Cooke* [1952] Ch. 95).

In *Universal Permanent Building Society* v. *Cooke*, Jenkins, L.J., expressed the opinion that an agreement that would be enforced under the doctrine of part performance may be registered although not evidenced by writing. The contrary view is expressed by Mr. R. Geoffrey Rowley in the *Conveyancer N.S.*, vol. 19, p. 99 *et seq.*

Contracts for sale likely to be completed quickly are often not registered, particularly if they relate to property of small value. Cases in which it is especially desirable to register are referred to *ante*, p. 39.

Where a memorandum of deposit of deeds contains a covenant or agreement to execute a legal mortgage when called on, it will be a wise precaution to register it as an estate contract. But if this were not done it would only mean that the agreement to execute a mortgage might not be enforceable. It would not make the security bad, and as the mortgagee would have the deeds he could, as it is termed, " sit " upon them until his claim was satisfied or obtain an order to sell and pass a legal estate under s. 90 of the L.P.A. 1925.

An estate contract cannot be overreached under the provisions of the " curtain clauses " (L.P.A. 1925, s. 2 (2), as amended by the Law of Property (Amendment) Act, 1926, and subs. (3)), as it would not be just to shift the charge to the purchase-money.

It is specially provided by s. 11 of the S.L.A. 1925 that a contract made or other liability created or arising after 1925 for the settlement of land, by the persons mentioned therein, shall be deemed an estate contract within the meaning of the L.C.A., and may be registered as a land charge.

It is provided by s. 6 (1) of the L.P.A. 1925 that nothing in Pt. I of the Act affects prejudicially the right to enforce a valid option to purchase or right of pre-emption over the reversion contained in a lease. Therefore, at first sight, this provision would seem to make it unnecessary to register the option or right as a land charge. But the above saving is only in connection with Pt. I of the L.P.A., and as such options or rights have not been excluded from the operation of the L.C.A., they must be registered as land charges.

Class D.—This class covers the following charges or obligations, namely—

    (i) Inland Revenue (death duty) charges ;

    (ii) restrictive covenants or agreements ;

    (iii) equitable easements (L.C.A. 1972, s. 2 (5)).

    (i) *Death duty charges.*—" a charge on land, being a charge acquired by the [Commissioners of Inland Revenue] under any enactment . . . for death duties leviable or payable on any death occurring on or after 1st January 1926 "(L.C.A. 1972, ss. 2 (5) (i), 17 (1)).

(ii) *Restrictive covenants.*—" a covenant or agreement (other than a covenant or agreement between a lessor and lessee) restrictive of the user of land and entered into [after 1925] " (L.C.A. 1972, s. 2 (5) (ii)).

It is not necessary to register as a land charge a covenant given by a purchaser to a vendor to indemnify him against breaches regarding restrictive covenants, whether such restrictive covenants are contained in a deed made before 1926 or after 1925. But a covenant purporting to be a covenant of indemnity may be so worded as to amount, in effect, to a fresh independent restrictive covenant, and so require registration. See *ante*, p. 559. It should be noted that there is no need to register a *positive* covenant ; the distinction etween positive and restrictive covenants is discussed *ante*, p. 551.

Where a vendor sells land and imposes restrictive covenants on that land, and the purchaser intends to mortgage the property to raise part of the purchase-money, it is necessary for the vendor to take advantage of s. 11 of the L.C.A. 1972, and give *a priority notice* at least fifteen days before the registration is to take effect. See further *post*, p. 610. The effect of the priority notice is to get the restrictive covenant on the register before the mortgage takes effect. Something of the sort was necessary because the restrictive covenant could not be registered before it was created. The priority notice having been given, then, if the formal application referring to the priority notice is presented within thirty days, the registration will take effect as if the registration had been made at the time when the matter arose.

It is provided by s. 200 of the L.P.A. 1925, in effect, that where land having a common title with other land is disposed of to a purchaser who does not get the deeds, such purchaser is entitled to require that a memorandum giving notice of any provision contained in the disposition to him restrictive of the user of any other land comprised in the common title, shall be indorsed on one of the deeds selected by him ; but that this provision is not to affect the obligation to register the restrictive covenants as a land charge. See *ante*, pp. 171, 172.

It will be noted that a covenant or agreement made between a lessor and lessee is not registrable. This is because is was assumed that such covenants or agreements will be contained in a lease or underlease which will be inspected by persons likely be to affected. On this subject see *Newman* v. *Real Estate Debenture Corporation* [1940] 1 All E.R. 131.

This rule causes particular difficulty where a lessor binds land other than that demised. A subsequent purchaser of the land restricted may have no knowledge of the covenant and so, on equitable grounds, the covenant may cease to be enforceable (except, perhaps, by a personal action against the lessor). It has been argued, for example, in the *Law Times*, vol. 227, pp. 243, 244, that a covenant " by a lessor as to user of land not included in the demise is not within the exception and can therefore be registered." This reasoning required that, in order to produce a sensible result, the words " affecting the land demised " be implied after the words " other than a covenant or agreement between a lessor and lessee " in the L.C.A. 1972, s. 2 (5), Class D (ii). It was thought not reasonable that the exemption from registration should exist merely because the covenant is made between two persons who are lessor and lessee if the covenant does not relate to the demised premises. Nonetheless, however, it has now been held that the argument in this paragraph is incorrect ; the courts will not imply the words mentioned. A covenant between lessor and lessee is incapable of registration (and so its enforceability depends on equitable rules as to notice) even if it relates to land not comprised in the demise (*Dartstone, Ltd.* v. *Cleveland Petroleum Co., Ltd.* [1969] 1 W.L.R. 1807).

Accordingly it is suggested that, to protect the lessee in such a case, the lessor should be asked to permit an endorsement of the covenant on an appropriate deed on the title to the premises restricted. Such endorsement would ensure notice to a subsequent purchaser but not necessarily to a lessee. Compare *Golden Lion Hotel (Hunstanton), Ltd.* v. *Carter* [1965] 1 W.L.R. 1189.

(iii) *Equitable easement.*—This class of charge is defined (L.C.A. 1972, s. 2 (5) (iii)) as :—

" an easement, right or privilege over or affecting land created or arising [after 1925], and being merely an equitable interest."

A legal easement is an easement held for an interest equivalent to an estate in fee simple absolute in possession, or a term of years absolute (L.P.A. 1925, s. 1 (2) (*a*)). A legal easement has not to be registered as a land charge for its protection. An equitable easement is an easement which is not a legal easement, for instance, an easement for life, or for an indefinite period until a certain length of notice is given. But the expression " equitable easement " would not include a licence, such as a licence to fish not connected with any land of the person having the right. Such a right is not an " easement " at all, although it is sometimes incorrectly called " an easement in gross ". See further, as to the nature of an easement, *ante*, p. 503 and particularly as to equitable easements, *ante*, p. 505.

In *Lewisham Borough Council* v. *Maloney* [1948] 1 K.B. 50, the Court of Appeal decided that the requisitioning of premises under reg. 51 of the Defence (General) Regulations, 1939, did not require registration as an equitable easement. The ground of the decision was that the words " right or privilege " bear a restricted meaning in their context, particularly because they follow the word " easement," and the charges comprised in the whole phrase are referred to as " equitable easements ". The court did not attempt to define the meaning of the phrase. A right of way enjoyed in equity consequent on mutual benefit and burden (*Hopgood* v. *Brown* [1955] 1W.L.R. 213) or on mutual acquiescence (*Inwards* v. *Baker* [1965] 2 Q.B. 29) may not be within this class (*E. R. Ives Investment, Ltd.* v. *High* [1967] 2 Q.B. 379), nor may a tenant's right under his lease to remove fixtures at the determination of the lease (*Poster* v. *Slough Estates, Ltd.* [1967] 1 W.L.R. 1515). Further the House of Lords has held not registrable within Class D (iii) a right of re-entry given by an assignee of a lease to the assignor where the assignee covenanted with the assignor to observe certain stipulations (*Shiloh Spinners, Ltd.* v. *Harding* [1973] 1 All E.R. 90). Thus, although an equitable interest, the right was not unenforceable for want of registration under the L.C.A. The word " right " in the definition was said not to have a meaning so different in quality from easement and privilege as to include the right of entry (*ibid.*).

Class E.—Register of old annuities.—See *post*, p. 609.

Class F.—This class of charge is created by the Matrimonial Homes Act, 1967 ; see L.C.A. 1972, s. 2 (7), and the discussion *ante*, p. 370 *et seq.*

Avoidance of unregistered charges.—A land charge of Class A created after 31st December, 1888, is void against a purchaser for value (including a mortgagee or lessee) of the land charged therewith or of any interest in such land unless registered before the completion of the purchase (L.C.A. 1972, ss. 4 (2) and 17 (1)). Accordingly as regards Class A, a search should (in theory) be made from 1888. As regards charges within Class B, as they could not be registered under the 1888 Act (*R.* v. *Land Registry* (1889), 24 Q.B.D. 178), no search need be made before 1926.

A land charge of Class A or Class B for securing money, when registered, takes effect as if it had been created by a deed of charge by way of legal mortgage, but without prejudice to the priority of the charge (L.C.A. 1972, s. 4 (1)). The effect of this provision is to give the person entitled to the benefit of the land charge a power of sale, and thus enable a sale to be made to realise the security without having to go to the court for an order.

The L.C.A. 1972, s. 4 (5) (6), provides that a land charge of Class B, Class C or Class D created or arising after 1925 shall (except as mentioned below) be void as against a purchaser of the land charged therewith, or of any interest in such land, unless the land charge is registered in the appropriate register before the completion of the purchase. " Purchaser " means a person who, for valuable consideration, takes any interest in land or in a charge on land, and includes a mortgagee or lessee (*ibid.*, s. 17 (1)). It is provided, however, that as respects an estate contract (Class C (iv)) and a land charge of Class D created or entered into after 1925, this provision only applies in favour of a purchaser of a legal estate for money or money's worth (L.C.A. 1972, s. 4 (6)). An estate contract (or a Class D land charge) will *not* be void for non-registration as against an equitable mortgagee since such a person is not a purchaser of a *legal estate* (*McCarthy & Stone, Ltd.* v. *Julian S. Hodge & Co., Ltd.* [1971] 1 W.L.R. 1547).

If a land charge of Class B or Class C was created before 1926, s. 4 (7) of the L.C.A. 1972 applies. This subsection provides that after the expiration of one year from the first conveyance, occurring after 1925, of a land charge of Class B or Class C created before 1926, the person entitled thereto shall not be able to enforce or recover the land charge or any part thereof as against a purchaser for value, including a mortgagee or lessee, of the land charged therewith, or of any interest in the land unless the land charge is registered in the appropriate register before the completion of the purchase.

Where the land charge has not been registered, the fact that the purchaser, as a matter of fact, may have notice thereof, is not material (L.P.A. 1925, s. 199 (1) (i) ; *ante*, p. 163). Further in favour of a purchaser (including mortgagee and lessee) an official certificate of search is conclusive, affirmatively or negatively, as the case may be, as to land charges registered (L.C.A. 1972, s. 10 (4), and see s. 11 (5) (6), *post*, p. 611 ; also *Stock* v. *Wanstead and Woodford Borough Council* [1962] 2 Q.B. 479, *post*, p. 633). However, this protection is only available if the application for the search gave no reasonable scope for misunderstanding (*Du Sautoy* v. *Symes* [1967] Ch. 1146). Accordingly, particular care should be taken on behalf of purchasers to search against correctly named persons and clearly described land. Registration to be effective must be in the correct full name of the estate owner ; if that is not done and a subsequent purchaser searches in such name but receives a clear certificate the registration will not bind him (*Oak Co-operative Building Society* v. *Blackburn* [1968] Ch. 730, C.A.). On the other hand registration in " what may fairly be described as a version of the full names of the vendor, albeit not a version which is bound to be discovered on a search in the correct full names . . . would not [be held] to be a nullity against someone who does not search at all, or who, as here, searches in the wrong name " (*ibid.*, at p. 737). It seems that names on the title can be assumed to be the correct full names for this purpose (*Diligent Finance Co., Ltd.* v. *Alleyne* (1972), 23 P. & C.R. 346).

Thus the rules would appear to operate as reasonably as possible although there is an almost insuperable problem in ensuring that registration is effective unless the deeds are available (e.g., on registering a Class F charge or, in many cases, an estate contract).

When a restrictive covenant or other land charge has become void against the purchaser because it has not been registered, it does not appear possible to revive it as against subsequent purchasers by late registration. By analogy to equitable rules a subsequent purchaser would be protected, otherwise the value of the estate to the purchaser against whom the land charge is by virtue of the above provisions void might be depreciated (*Wilkes* v. *Spooner* [1911] 2 K.B. 473). In any event, there would be a practical difficulty in registering because that must be done against the estate owner whose estate is intended to be affected (L.C.A. 1972, s. 3 (1)). By virtue of the statute the land charge is void against the owner and so cannot affect his estate. There is, however, the point that the restrictive covenant could revive against successors in title who are not purchasers, e.g., against squatters, so that registration might be effective to bind purchasers from such successors (cf. *St. Marylebone Property Co., Ltd.* v. *Fairweather* [1962] 1 W.L.R. 1020 and *Marten* v. *Flight Refuelling, Ltd.* [1962] Ch. 115).

Cancellation of land charges.—An application to cancel entry of a land charge (other than Class F) generally has to be made on Form L.C.8 accompanied by *either* sufficient evidence of the applicant's title to apply for cancellation (unless the registration was made on his behalf and for his benefit) *or* office copies of orders of the court or Lands Tribunal justifying cancellation (Land Charges (No. 2) Rules, 1972, r. 10). Form L.C.8 may be signed by the applicant's solicitor(s) (*ibid.*, Sched. 2). However, the rigour of Form L.C.8 may be departed from in special circumstances : if the registrar has *first* been consulted and satisfied that the applicant would " suffer exceptional hardship or expense " by complying with the above, then an application for cancellation (or rectification) on Form L.C.17 may be allowed, supported by sufficient evidence that the land charge has been " discharged or overreached or is of no effect " (*ibid.*, r. 10, proviso). This relaxation will prove convenient, for instance, on cancellation of registration of restrictive covenants. Where the original parties to the deed imposing the covenants have released them, and there is no building scheme, the registration is cancelled on production of (*a*) the deed containing the covenant *indicating the land benefited*, (*b*) evidence that the covenantee still owns the whole of that land, for instance, by a certificate of his solicitor, and (*c*) the deed of release between the same parties. In view of the difficulty of proving who is entitled to the benefit of covenants the registrar may refuse to cancel entries of restrictive covenants in other circumstances unless application is made pursuant to an order under the L.P.A. 1925, s. 84, or the L.C.A. 1972, s. 1 (6) (cf. *Law Society's Gazette*, vol. 44, p. 218).

The Council of The Law Society have expressed the opinion (Opinion No. 940 (*b*), published in the Fourth (Cumulative) Supplement to the *Law Society's Digest*) that, although a vendor cannot insist on such an action, as a matter of good practice a purchaser's solicitor should effect the cancellation of an estate contract upon completion of the purchase as the purpose has then been fulfilled.

Difficulty often arises where an estate contract has been registered and the vendor wishes to have it removed so that he can resell on default to the purchaser. If there is a dispute as to whether the vendor's right to

rescind and resell has arisen, then the vendor must take action for rescission
or specific performance. He may not attack the registration under the
L.C.A. 1972, s. 1 (6), until the substantial dispute is settled (*Re Engall's
Agreement* [1953] 1 W.L.R. 977). See also *Jones* v. *Browne* (1945), 146
Estates Gazette 9 (where the dispute was as to the existence of a contract) ;
Pedigree Stock Farm Developments, Ltd. v. *R. Wheeler & Co., Ltd.* (1950), 155
Estates Gazette 66 and *Holland New Homes* v. *A. J. Wait & Co.* (1971), 221
Estates Gazette 148, C.A. (where despite rescission by a purchaser, the contract
was held to subsist at least for the purposes of the return of the deposit and
the court in its discretion did not vacate the Class C (iv) charge). Nevertheless, vacation of registration by way of interlocutory relief will be ordered
where there is no *prima facie* evidence before the court establishing the
existence of a contract (*Heywood* v. *B.D.C. Properties, Ltd.* [1963] 1 W.L.R.
975 ; *Georgiades* v. *Edward Wolfe & Co., Ltd.* [1965] Ch. 487). *Heywood* v.
B.D.C. Properties, Ltd., was followed in *W. H. Phillips, Ltd.* v. *George Wimpey
& Co. Ltd.* (1967), 111 Sol. J. 457, where a letter had been registered as
creating a land charge Class C (iii) ; Pennycuick, J., ordered that the entry
be vacated, saying that the creation of the land charge was purely a question
of construction of the letter with which the court could deal on motion.
See also *Rawlplug Co., Ltd.* v. *Kamvale Properties, Ltd.* (1968), 112 Sol. J. 723,
and *Hooker* v. *Wyle* (1973), 117 Sol. J. 545 (expiry of notice to complete).

Again, an entry as a pending action of proceedings under the Married
Women's Property Act, 1882, s. 17, by which a wife asked for a declaration
as to beneficial shares in the matrimonial home will be vacated ; the wife's
interest is at most a share in proceeds of sale and not an interest in land
under the L.C.A. (*Taylor* v. *Taylor* [1968] 1 W.L.R. 378).

However, in a case in which entries in respect of two Class C (i) land charges
were found registered relating to a transfer of mortgage and to a legal charge,
which mortgage and legal charge had both been discharged, the Council of
The Law Society eventually expressed the opinion that the purchaser was
not entitled to insist that the vendor should obtain at the vendor's expense
the cancellation of the entries (*Law Society's Digest*, Opinion No. 136 as
explained in Fourth (Cumulative) Supplement). In their view " entries in
the register do no more than give notice to a purchaser . . . the notice is
rebutted in the circumstances mentioned . . . by the production of the
discharged mortgage and legal charge ". See also Opinions Nos. 130 and 131.
The Council consider that where entries relating to charges removable by
the vendor (for instance, equitable charges of Class C (iii)) have been found
on searching before completion the vendor should hand over on completion
the charges duly vacated (assuming they do not refer to other land retained
by the vendor) together with the necessary forms for removal of the entries
from the register (*Law Society's Digest*, Opinion No. 139).

(b) **Register of pending actions.**—In this register there may be registered
a *pending land action*, which means " any action or proceedings pending in
court relating to land or any interest in or charge on land," and *a petition in
bankruptcy* filed after 1925 (L.C.A. 1972, ss. 5 (1) and 17 (1)). Registration
is made in the name of the estate owner or other person whose estate or
interest is intended to be affected thereby (L.C.A. 1972, s. 5 (2)). But a
petition in bankruptcy is registered against the bankrupt, and in the case
of a firm, against each partner as well as against the firm (*ibid.*, subs. (5) ;
s. 19 (2) ; Bankruptcy Rules, 1952, rr. 147, 148). Bankruptcy petitions are
automatically registered, whether or not the debtor is known to own any

land, but any other pending action can only be registered if it relates to specified land.

The court may, during the pendency of proceedings if satisfied that they are not prosecuted in good faith, make an order vacating the registration (L.C.A. 1972, s. 5 (10)). Nevertheless, it is difficult for a defendant to prove the absence of good faith even if proceedings appear to be unjustified. It has been suggested by Roxburgh, J., that " opportunities for blackmail " are given by the rule that the burden of proof is on the defendant. See the discussion of an interlocutory application in *Smith* v. *Jones* in the *Law Journal*, vol. 105, p. 482.

However, for a case of an order vacating a registration on the ground that the proceedings were not prosecuted in good faith, see *Calgary & Edmonton Land Co., Ltd.* v. *Discount Bank (Overseas), Ltd.* [1971] 1 W.L.R. 81 (where the Court of Appeal had upheld a finding that the proceedings in question were frivolous and vexatious and an abuse of the process of the court but where a petition for leave to appeal to the House of Lords had been lodged). Further, where the court has no power to vacate the wrongful registration of a pending action under s. 5 (10) of the L.C.A. 1972, it may order the registration to be vacated under its inherent jurisdiction (*Heywood* v. *B.D.C. Properties, Ltd.* (*No.* 2) [1964] 1 W.L.R. 971). In this case the Court of Appeal held, as a matter of law, that a pending action was properly registrable only by the plaintiff or by a counter-claiming defendant.

The registration of a pending action remains effective for five years only, and must then be renewed (L.C.A. 1972, s. 8).

A pending action will not bind a purchaser for value (including a mortgagee or lessee) without express notice thereof unless it is for the time being registered in the register of pending actions (L.C.A. 1972, ss. 5 (7) (8) and 17 (1)). But as respects a petition in bankruptcy, s. 5 (8) applies only in favour of a purchaser of a legal estate in good faith for *money or money's worth*, without notice of an available act of bankruptcy.

Registration of pending actions by private persons will not often be necessary, because when an order has been made in the action such order can be registered in the register of writs and orders affecting land under s. 6, and, on such registration, the effect of the registration as a pending action will come to an end. At the same time, in view of the fact that registration gives notice under s. 198 of the L.P.A. 1925, it may sometimes, for this purpose, be wise to register actions such as foreclosure and administration actions before obtaining the order.

The object of registering a petition is to protect the trustee in bankruptcy *until* the receiving order is registered in the register of writs and orders. If a petition has been filed or a receiving order made, the purchaser may take it for granted that it will have been registered in its proper register, as this will be done automatically by the officials. But it is necessary to know what the effect would be if neither of them, by some unaccountable accident, were registered. If a petition filed after 1925 be not registered in the register of pending actions, it will not bind a purchaser of a legal estate in good faith for money or money's worth, without notice of an available act of bankruptcy *unless a receiving order has been duly registered*. The mere filing of the petition will not give notice or be evidence of any act of bankruptcy therein alleged. For it is provided by s. 5 (9) of the L.C.A. 1972, as respects any transfer or creation of a legal estate, that a petition in bankruptcy filed after the commencement of the Act, which is not for the time being registered as a pending action, *shall not be notice or evidence of any act of bankruptcy* therein alleged ;

and by s. 6 (6) it is provided that the title of a trustee in bankruptcy acquired after 1925 will be void as against a purchaser of a legal estate in good faith for money or money's worth without notice of an available act of bankruptcy claiming under a conveyance made after the date of registration of a petition in bankruptcy as a pending action, unless at the date of the conveyance, either the registration of the pending action is in force, or the receiving order is registered in pursuance of the Act.

As regards a conveyance of land to a purchaser *before* the receiving order, he will get a good title under s. 45 of the Bankruptcy Act, 1914, provided that he had no notice of an available act of bankruptcy. And this will be so, although the conveyance itself amounts to an act of bankruptcy (*Shears* v. *Goddard* [1896] 1 Q.B. 406).

As regards after-acquired property, both real and personal, a bankrupt will be able to give a good title to a purchaser, in good faith, for value, so long as the trustee has not intervened by virtue of s. 47 (1) of the Bankruptcy Act, 1914, even if he has notice of the bankruptcy. The fact, therefore, that registration under s. 198 of the L.P.A. 1925, gives him notice is immaterial.

(c) **Register of writs and orders affecting land.**—The writs and orders affecting land which can be registered in this register are as follows :—

" (*a*) any writ or order affecting land issued or made by any court for the purpose of enforcing a judgment or recognizance ;

(*b*) any order appointing a receiver or sequestrator of land ;

(*c*) any receiving order in bankruptcy made [after 1925], whether or not it is known to affect land " (L.C.A. 1972, s. 6 (1)).

" Judgment " in the L.C.A. 1972 includes any order or decree having the effect of a judgment (*ibid.*, s. 17 (1)).

The registration has to be made in the name of the estate owner or other person whose land is affected by the writ or order registered (*ibid.*, s. 6 (2)). But in the case of a receiving order the registration will be made in the name of the bankrupt, and in the case of a firm, in the name of each partner, as well as against the firm (L.C.A. 1972, s. 16 (2) ; Bankruptcy Rules, 1952, r. 178 ; and *ante*, p. 606).

The registration has to be renewed every five years (L.C.A. 1972, s. 8). The question whether application for renewal must be made before the expiration of the original registration was raised, but not decided, in *Re a Receiving Order* [1947] Ch. 498 ; in that case re-registration of a receiving order effected after discharge of the bankrupt was vacated by the court.

Every such writ or order and every delivery in execution or other proceeding taken pursuant to such writ or order will be void as against a purchaser for value, including a mortgagee or lessee, unless the writ or order is for the time being registered but, as respects a receiving order, only if he is a purchaser of a legal estate in good faith for money or money's worth, without notice of an available act of bankruptcy (L.C.A. 1972, s. 6 (4) (5) ; there is a special exception in the case of an appointment of a receiver following a registered charge, in the Administration of Justice Act, 1956, s. 36 (3)).

Section 195 of the L.P.A. 1925 enacted that a judgment entered up in the Supreme Court against a judgment debtor operated as an equitable charge upon every estate or interest (whether legal or equitable) in all land to which the debtor at the date of entry or at any time thereafter was or became beneficially entitled provided it was registered in the register of writs and orders (L.P.A. 1925, s. 195 (3)). However, the Administration of Justice Act, 1956, s. 34, abolished the writ of *elegit* and repealed the above provisions of the L.P.A. 1925. For enforcing a judgment or order for payment of money, both the High Court and a county court are now empowered to impose a charge on *specified* land of the judgment debtor, such charge having the same effect as an equitable charge created by the debtor and being registrable as a land charge (*ibid.*, s. 35 ; County Courts Act, 1959, s. 141). The High Court, or a county court, may appoint a receiver by way of equitable execution of legal estates as well as equitable interests in land (*ibid.*, s. 36 ; County Courts Act, 1959, s. 142).

The procedure for obtaining and enforcing a charging order is discussed in the *Solicitors' Journal*, vol. 102, pp. 317 and 318. It was there argued that, as a share in proceeds of sale may, for some purposes, be an " interest in land " (*Cooper* v. *Critchley* [1955] Ch. 431) it was possible that a charging order may be obtained against the beneficial interest of a joint tenant.

However, the Court of Appeal has now decided that the beneficial interest of a joint tenant (or of a tenant in common), being merely an interest in the proceeds of sale, is not an " interest in land " for the purposes of a charging order under s. 35 of the Administration of Justice Act, 1956 (*Irani Finance Ltd.* v. *Singh* [1971] Ch. 59). In that case separate judgments for separate amounts had been made against each of two brothers who were joint tenants of land, both at law and in equity ; nevertheless charging orders over the " land or interest in land " of each of the brothers were ineffective so far as their interests as joint tenants were concerned. However, that case has been distinguished by Waller, J., where a husband and wife were joint tenants of a lease both at law and in equity, on the ground that the judgments in question had not been made against them separately but jointly in respect of overdrawn joint bank accounts (*National Westminster Bank, Ltd.* v. *Allen* [1971] 2 Q.B. 218). The learned judge accepted the proposition that where the judgment debtors could themselves validly charge an interest in land (i.e., the legal estate) in respect of a joint liability, then it was proper to make a charging order. Whilst this would appear to be a reasonable and realistic distinction and proposition, it is difficult to find anything suggesting support for them in *Irani Finance, Ltd.* v. *Singh, ante*.

An order appointing a receiver requires registration pursuant to the L.C.A. 1972, s. 6 (1) (*b*), *ante*, p. 607. Nevertheless, if an order under the 1956 Act, s. 35, *ante*, imposing a charge has been registered, it is not necessary to register an order appointing a receiver made either in proceedings for enforcing the charge or by way of equitable execution (1956 Act, s. 36 (3)).

(d) Register of deeds of arrangement.—The expression " deed of arrangement " under the L.C.A. has the same meaning as in the Deeds of Arrangement Act, 1914 (L.C.A. 1972, s. 17 (1)). See next note.

It should be said at once that registration of a deed of arrangement under the L.C.A. 1972 : (i) is only necessary where the deed transfers or affects land, and (ii) does not exempt the deed from registration under the Deeds of Arrangement Act, 1914, as to which see below. The definition of the word " land " in s. 17 (1) of the L.C.A. 1972 is very wide, but it does not include an undivided share in land.

The effect of non-registration under the two Acts is different. The effect of non-registration under the 1914 Act is that the deed becomes absolutely void, but the effect of non-registration under the L.C.A. 1972 is only to make the deed void as against a purchaser for valuable consideration, including a mortgagee or lessee, of any land comprised therein or affected thereby (L.C.A. 1972, s. 7 (2)).

Registration of a deed of arrangement ceases to have effect at the expiration of five years from the date of registration, *but may be renewed from time to time,* and, if renewed, will have effect for five years from the date or renewal (L.C.A. 1972, s. 8).

Registration under Deeds of Arrangement Act, 1914.—An

assignment for the benefit of creditors *generally* must be registered at the Department of Trade and Industry (Administration of Justice Act, 1925, s. 22), under the Deeds of Arrangement Act, 1914, within seven clear days after its first execution by the debtor or any creditor ; otherwise it will be absolutely void (*ibid.*, s. 1).

The deed will also be void unless it is assented to by the majority in number and value of the creditors within twenty-one days after registration ; if security be not given by the trustee as provided by the Act or dispensed with by the creditors, the court may, on the application of a creditor, declare the deed to be void (*ibid.*, ss. 3 and 11).

By the Deeds of Arrangement Act, 1914, s. 1 (1) (*b*), it is provided that a deed of arrangement to which the Act applies shall include a deed made by a debtor *who was insolvent* at the date of the execution of the deed, for the benefit of any three or more of his creditors. But, except in this case, a deed of arrangement with some of the creditors, but not allowing the general body of creditors to come in, will not be a deed of arrangement within the Act (*Re Saumarez* [1907] 2 K.B. 170). See also *Re Allix* [1914] 2 K.B. 77 ; *General Furnishing and Upholstery Company* v. *Venn* (1863), 32 L.J. Ex. 220 ; *Re Rileys, Ltd.* [1903] 2 Ch. 590. The Act does not apply to arrangements with creditors made by limited companies (*Re Rileys, Ltd., ante*).

(e) Register of annuities created before 1926.—The "annuity" which had before 1926 to be entered in this register is " a rent-charge or an annuity for a life or lives, or for any term of years or greater estate determinable on a life or lives and created after 25th April, 1855, and before 1st January, 1926 but does not include an annuity created by a marriage settlement or will " (L.C.A. 1972, s. 17 (1)). No annuity may be entered in the register after 1925 (*ibid.*, Sched. 1, para. 1).

Any such annuity created before 1926 and not registered in the register of annuities should be registered as a land charge under s. 2 (6), Class E, of the L.C.A. 1972 ; Class E was provided specially for this purpose. For, before 1926, partly because an annuity created by a marriage settlement or will had not to be registered, and partly because of the decision in *Greaves* v. *Tofield* (1880), 14 Ch. D. 653, there were not many annuities registered. This case decided that if a purchaser or mortgagee took with notice of an unregistered annuity (and he would in practically every case have notice), he would be bound in equity. But the position is now quite different, for it is provided, in effect, that a purchaser will not be deemed to have notice of a matter which *ought* to have been registered and has not been registered under the L.C.A. *or an enactment replaced by the Act* (L.P.A. 1925, s. 199 (1) (i)).

It is also provided by Sched. 1, para. 4 of the L.C.A. 1972 that *an annuity which before 1926 was capable of being registered in the register of annuities* will be void as against a creditor or a purchaser for value, including a mortgagee or lessee, of any interest in the land charged therewith, unless the

20

annuity is for the time being registered in the register of annuities or in the register of land charges, that is, in Class E above referred to. However, even if an annuity is registered, this does not as a rule prevent the annuity being overreached (L.C.A. 1972, s. 13 (1)), and a disposition under the S.L.A. 1925 operates to do this (S.L.A. 1925, s. 72 (3) (*a*) ; by virtue of s. 1 of the Law of Property (Amendment) Act, 1926, conveyances may be made subject to a prior interest such as an annuity).

Rent-charges and annuities created after 1925.—These should be registered as general equitable charges under s. 2 (4), Class C (iii), of the L.C.A. 1972, unless secured by a deposit of documents relating to the legal estate affected, or affecting an interest arising under a trust for sale or a settlement. See *ante*, p. 599. Such a rent-charge or annuity created before 1926 and assigned after 1925 should also be registered under Class C (iii) (L.C.A. 1972, s. 4 (7)).

Register of agricultural charges.—It is provided by s. 5 of the Agricultural Credits Act, 1928, that it shall be lawful for a farmer by instrument in writing to create, in favour of a bank, a charge on his farming stock and other agricultural assets as security for sums advanced by the bank. An agricultural charge is not deemed to be a bill of sale, and is exempt from stamp duty. A register of agricultural charges containing prescribed particulars is kept at the Land Registry, and every agricultural charge must be registered within seven clear days after execution, but power is given to the High Court to extend the time on proof that omission to register was accidental or due to inadvertence (*ibid.*, s. 9). If not so registered it will be void as against any other person than the farmer. These provisions as to registration have been extended to a debenture issued under the Agricultural Marketing Act, 1931, s. 7 (4), or the Agricultural Marketing Act, 1958, s. 15 (5).

Provision has now also been made for official searches in the register of agricultural charges (s. 9 (7) and Schedule to 1928 Act, as amended by L.C.A. 1972, Sched. 4, para. 7).

Registration is deemed to constitute actual notice of the charge to all persons and for all purposes connected with the property comprised in the charge, as from the date of registration, provided that, where a charge is expressly made for securing a current account or other further advances, the bank, in relation to the making of further advances under the charge, is not deemed to have notice of another agricultural charge by reason only that it is so registered if it was not so registered at the time when the first-mentioned charge was created or when the last search (if any) by or on behalf of the bank was made, whichever last happened (*ibid.*, s. 9 (8)). There is no provision in the Act as to how long the registration is to remain in force, or as to priority notices, but power is given to the Lord Chancellor to make regulations ; see the Agricultural Credits Regulations, 1928, and the Agricultural Credits Fees Order, 1970.

Priority notices.—The L.C.A. 1972, s. 11 (replacing Law of Property (Amendment) Act, 1926, s. 4 (1), as amended) is chiefly useful when it is desired to get restrictive covenants on to the register on a sale, so as to bind a mortgagee from the purchaser or any person deriving title under him. At the same time it is not limited to this, and applies to " any contemplated charge, instrument, or other matter " in connection with the L.C.A. 1972 in respect of which it is desired to get priority of registration. Use of the procedure is not easy as it involves anticipation of the date of the coming into operation of the matter constituting the land charge. Nevertheless, the danger of avoidance of a land charge in favour of a subsequent purchaser or mortgagee who has obtained a clear certificate is such that it is wise to use the procedure, if possible, before creation of such interests as puisne mortgages or general equitable charges.

The procedure is that any person intending to make an application for the registration of any contemplated charge, etc., gives a priority notice in Form L.C. 16 at least fifteen working days before the registration is to take effect (L.C.A. 1972, s. 11 (1) (6) ; Land Charges (No. 2) Rules, 1972, r. 4 and Sched. 2). The priority notice is to be entered on the register appropriate to the intended application (L.C.A. 1972, s. 11 (2)). Then, if the intended application is actually presented within thirty working days and cites the official reference number allocated to the priority notice, the registration will take effect as at the time when the charge, etc., was created (L.C.A. 1972, s. 11 (3) (6) ; Land Charges (No. 2) Rules, 1972, r. 7). When two charges, etc., are contemporaneous and one of them is subject to or dependent on the other which is protected by a priority notice, then the former is deemed to have been created after the registration of the latter (L.C.A. 1972, s. 11 (4)).

Unless special provision had been made there would be danger that unless a conveyance is completed immediately after issue of a certificate of search some other document might have priority by registration in the meantime. Under the L.C.A. 1972, s. 11 (5) (6), provided a purchase (widely defined by the L.C.A. 1972, s. 17 (1)) is completed within fifteen working days the certificate is conclusive notwithstanding registration in the meantime of any adverse interest or matter.

There is a difference of opinion whether the making of a contract (preceded by search) is protected in the same way as completion. It is suggested that it is not as the contract creates a mere equitable interest and is itself registrable in the land charges register. See *Conveyancer N.S.*, vol. 20, p. 260.

Priority notices and applications for registration received in the registry between 15.00 hours on one day and 15.00 hours on the next day are deemed to have been given or made at the same time, namely immediately before 15.00 hours on the second of those days (Land Charges (No. 2) Rules, 1972, r. 8 (1)).

B. REGISTRATION OF DEEDS

Areas of Yorkshire affected.—The Yorkshire deeds registries are each to be closed as compulsory registration of title spreads to any part of their areas (s. 16 of the L.P.A. 1969). In consequence the L.P.A. 1925, s. 11, and the Yorkshire Deeds Registries Act, 1884, will not apply to any subsequently made instrument and will after two years be repealed. The position at October, 1973, is as follows :—

The North Riding Deeds Register has been closed as respects registration of instruments made on or after 1st September, 1970, and the West Riding Deeds Register has been closed as respects registration of instruments made on or after 1st October, 1970. These closures have resulted from the L.P.A. 1969, s. 16, which provides that a deeds register shall be closed as respects registration of instruments made on or after the " relevant date " for each registry. The " relevant date " is the coming into force of an order making registration of title compulsory as respects *any part* of the area of the deeds registry. The Registration of Title (Teesside, Leeds and Sheffield) Order, 1970, made registration compulsory as from 1st September, 1970, in the county borough of Teesside (part of which was in the area of the

North Riding Registry) and as from 1st October in the county boroughs of Leeds and Sheffield (both of which were in the area of the West Riding Registry).

Thus :—

(i) As from 1st September, 1970, registration of title was compulsory in the usual cases of conveyance and certain leases within the county borough of Teesside ; no deed operative thereafter was registrable in the deeds register.

(ii) As regards land in the North Riding but not within the county borough of Teesside registration of title is not compulsory but instruments operative on or after 1st September, 1970, do not require registration in the deeds register.

(iii) As from 1st October, 1970, registration of title was compulsory in the usual cases of conveyance and certain leases within the county boroughs of Leeds and Sheffield ; no deed operative thereafter was registrable in the deeds register.

(iv) As regards land in the West Riding but not within the county boroughs of Leeds or Sheffield registration of title is not compulsory but instruments operative on or after 1st October, 1970, do not require registration in the deeds register.

At the time of writing there has been no change affecting the East Riding register which affects an area including Kingston-upon-Hull.

Instruments registrable.—Before 1926 assurances and wills by which any lands within any of the three Ridings were affected might be registered at the deeds registry. Assurances entitled to be registered had, and still have, priority according to the date of registration thereof, and not according to the date of such assurances (Yorkshire Registries Act, 1884, s. 14). Priority is not lost as a result of actual or constructive notice of an assurance earlier in date except in cases of actual fraud (*ibid.*).

A great deal of controversy has arisen over the exact meaning of the L.P.A. 1925, s. 11, which provides as follows :—

" 11.—(1) It shall not be necessary to register a memorial of any instrument made after the commencement of this Act in any local deeds registry unless the instrument operates to transfer or create a legal estate, or to create a charge thereon by way of legal mortgage ; nor shall the registration of a memorial of any instrument not required to be registered affect any priority.

(2) Probates and letters of administration shall be treated as instruments capable of transferring a legal estate to personal representatives.

(3) Memorials of all instruments capable of transferring or creating a legal estate or charge by way of legal mortgage, may, when so operating, be registered."

It has been suggested that the words " it shall not be *necessary* to register . . ." mean that other documents dealing only with the *equitable* estate *may* be registered, provided they are allowed to be registered by the Yorkshire Registries Acts. The registrars of the three Ridings have not refused to accept for registration such instruments affecting equitable interests only.

Nevertheless, it is considered that the effect of the L.P.A. 1925, s. 11, was to restrict the documents of which memorials are properly registrable to those dealing with *legal* estates. It is suggested that the meaning of the words in s. 11 (3) that " memorials of all instruments capable of transferring or creating a legal estate . . . may, when so operating, be registered," is that such instruments are the only ones which may be registered. It is unfortunate that the draftsman did not expressly repeal or amend the provisions of the Yorkshire Registries Act, 1884, as to the documents which may be registered but it is clear that he intended that the L.P.A. 1925, s. 11, should amount to an amendment. This intention is shown, for instance, by the fact that there is no provision in the Yorkshire Registries Act, 1884, for registration of letters of administration without the will annexed. Just as the L.P.A. 1925, s. 11 (2), means that all letters of administration are registrable, so the L.P.A. 1925, s. 11 (1), (3), implies that documents not affecting a legal estate are not registrable. The intention of the draftsman was further shown by the exclusion of *legal* mortgages of land within the jurisdiction of a local deeds registry which are registered in the deeds register from the definition of a puisne mortgage (L.C.A. 1925, s. 10 (1), Class C (i)). It must have been intended that *equitable* mortgages should not be registrable in a deeds register, otherwise if so registered they would similarly have been excluded from the definition of a general equitable charge (L.P.A. 1925, s. 10 (1), Class C (iii)). In reliance on the L.P.A. 1925, s. 11, the officials of the former Middlesex Deeds Registry refused to register an instrument which did not affect a legal estate.

It must be noted that registration of a memorial not required to be registered does not affect priority (L.P.A. 1925, s. 11 (1)). The L.P.A. 1925, s. **197**, provides that the registration of a memorial of any instrument transferring or creating *a legal estate or charge by way of legal mortgage* shall be deemed to constitute actual notice to all persons and for all purposes, but does not constitute registration of an instrument affecting an equitable estate notice. The provision, in fact, will rarely have any effect because the doctrine of notice does not normally apply to legal estates. As the objects of registration are, first to secure priority (Yorkshire Registries Act, 1884, s. 14), and secondly to give notice, no useful purpose is served by registering, in the deeds register, an instrument affecting an equitable interest.

The view above advocated had the support of the late Sir Benjamin Cherry (Wolstenholme & Cherry's Conveyancing Statutes, 12th ed., vol. I, p. 252), and of the late J. M. Lightwood (see his " Conveyancer's Letter " in the *Law Journal*, vol. 69, pp. 261, 262). Whatever doubts may formerly have existed it is believed that solicitors in Yorkshire generally acted on the assumption that instruments affecting equitable interests need not be registered.

The L.P.A. 1925, s. 11, assumes that all instruments are registrable in the deeds registers by *memorial*. In fact certain instruments, such as a caveat or a memorandum (see next paragraph), were not registered in this way. The point does not seem to have any importance as the word " memorial " in the L.P.A. 1925, s. 11, is clearly intended to refer to the document by which registration in a deeds register is effected whether or not it is properly described as a " memorial."

Registration of memorandum accompanying deposit of deeds.— Such a memorandum creates an equitable interest only, but it cannot be registered in the land charges register as a " general equitable charge " because the definition of such a charge excludes a charge secured by a deposit of documents. If the view taken above of the effect of the L.P.A. 1925, s. 11, is correct it cannot be registered in a deeds register.

As possession of the deeds provides adequate protection no harm is done if it is not registrable, but it has been suggested that a memorandum of deposit is not within s. 11 of the L.P.A. 1925 at all. The section refers to registration by memorial. But under the Yorkshire Registries Act, 1884, such a memorandum had be to registered at full length, and by means of a document termed "a memorandum". It might therefore be contended that this was not the same thing as registration by memorial. If so, then we are thrown back on the provision in s. 7 of the Yorkshire Registries Act, 1884, that no such charge shall have any effect or priority as against any assurance for valuable consideration which may be registered under the Act, unless and until such memorandum has been so registered. It will be seen, therefore, that if s. 7 applies, the consequences of non-registration might be serious. Until, therefore, there is some decision, it may be considered advisable to register such a document at full length, although the better opinion appears to be that the word "memorial" in s. 11 of the L.P.A. 1925 includes a memorandum with the result that registration is unnecessary. It must be noted that if a memorandum of deposit contains an agreement to execute a legal mortgage this agreement amounts to an estate contract (L.C.A. 1972, s. 2 (4), Class C (iv)), and should be registered as such in the land charges register kept at the appropriate deeds registry.

Leases.—It is provided by s. 28 of the Yorkshire Registries Act, 1884, that "Nothing in this Act contained shall be deemed to extend . . . to any lease not exceeding twenty-one years, or any assignment thereof where accompanied by actual possession from the making of such lease or assignment". Consequently, leases of over twenty-one years, leases for twenty-one years or less, if not accompanied by actual possession, and assignments thereof must be registered in the appropriate deeds register, if they create legal estates (L.P.A. 1925, s. 11). An agreement for a lease, creating an equitable interest, is, of course, registrable as an estate contract in the land charges register kept at the appropriate registry (L.C.A. 1972, s. 2 (4), Class C (iv)).

It is provided by the L.P.A. 1925, s. 11 (3), that memorials of *all* instruments capable of transferring or creating a legal estate may, when so operating, be registered. A term of years absolute is a legal estate (L.P.A. 1925, s. 1 (1) (*b*)) ; and a term of years includes even a weekly tenancy (*ibid.*, s. 205 (1) (xxvii) ; compare *Sharp* v. *Coates* [1949] 1 K.B. 285). However that may be explained away, it is understood that the officials of the three Yorkshire registries were of the opinion that the Yorkshire Registries Act, 1884, s. 28, still remains in force and is not affected by s. 11 of the L.P.A. 1925, and it has certainly not been the practice to register leases not exceeding twenty-one years accompanied by possession.

Examples of instruments requiring registration :—

Adjudication.—An order of adjudication in bankruptcy should be registered.

Affidavit of intestacy.—It is thought that for all practical purposes the procedure of filing an affidavit of intestacy under s. 12 of the Yorkshire Registries Act, 1884, may be considered obsolete. It is stated in Flynn on Registration in Yorkshire, at pp. 18 and 48, that " having regard to the recent legislation, particularly the A.E.A. 1925, the use of this affidavit is considered as being of doubtful utility ". The author stated, however, that the affidavit was still accepted, if presented for enrolment, after the expiration of the required period of six months from the date of death of the intestate.

Appointment of new trustee.—Before 1926, a vesting declaration on the appointment of a new trustee under s. 34 of the Conveyancing Act, 1881, or s. 12 of the Trustee Act, 1893, required registration in the local registry. Although a deed appointing a new trustee made after 1925 does not contain a declaration that the property shall vest in the new trustees, the deed will, under s. 40 (1) (*b*) of the T.A. 1925, operate as if it contained such a declaration. It should, therefore, be registered as operating to transfer a legal estate.

Appointment of trustee in bankruptcy.—The certificate of appointment of a trustee in bankruptcy requires registration (Bankruptcy Act, 1914, s. 53 (4)).

Assent.—Under s. 36 (4) of the A.E.A. 1925, an assent to the vesting of a legal estate must be in writing, signed by the personal representatives, and must name the person in whose favour it is given, *and will operate to vest in that person the legal estate* to which it relates. See also ss. 7 (1) and 8 (1) of the S.L.A. 1925, as to assents under that Act. In these cases the document must be registered.

Compensation agreements under the Law of Property Act, 1922.—An agreement made to secure a gross sum under the L.P.A. 1922, s. 138 (7), is equivalent to a mortgage by deed and should be registered.

Easements, grants of.—The grant of a *legal* easement requires registration in the deeds register (L.P.A. 1925, s. 11 (3), as explained *ibid.*, s. 1 (1), (2), (4)). The grant of an *equitable* easement requires registration *as a land charge.*

Foreclosure.—An order for foreclosure of a legal mortgage operates to vest the legal estate in the mortgagee (L.P.A. 1925, ss. 88 (2), 89 (2)), and must now be registered.

Further Charge.—A further charge required registration (*Re Wight's Mortgage Trust* (1873), L.R. 16 Eq. 41) ; but *not*, it is thought, since 1925. It is, however, the practice, and a convenient practice, to register it.

Mortgages.—A legal mortgage of land wholly within the district of one of the Yorkshire registries, and not protected by deposit of documents originally fell outside the definition of a " puisne mortgage " if it was registered in the local deeds register (L.C.A. 1925, s. 10 (1), Class C (i) ; cp. L.C.A. 1972, s. 2 (4), Class C (i)). It appeared to follow, therefore, that such a mortgage was a puisne mortgage unless and until registration in the deeds register was effected. Consequently, the better view appeared to be that the mortgagee had an option either to register by memorial in the appropriate deeds register (whereupon the mortgage ceases to be a " puisne mortgage ") or to register as a puisne mortgage in the land charges department of the appropriate registry. Now, however, even in the East Riding, it is clear that registration under the L.C.A. 1972 alone suffices.

Probate and letters of administration.—Before the passing of the Land Transfer Act, 1897, a devisee of freehold property under the will of a testator dying within Great Britain had, by the Middlesex Registry Act, and s. 14 of the Yorkshire Registries Act, 1884, six months in which to register such will, and if registered within that time it had priority as if it were registered at the date of the death. After the six months a conveyance for value from the devisee, *if registered before a conveyance from the heir*, prevailed over the latter (Vendor and Purchaser Act, 1874, s. 8). It was very important, therefore, until the Land Transfer Act, 1897, came into operation, that a will of freeholds should be registered. But, since the passing of that Act, the real estate vested in the personal representatives and so in most cases, if not in all, it became impossible for an heir of freehold lands in Middlesex or Yorkshire to convey the same to a purchaser so as to defeat the title of an executor or devisee under an unregistered will. Therefore, if a will affecting freeholds, coming into operation before 1926, should not have been registered in Yorkshire, a purchaser cannot now require this to be done, and registration in Middlesex is now impossible anyway (Land Registration Act, 1936, s. 2 (2)).

A purchaser of leaseholds could not before 1926 ask for a will to be registered ; and it was not necessary to register letters of administration.

Since 1925 probates and letters of administration have to be registered as they are to be treated as instruments capable of transferring a legal estate to personal representatives (L.P.A. 1925, s. 11 (2)). But, as regards letters of administration *without the will annexed*, the curious position arises that there is no provision in the Yorkshire Registries Acts for registration thereof. Such letters of administration have been accepted for registration. If the suggested view that s. 11 of the L.P.A. 1925 was not only intended to act, but did act, as *an amendment* of the Yorkshire Acts, is correct, then s. 11 (2) would be sufficient authority to register such a document. There is no form appropriate to registration of probate or letters of administration but the practice is to make additions to Form 8 (memorial of a will) stating the date of the grant.

It will be noticed that it is the probate, and not the will, which has now to be registered. The reason is that as the whole of the estate of a deceased person passes to his personal representatives, a purchaser is not interested in the terms of the will, but only in *the evidence* of the passing of the legal estate to the personal representatives (which consist of the probate or letters of administration : A.E.A. 1925, ss. 1, 22–24), and the subsequent assent to the persons proposing to make title to the property, be they trustees for sale or the devisee under the will. If the personal representatives themselves are making title there will, of course, be no assent.

It does not seem necessary to register probate or letters of administration of a person who is mortgagee of land as his representatives can validly discharge the mortgage in any case and no question of priority arises.

Statutory receipts on discharge of mortgages.—Speaking strictly, it is not *necessary*, though desirable, to register a statutory receipt when, under s. 116 of the L.P.A. 1925, the mortgage term has, by reason of the money secured by the mortgage having been discharged, become a satisfied term and has ceased. This will be so except (i) in the case of a tenant for life or other person having only a limited interest in the equity of redemption, having discharged the mortgage, in which case he has a right to require the mortgage to be kept alive by transfer or otherwise, and (ii) where by the receipt the money appears to have been paid by a person who is not entitled to the immediate equity of redemption, in which case the receipt operates as if the benefit of the mortgage *had by deed been transferred* to him, unless it is otherwise provided, or the money is paid out of capital money or other money in the hands of a personal representative or trustee properly applicable for the discharge of the mortgage, *and it is not expressly provided* that the receipt is to operate as a transfer (L.P.A. 1925, s. 115 (2)). The result appears to be that a subsequent purchaser will not be able to object if a statutory receipt is not registered at a local registry, unless it acts as a transfer of mortgage under the above provisions.

Title under Statutes of Limitation.—Where a mortgagee acquires a title under the Limitation Acts, he, or the persons deriving title under him, may enlarge the mortgage term into a fee simple ; or in the case of a chargee by way of legal mortgage, may by deed declare that the fee simple is vested in him discharged from the mortgage, and the same will vest accordingly (L.P.A. 1925, s. 88 (3)). There is a similar provision in connection with the leasehold interest in s. 89 (3). In each case the document must be registered.

Vesting orders.—Vesting orders having the effect of transferring or creating a legal estate required to be registered in the local Yorkshire registry by memorial. There are many cases where a vesting order will be granted. See, for instance, L.P.A. 1925, ss. 3 (5), 9, 30, 50 (2), 88 (2), 89 (2), 90, 91, 181 ; T.A. 1925, ss. 44-49 ; S.L.A. 1925, ss. 12, 16 (7) ; A.E.A. 1925, ss. 38 (2), 43 (2).

Middlesex deeds register.—Registration at the Middlesex Deeds Registry was, after 1925, confined to registration by memorial under s. 11 of the L.P.A. 1925 (L.C.A. 1925, s. 18). The Middlesex authorities took the view that it was only necessary to register instruments which operated to transfer or create a legal estate. This view was supported by the wording of the Land Registry (Middlesex Deeds) Rules, 1926. Probates and letters of administration had to be registered.

Property within the City of London was not within the Middlesex Registry Act. Lands taken from Middlesex to make up the County of London in 1888 remained subject to the jurisdiction of the Middlesex Registry (Local Government Act, 1888, ss. 40 and 96).

Mortgages of land in Middlesex made after 1925 by deposit of deeds with or without any written memorandum did not require registration either by memorial or as a land charge (L.P.A. 1925, s. 13), unless the written memorandum contained an agreement to execute a legal mortgage when called on, in which case it was wise to register the agreement as " an estate contract."

The registration of leases in Middlesex was governed by s. 17 of the Middlesex Registry Act, 1708. This section provided for the registration of all leases except leases at a rack rent, and leases not exceeding twenty-one years where the actual possession and occupation went along with the lease. A lease which contained any engagement on the part of the lessee to build upon, or otherwise improve the property, was considered as a lease at a rack rent within the meaning of the exception.

It is unlikely that the rules regarding registration of puisne mortgages made before 1937 are now of interest ; reference may be made to the 14th Edition of this book, vol. I, pp. 589, 590.

Closing of Middlesex deeds register.—Compulsory registration of title was extended to Middlesex on 1st January, 1937, and it became neither necessary nor permissible to register under the Middlesex Deeds Acts a memorial of any instrument made after that date (Land Registration Act, 1936, s. 2 (2)). No memorial of any instrument made before that date

20A

might be registered after 1st January, 1939. By the Middlesex Deeds Act, 1940, s. 1 (1), the register was closed on 10th July, 1940. Official searches only could be made after 1st January, 1937 (Land Registration Act, 1936, s. 2 (5)), and no searches whatever can be made since 10th July, 1940 (Middlesex Deeds Act, 1940, s. 1 (1) (a)). The provision in the L.P.A. 1925, s. 197, that registration shall be deemed to constitute actual notice to all persons ceased to have effect as respects the Middlesex Deeds Register on 10th July, 1940, but the closing of the register did not affect the consequences flowing under the Middlesex Deeds Acts from any failure to register a memorial capable of registration (*ibid.*, s. 1 (1)), that is, a memorial of a deed made before 1937 (Land Registration Act, 1936, s. 2 (2), *ante*).

Where a memorial had been duly registered, a purchaser (that is, any person who for value acquires an interest in property, including a lessee and mortgagee), whose purchase took place after 10th July, 1940, and who at the time of purchase had no notice of the transaction to which the memorial related, has the same rights *as if the memorial had not been registered* (Middlesex Deeds Act, 1940, s. 1 (2)). As searches cannot be made, this provision is necessary, but it means that in certain circumstances the rights of a person who formerly had protection as a result of registration may be overridden. A person suffering loss as a result of this provision, or of s. 1 (1) (b) (which provides that registration shall no longer be notice), is entitled to an indemnity from public funds (Middlesex Deeds Act, 1940, s. 3 (1)), but no indemnity is payable in respect of any loss where the applicant has himself caused or substantially contributed to the loss by his act, neglect or default (*ibid.*, s. 3 (2)).

PART 2. REGISTERED LAND

Any person, other than the registered proprietor of registered land, who has an interest in that land which does not fall within the meaning of " overriding interest " (see Pt. 11 of Chapter 5, *ante*, p. 184), is liable to have that interest overridden by a registered disposition for value of the land (whether or not the purchaser has notice thereof) *unless* it is protected by entry on the register (L.R.A. 1925, ss. 20 and 23 (1)). Interests of this sort, which are generally incumbrances and adverse to the registered estate (see L.R.A. 1925, s. 3 (xv), defining " minor interest "), can be protected on the register by the entry of a notice, or a caution, or an inhibition, or a restriction. " These four devices exist not only to safeguard the equitable interests, that lie behind the curtain provisions of all the real property legislation of 1925 [see as to Overreaching, *ante*, p. 172] but also to protect the uncomfortably heterogeneous collection of interests which, in the case of unregistered land, are registrable under the Land Charges Act, 1925 [now 1972] " (Ruoff and Roper, Registered Conveyancing, 3rd ed., p. 233).

Before proceeding attention may be drawn to the question whether land charges, such as restrictive covenants, created on the conveyance or other grant leading to first registration ought to be protected immediately as in unregistered conveyancing by registration under the L.C.A. The argument was that protection by notice on the register of title (which will duly occur) does not validate an otherwise void claim (see below) and that such land charges might in the meantime have become void against, for example, a mortgagee. However, it is now provided that where an instrument conveys, grants or assigns an estate in land and creates a land charge affecting that estate, the L.C.A. 1972 does not apply to that land charge, so far as it affects that estate, if the instrument is one which should lead to compulsory registration of title within the L.R.A. 1925, s. 123, *post*, p. 637 (L.C.A. 1972, s. 14 (3), deriving from the Land Registration and Land Charges Act, 1971, s. 9, and only applying where the instrument was executed on or after 27th July, 1971).

Notices.—A disposition by the proprietor takes effect " subject to all estates, rights, and claims which are protected by way of notice on the register at the date of the registration or entry of notice of the disposition, but only if and so far as such estates, rights and claims may be valid and are not (independently of this Act) overridden by the disposition " (L.R.A. 1925, s. 52 (1)). Where notice of a claim is entered on the register, such entry does not operate to render the claim valid whether made adversely to or for the benefit of the registered land or charge (L.R.A. 1925, s. 52 (2)) ; for instance, an entry that land is subject to a positive covenant does not make the burden of the covenant run with the land (*Cator* v. *Newton* [1940] 1 K.B. 415).

Notices may be entered for the protection of limited classes of minor interests only which are as follows :—

(i) *Leases.*—A lessee or other person interested in a lease which is *not* an overriding interest (as to which, see *ante*, pp. 190, 194) may apply to register notice of the lease, and when so registered, every proprietor and the persons deriving title under him are affected with notice of the lease as being an incumbrance, although a proprietor of a charge or incumbrance registered or protected on the register prior to registration of the notice is not affected by it unless such proprietor is, by reason of the lease having been made under a statutory or other power or by reason of his concurrence or otherwise, bound by the terms of the lease (L.R.A. 1925, s. 48 (1)). If, for any reason, the lease is not binding on the proprietor, the consent in writing of the lessor or an order of the court authorising registration must be obtained (L.R.A. 1925, s. 48 (2)). It is important to note that certain leases must themselves be registered and that a notice protecting them is not adequate : see *post*, p. 637 ; if the lease is registered notice will automatically be entered

Application to register a notice must be made on Form 84 and accompanied by the lease or counterpart, or by the agreement or duplicate (or a statutory declaration by the applicant or his solicitor stating the reason for non-production and verifying the copy or abstract), and by a certified copy or full abstract thereof, and a copy or tracing of any plan, and (except where the application is by the proprietor) by the consent of the proprietor signed by himself or his solicitor or by an order of court authorising the registration of the notice (L.R.R. 1925, rr. 186, 189). The notice in the register must give the term and may include such other short particulars as can be conveniently entered (L.R.R. 1925, r. 188).

It must be remembered that the word " lease " normally includes an agreement for a lease (L.R.A. 1925, s. 3 (x)) ; in practice notices are of most importance in protecting agreements.

(ii) *Covenants.*—A person entitled to the benefit of a restrictive covenant or agreement (not made between lessor and lessee) with respect to the building on or other user of registered land may apply to the registrar to enter notice thereof on the register, and where any such covenant or agreement appears to exist at the time of first registration notice must be entered (L.R.A. 1925, s. 50 (1) ; L.R.R. 1925, r. 212). Such registration takes the place of registration as a land charge (L.R.A. 1925, s. 50 (1)). The effect of entry of a notice is that the proprietor and the persons deriving title under him (except incumbrancers or others who at the time when the notice is entered may not be bound by the covenant or agreement) are deemed affected with notice of it (L.R.A. 1925, s. 50 (2)). See also *White* v. *Bijou Mansions, Ltd.* [1937] Ch. 610, mentioned at p. 571. It should be noted that the L.R.A. 1925, s. 50 (2), gives notice only to the proprietor and persons deriving title under him. The wording is not as wide as that in the L.P.A. 1925, s. 198 (1), and so it seems that the decision in *Re Forsey and Hollebone's Contract* [1927] 2 Ch. 379 did *not* apply to registered land in any case (see now as to unregistered land L.P.A. 1969, s. 24, *ante*, p. 4 *et seq.*).

Where the terms of a covenant imposed before first registration are not known, a reference to the existence of the covenant may be made in the charges register. Registered Land Practice Notes 1972, p. 25, No. 28 explains the circumstances (where a purchaser has bought from a squatter ; where an applicant for first registration is unable to produce deeds ; where a purchaser has accepted a short title or, sometimes, where a title back to 1st January, 1926, cannot be shown and so complete land charge searches cannot be made) in which the registrar finds it necessary to make an entry to the effect that the land is subject to such restrictive covenants as may have been imposed before a certain date. Where restrictive covenants are to be imposed by a transfer of the registered land, the covenants should be set out in the transfer, in which case they will be noted in the charges register on registration of the transfer. If the covenants are imposed by some other deed, it should state the title number and a certified copy should be sent to the registry. It is advisable to supply a copy of any covenant, positive or restrictive, including introductory words, on stout paper foolscap size with a sufficient binding margin, so that it may be bound with the land or charge certificate ; see Registered Land Practice Notes 1972, pp. 27, 28, Nos. 31 and 32. See also *ibid.*, p. 26, No. 55, as to restrictive covenants unenforceable for non-registration at the time of first registration, *ante*, p. 571.

If the covenant or agreement is discharged or modified under the L.P.A. 1925, s. 84 (*ante*, p. 579), or if the court refuses to grant an injunction for enforcing it, the entry must be cancelled or a reference made to the order or other instrument, and a copy of the order, judgment, or instrument must be filed (L.R.A. 1925, s. 50 (3)). The notice must, where practicable, refer to the land, *whether registered or not*, for the benefit of which the restriction was made (L.R.A. 1925, s. 50 (4)).

The power of a registered proprietor to impose, release, or waive restrictive covenants is contained in the L.R.A. 1925, s. 40.

(iii) *Various other rights, interests and claims.*—The provisions of the L.R.A. 1925, s. 48, are extended to apply to (*a*) the grant or reservation of any annuity or rent-charge in possession, either perpetual or for a term of years absolute, (*b*) the severance of mines or minerals, except where they are *expressly* included in the registration, (*c*) land charges until registered as registered charges, (*d*) the right of any person interested under a trust for sale or a settlement to require that there shall be at least two trustees or a trust corporation, (*e*) the rights of any widow in respect of dower and similar rights, which now rarely arise, (*f*) creditors' notices and any other right, interest or claim which it is deemed expedient to protect by notice instead of by caution, inhibition, or restriction (L.R.A. 1925, s. 49 (1) ; L.R.R. 1925, r. 190). For example, an option or other estate contract may be protected under s. 49 (1) (c). Application should be made by letter accompanied by the documents creating the option, etc., a certified copy for filing and a fee of £1; the land certificate must be lodged, and, if a mortgagee is to be bound, the charge certificate (Registered Land Practice Notes 1972, p. 29, No. 2). See also *post*, p. 1027, as to the giving of notice of the deposit of a land or charge certificate.

A notice may not be registered in respect of any estate, right, or interest which, independently of the L.R.A. 1925, is capable of being overridden by the proprietor under a trust for sale or the powers of the S.L.A. 1925, or any other statute, or of a settlement, and of being protected by a restriction, although a notice may be lodged pending the appointment of trustees of a disposition on trust for sale or a settlement, such notice being cancelled when the appointment is made and the proper restriction entered (L.R.A. 1925, s. 49 (2)).

A notice in respect of a right, interest, or claim will not affect prejudicially the powers of disposition of personal representatives of the deceased under whose will or by the operation of whose intestacy the right, interest, or claim arose, or the powers of disposition of a proprietor holding on trust for sale (L.R.A. 1925, s. 49 (3)).

Cautions.—A caution provides a means whereby a person interested may be warned before registration of title is effected or before any disposition is registered which might adversely affect him. There are two types of caution —(i) against first registration, and (ii) against dealings with registered land or a registered charge.

Against first registration.—Any person having or claiming such an interest in land not already registered as entitles him to object to any disposition thereof being made without his consent, may lodge a caution to the effect that the cautioner is entitled to notice of any application that may be made for the registration of an interest in the land affecting the right of the cautioner (L.R.A. 1925, s. 53 (1)). The caution must be supported by affidavit or declaration in Form 14 in the Schedule to the L.R.R. 1925, which must state the nature of the interest of the cautioner and the land and estate therein to be affected (L.R.A. 1925, s. 53 (2) ; L.R.R. 1925, r. 66). The caution itself must be in Form 13 in that Schedule, signed by the cautioner or his solicitor, containing an address for service, and accompanied by sufficient particulars, by plan or otherwise, to identify on the ordnance map or land registry general map, the land to which it relates (L.R.R. 1925, r. 64). Forms 13 and 14 are, in practice, combined.

After such a caution has been lodged registration of the estate will not be made until notice has been served on the cautioner to appear and oppose registration, and fourteen days, or such other period (not being less than seven days) as the registrar may direct, has elapsed since service of such notice or the cautioner has entered appearance, as the case may be (L.R.A. 1925, s. 53 (3) ; L.R.R. 1925, r. 57). A caution may be withdrawn on application in Form 16 in the Schedule (L.R.R. 1925, r. 68), or the cautioner may, after notice has been served on him under s. 53 (3), by writing signed by himself or his solicitor, consent to registration absolutely or conditionally on some special entry being made in the register (L.R.R. 1925, r. 69).

Against dealings.—A caution against dealings has a similar effect, but is used in different circumstances. It is substantially a hostile action and the procedure is designed accordingly.

A person interested under an unregistered instrument, or interested as a judgment creditor or otherwise, in any land or charge registered in the name of another, may lodge a caution to the effect that no dealing with such land or charge is to be registered until notice has been served on him (L.R.A. 1925, s. 54 (1)). Such a caution must be in Form 63 in the Schedule to the L.R.R., signed by the cautioner or his solicitor and containing an address for service (L.R.R. 1925, r. 215 (1), (2), (3)). Sufficient particulars must be given, by plan or otherwise, to identify the land affected on the proper ordnance map or the general map (L.R.R. 1925, r. 216). It must be supported by declaration in Form 14, or to the like effect, containing a reference to the land or charge and to the registered number of the title, and stating the nature of the interest of the cautioner (L.R.R. 1925, r. 215 (4)).

A person whose interest has been registered or protected by a notice or restriction is not entitled to lodge a caution except with the consent of the registrar (L.R.A. 1925, s. 54 (1), proviso).

Normally options and other estate contracts are protected by notice ; see *ante*, p. 620. If, however, the registered proprietor refuses to lodge his land certificate protection may be obtained for the purchaser by lodging a caution against dealings. Protection in this way is not available in respect of an agreement giving first refusal to purchase land since this does not constitute even a minor interest (*Murray* v. *Two Strokes, Ltd.* [1973] 1 W.L.R. 823 ; cp. *ante*, p. 76).

Further, it has now been held that a beneficial tenant in common (or presumably a beneficial joint tenant) is entitled to lodge a caution as being " any person interested . . . howsoever, in any land " within the L.R.A. 1925, s. 54 (1), *ante*, notwithstanding that his interest necessarily subsists behind a trust for sale and is strictly in the proceeds of sale (*Elias* v. *Mitchell* [1972] 2 W.L.R. 740, distinguishing *Irani Finance, Ltd.* v. *Singh* [1971] Ch. 59 on grounds of context). Consequently, in appropriate circumstances, a caution is available as an alternative to the more normal protection of entry of a restriction (*post*, p. 623).

A purchaser may obtain an office copy of the declaration if he is not able otherwise to ascertain the nature of the interest protected. Often the contract will be subject to the interest protected by the caution or the interest will be financial (e.g., an equitable charge) such that it can be discharged on completion and the caution withdrawn. Otherwise the purchaser should refuse to complete until it is withdrawn.

After such a caution has been lodged the registrar may not, without the consent of the cautioner, register any dealing or make any entry on the register for protecting the rights acquired under a deposit of a land or charge certificate or other dealing by the proprietor until he has served notice warning the cautioner that his caution will cease to have effect after the expiration of fourteen days (or such other period, not being less than seven days, as the registrar may direct) from service of the notice unless an order to the contrary is made by the registrar (L.R.A. 1925, s. 55 (1) ; L.R.R. 1925, r. 218 (2)). If, before the expiration of that period, the cautioner appears before the registrar and gives security, if required, to indemnify every party, the registrar may delay registering any dealing or making any entry (L.R.A. 1925, s. 55 (2)). Before the expiration of the time limited by the notice, or of any extension granted by the registrar, the cautioner or his personal representative may show cause why the caution should continue to have effect or why the dealing should not be registered (L.R.R. 1925, r. 219), and cause may be shown either by the cautioner appearing before the registrar, or by his delivering a statement in writing, signed by him or his solicitor, setting forth the grounds on which cause is shown (L.R.R. 1925, r. 220). When the notice has been given and the period limited has expired the caution is cancelled unless the registrar directs otherwise (L.R.R. 1925, r. 221).

However, a cautioner does not lose the protection of a caution simply because a purchaser was ignorant of its existence even though such ignorance was due to a mistake, other than failure to register the caution, by the Land Registry (*Parkash* v. *Irani Finance, Ltd.* [1970] Ch. 101, where an official search had failed to disclose a caution which was nevertheless effective against the searcher who was left to pursue his remedies against the Land Registry's compensation fund).

A caution against dealings may be withdrawn by application on Form 71. As to mortgage cautions, see *post*, p. 1027.

Inhibitions.—The court, or, subject to an appeal to the court, the registrar, upon the application of any person interested, may, after directing such inquiries (if any) to be made and notices to be given and hearing such persons as the court or registrar thinks expedient, issue an order or make an entry inhibiting for a time, or until the occurrence of an event to be named in such order or entry, or generally until further order or entry, the registration or entry of any dealing with any registered land or registered charge (L.R.A. 1925, s. 57 (1)). An application must be accompanied by the consent in writing of the proprietor or must be supported by the statutory declaration of the applicant and such other evidence as the registrar may deem necessary ; the registrar may enter an inhibition pending any hearing (L.R.R. 1925, r. 230). The court or registrar may refuse to make such an order or entry, or annex conditions, and may discharge an order or entry and generally act as the justice of the case requires (L.R.A. 1925, s. 57 (2)). Alternatively, in lieu of an inhibition, the court or registrar may order a notice or restriction to be placed on the register (L.R.A. 1925, s. 57 (4)). It will be noted that the discretion left to the court or registrar is wide, the primary intention being that inhibitions should be used only when there is no satisfactory alternative, and particularly in cases of urgency.

When land is transferred to the incumbent of a benefice in his corporate capacity an inhibition is entered in Form 73 in the Schedule to the L.R.R. 1925 (r. 232). Except in this special case it is useless to attempt to complete a purchase so long as an inhibition remains on the register.

Restrictions.—Where the proprietor of any registered land or charge desires to place restrictions on transferring or charging the land or on disposing of or dealing with the land or charge, or on the deposit by way of security of any certificate, the proprietor may apply to the registrar to make an entry in the register " that no transaction to which the application relates shall be effected, unless the following things, or such of them as the proprietor may determine, are done :—

(*a*) unless notice of any application for the transaction is transmitted by post to such address as he may specify to the registrar ;

(*b*) unless the consent of some person or persons, to be named by the proprietor, is given to the transaction ;

(*c*) unless some such other matter or thing is done as may be required by the applicant and approved by the registrar " (L.R.A. 1925, s. 58 (1)).

If he is satisfied of the applicant's right to give the directions the registrar will enter the requisite restriction with the result that no transaction to which it relates may be effected except in conformity therewith, although the registrar is under no duty to enter a restriction which he deems unreasonable or calculated to cause inconvenience (L.R.A. 1925, s. 58 (2)). An application must be in Form 75 in the Schedule to the L.R.R. 1925 and must state the particulars of the restriction required and be signed by the applicant or his solicitor (L.R.R. 1925, r. 235 (1)). The fee is £1. Application may be made by a person other than the proprietor, in which case the form must be modified as required to meet the circumstances and must set out the grounds on which it is made, and be accompanied by such evidence as the registrar may direct (L.R.A. 1925, s. 58 (5) ; L.R.R. 1925, r. 236). This procedure might be used to protect an option or other estate contract, but it is more common to register a notice, as to which see *ante*, p. 619 (Registered Land Practice Notes 1972, p. 29, No. 2).

An application to withdraw or modify a restriction must be in Form 77, signed by all persons for the time being appearing by the register to be interested in the restriction, or their solicitors (L.R.R. 1925, r. 235 (2)).

In the case of joint proprietors a restriction is obligatory *where the survivor will not have power to give a valid receipt for capital or where the registrar considers an entry desirable*, unless it is shown to the registrar's satisfaction that the joint proprietors are entitled for their own benefit, or that one of them is a trust corporation (L.R.A. 1925, s. 58 (3) ; L.R.R. 1925, r. 213 (1)). Although r. 213 refers to an entry in Form 62 it is understood that the usual practice is to word the restriction: " No disposition by one proprietor of the land (being the survivor of joint proprietors and not being a trust corporation) under which capital money arises is to be registered except under an Order of the Registrar or of the Court." A similar entry may be made with the consent of joint proprietors entitled in their own right (L.R.R. 1925, r. 213 (2)).

Where such an entry has been made and the joint proprietors have been reduced to the number specified, the registrar must, before entering any disposition on the register, require the production of the equitable title (L.R.R. 1925, r. 214). Except where such a restriction is obligatory it may at any time be withdrawn or modified at the instance of all persons for the time being appearing by the register to be interested in the directions (L.R.A. 1925, s. 58 (4)). See further, the *Conveyancer N.S.*, vol. 13, p. 425 *et seq.*, and vol. 14, p. 2, particularly as to the unusual case where a sole trustee acquires on trust for sale. As to the use of restrictions where trustees for sale are registered as proprietors, see further, p. 770, and as to the use of restrictions in relation to settled land, see p. 759 *et seq*.

A purchaser need not be concerned about the existence of a restriction provided that his purchase is carried out in accordance with it. Thus, as in the case of unregistered land, if the land is settled, the purchase-money must be paid to at least two trustees or a trust corporation.

Dealings with minor interests.—The definition of " minor interests " (L.R.A. 1925, s. 3 (xv)) refers to them as " interests not capable of being disposed of or created by registered dispositions ". It follows that they are disposed of, or created, by the means which would be used if they affected unregistered land, although it may be necessary to protect them in one of the ways specified at p. 619 *et seq*. See also L.R.A. 1925, s. 101.

Special rules apply, however, with regard to the priority as between dealings with certain minor interests. It is provided by the L.R.A. 1925, s. 102 (2), that priorities as regards dealings after 1925 between assignees and incumbrancers of life interests, remainders, reversions and executory interests are regulated by the order of the priority cautions or inhibitions lodged against the proprietor of the registered estate. It will be noted that priority cautions and inhibitions are not entered on the register itself, but are entered in the minor interests index (L.R.R. 1925, r. 229) ; this index is maintained at the registry in London and not at any district land registry. They do not affect the powers of the registered proprietor (L.R.A. 1925, s. 102 (3)) ; they are quite different from the cautions and inhibitions mentioned *ante*, pp. 621, 623. The minor interests index is not a register of minor interests, but merely provides a means of determining the priority of dealings with such interests.

As respects registered land and registered charges, the registration of a priority caution or inhibition takes the place of notice to trustees under the L.P.A. 1925, s. 137 (L.R.R. 1925, r. 229 (4), (5)).

An inhibition is applicable where the applicant claims to have acquired an absolute interest, free from any right of redemption ; otherwise a caution should be used (L.R.R. 1925, r. 229 (6)). As to the procedure, see further, L.R.R. 1925, r. 229.

Except as regards *dealings as between assignees and incumbrancers* of the interests mentioned above, priorities as between persons interested in minor interests are not affected by the lodgment of cautions or inhibitions (L.R.A. 1925, s. 102 (2)). Consequently, the lodgment of a priority caution or inhibition is not necessary on the creation of minor interests by the execution of a trust for sale or settlement.

Searches.—The usual search in the local land charges registry must be made after contract, if not made before, as local land charges are overriding interests. See *ante*, p. 194. Also a search of the public index maps may in some cases be appropriate (L.R.R. 1925, rr. 12, 286). The only other search which is necessary is that in the register, which may be either official or personal, and must be accompanied by an authority to inspect the register. It is considered that there is no need to make a search in the land charges register where an absolute title is transferred (L.R.A. 1925, s. 110 (7)). Some words used by Evershed, M.R., in *City Permanent Building Society* v. *Miller* [1952] Ch. 840, at p. 850, implied that entries in the land charges register might affect registered land, but the reasoning is difficult to follow. See the convincing rebuttal by the present Chief Land Registrar in the *Conveyancer N.S.*, vol. 17, p. 39, disagreeing with the statement (made *obiter*) of Evershed, M.R.

As to searches in respect of developing building estates, see the procedure outlined *ante*, p. 139, and *post*, p. 648.

Complete protection to a purchaser is provided by an official search, which should relate to the period since the purchaser last inspected the register or the date on which the land certificate was last officially brought up to date or the date of issue of an office copy of the register. This protection is now given by the L.R. (Official Searches) Rules, 1969, r. 5, which provides that where a purchaser has applied under the rules for an official search " any entry which is made in the register during the priority period relating to that search shall be postponed to a subsequent application to register the instrument effecting the purchase ". The subsequent application will have to be (i) in order ; (ii) delivered to the proper office within the priority period ; and (iii) affect the same land or charge as the postponed entry (*ibid.*). The " priority period " means in effect fifteen working days (see *ibid.*, r. 2 (2)).

Further, the protection conferred by r. 5 of the 1969 Rules now explicitly covers any prior dealing on which the " purchase " is dependent provided that there is due subsequent application to register that dealing. In view of the wide meaning given to " purchaser " (and correspondingly to " purchase ") in the Rules (r. 2 (2)), it is now clear that a solicitor who is acting for both a purchaser (or lessee) and a mortgagee need only make an official search on behalf of the mortgagee which will automatically cover the transfer on sale (or lease) on which the mortgage will be dependent (see Registered Land Practice Notes 1972, p. 36, No. 25).

It will be seen, therefore, that it is important to make an official search and to ensure that application for registration accompanied by the certificate is delivered at the registry before the sixteenth working day after the date of the certificate. Form 94A is used for searches in respect of the whole and Form 94B for searches in respect of part of the land comprised in the title (see Sched. 1 to 1969 Rules). If the search is in respect of part only and that part is not adequately defined by walls or fences, the search must be accompanied by a plan giving the dimensions of the plot and its position in relation to physical features shown on the registry plan. As to searches which may be against the residue of land in a title, see Registered Land Practice Notes No. 63, published in the *Law Society's Gazette*, vol. 70, No. 29, p. 2142.

However, it is now provided that where it will not be possible to make the subsequent application within the initial priority period (e.g., on account of stamping delays) the period may be extended for a further period of fourteen working days (rr. 6 and 7 of the Land Registration (Official Searches) Rules, 1969). To achieve this, the solicitor acting for the purchaser (or mortgagee) should apply for the extension on printed Form 95 before the expiration of the existing search. The application should be accompanied by (i) the official certificate of search ; (ii) a certified copy of the instrument effecting the purchase ; (iii) if that instrument is dependent upon a prior dealing, a certified copy of the instrument effecting that dealing ; and (iv) a fee of £1.

It should be noted that an official search is much to be preferred to a personal inspection of the register. The comparative advantages of an official search include the absence of either attendance or payment of a fee as well as the presence of priority (see above) and of indemnity in case of error (i.e., under L.R.A. 1925, s. 83 (3)) ; see further *Law Society's Gazette*, vol. 56, at p. 395. However, searches by telephone or teleprinter (telex), but not by telegraph, may be made (Land Registration (Official Searches) Rules, 1969, rr. 9 and 10 and Sched. 2). The prescribed fee for each is £1 and each involves, *inter alia*, giving an undertaking to follow up with a proper official search forthwith.

As to the extent of the protection afforded by official searches, the priority conferred is only in respect of entries later made in the register and not in respect of existing entries erroneously undisclosed by the search (cf. *Parkash* v. *Irani Finance Ltd.* [1970] Ch. 101). Further observations both of Lord Denning, M.R., and in particular of Russell, L.J., in *Strand Securities, Ltd.* v. *Caswell* [1965] Ch. 958, suggested that the certificate of search does not cover the risk of there being binding entries, not on the register itself, but on the list of pending applications for first registration kept under L.R.R. 1925, r. 10. From this it would follow that forms 94A or 94B ought to be amended so as to include a request for a search also to be made in this list with a view to the result being included in the certificate. However, the Chief Land Registrar by explaining the registry practice in relation to the application book (or " day list ") kept under L.R.R. 1925, rr. 24 and 83, has convincingly, it is thought, demonstrated that such amendments would be unnecessary, unacceptable and unauthorised (*Law Society's Gazette*, vol. 62, p. 507 *et seq.*).

It is not thought that there is any need to search in the companies register on purchase from a limited company, registered with an absolute title, although this precaution is often taken. Although certain charges made by a company must be registered under the Companies Act, 1948, s. 95 (*post*, p. 633), they should thereafter be noted on the charges register at the Land Registry, and it seems clear that a purchaser is not concerned unless that has been done (L.R.A. 1925, s. 110 (7)). Further, the effect of the L.R.A. 1925, s. 60, appears to be that a purchaser will not be affected by any charge subject to which the company bought unless registered or protected under the L.R.A. 1925 ; see *ibid.*, s. 60. See *Conveyancer N.S.*, vol. 26, p. 408, and Ruoff and Roper, Registered Conveyancing, 3rd ed., pp. 355 and 527.

PART 3.   LOCAL LAND CHARGES

Matters registrable as local land charges.—The provisions as to local land charges are contained in s. 15 of the L.C.A. 1925 as amended and now reproduced in Sched. 4 to the L.C.A. 1972. The primary requirement of registration is defined in these terms :—

" 15.—(1) Any charge (hereinafter called ' a local land charge ') acquired either before or after the commencement of this Act by the council of any administrative county, London borough, or urban or rural district, or by the corporation of any municipal borough, or by any other local authority under the Public Health Acts, 1936 and 1937, the Highways Act, 1959 or the Public Health Act, 1961, or under any similar statute (public general or local or private) passed or hereafter to be passed, which takes effect by virtue of the statute, shall be registered in the prescribed manner by the proper officer of the local authority, *and shall* (except as hereinafter mentioned in regard to charges created or arising before the commencement of this Act) *be void as against a purchaser for money or money's worth of a legal estate in the land affected thereby, unless registered* in the appropriate register before the completion of the purchase.

For the purposes of this section any sum which is *recoverable* by a local authority under any of the Acts aforesaid *from successive owners or occupiers* of the property in respect of which the sum is recoverable shall, whether such sum is expressed to be a charge on the property or not, be deemed to be a charge.

*　　*　　*　　*　　*

(4) Where a local authority has expended money for any purpose which, when the work is completed, and any requisite resolution is passed or order is made, will confer a charge upon land, the proper officer of the local authority may in the meantime register a local land charge in his register against the land generally without specifying the amount, but the registration of any such general charge shall be cancelled within the prescribed time not being less than one year after the charge is ascertained and allotted, and thereupon the specific local land charge shall, unless previously discharged, be registered as of the date on which the general charge was registered.

*　　*　　*　　*　　*

(7) The foregoing provisions of this section shall apply to—

(a) . . .

(b) any prohibition of or restriction on the user or mode of user of land or buildings imposed by a local authority after the commencement of this Act by order, instrument, or resolution, or enforceable by a local authority under any covenant or agreement made with them after the commencement of this Act, or by virtue of any conditions attached to a consent, approval or licence granted by a local authority after that date, being a prohibition or restriction binding on successive owners of the land or buildings, and not being—

(i) a prohibition or restriction operating over the whole of the district of the authority or over the whole of any contributory place thereof ; or

(ii) . . .

(iii) a prohibition or restriction imposed by a covenant or agreement made between a lessor and lessee ;

as if the resolution, authority, prohibition, or restriction were a local land charge, and the same shall be registered by the proper officer as a local land charge accordingly."

It is further provided that if a matter is registrable both in a local land charges register and under the L.C.A. 1972, it is sufficiently protected by registration in one register only (s. 15 (7A) of the L.C.A. 1925, added in 1972).

"*shall . . . be void as against a purchaser.*"—Thus it is essential to search in the local land charges register. The requirement applies to registered land in the same way as unregistered land (L.C.A. 1925, s. 15 (8)).

"*recoverable . . . from successive owners or occupiers.*"—The provision that sums recoverable from successive owners or successive occupiers of property are to be registered, whether expressed to be a charge on the property or not, is necessary because a number of charges for street and sanitary works, for instance, are recoverable by statute from successive owners and occupiers, but are not charged directly on the land.

Section 15 (7) (a) of the L.C.A. 1925 formerly required town planning schemes, and resolutions to prepare schemes, to be registered, but town planning schemes are no longer prepared, and resolutions to prepare or adopt them are not passed. See further, *post*, p. 1181. Consequently, the provision formerly contained in s. 15 (7) (a) has been repealed, although there is doubt as to whether references to schemes made or resolutions passed prior to the operation of the 1947 Act should remain in registers.

In some areas it may be possible for the local authority to satisfy itself that no provision of a scheme now remains effective or that no enforceable obligation can now arise as a result of a resolution to prepare a scheme. If this is the case then it would be the duty of the clerk to the authority to delete any reference to the scheme or resolution in the register. It appears that the only action likely to be dependent on registration of a resolution is the remedying of a breach of planning law which occurred during the war period where the normal time limit has been extended because the Crown has been in possession (Building Restrictions (War-Time Contraventions) Act, 1946, s. 7 (6)). On the other hand, there is still some value in an entry which discloses to a purchaser whether there was in force before 1948 an operative scheme or a resolution to prepare a scheme under which an interim development permission may remain effective.

Section 15 (7) (*b*) (ii) provided that prohibitions or restrictions which were or might be enforceable by virtue of a town planning scheme were *not* registrable. This provision was also repealed by the Town and Country Planning Act, 1947, with the result that a condition attached to the grant of planning permission (such as one imposing a time limit) under the Town and Country Planning Act need not be registered as a local land charge, as it does not amount to a prohibition or restriction on the user or mode of user of land or buildings. Such a condition merely limits the extent of the permission granted and any prohibition or restriction on user is imposed by the Act itself, and not by the resolution of the authority which attached the condition (*Rose* v. *Leeds Corporation* [1964] 1 W.L.R. 1939). Nevertheless it is thought that prior to the last mentioned decision most clerks to local authorities took the precaution of registering as local land charges all resolutions which granted permission subject to conditions, and some may continue to do so pending legislation on the point (which is desirable) or a decision of the House of Lords. It has been argued that permissions imposing conditions other than time limits should be registered, although this argument seems difficult to reconcile with the judgment of Diplock, L.J., in *Rose* v. *Leeds Corporation*. The matter is discussed in the *Conveyancer N.S.*, vol. 29, p. 35 *et seq.* and pp. 161 and 162. It may be that a condition imposed under s. 30 of the 1971 Act, for regulating development of land under the control of the applicant but not the subject of the application, requires registration as a restriction ; it is most desirable that it should be registered against land affected otherwise it may not be ascertained by a purchaser. Conditions imposed on permissions granted by Ministers (for example, on appeal) have never been registrable.

A restriction contained in a mortgage made in favour of a local authority, for instance, under the Small Dwellings Acquisition Acts, would not appear to be registrable by virtue of s. 15 (7) (*b*), as it amounts to a covenant between lessor and lessee (L.P.A. 1925, s. 85).

Prohibitions or restrictions enforceable by a local authority under covenant or agreement may be registered both as local land charges and as land charges (L.C.A. 1972, s. 2 (5), Class D (ii)) ; but registration in one or other register will be sufficient (s. 15 (7A) of the L.C.A. 1925).

Statutes passed since 1926 have made various matters (of which the following are some of the more important) registrable in the register of local land charges :—

(i) With respect to ancient monuments, a preservation scheme or notice of intention to confirm a scheme, a notice of intention to include a monument in a list prepared by the Secretary of State for the Environment, an interim preservation notice, or a preservation order (Ancient Monuments Act, 1931, s. 11 ; Historic Buildings and Ancient Monuments Act, 1953, s. 19).

(ii) A charge in favour of a county council for expenses incurred in the improvement of a way over fenland (Agriculture (Miscellaneous Provisions) Act, 1941, s. 8).

(iii) A condition limiting the price for which a house disposed of by a local authority may be sold or the rent at which it may be let (Building Materials and Housing Act, 1945, s. 8 (1) ; Housing Act, 1949, s. 43 ; Housing Act, 1957, ss. 104, 105 and 106).

(iv) A prohibition or restriction on the use of land or buildings imposed by the Secretary of State for the Environment under certain statutes in relation to trunk and other roads : Trunk Roads Act, 1946, s. 8 (4) ; Highways Act, 1959, s. 72 (improvement lines) ; s. 73 (building lines) ; s. 81 (obstructions at corners).

(v) An order designating an area as the site of a proposed new town and a compulsory purchase order which could formerly be made under the Town and Country Planning Act, 1944, and the New Towns Act, 1946, but may now be made under the New Towns Act, 1965, ss. 1, 7 and 8 (Town and Country Planning Act, 1944, s. 17 ; New Towns Act, 1946, s. 23, Sched. 4 ; New Towns Act, 1965, ss. 1 (4) and 9 (1)).

(vi) Orders for obtaining rights over land and similar orders and directions for the purposes of an aerodrome (Civil Aviation Act, 1949, ss. 24, 25, 26, 33 ; Airports Authority Act, 1965, s. 17 (4), Sched. 4, Pt. II ; Civil Aviation Acts, 1968, ss. 21, 22, and 1971, s. 16).

(vii) Lists of buildings of special architectural or historic interest (Town and Country Planning Act, 1971, s. 54).

(viii) Notices that property is subject to the control of a Rural Development Board (s. 45 (6) of the Agriculture Act, 1967). As to consent of the Board being required to the transfer of land in its area, see ss. 49 and 50 of the 1967 Act. As to the establishment of the North Pennines Rural Development Board, see *Law Society's Gazette*, vol. 66, p. 764.

(ix) Rights in relation to government oil pipe-lines and accessory works (Requisitioned Land and War Works Act, 1948, s. 14 ; Land Powers (Defence) Act, 1958, s. 12).

(x) Conditions imposed on the use, letting and rent of a dwelling-house in respect of the provision or improvement of which assistance has been given under the Housing Acts (Housing (Financial Provisions) Act, 1958, s. 34 (9)).

(xi) Works schemes indicating land as contributory land made under the Coast Protection Act, 1949 (*ibid.*, ss. 8 (8), 13 (6)).

(xii) Agreements for the use of land for cattle-grids or by-passes (Highways Act, 1959, s. 92 (5)).

(xiii) Declarations that streets are likely to become maintainable highways for the purposes of the Public Utilities Street Works Act, 1950 (*ibid.*, Sched. 2). Where a street has been declared likely to become a maintainable highway, the powers and duties in the Act in relation to works of statutory undertakers are exercisable by, and imposed on, the highway authority ; in general this is to the advantage of frontagers. Incidentally, the entry in the register serves as a warning that private street works procedure is likely to be applied in the future if the street is not in a satisfactory state of construction or repair. See also *ante*, p. 24.

(xiv) Conditions applied to cottages under the Hill Farming Act, 1946, s. 10 (Hill Farming Act, 1954, s. 2 (1)).

(xv) Notices of compensation payments of £20 or more in respect of planning decisions (Town and Country Planning Act, 1971, s. 158) and notices of additional compensation payments of £20 or more made in respect of war-damaged land under the Town and Country Planning Act, 1947, s. 59 (1971 Act, Sched. 24, para. 80).

(xvi) Notices served by a local authority, pursuant to s. 193 (1) of the Highways Act, 1959 (that is, notices requiring payment or security on account of costs of street works before building commences), or pursuant to s. 193 (3) of that Act (that is, notices reducing or extinguishing a sum previously required to be paid or secured) ; determinations by the Minister on appeal under s. 193 (5) of that Act as to the sum to be paid or secured ; payments made or securities given pursuant to s. 192 of that Act ; notices served under s. 192 (3) (e), (f) or (h) of that Act exempting a building ; resolutions passed under s. 192 (3) (k) exempting a street or part of a street ; and refunds made and releases of securities granted under ss. 194, 195 or 196 of the Highways Act, 1959 (ibid., s. 197 (i)).

It is doubtful whether an order made pursuant to the Clean Air Act, 1956, s. 11, declaring a smoke control area should be registered as a local land charge. It can be argued that it is a " restriction on the user or mode of user of land or buildings " within the L.C.A. 1925, s. 15 (7). Nonetheless, against this it is suggested that it does not provide a restriction on the user of the building itself. It seems more likely, however, that expenses incurred by the local authority so far as they are recoverable, in taking action in default of compliance with a notice requiring adaptations to fireplaces, are registrable.

The Minister of Housing and Local Government by circular 54/63 advised that a smoke control order which does not cover the whole of a local authority district comes within the scope of the L.C.A. 1925, s. 15 (7) (b), as amended, and so should be registered as soon as ministerial confirmation has been obtained.

(xvii) Wayleave orders or draft orders for oil pipe-lines and accessory works and notices of restrictions on land immediately adjoining such lines and works (Land Powers (Defence) Act, 1958, s. 17).

(xviii) Compulsory rights orders granting temporary rights of use and occupation of land for opencast coal operations (Opencast Coal Act, 1958, s. 4) and compulsory purchase orders made by the National Coal Board under s. 16 of that Act (ibid., s. 11).

(xix) Charges on land in respect of the cost of preventing weeds from spreading where action has been taken on default of the occupier and the names or addresses of both owner and occupier cannot be ascertained (Weeds Act, 1959, s. 3 (3)).

(xx) Notices preventing the acquisition of rights to light (Rights of Light Act, 1959, s. 2).

(xxi) Certain undertakings and agreements with the Corporation of London (City of London (Various Powers) Act, 1960, s. 33 (2)).

(xxii) Notices requiring payment for expenses in respect of the sewering of a highway served after a building has been connected to the sewer (Public Health Act, 1961, ss. 12, 13, Sched. 2, para. 5). [Although the local authority have passed a resolution (i) under s. 12 to construct a sewer, or (ii) under s. 13 that a sewer constructed in land afterwards laid out as a street has increased the value of premises fronting the street, the cost is not charged on the land until a building is connected with the sewer.]

(xxiii) Management orders relating to houses let in lodgings or occupied by members of more than one family (Housing Act, 1961, s. 12 (7)).

(xxiv) Drainage schemes (Land Drainage Act, 1961, s. 30 (8)).

(xxv) Improvement notices, and immediate improvement notices and control orders (Housing Act, 1964, ss. 15, 19, 21 and 73). See further, Garner, Local Land Charges, 5th ed., p. 66.

(xxvi) Particulars of a storage area or protective area and of Ministerial consent relating to the underground storage of gas (Gas Act, 1965, ss. 5 (10), 27).

(xxvii) Notice of conditions applicable for a period of forty years to a unit of agricultural land which has been amalgamated pursuant to the Agriculture Act, 1967, ss. 26, 28, 29 or 48 (*ibid.*, Sched. 3, paras. 1 and 2). The provisions of s. 15 (1) of the L.C.A. 1925 avoiding an unregistered charge apply as if the conditions were a charge required to be registered under that subsection, and the other provisions of that Act have effect accordingly. The main conditions (i) restrict transfer of part or use other than for agriculture, without the Minister's consent, (ii) require information to be given regarding the unit.

Registration of a prescribed charge as a local land charge takes the place of registration at the Land Registry (L.C.A. 1925, s. 15 (3)). Except as expressly provided the provisions of the L.C.A. 1972 relating to land charges Class B (*ante*, p. 597), apply to a local land charge (L.C.A. 1925, s. 15 (2)). For instance, it is provided by s. 4 (1) of the L.C.A. 1972 that a land charge of Class B, when registered, takes effect as if it had been created by a deed of charge by way of legal mortgage. A local authority can, therefore, sell as if it was a mortgagee, without obtaining an order of court.

Effect of non-registration.—The L.C.A. 1925, s. 15 (1), provides that a local land charge shall be void as against a purchaser for money or money's worth of a legal estate in the land affected unless registered before completion. Further, the Local Land Charges Rules, 1966, r. 24 (6), provides that an official certificate of search should be conclusive, affirmatively or negatively as the case may be, in favour of a purchaser or intending purchaser as against authorities or persons interested under or in respect of charges required or allowed to be entered in the register (*except* in respect of control orders registered under s. 73 (5) of the Housing Act, 1964, in Pt. 4 of the register and charges registered in Pts. 6 to 12 of the register). By virtue of the Local Land Charges (Amendment) Rules, 1972, r. 2 (*a*), the 1966 rules apply fully to all registrable matters, whether or not strictly local land charges.

The Minister of Housing and Local Government who had registered a compensation notice was held to be within the class of " persons interested under . . . matters . . . whereof entries are allowed " (i.e., within L.C.A. 1925, s. 17 (3), the equivalent of which is now r. 24 (6) of the 1966 Rules). Consequently, where the registrar omitted from an official certificate of search a reference to such a notice which had been registered by the Minister, a person who subsequently purchased in reliance on the certificate was absolved from the statutory obligation to make repayment on development of the land (*Stock* v. *Wanstead and Woodford Borough Council* [1962] 2 Q.B. 479).

Further, by majority it was decided in the Court of Appeal that s. 17 (2) of the L.C.A. 1925 (which required the registrar to issue a certificate of search on requisition ; the equivalent provision here now is r. 24 (4) of the 1966 Rules) (i) did not impose on the registrar an absolute statutory duty but (ii) imposed a duty of care on the clerk who makes the search and if he is negligent in omitting an entry on the register when he prepares the certificate the local authority who employ him are liable (*Ministry of Housing* v. *Sharp* [1970] 2 Q.B. 223). Thus, the Minister (whose compensation notice became void against a purchaser because it was not disclosed on a search) recovered damages from the local authority. Compare *Coats Patons (Retail), Ltd.* v. *Birmingham Corporation* (1971), 115 Sol. J. 757, noted *ante*, p. 7.

PART 4.   COMPANIES REGISTER

Charge or mortgage for securing money.—It is provided by s. 95 of the Companies Act, 1948 (replacing s. 93 of the Companies (Consolidation) Act, 1908), that *every charge* created after 1st July, 1908, under the 1948 Act or previous Companies Acts by a company registered in England, being a charge of the nature specified in s. 95 (2), so far as any security on the company's property or undertaking is conferred thereby, shall be void against the liquidator and any creditor of the company, unless the same is registered within twenty-one days after the date of its creation, but without prejudice to any contract or obligation for repayment of the money thereby secured, and that when a charge becomes void under the section, the money secured thereby shall immediately become payable. The charges specified in s. 95 (2) include : charges for securing debentures ; charges which if executed by an individual would be bills of sale ; charges on land (not including a charge for rent or other periodical sum issuing out of land) ; floating charges ; charges on book debts (but not on contracts which may ultimately but have not yet resulted in a book debt : *Paul & Frank, Ltd.* v. *Discount Bank (Overseas), Ltd.* [1967] Ch. 348).

Where an equitable charge is avoided for non-registration under s. 95 (1) the chargee has no lien on documents of title deposited with him (*Re Molton Finance, Ltd.* [1968] Ch. 325).

Section 106 of the Companies Act, 1948, applies Pt. III of that Act to charges on property in England which are created, and to charges on property in England which are acquired, by a company incorporated outside England which has an established place of business in England. Both s. 93 and s. 104 are in Pt. III. Consequently, if a company incorporated outside England (for instance, in Scotland) has an established place of business in England the same searches and inquiries as to possible charges should be made as if it had been incorporated in England.

Where a vendor undertakes in a contract to lend to the purchaser part of the price to be secured by legal mortgage (i) he has an equitable mortgage between contract and completion, (ii) his lien as unpaid vendor merges in this mortgage and is lost except as to the part of the price to be paid in cash on completion, (iii) the equitable mortgage requires registration under s. 95. These rules provide a potential trap ; the solicitor for the vendor should register the equitable mortgage which arises on the signing of the contract (*Capital Finance Co., Ltd.* v. *Stokes* [1969] 1 Ch. 261 ; see further *ante*, p. 199).

It has been decided that an unpaid vendor's lien, resulting from a sale of land to a limited company, is not a charge *created* by a company, requiring registration within s. 95 ; such a lien arises by operation of law (*London and Cheshire Insurance Co., Ltd.* v. *Laplagrene Property Co., Ltd.* [1971] Ch. 499).

The court has jurisdiction to extend the time for registration if satisfied that the omission to register the charge was accidental, or due to inadvertence or to some other sufficient cause, or is not of a nature to prejudice the position of creditors or shareholders of the company, or that on other grounds it is just and equitable (Companies Act, 1948, s. 101). This section enables time to be extended notwithstanding that litigation challenging the validity of the charge is pending, but does not enable interim relief to be granted (*Re Heathstar Properties, Ltd.* [1966] 1 W.L.R. 993).

It is provided by the L.C.A. 1972, s. 3 (7), (8), that in the case of a land charge for securing money, created by a company before 1970 or at any time as a floating charge, registration in the companies register should be sufficient in place of registration under the L.C.A. and should have effect as if the land charge had been registered under the L.C.A. It will be noted that the subsection only applies to a land charge *for securing money*. Restrictive covenants, equitable easements and estate contracts affecting land of a company had to be registered as land charges under the L.C.A. Further, company charges for securing money (not being floating charges) created after 1969, in order to bind a purchaser for value, must be protected by deposit of documents or else by registration under the L.C.A. 1972. Registration within s. 95 of the Companies Act, 1948, is still required, but is not alone sufficient.

Again, where registered land is concerned the charge will have to be protected by registration both under the Companies Act, 1948, and under the L.R.A. 1925 to affect subsequent purchasers or mortgagees (*Re Overseas Aviation Engineering (G.B.), Ltd.* [1963] Ch. 24) notwithstanding that such persons need only search under the L.R.A. 1925 (see *ante*, p. 627).

The registrar's certificate of registration of a charge is *conclusive* evidence that the requirements as to registration have been complied with (Companies Act, 1948, s. 98 (2)), even though the particulars given to the registrar were inaccurate (*Re Mechanisations (Eaglescliffe), Ltd.* [1966] Ch. 20). This is so even though, in fact, the date was incorrectly stated and the particulars had not been delivered in time (*Re Eric Holmes (Property), Ltd.* [1965] Ch. 1052). The Court of Appeal has confirmed that a company's charge will be binding on a liquidator because the certificate of registration is by statute conclusive even though the application for registration not only misstated the date of creation of the charge but was made more than twenty-one days after the actual creation thereof (*Re C. L. Nye, Ltd.* [1971] Ch. 442). As the particulars sent to the registrar may have been inaccurate the entries in the register may be inaccurate or incomplete and so, on purchase or other dealing, the certificate should not be relied on and, if its contents may affect the transaction, the charge itself should be inspected.

The Companies Act, 1948, s. 97 (re-enacting the Companies Act, 1929, s. 81) requires registration of a charge subject to which property is acquired by a company within twenty-one days of acquisition. Failure to comply with this requirement does not invalidate the charge but penalties are imposed.

Where a company is wound up by or under supervision of the court every disposition after the commencement of the winding up is void unless the court orders otherwise (Companies Act, 1948, ss. 227, 313). Such winding up commences (i) where there has been a previous resolution for voluntary winding up, on the passing of the resolution, (ii) otherwise at the time of presentation of the petition. Consequently, it is usually advised that, if there is any reason to suspect winding-up proceedings, a purchaser should search the *London Gazette* for an advertisement of a petition.

Registration of rent-charges affecting lands held by companies.— There was formerly some doubt whether under ss. 81 and 91 of the Companies Act, 1929, deeds by which rent-charges had been created affecting lands belonging to limited companies required registration. The Board of Trade expressed the opinion that registration *was* necessary under the terms of the Companies Act, 1929, s. 79 (2) (*d*) and 10 (*a*). The Companies Act, 1929, has now been repealed and s. 79 (2) (*d*) thereof is replaced by s. 95 (2) (*d*) of the Companies Act, 1948, which expressly enacts that a charge for any rent or other periodical sum issuing out of land is *not* a charge which requires to be registered.

CHAPTER EIGHTEEN

MATTERS NECESSARY AFTER COMPLETION

THE important matter of stamping and producing conveyances and other documents must be borne in mind and is dealt with in chapter 24, p. 1151.

It is convenient in this chapter not only to deal with the major question of registration of title but also to draw attention to the post-completion points in the paragraphs immediately following.

Tithe redemption annuity.—On a conveyance of land charged with a tithe redemption annuity or any part of such land, the vendor must, within one month, furnish to the Board of Inland Revenue, on a prescribed form, particulars of the conveyance and the name and address of the purchaser (Tithe Act, 1951, s. 5 (3), (4) and Sched. 1, para. 3 ; Tithe (Change of Ownership of Land) Rules, 1962).

Where an estate or interest in land charged with an annuity is, after 1st October, 1962, for money or money's worth, disposed of or created in such a manner as to bring about a change in the person who is the owner, any annuity which is or thereafter becomes chargeable wholly in respect of land to which the change of ownership extends must be redeemed (F.A. 1962, s. 32). " Owner " is so defined that the section applies to the grant or transfer of a lease for a term of more than fourteen years at a rent less than two-thirds of the full net annual value (Tithe Act, 1936, s. 17 (1) (3)).

The present address of the Tithe Redemption Office is Inland Revenue (14), Tithe Redemption Office, East Block, Barrington Road, Worthing, Sussex.

Former rules as to charities.—The Education Act, 1944, s. 87 (2), stated that assurances of land to be used for educational purposes should be void unless the assurance or a copy was sent to the Minister of Education within six months. This step ceased to be necessary in respect of an assurance to a local education authority, a university, a university college, or a college of a university which took effect after 14th July, 1953. Similarly, other assurances of land to charities or copies were formerly required to be sent to the Charity Commissioners within six months (S.L.A. 1925, s. 29 (4)). The Education Act, 1944, s. 87, and the S.L.A. 1925, s. 29 (4), were repealed by the Charities Act, 1960, Sched. 7, and so production has not been necessary since 29th July, 1960. Section 28 (2) of the 1960 Act provides that no right or title to any property shall be defeated or impugned, and no assurance or disposition of property shall be treated as void or voidable by virtue of (*inter alia*) any of these repealed enactments if on 29th July, 1960, " the possession is in accordance with that right or title or with that assurance or disposition, and no step has been taken to assert a claim by virtue of any such enactment ". This subsection does not, however, validate any assurance or disposition so as to defeat a right or title acquired by adverse possession before the date mentioned (*ibid.*).

Miscellaneous.—It is important that all search certificates, inquiries of local authorities, inquiries before contract and requisitions on title should be placed with the deeds in order that all information may be available for the purposes of a future dealing with the property. This is a small point but one worthy of attention ; see *Law Society's Digest*, Opinion No. 200.

In the *Law Society's Gazette*, vol. 53, p. 155, a firm of solicitors drew attention to the advantages of endorsing on a conveyance the land charge registration number of an entry protecting a matter contained in the conveyance such as an option or a restrictive covenant. The adoption of this practice would facilitate reference later, for example, when a search disclosed the entry.

Simultaneous conveyance and mortgage.—When completion of a conveyance or transfer takes place simultaneously with a mortgage of the same property it is usual for the conveyance or transfer to be handed over to the mortgagee's solicitor as security and he attends to stamping (and, in the case of registered land, lodgment of necessary papers). That work, so far as the conveyance or transfer is concerned, falls within the responsibility of the purchaser's solicitor and the Council of The Law Society have pointed out that the mortgagee's solicitor performs it as agent for the purchaser's solicitor and accordingly may be entitled to make a reasonable charge against the purchaser's solicitor for doing it (*Law Society's Gazette*, vol. 53, p. 81).

REGISTRATION OF TITLE

Effect of compulsory registration.—In any area in which registration of title has been made compulsory " every conveyance on sale of freehold land and every grant of a term of years absolute not being less than forty years from the date of the delivery of the grant, and every assignment on sale of leasehold land held for a term of years absolute having not less than forty years to run from the date of delivery of the assignment, *shall* (save as hereinafter provided), *on the expiration of two months from the date thereof* or of any authorised extension of that period, *become void so far as regards the grant or conveyance of the legal estate* in the freehold or leasehold land comprised in the conveyance, grant or assignment, or so much of such land as is situated within the area affected, unless the grantee (that is to say, the person who is entitled to be registered as proprietor of the freehold or leasehold land) or his successor in title or assign has in the meantime applied to be registered as proprietor of such land " (L.R.A. 1925, s. 123 (1)). There is a proviso whereby the registrar, or the court on appeal, may extend the period if application cannot be made within two months, or can only be made in that time by incurring unreasonable expense, or application has not been made within that time by reason of accident or other sufficient cause.

Reference may be made to an article entitled " Compulsory Registration of Title—The Effect of Failure to Register," by Mr. D. G. Barnsley at *Conveyancer N.S.*, vol. 32, p. 391. There the original and unorthodox suggestion is made that the L.R.A. 1925, s. 123 (1), has the effect of creating a strict settlement of the land so that the inappropriately cumbersome conveyancing machinery of the S.L.A. 1925 would have to be operated. However, this suggestion is based entirely on equating a *legal estate* liable to be divested with a *fee simple* liable to be divested (see particularly *ibid.*, p. 401, where the argument proceeds as if the two expressions here italicised were synonymous). The true position would appear to be that the purchaser of unregistered freehold land in an area of compulsory registration of title obtains and retains *beneficially* the fee simple absolute in possession conveyed to him notwithstanding non-registration ; i.e., the purchaser has an estate which, although it may cease to subsist at law, remains *capable* of so doing within L.P.A. 1925, s. 1 (1) (*a*), and which does not fall within any of the paragraphs of S.L.A. 1925, s. 1 (1). Accordingly the better view must still be held that since there is nothing in L.R.A. 1925, s. 123 (1), to disturb the equitable position as to ownership, non-registration merely produces a bare trusteeship on the part of the vendor for the benefit of the purchaser. This more orthodox approach is also usefully considered in the article referred to.

The expressions " conveyance on sale " and " assignment on sale " in L.R.A. 1925, s. 123 (1), mean an instrument made on sale by virtue whereof there is conferred or completed a title under which an application for registration as first proprietor may be made, and include a conveyance or assignment by way of exchange *where money is paid for equality of exchange*, but do not include an assignment or surrender of a lease to the owner of the immediate reversion *containing a declaration that* the term is to merge in such reversion (L.R.A. 1925, s. 123 (3)). There is some doubt whether a conveyance by trustees to give effect to a partition agreement between persons entitled in undivided shares in which money is paid for equality or an appropriation by a personal representative under the A.E.A. 1925, s. 41, are conveyances on sale. Probably such a partition agreement is not, as the only interest transferred for value is in the proceeds of sale only and it would seem that the word " sale " in s. 123 (1) must refer to a sale of a legal estate ; it is understood that this is the view acted on in the registry. On the other hand, it would seem proper to regard an appropriation as a " sale " ; compare *Jopling* v. *I.R.C.* [1940] 2 K.B. 282.

Nothing in the L.R.A. 1925 or any order providing for compulsory registration renders compulsory the registration of title to an incorporeal hereditament, or to mines and minerals apart from the surface, or to corporeal hereditaments parcel of a manor and included in the sale of a manor as such (L.R.A. 1925, s. 120 (1), proviso).

There is an unfortunate doubt about the effect of the creation of a mortgage term. The wording of the L.R.A. 1925, s. 123 (1), if read literally, makes registration compulsory on the grant of such term. Nevertheless, a mortgagee cannot be registered as proprietor when there is a subsisting right of redemption (L.R.A. 1925, ss. 4 (*b*), 8 (1) (*a*)). Consequently, it is assumed in practice that the grant of a mortgage term can be made without registering the title affected.

Areas of compulsory registration.—Registration of title may by Order in Council be made compulsory on sale of land within any county or part of a county, or any county borough (L.R.A. 1925, s. 120 (1), (7)). Originally the L.R.A. 1925, ss. 120 (2), 121 and 122, provided in effect that compulsory registration of title could be extended to a new area only at the instance of the county council concerned or after notice to the county council followed, if the county council or a local law society so required, by a public inquiry. However, these provisions have been repealed by the L.R.A. 1966, s. 1 (1).

Souvenir land.—By virtue of the Land Registration and Land Charges Act, 1971, s. 4, an area may be declared subject to a " souvenir land scheme " (see the Land Registration (Souvenir Land) Rules, 1972). The effect of such a declaration is to exclude the area from the operation of s. 123 of the 1925 Act (see *ibid.*, rr. 5, 6 and 7, which in effect provide that souvenir land, whether or not already registered, can thereafter only be dealt with as unregistered). Land becomes " souvenir " for present purposes when the registrar believes that its disposal is in plots which " being of inconsiderable size and little or no practical utility, [are] unlikely to be wanted in isolation except for the sake of pure ownership or for sentimental reasons or commemorative purposes " (s. 4 (5) of the 1971 Act).

Voluntary registration.—As respects land outside an area of compulsory registration, voluntary applications for registration (under L.R.A. 1925, ss. 4 and 8, below) were originally not restricted. But now s. 1 (2) of the L.R.A. 1966 provides that such applications are not to be entertained except in such classes of cases as the Chief Land Registrar may, by notice published in such a way as appears to him appropriate, from time to time specify and in these cases the applicant may be required to show that there are special considerations which make it expedient to grant the application. The object of this restriction was to facilitate the rapid extension of compulsory registration of title on sale. The voluntary registration of estates to be developed for housing to consist of at least twenty plots or houses (or purpose-built flat developments of similar size) will be permitted on the lodging of certain certificates and undertakings. See the preliminary notice published in the *Law Society's Gazette*, vol. 63, p. 184 ; further guidance is given in leaflet E.295, copies of which can be obtained from the Chief Land Registrar. The fact that an application is based upon a Land Registry transfer purporting to be made pursuant to the provisions of r. 72 of the L.R.R. 1925 is *not* a reason which will induce the Land Registry to accept where the land is outside the compulsory areas (see Practice Note by Chief Land Registrar in *Solicitors' Journal*, vol. 115, p. 728). As to the interim extension of voluntary registration of title to certain districts now comprised in the new metropolitan counties created under the Local Government Act, 1972, see a statement by the Chief Land Registrar in *Solicitors' Journal* (1973), vol. 117, p. 684.

Subject to the above, the persons who may apply for registration in respect of a freehold estate are specified in the L.R.A. 1925, s. 4, which provides as follows :—

" 4. Where the title to be registered is a title to a freehold estate in land—

(a) any estate owner holding an estate in fee simple (including a tenant for life, statutory owner, personal representative, or trustee for sale) whether subject or not to incumbrances ; or

(b) any other person (not being a mortgagee where there is a subsisting right of redemption or a person who has merely contracted to buy land) who is entitled to require a legal estate in fee simple whether subject or not to incumbrances, to be vested in him ;

may apply to the registrar to be registered in respect of such estate, or, in the case of a person not in a fiduciary position, to have registered in his stead any nominee, as proprietor with an absolute title or with a possessory title."

Where the application is for registration in the name of a nominee the consent in writing of the nominee must be delivered with the application together with a statement that the applicant is not in a fiduciary position in regard to the land (L.R.R. 1925, r. 22).

Similarly, it is provided by the L.R.A. 1925, s. 8 (1), that where the title is to a leasehold interest any estate owner (including a tenant for life, statutory owner, personal representative or trustee for sale, but not including a mortgagee where there is a subsisting right of redemption) holding under a lease for a term of years absolute of which more than twenty-one are unexpired, or any other person (not being such a mortgagee and not being a person who has merely contracted to buy a leasehold interest) who is entitled to require a legal leasehold interest held under such a lease to be vested in him, may apply to be registered in respect of such estate, or, in the case of a person not being in a fiduciary position, to have registered any nominee.

Thus, it will be noted that a mortgagee cannot be registered as proprietor of a mortgage term if there is a subsisting right of redemption. Where the application is to register a mortgage term where there is no subsisting right of redemption, and it appears that the applicant is entitled in equity to the superior term, if any, out of which it was created, the registrar must register him as proprietor of the superior term, and on such registration the superior term vests in the proprietor and the mortgage term is merged therein (L.R.A. 1925, s. 8 (3)). This subsection does not apply, however, where the mortgage term does not comprise the whole of the land included in the superior term unless any rent payable in respect of the superior term has been apportioned, or the rent is of no money value, or no rent is reserved, and unless any covenants entered into for the benefit of the reversion have been apportioned (L.R.A. 1925, s. 8 (3), proviso).

Land held under a lease containing an absolute prohibition against all dealings *inter vivos* therewith is not registrable, and land held under a lease containing a restriction on any such dealings may not be registered until provision is made in the prescribed manner for preventing any dealing in contravention of the restriction (L.R.A. 1925, s. 8 (2)). It is provided by the L.R.R. 1925, r. 45, that on registration of leasehold land held under a lease containing a prohibition against alienation *without licence* all estates, interests and remedies under the lease arising by reason of any alienation without licence must be expressly excepted from the effect of registration.

Dealings prior to registration.—A person who has the right to apply for first registration may deal with the land in any way permitted by the L.R.A. 1925 before he is registered as proprietor, and in the case of a transfer the transferee will be deemed to be the applicant for first registration and will be entered on the register accordingly (L.R.A. 1925, s. 37 (3) ; L.R.R. 1925, r. 72 (1)). Any instrument for giving effect to a dealing prior to first registration by a person entitled to be registered as proprietor of any interest in land, or a charge, before he has been registered as such, must be in the same form as is required for a disposition by the proprietor, but with any modifications necessary to define clearly the land affected (L.R.R. 1925, r. 81), but no registration of such an instrument will be made until the person executing it has been registered as proprietor, or his right to be registered has been shown to the satisfaction of the registrar (*ibid.*). This means that a person intending to apply for registration may take his conveyance in the form of a transfer of registered land, although, in practice, this is rarely done.

A dealing made in this way, when completed by registration, has the same effect as if the person making it had been registered as proprietor, but subject to any prior rights obtained by registration (L.R.R. 1925, r. 72 (2)). A dealing other than a lease will not be accepted for registration until an application has been made for the registration of the estate to which it relates, and if the application for registration of the estate is refused, withdrawn or abandoned, the registration of the dealing will be annulled (L.R.R. 1925, r. 72 (3)).

Where a dealing takes place after a conveyance, grant, or assignment necessitating compulsory registration of land, but before application to register the title, the dealing will take effect as if it had taken place after the date of first registration, which must be effected as of the date of the application to register (L.R.A. 1925, s. 123 (2) ; L.R.R. 1925, r. 73 (1)). If the dealing in question is a charge or other incumbrance, capable of registration in the charges register, the person entitled to it has power to lodge an application on behalf of the proper applicant for the first registration of the estate on which the charge or incumbrance has been created (L.R.R. 1925, r. 73 (2)). If, for instance, land in a compulsory area is sold and immediately mortgaged this provision enables the mortgagee to make application for registration of the estate which, of course, he must do to ensure that the conveyance to the mortgagor does not become void, and such a mortgagee should obtain documents necessary for application for registration on completion of the mortgage.

The question whether a purchaser is bound to or should accept a title from a vendor who has the right to apply for first registration is considered in the *Solicitors' Journal*, vol. 109, pp. 838–9. The vital point to observe in practice is the provision of s. 123 (1) of the L.R.A. 1925 that the conveyance or grant to the vendor, enabling him to convey, will become void at law after two months (*ante*, p. 637).

Application for registration.—Application for registration of title to a freehold estate may be for either an absolute or possessory title, but even if the application is made only for a possessory title the registrar may, without the consent of the applicant, register an absolute title (L.R.A. 1925, s. 4).

It is usually advisable to apply for an absolute title unless there is a very clear defect. If there is a defect in title and objection may be taken to the registration there is a danger that costs of settling the dispute may be payable by the applicant. Consequently, it may be more convenient in such a case to apply for registration of a possessory title only.

The application must be made on the appropriate printed form (the forms in the Schedule to the L.R.R. 1925 have been revised ; see the list of the most commonly used forms in Registered Land Practice Notes 1972, p. 47). Cheques for the fees based on the value of the property in accordance with the Land Registration Fee Order, 1970, should be made payable to H.M. Land Registry.

The application form may be signed by the applicant or (except where a nominee is to be registered) by his solicitor, but where application is for registration in the name of a nominee the consent in writing of the nominee must be delivered with the application, together with a statement, which must be signed by the applicant himself, that the applicant is not in a fiduciary position. The documents which must be delivered with the application are specified in L.R.R. 1925, r. 20, as follows :—

" 20. The application shall (unless the Registrar shall otherwise direct) be accompanied by—

    (i) all such *original deeds and documents* relating to the title as the applicant has in his possession or under his control, including

21

opinions of counsel, abstracts of title, contracts for or conditions of sale, requisitions, replies and other like documents, in regard to the title,

(ii) a *copy or sufficient abstract of the latest document of title,* not being a document of record,

(iii) *sufficient particulars,* by plan or otherwise, *to enable the land to be fully identified* on the Ordnance Map or Land Registry General Map,

(iv) a *list* in triplicate *of all documents delivered."*

" *original deeds and documents."*—Abstracts of title should be marked as having been examined with the original documents (L.R.R. 1925, r. 306). If the applicant has no documents of title he must make a statutory declaration in Form 4 that he is in possession and explain the absence of the deeds. Where the land has been mortgaged, the original mortgage and a certified copy must be forwarded ; in the case of a building society, friendly society, or industrial society mortgage, the certificate must be that of the secretary or solicitor to the society. Official certificates of search should be forwarded.

" *copy . . . of the latest document of title."*—The copy of the latest document should be on foolscap certified by the applicant's solicitor as a true copy and endorsed with his name and address (L.R.R. 1925, r. 309). Where a land registry form was used on the last transaction in accordance with the L.R.R. 1925, r. 72, it is requested that the transfer should be lodged with a *certified* copy ; the original transfer will then be issued on completion of the registration (Registered Land Practice Notes 1972, p. 5, No. 14).

" *sufficient particulars . . . to enable the land to be fully identified."*—It is the practice for the registrar to require a certificate to be included in, or forwarded with, the application to the effect that the land is defined on all sides by fences or physical features on the ground. If the land is not defined by fences or physical features the registrar will require that fences or substantial boundary posts should be erected on the boundaries so that the land can be surveyed. See further, as to boundaries of land, *ante,* p. 490. In a compulsory area the land will be surveyed on behalf of the registrar without fee, but elsewhere the applicant must pay for the survey, the cost being quoted before it is incurred.

" *list . . . of all documents delivered."*—Form A.13 may, but need not, be used ; the list must be signed by or on behalf of the person lodging the documents.

Rent-charges.—As a result of the increase in compulsory areas forms of application for registration of rent-charges have now been provided. The forms are : 1F (application for first registration of a purchaser or original grantee immediately after sale or grant) ; 1H (same where the applicant is a company or corporation) ; 1G (application for first registration not immediately after sale or grant with a supporting statutory declaration) ; 1G (Co.) (same where the applicant is a company or corporation).

Where a conveyance to the applicant conveys more than one rent-charge the form may be adapted, but where corporeal land and rent-charges are comprised in a single assurance, and it is desired to register the rent-charges, a separate application must be made in one of these forms.

In addition to the documents required by L.R.R. 1925, r. 20, to be delivered with the application, the following should be provided :—

(i) detailed particulars of the deed which created the rent-charge, of any deed which formally apportioned it and of all deeds creating prior rent-charges.   Where the original of any such deed is in the applicant's possession and is lodged with the application, a certified copy should be lodged for filing in the registry.   If the applicant holds only an abstract or copy an additional abstract or copy should be furnished for filing.   All abstracts or copies should be marked by a solicitor as having been examined with the original deeds ;

(ii) on an application relating to an original grant, if the grantor's title is already registered, the land certificate must be lodged with the application or deposited at the registry.

It is stated that in addition to supplying a properly verified abstract of title, full information should be given on any points on which a well-advised purchaser would raise requisitions.   For example, all overriding rent-charges must be dislosed in the schedule of incumbrances in the application form and evidence of them lodged.   Where a document of title has been lost or destroyed a statutory declaration should be supplied giving an account of the incumbrances supported by any secondary evidence available including proof of uninterrupted possession of the rent-charge and an unequivocal declaration that the deeds have not been deposited as security for money.   Where the deeds have been destroyed by enemy action the statutory declaration must contain a clear statement that no person other than the applicant has any interest whatever in the rent-charge and a completed draft of the conveyance or grant in favour of the applicant should be produced together with a certified copy for filing (Practice Leaflet No. 9).

Examination of title.—After deposit of the necessary documents the title will be examined by the registrar and requisitions will be issued to the applicant's solicitor if necessary.   The procedure can be simplified, however, in the case of land of small value in a compulsory area by reason of the L.R.R. 1925, r. 29, which provides as follows :—

" 29. In cases of sale in a district where registration of title is compulsory on sale and

(a) the value of the land does not exceed £700, or

(b) where there has been a sale by or after public auction within two years previous to the application, and the value of the land does not exceed £1,000,

the Registrar may, if he thinks fit, register a title as absolute or good leasehold, on production of a certificate by a solicitor, at the expense of the applicant, to the effect that—

(a) he acted for the applicant on the purchase, which induced the registration,

(b) he investigated, or caused to be investigated, the title in the usual way on the applicant's behalf, and made, or caused to be made, all such searches or official certificates of search, as he considered necessary,

(c) the whole of the purchase money was paid to the person mentioned in that behalf in the conveyance or assignment,

(d) he believes, as the result of his investigation, that the conveyance or assignment validly conveyed or assigned to the applicant the estate and interest thereby purported to be conveyed or assigned, free from any adverse rights or incumbrances (including restrictive covenants affecting the land by way of notice actual or constructive or by reason of the registration of a land charge), which were not shown by the conveyance or assignment."

Before any registration is completed with absolute or good leasehold title an advertisement must be inserted in the *Gazette* and in such local or other newspapers as may be decided by the registrar (L.R.R. 1925, r. 31), but where the original lessee is registered as first proprietor, or if the land is situate in a compulsory area and the applicant is a purchaser on a sale completed within the year preceding the application, an advertisement is not issued unless the registrar thinks it advisable ; in practice he rarely requires advertisement in such cases (L.R.R. 1925, r. 33). Any person may object to the registration by notice delivered at the registry before the completion of registration, but such a notice must state concisely the grounds of the objection, and give an address for service of the person objecting (L.R.R. 1925, r. 34). The registrar has jurisdiction to hear and determine any objections subject to an appeal to the court (L.R.A. 1925, s. 13, proviso (b) ; L.R.R. 1925, r. 35).

Even though the registrar is of opinion that the title is open to objection if it is, nevertheless, a title the holding under which will, in his opinion, not be disturbed, he may approve of the title or may require the applicant to apply to the court, upon a statement signed by him, for sanction to the registration (L.R.A. 1925, s. 13, proviso (c)).

Where requisitions are sent, a time for answer is usually specified, for instance fourteen days, but if the replies cannot be completed within that period application may be made for an extension of time. If, however, the form is not returned within the specified or any extended time, the application will be cancelled and a fresh fee will have to be paid. Before completion of registration the registrar may require the applicant or his solicitor to make an affidavit or declaration that to the best of his knowledge and belief all deeds, wills, and instruments of title, and all charges and incumbrances affecting the title, and all facts material to the title have been disclosed (L.R.A. 1925, s. 14 (1)), and the registrar may require any person making such an affidavit or declaration to state therein what means he has had of becoming acquainted with such matters (L.R.A. 1925, s. 14 (2)). The registrar requires the applicant's solicitor to make a statutory declaration if the application is not founded on a sale and is for absolute or good leasehold title.

When the time fixed in any advertisement for delivery of objections has expired, and the registrar is satisfied with the title, registration will be completed with effect from the date of application A person cannot be registered as proprietor until, if required by the registrar, he has produced such documents of title as will, in the opinion of the registrar, when stamped or otherwise marked, give notice to any person dealing with the land of the fact of the registration (L.R.A. 1925, s. 16). All abstracts and copies of documents and all documents for registration delivered to the Land Registry are retained there, pending completion of the registration to which they relate (L.R.R. 1925, r. 306 (1)). Afterwards all deeds, applications and other documents on which any entry in the register is founded should be retained at the registry, and only taken away under a written order of the registrar or an order of the court (L.R.R. 1925, r. 90). Where such retention is not required, any documents are to be dealt with as the registrar directs (L.R.R. 1925, r. 306 (2)) which in practice means that they are returned to the applicant for registration or to the persons producing them (or their successors in title) although the registrar does in fact have power, apparently unexercised, to order their destruction in certain cases (see L.R.R. 1925, rr. 42 and 310 ; Ruoff and Roper, Registered Conveyancing, 3rd ed., p. 226). Original documents which are not usually retained at the registry include a transfer by a person having the right to apply for first registration (i.e., under L.R.R. 1925, r. 72), instruments of charge, leases and counterparts, grants of probate or letters of administration and noted deeds (i.e., under L.R.A. 1925, s. 49, and L.R.R. 1925, r. 190), provided in most cases a certified copy is filed. The registrar must mark the documents of title required to be produced under L.R.A. 1925, s. 16, *ante*, unless he is satisfied that even without such marking the fact of registration cannot be concealed. The registry's present practice on first registration is to place its official stamp with the title number, etc., in the case of a freehold title on the conveyance to the applicant and in the case of a leasehold title on the lease and on the assignment to the applicant. Unfortunately, staff difficulties appear to prevent the registry reverting to the original practice of stamping every document before returning them to the solicitors. It is pointed out in Registered Land Practice Notes 1972, p. 5, No. 15, that the real protection of the purchaser against any possible fraud or mistake lies in the existence of the index maps, which can be searched free of charge prior to completion. In the case of registration with a possessory title, the registrar may act on a statutory declaration by the solicitor of the applicant that the documents produced affect the land included in the application and are all the deeds necessary to be marked, or may dispense with the production of deeds on being furnished with a statutory declaration showing why they cannot be produced (L.R.A. 1925, s. 16, proviso ; L.R.R. 1925, r. 38).

An application by a person who claims to have acquired a title under the Limitation Act, 1939, by adverse possession should in any case take the form of an application for first registration supported by appropriate statutory declarations. As to the form and contents of such statutory declarations see the notes and suggestions for the assistance of practitioners in Ruoff and Roper, *op. cit.*, pp. 687–693 (reference may also be made to the full discussion of this topic, and in particular of the position of encroachments by lessees, by the present Chief Land Registrar in *Conveyancer N.S.*, vol. 27, p. 353).

On the first registration of a freehold or leasehold interest, or on the registration of a charge, a land certificate or charge certificate will be prepared stating whether the title is absolute, good leasehold, qualified or possessory and it will be either delivered to the proprietor or deposited in the registry as the proprietor prefers (L.R.A. 1925, s. 63 (1).

Applications for registration of title to leaseholds.—The procedure is similar to that on application for registration of title to freeholds, but there are a few differences. See L.R.A. 1925, ss. 8 to 12, inclusive, and L.R.R. 1925, rr. 21, 44 to 47, inclusive. Application may be for an absolute, good leasehold or a possessory title. An absolute leasehold title means that the registrar has investigated and approved the title not only to the leasehold but also to the freehold and to any intermediate leasehold (L.R.A. 1925, s. 8 (1), proviso (i)). Such a title has the clear advantage that any restrictive covenants or other entries on the superior title will also appear on the lease-hold title so that no problem should arise of a purchaser being affected by what he cannot discover (compare *White* v. *Bijou Mansions, Ltd.* [1937] Ch. 610, 621 ; on appeal [1938] Ch. 351). Notwithstanding this, applications for registration with an absolute leasehold title appear to be comparatively few (see Ruoff and Roper, Registered Conveyancing, 3rd ed., pp. 86–87). It is thought this is often because of the ordinary restriction on the right of a purchaser of a leasehold to investigate the title, but it may also be because there is an unjustifiable reluctance on the part of practitioners to apply for other than a good leasehold title, even where the superior titles themselves are already registered as absolute. Apparently following the decision in *White* v. *Bijou Mansions, Ltd., ante,* the registry adopted the admirable practice of granting absolute leasehold titles whenever the estate out of which the lease was granted was already registered with absolute title. Unhappily, however, this practice was abandoned simply because so many complaints were received about the restrictive covenants affecting the freehold title being set out in full (*Law Society's Gazette*, vol. 59, p. 481). However, the Chief Land Registrar has promulgated certain forms of application for an absolute leasehold title which contain indications of the particular evidence which is needed (Forms 3F, 3F (Co.), 2F, 2F (Co.) ; see Registered Land Practice Notes 1972, p. 5, No. 53).

Where a possessory title is applied for, the registrar may grant a good leasehold title, without the consent of the applicant, or he may, upon request in writing by the applicant, grant a qualified title. Application must be made on Form 2A, 2B, 2C, 2C (Co.), 2E, 3A, 3B or 3E as the case may require. If the lease affects land already registered, notice of registration is given to the proprietor of the freehold land or of the superior lease out of which the lease is derived, and if no valid objection is made within seven days, or if the proprietor of the freehold or such superior lease consents in writing to the application, the lease will be noted against the title to the freehold or to the superior lease (L.R.R. 1925, r. 46). The Court of Appeal has decided that in such a case production of the lessor's land certificate at the registry is not a requirement of the lessee's application for registration (*Strand Securities, Ltd.* v. *Caswell* [1965] Ch. 958 ; this concerned the comparatively rare case of a registrable rack-rent lease and may not be applicable where the grant of the lease is in consideration of a premium and in pursuance of a contract entitling the lessee to call for the lessor's land certificate). With regard to the decision the Chief Land Registrar has commented that " it is clearly far more convenient to the registry, and almost certainly to the parties also, if the long-established practice of producing the land certificate, or placing it upon deposit, is continued in all instances in which the registration of a lease of registered land is sought " (*Law Society's Gazette*, vol. 62, p. 507).

It may also be noted that the Court of Appeal also decided in *Strand Securities, Ltd.* v. *Caswell, ante,* that if a registered proprietor lodges his land certificate for one purpose, it is to be treated as lodged for any other application that has in fact been made, even one of which the proprietor is unaware. However, a proprietor is able to lodge his certificate with written directions that it is to be held for a specified purpose only which will effectively prevent its use for any other purpose without the written consent of himself, his successor in title or his solicitor (L.R.R. 1925, r. 269).

See further *post*, p. 805.

A certified copy of the lease or, if approved by the registrar, an abstract or other sufficient evidence of its content, must be deposited with the application if the original lessee is the applicant, and in other cases if required by the registrar ; and in all cases the lease itself must accompany the application if in the possession or control of the applicant (L.R.R. 1925, r. 21).

Applications following dealings with registered land.—The stamped transfer must be produced at the registry with the registry fee stamps affixed or with a remittance in payment of the fees, and accompanied by the land certificate. The solicitor for the applicant completes Form A.4 where the whole of the land is being transferred or Form A.5 where part only is being transferred. It is essential to forward also the official search certificate ; see *ante*, p. 625. If the transfer imposes restrictive covenants a copy certified by the purchaser's solicitor, or a partner in the firm, must be provided. Difficulty in producing the transfer (or a conveyance on first registration) may result from the delay which often occurs when it is necessary to have the stamp duty adjudicated. The transfer or conveyance should be sent to the registry with the application (marked in red ink ' please return transfer for adjudication '), together with a certified copy of the transfer or conveyance and a written request by the applicant's solicitor for the immediate return of the original, including an undertaking to lodge it in the registry as soon as the duty has been adjudicated. When the document is lodged, the application will be completed with effect from the date on which it was originally forwarded (L.R.R. 1925, r. 95 ; Registered Land Practice Notes 1972, pp. 31-32, No. 26 ; *Solicitors' Journal*, vol. 105, p. 677).

L.R.R. 1925, r. 89, under which notice of the transfer was required at this point to be sent to the vendor or the proprietor of the land, has been revoked by the L.R.R. 1964. Even before this, however, it is understood that it was not the registry's practice to send such notices, the registrar having power to relax the regulations (i.e., under L.R.R. 1925, r. 322 (1)). Despite the revocation, such notices may, it is assumed, still be sent whenever it is thought necessary. Where no notice is sent or no objection received, the registrar will then deliver to the purchaser a land certificate, and if the transfer was of part only of the vendor's holding, will deliver an amended land certificate to the vendor.

On application for registration of a company the memorandum and articles of association with a copy certificate of incorporation, all certified as true copies by the secretary or solicitor to the company, must be produced in order that any restriction on the power of dealing with land (for instance, a restriction on the power of charging where the borrowing powers of a company are limited) may be noted.

On application for registration of dealings by trustees of a friendly society, the registrar must be satisfied that the persons executing the disposition are the trustees for the time being. " When the trustees have changed since the date of registration a certificate by the secretary or solicitor of the society that the persons executing the disposition are the present duly appointed trustees of the society will always be accepted as sufficient evidence of their appointment. Again, where the persons executing a discharge of a registered charge are different persons from those named in the charge as being the trustees of the society, and their signatures are witnessed by the secretary, that attestation will be regarded as sufficient evidence that the executing parties are the present duly appointed trustees of the society. The same evidence will be accepted in the case of unincorporated Building Societies and Industrial and Provident Societies " (Registered Land Practice Notes 1972, pp. 34-35, No. 22).

If the vendor held the land subject to a registered charge, a discharge (Form 53) signed by the proprietor of the charge should be handed over on completion and forwarded to the registry with the charge certificate. Similarly, in appropriate cases, an application for withdrawal of a mortgage caution, or for withdrawal of notice of deposit of the land certificate, should be obtained, although if part only of the land affected by the mortgage or lien is sold a consent to the transfer, signed by the mortgagee or depositee, is the appropriate document (the charge certificate being deposited at the registry). There is no prescribed form for such a consent. Mortgagees (particularly building societies) often refuse to execute a discharge for some days. This difficulty can be avoided by obtaining the undertaking of the society's solicitors to have the mortgage discharged. This undertaking should be forwarded to the registry with the application for registration and the application will then be treated as valid if the discharged mortgage is lodged later.

Effect of registration.—On first registration, the proprietor of the land is deemed to have vested in him without any conveyance either the freehold or leasehold legal estates as appropriate, subject to any overriding or prior interests (L.R.A. 1925, s. 69 (1)). As to the detailed effects of first registration with an absolute, good leasehold, possessory or qualified title, see ss. 5-7 and 9-12 of the L.R.A. 1925. In the case of a freehold estate registered with an absolute title, a disposition of the registered land, including a lease, made for valuable consideration, when registered confers on the transferee or grantee an estate in fee simple or the term of years absolute or other legal estate expressed to be created " together with all rights, privileges, and appurtenances belonging or appertaining thereto, including (subject to any entry to the contrary in the register) the appropriate rights and interests which would, under the L.P.A. 1925, have been transferred if the land had not been registered, subject (a) to the incumbrances and other entries, if any, appearing on the register ; and (b) unless the contrary is expressed on the register, to the overriding interests, if any, affecting the estate transferred or created, but free from all other estates and interests whatsoever " (L.R.A. 1925, s. 20 (1)). In the case of a freehold estate registered with a qualified title or a possessory title a disposition has the same effect, save that it does not affect the enforcement of any right or interest excepted from registration, or, as the case may be, adverse to the title of the first registered proprietor and subsisting at the time of his registration (L.R.A. 1925, s. 20).

It is important to bear in mind that the legal estate does not pass to the purchaser until the transfer is registered (L.R.A. 1925, ss. 19 (1) and 22 (1)). Prior to that date the purchaser cannot, for instance, serve a valid notice to quit (*Smith* v. *Express Dairy Co., Ltd.* [1954] J.P.L. 45 ; *Lever Finance, Ltd.* v. *Needleman's Trustee* [1956] Ch. 375).

More accurately, the legal estate is passed retrospectively as on the day on which the application for registration was delivered to the Land Registry (L.R.R. 1925, s. 83 (2)).

Where any such disposition is made without valuable consideration, so far as the transferee or grantee is concerned it is subject to any minor interests subject to which the transferor or grantor held, but otherwise has the same effect as if made for valuable consideration (L.R.A. 1925, s. 20 (4)).

Developing building estates procedure.—In practice, the purpose of applying for voluntary registration of title often is to facilitate dispositions after the land has been developed as a building estate (and see the L.R.A. 1966, s. 1 (2), *ante*, p. 639). Equally, of course, the purchase of land in an area of compulsory registration or title to which is already registered may be with a view to development as a building estate. So, although this is not strictly a post-completion matter, it may be convenient here to draw attention to the procedure which may be used in cases of such development.

A general guide to solicitors acting for developers of estates containing ten or more plots, flats or maisonettes is given and explained by Registered Land Practice Leaflet No. 7 (obtainable without charge from any district land registry) ; see also Ruoff and Roper, Registered Conveyancing, 3rd ed., p. 358 *et seq.* The object of the procedure outlined is to enable the simplified form of verification by purchasers of plots, etc., of the vendor's title indicated *ante*, p. 139, with the particular advantages of overriding the necessity either for office copies of the filed plan or for providing separate plans for official searches.

The basic step, to be taken as early as possible, is to send two copies of the estate layout plan to the registry for approval. These copies must be fairly detailed and precise, showing plot or other reference numbers and the extent of the individual plots or flats or maisonettes and any garages should be clearly defined. In the case of blocks of flats, floor plans should also be lodged. After approval, one copy of the layout plan will be retained in the registry : the duplicate copy, marked as officially approved, will be returned to the vendor's solicitor.

After this, to avoid any confusion or delay, solicitors should ensure that any change in the estate layout is immediately notified with full details to the registry. The registry should also be informed of areas of new development, when fresh roads or fences are constructed, so that fresh surveys can be made.

Since the land (or charge) certificate may have to be deposited at the registry for a long period during the development of large estates, it is also recommended that the vendor should apply at the outset for an office copy of the filed plan.

It may incidentally be noted that each instrument of transfer will have to be accompanied by a plan of the property concerned. Mere reference to a plot number on the estate plan will not suffice. It would appear especially desirable that an extract from the approved estate plan be used for the instrument plan ; otherwise the plan used should show not only the property dealt with but also sufficient adjacent details to show its position on the vendor's filed plan.

It is also helpful if a draft of the standard form of transfer proposed for general use on the estate can be submitted for approval by the registry before development is commenced. This will ultimately facilitate the proof of easements over the estate as indicated *ante*, p. 139.

In the outlining of the above procedures, references to transfers of part should be taken as including leases of part of the land in a title and " vendor " and " purchaser " as having corresponding meanings.

CHAPTER NINETEEN

CUSTODY AND PRODUCTION OF DEEDS

PART 1. CUSTODY OF DEEDS GENERALLY

Right of an estate owner.—In *Clayton* v. *Clayton* [1930] 2 Ch. 12, the plaintiff sought to recover in an action of detinue three deeds of appointment of trustees, from the trustees who held them, on the ground that he was absolutely entitled to the property to which they had reference. The L.P.A. 1925, s. 45 (9) (*b*) (*post*, p. 654), had no bearing, because that paragraph is applicable only as between vendor and purchaser. Maugham, J., held that the right of an estate owner to the title deeds of the estate is not absolute. If no one else has any legal interest in the subjects dealt with in a title deed, the estate owner is generally entitled to recover it from a stranger, but there are numerous exceptions. The learned judge held that the right or title of the defendants to the deeds, so long as they had duties as trustees to perform, precluded the plaintiff from succeeding in the action.

Where the title of a mortgagee has become extinguished by lapse of time, the mortgagor is entitled to recover possession of title deeds relating to the land from the mortgagee without repaying the mortgage sum (*Lewis* v. *Plunket* [1937] Ch. 306).

Settled land.—Before 1926, in general both a legal and an equitable tenant for life were entitled to the custody of deeds, except where he had been guilty of misconduct whereby their safety might be endangered, or where it was necessary for the court to take charge of the deeds in order to carry out the administration of the property (*Garner* v. *Hannyngton* (1856), 22 Beav. 627 ; *Leathes* v. *Leathes* (1877), 5 Ch. D. 221 ; *Re Beddoe* [1893] 1 Ch. 547 ; *Re Richardson ; Richardson* v. *Richardson* [1900] 2 Ch. 778 ; *Re Bentley ; Wade* v. *Wilson* (1885), 54 L.J. Ch. 782 ; *Re Wythes ; West* v. *Wythes* [1893] 2 Ch. 369 ; *Re Money Kyrle's Settlement* [1900] 2 Ch. 839). If the trustees had active duties to perform which might make it desirable for them to retain the deeds, this was sufficient ground for refusing to hand them over to the equitable life tenant (*Re Newen ; Newen* v. *Barnes* [1894] 2 Ch. 297 ; see also *Re Burnaby's Settled Estates* (1889), 42 Ch. D. 621).

Since 1925 the tenant for life has the legal estate vested in him, and express provision as to the custody of deeds is contained in the following subsection of the S.L.A. 1925 :—

" 98.—(3) The trustees of the settlement shall not be liable in any way on account of any vesting instrument or other documents of title relating to the settled land, other than securities for capital money, being placed in the possession of the tenant for life or statutory owner :

Provided that where, if the settlement were not disclosed, it would appear that the tenant for life had a general power of appointment over, or was absolutely and beneficially entitled to the settled land, the trustees of the settlement shall, before they deliver the documents to him, require that notice of the last or only principal vesting instrument be written on one of the documents under which the tenant for life acquired his title, and may, if the documents are not in their possession, require such notice to be written as aforesaid, but, in the latter case, they shall not be liable in any way for not requiring the notice to be written."

If trustees hand the deeds over to the tenant for life without having first endorsed a memorandum of the vesting deed on one of the documents of title, they may, for instance, if the tenant for life should mortgage the land for his own benefit, be personally liable for their negligence.

Where the tenant for life is absolute owner subject to family charges he can, under s. 1 of the Law of Property (Amendment) Act, 1926, convey the legal estate subject to such family charges. As the purchaser in this case gets the legal estate it seems to follow that, if he buys the whole of the settled land, he would be entitled to the possession of the deeds. The same principle seems also to apply where the tenant for life creates a legal estate under s. 16 of the S.L.A. 1925.

It is provided by the S.L.A. 1925, s. 24 (1), in effect, that the court may direct that any documents of title in the possession of the tenant for life relating to the settled land be delivered to the trustees of the settlement, when an order is made enabling the trustees to exercise any powers of the tenant for life in relation to the settled land on the ground that the tenant for life has, by reason of bankruptcy, or otherwise, ceased to have a substantial interest in his estate or interest in the settled land, and has unreasonably refused to exercise any of the powers conferred on him by the Act, or has consented to an order. See further *post*, p. 742.

Where a tenant for life himself purchases part of the settled land under s. 68 of the S.L.A. 1925, he is entitled to any deeds relating solely to the land sold, not being trust instruments, as any other purchaser would be, and as regards other deeds, he is entitled to an acknowledgment. The position is that as tenant for life he is entitled to the custody of the deeds as the owner of the legal estate, but only as trustee, and as purchaser he is entitled to the deeds for his own benefit or to an acknowledgment which is given by the trustees acting on his behalf pursuant to the S.L.A. 1925, s. 68. The reason why this is important is that on his death his special executors will be entitled to the custody of deeds held by him in his capacity of tenant for life, and there might be other cases where the deeds would pass out of his hands.

It is provided by s. 111 of the S.L.A. 1925, in effect, that when a tenant for life sells his *beneficial interest* after 1925, he must not hand to the purchaser the documents of title to the settled land, unless the purchaser has purchased the whole of the settled land to which such documents relate ; and that the purchaser shall not, except in the case mentioned, have the right to require the deeds to be handed to him. This could not be otherwise, as the tenant for life is a trustee for the parties beneficially interested, and in that capacity must hold the deeds (S.L.A. 1925, ss. 16 and 107 (1)). But by the same section it is provided that the purchaser of the beneficial interest shall have the same rights with respect to the deeds as if the tenant for life had given to him a statutory acknowledgment of his right to production and delivery of copies thereof and a statutory undertaking for the safe custody thereof. Section 111 applies only on sale of a *beneficial interest ;* where the tenant for life sells the fee simple under his statutory powers the usual rules (*post*, p. 653) apply as to the deeds which should be handed over.

Section 111 of the S.L.A. 1925 has no application in the circumstances mentioned in s. 105 (1) of the same Act, as amended by the Law of Property (Amendment) Act, 1926, namely, where the estate or interest of the tenant for life under the settlement is absolutely assured with intent to extinguish the same to the person next entitled in remainder or reversion under the settlement, in which case the statutory powers of the tenant for life under the Act cease to be exercisable by him, and such powers thenceforth become exercisable as if he were dead, but without prejudice to any incumbrance affecting the estate or interest assured. In this case the person entitled to exercise the powers of the tenant for life will be entitled to the possession of the deeds, provided that he has obtained a vesting deed (S.L.A. 1925, s. 13).

As regards a purchaser of the beneficial interest of a tenant for life before 1926, as, by the transitional provisions of the L.P.A. 1925 (s. 39 and Sched. 1, Pts. I and II), the legal estate vested in the purchaser passed to the tenant for life, it would seem, at first sight, that the tenant for life would be entitled to ask the purchaser to return the deeds to him, but a doubt is raised by the words of the proviso to s. 111 of the S.L.A. 1925. They are : " Provided that, where the conveyance or dealing is effected *after the commencement of this Act*, the purchaser shall not be entitled to the possession of the documents of title to the settled land . . . ," suggesting that the rule is not to apply where the transaction took place before 1926.

Right of lessee to retain expired lease.—A *lessee* would appear to be entitled to the custody of an expired lease, at least for a time, since he may have occasion to use it in an action of covenant against the lessor ; but after a considerable interval it may be that the lessor is entitled to it (*Hall* v. *Ball* (1841), 3 Man. & G. 242 ; *Elworthy* v. *Sandford* (1864), 34 L.J. Ex. 42). The same rule applies to a lease surrendered in order that a new lease may be granted in lieu thereof (*Knight* v. *Williams* [1901] 1 Ch. 256) ; although, in practice, this is not insisted on.

Land held by several owners under a common title.—Generally, when land is held by several owners under a *common title*, he who can get possession of the deeds is entitled to keep them (*Foster* v. *Crabb* (1852), 12 C.B. 136). Accordingly, joint tenants have all an equal right to the custody of the deeds relating to the joint title, and one may justify the detention of the deeds against the other, but a court of equity will order the deeds in the hands of either to be produced for the other's inspection (*Wright* v. *Robotham* (1866), 33 Ch. D. 106). This rule also applies as between trustees. It was stated in *Re Sisson's Settlement* [1903] 1 Ch. 262 that there is no strict rule entitling one trustee to have the documents connected with the trust kept in a box which must not be in the physical possession of either trustee, but be placed in a bank in their joint names ; also, that there is no rule requiring title deeds and registered securities to be put in such a position that no trustee can even look at them without the concurrence of his co-trustee. Therefore, if the deeds of the trust happen to be in the possession of one trustee, the other trustee cannot (unless there are special circumstances) insist on such deeds being taken out of his possession and lodged with a bank in their joint names. See also *Re Jenkin's Contract* [1917] W.N. 49 ; *post*, pp. 660, 661.

Trustees may deposit deeds at bank, or with solicitors.—Trustees may now deposit any documents held by them relating to the trust, or to the trust property, with any banker or banking company or any other company whose business includes the undertaking of the safe custody of documents, and any sum payable in respect of such deposit is to be paid out of the income of the trust property (T.A. 1925, s. 21). Where it is necessary for the solicitors of the trust to be constantly referring to them, for instance, in connection with the development of a building estate, trustees would be justified in leaving the deeds with the solicitors for the trust (*Field* v. *Field* [1894] 1 Ch. 425).

Deeds not in proper custody.—If the deeds are not in the possession of the person who, the deeds show, ought to hold them, inquiry should be made by a purchaser as to the reason thereof, as the purchaser will be deemed to have notice of the facts which this inquiry would have disclosed. See *ante*, p. 164.

PART 2.   RIGHTS AS BETWEEN VENDOR AND PURCHASER

Documents handed over to a purchaser.—A purchaser is entitled to have *all* the deeds and documents, however ancient, in the possession or power of the vendor, and relating solely to the land, handed over to him on completion (*Parr* v. *Lovegrove* (1858), 4 Drew. 170 ; *Re Duthy and Jesson's Contract* [1898] 1 Ch. 419) ; and this is notwithstanding that the commencement of the title is limited by special condition. The documents should include " all documents produced for the purpose of verifying the abstract in proof of any fact stated therein ; such as certificates of baptism, marriage or burial, statutory declarations as to matters of pedigree or as to the identity of the property sold, or certificates of the result of an official search in the registers kept under the L.C.A. or otherwise " (Williams on Vendor and Purchaser, 4th ed., vol. 3, p. 695). Section 45 (4) of the L.P.A. 1925 referred to *ante*, p. 141, does not affect this right, and, therefore, the mere fact that obtaining the deeds for the purpose of handing them over on completion may cause the vendor trouble and expense is no answer to the purchaser (*Re Duthy and Jesson's Contract, ante*).

If the conveyance is executed under *a power of attorney* the purchaser is entitled, notwithstanding any stipulation to the contrary (except in the case of registered land), to have the original power or a copy thereof or of the material portions thereof delivered to him free of expense (L.P.A. 1925, s. 125 (2), as amended by the Law of Property (Amendment) Act, 1926, and the Powers of Attorney Act, 1971, s. 11 (3)).

Where the land purchased is leasehold and the lease contains a covenant by the lessee to build the house to the satisfaction of the lessor's surveyor, the certificate to this effect from the surveyor should be handed over to the purchaser on completion (*Re Moody and Yates' Contract* (1885), 30 Ch. D. 344). A purchaser is also entitled to require the vendor to hand him the *original certificate* under s. 11 of the F.A. 1894, that estate duty has been paid, when such estate duty would, if not paid, be a charge on the land (*Re Conlon and Faulkener's Contract* [1916] 1 Ir. R. 241), that is, if it has been registered under the L.C.A. 1972, s. 2 (5), Class D (i) ; but the purchaser would not be entitled to the *original accounts*, as those are in the nature of a voucher for the payment of duty.

It has been suggested that a planning permission, granted under the Town and Country Planning Acts, should be handed over on completion or included in an acknowledgment for production of deeds. It is not the practice to do this and it is not considered that a vendor is obliged to do so. A planning permission is not a document of title and its effect can be ascertained by the purchaser by inspecting the register of applications kept by the local authority. See Opinion No. 204 (*d*) in the *Law Society's Digest*, Fourth (Cumulative) Supplement, that a vendor is not obliged to supply a copy of a planning permission free of charge.

In the opinion of the Council of The Law Society a purchaser of a leasehold interest is entitled to custody of the licence to assign granted by the lessor pursuant to the lease (*Law Society's Digest*, Opinion No. 184). A licence to sub-let, however, should, in the opinion of the Council of The Law Society, be retained by the sub-lessor. The reason is that he may wish to assign his own interest, subject to the underlease, and so he may require to produce the licence to sub-let (Opinion No. 204 (*g*), *Law Society's Digest*, Second Supplement). A purchaser is entitled to custody of an order of the Charity Commissioners authorising sale (*Law Society's Digest*, Opinion No. 201).

Documents a vendor is entitled to retain.—It is provided by s. 45 (9) of the L.P.A. 1925 as follows :—

" 45.—(9) A vendor shall be entitled to retain documents of title where—

(*a*) he retains any part of the land to which the documents relate ; or

(*b*) the document consists of a trust instrument or other instrument creating a trust which is still subsisting, or an instrument relating to the appointment or discharge of a trustee of a subsisting trust.

(10)   *   *   *   *   *

Provided that this section shall apply subject to any stipulation or contrary intention expressed in the contract."

" Land " includes an easement (L.P.A. 1925, s. 205 (1) (x)) ; therefore deeds and documents relating to an easement can be required by the purchaser to be handed over, unless, of course, they also relate to land retained, when they come within para. (*a*), above. In *Re Lehmann and Walker's Contract* [1906] 2 Ch. 640, it was held that the vendor was entitled to retain documents showing the title to, and extinguishment by unity of possession of, an easement formerly appurtenant to the land sold, but over land retained by the vendor. It was held in *Re Williams and Newcastle's Contract* [1897] 2 Ch. 144 that under a provision replaced by s. 45 (9) (*a*) a vendor could only retain deeds relating to *land* retained by him, and as the deed in that case related to freehold land and life policies, and the vendor had sold the land, retaining the policies, the purchaser was entitled to the deed. It is arguable, however, that where a rentcharge is reserved on a sale of land the vendor is entitled to retain the documents on the ground that a rentcharge is included in the definition of " land " (L.P.A. 1925, s. 205 (1) (x) and (xxiii)). That this is a correct construction of the section would appear to follow from the decision in *Re Lehmann and Walker's Contract, ante* (compare *Solicitors' Journal*, vol. 106, p. 1059, where a contrary conclusion is reached, without considering that case ; also *Law Society's Digest*, Opinion No. 188, that a purchaser is entitled to the document in the absence of a local custom such as that in Manchester).

Where the last of the land comprised in a principal vesting deed is sold, it is doubtful whether the deed should be handed over, particularly if a subsidiary vesting deed has been executed pursuant to the S.L.A. 1925, s. 10 (1), as to which see *post*, p. 689.   If there has been a subsidiary vesting deed, or if further land may be purchased, a tenant for life would be well advised, on selling the last of the land comprised in the principal deed, to stipulate in the contract that he may retain that deed ; see further, *Law Times*, vol. 213, p. 148.

The vendor is not entitled to retain deeds merely because he has given an acknowledgment for production and undertaking for their safe custody. The reason is that a person who has given an acknowledgment for production of deeds, or an acknowledgment and undertaking for safe custody, is only liable thereunder so long as he has possession or control of the deeds (L.P.A. 1925, s. 64 (2), (9)).

Where the vendor is entitled to retain deeds he must give an acknowledgment of the right of the purchaser to production of such of the abstracted deeds as are necessary to show a good title (*Cooper* v. *Emery* (1844), 13 L.J. Ch. 275), except documents in public or official custody of which the purchaser can obtain copies (*ibid.*).   The practice (not settled by authority) is for persons selling as personal representatives, trustees or mortgagees to give an acknowledgment only and not an undertaking for safe custody.

Sale in lots.—Where the contract provides that the vendor shall hand over the common title deeds to the purchaser of the largest lot in amount, but is silent as to what is to take place if one lot is unsold, it would seem that s. 45 (9) (*a*) of the L.P.A. 1925, above, becomes excluded, and that the purchaser of the largest lot is entitled to the deeds (*Re Doherty* (1884), 15 L.R. Ir. 247).

As between different purchasers of lots, where all the lots have been sold, *in the absence of any condition* the deeds go to the purchaser whose aggregate purchase-money of land held under the same title amounts to the largest sum (*Griffiths* v. *Hatchard* (1854), 1 K. & J. 17).   If all the lots are not sold the vendor will, of course, retain the deeds.   But a *condition* that the purchaser of the largest lot, not mentioning " in value," shall have the title deeds, gives the deeds to the purchaser of the lot largest in *area*, not in value, and in preference to the purchaser of the largest aggregate area made up of several lots (*Griffiths* v. *Hatchard, ante ; Scott* v. *Jackman* (1855), 21 Beav. 110).

Indorsement of memorandum of sale of part.—The Council of The Law Society are of the opinion that on sale or mortgage of part of a property, the vendor or mortgagor retaining the documents of title, a memorandum giving short particulars of the transaction (accompanied, if necessary, by a plan), should be indorsed on the appropriate deed, i.e., normally the conveyance of the whole to the vendor or mortgagor (*Law Society's Digest*, Opinion No. 198).   A vendor's solicitor usually offers no objection to this being done, but it seems that a purchaser's solicitor cannot insist on its being done.   A statutory acknowledgment and undertaking is enforceable at law against all persons who have or may come into possession of the documents, whether they have or have not notice thereof, and therefore the old authorities on the point are not applicable. Before statutory acknowledgments came into being a purchaser might have had to rely on his equitable right to the production of the documents of title, and it was therefore then important when deeds were retained by the vendor to have a memorandum of the sale of the portion indorsed on the deeds retained, although a purchaser could not insist on its being done.

If the purchaser's solicitor wishes to make sure that he will have the right to insist on an indorsement he must insert a condition in the contract that such a memorandum shall be so indorsed. Even from the point of view of a vendor it is better to have such a memorandum indorsed, for it will always be a reminder that part of the land has been sold.

In the case of a mortgage of part of land, where the mortgagor retains the deeds, even assuming that the mortgagee has obtained an acknowledgment and undertaking from the mortgagor, and has seen that a memorandum of the mortgage has been endorsed on one of the material documents of title, it is also necessary to register the mortgage as a land charge under the L.C.A. 1972, s. 2 (4), Class C, unless the land is registered land.

Indorsement of restrictive covenants, etc.—Where a purchaser (not including a mortgagee or a lessee) does not get the deeds, he can ask the vendor to indorse or annex notice of any provision contained in the disposition to him restrictive of user of, or giving rights over, the land retained by the vendor, on one of the deeds (selected by the purchaser) retained by the vendor (L.P.A. 1925, s. 200 (1)). But it is expressly provided, by subs. (4) of the same section, that such an indorsement is not to affect the obligation to register a land charge in respect of—

(a) any restrictive covenant or agreement affecting freehold land ; or

(b) any estate contract ; or

(c) any equitable easement, liberty or privilege.

Indorsement on trust instrument of dealing with equitable interest.
—If, on a sale by a tenant for life or other person of his equitable interest in real or personal property, there are no trustees to whom notice of the transaction can be given, and also in the other cases referred to in the subsection given below, the purchaser may require a memorandum of the transaction to be indorsed on or annexed to the instrument creating the trust. This is provided for by s. 137 (4) of the L.P.A. 1925 :—

" 137.—(4) Where, as respects any dealing with an equitable interest in real or personal property—

(a) the trustees are not persons to whom a valid notice of the dealing can be given ; or

(b) there are no trustees to whom a notice can be given ; or

(c) for any other reason a valid notice cannot be served, or cannot be served without unreasonable cost or delay ;

a purchaser may at his own cost require that—

(i) a memorandum of the dealing be indorsed, written on or permanently annexed to the instrument creating the trust ;

(ii) the instrument be produced to him by the person having the possession or custody thereof to prove that a sufficient memorandum has been placed thereon or annexed thereto.

Such memorandum shall, as respects priorities, operate in like manner as if notice in writing of the dealing had been given to trustees duly qualified to receive the notice at the time when the memorandum is placed on or annexed to the instrument creating the trust."

In the case of settled land the " instrument " will be the trust instrument and not the vesting instrument, and in the case of a trust for sale, the instrument whereby the equitable interest is created ; and where the trust is created by statute or by operation of law the " instrument " will be the instrument under which the equitable interest is acquired or which is evidence of the devolution thereof (ibid., s. 137 (4), (5), (6)).

Lost or destroyed deeds.—The fact that the title deeds to property sold have been lost will not release the purchaser from the performance of his contract, and he can be compelled to complete if the loss be proved, and he is furnished in proper time with satisfactory secondary evidence as to the contents of the lost documents and (for example, by statutory declaration) as to their having been duly executed (Re Halifax Commercial Banking Co., Ltd. and Wood (1898), 79 L.T. 536).

Oral evidence of the execution and contents will be admitted, but the mere fact of a deed having been registered under the Yorkshire Registries Act was not evidence of its execution (Re Halifax Commercial Banking Co., Ltd. and Wood, ante). Secondary evidence may consist of a counterpart, a draft, or a copy, or an abstract proved to be correct. A recital may be good secondary evidence of the lost document when there has been long uninterrupted possession in accordance therewith (Moulton v. Edmonds (1859), 1 De G.F. & J. 246) ; also verified extracts from the books of the solicitors who prepared the document showing charges made for the preparation and execution of the document, where, after a considerable lapse of time, execution may be assumed (ibid.). Proof of title by evidence of possession is not admissible in such cases ; see ante, p. 147.

When a lost document has been proved to have been duly executed, it will be presumed to have been duly stamped in the absence of evidence to the contrary (Hart v. Hart (1841), 1 Hare 1 ; Marine Investment Co. v. Haviside (1872), L.R. 5 H.L. 624), although a contrary view was expressed (obiter) by Williams, L.J., in Re Halifax Commercial Banking Co., Ltd., and Wood, ante.

The same principles apply in the case of a destroyed instrument, for instance, one lost by fire. Cases may also happen where parties have deliberately destroyed a deed by tearing it up. It is stated in Norton on Deeds, 2nd ed., at p. 36 : " In Woodward v. Ashton (1676), 1 Vent. 296, the court said that a rent or other grant was not lost by the destruction of the deed, as a bond or chose in action was. The reporter adds, ' Quære, if the party himself cancels it,' but the answer is, it would make no difference." See also the cases referred to in Norton, op. cit., at pp. 36–38. In Hall v. Hall (1873), L.R. 8 Ch. 430, the court decreed the execution of the trusts of a voluntary settlement which the settlor had purposely burned. In Davidson v. Cooper (1843), 11 M. & W. 778, 800, Lord Abinger, C.B., said : " The moment after their execution, the deeds become valueless, so far as they relate to the passing of the estate, except as affording evidence of the fact that they were executed."

Right of purchaser of equitable interest to inspect deeds.—It is provided by s. 137 (9) of the L.P.A. 1925 that the liability of the estate owner of the legal estate affected to produce documents and furnish information to persons entitled to equitable interests therein is to correspond to the liability of a trustee for sale to produce documents and furnish information to persons entitled to equitable interests in the proceeds of sale of the land. The principle in equity is that in the absence of special circumstances any person who has any estate or interest in property is entitled to inspection of deeds (*Compton* v. *Grey* (1826), 1 Y. & J. 154, 158), and the same rule applies in favour of a person interested in proceeds of sale (*Re Cowin* (1886), 33 Ch. D. 179).

Where two parties are interested in a deed, no duplicate or counterpart thereof having been executed, it is thought that the holder of it is impliedly a trustee for the other party, and such holder may be ordered to produce it for the other's inspection.

PART 3.   ACKNOWLEDGMENT FOR PRODUCTION AND UNDERTAKING FOR SAFE CUSTODY

Acknowledgments and undertakings generally.—The L.P.A. 1925, s. 64 (re-enacting the Conveyancing Act, 1881, s. 9) provides :—

" 64.—(1) Where a person *retains possession* of documents, and *gives to another* an acknowledgment in writing of the right of that other to production of those documents, and to delivery of copies thereof . . . that acknowledgment shall have effect as in this section provided.

(2) An acknowledgment shall bind the documents to which it relates in the possession or under the control of the person who retains them, and in the possession or under the control of every other person having possession or control thereof from time to time, but shall bind each individual possessor or person as long only as he has possession or control thereof ; and every person so having possession or control from time to time shall be bound specifically to perform the obligations imposed under this section by an acknowledgment, unless prevented from so doing by fire or other inevitable accident."

"*retains possession.*"—An acknowledgment and undertaking must be given by the person *retaining* the deeds ; otherwise it will have no statutory effect. Consequently, when the property is in mortgage the mortgagee should give the acknowledgment, and the mortgagor vendor should give a covenant in the old form (for production *and* safe custody) to come into force when the deeds come into his possession on the payment off of the mortgage (*Re Pursell and Deakin* [1893] W.N. 152). An acknowledgment and undertaking by the mortgagor would have no operation. It has been suggested that the acknowledgment and undertaking (or acknowledgment alone) should contain words indicating that possession is retained. If this is not done a subsequent purchaser may feel obliged to inquire whether the deeds were retained by the person giving the acknowledgment ; in any case insertion of the words reminds the draftsman of the requirement.

"*gives to another.*"—An acknowledgment expressed to be in favour of the person giving it (for example in an assent by a personal representative in his own favour) is not given to " another " and so appears to be invalid (compare *Rye* v. *Rye* [1962] A.C. 496). There would seem to be no objection to an acknowledgment in favour of several persons of whom the grantor is one, but an acknowledgment by several persons in favour of one of themselves is probably invalid and an express covenant for production in the old form should be used. Suggestions have been made that these difficulties can be avoided by making acknowledgments in favour of " any successor in title " or an " estate owner for the time being " but the efficacy of these is doubtful. An acknowledgment *only* does not confer any right to damages for loss or destruction of, or injury to, the documents to which it relates, from whatever cause arising (L.P.A. 1925, s. 64 (6)).

The obligations imposed by an acknowledgment are to be performed at the request in writing of the person to whom it is given, or of any person, not being a lessee at a rent, having or claiming any estate, interest or right through or under that person, or otherwise becoming through or under that person interested in or affected by the terms of any document to which the acknowledgment relates (L.P.A. 1925, s. 64 (3)). As to the nature of those obligations, see *post*, p. 662.

An undertaking for safe custody, on the other hand, imposes on the person giving it and on every person having possession or control of the documents from time to time, but on each individual possessor or person as long only as he has possession or control thereof, an obligation to keep the documents safe, whole, uncancelled and undefaced, unless prevented from so doing by fire or other inevitable accident (L.P.A. 1925, s. 64 (9)). Any person claiming to be entitled to the benefit of such an undertaking may apply to the court to assess damages for any loss or destruction of, or injury to, the documents, and the court may direct an inquiry and order payment of the amount of damages by the person liable (*ibid.*, subs. (10)).

A purchaser can only ask for an acknowledgment, or an acknowledgment and undertaking, whichever he is entitled to, as to documents of title dated after the time fixed by law for the commencement of the title, in the case of an open contract, or by the contract when the time is fixed thereby (*Re Guest and Worth*, decided by Stirling, J., in chambers, on 20th May, 1889). An acknowledgment cannot be required of documents produced for the purpose of showing that they do not contain anything affecting the title.

The Council of The Law Society have expressed the opinion that the vendor of property sold subject to the reservation of a chief rent is entitled to insist upon the inclusion in the conveyance of an acknowledgment for production and undertaking for safe custody of the title deeds to the property (*Law Society's Digest*, Opinion No. 192). Although s. 64 (1) refers to a person who " retains " possession of a document, it is thought that a purchaser who acquires the document can give a valid statutory acknowledgment and undertaking ; see Opinion No. 204 (*a*) in Fourth (Cumulative) Supplement to the *Law Society's Digest*.

The Council are of opinion that certificates of search are not documents of title and so a purchaser cannot insist on their being included in any acknowledgment. Nevertheless, they advise that such inclusion is convenient practice and, no doubt, most vendors will agree if requested (*Law Society's Digest*, Opinion No. 90).

If a purchaser is entitled to an acknowledgment, etc., and the deeds are not in the vendor's possession, he (the purchaser) must obtain it from the person who has the custody of them (*Re Pursell and Deakin* [1893] W.N. 152).

Such acknowledgment, etc., as the purchaser can and shall require must be furnished at his own expense, but the vendor must bear the expense of perusal and execution on behalf of and by himself, and on behalf of and by necessary parties other than the purchaser (L.P.A. 1925, s. 45 (8), replacing Vendor and Purchaser Act, 1874, s. 2, r. 4, as modified by Conveyancing Act, 1881, s. 9 (8)).

Covenants and acknowledgments for production of deeds should be carefully examined, as they may give the purchaser notice of an incumbrance not abstracted.

The Council of The Law Society take the view that an acknowledgment for production of a mortgage in effect covers an indorsed receipt for which a separate acknowledgment is unnecessary (*Law Society's Digest*, Opinion No. 264).

Right of purchaser to acknowledgment and undertaking.—The primary rule is that the vendor must deliver to the purchaser all documents of title which are or should be in his possession and relate solely to the land conveyed; cf. *ante*, p. 653. Where, however, documents are not in the vendor's possession but he is entitled *at law* to the benefit of a covenant or statutory acknowledgment for their production, and the right to enforce such covenant or acknowledgment will pass to the purchaser (as will normally be the case, see *ante*, pp. 658 and 659), the purchaser must rely on the covenant or acknowledgment.

Although the authorities are conflicting, the better view appears to be that where the ownership of land held under one title is divided, and documents remain in the possession of owners of part, the owners of the remainder have an *equitable* right to production of the documents in proof of title, for instance, on sale or other disposition (*Barclay* v. *Raine* (1823), 1 Sim. & St. 449 ; *Fain* v. *Ayres* (1826), 4 L.J. (o.s.) Ch. 166 ; *Conveyancer N.S.*, vol. 13, p. 354 *et seq*.). Probably this expression of the rule is too limited ; it may well be that an equitable right exists if deeds were retained by a vendor who sold the whole of his land ; cf. *Solicitors' Journal*, vol. 98, p. 102. An equitable right to production of documents, like any other equity, would apparently be lost if the deeds should pass into the possession of a purchaser for value who has acquired a legal interest in them in good faith without notice of the right although in most cases it is probable that such a purchaser would have at least constructive notice of the equitable right from the deeds themselves as documents of title.

A purchaser appears to be entitled to the deeds or to a *legal* right to a covenant or to the benefit of an acknowledgment, if the vendor is able to obtain it. The *inability* of the vendor to furnish the purchaser with an acknowledgment, etc., is not an objection to title, in case the purchaser will, on completion, have an equitable right to the production of documents of title (L.P.A. 1925, s. 45 (7), replacing Vendor and Purchaser Act, 1874, s. 2, r. 3, as modified by Conveyancing Act, 1881, s. 9 (8)). The word " inability " implies that the vendor must procure a legal acknowledgment, if he can, and that it is only when he is unable to do so that the purchaser can rely on the Act. The point does not seem to have been considered in *Re Jenkin's Contract* [1917] W.N. 49. In *Re Jenkin's Contract* the title deeds common to two estates were held by solicitors on behalf of the owners for the time being. On a sale of one of the estates the purchaser was offered an undertaking by the solicitors, but insisted on the deeds being handed over. It was held by Neville, J., that the equitable right to the deeds possessed by the purchaser was an adequate protection, and that the purchaser's objection failed.

The decision in *Re Jenkin's Contract* is unsatisfactory as no reasons are given for it. In the present state of the authorities it appears that a vendor who is unable to hand over the deeds or to show that the purchaser will have the benefit of a legal covenant or acknowledgment for their production, will not be able, under an open contract, to require the purchaser to complete. In practice it will usually be difficult, if not impossible, for the vendor to show that the holder of the deeds is bound by any equitable obligation to produce them. Further, the authorities for the existence of such equitable obligations are so doubtful that it is thought the title could not be forced on the purchaser on the grounds discussed *ante*, p. 229. See the full discussion in the article in the *Solicitors' Journal* mentioned above where registration of title is suggested as a solution to a vendor's difficulty.

Undertakings by fiduciary vendors.—Trustees, personal representatives and mortgagees, when retaining deeds, usually give only an acknowledgment and not an undertaking; General Condition 11 (3) of The Law Society's Conditions of Sale, 1973 Revision, provides that this is all the purchaser may require. It is normally assumed that under an open contract a purchaser from a fiduciary owner is not entitled to an undertaking, but Mr. Richard C. Fitzgerald, writing in the *Solicitor* for February, 1947, at p. 28, gave very convincing reasons for a statement that " there is no rule of law exempting the fiduciary owner from giving an undertaking for safe custody and, in the absence of an express stipulation, it is thought that he could be compelled to give it." In Williams on Vendor and Purchaser, 4th ed., vol. I, p. 702, it is advised that trustees who sell as such should stipulate expressly that they will not be required to give an undertaking, and the opinion is expressed that a person who sells apparently as beneficial owner is bound to furnish a proper statutory undertaking. The opinion of the Council of The Law Society is that a tenant for life selling part of the settled land should give an acknowledgment only (*Law Society's Digest*, Opinion No. 191).

Probate and administration now included in acknowledgments.— Probates and letters of administration dated after 1925 should be included in statutory acknowledgments of documents on account of the indorsements thereon, made under the A.E.A. 1925, s. 36 (5), which will not be recorded at Somerset House. This has the effect of making them muniments of title on which a purchaser's title depends (*Re Miller and Pickersgill's Contract* [1931] 1 Ch. 511). " Whether a purchaser requires an acknowledgment in respect of [pre-1926] grants would seem to depend on when the grant was taken out and what subsequent dealings appear on the title between the date of the grant and 1926. Where the grant was taken out considerably before [1926] and it is clear that an assent was made and dealings in the property occurred before 1st January, 1926, then, as it is reasonably certain that no endorsements are on the grant and if there were any they would have no legal significance, a purchaser should not press for an acknowledgment in respect of such grant. The position is different in the case of grants taken out shortly before 1st January, 1936, where an assent or conveyance was made by personal representatives under the grant after that date. In that case . . . an acknowledgment should be obtained." (*Law Times*, vol. 230, p. 349). There is a difference of opinion as to whether an acknowledgment for production of probate or letters of administration should be given by personal representatives of a mortgagee in a statutory receipt for the mortgage money. On this occasion indorsements do not seem to have any importance and, consequently, the better opinion appears to be that an acknowledgment need not be given, the documents for this purpose being documents of record as they were before 1926. See the *Conveyancer*, vol. 16, p. 101. On a transfer of the mortgage, however, such an acknowledgment should be given (*Law Society's Digest*, Opinion No. 196).

Copying of deeds produced under acknowledgments.—Where a person (other than a mortgagor) is entitled to the benefit of an acknowledgment for the production of deeds, he cannot insist on making copies of the deeds himself (or, apparently, on making an abstract : *Law Society's Digest*, Opinion No. 80). Section 64 (4) of the L.P.A. 1925 provides that the obligation under an acknowledgment is to produce the documents at all reasonable times for the purpose of inspection by the person entitled to request production or by any person authorised by him in writing ; and an obligation " to deliver to the person entitled to request the same true copies of extracts, attested or unattested, of or from the documents or any of them " ; together with an obligation to produce the documents in court. By s. 64 (5), all costs of and incidental thereto are to be paid by the person making the request. See also *Ormerod, Grierson & Co.* v. *St. George's Ironworks, Ltd.* [1905] 1 Ch. 505.

On the other hand, it will be noted that the subsection defining the rights of a *mortgagor* in respect of copies, namely, s. 96 (1) of the L.P.A. 1925 (replacing s. 16 of the Conveyancing Act, 1881), *expressly* gives him the right to take copies. The words of the subsection are : " A mortgagor, as long as his right to redeem subsists, shall be entitled from time to time, at reasonable times, on his request, and at his own cost, and on payment of the mortgagee's costs and expenses in this behalf, to inspect *and make* copies or abstracts of or extracts from the documents of title relating to the mortgaged property in the custody or power of the mortgagee." The word " mortgagor," by the definition clause (s. 205 (1) (xvi)) of the L.P.A. 1925, includes any person from time to time deriving title under the original mortgagor or entitled to redeem a mortgage according to his estate, interest or right in the mortgaged property.

Acknowledgment and undertaking in registered conveyancing.— No clause of acknowledgment or undertaking is included in the prescribed forms of transfer of registered freehold or leasehold land (see L.R.R. 1925, Schedule, forms 19 and 32). However, if necessary, the variation of these forms to include such a clause would without doubt be permitted. But as a general rule this is *not* necessary ; in cases where the transferor is registered as proprietor with an absolute or good leasehold title, the past history of ownership has become irrelevant so that the inclusion of an acknowledgment or undertaking would be " mere verbiage " (Ruoff and Roper, Registered Conveyancing, 3rd ed., p. 354).

Two exceptions to this rule are recognised (*ibid.*). First, where the transferor has only a possessory title, an acknowledgment and undertaking will be necessary as to pre-registration documents as in unregistered conveyancing. Secondly, when part of the land comprised in a leasehold title is transferred, an acknowledgment and undertaking will be necessary in respect of the lease itself.

In addition to these two exceptions, three other cases have been suggested in which an acknowledgment and undertaking would be necessary or at least useful even in registered conveyancing (Potter, Registered Land Conveyancing, pp. 69–70). The first is if documents relating to overriding interests are retained. The second is if documents relating to interests referred to in the charges register are retained. And the third case suggested is in respect of the grant of representation where personal representatives of a deceased proprietor transfer without first themselves obtaining registration (i.e., under L.R.A. 1925, s. 37). In such a case the grant has to be lodged at H.M. Land Registry in order for the application for registration to be properly made (L.R.R. 1925, r. 170 (4)). It is thought that the better practice is to insist either on the deposit of the grant before completion or else on a solicitor's undertaking to make the deposit after completion.

CHAPTER TWENTY

SETTLED LAND

PART 1.   WHAT IS SETTLED LAND

The S.L.A. 1925, s. 2, provides that " *land* which is or is deemed to be the subject of a *settlement* is for the purposes of this Act settled land." As to the definition of " *land*," see *post*, p. 673. The definition of a *settlement* is to be found in the S.L.A. 1925, s. 1, which provides as follows :—

" 1.—(1) Any deed, *will*, agreement for a settlement or other agreement, Act of Parliament, or other instrument, *or any number of instruments*, whether made or passed before or after, or partly before and partly after, the commencement of this Act, under or by virtue of which instrument or instruments any land, after the commencement of this Act, stands for the time being—

(i) *limited in trust for any persons by way of succession ;* or

(ii) *limited in trust for any person in possession—*

(a) *for an entailed interest whether or not capable of being barred or defeated ;*

(b) *for an estate in fee simple or for a term of years absolute subject to an executory limitation, gift, or disposition over on failure of his issue or in any other event ;*

(c) *for a base or determinable fee or any corresponding interest in leasehold land ;*

(d) *being an infant, for an estate in fee simple or for a term of years absolute ;* or

(iii) *limited in trust for any person for an estate in fee simple or for a term of years absolute contingently on the happening of any event ;* or

(iv) [This paragraph was repealed by the Married Women (Restraint upon Anticipation) Act, 1949, Sched. 2. It formerly dealt with land held subject to a restraint ; see *post*, p. 670.]

(v) *charged, whether voluntarily or in consideration of marriage or by way of family arrangement, and whether immediately or after an interval, with the payment of any rent-charge for the life of any person, or any less period, or of any capital, annual, or periodical sums for the portions, advancement, maintenance, or otherwise for the benefit of any persons*, with or without any term of years for securing or raising the same ;

creates or is for the purposes of this Act a settlement and is in this Act referred to as a settlement, or as the settlement, as the case requires :

Provided that, where land is the subject of a compound settlement, references in this Act to the settlement shall be construed as meaning such compound settlement, unless the context otherwise requires. [See *post*, p. 675, as to compound settlements.]

(2) Where an infant is beneficially entitled to land for an estate in fee simple or for a term of years absolute and by reason of an intestacy or otherwise there is no instrument under which the interest of the infant arises or is acquired, a settlement shall be deemed to have been made by the intestate, or by the person whose interest the infant has acquired. [See *post*, p. 670, as to the effect of this subsection.]

(3) An infant shall be deemed to be entitled in possession notwith-standing any subsisting right of dower (not assigned by metes and bounds) affecting the land, and such a right of dower shall be deemed to be an interest comprised in the subject of the settlement and coming to the dowress under or by virtue of the settlement.

Where dower has been assigned by metes and bounds, the letters of administration or probate granted in respect of the estate of the husband of the dowress shall be deemed a settlement made by the husband.

[See *post*, p. 670, as to the effect of this subsection.]

(4) An estate or interest not disposed of by a settlement and remaining in or reverting to the settlor, or any person deriving title under him, is for the purposes of this Act an estate or interest comprised in the subject of the settlement and coming to the settlor or such person under or by virtue of the settlement.   [See *post*, p. 672, as to the effect of this subsection.]

(5) Where—

    (a) a settlement creates an entailed interest which is incapable of being barred or defeated [see *ante*, p. 436], or a base or determinable fee, whether or not the reversion or right of reverter is in the Crown, or any corresponding interest in leasehold land ; or

    (b) the subject of a settlement is an entailed interest, or a base or determinable fee, whether or not the reversion or right of reverter is in the Crown, or any corresponding interest in leasehold land ;

the reversion or right of reverter upon the cesser of the interest so created or settled shall be deemed to be an interest comprised in the subject of the settlement, and limited by the settlement.

(6) Subsections (4) and (5) of this section bind the Crown.

(7) *This section does not apply to land held upon trust for sale."* [This subsection was introduced by the Law of Property (Amendment) Act, 1926, and is considered *post*, p. 673.]

Notes on S.L.A. 1925, s. 1, as to what constitutes a settlement.— Romer, J., in *Re Ogle's Settled Estates* [1927] 1 Ch. 229, 233, drew attention to the fact that the word " settlement " may mean either the documents creating a settlement or, more often, the state of affairs brought about by the documents. It follows from this that the unintentional creation of a strict settlement is possible (indeed, today, due to taxation considerations, the intentional creation of a strict settlement is comparatively rare). This being so it is important not to overlook the S.L.A. 1925 conveyancing machinery in such a case. Thus in *Re Duce and Boots Cash Chemist (Southern) Ltd.'s Contract* [1937] 1 Ch. 642 a testator devised land upon trust " to permit his daughter to use and occupy the dwelling-house . . . during her life or spinster-hood should she wish to do so." The decision dealt primarily with the meaning of the words " sufficient evidence " in s. 36 (7) of the A.E.A. 1925, but it was quite clear that a strict settlement of the land had been created so that title could only be made by complying with the S.L.A. 1925 machinery, which had patently not been done.

Again in *Bannister* v. *Bannister* [1948] 2 All E.R. 133 the defendant had offered to sell two cottages to the plaintiff, her brother-in-law, at a certain price if he would let her rent the one in which she was then living and the plaintiff had replied : " I do not want to take any rent, but will let you stay as long as you like rent-free." The Court of Appeal held (*per* Scott, L.J., at p. 137, giving the judgment of the court) that " the plaintiff holds [the cottage] in trust during the life of the defendant to permit the defendant to occupy the same so long as she may desire to do so and subject thereto in trust for the plaintiff," adding " a trust in this form has the effect of making the beneficiary a tenant for life within the meaning of the S.L.A., and, consequently, there is very little practical difference between such a trust and a trust for life *simpliciter.*"

This decision was followed recently by a majority of the Court of Appeal in *Binions* v. *Evans* [1972] 2 W.L.R. 729, where estate trustees had made a written agreement with an employee's widow (the defendant) that she could make her home in a particular cottage " as tenant at will . . . free of rent for the remainder of her life " ; subsequently the estate trustees had sold the cottage to the plaintiffs expressly subject to the defendant's tenancy, but shortly afterwards the plaintiffs had given the defendant notice to quit. All members of the Court of Appeal were agreed that the agreement had not created a tenancy at will since it contained inconsistent provisions. The majority (Megaw and Stephenson, L.JJ.) followed *Bannister* v. *Bannister, ante,* albeit without enthusiasm, and held that the agreement had created a trust, so that the defendant had an equitable life interest, and would be a tenant for life within the S.L.A. 1925. In the result, the plaintiffs were held, as purchasers with notice, to be bound by the defendant's interest. However, it is suggested that it would be more accurate to say that the plaintiffs simply had no title because the S.L.A. 1925 conveyancing machinery had not been operated ; i.e., their transaction would have been " paralysed " by s. 13 of the S.L.A. 1925 (*post*, p. 686).

In *Binions* v. *Evans, ante,* Lord Denning, M.R., rejected the idea that an informal strict settlement might have arisen (although his reasons appear quite inadequate : see Brian W. Harvey in the *Solicitors' Journal* (1973), vol. 117, p. 23) and took the view that the agreement had conferred a contractual licence upon the defendant and that the sale had constituted the plaintiffs constructive trustees for her. Compare *Inwards* v. *Baker* [1965] 2 Q.B. 29 where a father's expressed intention that a bungalow was to be his son's " home for his life or, at all events, his home as long as he wished it to remain his home " (see *per* Lord Denning, M.R., at p. 37) was held by the Court of Appeal to create merely a licence coupled with an equity (the strict settlement aspect was not adverted to). See also *Centaploy, Ltd.* v. *Matlodge, Ltd.* [1973] 2 All E.R. 720, where a periodic tenancy was found.

These differing approaches are confusing and cause too much uncertainty for practitioners' purposes, since the result may not always be the same. For example, *Binions* v. *Evans, ante,* involved unregistered land, but had the title been registered the defendant's interest under the S.L.A. 1925 would have required protection on the register as a minor interest (see L.R.A. 1925, s. 86 (2)), neither notice nor occupation alone sufficing to bind the plaintiffs. However, had the defendant been a licensee rather than a tenant for life then, the title being registered, it is conceivable that the mere fact of her actual occupation would have sufficed to bind the plaintiffs (i.e., as an overriding interest under the L.R.A. 1925, s. 70 (1) (*g*)).

Further reference may be made here to a number of other modern cases in which it is thought that the circumstances created a strict settlement, inadvertently, within s. 1 of the S.L.A. 1925, but in which this consequence and its conveyancing implications were overlooked or disregarded by the courts : *Kingswood Estate Co., Ltd.* v. *Anderson* [1963] 2 Q.B. 169 ; *National Provincial Bank* v. *Moore* (1967), 111 Sol. J. 357 ; *Wakeham* v. *Mackenzie* [1968]

1 W.L.R. 1175 ; *Hughes* v. *Griffin* [1969] 1 W.L.R. 23 ; *Ottaway* v. *Norman* [1972] 2 W.L.R. 50 ; *Morss* v. *Morss* [1972] 2 W.L.R. 908 ; and *Hussey* v. *Palmer* [1972] 1 W.L.R. 1286. This last cited case involved a family arrangement under which a mother-in-law was to be given a home for life in her son-in-law's house, to the improvement of which she had contributed. It is not thought that these circumstances created simple concurrent interests (which would subsist behind a trust for sale : L.P.A. 1925, ss. 34–36) ; nor is it thought that the mother-in-law should have been regarded as a tenant for life of a home she was merely sharing ; instead it is suggested that the son-in-law had the powers of a tenant for life by virtue of s. 20 (1) (ix) of the S.L.A. 1925 (*post*, p. 729).

It will be noted that the S.L.A. 1925, s. 1, applies to instruments made before or after, or partly before and partly after the commencement of the Act. For the transitional provisions applicable to settlements made before 1926, see *post*, p. 695.

"*will.*"—Land limited as so described becomes settled land as from the testator's death and so the relevant powers exist even prior to a vesting assent (*Re Pennant's Will Trusts* [1970] Ch. 75).

"*or any number of instruments.*"—These words refer to the proviso at the end of s. 1 (1). See *post*, p. 675.

Section 1 (1) (i) : "*limited in trust for any persons by way of succession.*" These words must not be confused with a limitation of land on trust for sale and to stand possessed of the net proceeds for persons in succession. Land held on trust for sale is *not* settled land (S.L.A. 1925, s. 1 (7)).

In *Re Phillimore's Estate* [1904] 2 Ch. 460, at the date of a proposed sale the only trusts which could be said to create interests in succession were trusts for payment of annuities, and it was held that this was sufficient to support the claim that a compound settlement existed consisting of the original settlement providing for the payment of the annuities and later instruments. In *Re Trafford's Settled Estates* [1915] 1 Ch. 9, *S*, upon the death of his father, became tenant in tail in possession of land. This land was charged with certain annuities, but no term of years was limited to secure them as in *Re Ailesbury* (*Marquis*) [1893] 2 Ch. 345, and there was no trust for payment of them as in *Re Phillimore's Estate, ante. S* barred the entail, and then resettled part of the land upon himself for life with remainders over. It was held that as regards the part of the land included in the resettlement, notwithstanding that there was no term limited to secure and no trust for payment of the annuities, there was a *succession of interests* within the words of the Settled Land Act, 1882, and there was therefore a compound settlement constituted by the will, the disentailing deed, and the resettlement ; and *S*, as tenant for life, could sell the land freed from the annuities.

Reference might also be made to *Re Mundy and Roper's Contract* [1899] 1 Ch. 275 ; *Re Wimborne* (*Lord*) *and Browne's Contract* [1904] 1 Ch. 537 ; and *Re Monckton's Settlement* [1917] 1 Ch. 224.

In *Re Higgs and May's Contract* [1927] 2 Ch. 249, a house was vested in trustees on trust to permit the minister for the time being of a church to reside therein and have the use and enjoyment thereof, and it was held by Romer, J., that the house was not limited to the ministers " by way of succession " within the meaning of this paragraph, but was limited in trust for the church, and came within s. 29 of the S.L.A. 1925 as a charitable trust, the trustees having all the powers conferred on a tenant for life by the S.L.A. 1925.

Section 1 (1) (ii) : *" limited in trust for any person in possession—*

(a) for an entailed interest whether or not capable of being barred or defeated ; "

Entailed interests are discussed fully *ante*, p. 428 *et seq.*, and entails not capable of being barred are mentioned *ante*, p. 436 *et seq.*

Section 1 (1) (ii) (b) : *" for an estate in fee simple or for a term of years absolute subject to an executory limitation, gift, or disposition over on failure of his issue or in any other event ; "*

A person entitled to such an estate in possession, being of full age, has the powers of a tenant for life (S.L.A. 1925, s. 20 (1) (ii) ; see *post*, p. 725). A limitation over on failure of issue attached to such an estate becomes void as soon as there is living any issue who has attained the age of eighteen years (L.P.A. 1925, s. 134 (1) ; see *post*, p. 725).

Section 1 (1) (ii) (c) : *" for a base or determinable fee or any corresponding interest in leasehold land ; "*

A determinable fee is defined in the S.L.A. 1925, s. 117 (1) (iv), as " a fee determinable whether by limitation or condition." This definition must be read with the exceptions contained in s. 7 (1) of the L.P.A. 1925, which provides that " A fee simple which, by virtue of the Lands Clauses Acts, the School Sites Acts, or any similar statute, is liable to be divested, is for the purposes of this Act a fee simple absolute, and remains liable to be divested as if this Act had not been passed, *and a fee simple subject to a legal or equitable right of entry or re-entry is for the purposes of this Act a fee simple absolute.*"

The words in italics were added by the Law of Property (Amendment) Act, 1926, the reason for the amendment being that doubts had been raised as to whether a fee simple subject to a right of entry or re-entry annexed to a rent-charge, became a determinable fee, and therefore an *equitable* interest, by reason of which the land would, by virtue of the S.L.A. 1925, s. 1 (1) (ii) (*c*), have become settled land. This would, of course, have affected large tracts of land, e.g., around Manchester, traditionally developed by means of rent-charges. But a right of entry on breach is implied by conditions subsequent other than failure to pay a perpetual rent-charge and may be expressly reserved (for example, on marriage or on failure to reside on the land). In such a case, provided that exercise of the right of entry is restricted within the perpetuity rule (see s. 4 (3) of the L.P.A. 1925 ; compare s. 11 of the Perpetuities and Accumulations Act, 1964), then the fee simple should strictly be absolute within s. 1 (1) of the L.P.A. 1925 by virtue of the 1926 amendment to s. 7 of the L.P.A. 1925 with the result that the S.L.A. 1925 rules would not apply. It seems difficult to argue otherwise despite the inclusion as settled land of " land . . . limited in trust for any person in possession . . . for an estate in fee simple . . . subject to an executory limitation, gift, or disposition over on failure of his issue *or in any other event* " (S.L.A. 1925, s. 1 (1) (ii) (*b*)). However, this result clearly was not intended by the 1926 amendment but, in the absence of a decision, it is impossible to be certain whether the amendments to s. 7 will or will not be confined by the courts to rights of entry annexed to rent-charges.

Section 1 (1) (ii) (d) : *" being an infant, for an estate in fee simple or for a term of years absolute ; "*

This paragraph should be read with s. 1 (2) (*ante*, p. 665), whereby, if by reason of an intestacy or otherwise there is no instrument under which the interest of the infant arises or is acquired, a settlement shall be deemed to have been made by the intestate, or by the person whose interest the infant has acquired. Section 1 (2) would appear to apply only to the case where the infant became beneficially entitled to land *before* 1926, because, where an infant becomes beneficially entitled under an intestacy after 1925, his interest is not in the land but only in the proceeds of sale thereof, and as the land, in the hands of the personal representatives, becomes subject to a trust for sale under s. 33 (1) of the A.E.A., *it is not settled land* (S.L.A. 1925, s. 1 (7)). Moreover, an infant would not become entitled to the proceeds until he became eighteen or married before he was eighteen (A.E.A. 1925, ss. 33, 46, 47, as amended by the Family Law Reform Act, 1969).

Further, by s. 1 (3) (*ante*, p. 666), an infant was deemed to be entitled in possession notwithstanding any subsisting right of dower (not assigned by metes and bounds) affecting the land, and such right of dower was deemed to be an interest comprised in the subject of the settlement, and coming to the dowress under or by virtue of the settlement. Where dower has been assigned by metes and bounds, the letters of administration or probate granted in respect of the estate of the husband of the dowress was deemed " a settlement " made by the husband.

So long as the widow lived notwithstanding that the infant may have attained eighteen, the land remained settled land, because s. 3 of the S.L.A. 1925 provides that land which has been subject to a settlement shall be deemed to remain settled land so long as any limitation or charge subsists under the settlement.

Dower has been abolished in regard to the freehold property of a person dying after 1925, except in the case of estates of certain persons of unsound mind. As to the dowress being tenant for life when the dower has been assigned to her by metes and bounds, see 15th Edition, p. 357.

If the intestacy arose before 1926 and a settlement was deemed to exist by virtue of the S.L.A. 1925, s. 1 (2), then, if the infant died without having been married, his interest was treated as an entailed interest and the notional settlement construed accordingly (A.E.A. 1925, s. 51 (3) ; *Re Taylor ; Pullan v. Taylor* [1931] 2 Ch. 242 ; see *ante*, p. 347).

Section 1 (1) (iii) : " *limited in trust for any person for an estate in fee simple or for a term of years absolute contingently on the happening of any event ;* "

As a person contingently entitled might never obtain any interest in the land, he naturally will not be deemed to be a person having the powers of a tenant for life under s. 20 of the S.L.A. 1925. Until the event happens, the person nominated in the settlement to exercise the powers of a tenant for life, or, if none, then the trustees of the settlement, will be the persons to exercise the powers of a tenant for life (S.L.A. 1925, s. 23). See *Re Bird* [1927] 1 Ch. 210.

Section 1 (1) (iv) : This paragraph formerly referred to land " limited to or in trust for a married woman of full age in possession for an estate in fee simple or a term of years absolute or any other interest with a restraint on anticipation." When restraints ceased to be effective the paragraph was repealed (Married Women (Restraint upon Anticipation) Act, 1949, Sched. 2). The document containing the restraint was formerly deemed to be the settlement, and the married woman if of full age had the powers of a tenant for life (S.L.A. 1925, s. 20 (1) (x)). No restraint on anticipation could, however, be imposed by an instrument executed on or after 1st January, 1936, except in pursuance of an obligation imposed before that date to attach a restraint (Law Reform (Married Women and Tortfeasors) Act, 1935, s. 2 (2), (3)). Further, all restraints ceased to have effect on 16th December, 1949 (1949

Act, s. 1 (1)). Where land was formerly held in fee simple or for a term of years absolute by a married woman subject to a restraint, the effect of the 1949 Act was normally to bring the settlement to an end. If a vesting instrument had been made in her favour, the trustees should have executed a deed of discharge. Where the interest of the married woman was something other than an estate in fee simple or term of years absolute, it was most likely that the land remained settled land notwithstanding the removal of the restraint (e.g., under s. 1 (1) (i), *ante*, p. 668, or under s. 1 (1) (v), *post*).

Section 1 (1) (v) : " *charged whether voluntarily or in consideration of marriage or by way of family arrangement . . . with the payment of any rent-charge for the life of any person, or any less period, or of any . . . sums for the . . . benefit of any persons.*"

This paragraph made a great change in the law ; it made land which was not settled before 1926, settled land after 1925. Before 1926 when a person bought land subject to an annuity or family charge it was usual for the vendor to give him an indemnity against the charge. But it was most inconvenient that this paragraph should have made the land subject to the charge settled land.

It seems that land may be " charged " with a payment, for instance, of an annuity, even though no security is created (*Re Bird* [1927] Ch. 210). Thus the devise " subject to payment of £*x* per annum to *A* " for life would appear to create a settlement.

In the vast majority of cases it is not necessary to overreach the charge, because the estate owner takes advantage of the power to sell subject to the charge which was given to him by the Law of Property (Amendment) Act, 1926, with the object of avoiding these difficulties. This Act provided that a sale could be made as if the land was not settled land, that is, subject to the charge and with an indemnity against it, as was done before 1926, and without the necessity of having a vesting deed ; see further, *post*, p. 730.

If, before 1926, land formerly subject to a settlement vested in a person absolutely, but subject to a jointure rent-charge, the land, on such absolute vesting, ceased to be settled land under the old Settled Land Acts (*Re Carnarvon's (Earl) Settled Estates* [1927] 1 Ch. 138 ; followed in *Re Alington (Lord) and London County Council's Contract* [1927] 2 Ch. 253) ; but if the land continued to be subject to the jointure rent-charge after 1925, it became again settled land under this paragraph (*Re Alington, ante*). On the cesser of the jointure rent-charge after 1925, the land would cease to be subject to the settlement (S.L.A. 1925, s. 3 ; *Re Draycott Settled Estate* [1928] Ch. 371).

On 31st December, 1925, land was vested in two persons as joint tenants in fee subject to a charge, and it was held that the land had not become subject to a trust for sale under s. 36 of the L.P.A. 1925, as settled land was excepted from that section. There was nothing in the context to confine the expression " settled land " to land settled before 1926, and therefore the land was settled land under the above paragraph (*Re Gaul and Houlston's Contract* [1928] Ch. 689). But land vested, before 1926, in tenants in common, subject to a charge, did not, after 1925, come within the paragraph and was not settled land. In this case the land vested in the tenants in common on trust for sale, subject to the charge, and they would, as such trustees for sale, be the persons to make title (*Re Ryder and Steadman's Contract* [1927] 2 Ch. 62 ; *Re Catchpool* [1928] Ch. 429).

Settled land which, on the death of the tenant for life, still remains subject to outstanding family charges, remains settled land, notwithstanding that by the terms of the settlement the land is on the death of the tenant for life to be held by the trustees on trust for sale. And the land remains settled land until the whole legal estate, the subject of the settlement, becomes comprised in the trust for sale (*Re Norton* [1929] 1 Ch. 84 ; see further, *post*, p. 672) ; and a vesting instrument will be necessary (S.L.A. 1925, s. 13). But if on the death of the tenant for life all family charges have been cleared off or come to an end, and the land becomes subject to a trust for sale, the land then ceases to be settled land, and no vesting instrument is necessary (*Re Bridgett and Hayes' Contract* [1928] Ch. 163). See further *post*, p. 708.

Land charged by will with a legacy or an annuity, if not devised on trust for sale, becomes settled land by virtue of this subsection even if it was not previously settled. Consequently, the executors should convey such land to the person who becomes tenant for life or statutory owner by a vesting instrument (S.L.A. 1925, ss. 6 (*b*) and 8 (4) (*b*)). If, by inadvertence, the land is conveyed to a devisee by an ordinary assent it would seem that the assent would pass the legal estate to such devisee (A.E.A. 1925, s. 2 (1)), but that he will be unable to dispose of the legal estate except in favour of a purchaser without notice (S.L.A. 1925, s. 13), or under the Law of Property (Amendment) Act, 1926, subject to the legacy or annuity (see *post*, p. 730). Probably no difficulty would arise, as a purchaser would not inquire as to the contents of the will and so would not have notice that a vesting assent should have been executed, and in any case on the death of the devisee his personal representative could make a good title (S.L.A. 1925, s. 13).

"*or otherwise for the benefit.*"—In *Re Bird* [1927] 1 Ch. 210, Clauson, J., had to consider whether certain annuities charged on land came within the paragraph, so as to make the land settled land. The learned judge said, at p. 215 : " It was suggested that . . . ' benefit ' there means something *ejusdem generis* with portions, advancement and maintenance, and accordingly that the word ' benefit ' must be construed in some restricted sense. I do not see any reason for construing it in a restricted sense ; at all events, I see no reason to doubt that these annuities given, as they are, for the benefit of certain persons named in the will, are sums for the benefit of persons, and I accordingly decide as regards the residuary estate which has been appropriated to meet the annuities and is charged with the annuities, that in regard to that land the will operates as a settlement within the Settled Land Act."

Perpetual annuities created voluntarily, where they are merely equitable and not legal rent-charges, are within the paragraph (*Re Austen* [1929] 2 Ch. 155, also decided by Clauson, J.). In the same case the learned judge seemed to be of the opinion that legal and equitable rent-charges were on the same footing, but as the point did not arise in the case he gave no decision on it.

Estates not disposed of by a settlement.—It is provided by the S.L.A. 1925, s. 1 (4) (*ante*, p. 666), that a right of reverter, whether in favour of the settlor or any person deriving title under him, will be deemed for the purposes of the Act to be an estate or interest coming to such settlor or person deriving title under him *under or by virtue of the settlement*.

The object of subs. (4) is to provide that if, e.g., a testator seised of Whiteacre in fee simple devises it to *A* for life, with either no devise of the remainder in fee, or a devise which lapses, yet the subject-matter of the settlement, and therefore the settled land (see s. 2), is the entire fee simple of Whiteacre, and the undisposed-of estate in remainder is an estate under the settlement, which, by virtue of s. 72 (2), will be overreached by an exercise of the tenant for life's powers.

Undivided share in land.—The definition of the word "land" in s. 117 (1) (i) of the S.L.A. 1925 ends with the words "and any estate or interest in land not being an undivided share in land." There cannot, therefore, be a settlement of an undivided share in land (*Re Bird* [1927] 1 Ch. 210 ; *Re Stamford and Warrington (No.* 2) [1927] 2 Ch. 217 ; see also *Re Stevens and Dunsby's Contract* [1928] W.N. 187). If an attempt should be made to create a settlement of an undivided share in land, it would operate as a settlement of a corresponding share of the net proceeds of sale and of the rents and profits until sale of the entirety of the land (L.P.A. 1925, s. 34 (4)).

Trusts for sale.—Section 1 of the S.L.A. 1925, defines what constitutes a settlement, and subs. (7) thereof provides that " This section does not apply to land *held upon trust for sale*." For a definition of these words, the S.L.A. 1925, s. 117 (1) (xxx) refers to the L.P.A. 1925, s. 205 (1) (xxix), which provides that " ' Trust for sale,' in relation to land, means an immediate binding trust for sale, whether or not exercisable at the request or with the consent of any person, and with or without a power at discretion to postpone the sale."

A trust for sale to take effect at a *future* date would obviously not be an immediate trust for sale. Therefore, land subject to a future trust for sale will not thereby cease to be settled land until the time for exercising the trust arrives. A trust for sale must be distinguished from a power of sale, and this is dealt with *post* p. 674.

Romer, J., in *Re Parker's Settled Estates* [1928] Ch. 247, came to the conclusion that land was not settled land where the whole legal estate which would be otherwise subject to a settlement was held upon trust for sale, and that the land in question in that case was settled land, because there was outstanding in certain trustees a legal estate in a term of years for securing portions. The same question came again before Romer, J., in *Re Norton* [1929] 1 Ch. 84. After quoting the S.L.A. 1925, s. 3 (which, as amended, provides that land not held upon trust for sale which has become subject to a settlement shall be deemed to remain settled land so long as any limitation, charge, or power of charging under the settlement subsists), he said, at p. 88 : " Up to [Lord Norton's] death he had had the legal estate in fee simple, . . . which was the subject of the settlement. On his death it vested in his personal representatives, his special representatives to whom probate had been granted, and was not vested in the trustees for sale. I must accordingly turn to s. 7 of the Act, . . . I need only refer to subs. (5), which is in these terms : ' If any person of full age becomes absolutely entitled to the settled land . . . free from all limitations, powers, and charges, taking effect under the settlement, he shall be entitled to require the . . . persons in whom the settled land is vested, to convey the land to him.' But the trustees for sale in this case have not become absolutely entitled to the settled land free from all charges taking effect under the settlement. There are certain equitable rent-charges which take effect in priority to the trust for sale. That being so, it appears to me that not only was the whole legal estate the subject-matter of the settlement not held upon trust for sale upon the death of [Lord Norton], but that the trustees for sale as such had not,

22

and have not now, a right to call for the legal estate. So far, I must, as it seems to me, come to the conclusion that on the death of [Lord Norton] the land did not cease to be settled land, . . . and is still settled land."

In *Re Hanson* [1928] Ch. 96, the testator directed his trustees to purchase a house as a residence for his wife until a certain event, when the house was to fall into the residue. By s. 32 of the L.P.A. 1925, where a settlement of land held on trust for sale contains a power to invest money in the purchase of land, such land shall, unless the settlement otherwise provides, be held by the trustees on trust for sale. It was held that the testator's intention that the house should be his wife's residence was inconsistent with an immediate trust for sale, and so s. 32 was excluded, and the land was settled land. Contrast *Re Herklot's Will Trusts* [1964] 1 W.L.R. 583 where a provision that a person interested for life should be permitted to reside in a house was not regarded as inconsistent with a binding trust for sale.

The difficulty usually occurs when the land is already settled land and the question to be determined is whether the settlement has come to an end and the land has become subject to a trust for sale contained in the instrument which created the settlement. In *Re Parker's Settled Estates, ante,* it was held that land was not settled land where the whole *legal* estate was held upon trust for sale, and this decision was followed in *Re Norton, ante.* In *Re Beaumont Settled Estates* [1937] 2 All E.R. 353, where a trust for sale was created by a person who held the legal estate as estate owner under the S.L.A. 1925, but subject to equitable interests under an old settlement, it was decided that the land remained settled land. Similarly, in *Re Sharpe's Deed of Release* [1939] Ch. 51, Morton, J., held that the trust for sale was not " binding " and that the land was settled land, because the trustees held the legal estate, first, on trust to pay two equitable rent-charges, and, secondly, subject thereto on trust for sale. Thus, the whole legal estate was not held on trust for sale even though the trustees for sale were themselves the trustees of the annuities, and the decision followed *Re Parker, ante,* and *Re Norton, ante.* The result appears to be that, where interests, *whether legal or equitable,* under a prior settlement exist at the time of the creation of a trust for sale, the trust for sale is not " binding " and the land remains settled.

Unusual circumstances, involving a trust for sale already in existence, arose in *Bacon* v. *Bacon* [1947] P. 151, where a husband and wife were joint tenants of a house which they held on trust for sale. A consent order was made after decree *nisi* providing that the house should be secured to the wife for her life. It was held that the order created a settlement and that a vesting deed should be executed in favour of the wife. The life interest of the wife took effect *in priority* to the trust for sale, and so the S.L.A. 1925, s. 1 (7), did not apply. See also *Smith* v. *Smith* [1945] 1 All E.R. 584.

Trust for sale distinguished from power of sale.—Where a settlement or will before 1926 contained a trust either to retain or sell land it was often difficult to determine whether there was created what was then termed " an imperative trust for sale " or a mere power of sale when the land would be settled. Indeed, it was said by Swinfen-Eady, L.J., in *Re Newbold* (1913), 110 L.T. 6, that what was in form a trust for sale might be only a discretionary power, and what was in form a power might really be an imperative trust. The whole document had to be considered before coming to a decision ; see further *Re Hotchkys* (1886), 32 Ch. D. 408 ; *Re White's*

Settlement [1930] 1 Ch. 179 ; *Re Crips* (1906), 95 L.T. 865 ; *Re Johnson* [1915] 1 Ch. 435.

Where the settlement or will came into operation after 1925, the difficulties of construction caused by the insertion in the form of trust of the words " either to retain or sell the land " have been set at rest by s. 25 (4) of the L.P.A. 1925, which provides that " Where a disposition or settlement coming into operation after the commencement of this Act contains a trust either to retain or sell land the same shall be construed as a trust to sell the land with power to postpone the sale."

As to the duty on a purchaser to ascertain that old powers of sale remain exercisable, see *Re Holmes and Cosmopolitan Press, Ltd.'s Contract* [1944] Ch. 53.

Effect of giving trustees of settled land a power of sale.—It is provided by s. 108 of the S.L.A. 1925 that, notwithstanding anything in a settlement, any power (not being merely a power of revocation or appointment) relating to the settled land thereby conferred on the trustees of the settlement exercisable for any purpose shall be exercisable by the tenant for life or statutory owner, as if it were an additional power conferred on the tenant for life within s. 109 of the Act, and not otherwise. And by s. 109 it is provided that nothing in the Act precludes a settlor from conferring on the tenant for life any powers additional to or larger than those conferred by the Act.

The giving to trustees of a power of sale operates to make them S.L.A. 1925 trustees (S.L.A. 1925, s. 30 ; see *post*, p. 713).

PART 2. COMPOUND, REFERENTIAL AND DERIVATIVE SETTLEMENTS

These classes are not exclusive of one another, but are grouped together for convenience. For instance, one of the documents which forms part of a compound settlement may itself be a settlement by reference.

A. COMPOUND SETTLEMENT

Nature of compound settlement.—Under s. 1 (1) of the S.L.A. 1925 (*ante*, p. 665) any deed, will or other instrument *or any number of instruments*, under which any land, after 1925, *stands for the time being limited or charged* as therein mentioned, creates a settlement, but there is a proviso which is as follows :—

" Provided that, where land is the subject of a compound settlement, references in this Act to the settlement shall be construed as meaning such compound settlement, *unless the context otherwise requires.*"

" *stands for the time being limited or charged.*"—A document which merely declares the trusts on which an annuity is to be held is not one of the documents constituting the compound settlement, where the annuity was created by an earlier document which did form part of the compound settlement (*Re Sharpe's Deed of Release* [1939] Ch. 51, at p. 72).

" *unless the context otherwise requires.*"—These words mean the context of the Act, and not the context of the settlement (*Re Cowley's Settled Estates* [1926] Ch. 725).

The practical importance of determining whether or not a compound settlement exists is twofold : first, additional powers conferred by any instrument are additional powers for the whole settlement (*Re Cowley's Settled Estates* [1926] Ch. 725), and secondly, there must be trustees appropriate for the purposes of the compound settlement since failure to obtain a necessary execution by them, e.g., of a vesting deed, may render a title defective (*Re Cayley and Evans' Contract* [1930] 2 Ch. 143 ; see further at pp. 716 and 683, *post*).

However, there is no definition of a compound settlement in the S.L.A. 1925, but in *Re Ogle's Settled Estates* [1927] 1 Ch. 229, at p. 232, Romer, J., said : " In some parts of the Act no doubt ' settlement ' means merely the document or documents creating the settlement : see, for example, ss. 1 (4), 47 and 64. But in general a settlement, for the purposes of the Act, is a state of affairs in relation to certain land brought about, or deemed to have been brought about, by one or more documents, the particular state of affairs being one or more of those specified in subss. (i) to (v) of s. 1 (1). A document may, therefore, create more than one settlement. If by means of one and the same document, Blackacre and Whiteacre stand limited in trust for *A* and his children in strict succession, and for *B* and his children in strict succession respectively, there are two settlements. In one case the settled land is Blackacre, and *A* is the tenant for life under ' the settlement ' ; in the other the settled land is Whiteacre, and the tenant for life under ' the settlement ' is *B*. If the court appoints trustees for the purposes of the Act of the one settlement, they do not thereby become trustees for the purposes of the other. And all this is, I conceive, equally true, even if, by the document, both Blackacre and Whiteacre have been subjected to one and the same jointure rent-charge ranking in priority to the respective limitations in favour of *A* and his children and *B* and his children. But now suppose that, *A* and *B* being dead, their eldest sons disentail and resettle the two properties. Each of the properties is now the subject-matter of a compound settlement . . . If, now, trustees are appointed of the settlement of Blackacre created by the original document, which settlement is still deemed to be in existence by reason of s. 3 of the new S.L.A. 1925, or is actually in existence because that document brought about a state of affairs in relation to Blackacre such as is mentioned in s. 1 (1) (v), those trustees will, by virtue of s. 31, become trustees for the purposes of the Act of the compound settlement of Blackacre. But they will not thereby become trustees of the compound settlement of Whiteacre. For, though s. 31 of the Act in terms refers to persons who are ' trustees . . . of an instrument which is a settlement, or is deemed to be a subsisting settlement,' it can only mean trustees of a settlement which is created by the instrument, or which is deemed to be subsisting by virtue of that instrument."

In *Re Adair ; Adair* v. *Treherne* (1927), 71 Sol. J. 844, Sir F. Adair devised certain estates upon the same trusts and limitations as those in the will of Sir R. A. Adair. It was held by Russell, J., that the will of Sir R. A. Adair was no part of the compound settlement, any more than " Wolstenholme " would be if the testator had settled the land by reference to a form in " Wolstenholme." This decision was followed in *Re Shelton's Settled Estate* [1928] W.N. 27.

In *Re Symons* [1927] 1 Ch. 344, it was held that separate compound settlements may arise from distinct appointments made under the same power. There were two compound settlements, one constituted by the original will and the appointing will, and the other by the original will and the appointed codicil. The learned judge also decided that as there existed estates settled by different settlements, though on the same limitations, the two estates might be treated as one aggregate estate under s. 91 of the S.L.A. 1925. The advantage of an estate being an aggregate estate is that capital arising from one of the estates may be applied, by the direction of the tenant for life or statutory owner, as if the same had arisen from either of the estates. See further below.

Where all the limitations and charges arising under an instrument forming part of a compound settlement come to an end, that instrument ceases to be part of the compound settlement, and so the settlement may cease to be compound (*Re Draycott Settled Estate* [1928] Ch. 371).

Assignment by tenant for life of his interest.—Under s. 104 (1) of the S.L.A. 1925 the powers of a tenant for life under the Act are not capable of assignment or release, but remain exercisable by the tenant for life after an assignment. The result is that the assignment by a tenant for life of his life interest (with certain exceptions) does not become one of the instruments constituting a compound settlement (*Re Earl of Carnarvon's Settled Estates* [1927] 1 Ch. 138). One exception is where the tenant for life assigns his interest to the person next entitled in remainder or reversion under the settlement with intent to extinguish his interest, as in that case the statutory powers of the tenant for life will cease to be exercisable by him, and will thenceforth become exercisable as if he were dead, that is, by the person next entitled (S.L.A. 1925, s. 105). In this case the assignment will become part of the compound settlement. Section 104 (11) of the S.L.A. 1925 contains another exception, for it is thereby expressly provided that an instrument whereby a tenant for life, in consideration of marriage or by way of family arrangement, not being a security for the payment of money advanced, makes an assignment of or creates a charge upon his estate or interest under the settlement, *is to be deemed one of the instruments* creating the settlement, and not an assignment for value for the purposes of that section.

Compound settlements on disentailment.—A very frequent example of a compound settlement is the case where a tenant in tail under an old settlement (provided that any limitations or charges thereunder remain subsisting) disentails and resettles the land, with the concurrence of the tenant for life. The compound settlement will consist of the old settlement, the disentailing deed and the resettlement (*Re Cowley's Settled Estates* [1926] Ch. 725 ; *Re Cradock's Settled Estates* [1926] Ch. 944).

B. REFERENTIAL SETTLEMENT

A settlement by reference to another settlement means a settlement of property upon the limitations and subject to the powers and provisions of an existing settlement with or without variations (S.L.A. 1925, s. 32 (3)).

Section 91 (1) of the S.L.A. 1925 provides, in effect, that where estates are settled by different settlements *upon the same limitations*, whether by reference or otherwise, the estates or any two or more of them may be treated as one aggregate estate, in which case the aggregate estate shall be the settled land for the purposes of the Act. Where the *trustees* for the purposes of the S.L.A. 1925 of the two or several settlements *are the same persons* they are the trustees of the settlements of the aggregate estate, and all or any part of the capital money arising from one of the estates may be applied by the direction of the tenant for life or statutory owner as if the same had arisen from any other of the estates (*ibid.*, s. 91 (1) (ii)). On the other hand, where the *trustees* of the settlements *are not the same persons* (*a*) any notice required to be given by the Act to the trustees of the settlement and their solicitor must be given to the trustees of every settlement which comprises any part of the land to which such notice relates and to the solicitor of such trustees ; (*b*) any capital money arising on any disposition of land comprised in more than one settlement must be apportioned between the trustees of the different settlements in such manner as the tenant for life or statutory owner may think fit ; and (*c*) capital money arising from the land comprised in one of the settlements may be paid by the trustees, by such direction as aforesaid, to the trustees of any of the other settlements, to be applied as if the same had arisen from land comprised in that other settlement (*ibid.*, s. 91 (1) (iii)). The section has effect (*a*) without prejudice to any appointment by the court of trustees of the settlement of an aggregate estate, and (*b*) as if trustees so appointed and their successors were the trustees of each of the settlements constituting the settlement of the aggregate estate and there were no other trustees thereof (*ibid.*, s. 91 (3)).

"*upon the same limitations*" refers to the beneficial limitations. In *Re Symons* [1927] 1 Ch. 344, there were two compound settlements. The trustees of each settlement were the same, and the limitations were the same. A question arose as to the discharge of a sum of money affecting both settlements. Clauson, J., held that the estates might be treated as one aggregate estate under this section. It was also held that, there being two compound settlements, there should be two vesting deeds, one relating to the land settled by each of the two compound settlements. Estates are deemed to be settled upon the same limitations, notwithstanding that any of them may be subject to incumbrances, charges, or powers of charging to which others of them may not be subject, but in any such case the powers relating to the application of capital money must not, unless the settlement under which the capital money is held otherwise provides, be exercised without an order of the court (S.L.A. 1925, s. 91 (2)).

See s. 32 of the S.L.A. 1925, *post*, p. 717, as to who will be the trustees of a referential settlement.

If there are two estates settled upon the same beneficial limitations, and the trustees of the settlements are not the same, it will be *necessary* to have two vesting deeds ; and even if the trustees are the same it is better to have separate vesting deeds. In fact, save in very exceptional cases, separate independent settlements should be prepared, and no attempt be made to make the settlement by reference to an existing settlement. Difficulties have occurred in the past, and will do so in the future, where a settlement is made by reference. Some of the old difficulties were put right by s. 91, but not all. The main object of this section was to facilitate the interchange of capital money between the different estates to their advantage, so far as that is possible *without seriously affecting beneficial interests*, but it is seldom that such a settlement is satisfactory.

If a testator directs that property is to be held "upon the same trusts and for the same intents and purposes" as other property already settled, the property of the deceased will be held on the trusts affecting the settled property *at the date of the testator's death* (*Re Shelton* [1945] Ch. 158). For a case where a gift by will amounted to an accretion to a sum mentioned in a marriage settlement and did not constitute a referential trust, see *Re Playfair* [1951] Ch. 4.

Settlements of personalty by reference to capital money.—By s. 130 of the L.P.A. 1925 an entailed interest can be created in personal property. The whole section should be referred to (*ante*, p. 431), but subs. (3) is particularly useful, because it enables leaseholds and heirlooms to be settled by the same document as that settling freeholds.

Section 78 (1) of the S.L.A. 1925 also contains provision enabling trusts of personalty to be declared by reference to capital money, as follows :—

" 78.—(1) Where money or securities or the proceeds of sale of any property is or are by any instrument . . . directed to be held on trusts declared by reference to capital money arising under this Act from land settled by that instrument or any other instrument, the money securities or proceeds shall be held on the like trusts as if the same had been or represented money which had actually arisen under this Act from the settled land.

This subsection operates without prejudice to the rights of any person claiming under a disposition for valuable consideration of any such money securities or proceeds, made before the commencement of this Act."

The last paragraph was added by the Law of Property (Amendment) Act, 1926, in order to make it clear that the beneficial interest of a purchaser acquired before 1926 should not be affected.

It was decided in *Re Walker ; Macintosh-Walker* v. *Walker* [1908] 2 Ch. 705, that personalty could only be made to devolve as if it had been realty by the creation of an imperative trust for its conversion into realty and settlement of such realty ; and that a mere declaration that personalty should devolve as realty could only be regarded in so far as it might in cases of ambiguity help the court to construe the instrument as creating an imperative trust for conversion. The S.L.A. 1925, s. 78 (1), was intended to meet this case.

Subsection (2) of s. 78 provides as follows :—

" (2) Where money or securities or the proceeds of sale of any property is or are by any instrument *coming into operation after the commencement of this Act* directed to be held on the same trusts as, or on trusts corresponding as nearly as may be with the limitations of land settled by that instrument or any other instrument, the money, securities or proceeds shall be held on the like trusts as if the same had been or represented capital money arising under this Act from the settled land."

It will be noticed that this subsection only applies as regards instruments coming into operation after 1925. To some extent it may be said that this subsection covers the ground of s. 130 (3) of the L.P.A. 1925, but the explanation is that subs. (3) of s. 130 only deals with entailed property, and this subsection deals with land settled but not entailed.

C. DERIVATIVE SETTLEMENT

If a person has a future interest under a settlement and executes a settlement of such equitable interest, the second settlement becomes a derivative settlement, and the provision as to equitable interests contained in s. 9 (1) (iv) of the S.L.A. 1925 applies. Under this provision, a settlement made after 1925 of an equitable interest in land which is *capable, when in possession, of subsisting at law* shall be deemed to be a trust instrument for the purposes of the S.L.A. 1925 *but only if and when the interest settled takes effect free from all equitable interests and powers* under every prior settlement (if any). So that until the settlement becomes a trust instrument no effective action can be taken thereunder, as a vesting deed cannot be executed. The beneficial owner can, of course, sell and assign his future interest, but he cannot make a title to the settled land until all interests and powers prior to it have come to an end. When this has happened, that is, as soon as the settlement becomes a trust instrument, a new vesting instrument should be executed in favour of the tenant for life under the derivative settlement, under s. 9 (2), vesting the legal estate in the settled land in him, if not already so vested, and the trustees of the original settlement will execute a deed of discharge as regards that land under s. 17 (1) of the S.L.A. 1925.

An equitable interest capable of subsisting at law means such an equitable interest as could validly subsist at law, if clothed with the legal estate (S.L.A. 1925, s. 117 (1) (xi)).

PART 3. CREATION OF SETTLEMENTS

Custody and marking of documents of title, see *ante*, p. 650.

Contract for the settlement of land.—It is provided by s. 11 (1) of the S.L.A. 1925 as follows :—

" 11.—(1) A contract made or other liability created or arising after the commencement of this Act for the settlement of land—

(i) by or on the part of an estate owner ; or

(ii) by a person entitled to—

(*a*) an equitable interest which is capable when in possession of subsisting at law ; or

(*b*) an entailed interest ; or

(*c*) a base or determinable fee or any corresponding interest in leasehold land ;

shall, but in cases under paragraph (ii) only if and when the interest of the person entitled takes effect free from all equitable interests and powers under every prior settlement, if any, be deemed an estate contract within the meaning of the Land Charges Act, 1925 [now 1972], and may be registered as a land charge accordingly, and effect shall be given thereto by a vesting deed and a trust instrument in accordance with this Act."

It will seldom be necessary for a contract for a settlement to be registered as a land charge. It would, however, be necessary in the unusual event of a conveyance having been made of a *legal estate* in land to an infant or infants, beneficially, because such a conveyance would operate as an agreement for valuable consideration to execute a settlement by means of a principal vesting deed and a trust instrument in his or their favour, and in the meantime to hold the land in trust for him or them (S.L.A. 1925, s. 27 (1)). The document should be registered as an estate contract under the L.C.A. 1972, s. 2 (4), Class C (iv).

A. METHOD OF SETTLING LAND INTER VIVOS

Settlement by means of a vesting deed and a trust instrument.— The S.L.A. 1925, s. 4, provides as follows:—

" 4.—(1) Every *settlement of a legal estate* in land *inter vivos* shall, *save as in this Act otherwise provided*, be effected by two deeds, namely, a vesting deed and a trust instrument *and if effected in any other way shall not operate to transfer or create a legal estate.*"

"*settlement of a legal estate.*"—It will be noted that s. 4 (1) applies only to settlement of a *legal estate*. The settlement of equitable estates is dealt with by s. 9 (1) of the S.L.A. 1925. See *ante*, p. 679.

"*save as in this Act otherwise provided.*"—This refers to the provision in s. 29 of the S.L.A. 1925 as to charity lands, which are deemed to be settled; see *ante*, p. 271.

"*if effected in any other way shall not operate to transfer or create a legal estate.*" —This statement should be read with S.L.A. 1925, s. 9 (1) (iii), which provides, in effect, that an instrument *inter vivos* intended to create a settlement of a legal estate in land which is executed after 1925 *and does not comply with the requirements of the Act* with respect to the method of effecting such a settlement, will, for the purposes of the Act, be deemed to be a trust instrument. This means that a settlement of a legal estate in land cannot be effected merely by a conveyance, and that if such a method should be attempted it will only operate as a trust instrument, and so before the legal estate can be dealt with, it will be necessary to execute a vesting deed and appoint S.L.A. 1925 trustees. Thus, if an estate owner of a fee simple purports to grant a legal life interest to *B* with legal remainder to *C* in fee simple, and no trustees are appointed, the document operates as a trust instrument, trustees would be appointed by the court and, if necessary, the court would also make a vesting order under s. 12.

B. THE VESTING INSTRUMENT

Definitions.—There are several kinds of vesting instruments. The definitions given in the S.L.A. 1925 are set out below :—

Section 117 (1). " (xxxi) In relation to settled land ' *vesting deed* ' or ' vesting order ' means the instrument whereby settled land is conveyed to or vested or declared to be vested in a tenant for life or statutory owner ; ' *vesting assent* ' means the instrument whereby a personal representative, after the death of a tenant for life or statutory owner, or the survivor of two or more tenants for life or statutory owners, vests settled land in a person entitled as tenant for life or statutory owner ; ' *vesting instrument* ' means a vesting deed, a vesting assent or, where the land affected remains settled land, a vesting order ; ' *principal vesting instrument* ' includes any vesting instrument other than a *subsidiary vesting deed*."

Section 10 (1). " Where after [1925] land is acquired with capital money arising under this Act or in exchange for settled land, or a rent-charge is reserved on a grant of settled land, the land shall be conveyed to, and the rent-charge shall by virtue of this Act become vested in, the tenant for life or statutory owner, *and such conveyance or grant is in this Act referred to as a subsidiary vesting deed :* "

Section 10 (2) states what statements and particulars a subsidiary vesting deed must contain, and a form of a subsidiary vesting deed is given in Sched. I to the S.L.A., being Form No. 4.

Vesting deed for giving effect to a settlement.—It has been noted that a settlement *inter vivos* of a legal estate must be effected by a vesting deed and a trust instrument (S.L.A. 1925, s. 4 (1)). Section 4 (2) provides as follows :—

" (2) By the vesting deed the land *shall be conveyed* to the tenant for life or statutory owner (*and if more than one as joint tenants*) for the legal estate the subject of the intended settlement :

22A

Provided that, where such legal estate is already vested in the tenant for life or statutory owner, it shall be sufficient, without any other conveyance, if the vesting deed declares that the land is vested in him for that estate."

" *shall be conveyed.*"—Any covenant or provision in a settlement or other instrument having the object of interfering with the right of a tenant for life " to require the settled land to be vested in him," will be void (S.L.A. 1925, s. 106 (1) (*a*), (*b*)). Section 14 (1) of the S.L.A. 1925 provides that " any vesting effected under the powers conferred by this Act in relation to settled land shall not operate as a breach of a covenant or condition against alienation or give rise to a forfeiture."

" *and if more than one as joint tenants.*"—It is only in the case where two or more persons *of full age* are entitled as joint tenants for life that they will constitute the tenant for life for the purposes of the S.L.A. 1925 (s. 19 (2)). If there are two or more persons entitled as joint tenants, but not all of full age, the one (or more) of full age will be tenant for life (*ibid.*, s. 19 (3)). The land will not be held by the joint tenants for life on trust for sale under s. 36 (1) of the L.P.A. 1925 (which provides that, where a legal estate is beneficially limited to any persons as joint tenants, the same shall be held on trust for sale), because it is expressly stated in the subsection that this provision shall not apply to settled land.

If the two or more persons take as *tenants in common* for life, the case will come within s. 36 of the S.L.A. 1925 as to which see *ante*, p. 309 *et seq.*

It will be noted later that the object of having two deeds is to keep the equitable interests arising under the settlement off the title to the legal estate, and so the *legal* estate is dealt with by the vesting deed. By the S.L.A. 1925, s. 9 (1), *post*, p. 694, certain settlements and instruments are *deemed* to be trust instruments and so provision is made by s. 9 (2) for the execution of a vesting deed in order that the legal estate may be dealt with. The section, apart from subs. (1), reads as follows :—

" 9.—(2) As soon as practicable after a settlement, or an *instrument which for the purposes of this Act is deemed to be a trust instrument*, takes effect as such, *the trustees of the settlement* may, and on the request of the tenant for life or statutory owner shall, *execute a principal vesting deed*, containing the proper statements and particulars, declaring that the legal estate in the settled land shall vest or is vested in the person or persons therein named, being the tenant for life or statutory owner, and including themselves if they are the statutory owners, and such deed shall, unless the legal estate is already so vested, operate to convey or vest the legal estate in the settled land to or in the person or persons aforesaid and, if more than one, as joint tenants.

(3) If there are no trustees of the settlement, then (in default of a person able and willing to appoint such trustees) an application under this Act shall be made to the court for the appointment of such trustees.

(4) The provisions of the last preceding section with reference to a conveyance shall apply, so far as they are applicable, to a principal vesting deed under this section." [Thus a vesting assent may take the place of a deed.]

Contents of vesting deeds.—Section 5 (1) of the S.L.A. 1925 provides that every vesting deed for giving effect to a settlement or for conveying settled land to a tenant for life or statutory owner during the subsistence of the settlement shall contain the following statements and particulars, namely :—

"(a) A description, either specific or general, of the settled land ;

(b) A statement that the settled land is vested in the person or persons to whom it is conveyed or in whom it is declared to be vested upon the trusts from time to time affecting the settled land ;

(c) The *names of the persons who are the trustees* of the settlement ;

(d) *Any additional or larger powers conferred by the trust instrument relating to the settled land* which by virtue of this Act operate and are *exercisable as if conferred by this Act on a tenant for life ;*

(e) The name of any person for the time being entitled under the trust instrument to appoint new trustees of the settlement."

The statements or particulars required by the section may be incorporated by reference to an existing vesting instrument or to a pre-1926 settlement ; see *post*, p. 685.

It is not necessary that the whole of the settled land dealt with by the settlement should be contained in one vesting deed. Indeed, as many separate vesting deeds can be executed as there are separate parcels dealt with by the settlement (*Re Clayton's Settled Estates* [1926] Ch. 279).

"*names of the persons who are the trustees.*"—If there is a compound settlement care must be taken to see that the vesting deed contains a correct statement as to who are the trustees of such compound settlement. If they should not be so correctly stated the vesting deed would not be effective. In *Re Cayley and Evans' Contract* [1930] 2 Ch. 143, the relevant settlement was the compound settlement consisting of the original settlement, two other documents and a resettlement and it was decided that the vesting deed was ineffective as it was framed upon the footing that the only relevant settlement was the resettlement, and was executed by the trustees of that settlement in their capacity as such and without any reference to any other settlement. But see *Re Curwen* [1931] 2 Ch. 341, in which the vesting deed was executed by the trustees of the compound settlement but contained a statement that such trustees were the trustees of the principal settlement and contained no reference to the fact that they were the trustees of the compound settlement, and it was held that the trustees were sufficiently described, and that the vesting deed was valid in respect of the land comprised in the compound settlement constituted by the various documents.

"*Any additional or larger powers conferred by the trust instrument relating to the settled land.*"—It is important to note the exact words as they differ from the words of s. 4 (3) as to what powers are to be set out or referred to in the trust instrument. The additional or larger powers given by the vesting deed are limited to those *relating to the land*. The additional or larger powers set out or referred to in the trust instrument relate not only to the land but to the capital moneys, the latter of which do not concern a purchaser. The vesting deed is the document which will be produced to a purchaser, and it must therefore only contain such extra powers as affect him ; in other words, as affect the land. The trust instrument will not be produced to him except in a few special cases (see *post*, p. 689). Additional powers that may be inserted are discussed *post*, p. 751.

"*exercisable as if conferred by this Act on a tenant for life.*"—It should be noted that any additional or larger powers relating to the settled land (not being merely powers of revocation or appointment) given by the settlor to the trustees of the settlement will operate as if they were given to the tenant for life ; and, if there is no tenant for life, to the statutory owner (S.L.A. 1925, ss. 108 and 109). The reason, of course, is that as the legal estate will be vested in the tenant for life or statutory owner he is the person to exercise the powers in connection with it. In the case of a compound settlement, the tenant for life or statutory owner can exercise any such additional or larger powers contained in any of the documents which together constitute the compound settlement (*Re Cowley's Settled Estates* [1926] Ch. 725) and, in the case of such powers being contained in an earlier settlement, notwithstanding that the land has been resettled, and in the resettlement the life estate given by the earlier settlement has not been expressly restored (*ibid.*).

Under s. 22 (2) of the S.L.A. 1925, where by a resettlement of settled land any estate or interest therein *is expressed to be limited* to any person in restoration or confirmation of his estate or interest under the prior settlement, then that person is entitled to the estate or interest so restored or confirmed as of his former estate or interest, and, *in addition to the powers exercisable by him in respect of his former estate or interest,* he is capable of exercising all such further powers as he could have exercised by virtue of the resettlement, if his estate or interest under the prior settlement had not been so restored or confirmed, but he had been entitled under the resettlement only ; and s. 118 and Sched. 4, para. 8, of the S.L.A. 1925, made the subsection retrospective.

It was argued in *Re Cowley's Settled Estates, ante,* that the words " is expressed to be limited " operated as a condition or limitation, and that consequently the tenant for life or statutory owner could not exercise such further powers *unless the life estate had been expressly restored,* but it was held by Astbury, J., that there was no context in s. 1 or ss. 108 and 109 of the S.L.A. 1925 to exclude a compound settlement, and Earl Cowley, being a statutory owner under s. 23 of the S.L.A. 1925, could exercise such further powers. See also *Re Cradock's Settled Estates* [1926] Ch. 944, where it was pointed out that although the words " prior settlement " do not refer to a compound settlement, yet the word " settlement," where the context admits, means a compound settlement, if there is one, by virtue of the proviso to s. 1 of the S.L.A. 1925.

If the settlement is a compound settlement existing before 1926, and includes a resettlement restoring the life estate of the tenant for life under a previous instrument, then under s. 22 (2) the vesting instrument should refer to any additional powers, relating to the land, conferred by the resettlement, as well as those conferred by the prior instrument.

A form of vesting deed is given in the S.L.A. 1925, Sched. 1 ; as to stamp duty, see *post,* p. 1168.

Errors in principal vesting deeds.—The S.L.A. 1925, s. 5 (3), provides that a principal vesting deed shall not be invalidated by reason only of any error in any of the statements or particulars required to be contained therein by the Act (as to which, see *ante,* p. 683). This subsection must be read with s. 110 (2) of the S.L.A. 1925 (as to which, see *post,* p. 689), which requires a purchaser to satisfy himself that a first vesting deed executed for the *purpose of giving effect to* (a) *a settlement subsisting at the commencement of the S.L.A.* 1925 ; (b) an instrument deemed to be a settlement ; (c) a settlement deemed to be made by any person ; or (d) an instrument which was intended to create a settlement but which does not comply with the requirements of the S.L.A. 1925, correctly states certain matters therein referred to.

Also notwithstanding the definite words of subs. (3) of s. 5, as to an error not having the effect of invalidating the vesting deed, see *Re Cayley and Evans' Contract* [1930] 2 Ch. 143, and *Re Curwen* [1931] 2 Ch. 341.

Incorporation of particulars by reference.—Section 5 (2) of the S.L.A. 1925 provides that the statements or particulars required by s. 5 (1) may be incorporated by reference to an existing vesting instrument, and, where there is a settlement subsisting at the commencement of the Act, by reference to that settlement and to any instrument whereby land has been conveyed to the uses or upon the trusts of that settlement, but not (save as last aforesaid) by reference to a trust instrument nor by reference to a disentailing deed. This means that it will not be proper to incorporate the statements or particulars required to be made in a vesting deed by reference to a trust instrument or a disentailing deed, *except in the one case of a principal vesting deed made to give effect to a settlement created before the commencement of the Act*. But in a *subsequent* vesting deed, any statement or particular may be incorporated by reference to a previous vesting instrument. An example will be found in the L.P.A. 1925, Sched. 6, Specimen No. 3 of Abstracts of Title.

Vesting assent where land settled by will.—Where a settlement is created by the will of an estate owner who dies after 1925, the will is for the purposes of the S.L.A. 1925 a trust instrument ; and the personal representatives of the testator must hold the settled land on trust, if and when required so to do, to convey it to the person who, under the will, or by virtue of the Act, is the tenant for life or statutory owner, and if more than one, as joint tenants (S.L.A. 1925, s. 6). And it is provided by s. 8 of the S.L.A. 1925 that a conveyance by personal representatives under s. 6 may be made by an assent in writing signed by them, which shall operate as a conveyance. Such an assent is a " vesting assent " which must contain the particulars mentioned in s. 5 (1), *ante*, p. 683 (S.L.A. 1925, s. 8 (4), (6)).

This obligation to convey is subject, of course, to the rights and powers of the personal representatives for the purposes of administration (*ibid.*, s. 8 (3)). An assent is not properly postponed merely because death duty remains to be paid. The representatives have only to be satisfied (e.g., where the tenant for life has directed payment out of capital money or has executed a mortgage for raising the money as and when an instalment becomes due) that the duty will be paid.

A form of vesting assent is given in the S.L.A. 1925, Sched. 1. The statutory covenants implied by a person being expressed to convey as personal representative will be implied in the assent in like manner as in a conveyance by deed (A.E.A. 1925, s. 36 (3)). If under seal, the vesting assent will require a 50p deed stamp, but no stamp will be necessary if under hand only. It is to be noted that a memorandum of the assent must be endorsed on the probate or grant of administration (A.E.A. 1925, s. 36 (5)).

If an assent is executed in favour of the tenant for life which does not contain the prescribed information (S.L.A. 1925, s. 5 (1), *ante*, p. 683) it is thought that it does not pass the legal estate. If, however, it does not contain anything to indicate that the land is settled a purchaser for money or money's worth of the legal estate from the tenant for life may be justified in relying on it as an ordinary assent pursuant to the protection in the A.E.A. 1925, s. 36 (7), *ante*, p. 416. It is unlikely that a purchaser could safely accept title in this way if the person in whose favour the assent was executed had contracted to sell as tenant for life. See also S.L.A. 1925, s. 13, below.

Vesting instrument necessary.—As to special cases in which a vesting instrument is not necessary, see below. A tenant for life or statutory owner under a settlement cannot sell, mortgage, lease or otherwise deal with the settled land until a vesting instrument has been executed in his favour by the trustees of the settlement for the purposes of the S.L.A. 1925. The familiar section which provides that dispositions of the legal estate in land shall have no effect until a vesting instrument has been executed is s. 13 of the S.L.A. 1925, which is set out below, as amended by the Law of Property (Amendment) Act, 1926 (it is sometimes referred to as the " paralysing " section).

" 13. Where a tenant for life or statutory owner has become entitled to have a principal vesting deed or a vesting assent executed in his favour, then until a vesting instrument is executed or made pursuant to this Act in respect of the settled land, any purported disposition thereof *inter vivos* by any person, other than a personal representative (not being a disposition which he has power to make in right of his equitable interests or powers under a trust instrument), shall not take effect except in favour of a purchaser of a legal estate *without notice of such tenant for life or statutory owner having become so entitled as aforesaid*, but, save as aforesaid, shall operate only as a contract for valuable consideration to carry out the transaction after the requisite vesting instrument has been executed or made, and a purchaser of a legal estate shall not be concerned with such disposition unless the contract is registered as a land charge.

Nothing in this section affects the creation or transfer of a legal estate by virtue of an order of the court or the Minister or other competent authority."

Section 13 only applies to " settled land," and therefore if the settlement should determine before a vesting instrument has been executed then no vesting instrument will be required and no discharge. For instance, if on the death of a tenant for life, in whom the legal estate had become vested as a result of the transitional provisions of the L.P.A. 1925, the trust should have come to an end, either by parties becoming absolutely and beneficially entitled, or in consequence of the land at that date having become subject to a trust for sale, the general executors of the tenant for life can dispose of the land without a vesting instrument, or they can assent to the legal estate in the land vesting in the parties entitled beneficially or in trust respectively, and then such parties can dispose of the land without the necessity for a vesting instrument (*Re Alefounder's Will Trusts* [1927] 1 Ch. 360). The provision in s. 18 (1) of the S.L.A. 1925, *post*, p. 687 (that so long as the trustees of the settlement have not been discharged any disposition by the tenant for life or statutory owner other than a disposition authorised by the Act shall be void) only applies where a vesting instrument has been executed (note the words in the subsection " Where land is the subject of a vesting instrument and the trustees of the settlement have not been discharged "). Section 17 (1) of the S.L.A. 1925 (set out in full, *post*, p. 706) which contains the provisions as to discharge, also only applies where a vesting instrument has been executed ; this appears from the words " in the last or only principal vesting instrument " in the subsection.

Vesting instrument unnecessary.—A vesting instrument is only required in respect of land, and not in respect of capital money (*Re Clayton's Settled Estates* [1926] Ch. 279) ; but it is provided by the proviso to s. 10 (1) of the S.L.A. 1925 that where there is no land in respect of which a principal vesting deed is capable of being executed, the first deed after 1925 by which any land is acquired shall be a principal vesting deed and shall be framed accordingly.

The execution of a vesting deed is necessary on the creation of a settlement *inter vivos* after 1925 if the legal estate is to be transferred. See *ante*, p. 680. But if the settlement is created by will there is no necessity to have a vesting deed or assent executed unless it is desired that the tenant for life shall deal with the *legal estate* in the land. For instance, in the common case where a testator has devised land to his wife for life, and on her death to his children, the legal estate in the land vests in his personal representatives and remains in them until they have by a written assent vested such legal estate in some other person or persons. Thus by avoiding giving any assent they will during the life of the tenant for life continue to be the persons to make title. And on the death of the tenant for life no representation to her estate will have to be taken out so far as the settled land is concerned, as the legal estate will never have vested in her. Thus, it is often convenient not to execute a vesting assent but it is important to bear in mind that there may be a risk of death of all personal representatives (without operation of the " chain " of representation, *ante*, p. 391) so that the expense of a grant *de bonis non* is incurred.

Where land has become settled land under s. 1 (1) (v) of the S.L.A. 1925, *ante*, p. 671, because it is charged with the payment of certain sums for portions or otherwise for the benefit of any persons and before a vesting deed has been executed the person in whom the legal estate is vested can get the person entitled to the benefit of the charge to join in the deed and release the land therefrom, a title can be made that way, and no vesting deed will be required. It would perhaps be better to have the release by a separate document, as by this means the owner, at the time of sale, will have both the legal and equitable estates vested in him, and the incumbrance can be kept off the title. But if the owner of the incumbrance will not release the charge, then under the provisions of the Law of Property (Amendment) Act, 1926 (*post*, p. 730), the vendor can convey the land subject to the incumbrance as if the land had not been settled land, and a vesting deed will be unnecessary.

It is also possible for the parties to end a settlement by agreement and thus make the execution of a vesting deed unnecessary. For instance, there is nothing in the Acts to prevent a tenant for life and remainderman arranging to terminate the settlement by a surrender of the life interest and a conveyance or assent to themselves on trust for sale, the net proceeds and the income to be held on trusts corresponding to those formerly affecting the land. This course saves not only the cost of a vesting instrument, but possibly also the cost of taking out representation to the estate of the tenant for life, for they would become joint tenants, and if the remainderman survived he could make a good title although he may have to appoint a new trustee (L.P.A. 1925, s. 36 (2), as amended by the Law of Property (Amendment) Act, 1926 ; but see *ante*, p. 300). As a rule administration and the making of title under a trust for sale are more simple than under a strict settlement. But where there is a surrender of a life interest to a remainderman in fee, provision would have to be made for payment of estate duty if the tenant for life died within seven years.

Dispositions authorised after vesting instrument.—The S.L.A. 1925, s. 18 (1), provides that *where land* is the subject of a vesting instrument and th trustees of the settlement have not been discharged under the Act, then *an* *disposition by the tenant for life* or statutory owner of the land, *other than a disposition authorised by* the Act or *any other statute*, or made in pursuance of any additional or larger powers mentioned in the vesting instrument, will be *void*, except for the purpose of conveying or creating such equitable interests as he has power, in right of his equitable interest and powers under the trust instrument, to convey or create.

There are three exceptions given in subs. (2), namely :—

(*a*) The right of a personal representative in whom the settled land may be vested to convey or deal with the land for the purposes of administration.

(*b*) The right of a person of full age who has become absolutely entitled (whether beneficially or as trustee for sale or personal representative or otherwise) to the settled land, free from all limitations, powers, and charges taking effect under the trust instrument, to require the land to be conveyed to him.

(*c*) The power of the tenant for life, statutory owner, or personal representative in whom the settled land is vested to transfer or create such legal estates, to take effect in priority to the settlement, as may be required for giving effect to any obligations imposed on him by statute, but where any capital money is raised or received in respect of the transaction the money shall be paid to or by the direction of the trustees of the settlement or in accordance with an order of the court.

" *where land.*"—Section 18 uses this general expression whilst s. 13 (*ante*, p. 686) is expressed to apply only to " settled land." Consequently, unlike s. 13, this section will continue to be applicable where there has been a vesting instrument and no discharge notwithstanding the determination of the settlement itself.

" *any disposition by the tenant for life.*"—Although s. 112 (2) provides that, unless the contrary appears, a " disposition " refers only to a disposition under the S.L.A. 1925, a contrary intention does appear in s. 18 (1) ; the subsection would not otherwise make sense (*Weston* v. *Henshaw* [1950] Ch. 510).

" *other than a disposition authorised by . . . any other statute.*"—The most important exception arises where an absolute owner subject to family charges sells subject to the charges under the Law of Property (Amendment) Act, 1926, s. 1. See *post*, p. 730.

" *void.*"—In some statutory provisions the word void has been held to mean voidable, so saving the interest of a *bona fide* purchaser for value without notice (e.g., in s. 42 of the Bankruptcy Act, 1914 ; see *Re Carter and Kenderdine's Contract* [1897] 1 Ch. 776 and *Re Hart* [1912] 3 K.B. 6). However " void " in s. 18 has been held to mean void not voidable by Danckwerts, J., in *Weston* v. *Henshaw* [1950] Ch. 510. In that case the property in question was sold to a son by his father who then bought it back and settled it by will. When the son became tenant for life, with a vesting deed, he charged the property purporting to act as beneficial owner and showing the first conveyance from his father. The next tenant for life succeeded in obtaining a declaration that the charge was void against him. See also *Re Liberty's Will Trusts* [1937] Ch. 176.

Subsidiary vesting deed.—Section 10 (1) of the S.L.A. 1925 provides as follows :—

"10.—(1) Where after [1925] land is acquired with capital money arising under this Act or in exchange for settled land, or a rent-charge is reserved on a grant of settled land, the land shall be conveyed to, and the rent-charge shall by virtue of this Act become vested in, the tenant for life or statutory owner, and such conveyance or grant is in this Act referred to as a subsidiary vesting deed : "

Section 10 (2) states what statements and particulars a subsidiary vesting deed must contain, and a form of a subsidiary vesting deed is given in Sched. 1 to the S.L.A. 1925.

No vesting instrument is required, of course, in the case of capital money, but it is provided by the proviso to s. 10 (1), above, that, where there is no land in respect of which a principal vesting deed is capable of being executed, the first deed after the commencement of the Act by which any land is acquired as aforesaid shall be a principal vesting deed and shall be framed accordingly.

If all land comprised in the principal vesting deed has been, or may be, sold it may be convenient to ignore s. 10 (1) and use a principal vesting deed on purchase of further land. This procedure may simplify the title and avoid questions of custody of the original principal vesting deed without doing any harm ; a subsequent purchaser of land brought into settlement will not know of any breach of s. 10 (1). It is wise, in such a case, to avoid any recitals, or other statements, that indicate the existence of the original settlement, because they may put a subsequent purchaser on inquiry as to why s. 10 (1) has been ignored.

C. THE TRUST INSTRUMENT

Definition.—A trust instrument means the instrument whereby the trusts of settled land are declared, and includes any two or more of such instruments (S.L.A. 1925, s. 117 (1) (xxxi)). See also *ibid.*, Sched. 2, para. 1 (1), which states that " A settlement subsisting at the commencement of this Act is, for the purposes of this Act, a trust instrument," and s. 9 of the S.L.A. 1925, at p. 694, which sets out a list of settlements or instruments which, for the purposes of the Act, are to be deemed trust instruments.

Purchaser's concern with contents of trust instrument.—As regards a settlement *inter vivos*, created after 1925, in accordance with the provisions of s. 4 of the S.L.A. 1925, the intention was that a purchaser should not be concerned with the trust instrument, or its contents, or whether or not it is stamped. The object of making it necessary for the creation of a settlement *inter vivos* that there should be two deeds, namely, a vesting deed and a trust instrument, was to enable the trusts to be kept off the title, by being dealt with by the trust instrument alone. However, as will be seen, the statutory provision devised to curtain off the trust instrument is not without its difficulties.

The S.L.A. 1925, s. 110 (2), provides that " a purchaser of a *legal estate* in *settled land* shall not, except as hereby expressly provided [as to which see next paragraph], be bound or entitled to call for the production of the trust instrument or any information concerning that instrument . . . and whether or not he has notice of its contents he shall, save as hereinafter provided, be bound and entitled if the last or only principal vesting instrument contains the *statements and particulars required by this Act* to assume that—

   (a) the person in whom the land is by the said instrument vested or declared to be vested is the tenant for life or statutory owner and has all the powers of a tenant for life under this Act, including such additional or larger powers, if any, as are therein mentioned ;

   (b) the persons by the said instrument stated to be the trustees of the settlement, or their successors appearing to be duly appointed, are the properly constituted trustees of the settlement ;

   (c) the statements and particulars required by this Act and contained (expressly or by reference) in the said instrument were correct at the date thereof ;

   (d) the statements contained in any deed executed in accordance with this Act declaring who are the trustees of the settlement for the purposes of this Act are correct ;

   (e) the statements contained in any deed of discharge, executed in accordance with this Act, are correct."

" *legal estate.*"—The first difficulty appears to be that s. 110 (2) only applies to " a purchaser of a legal estate " whereas unless s. 4 has been complied with a purchaser cannot acquire a legal estate since none will have passed to the tenant for life. It would seem to follow that the purchaser should satisfy himself as to the trust instrument before he can rely on the vesting instrument under s. 110 (2) which would be a self-defeating consequence.

" *settled land.*"—These words probably include land which has ceased to be settled. For instance if land ceases to be settled and a deed of discharge is executed in favour of an absolute owner a purchaser from that owner is protected by s. 110 (2) (e) above. But compare *ante*, p. 688, as to the different wording in ss. 13 and 18.

" *statements and particulars required by this Act.*"—See s. 5 (1), *ante*, p. 683. Paragraph (c) above protects a purchaser against inaccurate statements and particulars in the vesting instrument, but difficulty may arise in connection with *omissions*, since s. 110 (2) only affords protection " if the last or only principal vesting instrument contains the statements and particulars required by this Act." For example, if the wrong persons were named as trustees in the document purporting to be a vesting instrument, it is arguable that the document did not constitute a vesting instrument within s. 110 (2) because it did not contain the names of the persons who are the trustees of the settlement as required by s. 5 (1) (c) (and see *Re Cayley and Evans' Contract* [1930] 2 Ch. 143). Again, it would seem to follow that, contradictorily, the purchaser must first satisfy himself as to the trust instrument.

To obtain protection in any case, the purchaser must pay the capital money to the trustees of the settlement (S.L.A. 1925, s. 94 (1)) ; and to satisfy himself who are the trustees, he should look at the endorsements on the vesting instrument, and at any deed executed supplemental to the last or only principal vesting instrument, which has to be executed in compliance with s. 35 of the S.L.A. 1925 on the appointment of a new trustee and which contains a declaration as to who were the trustees at the date thereof. See further *post*, pp. 720–721.

Cases in which purchaser is concerned with contents of trust instruments.—These cases arise under the proviso to s. 110 (2), which is as follows :—

" Provided that, as regards the first vesting instrument executed for the purpose of giving effect to—

(a) a settlement subsisting at the commencement of this Act ; or

(b) an instrument which by virtue of this Act is deemed to be a settlement ; or

(c) a settlement which by virtue of this Act is deemed to have been made by any person after the commencement of this Act ; or

(d) an instrument *inter vivos* intended to create a settlement of a legal estate in land which is executed after the commencement of this Act and does not comply with the requirements of this Act with respect to the method of effecting such a settlement ;

a purchaser shall be concerned to see—

(i) that the land disposed of to him is comprised in such settlement or instrument ;

(ii) that the person in whom the settled land is by such vesting instrument vested, or declared to be vested, is the person in whom it ought to be vested as tenant for life or statutory owner ;

(iii) that the persons thereby stated to be the trustees of the settlement are the properly constituted trustees of the settlement."

However, the question which may be asked here is how a purchaser is to know that a vesting instrument falls within the proviso. So far as concerns a first vesting instrument for giving effect to a settlement within para. (a), there will normally be no difficulty since the fact of there being a pre-1926 settlement should normally be recited (see Form No. 1, Sched. 1 to S.L.A. 1925). But with regard to first vesting instruments for giving effect to settlements or instruments within paras. (b), (c) and (d) difficulties could arise. These three paragraphs in effect cross-refer to and are governed by s. 9 of the S.L.A. 1925 (see subs. (1) (i), (ii) and (iii), *post*, p. 694). Therefore, for each the vesting instrument is required to be executed by the trustees of the settlement and not by the person who has a legal estate (subs. (2) of s. 9, *ante*, p. 682). If this requirement has in fact been complied with, then there will be no difficulty since execution by the trustees will indicate to the purchaser that the proviso to s. 110 (2) is applicable, so that he is concerned with (i), (ii) and (iii), above. But if instead the estate owner has purported to execute the vesting instrument it would appear that, in the absence of any express statement to that effect, the purchaser will not know that the proviso to s. 110 (2) is applicable. If, in such circumstances, a purchaser in his ignorance relies on the vesting instrument alone he would appear to be without any protection for two reasons. On the one hand, he will not have made the investigations called for by the proviso to s. 110 (2), the application of which is not made to depend in any way on a purchaser having knowledge or notice of the vesting instrument having been executed for giving effect to a settlement or instrument within paras. (b), (c) or (d). And on the other hand, if s. 9 (2) has not been complied with, he will simply not be a purchaser of a legal estate within s. 110 (2) (see s. 4 (1) of the Act).

The inconvenient consequence of this reasoning (and see the other difficulties mentioned above) is that a purchaser, in order to ascertain whether the vesting instrument is one on which he can rely, must *in all cases* inspect the trust instrument. If this inspection reveals that the trust instrument is in the form required by s. 4 (3) below, but that there are other irregularities on the title, the position is not clear. The as yet unanswered problem arising is whether a person with knowledge or notice of irregularities can claim the protection against them afforded by s. 110 (2) to a purchaser when " purchaser " is defined as involving good faith (s. 117 (1) (xxi) of the Act).

However, it must be said that the difficulties which have been mentioned, caused by the drafting of s. 110 (2), although theoretically of importance, are not thought to be felt in practice.

It is arguable that this proviso to the S.L.A. 1925, s. 110 (2), has no application where the first vesting instrument is at least twenty years old, since the purchaser must take the statements in it (which will necessarily cover (i), (ii) and (iii) above ; see the S.L.A. 1925, s. 5) as sufficient evidence of their own truth (L.P.A. 1925, s. 45 (6) ; *ante*, p. 446). Equally it is suggested that the proviso does not apply to vesting assents since A.E.A. 1925, s. 36 (7), which provides that assents are to be taken as sufficient evidence of their own propriety (see *ante*, p. 416), contains no saving reference to the proviso.

It seems that a first vesting instrument executed after 1925 for the purposes of a settlement existing before 1926 may now be a good root of title under an open contract if that instrument vested the legal estate (where the instrument merely declared that the legal estate was already vested in the tenant for life there may be more doubt : see, *ante*, p. 119). The question arises whether a purchaser from the tenant for life or statutory owners can call for evidence that the land was comprised in the settlement, that the person in whom the land was vested or declared to be vested by the vesting instrument was entitled to have it vested in him and that the persons stated to be trustees were in fact trustees.

The L.P.A. 1925, s. 45 (1), *ante*, p. 120, provides that a purchaser shall not be entitled to production, or any abstract, of a document made before the root of title nor shall he require any information with respect to any such document or the title prior to the root of title. Consequently, it is suggested that, where the first vesting instrument is the root of title, neither a purchaser from the tenant for life or statutory owners, nor a subsequent purchaser can call for evidence of the accuracy of the statements in the vesting instrument. It may be argued (as in the *Law Journal*, vol. 107, p. 335) that the proviso to the S.L.A. 1925, s. 110 (2), preserves the right of a purchaser to inquire as to the matters mentioned and that there is a conflict between the L.P.A. 1925, s. 45 (1), and the S.L.A. 1925, s. 110 (2), on a sale by a tenant for life if the first vesting deed after 1925 is the root of title. It is suggested, however, that the L.P.A. 1925, s. 45 (1), provides the rule governing the root of title. The S.L.A. 1925, s. 110 (2), exempts a purchaser from inquiring as to the trust instrument and obliges him to assume that certain statements in the last vesting instrument are correct. The proviso to that section requires a purchaser to inquire about the matters mentioned above in the case of the first vesting instrument after 1925 giving effect to an existing settlement. It is submitted that this proviso must be read as an exception to the benefits conferred on a purchaser by s. 110 (2) and that the proviso does not impose an obligation to make inquiries if they would not have been made even if s. 110 had not been enacted. Where the purchaser is prevented by the L.P.A. 1925, s. 45 (1), from making inquiries prior to the first vesting deed, which is the root of title, he does not need to resort to the S.L.A. 1925, s. 110 (2), and so the proviso to that subsection is not relevant.

As to the application of the S.L.A. 1925, s. 110 (2), proviso, to derivative settlements, see A. M. Prichard at *Society of Public Teachers of Law Journal* 1969, p. 237.

Contents of a trust instrument.—These will be found set out in the S.L.A. 1925, s. 4 (3), which provides as follows :—

" (3) The trust instrument shall—

    (*a*) declare the trusts affecting the settled land ;

    (*b*) *appoint or constitute trustees of the settlement* ;

    (*c*) contain the power, if any, to appoint new trustees of the settlement ;

    (*d*) *set out, either expressly or by reference, any powers intended to be conferred by the settlement in extension of those conferred by this Act* ;

    (*e*) bear any *ad valorem* stamp duty which may be payable (whether by virtue of the vesting deed or otherwise) in respect of the settlement."

" *appoint or constitute trustees of the settlement.*"—It will be seen that the trustees are appointed by the trust instrument, and that in the vesting deed it is only necessary to state the names of the trustees of the settlement.

" *set out . . . any powers intended to be conferred by the settlement in extension of those conferred by this Act.*"—The additional powers *relating to the land* set out in the vesting deed need not be copied out again in the trust instrument, but can be included in the trust instrument by reference to the vesting deed. In addition, the trust instrument is the proper place to set out any matters relative to family charges and equitable interests, and as regards the application or investment of capital money. These latter matters will not be set out in the vesting deed for the reasons mentioned *ante*, p. 683.

" *bear any ad valorem stamp duty.*"—The *ad valorem* stamp duty will be impressed on the trust instrument. The vesting deed will only be stamped with a 50p deed stamp ; but, as we have seen, a purchaser is not concerned with the stamp duty on the trust instrument (S.L.A. 1925, s. 110 (2)).

The description of the land should not be given in the trust instrument, but by reference to the vesting deed. A form of trust instrument is given in the S.L.A. 1925, Sched. 1.

Settlement by will.—It is provided by s. 6 of the S.L.A. 1925 as follows :—

" 6. Where a settlement is created by the will of an estate owner who dies after the commencement of this Act—

    (*a*) the will is for the purposes of this Act a trust instrument ; and

    (*b*) the personal representatives of the testator shall hold the settled land on trust, if and when required so to do, to convey it to the person who, under the will, or by virtue of this Act, is the tenant for life or statutory owner, and, if more than one, as joint tenants."

In the first instance the legal estate in the land vests in the general personal representatives and, so long as their duties as such remain unperformed, they will be the persons to make title to the land under s. 39 of the A.E.A. 1925.

Where a testator devises or bequeaths his land so as to make it settled land, he can, if he likes, appoint special executors in regard to that land, provided that he is at the time solvent, and general executors as regards his other estate. If he does, there should be two grants, one to his general executors, save and except the settled land, and a grant *caeterorum* to the special executors. Such a procedure would be most unusual.

If the testator does not by his will appoint special executors, the land at his death will vest in his general executors (A.E.A. 1925, s. 1 (1)) ; and they will be the S.L.A. trustees of the settlement created by his will (S.L.A. 1925, s. 30 (3)), unless and until other S.L.A. trustees are appointed. Such general executors can make a good title to a purchaser in the ordinary course of administration (A.E.A. 1925, ss. 1, 2). If there is no occasion to do this, they should execute a vesting assent in favour of the tenant for life or statutory owner (S.L.A. 1925, s. 6 (*b*)), the will becoming the trust instrument (*ibid.*, s. 6 (*a*)).

This case must not be confused with the case provided for by ss. 22 and 23 of the A.E.A. 1925, namely, land vested in the testator which was settled *previously to his death and not by his will*. In the latter case he will be deemed to have appointed the trustees of the settlement special executors of his will in respect of the land which he held as tenant for life, except where the settlement comes to an end on his death, when the land formerly settled will vest in his general personal representatives (*Re Bridgett and Hayes' Contract* [1928] Ch. 163). See further *post*, p. 708 *et seq.*

A purchaser of a legal estate in settled land from personal representatives is entitled to assume when capital money is paid to them that they are acting under their statutory or other powers, and require the money for purposes of administration (S.L.A. 1925, s. 110 (3)).

The form of vesting assent to be executed by the personal representatives is considered *ante*, p. 685.

Instruments deemed to be trust instruments.—Certain instruments are deemed to be trust instruments as a result of the S.L.A. 1925, s. 9 (1), which is as follows :—

" 9.—(1) Each of the following settlements or instruments shall for the purposes of this Act be deemed to be a trust instrument, and any reference to a trust instrument contained in this Act shall apply thereto, namely :—

(i) An instrument executed, or, in case of a will, coming into operation, after [1925] which by virtue of this Act is deemed to be a settlement [for instance, an instrument creating charitable trusts—S.L.A. 1925, s. 29 ; see *ante*, p. 271] ;

(ii) A settlement which by virtue of this Act is deemed to have been made by any person after [1925] [for instance, where an infant became entitled before 1926 by reason of an intestacy ; see *ante*, p. 669] ;

(iii) An instrument *inter vivos* intended to create a settlement of a legal estate in land which is executed after [1925] and does not comply with the requirements of this Act with respect to the method of effecting such a settlement [as to which, see *ante*, p. 680 *et seq.*] ; and

(iv) A settlement made after [1925] (including a settlement by the will of a person who dies after such [date]) of any of the following interests—

(*a*) an equitable interest in land which is capable, when in possession of subsisting at law ; or

(*b*) an entailed interest ; or

(c) a base or determinable fee or any corresponding interest in leasehold land,

but only if and when the interest settled takes effect free from all equitable interests and powers under every prior settlement (if any) [for an example, see *ante*, p. 679]."

Endorsement of dealings with the equitable interest on the trust instrument.—Where there are S.L.A. 1925 trustees, and they are persons to whom a valid notice of the dealing can be given, notice to such trustees will be sufficient, but if they or one of them is not such a person or there are no trustees, then a memorandum of the dealing (at the cost of the purchaser) should be endorsed or permanently attached to the instrument creating the trust, otherwise any right of priority will be lost (L.P.A. 1925, s. 137 (4)) ; and the purchaser is entitled to require the instrument to be produced to him by the person having the custody thereof to satisfy him that a sufficient memorandum has been so endorsed or annexed (*ibid.*). See further *ante*, p. 656.

PART 4. TRANSITIONAL PROVISIONS

Transitional provisions were necessary to deal with the vesting of the legal estate on 1st January, 1926, to accord with the policy of the 1925 legislation. The following circumstances require separate explanation :—

(i) Where settled land was, on or immediately before 1st January, 1926, vested in personal representatives or became so vested before a principal vesting deed was executed ; see next section.

(ii) Where an infant was, at or immediately after 1st January, 1926, entitled in possession for an estate in fee simple or for a term of years absolute ; see *post*, p. 698.

(iii) Where the entirety of settled land was, immediately before 1926, held in undivided shares in possession under one and the same settlement ; see *post*, p. 699.

(iv) Where on 1st January, 1926, the legal estate in settled land was not vested in personal representatives, and did not otherwise fall within the last mentioned classes ; see *post*, p. 700.

The S.L.A. 1925, Sched. 2, para. 1 (2), provides that as soon as practicable after the commencement of the Act the S.L.A. 1925 trustees must at the request of the tenant for life or statutory owner execute a principal vesting deed declaring that the legal estate in the settled land shall vest or is vested in such tenant for life or statutory owner, and if more than one, as joint tenants. See further, p. 700 *et seq.* As to the necessity for such vesting deed before the land can be dealt with, see S.L.A. 1925, s. 13, *ante*, p. 686.

A. SETTLED LAND VESTED IN PERSONAL REPRESENTATIVES

The provisions as to such land contained in the S.L.A. 1925, Sched. 2, para. 2, are as follows (the matters in italics being the subjects of notes) :—

" 2.—(1) Where settled land *remains at the commencement of this Act vested in the personal representatives of a person* who dies before such commencement, *or becomes vested in personal representatives before a principal vesting deed* has been executed pursuant to the last preceding paragraph, the personal representatives shall hold the settled land on trust, if and when required so to do, to convey the same to the person who, under the trust instrument, or by virtue of this Act, is the tenant for life or statutory owner and, if more than one, as joint tenants.

(2) A conveyance under this paragraph shall be made at the cost of the trust estate and *may be made by an assent in writing* signed by the personal representatives which shall operate as a conveyance. No stamp duty is payable in respect of a vesting assent.

(3) The obligation to convey settled land imposed on the personal representatives by this paragraph is *subject* and without prejudice—

(a) *to their rights and powers for purposes of administration*, and

(b) to their being satisfied that provision has been or will be made for the payment of any unpaid death duties in respect of the land or any interest therein for which they are accountable, and any interest and costs in respect of such duties, or that they are otherwise effectually indemnified against such duties, interest and costs.

(4) A conveyance under this paragraph shall—

(a) if by deed, be a principal vesting deed, and

(b) if by an assent, be a vesting assent, which shall contain the like statements and particulars as are required by this Act in the case of a principal vesting deed.

(5) Nothing contained in this paragraph affects the rights of personal representatives to transfer or create such legal estates to take effect in priority to a conveyance under this paragraph as may be required for giving effect to the obligations imposed on them by statute.

(6) A conveyance by personal representatives under this paragraph, if made by deed, may contain a *reservation to themselves of a term of years absolute* in the land conveyed upon trusts *for indemnifying them against any unpaid death duties* in respect of the land conveyed or any interest therein, and any interest and costs in respect of such duties.

(7) Nothing contained in this paragraph affects any *right which a person entitled to an equitable charge for securing money actually raised*, and affecting the whole estate the subject of the settlement, *may have to require effect to be given thereto by a legal mortgage*, before the execution of a conveyance under this section."

"*remains . . . vested in the personal representatives of a person.*"—The opening words referred to the case where a testator who had died before 1926 had by his will settled land which remained vested in his personal representatives on 1st January, 1926, and not to settled land of which he was in his lifetime tenant for life. It is important to remember that before 1926 an assent might be implied (see *ante*, p. 409). If the testator died before 1925 it is likely that the tenant for life would have entered into possession before 1926 and so the land would have ceased to be vested in the personal representatives. In such a case the S.L.A. 1925, Sched. 2, para. 2, has no application and the legal estate in the land vested in the tenant for life under the L.P.A. 1925, Sched. 1, Pt. II, para. 6 (c), *post*, p. 700.

Although the word " remains " implies that the legal estate in the settled land must have been vested in the personal representatives *previously* to 1st January, 1926, the paragraph would, it is thought, cover the case where the legal estate in the settled land only vested in them *on* 1st January, 1926, by virtue of paras. 3, 5, and 6 (c) of Pt. II of Sched. 1 to the L.P.A. 1925.

Under these paragraphs any outstanding legal estate in settled land which personal representatives could require to be vested in them on 1st January, 1926, vested in them on that date without any conveyance. For instance, if a person died before 1926 having, by his will, settled land which was vested in a nominee holding on his behalf, his personal representatives would be entitled to require the legal estate to be vested in them within the meaning of the above paragraphs, and accordingly the legal estate in the settled land would have vested in them on 1st January, 1926.

" *or becomes vested in personal representatives before a principal vesting deed.*"—When considering whether the legal estate in the settled land was vested in personal representatives at the date indicated, it must be remembered that a grant of administration operates only as from the date of the grant, and does not relate back to the date of the death, as does a probate of a will of a deceased testator. See *ante*, p. 395. The effect might be that if a person died intestate shortly before 1926, and the grant of administration was not made until after 1925, the legal estate in the settled land would not, on 1st January, 1926, have been vested in personal representatives, but it might have vested in them " before a principal vesting deed has been executed."

The sub-paragraph also applies where, on 1st January, 1926, a settlement was subsisting or where, on that date, a settlement was created by the S.L.A. 1925 (s. 117 (1) (xxiv)), and " before a principal vesting deed has been executed pursuant to the last preceding paragraph " the tenant for life thereunder (in whom the legal estate had vested under para. 6 (*c*) of Pt. II of Sched. 1 to the L.P.A. 1925) had died wholly intestate and the land remained settled land. In that case the legal estate would have vested in the trustees of the settlement as his special personal representatives on the grant being made to them ; see *post*, p. 711. During the period between the death of the tenant for life and the grant there would have been no personal representatives in existence in whom the legal estate in the settled land had become vested. And during this period power was given to the S.L.A. 1925 trustees by para. 1 (2) of Sched. 2 to the S.L.A. 1925 (as to which, see *post*, p. 701) to execute a vesting deed. But directly the grant of administration was made, the legal estate vested (if the trustees had not already executed a vesting deed under para. 1 (2), above) in such special personal representatives, and the provisions of para. 2 of Sched. 2 applied, and not the provisions of para. 1 of that Schedule.

This principle applies only in the case of an intestacy. It would not apply if the tenant for life had made a will, as the grant of probate to the special personal representatives would date back to the date of the death of the tenant for life.

" *may be made by an assent in writing.*"—In practice an assent is the document invariably used. An executor can give an assent before probate, but an administrator can only give an assent after the grant of administration. For other points in connection with an assent, see *ante*, p. 409 *et seq.*

" *subject . . . to their rights and powers for purposes of administration.*"—It is important that personal representatives should have control of the property until all death duties have been discharged or satisfactory arrangements have been made for their payment, because by s. 16 (1) of the L.P.A. 1925 personal representatives are made accountable for all death duties which may become leviable or payable on the death of the deceased in respect of land (*including settled land*) which devolves on them by virtue of any statute or otherwise. See also the A.E.A. 1925, ss. 36 (10) and 43 (1), *ante*, p. 413.

"*a reservation . . . of a term of years absolute . . . for indemnifying them against any unpaid death duties.*"—This power appears to be given *in terrorem*, and should seldom, if ever, be used ; and see s. 36 (10) of the A.E.A. 1925 mentioned above.

"*right which a person entitled to an equitable charge for securing money actually raised . . . may have to require effect to be given thereto by a legal mortgage.*"—There is a similar provision in the S.L.A. 1925, s. 8 (7).

B. SETTLED LAND TO WHICH INFANT BENEFICIALLY ENTITLED

Settled land vested in personal representatives.—Where an infant was, at or immediately after 1st January, 1926, entitled in possession for an estate in fee simple or for a term of years absolute, the land on that date became settled land, although it might not have been settled land before that date (S.L.A. 1925, s. 1 (1) (ii) (*d*), (2), (3)). Where such settled land was at that date vested in personal representatives, it remained in them, and, subject to their rights and powers for purposes of administration, they held the land on trust to convey the same, when required to do so, to the S.L.A. 1925 trustees as statutory owners (S.L.A. 1925, Sched. 2, para. 2 (1) ; *ante*, p. 695 ; *ibid.*, Sched. 2, para. 3 (2)). Under s. 26 (2) of the S.L.A. 1925, however, the trustees had the option to require the personal representatives, when they had done with the land for purposes of administration, to execute a vesting instrument in their favour, or to continue to hold the settled land, and act for the benefit of the infant under their direction, without a vesting instrument being executed in their favour. In practice, the trustees allowed the personal representatives to carry on until the infant attained twenty-one, when such personal representatives executed a vesting assent in the infant's favour (S.L.A. 1925, s. 7 (5)). The personal representatives and the trustees were usually the same persons. Subsection (2) of s. 26 applies whether the infant became entitled before or after the commencement of the Act, and has effect during successive minorities until a person of full age becomes entitled to require the settled land to be vested in him. The same subsection also provides that a purchaser dealing with the personal representatives and paying the capital money, if any, to them, shall not be concerned to see that the money is paid to trustees of the settlement or into court, or to inquire whether the personal representatives are liable to give effect to any such directions, or whether any such directions have been given. See further as to the S.L.A. 1925, s. 26, *ante*, p. 339.

Settled land not vested in personal representatives.—This case comes within para. 3 (1) of Sched. 2 to the S.L.A. 1925 which provides that where at the commencement of the Act an infant was beneficially entitled to land in possession for an estate in fee simple or for a term of years absolute, or would, if of full age, have been tenant for life, or have had the powers of a tenant for life, the settled land should, by virtue of the S.L.A. 1925, *vest in the trustees* (*if any*) *of the settlement* upon such trusts as might be requisite for giving effect to the rights of the infant and other persons (if any) interested. If there were no trustees the settled land vested in the Public Trustee upon the trusts aforesaid pending the appointment of trustees (S.L.A. 1925,

Sched. 2, para. 3 (1)), and if there was no other person able and willing to appoint trustees, the parents or parent or guardian of the infant might by deed appoint trustees of the settlement in the place of the Public Trustee (*ibid.*, para. 3 (1) proviso). The Public Trustee would not be made a party to the deed of appointment, and the settled land could be divested out of him, and vested in the trustees appointed in his place by express or implied declaration under the T.A. 1925, s. 40 (1) ; but if the appointment was made by the court, the settled land would automatically vest by the S.L.A. 1925 in the trustees by the mere appointment. Finally, the proviso states that if land to which an infant was beneficially entitled in possession for an estate in fee simple or for a term of years absolute vested in the Public Trustee, but he did not become the trustee of the settlement, and trustees of the settlement were not appointed in his place, then, if and when the infant attained the age of twenty-one years, the land should vest in him.

Paragraph 3 also applies where there were two or more infants entitled *jointly* (S.L.A. 1925, Sched. 2, para. 3 (5)), and the word " infant " may be construed as also meaning " infants." Consequently, if there were two or more infants, the land would not vest in each as he attained full age, but would only vest when both or all of them attained full age, and then in the two or in all of them. The word " jointly " must be noted, because if the infants were entitled as tenants in common, the land would not be settled land, and para. 3 would not apply. See *ante*, p. 292, and the next section as to settled land held in undivided shares.

Paragraph 2 also applies where there were two or more infants who would, if all of them had been of full age, together have constituted the tenant for life or had the powers of a tenant for life (S.L.A. 1925, Sched. 2, para. 3 (6)).

But if an infant was entitled jointly with a person of full age, or was tenant for life with a person of full age, para. 3 did not apply (*ibid.*, para. 3 (5) and (6)). In the first case the legal estate vested in the person of full age as trustee on trust for sale, and if he wished to deal with the land another trustee had to be appointed by the parents or parent or guardian of the infant (L.P.A. 1925, Sched. 1, Pt. III, para. 2). In the second case the person of full age would alone be tenant for life (S.L.A. 1925, s. 19 (3)) ; and the legal estate would have vested in him under the L.P.A. 1925, Sched. 1, Pt. II, para. 6 (c).

C. SETTLED LAND HELD IN UNDIVIDED SHARES

Where *immediately before* 1926 the entirety of settled land (as defined by the Settled Land Acts, 1882 to 1890) was held in undivided shares in possession, under one and the same settlement, the land vested in the trustees (if any) of the settlement as joint tenants upon the statutory trusts, free from incumbrances affecting undivided shares, and from any interests, powers and charges subsisting under the settlement which had priority to the interests of the persons entitled to the undivided shares (L.P.A. 1925, Sched. 1, Pt. IV, para. 1 (3), as amended by the Law of Property (Amendment) Act, 1926). This provision is considered *ante*, p. 290 *et seq.* ; in particular it will be noted that the expression " settled land ", as used in it, means settled land under the Settled Land Acts, 1882 to 1890, and does not apply to land held absolutely subject to a family charge (*Re Ryder and Steadman's Contract* [1927] 2 Ch. 62 ; *ante*, p. 287), and that the provision does not apply if there was only one trustee (*Re Price ; Price* v. *Price* [1929] 2 Ch. 400 ; *ante*, p. 291).

There is an important exception to the application of the L.P.A. 1925, Sched. 1, Pt. IV, para. 1 (3), created by the Law of Property (Amendment)

Act, 1926, *where, after cesser of interests of tenants for life entitled in undivided shares, land is limited to devolve together* (L.P.A. 1925, Sched. 1, Pt. IV, para. 4, inserted by Law of Property (Amendment) Act, 1926, Sched.). It is set out and discussed *ante*, p. 294.

D. SETTLED LAND VESTING IN TENANT FOR LIFE OR STATUTORY OWNERS

General provisions as to vesting.—These provisions are contained in Pt. II of Sched. 1 to the L.P.A. 1925, para. 6 (*c*) of which provides that " where at the commencement of this Act or by virtue of any statute coming into operation at the same time the land is settled land, the legal estate affected shall vest in the tenant for life or statutory owner entitled under the Settled Land Act, 1925, to require a vesting deed to be executed in his favour, or in the personal representative, if any, in whom the land may be vested or the Public Trustee, as the case may require but subject to any mortgage term subsisting or created by this Act." As to vesting in personal representatives, see *ante*, p. 695 ; the Public Trustee, see *ante*, p. 698 ; and as to mortgage terms, see below.

It is also provided by para. 5 of Pt. II of Sched. 1 to the L.P.A. 1925 that for the purposes of that Part a tenant for life or statutory owner was deemed to be entitled to require to be vested in him any legal estate in settled land which he was, by the S.L.A. 1925, given power to convey. The legal estate that such a person is given power to convey is set out in the S.L.A. 1925, s. 72 ; see *post*, p. 752.

The result is that where the settled land (i) did not remain vested or become vested in personal representatives (see *ante*, p. 695) ; (ii) was not held in undivided shares in possession (see *ante*, p. 699) ; (iii) was not the beneficial property of an infant (see *ante*, p. 698), then it vested in the tenant or tenants for life of full age, and if more than one as joint tenants, or, if there was no tenant for life, in the statutory owner or owners. The expression " statutory owners " is defined in the S.L.A. 1925, s. 117 (1) (xxvi), as meaning the trustees of the settlement or other persons who, during a minority, or at any time when there is no tenant for life, have the powers of a tenant for life under that Act.

Transitional provisions as regards mortgages.—The settled land might, of course, have been in mortgage on 1st January, 1926. Paragraph 6 (*c*) of Pt. II of Sched. 1 to the L.P.A. 1925 specially mentioned the fact that the persons in whom the settled land vested on 1st January, 1926, took " subject to any mortgage term subsisting or created by this Act." The transitional provisions as to mortgages are to be found in the L.P.A. 1925, Sched. 1, Pt. II, para. 6 (*a*), Pt. VII, and Pt. VIII, and are outlined *post*, p. 1033 *et seq*. But the fact that there was a mortgage on the settled land or on the estate or interest of the tenant for life therein did not affect the powers of such tenant for life, for it is expressly provided by s. 19 (4) of the S.L.A. 1925 that a tenant for life will be deemed to be such notwithstanding that, under the settlement or otherwise, the settled land, or his estate or interest therein, is incumbered or charged in any manner or to any extent.

First vesting deed.—Such a deed became necessary as a result of para. 1 of Sched. 2 to the S.L.A. 1925, but before dealing with the requirements of this paragraph it must be noted that sub-para. (5) provides that the paragraph does not apply where, at the commencement of the Act, settled land was held in undivided shares in possession (see *ante*, p. 699), and that sub-para. (7) provides that the paragraph does not apply where settled land was vested in personal representatives at the commencement of the Act, or where settled land became vested in personal representatives before a principal vesting deed had been executed pursuant to that paragraph. These cases have also been dealt with ; see *ante*, p. 695 *et seq.*

For all practical purposes, therefore, this paragraph continues the transitional narrative, and deals with the cases not dealt with by the provisions already considered. The important sub-paragraphs are given below, in full, as amended by the Law of Property (Amendment) Act, 1926 (the words in italics being the subjects of notes made below) :—

" 1.—(1) *A settlement subsisting at the commencement of this Act* is, for the purposes of this Act, a trust instrument.

(2) As soon as practicable after the commencement of this Act, *the trustees* for the purposes of this Act of every settlement of land subsisting at the commencement of this Act (whether or not the settled land is already vested in them), may and on the request of the tenant for life or statutory owner, *shall* at the cost of the trust estate, *execute a principal vesting deed* (containing the proper statements and particulars) declaring that the legal estate in the settled land shall vest or is vested in the person or persons therein named (being the tenant for life or statutory owner, and including themselves if they are the statutory owners), and such deed shall (unless the legal estate is already so vested) *operate to convey or vest the legal estate* in the settled land to or in the person or persons aforesaid and, if more than one, as joint tenants."

(3) If there are no trustees of the settlement then (in default of a person able and willing to appoint such trustees), an application shall be made to the court by the tenant for life or statutory owner, or by any other person interested, for the appointment of such trustees.

(4) *If default is made in the execution of any such principal vesting deed, the provisions of this Act relating to vesting orders of settled land* shall apply in like manner as if the trustees of the settlement were persons in whom the settled land is wrongly vested."

" *a settlement subsisting at the commencement of this Act.*"—This includes a settlement created by virtue of the Act immediately on the commencement thereof, and a " settlement " is stated to include an instrument or instruments which, under the Act *or the Acts which it replaces*, is or are deemed to be or which together constitute a settlement, and a settlement which is deemed to have been made by any person or to be subsisting for the purposes of the Act (S.L.A. 1925, s. 117 (1) (xxiv)).

The expression " trust instrument " in sub-para. (1) means the instrument whereby the trusts of the settled land are declared, and includes any two or more such instruments and a settlement or instrument which is deemed to be a trust instrument (S.L.A. 1925, s. 117 (1) (xxxi)). See also the proviso to s. 1 of the S.L.A. 1925, which states that where land is the subject of a compound settlement, references in the Act to the settlement shall be construed as meaning such compound settlement, unless the context otherwise requires.

" *the trustees . . . shall . . . execute a principal vesting deed.*"—The scheme of the post-1925 conveyancing is that the trusts of the settlement and

the title to the land shall be kept separate, and that a purchaser of a legal
estate shall only be concerned with the latter. This scheme is made
possible by providing that a settlement shall consist of a trust deed or
deeds whereby " the trusts of the settled land are declared," and a principal
vesting deed, the purpose of which is to vest the legal estate in the tenant
for life, or, if there is no tenant for life, in the statutory owner. A purchaser
will not be concerned with the trust deed or the contents thereof. Only the
vesting deed will appear on the title. Now, in the case of a settlement created
before 1926 by deed, there being already a deed in existence, whereby the
trusts of the settled land would already have been declared, it was obviously
unnecessary to require that another deed should be executed, and therefore
it was provided by sub-para. (1) that such existing deed should be the trust
instrument for the purposes of the general scheme. The only provisions
remaining necessary to make the old settlement workable according to
the new conveyancing scheme were—

   (i) For converting estates and interests which on 31st December, 1925,
       were legal, but which after that date were not capable of taking
       effect as legal estates, into equitable interests. This was done by
       the L.P.A. 1925, Sched. 1, Pt. I, and terms of years subsisting under
       settlements created before 1926 were also converted into equitable
       interests by the S.L.A. 1925, Sched. 2, para. 1 (6), as amended by the
       Law of Property (Amendment) Act, 1926 ; see below.

   (ii) For the execution of a principal vesting deed vesting the legal estate
        in the tenant for life, or, if there was then no tenant for life, in the
        statutory owner. If the legal estate had already become vested in
        such tenant for life or statutory owner, the vesting deed stated the
        fact, so as to form a written record of such legal estate being so vested.
        As a matter of fact the legal estate would then (on 1st January, 1926)
        have vested in such tenant for life or statutory owner by virtue of
        the L.P.A. 1925, Sched. 1, Pt. II, paras. 3, 5 and 6 (c).

It will be noted that the vesting deed had to be executed by the trustees
for the purposes of the S.L.A. 1925, even though the settled land was not then
vested in them. It is therefore extremely important, when investigating
a title, to be satisfied that the persons who purported to be the trustees for
the S.L.A. 1925 were, in fact, at the time, such trustees. For if they were
not the vesting deed would not be valid (Re Cayley and Evans' Contract [1930]
2 Ch. 143). Further, this is one of the cases where it is the duty of the
purchaser to see that the proper parties have executed the vesting deed
(S.L.A. 1925, s. 110 (2), proviso, ante, p. 691). (Nevertheless, this investigation is now not often necessary as, in practice, a principal vesting deed can be
made a root of title ; see ante, p. 119.) The persons who would be the
trustees for the purposes of the S.L.A. 1925, will be found defined in the
following subsections of the S.L.A. 1925, set out at p. 713 et seq. : s. 30 (1),
(3) ; s. 31 (1), as amended by the Law of Property (Amendment) Act, 1926
(compound settlement) ; and s. 32 (1), (2) and (3) (referential settlement).
If there were no trustees coming within the description contained in these
provisions, or there should then have been only one trustee, then trustees,
or an additional trustee, for the purposes of the S.L.A. 1925, had first to be
appointed under the provisions for appointment of trustees contained in the
T.A. 1925, made applicable by s. 64 of the T.A. 1925. If there was no person
able and willing to appoint trustees under the T.A. then an application
had to be made to the court.

By these means settlements by deed executed before 1926 were placed in exactly the same position as settlements by deed executed after 1925.

A will which came into operation before 1926, and which created a settlement, is for the purposes of the Act a trust instrument (S.L.A. 1925, s. 1 (1), Sched. 2, para. 1 (1)) and, therefore, within the express provision of sub-para. (1) of the paragraph we are now considering. And, on the execution of a principal vesting deed, such settlement by will was brought into the same position as a will coming into operation after 1925.

Lastly, in the case where the Act itself created the settlement, sub-para. (1) also applies, for it is provided by the definition section, s. 117 (1) (xxiv), of the S.L.A. 1925 that " a settlement subsisting at the commencement of this Act " includes a settlement created by virtue of the Act immediately on the commencement thereof. The document connected with the circumstances which will be deemed to constitute a settlement will be the trust instrument, and, after the vesting deed has been executed, the transition in this case also becomes complete.

It was decided by Russell, J., in *Re Clayton's Settled Estates* [1926] Ch. 279, that in the case of a settlement existing at the commencement of the S.L.A. 1925, separate vesting deeds could be executed for each separate parcel of land of the settled land, on the ground that under s. 1 of the Interpretation Act, 1889, words in the singular include the plural unless a contrary intention appears, and there was nothing in the S.L.A. 1925 to show that a " principal vesting deed " in that sub-paragraph meant only one vesting deed. In *Re Ogle's Settled Estates* [1927] 1 Ch. 229, O was before 1926 owner in fee subject to a jointure rent-charge created by an old settlement. He had sold part of the property before 1926 and applied (after 1925) to the court for the appointment of trustees for the purposes of the S.L.A. 1925, because the land *had then, because of the rent-charge, become settled land.* The question arose as to whether the trustees, when appointed, would be trustees not only of the land retained by him, but of the other portions sold to the several purchasers. Romer, J., held that the part remaining vested in O was the subject of one settlement, and that each part vested in the purchasers was the subject of another settlement, and, consequently, that trustees appointed of the one settlement would not become trustees of the other settlements. See also *Re Symons* [1927] 1 Ch. 344.

" *operate to convey or vest the legal estate.*"—All the estates, interests and powers limited by the settlements which are not by statute (for instance, the L.P.A. 1925, Sched. 1, Pt. I, which converts into equitable interests legal estates which under the L.P.A. 1925, s. 1 (3), were not capable of taking effect as legal estates after 1925) otherwise converted into equitable interests or powers, as from the date of the principal vesting deed or the vesting order, took effect only in equity (S.L.A. 1925, Sched. 2, para. 1 (6)). This sub-paragraph does not apply, however, to any legal estate or interest vested in a mortgagee or other purchaser for money or money's worth (*ibid.*, as amended) ; as to mortgages, see *ante*, p. 700.

" *if default is made in the execution of any such principal vesting deed.*"— These words refer to a case in which the tenant for life or statutory owner had requested the trustees to execute a principal vesting deed and such trustees had refused or neglected to execute it, and had therefore made " default." They do not refer to a case in which the tenant for life or statutory owner had made default by not obtaining a principal vesting deed, for there is nothing in the S.L.A. 1925 to compel a tenant for life or statutory owner to take a vesting deed unless he wants to do so. It was (and is) only necessary to obtain a vesting deed when he required to deal with the land by way of sale, mortgage or lease. In some cases (see *post*, p. 686) it may never be required at all. If the settlement came to an end the land would cease to be settled land. Section 13 of the S.L.A. 1925 only makes it necessary to have a vesting deed before dealing with the land whilst it remains settled land. See *Re Alefounder's Will Trusts* [1927] 1 Ch. 360, referred to *ante*, p. 686.

If the tenant for life died without having taken a vesting deed, and the land remained settled land, the legal estate which had vested in him by the L.P.A. 1925, Sched. 1, Pt. II, paras. 3, 5 and 6 (*c*), passed to his special personal representatives under s. 22 of the A.E.A. 1925, and they would be the S.L.A. 1925 trustees. But if the land ceased to be settled land on his death, the legal estate passed to his general personal representatives. See also *post*, p. 708 *et seq.*

" *the provisions of this Act relating to vesting orders of settled land.*"—See S.L.A. 1925, ss. 12 and 113 (9) ; T.A. 1925, ss. 44 to 51.

Necessity for vesting deed.—Although under the transitional provisions of Sched. 1 to the L.P.A. 1925, Pt. II, paras. 3, 5 and 6 (*c*), the legal estate in the settled land has vested in the tenant for life or statutory owner, he cannot convey, mortgage or otherwise deal with the land until he has obtained the execution of a vesting deed by the trustees of the settlement in his favour, as directed by Sched. 2 to the S.L.A. 1925, para. 1 (2) (*ante*, p. 701). This is made clear by s. 13 of the S.L.A. 1925, as amended by the Law of Property (Amendment) Act, 1926, which will be found set out in full *ante*, p. 686. But until the tenant for life or statutory owner wants to deal with the land there is no necessity for him to have a vesting deed. The fact that he has not taken a vesting deed will not in any way interfere with his enjoyment of the land. Indeed, he may die without having taken a vesting deed, and if on his death the land has ceased to be settled land no vesting deed will be required at all. In that case the position would be that the legal estate which had vested in him under the L.P.A. 1925, as above-mentioned, would vest in his general personal representatives, and they would be the persons to make title so long as their rights and powers as personal representatives remained in existence. Section 13, above, makes it clear that it is not necessary for personal representatives to take a vesting deed.

Section 13 of the S.L.A. 1925, is dealt with *ante*, p. 686, in connection with settlements created since 1925, and as its provisions apply equally to a vesting deed for giving effect to a settlement subsisting on 1st January, 1926, reference should be made to that page for the notes on the section.

PART 5. DURATION OF SETTLEMENT AND DEVOLUTION OF SETTLED LAND

A. DURATION OF SETTLEMENT

General rule.—It is provided by the S.L.A. 1925, s. 3, as amended by the Law of Property (Amendment) Act, 1926, as follows :—

" 3. Land not held upon trust for sale which has been subject to a settlement shall be deemed for the purposes of this Act to remain and be settled land, and the settlement shall be deemed to be a subsisting settlement for the purposes of this Act so long as—

(a) any limitation, charge, or power of charging *under the settlement* subsists, or is capable of being exercised ; or

(b) the person who, if of full age, would be entitled as beneficial owner to have that land vested in him for a legal estate is an infant."

As to the meaning of " land," and as to land held on trust for sale, see *ante*, p. 673.

Section 3 of the S.L.A. 1925 is not confined to land which has become subject to a settlement since 1925. Land which had ceased to be settled land under the Settled Land Acts, 1882 to 1890, might have become settled land under the S.L.A. (*Re Ogle's Settled Estates* [1927] 1 Ch. 229 ; see *ante*, p. 671). In *Re Alington (Lord) and London County Council's Contract* [1927] 2 Ch. 253, on 1st January, 1926, when the S.L.A. 1925 came into operation, the vendor was tenant in fee simple by virtue of a disentailing deed executed before 1926, subject to a jointure rent-charge. Before the disentailing deed the land had been subject to a compound settlement. Russell, J., held, following *Re Carnarvon's Highclere Settled Estates* [1927] 1 Ch. 138, that the land was not settled land before 1926. The learned judge also said that he saw no reason for limiting s. 3 of the S.L.A. 1925, by reading it as only referring to land which since the Act had been subject to a settlement, or to land which had been continuously subject to a settlement, and that as the land had been subject to a compound settlement under which the charge was still subsisting, the compound settlement must be deemed to be still subsisting by virtue of s. 3 of the S.L.A. 1925.

" *under the settlement.*"—In *Re Draycott Settled Estate* [1928] Ch. 371, Tomlin, J., held that the words " under the settlement " in s. 3 (a) of the S.L.A. 1925, above, " must mean under the settlement deemed to be subsisting " ; hence land subject to a compound settlement, by reason of the subsistence of a jointure rent-charge under an earlier settlement, will, on the cesser of the jointure after 1925, cease to be subject to such compound settlement, s. 3 being a section to facilitate, and not to impede, dealings with the land.

Termination of settlement.—If a conveyance or assent does not state who are the trustees of the settlement, a purchaser is entitled to assume that the settlement has come to an end. For it is provided by s. 110 (5) of the S.L.A. 1925, that " If a conveyance of or an assent relating to land formerly subject to a vesting instrument does not state who are the trustees of the settlement for the purposes of this Act, a purchaser of a legal estate shall be bound and entitled to act on the assumption that the person in whom the land was thereby vested was entitled to the land free from all limitations, powers and charges taking effect under that settlement, absolutely and beneficially, or, if so expressed in the conveyance or assent, as personal representative, or trustee for sale or otherwise, and that every statement of fact in such conveyance or assent is correct." Although the Act says that a purchaser is *bound* to act on the assumption that, in the circumstances mentioned, the person in whom the land is vested is so entitled, the S.L.A. 1925, s. 18 (*ante*, p. 687), provides that, if the land has been subject to a vesting instrument, a disposition other than one authorised by that Act or some other statute, or pursuant to powers in the vesting instrument, will be void as regards the legal estate. Consequently it seems, as was well argued

23

by a writer in the *Law Society's Gazette*, vol. 56, pp. 231 and 256, that a purchaser may not safely rely on the assumption specified in s. 110 (5) if the conveyance is void under s. 18. His conclusion is that " the only safe course for any purchaser of land formerly subject to a vesting instrument is never to complete unless there is on the title either a deed of discharge under s. 17 by the S.L.A. 1925 trustees or a clean conveyance or assent under s. 110 (5) *by personal representatives.*"

On the termination of a settlement on the death of a tenant for life (there being no family charges on foot), all that is required is an absolute assent (not naming any S.L.A. 1925 trustees) by the general representatives of the deceased ; no release or discharge is required as respects the legal title.

As regards deeds of discharge it is important to give subs. (1) of s. 17 of the S.L.A. 1925 in full :—

" 17.—(1) *Where the estate owner* of any *settled land* holds the land free from all equitable interests and powers under a trust instrument, the persons who in the last or only principal vesting instrument or the last or only endorsement on or annex thereto are declared to be the trustees of the settlement or *the survivors* of them shall, save as hereinafter mentioned, be bound to execute, at the cost of the trust estate, a deed declaring that they are discharged from the trust so far as regards that land :

Provided that, if the trustees have notice of any derivative settlement, trust for sale or equitable charge affecting such land, they shall not execute a deed of discharge until—

(*a*) in the case of a derivative settlement or trust for sale, a vesting instrument or a conveyance has been executed or made for giving effect thereto ; and

(*b*) in the case of an equitable charge, they are satisfied that the charge is or will be secured by a legal mortgage, or is protected by registration as a land charge, or by deposit of the documents of title, or that the owner thereof consents to the execution of the deed of discharge.

Where the land is affected by a derivative settlement or trust for sale, the deed of discharge shall contain a statement that the land is settled land by virtue of such vesting instrument as aforesaid and the trust instrument therein referred to, or is held on trust for sale by virtue of such conveyance as aforesaid, as the case may require."

" *Where the estate owner.*"—Personal representatives do not come within the subsection, for they hold the land as personal representatives for the purposes of administration and not as settled land. On the settlement coming to an end they are under an obligation, imposed by the S.L.A. 1925, s. 7 (5) (as to which, see next paragraph), to execute an assent in favour of the person of full age absolutely entitled, without nominating S.L.A. 1925 trustees. The effect of such an assent is that a purchaser will be entitled to assume that the settlement has come to an end (S.L.A. 1925, s. 110 (5), *ante*, p. 705).

" *settled land.*"—This section only applies to land (not to capital money) where a vesting instrument has been made and the settlement terminates during the lifetime of the trustee estate owner. This means that where a settlement ends otherwise than on death a deed of discharge is necessary. For the case where the settlement terminates on the death of the estate owner, see *post*, p. 708.

" *the survivors.*"—A sole survivor may execute a deed of discharge as no question arises of receipt of capital money (S.L.A. 1925, s. 94 (1), (2)).

If the trustees refuse to execute the deed of discharge, or if for any reason the discharge cannot be effected without undue delay or expense, an application may be made to the court and the court may make such order as it may think fit (S.L.A. 1925, s. 17 (2)).

Conveyance of legal estate to person absolutely entitled.—This is dealt with by the S.L.A. 1925, s. 7 (5), as follows :—

" 7.—(5) If any person of full age becomes absolutely entitled to the settled land (whether beneficially, or as personal representative, or as trustee for sale, or otherwise) free from all limitations, powers, and charges taking effect under the settlement, he shall be entitled to require the trustees of the settlement, personal representatives, or other persons in whom the settled land is vested, to convey the land to him, and if more persons than one being of full age become so entitled to the settled land they shall be entitled to require such persons as aforesaid to convey the land to them as joint tenants."

It will be noted that this subsection applies where the settlement has come to an end, and so the conveyance will be an ordinary conveyance or assent and not a vesting instrument. An example is where land was settled because it was subject to family charges (S.L.A. 1925, s. 1 (1) (v), *ante*, p. 671) which have ceased or been satisfied.

Land ceasing to be settled on infant attaining full age.—It frequently happens that land has become settled land by reason of a beneficiary being an infant (S.L.A. 1925, s. 1 (1) (ii) (*d*)), and has ceased to be settled land on account of the infant having attained full age. Under the provisions of s. 26 of the S.L.A. 1925, it is the practice, where an infant is entitled and the settled land thereby created is vested in personal representatives, for the trustees of the settlement to allow such personal representatives to act under their direction during the minority, and when the infant attains full age the personal representatives will, under S.L.A. 1925, s. 7 (5), above, sign a simple assent passing the legal estate to the former infant. No deed of discharge under s. 17 (1) of the S.L.A. 1925 will in that case be necessary. See *ante*, p. 706.

Land ceasing to be settled by reason of purchase of remainder.—
A tenant for life *who has obtained a vesting deed* and has purchased the interest of the remainderman under the settlement will, when all family charges and other equitable interests have come to an end, be an estate owner of settled land free from all equitable interests and powers within the S.L.A. 1925, s. 17 (1). Therefore, although he would have become the absolute owner, he cannot pass the legal estate to a purchaser or mortgagee (other than under his S.L.A. 1925 powers) until the S.L.A. 1925 trustees have executed a discharge (S.L.A. 1925, s. 18 (1), (2) (*b*)). But if the tenant for life *had not obtained a vesting deed* (as, for instance, if the settlement had been made before 1926 and no principal vesting deed was executed pursuant to the S.L.A. 1925, Sched. 2, para. 1 (2)), then after the purchase of the remainder has been effected neither a vesting deed nor a deed of discharge would be necessary, as s. 17 (1) applies only where there has been a vesting deed executed ; see

the words " in the last or only principal vesting instrument " in the subsection, and also the words of s. 18 (1) : " Where land is the subject of a
vesting instrument and the trustees of the settlement have not been
discharged " (*Re Alefounder's Will Trusts* [1927] 1 Ch. 360).

B. DEVOLUTION OF LAND CEASING TO BE SETTLED ON
DEATH OF TENANT FOR LIFE

If, on the death of the tenant for life in whom the legal estate was vested,
the land *ceases* to be settled land, whether he left a will or died intestate,
no *special* grant need be made (*Re Bridgett* and *Hayes' Contract* [1928]
Ch. 163 ; *Re Bordass Estates* [1929] P. 107 ; see also r. 28 (1) of the Non-
Contentious Probate Rules, 1954). In this case the land, formerly settled
land, will be included in the *general* grant of probate or administration of
the estate of the tenant for life. It should be sworn in the oath that there
was settled land, but that the settlement came to an end upon the death of
the deceased. In *Re Bordass, ante,* a tenant for life died intestate without
known next of kin, and the settlement came to an end on her death. The
persons interested had been cited and had not appeared, and Hill, J., made
a general grant of administration to the *remainderman* under the settlement,
following the decision in *Re Bridgett and Hayes' Contract.* See also *Re Birch's
Estate* [1929] P. 164, where it was decided, in effect, that where a tenant for
life, on whose death the settlement comes to an end, dies intestate, and by
reason of his own estate being of no value or for other reasons, no one desires
to take a grant of representation, a grant may be made to the *remainderman*
under the settlement *without citation of the intestate's next of kin.*

On a grant being made to general executors or administrators the legal
estate in the land vests in them, and they can be required by any person
of full age absolutely entitled to the land, formerly settled land (whether
beneficially, or as personal representative, or as trustee for sale, or otherwise)
free from all limitations, powers, and charges taking effect under the
settlement, *to convey the land* to him, and if more persons than one being of
full age become so entitled to the land, to convey the land to them as joint
tenants (S.L.A. 1925, s. 7 (5)). The land having ceased to be settled land,
the document will be either an ordinary conveyance or an ordinary assent,
and not a vesting instrument. In practice, an assent is used.

But even where the settlement comes to an end on the death of the tenant
for life the court has power under the Judicature Act, 1925, s. 155, to make
a grant limited to the settled land to one person and a grant " save and
except " settled land to another. Thus in *In the Estate of Mortifee* [1948]
P. 274, where the tenant for life died intestate without known kin, a grant
of letters of administration excepting settled land was, for convenience,
made to the Treasury Solicitor and a grant limited to land previously settled
to the remainderman. See the further discussion in the *Solicitors' Journal,*
vol. 94, p. 60.

General personal representatives have power to sell, mortgage or lease
the land (A.E.A. 1925, s. 39), but unless it is necessary to deal with the land
for the purpose of raising estate duty (they being the persons accountable
therefor : L.P.A. 1925, s. 16), or the parties request them to exercise their
powers, it will be best for them, when the duties have been paid, to transfer
the land, formerly settled land, to the persons entitled, and get rid of their

responsibility. If the personal representatives sell, the purchaser is not concerned to enquire whether they need to do so in order to pay estate duty and, although Sir Lancelot Elphinstone has argued to the contrary, the better opinion is that this is so even if the grant shows that no duty was payable (S.L.A. 1925, s. 110 (3)).

A difficulty is that a purchaser who has no right to investigate the equitable title shown by the trust instrument does not know whether the settlement has come to an end. It is generally accepted, in practice, that if a general grant including settled land has been made in favour of personal representatives of the tenant for life, a purchaser from those representatives or from a person in whose favour they have executed an ordinary (i.e., not a vesting) assent may safely assume that the settlement has come to an end and would get a good title even if in fact the land remained settled land. *Re Bridgett and Hayes' Contract, ante,* was a case in which the settlement had in fact come to an end, but one ground for the decision was that the grant of probate was an order of the court and therefore the title of the purchaser was valid even if the order was made without jurisdiction (see L.P.A. 1925, s. 204 (1) ; *In the Estate of Taylor* [1929] P. 260, 263). For a full discussion of the point see the *Conveyancer N.S.,* vol. 10, p. 137, vol. 11, pp. 91, 93 and 159, and the *Law Times,* vol. 201, p. 307.

It is important to remember that the decision in *Re Bridgett and Hayes' Contract* has no application unless the legal estate was vested in the tenant for life at the time of his death. Thus, if a testator devised land to his wife for life and after her death to a son absolutely, the legal estate will not pass to the wife unless an assent is executed in her favour (or unless it passed to her under the transitional provisions in the 1925 legislation). If the testator died after 1925 and no written assent has been executed, the persons to make title on her death will be the personal representatives of the husband, in whom the legal estate will have remained vested. As this may be convenient, a vesting assent in favour of the wife as tenant for life is frequently deliberately omitted.

Cases in which land ceases to be settled.—The land will cease to be settled land when on the death of the tenant for life a remainderman of full age becomes absolutely entitled free from all limitations, charges or powers f charging under the settlement (S.L.A. 1925, s. 3 ; *ante,* p. 704). Where the person absolutely and beneficially entitled to the land is an infant the land remains settled land, but it will cease to be such when the infant attains full age (S.L.A. 1925, ss. 1 (1) (ii) (*d*), 2, 3).

If, on the death of the tenant for life, the land becomes subject to an express trust for sale, it will cease to be settled (*Re Bridgett and Hayes' Contract* [1928] Ch. 163). This being the case, a general grant of probate or administration will be obtained without exception of settled land. After administration is complete the personal representatives must (unless they sell under their powers) then vest the legal estate in the trustees for sale (S.L.A. 1925, s. 7 (5)). If, however, a charge under the settlement having priority to the trust for sale continues after the death of the tenant for life, it appears that the land remains settled land, with the result that the trustees of the settlement must obtain a grant limited to the settled land (*Re Norton* [1929] 1 Ch. 84).

Where, on the death of the tenant for life, the land is limited in undivided shares, s. 36 (2) of the S.L.A. 1925 applies, with the result that the land is held upon the statutory trusts ; see further, *ante,* p. 310. This subsection creates a *statutory paramount trust for sale ;* there is no need in this case for the trustees to be approved by the court under L.P.A. 1925, s. 2 (2), as amended. See also L.P.A. 1925, Sched. 1, Pt. IV, para. 1 (3), as amended, which creates a correpsonding trust where the shares were vested in possession immediately before 1st January, 1926. A paramount trust for sale puts an end to the settlement : s. 3. It has been noted (p. 312) that the phrase " paramount trust for sale " may be misleading, but, as the statutory trust for sale under the S.L.A. 1925, s. 36 (2), overrides any interests, powers or charges under the trust instrument, even if they have priority to the trust for the persons entitled to the undivided shares, the trust for sale undoubtedly puts an end to the settlement. Consequently, if on the death of the tenant for life persons are entitled in undivided shares in possession, his general personal representatives can be required to execute a conveyance or assent to the trustees for sale (*Re Cugny's Will Trusts* [1931] 1 Ch. 305). It might be argued that because *Re Cugny* has decided that the land remains notionally settled so as to bring the S.L.A. 1925, s. 36 (2), into operation, then the land is also settled for the purposes of the A.E.A. 1925, s. 22, and a grant limited to the settled land should be made to the trustees of the settlement. Such does not seem to be the case, and apparently, for the purpose of deciding whether the A.E.A. 1925, s. 22, applies, we must assume that, on the authority of *Re Bridgett and Hayes' Contract, ante*, the settlement has come to an end. This appears to have been assumed in *Re Thomas* [1939] Ch. 513, in which *Re Cugny* was expressly approved, although the grant made on the death of the tenant for life was a general one. It is unsatisfactory that the settlement should be treated as being at an end for the purposes of the A.E.A. 1925, s. 22, but continuing for the purposes of the S.L.A. 1925, s. 36 (2), but no other conclusion seems possible so long as both *Re Bridgett and Hayes' Contract* and *Re Cugny* stand.

C. DEVOLUTION OF LAND WHICH REMAINS SETTLED LAND ON DEATH OF TENANT FOR LIFE

Where tenant for life left a will.—Where on the death of the tenant for life the land remains settled land, and he left a will, it is provided by s. 22 (1) of the A.E.A. 1925 that a testator may appoint, and in default of such express appointment shall be deemed to have appointed, as his special executors in regard to settled land, the persons, if any, who are at his death the S.L.A. 1925 trustees of the settlement, and probate may be granted to such trustees specially limited to the settled land. Where there is settled land within this subsection, there should be two grants, namely, first a *general grant* " save and except settled land vested in the deceased which was settled previously to his death and remains settled land notwithstanding his death " (see r. 28 (5) of the Non-Contentious Probate Rules, 1954), and a *special grant* as respects land vested in the deceased immediately before his death which was settled previously thereto (and not by his will) and remains settled land. If the general executors and the special executors happen to be the same persons, it would be possible to obtain one grant to cover both the general estate of the tenant for life and the settled land (see r. 28 (4) of the Non-Contentious Probate Rules, 1954). In many cases, however, this may be undesirable because it may be important to keep the title to the settled estate separate from that to the unsettled estate.

If a general grant has been made in respect of the general estate of the tenant for life in consequence of the executors being unaware of there being any settled land, and having sworn in the oath that there was no settled land, and it turns out that, in fact, there was settled land which remained settled land after his death, to be strictly correct a further grant to the settled land should be taken out. Before this can be done it will be necessary to amend the original grant, by the addition of the words " save and except settled land." But it seems that there is no necessity for a purchaser to take the objection, because when a general grant has been made (though in error) he is not entitled to go behind the grant. See *ante*, p. 709.

There is, however, one case in which real difficulty arises ; that is where the deceased was tenant for life of two estates, in one of which the settlement came to an end on his death and in the other it did not come to an end. In such circumstances a grant limited to settled land should be taken out by the trustees of the settlement which did not come to an end and, of course, a grant " save and except " settled land by the general personal representatives of the deceased. It might appear at first sight that the land comprised in the settlement which came to an end on the death of the tenant for life would pass under the grant limited to settled land, as such a grant does not describe any particular land as passing under it. But a purchaser would see that such limited grant was not made to the persons who were trustees of the settlement which had come to an end and he would then suspect that it did not apply to the land with which he was concerned and that such land had ceased to be settled land on the death of the tenant for life. Contrary to the general rule under the S.L.A. 1925, it appears that he would then have to investigate the equitable title to the land with which he was concerned, as shown in the trust instruments, to ensure that the settlement with which he was concerned had come to an end and that, as a result, such land had vested in the general personal representatives of the deceased tenant for life.

On the other hand, before the decision in *Re Bridgett and Hayes' Contract* [1928] Ch. 163, *ante*, p. 708, limited grants were often made when, on the death of the tenant for life, the land ceased to be settled. It has been customary to accept a title made by or through special personal representatives acting under such grants in reliance on the L.P.A. 1925, s. 204 (1), even if the purchaser knows that the settlement had come to an end.

In *In the Estate of Powell* [1935] P. 114, *P* owned land absolutely, subject to a family charge ; the land was, therefore, settled (S.L.A. 1925, s. 1 (1) (v)). *P* died, having appointed executors but not *special* executors in respect of the settled land. Probate was granted to his executors save and except settled land which remained so settled. It was desired to sell the land, but this could not be done until a further grant had been made limited to such settled land. The proper persons to apply for a special grant would be the executors of the original settlor, if they were living (S.L.A. 1925, s. .30 (3)), but it was found impossible to trace them, at any rate without excessive costs. An application to the court was therefore made under s. 155 of the Judicature Act, 1925, to clear off the representatives of the settlor, who, as they were not known, could not be cited to accept or refuse a grant, and a grant of probate of the will limited to such settled land was made to the executors of *P*.

Where there are no special executors.—If *at the date of death* of a tenant for life the land continues to be settled land, but there are no trustees, the land will vest in his general executors, unless settled land was excepted from the grant, in which case it would vest in the Probate judge. No grant will be made under s. 22 of the A.E.A. 1925 to persons who are appointed S.L.A.

1925 trustees *after the testator's death ;* nor can a trustee appointed after the death be joined in a grant to special executors. Where no grant of probate can be made under s. 22 of the A.E.A. 1925, the persons entitled to a grant of administration limited to settled land are to be determined in accordance with the following order of priority, namely :—

    (i) The trustees of the settlement at the time of the application for the grant ;

    (ii) Where there are no such trustees and the settlement arises under a will or intestacy, the personal representative of the settlor ;

    (iii) The personal representative of the deceased

(r. 28 (3) of the Non-Contentious Probate Rules, 1954 ; see also s. 162 of the Judicature Act, 1925, as amended by s. 9 of the Administration of Justice Act, 1928).

Vesting of land in the person next entitled.—Provision as to this will be found in ss. 7 and 8 of the S.L.A. 1925. Section 7 (1) provides that if, on the death of a tenant for life or statutory owner, or of the survivor of two or more tenants for life or statutory owners, in whom the settled land was vested, the land remains settled land, his *personal representatives* are to hold the settled land on trust, if and when required so to do, to convey it to the person who under the trust instrument or by virtue of the Act becomes the tenant for life or statutory owner and, if more than one, as joint tenants. The expression " personal representatives " includes special personal representatives for the purpose of settled land (*ibid.*, s. 117 (1) (xviii)).

They cannot, of course, be required to convey the settled land to the persons entitled until they have done with it in their capacity of special personal representatives. Their duty, however, is only to see that provision has been or will be made for the payment of any unpaid death duties in respect of the land or any interest therein and interest and costs, or that they are otherwise effectually indemnified therefrom. In carrying out their duties they may transfer or create such legal estates to take effect in priority to the conveyance to the tenant for life or statutory owner as may be required for giving effect to the obligations imposed on them by statute ; and such conveyance, if made by deed, may contain a reservation to the persons conveying of a term of years absolute in the land conveyed, upon trusts for indemnifying them against any unpaid death duties in respect of the land conveyed, or any interest therein, and interest and costs. This is all provided for in s. 8 of the S.L.A. 1925. It is also provided by subs. (7) of the same section that nothing is to affect any right which a person entitled to an equitable charge for securing money actually raised, and affecting the whole estate the subject of the settlement, may have to require effect to be given thereto by a legal mortgage, before the execution of the conveyance above referred to. See S.L.A. 1925, s. 16 (1) (iii) (*b*). The conveyance will be made at the cost of the trust estate and, in practice, will take the form of an assent.

Dispositions by special personal representatives.—Section 24 (1) of the A.E.A. 1925 provides that the special personal representatives may dispose of the settled land without the concurrence of the general personal representatives, who may likewise dispose of the other property and assets of the deceased without the concurrence of the special personal representatives.

PART 6. SETTLED LAND ACT TRUSTEES

A. GENERALLY

Persons who become S.L.A. trustees.—The persons who are S.L.A. 1925 trustees are specified in s. 30 of the S.L.A. 1925 ; subss. (1) and (2) are given below, and subs. (3) is quoted *post*, p. 714.

" 30.—(1) *Subject to the provisions of this Act*, the following persons are trustees of a settlement for the purposes of this Act, and are in this Act referred to as the ' trustees of the settlement ' or ' trustees of a settlement,' namely :—

(i) the persons, if any, who are for the time being under the settlement, *trustees with power of sale* of the settled land (*subject or not to the consent* of any person), or with power of consent to or approval of the exercise of such a power of sale, or if there are no such persons ; then

(ii) *the persons, if any, for the time being, who are by the settlement declared to be trustees thereof* for the purposes of the Settled Land Acts, 1882 to 1890, or any of them, or this Act, or if there are no such persons ; then

(iii) the persons, if any, who are for the time being under the settlement trustees with power of or upon trust for sale of any other land *comprised in the settlement* and subject to the same limitations as the land to be sold or otherwise dealt with, or with power of consent to or approval of the exercise of such a power of sale, or, if there are no such persons ; then

(iv) the persons, if any, who are for the time being under the settlement *trustees with future power of sale, or under a future trust for sale* of the settled land, or with power of consent to or approval of the exercise of such a future power of sale, and *whether the power or trust takes effect in all events or not*, or, if there are no such persons ; then

(v) *the persons, if any, appointed by deed to be trustees of the settlement* by all the persons who at the date of the deed were together able, by virtue of their beneficial interests or by the exercise of an equitable power, to dispose of the settled land in equity for the whole estate the subject of the settlement.

(2) Paragraphs (i), (iii) and (iv) of the last preceding subsection take effect in like manner as if the powers therein referred to had not by this Act been made exercisable by the tenant for life or statutory owner."

It is important to note the words " or if there are no such persons ; then " at the end of each paragraph. They make it clear that if there are persons who fall within the definition of an earlier paragraph the later paragraphs will not apply.

As to who will be S.L.A. 1925 trustees of a compound settlement and of a referential settlement, see *post*, pp. 716 and 717 respectively.

" *Subject to the provisions of this Act*."—See S.L.A. 1925, s. 31, *post*, p. 716, as to compound settlements, s. 32, *post*, p. 717, as to referential settlements and s. 34, *post*, p. 720, as to the power of the court to appoint trustees.

" *trustees with power of sale*."—It is not now the practice to give the trustees a power of sale, because it is expressly provided by s. 108 of the

23A

S.L.A. 1925 that if a power of sale is given to trustees it will be exercisable by the tenant for life.

To bring the case within this paragraph the power of sale must be general and not limited, that is, it must be exercisable at any time and for any purpose and not merely in a contingency and for a particular purpose. For instance, it was held that a power for the purpose of raising certain costs, charges and expenses was not within the similar section in the Settled Land Act, 1882 (*Re Coull's Settled Estates* [1905] 1 Ch. 712). The power must also be a present and not a future power of sale (*Wheelwright* v. *Walker* (1883), 23 Ch. D. 752), but trustees with a future power of sale will be trustees under para. (iv) of s. 30 (1). A general power of sale would be *inferred* from power being given to trustees to vary securities (*Re Tapp and London and India Docks Co.'s Contract* (1905), 74 L.J. Ch. 523).

" *subject or not to the consent.*"—These words cover the case where the words in the settlement are " at the request of " (*Re Ffennell's Settlement* [1918] 1 Ch. 91).

" *the persons . . . who are by the settlement declared to be trustees thereof.*"— If the trustees have been given a power of sale either expressly or by implication, then they would have become S.L.A. 1925 trustees by force of para. (i), above. Therefore if, in such a case, separate S.L.A. 1925 trustees should have been appointed, the latter appointment would be ineffectual.

" *comprised in the settlement.*"—These words mean " for the time being comprised in," and include land subsequently purchased and brought into the settlement (*Re Moore* [1906] 1 Ch. 789).

" *trustees with future power of sale, or under a future trust for sale.*"—Where land was devised to *A* and *B* upon trust for *A* for life, with power to sell on *A's* death, *A* sold the land as tenant for life. It was held that *A* and *B* were S.L.A. trustees under s. 16 (ii) of the Settled Land Act, 1890 (which this paragraph replaces), and that it was immaterial that some or one of them were persons who in all human probability would not, or, in fact, could not, ever exercise the trust, as for instance if one of them is a person who necessarily would be dead before the trust took effect (*Re Jackson's Settled Estate* [1902] 1 Ch. 258). This decision was followed in *Re Davies and Kent's Contract* [1910] 2 Ch. 35.

" *whether the power or trust takes effect in all events or not.*"—If, at the time of the sale by the tenant for life, there is a valid future trust for sale, the sale will be effectual, notwithstanding that, by the nature of the devise, some future act might be done which might render such trust for sale void as infringing the rule against perpetuities (*Re Davies and Kent's Contract, ante*).

" *the persons, if any, appointed by deed to be trustees of the settlement.*"— If there are no persons who come within paras. (i) to (iv) then the beneficiaries can by deed appoint trustees, but it must be clear that the beneficiaries are entitled beneficially to the *whole estate or interest* the subject of the settlement (*Re Spencer's Settled Estates* [1903] 1 Ch. 75). The paragraph would not apply to a case where the class of beneficiaries was still susceptible of increase.

Personal representatives of settlor as trustees.—Section 30 (3) is very valuable in practice but gives rise to some difficulty. It provides :—

" (3) Where a settlement is created by will, or a settlement has arisen by the effect of an intestacy, and *apart from this subsection there would be no trustees* for the purposes of this Act of such settlement, then the personal representatives of the deceased shall, until other trustees are appointed, be by virtue of this Act the trustees of the settlement, but *where there is a sole personal representative*, not being a trust corporation, *it shall be obligatory on him to appoint an additional trustee* to act with him for the purposes of this Act, and the *provisions* of the Trustee Act, 1925, *relating to the appointment of new trustees* and the vesting of trust property *shall apply* accordingly."

This subsection contains a provision first introduced by the S.L.A. 1925, but it applies whether the death occurred before 1926 or after 1925. It was held by Russell, J., in chambers ((1926), *Law Journal*, vol. 62, p. 436), that the executor would be the personal representative even though he had assented to the legal estate passing and had fully administered the estate and his duties as personal representative had come to an end, and that he could deal with the settled land when he had appointed another trustee to act with him under the provision in the subsection.

Personal representatives who become S.L.A. 1925 trustees by virtue of s. 30 (3) may retire and appoint new trustees under the T.A. 1925, s. 36, *post*, p. 790 *et seq.*, as they are trustees appointed under the provisions of an " instrument " (that is, in this case, an Act of Parliament : T.A. 1925, s. 68 (5)) and so have the necessary powers conferred on them by the T.A. 1925, s. 64 (1) (*Re Dark* [1954] Ch. 291).

In *Re Gibbings' Estates* [1928] P. 28 a settlor who died in 1890 appointed his wife and son executors and devised land to them on trust for his wife for her life, and subject thereto in trust for his children in such shares as his wife should appoint. She appointed to the children equally, and died in 1926. Her executor took general probate " save and except the settled land." Lord Merrivale held that the personal representatives of the settlor became the S.L.A. 1925 trustees by virtue of the above subs. (3), and were entitled to a grant as special executors of the tenant for life under s. 22 (1) of the A.E.A. 1925. It is now doubtful whether the decision was correct, because on the death of the wife, the children having become absolutely entitled, the land ceased to be settled land and the principle of *Re Bridgett and Hayes' Contract* [1928] Ch. 163, *ante*, p. 708, should be applied. It should also be noted that, in spite of this decision, the practice of the Probate Registry has been to refuse a grant of probate (as special executors under the A.E.A. 1925, s. 22 ; see *ante*, p. 710 *et seq.*) to personal representatives of the settlor who have become trustees under s. 30 (3) unless they have expressly appointed themselves trustees before the death of the tenant for life. A grant of letters of administration with the will annexed limited to the settled land will, however, be made ; see r. 28 (3) (ii) of the Non-Contentious Probate Rules, 1954.

" *apart from this subsection there would be no trustees.*"—These words cause some difficulty. Other trustees may be appointed after the personal representatives have commenced to act as S.L.A. 1925 trustees or even after they have appointed trustees to act jointly with themselves. In a full discussion of the problems arising, the late Dr. E. O. Walford wrote in the *Conveyancer N.S.*, vol. 15, p. 109 : " In my view s. 30 (3) establishes a special category of trustees who can act so long as certain conditions continue. Those conditions are :—

(1) That apart from s. 30 (3) no trustees can be found under other provisions contained in the Act ;

(2) That the trusteeship constituted by s. 30 (3) ceases when other trustees are appointed (i.e., validly appointed)."

Dr. Walford then expressed the opinion that an additional trustee appointed by a sole personal representative as required by the subsection will hold office only on the same conditions.

" *where there is a sole personal representative . . . it shall be obligatory on him to appoint an additional trustee.*"—If there was only one personal representative (not a trust corporation) who became a trustee for the purposes of the S.L.A. 1925 by virtue of the S.L.A. 1925, s. 30 (3), he would have to appoint an additional trustee to act with him in order to give a valid receipt for capital money (S.L.A. 1925, s. 94 (1)), but so long as he remained a pure personal representative he could act alone (L.P.A. 1925, s. 27 (2), as amended). The deed of appointment of the additional trustee may be executed before a vesting assent is made by the personal representative in favour of the tenant for life. It does not appear that the T.A. 1925, s. 40, *post*, p. 796, will vest the property in the new trustees and so the sole personal representative is still able to execute the assent. Compare *Re King's Will Trust* [1964] Ch. 542 and see the *Law Journal*, vol. 101, p. 282, quoting the unreported decision in *Re Springer*. Such a deed should expressly appoint the additional trustee as a trustee *for the purposes of the S.L.A.* 1925. It is doubtful whether an appointment merely as a new trustee of the will would be effective.

" *provisions . . . relating to the appointment of new trustees . . . shall apply.*" —These words are not necessary, as the provisions of the T.A. 1925 mentioned apply where either a sole representative or several representatives are trustees by virtue of s. 30 (3). The provisions of the T.A. 1925 with reference to the appointment of new trustees and the discharge and retirement of trustees apply to trustees for the purposes of the S.L.A. 1925 where (*inter alia*) such trustees are appointed in " any instrument " (T.A. 1925, s. 64 (1), *post*, p. 719) and " instrument " includes an Act of Parliament (*ibid.*, s. 68 (5)). It follows that personal representatives who are appointed trustees by s. 30 (3) of the S.L.A. 1925 have the powers in the T.A. 1925, s. 36 (1), *post*, p. 790 (*Re Dark* [1954] Ch. 291).

S.L.A. trustees of compound settlements.—As to compound settlements generally, see *ante*, p. 675. Section 31 of the S.L.A. 1925, as amended by the Law of Property (Amendment) Act, 1926, states who are S.L.A. 1925 trustees of a compound settlement, and provides as follows :—

" 31.—(1) Persons who are for the time being trustees for the purposes of this Act of an instrument which is a settlement, *or is deemed to be a subsisting settlement* for the purposes of this Act, shall be the trustees for the purposes of this Act of any settlement constituted by that instrument and any instruments subsequent in date or operation.

Where there are trustees for the purposes of this Act of the *instrument under which there is a tenant for life or statutory owner* but there are no trustees for those purposes of a prior instrument, being one of the instruments by which a compound settlement is constituted, those trustees shall, *unless and until trustees are appointed* of the prior instrument or of the compound settlement, be the trustees for the purposes of this Act of the compound settlement.

(2) This section applies to instruments coming into operation before as well as after the commencement of this Act, but shall have effect without

prejudice to any appointment made by the court before such commencement of trustees of a settlement constituted by more than one instrument, and to the power of the court in any case after such commencement to make any such appointment, and where any such appointment has been made before such commencement or is made thereafter this section shall not apply or shall cease to apply to the settlement consisting of the instruments to which the appointment relates."

" *is deemed to be a subsisting settlement.*"—These words refer to s. 3 of the S.L.A. 1925, as to which, see *ante*, p. 704.

" *instrument under which there is a tenant for life or statutory owner.*"— See S.L.A. 1925, ss. 19, 20, 23 and 26. See also s. 22 (2), *ante*, p. 684, and *Re Cradock's Settled Estates* [1926] Ch. 944. " Statutory owner " for this purpose does not appear to include the trustees of the settlement when they act as such under the S.L.A. 1925, s. 23 (1) (*b*) (*Re Sharpe's Deed of Release* [1939] Ch. 51, at p. 74 ; see the *Conveyancer N.S.*, vol. 3, p. 81).

" *unless and until trustees are appointed.*"—See *Re Ogle's Settled Estates* [1927] 1 Ch. 229, *ante*, p. 703, as to the separate settlements for which trustees can be appointed, and *Re Symons* [1927] 1 Ch. 344, referred to *ante*, p. 678.

It is important to remember that where there is a compound settlement, not only must a sale or other transaction be made thereunder, but any vesting deed required to be executed by the trustees (for instance, under the S.L.A. 1925, Sched. 2, para. 1 (2), *ante*, p. 701) must be executed by the trustees of the compound settlement as defined above ; see *ante*, p. 683.

Provision is made by the S.L.A. 1925, s. 33 (2) and (3), validating certain dispositions made under compound settlements of which trustees were irregularly appointed by the court.

Trustees of referential settlements.—It is provided by s. 32 (1) and (3) of the S.L.A. 1925 as follows :—

" 32.—(1) Where a settlement takes or has taken effect by reference to another settlement, the trustees for the time being of the settlement to which reference is made shall be the trustees of the settlement by reference, but this section does not apply if the settlement by reference contains an appointment of trustees thereof for the purposes of the Settled Land Acts, 1882 to 1890, or any of them, or this Act.

(3) In this section ' a settlement by reference to another settlement ' means a settlement of property upon the limitations and subject to the powers and provisions of an existing settlement, with or without variation."

By subs. (2) the section is to have effect without prejudice to any order of court appointing trustees of the settlement by reference or of a compound settlement including it.

See also s. 91 (1) of the S.L.A. 1925, which provides, in effect, that where estates are settled by different settlements upon the same limitations, *whether by reference* or otherwise, the estates or any two or more of them may be treated as one *aggregate estate*, in which case the aggregate estate shall be the settled land for the purposes of the Act ; and that where the S.L.A. 1925 trustees of the two or several settlements are the same persons, they shall be the trustees of the settlement of the aggregate estate. By subs. (2) of s. 91 it is provided that estates shall be deemed to be settled upon the same limitations, notwithstanding that any of them may be subject to incumbrances, charges or powers of charging to which the other or others of them may not be subject.

Devolution of office of trustee.—Where the trustees for the purposes of the S.L.A. 1925 have been appointed by the court under s. 34 (1) of the S.L.A. 1925 (*post*, p. 720), it is expressly provided by subs. (2) of the same section that the survivors and survivor of them, while continuing to be trustees or trustee, and, until the appointment of new trustees, the personal representatives or representative for the time being of the last surviving or continuing trustee, shall become and be the trustees or trustee of the settlement.

As regards S.L.A. 1925 trustees *not appointed by the court*, it is provided by s. 94 (2) of the S.L.A. 1925 that the provisions of the Act referring to the trustees of a settlement *apply to the surviving or continuing trustees or trustee* of the settlement for the time being ; and s. 18 (2) of the T.A. 1925 provides that until the appointment of new trustees the personal representatives or representative for the time being of a sole trustee, or, where there were two or more trustees, of the last surviving or continuing trustee, shall be capable of exercising or performing *any power or trust* which was given to, or capable of being exercised by, the sole or last surviving or continuing trustee or other the trustees or trustee for the time being of the trust. There seems to be no doubt but that the T.A. 1925, s. 18 (2), applies to the personal representatives of a S.L.A. 1925 trustee not appointed by the court.

As to the power of the personal representatives of the last surviving or continuing trustee to give receipts *as S.L.A. 1925 trustees*, see s. 95 of the S.L.A. 1925.

But all the above subsections, whether applying to trustees appointed by the court or not, must, of course, be read with s. 94 (1) of the S.L.A. 1925, that capital money must not be paid to fewer than two persons as trustees of a settlement, unless the trustee is a corporation. Therefore, if there should be only one personal representative, he would, *while acting as trustee*, have to appoint another trustee to act with him. A single personal representative can give a good receipt for purchase-money when selling *as personal representative* (L.P.A. 1925, s. 27 (2), as amended).

Where the personal representatives of a last surviving or sole trustee have become statutory trustees, their trusteeship is ousted immediately the donees of a power of appointing new trustees exercise their power (*Re Routledge's Trusts* [1909] 1 Ch. 280).

Continuation of office of trustee.—It is provided by s. 33 (1) of the S.L.A. 1925 as follows :—

" 33.—(1) Where any persons have been appointed or constituted trustees of a settlement, whether by an order of the court or otherwise, or have by reason of any power of sale, or trust for sale, or by reason of a power of consent to, or approval of, the exercise of a power of sale, or by virtue of this Act, or otherwise at any time become trustees of a settlement for the purposes of the Settled Land Acts, 1882 to 1890, or this Act, then those persons or their successors in office shall remain and be trustees of the settlement as long as that settlement is subsisting or *deemed to be subsisting* for the purposes of this Act.

In this subsection ' successors in office ' means the persons who, by appointment or otherwise, have become trustees for the purposes aforesaid."

" deemed to be subsisting."—See S.L.A. 1925, s. 3, *ante*, p. 704.

The above subsection has the effect of extending the term of office of trustees of a settlement which came to an end before 1926, but which by s. 3 of the S.L.A. 1925 became revived by reason of a charge under s. 1 (1) (v) of the S.L.A. 1925. Such a charge before 1926 did not make the land settled land, and therefore, when the settlement came to an end the office of the trustees also came to an end. See further, *ante*, p. 671 *et seq.*

B. APPOINTMENT OF NEW TRUSTEES OR ADDITIONAL TRUSTEES

Application of the provisions of the Trustee Act.—It is provided by s. 64 of the T.A. 1925 as follows :—

" 64.—(1) All the powers and provisions contained in this Act with reference to the appointment of new trustees, and the discharge and retirement of trustees, apply to and include trustees for the purposes of the Settled Land Act, 1925, and trustees for the purpose of the management of land during a minority, *whether such trustees are appointed by the court or by the settlement, or under provisions contained in any instrument.*

(2) Where, either before or after the commencement of this Act, trustees of a settlement have been appointed by the court for the purposes of the Settled Land Acts, 1882 to 1890, or of the Settled Land Act, 1925, then, after the commencement of this Act—

(*a*) the person or persons nominated for the purpose of appointing new trustees by the instrument, if any, creating the settlement, though no trustees for the purposes of the said Acts were thereby appointed ; or

(*b*) if there is no such person, or no such person able and willing to act, the surviving or continuing trustees or trustee for the time being for the purposes of the said Acts, or the personal representatives of the last surviving or continuing trustee for those purposes,

shall have the powers conferred by this Act to appoint new or additional trustees of the settlement for the purposes of the said Acts."

These subsections bring in (*inter alia*) s. 36 of the T.A. 1925 (*post*, p. 790) (general power of appointment of new trustees) and, particularly, s. 36 (6) of the same Act (power to appoint additional trustee or trustees), set out *post*, p. 795.

The statutory power of appointment of new trustees is satisfactory from a practical point of view and so it is not necessary to insert an express power in settlements and wills. See further, as to this, *post*, p. 790.

It will be noted that where *S.L.A.* 1925 *trustees* have been appointed by the court, the statutory power to appoint new or additional trustees is exercisable by a person nominated for the purpose of appointing new trustees (i.e., trustees generally and not S.L.A. 1925 trustees) by the instrument creating the settlement, though no *S.L.A.* 1925 *trustees* were thereby appointed (T.A. 1925, s. 64 (2) (*a*)). In other cases where there are no persons who will be S.L.A. 1925 trustees under the S.L.A. 1925, s. 30 (1), paras. (i) to (iv), it is provided by para. (v) of s. 30 (1), as we have seen *ante*, p. 713, that the beneficiaries may appoint S.L.A. 1925 trustees, provided they are entitled beneficially to the whole estate or interest the subject of the settlement. But unless trustees have been appointed by the beneficiaries in a case in which the settlement was created by will, the personal representatives of the testator will be the trustees of the settlement, by virtue of s. 30 (3) of the S.L.A. 1925, *until other trustees are appointed*, and the provisions of the T.A. 1925 relating to the appointment of new trustees and the vesting of trust property will apply accordingly. See further, *ante*, p. 714.

In dealing with S.L.A. 1925 trustees it must be remembered that s. 35 (3) of the S.L.A. 1925 provides that a statement in a deed of declaration, as defined by subs. (1) of the section, to the effect that the person named in the principal vesting instrument as the person for the time being entitled to appoint new trustees of the settlement is *unable or unwilling* to act, or that a trustee has *remained outside the United Kingdom* for more than twelve months, or *refuses* or is *unfit* to act, or is *incapable* of acting, shall, in favour of a purchaser of a legal estate, be conclusive evidence of the matter stated. The words in italics are similar to the words of the T.A. 1925, s. 36 (1), giving powers to appoint new trustees.

Power of court to appoint S.L.A. trustees.—This power is given by s. 34 of the S.L.A. 1925, which provides that if there are no trustees of a settlement, or where in any other case it is expedient that new trustees be appointed, the court may, on the application of the tenant for life, statutory owner, or of any other person having, under the settlement, an estate or interest in the settled land, or, in the case of an infant, of his testamentary or other guardian or next friend, appoint fit persons to be trustees of the settlement.

In view of the wide powers of appointing trustees given by the S.L.A. 1925 and the T.A. 1925, which we have been considering, it is seldom necessary to apply to the court for this purpose.

The Official Solicitor can be appointed as a judicial trustee to be trustee for the purposes of the S.L.A. 1925 (Judicial Trustees Act, 1896, s. 1 (1) ; *Re Marshall's Will Trusts* [1945] Ch. 217).

Persons who can be appointed trustees.—The appointment of a person beneficially interested, including a tenant for life, as a trustee for the purposes of the S.L.A. 1925 is undesirable, but it is not invalid, and will not therefore affect a purchaser from the tenant for life (*Forster* v. *Abraham* (1874), L.R. 17 Eq. 351) ; although the court would not appoint him, it will not revoke his appointment (*Re Harrop's Trusts* (1883), 24 Ch. D. 717 ; *Re Jackson's Settled Estate* [1902] 1 Ch. 258 ; *Re Davies and Kent's Contract* [1910] 2 Ch. 35 ; *Re Johnson's Settled Estates* [1913] W.N. 222). The husband of a tenant for life is also not considered a suitable person to be appointed a trustee, but if he was appointed the court would not revoke the appointment (*Re Earl of Stamford* [1896] 1 Ch. 288). The same applies to the case of an appointment of the solicitor of the tenant for life (*Wheelwright* v. *Walker* (1883), 23 Ch. D. 752, at p. 763 ; *Re Spencer's Settled Estates* [1903] 1 Ch. 75) ; or to the solicitor for a trustee (*Re Norris* (1884), 27 Ch. D. 333) ; or to two persons related to each other (*Re Knowles' Settled Estates* (1884), 27 Ch. D. 707). An unmarried lady will be appointed by the court if satisfied that she is capable of acting (*Re Dickinson's Trusts* [1902] W.N. 104). A married woman may be appointed a trustee (L.P.A. 1925, s. 170).

Procedure on appointment of new trustees or an additional trustee.—
The procedure is described in s. 35 of the S.L.A. 1925 and s. 35 (2) of the T.A.

1925. There must be : (1) a deed of appointment ; (2) a deed of declaration, consisting of a shorter deed made supplemental to the last or only vesting instrument, and containing merely a declaration as to who are the trustees (after the appointment) for the purposes of the S.L.A. 1925 of the settlement ; and (3) a memorandum endorsed on or annexed to such vesting instrument.

Section 35 (1) of the S.L.A. 1925 provides that whenever a new S.L.A. 1925 trustee is appointed of a trust instrument, a deed shall be executed supplemental to the last or only principal vesting instrument containing a declaration that the persons therein named, being the persons who after such appointment are the S.L.A. 1925 trustees of the trust instrument, are the S.L.A. 1925 trustees ; and a memorandum shall be endorsed on or annexed to the last or only principal vesting instrument *in accordance with the T.A. 1925.* Subsection (2) provides that such deed shall, if the trustee was appointed by the court, be executed by such person as the court may direct, and, in any other case, shall be executed by the person or persons therein mentioned.

"*in accordance with the T.A. 1925.*"—This refers to the provision in s. 35 of the T.A. 1925 that where new trustees of a settlement are appointed, a memorandum of the names and addresses of the persons who are for the time being the trustees thereof for the purposes of the S.L.A. 1925 must be endorsed on or annexed to the last or only principal vesting instrument by or on behalf of the trustees of the settlement, and that such vesting instrument must, for that purpose, be produced by the person having the possession thereof to the trustees of the settlement when so required.

The deed of declaration made to correct and complete the statement in the last or only principal vesting instrument as to who are the present S.L.A. 1925 trustees of the settlement, with the memorandum, is the document to be abstracted and produced to a purchaser. The actual deed of appointment does not affect a purchaser and will not be abstracted or produced to him. See s. 110 (2) (*d*) of the S.L.A. 1925, *ante*, p. 689, which provides that a purchaser of a legal estate in settled land shall be bound and entitled to assume that the statements contained in any deed executed in accordance with the Act declaring who are the trustees of the settlement for the purposes of the Act are correct, and S.L.A. 1925, s. 35 (3), *ante*, p. 720, as to the conclusive effect of certain statements in such a deed of declaration.

Failure to execute a deed of declaration and to make the necessary endorsement does not appear to invalidate the appointment. It appears, however, that a purchaser can and should insist on the execution of the deed and the making of the endorsement. The S.L.A. 1925, s. 110 (2) (*b*), *ante*, p. 689, refers to " successors appearing to be duly appointed " and so if the appointment itself is valid the purchaser would not seem to be entitled to treat the persons stated in the principal vesting deed as being still the trustees. It might be argued that he can safely treat persons declared to be trustees by an earlier deed of declaration as remaining such (S.L.A. 1925, s. 110 (2) (*d*)) but there is doubt. If it is too late to have a deed of declaration duly executed, for instance, because a trustee is dead, the purchaser would not have the protection of ss. 35 (3) and 110 (2) (*d*) and so would have to investigate the deed of appointment itself, which would become a document of title.

It was stated in the unreported case of *Re Grinnell* (1932) that no deed of declaration could be executed if there was no principal vesting instrument in existence. There may well be circumstances in which trustees must be appointed before a vesting instrument is executed. In such a case there can apparently be no deed of declaration or memorandum and a subsequent purchaser must rely on the deed of appointment ; see also the comments in the *Conveyancer N.S.*, vol. 13, p. 347 *et seq.*

Vesting of property on appointment of new S.L.A. trustees.— Vesting declarations on appointments of new trustees are dealt with by the T.A. 1925, s. 40, as to which, see *post*, p. 796. It is important to remember, however, that settled land is vested in the tenant for life or statutory owners and *not* in the trustees of the settlement, unless they are statutory owners. Where new S.L.A. 1925 trustees are appointed (there being a tenant for life or statutory owners who are not also the S.L.A. 1925 trustees) the appointment will not deal with the settled land ; that will remain vested in the tenant for life or independent statutory owners. But if the S.L.A. 1925 trustees and the statutory owners are the same persons, then on an appointment of a new trustee there will be a separate vesting deed pursuant to S.L.A. 1925, s. 7 (4). Further, where the statutory owners are also the trustees, and new trustees are appointed, the former statutory owners should, by a vesting instrument (s. 8), convey the land to the new and continuing trustees who become statutory owners. This keeps the appointment of new trustees off the title. The S.L.A. 1925, s. 7 (4), provides as follows :—

" (4) If by reason of forfeiture, surrender, or otherwise the estate owner of any settled land ceases to have the statutory powers of a tenant for life and the land remains settled land, he shall be bound forthwith to convey the settled land to the person who under the trust instrument, or by virtue of this Act, becomes the tenant for life or statutory owner and, if more than one, as joint tenants."

PART 7.   TENANTS FOR LIFE AND STATUTORY OWNERS

A.   TENANTS FOR LIFE

Who is tenant for life.—It is provided by s. 117 (1) (xxviii) of the S.L.A. 1925 that the expression " ' tenant for life ' includes a person (not being a statutory owner) who has the powers of a tenant for life under this Act ". The definition of a tenant for life given in s. 19 (1) of the S.L.A. 1925 (which is set out below) is more limited, but s. 20 (2) of the S.L.A. 1925 extends the meaning to each of the ten classes of persons mentioned in s. 20 (1) (*post*, p. 725), and s. 20 (1) gives each of them (if of full age), when his estate or interest is in possession, all the powers of a true tenant for life.

The S.L.A. 1925, s. 19, is as follows :—

" 19.—(1) *The person of full age* who is for the time being beneficially *entitled under a settlement to possession* of settled land for his life is for the purposes of this Act the tenant for life of that land and the tenant for life under that settlement.

(2) If in any case there are *two or more persons of full age so entitled as joint tenants*, they together constitute the tenant for life for the purposes of this Act.

(3) If in any case there are two or more persons so entitled as joint tenants and they are not of full age, such one or more of them as is or are for the time being of full age is or (if more than one) together constitute the tenant for life for the purposes of this Act, but this subsection does not affect the beneficial interests of such of them as are not for the time being of full age.

(4) A person being tenant for life within the foregoing definitions shall be deemed to be such *notwithstanding that, under the settlement or otherwise, the settled land, or his estate or interest therein, is incumbered or charged* in any manner or to any extent, and notwithstanding any *assignment by operation of law* or otherwise of his estate or interest under the settlement, whether before or after it came into possession, *other than an assurance which extinguishes that estate or interest.*"

So far as regards a purchaser, mortgagee or lessee, it is immaterial whether the person making title can do so as a true tenant for life as defined in s. 19 of the S.L.A. 1925, or under s. 20 (1), as a person having the powers of a tenant for life, as a good title can be obtained in either case. It may be that there is no person under the settlement who is either a tenant for life or a person having the powers of a tenant for life. In that case it is provided by s. 23 (1) of the S.L.A. 1925 that (*a*) any person of full age on whom such powers are conferred by the settlement, and (*b*) in any other case the trustees of the settlement, shall have the powers of a tenant for life under the Act. Such persons are the " statutory owners " (S.L.A. 1925, s. 117 (1) (xxvi) ; *post*, p. 733).

" *The person of full age.*"—It was held in *Re Carnarvon's Settled Estates* [1927] 1 Ch. 138, that these words mean " not being an infant," and that a corporation can be a tenant for life.

" *entitled . . . to possession.*"—" Possession " is defined by s. 117 (1) (xix) of the S.L.A. 1925 to include receipt of rents and profits, or the right to receive them, if any. Where the right to receive the rents is vested in trustees upon trust to manage the settled land and pay the surplus income to a person for life, that person is not a tenant for life, but a person having the powers of a tenant for life under s. 20 (1) (viii) of the S.L.A. 1925, *post*, p. 728 (*Re Sumner's Settled Estates* [1911] 1 Ch. 315, decided on a similar wording in the Settled Land Act, 1882, s. 58 (1) (ix)). A person having use of a house rent free during his life is a tenant for life (*Re Gibbons* [1920] 1 Ch. 372), but a person who has been granted an option to use and occupy a house as a personal residence is not unless and until he exercises the option (*Re Anderson* [1920] 1 Ch. 175). See also the decisions referred to *post*, p. 727.

In *Re Pollock* [1906] 1 Ch. 146, *A* gave real estate to trustees on trust for his wife during widowhood, for the benefit and maintenance of herself and her children, and for their proper bringing up, and it was held that although the widow's interest was charged with the maintenance of the children she had the powers of a tenant for life under the Settled Land Act, 1882. But when the trust is a discretionary trust, for instance, during the life of *A* to apply the rents and profits of an estate for the benefit of *A* and of his wife and children, if any, it would not constitute *A*, or *A* and his wife together, a tenant for life or persons having the powers of a tenant for life (*Re Atkinson* (1886), 31 Ch. D. 577 ; *Re Jemmett and Guest's Contract* [1907] 1 Ch. 629).

" *two or more persons . . . so entitled.*"—Two or more persons can together constitute the tenant for life, but if the legal estate is beneficially limited to, or held in trust for, any persons as joint tenants *absolutely*, the land is held on trust for sale and is not settled land (L.P.A. 1925, s. 36 (1) ; *Re Gaul and Houlston's Contract* [1928] Ch. 689).

" *notwithstanding . . . the settled land, or his estate or interest therein, is incumbered or charged.*"—These words must be read with s. 104 (3) of the S.L.A. 1925, which provides, in effect, that if the tenant for life had, before

1926, for value assigned his estate or interest, he must not exercise his powers so as to prejudice the rights of the assignee, without his consent. See *post*, pp. 735–736. See also S.L.A. 1925, s. 24, as regards the position of a tenant for life who has ceased to have a substantial interest in his estate or interest in the settled land (referred to *post*, p. 742).

" *assignment by operation of law.*"—These words refer to the bankruptcy of the tenant for life. See Bankruptcy Act, 1914, ss. 18 and 53 (1). The legal estate remains in the tenant for life notwithstanding his bankruptcy. His powers under the Act do not pass to the trustee in bankruptcy, but remain exercisable by him notwithstanding his bankruptcy (S.L.A. 1925, s. 104 (1)), and he cannot contract not to exercise his powers (*ibid.*, s. 104 (2)). The only case in which the powers pass from him is where he surrenders his life interest to the remainderman under the settlement with intent to extinguish it (S.L.A. 1925, s. 105, referred to in the next paragraph). If the tenant for life should have assigned his life interest to some person other than the remainderman, it can readily be seen that such life tenant, not having any further interest in developing the land to the best advantage, might refuse, without payment, to assist the assignee of his interest. Section 24 of the S.L.A. 1925 is intended to meet cases of this kind and it provides that, in certain circumstances, the court may order that the trustees may exercise the powers of the tenant for life on his behalf ; see further, *post*, p. 742.

" *other than an assurance which extinguishes,*" etc.—Section 105 of the S.L.A. 1925 provides that where the estate or interest of a tenant for life has been " assured " (for definition of this word see subs. (2)) with intent to extinguish the same to the person next entitled in remainder or reversion under the settlement, then his statutory powers under the Act will cease to be exercisable by him, and thenceforth become exercisable as if he were dead, without prejudice to any incumbrance on such interest. See further, *post*, p. 741. The persons next entitled under the settlement might be paramount trustees for sale, in which case, on the execution of the " assurance," the land would cease to be settled land (S.L.A. 1925, s. 7 (5), *ante*, p. 707) ; and title would be made by such trustees for sale under s. 28 of the L.P.A. 1925. If the remainderman should be an infant the land would remain settled land, and the S.L.A. 1925 trustees would be entitled to call for a vesting deed (S.L.A. 1925, s. 7) from the surrenderer, as they would be the persons to deal with the land under s. 26 of the S.L.A. 1925. It was decided in *Re Shawdon Settled Estates* [1930] 2 Ch. 1, that where the person entitled to the life tenant's interest has become bankrupt, his trustee in bankruptcy may surrender such interest with intent to extinguish the same, to the person next entitled in remainder or reversion under the settlement.

A person who is tenant for life under the settlement may purport to exercise statutory powers although there has been no vesting deed or assent and the legal estate has not otherwise passed to him. It appears that a purported sale or lease would operate as a contract to sell or let which would be binding not only on the tenant for life but on persons having the powers of tenant for life after his death. See, for instance, the county court decision in *Marshall and Read* v. *Chapman*, Current Law, May, 1955, para. 322.

Persons having the powers of a tenant for life.—As already mentioned (*ante*, p. 722), in the definition section—s. 117 (1) (xxviii)—of the S.L.A. 1925, the expression " tenant for life " includes a person (not being a statutory owner) who has the powers of a tenant for life under the Act. The persons who have the powers of a tenant for life are set out in s. 20 of the S.L.A. 1925, given below :—

"20.—(1) *Each of the following persons* being of full age shall, *when his estate or interest is in possession,* have the powers of a tenant for life under this Act (namely) :—

(i) *A tenant in tail,* including a tenant in tail after possibility of issue extinct, and a tenant in tail who is by Act of Parliament restrained from barring or defeating his estate tail, and although the reversion is in the Crown, but not including such a tenant in tail where the land in respect whereof he is so restrained was purchased with money provided by Parliament in consideration of public services ; "

"*Each of the following persons.*"—This means persons beneficially entitled, and does not include trustees (*Re Jemmett and Guest's Contract* [1907] 1 Ch. 629, decided on the same words in s. 58 of the Settled Land Act, 1882). It was therefore held that if trustees held land for the life of another upon discretionary trusts they could not exercise the powers of a life tenant under s. 58 (1) (v) of the Settled Land Act, 1882, which is now represented by s. 20 (1) (v) of the S.L.A. 1925 set out below. It was held, further, in *Re Atkinson* (1885), 30 Ch. D. 605, that the beneficiaries under discretionary trusts would not together constitute persons having the powers of a tenant for life under the section of the 1882 Act which is now represented by s. 20 (1) (viii) of the S.L.A. 1925.

"*when his estate or interest is in possession.*"—This means possession as distinguished from remainder or reversion (*Re Martyn* (1900), 69 L.J. Ch. 733).

"*A tenant in tail,*" etc.—See *ante,* p. 428.

S.L.A. 1925, s. 20 (1) (ii).—

"(ii) A person *entitled* to land for an estate in fee simple or for a term of years absolute with or *subject to,* in any of such cases, *an executory limitation, gift or disposition over on failure of his issue* or *in any other event* ; "

This paragraph is a reproduction of s. 58 (1) (ii) of the Settled Land Act, 1882, except that the old paragraph did not apply to leaseholds.

"*entitled.*"—That is, entitled in possession (*Re Bird* [1927] 1 Ch. 210).

"*subject to . . . an executory limitation . . . over on failure of his issue.*"— But an executory limitation over on failure of issue will become incapable of taking effect immediately there is any issue who attains eighteen. For it is provided by s. 134 (1) of the L.P.A 1925 (replacing but enlarging the scope of s. 10 of the Conveyancing Act, 1882, and as amended by the Family Law Reform Act 1969, s. 1 (7), Sched. 1, Pt. I), that where there is a person entitled to—

(a) an equitable interest in land for an estate in fee simple or for any less interest not being an entailed interest, or

(b) any interest in other property, not being an entailed interest,

with an executory limitation over on default or failure of all or any of his issue, whether within or at any specified period or time or not, that executory limitation will be or become void and incapable of taking effect, if and as soon as there is living any issue who has attained the age of eighteen years of the class on default or failure whereof the limitation over was to take effect.

Subsection (2) of s. 134 of the L.P.A. 1925 provides that the section is to apply where the executory limitation is contained in an instrument coming into operation after 31st December, 1882, save that, as regards instruments coming into operation *before* 1926, *it only applies to limitations of land* for an estate in fee, or for a term of years absolute or determinable on life, or for a term of life.

As the section only applies to the equitable interest, to make a title the owner of the interest will have to request the person in whom the legal estate is vested to carry out his wishes under the S.L.A. 1925, s. 16.

" *or in any other event.*"—In *Re Richardson* [1904] 2 Ch. 777, a freehold house was devised to a niece subject to the condition that she resided there during an aunt's life and kept a home for the latter, and in default there was a gift over to another niece on the same terms, and it was held that she was a person having the powers of a tenant for life under s. 58 of the Settled Land Act, 1882, now represented by s. 20 (1) (ii) of the S.L.A. 1925, and that the provision as to residence was a condition (not a trust for the aunt's benefit), and as such was void under s. 51 of the Act of 1882, now represented by s. 106 of the 1925 Act, and that the niece could sell the property as tenant for life, and was entitled to the proceeds absolutely. See further, *post*, p. 737 *et seq.*

Other cases decided on the 1882 paragraph are *Re Morgan* (1883), 24 Ch. D. 114 ; *Re Walmsley* (1911), 105 L.T. 332 ; *Re Dilks ; Godsell* v. *Hulse* (1924), 131 L.T. 533.

S.L.A. 1925, s. 20 (1) (iii).—

" (iii) A person entitled to a base or determinable fee, although the reversion or right of reverter is in the Crown, or to any corresponding interest in leasehold land ; "

As to a base fee, see *ante*, p. 438, and as to a " determinable fee," see *ante*, p. 669.

Leasehold land can now be entailed (L.P.A. 1925, s. 130, *ante*, p. 431).

S.L.A. 1925, s. 20 (1) (iv).—

" (iv) A tenant for years determinable on life, not holding merely under a lease at a rent ; "

It was held by Bennett, J., in *Re Catling* [1931] 2 Ch. 359, that a person who is a tenant of settled land under a lease at a rent is, as a matter of necessary implication from the language of this paragraph, excluded from the class of persons upon whom the section confers the powers of a tenant for life. The amount of the rent is immaterial. In that case the rent was the nominal one of £1 a year. For the facts of this case see *post*, p. 740.

Leases for years at a rent determinable on life created before or after the L.P.A. 1925 are now abolished and converted into terms of ninety years, determinable on notice as mentioned in s. 149 (6) of the L.P.A. 1925. See *post*, p. 941.

S.L.A. 1925, s. 20 (1) (v).—

" (v) A tenant for the life of another, not holding merely under a lease at a rent ; "

See under heading " Tenants *pur autre vie*," *ante*, p. 443.

S.L.A. 1925, s. 20 (1) (vi).—

" (vi) A tenant for his own or any other life, or for years determinable on life, whose estate is liable to cease in any event during that life, whether by expiration of the estate, or by conditional limitation, or otherwise, or to be defeated by an executory limitation, gift, or disposition over, or is subject to a trust for accumulation of income for any purpose ; "

An example occurs on a gift by a testator of land to trustees upon trust for his wife during widowhood, for the benefit and maintenance of herself and her children, and for their proper bringing up. In such a case it has been held that, although the widow's interest was charged with the main-tenance of the children, she had the powers of a tenant for life (*Re Pollock* [1906] 1 Ch. 146). See also *Re Edward's Settlement* [1897] 2 Ch. 412 ; *Re Eastman's Settled Estates* (1898), 68 L.J. Ch. 122n ; *Re Acklom* [1929] 1 Ch. 195, mentioned at p. 739. An example in which the paragraph did *not* apply is *Re Catling* [1931] 2 Ch. 359, *post*, p. 740.

In *Re Paget's Settled Estates* (1885), 30 Ch. D. 161, land was limited to the use of *A* so long as he should reside there, with a gift over on his ceasing to reside there, and it was held that such limitation gave him the powers of a tenant for life, and that if he sold the property under such powers he would be entitled to the income of the proceeds of sale during his life in spite of the gift over. See also *Re Trenchard* [1902] 1 Ch. 378 ; *Re Simpson* [1913] 1 Ch. 277 ; and *Re Patten* [1929] 2 Ch. 276. In *Re Carne's Settled Estates* [1899] 1 Ch. 324, the limitation was to trustees upon trust to permit a person to reside so long as he should desire to do so, and such trustees were given very full powers of management, and the power to pay outgoings out of the rent, and it was held that the limitation gave such person the powers of a tenant for life.

This paragraph will also apply if there is a trust to allow unmarried children to reside in a house so long as any one or more of them remain unmarried (*Re Boyer's Settled Estates* [1916] 2 Ch. 404).

The principle was also held to apply although the present interest of the tenant for life was subject to a term limited to trustees for the purpose of accumulation of rents after payment of interest on mortgages and annuities (*Re Clitheroe Estate* (1855), 31 Ch. D. 135 ; *Williams* v. *Jenkins* [1893] 1 Ch. 700 ; *Re Martyn* (1900), 69 L.J. Ch. 733 ; *Re Money Kyrle's Settlement* [1900] 2 Ch. 839 ; and *Re Earl of Stamford and Warrington* [1925] Ch. 162, not reversed on this point). But the paragraph would not apply where the interest of the tenant for life only arises *after* a trust for accumulation of rents has determined. Consequently, a trust to accumulate rents for a period of years, and at the end of that time to hold upon trusts under which an existing person, if then living, would be tenant for life, would not constitute him a tenant for life or person having the powers of a tenant for life (*Re Strangeways* (1886), 34 Ch. D. 423). But see *Re Beauchamp's Will Trusts* [1914] 1 Ch. 676, in which case a testator devised his mansion house and the whole of his real estate to trustees upon trust to permit his daughter during her life to have the personal use of the mansion house free from rent, rates and repair, *and to manage the remainder of the property* and to accumulate the rents for twenty years, *and upon the expiration of that period* to hold upon trust for the same daughter for life. It was held that the daughter was a person having the powers of a tenant for life in respect of such remainder

of the property as well as of the mansion house. It is thought that this case
was wrongly decided, and that it should have followed *Re Strangeways, ante.*

The paragraph does not apply where a person is only entitled to surplus
rents which are undisposed of during a limited period (*Re Baroness Llanover*
[1907] 1 Ch. 635). In *Re Musgrave* [1916] 2 Ch. 417, a testator devised lands
to four named grandsons as tenants in common for life with cross-remainders
between them and directed that after the death of the survivor such lands
should fall into the residue ; and by a codicil he directed his trustees to let
the lands and accumulate the rents for ten years to raise a fund for the
construction of a carriage road, and it was held that the grandsons were,
notwithstanding the term, persons who had the powers of a tenant for life,
as being a tenant for life whose estate is subject to a trust for accumulation
of income for payment of debts or other purposes within s. 58 (1) (vi) of the
Settled Land Act, 1882.

In *Re Higgs and May's Contract* [1927] 2 Ch. 249, a house was vested in
trustees on trust to permit the minister for the time being of a certain church
to reside therein and have the use and enjoyment thereof. It was decided
that the minister for the time being of the church was not a person having
the powers of a tenant for life, for the limitation was not for the benefit of
the minister, but for the benefit of the church, and the case came within
s. 29 of the S.L.A. 1925 (as to which, see *ante*, p. 271).

The above cases are not exhaustive, but they contain the principle on which
the court acts.

S.L.A. 1925, s. 20 (1) (vii)—

  " (vii) A tenant by the curtesy ; "

For the purposes of the Act, the estate or interest of a tenant by the
curtesy will be deemed to be an estate or interest arising under a settlement
made by his wife (S.L.A. 1925, s. 20 (3)).

Tenancy by the curtesy is abolished in the case of deaths occurring after
1925 (A.E.A. 1925, s. 45 (1)), except (i) as regards the descent or devolution of
an entailed interest (*ibid.*, s. 45 (2)), and (ii) as regards descent from a person of
unsound mind or defective, living and of full age on 1st January, 1926, who
afterwards died without recovering his or her sanity (*ibid.*, s. 51 (2)). See
further, *ante*, p. 428

S.L.A. 1925, s. 20 (1) (viii)—

  " (viii) *A person entitled to the income of land under a trust* or direction
    for payment thereof to him *during his own or any other life*, whether
    or not subject to expenses of management or to a trust for
    accumulation of income for any purpose, or until sale of the land,
    or until forfeiture, *cesser or determination* by any means of his interest
    therein, unless the land is subject to an immediate binding trust
    for sale ; "

A simple example of the application of this paragraph occurred in
Re Waleran Settled Estates [1927] 1 Ch. 522. In that case land was conveyed
to trustees for a term of ninety-nine years upon trust in the events which
happened to pay the income therefrom to *A* during the term if she should so
long live, with remainders over, and it was held by Clauson, J., that *A* was
a person having the powers of a tenant for life under this paragraph.

A person entitled to a *defined* part only of the income would not be a
person " entitled to the income of land " within this paragraph, and therefore
not a person having the powers of a tenant for life (*Re Frewen* [1926] Ch. 580 ;

Re Jefferys [1939] Ch. 205). But if the trust is to enter on the land and pay expenses, mortgage interest, and an annuity and the balance of the rents to a person for life, *and there should be no balance*, such person would nevertheless be a person having the powers of a tenant for life under this paragraph (*Re Jones* (1884), 26 Ch. D. 736).

" *A person entitled to the income of land under a trust.*"—The word " trust " includes a resulting trust (*Re Llanover Settled Estates* [1926] Ch. 626).

In *Re Alston-Roberts-West's Settled Estate* [1928] W.N. 41, the testator gave the trustees of his will a discretion to pay the income to a person for life, but did not deal with the balance of the income, and there was a resulting trust to the heir. The court decided that the heir was not a person having the powers of a tenant for life under this paragraph, as his interest was too shadowy, and, as there was no tenant for life, that the trustees could exercise the powers of a tenant for life under s. 23 of the S.L.A. 1925. Presumably this case is to be distinguished from *Re Jones*, ante, on the ground that the heir would benefit only if the trustees did not exercise their discretion, whereas the tenant for life in *Re Jones* was bound to benefit if the income was sufficient. *Re Alston-Roberts-West's Settled Estate*, ante, was followed in *Re Gallenga Will Trusts* [1938] 1 All E.R. 106 ; see also *Re Sharpe's Deed of Release* [1939] Ch. 51, mentioned at p. 674, and *Re Beaumont Settled Estates* [1937] 2 All E.R. 353.

" Land " does not include an undivided share in land (S.L.A. 1925, s. 117 (1) (ix)). In *Re Stamford and Warrington* [1927] 2 Ch. 217, at the end of 1925 land was vested in trustees for a term of 1,000 years, and, subject thereto, one-half was vested in one person for life and the other half was vested in another person for life. It was contended that these two persons were persons having the powers of a tenant for life under this paragraph, because their estate or interest was in possession as distinct from in reversion, but the court decided that the word " land " in the paragraph cannot be satisfied by producing and adding together two undivided moieties of land where undivided shares in land are in terms excluded from the definition of land in the Act. As in the result there was no tenant for life, the trustees were the persons to exercise the powers under s. 23 of the S.L.A. 1925. But during *the subsistence of a trust for accumulation of rents* for the purpose of paying off mortgages, the members of a class entitled in undivided shares to the income (if any) for their lives after payment off of the mortgages would be within this paragraph (*Re Stevens and Dunsby's Contract* [1928] W.N. 187). If, however, *there was no trust for accumulation*, such members would be entitled in equity in undivided shares *in possession* within Pt. IV of Sched. 1 to the L.P.A. 1925 and the land would be held upon the statutory trusts, and the case would not come within this paragraph (*ibid.*).

" *during his own or any other life.*"—These words are an essential part of the description and therefore a person, to be entitled to the benefit of the paragraph, must show that he is tenant for his own or some other life (*Re Astor* [1922] 1 Ch. 364, at p. 391). The objects for the time being of a discretionary power are not within this paragraph (*Re Atkinson* (1886), 31 Ch. D. 577 ; *Re Horne's Settled Estate* (1888), 39 Ch. D. 84).

S.L.A. 1925, s. 20 (1) (ix).—

" (ix) A person beneficially entitled to land for an estate in fee simple or for a term of years absolute subject to any estates, interests, charges, or powers of charging, subsisting or capable of being exercised under a settlement ; "

Joint tenants subject to a family charge are persons having the powers of a tenant for life within this paragraph (*Re Gaul and Houlston's Contract* [1928] Ch. 689). Section 36 (1) of the L.P.A. 1925, providing that a legal estate limited to or held in trust for persons as joint tenants shall be held on trust for sale, does not apply where the land is settled land. But the paragraph does not apply to land held by tenants in common (compare *Re Ryder and Steadman's Contract* [1927] 2 Ch. 62 ; S.L.A. 1925, ss. 1 (7) and 3).

This paragraph was not contained in the Settled Land Acts existing before the S.L.A. 1925. The person beneficially entitled to land under the above paragraph may sell the land subject to the charge ; in effect he has the option of treating the land as not settled. This option is given him by s. 1 (1) of the Law of Property (Amendment) Act, 1926. It is thought that this is the most convenient place to discuss this section, and it is therefore given below in full with some observations.

" 1.—(1) Nothing in the Settled Land Act, 1925, shall prevent a person on whom the powers of a tenant for life are conferred by paragraph (ix) of subsection (1) of section twenty of that Act from conveying or creating a legal estate subject to a prior interest as if the land had not been settled land.

(2) In any of the following cases, namely—

(*a*) where a legal estate has been conveyed or created under subsection one of this section, or under section sixteen of the Settled Land Act, 1925, subject to any prior interest, or

(*b*) where before the first day of January, nineteen hundred and twenty-six, land has been conveyed to a purchaser for money or money's worth subject to any prior interest whether or not on the purchase the land was expressed to be exonerated from or the grantor agreed to indemnify the purchaser against, such prior interest,

the estate owner for the time being of the land subject to such prior interest may, notwithstanding any provision contained in the Settled Land Act, 1925, but without prejudice to any power whereby such prior interest is capable of being overreached, convey or create a legal estate subject to such prior interest as if the instrument creating the prior interest was not an instrument or one of the instruments constituting a settlement of the land.

(3) In this section ' interest ' means an estate, interest, charge or power of charging subsisting, or capable of arising or of being exercised, under a settlement, and, where a prior interest arises under the exercise of a power, ' instrument ' includes both the instrument conferring the power and the instrument exercising it."

The above amendment was made to meet cases where portions of large estates had before 1926 been sold subject to a jointure rent-charge or other family charge, with an indemnity against such charge. Under these circumstances the land became, on 1st January, 1926, settled land under s. 1 (1) (v) (see *ante*, p. 671) and s. 3 of the S.L.A. 1925 (see *ante*, p. 704). It will be noticed that the amendment does not remove the land from the category of settled land. It merely enables the owner for the time being subject to the family charge to *sell or mortgage the land subject to the charge as if the land was not settled land.* The owner has the choice of dealing with the land in four different ways :—

(i) Subject to the family charge and with the benefit of the indemnity, under the above provision of the Law of Property (Amendment) Act, 1926.

(ii) As a person having the powers of a tenant for life, under the S.L.A. 1925 free from the charge. In this case he would have first to get a vesting deed from the trustees. It was thought at one time that these trustees would be the trustees of the original settlement under s. 31 (1) of the S.L.A. 1925. But it was decided by Romer, J., in *Re Ogle's Settled Estates* [1927] 1 Ch. 229, that, where property subject to a jointure rent-charge had been disentailed and sold in separate portions to separate purchasers subject thereto, and with an indemnity, each portion sold must be deemed to be the subject of a different settlement and that trustees could be appointed of one without those persons becoming the trustees of any of the other settlements. If this mode of sale were chosen, there would be the further disadvantage that the trustees of the settlement would have to receive the purchase money. In fact, the technical objections to this course are such that it has not often been adopted.

(iii) By arranging with the trustees of the settlement for a discharge of the charge. The land would then cease to be settled land, and the owner would be in a position to sell or mortgage as an ordinary beneficial owner, and thus avoid the necessity for obtaining a vesting deed, and all the other inconveniences attached to settled land (*Re Alefounder's Will Trusts* [1927] 1 Ch. 360). See also S.L.A. 1925, s. 112 (2).

(iv) By conveying his interest to trustees appointed by or approved by the court upon trust for sale under s. 2 (2) of the L.P.A. 1925. The effect would be to determine the settlement and enable him to over-reach the charge ; see *ante,* p. 176.

On the death of the owner for the time being, the persons who become his special representatives under s. 22 of the A.E.A. 1925 or s. 162 of the Judicature Act, 1925 (see *ante,* p. 710), will be entitled to take out probate or administration to the settled land. Probably it would be proper for the general representatives to take out a grant including settled land so as to avoid having a separate grant limited to settled land. See further *ante,* p. 111.

In the case of a sale subject to the charge, the provisions of s. 42 of the L.P.A. 1925 (*ante,* p. 110) must be borne in mind, and the vendor must expressly state in the contract that the land is sold subject to the charge. For if there is only an open contract, that is, a contract omitting to state that the land is sold subject to the charge, the purchaser could insist upon a title being made free therefrom under the S.L.A. 1925.

S.L.A. 1925, s. 20 (1) (x).—

" (x) *A married woman entitled to land for an estate in fee simple or for a term of years absolute subject to a restraint on anticipation."* ·

This paragraph was repealed by the Married Women (Restraint upon Anticipation) Act, 1949, Sched. 2 ; as restraints are no longer valid it is now unnecessary.

The instrument under which the land stood limited subject to the restraint was the settlement (S.L.A. 1925, s. 1 (1) (iv)). A restraint on anticipation did not prevent the exercise by a married woman of any power under the S.L.A. 1925 (S.L.A. 1925, s. 25). The paragraph applied where the married woman was entitled absolutely ; if she was entitled to the income of land under a trust or direction to pay it to her during her own or any other life, para. (viii), *ante*, p. 728, applied, and may continue to apply.

Devolution on death of persons having powers of tenant for life.— Settled land vested in a person having the powers of a tenant for life under the S.L.A. 1925, s. 20 (1), will devolve in the same manner as if it had been vested in a tenant for life. This is the result of the S.L.A. 1925, s. 20 (2), which provides as follows :—

" (2) In every such case as is mentioned in subsection (1) of this section, the provisions of this Act referring to a tenant for life, either as conferring powers on him or otherwise, shall extend to each of the persons aforesaid, and any reference in this Act to death as regards a tenant for life shall, where necessary, be deemed to refer to the determination by death or otherwise of the estate or interest of the person on whom the powers of a tenant for life are conferred by this section."

B. STATUTORY OWNERS

It often happens that there is a settlement, yet there is no tenant for life or person having the powers of a tenant for life under ss. 19 or 20 of the S.L.A. 1925. For instance, under s. 1 (1) (iii) of the S.L.A. 1925, a settlement is created when land is " limited in trust for any person for an estate in fee simple or for a term of years absolute *contingently* on the happening of any event," but such person is not a tenant for life or person having the powers of a tenant for life under s. 19 or 20 above (*Re Bird* [1927] 1 Ch. 210). Another case is where land is held by trustees during a life on discretionary trusts. In such a case there is a settlement, but the trustees are not persons having the powers of a tenant for life, and therefore there is no tenant for life of the settlement (*Re Atkinson* (1885), 30 Ch. D. 605 ; *Re Jemmett and Guest's Contract* [1907] 1 Ch. 629 ; *Re Beaumont Settled Estates* [1937] 2 All E.R. 353 ; see further *ante*, p. 729).

When, therefore, there is a settlement and there is no tenant for life, or person having the powers of a tenant for life, under s. 19 or 20, to carry out the general scheme of the S.L.A. 1925, someone must be found in whom the legal estate must be vested and who must be given the powers of a tenant for life. This position is dealt with by ss. 23 and 26 of the S.L.A. 1925.

Section 23 (1) of the S.L.A. 1925 is as follows :—

" 23.—(1) Where under a settlement there is no tenant for life, nor independently of this section, a person having by virtue of this Act the powers of a tenant for life then—

(a) any *person of full age* on whom such powers are by the settlement expressed to be conferred ; and

(b) in any other case the trustees of the settlement ;

shall have the powers of a tenant for life under this Act."

" *person of full age* " includes a corporation (*Re Carnarvon's Settled Estates* [1927] 1 Ch. 138).

If the powers are expressed to be conferred on a certain person by a re-settlement that person will have the powers of a tenant for life under the compound settlement of which the re-settlement is part (*Re Beaumont Settled Estates* [1937] 2 All E.R. 353).

The persons given the powers of a tenant for life under s. 23 are known as " statutory owners ". The definition of statutory owners given in s. 117 (1) (xxvi) is as follows :—

" 117.—(1) (xxvi) ' Statutory owner ' means the trustees of the settlement or other persons who, *during a minority*, or at any other time when there is no tenant for life, have the powers of a tenant for life under this Act, but does not include the trustees of the settlement, where by virtue of an order of the court or otherwise the trustees *have power to convey the settled land in the name of the tenant for life*."

" *during a minority.*"—Section 26 of the S.L.A. 1925 deals with the case where there is no tenant for life or person having the powers of a tenant for life, by reason of a person entitled beneficially being an infant.   As an infant cannot hold a legal estate, and as the scheme of modern conveyancing is that there must always be someone in whom the legal estate is vested with power to convey it to a purchaser, it follows that provision had to be made for someone to act for him during his minority.   See further, *ante*, p. 339.

" *have power to convey the settled land in the name of the tenant for life.*"— This refers to s. 68, *post*, p. 743, which contains provision for enabling dealings to be made with the tenant for life, and to s. 24, *post*, p. 742, under which, in certain circumstances, the court may make an order authorising the trustees to exercise the powers of the tenant for life.

A statutory owner has the right to insist that the legal estate shall be vested in him (S.L.A. 1925, ss. 4 (2), 7 (1), 106 (1) (*a*), (*b*)).

PART 8.   POWERS OF TENANT FOR LIFE

A.   GENERAL POSITION WHEN EXERCISING POWERS

Tenant for life a trustee for all parties interested.—It is provided by s. 107 (1) of the S.L.A. 1925 that—

" A tenant for life or statutory owner shall, in exercising *any power under this Act, have regard to the interests of all parties* entitled under the settlement, and shall, in relation to the exercise thereof by him, be deemed to be in the position and to have the duties and liabilities of a trustee for those parties."

The words " *any power under this Act* " include any additional or wider power under ss. 108 and 109 of the S.L.A. 1925 ; see *post*, p. 751.   There are also various provisions in the S.L.A. 1925 by virtue of which the tenant for life gets power to do certain acts which an ordinary trustee could not do without express power.   For instance, under s. 57 of the S.L.A. 1925, provision is made for selling land for small dwellings, smallholdings and dwellings for the working classes, notwithstanding that a better price might have been obtained if the land had been sold for another purpose.   So, although an ordinary trustee should not, without express power, grant an option to purchase in a lease, a tenant for life is expressly given such right by s. 51 (1) of the S.L.A. 1925.   See *post*, p. 737.

See also s. 16 (1) (i) of the S.L.A. 1925, the effect of which is to make the tenant for life or person or persons having the powers of a tenant for life an express trustee or express trustees of the settled land and the income thereof.

A tenant for life should not, being a trustee, sell at a price to be fixed by valuation (*Re Earl of Wilton's Settled Estates* [1907] 1 Ch. 50). See further, *ante*, p. 456.

Where there is doubt as to the powers of the tenant for life it may be advisable to apply to the court under the S.L.A. 1925, s. 93. This section enables the court to give a decision or directions if a question arises respecting the exercise or intended exercise of any of the powers conferred by the S.L.A. 1925, or as to the person in whose favour a vesting deed or assent ought to be executed or as to the contents thereof, or otherwise in relation to property subject to a settlement. The section cannot be used, however, merely for the solution of theoretical problems ; persons who wish to know their powers must explain the precise transaction they wish to undertake (*Re Holland House*, unreported but discussed in the *Law Times*, vol. 223, pp. 230, 231). Nor can s. 93 of the S.L.A. 1925 be used where joint tenants for life disagree as to the exercise of the power of sale vested in them ; in such circumstances the power simply cannot be exercised and therefore no question of doubt arises giving the court jurisdiction within s. 93 (*Re 90 Thornhill Road, Tolworth, Surrey* [1970] Ch. 261).

" *have regard to the interests of all parties.*"—The duty imposed by subs. (1) of s. 107 on the tenant for life or statutory owner will not affect the title of a purchaser (including a lessee, mortgagee or other person who acquires an interest for value : *ibid.*, s. 117 (1) (xxi)) dealing *in good faith* with him (S.L.A. 1925, s. 110 (1)) as such a purchaser is conclusively taken to have given the best consideration or rent reasonably obtainable and to have complied with all the requirements of the Act. As to what amounts to dealing in good faith, see *Mogridge* v. *Clapp* [1892] 3 Ch. 382. A person who has only contracted to take a lease may be a " purchaser " for the purposes of the S.L.A. 1925, s. 110 (1), the protection of which is not restricted to completed transactions (*Re Morgan's Lease* [1972] Ch. 1, where the contract arose from the exercise of an option to renew a lease). But the provision in s. 110 will not protect a purchaser with knowledge that the tenant for life is not acting fairly towards the remaindermen. For instance, the payment of a commission to the tenant for life would invalidate the sale (*Chandler* v. *Bradley* [1897] 1 Ch. 315). A person taking under a document, for instance, a lease, which is invalid on the face of it is apparently not regarded as taking in good faith and so cannot rely on s. 110 (1) (*Davies* v. *Hall* [1954] 1 W.L.R. 855, at p. 861). But this does not imply a general proposition that where an attack is made on a lease for reasons other than insufficiency of rent the lessee can never rely on s. 110 (1) : he can do so provided he acted in good faith (*Re Morgan's Lease* [1972] Ch. 1).

It used to be accepted that s. 110 (1) of the S.L.A. 1925 applies only to a person dealing with a tenant for life or statutory owner as such, and who knows him to be a limited owner ; that it does not apply where the purchaser is fraudulently led to believe that he is dealing with an absolute owner (*Weston* v. *Henshaw* [1950] Ch. 510 ; see *ante*, p. 650, for provisions as to the marking of deeds to prevent fraud). However, these propositions derived from *Weston* v. *Henshaw* now appear to be incorrect. Ungoed-Thomas, J., has held that s. 110 (1) applies whether or not the purchaser knows that the other party to the transaction is a tenant for life (*Re Morgan's Lease* [1972] Ch. 1, following *Mogridge* v. *Clapp* [1892] 3 Ch. 382, C.A., not cited in *Weston* v. *Henshaw*). Further, the learned judge held that a person who believed he was dealing with an absolute owner could not be said to lack good faith merely because he thought that the price or rent was not the best obtainable (*ibid.*).

A purchaser from a tenant for life is under no obligation to inquire whether he has had a valuation ; an immediate resale by the purchaser at an increased price is not alone sufficient evidence of bad faith on his part, and even if it turned out that the sale was made at an undervalue, that would not, of itself, be sufficient to invalidate the sale (*Hurrell* v. *Littlejohn* [1904] 1 Ch. 689). To affect the title of a purchaser it would have to be shown that he had notice of and was a party to such improper dealing (*Re Handman and Wilcox's Contract* [1902] 1 Ch. 599). As regards a purchaser from the first purchaser, the position would seem to be that it is doubtful whether the original transaction was void or merely voidable against the parties interested under the settlement. If it was void, then the title of the vendor would be bad, and he could not pass a title to a purchaser from him. But if the transaction was only voidable, then it may be that a subsequent purchaser for value without notice would get a good title, though, as notice is always a doubtful question of fact, the title would not be forced on an unwilling purchaser.

Notice to trustees before sale, mortgage or lease.—As between the tenant for life or statutory owner and the trustees, one month's previous notice of his intention to make a sale, exchange, lease (except in the case of leases for less than twenty-one years where no fine : S.L.A. 1925, s. 42 (5) ; see *post*, p. 815), mortgage, or charge, or to grant an option, must be given to each of the trustees of the settlement and their solicitor, if any such solicitor is known, by registered letter (S.L.A. 1925, s. 101 (1)). It will be sufficient if the notice is given one month before the completion of a sale (*Duke of Marlborough* v. *Sartoris* (1886), 32 Ch. D. 616). The trustees may also, by writing under their hand, accept less than a month's notice or waive altogether a notice being given (*ibid.*, s. 101 (4)). The notice of a proposed sale, exchange or lease or grant of an option may be a notice of a general intention in that behalf (S.L.A. 1925, s. 101 (22)), but this subsection does not apply to a *mortgage*, and therefore notice of intention to make the *specific* mortgage must be given to the trustees (*Re Ray's Settled Estates* (1884), 25 Ch. D. 464). Receipt of notice does not oblige the trustees to inquire, in the interest of a remainderman, whether the proposed sale is improvident (*England* v. *Public Trustee* (1967), 112 Sol. J. 70).

At the date of the notice there must (where capital money arises) be two trustees, unless the trustee is a trust corporation (S.L.A. 1925, s. 101 (1)). Where no capital money arises under a transaction, for instance, in the case of a lease, such transaction will have effect in favour of a purchaser of a legal estate, although there are no trustees (S.L.A. 1925, s. 110 (4)).

A purchaser is not concerned to inquire respecting the giving of any such notice, provided he is dealing in good faith (S.L.A. 1925, s. 101 (5)). But the purchaser should satisfy himself that there are trustees to whom notice may have been given (*Hatten* v. *Russell* (1888), 38 Ch. D. 334 ; *Mogridge* v. *Clapp* [1892] 3 Ch. 382).

If the purchaser *has actual knowledge* that no notice has been given the legal estate will not pass to him (*Hughes* v. *Fanagan* (1891), 30 L.R. Ir. 111).

Consent of, or notice to, a mortgagee or assignee of the life tenant's interest.—If the mortgage or assignment (for value) of the tenant for life's interest was made before 1926, such consent is necessary on a sale, mortgage or lease, except in the case of the grant of a lease by the tenant for life at the best rent without fine ; and even in that case notice is necessary if the assignee is actually in possession of the part of the settled land affected (S.L.A. 1925, s. 104 (3) ; *Re Dickin and Kelsall's Contract* [1908] 1 Ch. 213). Where the sale, mortgage or lease is made after 1925, a purchaser is not concerned to inquire whether consent has been obtained (S.L.A. 1925, s. 104 (5)).

A mortgage or assignment for value of the tenant for life's interest made after 1925 does not prevent him from exercising his powers under the S.L.A. 1925, s. 104 (2) (4)). The tenant for life must give notice to the mortgagee or assignee of the intended transaction but a purchaser is not concerned to see that the notice has been given (*ibid.*, s. 104 (4)).

An assignment by the operation of the law of bankruptcy where the assignment comes into operation after 1925 is deemed an assignment for value (S.L.A. 1925, s. 104 (10)). But an assignment or charge by a tenant for life of or upon his estate or interest under the settlement in consideration of marriage or by way of family arrangement, not being a security for money advanced, will be deemed to be one of the instruments creating the settlement and not an assignment for value (*ibid.*, s. 110 (11)). This is a reproduction of s. 4 of the Settled Land Act, 1890. See *Re Sebright's Settled Estates* (1886), 33 Ch. D. 429 ; *Re Du Cane and Nettleford's Contract* [1898] 2 Ch. 96.

Remedies of purchaser of beneficial interest of tenant for life.— It is provided by s. 111 of the S.L.A. 1925 that where, (*a*) on 1st January, 1926, the legal beneficial interest of a tenant for life under a settlement was vested in a purchaser, or (*b*) after 1925 a tenant for life conveys or deals with his beneficial interest in possession in favour of a purchaser, and the interest so conveyed or created would, but for the restrictions imposed by statute on the creation of legal estates, have been a legal interest, the purchaser shall (without prejudice to the powers conferred by the Act on the tenant for life) have all the same rights and remedies as he would have had if the interest had remained or been a legal interest and the reversion, if any, on any leases or tenancies derived out of the settled land had been vested in him. There is a proviso to the section, however, to the effect that, where the conveyance or dealing is effected after 1925, the purchaser shall not be entitled to the possession of the documents of title relating to the settled land, but shall have the same rights with respect thereto as if the tenant for life had given to him a statutory acknowledgment of his right to production and delivery of copies thereof, and a statutory undertaking for the safe custody thereof.

This section became necessary because the L.P.A. 1925 converted legal estates for life into equitable interests. To enable an owner to distrain for rent or to recover possession of land the subject of a lease when the lessee has forfeited his interest by breach of some covenant in the lease, he must have the legal estate vested in him. Where, therefore, before 1926, a legal tenant for life had assigned his life interest to a purchaser or mortgagee, such purchaser or mortgagee having the legal estate could distrain for the rent in arrear or recover possession on a forfeiture. After 1925 this was altered. In the case of para. (*a*) of s. 111 the legal estate passed on 1st January, 1926, from the purchaser or mortgagee to the tenant for life notwithstanding that he had assigned away his interest, and the assignee took only an equitable interest (L.P.A. 1925, s. 1 ; Sched. 1, Pts. I and II) ; and in the case of para. (*b*) the assignee also only acquires an equitable interest. In both cases, therefore, the assignee not having the legal estate, to enable him to exercise his rights over the property, subject to the statutory rights of the tenant for life, it was necessary to make the special provision contained in s. 111.

Power of tenant for life to make or confirm contracts.—Section 90 of the S.L.A. 1925 provides, in effect, that a tenant for life may contract to make any sale, exchange, mortgage, charge or other disposition *authorised by the Act* ; and may vary or rescind ; and may contract to make any lease so that it conforms with the Act, and generally may enter into a contract to do any act for carrying into effect any of the purposes of the Act. It is also provided by the same section that every contract, including a contract arising by reason of the exercise of an option, shall be binding on and shall enure for the benefit of the settled land, and shall be enforceable against and by every successor in title for the time being of the tenant for life, or statutory owner, and may be carried into effect by any such successor.

If a contract is not registered as a land charge under the L.C.A. 1972, s. 2 (4), Class C (iv), it will be void as against a purchaser of a legal estate for money's worth (L.C.A. 1972, s. 4 (6)). An option to purchase should always be registered as a land charge at once ; in other cases it may not be necessary to register, for reasons mentioned *ante*, p. 39.

A tenant for life may, either with or without consideration, grant by writing an option to purchase or take a lease of the settled land, or any part thereof, or any easement, right, or privilege over or in relation to the same at a price fixed at the time of the granting of the option (S.L.A. 1925, s. 51 (1)) ; and if any consideration is given it will have to be treated as capital money (*ibid.*, s. 51 (5)).

Prohibition or limitation against exercise of the powers is void.— The provision to this effect is contained in s. 106 of the S.L.A. 1925, which replaces ss. 51 and 52 of the Settled Land Act, 1882.

" 106.—(1) If in a settlement, will, assurance, or other instrument . . . a provision is inserted—

> (*a*) purporting or attempting, by way of direction, declaration, or otherwise, to forbid a tenant for life or statutory owner to exercise any power under this Act, *or his right to require the settled land to be vested in him ;* or
>
> (*b*) attempting, or tending, or intended, by a limitation, gift, or disposition over of settled land, or by a limitation, gift, or disposition of other real or any personal property, or by the imposition of any condition, or by forfeiture, or in any other manner whatever, to prohibit or prevent him from exercising, or to induce him to abstain from exercising, or to put him into a position inconsistent with his exercising, any power under this Act, *or his right to require the settled land to be vested in him ;*
>
> that provision, as far as it purports, or attempts, or tends, or is intended to have, or would or might have, the operation aforesaid, shall be deemed to be void."

For the purposes of s. 106 an estate or interest limited to continue so long only as a person abstains from exercising any power under the Act or right to require the land to be vested in him takes effect as an estate or interest

24

for the period for which it would continue if that person were to abstain
from exercising the power or right, discharged from liability to determination
or cesser by or on his exercising the same (*ibid.*, s. 106 (2)). Similarly, it
is provided by s. 106 (3) that, notwithstanding anything in a settlement,
the exercise by the tenant for life or statutory owner of any power under the
Act shall not occasion a forfeiture.

A gift over on bankruptcy or alienation is not void under this section, as
bankruptcy or alienation would not prevent the tenant for life exercising
his statutory powers (*Re Levy's Trusts* (1885), 30 Ch. D. 119).

Section 106 often has to be applied where there is a limitation over on
failure of the tenant for life to reside on the settled land; the matter is
discussed *post*, p. 739 *et seq*. The other circumstances in which the section
frequently causes difficulty are where provision is made for payment of the
costs of upkeep of the settled land on the terms that the provision will cease
to operate if the tenant for life exercises his statutory power of sale. The
question is whether a condition that such a benefit will cease on sale is one
tending to induce the life tenant to abstain from exercising his powers;
if it is, then s. 106 will make it void and so entitle the life tenant to continue
to enjoy the benefit of the provision even after sale.

Although the reasoning in the various decisions is difficult to follow,
the balance of authority appears to support the assertion that " it would
seem at least to be established that trusts for the upkeep of settled property,
which merely provide for the payment of outgoings and repairs, are not within
the scope of [the S.L.A. 1925, s. 106 (1) (*b*)], and, if a tenant for life sells, the
trust fund applicable to such purposes can be so made to go over to a
beneficiary other than the tenant for life " (*Law Times*, vol. 216, p. 406).
Thus, in *Re Burden* [1948] Ch. 160, a house was given to *A* for life with
remainder to *B* subject to a provision that, if the life tenant should cease to
reside in the house, it should pass to *B*. A capital sum was directed to be
held by trustees during the life-time of *A* on trust to pay rates, taxes and
cost of repairs, and after her death the balance was given to *B*. It was
held that the deprivation of the advantage of having rates, taxes and cost
of repairs paid was not within the S.L.A. 1925, s. 106 (1), and so was valid. It
will be noted that there was no provision for payment of the balance of the
income derived from the capital sum to the life tenant. See also *Re Patten*
[1929] 2 Ch. 276, mentioned at p. 720, and *Re Simpson* [1913] 1 Ch. 277.

The facts of *Re Aberconway's Settlement Trusts* [1953] Ch. 647 were
unusual, but the majority decision of the Court of Appeal suggests that,
where the tenant for life is not able to receive any part of the income of
the fund which is to be used for maintenance of the estate, a provision for
cesser of the application of that fund on sale is not a deterrent to the exercise
of powers under the S.L.A. 1925, and so is not caught by s. 106. " In my
judgment, neither s. 51 of the Act of 1882, nor s. 106 of the Act of 1925 (which
has replaced it) should be taken as operating to render void directions in a
settlement operating to determine other provisions in the settlement which are
neither for the benefit (properly speaking) of any *cestui que trust* nor even,
in strictness, ancillary to the enjoyment by a *cestui que trust* of the trust
property " (*ibid.*, per Evershed, M.R., at p. 664).

A different conclusion was reached in *Re Herbert* [1946] 1 All E.R. 421.
In that case a capital sum was given to trustees on trust to apply such part
of the income thereof as they should think fit towards maintenance of a
settled estate *and to pay the balance of such income to the tenant for life*.
On sale of the land the fund was directed to fall into residue, but it was

held, following *Re Ames* [1893] 2 Ch. 479 and *Re Smith* [1899] 1 Ch. 331, that this direction was void because it tended to induce the tenant for life not to exercise his statutory power of sale and that the income from the fund continued to be payable to the tenant for life after the sale.

" *or his right to require the settled land to be vested in him.*"—These words, in sub-paras. (*a*) and (*b*), do not prevent a statutory owner, having no beneficial interest and not being a S.L.A. 1925 trustee, from releasing his powers so as to enable the S.L.A. 1925 trustees under s. 23 of the S.L.A. 1925 to become statutory owners in his place (*Re Craven Settled Estates* [1926] Ch. 985) ; nor do they affect the right of a tenant for life to extinguish his beneficial interest under s. 105 of the S.L.A. 1925, *post*, p. 741. Section 155 of the L.P.A. 1925 provides that a person to whom any power, whether *coupled with an interest* or not, is given, may by deed release, or contract not to exercise, the power. But this section would not allow S.L.A. 1925 trustees to release the powers given to them as statutory powers ; the statutory powers are *powers coupled with a duty* which do not come within s. 155 above, and cannot be released (*Re Eyre* (1883), 49 L.T. 259).

Conditions as to residence.—The general effect of s. 106 of the S.L.A. 1925 (*ante*, p. 737) on gifts containing a condition as to residence would appear to be that the condition is void so far as it tends to prevent the exercise by the donee of his powers as tenant for life, but not otherwise (*Re Paget's Settled Estates* (1885), 30 Ch. D. 161 ; *Re Trenchard* [1902] 1 Ch. 378). In *Re Richardson* [1904] 2 Ch. 777, a testatrix devised real estate to her niece on condition that she resided there during an aunt's life and kept a home there for the latter whenever she should require it ; in default, there was a gift over on the same condition to another niece. It was held by Joyce, J., that the niece was a person having the powers of a tenant for life under the Act, and that, as the provision as to residence was a *condition* (not a trust for the aunt's benefit), it was void under s. 51 of the 1882 Act ; therefore, the niece could sell the house as tenant for life.

Therefore, if in such a case a sale of the subject-matter of the gift were made by the donee as tenant for life, such donee tenant for life would be entitled to the income of the purchase-money made by the sale (*Re Patten* [1929] 2 Ch. 276 ; *Re Orlebar* [1936] Ch. 147). This would not be so if the donee tenant for life had broken the condition as to residence definitely and finally, before exercising or attempting to exercise the power of the S.L.A. 1925, for in that case the forfeiture would already have operated, and the gift over would have taken effect (*Re Haynes* (1887), 37 Ch. D. 306). But before the forfeiture could take effect it would have to be shown that the donee *had* finally and irrevocably decided not to reside in the house. For instance, in *Re Acklom* [1929] 1 Ch. 195, a testator bequeathed a house to trustees for *A* for life or so long as she wished to continue to reside there, and directed that after her death, or during her life if she did not wish to reside there, the trustees should sell the house and divide the proceeds among charities. *A* went to reside in the house, but being taken ill later went to reside abroad and left the house in the charge of servants. As she was too ill to return she let the house and later sold it as a person having the powers of a tenant for life. It was held that the limitation over would take effect only if and when she decided not to continue to reside in the house, and that before she sold the house there was no evidence that she had finally and irrevocably decided not to continue to reside there. Consequently, she had not forfeited her interest in the proceeds of sale, namely, the income made thereby. The learned judge said that so long as she continued to let the house she was, in the very act of letting, exercising her powers as tenant for life, and this alone prevented the forfeiture becoming operative. The life tenant was entitled to give up possession if it was for the purpose of exercising her statutory powers, without forfeiting her interest.

As to the meaning of the word " residence," see *Re Coxen* [1948] Ch. 747. A condition that a person shall *occupy* settled property may be void for uncertainty (*Re Field's Will Trusts* [1950] Ch. 520 ; *Re Brace* [1954] 2 All E.R. 354 ; compare *Re Gape* [1952] 1 Ch. 743).

The difficulty caused by s. 106 was avoided in *Re Catling* [1931] 2 Ch. 359. The testator devised a house to his trustee on trust that his trustee should, if his wife so desired, let it to her on a yearly tenancy at a rent of £1 a year without power for her to assign, sub-let or part with possession, and provided that so long as his wife should be living and should duly observe and perform all the conditions, a notice to determine such tenancy should not be effectual unless given by his wife to his trustees, but on any default on her part in observing and performing the conditions such notice might be forthwith given by his trustees. He declared that in the event of such tenancy being determined she was to have an annuity. The question arose as to whether she was a tenant for life or person having the powers of a tenant for life under the S.L.A. 1925, because if she *was*, most of the above conditions would be void as tending to prevent her exercising her statutory powers. It was held that she was not a tenant for life or a person having the powers of a tenant for life. It might be thought that she came within s. 20 (1) (vi) of the S.L.A. 1925 (*ante*, p. 727), but it was decided that that paragraph must be construed as if it contained the words " not holding merely under a lease at a rent," so as to fit in with paras. (iv) and (v) of the same section, which contained such words. The result seems to be that an effective condition of residence may be created by the granting of a lease, even at a small rent, but perhaps at the present time £1 per annum would be so obviously nominal that the lease would not be regarded as a genuine one avoiding the application of s. 106. See the discussion in *Law Times*, vol. 227, pp. 48 and 49. Further, in order to make proper use of this method of avoiding s. 106, it should be appreciated that the decision in *Re Catling*, *ante*, although reaching a correct conclusion, was based on the false premise that a strict settlement had been created. In fact, the state of affairs in that case would not appear to be within s. 1 of the S.L.A. 1925 at all, but instead to be within s. 149 (6) of the L.P.A. 1925, i.e., the wife's interest should have taken effect as a lease for a term of ninety years determinable by notice after her death. Accordingly, the estate in fee simple absolute in possession (which of course includes receipt of rent : s. 205 (1) (xix) of the L.P.A. 1925) should have been vested in the person entitled thereto under the will, subject to the wife's term of years absolute, each of these interests being capable of subsisting as a legal estate (s. 1 (1) of the L.P.A. 1925). In other words, in this way, the S.L.A. 1925 can be avoided altogether.

Perhaps the simplest way of avoiding the S.L.A. 1925, however, is to give the house to trustees upon trust for sale, with power to postpone, directing such trustees to permit the widow to reside in the house until sale, and providing also that so long as she shall desire to reside in the house no sale shall take place without her consent. See *Re Herklot's Will Trusts* [1964] 1 W.L.R. 583, where the employment of this method was considered and upheld. Reference may also be made to articles, considering the suggestion that the

S.L.A. 1925 may be avoided by constituting the residing beneficiary a mere licensee rather than tenant for life, at *Conveyancer N.S.*, vol. 30, at p. 256 (A. J. Hawkins) and *New Law Journal*, vol. 116, pp. 1567 and 1591 (B. A. Bicknell).

The powers of a tenant for life are not assignable, and any contract not to exercise powers is void.—This is roughly the effect of s. 104 (1) and (2) of the S.L.A. 1925 given below :—

" 104.—(1) The powers under this Act of a tenant for life are not capable of assignment or release, and do not pass to a person as being, by operation of law or otherwise, an assignee of a tenant for life, and remain exercisable by the tenant for life after and notwithstanding any assignment, by operation of law or otherwise, of his estate or interest under the settlement.

This subsection applies notwithstanding that the estate or interest of the tenant for life under the settlement was not in possession when the assignment was made or took effect by operation of law.

(2) A contract by a tenant for life not to exercise his powers under this Act or any of them shall be void."

The question as to whether a tenant for life can disclaim his power as a tenant for life which he holds as trustee for all parties interested (S.L.A. 1925, s. 107) is not dealt with by s. 104 (1), but it could not very well arise, because a disclaimer of the office of trustee amounts to a disclaimer also of the legal estate and interest (*Re Birchall* (1889), 40 Ch. D. 436 ; see also *Re Lord and Fullerton's Contract* [1896] 1 Ch. 228).

It was held under s. 50 of the 1882 Act (now represented by s. 104 above) that the fact that a tenant for life received no income by reason of his having mortgaged his interest (*Re Jones* (1884), 26 Ch. D. 736) ; or even the fact of his having assigned his interest away altogether (*Re Mundy and Roper's Contract* [1899] 1 Ch. 275 ; *Re Barlow's Contract* [1903] 1 Ch. 382) ; or having become bankrupt (*Re Levy's Trusts* (1885), 30 Ch. D. 119), did not prevent him exercising his powers as tenant for life. As to bankruptcy of a tenant for life since 1925, see *post*, p. 742 *et seq*.

Surrender by tenant for life of estate to remainderman.—This is dealt with by s. 105 of the S.L.A. 1925 as amended by the Law of Property (Amendment) Act, 1926 :—

" 105.—(1) Where the estate or interest of a tenant for life under the settlement has been or is absolutely assured *with intent* to extinguish the same, either before or after the commencement of this Act, *to the person next entitled in remainder or reversion* under the settlement, then the statutory powers of the tenant for life under this Act shall, in reference to the property affected by the assurance, and notwithstanding the provisions of the last preceding section, cease to be exercisable by him, and the statutory powers shall thenceforth become exercisable as if he were dead, but without prejudice to any incumbrance affecting the estate or interest assured, and to the rights to which any incumbrancer would have been entitled if those powers had remained exercisable by the tenant for life.

This subsection applies whether or not any term of years or charge intervenes, or the estate of the remainderman or reversioner is liable to be defeated, and whether or not the estate or interest of the tenant for life under the settlement was in possession at the date of the assurance.

* * * * *

(2) In this section 'assurance' means any surrender, conveyance, assignment or appointment under a power (whether vested in any person solely, or jointly in two or more persons) which operates in equity to extinguish the estate or interest of the tenant for life, and 'assured' has a corresponding meaning."

It was held in *Re Shawdon Settled Estates* [1930] 2 Ch. 1, that s. 105 (1) applied to an assurance by any person in whom the life estate was vested, *including a trustee in bankruptcy of the tenant for life*. The "intent" referred to in the subsection was the intent of the assignor. It was further held that where the tenant for life was bankrupt, and his trustee in bankruptcy had assured the estate for life to the tenant in tail in remainder, but the tenant for life had refused to execute a vesting deed in his favour, the tenant in tail was entitled to a vesting order under s. 12 (1) (*a*) of the S.L.A. 1925.

The remaindermen to whom the tenant for life had surrendered his estate or interest with intent to extinguish it might be trustees for sale. In that case the effect of the surrender would be to bring the settlement to an end, and to use the words of the subsection, "the statutory powers shall thenceforth become exercisable as if he were dead," and the trustees for sale can require the tenant for life to convey the legal estate to them by virtue of s. 7 (5) of the S.L.A. 1925.

Section 105 (1) does not apply where there is any intervening limitation which may still take effect (*Re Maryon-Wilson's Settlements* [1971] Ch. 789).

Tenant for life who has ceased to have a substantial interest.— The fact that a tenant for life has become bankrupt does not prevent him exercising his powers as a tenant for life, and the legal estate in the settled land will not vest in his trustee in bankruptcy (S.L.A. 1925, s. 19 (4), *ante*, p. 723). The legal estate in settled land does not vest in the trustee in bankruptcy of an estate owner unless and until the estate owner becomes absolutely and beneficially entitled free from all limitations, powers and charges taking effect under the settlement (*ibid.*, s. 103).

It is provided by s. 24 (1) of the S.L.A. 1925 that : "If it is shown to the satisfaction of the court that a tenant for life, who has by reason of bankruptcy, assignment, incumbrance, or otherwise ceased in the opinion of the court to have a substantial interest in his estate or interest in the settled land or any part thereof, has unreasonably refused to exercise any of the powers conferred on him by this Act, or consents to an order under this section, the court may, on the application of any person interested in the settled land or the part thereof affected, make an order authorising the trustees of the settlement to exercise in the name and on behalf of the tenant for life, any of the powers of a tenant for life under this Act, in relation to the settled land or the part thereof affected, either generally and in such manner and for such period as the court may think fit, or in a particular instance, and the court may by the order direct that any documents of title in the possession of the tenant for life relating to the settled land be delivered to the trustees of the settlement."

The tenant for life should be made a party to the application or his consent obtained and proved (*Re Lady Francis Cecil's Settled Estates* [1926] W.N. 262).

Subsection (2) of s. 24 provides that : "While any such order is in force, the tenant for life shall not, in relation to the settled land or the part thereof affected, exercise any of the powers thereby authorised to be exercised in his name and on his behalf, but no person dealing with the tenant for life shall be affected by any such order, unless the order is for the time being registered as an order affecting land." (As to orders affecting land, see L.C.A. 1972, s. 6 : *ante*, p. 607.)

The section does not apply to a *statutory owner* (*Re Craven Settled Estates* [1926] Ch. 985). It should be contrasted with s. 7 (4) of the S.L.A. 1925, *ante*, p. 722, which deals with cases where, by reason of forfeiture, surrender or otherwise, the estate owner of any settled land *ceases to have the statutory powers* of a tenant for life.

An order cannot be made under the S.L.A. 1925, s. 24, merely because the tenant for life has allowed the settled land to become derelict, but if he has unreasonably refused to exercise his powers of leasing, an order may be made (*Re Thornhill's Settlement* [1941] Ch. 24). It should be noted that specified powers only, for instance of leasing, may be made exercisable by the trustees under this section and that different powers may be granted to them over various parts of the settled land (*ibid.*).

Transactions made by tenant for life in his personal capacity.—It is provided by s. 68 of the S.L.A. 1925 as follows :—

" 68.—(1) In the manner mentioned and subject to the provisions contained in this section—

(*a*) a sale, grant, lease, mortgage, charge or other disposition of settled land, or of any easement, right, or privilege over the same may be made to the tenant for life ; or

(*b*) capital money may be advanced on mortgage to him ; or

(*c*) a purchase may be made from him of land to be made subject to the limitations of the settlement ; or

(*d*) an exchange may be made with him of settled land for other land ; and

(*e*) any such disposition, advance, purchase, or exchange as aforesaid may be made to, from, or with any persons of whom the tenant for life is one.

(2) In every such case *the trustees of the settlement* shall, in addition to their powers as trustees, have all the powers of a tenant for life in reference to negotiating and completing the transaction, and shall have power to enforce any covenants by the tenant for life, or, where the tenant for life is himself one of the trustees, then the other or others of them shall have such power, and the said powers of a tenant for life may be exercised by the trustees of the settlement in the name and on behalf of the tenant for life.

(3) This section applies, notwithstanding that the tenant for life is one of the trustees of the settlement, or that an order has been made authorising the trustees to act on his behalf, or that he is [suffering from mental disorder ; Mental Health Act, 1959, Sched. 7], *but does not apply to dealings with any body of persons which includes a trustee of the settlement*, not being the tenant for life, unless the transaction is either previously or subsequently approved by the court."

" *the trustees of the settlement.*"—Where a tenant for life is one of the trustees he should be one of the conveying parties as well as the person in whose favour the conveyance is made (*Re Pennant's Will Trusts* [1970] Ch. 75).

" *but does not apply to dealings with any body of persons.*"—These words were necessary because, in the case mentioned, the trustees would have conflicting interests and duties.

B. VARIOUS POWERS OF TENANT FOR LIFE

Overreaching powers of tenant for life, see *ante*, p. 173 *et seq.*

Leasing powers of tenant for life, see *post*, p. 815 *et seq.*

Grant of option to renew lease, see *post*, p. 819.

Acceptance of surrender of lease, see *post*, p. 828.

Power to sell or exchange the settled land.—The power of a tenant for life to sell and exchange, as distinguished from his power to contract and to *convey*, is contained in ss. 38 and 39 of the S.L.A. 1925, given below.

" 38.　A tenant for life—

(i) *May sell the settled land, or any part thereof, or any easement,* right or privilege of any kind over or in relation to the land ; and

(ii) [This paragraph deals with the power of a tenant for life to sell the *seignory* of land within a manor.]

(iii) May make an exchange of the settled land, or any part thereof, or of any easement, right, or privilege of any kind, whether or not newly created, over or in relation to the settled land, or any part thereof, for other land, or for any easement, right or privilege of any kind, whether or not newly created, over or in relation to other land, including an exchange in consideration of money paid for equality of exchange."

" *May sell the settled land.*"—The court will not order exercise of a power unless *mala fides* is found ; thus if one joint tenant for life wishes to sell but the other does not the court will not interfere (*Re 90 Thornhill Road* [1970] Ch. 261). As to the power of a person absolutely entitled to freehold or leasehold land subject to a family charge (made settled land by the charge) to sell the land subject to the charge as if the land was not settled land, see the Law of Property (Amendment) Act, 1926, s. 1 (1), given *ante*, p. 730. If the settled land can be freed from the charge, the land will cease to be settled land. See S.L.A. 1925, s. 112 (2).

" *or any part thereof.*"—It was held under the Settled Land Act, 1882, that these words would cover the case of a sale to a railway company of sub-soil for the purpose of driving a tunnel (*Re Pearson's Will* (1900), 83 L.T. 626).

" *or any easement.*"—As to *release* of an easement with the consent in writing of the trustees of the settlement, see S.L.A. 1925, s. 58 (2). As to *reservation* of an easement, see *post*, p. 745.

Section 39 of the S.L.A. 1925 provides (*inter alia*) by subs. (1) that *save as thereinafter provided* every *sale* shall be made for the best consideration in money that can reasonably be obtained ; by subs. (2) that a sale may be made in consideration wholly or partially of a perpetual rent, or a terminable rent consisting of principal and interest combined, payable yearly or half-yearly, to be secured upon the land sold ; and by subs. (5) that the consideration on a sale to any *company incorporated by Act of Parliament* may, with the consent of the tenant for life, consist wholly or in part of fully paid securities of any description of the company, and that such securities shall be vested in the trustees of the settlement.

Save as thereinafter provided.—This refers to s. 54 (power to grant water rights to statutory bodies) ; s. 55 (power to grant land for public and charitable purposes) ; s. 57 (where land is sold for small dwellings, small-holdings and dwellings for the working classes), and s. 64 (empowering a tenant for life to effect any transaction under an order of the court ; see *post*, p. 753).

Sale to any company incorporated by Act of Parliament.—This does not apply to a limited company incorporated under the Companies Acts, as these companies are not incorporated by Act of Parliament but by registration.

Section 40 (1) of the S.L.A. 1925 provides that, save as in that Part of the Act provided, every *exchange* shall be made for the best consideration in land or in land and money that can reasonably be obtained. The saving refers to ss. 55 and 64, above referred to. Power is given by s. 71 (1) (iii) to a tenant for life to raise money by legal mortgage of the settled land for purposes of "equality of exchange," and it is provided by s. 73 (1) (v) that capital money may be applied in payment for equality of exchange of settled land.

As to the power of a tenant for life to carry out the transaction by deed, see p. 752.

Power to deal separately with the surface and the minerals.—It is provided by s. 50 of the S.L.A. 1925 that a sale, exchange, *lease or other authorised disposition* may be made by a tenant for life, either of land, with or without an exception or reservation of all or any of the mines and minerals therein, or of any mines and minerals, and in any such case with or without a grant or reservation of powers of working, wayleaves or rights of way, rights of water and drainage, and other powers, easements, rights, and privileges for or incident to or connected with mining purposes, in relation to the settled land, or any part thereof, or any other land.

It will be noted that in the above section there is no limitation of the word "lease" to mining leases, as was the case in s. 17 (1) of the Settled Land Act, 1882, and that it extends to any "other authorised disposition," which words were not in s. 17 (1) of the 1882 Act. With a view to making valid doubtful pre-1926 transactions, it is provided by para. 4 of Sched. 4 to the S.L.A. 1925 that s. 17 (1) of the Settled Land Act, 1882, is to be deemed always to have had effect as if the words "or mining" had not been contained therein, and the words "or other authorised disposition" had been inserted therein after the word "lease."

Power to impose restrictions, and to reserve easements.—It is provided by s. 49 (1) of the S.L.A. 1925 that on a sale or other disposition under the powers of the Act (*a*) any easement, right, or privilege of any kind may be reserved or granted over or in relation to the settled land or other land, including the land disposed of, and in the case of an exchange, the land taken in exchange ; and (*b*) any restriction with respect to building on or other use of land, or with respect to any other thing, may be imposed and made binding by covenant, condition or otherwise, on the tenant for life or statutory owner and the settled land, or on the other party, and any land disposed of to him. As to power of tenant for life to release restrictive covenants, see *ante*, p. 578.

24A

Power to dispose of mansion house.—Section 65 (1) of the S.L.A. 1925 provides, in effect, that a tenant for life may, *where the settlement was made or comes into operation after 1925 and does not contain any provision to the contrary*, dispose of the principal mansion house on the settled land, if any, and the pleasure grounds and parks and lands, if any, usually occupied therewith, without the consent of the trustees of the settlement or an order of court. But where the settlement was made or came into operation before 1926, and contains no provision to the contrary, the consent of the trustees or an order of court must still be obtained.

If there *is* any provision to the contrary which would affect a purchaser it should be referred to in the vesting instrument.

The consent of the trustees need not be in writing, but may be inferred from their acts (*Gilbey* v. *Rush* [1906] 1 Ch. 11).

Subsection (2) of s. 65 provides that—

" Where a house is usually occupied as a farmhouse, or where the site of any house and the pleasure grounds and park and lands, if any, usually occupied therewith do not together exceed twenty-five acres in extent, the house is not to be deemed a principal mansion house within the meaning of this section, and may accordingly be disposed of in like manner as any other part of the settled land."

Whether any particular house is the " principal mansion house " is a question of fact, and if circumstances change a different house may become the principal one (*Re Feversham Settled Estate* [1938] 2 All E.R. 210).

Sale of heirlooms.—A distinction must be drawn between a sale of heirlooms settled so as to devolve with settled land and heirlooms settled without reference to settled land. Section 67 of the S.L.A. 1925 deals with the first case and s. 130 (5) of the L.P.A. 1925, with the second case.

Where personal chattels are settled so as to devolve with settled land, or are settled together with land, or upon trusts declared by reference to the trusts affecting land, a tenant for life of the land (or, if there is no tenant for life, the statutory owner) may sell the chattels, but only under an order of the court (S.L.A. 1925, s. 67 (1), (3)). The money arising from the sale must be treated as capital money, and must be paid, invested or applied accordingly or invested in the purchase of other chattels (*ibid.*, s. 67 (2) and s. 75).

To get an order the tenant for life or statutory owner would have to satisfy the court that the sale would be for the benefit of all parties interested (*Re Hope* [1899] 2 Ch. 679).

Where personal chattels are settled *without reference to settled land* on trusts creating entailed interests therein, it is provided by s. 130 (5) of the L.P.A. 1925 that the trustees, with the consent of the usufructuary for the time being if of full age, may sell the chattels or any of them, and that the net proceeds of any such sale shall be held in trust for and shall go to the same persons successively, in the same manner and for the same interests, as the chattels would have been held if they had not been sold, and the income of investments representing such proceeds of sale shall be applied accordingly.

As heirlooms can, since 1925, be entailed, they can be settled on the same trusts as land (L.P.A. 1925, s. 130 (1), (3)). See further, *ante*, p. 431.

Condition that fixtures or timber shall be taken at a valuation.— It is provided by s. 49 (2) of the S.L.A. 1925 that a sale of land may be made subject to a stipulation that all or any of the timber or fixtures shall be taken by the purchaser at a valuation, and that the amount of the valuation shall form part of the price of the land, and shall be capital money accordingly. This last provision is very important, for if the purchaser by mistake paid the amount of the valuation to the tenant for life instead of to the trustees of the settlement the sale would be invalid. If such a mistake should be made it could not be rectified without payment of the amount of such purchase-money to the trustees of the settlement by the tenant for life or the purchaser, and an application to the court under subsection (3) of the same section.

The word " timber " in the subsection means " timber and other trees, pollards, tellers, underwood, saplings and plantations on the land sold."

General power to cut and sell timber.—Where there is on the settled land timber ripe and fit for cutting, the tenant for life, although impeachable for waste (as to which, see *post*, p. 754), may, on obtaining the consent of the trustees of the settlement or an order of the court, cut and sell that timber. He is entitled to one fourth part of the net proceeds of the sale but the other three fourth parts must be set aside as capital money arising under the Act (S.L.A. 1925, s. 66). This provision does not entitle the tenant for life to commit equitable waste ; for instance, he must not cut ornamental timber (L.P.A. 1925, s. 135 ; *Weld-Blundell* v. *Wolseley* [1903] 2 Ch. 664) ; nor must he cut down, except in proper thinning, any trees planted as an improvement under the provisions of the Act (S.L.A. 1925, s. 88).

Trees which are not timber, at common law or by the custom of the district, may be cut by the tenant for life, when they are ripe for cutting, and the tenant for life can keep the proceeds of sale without being bound to replant (*Re Harker's Will Trusts ; Harker* v. *Bayliss* [1938] Ch. 323).

Power to lease and accept surrenders of leases.—This subject will be found dealt with at pp. 815 and 828, *post*.

Power to mortgage the settled land.—As a tenant for life is a trustee for the parties beneficially interested in the settled land (S.L.A. 1925, s. 107), his powers to raise money are restricted. At the same time the S.L.A. 1925 contains an extremely useful provision, namely, s. 64 (*post*, p. 753), under which the court may give the tenant for life power to mortgage the settled land to raise money, when it will, in the opinion of the court, be for the benefit of the settled land or the persons interested under the settlement. And a settlor can always, if he so desires, give the tenant for life fuller powers of mortgage than are given him by the Act, but he cannot restrict the powers given him by the Act (S.L.A. 1925, ss. 108, 109 ; *Re Cowley's Settled Estates* [1926] Ch. 725). If, by the settlement, the further power to mortgage is given to the trustees of the settlement, and not to the tenant for life, such power will be exercisable as if it had been conferred on the tenant for life (S.L.A. 1925, s. 108).

The following specific powers of mortgaging the settled land are given by s. 71 (1) of the S.L.A. 1925 to the tenant for life ; that is to say, for—

  (i) *Discharging an incumbrance* on the settled land or part thereof ;

  (ii) *Paying for any impeachment* authorised by the Act or by the settlement ;

  (iii) Equality of exchange ;

(iv) Extinguishing any manorial incidents ;

(v) Compensating the steward on the extinguishment of manorial incidents and discharging the expenses incurred in connection with the extinguishment ;

(vi) Redeeming a compensation rent-charge in respect of the extinguishment of manorial incidents and affecting the settled land ;

(vii) Commuting any additional rent made payable on the conversion of a perpetually renewable leasehold interest into a long term ;

(viii) Satisfying any claims for compensation on the conversion of a perpetually renewable leasehold interest by any agent of the lessor ;

(ix) Payment of the costs of any transaction authorised by this section or by ss. 69 or 70 (which relate to the shifting or variation of incumbrances ; see *post*, pp. 749, 750).

" *Discharging an incumbrance.*"—A tenant for life may raise money by mortgage under this provision for the purpose of discharging expenses charged on the settled land by statutory provisions now re-enacted in the Highways Act, 1959, ss. 190 (as extended by s. 264) and 181 (2) ; *Re Smith's Settled Estates* [1901] 1 Ch. 689, and *Re Pizzi* [1907] 1 Ch. 67 ; or of discharging a charge under the Agricultural Holdings Act, 1948, s. 82 : also to repay himself sums paid for estate duty under the F.A. 1894, or for redemption of land tax (F.A. 1949, s. 40, as the redemption money is a charge on the estate), and for payment of coast protection charges (Coast Protection Act, 1949, s. 11 (2) (*a*)).

" *Paying for any improvement.*"—See s. 73 (1) of the S.L.A. 1925 (*post*, p. 755), which provides that capital money may be applied (*inter alia*) in payment for any improvement authorised by the Act, and in payment as for an improvement authorised by the Act of money expended by a landlord in the execution of certain improvements comprised in Pt. I or Pt. II of Sched. 1 to the Agricultural Holdings Act, 1923 (now Agricultural Holdings Act, 1948, Sched. 2). The improvements authorised by the S.L.A. 1925 are dealt with by ss. 83 to 89 and Sched. 3 ; a detailed discussion of improvements is not relevant to the purpose of this book, but an outline of the subject is given *post*, p. 754, and reference may also be made to the Agricultural Holdings Act, 1948, s. 81, and the Hill Farming Act, 1946, s. 11. The Town and Country Planning Act, 1971, s. 275, enables money to be raised under the S.L.A. 1925, s. 71, for the purpose of discharging certain sums payable under that Act ; for example, repayment of compensation in respect of subsequent development (under ss. 159, 168 or 279 (1)).

The payments for improvements provided for by s. 73 (1) of the S.L.A. 1925 do not authorise the reimbursement out of capital moneys of sums paid by a beneficiary by way of compensation to outgoing tenants of agricultural holdings in respect of improvements effected by the tenants (*Re Duke of Wellington's Parliamentary Estates* [1972] 1 Ch. 374). However, such sums may be recoverable by means of obtaining from the Minister an order charging the holding with repayment of compensation which charge the trustees can redeem out of capital moneys (see s. 82 of the Agricultural Holdings Act, 1948, and s. 73 (1) (ii) of the S.L.A. 1925).

Before a tenant for life can mortgage the settled land he must, of course, get a vesting deed vesting the legal estate in him, or stating that the legal estate is already so vested (S.L.A. 1925, s. 13). As to the necessity for the tenant for life to give one month's previous notice of his intention to make the specific mortgage to each of the trustees and their solicitor, see *ante*, p. 735.

As the mortgage money has to be paid to the trustees (except in the unusual case of the tenant for life wishing the money to be paid into court), they should be made parties to the mortgage to give the receipt (S.L.A. 1925, s. 18 (1) (*b*) ; ss. 75 and 94). See also s. 95 of the S.L.A. 1925, which provides that the receipt in writing of the trustees shall effectually discharge the mortgagee therefrom, and from being bound to see to the application or being answerable for any loss or misapplication thereof, or from being concerned to see that any money advanced by him is wanted for any purpose of the Act, or that no more than is wanted is raised.

Even pending the investigating of the title with a view to the tenant for life ultimately executing a legal mortgage, he has no power to give an equitable mortgage. The difficulty can be got over by the tenant for life entering into a contract to make a legal mortgage, under s. 90 (1) of the S.L.A. 1925, and a sum being paid him on account of such legal mortgage to be executed.

See also S.L.A. 1925, s. 16 (1) (iii), which provides for the raising of money for portions by legal mortgage subject to an existing jointure, but this is not an expedient transaction, nor a security on which money could be readily obtained. The money should, as a rule, be raised under s. 71, above.

Power to shift an incumbrance.—Section 69 of the S.L.A. 1925 provides that where there is an incumbrance affecting any part of the settled land, the tenant for life, with the consent of the incumbrancer, may charge that incumbrance *on any other part of the settled land*, or on all or any part of the capital money or securities representing capital money subject or to become subject to the settlement, whether already charged therewith or not, *in exoneration of* the first mentioned part, and, by a legal mortgage, or otherwise, make provision accordingly.

This section is a much improved form of s. 5 of the Settled Land Act, 1882, with amendments ; see also Sched. 4, para. 1, to the S.L.A. 1925.

" *in exoneration of.*"—As to equitable exoneration of the rest of the land, see S.L.A. 1925, s. 49 (1) (*c*). But now an absolute owner subject to a family charge may sell subject thereto and with an indemnity under the Law of Property (Amendment) Act, 1926, s. 1 (1), *ante*, p. 730, so that s. 49 (1) (*c*) is not likely to be used.

Substituted security for released charges.—It is provided by s. 82 of the S.L.A. 1925 that land acquired by purchase or otherwise under the powers of the Act, may be made a substituted security for any charge from which the settled land has theretofore been released on the occasion and in order to the completion of a sale, exchange or other disposition. Where, however, a charge does not affect the whole of the settled land, the land acquired may not be subjected thereto, unless it is acquired either by purchase with money arising from sale of land, which was before the sale subject to the charge, or by an exchange of land which was before the exchange subject to the charge (*ibid.*).

It is thought that s. 82 is not much used, as the object is generally better attained under s. 69 of the S.L.A. 1925, given above.

Power to vary the terms of an incumbrance.—It is provided by s. 70 (1) of the S.L.A. 1925, that where an incumbrance affects any part of the settled land the tenant for life may, with the consent of the incumbrancer, vary the rate of interest and any of the other provisions of the instrument creating the incumbrance, and with the like consent charge that incumbrance on any part of the settled land, whether already charged therewith or not, or on all or any part of the capital money or securities representing capital money subject or to become subject to the settlement, by way of additional security, or of consolidation of securities, and by a legal mortgage or otherwise make provision accordingly.

Discharge of mortgage by a tenant for life.—Where a tenant for life pays off a mortgage on the settled land, there arises a presumption that he intends to keep the charge alive, and it makes no difference in this respect whether the payment is made by a tenant for life in possession (*Wigsell* v. *Wigsell* (1825), 2 Sim. & St. 364) or in remainder (*Re Chesters* [1935] Ch. 77). See also *post*, pp. 1010, 1012.

Power to appropriate land for streets or open spaces.—It is provided by s. 56 (1) of the S.L.A. 1925 that on or after or in connection with a sale or grant for building purposes, or a building lease, or the development as a building estate of the settled land, or any part thereof, or at any other reasonable time, the tenant for life, for the benefit of residents on the settled land, may cause any parts of the settled land to be appropriated and laid out for streets, roads, paths, squares, gardens, or other open spaces, for the use, gratuitously or on payment, of the public or of individuals, with sewers, drains, watercourses, fencing, paving, or other works proper in connection therewith ; and may provide that the parts so appropriated be vested in the trustees of the settlement, or other trustees, or any company or public body, on trusts for securing the continued appropriation to such purposes. Section 16 of the Settled Land Act, 1882, contained similar provisions, except that the power was limited to the case of a sale or grant for building purposes, or a building lease, and the provision for dedication is new.

The cost of doing the work may be paid out of money being or representing or applicable as capital money under the S.L.A. 1925 (ss. 73 (1) (xx), 77, 78, 83, Sched. 3, Pt. I (xix), (xxi)).

Power to agree to the widening, etc., of a highway.—It is provided by s. 56 (3) of the S.L.A. 1925 that a tenant for life is to have power (*a*) to enter into any agreement for the recompense to be made for any part of the settled land required for the widening of a highway ; and (*b*) to consent to the diversion of a highway over the settled land. All money, not being rent, received on the exercise of any such power is capital money.

Miscellaneous powers.—A tenant for life may—

(i) enter into a forestry dedication covenant gratuitously or for consideration (Forestry Act, 1967, Sched. 2, para. 1) ;

(ii) enter into an access agreement under the National Parks and Access to the Countryside Act, 1949 (*ibid.*, s. 64 (4)) ;

(iii) enter into an agreement for use of land for cattle-grids (Highways Act, 1959, s. 92 (4)) ;

(iv) enter into an agreement with the Countryside Commission or a local authority under the Countryside Act, 1968 (*ibid.*, s. 45 (2)).

Reference may also be made to the ability of a tenant for life to execute a power of attorney : see ss. 8 and 9 of the Powers of Attorney Act, 1971 (amending s. 25 of the Trustee Act, 1925) noted *ante*, pp. 244–246.

Additional powers conferred by the settlement.—A tenant for life or statutory owner may have additional or larger powers outside the Act. It will be noticed that in the forms of vesting instruments and trust instruments given in the Act a blank is left for the practitioner to fill in any additional or larger powers. Few additions are necessary but possible ones are : (i) power with the consent of the trustees to lease generally upon such conditions as the tenant for life may think fit ; (ii) power with the consent of the trustees to sell or lease at a price or rent to be fixed by valuation or arbitration. This cannot be done without special power (*Re Wilton's (Earl) Settled Estates* [1907] 1 Ch. 50).

It is provided by s. 108 (2) of the S.L.A. 1925 as follows :—

" 108.—(2) *In case of conflict between the provisions of a settlement and the provisions of this Act*, relative to any matter in respect whereof the tenant for life or statutory owner exercises or contracts or intends to exercise any power under this Act, *the provisions of this Act shall prevail ;* and, notwithstanding anything in the settlement, *any power* (not being merely a power of revocation or appointment) *relating to the settled land* thereby *conferred on the trustees of the settlement* or other persons exercisable for any purpose, whether or not provided for in this Act, shall, after the commencement of this Act, *be exercisable by the tenant for life or statutory owner* as if it were an additional power conferred on the tenant for life within the next following section of this Act and not otherwise."

The words " any power . . . relating to the settled land " in s. 108 (2) have been held not to comprehend a testamentary power to appoint new trustees of a settlement (*Re Maryon-Wilson's Settlements* [1971] Ch. 789).

And s. 109 of the same Act provides as follows :—

" 109.—(1) *Nothing in this Act precludes a settlor from conferring* on the tenant for life, or (save as provided by the last preceding section) on the trustees of the settlement, *any powers additional to or larger than* those conferred by this Act.

(2) Any additional or larger powers so conferred shall, as far as may be, notwithstanding anything in this Act, operate and be exercisable in the like manner, and with all the like incidents, effects, and consequences, as if they were conferred by this Act, and, if relating to the settled land, as if they were conferred by this Act on a tenant for life."

It will, therefore, be seen that where the settlement confers on trustees larger or additional powers, the trustees will not be the persons to exercise such powers, but the tenant for life. The reason, of course, is that the legal estate is in the tenant for life, and he is therefore the person to make title. But although the settlor can enlarge the powers of a tenant for life he cannot restrict the powers given to him by the S.L.A. 1925, and any attempt to do so would be ineffectual. For instance, in *Re Jeffereys ; Finch* v. *Martin* [1939] Ch. 205, the trustees of a settlement had a power of sale under the settlement with the consent of an annuitant. The legal estate was vested in them as statutory owners and it was held that the power of sale with consent, given by the settlement, was in conflict with the power under the S.L.A. 1925 to sell without consent, and so the latter prevailed.

By s. 108 (1) of the S.L.A. 1925 nothing in the S.L.A. 1925 is to take away, abridge or prejudicially affect any power for the time being subsisting under a settlement, or by statute or otherwise, exercisable by a tenant for life, or (save as thereinafter provided ; see s. 108 (2), above) by trustees with his consent, or on his request, or by his direction *or otherwise*, and the powers given by the S.L.A. 1925 are declared to be cumulative. This subsection does not, in spite of the words " or otherwise," preserve powers exercisable by trustees with the consent of a person other than a tenant for life (*Re Jeffereys ; Finch* v. *Martin, ante*).

The Town and Country Planning Acts have made it advisable for settlements to contain a number of powers designed to assist in dealing with various matters arising under those Acts so far as they affect the settled land. See *post*, p. 756 *et seq.*

Powers of a tenant for life under a compound settlement.—As to what will constitute a " compound settlement," see *ante*, p. 675. Where a settlement consists of two or more documents and is therefore a compound settlement, the tenant for life or person having the powers of a tenant for life thereunder can exercise not only the statutory powers given to a tenant for life but he can also exercise all additional or larger powers than those created by the Act, given to the tenant for life or trustees by each of the documents constituting the compound settlement. In such a case it is immaterial, as regards a purchaser, whether or not the life interest has been restored. Notwithstanding the limitation contained in s. 22 (2) of the S.L.A. 1925 (which provides that where by a re-settlement of land any estate or interest *is expressed to be limited to any person in restoration or confirmation of his estate or interest* under a prior settlement, then that person is entitled to the estate or interest so restored or confirmed as of his former estate or interest), a tenant for life or person having the powers of a tenant for life has, under ss. 108 and 109 of the S.L.A. 1925, the additional or larger powers contained in each of the documents forming part of such compound settlement (*Re Cowley's Settled Estates* [1926] Ch. 725).

Power to execute deeds or carry out authorised transactions.—It is provided by s. 63 of the S.L.A. 1925, replacing s. 6 of the Settled Land Act, 1890, that a tenant for life may make any disposition which is necessary or proper for *giving effect to a contract entered into by a predecessor in title*, and which if made by that predecessor would have been valid as against his successors in title.

It is also provided by s. 72 (1) of the S.L.A. 1925 as follows :—

" 72.—(1) On a *sale, exchange, lease, mortgage, charge or other disposition*, the tenant for life may, as regards land sold, given in exchange, leased, mortgaged, charged, or otherwise disposed of, or intended so to be, or as regards easements or other rights or privileges sold, given in exchange, leased, mortgaged, or otherwise disposed of, or intended so to be, *effect the transaction by deed to the extent of the estate or interest vested or declared to be vested in him by the last or only vesting instrument affecting the settled land* or any less estate or interest, in the manner requisite for giving effect to the sale, exchange, lease, mortgage, charge, or other disposition, *but so that a mortgage shall be effected by* the creation of a term of years absolute in the settled land or by charge by way of legal mortgage, and not otherwise."

There is also a general power given by s. 112 (1) of the S.L.A. 1925 to the effect that where a power of sale, exchange, leasing, mortgaging, charging, or other power is exercised by a tenant for life, or statutory owner, or by the trustees of a settlement, he and they may respectively *execute, make, and do all deeds, instruments, and things necessary or proper in that behalf.*

Payment of purchase-money to two trustees or to a trust corporation.—To make a conveyance or other document executed by a tenant for life or statutory owner an *effective* document under the Act, capital money arising under the transaction must be paid to or by the direction of the trustees of the settlement, being two individual trustees or a trust corporation, or into court (S.L.A. 1925, s. 18). Section 18 pre-supposes that there are trustees for the purposes of the Act in existence, and it is thought that the tenant for life cannot require the purchaser to pay the money into court under s. 75 (1) of the S.L.A. 1925, where he, the purchaser, has notice of the fact that there are no trustees (*Re Fisher and Grazebrook's Contract* [1898] 2 Ch. 660).

But where no capital money arises under the transaction (for instance, a lease without fine), a disposition by a tenant for life or statutory owner will, in favour of a purchaser of a legal estate, have effect under the Act notwithstanding that at the date of the transaction there are no trustees of the settlement (S.L.A. 1925, s. 110 (4)).

General power to effect any transaction under order of the court.—Section 64 of the S.L.A. 1925 is a most useful provision :—

" 64.—(1) Any transaction affecting or concerning the settled land, or any part thereof, or any other land (not being a transaction otherwise authorised by this Act, or by the settlement) which in the opinion of the court would be *for the benefit* of the settled land, or any part thereof, or the persons interested under the settlement, may, *under an order of the court,* be effected by a tenant for life, if it is one which could have been validly effected by an absolute owner."

" *for the benefit* " will cover a benefit accruing to the tenants (*Re Ailesbury's (Marquis) Settled Estate* [1892] 1 Ch. 506).

Subsection (2) contains a long definition of the word " transaction " which, as amended, appears to include an application of capital money in payment for a permanent improvement even though that improvement is not one authorised by the S.L.A. 1925, Sched. 3 (Settled Land and Trustee Acts (Court's General Powers) Act, 1943, s. 2, which, although repealed, remains effective under the Interpretation Act, 1889, s. 11 (1)).

In *Re White-Popham Settled Estates* [1936] Ch. 725, it was held that the court had power to sanction a scheme providing for the sale or mortgage of part of the settled land in order to pay debts of the tenant for life incurred in the upkeep of the estate, provision being made for repayment by the tenant for life or on his death. The effect of the decision is that transactions may be sanctioned even if they cannot be said to benefit the settled land, if they will benefit the persons interested under the settlement. The power to order payment of management expenses contained in the Settled Land and Trustee Acts (Court's General Powers) Act, 1943, s. 1, below, does not show any intention to restrict the wide interpretation placed on the S.L.A. 1925, s. 64, in *Re White-Popham Settled Estates, ante* (*Re Scarisbrick Resettlement Estates* [1944] Ch. 229). See also *Re Mount Edgcumbe Settled Estate* [1950] Ch. 615.

A scheme was devised to minimise the incidence of estate duty in respect of settled land and the court was asked to authorise its adoption under s. 64 (1) or otherwise. It was found that in substance it amounted to a re-writing of the trusts. The Court of Appeal ([1953] Ch. 218) decided that it might properly be approved as a " compromise " in the wide sense of the word, but their decision on this point was reversed by the House of Lords in *Chapman* v. *Chapman* [1954] A.C. 429. The Court of Appeal further expressed the views (a) that the scheme was for the benefit of persons interested in that it would, if the tenant for life lived five years, relieve the settled land from death duties, and (b) that it was a " transaction " within the S.L.A. 1925, s. 64 (1), and, consequently, might be approved under that subsection (*Re Downshire Settled Estates* [1953] Ch. 218). In *Re Simmons, Simmons* v. *Public Trustee* [1956] Ch. 125, it was decided that a similar scheme by which a life tenant took half the capital and released a power of appointment over the other half might be authorised under s. 64 (1), that section applying to land held on trust for sale by reason of the L.P.A. 1925, s. 28 (1).

The jurisdiction of the court under the S.L.A. 1925, s. 64, includes power to order that management expenses shall be paid out of capital if the court is satisfied that it is for the benefit of the persons entitled under the settlement and either (i) the available income from all sources of the person who, as being beneficially entitled in possession, might otherwise have been expected to bear such expenses, has been so reduced as to render him unable to bear the expenses without undue hardship, or (ii) there is no such person, and the income available for such expenses has become insufficient (Settled Land and Trustee Acts (Court's General Powers) Act, 1943, s. 1 ; Emergency Laws (Miscellaneous Provisions) Act, 1953, s. 9).

Reference should also be made to the extensive jurisdiction conferred on the courts by the Variation of Trusts Act, 1958, which expressly does not limit the powers conferred by s. 64 of the S.L.A. 1925 (s. 1 (6)).

C. IMPROVEMENTS AND ALTERATIONS TO SETTLED LAND

Doctrine of waste.—The general rule is that a tenant for life is liable for voluntary waste, but not for permissive waste unless the settlement has imposed on him an obligation to repair (*Re Parry and Hopkin* [1900] 1 Ch. 160 ; *Woodhouse* v. *Walker* (1880), 5 Q.B.D. 404). [It should be noted that the phrase " tenant for life " is here used in its normal sense and not as defined for the purposes of the S.L.A. 1925. For instance, a person who is tenant for life for the purposes of the S.L.A. 1925 because he holds absolutely but subject to family charges is not liable for waste.] Voluntary waste consists of a positive act of injury to the land such as the pulling down of houses (*Marsden* v. *Edward Heyes, Ltd.* [1927] 2 K.B. 1) or changing the course of husbandry in a manner injuring the land (*Doherty* v. *Allman* (1878), 3 App. Cas. 709). Permissive waste, on the other hand, consists of an omission to repair or to take other steps whereby damage is caused to the property.

Many settlements provide that a tenant for life shall not be impeachable for waste, and in these cases he is not liable for either voluntary or permissive waste, although he will be restrained from committing what is known as " equitable " waste, that is, wanton acts of destruction such as dismantling a house (*Vane* v. *Barnard* (1716), 2 Vern. 738) or felling ornamental timber (*Downshire (Marquis)* v. *Sandys (Lady)* (1801), 6 Ves. 107).

Payment for improvements out of capital.—A tenant for life, as a result of the doctrine of waste, is left with wide powers to alter or improve the settled land. The difficulty which often arises is that he may be unable or unwilling to do so at his own expense. This is avoided to a large degree by the provision that capital money arising under the S.L.A. 1925 may be applied in payment for any improvement authorised by the S.L.A. 1925 or by the settlement (S.L.A. 1925, ss. 73 (1), 84 (1)), and that the land may be mortgaged to pay for such an improvement (S.L.A. 1925, s. 71 (1) ; cf. *Re Duke of Wellington's Parliamentary Estate* [1972] 1 Ch. 374 ; *ante*, p. 748). The improvements authorised by the S.L.A. 1925 are mentioned in Sched. 3, and, for example, include the following items : drainage (Pt. I, paras. (i) and (xix)), fencing (Pt. I, para. (vii)), roads (Pt. I, para. (xi)), additions to or alterations in buildings reasonably necessary or proper to enable the same to be let (Pt. I, para. (xxiii), and see *Re Calverley's Settled Estates* [1904] 1 Ch. 150 and *Re Lindsay's Settlement* [1941] Ch. 119), restoration or reconstruction of buildings damaged or destroyed by dry rot (Pt. II, para. (iv), structural additions to or alterations in buildings reasonably required, whether the buildings are intended to let or are already let (Pt. II, para. (v)). The following matters are also deemed to be improvements so authorised : improvements specified in the Hill Farming Improvements (Settled Land and Trusts for Sale) Regulations, 1949 (Hill Farming Act, 1946, s. 11) ; works specified by the Secretary of State for the Environment as being necessary for properly maintaining a building in relation to which a building preservation order is in force (Town and Country Planning Act, 1971, s. 275 (2)) ; improvements specified in the Agricultural Holdings Act, 1948, Sched. 3 (*ibid.*, s. 81 (1)). Regulations made under the Agriculture Act, 1970, s. 30, may extend the list of improvements in Sched. 3 to the S.L.A. 1925 to include works approved for the purposes of certain grants. Capital money may also be used for payment of coast protection charges and expenses (Coast Protection Act, 1949, s. 11 (2) (*b*)) and for repayment of certain sums mentioned *ante*, p. 748, under the Town and Country Planning Act, 1971, s. 275 (1).

The list of matters authorised by the S.L.A. 1925, Sched. 3, is long but as a rule they only involve *improvements* in the strict sense (although some of them may also involve an element of repair : see the examples mentioned above and *Re Gaskell's Settled Estates* [1894] 1 Ch. 485). However, it is important to note that Sched. 3 to the Agricultural Holdings Act, 1948, in the case of agricultural property, authorises as improvements to be paid for out of capital almost any *repairs*. This result is achieved by para. 23 of that Schedule which authorises " Repairs to fixed equipment, being equipment reasonably required for the proper farming of the holding other than repairs which the tenant is under an obligation to carry out " ; s. 94 (1) of the Act defines " fixed equipment " as including " any building or structure affixed to land and any works, on, in, over or under land." In *Re Duke of Northumberland* [1915] Ch. 202, it was held that para. 23 applied (i) even though the land was not comprised in a contract of tenancy, and (ii) even though the land did not fall within the definition of agricultural land in the Agrricultural Holdings Act, 1948, s. 1 ; (iii) the capital might be used to recoup expenditure by the tenant for life during the past six years ; (iv) the trustees were bound to comply with directions given by the tenant for life in the matter as provided by the S.L.A. 1925, s. 75 (2). This judgment shows how wide the powers to use capital now become as a result of somewhat unsatisfactory referential legislation. In giving a direction, however, the tenant for life must have regard to his position as trustee under s. 107 (*ante*, p. 733), and take into account the interests of remaindermen (*Re Sutherland Settlement Trusts* [1953] Ch. 792).

If the capital money is in the hands of the trustees they must not pay for an improvement unless they act under an order of the court or unless they have obtained from a competent engineer or able practical surveyor employed independently of the tenant for life a certificate that the improvement has been properly executed and of the amount properly payable (S.L.A. 1925, s. 84 (2)). If the capital money is in court, the court may act on a report of the Minister of Agriculture, Fisheries and Food or of a competent engineer or surveyor or on such other evidence as it may think sufficient (*ibid.*, s. 84 (3)). Even though capital paid to the tenant for life is not part of his income for tax purposes, nor a trade receipt of his farming, the trustees are apparently not able to deduct from the sum paid relief from tax recoverable by him in respect of the expenditure on improvements (*Re Pelly's Will Trusts* [1957] Ch. 1). The liability to tax and the benefit of reductions in liability are personal to the tenant for life (*ibid.*). In this case, however, the tenant for life paid for the improvements and later asked to be re-imbursed from capital ; the judgments reserved the question as to what would have happened if the improvements had been paid for in the first instance by the trustees.

The improvements specified in Sched. 3 to the S.L.A. 1925 form three classes. Those set out in Pt. I of the Schedule comprise improvements of a permanent nature, such as drainage and provision of farmhouses and cottages. Those set out in Pt. II may be of less permanent nature and include such matters as provision of houses for land agents and other persons employed on the estate, and buildings for religious, educational and similar purposes in connection with the development of the land as a building estate. In the case of improvements in Pt. II the trustees *may* (but are not obliged to) require that the money shall be repaid out of income by not more than fifty half-yearly instalments (S.L.A. 1925, s. 84 (2), proviso (*a*)). The improvements in Pt. III include the installation of heating or electric power or lighting apparatus for buildings and the purchase of lorries or machinery for farming purposes. In these cases the trustees *must* require repayment out of income by not more than fifty half-yearly instalments (S.L.A. 1925, s. 84 (2), proviso (*b*)).

The question whether a tenant for life of agricultural land may require capital money to be applied in payment of a tenant's claim for compensation for improvements or disturbance is considered in detail by E. H. Scammell in the *Conveyancer N.S.*, vol. 15, p. 415. See also Landlord and Tenant Act, 1927, s. 13, as to compensation for improvements to business premises.

PART 9. PLANNING MATTERS AFFECTING SETTLED LAND

Provisions in settlements.—There are various expenses which may arise but which cannot be paid for out of capital unless there is express provision in the settlement. Consequently a clause enabling the expenses of the following matters to be met out of capital or to be raised by mortgage may be usefully inserted in the trust instrument : (i) an application for planning permission ; (ii) the making of a claim for compensation under the Town and Country Planning Acts ; (iii) opposing the making of orders or other proposals of the local planning authority ; and (iv) complying with the requirements of the Acts such as enforcement notices.

Planning permission affecting settled land.—If the land has been let the tenant is entitled to apply for planning permission which will enure for the benefit of the land and of all persons for the time being interested therein except so far as it provides otherwise ; see *post*, p. 1194. If the land has not been let the tenant for life is entitled to apply for any necessary planning permission for development he wishes to carry out. Subject to the limits on his powers resulting from the doctrine of waste (as to which, see *ante*, p. 754), he will be able to carry out any development whether it takes the form of operations on the land or a material change of use of it. It would seem likely that any development carried out without obtaining a necessary planning permission would be held to amount to voluntary waste, although the application of the old doctrine of waste to modern planning contraventions is a matter of some difficulty. Where, however, the tenant for life is unimpeachable for waste it would appear that he would not be liable unless a contravention amounted to such a deliberate breach of the law as to be classed as equitable waste. See further, an article by the late Dr. Potter in the *Journal of Planning Law*, vol. I, p. 552 *et seq.* If, in due course, an enforcement notice (as to which see *post*, p. 1201) were served by the local planning authority it would have to be served on the then tenant for life who would be the " owner," that is, the person entitled to receive the rack rent (Town and Country Planning Act, 1971, ss. 87 (4), 290 (11)). Consequently, there would be no liability on the trustees of the settlement (unless at the time of service they came within the definition of " owner," for instance if they held the legal estate as statutory owners) to comply with the notice or to pay the cost of compliance out of capital.

Whether the cost of any development can be borne out of capital depends on whether the development is an improvement within the S.L.A. 1925, Sched. 3, as to which, see *ante*, p. 755.

Claims for planning compensation.—The right to compensation may arise if permission for the carrying out of " new " development is refused or is granted subject to conditions (Town and Country Planning Act, 1971, s. 146, *post*, p. 1205). In such cases the application for payment should be made by the trustees of the settlement and any payment will be made to them. To the extent that, as between the persons beneficially interested under the trusts of the settlement, moneys received ought to be treated as capital, they are applicable as capital money under the S.L.A. 1925. It is thought that the circumstances in which a payment has been made under Pt. I or a payment has been made, or may be made, in respect of a planning decision, will normally be such that it will represent part of the settled capital and so should be treated as such as between persons beneficially interested (*Re Meux* [1958] Ch. 154).

Compensation may be payable under various provisions of the Town and Country Planning Act, 1971 : for instance, on revocation or modification of planning permission (s. 164) ; on the making of an order requiring discontinuance of use of land (s. 170) ; for damage or expenditure consequent on refusal of consent under a tree preservation order (ss. 60, 174) ; for damage or expenditure consequent on refusal of consent under an order for preservation of buildings (see ss. 171–173) ; and on removal of certain existing advertisements (s. 176).

Compensation on revocation or modification of planning permission is payable where it is shown that any person interested in the land has incurred expenditure in carrying out work which is rendered abortive, or has otherwise sustained loss or damage which is directly attributable to the revocation or modification (*ibid.*, s. 164 (1)). Such expenditure may be incurred or loss or damage may be sustained by a person not interested under the settlement, for instance, a lessee. It may, however, be incurred or sustained by the tenant for life or even by the trustees of the settlement if an improvement was being made out of capital (see *ante*, p. 754). As it will normally be easy to determine who has incurred expenditure or sustained loss or damage there should be no difficulty in determining the person entitled to the compensation.

Compensation on the making of an order for discontinuance of an authorised use or for removal of buildings or works is payable if it is shown that " any person has suffered damage in consequence of the order or by depreciation of the value of an interest in the land to which he is entitled, or by being disturbed in his enjoyment of the land " (1971 Act, s. 170 (2)). It would seem possible for the tenant for life to recover on account of the legal estate vested in him, in which case the compensation would, apparently, be payable to the trustees as capital money (S.L.A. 1925, s. 81).

Compensation consequent on refusal of permission under a tree preservation order or under an order for preservation of buildings, is payable in respect of damage or expenditure caused or incurred (1971 Act, ss. 171–174). Such damage or expenditure is most likely to be suffered or made by the tenant for life, in which case he would recover and keep the compensation. It is just possible that damage may be suffered in respect of the whole settled interest, if, for instance, refusal of permission depreciated the value of the whole interest, and in such a case it seems that the tenant for life could recover compensation but should pay it to the trustees to be held as capital money under the S.L.A. 1925, s. 81.

Compensation under s. 176 of the 1971 Act is recoverable where works are carried out for removal of advertisements. Such works are not likely to be done by persons interested under a settlement, but if they are the compensation will be recoverable by the person incurring the expenditure.

Opposition to proposed orders and notices.—There are many occasions on which it will be advisable for the proposals of the local planning authority to be opposed. For instance, objections and representations may be made with regard to proposed development plans (1971 Act, Sched. 5, para. 6) ; appeal may be made against an enforcement notice (*ibid.*, s. 88) ; objections and representations may be made with regard to proposed tree preservation orders (*ibid.*, s. 60 (5) (*b*)). It is clear that a tenant for life will be able to take any such action but it is difficult to see how he could be compelled to do so, except perhaps in a very clear case in which failure to act might amount to a breach of his duties as trustee (S.L.A. 1925, ss. 16, 107 (1)).

It may be noted that the S.L.A. 1925, s. 73 (1) (xv), enabled the cost of opposing a town planning scheme to be paid out of capital, but schemes were so different from development (or structure) plans that this is unlikely to authorise the payment out of capital of the cost of opposing a development plan. What is more, there does not appear to be any power to pay out of capital the cost of opposing the other proposals mentioned above, unless there is provision in the settlement or an order of the court is obtained under the S.L.A. 1925, s. 92. This section enables the court to approve any action, defence or other proceeding taken or proposed to be taken for the benefit of the settled land and to direct that any expenses incurred in relation thereto be paid out of property subject to the settlement.

Recovery of cost of complying with notices.—The cost incurred by a local planning authority in complying with an enforcement notice on default of the persons on whom it was served is recoverable from the owner of the land, and " owner " for this purpose includes any person entitled to receive the rack rent (1971 Act, ss. 87 (4), 290 (1)). Thus, the tenant for life may, as owner, have complied with the notice, or in default the cost may have fallen on him, and in either case he has a right of action against the person by whom the breach of planning control was committed (*ibid.*, s. 91). If he is unable to obtain reimbursement in this way it seems that the loss must fall on him personally.

PART 10. REGISTERED CONVEYANCING AND SETTLED LAND

Generally.—The provisions of the S.L.A. 1925 as dealt with in the preceding parts of this Chapter apply to registered land but take effect subject to the provisions of the L.R.A. 1925 and the L.R.R. 1925 (s. 119 (3) of the S.L.A. 1925 ; the L.R.R. 1925 have the same authority as the L.R.A. 1925 : see s. 144 (2) of the L.R.A. 1925). These latter provisions are relatively few and are not comprehensive, but the machinery of the S.L.A. 1925 is, as will be seen, largely followed. Further, so far as a purchaser is concerned, in registered conveyancing the principle of the trust instrument curtailing the equities off the title is fully realised without apparent difficulties (see ss. 74 and 88 of the L.P.A. 1925, and compare the comments on s. 110 (2) of the S.L.A. 1925, *ante*, p. 689). What is more, it would appear that if a tenant for life where there has been a vesting instrument is registered as proprietor without any such restriction as mentioned below a purchaser would be able to deal with him safely as a beneficial owner (s. 18 of the S.L.A. 1925, and *Weston* v. *Henshaw* [1950] Ch. 510, *ante*, p. 688, making the transaction void, are taken not to prevail over the general provisions of the L.R.A. 1925).

Detailed provisions.—The legal estate in settled land is vested in the tenant for life or statutory owners ; see *ante*, p. 722 *et seq.* Consequently settled land is registered in the name of the tenant for life or statutory owner (L.R.A. 1925, s. 86 (1)). The interests arising under the settlement (except a legal estate which cannot be overreached under the powers of the S.L.A. 1925, or any other statute, as to which, see p. 172 *et seq.*) take effect as minor interests (as to which, see *ante*, p. 624) (L.R.A. 1925, s. 86 (2)). These interests are protected by restrictions on the register which are binding on the proprietor during his life, but do not affect a disposition by his personal representative (L.R.A. 1925, s. 86 (3)). Restrictions are dealt with *ante*, p. 623, but there are special rules affecting restrictions required in the case of settled land.

Where application is made for registration of settled land a statement of the proper restriction must be left with the application or the registrar must be furnished with the information necessary to enable him to frame the proper restriction (L.R.R. 1925, r. 56). In framing restrictions it is not the duty of the trustees or of the registrar to protect the interests of any person who would not have been a necessary party to a disposition under the S.L.A. 1925 if the land had been unregistered, but it is the duty of the trustees, or, if there are no trustees, of the registrar, to give notice of the restrictions to such of the beneficiaries (if any) as the registrar may direct, and any such person can lodge a caution or apply for an inhibition (L.R.R. 1925, r. 57).

Forms of restrictions are specified in Forms 9 to 11 in the Schedule to the L.R.R. 1925, which will be applied to various cases, but the forms may be modified according to the circumstances, as the parties require and the registrar may deem fit (L.R.R. 1925, r. 58 (1)). Thus, Form 9, which is used where the tenant for life is registered as proprietor, or when statutory owners who are *not* trustees are registered, is as follows :—

" No disposition under which capital money arises is to be registered unless the money is paid to *A B*, of etc., and *C D*, of etc. (the trustees of the settlement, of which there must be two and not more than four individuals, or a trust corporation), or into Court.

Except under an order of the Registrar, no disposition is to be registered unless authorised by the Settled Land Act, 1925."

A note is added to the form to the effect that if the settlement so provides a provision may be added that no transfer of the mansion house (shown on an attached plan or otherwise adequately described to enable it to be identified on the general map, ordnance map, or filed plan) is to be registered without the consent of the trustees or an order of the court. For the reason for this additional restriction, see *ante*, p. 746.

The restriction applicable where statutory owners who are trustees are registered is contained in Form 10, which is as follows :—

" Except under an order of the Registrar, no disposition is to be registered unless authorised by the Settled Land Act, 1925, and except where the sole proprietor is a trust corporation, no disposition under which capital money arises is to be registered unless the money is paid to at least two proprietors."

The heading to this form states that it is applicable also where trustees holding on trust for sale are interested as proprietors, but this appears to be an error as the relevant rules do not refer to trustees for sale.

Where land already registered is acquired with capital money, it must be transferred to the tenant for life or statutory owners by a transfer in Form 24 (L.R.A. 1925, s. 86 (4) ; L.R.R. 1925, r. 101). This form declares that the land is vested in the tenant for life upon the trusts for the time being affecting it by virtue of the trust deed ; it also states who are the trustees, whether there are any powers in the trust deed extending those in the S.L.A. 1925, and the person having power to appoint new trustees ; application is also made by the transfer for entry of restrictions corresponding to those in Form 9, above. A transfer made in this form is deemed to comply with the requirements of the S.L.A. 1925 respecting vesting deeds, as to which, see *ante*, p. 681 *et seq.*

A transfer of land into settlement is made by a vesting transfer in either Form 21 (which is used where the transfer is to a tenant for life), or Form 22 (which is used where the transfer is to trustees or statutory owners) in the Schedule to the L.R.R. 1925 (r. 99). Similarly, where registered land has been settled and the existing registered proprietor is the tenant for life the proprietor must make a declaration in Form 23 in that Schedule (*ibid.*, r. 100). On the creation of a settlement it is the duty of the proprietor, or of the personal representatives of a deceased proprietor, to apply to the registrar for the entry of such restrictions or inhibitions or notices as may be appropriate (L.R.R. 1925, r. 104 (1)) and the registrar must enter such restrictions, inhibitions or notices without inquiring as to the terms of the settlement, provided they are not, in his opinion, unreasonable or calculated to cause inconvenience (*ibid.*, r. 104 (2)).

On the death of the proprietor, or of the survivor of two or more joint proprietors of settled land (*whether the land is settled by his will or by an instrument taking effect on or previously to his death*), his personal representatives hold the land subject to payment of death duties, and other liabilities affecting the land, and having priority to the settlement, upon trust to transfer the same by an assent to the tenant for life or statutory owner ; and in the meantime on trust to give effect to the minor interests under the settlement (L.R.A. 1925, s. 87 (1)). A proprietor or the personal representative of a deceased proprietor may have power to create a legal estate in priority to the settlement ; see, for instance, *ante*, p. 175. He may do this by any document sufficient at law to create it (L.R.R. 1925, r. 103 (i)) ; such a document must be a registered disposition and completed by registration (L.R.R. 1925, r. 103 (ii)). On production of such a document the registrar, without inquiry as to the existence or terms of the power, must register notice of the estate created as an incumbrance on the land, and must inform all persons appearing to be interested (L.R.R. 1925, r. 103 (iii)).

Where a tenant for life or statutory owner who, if the land were not registered, would be entitled to have the settled land vested in him, is not the proprietor, the proprietor is bound at the cost of the trust estate to execute such transfers as may be required for giving effect on the register to the rights of the tenant for life or statutory owner (L.R.A. 1925, s. 87 (3)). Similarly, where a proprietor ceases in his lifetime to be a tenant for life, he must transfer the land to his successor in title, or if such successor is an infant, to the statutory owner, and on the registration of such successor or statutory owner it is the duty of the trustees, if the settlement remains subsisting, to apply for any alteration in the restrictions required for the protection of minor interests (L.R.A. 1925, s. 87 (6)). Where an order is made under the S.L.A. 1925, s. 24, *ante*, p. 742, authorising the trustees to exercise powers on behalf of a tenant for life who is registered, they may in his name and on his behalf do all such acts and things under the L.R.A. 1925 as are requisite for giving effect on the register to the powers authorised to be exercised as if they were registered as proprietors, but a copy of the order must first be filed (L.R.A. 1925, s. 87 (5)).

Notwithstanding any restriction, the registrar may certify that an intended disposition is authorised by the settlement or otherwise and will be registered, and a purchaser who obtains such a certificate is not concerned to see that the disposition is authorised ; but no such certificate may be required where capital money is paid according to the restriction or into court (L.R.A. 1925, s. 89).

The L.R.A. 1925, s. 91, lays down the following provisions affecting settled land during a minority. The personal representatives under the will or intestacy under which the settlement arises must be registered as proprietors during the minority and they have all the powers conferred by the S.L.A. 1925 on a tenant for life and on the trustees of the settlement. If the circumstances are such that the personal representatives would, if the infant had been of full age, have been bound to transfer the land to him, the personal representatives (unless themselves the statutory owners) must give effect on the register to the directions of the statutory owner and must apply for registration of the prescribed restriction (which is Form 76 in the Schedule to the L.R.R. 1925). They are not concerned with the propriety of a disposition if it appears to be proper and the capital money is paid to the trustees or into court ; a purchaser dealing with them who complies with any restrictions is not concerned to inquire whether any directions have been given.

Where an infant becomes entitled in possession, or will become entitled in possession on attaining full age, otherwise than on a death, the statutory owners during minority are entitled to require the settled land to be transferred to them (L.R.A. 1925, s. 91 (2)). If the registered land would, if not registered, have become vested in the trustees (pursuant to the L.P.A. 1925, s. 34 (3) or Sched. 1, Pt. III or Sched. 1, Pt. IV) the trustees, unless they are already registered, are entitled to be registered as proprietors (L.R.A. 1925, s. 91 (3)).

TRUSTS FOR SALE

PART 1. GENERAL PRINCIPLES

Creation of trust of land.—Section 53 (1) (*b*) of the L.P.A. 1925 provides that " a *declaration of trust* respecting *any land or any interest therein* must be *manifested and proved* by some writing signed by some person who is able to declare such trust or by his will." But the section does not affect the creation or operation of resulting, implied or constructive trusts (L.P.A. 1925, s. 53 (2)), and nothing in s. 53 is to invalidate dispositions by will (L.P.A. 1925, s. 55 (*a*)). It will be noted that this provision applies only to land and any interest therein and that there is no provision that signature by an agent will be sufficient. The words " person who is able to declare such trust " mean the owner of the beneficial interest (*Tierney* v. *Wood* (1854), 19 Beav. 330, and *Grey* v. *I.R.C.* [1958] Ch. 690, 709 ; affd. [1960] A.C.1) ; contrast para. (*a*) of s. 53 (1) and s. 40 (1) of the L.P.A. 1925. An apparently absolute voluntary transfer of a legal estate which was not intended to operate as a gift has given rise to a resulting trust of the beneficial interest which was within s. 53 (2) and not affected by s. 53 (1) of the L.P.A. 1925 (*Hodgson* v. *Marks* [1971] Ch. 892, C.A.).

Perhaps the most important point to note is that in s. 53 (1) (*b*) the words used are " *manifested and proved*." It is well established that this expression does not mean that the trust must be *created* by a signed writing, but only that evidence of it must exist in the form of a signed writing (*Forster* v. *Hale* (1798), 3 Ves. 696). The trust need not necessarily have been put into writing at the time the trust was created provided that a signed writing was in existence before action brought. It will be sufficient if the trust can be manifested by any subsequent acknowledgment by the settlor (*Rochefoucauld* v. *Boustead* [1897] 1 Ch. 196, 206). The fact of the *creation* of the trust may be found in a recital in a deed signed by the creator, or even in a letter to a third party, provided that it sufficiently shows who the parties are or gives the means of ascertaining who they are, and also shows the property and the trusts to which it is made subject, or a sufficient reference thereto. With regard to letters or unsigned memoranda, they will be admitted in evidence, but only if they can be clearly connected with and are referred to in the signed writing (*Forster* v. *Hale, ante*).

Disclaimer of a trust.—A disclaimer by a trustee, even of a freehold estate, may be by conduct, and need not be in writing (*Re Birchall* (1889), 40 Ch. D. 436). It was said by Sargant, L.J., in *Re Lister* [1926] Ch. 149, at p. 166, that a renunciation should be " of the totality of the office and estate and *ab initio*."

It is provided by s. 52 (2) (*b*) of the L.P.A. 1925 that a disclaimer not required to be evidenced in writing is excepted from the provisions therein contained that conveyances of land or any interest therein must be made by deed. Strictly speaking this exception does not apply to disclaimers by trustees of a will, because until they accept the trust no estate passes to them, and there is nothing under the section to disclaim.

In *Re Gordon* (1877), 6 Ch. D. 531, it was decided that although renunciation of probate by a person appointed executor and trustee of a will was not of itself a disclaimer of the trusts (unless the administration of the estate and the carrying out of the trusts were so combined that one could not be performed without the other), the renunciation of probate, coupled with the fact that such trustee had acted as trustee, was conclusive evidence of disclaimer. It was also held that three years' inaction would not be a sufficiently long period to infer disclaimer therefrom. When a person has been nominated both executor and trustee, he cannot disclaim the trusteeship after having proved the will, because his acceptance of the office of executor amounts to an acceptance of the office of trustee (*Mucklow* v. *Fuller* (1821), Jac. 198). See also *Re Sharman's Will Trusts* [1942] Ch. 311.

The fact of a nominated trustee doing nothing for many years must be taken as evidence of disclaimer. In *Re Clout and Frewer's Contract* [1924] 2 Ch. 230, an executor-trustee survived his testator for nearly thirty years without proving or acting or applying for or receiving a legacy given him in his official capacity, but he had not formally renounced or disclaimed, and it was decided that his conduct amounted to a disclaimer.

The disclaimer of the office of trustee has the effect of disclaiming the estate (*Re Birchall, ante*). The estate, before disclaimer, is deemed to be vested in the trustee, but the effect of the disclaimer is to relate back, and the trustee disclaiming is afterwards deemed never to have been a trustee (*ibid.* ; but see *Re Stratton's Deed of Disclaimer* [1958] 1 Ch. 42). If the sole trustee or all the trustees of a settlement disclaim, the trust property is by operation of law revested in the settlor, or his personal representative if dead, who is bound by the trust (*Mallott* v. *Wilson* [1903] 2 Ch. 494). The disclaimer of one trustee (either expressly or by conduct : *Re Birchall, ante*) of real estate has the effect of causing the legal estate and powers to vest in the remaining trustees or trustee, and operates retrospectively and makes the other trustees or trustee the only trustees or trustee *ab initio* (*Peppercorn* v. *Wayman* (1852), 5 De G. & Sm. 230).

A trustee can appoint a new trustee *before* he disclaims (T.A. 1925, s. 36 (8)).

A disclaimer does not require any stamp unless under seal, in which case it should be stamped 50p.

Definition of a trust for sale.—The L.P.A. 1925, s. 205 (1) (xxix), provides that " ' Trust for sale ' in relation to land, means an immediate binding trust for sale, whether or not exercisable at the request or with the consent of any person, and with or without a power at discretion to postpone the sale." The S.L.A. 1925, s. 117 (1) (xxx), provides that the same definition applies for the purposes of that Act and precisely the same definition is contained in the T.A. 1925, s. 68 (19), in the A.E.A. 1925, s. 55 (1) (xxvii) and in the L.R.A. 1925, s. 3 (xxviii). The question as to what amounts to an immediate binding trust for sale usually arises, in practice, in connection with settled land, and so it is discussed *ante*, p. 673 *et seq.* Perhaps it should be noted here that : " Where a disposition or settlement coming into operation after [1925] contains a trust either to retain or sell land the same shall be construed as a trust to sell the land with power to postpone the sale " (L.P.A. 1925, s. 25 (1)).

Trustees who have purchased land in breach of trust, hold on trust for sale. Before 1926 it was their duty to sell unless all beneficiaries were of full age and requested them to retain the land, and so a purchaser obtained a good title if one beneficiary concurred in the sale (*Re Jenkins and Randall's Contract* [1903] 2 Ch. 362). It seems that the L.P.A. 1925, s. 23, makes the concurrence of even one beneficiary unnecessary as it provides that where land has become subject to an *implied* trust for sale for the protection of a purchaser that trust is deemed to subsist until the land has been conveyed to, or under the direction of, the persons interested in the proceeds of sale.

The effect of a power of sale since 1925.—Since 1925, a mere power of sale in relation to land given to trustees for successive interests will not enable the trustees to sell the land. The only operation it will have will be—

(a) to confer such power on the tenant for life or statutory owners in addition to the powers given by the S.L.A. 1925 (ss. 108, 109 ; see *ante*, p. 751) ; and

(b) for the purposes of constituting trustees for the purposes of the S.L.A. 1925 (s. 30 (1)). See *ante*, p. 713, and note the mention of trustees with power of sale in s. 30 (1) (i), of trustees with power of sale of other land in s. 30 (1) (iii), and of trustees with future power of sale in s. 30 (1) (iv). By s. 30 (2) of the S.L.A. 1925, paras. (i), (iii) and (iv) of s. 30 (1) take effect as if the powers therein referred to had not been made exercisable by the tenant for life or statutory owners by s. 109 (2).

Therefore, if trustees with a mere power of sale were to attempt to convey land to a purchaser, the purchaser would get no title, because the legal estate would be in the tenant for life. It will be seen how important it is to distinguish a trust for sale from a mere power of sale.

Separate documents on creation of trust for sale of land.—A trust for sale may be contained in a document *inter vivos* or in a will, and a conveyance on trust for sale may consist of an assent on trust for sale (T.A. 1925, s. 68 (3)). When creating a trust for sale, *inter vivos*, it is considered better conveyancing to have two deeds, one for vesting the legal estate in the trustees and the other for declaring the trusts. By this means the trusts are kept off the title, and a purchaser from the trustees will only be entitled to an abstract of the one deed conveying the legal estate to them. At the same time there is nothing in the 1925 Acts or elsewhere which makes it necessary to have more than one deed, and, even where the conveyance of the estate and the trusts are contained in one deed, a purchaser from the trustees is entitled to an abstract of only that part of the deed conveying the legal estate to the trustees and declaring the trust for sale. It is provided by s. 27 (1) of the L.P.A. 1925 as follows :—

" 27.—(1) A purchaser of a legal estate from trustees for sale shall not be concerned with the trusts affecting the proceeds of sale of land subject to a trust for sale (whether made to attach to such proceeds by virtue of this Act or otherwise), or affecting the rents and profits of the land until sale, *whether or not those trusts are declared by the same instrument by which the trust for sale is created.*"

The words " made to attach by virtue of this Act " refer to implied statutory trusts for sale. Notwithstanding s. 27 (1) such a purchaser obtains a good receipt only if the price is paid to two trustees or a trust corporation ; see *ante*, p. 177.

Where the trust for sale is created by a will, there will be two instruments, namely, the probate and the assent to the trustees for sale. So, also, where the trust for sale arises under an intestacy, as under s. 33 of the A.E.A. 1925, there will be two instruments, the letters of administration and the assent (see *Re Yerburgh* [1928] W.N. 208, *ante*, p. 396). An assent made after 1925 must be in writing ; see *ante*, p. 410. A form of assent by executors in favour of themselves as trustees for sale under a will is given in Sched. 5 to the L.P.A. 1925. But there is a difference of opinion as to the form of an assent in such a case. One course of action is to make the assent to the trustees (who are usually the personal representatives themselves) on an independent trust for sale naming the persons having the power of appointing new trustees, if this is specified in the will. This is the course adopted in Form No. 9 in the L.P.A. 1925, Sched. 5, whereby the trustees thereunder take the land subject to the trust for sale given in the form and not subject to the trust for sale in the will. This course is also recommended, for all except very simple cases, in Hallett's Conveyancing Precedents, p. 112. There is no obligation to use this form, and it may in some cases be a serious objection to so doing that a power for a professional trustee to charge contained in the will may not be drawn so as to authorise work done under the independent trust for sale (see the discussions in *Law Journal*, vol. 63, pp. 247, 468, and *Solicitors' Journal*, vol. 71, pp. 343, 402). Similarly, it seems that other powers in the will, for instance, as to postponement of sale and as to appointment of new trustees, would not apply to the new trust for sale. Such an assent is in accordance with the principles of the L.P.A. 1925 as it keeps the will off the title, but it follows that on appointment of new trustees two instruments are necessary, one appointing new trustees of the assent and the other appointing new trustees of the trusts of the will. After an assent in this form, an appointment or discharge merely of a trustee of the will would not necessarily appoint or discharge that person as trustee of the legal estate. Further, a conveyance by the trustees should be made pursuant to the trust for sale created by the assent (that is, not pursuant to the trust for sale in the will).

The alternative course of action is to make the assent to the trustees on the trusts of the will. This certainly brings the will on to the title, but normally there is no harm in doing so because the trust for sale in the will operates as a " curtain," keeping equities affecting proceeds of sale from the title. The advantage is that only one document is needed when new trustees are appointed. Consequently, an assent on the trusts of the will seems adequate in simple cases (although the terms of the will would then have to be abstracted in so far as the trust for sale was constituted), but if there is any complication in the terms of the will, and particularly if there is any doubt as to whether an immediate binding trust for sale is imposed, an assent such as that given in Form No. 9 should be used.

The assent is itself sufficient evidence in favour of a purchaser that it is given in favour of the proper persons and upon the proper trusts (A.E.A. 1925, s. 36 (7)). See further, *ante*, p. 416.

It must also be remembered that where new trustees are appointed, a memorandum of the persons who are for the time being the trustees for sale must be indorsed on or annexed to the conveyance on trust for sale and be produced to the trustees when required (T.A. 1925, s. 35 (3)).

Where registered land is subject to a trust for sale, express or implied, title to the land must be registered in the names of the trustees for sale (L.R.A. 1925, ss. 94, 95), i.e., following the transfer or assent to them (see Ruoff, Land Registration Forms, pp. 165 *et seq.*, and 188 *et seq.*). Thereafter, no persons dealing with the land will be affected by the trust, references to which will so far as possible be excluded from the register (L.R.A. 1925, s. 74). Thus any person dealing with the persons registered as proprietors will be wholly protected provided only that he complies with any restriction or caution entered on the register (i.e., under L.R.A. 1925, s. 58 (3), in the case of joint proprietors not beneficially entitled as such or under *ibid.*, s. 54 (1), by a beneficial co-owner : *Elias* v. *Mitchell* [1972] Ch. 652). The equities are otherwise completely curtained off (see also ss. 20 (1) and 23 (1) of the L.R.A. 1925, but cp. *ibid.*, s. 70 (1) (*g*), *ante*, p. 188).

Trust for sale in deed of arrangement.—The special difference in this case from an ordinary trust for sale is that only one trustee need be appointed and that such trustee can give a valid receipt for capital moneys (Law of Property (Amendment) Act, 1926, s. 3). This is as it should be, because under the Deeds of Arrangement Act, 1914, the trustee has to give security. In reference to the appointment of a new trustee of a deed of arrangement, it is specially provided by s. 41 (2) of the T.A. 1925, replacing s. 18 of the Deeds of Arrangement Act, 1914, that whenever it is expedient to appoint *a new trustee*, and it is found inexpedient, difficult or impracticable to do so without the assistance of the court, then, in the case of a deed of arrangement within the meaning of the Deeds of Arrangement Act, 1914, the power may be exercised either by the High Court or by the court having jurisdiction in bankruptcy in the district in which the debtor resided or carried on business at the date of the execution of the deed.

Application of perpetuity rule to trusts for sale.—Section 23 of the L.P.A. 1925 provides that a trust for sale will, so far as regards the safety and protection of a purchaser, be deemed to be subsisting until the land has been conveyed to or under the direction of the beneficiaries. But it is thought that only immediate trusts for sale are within this section ; it does not give validity to a future trust, when too remote : *Re Wood* [1894] 3 Ch. 381. Consequently a trust for sale to *arise at a future time* will offend the rule against perpetuities if it is directed to take effect at a time which may be beyond the perpetuity period of a life or lives in being and twenty-one years afterwards or, alternatively, now of a specified period not exceeding eighty years (*Re Daveron ; Bowen* v. *Churchill* [1893] 3 Ch. 421 ; *Goodier* v. *Edmunds* [1893] 3 Ch. 455 ; *Re Appleby ; Walker* v. *Nesbit* [1903] 1 Ch. 565 ; *Re Davies and Kent's Contract* [1910] 2 Ch. 35 ; *Re Bewick ; Ryle* v. *Ryle* [1911] 1 Ch. 116 ; *Kennedy* v. *Kennedy* [1914] A.C. 215 ; *English* v. *Cliff* [1914] 2 Ch. 376 ; *Re Garnham ; Taylor* v. *Baker* [1916] 2 Ch. 413 ; Perpetuities and Accumulations Act, 1964, s. 1). In applying the rule, at common law the state of things existing at the testator's death, and not at the date of the will, was to be looked at (*Re Wood, ante*), but since 1964 regard must be had instead in this context to the " wait and see " rule introduced by s. 3 of the Perpetuities and Accumulations Act, 1964.

Assuming a trust for sale has been validly created within the perpetuity rule, considerable questions used to occur as to whether administrative powers conferred on the trustees throughout the duration of the trust would be void *ab initio* unless their exercise were restricted to the perpetuity period (see *Re Allott* [1924] 2 Ch. 498 ; *Law Society's Gazette*, vol. 60, p. 723 *et seq.*). Now, however, the question has been completely clarified by s. 8 (1) of the Perpetuities and Accumulations Act, 1964, which subsection applies notwithstanding that the power in question was conferred by an instrument taking effect before the commencement of the Act (subs. (2)) and which provides as follows :—

" 8.—(1) The rule against perpetuities shall not operate to invalidate a power conferred on trustees or other persons to sell, lease, exchange or otherwise dispose of any property for full consideration, or to do any other act in the administration (as opposed to the distribution) of any property . . ."

Transitional provisions affecting land held on trust for sale.— It is provided by para. 6 (*b*) of Pt. II of Sched. 1 to the L.P.A. 1925 that : " Where the land is at the commencement *or by virtue of this Act* or any Act coming into operation at the same time subject or is by virtue of any statute made subject to a trust for sale, the legal estate affected *shall vest* in the trustees for sale (including personal representatives holding land on trust for sale) but subject to any mortgage term subsisting or created by this Act."

" *or by virtue of this Act.*"—This includes the case of undivided shares (Pt. IV of same Schedule, as to which, see *ante*, p. 286 *et seq.*), and the case of an infant entitled to a legal estate with a person of full age (Pt. III, para. 2, of same Schedule, as to which, see *ante*, p. 335).

" *shall vest.*"—The paragraph should have said " shall vest or remain vested " ; if the legal estate was already vested in the trustees on 1st January, 1926, it merely remained so vested.

It is provided by s. 34 (1) of the T.A. 1925 that where, at the commencement of the Act, there were more than four trustees holding land on trust for sale, no new trustees shall (except where as a result of the appointment the number is reduced to four or less) be capable of being appointed until the number is reduced to less than four, and thereafter the number shall not be increased beyond four. Therefore although, on 1st January, 1926, there might have been more than four trustees for sale of land, they all could and can act. But when by death or other cause the number is reduced to four, this number must not be exceeded. But s. 34 does not apply (*a*) in the case of land vested in trustees for charitable, ecclesiastical or public purposes ; or (*b*) where the net proceeds of the sale of the land are held for like purposes ; or (*c*) to trustees of a term of years absolute limited by a settlement on trusts for raising money, or of a like term created under the statutory remedies relating to annual sums charged on land (*ibid.*, s. 34 (3)).

Devolution of trust estate and powers.—On the death of a sole or last surviving or continuing trustee before 1926, the trust estate devolved on his personal representatives by virtue of s. 30 of the Conveyancing Act, 1881, and on the death after 1925 the estate devolves on the personal representatives, under ss. 1 (1), (3), and 3 (1) (ii) of the A.E.A. 1925 and, in both cases, notwithstanding any testamentary disposition thereof.

In this connection s. 18 of the T.A. 1925 (replacing s. 22 of the Trustee Act, 1893), is a most important section :—

" 18.—(2) Until the appointment of new trustees, the personal representatives or representative for the time being of a sole trustee, or where there were two or more trustees, of the last surviving or continuing trustee, *shall be capable of exercising or performing* any power or trust which was given to, or capable of being exercised by, the sole or last surviving or continuing trustee, or other the trustees or trustee for the time being of the trust.

(3) This section takes effect subject to the restrictions imposed in regard to receipts by a sole trustee, not being a trust corporation. [As to these, see *ante*, p. 177.]

(4) In this section ' personal representative ' does not include an executor who has renounced or has not proved."

" *shall be capable of exercising or performing*."—Section 18 (2) does not say that the personal representatives are *compelled* to act, and they can insist on new trustees being appointed, and will be entitled to the cost of appointing new trustees (*Re Knight's Will* (1883), 26 Ch. D. 82 ; *Re Ridley* [1904] 2 Ch. 774; *Re Benett* [1906] 1 Ch. 216). On the other hand, they cannot insist on acting as trustees if their services are not required, and on the appointment of new trustees their powers cease (*Re Routledge's Trusts* [1909] 1 Ch. 280).

Personal representatives who exercise powers pursuant to s. 18 (2) are apparently not themselves trustees. Consequently, on death of a sole personal representative, or of the survivor of two or more, it is thought that his representatives are not capable of exercising the powers and trusts unless they are executors by representation of the sole or surviving trustee.

To construe this section properly it must be borne in mind that powers under a settlement may be broadly divided into two classes, namely :—

(i) Powers given to trustees *ex officio*, that is in their capacity as trustees, and as incident to their office of trustees. *Prima facie*, powers given to trustees which enable them to deal with the trust property, notwithstanding that they may have to exercise a wide discretion, are taken to be given to them *ex officio* as an incident of their office and pass with the office to the holders or holder thereof for the time being.

(ii) Bare powers given to *individuals* by name and not annexed to an estate or office. To bring the case within this class the settlor must have expressed his wishes and instructions in clear and apt language (Farwell, J., in *Re Smith* [1904] 1 Ch. 139).

The latter class of powers do *not* come within the section, i.e., they do not survive the named individuals (*Re Smith, ante ; Re Harding* [1923] 1 Ch. 182).

By s. 36 (7) of the T.A. 1925 it is also provided that every new trustee appointed under that section as well before as after all the trust property becomes by law, or by assurance, or otherwise, vested in him, shall have the same powers, authorities and discretions, and may in all respects act as if he had been originally appointed a trustee of the instrument, if any, creating the trust. Section 43 of the same Act contains similar provisions in regard to every trustee appointed by a court of competent jurisdiction.

It must be borne in mind that where the personal representative of a surviving or continuing or sole trustee for sale of land is himself a sole personal representative, and the parties wish him to act instead of appointing new trustees, and he is willing to do so, he must first appoint another trustee to act with him, so as to enable an effective receipt to be given for purchase-money of land. See next note.

25

Where registered land is held on trust for sale, the same problems as to the powers of the trustees for the time being do not appear to arise. " It is fundamental that any registered proprietor or proprietors can exercise all or any powers of disposition unless some entry on the register exists to curtail or remove these powers " (Ruoff & Roper, Registered Conveyancing, 3rd ed., p. 406).

Number of trustees for sale.—It is provided by s. 27 (2) of the L.P.A. 1925, as amended by the Law of Property (Amendment) Act, 1926, that, " notwithstanding anything to the contrary in the instrument (if any) creating a trust for sale of land or in the settlement of the net proceeds, the proceeds of sale or other capital money shall not be paid to or applied by the direction of fewer than two persons as trustees for sale, except where the trustee is a trust corporation, but this subsection does not affect the right of a *sole personal representative as such* to give valid receipts for, or direct the application of, proceeds of sale or other capital money, nor, except where capital money arises on the transaction, render it necessary to have more than one trustee." See also T.A., 1925, s. 34 (2).

"*sole personal representative as such.*"—A sole personal representative of a sole or last surviving trustee for sale, not being a trust corporation, cannot give a good receipt on sale in pursuance of the trust for sale. It is difficult to suggest any case in which sale would be necessary for purposes of administration. Such a personal representative may exercise the trusts (T.A. 1925, s. 18 (2)), but s. 18 (3) expressly states that the section takes effect subject to restrictions in regard to receipts by a sole trustee. Thus, on such a sale although the legal estate would pass the title would be a bad one because the rights of beneficiaries would not be overreached (L.P.A. 1925, s. 27 (2)) and equities would continue to be enforceable against subsequent purchasers.

Registered land.—Section 95 of the L.R.A. 1925 provides that the statutory restrictions affecting the number of persons entitled to hold land on trust for sale apply to registered land. It appears probable that this incorporates by reference not only s. 34 of the T.A. 1925 (limiting the maximum number of trustees to four) but also s. 27 (2) of the L.P.A. 1925 above (see Ruoff & Roper, Registered Conveyancing, 3rd ed., p. 403). In any case where trustees for sale are registered as proprietors of the land (L.R.A. 1925, s. 94) entry of a restriction is rendered obligatory by s. 58 (3) of the L.R.A. 1925, in the following form (L.R.R. 1925, Sched., Form 62, as amended under r. 74) :—

" Restriction registered on [date] : No disposition by one proprietor of the land (being the survivor of joint proprietors and not being a trust corporation) under which capital money arises is to be registered except under an order of the registrar or of the court "

(Ruoff & Roper, *op. cit.*, p. 408).

Planning matters affecting land held on trust for sale.—Most of the statements made *ante*, p. 409, as to the position of personal representatives apply also to trustees for sale. For instance, the liability of trustees to repay to the planning authority the cost of taking steps to ensure compliance with enforcement and similar notices is limited to the amount of moneys in their hands since a demand for repayment was made (Public Health Act, 1936, s. 294, as applied by the Town and Country Planning Act, 1971, s. 91 (3) (4)).

For the reasons given *ante*, p. 758, it does not appear that trustees for sale have power to pay out of capital the costs of opposing proposed orders and notices of the local planning authority.

In view of the provisions of the Town and Country Planning Acts, a few new clauses might be inserted in a settlement on trust for sale, similar to those recommended in the case of a strict settlement of land (*ante*, p. 756 *et seq*.). Such clauses do not seem necessary when a trust for sale is created merely in order that persons may hold beneficially as joint tenants or tenants in common. Suggestions are (i) a power to apply trust money in payment of costs of applications, opposition to orders, compliance with requirements, etc. ; (ii) a provision that trust money may be applied in payment of costs of obtaining planning permission or of claiming compensation, and that all compensation shall be capital.

Determination of trust for sale.—Where property formerly held on trust for sale has been conveyed to a beneficiary whether the conveyance is the result of a partition or the merger or determination of prior interests, it is necessary that the equitable title of the beneficiary should be abstracted. This is because a purchaser from the beneficiary will have notice of the existence of equitable interests under the trust for sale and so he must investigate the equitable title. It is possible to forget that this is the general rule as a purchaser is so often protected from its operation by " curtain " provisions of the 1925 legislation (such as those in the S.L.A. 1925, ss. 17 and 110, *ante*, pp. 706, 689) none of which applies in this particular case. Similarly, it may be necessary to bring equities on to the title to show that a sole trustee is the only person entitled beneficially and that a prior trust for sale has, in consequence, ceased to be operative. In such a case the person so shown to be solely entitled at law and in equity can make a good title. The difficulties caused by bringing the equitable interests on to the title to the legal estate may often make it advisable to keep a trust for sale in existence, even if one person is solely interested beneficially, new trustees being appointed if necessary. See further the discussion in *Law Times*, vol. 216, pp. 577, 650, vol. 217, p. 38.

No such problem arises with registered land since a purchaser from a registered proprietor should never need to investigate the equitable title (L.R.A. 1925, s. 74).

PART 2. POWERS OF TRUSTEES FOR SALE

Settled Land Act powers.—Section 28 (1) of the L.P.A. 1925, as amended, might almost be called the charter of trustees for sale, as it is the source of most of their statutory powers. The amendment is shown in italics :—

" 28.—(1) Trustees for sale shall, in relation to land or to manorial incidents and to the proceeds of sale, have all the powers of a tenant for life and the trustees of a settlement under the Settled Land Act, 1925, including in relation to the land the powers of management conferred by that Act during a minority : *and where by Statute settled land is or becomes vested in the trustees of the settlement upon the statutory trusts, such trustees and their successors in office, shall also have all the additional or larger powers (if any) conferred by the settlement on the tenant for life, statutory owner, or trustees of the settlement* ; and (subject to any express trust to the contrary) all capital money arising under the said powers shall, unless paid or applied for any purpose authorised by the Settled Land Act, 1925, be applicable in the same manner as if the money represented proceeds of sale arising under the trust for sale.

All land acquired under this subsection shall be conveyed to the trustees on trust for sale.

The powers conferred by this subsection shall be exercised with such consents (if any) as would have been required on a sale under the trust for sale, and when exercised shall operate to overreach any equitable interests or powers which are by virtue of this Act or otherwise made to attach to the net proceeds of sale as if created by a trust affecting those proceeds."

Subsection (2) provides, in effect, that, subject to any direction to the contrary in the disposition on trust for sale, the net rents and profits until sale, " after keeping down costs of repairs and insurance and other outgoings," shall be paid in like manner as if the sale had been made and the proceeds duly invested. See further, *post*, p. 777.

The amendment in s. 28 (1) was necessary because directly settled land becomes subject to a trust for sale it ceases to be settled land. See *ante*, p. 673. Consequently, it is provided that where the settlement contained special powers, such powers should not lapse, and that the persons who become trustees under the trust for sale shall have the benefit of these powers.

Trustees for sale, therefore, for all practical purposes, are in as good a position as a tenant for life under the S.L.A. 1925, but without the disadvantage of the formalities of the S.L.A. 1925, for instance of a vesting deed under s. 13 of that Act. For instance, it was held by Clauson, J., in *Re Gray* ; *Public Trustee* v. *Woodhouse* [1927] 1 Ch. 242 that the expression " repairs " in s. 28 (2) bears the same wide meaning as the word " repair " in the S.L.A. 1925, s. 102 (2) (*b*) ; and that although the powers under s. 102 are only exercisable by S.L.A. 1925 trustees during a minority or a contingency, they are exercisable *at any time* by trustees for sale. The powers given by the L.P.A. 1925, s. 28 (1), include all the powers conferred by the S.L.A. 1925, s. 73, both as to investment and as to administration (*Re Wellsted's Will Trusts* [1949] Ch. 296 ; see further, *post*, p. 778) and also include the power to effect, under order of the court, a transaction within the S.L.A. 1925, s. 64 (1), *ante*, p. 753, for the benefit of persons interested (*Re Simmons* [1956] 2 W.L.R. 16). For the powers of a tenant for life, see *ante*, p. 733 *et seq.*

However, trustees for sale, unlike a tenant for life under the S.L.A. 1925, may have the exercise of their powers inhibited (cp. s. 106 of the S.L.A. 1925). Thus s. 28 (1) of the L.P.A. 1925 (set out above, and see *post*, p. 777), expressly contemplates that consent may be required. Again, trustees for sale may be under a duty to consult beneficiaries and give effect to their wishes in the exercise of any of the powers (s. 26 (3) of the L.P.A. 1925, as substituted in 1926 ; see *Re Jones* [1931] 1 Ch. 375 according to which the subsection applies to all powers, not just sale). This duty to consult arises anyway with a statutory trust for sale but in other cases only if an appropriate intention appears in the disposition creating the trust, and the wishes of the majority of beneficiaries according to the value of their combined interests should prevail (*ibid.* ; see *post*, p. 774). Further, some of the statutory powers conferred on trustees for sale are subject to a contrary intention appearing (see, e.g., s. 25 (1) of the L.P.A. 1925 as to the power to postpone sale ; *Re Rooke* [1953] Ch. 716).

Apart from these permitted inhibitions of the powers of trustees for sale, it becomes a moot question whether a settlor can otherwise in any way restrict their statutory powers. There is no equivalent expressed in the L.P.A. 1925 of the general avoidance of restrictions effected by s. 106 of the S.L.A. 1925 (see *ante*, p. 737).   Nevertheless it can be argued that trustees for sale should be in this respect again in the same position as a tenant for life under the S.L.A. 1925.   Firstly, it can be said that s. 28 (1) of the L.P.A. 1925 is mandatory : " Trustees for sale *shall . . . have all the powers . . .* "   Secondly, it can be said that the reference to the S.L.A. 1925 powers incidentally incorporates s. 106 of the S.L.A. 1925.   And thirdly, it can be said that the general legislative policy must have been that all limited owners should have unlimited powers of management.   Therefore, for example, in the case of a trust for sale of a farm where a trustee is also a beneficiary entitled to income so long as he resides on and manages the property, it is suggested that the trustee/beneficiary ought not to lose his interest in income if the farm is sold or let.   There is decided authority which would support this suggestion, namely *Re Davies W.T.* [1932] 1 Ch. 530, but which is slightly peculiar in that it concerned a trust for sale subsisting before 1926 when it would have been subject to the predecessor of s. 106 of the S.L.A. 1925.

Trustees have an overriding duty to obtain the best price which they can for their beneficiaries.   Therefore they may have to accept a higher offer which it would be to the credit of an ordinary vendor to refuse on the ground that negotiations with someone else had proceeded so far that they ought not to be terminated, i.e., there appears to be a duty to " gazump " (*Buttle* v. *Saunders* [1950] 2 All E.R. 193).   The duty of trustees for sale to obtain the best price is discussed by Mr. E. H. Bodkin in the *Conveyancer N.S.*, vol. 14, p. 228.

Trustees for sale can dispose of leaseholds by way of underlease, retaining the original term themselves (*Re Judd and Poland's Contract* [1906] 1 Ch. 684).

Registered land.—Where trustees for sale are registered as proprietors of the land the accepted view is that they have all the powers of any other registered proprietor unless a restriction is entered on the register (Ruoff & Roper, Registered Conveyancing, 3rd ed., p. 406).   An appropriate restriction might appear to be in L.R.R. 1925, Sched., Form 10, which is headed " restriction where statutory owners *or trustees holding on trust for sale* are entered as proprietors " and which *inter alia* states that " no disposition is to be registered unless authorised by the Settled Land Act, 1925."   However, it is pointed out in Ruoff & Roper (*op. cit.*, p. 808) that the italicised part of the heading " has been responsible for some confusion ", that " it is certain that the restriction has no possible connection with a normal trust for sale " and that " this restriction is undoubtedly confined " to a " settled land context " (and see L.R.R. 1925, r. 58).

Protection of purchaser.—Section 23 of the L.P.A. 1925 provides that where land has become subject to an express *or implied trust for sale*, such trust shall, so far as regards the safety and protection of any purchaser thereunder, be deemed to be subsisting until the land has been conveyed to or under the direction of the persons interested in the proceeds of sale.   Therefore a purchaser from the trustees will now be protected although he has notice that the beneficiaries have obtained a vested interest in the proceeds of sale.

It is also provided by s. 27 (1) of the L.P.A. 1925 that a purchaser of a legal estate from trustees for sale shall not be concerned with the trusts affecting the proceeds of sale of land subject to a trust for sale (whether made to attach to such proceeds by virtue of this Act or otherwise), or affecting the rents and profits of the land until sale, whether or not those trusts are declared by the same instrument by which the trust for sale is created.

Contrast the comments, *ante*, p. 771, as to the position where land held on trust for sale is conveyed to a beneficiary under the trust. Nevertheless, the L.P.A. 1925, s. 27 (2), *ante*, p. 770, as to the number of trustees must not be overlooked (see also *ante*, p. 177).

Where a trust for sale has been created by a conveyance to the trustees upon trust for sale and by a separate trust instrument declaring the trusts a purchaser will be concerned only with the contents of the conveyance. Before 1926, in *Re Goodall's Settlement* [1909] 1 Ch. 440, a conveyance on trust for sale, when construed in the light of the trust instrument, was held not to create an effective trust for sale, and there is nothing in the 1925 legislation to alter this decision. Consequently, it is important, in such a case, for a purchaser from trustees for sale to ensure that the conveyance on trust for sale was executed, or was intended to take effect, *before* the trust instrument. If that was the case, the purchaser need not concern himself with the trust instrument which cannot have negatived the trust for sale. See an article by S. J. Bailey in the *Cambridge Law Journal*, vol. 8, p. 36.

In the case, however, of registered land the position is much simplified for purchasers by the fundamental provision that no person dealing with a registered estate or charge should be affected with notice of a trust express, implied or constructive (s. 74 of the L.R.A. 1925).

Implied power to postpone the exercise of a trust for sale.—It is provided by s. 25 of the L.P.A. 1925 that a power to postpone sale shall, in the case of every trust for sale of land, be implied unless a contrary intention appears ; also that the trustees for sale shall not be liable in any way for postponing the sale, in the exercise of their discretion, for any indefinite period ; nor shall a purchaser of a legal estate be concerned in any case with any directions respecting the postponement of a sale. But a trustee must exercise the power with discretion, for in the definition clause in s. 205 (1) (xxix) of the L.P.A. 1925, the expression " power to postpone a sale " means power to postpone in the exercise of a discretion.

In *Re Ball ; Jones* v. *Jones* [1930] W.N. 111, it was held that the above statutory power to postpone sale did not apply where there was an express power to postpone sale ; also that where there was an express power to postpone and the capital of the trust estate had become divisible, the power to postpone ceased ; and that even where the statutory power applies, it ceases when the capital fund becomes distributable.

Where a testator directed his trustees " as soon as possible after [his] death " to sell his farm, it was held that the trustees had no power to postpone sale under the L.P.A. 1925, s. 25, as a contrary intention was shown (*Re Rooke* [1953] Ch. 716). See also the discussion of *Re Ball* at [1953] Ch. 723.

Consultation with beneficiaries.—Section 26 (3) of the L.P.A. 1925, as re-enacted by the Law of Property (Amendment) Act, 1926, provides as follows :—

" 26.—(3) Trustees for sale shall *so far as practicable* consult the persons of full age for the time being beneficially interested in possession in the rents and profits of the land until sale, and shall, *so far as consistent with the general interest of the trust*, give effect to the wishes of such persons, or, in the case of dispute, of the majority (according to the value of their combined interests) of such persons, but a purchaser shall not be concerned to see that the provisions of this subsection have been complied with.

In the case of a trust for sale, not being a trust for sale created by or in pursuance of the powers conferred by this or any other Act, *this subsection shall not apply unless* the contrary intention appears in the disposition creating the trust."

It was held by Bennett, J., in *Re Jones ; Jones* v. *Cusack-Smith* [1931] 1 Ch. 375, that subs. (3), as amended, must not be limited to the case where the trustees proposed to exercise the trust for sale, but that the wishes of the beneficiaries should be consulted on the exercise of any of their *statutory trusts and powers* under the S.L.A. 1925 and the L.P.A. 1925, or on the exercise of additional or larger powers conferred by a settlement.

In practice, a contrary intention within the second paragraph of s. 26 (3) appears rarely if ever in express trusts for sale ; for a discussion of this, see A. M. Prichard in *Solicitors' Journal*, vol. 117, p. 518.

Consents to exercise of trust for sale.—If the trust for sale cannot be exercised without the consent of more than two persons, then, in favour of a purchaser, the consent of any two of such persons to the execution of the trust or to the exercise of any statutory or other powers vested in the trustees for sale will be sufficient (L.P.A. 1925, s. 26 (1)). But trustees will, no doubt, for their own protection, obtain all the consents.

A most useful provision in the L.P.A. 1925 is that where the person whose consent is required is an infant or subject to disability, so far as a purchaser is concerned, his consent will not be necessary. And, so far as the trustees are concerned, it will be sufficient if they obtain the consent of the parent or testamentary or other guardian of the infant or of the receiver (if any) of the person suffering from mental disorder (L.P.A. 1925, s. 26 (2), as amended by the Mental Health Act, 1959, Sched. 7).

In *Re Beale's Settlement Trusts* [1932] 2 Ch. 15, Maugham, J., held that where, in the case of a trust for sale, " any requisite consent cannot be obtained," because the person from whom it must be obtained refuses it, the court can, under the L.P.A. 1925, s. 30, and the T.A. 1925, s. 57, direct the trustees to sell.

Refusal to sell or to exercise certain powers.—If trustees for sale refuse to sell or to exercise any of the powers conferred on them by the L.P.A. 1925, s. 28 (that is, powers of management, see *ante*, p. 771), or by the L.P.A. 1925, s. 29 (that is, power to delegate management, see *post*, p. 821), or any requisite consent cannot be obtained, any person interested may apply to the court for a vesting or other order for giving effect to the proposed transaction or for an order directing the trustees to give effect thereto (L.P.A. 1925, s. 30). Where a person refuses to consent, the case is one in which " any requisite consent cannot be obtained " within this section (*Re Beale's Settlement, ante*). A judgment creditor, who has been appointed receiver by way of equitable execution of the debtor's interest in a house which is held by the debtor and his wife on trust for sale for themselves as tenants in common, is not a " person interested " within the L.P.A. 1925, s. 30 (*Stevens* v. *Hutchinson* [1953] Ch. 299 ; see also *Irani Finance, Ltd.* v. *Singh* [1971] Ch. 59, and compare *Cooper* v. *Critchley* [1955] Ch. 431). However, the trustee in bankruptcy of a beneficial joint tenant successfully made an application under s. 30 in *Re Solomon* [1967] Ch. 573, but *Stevens* v. *Hutchinson* was not apparently cited.

Whether sale ordered.—On such an application being properly made " the court may make such order as it thinks fit " (L.P.A. 1925, s. 30). As a *prima facie* rule, where the parties are not agreed on sale, the court will order sale in pursuance of " the simple and fundamental principle that in a trust for sale there is a duty to sell, and a power to postpone ; and, accordingly, one trustee may call upon the others to perform the duty, but all must be agreed if they are to exercise the power " (*per* Devlin, L.J., in *Jones* v. *Challenger* [1961] 1 Q.B. 176, at p. 181, referring to *Re Mayo* [1943] Ch. 302 ; see also *Re Steed* [1960] Ch. 407). But this *prima facie* rule can be displaced where the trust for sale subsists merely as a conveyancing device enabling the convenient co-holding of the property. Lord Justice Devlin continued (*ibid.*, pp. 181, 183) : " This simple principle cannot prevail where the trust itself, or the circumstances in which it was made, show that there was a secondary or collateral object besides that of sale . . . There is, as I have said, something akin to *mala fides* if one trustee tries to defeat a collateral object in the trust by arbitrarily insisting on the duty of sale. He should have good grounds for doing so and, therefore, the court will inquire whether, in all the circumstances, it is right and proper to order the sale." Thus sale was not ordered in *Re Buchanan-Wollaston* [1939] Ch. 738 where four persons had purchased land to preserve the amenities and had covenanted *inter se* to do so (see also *Re Hyde's Conveyance* (1952), *Law Journal*, vol. 102, p. 58, where the land was virtually partnership property). In practice the primary purpose of purchase of land by co-owners, who expressly or impliedly become trustees for sale, will mostly not be sale at all but simply to provide a home (as for a son and his mother in *Bull* v. *Bull* [1955] 1 Q.B. 234). In particular, the matrimonial home is often vested in the names of both husband and wife.

The position appears to be that so long only as the purpose other than sale (whether to provide a home or otherwise) remains extant the court will not order sale. Thus, in *Jones* v. *Challenger* [1961] 1 Q.B. 176 the sale of a house purchased as a matrimonial home was ordered by a majority of the Court of Appeal on the application of the wife after she had been divorced to enable her to realise her investment, since the end of the marriage was the end of the purpose ; it was said that the innocent spouse's protection lay in an application under the Married Women's Property Act, 1882, s. 17 (*ante*, p. 365) or under, now, the Matrimonial Proceedings and Property Act, 1970, s. 4 (*ante*, p. 368). Further in *Rawlings* v. *Rawlings* [1964] P. 398 such a majority ordered sale on the application of a wife in desertion since the marriage had in fact though not in law broken down. However, it was observed that there were no children to provide a home for despite the desertion, and reference by way of contrast may be made to *dicta* as to the position of an innocent party in *Stevens* v. *Hutchinson* [1953] Ch. 299 and *Bull* v. *Bull* [1955] 1 Q.B. 234. Also *Rawlings* v. *Rawlings*, *ante*, was distinguished by the Court of Appeal in *Bedson* v. *Bedson* [1965] 2 Q.B. 666, where the application for an order to sell made by a wife in desertion was refused, having regard to hardship to the husband if he lost the premises and to the possibility of either reconciliation or matrimonial proceedings in which an order varying the property rights could be made under, now, s. 4 of the 1970 Act.

With *Jones* v. *Challenger*, *ante*, contrast *Barclay* v. *Barclay* [1970] 2 Q.B. 677, C.A., where there was an express trust for sale in a will, the proceeds being held for tenants in common. An order for possession was made against one of the tenants in common to enable sale with vacant possession. See also *Re Solomon* [1967] Ch. 573, *Re John's Assignment Trusts, Niven* v. *Niven* [1970] 1 W.L.R. 955, *Jackson* v. *Jackson* [1971] 1 W.L.R. 1539, C.A., and *Irani Finance Ltd.* v. *Singh* [1971] Ch. 59 (in which the Court of Appeal explained certain aspects of *Bull* v. *Bull* and *Barclay* v. *Barclay*).

These cases are considered generally in a useful article by Gareth Miller in the *Conveyancer N.S.*, vol. 36, p. 99 *et seq.*

As to a married woman's rights in the matrimonial home generally, see *ante*, p. 364 *et seq.*

Powers of management.—Trustees for sale have wide powers of management under the L.P.A. 1925, s. 28 (1), *ante*, p. 771. There has been a certain amount of doubt as to what class of repairs has to be paid out of capital and what class of repairs has to be paid out of income. The point is obviously of the very greatest importance, for although by paying for repairs out of capital the income of the life tenant is reduced, by paying for repairs out of income the life tenant may be deprived of the whole of his income, perhaps, for several years. Before 1926 a court of equity had power to assist trustees in adjusting the cost on equitable lines as between the tenant for life and the remainderman, and this power extended not only to the cost of repairs necessary for the preservation of the property, but also to the cost of erecting buildings, necessary for making the property saleable. And, whatever the court could do, trustees for sale could do without the aid of the court, for, if the matter was brought before the court by a person interested, the court would have confirmed the acts of the trustees. See *Re Hotchkys* (1886), 32 Ch. D. 408 ; *Conway* v. *Fenton* (1888), 40 Ch. D. 512.

It is thought that since 1925 there has been no substantial alteration in the law, although the trustees may now have a wider discretion as a result of the grant to them of S.L.A. 1925 powers. In *Re Conquest* [1929] 2 Ch. 33, £727 had been expended on rebuilding which might be described as " alterations in buildings reasonably necessary or proper to enable the buildings to be let." The learned judge said that the effect of the L.P.A. 1925, s. 28 (1), is to give trustees for sale two sets of powers. One is set out in s. 102 (2) of the S.L.A. 1925, and the expenses incurred in exercising those powers may by virtue of the L.P.A. 1925, s. 28 (1), and the S.L.A. 1925, s. 102, be met out of income. The other set of powers is contained in the S.L.A. 1925, s. 84 and Sched. 3, and permits improvements to be made and paid for out of capital. Accordingly the effect of the L.P.A. 1925, s. 28 (1), is to confer power on the trustees to spend income for such purposes as are particularised in the S.L.A. 1925, s. 102 (2), and to spend capital for such purposes as are particularised in Pt. I of Sched. 3 to that Act. Those powers overlap, and there may be work which the trustees could carry out under s. 102, under the power given to them to erect, pull down, rebuild and repair houses, and could under that section pay for out of income, and which at the same time they could, under Pt. I of Sched. 3, carry out and pay for out of capital. He did not, however, consider whether the work in the particular case could be paid for out of income but decided that it was structural reconstruction and so fell within the class of work which the trustees might pay for out of capital. Clauson, J., added that his decision followed *Re Robins* [1928] Ch. 721 and *Re Whitaker* [1929] 1 Ch. 662 and then said : " Where, in such a case, the trustees have a choice of powers, they may, I venture to think, be properly guided in their choice by the equitable principles laid down and applied in *Re Hotchkys* (1886), 32 Ch. D. 408." In *Re Wynn* [1955] 1 W.L.R. 940, it was decided that trustees for sale have a discretion to pay out of capital for repairs to agricultural property, which amount to improvements within the Agricultural Holdings Act, 1948, Sched. 3, and, therefore, improvements within the S.L.A. 1925, Sched. 3 ; compare the remarks *ante*, p. 754 *et seq.* Nevertheless, if they properly pay for such

25A

repairs out of income the person interested for life in the proceeds of sale cannot insist on having repayment out of capital (*ibid.*). The trustees' discretion must be exercised reasonably : for example, they must not expend capital on repairs without regard to their duty to preserve the capital of the estate (*Re Boston's Will Trusts* [1956] Ch. 395). See further an excellent article in *Conveyancer N.S.*, vol. 20, at p. 351.

Power of trustees for sale to partition.—See *ante*, p. 310.

Power of trustees for sale to purchase land.—The L.P.A. 1925, s. 28 (1), as amended by the Law of Property (Amendment) Act, 1926, provides that trustees for sale shall in relation to land and to the proceeds of sale have all the powers of a tenant for life and the trustees of a settlement under the S.L.A. 1925, and that land acquired under this subsection shall be conveyed to the trustees on trust for sale. The S.L.A. 1925, s. 73 (1) (xi), provides that capital money arising under the S.L.A. 1925 may be invested or otherwise applied in purchase of land in fee simple or of leasehold land held for sixty years or more unexpired at the time of purchase. Trustees for sale may therefore invest the proceeds of sale in the purchase of other land as an investment, even if they have, in the meantime, been invested in another way (*Re Wellsted's Will Trusts* [1949] Ch. 296).

However, in *Re Wakeman* [1945] Ch. 177, Uthwatt, J., had held that where all the land held on trust for sale had already been sold and the proceeds invested the trustees ceased to be trustees for sale within the definition in the L.P.A. 1925, s. 205 (1) (xxix), and so had no power to invest in the purchase of land. In the Court of Appeal in *Re Wellsted's Will Trusts*, *ante*, Cohen, L.J., said that he reserved the question what the position would be if at the time when the question of investment arose no land was held on the trusts of the settlement. Consequently, until there is further authority, it must be accepted that once trustees for sale have disposed of all of the land, they have no power to invest in the purchase of further land. See further, comments by Mr. Desmond Pollock in the *Conveyancer N.S.*, vol. 17, p. 134 *et seq.*

It was held in *Re Power's Will Trusts* [1947] Ch. 572, that an express power to invest in the purchase of freehold property does not permit the purchase of a vacant freehold house for occupation by the testator's widow and children. The question raised in *Re Power's Will Trusts* was, however, whether the trustee might purchase, not as an investment, but for occupation by the widow, the tenant for life, on the terms that she should pay outgoings, do repairs, and insure. Although a negative answer was given to this general question it may be possible to carry out the proposal of the parties in another way. It is understood that the question has been raised by summons whether trustees might purchase a specified house at a valuation which they considered to be a proper investment (the house being conveyed to them on trust for sale) and might permit the tenant for life to occupy it on his undertaking to pay outgoings and to give vacant possession on three months' notice in writing. The undertaking to give possession avoids any objection on the ground that part of the purchase-money might be paid for the advantage of vacant possession which would be lost as soon as the tenant for life entered ; a licence is suggested so that there is no possibility of the acquisition of a protected tenancy. Apparently approval to this arrangement was granted in the application in question ; see the note by " D.P." in the *Conveyancer N.S.*, vol. 16, p. 316.

Alternatively it may be noted that the decision in *Re Power's Will Trusts* turned on the point that the express power extended only to purchases as an investment, whereas s. 73 (1) (xi) of the S.L.A. 1925 permits capital money to be "invested *or otherwise applied*" in such purchases. In other words, it is not obvious why the decision should apply at all to the statutory powers conferred on trustees for sale.

Power of appropriation of trustees for sale.—Very wide powers of appropriation are given to personal representatives by s. 41 of the A.E.A. 1925. See *ante*, p. 401 *et seq*. These powers are not given to trustees for sale, but in certain cases a trust for sale implies a power of appropriation. In *Re Beverley* [1901] 1 Ch. 681, Buckley, J., stated that where the trustees are directed to convert and to pay the beneficiary money, it must be competent to them to agree with the beneficiary that they will sell him the property and set off the purchase-money against the money which otherwise they would have to pay to him, and it is not necessary to go through the form of first converting the property and then giving the beneficiary the money which he may be desirous immediately of reinvesting in the property which has just been sold. The judge continued that if that was the principle, it was obvious that the doctrine of appropriation extends to chattels real, and also to real estate which is subject to a trust for sale and conversion. But in the case then under consideration there were three ninth shares which were settled, and as to these a different principle came in. The trustees of the settled shares could only consent to take, in satisfaction of what was given to them, such investments as were authorised by the instrument which created the settlement. The will in question contained certain clauses as to investment, and other investments could not be appropriated to those shares.

In *Re Brookes* (1897), 76 L.T. 771, Stirling, J., held that a direction in a will to the trustees, to continue the investments of the testator, meant that investments unauthorised by law were for the purposes of the will to be considered authorised investments, and consequently the trustees had power to make the appropriation which they had made to the settled shares. In *Re Craven* [1914] 1 Ch. 358, Warrington, J., held that a mere power to postpone the sale, that is to delay realisation, did not give trustees for sale an implied power of appropriation.

Power of trustees for sale to lease, see *post*, p. 820; **to delegate powers of leasing,** see *post*, p. 821; **to grant options to purchase,** see *ante*, p. 77.

Power to raise money for improvements and to pay compensation.— Trustees for sale have power under s. 13 of the Landlord and Tenant Act, 1927, to raise money and to apply the same—

"(*a*) in payment as for an improvement authorised by the Act of any money expended and costs incurred by a landlord under or in pursuance of this Part of this Act in or about the execution of any improvement;

(*b*) in payment of any sum due to a tenant under this Part of this Act in respect of compensation for an improvement, and any costs, charges and expenses incidental thereto;

(*c*) in payment of the costs, charges and expenses of opposing any proposal by a tenant to execute an improvement."

Subsection (2) of s. 13 provides that the satisfaction of such a claim for compensation shall be included among the purposes for which a trustee for sale may raise money under s. 71 of the S.L.A. 1925 (as applied to trustees for sale by the L.P.A. 1925, s. 28 (1)). There is *not* a similar power in the Landlord and Tenant Act, 1954 (compensation rarely being payable thereunder).

Power to fix value of trust property.—Trustees may, for the purpose of giving effect to a trust, or any of the provisions of an instrument, if any, creating a trust or of any statute, from time to time (by duly qualified agents) ascertain and fix the value of any trust property in such manner as they think proper, and any valuation so made in good faith will be binding upon all persons interested under the trust (T.A. 1925, s. 22 (3)).

Power to mortgage.—Trustees have no power to mortgage except—

   (i) so far as they are authorised by an express power contained in the instrument creating the trust ; or

   (ii) so far as they may be taken to be authorised by any other power or authority in such instrument, from which an intention can be gathered or implied that the trustees are to have such power ; or

   (iii) under some statute expressly conferring such power ; or

   (iv) where the mortgage is made at the request or with the consent of the beneficiaries, provided they are all of full age.

A power given to trustees to *sell* in order to raise a sum of money implies a power to mortgage when the purposes of the trusts will be answered by a mortgage, but not if the intention appears that a sale out and out shall be made (*Stronghill* v. *Anstey* (1852), 1 De G.M. & G. 635 ; *Devaynes* v. *Robinson* (1857), 27 L.J. Ch. 157). So, a power to make outlays in repairs or improvements out of income *or capital* impliedly authorises trustees to mortgage the property for that purpose (*Re Bellinger ; Durell* v. *Bellinger* [1898] 2 Ch. 534).

Trustees for sale have (i) by virtue of s. 28 (1) of the L.P.A. 1925, all the powers to mortgage given to a tenant for life by s. 71 of the S.L.A. 1925, *ante*, p. 747, but these powers are very limited ; (ii) power to raise the necessary money for the payment of death duties by mortgage, under the F.A. 1894, s. 9 ; S.L.A. 1925, s. 71 (1) (i) ; L.P.A. 1925, ss. 16 (3) and 28 ; and (iii) under s. 28 (3) of the L.P.A. 1925 power to raise money for the payment of equality money in cases of partition (and it is thought they have this power irrespective of that subsection). But the powers to mortgage which trustees principally rely on is contained in s. 16 (1) of the T.A. 1925, which provides that where trustees are authorised by the instrument, if any, creating the trust or by law to pay or apply capital money subject to the trust for any purpose or in any manner, they are to have power to raise the money required by sale, conversion, calling in *or mortgage* of all or any part of the trust property for the time being in possession. The section applies notwithstanding anything to the contrary contained in the instrument creating the trust, but does not apply to trustees of property held for charitable purposes, or to trustees of a settlement for the purposes of the S.L.A. 1925 not being also the statutory owners (T.A. 1925, s. 16 (2)).

Where there is power to mortgage as above, it is thought that a mortgage to a building society will be valid to the extent of the money actually advanced (compare *Thorne* v. *Thorne* [1893] 3 Ch. 196). However, it should perhaps be noted that the above powers do not include mortgaging to raise the initial purchase price of land, but that this limitation is mitigated in practice by the points mentioned in the following two paragraphs.

As regards protection to purchasers and mortgagees, it is provided by s. 17 of the T.A. 1925 that no purchaser or mortgagee, paying or advancing money on a sale or mortgage purporting to be made under any trust or power vested in trustees, is to be concerned to see that such money is wanted, or that no more than is wanted is raised, or otherwise as to the application thereof.

Where trustees hold the legal estate in land on trust for beneficiaries in possession, all of whom are of age, and are requested by such beneficiaries to raise money on mortgage for the private purposes of such beneficiaries, the trustees will be able to carry out their wishes, and such a mortgage would give a good title to the mortgagee. On this principle, if persons before 1926 were beneficially entitled to land as tenants in common or as joint tenants, and therefore at the beginning of 1926 became trustees for themselves holding such land on trust for sale under Sched. 1, Pt. IV, to the L.P.A. 1925, or where the land (other than settled land) is, since 1925, conveyed to persons beneficially as tenants in common or as joint tenants, and they thereby become trustees for sale thereof for themselves, under ss. 34 and 36 of the same Act, they can, if they like, mortgage the land by exercising their powers as trustees, provided that there are two of them to give the necessary receipt, but there is nothing to prevent them ignoring the trust for sale and mortgaging the property as freely as they could have done before 1926. They have both the legal estate and the beneficial interest and can give a mortgagee a perfect title. But there is just this difference, namely, that where the mortgage is made by the parties as beneficial owners, it is incumbent on the mortgagee to investigate the beneficial title, which he would not have to do if the mortgage were made by them in their capacity of trustees for sale.

There is power for the court to confer on trustees power to mortgage in exceptional cases given by s. 57 (1) of the T.A. 1925 set out *post*, p. 783 ; and, in the case of settled land, by s. 64 of the S.L.A. 1925, set out *ante*, p. 753.

Registered land.—The generally accepted view is that trustees who are registered as proprietors have all the powers of any other registered proprietor unless a restriction is entered on the register (Ruoff & Roper, Registered Conveyancing, 3rd ed., p. 406). These powers expressly include the power to charge the registered land (L.R.A. 1925, s. 25).

Power of trustees to advance money on mortgage.—The " narrower-range " investments specified in Sched. 1 to the Trustee Investments Act, 1961, include " mortgages of freehold property in England and Wales or Northern Ireland and of leasehold property in those countries of which the unexpired term at the time of investment is not less than sixty years". Consequently, trustees may lend on such mortgages even if they do not exercise their power to divide the trust fund and invest part in " wider-range " investments (1961 Act, ss. 1 and 2). They must first " obtain and consider proper advice on the question whether the investment is satisfactory having regard to [the need for diversification so far as appropriate and the suitability to the trust] " (*ibid.*, s. 6 (1) (2)). " Proper " advice is that of " a person who is reasonably believed by the trustees to be qualified by his ability in and practical experience of financial matters " and who may be one of the trustees (*ibid.*, s. 6 (4) (6)).

Apart from the 1961 Act, trustees were not able to lend on a second or
subsequent mortgage (*Chapman* v. *Browne* [1902] 1 Ch. 785), or on a contributory mortgage (*Webb* v. *Jonas* (1888), 39 Ch. D. 660), although they could
lend on the security of a legal sub-mortgage (*Smethurst* v. *Hastings* (1885),
30 Ch. D. 490), or on a charge or a mortgage of a charge under the Improvement
of Land Act, 1864 (T.A. 1925, s. 5 (1) (*b*)). It is arguable that these restrictions
are not applicable to the 1961 Act power, since there are no express restrictions
on it and the word " mortgage " is defined to " relate to every estate and
interest regarded in equity as merely a security for money " (s. 17 (4) of the
1961 Act and s. 68 (7) of the T.A. 1925). However, pending a decision of the
courts, it would appear better practice to assume that the 1961 Act has not
changed the law in this respect in disregard of the principles enunciated in the
decisions mentioned.

Protection to a trustee as regards the proportion of the loan to the value
of the property is given by the following subsection of the T.A. 1925 :—

" 8.—(1) A trustee lending money on the security of any property on
which he can properly lend shall not be chargeable with breach of trust
by reason only of the proportion borne by the amount of the loan to the
value of the property at the time when the loan was made, if it appears
to the court—

(*a*) that in making the loan the trustee was acting upon a report as
to the value of the property made by a person whom he reasonably
believed to be an able practical surveyor or valuer instructed and
employed independently of any owner of the property, whether such
surveyor or valuer carried on business in the locality where the
property is situate or elsewhere ; and

(*b*) that the amount of the loan does not exceed two-third parts of the
value of the property as stated in the report ; and

(*c*) that the loan was made under *the advice of the surveyor or valuer
expressed in the report*."

" *by reason only of the proportion*."—Competent advice as to the desirability
of the mortgage as an investment must be obtained in accordance with
s. 6 (1), (2) of the 1961 Act, *ante*, which advice need not extend to the
suitability of any particular loan on the security of freehold or leasehold
property in England and Wales or Northern Ireland (s. 6 (7) of the 1961 Act,
applying without prejudice to s. 8 of the 1925 Act above).

" *the advice of the surveyor or valuer expressed in the report*."—Care must
be taken to see that the report states that the surveyor advises the advance,
as this is sometimes omitted.

A trustee lending on the security of leaseholds is not chargeable with
breach of trust only upon the ground that he dispensed wholly or partly
with investigation of the lessor's title (T.A. 1925, s. 8 (2)), and a trustee is not
so chargeable only upon the ground that he accepted a shorter title than that
which a purchaser is entitled to require " if in the opinion of the court the
title accepted be such as a person acting with prudence and caution would
have accepted " (T.A. 1925, s. 8 (3)).

Trustees lending money on the security of any property on which they
can lawfully lend may contract that such money shall not be called in during
any period not exceeding seven years from the time when the loan was
made, provided interest be paid within a specified time not exceeding thirty
days after every half-yearly or other day on which it becomes due, and

provided there be no breach of any covenant by the mortgagor contained in the instrument of mortgage or charge for the maintenance and protection of the property (T.A. 1925, s. 10 (1)).

Power to leave money on mortgage without valuation.—Section 10 (2) of the T.A. 1925 provides that on a sale of land for an estate in fee simple or for a term having at least five hundred years to run by trustees or by a tenant for life or statutory owner, the trustees, or the tenant for life or statutory owner on behalf of the trustees of the settlement, may, where the proceeds are liable to be invested, contract that the payment of any part, not exceeding two-thirds, of the purchase-money shall be secured by a charge by way of legal mortgage or a mortgage by demise or sub-demise for a term of at least five hundred years (less a nominal reversion when by sub-demise), of the land sold. Such charge or mortgage, if any buildings are comprised in the mortgage, must contain a covenant by the mortgagor to keep them insured against loss or damage by fire to their full value. *The trustees are not bound to obtain any report as to the value of the land* or other property to be comprised in such charge or mortgage, or any advice as to the making of the loan, and will not be liable for any loss which may be incurred by reason only of the security being insufficient at the date of the charge or mortgage (*ibid.*). The powers conferred by the section are exercisable subject to the consent of any person whose consent to a change of investment is required by law, or by the instrument, if any, creating the trust (*ibid.*, s. 10 (5)).

Power to finance builders.—It is provided by s. 28 (1) of the L.P.A. 1925 that trustees for sale shall, in relation to the proceeds of sale, have all the powers of a tenant for life under the S.L.A. 1925. Therefore, they have the power to finance builders given by the S.L.A. 1925, s. 73 (1) (xviii). This paragraph provides that capital money arising under the Act, *subject to the application thereof for any special authorised object for which the capital money was raised*, may be invested or otherwise applied in financing any person who may have agreed to take a lease or grant for building purposes of the settled land, or any part thereof, by making advances to him in the usual manner on the security of an equitable mortgage of his building agreement.

In preparing a settlement it may be wise to consider in any particular case whether this provision should be negatived.

Power of court to authorise dealings with trust property.—It is provided by s. 57 of the T.A. 1925 as follows :—

" 57.—(1) Where in the *management or administration* of any property vested in trustees, any sale, lease, mortgage, surrender, release, or other disposition, or any purchase, investment, acquisition, expenditure, or other transaction, is in the opinion of the court expedient, but the same cannot be effected by reason of the *absence of any power for that purpose* vested in the trustees by the trust instrument, if any, or by law, the court may by order confer upon the trustees, either generally or in any particular instance, the necessary power for the purpose, on such terms, and subject to such provisions and conditions, if any, as the court may think fit and may direct in what manner any money authorised to be expended, and the costs of any transaction, are to be paid or borne as between capital and income."

" *management or administration.*"—" The alteration or remoulding as such of trusts declared by a settlement is not within the scope of s. 57, which only empowers the court to make orders, if it thinks it expedient so to do, with reference to the management or administration by trustees of the trust property which is vested in them " (Evershed, M.R., in *Re Chapman's Settled Estates* [1953] Ch. 218, 264 ; on appeal [1954] A.C. 429). " We are satisfied that the application of both words [' management ' and ' administration '] is confined to the managerial supervision and control of trust property on behalf of beneficiaries " (*ibid.*, at p. 247). In special circumstances, however, even the purchase of a life interest in a fund by the trustees may be a matter of administration which can be sanctioned under s. 57 (*Re Forster's Settlement* [1954] 1 W.L.R. 1450). If a settlement of a reversionary interest contains no power to sell that interest until it falls into possession, a sale, for instance, to the person entitled for life, with a view to saving estate duty, may be made with the leave of the court under s. 57 (*Re Cockerell* [1956] Ch. 372). It must be noted that the property settled was the reversionary interest itself ; a sale of a reversionary interest in settled property is a different matter as it may alter the trusts (*Re Heyworth's Contingent Reversionary Interest* [1956] Ch. 364). See further now the Variation of Trusts Act, 1958, for the general jurisdiction conferred on the courts as a consequence of the *Chapman* v. *Chapman* decision, *ante.*

" *absence of any power for that purpose.*"—The court has no jurisdiction under s. 57 (1) if the trustees have statutory power to take the action desired (*Re Pratt* [1943] Ch. 356). See also *Re Basden's Settlement Trusts* [1943] 2 All E.R. 11, and *Municipal and General Securities* v. *Lloyds Bank, Ltd.* [1950] Ch. 212.

The application can be made by the trustees or by any person beneficially interested under the trust, T.A. 1925, s. 57 (3)). A county court has jurisdiction under the T.A. 1925, s. 57, in a case where the trust estate or fund to be dealt with in the court does not exceed in amount or value £500 (County Courts Act, 1959, s. 52 (3), Sched. 1).

This extension of the jurisdiction of the court will enable the court to authorise dealings with the trust property which otherwise would amount to a breach of trust. For the court to exercise its power the proposed transaction must, in the opinion of the court, be expedient for the benefit of the whole trust and not for the benefit of one beneficiary only (*Re Craven's Estate (No.* 2) [1937] Ch. 431). For an example of the application of the section, see *Re Salting* [1932] 2 Ch. 57.

This particular section does not apply to S.L.A. 1925 trustees (T.A. 1925, s. 57 (4)), but the court can sanction transactions by a tenant for life (or trustees for sale) under s. 64 of the S.L.A. 1925. See *ante*, p. 753.

The jurisdiction of the court under the T.A. 1925, s. 57, so far as regards trustees for sale of land, includes a power to order that management expenses shall be paid out of capital if the court is satisfied that it is for the benefit of the persons entitled under the trust for sale and either (i) the available income from all sources of the person who, being beneficially entitled in possession, might otherwise have been expected to bear such expenses, has been so reduced as to render him unable to bear the expenses without undue hardship ; or (ii) there is no such person, and the income available for such expenses has become insufficient (Settled Land and Trustee Acts (Court's General Powers) Act, 1943, s. 1 ; Emergency Laws (Miscellaneous Provisions) Act, 1953, s. 9).

Power to pay money into a bank, and to lodge deeds.—Trustees may, pending the negotiation and preparation of any mortgage or charge, or during any other time while an investment is being sought for, pay any trust money into a bank to a deposit or other account, and all interest, if any, payable in respect thereof is to be applied as income (T.A. 1925, s. 11 (1)).

Trustees may deposit any documents held by them relating to the trust, or to the trust property, with any banker or banking company, or any other company whose business includes the undertaking of the safe custody of documents, and any sum payable in respect of such deposit will be paid out of the income of the trust property (T.A. 1925, s. 21).

Power to employ an agent.—Trustees or personal representatives may, instead of acting personally, employ and pay an agent, whether a solicitor, banker, stockbroker, or other person, to transact any business or do any act required to be transacted or done in the execution of the trust or the administration of the testator's or intestate's estate, including the receipt and payment of money, and are entitled to be allowed all charges so incurred and are not responsible for the default of any agent if employed in good faith (T.A. 1925, s. 23 (1) ; *Re Vickery* [1931] 1 Ch. 572, distinguished in *Re Lucking's Will Trust* [1968] 1 W.L.R. 866 ; see also *Modern Law Review*, vol. 22, p. 381). As to the delegation of *discretionary* powers, see *ante*, p. 244.

Whether trustees can require a release.—In practice, it is usual to require a release under seal on winding-up of the estate, but in strict right a trustee, in the absence of special circumstances, cannot insist upon a release under seal (*Re Wright's Trusts* (1857), 3 K. & J. 419) ; though it has been held that an executor, on the winding-up of the estate, has a right to a release from the residuary legatee. See *King* v. *Mullins* (1852), 1 Drew. 308. See also *post*, p. 1178, as to retention of assets to protect a trustee against possible future liability for estate duty.

Protection of trustees.—The following protection given to personal representatives is also given to trustees :—

(a) To free them from liability in respect of rents and covenants under a lease. See s. 26 of the T.A. 1925, *ante*, p. 406.

(b) To free them from responsibility on the winding-up of the estate, by advertisement for claims. See s. 27 of the T.A. 1925, *ante*, p. 407.

(c) To free them from any obligation to inquire as to adoption of children. See Adoption Act, 1958, s. 17 (3). Trustees are also freed from any obligation to inquire as to illegitimate relationships. See s. 17 of the Family Law Reform Act, 1969.

Purchase by trustee from himself or co-trustee.—An active trustee is not allowed to purchase from himself or from his co-trustee even though the purchase be thoroughly fair. The principle is that a trustee must not place himself in the position that his interest and his duty would clash, as would be the case if he were allowed to be both seller and buyer. Of course, if the settlement specially authorises him to purchase, or if all the persons interested are of age and of sound mind and join in the conveyance, that is another thing (see *Re Hayes' Will Trusts* [1971] 1 W.L.R. 758, where a power had been given to executors to sell realty to one of themselves for a price being the estate duty valuation). In all other cases where a trustee wishes to buy, he should apply to the court for an order to enable him to do so. A purchase not under an order of court would not be void *ab initio*, but would be liable to be set aside by any *cestui que trust*, provided that he applied to the court for that purpose without unreasonable delay ; and it would not be necessary to show that the trustee had taken any advantage (*Re Bulmer* [1937] Ch. 499). As an alternative to setting aside, the court may order the trustee to offer the property for resale at a reserve price equal to the price paid by the trustee plus the cost of any improvements, with any surplus over the reserve price belonging to the trust, and in certain circumstances purchase by auction by a co-trustee who has not influenced the sale may be upheld (see *Holder* v. *Holder* [1968] Ch. 353).

The defect may be cured by acts of confirmation by the parties, or lapse of time (*Nutt* v. *Easton* [1900] 1 Ch. 29), but no confirmation or lapse of time will bar the right of the *cestuis que trust* to set aside the sale unless it be shown that they were aware that the trustee had become the purchaser (*Randall* v. *Errington* (1805), 10 Ves. 423).

A purchase by a person who retired from the office of trustee twelve years before, without any intention of purchasing at the time of retirement, was held to be valid in *Re Boles and British Land Co., Ltd.* [1902] 1 Ch. 244. There is no objection to a trustee re-purchasing for his own benefit property sold by him as trustee, provided that the original sale was *bona fide* in all respects, and there was no understanding at the time that he was to re-purchase (*Re Postlethwaite* (1888), 37 W.R. 200).

The objection to a trustee purchasing part of the estate does not apply (i) where he is merely a *bare* trustee, that is, a person holding the legal estate without any duties to perform and compellable to transfer the same as directed by the beneficiaries (*Stacey* v. *Elph* (1833), 1 Myl. & K. 1965) ; (ii) to a person who is nominated a trustee, but declines to accept the trust (*Clark* v. *Clark* (1884), 9 App. Cas. 733) ; or (iii) if the contract was made before the fiduciary relationship arose, for instance, if the trustee was given an option to purchase by the testator under whose will the trust took effect (*Re Mulholland's Will Trusts* [1949] 1 All E.R. 460).

Taking a conveyance in the name of a nominee will vitiate the sale, although proper in other respects, in consequence of the act of concealment (*MacPherson* v. *Watt* (1877), 3 App. Cas. 254).

A purchaser with notice is in no better position than the trustee (*Bainbrigge* v. *Browne* (1881), 18 Ch. D. 188 ; *Silkstone and Haigh Moor Colliery Co.* v. *Edey* [1900] 1 Ch. 167 ; and see *Pilkington* v. *Wood* [1953] Ch. 770 as to the effect on the title). If the purchase is set aside, the purchaser is entitled to a return of his purchase-money (*Gresley* v. *Mousley* (1859), 28 L.J. Ch. 620). To put the title in order a confirmatory conveyance should be executed in which all persons beneficially interested should join after taking independent professional advice. For a discussion of such conveyances, see *Conveyancer N.S.*, vol. 18, p. 528, and for a precedent, see *ibid.*, p. 715 *et seq.*

Whether a trustee for the purposes of the S.L.A. 1925 may purchase the land is not clear ; as the discretion to sell lies with the tenant for life it would appear that he may do so just as a bare trustee may. In practice it would be wise to obtain the concurrence of all persons beneficially interested, if possible.

The opinion is widely held that statutory trustees holding land on trust for themselves only as joint tenants or tenants in common do not come within the general rule that a trustee is not able to buy from his co-trustee.

The reason is that the relationship is merely caused by a conveyancing device and the case is in reality one of buying from a co-beneficial owner. See *Green* v. *Whitehead* [1930] 1 Ch. 38, *ante*, pp. 244–245. In *Re Foot and Hall Beddall & Co., Ltd.'s Agreement* (1945), 174 L.T. 83, where a trust for sale arose from a transaction in the nature of a partnership affecting land, Cohen, J., permitted one person who was in the position of a trustee to purchase but appears to have treated the case as one in which the leave of the court was required for the purchase.

It is provided by s. 72 (4) of the L.P.A. 1925 that two or more persons (whether or not being trustees or personal representatives) may convey, and will be deemed always to have been capable of conveying, any property vested in them to any one or more of themselves in like manner as they could have conveyed such property to a third party ; provided that if the persons in whose favour the conveyance is made are, by reason of any fiduciary relationship or otherwise, precluded from validly carrying out the transaction, the conveyance will be liable to be set aside. A lease for three years or under made by parol may be a " conveyance " within the meaning of the word as used in s. 72 (4) (*Rye* v. *Rye* [1961] Ch. 70).

It would appear that a trustee who has power to mortgage (see *ante*, p. 780) may validly advance money on the security of trust property and exercise all the rights of a mortgagee (*A.-G.* v. *Hardy* (1851), 1 Sim. (N.S.) 338 ; but see *Re Mason's Orphanage and London and North Western Rail Co.* [1896] 1 Ch. 54, 59). Clearly, however, such a transaction would be closely scrutinised before enforcement by the courts.

Purchase by others in fiduciary position.—The rule that an active trustee is incapacitated from buying applies to mortgagees, solicitors, agents, and all other persons who, by being concerned or employed in the affairs of another, have acquired a knowledge of his property. As to a secretary of a building society not being able to purchase, see *Martinson* v. *Clowes* (1882), 21 Ch. D. 857 ; or a member of an investment committee of a building society, *Hodson* v. *Deans* [1903] 2 Ch. 647. As to a solicitor, see further *ante*, p. 426. Recently the rule was applied to an executor who had performed acts of administration before purporting to renounce, although in the special circumstances of the case the purchase was upheld (*Holder* v. *Holder* [1968] Ch. 357).

Neither the trustee nor any member of the committee of inspection of an estate in bankruptcy may, while acting as trustee or member of such committee, except by leave of the court, either directly or indirectly, by himself, or any partner, clerk, agent or servant, become purchaser of any part of the estate (*Re Bulmer* [1937] Ch. 499). Any such purchase made contrary to the provisions of this rule may be set aside by the court on the application of the Department of Trade and Industry or any creditor (Bankruptcy Rules, 1952, r. 349). But a partner of a member of the committee may purchase on his own private account (*Re Gallard* [1897] 2 Q.B. 8).

Although a tenant for life is deemed to be a trustee for all parties interested (S.L.A. 1925, s. 107 (1)), it is provided by s. 68 of the S.L.A. 1925, *ante*, p. 743, that he may buy the settled land.

Purchase by wife or other relative of trustee.—It may be that a trustee acting in good faith could grant a lease to his wife (*Dowager Duchess of Sutherland* v. *Duke of Sutherland* [1893] 3 Ch. 169), and, in the Scottish case of *Burrell* v. *Burrell's Trustees* [1915] S.C. 333 it was said that there is no absolute rule of law that the purchase of part of a trust estate from the trustees by the wife of one of them is illegal. Probably a purchase by the wife of a trustee would not be set aside unless it could be shown that it was carried out for the husband's benefit or at an undervalue. Consequently it is thought that a purchaser from the wife could safely accept the title unless he had notice that the consideration was inadequate, or of some other objection. It is thought that purchases by other members of the trustee's family are governed by similar rules, but there is no adequate authority. Discussion of these matters can be found in *Conveyancer N.S.*, vol. 13, p. 248, *Law Times*, vol. 217, pp. 16, 17, *Law Journal*, vol. 104, p. 262 *et seq.* and *Law Times*, vol. 228, p. 190 (referring to an unreported decision in *Re King's Will Trusts*, where Harman, J., held valid, on the facts, a sale by a trustee to his wife).

Purchase by trustee from beneficiaries.—The case of a trustee for the sale of property purchasing from his beneficiaries is quite different. Here he is not exercising his power and any objection is caused merely by the relation between the parties. But even in this case, to support the purchase, the trustee must prove that the parties were at arm's length, that the trustee had fully communicated to the beneficiaries all matters affecting the value of the land sold, and that the price was adequate. In the absence of such evidence, a title traced through such a trustee will not be forced on a purchaser (*Williams* v. *Scott* [1900] A.C. 499 ; *Dougan* v. *MacPherson* [1902] A.C. 197).

The general rule is that a trustee must not take advantage of his position to make a personal profit where to do so might create a conflict between his duty and his interest. Thus, if a trustee who holds a lease obtains a renewal of the lease for his own benefit he must hold it upon trust even if he had first attempted to renew for the benefit of the trust (*Keech* v. *Sandford* (1726), Cas. t. King 61 ; *Re Biss* [1903] 2 Ch. 40 ; *Re Knowles' Will Trusts* [1948] 1 All E.R. 866). The principle in *Keech* v. *Sandford, ante,* has been applied by the Court of Appeal to the purchase of the freehold reversion by one of the joint owners of a leasehold matrimonial home (*Protheroe* v. *Protheroe* [1968] 1 W.L.R. 519). This principle has also received a statutory application in the Leasehold Reform Act, 1967, s. 6 (2), (3).

Power to charge.—The *prima facie* strict rule is that trustees for sale, or otherwise, are not entitled to remuneration for their time and trouble but must act gratuitously (*Robinson* v. *Pett* (1734), 3 P. Wms. 249 ; *Re Doody* [1893] 1 Ch. 129 ; *Re Hill* [1934] Ch. 623 ; *Brown* v. *I.R.C.* [1965] A.C. 244) ; although they are, of course, entitled to reimbursement of out-of-pocket expenses (T.A. 1925, s. 30 (2)). This rule, however, is subject to contrary provision in the trust instrument, i.e., a charging clause, which should always be inserted in practice, is valid and effective (see generally G. B. Graham, *Conveyancer N.S.*, vol. 16, p. 13 ; also Hallett, Conveyancing Precedents, p. 774 *et seq.*). It need only be noted here that charging clauses are construed strictly (*Re Gee* [1948] Ch. 284) and may be confined in the case of a solicitor-trustee to charges for purely professional services (*Re Chalinder & Herington* [1907] 1 Ch. 58). Also such a clause is taken as conferring a gift and so is subject to abatement and to s. 15 of the Wills Act, 1837, but no longer to the perpetuity rule (s. 8 (1) of the Perpetuities and Accumulations Act, 1964). Reference may also be made to *Re Parry* [1969] 1 W.L.R. 614, in which a bequest of a share of residue to a solicitor " if he shall . . . act in the trusts thereof " was held only to require the doing of those acts which a non-professional trustee was obliged to do (there was, in addition, a charging clause in the will).

Certain other exceptions of less practical importance to the no-remuneration rule are recognised. Thus the court has inherent jurisdiction to order remuneration (see *Re Worthington* [1954] 1 All E.R. 677 and *Boardman* v. *Phipps* [1967] 2 A.C. 46), as well as where it appoints the trustee (T.A. 1925, s. 42). Again the beneficiaries may contract with the trustee for his remuneration, although this would be open to close scrutiny by the courts (*Ayliffe* v. *Murray* (1740), 2 Atk. 58, and see *Law Quarterly Review*, vol. 72, p. 490). Also there is the anomalous rule in *Cradock* v. *Piper* (1850), 1 Mac. & G. 664, that a solicitor-trustee employed by his co-trustees (and himself) to conduct legal proceedings on behalf of the trust may charge the usual profit costs provided that acting for himself as well has not increased the costs (and see *Re Worthington* [1954] 1 All E.R. 677, 679).

PART 3. APPOINTMENT OF NEW TRUSTEES

Number of trustees.—We have already (*ante*, p. 768) dealt with the case where there were more than four trustees on 1st January, 1926. As regards the number of trustees of settlements and dispositions (including wills) on trust for sale made or coming into operation after 1925, it is provided by s. 34 (2) and (3) of the T.A. 1925 as follows :—

" 34.—(2) In the case of settlements and dispositions on trust for sale of land made or coming into operation after [1925]—

(a) the number of trustees thereof shall not in any case exceed four, and where more than four persons are named as such trustees, the four first named (who are able and willing to act) shall alone be the trustees, and the other persons named shall not be trustees unless appointed on the occurrence of a vacancy ;

(b) the number of the trustees shall not be increased beyond four.

(3) This section only applies to settlements and dispositions of land, and the restrictions imposed on the number of trustees do not apply—

(a) in the case of land vested in trustees for charitable, ecclesiastical or public purposes ; or

(b) where the net proceeds of the sale of the land are held for like purposes ; or

(c) to the trustees of a term of years absolute limited by a settlement on trusts for raising money or of a like term created under the *statutory remedies* relating to annual sums charged on land."

" *statutory remedies* "—These are to be found in s. 121 (4) of the L.P.A. 1925.

It is also provided by s. 95 of the L.R.A. 1925 that the statutory restrictions affecting the number of persons entitled to hold land on trust for sale and the number of trustees of a settlement apply to registered land.

Powers of appointing new trustees.—New trustees of a settlement or will can be appointed—

(i) under an express power contained in the settlement ;

(ii) under the statutory power ;

(iii) by the court ;

(iv) by all the beneficiaries.

The statutory power of appointing new trustees (T.A. 1925, s. 36, below) is very satisfactory, and it is normally wise not to insert an express power in settlements and wills. If an express power does not refer to one of the occasions on which a new trustee could be appointed under the statutory power, then an appointment may be made under the statutory power unless it has been expressly negatived or modified (*Re Wheeler and de Rochow* [1896] 1 Ch. 315).

Usually, a power to appoint trustees is construed as a personal power, that is, a power given by reason of the settlor's trust in particular persons, as contrasted with a power which is deemed to be annexed to the office of trustee. If the power is given to persons by name it will usually be a personal power, with the consequence that it can only be exercised by the named persons, and will not be exercisable by the survivor notwithstanding the T.A. 1925, s. 18 (1) (see *ante*, p. 768).

Further, it is probable that the named person cannot appoint himself as a new trustee under an express power (*Re Skeats' Settlement* (1889), 42 Ch. D. 522, 527).

Statutory power of appointing new trustees.—The statutory power of appointment is contained in s. 36 (1) of the T.A. 1925, given below :—

"36.—(1) Where a trustee, either original or substituted, and whether appointed by a court or otherwise, *is dead*, or *remains out of the United Kingdom* for more than twelve months, or desires to be discharged from all or any of the trusts or powers reposed in or conferred on him, or refuses or is *unfit* to act therein, or is *incapable* of acting therein, *or is an infant*, then, subject to the restrictions imposed by this Act on the number of trustees,—

> (a) the *person or persons nominated* for the purpose of appointing new trustees by the instrument, if any, creating the trust ; or
>
> (b) if there is no such person, or no such person able and willing to act, then the surviving or *continuing trustees or trustee* for the time being, or the *personal representatives of the last surviving or continuing trustee ;*

may, *by writing*, appoint one or more other persons (*whether or not being the persons exercising the power*) *to be a trustee or trustees* in the place of the trustee so deceased, remaining out of the United Kingdom, desiring to be discharged, refusing, or being unfit or being incapable, or being an infant, as aforesaid."

Certain statements in an instrument of appointment as to the justification for the appointment are conclusive in favour of a purchaser of a legal estate (T.A. 1925, s. 38, *post*, p. 793).

"*is dead*."—The provisions of this section relating to a trustee who is dead include the case of a person nominated trustee in a will but dying before the testator (T.A. 1925, s. 36 (8)).

"*remains out of the United Kingdom*."—The twelve months' absence must be unbroken (*Re Walker* [1901] 1 Ch. 259 ; *Re Arbib and Class* [1891] 1 Ch. 601 ; *Re Earl of Stamford* [1896] 1 Ch. 288) ; if it is the absent trustee may be replaced without his concurrence and even against his will (*Re Stoneham's Settlement Trusts* [1953] Ch. 59). Notwithstanding this provision whereby a trustee abroad for twelve months may be supplanted, a new trustee residing out of the United Kingdom can still, in exceptional circumstances, properly and validly be appointed under s. 36 (1) (*Re Whitehead's Will Trusts* [1971] 1 W.L.R. 833).

"*unfit.*"—It was decided in *Re Roche* (1842), 2 Dr. & War. 287, that a bankrupt trustee is " unfit to act," but where the trustee has no money to receive, it would seem that he ought not to be removed. In *Re Barker's Trusts* (1875), 1 Ch. D. 43, 48, Jessel, M.R., said : " In my view it is the duty of the court to remove a bankrupt trustee who has trust money to receive, or deal with, so that he cannot misappropriate it. There may be exceptions, under special circumstances, to that general rule ; and it may also be that, where a trustee has no money to receive, he ought not to be removed merely because he has become bankrupt." In *Re Adams* (1879), 12 Ch. D. 634, the same learned judge said that where a trustee having, either solely or with others, control over the trust property had *recently* become bankrupt, and it was not shown that he had since become possessed of means, the court would, as a general rule, order his removal. It would not, therefore, be wise, just because a trustee has become bankrupt, to appoint another trustee in his place, unless the bankrupt trustee is willing to retire. It would be getter to get an order of court.

"*incapable.*"—This means personal incapacity, as in the case of a person of unsound mind (*Re Blake* [1887] W.N. 173). See further, *ante*, p. 423, and note, particularly, the restriction on an appointment of a new trustee in place of such a trustee who is entitled in possession to a beneficial interest (T.A. 1925, s. 36 (9) as re-enacted).

"*or is an infant.*"—An infant cannot now be a trustee under an express trust (L.P.A. 1925, s. 20), although he may become a trustee under an implied, constructive or resulting trust (*Re Vinogradoff* [1935] W.N. 68).

"*person or persons nominated.*"—There is no adequate authority as to the validity of the exercise by an infant of a power expressly granted to him to appoint a new trustee ; any appointment by him which is imprudent and which may prejudice his interests will be set aside (*Re Parsons* [1940] Ch. 973). If two or more persons are nominated jointly, it would appear that the power to appoint does not accrue to the survivor but ceases when the first nominee dies (*Re Harding* [1923] 1 Ch. 182).

"*continuing trustees or trustee.*"—The T.A. 1925, s. 36 (8), provides that : " The provisions of this section . . . relative to a continuing trustee include a refusing or retiring trustee, if willing to act in the execution of the provisions of this section." A trustee who is replaced under the power contained in the T.A. 1925, s. 36 (1), because he has remained abroad for more than twelve months is not " a refusing or retiring trustee " and so he cannot claim to be a " continuing trustee " whose concurrence in the appointment of a trustee to replace him is necessary under head (*b*) in the T.A. 1925, s. 36 (1) (*Re Stoneham's Settlement Trusts* [1953] Ch. 59).

"*personal representatives of the last surviving or continuing trustee.*"—It was decided, on s. 31 of the Conveyancing Act, 1881, that the executor of a sole trustee might appoint (*Re Shafto's Trusts* (1885), 29 Ch. D. 247) ; also the proving executor of a surviving trustee (*Re Boucherett* [1908] 1 Ch. 180).

But the personal representatives or representative of the last surviving or continuing trustee are not bound at the request of the *cestui que trust* to exercise the power of appointing a new trustee or new trustees (*Re Sarah Knight's Will* (1883), 26 Ch. D. 82). Section 36 (1) of the T.A. 1925, above, must be read with s. 18 of the same Act. Subsection (2) of s. 18 provides that, until the appointment of new trustees, the personal representatives or representative for the time being of a sole trustee, or, where there were two or more trustees, of the last surviving or continuing trustee, shall be capable of exercising or performing any power or trust which was given to, or capable of being exercised by, the sole or last surviving or continuing trustee, or other the trustees or trustee for the time being of the trust. At the same time they or he cannot insist on acting if their services are not required. If there should only be one personal representative of the last surviving or continuing or sole trustee, and the parties desire that he should act in the trust, and he is willing to do so, it will be necessary for him to appoint another trustee to enable an effective receipt to be given for purchase-money of land. See further, *ante*, p. 768, where s. 18 of the T.A. 1925 is considered.

The power given to the representatives of the last surviving or continuing trustee to appoint is, and is deemed always to have been, " exercisable by the executors for the time being (whether original or by representation) of such surviving or continuing trustee who have proved the will of their testator or by the administrators for the time being of such trustee without the concurrence of any executor who has renounced or has not proved " (T.A. 1925, s. 36 (4)), but a sole or last surviving executor intending to renounce, or all the executors where they all intend to renounce, have and are deemed always to have had power, at any time before renouncing probate, to exercise the power of appointment given by s. 36, or by a similar previous enactment, if willing to act for that purpose and without thereby accepting the office of executor (T.A. 1925, s. 36 (5)). It is thought that if such a non-proving executor makes the appointment by deed, the legal estate would without more be effectively vested in the new trustees by virtue of s. 40 of the T.A. 1925. In practice, however, it would clearly be desirable also to have an assent or conveyance in favour of the new trustees from the persons ultimately acting as personal representatives. See the discussion in the *Law Society's Gazette*, vol. 61, pp. 690 and 757 ; vol. 62, pp. 39, 40 and 235.

It seems that an appointment of new trustees executed by the representatives of a sole or last surviving trustee should contain an acknowledgment of the right of the new trustees to production of the grant. The implied vesting declaration (T.A. 1925, s. 40, *post*, p. 796) is a "conveyance " for the purposes of the A.E.A. 1925 (*ibid.*, s. 55), and so a memorandum of it should be indorsed on the grant ; a purchaser is entitled to have production of the grant to see that this has been done (but compare *Re King's Will Trusts* [1946] Ch. 542).

" *by writing.*"—The word " writing " does not include a will. Therefore, a sole surviving trustee of a will cannot by his will appoint, in continuation of himself, trustees of the will of the original testator (*Re Parker's Trusts* [1894] 1 Ch. 707). In practice it will be necessary, in almost all cases, to have a deed, but writing without a deed is sufficient if all securities are such that a vesting declaration will not transfer them. For, by s. 40 of the T.A. 1925, the provisions as to land vesting, whether or not the document contains a vesting declaration, only apply where such document is under seal ; see *post*, p. 796 and s. 30 (1) (v) of the S.L.A. 1925, *ante*, p. 713, which makes it necessary to have a deed where the appointment is made by the beneficiaries under that provision.

" *whether or not being the persons exercising the power.*"—Under the Trustee Act, 1893, this could not be done (*Re Sampson* [1906] 1 Ch. 435).

" *to be a trustee or trustees.*"—The following quotation from an article by " The Conveyancer " in the *Law Times*, vol. 214, p. 225, expresses clearly a rule sometimes overlooked :—

" It is wrong when appointing a new trustee to appoint the trustee to be such trustee in respect of the property specified in the schedule to the appointment. The new trustee should be appointed trustee of the trust instrument under which the property is held or of the trusts affecting the property. If this course is not adopted, since there is no power to appoint a new trustee of part of the trust property, it is necessary before the title can be taken from such new trustee for him to establish that the scheduled property is all the property then subject to the trusts. If any is omitted, the appointment is bad as not complying with the statutory power."

The beneficiaries cannot control the exercise of the power of appointing new trustees conferred on a continuing trustee by the T.A. 1925, s. 36 (1) (*b*), even if the beneficiaries are *sui juris* and able to direct the trustees to transfer the trust property to themselves (*Re Brockbank* [1948] Ch. 206).

Every new trustee appointed under s. 36 has the same powers, authorities, and discretions, and may in all respects act as if he had been originally appointed a trustee by the instrument, if any, creating the trust (T.A. 1925, s. 36 (7)). The result of this subsection taken with s. 18 (1) of the T.A. 1925 is that an elaborate definition of the trustees is unnecessary, and that a definition stating that the expression includes " the trustees for the time being hereof " is undesirable.

Dissolution of corporate trustee.—The possible dissolution of a corporation trustee is provided for by the T.A. 1925, s. 36 (3), as follows :—

" (3) Where a corporation being a trustee is or has been dissolved . . . then, for the purposes of this section and of any enactment replaced thereby, the corporation shall be deemed to be and to have been from the date of the dissolution incapable of acting in the trusts or powers reposed in or conferred on the corporation."

Generally, as to the effect of the dissolution of a corporation, see *ante*, p. 316.

Appointment in place of trustee removed.—The appointment of a new trustee in place of one removed under a power in the instrument creating the trust is authorised by the following provisions of the T.A. 1925, s. 36 (2) :—

" 36.—(2) Where a trustee has been removed, *under a power contained in the instrument* creating the trust, a new trustee or new trustees may be appointed in the place of the trustee who is removed, as if he were dead, or, in the case of a corporation, as if the corporation desired to be discharged from the trust, and the provisions of this section shall apply accordingly, but subject to the restrictions imposed by this Act on the number of trustees."

Evidence as to appointment.—A statement in an appointment of a new trustee as to the reason for the appointment is made conclusive evidence in favour of a purchaser, by the following section of the T.A. 1925 :—

" 38.—(1) A statement, contained in any instrument coming into operation after [1925] by which a new trustee is appointed for any purpose connected with land, to the effect that a trustee has remained out of the

United Kingdom for more than twelve months or refuses or is unfit to act, or is incapable of acting, or that he is not entitled to a beneficial interest in the trust property in possession, shall, in favour of a purchaser of a legal estate, be conclusive evidence of the matter stated.

(2) In favour of such purchaser any appointment of a new trustee depending on that statement, and any vesting declaration, express or implied, consequent on the appointment, shall be valid."

A corresponding provision, applicable to deeds of declaration, is contained in the S.L.A. 1925, s. 35 (3), see *ante*, p. 720.

Appointment of new trustees of trust for sale.—Section 35 of the T.A. 1925 and s. 24 of the L.P.A. 1925 deal with the *manner* of appointment of new trustees of conveyances on trust for sale, and are given below. It should be noted that different rules apply to the appointment of new trustees under the S.L.A. 1925 ; see *ante*, p. 719.

[T.A. 1925.] " 35.—(1) Appointments of new trustees of *conveyances on trust for sale* on the one hand and of the settlement of the proceeds of sale on the other hand, *shall*, subject to any order of the court, *be effected by separate instruments*, but in such manner as to secure that the same persons shall become the trustees of the conveyance on trust for sale as become the trustees of the settlements of the proceeds of sale."

[L.P.A. 1925.] " 24.—(1) The persons having power to appoint new trustees of a conveyance of land on trust for sale shall be bound to appoint the same persons (if any) who are for the time being trustees of the settlement of the proceeds of sale, but a purchaser shall not be concerned to see whether the proper persons are appointed to be trustees of the conveyance of the land."

Section 35 (1) of the T.A. 1925 appears to have been drawn on the assumption that there would always be two deeds when a trust for sale was created. But in practice it is only necessary to have two deeds of appointment where two deeds were used to create the trust for sale. There is nothing in this subsection, or in any Act, to make it necessary to have two deeds when *creating* a trust for sale (see note *ante*, p. 765), and when the conveyance of the estate and the trusts are contained in one deed, there is no object to be gained by having two deeds on the appointment of a new trustee. Where the beneficiaries and the trustees for sale are the same persons, it is sometimes convenient to declare the trusts of the proceeds by the conveyance. In such a case there will only be one deed when new trustees are appointed.

Where an assent on trust for sale is made after 1925 the form of the assent may affect the question whether one or two documents must be drawn up on the appointment of a new trustee. See *ante*, p. 766.

In order to prevent an appointment being overlooked, provision for an indorsement on the conveyance on trust for sale is made by the T.A. 1925, s. 35 (3), as follows :—

" (3) Where *new trustees* of a conveyance on trust for sale relating to a legal estate are appointed, a memorandum of the persons who are for the time being the trustees for sale shall be endorsed on or annexed thereto by or on behalf of the trustees of the settlement of the proceeds of sale, and the conveyance shall, for that purpose, be produced by the person having the possession thereof to the last-mentioned trustees when so required."

" *new trustees.*"—These words include additional trustees (T.A. 1925, s. 68 (17)).

Statutory power to appoint additional trustees.—This power was first introduced by the T.A. 1925, s. 36 (6), which provides as follows :—

" (6) Where a sole trustee, other than a trust corporation, is or has been originally appointed to act in a trust, or where, in the case of any trust, there are not more than three trustees (none of them being a trust corporation), either original or substituted and whether appointed by the court or otherwise, then and in any such case—

(*a*) the person or persons nominated for the purpose of appointing new trustees by the instrument, if any, creating the trust ; or

(*b*) if there is no such person, or no such person able and willing to act, then the trustee or trustees for the time being ;

may, *by writing*, appoint *another person* or other persons to be an additional trustee or additional trustees, but it shall not be obligatory to appoint any additional trustee unless the instrument, if any, creating the trust, or any statutory enactment, provides to the contrary, nor shall the number of trustees be increased beyond four by virtue of any such appointment."

" *by writing.*"—This should be effected by deed. See *post*, p. 796.

" *another person.*"—An appointor may not appoint himself as an *additional* trustee under this provision (*Re Power's Settlement* [1951] Ch. 1074) ; contrast the words of s. 36 (1), *ante*, p. 790.

Variation in number of trustees.—There are a number of rules as to this in the T.A. 1925, s. 37, whereby, on the appointment of a trustee :—

" (*a*) the number of trustees may, subject to the *restrictions imposed by this Act on the number of trustees*, be increased ; and

(*b*) a separate set of trustees, not exceeding four, may be appointed for any *part of the trust property held on trusts distinct from those relating to any other part* or parts of the trust property, notwithstanding that no new trustees or trustee are or is to be appointed for other parts of the trust property, and any existing trustee may be appointed or remain one of such separate set of trustees, or, if only one trustee was originally appointed, then, save as hereinafter provided, one separate trustee may be so appointed ; and

(*c*) it shall not be obligatory, save as hereinafter provided, to appoint more than one new trustee where only one trustee was originally appointed, or to fill up the original number of trustees where more than two trustees were originally appointed, but, except where only one trustee was originally appointed, and a sole trustee when appointed will be able to give valid receipts for all capital money, a trustee shall not be discharged from his trust unless there will be either a trust corporation or at least two individuals to act as trustees to perform the trust."

" *restrictions imposed by this Act on the number of trustees.*"—See *ante*, p. 789, as to the maximum number of S.L.A. 1925 trustees, and trustees holding land on trust for sale.

" *part of the trust property held on trusts distinct from those relating to any other part.*"—The trusts need not be permanently distinct (*Re Hetherington's*

Trusts (1886), 34 Ch. D. 211 ; *Re Moss's Trusts* (1888), 37 Ch. D. 513). It is important to note that the power to appoint a separate set of trustees applies only where the trusts are distinct.

Nothing in the T.A. 1925 authorises the appointment of a sole trustee, not being a trust corporation, where the trustee, when appointed, would not be able to give valid receipts for all capital money arising under the trust (T.A. 1925, s. 37 (2)).

Retirement of a trustee.—A trustee can retire without a new trustee being appointed in his place, provided that the conditions of the T.A. 1925, s. 39, are complied with. This section provides :—

" 39.—(1) Where a trustee is desirous of being discharged from the trust, and after his discharge there will be either a trust corporation or at least two individuals to act as trustees to perform the trust, then, if such trustee as aforesaid by deed declares that he is desirous of being discharged from the trust, and if his co-trustees and such other person, if any, as is empowered to appoint trustees, by deed consent to the discharge of the trustee, and to the vesting in the co-trustees alone of the trust property, the trustee desirous of being discharged shall be deemed to have retired from the trust, and shall, by the deed, be discharged therefrom under this Act, without any new trustee being appointed in his place.

(2) Any assurance or thing requisite for vesting the trust property in the continuing trustees alone shall be executed or done."

It must be borne in mind that if the object of the retirement is to enable a breach of trust to be effected, the retiring trustee will be equally liable for the breach (*Head* v. *Gould* [1898] 2 Ch. 250).

" If a deed of appointment is executed under [s. 39 (1)] and the consent to the vesting in the co-trustees alone is confined to the property specified in the schedule thereto, it has to be proved that such property is all the property subject to the trust, otherwise the whole deed is void " (" The Conveyancer," in *Law Times*, vol. 215, p. 225 ; compare *ante*, p. 793).

Vesting of trust property in new trustees.—This is now usually implied as a result of the T.A. 1925, s. 40, which is as follows :—

" 40.—(1) Where *by a deed* a new trustee is appointed to perform any trust, then—

(*a*) if the deed contains a declaration by the appointor to the effect that any estate or interest in any land subject to the trust, or in any chattel so subject, or the right to recover or receive any debt or other thing in action so subject, shall vest in the persons who by virtue of the deed become or are the trustees for performing the trust, the deed shall operate, without any conveyance or assignment, to vest in those persons as joint tenants and for the purposes of the trust the estate interest or right to which the declaration relates ; and

(*b*) if the deed is made after [1925] and does not contain such a declaration, the deed shall, subject to any express provision to the contrary therein contained, operate as if it had contained such a declaration by the appointor extending to all the estates interests and rights with respect to which a declaration could have been made."

" *by a deed*."—Section 36 (1), *ante*, p. 790, refers to the appointment being made " by writing," but s. 40 makes it necessary to have a deed if (as is usual) the provisions as to vesting are to apply. In practice, an express vesting declaration is not inserted. Not using an express declaration means that no risk is run as to the declaration being defective in form, and 50p in stamp duty is saved. See *post*, pp. 1154–1155.

It should be noted that the deed can operate to vest the legal estate in the new trustees even though it was not vested in the person making the appointment (see s. 9 (1) of the L.P.A. 1925). This facilitates the position, for example, where the appointor was not himself a trustee (see s. 36 (1) of the T.A. 1925). However, it is assumed that there would be no such operation where the legal estate is vested in some person whose interest is adverse and not subject to the trust. Again by the decision in *Re King's Will Trusts* [1964] Ch. 452 it appears that s. 40 (1) (*a*) and (*b*) is applicable only to estates and interests which form part of the existing trust property and not where an estate or interest is vested in an appointing trustee in some other capacity, e.g., as personal representative of the settlor ; i.e., a separate assent or conveyance is necessary under s. 36 (1) (4) of the A.E.A. 1925. This decision cannot be regarded as entirely satisfactory, particularly in relation to *Re Stirrup's Contract* [1961] 1 W.L.R. 449 which was not cited, but must be accepted in practice (see also *Re Pennant's Will Trusts* [1970] Ch. 75 and further, *ante*, p. 418).

Mortgage debts (as distinguished from the mortgaged land ; see s. 40 (4), below) would be included in the implied vesting declaration, and therefore (if the trust property includes mortgages) there should be a clause expressly stating that such implied declaration shall not apply to these. The mortgaged land and the debt will then be the subject of a separate transfer. In practice, this point is not always appreciated.

Section 40 (2) makes similar provision with regard to a vesting declaration in the case of a deed under which a retiring trustee is discharged under the statutory power without a new trustee being appointed.

In the case of certain types of property vesting declarations would be inconvenient and, therefore, s. 40 (4) of the T.A. 1925 provides :—

" 40.—(4) This section does not extend—

> (*a*) to land conveyed by way of mortgage for securing money subject to the trust, except land conveyed on trust for securing debentures or debenture stock ;
>
> (*b*) to land held under a lease which contains any *covenant* condition or agreement *against assignment* or disposing of the land without licence or consent, unless, prior to the execution of the deed containing expressly or impliedly the vesting declaration, the requisite licence or consent has been obtained, or unless, by virtue of any statute or rule of law, the vesting declaration, express or implied, would not operate as a breach of covenant or give rise to a forfeiture ;
>
> (*c*) to any share, stock, annuity or property which is only transferable in books kept by a company or other body, or in manner directed by or under an Act of Parliament.

In this subsection ' lease ' includes an underlease and an agreement for a lease or underlease."

" *covenant . . . against assignment*," etc.—Section 40 (4) (*b*) must be read
with the provision contained in s. 19 (1) (*b*) of the Landlord and Tenant Act,
1927, *post*, pp. 861, 862, whereby licences are not necessary as regards certain
building leases. Similarly, if application is made to vest leaseholds in new
trustees and consent is unreasonably withheld, contrary to the Landlord and
Tenant Act, 1927, s. 19 (1) (*a*), the vesting declaration will take effect.

Registered land.—A deed of appointment of new trustees in the ordinary
way as for unregistered conveyancing is all that is strictly required where the
trust property includes registered land. For s. 47 (1) of the L.R.A. 1925
provides *inter alia* that the registrar must give effect on the register to any
vesting declaration (express or implied) made on the appointment or discharge
of a trustee and that the provisions of the T.A. 1925 relating to the appointment and discharge of trustees and the vesting of trust property apply to
registered land subject to the proper entry being made on the register.
Section 47 (2) adds that the registrar must also give effect on the register in
the prescribed manner to any vesting instrument which may be made pursuant
to any statutory power.

However, notwithstanding the strict sufficiency of the above, it does not
represent the recommended procedure. Registered Land Practice Notes 1972,
pp. 35-36, No. 57, is in the following terms :

" When it becomes necessary to give effect to an appointment of new
or additional trustees of registered land which is held upon trust for sale,
there are three methods by which the requisite change in the proprietorship
register may be made. They are as follows :—

1. When the trust affects only registered land, the recommended
method is that a transfer (stamped 50p) in printed form 19 (freehold)
or form 32 (leasehold) should be used and that the registered proprietors,
whether they are retiring or continuing trustees, should transfer to the
continuing and new trustees. The printed deed may be prefaced by
the words : ' For the purpose of giving effect to an appointment of new
trustees . . . ', or some similar phrase. If one of the registered proprietors
(the trustees) has died, his death must be proved by the production of a
death certificate. If the reason for the appointment is that one of the
proprietors has remained out of the United Kingdom for more than
twelve months, his concurrence in the transfer is not required, but the
facts should be proved by statutory declaration. Similar proof is
needed when a proprietor refuses, or is unfit to act, or is incapable
of acting. The Chief Land Registrar is in no way concerned with the
title to make the appointment.

When this simple method is used the Land Registry fee will be payable
at the rate of 50p for every £1,000, or part of £1,000, on the capital
value of the interest affected, with a maximum of £2 for each title
affected, and a further maximum fee of £50 where numerous titles are
affected and are the subject of a single application (Land Registration
Fee Order, 1971, para. 3, operating from 1st August).

2. If the trust for sale comprises both registered and unregistered
land, clearly it will be necessary to have a deed of appointment in
unregistered form which may then embrace the registered land. So far
as the registered land is concerned, the necessary changes in the register
will be effected on production of a printed transfer made by the registered
proprietors as in para. 1 above. This may be introduced by wording

such as : ' Pursuant to a deed of appointment of new trustees of even date made between [inter alia] the same persons as are parties hereto and for the purposes of giving effect to the provisions thereof . . .'. The transfer need bear no stamp duty if the original deed of appointment, duly stamped 50p, is produced to the Chief Land Registrar. Here again, the Chief Land Registrar is not concerned with the title to make the appointment.

Fees are payable as in para. 1 above (Land Registration Fee Order, 1971, para. 3).

3. The third method is used when the parties decline to use a Land Registry transfer. On production of a normal deed of appointment of new trustees (with a certified copy for filing) the Chief Land Registrar will give effect on the register to any express or implied vesting declaration pursuant to the provisions of s. 47 of the Land Registration Act, 1925. However, this is a cumbersome method in which the parties do not use the simple available machinery of registered conveyancing. Therefore, since the Chief Land Registrar does not know who are the persons entitled to appoint new trustees, the entire title to the trust must be deduced to him and investigated by him.

This method involves the payment of Land Registry fees to a much higher maximum than the others. The fee is 50p for every £1,000, or part of £1,000, on the capital value of the interest affected, with a maximum fee of £250 (Land Registration Fee Order, 1970, Sched., para. VI (8))."

Appointment of new trustees by the court.—The provisions giving the court power to appoint new trustees are now contained in ss. 41, 58 (1), 59 and 60 of the T.A. 1925. The cases where the aid of the court will most often have to be sought will be in connection with the appointment of a new trustee in substitution for a trustee who has been convicted of felony, or is of unsound mind, or a bankrupt, or a corporation which is in liquidation or has been dissolved. In other cases, the court will only make an order when it can be shown that it is inexpedient, difficult, or impracticable to appoint a new trustee without the assistance of the court. For instance, where a trustee, through old age and infirmity, became incapable of exercising the trust, the court exercised its jurisdiction (Re Lemann's Trusts (1883), 22 Ch. D. 633 ; Re Phelps' Settlement Trusts (1885), 31 Ch. D. 351). So, where, by reason of death or other circumstances, there were never any trustees of the settlement, and no express power to appoint them, the court assisted (Re Williams' Trusts (1887), 36 Ch. D. 231). And, where there was a doubt as to whether an express power or the statutory power applied, the court appointed new trustees (Re Woodgate's Settlement (1856), 5 W.R. 448). Where there is no dispute of fact the court has jurisdiction under s. 41 (1) to displace a trustee against his will and appoint a new trustee in substitution for him (Re Henderson [1940] Ch. 764).

When a new trustee has been appointed by the court he will have the same powers, authorities and discretions, and may in all respects act as if he had been originally appointed by the instrument, if any, creating the trust (T.A. 1925, s. 43).

Vesting of trust property in new trustees by order of court.—This subject is not within the scope of this book, but it may be mentioned that the provisions in the T.A. 1925 codify the law, and there is thus the great convenience of having all the provisions together ; they are contained in ss. 44, 51, 54 (as substituted by the Mental Health Act, 1959, Sched. 7), 55 and 58 of that Act. The power given by s. 51 (1) (i) to make a vesting order when the trustee has been appointed out of court is most useful ; and see L.R.A. 1925, s. 47.

LEASES AND TENANCIES

26

LEASES AND TENANCIES

Special rules as to title to leaseholds, see *ante*, p. 143.

Implied grants of easements, see *ante*, p. 506 *et seq.*

PART 1. CREATION OF TENANCY

Contracts generally, see *ante*, p. 32 *et seq.*

Agreements for leases and leases.—It is essential to keep in mind the distinction between an agreement for a lease and a lease. A lease creates the relationship of landlord and tenant and grants a right of exclusive possession to the tenant. An agreement for a lease is, as its name indicates, a contract to execute a lease. The distinction is of importance in considering the formalities necessary to create the relationship of landlord and tenant. On the sale of a fee simple estate it is customary to execute both a contract and a conveyance. In the case of a building lease, an agreement is often executed to be followed by the grant of a lease when building is complete, but in other cases the transaction is carried out by the execution of a lease or by an agreement, but seldom by both. The reason why an agreement is usually sufficient is that a party to it, who is in a position to obtain specific performance of the agreement, is considered in equity, as between the parties to the agreement, as being in the same position as if a lease under seal had been made to him (*Walsh* v. *Lonsdale* (1882), 21 Ch. D. 9 ; *Manchester Brewery Co.* v. *Coombs* [1901] 2 Ch. 608 ; *Rickett* v. *Green* [1910] 1 K.B. 253 ; *Inland Revenue Commissioners* v. *Derby (Earl)* [1914] 3 K.B. 1186 ; *Brough* v. *Nettleton* [1921] 2 Ch. 25). Consequently, it is almost true to say that an agreement for a lease is as good as a lease (see, e.g., *Re Maughan* (1885), 14 Q.B.D. 956, 958, also *Crump* v. *Temple* (1890), 7 T.L.R. 120, deciding that distress for rent is equally available). This makes it the more important to remember that there are differences. The first major point to emphasise is that the effectiveness in equity of the agreement depends upon the availability of specific performance (see, e.g., *Cornish* v. *Brook Green Laundry, Ltd.* [1959] 1 Q.B. 394 where the tenant was in breach of a repairing agreement and so unable to obtain the equitable remedy). Here it should be noted that a county court has jurisdiction only in proceedings for the specific performance of a lease where the value of the property does not exceed £5,000 (County

Courts Act, 1959, s. 52 (1) (*d*), as amended by Administration of Justice Act, 1969, s. 5) and above that figure there is only common-law jurisdiction (*Foster* v. *Reeves* [1892] 2 Q.B. 255). However, this limit is not applicable *either* where the county court is not granting specific performance but only declaring the existence of equitable rights (*Cornish* v. *Brook Green Laundry, Ltd.* [1959] 1 Q.B. 394) *or* where the agreement in question is being pleaded by way of defence as distinct from a counter-claim (s. 74 of the 1959 Act as amended by s. 6 of the 1969 Act ; see also *Kingswood Estate Co., Ltd.* v. *Anderson* [1963] 2 Q.B. 169). The second major point is that an agreement in equity, unlike a lease at law, will not bind a *bona fide* purchaser for value of a legal estate without notice (see below as to registration as an " estate contract "). In addition a number of comparatively minor points may be noted. Thus where there is only an agreement for a lease there is no privity of estate, no " conveyance " within s. 62 of the L.P.A. 1925 (*Borman* v. *Griffith* [1930] 1 Ch. 494, see *ante*, p. 513), and no implication of " usual covenants ". Again, under an agreement, the tenant does not himself gain priority by being a *bona fide* purchaser of a *legal estate* without notice and runs the risk of others registering their land charges before completion by grant of a lease (see s. 4 (6) of the L.C.A. 1972).

It is advisable to register such an agreement as an estate contract (L.C.A. 1972, s. 2 (4), Class C (iv)) or, if title to the land is registered, by entry of a notice, a restriction or a caution as appropriate (L.R.A. 1925, ss. 49 (1) (*c*), 58 (1), 54). Then it will have the same protection against subsequent purchasers of the fee simple as if a legal estate had been granted. If not so protected it will be void against a purchaser of a legal estate for money or money's worth even if he has notice of it (L.C.A. 1972, s. 4 (6) ; L.P.A. 1925, s. 199 (1) (i) ; *Sharpe* v. *Coates* [1949] 1 K.B. 285) ; a disposition of registered land for valuable consideration when registered has much the same effect (L.R.A. 1925, ss. 20 (1) and 23 (1)). Failure to register will render the agreement void against such a purchaser of unregistered land even if the tenant has taken possession ; notwithstanding that the purchaser is deemed to have notice as a result of the tenant's possession the agreement is void against him by s. 4 (6) of the L.C.A. 1972 ; but if such a tenant paid rent which was accepted he would apparently have a yearly tenancy (or other periodic tenancy depending on what basis the rent was paid) at common law by implication, which would remain binding on a purchaser even if unregistered (see Megarry and Wade, Real Property, 3rd ed., p. 629). Further, in registered conveyancing, only where the tenant has *not* gone into possession does he require protection on the register (as in *City Permanent Building Society* v. *Miller* [1952] Ch. 840). For it has now been clearly established that a tenancy agreement together with possession of the land constitutes an overriding interest binding all comers (L.R.A. 1925, s. 70 (1) (*g*) ; *Woolwich Equitable Building Society* v. *Marshall* [1952] Ch. 1 ; *Mornington Permanent Building Society* v. *Kenway* [1953] Ch. 382 and *Grace Rymer Investments, Ltd.* v. *Waite* [1958] Ch. 831 ; see also *Bridges* v. *Mees* [1957] Ch. 475 and *Webb* v. *Pollmount* [1966] Ch. 584).

An agreement for a lease is enforceable only of the parties, the property the length of term, the rent and the date of commencement are fixed (*Harvey* v. *Pratt* [1965] 1 W.L.R. 1025 and earlier cited decisions). But the commencement of the term may be expressed by reference to the happening of an uncertain event, provided the event has taken place when the agreement is sought to be enforced (*Brilliant* v. *Michaels* [1945] 1 All E.R. 121). See, for instance, *Swift* v. *Macbean* [1942] 1 K.B. 375, where it was held that an agreement for a lease to commence on the declaration of war, if that should occur within one year, was valid. Such an agreement could be enforced against the grantor provided the event in fact occurs within the perpetuity period (see s. 10 of the Perpetuities and Accumulations Act, 1964). Also an agreement for a lease to contain such covenants and conditions as shall be reasonably required by the lessor has been held to be not too vague to be enforceable (*Sweet and Maxwell, Ltd.* v. *Universal News Services, Ltd.* [1964] 2 Q.B. 699). Again Lord Denning, M.R., has expressed the view that an agreement for a tenancy terminable " on or before " or " by " a fixed date is not invalid for uncertainty (*Joseph* v. *Joseph* [1967] Ch. 78, at p. 86, distinguishing *Lace* v. *Chandler* [1944] K.B. 368 where a tenancy " for the duration of the war " had been held invalid).

Lace v. *Chandler* has also been distinguished in *Re Midland Railway Co.'s Agreement* [1971] Ch. 764, where the Court of Appeal held valid a proviso that a notice determining the tenancy should be given by the landlord only if the premises were required for specified purposes. This last case has been followed in *Centaploy, Ltd.* v. *Matlodge, Ltd.* [1973] 2 All E.R. 720 by Whitford, J., in relation to a tenancy expressed to be at a weekly rent " to continue until determined by the lessee ", which was treated simply as a periodic tenancy, not subject to the certainty rule, and in fact the fetter on the lessor's right to determine was held void as repugnant.

Agreements for leases must be evidenced by writing.—It is provided by s. 40 (1) of the L.P.A. 1925 that no action may be brought upon any contract for the disposition (" disposition " includes a lease : L.P.A. 1925, s. 205 (1) (ii)) of any interest in land unless such contract, or some memorandum or note thereof, is in writing signed by or on behalf of the defendant. The effect of the L.P.A. 1925, s. 40 (1), is considered in detail *ante*, p. 40 *et seq.*

Even if there is no sufficient writing, an oral agreement to grant a lease is enforceable if the agreement has been followed by a sufficient act of part performance by the plaintiff. The doctrine of part performance is outlined *ante*, p. 52 *et seq.*

Leases should usually be made by deed.—The general rule is that interests in land created by parol and not put in writing have the effect of interests at will only (L.P.A. 1925, s. 54 (1)). As to the conflict in consequences between the rules governing the formation of contracts and those governing the execution of deeds, see *D'Silva* v. *Lister House Development, Ltd.* [1971] Ch. 17, considered *ante*, pp. 36, 37 and 592. But s. 54 (2) of the L.P.A. 1925 enables leases to be created by parol provided they (i) take effect in possession (not, e.g., in nineteen days' time : *Foster* v. *Reeves* [1892] 2 Q.B. 255, 257), and (ii) do so for a term not exceeding three years (e.g., a periodic tenancy : *Re Knight* (1882), 21 Ch. D. 442, but not a lease for more than three years determinable by the tenant at the end of any year : *Kushner* v. *Law Society* [1952] 1 K.B. 264), and (iii) do so at the best rent which can reasonably be obtained without taking a fine (i.e., not a premium ; see *Hughes* v. *Waite* [1957] 1 W.L.R. 713, where payment of rent in advance as a lump sum was held to be a fine). The legal assignment of such a lease must still be by deed (s. 52 (1) of the L.P.A. 1925, below, and *Botting* v. *Martin* (1808), 1 Camp. 317).

A valid oral lease is nevertheless not a " conveyance " within the L.P.A. 1925 (*Rye* v. *Rye* [1962] A.C. 496).

Also where the lease is made under statutory powers by a tenant for life, or by trustees or personal representatives, the lease must be in writing, although the term does not exceed three years (S.L.A. 1925, s. 42 (5) (ii)).

It is provided by s. 52 of the L.P.A. 1925 that, except in the case of leases or tenancies not required by law to be made in writing (as to which, see s. 54 (2), *ante*), leases will be void *for the purpose of creating a legal estate* unless made by deed. But, although void as a lease, if there is a sufficient memorandum or act of part performance, an invalid lease can be treated as an agreement for a lease and specific performance granted (*Zimbler* v. *Abrahams* [1903] 1 K.B. 577), and in the meantime the parties will be treated in equity in the same manner as if a lease had been executed (*Walsh* v. *Lonsdale* (1882), 21 Ch. D. 9). For the differing effects at common law and in equity, see *ante*, p. 802.

Where a term is expressed to commence prior to the execution of the lease there is some doubt as to how far the parties are bound by covenants in the lease during the period before its execution. In *Colton* v. *Becollda Property Investments, Ltd.* [1950] 1 K.B. 216, Denning, L.J., said, at p. 231, that the matter was one of construction of the lease ; see further, the discussion of the authorities in the *Conveyancer N.S.*, vol. 14, p. 367 *et seq.*

An owner of land is not able to grant a lease to himself, nor may two or more persons grant a lease to themselves (*Rye* v. *Rye* [1962] A.C. 496). But it may well be that the same person may be landlord and tenant in different capacities, for instance as personal representative and on his own behalf or as trustee of different estates. See the discussion in *Law Quarterly Review*, vol. 78, p. 176 *et seq.*

Leases of registered land.—Although there are prescribed forms for transfers of registered leasehold land (L.R.R. 1925, Sched., Forms 32–34), there is no prescribed form for the grant of a lease of registered land. However, s. 18 (1) (e) of the L.R.A. 1925 provides that leases may be granted " in any form which sufficiently refers, in the prescribed manner, to the registered land." In practice, therefore, ordinary unregistered forms of leases are used with the usual Land Registry heading, together with appropriate alterations to the parcels clauses.

Registered Land Practice Notes, 1972, pp. 14–15, No. 24, fully states the position as to the registration of leases as follows :—

" (a) *Where the freehold or superior leasehold is registered* (whether in the compulsory areas or not)

A grant of a term of more than twenty-one years by the registered proprietor must be completed by registration if the grantee is to obtain a legal estate (sections 20 and 23 [of the L.R.A. 1925]). It is emphasised that this refers to substantive registration of the lessee's term under section 19 (2) or 22 (2).

Notice of the grant should be entered against the freehold or superior leasehold title (section 48) and it is desirable that the Land Certificate of the title of the freeholder or superior leaseholder should be produced. The land certificate must be produced if the lessor takes a premium (section 64 (1) (c))."

At this point it must be interjected that the Court of Appeal have now considered the practice of the Chief Land Registrar (on which Note No. 24 was based) of requiring production of the lessor's land certificate in order for a lessee's application for registration to be regarded as sufficient and complete

(*Strand Securities, Ltd.* v. *Caswell* [1965] Ch. 958). The practice was unanimously held to be wrong. " In the absence of express agreement, a lessee has no right to call for his lessor's title. Likewise he has no right to call for his lessor's land certificate. The registrar should not insist on the lessee producing a document to which he has no right. The application is complete without it " (*per* Lord Denning, M.R., *ibid.*, p. 977). See further *ante*, p. 645.

" (*b*) *Where the freehold or superior leasehold is not registered* (*compulsory areas only*)

(i) A grant of a term of forty years or more or an assignment on sale of leasehold land where the lease has not less than forty years to run at the date of the delivery of the assignment *must* be completed by registration within two months from the date of the grant or the assignment, if the lessee or assignee is to obtain the legal estate (section 123).

(ii) A grant of a term of more than twenty-one years but less than forty years, or an assignment of a term having less than forty years but more than twenty-one years unexpired, *may* be registered.

(*c*) *Position where the lessee fails to register*

(i) As stated above, the lessee will not obtain the legal estate in the lease.

(ii) A lessee who has not protected himself in accordance with the foregoing provisions, may nevertheless have an overriding interest under section 70 (i) (*g*) if in actual occupation of the land or in receipt of the rents and profits thereof, but, if these circumstances change, the overriding interest may well cease (see *Strand Securities, Ltd.* v. *Caswell* [1965] Ch. 958).

(iii) If a lessee or assignee has failed to register in accordance with paragraph (*b*) (i) above, and application is made for the registration of the freehold or superior leasehold, the existence of the lease ought to be disclosed in the application, and if it is notice of it will be entered on the register automatically. If the grantee or assignee subsequently applies for registration, he will have no difficulty in obtaining an order under section 123 provided more than twenty-one years of his lease are unexpired (section 8 (1) (*a*)).

(iv) If a head lessee fails to register in any case where registration is compulsory, he cannot confer a legal estate on a sub-lessee (*British Maritime Trust* v. *Upsons, Ltd.* [1931] W.N. 7).

(*d*) *The following interests are incapable of registration :—*

(i) A lease with only twenty-one years (or less) to run at the time of application (section 8 (1) (*a*)).

(ii) A lease originally granted for twenty-one years (or less) (section 19 (2), proviso (*a*)).

(iii) A mortgage term where there is a subsisting right of redemption (section 8 (1) and section 19 (2), proviso (*b*)).

(iv) A lease containing an absolute prohibition against alienation *inter vivos* (section 8 (2)).

(v) An agreement for a lease (section 8 (1) (*b*)).

The interests referred to in items (i), (iv) and (v) should be protected on the register by notice, but such protection is not required in the case of the lease mentioned in (ii), if it was granted at a rent without taking a fine (section 19 (2), proviso (*a*), and section 70 (1) (*k*))."

Here it should be added also that all of items (i), (ii), (iv) and (v) in para. (d) above may enjoy adequate protection as an " overriding interest " without entry of a notice where there is actual occupation of the land or receipt of rents and profits (L.R.A. 1925, s. 70 (1) (g) ; *Grace Rymer Investments, Ltd.* v. *Waite* [1958] Ch. 831).

Distinction between lease and licence.—Legislation conferring on tenants security of tenure and other rights has increased the importance of the distinction between a lease and a licence and, in some circumstances, has provided a motive for creating a licence which grants a right of exclusive occupation ; often a document is described as a licence but it is argued that it is a lease because it confers on the person taking the benefit of it a right of exclusive possession. The following principles were stated by McNair, J., in *Finbow* v. *Air Ministry* [1963] 1 W.L.R. 697, at p. 706 : " (1) that the agreement must be construed as a whole and the relationship is determined by the law and not by the label which the parties put upon it, though the label is a factor to be taken into account in determining the true relationship : see *Facchini* v. *Bryson* [1952] 1 T.L.R. 1386 ; *Addiscombe Garden Estates, Ltd.* v. *Crabbe* [1958] 1 Q.B. 513 ; (2) that the grant of exclusive possession, if not conclusive against the view that there is a mere licence as distinct from a tenancy, is at any rate a consideration of the first importance : see Jenkins, L.J., in the *Addiscombe* case ; (3) that in all cases where an occupier has been held to be a licensee ' there has been something in the circumstances such as a family arrangement, an act of friendship or generosity, or such like to negative any intention to create a tenancy. In such circumstances it would be obviously unjust to saddle the owner with a tenancy, with all the momentous consequences that that entails nowadays, when there was no intention to create a tenancy at all ' : *per* Denning, L.J., in *Facchini* v. *Bryson* [1952] 1 T.L.R. 1386, 1389." *Addiscombe Garden Estates, Ltd.* v. *Crabbe, ante*, was a case in which parties to an agreement, described as a licence and relating to a tennis court and club house, were referred to as " grantors " and " grantees " but it was construed as a lease. See also *Errington* v. *Errington* [1952] 1 K.B. 290, *Bracey* v. *Reid* [1963] Ch. 88, *Crane* v. *Morris* [1965] 1 W.L.R. 1104, and *Leslie A. Parsons & Sons, Ltd.* v. *Griffiths* (1966), 11 C.L. 371a. In the case of premises not subject to rent restriction legislation, neither exclusive possession nor payment and acceptance of rent was conclusive of the existence of a tenancy where they can be explained otherwise (*Isaac* v. *Hotel de Paris, Ltd.* [1960] 1 W.L.R. 239).

Further consideration has been given to the distinction between leases and licences by the Court of Appeal in *Shell-Mex and B.P., Ltd.* v. *Manchester Garages, Ltd.* [1971] 1 W.L.R. 612. It was emphasised, first, that the fact of exclusive possession is no longer conclusive of a lease, and, second, that the description of the agreement as a licence is also not conclusive the other way. However, it was held that it is open to the parties to determine whether their agreement should constitute a lease or a licence and that in this case a licence was indicated because (a) the landowners retained rights of possession and control inconsistent with a lease, and (b) the agreement was in nature personal to the parties and for these reasons lacked the element of assignability normally characteristic of the interest in land created by a tenancy (see also *Barnes* v. *Barratt* [1970] 2 Q.B. 657). Also the motive of avoiding the protection otherwise conferred by the Landlord and Tenant Act, 1954, Pt. II, was expressly not treated as relevant in drawing the distinction between a lease and a licence. See also *Luganda* v. *Service Hotels, Ltd.*

[1969] 2 Ch. 209 and *Warder* v. *Cooper* [1970] Ch. 495, as to this distinction, and in addition *London Borough of Hounslow* v. *Twickenham Garden Developments, Ltd.* [1971] Ch. 233, in which Megarry, J., exhaustively examined the nature of contractual licences.

Variable rents.—The fall in the purchasing power of money in recent years has caused many owners to be reluctant to lease land for a long term unless the rent can be varied at intervals, and there has been controversy as to the most effective terms.   It has been argued (*Solicitors' Journal*, vol. 107, p. 924) that a provision to the effect that after a fixed period of years the rent shall be changed to an amount either to be agreed between the parties as a fair market rent or to be fixed by an arbitrator in default of agreement is uncertain. On this argument it follows that a sum so agreed or determined is not rent and so (although payable by an original party to the lease) is not valid and enforceable against an assignee.   The conclusions were challenged (*ibid.*, vol. 107, p. 1020, and vol. 108, p. 247) and the matter was discussed further *ibid.*, vol. 108, p. 47, and more recently was fully considered by John A. Franks at *ibid.*, vol. 115, p. 434 *et seq.*   The Law Society have taken the opinion of leading counsel who has advised (see *Law Society's Gazette*, vol. 61, p. 674) that in principle such clauses are effective provided " that there is sufficient machinery for determining the amount of each periodical payment of rent a reasonable time before it becomes due ".   If machinery for review had not taken effect before the due date for payment counsel advised that the payment would not be enforceable as rent but, when later quantified, a sum of money would be payable as between any parties *bound by privity of contract*.   Solicitors wishing to obtain further information on this subject have been invited to apply to The Law Society (*Law Society's Gazette*, vol. 61, p. 675).

These views have been fairly directly supported by Pennycuick, V.C., in *Re Essoldo (Bingo), Ltd.'s Underlease* (1971), 23 P. & C.R. 1, and it is difficult to justify an attack in principle on such clauses as Wynn-Parry, J., in *Re No. 88 High Road, Kilburn* [1959] 1 W.L.R. 279, at p. 284, in granting a new tenancy of business premises directed inclusion in the lease of a " right to have the rent reviewed " which was agreed by the parties to be by reference to an agreed surveyor or a surveyor to be nominated.

It is not sufficient merely to provide that a different rent shall be agreed ; see *King's Motors (Oxford), Ltd.* v. *Lax and Another* [1970] 1 W.L.R. 426 ; but cf. *Smith* v. *Morgan* [1971] 1 W.L.R. 803 and *Brown* v. *Gould* [1972] Ch. 53, noted *post*, p. 813.   However, rent is sufficiently certain where it can be calculated with certainty when it becomes payable, even though the increase be dependent on the whim of the landlord (*Greater London Council* v. *Connolly* [1970] 2 Q.B. 100, in which Lord Denning, M.R., spoke with approval of " the modern practice amongst conveyancers of providing for increases in rent as money falls in value ").   Further, in *Jenkin R. Lewis & Son, Ltd.* v. *Kerman* [1971] Ch. 477, the Court of Appeal decided that an agreement between landlord and tenant increasing the rent under a subsisting lease did not constitute a fresh demise.   From this it follows that the standard type of rent review clause resting on agreement or arbitration in default of agreement should be valid and effective.   Precedents are given in the *Conveyancer N.S.*, vol. 28, p. 662, and vol. 29, p. 722.   In general other clauses (such as " gold " clauses) having the same object seem less satisfactory.   For example, some leases have provided for variation of rent in accordance with changes in an Index of Retail Prices but there is a particular difficulty that the form of the Index may change or publication may cease. But on grant of a lease of land on which shops or similar premises are to be erected it may be convenient to arrange variation of the ground rent in accordance with changes in rack rents of the shops or other premises sub-let, and there is a useful precedent in the *Conveyancer N.S.*, vol. 29, p. 719.

Where there is a rent review provision in a lease, great care must be taken to comply with any dates or periods stipulated for the giving of notice to operate the review. The Court of Appeal has held that such time requirements are to be treated as inflexible and mandatory and a lessor who is late with his notice will get no relief (*Samuel Properties* (*Developments*), *Ltd.* v. *Hayek* [1972] 1 W.L.R. 1296 ; cf. the like position as to exercise of options to renew, *post*, p. 812 *et seq*).

Further, the implications of the currently fluctuating provisions of the counter-inflation legislation will have to be borne in mind in so far as it has application to rents.

Inquiries by lessee as to prior development.—Reasons are given *ante*, p. 6 *et seq.*, why certain inquiries should be made by a person who proposes to purchase land before he enters into a binding contract. An enforcement notice under s. 87 of the Town and Country Planning Act, 1971 (*post*, p. 1201), may be served on both owner and occupier and on any other person having an interest in the land in respect of development which has taken place in contravention of the Act. If steps required to be taken to comply with the notice (other than the discontinuance of any use of the land) are not taken and the local planning authority act in default, the expenses incurred by that authority are recoverable from the then *owner* of the land (*ibid.*, s. 91 (1)). Nevertheless an occupier such as a lessee may wish to comply with the notice in order to avoid action being taken by the local authority, and if he does so he may recover the expenses of so doing from the person by whom the breach of planning control was committed (*ibid.*, s. 91 (2)). If the enforcement notice requires any use of the land to be discontinued any person who uses the land or causes or permits it to be used in contravention of the notice is liable to a fine (*ibid.*, s. 89 (5), which deals also with breaches of conditions or limitations). The result is that a lessee may be seriously prejudiced by a contravention which occurred before the grant of the lease to him. In this respect it should be noted that for the purposes of this Act the word " owner " is defined as the person who is entitled to receive the rack rent (*ibid.*, s. 290 (1)), and consequently the word may include a lessee under a building lease or other lease reserving only a small rent.

To obtain full protection an intending lessee should make the same searches and inquiries as an intending purchaser. In the absence of express warranty a lessor does not undertake that the property may lawfully be used for any particular purpose even if that purpose is contemplated by both parties in the course of negotiations (*Edler* v. *Auerbach* [1950] 1 K.B. 359 ; *Best* v. *Glenville* [1960] 1 W.L.R. 1198 ; *Hill* v. *Harris* [1965] 2 Q.B. 601). Before a lease or an agreement for a lease is executed there is no obligation on the intending lessor to answer inquiries on planning matters, but he may be prepared to do so if the prospective lessee might otherwise refuse to proceed. Nevertheless, as a lessor does not normally prove his title he is not likely to be prepared to deal with planning matters. In the case of short tenancies at rack rents lessees will no doubt have to take a certain degree of risk. On the other hand, if the intention is to create a long term, and particularly if a premium is paid, a lessee would be well advised to insist on

26A

obtaining answers to the inquiries usually made by a purchaser. In any case inquiry can be made as to the contents of the register of planning applications, and as to the contents of the development plan, and a local land charges search can be made together with the usual additional inquiries, which include questions as to the register and as to some of the provisions of the development plan.

If there has been an earlier contravention of planning law by the lessor himself and, as a result, the enjoyment of the lessee is disturbed consequent on service of an enforcement notice, the lessee may possibly have an action on the lessor's covenant for quiet enjoyment (compare *ante*, p. 470). It is often stated that the implied covenant for quiet enjoyment does not extend to acts done before the granting of the lease, but there does not appear to be any authority which would prevent a tenant from recovering on this covenant where the act contravening planning control was that of the landlord himself. It is difficult to apply the technical rules as to covenants for quiet enjoyment to planning contraventions; in any case any right which may exist is probably of little value, as the lessee's right of indemnity under s. 91 (2), *ante*, covers very much the same ground. In any other circumstances the action of the planning authority would not be that of the lessor or any person claiming under him, and so would not entitle the lessee to sue under the covenant.

Where development, whether by way of building operations or change of use, is proposed, it is usual for planning permission to be obtained by the lessee. Such a permission may enure for the benefit of the lessor after surrender or determination of the term; see *post*, p. 1194, and compare the notes as to covenants on planning matters, *post*, p. 880 *et seq*. As is noted above, in the absence of express warranty a lessor does not undertake that the property may be used for a particular purpose. In *Best* v. *Glenville* [1960] 1 W.L.R. 1198 a room was let for use as a club and both landlord and tenant knew that planning permission would be necessary. The tenant commenced that use but permission was not granted and so he refused to pay rent on the ground that the agreement was illegal. In deciding that the rent could be recovered the Court of Appeal was influenced by the finding of fact that the parties had intended the tenant to obtain the permission. Ormerod, L.J., said (*obiter*), however : " If neither party took the trouble to take any steps to obtain planning permission, or if each party knew that no steps were to be taken, it might well be the case, if proved, that there was something unlawful in this agreement." Nevertheless, unless the lease stipulates that a particular use shall be made, and the parties intend that there shall thereby be a breach of planning law, it is doubtful whether there is any illegality. The Town and Country Planning Act, 1971, does not state that breach of planning law is itself an illegal act and the service of an enforcement notice following a breach is at the discretion of the planning authority. In any case of doubt a lessor should stipulate that the lessee shall make any necessary planning application.

Commencement of lease.—When a lease states that it is to operate from a certain date, it will operate from the day after. For instance, in *Raikes* v. *Ogle* [1921] 1 K.B. 576, the plaintiff, by an agreement dated 12th March, 1920, let to the defendant certain premises " from 25th March, 1920, for the term of three years thence next ensuing," and it was held that the rent began to accrue on 26th March, 1920. Where no date is mentioned in a *lease* for the commencement of the term, the term will commence on the date of delivery of the lease (*Marshall* v. *Berridge* (1881), 19 Ch. D. 233). The rule applying to an *agreement* not operating as a demise is different ; see *ante*, p. 803.

There is a limit on the date from which a lease may take effect in the future, as subs. (3) of s. 149 of the L.P.A. 1925 provides that a term at a rent or granted in consideration of a fine, limited after 1925 to take effect *more than twenty-one years* from the date of the instrument purporting to create it, will be void, and any contract to create such a term will likewise be void. In one case, a lease for thirty-five years provided that on written request made twelve months before the expiration of the term the lessor would grant a further term of thirty-five years from the expiration of the first term ; the renewal provision was not invalidated by the L.P.A. 1925, s. 149 (3), as that subsection relates to contracts to create terms which, *when created*, will take effect more than twenty-one years from the instrument creating them (*Re Strand and Savoy Properties, Ltd.* [1960] Ch. 582). This decision was discussed in *Weg Motors, Ltd.* v. *Hales* [1961] Ch. 176 ; [1962] Ch. 49 (C.A.) ; it was not necessary to state whether it was correct and no doubt was thrown on it. The subsection does not apply to any term *taking effect in equity* under a settlement or created out of an equitable interest under a settlement, or under an equitable power for mortgage, indemnity, or other like purposes ; for instance, for raising portions. These latter terms, being equitable, will not come on the title, at any rate not until the money is required.

It is provided by subs. (5) of the same section that nothing in the Act is to affect the rule of law that a legal term, whether or not being a mortgage term, may be created to take effect in reversion expectant on a longer term. A lease, therefore, may be granted of the reversion. The effect of such a lease will be that the reversionary lessee will stand in the shoes of the lessor during the term of the existing lease and will be entitled to the receipt of the rent and to distrain in default.

Rule against perpetuities.—The Perpetuities and Accumulations Act, 1964, s. 8 (1), provides that the rule against perpetuities " shall not operate to invalidate a power conferred on trustees or other persons to . . . lease . . . any property for full consideration." The subsection applies for the purpose of enabling a power to be exercised at any time after 16th July, 1964, notwithstanding that the power was conferred before that date (*ibid.,* s. 8 (2)). As protection is not expressly granted to a lessee it has been argued that he must ensure that the power was limited to leasing for full consideration. Otherwise, it is said, if the power is exercisable after the end of the perpetuity period, a disposition in exercise of it would be void (*Re Allott* [1924] 2 Ch. 498). However, the better view appears to be that there is no such restriction on the operation of s. 8. All powers exercisable by trustees must be exercised honestly and reasonably in the interests of beneficiaries, which includes, surely, obtaining full consideration. Therefore it seems that a lessee giving value and not having notice of anything improper would be protected under s. 8.

Construction of lease when differing from counterpart.—The general rule is that if there is a difference between the lease and the counterpart the lease will prevail, the lease being the principal document and the other but a counterpart. But, where the lease discloses a patent ambiguity, the counterpart may be looked at to rectify the terms of the lease (*Matthews* v. *Smallwood* [1910] 1 Ch. 777).

Option of renewal in a lease.—To enable a lessee to take advantage of an option of renewal in a lease he must conform very exactly to the terms set out in the lease. In *Finch* v. *Underwood* (1876), 2 Ch. D. 310, it was stated that landlords are entitled to stand on their strict rights and to insist that any condition precedent to granting such renewal must have been performed. In that case the lessor agreed to grant a fresh lease to two lessees on the condition that they performed the covenants in the lease. One of the lessees became bankrupt and the covenants in the lease had been broken by failure to carry out some very important repairs. In an action by the other lessee the Court of Appeal refused to help him on the grounds, first that the lessor's covenant was to grant the new lease to the two and, both being alive, he could not be called upon to grant a lease to one only ; and, secondly, it also held that the breach of the covenant to repair was also a bar to the exercise of the right of renewal. See also *Bastin* v. *Bidwell* (1881), 18 Ch. D. 238.

More recently *Finch* v. *Underwood*, *ante*, was followed by the Court of Appeal in *West Country Cleaners (Falmouth), Ltd.* v. *Saly* [1966] 1 W.L.R. 1485, where an option to renew was conferred on the tenant by a lease " providing all covenants herein contained have been duly observed and performed " ; one such covenant was to paint the inside of the premises every three years and in the last year of the term ; the tenant, although keeping the interior in fair decorative repair, had not painted the ceiling every three years and had done no painting in the last year ; it was held that these breaches of covenant, notwithstanding their triviality, rendered the option to renew unenforceable.

Also where a tenant has an option to purchase or renew, the notice of his desire to do so must be given in exact accordance with the terms of the lease. Thus where it was provided that the notice was to be given " to the lessors ", without specifying " or any of them ", a notice given to one of them only was held to be ineffectual (*Sutcliffe* v. *Wardle* (1890), 63 L.T. 329). Again in *Hollies Stores, Ltd.* v. *Timmis* [1921] 2 Ch. 202, the lease was to a company, and three guarantors joined in the document to covenant to pay the rent. The condition of renewal was that the three guarantors should again join to guarantee the payment of the rent. One of the guarantors died. The company offered to find a suitable guarantor to supply the place of the deceased guarantor or even to pay the rent in advance for the whole of the term of the new lease, but Russell, J., refused to help the tenants, on the ground that as one of the guarantors had died it was impossible for the condition precedent to be performed.

Where the grant of a renewal is conditional on performance of covenants the tenant can insist on renewal if any previous breaches of covenant have been remedied at the date when notice requiring renewal is served (*Robinson* v. *Thames Mead Park Estate, Ltd.* [1947] Ch. 334). In this case the lease was a building lease, and Evershed, J. (as he then was), suggested that an option for renewal in such a lease should not be construed as strictly as an option for renewal in a lease of an existing house. In *Biondi* v. *Kirklington and Piccadilly Estates, Ltd.* [1947] 2 All E.R. 59, an option was exercisable on request " made six calendar months before the expiration of the term." Roxburgh, J., decided that a request made shortly after the commencement of the term, which was for thirty years, was not a valid exercise of the option, but he refused to decide at exactly what time the option should have been exercised. As minor breaches of covenant are common a tenant may readily lose the benefit of an option if (as is usual) it is conditional on performance of covenants. From his point of view it is advisable to try to modify such terms ; a possible compromise is that renewal should be granted unless there is a breach and notice of it has been given by the landlord.

An option to take a further term at " such a rental as may be agreed upon between the parties " (without any arbitration clause or supplementary agreement fixing the rent) is void for uncertainty (*King's Motors (Oxford) Ltd.* v. *Lax and Another* [1970] 1 W.L.R. 426 ; but cf. *Smith* v. *Morgan* [1971] 1 W.L.R. 803 in which a covenant to offer land for sale " at a figure to be agreed upon " was *not* held void for uncertainty ; also, cf. *Brown* v. *Gould* [1972] Ch. 53, where an option to renew a lease " at a rent to be fixed " was held valid and enforceable since a sufficient formula for calculation was found ; see strong criticism by J. E. Adams in the *Law Society's Gazette*, vol. 68, at p. 529 ; also *ante*, p. 808).

An option for the renewal of a lease is not void as to perpetuity so long as the relation of landlord and tenant subsists between the person claiming to exercise the right of renewal and the person against whom the right is claimed (*Rider* v. *Ford* [1923] 1 Ch. 541). Whether this immunity from the perpetuity rule is limited to covenants which run with the land under the L.P.A. 1925, s. 142 (1), *post*, p. 848, was raised but not settled in *Weg Motors, Ltd.* v. *Hales* [1961] Ch. 176 ; [1962] Ch. 49 (C.A.). Further, the Perpetuities and Accumulations Act, 1964, s. 9 (1) provides that the rule against perpetuities shall not apply to a disposition made after 16th July, 1964, and consisting of an option to acquire for valuable consideration an interest reversionary (whether directly or indirectly) on the term of a lease if (*a*) the option is exercisable only by the lessee or his successors in title and (*b*) it ceases to be exercisable at or before the expiration of one year following the determination of the lease. The subsection applies also to agreements for leases and, in effect, removes options to renew in leases from danger of avoidance by the perpetuity rule.

A right of renewal contained in a lease of unregistered land is an " estate contract " within the meaning of the L.C.A. 1972, s. 2 (4), Class C (iv), and if not registered as a land charge thereunder it would not bind a purchaser of the legal reversion for money or money's worth (L.C.A. 1972, s. 4 (6)), notwithstanding that such purchaser may have express notice thereof (L.P.A. 1925, s. 199 (1) (i)). See *Sharp* v. *Coates* [1949] 1 K.B. 285, mentioned at p. 600, *ante*. Similarly, if the title is registered, a notice or caution should be registered, although the right will enjoy adequate protection as an " overriding interest " so long as the tenant remains in actual occupation of the land or in receipt of the rents and profits thereof (s. 70 (1) (*g*) of the L.R.A. 1925 ; *Webb* v. *Pollmount* [1966] Ch. 584). However, notwithstanding this last decision, Registered Land Practice Notes 1972, pp. 30-31, No. 50, expresses the view that it is still desirable for such options to be noted on the register. The Practice Note also points out that notice of the option will often be entered automatically by the registry on an application to register either the lessor's title or the lessee's title.

The passing of the benefit and burden of an option to renew is considered *post*, p. 845. It is important that a landlord should ensure protection by registration where necessary. If that step is not taken, then on sale by the landlord of his reversionary interest the purchaser will take free from the option (even if the contract of sale was expressed to be subject to the lease containing it) but the grantor of the option remains liable to the tenant under the covenant for renewal and so (being unable to perform it) is liable in damages (*Wright* v. *Dean* [1948] Ch. 686). However, this may not be so serious as it sounds in that the grantor (i.e., the original lessor) will in many cases be able to pass his liability in damages on to the purchaser by way of standard indemnity provisions against tenant's claims (*Eagon* v. *Dent* [1965] 3 All E.R. 334 ; see National Conditions of Sale, 18th ed., Condition 18 (3), and Law Society's Conditions of Sale, 1973 Revision, Condition 4 (2) (*d*)). See the discussion in *Law Society's Gazette*, vol. 61, p. 867, where it is suggested that the covenant for renewal might be expressed to be void if not registered within a stated time, which would prevent any of the above problems arising.

An agreement for a tenancy for a fixed period with an option to continue for a similar period at the expiration of the term on the same terms and conditions *including* the option clause, causes difficulty. It is doubtful whether the effect is (i) that the tenant on exercising the option may hold for a further period with a right to renew for one more period and no more, as was decided in *Green* v. *Palmer* [1944] Ch. 328, or (ii) to create a perpetually renewable tenancy, as was decided in *Parkus* v. *Greenwood* [1950] Ch. 644. See also *Plumrose, Ltd.* v. *Real and Leasehold Estates Investment Society, Ltd.* [1970] 1 W.L.R. 52, where a new lease granted in pursuance of a covenant for renewal and with the benefit of the covenants in the original lease was construed as not conferring any further right of renewal. And contrast *Re Hopkins's Lease* [1972] 1 All E.R. 248 where a lease was granted for a five years term with an option to renew for a further five years at the same rent and with the same covenant including, in parenthesis, the option to renew. The Court of Appeal held that the L.P.A. 1922, Sched. 15, para. 5 (*post*, p. 939) applied and converted the lease into one for a 2,000 year term. The court was not happy with this result, regarding it as a trap for unwary draftsmen which could not be understood by lay businessmen, especially since it produced a static rent for such a long term. Nevertheless a like conclusion was reached in *Caerphilly Concrete Products, Ltd.* v. *Owen* (1972), 116 Sol. J. 98, C.A. (but cp. *Centaploy, Ltd.* v. *Matlodge, Ltd.* [1973] 2 All E.R. 720).

A point of importance to solicitors was decided in *Yager* v. *Fishman & Co. and Teff & Teff* [1944] 1 All E.R. 552. Solicitors from time to time advised a client regarding certain leasehold property. The lease contained a " break " clause and the client claimed damages for negligence on the ground that the solicitors failed to remind him of the date on which the lease might be determined. The court decided that, in the absence of special instructions, it is not the duty of a solicitor to give such a reminder, and, no doubt, a similar decision would be given in the case of an option to renew.

Options to purchase contained in leases are discussed *ante*, p. 73 *et seq.*, and *post*, p. 832.

Position where tenant remains in occupation after expiration of fixed term.—The general rule is that a tenant who remains in possession after the termination of his lease with the consent of the landlord, for example pending negotiations for a new lease, becomes a tenant at will (*Wheeler* v. *Mercer* [1956] 1 Q.B. 274), although a tenant holding over may be a licensee only if he has a mere personal privilege, for instance if allowed to stay as a matter of humanity (*ibid.*). It should be observed that *Wheeler* v. *Mercer* was reversed at [1957] A.C. 416 on the question of the application of the Landlord and Tenant Act, 1954, to a tenancy at will and without affecting these propositions. But if a tenant, *with the consent of the landlord*, remains in occupation and pays rent with reference to a yearly holding then, in the absence of evidence showing that he holds on other terms, the law will imply that he holds as tenant from year to year upon such of the terms of the expired lease as are applicable to such a tenancy (*Wedd* v. *Porter* [1916] 2 K.B. 91 ; *Cole* v. *Kelly* [1920] 2 K.B. 106). The presumption of a yearly tenancy is based on the fact that rent has been expressed to be so much a year, although it may be payable weekly. Where, however, the rent was expressed to be so much a week during the tenancy which has ended, and it continues to be so paid, a weekly tenancy only is presumed (*Adler* v. *Blackman* [1953] 1 Q.B. 146).

A term in the lease providing for determination on six months' notice expiring at any time is consistent with a yearly tenancy and may continue to be valid after the holding over (*Godfrey Thornfield, Ltd.* v. *Bingham* [1946] 2 All E.R. 485). If, however, the parties have been in negotiation regarding the terms of a further tenancy it is a question of fact whether both parties have agreed to a continuance of the former tenancy and, if so, upon what terms (*Cole* v. *Kelly, ante* ; *Ladies' Hosiery and Underwear, Ltd.* v. *Parker* [1930] 1 Ch. 304). The best evidence that the landlord has consented to the holding over is that he has accepted rent (*Dougal* v. *McCarthy* [1893] 1 Q.B. 736 ; *Lowther* v. *Clifford* [1927] 1 K.B. 130).

A tenant of residential premises may, however, hold over by virtue of the protection of the Rent Restrictions Acts, *post*, pp. 916–917, or the Landlord and Tenant Act, 1954, Pt. I, *post*, p. 934, and a tenant of business or similar premises may remain under the protection of the Landlord and Tenant Act, 1954, Pt. II, *post*, p. 898 *et seq.*

PART 2. POWERS OF LEASING

A. TENANT FOR LIFE

General power.—It is provided by s. 41 of the S.L.A. 1925 that—" A tenant for life may lease the settled land, or any part thereof, or any easement, right, or privilege of any kind over or in relation to the land, for any purpose whatever, whether involving waste or not, for any term not exceeding—

(i) in case of a building lease, nine hundred and ninety-nine years ; [or such longer term as the court may allow (s. 46)]

(ii) in case of a mining lease, one hundred years ; [or such longer term as the court may allow (s. 46)]

(iii) in case of a forestry lease, nine hundred and ninety-nine years ; [as to such leases, see S.L.A. 1925, s. 48, and Forestry Act, 1967, s. 29 (7)]

(iv) in case of any other lease, fifty years."

" Tenant for life " includes a person who has the powers of a tenant for life under the S.L.A. 1925 (*ibid.*, s. 117 (1) (xxviii)) ; see *ante*, p. 722.

" Land " which a tenant for life has power to lease is by s. 117 (1) (ix) of the S.L.A. 1925 defined to include " buildings or parts of buildings (whether the division is horizontal, vertical or made in any other way)."

A tenant for life, when intending to make a lease (except where such lease is not to exceed the term of twenty-one years and no fine is paid : S.L.A. 1925, s. 42 (5)), must give notice of his intention to each of the trustees of the settlement, and to the solicitor for the trustees (S.L.A. 1925, s. 101 (1)); but a person dealing in good faith with the tenant for life will not be concerned to inquire respecting the giving of any such notice (*ibid.*, s. 101 (5)).

If no fine or money payment is made on the granting of the lease, then, in favour of a lessee, the lease will have legal effect notwithstanding that there were no trustees of the settlement (*ibid.*, s. 110 (4)). But where a fine is taken as part of the consideration for the granting of the lease there must be two trustees (unless the sole trustee is a trust corporation) to give a receipt therefor, unless the tenant for life prefers to pay the money into court (*ibid.*, ss. 18, 75 (1), 94 (1)), because a fine is deemed to be capital money (*ibid.*, s. 42 (4)).

The lease must be by deed except where the term does not exceed three years, and must be made to take effect in possession not later than twelve months after its date or in reversion after an existing lease having not more than seven years to run at the date of the new lease, and must contain a condition of re-entry on the rent not being paid within a time therein specified not exceeding thirty days (S.L.A. 1925, s. 42 (1), (5)). The lease must also reserve the best rent that can reasonably be obtained in the circumstances (*ibid.*, s. 42 (1) (ii)) ; as to the burden of proof that the best rent was charged, see *ibid.*, s. 110 (1), also *Kisch* v. *Hawes Brothers, Ltd.* [1935] Ch. 102, *Davies* v. *Hall* [1954] 1 W.L.R. 855 and *Re Morgan's Lease* [1972] Ch. 1. A lease which is invalid because it does not comply with one of these requirements—for instance, if it does not take effect in possession within twelve months— may take effect as a contract to grant a valid lease subject to such variation as is necessary to comply with the terms of the power of leasing in the S.L.A. 1925, s. 42 (L.P.A. 1925, s. 152). As to the construction and operation of s. 152 of the L.P.A. 1925 see the full discussion in *Pawson* v. *Revell* [1958] 2 Q.B. 360. A counterpart must be executed by the lessee and delivered to the tenant for life or statutory owner (S.L.A. 1925, s. 42 (2)).

Where the term does not extend beyond three years from the date of the writing, being at the best rent, without fine, the lessee not being exempted from punishment for waste, the lease may be made merely by writing under hand and may contain an agreement instead of a covenant by the lessee for payment of rent (*ibid.*, ss. 42 (5) (ii), 72 (4)). The better opinion is that s. 42 (5) (ii) provides a comprehensive code for leases for less than three years in which cases the requirements of s. 42 (1), for instance as to a proviso for re-entry, need not be complied with (*Davies* v. *Hall* [1954] 1 W.L.R. 855, at p. 860).

Contract to grant a lease.—A tenant for life " may contract to make any lease, and in making the lease may vary the terms, with or without consideration, but so that the lease be in conformity with this Act " (S.L.A. 1925, s. 90 (1) (iii). A preliminary contract under the Act for or relating to a lease, and a contract forming an option, do not form part of the title or evidence of the title of any person to the lease, or to the land the subject of the option (*ibid.*, s. 90 (4)).

A tenant for life may enter into an agreement pursuant to s. 90 (1) (iii) provided that the lease which he contracts to grant will be in conformity with the S.L.A. 1925 when granted. Thus the agreement may be valid even if the lease will not take effect within twelve months of the *agreement* (*Re Rycroft's Settlement* [1962] Ch. 263 ; S.L.A. 1925, s. 42 (1)). It has been held that s. 51 of the S.L.A. 1925 (see *post*, p. 819) prevails over s. 90 (1) (iii) so that the question of whether the best rent was obtained is to be determined as at the grant of the option and not as at the ultimate grant of the lease (*Re Morgan's Lease* [1972] Ch. 1 distinguishing *Re Rycroft's Settlement*).

Building leases.—A tenant for life may grant a building lease of the settled land for any term not exceeding 999 years (S.L.A. 1925, s. 41). " Building lease " is defined in s. 117 (1) (i) of the S.L.A. 1925 as being " a lease for any building purposes or purposes connected therewith " ; and " building purposes " is defined in the same paragraph as including " the erecting and the improving of, and the adding to, and the repairing of buildings ". It is thought that for a lease to be a building lease, the erecting or repairing, etc., of buildings must be the purpose or one of the purposes for which it is granted, and that what is commonly called a *repairing lease* is not a building lease within the meaning of the Act, save in so far as repairs are treated as improvements in Sched. 3 to the S.L.A. 1925. A further indication as to what " building lease " means is in s. 44 (1) of the S.L.A. 1925 which provides that every building lease shall be made partly in consideration of the lessee, or some person by whose direction the lease is granted, or some other person, having erected or agreed to erect buildings, new or additional, or having improved or repaired or agreed to improve or repair buildings, or having executed or agreed to execute on the land leased an improvement authorised by the S.L.A. 1925 (as to which see S.L.A. 1925, s. 83) for or in connection with building purposes. A peppercorn or nominal rent may be made payable for the first five years of the term (*ibid.*, s. 44 (2)) and this seems to imply that a building lease would not be valid if the rent were nominal only for the whole of the term (unless, perhaps, the term was short and so a nominal rent was the best that could be obtained). It was held in *Re Grosvenor Settled Estates (No. 1)* [1932] 1 Ch. 232 that the absence of a covenant to commence building operations within any specified time from a lease granted pursuant to the Act did not invalidate the lease.

Section 56 of the S.L.A. 1925 gives very full powers to a tenant for life to appropriate and lay out part of the settled land for streets and other purposes in connection with building leases. See *ante*, p. 750.

A very useful but somewhat dangerous provision is contained in s. 73 (1) (xviii) of the S.L.A. 1925. It provides that capital money may be applied in financing any person who may have agreed to take a lease for building purposes of the settled land, or any part thereof, by making advances to him in the usual manner on the security of an equitable mortgage of his building agreement. At the same time it is not as risky as at first sight might be thought, because the legal estate in the settled land agreed to be leased will still remain in the tenant for life until the lease is granted.

Mining leases.—A lease may be made either of land with an exception or reservation of mines and minerals therein, or of any mines and minerals ; in any such case there may be a grant or reservation of powers of working and other powers, easements, rights and privileges connected with mining purposes, in relation to the settled land or any other land (S.L.A. 1925, s. 50).

The manner of dealing with the rents and royalties is specified in s. 47 of the S.L.A. 1925 which provides that under a mining lease, whether the mines or minerals leased are *already opened or in work or not, unless a contrary intention* is expressed in the settlement, there must be from time to time set aside, as capital money where the tenant for life or statutory owner is impeachable for waste in respect of minerals, three-fourth parts of the rent, and otherwise one-fourth part thereof, the residue to go as rents and profits.

An express power in the settlement to open mines will amount to a contrary intention (*Re Bagot's Settlement* [1894] 1 Ch. 177 ; *Re Hanbury's Settled Estates* [1913] 2 Ch. 357). If the settlement gives power to lease, the rents have to be dealt with according to the terms of the settlement (*Re Duke of Newcastle's Estates* (1883), 24 Ch. D. 129 ; see also *Re Rayer* [1913] 2 Ch. 210 and *Re Chaytor* [1900] 2 Ch. 804).

A tenant for life may work *open mines* though impeachable for waste. Therefore, even if he is impeachable for waste, he is under an obligation to set apart only one fourth part of the rent as capital money if he grants a lease of mines which had been opened by the settlor, or if the mining lease was lawfully made by an earlier tenant for life (*Re Chaytor, ante ; Chaytor* v. *Trotter* (1902), 87 L.T. 36 ; *Re Morgan* [1914] 1 Ch. 910 ; *Re Fitzwalter* [1943] Ch. 285).

The provisions of the S.L.A. 1925, s. 47, apply only during the subsistence of the settlement which existed when the lease was granted. Consequently, after a resettlement of the land the tenant for life under that resettlement will be entitled to keep the whole of the rents (*Re Arkwright's Settlement* [1945] Ch. 195). See further, S.L.A. 1925, s. 59 ; *Re Savile Settled Estates* [1931] 2 Ch. 210 ; *Re Bruce* [1932] 1 Ch. 316.

It is noted *ante*, p. 501, that all coal and mines of coal are now vested in the National Coal Board. Interests in coal mining leases were usually " retained interests " which did not vest under the Coal Act, 1938, but the effect of the Coal Industry Nationalisation Act, 1946, is to cause coal mining leases to merge in the freehold reversion. Consequently, the detailed rules are not relevant to the present work. It may be noted that where a severance of the reversion expectant on a lease has been effected by the *vesting in the National Coal Board of part only of demised premises* (for instance, where part of the surface was demised with mines), and the lease did not reserve several rents for the separate parts of the premises, the Coal Act, 1938, s. 11, provides for the apportionment of the rent reserved. Compensation for compulsory acquisition of mines under settled land was payable to the trustees of the settlement (Coal Act, 1938, Sched. 3, Pt. IV, para. 18). As to apportionment of compensation between a tenant for life and remainderman, see *ibid.*, para. 21 (2) ; *Re Duke of Leeds' Will Trusts* [1947] Ch. 525 ; *Re Blandy-Jenkins* [1948] Ch. 322 ; *Williams* v. *Sharpe* [1949] Ch. 595.

Lease of mansion house.—The provisions as to this are contained in s. 65 of the S.L.A. 1925. If the settlement was made or came into operation before 1926, and it did not expressly provide to the contrary, the consent of the trustees of the settlement or an order of the court must be obtained before a lease can be granted. But if the settlement was made or came into operation after 1925, then neither the consent of the trustees nor an order of court is necessary to the granting of a lease, unless the settlement requires that such consent or order be obtained. As to the definition of the principal mansion house for this purpose, see *ante*, p. 746.

Duties of tenant for life when leasing.—It should be borne in mind that a tenant for life must, in exercising his powers of leasing under the S.L.A. 1925, have regard to the interests of all parties entitled under the settlement, and will, in relation to the exercise thereof by him, be deemed to be in the position and to have the duties and liabilities of a trustee for those parties (S.L.A. 1925, s. 107 (1)). It was said in *Re Hope's Settled Estates* (1910), 26 T.L.R. 413, that a tenant for life is bound to regard not his own interests only, but also those of the persons who are to follow him, and in considering those interests more weight must be given to those of persons nearest in succession than to the interests of those who are more remote.

A lease by a tenant for life to his wife, and *vice versa*, will be good if made in good faith (*Sutherland (Dowager Duchess)* v. *Sutherland (Duke)* [1893] 3 Ch. 169, 196 ; *Gilbey* v. *Rush* [1906] 1 Ch. 11, at pp. 17–20). But see *Middlemas* v. *Stevens* [1901] 1 Ch. 574 and *ante*, p. 787.

There are a few special provisions which may be considered somewhat in the nature of exceptions to the rule contained in s. 107 (1) of the S.L.A. 1925. For instance, under s. 57 (1) land may be leased for the erection of small dwellings, or for the purposes of small holdings *notwithstanding that a better rent* might have been obtained if the land were leased for another purpose; and, by subs. (2), land may be leased for the erection of dwellings or for small holdings or allotments for a nominal rent, or gratuitously, provided that not more than two acres are leased in an urban district, or ten acres in a rural district. Then by s. 54 of the S.L.A. 1925 a tenant for life may, for the general benefit of the settled land, grant a lease for a nominal rent, or gratuitously, in respect of water rights, to statutory bodies ; and by s. 55 of the same Act, the tenant for life may, for the same purpose, grant leases for public and charitable purposes, for less than the best rent, or for a nominal rent, or gratuitously, provided that not more than one acre is so leased where the land is in an urban district, or five acres where the land is in a rural district.

Power to vary or release the terms of a lease.—Full power is given to the tenant for life by s. 59 (1) of the S.L.A. 1925 to vary, release, waive or modify the terms of a lease, provided that every such lease shall after such variation be such a lease as might then have been lawfully made under the Act if the lease had been surrendered. See, for example, *Re Savile Settled Estates* [1931] 2 Ch. 210.

Options to grant or renew lease.—A tenant for life may, either with or without consideration, grant by writing an option to take a lease of the settled land or any part thereof, or any easement, right or privilege over or in relation to the same, at a rent to be fixed at the time of the granting of the option, which rent must be the best which can reasonably be obtained. If any consideration is obtained for the grant of the option it will be capital money payable to two individual trustees or a trust corporation (*ibid.*, s. 94 (1)). The option must be made exercisable within an agreed number of years not exceeding ten (S.L.A. 1925, s. 51 (1), (2), (3)). As to obtaining the best rent, see *Re Morgan's Lease* [1972] Ch. 1.

The general rules regarding options for renewal of leases are dealt with *ante*, p. 812.

Power of court to authorise any lease.—Section 64 of the S.L.A. 1925 provides that any transaction (including a lease) affecting or concerning the settled land or any other land (not being a transaction otherwise authorised by the Act, or by the settlement) which in the opinion of the court would be for the benefit of the settled land, or the persons interested under the settlement may, under an order of the court, be effected by a tenant for life, if it is one which could have been validly effected by an absolute owner.

Protection of lessee.—It is provided by s. 110 (1) of the S.L.A. 1925 that on a lease a lessee dealing in good faith with a tenant for life or statutory owner shall, as against all parties entitled under the settlement, be conclusively taken to have given the best consideration or rent that could reasonably be obtained by the tenant for life or statutory owner, and to have complied with all the requisitions of the Act. See further, as to this subsection, *ante*, p. 734. It is also provided by subs. (4) of the same section that when no capital money arises the lease will have effect under the Act notwithstanding that at the date of the lease there were no trustees of the settlement. It is thought that this protection is not available to a person who purports to take under a lease which is invalid on the face of it because it does not comply with the requirements of the S.L.A. 1925.

Power to accept a lease of land.—It is provided by s. 53 of the S.L.A. 1925 as follows :—

" 53.—(1) A tenant for life may accept a lease of any land, or of any mines and minerals or of any easement, right, or privilege, convenient to be held or worked with or annexed in enjoyment to the settled land, or any part thereof, for such period, and upon such terms and conditions, as the tenant for life thinks fit :

Provided that no fine shall be paid out of capital money in respect of such lease.

(2) The lease shall be granted to the tenant for life or statutory owner and shall be deemed a subsidiary vesting deed, and the statements and particulars required in the case of subsidiary vesting deeds shall either be inserted therein or endorsed thereon.

(3) The lease may contain an option to purchase the reversion expectant on the term thereby granted."

B. TRUSTEES FOR SALE

General power.—Before 1926, in the absence of an express power, trustees had an implied power to lease if the conditions of the trust made it necessary or proper that a lease should be granted, and it was considered that the implied power would not usually authorise a longer lease than one from year to year (*Re North* [1909] 1 Ch. 625 ; *Naylor* v. *Arnitt* (1830), 1 Russ. & M. 501 ; *Wood* v. *Patteson* (1847), 10 Beav. 541 ; *Re Shaw's Trusts* (1871), L.R. 12 Eq. 124). If there was an immediate trust for sale, the opinion was that trustees ought not to lease, unless it was absolutely impossible to sell (*Evans* v. *Jackson* (1836), 8 Sim. 217).

Now, by s. 28 of the L.P.A. 1925, it is provided that trustees for sale shall in relation to land have all the powers of a tenant for life and the trustees of a settlement under the S.L.A. 1925, including the powers of management conferred by that Act during a minority, and where by statute settled land is vested in the trustees of the settlement upon the statutory trusts, such trustees and their successors in office shall also have all the additional powers (if any) conferred by the settlement. It is also provided by the same section that such powers shall be exercised with such consents (if any) as would have been required on a sale under the trust for sale. The reference to powers of management during a minority is to s. 102 of the S.L.A. 1925, as to which, see *ante*, p. 345.

When the trust for sale is created by or pursuant to powers conferred by statute, or is created by a disposition made after 1925 containing a provision that the requirement is to apply, the trustees for sale should, when considering the desirability of granting a lease, at any rate a lease for any considerable period, first consult the beneficiaries. The L.P.A. 1925, s. 26 (3), as amended by the Law of Property (Amendment) Act, 1926, provides that trustees for sale shall in the above cases, so far as practicable, consult the persons of full age for the time being beneficially interested in possession in the rents and profits of the land until sale, and shall, so far as consistent with the general interest of the trust, give effect to the wishes of such persons, or, in the case of dispute, of the majority (according to the value of their combined interests) of such persons, but a purchaser (which includes a lessee) shall not be concerned to see that the provisions of this subsection have been complied with.

As regards the protection of a lessee, it is provided by s. 23 of the L.P.A. 1925 that where land has become subject to an express or implied trust for sale, such trust shall, so far as regards the safety and protection of any purchaser (which includes a lessee) thereunder, be deemed to be subsisting until the land has been conveyed to or under the direction of the persons interested in the proceeds of sale. It is also provided by s. 27 (1) of the L.P.A. 1925 that a purchaser (which includes a lessee) of a legal estate from trustees for sale shall not be concerned with the trusts affecting the rents and profits until sale, whether or not those trusts are declared by the same instrument by which the trust for sale is created.

The court has power to authorise trustees for sale to grant a lease where in the opinion of the court it is expedient, but cannot be effected by reason of the absence of any power for that purpose vested in the trustees (T.A. 1925, s. 57).

Delegation of powers.—Section 29 of the L.P.A. 1925 provides as follows :—

" 29.—(1) The powers of and incidental to leasing, accepting surrenders of leases and management, conferred on trustees for sale whether by this Act or otherwise, may, until sale of the land, be revocably delegated from time to time, by writing, signed by them, to any person of full age (not being merely an annuitant) for the time being beneficially entitled in possession to the net rents and profits of the land during his life or for any less period : and in favour of a lessee such writing shall, unless the contrary appears, be sufficient evidence that the person named therein is a person to whom the powers may be delegated, and the production of such writing shall, unless the contrary appears, be sufficient evidence that the delegation has not been revoked.

(2) Any power so delegated shall be exercised only in the names and on behalf of the trustees delegating the power.

(3) The persons delegating any power under this section shall not, in relation to the exercise or purported exercise of the power, be liable for the acts or defaults of the person to whom the power is delegated, but that person shall, in relation to the exercise of the power by him, be deemed to be in the position and to have the duties and liabilities of a trustee."

The tenant for life of the proceeds of sale can insist on the trustees (or personal representatives holding land on trust for sale, as the case may be) giving him this power. If they refuse, the tenant for life may apply to the court for an order to compel them to do so, and the court may make such order as it thinks fit (L.P.A. 1925, s. 30). So it may be said that a tenant for life of land held by trustees on trust for sale is practically in as good a position as a tenant for life of settled land, and without all the technicality connected therewith, which is so abhorrent to the lay mind and often to the professional mind also.

Administrators will hold land on trust for sale under s. 33 of the A.E.A. 1925 when their duties as administrators have been completed, and in such a case they should execute an assent to themselves as trustees for sale (*Re Yerburgh* [1928] W.N. 208). See further, *ante*, p. 393.

C. PERSONAL REPRESENTATIVES

General power.—The power of personal representatives to lease is now derived, primarily, from s. 39 of the A.E.A. 1925, which is set out *ante*, p. 395. This section provides, in effect, that in dealing with the real and personal estate of the deceased his *personal representatives* shall, *for the purposes of administration*, or *during a minority of any beneficiary* or the subsistence of any life interest, or until the period of distribution arrives, have (i) the same powers and *discretions*, including power to raise money by mortgage or charge, as a personal representative had before 1926 with respect to personal estate ; and (ii) all the powers, *discretions and duties* conferred or imposed by law on trustees holding land upon an effectual trust for sale ; and (iii) all the powers conferred by statute on trustees for sale.

"*personal representatives.*"—This term includes special representatives, such as " a person deemed to be appointed executor as respects settled land " (A.E.A. 1925, s. 55 (1) (i), (xi) ; s. 22).

"*for the purposes of administration.*"—Before 1926 it was considered that personal representatives ought not, in the absence of a special power in the will, to grant leases except where it was, at the time, the best way of dealing with the estate for the purposes of administration, and therefore for the benefit of the estate and the persons beneficially entitled (*Keating* v. *Keating* (1835), Ll. & G. 133). The primary duty of personal representatives, before distribution and after collection of assets, remains the same, namely, to discharge the liabilities against the estate, and in the meantime to manage it. This duty is referred to in s. 32 (1) of the A.E.A. 1925 as the duty to administer the property of the deceased for payment of the debts and liabilities ; and, in s. 33 (1) and (2), as the duty to sell and convert into money the real and personal estate of an intestate, and after payment of liabilities to distribute the balance. It will be noticed that in s. 39 of the A.E.A. 1925 the words " discretions " and " duties " occur.

It is quite clear, however, that none of these matters will concern a lessee. In the first place, personal representatives now have the powers of trustees for sale and it appears that such trustees may dispose of leaseholds by means of sub-leases if that procedure amounts to a conveyancing device for effecting a sale (A.E.A. 1925, s. 39 ; *Re Judd* [1906] 1 Ch. 684 ; *Re Chaplin and Staffordshire Potteries Waterworks Co.'s Contract* [1922] 2 Ch. 824). Indeed, even if the personal representatives in granting a lease exceed their powers, the lessee would be fully protected, provided he had inspected the probate or letters of administration and found thereon no endorsement of a previous dealing with the land, and had obtained from them a statement (usually given by way of recital in the lease) that they had not previously dealt with the legal estate in the land (A.E.A. 1925, s. 36 (6), (7)) ; and this will be so notwithstanding that the lessee had notice that all liabilities of the estate had been discharged (*ibid.*, s. 36 (8)). And, where the land is settled land, it is provided by s. 110 (3) of the S.L.A. 1925 that a purchaser (which includes a lessee) of a legal estate in settled land from a personal representative shall be entitled to act on the assumption that the personal representative is acting under his statutory or other powers. See also ss. 27 and 37 of the A.E.A. 1925, giving protection to persons acting on an invalid probate or letters of administration.

A sole personal representative can grant a lease when acting for the purposes of administration, *even though* a premium be charged (L.P.A. 1925, s. 27 (2), as re-enacted by the Law of Property (Amendment) Act, 1926); and also when acting as a trustee for sale, *unless* a premium is paid, in which case another trustee would have to be appointed to enable a good receipt to be given.

"*during a minority of any beneficiary.*"—Where there is a minority or a life interest, and personal representatives, having completed their administration, become trustees, whether under the will or by statute, they should execute an assent vesting the land in themselves as trustees for sale under s. 36 (4) of the A.E.A. 1925 (*Re King's Will Trusts* [1964] Ch. 542 ; see *ante*, p. 417).

In the case of settled land, during a minority, the personal representatives become statutory owners under the S.L.A. 1925, s. 26 (1), until they execute a vesting instrument in favour of the S.L.A. 1925 trustees and can act (subject to their rights and powers as pure personal representatives) under the directions of such S.L.A. 1925 trustees without executing a vesting instrument, by virtue of subs. (2) of the same section. See further, *ante*, p. 339. If trustees for sale are entitled to the land the personal representatives can similarly act under the directions of such trustees until they assent to the legal estate vesting in such trustees for sale.

All the proving personal representatives must join in any lease (A.E.A. 1925, s. 2 (2)) ; but special personal representatives may lease the settled land without the concurrence of the general personal representatives and *vice versa* (*ibid.*, s. 24).

D. RECEIVER OF ESTATE OF PERSON SUFFERING FROM MENTAL DISORDER

The Mental Health Act, 1959, s. 103, enables the judge nominated for the purposes of Pt. VIII of that Act to make orders for (*inter alia*) " the sale, exchange, charging or other disposition of or dealing with any property of the patient, the acquisition of any property in the name or on behalf of the patient " (*ibid.*, s. 103). " Property " includes any interest in real or personal property (*ibid.*, s. 119). These general powers replace earlier more specific powers as to such transactions as grants of leases.

The L.P.A. 1925, s. 22, as substituted by Sched. 7 to the 1959 Act, provides that where a legal estate (whether settled or not) is vested in a person suffering from mental disorder, either solely or jointly with any other person or persons, his receiver, or (if no receiver is acting) a person authorised shall, under an order of the authority under Pt. VIII, or of the court, or under any statutory power, make or concur in making all requisite dispositions for conveying or creating a legal estate in his name and on his behalf.

The powers of a patient who is tenant for life of settled land are exercised pursuant to an order under the Mental Health Act, 1959, s. 103 (1) (*j*) ; see *ante*, p. 422.

E. MORTGAGORS AND MORTGAGEES

At common law.—Apart from statute or special provision in the mortgage, a mortgagor, being in the position of a reversioner on a long term of years, can create no interests in the land otherwise than subject to the prior rights of the mortgagee. Thus the mortgagor cannot, by granting a lease, restrict the mortgagee's right to take possession (*Thunder d. Weaver* v. *Belcher* (1803), 3 East. 449) so that any lessee would have no protection at all as against the mortgagee (*Dudley and District Benefit Building Society* v. *Emerson* [1949] Ch. 707 ; *Rust* v. *Goodale* [1957] Ch. 33). However, any lease granted by the mortgagor will at least be binding as between the mortgagor and the lessee on a basis of estoppel (see *Rust* v. *Goodale*) so that the mortgagor may sue or distrain for rent (*Trent* v. *Hunt* (1853), 9 Ex. 14). But the mortgagee, as well as still being entitled to take possession, may require the rent to be paid to him (*Pope* v. *Biggs* (1829), 9 B. & C. 245 ; *Underhay* v. *Read* (1887), 20 Q.B.D. 209) including arrears (*Moss* v. *Gallimore* (1779), 1 Doug. 279). For this the mortgagee must first make an effective demand for payment in order to defeat the claims of the mortgagor (*Kitchen's Trustees* v. *Madders* [1950] Ch. 134).

On the other hand, the mortgagee, having the legal right to take possession, has the power to grant leases as one of the usual necessary powers of management. However, any such lease, like the mortgage itself, would as a rule be subject to the mortgagor's equity of redemption (*Chapman* v. *Smith* [1907] 2 Ch. 97 ; note that since 1925, such a lessee might defeat the equity by taking without notice under s. 44 (5) of the L.P.A. 1925, *ante*, p. 143). Accordingly, the lessee may again find himself without adequate protection. In other words, once land had been mortgaged a completely acceptable lease could only be granted with the concurrence of both the mortgagor and the mortgagee (unless the mortgage expressly conferred an appropriate power of leasing : *Carpenter* v. *Parker* (1857), 3 C.B. (N.S.) 206). This *prima facie* position was corrected by way of statutory powers.

By statute.—Power is conferred by s. 99 (1) and (3) of the L.P.A. 1925 on a mortgagor or mortgagee in possession to grant certain leases (or to make agreements for leases : subs. (17)) binding both the mortgagor and the mortgagee. This statutory power of leasing, however, is applicable only if and so far as a *contrary intention* is not expressed in the mortgage deed or otherwise in writing (subs. (13)) ; also the power may be similarly extended by agreement between the parties (subs. (14)). Under s. 99 where the mortgage was made before 1926, the mortgagor or mortgagee in possession have power to grant *agricultural* or *occupation leases* for a term not exceeding twenty-one years, and *building leases* for ninety-nine years ; but where the mortgage was made after 1925, they each have power to grant agricultural or occupation leases for a term not exceeding fifty years, and building leases for a term not exceeding 999 years. The word " mortgagor " in the section does not include an incumbrancer deriving title under the original mortgagor (*ibid.*, s. 99 (18)). Any such lease must take effect in possession within twelve months, and must reserve the best rent that can reasonably be obtained, be without any fine and contain a covenant by the lessee to pay rent and a condition of re-entry on rent being in arrear for thirty days (*ibid.*, s. 99 (5), (6), (7)). For a case in which it was claimed that the rent was not the best obtainable see *Coutts and Co.* v. *Somerville* [1935] Ch. 438 ; and note that " rent " in advance has been held to be a fine within the meaning of this section (*Hughes* v. *Waite* [1957] 1 W.L.R. 713, and see *Grace Rymer Investments, Ltd.* v. *Waite* [1958] Ch. 314).

In *Pawson* v. *Revell* [1958] 2 Q.B. 360, the mortgagors had orally agreed to lease a farm from year to year, but the agreement did not contain a condition for re-entry on non-payment of rent as required by the L.P.A. 1925, s. 99 (7).

The L.P.A. 1925, s. 99 (17) states that the provisions of the section apply " as far as circumstances admit," to any agreement for letting, whether in writing or not. The mortgage contained a clause excluding the leasing powers in s. 99 but as the mortgaged property was agricultural land the clause was not effective (Agricultural Holdings Act, 1948, Sched. 7, para. 2 ; see *post*, p. 827). It was argued that a parol agreement was valid even if it did not contain a condition for re-entry on non-payment of rent but the Court of Appeal did not decide as to this. The court considered that even if the agreement should have contained such a provision in order to comply with s. 99 the agreement was nevertheless validated by the L.P.A. 1925, s. 152. This section provides that a lease granted in intended exercise of a power of leasing which is invalid by reason of failure to comply with the terms of the power, if made in good faith and the lessee has entered into possession, takes effect as a contract to grant a lease in accordance with the terms of the power as against any person who is entitled to the land subject to any lease properly granted. *Iron Trades Employers Insurance Association, Ltd.* v. *Union Land and House Investors, Ltd.* [1937] Ch. 313, mentioned *post*, p. 826, was distinguished because in that case there was no power to lease without consent and s. 152 could not create a power which did not exist.

The relationship of an oral tenancy to the requirements of the L.P.A. 1925, s. 99, was considered by Goff, J., in *Rhodes* v. *Dalby* [1971] 1 W.L.R. 1325 ; he took the view that the reference in subs. (17) to " the circumstances admitting " meant that an oral tenancy need not have a condition for re-entry satisfying subs. (7), nor need there be delivery of a counterpart as required by subs. (11). Further in that case it was held that a clause excluding a mortgagor's power of leasing without consent did not lead to a breach of the mortgagor's obligation where there was a mere letting on a gentleman's agreement and not a tenancy.

A new tenancy of business or professional premises ordered to be granted under Pt. III of the Reserve and Auxiliary Forces (Protection of Civil Interests) Act, 1951, is deemed to be authorised by the L.P.A. 1925, s. 99 (1951 Act, s. 30 (6)). Notwithstanding any restrictions in the mortgage, a mortgagor might formerly have granted any such lease as would under Pt. I of the Landlord and Tenant Act, 1927, have relieved him from liability to pay compensation (*ibid.*, s. 14), and may grant a lease giving effect to an order of the court under the Landlord and Tenant Act, 1954, Pt. II, *post*, p. 898 *et seq.* (*ibid.*, s. 36 (4)).

" *contrary intention.*"—In practice, a proviso negativing the power of the mortgagor to lease is usually inserted in the mortgage deed. Whether or not this practice is a wise one is a matter of opinion. On the one hand such a clause tempts the mortgagor to lease without consent, with the result that if the mortgagee takes possession he cannot as of right claim the benefit of the lease. On the other hand, if no negativing clause is inserted and the mortgagee goes into possession, he may give notice to the lessee and become entitled to the benefit of the lease (*Municipal Permanent Investment Building Society* v. *Smith* (1888), 22 Q.B.D. 70).

It is considered that it is best to insert the negativing clause. For, if the mortgagor has granted a lease *after* the mortgage without consent the lease is void against the mortgagee and his assigns, and he may treat the lessee as a trespasser (*Towerson* v. *Jackson* [1891] 2 Q.B. 484). The mortgagee, being in this strong position as regards subsequent lessees, will invariably be able to arrange with any such lessee mutually suitable terms. Further, *Pawson* v.

Revell, ante, shows that a lease may be binding on a mortgagee if intended to be granted pursuant to the L.P.A. 1925, s. 99, even if all the conditions prescribed by that section were not complied with on the grant of the lease. This seems to be an additional reason for excluding the leasing power in s. 99 or at least making its exercise subject to the consent of the mortgagee (although such steps cannot be taken in a mortgage of agricultural land).

Of course, a lease granted by the mortgagor *before* the mortgage was granted is binding on the mortgagee in any case (*Moss* v. *Gallimore* (1779), 1 Doug. K.B. 279 : see also *District Bank, Ltd.* v. *Webb* [1958] 1 W.L.R. 148) ; also it must be remembered that this position may be reached by virtue of the doctrine of tenancy by estoppel and feeding the estoppel where the mortgagor has purported to grant leases before purchasing the legal estate with the aid of a mortgage (*Church of England Building Society* v. *Piskor* [1954] Ch. 553).

A restriction negativing the power to lease should refer to the premises *or any part* of them. If this is not done it is a question of construction of the mortgage whether the statutory power is avoided as regards leases of part only (*Westbourne Park Building Society* v. *Levermore* [1955] J.P.L. 351, referred to in *Current Law*, May, 1955, para. 222).

Where the statutory power is not be to exercised without the written consent of the mortgagee, a tenancy created without that consent will not bind him (*Parker* v. *Braithwaite* [1952] 2 All E.R. 837). If the mortgagee's written consent is necessary the onus is on the tenant to prove that it has been given (*Taylor* v. *Ellis* [1960] Ch. 368). In such a case the mortgagee's consent will not be inferred from the fact that, knowing of the tenancy, he has allowed the tenant to remain in possession for many years, no interest having been paid to him for some years (*ibid.*). On the other hand, where the statutory power has been negatived but the mortgagor nevertheless lets the premises, the mortgagee may so conduct himself as to confirm the tenancy. In the unreported case of *Bradford Permanent Building Society* v. *Cholmondeley,* referred to in *Parker* v. *Braithwaite,* a building society who had knowledge of a lease but stood by for a year or eighteen months without claiming to treat the tenant as a trespasser were held not to be thereby prevented from enforcing their right to possession. However, where a mortgage deed restricts the power of leasing of the mortgagor but also provides that a lessee should not be concerned to see that the mortgagee's consent has been given, the mortgagee would be estopped from asserting as against the lessee that a lease had been granted without his consent (*Lever Finance, Ltd.* v. *Needleman's Trustees* [1956] Ch. 375).

In *Iron Trades Employers' Insurance Association, Ltd.* v. *Union Land and House Investors, Ltd.* [1937] Ch. 313, the defendants had charged certain property by way of legal mortgage in favour of the plaintiffs and covenanted not to exercise the power of leasing contained in the L.P.A. 1925 without the consent of the plaintiffs. Defendants granted a yearly tenancy without plaintiffs' consent and in an action for a declaration that the defendants had committed a breach of covenant it was held that the tenancy could not have been created pursuant to the statutory power, as such power could, in the circumstances, be exercised only with the plaintiffs' consent. Therefore the lease must have been granted pursuant to the mortgagor's power to grant leases *not binding on the mortgagee* and so was not a breach of the covenant. If a clause is inserted excluding the mortgagor's leasing powers but the mortgagor grants a lease the tenant will not be lawfully in possession, and so will not be entitled to protection against the mortgagee under the

Rent Acts (*Dudley and District Benefit Building Society* v. *Emerson* [1949] Ch. 707) or under the Protection from Eviction Act, 1964 (*Bolton Building Society* v. *Cobb* [1966] 1 W.L.R. 1). This right of a mortgagee to treat a tenant as a trespasser passes without express assignment to his assignee on sale or foreclosure (*Rust* v. *Goodale* [1957] Ch. 33).

It is important to bear in mind that restrictions on leasing are enforceable only by the mortgagee and his assigns. " In our judgment . . . the mortgagor being the freeholder can create against all the world except his mortgagee any right or estate he chooses in the land so that even if an option was beyond the mortgagor's powers and could not have prevailed against the mortgagee . . . this is not a point which can be relied on except by the mortgagee himself " (Lord Evershed, M.R., in *Weg Motors, Ltd.* v. *Hales* [1962] Ch. 49, at p. 74).

A mortgage of agricultural land made after 1st March, 1948, cannot validly contain a provision restricting the leasing powers of a mortgagor or mortgagee under the L.P.A. 1925, s. 99 (Agricultural Holdings Act, 1948, Sched. 7, para. 2). However, provision which is invalid because of the Agricultural Holdings Act, 1948, will not be wholly void : it will have the residual effect of making a lease granted outside the statutory powers and under common-law powers a breach of the mortgagor's obligations to the mortgagee (*Rhodes* v. *Dalby* [1971] 1 W.L.R. 1325).

A mortgagee who has paid compensation under the Landlord and Tenant Act, 1927, will be entitled to obtain from the Minister of Agriculture, Fisheries and Food a charge on the holding and such charge will cover the amount of compensation and also all proper costs, charges and expenses incurred by him as " a landlord " within the Act, in connection therewith (*ibid.*, s. 12 ; Sched. 1, para. (1)). It is advised that in all mortgages of land on which buildings in which a business could be carried on are erected, a special power should be inserted requiring the mortgagor to repay the amount so expended and making such amount with interest thereon a charge on the premises, thereby saving the expense of having to get an order under the section.

The right of a tenant of agricultural land to enforce against a mortgagee taking possession such rights as he had against the mortgagor is considered *post*, p. 963.

PART 3. DETERMINATION OF TENANCY

A. SURRENDER AND MERGER OF LEASE

Surrender of lease generally.—There are two kinds of surrender : an express surrender and an implied surrender. An express surrender, for instance a surrender in writing of any interest in land, will be void *at law* unless made by deed (L.P.A. 1925, s. 52), but *in equity* a surrender, if made for valuable consideration, would pass the equitable interest, although the surrender was under hand only. It is sometimes stated that a surrender of an interest in land which might have been created without writing, that is, a lease in possession for not more than three years, at the best rent, need not be by deed. There would not appear to be any authority for this suggestion, as the L.P.A. 1925, s. 54 (2), which makes an exception with regard to the formalities required for such leases (see *ante*, p. 804), refers only to the *creation* of leases. It would seem unreasonable, however, that a mere weekly tenancy, for instance, should be capable of being expressly surrendered only by deed. But, in such a case, an oral surrender made for value and supported by a sufficient act of part-performance or by evidence in writing would probably be effective in equity as a contract to surrender.

One of two or more joint lessees cannot, in the absence of an express power in the lease, surrender the term without the authority of the other lessee or lessees (*Leek and Moorlands Building Society* v. *Clark* [1952] 2 Q.B. 788).

An implied surrender, that is, a surrender by operation of law, may be effected without writing. It is provided by s. 52 of the L.P.A. 1925 that all conveyances (this word includes " leases ") of land are void for the purpose of conveying a legal estate unless made by deed ; but the section does not apply to surrenders by operation of law, including surrenders which may, by law, be effected without writing. In fact, it would seem that no surrender may be effected without writing, other than a surrender by operation of law ; see L.P.A. 1925, s. 53 (1) (*a*), except that this section does not affect the operation of the law relating to part-performance (see L.P.A. 1925, s. 55 (*d*)).

For instance, if a lessor should grant a lease to begin during the currency of an existing lease held by the lessee, the existing lease would become surrendered by operation of law (*Fenner* v. *Blake* [1900] 1 Q.B. 426). Equally, the alteration of an existing lease to a longer term can operate in law only as a notional surrender and the grant of a new lease (*Baker* v. *Merckel* [1960] 2 W.L.R. 492). So, an effectual surrender would be made by the tenant consenting to any act inconsistent with the continuance of his tenancy, for instance, the acceptance by him of another lease, or his consenting to another lease being granted to a third person, and giving up possession to him (*Wallis* v. *Hands* [1893] 2 Ch. 75 ; *Gray* v. *Owen* [1910] 1 K.B. 622). If the new lease should be invalid, the old lease will revive (*Knight* v. *Williams* [1901] 1 Ch. 256 ; contrast the position where there has been an express surrender by deed which is not affected by the invalidity of the new lease : *Rhyl U.D.C.* v. *Rhyl Amusements, Ltd.* [1959] 1 W.L.R. 465) ; see also *Fredco Estates, Ltd.* v. *Bryant* [1961] 1 W.L.R. 76, where there was no new tenancy. Whether there is an implied surrender of the whole and grant of a new lease of the balance on surrender of part is a question dependent on the intention of the parties (*Baynton* v. *Morgan* (1888), 22 Q.B.D. 74 ; *Jenkin R. Lewis & Son, Ltd.* v. *Kerman* [1971] Ch. 477, C.A.). In *Foster* v. *Robinson* [1951] 1 K.B. 149 it was decided that a surrender by operation of law of the tenancy of premises within the Rent Acts occurs in the same circumstances as the surrender of any other tenancy, provided that there is an actual giving up of possession or its equivalent (*Collins* v. *Claughton* [1959] 1 W.L.R. 145). See further, *ante*, p. 59, as to surrender on purchase of the freehold by the tenant.

The surrender of a lease has not the effect of releasing the lessee from liability in respect of the breach of covenants committed before the date of the surrender (*Richmond* v. *Savill* [1926] 2 K.B. 530 ; *Dalton* v. *Pickard* [1926] 2 K.B. 545*n*). However, where surrender has determined a lease and the lessee has gone out of possession, the doctrine of estoppel no longer operates to prevent a denial of the lessor's title to grant the lease (*Harrison* v. *Wells* [1967] 1 Q.B. 267). If the lessee succeeds in showing that the lessor had no right to grant the lease, it follows that the covenants therein cannot be enforced even in respect of breaches committed before the surrender (*ibid.*, where the lease in question had been granted by a beneficiary with a life interest under a trust for sale but there had been no delegation of the power of leasing under s. 29 of the L.P.A. 1925).

Power of tenant for life to accept surrender.—Section 52 of the S.L.A. 1925 gives tenants for life the fullest powers to accept surrenders of leases.

Every new lease granted in place of a surrendered lease must be in conformity with the Act.

Power of mortgagor and mortgagee to accept surrender.—The general rule is that the surrender of a lease cannot validly be made to a mortgagor without the concurrence of the mortgagee (even though the lease was made by the mortgagor under his statutory powers : *Robbins* v. *Whyte* [1906] 1 K.B. 125), but special powers are contained in s. 100 of the L.P.A. 1925 if the mortgage was made after 31st December, 1911, and a contrary intention is not expressed by the mortgagor and mortgagee in the mortgage deed *or otherwise in writing*.

Section 100 is a very long one, consisting of thirteen subsections, and the reader is referred thereto ; the general effect is to give power, *but for the purpose only of enabling a lease to be granted*, to a mortgagor of land, *while in possession*, to accept a surrender of the mortgaged land comprised in the lease, against every incumbrancer, and either with or without an exception of the mines and minerals. For the same purpose, a mortgagee of land, while in possession, may, as against all prior or other incumbrancers, and as against the mortgagor, accept any such surrender as aforesaid. The section also gives power to vary the lease where only a part of the land or mines and minerals is surrendered.

Where any consideration is given, a surrender may not be made to a mortgagor without the consent of the incumbrancers, or to a second or subsequent incumbrancer without the consent of every prior incumbrancer (*ibid.*, s. 100 (4)).

It will be noticed that the section only enables the mortgagor to accept surrenders *while he is in possession*, and also only where there is no clause negativing the power. After the mortgagee (although he be only a second or third mortgagee) has taken possession *or appointed a receiver*, such mortgagee is the proper person to accept surrenders.

Where there is a surrender of an existing lease by operation of law, on the grant of a new lease, but the second lease is not effective, then the surrender is also ineffective and the original term continues (see *ante*, p. 828). This rule may apply where both surrender and new lease fail to bind a mortgagee because the statutory powers have been negatived with the result that the original term remains effective against the mortgagee (*Barclays Bank, Ltd.* v. *Stasek* [1957] Ch. 28).

Merger.—This is, in effect, the opposite of surrender : surrender involves the acquisition by the lessor of the lease ; merger involves the retention by the lessee of the lease and acquisition by him of the reversion. At common law a lease is determined by merger whenever the term and the reversion both vest, without any intervening estate, in the same person in the same right, for then the lesser interest merges in the greater. By s. 185 of the L.P.A. 1925 it is enacted that there shall not be any merger by operation of law only of any estate the beneficial interests in which would not be deemed to be merged or extinguished in equity.

A court of equity has always had regard not only to the *intention* of the parties but to the *duty* of the parties. Intention is a question of fact, and can be proved by any admissible evidence. The evidence of the parties at the moment when the two estates became vested in one person is not limited to what they said or did in executing the deed, and consequently the intention may be implied from the acts of the parties subsequent to the transaction

(*Re Fletcher ; Reading* v. *Fletcher* [1917] 1 Ch. 339). If it is to the interest of the party or consistent with his duty that merger should not take place, the court will, in the absence of direct evidence of intention, presume that merger was not intended (*Capital and Counties Bank, Ltd.* v. *Rhodes* [1903] 1 Ch. 631, 652) ; and, in the absence of such direct evidence, the court will inquire whether it was to the interest of the party or consistent with his duty that merger should take place (*Re Fletcher ; Reading* v. *Fletcher, ante*). If, however, the intention that merger should take place is expressly declared it will be effective to extinguish the lease even though this may not be in the interests of the party concerned (*Golden Lion Hotel (Hunstanton), Ltd.* v. *Carter* [1965] 1 W.L.R. 1189, where the right to enforce restrictive covenants conferred by the lease in respect of adjoining land was lost).

If no intention or duty can be shown either way, the common law will prevail, and there will be a merger (*Re Fletcher, per* Cozens-Hardy, M.R.). But in the case of a person having only a limited interest, such as a tenant for life, the presumption will be against merger (*Williams* v. *Williams-Wynn* (1915), 84 L.J. Ch. 801).

In practice it is not uncommon for the freehold to be acquired by a lessee whose leasehold estate is subject to a mortgage or charge. Some question has arisen recently as to the effect of this generally and in particular in relation to the mortgagee's or chargee's security (see the varied discussion in *Law Society's Gazette*, vol. 69, at pp. 469, 540, 562, 592, 617–618, 956–957, 1114, 1161–1162 and 1221–1222 where it was brought to a conclusion with a flash of academic clarity by Professor Graham Battersby). The short answer is thought to be that the mortgagee or chargee cannot be adversely affected and need take no further steps to protect his security.

Although there might well be held to be no merger by operation of law based on implied intention and duty where there is such a mortgage or charge, it appears clear that there can be merger as a result of an express declaration to that effect. The mortgage or charge, not being an intervening estate but a sub-interest, is not an absolute bar to merger. However, despite any merger, the mortgagee or chargee will remain protected by s. 139 of the L.P.A. 1925 (see below), whether the mortgage is actually by sub-demise (see L.P.A. 1925, s. 86) or is by charge by way of legal mortgage (see *ibid.*, s. 87 (1) (*b*)) ; i.e. in either case the mortgagee or chargee is protected as an underlessee.

Effect of surrender or merger where underlease exists.—The surrender or merger of a lease does not destroy the rights of underlessees, and the estate of the lessor is deemed to be the reversion on the underlease for the purpose of preserving the incidents and obligations of the leasehold reversion which has been surrendered or merged (L.P.A. 1925, s. 139).

It is provided by s. 150 (1) of the L.P.A. 1925 that a lease may be surrendered with a view to the acceptance of a new lease in place thereof, without a surrender of any underlease derived thereout ; and by subs. (2), that a new lease may be granted, in place of any lease so surrendered, without any surrender of an underlease, and the new lease operates as if all underleases derived out of the surrendered lease had been surrendered before the surrender of that lease was effected. The object of this section is to place parties, as nearly as may be, in the same position as if no surrender had taken place.

The lessee under such a new lease and any person entitled under him will be entitled to the same rights and remedies in respect of the rent and the covenants contained in any underlease as if the original lease had not been surrendered (*ibid.*, s. 150 (3)), and the underlessee will be entitled to hold the land comprised in the underlease as if the lease out of which the underlease was derived had not been surrendered (*ibid.*, s. 150 (4)). The lessor granting the new lease and any person deriving title under him will be entitled to the remedies by distress or entry upon the land comprised in such underlease for rent reserved by or for breach of any covenant contained in the new lease (but so far as the rents and covenants contained in the new lease do not exceed or impose greater burdens than those reserved by or contained in the original lease) as he would have had if the original lease had remained on foot, or if a new underlease derived out of the new lease had been granted to the underlessee or a person deriving title under him, as the case may require (*ibid.*, s. 150 (6)). See *Plummer and John* v. *David* [1920] 1 K.B. 326. The section is retrospective (L.P.A. 1925, s. 154). A tenant for life may accept a surrender and grant a new lease without obtaining the surrender of an underlease derived thereout, notwithstanding the wording of the S.L.A. 1925, s. 42 (1) (*Re Grosvenor Settled Estates ; Duke of Westminster* v. *McKenna* [1932] 1 Ch. 232).

B. DETERMINATION UNDER VARIOUS POWERS

Notices to determine fixed terms.—Leases frequently contain provision whereby either or both of the parties may determine the term before it has run its full course by a specified length of notice given to the other party. Such notices are documents of a technical nature and must be drawn with care. For instance, they must purport to terminate the lease on the correct date specified in the lease, and an error of a few days will be fatal to the validity of the notice (*Hankey* v. *Clavering* [1942] 2 K.B. 326), but an apparent ambiguity in the notice may be resolved by reading it in conjunction with the terms of the lease (*Winchester Court, Ltd.* v. *Holmes* [1941] 2 All E.R. 542). If provision is made for determination by notice after a specified date, the question whether the notice can be given before that date to expire afterwards, or whether it must be *given* on or after that date, depends on the construction of the words used (*Associated London Properties* v. *Sheridan* (1945), 62 T.L.R. 80 ; *British Iron & Steel Corporation* v. *Malpern* [1946] K.B. 171).

Where such a provision permits the tenant to determine the lease it is usually made subject to due payment of rent and performance of covenants. In such a case a notice to determine will be valid if any breaches of covenant are remedied before the expiration of the notice (*Simons* v. *Associated Furnishers, Ltd.* [1931] 1 Ch. 379). Where the tenant covenants to do an act, for instance, to paint, in the last quarter *of the term*, he is not obliged to do the act if, by reason of the exercise of an option to determine, that period of the term does not arrive (*Dickinson* v. *St. Aubyn* [1944] K.B. 454). The position would have been different if the covenant had referred to the last quarter of the *tenancy*.

A twenty-one years lease contained a clause whereby the lessors might determine the lease at the end of fourteen years if they required the premises for the purposes of their business. It was held that they might determine the term if they could show that they would require part of the premises for their business during the last seven years (*Parkinson* v. *Barclays Bank, Ltd.* [1951] 1 K.B. 368).

If the premises are business premises within Pt. II of the Landlord and Tenant Act, 1954, the landlord could take advantage of a determination clause only by serving notice under that Act ; the definition of notice to quit in s. 69 (1) includes a notice to terminate a tenancy for a term certain. See further, *post*, p. 898.

Options to purchase.—This subject is dealt with in general at p. 73, *ante*, but it may be convenient to mention here a few points regarding options in leases.

The grant of such an option for a lessee to purchase the reversion creates in favour of the grantee-lessee an equitable interest or chose in action. For the conditions of enforcement of the *burden* of this against the grantor-lessor and successors in title to the reversion (in particular as to the perpetuity rule and protection by registration) see at p. 812, *ante*. Nevertheless it should be noted here that even where an option is not directly enforceable against a successor in title, he may become indirectly liable for non-compliance with it by virtue of the usual contractual covenants for indemnity taken by the grantor (*Eagon* v. *Dent* [1965] 3 All E.R. 334).

So far as the *benefit* is concerned the equitable interest or chose in action created by the option is assignable by the lessee-grantee, unless this is prohibited or restricted by the terms of the grant or by some rule of law. This assignment of the option may be express or implied. Thus in *Griffith* v. *Pelton* [1958] Ch. 205, the benefit of an option to purchase the reversion was granted to the " lessee," defined to include " assigns," and held by the Court of Appeal to pass without mention on an assignment of the lease. Again in *Re Button's Lease* [1964] Ch. 263, an option to purchase the reversion was conferred on the " tenant " but there was no definition extending this to include assigns. Plowman, J., held that even though an implied assignment was not possible, the tenant was able to assign the benefit expressly and separately from an assignment of the lease. The learned judge added that the usual express definition of " tenant " might have the effect of restricting assignments of the benefit of the option to assignees of the lease but that otherwise the option would be assignable to anyone.

It is necessary to draw attention to the danger that the exercise of an option may form an open contract. A lessor should not grant an option without taking the same precautions, for instance in disclosure of restrictive covenants and defects in title generally, as he would take in making an unconditional offer to sell, because the grant of an option amounts to a continuing offer.

If there is delay in completing a purchase it is often difficult to decide whether rent continues to be payable after the time fixed for exercise of the option. In *Cockwell* v. *Romford Sanitary Steam Laundry, Ltd.* [1939] 4 All E.R. 370, there was provision for payment of interest from the expiration of the notice exercising the option until completion, and it was held that the tenancy ceased on such expiration and no rent was payable thereafter. Contrast *Weston* v. *Collins* (1865), 34 L.J. Ch. 353, where there was no provision for interest and it was held that there was no contract for purchase until the price was paid.

If a lease containing an option of purchase exercisable within a given time expires, and the lease is extended for a further period, the extension will not apply to the option, on the ground that it is a matter entirely outside the relation of landlord and tenant (*Re Leeds and Batley Breweries and Bradbury's Lease* [1920] 2 Ch. 548 ; *Sherwood* v. *Tucker* [1924] 2 Ch. 440). But if the agreement for the new lease provides in effect that the old lease is to be the model for the new lease and consequently that all the terms and conditions of the old lease are to be contained in the new lease the tenant would be entitled to have the option to purchase inserted in the new lease (*Batchelor* v. *Murphy* [1926] A.C. 63 ; *Hill* v. *Hill* [1947] Ch. 231).

If a lease contains an option to purchase the freehold " at any time " that option will be construed as exercisable during currency of the tenancy created by the agreement only ; it is not exercisable for instance at a time when the tenant has remained in occupation as statutory tenant (*Longmuir* v. *Kew* [1960] 1 W.L.R. 862).

Determination of lease under statutory powers.—Where a demolition or clearance order or a closing order has been made in respect of any premises subject to a lease, an underlease or a tenancy, the county court, on the application of the lessor or the lessee, may determine or vary the lease, conditionally or unconditionally (Housing Act, 1957, s. 162). It is also convenient to note that if a notice requiring execution of works has been served or a demolition order or clearance order made, if there is default in executing works or demolishing the house any " owner " (as defined, *ibid.*, s. 189 (1)) whose interests may be prejudiced can apply to a court of summary jurisdiction for authority to execute the works or demolish the house (*ibid.*, s. 163).

Similar powers are given to the High Court or the county court on application by a person entitled to an interest in land used as a site for housing. If premises on the land are, or may become, unfit for habitation, or it is proved that the applicant should be entrusted with the carrying out of a scheme of improvement, the applicant may be empowered to execute necessary works and any lease or agreement held from the applicant may be determined (*ibid.*, s. 164).

On an application by an owner or occupier of a factory for an order as to the liability for expenses of complying with the provisions of the Factories Act, 1961, the court, at the request of the owner or occupier, may determine the lease (Factories Act, 1961, s. 170). See also the power conferred on the county court, to set aside or modify agreements or leases, by s. 73 of the Offices, Shops and Railway Premises Act, 1963.

Where the tenant or occupier of premises is convicted of the offence of knowingly permitting the premises to be used as a brothel the landlord may require the tenant to assign the lease or other contract under which the premises are held to some person reasonably approved by the landlord (Sexual Offences Act, 1956, s. 35 (2) and Sched. 1, para. 1). If the tenant fails to do this within three months the landlord may determine the lease or contract (*ibid.*, Sched. 1, para. 2) and the court by which the tenant was convicted may order possession to be delivered (*ibid.*, Sched. 1, para. 3). These rules are, however, subject to any protection in the Rent Acts. A landlord who knows of such a conviction should exercise these rights. If he fails to do so, or, having done so, enters into a new tenancy with the same person without having all reasonable provisions to prevent the recurrence of the offence inserted in the new contract, he may be deemed a party to a future offence unless he can show that he took all reasonable steps to prevent its recurrence (Sexual Offences Act, 1956, s. 35 (3)).

C. NOTICES TO QUIT

Periodic tenancies.—The fact that a tenant pays his rent weekly, monthly or quarterly does not of itself make him a weekly, monthly or quarterly tenant. If a house is let *at so much a year*, notwithstanding that the rent is to be paid weekly or at any other period, it is a tenancy from year to year. To make a tenancy a weekly, monthly or quarterly tenancy it must be a letting for so much a week, a month, or a quarter. The Court of Appeal has held that a provision restricting or postponing, but not removing, the landlord's right to serve a notice to quit is *not* void as repugnant to the nature of a

27

periodical tenancy (*Re Midland Railway Co.'s Agreement* [1971] Ch. 764 ; cp. *Centaploy, Ltd.* v. *Matlodge, Ltd.* [1973] 2 All E.R. 720, where there was a purported removal of this right). In the case of a yearly tenancy it is possible that more than a half-year's (182 days) notice expiring at the time of entry may be necessary and also possible that less than a half-year's notice may be sufficient, for instance, if the tenancy is expressed to commence from a feast day, as from Michaelmas or Lady Day. If the tenancy should be made to commence from Michaelmas, notice would have to be given on or before the 25th March, but if the tenancy commenced from Lady Day, notice would only have to be given on or before the 29th September. In these cases, half-a-year means two quarters ; otherwise it means 182 days (*Anon.* (1575), 3 Dy. 345*a* ; the odd half day is ignored).

If a tenant enters in a broken quarter and pays rent for such broken quarter, the tenancy, so far as the notice to quit is concerned, will be considered to commence from the quarter day after the tenant first entered (*Doe d. King* v. *Grafton* (1852), 18 Q.B. 496). Where the demise is for more than a year and the tenant holds over and pays rent after the expiration of the original demise so as to create a yearly tenancy (see *ante*, pp. 814, 815), that tenancy is determinable on the anniversary of the determination and not of the commencement of the original term. Hence, notice to quit must be given for the anniversary of the determination of the term (*Croft* v. *Blay* [1919] 2 Ch. 343).

There is a difference between a tenancy commencing " on " and a tenancy commencing " from " a certain date. In the first case the tenancy would commence on the day, and in the second case it would commence on the following day.

A notice given by the landlord requiring the tenant to quit " on or before " the proper date of determination (*Dagger* v. *Shepherd* [1946] K.B. 215) or " by " that date (*Eastaugh* v. *Macpherson* [1954] 1 W.L.R. 1307) is valid. See also *Joseph* v. *Joseph* [1967] Ch. 78. These cases must be distinguished from *Gardner* v. *Ingram* (1889), 61 L.T. 729, in which an ambiguous statement by a tenant of his intention to surrender his tenancy on or before a certain date was held invalid. See also *De Vries* v. *Sparks* (1927), 137 L.T. 441.

In any periodic tenancy notice to quit must expire at the end of a current period ; this rule applies to yearly, quarterly, monthly or weekly tenancies (*Queen's Club Gardens Estates, Ltd.* v. *Bignell* [1924] 1 K.B. 117 ; *Lemon* v. *Lardeur* [1946] K.B. 613). A weekly tenancy, for example, beginning on a Monday expires at midnight on the following or any subsequent Sunday. Correctly a notice to quit should be expressed to expire on a Sunday, but in any such cases a notice to quit expressed to take effect on the " anniversary " either of the day on which the tenancy commenced or of the day before that date will be construed as a notice to quit when the current period ends and so will be a valid notice (*Queen's Club Gardens Estates, Ltd.* v. *Bignell, ante ; Crate* v. *Miller* [1947] K.B. 946). A notice to expire on the " anniversary " of the commencement of a tenancy is construed as expiring on the first moment of that day and so is valid (*Crate* v. *Miller, ante*). Thus, a notice expressed to take effect on a Monday and relating to a weekly tenancy from Monday to Sunday is effective. But if the notice expressly mentions a later time in the day of the " anniversary " of the commencement of the term it cannot be construed as expiring at the first moment of that day and so is ineffective (*Bathavon R.D.C.* v. *Carlile* [1958] 1 Q.B. 461). The burden is on the person alleging that a notice is valid to prove when a period of tenancy ends, and that accordingly the notice he has given is valid (*Lemon* v. *Lardeur*, *ante*).

The length of notice needed to determine a quarterly, monthly or weekly tenancy is one quarter, one month and one week respectively (*Queen's Club Gardens Estates, Ltd.* v. *Bignell, ante*). It is provided by s. 61 of the L.P.A. 1925 that in all documents executed, made, or coming into operation after 1925, unless the context otherwise requires, " month " means calendar month.

Where a tenancy of business premises has been continued under s. 24 of the Landlord and Tenant Act, 1954 (see *post*, p. 901) as a monthly tenancy, it is *not* necessary for a notice for termination of the tenancy within the period allowed by s. 25 (2) of that Act (see *ibid.*) to expire at the end of one of the monthly periods (*Commercial Properties, Ltd.* v. *Wood* [1968] 1 Q.B. 15).

The Rent Act, 1957, s. 16, provides that " no notice by a landlord or a tenant to quit any premises let . . . as a dwelling shall be valid unless it is given *not less than four weeks* before the date on which it is to take effect." The italicised words mean four weeks " inclusive of the day of service and exclusive of the day of expiry "; so a notice given on a Friday to expire on the fourth Friday thereafter would be valid (*Schnabel* v. *Allard* [1967] 1 Q.B. 627, where the Court of Appeal in effect overruled the contrary decision of the Divisional Court in *Thompson* v. *Stimpson* [1961] 1 Q.B. 195). It must be noted that the test as to whether premises are affected by this rule is provided by the purpose of letting of the premises. There is no provision, corresponding to that in the Rent Acts, that the letting must be as a " separate " dwelling. Pending a decision of the court, a notice to quit premises which include a part used as a dwelling should comply with s. 16. However, it has been held that, as a general rule, a tenancy arising under an attornment clause in a mortgage is not a genuine residential letting within s. 16 (*Alliance Building Society* v. *Pinwill* [1958] Ch. 788). It has further been decided by the Court of Appeal that s. 16 is only applicable to tenancies which require a notice to quit to terminate them ; thus it does not apply to a tenancy at will nor, of course, to a licence (*Crane* v. *Morris* [1965] 1 W.L.R. 1104).

Doubt has been expressed as to whether the common form of notice by which, in the alternative, it is expressed to take effect either on a day stated or at the expiration of the period of tenancy next after a given time from service, is valid (*per* Somervell, L.J., in *Crate* v. *Miller, ante*), but a similar notice was held to be valid in *Brothwood* v. *Murphy* (1944), 143 E.G. 465, one seems to have been accepted as valid in *Bathavon R.D.C.* v. *Carlile, ante*, and a notice to quit " at the expiration of your tenancy which will expire next after the end of one half-year from the service of this notice " was held to be valid in *Addis and Jenkins* v. *Burrows* [1948] 1 K.B. 444. In *Chez Auguste, Ltd.* v. *Cottat* [1951] 1 K.B. 292, the notice was expressed to expire in thirteen days " or at the expiration of the current period of your tenancy which shall expire next after the service upon you of this notice." Lord Goddard, C.J., found that the tenancy was a yearly one. As he considered that the notice was intended to put an end to a weekly tenancy, which the landlord alleged, he decided that it was ambiguous and invalid. Thus, although there is authority for considering notices so expressed in the alternative to be valid, there seems to be considerable doubt as to how far the alternative will be effective.

As to notices to quit after severance of the reversion, see *post*, p. 898.

By landlord only.—It appears that notice to quit cannot validly be given before the commencement of the tenancy to which it relates (*Lower* v. *Sorrell* [1963] 1 Q.B. 959). In that case, Donovan, L.J., said that in his opinion " a notice to quit is a notice given by an existing landlord to an existing tenant ; from which it follows, if that view be right, that a person cannot give a valid notice to quit before he has become a landlord, and the recipient of the notice his tenant, or before legal relations exist between them which otherwise permit such a notice." Equally a purchaser cannot until the legal estate is vested in him give a valid notice to quit to the tenants of the property purchased, unless he is expressly authorised to do so as agent of the vendor (*Graham* v. *M'Ilwaine* [1918] 2 Ir. R. 353) ; the fact that he holds a deed of conveyance delivered to him as an escrow only, will not enable him to give a valid notice (*Thompson* v. *McCullough* [1947] K.B. 447). Similarly, prior to registration of the transfer, a purchaser of registered land does not acquire the legal estate and so cannot serve a valid notice (*Smith* v. *Express Dairy Co., Ltd.* [1954] J.P.L. 45 ; *Lever Finance, Ltd.* v. *Needleman's Trustee* [1956] Ch. 375).

The Court of Appeal has held valid a notice to quit served on a tenant by solicitors stating that they did so " on behalf of your landlord, Mr. R. P. H.", even though Mr. R. P. H. was in fact only a director of the landlord company ; since Mr. R. P. H. was the company's general agent he was entitled to serve the notice to quit on its behalf, so that the notice bound the company, was not misleading and accorded with the tenant's understanding of the position (*Hammond Properties, Ltd.* v. *Gajdzis* [1968] 1 W.L.R. 1858).

Service of notice to quit.—On proof of posting of a notice, delivery is presumed in due course of post. But it is thought doubtful whether service by post would be held to be good where the tenant or his authorised agent is not in actual physical occupation of the premises to which the notice is addressed. In *Van Grutten* v. *Trevenen* [1902] 2 K.B. 82, the tenant, expecting the notice and guessing what the contents of a registered letter were, refused to sign the official receipt, and therefore the postman refused to leave the letter. It was held to be good service.

It is now expressly provided by s. 196 (4) and (5) of the L.P.A. 1925, in effect, that any notice required to be served by any instrument affecting property executed or coming into operation after 1925, unless a contrary intention appears, shall (*inter alia*) be sufficiently served if it is sent by post in a registered letter addressed to the lessee or lessor by name, at his place of abode or business, office or counting-house, and if that letter is not returned through the post-office undelivered ; and that service shall be deemed to be made at the time at which the registered letter would in the ordinary course be delivered. Posting by recorded delivery is now an alternative (Recorded Delivery Act, 1962, s. 1 ; and see *Re 88 Berkeley Road, N.W.9* [1971] Ch. 648). It is doubtful, however, whether a notice to quit is " required " to be served by a lease creating a periodic tenancy. See the discussion of this, and of many other doubtful points, by Mr. J. Montgomerie in the *Conveyancer N.S.*, vol. 16, p. 98 *et seq.*, where the view is expressed that the L.P.A. 1925, s. 196, " applies to a notice to quit expressly mentioned in the document but not where the document merely creates a periodic tenancy."

It may be impossible to effect service because a tenant's whereabouts are unknown. In such a case the procedure laid down in the Distress for Rent Act, 1737, s. 16, as amended by the Deserted Tenements Act, 1817, may be followed. If a tenant holding premises at a rack rent has deserted the premises

and left them unoccupied so that there is no sufficient distress, and one
half-year's rent is in arrear, two justices may, after viewing the premises
twice, put the landlord into possession. In London the procedure is laid
down by the Metropolitan Police Courts Act, 1840, s. 13. A more modern
remedy is contained in the Landlord and Tenant Act, 1954, s. 54. If the
landlord satisfies the county court (a) that he has taken all reasonable steps
to communicate with the person last known to be tenant but has failed,
(b) that during the last six months neither the tenant nor any person claiming
under him has been in occupation, and (c) that during that period no rent
has been paid, the court may, by order, determine the tenancy. As these
remedies are slow in operation, it is important to insert in leases and tenancy
agreements express provision as to methods of service which will be effective,
for instance by posting to the last known address.

A notice served on executors in whom a periodic tenancy has vested
would appear to be valid even if served before probate (*Brazier* v. *Hudson*
(1836), 8 Sim. 67), but if the tenant died intestate, until letters of administration have been obtained notice may validly be served on the President
of the Family Division (A.E.A. 1925, ss. 9 and 55, as amended by the
Administration of Justice Act, 1970, s. 1 (6), Sched. 2, para. 5 ; *Fred Long
and Son, Ltd.* v. *Burgess* [1950] 1 K.B. 115). A notice may be served on
the President by sending it by post to him c/o The Treasury Solicitor,
3 Central Buildings, Matthew Parker Street, London, S.W.1. In the case
of *Egerton* v. *Rutter* [1951] 1 K.B. 472, however, Lord Goddard, C.J., held
that a notice addressed to two persons as executors was valid although the
deceased had died intestate and those two persons did not obtain a grant of
administration until after they received the notice. The two grounds for the
decision were, first, that the intending administrators were acting as agents for
the President and so notice could be served on them under the A.H.A. 1948,
s. 92 (3) (see *post*, p. 960), and, secondly, that in the absence of a personal
representative the landlord could treat the party in possession as the tenant.
This second ground for the decision is most useful when a notice to quit a
small property has to be served and it is known that representation to the
estate of a former tenant has not been taken out, but it is not known whether
that tenant made a will. See also the similar decisions in *Harrowby* v. *Snelson*
[1951] 1 All E.R. 140, *Wilbraham* v. *Colclough* [1952] 1 All E.R. 979, and in
the Irish case *Hill* v. *Carroll* [1953] Ir. R. 52.

A valid notice to quit may be served and take effect during the currency of
a longer notice served earlier (*Thompson* v. *McCullough* [1947] K.B. 447).

Waiver of notice to quit.—A notice to quit may, with the consent of
the party to whom it was given, be withdrawn during its currency (*Davies*
v. *Bristow* [1920] 3 K.B. 428), but when it has taken effect the tenancy has
come to an end, and, strictly speaking, it cannot be " waived " (*Maconochie
Bros., Ltd.* v. *Brand* [1946] 2 All E.R. 778, *per* Henn Collins, J., at p. 779).
When a notice is withdrawn by agreement the withdrawal constitutes the
creation of a new tenancy, and *ad valorem* stamp duty is payable on that
agreement (*Freeman* v. *Evans* [1922] 1 Ch. 36).

A new tenancy may be impliedly created by the acts of the parties, for
instance, by payment and acceptance of rent due after the expiration of the
notice to quit. Receipt of rent by an agent, however, cannot have this
effect unless the agent is authorised by the landlord to receive it even after
the notice has expired (*Doe d. Ash* v. *Calvert* (1810), 2 Camp. 387). Payment

and receipt of rent will usually raise the implication of a new tenancy, but this may not be the case if the circumstances show that a new tenancy was not intended by the parties (*Thompsons* (*Funeral Furnishers*), *Ltd.* v. *Phillips* [1945] 2 All E.R. 49 ; *Clarke* v. *Grant* [1950] 1 K.B. 104). The acceptance of rent due before the expiration of the notice to quit, even though it be accepted after such expiration, will not have the effect of creating a new tenancy, nor will the acceptance of rent due after such expiration, by an agent, in the mistaken belief that it was due before the expiration (*Clarke* v. *Grant, ante*).

The case is different where a house is within the protection of the Rent Acts, in which case the acceptance of rent after expiration of a notice to quit does not of itself create a new contractual tenancy, because the tenant is entitled to remain as statutory tenant and the landlord may accept rent in respect of this statutory tenancy without any implication being raised of a new contractual tenancy (*Davies* v. *Bristow* [1920] 3 K.B. 428 ; *Felce* v. *Hill* (1923), 92 L.J.K.B. 974 ; *Shuter* v. *Hersh* [1922] 1 K.B. 438). The same rule applies if rent is accepted after the expiration of a tenancy for a fixed term if the tenancy of the house is governed by those Acts (*Morrison* v. *Jacobs* [1945] K.B. 577).

Distress for rent accruing after the expiration of a notice will constitute a new tenancy if the tenant acquiesces in it (*Panton* v. *Jones* (1813), 3 Camp. 372), but a mere demand for rent to which the tenant in no way consents will not (*Blyth* v. *Dennett* (1853), 13 C.B. 178). If a valid notice has been given and has expired a subsequent notice to quit is of no effect and does not itself raise the implication that a new tenancy has arisen after the expiration of the first notice (*Lowenthal* v. *Vanhoute* [1947] K.B. 342).

D. ENLARGEMENT OF LONG TERMS

Section 153 (1) of the L.P.A. 1925 enables the owner of a long term to enlarge it into a fee simple, provided that (*a*) the original term was for 300 or more years, and the residue unexpired is 200 or more years ; (*b*) there is no trust or right of redemption affecting the term in favour of the freeholder or other person entitled in reversion expectant on the term ; (*c*) the lease is not liable to be determined by re-entry for condition broken ; and (*d*) there is no rent, or merely a peppercorn rent or other rent having no money value (see exception below), or the rent must have become barred by lapse of time or otherwise ceased to be payable.

A rent of one shilling was a rent having a money value (*Blaiberg* v. *Keeves* [1906] 2 Ch. 175) ; but not a rent of a silver penny (*Re Chapman and Hobbs* (1885), 29 Ch. D. 1007). The exception referred to is where the original rent did not exceed £1, and such rent has not been collected or paid for a continuous period of twenty years (L.P.A. 1925, s. 153 (4)).

The section applies to mortgage terms, where the right of redemption has been foreclosed or barred by lapse of time since the mortgagee took possession (*ibid.*, s. 153 (3)), but not to any term created by a sub-demise out of a superior term, itself incapable of being enlarged into a fee simple, or to a term liable to be determined by re-entry for condition broken (*ibid.*, s. 153 (2)).

The document necessary to effect the enlargement into a fee simple is a deed declaring that from and after the execution thereof the term shall be enlarged into a fee simple (*ibid.*, s. 153 (6)). But where the term has been settled in trust by reference to other freehold land, or to go along with other freehold land, the fee simple so acquired will be conveyed by means of a subsidiary vesting instrument and settled in the same manner as the other freehold land (*ibid.*, s. 153 (9)). The persons who have power to execute the necessary document are described in subs. (6).

The effect of the enlargement is that " the person in whom the term was *previously* vested " acquires a fee simple instead of the term (including th⸲ fee simple in all mines and minerals which at the time of enlargement have not been severed in right or in fact), but such fee simple is subject to the same covenants and provisions relating to user and enjoyment and to all the same obligations of every kind as the term would have been subject to if it had not been enlarged (*ibid.*, s. 153 (7), (8), (10)). It is sometimes suggested that in view of the word " previously," as used in subs. (7) to describe the effect of an enlargement, it is not advisable to include a declaration of enlargement in the same deed as an assignment, conveyance or assent of the term. The enlargement of leaseholds is considered in detail in an article in the *Conveyancer N.S.*, vol. 22, p. 101 *et seq.* ; it is there suggested that the effect of s. 153 (8) is to " make the burden of positive covenants which touch and concern the land enforceable against successors in title of the grantee."

An unusual power to enlarge a term of years is contained in the Places of Worship (Enfranchisement) Act, 1920. Where premises are held under a lease upon trust to be used for the purposes of a place of worship, and the premises are so used, the trustees may enlarge their interest into a fee simple. This right does not extend to more than two acres and does not exist (*a*) if use as a place of worship is a breach of covenant ; (*b*) where the premises form part of land belonging to a local authority or certain transport undertakers ; or (*c*) where the lease was for less than twenty-one years.

E. DISCLAIMER

Disclaimer on bankruptcy.—A trustee in bankruptcy may disclaim a lease without leave of the court in the following cases :—

(1) Where the bankrupt has not sub-let the premises or any part of them or mortgaged or charged them and (i) the rent and Schedule A assessment are both less than £20 or (ii) the estate is being administered as a small bankruptcy or (iii) the trustee gives the landlord notice of intention to disclaim and the landlord does not within seven days give notice requiring the matter to be brought before the court.

(2) Where there is a sub-lease, mortgage or charge and notice has been served on the lessor and sub-lessee or mortgagee and none of the parties, within fourteen days, gives notice requiring the matter to be brought before the court (Bankruptcy Rules, 1952, r. 278).

In other cases leave is necessary, and in granting leave the court may impose conditions or make vesting orders for preserving the rights of sub-lessees, mortgagees or chargees (Bankruptcy Act, 1914, s. 54 (3), (6)). A disclaimer is not operative until it is filed (Bankruptcy Rules, 1952, r. 278 (3)).

Disclaimer does not affect the rights or liabilities of persons other than the trustee and the bankrupt, except so far as is necessary for releasing the bankrupt, his property and the trustee from liability (Bankruptcy Act, 1914, s. 54 (2)). Thus, if the bankrupt has assigned the lease, the trustee cannot disclaim (*Re Gee, ex parte Official Receiver* (1889), 24 Q.B.D. 65). On the other hand, if he was the assignee of the lease the disclaimer merely relieves the bankrupt and his estate from liability and leaves the original lessee under liability to pay the rent and perform the covenants in the lease (*Hill* v. *East and West India Dock Co.* (1884), 9 App. Cas. 448). If the bankrupt had sub-let the premises the sub-lessee may obtain a vesting order under the Bankruptcy Act, 1914, s. 54 (6), and if he does not he must pay the rent and perform the covenants in the lease ; otherwise the lessor may distrain or re-enter under the terms of the lease (*Re Finlay, ex parte Clothworkers' Co.* (1888), 21 Q.B.D. 475).

Disclaimer after war damage.—The common-law rule is that the destruction of a building situated on land the subject of a lease does not discharge the obligation of the tenant to pay rent or the obligation of either party to perform covenants such as those to repair the building (*Redmond* v. *Dainton* [1920] 2 K.B. 256 ; *Leighton's Investment Trust, Ltd.* v. *Cricklewood Property and Investment Trust, Ltd.* [1942] 2 All E.R. 580). The Landlord and Tenant (War Damage) Acts, 1939 and 1941, however, provided a number of rules applicable where " war damage," as defined in the War Damage Act, 1943, occurred. These rules have ceased to be of great practical importance ; they were stated in outline in the 14th Edition of this book, Vol. 2, p. 128.

Disclaimer on requisitioning of land.—Disclaimer was permitted, in certain circumstances, by the Landlord and Tenant (Requisitioned Land) Acts, 1942 and 1944, of certain short leases ; see the 14th Edition of this book, Vol. 2, p. 129.

F. REGISTERED LAND

The provisions applicable in registered conveyancing on determination of leases are not altogether satisfactory, mainly because determination may occur in a manner to which no rule applies directly. Where the title to a lease has been registered, the determination thereof may be notified on the register, upon the production of a surrender or other sufficient release or discharge, executed by the proprietor and every person appearing by the register to be interested (L.R.R. 1925, r. 200). Where the title is not so registered but a lease is noted on the register as an incumbrance, the determination may be notified on the register on production of the document (if any) creating it, with a sufficient release or discharge executed by the incumbrancer (L.R.R. 1925, r. 201) but if, in such a case, there has been a dealing with or transmission of the incumbrance the application must be accompanied by sufficient evidence of the applicant's title (L.R.R. 1925, r. 202).

Where the proprietor of any land comprised in a leasehold title becomes proprietor of the land comprised in the title against which the lease is noted or where a lease or agreement for a lease noted as an incumbrance is vested in such proprietor, the registrar may, unless the contrary appears, treat the lease as merged, in which case the title is closed or the note is cancelled, as the case requires (L.R.R. 1925, r. 206). Application for this to be done should be made by the proprietor of both estates and the form should be accompanied by both land certificates and the lease.

Where forfeiture occurs an order of the court may provide for rectification of the register, but otherwise the proper course would appear to be to ask the registrar to exercise his discretion, under the L.R.R. 1925, r. 16, to withdraw the lease from the register.

PART 4. COVENANTS AFFECTING LEASEHOLDS

Modification and discharge of restrictive covenants affecting leaseholds, see ante, pp. 585–586.

A. BENEFIT AND BURDEN

Restrictive covenants on reversionary title.—Before 1926, under the Vendor and Purchaser Act, 1874, and the Conveyancing Act, 1881, a lessee or assign, under an open contract, was not entitled to investigate the title to the freehold or the leasehold reversion. In spite of this, it was held in *Patman* v. *Harland* (1881), 17 Ch. D. 353, that a lessee or assign must be deemed to have constructive notice of, and therefore was bound by, any restrictive covenant on the freehold or leasehold reversionary title which he would have discovered had he specially contracted to investigate that title. This anomaly has been remedied by s. 44 (5) of the L.P.A. 1925 (*ante,* p. 143), which provides that in such a case the underlessee or assignee will not be deemed to be affected with notice. A lessee, underlessee, or assignee will, therefore, be affected by a covenant on the freehold or leasehold reversionary title, if made before 1926, only if he has actual or constructive notice thereof, but he will no longer be deemed to have constructive notice by reason of the decision in *Patman* v. *Harland, ante.* It may be observed in passing that remedying the anomaly as against underlessees and assignees has incidentally produced the rather more drastic anomaly as against covenantees and their successors that their rights may now be defeated to all intents and purposes by the simple grant or assignment of a lease in pursuance of an open contract.

This subsection (s. 44 (5)) would probably not protect an intending lessee or assign unless he is acting in good faith ; thus if he has reasonable grounds for suspecting some defect, or has notice in the same transaction (s. 199 (1) (ii) (*b*)), he ought to investigate the matter. If the covenant on the reversionary title was made before 1926 a person who alleges that a tenant is bound by it must prove that the tenant had notice of it (*Shears* v. *Wells* [1936] 1 All E.R. 832).

Although restrictive covenants between lessor and lessee, even if made after 1925, have not to be registered as land charges, the land, as against the lessee or occupier, may be subject to restrictive covenants created by the ground landlord or his predecessors. If such restrictive covenants were made after 1925 and registered under the L.C.A. 1925 or 1972, the lessee will be deemed to have actual notice of them (L.P.A. 1925, s. 198 (1) ; see *obiter per* Simonds, J., in *White* v. *Bijou Mansions, Ltd.* [1937] Ch. 610, at p. 621 ; on appeal [1938] Ch. 351). He should, therefore, search the register against the name of his lessor ; the difficulty is that he will not normally investigate title and so he will not know the names of any other persons against whom an entry might have been made on the register affecting the land, such as predecessors in title of the lessor. It is also advisable to make a local search, as entries on the local land charges register may affect a lessee (L.C.A. 1925, s. 15 ; Law of Property (Amendment) Act, 1926, Sched. ; *Re Forsey and Hollebone's Contract* [1927] 2 Ch. 379 ; *Re Middleton and Young's Contract* [1929] W.N. 70), and, in the case of a long lease, the additional inquiries mentioned *ante,* p. 6.

Covenants between lessor and lessee.—There are certain rules affecting the passing of the benefit and the burden of covenants entered into between

27A

lessor and lessee which do not apply to covenants imposed on the sale of a fee simple estate. Before dealing with these rules, we must first note that the benefit and the burden of *restrictive* covenants entered into between lessor and lessee may pass in equity in the same way as the benefit and the burden of *restrictive* covenants imposed on the sale of a fee simple estate. For this purpose, the lessor's reversion is an interest in the land to which the benefit of a restrictive covenant may be annexed in equity although not at common law (*Hall* v. *Ewin* (1887), 37 Ch. D. 74 ; *Teape* v. *Douse* (1905), 92 L.T. 319). The same rules, in connection with passing the burden, as to notice, are applicable, although the circumstances in which notice is held to exist may be different (see above). In particular, covenants made between lessor and lessee are not registrable as land charges, whether they are positive or negative (L.C.A. 1972, s. 2 (5), Class D (ii) ; and see *Dartstone, Ltd.* v. *Cleveland Petroleum Co., Ltd.* [1969] 1 W.L.R. 1807).

Thus a restrictive covenant can be enforced against an underlessee or a person claiming under an underlease of the whole or part of the premises contained in the lease (*Teape* v. *Douse* (1905), 92 L.T. 319), or against any purchaser for value of a legal estate in the land, provided that he has notice of the covenant (*Mander* v. *Falcke* [1891] 2 Ch. 554). As to these covenants, see *ante*, p. 555 *et seq.* As to the enforcement of mutual restrictive covenants in leases, equivalent to the creation of building schemes, see *ante*, p. 565.

It is in connection with *positive* covenants that the special rules applicable to leaseholds normally arise. Speaking generally, such covenants between lessor and lessee and persons claiming under them respectively cannot be enforced unless there is " privity of contract " or " privity of estate " between them.

Privity of contract.—This expression is used to denote the relation between the parties in regard to the actual covenants entered into between the lessor and lessee in the lease or underlease itself. Such covenants are binding by virtue of the direct contract (*Matthews* v. *Ruggles-Brise* [1911] 1 Ch. 194). The covenants remain binding on each and on the estate of each, during the whole of the term created, notwithstanding the assignment by either of his interest (*Stuart* v. *Joy* [1904] 1 K.B. 362). The fact that the document creating the tenancy containing the agreement sought to be enforced is under hand only appears to make no difference and will not prevent the lessor succeeding in his claim against the original lessee (*John Betts & Sons, Ltd.* v. *Price* (1924), 40 T.L.R. 589).

There is an exception in regard to the liability of the lessee or an underlessee in the case where they take a long term in lieu of a right to perpetual renewal of the lease. For it is provided by Sched. 15, para. 11 (1), to the L.P.A. 1922 (see *post*, p. 940), that in the case of every term or sub-term created by the Act or under any power conferred by the Act, each lessee or underlessee, although he may be the original lessee or underlessee, and notwithstanding any stipulation to the contrary, shall be liable only for rent accruing and for breaches of covenants or conditions occurring while he or his personal representatives shall have the term or sub-term vested in him or them, and in like manner, as respects an original lessee or underlessee, as if the term or sub-term had, immediately after its creation, been assigned to him.

Privity of estate.—Although there is no direct contractual relationship between a person claiming to enforce a covenant and a person against whom he seeks to enforce it, the covenant may be enforceable if (i) there is privity of estate between them, and (ii) it has reference to the subject-matter (as to which see *post*, p. 844).

" Privity of estate " exists when the persons in connection with whom it is said to exist are " of the same estate " as the original covenantor and covenantee. Thus, privity of estate exists between the lessor and his assigns and the person who for the time being is in possession of the term granted by the lease. If the lessor grants a lease of his reversion, i.e., a second concurrent lease of the same land, this constitutes a partial assignment and creates privity of estate between the second and first lessees (*Birch* v. *Wright* (1786), 1 T.R. 378, 384 ; *Cole* v. *Kelly* [1920] 2 K.B. 106). This is so whether the second lease is for a shorter or a longer period than the first lease. It is the person entitled to the next immediate reversion of the lease at any particular time who then has privity of estate with a lessee. It follows from this that where a lessee under-leases, whilst there is privity between the lessee and the under-lessee, there is no privity between the lessor and the under-lessee, since the former is not entitled to the immediate reversion in point. Consequently an under-lessee is not entitled to the benefit of, and cannot be sued on a positive covenant, as distinguished from a restrictive covenant, in the lease (*South of England Dairies, Ltd.* v. *Baker* [1906] 2 Ch. 631 ; *Westhoughton U.D.C.* v. *Wigan Coal & Iron Co., Ltd.* [1919] 1 Ch. 159). In other words, the under-lessee, not holding the whole estate of the assignee of the whole term, cannot be sued by and cannot sue the lessor in respect of the covenants in the lease. There is no privity of estate between them.

But an assign of the term is liable for breaches of a lessee's covenant by an underlessee, provided that such covenant is absolute and runs with the land (*Mumford* v. *Walker* (1901), 85 L.T. 518 ; *Wilson* v. *Twamley* [1904] 2 K.B. 99) ; but he is not necessarily liable if the covenant is not to suffer, or wilfully suffer, an act to be done (*Wilson* v. *Twamley, ante ; Bryant* v. *Hancock & Co., Ltd.* [1898] 1 Q.B. 716 ; [1899] A.C. 442). See further, *post*, p. 850.

Before 1882 only the legal reversioner or an assign of the legal reversion could enforce the covenants, but under s. 141 (2) of the L.P.A. 1925, such covenants can be " enforced and taken advantage of by the person from time to time entitled, subject to the term, *to the income of the whole or any part*, as the case may require, of the land leased." For instance, a mortgagor in possession will be " a person from time to time entitled " within the words of the subsection, so long as he has not received notice from the mortgagee of his intention to take possession (*Turner* v. *Walsh* [1909] 2 K.B. 484) ; and a mortgagee in possession may sue on the covenants in a lease granted by the mortgagor (*Municipal Permanent Investment Building Society* v. *Smith* (1888), 22 Q.B.D. 70).

It follows from the doctrine of privity of estate that an assign of the term is not liable for breaches of covenant which took place before the assignment to him (*Grescot* v. *Green* (1700), 1 Salk. 199 ; *St Saviour's, Southwark (Churchwardens)* v. *Smith* (1762), 3 Burr. 1271). Equally, liability (except, of course, under express covenant) ceases when the privity of estate ceases ; that is to say, after he has executed an assignment to another person, except for breaches of covenant which happened while he was an assignee (*Onslow* v. *Corrie* (1817), 2 Madd. 330 ; *Paul* v. *Nurse* (1828), 8 B. & C. 486) ; and in respect of such breaches there is an implied contract on the part of each successive assignee to indemnify the original lessee (*Moule* v. *Garrett* (1870), L.R. 5 Ex. 132 ; (1872), L.R. 7 Ex. 101). On the breach of a lessee's

27A

covenant the lessor may sue the lessee on his original contract, that is, by reason of privity of contract (see last note), or the assign who was in possession at the date of the breach by reason of privity of estate. As to covenants for indemnity by assignees, see *post*, p. 856.

Covenants having reference to the subject of the lease.—Covenants are enforceable by virtue of the doctrine of privity of estate (or, in other words, they " run with " the land or the reversion, as the case may be) only if they " *touch and concern* " the land. This was the common expression until the Conveyancing Act, 1881, but in that statute it was altered to " covenants having reference to the subject of the lease," and this latter expression is used in the L.P.A. 1925. Many definitions have been given of the expression " touch and concern " the land. Perhaps the one most often quoted is that of Russell, C.J., in *Horsey Estate, Ltd.* v. *Steiger* [1899] 2 Q.B. 79, 89, namely : " The true principle is that no covenant or condition which affects merely the person, and which does not affect the nature, quality or value of the thing demised or the mode of using or enjoying the thing demised, runs with the land." A very good definition is given in Cheshire's Modern Law of Real Property (see 11th ed., at p. 439), namely : " If a simple test is desired . . . it is suggested that the proper inquiry should be whether the covenant affects either the landlord *qua* landlord or the tenant *qua* tenant. A covenant may very well have reference to the land, but, unless is it reasonably incidental to the relation of landlord and tenant, it cannot be said to touch and concern the land so as to be capable of running therewith or with the reversion " (approved in the Court of Appeal in *Breams Property Investment Co., Ltd.* v. *Stroulger* [1948] 2 K.B. 1, at p. 7).

Covenants which do not " touch and concern the land " are merely personal covenants which bind only the persons entering into the covenants and their estates (*Ricketts* v. *Enfield* (*Churchwardens*) [1909] 1 Ch. 544 ; *Dewar* v. *Goodman* [1909] A.C. 72).

The following covenants have reference to the subject of the lease, or " touch and concern " the land, and therefore run with the land : implied covenants for title (L.P.A. 1925, s. 76 (6)) ; covenants for indemnity implied under s. 77 of the L.P.A. 1925 (*ibid.*, s. 77 (5)) ; a covenant not to assign without consent (*Goldstein* v. *Sanders* [1915] 1 Ch. 549 ; *Re Robert Stephenson & Co., Ltd.* [1913] 2 Ch. 201) ; a covenant to buy all beer from a lessor of a public-house (*Clegg* v. *Hands* (1890), 44 Ch. D. 503 ; *White* v. *Southend Hotel Co.* [1897] 1 Ch. 767 ; *Manchester Brewery Co.* v. *Coombs* [1901] 2 Ch. 608) ; a covenant to cultivate in a particular manner (*Chapman* v. *Smith* [1907] 2 Ch. 97) ; a covenant not to carry on a particular trade ; a covenant to pay a fixed sum to the landlord if that sum is not expended on repairs in any year (*Moss' Empires, Ltd.* v. *Olympia* (*Liverpool*), *Ltd.* [1939] A.C. 544) ; a covenant that a certain person should not be concerned in the business carried on at the demised premises (*Lewin* v. *American and Colonial Distributors, Ltd.* [1945] Ch. 225). Similarly, a term that the landlord will not, for a certain period, serve a notice to quit, constitutes a covenant with reference to the subject-matter which runs with the reversion under the L.P.A. 1925, s. 142, *post*, p. 848 (*Breams Property Investment Co., Ltd.* v. *Stroulger* [1948] 2 K.B. 1 ; *Re Midland Railway Co.'s Agreement* [1971] Ch. 764).

A covenant may touch and concern the land, although the subject-matter of the covenant is not a thing to be done *on* the demised premises, provided that it relates to the mode of their occupation and enjoyment (*Morris* v.

Kennedy [1896] 2 Ir. R. 247), or the support and maintenance of the property demised, as to insure and apply the insurance money in rebuilding the premises (*Vernon* v. *Smith* (1821), 5 B. & Ald. 1). In fact, a covenant not to do something on adjoining land, such as not to build beyond a certain building line, may affect the value of the land demised, and therefore be a covenant which touches and concerns the land demised (*Ricketts* v. *Enfield* (*Churchwardens*) [1909] 1 Ch. 544). An example of a personal covenant is a covenant or condition for forfeiture upon conviction of the tenant or occupier for an offence against the game laws (*Stevens* v. *Copp* (1868), L.R. 4 Ex. 20).

It is now settled that a covenant to renew a lease (unlike an option to purchase the freehold) does touch and concern the land (*per* Romer, L.J., in *Woodall* v. *Clifton* [1905] 2 Ch. 257, at p. 279 ; also *Weg Motors, Ltd.* v. *Hales* [1962] Ch. 49), but this rule is anomalous and will not be extended. Thus, in *Re Hunter's Lease* [1942] Ch. 124, it was agreed that the term might be renewed for a further period, but that in lieu of such renewal either party might insist on payment of £500 by the landlord to the tenant. Uthwatt, J., held that the burden of paying this sum of £500 did not "touch and concern" the thing demised and so did not pass to an assignee of the reversion. As to covenants granting options to purchase, see *ante*, p. 832.

The burden and benefit of covenants under a lease.—The general principles having been indicated, it may be convenient to consider in detail the persons on whom the burden of the covenants in a lease fall and the persons entitled to the benefit of such covenants. This will be done under the following four headings :—

(i) The burden on the persons claiming under the lessee.

(ii) The benefit to the persons claiming under the lessor.

(iii) The burden on the persons claiming under the lessor.

(iv) The benefit to the persons claiming under the lessee.

(i) *The burden on the persons claiming under the lessee.*—The question is whether, if the lessee assigns his interest under the lease to a purchaser, and if the purchaser in his turn assigns to someone else, and so on, the *burden* of observing and performing the covenants entered into by the lessee with the lessor in the lease falls upon the purchaser and subsequent assigns. That is, can the purchaser, or a subsequent assign, be sued on these covenants by the lessor or by his successors in title ? The answer is " Yes," provided that such covenants " touch and concern the land " (as to which, see *ante*, p. 844) and there is privity of estate between the parties (as to which, see *ante*, p. 843). There is one exception where the lease was executed before 1926. This exception is dealt with in *Spencer's Case* (1583), 5 Co. Rep. 16a, where it was laid down that in the case of a covenant by a lessee in connection with something not *in esse* on the land at the date of the lease (for instance, a covenant to build a new wall), such covenant was not binding on assigns *unless the lessee had covenanted in the lease for himself and his assigns to do so.* On the other hand, a covenant to do an act in connection with something already existing on the land, as, for example, a covenant to repair a wall *already built* on the land, was perfectly good and binding on the assigns, although the word " assigns " was not mentioned in the covenant. The point is not likely to occur, as it was the practice before 1926 to mention " assigns " in the covenant.

As regards leases made after 1925, the use of the word " assigns " strictly may be no longer necessary as the L.P.A. 1925, s. 79 (1), provides, in effect, that a covenant relating to any land of a covenantor, or *capable of being bound by him*, will be deemed to be made by the covenantor on behalf of himself and his successors in title and the persons deriving title under him or them, and the subsection is to extend to a covenant to do some act relating to the land, *notwithstanding that the subject-matter may not have been in existence when the covenant was made*. However, s. 79 applies only " unless a contrary intention is expressed ". This has been widely construed to mean : " unless an indication to the contrary is to be found in the instrument, and that such an indication may be sufficiently contained in the wording and context of the instrument, even though the instrument contains no provision expressly excluding successors in title from its operation " (*per* Pennycuick, J., in *Re Royal Victoria Pavilion, Ramsgate* [1961] Ch. 581, at p. 589). Consequently, for practical purposes it may not be entirely safe to rely on s. 79 and certainly this decision seems to suggest that the covenantor should be expressed to covenant, for example, " for himself, his successors and assigns ".

An *equitable* assignee is *not* liable on positive covenants in the lease even if he has entered into possession and paid the rent (*Cox* v. *Bishop* (1857), 8 De G.M. & G. 815), but he may by his conduct hold himself out as the tenant so that he is estopped from denying that he is the tenant and is liable to perform the covenants. Such estoppel arose in *Rodenhurst Estates, Ltd.* v. *Barnes, Ltd.* [1936] 2 All E.R. 3, where the lessor had consented to assignment but no assignment was actually executed in favour of the company which entered into possession and paid the rent ; but mere payment of rent and taking possession do not give rise to an estoppel (*Official Trustee of Charity Lands* v. *Ferriman Trust, Ltd.* [1937] 3 All E.R. 85).

(ii) *The benefit to the persons claiming under the lessor.*—The question in this case is whether the successors in title of the lessor can *enforce* the covenants in the lease entered into by the lessee in favour of the lessor, as against the lessee's assigns. Under the common law the remedy of the lessor was very limited (*Wedd* v. *Porter* [1916] 2 K.B. 91). The common law is remedied now by s. 141 of the L.P.A. 1925 (replacing earlier legislation), as follows :—

" 141.—(1) Rent reserved by a lease, and the benefit of every covenant or provision therein contained, *having reference to the subject-matter thereof*, and on the lessee's part to be observed or performed, and every condition of re-entry and other condition therein contained, shall be annexed and incident to and shall go with the reversionary estate in the land, or in any part thereof, immediately expectant on the term granted by the lease, *notwithstanding severance of that reversionary estate*, and without prejudice to any liability affecting a covenantor or his estate.

(2) Any such rent, covenant or provision shall be capable of being recovered, received, enforced, and taken advantage of, by the person from time to time entitled, subject to the term, to the income of *the whole or any part*, as the case may require, of the land leased.

(3) Where that person becomes entitled by conveyance or otherwise, such rent, covenant or provision may be recovered, received, enforced or taken advantage of by him notwithstanding that he becomes so entitled after the condition of re-entry or forfeiture has become enforceable, but this subsection does not render enforceable any condition of re-entry or other condition waived or released before such person becomes entitled as aforesaid.

(4) This section applies to leases made before or after the commencement of this Act, but does not affect the operation of—

(*a*) any severance of the reversionary estate ; or

(*b*) any acquisition by conveyance or otherwise of the right to receive or enforce any rent covenant or provision ;

effected before the commencement of this Act."

" *having reference to the subject matter thereof.*"—It will be noticed that the benefit of the covenants in favour of the lessor will only run with the land if they have reference to the subject-matter of the lease, or, to use the old expression, " touch or concern the land," as distinguished from being merely personal covenants. See more fully *ante*, p. 844.

" *notwithstanding severance of that reversionary estate.*"—Subsections (1) and (2) are not confined to cases where there had been a severance of the reversion, but apply in all cases, whether the reversion was severed or not ; a mortgagor in possession is " a person from time to time entitled " within the words of the section, so long as he has not received notice from the mortgagee of his intention to take possession, and he can sue a lessee for damages for breach of a covenant contained in a lease of the mortgaged land granted before the mortgage (*Turner* v. *Walsh* [1909] 2 K.B. 484).

Where a mortgagor grants a lease under s. 99 of the L.P.A. 1925 (*ante*, p. 824), as the benefit of the lessee's covenants runs with the reversion, a mortgagee in possession can enforce the covenants (*Municipal Permanent Investment Building Society* v. *Smith* (1888), 22 Q.B.D. 70, and *Re Ind Coope* [1911] 2 Ch. 223, 231–2) ; a legal chargee is in a similar position under s. 87 of the L.P.A. 1925.

The section applies to undertakings contained in a tenancy agreement not under seal or even in a parol lease as the L.P.A. 1925, s. 205 (1) (xxiii) defines the word " lease " to include " or other tenancy " ; s. 154 of the same Act has the same effect. And by s. 54 of the L.P.A. 1925, leases may be created by parol, provided that they take effect in possession for a term not exceeding three years, whether or not the lessee is given power to extend the term ; see *ante*, p. 804.

By virtue of subs. (3) of s. 141, a person entitled to the income can enforce a condition of re-entry or forfeiture for a breach of any covenant or condition contained in a lease, *although that person became entitled after the breach, provided that the condition of re-entry or other condition has not been waived or released before the person became entitled.* It is now clear that an assignment of the reversion " subject to and with the benefit of the lease " does *not* operate as a waiver by the lessor of any previous occasions for forfeiture of the lease for non-payment of rent or other breach of conditions (*London and County, Ltd.* v. *Wilfred Sportsman, Ltd.* [1971] Ch. 964, where the Court of Appeal disapproved *Davenport* v. *Smith* [1921] 2 Ch. 270, which was to the contrary). Russell, L.J., also expressed the view that the additional words " if and so far as subsisting " previously recommended, could not be regarded as necessary to avoid waiver.

On assignment of the reversion the right to sue in respect of breaches of covenant prior to that assignment has been said to be governed by the following propositions :—

(*i*) " If the cause of action accrued exclusively to the assignor during his time . . . then the assignor alone could sue and not the assignee."

(*ii*) " Failure to pay rent during the assignor's time was a breach which caused damage to the assignor exclusively. He alone could sue for it and not the assignee." [As to this proposition, see further below.]

(*iii*) " If there was a breach during the assignor's time which continued to depreciate the property during the assignee's time (as it would do in the case of a failure to repair or reinstate), then the assignee could sue in respect of the whole damage : for then it was annexed to the reversion and not severed from it."

(Lord Denning, M.R., in *Re King* [1963] Ch. 459, at p. 481).

The learned Master of the Rolls rested proposition (*ii*) above on *Flight* v. *Bentley* (1835), 7 Sim. 149, and concluded that s. 141 had not altered the previous law. However, Upjohn, L.J., said that he would not regard *Flight* v. *Bentley* as very satisfactory authority and that s. 141 might well as a matter of construction have altered the previous law, concluding " that I would regard it as open to any court, if satisfied that s. 141 leads to a different result (a matter on which I express no opinion), to say that *Flight* v. *Bentley* (assuming it correctly to interpret the law before 1881) no longer represented the law as to arrears of rent ". The other member of the court, Diplock, L.J., appeared rather to agree with Upjohn, L.J., that the question turned simply on the meaning of s. 141 unassisted by any earlier authority. And now proposition (*ii*) *per* Lord Denning, M.R., and *Flight* v. *Bentley* on which he rested it, have both been disapproved by the Court of Appeal in *London and County, Ltd.* v. *Wilfred Sportsman, Ltd.* [1971] Ch. 964. Accordingly, it now appears clear that an assignee of the reversion is entitled to sue and re-enter for rent in arrear at the date of the assignment even when the right of re-entry has arisen before the assignment. See also *Arlesford Trading Co., Ltd.* v. *Servansingh* [1971] 1 W.L.R. 1080, in which an assignee of the reversion successfully sued the original lessee for arrears of rent notwithstanding an assignment of the lease. However, propositions (*i*) and (*iii*) above still stand ; in *Re King, ante,* the court was unanimous on the main question, the decision that an assignor was unable to sue the tenant after an assignment of the reversion in respect of prior breaches of covenant.

(iii) *The burden on the person claiming under the lessor.*—The law as to when the burden of a lessor's covenants runs with the reversion (that is, when such covenants are binding on the assigns of the lessor) is now contained in s. 142 of the L.P.A. 1925 as supplemented by s. 140 of the same Act, except that when the lease was made before 1882 the position on severance of the reversion before 1926 is governed by s. 2 of 32 Hen. 8, c. 34.

Section 142 of the L.P.A. 1925 is as follows :—

" 142.—(1) The obligation under a condition or of a *covenant* entered into *by a lessor with reference to the subject-matter of the lease* shall, *if and so far as the lessor has power to bind the reversionary estate* immediately expectant on the term granted by the lease, be annexed and incident to and shall go with that reversionary estate, or the several parts thereof, notwithstanding severance of that reversionary estate, and may be taken advantage of and enforced by the person in whom the term is from time to time vested by conveyance, devolution of law, or otherwise ; and, *if and as far as the lessor has power to bind* the person from time to time entitled to *that reversionary estate,* the obligation aforesaid may be taken advantage of and enforced against any person so entitled.

(2) This section applies to leases made before or after the commencement of this Act, whether the severance of the reversionary estate was effected before or after such commencement ;

Provided that, where the lease was made before the first day of January eighteen hundred and eighty-two, nothing in this section shall affect the operation of any severance of the reversionary estate effected before such commencement.

This section takes effect *without prejudice to any liability affecting a covenantor or his estate."*

The section only applies where there is privity of estate between the parties. This means, in practice, that the section does not apply to under-lessees. For an underlessee is not an " assign " of the lessee. An assign of the reversion is only liable at the suit of the lessee or " an assign " of the lessee (*South of England Dairies, Ltd.* v. *Baker* [1906] 2 Ch. 631). See further *ante*, p. 843.

" *covenant.*"—In the law of landlord and tenant this word is not confined to its ordinary meaning of a contract under seal and so s. 142 applies to a contract under hand (*Weg Motors, Ltd.* v. *Hales* [1962] Ch. 49).

" *by a lessor.*"—The covenant need not be contained in the lease provided that it is entered into with reference to the subject matter (*Weg Motors, Ltd.* v. *Hales* [1962] Ch. 49).

" *with reference to the subject-matter of the lease.*"—This is the modern form of the expression " touching and concerning the land " ; as to the meaning of these expressions, see *ante*, p. 844.

" *if and as far as the lessor has power to bind the reversionary estate.*"— This expression refers to cases such as those in which a mortgagor has power to grant leases when in possession, although he holds subject to a mortgage term, or those in which a tenant for life has power to bind the reversion.

" *without prejudice to any liability affecting a covenantor.*"—A lessor remains liable on his express covenants notwithstanding that he may have assigned his reversion (*Stuart* v. *Joy* [1904] 1 K.B. 362).

Section 140 of the L.P.A. 1925, as amended, *post*, p. 898, deals with apportionment of conditions on severance, and should be borne in mind when considering the effect of s. 142. See also s. 79 (1) of the L.P.A. 1925, *ante*, p. 846, which provides that certain covenants are deemed to be made by the covenantor on behalf of himself and his successors in title.

(iv) *The benefit to persons claiming under the lessee.*—Where the lessee assigns his interest under the lease, can the assign and persons claiming under him enforce the covenants in the lease which were entered into by the lessor for the benefit of the lessee ? The answer is that he can, provided that the covenants " touch and concern the land," and there is privity of estate between the parties. As to the meaning of the expression " touch and concern the land," see at p. 844, and as to " privity of estate," see at p. 843. This is a common-law rule contained in the fourth resolution of *Spencer's Case* (1583), 5 Co. Rep. 16*a*, namely, " for the lessee and his assignee hath the yearly profits of the land, which shall grow by his labour and industry, for an annual rent ; and therefore it is reasonable when he hath applied his labour and employed his cost upon the land, and be evicted (whereby he loses all) that he shall take such benefit of the demise and grant as the first lessee might . . ."

As regards leases made before 1926, it was provided by s. 58 (2) of the Conveyancing Act, 1881 (the effect of which is continued by the L.P.A. 1925, s. 78 (2)), that a covenant relating to land not of inheritance was deemed to be made with the covenantee (that is, the lessee), his executors, administrators, and assigns, and had effect as if they were expressed. As regards leases made after 1925, it is provided by s. 78 (1) of the L.P.A. 1925 that a covenant relating to any land of the covenantee (that is, the lessee) will be deemed to be made with the covenantee and his successors in title and the persons deriving title under him or them, and will have effect as if such successors and other persons were expressed. These subsections do not make covenants run with the land, but provide that certain words are to be implied in such covenants in the same way as if they were expressed. (The Court of Appeal in *Smith* v. *River Douglas Catchment Board* [1949] 2 K.B. 500 appear to have decided that s. 78 (1) may make the benefit of a covenant pass to a person who would not at common law have taken that benefit, but the decision gives rise to many difficulties. See the discussion *ante*, p. 547 *et seq.*)

It would seem that the right of the assignee of the lease to sue in respect of breaches of covenant which occurred before the date of the assignment of the lease should be governed by much the same rules as apply to the assignment of the reversion (see *Re King* [1963] Ch. 459, *ante*, p. 848).

When lessee must compel his underlessee to observe covenants.— A covenant by a lessee not to permit or suffer premises to be used for a certain purpose will not bind him to do more than take reasonable steps to secure that the premises shall not be so used and will not make it necessary for him to take legal proceedings against the underlessee or other offending person *where there is a reasonable doubt* whether such legal proceedings would be successful (*Berton* v. *Alliance Economic Investment Co.* [1922] 1 K.B. 742) ; but otherwise where there could be no reasonable doubt that such proceedings would be successful (*Atkin* v. *Rose* [1923] 1 Ch. 522 ; *Barton* v. *Reed* [1932] 1 Ch. 362).

B. VARIOUS COVENANTS

Covenants to use premises as " private dwelling-house," see *ante*, p. 573.

What is a " business " and a " trade " ?, see *ante*, p. 574.

Covenants not to carry on offensive trade, see *ante*, p. 575.

Covenants as to erections, buildings and hoardings, see *ante*, p. 576.

" Usual covenants."—It becomes necessary to determine what are the " usual covenants " in leases from one of two points of view. Firstly, the question is important on the assignment of a lease where, notwithstanding the normal rule that notice of a document is notice of its contents, the vendor of leaseholds is under a duty to disclose any covenants in the lease which are unusually onerous for leases of that sort (*Re White and Smith's Contract* [1896] 1 Ch. 637 ; see also *per* Tomlin, J., in *Melzak* v. *Lilienfeld* [1926] 1 Ch. 480, at pp. 490–492). Secondly, the question is important on the grant of a lease following either an agreement expressly providing for the inclusion in the lease of in effect " the usual covenants and conditions " or an open contract which implies inclusion to the same effect (see *Charalambous* v. *Ktori* (1972), 116 Sol. J. 396, as to there always being room for argument as to what the usual covenants are in such cases).

In *Hampshire* v. *Wickens* (1878), 7 Ch. D. 555, the proposed lease (which was to contain all usual covenants and provisions) contained a covenant not to assign without the consent of the lessor, and it was held by Jessel, M.R., that such a covenant was not a " usual covenant," and the learned judge referred, with approval, to the statement in Davidson's Precedents that the only usual covenants in a lease of a dwelling-house were (1) to pay rent ; (2) to pay taxes, except such as are expressly payable by the landlord ; (3) to keep and deliver up the premises in repair ; and (4) to allow the lessor to enter and view the state of repair. At the same time the learned judge indicated his view that " usual covenants " may vary in different generations, and that the law declares what are usual covenants according to the then knowledge of mankind.

In *Allen* v. *Smith* [1924] 2 Ch. 308, the question was as to whether a covenant that the lessee should pay solicitors' and surveyors' charges in connection with the preparation and service of a notice under s. 14 of the Conveyancing Act, 1881, requiring the lessee to remedy a breach of covenant, was usual. Eve, J., said, at p. 314 : " I am not prepared to say that in the case of property of a nature likely to call for considerable repairs, and held for comparatively short terms, such a clause might not be regarded as a reasonable one to be insisted upon by the lessor, and in such circumstances be regarded as an ordinary one ; but, in my opinion, a very different state of things exists when a new house is being let for a term of 99 years at a moderate ground rent," and the judge held that the covenant was onerous and unusual. See also *Melzak* v. *Lilienfeld* [1926] 1 Ch. 480.

In *Flexman* v. *Corbett* [1930] 1 Ch. 672, Maugham, J., held : (i) that the question whether covenants in a lease are " usual covenants " is in each case a question of fact for the court to decide on the evidence ; (ii) that a covenant to do nothing to the " inconvenience of occupiers of neighbouring premises " is usual only in leases of properties on large estates and in a lease of one house is unusual and onerous ; and (iii) that the proviso for re-entry on breach of any of the covenants in the lease must be held to be an unusual and onerous provision.

In *Sweet and Maxwell, Ltd.* v. *Universal News Services, Ltd.* [1964] 2 Q.B. 699, clause 6 of an agreement for a lease provided for the inclusion of certain terms and concluded with para. (d) : " the lease shall contain such other covenants and conditions as shall be reasonably required by " the lessor. It was subsequently contended that this paragraph made the agreement too vague to be enforceable. This contention was dealt with by Harman, L.J., as follows : " I say at once that I cannot accept that view. It seems to me that if A agrees with B to grant him a lease at such a rent on such and such terms beginning on such a day and no more, that is a specifically enforceable agreement, and a court will insert in it what are called ' usual ' covenants. Those were defined in [*Hampshire* v. *Wickens, ante*], as being very *jejune* covenants indeed. In a later case [*Flexman* v. *Corbett, ante*], Maugham, J., said that what were ' usual covenants ' was a question of fact, and that the court would accept evidence, surveyors' or conveyancers', of the kind of covenants which were usual in leases of the kind of property which was the subject-matter of the agreement. Consequently, if this agreement had been merely an agreement for ' usual covenants ' the court could have completed it in ways that are well recognised. It is not that, of course ; but it gives the lessors further rights. It gives them rights beyond that which the law would give them in the way of usual covenants in reasonably requiring further covenants. The only limit is that the requirement must be reasonable. The court is constantly required to suggest as between *A* and *B* what is or is not reasonable, and in so far as the lessors demand things which are unreasonable the court will say ' You cannot have them ' : in so far as they are reasonable the court will say ' Those are conditions which you may impose and which must be accepted by the lessees and the lessees are contractually bound to accept them '. Therefore, in my judgment, there is nothing in this point that the agreement is not a specifically enforceable agreement." Consequently, draftsmen of agreements for leases should bear in mind the following observations, in the case, of Pearson, L.J.'s : " a formula such as that used in paragraph (*d*) is a convenient and effective means of dealing with the position where the parties agreed on the main points, but had not settled the details and wished to make a binding agreement immediately. By using a formula such as this, introducing the objective test of reasonableness the parties avoid making a mere agreement to agree which would be unenforceable."

Covenants affecting licensed premises.—On the principle stated *ante*, p. 844, if the object of a covenant in favour of a lessor who is a brewer is to benefit him and his successors in their capacity of *brewers* as distinguished from their character as *reversioners*, the covenant would not be considered as touching the land and could not be enforced by an assign of the reversion as such. See *White* v. *Southend Hotel Co.* [1897] 1 Ch. 767 ; *Birmingham Breweries, Ltd.* v. *Jameson* (1898), 78 L.T. 512 ; *Manchester Brewery Co.* v. *Coombs* [1901] 2 Ch. 608.

A covenant not to use premises as a public-house, tavern or beerhouse is not broken by the sale of beer in a grocer's shop by retail under an off-licence to be drunk off the premises (*London & North Western Railway Co.* v. *Garnett* (1869), L.R. 9 Eq. 26 ; *Holt & Co.* v. *Collyer* (1881), 16 Ch. D. 718) ; otherwise, if the word used is " beershop " (*London and Suburban Land & Building Co.* v. *Field* (1881), 16 Ch. D. 645 ; *Nicoll* v. *Fenning* (1881), 19 Ch. D. 258).

In *Holt & Co.* v. *Collyer*, *ante*, Fry, J., refused to admit evidence to show that the word " beerhouse " was understood in the trade in a technical sense, on the ground that there was nothing to show that the expression had not been used in its primary and popular sense. In *London and Suburban Land & Building Co.* v. *Field*, *ante*, Brett, L.J., said, at pp. 647, 648 : " Here two words are used which have a technical meaning, namely, ' public-house ' and ' tavern,' and if the third word had been ' beerhouse ' there again would have been a word which has acquired a technical meaning. But the word ' beershop ' has not acquired any such technical meaning, and I have no doubt that it means a shop where beer is sold. It includes a beerhouse, but it also includes a place where beer is sold, but which is not a beerhouse."

A lease contained a covenant that the demised premises should not be used for the trades of an alehouse keeper, beerhouse keeper, tavern keeper or licensed victualler, and it was held that the use of the premises as a restaurant, with a " restaurant licence " permitting the sale of beer and wines with food, was not a breach of the covenant (*Lorden* v. *Brooke-Hitching* [1927] 2 K.B. 237). The words " alehouse keeper . . . tavern keeper, licensed victualler," are to be read in their ordinary popular meaning, and " licensed victualler " accordingly means " publican " (*ibid.*). A grocer with an off-licence is not a publican (*Re Cullen and Riall's Contract* [1904] 1 Ir. R. 206).

" Not to use the premises as a public-house or beershop " will not prevent
the premises being used as an hotel, liquors being supplied only to the visitors
(*Duke of Devonshire* v. *Simmons* (1894), 11 T.L.R. 52). " Not to use premises
for the sale of spirituous liquors " is broken by a grocer selling wine or spirits
in bottles (*Feilden* v. *Slater* (1869), L.R. 7 Eq. 523) ; but see *Jones* v. *Bone*
(1870), L.R. 9 Eq. 674, deciding that a grocer with an off-licence was not
a seller by retail of wine and spirits. Although both decisions were by the
same judge (James, V.-C.), probably the later one would not now be followed.
" Not to permit the premises to be used for a public-house, inn, tavern, or
beershop, or otherwise for the sale of wine, malt liquor, or spirituous liquors "
is not broken by using the premises as a working men's club and supplying
beer to members (*Ranken* v. *Hunt* (1894), 38 Sol. J. 290).

The word " shop " does not include " a tavern " (*Coombs* v. *Cook* (1883),
Cab. & El. 75) ; or a public-house (*Hall* v. *Box* (1870), 18 W.R. 820).

Covenants in connection with outgoings.—The word " assessments "
and the word " charges," used by themselves, refer to payments of yearly
recurrence and not to expenses of permanent works (*Allum* v. *Dickinson*
(1882), 9 Q.B.D. 632 ; *George* v. *Coates* (1903), 88 L.T. 48 ; *Home and Colonial
Stores* v. *Todd* (1891), 63 L.T. 829 ; *Baylis* v. *Jiggens* [1898] 2 Q.B. 315 ;
Lyon v. *Greenhow* (1892), 8 T.L.R. 457 ; *Lumby* v. *Faupel* (1904), 90 L.T.
140), but the context may give them a much wider meaning. For instance,
" charged or assessed upon the premises or upon any person in respect
thereof " would give them the same meaning as " outgoings," a word of the
widest meaning (*Hartley* v. *Hudson* (1879), 4 C.P.D. 367).

Any of the words " duties," " outgoings," " impositions " or " burdens "
would cover the cost of road charges imposed under statutory authority
(*Wix* v. *Rutson* [1899] 1 Q.B. 474) ; or the cost of complying with an order
to abate a nuisance under the Public Health Act, 1936 (*Clayton* v. *Smith*
(1895), 11 T.L.R. 374). Indeed, it may be said, generally, that any of these
words will cover the cost of expenses incurred for making roads, drainage
and other matters which a local authority may require doing, although it
may incur considerable capital expense. The theory is that the parties, by
using words which have come to have a well-known meaning, must be taken
to have intended that they should have that meaning when they used the
words (*Brett* v. *Rogers* [1897] 1 Q.B. 525 ; *Farlow* v. *Stevenson* [1900] 1 Ch.
128 ; *Batchelor* v. *Bigger* (1889), 60 L.T. 416 ; *Stockdale* v. *Ascherberg* [1904]
1 K.B. 447 ; *Weld* v. *Clayton-le-Moors U.D.C.* (1902), 86 L.T. 584 ; *Greaves*
v. *Whitmarsh, Watson & Co., Ltd.* [1906] 2 K.B. 340 ; *Foulger* v. *Arding*
[1902] 1 K.B. 700 ; *Re Warriner* [1903] 2 Ch. 367 ; *Eastwood* v. *McNab*
[1914] 2 K.B. 361 ; *Lowther* v. *Clifford* [1926] 1 K.B. 185 ; [1927] 1 K.B. 130).

A covenant by the tenant to pay all rates, taxes and outgoings makes him
liable to discharge an owner's drainage rate (*Smith* v. *Smith* [1939]
4 All E.R. 312). Indeed, the word " outgoings " alone would appear to
cover any expense at all in respect of the premises since it has often been
judicially described as " the largest word which can be used " and " of the
largest possible signification " (see *Tubbs* v. *Wynne* [1897] 1 Q.B. 74 ; *Budd*
v. *Marshall* (1880), 50 L.J.Q.B. 24).

In *Lowther* v. *Clifford, ante,* McCardie, J. (whose judgment was affirmed
by the Court of Appeal), said ([1926] 1 K.B., at p. 188) : " The first question
which I have to decide is whether the words ' assessments, impositions and
outgoings ' as used in the covenant in the lease are sufficient to cover the
payment here claimed [a sum of £188 assessed upon land for the making up of

a road]. The word 'assessments' would be inadequate if taken by itself, because it imports a payment regularly repeated rather than one which is independent and casual. The meaning of 'outgoings' has been considered in many decisions, and the term has been held to apply in cases where it has been necessary to lay drains under the Public Health Act, to meet paving expenses, to reconstruct drains, and to meet expenses under the Private Street Works Act, 1892. I have no doubt that the words 'outgoings to be imposed on the tenant' include the burden here created. As regards the word 'impositions' it appears from the decisions that the meaning to be given is as wide as that given to 'outgoings': *Foulger* v. *Arding* [*ante*]; *Re Warriner* [*ante*]; and *George* v. *Coates* [*ante*]. It is true that in documents of this kind regard must be had to the context in order to see whether it cuts down the *prima facie* meaning of the words in question. But there is nothing in the context here which would cut down the meaning of the covenant."

Until the decision in *Lowther* v. *Clifford, ante*, there was considerable doubt as to whether the use of wide and comprehensive words in a tenancy agreement was inconsistent *with a short tenancy*, such as an annual tenancy. The decision of the court has, for the present, settled the question against the tenant. Sargant, L.J., said ([1927] 1 K.B., at p. 149) : "And however wide and sweeping the words of such a covenant may be, they are not, in my view, inconsistent with an annual tenancy." This judgment can be supported on the ground that when a tenant agrees to do something he must do it. But to say that an agreement in a yearly tenancy to make a road is not inconsistent with such a tenancy seems unreasonable. No tenant would sign such an agreement if he knew the effect of what he was signing. The fact is that printed agreements are sold, and filled up, and signed between the parties, with the object of saving expense, without their having the slightest idea of what the technical words contained in them really mean.

Covenant to insure.—If a covenant requires the lessee to insure with a company specified, or some other office approved by the lessor, the lessor has an absolute right to withhold approval without giving a reason (*Tredegar (Viscount)* v. *Harwood* [1929] A.C. 72).

The decision in *Halifax Building Society* v. *Keighley* [1931] 2 K.B. 248 is mentioned in the chapter on Mortgages (*post*, p. 979). It is thought that similar difficulties may arise if a lessee takes out a policy in addition to a joint policy in the names of lessor and lessee. So it is advisable to provide in a lease that the lessee shall apply any money he may receive on any policy, other than one taken out pursuant to the lease, in making good the loss or damage.

In considering whether covenants for insurance are necessary it should be borne in mind that a tenant who is under an unqualified covenant to repair must rebuild if the premises are destroyed by fire. If the tenant is required to take out a valid policy for an adequate sum it seems that the landlord could require the insurance company to lay out the insurance money in reinstating the premises under the Fires Prevention (Metropolis) Act, 1774, s. 83, but there are doubts about the application of this Act. Where the landlord is under obligation to insure and the tenant is required to pay the premiums as additional rent the insurance is for the benefit of both and so, if required by the tenant, the landlord must apply any insurance money received towards reinstatement (*Mumford Hotels, Ltd.* v. *Wheler* [1964] Ch. 117). It seems that this obligation does not arise where the landlord does not require the tenant to pay premiums ; in any event an express provision as to application of insurance money is advisable. As reinstatement is often impossible on account of planning or other restrictions it is often advisable, at least when dealing with valuable property, to provide for application of insurance money which cannot be so used. Compare *Re King* [1963] Ch. 459.

Statutory modification of covenant restricting improvements.—If a lease contains a covenant, condition or agreement against the making of improvements *without licence or consent*, it will be deemed to be subject to a proviso that such licence or consent is not to be unreasonably withheld ; but—

(i) this will not preclude the right of the landlord to require as a condition of such licence or consent the payment for damage to or diminution in the value of the premises or any neighbouring premises belonging to him and of any legal or other expenses properly incurred in connection with such licence or consent ; and

(ii) in the case of an improvement which does not add to the letting value of the holding, it will not preclude his right to require as a condition of such licence or consent, where such requirement would be reasonable, an undertaking by the tenant to reinstate the premises in the condition in which they were before the improvement was executed (Landlord and Tenant Act, 1927, s. 19 (2)).

The subsection does not apply to leases of agricultural holdings, or to mining leases (*ibid.*, s. 19 (2), (4)), but does apply to the common form of covenant against making alterations if the alteration proposed is, in fact, an improvement (*Lilley & Skinner, Ltd.* v. *Crump* (1929), 73 Sol. J. 366 ; *F. W. Woolworth & Co., Ltd.* v. *Lambert* [1937] Ch. 37 ; *Tideway Investment and Property Holdings, Ltd.* v. *Wellwood* [1952] W.N. 226 (affirmed [1952] Ch. 791)).

It will be noted that s. 19 (2) has no application if the covenant is *absolute* (that is, where the covenant does not mention licence or consent).

The Landlord and Tenant Act, 1927, s. 3 (4), permits tenants of holdings to which Pt. I of that Act applies (see at p. 934) to carry out certain improvements, " anything in any lease of the premises to the contrary notwithstanding." This provision applies where the tenant has served notice of his intention to make an improvement (*ibid.*, s. 3 (1)), and either the landlord has not served notice of objection or the tribunal has certified the improvement to be a proper one.

What is an " improvement " within the meaning of s. 19 (2), and when is consent withheld unreasonably, are two questions which arose in the cases of *F. W. Woolworth & Co., Ltd.* v. *Lambert* [1936] Ch. 415 ; on appeal [1937] Ch. 37 ; and *Lambert* v. *F. W. Woolworth & Co., Ltd.* (*No. 2*) [1937] 3 All E.R. 195, 334 ; on appeal [1938] Ch. 883. Premises were leased to Messrs. Woolworths subject to a covenant that no structural alterations would be made without the consent in writing of the landlords. The tenants wished to make such alterations in order to extend the shop over adjoining land, but the landlords would consent only on payment of £7,000. In the first action (*F. W. Woolworth & Co., Ltd.* v. *Lambert*) the Court of Appeal decided that the burden of proof that consent was unreasonably withheld was on the tenants, and in the absence of sufficient evidence as to the reasonableness or otherwise of the sum demanded they had failed to discharge this burden. Before the second action (*Lambert* v. *F. W.*

Woolworth & Co., Ltd. (No. 2)), Messrs. Woolworths offered an undertaking to reinstate the premises at the end of the lease, with security for the performance of such undertaking, and to pay all costs and expenses. On consent then being refused without reason given, the Court of Appeal held that the question whether an alteration is an improvement must be considered from the point of view of the tenant and that the alterations proposed were improvements, and also that if a landlord refuses consent without giving reasons the burden of proof will be on him that his refusal is reasonable. See also *Balls Brothers, Ltd.* v. *Sinclair* [1931] 2 Ch. 325.

If consent is unreasonably refused the lessee may proceed with the improvement. He may, however, prefer first to apply for a declaration that the refusal was unreasonable either in the High Court or in the county court whatever the net value for rating of the demised property is to be taken to be for the purposes of the County Courts Act, 1959 (Landlord and Tenant Act, 1954, s. 53 (1) as amended by County Courts Act, 1959, Sched. 2).

An undertaking (not under seal) to make a payment in the nature of a fine in return for consent cannot be enforced even if consent has been expressly granted, although, apparently, a sum paid could not be recovered (*Comber* v. *Fleet Electrics, Ltd.* [1955] 1 W.L.R. 566).

If works are reasonably necessary in order to enable a building to be used without contravention of the Clean Air Acts, 1956 and 1968, but they cannot be carried out without the consent of the owner or some other person interested by reason of a restriction affecting the interest of the occupier, the county court may, by order, enable the works to be carried out by the occupier, and if it thinks fit, order the whole or part of the cost to be met by the owner or other person (1956 Act, s. 28 ; 1968 Act, Sched. 1, para. 1). A similar provision is made by s. 73 (2) of the Offices, Shops and Railway Premises Act, 1963.

Statutory modification of covenant against alteration of user without consent.—Such covenants, as respects alterations not involving structural alteration of premises, are deemed subject to a proviso that no fine or sum of money in the nature of a fine, whether by increase of rent or otherwise, shall be payable for such consent, but the landlord is not precluded from requiring payment of a reasonable sum in respect of damage to or diminution in the value of the premises or neighbouring premises belonging to him, and legal or other expenses (Landlord and Tenant Act, 1927, s. 19 (3)). Once more it will be noted that if the covenant is absolute, that is, if it is a plain covenant against alteration in user not itself providing for grant of consent, the subsection has no application. In such cases it may, however, be possible, if the landlord will not waive the enforcement of the covenant, to proceed to obtain its discharge or modification under the L.P.A. 1925, s. 84, *ante,* p. 579. This subsection, also, does not apply to leases of agricultural holdings or to mining leases (Act of 1927, s. 19 (4)).

C. COVENANTS FOR INDEMNITY

Implied covenant by assignee.—It is provided by s. 77 (1) (*c*) of the L.P.A. 1925 that, in addition to the covenants for title dealt with in s. 76 of the L.P.A. 1925 (*ante,* p. 466 *et seq.*), there shall be deemed to be included and implied in a conveyance *for valuable consideration* made since 1925, other than a mortgage, *of the entirety of the land comprised in a lease, for the residue of the term* or interest created by the lease, a covenant by the assignee or joint and several covenants by the assignees (if more than one) with the conveying

parties and with each of them (if more than one) in the terms set out in
Pt. IX of Sched. 2 to the Act. These terms are that the assignees, or the
persons deriving title under them (i) will duly pay all rent becoming due
under the lease, and observe and perform all the covenants, agreements
and conditions therein contained and thenceforth on the part of the lessees
to be observed and performed, and (ii) will save harmless and keep indemnified
the conveying parties and their estates and effects, from and against all
proceedings, costs, claims and expenses on account of any omission to pay
the said rent or any breach of any of the said covenants, agreements and
conditions.

A purchaser was always impliedly bound to indemnify his vendor, but
his liability was limited to the time during which he remained assignee and
ceased on his assigning the property, except as regards breaches occurring
during the time he was in possession (*Crouch* v. *Tregonning* (1872), L.R.
7 Ex. 88, 93 ; *Moule* v. *Garrett* (1872), L.R. 7 Ex. 101). The express
covenant, which it was the practice to insert in assignments before 1926,
extended to the whole period of the remainder of the lease. The above
implied covenant, it will be noticed, also extends over the whole period of
the remainder of the lease. Therefore, a vendor can safely accept the implied
covenant, provided, as is usual, the assignment is for value.

A vendor will not be entitled to the benefit of the above wide covenant
of indemnity unless he, the vendor, is the original lessee or is under the
obligation of a similar covenant (*Moule* v. *Garrett, ante ; Bonner* v. *Tottenham
and Edmonton Permanent Investment Building Society* [1899] 1 Q.B. 161).
Therefore, where the vendor claims under a voluntary assignment (e.g., a
settlement), the purchaser from him would be entitled to insert a clause in
his assignment limiting the effect of the above indemnity to that which he
would have been bound to give if the assignment had been made before 1926.
Where a vendor holds in a fiduciary capacity it is advisable to provide that
the covenant implied by s. 77 (1) (c) shall extend for the protection of the
trust estate.

The view was formerly taken that the implied covenant of indemnity
should be construed as if it were prefaced with the words " with the object
and intent of affording the vendor and all persons claiming under him a
full and sufficient indemnity, but not further or otherwise " (*Harris* v. *Boots
Cash Chemists* (*Southern*), *Ltd.* [1904] 2 Ch. 376 ; *Reckitt* v. *Cody* [1920]
2 Ch. 452). If that is so, no liability arises on the implied covenant until
the lessor has made a claim. Nevertheless it was decided in *Ayling* v. *Wade*
[1961] 2 Q.B. 228, that a covenant by a sub-lessor " to pay the rent reserved
by and to observe the covenants contained in the lease . . . and to keep
the tenant indemnified " was not solely one of indemnity but also imposed
a separate obligation and so rendered the sub-lessor liable to the sub-lessee
for failing to repair in accordance with a covenant in the lease. This decision
casts doubt on the proposition that the implied covenant is one of indemnity
only ; see *Law Quarterly Review*, vol. 77, pp. 316, 317, 318. An *express*
covenant by the assignee of a lease to pay rent and observe covenants which
does not refer to indemnity is an absolute covenant and will not be construed
to be by way only of indemnity of the assignor (*Butler Estates, Ltd.* v. *Bean*
[1942] 1 K.B. 1).

A personal representative or trustee is able, by satisfying all claims up
to date, and setting aside a fund to provide for future ascertained claims,
to assign leasehold property to a purchaser and be free from any personal
liability (T.A., 1925, s. 26, as amended by the Law of Property (Amendment)

858 LEASES AND TENANCIES

Act, 1926). Personal representatives are entitled to make it a condition of assenting that security shall be given against liabilities affecting the estate.

Implied covenants in assignment of part of the property.—Where the rent has been *legally apportioned* in respect of any land, that is, apportioned with the consent of the lessor, the covenant mentioned in the last note will be implied in the assignment of that land in like manner as if the apportioned rent were the original rent reserved, and the lease related solely to that land (L.P.A. 1925, s. 77 (1) (c)). On the severance of the reversion, the rent becomes apportioned (*Mitchell* v. *Mosley* [1914] 1 Ch. 438 ; L.P.A. 1925, s. 141, *ante*, p. 846).

It is provided by the L.P.A. 1925, s. 77 (1) (d) and Sched. 2, Pt. X, para. (i), in effect, that where the *rent has been apportioned without the consent of the lessor*, a covenant will be implied *by the assignee* (not including a mortgagee) with the conveying parties that the assignee, or the persons deriving title under him, will pay the apportioned rent and observe and perform all the covenants, other than the covenant to pay the entire rent, agreements and conditions contained in the lease, and thenceforth on the part of the lessees to be observed and performed, so far as the same relate to the land conveyed ; and also will keep indemnified the conveying parties and their respective estates and effects from and against all proceedings, costs, claims and expenses on account of any omission to pay the said apportioned rent or any breach of any of the said covenants, agreements and conditions so far as the same relate as aforesaid.

Similarly, it is provided by the L.P.A. 1925, s. 77 (1) (d) and Sched. 2, Pt. X, para. (ii), in effect, that in such a case, that is, where the rent has been apportioned *without* the consent of the lessor, a covenant will be implied by a *person who conveys or is expressed to convey as " beneficial owner,"* if at the date of the conveyance any part of the land comprised in the lease is retained with the assignee that the conveying parties, or the persons deriving title under them, will pay the balance of the rent (after deducting the apportioned rent aforesaid and any other rents similarly apportioned in respect of land not retained) and observe and perform all the covenants, other than the covenant to pay the entire rent, agreements and conditions contained in the lease and on the part of the lessees to be observed and performed so far as the same relate to the land demised (other than the land comprised in the conveyance) and remaining vested in the covenantors ; and also will keep indemnified the assignee and his estate and effects from and against all proceedings, costs, claims and expenses on account of any omission to pay the aforesaid balance of the rent or any breach of any of the said covenants, agreements and conditions so far as they relate as aforesaid.

It should be particularly noticed that the covenants referred to in s. 77 (1) (d) *by the conveying party* will not be implied unless he conveys or is expressed to convey as " beneficial owner " ; but that the covenants by the *assignee* will be implied without the use of any technical expression.

The benefit of these covenants, when so implied, will run with the land, and it will not be necessary, therefore, on an assignment of the property, to include an assignment of the benefit of the covenants (L.P.A. 1925, s. 77 (5)). But the burden of such a covenant does not pass to the successors in title of the person giving the implied covenant ; the covenant being a positive one, the burden does not pass (*Austerberry* v. *Oldham Corporation* (1885), 29 Ch. D. 750). The successor in title of a person in whose favour one of these implied covenants operates who pays the whole of the rent under threat of distress may, however, on equitable principles, sue a successor in title of the implied covenantor for the appropriate proportion of the rent (*Whitham* v. *Bullock* [1939] 2 K.B. 81).

Any covenant which would be implied under s. 77 by reason of a person conveying as beneficial owner may, *but only by express reference* to the section, be implied in a conveyance, whether or not for valuable consideration, by a person who conveys as trustee, mortgagee, etc. (L.P.A. 1925, s. 77 (4)). Power is given to such a person to sell subject to an apportioned rent by s. 190 (5) of the L.P.A. 1925.

Power to charge implied covenants on the land.—It is provided by s. 77 (7) of the L.P.A. 1925, as regards conveyances made after 1925, that any covenant implied under the section *may be extended* by providing that the land conveyed, or the part of the land demised which remains vested in the covenantor, shall, as the case may require, stand charged with the payment of all money which may become payable under the implied covenant. As a covenant may not in all cases be effectual, it will be wise to include in the assignment to the purchaser a charge on the property retained and on the property assigned, to the effect mentioned in the section. A form will be found in Hallett's Conveyancing Precedents, p. 322.

It is not necessary to register such a charge under the L.C.A. 1972 : see s. 2 (4), Class C (iii) (c), thereof excluding " *a charge given by way of indemnity against rents equitably apportioned* or charged exclusively on land in exoneration of other land, and against the breach or non-observance of covenants or conditions."

Power to distrain.—Subsections (3) to (8) of s. 190 of the L.P.A. 1925 (applicable to assignments after 1925) confer on the person who is entitled to the benefit of the covenants implied by s. 77, who pays any rent which ought to have been paid by the person liable to pay it under such implied covenants, or who has to make other payments or incur costs through such person's default, a right to enter and distrain on the land of the defaulting person or to take possession of the income produced thereby until the claim is paid or satisfied.

When, before 1882, a legal apportionment of the rent and covenants could not by the terms of the contract have been asked for, it was customary for the parties to enter into mutual covenants for payment of the informally apportioned rent and to observe and perform the covenants of the lease so far as they affected the particular portion as apportioned, and to give cross-powers of entry and distress by way of indemnity, but after the passing of the Bills of Sale Act (1878) Amendment Act, 1882, it was thought that the power of distress would be void thereunder as an unregistered bill of sale, and the practice of taking cross-powers of distress was, to a great extent, discontinued.

It was also doubtful whether the power to distrain was within the rule against perpetuities. Both these points have now been cleared up. For it is provided by s. 189 (1) of the L.P.A. 1925 that such a power of distress given by way of indemnity against a rent or against the breach of a covenant or condition is not *and shall not be deemed ever to have been* a bill of sale. It is also provided by s. 162 of the L.P.A. 1925 that *for the purpose of removing doubts* the rule of law relating to perpetuities does not apply and *will be deemed never to have applied* to any power to distrain on or to take possession of land given by way of indemnity against a rent. See also s. 190 (8) of the L.P.A. 1925, *post*, p. 860.

Section 190 (3) is as follows :—

" 190.—(3) Where in a conveyance [made after 1925 : subs. (7)] for valuable consideration, other than a mortgage, of part of land comprised in a lease, for the residue of the term or interest created by the lease, the rent reserved by such lease or a part thereof is, *without the consent of the lessor, expressed to be—*

    (a) charged exclusively on the land *conveyed* or any part thereof in exoneration of the land retained by the assignor or other land ; or

    (b) charged exclusively on the land *retained* by the assignor or any part thereof in exoneration of the land conveyed or other land ; or

    (c) *apportioned* between the land conveyed or any part thereof and the land retained by the assignor or any part thereof ;

then, without prejudice to the rights of the lessor [and to anything in such conveyance to the contrary : s. 190 (6)], such charge or *apportionment* shall be binding as between the assignor and the assignee under the conveyance and their respective successors in title."

In case of default, the lessee for the time being of any other land comprised in the lease, in whom, as respects that land, the residue of the term or interest created by the lease is vested, who—

    (i) pays or is required to pay the whole or part of the rent which ought to have been paid by the defaulter ; or

    (ii) incurs any costs, damages or expenses by reason of the breach of covenant or condition ;

may (subject to anything in the conveyance to the contrary : L.P.A. 1925, s. 190 (6)), enter into and distrain on the land comprised in the lease in respect of which the default or breach is made or occurs, or any part of that land, and may take possession of the income of the same land until (so long as the term or interest created by the lease is subsisting) by means of such distress and receipt of income or otherwise, the whole or part of the rent (charged or apportioned as aforesaid) so unpaid and all costs, damages and expenses incurred by reason of the non-payment thereof or of the breach of the said covenants and conditions, are fully paid or satisfied (L.P.A. 1925, s. 190 (4)).

A trustee, personal representative, mortgagee, or other person in a fiduciary position has, and will be deemed always to have had, power to confer the same or like remedies as those conferred by the section (*ibid.*, s. 190 (5)).

The rule of law relating to perpetuities is not to affect the powers or remedies conferred by this section or any like powers or remedies expressly conferred by an instrument (*ibid.*, s. 190 (8)).

D. COVENANTS AGAINST ASSIGNMENT, ETC.

General note.—The consent of a lessor to an assignment, or to a sub-letting or a parting with the possession of the property, extends only to the permission actually given (L.P.A. 1925, s. 143 (1)).   And where the consent is granted to any one of two or more lessees, such licence is not to operate to extinguish the right of entry in the case of a breach by the co-lessees of the other shares or interests in the property (*ibid.*, s. 143 (3)).   The subsection does not, of course, authorise the grant of a licence to create an undivided share in a legal estate (*ibid.*). So an actual waiver by a lessor of one particular breach of covenant will only apply to that particular breach and will not operate as a general waiver (L.P.A. 1925, s. 148 (1)). It was held in *Muspratt* v. *Johnston* [1963] 2 Q.B. 383 by the Court of Appeal that if there has been a breach of a covenant against sub-letting and the breach has subsequently been waived by the lessor, the waiver only operates so as to render the sub-letting lawful as from the date of the waiver ; it does not relate back so as to make the sub-letting lawful *ab initio*.

A licence to assign need not be under seal and the lessor may not require a covenant by the assignee to perform the covenants of the lease (Opinion of the Council of The Law Society ; *Law Society's Digest*, vol. 1, Fourth Supplement, No. 306 (*a*)). A licence should be signed by the lessor, not his solicitor, but it need not be a formal document (*ibid.*, No. 160 (*b*)).

Statutory modification.—Under s. 19 (1) of the Landlord and Tenant Act, 1927, covenants against assigning, underletting, charging or parting with the possession of demised premises, or any part thereof, *without licence or consent*, are subject to certain statutory provisos. The exact words of the subsection are given below. It will be noticed that the subsection in terms only applies where there is in the lease a covenant against assigning, etc., *without consent* ; it has been assumed, therefore, that if the covenant is an *absolute covenant* against assigning, etc., the subsection will not apply. However, as to the application of s. 19 (1) to an absolute covenant against assigning, it is to be noted that Danckwerts, L.J., in *Property & Bloodstock, Ltd.* v. *Emerton* [1968] Ch. 94, concluded his judgment by observing : " Finally, I wish to reserve my opinion on the point whether the provisions of s. 19 (1) of the Landlord and Tenant Act, 1927, have no application to a covenant in simple terms against assignment, or assignment without the landlord's consent, of the property comprised in the lease. I am by no means convinced that that is so." See a note in *Law Quarterly Review*, vol. 84, p. 14.

It will also be noticed that subs. (1) (*a*) of s. 19 applies to leases for any length of term, whereas subs. (1) (*b*) applies only to certain leases *for more than forty years*.

" 19.—(1) In all leases whether made before or after the commencement of this Act containing a covenant, condition or agreement against assigning, under-letting, charging or parting with the possession of demised premises or any part thereof without licence or consent, such covenant, condition or agreement shall, notwithstanding any express provision to the contrary, be deemed to be subject—

(a) to a proviso to the effect that such licence or consent is not to be unreasonably withheld, but this proviso does not preclude the right of the landlord to require payment of a reasonable sum in respect of any legal or other expenses incurred in connection with such licence or consent ; and

(b) (if the lease is for more than forty years, and is made in consideration wholly or partially of the erection or the substantial improvement, addition or alteration of buildings, and the lessor is not a Government department or local or public authority, or a statutory or public utility company) to a proviso to the effect that in the case of any assignment, under-letting, charging or parting with the possession (whether by the holders of the lease or any under-tenant whether immediate or not) effected more than seven years before the end of the term *no consent or licence shall be required, if notice in writing* of the transaction *is given to* the lessor within six months after the transaction is effected.

* * * * *

(4) This section shall not apply to leases of agricultural holdings within the meaning of the [Agricultural Holdings Act, 1948, s. 1; see *ibid.*, s. 96 (2)], and paragraph (*b*) of subsection (1) . . . shall not apply to mining leases."

Paragraph (*a*) refers to "legal or other expenses," but no reference is made to legal expenses in para. (*b*). The question consequently arises whether, when notice is given in lieu of obtaining the lessor's consent, the lessor's solicitor can insist on the payment of a fee. It is thought that no fee can be asked for, provided that the notice is delivered or sent to the solicitor by registered post, *and no acknowledgment is asked for*. But, in the case of a building lease, the practice has been not only to provide for notice being given to the lessor, but for a fee to be paid, the object being to keep the lessor's register up to date.

A slight variation in the form of a covenant will take it out of s. 19 (1). In *Moat* v. *Martin* [1950] 1 K.B. 175, the covenant not to assign, etc., without consent was followed by the words "such consent will not be withheld in the case of a respectable and responsible person". The Court of Appeal decided that s. 19 (1) had no application as the landlord had precluded himself from withholding consent if the assignee was respectable and responsible ; the reasonableness of the refusal to consent did not arise. The parties cannot curtail the operation of s. 19 (1) by stipulating the circumstances in which the lessor's refusal should not be deemed unreasonable (*Re Smith's Lease* [1951] 1 All E.R. 346).

Adler v. *Upper Grosvenor Street Investment, Ltd.* [1957] 1 W.L.R. 227 indicates how the operation of s. 19 (1) may be curtailed. The lease contained a covenant against assignment without consent, such consent (subject to the proviso) not to be unreasonably withheld to an assignment to a responsible person. The proviso was to the effect that if the tenant should desire to assign or underlet he should first offer to surrender the lease. The landlords refused permission to assign on the ground that the tenant had not offered to surrender the lease. It was decided that the proviso to the covenant did not prevent the operation of the proviso incorporated into the lease by s. 19 (1) (*a*) of the 1927 Act as it did not purport to restrict the operation of that section. Hilbery, J., considered that the proviso in the lease dealt with a step prior to the question of consent to assignment, and so it did not negative s. 19 (1). This reasoning is criticised in the *Solicitors' Journal*, vol. 101, pp. 164, 165. See also *Cardshops, Ltd.* v. *Davies* [1971] 1 W.L.R. 591, C.A., noted *post*, p. 910.

Dispositions within a covenant against assigning, etc.—Such a covenant will not be broken by an alienation caused by operation of law ; e.g., by adjudication in bankruptcy of the lessee, even if on the lessee's own petition (*Re Riggs ; ex parte Lovell* [1901] 2 K.B. 16).

Where a tenant covenanted for himself and his successors in title not to assign, etc., without consent, and later became bankrupt, it was held that, although the lease vested in him by operation of law, the trustee was a successor in title and so was bound by the terms of the lease (*Re Wright* [1949] Ch. 729). In cases of this sort the lease may, and usually does, contain a power of re-entry in case the lessee is adjudicated bankrupt, or a receiving order is made against him, and this right could be exercised against the trustee in bankruptcy and against any assign from him. The lessor, however, would first have to give notice under s. 146 (1) of the L.P.A. 1925 and the trustee could apply for relief against forfeiture under the rules discussed *post*, p. 885.

The covenant is not broken by a judgment or order whereby the property becomes vested in a liquidator (*Re Birkbeck Permanent Benefit Building Society* [1913] 2 Ch. 34) ; or by the passing by a limited company of a resolution for voluntary winding up whereby the reconstructed company obtains possession of the property (*Horsey Estate, Ltd.* v. *Steiger* [1899] 2 Q.B. 79). It would be a breach for the liquidator of a lessee company which is being wound up, either voluntarily (*Cohen* v. *Popular Restaurants, Ltd.* [1917] 1 K.B. 480) or compulsorily (*Re Farrow's Bank, Ltd.* [1921] 2 Ch. 164), to assign without consent. An assignment on a compulsory sale to a company under the Lands Clauses Consolidation Act, 1845, was held not to require the lessor's consent, though the lease contained a covenant not to assign without such consent (*Baily* v. *De Crespigny* (1869), 38 L.J.Q.B. 98).

It is thought that where a mortgagee acquires a title by adverse possession under the Limitation Act, 1939, or obtains a foreclosure order absolute, notwithstanding that the vesting document or order operates as a conveyance under s. 9 of the L.P.A. 1925, no licence to assign is required.

Any vesting effected under the powers conferred by the S.L.A. 1925 in relation to settled land does not operate as a breach of a covenant or condition against alienation or give rise to a forfeiture (S.L.A. 1925, s. 14 (1)).

The better opinion is that a covenant not to assign or underlet without the lessor's consent is not breached by a bequest by will without consent (*Doe d. Goodbehere* v. *Bevan* (1815), 3 M. & S. 353), nor by the lease vesting in the lessee's personal representatives. Since 1925, wills operate only in equity and an equitable assignment does not breach the covenant (see *post*, p. 865), whilst personal representatives merely step into the shoes of the deceased lessee. However, it is arguable that any assent in favour of a beneficiary in respect of the lease by the personal representatives would come within the covenant on the ground that, since 1925, assents operate to pass the legal estate (A.E.A. 1925, s. 36 (2), (4)). This view is indicated in Megarry and Wade's Real Property, 3rd ed., p. 702, and is supported by the decision in *Re Wright* [1949] Ch. 729, where it was held that the trustee in bankruptcy for the lessee was a successor in title within such a covenant although the lease vested in him by operation of law, and as such was bound by the terms of the covenant. The question was fully argued by D. G. Barnsley in the *Conveyancer N.S.*, vol. 27, p. 159 *et seq.*, who also drew attention to the point that if the covenant extends also to parting with possession of the demised premises it will be breached in any case when the beneficiary takes possession. Consequently, it would appear clearly advisable for personal representatives to seek the lessor's consent before assenting in respect of a lease containing such a covenant.

On the appointment of new trustees, under which land vests in them by implication of law under s. 40 of the T.A. 1925, it must not be forgotten that subs. (4) provides that the section does not extend to land held under a lease (which includes an underlease and an agreement for a lease) which contains any covenant, condition or agreement against assigning or disposing of the land without licence or consent, unless prior to the execution of the deed containing expressly or impliedly the vesting declaration, the requisite licence or consent has been obtained, or unless, by virtue of any statute or rule of law, the vesting declaration, express or implied, would not operate as a breach of covenant or give rise to a forfeiture. This subsection now has to be read with s. 19 (1) of the Landlord and Tenant Act, 1927, set out *ante*, pp. 861, 862.

It was decided before 1926 that a covenant against assigning or underletting was broken by an assignment or sub-demise by way of mortgage (*Serjeant* v. *Nash, Field & Co.* [1903] 2 K.B. 304). Where, after 1926, a licence to sub-demise by way of mortgage is required, such licence is not to be unreasonably refused (L.P.A. 1925, s. 86 (1)) ; and where, after 1926, a mortgagee has exercised his power of sale, and in the ordinary way a licence to assign to the purchaser is required, the lessor must not unreasonably refuse to grant such licence (L.P.A. 1925, s. 89 (1)).

In the case of a charge by way of legal mortgage the mortgagee gets no term of years vested in him, and therefore the document does not come within the ordinary covenant unless, of course, the word " charge " is used in such covenant. See *post*, p. 972 as to the nature of such a charge. A covenant not to assign is not broken by the execution of an equitable mortgage (*Doe d. Pitt* v. *Laming* (1822), 27 R.R. 512).

Before 1926 the Council of The Law Society expressed the opinion that, as a statutory receipt endorsed on a building society mortgage operated as an assignment, it came within a covenant requiring all assignments and underleases to be registered. It is provided by s. 115 (1) of the L.P.A. 1925 that a receipt given on payment off of any mortgage of a legal estate will operate under the circumstances therein mentioned as a surrender, reconveyance or transfer. But, except where the mortgage is paid off by personal representatives or trustees or by a tenant for life or other person having only a limited interest (in which case the payment off operates as a transfer) *the mere payment of the money automatically causes the term to become a satisfied term and to cease* (L.P.A. 1925, s. 116). As, therefore, at the date of the signature of a statutory receipt there is no term in existence, the document cannot possibly operate as an assignment of something which is not in existence. Some covenants anticipate the point and contain the words " or by operation of law."

It is provided by s. 61 of the L.P.A. 1925 that " person " includes a corporation, when used in deeds executed after 1925. But before that date it had been held that a limited company might be " a responsible and respectable *person* " (*Willmott* v. *London Road Car Co., Ltd.* [1910] 2 Ch. 525).

An assignment by one of two joint tenants to the other is a breach of a covenant not to underlet or assign (*Corporation of Bristol* v. *Westcott* (1879), 12 Ch. D. 461) ; so also is an assignment from one partner to another (*Langton* v. *Henson* (1905), 92 L.T. 805 ; compare *Gian Singh & Co.* v. *Nahar* [1965] 1 W.L.R. 412 (P.C.), where a partnership deed between a tenant and others was not clear enough to constitute an assignment breaching such a covenant). Letting the premises from year to year is a breach of a covenant not to underlease (*Timms* v. *Baker* (1883), 49 L.T. 106 ; *Dymock* v. *Showell's Brewery Co., Ltd.* (1898), 79 L.T. 329).

A covenant not to underlet or part with the possession of the premises will not prevent the tenant from underletting or parting with a part of the premises (*Grove* v. *Portal* [1902] 1 Ch. 727 ; *Wilson* v. *Rosenthal* (1906),

22 T.L.R. 233 ; *Cottell* v. *Baker* [1920] W.N. 46 ; *Russell* v. *Beecham* [1924] 1 K.B. 525). In *Chatterton* v. *Terrell* [1923] A.C. 578, it was held that a covenant by a lessee not to sub-let, assign or part with possession of the premises without the lessor's consent was broken by a tenant who, after sub-letting part of the premises with consent, subsequently sub-let the remainder without consent, on the ground that the sub-letting of the final portion constituted a sub-letting of the whole premises without consent. In *Cook* v. *Shoesmith* [1951] 1 K.B. 752 a covenant " not to sub-let " was construed as meaning " not to sub-let *the premises* " and so was held not to prohibit a sub-lease of part ; this decision was followed in *Esdaile* v. *Lewis* [1956] 1 W.L.R. 709, where the words were " No sub-letting allowed without . . . written consent." Compare the results of a covenant not to use premises otherwise than as a dwelling-house, mentioned *post*, p. 897.

A covenant not to sub-let or part with the possession of the premises without the licence of the lessor on every occasion first had and obtained is not broken if the lessee, having sub-let with the consent of the lessor, afterwards consents to an assignment of the sub-lease by his lessee (*Mackusick* v. *Carmichael* [1917] 2 K.B. 581).

A lessee who is under a covenant not to assign or part with the possession without licence does not commit a breach of the covenant by permitting others to use the demised premises where he himself retains possession (*Peebles* v. *Crosthwaite* (1897), 13 T.L.R. 198 ; *Edwardes* v. *Barrington* (1901), 85 L.T. 650). And a covenant " not to part with the possession " is not broken by sharing the premises with another or others (*Jackson* v. *Simons* [1923] 1 Ch. 373). In *Chaplin* v. *Smith* [1926] 1 K.B. 198, a lessee assigned his business to a company, of which he was the managing director, and in which he held the bulk of the shares. He had the only key of the premises. A second company was afterwards formed, of which he was also the managing director, and it was stipulated upon the transfer that he was to remain in possession as actual tenant all the time. It was held that there was, on the part of the defendant, no parting with the possession of the premises within the meaning of the covenant not to " assign or underlet or part with the possession or otherwise dispose of the premises or any part thereof." See also *Gian Singh & Co.* v. *Nahar* [1965] 1 W.L.R. 412 (P.C.).

In *Stening* v. *Abrahams* [1931] 1 Ch. 470, Farwell, J., said that the meaning of " parting with possession " was a question of fact and of construction of the particular agreement in each case, and could not be determined by merely looking at the document. A lessee could not be said to part with possession unless his agreement with a licensee completely ousted him from the premises. The fact that the agreement was in the form of a licence was immaterial as it might well give the licensees so exclusive a right as to amount to parting with possession.

It has been decided that an assignment for the benefit of creditors, excepting leaseholds, containing a declaration that the assignor would stand possessed of such leaseholds for the trustee and would assign them to his nominee, was not a breach of a covenant not to assign without licence, as there was no dealing with the legal estate (*Gentle* v. *Faulkner* [1900] 2 Q.B. 267). The principle decided in this case is rather important, as it indicates a loophole by which a lessee can escape from his covenant unless the covenant is carefully drawn. See *Pincott* v. *Moorston's, Ltd.* [1937] 1 All E.R. 513, where a contract which provided that in the event of refusal by the lessor of consent to an assignment the vendors would procure a declaration of trust of the premises, or otherwise deal with them as the purchaser should

28

direct, was held to be valid. Another way by which a lessee might get out of his covenant would be to allow the person to whom he wished to give the benefit of the lease power to enter and use the premises as his (the lessee's) agent. See *Rainham Chemical Works Ltd.* v. *Belvedere Fish Guano Co.* [1921] 2 A.C. 465.

When refusal of consent to assignment is unreasonable.—This question arises when the covenant against assignment, etc., without consent is subject to a proviso that consent shall not be unreasonably withheld or when a similar proviso is implied by reason of the Landlord and Tenant Act, 1927, s. 19 (1), *ante*, p. 861.

It is not open to the parties to oust the discretion of the court under s. 19 (1) by inserting in the lease an express stipulation as to what shall be deemed reasonable (*Re Smith's Lease* [1951] 1 All E.R. 346). However, the landlord may validly insert into the lease a term to the effect that, before applying for consent, the lessee shall offer to surrender the lease to the lessor. This would impose a condition precedent to the coming into operation of the covenant not to assign without consent, so that unless the lessee has first offered to surrender the lease and the lessor has refused the offer, the covenant against assigning without consent and the expressed or implied proviso against unreasonably withholding consent never come into operation (*Adler* v. *Upper Grosvenor Street Investments, Ltd.* [1957] 1 W.L.R. 227). Again the covenant may be so worded that upon its proper construction no consent is required ; for example, " consent will not be withheld in the case of a respectable and responsible person " ; when once it is established that the proposed assignee fulfills these conditions, no question of reasonableness arises (*Moat* v. *Martin* [1950] 1 K.B. 175).

The principal place of reference in determining whether a lessor has withheld his consent to an assignment unreasonably is the judgments at first instance and in the Court of Appeal in *Houlder Bros and Co., Ltd.* v. *Gibbs* [1925] Ch. 198 and 575. Tomlin, J., said at p. 209 : " . . . It is by reference to the personality of the lessee or the nature of the user or occupation of the premises, that the court has to judge the reasonableness of the lessor's refusal." Also Sargant, L.J., said at p. 587 : " I was very much impressed by [counsel's] argument that in a case of this kind the reason must be something affecting the subject matter of the contract which forms the relationship between the landlord and the tenant and that it must not be something extraneous and completely disassociated from the subject matter of the contract." In the case it was held unreasonable to refuse consent because the proposed assignee would, if the assignment were permitted, probably terminate the tenancy of other premises held by him of the lessor, and for which the lessor might have great difficulty in finding another tenant.

The above comparatively narrow approach to what is reasonable has had some doubt cast upon it in the House of Lords. In *Viscount Tredegar* v. *Harwood* [1929] A.C. 72, Lord Dunedin said at p. 78 : " . . . I would like to say, that although it is unnecessary to consider whether that case was well decided, I am not inclined to adhere to the pronouncement, that reasonableness was only to be referred to something which touched both parties to the lease. I should read reasonableness in the general sense . . .". He indicated that he would have held that it was reasonable for a lessor to refuse to consent to the lessee insuring with other than a named office because of the administrative convenience of having one office to deal with all the business affecting the lessor's many lessees. Lord Phillimore shared the doubt (at p. 81) and Lord Shaw said (*ibid.*) that " it would be wrong to confine the reasons in such case to the particular house exclusive of all considerations as to the management of the estate to which it belonged." Notwithstanding these doubts, which were clearly expressed *obiter*, the approach in *Houlder Bros. & Co.* v. *Gibbs, ante*, has since been generally followed and treated by the Court of Appeal as binding upon it (see *Lee* v. *K. Carter, Ltd.* [1949] 1 K.B. 85, at p. 96, where it was held reasonable to refuse consent to an assignment shortly before the expiry of the lease from the lessee's company to an individual in whose favour a statutory tenancy would have arisen, so preventing the lessor from obtaining possession at the end of the lease ; see also *Swanson* v. *Forton* [1949] Ch. 143, at p. 149 ; contrast *Re Swanson's Agreement* [1946] 2 All E.R. 628 where a statutory tenancy would have arisen in favour of the assignor in any case). The most recent case in which the same approach was adopted by the Court of Appeal is *Pimms, Ltd.* v. *Tallow Chandlers in the City of London* [1964] 2 Q.B. 547. There the lessors withheld their consent to an assignment to a development company of the short remaining period of a lease of restaurant premises in an area due for comprehensive re-development on the ground that the object of the assignees was to share the profits which would be made out of re-development by using the nuisance value of the remainder of the term of the lease to force the lessors into letting them into the re-development scheme, so increasing its cost and reducing its profit to the lessors. Danckwerts, L.J., giving the judgment of the court, said : " these are matters which clearly relate to the personality of the proposed assignees, and affect the property which is the subject matter of the lease and the relations between the landlords and the tenants in respect of the lease and the property demised thereby. The landlords' apprehensions cannot be said to be unreasonable, and their refusal to consent to the assignment was justified " (*ibid.*, pp. 572–573).

Further examples by way of illustration may assist. Thus if the intended use of the premises by the proposed assignee would constitute a breach of a covenant in the lease the lessor will not be acting unreasonably in refusing consent, even if the breach would not be very serious, e.g., a lessor need not accept a commercial concern in premises for which the covenanted use is as offices for professional people (*Wilson* v. *Fynn* [1948] 2 All E.R. 40) ; *contra*, however, if a breach of covenant is not a necessary consequence of the proposed assignment (*Killick* v. *Second Covent Garden Property Co., Ltd.* [1973] 2 All E.R. 337). Again it is not unreasonable to refuse consent to an under-letting at a substantial premium and a low rent, since this might depreciate the value of the property and prejudice future negotiations for its sale or mortgage (*Re Town Investments Under-Lease* [1954] Ch. 301). However, it is not reasonable for the lessor to refuse his consent except on condition that the assignee agrees to terms as to personal residence or other terms not included in the lease and inconsistent with its provisions (*Mills* v. *Cannon Brewery Company* [1920] 2 Ch. 38). Equally it is unreasonable for the lessor to require a proposed under-lessee to enter into a direct covenant with him for payment of the rent reserved in the lease (*Balfour* v. *Kensington Garden Mansions* (1932), 49 T.L.R. 29). A lessor has been held unreasonable in objecting to an assignment to a diplomat because of the possibility of his claiming diplomatic immunity in the future, since the diplomat was *prima facie* a responsible person whose government would not allow him not to fulfil his obligations (*Parker* v. *Boggon* [1947] K.B. 346). In *Re Greater London Properties, Ltd., Lease* [1959] 1 W.L.R. 503, a lessor refused consent to an assignment to a company which was the wholly owned subsidiary of a large and well-known combine and whose liabilities included a large sum payable to the holding company on demand ; this was held unreasonable because as a practical matter the holding company would not, by demanding payment of the large sum, wreck the proposed assignee company, whose position as a subsidiary company in the combine was a source of strength rather than of weakness. Finally, it should be noted that the unreasonable withholding of consent by superior landlords does not make it reasonable for sub-lessors to withhold their consent (*Vienit, Ltd.* v. *W. Williams & Son (Bread Street), Ltd.* [1958] 1 W.L.R. 1267).

Effect of unreasonable refusal of consent to assignment.—If consent is refused by a lessor, the burden of proof is upon the lessee to satisfy the court that the refusal was unreasonable (see *Pimms, Ltd.* v. *Tallow Chandlers in the City of London* [1964] 2 Q.B. 547, at p. 564, and cases there cited). Further, it is not necessary for the lessors to prove that the conclusions which led them to refuse consent were justified, if they were conclusions which might have been reached by a reasonable man in the circumstances (*ibid.*). However, if the lessor gives no reason for refusing consent then the court is very ready to find that the refusal was unreasonable (see *Frederick Berry, Ltd.* v. *The Royal Bank of Scotland* [1949] 1 K.B. 619, *per* Goddard, L.C.J.). The lessor should put forward all his reasons for refusing consent as soon as possible because reasons put forward on his behalf for the first time in court may well be disregarded ; thus in *Lovelock* v. *Margo* [1963] 2 Q.B. 786, at p. 790, Lord Denning, M.R., said : " It seems to me that, when the tenant produced an assignee, a responsible person with good references to which no objection could be taken, the landlord had no good ground for objecting. She put forward a bad ground and she has not shown any other before the court, and, in those circumstances, the judge was perfectly justified in holding that consent had been unreasonably withheld and making a declaration accordingly."

Where a covenant in the lease requires consent to any assignment, the lessee must always ask the lessor for consent, notwithstanding that it may appear to be a mere formality because any refusal would be unreasonable (see *Barrow* v. *Isaacs & Son* [1891] 1 Q.B. 417). Assignment without asking consent would be a breach of covenant (*ibid. ; Eastern Telegraph Company* v. *Dent* [1899] 1 Q.B. 835). The lessor is entitled to have sufficient time to take up references and to consider whether or not to give his consent (*Lewis and Allanby, Ltd.* v. *Pegge* [1914] 1 Ch. 782 ; *Wilson* v. *Fynn* [1948] 2 All E.R. 40, at p. 43). Then if the lessor refuses consent unreasonably or delays unreasonably, the lessee may proceed with the assignment without consent (see *E. D. Lambert* v. *F. W. Woolworth & Co., Ltd.* [1938] Ch. 883, at p. 893). Nonetheless, the simplest course, where the lessor refuses his consent, is for the lessee to issue an originating summons to determine whether the refusal was unreasonable or not (see *Young* v. *Ashley Gardens Properties, Ltd.* [1903] 2 Ch. 112) or apply in the county court (whatever the net annual value for rating of the demised property) for a declaration (Landlord and Tenant Act, 1954, s. 53, as amended by County Courts Act, 1959, Sched. 2, para. 3). Also it is open to the assignee to apply for a declaration that the consent has been unreasonably withheld without joining the assignors of the lease as parties ; see *Theodorou* v. *Bloom* [1964] 1 W.L.R. 1152, where Ungoed-Thomas, J., said " if this lease were properly assigned without consent then the assignee is and has, ever since the assignment, been the lessee. Where there is a dispute between him and the landlord as to that title, he is entitled to have that dispute resolved and, if he is right, that title put beyond a doubt by a declaration in his favour."

The whole question of a lessor's refusal to consent to an assignment or sub-lease, and all the authorities, was very fully considered by Alec Samuels in the *Conveyancer N.S.*, vol. 28, p. 357.

What documents must be produced to the lessor.—It is frequently stipulated in leases that all assignments, underleases, probates or other instruments evidencing a devolution of the term shall be registered with the lessor or his solicitors. In *Portman* v. *J. Lyons & Co., Ltd.* [1937] Ch. 584, the covenant referred to " every assignment or underlease [except for short terms] of the demised premises or any part thereof." The lessees sub-let the premises and the sub-lessee further sub-let a part. It was held that the covenant required the lessees to produce the sub-lease of the part although they would not in the ordinary course of events possess that document.

No fine must be asked as a condition of giving consent.—The lessor must not require payment of a fine as a condition of giving his consent, *unless* the lease contains an express provision to the contrary. For s. 144 of the L.P.A. 1925 provides that in all leases containing a covenant, condition, or agreement against assigning, underletting, or parting with the possession, or disposing of the land or property leased *without licence or consent*, such covenant, condition, or agreement, unless the lease contains an express provision to the contrary, will be deemed to be subject to a proviso to the effect that no fine or sum of money in the nature of a fine shall be payable for or in respect of such licence or consent ; but this proviso will not preclude the right to require the payment of a reasonable sum in respect of any legal or other expense incurred in relation to such licence or consent. The section applies to all leases whenever executed (*West* v. *Gwynne* [1911] 2 Ch. 1). It will be noted that the section does not apply if the covenant against assigning, etc., is *absolute* (that is, it does not mention the granting of a licence or consent).

It would appear that it is not *illegal* for the lessor to demand a sum of money as a condition for giving leave to assign, and if a lessee has paid such a sum without protest, he cannot recover it (*Comber* v. *Fleet Electrics, Ltd.* [1955] 1 W.L.R. 566). Therefore there is no reason why the parties should not agree between themselves that a sum of money be paid (*Andrew* v. *Bridgman* [1908] 1 K.B. 596). Nevertheless, if the lessor refuses to give his consent unless such sum is paid, the lessee may disregard the covenant and assign without such consent (*Waite* v. *Jennings* [1906] 2 K.B. 11 ; *Andrew* v. *Bridgman, ante ; West* v. *Gwynne, ante*), and an undertaking (not under seal) to pay such a sum is not enforceable (*Comber* v. *Fleet Electrics, Ltd., ante*).

A requirement that a sum of money shall be deposited to secure the execution of certain agreed improvements as a condition of the giving of the licence is not within this section (*Re Cosh's Contract* [1897] 1 Ch. 9). But the lessor must not require the lessee to pay an increased rent as a condition of giving his consent, as this would clearly be only another mode of requiring the payment of a fine (*Jenkins* v. *Price* [1907] 2 Ch. 229). So, in *Gardner & Co.* v. *Cone* [1928] Ch. 955, it was held that where a landlord who was also a brewer made it a condition of giving his consent that for the remainder of the term the house should be a tied house, such stipulation was " a fine " or benefit " in the nature of a ' fine ' " within the meaning of the above section. The breach of covenant took place before the Landlord and Tenant Act, 1927, and therefore that Act did not apply.

Covenants to reside on premises.—A covenant against assignment often includes a covenant that the tenant shall reside personally on the premises, for instance, on a farm. The burden of such a covenant runs with the land and so a trustee under the tenant's will is bound by it (*Lloyd's Bank, Ltd.* v. *Jones* [1955] 2 Q.B. 298). It appears that " suspension of personal occupation for a reasonable time consequent on the death of the tenant would not amount to a breach of the covenant " (*ibid., per* Jenkins, L.J.).

E.　COVENANTS FOR QUIET ENJOYMENT

In a lease—or an agreement for a lease (*Robinson* v. *Kilvert* (1889), 41 Ch. D. 88)—a covenant or undertaking on the part of the landlord that the tenant (i) is entitled to be put into possession of the premises, and (ii) may remain quietly in possession thereof throughout the term, will be implied from the mere relationship of landlord and tenant (*Budd-Scott* v. *Daniell* [1902] 2 K.B. 351 ; *Jones* v. *Lavington* [1903] 1 K.B. 253 ; *Miller* v. *Emcer Products, Ltd.* [1956] Ch. 304) ; but only for such part of the term as the landlord's interest continues (*Baynes & Co.* v. *Lloyd & Sons* [1895] 2 Q.B. 610 ; *Jones* v. *Lavington, ante*). In several old cases it was said that the words " demise," " let," or similar words have the effect of extending such implied undertaking so as to make it a covenant for title, that is, so as to make the landlord responsible for the acts of all persons having a legal right to interfere with the tenant's possession. But in *Baynes* v. *Lloyd, ante*, the chief of these cases was discussed and Kay, L.J., doubted whether such an unlimited covenant was implied. See also *Markham* v. *Paget* [1908] 1 Ch. 697.

If there is an express covenant for quiet enjoyment it supersedes any implied covenant (*Mills* v. *United Counties Bank, Ltd.* [1912] 1 Ch. 231 ; *Miller* v. *Emcer Products, Ltd., ante*). The lessor's usual express qualified covenant for quiet enjoyment gives no remedy, even against the lessor personally, for an eviction by title paramount to that of the lessor's own predecessors in title (*Line* v. *Stephenson* (1838), 5 Bing. (N.C.) 183 ; *Williams* v. *Gabriel* [1906] 1 K.B. 155). So also the ordinary qualified covenant for quiet enjoyment in an *underlease* is no protection in case the superior lessor takes possession, as he is not a person claiming " by, through, or under " the underlessor (*Stanley* v. *Hayes* (1842), 3 Q.B. 105 ; approved and followed in *Kelly* v. *Rogers* [1892] 1 Q.B. 910 ; *Cohen* v. *Tannar* [1900] 2 Q.B. 609). Thus there is no breach if the tenant is evicted from part of the premises as a result of demolition by the local authority under their statutory powers to deal with dangerous structures (*Popular Catering Association, Ltd.* v. *Romagnoli* [1937] 1 All E.R. 167).

Generally, what will constitute a breach of a covenant for quiet enjoyment was laid down by the Court of Appeal in *Sanderson* v. *Berwick-upon-Tweed Corporation* (1884), 13 Q.B.D. 547, at p. 551, as follows : " But it appears to us to be in every case a question of fact whether the quiet enjoyment of the land has or has not been interrupted ; and where the ordinary and lawful enjoyment of the demised land is substantially interfered with by the acts of the lessor, or those lawfully claiming under him, the covenant appears to us to be broken, although neither the title to the land nor the possession of the land may be otherwise affected." The covenant may be broken by an act of *omission*, if it be the omission of some duty (*Anderson* v. *Oppenheimer* (1880), 5 Q.B.D. 602 ; *Harrison, Ainslie & Co.* v. *Muncaster* [1891] 2 Q.B. 680 ; *Cohen* v. *Tannar* [1900] 2 Q.B. 609 ; *Anderson* v. *Cleland* [1910] 2 Ir. R. 334 ; *Booth* v. *Thomas* [1926] 1 Ch. 397). In *Booth* v. *Thomas* the quiet enjoyment was interfered with by the bursting of a culvert over a brook on the adjoining land of the lessor which could have been prevented if the lessor had done the necessary repairs when they should have been done, it being his duty to do them. It was held that this *omission* was in the same category as the *commission* of an act in respect of the breach of the covenant for quiet enjoyment.

It was said in *Browne* v. *Flower* [1911] 1 Ch. 219 that to constitute a breach of a covenant for quiet enjoyment there must be some physical and substantial interference with the complainant's occupation of the premises, and that mere interference with the comfort of persons using the demised premises by the creation of a personal annoyance, such as might arise from noise, invasion of privacy, or otherwise, is not enough. But in *Matania* v. *National Provincial Bank, Ltd.* [1936] 2 All E.R. 633, it was held that there was a breach of the covenant where the floor of a flat was interfered with during structural alterations to another flat, with the result that unusual noise and dust had been admitted. See also *Jones* v. *Consolidated Anthracite Collieries, Ltd., and Lord Dynevor* [1916] 1 K.B. 123, *Lavender* v. *Betts* [1942] 2 All E.R. 72, and *Owen* v. *Gadd* [1956] 2 Q.B. 99, where it was held that erection of scaffold poles close to a shop window may be a breach.

F. COVENANTS TO REPAIR

Position in absence of covenant.—In the absence of express provision as to repairs the obligation to repair imposed on the tenant is ill-defined. It was stated in *Wedd* v. *Porter* [1916] 2 K.B. 91 that the obligation of a tenant from year to year is to keep the premises wind and water tight and to make fair and tenantable repairs and that the tenant is not liable to do substantial repairs, nor answerable for mere wear and tear. Nevertheless, in *Warren* v. *Keen* [1954] 1 Q.B. 15, it was doubted whether there is any greater obligation on a yearly tenant than to use the premises in a tenantlike manner, that is to avoid or repair wilful or negligent damage and to do minor acts necessary to keep the premises in a reasonable state, such as cleaning chimneys and mending fuses. It was decided in this case that a weekly tenant, and presumably a monthly or quarterly tenant, has no greater liability and is not liable for deterioration due to fair wear and tear or failure to paint.

Apart from express covenant or statutory provision (see below), under a lease " the landlords would clearly be under no liability to repair any part of the demised premises whether the required repairs were structural or internal and whether they had or had not noted the repair " (*per* Bankes, L.J., in *Cockburn* v. *Smith* [1924] 2 K.B. 119, at p. 128). Thus in *Sleafer* v. *Lambeth Metropolitan Borough Council* [1959] 3 All E.R. 378 the Court of Appeal held there to be no duty of repair on the landlords notwithstanding that the written agreement for a weekly tenancy both prohibited the tenant from doing repairs and gave the landlord a right of entry to do repairs, which in practice they exercised. Equally, apart from express covenant or statutory provision, the landlord will have no right to enter on the demised premises to do repairs even though non-repair may cause a forfeiture of his own lease (*Stocker* v. *Planet Building Society* (1879), 27 W.R. 877).

Notwithstanding any stipulations to the contrary, there is implied in certain contracts for letting houses for human habitation a condition that the house is at the commencement of the tenancy, and an undertaking that the house will be kept by the landlord during the tenancy, fit for human habitation (Housing Act, 1957, s. 6). This provision applies to :—

(i) a contract made before 31st July, 1923, for letting a house at a rent not exceeding £40 in the administrative county of London, or £26 in a borough or urban district which then had a population of 50,000 or upwards or £16 elsewhere ;

(ii) a contract made on or after 31st July, 1923, and before 6th July, 1957, for letting a house at a rent not exceeding £40 in the administrative county of London, or £26 elsewhere ;

(iii) a contract made on or after 6th July, 1957, for letting a house at a rent not exceeding £80 in the administrative county of London, or £52 elsewhere (Housing Act, 1957, s. 6).

The condition and undertaking are not implied, however, when a house is let for a term of not less than three years on terms that the lessee will put it in a condition reasonably fit for habitation (*ibid.*, s. 6 (2), proviso). Whether a house is fit for habitation must be determined by taking account of the matters specified in s. 4 (1), as extended by the Housing Act, 1969, s. 71.

The Court of Appeal has decided that the implied duties of a landlord referred to above only arise where the house is capable of being made fit for human habitation at reasonable expense (*Buswell* v. *Goodwin* [1971] 1 W.L.R. 92).

Further, a statutory obligation to repair a dwelling-house is imposed by the Housing Act, 1961, on a lessor who grants a lease (including a periodic tenancy) after 24th October, 1961, for a term of less than seven years. There is implied by s. 32 (1) a covenant by the lessor :—

" (*a*) to keep in repair the structure and exterior of the dwelling-house (including drains, gutters and external pipes) ; and

(*b*) to keep in repair and proper working order the installations in the dwelling-house—

(i) for the supply of water, gas and electricity, and for sanitation (including basins, sinks, baths and sanitary conveniences but not, except as aforesaid, fixtures, fittings and appliances for making use of the supply of water, gas or electricty), and

(ii) for space heating or heating water."

Any covenant by the lessee for repair is of no effect so far as it relates to these matters (*ibid.*, s. 31 (1)). The implied covenant does not require the lessor (i) to carry out works or repairs for which the lessee is liable by virtue of his duty to use the premises in a tenant-like manner ; (ii) to reinstate after fire, tempest, flood or other inevitable accident ; (iii) to maintain anything the lessee is entitled to remove (*ibid.*, s. 32 (2)). In determining the standard of repair regard must be had to the age, character and prospective life of the dwelling-house and to the locality (*ibid.*).

For this purpose " lease " includes an underlease, an agreement for a lease or underlease, and any other tenancy and " dwelling-house " means a building or part of a building let wholly or mainly as a private dwelling (*ibid.*, s. 32 (5)). A lease is treated as a lease for a term of less than seven years if it is determinable at the option of the lessor before the expiration of seven years from the commencement of the term, and, except where it is so determinable, is *not* so treated if it confers on the lessee an option for renewal for a term which, together with the original term, amounts to seven years or more (*ibid.*, s. 33 (2)). Section 32 does not apply to certain leases granted to persons who previously held tenancies, for example, if the new lease falls within the Landlord and Tenant Act, 1954, Pt. II (*post*, p. 898 *et seq.*) nor to a tenancy of an agricultural holding (*ibid.*, s. 33 (3), (4)).

The county court may, with the consent of the parties, authorise the exclusion or modification of these repairing obligations if, having regard to the other terms and to all the circumstances, it is reasonable to do so ; otherwise the statutory obligation may not be excluded or limited (*ibid.*, s. 33 (6), (7)).

Access path and steps have been treated as an integral part of a dwelling-house and so within this statutorily implied covenant for repair (*Brown* v. *Liverpool Corporation* [1969] 3 All E.R. 1345, C.A.).

A lessor's obligation to start carrying out repairs to premises occupied by his lessee, by virtue of the covenant implied by s. 32 of the 1961 Act, does not arise until he has information about defects such as would put a reasonable man on enquiry as to whether works of repair were needed (*O'Brien* v. *Robinson* [1973] 1 All E.R. 583, H.L.). This is so even where the lessee was unable to bring the defect to the attention of the lessor because it was latent (*ibid.*). The position is not settled where the lessor has received information about defects otherwise than from notice from the lessee. See also *Sheldon* v. *West Bromwich Corporation* (1973), 117 Sol. J. 486, C.A. (corroded water tank, but absence of weeping).

It should also be borne in mind that where a lessor has an obligation or right to repair the demised premises, he will be under a tortious duty of care in respect of defects in the premises owed to anyone who might reasonably be expected to be affected (see s. 4 of the Defective Premises Act, 1972). In consequence, the suggestion has been made that a provision in a lease reserving to the lessor a right to repair may no longer be worth inserting (see *Conveyancer N.S.*, vol. 37, pp. 1–2).

Construction of covenants to repair.—Covenants to repair are construed with due regard to the age and general condition of the premises at the commencement of the tenancy (*Gutteridge* v. *Munyard* (1834), 7 C. & P. 129 ; *Henman* v. *Berliner* [1918] 2 K.B. 236 ; *Pembery* v. *Lamdin* [1940] 2 All E.R. 434). So a tenant is not liable under such a covenant to restore old premises and bring them into an up-to-date condition (*Lurcott* v. *Wakely and Wheeler* [1911] 1 K.B. 905), or to undertake fundamental reconstruction works rendered necessary by an inherent defect in the premises (*Sotheby* v. *Grundy* [1947] 2 All E.R. 761). Nevertheless, in general a covenant to repair implies an obligation to put the premises into repair (*Proudfoot* v. *Hart* (1890), 25 Q.B.D. 42). It is often said that " repair " involves the restoration of subsidiary parts of the whole, and is to be distinguished from " renewal," which involves reconstruction of substantially the whole of the premises (*Lurcott* v. *Wakely and Wheeler, ante*). Thus in *Collins* v. *Flynn* [1963] 2 All E.R. 1068, it was necessary to construe a lessee's covenant " well and substantially to repair, amend, renew, uphold, support, maintain," etc., premises ; and at the end or sooner determination of the said term " to surrender and yield up the premises being so well and substantially repaired, amended, renewed," etc. After a full review of the relevant cases, the word " renew " was construed as adding nothing to the obligation imposed

28A

by a covenant to repair only, since " every repair does involve a degree of renewal (except, perhaps, tightening a loose screw, as counsel for the tenant suggested) . . . and I feel that I can give a separate meaning to the word ' renew ' only by holding that it includes re-building the whole property demised ; and I think that if this were intended, much stronger and specific words would have to be used ". But it was also found that the word " repair " was " apt to cover the renewal of a part of the premises, and, therefore, so far as the words of the covenant are concerned I regard the obligations of the defendant lessee as being similar to that in the cases cited where only the word ' repair ' is used ". The case in fact concerned subsidence due to defective foundations and the actual decision was that the re-building to remove an inherent defect was not part of the lessee's obligations as this would be " manifestly a most important improvement, which, if executed by the tenant, would involve him in rendering up the premises in different condition from that in which they were demised."

Whether work required to be done constitutes " repair " is a question of degree and it seems the correct approach is to determine (on a fair interpreta- tion of the lease in relation to the state of the property at the date of the lease) whether the work is fairly called " repair " (*Brew Brothers, Ltd.* v. *Snax (Ross), Ltd.* [1970] 1 Q.B. 612). In reaching a conclusion the court must look at the work as a whole and not at individual parts of it (*ibid.*).

It is doubtful if particular words such as " good tenantable repair " add much to the primary meaning of the word " repair " (*Anstruther-Gough- Calthorpe v. McOscar* [1924] 1 K.B. 716) ; this phrase has been said to mean " such repair as, having regard to the age, character and locality of the house, would make it reasonably fit for the occupation of a reasonably- minded tenant of the class who would be likely to take it " (*Proudfoot* v. *Hart* (1890), 25 Q.B.D. 42, at p. 52). Expressions such as " good repair " or " habitable repair " have similar meanings. As to the construction of the expression " structural repairs of a substantial nature," reference should be made to *Granada Theatres* v. *Freehold Investment* (*Leytonstone*) [1959] Ch. 592. See also *The Holiday Fellowship, Ltd.* v. *Viscount Hereford* [1959] 1 W.L.R. 211 where the Court of Appeal considered the question whether the windows might, in the context of a particular lease or in a particular building, be part of the main wall within the meaning of a landlord's covenant to repair. In *Ayling* v. *Wade* [1961] 2 Q.B. 228, the Court of Appeal held that an under-lessor's covenant to " observe " the covenants contained in the head-lease amounted to an express covenant to carry out the repairs and obligations in that lease and was not merely a covenant of indemnity.

Exception of fair wear and tear.—Leases very frequently impose on tenants the obligation to repair the premises " fair wear and tear excepted." The majority judgments in the House of Lords in *Regis Property Co., Ltd.* v. *Dudley* [1959] A.C. 370, reinstate as authoritative the following words of Talbot, J., in *Haskell* v. *Marlow* [1928] 2 K.B. 45 : " The tenant . . . is bound to keep the house in good repair and condition, but is not liable for what is due to reasonable wear and tear. That is to say, his obligation to keep in good repair is subject to that exception. If any want of repair is alleged and proved in fact, it lies on the tenant to show that it comes within the exception. Reasonable wear and tear means the reasonable use of the house by the tenant and the ordinary operation of natural forces. The exception of want of repair due to wear and tear must be construed as limited to what is directly due to wear and tear, reasonable conduct on the part of the tenant being assumed. It does not mean that if there is a defect originally proceeding from reasonable wear and tear the tenant is released from his obligation to keep in good repair and condition everything which it may be possible to trace ultimately to that defect. He is bound to do such repairs as may be required to prevent the consequences flowing originally from wear and tear from producing others which wear and tear would not directly produce." The decision in *Taylor* v. *Webb* [1937] 2 K.B. 283 (in which the Court of Appeal purported to overrule *Haskell* v. *Marlow*) must now be regarded as itself overruled to all intents and purposes. Reference may also be made to *Brown* v. *Davies* [1958] 1 Q.B. 117, where the Court of Appeal distinguished *Taylor* v. *Webb* and held that the onus was on the tenant to show that any dilapidations were attibutable to "reasonable wear and tear" and that such an exception from a repairing covenant did not entitle the tenant to do nothing at all in relation to repair and decoration.

Relief against notice to effect internal decorative repairs.—There is a special power in s. 147 of the L.P.A. 1925 whereby, after a notice is served on a lessee relating to *internal decorative repairs to a house or other building*, he may apply for relief, and if, having regard to all the circumstances, the court is satisfied that the notice is unreasonable, it may wholly or partially relieve the lessee from liability for such repairs. The section does not apply (i) where liability arises under an express agreement to *put* the property in a decorative state of repair which has never been performed ; (ii) to any matter necessary or proper for putting or keeping the property in a sanitary condition or for the maintenance or preservation of the structure ; (iii) to any statutory liability to keep a house in all respects reasonably fit for human habitation ; or (iv) to any stipulation to yield up the property in a specified state of repair at the end of the term (L.P.A. 1925, s. 147 (2)). It will be noticed that this section enables the court to grant relief from *liability* for repairs of the kind mentioned, and so, if such relief is granted, an action for damages will be avoided. Contrast s. 146 (2) of the L.P.A. 1925, *post* p. 890 which provides only for relief from *forfeiture* of the lease.

Relief against liability to repair.—Such relief may be granted by the court provided (i) the tenancy was granted for a term of years certain of not less than seven years ; (ii) that three years or more remain unexpired at the date of service of notice of dilapidations under the L.P.A. 1925, s. 146, *post*, p. 885, or, as the case may be, at the date of commencement of an action for damages, and (iii) the property is *not* an agricultural holding (Landlord and Tenant Act, 1954, s. 51 (1)).

If these conditions are fulfilled the lessee may claim the benefit of the Leasehold Property (Repairs) Act, 1938, either on the lessor proceeding to serve a notice under the L.P.A. 1925, s. 146 (1), *post*, p. 885, with a view to forfeiture, or on the lessor serving a notice under s. 1 (2) of the 1938 Act, with a view to claiming damages. The Leasehold Property (Repairs) Act, 1938, as materially amended by the Landlord and Tenant Act, 1954, s. 51 (2), provides as follows :—

" 1.—(1) Where a lessor serves on a lessee under [the L.P.A. 1925, s. 146 (1), *post*, p. 885] a notice that relates to a breach of a covenant or agreement to keep or put in repair during the currency of the lease all or any of the property comprised in the lease, and at the date of the service of the notice three years or more of the term of the lease remain unexpired, the lessee may within twenty-eight days from that date serve on the lessor a counter-notice to the effect that he claims the benefit of this Act.

(2) A right to damages for a breach of such a covenant as aforesaid shall not be enforceable by action commenced at any time at which three years or more of the term of the lease remain unexpired unless the lessor has served on the lessee not less than one month before the commencement of the action such a notice as is specified in [the L.P.A. 1925, s. 146 (1), *post*, p. 885] and where a notice is served under this subsection, the lessee may, within twenty-eight days from the date of the service thereof, serve on the lessor a counter-notice to the effect that he claims the benefit of this Act.

(3) Where a counter-notice is served by a lessee under this section, then, notwithstanding anything in any enactment or rule of law, no proceedings, by action or otherwise, shall be taken by the lessor for the enforcement of any right of re-entry or forfeiture under any proviso or stipulation in the lease for breach of the covenant or agreement in question, or for damages for breach thereof, otherwise than with the leave of the court."

Section 1 (3) " can only be invoked when the lessor is attempting to do that which the previous subsections dealt with—in this case to claim for damages for failure to repair when the unexpired period is as great as therein specified " (Sellers, L.J., in *Baker* v. *Sims* [1959] 1 Q.B. 114, at p. 130). The provision that " no proceedings shall be taken " for breach of covenant or for damages for breach thereof must be read as " no proceedings contemplated in the preceding subsections shall be taken." It follows that leave is only required where more than (now) three years of the term remain unexpired (*ibid.*).

It will be noted that, under s. 146 (1) of the L.P.A. 1925 (see *post*, p. 885), the lessor cannot proceed to enforce any right of re-entry or forfeiture until the appropriate notice has been served, and that by the Landlord and Tenant Act, 1927, s. 18 (2) (*post*, p. 889), in the case of repairing covenants, provision is made requiring that the notice has come to the knowledge of one of certain persons. It is not normally necessary for a lessor to serve any notice before suing for damages for breach of covenant ; therefore it was necessary to make particular provision, in subs. (2), above, that notice must be given in the case of covenants to which the Leasehold Property (Repairs) Act, 1938, applies. " The effect of s. 1 of the Act of 1938 is, in my view, to require that leave of the court be obtained before proceedings for re-entry, forfeiture or for damages for breach of covenant are brought by a landlord against the same category of persons upon whom the appropriate notice had to be served by the landlord before he took proceedings for re-entry or forfeiture under s. 146 of the Act of 1925 . . . the protection afforded by the Act of 1938 was intended to be confined to lessees in possession or lessees having a present estate or interest in the premises " (Pilcher, J., in *Cusack-Smith* v. *Gold* [1958] 1 W.L.R. 611, at p. 617). However, Lord Evershed, M.R., expressly left open the correctness of this decision in *Baker* v. *Sims* [1959] 1 Q.B. 114. Compare *post*, p. 887. It has, however, been held that leave to take action for forfeiture and damages can be properly granted, following a notice under the L.P.A. 1925, s. 146, and a counternotice under the 1938 Act, even though the name of the actual lessee has never been ascertained or disclosed (*Pascall* v. *Galinski* [1970] 1 Q.B. 38).

Where the lessee has served a counter-notice and leave to proceed against him has been obtained, it is still necessary to obtain leave to proceed against a person to whom the term has later been assigned (*Kanda* v. *Church Commissioners for England* [1958] 1 Q.B. 332).

The terms " lessor," " lessee " and " lease " have the meanings assigned to them by the L.P.A. 1925, ss. 146 and 154 (see *post*, pp. 885, 886), except that they do not refer to grants at fee farm rents or securing rents by condition, and except that " lease " means a lease for a term of seven years or more other than one of an agricultural holding (Act of 1938, s. 7 (1), as amended). *Thus the Leasehold Property (Repairs) Act, 1938, as amended, has no application to leases for less than seven years.*

Notices served under the L.P.A. 1925, s. 146 (1), in the circumstances specified in the Leasehold Property (Repairs) Act, 1938, s. 1 (1), and notices required to be served under s. 1 (2) of that Act, are not valid unless they contain a statement, in characters " not less conspicuous " than those used in any other part of the notice, to the effect that the lessee is entitled to serve such a counter-notice as is mentioned in those subsections, and a statement in the like characters specifying the time within which, and the manner in which, a counter-notice may be served, and specifying the name and address for service of the lessor (1938 Act, s. 1 (4)). The words " not less conspicuous " have been held to mean " equally readable " or " equally sufficient " to tell the lessee his entitlement, and not to depend solely upon the size and blackness of the print or type (*Middlegate Properties, Ltd.* v. *Messimeris* [1973] 1 All E.R. 645, C.A.). Also the notice is sufficient if it specifies one good manner of service ; it need not specify all (*ibid.*). Again, it is sufficient for the notice to specify an appropriate name and address for service (such as that of the lessor's solicitor) ; it need not specify the name and address of the lessor (*ibid.*). Further, a defective notice can be read with a later letter stating the entitlement to serve a counter-notice so as together to constitute a valid notice (*Sidnell* v. *Wilson* [1966] 2 Q.B. 67). Alternatively, if the tenant actually serves a counter-notice, he will be taken to have waived any defect in the original notice (*ibid.*). A counter-notice by the tenant may be served on the person to whom rent is paid (Landlord and Tenant Act, 1927, s. 23 (2) ; Landlord and Tenant Act, 1954, s. 51 (4)).

The circumstances in which leave can be given to enforce the right of re-entry or to sue for damages are specified in subs. (5) as amended :—

" 1.—(5) Leave for the purposes of this section shall not be given unless the lessor proves—

(a) that the immediate remedying of the breach in question is requisite for preventing substantial diminution in the value of his reversion, or that the value thereof has been substantially diminished by the breach ;

(b) that the immediate remedying of the breach is required for giving effect in relation to the premises to the purposes of any enactment, or of any byelaw or other provision having effect under an enactment, or for giving effect to any order of a court of requirement of any authority under any enactment or any such byelaw or other provision as aforesaid ;

(c) in a case in which the lessee is not in occupation of the whole of the premises as respects which the covenant or agreement is proposed

to be enforced, that the immediate remedying of the breach is
required in the interests of the occupier of those premises or of
part thereof;

(d) that the breach can be immediately remedied at an expense that is
relatively small in comparison with the much greater expense that
would probably be occasioned by postponement of the necessary
work; or

(e) special circumstances which in the opinion of the court render it
just and equitable that leave should be given."

Paragraphs (a) to (e) are alternatives; leave may be given if the landlord
proves the existence of facts complying with any one of them (*Phillips* v.
Price [1959] Ch. 181). In that case the property was included by the local
authority in a clearance area. Harman, J., exercised his discretion (available
because paras. (a) and (c) of s. 1 (5) were satisfied) to grant leave to commence
proceedings for damages. It should be noted that where s. 1 (5) is satisfied
the court is not bound, but has a discretion to give a lessor leave to sue; this
discretion " is of an interlocutory nature, not to be exercised to exclude the
lessor from his rights subject to the wide discretion given to the court under
s. 146, unless the court is clearly convinced that, despite compliance with the
requirements specified in the paragraphs of subsection (5) the application
should be refused " (*Re Metropolitan Film Studios' Application* [1962] 1 W.L.R.
1315, where the relevant types of proof under s. 1 (5) were also considered).
The court may, in granting or in refusing leave, impose such terms and
conditions on the lessor or on the lessee as it may think fit (*ibid.*, s. 1 (6)).
It follows from the interlocutory nature of the proceedings that the landlord
has only to show a *prima facie* (or arguable) case within one of the paragraphs
of s. 1 (5) in order to obtain leave (*Sidnell* v. *Wilson* [1966] 2 Q.B. 67).
The County Courts Act, 1959, Sched. 1, now provides that a county court
has jurisdiction under the Leasehold Property (Repairs) Act, 1938, s. 1 (3),
" in all cases, other than a case in which any proceedings by action for which
leave may be given would have to be taken in a court other than a county
court." A county court has jurisdiction to determine an action for the
recovery of land where the net annual value for rating of the land in question
does not exceed £1,000 (Administration of Justice Act, 1973, s. 6 and Sched. 2).
The Act of 1938 does not apply to a breach of a covenant or agreement in so
far as it imposes on a lessee an obligation to put premises in repair that is to
be performed upon the lessee taking possession of the premises or within a
reasonable time thereafter (*ibid.*, s. 3). The Act applies to leases made before
the Act (*ibid.*, s. 5), but see Landlord and Tenant Act, 1954, s. 51 (5), as to
cases in which a notice was served, or an action for damages commenced,
before 1st October, 1954.

Damages for breach of lessee's covenant to repair.—Apart from the
possibility of forfeiture, the landlord's remedy for breach of a repairing
covenant is an action for damages: ordinarily the remedy of specific
performance is not available (*Hill* v. *Barclay* (1810), 16 Ves. 402; but cp.
Jeune v. *Queens Cross Properties, Ltd.* [1973] 3 All E.R. 97, where specific
performance was ordered against a landlord in clear breach of a repairing
covenant). The common-law rule was that where an action was brought
during the term of a lease the measure of damages was the diminution of the
value of the reversion resulting from the breach, but that on termination of
the lease the measure was the sum which would be required to put the premises

in the state of repair in which the tenant should leave them (*Joyner* v. *Weeks* [1891] 2 Q.B. 31 ; *James* v. *Hutton* [1949] 2 All E.R. 243). The two classes of cases, namely, repairs during the term and repairs at the end of the term, are put on the same footing by the Landlord and Tenant Act, 1927, s. 18 (1), which provides that damages for breach of a covenant or agreement (i) to keep or put premises in repair during the currency of a lease ; or (ii) to leave or put premises in repair at the termination of a lease, are in no case to exceed the amount (if any) by which the value of the reversion in the premises is diminished owing to such breach. Further, no damages can be recovered in respect of breach of covenant or agreement number (ii) if—

(a) it can be shown that the premises, in whatever state of repair they might be, would at or shortly after the termination of the tenancy be pulled down ; or that

(b) such structural alterations are intended to be made therein as would render valueless the repairs covered by the covenant or agreement.

Even if a reversionary lease has been granted to the tenant damages will be based on the depreciation in the value of the reversion expectant on determination of the lease, and without taking into account the reversionary lease (*Terroni and Necchi* v. *Corsini* [1931] 1 Ch. 515). Damages will not be reduced because the lease has been forfeited for breach of the covenant, and the value to the landlord of the reversion in possession at the time of forfeiture exceeds the value of the reversion expectant on the expiration of the term (*Hanson* v. *Newman* [1934] Ch. 298). Nor will damages be reduced by the fact that the landlord has an undertaking from a new tenant to do the repairs (*Haviland* v. *Long* [1952] 1 All E.R. 463). Again the damages will not be reduced because a housing shortage has enabled the property to be re-let immediately at the same rent after only a small expenditure on partial repair (*Jaquin* v. *Holland* [1960] 1 W.L.R. 258). In *Lloyds Bank* v. *Lake* [1961] 1 W.L.R. 884 an under-lessor was held entitled to recover damages for an under-lessee's breaches of repairing covenants notwithstanding the fact that the under-lessor's reversion was only momentary and notional ; " as a matter of simple logic it will not do to say that because the value of property in repair is nil, therefore the value is still nil if it is out of repair due to the breaches of the outgoing tenant. Not at all. The value is minus *x* pounds, which is what the tenant must pay someone to take over, first, the fag end of the lease, and later the last moment of the lease."

In *Moss' Empires, Ltd.* v. *Olympia* (*Liverpool*), *Ltd.* [1939] A.C. 544, a lease contained a covenant by the lessees to expend a *fixed sum* each year on repairs and decorations or to pay to the lessors the difference between the amount expended and the fixed sum. The House of Lords decided that the obligation created a debt and was not a covenant to pay " damages for breach of covenant to repair " within the Landlord and Tenant Act, 1927, s. 18 (1), and, consequently, that the difference between the two amounts was recoverable.

Section 18 (1) does not mean that damages must necessarily be given in respect of repairs which were *not* rendered valueless by proposed structural alterations. If there is no proof of diminution in the value of the reversion nominal damages only will be given for breach of a covenant to repair irrespective of s. 18 (1) (*Landeau* v. *Marchbank* [1949] 2 All E.R. 172). Nevertheless, there are many cases in which it is obvious that the failure to repair has caused damage to the reversion to the extent of the proper cost of repair. In such cases damages can be awarded even though there is no direct evidence of diminution in the value of the reversion (*Jones* v. *Herxheimer* [1950] 2 K.B. 106). The landlord is not prevented from recovering the cost of repairs because he has arranged for them to be done by someone else, for instance a former sub-tenant to whom a new lease is granted (*Haviland* v. *Long* [1952] 2 Q.B. 80).

The relevant date at which it must be determined whether there was an intention to pull down or make structural alterations to the premises is the date of the termination of the tenancy (*Salisbury (Marquess)* v. *Gilmore* [1942] 2 K.B. 38 where the lessor changed his mind shortly afterwards because of the outbreak of war). Evidence as to events thereafter is not admissible as to the intention except that rarely they might be referred to in order to explain an ambiguity in what had gone before (*Keats* v. *Graham* [1960] 1 W.L.R. 30 where the building let had been erected under planning permission for a limited period, with a condition of removal at the end of that period, which period had in fact expired before the tenancy was determined, and the fact that some months later planning permission was granted to retain the building for another five years was disregarded). Compare *London County Freehold Properties* v. *Wallace-Whiddett* [1950] W.N. 180 where, before the expiration of the tenancy, a local authority had resolved to purchase the property compulsorily with a view to demolition, but the compulsory purchase order was not actually made until after the expiration of the tenancy and the house was regarded as not really being in the market when the lease ended. The tenant must be able to show that the intention to pull down the premises or to make structural alterations is a definite one. A conditional decision dependent, for instance, on the obtaining of a building licence is not enough (*Cunliffe* v. *Goodman* [1950] 2 K.B. 237). Further, s. 18 (1) contemplates the *lessor* making a decision to pull down or structurally alter the premises ; it cannot be construed as enabling a municipal corporation by its own failure as a tenant to comply with covenants to repair, so that the house has to be demolished, to claim relief (*Hibernian Property, Ltd.* v. *Liverpool Corporation* [1973] 2 All E.R. 1117).

The limitation on recovery of damages imposed by s. 18 (1) does not apply where the covenant broken was not a covenant to repair, for instance, where it restricted the use of the premises to that of a single private dwelling-house and the premises were turned into flats (*Eyre* v. *Rea* [1947] K.B. 567). In such a case the measure of damages is the actual loss suffered by the landlord (*Westminster (Duke)* v. *Swinton* [1948] 1 K.B. 524), which may be the full cost of restoring the premises to their former condition if it is reasonable, in the circumstances, for the landlord to reinstate them (*Eyre* v. *Rea, ante*).

Repair of war damage.—The Landlord and Tenant (War Damage) Acts, 1939 and 1941, permitted a tenant, in certain circumstances, to disclaim a lease. Further, an obligation to repair contained in a lease does not impose any obligation to make good war damage (1939 Act, s. 1 (1)). Where war damage had occurred, an obligation to repair was suspended until the war damage had been made good if compliance with the obligation would, having regard to the war damage, be impracticable except at unreasonable expense, or be of no substantial advantage to the person entitled to the benefit of the obligation (1939 Act, s. 1 (2)). See also 1941 Act, ss. 5 and 6, and 1943 Act, s. 12.

G. COVENANTS ON PLANNING MATTERS

Development during the currency of the lease.—It has already been noted, *ante*, p. 809, that ultimate liability for a contravention of planning control lies on the person who carried out the contravening development, but that both lessor and lessee may have an interest in ensuring that there is no contravention. It does not matter whether any necessary planning permission is obtained by the lessor or by the lessee, as in any case, except so far as it provides otherwise, it enures for the benefit of the land and of all persons for the time being interested therein (Town and Country Planning Act, 1971, s. 33 (1)).

During the currency of the lease the lessee will be the person in a position to carry out any development, and this may fall into one of two classes :—

(i) Development for which planning permission need not be obtained : see further, *post*, p. 1189 *et seq.* The lessor is not likely to wish to restrict any such development, and in the absence of any express provision it could be carried out by the lessee without the lessor's consent, unless it amounts to waste.

(ii) Development for which express permission is required. It has been noted above that any permission obtained by the lessee operates for the benefit of the land unless the permission provides otherwise. The main difficulty from the point of view of the lessor is that if development is carried out, whether by way of operations on the land or a material change of use of the land, planning permission will usually be necessary before the land can be restored to its former condition or use. A lessor may protect himself by inserting a covenant in the lease that the lessee will not carry out any operations or make any material change of use without the lessor's consent. For a precedent, see Hallett's Conveyancing Precedents, p. 467. A further covenant to obtain necessary permissions and to meet professional charges incurred by the lessor, as in Hallett, *op. cit.*, pp. 476, 477, is useful. It seems probable that the Landlord and Tenant Act, 1927, s. 19 (2), would prevent the lessor from withholding consent unreasonably to the carrying out of development which would amount to the making of an improvement. See further, *ante*, p. 855.

A possible solution to the difficulty that permission may be necessary on resumption of the former use, may be by requiring a lessee to apply for a planning permission for a limited period only. On the expiration of such a period no planning permission is necessary for resumption of the use of the premises which was the normal use before the permission was granted (Town and Country Planning Act, 1971, s. 27 (5)). See further, an article in the *Journal of Planning Law*, vol. 2, p. 169.

The usual condition of re-entry (*post*, p. 882) on breach of covenant should be made applicable. Where the lease was made before the Town and Country Planning Act, 1947, came into operation [1st July, 1948], such covenants will not be found, but it seems possible that many contraventions of planning law would break the customary covenant to use the premises in a tenant-like manner.

It is as well to obtain an indemnity from the lessee against the cost of complying with any enforcement notice served in respect of a contravention occurring during the currency of the lease, instead of relying on the provision in s. 91 (1) of the 1971 Act by which the cost is recoverable from the person who committed the breach of planning control.

Notice to lessor of service of notices and orders.—A covenant may be inserted that the lessee will at his own cost comply with all orders and requirements on planning matters and will notify the lessor of all orders and requirements and will deliver to him copies of all notices. See, for instance, *Journal of Planning Law*, vol. 1, p. 365. But it is doubtful if such covenants are really necessary. Enforcement notices (Town and Country Planning Act, 1971, s. 87 (4)), tree preservation orders (s. 60 (5)), listed building notices (s. 54 (7)), and notices requiring maintenance of waste land (s. 65 (1)) must all be served on the owner. An owner is defined (s. 290 (1)) as the person who is entitled to receive the rack rent or who would be entitled if the land were let at a rack rent. A lessee holding at a nominal rent may be the " owner " ; in such a case it would be advisable to stipulate that copies of such orders and notices should be forwarded forthwith to the lessor.

Power of lessor to carry out works on land.—Where steps are required to be taken by an enforcement notice served under s. 87 of the Town and Country Planning Act, 1971 (as to which see *post*, p. 1201), or by a notice requiring restoration of a building listed as of architectural or historic interest under s. 54 of the Town and Country Planning Act, 1971, or by a notice requiring maintenance of waste land under s. 65, a lessor may have difficulty in complying because he has no right to enter on the land. In such cases he may make complaint to a court of summary jurisdiction and the court may, if satisfied that any person having an interest in the premises other than the owner prevents the owner from taking steps that he is required to take by such a notice, order the occupier to permit the steps to be taken (Public Health Act, 1936, s. 289, as applied by the Town and Country Planning Act, 1971, ss. 91, 107). In order to avoid the necessity for application to the court it would be as well to insert in a lease the reservation of such a right.

Compensation for adverse planning decisions.—The general rules as to such compensation are discussed *post*, p. 1203 *et seq*. If a refusal of planning permission or a conditional grant of permission gives rise to a claim in respect of land subject to a lease, compensation will be payable to the lessee or to the reversioner, or to both, according to whether their respective interests are thereby depreciated in value (Town and Country Planning Act, 1971, s. 146). If the unexpended balance of established development value is not adequate to pay full compensation to both, then that balance is apportioned between them (*ibid.*, s. 152 (3)).

PART 5. FORFEITURE AND RE-ENTRY

Former rules.—The ordinary proviso giving power to the lessor to re-enter in case the rent should be in arrear for a specified time, or a breach be committed of any of the covenants and conditions in the lease, or in case the lessee should become bankrupt or a receiving order be made of his estate, is now so hedged in with statutory restrictions that quite a long process has to be gone through (except in certain special cases) before possession can be obtained. On the other hand it would be a serious thing if a lessor were allowed, unless for some very good and sufficient reason, to re-take possession of property on which the lessee may have spent much money. Before the passing of the Conveyancing Act, 1881, no relief could be given for forfeiture, except in the case of non-payment of rent, or failure to insure, or in the case of accident or surprise, and sometimes in the case of great hardship, but there was no general rule on which reliance could be placed. In these circumstances s. 14 of the Conveyancing Act, 1881, was passed, and is now replaced by s. 146 of the L.P.A. 1925 as amended by the Law of Property (Amendment) Act, 1929, and supplemented by s. 18 (2) of the Landlord and Tenant Act, 1927. Section 146 consists of twelve subsections, and it is proposed in the following notes, first, to deal with re-entry for non-payment of rent and then to consider each subsection in turn.

Forfeiture and relief in case of non-payment of rent.—This subject is introduced by the following subsection in s. 146 of the L.P.A. 1925 :—

" (11) This section does not, *save as otherwise mentioned*, affect the law relating to re-entry or forfeiture or relief in case of non-payment of rent."

" *save as otherwise mentioned*."—These words refer to the words " for non-payment of rent " in s. 146 (4), as to which see *post*, p. 891.

A proviso for re-entry, if rent is in arrear for a specified period, should be inserted in every lease for a term of years ; otherwise the lessor may find himself compelled to take a series of actions of arrears of rent against an unsatisfactory tenant who cannot be removed. Such a proviso almost invariably states that the lessor may re-enter *whether or not rent has been lawfully demanded.* If these, or similar, words were not inserted the landlord would not be able to enforce his right of re-entry without first making a formal demand on the premises for the exact amount of rent due (*Duppa* v. *Mayo* (1669), 1 Wms, Saund. 285) unless half a year's rent at least is due and there are not sufficient distrainable goods on the premises (Common Law Procedure Act, 1852, s. 210). The exact requirements of a formal demand were specified in the *Law Journal*, vol. 92, p. 189.

Forfeiture is not effected merely by the lessor issuing a writ for possession against the lessee in breach of covenant, but by the service thereof (*Canas Property Co., Ltd.* v. *K.L. Television Services, Ltd.* [1970] 2 Q.B. 433).

Provided that rent is six months in arrear a lessor's action of ejectment can be stopped by payment, tender or payment into court of all rent, arrears and costs (Common Law Procedure Act, 1852, s. 212 ; *Standard Pattern Co., Ltd.* v. *Ivey* [1962] Ch. 432). There is also power for the High Court (whether or not rent is in arrear for as long as six months) to give relief in a summary manner, and subject to the same terms and conditions in all respects as to payment of rent, costs and otherwise as could formerly have been imposed in the Court of Chancery, on payment of arrears of rent and costs before or within six months after execution under judgment of possession (Judicature Act, 1925, s. 46 ; *Standard Pattern Co., Ltd.* v. *Ivey, ante*). Relief can be given under the equitable jurisdiction of the court if the lessor has taken possession without bringing an action (*Lovelock* v. *Margo* [1963] 2 Q.B. 786). This case was followed in *Thatcher* v. *C. H. Pearce (Contractors), Ltd.* [1968] 1 W.L.R. 748 where it was held (doubting a *dictum* in *Howard* v. *Fanshawe, post*) that no rule of limitation is applied strictly to this equitable jurisdiction ; the court must consider whether in all the circumstances the plaintiff acted with reasonable promptitude and have regard to any hardships to the defendant by extension of relief. Although the statute does not expressly so provide, it appears that, by analogy, the court will require that payment should be made within six months of possession being taken (*Howard* v. *Fanshawe* [1895] 2 Ch. 581) ; and if the lessee, his executors, administrators or assigns are so relieved they will hold the demised premises according to the terms of the lease and without the necessity for any new lease (*ibid.*). See also *Nance* v. *Taylor* [1927] W.N. 257.

Where a lessor is proceeding by action in a county court to enforce a right of re-entry or forfeiture for non-payment of rent the County Courts Act, 1959, s. 191, contains special provisions for relief in favour of the lessee. In the first place (except where the lessor is also enforcing re-entry or forfeiture on any other ground or some other claim), if the lessee pays into court not less than five clear days before the return day all the rent in arrear and the costs of the action, the action ceases and the lessee thereupon holds the land according to the lease (but such payment must be made by or on behalf of the lessee : *Matthews* v. *Dobbins* [1963] 1 W.L.R. 217). Where the action does not so cease if the court is satisfied that the lessor is entitled to enforce the right of re-entry or forfeiture, possession must be ordered at the expiration of such period, not being less than four weeks, as the court thinks fit unless within that period the lessee pays into court all the rent in arrear and the costs (although the court can extend the period before possession is recovered : Administration of Justice Act, 1965, s. 23). On payment into court within that period the lease is reinstated, but otherwise the order is enforceable in the prescribed manner and, so long as it remains unreversed, the lessee is barred from all relief. As a consequence of s. 191 of the County Courts Act, 1959, an order for possession in any event not indicating that forfeiture might be avoided if the arrears of rent be paid was set aside by the Court of Appeal in *Spurgeons Homes* v. *Gentles* [1971] 1 W.L.R. 1514.

Where such an action is brought in a county court and, at the time of its commencement, a half-year's rent is in arrear and the lessor has a right to re-enter and no sufficient distress is to be found, the service of the summons is itself adequate demand and re-entry (County Courts Act, 1959, s. 191 (2)).

Similarly, if a lessor has enforced re-entry without action for non-payment of rent, provided that the net annual value for rating does not exceed £1,000 the lessee may, within six months from the re-entry, apply to the county court for such relief as the High Court could have granted (*ibid.*, s. 191 (3) ; Administration of Justice Act, 1973, s. 6 and Sched. 2).

In granting relief in cases of non-payment of rent the court regards the condition of re-entry as being merely security for payment and gives relief if the landlord can get his rent. If relief is given on terms the court may later extend the time for performance of the terms if it is equitable to do so, even if the order did not provide for liberty to apply (*Chandless-Chandless* v. *Nicholson* [1942] 2 K.B. 321). This jurisdiction is at the discretion of the court acting on equitable principles and so relief may be refused if the conduct of the plaintiff was such as to disqualify him. Breaches of other covenants would not normally result in refusal of relief (*Gill* v. *Lewis* [1956] 2 Q.B. 1) but might in an exceptional case and hardship to the landlord may be relevant (*Public Trustee* v. *Westbrook* [1965] 1 W.L.R. 1160, where twenty-two years had passed without any rent being paid in respect of sub-leases of houses which had been on a bombed site and everyone had treated the sub-leases as gone altogether, and the application for relief was an attempt at revival by speculators).

Leave of the court is necessary before enforcement of (a) a remedy by way of re-entry, or (b) a judgment for possession of land in default of payment of rent, where the special protection of the Reserve and Auxiliary Forces (Protection of Civil Interests) Act, 1951, applies.

As regards a sub-lessee or mortgagee the court can grant relief against forfeiture of the head-lease or the mortgagor's lease for non-payment of rent either under s. 146 (4) of the L.P.A. 1925, or under the equitable jurisdiction preserved by s. 46 of the Judicature Act, 1925, but the principles governing the court's discretion are the same in either case (*Belgravia Insurance Company, Ltd.* v. *Meah* [1964] 1 Q.B. 436, where the Court of Appeal held that relief would be granted to a sub-lessee or mortgagee on terms of paying all rent in arrear, making good breaches of lessee's covenants and paying costs, the order being such as would vest in him a legal term). Reference should also be made, however, to *Chatham Empire Theatre* (1955), *Ltd.* v. *Ultrans, Ltd.* [1961] 1 W.L.R. 817, where relief was granted to sub-lessees of part of the premises comprised in a head-lease on payment of that proportion of the total arrears of rent which the rent payable under their sub-lease bore to the rent payable under the head-lease, since the landlords were only entitled to be put back into the same position as they were in before the forfeiture *qua* that part of the premises let to the sub-lessees. But note also that Salmon, J., added : " I can certainly conceive of cases where it would be quite wrong to give a sub-lessee relief on this basis ; great hardship could be caused to the head lessor if granting relief to one or two of many sub-tenants would make it impossible for him to deal with the premises as a whole. Every case must be considered on its own facts." See also *Grangeside Properties, Ltd.* v. *Collingwood Securities, Ltd.* [1964] 1 W.L.R. 139, C.A.

It is most important to remember that where premises are let as a dwelling on a lease which is subject to a right of re-entry or forfeiture it is not lawful to enforce that right otherwise than by proceedings in the court while any person is lawfully residing in the premises or part of them (Rent Act, 1965, s. 31). As to an employee-licensee with exclusive possession being deemed to be a tenant for the purposes of s. 31 of the Rent Act, 1965, see *Warder* v. *Cooper* [1970] 1 Ch. 495. If the lease of a dwelling (not being a statutorily protected tenancy) has ended before the right is enforced but the occupier continues to reside in the premises, it is similarly unlawful to enforce the right of possession otherwise than by proceedings in the court (*ibid.*, s. 32, as amended by the Rent Act, 1968, Sched. 15).

Notice to be given before forfeiture other than for non-payment of rent.—The general rule with regard to notices is contained in the following provision of the L.P.A. 1925, s. 146 (1) :—

   " 146.—(1) A right of re-entry or forfeiture *under any proviso or stipulation in a lease* for a breach of any covenant or condition in the lease [other than for non-payment of rent, as to which see p. 883 : s. 146 (11)] shall not be enforceable, *by action or otherwise*, unless and until the lessor *serves on the lessee* a notice—

   (a) *specifying the particular breach* complained of ; and

   (b) if the breach is capable of remedy, *requiring the lessee to remedy the breach ;* and

   (c) *in any case, requiring the lessee to make compensation in money for the breach ;*

and the lessee fails, *within a reasonable time* thereafter, to remedy the breach, if it is capable of remedy, and to make reasonable compensation in money, to the satisfaction of the lessor, for the breach."

Plowman, J., has held unsuccessful a device adopted by landlords to avoid the s. 146 procedure which involved requiring the tenant to deliver in escrow a surrender of the lease, the condition of the escrow being the breach of certain covenants (*Plymouth Corporation* v. *Harvey* [1971] 1 W.L.R. 549).

"*under any proviso or stipulation in a lease.*"—Upon the breach of any *condition* the lessor or his assigns may re-enter or maintain an ejectment without there being any express proviso for re-entry in the lease ; but in the case of a breach of a *covenant* the lessor has this power only if the lease contains a condition or proviso for re-entry for a breach of such covenant. As covenants in leases are more common than conditions, this is an important rule and one which is sometimes overlooked. " Leases " includes " an underlease or other tenancy " (L.P.A. 1925, s. 154) and " an original or derivative underlease ; also an agreement for a lease where the lessee has become entitled to have his lease granted ; also a grant at a fee farm rent, or securing a rent by conditions " (L.P.A. 1925, s. 146 (5) (*a*)). The words " lessee " and " lessor " are defined accordingly, and include their successors in title (*ibid.*, s. 146 (5)).

"*by action or otherwise.*"—Thus the subsection applies where re-entry is peaceable and is made without first bringing an action (*Re Riggs ; ex parte Lovell* [1901] 2 K.B. 16). The restrictions on obtaining possession of dwelling-houses, otherwise than by action, mentioned *post*, p. 916, should be borne in mind.

When a forfeiture has been incurred by breach of a covenant or condition, the lease will not be determined until the landlord has re-entered upon the premises or done some act which in law will be considered as equivalent to re-entry. The issue of a writ of ejectment against the lessee will be deemed to be equivalent to actual re-entry (*Serjeant* v. *Nash, Field & Co.* [1903] 2 K.B. 304 ; *Moore* v. *Ullcoats Mining Co., Ltd.* [1908] 1 Ch. 575 ; see also *Calabar Properties, Ltd.* v. *Seagull Autos* [1969] 1 Ch. 451). But under the provisions of s. 146 (1), above, before the entry can be made whether peaceably or by action, the necessary step must be taken of giving the notice, and waiting a reasonable time, except in the cases referred to in subss. (8) to (10) of this section, dealt with at pp. 892–894. As a matter of practice, an action is almost invariably commenced and possession taken under a writ of possession (and, in the case of dwellings by virtue of the Rent Acts, this may be the only possible procedure).

The subject of taking possession by " *peaceable re-entry* " is fully discussed in *Hemmings* v. *Stoke Poges Golf Club* [1920] 1 K.B. 720. When a landlord is entitled to re-enter (that is when he has complied with the requirements of s. 146 (1), *ante*), he may take possession otherwise than by action except as specified in the Rent Acts. If he enters with more force than necessary it is a criminal offence and comes within 5 Rich. 2, stat. 1, c. 7, which provides that " none from henceforth make any entry into any lands and tenements, but in case where entry is given by the law ; and in such case not with strong hand, nor with multitude of people, but only in peaceable and easy manner. And if any man from henceforth do to the contrary, and thereof be duly convict, he shall be punished by imprisonment." It was said by Bankes, L.J., in the above case, at p. 737, however, that " Assuming . . . that the entry by the defendants was a forcible entry, the right to possession was in the defendants, and the acts which are alleged as giving the plaintiffs a right of action were done in defence of their right to possession, and of the possession which they had acquired by the alleged forcible entry . . . A person who makes a forcible entry upon lands and tenements renders himself liable to punishment, and he exposes himself also to the civil liability to pay damages in the event of more force being used than was necessary to remove the occupant of the premises, or in the event of any want of proper care in the removal of his goods." In the case, one of the occupants was a woman who refused to leave her chair, and the chair with the woman in it was taken out of the house, but with no more force than necessary. The action was dismissed. Even after he has obtained judgment for possession the landlord may enter without suing out a writ of possession, using no more force than necessary (*Aglionby* v. *Cohen* [1955] 1 Q.B. 558).

If the tenant is not in possession of the premises the action of the landlord in re-letting them may amount to the exercise by him of a right of re-entry (*Lewis & Son, Ltd.* v. *Morelli* [1948] 1 All E.R. 433).

Leave of the court is necessary before exercising a remedy by way of re-entry if the special protection of the Reserve and Auxiliary Forces (Protection of Civil Interests) Act, 1951, applies.

Where a notice served under the L.P.A. 1925, s. 146 (1), relates to a breach of a covenant or agreement (contained in a lease for seven years or more), to keep or put in repair premises, other than an agricultural holding, and at the date of the service of the notice three years or more of the term remain unexpired, the lessee may claim the protection of the Leasehold Property (Repairs) Act, 1938, as amended ; see *ante*, p. 875.

" *serves on the lessee.*"—The word " lessee " in s. 146 " can refer only to a lessee in possession or one who has a subsisting lease at the time when proceedings for forfeiture or re-entry are taken " (*Cusack-Smith* v. *Gold* [1958] 1 W.L.R. 611, 616). Thus, it is not necessary to serve notice on a lessee who has already assigned his whole interest in the lease and who is not in possession (*ibid.*). It is not necessary to serve a notice on a mortgagee of the term (*Church Commissioners for England* v. *Ve-Ri-Best Manufacturing Co., Ltd.* [1957] 1 Q.B. 238) or on a person to whom the term is later assigned (*Kanda* v. *Church Commissioners for England* [1958] 1 Q.B. 332).

" *specifying the particular breach.*"—When the breach consists of non-repair of the premises, *Fletcher* v. *Nokes* [1897] 1 Ch. 271 contains a good working rule. It decided that the notice ought to be such as to enable the tenant to know with reasonable certainty what he was required to do. The landlord need not go through every room and point out every defect, as he would incur needless expense which might fall on his own shoulders. But the notice ought to be sufficient to inform the tenant of the particular things of which the landlord complained, so that the tenant might have the opportunity of remedying them before an action was brought against him. *Fox* v. *Jolly* [1916] 1 A.C. 1 is also a useful case in which the extent of the particulars required was considered. On the other hand, to take an example of a case from the other extreme, it would obviously not be enough merely to require repairs to be done " in accordance with the covenants " in the lease (*Re Serle ; Gregory* v. *Serle* [1898] 1 Ch. 652).

" *requiring the lessee to remedy the breach.*"—It is important that the lessor should, in the notice, require the lessee to remedy the breach if it is capable of remedy (*North London Freehold Land & House Co.* v. *Jacques* (1883), 49 L.T. 659). As a matter of practice it is better in all cases to require the breach to be remedied, for it is not always apparent whether it is capable of remedy, and if it is not, such requirement will have done no harm. A notice may properly contain the words " if it is capable of remedy " (*Glass* v. *Kencakes* [1966] 1 Q.B. 611) ; after a reasonable time the landlord may claim (*a*) that the breach is incapable of remedy, or (*b*) that if capable of remedy it has not been remedied (*ibid.*). A breach involving immorality may be capable of remedy if the lessees neither know nor had reason to know of the user (*ibid.*, distinguishing *Rugby School* (*Governors*) v. *Tannahill* [1935] 1 K.B. 87 and other decisions ; see also *Central Estates* (*Belgravia*), *Ltd.* v. *Woolgar* (*No.* 2) [1972] 3 All E.R. 610 where relief against forfeiture was given despite immorality). A subletting in breach of covenant has been held to be a once and for all breach incapable of remedy, although in the circumstances relief against forfeiture was granted (*Scala House District Property Co., Ltd.* v. *Forbes* (1973), 117 Sol. J. 467, C.A.).

" *in any case, requiring the lessee to make compensation in money for the breach.*"—The subsection does not make it necessary for the lessor to claim compensation *if he does not desire compensation*, and, therefore, in such a case the absence of the requirement will not invalidate the notice (*Lock* v. *Pearce* [1893] 2 Ch. 271 ; *Rugby School* (*Governors*) v. *Tannahill, ante*). It follows that no compensation need be claimed where no compensation for the breach is possible (*Civil Serviee Co-operative Society* v. *McGrigor's Trustee* [1923] 2 Ch. 347).

" *within a reasonable time.*"—What is a reasonable time to wait will depend on the nature of the defects which have to be remedied. In *Civil Service Co-operative Society* v. *McGrigor's Trustee, ante*, fourteen days was under the circumstances considered reasonable. In most cases, however, it would be better to allow four weeks.

The effect of the Leasehold Property (Repairs) Act, 1938, s. 1 (4), as to which see *ante*, p. 875, is that a notice served under the L.P.A. 1925, s. 146 (1), if it refers to a covenant to repair premises, *may* be void unless it contains a statement of the rights of the lessee under that Act.

Service of notice.—It is provided by s. 196 (1) of the L.P.A. 1925 that the notice must be in writing and by s. 196 (2) that it will be sufficient service although the notice be only addressed to the lessee by that designation without his name, and notwithstanding that any person to be affected by the notice is absent, under disability, or unascertained. It is sufficient if the notice is affixed or left for the lessee on the land or any house or building comprised in the lease (*ibid.*, s. 196 (3)) ; or if it is sent by post in a registered letter or by the recorded delivery service (Recorded Delivery Act, 1962, s. 1 (1)), addressed to the lessee by name at his place of abode or business, provided that the letter is not returned through the post office undelivered, and the service will be deemed to be made at the time at which the registered letter would in the ordinary course be delivered (L.P.A. 1925, s. 196 (4)). It was held in *Cronin* v. *Rogers* (1884), 1 Cab. & El. 348, that service on an assignee will be sufficient if addressed to the original lessee and " all others whom it may concern " and left with the occupier. As to service by registered post, see *Van Grutten* v. *Trevenen* [1902] 2 K.B. 82, referred to *ante*, p. 836. As to the effect of service of a notice by recorded delivery, see *Re 88 Berkeley Road, London, N.W.9* [1971] 1 All E.R. 255, noted *ante*, p. 836. See also *Cannon Brewery Co., Ltd.* v. *Signal Press Ltd.* (1928), 139 L.T. 384, where it was held that a notice of a breach of covenant under s. 196 (3) of the L.P.A. 1925 was properly served on the tenant by being left with some person on the premises, where there was reasonable ground for supposing that that person would pass it on to the tenant, and *Gentle* v. *Faulkner* [1900] 2 Q.B. 267, in which service on the lessee's trustee for his creditors was held not to be sufficient.

Where the notice *is in respect of a breach of a covenant to repair*, s. 196 of the L.P.A. 1925 must be read with s. 18 (2) of the Landlord and Tenant Act, 1927, which provides as follows :—

" 18.—(2) *A right of re-entry or forfeiture* for a breach of [a covenant or agreement to keep or put premises in repair during the currency of a lease, or to leave or put premises in repair at the termination of a lease] shall not be enforceable by action or otherwise, unless the lessor proves that the fact that such a notice as is required by section one hundred and forty-six of the Law of Property Act, 1925, had been served on the lessee was known either—

(*a*) to the lessee ; or

(*b*) to an under-lessee holding under an under-lease which reserved a nominal reversion only to the lessee ; or

(*c*) to the person who last paid the rent due under the lease either on his own behalf or as agent for the lessee or under-lessee ;

and that a time reasonably sufficient to enable the repairs to be executed had elapsed since the time when the fact of the service of the notice came to the knowledge of any such person.

Where a notice has been sent by *registered post* addressed to a person at his last known place of abode in the United Kingdom, then, for the purposes of this subsection, that person shall be deemed, *unless the contrary is proved*, to have had knowledge of the fact that the notice had been served as from the time at which the letter would have been delivered in the ordinary course of post."

" *right of re-entry or forfeiture*."—A notice under s. 146 may have to be served before an action for damages for breach of covenant to repair may be brought (Leasehold Property (Repairs) Act, 1938, s. 1 (2), *ante*, p. 875). Nevertheless, s. 18 (2) of the 1927 Act has no application where damages only are claimed.

" *registered post*."—Posting by recorded delivery service has the same consequences (Recorded Delivery Act, 1962, s. 1 (1)).

When the notice has been sent by registered post, the person to whom it was addressed will be deemed to have knowledge of the fact that the notice has been served, " *unless the contrary is proved*." It might well happen that the lessee had not received the notice ; for instance, he might be able to prove that he had been away at the time for a holiday, and that the person who signed for the notice had left the address before his return and had forgotten to pass on the notice. It is thought that solicitors will be wise to adopt the practice of serving the notice personally in the case of the breach of a covenant to repair.

The lessor having given the lessee or assignee the necessary notice under s. 146 of the L.P.A. 1925, and, if necessary, in the manner provided for in s. 18 of the Landlord and Tenant Act, 1927, and having waited a reasonable time for the lessee to remedy the breach, if capable of remedy, and the lessee not having complied with the terms of the notice, the lessor has next to determine whether he shall enter and take possession of the property without obtaining an order of the court. It will be noticed that s. 146 (2), mentioned below, assumes that it is possible that the lessor might proceed to complete the forfeiture by entry without action, as it provides that " the lessee may, in the lessor's action, *if any*," apply for relief, and provides for this eventuality by giving the lessee power to bring an action himself if the lessor takes possession without bringing an action. But in the case of a dwelling, the lessor may have no alternative to commencing proceedings and even in connection with other property, except in very special circumstances, will commence an action for the reasons mentioned *ante*, p. 886.

Application for relief from forfeiture.—This is dealt with by s. 146 (2) of the L.P.A. 1925 as follows :—

" 146.—(2) Where a lessor is proceeding, by action or otherwise, to enforce such a right of re-entry or forfeiture, the lessee may, in the lessor's action, if any, or in any action brought by himself, apply to the court for relief ; and the court may grant or refuse relief, as the court, having regard to the proceedings and conduct of the parties under the foregoing provisions of this section, and to all the other circumstances, thinks fit and in case of relief may grant it on such terms, if any, as to costs, expenses, damages, compensation, penalty, or otherwise, including the granting of an injunction to restrain any like breach in the future, as the court, in the circumstances of each case, thinks fit."

This subsection must be read with subss. (8) to (10) of the section, as they limit the right to give relief conferred by this subsection. See *post*, pp. 892–894. The court may not grant relief where application is made by one only of joint lessees (*Equity and Law Life Assurance Society* v. *Gold and Holden* [1953] C.P.L. 149). Note also that s. 146 (2) is applicable only where there is a forfeiture under any proviso or stipulation in a lease, not where there is a forfeiture by operation of law (*Warner* v. *Sampson* (*No.* 2) [1958] 1 All E.R. 314, concerning a denial of lessor's title ; see further [1959] 1 Q.B. 297).

If relief is given the court may grant an injunction to restrain any like breach in the future. Relief may be given following breach of a restrictive covenant as well as breach of a positive covenant (*Harman* v. *Ainslie* [1904] 1 K.B. 698).

The effect of an order giving relief is to continue the original lease for all purposes. For instance, an underlessee would continue liable on the covenants in his derivative lease, notwithstanding the issue of the writ to recover possession by the superior landlord (*Dendy* v. *Evans* [1910] 1 K.B. 263).

The time within which the lessee may apply for relief is limited to the time during which the " *lessor is proceeding*," that is, it will be too late when the lessor has obtained possession (*Rogers* v. *Rice* [1892] 2 Ch. 170). See also *Lock* v. *Pearce* [1892] 2 Ch. 238.

It has been said by the House of Lords that the discretion to grant or refuse relief given by the statute is so wide that it is better not to lay down rigid rules for its exercise (*Hyman* v. *Rose* [1912] A.C. 623). It appears that the court will not normally grant relief unless the breach can be rectified and will grant relief only on terms that it shall be rectified (*Eyre* v. *Rea* [1947] K.B. 567), but in *Westminster* (*Duke*) v. *Swinton* [1948] 1 K.B. 524, although the breach could not immediately be rectified, relief was granted to a lessee and underlessee who were not parties to the breach, but refused to a sub-lessee from the underlessee, the sub-lessee having been guilty of a deliberate breach of covenant. See further *Borthwick-Norton* v. *Owens* (1949), 153 E.G. 165, *Borthwick-Norton* v. *Romney Warwick Estates, Ltd.* [1950] 1 All E.R. 798, and *Borthwick-Norton* v. *Dougherty* [1950] W.N. 481 ; also *Central Estates*

(*Belgravia*), *Ltd.* v. *Woolgar* (*No.* 2) [1972] 1 W.L.R. 1048, where relief was given even though the tenant had been convicted of keeping a brothel.

Persons who can enforce a proviso for re-entry.—It is provided by s. 141 (1) of the L.P.A. 1925, in effect, that every condition of re-entry contained in the lease is to be annexed and incident to and is to go with the reversionary estate in the land, or in any part thereof, immediately expectant on the term granted by the lease, notwithstanding severance of that reversionary estate. It is also provided by subs. (2) of the same section that any such provision is to be capable of being enforced by the person from time to time entitled, subject to the term, *to the income of the whole or any part*, as the case may require, of the land leased ; and by subs. (3) that where that person becomes entitled by conveyance or otherwise, then such provision may be enforced or taken advantage of by him, *notwithstanding that he becomes entitled after the condition of re-entry or forfeiture has become enforceable*, unless, of course, the same has been waived or released before such person became entitled. See also s. 140 of the L.P.A. 1925, *post*, p. 898.

Recovery of expenses on waiver of, or relief from, forfeiture.—This is provided for by the L.P.A. 1925, s. 146 (3), as follows :—

" 146.—(3) A lessor shall be entitled to recover as a debt due to him from a lessee, and in addition to damages (if any), all reasonable costs and expenses properly incurred by the lessor in the employment of a solicitor and surveyor or valuer, or otherwise, in reference to any breach giving rise to a right of re-entry or forfeiture which, at the request of the lessee, is waived by the lessor, or from which the lessee is relieved, under the provisions of this Act."

If, however, a counter-notice under the Leasehold Property (Repairs) Act, 1938, s. 1, *ante*, p. 875, is served by the lessee, the lessor is not entitled to the benefit of s. 146 (3) of the L.P.A. 1925 unless the lessor makes an application under the 1938 Act for leave to enforce a right of re-entry or to sue for damages. On any such application the court has power to direct to what extent the lessor may have the benefit of s. 146 (3) (Leasehold Property (Repairs) Act, 1938, s. 2). The restriction on the right to recover expenses under s. 146 (3) contained in s. 2 does not invalidate the common form provision in a lease to the effect that expenses incurred by the landlord in serving notice under s. 146 of the L.P.A. 1925 should be recoverable from the tenant notwithstanding that forfeiture is avoided (*Bader Properties, Ltd*. v. *Linley Property Investments, Ltd.* (1968), 112 Sol. J. 71).

Rights of underlessee when lessor proceeding to enforce right of re-entry.—The L.P.A. 1925, s. 146 (4), provides as follows :—

" (4) Where a lessor is proceeding by action or otherwise to enforce a right of re-entry or forfeiture under any covenant, proviso or stipulation in a lease, or *for non-payment of rent*, the court may, on application by *any person claiming as under-lessee* any estate or interest in the property comprised in the lease or any part thereof, either in the lessor's action (if any) or in any action brought by such person for that purpose, make an order vesting, for the whole term of the lease or any less term, the property comprised in the lease or any part thereof in any person entitled as under-lessee to any estate or interest in such property upon such conditions as to execution of any deed or other document, payment of rent, costs, expenses, damages, compensation, giving security, or otherwise, as the court in the circumstances of each case may think fit, but in no case shall any such under-lessee be entitled to require a lease to be granted to him for any longer term than he had under his original sub-lease."

"*for non-payment of rent.*"—An underlessee may apply under this subsection where his lessor does not pay the rent, instead of applying under the Judicature Act, 1925, s. 46. See *ante*, p. 883.

Before the Conveyancing and Law of Property Act, 1892, if the original lessee committed a breach and the superior lessor obtained an order and re-took possession, the underlessee lost his interest, except where the forfeiture took place by reason of non-payment of rent. This injustice was remedied by s. 4 of the Conveyancing and Law of Property Act, 1892. This section was an independent section, and did not contain any exceptions. The result was that an underlessee might get relief in cases where the lessee could not, for instance, on a forfeiture of a public-house by the lessee's bankruptcy. Then came subss. (8) to (10) of s. 146 of the L.P.A. 1925 (as to which, see below), creating various exceptions, which exceptions were made to apply not only to lessees but to underlessees as well, thereby taking away the right of such underlessees to relief in the cases where no relief would be granted to lessees, and altering the law as existing before 1926. The mistake was rectified by the Law of Property (Amendment) Act, 1929, which provides that nothing in subss. (8), (9) or (10) shall affect the provisions of subs. (4) of s. 146 of the L.P.A. 1925, the subsection we are now considering. The final result is that this Act restores the position as it was before 1926, and the court may therefore now grant relief to an underlessee for whatever cause the head lease is forfeited.

"*any person claiming as under-lessee.*"—A mortgagee of a leasehold interest is an underlessee who may apply for relief under the L.P.A. 1925, s. 146 (4). He need not have been joined by the lessor as a party to an action for possession, and if he subsequently joins in and obtains relief under s. 146 (4) he will normally be required to pay the lessor's solicitor's costs on a solicitor and client basis so far as they cannot be recovered from the lessee (*Egerton* v. *Jones* [1939] 2 K.B. 702 ; compare *Grangeside Properties, Ltd.* v. *Collingwoods Securities, Ltd.* [1964] 1 All E.R. 143). A mortgagee by way of legal charge has the same protection, powers and remedies as a mortgagee by sub-demise (L.P.A. 1925, s. 87 (1)) and so may obtain relief (*Grand Junction Co., Ltd.* v. *Bates* [1954] 2 Q.B. 160), as may an equitable chargee of the lease (*Re Good's Lease* [1954] 1 W.L.R. 309).

Subsection (6) of s. 146 is not of general interest. For subs. (7), see *post*, p. 894.

Covenants and premises to which special rules as to forfeiture apply.— Subsection (8) of s. 146 provides that s. 146 shall not extend, in the case of a mining lease, to a covenant or condition for allowing the lessor to have access to or inspect books, accounts, records, weighing machines or other things, or to enter or inspect the mine or the workings thereof.

The position of the parties on breach of such a covenant or condition is that the lessor can re-enter without the service of a notice and the court has no power to grant relief to a lessee, except in the rare case where, under its special equitable jurisdiction, it relieves on the ground of mistake. But, as we have seen, this paragraph does not apply in the case of *an underlessee* applying for relief against forfeiture for the breach of covenant by his lessor, the original lessee. See *ante*, p. 891.

Subsection (9) of s. 146 of the L.P.A. 1925 provides :—

" (9) This section does not apply to a condition for forfeiture on the bankruptcy of the lessee or on taking in execution of the lessee's interest if contained in a lease of—

(a) Agricultural or pastoral land ;

(b) Mines or minerals ;

(c) A house used or intended to be used as a public-house or beershop ;

(d) A house let as a dwelling-house, with the use of any furniture, books, works of art, or other chattels not being in the nature of fixtures ;

(e) Any property with respect to which the personal qualifications of the tenant are of importance for the preservation of the value or character of the property, or on the ground of neighbourhood to the lessor, or to any person holding under him."

It was decided in *Robert Ferguson & Co.* v. *Jane Ferguson* [1924] 1 Ir. R. 22, that land was agricultural land for this purpose if any substantial portion of the premises was of that character. In that case, the lease was of $37\frac{1}{2}$ acres of land on which a factory and certain other buildings were erected. The term " agricultural " must not be taken to mean " exclusively agricultural," and decisions on what is an agricultural holding are not necessarily relevant.

A proviso for re-entry if the lessee, his executors, administrators or assigns should become bankrupt refers only to the bankruptcy of the person holding the estate, and the lessor cannot re-enter on the bankruptcy of the lessee after he has assigned his interest away (*Smith* v. *Gronow* [1891] 2 Q.B. 394). " Bankruptcy " is defined in s. 205 (1) (i) of the L.P.A. 1925 to include liquidation by arrangement ; and, in relation to a corporation, to mean winding up.

Therefore, in these cases, the lessor can apply to the court without first giving the statutory notice and the court will not grant relief to the lessee.

Where there is a condition of forfeiture on bankruptcy of the lessee or taking in execution of his interest and the lease is *not one of those specified in s.* 146 (9) *above*, the position is governed by s. 146 (10), which is as follows :—

" (10) Where a condition of forfeiture on the bankruptcy of the lessee or on taking in execution of the lessee's interest is contained in any lease, other than a lease of any of the classes mentioned in the last subsection, then—

(a) if the lessee's interest is sold within one year from the bankruptcy or taking in execution, this section applies to the forfeiture condition aforesaid ;

(b) if the lessee's interest is not sold before the expiration of that year, this section only applies to the forfeiture condition aforesaid during the first year from the date of the bankruptcy or taking in execution."

The effect of the subsection is as follows :—

(a) if the lessor desires to enforce his right of re-entry within one year from the bankruptcy or taking in execution, this section applies ; that is to say, he must first give the statutory notice and relief can be given ;

(b) if the lessee's interest is sold during that year then the lessor cannot re-enter without first serving the statutory notice on the purchaser and waiting, and, in this case, the court can grant relief ;

(c) if the property is not sold within the year and the lessor has taken no step during that time, he may, after the expiration of the year, apply to the court for an order to enforce the forfeiture without going through the process of giving the statutory notice, and the court cannot give relief.

A compulsory winding-up order of a company was made and the company's interest was not sold within one year of its winding up, but within that year proceedings were commenced for relief from forfeiture which, however, were not before the court until after the expiration of the year, and it was held by the House of Lords that the jurisdiction of the court to deal with the application did not cease because the application was not dealt with before the year expired and, therefore, subs. (10) (b) was applicable (*Pearson* v. *Gee and Braceborough Spa, Ltd.* [1934] A.C. 272).

If the trustee in bankruptcy or, in the case of a company, the liquidator wishes to obtain relief against forfeiture on the ground that he has sold the property within the year, the sale must be a real sale. That is to say, there must be either an actual conveyance of the property or an absolute contract for sale (*Re Henry Castle & Sons, Ltd.* (1906), 94 L.T. 396 ; *Civil Service Co-operative Society* v. *McGrigor's Trustee* [1923] 2 Ch. 347) ; a conditional contract for sale will not be sufficient (*Robert Ferguson & Co., Ltd.* v. *Jane Ferguson* [1924] 1 Ir. R. 22).

Registration of proceedings for forfeiture.—A right of re-entry exercisable over a legal term of years absolute is a legal interest (L.P.A.1925, s. 1 (2) (e)) and does not require registration under the L.C.A. 1972; but if the lessor proceeds to action in the court it will be necessary to register the action as a pending action under s. 5 (1) of the L.C.A. 1972, as it is provided by s. 5 (7) of that Act that a pending action will not bind a purchaser without *express* notice thereof unless it is so registered.

Contract cannot avoid the provisions of s. 146.—It is provided by s. 146 (12) that the section has effect notwithstanding any stipulation to the contrary. It is also provided by s. 146 (7) that for the purposes of the section a lease limited to continue as long only as the lessee abstains from committing a breach of covenant shall take effect as a lease to continue for any longer term for which it could subsist, but determinable by a proviso for re-entry on such a breach. Thus evasion of the section by drafting a lease in a slightly different form is prevented. See also *Plymouth Corporation* v. *Harvey* [1971] 1 W.L.R. 549, noted *ante*, p. 885.

Waiver of breach.—" Waiver of a right of re-entry can only occur where the lessor, with knowledge of the facts upon which his right to re-enter arises, does some unequivocal act recognising the continued existence of the lease " (*per* Parker, J., in *Matthews* v. *Smallwood* [1910] 1 Ch. 777, at p. 786) ; or perhaps it would be more accurate to say that the act of the lessor will be taken as evidence from which, as a conclusion of fact, the intention to waive the forfeiture will be inferred, i.e., objectively but subjectively (*Abram Steamship Co., Ltd.* v. *Westville Shipping Co.* [1923] A.C. 773).

Where a lessor, with knowledge, acts in a way consistent only with the continued existence of the lease, it is immaterial that the lessor did not intend his action to waive forfeiture and also immaterial that the lesses knew that waiver was not intended (*Central Estates (Belgravia), Ltd.* v. *Woolgar (No.* 2) [1972] 1 W.L.R. 1048, C.A.).

The onus of proving that the lessor was aware of the facts which would amount to a forfeiture falls on the lessee or the assignee (*Matthews* v. *Smallwood, ante* ; *Fuller's Theatre & Vaudeville Co.* v. *Rolfe* [1923] A.C. 435).

An unqualified demand by the lessor on the lessee for payment of rent (*Doe d. Nash* v. *Birch* (1836), 1 M. & W. 402), or the acceptance by the lessor of rent from the lessee (*Price* v. *Worwood* (1859), 4 H. & N. 512), after a breach and with knowledge thereof, will amount to a waiver (*Creery* v. *Summersell and Flowerdew* [1949] Ch. 751 ; *Central Estates (Belgravia), Ltd.* v. *Woolgar (No.* 2), *ante*). The question was considered in *Windmill Investments London, Ltd.* v. *Milano Restaurant, Ltd.* [1962] 2 Q.B. 373 whether an acceptance of rent amounted to a waiver as a matter of law or whether the question was one of fact. Megaw, J., reconciled certain conflicting *dicta* as follows : " the explanation is that it is a question of fact whether the money tendered is tendered as, and accepted as, rent, as distinct, for example, from money tendered and accepted as damages for trespass. That is a question of fact. Once it is decided as a fact that the money was tendered and accepted as rent, the question of its consequences as a waiver is a matter of law." This statement was applied by the Court of Appeal in *Central Estates (Belgravia), Ltd.* v. *Woolgar (No.* 2), *ante*. To make acceptance of rent by the *agent* of the lessor a waiver, where it is not shown that the lessor has allowed it with knowledge of the breach, it would have to be shown that the agent had authority not only to receive the rent but to grant a new lease (*Doe d. Nash* v. *Birch, ante*). Acceptance of rent will amount to a waiver notwithstanding that the lease provides that waiver of a breach of covenant or condition shall not be operative unless expressed in writing (*R.* v. *Paulson* [1921] 1 A.C. 271).

The fact that the rent is accepted or demanded under protest or " without prejudice " will not prevent the receipt being a waiver (*Croft* v. *Lumley* (1858), 6 H.L. Cas. 672 ; *Segal Securities, Ltd.* v. *Thoseby* [1963] 1 Q.B. 887). An important point to bear in mind is that acceptance of rent only recognises the lease as existing *at the time when the rent accrued due*, and therefore will only amount to a waiver up to that date (*Atkin* v. *Rose* [1923] 1 Ch. 522).

The acceptance of rent by the lessor after he has commenced proceedings for ejectment will not amount to a waiver, for the fact of his issuing and serving the writ or summons would amount to an irrevocable election to put an end to the tenancy (*Serjeant* v. *Nash, Field & Co.* [1903] 2 K.B. 304 ; *Evans* v. *Enever* [1920] 2 K.B. 315). In the latter case the lease contained a proviso for re-entry in case the lessee should become bankrupt, or if the rent should be in arrear for twenty-one days. The lessee became bankrupt and the lessor, with knowledge of the bankruptcy, brought an action for possession on the ground that the lease was liable to forfeiture for non-payment of the rent. The action was settled by payment of rent and costs. Later the lessor sued the lessee for possession on the ground that the lease was forfeited by the bankruptcy. It was held that, notwithstanding that the rent which was accepted by the lessor in the first action had accrued due after the bankruptcy, its acceptance by the lessor did not amount to a waiver of the forfeiture. See also *Civil Service Co-operative Society, Ltd.* v. *McGrigor's Trustee* [1923] 2 Ch. 347, where the rent which had been accepted by the lessor had accrued due partly after the bankruptcy of the lessee and partly after the issue of the writ, and it was held that such acceptance did not operate as a waiver of the forfeiture. The point does not seem to have been taken that after action has been brought no act can set up the lease again, but that acceptance of rent after the writ becomes evidence of an agreement for a *new* tenancy from year to year upon the terms of the old lease. It might have been argued, therefore, that, if such agreement can be proved, the lessor cannot rely on the forfeiture to eject the lessee. See *Evans* v. *Wyatt* (1880), 43 L.T. 176. The question arose in *Segal Securities, Ltd.* v. *Thoseby* [1963] 1 Q.B. 887, of the effect of a demand for or an acceptance of rent where rent was payable in advance. Sachs, J., first held that a non-continuing breach in the past clearly could be waived and went on " as regards continuing breaches it seems to me that in the absence of express agreement the acceptance of rent in advance can, at highest, only waive those breaches that are at the time of demand continuing and to waive them for such period as it is definitely known that they will continue . . . The object of a covenant by which rent has to be paid in advance is to obtain a certain security for that payment . . . A landlord cannot, to my mind, lightly be deprived of the benefit of such rights : he cannot be put in the position of having to wait until the end of the period covered by the rent before demanding or accepting it, merely because there are chances that the tenant may so break or continue in breach of covenant as to render himself liable to forfeiture."

Acceptance of rent will not necessarily amount to a waiver of a breach of covenant if the premises are within the Rent Acts, and the tenant is entitled to remain in occupation as statutory tenant, provided that the landlord states that he accepts rent without prejudice to his right to obtain possession and that he takes proceedings within a reasonable time (*Oak Property Co., Ltd.* v. *Chapman* [1947] K.B. 886).

A distraint for rent will amount to a waiver, on the ground that, except in a few instances, a distraint can only be made on the assumption that the tenancy is in existence.

It has been held that some *positive act* is necessary on the part of the lessor, and that mere standing by will not amount to a waiver, though the lessee may spend money on the property with the knowledge of the lessor (*Doe d. Sheppard* v. *Allen* (1810), 3 Taunt. 78 ; *Perry* v. *Davis* (1858), 3 C.B. (N.S.) 769) ; but there will be a waiver if the lessor encourages the lessee to spend money (*North Stafford Steel, Iron and Coal Co. (Burslem), Ltd.* v. *Camoys (Lord)* (1865), 11 Jur. (N.S.) 555).

Where a waiver by a lessor or any persons deriving title under him of the benefit of any covenant or condition in a lease is proved to have taken place in any particular instance, such waiver will not be deemed to extend to *any* instance, or to *any* breach of covenant or conditions, save that to which such waiver specially relates, nor operate as a *general* waiver of the benefit of any such covenant or condition (L.P.A. 1925, s. 148 (1)). See also s. 143 (1) of the L.P.A. 1925, which provides that where a licence is granted to a lessee to do any act, the licence, unless otherwise expressed, will extend only to the specific breach of any provision or covenant referred to, and the licence will not prevent any proceeding for any subsequent breach, unless otherwise specified in the licence.

If there has been a long course of usage inconsistent with the covenant relied on, the court will presume (although the covenant is a continuing covenant) an actual waiver or release by the lessor (*Re Summerson* [1900] 1 Ch. 112*n ; Gibbon* v. *Payne* (1905), 22 T.L.R. 54) ; unless it can be proved that the lessor had not during the period, as a matter of fact, notice of the

breach. For instance, in *Ashcombe* v. *Mitchell* (1895), 12 T.L.R. 17, there
was a breach of covenant for twenty years without the actual knowledge
of the lessor, and it was held that there was no waiver.

Waiver of continuing breach.—There is a difference in the effect of a
breach made once and for all, and a continuing breach. Waiver does not
prevent a lessor from taking advantage of a breach which continues thereafter
(*Creery* v. *Summersell and Flowerdew & Co.* [1949] Ch. 751). It may be said,
generally, that if the lessee has it in his power to remedy the breach, it is a
continuing breach, but if he has not, then it will not be a continuing breach.
For instance, if the lessee sublets for a term in breach of his covenant, he has no
power to alter things, and the waiver will practically amount to a licence
for the sub-letting for the remainder of the term of the sub-letting. If a
covenant not to use the premises for a purpose other than that of a private
dwelling-house is broken as a result of a sub-lease, the landlord cannot rely
on the continuing character of this breach of covenant if he has waived the
breach constituted by the sub-letting. In such a case the two breaches are
no more than different aspects of the same act (*Downie* v. *Turner* [1951]
2 K.B. 112; also *Windmill Investments, Ltd.* v. *Milano Restaurant, Ltd.*
[1962] 2 Q.B. 373).

But in the case of sub-letting for short periods a new breach occurs on
every separate sub-letting, for where a breach is of a continuing nature
the waiver of any forfeiture up to a certain day will afford no defence to an
ejectment for a subsequent breach (*Laurie* v. *Lees* (1881), 7 App. Cas. 19).
Other instances of a continuing covenant are a covenant to repair (*New
River Co.* v. *Crumpton* [1917] 1 K.B. 762) and a covenant to insure (*Price* v.
Worwood (1859), 4 H. & N. 512). But a covenant to build within a fixed
time can only be broken once, and therefore is not of a continuing nature,
and the acceptance thereafter of rent would be a waiver (*Jacob* v. *Down*
[1900] 2 Ch. 156). In the last case there was also a covenant to keep the
buildings to be erected in repair, and the judge (Stirling, J.) stated that he
considered that such covenant was a continuing covenant and could be
enforced although the covenant to build had been waived. This *dictum*
was disapproved in *Stephens* v. *Junior Army and Navy Stores, Ltd.* [1914]
2 Ch. 516. See also *Powell* v. *Hemsley* [1909] 1 Ch. 680. The conversion
of a house into a shop is a breach complete *at once* and not a continuing
breach (*Bridges* v. *Longman* (1857), 24 Beav. 27).

In *City and Westminster Property, Ltd.* v. *Mudd* [1959] Ch. 129 (which
concerned a lessee's covenant to use the premises " as showrooms, workrooms,
and offices only "), Harman, J., *inter alia*, considered the question of waiver;
he said : " Now, residence contrary to the covenants of the lease is a continuing
breach and, therefore, *prima facie*, it is only waived by the acceptance of
rent down to the date of that acceptance and there is a new breach immediately
thereafter which is not waived. My attention was called to a number of
cases which show that acts of waiver may be so continuous that the court is
driven to the conclusion that there has been a new agreement or letting or a
licence or a release of the covenant. The cases cited on this subject show
acquiescence continuing for a very long period of years . . . [20 to 40
years] . . . I cannot think that anything proved here amounts to a release
by the landlord of his rights. He knew, indeed, that the tenant was using
the property to sleep in, but I do not think that he knew more than that.
At that he was willing to wink, but I am unable to find a release of the
covenant or an agreement for a new letting."

29

Apportionment of conditions on severance of reversion.—It is provided by the L.P.A. 1925, s. 140 (1), that, notwithstanding the severance by conveyance, surrender or otherwise of a reversionary estate and notwithstanding the avoidance or cesser in any other manner of the term granted by a lease as to part only of the land comprised therein, every condition or right of re-entry shall remain annexed to the severed parts of the reversionary estate as severed, and shall be in force with respect to the term whereon each severed part is reversionary, or the term in the part of the land as to which the term has not been surrendered, or has not been avoided or has not otherwise ceased. For this purpose " right of re-entry " includes a right to determine the lease by notice to quit or otherwise ; but where the notice is served by a person entitled to a severed part of the reversion so that it extends to part only of the land demised, the lessee may within one month determine the lease in regard to the rest of the land by giving to the owner of the reversionary estate therein a counter notice expiring at the same time as the original notice (L.P.A. 1925, s. 140 (2) ; for an example of the operation of this subsection, see *Smith* v. *Kinsey* [1936] 3 All E.R. 73).

For the special rules affecting notices to quit part of an agricultural holding see *post,* p. 958.

PART 6. BUSINESS PREMISES

Part I of the Landlord and Tenant Act, 1927, as amended, contains those sections which, together with miscellaneous sections in Pt. III, deal with the subject of compensation for improvements. The general effect of the Landlord and Tenant Act, 1954, Pt. II is to provide security of tenure for business, professional and other tenants or a right to compensation when, in special cases, an order for a new tenancy cannot be obtained.

It is thought not appropriate to attempt to deal in a book of this nature with the fluctuating and temporary control of business rents imposed now by the Counter-Inflation Act, 1973, and reference should be made to the Counter-Inflation (Business Rents) Order, 1973, made thereunder. By s. 4 of that Act, the provisions are to cease to operate by 31st March, 1976. However, in the meantime, practitioners will no doubt be bearing in mind that, in general, rents are frozen at the rate payable on 5th November, 1972, under any business tenancy then subsisting (or if no such tenancy was then subsisting, under any earlier one subsisting on or after 5th November, 1971).

A. SECURITY OF TENURE

Tenancies protected.—Part II of the Landlord and Tenant Act, 1954, provides security of tenure for certain occupying tenants of business and similar premises. The tenancies affected are widely defined by the Act as follows :—

" 23.—(1) *Subject to the provisions of this Act,* [Part II] of this Act *applies to any tenancy* where the property comprised in the tenancy is or includes *premises* which are *occupied by the tenant* and are so occupied for the purposes of a *business* carried on by him or for those and other purposes."

" *Subject to the provisions of this Act.*"—Part II does not apply :—

(a) to a tenancy of an agricultural holding or a tenancy which would be a tenancy of an agricultural holding if the proviso to s. 2 (1) of the Agricultural Holdings Act, 1948 (as to which see *post,* p. 943) did not have effect or, in a case where the approval of the Minister

of Agriculture, Fisheries and Food was given as mentioned in
s. 2 (1), if that approval had not been given (1954 Act, s. 43 (1), as
amended by the Agriculture Act, 1958, Sched. 1, Pt. I, para. 29) ;

(b) to a tenancy created by a mining lease (as to which see *O'Callaghan*
v. *Elliott* [1966] 1 Q.B. 601) ;

(c) to a tenancy where the property comprised therein is let under a
tenancy which either is a controlled tenancy or would be such a
tenancy if it were not a tenancy at a low rent (Rent Act, 1968,
s. 9 (3), Sched. 15) ;

(d) to a tenancy of a public-house (although there is protection for a
licensed restaurant or hotel).

Further, Part II does not apply to " a tenancy granted by reason that the
tenant was the holder of an office, appointment or employment from the
grantor thereof and continuing only so long as the tenant holds the office,
appointment or employment, or terminable by the grantor on the tenant's
ceasing to hold it, or coming to an end at a time fixed by reference to the
time at which the tenant ceases to hold it " (*ibid.*, s. 43 (2)). There is a proviso
to this subsection, however, that the subsection shall not have effect in
relation to a tenancy granted after 1st October, 1954, unless granted by an
instrument in writing " which expressed the purpose for which the tenancy
was granted." Nor does the protection of Pt. II apply to a fixed term not
exceeding six months unless (a) it contains provision for renewal beyond
six months, or (b) the tenant, or his predecessor in the business, has occupied
for over six months (*ibid.*, s. 43 (3) ; as amended by L.P.A. 1969, s. 12).

" *applies to any tenancy.*"—It is not assumed that the rules set out below
will always have to be applied. The landlord and tenant will often agree for
the grant of a further tenancy of the " holding " (as to which see *post*, p. 909),
possibly with other land, on terms and from a date specified. If this happens,
the current tenancy is continued until that date but no longer, and is *not* a
tenancy to which the protection of Pt. II applies (*ibid.*, s. 28). A tenancy at
will arising by implication of law on holding over is not a tenancy to which the
Act applies (*Wheeler* v. *Mercer* [1957] A.C. 416) ; Viscount Simonds expressed
the view that the Act might apply to a tenancy at will created by express
contract, but it is doubtful whether other members of the House of Lords
shared this view. Consequently, even if a prospective purchaser became a
tenant at will it seems that he could not claim the protection of the Act
(*ibid.*, at p. 425). However, it has now actually been held that an agreement
expressly creating a tenancy at will (for example, a letting until the landlord
can obtain planning permission to develop) avoids the 1954 Act, as such a
tenancy does not fall within Pt. II of the Act (*Manfield* v. *Sons, Ltd.* v.
Botchin [1970] 2 Q.B. 612 ; see further Trevor M. Aldridge at *Solicitors'
Journal*, vol. 114, p. 898).

Also an agreement expressly and effectively creating a licence to occupy
premises, rather than a tenancy, is outside the protection of the 1954 Act
(*Shell-Mex and B.P., Ltd.* v. *Manchester Garages, Ltd.* [1971] 1 W.L.R. 612 ;
see *ante*, p. 807).

The question whether there is a " holding " within the definition is to be
decided at the date of an order for a new tenancy (*I. and H. Caplan, Ltd.* v.
Caplan [1962] 1 W.L.R. 55).

Where a tenancy ceases to fall within Pt. II it does not thereby come
to an end. If it was granted for a term certain and has been continued by

s. 24 (1), *post*, p. 901, it may be terminated by not less than three nor more than six month's notice in writing given by the landlord to the tenant (1954 Act, s. 24 (3) (*a*)). On the other hand, where a landlord gives notice to quit at a time when the tenancy is not one to which the Part applies, the notice is not affected if the tenancy later falls within the protection of Pt. II (*ibid.*, s. 24 (3) (*b*)).

It is most important to note that a tenancy granted under Pt. II of the 1954 Act is itself protected by the Act. Thus new tanancies may be granted in succession in respect of the same premises.

Where the landlord is a Government department, local authority, hospital board or committee, statutory undertaker or development corporation, the Minister or board in charge of a Government department may certify that it is requisite for the purposes of the landlord that the use of property should be changed. The effect of such a certificate is to exclude the provisions of the Act as to continuance of tenancies and grant of new tenancies beyond the date stated in the certificate (*ibid.*, s. 57), even if the landlord purchased after the tenant had claimed a new tenancy (*X.L. Fisheries Ltd.* v. *Leeds Corporation* [1955] 2 Q.B. 636). Similarly, a certificate may require any new tenancy to be subject to a term that it shall be terminable by six month's notice given by the landlord (*ibid.*, s. 57 (5)).

" *premises.*"—This word may include land on which buildings are erected, the land immediately surrounding them and easements appurtenant (*Bracey* v. *Read* [1963] Ch. 88).

" *occupied by the tenant.*"—The word " occupied " in s. 23 (1) of the 1954 Act is to be given its ordinary and natural meaning (*Lee-Verholst* (*Investments*) *Ltd.* v. *Harwood Trust* [1972] 3 W.L.R. 772, C.A.). Accordingly, a tenant was held to occupy the whole of premises in which were situated some twenty separate fully-furnished apartments each with its own resident, in particular because the tenant enjoyed a right of access to all parts of the premises in order to run the business of letting apartments and to provide services to the residents (*ibid.*).

Occupation by all or any of the beneficiaries under a trust, and the carrying on by them of a business is equivalent to occupation or carrying on of a business by the tenant ; in such a case a change in the trustees is not treated as a change of tenant (*ibid.*, s. 41 (1) ; compare *Frish, Ltd.* v. *Barclays Bank, Ltd.* [1955] 2 Q.B. 541, *post*, p. 909). Special rules exist for cases where a tenancy is held by one of a group of companies (*ibid.*, s. 42). The tenant does not lose the protection of Pt. II of the Landlord and Tenant Act, 1954, simply by ceasing physically to occupy the premises, for example, if there were a need for urgent structural repairs and the tenant had to go out of physical occupation in order to enable them to be effected. Where premises are only occupied by a tenant during seasonal periods it is a question of fact and degree whether he has protection during the gap between the intermittent activities (*Teasdale* v. *Walker* [1958] 1 W.L.R. 1076). Again, a tenant may be regarded as in occupation of the premises despite going out of physical occupation during proceedings under the 1954 Act (*I. and H. Caplan, Ltd.* v. *Caplan* (*No.* 2) [1963] 2 All E.R. 930). The tenant will not be able to base his occupation on acts that are in breach of covenant (see *Naccriss* v. *Wolfe* [1916] Ch. 10, and below).

" *business.*"—This includes (i) a trade, profession or employment, and (ii) any activity carried on by a body of persons, whether corporate or unincorporate (*ibid.*, s. 23 (2)). The courts have not placed any artificial limit on the meaning of the word "activity" which includes a hospital carried on by governors (*Hills (Patents), Ltd.* v. *University College Hospital* [1956] 1 Q.B. 90), a lawn tennis club (*Addiscombe Garden Estates, Ltd.* v. *Crabbe* [1958] 1 Q.B. 513) and the provision of accommodation, equipment and staff to the Universities Central Council on Admissions which also occupied the same premises for the purposes of its activities (*Willis* v. *Association of Universities of the British Commonwealth* [1965] 1 Q.B. 140). As to the meaning of the word "business," see also *ante*, p. 574. The sub-letting of parts of premises as flats has been treated as not a business for this purpose (*Bagettes, Ltd.* v. *G.P. Estates, Ltd.* [1956] Ch. 290), but this appears open to re-consideration in the light of subsequent decisions (see *Lee-Verhulst (Investment), Ltd.* v. *Harwood Trust* [1972] 3 W.L.R. 772, noted *ante*, p. 900 ; also *Luganda* v. *Service Hotels, Ltd.* [1969] 2 Ch. 209). Held not to be a business is the carrying on of a Sunday school by the tenant alone (*Abernethie* v. *A.M. & J. Kleiman, Ltd.* [1970] 1 Q.B. 10).

Part II does not apply, however, where the tenant is carrying on a business in breach of a prohibition (however expressed) of use for business purposes which subsists under the terms of the tenancy and extends to the whole of the property unless (i) the immediate landlord or his predecessor in title has *consented* to the breach or (ii) the immediate landlord has *acquiesced* therein (*ibid.*, s. 23 (4)). " The reference to a prohibition of use for business purposes does not include a prohibition of use for the purposes of a specified business, or of use for purposes of any but a specified business, but save as aforesaid, includes a prohibition of use for the purposes of some one or more only of the classes of business specified in the definition of that expression in [s. 23 (2), *ante*] " (*ibid.*, s. 23 (4)). Thus it would seem that a tenant carrying on business contrary to a covenant not to carry on, for instance, an offensive business, is not able to claim the protection of the Act.

Section 23 (4) does not prevent the protection of Pt. II of the 1954 Act applying as between an occupying sub-tenant and his intermediate landlord where the only prohibition of use for business purposes is contained in the head lease (*D'Silva* v. *Lister House Developments, Ltd.* [1971] Ch. 17).

Continuation of tenancies.—A business tenancy as defined above does not come to an end in the normal way at the expiration of a fixed term, or in the case of a periodic tenancy on service by the landlord of a notice to quit (1954 Act, s. 24 (1)). On the other hand, there is no change in the common-law rules governing the termination of a tenancy (i) by notice to quit given by the *tenant*, or (ii) by surrender or forfeiture or by the forfeiture of a superior tenancy (*ibid.*, s. 24 (2)). Devices whereby the protection of the 1954 Act could be avoided have now been countered by provisions that a notice to quit or surrender will not be effective if given (or agreed) before or during the first month of occupancy under the tenancy (s. 4 of the L.P.A. 1969). However, such devices should no longer be required in any case in view of the fact that contracting-out may now be authorised (see *post*, p. 912).

Any such "business" tenancy, whether for a fixed term or a periodic tenancy, may be terminated by the *landlord* by a notice given to the tenant in the form prescribed by the Landlord and Tenant (Notices) Regulations, 1969 and 1973, specifying the date at which the tenancy is to come to an end (1954 Act, s. 25 (1)). Such a notice must be given not more than twelve nor less than six months before the date of termination specified (*ibid.*, s. 25 (2)) although it may be more than twelve months prior to that date in an exceptional case in which more than six months' notice would have been required to terminate the tenancy apart from the provisions of the 1954 Act (*ibid.*, s. 25 (3) (*b*)). The intention is that the protected tenancies shall continue until brought to an end by the special notice prescribed, but that they shall not be terminated earlier than would have been possible under the common-law rules. Thus, if the tenancy could have been brought to an end by notice to quit (which includes a notice to break a fixed term : s. 69 (1)) given by the landlord, the date of termination specified in the notice given pursuant to the 1954 Act must not be earlier than the earliest date on which the tenancy could have been ended by notice served by the landlord on the date when the 1954 Act notice was served (*ibid.*, s. 25 (3)). In the case of a tenancy for a fixed term, not terminable by notice, the earliest date of operation of a notice under the Act is the date on which the tenancy would otherwise end by effluxion of time (*ibid.*, s. 25 (4)). If there is a break clause, see *Scholl Manufacturing Co., Ltd.* v. *Clifton* (*Slimline*), *Ltd.* [1967] Ch. 41. A notice for termination of a periodical tenancy served within s. 25 of the 1954 Act need not expire on the same day as a like contractual notice to quit would have had to at common law (*Commercial Properties, Ltd.* v. *Wood* [1968] 1 Q.B. 15).

Where a lease for a fixed term enables the landlord by notice to terminate the term at some intermediate date, he may (subject to the statutory prolongation of the term mentioned below), do so notwithstanding the Landlord and Tenanct Act, 1954. After the landlord has broken the contractual term in this way the tenancy may hold over by virtue of s. 24 (1), which prevents the term from coming to an end. Nevertheless, the landlord could serve a statutory notice under s. 25 to determine the term or the tenant could at any time apply for a new tenancy under s. 26 mentioned below (*Weinbergs Weatherproofs, Ltd.* v. *Radcliffe Paper Mills Co., Ltd.* [1958] Ch. 437).

In order that the tenant shall know of his rights a notice is not effective unless it requires the tenant within two months after service to notify the landlord in writing whether or not at the date of termination the tenant will be willing to give up possession of the property comprised in the tenancy (*ibid.*, s. 25 (5)). A notice which wrongly states the date for service of such a counter notice is invalid (*Price* v. *West London Building Society* [1964] 1 W.L.R. 616). Further, the notice is not effective unless it states whether the landlord would oppose an application to the court for the grant of a new tenancy and, if so, also states on which of the grounds, set out *post*, p. 905, he would do so (*ibid.*, s. 25 (6)).

Tenant's power to terminate fixed term.—It is noted above that a protected business tenancy does not now come to an end, even if granted for a fixed term, unless terminated in accordance with the Act. The tenant may, however, have no desire either to allow it to continue or to apply for a new tenancy. He is given the right, therefore, to serve on his immediate landlord, not later than three months before the date on which it would, apart from the 1954 Act, end, a notice (for which a form is *not* prescribed) that he does not desire the tenancy to be continued. The tenancy will then end as at common law (*ibid.*, s. 27 (1)). But see the provision of s. 4 of the L.P.A. 1969, noted *ante*, p. 901.

Similarly, a tenant who formerly held a fixed term may wish to bring to an end a tenancy which continues under s. 24 (*ante*, p. 901) after the expiration of that fixed term. This he may do on any quarter day by giving to the immediate landlord three months' notice in writing (for which a form is *not* prescribed) ; such notice may even be given *before* the date on which, apart from the Act, the tenancy would have ended (*ibid.*, s. 27 (2)).

Where the tenancy is a periodic one, or a fixed term containing provision enabling the tenancy to terminate the term by notice, these rules do not apply. The tenant may terminate by ordinary notice to quit or by notice in accordance with the provision, as the case may be (*ibid.*, s. 24 (2), *ante*, p. 901 ; s. 69 (1)).

Request for new tenancy.—It is necessary to bear in mind that a tenancy to which Pt. II of the 1954 Act applies does not (even if granted for a fixed term) come to an end unless terminated in accordance with Pt. II. Where the tenancy was granted for a term of years certain exceeding one year, whether or not continued by s. 24, *ante*, or granted for a term certain and thereafter from year to year, the tenant may request a new tenancy (*ibid.*, s. 26 (1)). One of two or more joint tenants was held not to be " the tenant " within the meaning of s. 24 (1) and so was unable validly to apply for a new tenancy (*Jacobs* v. *Chaudhuri* [1968] 2 Q.B. 470). This position has now been remedied in the case of partnerships by s. 9 of the L.P.A. 1969. The position if the original term had been for a term certain and thereafter, for instance, from quarter to quarter, is doubtful. It will be noted that this section is concerned with fixed terms of over one year ; it does not apply, for instance, to yearly or other periodic tenancies. Where the original tenancy is a periodic one it continues until duly determined, for instance, by the landlord's notice mentioned *ante*, p. 901. The tenant may, if the landlord serves such a notice, apply to the court under the rules specified below. Where the original tenancy was for a fixed term, however, the tenant may suffer hardship unless he can ascertain whether he may stay in possession for a further fixed term and so he is given the right to apply under s. 26.

Such a request must be for a tenancy to begin at a date not more than twelve nor less than six months after the making of the request, and must specify such date ; such date may not be earlier than that on which, apart from the 1954 Act, the current tenancy would end by effluxion of time or could be terminated by notice given by the tenant (*ibid.*, s. 26 (2)). The request must be in the form set out in the Landlord and Tenant (Notices) Regulations, 1969 and 1973, and must state the tenant's proposals as to (i) the property to be comprised in the new tenancy (being either the whole or part of that comprised in the current tenancy) ; (ii) the rent to be payable under the new tenancy ; and (iii) the other terms of the new tenancy (*ibid.*, s. 26 (3)).

The request must include a proposal as to the duration of the new tenancy, but the request will not be invalid if it asks that the new lease shall be " upon the terms of the current tenancy " (*Sidney Bolsom Investment Trust, Ltd.* v. *E. Karmios & Co. (London), Ltd.* [1956] 1 Q.B. 529).

If the landlord has already given an effective notice of termination of the current tenancy under s. 25, *ante*, the tenant has the right specified below to apply to the court for a new tenancy, and so he has no right to make a request under s. 26. Further, he may not make such a request if he has already given notice to quit, or the prescribed notice mentioned above for termination of a fixed term (1954 Act, s. 26 (4)).

The effect of a request by the tenant for a new tenancy is that the current tenancy will terminate immediately before the date specified in the request for the beginning of the new tenancy, subject, however, to certain rules for the interim continuance of tenancies pending determination by the court. A period of two months from the making of the tenant's request is allowed to the landlord, during which he may give notice to the tenant (the form not being prescribed) that he will oppose an application to the court for the grant of a new tenancy, but his notice must state on which of the grounds mentioned in s. 30, *post*, p. 905, he will oppose the application (*ibid.*, s. 26 (5), (6)).

Application to court for new tenancy.—Application may be made by the tenant—

(*a*) if the landlord has given notice to terminate the tenancy under s. 25, *ante*, p. 901 ; or

(*b*) if the tenant has requested a new tenancy under s. 26, above.

The landlord may have given notice under s. 25 either where the original tenancy was for a fixed term or where it was a periodic tenancy. The tenant will not then be able to apply to the court for a new tenancy unless the tenant, within the period of two months from the giving of the landlord's notice, has notified the landlord (the form not being prescribed) that he will not be willing to give up possession (*ibid.*, s. 29 (2)). An application must be made not less than two nor more than four months after the giving of the landlord's notice under s. 25 (*ibid.*, s. 29 (3)). By a majority, the House of Lords has decided that the s. 29 (3) time-limits do not go to the jurisdiction of the court and are merely procedural, and so capable of being waived by a landlord (*Kammins Ballrooms Co., Ltd.* v. *Zenith Investments (Torquay), Ltd.* [1971] A.C. 750 ; on the facts it was held, by a different majority, that there had been no waiver where the point that the tenant's application had been made too soon was not taken until it was too late).

The procedure where the tenant requests a new tenancy under s. 26 is different ; in that case there was formerly a tenancy for a term of years certain and the initiative is taken by the tenant serving notice claiming a new tenancy. On receipt of such a notice the landlord must, if he wishes to oppose the grant of a new tenancy, within two months serve a notice on the tenant : see above. Only if he does this will he be able to sustain that opposition on the ground he states. The application to the court must be made by the tenant not less than two nor more than four months after the making of the tenant's request for a new tenancy (*ibid.*, s. 29 (3)). If the premises are sold by the landlord within the two-month period after the tenant served his notice claiming a new tenancy, it appears that the purchaser may serve notice opposing the grant of a new tenancy on any of grounds (*a*) to (*f*) of s. 30 (1) mentioned below, provided the vendor has not already served such a notice (*X.L. Fisheries, Ltd.* v. *Leeds Corporation* [1955] 2 Q.B. 636).

On the making of an application the existing tenancy is continued until three months after the application has been finally disposed of (*ibid.*, s. 64). An out-of-time application where there has been no waiver or acquiescence by the landlord is still an application effecting a continuance of the tenancy within s. 64 of the 1954 Act (*Zenith Invsetments (Torquay), Ltd.* v. *Kammins Ballrooms Co., Ltd. (No. 2)* [1971] 1 W.L.R. 1751). With a view to mitigating possible hardship to the landlord caused by the continuation of the existing tenancy at less than the current market rent, it is now provided that the landlord may apply to the court to determine a reasonable rent while the tenancy continues (s. 3 of the L.P.A. 1969, inserting a new section, s. 24A, into the 1954 Act ; see *Regis Property Co., Ltd.* v. *Lewis & Peat, Ltd.* [1970] Ch. 695, and compare *English Exporters (London), Ltd.* v. *Eldonwall, Ltd.*

[1973] 1 All E.R. 726). The interim rent will generally be payable from the date on which the proceedings to determine it were commenced, if later than the date specified in the landlord's notice or the tenant's request (*Stream Properties, Ltd.* v. *Davis* [1972] 1 W.L.R. 645).

Grounds on which landlord may oppose new tenancy.—As noted, *ante*, p. 902, where the landlord serves a notice under s. 25 he must state the grounds on which he would oppose an application. Similarly, where the tenant requests a new tenancy under s. 26 the landlord may give notice that he will oppose an application and such a notice must state the grounds ; see *ante*, p. 904. The landlord may not oppose an application, in either case, other than on such of the grounds, set out in s. 30 (1), as were stated in the appropriate notice.

" It is sufficient for the landlords in their notice of opposition to specify the particular paragraph (*a*), (*b*), (*c*), (*d*), (*e*), (*f*) or (*g*) of s. 30 (1)—upon which they rely. It is not necessary for them to specify any of the subsidiary portions of a paragraph, so long as they make clear which is the paragraph on which they rely " (Denning, L.J., in *Biles* v. *Caesar* [1957] 1 W.L.R. 156, followed in *Bolton's (House Furnishers), Ltd.* v. *Oppenheim* [1959] 1 W.L.R. 913 and in *Sevenarts, Ltd.* v. *Busvine* [1969] 1 W.L.R. 1928).

The grounds specified in s. 30 (1) are as follows :—

" (*a*) where under the current tenancy the tenant has any obligations as respects the repair and maintenance of the holding, that the tenant ought not to be granted a new tenancy in view of the state of repair of the holding, being a state resulting from the tenant's failure to comply with the said obligations ;

(*b*) that the tenant ought not to be granted a new tenancy in view of his persistent delay in paying rent which has become due ;

(*c*) that the tenant ought not to be granted a new tenancy in view of other substantial breaches by him of his obligations under the current tenancy, or for any other reason connected with the tenant's use or management of the holding ;

(*d*) that the landlord has offered and is willing to provide or secure the provision of alternative accommodation for the tenant, that the terms on which the alternative accommodation is available are reasonable having regard to the terms of the current tenancy and to all other relevant circumstances, and that the accommodation and the time at which it will be available are suitable for the tenant's requirements (including the requirement to preserve goodwill) having regard to the nature and class of his business and to the situation and extent of, and facilities afforded by, the holding ;

(*e*) where the current tenancy was created by the sub-letting of part only of the property comprised in a superior tenancy and the landlord is the owner of an interest in reversion expectant on the termination of a superior tenancy, that the aggregate of the rents reasonably obtainable on separate lettings of the holding and the remainder of that property would be substantially less than the rent reasonably obtainable on a letting of that property as a whole, that on the termination of the current tenancy the landlord requires possession of the holding for the purpose of letting or otherwise disposing of the said property as a whole, and that in view thereof the tenant ought not to be granted a new tenancy ;

(f) that on the termination of the current tenancy the landlord *intends* to *demolish or reconstruct* the premises comprised in the holding or a substantial part of those premises or to carry out substantial work of construction on the holding or part thereof *and that he could not reasonably do so without obtaining possession* of the holding ;

(g) subject as hereinafter provided, that on the termination of the current tenancy the landlord *intends* to *occupy the holding* for the purposes, or partly for the purposes, of a business to be carried on by him therein, or as his residence."

Under heads (a), (b) and (c) the court is entitled to consider all the circumstances in connection with the breaches of covenant and to consider the conduct of the tenant as a whole in regard to his obligations under the tenancy and is *not* confined only to those breaches specified in the landlord's notice of opposition (*Eichner* v. *Midland Bank Executor & Trustee Co. Ltd.* [1970] 1 W.L.R. 1120).

" *intends.*"—The relevant date for determining whether the landlord has the required intention is the date of the hearing and not the date of service of the landlord's notice of opposition (*Betty's Cafés, Ltd.* v. *Phillips Furnishing Stores, Ltd.* [1959] A.C. 20). " The decision means in effect that when a landlord serves his notice he must have a genuine expectation that at the trial he will be able to establish that he then has a genuine desire to carry out the work stated, coupled with reasonable prospects of giving effect to that wish ; at the trial he must prove this. The mere fact that he has not obtained all the necessary consents and approvals (e.g., planning permission) will not bring him to grief if there is a reasonable prospect of removing the remaining obstacles " (R. E. Megarry, Q.C., in *Law Quarterly Review*, vol. 74, p. 346). As to ascertaining the necessary intention from any relevant evidence (a resolution not being essential) where the landlord is a local authority or other body corporate, see *Poppett's Caterers, Ltd.* v. *Maidenhead Borough Council* [1971] 1 W.L.R. 69.

The person who is " landlord " within the meaning of s. 44 of the 1954 Act, *post*, p. 911, at the date of the hearing may oppose by virtue of para. (g) even if the notice of opposition was given by a previous landlord (*A. D. Wimbush & Son, Ltd.* v. *Franmills Properties, Ltd.* [1961] Ch. 419 ; *Morris Marks* v. *British Waterways Board* [1963] 1 W.L.R. 1008).

A landlord who has purchased within the last five years and so cannot rely on head (g) (see *post*, p. 908) may be tempted to endeavour to obtain possession for his own use by putting forward an insincere case of reconstruction. " In such circumstances the court must be careful to see that s. 30 (1) (f) is fully satisfied before it allows him to get possession. For this purpose the court must be satisfied that the intention to reconstruct is genuine and not colourable ; that it is a firm and settled intention, not likely to be changed ; that the reconstruction is of a substantial part of the premises, indeed so substantial that it cannot be thought to be a device to get possession ; that the work is so extensive that it is necessary to get possession of the holding in order to do it ; and that it is intended to do the work at once and not after a time . . . nevertheless I think it is going too far to say that the work of reconstruction must be the primary purpose " (Denning, L.J., in *Fisher* v. *Taylors Furnishing Stores, Ltd.* [1956] 2 Q.B. 78, at pp. 84, 85, explaining *Atkinson* v. *Bettison* [1955] 1 W.L.R. 1127). See also *Craddock* v. *Hampshire*

County Council [1958] 1 W.L.R. 202 ; *Betty's Cafes, Ltd.* v. *Phillips Furnishing Stores, Ltd.* [1959] A.C. 20 ; *Morris Marks* v. *British Waterways Board* [1963] 1 W.L.R. 1008.

Where the landlord is a limited company its intention can, in some circumstances, be inferred from the intention of its officers and agents. This was done in *H. L. Bolton (Engineering) Co., Ltd.* v. *T. J. Graham & Sons, Ltd.* [1957] 1 Q.B. 159 having regard to the nature of the proposal, to the relative position of the directors, and other relevant circumstances. Nevertheless, a formal resolution at a board meeting to take a particular course of action may sometimes be essential to record the intention of the company ; this was done, for example, in *Espresso Coffee Machine Co., Ltd.* v. *Guardian Assurance Co.* [1959] 1 W.L.R. 250.

" *demolish or reconstruct.*"—In determining whether works will amount to reconstruction one must have regard only to the demised premises and not to a larger unit including them (*Percy E. Cadle & Co., Ltd.* v. *Jacmarch Properties, Ltd.* [1957] 1 Q.B. 323). Ormerod, L.J., said in that case, at p. 329, " the ' reconstruction ' must mean . . . in the first place, a substantial interference with the structure of the premises and then a rebuilding, probably in a different form, of such part of the premises as had been demolished by reason of the interference with the structure." Proof of intention to change the identity or character of the premises by a lesser amount of work is not "reconstruction" (*ibid.*). In *Joel* v. *Swaddle* [1957] 1 W.L.R. 1094 it was decided that in applying this test one should look at the position as a whole and compare the results of the work proposed with the existing state of the premises.

The court is not obliged to grant a new lease merely because demolition, if regarded in isolation, would not be of a substantial part of the premises and construction or reconstruction itself would affect an insubstantial part only. A landlord who proposes to carry out both demolition of part and reconstruction of part may satisfy the requirements of head (*f*) if, looking at " the totality of what is proposed to be done," the proposal involves demolition or reconstruction of a substantial part or carrying out of substantial construction (*Bewlay (Tobacconists), Ltd.* v. *British Bata Shoe Co., Ltd.* [1959] 1 W.L.R. 45). Further, a landlord will satisfy head (*f*) if he shows an intention to demolish all the buildings on the holding, even though such buildings cover only a comparatively small part of the holding (*Housley's, Ltd.* v. *Bloomer-Holt, Ltd.* [1966] 1 W.L.R. 1244). Also it appears that the concreting of the whole of the holding may be to carry out " substantial work of construction " within para. (*f*) (*ibid.*).

If the landlord cannot oppose under head (*g*) because he bought within five years (see below), he may not rely on proposed work of reconstruction which is ancillary only to his main purpose of obtaining possession (*Atkinson* v. *Bettison* [1955] 1 W.L.R. 1127). A landlord who proposes to grant a building lease may satisfy the paragraph (*Gilmour Caterers, Ltd.* v. *St. Bartholomew's Hospital Governors* [1956] 1 Q.B. 387).

" *and that he could not reasonably do so without obtaining possession.*"—The word " possession " here means the legal right to possession of land and " obtaining possession " means putting an end to such rights of possession of the holding as were vested in the tenant under the terms of his current tenancy (*Heath* v. *Drown* [1972] 2 W.L.R. 1306, H.L., where the reservation of a right to enter and repair made it not necessary for the landlord to obtain possession in this sense). Thus an offer by the tenant of unspecified facilities will not defeat the landlord (*Whittingham* v. *Davies* [1962] 1 W.L.R. 142). *Whittingham* v. *Davies* was not followed in *Little Park Service Station* v. *Regent Oil* [1967] 2 Q.B. 655, where it had been found as a fact that the landlords could reasonably carry out the works without obtaining possession and the Court of Appeal held that regard could be paid to a clause in the old lease likely to be repeated in the new lease providing for the landlords to be permitted to enter the premises to carry out structural alterations. Also it had been held that a landlord could obtain possession of the whole by virtue of para. (*f*) even though intended reconstruction requires possession of part only of the holding (*Fernandez* v. *Walding* [1968] 2 Q.B. 606). But it is now expressly provided that a landlord's opposition under para. (*f*) shall not succeed if—

(*a*) the tenant agrees to the inclusion of terms giving the landlord, in effect, reasonable and satisfactory access facilities for carrying out the intended works ; or

(*b*) the tenant is willing to accept an economically (as to rents obtainable) separable part of the holding and either (*a*) above applies to that part or else possession of the remainder suffices for the landlord (s. 7 of the L.P.A. 1969).

These 1969 provisions will hardly be relevant in the ordinary case where a landlord intends to demolish substantially the whole of the premises. No statutory indication is afforded as to the form in which the tenant's agreement or willingness within (*a*) or (*b*) is to be evidenced. Also condition (*b*) raises awkward questions of rents where demolition was otherwise the real issue of fact.

" *occupy the holding.*"—A landlord cannot succeed under head (*g*) if he intends that a company shall occupy even if he holds all the shares except two which are held by nominees ; the company is a separate entity (*Tunstall* v. *Steigman* [1962] 2 Q.B. 593). A landlord who intends to demolish the buildings comprised in the tenancy and then occupy the site must rely on para. (*f*) ; he does not intend to occupy " the holding," which is defined by s. 23 (3) as the property comprised in the tenancy (*Nursery* v. *P. Currie* (*Dartford*), *Ltd.* [1959] 1 W.L.R. 273). Although the " holding " is defined as the *whole* of the premises comprised in the lease it seems that the landlord will succeed if he establishes an intention to occupy a substantial part of the holding within a reasonable time after the lease comes to an end (*Method Development, Ltd.* v. *Jones* [1971] 1 W.L.R. 168, C.A.). The law on this point may not yet be clearly settled and much may depend on the facts.

It is now provided that where a landlord has a " controlling interest " (which is fairly generously defined) in a company any business to be carried on by the company shall be treated for the purposes of head (*g*) as a business carried on by the landlord (s. 6 of the L.P.A. 1969, inserting a new subs. (3) into s. 30 of the 1954 Act).

A landlord is not entitled to oppose an application on the ground specified in para. (*g*) if he purchased his interest within the period of five years before the termination of the current tenancy or after the time when the holding became a business tenancy whichever is the later (1954 Act, s. 30 (2)) ; an interest under successive head leases is to be regarded as a single interest (*Artemiou* v. *Procopiou* [1966] 1 Q.B. 878, distinguishing *Cornish* v. *Brook Green Laundry* [1959] 1 Q.B. 392, as to a landlord having an earlier equitable interest). Where the landlord's interest is held on trust, references in para. (*g*) to the landlord include references to the beneficiaries under the trust or any of them, and, except in the case of a trust arising under a will or on intestacy, the reference to purchase is construed as including the creation of the trust (*ibid.*, s. 41 (2) ; and *Sevenarts, Ltd.* v. *Busvine* [1969] 1 W.L.R. 1929). Such a beneficiary intending to occupy must have such interest under the trusts as to entitle him to possession or, at least, to justify the trustees in letting him in to occupation on his application to do so ; an example is a life tenant either of the land or, apparently, of the proceeds of sale (*Frish, Ltd.* v. *Barclays Bank, Ltd.* [1955] 2 Q.B. 541). The word " purchased " is used in its popular sense of " bought for money " and not as a technical word. Consequently, it does not include surrender of a lease (*H. L. Bolton (Engineering) Co., Ltd.* v. *T. J. Graham & Sons, Ltd.* [1957] 1 Q.B. 159).

As to the date of creation of a landlord's interest, see *Northcote Laundry, Ltd.* v. *Frederick Donnelly* [1968] 1 W.L.R. 562 (date of execution of head lease is relevant, not later date of commencement of its term).

For the purposes of para. (*g*), members of a group of companies are, in effect, to be treated as the landlord, both as to occupying the holding and as to purchase of the interest (s. 10 of the L.P.A. 1969, substituting a new subs. (3) of s. 42 of the 1954 Act).

The court may not order a new tenancy if the landlord establishes one of the grounds specified in s. 30 (1) (1954 Act, s. 31 (1)). Where the court is not satisfied that one of the grounds (*d*), (*e*) or (*f*) exists, but would have been satisfied if the date of termination in the landlord's notice (*ante*, p. 901), or the date for the new tenancy in the tenant's request (*ante*, p. 903), had been *not more than one year later* the court may make a declaration to that effect. The result of such a declaration is that, within fourteen days, the *tenant* may require the court to substitute the later date and so the tenancy will continue until that date but no longer (*ibid.*, s. 31 (2)). The effect is to enable the tenant to continue the existing tenancy as long as reasonably possible having regard to the court's decision.

In the absence of agreement as to the property constituting the holding, the court must designate it by reference to circumstances existing at the date of the order (*ibid.*, s. 32 (1)). The " holding " means the property comprised in the tenancy *less* any part which is not occupied either by the tenant or by a person employed by him for business purposes (*ibid.*, s. 23 (3)). Nevertheless, where the current tenancy includes other property besides the holding the landlord may require the new tenancy to be of the whole property in the current tenancy (*ibid.*, s. 32 (2)). If the landlord and tenant do not agree otherwise the court must determine what is a reasonable length for the new tenancy " in all the circumstances," although if it is a term certain, the period may not exceed fourteen years (*ibid.*, s. 33 ; *Upsons, Ltd.* v. *E. Robins, Ltd.* [1956] 1 Q.B. 131 shows that the court has a wide discretion and may consider grounds of opposition which the landlord failed to establish as of right under ss. 30 and 31). A new lease ordered by the court must begin " on the coming to an end of the current tenancy " (1954 Act, s. 33). By virtue of s. 64, *ante*, p. 904, this may be three months after the termination of all proceedings relating to the application. This rule may cause injustice to the landlord by the continuation of the rent payable under the original lease but the court may reduce the term it would otherwise have fixed for the new lease by the period between the date fixed for expiration of the old lease and the date to which it was extended by statute (*Re No. 88 High Road, Kilburn* [1959] 1 W.L.R. 279). In this case the court, in granting a new lease for about fourteen years, as a guard against inflation, inserted a term that halfway through the term the landlord should have a right to have the rent reviewed if the rental value had by then increased.

If premises are dilapidated and ripe for development, and it is genuinely proposed to develop them, any new tenancy ordered should be for a short term (*London and Provincial Millinery Stores, Ltd.* v. *Barclays Bank, Ltd.* [1962] 1 W.L.R. 510) ; a new lease may contain a power for the lessor to determine it after a certain number of years (*McCombie* v. *Grand Junction Co., Ltd.* [1962] 1 W.L.R. 581).

The rent, in the absence of agreement, is also determined by the court as that at which, having regard to the other terms of tenancy, " the holding might reasonably be expected to be let in the open market by a willing lessor " but disregarding (a) the effect of the occupation by the tenant or his predecessors in title ; (b) goodwill resulting from the tenant's business, whether carried on by him or by a predecessor in the business ; (c) improvements other than those made by the tenant or a predecessor in title in pursuance of an obligation to his immediate landlord ; (d) the benefit of a licence belonging, in effect, to the tenant (*ibid.*, s. 34). In determining the rent the court may, in estimating at what rent the property might be let, admit evidence of the tenant's trading accounts as an indication of the earning capacity of the premises to a potential lessee but not for any other purpose (*Harewood Hotels, Ltd.* v. *Harris* [1958] 1 W.L.R. 108). Originally the only improvements disregarded were those made during the current tenancy to which Pt. II of the 1954 Act applies ; the value of improvements during an earlier tenancy could be taken into account even if it was between the same parties (*Re " Wonderland " Cleethorpes* [1965] A.C. 58). The L.P.A. 1969, s. 1, has widened the class of tenant's improvements which are to be disregarded under s. 34 (c) of the 1954 Act and has also reversed in part *Re " Wonderland " Cleethorpes*. In effect, in determining the rent, the tenant is now additionally entitled to the rent-free benefit of improvements carried out during an earlier tenancy provided then however that (a) the improvements are not more than twenty-one years old ; (b) the holding affected has ever since been within a business tenancy ; and (c) no tenant since has quit (s. 1 of the 1969 Act).

Also, by s. 2 of the L.P.A. 1969, power is expressly conferred on the court to fix a variable rent.

Other terms of the new tenancy, in absence of agreement, are determined by the court having regard to the terms of the current tenancy and other relevant circumstances (*ibid.*, s. 35 ; see also s. 32 (3) as amended by s. 8 of the L.P.A. 1969). A covenant against assignment in the terms indicated on p. 862, *ante*, has been held to be a more drastic change in the tenancy terms than that in *Gold* v. *Brighton Corporation, post*, and to be so novel and burdensome a change as to be not permissible under s. 35 (*Cardshops, Ltd.* v. *Davies* [1971] 1 W.L.R. 591, C.A.). On the grant of a new tenancy restrictions on user may be imposed, even if they were not contained in the former tenancy, provided they do not restrict the existing business (*Gold* v. *Brighton Corporation* [1956] 1 W.L.R. 1291). Unless they agree otherwise, the parties must enter into a lease or agreement embodying the terms agreed or determined by the court, and if requested the tenant must execute a counterpart (*ibid.*, s. 36 (1)). Even at this stage, however, the tenant may withdraw as he has the right, within fourteen days of the making of an order for a new tenancy, to require the court to revoke the order (*ibid.*, s. 36 (2)), although the court may then vary an order as to costs (*ibid.*, s. 36 (3)).

Compensation where new tenancy precluded.—Where *on the making of an application* the court is precluded from ordering a new tenancy on grounds (*e*), (*f*) and (*g*), stated *ante*, pp. 905, 906, but not on any other ground, the tenant is entitled on quitting the holding to compensation (1954 Act, s. 37 (1)). Such compensation cannot be claimed, however, where the tenancy existed on 1st October, 1954, unless, at the date of quitting, the holding has been continuously occupied for the purposes of the tenant's business for at least five years (*ibid.*, Sched. 9, para. 5 ; *Cramas Properties, Ltd.* v. *Connaught Fur Trimmings, Ltd.* [1965] 1 W.L.R. 892). Originally there was no right to compensation unless the tenant applied for a new tenancy, although the matter could be negotiated. Now, however, by virtue of s. 11 of the L.P.A. 1969 (amending s. 37 of the 1954 Act), a right to compensation will arise if the tenant simply quits the holding in response to a landlord's notice under s. 25 or counter-notice under s. 26 (6) if the grounds of opposition specified are limited to those specified in paras. (*e*), (*f*) and (*g*).

The amount of the compensation is normally the rateable value of the holding (or net annual value if that differs from rateable value ; s. 37 (7)), but it is twice that amount if, for the whole of the fourteen years before the termination of the current tenancy, (i) the premises have been occupied wholly or in part for business purposes by the occupier, and (ii) each successive occupier has succeeded to the same business (*ibid.*, s. 37 (2), (3)).

The right to compensation may be excluded by agreement in cases where, at the date of quitting, the business occupation will have been for less than five years (*ibid.*, s. 38 (3)) ; otherwise an agreement purporting to exclude or reduce compensation is void (*ibid.*, s. 38 (2)).

Reversions.—It will often happen that a tenancy is continued by the 1954 Act, or a new tenancy is granted pursuant to the Act, so that it will extend beyond the term of the immediate reversioner. Where a tenancy is so continued the superior tenancy is, nevertheless, so long as it subsists, deemed to be an interest in reversion expectant on the termination of the inferior tenancy (1954 Act, s. 65 (1)). Further, after such superior tenancy has come to an end, the next subsisting superior tenancy, or the freehold reversion, as the case may be, is deemed to be the reversion on the continued tenancy for the purpose of preserving the incidents and obligations thereof (1954 Act, s. 65 (2) ; L.P.A. 1925, s. 139 (1)).

Reversionary tenancies take effect subject to any tenancy continued by, or granted under, the 1954 Act (1954 Act, s. 65 (3), (4)).

Where sub-tenancies exist it is important to consider who is the " landlord" on whom notices must be served and who has various rights under the 1954 Act. For the purposes of Pt. II of that Act, he is the person (whether or not the immediate landlord) who is the owner of that interest which (*a*) is in reversion (whether immediately or not) on the termination of the relevant tenancy ; (*b*) is the fee simple or a tenancy which will not end within fourteen months by effluxion of time and no notice has been given by virtue of which such a tenancy will end within fourteen months (or any continued time under the Act), and (*c*) is not itself a reversion expectant on an interest within (*a*) and (*b*) (1954 Act, s. 44, as amended by L.P.A. 1969, s. 14 (1) ; cf. *Rene Claro (Haute Coiffure), Ltd.* v. *Hallé Concerts Society* [1969] 1 W.L.R. 909). A person who occupies premises as statutory tenant under the Rent Acts has no interest in the premises but merely a personal right to be allowed to remain in occupation. It follows that even if he allows some other person to use part of the premises for business purposes he is not a " landlord " within s. 44 of the 1954 Act (*Piper* v. *Muggleton* [1956] 2 Q.B. 569).

References to a notice to quit (*not* including a notice of termination under s. 25, *ante*, p. 901 ; see s. 69) given by the landlord are to notices given by the *immediate* landlord (*ibid.*, s. 44 (2)). Otherwise the definition given in the last paragraph applies. Thus a tenant wishing to request a new tenancy must serve his notice under s. 26 (*ante*, p. 903) on the person who is the landlord within that definition. To assist the tenant who requires to know who is the landlord as so defined, it is provided that he may (within two years before the expiration of his term) serve on *any* reversioner, or on a mortgagee of a reversion, a notice in the form prescribed in the Landlord and Tenant (Notices) Regulations, 1969 and 1973, asking as to the ownership in fee simple or as to the tenancy of the person served or his mortgagor (1954 Act, s. 40 (2)).

The landlord as so defined is known as the " competent landlord " ; there may be a " mesne landlord," whose interest is intermediate between the relevant tenancy and the interest of the competent landlord, and a " superior landlord " whose interest (whether in fee simple or as tenant) is superior to that of the competent landlord. In any such case the effect of Sched. 6 is, broadly, as follows :—

    (i) the court may order a new tenancy to take effect in reversion to make up a tenancy for the period it considers proper ;

    (ii) a notice given by the competent landlord and any agreement for a new lease binds any mesne landlord ; the mesne landlord may not withhold consent unreasonably, but if he has not consented he is entitled to compensation for any loss ;

    (iii) an agreement between the competent landlord and the tenant does not operate after the end of the interest of that landlord unless every superior landlord who is affected is a party to it.

Contracting-out prohibited.—Any agreement relating to a tenancy to which Pt. II applies is void so far as it " purports " to preclude the tenant from making an application or request under that Part or provides for the termination or surrender of the tenancy or the imposition of a penalty or disability if he does so (1954 Act, s. 38 (1)). However, contracting-out may now be authorised by the court on the joint application of the landlord and tenant in the form of an agreement which either excludes the 1954 provisions as to the continuation and renewal of tenancies or else provides for surrender in specified circumstances (s. 5 of the L.P.A. 1969). This new provision (which becomes s. 38 (4) of the 1954 Act) is expressed as applying on the grant of a " term of years certain " which has been construed as extending not only to a term of one year or more but also to a term for a period certain of less than one year (*Re Land and Premises at Liss, Hants* [1971] Ch. 986). Accordingly contracting-out is enabled in this way on the grant of a business tenancy for a period of six months. See also cases noted *ante*, p. 899, and for cases of urgency a *Practice Direction* at [1973] 1 All E.R. 796.

Mortgaged property.—Anything authorised or required by the 1954 Act to be done by, to or with the landlord shall, if the interest of the landlord is subject to a mortgage and the mortgagee is in possession or a receiver is in receipt of rents and profits, be deemed to be authorised or required to be done by, to or with the mortgagee (1954 Act, s. 67 ; *Meah* v. *Mouskos* [1964] 2 Q.B. 23) ; see also s. 36 (4), *ante*, p. 825.

B. IMPROVEMENTS

Premises in respect of which compensation may be claimed.—The premises to which Pt. I of the Landlord and Tenant Act, 1927, applies are premises held under a *lease* and used wholly or partly for carrying on any trade or business (*ibid.*, s. 17 (1)) including a profession (*ibid.*, s. 17 (3) proviso). But if the premises are used partly for the purposes of a trade or business and partly for other purposes, Pt. I will apply to improvements only if and so far as they are improvements in relation to the trade or business (*ibid.*, s. 17 (4)).

The above statements are subject to the following exceptions, that is to say, Pt. I does not apply in the following cases :—

(*a*) Mining leases (*ibid.*, s. 17 (1)).

(*b*) Agricultural holdings within the meaning of the Agricultural Holdings Act, 1948, s. 1 (1927 Act, s. 17 (1) ; Agricultural Holdings Act, 1948, s. 96 (2)).

(*c*) Premises let to a tenant (but in the case of a tenancy created after 25th March, 1928, only if the contract is in writing and the purpose for which the tenancy has been created is expressed) as the holder of any office, appointment or employment from the landlord (1927 Act, s. 17 (2)).

(*d*) Premises used by the tenant for carrying on the business of sub-letting the premises as residential flats (1927 Act, s. 17 (3) (*b*) ; *Barton* v. *Reed* [1932] 1 Ch. 362).

The word " lease " in the Act has a very wide meaning. It is defined in s. 25 as " a lease, under-lease *or other tenancy*, assignment operating as a lease or under-lease, or an agreement for such lease, under-lease, tenancy, or assignment." The definition would appear to include a weekly tenancy.

The meaning of the words " trade " and " business " is considered *ante*, p. 574.

In *Inland Revenue Commissioners* v. *Maxse* [1919] 1 K.B. 647, Scrutton, L.J., said that the word " profession " used to be confined to the three learned professions : the church, medicine and the law. But he thought that it had now a wider meaning, and that a journalist would carry on a profession. A schoolmaster is a professional man (*Inland Revenue Commissioners* v. *North & Ingram* [1918] 2 K.B. 705), but perhaps not a stockbroker (*Barber & Sons* v. *Inland Revenue Commissioners* [1919] 2 K.B. 222).

Compensation for improvements.—The Landlord and Tenant Act, 1927, provides that a tenant shall be entitled at the termination of his tenancy, on quitting the holding, to be paid by his landlord compensation for any improvement (including the erection of a building) made by him or his predecessors in title which *adds to the letting value of the holding* (*ibid.*, s. 1 (1)). The burden of proof that any increased value is the direct result of the improvement is on the tenant (*ibid.*, s. 1 (1), proviso (*a*)), and in any case compensation must not exceed the amount that the improvement would have cost at the end of the tenancy, allowance being made for necessary repairs (*ibid.*, s. 1 (1), proviso (*b*)). Demolition and rebuilding may amount to " improvement " ; see *National Electric Theatres, Ltd.* v. *Hudgell* [1939] Ch. 553.

A tenant is not entitled to compensation in respect of trade or other fixtures which the tenant is by law entitled to remove (*ibid.*, s. 1 (1)) ; or for improvements—

(*a*) made before 25th March, 1928 (*ibid.*, s. 2 (1) (*a*)) ;

(*b*) begun before 1st October, 1954, in pursuance of a statutory obligation (*ibid.*, s. 2 (1) (*b*) ; Landlord and Tenant Act, 1954, s. 48 (1)) ;

(*c*) made in pursuance of a contractual obligation for value whether or not that obligation is in favour of the landlord (1927 Act, s. 2 (1) (*b*) ; *Owen Owen Estate, Ltd.* v. *Livett* [1956] Ch. 1) ;

(*d*) made less than three years before the termination of the tenancy and begun before 1st October, 1954 (*ibid.*, s. 2 (1) (*c*) ; Landlord and Tenant Act, 1954, s. 48 (2)) ;

(*e*) if the landlord can show that the proposed improvement will be of no advantage to him, for instance, on the ground that he intends on the termination of the tenancy to demolish the premises, or to make structural alterations in the premises or to use the premises for a different purpose ; in such cases he may have to pay no compensation or only a reduced amount of compensation (1927 Act, s. 1 (2), (3)).

As the tenant is not entitled to be paid compensation for improvements until the termination of the tenancy, it is important that the tenant should, on completing his improvement, get a certificate of completion from his landlord under s. 3 (6), because when the claim arises the landlord may have parted with the premises and the new landlord will naturally require evidence of the making of the improvement. The tenant also may have assigned his interest and his assignee will require the certificate.

Compensation cannot be claimed unless, before commencing the work, the tenant notified the landlord of his intention and sent a specification and plan showing the nature of the improvement and the part of the premises affected. If, within three months, the landlord objects to the proposal, the tenant, to obtain any right to compensation, must (except where the improvement is made in pursuance of a statutory obligation) apply to the tribunal for a certificate that the improvement (*a*) is calculated to add to the letting value, (*b*) is reasonable and suitable to the premises, and (*c*) will not diminish the value of other property belonging to the same landlord ; and no certificate may be given if the landlord has offered to execute the improvement in consideration of a reasonable increase of rent (*ibid.*, s. 3 ; Landlord and Tenant Act, 1954, s. 48 (1)).

" Tenant " is defined as a person entitled in possession under a contract of tenancy, whether his interest was acquired by original contract, assignment, operation of law or otherwise (1927 Act, s. 25 (1)). It appears that a tenant can claim for improvements made during the term of a new lease granted under s. 5 (now repealed) in lieu of compensation for goodwill. Compare *Lawrence* v. *Sinclair* [1949] 2 K.B. 77.

Time for claim.—A claim for compensation must be made within the appropriate one of the following periods :—

(i) Where the tenancy is terminated by notice to quit, or by a notice given under Pt. I (*post*, p. 934 *et seq.*) or Pt. II (*ante*, p. 898 *et seq.*) of the 1954 Act, within three months from the giving of the notice.

(ii) Where the tenancy is terminated by the tenant's request for a new tenancy under s. 26 of the 1954 Act (*ante*, p. 903), within three months from the date when the landlord gives notice of opposition under s. 26 (6), or could have given such notice.

(iii) Where the tenancy comes to an end by effluxion of time, not earlier than six nor later than three months before the end of the tenancy.

(iv) Where the tenancy is terminated by forfeiture or re-entry, within three months from the effective date (that is, the date on which it is expressed to take effect or on which it ceases to be subject to appeal, whichever is the later) of an order for possession, or on re-entry without such an order, within three months from the date of re-entry (Landlord and Tenant Act, 1954, s. 47).

Persons from whom compensation may be claimed.—The claim is against the " landlord," that is, " Any person who under a lease is, as between himself and the tenant or other lessee, for the time being entitled to the rents and profits of the demised premises payable under the lease " (1927 Act, s. 25). Therefore, a trustee and not the beneficiaries would be the landlord. A mortgagee in possession would be the landlord, but not a receiver, as he would be deemed to be the agent of the mortgagor. A mortgagee who becomes the owner under the Limitation Act, 1939, or under an order of foreclosure, would also be the landlord. As to the power of a mortgagee, who has paid compensation, to obtain a charge on the premises, see *ante*, p. 827. Until a mortgagee takes possession of the property there seems to be nothing in the Act to give the tenant who has become entitled to compensation for improvements a claim against him or a charge on the property.

If an immediate landlord has omitted to send to the superior landlord copies of all documents and claims which have been sent to him by the tenant, he may not be able to get back the compensation which he has paid to the tenant. It will be better to give s. 8, which deals with the matter, in full as amended by the 1954 Act :—

" 8.—(1) Where, in the case of any holding, there are several persons standing in the relation to each other of lessor and lessee, the following provisions shall apply :—

Any mesne landlord who has paid or is liable to pay compensation under this Part of this Act shall, at the end of his term, be entitled to compensation from his immediate landlord in like manner and on the same conditions as if he had himself made the improvement in question except that it shall be sufficient if the claim for compensation is made at least two months before the expiration of his term."

[It would seem that the mesne landlord will not be entitled to obtain compensation from his landlord unless he has actually paid compensation to the tenant. Therefore if he has compromised the claim by renewing the tenancy, he will have no claim against the superior landlord. The immediate landlord can only get the compensation repaid at the end of his tenancy. The amount he will be entitled to will, it is assumed, be the unexhausted value of the improvement.]

" A mesne landlord shall not be entitled to make a claim under this section unless he has, within the time and in the manner prescribed, served on his immediate superior landlord copies of all documents relating to proposed improvements and claims which have been sent to him in pursuance of this Part of this Act :

Where such copies are so served, the said superior landlord shall have, in addition to the mesne landlord, the powers conferred by or in pursuance of this Part of this Act in like manner as if he were the immediate landlord of the occupying tenant, and shall, in the manner and to the extent prescribed, be at liberty to appear before the tribunal and shall be bound by the proceedings :

(2) In this section, references to a landlord shall include references to his predecessors in title."

The provisions applicable where the landlord is a tenant for life, statutory owner, trustee for sale or personal representative are contained in ss. 12 and 13 of and Sched. 1 to the 1927 Act. Section 13 (1) provides, in effect, that capital money arising under the S.L.A. 1925 (either as originally enacted or as applied in relation to trusts for sale by s. 28 of the L.P.A. 1925) may be applied (a) in payment as for an improvement authorised by the S.L.A. 1925 of money expended by a landlord in the execution of an improvement ; (b) in payment to a tenant for compensation for an improvement ; (c) in payment of costs of opposing any proposal by a tenant to execute an improvement. It is also provided that the satisfaction of a claim for compensation shall be included amongst the purposes for which a tenant for life, statutory owner, trustee for sale, or personal representative may raise money under s. 71 of the S.L.A. 1925, and that, where the landlord is a tenant for life or in a fiduciary position, he is entitled to require the compensation to be paid out of any capital money held on the same trusts as the settled land.

Section 12 of, and Sched. 1 to, the Act, provide for an amount expended or paid as compensation being made a charge on the premises by means of an application to and an order from the Minister of Agriculture, Fisheries and Food.

Contracting out.—Section 9 of the 1927 Act provides that Pt. I " shall apply notwithstanding any contract to the contrary, being a contract made at any time after the 8th day of February, 1927 : Provided that if, on the hearing of a claim or application under this Part of this Act it appears to the tribunal that a contract made after such date as aforesaid, so far as it deprives any person of any right under this Part of this Act, was made for adequate consideration, the tribunal shall in determining the matter give effect thereto." As to the meaning of the word " adequate," see *Holt* v. *Cadogan* (1930), 46 T.L.R. 271 and *Etam, Ltd.* v. *Forte* [1955] 1 Q.B. 239. By the Landlord and Tenant Act, 1954, s. 49, however, this proviso has effect only in the case of a contract made before 10th December, 1953.

PART 7.   RESIDENTIAL PREMISES

It is impossible to give a summary of the statutes on this subject in this book and discussion is limited to matters of direct concern in conveyancing as such. Accordingly it is only intended to deal with the statutory provisions relating to long leases at low rents (i.e., under two-thirds rateable value) on the basis that these do come within the scope of a treatise " on title," unlike the rules controlling and regulating unfurnished and furnished lettings which are now largely consolidated in the Rent Act, 1968 (as supplemented by the Housing Finance Act, 1972, and also the Counter-Inflation Act, 1973). This is a somewhat artificial division but it is considered preferable not to include any necessarily superficial and therefore potentially misleading outline of these latter extremely complicated rules. It is important, however, that on purchase of a house that is, or may be, affected by the restrictions in the Rent Acts, the inquiries mentioned below are made for the protection of the purchaser. The duty of a purchaser's solicitor to make inquiries as to regulated (or controlled) rents was confirmed in *Goody* v. *Baring* [1956] 1 W.L.R. 448. Thus normally the inquiries should ask at least whether the house is subject to the Rent Acts' protection, and if so whether the tenancy is contractual or statutory ; whether a fair rent has been registered ; whether there is any rent agreement.

A. THE LEASEHOLD REFORM ACT, 1967

Statutory rights of novelty and substance may now arise out of the landlord and tenant relationship in recognition of the somewhat controversial concept " that the land belongs in equity to the landowner and the house belongs in equity to the occupying leaseholder " (White Paper on Leasehold Reform in England and Wales, Cmnd. 2916, para. 4). The Leasehold Reform Act, 1967, according to its long title is primarily : " An Act to enable tenants of houses held on long leases at low rents to acquire [on fair terms] the freehold or an extended lease ; . . ." (the bracketed words are borrowed from s. 1 (1) of the Act). The four requisites for the operation of the Act indicated by this quotation are considered *seriatim* below. But first it should be mentioned that the provisions in point (i.e., Part I of the Act) came into force on 1st January, 1968 (s. 41 (4) and Leasehold Reform Act, 1967, Commencement Order, 1967), although certain transitional provisions (ss. 34–36) came into force on 27th October, 1967 (s. 41 (4)). The Act is, of course, capable of applying to then existing landlord and tenant relationships.

Readers may with advantage refer to the very full review of the cases, problems and literature inspired by the 1967 Act carried out by Alec Samuels in the *Solicitors' Journal*, vol. 115, p. 275.

Contracting out prohibited.—Any agreement relating to a tenancy (whether contained in the instrument creating the tenancy or not and whether made before the creation of the tenancy or not) is void in so far as it purports to exclude or modify any right to acquire the freehold or an extended lease or provides for the termination or surrender of the tenancy or the imposition of any penalty or disability in the event of a tenant acquiring or claiming such a right (s. 23 (1)). The wording of this provision follows that of s. 38 (1) of the Landlord and Tenant Act, 1954, which is considered *ante*, p. 912, as relaxed by s. 5 of the L.P.A. 1969.

This prohibition does not preclude a tenant from surrendering his tenancy and does not invalidate three specified sorts of agreement (s. 23 (2)). These excepted agreements are (*a*) an agreement for a tenant to acquire a superior interest or an extended lease on other than statutory terms ; (*b*) an agreement between landlord and tenant that the tenant's statutory notice (see *post*, p. 924) shall cease to be binding and restricting any further notice for five years ; (*c*) an agreement as to the amount of a tenant's compensation (see *post*, p. 932). However, the Act goes on to provide that an agreement for the surrender of a tenancy or an agreement within (*a*) above may be set aside or varied by the court unless entered into with the court's prior approval (s. 23 (3)). The test the court is to apply to such an agreement is whether the tenant is adequately recompensed for his statutory rights (*ibid.*). Nevertheless it appears clear from subs. (3) that only agreements are open to the court's scrutiny ; no jurisdiction would appear to be conferred to set aside or vary either an actual surrender, by deed or operation of law, or the completed grant of a superior interest or extended lease.

Four requisites.—The cumulative requirements for the right of enfranchisement or extension to arise are as follows :—

(1) **Tenant.**—The ordinary meaning of the word " tenant " is qualified for the purposes of operating the Act. Principally, in order to claim the statutory rights, a tenant must at the time of giving notice of his claim, first, actually be " *occupying the house as his residence*," and secondly, have been so occupying it under a long tenancy at a low rent for the preceding five years or for periods amounting to five years in the preceding ten years (s. 1 (1) (*b*)). Further, references to the tenant occupying as his residence mean that the tenant is occupying the house, in right of his tenancy, " as his only or main residence " (s. 1 (2)). However, it has been decided that a husband and wife may each have a main residence for present purposes despite being happily married and cohabiting when possible (*Fowell* v. *Radford* (1970), 21 P. & C.R. 99, C.A.). Nevertheless, in any case of an individual having multiple residences, a potentially difficult question of fact will arise ; no right of election is conferred on the tenant (contrast s. 29 of the Finance Act, 1965, relating to exemption from capital gains tax).

However, neither the fact that the main residence is used also for other purposes nor the fact that the tenant occupies part only of the house is a disqualification (s. 1 (2) (*a*)). Thus a tenant who occupies part only of the house and sub-lets the rest is still entitled to acquire the freehold of the whole (*Harris* v. *Swick Securities, Ltd.* [1969] 1 W.L.R. 1604, C.A.). Again, in determining in what right the tenant occupies, any mortgage terms and attornment clauses are to be disregarded (s. 1 (2) (*b*)). But the Act does not treat a tenant as occupying a house at any time when it is (*a*) let to and occupied by him with other land or premises to which it is ancillary ; or (*b*) comprised in an agricultural holding (s. 1 (3)). Also the occupation of a company or other artificial person is not to be taken to be the occupation by any person of the property as his residence ; and a corporation sole is not to be treated as an occupying tenant (s. 37 (5)).

Beneficiaries.—Occupation by a person as beneficiary under a trust or strict settlement of the leasehold house in question can be counted towards the qualifying period of occupation mentioned above (s. 6). If the occupying beneficiary has become absolutely entitled to the house then he may claim the statutory rights for himself as tenant in the ordinary way (s. 6 (1)). If the trust or strict settlement still subsists, the statutory rights are exercisable by the trustees or tenant for life as appropriate for the benefit of the trust (s. 6 (2) (3)). This last involves a statutory enunciation of the rule in *Keech* v. *Sandford* (1726), Cas. t. King 61 (see *ante*, p. 788) and the section also extends the powers of trustees and tenants for life and indicates the conveyancing machinery as far as necessary (s. 6 (2) (*a*) (*b*), (4) and (5)).

Succession on death.—Another extension arises where a tenant has died within, in effect, the previous five years. The present tenant may count towards his qualifying period of occupation any time when the house was his only or main residence provided (i) that the then tenant, now deceased, was also in occupation under the tenancy, (ii) he became entitled on the death to the same tenancy, and (iii) he is a member of the deceased tenant's family (s. 7). It is entirely immaterial how the present tenant became entitled on the death (even a purchase from the deceased tenant's personal representatives suffices), provided only, it would appear, that there has been no intermediate assent or conveyance to any other person (s. 7 (2)). Further, the section applies whether the occupation of the deceased and present tenants was because they were entitled absolutely or beneficially under a trust (s. 7 (3), (4), (5), (6)). The members of a tenant's family for present purposes are his spouse, children, children-in-law and spouse's children, expressly including illegitimate, adopted and step-children, and his or his wife's parents (s. 7 (7)). Lastly, the section applies whenever the tenant died, even if it were before the passing of the Act (s. 7 (9)).

A case likely to arise frequently in practice involves a combination of the preceding two paragraphs. If the tenant occupying under a long lease dies leaving his estate (including the tenancy) on trust for sale with a life interest for his widow, and if the widow is permitted by the trustees to occupy the house (whether or not in pursuance of a testamentary direction), then the *trustees* will as a rule be able to exercise the statutory rights (ss. 6 (3) and 7 (6) of the 1967 Act.)

Sub-tenancies.—The rights created by the Act are available also to sub-tenants, assuming that the other requisites of occupation, etc., are all satisfied (s. 5 (4)). However, this will not be so if the sub-tenancy has been granted in breach of covenant in the superior lease, the breach not having been waived, *unless* the superior lease happens itself to be a long tenancy at a low rent when apparently the breach of covenant is simply irrelevant (s. 5 (4)). Schedule 1 to the Act contains the detailed provisions governing the position where a sub-tenant wished to acquire the freehold or an extended lease. In essence, the scheme of the Schedule is to identify one of the persons with superior interests, freehold or leasehold, as " the reversioner " ; that person is then to take all steps, conduct all proceedings and execute all documents for giving effect to (or resisting) the sub-tenant's claim (paras. 1 and 4). The reversioner will do all this on behalf of the " other landlords " ; his acts within his authority will bind them and their interests, and provided he acts in good faith and with reasonable care and diligence he will incur no liability (paras. 1 (1) (*b*) (2) and 4 (2) (4)). Nevertheless provision is made to enable any of the other landlords to act separately in relation to legal proceedings, deduction of his title, and ascertainment and payment of the price (para. 5). Apart from this, a duty of co-operation and contribution is imposed on the other landlords (paras. 5 (5) and (6)).

" The reversioner " who needs must assume these somewhat invidious responsibilities is the person whose reversionary leasehold interest would give him : " an expectation of possession of thirty years or more," which is apparently to be construed as meaning that, but for the Act, he would have got *occupation* (not just receipt of rent) for such a period after due termination of the sub-tenancy (paras. 2, 13). If there happens to be more than one such person, then those with the more superior leasehold interests (if one can so say) are relieved from being the reversioner (para. 2 (*a*)), i.e., the first who would have got occupation is identified. If no person enjoys such a leasehold interest, then the freeholder is to be identified as the reversioner (para. 2 (*b*)). Provision is made for the court to appoint some other person as the reversioner or to replace the reversioner in specified circumstances (para. 3).

(2) **House.**—For the purposes of the Leasehold Reform Act, 1967, there are two aspects of this requisite. The first, more simply stated, is that the rateable value of the house on 23rd March, 1965 (or the later date on which such a value is first shown in the valuation list) must not exceed £200 or in Greater London £400 (s. 1 (1) (*a*), (4)).

A tenant in London who made a first floor opening between two adjoining residential properties which were together rated at over £600 was nevertheless held entitled to acquire the freehold of one as a separate house of rateable value £326 (*Wolf* v. *Crutchley* [1971] 1 W.L.R. 99, C.A. ; but cp. *Parsons* v. *Trustees of Henry Smith's Charity* [1973] 3 All E.R. 23, C.A., where a sub-let lock-up garage in the house meant an excessive rateable value).

The second more complex aspect is the meaning to be given to " house " itself : the word is to include " any building designed or adapted for living in and *reasonably so called*, notwithstanding that the building is not structurally detached, or was or is not solely designed or adapted for living in, or is divided horizontally into flats or maisonettes " (s. 2 (1)). It appears clear from this definition that, although the original purpose of a building may not be material, not every building actually lived in will qualify. " Temporary accommodation such as mobile caravans, boats houses and tents are not ' houses ' because they cannot reasonably be called such ; if immobilised, it must be doubtful whether they are buildings. Stables, barns, garages and workshops, though ' buildings,' are not ' houses ' if not adapted to living in ; but if they are so adapted, they are ' houses ' if on the facts they can be reasonably so called " (Woodfall, Landlord and Tenant, 27th ed., vol. 2, p. 1654). Equally a single house converted into flats is clearly included as a " house," but what is not quite so clear is whether a purpose-built block of flats or a lock-up shop with flats over would come within the definition. An intention to exclude such buildings from being treated as a " house " can be inferred from the phrase " reasonably so called," but it is thought by no means certain that this intention is fulfilled (cp. the width of any dictionary definition of " house "). However, some assistance with these queries can now be derived from judgments in *Lake* v. *Bennett* [1970] 1 Q.B. 663, C.A. There Salmon, L.J., (at p. 672) observed that : " It is quite plain that the definition of ' house ' including ' any building designed or adapted for living in ' must need some qualification. Otherwise it would apply to the Ritz Hotel and to Rowton House, and a large purpose-built block of flats, when quite obviously this Act was not intended to apply to such edifices." Again, Lord Denning, M.R. (at p. 671), without attempting a definition, said : " I do not think that a tower block of flats would reasonably be called a ' house.' But I think a four-storeyed building like the present one is reasonably called a ' house.' Take it in stages. First, if the tenant occupied the building entirely by himself, using the ground floor for his shop premises, that would plainly be a ' house ' reasonably so-called. Second, if the tenant, instead of using the ground floor himself for business purposes, sub-lets it, that does not alter the character of the building. It is still a ' house ' reasonably so-called. And that is this case." See further an article by Trevor M. Aldridge in *Solicitors' Journal*, vol. 114, p. 947.

The Act goes on to explain that in any case the individual flats (or other units of horizontal division) are not themselves separate " houses " although the building as a whole may be (s. 2 (1) (*a*) ; remember that whilst the claimant must be tenant of the whole he need only occupy part : see *ante*, p. 918). Conversely, where there is a vertical division, the building as a whole is not a " house " although any of the individual semi-detached or terraced units produced may be (s. 2 (1) (b) and see *Harper* v. *Harris* noted at (1968), 112 Sol. J. 954). By way of a further explicit exclusion, it is also provided that for present purposes a house is not a house if it is not structurally detached and a material part of it lies above or below a part of the structure not comprised in the house (s. 2 (2)). Since flats and semi-detached houses have already been dealt with, this subsection can only be directed at irregularly divided buildings, when it could be a difficult question of construction and fact to determine what is or is not a " material part " of a house. In one case, a tenant of premises consisting of a ground-floor shop and three floors of living accommodation above who had years ago physically joined the shop with the next door shop was not prevented by s. 2 (2) from acquiring the freehold of the original premises (*Peck* v. *Anicar Properties, Ltd.* [1971] 1 All E.R. 517, C.A. ; i.e., the hole in the shop wall was not a way out of the Act for the landlord). But in another the Act was held not to apply where part of a " house " overhung a garage used by an adjoining house even though the overhanging part had at one time belonged to the adjoining house (*Parsons* v. *Trustees of Henry Smith's Charity* [1973] 3 All E.R. 23, C.A.). In this case the overhanging part consisted substantially of two rooms and a w.c. and a bathroom so that it was found impossible not to say that it was a " material part " on any test. However, Stephenson, L.J., expressed the view (at *ibid.*, p. 30) that " Assuming ' material ' does not simply point the contrast with ' trivial ' or ' insignificant,' I think that it must mean material to the tenant or to his enjoyment of the house and that if it is material in that sense it will be of such significance as to alter the house into a flat, and so take it outside the Act." See also *Wolf* v. *Crutchley* [1971] 1 W.L.R. 99, C.A., *ante.*

It is important to note that the statutory rights conferred on the tenant of a house as above are to acquire the freehold or an extended lease of " the house and premises " (s. 1 (1)). The reference to premises is to be taken as meaning " any garage, outhouse, garden, yard and appurtenances " which, at the time the tenant gave his statutory notice (see *post*, p. 924), are " let to him with the house and are occupied with and used for the purposes of the house or any part of it by him or by another occupant " (s. 2 (3)). This latter " let . . . with " requirement could cause much the same difficult questions of construction and fact that already arise with the phrase " let together with " in, now, s. 1 (2) of the Rent Act, 1968. Following the cases on that phrase, there would appear no absolute necessity for the premises to have been let by the same instrument or at the same time as the house or at a single rent (see *Wimbush* v. *Cibulia* [1949] 2 K.B. 564) ; but then the parties must at least have intended that the two lettings should be inter-dependent, which presumably will not be so, for example, if there are different terms (cp. *Metropolitan Properties Co. (F.G.C.), Ltd.* v. *Barder* [1968] 1 W.L.R. 286). However, in the present context, this " let . . . with " requirement as a limit on the tenant's statutory rights may well be found to beat the air in many cases. The point is that the ultimate conveyance to the tenant will have the general words implied into it by s. 62 of the L.P.A. 1925, and these words are not only wide enough to include most of the premises as defined (see s. 62 (1) and (2) set out *ante*, pp. 511–512) but cannot be excluded or restricted (s. 10 (1) of the 1967 Act).

In addition, certain other inclusions into and exclusions from the house and premises for present purposes are allowed. Thus the landlord may insist on the inclusion of any other premises once but no longer " let with " the house if he objects to further severance, e.g., if he would be left with a useless piece of land or part of a building (s. 2 (4)). Conversely, at the landlord's

instance, there may be excluded any part of the house or premises which lies
above or below other premises belonging to the landlord, he objecting to
further severance (s. 2 (5)) ; it will be appreciated that this excluded part
cannot be material, for if it is the statutory rights will not have arisen anyway
(s. 2 (2)). Underlying mines and minerals do not count as other premises
within s. 2 (5) and the landlord is always entitled to have these excepted
from the conveyance or extended lease, provided proper provision be made
for support of the house and premises (s. 2 (6)). This last proviso would
appear to involve the grant of full rights of support (see *ante*, p. 520 *et seq.*)
and not to permit the reservation of a right to let down the surface even
subject to full compensation.

(3) **Long lease.**—It will be recalled that, to enjoy the statutory rights,
the tenant must not only hold presently on a long lease but must also have
so held throughout the five-year qualifying period (s. 1 (1) (*b*) ; see *ante*,
p. 918). A long lease in this context means " a tenancy *granted* for a term of
years certain exceeding twenty-one years " (s. 3 (1)). For the purposes of
this Part of the Act, the word " tenancy " means " a tenancy at law or *in
equity* " (s. 37 (1) (*f*)), which also expressly excludes tenancies at will, mortgage
terms and interests under trusts or settlements (see also *Curtin* v. *Greater
London Council* (1970), 114 Sol. J. 932, C.A., as to the ineligibility of a tenant
at will).

Not clear at all is the position of a tenant occupying a house under an
agreement for a long lease. The word " granted " as in s. 3 (1) would
ordinarily be taken as excluding a tenancy agreement (see *City Permanent
Building Society* v. *Miller* [1952] Ch. 840, as to s. 70 (1) (*k*) of the L.R.A. 1925 ;
ante, p. 195). Yet the definition section of the Leasehold Reform Act, 1967
(s. 37 (1) (*f*)), expressly includes a tenancy " in equity " and is not made
subject to the context otherwise requiring (cp. s. 3 (x) of the L.R.A. 1925).
An agreement for a lease can almost always be regarded as a lease in equity
(*Walsh* v. *Lonsdale* (1882), 21 Ch. D. 9 ; see *ante*, p. 802 *et seq.*). Nevertheless
it is arguable that the actual wording of s. 3 (1) of the 1967 Act still calls
for there to be a grant of a tenancy rather than merely an agreement therefor,
but that by virtue of the definition section it will suffice for present purposes
if the grant operates not in law but only in equity (e.g., for non-registration
under s. 123 (1) of the L.R.A. 1925, or because the formality of being made
by deed is lacking ; see s. 52 (1) of the L.P.A. 1925, and *Zimbler* v. *Abrahams*
[1903] 1 K.B. 577).

In recognising the length of the term, the possibility of premature termination by notice, re-entry, forfeiture or otherwise is to be ignored (s. 3 (1)).
A perpetually renewable lease (which is turned into a term of 2,000 years ;
see *post*, p. 939 *et seq.*) is to be treated as a long tenancy, *unless* it is a sub-lease
and the superior lease is not a long tenancy (s. 3 (1)). Also, perhaps rather
oddly, tenancies terminable on death or marriage are excluded (s. 3 (1) ;
cp. *post*, p. 941). If after a long tenancy at a low rent, the tenant holds
over under another tenancy of the property or part of it, then the immediate
and all subsequent new tenancies are also deemed to be long tenancies
irrespective of their terms (s. 3 (2) ; cf. *post*, p. 924). If the tenant's new
tenancy after a long tenancy is also itself a long tenancy, then the consecutive
tenancies are to be treated as a single long tenancy for the total term (s. 3 (3)).
A " short " tenancy which is renewable and renewed without payment of a
premium so as to bring the total term to more than twenty-one years is to
be treated as a long tenancy (s. 3 (4)) ; but a tenancy granted to continue

as a periodical tenancy is to be treated as two tenancies, one for the original term and the other for the continued term (s. 37 (4) which appears only applicable if the original was not a long tenancy : cp. s. 3 (2) above). Extensions of tenancies under the Leasehold Property (Temporary Provisions) Act, 1951, or Pts. I or II of the Landlord and Tenant Act, 1954, are included in the 1967 Act's references to long tenancies (s. 3 (5)).

The provisions mentioned above for totalling successive periods of right as a tenant are available only when the subsequent periods stem from a right of renewal or extension (*Roberts* v. *Church Commissioners for England* [1972] 1 Q.B. 278, C.A.). Thus the Act does not extend to a relationship which, not as of right, but merely in fact, ultimately turns out to have produced a continuous relationship of landlord and tenant for over twenty-one years (*ibid.*). Nor does the Act apply where the term of years granted exceeds twenty-one years only because the habendum expressed the term as commencing before the date of the grant of the lease (*ibid.*). Russell, L.J., suggested the test that, to satisfy this statutory meaning of a long lease, " a tenant must at some point of time be, or have been, in a position to say that, subject to options to determine, rights of entry and so forth, he is entitled to remain tenant for the next twenty-one years, whether at law or in equity " (*ibid.*, p. 284).

Provision is also made for a tenant's concurrent tenancies to be treated as a single tenancy, in the following terms : " Where at any time there are separate tenancies, with the same landlord and the same tenant, of two or more parts of a house, or of a house or part of it and land or other premises occupied therewith . . ." they are to be taken together (s. 3 (6)). But the word " premises " is not used here in such a wide sense as to include another house ; it is used in a narrow sense to denote a garage or out-building or such like, ancillary to the house (*Wolf* v. *Crutchley* [1971] 1 W.L.R. 99, C.A.). Accordingly two houses originally let separately but since physically joined are not to be treated as comprised in a single tenancy (*ibid.*).

Termination of tenancy.—Since the Act requires that the tenant should hold presently under a long tenancy, it also contains provisions relating to the premature ending of the term by notice or otherwise. Firstly, no claim to acquire the freehold or an extended lease can be made *either* after a tenant's notice *or* more than two months after a landlord's notice terminating the tenancy (s. 22 (1) (c) and Sched. 3, Pt. I, paras. 1 (1), 2 (1)). This restriction is not applicable if the tenant's notice has been superseded by a new tenancy (para. 1 (1)). For the restriction to apply the landlord's notice must have been given under ss. 4 or 25 of the Landlord and Tenant Act, 1954 (see *post,* p. 935, and *ante,* p. 901) and it is irrelevant that the notice may not have had effect to terminate the tenancy ; but in any case this restriction does not preclude the landlord from consenting to an out-of-time claim or the tenant from claiming, after the two months, an extended lease instead of the freehold if he has found the price of the latter too high (1967 Act, Sched. 3, Pt. I, para. 2 (1), proviso ; s. 9 (3)). However, where a continuation tenancy has been surrendered, although by operation of law and in consequence of a mutual mistake, no claim can be made by the tenant under the 1967 Act (*Curtin* v. *Greater London Council* (1970), 114 Sol. J. 932).

Secondly, no notice by landlord or tenant terminating the tenancy will be of any effect if given during the currency of a claim to statutory rights (paras. 1 (2), 2 (2)). Also, during such currency and for three months thereafter the tenancy is not to terminate by effluxion of time, by landlord's notice to quit or by termination of a superior tenancy (para. 3). Further, during the currency of a claim, no proceedings to enforce a right of re-entry or forfeiture may be brought without leave of the court which must not be granted if the claim was made in good faith (para. 4). The claim will be in good faith only if it is made honestly and with no ulterior motive and not, for example, where the tenant desires to buy the freehold in order to avoid forfeiture of his lease after a conviction for keeping a brothel (*Central Estates (Belgravia), Ltd.* v. *Woolgar* [1972] 1 Q.B. 48, C.A.). This was applied also where a tenant claiming an extended lease was in breach of repairing covenants and would not be able in the future to carry out repairs to the property (*Liverpool Corporation* v. *Husan* [1972] 1 Q.B. 48, C.A.). *Sed quaere :* would the question of repairs have been relevant to good faith if the tenant had been claiming enfranchisement rather than extension ? See comment at *Solicitors' Journal,* vol. 115, p. 645.

(4) **Low rent.**—For present purposes, a lease or tenancy will be at a low rent " at any time when rent is not payable under the tenancy in respect of the property at a yearly rate equal to or more than two-thirds of the rateable value of the property " (s. 4 (1)). The relevant rateable value is that on the latest of (i) 23rd March, 1965, (ii) its first appearance in the valuation list, and (iii) the first day of the term (s. 4 (1)). Deemed *not* low, however, is the rent of a lease granted after August, 1939, and before April, 1963, provided, first, it was not a building lease, and second, its rent exceeded two-thirds of the letting value of the property at its commencement (s. 4 (1), proviso, which takes some notice of inflation ; note that s. 4 (5) establishes a rebuttable presumption that the proviso does not apply, i.e., the onus is put on the landlord).

Subsection 4 (1) also provides that " rent " means " rent reserved as such " and that there must be disregarded " any part of the rent expressed to be payable in consideration of services to be provided, or for repairs, maintenance or insurance " (s. 4 (1) (*b*)). Also to be disregarded is any provision either for a penal addition to the rent in the event of a breach of the terms of the tenancy or for suspension or reduction of rent in the event of damage to the property demised (s. 4 (1) (*c*)). Incidentally, in view of the negative wording adopted in s. 4 (1) for defining a low rent, the expression would appear to include leases under which no rent or a peppercorn rent or other rent having no money value is reserved. Equally the payment of a premium seems irrelevant, except that presumably it would be possible to contend in appropriate circumstances that there was really a lump sum payment in advance of rent.

Finally, as to the requisites for the statutory rights to arise, it should be observed that the Act contains a transitional provision (applicable only where the tenant gave notice on or before 27th January, 1968), whereby any tenancy, on whatever terms, granted by way of continuation of a long tenancy at a low rent which has terminated after 8th December, 1964 (the date of a parliamentary pledge), but before the passing of the Act (27th October, 1967), should also itself be treated as a long tenancy at a low rent (s. 34, extending to statutory tenancies arising on such a termination).

Notices.—Assuming the presence of all the qualifying requirements set out above, the statutory rights become operative only if the tenant gives written notice of his desire to have either the freehold or an extended lease (ss. 5, 8, 14). The procedure generally is regulated by the provisions of Sched. 3, Pt. II (s. 22 (1) (*d*)) which make mandatory the use of a prescribed form containing specified particulars for the tenant's notice (para. 6 (1)). Since such a form, with notes, is set out in the Leasehold Reform (Notices) Regulations, 1967, and is readily obtainable from law stationers, nothing further need be said here as to its details. However, it should be noted that the notice will not be invalidated by any inaccuracy in the specified particulars or any misdescription of the property, and it may be amended as to extent with the court's leave (para. 6 (3)). Nevertheless the notice will be a nullity if it fails to make the tenant's wishes unambiguously clear (*Byrnlea Property Investments, Ltd.* v. *Ramsay* [1969] 2 Q.B. 253, C.A., where the tenant had left intact the phrase " the freehold or an extended lease " in disregard of the marginal instruction " Delete whichever is inapplicable " ; contrast *Lewis* v. *Harries* (1971), 115 Sol. J. 508, C.A., in which a tenant's notice was held valid where an appropriate deletion made in one part only of the prescribed form sufficed to make the tenant's claim clear.)

Although the tenant's notice is to be given to the landlord (ss. 8 and 14) it will be regarded as served on him if it is served on any person having a superior interest in the house and premises (para. 8, which also provides for copies to reach all persons having such an interest). In addition it may be observed in particular that provision is made for a mortgagee in possession or, more likely, his receiver in receipt of rents and profits, to step into the shoes of the mortgagor landlord (Sched. 3, para. 9 ; s. 25). Also, by way of stop gap a procedure is laid down, involving application to the High Court, for dealing with the situation arising where no person (i.e., immediate or superior landlord) can be found or identified to be served (s. 27 ; see generally *Re Robertson's Application* [1969] 1 W.L.R. 109 and *Re Frost's Application* [1970] 1 W.L.R. 1145 ; also *Re Howell's Application* [1972] Ch. 509, as to the payment into court of only six years arrears of rent).

Where a tenant has duly given notice as above, the landlord is obliged within two months to give the tenant notice in reply either admitting the tenant's claim or else stating the ground for not admitting it (para. 7 (1)). Again this notice must be in the prescribed form set out, with notes, in the Leasehold Reform (Notices) Regulations, 1967, and obtainable from law stationers. If the landlord admits the tenant's claim, i.e., his right to have the freehold or an extended lease, the admission is binding as to the presence of the qualifying requirements, unless he shows misrepresentation or conceal-ment of material facts (para. 7 (4)).

Effect of notice.—Once the tenant has duly given his statutory notice to the landlord, then according to the Act the rights, obligations and remedies which arise and are available are the same as if there were a contract for a sale or lease " freely entered into " between the landlord and tenant (s. 5 (1) and (3) ; see also an article by John Tiley in *Conveyancer N.S.*, vol. 33, pp. 43, 141, as to the application of the doctrine of conversion). However, this does not mean that there is to be the equivalent of an entirely open contract between the parties : there is, in effect, a prescribed statutory set of general conditions of sale made under the authority of s. 22 (2) and (3) of the 1967 Act and contained in the Leasehold Reform (Enfranchisement and Extension) Regulations, 1967. Only as to matters not covered by these is the position between the parties analogous to an open contract (s. 22 (2)). The conditions cover much the same ground as the standard sets of conditions of sale used in ordinary conveyancing practice. Thus the various steps in the deduction of title, requisitions, preparation and completion of the conveyance, with time-limits, are dealt with, as also are such aspects as apportionment of outgoings, payment of interest and cancellation of land charges. Two provisions call for comment. Firstly, the landlord in case of enfranchisement may by notice in writing call for payment of a deposit of a sum equal to three times the annual rent or £25, whichever is greater, which will operate as security for costs in case, for example, the tenant withdraws (1967 Regulations, Pt. I, Condition 1). Secondly, a provision is made for service of, in effect, a notice to complete (*ibid.*, Pt. I, Condition 10 ; Pt. II, Condition 5), but the drafting would appear to be inferior to that in Condition 22 of the National Conditions of Sale, 18th ed. (or in Condition 19 of The Law Society's Conditions of Sale, 1973 Revision ; see *ante*, pp. 216–217), in that time is not expressly made of the essence and the period of notice is to be " *at least* two months " ; i.e., the question of whether any particular notice is reasonable can arise and cause uncertainty. However, despite the apparently mandatory imposition of these conditions by the Act (see s. 22 (2)), the regulations themselves expressly permit the landlord and the tenant to " otherwise agree " (paras. 2 and 3), so that it would seem possible to use, suitably adapted, other sets of general conditions of sale.

The benefit and burden of the statutory rights made operative by the tenant's notice may pass to the personal representatives and assigns of the tenant and landlord to the same extent, but no further, as with contractual rights (s. 5 (1)). However, the benefit of these statutory rights is not assignable except with the tenancy, with which such benefit must apparently be expressly assigned or the tenant's notice will cease to have effect (s. 5 (2)).

So far as concerns purchasers of the freehold or other reversion from the landlord, it is made clear by the Act that the tenancy itself does not become registrable, as being an estate contract under the L.C.A. 1972, merely because of the inchoate statutory rights conferred by the 1967 Act (s. 5 (5)). But the tenant's notice, bringing these rights to life as it were, expressly can be protected, as if there were an estate contract, by registration under the L.C.A. 1972, or by an entry of a notice or caution under the L.R.A. 1925 (s. 5 (5) of the 1967 Act). Further, it is expressly declared that no right arising from the statutory notice will be an " overriding interest " within the meaning of the L.R.A. 1925 (i.e., notwithstanding the tenant's actual occupation). These are slightly puzzling provisions. No doubt if not protected as indicated any already served notices may be disregarded by the purchaser from the landlord. Yet there is nothing in the Act to take away the tenant's inchoate statutory rights or to prevent him from at once serving a fresh notice on the new landlord. Thus the consequences of there being no protection by registration appear not very serious, although having to start again may make a difference in individual cases.

Landlords are saved from potential embarrassment, financial or otherwise, as to their contractual relations with others by the provision that the due giving of notice by a tenant will discharge " the landlord and all other persons . . . from the further performance, so far as relates to the disposal in any manner of the landlord's interest in the house and premises or any part thereof, of any contract previously entered into and not providing for the eventuality of such a notice " (s. 5 (7) which has also inserted the cryptic parenthesis : " without prejudice to the general law as to the frustration of contracts "). But if the tenant's notice is of his desire to have an extended lease, this general discharge will only be available if the contract in question (presumably for sale of the reversion) had been entered into on the common basis that vacant possession could be obtained on the termination

of the existing tenancy (s. 5 (7), proviso). In view of the very existence
of the present Act, it is thought that such a common basis will be very
difficult to find.

Notice to treat served under a compulsory purchase order will render a
tenant's statutory notice of no effect, except for the purpose of ascertaining
the compensation payable (s. 5 (6)).

Enfranchisement.—Where all the statutory requirements are satisfied
and the tenant has duly given notice of his desire to acquire the freehold,
the result is that " the landlord shall be bound to make to the tenant, and the
tenant to accept . . . a grant of the house and premises for an estate in fee
simple absolute, subject to the tenancy and to tenant's incumbrances, but
otherwise free from incumbrances " (s. 8 (1)). It is clear from this that there
will not necessarily be any merger of the tenancy although equally clearly
this is not precluded by the Act (see further, *ante*, p. 829). " Tenant's
incumbrances " extend to interests derived out of the tenancy (such as a
sub-tenancy or mortgage of the lease) and to incumbrances binding the
tenancy, even though these may also bind superior interests (s. 8 (2)). The
word " incumbrances " itself is rather peculiarly defined for present purposes
simply as including rent-charges and " personal liabilities attaching in
respect of the ownership of land or an interest in land though not charged
on that land or interest " (s. 8 (2)). This suggests that the word is to be
confined to matters involving the payment of money and does not cover,
e.g., easements or restrictive covenants (see further, *ante*, pp. 105–107).
Support for this view may be found also in the express exclusion from the
meaning of incumbrance of " burdens originating in tenure [presumably
intending to cover any subsisting manorial incidents ; see *ante*, p. 150 *et
seq.*], and burdens in respect of the upkeep or regulation for the benefit of
any locality of any land, building, structure, works, ways or watercourses "
(s. 8 (3)). Although the conveyance to the tenant must be made subject
to these latter burdens (*loc. cit.*), it is not thought that they will thereby
become enforceable directly against him if, as positive burdens, they would
not otherwise run with the land (see *ante*, p. 552).

Thus, generally speaking, the tenant will at least take free of any liabilities
to spend money. But the converse of this is that the conveying landlord
may well remain subject to any such liabilities, either as an original
covenantor or as being bound to indemnify a predecessor in title. Nevertheless, there is nothing in the Act enabling the landlord to call for any
indemnity covenant from the tenant.

However, as to easements and restrictive covenants, whether or not these
are comprehended by the Act's expression " otherwise free of incumbrances "
(in s. 8 (1)), obviously the landlord cannot actually convey free of subsisting
legal interests or equitable interests properly protected by registration.
Nor can he magically rectify a bad or doubtful title. So the questions arise :
Is there any equivalent here to the ordinary vendor's duty to disclose latent
defects in his title (see *ante*, p. 97 *et seq.*)? What remedy has the tenant-
purchaser if an irremoveably incumbered or otherwise defective title is
deduced ? No doubt the statutory obligation to take a conveyance could be
avoided as if a contract for sale were involved (see s. 5 (3) and *ante*, p. 925). But
this course clearly would render the statutory rights conferred on the tenant
particularly fruitless. So, in effect, all that the tenant can usefully require
is that the price be abated by " such deduction (if any) in respect of any

defect in the title to be conveyed to the tenant as on a sale in the open market
might be expected to be allowed between a willing seller and a willing buyer "
(s. 9 (2)). This could raise difficult questions of assessment and of construction, particularly of the phrase " defect in the title." However, it is
important that this point be pursued by the tenant before completion since
he would not appear thereafter to enjoy the benefit of any covenants for
title by the landlord (see below).

Price.—The definition of the consideration which the tenant will have
to give for the conveyance is, of course, of prime importance ; unless he can
get a bargain the statutory right will be of little advantage. The government
idea was that " the price of enfranchisement must be calculated in accordance
with the principle that in equity the bricks and mortar belong to the qualified
leaseholder and the land to the landlord " (White Paper, Cmnd. 2916).
This has been achieved by providing that essentially the price payable is
to be the open market value of the fee simple subject to the tenancy as
extended under the 1967 Act (i.e., for fifty years at a site value rent ; see
below) but disregarding the enfranchisement (s. 9 (1)). The market value
is to be ascertained as at the time the tenant gave his statutory notice and
on the basis of the landlord being a willing seller (ss. 9 (1), 37 (1) (d)). It is
also to be assumed that the sale in the open market would be subject to and
with the benefit of the same rights and obligations as the tenant will take
(s. 9 (1) (c) ; see as to the contents of the conveyance below). The tenant
(or any of his family living with him) is *not* to be regarded as a competitor
in the open market for the purposes of calculating the price (s. 82 of the
Housing Act, 1969, reversing *Custins* v. *Hearts of Oak Benefit Society* [1969]
R.V.R. 58).

For the computations involved, reference should be made to decisions
of the Lands Tribunal, *Jenkins* v. *Bevan-Thomas* and *Barber* v. *Eltham
United Charities* (*Trustees*) (1972), 116 Sol. J. 333, 334, which indicate that
ten years purchase of the ground rent will be appropriate where the reversion
is distant ; see also *Mimmack* v. *Solent Land Investments, Ltd.* (1973), 226 E.G.
1771, and as to shorter reversions *Official Custodian for Charities* v. *Goldridge*
(1973), *The Times*, 25th July.

The reference to the open market might appear to raise like problems to
those which occur with valuation for estate duty purposes (i.e., under s. 7 (5)
of the F.A. 1894). Thus, must a price be calculated for the house
and premises as a whole or should natural subdivisions be taken into account
(cp. *Buccleuch* v. *I.R.C.* [1967] 1 A.C. 506) ? This question is unlikely to
arise often in the present context, but remember for example, that a " house "
within the 1967 Act may be a building converted into flats (s. 2 (1) (a)).
Equally, the estate duty question of restrictions on sale (such as subsisting
options to purchase or rights of pre-emption over the freehold) which may
reduce the market value (*I.R.C.* v. *Crossman* [1937] A.C. 26) could raise
moot problems here. The tenant's notice will discharge " the landlord and
all other persons . . . from the further performance " of such restrictions,
relating to the disposal of the landlord's interest (s. 5 (7)), but is this discharge
to be envisaged before or after the time of valuation ? And, indeed, is the
tenant also discharged ? Conversely, the possibility of a so-called " special
purchaser " (i.e., a person with a particular interest in purchasing) notionally
putting up the market value may have to be faced (cf. *I.R.C.* v. *Clay* [1914]
3 K.B. 466). Also it should be mentioned that the purchase price is apparently

to be increased by any development value the site may have (see s. 9 (1) (*a*) referring to s. 17). If the parties fail to agree on the price payable, it will be determined by the Lands Tribunal (s. 21 (1) (*a*)).

If the tenant feels that the price when finally ascertained is too much for him, he is enabled, by written notice within one month, to opt out of the acquisition of the freehold (s. 9 (3)). If he does, he must pay the landlord such compensation (if any) as may be just and may serve no further notice to acquire the freehold within the next five years, although his right to an extended lease remains unaffected (s. 9 (3)).

In any case, the tenant will be obliged to bear all the landlord's ordinary and reasonable conveyancing and valuation costs (s. 9 (4)) and the landlord will have a lien on the property for these and also for rent up to the date of conveyance (s. 9 (5)).

Conveyance.—As far as form is concerned, the conveyance is to be prepared by the tenant-purchaser so that presumably he has an entirely free choice in the ordinary way so long as no matter of substance affecting the vendor-landlord is concerned (Leasehold Reform (Enfranchisement and Extension) Regulations, 1967, Schedule, Part I, para. 9 (1)). As to what of substance should go in the conveyance, generally this will simply be determined as if the transaction were in pursuance of an ordinary contract for sale, subject to its general conditions of sale (see *loc. cit.*). But the Act does in addition contain certain specific provisions governing the contents of the conveyance (or, it is only safe to assume in practice, land registry transfer).

Firstly, it is in effect provided that, unless the tenant consents, the conveyance must not be framed so as to exclude or restrict the implied general words or all-estate clause (i.e., under ss. 62, 63 of the L.P.A. 1925 ; see *ante*, p. 511 *et seq.* and p. 542 *et seq.* ; s. 10 (1) of the 1967 Act). Secondly, the provision is added that " the landlord shall not be bound to convey any better title than that which he has or could require to be vested in him " (s. 10 (1)). From this it would appear that the vendor-landlord could insist on conveying expressly only such title as he has or at least on the omission of any words of limitation so that s. 60 (1) of the L.P.A. 1925 has to be relied on (see *ante*, pp. 532, 537). The adverse effect of this on the implied covenants for title, however, is not so serious here since in any case the landlord need only convey " as trustee " (s. 10 (1) of the 1967 Act ; see *ante*, p. 472).

Going beyond these rather general provisions, the implied grant and reservation of certain particular rights is also provided for. Thus such rights as rights of support, to access of light, to passage of water, gas, sewage, etc., or for the supply of electricity as may have been enjoyed by the landlord or the tenant will automatically be granted or reserved as easements to the appropriate party by the conveyance (s. 10 (2)). For this to happen the rights must have been enjoyed at the time of the tenant's notice and under or in connection with the tenancy and be capable of being granted in law (s. 10 (2)). Similar provision is made for the reciprocal creation of rights of way (s. 10 (3)). So far as the tenant is concerned, these particular implications will normally give him no more than he would get anyway by virtue either of s. 62 of the L.P.A. 1925 or of the rules in *Wheeldon* v. *Burrows* (1879), 12 Ch. D. 31 (*ante*, p. 506 *et seq.*) which it is presumed will apply to the conveyance to the tenant. But the landlord may need to rely considerably

30

on these particular implications of the 1967 Act to justify express reservations, since s. 62 of the 1925 Act does not benefit the grantor and only in exceptional cases may reservations be implied under *Wheeldon* v. *Burrows*.

A lengthy subsection in the 1967 Act further provides for the treatment of restrictive covenants in the conveyance to the tenant. First, the conveyance is to include any provisions required by the landlord " to secure that the tenant is bound by, or to indemnify the landlord against breaches of, restrictive covenants " affecting the house and not connected with the tenancy (s. 10 (4) (*a*)). *Prima facie*, this simply means that the conveyance will be made subject to existing restrictive covenants binding the freehold and that the usual indemnity covenant may be inserted. But, since the tenant would presumably be bound anyway by any enforceable (and duly protected by registration) restrictive covenants without additional provision, it is arguable that the landlord is enabled to compel the tenant to become bound by restrictive covenants which would not otherwise bind him, e.g., because the burden was personal to the covenantor or because of non-registration ; and it would follow that as an alternative only to this could an indemnity covenant be required.

Secondly, the conveyance is to include, in effect, any of the restrictions (suitably adapted) contained in the tenancy or any collateral agreement which the landlord or the tenant may require and which materially enhance the value of the house and premises or of other property as appropriate (s. 10 (4) (*b*)). If the element of material enhancement is lacking, the landlord may still require inclusion of the restriction provided it would be enforceable by some third party (e.g., under s. 56 of the L.P.A. 1925 ; *ante*, p. 546). The tenant in any case of doubt can, it would seem, maintain his position simply by inserting a declaration against merger into the conveyance (cp. *Golden Lion Hotel (Hunstanton), Ltd.* v. *Carter* [1965] 1 W.L.R. 1189 ; see further *ante*, p. 830). Thirdly, the landlord is enabled to impose on the tenant any new restrictive covenants he wishes provided these will materially enhance the value of other property belonging to the landlord and will not interfere with the continued reasonable enjoyment of the house and premises as under the tenancy (s. 10 (4) (*c*)).

Three other observations may be made upon this inclusion of restrictive covenants in the conveyance to the tenant. One is that there is a general test of being reasonable in all the circumstances which limits the landlord or the tenant in requiring such inclusion (s. 10 (5)). The second is that if the landlord is required to enter into any restrictive covenant under these provisions he is entitled to limit his personal liability to breaches for which he is responsible (s. 10 (6)) ; the tenant is *not* so entitled. And the third observation is that these provisions are confined entirely to restrictive covenants : there is nothing to enable the creation or the carrying over from the tenancy of positive covenants. See further an article at *Solicitors' Journal*, vol. 112, p. 831.

Lastly, as to the conveyance and its contents, note that the landlord may be required to give to the tenant an acknowledgement in respect of any retained document within s. 64 of the L.P.A. 1925 (*ante*, p. 658), but *not* an undertaking as to safe custody (s. 10 (6) of the 1967 Act). The legislature clearly regard the landlord as being a fiduciary as well as a compulsory vendor and have recognised conveyancing practice (see *ante*, pp. 650–663). Where the landlord's interest is held under the S.L.A. 1925, or on trust for sale, the conveyance to the tenant can have the ordinary overreaching effect provided the proper conveyancing machinery is followed (s. 8 (4) of the 1967

Act ; see *ante*, p. 172 *et seq.*). In addition, provision is made for the compulsory redemption of rentcharges and discharge of mortgages so that the conveyance to the tenant will be made free of such interests, they being in effect over-reached also (ss. 11, 12, 13 ; cp. s. 8 (4) (*b*)).

Extension.—Where all the statutory requirements are satisfied the tenant may give the landlord due notice of his desire to have an extended lease rather than the freehold. If so, the result is that the landlord is bound to grant, and the tenant to accept, in substitution for the existing tenancy, a new tenancy of the house and premises for a term expiring fifty years after the expiry date of the existing tenancy (ss. 14 (1), 37 (1) (*g*), (2), (3), (4)). The new tenancy is to be on the same terms essentially as the existing tenancy, account being taken of changes in the property and of multiple tenancies (s. 15 (1)) ; any agreement collateral to the existing tenancy must also be continued (s. 15 (4)). However, provisions for the renewal or premature termination of the tenancy, and options to purchase or rights of pre-emption over the house and premises are *not* to be carried over from the existing to the new tenancy (s. 15 (5)). Again the landlord and tenant are free to agree as to the terms of the new tenancy and either of them may require the exclusion or modification of any term that has become unreasonable in the circumstances (s. 15 (7)).

The rent under the new tenancy, according to the Act, is to be a ground rent in the sense that it is to represent the letting value of the site, ignoring any buildings, as used under and without any breach of the existing tenancy (s. 15 (2) (*a*)). This rent only becomes payable as from, and is to be assessed during the year before, as at the expiry date of the existing tenancy and may be revised after twenty-five years on the landlord giving written notice in the twenty-fifth year (s. 15 (2) (*b*), (*c*)). If the parties fail to agree, the rent is determinable by the Lands Tribunal (s. 21 (1) (*b*) ; and see comments in *Solicitors' Journal*, vol. 115, p. 922 *et seq.*, and vol. 116, pp. 40–41). In addition to this rent, the tenant will have to pay or contribute such sums as may be just towards the cost of any services, repairs, maintenance or insurance which the landlord will be obliged to provide during the new tenancy, whether or not there is a term requiring such payment in the existing tenancy (s. 15 (3)).

The new tenancy must be granted and will be deemed authorised, notwith-standing that the existing tenancy had been granted *before* 1968 in breach of a prior mortgage by the landlord (s. 14 (4)). On the other hand, if the existing tenancy be granted *after* 1967 and does not bind the landlord's mortgagees, nor will the new tenancy (s. 14 (4) proviso), but the landlord is obliged to take such steps as necessary to secure that the tenancy is not liable to be defeated by his mortgagees (s. 14 (7)). This last obligation is subject to the qualification that the landlord need not " acquire a better title than he has or could require to be vested in him " (s. 14 (7)). Nevertheless it would appear that this still permits the tenant to insist, if necessary, that the landlord either obtain his mortgagee's consent or else redeem the mortgage for the purposes of granting a completely binding new tenancy. There is also provision for the new lease and its counterpart to be handed, as and where appropriate, to the tenant's and the landlord's mortgagees so that it will continue protected despite any surrender of the existing tenancy being effective against them (s. 15 (5), (6)).

As with enfranchisement, the tenant must in any case bear all the landlord's reasonable conveyancing and valuation costs (s. 14 (2)) and will not be entitled to require the execution of the new lease until all sums due from him to the landlord, by way of rent or otherwise, have been paid (s. 14 (3)).

The grant of a new extended tenancy will also be at the cost to the tenant of the loss of any further rights. Thus, the statutory right to acquire the freehold is no longer exercisable once the expiry date of the original tenancy has passed (s. 16 (1) (a)) and there can be no second statutory extension of the tenancy (s. 16 (1) (b)). This loss of rights after an extension applies also to any sub-tenant (s. 16 (4)). In connection with the loss of rights, a somewhat odd provision is made that " where an instrument extending a tenancy," in effect, under the 1967 Act, contains a statement that the extension is under the 1967 Act, that statement is to be conclusive as to the loss of rights " in favour of any person not being a party to the instrument, unless the statement appears from the instrument to be untrue " (s. 16 (7)). The intention obviously is to limit the investigation and inquiries as to the risk of future statutory enfranchisement or extension which a purchaser of the reversion from the landlord might otherwise make ; the statement can hardly " favour " a purchaser from the tenant. But the subsection is drafted in a curiously question-begging way : as it stands, only if a lease was in fact granted under the Act is a statement that it was so granted conclusive !

Landlord's rights.—An overriding right to possession of the house and premises can be obtained by a landlord satisfying the court as to one or other of the following two grounds. The first, applying only to extended leases and *not* where the tenant has given notice to acquire the freehold, is that " for purposes of redevelopment he proposes to demolish or reconstruct the whole or a substantial part of the premises " (s. 17 (1), (6) ; an application relying on this ground cannot be made earlier than one year before the expiry date of the original term). Much the same problems of construction and fact would appear possible here as with s. 30 (1) (*f*) of the Landlord and Tenant Act, 1954 (as to which, see *ante*, pp. 905–908).

The second ground, overriding enfranchisement or extension, is that the property or part of it " is or will be reasonably required by him for occupation as the only or main residence of the landlord or of . . . an adult member of the landlord's family " (s. 18 (1)) ; for the meaning of member of family, see *ante*, p. 919. Here, however, the court has also to be satisfied that " having regard to all the circumstances of the case, including the question whether other accommodation is available for the landlord or the tenant, [no] greater hardship would be caused by making the order than by refusing to make it " (s. 18 (4) proviso). Further, the landlord's requirements have to be judged, on a balance of probabilities, as at the date when the lease would otherwise end and not at the date of the hearing (*Gurvidi* v. *Mangant* (1972), 116 Sol. J. 255, C.A.).

Assuming the court to be satisfied as to either ground, it will make a declaratory order that the landlord is entitled to possession and that the tenant is entitled to compensation (ss. 17 (2), 18 (4)). The amount of compensation is to be calculated in accordance with provisions set out in Sched. 2 to the 1967 Act (ss. 17 (3), 18 (5)). In essence, the measure is the open market value of the tenancy of the house and premises (Sched. 2, para. 5) with determination by the Lands Tribunal in default of agreement (s. 21 (1) (c)). Only when the amount of compensation is known can a second application be made to the court for an order actually terminating the tenancy and making the compensation payable (Sched. 2, para. 2). The provisions against contracting out of the Act, already mentioned, apply also to this right to compensation (s. 23 (1)).

Management scheme.—Provision has been made with a view to preserving the amenities of large, well-run leasehold estates by way of establishing management schemes. In the case of any area which is occupied directly or indirectly under tenancies from one landlord, the first essential step was for the landlord or a representative body of tenants to apply before 1st January, 1970, for a certificate from the appropriate Minister (i.e., now the Secretary of State for the Environment) that, " in order to maintain adequate standards of appearance and amenity and regulate redevelopment in the area," it is in his opinion " likely to be in the general interest that the landlord should retain powers of management in respect of the house and premises " (s. 19 (1) ; the procedure and criteria to be observed by the Minister are set out in subss. (2) and (3)). The next step is for an application to be made to the High Court within one year of the giving of the certificate for approval of a scheme giving the landlord appropriate rights and powers (s. 19 (1)). The High Court's approval will depend basically upon whether the scheme appears to be fair, practicable and reasonable (s. 19 (3), (4), (5)). However, normally expert evidence should be given by a surveyor or estate agent so as to assist the court in deciding whether a proposed scheme was likely to benefit the area as a whole (*Re Sherwood Close (Barnes) Management Co. Ltd.'s Application* [1972] Ch. 208). In that case, a provision requiring new owners to become members of the landlord company was excluded as being outside the contemplation of s. 19 (1), however desirable it might otherwise be, but in this respect it has since been distinguished and doubted (see *Re Abbots Park Estate* [1972] 1 W.L.R. 598). Once approved, the management scheme should be registered as a local land charge, after which its provisions will become enforceable by the landlord against the persons occupying or interested in the property from time to time as if they had covenanted to be bound by the scheme (s. 19 (10)). See further an article by Donald Keating in *Law Guardian*, No. 56, p. 9 ; also *St. Mary Abbot's Place Properties Application* (1970), 214 *Estates Gazette* 413 ; *Cadbury* v. *Woodward* (1972), 23 P. & C.R. 281 and 24 P. & C.R. 335 ; *Re Abbots Park Estate (No. 2)* [1972] 1 W.L.R. 1597.

Privileged landlords.—Where the landlord is a local authority, the Commission for New Towns, a development corporation, a university body, a hospital board, a nationalised industry or one of certain other public bodies, it may seek a certificate from a Minister that within ten years the property will be required for redevelopment for its non-investment purposes ; if such a certificate be obtained the tenant's claim to enfranchisement or extension is to be of no effect (s. 28). Again, where the landlord is a local authority, a new town authority or a university body, it may on the tenant's acquisition of the freehold or an extended lease by means of covenants reserve to itself future development rights (s. 29 ; as to the form of such a covenant, see an article by G. V. Tew in the *Solicitors' Journal*, vol. 116, at pp. 658–9). Further, when the landlord is a new town authority or has responsibility for an overspill area it may reserve to itself a right of pre-emption (s. 30).

Enfranchisement cannot be claimed as of right by a tenant from the National Trust or from the Crown (ss. 32, 33).

Relief against mortgages.—Finally, wide powers have been given to the court to relieve landlords whose estate at the passing of the Act (27th October, 1967) was subject (*a*) to a long tenancy with not more than twenty years to run, and (b) to a mortgage (s. 36). The idea appears to be that the new statutory rights conferred on tenants could well cause a drastic depreciation of reversionary interests and consequent financial hardship to mortgagors. Accordingly, the court may discharge or modify any liability or restrict the exercise of any right or remedy under the mortgage (s. 36 (1), (2)).

Jurisdiction.—All the principal issues which arise under the 1967 Act have been put within the jurisdiction of the county court, except those concerning the assessment of money payments (ss. 20, 21). However, the vendor and purchaser summons procedure is preserved for appropriate questions (s. 22 (4) ; see *ante*, pp. 230–232).

Registered conveyancing.—A booklet has been prepared by and is available free from H.M. Land Registry containing questions and answers on the Leasehold Reform Act, 1967, illustrating broadly the practice where the title to the land is registered.

B. PART I OF THE LANDLORD AND TENANT ACT, 1954

Continuance of tenancies.—The Landlord and Tenant Act, 1954, Pt. I, provides protection for certain tenants of dwelling-houses who would have been protected by the Rent Acts if it had not been for the rule (1920 Act, s. 12 (7), now 1968 Act, s. 2 (1) (a)) that those Acts do not apply where the rent is less than two-thirds of the rateable value. However, the practical significance of this protection has now much diminished in view of the general availability of wide rights conferred by the Leasehold Reform Act, 1967. The right to the 1954 Act protection was not affected by the decontrol provisions of the Rent Act, 1957, and has since been extended. In consequence, it applies if the rateable value on 23rd March, 1965, is £400 or less in Greater London or £200 or less in other parts of the country (1954 Act, s. 1 ; Rent Act, 1968, s. 1, Sched. 2, para. 1 (c)). A tenant who has a long lease at a low rent of a house which exceeds the prescribed rateable value cannot obtain protection for himself by sub-letting parts to others, so that the part retained is within the rateable value limits, because that part is not let as a dwelling separate from the rest (*Crown Lodge (Surbiton) Investments, Ltd.* v. *Nalecz* [1967] 1 W.L.R. 647).

By the 1954 Act, as amended, a tenancy is continued after the date at which it would otherwise expire if the following conditions are fulfilled :—

(1) The tenancy is a " long tenancy," that is " a tenancy granted for a term of years certain exceeding twenty-one years, whether or not subsequently extended " (*ibid.*, s. 2 (4)). A tenant who formerly held under a long tenancy continues to be protected, however, during any period for which he holds over and during any subsequent tenancy at a low rent, however short (*ibid.*, s. 19).

(2) The " qualifying condition " is fulfilled, that is the circumstances as respects the property, its use and all other relevant matters, are such that on the coming to an end of the tenancy the tenant would, if the tenancy had not been a long tenancy (and in the case of a tenancy at a low rent had not been a tenancy at a low rent), be entitled by virtue of the Rent Acts to retain possession of the whole or part of the property (1954 Act, s. 2 (1) as amended). Thus, the premises must be residential and the tenant must be in occupation. To prevent a claim

by a tenant resuming occupation a few days before the expiry of the term, the landlord may apply to the court at any time within the last twelve months for a declaration that the tenancy does not qualify.

Where premises comply with these conditions the tenancy is continued after the " term date " (*ibid.*, s. 3 (1)). The term date is the date of expiry of the term of years (*ibid.*, ss. 2 (6), 3 (1)), except where the tenant held over by consent, in which case the term date is the first day on which the landlord could have terminated the tenancy by notice (*ibid.*, s. 19, Sched. 4). If the premises so qualifying for protection (that is, the residential premises that would be protected by the Rent Acts : s. 3 (3)) are the whole of the property comprised in the tenancy, the tenancy continues at the same rent, and in all other respects on the same terms (*ibid.*, s. 3 (2)). On the other hand, if the premises qualifying for protection are only part of the property comprised in the tenancy, the tenancy continues after the term date as regards the premises qualifying only. In this case the rent is ascertained by apportioning the rent payable, but other terms (subject to any necessary modifications) remain applicable (*ibid.*). Where the parties are unable to agree as to the part of the premises which qualifies for protection, or as to any terms of such a tenancy, the matter may be determined by the court (*ibid.*, s. 3 (4)).

As the existing rent is likely to be low the tenant will probably not wish to terminate the tenancy which is prolonged in the manner stated above. If he does, however, he may give notice to the immediate landlord at least one month before the term date (*ibid.*, s. 5 (1)). Where the tenancy has continued after the term date the tenant may put an end to it at any time by not less than one month's notice in writing (*ibid.*, s. 5 (2)), notwithstanding that the landlord has taken steps to terminate the tenancy, or that the tenant has elected to retain possession following a notice by the landlord (*ibid.*, s. 5 (3)).

Any protected tenancy may be terminated by the landlord by notice given to the tenant in the form prescribed by the Landlord and Tenant (Notices) Regulations, 1969 and 1973, specifying the date at which the tenancy is to come to an end, which date may be either the term date or a later date (*ibid.*, s. 4 (1)). Such notice must be given not more than twelve nor less than six months before the date of termination specified in it (*ibid.*, s. 4 (2)). It will not have effect unless—

(i) it requires the tenant within two months to notify the landlord in writing whether or not at the date of termination of the tenancy the tenant will be willing to give up possession, and specifies the premises which the landlord believes to be, or to be likely to be, the premises qualifying for protection (*ibid.*, s. 4 (3), (4)) ;

(ii) it either (*a*) contains proposals for a statutory tenancy (in which case it is known as a " landlord's notice proposing a statutory tenancy "), or (*b*) contains notice that if the tenant is not willing to give up possession the landlord proposes to apply to the court, and states the ground on which the landlord alleges that he is entitled to possession, such grounds being specified *post*, p. 937 (in which case it is known as a " landlord's notice to resume possession ") (*ibid.*, s. 4 (3), (5)).

Statutory tenancies under the 1954 Act.—Where the tenancy is terminated by service of a landlord's notice proposing a statutory tenancy, then as from the termination of the tenancy a statutory tenancy under the Rent Act arises on the following terms :—

(1) The premises affected are those qualified for protection, or likely to be qualified for protection (*ibid*., s. 6 (3)).

(2) The tenancy is at a fixed rent, and on the terms agreed between the parties or determined by the court (*ibid*., s. 6 (1)). A reasonable rent is to be determined in the absence of agreement (1954 Act, s. 9 (5)).

This statutory tenancy has the characteristics of such a tenancy arising under the Rent Acts, with a slight modification as to the circumstances in which possession can be obtained (*ibid*., s. 6 (4)). It is envisaged that the standard rent and the terms of the tenancy will normally be agreed between the landlord and tenant, but otherwise they are to be determined by the county court.

It is the landlord's duty to make an application for determination by the court if relevant matters are not agreed. Such application must be made during the currency of his notice proposing a statutory tenancy and not earlier than two months after the giving thereof except where the tenant has already elected to retain possession (*ibid*., s. 7 (5)).

Where the landlord has proposed a statutory tenancy it is essential that he should, if necessary, apply to the court in proper time. If, at the expiration of two months from service of his notice *either* the tenant has given notice electing to retain possession *or* the tenant remains in occupation and the other qualifying conditions exist, then not later than two months before expiration of the landlord's notice (that is, within four months from service of the landlord's notice if it was of minimum length of six months) the landlord's notice ceases to have effect (and so the former tenancy continues : s. 3 (1)) unless the necessary conditions have been fulfilled. These conditions are that either :—

(1) the following matters have been agreed (*in writing :* s. 69 (2)), namely (*a*) what premises constitute the dwelling-house ; (*b*) the rent, the intervals at which it is payable, and whether or not it is payable in advance ; (*c*) whether any, and, if so, what initial repairs are to be carried out ; (*d*) by whom those repairs are to be carried out ; and (*e*) the questions as to initial repairs specified in s. 8 (4), below ; or

(2) an application has been made by the landlord for determination by the court of such of these matters as have not been agreed (*ibid*., s. 7 (2)).

The following matters in relation to repairs must be agreed or determined by the court—

(*a*) which of the initial repairs (if any) are required in consequence of the tenant's failure to fulfil his obligations under the former tenancy ;

(*b*) the estimated cost of repairs so required so far as they are to be carried out by the landlord ;

(*c*) whether any payment for accrued tenant's repairs is to be by instalments and, if so, the number and times of instalments ;

(*d*) whether there are to be any, and, if so, what obligations as respects the repair of the dwelling during the statutory tenancy (*ibid*., s. 8 (4)).

Carrying out of repairs.—It is likely that at the end of a long term substantial repairs may be necessary, but the Act does not envisage that the property shall necessarily be brought up to the standard of repair required by the covenants contained in the former lease. Consequently, the Act deals only with what are known as " initial repairs," that is such repairs as may be agreed between the landlord and tenant, or in default determined by the court. As respects such of the initial repairs as are required in consequence of the failure of the tenant to fulfil his obligations under the former tenancy, the landlord is entitled as one of the terms of a statutory tenancy to a payment (known as " payment for accrued tenant's repairs ") equal to the cost of carrying them out, excluding any part of the cost recoverable by the landlord otherwise than from the tenant or his predecessors in title (*ibid.*, s. 8 (1)). As payment of this capital sum might cause hardship to the tenant, it is provided that a payment may be made, either by instalments or otherwise, as may be agreed or determined by the court (*ibid.*, s. 8 (2)).

Provisions as to the time for, and method of recovery of, such payments are contained in Sched. 1 to the Act, with regard to lump sum payments and payments by instalments respectively ; there is also provision for the variation by the court, on certain grounds, of any agreement or determination for the making of a payment.

Where the tenant retains possession, and by virtue of an agreement or determination the landlord is required to carry out initial repairs but fails to do so within a reasonable time, the court may, on application of the tenant, reduce the rent (*ibid.*, Sched. 2). Such an order may be discharged if the landlord satisfies the court that the initial repairs have been carried out (*ibid.*, para. 2) or by agreement (*ibid.*, para. 3).

Hardship might be caused if a landlord insisted on the carrying out of repairs at the end of a lengthy tenancy in accordance with the lease. Consequently, it is provided that where the tenant retains possession by virtue of s. 6, *ante*, any liability of his, or of any predecessor in title, shall be extinguished, except as regards failure to pay rent or rates, or to insure or keep insured, or in respect of any use of the premises for immoral or illegal purposes (*ibid.*, s. 10).

Grounds on which landlord entitled to possession.—The grounds on which a landlord may apply to the court for possession of the property comprised in a protected long tenancy were originally as follows :—

(1) That the landlord proposes to demolish or reconstruct the whole, or a substantial part, of the protected premises for purposes of redevelopment.

(2) The grounds specified in Sched. 3 to the Act, which corresponds to the grounds on which a court may make an order for possession under the Rent Acts (1954 Act, s. 12).

However, by s. 38 of the Leasehold Reform Act, 1967, a landlord may no longer rely on the first ground for obtaining possession mentioned, namely for purposes of redevelopment (with a saving for local and certain other public authorities).

Where the landlord serves notice to resume possession (as to which see *ante*, p. 935), but either (i) the tenant elects to retain possession, or (ii) two months after service the " qualifying condition " (*ante*, p. 934) is fulfilled, the landlord may (within two months of the tenant's election, or four months of the landlord's notice if the tenant does not elect) apply to the court for an order for possession on such of the grounds mentioned above as were

30A

specified in the landlord's notice (*ibid.*, s. 13 (1)). If the ground is the first above mentioned, the court must be satisfied that possession will be required by the landlord by the date of termination of the tenancy, and that he has made reasonable preparations for redevelopment, including the obtaining of planning and other permissions (*ibid.*, s. 13 (2)). Where the court is satisfied that a later date (not being more than a year later than the date of determination specified in the landlord's notice) would be more appropriate, it must, if the landlord so requires, order that possession be given at such date, and that the tenancy shall continue at the same rent and on the same terms in the meantime (*ibid.*, s. 13 (3).

Where the landlord fails to apply to the court within the time specified, or where no order is made by the court, or where the notice is withdrawn, the landlord's notice to resume possession ceases to have effect ; the landlord may then serve a notice proposing a statutory tenancy (*ibid.*, s. 14).

Protection of sub-tenants.—In the past there has been a difficulty in that a tenant holding under a sub-lease at a rack rent could not claim protection on termination of the head lease if that head lease was at so low a rent as not to be protected by the Rent Acts (*Knightsbridge Estates Trust, Ltd.* v. *Deeley* [1950] 2 K.B. 228). This state of affairs has been reversed by s. 15 of the 1954 Act (replaced by s. 18 (3) (4) of the Rent Act, 1968), provided that the sub-lease was lawful.

Relief against forfeiture or damages.—The protection given to a resident tenant holding under a long lease is such that a landlord may be tempted to endeavour to forfeit the tenancy or claim substantial damages for breach of covenant if he can find grounds for so doing. Section 16 of the 1954 Act, therefore, makes two new rules. During the last seven months of a tenancy, on application by the tenant for relief, the court may not make an order for recovery from the tenant of possession of the property or for payment of damages for breach of covenant. Secondly, even if the order is made earlier than seven months before the expiration of the tenancy, the tenant may apply for relief in any action brought by the landlord, to enforce a right of re-entry or a right to damages for breach of covenant. Such an order is suspended for a period of fourteen days, and if, during that time, the tenant serves notice in writing on his landlord, and lodges a copy in court, the order is not enforceable except as to costs, and the tenancy has effect as if it had been granted for a term expiring seven months after the making of the order. After such expiration the tenancy will continue by virtue of s. 3, *ante*, p. 935, but the landlord will then be able to serve a notice proposing a statutory tenancy (under which obligations will become enforceable against the tenant), or, if the grounds exist, a notice to resume possession.

This protection does not apply, however, to proceedings consequent on failure to comply with a term of the tenancy as to payment of rent or rates, or as to insuring, or any term restricting the use of premises for immoral or illegal purposes.

Reversionary leases.—Complication arises if the tenancy for which protection is claimed is a subtenancy and there are several superior leases of varying terms of years. In the first place the " landlord " on whom the tenant may serve notice to terminate (s. 5, *ante*, p. 935) is invariably the immediate landlord. In general, however, the " landlord " is the owner of that interest which, for the time being, (a) is in reversion expectant (whether immediately or not) on the termination of the relevant tenancy, and (b) is either the fee simple or a tenancy for at least five years longer than the relevant tenancy (*ibid.*, s. 21 (1), (3)). Thus, in effect, the rights and obligations of landlord usually fall on the next superior reversioner whose term exceeds a further five years or who holds the fee simple. There may, however, be an intermediate lessee whose term has less than five years to run who may be next entitled to possession subject to the statutory tenancy. It is, therefore, provided that during the period of a statutory tenancy the expression " the landlord " means the landlord as defined in the Rent Acts, that is, usually, the person entitled to possession subject to the statutory tenancy ; there is an exception as regards the carrying out of initial repairs and payment therefor (1954 Act, s. 21 (4)).

Detailed provisions as to the rights and liabilities, between themselves, of the various reversioners are contained in Sched. 5 to the 1954 Act.

PART 8. MISCELLANEOUS TENANCIES

A. PERPETUALLY RENEWABLE LEASES

The L.P.A. 1922 is referred to throughout this note as " the 1922 Act." Section 190 (iii), (iv), of the 1922 Act defines a perpetually renewable lease or underlease as " a lease or underlease, the holder of which is entitled to enforce (whether or not subject to the fulfilment of any condition) the perpetual renewal thereof, and includes a lease or underlease for a life or lives or for a term of years, whether determinable with life or lives or not, which is perpetually renewable as aforesaid," and " underlease," unless the context otherwise requires, is defined as including a sub-term created out of a derivative leasehold interest.

Transitional provisions.—Perpetually renewable leases or underleases existing on 1st January, 1926, became on that date terms of 2,000 years calculated as from the date when the original term commenced, at the rent and subject to the lessee's covenants and conditions which under the lease would have been payable or enforceable during the subsistence of such term, but without any right of renewal. Similarly, perpetually renewable *underleases* derived out of perpetually renewable head terms became sub-terms of 2,000 years less one day, at the rent and subject to the underlessee's covenants and conditions, but without any right of renewal. The same principle applied to any perpetually renewable sub-term derived out of any other sub-term, but so that in every case the sub-term would be one day less in duration than the derivative term created by the 1922 Act out of which it took effect (1922 Act, Sched. 15, paras. 1 and 2). Every term or sub-term created by Sched. 15 is subject to the same trusts, powers, rights and equities (if any) and to all the same incumbrances and obligations of every kind, as the term, sub-term or other interest which it replaced.

Such legal terms created by the 1922 Act vested in the persons entitled to call for them under the provisions of the L.P.A. 1925, Sched. 1, and the S.L.A. 1925, Sched. 2, as the conversion into long terms is deemed to have been effected immediately before the commencement of the L.P.A. 1925. Thus, if the renewable interest was, immediately before 1926, vested in trustees of a settlement, the term by virtue of Sched. 1, Pt. II, paras. 5 and

6 (c) of the L.P.A. 1925 vested in the tenant for life or statutory owner entitled under the S.L.A. 1925 to require a vesting deed to be executed in his favour, but subject to any mortgage term subsisting or created by the Act.

Where under the lease or underlease a fine or other payment is payable on renewal, then an amount becomes payable annually as additional rent in lieu thereof (1922 Act, Sched. 15, paras. 12 to 17 ; Law of Property (Amendment) Act, 1924, Sched. 2, para. 5). The amount should be endorsed on the lease or counterpart, preferably on both, and signed by both the lessor and lessee. Such an endorsement is, as regards a purchaser, by para. 14 (2) of Sched. 15, to be deemed conclusive evidence of the matters stated.

Nothing in the 1922 Act is to affect prejudicially any right of renewal conferred by the Small Holdings and Allotments Act, 1908, s. 44, or the power conferred by s. 40 of that Act (amended by the Agriculture Act, 1947, s. 67 and Sched. 8) to grant leases for the purposes of that Act with a similar right of renewal (1922 Act, Sched. 15, para. 9). As to smallholdings, see now Pt. III of the Agriculture Act, 1970.

Mortgages of perpetually renewable leases existing before 1925 were converted into long terms by the L.P.A. 1925, Sched. 1, Pt. VIII, para. 6.

Implied terms of leases created by the 1922 Act.—The following powers and covenants are deemed to be contained in every lease or underlease taking effect by virtue of the 1922 Act :—

   (i) Where the lease or underlease would have expired but for the 1922 Act, the lessee or underlessee may give notice in writing to the lessor at least ten days before such expiration (with the consent of persons interested in any derivative interest) to determine the lease or underlease.

  (ii) A covenant by the lessee or the underlessee to register every assignment or devolution of the term or sub-term, including all probates and letters of administration affecting the same, with the lessor or his solicitor or agent, within six months thereof, and to pay a guinea fee ; this implied covenant to be in substitution for any express covenant to register with the lessor or his solicitor or agent.

 (iii) A covenant by the lessee or underlessee within one year from the commencement of the 1922 Act to produce his lease or underlease (including an assignment of a part of the land), with any particulars required to show that a perpetual right of renewal was subsisting at such commencement, to the lessor or his solicitor or agent, who must endorse notice of the fact on the document produced. Such endorsement signed by or on behalf of the lessor will, in favour of a purchaser, be sufficient evidence that the right of renewal was subsisting (Sched. 15, para. 10).

It is also provided by para. 11 (1) of the same Schedule that in the case of every term or sub-term created by the 1922 Act, or under any power conferred by Sched. 15, each lessee or underlessee, although he may be the original lessee or underlessee, and notwithstanding any stipulation to the contrary, will be liable only for rent accruing and for breaches of covenants or conditions occurring while he or his personal representatives have the term or sub-term vested in him or them. So that even an original lessee will not be liable on his express covenants after assignment.

Grant of a perpetually renewable lease after 1925.—A grant after 1925 of a term, sub-term, or other leasehold interest with a covenant or obligation for perpetual renewal, which would have been valid if the 1922 Act had not been passed, will take effect as a demise for a term of 2,000 years or, in the case of a sub-demise, for a term less in duration by one day than the term out of which it is derived, to commence from the date fixed for the commencement of the term, sub-term or other interest, and in every case free from any obligation for renewal or for payment of any fines, fees, costs, or other money in respect of renewal (1922 Act, Sched. 15, para. 5).

Any contract entered into after 1925 for the grant of a lease, sub-term or other leasehold interest with a covenant for perpetual renewal will operate as an agreement for a demise for a term of 2,000 years, or a sub-term less than the term in the head lease by one day (*ibid.*, Sched. 15, para. 7 (1)). Such a contract should be registered as a land charge (L.C.A. 1972, s. 2 (4), Class C (iv)). But any contract entered into after 1925 for the renewal of a lease or underlease for a *term exceeding sixty years* from the termination of the lease or underlease, whether or not contained in the lease or underlease, will be void (1922 Act, Sched. 15, para. 7 (2)).

An agreement to let premises for a period of a year with an option to renew the tenancy from year to year by notice in writing amounts to an agreement for a perpetually renewable lease which is converted by the L.P.A. 1922 into an agreement for a term of 2,000 years (*Northchurch Estates, Ltd.* v. *Daniels* [1947] Ch. 117). A lease containing a covenant for renewal for a similar term on the same conditions (including the covenant for renewal) constitutes a perpetually renewable lease (*Parkus* v. *Greenwood* [1950] Ch. 644, where *Green* v. *Palmer* [1944] Ch. 328 was distinguished and criticised). See further the more recent cases outlined *ante*, p. 814.

B. LEASES FOR LIVES

Any lease or underlease, at a rent, or in consideration of a fine, for life or lives or for any term of years determinable with life or lives, or on the marriage of the lessee, or any contract therefor, *made before or after the commencement of the L.P.A.* 1925, takes effect as a lease, underlease or contract therefor, *for a term of ninety years, determinable* after the death or marriage (as the case may be) of the original lessee, or of the survivor of the original lessees, by at least one month's notice in writing given to determine the same on one of the quarter days applicable to the tenancy (or if none, then on one of the usual quarter days) either by the lessor or the persons deriving title under him, to the person entitled to the leasehold interest, or if no such person is in existence, by affixing the same to the premises, or by the lessee or other persons in whom the leasehold interest is vested to the lessor or the persons deriving title under him (L.P.A. 1925, s. 149 (6)).

If the lease, underlease, or contract therefor is made determinable on the dropping of the lives of *persons other than or besides the lessees*, then the notice is to be capable of being served after the death of any person or of the survivor of any persons (whether or not including the lessees) on the cesser of whose life or lives the lease, underlease, or contract is made determinable, instead of after the death of the original lessee or of the survivor of the original lessees (*ibid.*, s. 149 (6), proviso (c)).

The subsection is not to apply to any term taking effect in equity under a settlement or created out of an equitable interest under a settlement for mortgage, indemnity or other like purposes (*ibid.*, s. 149 (6), proviso (a)).

(Such terms do not affect the legal estate.) Every *power to grant* a lease for life or otherwise as stated above, has effect after 1925 as if it authorised the grant of a lease for a term not exceeding ninety years determinable in similar manner (1922 Act, Sched. 15, para. 8 (2)).

It will be seen, therefore, that a legal estate may not now be granted for a term of years terminable with life. This can, however, be done indirectly by granting a term for any number of years, say, for ninety-nine years, terminable by either party by a specified notice to be given at any time after the death of that person. Mortgages of leases for lives, existing before 1926, were converted into terms of years absolute by the L.P.A. 1925, Sched. 1, Pt. VIII, para. 6.

PART 9. AGRICULTURAL TENANCIES

A. INTRODUCTORY

General note.—Most of the general rules already stated apply to agricultural holdings, but there are now so many statutory provisions governing agricultural tenancies that it is necessary to devote a separate part to the subject. The general effect of the Agricultural Holdings Act, 1948, is to enable a farmer who cultivates the land properly to remain in possession at a fair rent for life if he wishes. Freedom of contract is further restricted as a result of s. 6 of the Act (*post*, p. 947), which may limit the power of the parties to enter into a binding agreement as to the terms of tenancy, and in many other ways. Very great care is necessary, therefore, in carrying out transactions affecting agricultural holdings, and the present part deals with the matters which may arise in conveyancing practice, mainly as a result of provisions of the Agricultural Holdings Act, 1948, which will be referred to as the A.H.A. 1948.

What is an "agricultural holding"?—The A.H.A. 1948 provides that "the expression 'agricultural holding' means the aggregate of the agricultural land comprised in a contract of tenancy, not being a contract under which the said land is let to the tenant during his continuance in any office, appointment or employment held under the landlord" (*ibid.*, s. 1 (1)). As to what will constitute an "appointment" within the exception to this subsection, see *Verrall* v. *Farnes* [1966] 1 W.L.R. 1254. For this purpose "agricultural land" means land "used for agriculture which is so used for the purposes of a trade or business," and includes any other land which is designated as such by the Minister of Agriculture, Fisheries and Food under the Agriculture Act, 1947, s. 109 (1) (A.H.A. 1948, s. 1 (2)). Further "'agriculture' includes horticulture, fruit growing, seed growing, dairy farming and livestock breeding and keeping, the use of land as grazing land, meadow land, osier land, market gardens and nursery grounds, and the use of land for woodlands where that use is ancillary to the farming of land for other agricultural purposes" (A.H.A. 1948, s. 94 (1)). In *Steyning and Littlehampton Building Society* v. *Wilson* [1951] Ch. 1018, mentioned *post*, p. 982, Danckwerts, J., said, at p. 1025 : "It seems to me that the [A.H.A. 1948] cannot have been intended to apply to anything other than true transactions between landlord and tenant in respect of agricultural holdings." Land may be agricultural within s. 1 (2) even though the business for which it is used is not agricultural. Land used for grazing horses for the purposes of a riding school was held to be an agricultural holding because (i) grazing is within the definition of agriculture and (ii) a riding school is a business (*Rutherford* v. *Maurer* [1962] 1 Q.B. 16). Contrast *Deith* v. *Brown* mentioned below.

An agricultural holding is the aggregate of agricultural land comprised in a " contract of tenancy," which is defined by s. 94 (1) as " a letting of land, or agreement for letting land, for a term of years or from year to year." It was held, in *Land Settlement Association, Ltd.* v. *Carr* [1944] 1 K.B. 675, that a letting for successive periods of 364 days did not fall within a similar definition in the 1923 Act. Avoidance of the Acts by creation of such tenancies has been prevented by the A.H.A. 1948, s. 2, which provides that in the case of agreements made on or after 1st March, 1948, if land is let to a person for use as agricultural land (as defined above) for an interest *less than a tenancy from year to year*, or a person is licensed to occupy land as agricultural land, and he would, if a tenant from year to year, be tenant of an agricultural holding, then, unless the Minister's approval is *first* obtained the agreement will take effect as if it were a letting from year to year. The Minister's approval is not limited to *ad hoc* consent to one agreement at a time, but may be a general approval of agreements by a specified person or authority (*Finbow* v. *Air Ministry* [1963] 1 W.L.R. 697). There are exceptions to this section where the grant is for grazing or mowing " during some specified period of the year " or is made by a person whose interest is less than a tenancy from year to year and has not been converted by the section (*ibid.*, s. 2 (1), proviso : *Reid* v. *Dawson* [1955] 1 Q.B. 214 ; *Scene Estate, Ltd.* v. *Amos* [1957] 2 Q.B. 205) ; a letting for grazing " for six months periods " has been held to be a letting for at least one year not within the exception (*Rutherford* v. *Maurer* [1962] 1 Q.B. 16). A tenancy agreement for one year less one day under which the land was to be occupied expressly for the grazing of animals but where there was a subsidiary obligation for ploughing " in the interests of good husbandry on a crop rotation basis," has been held not to be for grazing only and so not within the exception (*Lory* v. *Brent London Borough Council* [1971] 1 W.L.R. 823).

The Court of Appeal has held that a tenancy for one year certain is an interest less than a tenancy from year to year and so within s. 2 of the 1948 Act (*Lower* v. *Sorrell* [1963] 1 Q.B. 959 ; *Bernays* v. *Prosser* [1963] 2 Q.B. 592). However, in these cases the earlier decision of the Court of Appeal in *Gladstone* v. *Bower* [1960] 2 Q.B. 384, had to be distinguished. There a tenancy for a term certain of eighteen months was held to create an interest greater, not less, than a tenancy from year to year, so coming within neither s. 2 nor s. 3 (as to which see *post*, p. 945). This, of course, reveals a considerable gap in the protection afforded by the A.H.A. 1948 in the case of a term certain of more than one but less than two years.

Where premises are used partly for agricultural and partly for other purposes, there is no severance between the agricultural and the non-agricultural land. The A.H.A. 1948 applies only if the tenancy as a whole is in substance a tenancy of agricultural land (*Monson* v. *Bound* [1954] 1 W.L.R. 1321, followed in *Deith* v. *Brown* (1956), L.T. News, 306, where it was held that land and premises expressly let as a riding school did not constitute an agricultural holding.) Thus, in *Howkins* v. *Jardine* [1951] 1 K.B. 614 it was decided that the Act will apply to a tenancy which is, in substance, a tenancy of agricultural land, and if this is the case it is impossible to sever a part, for instance cottages occupied by non-agricultural tenants, and treat that part as not affected by the Act. See also *Dunn* v. *Fidoe* [1950] 2 All E.R. 685 as explained in *Monson* v. *Bound, ante*.

944 LEASES AND TENANCIES

A cottage and garden may itself form an agricultural holding if, although let separately, it is used for agricultural purposes, for instance for occupation by a worker on a neighbouring farm let to the person who is also tenant of the cottage (*Blackmore* v. *Butler* [1954] 2 Q.B. 171 ; see also the comments in *Law Quarterly Review*, vol. 70, p. 311 *et seq.*).

By the A.H.A. 1948, s. 2 (2), any dispute as to the operation of s. 2 (1) is to be determined by arbitration. Nevertheless, the courts have power to decide whether any transaction is or is not within the proviso to s. 2 (1) (*Goldsack* v. *Shore* [1950] 1 K.B. 708). A mere licence granted orally without valuable consideration is not an " agreement " within s. 2 (1) and so it is not converted into a letting from year to year (*ibid.*) ; for a licence to come within the statute it must be a " transaction enforceable by law, a contract for valuable consideration " (*Harrison Broadley* v. *Smith* [1963] 1 W.L.R. 1262, at p. 1272, reversed on other grounds [1964] 1 W.L.R. 456). In the Court of Appeal in this last-mentioned case, Pearson, L.J., said that what is " to take effect [i.e., under s. 2] is the original agreement, with the necessary modifications. It is not permissible to substitute for the original agreement a radically different agreement and make that take effect instead of the original agreement." However, this reference to a radical difference was explained by Cross, J., in *Verrall* v. *Farnes* [1966] 1 W.L.R. 1254, at p. 1268, as having in mind " the difference between the party to whom the licence to occupy was given and the parties who would become tenants of the land under the tenancy into which the agreement was said to have been converted. He did not allude in any way to the fact that the tenancy from year to year which was contended for would be free of rent, and I cannot read his words as meaning that the court has a discretion to exclude from the operation of the section cases where the application of it produces surprising results which Parliament may not have contemplated." See also *Holder* v. *Holder* [1968] Ch. 353.

Person who is " landlord " of holding.—It is provided by s. 94 (1) of the A.H.A. 1948 that " landlord " means " any person for the time being entitled to receive the rents and profits of any land." The position where the reversion has changed hands is dealt with by s. 92 (5) as follows :—

" Unless or until the tenant of an agricultural holding has received notice that the person theretofore entitled to receive the rents and profits of the holding (hereinafter referred to as ' the original landlord ') has ceased to be so entitled, and also notice of the name and address of the person who has become entitled to receive the rents and profits, any notice or other document served upon or delivered to the original landlord by the tenant shall be deemed for the purposes of this Act to have been served upon or delivered to the landlord of the holding."

It will be appreciated, therefore, that when preparing conditions of sale of land, it is advisable to state therein whether the vendor or the purchaser has to pay the tenant compensation for unexhausted improvements and for disturbance. For the " landlord " or person entitled to receive the rents, when the notice to quit was given or received, will not necessarily be the " landlord " or person entitled to receive the rents and therefore the person to pay the compensation, when the notice to quit determines (*Bradshaw* v. *Bird* [1920] 2 K.B. 144 ; *Dale* v. *Hatfield Chase Corporation* [1922] 2 K.B. 282 ; *Tombs* v. *Turvey* (1923), 93 L.J.K.B. 785 ; *Richards* v. *Pryse* [1927] 2 K.B. 76).

In *Bennett* v. *Stone* [1902] 1 Ch. 226 ; [1903] 1 Ch. 509, the tenant gave notice to quit *after* the date of the contract, and as the property was sold subject to the tenancy it fell on the purchaser to pay the compensation. As it happened, the notice expired before the actual completion of the purchase, and the vendor, being at that time " the landlord " within the Act, had to pay the compensation ; it was held that the purchaser must recoup the vendor the amount he had paid.

It must be remembered that a notice to quit given by a landlord to the tenant may become void on execution of a contract for sale of the land. See p. 958.

Precautions to be taken on purchase of agricultural land.—Before advising a client to enter into a contract for the purchase of agricultural land it is very important to ascertain the rights of the tenant. It is apparent from the provisions as to the rights of the tenant to compensation mentioned in the present part that careful inquiry is essential. For instance, the purchaser will wish to know whether the vendor has consented to the carrying out of any improvements specified in the A.H.A. 1948, Sched. 2, Pt. I, or whether he has received notice of the tenant's intention to carry out the improvement specified in Sched. 2, Pt. II. See further, *post*, p. 960 *et seq.*

Where a landlord has paid compensation to an outgoing tenant for improvements or for disturbance, he may, if for instance he is a tenant for life or other limited owner, obtain a charge on the land under the A.H.A. 1948, s. 82. Similarly, the tenant may have obtained a charge in respect of compensation due to him (*ibid.*, ss. 72, 73, 74). See further, *post*, p. 960. Such charges are registrable under the L.C.A. 1972, s. 2 (2), Class A ; see *ante*, p. 597.

It was decided in *Farrow* v. *Orttewell* [1933] 1 Ch. 480 that a purchaser of a farm could not give a good notice to quit to the tenant before the completion of the purchase, because although he was equitably entitled to the rents, he was not legally so entitled. But as the tenant had acted on the notice, the proposed purchaser was, as regards the tenant, estopped from denying that he had power to give such notice, and so it was held that he was the " landlord " within the 1923 Act, and that the tenant was entitled to recover compensation from him. See also *ante*, p. 944.

It is necessary again to add a warning that a notice to quit given by a landlord may become void on the execution of a contract of sale ; see *post*, p. 958.

B. TERMS OF TENANCY

Extension of tenancy for fixed term.—Such tenancies continue as tenancies from year to year unless terminated by notice. This is the result of the A.H.A. 1948, s. 3 (1), which is as follows :—

" 3.—(1) A tenancy of an agricultural holding for a term of two years or upwards shall, instead of terminating on the expiration of the term for which it was granted, continue (as from the expiration of that term) as a tenancy from year to year, but otherwise on the terms of the original tenancy so far as applicable, unless, not less than one year nor more than two years before the date fixed for the expiration of the term, a written notice has been given by either party to the other of his intention to terminate the tenancy."

A notice given under this subsection is deemed to be a notice to quit (*ibid.*, s. 3 (2)), and consequently the special rules mentioned *post*, p. 951 *et seq.* will apply to it and compensation can be claimed as in the case of any other notice to quit. The section does not apply to a tenancy created before 1st January, 1921, or one operating under the L.P.A. 1925, s. 149 (6) ; see *ante*, p. 941 (A.H.A. 1948, s. 3 (3)). The section applies notwithstanding any contrary agreement (*ibid.*, s. 3 (4)).

This section should be read with s. 2 (*ante*, p. 943), which turns tenancies *less* than from year to year into lettings from year to year, necessarily lasting at least two years and so within s. 3. A tenancy for over one year but under two years does not fall within either s. 2 or s. 3 and so no notice is needed to determine it and the tenant will not be able to claim compensation for disturbance ; compare the remarks *ante*, p. 943.

It was decided in *Edell* v. *Dulieu* [1924] A.C. 38 that the words " a notice to quit " must be taken to include a notice to determine the tenancy, and therefore, in the case of a lease for twenty-one years with an option to either party to determine it on six months' notice at the end of the first seven or fourteen years of the term, it was necessary to give twelve months' notice according to s. 28 of the Agriculture Act, 1920, which is now replaced by s. 23 of the A.H.A. 1948, *post*, p. 951 *et seq.*

Similarly, where the tenancy, held at a rack rent, determines by the death or cesser of the interest of a landlord entitled for his life, or for any other uncertain interest, instead of a claim to emblements, the tenant will continue to occupy the holding until the occupation is determined by twelve months' notice to quit expiring at the end of a year of the tenancy (A.H.A. 1948, s. 4 (1)).

Arbitration as to rent.—Even the rent of a holding is not a matter solely of bargaining between the parties, but may be determined by arbitration. Also it must be borne in mind that agricultural rents are temporarily subject to control under the Counter-Inflation Act, 1973. Section 8 (1) of the A.H.A 1948, as amended by the Agriculture Act, 1958, s. 2, provides :—

" 8.—(1) Subject to the provisions of this section, the landlord or the tenant of an agricultural holding may, whether the tenancy was created before or after the commencement of this Act, by notice in writing served on his tenant or landlord demand a reference to arbitration under this Act of the question what rent should be payable in respect of the holding as from the next ensuing day on which the tenancy could have been determined by notice to quit given at the date of demanding the reference [as to this, see *Sclater* v. *Horton* [1954] 2 Q.B. 1], and on a reference under this sub-section the arbitrator shall determine what rent should be properly payable in respect of the holding at the date of the reference and accordingly shall, as from the day aforesaid, increase or reduce the rent previously payable or direct that it continue unchanged.

For the purposes of this subsection the rent properly payable in respect of a holding shall be the rent at which, having regard to the terms of the tenancy (other than those relating to rent), the holding might reasonably be expected to be let in the open market by a willing landlord to a willing tenant, there being disregarded (in addition to the matters referred to in the next following subsection) any effect on rent of the fact that the tenant who is a party to the arbitration is in occupation of the holding."

The arbitrator may not (i) increase the rent on account of improvements which were executed at the expense of the tenant without equivalent benefit given by the landlord in consideration of their execution, and which were not executed under an obligation in the tenancy contract ; (ii) reduce the rent by reason of deterioration or damage to buildings or land caused or permitted by the tenant (*ibid.*, s. 8 (2)). For this purpose a system of farming more beneficial than that required by the tenancy contract, or that normally practised on comparable holdings, is deemed an improvement executed at the expense of the tenant (*ibid.*, s. 8 (4)).

With certain exceptions (as to which see s. 8 (3), proviso), an increase or reduction in rent cannot take effect within three years from the commencement of the tenancy, or from a previous increase or reduction, or from a previous direction of an arbitrator that the rent shall remain unchanged (*ibid.*, s. 8 (3)). However, where the rent is calculated by reference to a formula it appears that s. 8 (3) does not apply so as to prohibit an alteration of the method of calculation (see the decision of the county court in *Bolesworth Estate Co., Ltd.* v. *Cook*, reported in *New Law Journal*, vol. 116, p. 1318).

Although the section does not expressly so provide, its wording is such that an award under it would appear to involve a compulsory variation in the rent, which the tenant is bound to pay and the landlord to accept.

In certain circumstances a landlord who carried out improvements (not necessarily limited to those for which compensation is provided in the A.H.A. 1948) may, by notice in writing served on the tenant within six months from the completion of the improvement, claim that the rent be increased by an amount " equal to the increase in the rental value of the holding attributable to the carrying out of the improvement " (*ibid.*, s. 9 (1)). The improvements in question include any improvement carried out at the request of, or in agreement with, the tenant, or one carried out by the landlord under s. 50 (3) (see *post*, p. 965), or in compliance with a direction given by the Minister, or at the cost of the landlord in pursuance of a direction given under the Agriculture Act, 1958, s. 4 (A.H.A. 1948, s. 9 (1) ; Agriculture Act, 1958, s. 4 (5)).

Regulations fixing terms of tenancy.—The Minister may make regulations prescribing terms " as to the maintenance, repair and insurance of fixed equipment which shall be deemed to be incorporated in every contract of tenancy of an agricultural holding . . . except in so far as they would impose on one of the parties to an agreement *in writing* a liability which under the agreement is imposed on the other " (A.H.A. 1948, s. 6 (1)). " Fixed equipment " is given a very wide definition by s. 94 (1) and includes any building and any works on land and anything grown on land for a purpose other than use after severance, consumption of the thing grown or of produce thereof, or amenity. Thus the term includes drains, hedges and ditches.

These terms apply even though the parties have agreed to other terms, if the agreement has not been reduced to writing ; even if there is an agreement in writing the statutory terms will apply except so far as that agreement deals with the liability in question. If the written agreement deals with that liability in a manner differing from the regulations, the agreement may be altered by the procedure mentioned at p. 949, *post*, but otherwise in any conflict between a statutory clause and a contractual clause the contractual clause has effect (*Burden* v. *Hannaford* [1956] 1 Q.B. 142).

The regulations which have been made are the Agriculture (Maintenance, Repair and Insurance of Fixed Equipment) Regulations, 1948 ; the following is a summary only and as from 29th September, 1974, these 1948 regulations are to be superseded by like regulations of 1973 (S.I. 1973 No. 1473).

Rights and Liabilities of the Landlord

1.—(1) To execute all repairs to the undermentioned parts of the farmhouse, cottages and farm buildings, namely, main walls and exterior walls, but excluding the interior covering of exterior walls save where such interior covering is affected by structural defect of the wall ; roofs, including eaves-guttering and downpipes ; and floors, doors and windows (excepting glass, locks and fastenings) ; provided that in the case of repairs to floorboards, doors, windows, eaves-guttering and downpipes, the landlord may recover one-half of the reasonable cost thereof from the tenant.

(2) To execute all repairs to the water mains, the sewage disposal systems (excepting the cleaning thereof and excepting the drains) and to the structure of reservoirs or pump houses of a water supply system.

2. To keep the farmhouse, cottages and farm buildings insured to their full value against damage by fire and to make good damage by fire, being damage not due to the wilful act or negligence of the tenant.

3. As often as may be necessary, and in any case at intervals of not more than five years, properly to paint or gas-tar or creosote all outside wood and ironwork of the farmhouse, cottages and farm buildings which have been previously painted, etc., or which it is necessary so to paint, etc. ; provided that in respect of doors, windows, eaves-guttering and downpipes, the landlord may recover one half of the reasonable cost from the tenant, subject nevertheless to para. 12 (2) hereof.

4.—(1) The landlord is under no liability to execute repairs or to insure buildings or fixtures which are the property of the tenant, or to execute repairs rendered necessary by the wilful act or negligence of the tenant, or any members of his household or his employees.

(2) If the tenant fails to execute repairs for which he is liable within one month of receiving from the landlord a written request specifying the necessary repair, and calling on him to execute them the landlord may enter and execute such repairs and recover the cost from the tenant.

Rights and Liabilities of the Tenant

Except in so far as such liabilities fall to be undertaken by the landlord :

5. To repair and to keep and leave clean in a good tenantable repair the farmhouse, cottages and farm buildings together with all fixtures and fittings, drains, sewers, water supplies, pumps, fences, live and dead hedges, gates, field walls, posts, stiles, bridges, culverts, ponds, water courses, ditches, roads and yards, and to keep in good order all eaves-guttering and down pipes, gulleys and grease-traps ; and also to use carefully all items for the repair of which the landlord is responsible, and also to report in writing immediately to the landlord any damage to such items. [The obligation to repair is not restricted to an obligation to leave items in as good repair as they were at the beginning of the tenancy, but in determining whether the obligation has been complied with regard must be had to the age, character and condition of the items at the beginning of the tenancy and to the length of the tenancy (*Evans* v. *Jones* [1955] 2 Q.B. 58).]

6. To replace or repair all items of fixed equipment, and to do any work, where such replacement, repair or work is rendered necessary by the wilful act or negligence of the tenant or any members of his household or his employees.

7. As often as may be necessary, and in any case at intervals of not more than seven years, properly to clean, colour, whiten, paper and paint the inside of the farmhouse, cottages and buildings which have been previously so treated, and in each year to limewash the inside of all farm buildings which previously have been limewashed.

8. Notwithstanding the general liability of the landlord for repairs, to renew all broken or cracked tiles or slates and replace all slipped tiles or slates, but so that the cost shall not exceed five pounds in any one year of the tenancy.

9. To cut and lay a proper proportion of the hedges in each year so as to maintain them in good and sound condition.

10. To dig out and cleanse all ponds, ditches, etc., and to keep clear from obstruction all field drains.

11. To provide suitable straw or reed for the repair of thatch.

12.—(1) If the last year of the tenancy is not a year in which such cleaning, etc., as is mentioned in para. 7 hereof is due, the tenant must pay at the end of such last year one seventh part of the estimated cost thereof in respect of each year that has elapsed since such last cleaning, etc., and in such a case the landlord must pay to the tenant at the time of the next subsequent occasion that such work is carried out, the reasonable cost thereof less one seventh part in respect of each year that has elapsed since the commencement of the tenancy.

(2) If the last year of the tenancy is not a year in which the landlord is liable, under para. 3 hereof, to paint the doors, etc., the tenant must then pay at the end of such last year one tenth part of the estimated cost thereof in respect of each year that has elapsed since such last painting, etc., and in such a case the landlord shall be entitled to recover from the tenant at the time of the next subsequent occasion that such work is carried out, one tenth part only of the reasonable cost thereof in respect of each year that has elapsed since the commencement of the tenancy.

13. If the landlord fails to execute repairs which are his liability within three months of receiving a written request specifying the repairs and calling on him to execute them, the tenant may execute them and recover the reasonable cost from the landlord.

General Proviso

14. Nothing in the regulations creates any liability (1) to maintain obsolete equipment which the landlord and the tenant agree in writing that neither party shall be liable to maintain, or (2) to execute any work so far as execution is rendered impossible (except at unreasonable expense) by reason of subsidence or by the blocking of outfalls not under the control of either party.

Variation of agreement.—Where an agreement in writing relating to tenancy of a holding effects substantial modifications in the operation of the regulations mentioned in the last paragraph, the landlord or tenant may, if the other fails on request to agree to bring the agreement into conformity with the regulations, refer to arbitration under the A.H.A. 1948, the terms of tenancy with respect to the maintenance, repair and insurance of fixed equipment (A.H.A. 1948, s. 6 (2)) ; provision is to be made for arbitration of any matter arising under the regulations : s. 15 (2) of the

Agriculture (Miscellaneous Provisions) Act, 1972. The arbitrator must disregard the rent payable but must consider whether the " modifications " effected by the agreement " are justifiable having regard to the circumstances of the holding and of the landlord and the tenant," and, if he determines that they are not justifiable, he may vary them in such manner as appears to him reasonable (A.H.A. 1948, s. 6 (3)). References cannot be made more often than once in three years (*ibid.*, *s.* 6 (2), proviso). These subsections come near to imposing standard terms of tenancy whilst retaining the semblance of an agreement between landlord and tenant.

Conditions applicable for forty years to an agricultural unit which has been amalgamated pursuant to the Agriculture Act, 1967, are, so far as applicable, deemed to be terms of any lease, agreement for lease or tenancy of the unit of land, or any part of it, and are enforceable accordingly (*ibid.*, Sched. 3, para. 1).

Where under the contract for a tenancy of an agricultural holding provision is made for the maintenance of specified land, or a specified proportion of the holding, as permanent pasture, the landlord or the tenant may demand a reference to arbitration of the question whether it is expedient in order to secure the full and efficient farming of the holding that the amount of land required to be maintained as permanent pasture should be reduced. The arbitrator may direct that the contract of tenancy shall be modified as to the land which is to be maintained as permanent pasture or is to be treated as arable land and as to cropping (A.H.A. 1948, s. 10, as substituted by Agriculture Act, 1958, Sched. 1, Pt. I, para. 6).

Provisions for securing written tenancy agreements.—Where there is not in force in respect of any tenancy of a holding an agreement in writing embodying the terms of the tenancy or the agreement contains no provision for one or more of the matters specified in Sched. 1 to the A.H.A. 1948, the landlord or tenant may, if no agreement can be reached with the other as to such matters, refer the terms of tenancy to arbitration (*ibid.*, s. 5 (1)). The arbitrator must specify the existing terms of tenancy, subject to any variation agreed between the parties, and if the terms do not provide for any matters specified in Sched. 1, make such provision for those matters as is agreed between landlord and tenant, or, in default of agreement, as appears to the arbitrator to be reasonable and just (*ibid.*, s. 5 (2)).

The matters specified in Sched. 1 are : (i) the names of the parties, (ii) particulars of the holding with a sufficient description *by reference to a map or plan*, (iii) the term, (iv) the rent and the dates on which it is payable, (v) liability for rates, (vi) a covenant as to maintenance and repair of fixed equipment, (vii) a covenant by the landlord to reinstate following damage by fire and (except where the landlord is a Government department or the Minister approves a different arrangement) a covenant by the landlord to insure against damage by fire, (viii) a covenant by the tenant to insure dead stock and harvested crops, and (ix) a power of re-entry in the event of the tenant not performing his obligations.

There are also various supplementary provisions as to the rights of the parties if liability for maintenance or repair of fixed equipment is transferred from one party to the other under ss. 5 or 6 of the A.H.A. 1948, including power for the arbitrator to vary the rent if it appears equitable to do so (*ibid.*, s. 7). In particular, it is provided that the award of an arbitrator under ss. 5 or 6 shall have effect as if its terms were contained in an agreement in writing entered into by the landlord and the tenant.

Equipment necessary to comply with statutory requirements.— Section 4 of the Agriculture Act, 1958, enables the tenant to call on the landlord to provide, alter or repair fixed equipment necessary to comply with statutory requirements. The tenant must first make a request in writing but if the landlord refuses to comply or fails to agree to do so within a reasonable time the tenant may apply for a direction of the Agricultural Land Tribunal. Failure to comply with a direction gives the tenant the same remedies as if the contract of tenancy had contained an undertaking by the landlord to do the work and the tenant may carry out the work and recover the cost. There are certain limits on the power of the Tribunal to make a direction, for instance (i) work may not be required for the purposes of an agricultural activity which has not been carried on in the last three years if it involves a substantial alteration of the type of farming ; (ii) the work must be reasonable having regard to the landlord's responsibilities to manage the holding in accordance with the rules of good estate management ; (iii) no direction must be given if there is already an agreement for the carrying out of the work by either the landlord or the tenant.

Rights of tenant to remove fixtures.—Any fixture affixed to a holding by the tenant and any building (*other than one in respect of which the tenant is entitled to compensation*) erected by him, not being affixed or erected pursuant to an obligation in that behalf or instead of a fixture or building belonging to the landlord, is removable by the tenant during the tenancy or within two months after its termination (A.H.A. 1948, s. 13 (1)). Before this right may be exercised the tenant must have paid all rent owing and performed all other obligations, and must, at least one month before both the exercise of the right *and* the termination of the tenancy, give the landlord notice of his intention to remove the fixture or building (*ibid.*, s. 13 (2)). The landlord may serve a counter-notice electing to purchase the fixture or building at a fair value to an incoming tenant (*ibid.*, s. 13 (3)). In removing the fixture or building the tenant must not do any avoidable damage and must make good any damage done (*ibid.*, s. 13 (4)).

C. NOTICE TO QUIT

Length of notice.—The general rule is that, notwithstanding any contrary provision in a tenancy contract, a notice to quit a holding or part of a holding will be invalid if it purports to terminate the tenancy before the expiration of twelve months from the end of the then current year of tenancy (A.H.A. 1948, s. 23 (1)). This rule does not apply (and the length of notice must be that specified in the tenancy contract, or if the length is not specified, must be that required in the case of other land, as to which see *ante*, p. 833) in the following cases :—

(i) Where a receiving order has been made against the tenant.

(ii) Where the notice is given in pursuance of a provision in the tenancy contract authorising resumption of possession for a specified purpose other than agriculture. Such a provision cannot validly specify a length of notice of one month or less, because if it did specify so short a notice the tenant would not have time to give notices regarding compensation, for instance notice of his intention to claim more than the minimum compensation for disturbance under s. 34 (2), proviso (*c*) (*Re Disraeli's Agreement* [1939] Ch. 382 ; *Coates* v. *Diment* [1951] 1 All E.R. 890).

(iii) Where the notice is given by a tenant to a sub-tenant.

(iv) Where the tenancy was made before 25th March, 1947, and (a) the notice is given by the Admiralty, War Department or Air Council where possession is required for naval, military or air force purposes, or (b) the notice is given by a statutory undertaking in respect of land acquired for the purposes of the undertaking or by a government department or local authority where possession is required for the purpose (not being agriculture) for which the land was acquired or has been appropriated (special rules as to land of the British Transport Commission are contained in s. 23 (2) ; see now as to the appropriate Board, s. 1 of the Transport Act, 1962).

(v) Where the tenancy has taken effect under the L.P.A. 1925, s. 149 (6) ; see *ante*, p. 914 (A.H.A. 1948, s. 23 (1), proviso).

It often happens that for the purposes of cultivation, and in accordance with the custom of the country, different parts of a farm, although under a tenancy at one entire rent, have been entered at different times and therefore the tenancy will have different times of ending. The question arises in such cases as to when the notice to quit must be given. In *Swinburne* v. *Andrews* [1923] 2 K.B. 483, the tenancy of the main portion of the land expired on the 6th April, and the tenancy of the farmhouse, buildings, and the remainder of the land expired on the 13th May, and it was held that the latter was the material date, as the contract of tenancy did not cease until then. The decision was in reference to the question of compensation for disturbance, and it is doubtful whether the same rule applies to notices to quit. The safest course is to give notice to quit expressed to take effect at the proper times applicable to each part and this would seem to be good if given in time to allow the proper length of notice with regard to the principal part of the land (*Doe d. Bradford* v. *Watkins* (1806), 7 East 551 ; *Doe d. Davenport* v. *Rhodes* (1843), 11 M. & W. 600). See further, Woodfall, Landlord and Tenant, 26th ed., p. 1000.

Restrictions on operation of notice.—These restrictions are of great importance because they confer a considerable measure of security of tenure on tenants of agricultural land. This is done by providing that if the tenant serves a counter-notice then the notice to quit shall have no effect unless the Agricultural Land Tribunal consents to its operation (A.H.A. 1948, s. 24 (1) ; Agriculture Act, 1958, Sched. 1, Pt. I, para. 8). The tenant's right to object by serving a counter-notice is excluded in certain cases (*ibid.*, s. 24 (2)), and there are circumstances in which the Tribunal must consent (*ibid.*, s. 25 (1) as re-enacted by the Agriculture Act, 1958, s. 3 (2)). The restrictions mentioned in this paragraph apply only where notice to quit has been given, and they have no application to forfeiture of a lease containing a proviso for re-entry (as to which, see *ante*, p. 882 *et seq.*). The effect of a notice to quit land used partly for agricultural purposes is mentioned *ante*, p. 943. These rules must now be considered in some detail.

Section 24 (1) of the A.H.A. 1948, provides as follows :—

"Where notice to quit an agricultural holding or part of an agricultural holding is given to the tenant thereof, and not later than one month from the giving of the notice to quit *the tenant serves* on the landlord *a counter-notice* in writing requiring that this subsection shall apply to the notice to quit, then, *subject to the provisions of the next following subsection*, the notice to quit shall not have effect unless the [Agricultural Land Tribunal : Agriculture Act, 1958, Sched. 1, Pt. I, para. 8] consents to the operation thereof."

" *the tenant serves . . . a counter-notice.*"—If the tenant is doubtful whether a notice served on him is valid he has the option of (i) serving counter-notice under s. 24 (1) or (ii) resisting any proceedings on the ground that the notice is invalid. There would appear to be no objection to keeping both lines of defence open by serving a counter-notice, and, if the Tribunal grants consent, relying on the invalidity of the notice. It would be advisable, on serving the counter-notice, to state that it is without prejudice to the contention that the notice is invalid. See the discussion in the *Conveyancer N.S.*, vol. 16, p. 319.

A counter-notice is effective, whatever its form, if it indicates so clear an intention to invoke the rights granted by the Act that the landlord could not reasonably mistake what was meant. Nevertheless, a letter merely stating " I don't intend to go I shall appeal against it and take the matter up with " the then appropriate committee was held not clear enough and so was not an effective counter-notice (*Mountford* v. *Hodkinson* [1956] 1 W.L.R. 422).

" *subject to the provisions of the next following subsection.*"—The next following subsection (s. 24 (2)) provides that the tenant may not object to the notice in the following cases :—

(*a*) If the Tribunal has consented to the notice before it was given. Application for such consent must be made not less than three nor more than twelve months before the commencement of the twelve months for which the notice will run (Agriculture (Notices to Remedy and Notices to Quit) Order, 1964).

(*b*) Where the notice is given on the ground that the land is required for a use, other than agriculture, for which planning permission has been granted or for which such permission is not required *otherwise* than by virtue of any provision of the enactments relating to town and country planning. Thus, if planning permission is unnecessary by virtue of an exemption in town planning legislation, the tenant has the right to object to the notice, but not, e.g., if the notice is given by the Crown or a government department to which the legislation does not apply (*Ministry of Agriculture, Fisheries and Food* v. *Jenkins* [1963] 2 Q.B. 317). The burden of proving that land is " required " for such a use is on the landlord ; see the county court case of *Branston Gravels, Ltd.* v. *Samuel Durose, Solicitors' Journal*, vol. 97, p. 125, and *Jones* v. *Gates* [1954] 1 W.L.R. 222. However, the words " required for a use, other than agriculture " in s. 24 (2) (*b*) do not refer only to requirements of the landlord, but refer also to any person requiring the land, including one who, having obtained planning permission, intended to make a compulsory purchase of the landlord's interest (*Rugby Joint Water Board* v. *Foottit* [1972] 2 W.L.R. 757, H.L.).

(*c*) Where the Tribunal, pursuant to an *application made not more than six months* before the giving of the notice, gave a certificate of bad husbandry. See further, p. 958.

(*d*) Where the tenant has failed to comply with a notice in writing served on him requiring him to pay within two months any rent due or requiring him within such reasonable period as was specified in the notice (where the notice is to do work, a period of six months is not to be treated as a reasonable period) to remedy any breach of the term of a tenancy contract which is capable of remedy and which term is consistent with good husbandry. Notices to remedy must be in the prescribed form, and any further notice requiring the doing of any work of repair, maintenance or replacement (although different in detail from an earlier notice) served on the tenant less than twelve months after the earlier notice requiring such work is to be disregarded, except in the case where the earlier notice was withdrawn with the tenant's agreement in writing. See s. 24 (2) (d) of the 1948 Act as amended by s. 19 (6) of the Agriculture (Miscellaneous Provisions) Act, 1963 ; in addition certain provisions as to the form of notices and relating to time and arbitration machinery are made by the Agriculture (Notices to Remedy and Notices to Quit) Order, 1964, fully discussed by J. Muir Watt in the *Conveyancer N.S.*, vol. 28, p. 41. If the notice specifies several breaches for remedying, failure to remedy any of them, subject to the *de minimis* rule, entitles the landlord to serve an effective notice to quit (*Price* v. *Romilly* [1960] 1 W.L.R. 1360 ; *Shepherd* v. *Lomas* [1963] 1 W.L.R. 962). However, if a tenant allows a notice to pay rent within two months to expire, his security of tenure is at an end notwithstanding that he may pay the rent before a notice to quit is served (*Stoneman* v. *Brown* [1973] 1 W.L.R. 459, C.A.). Nonetheless, Lord Denning, M.R., indicated that in suitable circumstances there might be jurisdiction to relieve the tenant from forfeiture (*ibid.*, p. 462).

(e) Where the interest of the landlord has been materially prejudiced by a breach of a term of the tenancy contract which was not capable of remedy, and which term is consistent with good husbandry.

(f) Where the tenant has become bankrupt or has compounded with his creditors.

(g) Where the tenant *with whom the contract of tenancy was made* (or the survivor or last survivor of joint tenants (Agriculture (Miscellaneous Provisions) Act, 1954, s. 7)) has died within three months before the service of the notice. After assignment of the tenancy, and subsequent death of the original tenant, a notice may be served within three months on the assignee pursuant to this sub-clause and he will be unable to object (*Clarke* v. *Hall* [1961] 2 Q.B. 331). Correspondingly, a notice cannot validly be served on this ground on the death of the executor of the tenant with whom the contract was made (*Costagliola* v. *Bunting* [1958] 1 W.L.R. 580). See also *Jenkin R. Lewis & Son, Ltd.* v. *Kerman* [1971] Ch. 477, where it was held that a valid and effective notice could be given within this paragraph notwithstanding that intervening increases in rent may have involved a new letting to a new tenant.

In each of the above-mentioned cases the provisions of s. 24 (1) will be excluded *only if the notice states the appropriate reason for which it is given.* The notice must make clear what the reason is and, in particular, when the landlord complains of a breach of covenant which might or might not be capable of remedy, must make clear whether it is given under para. (d) or (e) of subs. (2), above (*Budge* v. *Hicks* [1951] 2 K.B. 335). Nevertheless, a notice giving reasons similar to those in s. 24 (2) but not falling precisely within the conditions (for instance, that the rent is in arrear and the property has not been kept in repair), may be a valid notice taking effect under s. 24 (1) (*Hammon* v. *Fairbrother* [1956] 1 W.L.R. 490, but see further below). A notice which states a good reason within s. 24 (2) is not rendered invalid because it also states a reason which is not a valid one (*French* v. *Elliott* [1960] 1 W.L.R. 40).

A notice to quit served expressly under s. 24 (2) (*d*) before the expiration of the prior notice requiring the remedying of a breach of a term of the tenancy is invalid and cannot be treated as a notice to quit operating at common law in default of service of a counter-notice under s. 24 (1) (*Cowan* v. *Wrayford* [1953] 1 W.L.R. 1340). If a landlord wishes to rely on a notice, in the alternative, as a general common-law unqualified notice should he fail under s. 24 (2), that must appear on the face of the notice, or two notices should be served (*ibid.*, *per* Somervell, L.J., at p. 1344).

Hammon v. *Fairbrother* has been doubted, and *Cowan* v. *Wrayford* applied, by the Court of Appeal in *Mills* v. *Edwards* [1971] 1 Q.B. 379, where a notice to quit which did not make plain that it was served under s. 24 (1), and not s. 24 (2), was held to be ambiguous and therefore wholly invalid. In this case the view was expressed that it is unnecessary and undesirable, but not necessarily invalidating, to give reasons where the notice is intended to come under s. 24 (1). It was also indicated that, whilst an unsuccessful s. 24 (2) notice cannot be converted to a good s. 24 (1) notice, a landlord is not precluded from serving two notices, one under each subsection, and may even be able to rely on both subsections through an appropriately worded combined notice.

If the notice to quit states that it is given for one or more of the reasons specified in paras. (*b*), (*d*) or (*e*), the tenant may contest the reason stated by serving on the landlord, within one month of the notice to quit, a notice in writing requiring the question to be determined by arbitration (Agriculture (Notices to Remedy and Notices to Quit) Order, 1964, arts. 5, 6, 7, 8 and 9 ; revised by the Agriculture (Notices to Quit) (Miscellaneous Provisions) Order, 1972). Where this has been done and, in consequence of the arbitration, s. 24 (1), *ante*, p. 952, applies, the time within which a counter notice may be served by the tenant on the landlord under that subsection is one month from the termination of the arbitration (*ibid.*, art. 10 ; revised by the Agriculture (Notices to Quit) (Miscellaneous Provisions) Order, 1972). Where a notice to quit has effect in consequence of any such arbitration or of consent granted under s. 24 (1), *ante*, p. 952, and would otherwise come into operation on or within six months after the termination of the arbitration or the giving of the consent, the arbitrator or the tribunal may postpone the termination of the tenancy for a period not exceeding twelve months (*ibid.*, art. 12 ; revised by the Agriculture (Notices to Quit) (Miscellaneous Provisions) Order, 1972).

In *Attorney General (Duchy of Lancaster)* v. *Simcock* [1966] Ch. 1, Pennycuick, J., held that, in view of the mandatory terms of the relevant regulations, the validity of a landlord's reasons for giving a notice to quit an agricultural holding can be decided only by arbitration, the jurisdiction of the court being entirely excluded (the case concerns the construction of art. 6 of the Agricultural Land Tribunals and Notices to Quit Order, 1959 (replaced by art. 9 of the 1964 Order which, as the learned judge observed, " does not differ in substance from art. 6 ")). It is clear, therefore, that questions of law can only be brought before the court by way of a special case stated by the arbitrator to the county court, with appeal in the usual way thereafter. However, this decision does not appear to apply to other objections, such as challenging the notice as to adequacy of form.

In *Public Trustee* v. *Randag* [1966] Ch. 649, Plowden, J., held that it is *ultra vires* for an arbitrator under the A.H.A. 1948 to make an award which was conditional, with the consequence that in effect no award could be made and the operation of a landlord's notice to quit was still suspended.

If it is necessary for the landlord to have consent to the notice, he *must apply to the Tribunal within one month of the service on him of the counter-notice* by the tenant, and application must be made on Form 1 set out in the Appendix to the Agricultural Land Tribunals and Notices to Quit Order, 1959, which must be signed by the applicant and served on the secretary to the county agricultural executive committee (*ibid.*, art. 2).

The circumstances in which consent is to be given are set out in the A.H.A., 1948, s. 25 (1), as re-enacted by the Agriculture Act, 1958, s. 3 (2) :—

" 25.—(1) The Agricultural Land Tribunal shall consent under the last foregoing section to the operation of a notice to quit an agricultural holding or part of an agricultural holding if, but only if, they are satisfied as to one or more of the following matters, being a matter or matters specified by the landlord in his application for their consent, that is to say—

(a) that the carrying out of the purpose for which the landlord proposes to terminate the tenancy is desirable in the interests of good husbandry as respects the land to which the notice relates, treated as a separate unit ; or

(b) that the carrying out thereof is desirable in the interests of *sound management* of the estate of which the land to which the notice relates forms part or which that land constitutes ; or

(c) that the carrying out thereof is desirable for the purposes of agricultural research, education, experiment or demonstration, or for the purposes of the enactments relating to smallholdings or allotments ; or

(d) that *greater hardship* would be caused by withholding than by giving consent to the operation of the notice ; or

(e) that the landlord proposes to terminate the tenancy for the purpose of the land's being used for a use, other than for agriculture, not falling within paragraph (b) of subsection (2) of the last foregoing section [as to which see p. 953] :

Provided that, notwithstanding that they are satisfied as aforesaid, the Tribunal shall withhold consent to the operation of the notice to quit if in all the circumstances it appears to them that a fair and reasonable landlord would not insist on possession."

" *sound management*."—This refers to the landlord's obligation to manage the estate properly and does not comprehend the financial interest of the landlord in isolation (*National Coal Board* v. *Naylor* [1972] 1 W.L.R. 908).

" *greater hardship*."—The court may consider hardship at large ; the word is not restricted to hardship which is referable to the holding (*Purser* v. *Bailey* [1967] 2 Q.B. 500).

Where an application for arbitration is made the operation of the notice to quit is suspended, and if no decision is come to until the notice to quit has less than six months to run the Tribunal may postpone the date on which the notice takes effect for a period not exceeding twelve months (Agriculture (Notices to Remedy and Notices to Quit) Order, 1964, arts. 11 and 12).

Notices to quit served on sub-tenants.—At common law a notice to quit served on a tenant is conclusive against him and against any sub-tenant, and nothing in the Act or regulations alters this rule (*Sherwood* v. *Moody* [1952] 1 All E.R. 389). In that case a notice to quit was served by the head landlord on his tenant which became effective (being confirmed by the Minister, who then had power to do so, after objection by the tenant). The tenant had served on a sub-tenant a notice which did not state why it was served. It was held that although the sub-tenant had successfully objected to the notice served on him the head landlord could recover possession from the sub-tenant.

For the avoidance of disputes, however, a special procedure is laid down for cases in which notice is served by the landlord on the tenant and a sub-tenancy exists. If a notice to quit is served by a tenant on a sub-tenant after the tenant has himself received a notice to quit the same land, and that fact is stated in the notice served on the sub-tenant, the sub-tenant has no right to require the Minister's consent to the notice to be obtained (A.H.A. 1948, s. 26 (1) (*e*) as re-enacted by the Agriculture Act, 1958, Sched. 1, para. 10 (1); Agriculture (Notices to Remedy and Notices to Quit) Order, 1964, art. 14). In such a case the notice given to the sub-tenant will not take effect if the notice given to the tenant does not have effect, for instance, if the Tribunal refuses consent to the notice (*ibid.*, art. 14 (2)); but if the notice to the tenant takes effect so will the notice to the sub-tenant. It should be noted that unless the case is one in which the tenant can serve a counter-notice under s. 24 (1), *ante*, p. 952, and the tenant does in fact serve such a notice, the sub-tenant has no means of preventing the notice served on him from taking effect. The consequence is that a landlord may be able to evade the security of tenure provided by the Act by interposing a tenancy in favour of a nominee between himself and his tenant. The tenant would then become a sub-tenant who would have no redress (except, possibly, an action on a covenant for quiet enjoyment) if the nominee tenant failed to challenge a notice to quit served on him, but gave notice to the sub-tenant.

These special rules as to sub-tenancies apply only if the tenant has himself received a notice to quit. If the tenant has not received a notice the sub-tenant has the usual right under s. 24 (1), *ante*, to require consent of the Tribunal to be obtained to any notice served on him. Difficulties are likely to arise, however, if the principal tenant serves notice to quit on the landlord. If he also serves notice on the sub-tenant the sub-tenant will be entitled to require, in an appropriate case, that the Tribunal's consent be obtained to the notice. If the Tribunal grants consent the sub-tenant will, of course, be obliged to quit. If, on the other hand, the principal tenant fails to refer the matter of the notice to the Tribunal, or if the Tribunal refuses to grant consent, it seems that the sub-tenant can lawfully remain in possession. The reason is that the sub-tenancy remains valid even though the head tenancy ceases; the principal tenant, by giving notice to the landlord, cannot determine the sub-tenancy. See the decision of Hilbery, J., in *Brown* v. *Wilson* discussed in the *Law Times*, vol. 208, p. 144. The same rule would apply if the principal tenant gave notice to the landlord but not to the sub-tenant.

Certificates of bad husbandry.—One of the cases in which the Tribunal's consent to a notice to quit is not required is where a certificate of bad husbandry has been given on application made not more than six months before the giving of the notice (A.H.A. 1948, s. 24 (2) (c) ; *ante,* p. 953).

Application for a certificate must be made to the Agricultural Land Tribunal in accordance with the procedure specified in the Schedule to the Agricultural Land Tribunals and Notices to Quit Order, 1959 ; forms are prescribed for the application and for the tenant's reply. The A.H.A. 1948, s. 27 (as re-enacted by the Agriculture Act, 1958, Sched. 1, Pt. I, para. 11) provides as follows :—

" 27. For the purposes of paragraph (c) of subsection (2) of section 24 of this Act, the landlord of an agricultural holding may apply to the Agricultural Land Tribunal for a certificate that the tenant is not fulfilling his responsibilities to farm in accordance with the rules of good husbandry, and the Tribunal, if satisfied that the tenant is not fulfilling his said responsibilities, shall grant such a certificate."

If consent is given to a notice to quit conditions may be attached for securing that the land will be used for the purposes for which the landlord proposes to terminate the tenancy (A.H.A. 1948, s. 25 (5)), and if any such condition is not complied with the Crown may apply to the Tribunal who may impose on the landlord a penalty not exceeding two years' rent payable to the Exchequer (A.H.A. 1948, s. 29, as substituted by the Agriculture Act, 1958, Sched. 1, Pt. I, para. 13). There is no provision for compensating the tenant nor can the tenant refuse to give up possession on account of the breach of condition.

Sale during currency of notice to quit.—A notice to quit land being or comprised in an agricultural holding given to a tenant may become of no effect if a contract is made for the sale of the landlord's interest in the land or any part thereof while the notice is current (A.H.A. 1948, s. 30 (1)). The landlord and tenant may agree *in writing* within the three months before the making of the contract that the notice shall continue in force. The agreement that the notice shall continue in force need not be in express words if the intention of the tenant to comply with the notice is clear (*Rigby* v. *Waugh's Executors* (1931), 100 L.J.K.B. 259). If this is not done the landlord must within one month from the making of the contract, or, where the notice to quit expires within that period, before it expires, give notice in writing to the tenant of the contract (A.H.A. 1948, s. 30 (2) (a) ; Agriculture (Miscellaneous Time-Limits) Regulations, 1959, reg. 2 (1)). The tenant may then notify the landlord in writing that the tenant elects that the notice to quit shall continue in force, but this must be done *both* (i) before the expiration of the notice *and* (ii) within one month from receipt of notice of the contract (A.H.A. 1948, s. 30 (2) (b)). If the tenant does not so elect that the notice shall remain valid, and in the absence of the agreement mentioned above, the notice to quit will be of no effect unless the landlord failed duly to give notice of the contract and the tenant quits the holding in consequence of the notice (*ibid.,* s. 30 (3)). Reference may be made to *Conveyancer N.S.,* vol. 24, p. 143, where certain difficulties arising from these particular provisions are outlined by J. Muir Watt.

Notice to quit part.—In the absence of a special provision in the lease, a landlord cannot serve a notice to quit part only of the land comprised in the lease (*Re Bebington's Tenancy* [1921] 1 Ch. 559). But if the reversion has been severed the assignee of part may serve a valid notice in respect of that part (L.P.A. 1925, s. 140, *ante*, p. 898). Further, a notice to quit part of an agricultural holding *held on a tenancy from year to year* is not invalid on the ground that it relates to part only of the holding if it is given, and states that it is given, (i) for the purpose of adjusting boundaries between agricultural units or amalgamating agricultural units or parts thereof, or (ii) with a view to the use of the land to which it relates for erection of labourers' cottages, provision of gardens for cottages, provision of allotments or smallholdings, planting of trees, opening or working of mines or quarries, making of watercourses or reservoirs, or roads, railways, etc. (A.H.A. 1948, s. 31).

Where a notice to quit part of a holding is given under the above-mentioned provisions of s. 31 or by a person entitled to a severed part of the reversion under the L.P.A. 1925, s. 140 (*ante*, p. 898), then within twenty-eight days after the giving of the notice, or if the operation of the notice depends on any proceedings under the Act within twenty-eight days after the determination of those proceedings, the tenant may give a counter-notice to the landlord or to the persons entitled to the severed parts of the reversion, to the effect that he accepts the notice as a notice to quit the entire holding (A.H.A. 1948, s. 32).

A tenant who has given a counter-notice to quit the whole holding does not necessarily become entitled to compensation in respect of the whole. If the part affected by the landlord's notice, together with any part affected by a previous notice given under s. 31, is less than one-fourth of the original holding and the diminished holding is reasonably capable of being farmed separately, compensation is payable only in respect of the part to which the notice relates (A.H.A. 1948, s. 34 (4), as amended by the Agriculture (Miscellaneous Provisions) Act, 1963, Sched.). A tenant who quits part of a holding in consequence of a notice served pursuant to s. 31, *ante*, or pursuant to a provision in the contract of tenancy is entitled to compensation for disturbance assessed as if the part were a separate holding (A.H.A. 1948, s. 60). Where, however, notice in respect of a severed part of the holding was served by the reversioner under the power granted to the reversioner by the L.P.A. 1925, s. 140 (mentioned above and discussed *ante*, p. 898), but the tenant has *not* exercised his right to serve a counter-notice under s. 32, *ante*, accepting it as a notice to quit the entire holding, there appears to be an unusual gap in the compensation provisions. The tenancy of the " holding " as defined in the A.H.A. 1948, s. 1 (1), *ante*, p. 942 *et seq.*, has not been terminated and so the general compensation provision contained in s. 34 (*post*, p. 962), does not apply and there does not seem to be any other provision enabling the tenant to claim compensation for disturbance in respect of the part affected by the notice (unless, possibly, a new tenancy of the part as a separate holding can be inferred from the actions of the parties since the severance).

Service of notice to quit.—Service of any notice, request, demand or other instrument under the A.H.A. 1948 may be effected by delivering it to the person served, or by leaving it at his last known address or by sending it by registered post or recorded delivery (*ibid.*, s. 92 (1) ; Recorded Delivery Service Act, 1962). A notice served by ordinary post will be valid if it is actually received (*Sharpley* v. *Manby* [1942] 1 K.B. 217 ; *Re Poyser and*

Mills' Arbitration [1964] 2 Q.B. 467). In the case of an incorporated company, service may be effected on the secretary or clerk, at the registered or principal office (A.H.A. 1948, s. 92 (4)).

Service on a landlord or tenant may be effected on an agent or servant who is responsible for the control of the management or farming of the holding (*ibid.*, s. 92 (3)). A notice to quit addressed to persons who were mistakenly thought to be executors of a deceased tenant has been held to be valid by virtue of s. 92 (3) on the ground that they were in possession (*Egerton* v. *Rutter* [1951] 1 K.B. 472 ; *Wilbraham* v. *Colclough* [1952] 1 All E.R. 979 ; see also *ante*, p. 837). Unless the tenant has received notice that the landlord has ceased to be entitled to the reversion, and of the name and address of the person who has become entitled, a notice served on the original landlord will be valid (*ibid.*, s. 92 (5)). Service of notice on one only of joint tenants has not sufficed (*Jones* v. *Lewis* (1973), 117 Sol. J. 373, C.A.).

D. CLAIMS FOR COMPENSATION

Claims by contract and by custom.—The general rule is that where compensation is provided for by the A.H.A. 1948, it is payable according to that Act and *not otherwise* (for instance, by custom or contract), and it is payable notwithstanding any contrary agreement (*ibid.*, s. 65 (1)). Compensation may still be claimed by contract for tenant-right matters (as to which see *post*, p. 966) ; there may also be a claim for tenant-right matters by custom if the tenant was in possession on 1st March, 1948 ; and there may be a claim by custom for improvements begun before 1st March, 1948, provided those improvements are of a kind specified in Sched. 3 or Sched. 4, Pt. I (*ibid.*, ss. 51 (2), 64, 65).

Charges on holdings for compensation.—A tenant may apply to the Minister for an order charging the holding with payment of compensation in the following cases :—

(i) If the landlord fails to discharge his liability within one month from the date on which the sum becomes due (A.H.A. 1948, s. 72).

(ii) If the landlord is entitled to the rents and profits otherwise than for his own benefit, for instance as trustee, and he fails to pay any sum for one month after it becomes due (*ibid.*, s. 73). [In such cases the landlord is not under any personal liability to pay compensation.]

(iii) If the holding is subject to a mortgage, and the contract of tenancy is not binding on the mortgagee, any amount due for compensation under the A.H.A. 1948, s. 66, which is not set off against rent due from the occupier may be charged on the holding (*ibid.*, s. 74).

A charge under ss. 72, 73 or 74 ranks in priority to any other charge, however created (*ibid.*, s. 83 (5)).

A landlord, such as a tenant for life, who has paid to a tenant sums due as compensation for improvements or disturbance, may obtain from the Minister an order charging the holding (*ibid.*, s. 82 (1)). If the landlord is entitled to the rents and profits otherwise than for his own benefit, for instance as trustee, he can obtain such an order *either before or after* paying to the tenant any compensation (*ibid.*, s. 82 (2)). Similarly, a landlord who has paid the cost of an improvement executed by him under the Agricultural Holdings Act, 1923, s. 3, or under the A.H.A. 1948, s. 50 (3) (*post*, p. 965), may obtain from the Minister a charge on the holding (*ibid.*, s. 82 (1) (*b*)). A charge under s. 82 (1) affects the landlord's interest in the holding and all subsequent interests, but does not affect, for instance, the rights of a prior mortgagee (*ibid.*, s. 83 (3) (*b*)).

All the above-mentioned charges are registrable as land charges Class A (see *ante*, p. 597), and if not registered will be void against a purchaser for value (L.C.A. 1972, ss. 4 (2), 17 (1)).

Time limits for claims for compensation.—Any claim for compensation by a tenant or by a landlord of a holding arising on or out of the termination of the tenancy, whether under the A.H.A. 1948 or any custom or agreement, must, in the absence of agreement, be determined by arbitration (A.H.A. 1948, s. 70 (1)) and will not be enforceable unless before the expiration of two months from the termination of the tenancy the claimant has served notice in writing on the landlord or tenant, as the case may be, of his intention to make the claim (*ibid.*, s. 70 (2)). Such a notice must specify the nature of the claim, and it is a sufficient specification if it refers to the statutory provision, custom or term of an agreement under which the claim is made (*ibid.*).

It is important not to overlook that if there is no agreement *in writing* settling a claim within four months from the termination of the tenancy, or such extended period as the Minister may allow, then, within one month thereafter, or within such extended period as the Minister may, *in special circumstances*, allow, an arbitrator must be appointed by agreement or an application for an appointment must be made, otherwise the claim will cease to be enforceable (*ibid.*, s. 70 (3), (4)).

If, however, the tenant lawfully remains in occupation of *part* of a holding after termination of his tenancy, the time limits refer to termination of that occupation *in the case of a claim relating to that part* (*ibid.*, s. 70 (5)).

Compensation to landlord for deterioration of holding.—Where the holding has deteriorated as a result of the "non-fulfilment by the tenant of his responsibilities to farm in accordance with the rules of good husbandry," the landlord may have a claim for the cost of making good the damage, for instance, as a set-off against the claims of the tenant (A.H.A. 1948, s. 57 ; *Barrow Green Estate Co.* v. *Walker's Executors* [1954] 1 W.L.R. 231).

Instead of pursuing this right, the landlord may be able to sue for compensation under the terms of the contract of tenancy, but he can do so only on the tenant's quitting the holding on the termination of the tenancy (*ibid.*, s. 57 (3)). In *Kent* v. *Conniff* [1953] 1 Q.B. 361, it was decided that a landlord may sue for damages on account of dilapidations which constitute a breach of a written contract of tenancy even during the currency of the term, but this decision has been criticised. A notice may be valid even though it claims compensation in the alternative under the contract of tenancy and under s. 57 (1) (*Boyd* v. *Wilton* [1957] 2 Q.B. 277).

If the value of the holding has been reduced by reason of the non-fulfilment of such responsibilities and the landlord is not adequately compensated under s. 57, above (for instance, if the letting value will be reduced for some years after the damage has been made good), the landlord is entitled to recover compensation equal to the decrease in the value of the holding (*ibid.*, s. 58), but he must give notice to the tenant of his intention to make such a claim not later than one month *before* the termination of the tenancy (*ibid.*).

31

Compensation for disturbance.—This is payable by virtue of the A.H.A. 1948, s. 34 (1), which provides as follows :—

" Where the tenancy of an agricultural holding terminates by reason either—

    (a) of a notice to quit the holding given by the landlord ; or

    (b) of a counter-notice given by the tenant under section thirty-two of this Act [*ante*, p. 959] after the giving to him of such a notice to quit part of the holding as is mentioned in that section ;

and in consequence of the notice or counter-notice, as the case may be, the tenant quits the holding, then, subject to the provisions of this section, compensation for the disturbance shall be payable by the landlord to the tenant in accordance with the provisions of this section :"

There is a proviso to the subsection excluding the right to compensation in the circumstances mentioned in s. 24 (2) (c), (d), (e) (f) or (g) to be found *ante*, pp. 953, 954. (These are some of the cases in which the Minister's consent to notice to quit is not necessary.)

Compensation is payable only if the tenant actually quits *in consequence* of the notice. If the tenant holds over after the expiration of the notice and subsequently quits, whether he did so in consequence of the notice is a question of fact. For instance, where he disputed the validity of the notice and quitted after a decision had been given against him, the inference was drawn that he quitted in consequence of the notice (*Preston* v. *Norfolk County Council* [1947] K.B. 775). If a tenant quits in consequence of a notice, he is entitled to compensation even though the notice was void because a necessary consent had not been given (*Kestell* v. *Langmaid* [1950] 1 K.B. 233).

If a tenant has sub-let his holding and becomes liable to pay compensation to a sub-tenant in consequence of a notice to quit given by his landlord, the tenant can recover compensation from that landlord although the tenant does not actually quit the holding because he was not in occupation (A.H.A. 1948, s. 34 (3)).

Compensation payable to the tenant for disturbance will be in addition to any other claim, for instance, in respect of improvements (*ibid.*, s. 34 (5)).

Amount of compensation.—The amount is laid down by s. 34 (2) as being " the amount of the loss or expense directly attributable to the quitting of the holding which is unavoidably incurred by the tenant upon or in connection with the sale or removal of his household goods, implements of husbandry, fixtures, farm produce or farm stock on or used in connection with the holding, and [includes] any expenses reasonably incurred by him in the preparation of his claim for compensation (not being costs of an arbitration to determine any question arising under this section)." The effect of the proviso to s. 34 (2) is, however, that (a) compensation is payable of an amount equal to one year's rent of the holding without proof by the tenant of any such loss or expense as aforesaid ; (b) the tenant is not entitled to claim any greater amount than one year's rent unless before the sale of any such goods, etc., he has given to the landlord a reasonable opportunity of making a valuation thereof ; (c) the tenant is not entitled to claim any greater amount than aforesaid unless not less than one month before the termination of the tenancy he has given to the landlord notice in writing of his intention to make such a claim ; and (d) the tenant is not *in any case* entitled to compensation in excess of two year's rent of the holding.

A further sum is now payable by the landlord to the tenant " to assist in the reorganisation of the tenant's affairs," notwithstanding any agreement to the contrary (Agriculture (Miscellaneous Provisions) Act, 1968, ss. 9 (1), 10 (2)). The amount is four times the annual rent of the holding or, in the case of part of a holding, the appropriate portion (*ibid.*, s. 9 (1) (4)).

No such additional sum is payable where—

(a) the Agricultural Land Tribunal have consented (pursuant to s. 24 (2) (a), *ante*, p. 953), to a relevant notice stating the reason and certified they are satisfied as to any of the matters in paras. (a) to (d) of s. 25 (1) of the 1948 Act (as to which see *ante*, p. 956) ;

(b) the notice was one under paras. (a) to (c) of s. 25 (1) and the tribunal have consented and certified they are satisfied as to the relevant matter ;

(c) the notice states that the landlord will suffer hardship and the tribunal have consented and certified they are so satisfied (1968 Act, s. 10 (1)).

Notwithstanding these exceptions the additional compensation *is* payable if a tribunal certifies they are satisfied also as to the application of s. 25 (1) (e), *ante*, p. 956 (*ibid.*, s. 10 (2)). The additional compensation is not payable unless the notice to quit is served after 1st November, 1967, and termination of tenancy is after 3rd July, 1968 (*ibid.*, s. 10 (6)), although there are transitional provisions applicable where certain notices were served before 4th July, 1968 (*ibid.*, Sched. 1).

Corresponding additional compensation may be payable where by reason of a compulsory purchase order the interest of the tenant of an agricultural holding is acquired or the acquiring authority take possession (*ibid.*, ss. 12, 13, 15 and Sched. 3). Section 42 provides for assessment of compensation without regard to the tenant's prospects of remaining in possession.

The rules as to compensation where, under s. 32 of the A.H.A. 1948, a tenant accepts a notice to quit part of a holding as a notice to quit the whole are mentioned *ante*, p. 959.

Compensation when tenancy is not binding on a mortgagee.— Section 66 of the A.H.A. 1948 provides that when a person occupies a holding under a *contract of tenancy with a mortgagor*, which is not binding on the mortgagee, the occupier will, as against the mortgagee who takes possession, be entitled to any compensation which is, or would but for the mortgagee taking possession, be due to the occupier from the mortgagor as respects crops, improvements, tillages or other matters connected with the holding, whether under the Act or custom or an agreement authorised by the Act. The mortgagee is not under a personal liability to pay any sum due under this section, but such a sum may be set off against any rent due from the occupier and any balance charged on the holding (*ibid.*, s. 74 ; see also *ante*, p. 960).

If the tenancy is from year to year or for a term not exceeding twenty-one years at a rack rent, the mortgagee must give the occupier six months' notice in writing before he can deprive him of possession otherwise than in accordance with the contract of tenancy ; and the occupier, if deprived of possession, is entitled to compensation for his crops and for unexhausted improvements (*ibid.*, s. 66 (b)).

As has been noted, *ante*, p. 825, the leasing power of a mortgagor of agricultural land cannot now be restricted by the mortgage. Consequently, in the case of mortgages after 1st March, 1948, the only occasion on which a lease will not be binding on the mortgagee will be where it does not comply with the conditions in the L.P.A. 1925, s. 99 (*ante*, p. 824), and so the A.H.A. 1948, s. 66, will rarely operate.

Compensation for " old " improvements.—The improvements which are known as " old " improvements are those specified in the A.H.A. 1948, Sched. 2, being improvements begun before 1st March, 1948 (*ibid.*, s. 35). The list is the same as that contained in the Agricultural Holdings Act, 1923, Sched. 1. " New " improvements, on the other hand, are those begun on or after 1st March, 1948, which fall within the lists in Sched. 3 and Sched. 4, Pt. I, of the A.H.A. 1948 (*ibid.*, s. 46).

The result is that if compensation is claimed for an improvement commenced before 1st March, 1948, it must be ascertained whether it falls within Sched. 2, in which case a compensation claim must be based on the rules in the A.H.A. 1948, ss. 35 to 45, which are, in fact, the same as those in the Agricultural Holdings Act, 1923.

The tenant is entitled on termination of the tenancy, on quitting the holding, to obtain compensation for an old improvement unless he was required to carry it out by the terms of a tenancy agreement *made before* 1st January, 1921 (A.H.A. 1948, s. 36 (1)). Alternatively, he may claim under custom or agreement (*ibid.*, s. 36 (2)). The amount of compensation is such a sum as fairly represents the value of the improvement to an incoming tenant (*ibid.*, s. 37).

In the case of an old improvement specified in the A.H.A. 1948, Sched. 2, Pt. I, for instance the erection of buildings or laying down of permanent pasture, compensation is not payable unless, before the execution thereof, the landlord consented in writing to the execution (A.H.A. 1948, s. 38 (1)), and if consent was given on agreed terms as to compensation these terms are substituted for any claim under the Act (*ibid.*, s. 38 (2)), but it was not permissible to provide that no compensation should be paid (*Mears* v. *Callender* [1901] 2 Ch. 388). Where the old improvement consisted of drainage, the tenant had to give the landlord not more than three nor less than two months' notice before commencing the improvement, and the landlord had the option of carrying out the work himself (A.H.A. 1948, s. 39 (1), Sched. 2, Pt. II) ; further, the landlord and tenant might agree on compensation payable (*ibid.*, s. 39 (2)).

Necessary repairs, other than those which the tenant was obliged to execute, are the subject of a claim for compensation provided that the tenant first gave notice of his intention to execute them and the landlord failed to execute them within a reasonable time (Agricultural Holdings Act, 1923, Sched. 1, para. 29 ; A.H.A. 1948, s. 40 and Sched. 2, para. 29). An agreement as to the amount of compensation payable for improvements in the A.H.A. 1948, Sched. 2, Pt. III, is valid only if made before 1st January, 1921, and if it provides fair and reasonable compensation (A.H.A. 1948, s. 41).

Where a tenant has remained in the holding during two or more tenancies he is not deprived of his right to compensation for an improvement made during a tenancy, other than the one at the termination of which he quits the holding (A.H.A. 1948, s. 44). If an incoming tenant, *with the consent in writing of the landlord*, has paid compensation to an outgoing tenant, the incoming tenant will, at the end of his tenancy, have the right to compensation which the outgoing tenant would have had (*ibid.*, s. 45).

Compensation for " new " improvements.—Such improvements are those begun on or after 1st March, 1948, being of the kinds specified in the A.H.A. 1948, Sched. 3 or Sched. 4, Pt. I (*ibid.*, s. 46 (1)). The Minister, after consultation with representative bodies, may, by order approved by each House of Parliament, vary the provisions of Scheds. 3 and 4, and an order may make *such provision as to the operation* of the Act and of such Schedules in relation to current tenancies *as appears to the Minister to be just* (*ibid.*, s. 78). One order has been made under s. 78 in respect of the acclimatisation, hefting or settlement of hill sheep on hill land (Agricultural Holdings Act (Variation of Fourth Schedule) Order, 1951). Such flexibility of legislation may have value, but one is left in doubt whether the confusion which is likely to arise, if a number of such orders are made, will be justified.

It is provided by s. 47 (1) of the A.H.A. 1948 that a tenant of a holding shall be entitled *on the termination of the tenancy, on quitting the holding*, to obtain from his landlord compensation for a new improvement carried out by the tenant on the holding.

The A.H.A. 1948, Sched. 3, contains a list of long term improvements and for these the amount of compensation recoverable by the tenant is a sum " equal to the increase attributable to the improvement in the value of the agricultural holding as a holding, having regard to the character and situation of the holding and the average requirements of tenants reasonably skilled in husbandry " (A.H.A. 1948, s. 48). No compensation can be recovered for any improvement specified in Sched. 3 unless the landlord has given his consent in writing to the carrying out thereof, and such *consent may be given on such terms as to compensation or otherwise as may be agreed upon in writing* (A.H.A. 1948, s. 49 (1)). It would seem that the landlord cannot validly impose a condition that no compensation shall be paid, but that if there is some provision for compensation, the court cannot inquire as to its adequacy (*Mears* v. *Callender* [1901] 2 Ch. 388). If the landlord will not consent or agreement cannot be reached as to the terms of consent then, *in the case of the improvements specified in Pt. II* of Sched. 3, the tenant may apply to the Agricultural Land Tribunal for approval, which may be conditional or unconditional, of the carrying out of the improvement (A.H.A. 1948, s. 50 (1), (2) ; Agriculture Act, 1958, Sched. 1, Pt. I, para. 14). If the Tribunal grants such approval then the landlord may, within one month from the date on which he receives notice in writing of the approval (Agricultural Land Tribunals and Notices to Quit Order, 1959, art. 11), serve a notice in writing on the Tribunal and the tenant that the landlord proposes himself to carry out the improvement (A.H.A. 1948, s. 50 (3), as amended by the Agriculture Act, 1958). If the landlord does not take this step the approval of the Tribunal has the same effect in entitling the tenant to compensation as consent of the landlord (A.H.A. 1948, s. 50 (4)).

It is not necessary for the tenant to obtain consent before carrying out any of the short-term improvements mentioned in the A.H.A., Sched. 4, Pt. I, but in the case of one such improvement, that is, mole drainage, the tenant must give the landlord one month's notice of his intention to carry out the work (A.H.A. 1948, s. 52). The compensation recoverable in respect of improvements within Sched. 4, Pt. I, is the value to an incoming tenant (*ibid.*, s. 51 ; Agriculture (Calculation of Value for Compensation) Regulations, 1969). There is no provision enabling the parties to vary such compensation by agreement and so any agreement purporting to do this would be void (*ibid.*, s. 65 (1)). On the other hand, if an agreement has been made giving a benefit to the tenant in consideration of his carrying out such an improvement such benefit is taken into account in assessing compensation (*ibid.*, s. 51 (3)), and any grant to the tenant out of public moneys must be taken into account (*ibid.*, s. 53).

Provision is made for claims for compensation in respect of new improvements made during any tenancy of a series of tenancies (*ibid.*, s. 54) and for the right of a tenant who has, with the written consent of the landlord, paid compensation to an outgoing tenant (*ibid.*, s. 55).

Compensation for tenant-right matters.—The right to compensation for such matters as growing crops and seeds sown was first made statutory by the A.H.A. 1948, although it had previously been possible to claim by contract or custom. The tenant-right matters which may be the subject of claim are set out in the A.H.A. 1948, Sched. 4, Pt. II, to which an addition has been made by the Agricultural Holdings Act (Variation of Fourth Schedule) Order, 1951.

If the tenant entered into occupation before 1st March, 1948, he may claim under the statute only if he elects so to do before termination of the tenancy (*ibid.*, s. 47 (1), proviso (c)); if a tenant does not so elect his only claim will be any contractual claim (*ibid.*, s. 65 (2)) or any customary claim *in respect of matters corresponding to the ones specified in Sched. 4, Pt. II.* See further, A.H.A., 1948, ss. 47 (1) (c), 64.

The measure of compensation for the tenant-right matters specified in Sched. 4, Pt. II, is the value to an incoming tenant (A.H.A. 1948, s. 51 (1); Agriculture (Calculation of Value for Compensation) Regulations, 1969), but the parties may agree in a written tenancy contract on such measure of compensation, to be calculated according to such method, as they think fit (A.H.A. 1948, s. 51 (2)). The tenant is not entitled to compensation for such matters as seeds sown, if the act was done in contravention of a written contract of tenancy, unless (i) the act was done in consequence of a direction, or (ii) the term contravened was inconsistent with the rules of good husbandry (*ibid.*, s. 47 (1), proviso (b)).

It will be noticed that there is a difference between the basis of compensation for long-term improvements mentioned in Sched. 3, and short-term improvements and other matters mentioned in Sched. 4. In the first case the tenant is entitled to an amount equal to the increase attributable to the improvement in the value of the holding as a holding, having regard to certain matters. In the second case the tenant is entitled to the value of the improvement or other matter to an incoming tenant—a basis of compensation similar to that formerly provided by the 1923 Act for all improvements specified in that Act.

Compensation for adoption of special system of farming.— If the value of the holding has been increased by continuous adoption of a system of farming more beneficial to the holding than that required by the contract of tenancy, or that normally practised on comparable holdings, then the tenant is entitled on quitting the holding to obtain compensation equal to the increase. Such a claim is conditional, however, on the tenant giving notice of it not later than one month before the termination of the tenancy, and on a record having been made under the A.H.A. 1948, s. 16, of the condition of the holding (A.H.A. 1948, s. 56).

E. MARKET GARDENS

The parties may agree in writing that a holding shall be treated as a market garden ; as to what amounts to such agreement, see *Saunders-Jacobs* v. *Yates* [1933] 2 K.B. 240, and *Re Masters and Duveen* [1923] 2 K.B. 729. If this is done—

(i) the improvements specified in Sched. 5 are deemed to be included in Sched. 2, Pt. III (as to which, see *ante*, p. 964), if begun before 1st March, 1948, and in Sched. 4, Pt. I (as to which, see *ante*, p. 965), if begun on or after that date (the result is that compensation can be obtained for such improvements, although the consent of the landlord to their execution was not obtained, and even if no notice was given to him) ;

(ii) the tenant may remove fruit trees and fruit bushes planted by him *and not permanently set out* provided he does so before the termination of the tenancy ;

(iii) an incoming tenant is entitled to compensation in respect of an improvement he has purchased *whether or not the landlord has consented to the purchase* (compare *ante*, pp. 964, 965) (A.H.A. 1948, s. 67 (1)).

Where the tenant desires to make an improvement specified in Sched. 5, and the landlord fails to agree that the holding shall be treated as a market garden, the Agricultural Land Tribunal may, if satisfied that the holding is suitable for the purposes of market gardening, direct that s. 67 shall apply to the holding in respect of any of the improvements specified in Sched. 5 (*ibid.*, s. 68 (1) ; Agriculture Act, 1958, Sched. 1, Pt. I, para. 17).

The parties may agree in writing for the substitution of " fair and reasonable " compensation in lieu of that payable under the Act for improvements for which compensation is payable by virtue of ss. 67 and 68 above (A.H.A. 1948, s. 69 (1)).

F. ALLOTMENTS

This subject involves some very detailed and difficult rules, and only a few notes can be given of the matters arising most often in practice.

" *Allotment* " is defined by the Allotments Act, 1925, s. 1, as an allotment garden (as defined below) *or* a parcel of land not more than five acres in extent, cultivated or intended to be cultivated as a garden or farm, or both. The word is specially defined, however, for the purposes of s. 3 of the Allotments Act, 1922, as " any parcel of land, whether attached to a cottage or not, of not more than two acres in extent, held by a tenant under a landlord and cultivated as a farm or a garden, or partly as a garden and partly as a farm." This definition is given for the purposes only of s. 3, which provides for payment of compensation to the tenant of such an allotment (not being an allotment garden as defined below) notwithstanding any agreement to the contrary for (i) growing crops, labour expended, manure, and (ii) fruit trees planted and certain erections made on the land *with the consent in writing of the landlord*. In the case of such allotments, provided they comply with the definition of an agricultural holding (*ante*, p. 942), compensation may be claimed either under the A.H.A. 1948 or under this provision, but not under both (Allotments Act, 1922, s. 3).

Allotments (not being allotment gardens) are normally held for purposes of trade or business in which case they are agricultural holdings within the A.H.A. 1948, s. 1 (1), *ante*, p. 942, and the appropriate rules, for instance, as to notices to quit, apply (*Stevens* v. *Sedgeman* [1951] 2 K.B. 434).

" *Allotment garden* " is defined by s. 22 (1) of the Allotments Act, 1922, as an allotment not exceeding forty poles in extent which is wholly or mainly cultivated by the occupier for the production of vegetable or fruit crops for consumption by himself or his family. An allotment garden will not be used for the purposes of a trade or business and so will not be an agricultural holding.

Section 1 (1) of the 1922 Act, as amended by the Allotments Act, 1950, s. 1 (1), provides that where land is let on a tenancy for use by the tenant as an a*llotment garden* or is let to any local authority or association for the purpose of being sub-let for such use, the tenancy of the land or any part will not (except as thereinafter provided) be terminable by the landlord by notice to quit or re-entry, *notwithstanding any agreement to the contrary*, except by (i) a twelve months' or longer notice to quit expiring on or before the 6th April, or on or after the 29th September in any year ; or (ii) re-entry, after three months' previous notice in writing to the tenant, under a power of re-entry on account of the land being required for building, mining or any other industrial purpose or for roads or sewers necessary in connection with any of those purposes ; or (iii) re-entry for non-payment or rent or breach of any term or condition of the tenancy or on account of the tenant becoming bankrupt or compounding with his creditors, or under a few other special powers mentioned in the section. These statutory provisions entirely supersede any contractual terms of the tenancy agreement as to notices to quit, so that a notice which complies with s. 1 (1) above will be valid and effective even though it may not also comply with the tenancy agreement, e.g., as to date of expiry (*Wombwell U.D.C.* v. *Burke* [1966] 2 Q.B. 149). By s. 11 of the 1922 Act, it is provided that where land has been let to a local authority or association, and the landlord is proposing to resume possession in accordance with the provisions of the Act for any particular purpose, notice in writing of the purpose for which resumption is required must be given to the local authority or association, who may by a counter-notice demand that the question whether resumption of possession is required in good faith for the purpose specified in the notice shall be determined by arbitration.

Where land is let for use as an allotment garden the tenant is entitled to compensation for growing crops and manure on quitting the land if the tenancy is teminated by notice served by the landlord (Allotments Act, 1922, s. 2, as amended by Allotments Act, 1950, s. 2 (1)). Where the tenancy is terminated pursuant to certain of the powers of re-entry specified in s. 1 (1) of the 1922 Act, *ante*, additional compensation for disturbance equivalent to one year's rent is payable (1950 Act, s. 3).

Section 10 of the Allotments Act, 1922, as amended by the Allotments Act, 1925, s. 6, gives power to a local authority, after giving fourteen days' notice to the owner, to take possession of unoccupied land for the purpose of providing allotment gardens, and also provides that the right of occupation of the authority may be terminated by the council giving to the owner not less than six months' notice expiring on or before the 6th April, on or after the 29th September in any year, or by the owner giving to the council not less than three months' notice in any case where the land is required for any purpose other than the use of the land for agriculture, sport or recreation.

There is provision for payment of compensation to a tenant by the council if the tenancy is terminated by termination of the right of occupation of the council (1922 Act, s. 10 (4)). Any person who is interested in land on which entry is made under this section and who suffers loss by reason of the exercise of these powers is entitled to compensation, provided he claims not later than one year after the termination of the right of occupation (*ibid.*, s. 10 (5)).

CHAPTER TWENTY-THREE

MORTGAGES

PART 1. FORM OF MORTGAGE

Mortgages of freeholds.—Section 85 (1) of the L.P.A. 1925 provides that " a mortgage of an estate in fee simple shall only be capable of being effected at law either by a demise for a term of years absolute, subject to a provision for cesser on redemption, or by a charge by deed expressed to be by way of legal mortga*ga* " (as to which, see *post*, p. 972).

The lngeth of the term of years is not mentioned, and therefore the mortgagee can choose his own term. In the first specimen of abstracts of title in Sched. 6 to the L.P.A. 1925 a first mortgagee is given a term of 1,000 years, a second mortgagee a term of 2,000 years, and a third mortgagee a term of 3,000 years. Many solicitors follow the example of the L.P.A. 1925, s. 85 (2), mentioned below, and give a first mortgagee a term of 3,000 years and subsequent mortgagees terms each one day longer than the term of the immediately preceding mortgage.

As regards successive terms there is no necessity that one should be shorter than another ; they can, at law, all be of the same length : the L.P.A. 1925, s. 149 (5), provides that " Nothing in this Act affects the rule of law that a legal term, whether or not being a mortgage term, may be created to take effect in reversion expectant on a longer term, which rule is hereby confirmed".

Section 85 of the L.P.A. 1925 also contains provisions to prevent the Act being evaded, some of which are indicated below :—

" 85.—(2) Any purported conveyance of an estate in fee simple *by way of mortgage* made after [1925] shall (to the extent of the estate of the mortgagor) operate as a demise of the land to the mortgagee for a term of years absolute, without impeachment for waste, but subject to cesser on redemption, in manner following, namely :—

(a) A first or only mortgagee shall take a term of three thousand years from the date of the mortgage :

(b) A second or subsequent mortgagee shall take a term (commencing from the date of the mortgage) one day longer than the term vested in the first or other mortgagee whose security ranks immediately before that of such second or subsequent mortgagee."

" *by way of mortgage.*"—See the note on these words in s. 86 (2) below ; it is assumed that the position is the same.

Subsection (3) provides, *inter alia,* that the section applies where the mortgage is expressed to be made by way of trust for sale (for instance, a trust deed to secure debentures or debenture stock).

Mortgages of leaseholds.—Section 86 (1) of the L.P.A. 1925 provides that " a mortgage of a term of years absolute shall only be capable of being effected at law either by a sub-demise for a term of years absolute, less by one day at least than the term vested in the mortgagor, and subject to a provision for cesser on redemption, or by a charge by deed expressed to be by way of legal mortgage ; and where a licence to sub-demise by way of mortgage is required, such licence is not to be unreasonably refused."

To prevent evasion, it is provided by subs. (2) of s. 86 of the L.P.A. 1925 that " any purported assignment of a term of years absolute *by way of mortgage* made after [1925] shall (to the extent of the estate of the mortgagor) operate as a sub-demise of the leasehold land to the mortgagee for a term of years absolute, but subject to cesser on redemption, in the manner following, namely :—

(a) The term to be taken by a first or only mortgagee shall be ten days less than the term expressed to be assigned :

(b) The term to be taken by a second or subsequent mortgagee shall be one day longer than the term vested in the first or other mortgagee whose security ranks immediately before that of the second or subsequent mortgagee, if the length of the last mentioned term permits, and in any case for a term less by one day at least than the term expressed to be assigned."

" *by way of mortgage.*"—The subsection operates if an assignment was intended to be by way of mortgage even though it was not so expressed (*Grangeside Properties, Ltd.* v. *Collingwoods Securities, Ltd.* [1964] 1 W.L.R. 139).

Subsection (3) provides that the section applies, *inter alia,* to a mortgage made by way of sub-mortgage of a term of years absolute, or to a mortgage expressed to be made by way of trust for sale or otherwise.

A mortgagee runs a risk if he advances money on the security of a lease containing a condition for forfeiture, for instance on bankruptcy or liquidation of the lessee. While the lessor is proceeding to enforce a right of re-entry the mortgagee may obtain relief under the L.P.A. 1925, s. 146 (4), *ante,* p. 891. The danger is, however, that the lessor may re-enter without taking proceedings or that proceedings do not come to the knowledge of the mortgagee in time for him to apply for relief. See further, *Law Society's Gazette,* vol. 51, p. 239.

Charge by way of legal mortgage.—The exact wording of the subsection dealing with this alternative form of security is important :—

" 87.—(1) Where a legal mortgage of land is created by a charge by deed expressed to be by way of legal mortgage, the mortgagee shall have the same *protection, powers and remedies* (including the right to take proceedings to obtain possession from the occupiers and the persons in receipt of rents and profits, or any of them) as if—

> (*a*) where the mortgage is a mortgage of an estate in fee simple, a mortgage term for three thousand years without impeachment of waste had been thereby created in favour of the mortgagee ; and

> (*b*) where the mortgage is a mortgage of a term of years absolute, a sub-term less by one day than the term vested in the mortgagor had been thereby created in favour of the mortgagee."

" *protection, powers and remedies.*"—" I see no ground for confining s. 87 to protection, powers and remedies merely as between the mortgagor and the mortgagee ; it extends to protections, powers and remedies against all persons " (Upjohn, J., in *Grand Junction Co., Ltd.* v. *Bates* [1954] 2 Q.B. 160, at p. 168).

This view was expressly approved by the Court of Appeal in *Regent Oil Co., Ltd.* v. *J. A. Gregory (Hatch End), Ltd.* [1966] Ch. 402, which rejected a submission that the protection, powers and remedies referred to meant only those relating to the security itself. As Harman, L.J., said (at p. 431) : " In my opinion, the new charge by way of legal mortgage created by s. 87 (1) was intended to be a substitute in all respects for a mortgage by demise, and anything which would be good in the one is good in the other. It would indeed be a trap if the rights of the mortgagee depended on whether his charge were created in one way or the other " (see also *per* Salmon, L.J., at p. 434). Nevertheless, although the chargee has the same protection as if he held a term of years, he does not in fact hold such a term (*Weg Motors, Ltd.* v. *Hales* [1962] Ch. 49).

This last case was followed by Ungoed-Thomas, J., in *Cumberland Court (Brighton), Ltd.* v. *Taylor* [1964] Ch. 29, who, however, expressed the wider view that " a charge by way of legal mortgage does not create *a legal estate* " although he held that the doctrine of feeding the estoppel would nonetheless apply. Again in the *Regent Oil* case, *ante*, Willmer, L.J., said that " . . . a chargee by way of legal mortgage is to be deemed to have a charge by way of sub-demise, and therefore a legal estate in the property charged. If so, I see no difficulty in holding that the chargee, though not actually clothed with any legal estate himself is notionally so clothed, and is therefore competent to create a legal estate in his tenant by attornment." Incidentally, these *dicta* would appear to overlook ss. 1 (2) (*c*) and (4) and 205 (1) (x) of the L.P.A. 1925, which extend the basic meaning of the term " legal estate " beyond that in s. 1 (1) of that Act.

A form of a charge by way of legal mortgage, and also a form of a further charge by way of legal mortgage, are given in the L.P.A. 1925, Sched. 5. The form does not contain a proviso for redemption, and it is convenient to add one.

It has been suggested (see *per* Upjohn, J., in *Grand Junction Co., Ltd.* v. *Bates, ante*) that where leaseholds ar held subject to a covenant not to assign or sub-let without consent it may be possible to charge them in this way without obtaining consent. But if the covenant provides that consent must be obtained to a " mortgage " then probably it is necessary to a charge by way of legal mortgage. Again, if the covenant extends to parting with possession of the property, there would be a breach if the mortgagee were to enforce his right to possession. Of course, if the covenant expressly refers to charging, then the creation of a charge by way of legal mortgage would be a breach. See *ante*, p. 864 and *Gentle* v. *Faulkner* [1900] 2 Q.B. 267.

See also as to the nature of a charge within s. 87 of the L.P.A. 1925 the observations of Megarry, J., in *Thompson* v. *Salah* [1972] 1 All E.R. 530, at p. 533 e/f.

Although offering two alternative forms of security, the L.P.A. 1925 nowhere contains any clear indication as to which should be preferred (but see s. 87 (2)). However, it is thought that the legal charge has the advantage over the ordinary mortgage by demise in offering, first, a short and simple form, and second, the mortgaging of freeholds and leaseholds together conveniently.

Statutory charges by way of legal mortgage.—Section 117 of the L.P.A. 1925 (reproducing Conveyancing Act, 1881, with slight amendments) provides that a mortgage of freehold or leasehold land may be made by a deed expressed to be made by way of statutory mortgage, in one of the forms set out in Sched. 4 to the L.P.A. 1925, with such variations and additions, if any, as circumstances may require.

There is implied in such a mortgage deed (i) a covenant with the mortgagee by the person therein expressed to charge as mortgagor that the mortgagor will, on the stated day, pay the mortgage money, with interest at the stated rate, and will thereafter, as long as the mortgage money or any part thereof remains unpaid, pay interest thereon, or on the unpaid part thereof, at the stated rate, by equal half-yearly payments, the first thereof to be made at the end of six months from the day stated for payment of the mortgage money ; (ii) a provision that if the mortgagor on the stated day pays to the mortgagee the stated mortgage money with interest, the mortgagee at any time thereafter, at the request and cost of the mortgagor, shall discharge the mortgaged property or transfer the benefit of the mortgage as the mortgagor may direct (*ibid.*, s. 117 (2)).

These forms constitute " charges by way of legal mortgage " within ss. 85 and 86 of the L.P.A. 1925.

Registered land.—A form of charge is provided by the L.R.R. 1925, r. 139 (being Form 45) but it is not essential to follow this form because it is provided by the L.R.A. 1925, s. 25 (2), that a charge may be in any form provided the registered land comprised in it is described by reference to the register or in any other manner sufficient to enable the registrar to identify it without reference to any other document, and provided that the charge does not refer to any other interest or charge affecting the land which (i) would have priority over it and is not registered or protected on the register, and (ii) is not an overriding interest. A provision in a charge which purports to take away from the proprietor the power of transferring it by registered disposition, or which purports to affect any registered land or charge other than that in respect of which the charge is to be expressly registered, is void (L.R.A. 1925, s. 25 (3)).

The charge must be completed by entry on the register of the person in whose favour it is made as proprietor, and the particulars of the charge (L.R.A. 1925, s. 26 (1)). Until completed in this way, the charge does not take effect to create a legal estate or interest (L.R.A. 1925, s. 19 (2)). The provision of s. 27 (3) of the L.R.A. 1925 that a charge should " take effect from the date of delivery of the deed containing the same " has been held only to give the chargee protection *inter partes* as from that date, and not the legal estate (*Grace Rymer Investments, Ltd.* v. *Waite* [1958] Ch. 831).

Unless made by demise or sub-demise, and subject to any contrary provision in it, a registered charge takes effect as a charge by way of legal mortgage (L.R.A. 1925, s. 27 (1)) ; as to the effect of this, see *ante*, p. 972. It is desirable but not strictly necessary to express the charge as being " by way of legal mortgage " (*Cityland and Property* (*Holdings*), *Ltd.* v. *Dabrah* [1968] Ch. 166).

On registration of a charge a certified copy on foolscap must be supplied. In the case of a building society or friendly society or provident society mortgage the certificate must be given by the secretary or solicitor to the society and he must certify that the mortgage is in accordance with the rules of the society.

If application for registration of a charge is made with an application for first registration of the title, or with a transfer for value, no fee is charged in respect of it (Land Registration Fee Orders, 1970 and 1973, Abatement No. 1 and No. 2). In other cases the fees are those payable on transfer. An application form (A.4) should be used, but if the charge accompanies an application for first registration, or a transfer, the same form may be used. The land certificate should be forwarded with the charge unless it is already deposited at the registry.

A charge created by a company registered under the Companies Acts should be registered first in the companies register and on forwarding it to the Land Registry it should be accompanied by a copy of the memorandum and articles of association certified by the secretary or solicitor of the company, and by a certificate by the secretary or solicitor that the charge does not contravene the memorandum or articles (Ruoff & Roper, Registered Conveyancing, 3rd ed., pp. 530, 531). A floating charge may be protected by a notice if the land certificate can be produced, and otherwise by a caution, but cannot be registered.

A charge to a company requires production, with the application for registration, of evidence of incorporation and of the power to deal with the charge (L.R.R. 1925, r. 259). If the power of dealing is limited, e.g., subcharging, then a restriction will be entered. Where the company is registered for profit under the Companies Acts strictly a copy of the memorandum and articles of association should be provided, but no other evidence of powers is normally necessary (L.R.R. 1925, r. 259 proviso). However, in lieu of such copy, the confirmation of the company's solicitors as follows will be accepted :

(i) of trading for profit ;

(ii) of incorporation in England under the Companies Act ;

(iii) that the memorandum and articles of association fully enable the company to deal with land and to lend money ;

(iv) that the company is not a moneylender (as defined in s. 6 of the Moneylenders Act, 1900), or, if it is, it holds an appropriate excise licence (see Ruoff & Roper, Registered Conveyancing, 3rd ed., pp. 537 and 236).

Unregistered mortgages of registered land.—It is provided by the L.R.A. 1925, s. 106 (1), that the proprietor may, subject to any entry to the contrary on the register, mortgage the land or any part thereof in any manner which would have been permissible if the land had not been registered and with like effect, provided that the registered land comprised in the mortgage is described (whether by reference to the register or in any other manner) in such a way as is sufficient to enable the registrar to identify it without reference to any other document.

A mortgage made in this way " may, if by deed, be protected by a caution in a specially prescribed form *and in no other way*, and if not by deed, by a caution " (L.R.A. 1925, s. 106 (2)). The form prescribed specially for mortgage cautions is Form 64 in the Schedule to L.R.R. 1925 (see r. 223) ; as to other cautions, see *ante*, pp. 621–623. Until protected on the register as provided, the mortgage is " capable of taking effect only in equity and of being overridden as a minor interest " (L.R.A. 1925, s. 106 (4)). Nevertheless, even though not so protected, such a mortgage will not be postponed to a subsequent minor interest ; the ordinary rules of priority between equitable interests apply notwithstanding that the person entitled to the later interest has lodged a caution (*Barclays Bank, Ltd.* v. *Taylor* [1973] 1 All E.R. 752, C.A., relating to a later, uncompleted contract for sale).

However, it still appears that such a mortgage would be postponed to a subsequent interest which, being completed by registration, takes effect at law. This was the view taken by Goulding, J., at first instance with regard to a mortgage by deed which had been purportedly protected only by entry of notice of deposit of the land certificate ; he adopted the strict construction that a mortgage was made under s. 106 of the L.R.A. 1925 if it was within the scope of that section, whatever the intention of the parties, and that " the statutory words ' in no other way ' [italicised above] are inflexible and not to be disregarded " (see *Barclays Bank, Ltd.* v. *Taylor* [1972] 2 All E.R. 752, at p. 758*d*). This strict construction was expressly not approved or disapproved by the Court of Appeal (see *ibid.*, [1973] 1 All E.R. 752, at pp. 757*c* and 758), but it was indicated that the mortgagee's possession of the land certificate would confer a *de facto* protection by effectively preventing any entry on the register for which production of the land certificate is required (*loc. cit.*, pp. 755 f/g and 757 f/g). Even so, some unacceptable risks are thought to remain for the practise (widely used by banks) of taking a full mortgage and, instead of registering it substantially, holding it undated and unstamped protected only by the entry of a notice of deposit. For example, the mortgagor could grant a long lease with priority, for the lessee's application for registration would not require production of the mortgagor's land certificate (see *ante*, p. 646). Further, the priority position of subsequently created overriding interests is not clear : on principle, the eventual registration of the mortgage should be subject to any then subsisting overriding interests (see L.R.A. 1925, ss. 69 and 70) ; but the persons entitled to the later minor equitable interest in *Barclays Bank, Ltd.* v. *Taylor*, *ante*, appear also to have had an overriding interest by virtue of their actual occupation (see [1973] 1 All E.R., at p. 756 f) and no reference was made to the point in the judgment at first instance or on appeal. Finally, however, it must be emphasised that these risks all stem from the view taken by Goulding, J., at first instance, a view which might not survive a direct scrutiny by the Court of Appeal ; thus it may be regarded as inconsistent by implication with *Re White Rose Cottage* [1965] Ch. 940 (which was cited) in which it did not apparently occur to the Court of Appeal that an equitable charge created by deed could only be effectively protected by a mortgage caution (see further *post*, p. 1027).

On devolution of such an unregistered mortgage on the death of the cautioner the personal representatives may be registered in his place on application on Form 65. A transfer may be protected similarly by application on Form 66.

Such unregistered mortgages are sometimes created in areas where registered titles are still rare, and where solicitors are more familiar with forms of mortgage affecting unregistered land. However, it is said in Ruoff & Roper, Registered Conveyancing, 3rd ed., at p. 554, that the procedure involving the mortgage caution is " expensive, cumbersome, inconvenient, relatively unsafe, and never now used in practice." Yet so long as the strict construction of s. 106 of the L.R.A. 1925 indicated above still stands, there are of course quite common circumstances in which the procedure should be used in the interests of safety. Where a mortgage by deed has been protected by caution in the prescribed form, the mortgagee, or the persons deriving title under him, may, subject to furnishing sufficient evidence of title, require the mortgage to be registered as a charge with the same priority as the caution (L.R.A. 1925, s. 106 (5)). Where this is done the proprietor, subject to any entry on the register, has all the powers conferred on the proprietor of a registered charge (L.R.A. 1925, s. 106 (6)). So long as the mortgage is protected only by a caution the mortgagee is not capable of dealing with the registered land by a registered disposition (*ibid.*).

Promise to pay principal and interest implied.—It was said by Jessel, M.R., in *Sutton* v. *Sutton* (1882), 22 Ch. D. 511, at p. 515, that " it has been decided that if there is no covenant and no accompanying bond, there is still the implied promise to pay ; and if there is a time fixed by recital or otherwise for the repayment in many cases depending upon the construction of the instrument, the court will imply even a covenant to pay. That being so, every mortgage contains within itself, so to speak, a personal liability to repay the amount advanced " including interest (*Duke of Ancaster* v. *Mayer* (1785), 1 Bro. C.C. 454) ; but if the mortgage contained an express covenant to pay in some qualified manner, no contract by parol will be implied for the repayment in any other manner (*Mathew* v. *Blackmore* (1857), 1 H. & N. 762).

In the case of registered land, s. 28 (1) of the L.R.A. 1925 provides that, in the absence of any entry on the register negativing such implication, there is implied, in a registered charge, a covenant on the part of the proprietor of the land to pay the principal sum charged, and interest, at the appointed time and rate, and if the principal sum or any part thereof is unpaid at the appointed time, to pay half-yearly at the appointed rate as well after as before any judgment is obtained in respect of the charge on so much of the principal sum as for the time being remains unpaid. Further, where the charge is on leasehold land, there is implied, in the absence of any entry to the contrary, a covenant that the proprietor of the land or the persons deriving title under him will pay, perform, and observe the rent, covenants, and conditions reserved and contained in the registered lease, and on the part of the lessee to be paid, performed, and observed, and will keep the proprietor of the charge, and the persons deriving title under him, indemnified (L.R.A. 1925, s. 28 (2)).

Clog on equity of redemption.—The rule against clogging the equity of redemption is expressed in the maxim, " once a mortgage, always a mortgage," and must be borne in mind when drafting mortgages. " The meaning of that is," explained Lord Davey, in *Noakes and Co., Ltd.* v. *Rice* [1902] A.C. 24, at p. 33, " that the mortgagee shall not make any stipulation which will prevent a mortgagor, who has paid principal, interest, and costs, from getting back his mortgaged property in the condition in which he parted with it." There is no rule, however, which precludes a mortgagee, whether the mortgage is made upon the occasion of a loan or otherwise, from stipulating for any *collateral* advantage, provided that such collateral advantage is not either (1) unfair and unconscionable, or (2) in the nature of a penalty clogging the equity of redemption, or (3) inconsistent with or repugnant to the contractual and equitable right to redeem (*Kreglinger* v. *New Patagonia Meat and Cold Storage Co., Ltd.* [1914] A.C. 25). Those principles were applied in *Cityland and Property (Holdings), Ltd.* v. *Dabrah* [1968] Ch. 166, where the collateral advantage was a premium amounting to 57 per cent. of the sum lent ; this was held unreasonable and it was ordered that the charge should stand as security only for the principal lent and interest at 7 per cent. Equally, however, a provision in a mortgage of a public house to a brewer that the mortgagor will not buy beer from any other brewer *during the continuance of the security* is valid (*Biggs* v. *Hoddinott* [1898] 2 Ch. 307). This case should be contrasted with *Noakes* v. *Rice, ante,* in which it was held that a covenant to buy all beer from the mortgagee even after repayment of the mortgage was a clog on the equity and could not be enforced after repayment.

These " beer " cases have been considered by the Court of Appeal in connection with " tied petrol stations " (see *Petrofina (Great Britain), Ltd.* v. *Martin* [1966] Ch. 146) and then also by the House of Lords (see *Esso Petroleum Co., Ltd.* v. *Harpers Garage (Stourport), Ltd.* [1968] A.C. 269). It appears (1) that a provision postponing redemption throughout the duration of an unreasonable tie will amount to a clog on the equity and (2) that a tie in a mortgage will not be held unreasonable if there is no such clog. See further " restraint of trade," *post,* p. 978.

The principle that a clog on the equity is void applies where it is imposed on a transfer of a mortgage arranged between the mortgagor and the transferee (*Lewis* v. *Frank Love, Ltd.* [1961] 1 W.L.R. 261). An option for the transferee to purchase part of the mortgaged property is void as it prevents the mortgagor from recovering that part on redemption (*ibid.*).

The question arises whether an agreement by a mortgagor not to redeem the mortgage for a fixed period of years may be void. There does not appear to be any reported case in which a mere postponement of the right of redemption, without other oppressive conditions, has been held to be void, and there is no doubt but that postponement for a period of five or seven years is valid (*Teevan* v. *Smith* (1882), 20 Ch. D. 724). It was formerly stated that the mortgagor may be prevented from redeeming for a reasonable period, and that in estimating what is reasonable it is material to consider whether the mortgagee is precluded from calling in the mortgage for the same period. Thus, in *Morgan* v. *Jeffreys* [1910] 1 Ch. 620, where the mortgagor had built an hotel and mortgaged it to a brewer, and covenanted to buy all beer and other liquors from him for twenty-eight years, it was held that, even if it might be supported in a case where there was a similar provision against calling in the mortgage, the postponement exceeded all reasonable limits, and could not be enforced. In *Fairclough* v. *Swan Brewery Co., Ltd.* [1912] A.C. 565, it was held that a proviso in a mortgage of a lease that the mortgagor should not be at liberty to pay off the principal except by specified instalments was void, as the last instalment was payable only six weeks before the expiration of the lease.

In *Knightsbridge Estates Trust, Ltd.* v. *Byrne* [1940] A.C. 613, a limited company mortgaged properties on the terms that the advance should be repaid by eighty half-yearly instalments, the whole to be due on default in payment of any instalment. The mortgagee's statutory power of sale was exercisable on breach of covenant and also if the mortgagor should transfer the equity of redemption in any part of the mortgaged property without the consent of the mortgagee, consent not to be unreasonably withheld. The Court of Appeal held ([1939] Ch. 441) that postponement of the time for redemption does not amount to a clog on the equity of redemption, as it merely defers the contractual right to redeem and the equity to redeem does not arise until after the money has become due at law under the contract. The court considered that a right to redeem was essential to a mortgage and consequently if, as in *Fairclough* v. *Swan Brewery Co., Ltd., ante,* the contractual right to redeem was illusory, equity would permit the mortgage to be redeemed. On the other hand, the court held that on the facts before them there was nothing inconsistent with a mortgage transaction nor was the contract so oppressive that it could not be enforced in equity, and so decided that the company could redeem only on the terms specified in the mortgage. The court rejected the view previously expressed that a mortgage cannot be made irredeemable for more than a " reasonable " period.

The House of Lords decided that an ordinary mortgage by a limited company was a debenture as defined by the Companies Act, 1929, s. 380, and so an irredeemable mortgage could validly be issued (Companies Act, 1929, s. 74 ; see now Companies Act, 1948, s. 89). As a result it was not necessary to consider the rules which would have applied if the mortgage had not been made by a limited company. On the authority of the decision of the Court of Appeal the present rule appears to be that the right to redeem can be postponed, although equity will grant relief if the result is to make the contractual right of redemption illusory or if the terms as a whole are oppressive, taking into consideration any postponement of the right of redemption.

Restraint of trade.—It has been decided by the House of Lords that the common-law doctrine by which a covenant in restraint of trade is void unless reasonable applies also to mortgages of land (*Esso Petroleum Co., Ltd.* v. *Harper's Garage (Stourport), Ltd.* [1968] A.C. 269 ; filling station tied to petrol supplier). Diplock, L.J., said in the Court of Appeal : " What magic is there in a mortgage of land to exclude it from the ambit of the general principle of public policy that no one can lawfully interfere with another in the free exercise of his trade or business unless there exist some just cause or excuse for such interference ? The only real interest which a mortgagee has in the land by virtue of his mortgage is as security for his loan ; that if the mortgagor defaults, it should produce sufficient rents and profits to pay the interest if the mortgagee takes possession, that it should realise enough to repay the capital and arrears of interest if the mortgagee exercises his power of sale. In my view, covenants in restraint of trade, which would be invalid if contained in a simple contract such as a sales agreement, do not become enforceable where incorporated in a mortgage unless they are no more than is reasonably necessary to protect the mortgagee's interest in the value of the land as security for his loan." The covenant in question was held unreasonable because the duration of the restraint (twenty-one years) was too long, especially since redemption was also precluded for that period, and because there were other oppressive provisions in the mortgage. The case followed and extended a decision of the Court of Appeal in *Petrofina (Great Britain), Ltd.* v. *Martin* [1966] Ch. 146, establishing that the doctrine of restraint of trade did apply to a naked covenant limited to a particular property (i.e., in a sales agreement tying a petrol filling station). The court expressly left for decision when it arises the question of the further extension of the doctrine to covenants (ties) in leases and tenancy agreements or even in conveyances on the sale of land. It is of interest to compare with these decisions the Court of Appeal's earlier decision in *Regent Oil Co., Ltd.* v. *J. A. Gregory (Hatch End), Ltd.* [1966] Ch. 402. This also concerned a covenant in a mortgage tying a filling station to a particular petrol supplier in very similar terms and it was held enforceable entirely on the basis of a mortgagee's rights to protect his security without any express mention of the doctrine of restraint of trade. This case was not reported until after nor cited to the Court of Appeal in the *Esso Petroleum* decision, although Harman, L.J., was a member of both courts. Certainly the later decision will now prevail.

Insurance of mortgaged property.—In *Halifax Building Society* v. *Keighley* [1931] 2 K.B. 248, the society as mortgagees and the mortgagors of certain property were jointly interested in two policies of fire insurance. The policies contained the usual condition that if there were any other insurance effected on the property, the liability of the insurance company was to be limited to the rateable proportion of the damage suffered. The mortgagors had a separate policy in another office. On a fire happening the society and the mortgagors each received their due proportion under the two policies. In the action the society claimed the balance received by the mortgagors under the latter's separate policy. Wright, J., held that the mortgagors were not liable to pay it.

In view of this decision it is desirable to insert in a mortgage a covenant that the mortgagor shall not insure himself, but if he does he must hold any moneys received from the insurers as trustee for the mortgagee and hand them over on demand in or towards discharge of the mortgage. A form is to be found in Hallett's Conveyancing Precedents, p. 607.

The statutory power to insure of a mortgagee whose mortgage is by deed is contained in the L.P.A. 1925, s. 101 (1) (ii). This power is not always sufficient and most mortgages contain an express power. The statutory power enables the mortgagee to insure, and to charge premiums on the mortgaged property, provided the insurance does not exceed the amount specified in the mortgage, or, if no amount is specified, two-thirds of the sum it would require to restore the premises in case of total destruction, but the power does not exist if (i) the mortgagor states that insurance is not required, or (ii) an insurance is kept up by the mortgagor in accordance with the mortgage, or (iii) the mortgage contains no provision and the mortgagor insures up to the statutory amount (L.P.A. 1925, s. 108).

In connection with a mortgage of leaseholds it is important to remember that the lease will normally contain a covenant as to insurance and a provision that moneys received will be applied in making good any damage. Usually, it will not be necessary to provide in the mortgage for further insurance unless the mortgagee insists that insurance moneys should be applied in satisfaction of the mortgage debt, in which case an independent policy may be required. See, further, an article in the *Law Journal*, vol. 103,

p. 230, in which it is pointed out that rules of a building society may contain provision as to insurance demanding attention ; this is particularly so when the property is leasehold.

Notes on mortgage interest.—Where a mortgagor fails to pay principal and interest at the expiration of notice to redeem, the mortgagee is not entitled to a further six months' notice to redeem. All that he can require is reasonable notice. Reasonable notice may be three months' notice, or three months' interest in lieu thereof (*Cromwell Property Investment Co., Ltd.* v. *Western and Toovey* [1934] Ch. 322).

Although an agreement in a mortgage deed that, if the interest is *punctually* paid, a lower rate of interest will be accepted, is good, a covenant that if the interest is not punctually paid an increased rate of interest must be paid will be relieved against on the ground that it is in the nature of a penalty (*Wallingford* v. *Mutual Society* (1880), 5 App. Cas. 685). In an agreement of this kind the word " punctually " means payment on the day fixed for payment (*Maclaine* v. *Gatty* [1921] 1 A.C. 376).

A mortgagee is not entitled to notice from the mortgagor when he, the mortgagee, has demanded payment, or taken proceedings to realise his security, or entered into possession, but must accept the principal with interest to date of tender (*Bovill* v. *Endle* [1896] 1 Ch. 648 ; *Edmondson* v. *Copland* [1911] 2 Ch. 301).

After six years an action by a mortgagee for arrears of mortgage interest becomes statute-barred (s. 18 (5) of the Limitation Act, 1939). Nevertheless, a mortgagor who seeks to redeem is only allowed to do so on the equitable basis of paying all arrears of interest, however longstanding (*Holmes* v. *Cowcher* [1970] 1 W.L.R. 834). Further, a mortgagee who exercises a power of sale is also entitled to retain all arrears of interest, however longstanding, on the basis that this is not recovery by action (*Re Lloyd* [1903] 1 Ch. 385).

Purchaser of equity must indemnify vendor from mortgage.—A purchaser of an equity of redemption will be bound to indemnify the vendor against the mortgage debt (*Waring* v. *Ward* (1802), 7 Ves. 332 ; *Re Law Courts Chambers Co., Ltd.* (1889), 61 L.T. 669). If the purchaser is asked to enter into an express covenant with his vendor to indemnify him, and he refuses, a court of equity would compel him to do so (*Bridgman* v. *Daw* (1891), 40 W.R. 253).

It is, however, important to note that the principle in *Waring* v. *Ward*, *ante*, is to be confined to cases of a *sale* of the *whole* of the mortgaged property *expressly* subject to the mortgage. On a gift of property subject to a mortgage created by the donor, the assignee is entitled to be indemnified by the donor (see *Re Best* [1924] 1 Ch. 42). On a sale of part of the mortgaged property expressly subject to the mortgage, the mortgage debt is to be rateably apportioned between the parts sold and retained (*Re Mainwaring* [1937] 1 Ch. 96).

Right of mortgagee to recover compensation paid to a tenant of business premises.—A mortgagee who takes possession may become a " landlord " of property within the definition in the Landlord and Tenant Act, 1927 (see *ante*, p. 915), or within the Landlord and Tenant Act, 1954 (*ibid.*, ss. 44 (1), 69 (1), 67), and so may be obliged to pay compensation to

a tenant. If the property is of a nature likely to cause such a claim to be
made, some such provision as that set out below should be inserted in the
mortgage :—

" That should the mortgagee by reason of his having taken possession
of the property, or by reason of the appointment of a receiver become
' a landlord ' within the meaning of the word ' landlord ' in the Landlord
and Tenant Act, 1927, or be deemed to be authorised or required to act
as such by virtue of s. 67 of the Landlord and Tenant Act, 1954, and by
reason thereof have to pay compensation to any tenant under either of
the said Acts such amount so paid together with all costs incurred in
connection therewith shall be repaid to him by the borrower [or other word
used] or the persons deriving title under him on demand and until so
repaid shall be a charge on the premises hereby mortgaged in addition to
the principal money hereby secured and shall have the same priority and
shall bear interest at the same rate as the principal money hereby secured."

Sub-mortgages.—A sub-mortgage is in substance a mortgage of a
mortgage. Such a security is not very often created, but it may be convenient to do so if a mortgagee requires to borrow a sum of money, but does
not wish to disturb a profitable mortgage which he holds.

If the head mortgage was created by demise, or was converted by the
L.P.A. 1925 into a term of years, the sub-mortgage can be created by a sub-
demise or by a charge by way of legal mortgage (L.P.A. 1925, s. 86 (1)). If, on
the other hand, the head mortgage is a charge by way of legal mortgage,
the sub-mortgage will take the form of a transfer of the benefit of the head
mortgage. As there is some doubt whether the L.P.A. 1925, s. 114 (1), applies
to the creation of a sub-mortgage, it is as well to provide also for the transfer
of the benefit of all the powers and provisions contained in the head mortgage ;
see further, an article by H. Woodhouse in the *Conveyancer N.S.*, vol. 12,
p. 171.

It is advisable, if possible, that the original mortgagor should join in the
sub-mortgage and acknowledge the state of the mortgage debt by means
of a recital. If this is not done immediate notice should be given to him
of the execution of the sub-mortgage, because the sub-mortgagee takes
subject to any equities which have arisen between the mortgagor and
mortgagee up to the time when the mortgagor received notice (*Parker* v.
Jackson [1936] 2 All E.R. 281).

A sub-mortgagee can sell the mortgage debt and transfer the mortgage
term *if default has been made under the sub-mortgage* (L.P.A. 1925, s. 89 (1) and
(5)). In addition, *if default is made under the original mortgage,* he is able to
exercise the power of sale of the original mortgagee, as he is transferee of the
powers of the original mortgagee ; the conveyance will then pass the whole
fee simple the subject of the original mortgage (L.P.A. 1925, s. 88 (5) ; see also
s. 89 (5), applicable where the original mortgage was of a leasehold interest).
If the sale is expressed to be made under both the original mortgage and the
sub-mortgage, the purchaser will have a good title even if there has been no
default under the sub-mortgage (L.P.A. 1925, s. 104), although the original
mortgagee may have a right of action against the sub-mortgagee. A sub-
mortgage may be discharged by a statutory receipt taking effect under
the L.P.A. 1925, s. 115.

Mortgagee's costs.—It is advisable to include in a mortgage a term that
the mortgagor will pay the mortgagee's costs, charges and expenses, including

the costs of any proceedings for the protection or enforcement of the security, whether involving litigation or not, *on a solicitor and own client basis*, and that they shall be a charge on the property. See the comments of " the Conveyancer " in the *Law Times*, vol. 216, p. 391, although doubts are expressed in the *Conveyancer N.S.*, vol. 17, p. 325 (replied to at *ibid.*, vol. 18, p. 149). If this is not done, costs on enforcement of the security will be taxed on a party and party basis only (*Re Adelphi Hotel (Brighton), Ltd.* [1953] 1 W.L.R. 955).

Costs to be charged by private firms of solicitors acting on mortgage advances by the Agricultural Mortgage Corporation, Ltd., or by the Minister of Agriculture are explained in *Law Society's Gazette*, vol. 65, p. 468.

Attornment clause.—Formerly attornment clauses were inserted in order to create the relationship of landlord and tenant between mortgagee and mortgagor (with the rent reserved at an amount equivalent to the annual interest), and so to give the mortgagee a right to distrain in respect of arrears. But it was held in *Re Willis* (1888), 21 Q.B.D. 384, that the Bills of Sale Act, 1878, made the power of distress inoperative unless registered under that Act. As it is usually undesirable that it should be so registered, this reason for inserting the clause no longer exists. However, non-registration as a bill of sale does not invalidate the mortgage as far as the land is concerned (*Re Burdett* (1888), 20 Q.B.D. 310) nor prevent creation of the relationship of landlord and tenant (*Mumford* v. *Collier* (1890), 25 Q.B.D. 279 ; *Kemp* v. *Lester* [1896] 2 Q.B. 162).

Accordingly one suggested advantage of such a clause was that the tenancy thereby created can be made at a nominal rent and determinable on short notice by the mortgagee. If this was done in a mortgage of a house the mortgagee might have been able to use the cheap and speedy procedure provided by the Small Tenements Recovery Act, 1838, s. 1, to recover possession from the mortgagor (*Dudley and District Benefit Building Society* v. *Gordon* [1929] 2 K.B. 105). However, that Act has been repealed as from 1st October, 1972 (Rent Act, 1965, s. 35 (5) ; Small Tenements Recovery Act 1838 (Repeal) (Appointed Day) Order, 1972). This is, therefore, no longer a reason to insert the clause.

It appears that an attornment clause will not create a tenancy which is protected under the Rent Acts. In the case of *Portman Building Society* v. *Young* [1951] 1 All E.R. 191 it was pointed out that the clause in question allowed the tenancy to be determined at any time without notice. The Court of Appeal decided that the commencement of proceedings for possession operated as a determination and so there could be no tenancy after the commencement of the proceedings which might be protected. The case is not a clear authority for the assertion that such a clause will never give the mortgagor a protected tenancy of a house.

Where the clause requires notice for determination of the tenancy the mortgagee may not re-enter until the notice has been duly given (*Hinckley and Country Building Society* v. *Henny* [1953] 1 W.L.R. 352). An attornment clause does not create an agricultural tenancy for the purposes of the A.H.A. 1948, and so the restrictions on service of notices to quit contained in that Act do not apply to a notice to determine the tenancy created by such a clause (*Steyning and Littlehampton Building Society* v. *Wilson* [1951] Ch. 1018).

The Rent Act, 1957, s. 16 (which requires a notice to quit a dwelling to be at least four weeks' notice) does not normally apply to a notice to terminate the tenancy created by an attornment clause in a mortgage (*Alliance Building*

Society v. *Pinwill* [1958] Ch. 788). However, Vaisey, J., said that s. 16 might be held to apply in some special cases, for instance where the rent reserved by the attornment clause was a full rack-rent or where the mortgage required the mortgagor to reside on the premises.

In view of the possibility that occasionally s. 16 might apply it would seem advisable, if it is desired to insert such a clause, that it should be in a form enabling the mortgagee to take possession without previous notice ; in this case no notice to quit is necessary and so s. 16 could not operate (*Woolwich Equitable Building Society* v. *Preston* [1938] Ch. 129 ; *Portman Building Society* v. *Young, ante*).

Despite the possible advantage in recovering possession under the now repealed 1838 Act, attornment clauses had acquired some disfavour (Danckwerts, J., described them as " entirely obsolete " in *Steyning and Littlehampton Building Society* v. *Wilson, ante*, at p. 1020). Thus no attornment clause is included in any form of mortgage in Hallett's Conveyancing Precedents, it being observed that possession is easily and cheaply obtainable under R.S.C., 1965, Ord. 88 (see also Parker's Modern Conveyancing Precedents, at p. 151, note 1). However, a new lease of life may have been given to the attornment clause by the Court of Appeal in *Regent Oil Co., Ltd.* v. *J. A. Gregory (Hatch End), Ltd.* [1966] Ch. 402. There it was held that the clause enabled a mortgagee to enforce a mortgagor's covenants against the latter's successors in title as a landlord by privity of estate [the particular covenants in question may now be void, if unreasonable, as being in restraint of trade ; the decision must be read with that in *Esso Petroleum Co., Ltd.* v. *Harper's Garage (Stourport), Ltd.* [1968] A.C. 269 ; see *ante*, p. 978]. In the *Regent* case, the Court of Appeal also held that an attornment clause in a charge by way of legal mortgage was as effective as one in a mortgage by demise to create more than a mere tenancy at will. Willmer, L.J., said that the effect was " to create a tenancy during the continuance of the security, so long as the property remained in the occupation of [the mortgagor] (which included persons deriving title under him) subject to [the mortgagor's] right to determine the tenancy on seven days' notice " (*ibid.*, pp. 438–9). This decision settles doubts that had been held (see *Conveyancer N.S.*, vol. 13, p. 31) but has been criticised incidentally on the ground that the term created may not be sufficiently certain to be " absolute "—and so a legal estate—within L.P.A. 1925, ss. 1 and 205 (1) (xxvii) (*ibid.*, vol. 30, p. 59).

PART 2. INVESTIGATION BY MORTGAGEE

Investigation of title by a solicitor acting for an intending mortgagee is normally carried out in much the same way as investigation on behalf of a purchaser. An important point is to ensure that a good title can be deduced if the mortgagee is obliged to exercise his power of sale. But a mortgagee is rarely under any obligation to make an advance. It follows that he may at any time withdraw from the transaction if he is not satisfied with the title even though it is one that would be forced on a person who had contracted to purchase.

Consequently, it is not necessary to consider further the rules as to investigation of title. Two matters have, however, caused some difficulty, namely (i) the effect of planning restrictions and the right to compensation, and (ii) the effect of tenancies granted before the mortgage ; these matters are therefore considered specially here.

A. PLANNING MATTERS

Claims for compensation.—The making of claims under the Town and Country Planning Acts, and the devolution of such claims are discussed *post*, at p. 1203 *et seq.* Certain particular rules affect land subject to a mortgage, however.

In cases in which compensation becomes payable under the Town and Country Planning Act, 1971, s. 146 (replacing earlier provisions) in respect of a planning decision whereby permission for the carrying out of " new " development is refused, or is granted subject to conditions, the obligation of the Minister to notify a known mortgagee, the right of a mortgagee to require payment to him of the compensation and his right to make a claim on default of the mortgagor arise not only with regard to mortgages created before 1st July, 1948, but also (unless the mortgage provides otherwise) with regard to mortgages created on or after 1st January, 1955 (Town and Country Planning (Mortgages, Rentcharges, etc.) Regulations, 1955). Apparently any mortgagee who lent money on mortgage between those dates is assumed to have relied only on the existing use value of the land (unless he made express provision otherwise) so that no rule is needed for his benefit. See, further, *Law Society's Gazette*, vol. 52, pp. 45, 217. The benefit of the established claim under the 1947 Act may, however, have been transferred to the mortgagee with the result that the following may apply.

Compensation may also become payable on the occasion of—

(i) refusal of planning permission in a few special cases (Town and Country Planning Act, 1971, s. 169 ; see *post*, p. 1204) ;

(ii) revocation or modification of planning permission (*ibid.*, s. 164 ; see *post*, p. 1199) ;

(iii) an order requiring discontinuance of an existing use or alteration or removal of buildings or works (*ibid.*, s. 170 ; see *post*, p. 1200).

Any such compensation payable in respect of the depreciation in the value of an interest in land which is subject to a mortgage (which includes any charge or lien on any property for securing money or money's worth : *ibid.*, s. 290 (1)) is assessed as if the interest were not subject to the mortgage, and a mortgagee is not entitled to claim any such compensation in respect of his interest *as such* (*ibid.*, s. 178 (3) (*c*)). But the claim for any such compensation may be made by *any* mortgagee without prejudice to the making of a claim by the person entitled to the interest (*ibid.*, s. 178 (3) (*b*)), and compensation payable in respect of the interest subject to the mortgage is *payable to the mortgagee*, or, where there is more than one, to the *first mortgagee* to be applied by him as if it were proceeds of sale, as to which, see *post*, pp. 995, 996 (*ibid.*, s. 178 (3) (*d*)).

Inquiries by persons proposing to lend on mortgage.—The essential requirement of such a person is invariably that he shall have adequate security. Consequently, full inquiries should be made on planning matters, the intended mortgagee being in a position to refuse to lend the money if he is not satisfied with any answer given. The questions on planning matters to be answered by a solicitor making a report to a bank on title are specified in the *Law Society's Gazette*, vol. 53, p. 79.

Particular attention should be paid to the following points :—

(i) The usual searches should be made ; see Chapter 1, *ante*, p. 6.

(ii) Inquiry should be made as to the contents of the register of planning applications. It is important to know, for instance, whether a planning permission was granted for a limited period only. The necessity, in the future, to remove a building or to cease making a particular use of land may affect the security adversely. If the security is dependent on development being carried out, planning permission should be obtained before completion.

(iii) The structure and development plan should be inspected and inquiry should be made of the local planning authority as to whether any proposals for amendment have been formulated affecting the land in question. A matter which may appear and which may adversely affect the proposed security is designation, or proposed designation, of the land for compulsory purchase.

(iv) Inquiry should be made as to the user on 1st July, 1948, and whether that was in accordance with previous planning restrictions. If any subsequent changes of use have taken place or subsequent building or other operations have been carried out for which planning permission was necessary a reference to the register of applications will show whether it has been obtained. If there is any doubt about the use to which the property was put at any time the mortgagee may wish to insist on production of a statutory declaration.

(v) If inquiries as to planning permission show that a development charge should have been paid, proof of payment need not be required.

Provisions in mortgages as to planning matters.—In some mortgages the mortgagor has covenanted to comply with and not to commit any breach of the Town and Country Planning Acts or any regulations, directions or notices made or served thereunder. See, for instance, precedents in Hallett's Conveyancing Precedents at p. 607. From the point of view of a mortgagee this is a useful covenant but a mortgagor should consider its effect carefully before agreeing to it. Trivial breaches of the Act or regulations may be made inadvertently, and, if such a covenant has been inserted in the mortgage, the effect of any such breach would be to make the mortgagee's power of sale exercisable immediately (L.P.A. 1925, s. 103 (iii)). Another covenant which mortgagees may require is one to the effect that the mortgagor will not carry out any operation on the land or make any change of use of it constituting developments without the consent of the mortgagee. A precedent of this covenant is contained in Hallett's Conveyancing Precedents at p. 607. It is doubtful whether it is really necessary in the interest of the mortgagee to make his consent a condition precedent to the carrying out of development ; provided the mortgagor obtains any necessary planning permission there does not seem to be any necessity for such a provision. The danger against which the mortgagee may wish to guard himself is that development may take place without permission and so a suitable covenant is one to the effect that no development within the meaning of the 1971 Act shall be carried out without first obtaining any necessary planning permission. But it must be noted that the danger is not a serious one as an enforcement notice would have the object of restoring the land to its condition before contravention occurred and, consequently, it must be acknowledged that the value of the security as it existed at the time of the mortgage is not likely to be adversely affected. A useful provision is that requiring the mortgagor to forward to the mortgagee particulars of any notice, order or proposal served on him.

If it is known that the land has an unexpended balance of established development value it may be as well to require the mortgagor to covenant that he will notify the mortgagee of any adverse planning decision (as to which, see *post*, p. 1204 *et seq.*). The mortgagee would then be in a position to claim the compensation under s. 146 of the 1971 Act as provided in the rules mentioned *ante*, p. 984.

B. TENANCIES GRANTED BEFORE MORTGAGE

A mortgagee may negative the power of the mortgagor to lease by inserting an appropriate clause in the mortgage, and so may prevent the grant of any tenancy which would be binding on him ; see *ante*, p. 823 *et seq*. Questions have arisen, however, as to how the rights of a person lending money on mortgage to enable a purchase of property are affected by a tenancy which the purchaser purports to grant or agrees to grant before completion. Where the tenancy is one which may be protected by the Rent Acts, there is a grave danger that the mortgagee may lend money on the mistaken assumption that he can obtain vacant possession. In what follows it is assumed that there was no intent to defraud the mortgagee (or else that the lessee took in good faith), for otherwise the lease would be voidable under s. 172 of the L.P.A. 1925 (see *Lloyds Bank* v. *Marcan* [1973] 1 W.L.R. 339).

Purported grant.—If the intending purchaser-mortgagor purports to grant a tenancy so that the tenant would have a legal estate were it not for the sole fact that his landlord had no legal estate, nonetheless a tenancy by estoppel is effectively created as between the parties (Megarry and Wade, Real Property, 3rd ed., p. 652). This presupposes that the grant was either under seal or capable of being a valid parol lease (ss. 52 and 54 (2) of the L.P.A. 1925 ; and see *Hughes* v. *Waite* [1957] 1 W.L.R. 713). Then when the purchaser-mortgagor-landlord later actually acquires a legal estate on completion of his purchase it is said to " feed the estoppel " so that a legal tenancy at once arises in place of the mere tenancy by estoppel (Megarry and Wade, Real Property, 3rd ed., p. 652). In the result the tenant, it is now settled, acquires a legal estate immediately on execution of the conveyance which is necessarily prior to the grant of the mortgage so that the tenancy binds the mortgagee. This will be so notwithstanding the absence of any recital of ownership in the mortgage deed and notwithstanding that the conveyance and mortgage deed, as is usual in practice, form substantially one transaction and bear the same date (*Church of England Building Society* v. *Piskor* [1954] Ch. 553, the leading case, a decision of the Court of Appeal, in which the earlier unsettled authorities were cited).

This operation of feeding the estoppel would appear to be applicable to registered land despite the fact that no purchaser gets a legal estate before registration (L.R.A. 1925, ss. 19 (1), 22 (1)) and that the conveyance or transfer and mortgage are in practice likely to be lodged for registration simultaneously. It would seem that the *scintilla temporis* conferring priority either exists as a matter of law or can be found as a matter of fact in the order in which the column headed " nature and priority of applications " has necessarily to be completed on the cover form (see L.R.R. 1925, rr. 83 and 84). Indeed the doctrine of tenancy by estoppel and feeding the estoppel have been applied to confer priority on a tenant in respect of registered land at first instance, but only on the basis of a recital in the mortgage (*Woolwich Equitable Building Society* v. *Marshall* [1952] Ch. 1). The theoretical problem created by simultaneous registration of the transfer and mortgage has received only judicial mention without decision from the Court of Appeal (in *City Permanent Building Society* v. *Miller* [1952] Ch. 840 ; see also *Grace Rymer Investments, Ltd.* v. *Waite* [1958] Ch. 831 deciding, *inter alia*, that L.R.A. 1925, s. 27 (3), which provides that a legal charge " shall take effect from the date of the delivery of the deed containing the same, but subject to the . . . interest of any person . . . whose . . . interest . . . is registered or noted on the register before the date of registration of the charge," does not give the chargee any priority over a tenancy by estoppel). It will be appreciated that where a grant creates a tenancy by estoppel which is fed in this way to create a legal tenancy not exceeding twenty-one years the tenant will be protected in registered conveyancing as having an overriding interest (s. 70 (1) (*k*) of the L.R.A. 1925 ; if there is occupation it will also be within para. (*g*) ; compare *City Permanent Building Society* v. *Miller* [1952] Ch. 840).

Tenancy agreement.—If the intending purchaser-mortgagor, instead of purporting to make a grant, only contracts to grant a tenancy, then there is no question of a tenancy by estoppel subsisting to be fed as above. The position is the same, of course, if there is a purported grant which is ineffective in any case in point of form (i.e., neither under seal nor within L.P.A. 1925, s. 54 (2)). In *un*registered conveyancing the prospective tenant can only protect his interest against the mortgagee by registering his " estate contract " (L.C.A. 1972, s. 2 (4), Class C (iv), and s. 4 (6) ; L.R.A. 1925, s. 109 ; but see *Solicitors' Journal*, vol. 101, p. 439, arguing that a tenancy agreement in such circumstances is not registrable as the purchaser is not entitled to have the legal estate conveyed to him *until* he has paid the price ; it is thought, however, that the purchaser is in reality so entitled *subject* to paying the price). If the agreement is protected by being registered, it will be discovered by the mortgagee when searches are made before completion (registration will be in the name of the vendor : s. 3 (1) of the L.C.A. 1972).

In registered conveyancing, the legislative intention probably was that agreements for tenancies of registered land should create at most mere minor interests not binding a subsequent mortgagee unless protected on the register (i.e., to equate exactly with the *un*registered position ; see, e.g., s. 107 (1) of the L.R.A. 1925). However, it is now settled that only where a prospective tenant has *not* gone into occupation of the land does his interest need protection on the register (as in *City Permanent Building Society* v. *Miller* [1952] Ch. 840). This difference from the unregistered position first emerged in 1951 when Danckwerts, J., held that a tenancy agreement plus occupation constituted an overriding interest within s. 70 (1) (*g*) of the L.R.A. 1925, binding a subsequent mortgagee (*Woolwich Equitable Building Society* v. *Marshall* [1952] Ch. 1). This decision has since been followed by Vaisey, J. (*Mornington Permanent Building Society* v. *Kenway* [1953] Ch. 382), and adopted by the Court of Appeal (*Grace Rymer Investments, Ltd.* v. *Waite* [1958] Ch. 831 ; see also *Bridges* v. *Mees* [1957] Ch. 475 and *Webb* v. *Pollmount* [1966] Ch. 584). Consequently, with registered land, taking possession is for the tenant a simple and effective alternative as against mortgagees to both protection by registration and reliance on the estoppel doctrines.

Protection of mortgagee.—So far as concerns tenancy agreements entered into by an intending purchaser-mortgagor, a mortgagee can protect himself sufficiently by making the usual land charges or official searches and by enquiring of the persons in possession of the land as to their rights. Accordingly the risk which is hardest to cover is that there may have been a purported grant of a tenancy, to a person not in possession, which will become a legal or overriding interest with priority.

In the absence of fraud in which the tenant has been concerned, such a tenancy is unlikely, but it may be advisable to obtain an express statement from the purchaser that he has not created any tenancy on which a charge of obtaining money by false pretences might be based.

One suggested method of protecting the mortgagee is to include both the conveyance and mortgage in one document, the vendor demising the house to the mortgagee subject to redemption and conveying the fee simple to the purchaser subject to the mortgage. If this is done, it is argued, the purchaser cannot obtain a legal estate prior to that of the mortgagee and so the tenant could not, in the absence of registration of an estate contract or an overriding interest, take precedence over the mortgagee. There may, of course, be practical difficulties if the mortgage is to be in favour of a building society under a standard form. It is also worth noting that if restrictive covenants are to be imposed in connection with such a sale the mortgage term should be made subject to them in order to bind any purchaser from the mortgagee, and the covenants should be registered against both purchaser and mortgagee. See further, *Law Times*, vol. 217, p. 284 *et seq.*, and the precedent in the *Conveyancer N.S.*, vol. 18, p. 723.

However, the efficacy of this method of protecting a mortgagee was challenged by " L.H.E." in the *Solicitors' Journal*, vol. 101, p. 439. He argues that " a conveyance by the vendor (by the direction of the purchasers) to the mortgagees would have the same effect as would a conveyance by the vendor to the purchasers and by the purchasers to the mortgagees." The argument is based on the principle that a purchaser cannot escape his obligation to a tenant by directing the property to be conveyed to a mortgagee and is supported by the decision in *Carpenter* v. *Parker* (1857), 3 C.B. (N.S.) 206. " L.H.E.'s " alternative suggestion is that reliance should be placed on inspection as to possession and, if necessary, the mortgagee might take an assignment of the vendor's lien for the purchase money and register it as an equitable charge.

The same writer, however, makes a further suggestion in the *Solicitors' Journal*, vol. 101, p. 822 *et seq.* He points out that (assuming the facts to be as in *Church of England Building Society* v. *Piskor*) on paying the purchase money to the vendors at the request of the purchasers, the mortgagees became transferees of the vendor's lien, and that they also acquired a contractual equitable charge on the interest of the purchasers which, being protected by possession of the deeds, did not require registration. Consequently, it is alleged that " the title of the vendors and the mortgagees claimed through them was in inception paramount to the title of the tenants." The conclusions are drawn (i) " that the conveyance and mortgage should be made by one deed, the vendor's lien being reserved and the conveyance to the purchaser being expressed to be ' upon trust to create such legal mortgage as is hereinafter contained ' or words to that effect " and (ii) (in the case of registered land) " the vendor's lien [can be kept alive] by retaining possession of the land certificate—but it will be safer to give notice of the deposit to the registrar under r. 239."

These arguments and suggestions seem to be based on sound reasoning. But it is doubtful whether solicitors will often consider that the adoption of so complicated a procedure is justified if other precautions of inspection and inquiry are taken on behalf of a mortgagee.

PART 3. REMEDIES OF MORTGAGEE

Remedies of equitable mortgagees, see p. 1029.

Overreaching effect of sale by mortgagee, see p. 181 *et seq.*

A. POWER OF SALE

General rule.—The general statutory power of sale of a mortgagee is now contained in s. 101 (1) (i) of the L.P.A. 1925, set out below. It is only when the conditions there specified have been fulfilled that the power of sale is said to have *arisen*. As to when it becomes *exercisable*, see s. 103, *post*, p. 991.

" 101.—(1) A mortgagee, *where the mortgage is made by deed*, shall, by virtue of this Act, have the following powers, to the like extent as if they had been in terms conferred by the mortgage deed, but not further (namely) :

(i) A *power*, when the mortgage money has *become due, to sell*, or to concur with any other person in selling, the mortgaged property, *or any part thereof*, either subject to prior charges or not, and either together or in lots, by public auction or by private contract, subject to such conditions respecting title, or evidence of title, or other matter, as the mortgagee thinks fit, with power to vary any contract for sale, and to buy in at an auction, or to rescind any contract for sale, and to re-sell, without being answerable for any loss occasioned thereby."

" *where the mortgage is made by deed*."—In other cases there is no statutory power to sell without application to the court.

" *become due*."—That is, the legal date for redemption has passed ; the *whole* of the money need not be due (*Payne* v. *Cardiff Rural District Council* [1932] 1 K.B. 241).

" *power . . . to sell*."—The power to sell (s. 101 (1)) and the power to convey (s. 104 (1), *ante*, p. 181) are given separately. It has always been clear that the conveyance of the mortgagee under his power of sale automatically extinguished the right of the mortgagor to redeem, and it has been decided in *Waring* v. *London and Manchester Assurance Co., Ltd.* [1935] Ch. 310 that a contract for sale by the mortgagee under his power of sale has the same effect, provided that in the sale there was no lack of *bona fides* ; for as the learned judge (Plowman, J.) said, if this were not so, every sale by such a mortgagee would have to be conditional. Further, in *Property and Bloodstock, Ltd.* v. *Emerton* [1968] Ch. 94, the Court of Appeal held that the standard provision in a contract by a mortgagee for the sale of leasehold property that the landlord's consent should be obtained did not constitute a condition precedent to the creation of the relationship of vendor and purchaser ; consequently the contract for sale was to be regarded as unconditional, and so precluding from its date the mortgagor-lessee from exercising the right of redemption (following *Waring* v. *London and Manchester Assurance Co., Ltd., ante*). These decisions have more recently been followed where, before the mortgagee contracted to sell, the mortgagor had entered into a contract of sale and the purchaser had offered to put the total sum owing to all incumbrancers (with an upper limit) into the joint names of his solicitor and of the mortgagees' solicitor (*Duke* v. *Robson* [1973] 1 All E.R. 481, C.A.). The reasoning was that no transaction by a mortgagor short of redemption can affect a mortgagee's power of sale and that the purchaser's offer was not equivalent to a tender of the redemption money.

The duty of a mortgagee exercising his power of sale is to take reasonable care to obtain a proper price (*Cuckmore Brick Co. Ltd.* v. *Mutual Finance, Ltd.* [1971] Ch. 949). It was held in *Kennedy* v. *De Trafford* [1897] A.C. 180 that a mortgagee discharges his duty towards the mortgagor if he exercises his power of sale in good faith, but that if he wilfully and recklessly deals with the property in such a manner that the interests of the mortgagor are sacrificed, he cannot be said to have exercised his power of sale in good faith. And, in *Belton* v. *Bass, Ratcliffe & Gretton, Ltd.* [1922] 2 Ch. 449, it was held that, the sale in the case being otherwise proper, the mortgagor could not inquire as to the motive of the mortgagee. However, *Kennedy* v. *De Trafford, ante,* has been reconsidered by the Court of Appeal : a mortgagee will be liable to account to the mortgagor for any loss resulting merely from negligence in exercising the power of sale, notwithstanding that it was exercised in good faith (*Cuckmere Brick Co., Ltd.* v. *Mutual Finance, Ltd.* [1971] Ch. 949, where the mortgagee negligently failed to obtain the true market value of the mortgaged property on sale). See also *Palmer* v. *Barclays Bank, Ltd.* (1971), 23 P. & C.R. 30, as to the extent of the powers and duties of sale of a mortgagee of business premises in respect of goodwill.

For the similar statutory rule as to sales by building society mortgagees see *ante*, p. 262.

" *or any part thereof.*"—These words do not allow the mortgagee to sell the fixtures apart from the land (*Re Yates* (1888), 38 Ch. D. 112).

The section applies where the deed was executed after 31st December, 1881, but only if and as far as a contrary intention is not expressed in the mortgage deed (s. 101 (4), (5)). The statutory power of sale will not be excluded by reason of there being an express power of sale in the mortgage (*Life Interest and Reversionary Securities Corporation* v. *Hand-in-Hand Fire & Life Insurance Society* [1898] 2 Ch. 230).

The overreaching effect of a conveyance is discussed *ante*, p. 181 *et seq.* ; see particularly, p. 182 as to conveyance of leaseholds.

Subject to any entry on the register to the contrary, the proprietor of a registered charge has all the powers conferred by law on the owner of a legal mortgage (L.R.A. 1925, s. 34 (1)). If he exercises his power of sale the registered chargee will execute a transfer in favour of the purchaser in Form 31A (if it affetcs the whole of the land) or Form 31B (if it affects only part) and the transaction will be completed by registration ; the charge and all subsequent incumbrances will then be cancelled (L.R.A. 1925, s. 34 (4) ; L.R.R. 1925, r. 114). Such a transfer operates to transfer the registered estate and the mortgage term is merged (L.R.A. 1925, s. 34 (5)).

When power of sale exercisable.—Notwithstanding that the power of sale may have *arisen* as above, it may not yet be *exercisable*.   It is provided by s. 103 of the L.P.A. 1925 as follows :—

" 103. A mortgagee shall not exercise the power of sale conferred by this Act unless and until—

(i) *Notice requiring payment of the mortgage money has been served on the mortgagor* or one of two or more mortgagors, and *default* has been made *in payment of the mortgage money*, or of part thereof, for three months after such service ; or

(ii) Some interest under the mortgage is in arrear and unpaid for two months after becoming due ; or

(iii) There has been a *breach of some provision* contained in the mortgage deed or in this Act, or in an enactment replaced by this Act, and on the part of the mortgagor, or of some person concurring in making the mortgage, to be observed or performed, other than and besides a covenant for payment of the mortgage money or interest thereon."

" *Notice . . . served on the mortgagor.*"—The expression " mortgagor " is defined in s. 205 (1) (xvi) of the L.P.A. 1925 as including " any person from time to time deriving title under the original mortgagor or entitled to redeem a mortgage according to his estate, interest or right in the mortgaged property." Therefore, if a mortgagor has executed a second mortgage, notice of intention to exercise the power of sale ought to be given to the second mortgagee as well as to the mortgagor, and the mortgagee neglecting to do this will be liable in damages to the second mortgagee : see *Hoole* v. *Smith* (1881), 17 Ch. D. 434. And, as registration is now notice, a search should be made to make sure there is no subsequent mortgage. But a *purchaser* cannot take the objection that the mortgagee has not served notice on a second mortgagee as well as on the mortgagor (*Re Thompson and Holt* (1890), 44 Ch. D. 492).

There is a difference of opinion as to whether, if the mortgagor has created a third or subsequent mortgage, it is necessary to give notice to the third or subsequent mortgagee, but it would seem advisable to do so.

The notice should require payment of the mortgage money and should not fix any date on which this must be done. But in *Barker* v. *Illingworth* [1908] 2 Ch. 20, default had been made in payment at the expiration of six months from the date of the mortgage deed and the mortgagee gave notice requiring payment of principal and interest *at the expiration of three calendar months from the date of the notice*, and added that if the mortgagor made default in such payment he would sell. It was held that s. 20 (1) of the Conveyancing Act, 1881 (now replaced by s. 103 (i) of the L.P.A. 1925), only required the service of the notice and three months' default in payment after such service, and as such period had expired the power of sale had become exercisable.

The day of giving the notice is excluded from the computation of the three months' notice (*Re Railway Sleepers Supply Co.* (1885), 29 Ch. D. 204).

" *default . . . in payment of the mortgage money.*"—If mortgage moneys are made repayable by instalments consisting of principal and interest lumped together, then, upon two months' default in payment of any instalment after it has become due, the statutory power of sale will be exercisable (*Walsh* v. *Derrick* (1903), 19 T.L.R. 209). The reason is that " the mortgage money has become due " within the meaning of the words of s. 101 (1) (i) of the L.P.A. 1925 (see *ante*, p. 989) as regards any instalment or instalments in arrear (*Payne* v. *Cardiff Rural District Council* [1932] 1 K.B. 241).

" *breach of some provision.*"—It is provided by s. 110 of the L.P.A. 1925 that :—

" 110.—(1) Where the statutory or express power for a mortgagee either to sell or to appoint a receiver is made exercisable by reason of the mortgagor committing an act of bankruptcy or being adjudged a bankrupt, such power shall not be exercised only on account of the act of bankruptcy or adjudication, without the leave of the court.

(2) This section applies only where the mortgage deed is executed after [1925] ; and in this section ' act of bankruptcy ' has the same meaning as in the Bankruptcy Act, 1914."

As regards the exercise of the power of sale on the ground of the bankruptcy of the mortgagor, *the title of the purchaser* would not be impeachable on the ground (where the mortgage was made atfer 1925) that leave of the court had not been obtained (L.P.A. 1925, s. 104 (2) (c), set out *post*, p. 993).

Powers to sell mines and to impose restrictions.—Section 101 of the L.P.A. 1925 provides that where the mortgage *deed* is executed after 31st December, 1911, the mortgagee's statutory power of sale includes (i) a power to impose or reserve by covenant, condition or otherwise, on the unsold part of the mortgaged property, or on the purchaser and any property sold, any restriction or reservation with respect to building on or other user of land, or with respect to mines and minerals, or with respect to any other thing, and (ii) a power to sell the mortgaged property, or any part thereof, or all or any mines and minerals apart from the surface with or without a grant or reservation of easements and privileges, and with or without an exception or reservation of mines and minerals, and with or without covenants by the purchaser to expend money on the land sold. These provisions may be varied or extended by the mortgage deed, and, as so varied or extended, operate in the like manner and with all the like incidents, effects and consequences, as if such variations or extensions were contained in the L.P.A. 1925. Section 101, however, applies only if and as far as a contrary intention is not expressed in the mortgage deed, and has effect subject to the terms of the mortgage deed and to the provisions contained in it.

If the section does not apply to the particular mortgage, for instance, where the mortgage was not made by deed, or was made before 1912, then an application may be made to the court under s. 92 of the L.P.A. 1925 to grant authority to dispose (a) of the land, with an exception or reservation of mines and minerals, and with or without rights and powers of or incidental to the working, getting or carrying away of minerals, or (b) of all or any mines and minerals, with or without the said rights or powers separately from the land.

Sale by mortgagee to himself or to a person interested.—A mortgagee, in exercising his power of sale, is not deemed to be a trustee for his mortgagor, as he is of the surplus money after a sale (*Warner* v. *Jacob* (1882), 20 Ch. D. 220). But " he is bound to sell fairly, and to take reasonable steps to obtain a proper price ; and for this reason and because his authority is to *sell* and not to make himself full owner of the mortgaged property, he cannot sell to himself or to a trustee or an agent for himself, or rightly pursue any scheme for getting the property into his own hands under the guise of sale " (Williams, Vendor and Purchaser, 4th ed., vol. I, p. 391). Although a mortgagee may not buy from himself (*Farrar* v. *Farrars, Ltd.* (1888), 40 Ch. D. 395 ; *Henderson* v. *Astwood* [1894] A.C. 150, at p. 162), he may purchase from his mortgagor, and the purchase will be regarded in the same way as a purchase and sale between parties having no connection with each other (*Knight* v. *Marjoribanks* (1849), 2 Mac. & G. 10 ; *Melbourne Banking Corporation* v. *Brougham* (1882), 7 App. Cas. 307 ; *Reeve* v. *Lisle* [1902] A.C. 461), unless the mortgagor is in embarrassed circumstances and the mortgagee exercises coercion (*Ford* v. *Olden* (1867), L.R. 3 Eq. 461). So a second mortgagee may purchase from the first mortgagee under his power of sale (*Kirkwood* v. *Thompson* (1865), 2 De G. J. & Sm. 613 ; *Shaw* v. *Bunny* (1865), 2 De G. J. & Sm. 468) ; and a mortgagee may sell to one of two mortgagors, and the transaction cannot be upset by the other mortgagor (*Kennedy* v. *De Trafford* [1897] A.C. 180).

An agent appointed by the mortgagee to collect the rents and to find a purchaser cannot buy from the mortgagee (*Guest* v. *Smythe* (1870), L.R. 5 Ch. 551) ; nor can a receiver, even although appointed by a court, buy from the mortgagee under his power of sale (*Nugent* v. *Nugent* [1908] 1 Ch. 546) ; nor a secretary of a building society from the society under its power of sale (*Martinson* v. *Clowes* (1882), 21 Ch. D. 857).

Protection of purchaser buying from mortgagee.—The provisions as to this are contained in s. 104 (2) of the L.P.A. 1925, set out below :—

" 104.—(2) Where a conveyance is made in exercise of the power of sale conferred by this Act, or any enactment replaced by this Act, the title of the purchaser shall not be impeachable on the ground—

(*a*) that no case had arisen to authorise the sale, or

(*b*) that due notice was not given ; or

(*c*) where the mortgage is made after [1925], that leave of the court, when so required, was not obtained ; or

(*d*) . . . that the power was otherwise improperly or irregularly exercised ;

and a purchaser is not, either before or on conveyance, concerned to see or inquire whether a case has arisen to authorise the sale, or due notice has been given, or the power is otherwise properly and regularly exercised ; but any person damnified by an unauthorised, or improper, or irregular exercise of the power shall have his remedy in damages against the person exercising the power."

It is necessary to distinguish between the power of sale having *arisen* (i.e., within L.P.A. 1925, s. 101 (1) (i), *ante*, p. 989) and having become *exercisable* (i.e., within L.P.A. 1925, s. 103, *ante*, p. 991). If the power has not yet arisen, the mortgagee has neither the right nor the power to sell at all ; at most he can transfer his mortgage. If the power of sale has arisen, even though it may not yet be exercisable, the mortgagee can convey a good title to a purchaser free from the equity of redemption. He still has no right to sell, but the only remedy of any person injured is in damages against the mortgagee (s. 104 (2), above). " Thus while a purchaser from a mortgagee must satisfy himself that the power of sale has arisen, he need not enquire whether it has become exercisable. Proof of title is thereby simplified, for the existence of the power of sale is proved by the form of mortgage

32

and the redemption date specified in it ; the purchaser's title does not depend
on the fact of some later default by the mortgagor " (Megarry and Wade,
Real Property, 3rd ed., p. 904). From this, therefore, it would appear that
there is no question of a purchaser from a mortgagee being affected with
constructive notice in the ordinary sense and that he should abstain from
making any inquiries at all as to the exercisability of the power (*Bailey* v.
Barnes [1894] 1 Ch. 25 ; *Life Interest and Reversionary Securities Corporation*
v. *Hand-in-Hand Fire & Life Insurance Society* [1898] 2 Ch. 230).

The However, it is to be observed that the word " purchaser " in the L.P.A.
1925 is defined to involve " good faith." Consequently, s. 104 (2) of the
L.P.A. 1925 would not appear to protect a purchaser who has actual notice
that the mortgagee has no right to sell even though the power of sale may
have arisen. Thus, Crossman, J., in *Waring* (*Lord*) v. *London and
Manchester Assurance Co.* [1935] Ch. 310, at p. 318, after quoting s. 104 (2),
said : " If the purchaser becomes aware, during that period, of any facts
showing that the power of sale is not exercisable, or that there is some
impropriety in the sale, then in my judgment, he gets no good title on taking
the conveyance." For example, it will usually be clear on the face of the
mortgage whether or not sufficient time has elapsed for the power of sale
to become exercisable ; i.e., if the specified redemption date is six months
after the date of the mortgage deed, then the earliest time at which the
statutory power can become exercisable is eight months after the date of
the deed by the interest being two months in arrear (see *Selwyn* v. *Garfit*
(1888), 38 Ch. D. 273, and *Re Thompson and Holt* (1890), 44 Ch. D. 492,
decided in respect of express powers).

A purchaser from a mortgagee is absolved from being concerned with any
trust affecting the mortgage money ; see *ante*, p. 168.

The protection given to a purchaser by s. 21 of the Conveyancing Act,
1881, as amended by s. 5 of the Conveyancing Act, 1911, was subject to the
condition that the conveyance was made " *in professed exercise of the power
of sale conferred by this Act.*" Under the L.P.A. 1925, s. 104 (3), a conveyance by a mortgagee after 1925 is *deemed to have been made* in exercise
of the statutory power of sale unless a contrary intention appears, and it
will therefore no longer be necessary expressly to state that the conveyance
was made in exercise of such power.

The overreaching powers of mortgagees are referred to in the L.P.A. 1925,
ss. 2 (1) (iii), 42 (4) and (5), 88 and 89, mentioned *ante*, p. 181 *et seq.*

Power of mortgagee to give receipts.—Section 107 (1) of the L.P.A.
1925, given below, replaces s. 22 of the Conveyancing Act, 1881 :—

" 107.—(1) The receipt in writing of a mortgagee shall be a sufficient
discharge for any money arising under the power of sale conferred by this
Act, or for any money or securities comprised in his mortgage, or arising
thereunder ; and a person paying or transferring the same to the mortgagee
shall not be concerned to inquire whether any money remains due under
the mortgage."

It will be noticed that the words of the subsection are very wide and
cover not only money received by a mortgagee under his power of sale, but
any money paid to him under his mortgage. For instance, it would enable a
second mortgagee to give a good receipt to a first mortgagee for any balance
of money such first mortgagee might have in hand after paying himself all
that was due to him. This is emphasised by the words of s. 107 (2),

namely : " Money received by a mortgagee under his mortgage or from the proceeds of securities comprised in his mortgage shall be applied," etc.

Even if the mortgage had been paid off, this fact would not affect a purchaser in good faith (*Dicker* v. *Angerstein* (1876), 3 Ch. D. 600 ; see also s. 104 (2), *ante*, p. 993, and s. 113, *ante*, p. 169).

According to equitable rules where two or more persons lent money on mortgage there was a presumption that they were tenants in common of the mortgage money even if the legal estate was conveyed to them as joint tenants. This was inconvenient because on the death of one it was necessary for his personal representatives to join in to give a good receipt. Accordingly it became usual to insert a " joint account clause " which protected a transferee or the mortgagor on assignment or re-conveyance by the survivor or survivors. Such clauses are now unnecessary because it is provided by s. 111 (1) of the L.P.A. 1925, in effect, as follows:—

" 111.—(1) Where—

(a) in a mortgage, . . . or a transfer of a mortgage . . . the sum, or any part of the sum, advanced or owing is expressed to be advanced by or owing to more persons than one out of money, or as money, belonging to them on a joint account ; or

(b) *a mortgage, . . . or such a transfer is made to more persons than one, jointly ;*

* * * * *

the receipt in writing of the survivors or last survivor of them, or of the personal representative of the last survivor, shall be a complete discharge for all money or money's worth for the time being due, notwithstanding any notice to the payer of a severance of the joint account."

Section 111 of the L.P.A. 1925 (which substantially reproduces the Conveyancing Act, 1881, s. 61), applies to all mortgages or transfers made after 31st December, 1881, unless a contrary intention is expressed therein (L.P.A. 1925, s. 111 (2) and (3)).

In practice, where the money is advanced by persons in unequal shares it is better to have a short separate declaration of trust executed by the mortgagees stating in what proportions the money was lent.

It will be remembered that trustees ought not to lend on a contributory mortgage unless their trust instrument so allows (*Re Dive* [1909] 1 Ch. 328).

Person to whom the mortgagee should pay any balance.—The provision as to this is contained in s. 105 of the L.P.A. 1925 as follows :—

" 105. The money which is received by the mortgagee arising from the sale, after discharge of prior incumbrances to which the sale is not made subject, if any, or after payment into court under this Act of a sum to meet any prior incumbrance, *shall be held by him in trust* to be applied by him, first, in payment of all costs, charges, and expenses properly incurred by him as incident to the sale or any attempted sale, or otherwise ; and secondly, in discharge of the mortgage money, interest, and costs, and other money, if any, due under the mortgage ; and the residue of the money so received shall be paid to *the person* entitled to the mortgaged property, or *authorised to give receipts* for the proceeds of the sale thereof."

The rights of a subsequent mortgagee to any surplus proceeds of sale in the hands of a prior mortgagee, up to the amount properly due under the subsequent mortgage, are not discharged or defeated by a counterclaim by the mortgagor (*Samuel Keller (Holdings), Ltd.* v. *Martin's Bank, Ltd.* [1971] 1 W.L.R. 43, C.A., actually relating to a counterclaim for *un*liquidated damages).

Under this section a mortgagee is an express trustee of the residue in his hands, and he must therefore be careful to pay it to the right person. If there is any serious doubt it might be wise to pay the money into court under the general power given to trustees by s. 63 of the T.A. 1925. It is provided by s. 63 (1) that trustees having under their control money or securities belonging to a trust, may pay them into court ; and they shall, subject to rules of court, be dealt with according to the orders of the court.

A mortgagee who, as the result of a sale, has a balance in hand, should always search the land charges register. Suppose that he ascertained that there was a second and a third mortgagee, he would be justified in paying such balance to the second mortgagee and leaving him to settle with the third mortgagee. For the words in s. 105, " or authorised to give receipts for the proceeds of the sale thereof," would include the second mortgagee, such second mortgagee being authorised to give a receipt for the surplus on a sale by a first mortgagee by s. 107 (1) of the L.P.A. 1925 given in full *ante*, p. 994. See also *Re Thomson's Mortgage Trusts* [1920] 1 Ch. 508. The second mortgagee must deal with sums so paid to him as if they were proceeds of sale by him (L.P.A. 1925, s. 107 (2)).

The opinion was expressed in Curtis and Ruoff, Registered Conveyancing, 2nd ed., p. 614, that a first mortgagee who has a balance in hand after sale is not obliged to search the register to discover the identity of subsequent chargees, but such a step was advised. This opinion no longer appears in the 3rd ed. (Ruoff and Roper ; cf. at p. 569) and the point is not referred to. Nevertheless, such a search must still be advised.

The first mortgagee must pay to a second mortgagee a surplus in the hands of the first mortgagee even though the claim of the second mortgagee is for interest which is statute barred (*Re Thomson's Mortgage Trusts* [1920] 1 Ch. 508). If, however, the rights of the mortgagor and of a second mortgagee have been barred by lapse of time, *the first mortgagee having been in possession for twelve years* without acknowledgment or part payment, the first mortgagee is not bound to hand over to the second mortgagee any balance of the proceeds of sale (*Young* v. *Clarey* [1948] Ch. 191). Where the second mortgagee is a moneylender whose claim is barred under the Moneylenders Act, 1927, s. 13 (1), he cannot recover from the first mortgagee (*Matthews (C. & M.), Ltd.* v. *Marsden Building Society* [1951] Ch. 758).

B. TAKING POSSESSION

Power of mortgagee in possession to grant leases and accept surrenders, see *ante*, p. 823 *et seq.* and p. 829.

Right of mortgagee to take possession.—Where a mortgage is made by demise or sub-demise, the mortgagee obtains a term of years which gives him the right to take possession of the land at any time, even though the mortgagor is not in default (*Hughes* v. *Waite* [1957] 1 W.L.R. 713 ; *Fourmaids, Ltd.* v. *Dudley Marshall (Properties), Ltd.* [1957] Ch. 317 ; *R.* v. *Judge Dutton Briant* [1957] 2 Q.B. 497), provided that any tenancy created by an attornment clause has been terminated (*Hinckley and Country Building Society* v. *Henny* [1953] 1 W.L.R. 352). This right is rarely exercised (unless the mortgagor is in default and possession is required as a preliminary to sale) because a mortgagee in possession is required to account strictly (*White* v. *City of London Brewery* (1889), 42 Ch. D. 237). A chargee by way of legal mortgage has the same remedies (L.P.A. 1925, s. 87 (1)), as does the proprietor of a registered charge (L.R.A. 1925, s. 34 (1)). A special limitation is placed on the right of a mortgagee to obtain possession by the Reserve and Auxiliary Forces (Protection of Civil Interests) Act, 1951, s. 6 (5), where the mortgagor has the protection of that Act ; see also *ibid.*, s. 3 (8).

Where a mortgagee brings an action for possession in the Chancery Division, some doubts had existed as to the court's jurisdiction to postpone the order for possession due to the terms of a Practice Direction issued in 1936. Then in *Birmingham Citizens Permanent Building Society* v. *Caunt* [1962] Ch. 883, Russell, J., reviewed the authorities and held :—" . . . where, as here, the legal mortgagee under an instalment mortgage under which, by reason of default, the whole money has become payable, is entitled to possession, the court has no jurisdiction to decline to make the order or to adjourn the hearing, whether on terms of keeping up payments or paying arrears, if the mortgagee cannot be persuaded to agree to this course. The sole exception to this is that the application may be adjourned for a short time to afford to the mortgagor a chance of paying off the mortgagee in full or otherwise satisfying him ; but this should not be done if there is no reasonable prospect of this occurring. When I say the sole exception, I do not, of course, intend to exclude adjournments which in the ordinary course of procedure may be desirable in circumstances such as temporary inability of a party to attend, and so forth. The Practice Direction on which the district registrar, very understandably, relied does not assume such a jurisdiction, and if it had it would have been an erroneous assumption." The learned judge expressly came to no conclusion as to the court's jurisdiction, where there is an instalment mortgage with no provision for the whole sum to become payable, to keep the mortgagee out of possession by redemption spread over the period of the mortgage instalments.

However, at first sight it appeared that the decision in *Birmingham Citizens Permanent Building Society* v. *Caunt* had been reversed by the Administration of Justice Act, 1970, Pt. IV, following recommendation of the Payne Committee Report on the Enforcement of Judgment Debts (Cmnd. 3909, paras. 1345–1433). Part IV (ss. 36–39) of the Act came into operation on 1st February, 1971 (s. 54 (4); Administration of Justice (Commencement No. 3) Order, 1970). The court was given power, where a mortgagee brings an action claiming possession of mortgaged land which includes a dwelling-house, to adjourn the proceedings or to stay or suspend execution or to postpone the date of delivery of possession " for such period or periods as the court thinks reasonable " (s. 36 (1), (2) of the Administration of Justice Act, 1970).

Unfortunately, as drafted, this power could only be exercised on the ground that as a result the mortgagor would appear likely to be able " to pay any sums due," or remedy any other default, arising " under the mortgage," and the mortgagor could be put on terms as to this (s. 36 (1) (3), *ibid.*). That this was a condition precedent to exercise of the power was decided by Pennycuick, V.-C., in *Halifax Building Society* v. *Clarke* [1973] 2 W.L.R. 1, who also construed the words " any sums due under the mortgage " as meaning (where the mortgage provided that the whole debt becomes due on default) the entire redemption moneys and not just any arrears of instalments due. Accordingly the position before the 1970 Act as enunciated by Russell, J., could be seen as in substance still standing. Consequently, s. 8 of the

Administration of Justice Act, 1973, was considered necessary, in effect, to revive retrospectively the intent of the 1970 Act. Now in substance the court need look only to the likely payment of arrears of instalments and not of the whole redemption moneys, although the mortgagor's ability to keep up future instalments must also be considered (s. 8 (1) (2) of the 1973 Act). In addition the court's powers of postponement have been largely extended to foreclosure actions as well as possession actions (s. 8 (3) of the 1973 Act).

The county court has exclusive and complete jurisdiction in actions by mortgagees claiming possession where the mortgaged land includes a dwelling-house and is outside Greater London or the county palatine of Lancaster (ss. 37, 38 of the 1970 Act). In other cases the action may be brought in the High Court. See also *Corbiere Properties, Ltd.* v. *Taylor* (1972), 116 Sol. J. 101, and Practice Direction published (1972), 116 Sol. J. 108.

Title to realty by possession.—The Limitation Act, 1939, s. 12, provides as follows:—

" 12. When a mortgagee of land has been in possession of any of the mortgaged land for a period of twelve years, no action to redeem the land of which the mortgagee has been so in possession shall thereafter be brought by the mortgagor or any person claiming through him."

At the expiration of the period fixed by this section (as extended in cases of disability, etc.), the title of the mortgagor and of persons claiming through him is extinguished (*ibid.*, s. 16). A proprietor of a registered charge who takes possession and acquires a title under the Limitation Act, 1939, may, subject to any entry to the contrary on the register, and subject to the right of any persons appearing on the register to be prior incumbrancers, execute a declaration that the right of redemption is barred. Subject to furnishing evidence he may then be registered as proprietor of the land with the same consequence as if he had been a purchaser for value under the power of sale (L.R.A. 1925, s. 34 (2) ; L.R.R. 1925, r. 149).

By s. 22 of the Limitation Act, 1939, if at the date when the right to redeem the mortgage accrued the person to whom it accrued was under a disability, the action may be brought at any time before the expiration of six years from the date when the person ceased to be under disability or died, whichever event first occurred ; but if the right accrued to a person under disability and on his death, while still under disability, it accrues to another person under disability, then there will be no further extension by reason of the disability of the second person (*ibid.*, s. 22, proviso (*b*)). " Disability " exists while a person is an infant or of unsound mind (*ibid.*, s. 31 (2) and (3) as amended by the Mental Health Act, 1959, Sched. 7, and Statute Law (Repeals) Act, 1969, Sched., Pt. VII.

It will be noted that the possession must be by the mortgagee (which includes any person for the time being entitled to the mortgage) ; adverse possession by a stranger for a part of the period would not bar the right of redemption. " Possession " would appear to include receipt of the rents and profits from a tenant ; that is the normal meaning of the word.

The Limitation Act, 1939, s. 23 (3), provides for the fresh accrual of a right of action on acknowledgment or part payment :—

" 23.—(3) Where a mortgagee is by virtue of the mortgage in possession of any mortgaged land and either receives any sum in respect of the principal or interest of the mortgage debt or acknowledges the title of the mortgagor, or his equity of redemption, an action to redeem the land in his possession may be brought at any time before the expiration of twelve years from the date of the payment or acknowledgment."

Any such acknowledgment must be in writing signed by the person making it (*ibid.*, s. 24 (1)) ; any such acknowledgment or payment may be made by the agent of the one party and to the agent of the other party (*ibid.*, s. 24 (2)). An acknowledgment by the mortgagee to a third party is not sufficient (*Markwick* v. *Hardingham* (1880), 15 Ch. D. 339 ; *Ellis* v. *Ellis* [1905] 1 Ch. 613 ; *Re Metropolis and Counties Permanent Investment Building Society ; Gatfield's Case* [1911] 1 Ch. 698). After a mortgagor had become bankrupt a letter written to him by the mortgagee was held not to operate as an acknowledgment (*Markwick* v. *Hardingham, ante*), and where the mortgagee conveyed the land to a purchaser expressly subject to the equity of redemption of the mortgagor, it was held that this was not a sufficient acknowledgment of the title of the mortgagor (*Lucas* v. *Dennison* (1843), 13 Sim. 584).

Where two or more mortgagees are, by virtue of the mortgage, in possession, an acknowledgment by one of the mortgagees binds him and his successors, but not the other mortgagee and his successors. The receipt by the mortgagee of rent from a tenant is not deemed to be a part payment (*Harlock* v. *Ashberry* (1882), 19 Ch. D. 539).

Any " *person claiming through* " the mortgagor is barred if time has elapsed against the mortgagor ; there is no extension in favour of a remainderman. Thus, if an estate in fee simple is mortgaged and the right to redeem is barred against the mortgagor then it is also barred against a person entitled to a future interest (e.g., a remainderman under a settlement of the land). Contrast a case in which the mortgage comprises only a limited interest (e.g., the equitable interest of a tenant for life) ; in such a case the interest of a remainderman is not affected.

Possession of mortgage of pure personal property.—The Real Property Limitation Act, 1874, did not, nor does the Limitation Act, 1939, contain any provision as to time barring the right of a mortgagor to redeem pure personalty. These statutes cannot be applied by analogy to property of an entirely different nature, viz., to pure personalty (*Weld* v. *Petre* [1929] 1 Ch. 33).

In *Charter* v. *Watson* [1899] 1 Ch. 175, freehold property and a policy of life assurance were included in one mortgage as one indivisible security and subject to one and the same proviso for redemption, and the mortgagee had been in possession of the freehold property for more than twelve years without acknowledgment, and it was held that when the right to redeem the realty had been barred the right to redeem the policy had also gone, as the mortgagor could not redeem part without redeeming the whole.

Enlargement of term by mortgagee who has obtained title.—It is provided by s. 88 (3) of the L.P.A. 1925 that where an estate in fee simple has been mortgaged by the creation of a term of years absolute or by a charge by way of legal mortgage and the mortgagee acquires a title under the Limitation Acts, he, or the persons deriving title under him, may enlarge the mortgage term into a fee simple under *the statutory power* for that purpose discharged from any legal mortgage affected by the title so acquired, or in the case of a chargee by way of legal mortgage may by deed declare that the fee simple is vested in him discharged as aforesaid, and the same shall vest accordingly. The section does not operate to confer a better title to the fee simple than would have been acquired if the same had been conveyed by the mortgage (*ibid.*, s. 88 (6)).

" The statutory power for that purpose " refers to s. 153 (3) of the L.P.A. 1925. The effect of an enlargement deed or declaration appears to be to put the mortgagee in the same position as if a foreclosure order had been made. The effect of an order for foreclosure is stated in s. 88 (2) of the L.P.A. 1925, namely, that it will operate to vest the fee simple in the mortgagee (subject to any legal mortgage having priority to the mortgage in right of which the foreclosure is obtained) and thereupon the mortgage term (if any) shall thereby be merged in the fee simple, and any subsequent mortgage term or charge by way of legal mortgage bound by the order shall thereupon be extinguished.

Whether prior equitable mortgages will be overreached depends on whether, when made before 1926, the mortgagee had notice of them or not at the date of the mortgage (L.P.A. 1925, s. 2 (5)) ; and when made after 1925, whether they had been registered as land charges (L.C.A. 1972, s. 2 (4), Class C (iii) ; s. 4 (5)).

As regards leasehold property, it is provided by s. 89 (3) of the L.P.A. 1925 in effect that where a mortgage has been created by sub-demise or by charge by way of legal mortgage and the mortgagee acquires a title under the Limitation Acts, he, or the persons deriving title under him, may by deed declare that the leasehold reversion affected by the mortgage and any mortgage term affected by the title so acquired shall vest in him, free from any right of redemption which is barred, and the same shall (without giving rise to a forfeiture for want of a licence to assign) vest accordingly, and thereupon any mortgage term or charge by way of legal mortgage affected by the title so acquired shall merge in such leasehold reversion or be extinguished, but (subs. (6)) subject to any incumbrance or trust affecting the leasehold reversion which has priority over the mortgage in right of which the title is acquired. The section, however, is not to apply where the mortgage term does not comprise the whole of the land included in the leasehold reversion, unless the rent (if any) payable in respect of that reversion *has been apportioned* as respects the land affected or the rent is of no money value or no rent is reserved, and unless the lessee's covenants and conditions (if any) *have been apportioned*, either expressly or by implication, as respects the land affected (*ibid.*, s. 89 (6)). This subsection must now be read with the provision in the Law of Property (Amendment) Act, 1926, that at the end thereof shall be inserted the words " In this subsection references to an apportionment include an equitable apportionment made without the consent of the lessor." It will be noticed that no licence to assign will be required.

As to sub-mortgages by sub-demise, see s. 89 (5) ; and as to fixtures see the same section, subs. (4), below.

Section 205 (1) (xii) of the L.P.A. 1925 defines the words " Limitation Acts " to mean the Real Property Limitation Acts, 1833, 1837 and 1874, but they will now refer to the Limitation Act, 1939.

It is advisable, at the same time, to execute a statutory declaration stating the facts which show how the right of redemption has been barred.

Sections 88 and 89 above will be found useful when the mortgagee who has got a title by possession intends to keep the property as an investment, for by means of the deed of enlargement or declaration he becomes the absolute owner, free from all subsequent legal mortgages, but subject, of course, to any prior mortgages. If, however, he desires to sell the property and not keep it as an investment, he should sell under his power of sale, for his obtaining a possessory title does not prevent him taking this course. He could not exercise his power of sale if he had already executed a deed of enlargement or made a declaration.

C. FORECLOSURE

Effect of order for foreclosure.—The case of a freehold mortgage is dealt with by s. 88 (2) and (6) of the L.P.A. 1925, the effect of which, read together, is that where a mortgagee obtains an order for foreclosure absolute, *the order will operate to vest the fee simple in him* (subject to any legal mortgage having priority to his mortgage), and thereupon the mortgage term, if any, will thereby be merged in the fee simple, and any subsequent mortgage term or charge by way of legal mortgage bound by the order will thereupon be extinguished.

Similar provisions are contained in s. 89 (2) of the L.P.A. 1925 as regards a mortgagee of leasehold property who has obtained an order for foreclosure absolute. Such an order will operate (without giving rise to a forefeiture for want of a licence to assign) to vest the leasehold reversion affected by the mortgage and any subsequent mortgage term in him, subject to any legal mortgage having priority to his mortgage, and thereupon the mortgage term and any subsequent mortgage term or charge by way of legal mortgage bound by the order will merge in the leasehold reversion or be extinguished.

" Where the mortgage includes fixtures or chattels personal any statutory power of sale and any right to foreclose or take possession shall extend to the absolute or other interest therein affected by the charge " (L.P.A. 1925, ss. 88 (4), 89 (4)).

Subsection (5) of s. 89 provides for the case of a sub-mortgage by sub-demise of a term (less a nominal period) itself limited out of a leasehold reversion.

It may be said that the effect of an order absolute for foreclosure is to make the mortgagee absolute owner of the property, that is, assuming that all the persons interested in the equity of redemption were made parties to or were represented in the action (*Wallace* v. *Evershed* [1899] 1 Ch. 891).

Proceedings for foreclosure can be taken in the usual way by the proprietor of a registered charge and the order will be completed by the registration of the proprietor of the charge, or such other person as may be named in the foreclosure order, as the proprietor of the land, the charge and all subsequent incumbrances and entries being cancelled (L.R.A. 1925, s. 34 (3)). Application for registration as proprietor of the land should be accompanied by the foreclosure order or an office copy of it, and the charge certificate (L.R.R. 1925, r. 147).

A mortgagee, although he has obtained an order *nisi* for foreclosure, may still exercise his power of sale, but first he would have to obtain the leave of the court (*Stevens* v. *Theatres, Ltd.* [1903] 1 Ch. 857). The court has statutory jurisdiction in a foreclosure action to order a sale instead of a foreclosure, on the request of the mortgagee, or any person interested in the mortgage money or the equity of redemption, notwithstanding the dissent of any other person (L.P.A. 1925, s. 91 (2)). As to the court's power of postponement by virtue of s. 8 (3) of the Administration of Justice Act, 1973, see *ante*, pp. 997, 998.

As to foreclosure in the case of an equitable charge, see at p. 1029.

Position of trustee mortgagees obtaining title.—As regards trustee mortgagees, it is provided by s. 31 of the L.P.A. 1925 that where any property vested in trustees by way of security becomes, by virtue of the *Statutes of Limitation*, or of *an order for foreclosure* or otherwise, discharged from the right of redemption, it shall be held by them *on trust for sale*, and the net proceeds of sale shall be applied in like manner as the mortgage debt, if received, would have been applicable, and the income of the property until sale shall be applied in like manner as the interest, if received, would have been applicable ; but the section operates without prejudice to any rule of law relating to the apportionment of capital and income between tenant for life and remaindermen. The section does not affect the right of any person to require that, instead of a sale, the property shall be conveyed to him or in accordance with his directions ; and where the mortgage money is capital money for the purposes of the S.L.A. 1925 the trustees shall, if the tenant for life or statutory owner so requires, instead of selling any such property, execute such subsidiary vesting deed as would have been required if the land had been acquired on a purchase with capital money.

As to the meaning of the expression " Statutes of Limitation," see *ante*, p. 1000.

The words " without prejudice to any rule of law " appear to have been taken from s. 9 of the Conveyancing Act, 1911. It was pointed out in *Re Horn's Estate ; Public Trustee* v. *Garnett* [1924] 2 Ch. 222, that there was no such rule of law and that the effect of s. 9 was to place the property which had been foreclosed, so far as practicable, in the same position as if it had originally formed part of the estate of the testator, and that consequently the tenant for life was entitled to the whole of the net rents, pending the sale of the properties, notwithstanding that they amounted to more than the interest on the mortgage.

There is nothing in s. 31 of the L.P.A. 1925 to prevent trustees, where the right of redemption has been barred by the Statutes of Limitation, from selling under their power of sale (*Re Alison* (1879), 11 Ch. D. 284).

Reopening foreclosure.—If the mortgagee sues on the personal covenant in the mortgage after obtaining an order absolute the foreclosure is reopened and the mortgagor is once more entitled to redeem the mortgage (*Lockhart* v. *Hardy* (1846), 9 Beav. 349). Even if the mortgagee does not do this, the court may, in special circumstances, allow the mortgagor to redeem. Such circumstances might exist if, shortly after foreclosure, the mortgagor asked to be allowed to redeem because he had been unable to do so in time through no fault of his own, and he could show that the property was worth considerably more than the amount due on the mortgage (*Campbell* v. *Hoyland* (1877), 6 Ch. D. 166, at pp. 172 to 174). If it would be equitable to do so, the foreclosure might even be reopened against a purchaser from the mortgagee if the purchaser bought, for instance, soon after foreclosure with notice that the circumstances were such that it might be reasonable to allow the mortgagor a further opportunity to redeem (*ibid.*).

D. APPOINTMENT OF RECEIVER

Mortgages sometimes contain express provision for the appointment of a receiver, but in the absence of such provision the mortgagee has a statutory power to appoint a receiver if the mortgage was made by deed and an event has occurred (as to which see *ante*, p. 991) which would entitle the mortgagee to exercise his power of sale (L.P.A. 1925, ss. 101 (1) (iii), 103, 109 (1)). Such a receiver is deemed to be the agent of the mortgagor (*ibid.*, s. 109 (2)), and so the mortgagee appointing a receiver avoids the very strict liability imposed on a mortgagee in possession to account for rents and profits which he receives or which, but for his wilful neglect or default, he would receive (*White v. City of London Brewery Co.* (1889), 42 Ch. D. 237). It appears that, as the receiver is agent of the mortgagor, receipt of rent by the receiver does not create a tenancy by estoppel as against the mortgagee (*Lever Finance Ltd. v. Needleman's Trustee* [1956] Ch. 375), but other acts of the mortgagee even after the appointment may accept the tenancy (*Stroud Building Society v. Delamont* [1960] 1 W.L.R. 431 ; followed by the Court of Appeal in *Chatsworth Properties, Ltd. v. Effiom* [1971] 1 W.L.R. 144).

The receiver has power to recover the income of the property by action, distress or otherwise to the full extent of the estate or interest which the mortgagor could dispose of (L.P.A. 1925, s. 109 (3)). The receiver must apply money received by him as follows :—

(i) In discharge of rents, taxes, rates and outgoings.

(ii) In payment of sums due in priority to the mortgage.

(iii) In payment of his commission and premiums on insurances payable under the mortgage or the L.P.A. 1925 and the cost of repairs directed in writing by the mortgagee.

(iv) In payment of interest (including arrears, provided they are not statute barred : *National Bank v. Kenney* [1898] 1 Ir. R. 197 ; *Hibernian Bank v. Yourell* [1919] 1 Ir. R. 310).

(v) In or towards discharge of the principal money *if so directed in writing by the mortgagee.*

(vi) As to any balance, in payment to the person who, but for the possession of the receiver, would be entitled to the income (L.P.A. 1925, s. 109 (8)).

The statutory power to appoint a receiver may be exercised even after the mortgagee has taken possession, and thereupon the mortgagee must be treated as having gone out of possession (*Refuge Assurance Co., Ltd. v. Pearlberg* [1938] Ch. 687).

If the mortgagor is a company another body corporate cannot be appointed as receiver (Companies Act, 1948, s. 366 ; *Portman Building Society v. Gallwey* [1955] 1 W.L.R. 96).

The transferee of a registered charge does not become proprietor until his name is entered into the register and so cannot exercise statutory powers, such as that of appointing a receiver, until that has been done (*Lever Finance, Ltd. v. Needleman's Trustee* [1956] Ch. 375).

PART 4. TRANSFER OF MORTGAGE

Form of transfer.—The L.P.A. 1925 deals with transfers of ordinary mortgages as follows :—

" 114.—(1) A deed executed by a mortgagee purporting to transfer his mortgage or the benefit thereof shall, unless a contrary intention is therein expressed, and subject to any provisions therein contained, operate to transfer to the transferee—

(*a*) the right to demand, sue for, recover, and give receipts for, the mortgage money or the unpaid part thereof, and the interest then due, if any, and thenceforth to become due thereon ; and

(b) the benefit of all securities for the same, and the benefit of and the right to sue on all covenants with the mortgagee, and the right to exercise all powers of the mortgagee ; and

(c) all the estate and interest in the mortgaged property then vested in the mortgagee subject to redemption or cesser, but as to such estate and interest subject to the right of redemption then subsisting.

(2) In this section ' transferee ' includes his personal representatives and assigns.

(3) A transfer of mortgage may be made in the form contained in the Third Schedule to this Act with such variations and additions, if any, as the circumstances may require.

(4) This section applies, whether the mortgage transferred was made before or after the commencement of this Act, but applies only to transfers made after the commencement of this Act.

(5) This section does not extend to a transfer of a bill of sale of chattels by way of security.''

Before 1926, to make a transfer of mortgage effective to pass the legal estate in the land it was necessary that there should be a conveyance of the land, as well as an assignment of the mortgage debt, except in the case of a statutory transfer of a statutory mortgage (*Re Beachey* [1904] 1 Ch. 67). By virtue of s. 114 this is not so where the transfer is executed after 1925, notwithstanding that the mortgage is dated before 1926.

Where the mortgagor is not made a party to the transfer, it is not necessary in order to complete the title of the transferee that notice should be given to the mortgagor, but notice should be given to ensure that interest is paid to the proper person.

If the equity of redemption has been transferred it is desirable to have a covenant by the transferee for payment of principal and interest, and the transferee should be joined in the deed and the covenant inserted, except in the case of a transfer of a statutory mortgage, in which case, if the holder of the equity is joined in the transfer, the covenant will be implied (L.P.A. 1925, s. 118 (3)).

A mortgagee cannot add the costs of transfer to the security if the mortgagor does not join in the transfer (*Re Radcliffe* (1856), 22 Beav. 201).

The transfer of a statutory mortgage may be made by deed in one of the Forms Nos. 2, 3 or 4, set out in Sched. 4 to the L.P.A. 1925 (s. 118). The statutory form of transfer given by the Conveyancing Act, 1881, could not be used to transfer an ordinary mortgage, but only to transfer a statutory mortgage (Conveyancing Act, 1881, ss. 26 and 27 ; *Re Beachey* [1904] 1 Ch. 67), but it would appear that a transfer made after 1925 would be effective under the L.P.A. 1925, s. 114.

These new forms of statutory transfer can be used to transfer a statutory mortgage made under s. 26 of the Conveyancing Act, 1881 (L.P.A. 1925, s. 118 (5)). But it is thought that the form of transfer given in Sched. 3 to the Act (as to which see s. 114 (3), *ante*), would also be quite effective.

Where there is more than one transferee the transfer should be to them on a joint account, and they should execute a declaration of trust that the various lenders are entitled in specified amounts. See also L.P.A. 1925, s. 113 (1) and (2), *ante*, p. 169.

Transfer of registered charge.—The proprietor of a registered charge may transfer it, using Form 54, and the transfer will be completed by the registrar entering the transferee on the register as proprietor of the charge (L.R.A. 1925, s. 33 (1), (2)). Form A.4 should be forwarded as cover for the documents and the charge certificate lodged. A registered transferee for value and his successors are not affected by any irregularity or invalidity in the original charge of which the transferee did not have notice (L.R.A. 1925, s. 33 (3)). The effect of registration of the transfer is that the term granted vests in the proprietor for the time being of the charge without any conveyance or assignment (L.R.A. 1925, s. 33 (4), (5)). The transferee of a registered charge does not become proprietor of that charge until registration is effected ; consequently, until that is done, he cannot exercise statutory powers, such as that of appointing a receiver (*Lever Finance, Ltd.* v. *Needleman's Trustee* [1956] Ch. 375).

Assent as transfer.—There has been some controversy as to whether an assent by personal representatives will effectually pass a mortgage debt and the legal estate in the property. Curiously, most of the writers in support of the contention that it will be effective found their argument on the old law, but the new law makes a distinction. Under the pre-1926 law a will operated as a gift subject to the executor's assets. The assent was only needed to complete the gift. Under the post-1925 law the assent itself passes the estate and not the will. The difficulty arises because the A.E.A. 1925, s. 36 (1), provides that a personal representative may assent to the vesting of " any estate or interest in real estate." A mortgage debt is not " an estate or interest in real estate " from which it would follow that mortgages should, as a rule, be transferred in the short form (L.P.A. 1925, Sched. 3, Form 1) and not by an assent. But a mortgage term is such an estate and a mortgage debt passes without mention if there is a clear intention that it shall pass (*Re Culverhouse* [1896] 2 Ch. 251). Similarly, a charge by way of legal mortgage is a legal interest. For these reasons it appears that an assent is sufficient, although many conveyancers consider it advisable to use the statutory form of transfer.

Right to require a transfer on repayment of mortgage debt.—The right of a mortgagor or incumbrancer to require a mortgagee to transfer his mortgage instead of reconveying, given by s. 15 of the Conveyancing Act, 1881, and s. 12 of the Conveyancing Act, 1882, is reproduced in s. 95 of the L.P.A. 1925 in the following words :—

" 95.—(1) Where a mortgagor is entitled to redeem, then subject to compliance with the terms on compliance with which he would be entitled to require a reconveyance or surrender, he shall be entitled to require the mortgagee, instead of reconveying or surrendering, to assign the mortgage debt and convey the mortgaged property to any third person, as the mortgagor directs ; and the mortgagee shall be bound to assign and convey accordingly.

(2) The rights conferred by this section belong to and are capable of being enforced by each incumbrancer, or by the mortgagor, notwithstanding any intermediate incumbrance ; but a requisition of an incumbrancer prevails over a requisition of the mortgagor, and, as between incumbrancers, a requisition of a prior incumbrancer prevails over a requisition of a subsequent incumbrancer.

(3) The foregoing provisions of this section do not apply in the case of a mortgagee being or having been in possession."

Where a first mortgagee has notice of a subsequent mortgage he can and should refuse to transfer his mortgage to the nominee of the mortgagor without the consent of the subsequent mortgagee (*Re Magneta Time Co., Ltd.; Molden* v. *The Company* [1915] W.N. 318).

It is doubtful whether s. 95 applies in the case of building society mortgages unless the mortgage deed showed that it was intended that the assigns of the society should have the same rights as the society. See *ante*, p. 263.

As to the necessity of searching before executing a transfer, see *post*, p. 1013.

The circumstances in which a statutory receipt will operate as a transfer are mentioned *post*, p. 1010 *et seq.*

PART 5. DISCHARGE OF MORTGAGE

Presumption of reconveyance.—Before 1926, it was assumed that a reconveyance had been executed, even though the mortgage was not shown to have been paid off, when the mortgagor had long dealt with the property as his own, and the circumstances were such as to lead strongly to the conclusion that it had been paid off (*Cooke* v. *Soltau* (1824), 2 S. & S. 154 ; *Bennett* v. *Cooper* (1846), 9 Beav. 252) ; but not unless the circumstances were strongly in favour of the presumption (*Pickett* v. *Packham* (1868), L.R. 4 Ch. 190). The fact of an equitable charge being found in the possession of the mortgagor, although no receipt was endorsed thereon, was considered strong evidence that the charge had been paid off (*Nicoll* v. *Chambers* (1852), 11 C.B. 996, at p. 1004 ; *Farmer* v. *Turner* (1899), 15 T.L.R. 522).

When it was known that the mortgage had been paid off, and a long time had elapsed without obtaining a reconveyance, the Statutes of Limitation sometimes rendered one unnecessary. For instance, a mortgage of freeholds was paid off in 1856, but no reconveyance was taken of the legal estate. It was held (in 1883) that by the operation of the Real Property Limitation Act, 1833, s. 34, and the Real Property Limitation Act, 1874, s. 1, the legal title of the mortgagee had become extinguished, and the fact of there having been no reconveyance ceased to be a flaw on the title (*Sands to Thompson* (1883), 22 Ch. D. 614 ; see also *Kibble* v. *Fairthorne* [1895] 1 Ch. 219).

If the twelve years had not elapsed on 1st January, 1926, since the payment off of the mortgage, the legal estate vested in the mortgagor or the persons claiming under him by virtue of the transitional provisions of the L.P.A. 1925, Sched. 1, Pt. II, paras. 3 and 6 (*d*).

Since 1925, immediately a mortgage by demise is paid off, the term becomes a satisfied term and ceases to exist under ss. 5 and 116 of the L.P.A. 1925. See below.

Preliminary remarks as to receipts.—On the payment off of a legal mortgage (as opposed to a charge by way of legal mortgage), be it a building society mortgage, a friendly society mortgage, or any other mortgage by demise or sub-demise, by a person entitled to the immediate equity of redemption, it is necessary, of course, to have written evidence of the discharge (preferably witnessed by a solicitor) but it is not necessary, technically speaking, to have a statutory receipt. For under ss. 5 and 116 of the L.P.A. 1925 the mortgage term will, when the mortgage has been paid off, become a satisfied term and will cease. Even while the mortgage existed the mortgagor had in him a legal estate, but it was subject to the term, and therefore, when such term came to an end the legal estate still remained in him freed from the term. Consequently he then got an unincumbered title and could make a perfect title to a purchaser. It is true that s. 115 (1) says that when the mortgage takes effect by demise or sub-demise a statutory receipt shall operate as a surrender of the term so as to determine the term or merge the same in the reversion immediately expectant thereon, and this is sometimes said to be one of the few lapses which occur now and then in the 1925 legislation. For it is evident on the face of it that as, under s. 116 of the L.P.A. 1925, the mortgage term, when the money secured by the mortgage had been discharged, became a satisfied term and ceased, a statutory receipt could not cause a non-existent term to cease. However, it is also true that evidence of such discharge is requisite and that the statutory receipt fulfils this function better than a simple receipt which is not conclusive of payment. In other words, it appears possible for the statutory receipt to operate as provided by s. 115 (1) despite actual non-payment.

In discussing the use of a simple receipt as against a formal statutory receipt it should be mentioned that by using a simple receipt the mortgagor would not get the benefit of the implied covenant provided for by subs. (6) of s. 115 of the L.P.A. 1925 set out below, but that covenant could be well done without, as it is never of much value.

Notwithstanding the above reasoning, the almost universal practice is to take a formal statutory receipt, and pay the stamp duty thereon, except where the receipt is exempt therefrom. Further, it is to be noted that ss. 5 and 116 of the L.P.A. 1925 are only expressly applicable where there is a mortgage by demise ; i.e., a chargee by way of legal mortgage does not actually take a term (or sub-term) to be satisfied, but the charge, which is a legal interest, must be cleared and the only methods provided appear to be by s. 115 of the L.P.A. 1925 below, or by release under seal (ss. 52 (1) and 205 (1) (ii) of the L.P.A. 1925).

These remarks apply where the person paying off the mortgage is entitled to the immediate equity of redemption. Where the receipt shows that the money was paid by a person not so entitled, a very different position arises. In this case subs. (2) of s. 115 if the L.P.A. 1925 applies, with the result that the receipt will not operate as a discharge of the mortgage, but as a transfer of the mortgage, except (i) where it is otherwise expressly provided ; (ii) where payment is made out of capital money or certain other money applicable for the purpose, and the receipt does not expressly provide that it is to operate as a transfer. See fully, *post*, p. 1010.

It is now proposed to consider s. 115 of the L.P.A. 1925 in detail.

Payment by person entitled to the immediate equity.—The position is governed by the following provisions of the L.P.A. 1925, s. 115 :—

"115.—(1) A receipt *endorsed on, written at the foot of, or annexed to,* a mortgage for all money thereby secured, *which states the name of the person who pays the money* and is *executed by the chargee by way of legal mortgage or the person in whom the mortgaged property is vested* and who is legally entitled to give a receipt for the mortgage money shall operate, without any reconveyance, surrender, or release—

(a) *Where a mortgage takes effect by demise or sub-demise,* as a surrender of the term, so as to determine the term or merge the same in the reversion immediately expectant thereon ;

(b) Where the mortgage does not take effect by demise or sub-demise, as a reconveyance thereof to the extent of the interest which is the subject matter of the mortgage, to the person who immediately before the execution of the receipt was entitled to the equity of redemption ;

and in either case, as a discharge of the mortgaged property from all principal money and interest secured by, and from all claims under the mortgage, but without prejudice to any term or other interest which is paramount to the estate or interest of the mortgagee or other person in whom the mortgaged property was vested.

* * * * *

(5) A receipt may be given in the form contained in the Third Schedule to this Act, with such variations and additions, if any, as may be deemed expedient ; and where it takes effect under this section, it shall (subject as hereinafter provided) be liable to the same stamp duty as if it were a reconveyance under seal.

(6) In a receipt given under this section the same covenants shall be implied as if the person who executes the receipt had by deed been expressed to convey the property as mortgagee, subject to any interest which is paramount to the mortgage."

Section 115 applies to the discharge of a mortgage, including a charge by way of legal mortgage, and to the discharge of a statutory mortgage whether executed before or after 1st January, 1926, but only as respects discharges effected after 1925 (subs. (8)). The section does not (subs. (10)) apply to the discharge of a charge or incumbrance registered under the L.R.A. 1925, as to which see *post*, p. 1012.

" *endorsed on, written at the foot of, or annexed to.*"—If the receipt is taken separately, that is, is not endorsed on, or written at the foot of, the mortgage, it should be annexed to it at the time of signature or execution ; otherwise it would not comply with the terms of the subsection, and consequently would not operate under the Act, but merely as evidence of the discharge of the mortgage.

The better opinion appears to be that a receipt endorsed on a transfer of the mortgage is not effective under s. 115 unless the mortgagor entered into a new covenant to pay the mortgage money in the transfer in which case it might be argued that the mortgage consists of more than one deed and that the transfer is one of them (compare s. 115 (7), *post*, p. 1010).

" *which states the name of the person who pays the money.*"—The name of the person paying must be stated, and it is best to add the words " the person entitled to the immediate equity of redemption in the within mentioned property."

" *executed by the chargee by way of legal mortgage or the person in whom the mortgaged property is vested.*"—It is not strictly necessary that an ordinary statutory receipt given by an individual should be under seal (*Simpson* v. *Geoghegan* [1934] W.N. 232), but it appears desirable that it should be a deed, e.g., to constitute authority for payment to a solicitor (see s. 69 of the L.P.A. 1925, also s. 68).

If the mortgagee should die before signing the receipt, his personal representatives would be the persons to sign it ; and, in the case of executors, all of the proving executors should sign the document (A.E.A. 1925, ss. 1 (1), 2 (2)).

It is sometimes the practice of solicitors to refuse to get a receipt or reconveyance executed until the money has actually been paid, the idea being that if the deed was executed and then by some accident the money was not paid the estate would have passed to the mortgagor. But this would not be so, as the executed receipt would only operate as an escrow (*Lloyd's Bank, Ltd.* v. *Bullock* [1896] 2 Ch. 192). In fact a mortgagor is entitled to have an executed receipt or surrender of the mortgage term or release handed over to him at the time when he repays what is due on the mortgage (*Rourke* v. *Robinson* [1911] 1 Ch. 480). See further, *ante*, p. 266.

For the suggestion that a mortgagee should instead provide the solicitor with a power of attorney authorising the giving of a vacating receipt, see J. E. Adams in *Law Society's Gazette*, vol. 68, p. 175 (where the risks of making repayment on completion otherwise are indicated, e.g., that the mortgagee may die).

" *Where a mortgage takes effect by demise or sub-demise.*"—It is stated in the L.P.A. 1925, s. 115 (1) (*a*), that the receipt operates as a surrender of the term, so as to determine the term or merge it in the reversion immediately expectant thereon. That is to say, it becomes a satisfied term and merges in the reversion (L.P.A. 1925, s. 5 ; see also L.P.A. 1925, Sched. 1, Pt. II, para. 1). See further the remarks *ante*, pp. 1006–1007.

Mortgagor's right to insist on reconveyance, release or transfer.—The L.P.A. 1925, s. 115 (4), provides as follows :—

" (4) This section does not affect the right of any person to require a reassignment, surrender, release, or transfer to be executed in lieu of a receipt."

This provision must be read subject to s. 115 (3), which is as follows :—

" (3) Nothing in this section confers on a mortgagor a right to keep alive a mortgage paid off by him, so as to affect prejudicially any subsequent incumbrancer ; *and where there is no right to keep the mortgage alive, the receipt does not operate as a transfer.*"

The words in italics relate only to a case falling within the earlier words of the subsection and do not in any circumstances decide the question as to whether a receipt operates as a transfer (*Cumberland Court (Brighton), Ltd.* v. *Taylor* [1964] Ch. 29).

Section 115 (3) is only confirmatory of the law before 1926, for it was then well settled that where a mortgagor had executed a first mortgage and subsequent mortgages he would not have been allowed to pay off the first mortgage and take a transfer to himself or to a nominee on his behalf, and thus squeeeze out an intermediate mortgage or mortgages (*Watts* v. *Symes* (1851), 1 De G. M. & G. 240 ; *Otter* v. *Lord Vaux* (1856), 6 De G. M. & G. 638 ; *Grierson* v. *National Provincial Bank of England, Ltd.* [1913] 2 Ch. 18). The point decided in *Otter* v. *Lord Vaux* was that where a first mortgagee sells under his power of sale to the mortgagor, the mortgagor will take the property subject to any subsequent incumbrance which he himself may have created (followed in this respect in *Parkash* v. *Irani Finance, Ltd.* [1970] Ch. 101). This principle does not, of course, apply where the purchaser is not the mortgagor. For, as said by Lord Haldane, L.C., in *Whiteley* v. *Delaney* [1914] A.C. 132, 145, " It is now quite plain that a purchaser from a mortgagor and the first mortgagee can always, if he chooses, keep the first mortgage alive and so protect himself against subsequent incumbrancers whether he had notice of them or not."

In *Holme* v. *Fieldsend* [1911] W.N. 111, it was decided by Warrington, J., that where a mortgagee refuses, upon payment off of the mortgage debt, to reconvey the mortgage property, the court may appoint a master to execute the reconveyance on his behalf.

Statutory receipt where there is a further charge.—Before 1926 it was always a question, where there had been further charges and transfers, whether a separate statutory receipt should be put on each document, or, in the alternative, whether it would be allowable to insert in the receipt words indicating that it was in discharge, not only of the amount secured by the mortgage, but of any amount secured by the further charges or transfers. It may be that the L.P.A. 1925, s. 115 (7), makes a receipt on a transfer valid if the transfer contained a new covenant to pay the mortgage money ; a receipt on a further charge is valid. Section 115 (7) provides :—

" (7) Where the mortgage consists of a mortgage and a further charge or of more than one deed, it shall be sufficient for the purposes of this section, if the receipt refers either to all the deeds whereby the mortgage money is secured or to the aggregate amount of the mortgage money thereby secured and for the time being owing, and is endorsed on, written at the foot of, or annexed to, one of the mortgage deeds."

The better opinion is that s. 115 (7) does not apply to a receipt on a building society mortgage in the form prescribed by the Building Societies Act, 1962, s. 37 (and Sched. 6), since s. 37 (3) of that Act expressly excludes subs. (9) of s. 115 which otherwise would have applied the provisions of s. 115 to such receipts (see also s. 37 (2) which omits reference to s. 115 (7)). If the receipt is *not* in the form prescribed by the 1962 Act, then the provisions of s. 115 may be applicable (s. 37 (3)).

Payment by person not entitled to the immediate equity.—In this case if the receipt shows that payment was by such a person, it operates not as a discharge of the mortgage but as a transfer of the mortgage, except in the special cases mentioned in subs. (2) of s. 115 of the L.P.A. 1925. This subsection is as follows :—

" (2) Provided that, where by the receipt the money *appears to have been paid* by a person who is not entitled to the immediate equity of redemption, the receipt shall operate as if the benefit of the mortgage had by deed been transferred to him ; unless—

(*a*) it is otherwise expressly provided ; or

(*b*) the mortgage is paid off out of capital money, or other money in the hands of a personal representative or trustee properly applicable for the discharge of the mortgage, and it is not expressly provided that the receipt is to operate as a transfer."

Section 116 of the L.P.A. 1925 also makes it clear that the provision therein that when the money secured by the mortgage has been discharged the mortgage term shall become a satisfied term and shall cease, is without prejudice to the right of a tenant for life or other person having only a limited interest in the equity of redemption to require the mortgage to be kept alive by transfer or otherwise.

Further, it appears to happen comparatively frequently in practice that the receipt for the mortgage money is inadvertently dated *after* the conveyance on sale, the proceeds of which have been used to make payment to the mortgagee. It is therefore arguable that " by the receipt the money appears to have been paid by a person who is not entitled to the immediate equity of redemption," i.e., by the vendor and not, after the conveyance, by the purchaser, and so operates as a transfer within s. 115 (2). Precisely this problem arose, in connection with a vacating receipt on a charge by way of legal mortgage, in *Cumberland Court (Brighton), Ltd.* v. *Taylor* [1964] Ch. 29, but in the result was found *not* to constitute a defect in title. Ungoed-Thomas, J., first decided that the receipt had operated as a transfer of the charge to the vendor, but went on to hold that an estoppel arose from the recital in the conveyance that the vendor was seised in fee simple *free from incumbrances* and that this estoppel was " fed " immediately on the transfer of the charge so as to pass the interest on to the purchaser. The learned judge quoted a statement of the relevant doctrines of estoppel from Williams on Vendor and Purchaser, 4th ed., vol. II, p. 1096, and held them applicable despite the fact that no legal estate was involved (i.e., since a chargee by way of legal mortgage does not actually get a term of years, see *ante*, p. 972). However, a legal charge is both called and has the same incidents as a legal estate by virtue of the L.P.A. 1925 which created it (ss. 1 (2), (4) and 205 (1) (x)) and so might well have been regarded as within the doctrine in any case.

Of course, this decision does not leave the position free from difficulty. Thus it depends on the insertion of an appropriate recital. Also the point has been suggested that an estoppel is not " fed " if the grantor had *some* legal estate at the time of the grant (see *Conveyancer N.S.*, vol. 27, p. 298, referring to *Universal Permanent Building Society* v. *Cooke* [1952] Ch. 95, but this was a case concerning landlord and tenant where the only estoppel arose from the grant itself and not from any recital of other matters). However, it is thought that neither the courts nor conveyancers should be astute to see defects in title in what are in reality merely technical mistakes (see as to this approach *Re Stirrup's Contract* [1961] 1 W.L.R. 449). In addition, the alternative argument in such a case may be noted that the transferred mortgage is void against purchasers for value anyway on the ground that it had become registrable under the L.C.A. 1972 as being no longer protected by deposit of documents. Also a remedy may be found under the implied covenants for title. See further an excellent article by M. J. Goodman at *Law Society's Gazette*, vol. 60, p. 865.

However, these problems would appear to be all avoided where the practice is adopted when acting for institutional mortgagees of giving a solicitor's undertaking at completion to vacate, then dating the vacating receipt when it is actually sealed some days later but also stating the actual date of payment and receipt in the vacating receipt. It is considered that s. 115 (2) of the L.P.A. 1925 would not then be even *prima facie* applicable.

Subsection (2) of s. 115 is not necessary, and it would have been better if it had been left out of the section, as it only creates confusion (it may be noted it is not applicable to a receipt on a building society mortgage in the prescribed form : Building Societies Act, 1962, s. 37 (2), (3)). When a person having paid off a mortgage wants a transfer he will seldom use the machinery of a statutory receipt to effect his purpose, but will take a transfer, for instance, in the form given in Sched. 3 to the L.P.A. 1925. This form is very little longer than a statutory receipt, and he will avoid the pitfalls which await the use of the statutory receipt form, and particularly the question whether such form is prepared so as to operate as an effectual transfer. This question arose in *Simpson* v. *Geoghegan* [1934] W.N. 232 ; the mortgage

had been made by *G*, and the receipt endorsed on it stated that payment had
been made by the plaintiff and that it was intended that the receipt should
operate as a transfer. Clauson, J., held that the receipt showed, *prima facie*,
that the person entitled to the equity of redemption was the mortgagor *G*,
and not the plaintiff; that s. 115 (2) did not require that the receipt should
state that the person who paid the money to the mortgagees was not entitled
to the immediate equity of redemption and that the receipt executed in favour
of the plaintiff operated to transfer the benefit of the mortgage to him.
The result might appear to be that in determining whether a receipt operates
as a transfer, one need not inquire whether or not the person making the
payment was entitled to the immediate equity of redemption, but can rely
on the words " appears to have been paid " in s. 115 (2) and take the receipt
at its face value. But this would not appear to be entirely safe since the
receipt may be within para. (*b*) of s. 115 (2), particularly since some mortgagees
object to the inclusion of a statement as to payment out of capital money,
etc., on the ground that this is not a matter within their knowledge ; see
also *Cumberland Court (Brighton), Ltd.* v. *Taylor, ante.* In the case of
Pyke v. *Peters* [1943] 1 K.B. 242, 251, Asquith, J., stated that " when a
stranger pays off the mortgage he becomes the transferee of it and of the
benefit of its covenant, ' unless it is otherwise expressly provided '." It is
submitted that this is not the case unless *it appears from the receipt* that the
money was paid by a person not entitled to the immediate equity of
redemption. The decision does not seem satisfactory on this point.

In view of the doubts on the matter solicitors are advised not to rely on a
statutory receipt to effect a transfer, but to make a proper transfer. This
is particularly so where payments are made by a second mortgagee, as such
a mortgagee is the person entitled to the immediate equity of redemption
of the first mortgage. It is arguable that a statutory receipt stating that
payment was made by a person who was in fact second mortgagee operates
as a discharge, and not a transfer, of the first mortgage. The second
mortgagee undoubtedly has power to add the amount paid to his own
mortgage, but this is not a very satisfactory remedy and it is far better to
take a transfer of the first mortgage.

Where a tenant for life has paid off a mortgage out of his own money,
he should most certainly take an express transfer, because he would be a
person entitled to the equity of redemption, and a statutory receipt would
not act as a transfer (L.P.A. 1925, s. 115 (1), (2)). It was decided in
Re Chesters ; Whittingham v. *Chesters* [1935] Ch. 77 that the presumption
which arose in the case where a tenant for life in possession paid off a
mortgage out of his own moneys, that he intended to keep the charge
alive for his own benefit, arose where the tenant for life's interest was in
remainder.

Discharge of registered charges.—On requisition of the proprietor of a
charge or on due proof of the satisfaction thereof, the registrar must notify
on the register, by cancelling or varying the original entry or otherwise,
the cessation (whole or partial) of the charge, and thereupon the charge is
deemed to have ceased in whole or in part accordingly (L.R.A. 1925,
s. 35 (1)). On notification of entire cessation, whether as to the whole or
part only of the land affected, the term or sub-term implied in or granted
by the charge merges in the registered estate, so far as it affects the land to
which the discharge extends (L.R.A. 1925, s. 35 (2)). A discharge should
be in Form 53 in the Schedule to the L.R.R. 1925 (r. 151). The charge

certificate and discharge must be lodged at the registry with Form A.4 ; the
land certificate will not usually be issued to the person entitled to it unless
application for it is made by that person or his solicitor. See also *ante*,
p. 648, as to discharge on sale of the land.

A discharge by a building society may also be in Form 53 (L.R.R. 1925,
r. 152 ; Building Societies Act, 1962, s. 37 (4)) ; and was always exempt
from stamp duty (s. 117 of the 1962 Act). There is some conflict as to how
the receipt ought to be executed (cp. L.R.R. 1925, r. 152 (2) and s. 37 (1) (*a*)
of and Sched. 6 to the 1962 Act), but in practice H.M. Land Registry attach
no significance to the conflict (Ruoff and Roper, Registered Conveyancing,
3rd ed., p. 575).

Precautions before handing over the deeds.—It is provided by the
L.P.A. 1925, s. 96 (2), as amended by the Law of Property (Amendment)
Act, 1926, that :—

" 96.—(2) A mortgagee, whose mortgage is surrendered or otherwise
extinguished, shall not be liable on account of delivering documents of
title in his possession to the person not having the best right thereto,
unless he has notice of the right or claim of a person having a better right,
whether by virtue of a right to require a surrender or re-conveyance or
otherwise. In this subsection notice does not include notice implied by
reason of registration under the Land Charges Act, 1925 [now 1972], or in
a local deeds register."

There is nothing in the above subsection as amended to alter the law
that if a first mortgagee has notice of a second mortgage he can and should
refuse to reconvey the mortgaged property to the mortgagor or to transfer
it to the mortgagor's nominee (*Re Magneta Time Co., Ltd. ; Molden* v. *The
Company* [1915] W.N. 318 ; see also *West London Commercial Bank* v.
Reliance Permanent Building Society (1885), 29 Ch. D. 954). So that, quite
outside the question of registration being or not being notice, it is possible
that a mortgagee may have had actual notice of a second mortgage and have
forgotten it, and on this ground alone it is sometimes considered advisable
to search, although it is difficult to see how the cost of searches can be imposed
on the mortgagor.

Extinction of mortgage by lapse of time.—By the Limitation Act, 1939,
s. 18 (4), the provisions of that Act relating to actions to recover land apply
to a foreclosure action in respect of the land. The result is that if no payment
on account of principal or interest is made for twelve years and the mortgagor
does not during that period acknowledge the title of the mortgagee (as to
which see *ibid.*, s. 23 (1)), the mortgagee's right of action is extinguished.
When that has happened the mortgagee ceases to have any estate in the
land and must hand over the title deeds to the mortgagor without payment
of the sums due to him (*Lewis* v. *Plunket* [1937] Ch. 306). The effect of
judgment in a foreclosure action is to give the mortgagee a new right to
possession, with the result that time begins to run from the date of judgment
(*Pugh* v. *Heath* (1882), 7 App. Cas. 238).

Payment into court when mortgagee cannot be found.—It sometimes
happens that a mortgagor wishes to redeem a mortgage and sell the property
but he cannot trace the mortgagee and so cannot obtain a discharge of the
mortgage. In such a case he may apply to the court under the L.P.A. 1925,
s. 50, to direct payment into court of an amount sufficient to meet the

incumbrance and any interest thereon, and thereupon the court may, without any notice to the mortgagee, declare the land to be freed from the mortgage. A declaration that the land is freed from the mortgage cannot be given until the money has been paid into court (*Re Uplands* [1948] W.N. 165).

Liability to discharge mortgage on property of a deceased mortgagor. —This subject was formerly dealt with by the Real Estate Charges Acts, 1854, 1867 and 1877, generally known as the Locke-King Acts. As regards deaths occurring after 1925 they have been repealed by the A.E.A. 1925, s. 56, and replaced by the A.E.A. 1925, s. 35, which extends also to pure personalty. Section 35 is as follows :—

" 35.—(1) Where a person dies possessed of, or entitled to, or under a general power of appointment (including the statutory power to dispose of entailed interests) by his will disposes of, *an interest in property*, which at the time of his death is charged with the payment of money, whether by way of legal mortgage, equitable charge or otherwise (including a lien for unpaid purchase-money), and the deceased has not *by will deed or other document signified a contrary or other intention*, the interest so charged shall, as between the different persons claiming through the deceased, be primarily liable for the payment of the charge ; and every part of the said interest, according to its value, shall bear a proportionate part of the charge on the whole thereof.

(2) Such contrary or other intention shall not be deemed to be signified—

(a) by a general direction for the payment of debts or of all the debts of the testator out of his personal estate, or his residuary real and personal estate, or his residuary real estate ; or

(b) by a charge of debts upon any such estate ;

unless such intention is further signified by words expressly or by necessary implication referring to all or some part of the charge.

(3) Nothing in this section affects the right of a person entitled to the charge to obtain payment or satisfaction thereof either out of the other assets of the deceased or otherwise."

In *Re Nicholson ; Nicholson* v. *Boulton* [1923] W.N. 251, a testatrix devised her house to her nephew and afterwards borrowed money on the security of a mortgage thereon. About a year after she instructed her solicitors to give notice of her intention to pay off the mortgage, but died before the expiration of the notice. It was held that the notice was not another document signifying a contrary intention within the meaning of the Real Estate Charges Act, 1854. It was held in *Re Beirnstein ; Barnett* v. *Beirnstein* [1925] Ch. 12, that the word " mortgage " in a will does not include a vendor's lien for unpaid purchase-money. See also *Re Fegan* [1928] 1 Ch. 45 as to a contrary intention being implied by a direction of a testator that his debts should be paid out of a special fund (also *Allie* v. *Katah* [1963] 1 W.L.R. 202).

In *Re Birmingham* [1959] Ch. 523, it was held that a codicil reciting a contract to purchase a house and making a specific devise of the house did not show an intention contrary to s. 35 and so on death of the testatrix before completion, the devisee took subject to the vendor's charge for the unpaid balance of the purchase-money. It is difficult to believe that this decision carried out the true intention of the testatrix. The fact that part of property mortgaged was specifically devised and the balance fell into residue does not indicate an intention that the part specifically devised shall be exonerated from its proportion of the charge (*Re Neeld* [1962] Ch. 643).

Consolidation of mortgages.—Section 93 of the L.P.A. 1925, given below, replaced s. 17 of the Conveyancing Act, 1881, with some alterations.

" 93.—(1) *A mortgagor* seeking to redeem any one mortgage is entitled to do so without paying any money due under any separate mortgage made by him, or by any person through whom he claims, solely on property other than that comprised in the mortgage which he seeks to redeem.

This subsection applies only if and as far as a contrary intention is not expressed in the mortgage deeds *or one of them.*

(2) This section does not apply where all the mortgages were made before the first day of January, eighteen hundred and eighty-two.

(3) Save as aforesaid, nothing in this Act, in reference to mortgages, affects any right of consolidation or renders inoperative a stipulation in relation to any mortgage made before or after the commencement of this Act reserving a right to consolidate."

" *mortgagor.*"—This includes any person from time to time deriving title under the original mortgagor or entitled to redeem a mortgage according to his estate, interest or right in the mortgaged property (L.P.A. 1925, s. 205 (1) (xvi)).

" *or one of them.*"—It will be noticed that subs. (1) provides that the contrary intention need only be expressed in *one* of the deeds. Also note that s. 93 does not apply where there are several mortgages on the same property, even though one of them comprises other property (*Re Salmon* [1903] 1 K.B. 147 ; and see the word " solely ").

In practice, s. 93 is almost invariably excluded by the mortgage deed, and so it is still necessary to know the old law.

The principle is that, the right to redeem being an *equitable* right, the person who seeks to redeem must on his part do equity towards the mortgagee and redeem him entirely, not taking one of his securities and leaving him exposed to the risk of deficiency as to the other (*Willie* v. *Lugg* (1761), 2 Eden 78).

The doctrine of consolidation arising out of this principle will be best explained by a few examples. The simplest case would be that of the owner of a house who had mortgaged it and, at the same time or afterwards, had mortgaged another house belonging to him to the same mortgagee for another sum. In this case the mortgagee would be entitled to refuse to accept payment off of one mortgage without payment off of both mortgages. A variation is where a mortgagor mortgages one house to one mortgagee and another house to another mortgagee, and afterwards these two mortgages become vested in one person. The position here is the same, and the mortgagor cannot insist on paying off one of the mortgages without paying off the other.

Now, suppose that in either of the above cases the mortgagor should have sold the houses subject to the respective mortgages, or one of the houses subject to the particular mortgage thereon. The purchaser or purchasers would be in no better position than the mortgagor was in, for the mortgagor could only sell the equity of redemption of each mortgage on each house subject to the equities on which he himself held it. The rule as to this is that if at the time of the purchase of one equity of redemption the right of consolidation of the mortgagee could then have been enforced against that particular equity, the purchaser will take subject to that right. To make this point clear the case may be instanced where a person mortgages one house to a mortgagee, and then sells it subject to the mortgage, and then mortgages another house to the same mortgagee. In this case the mortgagee would have no right to consolidate, and the purchaser could pay off the mortgage on his house without having to pay off the other mortgage, for at the time he purchased *there was no right to consolidate in existence* (*Jennings* v. *Jordan* (1881), 6 App. Cas. 698). On the same principle, where a person has mortgaged one house to one mortgagee and another house to another mortgagee, and then sells one or both of the houses subject to the mortgage or mortgages, and after such sale or sales the two mortgages become vested in one mortgagee, the new mortgagee has no right to consolidate (*Harter* v. *Colman* (1882), 19 Ch. D. 630 ; *Minter* v. *Carr* [1894] 3 Ch. 498). But a mortgagee would be allowed to consolidate against a purchaser of *both* equities of redemption, although the two mortgages became vested in one mortgagee after the purchase (*Pledge* v. *White* [1896] A.C. 187). The reason is that the courts have made the further rule that where all the equities of redemption become united in one person, and all the mortgages also become united in one mortgagee, that mortgagee can require the one owner of all the equities to pay off all the mortgages or none. This principle applies whether there are two mortgages or a dozen. It is a principle which most writers simply state, but do not attempt to justify. But it is well established and no useful purpose can be served by discussing it. The reason given for the rule by Lord Davey in *Pledge* v. *White, ante*, is not convincing. He said : " It appears to me, my lords, that an assignee of two or more equities of redemption from one mortgagor stands in a widely different position from the assignee of one equity only. He knows, or has the opportunity of knowing, what are the mortgages subject to which he has purchased the property and he knows they may become united by transfer in one hand."

Where the equities of redemption are vested in separate persons the rule is that where several mortgages of different properties have been made to different persons by the same mortgagor (*Cummins* v. *Fletcher* (1880), 14 Ch. D. 699), if at any time while the equity of redemption in all the mortgages is vested in the same person the mortgages all become vested in the same mortgagee, *or where, after that state of things has once existed* the equities of redemption have become separated, the mortgagee can consolidate ; and notwithstanding that the union of mortgages may have occurred *after* the assignment of the equities. See *Pledge* v. *White* [1896] A.C. 187 ; *Riley* v. *Hall* (1898), 79 L.T. 244 ; *Farmer* v. *Pitt* [1902] 1 Ch. 954.

The rule does not apply where the mortgages were made by different mortgagors (*Sharp* v. *Rickards* [1909] 1 Ch. 109).

Hughes v. *Britannia Permanent Benefit Building Society* [1906] 2 Ch. 607 is a most instructive case. There A mortgaged No. 1 property for £87 to B ; then shortly afterwards he mortgaged No. 2 property to B for £900 ; then he executed a second mortgage of No. 2 property to C for £7,000 ; and then mortgaged No. 3 property to B for £687 ; and then sold No. 2 property. It was decided that B was entitled to require not only that the £900 due on his mortgage of the property sold should be paid off, but that the £87 due on his mortgage of No. 1 property should also be paid before the second mortgage to C was discharged, *on the ground that the right to consolidate had accrued on the execution of the mortgage to him* of the property sold, and that the benefit of this right could not be prejudicially affected by the subsequent mortgage to *C* of the equity of redemption. Also that *B* would not be entitled to consolidate his mortgage on property No. 3 because *C's* mortgage on the property sold was made first. *C* therefore was entitled to the balance of the purchase-money on account of his second mortgage for £7,000.

As the doctrine of consolidation is based on principles of equity, it follows that the doctrine applies although the interest of the mortgagee is merely equitable. A condition contained in an equitable mortgage that the mortgagor will execute a legal mortgage when called on in such form as the mortgagee shall require will not authorise the insertion of a clause in the mortgage excluding s. 93, *ante* (*Farmer* v. *Pitt* [1902] 1 Ch. 954).

It has been suggested in the *Solicitors' Journal*, vol. 92, p. 736, that the right to consolidate amounts to a " general equitable charge " as it is an equitable charge not secured by a deposit of documents *relating to the legal estate affected* (L.C.A. 1972, s. 2 (4), Class C (iii)). This contention does not appear to have been made earlier and there is no authority on the matter. The words of the L.C.A. seem to justify the contention, although opinion is divided ; for instance, it can be argued that the right to consolidate does not amount to a " charge." Consequently, if a right to consolidate has arisen it is advisable to register it ; otherwise it may become void against a purchaser for value from the mortgagor of the property against which the right is claimed, even if that purchaser had notice of the right (L.P.A. 1925, s. 13).

Registered charges.—The right to consolidate cannot be clearly defined in the case of charges of registered land. By the L.R.A. 1925, s. 25 (3), any provision in a charge which purports to affect any registered land other than that in respect of which the charge is expressly registered is void. The right to consolidate arises only if it is expressly reserved (L.P.A. 1925, s. 93 (1)), and so it follows that there can be no right of consolidation except where the right is *registered against* the land affected by consolidation of charges. It is provided by the L.R.R. 1925, r. 154 (1), that where a charge reserves the right to consolidate it shall not on that account only be registered against any other land than that expressly described in it. On the other hand, where the right reserved is to consolidate with a specified charge, or where an application is made to register the right in respect of a specified charge, the registrar will require production of the land certificates of all titles affected, and, on production thereof, will *enter in the register a notice* that the specified charges are consolidated (L.R.R. 1925, r. 154 (2)). It can be argued, therefore, first that if an earlier charge exists in respect of which consolidation may be possible, a later charge should reserve the right *specifying the earlier charge*, and, secondly, that if the right arises later (for instance, under the doctrine in *Pledge* v. *White* [1896] A.C. 187, *ante*, p. 1016, when both mortgages first come into the hands of one person), it may be protected, provided (i) the right was reserved in general terms by one of the charges, and (ii) application is made to have the right noted. On the other hand it is doubtful whether a note of consolidation under r. 154 is equivalent to *registration against the land affected* as required by s. 25 (3) and it may be that this subsection has no application to the doctrine of consolidation. If this be the case, consolidation occurs in the same circumstances as it would if the title were not registered. For further discussion and a statement of the present Land Registry practice, see Ruoff and Roper, Registered Conveyancing, 3rd ed., pp. 549–552.

Discharge by county court.—The county court has a statutory power to discharge or modify a mortgage of a house affected by slum clearance procedure which involves compensation under the Housing Act, 1957, Sched. 2, Pt. II (*ibid.*, Sched. 2, para. 5).

Discharge of mortgage of land and life policy.—The Council of The Law Society (*Law Society's Gazette*, vol. 55, p. 149) have pointed out the difficulties which may arise where land and a life policy are mortgaged by a single deed and, after the mortgage has been discharged, application is made for payment of moneys under the policy or the assured wishes to raise another loan on the security of the policy. In such cases the life office requires production of the mortgage deed and its discharge, and there may be difficulty if the documents have passed to a purchaser of the land. Consequently, it is advisable that the policy and the land should be charged by separate deeds. If this has not been done the mortgage and discharge should be produced to the life office as soon as the mortgage is discharged and the Council of The Law Society advise that on doing so one should ask the life office to state its future requirements so far as possible. If the common mortgage and discharge are handed over to a purchaser of the land an express right to production of them should be obtained and, if possible, an undertaking for safe custody, in case they are required later in proof of title to policy moneys.

Partial release of bank mortgages.—This subject is discussed in some detail in the *Solicitors' Journal*, vol. 97, p. 661, and in the *Law Times*, vol. 216, p. 538. The following points emerge on the form of a conveyance to which a bank becomes a party in order to release a part of the mortgaged property : (i) as such a mortgage is to secure an unspecified sum, a recital that the mortgage was made to secure a specific sum is mistaken ; (ii) if no payment is made to the bank " it is unnecessary to recite what moneys are owing or that the bank has sufficient security apart from the property sold ; " (iii) where the vendor is not an absolute owner recitals indicating that the amount owing exceeds the amount paid to the bank are essential in order to show that the vendor is justified in directing payment of part of the purchase price to the bank.

PART 6.   PRIORITY OF MORTGAGES

Priority before 1926.—According to the old law, a mortgagee who got the legal estate took precedence over all prior equitable mortgages of which he had neither express nor constructive notice when he made the advance (*Walker* v. *Linom* [1907] 2 Ch. 104 ; *Grierson* v. *National Provincial Bank of England, Ltd.* [1913] 2 Ch. 18). He also had priority over all subsequent equitable mortgages unless he had contributed by his fraud to the creation of an equitable mortgage without disclosure of the prior legal mortgage ; or by his actions had estopped himself from asserting his priority ; or had been guilty of such gross negligence as to be akin to fraud, for instance in failing to obtain the deeds (*Colyer* v. *Finch* (1856), 5 H.L. Cas. 905 ; *Berwick & Co.* v. *Price* [1905] 1 Ch. 632).

First mortgages of a legal freehold estate were usually made by conveyance of the fee simple, and so there could not normally be more than one legal mortgagee. Equitable mortgagees, between themselves, took priority in order of the date of their respective mortgages (*Taylor* v. *London and County*

Banking Co. [1901] 2 Ch. 231 ; *Perham* v. *Kempster* [1907] 1 Ch. 373) ; but an earlier equitable mortgagee would be postponed to a later one if he had been guilty of negligence, such as omission to make inquiries as to the title deeds (*Farrand* v. *Yorkshire Banking Co.* (1888), 40 Ch. D. 182).

As regards the present-day priority of mortgages created before 1926, if the mortgagee holds the deeds, he will normally have had first claim and he will retain his claim. As regards subsequent mortgages, whether legal or equitable, they were converted by the L.P.A. 1925, Sched. 1, Pt. VII, into legal terms of years, but their priority is not affected. See *post*, p. 1034. Further, s. 94 (3) of the L.P.A. 1925 provides that " nothing in this Act shall affect any priority acquired before the commencement of this Act by tacking, or in respect of further advances made without notice of a subsequent incumbrance or by arrangement with the subsequent incumbrancer." A puisne mortgage (i.e., a legal mortgage not protected by deposit of the deeds) created before 1926 may be registered as a land charge (L.C.A. 1972, s. 3 (3)), and if it is acquired under a transfer made after 1925 it must be registered within one year after the transfer, otherwise it will be void against a purchaser for value (including a mortgagee) of the land or any interest in the land (L.P.A. 1925, s. 2 (5) ; L.C.A. 1972, s. 4 (7)).

Priority after 1925.—Since 1925 there may be many legal mortgages of the same property, as well as equitable mortgages. It is obvious, therefore, that possession of the legal estate could not now form the basis of priority ; instead possession of the deeds forms that basis, whether the mortgage is legal or equitable.

This new law of priority of mortgages (so far as it applies to legal estates in land which is not registered land and which is not land within the jurisdiction of a local deeds registry) is based principally on the L.P.A. 1925, ss. 13 and 97, and the L.C.A. 1972, ss. 2 (4) and 4 (5). The relevant parts of the provisions of the L.P.A. 1925 are as follows :—

" 13. This Act shall not prejudicially affect the right or interest of any person arising out of or consequent on the possession by him of any documents relating to a legal estate in land, nor affect any question arising out of or consequent upon any omission to obtain or any other absence of possession by any person of any documents relating to a legal estate in land."

" *Priorities as between puisne mortgages*

97. Every mortgage affecting a legal estate in land made after [1925] whether legal or equitable (not being a mortgage protected by the deposit of documents relating to the legal estate affected) shall rank according to its date of registration as a land charge pursuant to the Land Charges Act, 1925 . . .".

We may first notice that the marginal note to s. 97 (which is printed above in italics) is confusing. It suggests that the operation of the section is limited to *puisne mortgages*, whereas it is not. A puisne mortgage is a *legal* mortgage not protected by possession of the deeds relating to the legal estate mortgaged (L.C.A. 1972, s. 2 (4), Class C (i)), and a legal mortgage means a mortgage by demise or sub-demise or a charge by way of legal mortgage (L.P.A. 1925, s. 205 (1) (xvi)). But the operation of s. 97 includes *equitable* mortgages affecting a legal estate (which come within the description " general equitable charges " : L.C.A. 1972, s. 2 (4), Class C (iii)).

It may be assumed that there can, in practice, be only one mortgagee who holds the deeds ; possibly one mortgagee might hold some of the deeds and another mortgagee the remainder, but this is not a likely eventuality with which we need deal (although priority would appear to depend on the basic principle that mortgages rank in the chronological order of their creation : cf. *Beddoes* v. *Shaw* [1937] Ch. 81). A mortgagee who holds the deeds does not depend for his priority on registering his mortgage ; he has no power to do so (L.C.A. 1972, s. 2 (4)). The problem then is, in what circumstances will he be affected by mortgages not protected by deposit of the deeds ? So far as subsequent mortgages are concerned there is no provision in the 1925 legislation, and it appears that a *legal* mortgagee who has a deposit of the deeds will be postponed to a subsequent mortgagee only in those special cases in which he has been guilty of such fraud, negligence or other conduct as would, before 1926, have postponed his mortgage in favour of a later one (see *ante*, p. 1018). So far as mortgages prior in time to his own are concerned, the answer is that a *legal* mortgagee who obtains the deeds will be bound by them, assuming them to have been created after 1925, only if they were registered as puisne mortgages or general equitable charges, as the case may be, at the time when the mortgage accompanied by deposit of the deeds was made (L.P.A. 1925, s. 97 ; L.C.A. 1972, s. 4 (5)).

The case of an *equitable* mortgagee by deposit is not quite so clear. Before 1926 a purchaser or mortgagee who obtained a legal estate without notice of an earlier equitable interest and who had received a reasonable excuse for non-production of the deeds obtained priority. This rule is continued by the L.P.A. 1925, s. 13. Consequently, it appears possible, although unlikely, that an equitable mortgagee may lose his priority, in favour of a later legal mortgagee, even if he holds the title deeds.

We are left, then, to consider the question of priority between themselves of two or more mortgages, whether legal or equitable, none of which is protected by deposit of the title deeds. The L.C.A. 1972, s. 4 (5), provides as follows :—

" 4.—(5) A land charge of . . . Class C . . . created or arising on or after 1st January, 1926, shall be void as against a purchaser of the land charged with it, or of any interest in such land, unless the land charge is registered in the appropriate register before the completion of the purchase."

A legal mortgage not protected by a deposit of documents relating to the legal estate affected (a puisne mortgage) is a land charge Class C (i) ; an equitable mortgage not so secured (a general equitable charge) is a land charge Class C (iii) (L.C.A. 1972, s. 2 (4)). Therefore, mortgagees holding either of these kinds of security should, to preserve priority, immediately register their security as a land charge. What, then, is the position if one or both of them fails to register or delays registration ?

If the mortgagee who was first in time had registered his mortgage before the other or others were created, then that first mortgagee has priority, because the mortgages rank according to date of registration (L.P.A. 1925, s. 97). And it is, in such circumstances, immaterial whether any of the mortgagees were legal or equitable.

The difficulty arises if the mortgage first in point of time was not registered when a mortgage second in point of time was created. (We are still considering, of course, mortgages affecting a legal estate in land, not being protected by deposit of the deeds.) If we apply the L.P.A. 1925, s. 97, we shall conclude that priority depends on priority of registration. Thus, if the earlier mortgagee (*A*) has not registered his mortgage until after registration is effected by the later mortgagee (*B*), then *B* will have priority over *A* (L.P.A. 1925, s. 97). If we apply the L.C.A. 1972, s. 4 (5), we shall come to the same conclusion, because *A's* mortgage, being unregistered, was void as against *B* (who is a " purchaser " : L.C.A. 1972, s. 17 (1)). If, however, *A* registered his mortgage *after the creation of B's mortgage but before B had effected registration* of that mortgage, we find a contradiction in the Acts. According to the L.P.A. 1925, s. 97, *A*, having registered first, will have priority. But we are met with the provision of the L.C.A. 1972, s. 4 (5), that *A's* mortgage, being unregistered at the time of *creation* of *B's* mortgage, is void against *B*. How then can *A* have priority over *B* if his mortgage is void against *B* ? The solution to the problem must await a judicial decision. The general opinion appears to be that probably priority will depend on the date of registration as mentioned in the L.P.A. 1925, s. 97, because that section deals expressly with priority of mortgages, whereas the L.C.A. 1972, s. 4 (5), deals with the avoidance of charges as against purchasers, and mortgagees are brought in only by reference to the L.C.A. 1972, s. 17 (1) (but the contrary view appears to be preferred in Megarry and Wade, Real Property, 3rd ed., p. 965 *et seq.*, where other insoluble problems of priority are also raised ; see further W. A. Lee in *Conveyancer N.S.*, vol. 32, p. 325 *et seq.*).

If both or all mortgages, not being protected by deposit of the deeds, are unregistered, then the one first in time is void against a later mortgage (L.C.A. 1972, s. 4 (5)), and so the later one has priority. Once more it is unimportant whether the mortgages are legal or equitable.

As to when *further advances* can be made by a mortgagee to rank in priority to subsequent mortgages, see below.

As to registration under the Companies Act, 1948, see *ante*, p. 633.

Priority of registered charges.—A further charge of registered land, following a first charge, may be made by use of the ordinary charge form, and it is provided by the L.R.A. 1925, s. 29, that, subject to any entry to the contrary on the register, registered charges rank according to the order in which they are entered on the register. As to possible entries to the contrary on the register, see Ruoff and Roper, Registered Conveyancing, 3rd ed., p. 547. In this connection, the effect of priority conferred by an official search should not be overlooked (Land Registration (Official Searches) Rules, 1969). As between registered and unregistered charges of registered land, the priorities are entirely governed by the fact that the unregistered ones take effect as mere minor interests which are overridden by registered dispositions for valuable consideration (L.R.A. 1925, s. 101 (2)).

"Tacking" of further advances.—Save in regard to further advances, the right to tack was abolished by the L.P.A. 1925. Before 1926 tacking arose under two different sets of circumstances. First, where a mortgagee, having made an advance on first mortgage of property and obtained a *legal* estate, afterwards made a further advance on the security of the property but without notice of an intervening mortgage executed by the mortgagor, the mortgagee was entitled to squeeze out and obtain priority over the intervening mortgage which was then necessarily *equitable*, as there could, before 1926, be only one *legal* mortgage. But if the first mortgagee, even though his mortgage was taken to cover future advances on the security of the property, had at the time of making a further advance notice of a second mortgage, he could not claim in respect of such future advance in priority to the second mortgagee (*Hopkinson* v. *Rolt* (1861), 9 H.L. Cas. 514). The principle of this decision applied, even if the first mortgage contained a covenant to make further advances (*West* v. *Williams* [1899] 1 Ch. 132) : this decision has ceased to have effect as a result of s. 94 (1) (c) of the L.P.A. 1925.

The other case before 1926 was where a third mortgagee lent money with knowledge of the existence of a first legal mortgage but without knowledge of a second mortgage, and paid off the first mortgage. In that case he was entitled to require payment of the amount due under the mortgage he had paid off as well as of the amount due on his own mortgage before anything was paid to the second mortgagee. Although it was essential that the mortgagee must have advanced the money without notice of the intervening mortgage it was not necessary that he should have been without notice at the time when he acquired the legal estate. This mode of tacking has been abolished by s. 94 (3) of the L.P.A. 1925.

Any priority obtained in either of these cases before 1926 is preserved by the L.P.A. 1925, s. 94 (3), set out below.

The post-1925 law is contained in s. 94 of the L.P.A. 1925 which, as amended by the Law of Property (Amendment) Act, 1926, is given below.

" 94.—(1) After [1925], *a prior mortgagee shall have a right to make further advances to rank in priority to subsequent mortgages* (whether legal or equitable)—

(a) *if an arrangement has been made to that effect* with the subsequent mortgagees ; or

(b) if he had *no notice of such subsequent mortgages* at the time when the further advance was made by him ; or

(c) whether or not he had such notice as aforesaid, *where the mortgage imposes an obligation on him to make such further advances.*

This subsection applies whether or not the prior mortgage was made expressly for securing further advances.

(2) In relation to the making of further advances after [1925] a mortgagee shall not be deemed to have notice of a mortgage merely by reason that it was registered as a land charge or in a local deeds registry, if it was not so registered at the time when the original mortgage was created or when the last search (if any) by or on behalf of the mortgagee was made, whichever last happened.

This subsection only applies *where the prior mortgage was made expressly for securing a current account or other further advances.*

(3) Save in regard to the making of further advances as aforesaid, the right to tack is hereby abolished :

Provided that nothing in this Act shall affect any priority acquired before [1926] by tacking, or in respect of further advances made without notice of a subsequent incumbrance or by arrangement with the subsequent incumbrancer.

(4) This section applies to mortgages of land made before or after the commencement of this Act, but not to *charges registered under the Land Registration Act*, 1925, or any enactment replaced by that Act."

" *a prior mortgagee.*"—Before 1926, although a mortgagee had not the legal estate, if he had the best right to call for it, he was, by virtue of that right, entitled to tack a further advance made without notice of any other advance. Section 94 of the L.P.A. 1925 is not limited to a first mortgagee or to a legal mortgagee but extends to any " prior " mortgagee ; in this respect the doctrine of tacking is extended.

" *if an arrangement has been made to that effect.*"—We can pass over this provision as anything can be done by arrangement.

" *no notice of such subsequent mortgages.*"—As regards further advances not made in pursuance of an obligation to make them, and not being further advances analogous to current accounts, a mortgagee may safely make them so long as he has no notice of any subsequent mortgage at the time when the further advance is made. This confirms the old law as contained in the decision of *Hopkinson* v. *Rolt*, above referred to. But there is this difference, namely, that registration as a land charge is now to be deemed actual notice (L.P.A. 1925, ss. 197, 198). This means that such a mortgagee (unless his mortgage was made *expressly* for securing a current account or other further advances, as to which, see below) must make a search every time before he makes a further advance to satisfy himself that he will not be deemed to have notice. An unregistered mortgage will not affect him unless he has actual notice of it.

" *where the mortgage imposes an obligation on him to make such further advances.*"—In this case further advances can be tacked to the original mortgage, although the mortgagee has notice, either express or implied, of a subsequent mortgage.

" *where the prior mortgage was made expressly for securing a current account or other further advances.*"—Subsection (2) was enacted principally for the protection of banks. The effect is that, where the document of security states (as all such documents do) that it is made to secure a current account, the bank may continue to make advances until it receives *express notice* of another incumbrance, and, under the provision in subs. (2), registration of such incumbrance as a land charge, or by memorial in a local deeds registry, will not be deemed for this purpose to be express notice, *provided that* (and this is important) such other incumbrance was not registered at the date of the original security to the bank, or when the last search (if any) was made.

There is difference of opinion as to whether the words " for securing a current account or other further advances " apply to the ordinary case where one person lends money to another on security of mortgage by way of investment. *Prima facie* they seem to mean " further advances " *of the same kind* as those which are made by bankers in the case of current accounts ; an example would be the case of an advance to a builder by instalments as a building progresses. That their meaning is not so restricted is argued by R. Geoffrey Rowley in the *Conveyancer N.S.*, vol. 22, p. 49.

As regards banks there is another point to be borne in mind, namely, the rule in *Clayton's Case* (1816), 1 Mer. 572. This rule as applied to banks is that, where a person keeps an account at a bank, and in the ordinary course of business pays sums to the credit of his account, the bank must appropriate such sums to liabilities in order of priority. In *Deeley* v. *Lloyds Bank* [1912]

A.C. 756, *G*, a customer, gave a mortgage of some property to the bank, and afterwards executed a second mortgage to *D*, who gave due notice thereof to the bank. *G's* account was continued as an ordinary bank account to the credit of which payments were made from time to time, with the result that the amount owing on the mortgage at the date of the notice became discharged. It was held that the rule in *Clayton's Case* applied, and that the second mortgagee became entitled on the bankruptcy of *G* to priority over the bank's mortgage. See also the Irish case of *Re Chute's Estate* [1914] 1 Ir. R. 180. This was before 1926. But, if the mortgage to the bank in circumstances similar to those in *Deeley* v. *Lloyds Bank* had been made after 1925, and imposed *an obligation* to make further advances, as mentioned in s. 94 (1) (*c*), above set out, then, to the extent of the amount agreed to be further advanced, the bank's mortgage would now have priority.

The second kind of tacking which was referred to *ante*, p. 1021, occurred where, before 1926, a third mortgagee had lent money with the knowledge of the existence of a first legal mortgage, but without knowledge of the second mortgage, and paid off the first mortgage, in which case he was entitled to " tack." This method of tacking was abolished by subs. (3) above.

It should be noted that the L.P.A. 1925, s. 94, gives further advances priority only to subsequent *mortgages*. There may, however, be other matters registered after the date of a mortgage, but before the date of a further advance, for instance, a receiving order in bankruptcy, or an estate contract. To take the example of an estate contract, the mortgagee would be deemed to make the further advance with notice of it (L.P.A. 1925, s. 198 (1)), and so it would appear that he could be compelled to release his security in favour of the purchaser on receiving the amount of the original advance without including the whole of the further advance, if by chance the purchase price was not sufficient to repay both. Consequently, it would appear that there is a slight risk in not searching before making a further advance even though the original mortgage was made expressly for securing a current account or other further advances. See further R. Geoffrey Rowley in the *Conveyancer N.S.*, vol. 22, at p. 56.

" *charges registered under the Land Registration Act*, 1925."—In the case of registered land, the L.P.A. 1925, s. 94, does not apply to registered charges (subs. (4)) and special rules are made by the L.R.A. 1925, s. 30, with regard to further advances. If there is an obligation in the charge to make further advances, and that obligation is entered on the register, further advances will be protected as against a later registered charge (L.R.A. 1925, s. 30 (3), added by the Law of Property (Amendment) Act, 1926, s. 5). Where no obligation to make further advances is noted but the registered charge was made for securing further advances, the registrar must, before making any entry on the register which would prejudicially affect the priority of any further advance, give notice to the proprietor of the registered charge by registered post of the intended entry. The proprietor of the charge will not, in respect of any further advance, be affected by such entry, unless the advance is made after the date when the notice ought to have been received in due course of post (L.R.A. 1925, s. 30 (1)). A proprietor who suffers any loss in relation to a further charge by failure on the part of the registrar or the Post Office in reference to any notice is entitled to be indemnified (L.R.A. 1925, s. 30 (2)). See further Ruoff and Roper, Registered Conveyancing, 3rd ed., pp. 547–549.

PART 7. EQUITABLE MORTGAGES

A. GENERALLY

Nature and form of equitable mortgages.—Before 1926 a first mortgage of a legal estate in fee simple was made by a conveyance of that estate to the mortgagee subject to a proviso for reconveyance on repayment. Consequently, there could be *only one legal mortgage ;* second and subsequent mortgages were necessarily equitable. After 1925, as we have seen, mortgages by conveyance of the fee simple are prohibited ; there can, however, now be any number of legal mortgages of the same land by demise or charge. On the other hand, before 1926 a mortgage of a reversionary interest in settled land could be a legal mortgage. But now, the legal estate would be in the tenant for life, and the mortgage on the reversion will only be an equitable mortgage. The S.L.A. 1925, Sched. 2, para. 1 (6), provided for conversion of legal estates under pre-1926 settlements into equitable interests, but preserved any legal estate of a mortgagee.

An equitable mortgage or charge may be effected by the mere deposit of the deeds relating to the legal estate, or of the material deeds providing that such deeds show the present title to the land, and there is evidence of the purpose for which they were deposited, as in such a case the deposit amounts to part performance (*Dixon* v. *Muckleston* (1872), L.R. 8 Ch. 155 ; see generally Megarry and Wade, Real Property, 3rd ed., p. 893 *et seq.*). If there is no deposit of deeds to constitute part performance, then there must be evidence in writing signed by the party to be charged so as to comply with s. 40 of the L.P.A. 1925 (as to which, see *ante*, p. 40).

The writing need not be made at the time of the agreement and where the writing shows that the intention of the parties was that a security should be created, it is not necessary that the document should contain words of charge (*Cradock* v. *Scottish Provident Institution* (1894), 70 L.T. 718). In modern practice, equitable mortgages unsupported by any writing are infrequently encountered, even though the title deeds are deposited (see below). Instead the deposit will usually be accompanied by a memorandum under seal defining the position of the parties and reinforcing the lender's security by including, e.g., an undertaking to execute a legal mortgage, a declaration of trusteeship and power to appoint new trustees, and even a power of attorney (see *Re White Rose Cottage* [1965] Ch. 940). In this form, of course, the equitable mortgage is at least as formal as a proper legal mortgage or charge. Nonetheless it is still often used, in particular for temporary loans by bankers.

As regards a security formed by a deposit of documents without any writing, parol evidence will be allowed to prove the terms of the security (*Russel* v. *Russel* (1783), 1 Bro. C.C. 269). It was said by Lord Macnaghten in *Bank of New South Wales* v. *O'Connor* (1889), 14 App. Cas. 273, at p. 282, that " it is a well-established rule of equity that a deposit of a document of title without either writing or word of mouth will create in equity a charge upon the property to which the document relates to the extent of the interest of the person who makes the deposit. In the absence of consent that charge can only be displaced by actual payment of the amount secured." But there must be something to connect the deposit with the advance. For, as was said by Lord Selborne in *Dixon* v. *Muckleston* (1872), L.R. 8 Ch. 155, at p. 162, " the mere possession of deeds, without evidence of the contract

33

upon which the possession originated, or at least of the manner in which that possession originated, so that you may infer a contract, will not be enough to create an equitable security."

In *Fullerton* v. *Provincial Bank of Ireland* [1903] A.C. 309, *S* was being pressed by the bank to give security for his overdraft. He wrote to the bank that he was buying some property and that as soon as the matter was completed he would lodge the deeds with the bank. *S* in due course kept his promise and lodged the deeds with the bank, but there was no memorandum at the date of the deposit. It was held that the letter from *S* to the bank amounted to an agreement to execute a legal mortgage. But in *Re Beetham* (1887), 18 Q.B.D. 766, a man made an oral promise to his bankers to give them, when required, security for his debt. He was entitled to a reversionary interest in one-fifth of a farm subject to the life interest of his mother. The mother died, and the brother of the debtor, who was the manager of the bank, became possessed of the deeds of the farm in his private capacity. This brother then told the debtor that he would consider himself as trustee of the deeds for the bank, so far as they affected the one-fifth share, to secure the debt owing to the bank, and the debtor agreed. On the bankruptcy of the debtor, it was held that the bank had not a valid equitable mortgage of the bankrupt's share in the farm, on the ground that there was no sufficient memorandum in writing to satisfy the Statute of Frauds, nor was there part performance of the oral promise to give security.

An equitable *mortgage* exists where the mortgagor has agreed to create a legal mortgage, and that agreement is evidenced by a sufficient memorandum or by an act of part performance, or where the title deeds have been deposited, in which case the deposit is regarded as implying an agreement to execute a legal mortgage (*Carter* v. *Wake* (1877), 4 Ch. D. 605). An equitable *charge* exists where there is no such agreement to execute a legal mortgage but a mere written agreement that property is to become security for performance of an obligation (*London County and Westminster Bank, Ltd.* v. *Tompkins* [1918] 1 K.B. 515). The distinction is important in dealing with the remedies available to the parties. Where there is an express or implied promise to execute a legal mortgage an action for specific performance can be brought and the court can make an order vesting in the mortgagee a legal term of years under which he can realise his security, or he can apply to the court for an order for foreclosure (see further at p. 1029). But in the case of a mere charge on the land the proper remedy would not be an action for specific performance, because in such a charge there is no express or implied agreement to execute a legal mortgage. The proper remedy would be an order for the sale or mortgage of the property to raise the money to pay off the security (*Matthews* v. *Goodday* (1861), 31 L.J. Ch. 282).

Since an equitable mortgage by deposit (or not) necessarily contains or implies an agreement to create a legal mortgage it is arguable that it is an estate contract within the L.C.A. 1972, s. 2 (4), Class C (iv), and so void against a purchaser of a legal estate for money or money's worth unless registered. Of this it is said in Megarry and Wade, Real Property, 3rd ed., at p. 964 : " This argument is logically strong, but its weakness is that it would upset the scheme of the Act [i.e., of the L.P.A. 1925 that deposit of documents should be an alternative to registration] and destroy the security of many equitable mortgages. For these reasons it is probable that the courts would resist it." In practice where the agreement to execute a legal mortgage is merely implied registration as an estate contract is often not effected. It would appear that failure to register would only avoid the contract to create the legal estate, and the mortgagee would still have the remedies of an equitable chargee (*Pryce* v. *Bury* (1853), 2 Drew. 41). However, there is the further point that an equitable mortgagee or chargee who is not protected by registration under the L.C.A. 1972 but only by deposit of documents may well lose priority as against a lessee by virtue of s. 44 (5) of the L.P.A. 1925 (see *Conveyancer N.S.*, vol. 8, p. 145 *et seq.*). Consequently, the safest course clearly is to effect registration in all cases (see L.P.A. 1925, s. 198 (1), and *White* v. *Bijou Mansions, Ltd.* [1937] Ch. 610, 619).

Conversely it must be observed that estate contracts and Class D land charges will *not* be void for non-registration as against an equitable mortgagee since he is not a purchaser of a legal estate (*McCarthy & Stone, Ltd.* v. *Julian S. Hodge Co., Ltd.* [1971] 1 W.L.R. 1547).

Transitional provisions affecting equitable mortgages.—The transitional provisions contained in Pts. VII and VIII of Sched. 1 to the L.P.A. 1925 dealt with *post*, p. 1033 *et seq.*, only apply where the mortgage conveyed to the mortgagee *an estate* in the land for a fee simple or term of years absolute. Such estate might have been a legal or equitable estate, provided it was an estate. These provisions did not apply to an equitable mortgage created by a mere deposit of deeds, or by a writing agreeing to execute a legal mortgage, or an agreement in which such an agreement would be implied, or to a mere charge on the land (L.P.A. 1925, Sched. 1, Pt. II, para. 6 (*a*); *ibid.*, Pt. II, para. 7 (*j*)).

As regards an equitable security created by a deposit of deeds, it is expressly provided by s. 13 of the L.P.A. 1925 that " this Act shall not prejudicially affect the right or interest of any person arising out of or consequent on the possession by him of any documents relating to a legal estate in land." Indeed, after 1925, the possession of the deeds puts the mortgagee in a better position than he was in before 1926. For, in the absence of gross negligence, which would have to amount almost to fraud, he gets priority to both legal and equitable mortgagees who have not got the deeds. See further *ante*, pp. 1018, 1019. But it is thought that s. 13 will not prevail over the specific provision of s. 44 (5) protecting lessees and abolishing the rule in *Patman* v. *Harland* (1881), 17 Ch. D. 353 (see *ante*, p. 143).

Registered land.—The proprietor of any registered land or charge may, subject to overriding interests, to any entry to the contrary on the register, and to any interests registered or protected on the register, create a lien on the registered land or charge by deposit of the land certificate or charge certificate, and such a lien is (subject as aforesaid) equivalent to that created in the case of unregistered land by the deposit of documents of title or of the mortgage deed by an owner entitled for his own benefit to the registered estate or a mortgagee beneficially entitled to the mortgage, as the case may be (L.R.A. 1925, s. 66). Also, of course, such deposit may be accompanied by writing as in unregistered conveyancing.

The methods of protection available to an equitable mortgagee or chargee of registered land were considered by the Court of Appeal in *Re White Rose Cottage* [1965] Ch. 940, where there was both a deposit of the land certificate and a memorandum of equitable charge to a bank under seal. It emerges from the judgment of Lord Denning, M.R., that the bank could *not* register the charge as a registered charge as this required a legal charge (referring to L.R.A. 1925, ss. 25 to 36), but the bank could protect it (1) by applying for registration of a *notice* of the charge as a land charge (referring to L.R.A. 1925, ss. 48 (1), 49 (1) (*c*), 64 (1)) ; or (2) by lodging a *caution* (under L.R.A. 1925, ss. 54, 59 (2)) ; or (3) by giving a *notice of deposit* of the land certificate, which operates as a caution (i.e., under L.R.R. 1925, r. 239). In fact method (3) had been adopted and, notwithstanding that the memorandum and not the deposit created the charge (so that method (1) was regarded as the more correct), the entry on the register was sufficient to preserve priority. See further, however, the notes relating to *Barclays Bank, Ltd.* v. *Taylor* [1973] 1 All E.R. 752, *ante*, p. 975.

A form of notice of deposit is available (Form 85A) ; it is desirable, but not essential, to lodge the land charge certificate with it. Form 85B may be used where the borrower is applying for first registration and the land certificate has not yet been issued, and Form 85c where the borrower has just acquired the property and that certificate has not yet been issued.

The notice may be withdrawn by application in Form 86 (a copy of which is printed on the back of the duplicate Form 85A) which must be accompanied by Form A.4 and the land or charge certificate. Form 85 may be signed by the lender's solicitor, but Form 86 must be signed by the lender personally.

Incidentally, it may be observed that apparently the entry of a notice of deposit on the register actually precludes the subsequent registration of a legal charge as a registered charge until the notice has been withdrawn (this proposition was doubted in the *Conveyancer N.S.*, vol. 26, p. 169, but the objections are answered, in effect, in Ruoff & Roper, Registered Conveyancing, 3rd ed., at pp. 586–588).

Equitable mortgage with deposit of deeds cannot be overreached.— This is another instance of the favour given by the 1925 legislation to a person holding the deeds. Such an equitable mortgage cannot even be overreached under the machinery provided by s. 2 (2) of the L.P.A. 1925 or s. 21 of the S.L.A. 1925. Where the legal estate is subject to a trust for sale and the trustees have been approved or appointed by the court, they can, on a sale, by virtue of s. 2 (2) of the L.P.A. 1925 overreach many equitable interests and powers. An estate owner can also under s. 21 of the S.L.A. 1925, by creating the necessary machinery, overreach most equitable interests and powers. But it is specially provided by s. 2 (3) (i) of the L.P.A. 1925 and by s. 21 (2) (i) of the S.L.A. 1925 that " Any equitable interest protected by a deposit of documents relating to the legal estate affected " is excepted from these provisions, in other words, that, *inter alia*, an equitable mortgage protected by the possession of the deeds cannot be overreached under the above provisions. There is no injustice in this, because it is clearly the duty of a purchaser to inquire as to the custody of the deeds, and such an inquiry would inform him of the true position. See further, *ante*, p. 178.

Receipt on discharge of an equitable charge.—Section 115 (1) of the L.P.A. 1925 (*ante*, p. 1007) does not apply to equitable charges not passing any estate, such as are often given to banks, for instance, by a mere deposit of deeds. The words of the section " executed by the chargee by way of legal mortgage or the person in whom the mortgaged *property is vested* " do not apply when there is no estate vested in the mortgagee. A simple receipt is sufficient to show that the charge has ceased.

Notice of repayment of equitable charge.—An equitable chargee, by deposit of title deeds, is not entitled to six months' notice of the chargor's intention to pay off the mortgage, but only to a reasonable time to enable him to look up the deeds (*Fitzgerald's Trustee* v. *Mellersh* [1892] 1 Ch. 385). But the chargor is entitled to six months' notice before he can be required to pay off the mortgage (*Parker* v. *Housefield* (1834), 2 Myl. & K. 419).

Priorities between mortgagees of an equitable estate in land.— Mortgages of an equitable interest not affecting a legal estate, that is, equitable mortgages or charges of an interest arising under a trust for sale or settlement, cannot be registered as land charges (L.C.A. 1972, s. 2 (4), Class C (iii)). The reason is that the mortgagee will be sufficiently protected by the fact that all capital money has to be paid to two trustees or to a trust corporation. The priority between mortgages of such an equitable interest is governed by the rule in *Dearle* v. *Hall* (1828), 3 Russ. 1, as extended by the L.P.A. 1925, s. 137 (1), to equitable interests in real and leasehold property, or, in the case of registered land, by the minor interests index (L.R.R. 1925, rr. 11, 229). Consequently, the mortgagee who first gives notice of his mortgage to the trustees or lodges a priority caution gets priority.

B. REMEDIES OF EQUITABLE MORTGAGEE

Where the security takes the form merely of an equitable charge and there is no agreement to create a legal mortgage, either express, or implied from a deposit of the title deeds (*Backhouse* v. *Charlton* (1878), 8 Ch. D. 444 ; *Carter* v. *Wake* (1877), 4 Ch. D. 605), then the remedies of the chargee are to sue the mortgagor personally or to apply to the court for an order for sale of the property (*Re Owen* [1894] 3 Ch. 220). In practice there is almost invariably an agreement to create a legal mortgage, and so the remedies of an equitable mortgagee having the benefit of such an agreement will be discussed more fully.

An equitable mortgagee may not claim rent payable under a tenancy binding on him as his interest in the reversion is equitable only (*Vacuum Oil Co., Ltd.* v. *Ellis* [1914] 1 K.B. 693) ; his remedy is to appoint a receiver or to apply to the court for an appointment. In the past the general opinion has been that if the mortgagor is in possession an equitable mortgagee may not take possession without an order of the court ; see, for instance, *Barclays Bank, Ltd.* v. *Bird* [1954] Ch. 274. H. W. R. Wade has drawn attention in the *Law Quarterly Review*, vol. 71, p. 204 *et seq.*, to the weakness of the authorities quoted in support of this opinion and argued convincingly that an equitable mortgagee may take possession against the mortgagor without an order of the court (see also Megarry and Wade, Real Property, 3rd ed., p. 901 *et seq.*).

Such a mortgagee, in addition to a personal action against the mortgagor, may have one or more of the following remedies, each of which will be discussed separately :—

   (i) Foreclosure.

   (ii) Sale.

   (iii) Appointment of receiver.

Foreclosure.—Foreclosure proceedings may be taken wherever there is an express or implied agreement to create a legal mortgage. In such proceedings the foreclosure decree will declare that in default of payment the mortgagor is trustee of the legal estate for the mortgagee and that he must convey that estate to the mortgagee (*Marshall* v. *Shrewsbury* (1875),

L.R. 10 Ch. 250). If the mortgagor then neglects to convey the property for twenty-eight days after request he is a trustee who has neglected to convey within the meaning of the T.A. 1925, s. 44 (vi), and the court may make a vesting order (*Jones* v. *Davies* [1940] W.N. 174).

Sale.—In practice, it is not often that an equitable mortgage by deposit of deeds is left to depend upon an oral or implied agreement that the mortgagor shall execute a legal mortgage when called on to do so. The proper and usual way is to have an agreement under seal. The advantage of the agreement's being under seal is that there will be implied in it the statutory power of sale given to mortgagees by s. 101 (1) (i) and s. 104 (1) of the L.P.A. 1925. This power enables a mortgagee, where the mortgage is made by deed, and the mortgage money has become due, to sell *the property the subject of the mortgage*. The subject of the mortgage in this case has long been regarded as an equitable interest in the land so that the statutory power would not enable the mortgagee to convey the legal estate (*Re Hodson and Howes Contract* (1887), 35 Ch. D. 668). Consequently it was and is the practice for the instrument of charge to contain a *power of attorney* by virtue of which the mortgagee can sell and convey to a purchaser the legal estate in the mortgaged property without first going through the form of calling for the execution by the mortgagor of a legal mortgage (*per* Harman, L.J., in *Re White Rose Cottage* [1965] Ch. 940, at p. 956). However, it is to be observed that in this last-mentioned case Lord Denning, M.R., went further and expressed the view that s. 104 (1) of the L.P.A. 1925 even without a power of attorney would be sufficient, saying : " The subject of the [equitable] mortgage here was the property itself, both the legal and equitable estate in it and I see no reason why a mortgagee, exercising his power of sale, should not be able to convey the legal estate " (he added that he did not regard *Re Hodson and Howes, ante,* as an authority on the different wording in the present Act). It is doubted whether s. 104 (1) can properly have such an extended effect having regard to the express provision in ss. 88 and 89 of the L.P.A. 1925, which must be read with s. 104, that conveyances by *legal* mortgagees vest in the purchaser the legal estate of the mortgagor. Clearly therefore the better practice remains for equitable mortgagees to continue to take, and convey in exercise of, the usual power of attorney. In doing so, it is important that the mortgagee and his purchaser avoid the pitfall illustrated in *Re White Rose Cottage, ante.* There the conveyance in form purported to be a sale by the mortgagor (albeit by its attorney) and a release by the mortgagee with the result that the purchaser took only that title which the mortgagor could convey, i.e., the legal estate freed from the mortgage but subject to certain subsequent equitable charges which were protected by cautions on the register. This need not cause difficulty in the future if the form adopted accords also with the substance of the transaction, namely, a conveyance on sale of the legal estate by the mortgagee in exercise of his powers, statutory or by attorney, as mortgagee. See further, and as to the Powers of Attorney Act, 1971, *ante,* p. 239 *et seq.*

Another way to enable an equitable mortgagee whose security is under seal, when the mortgage money has become due, to pass the legal estate, is that employed in *London & County Banking Co., Ltd.* v. *Goddard* [1897] 1 Ch. 642. There, the title deeds were deposited with a bank to secure an overdraft. The memorandum of deposit contained a declaration that the customer would stand possessed of his estate in the property *in trust* for the bank, and would convey it as they should direct, and that it should be lawful for the bank to remove him from being a trustee and to appoint new trustees and thereupon to make a declaration vesting all his estate in the new trustees. The bank afterwards executed a deed appointing trustees, containing a declaration that the legal estate in the mortgaged premises should vest in them, and it was held that the vesting declaration was effectual to pass to the new trustees the legal estate. See now T.A. 1925, s. 40, mentioned *ante*, p. 796.

As to whether further advances can be recovered under an equitable mortgage, it would seem that parol evidence will be admissible to prove that at the time when the deeds were deposited or the advance agreed to be made, it was agreed that the equitable mortgage created by such deposit should cover not only the original advance but further advances (*Ex parte Kensington* (1813), 2 Ves. & B. 79).

If there is no agreement under seal, and as a result the mortgagee has no statutory power of sale, a sale can be ordered by the court. Provision to this effect is made in the following subsections of s. 91 of the L.P.A. 1925 :—

" 91.—(1) Any person entitled to redeem *mortgaged property* may have a judgment or order for sale instead of for redemption in an action brought by him either for redemption alone, or for sale alone, or for sale or redemption in the alternative.

(2) In any action, whether for foreclosure, or for redemption, or for sale, or for the raising and payment in any manner of mortgage money, the court, on the request of the mortgagee, or of any person interested either in the mortgage money or in the right of redemption, and, notwithstanding that—

(a) any other person dissents ; or

(b) the mortgagee or any person so interested does not appear in the action ;

and without allowing any time for redemption or for payment of any mortgage money, may direct a sale of the mortgaged property, on such terms as it thinks fit, including the deposit in court of a reasonable sum fixed by the court to meet the expenses of sale and to secure performance of the terms.

(3) But, in an action brought by a person interested in the right of redemption and seeking a sale, the court may, on the application of any defendant, direct the plaintiff to give such security for costs as the court thinks fit, and may give the conduct of the sale to any defendant, and may give such directions as it thinks fit respecting the costs of the defendants or any of them.

(4) In any case within this section the court may, if it thinks fit, direct a sale without previously determining the priorities of incumbrancers."

" *mortgaged property.*"—This phrase includes the estate or interest which a mortgagee would have had power to convey if the statutory power of sale were applicable (L.P.A. 1925, s. 91 (6)).

For the purposes of s. 91 the court may, in favour of a purchaser, make a vesting order conveying the mortgaged property, subject or not to any incumbrance ; *or, in the case of an equitable mortgage, may create and vest a mortgage term in the mortgagee to enable him to carry out the sale as if the mortgage had been made by deed by way of legal mortgage* (*ibid.*, s. 91 (7)). In the case of registered land, the order should contain a direction to the applicant to produce it to the registrar for the necessary alteration in the register to be made (L.R.A. 1925, s. 47 ; L.R.R. 1925, r. 30 ; Practice Note [1932] W.N. 6).

There is also an express power in the L.P.A. 1925, s. 90, enabling the court to confer power on an equitable mortgagee to carry out a sale in like manner as if the mortgage had been created by deed by way of legal mortgage pursuant to the L.P.A. 1925.

Appointment of receiver.—A mortgagee, including an equitable mortgagee, when the mortgage is made *by deed* has power, when the mortgage money has become due, to appoint a receiver of the income of the mortgaged property (L.P.A. 1925, s. 101 (1) (iii)). If the mortgage is not by deed, application must be made to the court for an appointment.

Remedies where the interest charged was itself equitable.—In dealing with the above-mentioned remedies it has been assumed that the mortgagor or chargor was himself entitled to a legal estate, but an equitable charge may be created on the security of an equitable interest, for instance, an interest arising under a strict settlement or a trust for sale.

Before 1926 a mortgagee of a reversion in settled land, assuming that the limitations were legal, held a legal estate in remainder, and on the death of the tenant for life his estate became a legal estate in possession, and he could exercise his power of sale and convey the legal estate to a purchaser. The mortgagee ran the risk that the tenant for life might sell the land under his statutory power (*Re Davies & Kent's Contract* [1910] 2 Ch. 35), and in that case his security would have been transferred to the capital moneys in the hands of the trustees. But since 1925 all this has been changed. The legal estate is in the tenant for life, and the mortgage on the reversion can only be equitable. Since it affects an interest which arises under a settlement, it cannot be registered as a land charge (L.C.A. 1972, s. 2 (4), Class C (iii)), but it can be protected by notice to the trustees under s. 137 of the L.P.A. 1925. When the tenant for life dies the land may have ceased to be settled land under *Re Bridgett and Hayes' Contract* [1928] Ch. 163. Section 3 (1) (*c*) of the L.P.A. 1925 provides that where the legal estate is neither settled land nor vested in trustees for sale, the estate owner will be bound to give effect to the equitable mortgages of which he has notice according to their respective priorities. There is nothing, therefore, to prevent the equitable mortgagees requiring the personal representatives of the tenant for life in whom the legal estate will be vested to create a legal term to secure the amount owing. In the meantime, and until this has been done, it will be wise for the mortgagee to register his security as a land charge.

If an equitable charge affects the whole settled estate, then effect can be given to it under s. 16 of the S.L.A. 1925 which provides that, whether it was created before or after the date of any vesting instrument affecting the legal estate, it is enforceable against the estate owner in whom the settled land is vested (but in the case of personal representatives without prejudice to their rights and powers for purposes of administration) in manner following :—

" Where . . . the settled land is subject to any equitable charge for securing money actually raised and affecting the whole estate the subject of the settlement, the estate owner shall be bound, if so requested in writing, to create such legal estate or charge by way of legal mortgage as may be required for raising the money or giving effect to the equitable charge " (S.L.A. 1925, s. 16 (1) (iii) (*b*)).

Then follows a proviso that so long as the settlement remains subsisting such legal estate or charge so created is to take effect subject to any equitable charges which have priority to the interests of the persons by or on behalf of whom the money is required to be raised or legal effect is required to be given to the equitable charge, unless, of course, the persons entitled to the prior charges consent in writing to their being postponed. But as regards a purchaser the legal estate or charge will take effect in priority to all the trusts of the settlement except those to which it is expressly made subject.

There are also general provisions in subss. (4), (6) and (7) of s. 16 to the effect that *if the equitable mortgage ought to have priority* over the settlement the mortgagee may give notice to the estate owner requesting that effect may be given to his equitable mortgage by the creation of a legal mortgage in his favour. If the estate owner refuses or neglects for one month to create such a legal mortgage, or if for any other reason the court is satisfied that the transaction cannot be otherwise effected, the court may, on the application of the person interested, make a vesting order creating the requisite legal estate. There is also provision that if a question arises or a doubt is entertained whether a legal estate ought to be created, an application may be made to the court for directions.

An equitable mortgage of a life interest in settled land may still be effected. The tenant for life is not thereby prevented from exercising his powers of disposition under the S.L.A. 1925, but the mortgage should provide that, except with the consent of the mortgagee, capital moneys arising should be invested in trustee securities (S.L.A. 1925, s. 104 (4), proviso (b)). On the making of such a mortgage the title deeds relating to the legal estate may not be handed over; see *ante*, p. 651. Provided that the assignment of the equitable life interest is such that a legal estate would have passed before 1926, the mortgagee will have all the remedies he would have had if his interest had been legal, for instance, he will be able to take proceedings against tenants (S.L.A. 1925, s. 111). See further, an article by A. H. Withers in the *Law Times*, vol. 215, p. 258.

If the legal estate is vested in trustees for sale a mortgage of an equitable interest arising under the trust for sale will be protected by notice given to the trustees for sale (L.P.A. 1925, s. 137 (1)), or by entry of a priority caution or inhibition in the minor interests index (L.R.A. 1925, s. 102 (2) ; L.R.R. 1925, r. 229). If the mortgage was made by all persons entitled to the proceeds of sale the mortgagee would be entitled to call on the trustees for sale to give effect to it by means of a legal mortgage (L.P.A. 1925, s. 3 (2)). See also L.P.A. 1925, s. 3 (5).

Where the legal estate is neither settled land nor vested in trustees for sale, the estate owner will be bound to give effect to the equitable mortgages of which he has notice according to their respective priorities (*ibid.*, s. 3 (1) (c)).

PART 8.   TRANSITIONAL PROVISIONS

First mortgages of freehold land.—The provisions affecting mortgages existing on 31st December, 1925, are contained in Sched. 1, Pt. VII, to the L.P.A. 1925 as extended by para. 6 of Pt. II of Sched. 1 to the same Act. The general effect is that all land which immediately before 1926 was vested in a first or only mortgagee for either a legal or an equitable *estate* in fee simple in possession, and *in respect of which a right of redemption was then subsisting*, vested, on 1st January, 1926, in such mortgagee for a term of 3,000 years subject to a proviso for cesser corresponding to the right of redemption then subsisting. The legal or equitable estate in fee simple which was then vested in the mortgagee vested in the mortgagor or tenant for life, statutory owner, trustee for sale, personal representative or other person of full age who, if all money owing on the security had been then discharged, would have been entitled to have the fee simple conveyed to him, but subject, of course, to the mortgage term created by the Act and the money thereby secured.

This applied to land enfranchised by statute as well as to land which was freehold before 1926 (L.P.A. 1925, Sched. 1, Pt. VII, para. 5). The above rules also applied to mortgages made by way of trust for sale (*ibid.*). The point here is that this brought in trust deeds to secure debentures.

It will be noted that a mortgagee got a term of years, and therefore a legal estate, by the automatic effect of the L.P.A. 1925 *if he had an estate in the land*, that is, either a legal or an equitable estate in fee simple. If he had no estate, for instance if his security consisted of a deposit of deeds, with or without an agreement to execute a legal mortgage, or only a charge, then he got no term. This is brought out very definitely by para. 6 of Pt. II of Sched. 1 to the L.P.A. 1925 which states that—" (*a*) Where at the commencement of this Act land is subject to a mortgage (*not being an equitable charge unsecured by any estate*), the legal estate affected shall vest in accordance with the provisions relating to mortgages contained in this Schedule." But a mere holder of the deeds, although he had no estate, did not lose any advantage he had before 1926 by reason of such holding, and he need not even register his security as a land charge to keep his protection.

The above provisions applied only where a right of redemption was then subsisting. Therefore, if the fee simple was vested in the mortgagee free from redemption because it was barred under the Statutes of Limitation, or extinguished by a foreclosure order, the estate remained unaffected.

Subsequent mortgages of freehold land.—As regards second and subsequent mortgages of freehold land, it is provided by the L.P.A. 1925, Sched. 1, Pt. VII, para. 2, that all land which immediately before 1926 was vested in a second or subsequent mortgagee for an estate in fee simple in possession, whether legal or equitable, should vest, on 1st January, 1926, in the second or subsequent mortgagee for a term one day longer than the term vested in the first or other mortgagee whose security ranked immediately before that of such second or subsequent mortgagee, without impeachment for waste, but subject to the term or terms vested in such first or other prior mortgagee and to a proviso for cesser on redemption corresponding to the right of redemption then subsisting. And by para. 3 of the same Part it is provided that the estate in fee simple which before 1926 was vested in such mortgagee should vest on 1st January, 1926, in the mortgagor or tenant for life, statutory owner, trustee for sale, personal representative, or other person of full age who would have been entitled to have the fee simple conveyed to him if all moneys then due had been paid, but subject to the mortgage term created by the Act and all money thereby secured.

If a sub-mortgage by conveyance of the fee simple was subsisting on 31st December, 1925, the principal mortgagee took the principal term created by para. 1 or 2 (as the case might require) and the sub-mortgagee took a derivative term less by one day than the term created, without impeachment of waste, and subject to a provision for cesser on redemption (L.P.A. 1925, Sched. 1, Pt. VII, para. 4).

One result of the above rules was that a second and subsequent mortgagee who before 1926 had only an equitable estate got a legal estate ; but it is provided by para. 6 of Pt. VII of Sched. 1 to the L.P.A. 1925 that such a mortgage which is not protected, either by a deposit of documents of title relating to the legal estate *or by registration as a land charge*, will not, as against a purchaser in good faith without notice thereof, obtain any benefit by reason of being converted into a legal mortgage by this Schedule, but will, in favour of such purchaser, be deemed to remain an equitable interest. This paragraph does not apply to mortgages or charges registered or protected under the L.R.A. 1925, or formerly to mortgages or charges registered in a Yorkshire deeds register, or in the Middlesex deeds register (*ibid.*). The power to register such a second or subsequent mortgage created before 1926 is now given by the L.C.A. 1972, s. 3 (3), which provides that " a puisne mortgage created before 1st January, 1926, may be registered as a land charge before any transfer of the mortgage is made."

But if such puisne mortgagee should not have registered his mortgage as a land charge it is absolutely essential that it should be registered as a land charge under s. 2 (4), Class C (i), of the L.C.A. 1972, within a year after the first transfer made after 1926, for it is expressly provided by s. 4 (7) of the L.C.A. 1972 that after the expiration of one year from the first conveyance, occurring after 1st January, 1926, of a land charge of this nature created before 1st January, 1926, the person entitled thereto shall not be entitled to enforce or recover the land charge as against a purchaser of the land charged therewith, or of any interest in the land, unless the land charge is registered in the appropriate register before the completion of the purchase.

The creation of mortgages for a term of years was entirely automatic, but a mortgagee can, if he so desires, change his mortgage into " a charge by way of legal mortgage," by signing a declaration in writing to that effect. In that case the mortgage term would be extinguished in the inheritance or in the head term, as the case might be, and the mortgagee would have the same protection, powers and remedies as if the mortgage term or sub-term had remained subsisting (L.P.A. 1925, s. 87 (2)).

It is expressly provided by para. 7 of Pt. VII of Sched. 1 that this change from a fee simple estate to a term of years is not to affect priorities or the right of any mortgagee to retain possession of documents or his title to or rights over any fixtures or chattels personal comprised in the mortgage.

Mortgages of leaseholds.—The provisions of the L.P.A. 1925 as to mortgages of leaseholds existing on 31st December, 1925, are contained in Pt. VIII of Sched. 1 to the L.P.A. 1925, as extended by para. 6 of Pt. II of the same Schedule. All leasehold land which was on 31st December, 1925, vested in a first or only mortgagee *by way of assignment* of a term of years absolute, and in respect *of which a right of redemption was subsisting*, vested on 1st January, 1926, in him for a term equal to the term assigned by the mortgage, less the last ten days thereof, subject to a provision for cesser on redemption (*ibid.*, paras. 1 and 8).

Further, all leasehold land which was on 31st December, 1925, vested in a second or subsequent mortgagee by way of assignment of a term of years absolute (whether legal or equitable), vested on 1st January, 1926, in such mortgagee for a term one day longer than the term vested in the first or other mortgagee whose security ranked immediately before that of such mortgagee if the length of the last-mentioned term permitted, and in any case for a term less by one day at least than the term assigned by the mortgage, but subject to the term or terms vested in such first or other prior mortgagee, and subject to a provision for cesser on redemption (*ibid.*, para. 2).

The term of years absolute which was assigned by the mortgage vested on 1st January, 1926, in the mortgagor or tenant for life, statutory owner, trustee for sale, personal representative, or other person of full age, who, if all the money owing on the security of the mortgage and all other mortgages or charges, if any, had been discharged at the commencement of the Act, would have been entitled to have the term assigned or surrendered to him, but subject to any derivative mortgage term created by Pt. VIII of the Schedule or otherwise and to the money thereby secured (*ibid.*, para. 3).

If a sub-mortgage by assignment of a term was subsisting immediately before 1926, the principal mortgagee took the principal derivative term created by para. 1 or 2 of Pt. VIII of the Schedule or the derivative term created by his mortgage (as the case required), and the sub-mortgagee took a derivative term less by one day than the term so vested in the principal mortgagee, subject to a provision for cesser on redemption (*ibid.*, para. 4).

Part VIII also contains paragraphs similar to paras. 5 (except as to enfranchisement), 6 and 7 of Pt. VII given *ante*, pp. 1034, 1035, and the observations made in those pages equally apply to mortgages of leaseholds existing on 31st December, 1925.

It will be noticed that the above provisions *applied only where the mortgage was by assignment of the term, and the right of redemption was subsisting.* So that where the mortgage was made by sub-demise with a view to preventing the mortgagee becoming liable to the lessor on the covenants in the lease, such mortgage was not affected by these provisions. If the mortgage was by sub-demise, and there was a trust of the nominal reversion in favour of the mortgagee but the mortgagee had before 1926 become entitled under the Statutes of Limitation to the property free from the equity of redemption the head term on 1st January, 1926, vested in him (L.P.A. 1925, Sched. 1, Pt. II, para. 3). The result of this was that the mortgagee became liable to the lessor under the lease, but he may be able to avoid such liability by disclaimer; see next paragraph. On the other hand, if there was no trust of the nominal reversion (for instance, if the mortgage deed contained a power of attorney to get it in) the head term did not vest in the mortgagee on 1st January, 1926 (*St. Germans (Earl)* v. *Barker* [1936] 1 All E.R. 849).

Disclaimer of nominal reversion where leaseholds mortgaged before 1926.—Before 1926 it was usual to take a mortgage of leasehold property by sub-demise, that is, by a demise of the term less the last few days, and for the mortgagor to declare that he would stand possessed of such nominal reversion on trust for the mortgagee or a purchaser from him. The object was to prevent there being any privity of estate between the mortgagee and the lessor, and the mortgagee becoming liable to the lessor on the covenants in the lease. It would not have been fair to allow the transitional provisions of the L.P.A. 1925 to vest the reversion in the mortgagee, making him liable to the lessor. It was, therefore, provided by the L.P.A. 1925, Sched. 1, Pt. II, para. 7 (a), that " Nothing in this Part of this Schedule shall operate— (a) To vest in a mortgagee of a term of years absolute any nominal leasehold reversion which is held in trust for him subject to redemption."

It will be noticed that the exception limits the case to where the reversion is *held in trust subject to redemption.* But a purchaser from the mortgagee, although he would be a person entitled, as an assign of the mortgagee, to have the nominal reversion assigned to him, could not say that such right was, in the words of the paragraph, " subject to redemption," because the right of redemption had gone. The result was that, on 1st January, 1926, such nominal reversion became automatically vested in the purchaser under the L.P.A. 1925, Sched. 1, Pt. II, paras. 3 and 6 (*d*). This was not fair to the purchaser, and the Law of Property (Amendment) Act, 1926, partially cured such unfairness by providing that at the end of para. 7 of Pt. II of Sched. 1, the following paragraph shall be inserted :—

" 7.   Nothing in this Part of this Schedule shall operate—

(*m*) To vest in any person any legal estate affected by any rent covenants or conditions if, before any proceedings are commenced in respect of the rent covenants or conditions, and before any conveyance of the legal estate or dealing therewith *inter vivos* is effected, he or his personal representatives *disclaim it in writing signed by him or them.*"

It will be noticed that the purchaser who has become entitled to the property free from the equity of redemption can only disclaim the head term on condition that such disclaimer is made by him or his personal representatives *before any proceedings* have been commenced in respect of the rent or covenants *and before any dealing with the property :* see *Peachy* v. *Young* [1929] 1 Ch. 449.

The above principle applied not only to a purchaser, but also to a *mortgagee* who had become entitled to the property free from the equity of redemption on 31st December, 1925.   He might have become so entitled under the Statutes of Limitation or under a foreclosure decree.

It will be seen that the principle of *Peachy* v. *Young* only applies where the equity of redemption had become extinguished before 1926.   If the mortgage by sub-demise remained in force, and the relation of mortgagor and mortgagee still continued *after 1926, then on a sale by the mortgagee under this power of sale* after 1925, s. 89 of the L.P.A. 1925 operates to convey to the purchaser not only the mortgage term *but also the leasehold reversion of the last few days.* It follows that *the purchaser will become liable* to the lessor on the covenants in the lease and the provision as to disclaimer does not apply.

CHAPTER TWENTY-FOUR

TAXATION

IN this Chapter is offered a consideration of the particular implications to conveyancers of the principal taxes. Clearly it would be inappropriate to attempt here any general account of revenue law. Instead an attempt is made to examine in suitable detail the actual and potential taxation consequences of most of the less esoteric conveyancing dispositions of land. It will be appreciated that this is far from being a straightforward matter. Indeed, however practical a writer's aspirations may be, he will rarely have open to him the robust approach adopted by Megarry, J., in saying : " where the technicalities of English conveyancing and land law are brought into juxtaposition with a United Kingdom taxing Statute, I am encouraged to look at the realities at the expense of the technicalities " (in *Sargaison* v. *Roberts* (1969), 45 T.C. 612, at p. 618). Fortunately the task has been substantially eased by the abolition, firstly, of betterment levy (Land Commission (Dissolution) Act, 1971, s. 1 (1)) and secondly, of the so-called " short-term capital gains tax ", i.e., Case VII of Schedule D (F.A. 1971, s. 56).

Obviously the outright sale of land for a lump sum consideration is the commonest disposition of concern to conveyancers. In Parts 1 and 2 the sale of land by way of conveyance of the freehold or assignment of a subsisting leasehold is primarily considered although certain transactions incidental to sales are included, and also the rules relating to some other commonplace dispositions, such as gifts and settlements, are outlined in Part 1 ; for the " sale " of land by means of the grant of a lease at a premium, see Part 3— A. Leases, *post*, p. 1115.

The principal taxation possibilities affecting the price received by the vendor following such a conveyance or assignment are three : (i) *capital gains tax* under the F.A. 1965, as amended ; or (ii) income tax under Case I of Schedule D, i.e., in respect of a *trade* (ss. 108, 109 of the I.C.T.A. 1970) ; or (iii) income tax under Case VI of Schedule D in consequence of an *artificial transaction in land* (s. 488 of the I.C.T.A. 1970). The relevant elements of these three topics are dealt with separately, the first in Part 1 and the other two in Part 2, *post*, p. 1091.

First, however, it must be mentioned that if the vendor is a company, its profits will be subject to corporation tax and not income and capital gains tax (s. 238 of the I.C.T.A. 1970). Nevertheless, as a general principle, the rules of income tax and of capital gains tax have simply been adopted for the purposes of corporation tax computations (*ibid.*, ss. 250 (3), 265 (2) ; as to reduced rates of corporation tax, see F.A. 1972, ss. 93, 95). Accordingly, it appears unnecessary to direct any particular attention to corporation tax whilst considering the taxation possibilities arising in ordinary conveyancing.

PART 1.   CAPITAL GAINS TAX

Essentially, capital gains tax is charged in respect of gains " accruing to a person on the disposal of assets " (F.A. 1965, s. 19 (1)). A current year basis of assessment applies (F.A. 1965, s. 20 (4) ; compare the preceding year basis which applies for the income tax of traders under Case I of Schedule D, *post*, p. 1091). The rate of capital gains tax for individuals is a flat 30 per cent. (F.A. 1965, s. 20 (3)), except that the so-called " half-income " alternative is available in respect of aggregate gains not exceeding £5,000 with marginal relief (F.A. 1965, s. 21 : in effect, the income tax rate appropriate may be paid on half the gains treated as " top slice " income, assuming this rate comes to less than 30 per cent. of all the gains). Companies will, of course, be liable to the corporation tax rate which for capital gains is expected to be about 30 per cent. (see F.A. 1972, s. 93).

It will be convenient to consider, first, who is a chargeable person, second, what amounts to a disposal of assets, and third, how gains are computed.

A.   CHARGEABLE PERSONS

The charge is imposed primarily upon persons who were resident or ordinarily resident in the United Kingdom in the year of assessment in which the gains accrued to them (F.A. 1965, s. 20 (1) ; the meaning of " resident " and " ordinarily " resident here is the same as for income tax purposes : *ibid.*, s. 43 (1), (2)). By concession, disposals made before or after (as appropriate) the actual commencement or cessation of ordinary residence are disregarded even though the two events occur in the same year of assessment (Extra-Statutory Concession D.2, I.R. 1 (1970)).

In the normal way, there will be no charge to this tax merely on the ground that the gains accrue from the disposal of assets which are situated in the

United Kingdom. There will only be a charge in such a case where the non-resident happened to be carrying on a trade in the United Kingdom through a branch or agency and the assets were used for the trade or for the branch or agency (F.A. 1965, s. 20 (2), which is subject to double taxation agreements). So far as concerns land (i.e., immovable property), the situation of all rights or interests (not being by way of security only) in or over the land is that of the land itself (F.A. 1965, s. 43 (3) (a)). Accordingly, in a conveyancing context, a charge to capital gains tax could arise, for example, where a non-resident U.K. trader disposes of his premises.

When gains accrue from the disposal of assets situated outside the United Kingdom (such as foreign land), there are only two reliefs to note. Firstly, if such gains accrue to a U.K. resident who is domiciled abroad, then the tax is charged on a remittance basis (F.A. 1965, s. 20 (7), which similarly provides that foreign losses should not be allowable). Secondly, if such gains accrue to a person both resident and domiciled in the U.K. (so that the remittance basis is unavailable) but he was unable to remit the gains to the U.K. (e.g., because of exchange control restrictions in the foreign country), then he may claim, in effect, a delay in the charge to tax until it became possible to remit the gains (F.A. 1965, s. 40).

B. DISPOSAL OF ASSETS

It is of the very essence of the charge to tax that the capital gain accrued " *on the disposal of assets* " (F.A. 1965, s. 19 (1)). Therefore a close scrutiny of the meaning of this short phrase is necessary, with particular reference to its applicability to the various transactions which may be incidental to a sale of land.

"Assets."—This word is defined first as meaning " all forms of property " (whether situated in the United Kingdom or not) and then as specifically including—

" (a) options, debts and incorporeal property generally, and

(b) any currency other than sterling, and

(c) any form of property created by the person disposing of it, or otherwise coming to be owned without being acquired "

(F.A. 1965, s. 22 (1)). One wonders in passing why the draftsman of the 1965 Act could not have used the word " property " to start with in the charging provision itself, since the word already enjoyed several satisfactorily wide statutory definitions which might have served as precedents (see, e.g., L.P.A. 1925, s. 205 (1) (xx), and F.A. 1894, s. 22 (1) (f)), but no doubt the word " assets " more appropriately carried the flavour of the new tax.

Clearly land and any estate, interest or charge, whether legal or equitable, real or personal, in or over land are all " assets " for present purposes (but see the exemption for beneficiaries' interests *post*, p. 1080). Both corporeal and incorporeal hereditaments must be included (compare the definition of " land " in L.P.A. 1925, s. 205 (1) (ix)). Thus, so far as concerns land in its physical sense, mines and minerals below and fixtures above the surface will be " assets " whatever the division of ownership (see *post*, p. 1051 *et seq.*, however, as to " part disposals "). In particular, it should be observed that para. (c), *ante*, expressly comprehends such things as buildings constructed or crops grown by a landowner. Also, of course, any tangible movables included in the sale will be " assets." However, it will still often be necessary to consider whether caravans or carpets, garages and greenhouses, and such like included in the arrangements for a sale of land amount to fixtures or are merely chattels. The reason lies in the existence of an exemption where a tangible movable is disposed of for a consideration not exceeding £1,000 (F.A. 1965, s. 30 ; see also F.A. 1968, Sched. 12, para. 1, as to the exemption for tangible movables which are wasting assets). This talk of exemptions makes it expedient perhaps to mention the main exemption of interest to conveyancers relating to a dwelling-house and garden which was an individual's only or main residence (F.A. 1965, p. 29, fully considered *post*, p. 1083 *et seq*).

Concurrent interests.—Further, it is equally clear that interests in the proceeds of sale of land, whether vested in joint tenants or in tenants in common, are also " assets " here (compare *Irani Finance, Ltd.* v. *Singh* [1971] Ch. 59). Accordingly, a disposition by a beneficiary of such an equitable interest (i.e., of his undivided share) could give rise to a charge to capital gains tax (*Kidson* v. *Macdonald* (1973), *The Times*, 27th November, not applying the exemption *post*, p. 1080). However, the much more frequently encountered case, where there is a trust for sale due to concurrent equitable interests (see L.P.A. 1925, ss. 34–36), will usually produce a disposition of the land itself by the trustees for sale. It is provided that " in relation to assets held by a person . . . as trustee for another person absolutely entitled as against the trustee . . . (or for two or more persons who are . . . jointly so entitled) . . . " the capital gains tax provisions apply as if the beneficiaries had " the property " (*sic*) vested in them and as if the trustee's acts were their acts (F.A. 1965, s. 22 (5)). Thus, for present purposes, the statutory conveyancing device of the trust for sale where there is beneficial co-ownership of land will be disregarded. If this was not so, the position would be governed by the special provisions as to settled property (see F.A. 1965, ss. 25 and 45 (1) ; also *post*, p. 1056).

Nevertheless, one question has been raised by the fact that the provision quoted above (i.e., F.A. 1965, s. 22 (5)) only refers expressly to persons " jointly so entitled." Does it apply also to tenants in common, who are persons technically entitled not jointly but in undivided shares ? This question has now received a direct answer : Foster, J., has held that the word " jointly " in s. 22 (5) should not be treated as a term of art but given " its ordinary and commonsense meaning—' concurrently ' or ' in common ' " (*Kidson* v. *Macdonald* (1973), *The Times*, 27th November). It followed that land owned beneficially by tenants in common subject to the statutory trust for sale was not settled property for capital gains tax purposes. Consequently, the gain on the assignment of the undivided share of one (deceased) tenant in common to the other (surviving) tenant in common was chargeable. See also *Tomlinson* v. *Glyns Executor and Trustee Co.* [1970] Ch. 112, at pp. 118 and 125.

Rights.—In addition to the land and interests mentioned above, it is considered that any rights, however arising (i.e., whether from statute, common law or equity), enjoyed by any person must be regarded as " assets " for capital gains tax purposes (cp. F.A. 1965, s. 43 (3) (*a*), as to the situation of " rights . . . in or over immovable property "). In this conveyancing context, the consideration is naturally confined to rights having some relation to land, although this is not a necessary element. It is also assumed that the rights being considered are enforceable in some manner, although not necessarily specifically against the land (which would normally convert rights into interests anyway).

This wholesale inclusion of rights as assets would appear to follow from the ordinary meaning of the phrase " all forms of property shall be assets " (F.A. 1965, s. 22 (1) ; cp. the assumption made for estate duty purposes in *Feay* v. *Barnwell* [1938] 1 All E.R. 31, 36). It is also supported by the express reference to " debts and incorporeal property generally " (F.A. 1965, s. 22 (1) (*a*) ; see *ante*, p. 1040). Further, the point would seem to be put beyond argument by the subsequent particular provision that there is a disposal of assets where " capital sums [are] received in return for forfeiture or surrender of rights, or for refraining from exercising rights " (F.A. 1965, s. 22 (3) (*c*)). In this connection reference may with especial relevance be made to the so-called miscellaneous rule that—

> " If an asset is subject to any description of right or restriction the extinction or abrogation, in whole or in part, of the right or restriction by the person entitled to enforce it shall be a disposal by him of the right or restriction "

(F.A. 1965, Sched. 7, para. 15 (4) ; see also *ibid.*, para. 15 (3), as to the variation of rights and liabilities under a lease being treated as the disposal of an interest in the property). Further, if personal rights could not be regarded as assets, it would have been both totally unnecessary and oddly limited for the statute to declare that " sums obtained by way of compensation or damages for any wrong or injury suffered by an individual in his person or in his profession or vocation are not chargeable gains " (F.A. 1965, s. 27 (8) ; marginal note : " Miscellaneous exemptions to certain kinds of property ").

Therefore, there is thought to be *no* justification to be found in the legislation on capital gains tax for the view that " purely personal " rights (as of a deserted wife or statutory tenant) not being of a " proprietary nature " are therefore not " assets " (see George, Taxation and Property Transactions, 3rd ed., pp. 192–193, where, rather in contradiction to himself, a right to damages in contract or tort is said to be property ; also Mellows, Taxation of Land Transactions, 1st ed., p. 67). This view would only be supportable, it is suggested, if " assets " were defined as interests in property instead of simply as property (see also Edo de Vries at [1972] B.T.R., pp. 329 and 331).

In accordance with the reasoning above, the following would appear to be examples of transactions incidental to a sale of land which do give rise to a potential charge to capital gains tax. The first fairly common example occurs where a separate payment is made (in particular to a third party) for the grant or for the release or modification of an easement, *profit à prendre* or restrictive (or other) covenant (compare the now repealed s. 34 of the Land Commission Act, 1967). Again the position would seem to be the same where a sum is paid for the redemption of a rent-charge (see L.P.A. 1925, s. 191). Equally within this tax would be payments to tenants to leave so as to enable sale with vacant possession, and it should make no difference whether this involves the surrender of a lease or tenancy agreement or the abandonment of some statutory security of tenure (e.g., under the Rent Act, 1968, the Landlord and Tenant Act, 1954, or the Agricultural Holdings Act, 1948). There is no reason why payments to occupational licensees (whether or not the licence is irrevocable or binding on third parties) should not be treated alike (indeed a " lease " is actually defined as including any licence or agreement for a licence : see F.A. 1965, s. 45 (1)). Further, any sums paid to a deserted spouse to leave a matrimonial home to facilitate a sale must surely be potentially chargeable on the same footing, *a fortiori* in view of

the rights conferred by the Matrimonial Homes Act, 1967 (but as to the
" private residences " exemption, see *post*, p. 1083).

In contrast to the above examples, there would appear to be *no* potential
charge to capital gains tax where there is a payment to effect the release of the
land wholly or partially from a mortgage. The reason is that the subsection
which provides in effect that a mortgage is not to be treated as involving a
disposal of an asset in parenthesis extends the exemption to " a retransfer
on redemption of the security " (F.A. 1965, s. 22 (6)). Although this wording
is strictly inapt anyway for legal mortgages of land since 1925 (where repayment produces not retransfer but cesser of a term : L.P.A. 1925, s. 116),
there can be little doubt that the subsection should be construed as intending
a general exemption in all aspects of security cases. If so, it would cover the
situation where the land sold is released from a mortgage which involves a
larger area and which is therefore not redeemed.

Also, a much wider proposition, it is suggested that there ought to be *no*
potential charge to capital gains tax where there was no enforceable right
(this appears to be assumed in George, Taxation and Property Transactions,
3rd ed., at p. 192). After all the expression " unenforceable right " very
nearly, but not quite, involves a direct contradiction in terms (see also F.A.
1967, Sched. 7, para. 15 (4), quoted *ante*, p. 1042, which refers to the person
" entitled to enforce " the right or restriction). Nevertheless this common-
sense reliance on the apparently ordinary meaning of words does not always
prove conclusive in taxing contexts (see *A.-G.* v. *Murray* [1904] 1 K.B. 165,
C.A., where a void policy of insurance was held to be " property " for estate
duty purposes). However, the suggestion that no tax should be payable
may be more strongly supported on the basis that any money payment made
was necessarily gratuitous. Such payments escape tax (even though gifts
generally may be caught : F.A. 1965, s. 22 (4) (*a*)), for the odd reason that
money (i.e., sterling) is not an asset (F.A. 1965, s. 22 (1) (*b*)).

Accordingly a payment to an admitted trespasser to leave the land vacant
should be an example of a tax-free receipt. In *Dickinson* v. *Abel* [1969]
1 W.L.R. 295 a " go-between " received £10,000 in pursuance of an
unenforceable promise by a prospective purchaser of land to make the
payment if an offer to buy at a certain price were accepted by the owner ;
the £10,000 was held to be free of income tax and it is thought that it would
also be free of capital gains tax. Not so obvious is the position of any payment
made to a landlord on a sale of leasehold land as a condition of giving a
licence to assign : such a payment if made would, in effect, normally be
gratuitous (see L.P.A. 1925, s. 144, and *ante*, pp. 860 *et seq.*, 869) when it
should also be free of capital gains tax (but there may be a liability to income
tax under Schedule A : I.C.T.A. 1970, s. 80 (4) ; see *post*, p. 1129). Against
this, any payment to a landlord to secure the release or waiver of any
enforceable right (e.g., in respect of past breaches of covenant) could give
rise to a capital gains tax charge (see F.A. 1965, Sched. 7, para. 15 (3) ;
again Schedule A liability might have to be considered first).

Somewhat less clear is the status here of rights which certainly exist but
which are subject to some procedural bar. Would capital gains tax be
chargeable where payments are made for the release of rights otherwise
unenforceable by action, e.g., because of the limitation period (i.e., under the
Limitation Act, 1939) or because of an absence of evidence in writing (see
especially the L.P.A. 1925, s. 40 (1)) ? The answer, it is considered, should
be that tax is chargeable on the basis that such rights remain both property
and assets : they retain their essential validity (see *Leroux* v. *Brown* (1852),

12 C.B. 801 ; *Monnickendam* v. *Leanse* (1923), 39 T.L.R. 445 ; and cf. *Holmes* v. *Cowcher* [1970] 1 W.L.R. 834 ; the reasoning in *A.-G.* v. *Murray* [1904] 1 K.B. 165, *ante*, is, in fact, on these lines).

Much less clear, and rather more likely to occur, is the situation where payments are made in respect of doubtful and disputed rights. Thus, whilst the doctrine of notice and the fact of registration may mean that land could only be offered for sale subject to the burden of unacceptable restrictive covenants, it is difficult to know that the benefit has actually passed to the claimant who is being bought off (see *ante*, p. 544 *et seq.*). Again, going beyond rights over land, it is by no means unknown for purchasers to accept a sale of "such title right and interest (if any) as the vendor may have " (cf. *Re Haedicke and Lipski's Contract* [1901] 2 Ch. 666 and *George Wimpey & Co., Ltd.* v. *Sohn* [1967] Ch. 487). Indeed, a mere possession can be sold (*Rosenberg* v. *Cook* (1881), 8 Q.B.D. 162).

Do such transactions in uncertainty constitute disposals of assets within the capital gains tax legislation ? The payments made cannot be treated as gratuitous : a promise to abandon a claim which is doubtful in law is good consideration (*Haigh* v. *Brooks* (1839), 10 Ad. & El. 309) and this appears to be true too of a claim which is bad but which is believed to be valid (*Cook* v. *Wright* (1861), 1 B. & S. 559 ; *Callischer* v. *Bischoffsheim* (1870), L.R. 5 Q.B. 449). Equally, the vendor's conveyance of " such title as he may have " must always be at least as good consideration as three chocolate wrappers or a peppercorn (see *per* Lord Somervell in *Chappell & Co., Ltd.* v. *The Nestle Co., Ltd.* [1960] A.C. 87, 114). So the question is : do doubtful and disputed rights amount to " assets " ?

Considerable assistance in suggesting an answer can be deduced from an income tax case. In *Scott* v. *Ricketts* [1967] 1 W.L.R. 828, one of the parties to some rather complicated dealings with certain development sites paid £39,000 to an estate agent " in consideration of your withdrawing any claim you might have had to participate " ; in fact all that the estate agent was found to have was " a moral claim or a nuisance value." The question in the case was whether the sum paid was taxable as " annual profits and gains " within Case VI of Schedule D, which it was already well established does not catch either gratuitous payments or gains made on the sale and purchase of an asset (these latter being capital gains or else trading profits within Case I of Schedule D). The Court of Appeal accepted that the payment was not gratuitous (and was criticised for this at [1967] B.T.R. 214) but decided that it also had not the quality of income since the transaction was analogous to the sale of an asset. As Lord Denning, M.R., explained (at [1967] 1 W.L.R. 831-2) :—

" Take the case where a man has a good legal claim which he agrees to forego in return for a sum of money . . . That is not an annual profit or gain within Case VI. It is the sale of an asset—namely, his legal claim— for a price. Next suppose that the man has a claim which he believes to be good but which is in fact unfounded—and he agrees to forgo it in return for a sum of money . . . It is not strictly an ' asset ', because it would not stand up in the courts ; but the compromise is binding. The payment has the same quality as if the claim were well-founded. It is not an annual profit or gain within Case VI. Finally, take a man who has a moral claim but knows that he has no legal claim. He tries it on so as to see if the defendants will pay him something. They agree to buy him out so as to save the cost of fighting it. It seems to me that the payment has the same quality as that in a compromise. It is not an annual profit or gain within Case VI."

At first sight this decision may render attractive the simplistic approach that if a payment made in respect of doubtful or disputed claims is not income then it must be a capital gain. But this would be too logical for tax purposes—after all, gratuitous payments escape both nets. For a capital gains tax charge it is essential that the disposal of an *asset* be shown. These claims are not strictly assets unless they are actually well-founded (see *per* Lord Denning, M.R., *ante*). Accordingly, the answer might appear to be that in these cases a condition precedent to the capital gains tax charge should be an inconvenient inquiry to establish that the claims and rights released or sold really would stand up in court. But this would not alter the fact that as at the time of the disposition the claims and rights remained doubtful and so were then still strictly not assets.

One other point to note in connection with the release of rights or restrictions generally on the sale of land is that consideration for the release need not be present for capital gains tax purposes. It is provided that if between parties at arm's length consideration (or additional consideration) could have been obtained for the release, then it shall be treated as a disposal at the market value of what is acquired (F.A. 1956, Sched. 7, para. 15 (1) and (4)). This is naturally important when it comes to computing the gains or losses (see *post*, p. 1057 *et seq.*).

Lastly, with regard to payments in respect of rights and claims, particularly unenforceable or uncertain rights and claims, in connection with the sale of land, it might be advisable to mention the position of the person making the payment. So far, only the potential liability to capital gains tax of the recipient of the payment has been considered. But of no little practical importance is the question whether the person making the payment (i.e., usually the vendor) will be allowed to deduct the amount from any gains for the purposes of this tax. This anticipates the topic of computation of gains which is dealt with fairly fully later. Nevertheless, it would probably be helpful to say here that the answer appears to depend entirely upon whether the payment can be regarded as—

"expenditure wholly and exclusively incurred by him in establishing, preserving or defending his title to, or to a right over, the asset"

(F.A. 1965, Sched. 6, para. 4 (1) (*b*) ; see *post*, p. 1066). It is thought that any payments for the release of rights or claims relating to land should be allowable as being within these quoted words. A title can properly be defended even (or especially) against unenforceable or uncertain rights and claims.

" **Disposal of** ".—The opening words of the essential expression, " the disposal of assets," enjoy no general statutory definition for the purposes of capital gains tax (although there are a number of special provisions, not of explanation, but of particular application as indicated below). Accordingly the words primarily bear their ordinary meaning—whatever that may be. Reference to the Oxford English Dictionary (Compact Edition 1971 ; cf. *per* Morton, L.J., in *McVittie* v. *Bolton Corporation* [1945] 1 K.B. 281, at p. 288, *re* " rubbish " in that work) reveals a strong if inapt original sense of " arranging in order " or " managing," which has been largely replaced by the more modern popular interpretation of " getting rid of," which in turn obviously leads directly to the presently relevant meanings of :

" The action of bestowing, giving, or making over ; bestowal, assignment "
and " Alienation, making over, or parting with, by sale or the like." From
all of this the general idea may emerge without too much difficulty.
Nevertheless a fairly high degree of precision in definition would surely have
been not just desirable but only proper in a taxing statute (compare I.C.T.A.
1970, ss. 488 (4) and 489 (2), (3)).

Generally.—As far as conveyancing is concerned, all the common transactions in land, such as sales, leases, exchanges, gifts and settlements, are
undoubtedly covered by the words, " the disposal of assets." Indeed, the
meaning must be much the same as that attributed to the word " assurance "
in this context, namely : " something which operates as a transfer of
property " (*per* Kay, L.J., in *Re Ray* [1896] 1 Ch. 468, at p. 476 ; cp. L.P.A.
1925, s. 205 (1) (ii) which defines " dispose of," " disposition " and " conveyance " all as ultimately including " every other assurance of property ").
This approach receives support from the assumption evidently made
throughout the capital gains tax legislation that every disposal of assets
will involve also an " acquisition " of assets except where the contrary is
specifically provided (e.g., in F.A. 1965, s. 22 (3)).

Some doubt may be felt in other contexts over the question whether the
words " disposal of " comprehend the creation as opposed to the transfer of
assets (bearing in mind that " all forms of property " are included : F.A. 1965,
s. 22 (1) ; see *ante*, p. 1040). But here, where we are dealing primarily with
estates, interests and rights which do not subsist alone but in or over property,
the question has been forestalled : the creation is to be treated as " a part
disposal of an asset " (F.A. 1965, s. 22 (2) (*b*) ; " part disposals " are considered *post*, pp. 1051–1055). Otherwise it is suggested that there is no
disposal of assets where a right is created, e.g., by contract, which is purely
personal in the sense of not being enforceable against property ; subsequently
there can, it is thought, be a disposal of that right (e.g., by assignment or
release ; see *ante*, p. 1043). But even this suggestion can offer, in itself, no
answer where rights are created which are, as yet, neither clearly proprietary
nor purely personal. Thus would the grant of a licence to use land ordinarily
be seen as a part disposal ? However, in this particular instance there is a
statutory answer : the definition of " lease " includes a licence and even an
agreement for a licence (F.A. 1965, s. 45 (1)), so that a part disposal will
usually be involved for capital gains tax purposes (see Part 3—A. Leases,
post, p. 1115).

The one common conveyancing transaction which might conceivably escape
is a disclaimer. The Court of Appeal has pronounced, in another context,
that " a disclaimer operates by way of avoidance and not by way of disposition " (see *per* Danckwerts, L.J., in *Re Paradise Motor Co., Ltd.* [1968]
1 W.L.R. 1125, at p. 1143, where the particularly relevant provision, L.P.A.
1925, s. 205 (1) (ii), defining a " disposition " as including a conveyance and
defining a " conveyance " as including a disclaimer was apparently overlooked).
Accordingly, in the absence of any relevant special provision, it can be
contended that a disclaimer does not fall within the ordinary meaning of
" the disposal of assets " (cf. *Re Stratton's Disclaimer* [1958] Ch. 42, where an
estate duty charge under the F.A. 1894, s. 2 (1) (*c*), *post*, p. 1176, depended
on the special provision made by the F.A. 1940, s. 45). In this capital gains
tax context there seem to be only two remotely relevant special provisions.
The first could only apply where payment is made as consideration for the
disclaimer : there is a disposal of assets where " capital sums [are] received by

way of compensation . . . for the loss . . . of assets . . ., [or] in return for forfeiture or surrender of rights, or for refraining from exercising rights" (F.A. 1965, s. 22 (3) (*a*) and (*c*)). The second could be especially available where, as is usual, a voluntary disclaimer takes place : " the occasion of the entire loss . . . or extinction of an asset shall . . . constitute a disposal of the asset whether or not any capital sum by way of compensation or otherwise is received . . ." (F.A. 1965, s. 23 (3)). Each of these provisions could well be regarded as comprehending a disclaimer in the sense of avoidance of a right or asset, and the latter would actually enable the person disclaiming to claim a capital loss. It is thought that a disclaimer in this sense cannot properly be fitted within the provision that " a person's acquisition of an asset and the disposal of it to him shall . . . be deemed to be for a consideration equal to the market value of the asset—where he acquires the asset otherwise than by way of a bargain made at arm's length and in particular where he acquires it by way of gift . . ." (F.A. 1965, s. 22 (4) (*a*)). These are not apt words for an avoidance, even if construed in the light of the two other special provisions mentioned above.

Contract or conveyance.—The problem, particularly acute with sales of land, was to decide when the disposal occurred : on the making of the contract or on completion by conveyance ? This was not an entirely academic quibble, since the exact time of a disposal could affect, e.g., the year of assessment in which the gains or losses occurred or else the variable factors governing market value in certain cases. The initial instinctive reaction of many seemed to be to say that the conveyance, and not the contract, was the disposal (see, e.g., George, Taxation and Property Transactions, 3rd ed., p. 195 ; cp. P.L. [1971] B.T.R. 131, 132). This reaction stemmed principally from the fact that an express provision to the contrary had been considered necessary for the purposes of the now-repealed " short-term " capital gains tax (F.A. 1962, s. 12 (2) ; see *Beattie* v. *Jenkinson* [1971] 1 W.L.R. 1419 ; also *Thompson* v. *Salah* [1972] 1 All E.R. 530), whereas no like provision at all had been adopted in the " long-term " capital gains tax legislation. What is more, the reaction could well have been supported on reflection as analogous to the argument for not treating even a specifically enforceable contract as amounting to a " conveyance " (see e.g., at [1962] B.T.R., pp. 36–46).

All this notwithstanding, it is understood that the Revenue practice was to treat a binding contract as a disposal. It is now laid down, as a general rule for capital gains tax, that—

" . . . where an asset is disposed of and acquired under a contract the time at which the disposal and acquisition is made is the time the contract is made (and not, if different, the time at which the asset is conveyed or transferred) "

(F.A. 1971, Sched. 10, para. 10 (1)). However, this provision does not purport to be declaratory, was expressly passed for making " modifications " to capital gains tax (*ibid.*, s. 56 (2)), and is not made retrospective in operation. Accordingly an admission may be deduced that the former Revenue practice was wrong and that a contract without a conveyance was not a disposal.

This last reiteration of the position apart from statute is not pointless. The new rule quoted above can, it is thought, only be construed as applying to completed contracts. It conspicuously fails to say that the contract alone should be deemed to be a disposal (cp. F.A. 1962, s. 12 (2) ; also F.A. 1965, Sched. 7, para. 14 (1), as to options, *post*, p. 1049). Thus if a contract for the sale of land is not performed, through rescission or breach, there would appear to be no disposal of the land so that the time of disposal does not arise. A comparison may usefully be made with the familiar equitable rule whereby the vendor becomes a trustee for the purchaser as from the date of a specifically enforceable contract (see *Lysaght* v. *Edwards* (1876), 2 Ch. D. 499). This too is a rule which can only be applied retrospectively to determine the rights and liabilities of the parties between contract and completion : if the transaction be never completed, even though the discharge of the contract does not occur for months or even years, the vendor can never be held liable to the purchaser for breach of his duty as a trustee (see *Plews* v. *Samuel* [1904] 1 Ch. 464 ; *Ridout* v. *Fowles* [1904] 1 Ch. 658 ; 2 Ch. 93). However, it is suggested that completion here need not involve actual execution of a conveyance and that full payment of the purchase price would suffice for a disposal since then the whole equitable estate would have been passed from the vendor to the purchaser (see *Bridges* v. *Mees* [1957] Ch. 475 ; also George, Taxation and Property Transactions, 3rd ed., p. 196).

Uncompleted contracts.—Accordingly, it is contended that where a contract for the sale of land is never completed, so that the purchaser never becomes absolutely entitled as against the vendor, there will be no disposal of an asset. The asset envisaged as not being disposed of is the estate or interest in the land which was the subject of the contract for sale. It is true that contracts for the sale of land are, as a rule, specifically enforceable and that " Equity looks on that as done which ought to be done ", which produces the proposition that beneficial ownership passes to the purchaser as from the contract. But this is, of course, a qualified proposition :—

" . . . the vendor, whom I have called the trustee, was not a mere dormant trustee, he was a trustee having a personal and substantial interest in the property, a right to protect that interest, and an active right to assert that interest if anything should be done in derogation of it "

(*per* Lord Cairns in *Shaw* v. *Foster* (1872), L.R. 5 H.L. 321, at p. 338 ; see also *per* Jessel, M.R., in *Lysaght* v. *Edwards* (1876), 2 Ch. D. 499, at p. 506). In other words, the whole equitable estate or interest does not pass on contract and is not then disposed of.

Nevertheless, it is clear that such a contract creates an equitable interest in the purchaser. Therefore, it is further contended that the contract, although not on its own a disposal, must be treated as a " part disposal " of the land (i.e., within the F.A. 1965, s. 22 (2) (*b*) ; see *post*, p. 1052). Thus what has been disposed of and acquired is simply the benefit of the contract for sale, itself an asset capable of valuation (e.g., at the amount of any deposit paid : see *Philipson-Stow's Special Representative* v. *I.R.C.* [1959] T.R. 23, an estate duty case which affords considerable comfort in pursuing this line of reasoning). Then if the contract be completed it will disappear into one full disposal as at the date of the contract (see F.A. 1971, Sched. 10, para. 10 (1) ; cf. the rules as to exercised options in F.A. 1965, Sched. 7, para. 14 (2) (3), *post*, p. 1050). But if the contract is never completed, the part disposal remains extant and able to produce chargeable gains.

Forfeiture of deposit.—In the preceding paragraph the contention was put that a contract for the sale of land which is never completed constitutes a part disposal. However, a not uncommon accompaniment to the non-completion of such a contract is the forfeiture of the purchaser's deposit to the vendor. *Prima facie* this clearly would involve another chargeable capital gain to the vendor, plus an allowable capital loss to the purchaser, but fortunately or otherwise there is express provision made that such a forfeiture does *not* constitute the disposal of an asset (F.A. 1965, Sched. 7, para. 14 (3) (8)). This would appear to be no more than a logical corollary to the notion that the contract had already " partly disposed " of an interest equal in value to the benefit of the contract which benefit in turn might be treated as equal in value to the amount of the deposit (see *Philipson-Stow's Special Representative* v. *I.R.C.* [1959] T.R. 23).

Thus the " forfeited deposit " is excluded from the reckoning (F.A. 1965, Sched. 7, para. 14 (3) (8)). Of course, the question may arise whether the accompanying loss of the benefit of the contract could independently be treated as another " part disposal " by the purchaser back to the vendor. But this particular question should only arise briefly, the answer to it seeming to be a simple negative, since only the creation, and not the extinction, of rights is included in the " part disposal " provision (F.A. 1965, s. 22 (2) (*b*)). However, the loss of the benefit of the contract, although not a part disposal, might very well be treated as a full disposal of an asset by the purchaser, the asset being his contractual right. It is pertinently provided that " the occasion of the entire loss . . . or extinction of an asset shall . . . constitute a disposal of the asset " even though no compensation is received (F.A. 1965, s. 23 (3)). Consequently, it is suggested that a defaulting purchaser who forfeits his deposit incurs an allowable loss which may be set against any chargeable gains he may have (see further as to Losses, *post*, p. 1077).

Conditional contracts.—The general rule that the disposal occurs when the contract is made (see *ante*, p. 1047) is subject to the qualification that—

" If the contract is conditional (and, in particular, if it is conditional on the exercise of an option) the time at which the disposal and acquisition is made is the time when the condition is satisfied "

(F.A. 1971, Sched. 10, para. 10 (2)). Presumably this qualification calls for the sometimes difficult distinction between a conditional contract and the ordinary absolute contract for the sale and purchase of land which incorporates what are traditionally called " conditions of sale " but which are really no more than terms of that contract (see *per* Danckwerts and Sachs, L.JJ., in *Property and Bloodstock, Ltd.* v. *Everton* [1968] Ch. 94, at pp. 112 and 121 ; also *Eastham* v. *Leigh London Properties, Ltd.* [1971] Ch. 871, C.A. ; as to the difficulty of the distinction, compare *Lipman's Wallpaper, Ltd.* v. *Mason & Hodghton, Ltd.* [1969] 1 Ch. 20).

Options.—Specific provision has been made that " the grant of an option . . . is the disposal of an asset (namely of the option) " (F.A. 1965, Sched. 7, para. 14 (1)). It will be recalled that " options " were particularly included in the enumeration of the forms of property amounting to assets (F.A. 1965, s. 22 (1) (*a*)). Accordingly the grant of an option is simply put on the same footing as a dealing with an already existing option. Thus the grant of an option relating to land is *not* to be treated as a part disposal of the land itself (i.e., under F.A. 1965, s. 22 (2) (*b*), as to the creation of an interest or right in or over an asset).

The Act speaks first in terms of an option to buy and to sell but then expressly includes " an option binding the grantor to grant a lease for a premium, or enter into any other transaction which is not a sale " (F.A. 1965, Sched. 7, para. 14 (1) (7)). Apart from the inescapable inference that an option for a lease at a rack rent falls outside these specific provisions, other problems may be raised by this vague non-definition. For example, is a right of pre-emption to be treated as an option ? (cp. L.C.A. 1972, s. 2 (4), Class C (iv)). Would the unusual agency agreements considered in *Turley* v. *Mackay* [1944] Ch. 37 and *Thomas* v. *Rose* [1968] 1 W.L.R. 1797 (see *ante*, p. 599) be regarded as options for present purposes ? What should the position be if the " any other transaction " is not only " not a sale " but also not a disposal ?

Notwithstanding the rule that a granted option is itself a disposal of an asset, once it is exercised by the grantee a merger occurs : " the grant of the option and the transaction entered into by the grantor in fulfilment of his obligations under the option shall be treated as a single transaction " (F.A. 1965, Sched. 7, para. 14 (2)). The point is that the price of the option and the price of the transaction are to be totalled together in computing the capital gains and losses of the parties (*ibid.*). Again one must observe that the introduction of the word " transaction " begs the question whether there is a disposal of assets. There is also the problem of saying *when* there is a disposal of assets—at the time of the grant or of the exercise of the option, or on completion of the single transaction ? For example, assume that an option is granted for £50 to purchase Blackacre for £10,000, which option is duly exercised and Blackacre eventually conveyed to the purchaser. It is clear that there is a disposal of Blackacre for a consideration of £10,050 for capital gains tax purposes, and it is thought that the time of the disposal occurred on the exercise of the option, this being regarded as the " contract " under which Blackacre was disposed of and acquired (i.e., within F.A. 1971, Sched. 10, para. 10 (1), *ante*, p. 1047). But what would be the consequences in this case if the option was exercised but the contract was never completed (and a 10 per cent. deposit forfeited) ? It is suggested that there can only be a capital gains tax charge on the basis of a " part disposal." The option on exercise was lost in the " transaction " (F.A. 1965, Sched. 7, para. 14 (2)) ; this transaction was the contract of sale and purchase ; and an uncompleted contract for the sale of land has already been found to be a part disposal of assets, i.e., the benefit of the contract (see *ante*, pp. 1048, 1049). Against this suggestion, however, reference may be made to the sub-paragraph next mentioned (i.e., F.A. 1965, Sched. 7, para. 14 (3)) which in terms stipulates that " the exercise . . . of an option . . . shall not constitute the disposal of an asset " (and which then applies the single transaction rule). If the option has gone, and the conveyance never came and the exercise does not count, what is left to be a disposal ?

It is further provided that the " abandonment " of an option does not constitute the disposal of an asset (F.A. 1965, Sched. 7, para. 14 (3), which is subject to F.A. 1971, s. 58, relating only to company shares and trader's assets). It is suggested, despite doubts, that this provision should be applied both to a mere failure duly to exercise an option and to an express abandonment of an option for a consideration (cf. George, Taxation and Property Transactions, 3rd ed., p. 218, *n.* 137). Unlike an exercise, however, the abandonment of an option effects no merger : the grant of the option remains the disposal of an asset (namely of itself).

Sub-sales.—The situation envisaged is that (i) the vendor contracts to sell land to the purchaser at a certain price, (ii) the purchaser contracts to sell the same land to a sub-purchaser at a higher price and (iii) the vendor ultimately conveys the land directly to the sub-purchaser. It is thought that for capital gains tax purposes this common transaction produces two disposals—one by the vendor to the purchaser at the first contract price and the other by the purchaser to the sub-purchaser at the second contract price. Each of these disposals would occur at different times, namely at the times of the respective contracts (F.A. 1971, Sched. 10, para. 10 (1)). Even though in practice there is virtually bound to be only one completion ceremony, the suggestion is that the law would deem completion of the contracts in proper order with a *scintilla temporis* between them (cp. *Church of England Building Society* v. *Piskor* [1954] Ch. 553). Accordingly, it would be assumed that the purchaser paid the whole of his purchase price to the vendor before the conveyance to the sub-purchaser. On such payment being made the whole equitable estate would have passed to the purchaser, i.e., on disposal. Thereafter the purchaser would be absolutely entitled as against the vendor whose acts as a nominee (including the conveyance to the sub-purchaser) would be attributed to the purchaser (F.A. 1965, s. 22 (5)), i.e., the second disposal. Some support for this view can be derived from the observation that the result would be exactly the same for stamp duty purposes (i.e., duty on both the original price and the sub-sale price) were it not for a special statutory relief (Stamp Act, 1891, s. 58 (4) (5) ; see *per* Lord Somervell in *Escoigne Properties, Limited* v. *I.R.C.* [1958] A.C. 549 at p. 563).

No contract.—Occasionally it happens that a conveyance on sale of land is not preceded by any contract, or much more probably not by any binding contract. In such a case the time of the disposal for capital gains tax purposes can only be the time of the conveyance (cp. F.A. 1971, Sched. 10, para. 10 (1)). However, it must be remembered that a contract can be valid and binding even though unenforceable by action. Thus an oral agreement for the sale of land, supported neither by written evidence nor by part-performance, remains a contract so that the time of its making will be the time of the disposal (see *Thompson* v. *Salah* [1972] 1 All E.R. 530).

The lack of a contract for sale should rarely give rise to any real difficulties. Nevertheless two queries might be mentioned in passing : first, what is the time of disposal where the conveyance was delivered as an escrow (see *ante*, pp. 591–593). It is thought that the answer would be at the time not of delivery but of fulfilment of the condition of the escrow (cp. F.A. 1971, Sched. 10, para. 10 (2), as to conditional contracts). Second, where title is registered, is the time of disposal the date of the transfer or of registration ? Again, the answer is thought to be that the date of transfer should be chosen as the time at which the whole equitable estate was disposed of.

Compulsory purchase.—A particularly frequent instance of there being no contract preceding the conveyance is where an interest in land is acquired by an authority possessing compulsory purchase powers. For this instance it is especially provided that the disposal is made at the time at which the compensation for the acquisition is agreed or otherwise determined (variations on appeal being disregarded) or, if earlier (but after 20th April, 1971), at the time when the authority enter on the land in pursuance of their powers (F.A. 1971, Sched. 10, para. 11). See further the consideration of " Taxation Aspects of the Compulsory Purchase of Land," by D. A. Chaffey at [1969] B.T.R., pp. 295 and 392 ; also Inland Revenue Statement published at [1972] B.T.R., pp. 403–404.

Sale of part.—It would be unduly optimistic to suppose that the capital gains tax legislation might be confined to the situation where the landowner sells, or otherwise disposes, of all that he has. On the contrary, references in the charging provisions to " a disposal of an asset " are to be construed (subject to the context) as including " a part disposal of an asset " (F.A. 1965, s. 22 (2) (*a*)). Then, although the basic word " disposal " is not defined, the meaning of the derivative expression " part disposal " enjoys extensive description, as follows :—

"there is a part disposal of an asset where an interest or right in or over the asset is created by the disposal, as well as where it subsists before the disposal, and generally, there is a part disposal of an asset where, on a person making a disposal, any description of property derived from the asset remains undisposed of "

(F.A. 1965, s. 22 (2) (*b*) ; cp. *ibid.*, s. 25 (2), as to a settlement with a reservation being a disposal of the whole of the settled property).

Thus, so far as concerns transactions involving land, there are two sorts of " part disposal." First, there is the case where the landowner creates a lesser interest in the land, as by granting a lease, a restrictive covenant, an easement or even a licence. Secondly, the landowner may sell his whole estate or interest in a physical part of his land, such as one field from his farm or a flat in his house or a strip off his garden.

The recognition of the breed known as " part disposal," and its distinction from the parent species " disposal," becomes of great importance in the computation of gains and losses. Generally computation questions are discussed later, but it appears convenient to anticipate that discussion here in order to indicate why it is important to recognise a part disposal.

Briefly, to calculate the chargeable gain accruing on a disposal it is necessary to know how much money has been spent on the asset, both initially as the consideration and costs of acquisition and subsequently on enhancing its value and preserving (see *post*, p. 1063 *et seq.*). This money obviously will have to be apportioned in some way if only part of the whole asset on which it was spent is being disposed of. The way of apportionment laid down is through the disconcerting formula $\dfrac{A}{A+B}$, where A = the consideration for the part disposal and B = the then market value of what is left (F.A. 1965, Sched. 6, para. 7). Thus if the money spent on the whole asset totalled £10,000 and part of it is now being sold for £3,000 and the market value of the remainder retained comes to £9,000, then the sum is—

$$\frac{£3,000}{£3,000 + £9,000} \times £10,000 = £2,500.$$

This enables the eventual answer that the gain on the sale of the part is £500 (i.e., £3,000 − £2,500). Also, thereafter on a disposal of the retained remainder, the gain will be calculated from the apportioned value of £7,500 (i.e., £10,000 − £2,500). Of course, no such apportionment by formula is required of any expenditure which was not on the whole asset but which was wholly attributable to the part disposed of or to the part retained (F.A. 1965, Sched. 6, para. 7 (4)).

This formula has suffered some respectable criticism. The Law Commission and the Scottish Law Commission have together commented that " Although that formula generally produces an acceptable answer, it is somewhat cumbersome and may involve the taxpayer in considerable expense " (Report on Taxation of Income and Gains Derived From Land, para. 36 ; Law. Com. No. 43 ; Scot. Law Com. No. 21 ; 1971 Cmnd. 4654). The complaint in practice was against the necessity of ascertaining the market value of the rest on the disposal of, perhaps, a very small part of a large estate. However, this complaint has been accepted by our legislators and two (complicated) mitigations offered which apply only to part disposals of land.

The first mitigation applies, essentially, where the consideration for the disposal of part of a holding of land is " small " (F.A. 1969, Sched. 19, para. 10 (1) (a)). Here the word " small " enjoys two connotations. One connotation is that the consideration must not exceed £2,500 (F.A. 1969, Sched. 19, para. 10 (3), which applies this limit to the consideration for all disposals of land in the year of assessment and so forestalls the splitting of transactions). The other connotation is that the consideration should be small as compared with the then market value of the whole holding (F.A. 1969, Sched. 19, para. 10 (1) (a)) and 5 per cent. or less is normally regarded as " small " in this sense (see Inland Revenue Booklet CGT8, February, 1973, para. 126).

If the consideration for the part disposal is " small," then the transferor may simply choose not to have the transfer treated as a disposal at all for capital gains tax purposes (F.A. 1969, Sched. 19, para. 10 (2)). This choice does not mean that the part disposal will be completely ignored. Instead the small consideration received will be deducted from the allowable expenditure on the holding for the purpose of computing the gain on a subsequent disposal of the retained remainder (*ibid.*). Thus the charge is postponed until the calculations become convenient (a so-called " roll-over " relief). For example, if the money spent on acquiring, etc., a holding of land totalled £40,000 and the market value of the holding is now £50,000, the sale of a part for £2,500 (or less) would give rise to no charge, but when subsequently the remainder is disposed of, e.g., for £49,000, the gain will be computed as from £37,500 (i.e., £40,000 −£2,500) producing a chargeable sum, in this example, of £11,500 which in effect includes the gain from the earlier part disposal. This appears to be a helpful relief, but it has nevertheless been strongly criticised for pitching its £2,500 small ceiling too low in relation to the value of most properties, and the hope has been expressed that a review would lead to an immediate and substantial raising of this ceiling and of the percentage accepted as small (Law Commission, Report on Taxation of Income and Gains Derived from Land, para. 39 ; 1971 Cmnd. 4654).

The second mitigation runs along essentially the same " roll over " lines. It is available, if claimed, where there is a part disposal of land to an authority with compulsory powers of acquisition for a consideration which is comparatively small (in the 5 per cent. or less sense indicated above) (F.A. 1966, Sched. 10, para. 4 ; see also F.A. 1967, Sched. 14, para. 5 (6), and F.A. 1969, Sched. 19, para. 11). Whilst there is here no ceiling of £2,500 for the part consideration, there is the additional condition that no steps should have been taken indicating a willingness to dispose of any part of the holding (F.A. 1966, Sched. 10, para. 4 (1) (b)).

Apart from these two mitigations, room for argument at least is afforded by a more general provision which is certainly of application to some part disposals of land. The provision applies :—

" If and so far as, in a case where assets have been merged or divided or have changed their nature or rights or interests in or over assets have been created or extinguished, the value of an asset is derived from any other asset in the same ownership . . . "

(F.A. 1965, Sched. 6, para. 8). Then the consequence is that " an appropriate proportion " of the money spent on the *other* asset may be attributed to the asset deriving value from it (*ibid.*). To take a simple example, a man might purchase adjoining plots of land and then sell one together with the benefit of valuable rights over the other (e.g., a right of way, as in *Croft* v. *Land Commission* (1971), 22 P. & C.R. 546, C.A.). Or the merger of ownership might have enabled the sale of one plot free from burdens otherwise enuring for the benefit of the other plot. Either way the resale price of each plot could be substantially affected. This provision would enable some of the allowable expenditure on the plot losing rights and value to be passed over to the plot gaining rights and value so as to reduce the chargeable capital gains on a disposal of the latter. The " appropriate proportion " here, however, will be whatever appears to be " just and reasonable " to the inspector of taxes or appeal commissioners (F.A. 1965, Sched. 6, para. 21 (4)).

Thus far the computation of gains on a part disposal of land has been seen to attract a formula, or one of two " roll-over " reliefs, or an appropriate proportion provision. None of these complicated consequences will exactly commend the part disposal concept to the practitioner. Nor, happily, has it commended itself to the Board of Inland Revenue, which instead offers a " confirmation or clarification of views " on, in effect, the avoidance altogether of *part* disposals in the following terms :—

" Unless it appears from the facts at the time of acquisition that more than one asset (given its natural meaning) was acquired, a single acquisition of land (with or without buildings) whether obtained by purchase under one contract at an inclusive price or by gift or inheritance as a whole, should normally be regarded as a single asset (even though it comprises distinguishable elements such as a house and garden, farm-houses, buildings, woodlands, cottages, etc.).

On the other hand, in the case of acquisitions by purchase, there may be contemporary evidence showing that the acquisition comprised more than one asset. For example, correspondence, etc., during negotiations leading up to a purchase may show that the contract price was based upon the sum rounded up or down of a number of valuation units ; the land may have been offered for sale by auction in lots ; or the rent roll of an estate may show separate tenants paying substantial rents for individual properties such as farms. In such cases it may be possible to make a satisfactory apportionment of the purchase price.

Where estates of small let properties (e.g., terraced urban dwelling-houses) are acquired, blocks of a size convenient to hold as investments are normally regarded as single assets, but in practice no objection is taken to treating individual dwelling-houses as separate assets and apportioning the cost of the larger unit on the basis of such evidence as is available. As a general rule single buildings in multiple occupation such as blocks of flats or office suites are regarded as single assets, but again no objection is normally taken to treating individual flats, etc., as separate assets if it appears that similar flats, etc., in the same ownership or in the locality have commonly been sold as independent dwellings "

(see [1967] B.T.R. 438). This statement represents a general acceptance of the " natural units " idea already established, e.g., for the purposes of estate duty valuations (see *Duke of Buccleugh* v. *I.R.C.* [1967] A.C. 506). Accordingly the disposal of a " natural unit " of land, such as a single farm out of a large estate, need not be treated as involving the part disposal provisions. Instead the computation of chargeable gains will merely call for a retrospective valuation of the natural unit, a process to which valuers are apparently becoming accustomed.

Further it is understood that this simpler approach may even be extended, under certain conditions, to the disposal of unnatural units, i.e., property which is not itself a natural unit for sale purposes, e.g., part of a field belonging to a farm. The conditions for this extension are two : first, that the taxpayer and the Revenue agree ; and second, that there has been no previous use of the statutory part disposal formula. This robust extension, an injection of simplicity despite the statute, is surely welcome (see The Law Commission Report on The Taxation of Income and Gains Derived From Land, paras. 49–54 ; 1971 Cmnd. 4654).

Sale and leaseback.—A conveyancing transaction which has become by no means uncommon is the sale of land (and premises) by one person to another and the immediate lease-back of that land to the original owner. The object of the exercise has usually been to realise the capital represented by a fixed asset whilst retaining use and occupation. As to restrictions in an income tax context directed at the deductibility of the rent reserved by the lease-back, see I.C.T.A. 1970, s. 491, and F.A. 1972, s. 80 ; for general considerations, see also Philip Lawton at [1972] B.T.R., p. 269, and David Pyott and Jonathan Ody at *Law Society's Gazette* (1973), vol. 70, p. 1336.

For capital gains tax purposes it is thought that this transaction should technically be treated as two in one : first, a disposal of the freehold by the vendor to the purchaser ; second, a notional instant later, a part disposal (i.e., a lease) of the freehold by the purchaser-lessor back to the vendor-lessee. Nevertheless, it is quite conceivable that these contemporaneous and connected transactions should be treated as a single part disposal by the vendor of a freehold reversion only to the purchaser. This latter treatment would be entirely in accord with the robust reasoning emanating from Megarry, J., with regard to a similar transaction in a different taxing context, which reasoning enabled substance to prevail over form and which the learned judge seems to have envisaged as applicable more generally (see *Sargaison* v. *Roberts* (1969), 45 T.C. 612). For the present, nevertheless, it is simply not possible to be certain which treatment would be ruled to be correct. Compare, for example, *Coren* v. *Keighley* [1972] 1 W.L.R. 1556, where a contract for the sale of land had provided that the vendor should lend the purchaser part of the price but the sale and mortgage-back were held by Ungoed-Thomas, J., to be two distinct transactions.

Gifts.—Although the central theme of this Part is the sale of land, the present transaction and the next (i.e., settlements) are hardly outside the scope of ordinary conveyancing and so call for, at least, an outline of the capital gains tax position.

A gift of land (i.e., a voluntary conveyance or assignment of an estate or interest therein) is clearly included within the vital charging expression " disposal of assets " (i.e., in s. 19 (1) of the F.A. 1965). This proposition has indeed been tested and found to be true notwithstanding that in the result a gift tax might be seen masquerading as a capital gains tax (see *Turner* v. *Follett* (1973), 48 T.C. 614, C.A.). The voluntary disposal will be deemed to be for a consideration equal to the market value of the land (F.A. 1965, s. 22 (4)) and so may produce a notional but nonetheless taxable gain for the donor (although in certain circumstances the Revenue can recover the tax from the donee who is then entitled, if he has the face, to recover it in turn from the donor : see F.A. 1965, Sched. 7, para. 19).

Incidentally, it should be noticed that this deemed market value applies equally to the donee's acquisition, so that when the donee comes to dispose of the land his gain will be calculated basically as from that value and not as from nil.

The only real relief available to the donor of land or an estate or interest in land is the lately introduced privilege of paying the tax by instalments over eight years (see F.A. 1965, Sched. 10, para. 4, substituted by F.A. 1972, s. 117). Otherwise there is a derisory exemption applicable where the asset given was worth £100 or less (F.A. 1965, s. 27 (2)), and reference may also be made to the general exemptions and reliefs mentioned *post*, p. 1079.

It is also provided that where the gift is made by means of a settlement then " the whole of the property thereby becoming settled property " is disposed of despite the fact that the settlement may be revocable or that the donor has some interest as a beneficiary or is a trustee or the sole trustee (F.A. 1965, s. 25 (2) ; contrast the stamp duty provision, *ibid.*, s. 90 (5)). Some problems could be encountered with transactions akin to the sale and lease-back already discussed (see *ante*, p. 1055), for example where advantage is to be taken of s. 35 of the F.A. 1959 (see *post*, p. 1176). It might then similarly be argued that notwithstanding that technically there are two transactions, i.e., the gift and the lease-back, in substance only the freehold reversion thereby becomes settled (cf. *Nichols* v. *I.R.C.* [1973] 3 All E.R. 632).

Settlements.—In essence, there will be a disposal of assets, and in consequence a potential charge to capital gains tax, on four occasions :—

(1) on the creation of the settlement (F.A. 1965, s. 25 (2), in effect discussed in the immediately preceding paragraph) ;

(2) on changes of investments by the trustees (F.A. 1965, s. 25 (1)) ;

(3) on the termination of a life interest in possession where the settlement itself continues (F.A. 1965, s. 25 (4), as amended by F.A. 1971, Sched. 12, paras. 7 and 8, and applied by F.A. 1966, Sched. 10, para. 1), *but* no chargeable gain now accrues if the termination was due to death (F.A. 1971, Sched. 12, paras. 9, 10 and 11) ;

(4) on the ending of a settlement in whole or in part (F.A. 1965, s. 25 (3) ; see further immediately below).

To be more precise as to (4) above, the statutory wording actually is :—

" On the occasion when a person becomes absolutely entitled to any settled property as against the trustee all the assets forming part of the settled property to which he becomes so entitled shall be deemed to have been disposed of by the trustee, and immediately re-acquired by him in his capacity as a trustee within s. 22 (5) of this Act, for a consideration equal to their market value "

(F.A. 1965, s. 25 (3) ; as to s. 22 (5) see below). Thus without any actual distribution occurring (e.g., where there has merely been a deed of family arrangement) a notional gain can be made by trustees with the incidence of capital gains tax ultimately, of course, falling on the beneficiary. However, it must be appreciated that no chargeable gain now accrues where the absolute entitlement is due to the termination of a life interest by death (see F.A. 1971, Sched. 12, para. 6).

Some question used to arise whether a beneficiary could be regarded as absolutely entitled (i.e., within s. 25 (3) of the 1965 Act) before the trustees had reached the point of distribution by clearing the estate. This question was answered (F.A. 1969, Sched. 19, para. 9) by the declaration that the reference to absolute entitlement to an asset means cases where a person has " the exclusive right, subject only to satisfying any outstanding charge, lien or other right of the trustee to resort to the asset for payment of duty, taxes, costs or other outgoings, to direct how that asset shall be dealt with."

Section 22 (5) of the 1965 Act, which received mention in the subsection quoted above (i.e., s. 25 (3)) as governing the trustee's future capacity, provides that—

" In relation to assets held by a person as nominee for another person, or as trustee for another person absolutely entitled as against the trustee, or for any person who would be so entitled but for being an infant or other person under disability (or for two or more persons who are or would be jointly so entitled), . . . [the capital gains tax legislation] shall apply as if the property were vested in, and the acts of the nominee or trustees in relation to the assets were the acts of, the person or persons for whom he is the nominee or trustee (acquisition from or disposals to him by that person or persons being disregarded accordingly)."

Thus the reality is regarded and the beneficiary becomes, in substance, the chargeable person. In consequence, indeed, property within this provision is excluded for present purposes from the statutory meaning of " settled property " (F.A. 1965, s. 45 (1)).

The uncertainty caused by the reference, in the first parenthesis of s. 22 (5), to being " jointly so entitled " has already been considered (see ante, p. 1041). Another uncertainty has been resolved by a judicial decision that the subsection applies where infancy (or other disability) is the only bar to absolute entitlement and therefore does not apply where the beneficiary's interest has been made contingent on attaining a specified age, even though that age happens to coincide with the age of majority (*Tomlinson* v. *Glyns Executor & Trustee Co.* [1970] Ch. 112, C.A., where, since the trustees were chargeable, the " half-income " relief was not available for the unfortunate infant beneficiary).

Lastly it should be said that no disposal of assets occurs on a mere change of trustees, since the trustees from time to time are to be regarded as a single and continuing body of persons (F.A. 1965, s. 25 (1)). This remains true even though property comprised in one settlement may at any one time be vested in different trustees, for example, where there is a strict settlement within the S.L.A. 1925 and land is vested in the tenant for life whilst investments are held by the trustees (F.A. 1965, s. 25 (11)).

As to the disposal of beneficiaries' interests, see *post*, p. 1080.

C. CHARGEABLE GAINS

It will be recalled that the capital gains tax simply cannot bite at all in the absence of " chargeable gains computed in accordance with this Act and accruing to a person on the disposal of assets " (F.A. 1965, s. 19 (1)). Now, taking for granted the person, the disposal and the assets, and envisaging still the central theme of a sale of land, the time has arrived to consider the computation of the chargeable gains

A considerable number of rules governing the computation of gains may be discovered secreted in detailed Schedules (see F.A. 1965, s. 22 (9) and (10), which refer primarily to Sched. 6 but also to Scheds. 7 and 8). But nowhere at all is any general principle actually stated. Accordingly it is necessary (and fortunately possible) to infer the basic proposition that a chargeable

34

gain is the difference between (1) the *consideration* for the disposal, and
(2) the *allowable expenditure* on the asset. In *Coren* v. *Keighley* (1972),
48 T.C. 370, at p. 378, Ungoed-Thomas, J., appeared to find this proposition,
in effect, hidden in subss. (3) and (9) of s. 22 of the F.A. 1965 : subs. (3),
which at first sight only extends the meaning of " disposal of assets ", has
reference to " any capital sum derived from assets " ; subs. (9) then defines
" capital sum " as meaning " any money or money's worth which is not
excluded from the consideration taken into account in the computation under
[Schedule 6] ".

To this proposition, three sub-principles may be appended before
descending to the detailed rules. The first is that, ordinarily, allowable
losses accruing on a disposal are to be arrived at in exactly the same way
as chargeable gains (F.A. 1965, s. 23). The second sub-principle is that
income tax profits and expenditure are to be excluded from the computation
(see F.A. 1965, Sched. 6, paras. 2 and 5). The third sub-principle is that the
consideration and expenditure are to be included in terms of money at the
time it was spent without any adjustment designed to reflect subsequent
changes in the value of money (*Secretan* v. *Hart* [1969] 1 W.L.R. 1599, relating
particularly to inflation ; cp. *Wisdom* v. *Chamberlain* [1969] 1 W.L.R. 275).

In addition, notice should be given here of two extraordinary aspects
calling for subsequent separate treatment. One flows from the fact that the
tax was not made retrospective so that only capital gains accruing after
6th April, 1965, are chargeable (F.A. 1965, s. 22 (1)). In consequence,
special rules have been made for computing the gains accruing on the disposal
of assets which were acquired before that date (F.A. 1965, Sched. 6, Pt. II).
The other extraordinary aspect is the treatment of " wasting assets " which
includes especially leases of land with fifty years or less to run (F.A. 1965,
Sched. 6, paras. 9, 10 and 11, and Sched. 8). Each of these is considered later
(see *post*, pp. 1076, 1073).

Consideration.—*Prima facie* the consideration for a disposal of assets,
for capital gains tax purposes, must certainly be the gross money price
paid or payable. The legislation contains no definition of the word
" consideration " but there are several rules of specific inclusion or exclusion
which may be regarded as inconsistent with any general application here of
commercial accounting principles (see *per* Ungoed-Thomas, J., in *Coren* v.
Keighley (1972), 48 T.C. 370, at p. 380, referring particularly to F.A. 1965,
Sched. 6, para. 14 (5), *post*, p. 1061 ; and see F.A. 1965, Sched. 6, para. 4 (1) (*c*),
(2), as to deducting the expenses of sale, *post*, p. 1070). Presumably also a
consideration in money's worth which can be valued is to be brought into
the computation (this has to be deduced from the F.A. 1965, s. 22 (4) (*b*) which,
in effect, deems the price for the disposal to be equal to the market value of
the asset where the consideration cannot be valued ; see also *ibid.*, s. 22 (9),
which mentions " money's worth," and Sched. 6, para. 4 (1) (*a*), as to the
acquisition consideration, *post*, p. 1063, and para. 2 (3) referring to the
exchange of a rent-charge for some other asset, *post*, p. 1059). Thus it would
seem clear that an exchange of assets could give rise to chargeable gains on
each side—being treated, in effect, as two disposals (cp. *Littlewoods Mail
Order Stores, Ltd.* v. *I.R.C.* [1963] A.C. 135 ; also *Portman* v. *I.R.C.* (1956),
35 A.T.C. 349).

Further, it is expressly provided that, where an asset is acquired subject
to any subsisting " interest or right by way of security " (e.g., a mortgage
or lien), then " the full amount of the liability thereby assumed by the person

acquiring the asset " is to form part of the consideration for the disposal (F.A. 1965, s. 22 (8) ; cf. *Marquess of Bristol* v. *I.R.C.* [1901] 2 K.B. 336 concerning the consideration for a conveyance on sale for stamp duty purposes). The intent of this provision appears clear : the amount outstanding on the mortgage for principal and interest is to be added to the price. But this apparent clarity is slightly obscured by the reference to " the liability thereby assumed." The purchaser of an equity of redemption does *not* thereby become liable in contract to the mortgagee at all (*Re Errington* [1894] 1 Q.B. 11). What is more, such a purchaser only becomes thereby liable to indemnify his vendor against the mortgage debt if the property is expressly conveyed subject to the mortgage or there is an express indemnity covenant (*Waring* v. *Ward* (1802), 7 Ves. 332 ; see *ante*, p. 980). So a simple conveyance of land which happens to be subject to a duly protected mortgage should *not* cause any addition to the consideration for present purposes. Also not clear is the position where land is conveyed subject to a pecuniary interest or right which is *not* " by way of security " (e.g., subject to a family charge by virtue of s. 1 of the Law of Property (Amendment) Act, 1926 ; *ante*, p. 730). Presumably, no addition to the consideration is called for.

Income excluded.—Against this, the sub-principle must be repeated that speaking generally there must be excluded from the capital gains tax computation any money or money's worth which is chargeable to income tax " as income of, or taken into account as a receipt in computing income or profits or gains or losses of, the person making the disposal for the purposes of the Income Tax Acts " (F.A. 1965, Sched. 6, para. 2 (1)). Thus property dealers or traders in land will normally not be concerned with capital gains tax. This general exclusion extends also to sums which would be taken into account for income tax purposes " but for the fact that any profits or gains of a trade, profession, employment or vocation are not chargeable to income tax " (*ibid.*, para. 21 (2)). No doubt this oddly drafted provision merely envisages the exclusion of sums which are of an income nature but which come within some income tax exemption, allowance or relief ; it could hardly be taken as applying to sums which are not chargeable to income tax because they constitute capital gains ! Also excluded, as one would expect, from the capital gains tax computation on this same basis are sums which suffer income tax by deduction at source (*ibid.*, para. 21 (3)).

However, *not* so excluded as above are any sums which happen to be taken into account in the making of a balancing charge in connection with capital allowances against income tax (F.A. 1965, Sched. 6, para. 2 (2)). Nor does this general exclusion of sums chargeable to income tax preclude the inclusion in a capital gains tax computation, as consideration for the disposal of an asset :—

" of the capitalised value of a rent-charge (as in a case where a rent-charge is exchanged for some other asset) or of the capitalised value of a ground annual or feu duty, or of a right of any other description to income or to payments in the nature of income over a period, or to a series of payments in the nature of income "

(F.A. 1965, Sched. 6, para. 2 (3)). This provision does not require the inclusion in all cases of the sums to which it applies ; it merely makes plain that their inclusion is not precluded in, presumably, proper cases. It is suggested that the provision should be confined to cases where the right to the rent-charge or other periodic payments subsists separately and is not created as an element in the disposal of assets in question. In other words, the right to income is itself an asset which can be sold or exchanged for capital gains tax purposes even though the income remains chargeable to income tax. Thus this provision enabling the inclusion of capitalised values should not be applicable, for example, to the grant of a lease (or licence) at a rack rent (or for other periodic payments). Indeed this must surely be so in view of the special rules for leases considered later (*post*, p. 1074 ; see in particular F.A. 1965, Sched. 8, para. 2 as to premiums). Again, this provision should not be applicable where property is sold simply at a price payable by instalments by the purchaser. Here, too, there are special rules which would tend to contradict the simple inclusion of the capitalised value (see the next following paragraphs).

Instalments.—If the consideration (or part of it) for the disposal of an asset is payable by instalments, a limited provision is made for deferring the payment of capital gains tax so as to match the actual receipt of the instalments. The provision applies where the instalments are payable over a period which begins not earlier than the time of the disposal and lasts longer than eighteen months (F.A. 1965, Sched. 6, para. 14). Incidentally, the fact that the deposit paid on exchange of contracts for sale may become the first instalment of the consideration does *not* mean that the period for payment begins before the time of the disposal *unless* the contract is conditional (see F.A. 1971, Sched. 10, para. 10 ; *ante*, p. 1047). Then, as the provision was originally enacted, any gain was to be regarded as accruing proportionately in the years of assessment covered by the whole period for payment of the instalments. But it seems that this dispensation was abused by tax avoiders (see the notice published by H.M. Treasury at (1971), 115 Sol. J. 676). Consequently, instead of a right to spread the gain across all the years, the recipient of instalments now finds that he must throw himself upon the uncertain mercy of the Revenue. The F.A. 1972, s. 116, has amended Sched. 6, para. 14, to the 1965 Act with the result in substance that capital gains tax will as a general rule become payable immediately notwithstanding any instalments of the consideration. Only if the Revenue can be convinced that otherwise " undue hardship " would be suffered does the taxpayer have an option to pay his tax also by instalments and then only by such instalments as the Revenue may allow with a maximum spread of eight years (F.A. 1965, Sched. 6, para. 14 (1), as amended by F.A. 1972, s. 116 (1)). These 1972 amendments came into force as on 11th April, 1972, and then applied even to existing balances of instalments (F.A. 1972, s. 116 (2), (3)). As to what application might be given by the Revenue to the undefined concept of " undue hardship," the Chief Secretary to the Treasury said during the Committee Stage of the Finance Bill, 1972, that—

" in considering whether undue hardship would arise, the Revenue would look primarily to the question whether the vendor or disponer could reasonably be expected to pay the tax on the full amount immediately, in the light of the resources made available by the particular transaction involved. Regard would not normally be paid to the other resources of the taxpayer if it could be shown that the instalment arrangement was in the circumstances, and apart from any tax considerations, a normal commercial arrangement, and reflected a genuine deferment of the enjoyment of the consideration "

(Standing Committee E, 22nd June, 1972, col. 1358).

In computing the gain from a disposal where the consideration is payable by instalments (or otherwise in the future) *no* discount is allowable on account of (i) the postponement of the right to receive any part of it, or (ii) the risk of any part being irrecoverable, or (iii) any contingency attached to the right to receive any part of it (F.A. 1965, Sched. 6, para. 14 (5)). Thus, in the first instance, the consideration has to be brought in at the full totalled amount of the instalments. However, if subsequently the inspector of taxes can be satisfactorily shown that any part of the consideration has become irrecoverable, then " such adjustment, whether by way of discharge or repayment of tax or otherwise, shall be made as is required in consequence " (F.A. 1965, Sched. 6, para. 14 (5)).

Before any of the above provisions can be applied, it must be shown that the consideration for a sale really is payable by instalments. Thus in *Coren* v. *Keighley* (1972), 48 T.C. 370, the taxpayer had contracted to sell land for £3,750 and the contract provided that he would on completion advance to the purchaser £2,250 at 9½ per cent. p.a. payable over ten years ; it was held that this resulted in two distinct transactions—a transfer on sale by a vendor to a purchaser and a charge by a borrower to a lender—and not a simple contract for the payment of the purchase price by instalments. Consequently the whole £3,750 was brought into the capital gains tax computation at once ; the capitalised value of the interest was, however, to be left out of account as it represented consideration for the loan rather than for the disposal.

Interest element.—Even where there is no distinct mortgage-back, the discussion above about instalments *simpliciter* has involved some over-simplification. It has been seen that the capital gains tax legislation allows no discounts because payments are postponed, risky or contingent. But who would agree to such payments without interest ? This leads directly that difficult problem, often litigated for income tax purposes, of deciding whether annual instalments are to be treated as wholly capital, wholly income or mixed capital and income. If the whole price was from the beginning payable by instalments, there might be found to be no " interest content " (see *I.R.C.* v. *Land Securities Investment, Ltd.* [1969] 1 W.L.R. 604, H.L. ; also *Littlewoods Mail Order Stores* v. *I.R.C.* [1969] 1 W.L.R. 1241, C.A.). If, however, *V* had contracted to sell the land to *P* for, say, £10,000, and then agreed to accept twelve annual instalments of £1,000, it would clearly be possible to draw the inference that a capital sum was being paid with interest (see *Secretary of State in Council of India* v. *Scoble* [1903] A.C. 299 ; also *Vestey* v. *I.R.C.* [1962] Ch. 861). Again it might be that the " land " sold by *V* to *P* is really a lease with eleven years to run at a ground rent of £100 per annum but is sub-let for £1,000 per annum ; here it is conceivable that all the instalments, except the first one, should be treated as wholly income (see *Chadwick* v. *Pearl Life Insurance Co.* [1905] 2 K.B. 507).

The present question in this sort of situation would seem to be what amount of consideration should be brought into the computation for capital gains tax purposes ? The answer it is submitted ought to be that any income element, the " interest content," in the instalments should be simply excluded from the consideration as chargeable to income tax (F.A. 1965, Sched. 6, paras. 2 (1) and 21 (3) ; see *ante,* p. 1059). Against this submission, however, it could be argued that statute indicates that the capitalised value of the income element is to be brought into the computation (see F.A. 1965, Sched. 6, para. 2 (3), *ante,* p. 1059). Nevertheless for the reasons already outlined (*ante*, pp. 1059–1060) it is thought that this counter-argument is unsound (see also *per* Ungoed-Thomas, J., in *Coren* v. *Keighley* (1972), 48 T.C. 370, at p. 379, for the suggestion that interest paid on deferred payments of purchase money is consideration for the deferment and not for the disposal).

Contingency principle.—Where the amount of the consideration is not certain at the time of the disposal, it could be suggested that whatever sum may be then calculable as the maximum consideration in any contingency should be brought into the capital gains tax computation. That there can be no reduction simply because there is a contingency that a lesser consideration than that stated may become payable is actually stipulated (F.A. 1965, Sched. 6, para. 14 (5), which also provides for later adjustment). Open to doubt, however, is the position where there is only a calculable minimum consideration plus the contingency of more becoming payable (cp. *Jones* v. *I.R.C.* [1965] 1 Q.B. 484) ; or worse where the calculable sum is neither a maximum nor a minimum but simply a sum payable subject to variation (cp. *Independent Television Authority* v. *I.R.C.* [1961] A.C. 427). The suggestion at the beginning of this paragraph, that whatever sum is calculable should be included, would be supportable by analogy with the two stamp duty cases cited. There is, however, an alternative suggestion, which would certainly commend itself where no sum at all is calculable (cp. *Underground Electric Railways Co.* v. *I.R.C.* [1916] 1 K.B. 484), namely, that these contingent increases are all cases in which an asset is acquired " wholly or partly for a consideration that cannot be valued " with the consequence that the consideration will be deemed to be equal to the market value of the asset (F.A. 1965, ss. 22 (4) (*b*) and 44).

Artificial price.—It may happen that the parties to a sale of land deliberately agree a price, for reasons of their own, which is either too low or too high. However, the price agreed is by no means always conclusive for capital gains tax purposes. It is provided that where a person " acquires the asset otherwise than by way of a bargain made at arm's length " then the disposal is again deemed to be for a consideration equal to the market value of the asset (F.A. 1965, s. 22 (4) (*a*)). For the purpose of capital gains tax, " market value " is defined as meaning " the price which the asset might reasonably be expected to fetch on a sale in the open market " (F.A. 1965, s. 44 (1) ; cp. F.A. 1894, s. 7 (5), as to the estate duty value, explained generally in *Duke of Buccleugh* v. *I.R.C.* [1967] 1 A.C. 506, H.L.). There seems to be no reason why a lower market value should not be substituted for a higher artificial price in appropriate circumstances.

Little statutory assistance is given over the meaning of the colloquialism " a bargain made at arm's length " except for two particular illustrations, namely, gifts and company distributions, from which it might be difficult to generalise (see F.A. 1965, s. 22 (4) (*a*)). As to gifts, see generally *ante*, p. 1055. At first sight, one could take it that strangers would be " at arm's length " so that the market value imposition operates here only where " some element of connection or relationship between the parties " existed (see, to this effect, Wheatcroft and Whiteman, Capital Gains Taxes, 2nd ed., para. 7–02 ; also Booklet CGT 8 (1973), para. 155, issued by the Board of Inland Revenue). Nevertheless, it is suggested that this ought not to be the correct interpretation in the context, for two reasons. On the one hand, neither of the two particular illustrations necessarily involves any connection or relationship between the parties. On the other hand, there are special, precise provisions relating to transactions between connected persons (see below) which would render unnecessary the use of the general colloquialism if they purported (which they do not) to be exhaustive as to parties not at arm's length. Accordingly, it is tentatively thought that a bargain should be treated as being otherwise than at arm's length for present purposes if there was present some non-commercial factor, some ulterior motive or object, which was not purely a part of the transaction of disposal and acquisition of the asset. For example, the parties without being in any way connected or related may have consciously adjusted the price to suit their separate taxation liabilities, financial positions or even moral obligations.

Expressly without prejudice to the generality of the provisions above mentioned, it is also provided that where a person acquires an asset and the person making the disposal is " connected with him," then they are to be treated as parties to a transaction otherwise than by way of bargain made at arm's length (F.A. 1965, Sched. 7, para. 17 (1), (2)). The result is that the market value will become the price for capital gains tax purposes. The explanation of "connected persons " is fairly wide (covering spouses and relatives, trustees and settlors, partners and controlled companies) being similar to the definition adopted for various anti-avoidance provisions in income tax and estate duty legislation (see F.A. 1965, Sched. 7, para. 21).

It is further provided that where there is a disposal to a connected person of an asset which is subject to any right or restriction enforceable by the person making the disposal then the right or restriction is either ignored altogether or limited in its effect in arriving at the market value (F.A. 1965, Sched. 7, para. 17 (5)). This provision does *not* apply to rights exercisable on breach of a covenant in a lease or to rights or restrictions under a mortgage or other charge (*ibid.*), but it would apply, for example, to restrictive or other covenants imposed on a sale of land between connected persons.

Finally, it should be emphasised that there is no provision for substituting market value, to compute capital gains or losses, where a bad bargain has been made at arm's length. Nor does there seem to be anything to prevent a collusive sale and repurchase of a depreciated asset actually at market value in order simply to realise in that tax year an allowable loss so as to cancel out or at least reduce any gains accruing on the disposal of other assets (but see F.A. 1965, Sched. 7, para. 7 (3), as to connected persons and losses : *post*, p. 1078).

Allowable expenditure.—The sums allowable as a deduction from the consideration in the computation of capital gains are expressly restricted to three heads (F.A. 1965, Sched. 6, para. 4 (1)), as follows :—

(*a*) *Initial expenditure.*—The first allowable head comprises :—

" the amount or value of the consideration, in money or money's worth, given by him [i.e., the person now disposing of the asset] or on his behalf wholly and exclusively for the acquisition of the asset, together with the incidental costs to him of the acquisition or, if the asset was not acquired by him, any expenditure wholly and exclusively incurred by him in providing the asset "

(F.A. 1965, Sched. 6, para. 4 (1) (*a*)).

Clearly this initial allowable expenditure must normally be closely related to an " acquisition." This vital word is not defined but there can be little doubt that its construction will be controlled in the present context by the meaning of " disposal " (which is also undefined, of course, but was considered

ante, p. 1045).   The reference to " providing " but not acquiring an asset must
equally be read with the specific inclusion in the definition of " assets " of :—

> " any form of property created by the person disposing of it, or otherwise
> coming to be owned without being acquired "

(F.A. 1965, s. 22 (1) (*c*) ; *ante*, p. 1040).   This reference to providing assets
bears some of the marks of an afterthought.   Was any significance intended
by the failure to repeat, where assets are provided, the words " on his
behalf " and " together with incidental costs " ?

It will be appreciated that this head of allowable expenditure has attached
a much more explicit scope to the word " consideration " for the purposes
of deduction than could be found for the purposes of inclusion (see *ante*,
p. 1058).   Thus the value of money's worth certainly figures in the computation.   Nevertheless this explicit scope is not as definitive as it appears on
the face of it.   There are other relevant provisions.   Thus, if the asset had
been acquired for a consideration which could not be valued, perhaps because
it was not even in money's worth (e.g., marriage), then the acquisition will
be deemed to be for a consideration equal to the then market value of the
asset (F.A. 1965, s. 22 (4) (*b*)).   This insertion of the market value into the
computation also operates where no consideration at all was given for the
acquisition (i.e., a gift) and indeed applies generally where the acquisition
was " otherwise than by way of a bargain made at arm's length " (F.A. 1965,
s. 22 (4) (*a*), whereby, *semble*, too high as well as too low a price agreed
between friends or relatives may be disregarded).

It should also be noticed that where an asset was acquired subject to any
security interests or rights (e.g., a mortgage or lien), then again the full
amount of the liability assumed is to be added to the consideration (F.A. 1965,
s. 22 (8) ; see *ante*, pp. 1058–1059).   As to a " liability " to repair the
property, see under head (*b*) (*post*, p. 1066).

The reference in head (*a*) (quoted *ante*, p. 1063) to " the *amount or value* of
the consideration " could at first sight cause difficulties if the amount and
the value were shown to come to different figures—e.g., if the consideration
was a lump sum but payment was postponed for a period without interest.
However it is thought that in any such cases the amount of the consideration
(i.e., the lump sum) will prevail over the value (cp. F.A. 1965, Sched. 6,
para. 14 (5), *ante*, p. 1061, which deals in this way with the consideration for
a disposal ; see also *Hotung* v. *Collector of Stamp Revenue* [1965] A.C. 766,
and cp. *Coren* v. *Keighley* (1972), 48 T.C. 370).

It will also be observed that the allowable expenditure under head (*a*)
(and also head (*b*), *post*) may have been given or incurred by the person now
disposing of the asset " *or on his behalf* ".   The significance of this is not
entirely plain.   Presumably, a person who bears the incidence of a payment,
whether he makes the payment directly or indirectly, must be regarded
anyway as incurring the expenditure himself.   Thus if a bare trustee or
nominee, with an undisputed right of reimbursement, were to purchase land,
the beneficial owner would have to be treated as paying the price himself
(see F.A. 1965, s. 22 (5), to this effect).   Therefore it can be contended that
the words " or on his behalf " envisage the situation where the asset was
acquired beneficially by a person who did not pay for it, who did not give the
consideration or incur the expenditure himself at all.   For example, one
person, *C* (e.g., a wife or child), may contract to buy land and take a conveyance of it from *B* with another person, *A* (e.g., a husband or father),
actually paying for it without giving rise to a resulting trust (e.g., because of

the presumption of advancement) ; when C decides to dispose of the land, the consideration given by A on $C's$ behalf should be treated as allowable expenditure (compare the examples considered by Goff, J., in the estate duty case *Ralli Brothers Trustee Co., Ltd.* v. *I.R.C.* [1968] Ch. 215, at p. 235). If this example was treated as constituting a gift by A to C, then an additional acquisition (at the price paid) and disposal (at market value) by A would have occurred, presumably producing an allowable loss for A, if only on account of the incidental costs. A similar example would occur where a third party contributes to the cost of improvements to property, the benefit of which accrues, immediately or ultimately, to the owner of the property (consider the position on sale in *Hussey* v. *Palmer* [1972] 1 W.L.R. 1268, C.A.) ; the contributions should be allowable subsequent expenditure within head (*b*), *post*, p. 1066.

The point laboured in the previous paragraph may have some practical importance, since it should indicate the answer in one extremely common situation, namely the sale of land by a sole surviving beneficial joint tenant. What expenditure is allowable on the assumption that all the original beneficial joint tenants contributed to the purchase price and to any subsequent expenditure? Does only the survivor's own expenditure enter into the computation ? On the contrary it is submitted that the very nature of a joint tenancy involves the conclusion that all money spent by any joint tenant must be regarded as expenditure incurred on behalf of all the joint tenants—after all, to the world they are as a single owner (see Megarry and Wade, Real Property, 3rd ed., p. 403). In other words all of the consideration given and all of the subsequent expenditure should be allowable deductions as being either by the survivor " or on his behalf " (but see George, Taxation and Property Transactions, 3rd ed., at p. 213, accepting an opposite view).

However, the application of this seemingly simple proposition is complicated by the capital gains tax provisions relating to the death of a beneficial joint tenant. These are that the deceased's " severable share " is deemed to be acquired by the surviving beneficial joint tenant(s) for a market value consideration but without any disposal by the deceased (F.A. 1971, Sched. 12, paras. 1 and 2, amending F.A. 1965, s. 24 (1) and (9)). Accordingly no gain (or loss) has to be computed for the deceased and, when the survivor sells, his gain on the " severable share " must be computed from the deemed acquisition at market value whilst his gain on the rest will be computed in the ordinary way. Presumably, therefore, the total expenditure of all the joint tenants before decease both initially and subsequently should be spread across their severable shares.

For example, assume that X and Y owned Blackacre expressly as beneficial joint tenants and that X has spent altogether £7,000 on the property both for its acquisition and subsequently, whilst Y has only spent £1,000. Then one of the joint tenants died when the market value of Blackacre was £12,000 and now the survivor is selling for £15,000. *Prima facie* the chargeable gain will be arrived at by imagining that two severable shares have been sold : (i) the deceased's share which was acquired by the survivor at market value (i.e. £6,000) and sold for a gain of £1,500 (i.e., £7,500–£6,000) ; (ii) the survivor's own share which has half the allowable expenditure by both X and Y apportioned to it (i.e., £4,000) and is therefore sold for a gain of £3,500 (i.e., £7,500 – £4,000).

But it cannot be so straightforward. On the one hand, if X is the survivor he can certainly contend that all his own expenditure (i.e., £7,000) should be

allowable in computing the gain on his severable share (i.e., £500 rather than
£3,500). On the other hand, the market value of the deceased's severable
share should not be taken to be an exact half of the market value of Blackacre.
The estate duty value will apply also for capital gains tax purposes (F.A. 1965,
s. 26, as substituted by F.A. 1971, Sched. 12, para. 15) and the practice is to
value the share independently and ignoring any vacant possession element
(see Dymond's Death Duties, 15th ed., pp. 1452-1454). This would produce
a lesser figure than £6,000 and in consequence a greater chargeable gain.
Further, however, one may very well argue that the survivor should be
allowed to deduct the amount of any estate duty payable in respect of the
deceased's severable share (i.e., under the F.A. 1894, s. 2 (1) (a) ; see F.A.
1969, s. 36 (7)). After all such estate duty will be a charge on the property
acquired by the survivor (see F.A. 1894, s. 9 (1)), so that " the full amount
of the liability thereby assumed shall form part of the consideration . . .
in addition to any other consideration " (F.A. 1965, s. 22 (8)). According to
this the amount of estate duty borne by the survivor should be added to the
market value of the deceased's severable share in ascertaining the consideration for its acquisition, thus producing a lesser, and more real, chargeable
gain.

This argument for the allowance of estate duty should be of general
applicability whenever an asset (in particular, land) has been acquired on a
death subject to a charge for estate duty. In the case of other assets,where
estate duty is treated as a testamentary expense rather than a charge, the
argument for a deduction to be allowed would have to be (and has been)
put on the basis of subsequent and not initial expenditure (see *I.R.C.* v.
Executors of Dr. Robert Richards [1971] 1 W.L.R. 571, *post*, p. 1069).

Lastly, here, to know what items are comprehended by " the incidental
costs . . . of the acquisition," see head (c), *post*, p. 1070.

(b) *Subsequent expenditure.*—Allowable as a deduction under this head
from the consideration for a disposal of an asset by a person is :—

" the amount of any expenditure wholly and exclusively incurred on the
asset by him or on his behalf for the purpose of enhancing the value of the
asset, being expenditure reflected in the state or nature of the asset at the
time of the disposal, and any expenditure wholly and exclusively incurred
by him in establishing, preserving or defending his title to, or to a right over,
the asset "

(F.A. 1965, Sched. 6, para. 4 (1) (b)). Obviously this head embraces two
distinct sorts of subsequent expenditure, one as respects value and the other
as respects title, which call for some separate discussion.

First, the reference to " enhancing the value " seems, in effect, to incorporate
into this legislation the familiar but occasionally difficult distinction between
" improvements " and " repairs " (compare, e.g., the powers of a tenant for
life or of trustees for sale, *ante*, pp. 754, 777). Expenditure on improvements
would be allowable here, whilst that on repairs would not. In the context
of taxation there is a tendency, recently confirmed by the Court of Appeal,
to equate this distinction with that between " capital " and " revenue "
expenditure and then to decide any issues in accordance with " the ordinary
principles of commercial accountancy " (see *Odeon Associated Theatres, Ltd.*
v. *Jones* [1972] 2 W.L.R. 331, but compare *Heather* v. *P-E Consulting Group,
Ltd.* [1972] 3 W.L.R. 833).

The *Odeon Associated Theatres* case, it is true, concerned not capital gains but the expenses of a trade within Sched. D, Case I, and it is also true that expenditure on repairs, as well as on improvements, may be said to enhance the value of assets (does not a redecorated house fetch more ?). Nevertheless, despite any contrary appearances, the applicable principles must be substantially the same because it is elsewhere provided that expenditure is *not* allowable here if it would have been a deductible trading expense had the asset been part of the fixed capital of a trade (F.A. 1965, Sched. 6, para. 5 (2)). This would seem to justify the complete adoption of the income tax distinction between " capital " and " revenue " for capital gains tax purposes also, where it is surely rather apt. Whether one should then go on and decide any doubtful questions by reference to the principles of accountancy, instead of, say, the practice of surveyors, is hardly clear at present (cp. *per* Ungoed-Thomas, J., in *Coren* v. *Keighley* (1972), 48 T.C. 370, at p. 380F).

The *Odeon* case, *ante*, concerned a particular aspect of the " improvements " versus " repairs " problem which could well prove difficult here. It has been a well established rule for income tax purposes that where a trader purchases a capital asset in a state of disrepair then expenditure on repairs is " capital " and not " revenue " (*Law Shipping Co., Ltd.* v. *I.R.C.* (1923), 12 T.C. 621 ; see also *Jackson* v. *Laskers Home Furnishers, Ltd.* [1957] 1 W.L.R. 69). Indeed, so well established was this rule for Sched. D, Case I, purposes that it was also applied and eventually even given statutory force for Sched. A purposes (see I.C.T.A. 1970, s. 72 (2) (*b*) ; see also *ibid.*, s. 57 (4) as to relief from income tax in respect of interest). If followed here too, the rule would mean that such expenditure on " deferred repairs ", as they are often called, would be allowable expenditure in computing capital gains. However, the rule has now been disestablished, if not demolished, for Sched. D, Case I, purposes by the Court of Appeal which held that certain deferred repairs referable to the pre-acquisition period were deductible as trading expenses of the purchaser (*Odeon Associated Theatres, Ltd.* v. *Jones* [1972] 2 W.L.R. 331). The *Law Shipping* case, *ante*, appears distinguishable on two grounds ; first, because in it no evidence of accountancy practice had been given ; and second, because the assets in question in it were not commercially viable until repaired.

Although the *Odeon Associated Theatres* case favoured its own taxpayer, if it were followed here it would mean that capital gains taxpayers strictly could not claim as allowable any expenditure on deferred repairs unless the asset in question was virtually unusable until repaired. There is, of course, already an irreconcilable difference in approach to deferred repairs between Sched. D and Sched. A ; it appears generally thought that the new Sched. D approach is to be preferred (see F.A. 1965, Sched. 6, para. 5 (2) ; also Law Commission Report on Taxation of Income and Gains Derived from Land, para. 33 ; Law Com. No. 43 ; 1971 Cmnd. 4654). Nevertheless, there is some reason to suppose that the Revenue may be content to let the *Law Shipping* (and Sched. A) approach be adopted here too (study the dilapidated country cottage example given in the Inland Revenue Booklet CGT 8 (1973), at para. 144).

It will have been observed that the expenditure, to be allowable, must not only be intended to enhance the value of the asset but also actually be reflected in its state and nature at disposal. Therefore, not allowable would be any expenditure which proves abortive (e.g., payments in advance to a builder who goes bankrupt or to an unsuccessful oil prospector or water diviner) or which produces only temporary improvements (e.g., payments for the benefit of an easement for a period which has expired or to sink a well which has dried up).

However, some care must be taken with such abortive or temporary expenditure not to overlook altogether the existence of an earlier disposal. Thus, in discussing the point that allowable expenditure under this head must be reflected in the state or nature of the asset at the time of the disposal, Edward F. George comments (Taxation and Property Transactions, 3rd ed., at p. 221) :—

> " For example, if a wing is added to a building at a cost of £10,000 and subsequently the wing is demolished and superseded by a new wing at a cost of £20,000, the latter figure but not the former is allowable."

Whilst this is true on an eventual sale of the building, it fails to appreciate that the £10,000 wing was itself an asset and that its demolition may be treated as a disposal giving rise then and there to an allowable loss which could be carried forward and set against the eventual gain (see F.A. 1965, ss. 20 (4), 22 (1) (c) and 23 (3) (4) (5) ; the disposal would involve also the site of the wing and its market value). Oddly enough a like oversight occurs in Mellows, Taxation of Land Transactions, 1st ed., at p. 75.

Of particular relevance in connection with expenditure which proves abortive is the posthumous opinion of Lord Upjohn that the word " purpose " in this head must be read in an objective sense (in *I.R.C.* v. *Executors of Dr. Robert Richards* [1971] 1 W.L.R. 571, at p. 580). Accordingly it is not what the individual capital gains taxpayer intended by and expected from his expenditure that is relevant ; it is whether he actually achieved some lasting enhancement of value which matters.

As with head (a), the expenditure may be incurred by the person now disposing of the asset " or on his behalf " (see *ante*, p. 1064). Thus expenditure by joint tenants may be allowable, whilst expenditure by bare trustees, nominees or mortgagees is certainly allowable (F.A. 1965, s. 22 (5) and (7)).

Incidentally, attention may be drawn to the fact that interest on a loan to pay for improvements to land is *not* generally allowable expenditure for capital gains tax purposes since it would be a deduction in full for income tax purposes (see F.A. 1965, Sched. 6, para. 5 (1) and F.A. 1972, s. 75 and Sched. 9, Pt. I).

The second sort of subsequent expenditure allowable under head (b) relates primarily to matters of title rather than of value. Thus clearly the costs of any legal proceedings undertaken to resolve any title dispute would be a permissible deduction (see *per* Lord Reid in *I.R.C.* v. *Executors of Dr. Robert Richards* [1971] 1 W.L.R. 571, at p. 573). Equally allowable should be any costs incurred, without involving the courts, for similar purposes. For example, no question should be caused by the costs of correcting conveyancing mistakes or of any other form of further assurance. Again, the expense of settling boundary squabbles, doubtful claims and the like out of court should be allowable. Also any steps taken to protect title in the strict sense of evidence of ownership should give rise to allowable expenditure, e.g., the cost of obtaining statutory declarations and even of effecting out of time stamping of title deeds (cp. s. 14 (4) of the Stamp Act, 1891). Further, it is thought that any steps taken to preserve priorities, as by registering or giving notice, or to prevent adverse interests arising, as by actually or notionally obstructing quasi rights of way or light, should all be treated as allowable in the same way (and see *ante*, p. 1045).

Some rather unexpected light has been thrown on this sort of allowable expenditure by the House of Lords in *I.R.C.* v. *Executors of Dr. Robert Richards* [1971] 1 W.L.R. 571. The short majority decision was that expenditure by Scottish executors in obtaining the valuations necessary for estate duty purposes was an allowable deduction since this was only ancillary to the main purpose of obtaining an English confirmation which established their title. The case concerned the gain accruing on an actual sale of assets (shares) by the executors after the death and it is thought that it should be applied to any similar expenditure leading directly to the grant of probate or letters of administration (i.e., even though death is no longer a deemed disposal, a sale after death can give rise to a gain as from the death and personal representatives do have to show title: cf. F.A. 1971, s. 59 and Sched. 12).

The suggestion that estate duty itself should logically be treated in the same way as the expense of valuations, or of anything else leading to the grant of representation which establishes title, received a little illogical consideration from their lordships. It was first reasoned that estate duty is a stamp duty (F.A. 1894, s. 6) and that stamp duties should be deductible, but it was then concluded that estate duty would not be allowable because the rates were now so high, although if only a small amount of estate duty was involved it might perhaps be allowable (see *per* Lord Reid, Lord Morris and Lord Guest in *I.R.C.* v. *Executors of Dr. Robert Richards* [1971] 1 W.L.R. 571, at pp. 574, 578–9 and 582–3). All this was undoubtedly *obiter* and it must surely be assumed by practitioners that the legislature never intended, nor even imagined, that estate duty might be a deduction for capital gains tax purposes.

Nevertheless, there are certain situations which would seem to render the contention that estate duty should be deductible, even harder to resist. For example, envisage a gift *inter vivos* of Blackacre followed immediately by the death of the donor so that estate duty became payable by the donee (i.e., by virtue of the F.A. 1894, s. 2 (1) (c)). For capital gains tax purposes, the death of the donor caused an instant disposal and reacquisition of Blackacre by the donee for a consideration equal to its market value but without any chargeable gain accruing (F.A. 1965, s. 25A, as inserted by F.A. 1971, Sched. 12, para. 14). Consequently, when the donee sells Blackacre his gain will be computed *prima facie* from the market value at the donor's death. However, the writer suggests that the amount of estate duty paid by the donee should in this situation clearly count as a deduction in the computation. This suggestion need rest neither on the argument of substance that it produces the donee's real gain nor on the technical point already mentioned that estate duty is a stamp duty and therefore as such explicitly deductible as an incidental expense (see F.A. 1965, Sched. 6, para. 4 (2)). Instead the suggestion simply flows smoothly from the fact that the estate duty constitutes a first charge on Blackacre (i.e., by virtue of F.A. 1894, s. 9 (1)). As a direct result of this, the payment of the estate duty by the donee not only comes within the present head (*b*) of allowable (subsequent) expenditure but also actually comes within head (*a*) as initial allowable expenditure. It comes within head (*b*) because the charge must surely be regarded as a defect in title so that its discharge becomes a matter of preservation of title (see *Manning* v. *Turner* [1957] 1 W.L.R. 93). It comes within head (*a*) because statute itself provides that where an asset is acquired subject to a charge (i.e., " any interest or right by way of security ") then " the full amount of the liability thereby assumed by the person acquiring the asset shall form part of the consideration for the acquisition and disposal in addition to any other consideration " (F.A. 1969, s. 22 (8)). Therefore, the price of the donee's deemed re-acquisition following the donor's death was the estate duty liability in addition to the market value so that his gain on a subsequent sale should be calculated from that total. It would appear that these arguments for the deduction of estate duty in a capital gains tax computation ought all to be usable, *mutatis mutandis*, whenever the asset concerned is land. However, certainly incontestable is the existence of a lacuna in the legislation, namely an answer one way or the other to this estate duty question.

At this point attention may also be drawn to a latent contradiction in terms. In one paragraph, deduction of expenditure incurred in defending title to an asset is specifically allowed (F.A. 1965, Sched. 6, para. 4 (1) (*b*)). Then in the following paragraph, expressly excluded is any expenditure which would be deductible for income tax purposes if the asset had been part of the fixed capital of a trade (*ibid.*, para. 5 (2)). But expenditure incurred in defending title would clearly be so deductible for income tax purposes (see *Southern* v. *Borax Consolidated, Ltd.* [1941] 1 K.B. 111, a direct decision to this effect in respect of legal expenses which was applied by the House of Lords in *Morgan* v. *Tate & Lyle, Ltd.* [1955] A.C. 21). One trusts that the specific allowance will prevail over the general exclusion.

(*c*) *Incidental costs.*—Allowable under this head as a deduction from the consideration for the purposes of computing the gains accruing to a person on disposing of assets is simply :—

" the incidental costs to him of making the disposal "

(F.A. 1965, Sched. 6, para. 4 (1) (*c*)). Also it will be recalled that deduction is allowed under head (*a*) of " the incidental costs to him of the acquisition " (see *ante*, p. 1063). So the question is the precise scope of a person's " incidental costs " of an acquisition or of a disposal, and the answer, very precisely, is that these costs :—

" shall consist of expenditure wholly and exclusively incurred by him for the purposes of the acquisition or, as the case may be, the disposal, being fees, commission or remuneration paid for the professional services of any surveyor or valuer, or auctioneer, or accountant, or agent or legal adviser and costs of transfer or conveyance (including stamp duty) together—

(*a*) in the case of the acquisition of an asset, with costs of advertising to find a seller, and

(*b*) in the case of a disposal, with costs of advertising to find a buyer and costs reasonably incurred in making any valuation or apportionment required for the purposes of the computation under this Schedule, including in particular expenses reasonably incurred in ascertaining market value where required by this Part of this Act "

(F.A. 1965, Sched. 6, para. 4 (2)).

This is such a full description of what is allowable that very little, if any, room for uncertainty is left. Almost everything that one can think of would seem, on the face of it, to be allowable. Nevertheless it is believed that the

Revenue are endeavouring to construe this description of allowable incidental costs as strictly as possible ; for example, it is understood that fees incurred in connection with a mortgage are not allowed as a deduction.

Two reported cases have touched upon the question of incidental costs. In *I.R.C.* v. *Executors of Dr. Robert Richards* [1971] 1 W.L.R. 571, certain commission payable to stockbrokers and to solicitors in connection with the sale of stocks and shares had at first been challenged as a deduction but the challenge was abandoned in the House of Lords (see at p. 577). Then in *I.R.C.* v. *Chubb's Settlement Trustees* (1971), 47 T.C. 353, the deduction of sums spent upon solicitors' and actuary's fees, counsel's advice and stamp duty on an eventual transfer to beneficiaries absolutely entitled was allowed by the Court of Session even though a notional disposal had been involved.

It will be observed that stamp duty itself is expressly if parenthetically included. One assumes that the incidental costs of the stamping are equally allowable, and also trusts that the costs of and incidental to other necessary post-completion steps will be permitted within this head or (perhaps more appropriately) within the second part of head (*b*), *ante*.

Expenditure not allowable.—It might be most convenient to collect and list the principal instances of expenditure which, for one reason or another, is *not* allowable in the computation of capital gains. These instances are additional to those already mentioned in appropriate places (e.g., abortive expenditure).

(i) *Dual purpose.*—All three of the allowable heads rely restrictively on the phrase " wholly and exclusively." This is, of course, the very phrase which limits the allowable trading expenses for income tax purposes (see I.C.T.A. 1970, s. 130 (*a*)). And one thing that has become increasingly well established is that dual purpose expenditure (mixing business with pleasure say) does not qualify and that no apportionment is permissible (see, e.g., *Bowden* v. *Russell and Russell* [1965] 1 W.L.R. 711, combined conference and holiday). Accordingly, it would follow that any expenditure for purposes both within and outside the three allowable heads should not be deductible at all for capital gains tax purposes. Fortunately, however, some mitigation of this Revenue approach is now to be found.

In *I.R.C.* v. *Executors of Dr. Robert Richards* [1971] 1 W.L.R. 571, it was inferred " that ' wholly and exclusively ' must not be read too literally . . . one is entitled to construe ' wholly and exclusively ' not strictly but so as to give a reasonable result " (*per* Lord Reid at p. 574 ; see also *per* Lord Guest at pp. 582–3). This inference was drawn from two factors : first, the express inclusion amongst the incidental expenses of items (such as stamp duty) which would not meet the strict test ; and second, the provision for making any necessary apportionments of expenditure (i.e., F.A. 1965, Sched. 6, para. 21 (4)). Thus it is strongly arguable that dual purpose expenditure is not totally disqualified as a deduction for capital gains tax purposes and that an apportionment between the purposes, to produce allowable and non-allowable portions of expenditure, may be required by such method as may appear to the inspector of taxes " to be just and reasonable " (see *ibid.*).

It should incidentally be noticed that specific provision is made whereby expenditure on *another* asset may be allowable as a deduction. This is where the asset being disposed of has derived some of its value from another asset in the same ownership, it being a case " where assets have been merged or divided or have changed their nature or rights or interests in or over assets have been created or extinguished " (F.A. 1965, Sched. 6, para. 8). In such a case " an appropriate proportion " of the sums spent on the other asset within heads (*a*) or (*b*) of the allowable expenditure are to be attributed to the asset disposed of (*ibid.*) ; the apportionment will be whatever appears to be " just and reasonable " to the inspector of taxes or appeal commissioners (*ibid.*, para. 21 (4)).

An example would occur where a plot of land is sold together with the benefit of a right of way over an adjoining plot which had had to be purchased by the vendor so that he could grant the right of way (see *Croft* v. *Land Commission* (1971), 22 P. & C.R. 596, C.A.). Again, if a tenant were to acquire the freehold reversion with intent to merge, this present provision would appear applicable so that expenditure on the merged lease would be allowable on disposal of the freehold (see further P.L., [1972] B.T.R., p. 4).

(ii) *Income tax deductions.*—The principle that any money which counts for income tax purposes is to be ignored for capital gains tax purposes is consistently observed for deductions as for the consideration. It is provided that expenditure allowable for income tax (including any which would be so allowable but for an insufficiency of income or profits or gains) is to be excluded from the capital gains tax computation (F.A. 1965, Sched. 6, para. 5 (1) ; as to *ibid.*, para. 5 (2), see *ante*, p. 1067). However, this general principle does *not* prohibit the deduction of expenditure which qualifies for a capital or renewals allowance (*ibid.*, para. 6).

(iii) *Contingent liabilities.*—To begin with, the existence of any of certain contingent liabilities to the person disposing of an asset is *not* to be regarded as reducing his gains (F.A. 1965, Sched. 6, para. 15 (1)). But if the liability subsequently becomes enforceable then, on the inspector of taxes being satisfied of this, consequential adjustments in the tax are to be made (*ibid.*, para. 15 (2)).

The particular contingent liabilities specified have a peculiar relevance to sales of land. There is to be no reduction in gains on account of any liability, in effect—

(*a*) of the assignor of a lease for a default by the assignee ;

(*b*) of a vendor of land or lessor under " any covenant for quiet enjoyment or other obligation " assumed in that capacity ;

(*c*) in respect of " a warranty or representation made on a disposal by way of sale or lease of any property *other than land* "

(F.A. 1965, Sched. 6, para. 15 (1) ; italics supplied).

It may in practice be important to remember that a reduction in gains *can* be caused because of any contingent liabilities *other than* those specified. Especially worth remembering is the fact that a warranty or representation made on the sale or lease of land may enable a reduction (cp. para. (*c*), *ante*) and that the reduction in such a case could well be substantial in view of the pecuniary liabilities potentially imposed by the Misrepresentation Act, 1967.

(iv) *Insurance premiums.*—Not allowed as a deduction in computing gains are " any premiums or other payments made under a policy of insurance of the risk of any kind of damage or injury to, or loss or depreciation of, the asset " (F.A. 1965, Sched. 6, para. 12). So the premiums payable by either vendor or purchaser in respect of the near-obligatory fire insurance policy are to be disregarded. Against this it must be appreciated that the unhappy eventuality of the insurance money being received will by itself constitute a disposal of the asset for present purposes (F.A. 1965, s. 22 (3) (*b*) ; but see *ibid.*, Sched. 6, para. 13, as to the position if the money is applied in restoring the asset).

(v) *Expenditure reimbursed out of public money.*—This exclusion virtually speaks for itself. It covers indirect as well as direct reimbursement " by the Crown or by any Government, public or local authority whether in the United Kingdom or elsewhere " (F.A. 1965, Sched. 6, para. 17). For example, it would apply where there are investment grants (e.g., under the Industrial Development Act, 1966).

(vi) *Twice.*—This exclusion does not speak for itself, but is only intended to indicate the inevitable provision that : " No deduction shall be allowable in a computation . . . more than once from any sum or from more than one sum " (F.A. 1965, Sched. 6, para. 21 (1)).

Wasting assets.—This is one of the two extraordinary aspects of the computation of capital gains of which notice has been given (see *ante*, p. 1058). It is extraordinary in that there are special rules for " writing-down " the allowable expenditure (i.e., under heads (*a*) and (*b*), *ante*, pp. 1063, 1066) where a wasting asset is disposed of (see F.A. 1965, Sched. 6, paras. 9, 10 and 11, and Sched. 8). The object, of course, is to reduce the amount of deductions in the computation so as to increase the amount of any chargeable gain (or, more likely, to restrict the amount of any allowable loss). The justification appears to rest on the deliberate choice a person makes on the acquisition of a wasting asset " to invest his capital in an asset which he knows will depreciate (eventually to nothing) " and on the fact that " what is disposed of is not in reality the whole of what was acquired ", so that " by analogy with part disposals, he should not be able to deduct the whole of the acquisition cost from the consideration received " (see The Law Commission's Report on Taxation of Income and Gains Derived from Land, para. 44 ; Law Com. No. 43 ; 1971 Cmnd. 4654). Naturally, not everyone accepts this as any justification at all, rather regarding the taxation of deliberate appreciation whilst not allowing deliberate depreciation as " the most unreasonable aspect of capital gains tax " (see Edward F. George, Taxation and Property Transactions, 3rd ed., at p. 204 ; even the Law Commission had no suggestions to offer on the wasting assets rules because " it was the only major topic on which we were unable to reach general agreement on principles " : *loc. cit.*, para. 43). However, the rules are with us and must be considered in so far as they relate to sales of land.

The rules apply to a " wasting asset ", which primarily means " an asset with a predictable life not exceeding fifty years " (F.A. 1965, s. 45 (1) and Sched. 6, para. 9 (1)). This is not the place to be concerned with animals, immature or not, with plant and machinery or with other tangible moveable property (see *ibid.*, para. 9 (1) (*c*) and (*d*) ; also *ibid.*, para. 11, as to the exclusion of assets qualifying for capital allowances, and F.A. 1968, Sched. 12, para. 1, as to the complete " exemption " of wasting chattels). It is, however, the proper place to point out three particular provisions. Firstly, there is the sweeping pronouncement that—

" freehold land shall not be a wasting asset whatever its nature, and whatever the nature of the buildings or works on it "

(F.A. 1965, Sched. 6, para. 9 (1) (a)). Thus no question about the wasting asset rules for " writing down " the allowable expenditure can ever arise on the sale of freeholds, even of cliff lands due to fall into the sea (this represents a convenient revival of the so-called " magic gravel pit " type of case : see *Re Wood* [1894] 2 Ch. 310).

Secondly, it is provided that—

" a life interest in settled property shall not be a wasting asset until the predictable expectation of life of the life tenant is fifty years or less "

(F.A. 1965, Sched. 6, para. 9 (1) (e)). The prediction here will be based on the a(55) Tables for Annuitants, published in 1953 at the University Press, Cambridge, for the Institute of Actuaries and the Faculty of Actuaries (see *ibid.*, and CGT 8, para. 169, issued in 1973 by the Board of Inland Revenue). This provision does *not* envisage the sale of settled land by the tenant for life *nor* can it be relevant to the sale by an original tenant for life of his life interest ; it only becomes applicable on the re-sale of a purchased interest *pur autre vie* (see F.A. 1965, Sched. 7, para. 13 ; also *ibid.*, s. 25 (10) ; F.A. 1966, Sched. 10, para. 1 (3), and F.A. 1971, Sched. 12, para. 8). Accordingly, the provision can hardly be of vast importance to conveyancers.

Leases.—Thirdly, producing much the commonest case, is the provision that :—

" A lease of land shall not be a wasting asset until the time when its duration does not exceed fifty years "

(F.A. 1965, Sched. 8, para. 1 (1)). Thus the sale of leasehold land where the unexpired term is fifty years or less can cause an application of the wasting assets rules. But this is too simple a statement. There are four complicating factors. One is the extended definition of the word " lease " which includes sub-leases and licences and also agreements for any of these (F.A. 1965, s. 45 (1), which in addition brings in corresponding interests in foreign land). The second lies in the refinements attached to the duration of leases : in effect, the Schedule A rules for ascertaining the duration of terminable and renewable leases have been adopted (F.A. 1965, Sched. 8, para. 8 ; see *post*, p. 1130, as to, now, the I.C.T.A. 1970, s. 84). Also to be noted is the odd exception whereby a lease may not be treated as a wasting asset at all so long as it remains subject to a sub-lease not at a rack rent which subsisted when the lease was acquired (F.A. 1965, Sched. 8, para. 1 (2) ; the point is that as the sub-lease nears its end, the lease rather than " wasting " should increase in value). The third rests in principle : the part of a premium for a lease which is chargeable to income tax under Schedule A is excluded from liability to capital gains tax (F.A. 1965, Sched. 8, para. 5 ; see further *post*, p. 1126). The fourth complicating factor is the rate at which the allowable expenditure on such short leases is to be " written-down ". This rate is not straightforward or straightline (as with other wasting assets : see F.A. 1965, Sched. 6, para. 10) ; on the contrary it is curved. Instead of a uniform rate, the rate is to be fixed in accordance with the Table immediately below (F.A. 1965, Sched. 8, para. 1 (3)) :—

Years	Percentage	Years	Percentage
50 (or more)	100	25	81·100
49	99·657	24	79·622
48	99·289	23	78·055
47	98·902	22	76·399
46	98·490	21	74·635
45	98·059	20	72·770
44	97·595	19	70·791
43	97·107	18	68·697
42	96·593	17	66·470
41	96·041	16	64·116
40	95·457	15	61·617
39	94·842	14	58·971
38	94·189	13	56·167
37	93·497	12	53·191
36	92·761	11	50·038
35	91·981	10	46·695
34	91·156	9	43·154
33	90·280	8	39·399
32	89·354	7	35·414
31	88·371	6	31·195
30	87·330	5	26·722
29	86·226	4	21·983
28	85·053	3	16·959
27	83·816	2	11·629
26	82·496	1	5·983
		0	0

This Table enables certain formulae to be operated in order to apportion the expenditure allowable under head (a) (initial expenditure) or head (b) (subsequent expenditure). The formulae are, for head (a) :—

$$\frac{P(1) - P(3)}{P(1)} \times \text{initial expenditure}$$

and for head (b) :-

$$\frac{P(2) - P(3)}{P(2)} \times \text{subsequent expenditure}$$

where P(1) = percentage appropriate for years of duration remaining at time of acquisition of the lease,

and P(2) = percentage appropriate for years of duration remaining at time of each item of subsequent expenditure,

and P(3) = percentage appropriate for years of duration remaining at time of disposal

(F.A. 1965, Sched. 8, para. 1 (4)).

A simple example can hardly make matters worse. Assume that a taxpayer purchased for £10,000 a lease having thirty years left to run and sold the lease for £11,000 when it had twenty-one years left to run, then the arithmetic should look something like this :—

		£
Consideration for disposal		11,000
Less	£10,000	

$$\text{Exclude } \frac{87\cdot330 - 74\cdot635}{87\cdot330} \times £10,000 = \text{(approx.)} \quad 1,680$$

		8,320
Chargeable gain		£2,680

It is to be hoped that only sales of leases with whole numbers of years to run are ever encountered. Otherwise it is provided (at the foot of the Table set out above) that :—

"If the duration of the lease is not an exact number of years the percentage to be derived from the Table above shall be the percentage for the whole number of years plus one-twelfth of the difference between that and the percentage for the next higher number of years for each odd month counting an odd 14 days or more as one month"

(F.A. 1965, Sched. 8, para. 1 end). A very odd provision indeed.

More sensible is the point that no expenditure, whether initial or subsequent, is to be written down under these rules in respect of any period before the lease became a wasting asset, i.e., whilst it still had more than fifty years to run (F.A. 1965, Sched. 8, para. 1 (5)). This point is achieved by the Table attributing 100 per cent. to any number of years over fifty, as to fifty itself, with the result that the writing down only begins when the "fag-end" of the lease becomes less than fifty years.

Finally, as to this extraordinary aspect, it should be mentioned that only sales of subsisting leases have been considered here. The rules outlined above do apply similarly on the grant of short leases at a premium, with provisions to avoid an overlap with Schedule A taxation, and all of this is looked at under the general heading of Leases, *post*, p. 1124 *et seq.*

Assets held on 6th April, 1965.—The other extraordinary aspect of which notice was given (see *ante*, p. 1058) is contributed by the special rules for computing the gains accruing on the disposal of assets which were acquired before 6th April, 1965. These rules are a necessary consequence of the fact that capital gains tax, introduced on the date mentioned, was in no way retrospective so that gains already accrued were not to be caught (F.A. 1965, s. 22 (10), Sched. 6, para. 24 (2)).

The *general rule* is that the gains in such cases should be apportioned by reference to "straightline growth" (F.A. 1965, Sched. 6, para. 25). In other words the gain will be assumed to have accrued at a uniform rate over the period of ownership so that only the post-6th April, 1965, fraction will be chargeable. This is easy enough where only initial expenditure under head (*a*) is involved but it becomes somewhat complicated if there happens also to be pre-1965 subsequent expenditure to be allowed under head (*b*). The legislation provides various formulae for this case (see F.A. 1965, Sched. 6, para. 24 (4)), but in effect the total gain on disposal is first apportioned between the various items of expenditure and then treated as accruing uniformly as from the date each item was incurred. Thus assume a taxpayer purchased freehold land for £1,000 in 1955, then built a house on it for £4,000 in 1960 and eventually sells the land and house for £20,000 in 1980 (also assume that only whole years are involved and that the house was not a private residence). The result is that the total gain of £15,000 is first apportioned as to 1/5th to the initial expenditure in 1955 (i.e., £3,000) and as to 4/5ths to the subsequent expenditure in 1960 (i.e., £12,000) ; then the chargeable gains are 15/25ths × £3,000 = £1,800 *plus* 15/20ths × £12,000 = £9,000, together totalling £10,800 (in the fractions, the 15 is the number of years after 1965, the 25 is the number of years after the initial expenditure, and the 20 is the number of years after the subsequent expenditure).

It should be observed that the earliest date at which such straightline growth may be treated as beginning is 6th April, 1945 (F.A. 1965, Sched. 6, para. 24 (6), which neglects to indicate what it is one then begins with, actual acquisition cost or market value in 1945). Again, if there has been a part-disposal of an asset before 6th April, 1965, the growth of the part retained will be treated as beginning then (*ibid.*, para. 25 (7), which appears to overlook that the part disposal rules, whereby the market value of the part retained now requires ascertainment, would hardly have been operated before 1965 ; cp. *ante*, p. 1051).

Incidentally, so far as concerns short leases, there appears to be nothing in the legislation which says that the wastage of the allowable expenditure does not begin until 6th April, 1965 (see *ante*, p. 1074).

As an alternative to the general " straightline growth " rule, the taxpayer can elect to have his gain computed as from the market value of the asset on 6th April, 1965 (F.A. 1965, Sched. 6, para. 25 (1)). Such an election will be irrevocable (*ibid.*, para. 25 (3)), but the taxpayer does have two years from the date of the disposal (*ibid.*, para. 25 (1)) in which to work out which method of computation will be to his advantage—i.e., whether or not an election would produce a smaller gain (or larger loss). However, the taxpayer will not be permitted to turn a " straight line " gain into a loss as a result of an election for the 1965 market value : in such a case there will simply be deemed to be neither a loss nor a gain accruing on the disposal (*ibid.*, para. 25 (2)). These alternative provisions are not available following a part-disposal where the market value of the part of the asset retained has already been ascertained (*ibid.*, para. 25 (4) ; see *ante*, p. 1052).

Further, in one presently important case the " straightline growth " rule does not apply at all. This case concerns land in the United Kingdom having development value in the sense of fetching a price in excess of its market value for its existing use at the time of disposal (F.A. 1965, Sched. 6, para. 23). If there has been otherwise allowable expenditure on such land before 6th April, 1965, then the gain will be computed by reference to the market value of the land on 6th April, 1965 (*ibid.*,) unless this happens to produce a greater gain (or a loss) than was actually incurred (*ibid.*, para. 23 (4), which again prevents the substitution of a notional loss for an actual gain).

For the purposes of capital gains tax, " market value " is defined as meaning " the price which these assets might reasonably be expected to fetch on a sale in the open market " (F.A. 1965, s. 44 (1) ; cp. F.A. 1894, s. 7 (5), as to estate duty valuations, explained generally in *Duke of Buccleugh* v. *I.R.C.* [1967] 1 A.C. 506, H.L.).

D. LOSSES

Capital gains tax is charged on the total chargeable gains accruing in a tax year " after deducting any allowable losses " (F.A. 1965, s. 20 (4)).

If such losses exceed gains they can be carried forward to be deducted from the gains of future tax years until exhausted (*ibid.*, not applying to pre 1965–66 losses), but they *cannot* be carried back to be deducted from the gains of earlier tax years (*ibid.*, s. 23 (7)). It seems unnecessary to add, as the statute does, that no particular loss may be deducted from gains more than once (*ibid.*). Nor may there be any deduction from gains where relief for the loss has been or may be given for income tax (*ibid.*), except that any unrelieved losses under Case VII (i.e., the repealed " short-term " capital gains tax) accruing before 1971–72 may now be deducted for capital gains tax purposes (F.A. 1971, Sched. 10, para. 2). Incidentally, it should be noticed that spouses living together may, if they wish, set-off their losses against each other's gains (F.A. 1965, s. 30 (5) ; see further, as to spouses, *post*, p. 1079).

The principle has already been indicated (*ante*, p. 1058), that " allowable losses " are computed and ascertained in general in the same way as chargeable gains (F.A. 1965, s. 23 (1) (2)). Thus losses accruing to foreigners, not being chargeable persons (see *ante*, p. 1039), are not allowable (F.A. 1965, s. 23 (6)). Again a loss accruing on a disposal to a connected person can only be deducted from a gain accruing on another disposal to the same connected person (F.A. 1965, Sched. 7, para. 7 (3), which appears rather unreasonable since in each case the loss and gain must depend on a compulsory substitution of market value for price, see *ante*, p. 1063).

Certain special provisions as to losses may be of especial concern to conveyancers. First it is provided that " the occasion of the entire loss, destruction, dissipation or extinction of an asset " constitutes a disposal of the asset (F.A. 1965, s. 23 (3)). Accordingly if no compensation is received for the loss, etc., then the disposal being for a nil consideration will almost inevitably cause an allowable loss to be computed. But any capital sum received as compensation, e.g., under a policy of insurance or by way of damages, would have to be brought into the computation, in effect, as consideration for the disposal (F.A. 1965, s. 22 (3) (*a*) and (*b*) ; but see *ibid.*, Sched. 6, para. 13, where the compensation is used to restore or replace the lost or destroyed asset).

Second, provision is also made for assets which, although not entirely lost etc., have depreciated to virtually nothing ; if the owner claims and the inspector of taxes is satisfied that " the value of an asset has become negligible " then the owner will be treated as having sold and immediately repurchased the asset at its negligible value (F.A. 1965, s. 23 (4)). Thus the unfortunate owner will, with official approval, realise an allowable loss whilst retaining his poor asset. However, if the asset's value has not quite sunk to negligible, the owner could still realise his loss and keep his asset, without official approval, by actually selling and repurchasing it at market value. This would cost something in (allowable) expenses and, perhaps, in securing co-operation but it might well be worth while to minimise other chargeable gains accruing in that tax year (but see F.A. 1965, Sched. 7, para. 17 (3), as to connected persons).

The draftsman apparently assumed that the provisions mentioned in the previous paragraph would be found inapplicable to land and buildings, since the physical and legal land would remain, not lost, destroyed or negligible in value, whatever might happen to the buildings. Of course, it is possible to lose land altogether without compensation, either legally, e.g., through a title paramount claim or by squatter's rights, or even physically, e.g., if cliff land falls into the sea. Nevertheless, the assumption that land and buildings would be excluded would normally prove correct. Accordingly, it is provided for the purpose of these provisions that " a building and any permanent or semi-permanent structure in the nature of a building, may be regarded as an asset separate from the land on which it is situated " (F.A. 1965, s. 23 (5)). Thus a lost, destroyed, or negligible in value building may be brought within the provisions to give rise to an allowable loss despite the continued existence of the land. However, the land is not completely ignored : the owner must be treated " as if he had also sold, and immediately re-acquired, the site of the building or structure (including in the site any land occupied for purposes ancillary to the use of the building or structure) for a consideration equal to its market value at that time " (*ibid.*). Thus any consequent gain in site value comes into the computation.

E. EXEMPTIONS AND RELIEFS

The charge to capital gains tax, considered in the preceding pages in more or less general terms, is qualified by a considerable collection of miscellaneous exemptions and reliefs available with regard to particular persons, assets or transactions. What follows is a restricted list, confined to those of relevance to conveyancers *qua* conveyancers. By this test, the most important exemption will surely be the one applicable to private residences. However, the other relevant exemptions and reliefs will first be listed fairly briefly.

Small disposals.—If the aggregated net consideration for all of an individual's disposals of assets in one tax year does not exceed £500, then he will not be chargeable anyway to capital gains tax (F.A. 1971, s. 57 and Sched. 11). In the present context (and perhaps any other, too), this appears a totally trivial exemption. It is difficult indeed nowadays to imagine a consideration of only £500 in connection with sales of land, and the exempted gain element is in any case likely to be slight. The possibility of taking advantage of this exemption by arranging for a price exceeding £500 to be paid by appropriate annual instalments which would be treated as consideration of the years of payment has been promptly nipped in the bud (by F.A. 1972, s. 116 (1), repealing F.A. 1971, Sched. 11, para. 5 ; see *ante*, p. 1060). Provision is also made for marginal relief (F.A. 1971, s. 57 (2) : in effect, the tax is limited to one-half of the excess over £500) and for spouses living together (*ibid.*, s. 57 (3) : in effect, disposals *inter se* are disregarded and others aggregated).

Husband and wife.—A disposal and acquisition of an asset between spouses living together is to be treated as being " for a consideration of such amount as would secure that on the disposal neither a gain nor a loss would accrue to the one making the disposal " (F.A. 1965, Sched. 7, para. 20 (1), not applying to trading stock, *ibid.*, para. 20 (2)). Although spouses are " connected persons ", this particular provision prevails over the general market value rule (*ibid.*, para. 20 (2) ; cp. *ibid.*, s. 22 (4) ; Sched. 7, paras. 17 and 21, discussed *ante*, p. 1063). In the result this provision does not constitute an exemption at all : in substance it merely postpones the liability to pay capital gains tax (or the ability to claim an allowable loss) until the next disposal of the asset, which may no doubt be described as some relief. As to the joint or separate assessment of such spouses, and the collection of tax, see F.A. 1965, Sched. 10, para. 3.

Mortgages.—No acquisition or disposal is involved, for capital gains tax purposes, in " the conveyance or transfer by way of security of an asset . . .

(including a retransfer on redemption of the security) . . ." (F.A. 1965, s. 22 (6)). It appears fairly clear that attempts to disguise a sale of land as a mortgage, so as to obtain this exemption, will not be received with sympathy or encouragement in the courts (cp. *Beattie* v. *Jenkinson* [1971] 1 W.L.R. 1419 and *Thompson* v. *Salah* [1972] 1 All E.R. 530). Further, a mortgagee dealing with the mortgaged property in order to realise his security is to be treated as doing so as nominee for the mortgagor (F.A. 1965, s. 22 (7), applying also to the dealings of a receiver). As to the effect of a subsisting mortgage on the consideration, see *ante*, pp. 1058–1059.

It will be appreciated that the mortgage debt itself can be treated as an asset for capital gains tax purposes (see F.A. 1965, s. 22 (1) (*a*)), so that the transfer of a mortgage by the mortgagee could theoretically give rise to a chargeable gain or allowable loss. However, it is actually provided that the disposal of a debt by the original creditor (or his legatee) is not to give rise to a chargeable gain (F.A. 1965, Sched. 7, para. 11, which does not expressly preclude allowable losses, but this is achieved by *ibid.*, s. 25 (2)).

Beneficiaries' interests.—A beneficial equitable interest under a trust or settlement of land (or indeed, other property) is undoubtedly an asset for capital gains tax purposes (see *ante*, p. 1040). However, it is provided that chargeable gains should only accrue on the disposal of such an interest by someone who acquired the interest for a consideration in money or money's worth (F.A. 1965, Sched. 7, para. 13 (1), applying equally to successors in title of such a purchaser). Thus the original beneficiary does not become liable to capital gains tax on assigning his interest and nor does anyone who has acquired it through him otherwise than for value (not counting marriage). The exemption, in effect, ends only with the second sale. Incidentally, a consideration consisting of another interest under the same settlement is to be ignored (F.A. 1965, Sched. 7, para. 13 (1)). Accordingly, a re-arrangement or variation of the trusts will not cause a loss of this exemption for the future.

The purchaser of a beneficiary's interest will be liable to capital gains tax not only when he disposes of the interest, but also if he becomes, as the holder of that interest, absolutely entitled to the trust property as against the trustee (F.A. 1965, Sched. 7, para. 13 (2), applying particularly to reversionary interests). In this latter case, the purchaser is treated as if he had disposed of the interest for a consideration equal to the value of the trust property (*ibid.*). Thus his chargeable gain (or allowable loss) will be the difference between the price he paid for the interest and the value of the property distributable to him by the trustees.

Some difficulty has been experienced here over the interests of beneficial co-owners. Is the assignment of an undivided share by a tenant in common, or of a " severable " share by a joint tenant, within this exemption ? With land, of course, these interests necessarily subsist under trusts for sale (see L.P.A. 1925, ss. 34–36), but are they interests under " a settlement " (i.e., within F.A. 1965, Sched. 7, para. 13 (1)) ? Whilst the word " settlement " is not defined, it must surely be construed as conditioned by the meaning given to the words " settled property," namely " any property held in trust *other than* property to which section 22 (5) of this Act applies " (F.A. 1965, s. 45 (1) : italics supplied). Section 22 (5), so far as relevant, applies to " assets held by a person . . . as trustee for another person absolutely entitled as against the trustee . . . (or for two or more persons who are . . . jointly so entitled) . . .". This obscure subsection has already been considered in some detail (see *ante*, pp. 1041 and 1057) and the judicial answer indicated that both tenancies in common and joint tenancies were covered (*Kidson* v. *Macdonald* (1973), *The Times*, 27th November).

Previously, one could only answer in the alternative. If tenancies in common are outside s. 22 (5) then they are within this exemption so that the assignment of an undivided share by an original beneficiary will attract no capital gains tax. However, if tenancies in common, like joint tenancies, are within s. 22 (5), then the assignment of an undivided share, or of a severable share, should be treated as a part disposal of the trust property itself, without any applicable exemption. The latter answer, now given in *Kidson* v. *Macdonald*, *ante*, must be preferable. This distinction in position between joint tenancies and tenancies in common would be too irrational to be supportable—after all the former readily becomes the latter merely by an act of severance, which would be effected automatically by the simple assignment of a joint tenant's " severable " share.

Of course, all these answers depend anyway on the word " settlement " being construed in the qualified light thrown by the limited meaning given to the words " settled property " (i.e., by F.A. 1965, s. 45 (1), referring to s. 22 (5)). This is by no means a necessary approach, but it is felt that the tenor of the exemption evinces no intention of extending to concurrent interests at all. Thus after the mention of interests under a settlement is added the parenthesis " (including, in particular, an annuity or life interest, and the reversion to an annuity or life interest)." Consequently it is arguable that only successive interests are envisaged by the exemption and that the word " settlement " should be construed in any case as so confined by the context (cp. as to settlements for estate duty purposes, the dreaming of F. R. Davies at [1971] B.T.R., pp. 121–124).

Business premises.—There is no exemption from capital gains tax for business assets as such, but some relief is available where certain classes of business assets are sold and replaced. The relief in substance takes the form of deferring the tax until such time as business assets are sold and not replaced : if one such asset, having been purchased for £7,000, was sold for £10,000 and the money used towards purchasing a new asset costing £12,000, then no tax is payable but the cost of the second asset is regarded as reduced by the gain on the sale of the first asset, i.e., £12,000 − £3,000 = £9,000, so that, if the second asset be eventually sold for £14,000 and not replaced, then a chargeable gain of £5,000 accrues (see for details F.A. 1965, s. 33, as amended by F.A. 1967, Sched. 13, para. 2 ; F.A. 1968, Sched. 12, para. 3 ; F.A. 1969, Sched. 19, paras. 16 and 17 ; F.A. 1971, s. 60, and F.A. 1972, s. 118).

This relief is relevant here because one of the classes of business assets to which it applies comprises :—

" (*a*) any building or part of a building and any permanent or semi-permanent structure in the nature of a building, occupied (as well as used) only for the purposes of the trade, and

(*b*) any land occupied (as well as used) only for the purposes of the trade "

(F.A. 1965, s. 33 (6) ; the other business assets within the relief are fixed plant and machinery ; ships ; aircraft ; goodwill ; and hovercraft). Even buildings and land of the sort specified, however, will not qualify for the relief if the trade is " of dealing in or developing land or of providing services for the occupier of land in which the person carrying on the trade has an estate or interest " (*ibid.*). Otherwise " trade " here includes " a profession,

vocation, office or employment " and also extends to public authority
functions, commercial woodlands and certain non-profit making institutions
(*ibid.*, s. 33 (10), as amended by F.A. 1972, s. 118).

The relief is only available if the replacement by new premises takes place
within three years of the disposal of the old premises (F.A. 1965, s. 33 (3) ;
F.A. 1973, s. 37). The period, it would appear, must be calculated as being
between two unconditional contracts, one to sell the old premises and the
other to purchase the new (see *ibid.*, and F.A. 1971, Sched. 10, para. 10 ;
ante, p. 1047).

It should be observed that the relief will not be allowed if the purpose,
wholly or partly, of acquiring new premises was to realise a gain on their
disposal (F.A. 1965, s. 33 (5)). There are, however, provisions for apportionment where premises were not used wholly for the purposes of the trade,
whether as to parts of buildings or as to parts of the period of ownership
(F.A. 1965, s. 33 (7) (8) ; see also subs. (12) as to apportionment where a price
is paid for assorted assets, some within and some without this relief).

Incidentally, a brief reference should also be made to the businessman's
retirement exemption. A trader, etc., is allowed to dispose of his business
assets (which would include the premises) by sale or gift without paying
capital gains tax until the gains accruing exceed £10,000 provided (1) he
has owned the business (*not* necessarily the particular asset) for the previous
ten years, and (2) he has attained the age of 65 years (F.A. 1965, s. 34 (1) ;
in effect, £2,000 is deducted for each year short of 65 ; see also Inland
Revenue statement at (1973), 117 Sol. J. 40).

Charities.—A gain will not be chargeable to capital gains tax " if it accrues
to a charity and is applicable and applied for charitable purposes " (F.A.
1965, s. 35 (1)). However gains (or losses) may accrue when property ceases
to be subject to charitable trusts (*ibid.*, s. 35 (2)).

An encouraging relief has also now been made available for donors. By a
provision applying to dispositions of assets " otherwise than under a bargain
at arm's length " to charities or to certain listed bodies concerned with the
national heritage, the relief takes the general form of neither notional gain nor
actual loss accruing : F.A. 1972, s. 119. The charity or other body steps
into its donor's shoes for capital gains tax purposes as to acquisition date and
base value, which would be relevant on subsequent disposal of the asset :
ibid., s. 119 (2) (*b*). If, however, there is a consideration for the disposition,
although not at arm's length, which does, in effect, produce a capital gains
tax gain for the " donor " then liability to the tax will be calculated by
reference to that actual consideration rather than to the (higher) market value.
Further in all cases, the actual consideration (if any) will always be counted for
the purposes of the " small disposals " relief mentioned above.

A useful peculiarity to remember is that " charity " bears no special
restrictive definition for tax purposes. Accordingly advantage might well
be taken of this relief in somewhat unexpected ways. For one example only,
a testamentary gift on discretionary trusts for " the maintenance and benefit
of any relatives of mine whom my Trustees shall consider to be in special
need " has recently been held to create a valid charitable trust for the relief
of poverty (*Re Cohen* [1973] 1 All E.R. 889 ; see also *Dingle* v. *Turner*
[1972] 2 W.L.R. 523, H.L.). This certainly suggests an easy means whereby
donors may not only escape any tax on their notional capital gains (cp.
ante, p. 1055) but also avoid estate duty up to a limit of £50,000 (F.A. 1972,
s. 121 (1) (*b*)).

Woodlands.—The principle appears to be that the price of trees should be completely ignored for capital gains tax purposes (i.e., that income tax under Schedule B is to suffice : see F.A. 1965, Sched. 6, para. 19 (1)). Accordingly, in computing gains on the disposal of woodland in the United Kingdom, any part of the acquisition cost or disposal consideration which is attributable to trees growing on the land is to be disregarded (F.A. 1965, Sched. 6, para. 19 (2) and (3)).

See further as to the taxation of profits from Woodlands, Part 3.–E., *post*, p. 1141.

Private residences.—In our owner-occupier orientated society we have begun to expect the benevolent treatment accorded to dwelling-houses by the tax laws. This present exemption from capital gains tax should cover a very great deal of the bread and butter work of conveyancers.

Essentially, the exemption provides that a gain accruing to an individual is not chargeable " so far as attributable to the disposal of, or of an interest in—

(*a*) a dwelling-house or part of a dwelling-house . . ., or

(*b*) land which he has for his own occupation and enjoyment with that [dwelling-house] as its garden or grounds . . . ."

(F.A. 1965, s. 29 (1) (2)). Pausing here before proceeding to certain other conditions of the exemption, attention may be drawn to four not completely obvious points. First, this exemption also excludes the possibility of an allowable loss being incurred (see *ibid.*, s. 23 (1) (2)) which with inflation at its current rates should not cause widespread concern. Second, it is conceivable that the use of the word " attributable to " (rather than the word " on " as elsewhere in the statute) should be taken as extending the scope of this exemption to cover the gains from collateral transactions. For example, it is not uncommon for leasehold ownership to involve the holding of shares in the landlord company which must be sold with the lease, so that a gain on disposal of the shares could be said to be attributable to disposal of the dwelling-house.

The third point is the implications of the word " interest." Much earlier it was argued that " assets " for capital gains tax purposes include any enforceable rights, even though purely personal (see *ante*, pp. 1040–1045). This exemption, however, appears clearly restricted to the owners of estates or interests in land (i.e., in the dwelling-house and garden) and so should not be available to anyone merely having a right of a non-proprietary nature even though relating to the land. Consequently, for example, a payment to a contractual licensee to leave a home vacant ought to enjoy no exemption. Strictly no doubt this consequence should apply also to payments to vacate made to statutory tenants (who enjoy no more than " a status of irremovability " : *Keeves* v. *Dean* [1924] 1 K.B. 685) or even to deserted wives (although for their sake it is arguable that an interest for present purposes exists in the charge conferred by s. 2 of the Matrimonial Homes Act, 1967). Further it will have been observed that " an interest in . . . a dwelling-house " is required. Accordingly the question must be asked : does the exemption cover the disposal of an interest in the proceeds of sale of a dwelling-house ? There is authority which would indicate a negative answer (see *Irani Finance, Ltd.* v. *Singh* [1971] Ch. 59). Thus an assignment on sale of the undivided share of a tenant in common, or of the " severable " share of a joint tenant, in the dwelling-house in which he resides might give rise to a chargeable gain (compare the beneficiaries' interests exemption, *ante*, p. 1080). There would appear to be no question, however, of losing the exemption where beneficial co-owners dispose of the legal estate in their dwelling-house as trustees for sale (see F.A. 1965, s. 29 (9), *post*, p. 1089).

The fourth point turns on the insertion of the word " or " between the (*a*) (dwelling-house) and the (*b*) (garden) of the exemption. If construed strictly disjunctively, the unlikely result would be produced that this exemption would not cover gains attributable to the disposal of house and garden together. Such a strict construction is hardly to be feared, but the use of the disjunctive does enable the argument to be put where appropriate that any conditions of the exemption which apply in terms only to dwelling-houses should not necessarily be applied also to gardens (see further below).

"*Only or main residence.*"—The exemption is enacted as subject to two separate but rather repetitious conditions which do not exactly overlap. It is available to an individual where the dwelling-house (or part), first, " is, or has at any time, been his only or main residence " (F.A. 1965, s. 29 (1) (*a*)) and second, " has been the individual's only or main residence throughout the period of ownership, or throughout the period of ownership except for all or any part of the last twelve months of that period " (*ibid.*, s. 29 (2)). If the second condition is satisfied, the first must be and may therefore be thought superfluous. However, some unintentional sense could be drawn from the fact that the second condition in terms only applies to the dwelling-house, whilst the first is applied by reference also to the garden (*ibid.*, s. 29 (1) (*b*) ; see above as to the disjunctive between (*a*) and (*b*) of subs. (1)). Thus it can be argued that the exemption should be wholly available on the sale of the garden (or part of it) of a dwelling-house which was at any time the vendor's only or main residence even though not being such throughout the period of ownership (a thin argument but due entirely to tautologous draftsmanship). However, it does appear clear that, for the exemption to apply on the separate sale of a garden, the relevant dwelling-house must still be unsold (see para. (*b*) of s. 29 (1) of the 1965 Act : " . . . land which he has for his own occupation and enjoyment with that residence as its garden . . . ").

"*Period of ownership.*"—The expression " the period of ownership " is defined only so as to cater for individuals who have had different interests in the dwelling-house at different times : in such a case the period begins from the first acquisition on which was incurred expenditure deductible in computing the (exempted) gain on the present disposal (F.A. 1965, s. 29 (13) (*a*)). For example, if a person first occupied the dwelling-house as a tenant and later acquired the freehold reversion, his period of ownership would normally begin with the grant of the tenancy to him since this would normally involve some allowable expenditure if only in the form of incidental costs (i.e., within *ibid.*, Sched. 6, para. 4 (1) (*a*) and (*c*) ; cp. a note by P.L. in [1972] B.T.R., p. 5). Also the period of ownership normally excludes any period before 6th April, 1965 (*ibid.*, s. 29 (13) (*b*), applying to subs. (2) but not to subs. (1) (*a*), which renders the distinction between the two conditions mentioned in the previous paragraph even more peculiar). The last twelve months is excluded in obvious recognition of the travails of moving house— the purchase of the new house can be completed and the old house vacated for a year without adversely affecting this exemption.   To this, the Revenue have actually added the concession :—

"Similarly, where there is a delay (normally of not more than twelve months) in taking up residence in a newly-acquired property so that building work or redecoration can be carried out, or while the necessary steps are taken to dispose of a previous residence this period of absence will be ignored when the house is subsequently disposed of"

(see Inland Revenue Booklet CGT 8, February, 1973, para. 67).

However, the section fails to define exactly what "the period of ownership" relates to : is it ownership of the interest in land now sold or is it ownership of the dwelling-house ?   For example, if one first purchases freehold land and then much later builds on it a dwelling-house as a residence, has one resided "throughout the period of ownership" as required for the exemption (see s. 29 (2) of the 1965 Act) ?   The Inland Revenue clearly assume that it is ownership of the interest in the land which is in question, and have issued the following statement of practice :—

"Where an individual acquires land and has a house built on it, and he thereupon goes into occupation of the house as his only or main residence, then, provided that the period of ownership of the land up to the date of occupation of the house does not exceed a year, or somewhat longer if there are good reasons for exceptional delay, the Inland Revenue will regard that period as part of his period of occupation of the house as his only or main residence within s. 29"

(see *Law Society's Gazette* (1972), vol. 69, p. 851).   Nevertheless, the inexact drafting of s. 29 does allow the argument that the relevant "period of ownership" does not begin until the land with building and fixtures achieves the privileged status of dwelling-house (see correspondence between B. W. Turner and others at *Law Society's Gazette* (1972), vol. 69, p. 1026 ; (1973), pp. 1260, 1343, 1430 and 1480).   Unhappily, the present writer does not feel compelled to accept the central submission that the ownership must be of the dwelling-house rather than the land.   The section simply does not in terms say what ownership is meant, with the result that whilst this remains a possible construction so does the Revenue's view and there should here be no case for a strict construction in favour of the taxpayer who is, after all, claiming a generous exemption.

"*Residence.*"—The essential word "residence" is also not defined (as to determining "main" residence, see F.A. 1965, s. 29 (7), *post*).   However, judicial views expressed in a taxation context that residence is a question of fact will surely be followed (see *I.R.C.* v. *Lysaght* [1928] A.C. 234).   Further the word "reside" has in the same context been defined as "to dwell permanently or for a considerable time, to have one's settled or usual abode, to live in or at a particular place" (*per* Viscount Cave, L.C., in *Levene* v. *I.R.C.* [1928] A.C. 217, at p. 222).   It would appear clear that residence, in this sense, in fact by the individual himself is necessary for this exemption, and that constructive residence would not suffice (cp. George, Taxation and Property Transactions, 3rd ed., p. 202, where it is suggested that only a mere purpose of residence is required, criticised by P.L. at [1971] B.T.R., p. 132).

If the dwelling-house has not been the only or main residence throughout the period of ownership (excepting the last twelve months) then all is not lost.

Provision is made for apportionment : a fraction of the gain will be exempt corresponding, in effect, to the period(s) of residence (including the last twelve months) divided by the period of ownership (F.A. 1965, s. 29 (3) ; see also subs. (11)). This would be particularly applicable where the house has been let (or sub-let) to a tenant for a period.

Absence.—Further, certain periods of absence are to be treated as periods of residence subject to certain conditions (F.A. 1965, s. 29 (4)). These periods of absence are—

(a) any period(s) " not exceeding three years ; " if the periods of absence exceed three years (and do not come within (b) or (c) below), then the Board of Inland Revenue have taken the view that no part of the periods should count as a period of residence (see Booklet G.G.T. 8, para. 73 in November, 1968, version, which was, perhaps significantly, *not* repeated in the February, 1973, version), and lacking anything resenbling a marginal relief provision, this would appear to be the better construction (see Wheatcroft and Whiteman, Capital Gains Taxes, 2nd ed., para. 13–06) ;

(b) any period(s) throughout which the individual worked in an employment or office all the duties of which were performed outside the United Kingdom ; thus unlimited periods of absence, without loss of this exemption, are allowed to missionaries, diplomats and other such exiled mercenaries, so long as they are not self-employed ; by concession, these periods are also allowed where spouses are living together, one owns the residence and the other is employed abroad (Extra Statutory Concessions Supplement (1971) I.R. 1 (Insert) No. D.7) ;

(c) any period(s) " not exceeding four years . . . throughout which the individual was prevented from residing in the dwelling-house in consequence of the situation of his place of work or in consequence of any condition imposed by his employer requiring him to reside elsewhere, being a condition reasonably imposed to secure the effective performance by the employee of his duties " ; again if the four years is even slightly exceeded (and neither (a) nor (b) is applicable) all of the period of absence will remain a period of absence (see note to (a) above) ; however, unlike (b) above, this present period would seem to be available to a self-employed individual with a place of work away from home ; Concession D.7, referred to under (b) above, appears to be allowed here too but is in terms restricted to employments.

These three types of period(s) of absence may, in appropriate cases, be cumulatively treated as periods of residence (F.A. 1965, s. 29 (4)). However there are two overriding conditions to be satisfied in any case. One is that the dwelling-house must have been at some time the individual's only or main residence " both before and after " the period of absence (*ibid.* ; the word " immediately " is significant by its omission). Despite the definition of " period of ownership " as not including any period before 6th April, 1965 (*ibid.*, s. 29 (13) (b)), it is thought that residence before that date should nevertheless be within this first condition. The other overriding condition is that there must not have been any other residence eligible for this exemption during the period of absence (*ibid.*, s. 29 (4)).

Apportionment.—Apart from apportionments on a time basis, provision is made for apportioning the gain where part of the dwelling-house " is used exclusively for the purposes of a trade or business or of a profession or vocation " (F.A. 1965, s. 29 (5) ; notice that employments are not mentioned). This provision appears intended as a logical corollary to the practice in relation to deductions for the purposes of income tax.

" This practice is very old, works great justice between the Crown and the subject and I trust will never be disturbed.   Thus, speaking generally, the grocer living above his shop, the doctor who has a surgery in his house and the barrister who works in his house where he keeps or brings his law books and works on his briefs in the evenings and at weekends is allowed by the Crown a reasonable sum in respect of the necessary upkeep of his dwelling as being properly attributable to his trading or professional activities."

(*per* Lord Upjohn in *I.R.C.* v. *Korner* [1969] 1 W.L.R. 554, at p. 558).

Obviously the idea is that what you gain on the income tax expenses you lose on the capital gains tax exemption. It is understood that the Revenue seek to apportion the exemption so as to accord with the taxpayer's claim in respect of rates.   Thus if a writer has been claiming one-fifth of his rates as an expense of his profession, then one-fifth of his gain on sale will be subjected to capital gains tax.   However, apart altogether from the point that rateable values and capital values have different bases, it is possible to discern no less than four flaws in this Revenue approach.

First, no great insistence on the exclusiveness of use for trade or professional purposes has hitherto been encountered for income tax deduction purposes.   Thus a room that doubles, for example, as a study and occasional lounge may well enable an expenses claim without attracting capital gains tax.   Second, the subsection quoted at the beginning of the preceding paragraph is couched in the present tense (i.e., F.A. 1965, s. 29 (5)).   Therefore, it is arguable that no apportionment need be made where a part of the dwelling-house has been but no longer is used for trade, etc., purposes (but see here the next paragraph).   Third, the apportionment should in any case be restricted to the gain accruing from disposal of the dwelling-house (or part) itself and should not take into account at all any gain due to disposal of the garden (the subsection refers only to a dwelling-house and, anyway, the garden is unlikely to be used exclusively for trade, etc., purposes).   And fourth, even if this exemption from capital gains tax should be partly lost, there appears no reason why the " replacement of business premises " relief (see *ante*, p. 1081) could not be properly claimed.

Not all dwelling-houses remain static in the extent of their occupation and user : reconstruction or conversion of the building (e.g., into flats with one or more let) may take place or there may be changes as regards the use of part of it for trading, etc., purposes.   In such cases, this exemption " may be adjusted in such manner as the Commissioners concerned may consider to be just and reasonable " (F.A. 1965, s. 29 (6).

Multiple dwelling-houses.—Those fortunate enough to own and occupy two dwelling-houses (e.g., a town mansion and country cottage)—or even more than two—also enjoy the privilege of choosing which should be treated as their main residence for the purposes of this exemption (F.A. 1965, s. 29 (7)). The choice might sensibly be dictated by an estimate as to which will produce the greater or greatest gain on disposal.   Failing any such choice (by notice in writing to the inspector of taxes which may be varied and which may, in effect, operate retrospectively for up to two years) the question will ultimately be determined, subject to appeal, by the inspector (*ibid.*). Presumably, the inspector, unlike the taxpayer, will have to relate his determination to the facts of residence rather than to the amount of exempted gains. Incidentally, it is surprisingly arguable that the exemption, although confined to one dwelling-house, may actually cover any number of gardens : provided the garden is occupied and enjoyed with a dwelling-house which has at any time been the individual's only or main residence it falls fairly and squarely within the words of the section (see F.A. 1965, s. 29 (1) (*b*)).

A man and his wife living with him are again to be regarded, in effect, as one individual. There can only be one (main) residence for both so long as they are living together (F.A. 1965, s. 29 (8) (*a*)). A choice of residence, where it affects both spouses, must be exercised by both (*ibid.* ; see the preceding paragraph) and notice of the inspector's determination in default must be given to each where it affects residences owned by each, either of whom may appeal (*ibid.*, s. 29 (8) (*c*)). Further, where one spouse disposes of his or her interest in a dwelling-house to the other spouse, then for the purposes of this exemption the period of ownership of the latter is to be taken as beginning when the former's did (*ibid.*, s. 29 (8) (*b*), applying where the spouses are living together and the dwelling-house is the only or main residence). Where this last provision applies, it is possible that the period of ownership and residence of the former spouse was not also a period of residence of the latter (e.g., where a husband had owned the house before marriage) ; nevertheless, in effect, the spouses will be deemed both resident whilst the former alone was resident (*ibid.*, s. 29 (8) (*bb*), added by F.A. 1969, Sched. 10, para. 7). Reference should also be made generally to the relief available for disposals between spouses (*ante*, p. 1079). It should also be observed that in the unhappily common situation where a husband has deserted his wife, they will no longer be living together within these exemptions and the dwelling-house will have ceased to be his only or main residence (this latter point will not deprive him of any of the exemption if he manages to sell within twelve months : F.A. 1965, s. 29 (2) (3) ; see also, as to transfers in the course of matrimonial proceedings or under a separation agreement, a note by P.L. at [1973] B.T.R. 193).

Garden.—The garden or grounds of a dwelling-house within the exemption (see *ante*, p. 1083) is subject to the general limitation of being up to an area (inclusive of the site of the dwelling-house) of one acre (F.A. 1965, s. 29 (1) (*b*)). However, the Commissioners may allow a larger area to qualify in any particular case on being satisfied that the larger area is required for the reasonable enjoyment of the dwelling-house, regard being had to its size and character (*ibid.*, cf. S.L.A. 1925, s. 65 (2), under which a principal mansion house must have more than twenty-five acres of pleasure grounds and park and land usually occupied with it). It would seem unlikely that a larger area would be allowed if the garden, or part of it, were to be sold separately from the dwelling-house, since this surely indicates that what is being sold was *not* required for the reasonable enjoyment of the dwelling-house. If the area of the garden is larger than one acre, and is not all allowed by the Commissioners, then the problem arises of determining which part of the garden is covered by the exemption. According to statute, in such a case, it is that part of the garden, " which, if the remainder were separately occupied, would be the most suitable for occupation and enjoyment with the residence " (*ibid.*). Normally, no doubt, this will mean that the nearest, surrounding part of a large garden is covered by the exemption, i.e., the acre with the dwelling-house on it, but it could produce difficult questions of fact. See further the useful discussion by Robert Argles in *Solicitors' Journal* (1972), vol. 116, p. 575.

Trustees.—In form, though not in substance, a separate exemption becomes available where a dwelling-house (or part or garden) is being disposed of not by an owner-occupier but by trustees. The exemption then depends on whether the dwelling-house has been the only or main residence of " a person entitled to occupy it under the terms of the settlement " (F.A. 1965, s. 29 (9)). This is inaptly drafted since the commonest case of a beneficiary being entitled to occupation of trust property is the tenant for life of a strict settlement who would also be the individual disposing of the dwelling-house under his statutory powers. In the case of other trusts in practice it is more common for beneficiaries merely to be permitted occupation at the discretion of the trustees (cp. *Re Herklots' Will Trusts* [1964] 1 W.L.R. 583, where there was a direction as to occupation). However, by concession the exemption is also available " in respect of a residence occupied by permission of the trustees of a settlement by an individual who is entitled, under the terms of the settlement, to the whole income from the residence or from its proceeds on sale " (Extra-Statutory Concession D 3 I.R. 1 (Insert) (1972)). Clearly a discretionary trust, properly so-called, will not satisfy even the concession. One wonders whether the exemption would be allowed where trustees permit more than one individual to reside, they being the beneficiaries together entitled to the whole income. However, the concession (*loc. cit.*) does expressly apply where personal representatives dispose of a house which before and after the deceased's death has been used as the only or main residence of individuals who under the will or intestacy are entitled to the whole or substantially the whole of the proceeds of the house either absolutely or for life. See further A. M. S. Alexander at *Law Society's Gazette* (1972), vol. 69, No. 11, at p. 8.

Dependent relative.—An extra exemption of similar substance is available in respect of a dwelling-house (or part and its garden) which the owner has provided " rent-free and without any other consideration " as the sole residence of a dependent relative (F.A. 1965, s. 29 (10)). For this purpose, a dependent relative is a relative of the owner, or of his spouse, " who is incapacitated by old age or infirmity from maintaining himself, or the mother of the individual or of his or her wife or husband, if the mother is widowed or living apart from her husband, or, in consequence of dissolution or annulment of marriage, a single woman " (*ibid.* ; thus unmarried mothers, like all fathers, must be incapacitated). This extra exemption has to be claimed and only one dwelling-house will qualify at any one time *per* individual and *per* spouse living together (*ibid.*, proviso (*a*)). Any rival claims in respect of the dependent relatives of each spouse may have to be settled to the satisfaction of the inspector of taxes before any exemption at all is allowed (*ibid.*, proviso (*b*)).

One question which could well arise here is the scope of the words " without any other consideration ". In practice it is surely most common for people housed rent-free to agree to pay all or some of the outgoings and to undertake the maintenance of the property (cf. *Binions* v. *Evans* [1972] Ch. 359). Strictly, any such arrangements would appear to lead to loss of this capital gains tax exemption. The Revenue may well not take a strict view, but the risk can be avoided by making it clear that any such arrangements are non-binding.

35

Purposeful gains.—No doubt in anticipation of attempts to abuse this private residence exemption, provision is made that it should not apply :

" in relation to a gain if the acquisition of, or of the interest in, the dwelling-house or the part of a dwelling-house was made wholly or partly for the purpose of realising a gain from the disposal of it, and shall not apply in relation to a gain so far as attributable to any expenditure which was incurred after the beginning of the period of ownership and was incurred wholly or partly for the purpose of realising a gain from the disposal "

(F.A. 1968, Sched. 12, para. 2, which has effect in substitution for subs. (11) of s. 29 of the F.A. 1965).

The intention of this provision is clear : no capital gains tax exemption should be obtainable merely by the device of interposing residence between acquisition and disposal. The effect is less clear. On the one hand, if the realisation of a gain was really the purpose of the acquisition then the profit on sale should in any case be liable to income tax (i.e., as arising from an adventure in the nature of trade ; see *Page* v. *Pogson* (1954), 35 T.C. 545, which is precisely in point ; cf. *Eames* v. *Stepnell Properties, Ltd.* [1967] 1 W.L.R. 593 ; but not as an artificial transaction in land ; see s. 488 (9) of the I.C.T.A. 1970). On the other hand, every purchaser of a dwelling-house these days must surely expect to be able to re-sell at an increased price keeping in step with inflation. Accordingly the purpose of the acquisition must almost always be at least *partly* to realise a gain on disposal. It will be appreciated that an increased nominal value due only to inflation nevertheless constitutes a capital gain (see *Secretan* v. *Hart* [1969] 1 W.L.R. 1599) and that the whole exemption would be lost where gain was even partly the purpose of acquisition (see F.A. 1968, Sched. 12, para. 2, *ante*).

However, some realistic line must certainly be drawn to give the exemption some meaning in *bona fide* private residence situations. Indeed a practical limit is to be found in the fact that the onus appears to be on the Revenue of showing that gain was the (or a) purpose of the acquisition (see *ibid.*, and compare the terms of the replaced subs. (11) of s. 29 of the F.A. 1965, under which this onus would have been on the tax payer). Interesting, in this connection, therefore, is the example given by the Board of Inland Revenue (Capital Gains Tax Booklet C.G.T. 8, para. 78 in Feb. 1973 revision) as follows : " If, for example, an individual who was the lessee of a private house under the terms of a lease which still had thirty years to run purchased the freehold because he was on the point of leaving the house and thought that he would make a larger gain, over and above the additional cost of acquiring the freehold, if he could dispose of it as a freehold property, the additional part of the gain which related to his ability to dispose of the freehold interest, would be outside the scope of the exemption ". Thus the exciting benefits of enfranchisement under the Leasehold Reform Act, 1967, might be rather dampened by a later capital gains tax liability (but cp. George, Taxation and Property Transactions, 3rd ed., pp. 291–2, as to the abolished short term capital gains tax).

Further, it should be observed that this provision for loss of the private residence exemption in terms refers solely to the dwelling-house and does not anywhere mention the garden or grounds (see F.A. 1968, Sched. 12, para. 2, quoted above). Accordingly, certain obvious arguments are open to tax-payers (and see *ante*, p. 1084, as to the distinction between paras. (*a*) and (*b*) of s. 29 (1) of the F.A. 1965). For example, it should strictly be possible to purchase a dwelling-house and large garden intending not only residence and enjoyment for a time but also the eventual profitable sale of a building plot all beneath the cover of this exemption. Nevertheless, it seems unlikely that the Revenue would ever quietly accept this contention, however arguable it might be.

A connected point arises from a query as to the scope of expenditure which leads to exclusion of gains by Sched. 12, para. 2, to the 1968 Act (see above). Does this mean only expenditure which was actually on the land ? For example, if money is spent in obtaining planning permission for part of a garden which is then sold as a building plot at a handsome profit, does Sched. 12, para. 2, apply ? It is understood that the Revenue view is that the profit must be apportioned with the gain attributable to the planning permission being taxable. But, as almost always, this appears arguable : even though the gain might not have been obtainable without the planning permission, it does not necessarily follow, according to the ordinary usage of words, that the gain can really be regarded as *attributable* to that permission.

PART 2.   SCHEDULE D, CASE I—INCOME TAX

A. TRADERS

A sale of land will normally nowadays produce a profit. Such a profit will be potentially taxable. It may be a capital profit ; if so, reference should be made either to Capital Gains Tax (*ante*, p. 1039) or to " artificial transactions in land " (*post*, p. 1106). Or else it may be an income profit, the vendor being classified as a " trader." This possibility is considered in the following pages which, however, do not attempt anything like a full survey of the law of income tax even as relating only to traders. What do follow are some notes which could only be described as miscellaneous were it not for the connecting factor that they all bear some more or less direct relevance to sales of land.

Of course, the question precedent is whether the profit is capital or income, for if the former what follows will be by definition inapplicable. However, the traditional approach (established before the imposition of any capital gains tax) has always been to enquire first whether the profit was income, or more precisely whether the vendor was a trader, without considering the nature of capital as such. This approach was necessarily adopted because there were statutory provisions upon which a positive answer could hang and which had always to be considered. Until the early- to mid-1960's the alternative negative answer (i.e., not income) merely led to a legislative vacuum into which profits or gains escaped tax-free if they could. Accordingly, capital *versus* income in this context can only be decided through the twofold process of first collecting the few statutory provisions which might charge income tax on the profit from a sale of land and of then examining these provisions in the light of judicial interpretation.

Charging provisions.—The charge to income tax is by reference to six mutually exclusive Schedules which describe various sources of income (I.C.T.A. 1970, s. 1 ; *Mitchell and Eden* v. *Ross* [1962] A.C. 1). It is Schedule D which covers traders by virtue of its Case I (I.C.T.A. 1970, ss. 108, 109). The bare essential words may be extracted straight from the statute as follows : " Tax . . . shall be charged in respect of—the annual profits or gains arising or accruing—to any person . . . in respect of any trade carried on in the United Kingdom or elsewhere " (Schedule D, para. 1 (a), Case I, I.C.T.A. 1970, ss. 108, 109 ; if the trade be carried on elsewhere residence in the United Kingdom is a requirement). The vital word " *trade* " has in addition had a circular explanation extended to it by which it " includes every trade, manufacture, adventure or concern in the nature of trade " (I.C.T.A. 1970, s. 526 (5)). As a definition this has been authoratively stigmatised as " not worth very much " (*per* Lord Donovan in *J. G. Ingram & Son, Ltd.* v. *Callaghan* (1969), 45 T.C. 151, at p. 166) ; and as being of " baffling simplicity " (*per* Megarry, J., in *Ransom* v. *Higgs* [1972] 2 All E.R. 817, at p. 838 ; on appeal [1973] 2 All E.R. 657).

By way of narrowing down the present consideration to focus upon the statutory words, two preliminary points may be made. First, Schedule A tax is directed particularly to rents and similar receipts from land (I.C.T.A 1970, s. 67) and where it applies (see Leases, *post*, p. 1115), it does so strictly to the exclusion of Schedule D, Case I, over which it prevails (see *Fry* v. *Salisbury House Estate, Ltd.* [1930] A.C. 432, although in practice the differentiation may not be quite so rigid : see George, Taxation and Property Transactions, 3rd ed., p. 46). Second, the seemingly " sweeping-up " Case VI of Schedule D (which catches, in effect, income not otherwise caught : I.C.T.A. 1970, s. 109 (2)), does *not* apply to a profit on the sale of property—such a profit must be either attributed to trade or else treated as a capital gain (see *per* Lawrence, L.J., in *Leeming* v. *Jones* [1930] 1 K.B. 279, at p. 302 ; affirmed *sub nom. Jones* v. *Leeming* [1930] A.C. 415). However, certain specific profits from land have been especially assigned to Case VI, e.g., gains from " artificial transactions in land " (I.C.T.A. 1970, s. 488 (3)), rent from furnished lettings (*ibid.*, s. 67 (1)) and certain premiums payable otherwise than to the landlord (*ibid.*, s. 80 (5)).

What is trading ?—With only the circular statutory explanation for a guide, the concept of " trade " tends to prove elusive. Of course, there are obvious applications—the baker, the butcher, the candle-stick maker should all use the tradesmen's entrance—but the imaginative range of mankind's profitable activities can certainly cause difficult questions (e.g., " Is Dividend Stripping a Trade ? " at [1970] B.T.R., p. 211 ; see also [1972] B.T.R., p. 6). And when the question has become difficult there is simply no rule of thumb test which will supply the answer. Indeed the nature of the question itself is not entirely uncomplicated : whilst it is a question of law what meaning is to be given to the statutory words " trade, manufacture, adventure or concern in the nature of trade," it is a question of fact whether any particular transaction comes within that meaning (see *Edwards* v. *Bairstow & Harrison* [1956] A.C. 14). Thus the courts only allow themselves, with respectful expressions of reluctance, to interfere with a decision of the General or Special Commissioners when it is considered that that decision is contradicted by the one reasonable conclusion from the facts in the stated case, since then the Commissioners must have misdirected themselves as to the law (*ibid.*). This near sophistry hardly helps the candidate taxpayer or his advisers, especially as the courts have conspicuously failed to provide any answer which even approaches general adequacy to the question of law (see, e.g., the judgment of Scott, L.J., in *Barry* v. *Cordy* [1946] 2 All E.R. 396, at pp. 398–399, making extensive reference to the Oxford English Dictionary in order to conclude that the word " trade " is of the very widest import). In consequence, the reported cases remain in reality mere factual illustrations rather than legal precedents. When it is borne in mind that, once an assessment has been made by an inspector of taxes, any appeal before the Commissioners must be conducted on the basis of guilty of trading unless proved innocent (see Taxes Management Act, 1970, s. 50 (6)), the plight of a citizen caught in this morass of uncertainty is potentially and often actually appalling.

Happily, however, the possibilities arising from a profitable sale of land, not being a transaction of infinite variety, cannot stretch the imagination as much as transactions in other contexts might (although saying this means turning a blind eye to the " novel transactions of considerable intricacy " involving land and defying summary considered in *Ransom* v. *Higgs* [1972] 2 All E.R. 817, 836, on appeal [1973] 2 All E.R. 657). Where a man has bought land only three basic possibilities would appear open :—

(1) He may have bought the land for his own use and occupation, either actually or constructively, for example as a private residence or as business premises. Unlike certain other commodities or manufactured articles of which only commercial disposal could be envisaged, land is clearly capable of personal enjoyment by virtue of ownership (cp. *Rutledge* v. *I.R.C.* (1929), 14 T.C. 490). In this common case, there is no trading and eventual re-sale at a profit would simply produce a capital gain (as to the taxation of which see *ante*, p. 1090).

(2) He may have bought the land for the sake of the income produced by it, i.e., as an investment as where the property is let at a rent. This again does not lead to trading but to a capital gain on the change of investments (see *I.R.C.* v. *Reinhold* (1953), 34 T.C. 389 ; cp. *Cooke* v. *Haddock* (1960), 39 T.C. 64).

(3) He may have bought the land with the idea of realising a profit on re-sale. Stated baldly in this way, without any circumstantial detail, the most plausible and likely inference would be that " an adventure in the nature of trade " had been undertaken leading to an income tax charge under Sched. D, Case I. This inference would become irresistible if, for example, the purchase and re-sale was one of a series of such transactions. One of the so-called " badges of trade " is " the frequency or number of similar transactions by the same person " (Royal Commission on the Taxation of Profits and Income Final Report, para. 116, 1955 Cmnd. 9474). To put it another way, land may simply be stock in trade :—

" The determining factor must be the nature of the trade in which the asset is employed. The land upon which a manufacturer carries on his business is part of his fixed capital. The land with which a dealer in real estate carries on his business is part of his circulating capital "

(*per* Romer, L.J., in *Golden Horse Shoe* (*New*), *Ltd.* v. *Thurgood* [1934] 1 K.B. 548, at p. 563). And more graphically :

" The price of a sale of a factory is ordinarily a capital receipt, but it may be an income receipt in the case of a person whose business it is to buy and sell factories "

(*per* Lord Macmillan in *Van der Berghs, Ltd.* v. *Clark* [1935] A.C. 431, at p. 441 ; see also *W. M. Robb, Ltd.* v. *Page* (1971), 47 T.C. 465, where the taxpayer's business was found in fact to involve the building and selling of factories).

Unhappily, the clarity of these basic possibilities can become blurred by changes of mind. A purchase of land which comes clearly and comfortably within possibilities (1) or (2) above does not thereby confer an immutable immunity from income tax on re-sale. The initial intention not to trade may be displaced by a subsequent intention in the course of ownership to embark upon an adventure in the nature of trade (see *Mitchell Bros.* v.

Tomlinson (1957), 37 T.C. 224, C.A., where the taxpayer was found to have departed from a policy of holding houses as an investment fund ; also *W. M. Robb, Ltd.* v. *Page, ante,* where the factory in question had been held for some twelve years as a fixed asset of the business). Thus in a recent imaginative example, a council flat tenant bought a 17-bedroom mansion for £5,100 with an idea of living there but soon abandoned the idea and instead obtained planning permission for comprehensive redevelopment, eventually selling for £54,500 ; he was found to have been trading and therefore liable to income tax (*Taylor* v. *Good* [1973] 2 All E.R. 785). As to changes of mind generally, and the other way, see *Appropriations, post,* p. 1102.

However, the carrot of tax-free capital gains has over the years been a considerable incentive for resistance to the " trader " inference on sales of land. Indeed, the two quotations in the paragraph before last, although generally helpful, do point to one particular problem : persons who are indubitably traders are capable of having, and would usually prefer to have, capital receipts. Even admitted traders in land can contend that, in addition to their stock in trade, they hold land for use and occupation or at least as an investment. Such contentions are sometimes successful (as in *West* v. *Phillips* (1958), 38 T.C. 203, C.A.), sometimes—and it has seemed more often— not (as in *Eames* v. *Stepnell Properties, Ltd.* [1967] 1 W.L.R. 593, C.A. ; see also *Snell* v. *Rosser, Thomas & Co., Ltd.* [1967] 1 W.L.R. 295, *W. M. Robb, Ltd.* v. *Page, ante,* p. 1093 ; and *Speck* v. *Morton* (1972), 48 T.C. 476).

Another apparently perennial problem has been caused by the "isolated transaction," where there is no series but a single purchase and re-sale of property at a profit. Although the House of Lords once decided that such a transaction gave rise only to a capital gain (i.e., in *Jones* v. *Leeming* [1930] A.C. 415, which concerned land), recent years have seen this decision consistently bypassed (see, e.g., *Wisdom* v. *Chamberlain* [1969] 1 W.L.R. 275, where the Court of Appeal upheld the assessment of a well-known comedian as a dealer in silver following one profitable adventure—as Harman, L.J., said at p. 281, this " would take most of the gilt off the gingerbread) ". Sales of land have not been allowed to escape from this approach ; isolated transactions in land have been condemned as trading (see *Turner* v. *Last* (1965), 42 Tax Cas. 517, and *Johnston* v. *Heath* [1970] 1 W.L.R. 1567). Just how difficult such escape would be was recently underlined by Megarry, J., who, in a case concerning profits from transactions in land, said :—

> " No doubt from time to time human ingenuity conjures up some new money-making venture which does not fit into any of the ordinary categories of trade. But activities which exhibit the characteristics of trade do not fail to be trades merely because they are rare or innominate or, for that matter, do not consist of any regular business of buying and selling "

(in *Ransom* v. *Higgs* [1972] 2 All E.R. 817, at p. 838 ; on appeal [1973] 2 All E.R. 657). In the result, the Commissioners' finding that Mr. Higgs was a trader was not disturbed by the facts that he had acted as controlling shareholder of certain land-owning companies and that the profits had all been received by trustees who were assessable.

No further exposition of deducible principles will be attempted since it is thought that all the decision ultimately and essentially depended on considerations of fact :—

> " There is [a great deal of] danger . . . of exalting to the status of propositions of law what really are particular applications to special facts of propositions of ordinary good sense "

(*per* du Parcq, L.J., in *Easson* v. *London North Eastern Railway Co.* [1944] K.B. 421, at p. 426 ; see also [1944] 2 All E.R. 425, at p. 430 ; consider further the judgments of Lord Somervell of Harrow and Lord Denning in *Qualcast (Wolverhampton), Ltd.* v. *Haynes* [1959] A.C. 743, at pp. 758 and 759, as to the precedent system dying of a surfeit of authorities if decisions on facts are treated as citable). It is true that the courts have had to pretend that a question of law was involved in some cases in order that decisions of the Commissioners could be reconsidered and reversed on appeal (see *Edwards* v. *Bairstow & Harrison* [1956] A.C. 14). But since such reconsiderations always turn on the one reasonable conclusion to be drawn from the facts (*ibid.*), no real question of law is ever involved in the decision " trade " or " no trade " in any particular case, and strictly speaking none of the cases constitute binding precedents. It is only a failure to appreciate this vital distinction in significance between decisions of fact and decisions of law which can lead to such misapprehensions as the suggestion that any subsequent case ought to be reconcileable " with the undoubted principle established authoritatively in *Jones* v. *Leeming*" (George, Taxation and Property Transactions, 3rd ed., at p. 30).

There are additional entirely practical reasons for not pursuing the search for principles lurking within the question of " trade " or " no trade ". More precisely the question would be : when is a vendor of land to be treated as a trader and the profit assessable to income tax under Sched. D, Case I ? And the answer in practice must surely be : only when it is literally clear beyond argument that he was trading.

Hitherto the argument has been due to the fact that "trade " *versus* " no trade " actually meant " tax " *versus* " tax free." This is no longer so. The capital gains tax provisions will now catch most if not all of the arguable transactions in property. Thus the case stated in *Johnston* v. *Heath* [1970] 1 W.L.R. 1567, at p. 1570E, includes the line : " it was also admitted that capital gains taxes were introduced in 1962 and 1965 to cover this type of [isolated] transaction." There appear to be no reported cases involving the " trade " *versus* " no trade " argument with regard to the sale of property where the profits arose appropriately in a tax year after the introduction in 1965 of capital gains tax although cases concerning earlier tax years still reach the reports. Thus recently in *Ransom* v. *Higgs* [1972] 2 All E.R. 817, virtually all the relevant steps were taken during " what must have been a busy period of eight days ending on 5th April, 1961 " : *per* Megarry, J., at p. 837 ; on appeal, [1973] 2 All E.R. 657. Again, there have been a number of cases where the profits accrued on a sale after 1962 (but before 1965) of property purchased several years earlier so that the short-term capital gains tax could not have bitten (see, e.g., *W. M. Robb, Ltd.* v. *Page* (1971), 47 T.C. 465 ; *Taylor* v. *Good* [1973] 2 All E.R. 785 ; also *Speck* v. *Morton* (1972), 48 T.C. 476, and *Parkin* v. *Cattell* (1971), 48 T.C. 462, C.A. ; but cp. *Clark* v. *Follett* [1973] T.R. 43).

Apart from capital gains tax, very wide provisions were enacted in 1969 expressly " to prevent the avoidance of tax by persons concerned with land or the development of land " (F.A. 1969, s. 32 and Sched. 16, replacing some too specialised sections of the F.A.'s 1960 and 1962, and now consolidated into ss. 488 to 490 of I.C.T.A. 1970). These provisions, in general, will catch for income tax any profit from a sale of land which might otherwise be within reach of, although liable to be missed by, the " trader " concept. They are considered later under " Artificial Transactions in Land " (*post*, p. 1106).

In view, therefore, of the provisions referred to in the two preceding paragraphs, there can be little doubt that, for sales of land at least, the battle-scarred borderline between " trade " and " no trade " should now be abandoned by both sides as fruitless neutral ground. And were it not for the loss of the tax-free chance, the abandonment would be attended only by relief :

> " There have been many cases which fell on the borderline. Indeed, in many cases it is almost true to say that the spin of a coin would decide the matter almost as satisfactorily as an attempt to find reasons "

(*per* Greene, M.R., in *I.R.C.* v. *British Salmson Aero Engines, Ltd.* [1938] 2 K.B. 482, at p. 498). No longer need coins be spun : only when it is literally clear beyond argument that a vendor of land was trading will any reliance have to be placed by the Revenue on the magic words of Schedule D, Case I.

However, the present position in substance and rather surprisingly would appear to be that the *taxpayer* is able to choose whether or not to be treated as a trader. Why might a person prefer income profits to capital gains ? It depends entirely on his fiscal circumstances. Of course, the main, often overwhelming disadvantage of being treated as a trader is the higher rate(s) of income tax. Notwithstanding this, however, potential advantages may be perceived. Thus all the " trade " expenses and any resulting losses will be allowable against income generally. Also some benefit may be derived from the preceding year basis of assessment. Again it may be desirable to escape some of the more irksome rules of capital gains tax, e.g., those relating to short leases as wasting assets. Accordingly, only a careful consideration of the circumstances, both known and predicted, of a particular taxpayer can indicate whether or not it would prove favourable to be a trader in relation to land.

The choice was said to be in substance the taxpayer's for it can hardly be doubted that the Revenue would be unable and unwilling in practice to contest a claim to be a trader made by a landowner who has supplied sufficiently clear evidence of an intention to trade in land. Such evidence calls for some foresight and goes beyond merely completing appropriately an income tax return, but it should be by no means difficult to establish (see *Reeves* v. *Evans, Boyce and Northcote Syndicate* (1971), 48 T.C. 495, where the trappings of trade had been effectively assumed by means of a partnership deed declaring the taxpayer's intentions). Against this, if the taxpayer does not wish to be treated as a trader, he might well leave his intentions obscure and his status a matter of argument in the expectation that the Revenue will then rely on the certainty of the alternative taxing provisions (but see *per* Megarry, J., at *ibid.*, p. 514, as to the standards expected of solicitors).

Computation.—On the assumption that the vendor of land is, in fact, found to be a trader, what precisely is his tax liability ? The answer is provided in the form of an extremely general rule as follows :

> " . . . income tax shall be charged under Case I . . . of Schedule II on *the full amount of the profits or gains* of the year preceding the year of assessment "

(I.C.T.A. 1970, s. 115 (1) ; italics supplied). Thus the words italicised indicate what has to be computed, but beyond this the statute offers no further assistance with the computation—there is not even any definition of " profits or gains ".

However, the courts have established the equally general proposition that the computation of profits and gains must be in accordance with the ordinary principles of commercial accounting unless these happen to conflict with some specific provision of the Income Tax Acts (see *Odeon Associated Theatres, Ltd.* v. *Jones* [1972] 2 W.L.R. 331, C.A., and the numerous cases cited therein). Therefore everything can turn in the end on expert evidence as to accountancy principles. This is not the place to speculate about the position where there appears to be an absence of such principles or a conflict of evidence (cf. *B.S.C. Footwear, Ltd.* v. *Ridgway* [1972] A.C. 544). Nor is there space to discuss the questions of whether changes in accountancy principles automatically alter otherwise established tax consequences, and of whether accepted accountancy principles are conclusive as to profits and gains for tax purposes (cf. *Heather* v. *P-E Consulting Group, Ltd.* [1973] 1 All E.R. 8, where the Court of Appeal pronounced that such principles were not conclusive as to what was capital and what was revenue expenditure, this remaining a question of law, although the decision actually did accord with the evidence given by accountants ; see also Buckley, L.J., in *Odeon Associated Theatres, Ltd.* v. *Jones* [1972] 2 W.L.R. 331, at p. 340). In point here alone is the application of these principles to sales of land so as to define (1) the taxable receipts, and (2) the deductible expenditure—the difference between these producing the " profits and gains " within Case I of Schedule D (losses are arrived at in the same way).

Traders in land, in the tax sense, are only likely to be one or other of two sorts. On the one hand there will be the admitted traders, persons who are, and were from the beginning of their transactions, by both intention and act, property dealers, builders or developers. This sort should have properly kept accounts for the whole period of their trading which, just as with any other traders, would incidentally throw up their tax liability. On the other hand there may still be persons found retrospectively to be traders, i.e., persons who have made a profit from one or more transactions in land and have been successfully assessed as traders. This latter sort may be a declining breed for the reasons indicated earlier, but if encountered the result will usually be that trading accounts will have to be constructed for the relevant period. With either sort, however, there is usually little of practice or principle that is peculiar to traders in land. For example, of no special concern to conveyancers is the preceding year basis of assessment or the commencement and discontinuance rules (I.C.T.A. 1970, ss. 115 to 118). Accordingly what follows does not in any way purport to be a comprehensive account of trader's tax computations. Instead, it is confined to what little there is of peculiar relevance to land dealings. Within these confines, therefore, what is offered are a few rather miscellaneous notes on (1) the taxable receipts, and (2) the deductible expenditure of traders in land.

Taxable receipts.—*Prima facie*, of course, there would seem to be no real problem here : if a vendor of land is assessable as a trader, then obviously the purchase price will be the primary taxable receipt. However, even this apparently elementary proposition has about it a few noteworthy points of elaboration. In particular, two well-established sub-rules need to be applied. Firstly, in accordance with accepted accountancy principles, a trader's profits are ordinarily computed by reference to his earnings, rather than his actual cash receipts, in the relevant period (see *Gardner, Mountain and D'Ambrumenil, Ltd.* v. *I.R.C.* [1947] 1 All E.R. 650, H.L.). On this earnings basis, therefore, sums of money would be treated as taxable receipts when payment is due (an allowance may be claimed later for bad debts: I.C.T.A. 1970, s. 130 (*i*)). Secondly, if a trader receives payment not in money but in money's worth, this should be included in the computation at " the best valuation possible " (*Gold Coast Trust, Ltd.* v. *Humphrey* [1948] A.C. 459, see *per* Viscount Simon at p. 473). This would cover exchanges of land whether for different land or for other assets, such as shares.

Instalments.—So far as concerns sales of land, the earnings basis will usually coincide with the alternative cash basis since completion will normally involve actual payment of the purchase money which was not previously due (see, e.g., *per* Vaisey, J., in *Palmer* v. *Lark* [1945] Ch. 182, at pp. 194–195). Nevertheless, it is not too uncommon, especially with builders' sales, for some part of the purchase price to be left outstanding on completion and for that unpaid balance to be payable by future instalments, no doubt with interest, and on the security of a (second) mortgage. The question then is how that balance should appear in any computation of profits. Exactly this case has been considered in the House of Lords where (by a bare majority) no very satisfactory decision was reached (in *Absalom* v. *Talbot* [1944] A.C. 204). The majority, although firmly rejecting the Crown's contention that the balance of the purchase price (*less* interest) should be included at full face value, actually suggested various methods of calculating the profits in such cases before finally indicating no less than two methods. Of these two methods, the one apparently preferred by a majority of the majority was valuation : that is to say, the balance of the price should be brought into the computation as at the time of the sale but at a valuation " which takes into account all the risks which a creditor runs who . . . gives very long credit on doubtful security " (*per* Lord Russell of Killowen at *ibid.*, p. 222). The other method is simply to include the instalments in the computations for the years in which they are payable (which would generally be the whole of the balance if and when any default occurred).

However, it must be said that the preference shown for the former, valuation method is highly suspect for certain intrinsic reasons. To begin with, the case was in fact sent back to the Commissioners with the direction—

" . . . it will be sufficient to leave it to them to settle the right method of adjusting the assessment, feeling that the method of valuation affords least scope for legal doubt, and that, in default of satisfactory valuation being possible, they may have to fall back upon the method of taxing instalments in each year as they fall due "

(*per* Lord Atkin, whose speech led the majority, in *Absolom* v. *Talbot* [1944] A.C. 204, at p. 218). Can an instruction in these terms be described as a decision at all ? Is the question not shown to be rather one of fact than of law ? Then the preference for the valuation method was couched in strange terms : it was called " a rough method of adjusting profit " in contrast to the " more accurate method " of taxing the instalments (*per* Lord Atkin, *loc. cit.*, pp. 217–8). However, the true and only explanation for preferring the valuation method is rendered explicit throughout the speeches : it was the base fear that otherwise instalments payable after a discontinuance of the trade would not be chargeable to tax (see *ibid.*). This would almost certainly have been correct as at the date of the case but has not been any sort of factor since so-called " post-cessation receipts " were brought into charge by various provisions of the 1960 and 1968 Finance Acts (now consolidated into I.C.T.A. 1970, ss. 143–151). Accordingly, it is strongly submitted that the proper method to be adopted today in the sort of case under discussion is to compute profits as and when the balance of the price, or any instalment of it, becomes due and payable. There appears no longer to be any valid reason for preferring the valuation method which it was conceded suffered from the inherent defect of permitting " no means of subsequent correction by actual results " (*per* Lord Atkin, *loc. cit.*).

Building society deposits.—A very similar sort of situation which has come before the courts is the following : a builder sells a house to a purchaser to whom a building society makes an excessive advance (i.e., beyond the normal proportion of its valuation) ; in consideration for this the builder not only guarantees the repayment of the excess but also deposits a sum of money (at interest) with the building society in support of the guarantee, which sum is only releasable on the fulfilment of certain specified conditions by the purchaser (see further *ante*, p. 259). The situation will probably be complicated by the fact that, although in theory the sum deposited would represent a part of the excess advance, in practice total sums would be deposited to cover numerous such transactions. Nevertheless, in substance the situation can be seen to be that a part of the sale price is neither received by nor due to the builder-vendor at the time of completion. The question then, as before, is how to treat these deposited sums in the computation of his profits. The answer offered by the courts starts from the premise that the deposit should not be regarded as simply constituting a debt of money but as representing an asset consisting of various contractual rights and obligations subsisting between the builder and the building society. This being so, that asset should be brought into the computation of the builder's profits as at the time of the sale at a proper valuation *if practicable*. But if a proper valuation is *not* practicable, then the sum deposited should only be included in the computation when it is released to or otherwise becomes receivable by the builder. The principal authority for this answer is the Court of Appeal decision in *Chibbett* v. *Harold Brookfield & Son, Ltd.* [1952] 2 Q.B. 677 in which was explained the House of Lords' decision in *Harrison* v. *John Cronk & Sons, Ltd.* [1937] A.C. 185. However it is thought essential to appreciate that both the Court of Appeal and the House of Lords in these cases evinced a complete absence of belief that the valuation indicated would ever prove practicable. Accordingly, it can fairly safely be assumed that the latter method, whereby the deposits are taxable only when receivable, will be adopted in practice (see George, Taxation and Property Transactions, 3rd ed., at p. 131). Again the point may be noticed that the position can no longer be prejudiced, as in the cited cases, by the risk of post-cessation receipts escaping tax.

It should incidentally be observed that the valuation methods indicated by the *Absalom* and *Cronk* cases above have been held inappropriate for capital gains tax purposes (*Coren* v. *Keighley* (1972), 48 T.C., at p. 381). One consequence of this is that any difference between the amount treated as a trading receipt and the (higher) total purchase price might be subject to capital gains tax (see *per* Ungoed-Thomas, J., at *ibid.*, p. 381F).

Notwithstanding the preceding paragraphs, the basic principle remains that if the purchase price on a sale of land by a trader is due in full on completion then the whole sum should be included in the computation of profits in that period. The fact that the vendor-trader may deal with the price without actually receiving it should make no difference, and this may be so even though the dealing takes the form of a loan back to the purchaser (see, e.g., *Lock* v. *Jones* (1941), 23 T.C. 749 ; cf. *Coren* v. *Keighley* (1972), 48 T.C. 370).

Rentcharges.—The somewhat uncertain references in the cases cited in the preceding paragraphs to the valuation of future instalments and of deferred deposits really involve examples of the computation of trader's profits needing to include money's worth rather than merely money. A rather hardier variant by no means infrequently encountered in practice arises where freehold land is sold for a lump sum payment plus the reservation of a perpetual rent-charge. In such a case it has been held that the computation for the period covering the sale should include, in addition of course to the lump sum, the capitalised value of the rentcharge, as being a profit in money's worth (*Emery & Sons* v. *I.R.C.* [1937] A.C. 91, H.L.). A later sale of the rentcharge ought in consequence to attract no further income tax, but could give rise to a capital gains tax charge (see F.A. 1965, Sched. 6, para. 2 (3)). Consequently, it is suggested that the Revenue practice of permitting the treatment of rentcharges in the same way as ground rents (see below), should be accepted as a concession (compare George, Taxation and Property Transactions, 3rd ed., at p. 129). In any case, the point should not be overlooked that this practice may now not be a concession at all but strict necessity : rent-charges fall fairly and squarely within the new and virtually exclusive Schedule A for income tax purposes and may therefore not be otherwise taxable at all (see I.C.T.A. 1970, s. 67 (1), para. 1 (*b*) ; also further Part 3, A. Leases, *post*, p. 1115, and B. Other Schedule A Receipts, *post*, p. 1132).

Long leases.—Where land is disposed of in the course of trade, not by sale of the freehold but by the grant of a long lease in consideration of the payment of a premium plus the reservation of a ground rent, then in reality the position might well appear no different from that considered in the previous paragraph. However, in law distinctions must be drawn. The House of Lords has decided that in such a case only the premium is to be treated as a taxable receipt (*Hughes* v. *Utting* [1940] A.C. 463 ; cp. I.C.T.A. 1970, s. 488 (6) (*a*), which appears to adopt this position for " artificial transactions in land " also). The distinguishing point is that here the taxpayer has not parted with his whole property, namely, the freehold estate in the land, in exchange for other property, namely, the rent-charge. Instead he has only disposed of part of his property, namely, the leasehold interest, retaining the rest of the property, namely, the freehold reversion with the benefit of the ground rents. Accordingly, it follows logically that the value of this retained property should not be regarded as a taxable receipt but simply treated as part of the trader's stock-in-trade (as to which see further below). In effect, a profit within Case I of Schedule D will only arise on a sale of the reversion. It should be mentioned in passing that where the grant is of a short lease (i.e., for a term not exceeding fifty years), the premium will be chargeable primarily under Schedule A and to that extent will be excluded from the present trader's computation under Schedule D, Case I (see I.C.T.A. 1970, s. 142 (2)–(4)). See further also Part 3, A. Leases, *post*, p. 1115 ; also as to ground rents as stock-in-trade, see *post*, p. 1101.

Stock-in-trade.—It may very well happen that an admitted trader, having purchased (or otherwise acquired) land as such, does not sell it so as to realise his profit (or loss) for more than a year (whether a tax or accounting year). That land, which is held as " stock-in-trade ", will not in the meantime be entirely ignored for income tax purposes. Although the Income Tax Acts say nothing to speak of about " stock-in-trade ", there has evolved from the practice of accountants, as accepted by the courts, a well-nigh sacrosanct general rule. This rule may be expressed as follows : " stock-in-trade " should be included in the trader's accounts for tax purposes both at the beginning and at the end of his accounting year, each item being valued at either cost or market price whichever is the lower (see more particularly *B.S.C. Footwear, Ltd.* v. *Ridgway* [1972] A.C. 544). The practical effect of this rule is that where the stock-in-trade depreciates in value below cost, the trader can obtain relief almost immediately, whereas an appreciation above cost will still not produce a taxable profit until actual realisation on sale.

As regards land, this topic is most likely to be of concern to builders and other developers who will be carrying out operations in relation to the land before sale. Accordingly it must be noticed that a virtually identical rule applies to " work-in-progress " which consequently should figure in the accounts at a cost valuation (as to any consistent method of valuation being proper, see *Ostime* v. *Duple Motor Bodies, Ltd.* [1961] 1 W.L.R. 739, H.L. ; see also I.C.T.A. 1970, s. 137 (4), which defines " trading stock " as including work in progress for the purposes of the discontinuance rules).

Ordinarily, of course, the price of land, whether developed or not, rises so rapidly that the cost, remaining below market value, will be the appropriate figure for the accounts. Occasionally, however, this will not be so, in particular where land purchased as one lot has been divided. Another more experienced writer has picturesquely observed that—

" . . . a parcel of land bears closer resemblance to the curate's egg than to a bolt of cloth it is good in parts and variable in quality and value "

(George, Taxation and Property Transactions, 3rd ed., at p. 120). Thus a high price may have been paid for land because part of it enjoyed the benefit of planning permission for building ; what is left may have merely a nominal value well below the cost apportioned according to area.

Ground rents.—A particular example of apportioning the cost of stock-in-trade where land has been divided is commonly encountered where the division is not physical but legal. It has already been noted (*ante*, p. 1100) that where a trader disposes of land by granting a lease at a premium and a ground rent, the reversion plus ground rent should be treated as stock-in-trade. This calls for an apportionment of the cost of the land in order that appropriate figures may appear in the accounts. This apportionment will be made by reference to what is normally known as the Emery formula (although sometimes called the Macnaghten formula) as follows—

$$\frac{A}{A + B} \times C = D$$

—where A equals the market value of the reversion with ground rents

B equals the amount of the premium

C equals the cost of the whole land (i.e., price plus development)

D equals the apportioned cost of the reversion with ground rents (i.e., the retained land).

This formula was determined by the Special Commissioners in *John Emery & Sons, Ltd.* v. *I.R.C.* (1937), 20 T.C. 213 (not reported on this aspect at [1937] A.C. 91) and referred to by Macnaghten, J., in *Heather* v. *A. Redfern &*

Sons (1944), 26 T.C. 119, at p. 124 (see also the apparent approval in I.C.T.A. 1970, s. 488 (6) (*a*)). The Revenue appear to take the view that the application of this formula to suitable circumstances is compulsory. This view, however, may be open to query in the light of the flexible attitude more recently displayed by the House of Lords towards the variety of methods whereby stock in trade may be valued (see especially *Ostime* v. *Duple Motor Bodies, Ltd.* [1961] 1 W.L.R. 739 ; cf. *B.S.C. Footwear, Ltd.* v. *Ridgway* [1972] A.C. 544). Further, the query may be reinforced, if need be, by pointing out that the formula has never in fact received the accolade of a decision of the courts. In the *Emery* case, the formula appears as part of the determination of the Commissioners which was unanimously held by the Court of Session and the House of Lords to be erroneous in law on the main question so that other aspects were not considered (*John Emery & Sons, Ltd.* v. *I.R.C.* (1937), 20 T.C. 213). And in Macnaghten, J.'s case, the parties had agreed that the formula should be adopted so that no decision was necessary or made as to the basis on which the cost of the reversions should be ascertained (*Heather* v. *A. Redfern & Sons Ltd.* (1944), 26 T.C. 119).

Appropriations.—Traders, even in land, do not always sell their stock-in-trade so as to produce a recognisable trading receipt. For example, a builder who has developed an estate may in the end appropriate one of the houses for his own use and enjoyment. The established rule in such a case now is that the appropriate item of stock-in-trade must be credited in the trader's accounts at market value, rather than cost (*Sharkey* v. *Wernher* [1956] A.C. 58, H.L.). As a result a notional but nevertheless taxable trading receipt will normally be produced (although a loss is equally possible : see *Watson Bros.* v. *Hornby* (1942), 24 T.C. 506). This rule is applicable where stock-in-trade is appropriated for retention as an investment, for example, where the method selected for the disposal of a developed estate leaves some physical part or legal interest in the hands of the developer (e.g., reversions plus ground rents). In this sort of case, in practice, the appropriation appears unwise : it will cause an immediately taxable receipt by virtue of the rule just mentioned and eventual sale will produce a capital gain liable to income tax (i.e., under I.C.T.A. 1970, s. 488 (2) (*b*)).

The rule will also catch a trader who gives away his stock-in-trade, whether as a gratuitous appropriation to a third party or through a sale at undervalue (see *Petrotim Securities, Ltd.* v. *Ayres* [1964] 1 W.L.R. 190, C.A.). So far as sales at undervalue are concerned, difficult questions might be envisaged of whether the explanation was a bad bargain or an element of bounty. But these questions should not arise. The testing principle in all cases is simply this : was the transaction outside the course of trade? If so, the rule applies (*ibid.*). A sale of stock at a gross undervalue may itself be sufficient evidence that the transaction fell outside the course of trade (see *ibid.* ; also *Skinner* v. *Berry Head Lands, Ltd.* [1970] 1 W.L.R. 1441, where the taxpayer company sold land to a parent company for £4,175 and the parent company resold it on the same day for £40,000 ; Goff, J., applied the present rule). Reference may also be made to a substantially similar statutory rule applying to transactions between certain associated persons (I.C.T.A. 1970, s. 485).

Incidentally, this rule can be displaced by a discontinuance of the trade. Then the primary statutory rule is that if " any trading stock belonging to the trade at the discontinuance " is sold to another U.K. trader then the actual price should be included in the income tax computation (I.C.T.A. 1970, s. 137 (1) (*a*)). This statutory rule applies even though the *Sharkey* v.

Wernher rule might otherwise be applicable because the transaction was outside the ordinary course of trade (see *Moore* v. *Mackenzie & Sons, Ltd.* [1972] 1 W.L.R. 359, where an actual price of £27,686 prevailed over the market value of £95,000 of two blocks of flats ; but as to this decision, see now I.C.T.A. 1970, s. 488 (4), Artificial Transactions in Land, *post*, p. 1106).

Conversely, land may be appropriated *to* stock-in-trade. For example, a beneficiary receiving a devise of land may decide to become a trader by developing and selling the land. Or a donee or purchaser at undervalue of land may make the same decision. Then the normal rule is that the appropriation will be treated as being at market value for the purposes not only of the trading accounts but also for the capital gains tax charge (see F.A. 1965, Sched. 7, para. 1 (1) ; also *per* Lord Denning, M.R., in *Petrotim Securities, Ltd.* v. *Ayres* (1963), 41 T.C. 389, at p. 407). Alternatively, however, the trader may elect to have the market value of the appropriated asset reduced by the amount of any capital gain (or increased by the amount of any capital loss), so that no capital gains tax consequences will arise from the appropriation but so that eventually the trading computation for income tax will be affected (see F.A. 1965, Sched. 7, para. 1 (3)).

Compensation.—Lastly with regard to trading receipts it should be noticed that sums received otherwise than as the consideration for dispositions of a trader's land have been held to be an element in the computation of his profits. In particular it has been decided that where land forms part of the taxpayer's stock-in-trade, just as the price on sale is a trading receipt so likewise is any compensation for injurious affection (*Johnson* v. *W. S. Try* (1945), 27 T.C. 167 ; see particularly *per* Macnaghten, J., at *ibid.*, p. 173 ; on appeal (1946), 27 T.C. 174). The case just cited concerned a sum of £4,800 received by a building contractor and estate developer as compensation for the refusal of consent to further development proposals in respect of certain land under the Restriction of Ribbon Development Act, 1935, and, as indicated, that sum was held to constitute a trading receipt. Reference may also be made to a case in which the sum of £5,000 was paid to a builder in consequence of the variation of an agreement which caused the builder to lose the right to build on certain plots of land ; Macnaghten, J., held that this right to build was as much part of the builder's stock-in-trade as the plots themselves would have been so that the £5,000 was also as much a trading receipt as the sale price of the plots would have been (*Shadbolt* v. *Salmon Estate (Kingsbury), Ltd.* (1943), 25 T.C. 52). Of course, these cases will not be applicable if the compensation payment is of a capital nature, that is if it relates not to land as stock-in-trade but to land as a fixed asset (see *Watson* v. *Samson Bros.* (1959), 38 T.C. 346).

Deductible expenditure.—On the other side of the computation account from trading receipts are the various items of deductible expenditure. It is provided that " in arriving at the amount of profits or gains for tax purposes no other deductions shall be made than such as are expressly enumerated in the Tax Acts " (I.C.T.A. 1970, s. 519 (1) (*a*)). But so far as those Acts are concerned we can only find " General rules as to deductions *not* allowable." This is the marginal note to I.C.T.A. 1970, s. 130, which lists fifteen items of expenditure in respect of which *no* sum may be deducted from Case I Schedule D profits. There are virtually no positive provisions whereby any expenditure is specifically allowed and there is certainly no express enumeration of deductions.

Yet most of the items listed in s. 130 are qualified by words of exception ;
for example : "any debts, except bad debts" (para. (*i*)), or "any sum
expended for repairs . . . beyond the sum actually expended" (para. (*d*)).
Consequently by virtue of this curious double-negative form the section does
actually indicate various miscellaneous items of expressly deductible
expenditure. Thriving on this, the courts have managed a complete reversal
of the statutory approach. Instead, the general rule has been adopted that
all expenditure which would be deductible from income according to the
accepted principles of accountancy will be allowable for income tax purposes
unless there is some specific statutory prohibition (see *per* Lord Sumner in
Usher's Wiltshire Brewery, Ltd. v. *Bruce* [1915] A.C. 433, at p. 467 ; also the
dicta referred to by Salmon, L.J., in *Odeon Associated Theatres, Ltd.* v. *Jones*
[1972] 2 W.L.R. 331, at p. 335 ; but cf. *Heather* v. *P-E Consulting Group, Ltd.*
[1973] 1 All E.R. 8, C.A., as to the weight to be attached to accountancy
principles).

Further, the principles of accountancy can be said to coalesce with the
statutory prohibitions so as to produce two simply stated qualifying conditions
for deductible expenditure. The expenditure must be (1) solely from a
trading activity and (2) not of a capital nature. In effect, such expenditure
is required to be the exact converse of trading receipts. As to condition (1),
the statute itself primarily prohibits the deduction of—

"any disbursements or expenses, *not* being money wholly and exclusively
laid out for the purposes of the trade . . ."

(I.C.T.A. 1970, s. 130 (*a*) ; the other paragraphs of the section often only
elaborate or illustrate the scope of this first paragraph). Again as to
condition (2) the statute has expressly precluded the deduction of—

"any capital withdrawn from, or any sum employed or intended to be
employed as capital in, the trade . . ."

(*ibid.*, para. (*f*) ; see also para. (*g*)). It has been observed that, although
these last mentioned paragraphs exclude capital expenditure, "no help can
be derived from the Act in deciding the question of what is capital expenditure" (*per* Salmon, L.J., in *Odeon Associated Theatres, Ltd.* v. *Jones* [1972]
2 W.L.R. 331, at p. 336). Against this it will be appreciated that capital
allowances are available in certain cases.

Although simply stated, these two conditions have not always proved
easy to apply in practice (see the "spin of a coin" comment of Lord Greene,
M.R., in *British Salmson Aero Engines, Ltd.* v. *I.R.C.* [1938] 2 K.B. 482, at
p. 498). Nevertheless, not much difficulty should be experienced in any
discussion which is deliberately confined to traders in land. The vital point
to remember is that the land in question is by definition stock-in-trade
rather than business premises or other fixed assets. Consequently, for
example, the troublesome distinction between repairs and improvements
becomes irrelevant : expenditure of either sort in respect of stock-in-trade
is clearly allowable (cp. *Odeon Associated Theatres, Ltd.* v. *Jones* [1972]
2 W.L.R. 331).

Bearing in mind that the deductible expenditure is essentially the converse
of trading receipts, it is obvious that any sums initially spent on or in
connection with the acquisition of the land will be properly deductible.
The same applies to any sums spent towards preserving and preparing the
land (e.g., by building) with a view to profitable disposition in the course of
trade, or indeed to those sums spent on actually achieving such a disposition.
To mention a particular example, professional fees and costs, whether of

lawyers or others, incurred in connection with the purchase or sale of the
land or with its improvement or preservation will be deductible (see *Southern
v. Borax Consolidated, Ltd.* [1941] 1 K.B. 111, defence of title ; cp. *Owen
and Galsden* v. *Brook* (1951), 32 T.C. 206, where the purchase and sale was
not a trading activity, also *Smith's Potato Estates, Ltd.* v. *Bolland* [1948]
A.C. 503 and *Meredith* v. *Roberts* (1968), 44 T.C. 559). Another particular
point worth mentioning concerns borrowings for the purpose of carrying on
the trade : the interest payable will be an allowable deduction from profits
(see *Farmer* v. *Scottish North American Trust, Ltd.* [1912] A.C. 118 ; also
I.C.T.A. 1970, s. 130 (*l*) and (*m*)). Also it will be appreciated that the
deductible expenditure need not be directly tied to any particular trading
receipt, whether or not in the same tax year. Thus Lord Reid has observed—

" If you manure the field in year one in order to reap the harvest in
year two, no one now doubts that the cost of the manure is a proper charge
against the receipts in year one although that cost produces no return
until the next year "

(in *B.S.C. Footwear, Ltd.* v. *Ridgway* [1972] A.C. 544, at p. 552 ; see also
Vallambrosa Rubber Co., Ltd. v. *Farmer* (1910), 5 T.C. 529, as to the costs
of cultivating trees which yield a profit only after six years).

Business premises.—Presumably all traders in land will operate from
somewhere, even if the scale of their activities calls only for the use of a
study/lounge at home. Consequently, it may be worthwhile to conclude
by noticing that expenditure upon the business premises of traders, even in
land, can be an allowable deduction from profits. Not the purchase price
(see *I.R.C.* v. *Land Securities, Ltd.* (1969), 45 T.C. 495, H.L.), nor the cost of
improvements (see *Odeon Associated Theatres, Ltd.* v. *Jones* [1972] 2 W.L.R.
331, C.A.), but certainly the expenses of maintenance and upkeep should be
included in the computation (see I.C.T.A. 1970, s. 130 (*d*)). Again, for
example, any rent paid for business premises will be properly deductible
(see *I.R.C.* v. *Falkirk Iron Co., Ltd.* (1933), 17 T.C. 625 ; also *Hyett* v. *Lennard*
[1940] 2 K.B. 180 ; provided it really is " rent " and not price : see
Littlewoods Mail Order Stores, Ltd. v. *McGregor* (1969), 45 T.C. 519, and
subject to the sale and lease-back restrictions : see I.C.T.A. 1970, s. 491, and
F.A. 1972, s. 80). Premiums paid for leasehold business premises, being
capital costs, are generally not deductible (see *Watney & Co.* v. *Musgrove*
(1880), 1 T.C. 272 ; also *Green* v. *Favourite Cinemas, Ltd.* (1930), 15 T.C. 390,
where the premium was payable by quarterly instalments over the whole
term of the lease). But if such premiums happen to be taxable in part as
rent (see Part 3, A. Leases, *post*, p. 1115 *et seq.*), then appropriate deductions
are allowed in the computation of trading profits (I.C.T.A. 1970, s. 134).

Further, so far as concerns such expenditure on business premises, the
strict " wholly and exclusively " requirement is relaxed. Instead of the
customary total disqualification where purposes other than the trade alone
are involved (see e.g., *Prince* v. *Mapp* (1969), 46 T.C. 169 ; also *Ransom* v.
Higgs [1972] 2 All E.R. 817 ; on appeal [1973] 2 All E.R. 657), here
appropriate apportionments are permitted. Thus statute itself provides
that " no sum shall be deducted in respect of . . . the rent of any dwelling-house
or domestic offices or any part thereof, *except such part* thereof as is used for
the purposes of the trade . . . " (I.C.T.A. 1970, s. 130 (*c*), with a two-thirds
limit). Equally a proportion of the expenditure on the maintenance and
upkeep of premises which are used both domestically and for trade activities

is deductible, not by statute, but by a long standing practice which has received express approval in the House of Lords (see *per* Lord Upjohn in *Korner* v. *I.R.C.* (1969), 45 T.C. 287, at p. 297).

Finally, two things may be noted. The first is that the business premises of traders in land are not covered by the meaning given to " industrial building or structure " by s. 7 of the Capital Allowances Act, 1968. And the second is that the trader who conducts his activities from his dwelling-house risks a subsequent capital gains tax charge on its disposal (see F.A. 1965, s. 29, as amended by F.A. 1968, Sched. 12, para. 2 ; see *ante*, p. 1090).

B. ARTIFICIAL TRANSACTIONS IN LAND

This heading simply reproduces the marginal note to s. 488 of the I.C.T.A. 1970, the avowed intention of which is indicated in subs. (1) as follows :—

" This section is enacted to prevent the avoidance of tax by persons concerned with land or the development of land."

The marginal note is misleading : the section itself does not use the word " artificial " and certainly it is wide enough to catch the most natural of transactions involving land. Further, subs. (1) quoted above is no more than a declaration of intent : the avoidance of tax does not constitute either a condition precedent to or even an element in the application of the section. Some explanation may be sought in the section's origin which was to replace (as s. 32 of the F.A. 1969) certain earlier, much narrower and apparently too easily avoided provisions (i.e., substantially ss. 21 to 26 of the F.A. 1960 as extended by ss. 23 to 25 of the F.A. 1962).

The result and object of applying s. 488 is that " any gain of a capital nature " from a transaction within the section should be treated for all tax purposes as *income* chargeable under Case VI of Schedule D (subs. (3)). Thus this complicated exercise is all occasioned by the variable to strong discrimination in rates between the progressive income tax and the flat capital gains tax. Ironically, there is now some evidence that the exercise was prompted by a fear of shadows : *Ransom* v. *Higgs* [1972] 2 All E.R. 817 ; on appeal [1973] 2 All E.R. 657, concerned some of the most artificial transactions in land imaginable but nonetheless produced a trading profit attracting income tax. However, if the section operates as a deterrent from further such extreme transactions, it may be thought worth its place on that account alone (and see *Moore* v. *Mackenzie & Sons, Ltd.* [1972] 1 W.L.R. 359 where an application of the section, had it been available, might have attracted more income tax).

Conditions.—The conditions precedent to the application of the section are set out as follows :—

" This section applies wherever :—

    (*a*) land, or any property deriving its value from land, is acquired with the sole or main object of realising a gain from disposing of the land, or

    (*b*) land is held as trading stock, or

    (*c*) land is developed with the sole or main object of realising a gain from disposing of the land when developed,

and any gain of a capital nature is obtained from the disposal of the land . . ."

(I.C.T.A. 1970, s. 488 (2), which goes on in an all-embracing way to say who must obtain the gain, as to which see below).

Some initial assistance with these conditions can be found in certain definitions provided by the section. Thus the references to " land " include " all or any part of the land " together with " buildings, and any estate or interest in land or buildings " (I.C.T.A. 1970, s. 488 (12) (*a*)). It might be thought that the section could actually be avoided through the artificiality of adopting non-proprietary rights or interests in the proceeds of sale (cf. *Irani Finance, Ltd.* v. *Singh* [1971] Ch. 59). But this is precluded by the extended explanation of the reference to " any property deriving its value from land " as including :—

" (i) any shareholding in a company, or any partnership interest, or any interest in settled property, deriving its value directly or indirectly from land, and

(ii) any option, consent or embargo affecting the disposition of land "

(I.C.T.A. 1970, s. 488 (12) (*b*) ; see also *ibid.*, s. 489 (5), as to " tracing " the value back to the land through multiple companies, partnerships and trusts). All this is so wide that the only possible escape is the one envisaged by the section itself, namely, via wholly foreign immovable property ; i.e., the section applies if any part of the land in question is situated in the United Kingdom (I.C.T.A. 1970, s. 488 (13)—the foreign residence of anyone is expressly quite irrelevant).

The only other statutory assistance with these conditions is directed to the word " disposal." This word appears also as an essential element in the charge to capital gains tax (F.A. 1965, s. 19 (1), " the disposal of assets "), and in that context it was left virtually to speak for itself (see *ante*, p. 1045). Here, however, there is first an elaborate explanation—

" . . . land is disposed of if, by one or more transactions, or by any arrangement or scheme, . . . the property in the land, or control over the land, is effectually disposed of . . ."

(I.C.T.A. 1970, s. 488 (4)). This is then further elaborated in a supporting section: —

" . . . account shall be taken of any method, however indirect, by which—

(*a*) any property or right is transferred or transmitted, or

(*b*) the value of any property or right is enhanced or diminished . . . "

(I.C.T.A. 1970, s. 489 (2)). This is itself even more lengthily and particularly elaborated (by *ibid.*, subs. (3)).

Thus it appears clear that a " disposal " can be detected in anything beyond a mere non-binding, gentleman's agreement relating in any way to land. For example, no question can arise here surely that the contract and not the conveyance constitutes the disposal. But happily the question would miss the mark : the section is aimed entirely at the gain obtained or realised by any person (see I.C.T.A. 1970, s. 488 (2), (3) ; see further below). Consequently the vital moment and event will undoubtedly be the payment of the purchase price or other consideration money. This fact of payment alone would certainly create sufficient rights over the land to satisfy the section's need for a disposal whatever may be the state otherwise of the transaction. So no escape is available through the simple expedient of dispensing with contracts or other documents.

None of these elaborate explanations of the word disposal appears, in terms at least, to govern the construction of its sibling, the word " acquired " (in condition (*a*) of I.C.T.A. 1970, s. 488 (2), *ante*). Although in general this may seem unlikely to cause difficulty, one must not overlook the potential importance of ascertaining the time of acquisition. The point is that the object of realising a gain obviously must exist when the land is acquired ; a subsequent change of object (without development within condition (*c*)) does not bring the section into play. For a simple example, a man might have entered into a contract to purchase a plot of land with the object of building a bungalow to retire to, but before completion a developer makes him an irresistibly higher offer for a re-sale. Acceptance of the offer may turn entirely on whether the resultant gain will be subject to income tax under the present section or to capital gains tax. Unfortunately, no sufficiently certain answer to be worth suggesting as to the time of acquisition is to be found in the legislation. Instead, the unanswerable question can be found of whether the words " is acquired " are apt to catch gains where the acquisition occurred before the section was passed (i.e., originally as s. 32 of the F.A. 1969 ; see further, A. J. Chadwick Sumption at [1972] B.T.R. 129, 264).

" *sole or main object . . . gain.*"—There can be no doubt that the heart of s. 488 lies in the condition whereby it applies when the realisation of a gain was the " sole or main object " of the acquisition of the land (I.C.T.A. 1970, s. 488 (2) (*a*)). Thus a man who purchased farmland in order simply to farm it, but who eventually sells it at a profit, will obviously not fall within this section —gain was not the sole or main object with which he acquired the land. It will be observed that a purchaser of land is permitted with impunity subsequently to change his mind towards gain, so long as he does not develop the land for the purpose of a profitable sale (see I.C.T.A. 1970, s. 488 (2) (*c*)). Against this, a man who contracts to sell a piece of land for £25,000 a week *before* he contracts to buy it for £15,000 would come as clearly as could be within s. 488 (cp. *Johnston* v. *Heath* [1970] 1 W.L.R. 1567 where, with these facts but without benefit of the section, the isolated transaction was miraculously converted into trade). But not all the examples will be as elementary and one day a court will have to decide what exactly is meant by a person's " sole or main object " and precisely how it is to be ascertained.

There would appear to be two aspects to this problem. The first stems from the truism that most people act with mixed motives. Does the section apply where land is acquired (or developed) with two (or more) main objects ? Since the section refers simply to " *the* sole or main object " (italics supplied), the question should surely receive a negative answer even though one main object was to realise a gain. However, the other aspect of the problem must be examined first as being the more fundamental : is a person's object to be ascertained objectively or subjectively ? Should he be taxed otherwise than on account of his own actual intention ?

This very question was inherent in the concept of " trade " (i.e., for Schedule D, Case I). Thus the sixth and last of the " badges of trade " set out in 1955 by the Royal Commission on The Taxation of Profits and Income (Report, para. 116, Cmd. 9474) reads as follows :—

  " (6) *Motive.* There are cases in which the purpose of the transaction of purchase and sale is clearly discernible. Motive is never irrelevant in any of these cases. What is desirable is that it should be realised

INCOME TAX: SCHEDULE D, CASE I

clearly that it can be inferred from surrounding circumstances in the absence of direct evidence of the seller's intentions and even, if necessary, in the face of his own evidence."

Again, ten years more recently, Lord Reid summarised the same position as follows :—

"If, in order to get what he wants, the taxpayer has to embark on an adventure which has all the characteristics of trading, his purpose or object alone cannot prevail over what he, in fact, does. But if his acts are equivocal, his purpose or object may be a very material factor when weighing the total effect of all the circumstances "

(in *Iswera* v. *Ceylon Commissioners of Taxation* [1965] 1 W.L.R. 663, at p. 668 ; see also *per* Lord Simon of Glaisdale in *Lupton* v. *F.A. & A.B., Ltd.* [1972] A.C. 634, pp. 660–661).

Mutatis mutandis, the approach adopted towards motive in these quotations will, it must be assumed, likewise be adopted in the present context for ascertaining a person's sole or main object. In other words, the object of realising a gain will be deduced in the first place objectively from what has in fact been done. Only if no adequate deduction can be made in this way will a person's actual intentions, his subjective object, have any real influence. In this particular connection, however, mention must be made of certain limited but negative assistance afforded by statute. It is provided that :—

"In ascertaining . . . the intention of any person, the objects and powers of any company, partners or trustees, as set out in any memorandum, articles of association or other document, shall not be conclusive "

(I.C.T.A. 1970, s. 489 (4)). Unhappily this does not seem quite to justify the inference that in the case of other persons documentary statements of intention will be conclusive—companies, partners and trustees, unlike other persons, are usually restricted in all respects to their written objects and powers. Consequently, the insertion of a recital into a conveyance expressly declaring that the purchaser has no intention at all of ever making any gain from a disposal of the land is unlikely to cut much ice, especially if a gain is in fact fairly promptly realised. Nevertheless a positive recital of the real object of the acquisition (other than gain)—whether it be investment, farming, residence, retirement or even pride of possession (see *per* Lord Normand in *I.R.C.* v. *Frazer* (1942), T.C. 502, at p. 503)—would appear to be a highly desirable expedient in practice. Thereby at least one unambiguous piece of evidence can be presented which may well prevail if other circumstances happen to be equivocal.

The references to recitals of intention when acquiring land in the previous paragraph bring one back to the aspect of mixed motives. Few people can acquire land today without the (to use a neutral word) expectation of being able one day to sell at an increased price. And since even fewer people nowadays will expect to keep this land " in the family " (or business) during their own lifetime, still less in perpetuity, it would seem to follow that the object of eventually realising a gain on disposal must almost always be present. But this will not suffice for s. 488. Gain, as was said before, must be *the* sole or main object " (*ibid.*, subs. (2) (*a*) and (*c*)). So if there is present some other object of the acquisition, which can also be called a main if not dominant object, then the section should not apply. Support for this singular construction can be derived directly from a comparison with s. 460 of I.C.T.A.

1970, which is also in Pt. XVII of that Act concerned with " Tax Avoidance " and which refers to transactions which have " as their main object, *or one of their main objects*," the obtaining of tax advantages (italics supplied ; s. 460 pre-dates s. 488 ; cp. *Haslock* v. *I.R.C.* (1971), 47 T.C. 50).

However, there is an express exemption where a gain accrues on the disposal of an individual's " only or main " residence even though it was acquired " wholly or partly " for the purpose of realising a gain (I.C.T.A. 1970, s. 488 (9), referring to the capital gains tax provisions as to private residences, i.e., F.A. 1965, s. 29, as amended, which incidentally recognises the possibility of two " main " residences and calls for a choice ; see *ante*, p. 1083 *et seq.*). This express exemption would be pure surplusage if the narrow construction of the phrase " *the* sole or main object " suggested in the previous paragraph were correct. Of course, the point is academic so far as private residences are concerned : a dwelling-house clearly can be acquired with the dual objects of occupation and of eventual gain without being caught by this section (although it should be by capital gains tax). But if a farm, a shop, a garage or such like be substituted for a dwelling-house and coupled with the same dual objects, then the express exemption of private residences may be seen to assume significance. *Exclusio unius est inclusio alterius !*

Another sort of mixed motive will not infrequently be encountered. Land may be acquired with the object of retaining and using part (e.g., as a residence or business premises) and of re-selling the remainder at a proportionate profit. Thus in one case a lady, wishing to live near the school which her daughters were attending, tried to purchase a site sufficient for the erection of a house, but was forced by the vendor to acquire a larger area and afterwards disposed of the excess to nine sub-purchasers (*Iswera* v. *I.R.C.* [1965] 1 W.L.R. 663). That lady was found by the Privy Council to have the dominant motive of making a profit and was treated as a trader. It is thought, however, that such people can now be brought more readily within s. 488. Even though the object of realising a gain in such cases does not relate to the whole of the land acquired, the word " land " is defined as including " all or any part of the land " (s. 488 (12) (*a*)) and provision is made for apportionments of expenditure and appropriate valuations (s. 489 (6)).

Again mixed motives may be encountered where more than one person is involved in the acquisition of the land. Indeed it is notable that the section conspicuously fails to say who has to have the object of realising a gain. One could not too unreasonably read condition (*a*), *supra* (i.e., s. 488 (2) (*a*)) as simply applying whenever land is sold : the purchaser makes the acquisition and the vendor has the sole object of realising a gain from the disposal ! However, it must surely be assumed that the requisite gainful object of the acquisition was intended to mean the object of the person acquiring the land.

Thus donees and beneficiaries, receiving land through someone else's bounty, would appear to be quite untainted by the profit motive in their acquisition. This is so submitted in George, Taxation and Property Transactions, 3rd ed., at p. 35, and it may be supported by reference to the majority Privy Council decision in *McClelland* v. *Taxation Commissioner* [1971] 1 W.L.R. 191 (where, *inter alia*, an acquisition of an interest in land by testamentary disposition was held not to be " for the purpose of profit-making by sale " within the Australian Income Tax Acts, 1936–63, s. 26 (*a*)). Of course, a donee or beneficiary clearly can bring himself within s. 488 (2) (*c*) by developing the land, by constructing roads and installing drains and services before selling in lots (see *Pilkington* v. *Randall* (1966), 42 T.C. 662, C.A., where a beneficiary acting in this way was, in fact, treated as a trader).

But other awkward cases can be imagined.   Should not a donee or beneficiary who asked to be given or left that particular land so that he could make a profit on sale come within s. 488 ?   Or what of the donee or beneficiary of a house who already has a house—are not the alternatives open to him virtually limited to disclaimer or else acceptance and acquisition with the object of realising a gain on sale ?   Further, indeed, reference may be made to *Williams* v. *Davies* [1945] 1 All E.R. 304, for a very likely case of a donee acquiring land with the sole object of realising a gain (in effect, a property-dealer husband made a genuine gift of certain just-purchased plots of land to his wife who promptly re-sold them profitably ; she was found not to be a trader).

Beyond even these queries there is a peculiar quirk provided by the statute itself.   Imagine a gift of land where the *donor* has the sole or main object of enabling the *donee* to realise a gain by selling, and assume that the *donee* acquires the land without any such object but does in fact make a profitable sale.   The section seems to say that the *donor* should pay income tax on the *donee's* gain on sale and this would be in addition to any capital gains tax charge because of the original gift (see F.A. 1965, s. 22 (4) (*a*)).   Inconceivable, one exclaims, but read more of s. 488—

" . . . where, whether by a premature sale or otherwise, a person directly or indirectly transmits the opportunity of making a gain to another person, that other person's gain is obtained for him by the first-mentioned person . . . "

and—

" . . . If all or any part of the gain accruing to any person is derived from value, or an opportunity of realising a gain, provided directly or indirectly by some other person, whether or not put at the disposal of the first-mentioned person, subsection (3) (*b*) of this section [which provides that for all income tax purposes the gain shall be treated as income of the person by whom the gain is realised] shall apply to the gain, or that part of it, with the substitution of that other person for the person by whom the gain was realised "

(I.C.T.A. 1970, s. 488 (5) (*a*) and (8)).   These subsections create fragile overstretched concepts—premature sale, opportunity of gain—which one fears to touch overmuch lest they be seen to crumble away (cp. D. C. Potter at [1969] B.T.R., p. 207).   But they must certainly be capable of covering a gift of the land itself, whether direct or indirect, as by a purchase in the name of another with the intention of an advancement.   Presumably also conveyances of land at undervalue, or in consideration of marriage or even merely with the benefit of planning permission could be caught.

One other instance of mixed motives may be considered here, that is, where the acquisition of the land is made by co-owners who have different objects.   The only real difficulty should be in establishing their individual intentions at the time : recitals or other declarations in writing will not be conclusive (see s. 489 (4)—the co-owners would necessarily be trustees of the legal estate : L.P.A., 1925, ss. 34–36) although any covenants *inter se* may be conclusive (see *Re Buchanan-Wollaston* [1939] Ch. 738).   Once it is established that any one of the co-owners entered into the acquisition with the sole or main object of realising a gain, then the section can apply with regard to his interest alone just as it is applicable to physical parts of the land (see ss. 488 (12) and 489 (6) as to the definition of " land " and as to apportionments and valuations). Of course co-owners, even though unanimously having non-gainful objects, could find themselves in theoretical difficulties in avoiding this section. They are, after all, under a duty to sell at the best price possible which ought to put the onus of establishing the non-gainful object heavily upon them. Again, if they deliberately purchased as beneficial joint tenants, one main object may be said to involve the right of survivorship, the operation of which would seem to be not only gainful to the survivor but also a disposal within the section.

" *developed*."—After consideration of the meaning of the words " sole or main object " which appear in both condition (*a*) and condition (*c*) for the application of the section (i.e., I.C.T.A. 1970, s. 488 (2)), it remains to consider condition (*c*), which brings the section into play wherever " land is developed " (*ibid.*). The intention appears plain. *Dicta* such as the following are to be neutralised for income tax purposes—

" Again, a landowner may lay out part of his estate with roads and sewers and sell it in lots for building, but he does this as owner, not as a land speculator "

(*per* Farwell, L.J., in *Hudson's Bay Co., Ltd.* v. *Stevens* (1909), 5 T.C. 424, at p. 437) ; and—

" If a land-owner, finding his property appreciating in value, sells part of it, and uses part of his money still further to develop the remaining parts, and so on, he is not carrying on a trade or business ; he is only properly developing and realising his land "

(*per* Rowlatt, J., in *Rand* v. *Alberni Land Co., Ltd.* (1920), 7 T.C. 629, at pp. 638–9, adding pessimistically that " if that is to make him liable to income tax as well as to greater death duties . . . nobody would do it "). Although these cases have been held not to establish any proposition of law completely negativing trading in such circumstances—" This would be opening the door very wide to modern property developers "—nevertheless usually the property owner would be found not to be carrying on a trade, as a question of fact and degree (see *per* Salmon, L.J., in *Pilkington* v. *Randall* (1966), 42 T.C. 662, at pp. 673–4). But now the liability to income tax in such cases has been put beyond any question of trading by s. 488.

However, no definition is offered of the vital word " developed." Will it be construed in accordance with the meaning given to " development " for planning purposes (i.e., in, now, s. 22 of the Town and Country Planning Act, 1971) ? This is " hardly likely " according George, Taxation and Property Transactions, 3rd ed., at p. 268, but it would seem only too natural to the present writer for the technical planning meaning to be intended and adopted here. Reference to the Oxford English Dictionary will reveal a sad lack of any apt ordinary meanings !

" *Gain*."—After setting out the three conditions quoted above, the section continues—

" and any gain of a capital nature is obtained from the disposal of the land—

(i) by the person acquiring, holding or developing the land, or by any connected person, or . . ."

(I.C.T.A. 1970, s. 488 (2)). This turns out to be grammatically ambiguous. The present writer reads the words as meaning that the gain has to be obtained by one or other of the persons enumerated. But in George, Taxation and

Property Transactions, 3rd ed., at p. 269, the word "by" has obviously been read with the word "disposal," so that the subsection has been taken as listing the disponers rather than merely the gainers (see also Pinson, Revenue Law, 7th ed., para. 44). It is thought that this latter interpretation although open ought not to be regarded as really tenable for two reasons. Firstly, a wider meaning is given to the word "disposal" for the purpose of the section generally than would comprehend merely the people listed as disponers (see *ibid.*, subs. (4) and s. 489 (2) (3)). Secondly, the subsection concludes by saying that "this *subsection*"—not "this section" as stated in George, *loc. cit.*—"applies whether any such person obtains the gain for himself or for any other person" (i.e., *ibid.*, s. 488 (2)).

Paragraph (ii) adds to the short list of potential gainers who bring the section into play "any person who is a party to or concerned in" any arrangement or scheme enabling a gain to be realised by any indirect method or by any series of transactions (I.C.T.A. 1970, s. 488 (2)). In the combined light of this and of the concluding words already quoted, it is clearly almost irrelevant who gets the capital gain, for if someone not listed gets it, he can only do so if someone listed has given it to him—unless he steals it! Reference should also be made to the subsection already mentioned concerning the transmission of the opportunity of gain (i.e., *ibid.*, subs. (5) (*a*) and (8)).

Computation.—It has just been said to be almost irrelevant who gets the capital gain. This is only so in deciding initially whether or not s. 488 applies. If the section does apply, then it certainly matters which person has realised the gain, for it is he who will be chargeable to income tax in respect of it (I.C.T.A. 1970, s. 488 (3) ; i.e., under Case VI of Sched. D). For his benefit, the question of computation must be considered and here one cannot help remarking upon the differences in approach between the capital gains tax legislation and the present provisions. The F.A. 1965, dealing with the former, says next to nothing about the meaning of "disposal" but contains very many detailed rules governing the calculation of gains. Section 488 (with s. 489) elaborates upon the word "disposal" but provides that—

> ". . . such method of computing a gain shall be adopted as is just and reasonable in the circumstances, taking into account the value of what is obtained for disposing of the land, and allowing only such expenses as are attributable to the land disposed of . . ."

(*ibid.*, subs. (6), although a very few special provisions are noticed below).

It is difficult to predict which approach will cause more particular problems, although the generality of the present section will probably create larger uncertainties. Incidentally, it is immediately unclear whether the final words quoted mean that allowable expenses here are confined to those attributable to the land itself (e.g., not legal costs) or only, preferably, that expenses attributable to other land are not allowable. Reference should also be made to the fact that general authority is given for just and reasonable apportionments and for appropriate valuations (*ibid.*, s. 489 (6)).

Having computed a just and reasonable gain, the whole of it will be treated as "income which arises [in the tax year] when the gain is realised" (I.C.T.A. 1970, s. 488 (3) (*a*)). As it is chargeable under Case VI of Sched. D, there is no preceding year basis of assessment, and any losses can as a rule only be set off or carried forward against other Case VI income (I.C.T.A. 1970, ss. 125 and 176). The only question which springs to mind is to ask when a gain is to be regarded as realised if, e.g., payment of the price is postponed or by instalments. The question is caused by the undefined word " realised ", but presumably it should be construed as synonymous with receivable. This being so, the provision that the section " shall not apply to any gain realised before 15th April, 1960 " (*ibid.*, s. 488 (14)) means that it does apply where a gain realised later had begun to accrue before that date : cf. the strictly non-retrospecive operation of the capital gains tax legislation (F.A. 1965, s. 22 (10)) ; and see further, as to the significance of " is acquired," A. J. Chadwick Sumption at [1972] B.T.R. 129, 264.

Special computational provisions.—Beyond the general, just and reasonable rule for computations under the section, there are four special provisions which should be noticed.

First, where a freehold is acquired and the reversion is retained on disposal, it is simply provided that account should be taken of the way in which a trader's profits would be computed in such a case (I.C.T.A. 1970, s. 488 (6) (*a*) ; i.e., under Case I, Sched. D, see *Hughes* v. *Utting* [1940] A.C. 463; see *ante*, p. 1100).

Secondly, also by virtue of a similar cross reference, premiums on leases may be taxed, in effect, not only under Sched. A but also, as to the balance, under this section (I.C.T.A. 1970, s. 488 (6) (*b*), referring to *ibid.*, s. 142 (2)–(4)).

Thirdly, if the section applies only because the land has been developed with the object of gain, " So much of any gain as is fairly attributable to the period, if any, before the intention to develop the land was formed " is to be disregarded (I.C.T.A. 1970, s. 488 (7)). Presumably this envisages the making of appropriate valuations and apportionments (*ibid.*, s. 489 (6)). Nevertheless the mind tends to boggle rather at the need to ascertain not only the main object of an equivocal development but also exactly when the intention to develop was formed.

Fourthly, there is an odd exemption applicable to a sale of shares in a company which holds land as trading stock, whether directly or through a subsidiary. *Prima facie* the gain on the sale of the shares would come within the section, but it will be exempted if it is shown that all the land " is disposed of in the normal course of its trade by the company . . . so as to procure that all opportunity of profit in respect of the land arises to that company " (I.C.T.A. 1970, s. 488 (10)). For example, if *A* and *B*, the only shareholders of *AB* Ltd., a property dealing company which owns certain parcels of land, were to sell their shares to *C* Ltd., then their gains would be liable to income tax under s. 488 ; if subsequently *AB* Ltd. sells all the parcels of land in the normal course of trade, then *A* and *B* would appear entitled to reclaim the income tax paid in respect of the sale of shares. This seems simple, but there are one or two practical problems. Thus the exemption itself contains no time limit, but it is possible that a six-year period will limit the repayment claim (cf. Taxes Management Act, 1970, ss. 33 and 34). If so, *A* and *B* would be well advised to oblige *C* Ltd. to procure the sale of the land within that period. Also *A* and *B* should secure that *all* the parcels of land are sold and in the normal course of *AB* Ltd.'s trade (e.g., not taken out of *AB* Ltd. at book value and sold by another subsidiary of *C* Ltd.).

Clearance.—What has been written so far will at least serve to demonstrate the difficulty which will be experienced in advising whether or not s. 488 is going to be applicable. It has been observed that " the section seems, in parts, designed to terrorise by its obscurity " (D. C. Potter at [1969] B.T.R., p. 207). However, a useful clearance procedure is provided whereby an

application, supported by full and accurate written particulars, may be
made to the inspector of taxes to be notified whether or not a gain (actual
or potential) would be chargeable ; a negative notification is conclusive
(I.C.T.A. 1970, s. 488 (11)), as also apparently is a failure to reply within
thirty days (see [1972] B.T.R. 850). The only pity about this procedure is
that the inspector need give no reasons for refusing to provide a negative
notification.

PART 3.   SCHEDULES A AND B (AND ASSOCIATED CHARGES)—INCOME TAX

A.   LEASES

In this section attention is directed essentially towards the taxation
consequences of that conveyancing transaction which is very often called
" a sale by way of lease." Although this expression may strictly constitute
a blatant contradiction in terms (see *per* Lord Romer in *Utting & Co., Ltd.* v.
Hughes (1940), 23 T.C. 174, at p. 196), the sense is readily understood. What
is envisaged by the expression is that the vendor-landlord will be paid not
only the *rent* reserved by the lease but also a lump sum *premium*. Each of
these payments attracts a liability to income tax or to capital gains tax
(and sometimes to both). So far as the former is concerned, the tax position
generally remains the same whether or not a premium was also involved
(i.e., even though the lease was simply granted at a rent without any pretence
of being a sale). Therefore what follows should cover most forms of lease,
with the exception of such special aspects as furnished lettings and mineral
royalties, which will be looked at later (*post*, pp. 1135 and 1137). Almost all
the tax rules now applicable to leaseholds are of comparatively modern
origin : apart from those few which apply to traders in land, everything else
basically stems at the earliest from the F.A. 1963, although now consolidated
of course into I.C.T.A. 1970 (see a commentary at [1963] B.T.R. 500 ; also
A. E. W. Park and D. A. Landau at [1969] B.T.R. 265 and 368).

Rents.—Income tax is chargeable under Schedule A—

" . . . on the annual profits or gains arising in respect of any such rents
or receipts as follow, that is to say—

(*a*) rents under leases of land in the United Kingdom, . . . "

(I.C.T.A. 1970, s. 67 (1) ; see s. 90 (1) which defines " lease " as including an
agreement for a lease, and any tenancy, but not a mortgage). It is now
well-established at House of Lords level that the various Schedules are
mutually exclusive (see most recently *Mitchell and Eden* v. *Ross* [1962]
A.C. 814 and *I.R.C.* v. *Brander & Cruickshank* [1971] 1 W.L.R. 212).
Accordingly it is not open to the Revenue to choose to assess any person
whose trade or business happens to be or to involve the letting of land under
any other Schedule in respect of the rents (*Fry* v. *Salisbury House Estate, Ltd.*
[1930] A.C. 432 ; but see I.C.T.A. 1970, s. 67 (1), para. 3, and s. 140 as to tied
premises).

One odd point, however, is that this last cited case concerned the relationship between Schedule D, Case I, and Schedule A in its original form, which
form was repealed in 1963 and replaced by the present charge as a new
Case VIII of Schedule D (F.A. 1963, s. 15). The point is that it is also
established in the House of Lords that the Revenue can choose between

different Cases of the same Schedule (see *Liverpool & London & Globe Insurance Co.* v. *Bennett* (1913), 6 T.C. 327, at pp. 376 and 378 ; also *Fry* v. *Salisbury House Estate, Ltd., ante ;* cf. *Jones* v. *Leeming* [1930] A.C. 415). Then in 1970, for the purposes of consolidation this charge was changed from Case VIII of Schedule D to the present Schedule A (F.A. 1969, Sched. 20, para. 1 ; I.C.T.A. 1970, s. 67 (1)). As an incidental consequence of this change, which appeared to be merely one of name, the Revenue seems to have lost its freedom, enjoyed presumably between 1963 and 1970, to choose to make an assessment under Case I of Schedule D where possible on the facts.

Thus in *Lowe* v. *J. W. Ashmore, Ltd.* [1971] 1 Ch. 545, concerning profits from the sale of turves in the years 1964–66, assessments made in the alternative under both Case I and Case VIII of Schedule D were simply upheld by Megarry, J., without any apparent thought being directed to which should prevail. The choice would have been material even then (i.e., between 1963 and 1970) to the taxpayer's liability because of differences between the Cases in the rules, for example, as to preceding or current year bases of assessment and as to allowable expenditure. Now, on the facts of the case, only a Schedule A and not a Schedule D, Case I, assessment should be open to Revenue and taxpayer.

However, a landlord may in addition to receiving rents within Schedule A, also carry on a connected trade giving rise to trading receipts properly and only within Schedule D, Case I. A common example of this would be where property such as flats or offices is leased and services such as cleaning and heating, are provided by the landlord for a separate consideration (see *Fry* v. *Salisbury House Estate, Ltd.* [1930] A.C. 432). Further, in practice, where rents are merely incidental to the trade and are small in relation to the trading profits inspectors of taxes will permit all the rents (and deductions) to be brought into the Schedule D, Case I, computation. This practice can usually be approved and accepted by the taxpayer as constituting a useful simplification (see Law Commission Report on Taxation of Income and Gains Derived from Land, para. 60 ; 1971 Cmnd. 4654).

Rents: basis of assessment.—The basis of assessment under Schedule A is " by reference to the rents or receipts to which a person becomes entitled in the chargeable period " (I.C.T.A. 1970, s. 67 (1), para. 2). Thus the assessment is to accord with the general tax rule of depending on " earnings " rather than " cash " (see Traders, *ante,* p. 1091 ; for the relief available in the event of non-payment, see *ibid.,* s. 87, dealt with *post,* p. 1123). But in contrast to the preceding year basis of Schedule D, Case I, here the assessment is put *prima facie* on a current year basis. Despite this, assessments are actually to be made, in effect, during the course of a tax year on the basis of the final figures for the preceding year with any necessary adjustments up or down being made after the tax year has ended (see I.C.T.A. 1970, s. 69 (2)). In practice, the Revenue appear willing to accept a taxpayer's annual accounts ending in the preceding tax year as a basis of the provisional assessment rather than insisting on the statutory reference to the income for that preceding year of assessment (i.e., in *ibid.,* para. (*a*) ; see Inland Revenue Booklet No. 530, Notes on the Taxation of Income from Real Property, paras. 138–140). The Law Commission, observing that rental income tends to be fairly steady, saw no reason to change this unusual mixture of " current-year " and " preceding-year " bases (Report on Taxation of Income and Gains Derived from Land, para. 55 ; 1971 Cmnd. 4654).

Chargeable persons.—Schedule A income tax is to be paid by " the persons receiving or entitled to the profits or gains " within the charging provisions (I.C.T.A. 1970, s. 68 (1)). This alternative form of wording permits a potential dual liability, as where one person in fact receives rents to which another person is entitled. An application of this could have been to a vendor or purchaser of land where rent is payable in advance or in arrear, but special provision has been made, in effect, for the Schedule A liability to follow the apportionments of receipts and outgoings made on completion of the contract (I.C.T.A. 1970, s. 86). Consequently there is no need to make any apportionment of the tax liability itself on completion in such a case *unless* completion was not for some reason preceded by any contract for sale (as to Apportionments, see *ante*, p. 205).

It may be contended that any potential dual liability should be resolved by construing the words quoted as meaning the persons *beneficially* entitled to the rents and profits of land (see *Soul* v. *Irving* (1963), 41 T.C. 517, C.A., where " landlord " in s. 109 of the Income Tax Act, 1952, was applied to the reluctant beneficiary under a number of resulting trusts). But recently the very same words (i.e., " receiving or entitled ") in a different charging provision have actually been held to make assessable to tax a person, trustee or agent, who received money to which other persons were beneficially entitled (*Aplin* v. *White* [1973] 2 All E.R. 637, concerning Case III of Schedule D and applying s. 148 of the Income Tax Act, 1952, which was the predecessor of s. 68 (1) as well as s. 114 (1) of I.C.T.A. 1970). In that case, an estate agent collected rents on behalf of clients and placed the money on deposit; he was assessed on the interest notwithstanding that it belonged beneficially to his clients. It does not appear, however, from the report whether the rents themselves were treated in the same way, although it is thought that by parity of reasoning they could have been (but compare s. 70 (2) of I.C.T.A. 1970 as to collecting unpaid tax from agents). Ultimately, of course, in this sort of case, the person beneficially entitled should bear the burden of the tax in effect by way of deduction at source (see *Pyne* v. *Stallard-Penoyre* [1965] Ch. 705, *post*, p. 1121, for the position following misappropriation).

Where a chargeable person fails to pay his Schedule A tax, then in certain circumstances the tax can be collected from his lessees or agents (I.C.T.A. 1970, s. 70). So far as concerns lessees, this collection provision only applies if his " interest is derived (directly or indirectly) from that held by the person in default " (*ibid.*, subs. (1) (*a*)). The words in parenthesis clearly cover sub-lessees, but what is not quite so clear is the position where the lessor in default actually has no title since the section seems to assume that the person in default must have an interest (presumably the lessee is not estopped as against the Revenue ; cf. *Warner* v. *Sampson* [1959] 1 Q.B. 297). The tax collected from such a lessee may not exceed the rent due from him by the end of the relevant period (I.C.T.A. 1970, s. 70 (1) (*b*)) and the lessee will be entitled to recoup himself by deduction from the subsequent payments of rent (*ibid.*, para. (*d*)).

As to agents, the only requirement of this collection provision is that they should be " in receipt of rents or receipts from land on behalf of " a chargeable person in default (*ibid.*, subs. (2)). It does not appear necessary that the particular rents and land are not related to the default in question.

Profits.—It should be emphasised that the Schedule A charge is not on rents as such but rather " on the annual profits or gains arising in respect of such rents " (I.C.T.A. 1970, s. 67 (1)). Accordingly this can be regarded as a statutory justification, if not indeed requirement, that assessments should be based on computations complying with accountancy practice in much the same way as Schedule D, Case I, has reference to traders' accounts. However, whilst rents (and certain other receipts) are obviously entered on the credit side, the statute is fairly specific as to the deductions which may be debited (see I.C.T.A. 1970, s. 71 *et seq.*).

Before turning to the topic of deductions, two last points as to the credit side need to be noted. First, the word " annual " in the charging provision must be taken as merely intended to connote profits of an income and not capital nature (see *per* Lord Inglis in *Scottish Provident Institution* v. *Farmer* (1912), 6 T.C. 34, at p. 38). Second, it is thought that a Schedule A charge should arise also in respect of rents (or other receipts) in money's worth. Thus the value to the lessor of property or services provided by the lessee as rent should be included in the computation of profits (see as to valuation *Gold Coast Trust, Ltd.* v. *Humphrey* [1948] A.C. 459 ; cp. I.C.T.A. 1970, s. 156 (2), as to the value of mining, etc. rents " rendered in produce of the concern " being charged under Schedule D, Case III).

Rents: deductions.—The statute is not simple about this. It begins by saying that in Schedule A computations " such deductions shall be made ... as are provided for by sections 72 to 77 below " (I.C.T.A. 1970, s. 71 (1)). This positive provision, apparently mandatory, must really be read as a negative rule : no other deductions than those specified are permitted. Then the statute proceeds with a section (*ibid.*, s. 72) to which is attached the marginal note : " Deductions from rents : general rules " (although " miscellaneous details " might be more apt). The primary subsection then lists four groups of items ((a)–(d), see below) in respect of which the lessor liable to the tax may deduct " the amounts of payments made by him " from " rent " to which he is entitled under a " lease " (*ibid.*, s. 72 (1)).

" *Lease.*"—In these deductions provisions the words " lease " and " rent " each purport to enjoy a special meaning. References to a lease " extend only to a lease conferring a right, as against the person whose interest is subject to the lease, to the possession of premises " (I.C.T.A. 1970, s. 71 (2)). This odd restriction can only be taken as excluding leases which are not actually of " premises " since, as a general proposition, all lessees are entitled to " possession " as against their lessors (cp. the definition of " possession " in L.P.A. 1925, s. 205 (1) (xix), as including the right to receive any rents and profits). And the word " premises " is defined as including " any land " (I.C.T.A. 1970, s. 90 (1)), but the word " land " is not defined for present tax purposes (cp. L.P.A. 1925, s. 205 (1) (ix)). So, accepting this sense, what " leases of land " are excluded ? The suggestion has been made that the exclusion of leases of incorporeal rights was intended (see George, Taxation and Property Transactions, 3rd ed., p. 50). Nevertheless the present writer feels not only that the language employed is strictly inappropriate to have this effect but also that such an exclusion would be so negligible in consequence as to be not worthwhile.

" *Rent.*"—In contrast to the restrictive references to leases, the meaning of " rent " is extended (for the deductions provisions) to include—

" a payment made by the tenant to defray the cost of work of maintenance of, or repairs to, the demised premises, not being work required by the lease to be carried out by the tenant."

(I.C.T.A. 1970, s. 71 (2)). Since in practice any such (and other) " service " contributions by tenants have often been reserved as rent, this extension will surely prove of maximum unimportance ! After all, if services are provided by the landlord for a separate consideration, then the Schedule D, Case I, deductions rules, rather than the present ones, will become relevant (see *Fry* v. *Salisbury House Estate, Ltd.* [1930] A.C. 432).

" *By lessor.*"—Deductions are allowed by a lessor " of payments made by him " in respect of the various items (I.C.T.A. 1970, s. 72 (1)). Accordingly actual expenditure appears required, the mere incurring of a liability not sufficing. Also there must be expenditure by the lessor himself, although presumably this need not be directly on the items mentioned: the words " in respect of " must allow indirect payments. This being so, one wonders why the deduction should not be allowed of payments made by a lessor (e.g., year by year into a special " sinking " fund) towards *future* expenditure (e.g., eventual and inevitable renewals and replacements, even decoration). It is, however, particularly provided, in effect, that deductions of expenditure are not permitted where the incidence falls on someone else, e.g., insurance moneys (I.C.T.A. 1970, s. 77 (3)).

Items.—The statutory list of items in respect of which a lessor may make deductions is as follows—

" (*a*) . . . maintenance, repairs, insurance or management,

(*b*) . . . any services provided by him otherwise than by way of maintenance or repairs, being services which he was obliged to provide but in respect of which he received no separate consideration,

(*c*) . . . rates or other charges on the occupier which [the lessor] . . . was obliged to defray,

(*d*) . . . any rent, rentcharge, . . . or other periodical payment reserved in respect of, or charged on or issuing out of, land "

(I.C.T.A. 1970, s. 72 (1)). This list is followed by a proviso whereby it does not apply to " any payment of interest " (*ibid.*), but it will be appreciated that tax relief for interest on loans is anyway otherwise available, especially for loans in connection with the purchase or improvement of land (see I.C.T.A. 1970, s. 57, and F.A. 1972, s. 75). These items of expenditure are not restricted to the demised premises but expressly may extend to the common parts of the premises (I.C.T.A. 1970, s. 72 (6)).

Repairs.—In practice, very much of that list will be applied to the facts in a largely self-explanatory manner. Nevertheless, some observations are occasioned by certain of the items. In particular the opening words " maintenance " and " repairs " can give rise to difficult practical distinctions —not *inter se* for they are substantially synonymous but from improvements, renewals and additions, expenditure which is not allowable. This is a distinction which arises in many contexts and which does not appear readily soluble by reference to any precise and all-purpose definitions (certainly the taxing statutes provide none). Accordingly the courts have tended instead to have resort to a few helpful illustrations ; an often cited example is the following :—

" ' Repair ' and ' renew ' are not words expressive of a clear contrast. Repair always involves renewal ; renewal of a part ; of a subordinate part. A skylight leaks ; repair is effected by hacking out the putties,

putting in new ones, and renewing the paint. A roof falls out of repair ;
the necessary work is to replace the decayed timbers by sound wood ;
to substitute sound tiles or slates for those which are cracked, broken or
missing ; to make good the flashings and the like. Part of a garden wall
tumbles down ; repair is effected by building it up again with new mortar,
and, so far as necessary, new bricks or stone. Repair is restoration by
renewal or replacement of subsidiary parts of a whole. Renewal, as
distinguished from repair, is reconstruction of the entirety, meaning by
the entirety not necessarily the whole but substantially the whole subject-
matter under discussion "

(*per* Buckley, L.J., in *Lurcott* v. *Wakely & Wheeler* [1911] 1 K.B. 905, at
p. 923 ; see also *per* Fletcher Moulton, L.J., *ibid.*, p. 918). However, rather
more recently, Denning, L.J., having given the customary illustrations,
concluded—

" It seems to me that the test, so far as one can give any test in these
matters, is this : If the work which is done is the provision of something
new for the benefit of the occupier, that is, properly speaking, an improvement ; but if it is only the replacement of something already there, which
has become dilapidated or worn out, then, albeit that it is a replacement by
its modern equivalent, it comes within the category of repairs and not
improvements "

(in *Morcom* v. *Campbell-Johnson* [1956] 1 Q.B. 106, at p. 115).

Neither of these illuminating observations was made in an income tax
context, but there can be little doubt that they are applicable here too.
However, in this context there are three additional considerations to be
especially noticed. One is that the vital distinction between repairs and
improvements is very frequently treated by the courts as a question of fact
on which the Commissioners' determination is final (see, e.g., *Thomas Wilson*
(*Keighley*), *Ltd.* v. *Emmerson* (1960), 39 T.C. 360, and *Conn* v. *Robins Brothers,
Ltd.* (1966), 43 T.C. 266). The second is that the courts display a tendency
in taxation matters to let the major distinction between capital and income
(whether of receipts or of expenditure) colour all lesser distinctions with the
consequence that reliance can then simply be placed on the touchstone of
" established principles of sound commercial accounting " (see *Odeon
Associated Theatres, Ltd.* v. *Jones* [1972] 2 W.L.R. 331, C.A. ; but cp. *Heather*
v. *P-E Consulting Group, Ltd.* [1973] 1 All E.R. 8, C.A.). There seems no
valid reason to suppose that this approach *via* accountants should not properly
be adopted for Schedule A as well as for Schedule D, Case I.

However, this wider view may be contradicted by the narrower inferences
to be drawn from the terms of Extra-Statutory Concession B4—which
constitutes the third additional consideration mentioned in the preceding
paragraph. The terms of this concession are as follows :—

" Where maintenance and repairs of property are obviated by improvements, additions and alterations, so much of the outlay as is equal to the
estimated cost of the maintenance and repairs is allowed as a deduction
in computing liability in respect of rents under Schedule A. This concession
does not apply where—

(i) the alterations, etc., are so extensive as to amount to the
reconstruction of the property, or

(ii) there is a change in the use of the property which would have made
such maintenance or repairs unnecessary "

(Booklet IR 1 (1970), p. 9). This concession was no doubt designed so as not to discourage expenditure on property. It also has the inestimable merit of rendering unnecessary in practice most of the arguments around the borderline between repairs and improvements.

Insurance.—The statute includes the simple unexplained word "insurance" amongst the deductible items (i.e., in I.C.T.A. 1970, s. 72 (1) (*a*)). The view has been expressed judicially that the insurance referred to " is insurance of the premises, the expense of insuring the continued existence of the premises against loss by fire or in other ways " (*per* Atkinson, J., in *Pearce* v. *Doulton* (1947), 27 T.C. 405, at p. 408 ; a case relating to identically worded provisions of the original Schedule A tax and concerning premiums on a leasehold redemption policy ; deduction was not allowed). In the result, so long as the insurance relates to the property in a similar way to maintenance, repairs and management (which represent a controlling context) the premiums should be deductible whatever form the policy takes (e.g., fire cover only or comprehensive). However, apparently the Revenue opinion is that neither insurance of the contents (e.g., furniture) nor insurance against loss of rent are allowable (see Inland Revenue Booklet No. 530, Notes on the Taxation of Income from Real Property, Appendix I, at p. 58). This opinion, especially as to rent, may well be arguable (cp. George, Taxation and Property Transactions, 3rd ed., p. 62).

Management.—The scope of the word " management " in an almost identical tax context was thoroughly and judicially considered by the Court of Session in *I.R.C.* v. *Wilson's Executors* (1934), 18 T.C. 465. Lord Sands said he would include " all charges fairly as business charges incident to the prudent management of the estate . . . not being charges incident to the business in connection with capital matters of a substantial character " (at p. 476). And Lord Clyde instanced as particular inclusions " any cost in having the estate accounts properly kept, in collecting the rents and in making the necessary disbursements " (at p. 473). In the case, in fact, compensation for disturbance paid to a tenant and the expenses of connected litigation were disallowed, although in practice it is understood that the Revenue do accept all costs arising out of renewals of leases including the expenses of determining the rent and other terms of the new leases (see George, Taxation and Property Transactions, 3rd ed., p. 64).

Examples of expenditure which has been held to come within the word " management " in the present context include surveyor's fees, even in the form of a retainer (*London & Northern Estates Co., Ltd.* v. *Harris* (1937), 21 T.C. 197) and the costs of advertising for tenants of unlet flats (*Southern* v. *Aldwych Property Trust, Ltd.* [1940] 2 K.B. 266). Outside the word fell the amount of rents misappropriated by the estate agent who collected them for the lessor (*Pyne* v. *Stallard-Penoyre* [1965] Ch. 705) but in such a case now the lessor, charged to tax on the basis of his entitlement to the rents, would presumably be able to claim relief simply because he had not received the rents (i.e., under I.C.T.A. 1970, s. 87 (1) ; in the *Pyne* case, some support was sought by counsel for the Crown in the fact that the Schedule A tax then related to the annual value of the land and not to receipt of rents).

Capital allowances.—Certain capital allowances are available in relation to machinery or plant used for the maintenance, repair or management of premises producing Schedule A rents (I.C.T.A. 1970, s. 78). Capital allowances are also available where machinery or plant is " let by any person otherwise than in the course of a trade . . . whether or not it is used for the purposes of a trade carried on by the lessee " (F.A. 1971, s. 46). This would apply where there is a lease of a building including, for example, lifts and central heating equipment (cf. *Lupton* v. *Cadogan Gardens Developments, Ltd.* [1971] 3 All E.R. 460, C.A.).

Services.—Group (*b*) of the deductible items calls for some comment (i.e., I.C.T.A. 1970, s. 72 (1)). It relates to " services " provided by the lessor going beyond maintenance and repair. The two essential points to note are that the provision of these services must be (1) obligatory and (2) for no separate consideration (*ibid.*). As to (1), the statute makes no reference to a source of the obligation and in practice the Revenue liberally accept that it need not arise from any provision in the lease but may depend merely upon commercial expediency (see George, Taxation and Property Transactions, 3rd ed., pp. 65–66). As to (2), if there *is* separate consideration for the services, the charge to tax should normally be made not under Schedule A but under Schedule D, Case I (*Fry* v. *Salisbury House Estate, Ltd.* [1930] A.C. 432) ; see also as to V.A.T., *post*, p. 1143.

The precise meaning of the central word " services," lacking any statutory definition, is left in obscurity. In practice, it is not treated restrictively but appears allowed to cover virtually all incidental amenities provided by a lessor in relation to the demised premises or to other property, such as the common parts of the building and grounds. Thus the cost of cleaning, heating, hot water, lifts, porters and such like would all be deductible. Further, it appears that the Revenue will allow within this group (*b*) certain expenditure which is not actually on the lessor's premises, either demised or in common use, but which can be regarded as " in respect of " the premises. For example, payments to third parties for the use of their land as a means of access or as a garden to the premises may be treated as comprehended by " services " (see George, Taxation and Property Transactions, 3rd ed., pp. 52 and 65 ; cp. I.C.T.A. 1970, s. 72 (6)).

Period of deductions.—Payments in respect of any of the above items may, as a general rule, only be deducted from rents if they became due during the period in which the person chargeable to the tax has been the lessor of the lease (I.C.T.A. 1970, s. 72 (2)). In particular payments for maintenance or repairs are not deductible if incurred by reason of dilapidation before that period (*ibid.*, para. (*b*)). This necessarily excludes, for Schedule A purposes, deferred repairs attributable to a pre-acquisition period (i.e., in accordance with *Law Shipping Co., Ltd.* v. *I.R.C.* (1924), 12 T.C. 621, but cp. *Odeon Associated Theatres, Ltd.* v. *Jones* [1972] 2 W.L.R. 331 ; the Law Commission has suggested that this should be reviewed : Report on Taxation of Income and Gains Derived from Land, para. 33 : 1971 Cmnd. 4654).

As an exception to the general rule, the period during which deductible payments can become due is extended, in effect, so as to include (*a*) previous leases at a full rent and (*b*) any intervening time when the premises were not occupied by either tenant or owner, provided that the chargeable person was the lessor and owner throughout (I.C.T.A. 1970, s. 72 (2)). In other words, there may be a " carry-forward " of deductible items to be set against future full rents from future leases. For this purpose, a rack-rent is not required ; a lease will be at a full rent—

" . . . if the rent reserved under the lease (including an appropriate sum in respect of any premium under the lease) is sufficient, taking one year with another, to defray the cost to the lessor of fulfilling his obligations under the lease and of meeting any expenses of maintenance, repairs, insurance and management of the premises subject to the lease which fell to be borne by him . . . "

(I.C.T.A. 1970, s. 71 (2)).   Thus a profit is not necessary to a full rent, only the expectation of an overall absence of loss.   However, something of a problem is caused by the use of the present tense—" is sufficient "—which fails to cater for the case of a fixed rent, initially sufficient, which cannot keep pace with the galloping inflation of costs.

There is also a restricted provision for " setting-off " or " pooling " expenditure on various premises all let on leases which are at a full rent as above and which are not tenant's repairing leases (I.C.T.A. 1970, s. 72 (4)). A tenant's repairing lease here is one " where the lessee is under an obligation to maintain and repair the whole or substantially the whole, of the premises comprised in the lease " (ibid., s. 71 (2)).   Thus these provisions have thrown up three distinct sorts of leases—(i) at a full rent and not tenant's repairing, (ii) tenant's repairing, and (iii) not at a full rent—which each have separate rules as to " set-off " and " carry-forward." The Law Commission has expressed the view that the complications introduced by these distinctions are not justified and has recommended their abolition (see Report on Taxation of Income and Gains Derived from Land, paras. 12–17 : 1971 Cmnd. 4654).

Non-receipt relief.—It will be recalled that the Schedule A assessments essentially have reference to entitlement to rent.   But even taxpayers do not always get what they are entitled to.   Accordingly, appropriate relief is made available to a lessor who claims and proves that he has not received any part of the rents (I.C.T.A. 1970, s. 87 (1) (a) ;   cp. *Pyne* v. *Stallard-Penoyre* [1965] Ch. 705, concerning misappropriation by an estate agent). However, if the non-receipt was due to someone's default, he must also show that any reasonable steps to enforce payment have been taken (ibid., para. (b)).   Again, if the non-receipt was due to waiver, it must have been without consideration and reasonable in order to avoid hardship (ibid., para. (c) ;   if hardship is not involved, thought might well be given to a suitable advance variation of the lease).   Also, of course, if the rents in question are, in fact, subsequently received, equally appropriate tax adjustments are to be made (ibid.; the lessor has six months in which to own-up to an inspector).   Incidentally, if an increase in rent is waived because of the " freeze," then the above provisions of s. 87 will apply by concession (see statement at (1973), 117 Sol. J. 76).

Premiums.—If only rents and income receipts from land had been made liable to income tax, most people would have preferred to take premiums and other capital payments instead.   Of course, traders in land and property dealers would be caught anyway for an income tax assessment under Schedule D, Case I, but when the old Schedule A was replaced in 1963 by what is now the new Schedule A (via a change of name) there was no capital gains tax in its present all-embracing form to rely on or to worry about. Accordingly certain complicated sections were enacted, directed at premiums for short leases, which must be regarded and understood as anti-avoidance legislation (i.e., a comprehensively detailed and imaginatively penal approach appears to have been adopted).

In essence and intent, the result of the legislation seems straightforward : any premium required under any lease not exceeding fifty years is to be treated, at least in part, as (additional) rent which therefore comes within the Schedule A charge (see now I.C.T.A. 1970, ss. 80 to 84). There is much more to it than this, of course, mostly because of the need felt to anticipate avoidance devices, but partly also because of those attempts at equity in the operation of a new tax which always militate against simplicity. Consequently it can be suggested all the more strongly that these complications have become totally otiose since 1965. Had there been the present capital gains tax in 1963, surely they would never have been enacted. Nevertheless, the Law Commission has fairly recently expressed the view that

" it would be going too far to abolish the taxation of premiums (as income) altogether : a premium for a very short lease is not sensibly distinguishable from rent in advance and should be taxed as such at income tax rates "

(Report on Taxation of Income and Gains from Land, para. 20 : 1971 Cmnd. 4654 ; a supposed simplification was recommended in para. 22 involving principally a reduction to 7–10 years of the relevant duration of leases). But even granting what the Law Commission says, the case for special provisions for premiums still does not seem to be completely made. Can it have been overlooked that the persistent receiver of premiums would be liable to income tax as a trader within Schedule D, Case I, and that even the less-persistent profit-maker would now very likely be caught by the so-called " artificial transactions in land " net (i.e. I.C.T.A. 1970, s. 488) ?

Nothing further will be said here generally about either traders or artificial transactions in relation to premiums since the applicable principles have already been sufficiently indicated (see pp. 1091–1123). But brief mention should be made of the inter-relationship of the income tax liability in respect of premiums under Schedule A and under Schedule D, Case I (traders) or Case VI (artificial transactions). The position in both cases is the same (see I.C.T.A. 1970, s. 488 (6) (b)). In essence, the premium will first attract tax under Schedule A (assuming a short lease, etc.) and must then be brought into the Schedule D computation reduced only by the amount on which Schedule A tax has been paid (I.C.T.A. 1970, s. 142 (2)–(4) ; it will be seen below that Schedule A tax is not paid on premiums in full but as discounted in accordance with the length of the term).

Premiums and capital gains tax.—The application of capital gains tax to the sale of subsisting leaseholds has already been fairly fully considered (see *ante*, pp. 1074–1076). The so-called sale by way of the grant of a lease at a premium should be thought of also in that context since the general principles of the charge and many of the detailed rules are obviously equally relevant (e.g., short leases as " wasting assets "). Accordingly what follows is an outline indication only of the capital gains tax provisions which should be borne in mind by or on behalf of an intending lessor.

The F.A. 1965 (which imposes the capital gains tax charge) deals especially with leases in Sched. 8, para. 2 (1) of which provides that—

" . . . where the payment of a premium is required under a lease of land, or otherwise under the terms subject to which a lease of land is granted, there is a part disposal of the freehold or other asset out of which the lease is granted . . ."

Thus a premium produces a part disposal and there are provisions for the recognition in certain cases of deemed or notional premiums (*ibid.*, para. 3). These cases, in effect, cover payments made (i) in lieu of rent, (ii) for the surrender of the lease and (iii) for the variation or waiver of any of the terms of the lease. Further the word " premium " is first widely defined as including " any like sum, whether payable to the intermediate or a superior landlord " and then a presumption is attached that " any sum (other than rent paid on or in connection with the granting of a tenancy) " constitutes a premium (*ibid.*, para. 10 (1) ; the presumption can only be rebutted by showing other sufficient consideration for the payment).

This catchment area extending around the word " premium " for capital gains tax purposes has been lifted almost intact from the Schedule A provisions which are discussed in more detail below. But there are three differences worth noting. First, the present provisions do not appear to cover payments to a person other than a landlord (cp. I.C.T.A. 1970, s. 80 (5), imposing liability under Schedule D, Case VI). Second, the enhanced value of the premises due to work which the tenant is obliged to do is not here turned into a premium (cp. I.C.T.A. 1970, s. 80 (2)). And third, the definition of " lease " for capital gains tax purposes includes a mere licence (F.A. 1965, s. 45 (1)) ; this is not so in the Schedule A provisions (see I.C.T.A. 1970, s. 90 (1)).

It is thought that the grant of a lease at a rack rent without any premium should not be treated as a part disposal. Although such a grant would clearly come within the general meaning given to part disposals (i.e., by F.A. 1965, s. 22 (2) (*b*) as including the creation of an interest in an asset), the particular provisions directed at leases expressly bring in only a lease plus premium (see *ibid.*, Sched. 8, para. 2 (1), quoted above ; cf. also *ibid.*, Sched. 7, para. 14 (7)). Surely the particular should be allowed to prevail over the general. However, the point is hardly of great practical importance since the consideration for the disposal and for the acquisition of a rack rent lease will be virtually nil (i.e., the capitalised value of the rent should not be included in the capital gains tax computation : see *ibid.*, Sched. 6, para. 2).

If a lease is granted neither at a rack rent nor for any (adequate) premium, then for capital gains tax purposes thought must be given to the application of the general rules relating to dispositions not at arm's length and by way of gift (see F.A. 1965, s. 22 (4) ; see also *ibid.*, Sched. 7, para. 17, as to transactions between connected persons). Under these rules the lease would, in effect, be deemed to be granted " for a consideration equal to the market value of the asset " (*ibid.*), which means " the price . . . on a sale in the open market " (*ibid.*, s. 44). At first sight these provisions seem to justify the assumption that a market value premium for the lease should figure in the capital gains tax computations. But there are two possible objections to this. One is that if there is no other premium (even of an inadequate amount) then it is arguable that there is simply no disposal or part disposal to attract the tax at all (see above as to *ibid.*, Sched. 8, para. 2 (1)). The other objection is that the " consideration equal to the market value " might just as well be a full rack rent as a premium (although the reference to " price . . . on a sale " may militate against this view).

Where there really is a part disposal because of the grant of a lease at a premium, then the result is that a capital gains tax computation must be made in accordance with the ordinary apportionment formula governing part disposals (see F.A. 1965, Sched. 6, para. 7, discussed *ante*, p. 1052). However, it is expressly provided that for this purpose—

" . . . the property which remains undisposed of includes a right to any rent or other payments, other than a premium, payable under the lease, and that right shall be valued as at the time of the part disposal . . ."

(*ibid.*, Sched. 8, para. 2 (2)). In substance, therefore, this imports the " Emery " (or " Macnaghten ") formula which is used for traders in land with reversions and ground rents as stock-in-trade (see *Heather* v. *A. Redfern & Sons* (1944), 26 T.C. 119, at p. 124, and *ante*, p. 1101).

Lastly the interrelationship with regard to premiums of capital gains tax and of Schedule A tax must be mentioned. The position is essentially the same as for traders and artificial transactions (see above). First, the premium will be subjected to any Schedule A tax liability, then the amount of the premium so subjected will be excluded from the capital gains tax computation (except from the denominator of the apportionment fraction) and the balance only brought in (see F.A. 1965, Sched. 8, para. 5, and F.A. 1967, Sched. 13, para. 8). It will be appreciated that these interrelationship rules are never relevant if the duration of the lease exceeds fifty years since then there is no Schedule A tax liability and only a potential capital gains tax charge.

Premiums as rent.—Where a premium is payable under a short lease, the charging provisions proceed by way of implied cross-reference. The statute simply says that in such a case—

> ". . . the landlord shall be treated for the purposes of the Tax Acts as becoming entitled when the lease is granted to an amount by way of rent (in addition to any actual rent) equal to the amount of the premium reduced . . ."

(I.C.T.A. 1970, s. 80 (1) ; the reduction by discount is dealt with below). A landlord treated in this way will be brought fairly and squarely within the ambit of the Schedule A charge already considered (*ibid.*, s. 67 (1)). Generally speaking, if the premium is payable to a person other than the landlord, then instead of the Schedule A charge, the amount in question will be treated as profits or gains of that other person chargeable under Schedule D, Case VI (*ibid.*, s. 80 (5)).

Top-slicing relief.—The charge to tax arises in full in the year when the lease was granted. This could be thought to cause injustice to an individual taxpayer through the higher rates of tax which would be produced by cramming all of the premium-cum-rent into one tax year. Consequently certain so-called " top-slicing " relief may be claimed (I.C.T.A. 1970, s. 85 (2) and Sched. 3). Needless to say, as statutorily stated, this relief seems to call for a calculation complex to the point of incomprehensibility. Yet in simple arithmetic terms, the sum is as follows : divide the premium (discounted as below) by the number of years of the term, *add* the resulting figure to the taxpayer's other income for the current tax year, ascertain his highest rate of tax on the resulting total for that year, and finally apply that rate to the whole of the premium. It would not be sensible or even practicable to do more here than refer the reader to the statute (*loc. cit.*) for the more precise details of this relief.

Discounted.—The charge to tax under Schedule A where a premium is treated as rent is not on the whole amount. Instead the amount of the premium is to be taken as reduced by 1/50th for every full year of the lease other than the first year (I.C.T.A. 1970, s. 80 (1)). Resorting to simple arithmetic again : deduct one from the term and multiply by two ; the answer represents the percentage discount on the premium (e.g., a 21-year **lease** produces a 40 per cent. discount).

Instalments.—Where the premium within these provisions is made payable by instalments, the taxpayer was initially allowed to choose to have each instalment simply treated for tax purposes as a payment of rent (or as an annual profit or gain under Schedule D, Case VI, if and when he was no longer the landlord : I.C.T.A. 1970, s. 80 (6)). This appeared at first sight to be something of a Morton's fork : the choice was either to pay the full tax immediately on a premium not yet receivable or to lose the discount available for a premium but not for rents. A later look, however, apparently revealed some elaborate tax avoidance devices springing directly from the treatment of instalments as rent (see the reproachful notice issued by H.M. Treasury at (1971), 115 Sol. J. 676). Consequently the taxpayer's choice has been substantially restricted. Now, where a premium is payable by instalments, the only option is to pay the tax by instalments over not more than eight years and this option depends entirely on the Revenue being first satisfied that otherwise undue hardship would be suffered (see F.A. 1972, s. 81 (1), amending I.C.T.A. 1970, s. 80 (6) ; see further Philip Lawton at [1972] B.T.R. pp. 272–274).

" *Premium* " *defined.*—It will be appreciated that the precise scope of the central word " premium " in all these provisions is of vital importance. The ordinary legal meaning of this word in the context of leases must be fairly well understood as—

" a cash payment made to the lessor, and representing, or supposed to represent, the capital value of the difference between the actual rent and the best rent that might otherwise be obtained "

(*per* Warrington, L.J., in *King* v. *Earl of Cadogan* [1915] 3 K.B. 485, at p. 492). This clear concept has, of course, become considerably obscured by decisions depending on the meaning of the word as conditioned by the special definitions in the Rent Acts and similar protective legislation in cases where there have been attempts to disguise premiums as rents in advance or as other things altogether (see, e.g., *Elmdene Estates, Ltd.* v. *White* [1960] A.C. 528, which concerned a requirement that a tenant sell property at an undervalue to a third party). It is thought that the wide construction and approach favouring tenants adopted in these cases should not prove of any help here. The present statute, which has its own specially extended definition, is a taxing Act and so, theoretically at least, should be approached narrowly.

Apparently assuming that there is a well understood ordinary meaning, the statute begins by providing (subject to context) that—

" ' premium ' includes any like sum, whether payable to the immediate or a superior landlord " [or to a " connected person "]

(I.C.T.A. 1970, s. 90 (1), as amended by F.A. 1972, s. 81 (3)). Presumably recipients other than the immediate landlord come within the Schedule D, Case VI, liability (see *ibid.*, s. 80 (5)). But there appears a pretty strong inference to be drawn that payments to persons other than those actually specified should not be regarded as premiums. Consequently a payment to a third party not " connected " with any landlord as in *Elmdene Estates, Ltd.* v. *White* [1960] A.C. 528, although possibly constituting a premium for some other purposes, should not be caught by the present legislation. Then, wider still and wider, the statute proceeds—

" . . . any sum (other than rent) paid on or in connection with the granting of a tenancy shall be presumed to have been paid by way of premium except in so far as other sufficient consideration for the payment is shown to have been given "

(I.C.T.A. 1970, s. 90 (2)).   The reference to " tenancy," rather than " lease "
as elsewhere, is no doubt meaningless.   However the use of " sufficient "
would seem to be a potentially significant slip in terminology : the elementary
rule of the law of contract is that consideration need not be adequate to be
sufficient (see, e.g., *Chappell & Co., Ltd.* v. *Nestlé Co., Ltd* [1960] A.C. 87
as to the sufficiency of peppercorns and chocolate wrappers ; cp. *Ball* v.
National and Grindlays Bank, Ltd. [1972] 3 W.L.R. 17, where this very point
was taken unsuccessfully in another taxation context but which may be
distinguishable since the relevant statutory phrase was " valuable and
sufficient consideration ").   Another slip, the word " sum " with its purely
monetary implications, has now been rectified by the provision that—

> " References in this section to a sum shall be construed as including the
> value of any consideration, and references to a sum paid or payable or to
> the payment of a sum shall be construed accordingly "

(I.C.T.A. 1970, s. 90, subs. (2B), inserted by F.A. 1972, s. 81 (4)).   Thus
money's worth clearly may be caught as a premium.

It is thought that this presumption, applying to sums, etc., paid on the
granting of tenancies, must still be read with the earlier definition of premiums
so as to be confined to sums, etc., paid to the landlord, immediate or superior,
or to connected persons (as to whom see I.C.T.A. 1970, s. 533).   Consequently,
the view has been expressed that the all too common requirement that a lessee
should pay the lessor's legal costs (i.e., despite the Costs of Leases Act, 1958)
does not amount to a premium because the payment is made to a third party
(see George, Taxation and Property Transactions, 3rd ed., p. 71).   But this
view seems unsound : such a requirement must obviously be of direct value
to the lessor, since otherwise he would have to meet the costs himself (see
I.C.T.A. 1970, s. 90 (2B), quoted above).   As Lord Radcliffe has put it :—

> " The landlord . . . gets his benefit out of the tenant if the premium is
> paid at his order to his creditor, to his son or to any other person or purpose
> he nominates no less than if he receives what is paid directly into his own
> hands "

(in *Elmdene Estates, Ltd.* v. *White* [1960] A.C. 528, at p. 541).   A second
reason given for the view that payment of the lessor's legal costs does not
amount to a premium is that " there is sufficient consideration, namely, the
legal work done " (George, *loc. cit.*).   But surely this ignores the essential
objection that the work in question is simply not done for the payer, the lessee,
but for the lessor, so that no consideration other than the grant of a lease
can be shown for the payment.   Therefore, it is suggested that the pecuniary
value to the lessor of the payment of his legal costs by the lessee should be
treated as a premium due to the lessor and chargeable as such.   This would
accord with the real substance of what happens.   However, equally in accord
with substance, the lessor will no doubt be able to deduct these legal costs
in the computation from chargeable rents as being expenses of management
(see *ante*).   Thus it will actually be advantageous to a lessor to require legal
costs to be included in the premium since the total amount will be discounted
as a receipt with no corresponding discount as a deduction.

Deemed premiums.—In addition to the extension by definition of the
meaning of " premium," there are certain other provisions elsewhere deeming
other sums to be premiums.   First, if the tenant is obliged to make any
improvements to the premises, then the amount of the immediate increase in
the value of the reversion will be treated as a premium (I.C.T.A. 1970, s. 80 (2)).

Obviously, this amount will lessen with the length of the lease and it will also be subject to the usual reduction by discount (see *ante*). Apart from this double discount, the provision ought to be readily avoidable if wished. Thus it will not apply to improvements of a temporary nature or where there is no obligation but only an expectation of work being done by the tenant. Again, it is arguable that work done either to other premises of the landlord or before the grant of the lease might not be covered. However, in these latter cases there would appear to be some clear value to the lessor, which could itself constitute a premium within the extended statutory definition.

A second sort of deemed premium occurs where, in effect, the lease itself provides in advance for sums to be paid in lieu of rent for any period or as consideration for its surrender (I.C.T.A. 1970, s. 80 (3)). Again, another deemed premium is to be found where sums become payable as consideration for the variation or waiver of any of the terms of the lease (*ibid.*, s. 80 (4) ; note that no provision for this payment need be present in the lease, also that waiver does not necessarily require total abandonment of a term : *Banning* v. *Wright* [1972] 1 W.L.R. 972, H.L.).

Deductions from premiums.—There is only one provision directed expressly towards deductions from premiums. This is an extraordinarily complex section designed to afford relief to *sub*-lessors who have paid a premium for their own lease (see I.C.T.A. 1970, s. 83). In effect, the discounted amount of the premium for the head lease is regarded as spread evenly over the term and may then by appropriate apportionment be set off against any premium or rents receivable in respect of the sub-lease.

Otherwise, since a premium is chargeable to tax as rent, it follows that any of the items deductible from rents are equally deductible from the chargeable amount of the premium (see I.C.T.A. 1970, ss. 71 (1), 72 (1) and 80 (1)). However, this would only appear relevant to the first tax year of the lease since that is normally the only chargeable period for which the computation will include the premium (see *ibid.*, s. 71 (1)). It must further be appreciated that there is no provision by which the capital costs, as of acquisition or improvement, can be set against premiums chargeable within the present provisions (i.e., as rents under Schedule A or income under Schedule D, Case VI), although such capital costs will quite properly figure in any computation for capital gains tax purposes.

Duration of lease.—The present charge on premiums is only imposed in the case of so-called " short-leases ", that is where " the duration of the lease does not exceed fifty years " (I.C.T.A. 1970, s. 80 (1)). A conveyancer, believing that a lease will be invalid unless its duration be certain (see *Lace* v. *Chandler* [1944] K.B. 368), might think that nothing further need be said. This would be a naïve view. Very little ingenuity used to be called for, even under the original Schedule A, to make effective short leases look like long leases. Accordingly, certain sweeping provisions appear in the legislation with intent to frustrate any such ingenuity. These provisions, considered below, are relevant not only to the question of whether a lease is long or short in duration but also to the amount of reduction in the chargeable premium (i.e., the longer the short lease, the greater the discount : see I.C.T.A. 1970, s. 80 (1)). One incidental point worth noticing is that these provisions for restricting the duration of leases have suffered several amendments from their original form largely because they allowed ingenuity to operate in reverse : apparently artificial income losses were produced via making long leases look like short leases ! This is the brief explanation for the present rather ambivalent form of the provisions.

Basically, the duration of a lease is restricted to a term ending on that date beyond which any circumstances at all render it " unlikely " that the lease will continue (I.C.T.A. 1970, s. 84 (1) (*b*), as amended by F.A. 1972, s. 81 (2)). In particular the substantial size of the premium may be taken as indicating a longer lease than indicated by other circumstances (*ibid.*). Also, if the lease includes a provision for extension by a tenant's notice, then account may be taken of any circumstances making the extension " likely " (*ibid.*, subs. (1) (*c*)). Again, if the tenant (or a " connected person ") may become entitled to a further lease, then the terms may be added together (*ibid.*, subs. (1) (*d*), added by F.A. 1972, s. 81 (2)). All these " likelihoods " are to be judged in the light of the facts " known or ascertainable " at the time of the grant of the lease and on the assumption that all the parties concerned will behave as if at arm's length (*ibid.*, subs. (2)). Further, a very strange provision has been added whereby, in effect, if extra benefits beyond those ordinarily enjoyed by a tenant were actually conferred or apparently paid for, then it is to be rebuttably assumed that the lease will end on some other date than the likely one (*ibid.*, subs. (2) as amended by F.A. 1972, s. 81 (2) ; no doubt this envisages a longer lease, but it nowhere says so).

Grant at undervalue.—As well as dealing with attempts to adjust the duration of leases, the statute also anticipates two other avoidance devices. The first, in essence, involves the grant of a lease at undervalue to a co-operative person who will later assign it for full value to the real tenant. This device has been countered by providing that on assignments of such leases the excess of the consideration given over the original premium (if any) should, in effect, be treated as a premium to be treated and taxed, in turn, as rent, except that the charge is to be under Schedule D, Case VI, as if the amount were profits or gains of the assignor, not the lessor (I.C.T.A. 1970, s. 81 (1)). Not necessarily all the excess, however, is to be so treated but only up to " the amount forgone ", that is, the additional premium which could have been required for the lease " having regard to values prevailing at the time it was granted, and on the assumption that the negotiations for the lease were at arm's length " (*ibid.*). If the excess on the first assignment does not cover " the amount forgone ", then the charge similarly catches so much of the consideration for later assignments as exceeds the last consideration given until the balance of " the amount forgone " is covered (*ibid.*).

This last point produces a practical problem for prospective assignors and assignees : each will wish to know whether or not a charge to tax may arise, the former in respect of the present assignment and the latter in respect of the next. It is suggested, therefore, that preliminary inquiries should always be directed to this problem (where the assignment will be of a lease granted in or after 1963–64), with a view to having the facts submitted to the inspector of taxes who then has to commit himself as to what if any potential charge there is (I.C.T.A. 1970, s. 81 (2)).

One query occurs with this anti-avoidance provision. In terms it imposes a charge to tax " on any assignment of the lease " (I.C.T.A. 1970, s. 81 (1)). But the vital word " assignment " is not defined by the statute, and its ordinary meaning is nowhere extended. Conveyancers will be well aware that lessees' covenants against assignment are cautiously drafted much more widely, as being also against underletting or parting with possession of the premises or any part thereof (cf. *ante*, p. 860 *et seq.*). Even so not everything would be covered. Accordingly, it may be queried whether this anti-avoidance provision would apply to the grant of a lease at undervalue followed, for example, by a declaration of trust, or even by an irrevocable licence, for an appropriate consideration, instead of an assignment (cp. *Gentle* v. *Faulkner* [1900] 2 Q.B. 267 and *Pincott* v. *Moorston's, Ltd.* [1937] 1 All E.R. 513).

Right to reconveyance.—The second avoidance device anticipated by statute involves essentially " sale of land with right to reconveyance." This is the marginal note to a section which begins more broadly :—

" Where the terms subject to which an estate or interest in land is sold provide that it shall be, or may be required to be, reconveyed at a future date to the vendor or a person who is . . . connected with him . . ."

(I.C.T.A. 1970, s. 82 (1)). This wording would appear clearly to cover an option to re-purchase, but not a mere right of pre-emption in favour of the vendor where reconveyance cannot be "required" without some co-operation. The result of applying the section is that the vendor becomes at once chargeable to tax under Schedule D, Case VI, on the excess (if any) of the sale price over the reconveyance price (*ibid.*, which includes a discount reduction provision). In effect, therefore, a sale of land for £50,000 to be reconveyed in seven years' time for £20,000 equals a seven years' lease for a premium of £30,000. If the reconveyance price is variable with the date, then the lowest possible price is to be taken, the vendor being able eventually to make a repayment claim based on the actual reconveyance price (*ibid.*, s. 82 (2)). Where, instead of a reconveyance, there may be a grant back of a lease at a premium, then this is to count as a reconveyance at a price equal to the premium plus the value of the reversion (*ibid.*, s. 84 (3), not applying if the grant back is within one month).

Conveyancers will probably appreciate that " sale of land with right to reconveyance " was the customary pre-1926 method of mortgaging freeholds and that its post-1925 use has been suppressed in favour of automatic conversion into a mortgage term (see L.P.A. 1925, s. 85 (2)). Yet it must surely be assumed that the taxing provisions under consideration do not apply to mortgages (see I.C.T.A. 1970, s. 90 (1), defining " lease " for present purposes as not including a mortgage). Of course, the conversion into a mortgage term will only occur if the conveyance was " by way of mortgage " which need only be intended and not necessarily expressed (*Grangeside Properties, Ltd.* v. *Collingwood Securities, Ltd.* [1964] 1 W.L.R. 139). Since the essence of the present anti-avoidance provision is that the reconveyance price should be less than the sale price, transactions within it are unlikely, without more, to be found to be intended to be by way of mortgage (cp. *Lewis* v. *Frank Love, Ltd.* [1961] 1 W.L.R. 261). But the adjustment involved here seems fairly straightforward. For example, land could be expressly mortgaged in the ordinary form to secure the repayment by the mortgagor of an interest-free loan of £20,000, with the mortgagee both paying an additional £30,000 as consideration for the postponement of the legal redemption date until seven years hence and also taking immediate possession of the land (mortgagees are generally entitled to possession and the £30,000 would prevent there being a clog on the equity). This transaction, with the substitution of vendor-lessor for mortgagor and of purchaser-lessee for mortgagee, might be seen to be simply the same as before—a seven years' lease at a £30,000 premium. But, according to legal substance, it should be difficult for the Revenue to treat it otherwise than as a mortgage (see *I.R.C.* v. *Duke of Westminster* [1936] A.C. 1 ; but cp. *Beattie* v. *Jenkinson* [1971] 1 W.L.R. 1419).

Agreement for lease.—The avoidance devices discussed as anticipated by statute in the immediately preceding paragraphs are distinctly elaborate. In contrast, there appears to be a method of avoidance, not touched by statute, which is simplicity itself. The suggestion is that no charge to tax should arise under the present provisions where a premium is taken for a mere agreement for a lease, i.e., a common or garden tenancy agreement, without there being any actual lease. It is true that for Schedule A purposes generally a lease is defined as including an agreement for a lease (I.C.T.A. 1970, s. 90 (1)) but this definition applies only " except where the context otherwise requires " (*ibid*). The charge to tax in respect of premiums arises " when the lease is *granted* " (*ibid.*, s. 80 (1)) and throughout the sections dealing with premiums (*ibid.*, ss. 80–85), but not elsewhere, this word " granted " almost invariably appears with the word " lease ". There is indisputable Court of Appeal authority for the proposition that this constitutes a context which excludes a mere agreement for a lease (*City Permanent Building Society* v. *Miller* [1952] Ch. 840). Accordingly, the (pecuniary) persuasion of lessees that an agreement for a lease really is as good as a lease would seem eminently desirable for lessors taking premiums.

B. OTHER SCHEDULE A RECEIPTS

The word " other " in the heading indicates the exclusion from the present consideration of the primary charge under Schedule A which is in respect of " rents under leases of land in the United Kingdom " since this topic has already received sufficient coverage (*ante*, pp. 1115–1132). Apart from such rents, income tax is chargeable under Schedule A—

" . . . on the annual profits or gains arising in respect of any such rents or receipts as follows, that is to say—

    (a) . . .

    (b) rent charges . . . and any other annual payments received in respect of, or charged on or issuing out of [land in the United Kingdom], and

    (c) other receipts arising to a person from, or by virtue of, his ownership of an estate or interest in or right over such land or any incorporeal hereditament . . . in the United Kingdom "

(I.C.T.A. 1970, s. 67 (1), para. 1.). Assuming a rent or receipt within paras. (b) or (c) above, then the observations already made in connection with rents as to the basis of assessment, the chargeable persons and the computation of profits (*ante*, pp. 1116–1118) are equally applicable here.

Rentcharges and annual payments.—Little difficulty is ever likely to be experienced in practice in recognising rentcharges within para. (b). However, the " other annual payments " within that paragraph could on occasion cause some small trouble. It is clear not only that they must be of an income nature (anyway because of the earlier reference to " annual profits or gains ") but also that they attract the *ejusdem generis* principle of construction (see *per* Megarry, J., in *Lowe* v. *J. W. Ashmore, Ltd.* [1971] Ch. 545, at p. 558). Accordingly para. (b) will not catch annual payments of a capital nature even though charged on or issuing out of land, such as instalments of the purchase price. But it is not always easy to distinguish between income and capital natures. Nor would para. (*b*) appear to cover payments, even though of an income nature, and even though made by a lessee to a lessor, where the obligation rests merely in a contract or covenant, without any reservation or charge (although this seems a purely academic point since para. (*c*) would almost certainly be applicable).

"Other receipts . . .".—The only real difficulty raised by para. (*c*) is in finding anything which might limit the application of the wide and general words used. The Act itself contains certain specific exclusions from the Schedule A charge, in brief, as follows : (i) yearly interest ; (ii) mining, etc., profits, rents and royalties ; (iii) rents from tied premises, and (iv) rents from furnished lettings (see I.C.T.A. 1970, s. 67 (1), paras. 3 and 4). These are, of course, all charged to income tax elsewhere in the statute (see *post*, pp. 1135–1141). Apart from such exclusions, the statute appears to contain nothing else designed to limit para. (*c*). Indeed, in the only reported case on the construction of the paragraph, Megarry, J., observed : " This seems to me to be wide and relatively simple language, and I do not not find the attempt to cut down its meaning at all persuasive " (in *Lowe* v. *J. W. Ashmore, Ltd.* [1971] Ch. 545, at p. 561).

In this last cited case, two general principles governing the construction of para. (*c*) were indicated which cannot be disputed. One was that receipts within it, as with Schedule A overall, must be of an income nature (*ibid.*, at p. 554). The other was that the receipts must arise from a retained ownership rather than from the disposal of the estate, interest or right which was owned (*loc. cit.*). These are, of course, connected principles in that the disposal of an asset more aptly attracts capital gains tax than income tax.

In addition, in the same case, two particular points of construction were determined. On the one hand the contention was rejected that para. (*c*) should be construed *ejusdem generis* with the other two paragraphs : this principle of construction was found to be exhausted by the inclusion of " other annual payments " in para. (*b*) (see *ibid.*, at p. 558). On the other hand, the scope of para. (*c*) was held to be illustrated to some extent by what is now s. 67 (3) of the I.C.T.A. 1970. This subsection deals with possible overlaps of charge between Schedules A and B in respect of " payments for any easement over or right to use any land." Megarry, J., accepted the contention that this assumed and indicated that the payments mentioned did come within para. (*c*) (see *ibid.*, at pp. 558 and 561). Further he cited binding authorities showing that the expression " right to use any land " in this context embraces all *profits à prendre* (see *ibid.*, at p. 559, referring to *Russell* v. *Scott* [1948] A.C. 422 and *Smethurst* v. *Davy* (1957), 37 T.C. 593).

Thus receipts arising from the grant of legal interests over land such as easements and *profits à prendre* are clearly covered by para. (*c*), even though in a sense they involve a disposal. Equally, receipts on account of equivalent equitable interests must certainly be covered. However, the language of para. (*c*) would appear even more naturally to envisage receipts under contracts relating to the user of the land in question, where the taxpayer's ownership is not disturbed at all. For example, fees from licences to park cars or exhibit advertisements should be caught here. There are, in fact, two decided cases where particular receipts were held to be within the paragraph which should be mentioned although neither concerned circumstances frequently encountered except by farmers. In *Lowe* v. *J. W. Ashmore, Ltd.* [1971] Ch. 545, sums paid under an oral agreement to a landowner for the sale of turf two inches thick from certain farm acres were held by

Megarry, J., to be within the paragraph ; the contention that the transaction constituted a sale of freehold land was rejected. And in *Bennion* v. *Roper* (1970), 46 T.C. 613, sums received from granting the grass-keeping of part of a farm were likewise held by Pennycuick, J., not to be capital receipts but to be within the present paragraph (the decision was affirmed by the Court of Appeal on another point).

Deductions.—Having considered what receipts fall within paras. (*b*) and (*c*) of Schedule A, it must still be remembered that this represents only one side of the computation which is necessary to produce the taxable profits and gains (see I.C.T.A. 1970, s. 67 (1)). The other side is represented by certain deductions which appear in terms to be both exclusive and mandatory (see *ibid.*, ss. 71 (1) and 74 (1)). These statutory deductions are set out under four heads as follows :—

" (*a*) so much of any payment made by that person as was made in respect of maintenance, repairs, insurance or management of premises to which the said sum relates and constituted an expense of the transaction under which he became entitled to that sum ;

(*b*) so much of any rent, rentcharge, ground annual, feu duty or other periodical payment made by that person as was reserved in respect of, or was charged upon or issued out of, premises to which the sum relates and constituted an expense of that transaction ;

(*c*) so much of any other payment made by that person as constituted an expense of that transaction, not being an expense of a capital nature ; and

(*d*) where, in or before the chargeable period, that person entered into any like transaction, any amount which, under paragraphs (*a*) to (*c*) above, is deductible from a sum to which he is entitled under that like transaction in the period, or was deductible from a sum to which he was so entitled in a previous chargeable period but had not been deducted "

(I.C.T.A. 1970, s. 74 (2)). From this it is plain that almost everything turns on the thrice repeated qualifying phrase " an expense of the transaction," for otherwise the scope of these heads of deduction is quite comprehensive. So far the phrase remains untested in reported cases. However, the suggestion has been made that this is not such a stringent test as the " wholly and exclusively " rule which qualifies expenditure for Schedule D, Cases I and II, computations (see commentary to the section in Current Law Statutes Annotated, 1970). In particular it has been suggested that " duality of purpose, which is fatal under the latter rule, would under the rule at present under consideration, merely result in an apportionment " (*loc. cit.*). This is largely true, but these suggestions do seem to overlook the fact that it is necessarily expenditure in respect of land which is under consideration and that a proportion of expenditure generally in respect of business premises should be deductible for the purposes of Schedule D, Cases I and II, notwithstanding duality of purpose (see *per* Lord Upjohn in *Korner* v. *I.R.C.* (1969), 45 T.C. 287, at p. 297). Also, unlike Schedule D, Cases I and II, expenditure, it would appear that deductions are only allowed here if the payment (1) has actually been made (i.e., not merely a liability incurred) and (2) was directly related to one productive transaction. Read strictly, the language of the heads of deduction (*a*) to (*c*), quoted above, does not seem to cover expenditure, for example, in between transactions or for the purposes of an abortive transaction. Consequently, it is thought that the present " expense of the transaction " rule should be regarded as stricter overall than the Schedule D, Cases I and II, rule (and see the illustrations given in George, Taxation and Property Transactions, 3rd ed., pp. 66–67).

C. FURNISHED LETTINGS

The leases or lettings about to be considered constitute for income tax purposes hybrid creatures. This is because the rents will be received partly in respect of land (i.e., the building or some of it) and partly in respect of chattels (i.e., the furniture and fittings). In other words, the receipts as a whole come from a source not falling comfortably into any one of the income tax Schedules. However, this theoretical difficulty has not been allowed to produce an *impasse*. Such rents have been assigned through the good offices of revenue practice to the sweeping-up Case VI of Schedule D—" tax in respect of any annual profits or gains not falling under any other Case of Schedule D, and not charged by virtue of Schedule A, B, C or E " (I.C.T.A. 1970, s. 109 (2)). Thus, in the course of discussing generally the scope of Case VI, Rowlatt, J., observed—

" One is not left entirely without guidance, at any rate as a matter of practice. Take the case of letting a furnished house. It is inveterate now that the letting of a furnished house for a few weeks in one year will attract income tax under this Case, upon the profits made by the letting. That is the inveterate practice, and although it has never been ruled upon in principle by the courts, it has been tacitly assumed by the courts in Scotland, and it seems out of question that a court of first instance, at any rate, could possibly say that that is wrong "

(in *Ryall* v. *Hoare* (1923), 8 T.C. 521, at p. 526 ; the Scottish assumption mentioned must mean the one made by the Court of Session in *Wylie* v. *Escott* (1912), 6 T.C. 128, see *per* Lord Johnston at p. 131).

Basis of assessment.—This practice of assigning furnished lettings to Case VI of Schedule D has still not been judicially " ruled upon in principle " although there have since been some English decisions also tacitly assuming that this was correct (see *Shop Investments, Ltd.* v. *Sweet* (1940), 23 T.C. 38, and *Smith* v. *Irvine* (1946), 27 T.C. 381) and there is now actually a statutory provision embodying the same assumption (i.e., I.C.T.A. 1970, s. 67 (1), para. 4). In the first of the two cases just cited, it was established that strictly the Case VI of Schedule D assessment was applicable only to the proportion of the rent attributable to the use of the furniture and fittings, the rest of the rent being covered by a Schedule A assessment (pre-1963 type). Since then, this odd duality of assessment has been rendered avoidable by law. It is provided that in such cases the whole of the rent is to be chargeable under Case VI of Schedule D *unless* the landlord elects otherwise (I.C.T.A. 1970, s. 67 (1), para. 4 ; the election must be made by notice in writing within the following two tax years : *ibid.*, s. 67 (2)). Accordingly, only if the landlord so elects will there now have to be proportionate assessments of the rent, as above, under the two Schedules. There would be good reason in practice for so electing only if the landlord has other Schedule A losses to be set off against the proportion of the rent attributable to the premises. The proportion of rent attributable to the use of furniture will remain within Case VI of Schedule D notwithstanding the election for Schedule A.

Apart from the possibilities of assessment under Case VI of Schedule D and under Schedule A, if the landlord in addition provides services, such as cleaning and heating, even meals, then an apportioned assessment may also be made on him as a trader within Case I of Schedule D (see *Fry* v. *Salisbury House Estate, Ltd.* [1930] A.C. 321). Further, in practice, where services are provided, the Revenue may agree to the transfer of all the liability in respect of receipts from the furnished letting to Case I of Schedule D on a trading basis, which will usually be to the taxpayer's advantage.

Assuming, however, liability under Case VI of Schedule D as the norm for furnished lettings, then the general rule applicable is that the assessment should be made on a current year basis unless, in effect, the inspector of taxes otherwise directs (I.C.T.A. 1970, s. 125, which also provides for the inspector's direction to be reviewed on appeal by the General or Special Commissioners). Of course, rents from furnished lettings have a tendency towards irregularity between years so that the flexibility of the current year basis will often prove most appropriate. But if average regularity can be shown then an annual accounts basis should be acceptable.

Computation.—The statute provides that income tax under Case VI of Schedule D " shall be computed . . . on the full amount of the profits or gains arising . . ." (I.C.T.A. 1970, s. 125 (1)). The terms of this clearly call for an account in the ordinary way balancing income receipts against expenditure to produce the taxable profit (or allowable loss : see *ibid.*, s. 176 (1)). So far as the receipts are concerned, in the present context, these are essentially the rents or other consideration for the letting of the premises and the use of the furniture. However, it is important to appreciate that the word " arising " signifies that actual payment is required ; i.e., the assessment here is on a cash received rather than on an entitlement or earnings basis (see *Grey* v. *Tile* (1932), 16 T.C. 414 ; also *Whitworth Park Coal Co., Ltd.* v. *I.R.C.* [1961] A.C. 31).

On the other side of the computation will appear deductible expenditure. However, no precise or restrictive statutory definition of the scope of such expenditure has been made available. Nevertheless, the scope can be fairly well illustrated for present purposes from the few reported cases directly relevant to furnished lettings. Thus in *Wylie* v. *Escott* (1912), 6 T.C. 128, where a house was let furnished for two months, deductions had been allowed (and were not in dispute) for the following items : proportion of rates ; wear and tear of furniture ; cleaning ; and " agency ". Again in *Smith* v. *Irvine* (1946), 27 T.C. 381, also concerning the furnished letting of a house, but over three years, the landlord had been allowed in the assessments as a deduction the annual rent which he himself paid for the house, rates, estate agents' commission, wear and tear, and also the costs incurred in recovering the rent due from one tenant. *Not* allowed as a deduction in either case (and this is what they were both about) were the costs to the landlord of obtaining alternative accommodation to live in whilst his house was let. In other words, rent paid for other premises is not deductible whilst rent paid for the premises sub-let furnished is deductible (see *Smith* v. *Irvine, ante ;* also *Barron* v. *Littman* [1953] A.C. 96).

In addition to these illustrations from cases, other indisputable examples of deductible expenditure will come to mind. For example, the costs of " maintenance, repairs, insurance and management " of the premises and contents must be allowable (see I.C.T.A. 1970, s. 72 (1) as to the Schedule A deductions). And these costs may be extended to the gardens, grounds and other common parts of the premises. Also, with furnished lettings of the " bed-sit " or thereabouts variety, a landlord may be expected to provide numerous facilities on the borderline of services—gas, electricity, telephone, television, washing machines, etc.—and the expenses should be included as a deduction in the computation.

Finally, where the deductible expenditure manages to exceed the rents received from furnished lettings, the rule in general is that Case VI losses can be set off only against Case VI profits of the same or subsequent tax years (I.C.T.A. 1970, s. 176, i.e., *not* against income from other sources, which is harsher than the Case I of Schedule D rule).

Thus if the rent from a furnished sub-letting is for some reason less than the head rent for the premises the result clearly is a Case VI loss within that general rule (unless the sub-landlord elects to have a proportionate Schedule A assessment and loss, see above). Not quite so clear is the consequence of abortive expenditure : do costly but unsuccessful efforts to let property furnished produce Case VI losses ? The section governing relief applies where " a person sustains a loss in any transaction " and any profits would have been assessable under Case VI (see I.C.T.A. 1970, s. 176 (1)). These quoted words have been considered in the House of Lords where the view was definitely taken, on the facts of the case, that they cover the situation where a taxpayer acquires by purchase a lease of property with intent to re-let but fails in an attempt to do so ; in other words, all of this together constitutes a " transaction " within the section (*Littman* v. *Barron* (1952), 33 T.C. 373). However, as Viscount Simon put it—

" If all that could be said was that an owner of property, freehold or leasehold, had tried to find a tenant for it and had failed, it would be a question whether his unsuccessful effort could be regarded as a transaction. A similar difficulty would arise if the taxpayer had become the owner of property by bequest or inheritance, which he failed to re-let "

(*ibid.*, at p. 402 ; see also *per* Lord Normand at *ibid.*, p. 405, and *per* Jenkins, L.J., in the Court of Appeal at *ibid.*, pp. 392–3). No answers were indicated. Consequently, it remains arguable that all expenditure which would have been deductible had there actually been a furnished letting during any period may simply be totalled to produce an allowable loss provided some attempt to achieve such a letting can be shown.

D. MINING, ETC., RENTS AND ROYALTIES

The essential situation envisaged here is that an owner of land, for a suitably regular consideration, allows another person to exploit the land in any of various potentially profitable ways. The taxation consequences for each person are contained in certain sections statutorily sub-headed " Mines, quarries and other concerns " and " Mining, etc., rents and royalties " (see I.C.T.A. 1970, ss. 112 and 156), but the ways of exploitation comprehended by the provisions extend fairly far beyond the mere extraction of minerals.

The general Schedule A charge in respect of rents, annual payments and other receipts from land expressly does not apply, *inter alia*, either to the profits or gains from " mines, quarries and other concerns " or to " mining, etc. rents and royalties " (I.C.T.A. 1970, s. 67 (1), para. 3). Accordingly, the charge to tax must be found elsewhere.

" Mines, quarries and other concerns ".—It is provided first that the profits or gains " arising out of land " in the case of any of the concerns listed below are to be charged to tax under Case I of Schedule D (I.C.T.A. 1970, s. 112 (1)). Thus in effect the person actually exploiting the land, whether his own or someone else's, is treated for tax purposes as a trader subject to all the ordinarily applicable rules (and see the Capital Allowances Act, 1968, s. 60). The concerns specified in the statute are—

(a) Mines and quarries (including gravel pits, sand pits and brickfields) ;

(b) Ironworks, gasworks, salt springs or works, alum mines or works (not being mines falling within the preceding paragraph), and waterworks and streams of water ;

(c) Canals, inland navigations, docks, and drains or levels ;

(d) Fishings ;

(e) Rights of markets and fairs, tolls, bridges and ferries ;

(f) Railways and other ways ;

(g) Other concerns of the like nature as any of the concerns specified above (see I.C.T.A. 1970, s. 112 (2)). It would appear that the words " arising out of land " must be taken as adding the qualification that to come within this list the concern in question must involve an interest in land in the strict sense (see *I.R.C.* v. *Forth Conservancy Board* [1929] A.C. 213). However the point must be regarded as almost entirely academic since the profits of the concern will virtually inevitably be taxable either simply as those of a trader anyway or else under Case VI of Schedule D (see *Forth Conservancy Board* v. *I.R.C.* [1931] A.C. 540).

Apart from that qualification, the inquiry may be made as to what inherent limitations there are on the scope of head (g) : " other concerns of the like nature as any of the concerns specified . . ." (I.C.T.A. 1970, s. 112 (2)). These words have received some critical scrutiny by the House of Lords (see *Russell* v. *Scott* (1948), 30 T.C. 394) but in a statutory setting which has since been modified, in particular by the mention in head (a) of sand pits (which was what the case was about) and by the insertion of the magic words " any of " in head (g) itself. This latter insertion was to meet the objections uttered in the House of Lords against having to attempt an *ejusdem generis* construction in respect of the whole of a heterogeneous collection of items. Now a like nature to any one other specified concern will suffice. But what is a concern ? Viscount Simon explained—

" ' Concern ' is a very wide word, and appears to imply an adequate degree of business organisation for the purpose of carrying on the undertaking. But the amount of organisation needed must depend upon the character of the ' concern ' itself. It will be noted from the language . . . that all the various enterprises . . . are spoken of as ' concerns ', and it is obvious that the amount of organisation needed for a toll or for streams of water would be vastly less than for a mine of coal or for gasworks "

(in *Russell* v. *Scott* (1948), 30 T.C. 394, at p. 421). Accordingly for there to be a " concern " within the present provisions it appears that there must be some organisation going beyond the mere receipt of profits.

" Mining, etc., rents and royalties ".—Apart from the taxpayer who exploits the land himself, it remains to consider a person who allows another to exploit his land. It is provided that " where rent is payable in respect of any land or easement " which, in effect, is " used, occupied or enjoyed in connection with any of the concerns specified " above, then the rent is charged to tax under Schedule D (I.C.T.A. 1970, s. 156 (1)). This subsection does not state which Case of Schedule D is applicable but does lay down the general rule that the tax should be collected by means of deduction at source (i.e., within *ibid.*, ss. 52 and 53). In other words, the rent is payable less tax and the payer becomes unable to claim the payment as deductible expenditure (see *Earl Fitzwilliam's Collieries Co.* v. *Phillips* [1943] A.C. 470). As an exception to this general rule, however, where the rent is " rendered in produce of the concern "—i.e., money's worth rather than money—then it is charged under Case III of Schedule D, with the value of the produce being brought into the computation and deduction at source not applying as inappropriate (*ibid.*, s. 156 (2)). Further it should be noted that mineral royalties otherwise within these provisions have been subjected to certain special relieving rules outlined below.

It will be appreciated that the application of the provisions partly quoted above (i.e., I.C.T.A. 1970, s. 156 (1) (2)) depends upon there being a " concern " in the heterogeneous sense already discussed. In the absence of such a concern, however, the rent payable will certainly not escape tax but would appear chargeable instead under Schedule A (see *ibid.*, s. 67 (1)). Also it is an essential that the rent be payable " in respect of any land or easement " (*ibid.*, s. 156 (1)). The word " land " is not defined for the purposes of the section but the inference that it is used in the purely physical rather than legal sense may be drawn from the fact that easements are separately mentioned (cp. L.P.A. 1925, s. 205 (1) (ix)). The word " easement " is specially defined for the section as including " any right, privilege or benefit in, over or derived from land " (I.C.T.A. 1970, s. 156 (3) (*a*)). This bears a suspicious similarity to the phraseology used in the property statutes (cp. L.P.A. 1925, ss. 1 (2) (*a*), 62 (1)–(3) and 205 (1) (ix)) which the courts are tending to restrict to interests capable of subsisting as legal easements or *profits à prendre* (see, e.g., *Phipps* v. *Pears* [1965] 1 Q.B. 76, 84). Nevertheless it appears quite clear that the present context affords no justification for such a strictly restrictive construction. Thus in the House of Lords it has been said that the words used (i.e., to define easements) are—

" not words of art or such as a conveyancer would use. They are popular in character ; they do not suggest the idea of an easement or interest in land. The words, in my opinion, would be satisfied by a merely personal right, privilege or benefit, so long as it concerns or affects a piece of land. So far as the fair meaning of the words requires, such a right, benefit or privilege might be created by deed or by simple contract. The definition seems to me to be inconsistent with the idea of its being limited to what could properly be called an estate or interest in land. The word ' any ' preceding ' right, privilege or benefit ' points in the direction of a wide construction "

(*per* Lord Wright in *Earl Fitzwilliam's Collieries Co.* v. *Phillips* (1943), 25 T.C. 430, at p. 441, where the liberty to let down the surface was held to be a " privilege " within the statutory definition ; distinguish *Elliott* v. *Burn* [1934] 1 K.B. 109 ; see also *I.R.C.* v. *New Sharlston Collieries Co., Ltd.* [1937] 1 K.B. 583 and *I.R.C.* v. *Hope* (1937), 21 T.C. 116).

The word " rent " is also defined for the section as including—

" a rent service, rent charge, fee farm rent, feu duty or other rent, toll duty, royalty or annual or periodical payment in the nature of rent, whether payable in money or money's worth or otherwise "

(I.C.T.A. 1970, s. 156 (3) (b)). As was said in the Court of Session " the draftsman has invented for the purposes of the section a unique vocabulary of quite exceptional comprehensiveness " which " spreads so wide a net that escape . . . is impossible " (see *Craigenlow Quarries, Ltd.* v. *I.R.C.* (1951), 32 T.C. 326, at p. 331 ; also *per* Lord Wright in *Earl Fitzwilliam's Collieries Co.* v. *Phillips* (1943), 25 T.C. 430, at p. 442). And if this width of statutory definition were not enough, the courts have reinforced the net by looking directly to the substance of the transaction. Thus in the two cases just cited there was held to be " rent " notwithstanding the documentary description of the payments, in the first case, as the price for the sale of stone, and in the second case, as liquidated damages for loss of surface support (but cp. *I.R.C.* v. *Broomhouse Brick Co., Ltd.* (1952), 34 T.C. 1, as to the purchase of " blaes from bings "—which translates roughly as pit refuse from heaps). Reference should also be made to a decision that the provision free of such coals as may be required constituted a rent payable in money's worth within the present definition (*I.R.C.* v. *Baillie* (1936), 20 T.C. 187).

Management expenses of lessor.—The allowable expenditure of the person, the tenant, actually carrying on the " concern " will be governed by the reasonably liberal rules applying to traders within Case I of Sched. D (see I.C.T.A. 1970, ss. 112, 130). Against this, it is less liberally provided that where " rights to work minerals in the United Kingdom are let " the lessor is entitled, in effect, to deduct " any sums proved to have been wholly, exclusively and necessarily disbursed by him as expenses of management or supervision of those minerals " (I.C.T.A. 1970, s. 158 (1)). In fact, since tax will normally be deducted at source, the lessor's entitlement is to make a repayment claim. It will be observed that the insertion of the word " necessarily " imports the notoriously stricter Sched. E test of allowable expenditure (cp. s. 130 (a) and s. 189 (1) of I.C.T.A. 1970).

Mineral royalties.—The subjection to income tax of profits arising from the exploitation of minerals has always involved an inherent injustice. What is taxed is the proceeds of selling the exhaustible and irreplaceable ; there is a substantial element of capital in the receipts. So far as regards the taxpayer actually carrying on the mining concern, some mitigation has been available since 1963 in the form of capital allowances (see now the Capital Allowances Act, 1968, s. 60). Only in 1970, however, was the injustice recognised with regard to the owner of the land leased for exploitation by another. By virtue of some lengthy and complex provisions, a novel rule of thumb form of relief was introduced (see F.A. 1970, s. 29 and Sched. 6). In essence, one half only of the mineral royalties will be taxed as income (less half only of the management expenses) whilst the other half becomes subject to capital gains tax. The provisions are of extremely wide scope in consequence of the all-inclusive definition conferred on the expressions " mineral royalties," " minerals " and " mineral lease or agreement " (see F.A. 1970, s. 29 (6) and (7)). Otherwise, the precise complexities of the section and Schedule defy any explanatory outline, so that reference to the statute must be made (see also Philip Lawton at [1970] B.T.R. 250).

Wayleaves.—Similar provisions to those applying to " mining, etc., rents and royalties " (see above) govern the taxation of " rent, etc., payable in respect of electric line wayleaves ", which are equally taken out of Sched. A (see I.C.T.A. 1970, s. 67 (1), para. 3 (c)). These last quoted words are the marginal note to a section charging tax under Schedule D generally " where rent [widely defined as above] is payable in respect of any easement [again defined as above] enjoyed in the United Kingdom in connection with any electric, telegraphic or telephonic wire or cable " (I.C.T.A. 1970, s. 157 (1)). Here too the collection of tax is by way of deduction at source, unless the rent does not exceed £2·50 per year. (*ibid.*, s. 157 (1) and (2) ; see also subs. (3) as to direct assessment under Case III of Sched. D wherever tax has not been deducted). There is also a provision whereby the gross payment of rent may be deducted from the trading profits of a " radio relay service " (*ibid.*, s. 157 (4) (5)).

E. WOODLANDS

The occupation of woodlands on a commercial basis is another form of the exploitation of land for profit which is less exhaustive in its effects than mining but which nevertheless attracts special treatment for income tax purposes. Trees can be cut and sold but unlike minerals they can also be replaced, whilst unlike other crops they take so long to mature as to bear strong resemblance to capital assets. Hence the special treatment.

Schedule B.—The primary charge to tax is under Schedule B " in respect of the occupation of woodlands in the United Kingdom managed on a commercial basis and with a view to the realisation of profits " (I.C.T.A. 1970, s. 91, para. 1 ; as to election for Schedule D instead, see below). The amount chargeable as income is, in effect, a fixed one-third of the woodlands' annual value (*ibid.*, s. 92 (1) and (1) (*a*) ; the annual value is essentially determined as for rating purposes, but as if the land, instead of being woodlands, was let in its natural and unimproved state : see *ibid.*, ss. 92 (2) (*b*) and 531). The taxpayer chargeable is " the occupier of the woodlands " but it is added that here " every person having the use of lands shall be deemed to be the occupier thereof " (*ibid.*, s. 92 (1) and (3) ; cp. as to the general exclusion otherwise of representative occupancy, *Coomber* v. *Justices of County of Berk* (1883), 2 T.C. 1 ; also *Commissioner of Valuation for Northern Ireland* v. *Fermanagh Protestant Board of Education* [1969] 1 W.L.R. 1708).

The assessment under Schedule B covers, as a general proposition, all the profits made from the sale of the timber and other produce from the woodlands (see *Christie* v. *Davies* (1945), 26 T.C. 398). This remains true even though the taxpayer, rather than merely selling untouched timber, carries on activities in relation to the timber and woodlands which would otherwise bear all the badges of trade within Case I of Schedule D (see *ibid.*, as to profits of a sawmill). The language of Schedule B contemplates such activities by referring to management on a commercial basis with a view to profit. However, the position becomes more difficult where the taxpayer actually makes things from the timber and then sells them—are the profits still covered by the Schedule B assessment ?

The answer in principle may appear clear : " so long as all that is done can fairly be said to be done in order to make the produce of the soil marketable in some shape or form " then Schedule B covers that activity (see *per* Megarry, J., in *Collins* v. *Fraser* [1969] 1 W.L.R. 823, at p. 830). Nevertheless drawing the line on the facts of a particular case may not be so easy. Thus in the cited case, the activities passed through various stages : the occupier of the woodlands had felled timber, then converted it on the site to felled round timber, then stripped, cut and hauled it to the roadside, then transported it to his mill twelve miles away, then converted it into planking then converted the planking into boxes which he sold. The Crown contended that the Schedule B assessment only covered the activities up to the roadside stage, but Megarry, J., accepted the counter-contention that up to and including the planking no more had been done than market the timber. Accordingly the case was sent back to the Commissioners, in effect, to determine what proportion of the ultimate profits came within Schedule B and what within Case I of Schedule D. Incidentally, Megarry, J., took the view that applying the stated principle governing the Schedule B coverage to the facts was not a pure question of fact on which there could be no appeal.

Schedule A.—The occupier of woodlands may be in receipt of payments for easements, *profits à prendre* or other rights granted or given to other persons to use the land. Such receipts would *prima facie* attract a Schedule A assessment (I.C.T.A. 1970, s. 67 (1), para. 1 (c) ; see also *Lowe* v. *J. W. Ashmore, Ltd.* [1971] Ch. 545). The fact of a Schedule B assessment will not cause a total exclusion of the receipts from Schedule A, but it will cover them up to the amount of the assessable value for Schedule B purposes ; i.e., only the excess receipts remain chargeable under Schedule A (I.C.T.A. 1970, s. 67 (3)).

Schedule D.—As an alternative to the charge under Schedule B, the taxpayer is entitled to elect to be assessed in respect of the woodlands under Schedule D (I.C.T.A. 1970, s. 91, para. 2, and s. 111 (1)). The result of making such an election is that " the profits or gains arising to him from the occupation of the woodlands shall for all purposes be deemed to be profits or gains of a trade chargeable under that Schedule " (*ibid.*, s. 111 (2)). Accordingly, all the ordinary Case I of Schedule D rules as to the preceding year basis of assessment and such like for traders become applicable (see also s. 68 of the Capital Allowances Act, 1968). However, this treatment of the profits does not mean that the activities themselves—that is, the occupation and management of woodlands on a commercial basis—are also to be regarded as trading (see *Coates* v. *Holker Estates Co.* (1961), 40 T.C. 75). For example, the standing timber does not become stock-in-trade (*ibid.*).

The election for Schedule D must be signified to the inspector of taxes by notice in writing within two years after the tax year in question (I.C.T.A. 1970, s. 111 (2)). Thereafter the election remains irrevocably in force through subsequent tax years " so long as the woodlands are occupied by the person making the election " (*ibid.*, s. 111 (4) ; on a change of occupier Schedule B will automatically become applicable again pending a fresh election). Also any such election has to extend to all woodlands on the same estate which are managed on a commercial basis with a view to the realisation of profits (*ibid.*, s. 111 (3), with a proviso as to any woodlands planted within the last ten years). The concept of " the same estate " here would appear to involve some physical unity rather than merely the fact of management by the same person (see *Scottish Heritable Trust, Ltd.* v. *I.R.C.* (1945), 26 T.C. 414).

Election.—The choice open to the occupier of woodlands thus lies between (1) remaining with Schedule B, which produces a relatively low assessment all the time (i.e., completely ignoring the maturity or not of the trees on which actual profit or loss will depend), and (2) electing instead for Schedule D, which produces a relatively high assessment but only on actual profits, if any, and with the availability of the usual reliefs for losses and of certain capital allowances. Accordingly, it is clearly in a taxpayer's best interests to

enjoy a Schedule D assessment during, as it were, the immature years and
then turn to a Schedule B assessment when the trees have matured and the
losses turn to profits.   One hurdle in the way of achieving this ideal is the
provision already noted that an election for Schedule D is irreversible by the
same occupier or taxpayer (I.C.T.A. 1970, s. 111 (4)).   But this hurdle seems
easily surmountable by means of a simple change of occupier : the woodlands
plus standing timber could be sold.   This would be a capital transaction and
receipt for the vendor, not a sale of stock-in-trade assessable under Schedule D
(see *Coates* v. *Holker Estates Co.* (1961), 40 T.C. 75).   The purchaser, the new
occupier, who might happen to be a company, trustee or wife belonging to
the old occupier, will automatically be entitled to market the timber under
the benevolent cover of Schedule B.

See also as to the capital gains tax and the estate duty advantages attaching
to the ownership of timber and woodlands, *ante*, p. 1083, and *post*, p. 1180,
respectively.   Reference may also be made to a note on the " Tax planning
aspects of forestry investment " by K. N. Rankin at *Law Society's Gazette*
(1972), vol. 69, No. 47, p. 1231.

PART 4.   VALUE ADDED TAX

The imposition of value added tax (as from 1st April, 1973 : F.A. 1972,
ss. 1 (1) and 47 (1)), raises the question how far VAT has any application
to the principal conveyancing transactions of sales and leases of land.   This
question is examined below.

Charging words.—The very few relevant words of charge to this new tax
may be extracted as follows :—

"A tax . . . shall be charged . . . on the supply of goods and
services . . . in the course of a business carried on by [the supplier] "

(F.A. 1972, ss. 1 (1) and 2 (2) (*b*)).   These are merely the words thought to
be of direct relevance to the present question of the application of VAT
to conveyancing.   There are, naturally, other elements of the charge.   Thus
the supply must be in the United Kingdom (see *ibid.*; also ss. 8 and 46 (4)),
it must be " taxable " (i.e., not exempt : s. 46 (1)), and the supplier also
must be " taxable " (i.e., liable to be registered : s. 4 and Sched. 1—in effect
having a turnover exceeding £5,000 p.a.).   Also there is a charge to VAT
on the " importation " of goods into the United Kingdom (s. 1 (1)).   But all
of these extra elements appear to be of no especial concern to conveyancers.

The first phrase of the charge—" the supply of goods and services "—has
to be construed as a whole since the statute offers no divisive definitions of
the individual words.   Words less apt to catch the ordinary sale or lease of
land would be hard to find, but it is specifically enacted that—

" The granting, assignment or surrender of a major interest in land
shall be treated as a supply of goods "

(F.A. 1972, s. 5 (6)).   Thus real property lawyers, already familiar with the
established scheme of legal or equitable estates and interests in land, may now
be confronted with the novel concept of a " major interest " in land.   This
newly conceived interest has been loosely defined as meaning " the fee
simple or a tenancy for a term certain exceeding twenty-one years " (*loc. cit.*).
Although consideration, valuable or otherwise, is not made an element, it
is doubted whether a gratuitous grant of such an interest could ever be
" in the course of a business " which would be required for VAT purposes.

Again, the use of the word " granting " would appear to exclude from the provision any mere contract or agreement to grant a fee simple or tenancy (cf. *City Permanent Building Society* v. *Miller* [1952] Ch. 840). Also the failure to use the technical language of the property statutes causes some uncertainties (cp. L.P.A. 1925, ss. 1 (1) and 205 (1) (ix) (x) and (xxvii), as to " land ", " legal estates " and " term of years absolute "—not " term certain " as in F.A. 1972, s. 5 (6)). Thus it can pertinently be asked : " Does a term certain exceeding 21 years include a lease for 22 years with a break clause, a lease of life, or a perpetually renewable lease ? The answers to these questions could be important as the grant of a term certain exceeding 21 years is zero-rated if granted by a person constructing a building " (P. G. Willoughby in *Law Society's Gazette* (1973), vol. 70, No. 34, at p. 2236). These questions, on the authorities available, are still strictly unanswerable. Nevertheless, H.M. Customs and Excise take the unsupported view that " Long leases providing for periodic rent revisions, or giving either party the right to terminate within 21 years would count as ' major interests ' " (VAT Notice No. 708, para. 17 ; Construction Industry ; Revised June, 1973).

It is further specifically enacted that—

" . . . anything which is not a supply of goods but is done for a considera-tion (including, if so done, the granting, assignment or surrender of the whole or part of any right) is a supply of services "

(F.A. 1972, s. 5 (8)). Thus it seems that any disposition for value of any interest in or right over land (other than a " major interest ") is to constitute the supply of services. It appears an abuse of language so to describe, for example, the grant of an easement or even of a lease for a term of twenty-one years or less. Of course, leases of whatever length of term not infrequently do contain incidental covenants which undeniably involve the supply of services, such as repairs and cleaning on a lessor's part. Notice, however, that " the supply of any form of power, heat, refrigeration or ventilation is a supply of goods and not of services " (F.A. 1972, s. 5 (4) ; could this lead to a resurrection of the window tax ?).

Receipt of rents.—It should be appreciated from the quoted statutory words that neither payment nor receipt of rent was made a supply of goods or services within the VAT provisions. Ignoring the effect of exemptions and zero-rating, only the grant of the lease was a chargeable supply (s. 5 (6), (8) of the F.A. 1972) ; VAT is charged on the value of that supply (s. 9 (1) (*a*)) ; the total rent reserved throughout the term (and any premium) was merely taken into account in determining that value (s. 10 (2), (3)). In other words, the grant alone was the supply and its value and the charge were, *prima facie*, calculated once and for all at that time (see s. 7 (2), (3)). The only qualification of this was that regulations may be made (under s. 7 (8)) relating to cases where the consideration for a supply is payable periodically under which regulations a single supply of goods or services may be treated as successive supplies, " but to apply this to the rents of long leases would seem to be stretching the language too far " (see Trevor M. Aldridge at *Solicitors' Journal* (1973), vol. 117, p. 5). But now a relevant regulation has been made (" for the removal of doubt " according to its Explanatory Note), in the following terms :—

" Where, pursuant to the provisions of section 5 (6) of the Act, the granting of a tenancy . . . is treated as a supply of goods and payments in respect thereto are to be made periodically, that supply shall be treated as taking place when each payment is received or a tax invoice relating thereto is issued by the supplier, whichever is the earlier, to the extent covered by the payment or invoice "

(Value Added Tax (General) (Amendment) Regulations, 1973 (S.I. 1973 No. 244), para. 3). In the result, the grant of a lease at a rent for a term certain exceeding twenty-one years (i.e., within s. 5 (6) of the Act) can be broken down into periodical supplies of goods by the landlord from time to time rather than by the original grantor. In contrast, any other lease must still be seen as a once and for all supply of services.

" *in the course of business.*"—*Prima facie*, therefore, all conveyancing transactions appear to be brought within the scope of VAT as the supply of goods or services, but subject to the proviso that they occur " in the course of a business " (i.e., within the other phrase of the extracted words of charge ; see F.A. 1972, s. 2 (2) (*b*)). For present purposes, "business" primarily "includes any trade, profession or vocation " (F.A. 1972, s. 45 (1)). This seems at best a throw-back to the uncertainties already experienced for income tax purposes (see " Traders ", *ante*, p. 1091), but without benefit of the circular explanation referring to an adventure in the nature of trade which was relied on to catch the isolated transaction (I.C.T.A. 1970, s. 536 (5)). At worst everything still turns on the essentially undefined word " business ", since where the word "includes " appears in a definition clause it is in construction to be replaced by the words " in addition to its ordinary meaning means " (see *Rodger* v. *Harrison* [1893] 1 Q.B. 161, 167 ; also *Deeble* v. *Robinson* [1954] 1 Q.B. 77, 81–83). So what is the ordinary meaning of " business " ? This is not easy to pin down. As Lindley, L.J., once said :

" When we look into the dictionaries as to the meaning of the word ' business ', I do not think they throw much light upon it. The word means almost anything which is an occupation and not a pleasure ; anything which is an occupation or duty which requires attention is a business "

(in *Rolls* v. *Miller* (1884), 27 Ch. D. 71, at p. 88 ; concerning a lessees' covenant). There are cases in other contexts supporting the proposition that "business " essentially involves continuous and commercial activity (see *I.R.C.* v. *Marine Steam Turbine Co., Ltd.* [1920] 1 K.B. 193 and *Carr* v. *I.R.C.* [1944] 2 All E.R. 163, C.A., both concerning excess profits tax ; also *Abernethie* v. *A. M. & J. Kleiman, Ltd.* [1970] 1 Q.B. 10, C.A., concerning the Landlord and Tenant Act, 1954, Pt. II). Yet cases can be found emphasising that " neither the making of profit nor any commercial activity is an essential " of the course of business (see *per* Widgery, J., in *Rael-Brook, Ltd.* v. *Minister of Housing and Local Government* [1967] 2 Q.B. 65, at p. 76 ; also *per* Cotton, L.J., in *Rolls* v. *Miller* (1884), 27 Ch. D. 71, at p. 85).

Accordingly, the only thing clear is that the tax has been largely founded on this imprecise notion of " business ". However, the Act does add a few touches of elaboration to the notion (see F.A. 1972, s. 45 generally). One only of these touches may be worth mention here as of remotely possible interest to conveyancers. It is provided that " the admission, for a consideration, of persons to any premises . . . shall be deemed to be the carrying on of a business " (*ibid.*, subs. (1) (*d*)). Although not much imagination is needed to see that theatres, casinos and such like are aimed at, one wonders what may actually be hit. For example, any vendor of land who lets a purchaser into possession before completion on the usual terms (see Law Society's Conditions of Sale, 1973 Revision, No. 14, and National Conditions of

Sale, 18th ed., No. 7) would seem to be indulging in business. Nevertheless trivial admissions of this sort may perhaps be ignored as unlikely to reach the turnover limit necessary for the VAT charge (i.e., £5,000 p.a. ; see F.A. 1972, ss. 2 (2) (*b*) and 4, referring to Sched. 1).

Exemptions.—It can so far be said that all conveyancing transactions in the course of a business are *prima facie* within the scope of VAT. But the charge will only apply where the supply is " taxable " (F.A. 1972, s. 2 (2) (*a*)) which means any supply " other than an exempt supply " (*ibid.*, s. 46 (1)). The exempt supplies are listed and described in Sched. 5 to the Act (*ibid.*, s. 13, which permits variations by Treasury order). This Schedule's list of exemptions begins with—

" GROUP 1—LAND

Item No.

1. The grant, assignment or surrender of any interest in or right over land or of any licence to occupy land, other than—

   (*a*) the provision of accommodation in a hotel, inn, boarding house or similar establishment or in a house, flat or caravan used wholly or mainly for the provision of holiday accommodation ;

   (*b*) the granting of facilities for camping in tents or caravans ;

   (*c*) the granting of facilities for parking a vehicle ; and

   (*d*) the granting of any right to take game or fish ".

Aside from the special or marginal matters in paras. (*a*)–(*d*), all conveyancing transactions, by property dealers and by others, may seem to have been exempted from VAT. However, it is no great privilege to receive exemption ; it is, indeed, usually preferable to be " zero-rated " (see below). The short point is that a person who makes exempt supplies is precluded from recovering by repayment (or, of course, deduction) any of the tax he may himself have borne on the supply to him of goods or services for the purpose of the business (see F.A. 1972, s. 3 (2), which refers to the " input tax " exceeding the " output tax "). Nevertheless it is thought that any irrecoverable " input " VAT suffered by an exempt land or property dealer should generally be treated as deductible expenditure to be set against profits for the purposes of income tax or corporation tax.

Three other observations as to exemptions may be offered. First, if not all of the transactions of a land dealer are exempt, then provision is made for an appropriate proportion only of the " input tax " to be recovered (see F.A. 1972, s. 3 (3) (4)). For example, a person might grant a lease (exempt) containing covenants for the supply of services or goods, such as cleaning (fully taxable) or heating (zero-rated) ; in this sort of case it may be necessary initially to apportion the rent so as to facilitate recovery of any " input tax " (see F.A. 1972, s. 10). However, H.M. Customs and Excise have issued the following relevant guidance :

" In general, rents for accommodation are exempt from VAT under Schedule 5, Group 1, of the Finance Act, 1972. An inclusive rental will normally be regarded as exempt from the tax whether the accommodation is furnished or unfurnished, and exemption will also extend to the costs of the general maintenance and upkeep of a building and its grounds, and the payment of caretakers' and porters' wages, etc., provided that these costs and payments are covered by an inclusive rental and no separate service charge for them is made by the landlord. But where a rental for industrial or commercial premises includes payment for the hire of plant or machinery or other equipment the rental should be apportioned and tax applied as appropriate. In certain circumstances a landlord of residential premises may also apportion an inclusive rental and not regard it as wholly exempt. This would happen for example when the inclusive rental covers not only the right to occupy the premises but also the supply of other goods or services direct to the tenant, such as central heating. In these circumstances the rent may be apportioned in respect of the value of those other supplies, but as heating is zero-rated this will in most cases not cause any tax to be payable, but will only affect the proportion of the landlord's input tax which he may recover.

" If a landlord makes a separate charge or charges for the supply of services, these supplies will be taxable at the standard rate unless they are of a type (e.g., lighting and heating) to which the zero-rate applies. But in the latter case only clearly identifiable supplies to the tenant, e.g., the heating of a flat, would be zero-rated."

(see VAT Bulletin No. 7 with *Law Society's Gazette* (1973), vol. 70, No. 34). In consequence, therefore, it appears desirable to continue the practice of reserving payments in respect of such matters as part of the rent.

Second, this Group 1 exemption relating to Land contains no item covering the services of professional people, such as solicitors, surveyors, or even estate agents, who may be instructed to achieve a conveyancing transaction within the exemption. Thus the client, whether or not a property dealer, will have to bear an irrecoverable " input tax " on these professional services. Incidentally other groups of exemptions in Sched. 5 do have items which would cover connected professional services (e.g., Group 2—Insurance, Item No. 2 ; Group 8—Burial and Cremation, Item No. 2).

The third and last observation is that any financial arrangements, especially a mortgage advance, involved with conveyancing transactions, or otherwise, appear to be covered by the first three items in the following exemption :

" GROUP 5—FINANCE

Item No.

1. The issue, transfer or receipt of, or any dealing with, money, any security for money or any note or order for the payment of money.
2. The making of any advance or the granting of any credit.
3. The making of arrangements for any transaction comprised in item 1 or 2 . . ."

This last item gives rise to the query whether the services of a solicitor on behalf of mortgagor or mortgagee are thereby exempted. Arguably they are not since the mortgage itself must strictly be the grant of an interest in land within the " Group 1—Land " exemption, only the actual advance or loan coming within the present exemption. Against this it can only be urged, rather feebly, that a mortgage should properly be treated as a " security for money " within Item No. 1 of this exemption.

Zero-rating.—As already mentioned, it is generally preferable to be not exempt but zero-rated for VAT purposes so as to enable full recovery of any necessarily excess " input tax " (i.e., under F.A. 1972, s. 3). Zero-rating means, in effect, that the supply of goods or services is taxable but at a nil rate and this privileged status clearly prevails, in cases of conflict, over the somewhat less desirable exempt status (see F.A. 1972, s. 12 (1)). The items enjoying zero-rating are listed in groups in Sched. 4 to the Act (with some explanatory notes which have statutory effect: F.A. 1972, s. 46 (2) ; the list is subject to variation by Treasury order: F.A. 1972, s. 12 (4)). Of obvious and especial interest to conveyancers will be the following :—

" GROUP 8—CONSTRUCTION OF BUILDINGS, ETC.

Item No.

1. The granting, by a person constructing a building, of a major interest in, or in any part of, the building or its site.
2. The supply, in the course of the construction, alteration or demolition of any building or of any civil engineering work, of any services other than the services of an architect, surveyor or any person acting as consultant or in a supervisory capacity.
3. The supply, in connection with a supply of services falling within item 2, of materials or of builder's hardware, sanitary ware or other articles of a kind ordinarily installed by builders as fixtures.

Notes :

(1) Item 2 does not include any work of repair or maintenance or the supply of any services to a person who himself supplies such services as are mentioned therein or who, in the course of a business consisting wholly or mainly in the construction, alteration or demolition of buildings or civil engineering works, carries out the construction, alteration or demolition on land in which he owns a major interest.

(2) 'Major interest' has the same meaning as in section 5 (6) of this Act.

(3) Section 12 (3) of this Act does not apply to goods forming part of a description of supply in this Group."

A number of comments are called for. In the first place the meaning of the novel concept of a " major interest " in land was indicated earlier and it will be recalled that it is to be treated as goods (i.e., by virtue specifically of F.A. 1972, s. 5 (6) ; see *ante*, p. 1143).

It may also be recalled that the grant of a lease for a term certain exceeding twenty-one years (i.e., within s. 5 (6)) must be treated as periodical supplies of goods taking place, in effect, at the time of each payment of rent (see *ante*, p. 1144). Accordingly, if the reversion or a lease which was originally granted within this zero-rating group changes hands, it would appear to follow that the zero-rating then ends. Thereafter, presumably, the new, non-constructing landlord should be regarded as a supplier within the exemption " Group 1— Land " (see *ante*, p. 1146). However, none of this is clear. It seems almost equally arguable that, notwithstanding the provision as to rents becoming periodical supplies of goods, the lease remains granted within the terms of this zero-rating group which will therefore continue to apply throughout the term whoever might be the landlord from time to time If so, an artificial difference will exist between the rents of buildings which were leased from constructors and of those which were leased second-hand and consequently records will have to be kept of the circumstances (see Trevor M. Aldridge in *Solicitors' Journal* (1973), vol. 117, p. 5).

Zero-rating applies only to the " granting " of such an interest and not also, as elsewhere, to its " assignment or surrender," i.e., even though by a builder. However, no competent conveyancer should experience any difficulty in drafting documents which indisputably grant appropriate interests (e.g., sub-leases) where this would be to the financial advantage of the parties.

Another peculiarity to be mentioned now is the present tense of the vital words " by a person constructing " in Item No. 1. Does this signify, surely whimsically, that zero-rating is not available for the sale of an already completed building ? Perhaps builder-vendors should carefully and deliberately (for a change) leave something still to be done after the conveyance just in case a strict construction is adopted (cp. *Hoskins* v. *Woodham* [1938] 1 All E.R. 692 where the implied warranty of fitness for human habitation was held not applicable to the sale of a very recently completed house ; see *ante*, p. 72). However, H.M. Customs and Excise appear to accept a subsequent grant by a person who has constructed a building as being zero-rated (see VAT Notice No. 708, para. 20 ; Construction Industry ; Revised June, 1973). The official view also is that the words " a person constructing " do not mean that a property developer must actually undertake the building work himself : he may commission a builder or builders provided contracts for the building are made before the work has progressed beyond the foundation stage (*loc. cit.*, para. 18 (*b*) ; no authority is offered in support of the proviso).

Further, the official view stretches sufficiently to allow " constructing " to include " a work of substantial reconstruction," the test of substantial being put at over half the cost of an actual construction (*loc. cit.*, para. 19). Also the word " building " is permitted to comprehend only a structure attached to its site by a builder as a " permanent fixture," and this tautology means that it must have a permanent, e.g., concrete, base (*loc. cit.*, para. 6). Thus garden sheds, domestic glass-houses and workmen's huts will be zero-rated when supplied and erected by a builder on such a base but not otherwise.

Item No. 2 in Group 8 presumably excludes not only the professional persons mentioned but also such legal or property consultants as solicitors or estate agents. Otherwise that Item coupled with Note (1) introduces a new distinction : instead of drawing the customary line between repairs and improvements, we have to separate off alterations and demolitions (cf. *Conn* v. *Robins Bros. Ltd.* (1966), 43 T.C. 266, in which repairs and alterations were together distinguished from improvements for income tax purposes). H.M. Customs and Excise have pronounced that a work will only be regarded eligible for zero-rating as an alteration " if it involves structural changes to a building," giving the examples of the conversion of a house into shops or flats, or of a bedroom into a bathroom or of a loft into a habitable room, or the installation of a lift or a central heating system, other than by way of replacement (VAT Notice No. 708, para. 5, supplemented by VAT Notice No. 715 generally). However, like many of the official views, this seems merely a plausible approach and by no means a necessary construction of the statutory words. It is also indicated that " civil engineering work " means any work forming, or intended to form, part of the land, including walls, roadworks, bridges, docks and harbours, railways and sewers, provided it is of a permanent nature (*loc. cit.*, para. 7).

Note (1) beneath Group 8, *ante*, also seems effective for withholding zero-rating from sub-contractors just as Item No. 3 only covers supplies of fixtures (but *semble* not fittings) *by* the builder and not supplies *to* the builder by a builders' merchant. With regard to this last Item, it may not always be easy to say what articles are " of a kind ordinarily installed by builders as fixtures," since there are judicial suggestions that this must depend on the current practice of builders which may change (see *F. Austin (Leyton), Ltd.* v. *Commissioners of Customs and Excise* [1968] Ch. 529, which concerned the application of identical wording in the purchase tax legislation to built-in dressing table units). The Treasury has power by order to disallow the deduction of " input tax " on specified supplies (F.A. 1972, s. 3 (6)) and it was indicated that this power would be used in respect of such luxury (*sic*) fittings as washing-machines, cookers, refrigerators, and fitted carpets (see Standing Committee E, 24th May, 1972, col. 132). But oddly enough the whole question has now been begged by the Input Tax (Exceptions) (No. 1) Order, 1972 (S.I. 1972 No. 1165) which is again only made applicable where " goods other than materials . . . ordinarily installed by builders as fixtures " are incorporated during construction (para. 3). Accordingly this wording read in the light of the case cited can be seen as an encouragement to builders in general to increase the standard and number of things they ordinarily instal as fixtures (cp. VAT Notice No. 708, paras. 11 and 12, for " official " examples). Incidentally, the effect of Note (3) is simply to charge VAT on imported builders' materials or hardware, etc.

Two other zero-rated groups may also be of passing interest to conveyancers. The first of these is—

" GROUP 11—CARAVANS

Item No.

   1. Caravans exceeding the limits of size for the time being permitted for the use of trailers on roads.

   Note : This item does not include removable contents other than goods of a kind mentioned in Item 3 of Group 8 ".

Thus immoveable, permanently sited caravans are, appropriately, put in much the same position in relation to VAT as buildings. The other group of interest really is one item only—

" GROUP 7—FUEL AND POWER

Item No.

   5. Electricity, heat and air-conditioning ".

Thus a lessor who, under covenant or otherwise, supplies such goods as these will be zero-rated (supply of " goods " is correct : F.A. 1972, s. 5 (4)).

Other taxes.—Presumably, a trader, in land or otherwise, whose supplies are zero-rated, so that his " input tax " can be recovered, will simply ignore VAT in computing his profits or losses for the purposes of income tax (or corporation tax). Indeed the Board of Inland Revenue has issued a notice, purporting to set out the applicable general principles, which includes the presently relevant statement : " In computing income for direct tax purposes in these circumstances it would be correct to take into account both income and expenditure exclusive of the related VAT " (see " VAT and Tax Practice " in *Solicitors' Journal* (1973), vol. 117, p. 380 ; cf. *ibid.*, p. 291). But this statement is accompanied neither by authority nor reasoning in support and the position may not be so simple or sensible. Instead it could be that the full cost (including the VAT percentage) of stock in trade or other supplies of goods or services would be properly deductible as " money wholly and exclusively laid out or expended for the purposes of the trade " (see I.C.T.A. 1970, s. 130 (*a*) ; also *Harrods (Buenos Aires), Ltd.* v. *Taylor-Gooby* (1963), 41 T.C. 450). This is actually accepted by the Board of Inland Revenue where a trader is *not* a taxable person for VAT (*loc. cit.*). Thereafter it could be contended that the repayment of VAT (i.e., by the Commissioners of Customs and Excise under F.A. 1972, s. 3 (3)) is not made

a trading receipt by statute or otherwise for income tax purposes. This
contention might contain little of merit, but the blame must be laid on the
lack of any express provisions accompanying the imposition of VAT dealing
with its relationship with other taxes.

Conclusion.—Unless the grantor (vendor or lessor) is a trader disposing of the
property in the course of his business with a turnover exceeding £5,000 p.a.,
the VAT provisions will have no relevance at all. In other words, for the
purposes of everyday conveyancing of houses, the new tax can be ignored
(except, of course, as an element increasing the bills of those more or less
professional gentlemen who arranged, advised and carried out the transaction).

If a trader and his large enough business is involved, then the primary
matter of substance seems to be to distinguish the zero-rated builder from the
generally exempt property dealer with a view to reclaiming any excess " input
tax ".

Supplies of services or goods under covenant by a lessor may be within the
VAT charge, although again the supply would have to be in the course of a
large enough business. Otherwise, VAT seems to have almost as little to
do with conveyancing as did purchase tax.

PART 5. STAMPS

A. STAMP DUTIES GENERALLY

Questions on title.—Under an open contract, the vendor can be called
upon to stamp all deeds *on which his title depends* at his own expense, including
even a discharged mortgage (*Whiting to Loomes* (1881), 17 Ch. D. 10). The
rule extends not only to instruments disposing of the estate sold but also to
those relating to interests to which the estate sold is or has been subject, such
as a lease (*Coleman* v. *Coleman* (1898), 79 L.T. 66) or a mortgage (*Whiting to
Loomes, ante*). But if a good title can be made without recourse to a particular
deed, the purchaser cannot insist on such deed being properly stamped
(*Ex parte Birkbeck Freehold Land Society* (1883), 24 Ch. D. 119). And,
notwithstanding any stipulation to the contrary, a purchaser can require the
vendor to stamp any unstamped or insufficiently stamped deeds executed
after 16th May, 1888 (Stamp Act, 1891, s. 117). A stipulation that a
purchaser of a legal estate in land is to pay or contribute towards the cost of or
incidental to the stamping of a conveyance on trust for sale, or of a vesting
instrument for bringing into force the provisions of the S.L.A. 1925, will be
void (L.P.A. 1925, s. 42 (2)). A purchaser cannot be compelled to accept a
statutory declaration as sufficient evidence to contradict statements appearing
in the documents of title. Thus, he need not accept a statutory declaration
which shows that the consideration stated in a deed was mistaken and,
consequently, that a deed appearing to be insufficiently stamped was in fact
adequately stamped (*Re Spollon and Long's Contract* [1936] Ch. 713).

An undertaking to pay the penalty if at any time it should become necessary
to stamp a deed would be void (Stamp Act, 1891, s. 117).

Principles.—If an instrument is stamped for its leading object, the stamp
covers everything accessory to that object (*Limmer Asphalte Paving Co.* v.
Commissioners (1872), 41 L.J. Ex. 106). For instance, a lease does not
require an extra stamp on account of its containing an option to purchase the
property the subject thereof. So an acknowledgment for production of a

probate or letters of administration, contained in an assent, will not make the
assent liable to stamp duty. On the other hand, the general rule is that an
instrument relating to " several distinct matters " is separately charged, as if
it were a separate instrument, with duty in respect of each of those matters
(Stamp Act, 1891, s. 4). The construction of this section may prove difficult
in practice, but in the absence of a statutory definition " matters " may be
taken to mean transactions, whether or not within one head of charge.
For instance, a transfer of shares by executors to four residuary legatees, to
hold to them respectively, has been held to be liable to four stamps (*Freeman*
v. *Commissioners* (1871), L.R. 6 Ex. 101) ; and similar decisions were reached
where one instrument both conveyed property and contained a further
agreement between the parties (*John Foster & Sons* v. *I.R.C.* [1894] 1 Q.B.
516) and where one instrument passed property of different classes for stamp
duty purposes (*Ansell* v. *I.R.C.* [1929] 1 K.B. 608).

Where a deed is altered with the consent of the parties after execution,
so as to form a new contract between the parties, a new stamp is required
(*London, Brighton and South Coast Railway Co.* v. *Fairclough* (1841),
2 Man. & G. 674).

An agreement to sell property and give the purchaser " a free conveyance,"
according to the view of the Council of The Law Society, includes the stamp
duty.

In many cases there may be doubt whether a deed was adequately stamped
even though it was stamped in accordance with the consideration stated in it.
For instance, a conveyance of a plot of land for a small price may be followed
immediately by a mortgage of the land with a house erected on it or the
consideration in a conveyance may apparently be less than the true value.

Normally, a solicitor must assume that the consideration was adequately
stated as required by the Stamp Act, 1891, s. 5 (*ante*, p. 454). The Council
of The Law Society have expressed the opinion (*Law Society's Digest*, Opinion
No. 268) that a purchaser is not entitled to inquire whether a mortgage
to secure sums not ascertained at the date of the mortgage was adequately
stamped to cover further advances. Where, however, doubt arises on the
face of the title, for instance, where a conveyance stating a low consideration
is followed at once by a mortgage for a larger sum, a purchaser's solicitor may
be obliged to call for evidence of proper stamping or adjudication (*Law
Society's Digest*, Opinion 209 (*a*), Fourth Supplement). *Re Weir and
Pitt's Contract* (1911), 55 Sol. J. 536, is often quoted as authority for stating
that a subsequent purchaser is not concerned with the adequacy of the stamp
on a conveyance. The decision was concerned solely with the application
of the Finance (1909–10) Act, 1910, s. 74 (5), which provides that a transfer
is deemed voluntary if, in the opinion of the Commissioners, the consideration
was inadequate or the transferee received a substantial benefit. It was
decided that the Commissioners could raise the question of adequacy of the
consideration only when the deed was presented for stamping and not at a
later date. Consequently after stamping according to the apparent consideration, a subsequent purchaser could not be prejudiced even if there was an
element of gift. It seems, therefore, that the decision does not provide
authority for the assertion often based on it. Even if a doubt does arise on
the face of the title whether the stamp was adequate, it seems that the
purchaser would be obliged to accept a reasonable explanation consistent
with the known facts. In practice the best solution is to have the stamp
adjudicated. The Stamp Act, 1891, s. 12, enables any person interested to
require the Commissioners to do this, but apparently they insist on production

of the original document so the necessary steps cannot be taken by a purchaser without the vendor's concurrence.

If a consideration is inadequate and thereby the conveyance is a voluntary disposition within the Finance (1909–10) Act, 1910, s. 74, adjudication is essential (*Re Robb's Contract* [1941] Ch. 463). The purchaser's difficulty usually lies in proving that the consideration is inadequate.

It is suggested that, in view of present doubts, purchasers' solicitors should accept a reasonable explanation of any apparent deficiency of stamp duty particularly if the amount is small. Where, however, there is no explanation, or an unsatisfactory one, and the amount involved may be substantial, they should insist on adjudication on the ground that the vendor cannot require the purchaser to accept a doubtful title.

Production to Commissioners.—By the Finance (1909–1910) Act, 1910, s. 4 (3), a conveyance in fee simple or a lease for over fourteen years was deemed not to be duly stamped unless it had on it a stamp showing that Increment Value Particulars had been delivered. This requirement took effect on 30th April, 1910, but was repealed as from 18th July, 1923, by the F.A. 1923, s. 28. The provisions as to increment value (for the purpose of which the particulars were required) were repealed by the F.A. 1920, and sums which had been paid were repayable. Consequently, it is thought that the absence of the Particulars Delivered stamp required by the 1910 Act is not now a defect in title.

On the sale of the fee simple of land, the grant of a lease for seven years or more or the transfer on sale of any such lease, on or after 1st September, 1931, the transferee or lessee must produce to the Commissioners the instrument by which the transfer is effected or the lease granted (F.A. 1931, s. 28). At the same time he must furnish with the instrument a document giving certain prescribed particulars (*ibid.*, Sched. 2 ; cf. *Law Society's Gazette* (1973), vol. 70, No. 3, p. 1315, as to revision of the form to exclude the " betterment levy " questions). Failure to comply with these requirements within thirty days after execution of the instrument, if executed in Great Britain, renders a transferee or lessee liable to a fine of £50. It is understood, however, that the practice of the Commissioners is to add the " Produced " stamp on production of the document at any time, without payment of any penalty.

Although stamp duty has been abolished on conveyances for considerations not exceeding £10,000, it is still necessary that they should obtain the " Produced " stamp. The Council of The Law Society has asked solicitors, unless there is some special reason for sending documents direct to the Direct Post Section (now at West Block, Barrington Road, Worthing, Sussex), to adopt the practice of lodging documents for stamping through a local post office (*Law Society's Gazette*, vol. 56, p. 397).

It is not necessary to produce a deed of exchange where no consideration passes as it is not a " sale ".

An agreement for a lease for seven years or more must be produced, but if that is done it is not necessary to produce an instrument granting the lease in pursuance of that agreement unless that instrument is inconsistent with the agreement (*ibid.*, s. 28 (2)). The section does not apply to an instrument relating solely to incorporeal hereditaments or to a grave or right of burial, or to a mining lease or transfer of a mining lease (*ibid.*, s. 28 (3)).

A purchaser must see that the " Produced " stamp is on any documents within the section, otherwise he may not be able to give them in evidence (*ibid.*, s. 28 (4) ; Stamp Act, 1891, ss. 12 and 14).

A foreclosure order which vests the property in the mortgagee is a transfer on sale within the meaning of the section and must be produced (F.A. 1898, s. 6 ; L.P.A. 1925, ss. 88 and 89). A counterpart lease for seven or more years executed by the grantee alone is not required to be produced ; if the instrument is executed in duplicate by all parties the Commissioners' view is that *both* parts must be produced.

Where any person is authorised by statute to purchase property such person must within three months of completion of the purchase produce to the Commissioners an instrument of conveyance of the property duly stamped (F.A. 1985, s. 12). Such instruments are then stamped as having been produced under this Act. The Commissioners consider production under s. 12 obligatory only if an Act or order (e.g., a compulsory purchase order) authorises the purchase of *specific* property. If there is such an Act or order, it is immaterial whether the acquisition is ultimately carried out by agreement or compulsion. Most local authorities produce *all* conveyances, as the rubber-stamped note indicating production is added on request when a conveyance is sent for stamping. See further, *Solicitors' Journal*, vol. 94, p. 123, and *Law Society's Gazette*, vol. 51, p. 538.

Stamp on lost or destroyed instrument.—The presumption is that an instrument that has been lost or destroyed was duly stamped, unless some evidence is given to the contrary, and the onus of proving it to have been unstamped lies on the party taking the objection ; but, if evidence is given that it *was* unstamped at a particular time, the onus of proof is shifted and the party who relies on the unstamped document must prove it to have been duly stamped (*Marine Investment Co.* v. *Haviside* (1872), 42 L.J. Ch. 173). As a concession, the Revenue allow the stamp duty on lost documents either by repayment, where replicas have been stamped, or by free stamping of the replicas.

Duplicates and counterparts.—It is important to bear in mind the provisions of the Stamp Act as to when denoting is required. A duplicate or counterpart has to be stamped with 25p, and the general rule is that when so stamped the document will not be deemed duly stamped unless it is also denoted. The point to remember is that there is an exception to the general rule in the case of a counterpart of a lease, which does not require denoting as well as stamping, *provided that it is not executed by the lessor*. If it is executed by the lessor it requires denoting (Stamp Act, 1891, s. 72). In theory, a denoting stamp does not guarantee that the original is properly stamped, but in practice it is found that the authorities before affixing the denoting stamp look to see whether the original is properly stamped.

B. STAMPS ON PARTICULAR INSTRUMENTS

Acknowledgment and undertaking.—If under hand only, the document should not be stamped, but if under seal is stamped 50p. Such duty is not payable, however, if the acknowledgment and undertaking are contained in a document carrying out a transaction for the purposes of which the acknowledgment and undertaking are given. See *ante*, p. 658.

Appointment of trustees.—A conveyance or transfer made for effectuating the appointment of a *new* trustee is not to be charged with any higher duty than 50p (Stamp Act, 1891, s. 62). Section 62 was, by s. 9 of the F.A. 1902,

made to apply to any conveyance or transfer for effectuating the retirement
of a trustee, although no new trustee has been appointed. See also Finance
(1909–10) Act, 1910, s. 74 (6).

A deed or order appointing new trustees and containing an express vesting
declaration would appear to require two 50p stamps (Stamp Act, 1891,
ss. 4 and 62 ; *Hadgett* v. *Commissioners* (1877), 37 L.T. 612). In this case
Kelly, C.B., indicated that if there was a document which *of itself* had the
effect of appointing new trustees and also of vesting the property in them
without a vesting order, only one stamp would have been necessary. As this
is exactly what s. 40 (1) (*b*) of the T.A. 1925 does, by providing that, where
the appointment is made after 1925 and does not contain a vesting declaration,
the appointment will operate as if it contained a vesting declaration, it is
thought that the appointment under such circumstances need only be stamped
with one 50p stamp, and the Board of Inland Revenue have expressed this
view (see *Law Society's Digest*, Opinion No. 268).

The appointment of a trustee for the purposes of the S.L.A. is not
chargeable with duty unless such trustee is a *new trustee*, that is, a trustee
in place of another (*Re Potter* [1889] W.N. 69 ; *Re Kennaway* [1889] W.N. 70).

A record upon minutes of the election or appointment of a trustee by
resolution at a meeting is not chargeable with duty.

Other matters expressed in the deed of appointment, such as a release
(unless from a breach of trust) or a declaration that the trusts of an existing
instrument apply, are regarded as accessory and not chargeable.

Appointment of new trustee; transfer of mortgage.—By s. 62 of
the Stamp Act, 1891, a transfer made for effectuating the appointment of
a new trustee is not to be charged with any higher duty than 50p. By s. 112
of the L.P.A. 1925 it is provided that where, on the transfer of a mortgage,
the stamp duty, if payable according to the amount of the debt transferred,
would exceed the sum of 50p, a purchaser is not, by reason only of the transfer
bearing a 50p stamp, whether adjudicated or not, to be deemed to have or
to have had any notice of any trust, *or that the transfer was made for effectuating
the discharge of a trustee or the appointment of a new trustee.* In practice the
Commissioners have required the document to be adjudicated, notwithstanding
the words in the section " whether adjudicated or not." However, the
better view now appears to be that no duty is payable on a transfer of
mortgage on the appointment of a new trustee, the mortgagees being trustees,
because of the abolitions effected by s. 64 (1) (*c*) of the F.A. 1971 (see a note
at *Solicitors' Journal* (1972), vol. 116, p. 381).

Appropriation.—Under the A.E.A. 1925, s. 41, personal representatives
may appropriate any part of the real or personal estate of the deceased in
satisfaction of a legacy or any other interest or share in his property, but if
such appropriation is for the benefit of a person absolutely and beneficially
entitled in possession his consent must be obtained. As an appropriation,
for instance, in satisfaction of a pecuniary legatee, is dependent on the consent
of the legatee, it amounts to a conveyance and in consequence the general rule
is that an appropriation is liable to *ad valorem* duty under the heading
" Conveyance or Transfer on Sale " in Sched. 1 to the Stamp Act, 1891
(*Jopling* v. *Commissioners* [1940] 2 K.B. 282). No such duty is claimed where
appropriation is in satisfaction of a share in *residue*.

Solicitors are advised, when taking instructions for a will, to suggest to
the testator that a clause should be inserted in the will that it shall not be

necessary to obtain the consent of any beneficiary to the making of an appropriation. The result of this is that the Commissioners cannot contend that there is a " bargain," and therefore *ad valorem* duty would not be payable.

An assent made in full or part satisfaction of the claim of a surviving spouse on an intestacy to a statutory legacy (£15,000, or, if no issue survive, £40,000) is regarded by the Commissioners as a conveyance, and is alleged by them to be chargeable with *ad valorem* duty under the Stamp Act, 1891, s. 54. Where, however, the value of the estate of the deceased does not exceed the amount of the statutory legacy, the Commissioners take the view that an assent to the surviving spouse on an intestacy is not liable to *ad valorem* duty, on the ground that the surviving spouse is entitled to elect for an appropriation of the estate unconverted, and if such election is exercised no question of a sale arises. See *Law Society's Gazette*, vol. 28, p. 79. It is understood that the Commissioners take a similar view even where the estate exceeds the amount of the appropriate statutory legacy, if the surviving spouse has become entitled to the whole of the estate. Thus, where the interests of children in the remainder of the estate are assigned to a surviving spouse by a deed of gift stamped *ad valorem* on the total value of those interests, an assent in favour of the surviving spouse of any part of the estate does not attract *ad valorem* duty.

Similarly, where a surviving spouse is sole administrator an assent in his or her own favour by way of appropriation does not attract *ad valorem* duty as there can be no question of sale. Further, it is understood that where a surviving spouse elects to take an appropriation of the matrimonial home pursuant to the Intestates' Estates Act, 1952, Sched. 2, in part or full satisfaction of his or her statutory legacy the Commissioners do not claim *ad valorem* duty ; where there is a right to appropriation there cannot be a " sale." If such a transfer is made partly in satisfaction of the statutory legacy, however, and partly in consideration of payment by a surviving spouse the transaction is regarded as a sale to the extent of the cash payment.

Even though the Commissioners would claim duty a purchaser may not be concerned as he may have to accept that an assent is made in favour of the correct person (A.E.A. 1925, s. 36 (7) ; compare *Re Duce and Boots Cash Chemists (Southern), Ltd.* [1937] Ch. 642).

Assents.—An assent in writing, but not under seal, of an executor to a devise of real estate, made under the Land Transfer Act, 1897, s. 3 (1), was not chargeable with *ad valorem* duty as a conveyance (*Kemp* v. *Commissioners* [1905] 1 K.B. 581). The A.E.A. 1925, s. 36 (11), provides that s. 36 (which makes an assent operate as a conveyance) shall not operate to impose any stamp duty in respect of an assent. The result is that no duty is payable on assents under hand made in favour of specific or residuary devisees or legatees under a will (*G. H. R. Co., Ltd.* v. *Commissioners* [1943] 1 K.B. 303). Any such assent made under seal will be liable to a 50p stamp.

Assents often contain ancillary provisions, such as an acknowledgment for production of probate or letters of administration, or an undertaking to indemnify the personal representatives against a mortgage or against covenants in a lease. The Commissioners of Inland Revenue take the view that neither an acknowledgment of the right to production of the grant or other documents of title, nor an undertaking to indemnify the personal representatives, will make an assent under hand liable to duty or will increase the liability to duty of an assent under seal.

An assent given under the A.E.A. 1925, s. 36 (1), by the executor of a vendor in favour of a purchaser to whom the vendor, before his death, had agreed to sell the property, is chargeable with *ad valorem* duty as a " conveyance on sale " (*G. H. R. Co., Ltd.* v. *Commissioners, ante*). If an executor purported to assent to a purchaser from himself *ad valorem* duty would similarly be payable on the assent (*Jopling* v. *Commissioners* [1940] 2 K.B. 282).

If a devisee had sold his equitable interest the executor might vest the legal estate in the purchaser by means of an assent, in which case such assent would not appear to be liable to *ad valorem* duty if such duty had been paid on the transfer to the purchaser of the equitable interest ; otherwise it is thought that the assent should be stamped *ad valorem*. In any event it would appear that a subsequent purchaser could not inquire as to the manner in which the person to whom assent was made became entitled and so could not raise the question whether the assent was duly stamped (A.E.A. 1925, s. 36 (7) ; compare *Re Duce and Boots Cash Chemists (Southern), Ltd.* [1937] Ch. 642).

If the value of the property in respect of which the assent is made exceeds the value of the share of the beneficiary in whose favour the assent is made and a sum is paid to make up the difference, duty is normally claimed on the excess value. Such duty is not claimed, however, if the devisee paying the difference is himself the sole personal representative, and if the devisee is one of several personal representatives an assent under seal will apparently be stamped 50p as a deed of partition. See *Law Notes*, vol. 70, pp. 51, 52, and vol. 71, p. 27. Compare the notes as to appropriation, *ante*, p. 1155.

It is provided by s. 14 (2) of the S.L.A. 1925 that nothing in that Act shall operate to impose any stamp duty on a vesting or other assent.

Bankrupt's property, exemption from duty.—A conveyance or other assurance relating solely to property which is part of the estate of a bankrupt, and which after the execution of the assurance remains the estate of the bankrupt or of the trustee in bankruptcy, is exempt from stamp duty (Bankruptcy Act, 1914, s. 148).

Bank securities.—The relevant head of charge (i.e., Mortgage, Bond, Debenture, Covenant) was abolished with effect from 1st August, 1971 (F.A. 1971, s. 64).

Contracts.—The duty of 6d. (2½p) under the heading Agreement was abolished as from 1st August, 1970 (F.A. 1970, s. 32, Sched. 7, Pt. I, para. 1).

Contract for sale of a business with a view to turning it into a limited company.—The effect of s. 59 of the Stamp Act, 1891, is that the contract must bear the stamp on that part of the consideration liable to duty which represents the property which will not be subsequently included in a separate conveyance. Unless this is done the registrar will not file it. It is provided by the same section that for the purpose of proceedings to enforce specific performance or to recover damages for the breach thereof, the document will be regarded as being duly stamped, in effect now, if it is either under hand only or bears a deed stamp (50p).

Sometimes the consideration is referred to in the contract as a lump sum without giving any particulars showing how it is arrived at, in which case, to enable the contract to be properly stamped, it will be necessary to prepare a statement apportioning the consideration money to the several classes of property which it covers. But it is much better to state in the contract itself exactly how the purchase-money is made up, putting the price against each item.

Before preparing the contract for the sale of the business to the new company it is important to consider whether by a proper and legal arrangement the terms of the sale can be so arranged as to save as much stamp duty as possible. No stamp duty is payable on property which will pass by delivery such as loose fixtures, loose plant, stock-in-trade, furniture and other goods and chattels, or on cash and money in the bank on current account. But money on deposit in a bank will attract duty (*Troup* v. *Commissioners* (1891), 7 T.L.R. 610). If it is intended that the company is to have the benefit of the money on deposit, the best way is not to include it in the sale, but after the company is registered to take up debentures for the amount, and thus save the difference between a stamp duty of £1 per £100 and no duty at all (F.A. 1971, s. 64). Alternatively, the amount on deposit may be transferred to a current account.

If book debts are included in the sale and purchase, stamp duty will have to be paid on the amount thereof, but, in practice, this is never done. The agreement for sale should contain a clause to the effect that the company shall collect, on behalf of the vendor, all the book debts. If it is important that the company shall have the money received from the debts to enable them to carry on, it can be arranged for them to keep the money, less the amount of the debts owing by the vendor, and give the vendor debentures or allot shares in place thereof.

If the owner of the business is also the owner of the property where the business is carried on, and the company purchases the property, stamp duty will, of course, attach. It may sometimes be well to consider whether it would suit the parties equally well if the vendor leased the property to the company instead of selling it. The lease could contain an option of purchase, fixed for a time when the company could better afford to pay for the property. This arrangement would probably reduce considerably the duty payable immediately. If the property is included in the sale the stamp duty will be impressed on the conveyance to the company. If the property is freehold and is sold or leased, attached fixtures form part of the land and will pass with the conveyance or lease. Where the vendor has only a leasehold interest in the land, and, as against the landlord, has a right to remove tenant's or trade fixtures, and proposes to include such fixtures in the sale to the company, a separate price should be fixed for them and the stamp on the amount should be affixed on the contract, on the ground that such fixtures are not an interest in land, nor " goods, wares or merchandise " within s. 59 of the Stamp Act, 1891 (*Lee* v. *Gaskell* (1876), 1 Q.B.D. 700). See further *post*, p. 1162.

There will be no separate conveyance of goodwill and so the stamp on the purchase price for the goodwill (if any) will be put on the contract (Stamp Act, 1891, s. 54 (1)).

Conveyances on sale generally.—Every instrument, and every decree or order of any court (other than an appointment of a new trustee), whereby any property on any occasion except a sale or mortgage is transferred to or vested in any person, is charged with duty as a conveyance or transfer (Stamp Act, 1891, s. 62). Further, a contract for the sale of an *equitable* estate is chargeable with *ad valorem* duty as if it were an actual conveyance (Stamp Act, 1891, s. 59). A father was tenant for life of settled estates and his son was tenant in tail in remainder. An arrangement was made by which the son was to disentail and the father to purchase from him the absolute reversion. The only document relating to the sale was an acknowledgment by the son of the receipt from the father of the purchase price agreed. It was held that the acknowledgment was chargeable as a conveyance on sale within s. 59 (*Fleetwood-Hesketh* v. *Commissioners* [1936] 1 K.B. 351).

An unexpected liability to duty may arise on the execution of a release to trustees of a settlement where the settlement has been brought to an end as a result of the purchase by the life-tenant of the reversion. If he gives a release to the trustees reciting the purchase there is a strong argument that the release should be stamped *ad valorem* as a conveyance. See the discussion in the *Law Times*, vol. 215, p. 260.

The rates of duty and, particularly, the exemptions for transactions for relatively small considerations have changed so much in recent years that the only convenient method of indicating the earlier rates and exemptions is by means of a table, such as that on pp. 1160–1161.

However, the position at present is that *ad valorem* duty is charged on a conveyance on sale at the ordinary rate of 50p per £50 or part of £50 of the consideration (F.A. 1963, s. 55 (1), Sched. 11, Pt. I ; F.A. 1967, s. 27 (1) ; F.A. 1970, Sched. 7, para. 10 ; F.A. 1972, s. 125) ; for the steps applying if the consideration is less than £300 see the table in the Appendix (*post*, p. 1220). This ordinary rate is subject to the following special rates : where the consideration is £10,000 or under, the duty is nil ; where the consideration is £15,000 or under, the rate is 25p per £50 or part of £50. These special rates are not available unless the instrument has an appropriate " certificate of value " as follows : " It is hereby certified that the transaction hereby effected does not form part of a larger transaction or of a series of transactions in respect of which the amount or value or the aggregate amount or value of the consideration exceeds [£10,000] [£15,000] " (see F.A. 1972, s. 125 (1) ; F.A. 1963, s. 55 (1) (*a*), (*b*) ; and F.A. 1958, s. 34 (4)). It appears that the Controller of Stamps will accept only the slightest variations from the above statutory form (see *Conveyancer N.S.*, vol. 26, p. 250 ; *Law Society's Gazette*, vol. 61, pp. 351 and 418 ; also *Solicitors' Journal*, vol. 108, pp. 1009–1010).

Whether a transaction forms part of a larger transaction or of a series of transactions is often difficult to decide. In *A.-G.* v. *Cohen* [1937] 1 K.B. 478, the Court of Appeal decided that where four lots were bought by auction, separate contracts being signed, separate deposits paid and separate conveyances taken, each of the four sales did not form part of a larger transaction or of a series of transactions. Where several lots are purchased by auction, whether the transactions constitute a series depends on circumstances. If separate independent bids were made and separate conveyances are taken a certificate may properly be inserted even if, after the bidding, one memorandum only of the contracts was prepared. On the other hand, if the lots were not bought separately, for instance if the bids were dependent on obtaining a good title to all lots, preparation of separate memoranda would not justify an argument that there was not a series of transactions. Where several conveyances are negotiated by private treaty about the same time, even if there are separate memoranda, there is a strong presumption that the conveyances form part of a series. See further, *Law Society's Gazette*, vol. 51, p. 369.

By the F.A. 1949, s. 36, as amended by the F.A. 1952, s. 73 (4), any sale or agreement for the sale of goods, wares or merchandise was disregarded for the purpose of determining whether an aggregate consideration exceeded

CONVEYANCE ON SALE DUTY

Instruments executed on or after 1st January, 1892, but before 1st August, 1972

The table below shows the rates of duty applicable between 1st January, 1892, and 31st July, 1972, according to the date of execution and whether any and if so what certificate of value* is included in the instrument. Duty is calculated at intervals of £50, except where the consideration is under £300 (see note † below).

Consideration £	DATE OF EXECUTION							
	1st January, 1892, to 28th April, 1910	29th April, 1910,* to 31st July, 1947	1st August, 1947, to 9th July, 1952	10th July, 1952, to 31st July, 1956	1st August, 1956, to 31st July, 1958	1st August, 1958, to 31st July, 1963	1st August, 1963, to 31st July, 1967	1st August, 1967, to 31st July, 1972
500 or under	£½%	£500 : £½% — No certificate : £1%	£500 : £½% — £1,500 : £1% — No certificate : £2%‡	£500 : £½% — £3,000 : £1% — £3,450 : £1½%‡ — No certificate : £2%‡	£3,500 : £½% — £4,250 : £1% — £5,000 : £1½%‡ — No certificate : £2%‡	£3,500 : Nil — £4,500 : £½% — £5,250 : £1% — £6,000 : £1½%‡ — No certificate : £2%‡	£4,500 : Nil — £6,000 : £½% — No certificate: £1%	£5,500 : Nil — £7,000 : £½% — No certificate : £1%
501–1,500	£½%	£1%	£1,500 : £1% — No certificate : £2%‡	£3,000 : £1% — £3,450 : £1½%‡ — No certificate : £2%‡	(as above)	(as above)	(as above)	(as above)
1,501–1,950	£½%	£1%	"Single transaction" certificate (F.A., 1947, s. 54 (3)): see note ¶ — No certificate : £2%‡	(as above)	(as above)	(as above)	(as above)	(as above)
1,951–3,000	£½%	£1%	£2%‡	(as above)	(as above)	(as above)	(as above)	(as above)
3,001–3,450	£½%	£1%	£2%‡	£3,450 : £1½%‡ — No certificate : £2%‡	(as above)	(as above)	(as above)	(as above)
3,451–3,500	£1%	£1%	£2%‡	£2%‡	(as above)	(as above)	(as above)	(as above)

3,501–4,250	£½%	£1%	£2%‡	£2%‡	C£4,250 : £1% — C£5,000 : £1½%‡ — No certificate : £2%‡	C£4,500 : £½% — C£5,250 : £1% — C£6,000 : £1½%‡ — No certificate : £2%‡	(as above)	(as above)
4,251–4,500	£½%	£1%	£2%‡	£2%‡	C£5,000 : £1½%‡ — No certificate : £2%‡	(as above)	(as above)	(as above)
4,501–5,000	£½%	£1%	£2%‡	£2%‡	(as above)	C£5,250 : £1% — C£6,000 : £1½%‡ — No certificate : £2%‡	C£6,000 : £½% — No certificate : £1%	(as above)
5,001–5,250	£½%	£1%	£2%‡	£2%‡	£2%‡	(as above)	(as above)	(as above)
5,251–5,500	£½%	£1%	£2%‡	£2%‡	£2%‡	C£6,000 : £1½%‡ — No certificate : £2%‡	(as above)	(as above)
5,501–6,000	£½%	£1%	£2%‡	£2%‡	£2%‡	(as above)	(as above)	C£7,000 : £½% — No certificate : £1%
6,001–7,000	£½%	£1%	£2%‡	£2%‡	£2%‡	£2%‡	£1%	(as above)
Over 7,000	£½%	£1%	£2%‡	£2%‡	£2%‡	£2%‡	£1%	£1%

*Certificates of value are denoted by the prefix C followed by the amount mentioned in the certificate in question (viz., £500 : F. (1909–10) A., 1910, s. 73 ; (leases) Revenue Act, 1911, s. 15 ; £1,500 : F.A., 1947, s. 54 (3) ; £3,000 : F.A., 1952, s. 73 ; £3,450 : F.A., 1952, s. 73 ; £3,500 : F.A., 1956, s. 37, and F.A., 1958, s. 34 ; £4,250 : F.A., 1956, s. 37 ; £4,500 : F.A., 1958, s. 34, and F.A., 1963, s. 55 ; £5,000 : F.A., 1956, s. 37 ; £5,250 : F.A., 1958, s. 34 ; £5,500 : F.A. 1967, s. 27 ; £6,000 : F.A., 1958, s. 34, and F.A., 1963, s. 55 ; £7,000 : F.A., 1967, s. 27. Note that the £500 certificate of value in relation to leases introduced by the Revenue Act, 1911, operated from 31st March, 1911.

†For amounts up to £300, duty is calculated at intervals of less than £50, viz. :—

(*a*) for instruments executed before 1st August, 1970, at £5 intervals up to £25, then at £25 intervals to £300 ; and if the consideration is less than £5 and the instrument is executed on or after 1st August, 1959, duty payable is limited to 6d. for every 25s. or part of 25s. of the consideration ;

(*b*) for instruments executed on or after 1st August, 1970, at £10 intervals up to £100, then at £20 intervals to £300 ; and if the consideration does not exceed £5, duty is 1s.

‡Not applicable to conveyances to charities, etc.—see F.A., 1947, s. 54, and F.A., 1958, s. 34 (6).

¶Sliding scale applicable as follows :—

Consideration	£1,550	£1,600	£1,650	£1,700	£1,750	£1,800	£1,850	£1,900	£1,950
Duty (see note ‡ above)	£17 10s.	£20	£22 10s.	£25	£27 10s.	£30	£32 10s.	£35	£37 10s.

£500, £3,000 or £3,450 (or £1,500 in the case of instruments made before 10th July, 1952), in regard to a conveyance which is not an actual conveyance or transfer of the goods, wares or merchandise.

The corresponding rule applicable between 1st August, 1956, and 31st July, 1958, and also to transactions on or after 1st August, 1958, is that, for the purposes of determining the relevant consideration, any sale or agreement for the sale of goods, wares or merchandise is disregarded unless the instrument is an actual conveyance or transfer of the goods, wares or merchandise (with or without other property) (1956 Act, s. 37 (4) ; 1958 Act, s. 34 (4)).

This rule will operate, for instance, where goods pass by delivery. Chattel property only (in an actual state of severance at the date of sale) can be excluded ; any sum paid for fixtures forms part of the consideration for the purposes of the certificate.

Cases often arise in which there is a sale of freehold property with the goodwill of a business and fittings. Where the freehold was sold for £1,200 and, by a separate contract, the vendor agreed to sell goodwill for £900 and fittings for £500, the Council of The Law Society expressed the opinion that the two transactions formed a series and that the certificate of value then relevant could not properly be inserted in the conveyance of the freehold although it was not proposed to take an assignment of the goodwill (*Law Society's Digest*, Opinion No. 215).

If a certificate has been omitted from a conveyance the Commissioners allow it to be written on the document and signed by the parties to the conveyance.

A conveyance from one joint tenant or tenant in common to a co-tenant should be stamped *ad valorem* on the consideration ; it is not necessary to pay additional duty of 50p in respect of any conveyance of the legal estate (*Law Society's Gazette*, vol. 37, p. 157).

Conveyance including standing timber or fixtures.—Fixtures and standing timber pass by the conveyance without mention, but the amount of their valuation should be included in the statement of the consideration. Loose plant or machinery, also any articles which, although fixed, do not pass with the land, may be handed over and receipts given for them and their price, and they need not be mentioned in the conveyance or *ad valorem* stamp duty paid thereon. But where such chattels have not been delivered before the execution of the conveyance and such conveyance contains a recital that they have been sold, the recital may operate as an assurance of them so as to attract duty (*Garnett* v. *Commissioners* (1899), 81 L.T. 633). If the chattels have once *passed* by delivery, neither a recital nor a receipt can possibly operate as an assurance (*Ramsay* v. *Margrett* [1894] 2 Q.B. 18, at p. 24).

Conveyance of land on which building to be erected.—The stamp duty on a conveyance on sale is calculated by reference to the amount or value of the consideration. Where a purchaser of land enters into a contract for the erection of buildings on land purchased it is often difficult to decide whether sums payable under the building contract form part of the consideration for the sale on which stamp duty must be paid. In the Scottish case of *M'Innes* v. *Commissioners* [1934] S.C. 425, a purchaser entered into an agreement with a building company to build a house, and, at the same time, contracted to acquire the site of the house from a person who held a controlling interest in the building company. After the house had been erected a feu-contract was entered into with reference to the land. The Inner House decided that stamp duty was payable on the feu-contract on both the feu-duty capitalised and the price of the house.

This case was distinguished by Finlay, J., in *Kimbers & Co.* v. *Commissioners* [1936] 1 K.B. 132, in which a contract for sale of a site for £500 was made, to be completed in three weeks, and, at the same time, a contract was made between the same parties *conditional on the completion of the contract of sale*, whereby the vendor contracted to build a house for £1,350. The building work was in progress when the conveyance of the land was executed. Finlay, J., held that the conveyance might properly contain a certificate that the transaction did not form part of a larger transaction or of a series of transactions in respect of which the total consideration exceeded £500, and was properly stamped on a consideration of £500. Finlay, J., stated that *M'Innes* v. *Commissioners* was to be distinguished on the ground that in that case the house was on the site when the feu-contract was executed and in consequence the transaction was substantially a sale of both house and site. He also held that the F.A. 1900, s. 10 (see next paragraph), supported the case that duty should be charged on £500 only.

A purchaser who proposes to carry out a transaction in a manner which will enable him to save stamp duty by relying on this case should bear in mind the warning of the learned judge, at p. 140, that such cases to a certain extent depend on their facts and the facts in any other case are not likely to be exactly the same, and consider his statement that " the substance of the matter has to be looked at, and in order to determine whether the reality of it is a contract for the sale of a house, it has to be ascertained whether the transaction is really all one."

The Board of Inland Revenue have issued a statement of their views as to the stamp duty chargeable on conveyances or leases of building plots in cases where at the date of the contract no house has been erected or a house has been partly erected on the site and at the date of the conveyance or lease a house has been wholly or partly erected. This statement is printed in the *Law Society's Gazette*, vol. 54, pp. 450, 451, but the Council of The Law Society state that they " wish it to be understood that they express no opinion on the legal validity of the statement," and recommend that in the type of cases covered by the statement the duty should be adjudicated. The Board's statement itself concludes by commenting that their observations " have not, of course, the force of law. The Board are not bound by them, and the circumstances of any particular case may call for special consideration." The statement contains the following rules :—

" (i) Subject to what is said under para. (iv) below, if under the contract for the sale or lease the purchaser or lessee is entitled to a conveyance or lease of the land in consideration only of the purchase price or rent of the site, the *ad valorem* duty on the conveyance or lease will be determined only by the amount of the purchase price or rent, although it may have been agreed that a house is to be built on the site at the expense of the purchaser or lessee. In such a case, the concurrent existence of a contract with the vendor or lessor or any other person for the building of a house on the site will not increase the stamp duty chargeable on the conveyance or lease. [This seems to be decided by *Kimbers & Co.* v. *Inland Revenue Commissioners*, above.]

(ii) If under the contract the purchaser or lessee is not entitled to a conveyance or lease until a house has been built on the site at his expense and if the house is to be built by the vendor or lessor or by his agent or nominee, the payment of the building price by the purchaser or lessee will be part of the consideration for the conveyance or lease and the building price will be liable to *ad valorem* duty accordingly. (If the house is to be built by a person who is not the vendor or lessor or his agent or nominee the payment of the building price will not form part of the consideration for the sale or lease except in so far as para. (iv) below applies.) [It is doubtful whether the first of these two rules is stated in words consistent with the authorities. Scottish decisions suggest that the two contracts are regarded as one bargain and duty is leviable on the total consideration only if, in addition to the builder being the vendor or his agent, ' the contracts are so interlocked that if default is made on either, the other is not enforceable by either side ' (Lord Normand in *Paul* v. *Inland Revenue Commissioners* [1936] S.C. 443).]

(iii) When the position is as in para. (ii) above, and a purchaser or lessee not entitled to a conveyance or lease until a house has been erected at his expense in fact obtains a conveyance or lease when the house has been only partly erected, *ad valorem* duty is payable on the conveyance or lease on the proportionate amount of the building price attributable to the partial erection of the house computed as at the date of the conveyance or lease. [This rule does not appear to be in accordance with the decision in *Paul* v. *Inland Revenue Commissioners, ante*. It has been criticised on the ground that there is no authority for apportioning duty according to work done at the date of the conveyance ; see *Law Times*, vol. 222, p. 246, and vol. 224, pp. 115, 116.]

(iv) (*a*) If at the date of the contract, a house has been wholly or partly erected by the vendor or lessor or by his agent or nominee or by a builder not employed by the purchaser or lessee, it normally forms part of the subject-matter of the sale or lease and the consideration or apportioned consideration for that building (as existing at the date of the contract) is accordingly liable to *ad valorem* duty.

(*b*) If, at the date of the contract, a house has been wholly or partly erected by the purchaser or lessee or by any person on his behalf the consideration or apportioned consideration for the house wholly or partly erected will not normally form part of the consideration for the sale or lease and accordingly will not be liable to *ad valorem* duty.

(*c*) This paragraph is subject to what is said in paras. (ii) and (iii) above. [These rules should be applied with caution. It is not easy to suggest what cases would not be regarded as ' normal '.]

(v) The contract referred to above may be contained in more than one instrument or it may be partly written and partly verbal. It includes any contractual arrangement between the parties."

Conveyance in part consideration of improvements.—Section 10 of the F.A. 1900, is not so well known as it should be. It provides that " A conveyance on sale made for any consideration in respect whereof it is chargeable with *ad valorem* duty, and in further consideration of a covenant by the purchaser to make, or of his having previously made, any substantial improvement of or addition to the property conveyed to him, or of any covenant relating to the subject-matter of the conveyance, *is not chargeable*, and shall be deemed not to have been chargeable, with any duty in respect of such further consideration."

Conveyance in consideration of covenant to pay apportioned rent.—Where land is sold subject to a rent-charge or ground rent, and the purchaser resells a portion of such land in consideration of a sum of money and a covenant by the assignee to pay an apportioned rent, *ad valorem* duty is not chargeable on such rent-charge or ground rent as well as on the consideration money (*Swayne* v. *Commissioners* [1900] 1 Q.B. 172).

Conveyance on compulsory purchase.—Where land is acquired under compulsory powers and the payment made by the purchasing authority includes compensation for damage by severance or other injury to other lands of the vendor, stamp duty has been claimed since 22nd April, 1953, on the total price, including the compensation. Formerly *ad valorem* duty was not charged on any part of the payment expressed in the conveyance to represent such compensation. To obviate any question as to sufficiency of the stamp on documents stamped according to the former rule they will, on request, be marked " adjudged duly stamped."

Compensation for disturbance is an element in the purchase price to be stated in the conveyance (*Horn* v. *Sunderland Corporation* [1941] 2 K.B. 26) and so it appears that stamp duty is payable on it.

Special company exemptions.—Attention must be drawn to two special exemptions from conveyance on sale duty, although these are generally more a matter of company law and practice than of conveyancing.

First, where for the purposes of amalgamation or reconstruction a company is either formed or has its capital increased expressly to acquire the undertaking (or part thereof) or at least 90 per cent. of the issued share capital of another company, then any conveyance of the undertaking or transfer of the shares acquired is exempt, if adjudicated, from conveyance on sale duty (F.A. 1927, s. 55, as amended by F.A. 1928, s. 31). The statutory conditions to be satisfied are lengthy and complex, and further reference should be made to the sections. See also *E. Gomme, Ltd.* v. *Inland Revenue Commissioners* [1964] 1 W.L.R. 1348, and *Central and District Properties, Ltd.* v. *Inland Revenue Commissioners* [1966] 1 W.L.R. 1015.

Second, *ad valorem* stamp duty is not chargeable on a conveyance the effect of which is to convey a beneficial interest from one body corporate to another if (i) one corporation is beneficial owner of not less than 90 per cent. of the issued share capital of the other ; and (ii) the Commissioners are satisfied that there was no arrangement whereby the consideration was provided by someone other than an associated corporation (F.A. 1930, s. 42, as amended by F.A. 1967, s. 27 (2) (3)). Further reference should be made to the detailed discussion by Robert R. Pennington in *Solicitors' Journal* (1973), vol. 117, at pp. 235 and 255.

Equitable mortgages.—The duty previously dealt with under this subheading has been abolished as from 1st August, 1971 (F.A. 1971, s. 64).

Equity of redemption, conveyance of.—In a conveyance of an equity of redemption, the amount owing on the mortgage for principal *and interest*

to the date of contract must be included in the consideration, unless interest
to date be paid by the vendor. In a conveyance of property subject to a
mortgage to a building society, the amount for which the mortgage could
be redeemed by immediate payment is the amount which should be included
in the consideration.

Foreclosure orders.—In the case of a legal mortgage of freehold or
leasehold land a foreclosure order vests the fee simple, or the residue of the
lease as the case may be, in the mortgagee (L.P.A. 1925, ss. 88 (2) and 89 (2)).
Consequently an order for foreclosure of a legal mortgage must be stamped
as a conveyance on sale (Stamp Act, 1891, ss. 54 and 57 ; F.A. 1898, s. 6 ;
Re Lovell and Collard's Contract [1907] 1 Ch. 249). The amount of the duty
is based on the sum payable on redemption as certified by the master, less
costs (Stamp Act, 1891, s. 57) provided that sum does not exceed the value
of the property to which the order relates (F.A. 1898, s. 6).

In the case of an equitable mortgage the foreclosure order does not itself
operate to transfer the legal estate and, consequently, *ad valorem* stamp duty
is not payable on the order but is payable on a subsequent conveyance of
the legal estate to the mortgagee.

Exchange or partition.—Fixed duty of 50p is charged on instruments
effecting either an exchange or partition of real property only (Stamp Act,
1891, s. 1, Sched. 1), except that where there is equality consideration
exceeding £100 *ad valorem* conveyance on sale duty is charged on the equality
consideration (*ibid.*, s. 73). In this latter case, the ordinary and special rates
of conveyance on sale duty and the certificate of value apply and have
reference to the equality consideration disregarding the value of the properties
exchanged or partitioned. If there is inequality in the value of the properties
exchanged or partitioned not balanced by equality consideration, the
instrument may be treated as a voluntary disposition (see *post*, p. 1168).
If the exchange or partition involves personal property (e.g., leaseholds),
the instrument attracts fixed duty of 50p, not as an exchange or partition
but as a " conveyance of any other kind " (Stamp Act, 1891, s. 1, Sched. 1 ;
Littlewoods Mail Order Stores, Ltd. v. *Inland Revenue Commissioners* [1963]
A.C. 135). If, in this case, there is equality consideration, the instrument
to that extent attracts *ad valorem* duty as a conveyance on sale (*ibid.*). An
exchange of property for shares, stocks or marketable securities (or, of course,
money), is a sale for stamp duty purposes (Stamp Act, 1891, s. 55 (1)), and
where shares, etc., are exchanged for shares, etc., conveyance on sale duty
is claimed twice (*J. & P. Coates, Ltd.* v. *Inland Revenue Commissioners*
[1897] 2 Q.B. 423 ; *Littlewoods Mail Order Stores, Ltd.* v. *Inland Revenue
Commissioners, ante*). An instrument implementing two contracts for sale
is not treated as a deed of exchange but as two conveyances on sale (see
Portman v. *Inland Revenue Commissioners* (1956), 35 A.T.C. 349).

Leases.—Sometimes a builder builds a house without taking a lease,
and when he has sold the house gets the owner of the land to grant the lease
direct to the purchaser. Such a lease should be stamped as a conveyance
on the purchase-money, and in addition as a lease on the rent (*A.-G.* v. *Brown*
(1849), 3 Ex. 662 ; see Stamp Act, 1891, Sched. 1, under the head " Lease
or Tack " where the words used are " consideration moving either to the
lessor *or to any other person* "). Where a contract is made between lessor
and lessee whereby the lessor is to erect a building on the land the sum

payable under the contract may form part of the consideration for which the lease is granted. Whether this was the case must be decided in accordance with the rules applicable to conveyances of plots of land in similar circumstances, as to which see *ante*, p. 1162.

A lease containing an option to purchase the property comprised in the lease does not require an extra stamp (*Worthington* v. *Warrington* (1848), 17 L.J.C.P. 117).

Leases are now charged with fixed duties in one minor case and otherwise with *ad valorem* duties (Stamp Act, 1891, s. 1, Sched. 1, as amended by Finance Act, 1963, s. 56, and F.A. 1972, s. 125 (3)).

Fixed duties. First, on a lease for a definite term less than one year of a furnished dwelling at a total rent for the term exceeding £250, the charge is a fixed duty of 50p. Secondly, on a lease of any other kind than either the above or those attracting *ad valorem* duty below, there is a fixed duty of £1.

Ad valorem duties. When a lease is for a definite period other than as above or is a periodic tenancy, then *ad valorem* duties are charged as follows :—

(1) On any premium : conveyance on sale duty at the ordinary rate (see *ante*, p. 1159) ; the special rates are applicable only if the rent does not exceed £150 per annum (F.A. 1963, s. 55 (2), as amended by F.A. 1972, s. 125 (2)) and then the certificate of value has reference to the amount or value of the consideration other than rent ;

(2) On any rent : the following rates are now calculated on the average rent per annum—

  (*a*) term not exceeding seven years or periodic : rent not exceeding £250 per annum—duty nil ; otherwise—rate £½ per cent. ;

  (*b*) term exceeding seven years but not exceeding thirty-five years : rate £1 per cent. ;

  (*c*) term exceeding thirty-five years but not exceeding one hundred years : rate £6 per cent. ;

  (*d*) term exceeding one hundred years : rate £12 per cent.

(F.A. 1963, s. 56 (1), Sched. 11, Pt. II ; F.A. 1972, s. 125 (3)).

See further, Tables I and II in the Appendix, *post*, pp. 1220, 1223.

Lessor's consent.—The consent of a lessor does not require a stamp (*Hill* v. *Ransom* (1843), 5 Man. & G. 789) unless under seal, when a 50p stamp is necessary.

Mortgages—transfers, reconveyances and receipts.—The duties charged under the general head Mortgages have been abolished as from 1st August, 1971 (F.A. 1971, s. 64).

Instruments freed from duty by this abolition are expressly *not* to be charged either as a " Conveyance of any other kind " or as a " Deed of any other kind " (*ibid.*).

Sub-conveyance.—Where a person having contracted for the purchase of property, but not having obtained a conveyance, contracts to sell " *the same* " to any other person, and the property is conveyed immediately to the sub-purchaser, the conveyance is charged with *ad valorem* duty in respect of the consideration moving from the sub-purchaser (Stamp Act, 1891,

s. 58 (4)). Apart from this relief, duty would be payable on the original consideration as well as on the sub-sale consideration (*Escoigne Properties, Ltd.* v. *Commissioners* [1958] A.C. 549). The relief does not apply if the property sub-sold is not " the same " as that which the original purchaser contracted to buy ; for example, there must be no change in the character of the property (*Fitch Lovell, Ltd.* v. *Commissioners* [1962] 1 W.L.R. 1325 ; shares reduced to a negligible value by the creation of " master shares "). And where a person, having contracted for the purchase of a property, but not having obtained a conveyance, contracts to sell the whole or any part to any other person or persons, and the property is in consequence conveyed by the original vendor to different persons in parts, the conveyance of each part is charged with *ad valorem* duty in respect only of the consideration moving from the sub-purchaser, without regard to the amount of the original consideration (*ibid.*, s. 58 (5)). In *Maples* v. *Commissioners* [1914] 3 K.B. 303, a purchaser resold part of the property purchased without having obtained a conveyance, and then obtained a conveyance of the remainder. The case lays down the principle that the conveyance of the remainder, in such circumstances, is liable to duty on such part of the original purchase price as is apportionable to the property remaining having regard to its value compared with that of the property resold.

The Council of The Law Society have expressed the opinion that " in the case of a sub-sale of part of the property, the amount paid by the sub-purchaser is the relevant factor so far as the inclusion of a certificate of value in his conveyance is concerned, but as regards the conveyance of the other part of the property to the purchaser the contract to purchase the whole property must be looked at as one transaction " (*Law Society's Digest*, p. 62, and Opinion No. 211, p. 63).

Trust, stamp on conveyance to beneficiary under.—A transfer for a nominal consideration to a beneficiary under a trust of the proportion of the trust funds to which he is entitled upon distribution is exempt from duty, other than the fixed duty of 50p (Finance (1909–10) Act, 1910, s. 74 (6)).

Voluntary conveyances.—A voluntary conveyance or transfer is liable to the same duty as a conveyance on sale, on the amount of the value of the property, which value has to be adjudicated by the Commissioners of Inland Revenue (Finance (1909–10) Act, 1910, s. 74 (1), (2)). Section 74 (1) provides that " Any conveyance or transfer operating as a voluntary disposition *inter vivos* shall be chargeable with the like stamp duty as if it were a conveyance or transfer on sale, with the substitution in each case of the value of the property conveyed or transferred for the amount or value of the consideration for the sale."

Adjudication is not necessary, however, in the case of conveyances or transfers exempt from *ad valorem* duty under the Finance (1909–10) Act, 1910, s. 74 (6), as to which see *post*, pp. 1169–1170, because they are made for securing repayments of advances and loans or connected with trusts or not passing any beneficial interest (F.A. 1942, s. 44). The words " conveyance or transfer " have a wide meaning ; see Stamp Act, 1891, s. 62, *ante*, p. 1158. Further, a conveyance is deemed to operate as a voluntary disposition *inter vivos* both where it is not in favour of a purchaser or incumbrancer in good faith for valuable consideration, and where in the opinion of the Commissioners it confers a substantial benefit on the grantee by reason of the consideration being inadequate or otherwise (Finance (1909–10) Act, 1910,

s. 74 (5) ; see *Re Weir & Pitt's Contract* (1911), 55 Sol. J. 536, *ante*, p. 1152).
A substantial benefit means one over and above what is paid for (*Wigan Coal & Iron Co., Ltd.* v. *Commissioners* [1945] 1 All E.R. 392, 395).   In this latter case, where the consideration is inadequate, duty is still calculated on the value of the property conveyed, not merely on that of the benefit conferred (*Baker* v. *Commissioners* [1924] A.C. 270).

The effect of a power of revocation on the stamp duty payable on a settlement is not easy to determine.   If the property is already settled on trusts which are subject to an existing power of revocation, the value of the property transferred is seriously diminished by the existence of that power so that the value may be nominal only (*Stanyforth* v. *Commissioners* [1930] A.C. 339).   Whether, on the creation of a settlement on trusts which include a power of revocation by the settlor or the trustees (which power can later be released), the value of the property transferred is similarly reduced for stamp duty purposes by the power of revocation seems to be a question on which there is no authority.   However, notwithstanding arguments to the contrary, this is a device which appears effective in practice in minimising stamp duty.

The words " conveyance or transfer " are held by the Commissioners to include an appointment under a general power of appointment, but not an appointment under a special power.   For a discussion as to what amounts to a general power and of the effect of the Stamp Act, 1891, s. 62 (*ante*, p. 1158), see *Fuller* v. *Commissioners* [1950] 2 All E.R. 976.   Where a transaction which is in substance a sale is carried out by means of a declaration of trust, the declaration attracts *ad valorem* duty as a conveyance (*West London Syndicate* v. *Commissioners* [1898] 1 Q.B. 226, at p. 240 ; [1898] 2 Q.B. 507, at p. 522).

In *Grey* v. *Inland Revenue Commissioners* [1960] A.C. 1, the settlor had transferred shares to trustees.   A few days later he *orally* directed the trustees to hold the shares on the trusts of certain settlements executed several years earlier.   A month after this oral direction the trustees executed declarations of trust accordingly which the settlor executed (to testify that he had given the direction) but he was not made a party to them.   The House of Lords decided that the written declarations were chargeable to duty.   The reason was that the oral directions were " dispositions " of equitable interests within the L.P.A. 1925, s. 53 (1) (c), and so were ineffective because they were not in writing.   Consequently, the written declarations were chargeable as voluntary dispositions.

Similar reasoning was applied in *Oughtred* v. *Inland Revenue Commissioners* [1960] A.C. 206, where a reversioner of shares agreed orally to transfer his interest to a life tenant and both parties subsequently executed a deed of release in favour of the trustees who transferred the shares to the life tenant. The transfer was held to be liable to *ad valorem* duty as it was an instrument whereby the shares were transferred " upon a sale thereof."   Although the oral contract gave rise to a constructive trust in favour of the former life tenant the full title could be transferred only by an instrument and so that instrument ranked for duty as a conveyance on sale.

Other exceptions to s. 74 are a conveyance made for nominal consideration for the purpose of securing the repayment of an advance, or made for effectuating the appointment of a new trustee, or the retirement of a trustee, or made to a beneficiary by a trustee under any trust, or a disentailing assurance not limiting any new estate other than an estate in fee simple in the person disentailing the property ; in these cases the stamp is the fixed one of 50p (subs. (6)).

A voluntary conveyance of property subject to a mortgage attracts duty on the value of the equity of redemption only, but if the grantee covenants to pay the mortgage debt then duty is alternatively chargeable on the amount payable as being the consideration for a conveyance on sale (Stamp Act, 1891, s. 57). In practice, the Commissioners claim whichever duty is higher (see *Speyer* v. *Commissioners* [1908] A.C. 92).

In order to avoid payment of the increased rate of *ad valorem* stamp duty on a voluntary conveyance, when the value of the property does not exceed £10,000 or £15,000, as the case may be, a similar certificate should be inserted in the voluntary conveyance as in an ordinary conveyance, except that the words " the amount or value, or the aggregate amount or value of the property *conveyed or transferred* " should be substituted in the certificate for the words " amount or value or the aggregate amount or value of the consideration " (Finance (1909–10) Act, 1910, s. 74 (1) ; F.A. 1952, s. 73 (3)). Where the value of the property is not known at the time of completion it is understood that a certificate may be inserted that the transaction " does not form part of a larger transaction or of a series of transactions." The appropriate duty will be charged when the value of the property has been ascertained by adjudication (see [1954] C.L.Y. 3190).

A settlement liable to *ad valorem* duty requires an extra stamp of 50p if the deed contains a covenant to settle after-acquired property (Finance (1909–10) Act, 1910, s. 4).

It is provided by s. 4 (1) of the S.L.A. 1925 that a settlement of a legal estate in land must (except as therein mentioned) be effected by a vesting deed and a trust instrument ; and by subs. (3) of the same section, that the trust instrument is to bear any *ad valorem* stamp duty which may be payable (whether by virtue of the vesting deed or otherwise) in respect of the settlement. The vesting deed itself will bear a 50p deed stamp. A purchaser dealing with settled land is not concerned as to the *ad valorem* duty (S.L.A. 1925, s. 110 (2)).

Marriage consideration.—A conveyance in consideration of marriage does not attract *ad valorem* duty since it is neither " on sale " nor voluntary and is also expressly excepted from the " deeming " provision (Finance (1909–10) Act, 1910, s. 74 (5)). This exception does *not* apply—

(*a*) in the case of an outright gift, if or in so far as it is a gift to a person other than a party to the marriage ;

(*b*) in the case of any other disposition, if the persons who are or may become entitled to any benefit under the disposition include any person other than—

(i) the parties to the marriage, issue of the marriage, or a wife or husband of any such issue ;

(ii) persons becoming entitled on the failure of trusts for any such issue under which trust property would vest indefeasibly on the attainment of a specified age or either on the attainment of such an age or on some earlier event, or persons becoming entitled on the failure of any limitation in tail ;

(iii) a subsequent wife or husband of a party to the marriage or any issue, or the wife or husband of any issue of a subsequent marriage of either party ;

(iv) persons becoming entitled under the trusts specified in
s. 33 (1) of the Trustee Act, 1925 (" protective trusts "), the principal
beneficiary being a person falling within (i) or (iii), *ante,* or under
such trusts modified by the enlargement, as respects any period
during which there is no such issue as aforesaid in existence, of the
class of potential beneficiaries specified in s. 33 (1) (ii) ;

(v) persons becoming entitled under Scottish trusts corresponding
with those mentioned in (iv), *ante* ;

(vi) as respects a reasonable amount by way of remuneration,
the trustees of the settlement

(F.A. 1963, ss. 53 (1), 64, reversing the effect of *Inland Revenue Commissioners*
v. *Rennell* [1964] A.C. 173 for conveyances on or after 1st August, 1963 :
F.A. 1963, s. 73 (2)). Note that " issue " above includes issue legitimated
by the marriage or persons adopted jointly by the spouses (F.A. 1963, s. 53 (3)) .

Settlement.—This head of charge has been repealed in relation to instruments made after July, 1962 (F.A. 1962, s. 34 (7), Sched. 11, Pt. V).

PART 6. ESTATE DUTY

It is not possible to deal with this subject in general in this book ; the
purpose of the present Part is to draw attention to certain rules which are of
particular concern to conveyancers.

Purchaser's concern with death duties.—A purchaser or mortgagee is
not now concerned to see that duty has been paid on death before 1926
(Customs and Inland Revenue Act, 1889, s. 12 ; F.A. 1894, s. 8 (2)). Where
the death occurred after 1925, a purchaser, mortgagee or lessee, in good
faith for valuable consideration, of a legal estate in unregistered freeholds
will not take subject to any death duty unless the charge for duty is registered
as a land charge (ss. 17 (1) and 205 (1) (xxi) of the L.P.A. 1925). If not so
registered, the charge is attached instead to the proceeds of sale (s. 17 (2) of
the L.P.A. 1925). Section 2 (5), Class D (i), of the L.C.A. 1972 provides, in
effect, that any charge acquired by the Commissioners of Inland Revenue
under any statute for death duties leviable or payable on any death after 1925
may be registered as a land charge ; and s. 4 (6) of the same Act provides that
a land charge of Class D, created or arising after 1925, is to be void as against
a purchaser of a legal estate for money or money's worth, of the land charged
therewith, or of any interest in such land, unless the land charge is registered
in the appropriate register before the completion of the purchase. Thus, a
purchaser or mortgagee will be concerned only if death took place within
the last twelve years (Customs and Inland Revenue Act, 1889, s. 12 ; F.A. 1894,
s. 8 (2)), and the Commissioners have registered a charge.

If, on a search in the land charges register, the purchaser of property on
which the duty is a charge should find that a charge for death duties has
been registered, he should require the vendor to pay or commute the duty
and produce to him a certificate of the Commissioners of Inland Revenue
that it has been so paid or commuted under s. 11 of the F.A. 1894, which
applies to estate duty, or s. 16 (7) of the L.P.A. 1925, which, in relation to
deaths occurring before 30th July, 1949, applies to the other death duties.
This certificate he is entitled to at the expense of the vendor (*Re Conlon and
Faulkener's Contract* [1916] 1 Ir. R. 241). However, it is understood not to

be the Commissioners' practice to register a land charge unless there is some doubt or difficulty about recovery of the duty.

In the case of registered land, purchasers, etc., are never concerned with death duties since a registered disposition always overreaches the charge (L.R.A. 1925, s. 73). If it appears to the registrar that a charge has arisen he must enter notice thereof on the register; and after that has been done, before registering or entering notice of any disposition which would override the charge, he must give notice to the Commissioners and cancel the notice of claim. If all claims have been satisfied, or no such claims arise, or the Commissioners are satisfied that the duties will be paid, they must notify the registrar, who will then cancel any notice of claim. The effect of s. 73 (1) and (15) is that a registered disposition in favour of a purchaser for money or money's worth operates to vest in him the estate or interest transferred or created by the disposition *free from all claims for death duties, notwithstanding* that a claim has been noted on the register, although a disposition to a person other than such a purchaser takes effect subject to any charge for death duties *whether or not* a claim has been noted (L.R.A. 1925, s. 73 (2)). As a purchaser for money or money's worth takes free from any charge for duties, the section provides for the liability of the personal representative or other person in whom the registered estate vested on the death, and gives to such a person powers for the purpose of raising the duty and costs.

Although, under the F.A. 1894, the rule is that estate duty becomes a first charge on the property in respect of which it is leviable, there is an exception in the case of property passing to the executor or administrator as such (*ibid.*, s. 9 (1); s. 8 (18)). Freeholds do not pass to the executor or administrator " as such " (*Re Palmer* [1900] W.N. 9; and see s. 53 (3) of the A.E.A. 1925) but leasehold property, even although specifically bequeathed, does so pass, consequently estate duty does not become a charge on leaseholds and a purchaser or mortgagee is not concerned as to the payment of the duty (*Re Culverhouse; Cook* v. *Culverhouse* [1896] 2 Ch. 251). This freedom from charge of leasehold property is confirmed by the statement in s. 16 (6) of the L.P.A. 1925 that nothing in Pt. I of the Act is to impose a charge for duties on leasehold land. But leasehold property escapes the charge only where it forms part of the *free estate* of the deceased, devolving under his will or intestacy. If it becomes liable to duty on the death of a person who was not absolute owner, it cannot pass to *his* executor as such and therefore will not escape.

The principal cases in which estate duty is a charge on leaseholds are where the duty is payable in connection with the death of—

(1) a person who has exercised a general power of appointment (it was held in *O'Grady* v. *Wilmot* [1916] 2 A.C. 231 that the property in this case did not pass to the executor *as such*; of course, if such a power is not exercised by will, the property does not pass to the executor at all);

(2) a life tenant, or a former life tenant who surrendered his interest;

(3) a donor who made a gift of the property in his lifetime (but see *post*, p. 1176, for the position where the donee has sold *before* the death of the donor);

(4) a joint tenant.

Entailed property does not pass to the executor " as such "; nor, apparently, does entailed personal property disposed of by a testator under the provisions of s. 176 of the L.P.A. 1925. As to foreign immovable property, see s. 28 (1) of the F.A. 1962, amending s. 28 (2) of the F.A. 1949.

Where freeholds are held on trust for sale or are subject to a contract for sale, the equitable doctrine of conversion applies (*In the Goods of Gunn* (1884), 9 P.D. 242) and it is accepted that the beneficial interests are therefore personalty and that no charge arises. This does not apply, and there is a charge, if the conversion to personalty (i) only takes place on the death, e.g., by virtue of a trust for sale arising under the deceased's will or intestacy, or (ii) under a statutory (as opposed to an express) trust for sale (L.P.A. 1925, s. 16 (4) ; A.E.A. 1925, s. 53 (3) ; and see *Re Tuck* [1929] 2 K.B. 77 and *Re Previte* [1931] 1 Ch. 447). However, it may be observed that where freeholds have been settled on an express trust for sale the doctrine of conversion strictly may have no relevance for estate duty purposes since it is not the equitable interests (personalty) which pass on the death of a beneficiary but the trust fund (realty). Compare *Philipson-Stow* v. *I.R.C.* [1961] A.C. 727 ; and *Burdett-Coutts* v. *I.R.C.* [1960] 1 W.L.R. 1027. Again, if freeholds which have been notionally converted to personalty have been reconverted in the deceased's lifetime (e.g., by the ending of a trust for sale at the direction of a beneficiary or beneficiaries of full capacity and absolutely entitled) then the property passes as freeholds anyway and is subject to a charge for estate duty (*Re Lord Grimthorpe* [1908] 2 Ch. 675 ; and see *Re Cook* [1948] Ch. 212).

As to payment of estate duty by instalments in respect of land whether it is real property or leasehold or personal property because of a trust for sale, see F.A. 1894, s. 6 (8) and F.A. 1971, s. 62 (1) (*c*).

Incidence of estate duty.—In deciding which beneficial interests are to bear any estate duty payable, it is necessary to distinguish again property passing to the deceased's personal representatives as such from all other property. Estate duty on the latter, which particularly includes real property as already noted *ante*, p. 1172, is a first charge thereon (F.A. 1894, s. 9 (1)) ; it is therefore borne by the beneficiaries taking such property, if more than one, according to their respective interests (*Re Rosenthal* [1972] 1 W.L.R. 1273 ; see also *Re Orford* [1896] 1 Ch. 257 ; *Re Buesst's Will Trusts* [1963] Ch. 419).

Estate duty attributable to property passing to the deceased's personal representatives as such (i.e., the deceased's free personal estate in Great Britain) must be discharged in due course of administration as a testamentary expense (*Re Clemow* [1900] 2 Ch. 182 ; *Re Buesst's Will Trusts, ante*). Accordingly the incidence of estate duty in the case of such property is governed entirely by the order of application of assets provided by A.E.A. 1925, s. 34 (3), Sched. 1, Pt. II, which may, of course, be varied by testamentary direction (see below).

Where pecuniary legacies are payable out of a mixed fund of property passing to the personal representatives as such (personalty) and of other property (e.g., realty), they must bear their proportion of the estate duty charged on the latter (*Re Owers* [1941] Ch. 17, approving *Re Spencer Cooper* [1908] 1 Ch. 130 ; and see *Re Paterson's Will Trusts* [1963] 1 W.L.R. 623).

It may be noted that no part of the estate duty on property passing to personal representatives as such is cast on other property, nor *vice versa* (*Re Buesst's Will Trusts, ante*). In particular, estate duty in respect of real estate cannot be treated as a testamentary expense payable out of residue (*Re Rosenthal, ante*).

Express directions as to incidence.—Whether the effect of a general direction by a testator that settled legacies are to be free of death duties, or that all death duties are to be paid out of his residuary estate, or any direction of a similar nature, is to make the gift free of death duties payable on his death alone, or free also of duties payable on the death of the tenant for life or other future event, depends on discovery of the intention of the testator from the language of the will (*Re Palmer* (1912), 106 L.T. 319). In *Re Wedgwood* [1921] 1 Ch. 601, it was held that the *prima facie* effect of such words was to throw on the residue the duties payable only at the testator's own death. The inconvenience of having to keep a sum in hand the amount of which cannot accurately be judged influences the court in favour of this construction (*Re Duke of Sutherland* [1922] 2 Ch. 782 ; *Re Fenwick ; Lloyds Bank, Ltd.* v. *Fenwick* [1922] 2 Ch. 775 ; *Re Beecham* (1923), 130 L.T. 558 ; *Re Sarson* [1925] Ch. 31 ; *Re Jones* [1928] W.N. 227 ; *Re Laidlaw* [1930] 2 Ch. 392 ; *Re Trimble* [1931] 1 Ch. 369 ; *Re Hicks* [1933] Ch. 335 ; *Re Howell* [1952] Ch. 264 ; *Re Embleton's Will Trusts* [1965] 1 W.L.R. 840). However, in *Re Stoddart* [1916] 2 Ch. 444 where the words were " All the legacies (whether settled or otherwise) " to be " paid and enjoyed free of all death duties " and the trustees to " pay or provide for the legacies . . . and the duties thereon," it was held that they threw all prospective claims for death duty upon the residue in relief of the settled legacies.

Estate duty on death of joint tenant.—A deceased beneficial joint tenant, notwithstanding the right of survivorship, is to be treated as competent to dispose of his severable share at death (F.A. 1969, s. 36 (7)). Consequently the principal estate duty charge is under s. 2 (1) (*a*) of the F.A. 1894.

The point is constantly arising as to what estate duty has to be paid on the death of a person who has invested property in the joint names of himself and his wife or child, or a person to whom the deceased stood *in loco parentis*. In such a case, whatever the nature of the property, there is a *prima facie* presumption of law that the deceased in placing the property in the joint names intended " an advancement." Such presumption, like any other presumption, can be rebutted. But assuming that an advancement was intended, then the estate duty to be paid appears to depend on the class of property of which the gift consisted. If the property was pure personal property, the presumption is that the deceased intended to enjoy the entire income during the joint lives, the gift to the other person only to take effect in the event of him or her surviving the donor. Therefore, assuming the investment of personal property was made by the husband in the name of himself and wife, and the wife survived, the whole fund would become the property of the wife by survivorship, and estate duty would be payable on the whole of the fund. See Customs and Inland Revenue Act, 1881, s. 38, as amended by s. 11 of the Customs and Inland Revenue Act, 1889, and incorporated as s. 2 (1) (*c*) of the F.A. 1894 ; also *Fowkes* v. *Pascoe* (1875), L.R. 10 Ch. 343, and *Re Eykyn's Trusts* (1877), 6 Ch. D. 115. As the advancement would only be contingent on the wife surviving her husband it follows that if the wife died in the lifetime of the husband her interest never became an interest in possession, and therefore no estate duty would be payable on the death of the wife (F.A. 1894, s. 5 (3)). But if it can be proved that the wife actually received part of the income during the joint lives as an enforceable right, the presumption is to that extent rebutted. If, therefore, the husband survives for seven years or more, estate duty is not payable on the proportion of the fund from which the wife received the income, but if she dies first duty is payable on her portion.

If the property consists of freehold or leasehold property other considerations apply. In the case of pure personalty property parol trusts are permitted, but in the case of freehold and leasehold property a trust cannot be created except by writing (see s. 53 of the L.P.A. 1925). The practical result is that where land is paid for by a husband but conveyed into joint names the conveyance is regarded as establishing an *immediate* advancement to the wife, each party on the execution of the deed becoming a true joint tenant with the other. In these circumstances, on the death of the husband, provided he survived the conveyance by seven years, estate duty is only claimed on the moiety then passing to the wife ; the Crown could claim duty on the whole under the Customs and Inland Revenue Act, 1881, s. 38 (2) (b), although a concession is made in practice. But if in such circumstances the wife should die before the husband, estate duty would be payable on the death of the wife on one moiety. This must follow from the fact that the effect of the conveyance operated as an immediate gift in favour of the wife. See also *Dunbar* v. *Dunbar* [1909] 2 Ch. 639.

In the past it has been accepted that even though a husband continued to live in the matrimonial home after it had been conveyed to husband and wife jointly no duty would be payable on the wife's half share if he survived for seven years. Although he lived in the house it was thought that, as regards the wife's share, possession was taken by her to the exclusion of the husband ; compare the statutory provisions mentioned *post*, p. 1176.

Some doubt has been thrown on this view by the Privy Council in *Chick* v. *Commissioner of Stamp Duties* [1958] A.C. 435. A father gave land to his son and some months later the land became used by a partnership consisting of the father, the donee and another son. On similar wording of a New South Wales statute it was held that duty was payable as the father had not been excluded from possession. It is understood not to be the practice of the Commissioners to seek to apply this decision to a gift by a husband to his wife of the matrimonial home or a share in it.

Now the converse case may be considered, namely, where the wife provides the price. It is understood that on such a purchase of freehold property and conveyance into joint names where the husband dies first, the Revenue claim estate duty on half the value of the property. The ground of their claim is that a conveyance to joint tenants normally contains an express trust for sale and trust to hold the proceeds for the two joint tenants. Therefore, it is argued, there is an express trust and liability must be determined on that footing, the equitable doctrine of resulting trusts being displaced. If, on the other hand, freehold property was conveyed to joint tenants without the usual joint tenancy clauses, it seems clear that no duty would be payable on the death of the husband (this would appear particularly applicable to registered land where joint tenancy clauses are not usual). It is doubtful whether the L.P.A. 1925, s. 36 (1), *ante*, p. 295, would apply, but even if it did, it would not affect death duties (L.P.A. 1925, s. 16 (4)). Similarly, no duty would be payable if the property were pure personalty. On the *wife's* death (there being no joint tenancy clause) the husband would not obtain any beneficial interest ; such interest would pass as part of the wife's estate and duty would be payable accordingly. In this case there is no presumption of advancement and so the husband would be deemed to be a trustee of the property for his wife. On the death of the wife, however, estate duty on the whole would be payable, she being absolutely entitled to the whole under a resulting trust. Section 53 of the L.P.A. 1925 above referred to, does not affect resulting trusts.

If the person paying for the property was a child, the father would be deemed to be a trustee for such child, and the same consequences would follow as in the case of a wife.

If the parties to a joint purchase are strangers to each other, then on the death of the one, in the absence of express provision as to the beneficial interests and of evidence of a contrary intention, the presumption of a resulting trust arises. Consequently, a calculation has to be made as to the value of the capital which the deceased had contributed.

Estate duty on gifts.—Estate duty is payable in respect of property taken under a disposition " purporting to operate as an immediate gift *inter vivos* " which is not *bona fide* made seven years, or, if for public or charitable purposes, one year, before the donor's death (Customs and Inland Revenue Act, 1881, s. 38 (2) (*a*), as amended and extended). Further, duty is payable, even if the gift was more than seven years before the death, if *bona fide* possession and enjoyment were not assumed by the donee immediately upon the gift and thereafter retained to the entire exclusion of the donor, or of any benefit to him by contract or otherwise (Customs and Inland Revenue Act, 1889, s. 11 (1) ; F.A. 1894, s. 2 (1) (*c*) ; Finance (1909–10) Act, 1910, s. 59 (3)). The application of these rules is too detailed for consideration here, but it may be noted that on death after 29th July, 1959, retention or assumption of actual occupation of land or actual enjoyment of an incorporeal right over the land is disregarded if for full consideration in money or money's worth (F.A. 1959, s. 35 (1), (2)) ; but, in the case of a gift, a benefit obtained by virtue of associated operations, of which the gift is one, is treated as a benefit by contract or otherwise (*ibid.*, s. 35 (3) ; as to this, see *Nichols* v. *I.R.C.* [1973] 3 All E.R. 632). On death after 19th March, 1968, the principal value of the property deemed to pass by virtue of a gift, etc., is reduced for estate duty purposes by (i) 15 per cent. if death takes place in the fifth year ; (ii) 30 per cent. if death takes place in the sixth year ; and (iii) 60 per cent. if death takes place in the seventh year (F.A. 1968, s. 35 (2)).

For the purposes of this charge the " property taken " originally meant the actual property given, whether absolutely or by way of settlement, and no regard was paid to any change of investment made before the death of the donor (*Sneddon* v. *Lord Advocate* [1954] A.C. 257) ; such property was valued as at the time of the donor's death (*ibid.*). This led to certain estate duty avoidance devices being adopted and as a result the F.A. 1957, s. 38, laid down complicated rules for identifying the property dutiable taking changes of investment into account. The particular interest of these rules for conveyancers is that they have incidentally removed a difficulty which formerly arose where land comprised in a gift was sold by the donee within five (now seven) years of the gift. For instance, land might have been given to *B*, who sold it to *A*. If the donor died after the sale but within five years of the gift, *A* had notice of the potential liability to pay duty in the event of the donor dying within the five-year period and so he was not protected against a claim for duty on the ground that he was a *bona fide* purchaser for value without notice and so protected by the F.A. 1894, ss. 8 (18), 9 (1). If the land was registered it appeared that duty would be claimed from a purchaser who had notice of the facts. However, the F.A. 1957, s. 38, has enacted, in effect, that where there has been an absolute gift of property other than money but, prior to the death of the donor, the donee ceased to have possession and enjoyment of it, liability to estate duty on the death of the donor after 31st July, 1957, is to be determined as if the property given was the property received by the donee in substitution for the gift. The fortunate result of this change is that on the death of a donor after 31st July, 1957, but within now seven years of the gift, a purchaser from the donee before the donor's death is not concerned with the duty, which is no longer a charge on the property given ; the charge is imposed on the proceeds of sale by s. 38. Provided that the donee sells the land or otherwise disposes of it for full value before the death of the donor and the donor dies after 31st July, 1957, the former difficulty no longer arises. Where death has already occurred the land charges search against the name of the donor will indicate whether a charge may be enforceable (*see ante*, p. 600).

The former problem may still arise when a donee has disposed of the property otherwise than by sale at full value, for instance, by gift. Similarly if the donee has mortgaged the property the problem may arise on the death of the donor because the mortgage does not remove from the property the potential charge for duty. How that problem could be dealt with was illustrated in *Manning* v. *Turner* [1957] 1 W.L.R. 91 where the purchaser demanded, and the vendor eventually agreed to provide, an indemnity policy.

Gifts and settlements made in consideration of marriage (not necessarily the marriage of the deceased) may be exempt from estate duty. Where made on or after 4th April, 1963, exemption is obtained for an outright gift only if it is in favour of a party to the marriage (F.A. 1963, s. 53 (1) (*a*)) and for any other disposition only if the persons who are or may become entitled to any benefit are parties to the marriage, issue or a spouse of such issue and certain others such as persons entitled under protective trusts (*ibid.*, s. 53 (1) (*b*), (2)).

The exemption for gifts made in consideration of marriage is now restricted to a total of £5,000 where the donor was a party to or an ancestor of a party to the marriage, and to £1,000 in any other case (F.A. 1968, s. 36, applying to gifts made after 19th March, 1968).

It is often difficult to be certain whether a gift is in fact made in consideration of marriage within the exemption, or whether marriage is merely the occasion of the gift. Great care is necessary in advising a settlor, not least because in deciding the question the court may look at the settlement in the light of surrounding circumstances (see generally *Re Park* (*No.* 2) [1972] Ch. 385, C.A.).

Disclaimer of an absolute gift in a will amounts to a gift to the person who thereby becomes entitled and so duty may be claimed under the F.A. 1940, s. 45 (2), on death of the person disclaiming within seven years (*Re Stratton's Disclaimer* [1958] Ch. 42). Contrast the rule as to life interests mentioned *post*, p. 1178.

All property chargeable to estate duty by virtue of s. 2 (1) (*c*) of the F.A. 1894 (i.e., primarily the subject-matter of gifts *inter vivos*) is now made aggregable as being property in which the deceased had an interest (F.A. 1968, s. 38). This provision applies to deaths after 19th March, 1968, whenever the gift was made, and appears principally directed to policies nominated under the Married Women's Property Act, 1882.

Duty on breaking settlements.—It is provided by the F.A. 1894, s. 2 (1) (*b*) (as substituted by s. 36 (2) of the F.A. 1969), in effect that property in which the deceased person had a beneficial interest in possession shall pass on the death of the deceased, notwithstanding that that interest has been surrendered or otherwise disposed of, whether for value or not, and irrespective of the person to whom surrender was made, but not where the surrender was *bona fide* effected seven years before death, and *bona fide* enjoyment and possession was immediately assumed thereunder to the entire exclusion of the person who had the estate or interest limited to cease as aforesaid. The property liable to duty is in effect that which constituted the fund at the time of the termination of the settlement or of the former tenant for life's death valued at that date (F.A. 1957, s. 38 (12)). The proportionate reductions mentioned *ante*, p. 1176, may apply to cases falling within this provision. Where a life tenant and remainderman break a settlement and divide the assets in proportion to the actuarial value of their interests estate duty is nevertheless payable under this section on the full value of the assets if the life tenant dies within seven years (*A.-G.* v. *Llewelyn* [1935] 1 K.B. 94).

The effect of the F.A. 1969, s. 38, is that the purchase of interests in remainder by the life tenant also attracts a liability to estate duty in the event of the death of the life tenant within seven years. The duty would be payable ultimately out of the life tenant's estate but it is a charge on the settled fund. Even if there is a material risk of the death of the life tenant within seven years (which can usually be covered by insurance) the breaking of the settlement may often result in substantial saving of estate duty (for instance, because a lower rate may become payable on the life tenant's aggregable estate).

Where a beneficial interest in possession is disposed of, there may be difficulty in providing for estate duty payable in the future, as also there may be under s. 38 of the F.A. 1969, where the settlement is ended before the life tenant's death. The F.A. 1950, s. 44 (as slightly amended in 1969), states who is accountable and, where the trustees of the settlement may be accountable, the Commissioners may certify the sum which should be retained. The obtaining of such a certificate may not, however, provide complete protection to trustees if a part only of the settled fund is subject to an arrangement which may be caught by s. 2 (1) (*b*). The effect of s. 44 (4) is to give the trustees a lien for the prospective duty and costs on the property remaining in their hands. (Although the primary liability to recoup the trustees is on the persons taking the share of capital involved in the arrangement the property may be disposed of by them so that they cannot be made to repay.) It follows that where, for instance, a life interest is released in part of settled property all persons interested in the whole of the property should give a satisfactory indemnity to the trustees. Otherwise the trustees must retain an adequate part of the property in respect of which the release is given. Normally it is sufficient to retain for seven years the amount certified by the Commissioners under s. 44 (3); one must note, however, that in theory even this action may not give full protection as the certificate may be an underestimate and there is nothing to prevent the Commissioners claiming the additional duty out of the part of the fund retained, thereby causing difficulty to the trustees who may be met by a claim from persons interested in the part retained. On this problem, see further, *Re Joynson's Will Trusts* [1954] Ch. 567, and *Law Times*, vol. 218, pp. 4 and 5.

There is a further problem that even after seven years a claim may arise if the life tenant who released his interest has resumed possession or taken any benefit in the property within seven years of his death. It is understood, however, that if the Commissioners are satisfied that the life tenant has been excluded for a period of seven years they will certify that no claim for duty will be made and thereupon the trustees will be safe in distributing sums retained.

Where a settlement is broken during the lifetime of the tenant for life trustees must for their own protection ensure, before they part with substantial portions of the trust funds, that the settlement had been validly determined. If they do not they may remain liable for heavy estate duty. See the discussion in the *Law Times*, vol. 214, pp. 260, 261, where the necessity for obtaining a certificate under the F.A. 1950, s. 44, is emphasised and the necessity for ensuring due payment of stamp duty is mentioned.

Exemption for certain property passing by reason of purchase.— The basic rule is that estate duty is imposed on property which passes on the death of the deceased (F.A. 1894, ss. 1 and 2). No duty is payable, however, in respect of property passing on death by reason only of a *bona fide* purchase from the person under whose disposition the property passes, nor in respect of the falling into possession of the reversion on any lease for lives, nor in respect of the determination of any annuity for lives, where such purchase was made, or such lease or annuity granted, for full consideration in money or money's worth paid to the vendor or grantor for his own use or benefit, or in the case of a lease for the use or benefit of any person for whom the grantor was a trustee (F.A. 1894, s. 3 (1)) ; and when such consideration is only partial, the value of the consideration will be allowed as a deduction from the value of the property for the purpose of estate duty (*ibid.*, s. 3 (2)). For instance, if a person sells his house for its full reversionary value, reserving to himself a life interest, no estate duty will be payable thereon on his death (*A.-G.* v. *Dobree* [1900] 1 Q.B. 442, 450). It has also been held that where a husband bequeathed an annuity to his wife subject to the condition precedent that she agreed to dispose testamentarily of certain property in a specified way, which she did, the property was *prima facie* exempt from duty on her death as passing under a purchase (*Re Harmsworth* [1967] Ch. 826, C.A. ; since the wife's disposition was in favour of relatives, it was deemed to be a gift *inter vivos* despite the annuity). As to cesser of annuity, see *A.-G.* v. *Sandwich* [1922] 2 K.B. 500 ; as to partial consideration, see *Re Bateman ; A.-G.* v. *Wreford Brown* [1925] 2 K.B. 429 ; and as to purchase of annuities from relatives, see F.A. 1940, s. 44, F.A. 1944, s. 40, and F.A. 1950, s. 46.

Where an interest in expectancy has been *bona fide* sold or mortgaged for full consideration in money or money's worth and the rates of estate duty in force in the case of a person dying when the interest falls into possession are higher than the rates in force in the case of a person dying at the time of the sale or mortgage, then no other duty is payable by the purchaser or mortgagee than would have been payable if the rates had remained the same (Finance (No. 2) Act, 1940, s. 17). The mortgagor is only protected if the mortgagee has foreclosed, or if the equity of redemption is valueless, but even then the mortgagor may remain technically liable for duty at the higher rate.

Agricultural relief.—The agricultural value of agricultural property is charged to estate duty on a scale where each rate is 55 per cent. of the normal rate, i.e., this value bears duty at 55 per cent. of the estate rate (F.A. 1925, s. 23, as amended by F.A. 1949, s. 28, and by F.A. 1969, Sched. 17, Pt. III, and Sched. 21, Pt. V). " Agricultural property " is widely defined to include appropriate buildings (F.A. 1894, s. 22 (1) (g)) and the agricultural value thereof is its value if it were subject to a perpetual covenant prohibiting use otherwise than as agricultural property (F.A. 1925, s. 23 (2)). Thus the special scale does not necessarily apply to the actual value. Further, timber, trees and wood are not to be included, although the land on which they grow is, as part of the agricultural value (*ibid.* ; as to timber, etc., see below). Mortgages on agricultural property are apportioned, for the purposes of deduction, between the agricultural and non-agricultural values in the proportion these bear to each other (F.A. 1925, s. 23 (3)).

In *Philipson-Stow's Special Personal Representatives* v. *I.R.C.* (1959), 38 A.T.C. 21, the deceased had contracted to buy agricultural land, paid a 10 per cent. deposit, but died before completion ; Upjohn, J., held that agricultural relief was available not on the full value of the land but only in respect of the value of the benefit of the contract (i.e., the amount of the 10 per cent. of the deposit paid).

Agricultural relief is available where there is an " assets valuation " of shares (or debentures) in a company holding and occupying (i.e., not letting) agricultural land (F.A. 1954, s. 28 (2) (b)) but is not otherwise available where such land is vested in a company. In practice, agricultural relief is accorded by the Revenue on the death of a partner where the partnership held agricultural land (compare *Burdett-Coutts* v. *I.R.C.* [1960] 1 W.L.R. 1027 and see *Law Society's Gazette*, vol. 58, p. 49). For this purpose, it would appear possible to find a partnership in most cases of co-ownership of agricultural land.

Timber, etc.—Where an estate comprises land on which timber, trees, wood or underwood are growing, then the value of such timber, etc., is in the first place not to be taken into account in estimating the principal value of the estate or the amount of estate duty and the timber, etc., is not itself dutiable (Finance (1909–10) Act, 1910, s. 61 (5), as amended by F.A. 1969, Sched. 17, Pt. III, para. 7). As to the land, see the note above on agricultural relief. However, the timber, etc., becomes dutiable when sold, in effect, at the estate rate without aggregation of the most recent death (*ibid.*) except that underwood is exempt from duty in any event (F.A. 1912, s. 9). If the timber, etc., is sold, felled or cut, the duty is payable " on the net moneys (if any) after deducting all necessary outgoings since the death " received from the sale (s. 61 (5) of the 1910 Act, as amended). If the timber, etc., is sold standing, with or without the land, the duty is payable, in effect, on its principal value as at the death (proviso to *ibid.*).

PLANNING AND COMPULSORY ACQUISITION

PART 1. TOWN AND COUNTRY PLANNING

The Town and Country Planning Act, 1947, made necessary certain changes in conveyancing practice, and a solicitor may be expected to advise his clients as to the effect of the Town and Country Planning Act, 1971 (which repeals and consolidates virtually all of the provisions of earlier Town and Country Planning legislation, with some minor adjustments, and which has already been amended) on land which is the subject of transactions being carried out. For the commonest instance of concern to conveyancers, a person intending to buy land will often wish to know whether he can make a certain use of it without applying for planning permission. Planning law is the subject of a number of text-books and cannot be stated adequately in a few pages. Nevertheless, the effects of the Town and Country Planning Acts on conveyancing transactions cannot be appreciated without a consideration of the provisions of the Acts and of many of the orders and regulations made under them, and many planning problems are so closely related to transactions affecting the land that they must be dealt with at the same time. This chapter, therefore, deals with those aspects of the subject most concerning conveyancing practice. No attempt will be made to give, for example, an historical introduction or an account of the public and administrative procedures for development plans and structure plans, whether " old style " or " new style " (to adopt the terminology used in Heap, Planning Law, chaps. 3 and 4).

A. WHAT AMOUNTS TO DEVELOPMENT

Definitions.—With certain exceptions, planning permission is required in respect of any development of land carried out after 1st July, 1948 (1947 Act,

s. 12 (1) ; 1971 Act, s. 23 (1) ; see further, p. 1192). Thus it is apparent that
the definition of the word " development " is of fundamental importance.
This definition is to be found in s. 22 (1) of the 1971 Act, which states that :—

" (1) In this Act, except where the context otherwise requires, ' development,' subject to the following provisions of this section, means the carrying
out of building, engineering, mining or other operations in, on, over or under
land, or the making of any material change in the use of any buildings or
other land ; "

In order to arrive at the precise meaning of the word we must note the
meaning of certain terms referred to in s. 290 (1) :—

" ' building ' . . . includes any structure or erection and any part of a
building, as so defined, but does not include plant or machinery comprised
in a building ;

' building operations ' includes rebuilding operations, structural alterations of or additions to buildings, and other operations normally undertaken
by a person carrying on business as a builder ;

' engineering operations ' includes the formation or laying out of means
of access to highways ;

' land ' means any corporeal hereditament, including a building, and in
relation to the acquisition of land . . . includes any interest in or right over
land ;

' means of access ' includes any means of access, whether private or
public, for vehicles or for foot passengers, and includes a street ; "

It is clear that there are two aspects to the meaning of the word
" development " ; first, the carrying out of certain operations and, secondly,
the making of material changes in the use of land, and these two aspects are
considered below. An initial problem, however, may be to recognise what is
the relevant " planning unit " for the purposes of development and planning
permission (see *Trentham (G. Percy), Ltd.* v. *Gloucestershire C.C.* [1966]
1 W.L.R. 506 ; also *Petticoat Lane Rentals, Ltd.* v. *Secretary of State for the
Environment* [1971] 1 W.L.R. 1112). After a helpful consideration of the
problem in the Queen's Bench Division it was said to be " a useful working
rule to assume that the unit of occupation is the appropriate planning unit,
unless and until some smaller unit can be recognised as the site of activities
which amount in substance to a separate use both physically and functionally "
(*per* Bridge, J., in *Burdle* v. *Secretary of State for the Environment* [1972]
1 W.L.R. 1207, at p. 1212 ; see also *Thomas David (Porthcawl), Ltd.* v.
Penybont R.D.C. [1972] 1 W.L.R. 1526 ; further reference may usefully be
made to an article by Simon N. L. Palk at *Conveyancer N.S.*, vol. 37, p. 154).

Development by carrying out of operations.—When read with the
definitions of building and engineering operations it is clear that this will
cover almost any substantial work on land ; even a fence may be a "building".

The test is whether, in all the circumstances, the physical character of the
land is altered (*Cheshire County Council* v. *Woodward* [1962] 2 Q.B. 126).
The placing of a structure affixed to land is usually development, whereas one
not affixed does not normally involve development, but that is one only of the
matters to be considered (*ibid.*).

It is not easy to say precisely what is an operation " normally undertaken
by a person carrying on business as a builder ". Demolition of a building
has been held not itself development (*London County Council* v. *Marks &*

Spencer, Ltd. [1953] A.C. 535 ; *Howell* v. *Sunbury-on-Thames U.D.C.* (1963), 107 Sol. J. 909) but subsequent use of the site may be. However, the question whether total demolition of a building amounts to " development " has now been considered in the House of Lords and has been said to be improperly put as a generalisation : instead the actual operations in the particular case should be considered, without any labelling word, and a decision made as a question of fact whether they come within the statutory definition (*Coleshill and District Investment Co., Ltd.* v. *Minister of Housing and Local Government* [1969] 1 W.L.R. 746 ; see also *Iddenden* v. *Secretary of State for the Environment* [1972] 1 W.L.R. 1433). Reference should now be made to the Town and Country Planning (Amendment) Act, 1972, s. 8 and Sched. 2, as to the control of demolition in conservation areas. It should be noted that the definition of engineering operations is such as to include so small a matter as the construction of a gateway giving access to a highway. In relation to mining operations, it has been held that each shovelful of earth extracted is itself a mining operation constituting a separate act of development (*Thomas David (Porthcawl), Ltd.* v. *Penybont R.D.C.* [1972] 1 W.L.R. 1526).

Section 22 (2) of the 1971 Act sets out three operations which do *not* constitute development, as follows :—

" The following operations . . . shall not be taken for the purposes of this Act to involve development of the land, that is to say :—

(*a*) the carrying out of works for the *maintenance*, improvement or other alteration of any building, being works which affect only the interior of the building or which do not materially affect the external appearance of the building and (in either case) are not works for making good war damage or works begun after 5th December, 1968, for the alteration of a building by providing additional space therein below ground ;

(*b*) the carrying out by a local highway authority of any works required for the maintenance or improvement of a road, being works carried out on land within the boundaries of the road ;

(*c*) the carrying out by a local authority or statutory undertakers of any works for the purpose of inspecting, repairing or renewing any sewers, mains, pipes, cables or other apparatus, including the breaking open of any street or other land for that purpose ; "

Once more, there is difficulty in applying the rules ; for instance, whether the alteration of exterior doors and windows *materially* affects the external appearance of a building is a question of fact. In this respect it must not be overlooked that the *use* of a dwelling-house as two or more separate dwelling-houses is development for which consent is needed (1971 Act, s. 22 (3) (*a*) ; see below).

Development by making a material change in use.—Probably the most troublesome matter of all is to determine what is a " *material* " change in the use of land. The real question is whether the new use is substantially different from the old one, although use of the word " substantial " does not carry one very far (compare, for instance, *Palser* v. *Grinling* [1948] A.C. 291) ; the question is one of fact and degree (*Birmingham Corporation* v. *Habib Ullah* [1964] 1 Q.B. 178). For example, it follows from the decision in *Central Land Board* v. *Saxone Shoe Co., Ltd.* [1956] 1 Q.B. 288 that the change of use from an ordinary public house, where sale of intoxicating liquor predominates, to a retail shop is a material change.

The then responsible Minister stated (Circular 67 of 1949) " that in considering whether a change is a material change, comparison with the previous use of the land or building in question is the governing factor and the effect of the proposal on a surrounding neighbourhood is not relevant to the issue," and, in the same circular, that a change in *kind*, e.g., from shop to factory, will always be material, whereas a change in the *degree* of an existing use will be material only if it is very marked.   A further indication of the views of the Secretary of State for the Environment can be gained from the Town and Country Planning (Use Classes) Order, 1972 (replacing earlier similar Orders of 1950 and 1963) (*post*, p. 1186).   The distinction between the various purposes within several of the classes is so narrow that one is led to suppose that Ministers considered that almost any change of user would be held to be " material," and subsequent decisions of Ministers and the courts indicate that such is the case.   See, further, " Development and the Use Classes Order," [1966] J.P.L. 504, 569, and note thereon, *ibid.*, p. 497 ; also " Permission Granted by Order " by W. A. Leach at [1972] J.P.L. 297.   It was decided in *Marshall* v. *Nottingham Corporation* [1960] 1 W.L.R. 707 that a change of use of land from manufacture and sale of portable buildings such as garages and greenhouses to display and sale of caravans was *not* a material change.   What should be considered is the character of the use of the land and not the particular purpose of the particular occupier (*East Barnet U.D.C.* v. *British Transport Commission* [1962] 2 Q.B. 484).

An increase in intensity of use (for example, by placing more caravans on the same area of land) may amount to a sufficiently material change as to be development (*Guildford R.D.C.* v. *Fortescue* [1959] 2 Q.B. 112 ; *Glamorgan C.C.* v. *Carter* [1963] 1 W.L.R. 1 ; *Hartnell* v. *Minister of Housing* [1964] 2 Q.B. 510 ; *James* v. *Minister of Housing* [1968] A.C. 409).

For planning purposes a use may be considered as continuing even though the physical use has been discontinued and there has been thought to be a presumption against abandonment (see " Abandonment of a Use " by Anthony R. Mellows, *Conveyancer N.S.*, vol. 27, p. 250).   However, it has been held that where a use has ceased for a considerable period (for example, four years) with no indicated intention of resuming it at a particular time, the Minister is entitled to find that it has been abandoned, with the result that resumption will be a material change of use requiring permission (*Hartley* v. *Minister of Housing* [1970] 1 Q.B. 413, C.A.).

Where open land is developed by the erection of a building on the whole of it, any former use of the land is automatically extinguished and there is a new planning unit (i.e., the land merged with the building) with a nil use for purposes of planning permission (*Petticoat Lane Rentals, Ltd.* v. *Secretary of State for the Environment* [1971] 1 W.L.R. 1112).   The position if the open land was not wholly built on was expressly reserved for future consideration.

It is stated that the following three uses *shall* be deemed to constitute development, namely :—

    (i) Use as two or more separate dwelling-houses (for instance, as flats) of any building previously used as a single dwelling-house (1971 Act, s. 22 (3) (*a*) ; see *Birmingham Corporation* v. *Habib Ullah* [1964] 1 Q.B. 178 ; also *Ealing Corporation* v. *Ryan* [1965] 2 Q.B. 486).   The result is that permission is necessary for conversion of a house into independent flats or maisonettes or for multiple occupation amounting to a material intensification of use.

(ii) Deposit of refuse on a site already used for the purpose if the area or height of deposit is extended (1971 Act, s. 22 (3) (*b*)). Thus continued deposit up to ground level in a quarry having vertical sides does not require permission. On the other hand, the Town and Country Planning General Development Order, 1973, Sched. 1, Class VIII, para. 2, permits deposits of refuse from an industrial process on a site used for such deposit on 1st July, 1948, *whether or not the area or height is extended.*

(iii) Display of advertisements on any external part of a building not normally used for that purpose (1971 Act, s. 22 (4) ; cf. *Mills and Rockleys* v. *Leicester City Council* [1946] K.B. 315). Generally the control of advertisements is by means of regulations made under s. 63 of the 1971 Act. Where an advertisement is displayed in accordance with the Town and Country Planning (Control of Advertisements) Regulations, 1969 and 1972, planning permission is deemed granted : s. 64 of the 1971 Act. As to the construction of these regulations, see *McDonald* v. *Howard Poole Advertising, Ltd.* [1972] 1 W.L.R. 90 and *Heron Service Stations, Ltd.* v. *Coupe* [1973] 2 All E.R. 110.

Section 22 (2) of the 1971 Act specifies three uses of land which do *not* constitute development, as follows :—

" The following . . . uses of land shall not be taken for the purposes of this Act to involve development of the land, that is to say :—

*   *   *   *   *

(*d*) the *use of* any buildings or other *land within the curtilage of a dwelling-house* for any purpose incidental to the enjoyment of the dwelling-house as such ;

(*e*) the *use of any land for the purposes of agriculture* [which as defined in s. 290 (1) includes horticulture, seed growing and other matters] or forestry (including afforestation), and the use for any of those purposes of any building occupied together with land so used ;

(*f*) in the case of buildings or other land which are used for a purpose of any class specified in [the Town and Country Planning (Use Classes) Order, 1972 ; see below] the use thereof for any other purpose of the same class."

" *curtilage.*"—In the Scottish case of *Sinclair-Lockhart's Trustees* v. *Central Land Board* [1951] S.L.T. 121, this word was stated to include " ground which is used for the comfortable enjoyment of a house or other building . . . although it has not been marked off or enclosed in any way ". See further, *Journal of Planning Law*, vol. 4, p. 14.

" *use of . . . land within the curtilage of a dwelling-house.*"—The word " use " in relation to land does not include the use of land for the carrying out of any building or other operations thereon (1971 Act, s. 290 (1)). Therefore *even though change of user is permitted, any necessary building work may require permission.* But in the case of buildings within the curtilage of a dwelling-house, see the exemptions from the necessity for obtaining permission contained in Class I of Sched. 1 to the Town and Country Planning General Development Order, 1973, at p. 1190.

" *use of any land for the purposes of agriculture.*"—Building work on agricultural or forest land may require permission, but see the exemptions contained in Class VI and VIII of Sched. 1 to the Town and Country Planning

38

General Development Order, 1973, at p. 1191. It is noteworthy that development does not occur on change of use to agricultural purposes however different the former use may have been.

Changes of use permitted by the Use Classes Order.—It has already been noted that buildings or other land used for a purpose of any class specified by an order made by the Minister may be used for any other purpose of the same class without the change amounting to development (1971 Act, s. 22 (2) (*f*)). The order now in force is the Town and Country Planning (Use Classes) Order, 1972. Before mentioning the main classes attention is drawn to the fact that the order does not necessarily mean that permission is needed for a change of user from one class to another. Even though it is from one class to another a change will require permission only if it is held to be a " material " change (1971 Act, s. 22 (2), *ante*, p. 1183 *et seq.*).

The order is lengthy and the following is a summary of its effect :—

(i) *Shops.*—Class I permits a shop of one kind (e.g., a grocer's) to be used as a shop of a different kind (e.g., a butcher's), *but not* as a hot food shop, a tripe shop, a shop for the sale of pet animals or birds, a cat's-meat shop or a shop for the sale of motor vehicles. Use of a shop for one of the special purposes, such as a fried-fish shop (i.e., hot food), would appear to be a material change for which permission would be necessary. On the other hand the change from one of these special purposes to that of an ordinary shop, such as a butcher's, can be carried out without consent under the Town and Country Planning General Development Order, 1973, Sched. 1, Class III (*post*, p. 1191). The 1972 Order definition of a shop is as follows :—

" ' shop ' means a building used for the carrying on of any retail trade or retail business wherein the primary purpose is the selling of goods by retail, and includes a building used for the purposes of a hairdresser, undertaker, travel agency, ticket agency or post office, or for the reception of goods to be washed, cleaned or repaired, *or for any other purpose appropriate to a shopping area*, but does not include a building used as a funfair, amusement arcade, pintable saloon, garage, launderette, petrol filling station, office, betting office, hotel, restaurant, snackbar or café or premises licensed for the sale of intoxicating liquors for consumption on the premises."

The definition does not include an ordinary public house in which the sale of intoxicating liquor predominates ; compare *Central Land Board* v. *Saxone Shoe Co., Ltd.* [1956] 1 Q.B. 288. See also *Marshall* v. *Nottingham Corporation* [1960] 1 W.L.R. 707, as to an office/hut constituting a shop.

(ii) *Offices.*—Class II relates to use as an office (including a bank, estate agency or building society or employment agency but not a post office or betting office) for any purpose. Thus a solicitor's office may be used as an accountant's office, or a bank, without permission.

(iii) *Industrial Buildings.*—Class III relates to use as a light industrial building for any purpose, and Class IV as a general industrial building for any purpose. " Industrial Building " means a building (not belonging to a quarry or mine and other than a shop) used for any process in making articles, altering, repairing, cleaning, packing or breaking up articles or the getting or treatment of minerals, being a process carried on in the course of trade or business other than agriculture. A light industrial building is one in which the processes or machinery are " such as could be carried on or installed in any residential area without detriment to the amenity of that area by reason of noise, vibration, smell, fumes, smoke, soot, ash, dust or grit." A general industrial building is one which is not within the definitions of light or special industrial buildings. Change from a general to a light industrial building without permission is authorised by the Town and Country Planning General Development Order, 1973, Sched. 1, Class III, *post*, p. 1191.

Special industrial buildings fall into five groups, Classes V–IX, which should be referred to as recast by the 1972 Order. It should be noted that there is no exemption from the necessity for obtaining planning permission for a change from one group to another.

(iv) *Other uses*.—Each of the remaining classes is narrow in content ; examples are wholesale warehouses (Class X) ; boarding houses and hotels (Class XI) ; certain hospitals and institutions (Class XIV) ; theatres, cinemas and concert halls (Class XVII); and dance halls or buildings for indoor sports and games (Class XVIII).

It should not be overlooked that even if permission is not necessary for a change of user that change may involve building or other works for which permission may be needed. Further, even if a change is apparently permitted by the Use Classes Order, it may involve the breach of a condition contained in a planning permission previously granted and so it may be necessary to inquire as to the terms of any such permission.

Application to determine whether permission required.—The complications of the Act and Orders are such that it is often most difficult to be certain whether permission is required. There is a very useful provision in s. 53 (1) of the 1971 Act which enables any person who proposes to carry out any operation on land or to make any change in the use of land to apply to the district planning authority to determine " whether the carrying out of those operations, or the making of that change, would constitute or involve development of the land, and, if so, whether an application for planning permission in respect thereof is required," and the application may (but need not) form part of an application for permission. There is a right of appeal to the Secretary of State in the same manner as in the case of an application for planning permission (1971 Act, ss. 53 (2), 36). The decision of the Secretary is final except that there is a right of appeal on a point of law from the decision of the Secretary to the High Court (*ibid.*, s. 247). The form of applications and of determinations under this section is laid down by the Town and Country Planning General Development Order, 1973 (see arts. 6 (2), 7).

The answer of an official to the effect that there is a valid existing use and planning permission need not be applied for, it has been held, does not estop the authority from challenging the use by an enforcement notice (*Southend-on-Sea Corporation* v. *Hodgson* (*Wickford*), *Ltd.* [1962] 1 Q.B. 416) and so formal procedure for determination of the issue should be used in cases of doubt.

However, against this, it has also been held that a local planning authority may make a determination under the predecessor of s. 53 even though no formal application for such determination has been made to them, for example when application is made for permission to carry out works which they do not consider to amount to development or they consider is " permitted " development under a development order (*Wells* v. *Minister of Housing* [1967] 1 W.L.R. 1000, where the " determination " was by letter only and in which the *Southend-on-Sea* case was not apparently cited ; see further the discussion in *Solicitor's Journal*, vol. 112, p. 304).

The *Wells* case was followed, whilst the *Southend-on-Sea* case was to be " taken with considerable reserve," by the Court of Appeal in *Lever* (*Finance*), *Ltd.* v. *Westminster Corporation* [1971] 1 Q.B. 222. In this case a planning officer by telephone erroneously informed a developer's architect that a variation to the detailed plan already submitted was not material and that no further permission was required. This was held to constitute a valid planning permission for the variation as a matter of agency : the planning officer had made a representation within the ostensible (or implied) authority which he had by virtue of s. 64 of the Town and Country Planning Act, 1968 (see now s. 4 of the 1971 Act, *post*, p. 1194). See further *Law Society's Gazette*, vol. 67, p. 673 and [1971] J.P.L. 143. The *Lever* case has since been applied by the Court of Appeal (in *R.* v. *Liverpool Corporation* [1972] 2 W.L.R. 1262) but distinguished by a Divisional Court (*Bedfordshire C.C.* v. *Secretary of State for the Environment* (1972), 71 L.G.R. 420). Reference should also be made here to the decision that planning permission is of no effect until it is put into writing (*R.* v. *Yeovil B.C.* (1971), 23 P. & C.R. 39, D.C. ; see further Professor J. F. Garner at [1972] J.P.L. 194). See also *Norfolk C.C.* v. *Secretary of State for the Environment* [1973] 3 All E.R. 673, where a planning officer by mistake had sent notice of permission instead of notice of refusal of permission and this was held to be outside his authority and not to estop the planning authority.

Procedure under s. 53 (1) did not enable the Minister to determine whether a grant of planning permission is valid ; to ascertain that before development is carried out application must be made to the High Court for a declaration (*Edgwarebury Park* v. *Minister of Housing* [1963] 2 Q.B. 408).

Established use certificate.—In view of the abolition in 1968 of the general rule that development by way of a change of use cannot be challenged after four years it may be difficult years later to prove that a certain use has become established. Accordingly as from 1st April, 1969, i.e., the date on which the provisions of the 1968 Act came into operation in relation to enforcement notices a person interested in land can apply to the district planning authority for what is known as an " established use certificate." No such application may be made in respect of the use of land as a single dwelling-house or of any use not subsisting at the time of the application (Town and Country Planning Act, 1971, s. 94 (1), (2)). No application may be made in the former case (change to a single dwelling-house) because the four year rule still applies to it. But it has been pointed out that an application for a certificate is similarly excluded where there has been a change in the occupation of a single dwelling-house, which change constitutes a breach of the condition of a planning permission (e.g., limiting the class of occupier to agricultural workers) although the four year rule does not apply to such a case (see an article by David Woolley at [1971] J.P.L. 257). A use of land is established if (a) it was begun before 1964 without planning permission and has continued since the end of 1963 (i.e., continuously throughout in breach of planning control : *Bolivian and General Tin Trust, Ltd.* v. *Secretary of State for the Environment* [1972] 1 W.L.R. 1481, where a temporary planning permission precluded a certificate) ; or (b) it was begun before 1964 under a permission granted subject to conditions or limitations which either have never been complied with or have not been complied with since the end of 1963 ; or (c) it was begun after the end of 1963 as the result of a change of use not requiring planning permission and there has been, since the end of 1963, no change of use requiring planning permission (*ibid.*). The procedure as to applications and appeals, and forms, is specified in the 1971 Act, Sched. 14 and the Town and Country Planning General Development Order, 1973, art. 18, Sched. 9.

On application the local planning authority must, if they are satisfied that the claim is made out, grant a certificate. Unless within a prescribed period, or any extended period agreed in writing, the authority give notice of their decision, the application is deemed to be refused (*ibid.*, s. 94 (5)). The certificate is conclusive for the purposes of an appeal to the Secretary of State against an enforcement notice served after the date of the application (*ibid.*, s. 94 (7)). The Secretary of State may require applications for such certificates to be referred to him and on refusal by a local planning authority there is a right of appeal to him (*ibid.*, s. 95).

An intending purchaser who is doubtful as to whether a use had been established might well consider requiring a vendor to apply for such a certificate and there seems to be no objection to an owner of land applying to record a change of use made by a predecessor in title. An application for an established use certificate will be recorded in the register of planning applications (1971 Act, Sched. 14, para. 6).

B. DEVELOPMENT FOR WHICH EXPRESS PERMISSION IS NOT NECESSARY

Development for which permission unnecessary.—So far we have considered various changes of use which do not constitute development ; it is now necessary to note certain cases in which the 1971 Act, s. 23, provides that planning permission need not be obtained even if development is involved. These cases are as follows :—

(a) in the case of land which, on 1st July, 1948, was being used temporarily for a purpose other than the purpose for which it was normally used, in respect of the resumption of the use of the land for the last-mentioned purpose ;

(b) in the case of land which, on 1st July, 1948, was normally used for one purpose and was also used on occasions, whether at regular intervals or not, for any other purpose, in respect of the use of the land for that other purpose on similar occasions ;

(c) in the case of land which on 1st July, 1948, was unoccupied but had been occupied on or after 7th January, 1937, in respect of the use of the land for the purpose for which it was last used.

Cases (a) and (c) do not operate unless resumption of the relevant user has taken place before 6th December, 1968 ; similarly case (b) will operate only if the occasional use has been made on at least one occasion between 1st July, 1948, and the end of 1968.

In determining for the purposes of paragraph (a) the purposes for which land was normally used and for the purposes of paragraph (c) the purposes for which land was last used, *no account is to be taken of any use of the land begun in contravention of Pt. III of the 1947 Act* and such last use must be a lawful one (*Glamorgan County Council* v. *Carter* [1963] 1 W.L.R. 1). Paragraphs (a) and (c) do not provide exemption from the need for planning permission for a caravan site unless the land was so used on one occasion at least during the period of two years ending 9th March, 1960.

Case (a) might apply, for instance, to land used temporarily on 1st July, 1948, for storage of building materials ; case (b) to agricultural land used once a year for a show.

The date 6th December, 1968, is relevant on account of the abolition by the 1968 Act of the " four year " rule regarding service of enforcement notices in respect of changes of use ; see p. 1202.

" *unoccupied on the seventh day of January nineteen hundred and thirty-seven.*" —The then Minister of Town and Country Planning stated that he was not able to accept the view that permission is *necessarily* required to resume a use merely because the premises have been unoccupied since 7th January, 1937. In his view the requirement would only arise if it were shown that the last use had been abandoned. See further, *Journal of Planning Law*, vol. 3, pp. 799, 843, 844.

Development for which permission granted by the Development Order.—The Town and Country Planning Act, 1971, s. 24 (1), requires the Secretary of State for the Environment by development order to provide for the granting of planning permission. The general order now in force is the Town and Country Planning General Development Order, 1973 (as amended). Further, certain *special* development orders have been made applying to limited areas, such as new towns or specified areas of natural beauty.

It must be noted that the Act does *not* state that the changes specified in these orders shall not be " development," nor does it state that planning permission need not be obtained. The effect of the orders is to *grant permission* for certain development *without application being made* to the local planning authority or the Secretary of State for the Environment (General Development Order, 1973, art. 3 (1)).

There are two important limitations to the effect of the 1973 General Development Order. First, it does not, with slight exceptions, authorise any development involving the formation, laying out or material widening of means of access to a trunk or classified road, or authorise any development which would obstruct the view of persons using roads in a way likely to cause danger (Town and Country Planning General Development Order, 1973, art. 3 (3)). Secondly, the Secretary of State for the Environment, or the local planning authority with in some cases his approval, may direct that application must be made for permission for any specified class of development in any particular area, or for any particular development (*ibid.*, art. 4 ; *Cole* v. *Somerset County Council* [1957] 1 Q.B. 23). The forms of inquiry approved by The Law Society to accompany searches in local land charges registers ask whether any such direction is in force which may affect the property.

It is impossible in the space available to set out in full the various classes of permitted development in Sched. I to the General Development Order, but the following are the most likely to arise in practice :—

Class I.—First, the enlargement, improvement or other alteration of a dwelling-house so long as the cubic content of the original dwelling-house is not exceeded by more than 50 cubic metres or one-tenth, whichever is the greater, subject to a maximum of 115 cubic metres (and provided height and forward projection are not increased). The erection of a garage or stable within the curtilage is treated as an enlargement for this purpose. Permission is now additionally granted for the construction of an outside porch, up to 3 metres high, 2 square metres floor area, and at least 2 metres away from highways. Secondly, the erection or alteration, *within the curtilage of a dwelling-house*, of a building, *other than a dwelling or garage*, incidental to the enjoyment of the dwelling-house including the erection of sheds for poultry or pet animals (subject to limitations as to projection forward, height and area). An addition to a building permitted within this Class becomes part of the original building, and takes on its characteristics in all respects including particularly its use (*Wood* v. *Secretary of State for the Environment* [1973] 2 All E.R. 404).

Class II.—The erection of gates, fences, and walls not exceeding 1 metre in height when abutting on a highway used by vehicular traffic or 2 metres in height in any other case. Also now permitted is the laying out and constructing of means of access to a highway *not* being a trunk or classified road. Painting the exterior of a building otherwise than as an advertisement is also allowed.

Class III.—Change of use from a general to a light industrial building or from a hot food shop, tripe shop, shop for the sale of pet animals, cat's meat shop, or shop for the sale of motor vehicles, to any other type of shop. Compare the definitions and discussion, *ante*, p. 1186.

Class IV.—(i) The erection of buildings, works, plant and machinery required temporarily for the purpose of operations (other than mining operations) for which planning permission has been granted or is deemed to have been granted or is not required ; (ii) use of land (other than a building or the site of a building demolished in consequence of war damage) for any purpose, except as a caravan site, for not more than twenty-eight days in any calendar year in total for all such purposes.

Class V.—Use of land other than buildings by members of a recreational organisation which holds a certificate of exemption under the Public Health Act, 1936, s. 269.

Class VI.—The carrying out on agricultural land having an area of more than one acre and comprised in an agricultural unit of building or engineering operations requisite for the use of that land for the purposes of agriculture, other than the placing on land of structures not designed for those purposes or the provision and alteration of dwellings. The ground area must not exceed 465 square metres including the area of buildings erected in the preceding two years within 90 metres, and there are restrictions as to height and near trunk or classified roads. Nevertheless, much building work for agricultural purposes on a farm, other than the erection of a house, can be carried out without applying for permission. In certain areas of special beauty (including the Lake District and parts of the Counties of Caernarvon, Merioneth and Derby) building works may not be carried out pursuant to this authority unless fourteen days' notice has been given to the local planning authority, who may require the applicant to obtain their approval to the design and external appearance of the building (Town and Country Planning (Landscape Areas Special Development) Order, 1950). There is also a limited permission for the working of minerals for agricultural purposes.

Class VIII.—Development on land used for an industrial process by (i) provision of private ways or railways, pipes and cables, or (ii) addition or replacement of plant or machinery or limited extension of buildings not substantially affecting the external appearance of the premises.

C. APPLICATION FOR PLANNING PERMISSION

Authority to which application should be made.—Where it is intended
to carry out works or make a change of user which will amount to development as previously defined, and that development is not authorised by the
General Development Order or a special development order, *ante*, p. 1190,
it is necessary to make application to the appropriate planning authority.
The application must be lodged, in effect, (i) if the land is in the City of
London, with the Common Council ; (ii) if the land is elsewhere in London,
with the council of the London borough ; (iii) if the land is elsewhere, with
the district planning authority (1971 Act, s. 5 and Sched. 3 ; Local
Government Act, 1972, Sched. 16, para. 15).

Form of application.—Application for planning permission must be made
on a form issued by the planning authority and must include the particulars
required by the form and be accompanied by the plans and drawings
necessary to identify the land and describe the development, together with
such additional number of copies (not exceeding three) of the forms, plans
and drawings as are required by the directions printed on the form (Town
and Country Planning General Development Order, 1973, art. 5 (1)). The
planning authority may require such further information as may be requisite
to enable them to determine the matter or such evidence as they may
reasonably call for to verify any information given to them (*ibid.*, art. 5 (1)
and (4)).

If it is not desired to make a detailed application until it is known that
proposals for the erection of buildings are at least acceptable in principle,
an " outline " application may be made (*ibid.*, art. 5 (2)). Such an application
is for permission for the erection of the buildings subject to the subsequent
approval of the authority with respect to any matters relating to the siting,
design or external appearance of the buildings, or the means of access thereto,
or landscaping. If permission is granted, it is expressed to be granted on an
outline application and the approval of the authority with respect to the
matters reserved in the permission is required before any development is
commenced. An application for subsequent approval in respect of matters
reserved must include the particulars, and be accompanied by the plans and
drawings, necessary to deal with the matters reserved (Town and Country
Planning General Development Order, 1973, art. 6 (1)). Such an application
is not itself a planning application requiring submission of a certificate under
s. 27 of the 1971 Act, below (*R.* v. *Bradford-on-Avon U.D.C.* [1964] 1 W.L.R.
1136). Where a planning authority reserve matters when considering an
outline application they cannot refuse final permission on other grounds
which they could have taken into account on the outline application.
Consequently, if they purport to refuse permission on the final detailed
application, notwithstanding that they approve it so far as it concerns the
matters previously reserved, they will be considered to have granted approval
(*Hamilton* v. *West Sussex County Council* [1958] 2 Q.B. 286). Time limits on
grants of permission pursuant to outline applications are dealt with *post*,
p. 1201.

Notices of applications.—Applications for permission to carry out certain
classes of development likely to cause disturbance to neighbours cannot be
entertained unless accompanied by a copy of a notice of the application
certified by or on behalf of the applicant as having been published in a named

newspaper circulating in the neighbourhood. Further an applicant for permission for one of the classes of development considered likely to cause disturbance will have to certify either :—

(a) that he has posted on the land a notice of the application for permission for at least seven days, or

(b) that he has been unable to do so (Town and Country Planning Act, 1971, s. 26).

Forms for certificates and site notices are prescribed by the Town and Country Planning General Development Order, 1973, Sched. 3. These disturbing classes of development include construction of buildings to a height exceeding 20 metres and construction of, or use of land for, public conveniences, disposal of refuse or waste material, slaughterhouses, fun fairs, bingo halls, theatres, cinemas and dance halls (Town and Country Planning General Development Order, 1973, art. 8 (1), list the designated purposes).

No application for planning permission may now be entertained unless accompanied by one or other of the following certificates :—

(a) that the applicant is the estate owner in respect of the fee simple or is entitled to a tenancy ;

(b) that the applicant has given the requisite notice to the owners ;

(c) that the applicant is unable to issue either of the foregoing certificates but he has given the requisite notice to specified owners and that he has taken reasonable steps (which are specified) to ascertain the names and addresses of the remainder but he has been unable to do so ;

(d) that the applicant is unable to issue a certificate in accordance with (a), that he has taken reasonable steps (which are specified) to ascertain the names and addresses of owners, and he does not know the names and addresses of any of the owners.

Every certificate must state either (i) that none of the land constitutes or forms part of an agricultural holding, or (ii) that notice has been given to a tenant of an agricultural holding. For these purposes " owner " means the estate owner in respect of the fee simple or a tenant for a term of which not less than ten years remain unexpired (Town and Country Planning Act, 1971, s. 27 ; Town and Country Planning General Development Order, 1973, art. 9). The authority have jurisdiction if the application is accompanied by a genuine certificate signed by the actual applicant even though it contains a factual error on an important point such as ownership (*R.* v. *Bradford-on-Avon U.D.C.* [1964] 1 W.L.R. 1136).

Where the application (i) is for development which would affect the character or appearance of a conservation area, or (ii) is of a kind specified by the Secretary of State and in respect of land in or adjacent to a conservation area the local planning authority must advertise the application and display on or near the land a notice of the application (1971 Act, s. 28).

Persons who may apply for planning permission.—The Town and Country Planning Act, 1971, s. 23 (1), provides that planning permission is required for the carrying out of any development of land (subject to the various exceptions mentioned earlier), and the Act does not specify the person by whom the application must be made. In *Hanily* v. *Minister of Local Government and Planning* [1952] 2 Q.B. 444 it was decided that anyone who genuinely hopes to acquire an interest in land may apply for planning permission. At the time of that decision it was not necessary even to give notice to the owner of the land but subsequent legislation (*ante,* p. 1192)

38A

has made certain provisions as to this. It is normally advisable that an
option or a provisional contract should be obtained before applying for
planning permission, because the only persons who are entitled to appeal to
the Secretary of State for the Environment against an adverse decision are
those who are " aggrieved " by the decision (1971 Act, s. 36 (1)), and it is
difficult to see how a person who has no interest in the land can be aggrieved.
Probably a person whose only interest is that he may be concerned as a
contractor in building may not make a valid application (*Ayles* v. *Romsey
and Stockbridge R.D.C.* (1944), 88 Sol. J. 135, decided on an earlier Act).
These rules clearly require to be better defined by the courts.

Any grant of planning permission " shall (except in so far as the permission
otherwise provides) enure for the benefit of the land and of all persons for the
time being interested therein " (1971 Act, s. 33 (1)) ; but this is without
prejudice to the rules as to duration of permissions and as to the powers of
revocation and modification of permission, or to time limits attached, as to
which, see p. 1199 and p. 1201.

Determination of applications.—The local planning authority must give
notice to the applicant of their decision, or of the reference of the application
to the Secretary of State for the Environment, within a period of two months,
unless the applicant agrees in writing to an extended period (Town and
Country Planning General Development Order, 1973, art. 7 (3)). There is
a very important provision that where the local planning authority decide
to grant permission subject to conditions or to refuse permission *they must
state their reasons in writing* (*ibid.*, art. 7 (4)) ; this rule is of great assistance
in deciding whether an appeal is likely to be successful. Failure to give a
reason does not render a condition void (*Brayhead (Ascot), Ltd.* v. *Berkshire
County Council* [1964] 2 Q.B. 303). If the applicant is not notified of the
decision, or that the application has been referred to the Secretary, within the
prescribed period, the applicant has the right to appeal to the Secretary as
if permission had been refused and notification of the decision received by the
applicant at the end of the prescribed period, as extended if that was done
(1971) Act, s. 37).

A grant of planning permission is effective if acted upon by the applicant
even if it was given after the expiration of the period specified in the General
Development Order (*James* v. *Secretary of State for Wales* [1968] A.C. 409).

It has been held that the resolution of a planning committee of a local
planning authority is not a grant of planning permission : permission is not
granted until a notice in writing has been issued (*Re R.* v. *Yeovil B.C.* (1971),
23 P. & C.R. 39, D.C. ; see further Professor J. F. Garner at [1972] J.P.L. 194).

The local planning authority may delegate to one of its officers the right
to determine applications for planning permission and certain other applications (Town and Country Planning Act, 1971, s. 4). The determination will
then be treated as that of the authority, for all purposes, *provided* it is notified
to the applicant in writing (*ibid.*, subs. (5) ; but cf. *Lever (Finance), Ltd.* v.
Westminster Corporation [1971] 1 Q.B. 222, in which a telephone representation
sufficed).

In dealing with applications for planning permission, a local planning
authority " shall have regard to the provisions of the development plan,
so far as material to the application, and to any other material considerations "
(s. 29 (1) of the 1971 Act).

As to the " material considerations " to which a planning authority must
have regard in determining a planning application (i.e., under s. 29 (1) of the

1971 Act), reference may be made to *Stringer* v. *Minister of Housing and Local Government* [1970] 1 W.L.R. 1281, where it was held that although these must be of a planning nature, they are not limited to amenity matters (Jodrell Bank radio telescope prevailed over the erection of local dwellings). See also *H. Lavender & Son, Ltd.* v. *Minister of Housing and Local Government* [1970] 1 W.L.R. 1231 (where regard had been paid not to planning considerations but to the objections of the Minister of Agriculture, etc.) and *J. Murphy & Sons, Ltd.* v. *Secretary of State for the Environment* [1973] 2 All E.R. 26 (cost of developing a site, and the wisdom of a commercial venture generally, are not material considerations).

In *Westminster Bank, Ltd.* v. *Minister of Housing and Local Government* [1971] A.C. 508, H.L., planning permission for building had been refused by the Minister on appeal so that a scheme for road widening was not prejudiced. No improvement line or building line had been prescribed under s. 72 or 73 of the Highways Act, 1959 (under which compensation would have been payable). Although the consequence of the refusal was to avoid payment of compensation the decision was upheld by the House of Lords. This authority settled a practical point on which previously there was doubt and applies to many properties which lie on streets in town centres.

The Town and Country Planning Act, 1971, s. 29 (1), states that the local planning authority may grant permission " either unconditionally or subject to such conditions as they think fit ". Nevertheless, in the words of Lord Denning in *Pyx Granite Co., Ltd.* v. *Ministry of Housing and Local Government* [1958] 1 Q.B. 554, the conditions, to be valid, " must fairly and reasonably relate to the permitted development. The planning authority are not at liberty to use their powers for an ulterior object, however desirable that object may seem to them to be in the public interest." The conditions must be imposed having regard to the authority's statutory duties and to local planning considerations. Further, they must be capable of being given a sensible and ascertainable meaning, otherwise they will be void for uncertainty. Nevertheless, a condition may prescribe permitted classes of occupants if it is, in the circumstances, intelligibly and sensibly related to planning considerations and proposals for the area. Thus, a condition imposed on a permission granted for the building of cottages that the occupation of them should be limited to persons whose employment was in agriculture, or in forestry or in an industry mainly dependent on agriculture, or to the dependants of such persons, was held to be valid in *Fawcett Properties, Ltd.* v. *Buckingham County Council* [1961] A.C. 636. Although the condition was not clearly expressed, it was not void for uncertainty. As to time limits on permissions, see *post*, p. 1201.

Conditions may regulate the development or use of land under the control of the applicant even though the application does not concern that land (*ibid.*, s. 30 (1) (*a*)). A very common condition is one requiring the removal of a building or the discontinuance of a use authorised by the permission at the end of a specified period ; this amounts to a " planning permission granted for a limited period " (*ibid.*, s. 30 (2)). As to registers of planning determinations, see *ante*, p. 7, and as to registration of *conditional* planning permissions as local land charges, see *ante*, p. 629.

Conditions may be invalid because they are *ultra vires*. Broadly, the test is whether the condition fairly and reasonably relates to a planning consideration (*Fawcett Properties, Ltd.* v. *Buckingham County Council*, *ante*) although it will nevertheless be invalid if it is so unreasonable that Parliament cannot have intended it should have been imposed (*Hall & Co., Ltd.* v. *Shoreham-by-Sea U.D.C.* [1964] 1 W.L.R. 240, where a condition requiring provision of a service road was held *ultra vires*).

It has been indicated in the House of Lords (see particularly *per* Lord Guest) that if a condition of the grant of planning permission is invalid, then it cannot be severed off and the permission itself will also be void (*Kent County Council* v. *Kingsway Investments (Kent), Ltd.* [1971] A.C. 72; noted *post*, p. 1201). See further an article by D. R. P. Mole at [1970] J.P.L. 306. See also " Planning Conditions and Existing Rights " by J. E. Alder, *Conveyancer N.S.*, vol. 36, p. 421.

The power to grant permission to develop land includes power to grant permission for the retention of buildings or works constructed or carried out or for continuance of any use instituted before the application (*ibid.*, s. 32). Application may be made under this provision where the necessity for planning permission has been overlooked.

A permission granted by a local planning authority for the purposes of another Act, for instance, the Public Health Act, 1936, s. 269, will not amount to a planning permission (*Higham* v. *Havant and Waterloo U.D.C.* [1951] 1 K.B. 509, affirmed [1951] 2 K.B. 527).

Construction of permission.—As the benefit of a permission runs with the land it is important to bear in mind that the reasons in it may be considered in construing it but that the effect of the permission cannot normally be restricted by reference to the terms of the application (*Miller-Mead* v. *Minister of Housing* [1963] 2 Q.B. 196). On the other hand, if the permission specifically incorporates the terms of the application reference may be made to it in order correctly to construe the permission (*Wilson* v. *West Sussex County Council* [1963] 2 Q.B. 764).

The House of Lords has held that in construing a public document, such as a planning permission, the court should not admit evidence of facts known to the maker of the document, but which were not common knowledge, to alter or qualify the apparent meaning of the words in the document (*Slough Estates, Ltd.* v. *Slough Borough Council (No. 2)* [1971] A.C. 958). It was found unnecessary for the House of Lords to consider whether the planning permission in this case had been abandoned by inconsistent acts (as the Court of Appeal had held : [1969] 2 Ch. 305) or, indeed, whether a planning permission could be abandoned.

Where permission for construction of a building does not specify the purpose for which it may be used then it may be used " for the purpose for which it is designed " (Town and Country Planning Act, 1971, s. 33 (2)). The word " designed " is not here used in a technical sense. Thus permission for an agricultural cottage " limits the intended building to one intended for an agricultural worker. It specifies the purpose but even if it did not the operation of [s. 33 (2)] would limit the use to occupation by someone engaged in agriculture " (*Wilson* v. *West Sussex County Council, ante*).

Appeals to the Secretary of State.—A person who desires to appeal against a decision refusing permission or granting permission subject to conditions, or on the failure of the authority to give notice of their decision within the prescribed period, must give notice of appeal to the Secretary within six months of receipt of the notice of the decision or of the expiry of the appropriate period specified in art. 7 (3), above, or such longer period as the Secretary may allow (1971 Act, s. 36 ; Town and Country Planning

General Development Order, 1973, art. 16). There are prescribed forms (obtainable from the Secretary) in which such appeal must be made (see (Sched. 4, Pt. III, to the 1973 Order).

The Town and Country Planning Act, 1971, provides that certain appeals may be decided by an inspector and not the Secretary of State himself (*ibid.*, Sched. 9 ; Determination of Appeals by Appointed Persons (Prescribed Classes) Regulations, 1970).

Obligation to purchase on refusal or conditional grant of permission.— Although this obligation arises only in limited circumstances, it is one which is often useful to a landowner. Where permission to develop any land is refused, or granted subject to conditions, whether by the local planning authority or by the Secretary of State, then in certain cases the *owner* of the land may require the council of the county district in which the land is situated to purchase his interest in the land (Town and Country Planning Act, 1971, s. 180). The " owner " is the person entitled to receive the rack rent, and so a freeholder who let the land at a rent less than its value at the time of letting is not able to use this procedure (1971 Act, s. 290 (1) ; *London Corporation* v. *Cusack-Smith* [1955] A.C. 337). This right arises where it can be shown (*a*) that the land has become *incapable of reasonably beneficial use in its existing state ;* (*b*) (if permission was conditional) that the land cannot be rendered capable of such use by development in accordance with those conditions, and (*c*) that the land cannot be rendered capable of reasonably beneficial use by development for which permission has been granted or for which the local planning authority or the Minister has undertaken to grant permission (*ibid.*, s. 180 (1)). In considering what is or would be a reasonably beneficial use of land no account is taken of any prospective use of that land which " would involve the carrying out of new development " or which would contravene the conditions in Sched. 18 to the Act (*ibid.*, s. 180 (2)). The substantial result of this complex wording is that one must disregard the possibility of development other than such as falls within the limited classes in Sched. 8 and even the assumption of permission within these classes is not made if Sched. 18 would be contravened (e.g., by excessive increase of floor space on rebuilding).

Land is not " incapable of reasonably beneficial use " merely because it is of less use in its present state than it would be if developed (*R.* v. *Minister of Housing and Local Government, ex parte Chichester R.D.C.* [1960] 1 W.L.R. 587).

Notice must be served on the council within twelve months from the date of the decision on the planning application or such longer period as the Secretary of State may permit (Town and Country Planning General Regulations, 1969, reg. 19 (2)). Local authorities have been requested to make available model forms of notice. The council on whom notice is served may state that they or another local authority agree to comply (1971 Act, s. 181 (1)). Alternatively, they may serve notice that they are unwilling and refer the matter to the Secretary of State. If the Secretary of State is satisfied that the above-mentioned conditions exist, he must confirm the notice (1971 Act, s. 183 (1)).

The Town and Country Planning Act, 1971, s. 184, provides a ground on which the Secretary of State may refuse to confirm a purchase notice. This occurs where, prior to the refusal or conditional grant of planning permission on which the purchase notice is based, there had been an earlier planning permission to develop the land with " a restricted use ". Land is treated as having a restricted use if it is part of a larger area in respect of which planning permission was previously granted and either (*a*) it is a condition of that permission that the part shall remain undeveloped or be preserved or laid out in a particular way as amenity land in relation to the remainder, or (*b*) the permission was granted on an application which contemplated (expressly or by necessary implication) that the parts should not be comprised in the development for which the planning permission was sought, or should be preserved or laid out in such particular way. Even though the Secretary of State is satisfied that the land has become incapable of reasonably beneficial use he may refuse to confirm the notice if it appears to him that the land ought, in accordance with the previous planning permission, to remain undeveloped or remain as amenity land in relation to the remainder of the larger area. The primary purpose of this rule is to deal with cases where a planning permission has been granted on condition that a part of the land shall be kept as public open space. It is considered to be unfair that at a later date the owner should be able to apply for planning permission and, on refusal, insist on the local authority purchasing. It has been held that for this rule to apply the *whole* of the land within the purchase notice must have a restricted use, not just part of it (*Plymouth Corporation* v. *Secretary of State for the Environment* [1972] 1 W.L.R. 1347).

If an authority agrees to comply with a notice or the Secretary of State has confirmed it the council are deemed to be authorised to purchase the interest compulsorily and to have served a notice to treat in respect thereof (*ibid.*, s. 186 (1)). The Secretary of State may, instead of confirming the purchase notice (i) grant permission for development, or amend the conditions so far as necessary to enable the land to be rendered capable of reasonably beneficial use, or (ii) direct that, in the event of an application being made, permission shall be granted for development which would render the land capable of reasonably beneficial use within a reasonable time, or (iii) confirm the notice but substitute any other local authority for the council on which the notice is served (*ibid.*, s. 183 (2), (3), (4)). The compensation payable is, in general, that payable on compulsory acquisition. Where the Secretary of State exercises his power under head (ii) above compensation is the amount (if any) by which the value of the land if the only development permitted is that mentioned in the Secretary of State's direction falls short of the value if the only development permitted is of the limited types specified in Sched. 8 (*ibid.*, s. 187 (2)).

Purchase of land affected by planning blight.—Broadly, the procedure is available only to owner-occupiers of houses, agricultural units and business premises of limited rateable value which are unsaleable by reason of well-defined planning proposals and is intended merely to avoid substantial hardship. It is worth noting that even where the case is not precisely within the limits defined the Secretary of State may press an authority to acquire in advance of requirements if that is necessary to avoid hardship (see Ministry Circular No. 46/70, para. 6). The procedure has effect in relation to land which comes within any of ten precise paragraphs set out in s. 192 (1) of the Town and Country Planning Act, 1971 (as extended by the Land Compensation Act, 1973, Part V, ss. 68–83). These paragraphs, which are too detailed for examination here, include land indicated in a structure plan or allocated by a local plan for functions of a government department, local authority or statutory undertakers ; land indicated in a development plan or certain orders or sections or by resolution of a highway authority for a highway ; land to be acquired under housing powers as a general improvement area ; land subject to a compulsory purchase order under which a notice to treat has not yet been served (1971 Act, ss. 192 to 208).

It has been observed that the basic feature of all the paragraphs is the known tentative prospective compulsory purchase and that it is this alone which causes blight leading to " compulsory purchase in reverse " (see Heap, Planning Law, 6th ed., at p. 244). The result where land comes within one of the paragraphs is that a person holding an interest therein which " qualifies for protection " and who has made reasonable endeavours to sell that interest but has been unable to do so except at a price substantially lower than that for which it might reasonably have been expected to sell if no part were comprised in land of any of the " specified descriptions " may then require the appropriate authority to purchase his interest (Town and Country Planning Act, 1971, s. 193). An interest qualifies for protection if either (a) the annual value of the hereditament does not exceed £2,250 and it is the interest of an owner-occupier of six months' standing ; or (b) it is the interest of a *resident* owner-occupier of six months' standing ; or (c) it is the interest of an owner-occupier of an agricultural unit (*ibid.*, ss. 192 (4), (5), 203). Also provision is made for mortgagees to take advantage of the blight notice procedure (s. 201 of the 1971 Act).

The claimant must serve on the appropriate authority (that is, the authority who propose eventually to acquire) a notice in the form prescribed in the Town and Country Planning General Regulations, 1969, and the authority may, in turn, serve a counter-notice objecting on certain grounds (*ibid.*, s. 194). If they do so the dispute may be determined by the Lands Tribunal (*ibid.*, s. 195).

If no counter-notice is served, or it is withdrawn, or not upheld by the Lands Tribunal, the appropriate authority are deemed to be authorised to acquire compulsorily and to have served a notice to treat (*ibid.*, s. 196). As compensation is now normally based on market value, this procedure may be advantageous to a person whose land is adversely affected by threatened (but not immediate) action by a public authority.

D. EXTENT AND EFFECT OF PERMISSION

Revocation or modification of planning permission.—The local planning authority (normally the district planning authority) have power by order, confirmed by the Secretary of State (unless unopposed), to revoke or modify any planning permission to such extent as they consider expedient (1971 Act, ss. 45, 46), but only (i) if it relates to the carrying out of building or other operations, at any time before those operations have been *completed* ; (ii) if it relates to a change of user, at any time before the change has taken place ; and revocation or modification does not affect so much of such operations as have been previously carried out (*ibid.*, s. 45 (4)). On submitting an order for confirmation the authority must serve notice on the owner and occupier of the land affected and on any other person who will be affected by the order, and any person on whom it is served may require the Secretary of State to afford to him an opportunity of being heard by a person appointed by the Secretary of State (*ibid.*, s. 45 (3)).

A right to compensation exists where permission is so revoked or modified. A claim may be delivered to the authority within six months from the date of the order or such later period as the Secretary of State may permit (Town and Country Planning General Regulations, 1969, reg. 19). Compensation is payable to any person interested in the land in respect of (i) expenditure incurred in carrying out " work which is rendered abortive by the revocation or modification," or (ii) loss or damage sustained otherwise " which is directly attributable to the revocation or modification " (1971 Act, s. 164 (1)).

Where compensation is payable *in respect of depreciation* in value of an interest in land exceeding £20 the local authority must, if practicable, apportion it between different parts of the land to which the claim relates (1971 Act, s. 166 (1)) ; there is an appeal to the Lands Tribunal in respect of the apportionment (*ibid.*, s. 166 (3), (4)).   Particulars of such compensation are then entered in the local land charges register (*ibid.*, ss. 166 (5), 112 (5)).   The purpose of such registration is to give notice to a subsequent purchaser.

Expenditure in the preparation of plans and similar matters preparatory to work is deemed to be incurred in carrying out the work, but otherwise no compensation is payable in respect of work carried out before the grant of the permission which is revoked or modified (1971 Act, s. 164 (2), (3)). It was decided in *Holmes* v. *Bradfield R.D.C.* [1949] 2 K.B. 1, on similar words in an earlier statute, that expenditure incurred in preparation of plans might be recovered although no work for the purposes of which the plans were prepared was begun before revocation of the planning permission.

The provisions (*ante*, p. 1197) which enable a landowner to compel the local authority to purchase his interest if it has become incapable of reasonably beneficial use, are made applicable if revocation or modification of permission has a similar effect (*ibid.*, s. 188).

Power to require discontinuance of an authorised use.—If it appears to a local planning authority that it is expedient in the interests of the proper planning in their area " (*a*) that any use of land should be discontinued, or that any conditions should be imposed on the continuance of a use of land ; or (*b*) that any buildings or works should be altered or removed," they may by order confirmed by the Secretary of State require the discontinuance of that use, or impose conditions on the continuance thereof, or require steps to be taken for the alteration or removal of the buildings or works (1971 Act, s. 51).   Notice must be served on the " owner " (as defined below) and occupier of the land affected and on any other person who will be affected by the order and any such person may, within the period specified in the notice (not being less than twenty-eight days from the service thereof) require the Secretary to give him an opportunity of being heard by a person appointed by the Secretary (*ibid.*, s. 51 (6)).   Where an order has been confirmed a copy must be served on the " owner " and occupier of the land (*ibid.*, s. 51 (7)).   Where the requirements of an order involve displacement of persons residing in any premises, the local planning authority must secure alternative accommodation so far as it is not reasonably available (*ibid.*, s. 51 (8)).

Where any such order is made a claim for compensation may be delivered to the authority or sent by post addressed to the clerk within six months from the date of the order or such extended period as the Secretary of State may allow (Town and Country Planning General Regulations, 1969, reg. 19). Compensation is payable if it can be shown that damage has been suffered in consequence of the order by depreciation of any interest in the land *or by disturbance in enjoyment of the land* (1971 Act, s. 170).   If any person entitled to an interest in land in respect of which an order is made claims that by reason of the order the land is incapable of reasonably beneficial use and that it cannot be rendered capable of such use by development for which permission has been granted, he may serve a purchase notice under s. 180, *ante*, p. 1197 (*ibid.*, s. 189).

Time limit on permission.—As from 1st April, 1969, there are important limits on the periods for which permissions will remain available. Difficulties have occurred in the past because a permission might not be acted on for very many years but remained available.

Every permission granted or deemed to be granted must be granted, or is deemed to be granted, subject to a condition that the development must be begun not later than (i) five years from grant or (ii) such other dates as the authority direct (Town and Country Planning Act, 1971, s. 41 (1)). These provisions do not apply to outline permission (referred to below), to permission granted by a development order (as to which see p. 1190 *et seq.*), to permissions previously granted subject to an express condition as to time for commencement or completion of development, to permissions granted for a limited period, or to permissions granted under s. 32 of the 1971 Act (referred to at p. 1196 (1971 Act, s. 41 (3)).

Outline planning permissions (which are explained at p. 1192), for *development consisting in or including building or other operations* are deemed to have been granted subject to conditions: (i) that application for approval of any reserved matter must be made within three years of the grant of outline permission and (ii) that the development must be begun not later than five years from the outline permission or two years from final approval, whichever is the later, although these periods may be varied on grant of the outline permission (*ibid.*, s. 42). In addition to the time limits mentioned above on the commencement of development there is a possibility that development begun in time may not be completed quickly. Accordingly the local planning authority have power to serve a "completion notice" if development has not been *completed* within the relevant time limit and they consider it is unlikely to be completed within a reasonable period thereafter (*ibid.*, s. 44). Such a notice must be confirmed by the Secretary of State and there is a right to a hearing before an inspector.

An outline permission granted before 1st April, 1969, on condition that it should cease to have effect after the expiration of a specified period unless within that time approval of the authority to reserved matters had been *notified* was valid (*Kent County Council* v. *Kingston Investments (Kent), Ltd.* [1971] A.C. 72).

Where permission was granted before 1st April, 1969, without imposition of any express time limit for commencement or completion of development (and development had not begun before 1968) statutory conditions as to the time within which development must be commenced and (in the case of outline permission) within which application had to be made for approval of a reserved matter are contained in paras. 18 to 21 of Sched. 24 to the 1971 Act.

E. ENFORCEMENT OF PLANNING CONTROL

Enforcement notice.—Where it appears to a local planning authority that there has been a breach of planning control after the end of 1963, then subject to any directions given by the Secretary of State, the authority, if they consider it expedient to do so having regard to the provisions of the development plan and to any other material consideration, may serve an enforcement notice requiring the breach to be remedied (Town and Country Planning

Act, 1971, s. 87 (1)). There is a breach of planning control if development has been carried out (whether before or after the commencement of the 1971 Act) without the grant of planning permission required in that behalf, or if any conditions or limitations subject to which planning permission was granted have not been complied with (*ibid.*, s. 87 (2)).

Subsection (3) of s. 87 provides that an enforcement notice relating to a breach of planning control may be served only within the period of four years from the date of the breach if that breach consists in " (*a*) the carrying out without planning permission of building, engineering, mining, or other operations, in, on, over or under land ; or (*b*) the failure to comply with any condition or limitation which relates to the carrying out of such operations and subject to which planning permission was granted for the development of that land ; or (*c*) the making without planning permission of a change of use of any building to use as a single dwelling-house."

It must be noted that December, 1963, was four years before publication of the Bill which became the 1968 Act, and so the broad rule (following that under the 1962 Act), is that any contravening development which persisted for four years before the end of 1967 remains free from the possibility of challenge by the local planning authority. On the other hand, development by way of change of use which had not completed the four-year period by the end of 1967 may be challenged now that the new procedure is in operation even if four years have expired before 1st April, 1969. Further, the four-year limit still applies to building and engineering works and to the one exceptional case of change of use. In general, however, the future rule will be that *development by way of change of use only* will never be made lawful by lapse of time.

An enforcement notice must be served on the owner and on the occupier of the land to which it relates and on any other person having an interest in that land which is materially affected by the notice (1971 Act, s. 87 (4)). The notice must specify—

(*a*) the matters alleged to constitute a breach of planning control ;

(*b*) the steps required by the authority to be taken in order to remedy the breach . . . ; and

(*c*) the period for compliance with the notice (*ibid.*, s. 87 (6)).

Subject to the provisions as to appeal a notice takes effect at the end of a specified period, not less than twenty-eight days after the service of the notice (*ibid.*, s. 87 (8)).

A person on whom a notice is served or any other person having an interest in the land may, at any time within the period specified as that at the end of which it is to take effect, appeal to the Secretary of State on any of the following grounds :—

(*a*) that planning permission ought to be granted for development or that a condition or limitation alleged not to have been complied with ought to be discharged ;

(*b*) that the matters alleged do not constitute a breach of planning control ;

(*c*) in the case of a notice to which that rule applies, that the four-year period has elapsed ;

(*d*) in any other case, that the breach of planning control alleged occurred before 1964 ;

(*e*) that the notice was not served as required ;

(*f*) that the steps required exceed what is necessary to remedy any breach of planning control ;

(*g*) that the specified period for compliance was too short (*ibid.*, s. 88 (1)).

The detailed rules regarding enforcement notices (as to which there are many decisions of courts) are not within the scope of this book. The following points should be noted by conveyancers :—

(i) The limit of time within which an enforcement notice may be served is most important in some cases and should be kept in mind on investigation of title. The implications are discussed *ante*, p. 13.

(ii) On default in compliance with a notice :

(*a*) If the steps required to be taken are discontinuance of a use or observance of a condition or limitation then any person who uses the land or causes or permits it to be used or carries out or causes or permits to be carried out operations in contravention is liable to a fine ;

(*b*) Except where the steps required consist of discontinuance of a use (i) the " owner " may be prosecuted for failure to comply, but " owner " does *not* include an agent, or (ii) the authority may take the necessary steps to secure compliance and recover reasonable expenses from the owner (*ibid.*, ss. 89, 91).

(iii) The owner and any occupier who is not personally responsible for the continuation is to some extent protected because expenses incurred in complying with a notice and sums paid by the owner in respect of expenses of steps taken by the authority to secure compliance are " deemed to be incurred or paid for the use and at the request of the person by whom the breach of planning control was committed " and so can be recovered (*ibid.*, s. 91 (2)).

Stop notices affecting development.—A new power was introduced by the Town and Country Planning Act, 1968, s. 19 (now contained in s. 90 of the 1971 Act) which enables a local planning authority who have served an enforcement notice to serve a " stop notice " at any time before the enforcement notice takes effect prohibiting the carrying out or continuing of specified operations alleged to constitute breach of planning control or closely associated therewith. It may be served on any person who appears to have an interest in the land or to be concerned with the carrying out or continuance of any operation. Breach of such a notice is an offence. There is provision in s. 177 of the 1971 Act and the Town and Country Planning General Regulations, 1969, reg. 19, for payment of compensation for loss due to a stop notice, for instance, if the enforcement notice is quashed. Procedure by means of a stop notice does not apply to development which is nothing more than change of use except in the case of deposit of refuse or waste materials (*ibid.*, s. 90 (2)).

Agreements regulating development of land.—A local planning authority may enter into an agreement restricting or regulating the development or use of land, and any such agreement may contain financial provisions (1971 Act, s. 52 (1)). The agreement may be enforced by the authority against the successors in title of the person entering into it as if the authority were possessed of adjacent land and the agreement was expressed to be for the benefit of that land (*ibid.*, s. 52 (2)). Thus the terms may operate substantially as restrictive covenants but there is no provision whereby positive obligations may be enforced against successors in title. An agreement should be registered *either* as a local land charge or as a restrictive covenant under the L.C.A., 1972, s. 2 (5), Class D (ii) (if title is not registered) or (if title is registered) notice should be entered on the register. Such an agreement does not prejudice the powers of the Secretary of State or of the local planning authority so long as they are exercised in accordance with the provisions of the development plan or in accordance with directions given by the Secretary of State (1971 Act, s. 52 (3)).

F. COMPENSATION PROVISIONS

Problems relating to the (very limited) right to compensation on refusal of planning permission now rarely arise in conveyancing practice. They were fully discussed in the 14th edition of this book, vol. 2, p. 314 *et seq.*, and the 15th edition, p. 1222 *et seq.* The following brief summary is intended to indicate the few cases in which it remains necessary to make further inquiries and (occasionally) to investigate the right to claim compensation. The two classes of claim for compensation are :—

(i) On refusal of permission for development within the " existing use."

(ii) On refusal of permission for " new development."

Compensation on refusal of permission for development within the existing use.—Certain very limited classes of development are regarded (for compensation purposes) as falling within the existing use. Consequently an owner is entitled to compensation if permission is refused (or granted subject to conditions) by the Secretary of State for the Environment on an application for permission for such development (1971 Act, s. 169). These classes were first specified in Sched. 3 to the 1947 Act and are now set out in Part 2 of Sched. 8 to the 1971 Act. A claim arises only if it is shown that the value of the interest is less than it would have been if the permission had been granted unconditionally. The right follows an adverse decision of the Secretary and so it is essential to appeal against a decision of the local planning authority.

The classes of development in Sched. 8 are detailed. Those in Part 1 do *not* rank for compensation under s. 169 but are relevant for the purposes of defining the limited right to compensation for " new development " referred to *post*, pp. 1205–1207, and may enable a purchase notice to be served under s. 180, *ante*, p. 1197. Part 1 contains two classes of development :—

(i) Rebuilding of existing buildings.

(ii) Use as separate houses of a building formerly used as a separate dwelling-house.

Part 2 of Sched. 8 (which may give rise to a right to compensation under s. 169) contains, broadly, the following classes :—

(iii) Alteration of buildings (including erection of an additional building in the same curtilage) provided any enlargement is small.

(iv) Building or other operations for agricultural purposes (other than erection or alteration of dwelling-houses or buildings used for the purposes of market gardens).

(v) Working of minerals for agricultural purposes.

(vi) In the case of a building or other land used for a purpose falling within any class specified in the Schedule to the Town and Country Planning

(Use Classes for Third Schedule Purposes) Order, 1948, the use of that building or land for any other purpose falling within the same general class is deemed to be within the limits of the existing user. The classes in this order are somewhat similar to (but rather broader than) those in the Town and Country Planning (Use Classes) Order, 1972, *ante*, p. 1186.

(vii) The use of an additional (relatively small) part for a purpose for which some other part was used.

(viii) Deposit of refuse in connection with the working of minerals on a site used for that purpose.

Compensation is, in general, the difference between the value subject to the refusal or conditional permission, and the value if an unconditional permission had been given (1971 Act, s. 169 (2)).

Compensation on refusal of permission for new development.—In practice compensation is rarely payable because a claim is dependent on the land having the benefit of an " unexpended balance of established development value " and the amount of compensation is limited to that balance. As the basic assessment of development value was related to projects of development in 1948 and to values at that time, very few areas of land remain affected and even in those cases sums involved are likely to be very small in relation to present day values.

The reason for this artificial state of affairs is as follows :—

(i) The policy of the 1947 Act was that a development charge became payable on carrying out of most development. Any increase in value of the land was assumed to be taken up by this charge ; refusal of permission would not (on this reasoning) cause loss and so compensation was not normally payable on refusal. However, a fund of £300,000,000 was set up out of which payments were to be made in respect of depreciation of land values to persons who were owners on 1st July, 1948.

(ii) The Town and Country Planning Act, 1953, abolished development charges in respect of development begun on or after 18th November, 1952. Thus, development value (if any) was restored to landowners and it became unnecessary to make the compensation payments envisaged by the 1947 Act. It followed that refusal of permission might cause hardship by preventing an owner from realising the development value of his land.

(iii) To meet this problem the Town and Country Planning Act, 1954, set up complicated provisions (now re-enacted in the 1971 Act) and for purposes of compensation *adopted the amount of any claim for depreciation of land value established under the 1947 Act as the limiting factor.*

It follows that to ascertain whether there is still an " unexpended balance of established development value " and, if so, its amount, a complex history may have to be traced. Broadly the steps are :—

(*a*) Ascertain whether there was an original established development value pursuant to Part IV of the 1947 Act.

(*b*) Consider whether such amount was reduced or extinguished by ss. 63 or 82 to 85 of the 1947 Act (e.g., because the land belonged to a local authority).

(*c*) Determine whether there remained an " original unexpended balance of established development value." This was (subject to the increase mentioned below) the balance after adjustment of claim holdings to give effect to the consequences of earlier legislation (1971 Act, ss. 136, 138 and Sched. 15). Examples of the adjustments—which might extinguish or reduce a claim holding were (i) where it had been set off against a development charge ; (ii) where compensation was paid under the 1954 Act to someone who had already incurred a development charge or to someone who had (in accordance with the policy of the 1947 Act) sold his land at existing use value ; (iii) where compensation had been paid under the 1954 Act on account of an earlier planning refusal. The balance was, however, increased by one-seventh (to represent, broadly, interest from 1948 to 1955).

Some assistance is gained by the provision (now 1971 Act, s. 145) that (now) the Secretary of State may issue on application a certificate as to whether land has an original unexpended balance of established development value and specifying its amount. The value of this certificate is not as great as first appears because it is *subject to any outstanding claims* under Part I or Part V of the 1954 Act in respect of acts, events and planning decisions before 1955. Even after these have been satisfied a certificate does not give a purchaser all the information he requires. To ascertain the balance remaining available at the time of a purchase it is necessary to make the further deductions mentioned below (and there are complex provisions as to apportionment).

(d) The unexpended balance of established development value as at 1st January, 1955 (as so ascertained) continues to be available (1971 Act, s. 139) but it may have been reduced or extinguished more recently. This may have occurred because—

    (i) compensation has already been paid for depreciation on account of a planning decision pursuant to the 1954 or 1962 or 1971 Acts (1971 Act, s. 140) or

    (ii) " new " development has actually been carried out on or after 1st July, 1948, in which case (with minor exceptions most of which relate to development shortly after 1948) the value of the development (ascertained in accordance with Sched. 16 to the 1971 Act) is to be deducted from the original unexpended balance (1971 Act, s. 141) ; or

    (iii) the balance has been extinguished on compulsory acquisition (1971 Act, s. 142 and Sched. 17) ; or

    (iv) compensation exceeding £20 has been paid in respect of revocation or modification of planning permission (1971 Act, s. 167).

In the rare cases in which application of these rules shows that land has the benefit of an unexpended balance compensation is payable (subject to the exceptions mentioned in the next paragraph) in respect of a planning decision which refuses permission for " new development " or grants it subject to conditions (1971 Act, s. 146, re-enacting earlier provisions). " New " development means (1971 Act, s. 22 (1) any development (defined *ante*, p. 1182) other than that of a class specified in Sched. 8 to the 1971 Act (as to which see *ante*, p. 1204). (The phrase " new development " is not well chosen and is not readily understood. It is important to bear in mind that compensation may be payable under s. 169 on refusal of permission for development within Pt. 2 of Sched. 8 irrespective of any unexpended balance of development value : see *ante*, p. 1204).

In certain cases even this limited compensation is not payable. They are set out in detail in s. 147 of the 1971 Act ; the main ones are :

    (i) where the development intended consists of or includes change of use ;

    (ii) in relation to conditions as to number or disposition of buildings, design, structure or external appearance of buildings, means of access or as to working of minerals ;

(iii) in relation to time limits on duration of permission ;

(iv) where refusal is premature ;

(v) where the land is unsuitable on account of liability to flooding or subsidence.

Moreover, there is normally no right to compensation (notwithstanding the refusal) if planning permission is available for development of a residential, commercial or industrial character (i.e. broadly separately remunerative development is possible) (*ibid.*, s. 148).

The measure of compensation (assuming there is a sufficient unexpended balance of established development value) is normally the extent to which the interest in the land is of less value immediately after the relevant planning decision than it would have been if the decision had been to the contrary effect (1971 Act, s. 153). If, however, permission has been granted, or undertaken to be granted for other development or the Secretary of State replaces the decision by one more favourable to the applicant or grants permission for some other development, account must be taken of the permission so granted in assessing compensation for the unfavourable decision (1971 Act, s. 153).

Compensation exceeding £20 must be notified to the council of the county district in which the land is situated and that council must register the notice in the register of local land charges (*ibid.*, s. 157 (4), (5), as amended). The registration is of the utmost importance in view of the liability to repay the compensation mentioned in the following paragraph.

Repayment of compensation on subsequent development.—Even where permission has been refused, it may be granted on a subsequent application if conditions have changed. Therefore, the 1971 Act, s. 159, makes provision for the recovery by the Secretary of State of compensation previously paid *and in respect of which a notice has been registered in the local land charges register.* No " new " development (as to which see *ante*, p. 1206), which consists of either (i) development of a residential, commercial or industrial character being development which consists wholly or mainly of the construction of houses, flats, shop or office premises, or industrial buildings, or (ii) the winning or working of minerals, or (iii) development to which the Secretary considers the rule should apply, having regard to its probable value, may be carried out on land in respect of which a compensation notice is registered, until the recoverable sum has been paid or secured to the Secretary's satisfaction. There is provision for repayment of part only if the new development covers a larger area than that comprised in the notice ; there is no obligation to repay on the second subsequent development of the same land (*ibid.*, s. 160). As might be expected, any compensation repaid under s. 159 is restored to the " unexpended balance of established development value " that will remain available for the future (*ibid.*, s. 161).

The result is that a prospective purchaser who discovers, for instance from the local search, that compensation under Part VII of the 1971 Act or earlier similar enactments has been paid will be concerned to know whether any development he proposes to carry out will give rise to a liability to make a repayment. If it does he may consider the possibility of obtaining remission from the Secretary of State on the ground that the obligation would prevent development (1971 Act, s. 160 (2)). A particular difficulty is to know whether development which does not fall within one of the two specified classes would be considered by the Secretary to have such value that the liability to repayment should exist.   To settle this point application may be made to the Secretary for his certificate that it is *not* reasonable that s. 159 should apply (*ibid.*, s. 159 (3)).

PART 2.   COMPULSORY ACQUISITION

A.   POWERS OF COMPULSORY ACQUISITION

General principles.—Until comparatively recent years, power to acquire land compulsorily was rarely granted except by private Act of Parliament. The provisions for such matters as compensation, entry on land, and conveyances, which had previously been included in each Act giving compulsory powers, were consolidated in the Lands Clauses Consolidation Act, 1845.   This Act did not itself grant to any person or body a power of compulsory acquisition but thereafter it was possible to incorporate its provisions in any Act granting such powers.

In more recent years local authorities, statutory undertakers, and certain Government departments have been empowered by public general Acts to obtain orders enabling them to acquire land compulsorily without obtaining a private Act.   The procedure which had to be adopted to obtain an order formerly varied greatly, but the Acquisition of Land (Authorisation Procedure) Act, 1946, specified procedure applicable in almost all cases in which land is sought to be acquired under compulsory powers by a local authority or a body such as an electricity board (see further, *post*, p. 1209 *et seq.*).

Thus, the first essential is to find the Act which grants a power of compulsory acquisition.   For instance, the Education Act, 1944, s. 90, provided that a local education authority might be authorised by the Minister to acquire compulsorily for the purposes of a school which is to be maintained by them.   Orders made under such Acts are made for purposes defined by the respective Acts and will not be valid if they contravene the statutory power (*London and Westcliff Properties, Ltd.* v. *Minister of Housing* [1961] 1 W.L.R. 519).   An authority cannot proceed to acquire land if their intentions have changed in such a manner that the purpose for which they propose to use the land differs from the purpose for which the compulsory purchase order was made (*Grice* v. *Dudley Corporation* [1958] Ch. 329).

The second important aspect of the subject of compulsory acquisition is the procedure to be adopted in the making and confirmation of compulsory purchase orders, and for the purposes of the present book those steps which affect a landowner or give him a right of objection are of particular importance. The procedure now almost invariably applicable is that set out in Sched. 1 to the Acquisition of Land (Authorisation Procedure) Act, 1946, which is discussed below at p. 1209 *et seq.*

When a compulsory power exists (either because it is conferred directly by a private Act or it has been obtained by a compulsory purchase order as mentioned above) detailed rules apply to such matters as service of notices to treat, entry on the land, conveyances and acquisition of special interests. If (as is usual), the procedure under Sched. 1 to the 1946 Act applies to the compulsory acquisition these rules are to be found in Pt. I of the Compulsory Purchase Act, 1965 (*ibid.*, s. 1 (1)) ; they are outlined below, p. 1210 *et seq.*

The assessment of compensation is a detailed matter not directly relevant to the subject of this volume.   Also it is not possible to set out here a list of all statutory powers to purchase land compulsorily.   If any question as to these powers arises the purpose for which the land is required will usually be known and so the appropriate statutory power can be traced.

Acquisition for planning purposes.—Section 112 of the Town and Country Planning Act, 1971, enables the Secretary of State for the Environment to authorise a local authority to acquire compulsorily any land if he is satisfied— " (a) that the land is required in order to secure the treatment as a whole, by development, redevelopment or improvement, or partly by one and partly by another method, of the land or of any area in which the land is situated ; or (b) that it is expedient in the public interest that the land should be held together with land so required ; or (c) that the land is required for development or redevelopment, or both, as a whole for the purpose of providing for the relocation of population or industry or the replacement of open space in the course of the redevelopment or improvement, or both, of another area as a whole ; or (d) that it is expedient to acquire the land immediately for a purpose which it is necessary to achieve in the interests of the proper planning of an area in which the land is situated."

The Acquisition of Land (Authorisation Procedure) Act, 1946, applies to compulsory acquisition under this section as if it had been in force before the commencement of that Act (1971 Act, s. 112 (4) ; see below). A local authority for the present purpose is the council of a county or county district, Greater London Council and councils of London Boroughs (*ibid.*, s. 112 (5), as amended by the Local Government Act, 1972).

The Secretary of State for the Environment is given power to acquire compulsorily " any land necessary for the public service " ; this is a novel provision potentially of considerable scope (*ibid.*, s. 113 (1)) ; a similar power was also conferred on the Postmaster General (see s. 29 (2) of the 1968 Act), replaced now by the Post Office (see Post Office Act, 1969).

B. COMPULSORY PURCHASE ORDERS

Procedure applicable.—By the Acquisition of Land (Authorisation Procedure) Act, 1946, s. 1 (1) (a), the authorisation of any compulsory purchase of land " by a local authority where, apart from this Act, power to authorise the authority to purchase land compulsorily is conferred by or under any enactment contained in a public general Act and in force immediately before the commencement of this Act, other than any enactment specified in sub-section (4) of this section " is conferred by a compulsory purchase order in accordance with the provisions of Sched. 1 to the Act. The exceptions specified in subs. (4) are the Light Railways Acts, 1896 and 1912, and (now) the Housing Act, 1957, Pt. III. The 1946 Act referred to purchase by local authorities under an Act *in force before* the 1946 Act, but the same procedure has been applied by numerous Acts passed more recently. The result is that the procedure laid down by the 1946 Act is the procedure which is applicable to most compulsory purchase orders, but there are still a number of exceptions. The exceptions occurring with any frequency refer to housing, acquisition by Government departments, new towns and pipe-lines.

Acquisition by a local authority under [the 1946 Act.—The local authority first make a compulsory purchase order in the form prescribed by the Compulsory Purchase of Land Regulations, 1972, which must describe the land to which it applies by reference to a map (1946 Act, s. 1 (1), Sched. 1, Pt. I, para. 2). A notice of the making of the order must be advertised and, except so far as the confirming authority directs otherwise in any particular case, a notice must be served on every owner, lessee and occupier (except tenants for a month or any period less than a month, and except statutory tenants (Housing Repairs and Rents Act, 1954, s. 50)) stating the effect of the order and the time within which objections can be made (1946 Act, Sched. 1, Pt. I, para. 3). If the confirming authority directs that notices need not be served on owners, lessees or occupiers, then a notice must be fixed on a conspicuous object on the land addressed to " owners and any occupiers " (*ibid.*, para. 3 (1) (c)). If no objection is made, or if all objections are withdrawn, the confirming authority may, if it thinks fit and if satisfied that proper notices have been published and served, confirm the order.

If an objection is made and not withdrawn the confirming authority may not confirm the order until a public local inquiry has been held or an opportunity has been given to any person by whom an objection has been made of appearing before a person appointed by the confirming authority for the purpose (*ibid.*, para. 4 (2)). The confirming authority may, however, require any person who has made an objection to state the grounds of his objection in writing, and may disregard an objection if satisfied that it relates exclusively to matters which can be dealt with by the Lands Tribunal on assessment of compensation (*ibid.*, para. 4 (4)). Procedure at a public local inquiry or hearing is governed by the Compulsory Purchase by Local Authorities (Inquiries Procedure) Rules, 1962.

An order may be confirmed with or without modification (*ibid.*, para. 4 (1)), but unless all persons interested consent, it may not authorise the purchase of any land not comprised in the order before modification (*ibid.*, para. 5). After confirmation a notice thereof must be published and a similar notice and a copy of the order as confirmed must be served on the persons on whom notice of the order had to be served.

Operation of orders made under the 1946 Act.—Any person aggrieved by a compulsory purchase order may question the validity thereof on the ground that there is no statutory authority for it, or that any requirement of the Acquisition of Land (Authorisation Procedure) Act, 1946, has not been complied with and, as a result, his interests have been *substantially* prejudiced. To do this an application must be made to the High Court within six weeks from the date on which notice of confirmation or making of the order is first published (*ibid.*, Sched. 1, Pt. IV, para. 15). Otherwise a compulsory purchase order cannot, either before or after it has been confirmed or made, be questioned in any legal proceedings whatsoever, and it becomes operative on the date on which notice is first published (*ibid.*, para. 16).

C. ENTRY ON LAND AND COMPLETION OF PURCHASE

General note.—In relation to any compulsory purchase to which the provisions of the Acquisition of Land (Authorisation Procedure) Act, 1946, Sched. 1, apply (see *ante*, p. 1209) such matters as the service of notices to treat, entry on the land, acquisition of special interests and particular rules as to conveyances are now governed by the Compulsory Purchase Act, 1965, provided that the order was confirmed or made after 1965 (*ibid.*, ss. 1 (1), 39, 40, Sched. 8, Pt. I). It must be noted, however, that some Acts giving powers of compulsory purchase modify these rules. The following passages deal with the normal cases of compulsory acquisition by local authorities in respect of which the 1965 Act applies.

Notice to treat.—After a compulsory purchase order has taken effect, the next step is for the acquiring authority to serve, within three years from the date on which the order became operative (*ante*, p. 1210), what is known as a " notice to treat " (Compulsory Purchase Act, 1965, s. 4). Nevertheless, after service of such a notice the authority may delay acquisition as long as six or seven years (*Simpson's Motor Sales (London)* v. *Hendon Corporation* [1964] A.C. 1088) unless there is evidence from which they can be presumed to have abandoned the acquisition (*Grice* v. *Dudley Corporation* [1958] Ch. 329).

A notice to treat must be served on all persons interested in, or having power to sell and convey or release, the land, so far as known to the acquiring authority after making diligent inquiry (1965 Act, s. 5) ; the authorised methods of service are specified in s. 30. There is no clear authority on the matter, but it does not seem necessary to serve a notice to treat on persons whose interests would be overreached on conveyance of the legal estate. Thus, service should be on an owner of a legal estate in fee simple, trustees for sale holding such an estate, a tenant for life under the S.L.A. 1925, a leaseholder holding a term greater than that of a tenant from year to year, and on mortgagees who can " release." A person holding an interest as tenant for a year or from year to year or for a shorter period may be required to give up possession before the expiration of the interest on payment of compensation (Compulsory Purchase Act, 1965, s. 20).

There is no right to compensation under s. 20 of the 1965 Act unless possession is required to be given before the expiration of the term ; a notice to treat may conveniently be served but it does not justify a claim for compensation (*Newham London Borough Council* v. *Benjamin* [1968] 1 W.L.R. 694 decided on the similar provisions of the 1845 Act).

The statutory rights of occupation of a spouse in the matrimonial home created by the Matrimonial Homes Act, 1967 (whether or not protected by registration) appear to be such that notice of entry should be served on that spouse pursuant to s. 5 of the Compulsory Purchase Act, 1965 ; see the discussion in *New Law Journal*, vol. 118, p. 200.

The effect of service of a notice to treat is to create a relationship similar to that of vendor and purchaser, but there is not an enforceable contract of which specific performance will be granted until the purchase price has been ascertained and service does not give the acquiring authority any interest in the land (*Harding* v. *Metropolitan Railway* (1872), L.R. 7 Ch. 154 ; *Re Cary-Elwes' Contract* [1906] 2 Ch. 143). As service does not give rise to a contract, the notice is not registrable as an estate contract or, in the case of registered land, capable of being protected by notice (*Capital Investments, Ltd.* v. *Wednesfield U.D.C.* [1965] Ch. 774). Thereafter, the owner may convey or otherwise deal with his land, but the rights and obligations created by the notice are legal and so bind all persons, whether or not they have notice ; an interest created after the service of the notice is not the subject of compensation. Nevertheless, after compensation has been agreed or determined it appears that either party could seek an order for specific performance (*Harding* v. *Metropolitan Railway Co.* (1872), 7 Ch. App. 154).

Taking of part of premises.—Where the 1946 Act is applicable no person can be required to sell a part only of any house or building, or of a park or garden belonging to a house, if he is willing and able to sell the whole, unless the Lands Tribunal determines that the part can be taken without material detriment to the house or building concerned (1965 Act, s. 8).

If the 1946 Act is not applicable, but the Lands Clauses Consolidation Act, 1845, s. 92, is incorporated in the enactment giving the power of compulsory purchase, then there is a similar provision that no party shall be required to sell a part only of a house or other building if he is willing and able to sell the whole. The owner may, by counter-notice, require the acquiring authority to take the whole or nothing (*Richards* v. *Swansea Improvement Co.* (1878), 9 Ch. D. 425), in which case the authority can withdraw the notice. After withdrawal of the notice, the authority can give a fresh notice (*Ashton Vale Iron Co., Ltd.* v. *Corporation of Bristol* [1901] 1 Ch. 591).

Entry on lands.—As the assessment of compensation may take some time there are special provisions enabling acquiring authorities to enter on the land before it is actually conveyed to them. Where the compulsory purchase has been authorised under s. 1 of the 1946 Act the acquiring authority may, after service of the notice to treat, and after serving on the owner, lessee and occupier not less than fourteen days' notice, enter on the land subject to payment of compensation and interest (Compulsory Purchase Act, 1965, s. 11 (1)). The rate of interest payable on compensation is changed frequently; reference should be made to the most recent Acquisition of Land (Rate of Interest after Entry) Regulations. If the 1946 Act is not applicable, entry will have to be made under the provisions of the Lands Clauses Consolidation Act, 1845, ss. 84 and 85 (if incorporated in the statute giving the power of purchase). In this case the acquiring authority cannot enter on the land without the consent of the owner and occupier unless compensation has been paid to all persons interested or an appropriate sum has been deposited in court. Where the compulsory purchase order was made under the Housing Act, 1957, Pt. III, a special notice of entry may be given under *ibid.*, Sched. 3, para. 9.

Completion of conveyance.—In practice, purchases are completed in the same manner as if no compulsory purchase order had been made but a contract existed. Title is investigated in the usual way and the vendor or vendors execute a conveyance or transfer. It is provided by s. 42 (7) of the L.P.A. 1925 that where on compulsory purchase title can be made without payment of the compensation money into court, title shall be made in that way unless the purchaser otherwise elects. Subject to this subsection power to sell and convey is conferred on all persons seised or possessed of or entitled to land subject to compulsory purchase or any estate or interest therein, such as corporations, tenants in tail or for life, trustees for charitable or other purposes, and persons entitled to rents and profits (1965 Act, Sched. 1). Normally s. 42 (7) will prevent use of these special powers, but if they are available a person, other than a lessee for a term of years, or for any less interest, may exercise the powers to sell and convey not only on behalf of himself and his successors, but also for and on behalf of every person entitled in reversion, remainder or expectancy after him, or in defeasance of his estate (*ibid.*, Sched. 1, para. 2 (3)).

Certain statutory forms of conveyance are specified in the Compulsory Purchase Act, 1965, Sched. 5, but these are rarely used. It is customary to use an ordinary form of transfer of registered land or of conveyance containing recitals showing how the compulsory power arises and how the compensation has been assessed.

If the owner of the land or any interest in it on tender of the compensation agreed or awarded to be paid refuses to accept it, or neglects or fails to make out a title to the satisfaction of the acquiring authority, or refuses to convey or release the land as directed by the acquiring authority, the authority may pay the compensation into court (Compulsory Purchase Act, 1965, s. 9 (1)). It is then lawful for the authority to execute a deed poll " containing a description of the land in respect of which the payment into court was made, and declaring the circumstances under which, and the names of the parties to whose credit, the payment into court was made " (*ibid.*, s. 9 (3)). On execution of such a deed " all the estate and interest in the land of the parties for whose use and in respect whereof the compensation was paid into court shall vest absolutely in the acquiring authority and as against those persons the acquiring authority shall be entitled to immediate possession of the land " (*ibid.*, s. 9 (4)). If a person entitled to compensation is prevented from treating on account of absence from the United Kingdom or cannot be found after diligent inquiry compensation may be determined by a surveyor member of the Lands Tribunal and, on payment into court of the amount, the acquiring authority may similarly vest the estate or interest in themselves by deed poll (*ibid.*, s. 5, Sched. 2).

Vesting declarations.—The Town and Country Planning Act, 1968, s. 30 and Sched. 3 (not repealed by the 1971 Act), enables Ministers or local or other public authorities to vest in themselves, by a declaration, land which they are authorised by a compulsory purchase order to acquire. The authority may execute a declaration in prescribed form (known as " A general vesting declaration ") vesting the land in themselves as from the end of a prescribed period not being less than twenty-eight days from the date of service of notices. To enable them to do this the authority must include in the notice of the making or confirmation of the compulsory purchase order or in a notice given subsequently, a statement of the effect of the vesting declaration and a statement as to compensation (1968 Act, Sched. 3, paras. 1 and 2). The notice must be registered in the register of local land charges and must be served on every occupier of land (other than land in which there subsists a minor tenancy or a long tenancy which is about to expire) and on every other person who has given certain information (*ibid.*, para. 4).

A general vesting declaration must not be executed before the expiration of two months beginning with the date of the first publication of such a notice (except with the consent of every occupier) (*ibid.*, para. 3). A certificate by the acquiring authority as to the date on which service of such notices was completed is *conclusive* (*ibid.*, para. 5).

The effect of a general vesting declaration is that at the end of the period specified in the general vesting declaration—

(i) the provisions of the Land Compensation Act, 1961 (as modified by Sched. 2 to the Acquisition of Land (Authorisation Procedure) Act, 1946) and of the Compulsory Purchase Act, 1965, apply as if on the date on which the declaration was made, a notice to treat had been served ;

(ii) the land specified in the declaration, together with the right to enter upon and take possession of it vests in the acquiring authority as if they had executed such a deed poll as is mentioned above (1968 Act, Sched. 3, paras. 6 and 7).

The acquiring authority may also, by serving both a notice to treat and a notice of intention to enter, put an end to a minor tenancy or a long tenancy which is about to expire (*ibid.*, para. 9).

The forms of general vesting declaration and of other documents required to be published are specified in the Compulsory Purchase of Land Regulations, 1972.

It still remains to be seen to what extent local authorities will take advantage of this procedure which enables them to acquire the legal estate in land within a compulsory purchase order without conveyance. They will find the procedure particularly advantageous if they wish to dispose of the land quickly but there are a number of titles and possible delay in obtaining conveyances.

Restrictive covenants affecting land purchased.—The general effect of the compulsory purchase of land under statutory powers is to permit the land to be used in contravention of restrictive covenants so far as is necessary to enable the statutory powers to be carried out, and this is so even if the acquiring authority had notice of the covenants before the purchase. Any person injuriously affected by the execution of works contrary to a restrictive covenant may claim compensation under the Compulsory Purchase Act, 1965, s. 10, or (if still applicable to the particular compulsory power), the Lands Clauses Consolidation Act, 1845, s. 68, but will not have a right of action for damages or an injunction (*Kirby* v. *Harrogate School Board* [1896] 1 Ch. 437 ; *Long Eaton Recreation Grounds Co.* v. *Midland Railway* [1902] 2 K.B. 574). Unless compensation is paid the burden of the covenants will revive again if the land is sold as superfluous (*Bird* v. *Eggleton* (1885), 29 Ch. D. 1012). The authorities are not altogether clear, but the better view appears to be that the effect of compulsory acquisition is to suspend the operation of covenants and that they are not extinguished unless compensation is paid.

Acquiring authorities may refuse to give a covenant for indemnity against existing restrictive covenants on the ground that any action by the authority which might be a breach will not involve the person who entered into the covenants in liability. The case of *Bailey* v. *De Crespigny* (1869), L.R. 4 Q.B. 180, appears to provide some authority for saying that no liability can, after compulsory acquisition, fall on a vendor who entered into restrictive covenants, or who gave a covenant for indemnity in respect of them, but the reasoning is not altogether satisfactory, and so there is ground for arguing that the acquiring authority should covenant to indemnify a vendor who may remain under a liability for a positive or restrictive covenant. See *Harding* v. *Metropolitan Railway Co.* (1872), L.R. 7 Ch. 154, and *Conveyancer N.S.*, vol. 15, p. 8 *et seq.* Even if a covenant for indemnity cannot be obtained any liability which may fall on a vendor would seem to give rise to a claim by him for compensation pursuant to s. 10 (2) of the 1965 Act.

It is often stated that compensation can be recovered only in respect of damage or loss occasioned by the construction of authorised works, and not in respect of damage or loss arising from their use ; the authorities are not satisfactory, see *Long Eaton Recreation Grounds Co.* v. *Midland Railway* [1902] 2 K.B. 574 ; *Re Simeon and Isle of Wight R.D.C.* [1937] Ch. 525 and *Conveyancer N.S.*, vol. 15, p. 13 *et seq.*

Restrictive covenants after purchase by agreement.—Authorities having powers of compulsory purchase invariably have the same or wider powers of acquiring land by agreement, and even where compulsory powers exist land is usually acquired by agreement. Express authority for this practice is contained in the Compulsory Purchase Act, 1965, s. 3.

The following alternatives exist :—

(i) A purchase may be by agreement even if the purchaser has a compulsory power.

(ii) A compulsory purchase order may be made but the purchase completed by agreement under s. 3.

If an order has been made to which the procedure in the Acquisition of Land (Authorisation Procedure) Act, 1946, applies then the Compulsory Purchase Act, 1965, s. 10 (*ante*) applies. In such a case restrictive covenants are affected in the same way as if compulsory powers had been used throughout. Unfortunately there is much doubt as to the effect of some purchases which have been entirely by agreement. Some statutory powers enabling such purchases by agreement incorporate either the Lands Clauses Consolidation Act, 1845, s. 68, or the Compulsory Purchase Act, 1965, s. 10, in which cases restrictive covenants are affected as if the purchase had been by compulsion incorporating those powers. However, the wording of other statutes giving power to acquire by agreement has caused doubt whether s. 68 or s. 10 has been incorporated.

D. VESTING OF LAND ON NATIONALISATION

Considerable areas of land have vested in various bodies without the execution of a conveyance as a result of the policy of nationalisation. The rules relating to such vesting are rather different from compulsory acquisition in the normal sense of the phrase, but it is thought to be convenient to give a brief reference to some of the statutory provisions as they will often have to be considered in the course of investigation of title.

Coal.—As to the statutory vesting of coal and rights of support, see *ante*, p. 501.

Under the Coal Industry Nationalisation Act, 1946, s. 5 (1) and Sched. 1, Pt. I, interests of colliery and similar concerns in land used for colliery activities, coal carbonisation and similar activities, vested in the National Coal Board on 1st January, 1947, unless excluded by order of the Minister of Fuel and Power (*ibid.*, s. 5 (8)). The interests of colliery concerns in certain other land, such as that used for the purposes of water works, dwelling-houses for staff and farms, might be made to vest in the Board on the same date at the option of the Board or the owners (*ibid.*, s. 5 (2) ; Sched. 1, Pt. II). The question whether any particular land vested is one to be decided only by applying the detailed rules in the Coal Industry Nationalisation Act, 1946, the Coal Industry Nationalisation (Vesting of Easements, etc.) Regulations, 1946, and the Coal Industry Nationalisation (Apportionments, Documents, etc.) Regulations, 1946, which rules cannot be set out in full here. See, for instance, *National Coal Board* v. *Hornby* [1949] 2 All E.R. 615.

Electricity undertakings.—All land which, immediately before 1st April, 1948, was the property of authorised undertakers or of a similar company, within the definition in the Electricity Act, 1947, s. 13, vested on that date in the appropriate electricity board (*ibid.*, s. 14). In the case of authorised undertakers who were a local authority, property held or used by the local authority *wholly or mainly in their capacity as authorised undertakers* vested in the board (*ibid.*, s. 15 (1)). Provision has been made for excluding from, or, as the case may be, including in the land which so vested any land used by a local authority partly in their capacity as authorised undertakers and partly in other capacities (*ibid.*, s. 15 (2) ; Electricity (Vesting of Assets)

Regulations, 1948). Consequently, the determination of whether any property formerly belonging to a local authority vested in an electricity board depends (i) on whether it was wholly or partly so used, and (ii) if partly so used on subsequent agreement between the local authority and the board, or, in the absence of agreement, on the determination of the appropriate Minister.

On 1st January, 1958, such property and rights of the Central Electricity Authority as were agreed in writing by the Central Electricity Council and the Central Electricity Generating Board (or, in default of agreement, were specified by the Minister of Power), were transferred to the Electricity Council without further assurance (Electricity Act, 1957, s. 25 (1), (2)). The remaining property and rights of the Authority were similarly transferred to the Central Electricity Generating Board (*ibid.*, s. 25 (5)).

Gas undertakings.—The rules as to vesting are very similar to those which relate to electricity undertakings. All land which, immediately before 1st May, 1949, was the property of a statutory undertaker, a non-statutory undertaker, a gas-holding company or an ancillary gas undertaker, as those terms are defined in the Gas Act, 1948, ss. 15 and 16, vested on that date in the appropriate area board (*ibid.*, s. 17 (1)). Where an undertaker was a local authority, a composite company supplying water as well as gas, an ancillary gas undertaker, or was not a body corporate, or was an electricity board, only property held or used wholly or mainly for the purpose of the gas undertaking or wholly or mainly in its capacity as a gas undertaker vested (*ibid.*, s. 18 (1)). There is similar provision for excluding or including land used by the undertaker partly as a gas undertaker and partly in another capacity within the property which vested and for agreement or determination by the appropriate Minister as in the case of electricity assets (Gas Act, 1948, s. 18 ; Gas (Vesting of Assets) Regulations, 1949 ; Gas (Vesting of Assets) (Amendment) Regulations, 1949).

Hospitals.—Under the National Health Service Act, 1946, s. 6 (1), interests in premises forming part of a voluntary hospital or used for the purposes of a voluntary hospital, and rights to which a governing body or trustees were entitled, which were then held *solely* for the purposes of that hospital, *but not including any endowments*, vested on 5th July, 1948, in the Minister of Health subject to any existing liabilities. Similarly, on the same date, all hospitals vested in a local authority and all property held by a local authority *solely* for the purposes of those hospitals were vested in the Minister (*ibid.*, s. 6 (2)). If, however, it appeared to the Minister that the transfer of a hospital was not required for the purpose of providing hospital and specialised services he might serve a notice to that effect on the governing body or the local authority concerned, and thereupon the hospital would not vest in the Minister unless a counter-notice was served on him by the governing body or local authority (*ibid.*, s. 6 (3)). If the Minister sells any land which vested in him under these provisions the title may be simplified because such vesting took effect free from any trust then existing (*ibid.*, s. 6 (4)). The word " hospital " for this purpose includes any institution for the reception and treatment of persons suffering from any disability requiring nursing (*Minister of Health* v. *Royal Midlands Counties Home for Incurables* [1954] Ch. 530).

Where premises were used partly for the purposes of a hospital and partly for other purposes an apportionment might be made between the Minister and the board of governors or other persons concerned, and the effect thereof is that on the date of it the part of the premises apportioned to the Minister vested in him without any conveyance (*ibid.*, s. 6 (5) ; National Health Service (Apportionment and Transfer) Regulations, 1948). In the absence of agreement as to apportionment the matter had to be determined by arbitration.

Property given to a hospital by will which had been handed over to the governors or trustees before 5th July, 1948, and applied by them for hospital purposes, probably passed to the Minister under s. 6 (1). In *Re Kellner's Will Trusts* [1950] Ch. 46 it was decided that the " rights " referred to did not include the right of a beneficiary in an unadministered estate.

Where any hospital has been designated as a teaching hospital, all " *endowments* " held immediately before 5th July, 1948, were transferred to the board of governors constituted under the Act for the teaching hospital. They vested in the board free of any trust existing before that date, and must be held on trust for such purposes relating to hospital services or to the functions of the board with respect to research as the board think fit (*ibid.*, s. 7 (1), (2)). All endowments of a nationalised hospital, other than a teaching hospital, held immediately before 5th July, 1948, were transferred on that date to the Minister of Health free of any trust existing immediately before that date (*ibid.*, s. 7 (4)). The expression " endowment " means property (which includes " rights " : s. 79) held by the governing body of a hospital or by trustees solely for the purposes of that hospital, being property of certain descriptions, such as investment land, securities or money (*ibid.*, s. 7 (10)).

It is expressly provided that an equitable interest held for the purposes of a voluntary hospital in trust property in which there are other equitable interests is *not* deemed to be an endowment (*ibid.*, s. 7 (10) proviso ; *Re Kellner, ante* ; *Re Buzzacott* [1953] Ch. 28).

Sections 6 and 7 deal with property and endowments held on 5th July, 1948, and other provisions affect property to which a nationalised hospital may become entitled after that date. By s. 59 (1) a regional hospital board, the board of governors of any teaching hospital or a hospital management committee have power to accept any property upon trust for purposes relating to hospital services or the functions of the board or committee with respect to research. Where property which was not transferred to the Minister or to a board of governors or hospital management committee under s. 6 or 7 was held on trust immediately before 5th July, 1948, and the terms of the trust authorised or required the trustees to apply any part of the capital or income for the purposes of any nationalised hospital, the trust instrument is construed as authorising or requiring the trustees to apply the property for the purpose of making payments, in the case of a teaching hospital, to the board of governors, and, in any other case, to the regional hospital board for the area or to the hospital management committee for the particular hospital (*ibid.*, s. 60 (1)).

If a testator died before 5th July, 1948, and his estate was fully administered, then a bequest to, or a trust in favour of, a single hospital became an endowment under s. 7. On the other hand, if in such a case there was a direction to trustees to pay a *part* of income or capital of a fund for the benefit of a hospital the bequest took effect as determined by s. 60 (1) (*Re Gartside* [1949] 2 All E.R. 546). If the estate had not been fully administered on that day, a bequest would in any case fall within s. 60 (1) (*Re Kellner, ante*).

39

Where a testator made a will after 5th July, 1948, containing a bequest to a hospital, it would be assumed that he knew of the terms of the National Health Service Act, 1946, and so he must be taken to have intended a gift either to the regional hospital board or to the hospital management committee or (in the case of a teaching hospital) to the board of governors.

The most difficult case is that in which the testator made a will before 5th July, 1948, but died later. Assuming that the work of the hospital has been carried on after that date in the same way as that in which it was carried on previously, the gift will take effect as a gift to the hospital management committee, or, in the case of a teaching hospital, to the board of governors. In many cases such committees control several hospitals, but it appears that they must hold the gift on trust for the particular hospital specified (*Re Morgan's Will Trusts* [1950] Ch. 637). In the case of *Re Morgan* the gift was " for the benefit of " the hospital, and it is reasonable to assume that a gift in these terms should now pass to the body controlling the hospital. In *Re Glass* [1950] Ch. 643*n*, where the will giving a legacy " to the King Edward VII Memorial Hospital " was made before 5th July, 1948, but the testator died afterwards, it was decided that the legacy should be paid to the management committee to be applied for the purposes of the hospital. See also *Re Meyers* [1951] Ch. 534. Even though the gift is expressed to be in favour of the former trustees, who no longer control the hospital, it operates in favour of the hospital management committee (*Re Little* [1953] 1 W.L.R. 1132).

In *Re Frere* [1951] Ch. 27 it was held that a gift in a will made before 1948 to a hospital " for endowment purposes " is still a good charitable gift and operates as a gift to the committee under s. 59 (1). As to the circumstances in which a hospital is considered to have been " nationalised," see *Royal College of Surgeons* v. *National Provincial Bank, Ltd.* [1952] A.C. 631 ; as to conditions requiring trustees to be satisfied that a hospital has not been taken over by the State, see *Dundee General Hospitals Board* v. *Walker* [1952] W.N. 180 ; and as to provisions for the withholding of benefits from institutions which have been " amalgamated " with others, see *Re Bawden's Settlement* [1954] 1 W.L.R. 33*n*, and *Re Hayes' Will Trusts* [1954] 1 W.L.R. 22 ; and as to a provision for independent existence, see *Re Lowry's Will Trusts* [1967] Ch. 638.

It is still possible to make a gift for the endowment of a bed. This may be done by making a gift in the will which should be of an amount acceptable to the management committee, or, as the case may be, board of governors, of the hospital, on the condition that the bed will be named as required. A gift of such a sum as may be necessary for the purpose is effective provided that the management committee or board of governors are prepared to fix a sum (which need not be determined by reference to the cost of running the hospital) on receipt of which they will undertake to name the bed (*Re Ginger* [1951] Ch. 458 ; *Re Mills* [1953] 1 W.L.R. 554 ; see further, *Solicitors' Journal*, vol. 97, p. 291). As to the effect of a gift for " endowing beds for paying patients," see *Re Adams* [1967] 1 W.L.R. 162.

Transport undertakings.—A brief note on the nationalisation of railways is contained at p. 424. Some difficulty may be anticipated in investigating title to land held by road transport undertakings which were acquired by the British Transport Commission pursuant to the Transport Act, 1947. The vesting was effected by ss. 39 to 51 of the 1947 Act ; see the brief notes in the 13th Edition of this book, at p. 1002. Although these sections were repealed by the Transport Act, 1953, their operation in connection with any transfer *effected before* 6th May, 1953, in consequence of a notice of acquisition is not affected (1953 Act, s. 1 (3) proviso). The 1953 Act contained provision for the disposal of the British Transport Commission's existing road haulage undertaking; see s. 3 as to disposal of property as part of a transport unit and s. 6 as to disposal of other property.

Consequent on the winding up of the London Transport Board by the Transport (London) Act, 1969, s. 39, all property rights and liabilities of the Board were transferred to the Executive (without any need for a conveyance or other instrument) on 1st January, 1970 (*ibid.*, s. 16 (1); Sched. 2). However, property which immediately before that date was used or appropriated for use solely for the part of the undertaking known as " country buses and coaches " and certain property situate outside Greater London vested in a subsidiary of the National Bus Company (*ibid.*, s. 16 (2); Sched. 2).

Further problems may arise as a result of the Transport Act, 1968. If the Minister of Transport designates any area (outside Greater London) and establishes for it a Passenger Transport Authority and a Passenger Transport Executive (which will be a body corporate : Transport Act, 1968, s. 9 (1)) then the Minister must by order make provision for the transfer to the Executive of property (determined by the order) which has been used in connection with a road passenger transport, ferry or railway undertaking of (i) a council of a constituent area or (ii) a body members of which fall to be appointed by such a council (*ibid.*, s. 17 (1)). The order may also transfer to the Executive all property of such a body if the Executive or persons appointed by the Executive would be sole members; this provision is apparently designed to deal with joint boards of local authorities (*ibid.*). There is provision for exclusion from transfer to or disclaimer by the Executive (*ibid.*, s. 17 (2)).

Certain property of the Railways Board concerned with specified local road passenger transport services may be transferred to the National Bus Company (*ibid.*, s. 29).

Miscellaneous statutory bodies.—Statutes continue to vest property in new or different bodies without any transfer or deed of conveyance. For example. parts of the undertaking and property of the United Kingdom Atomic Energy Authority were so vested by the Atomic Energy Authority Act, 1971, in British Nuclear Fuels Limited and The Radiochemical Centre Limited.

APPENDIX

AD VALOREM STAMP DUTIES

TABLE I : CONVEYANCE ON SALE DUTY

Instruments executed on or after 1st August, 1972

No duty is chargeable on instruments containing a certificate of value at £10,000.

Consideration not exceeding	Certificate of value £15,000	No Certificate of value	Consideration not exceeding	Certificate of value £15,000	No Certificate of value
£	£	£	£	£	£
5	0·05	0·05	1,400	7·00	14·00
10	0·05	0·10	1,450	7·25	14·50
20	0·10	0·20	1,500	7·50	15·00
30	0·15	0·30	1,550	7·75	15·50
40	0·20	0·40	1,600	8·00	16·00
50	0·25	0·50	1,650	8·25	16·50
60	0·30	0·60	1,700	8·50	17·00
70	0·35	0·70	1,750	8·75	17·50
80	0·40	0·80	1,800	9·00	18·00
90	0·45	0·90	1,850	9·25	18·50
100	0·50	1·00	1,900	9·50	19·00
120	0·60	1·20	1,950	9·75	19·50
140	0·70	1·40	2,000	10·00	20·00
160	0·80	1·60	2,050	10·25	20·50
180	0·90	1·80	2,100	10·50	21·00
200	1·00	2·00	2,150	10·75	21·50
220	1·10	2·20	2,200	11·00	22·00
240	1·20	2·40	2,250	11·25	22·50
260	1·30	2·60	2,300	11·50	23·00
280	1·40	2·80	2,350	11·75	23·50
300	1·50	3·00	2,400	12·00	24·00
350	1·75	3·50	2,450	12·25	24·50
400	2·00	4·00	2,500	12·50	25·00
450	2·25	4·50	2,550	12·75	25·50
500	2·50	5·00	2,600	13·00	26·00
550	2·75	5·50	2,650	13·25	26·50
600	3·00	6·00	2,700	13·50	27·00
650	3·25	6·50	2,750	13·75	27·50
700	3·50	7·00	2,800	14·00	28·00
750	3·75	7·50	2,850	14·25	28·50
800	4·00	8·00	2,900	14·50	29·00
850	4·25	8·50	2,950	14·75	29·50
900	4·50	9·00	3,000	15·00	30·00
950	4·75	9·50	3,050	15·25	30·50
1,000	5·00	10·00	3,100	15·50	31·00
1,050	5·25	10·50	3,150	15·75	31·50
1,100	5·50	11·00	3,200	16·00	32·00
1,150	5·75	11·50	3,250	16·25	32·50
1,200	6·00	12·00	3,300	16·50	33·00
1,250	6·25	12·50	3,350	16·75	33·50
1,300	6·50	13·00	3,400	17·00	34·00
1,350	6·75	13·50	3,450	17·25	34·50

CONVEYANCE ON SALE DUTY

Consideration not exceeding	Certificate of value £15,000	No Certificate of value	Consideration not exceeding	Certificate of value £15,000	No Certificate of value
£	£	£	£	£	£
3,500	17·50	35·00	6,450	32·25	64·50
3,550	17·75	35·50	6,500	32·50	65·00
3,600	18·00	36·00	6,550	32·75	65·50
3,650	18·25	36·50	6,600	33·00	66·00
3,700	18·50	37·00	6,650	33·25	66·50
3,750	18·75	37·50	6,700	33·50	67·00
3,800	19·00	38·00	6,750	33·75	67·50
3,850	19·25	38·50	6,800	34·00	68·00
3,900	19·50	39·00	6,850	34·25	68·50
3,950	19·75	39·50	6,900	34·50	69·00
4,000	20·00	40·00	6,950	34·75	69·50
4,050	20·25	40·50	7,000	35·00	70·00
4,100	20·50	41·00	7,050	35·25	70·50
4,150	20·75	41·50	7,100	35·50	71·00
4,200	21·00	42·00	7,150	35·75	71·50
4,250	21·25	42·50	7,200	36·00	72·00
4,300	21·50	43·00	7,250	36·25	72·50
4,350	21·75	43·50	7,300	36·50	73·00
4,400	22·00	44·00	7,350	36·75	73·50
4,450	22·25	44·50	7,400	37·00	74·00
4,500	22·50	45·00	7,450	37·25	74·50
4,550	22·75	45·50	7,500	37·50	75·00
4,600	23·00	46·00	7,550	37·75	75·50
4,650	23·25	46·50	7,600	38·00	76·00
4,700	23·50	47·00	7,650	38·25	76·50
4,750	23·75	47·50	7,700	38·50	77·00
4,800	24·00	48·00	7,750	38·75	77·50
4,850	24·25	48·50	7,800	39·00	78·00
4,900	24·50	49·00	7,850	39·25	78·50
4,950	24·75	49·50	7,900	39·50	79·00
5,000	25·00	50·00	7,950	39·75	79·50
5,050	25·25	50·50	8,000	40·00	80·00
5,100	25·50	51·00	8,050	40·25	80·50
5,150	25·75	51·50	8,100	40·50	81·00
5,200	26·00	52·00	8,150	40·75	81·50
5,250	26·25	52·50	8,200	41·00	82·00
5,300	26·50	53·00	8,250	41·25	82·50
5,350	26·75	53·50	8,300	41·50	83·00
5,400	27·00	54·00	8,350	41·75	83·50
5,450	27·25	54·50	8,400	42·00	84·00
5,500	27·50	55·00	8,450	42·25	84·50
5,550	27·75	55·50	8,500	42·50	85·00
5,600	28·00	56·00	8,550	42·75	85·50
5,650	28·25	56·50	8,600	43·00	86·00
5,700	28·50	57·00	8,650	43·25	86·50
5,750	28·75	57·50	8,700	43·50	87·00
5,800	29·00	58·00	8,750	43·75	87·50
5,850	29·25	58·50	8,800	44·00	88·00
5,900	29·50	59·00	8,850	44·25	88·50
5,950	29·75	59·50	8,900	44·50	89·00
6,000	30·00	60·00	8,950	44·75	89·50
6,050	30·25	60·50	9,000	45·00	90·00
6,100	30·50	61·00	9,050	45·25	90·50
6,150	30·75	61·50	9,100	45·50	91·00
6,200	31·00	62·00	9,150	45·75	91·50
6,250	31·25	62·50	9,200	46·00	92·00
6,300	31·50	63·00	9,250	46·25	92·50
6,350	31·75	63·50	9,300	46·50	93·00
6,400	32·00	64·00	9,350	46·75	93·50

CONVEYANCE ON SALE DUTY

Consideration not exceeding	Certificate of value £15,000	No Certificate of value	Consideration not exceeding	Certificate of value £15,000	No Certificate of value
£	£	£	£	£	£
9,400	47·00	94·00	12,350	61·75	123·50
9,450	47·25	94·50	12,400	62·00	124·00
9,500	47·50	95·00	12,450	62·25	124·50
9,550	47·75	95·50	12,500	62·50	125·00
9,600	48·00	96·00	12,550	62·75	125·50
9,650	48·25	96·50	12,600	63·00	126·00
9,700	48·50	97·00	12,650	63·25	126·50
9,750	48·75	97·50	12,700	63·50	127·00
9,800	49·00	98·00	12,750	63·75	127·50
9,850	49·25	98·50	12,800	64·00	128·00
9,900	49·50	99·00	12,850	64·25	128·50
9,950	49·75	99·50	12,900	64·50	129·00
10,000	50·00	100·00	12,950	64·75	129·50
10,050	50·25	100·50	13,000	65·00	130·00
10,100	50·50	101·00	13,050	65·25	130·50
10,150	50·75	101·50	13,100	65·50	131·00
10,200	51·00	102·00	13,150	65·75	131·50
10,250	51·25	102·50	13,200	66·00	132·00
10,300	51·50	103·00	13,250	66·25	132·50
10,350	51·75	103·50	13,300	66·50	133·00
10,400	52·00	104·00	13,350	66·75	133·50
10,450	52·25	104·50	13,400	67·00	134·00
10,500	52·50	105·00	13,450	67·25	134·50
10,550	52·75	105·50	13,500	67·50	135·00
10,600	53·00	106·00	13,550	67·75	135·50
10,650	53·25	106·50	13,600	68·00	136·00
10,700	53·50	107·00	13,650	68·25	136·50
10,750	53·75	107·50	13,700	68·50	137·00
10,800	54·00	108·00	13,750	68·75	137·50
10,850	54·25	108·50	13,800	69·00	138·00
10,900	54·50	109·00	13,850	69·25	138·50
10,950	54·75	109·50	13,900	69·50	139·00
11,000	55·00	110·00	13,950	69·75	139·50
11,050	55·25	110·50	14,000	70·00	140·00
11,100	55·50	111·00	14,050	70·25	140·50
11,150	55·75	111·50	14,100	70·50	141·00
11,200	56·00	112·00	14,150	70·75	141·50
11,250	56·25	112·50	14,200	71·00	142·00
11,300	56·50	113·00	14,250	71·25	142·50
11,350	56·75	113·50	14,300	71·50	143·00
11,400	57·00	114·00	14,350	71·75	143·50
11,450	57·25	114·50	14,400	72·00	144·00
11,500	57·50	115·00	14,450	72·25	144·50
11,550	57·75	115·50	14,500	72·50	145·00
11,600	58·00	116·00	14,550	72·75	145·50
11,650	58·25	116·50	14,600	73·00	146·00
11,700	58·50	117·00	14,650	73·25	146·50
11,750	58·75	117·50	14,700	73·50	147·00
11,800	59·00	118·00	14,750	73·75	147·50
11,850	59·25	118·50	14,800	74·00	148·00
11,900	59·50	119·00	14,850	74·25	148·50
11,950	59·75	119·50	14,900	74·50	149·00
12,000	60·00	120·00	14,950	74·75	149·50
12,050	60·25	120·50	15,000	75·00	150·00
12,100	60·50	121·00			
12,150	60·75	121·50	Exceeding	——	50p for
12,200	61·00	122·00	15,000		every £50
12,250	61·25	122·50			and fraction
12,300	61·50	123·00			of £50 of
					the total

TABLE II : LEASE DUTY

A. Instruments executed on or after 1st August, 1972

Rent not exceeding	TERM OF LEASE			
	Not exceeding 7 years or indefinite	Exceeding 7 years but not exceeding 35 years	Exceeding 35 years but not exceeding 100 years	Exceeding 100 years
£	£	£	£	£
5		0·05	0·30	0·60
10		0·10	0·60	1·20
15		0·15	0·90	1·80
20		0·20	1·20	2·40
25		0·25	1·50	3·00
50	Nil	0·50	3·00	6·00
75		0·75	4·50	9·00
100		1·00	6·00	12·00
150		1·50	9·00	18·00
200		2·00	12·00	24·00
250		2·50	15·00	30·00
300	1·50	3·00	18·00	36·00
350	1·75	3·50	21·00	42·00
400	2·00	4·00	24·00	48·00
450	2·25	4·50	27·00	54·00
500	2·50	5·00	30·00	60·00
550	2·75	5·50	33·00	66·00
600	3·00	6·00	36·00	72·00
650	3·25	6·50	39·00	78·00
700	3·50	7·00	42·00	84·00
750	3·75	7·50	45·00	90·00
800	4·00	8·00	48·00	96·00
850	4·25	8·50	51·00	102·00
900	4·50	9·00	54·00	108·00
950	4·75	9·50	57·00	114·00
1,000	5·00	10·00	60·00	120·00
1,050	5·25	10·50	63·00	126·00
1,100	5·50	11·00	66·00	132·00
1,150	5·75	11·50	69·00	138·00
1,200	6·00	12·00	72·00	144·00
1,250	6·25	12·50	75·00	150·00
1,300	6·50	13·00	78·00	156·00
1,350	6·75	13·50	81·00	162·00
1,400	7·00	14·00	84·00	168·00
1,450	7·25	14·50	87·00	174·00
1,500	7·50	15·00	90·00	180·00
1,550	7·75	15·50	93·00	186·00
1,600	8·00	16·00	96·00	192·00
1,650	8·25	16·50	99·00	198·00
1,700	8·50	17·00	102·00	204·00
1,750	8·75	17·50	105·00	210·00
1,800	9·00	18·00	108·00	216·00
1,850	9·25	18·50	111·00	222·00
1,900	9·50	19·00	114·00	228·00
1,950	9·75	19·50	117·00	234·00
2,000	10·00	20·00	120·00	240·00
2,050	10·25	20·50	123·00	246·00
2,100	10·50	21·00	126·00	252·00
2,150	10·75	21·50	129·00	258·00
2,200	11·00	22·00	132·00	264·00
2,250	11·25	22·50	135·00	270·00

APPENDIX: STAMP DUTY

LEASE DUTY

Rent not exceeding	TERM OF LEASE			
	Not exceeding 7 years or indefinite	Exceeding 7 years but not exceeding 35 years	Exceeding 35 years but not exceeding 100 years	Exceeding 100 years
£	£	£	£	£
2,300	11·50	23·00	138·00	276·00
2,350	11·75	23·50	141·00	282·00
2,400	12·00	24·00	144·00	288·00
2,450	12·25	24·50	147·00	294·00
2,500	12·50	25·00	150·00	300·00
2,550	12·75	25·50	153·00	306·00
2,600	13·00	26·00	156·00	312·00
2,650	13·25	26·50	159·00	318·00
2,700	13·50	27·00	162·00	324·00
2,750	13·75	27·50	165·00	330·00
2,800	14·00	28·00	168·00	336·00
2,850	14·25	28·50	171·00	342·00
2,900	14·50	29·00	174·00	348·00
2,950	14·75	29·50	177·00	354·00
3,000	15·00	30·00	180·00	360·00
3,050	15·25	30·50	183·00	366·00
3,100	15·50	31·00	186·00	372·00
3,150	15·75	31·50	189·00	378·00
3,200	16·00	32·00	192·00	384·00
3,250	16·25	32·50	195·00	390·00
3,300	16·50	33·00	198·00	396·00
3,350	16·75	33·50	201·00	402·00
3,400	17·00	34·00	204·00	408·00
3,450	17·25	34·50	207·00	414·00
3,500	17·50	35·00	210·00	420·00
3,550	17·75	35·50	213·00	426·00
3,600	18·00	36·00	216·00	432·00
3,650	18·25	36·50	219·00	438·00
3,700	18·50	37·00	222·00	444·00
3,750	18·75	37·50	225·00	450·00
3,800	19·00	38·00	228·00	456·00
3,850	19·25	38·50	231·00	462·00
3,900	19·50	39·00	234·00	468·00
3,950	19·75	39·50	237·00	474·00
4,000	20·00	40·00	240·00	480·00
4,050	20·25	40·50	243·00	486·00
4,100	20·50	41·00	246·00	492·00
4,150	20·75	41·50	249·00	498·00
4,200	21·00	42·00	252·00	504·00
4,250	21·25	42·50	255·00	510·00
4,300	21·50	43·00	258·00	516·00
4,350	21·75	43·50	261·00	522·00
4,400	22·00	44·00	264·00	528·00
4,450	22·25	44·50	267·00	534·00
4,500	22·50	45·00	270·00	540·00
4,550	22·75	45·50	273·00	546·00
4,600	23·00	46·00	276·00	552·00
4,650	23·25	46·50	279·00	558·00
4,700	23·50	47·00	282·00	564·00
4,750	23·75	47·50	285·00	570·00
4,800	24·00	48·00	288·00	576·00
4,850	24·25	48·50	291·00	582·00
4,900	24·50	49·00	294·00	588·00
4,950	24·75	49·50	297·00	594·00
5,000	25·00	50·00	300·00	600·00
Exceeding £5,000	25p for every £50 or part of £50	50p for every £50 or part of £50	£3 for every £50 or part of £50	£6 for every £50 or part of £50

B. Instruments executed on or after 1st August, 1963, but before 1st August, 1972

As Table II A above, except that exemption from duty where the term does not exceed seven years or is indefinite is not available where the rent exceeds £100, and in such a case duty is charged at 25p per £50 or part of £50 of the rent.

C. Instruments executed on or after 1st January, 1892, but before 1st August, 1963

The table below shows the rates of duty applicable between 1st January, 1892, and 31st July, 1963, according to date of execution. Duty is calculated at £5 intervals up to £25 rent, then at £25 intervals up to £100 rent, and thereafter at £50 intervals.

DATE OF EXECUTION	TERM OF LEASE		
	Not exceeding 35 years or indefinite	Exceeding 35 years but not exceeding 100 years	Exceeding 100 years
1st January, 1892, to 28th April, 1910	£½%	£3%	£6%
29th April, 1910, to 31st July, 1947	£1%	£6%	£12%
1st August, 1947, to 31st July, 1963	£2%* or if rent does not exceed £100 and no consideration in addition to rent, £1%	£12%*	£24%*

* Not applicable where the letting is made or agreed to be made to a body of persons established for charitable purposes only or to the trustees of a trust so established. In such cases the rates of duty in force before 1st August, 1947, remain applicable provided the instrument is adjudicated.

D. Premiums charged at conveyance rates

1. *Instruments executed on or after 1st August, 1972*

See Table I, p. 1220. Special rates dependent on the inclusion of a certificate of value are not available where the rent exceeds £150 per annum.

2. *Instruments executed on or after 1st January, 1892, but before 1st August, 1972*

In the case of leases at a rent and a premium the premium bore duty at the rates applicable to a conveyance on sale (*ante*, p. 1160) subject to the following qualifications:

    (i) the special rate introduced on 29th April, 1910, for conveyances containing a certificate of value did not apply to premiums under leases executed before 31st March, 1911 ;

    (ii) the special rates dependent on the inclusion of a certificate of value in instruments executed between 31st March, 1911, and 31st July, 1958, inclusive, did not apply where the rent exceeded £20 per annum ;

    (iii) the special rates dependent on the inclusion of a certificate of value in instruments executed between 1st August, 1958, and 31st July, 1972, inclusive, did not apply where the rent exceeded £50 per annum.

39A

INDEX

ENTAILED INTEREST—*continued.*
    protector of settlement, consent of, 440, 441.
    remainder, in, barring of, 438, 439.
            settlement of, 435.
    special protector abolished, 430, 431.
    tenant in tail, meaning of, 442.
    transitional provisions affecting, 430, 431.
    trust for sale, creation by way of, 433.
    undivided share in proceeds of sale, in, 433, 434.
    will, barred by, 441, 442.
        created by, 435.
    words of limitation before 1926, 429.
        in deeds, 429.
        necessary after 1925, 431, 432.

EQUITABLE CHARGE—*see* CHARGE ; MORTGAGE.

EQUITABLE EASEMENTS—*see* EASEMENTS.

EQUITABLE INTEREST—
    absence of words of limitation in transfer of, 538.
    capable of subsisting at law, 680.
    constructive notice of, 167.
    effect of enfranchisement on, 158.
    heirs by purchase taking, 330, 331.
    indorsement on trust instrument of dealing with, 656, 657, 695.
    infant's power to deal with, 348, 349.
    inspection of deeds by purchaser of, 657, 658.
    overreached by statutory trust for sale, 312.
        tenant for life selling, 112.
    overreaching of, generally, 173–184 ; *see also* OVERREACHING.
    prior, overreaching of, 177–179.
    priority of mortgages of, 1029.
    protected by registration, overreaching of, 179.
    purchaser of, right to inspect deeds, 657, 658.
    requirement that registration of, be cancelled, 57.

EQUITY OF REDEMPTION—
    clog on, 976–978.
    purchaser of, must indemnify vendor from mortgage, 980.
    root of title, as, 115.
    stamp duty on conveyance of, 1165, 1166.
    transfer of, by mortgagor, 263.

ERECTION—
    items falling within meaning of, 576.

ESCHEAT—
    abolition of, 153.
    bona vacantia replaces right of, 333.
    dissolution of corporation, on, 316.
    want of heirs, for, 328–333.

ESCROW—
    delivery of deed as, 591–593.
    effective date of, 233.

ESTATE AGENT—
    deposit held by, 61.

ESTATE CONTRACT—
    agreement for lease registered as, 803.
    definition of, 599.
    indorsement of existence of, on title deeds, 656.
    option to purchase may be registered as, 75.
    overreached, cannot be, 600.
    registration of, 599, 600.
        removal of, 604, 605.

40A

PATENT DEFECT—
  distinguished from latent defect, 97, 98.
  quality of freehold land, in, 101.

PERPETUALLY RENEWABLE LEASE—*see* Lease.

PERPETUITY RULE—
  administrative power of trustees not affected, 297.
  agreement for lease, 804.
  easement, application to, 526.
  lease, effect on, 811.
  option to purchase, effect on enforceability of, 73–75.
  rent-charge, fluctuating, 554.
  trust for sale, application to, 767, 768.

PERSON—
  meaning of, 56.

PERSONAL REPRESENTATIVES—
  acknowledgment for production of deeds by, 661.
  administrators, *see* Administrators.
  advertisements by, before distribution, 407, 408.
  appointment of additional, 388.
  appropriation by, 401–403.
  assent by, in their own favour, 417, 418 ; *see also* Assent ; Vesting
    Assent.
  covenants by, 546, 547.
  death of all, 687.
  definition of, 416.
  duties of, generally, 394.
  estate duty attributable to property passing to, 1173.
  executors, *see* Executors.
  fiduciary position of, 397, 398.
  general, powers over settled land, 708, 709.
              when land ceases to be settled, 404, 405.
  indorsement of grant on sale by, 415, 416.
  infant's interest held by, 343, 344.
  last surviving, power of, 791, 792.
  leaseholds, liabilities in respect of, 406, 407.
  matrimonial home, restrictions on sale of, 403–404.
  mines and minerals, sale by, 499.
  mortgage by, 259, 398, 399.
  notice not imputed to, 166, 408.
  number of, 386, 387.
  overreaching powers of, 179–181.
  parties to deeds, as, 383–418.
  planning law, position as regards contraventions of, 409.
  powers of, date exercisable from, 394, 395.
              leasing, 399, 822, 823.
              management, of, 345, 346, 395–397.
              single, 397, 462.
              to carry on deceased's business, 399–401.
                make appropriations, 401–403.
                raise money by mortgage, 259, 398, 399.
  prohibited from purchasing deceased's estate, 384.
  protection of, against claim for estate duty, 409.
              by advertising, 407, 408.
              persons dealing with, 405, 406, 415, 416.
  purchase from estate by, 397, 398.
  receipt by, 397, 405, 406, 461–463.
  recital by, that no assent given, 396, 452.
  registered land, may dispose of, 390, 391.
  restrictive covenants, power to release, 578, 579.
  sale of mines and minerals by, 499.
  security required by, prior to giving assent, 413.
  separate representation for real and personal property, 388.
  Settled Land Act trustees, as, 694, 714–716.